Oxford Dictionary of
National Biography

Volume 43

Oxford Dictionary of National Biography

IN ASSOCIATION WITH

The British Academy

From the earliest times to the year 2000

Edited by

H. C. G. Matthew

and

Brian Harrison

Volume 43

Patel–Phelips

UNIVERSITY PRESS

OXFORD
UNIVERSITY PRESS

Great Clarendon Street, Oxford OX2 6DP

Oxford University Press is a department of the University of Oxford.
It furthers the University's objective of excellence in research, scholarship,
and education by publishing worldwide in

Oxford New York

Auckland Bangkok Buenos Aires Cape Town
Chennai Dar es Salaam Delhi Hong Kong Istanbul Karachi
Kolkata Kuala Lumpur Madrid Melbourne Mexico City Mumbai Nairobi
São Paulo Shanghai Taipei Tokyo Toronto

Oxford is a registered trade mark of Oxford University Press
in the UK and in certain other countries

Published in the United States
by Oxford University Press Inc., New York

© Oxford University Press 2004

Illustrations © individual copyright holders as listed in
'Picture credits', and reproduced with permission

Database right Oxford University Press (maker)

First published 2004

All rights reserved. No part of this material may be reproduced,
stored in a retrieval system, or transmitted, in any form or by any means,
without the prior permission in writing of Oxford University Press,
or as expressly permitted by law, or under terms agreed with the appropriate
reprographics rights organization. Enquiries concerning reproduction
outside the scope of the above should be sent to the Rights Department,
Oxford University Press, at the address above

You must not circulate this book in any other binding or cover
and you must impose this same condition on any acquirer

British Library Cataloguing in Publication Data
Data available

Library of Congress Cataloging in Publication Data
Data available: for details see volume 1, p. iv

ISBN 0-19-861393-8 (this volume)
ISBN 0-19-861411-X (set of sixty volumes)

Text captured by Alliance Phototypesetters, Pondicherry
Illustrations reproduced and archived by
Alliance Graphics Ltd, UK
Typeset in OUP Swift by Interactive Sciences Limited, Gloucester
Printed in Great Britain on acid-free paper by
Butler and Tanner Ltd,
Frome, Somerset

LIST OF ABBREVIATIONS

1 General abbreviations

AB	bachelor of arts
ABC	Australian Broadcasting Corporation
ABC TV	ABC Television
act.	active
A$	Australian dollar
AD	*anno domini*
AFC	Air Force Cross
AIDS	acquired immune deficiency syndrome
AK	Alaska
AL	Alabama
A level	advanced level [examination]
ALS	associate of the Linnean Society
AM	master of arts
AMICE	associate member of the Institution of Civil Engineers
ANZAC	Australian and New Zealand Army Corps
appx *pl.* appxs	appendix(es)
AR	Arkansas
ARA	associate of the Royal Academy
ARCA	associate of the Royal College of Art
ARCM	associate of the Royal College of Music
ARCO	associate of the Royal College of Organists
ARIBA	associate of the Royal Institute of British Architects
ARP	air-raid precautions
ARRC	associate of the Royal Red Cross
ARSA	associate of the Royal Scottish Academy
art.	article / item
ASC	Army Service Corps
Asch	Austrian Schilling
ASDIC	Antisubmarine Detection Investigation Committee
ATS	Auxiliary Territorial Service
ATV	Associated Television
Aug	August
AZ	Arizona
b.	born
BA	bachelor of arts
BA (Admin.)	bachelor of arts (administration)
BAFTA	British Academy of Film and Television Arts
BAO	bachelor of arts in obstetrics
bap.	baptized
BBC	British Broadcasting Corporation / Company
BC	before Christ
BCE	before the common (*or* Christian) era
BCE	bachelor of civil engineering
BCG	bacillus of Calmette and Guérin [inoculation against tuberculosis]
BCh	bachelor of surgery
BChir	bachelor of surgery
BCL	bachelor of civil law

BCnL	bachelor of canon law
BCom	bachelor of commerce
BD	bachelor of divinity
BEd	bachelor of education
BEng	bachelor of engineering
bk *pl.* bks	book(s)
BL	bachelor of law / letters / literature
BLitt	bachelor of letters
BM	bachelor of medicine
BMus	bachelor of music
BP	before present
BP	British Petroleum
Bros.	Brothers
BS	(1) bachelor of science; (2) bachelor of surgery; (3) British standard
BSc	bachelor of science
BSc (Econ.)	bachelor of science (economics)
BSc (Eng.)	bachelor of science (engineering)
bt	baronet
BTh	bachelor of theology
bur.	buried
C.	command [identifier for published parliamentary papers]
c.	*circa*
c.	*capitulum pl. capitula*: chapter(s)
CA	California
Cantab.	Cantabrigiensis
cap.	*capitulum pl. capitula*: chapter(s)
CB	companion of the Bath
CBE	commander of the Order of the British Empire
CBS	Columbia Broadcasting System
cc	cubic centimetres
C$	Canadian dollar
CD	compact disc
Cd	command [identifier for published parliamentary papers]
CE	Common (*or* Christian) Era
cent.	century
cf.	compare
CH	Companion of Honour
chap.	chapter
ChB	bachelor of surgery
CI	Imperial Order of the Crown of India
CIA	Central Intelligence Agency
CID	Criminal Investigation Department
CIE	companion of the Order of the Indian Empire
Cie	Compagnie
CLit	companion of literature
CM	master of surgery
cm	centimetre(s)

Cmd	command [identifier for published parliamentary papers]		edn	edition
CMG	companion of the Order of St Michael and St George		EEC	European Economic Community
			EFTA	European Free Trade Association
Cmnd	command [identifier for published parliamentary papers]		EICS	East India Company Service
			EMI	Electrical and Musical Industries (Ltd)
CO	Colorado		Eng.	English
Co.	company		enl.	enlarged
co.	county		ENSA	Entertainments National Service Association
col. *pl.* cols.	column(s)		ep. *pl.* epp.	*epistola(e)*
Corp.	corporation		ESP	extra-sensory perception
CSE	certificate of secondary education		esp.	especially
CSI	companion of the Order of the Star of India		esq.	esquire
CT	Connecticut		est.	estimate / estimated
CVO	commander of the Royal Victorian Order		EU	European Union
cwt	hundredweight		ex	sold by (*lit.* out of)
$	(American) dollar		excl.	excludes / excluding
d.	(1) penny (pence); (2) died		exh.	exhibited
DBE	dame commander of the Order of the British Empire		exh. cat.	exhibition catalogue
			f. *pl.* ff.	following [pages]
DCH	diploma in child health		FA	Football Association
DCh	doctor of surgery		FACP	fellow of the American College of Physicians
DCL	doctor of civil law		facs.	facsimile
DCnL	doctor of canon law		FANY	First Aid Nursing Yeomanry
DCVO	dame commander of the Royal Victorian Order		FBA	fellow of the British Academy
DD	doctor of divinity		FBI	Federation of British Industries
DE	Delaware		FCS	fellow of the Chemical Society
Dec	December		Feb	February
dem.	demolished		FEng	fellow of the Fellowship of Engineering
DEng	doctor of engineering		FFCM	fellow of the Faculty of Community Medicine
des.	destroyed		FGS	fellow of the Geological Society
DFC	Distinguished Flying Cross		fig.	figure
DipEd	diploma in education		FIMechE	fellow of the Institution of Mechanical Engineers
DipPsych	diploma in psychiatry			
diss.	dissertation		FL	Florida
DL	deputy lieutenant		*fl.*	*floruit*
DLitt	doctor of letters		FLS	fellow of the Linnean Society
DLittCelt	doctor of Celtic letters		FM	frequency modulation
DM	(1) Deutschmark; (2) doctor of medicine; (3) doctor of musical arts		fol. *pl.* fols.	folio(s)
			Fr	French francs
DMus	doctor of music		Fr.	French
DNA	dioxyribonucleic acid		FRAeS	fellow of the Royal Aeronautical Society
doc.	document		FRAI	fellow of the Royal Anthropological Institute
DOL	doctor of oriental learning		FRAM	fellow of the Royal Academy of Music
DPH	diploma in public health		FRAS	(1) fellow of the Royal Asiatic Society; (2) fellow of the Royal Astronomical Society
DPhil	doctor of philosophy			
DPM	diploma in psychological medicine		FRCM	fellow of the Royal College of Music
DSC	Distinguished Service Cross		FRCO	fellow of the Royal College of Organists
DSc	doctor of science		FRCOG	fellow of the Royal College of Obstetricians and Gynaecologists
DSc (Econ.)	doctor of science (economics)			
DSc (Eng.)	doctor of science (engineering)		FRCP(C)	fellow of the Royal College of Physicians of Canada
DSM	Distinguished Service Medal			
DSO	companion of the Distinguished Service Order		FRCP (Edin.)	fellow of the Royal College of Physicians of Edinburgh
DSocSc	doctor of social science			
DTech	doctor of technology		FRCP (Lond.)	fellow of the Royal College of Physicians of London
DTh	doctor of theology			
DTM	diploma in tropical medicine		FRCPath	fellow of the Royal College of Pathologists
DTMH	diploma in tropical medicine and hygiene		FRCPsych	fellow of the Royal College of Psychiatrists
DU	doctor of the university		FRCS	fellow of the Royal College of Surgeons
DUniv	doctor of the university		FRGS	fellow of the Royal Geographical Society
dwt	pennyweight		FRIBA	fellow of the Royal Institute of British Architects
EC	European Community		FRICS	fellow of the Royal Institute of Chartered Surveyors
ed. *pl.* eds.	edited / edited by / editor(s)			
Edin.	Edinburgh		FRS	fellow of the Royal Society
			FRSA	fellow of the Royal Society of Arts

FRSCM	fellow of the Royal School of Church Music	ISO	companion of the Imperial Service Order
FRSE	fellow of the Royal Society of Edinburgh	It.	Italian
FRSL	fellow of the Royal Society of Literature	ITA	Independent Television Authority
FSA	fellow of the Society of Antiquaries	ITV	Independent Television
ft	foot *pl.* feet	Jan	January
FTCL	fellow of Trinity College of Music, London	JP	justice of the peace
ft-lb per min.	foot-pounds per minute [unit of horsepower]	jun.	junior
FZS	fellow of the Zoological Society	KB	knight of the Order of the Bath
GA	Georgia	KBE	knight commander of the Order of the British Empire
GBE	knight or dame grand cross of the Order of the British Empire	KC	king's counsel
GCB	knight grand cross of the Order of the Bath	kcal	kilocalorie
GCE	general certificate of education	KCB	knight commander of the Order of the Bath
GCH	knight grand cross of the Royal Guelphic Order	KCH	knight commander of the Royal Guelphic Order
GCHQ	government communications headquarters	KCIE	knight commander of the Order of the Indian Empire
GCIE	knight grand commander of the Order of the Indian Empire	KCMG	knight commander of the Order of St Michael and St George
GCMG	knight or dame grand cross of the Order of St Michael and St George	KCSI	knight commander of the Order of the Star of India
GCSE	general certificate of secondary education	KCVO	knight commander of the Royal Victorian Order
GCSI	knight grand commander of the Order of the Star of India	keV	kilo-electron-volt
GCStJ	bailiff or dame grand cross of the order of St John of Jerusalem	KG	knight of the Order of the Garter
		KGB	[Soviet committee of state security]
GCVO	knight or dame grand cross of the Royal Victorian Order	KH	knight of the Royal Guelphic Order
		KLM	Koninklijke Luchtvaart Maatschappij (Royal Dutch Air Lines)
GEC	General Electric Company	km	kilometre(s)
Ger.	German	KP	knight of the Order of St Patrick
GI	government (*or* general) issue	KS	Kansas
GMT	Greenwich mean time	KT	knight of the Order of the Thistle
GP	general practitioner	kt	knight
GPU	[Soviet special police unit]	KY	Kentucky
GSO	general staff officer	£	pound(s) sterling
Heb.	Hebrew	£E	Egyptian pound
HEICS	Honourable East India Company Service	L	lira *pl.* lire
HI	Hawaii	l. *pl.* ll.	line(s)
HIV	human immunodeficiency virus	LA	Lousiana
HK$	Hong Kong dollar	LAA	light anti-aircraft
HM	his / her majesty('s)	LAH	licentiate of the Apothecaries' Hall, Dublin
HMAS	his / her majesty's Australian ship	Lat.	Latin
HMNZS	his / her majesty's New Zealand ship	lb	pound(s), unit of weight
HMS	his / her majesty's ship	LDS	licence in dental surgery
HMSO	His / Her Majesty's Stationery Office	*lit.*	literally
HMV	His Master's Voice	LittB	bachelor of letters
Hon.	Honourable	LittD	doctor of letters
hp	horsepower	LKQCPI	licentiate of the King and Queen's College of Physicians, Ireland
hr	hour(s)	LLA	lady literate in arts
HRH	his / her royal highness	LLB	bachelor of laws
HTV	Harlech Television	LLD	doctor of laws
IA	Iowa	LLM	master of laws
ibid.	*ibidem*: in the same place	LM	licentiate in midwifery
ICI	Imperial Chemical Industries (Ltd)	LP	long-playing record
ID	Idaho	LRAM	licentiate of the Royal Academy of Music
IL	Illinois	LRCP	licentiate of the Royal College of Physicians
illus.	illustration	LRCPS (Glasgow)	licentiate of the Royal College of Physicians and Surgeons of Glasgow
illustr.	illustrated		
IN	Indiana	LRCS	licentiate of the Royal College of Surgeons
in.	inch(es)	LSA	licentiate of the Society of Apothecaries
Inc.	Incorporated	LSD	lysergic acid diethylamide
incl.	includes / including	LVO	lieutenant of the Royal Victorian Order
IOU	I owe you	M. *pl.* MM.	Monsieur *pl.* Messieurs
IQ	intelligence quotient	m	metre(s)
Ir£	Irish pound		
IRA	Irish Republican Army		

m. *pl.* mm.	membrane(s)
MA	(1) Massachusetts; (2) master of arts
MAI	master of engineering
MB	bachelor of medicine
MBA	master of business administration
MBE	member of the Order of the British Empire
MC	Military Cross
MCC	Marylebone Cricket Club
MCh	master of surgery
MChir	master of surgery
MCom	master of commerce
MD	(1) doctor of medicine; (2) Maryland
MDMA	methylenedioxymethamphetamine
ME	Maine
MEd	master of education
MEng	master of engineering
MEP	member of the European parliament
MG	Morris Garages
MGM	Metro-Goldwyn-Mayer
Mgr	Monsignor
MI	(1) Michigan; (2) military intelligence
MI1c	[secret intelligence department]
MI5	[military intelligence department]
MI6	[secret intelligence department]
MI9	[secret escape service]
MICE	member of the Institution of Civil Engineers
MIEE	member of the Institution of Electrical Engineers
min.	minute(s)
Mk	mark
ML	(1) licentiate of medicine; (2) master of laws
MLitt	master of letters
Mlle	Mademoiselle
mm	millimetre(s)
Mme	Madame
MN	Minnesota
MO	Missouri
MOH	medical officer of health
MP	member of parliament
m.p.h.	miles per hour
MPhil	master of philosophy
MRCP	member of the Royal College of Physicians
MRCS	member of the Royal College of Surgeons
MRCVS	member of the Royal College of Veterinary Surgeons
MRIA	member of the Royal Irish Academy
MS	(1) master of science; (2) Mississippi
MS *pl.* MSS	manuscript(s)
MSc	master of science
MSc (Econ.)	master of science (economics)
MT	Montana
MusB	bachelor of music
MusBac	bachelor of music
MusD	doctor of music
MV	motor vessel
MVO	member of the Royal Victorian Order
n. *pl.* nn.	note(s)
NAAFI	Navy, Army, and Air Force Institutes
NASA	National Aeronautics and Space Administration
NATO	North Atlantic Treaty Organization
NBC	National Broadcasting Corporation
NC	North Carolina
NCO	non-commissioned officer
ND	North Dakota
n.d.	no date
NE	Nebraska
nem. con.	*nemine contradicente*: unanimously
new ser.	new series
NH	New Hampshire
NHS	National Health Service
NJ	New Jersey
NKVD	[Soviet people's commissariat for internal affairs]
NM	New Mexico
nm	nanometre(s)
no. *pl.* nos.	number(s)
Nov	November
n.p.	no place [of publication]
NS	new style
NV	Nevada
NY	New York
NZBS	New Zealand Broadcasting Service
OBE	officer of the Order of the British Empire
obit.	obituary
Oct	October
OCTU	officer cadets training unit
OECD	Organization for Economic Co-operation and Development
OEEC	Organization for European Economic Co-operation
OFM	order of Friars Minor [Franciscans]
OFMCap	Ordine Frati Minori Cappucini: member of the Capuchin order
OH	Ohio
OK	Oklahoma
O level	ordinary level [examination]
OM	Order of Merit
OP	order of Preachers [Dominicans]
op. *pl.* opp.	opus *pl.* opera
OPEC	Organization of Petroleum Exporting Countries
OR	Oregon
orig.	original
OS	old style
OSB	Order of St Benedict
OTC	Officers' Training Corps
OWS	Old Watercolour Society
Oxon.	Oxoniensis
p. *pl.* pp.	page(s)
PA	Pennsylvania
p.a.	per annum
para.	paragraph
PAYE	pay as you earn
pbk *pl.* pbks	paperback(s)
per.	[during the] period
PhD	doctor of philosophy
pl.	(1) plate(s); (2) plural
priv. coll.	private collection
pt *pl.* pts	part(s)
pubd	published
PVC	polyvinyl chloride
q. *pl.* qq.	(1) question(s); (2) quire(s)
QC	queen's counsel
R	rand
R.	Rex / Regina
r	recto
r.	reigned / ruled
RA	Royal Academy / Royal Academician

RAC	Royal Automobile Club
RAF	Royal Air Force
RAFVR	Royal Air Force Volunteer Reserve
RAM	[member of the] Royal Academy of Music
RAMC	Royal Army Medical Corps
RCA	Royal College of Art
RCNC	Royal Corps of Naval Constructors
RCOG	Royal College of Obstetricians and Gynaecologists
RDI	royal designer for industry
RE	Royal Engineers
repr. *pl.* reprs.	reprint(s) / reprinted
repro.	reproduced
rev.	revised / revised by / reviser / revision
Revd	Reverend
RHA	Royal Hibernian Academy
RI	(1) Rhode Island; (2) Royal Institute of Painters in Water-Colours
RIBA	Royal Institute of British Architects
RIN	Royal Indian Navy
RM	Reichsmark
RMS	Royal Mail steamer
RN	Royal Navy
RNA	ribonucleic acid
RNAS	Royal Naval Air Service
RNR	Royal Naval Reserve
RNVR	Royal Naval Volunteer Reserve
RO	Record Office
r.p.m.	revolutions per minute
RRS	royal research ship
Rs	rupees
RSA	(1) Royal Scottish Academician; (2) Royal Society of Arts
RSPCA	Royal Society for the Prevention of Cruelty to Animals
Rt Hon.	Right Honourable
Rt Revd	Right Reverend
RUC	Royal Ulster Constabulary
Russ.	Russian
RWS	Royal Watercolour Society
S4C	Sianel Pedwar Cymru
s.	shilling(s)
s.a.	*sub anno*: under the year
SABC	South African Broadcasting Corporation
SAS	Special Air Service
SC	South Carolina
ScD	doctor of science
S$	Singapore dollar
SD	South Dakota
sec.	second(s)
sel.	selected
sen.	senior
Sept	September
ser.	series
SHAPE	supreme headquarters allied powers, Europe
SIDRO	Société Internationale d'Énergie Hydro-Électrique
sig. *pl.* sigs.	signature(s)
sing.	singular
SIS	Secret Intelligence Service
SJ	Society of Jesus
Skr	Swedish krona
Span.	Spanish
SPCK	Society for Promoting Christian Knowledge
SS	(1) Santissimi; (2) Schutzstaffel; (3) steam ship
STB	bachelor of theology
STD	doctor of theology
STM	master of theology
STP	doctor of theology
supp.	supposedly
suppl. *pl.* suppls.	supplement(s)
s.v.	*sub verbo	sub voce*: under the word / heading
SY	steam yacht
TA	Territorial Army
TASS	[Soviet news agency]
TB	tuberculosis (*lit.* tubercle bacillus)
TD	(1) *teachtaí dála* (member of the Dáil); (2) territorial decoration
TN	Tennessee
TNT	trinitrotoluene
trans.	translated / translated by / translation / translator
TT	tourist trophy
TUC	Trades Union Congress
TX	Texas
U-boat	*Unterseeboot*: submarine
Ufa	Universum-Film AG
UMIST	University of Manchester Institute of Science and Technology
UN	United Nations
UNESCO	United Nations Educational, Scientific, and Cultural Organization
UNICEF	United Nations International Children's Emergency Fund
unpubd	unpublished
USS	United States ship
UT	Utah
v	verso
v.	versus
VA	Virginia
VAD	Voluntary Aid Detachment
VC	Victoria Cross
VE-day	victory in Europe day
Ven.	Venerable
VJ-day	victory over Japan day
vol. *pl.* vols.	volume(s)
VT	Vermont
WA	Washington [state]
WAAC	Women's Auxiliary Army Corps
WAAF	Women's Auxiliary Air Force
WEA	Workers' Educational Association
WHO	World Health Organization
WI	Wisconsin
WRAF	Women's Royal Air Force
WRNS	Women's Royal Naval Service
WV	West Virginia
WVS	Women's Voluntary Service
WY	Wyoming
¥	yen
YMCA	Young Men's Christian Association
YWCA	Young Women's Christian Association

2 Institution abbreviations

All Souls Oxf.	All Souls College, Oxford
AM Oxf.	Ashmolean Museum, Oxford
Balliol Oxf.	Balliol College, Oxford
BBC WAC	BBC Written Archives Centre, Reading
Beds. & Luton ARS	Bedfordshire and Luton Archives and Record Service, Bedford
Berks. RO	Berkshire Record Office, Reading
BFI	British Film Institute, London
BFI NFTVA	British Film Institute, London, National Film and Television Archive
BGS	British Geological Survey, Keyworth, Nottingham
Birm. CA	Birmingham Central Library, Birmingham City Archives
Birm. CL	Birmingham Central Library
BL	British Library, London
BL NSA	British Library, London, National Sound Archive
BL OIOC	British Library, London, Oriental and India Office Collections
BLPES	London School of Economics and Political Science, British Library of Political and Economic Science
BM	British Museum, London
Bodl. Oxf.	Bodleian Library, Oxford
Bodl. RH	Bodleian Library of Commonwealth and African Studies at Rhodes House, Oxford
Borth. Inst.	Borthwick Institute of Historical Research, University of York
Boston PL	Boston Public Library, Massachusetts
Bristol RO	Bristol Record Office
Bucks. RLSS	Buckinghamshire Records and Local Studies Service, Aylesbury
CAC Cam.	Churchill College, Cambridge, Churchill Archives Centre
Cambs. AS	Cambridgeshire Archive Service
CCC Cam.	Corpus Christi College, Cambridge
CCC Oxf.	Corpus Christi College, Oxford
Ches. & Chester ALSS	Cheshire and Chester Archives and Local Studies Service
Christ Church Oxf.	Christ Church, Oxford
Christies	Christies, London
City Westm. AC	City of Westminster Archives Centre, London
CKS	Centre for Kentish Studies, Maidstone
CLRO	Corporation of London Records Office
Coll. Arms	College of Arms, London
Col. U.	Columbia University, New York
Cornwall RO	Cornwall Record Office, Truro
Courtauld Inst.	Courtauld Institute of Art, London
CUL	Cambridge University Library
Cumbria AS	Cumbria Archive Service
Derbys. RO	Derbyshire Record Office, Matlock
Devon RO	Devon Record Office, Exeter
Dorset RO	Dorset Record Office, Dorchester
Duke U.	Duke University, Durham, North Carolina
Duke U., Perkins L.	Duke University, Durham, North Carolina, William R. Perkins Library
Durham Cath. CL	Durham Cathedral, chapter library
Durham RO	Durham Record Office
DWL	Dr Williams's Library, London
Essex RO	Essex Record Office
E. Sussex RO	East Sussex Record Office, Lewes
Eton	Eton College, Berkshire
FM Cam.	Fitzwilliam Museum, Cambridge
Folger	Folger Shakespeare Library, Washington, DC
Garr. Club	Garrick Club, London
Girton Cam.	Girton College, Cambridge
GL	Guildhall Library, London
Glos. RO	Gloucestershire Record Office, Gloucester
Gon. & Caius Cam.	Gonville and Caius College, Cambridge
Gov. Art Coll.	Government Art Collection
GS Lond.	Geological Society of London
Hants. RO	Hampshire Record Office, Winchester
Harris Man. Oxf.	Harris Manchester College, Oxford
Harvard TC	Harvard Theatre Collection, Harvard University, Cambridge, Massachusetts, Nathan Marsh Pusey Library
Harvard U.	Harvard University, Cambridge, Massachusetts
Harvard U., Houghton L.	Harvard University, Cambridge, Massachusetts, Houghton Library
Herefs. RO	Herefordshire Record Office, Hereford
Herts. ALS	Hertfordshire Archives and Local Studies, Hertford
Hist. Soc. Penn.	Historical Society of Pennsylvania, Philadelphia
HLRO	House of Lords Record Office, London
Hult. Arch.	Hulton Archive, London and New York
Hunt. L.	Huntington Library, San Marino, California
ICL	Imperial College, London
Inst. CE	Institution of Civil Engineers, London
Inst. EE	Institution of Electrical Engineers, London
IWM	Imperial War Museum, London
IWM FVA	Imperial War Museum, London, Film and Video Archive
IWM SA	Imperial War Museum, London, Sound Archive
JRL	John Rylands University Library of Manchester
King's AC Cam.	King's College Archives Centre, Cambridge
King's Cam.	King's College, Cambridge
King's Lond.	King's College, London
King's Lond., Liddell Hart C.	King's College, London, Liddell Hart Centre for Military Archives
Lancs. RO	Lancashire Record Office, Preston
L. Cong.	Library of Congress, Washington, DC
Leics. RO	Leicestershire, Leicester, and Rutland Record Office, Leicester
Lincs. Arch.	Lincolnshire Archives, Lincoln
Linn. Soc.	Linnean Society of London
LMA	London Metropolitan Archives
LPL	Lambeth Palace, London
Lpool RO	Liverpool Record Office and Local Studies Service
LUL	London University Library
Magd. Cam.	Magdalene College, Cambridge
Magd. Oxf.	Magdalen College, Oxford
Man. City Gall.	Manchester City Galleries
Man. CL	Manchester Central Library
Mass. Hist. Soc.	Massachusetts Historical Society, Boston
Merton Oxf.	Merton College, Oxford
MHS Oxf.	Museum of the History of Science, Oxford
Mitchell L., Glas.	Mitchell Library, Glasgow
Mitchell L., NSW	State Library of New South Wales, Sydney, Mitchell Library
Morgan L.	Pierpont Morgan Library, New York
NA Canada	National Archives of Canada, Ottawa
NA Ire.	National Archives of Ireland, Dublin
NAM	National Army Museum, London
NA Scot.	National Archives of Scotland, Edinburgh
News Int. RO	News International Record Office, London
NG Ire.	National Gallery of Ireland, Dublin

NG Scot.	National Gallery of Scotland, Edinburgh
NHM	Natural History Museum, London
NL Aus.	National Library of Australia, Canberra
NL Ire.	National Library of Ireland, Dublin
NL NZ	National Library of New Zealand, Wellington
NL NZ, Turnbull L.	National Library of New Zealand, Wellington, Alexander Turnbull Library
NL Scot.	National Library of Scotland, Edinburgh
NL Wales	National Library of Wales, Aberystwyth
NMG Wales	National Museum and Gallery of Wales, Cardiff
NMM	National Maritime Museum, London
Norfolk RO	Norfolk Record Office, Norwich
Northants. RO	Northamptonshire Record Office, Northampton
Northumbd RO	Northumberland Record Office
Notts. Arch.	Nottinghamshire Archives, Nottingham
NPG	National Portrait Gallery, London
NRA	National Archives, London, Historical Manuscripts Commission, National Register of Archives
Nuffield Oxf.	Nuffield College, Oxford
N. Yorks. CRO	North Yorkshire County Record Office, Northallerton
NYPL	New York Public Library
Oxf. UA	Oxford University Archives
Oxf. U. Mus. NH	Oxford University Museum of Natural History
Oxon. RO	Oxfordshire Record Office, Oxford
Pembroke Cam.	Pembroke College, Cambridge
PRO	National Archives, London, Public Record Office
PRO NIre.	Public Record Office for Northern Ireland, Belfast
Pusey Oxf.	Pusey House, Oxford
RA	Royal Academy of Arts, London
Ransom HRC	Harry Ransom Humanities Research Center, University of Texas, Austin
RAS	Royal Astronomical Society, London
RBG Kew	Royal Botanic Gardens, Kew, London
RCP Lond.	Royal College of Physicians of London
RCS Eng.	Royal College of Surgeons of England, London
RGS	Royal Geographical Society, London
RIBA	Royal Institute of British Architects, London
RIBA BAL	Royal Institute of British Architects, London, British Architectural Library
Royal Arch.	Royal Archives, Windsor Castle, Berkshire [by gracious permission of her majesty the queen]
Royal Irish Acad.	Royal Irish Academy, Dublin
Royal Scot. Acad.	Royal Scottish Academy, Edinburgh
RS	Royal Society, London
RSA	Royal Society of Arts, London
RS Friends, Lond.	Religious Society of Friends, London
St Ant. Oxf.	St Antony's College, Oxford
St John Cam.	St John's College, Cambridge
S. Antiquaries, Lond.	Society of Antiquaries of London
Sci. Mus.	Science Museum, London
Scot. NPG	Scottish National Portrait Gallery, Edinburgh
Scott Polar RI	University of Cambridge, Scott Polar Research Institute
Sheff. Arch.	Sheffield Archives
Shrops. RRC	Shropshire Records and Research Centre, Shrewsbury
SOAS	School of Oriental and African Studies, London
Som. ARS	Somerset Archive and Record Service, Taunton
Staffs. RO	Staffordshire Record Office, Stafford
Suffolk RO	Suffolk Record Office
Surrey HC	Surrey History Centre, Woking
TCD	Trinity College, Dublin
Trinity Cam.	Trinity College, Cambridge
U. Aberdeen	University of Aberdeen
U. Birm.	University of Birmingham
U. Birm. L.	University of Birmingham Library
U. Cal.	University of California
U. Cam.	University of Cambridge
UCL	University College, London
U. Durham	University of Durham
U. Durham L.	University of Durham Library
U. Edin.	University of Edinburgh
U. Edin., New Coll.	University of Edinburgh, New College
U. Edin., New Coll. L.	University of Edinburgh, New College Library
U. Edin. L.	University of Edinburgh Library
U. Glas.	University of Glasgow
U. Glas. L.	University of Glasgow Library
U. Hull	University of Hull
U. Hull, Brynmor Jones L.	University of Hull, Brynmor Jones Library
U. Leeds	University of Leeds
U. Leeds, Brotherton L.	University of Leeds, Brotherton Library
U. Lond.	University of London
U. Lpool	University of Liverpool
U. Lpool L.	University of Liverpool Library
U. Mich.	University of Michigan, Ann Arbor
U. Mich., Clements L.	University of Michigan, Ann Arbor, William L. Clements Library
U. Newcastle	University of Newcastle upon Tyne
U. Newcastle, Robinson L.	University of Newcastle upon Tyne, Robinson Library
U. Nott.	University of Nottingham
U. Nott. L.	University of Nottingham Library
U. Oxf.	University of Oxford
U. Reading	University of Reading
U. Reading L.	University of Reading Library
U. St Andr.	University of St Andrews
U. St Andr. L.	University of St Andrews Library
U. Southampton	University of Southampton
U. Southampton L.	University of Southampton Library
U. Sussex	University of Sussex, Brighton
U. Texas	University of Texas, Austin
U. Wales	University of Wales
U. Warwick Mod. RC	University of Warwick, Coventry, Modern Records Centre
V&A	Victoria and Albert Museum, London
V&A NAL	Victoria and Albert Museum, London, National Art Library
Warks. CRO	Warwickshire County Record Office, Warwick
Wellcome L.	Wellcome Library for the History and Understanding of Medicine, London
Westm. DA	Westminster Diocesan Archives, London
Wilts. & Swindon RO	Wiltshire and Swindon Record Office, Trowbridge
Worcs. RO	Worcestershire Record Office, Worcester
W. Sussex RO	West Sussex Record Office, Chichester
W. Yorks. AS	West Yorkshire Archive Service
Yale U.	Yale University, New Haven, Connecticut
Yale U., Beinecke L.	Yale University, New Haven, Connecticut, Beinecke Rare Book and Manuscript Library
Yale U. CBA	Yale University, New Haven, Connecticut, Yale Center for British Art

3 Bibliographic abbreviations

Adams, *Drama* W. D. Adams, *A dictionary of the drama*, 1: *A–G* (1904); 2: *H–Z* (1956) [vol. 2 microfilm only]

AFM J O'Donovan, ed. and trans., *Annala rioghachta Eireann* / *Annals of the kingdom of Ireland by the four masters*, 7 vols. (1848–51); 2nd edn (1856); 3rd edn (1990)

Allibone, *Dict.* S. A. Allibone, *A critical dictionary of English literature and British and American authors*, 3 vols. (1859–71); suppl. by J. F. Kirk, 2 vols. (1891)

ANB J. A. Garraty and M. C. Carnes, eds., *American national biography*, 24 vols. (1999)

Anderson, *Scot. nat.* W. Anderson, *The Scottish nation, or, The surnames, families, literature, honours, and biographical history of the people of Scotland*, 3 vols. (1859–63)

Ann. mon. H. R. Luard, ed., *Annales monastici*, 5 vols., Rolls Series, 36 (1864–9)

Ann. Ulster S. Mac Airt and G. Mac Niocaill, eds., *Annals of Ulster (to AD 1131)* (1983)

APC *Acts of the privy council of England*, new ser., 46 vols. (1890–1964)

APS *The acts of the parliaments of Scotland*, 12 vols. in 13 (1814–75)

Arber, *Regs. Stationers* F. Arber, ed., *A transcript of the registers of the Company of Stationers of London, 1554–1640 AD*, 5 vols. (1875–94)

ArchR *Architectural Review*

ASC D. Whitelock, D. C. Douglas, and S. I. Tucker, ed. and trans., *The Anglo-Saxon Chronicle: a revised translation* (1961)

AS chart. P. H. Sawyer, *Anglo-Saxon charters: an annotated list and bibliography*, Royal Historical Society Guides and Handbooks (1968)

AusDB D. Pike and others, eds., *Australian dictionary of biography*, 16 vols. (1966–2002)

Baker, *Serjeants* J. H. Baker, *The order of serjeants at law*, SeldS, suppl. ser., 5 (1984)

Bale, *Cat.* J. Bale, *Scriptorum illustrium Maioris Brytannie, quam nunc Angliam et Scotiam vocant: catalogus*, 2 vols. in 1 (Basel, 1557–9); facs. edn (1971)

Bale, *Index* J. Bale, *Index Britanniae scriptorum*, ed. R. L. Poole and M. Bateson (1902); facs. edn (1990)

BBCS *Bulletin of the Board of Celtic Studies*

BDMBR J. O. Baylen and N. J. Gossman, eds., *Biographical dictionary of modern British radicals*, 3 vols. in 4 (1979–88)

Bede, *Hist. eccl.* *Bede's Ecclesiastical history of the English people*, ed. and trans. B. Colgrave and R. A. B. Mynors, OMT (1969); repr. (1991)

Bénézit, *Dict.* E. Bénézit, *Dictionnaire critique et documentaire des peintres, sculpteurs, dessinateurs et graveurs*, 3 vols. (Paris, 1911–23); new edn, 8 vols. (1948–66), repr. (1966); 3rd edn, rev. and enl., 10 vols. (1976); 4th edn, 14 vols. (1999)

BIHR *Bulletin of the Institute of Historical Research*

Birch, *Seals* W. de Birch, *Catalogue of seals in the department of manuscripts in the British Museum*, 6 vols. (1887–1900)

Bishop Burnet's History *Bishop Burnet's History of his own time*, ed. M. J. Routh, 2nd edn, 6 vols. (1833)

Blackwood *Blackwood's [Edinburgh] Magazine*, 328 vols. (1817–1980)

Blain, Clements & Grundy, *Feminist comp.* V. Blain, P. Clements, and I. Grundy, eds., *The feminist companion to literature in English* (1990)

BL cat. *The British Library general catalogue of printed books* [in 360 vols. with suppls., also CD-ROM and online]

BMJ *British Medical Journal*

Boase & Courtney, *Bibl. Corn.* G. C. Boase and W. P. Courtney, *Bibliotheca Cornubiensis: a catalogue of the writings … of Cornishmen*, 3 vols. (1874–82)

Boase, *Mod. Eng. biog.* F. Boase, *Modern English biography: containing many thousand concise memoirs of persons who have died since the year 1850*, 6 vols. (privately printed, Truro, 1892–1921); repr. (1965)

Boswell, *Life* *Boswell's Life of Johnson: together with Journal of a tour to the Hebrides and Johnson's Diary of a journey into north Wales*, ed. G. B. Hill, enl. edn, rev. L. F. Powell, 6 vols. (1934–50); 2nd edn (1964); repr. (1971)

Brown & Stratton, *Brit. mus.* J. D. Brown and S. S. Stratton, *British musical biography* (1897)

Bryan, *Painters* M. Bryan, *A biographical and critical dictionary of painters and engravers*, 2 vols. (1816); new edn, ed. G. Stanley (1849); new edn, ed. R. E. Graves and W. Armstrong, 2 vols. (1886–9); [4th edn], ed. G. C. Williamson, 5 vols. (1903–5) [various reprs.]

Burke, *Gen. GB* J. Burke, *A genealogical and heraldic history of the commoners of Great Britain and Ireland*, 4 vols. (1833–8); new edn as *A genealogical and heraldic dictionary of the landed gentry of Great Britain and Ireland*, 3 vols. [1843–9] [many later edns]

Burke, *Gen. Ire.* J. B. Burke, *A genealogical and heraldic history of the landed gentry of Ireland* (1899); 2nd edn (1904); 3rd edn (1912); 4th edn (1958); 5th edn as *Burke's Irish family records* (1976)

Burke, *Peerage* J. Burke, *A general [later edns A genealogical] and heraldic dictionary of the peerage and baronetage of the United Kingdom [later edns the British empire]* (1829–)

Burney, *Hist. mus.* C. Burney, *A general history of music, from the earliest ages to the present period*, 4 vols. (1776–89)

Burtchaell & Sadleir, *Alum. Dubl.* G. D. Burtchaell and T. U. Sadleir, *Alumni Dublinenses: a register of the students, graduates, and provosts of Trinity College* (1924); [2nd edn], with suppl., in 2 pts (1935)

Calamy rev. A. G. Matthews, *Calamy revised* (1934); repr. (1988)

CCI *Calendar of confirmations and inventories granted and given up in the several commissariots of Scotland* (1876–)

CClR *Calendar of the close rolls preserved in the Public Record Office*, 47 vols. (1892–1963)

CDS J. Bain, ed., *Calendar of documents relating to Scotland*, 4 vols., PRO (1881–8); suppl. vol. 5, ed. G. G. Simpson and J. D. Galbraith [1986]

CEPR letters W. H. Bliss, C. Johnson, and J. Twemlow, eds., *Calendar of entries in the papal registers relating to Great Britain and Ireland: papal letters* (1893–)

CGPLA *Calendars of the grants of probate and letters of administration [in 4 ser.: England & Wales, Northern Ireland, Ireland, and Éire]*

Chambers, *Scots.* R. Chambers, ed., *A biographical dictionary of eminent Scotsmen*, 4 vols. (1832–5)

Chancery records chancery records pubd by the PRO

Chancery records (RC) chancery records pubd by the Record Commissions

CIPM	Calendar of inquisitions post mortem, [20 vols.], PRO (1904–); also Henry VII, 3 vols. (1898–1955)
Clarendon, Hist. rebellion	E. Hyde, earl of Clarendon, The history of the rebellion and civil wars in England, 6 vols. (1888); repr. (1958) and (1992)
Cobbett, Parl. hist.	W. Cobbett and J. Wright, eds., Cobbett's Parliamentary history of England, 36 vols. (1806–1820)
Colvin, Archs.	H. Colvin, A biographical dictionary of British architects, 1600–1840, 3rd edn (1995)
Cooper, Ath. Cantab.	C. H. Cooper and T. Cooper, Athenae Cantabrigienses, 3 vols. (1858–1913); repr. (1967)
CPR	Calendar of the patent rolls preserved in the Public Record Office (1891–)
Crockford	Crockford's Clerical Directory
CS	Camden Society
CSP	Calendar of state papers [in 11 ser.: domestic, Scotland, Scottish series, Ireland, colonial, Commonwealth, foreign, Spain [at Simancas], Rome, Milan, and Venice]
CYS	Canterbury and York Society
DAB	Dictionary of American biography, 21 vols. (1928–36), repr. in 11 vols. (1964); 10 suppls. (1944–96)
DBB	D. J. Jeremy, ed., Dictionary of business biography, 5 vols. (1984–6)
DCB	G. W. Brown and others, Dictionary of Canadian biography, [14 vols.] (1966–)
Debrett's Peerage	Debrett's Peerage (1803–) [sometimes Debrett's Illustrated peerage]
Desmond, Botanists	R. Desmond, Dictionary of British and Irish botanists and horticulturists (1977); rev. edn (1994)
Dir. Brit. archs.	A. Felstead, J. Franklin, and L. Pinfield, eds., Directory of British architects, 1834–1900 (1993); 2nd edn, ed. A. Brodie and others, 2 vols. (2001)
DLB	J. M. Bellamy and J. Saville, eds., Dictionary of labour biography, [10 vols.] (1972–)
DLitB	Dictionary of Literary Biography
DNB	Dictionary of national biography, 63 vols. (1885–1900), suppl., 3 vols. (1901); repr. in 22 vols. (1908–9); 10 further suppls. (1912–96); Missing persons (1993)
DNZB	W. H. Oliver and C. Orange, eds., The dictionary of New Zealand biography, 5 vols. (1990–2000)
DSAB	W. J. de Kock and others, eds., Dictionary of South African biography, 5 vols. (1968–87)
DSB	C. C. Gillispie and F. L. Holmes, eds., Dictionary of scientific biography, 16 vols. (1970–80); repr. in 8 vols. (1981); 2 vol. suppl. (1990)
DSBB	A. Slaven and S. Checkland, eds., Dictionary of Scottish business biography, 1860–1960, 2 vols. (1986–90)
DSCHT	N. M. de S. Cameron and others, eds., Dictionary of Scottish church history and theology (1993)
Dugdale, Monasticon	W. Dugdale, Monasticon Anglicanum, 3 vols. (1655–72); 2nd edn, 3 vols. (1661–82); new edn, ed. J. Caley, J. Ellis, and B. Bandinel, 6 vols. in 8 pts (1817–30); repr. (1846) and (1970)
DWB	J. E. Lloyd and others, eds., Dictionary of Welsh biography down to 1940 (1959) [Eng. trans. of Y bywgraffiadur Cymreig hyd 1940, 2nd edn (1954)]
EdinR	Edinburgh Review, or, Critical Journal
EETS	Early English Text Society
Emden, Cam.	A. B. Emden, A biographical register of the University of Cambridge to 1500 (1963)
Emden, Oxf.	A. B. Emden, A biographical register of the University of Oxford to AD 1500, 3 vols. (1957–9); also A biographical register of the University of Oxford, AD 1501 to 1540 (1974)
EngHR	English Historical Review
Engraved Brit. ports.	F. M. O'Donoghue and H. M. Hake, Catalogue of engraved British portraits preserved in the department of prints and drawings in the British Museum, 6 vols. (1908–25)
ER	The English Reports, 178 vols. (1900–32)
ESTC	English short title catalogue, 1475–1800 [CD-ROM and online]
Evelyn, Diary	The diary of John Evelyn, ed. E. S. De Beer, 6 vols. (1955); repr. (2000)
Farington, Diary	The diary of Joseph Farington, ed. K. Garlick and others, 17 vols. (1978–98)
Fasti Angl. (Hardy)	J. Le Neve, Fasti ecclesiae Anglicanae, ed. T. D. Hardy, 3 vols. (1854)
Fasti Angl., 1066–1300	[J. Le Neve], Fasti ecclesiae Anglicanae, 1066–1300, ed. D. E. Greenway and J. S. Barrow, [8 vols.] (1968–)
Fasti Angl., 1300–1541	[J. Le Neve], Fasti ecclesiae Anglicanae, 1300–1541, 12 vols. (1962–7)
Fasti Angl., 1541–1857	[J. Le Neve], Fasti ecclesiae Anglicanae, 1541–1857, ed. J. M. Horn, D. M. Smith, and D. S. Bailey, [9 vols.] (1969–)
Fasti Scot.	H. Scott, Fasti ecclesiae Scoticanae, 3 vols. in 6 (1871); new edn, [11 vols.] (1915–)
FO List	Foreign Office List
Fortescue, Brit. army	J. W. Fortescue, A history of the British army, 13 vols. (1899–1930)
Foss, Judges	E. Foss, The judges of England, 9 vols. (1848–64); repr. (1966)
Foster, Alum. Oxon.	J. Foster, ed., Alumni Oxonienses: the members of the University of Oxford, 1715–1886, 4 vols. (1887–8); later edn (1891); also Alumni Oxonienses … 1500–1714, 4 vols. (1891–2); 8 vol. repr. (1968) and (2000)
Fuller, Worthies	T. Fuller, The history of the worthies of England, 4 pts (1662); new edn, 2 vols., ed. J. Nichols (1811); new edn, 3 vols., ed. P. A. Nuttall (1840); repr. (1965)
GEC, Baronetage	G. E. Cokayne, Complete baronetage, 6 vols. (1900–09); repr. (1983) [microprint]
GEC, Peerage	G. E. C. [G. E. Cokayne], The complete peerage of England, Scotland, Ireland, Great Britain, and the United Kingdom, 8 vols. (1887–98); new edn, ed. V. Gibbs and others, 14 vols. in 15 (1910–98); microprint repr. (1982) and (1987)
Genest, Eng. stage	J. Genest, Some account of the English stage from the Restoration in 1660 to 1830, 10 vols. (1832); repr. [New York, 1965]
Gillow, Lit. biog. hist.	J. Gillow, A literary and biographical history or bibliographical dictionary of the English Catholics, from the breach with Rome, in 1534, to the present time, 5 vols. [1885–1902]; repr. (1961); repr. with preface by C. Gillow (1999)
Gir. Camb. opera	Giraldi Cambrensis opera, ed. J. S. Brewer, J. F. Dimock, and G. F. Warner, 8 vols., Rolls Series, 21 (1861–91)
GJ	Geographical Journal

Gladstone, *Diaries* — *The Gladstone diaries: with cabinet minutes and prime-ministerial correspondence*, ed. M. R. D. Foot and H. C. G. Matthew, 14 vols. (1968–94)

GM — *Gentleman's Magazine*

Graves, *Artists* — A. Graves, ed., *A dictionary of artists who have exhibited works in the principal London exhibitions of oil paintings from 1760 to 1880* (1884); new edn (1895); 3rd edn (1901); facs. edn (1969); repr. [1970], (1973), and (1984)

Graves, *Brit. Inst.* — A. Graves, *The British Institution, 1806–1867: a complete dictionary of contributors and their work from the foundation of the institution* (1875); facs. edn (1908); repr. (1969)

Graves, *RA exhibitors* — A. Graves, *The Royal Academy of Arts: a complete dictionary of contributors and their work from its foundation in 1769 to 1904*, 8 vols. (1905–6); repr. in 4 vols. (1970) and (1972)

Graves, *Soc. Artists* — A. Graves, *The Society of Artists of Great Britain, 1760–1791, the Free Society of Artists, 1761–1783: a complete dictionary* (1907); facs. edn (1969)

Greaves & Zaller, *BDBR* — R. L. Greaves and R. Zaller, eds., *Biographical dictionary of British radicals in the seventeenth century*, 3 vols. (1982–4)

Grove, *Dict. mus.* — G. Grove, ed., *A dictionary of music and musicians*, 5 vols. (1878–90); 2nd edn, ed. J. A. Fuller Maitland (1904–10); 3rd edn, ed. H. C. Colles (1927); 4th edn with suppl. (1940); 5th edn, ed. E. Blom, 9 vols. (1954); suppl. (1961) [see also *New Grove*]

Hall, *Dramatic ports.* — L. A. Hall, *Catalogue of dramatic portraits in the theatre collection of the Harvard College library*, 4 vols. (1930–34)

Hansard — *Hansard's parliamentary debates*, ser. 1–5 (1803–)

Highfill, Burnim & Langhans, *BDA* — P. H. Highfill, K. A. Burnim, and E. A. Langhans, *A biographical dictionary of actors, actresses, musicians, dancers, managers, and other stage personnel in London, 1660–1800*, 16 vols. (1973–93)

Hist. U. Oxf. — T. H. Aston, ed., *The history of the University of Oxford*, 8 vols. (1984–2000) [1: *The early Oxford schools*, ed. J. I. Catto (1984); 2: *Late medieval Oxford*, ed. J. I. Catto and R. Evans (1992); 3: *The collegiate university*, ed. J. McConica (1986); 4: *Seventeenth-century Oxford*, ed. N. Tyacke (1997); 5: *The eighteenth century*, ed. L. S. Sutherland and L. G. Mitchell (1986); 6–7: *Nineteenth-century Oxford*, ed. M. G. Brock and M. C. Curthoys (1997–2000); 8: *The twentieth century*, ed. B. Harrison (2000)]

HJ — *Historical Journal*

HMC — Historical Manuscripts Commission

Holdsworth, *Eng. law* — W. S. Holdsworth, *A history of English law*, ed. A. L. Goodhart and H. L. Hanbury, 17 vols. (1903–72)

HoP, *Commons* — *The history of parliament: the House of Commons* [*1386–1421*, ed. J. S. Roskell, L. Clark, and C. Rawcliffe, 4 vols. (1992); *1509–1558*, ed. S. T. Bindoff, 3 vols. (1982); *1558–1603*, ed. P. W. Hasler, 3 vols. (1981); *1660–1690*, ed. B. D. Henning, 3 vols. (1983); *1690–1715*, ed. D. W. Hayton, E. Cruickshanks, and S. Handley, 5 vols. (2002); *1715–1754*, ed. R. Sedgwick, 2 vols. (1970); *1754–1790*, ed. L. Namier and J. Brooke, 3 vols. (1964), repr. (1985); *1790–1820*, ed. R. G. Thorne, 5 vols. (1986); in draft (used with permission): *1422–1504*, *1604–1629*, *1640–1660*, and *1820–1832*]

IGI — *International Genealogical Index*, Church of Jesus Christ of the Latterday Saints

ILN — *Illustrated London News*

IMC — Irish Manuscripts Commission

Irving, *Scots.* — J. Irving, ed., *The book of Scotsmen eminent for achievements in arms and arts, church and state, law, legislation and literature, commerce, science, travel and philanthropy* (1881)

JCS — *Journal of the Chemical Society*

JHC — *Journals of the House of Commons*

JHL — *Journals of the House of Lords*

John of Worcester, *Chron.* — *The chronicle of John of Worcester*, ed. R. R. Darlington and P. McGurk, trans. J. Bray and P. McGurk, 3 vols., OMT (1995–) [vol. 1 forthcoming]

Keeler, *Long Parliament* — M. F. Keeler, *The Long Parliament, 1640–1641: a biographical study of its members* (1954)

Kelly, *Handbk* — *The upper ten thousand: an alphabetical list of all members of noble families*, 3 vols. (1875–7); continued as *Kelly's handbook of the upper ten thousand for 1878* [1879], 2 vols. (1878–9); continued as *Kelly's handbook to the titled, landed and official classes*, 94 vols. (1880–1973)

LondG — *London Gazette*

LP Henry VIII — J. S. Brewer, J. Gairdner, and R. H. Brodie, eds., *Letters and papers, foreign and domestic, of the reign of Henry VIII*, 23 vols. in 38 (1862–1932); repr. (1965)

Mallalieu, *Watercolour artists* — H. L. Mallalieu, *The dictionary of British watercolour artists up to 1820*, 3 vols. (1976–90); vol. 1, 2nd edn (1986)

Memoirs FRS — *Biographical Memoirs of Fellows of the Royal Society*

MGH — Monumenta Germaniae Historica

MT — *Musical Times*

Munk, *Roll* — W. Munk, *The roll of the Royal College of Physicians of London*, 2 vols. (1861); 2nd edn, 3 vols. (1878)

N&Q — *Notes and Queries*

New Grove — S. Sadie, ed., *The new Grove dictionary of music and musicians*, 20 vols. (1980); 2nd edn, 29 vols. (2001) [also online edn; see also Grove, *Dict. mus.*]

Nichols, *Illustrations* — J. Nichols and J. B. Nichols, *Illustrations of the literary history of the eighteenth century*, 8 vols. (1817–58)

Nichols, *Lit. anecdotes* — J. Nichols, *Literary anecdotes of the eighteenth century*, 9 vols. (1812–16); facs. edn (1966)

Obits. FRS — *Obituary Notices of Fellows of the Royal Society*

O'Byrne, *Naval biog. dict.* — W. R. O'Byrne, *A naval biographical dictionary* (1849); repr. (1990); [2nd edn], 2 vols. (1861)

OHS — Oxford Historical Society

Old Westminsters — *The record of Old Westminsters*, 1–2, ed. G. F. R. Barker and A. H. Stenning (1928); suppl. 1, ed. J. B. Whitmore and G. R. Y. Radcliffe [1938]; 3, ed. J. B. Whitmore, G. R. Y. Radcliffe, and D. C. Simpson (1963); suppl. 2, ed. F. E. Pagan (1978); 4, ed. F. E. Pagan and H. E. Pagan (1992)

OMT — Oxford Medieval Texts

Ordericus Vitalis, *Eccl. hist.* — *The ecclesiastical history of Orderic Vitalis*, ed. and trans. M. Chibnall, 6 vols., OMT (1969–80); repr. (1990)

Paris, *Chron.* — *Matthaei Parisiensis, monachi sancti Albani, chronica majora*, ed. H. R. Luard, Rolls Series, 7 vols. (1872–83)

Parl. papers — *Parliamentary papers* (1801–)

PBA — *Proceedings of the British Academy*

Pepys, *Diary*	*The diary of Samuel Pepys*, ed. R. Latham and W. Matthews, 11 vols. (1970–83); repr. (1995) and (2000)
Pevsner	N. Pevsner and others, Buildings of England series
PICE	*Proceedings of the Institution of Civil Engineers*
Pipe rolls	*The great roll of the pipe for . . .*, PRSoc. (1884–)
PRO	Public Record Office
PRS	*Proceedings of the Royal Society of London*
PRSoc.	Pipe Roll Society
PTRS	*Philosophical Transactions of the Royal Society*
QR	*Quarterly Review*
RC	Record Commissions
Redgrave, *Artists*	S. Redgrave, *A dictionary of artists of the English school* (1874); rev. edn (1878); repr. (1970)
Reg. Oxf.	C. W. Boase and A. Clark, eds., *Register of the University of Oxford*, 5 vols., OHS, 1, 10–12, 14 (1885–9)
Reg. PCS	J. H. Burton and others, eds., *The register of the privy council of Scotland*, 1st ser., 14 vols. (1877–98); 2nd ser., 8 vols. (1899–1908); 3rd ser., [16 vols.] (1908–70)
Reg. RAN	H. W. C. Davis and others, eds., *Regesta regum Anglo-Normannorum, 1066–1154*, 4 vols. (1913–69)
RIBA Journal	*Journal of the Royal Institute of British Architects* [later *RIBA Journal*]
RotP	J. Strachey, ed., *Rotuli parliamentorum ut et petitiones, et placita in parliamento*, 6 vols. (1767–77)
RotS	D. Macpherson, J. Caley, and W. Illingworth, eds., *Rotuli Scotiae in Turri Londinensi et in domo capitulari Westmonasteriensi asservati*, 2 vols., RC, 14 (1814–19)
RS	Record(s) Society
Rymer, *Foedera*	T. Rymer and R. Sanderson, eds., *Foedera, conventiones, literae et cuiuscunque generis acta publica inter reges Angliae et alios quosvis imperatores, reges, pontifices, principes, vel communitates*, 20 vols. (1704–35); 2nd edn, 20 vols. (1726–35); 3rd edn, 10 vols. (1739–45), facs. edn (1967); new edn, ed. A. Clarke, J. Caley, and F. Holbrooke, 4 vols., RC, 50 (1816–30)
Sainty, *Judges*	J. Sainty, ed., *The judges of England, 1272–1990*, SeldS, suppl. ser., 10 (1993)
Sainty, *King's counsel*	J. Sainty, ed., *A list of English law officers and king's counsel*, SeldS, suppl. ser., 7 (1987)
SCH	Studies in Church History
Scots peerage	J. B. Paul, ed. *The Scots peerage, founded on Wood's edition of Sir Robert Douglas's Peerage of Scotland, containing an historical and genealogical account of the nobility of that kingdom*, 9 vols. (1904–14)
SeldS	Selden Society
SHR	*Scottish Historical Review*
State trials	T. B. Howell and T. J. Howell, eds., *Cobbett's Complete collection of state trials*, 34 vols. (1809–28)
STC, 1475–1640	A. W. Pollard, G. R. Redgrave, and others, eds., *A short-title catalogue of . . . English books . . . 1475–1640* (1926); 2nd edn, ed. W. A. Jackson, F. S. Ferguson, and K. F. Pantzer, 3 vols. (1976–91) [see also Wing, *STC*]
STS	Scottish Text Society
SurtS	Surtees Society
Symeon of Durham, *Opera*	*Symeonis monachi opera omnia*, ed. T. Arnold, 2 vols., Rolls Series, 75 (1882–5); repr. (1965)
Tanner, *Bibl. Brit.-Hib.*	T. Tanner, *Bibliotheca Britannico-Hibernica*, ed. D. Wilkins (1748); repr. (1963)
Thieme & Becker, *Allgemeines Lexikon*	U. Thieme, F. Becker, and H. Vollmer, eds., *Allgemeines Lexikon der bildenden Künstler von der Antike bis zur Gegenwart*, 37 vols. (Leipzig, 1907–50); repr. (1961–5), (1983), and (1992)
Thurloe, *State papers*	*A collection of the state papers of John Thurloe*, ed. T. Birch, 7 vols. (1742)
TLS	*Times Literary Supplement*
Tout, *Admin. hist.*	T. F. Tout, *Chapters in the administrative history of mediaeval England: the wardrobe, the chamber, and the small seals*, 6 vols. (1920–33); repr. (1967)
TRHS	*Transactions of the Royal Historical Society*
VCH	H. A. Doubleday and others, eds., *The Victoria history of the counties of England*, [88 vols.] (1900–)
Venn, *Alum. Cant.*	J. Venn and J. A. Venn, *Alumni Cantabrigienses: a biographical list of all known students, graduates, and holders of office at the University of Cambridge, from the earliest times to 1900*, 10 vols. (1922–54); repr. in 2 vols. (1974–8)
Vertue, *Note books*	[G. Vertue], *Note books*, ed. K. Esdaile, earl of Ilchester, and H. M. Hake, 6 vols., Walpole Society, 18, 20, 22, 24, 26, 30 (1930–55)
VF	*Vanity Fair*
Walford, *County families*	E. Walford, *The county families of the United Kingdom, or, Royal manual of the titled and untitled aristocracy of Great Britain and Ireland* (1860)
Walker rev.	A. G. Matthews, *Walker revised: being a revision of John Walker's Sufferings of the clergy during the grand rebellion, 1642–60* (1948); repr. (1988)
Walpole, *Corr.*	*The Yale edition of Horace Walpole's correspondence*, ed. W. S. Lewis, 48 vols. (1937–83)
Ward, *Men of the reign*	T. H. Ward, ed., *Men of the reign: a biographical dictionary of eminent persons of British and colonial birth who have died during the reign of Queen Victoria* (1885); repr. (Graz, 1968)
Waterhouse, *18c painters*	E. Waterhouse, *The dictionary of 18th century painters in oils and crayons* (1981); repr. as *British 18th century painters in oils and crayons* (1991), vol. 2 of *Dictionary of British art*
Watt, *Bibl. Brit.*	R. Watt, *Bibliotheca Britannica, or, A general index to British and foreign literature*, 4 vols. (1824) [many reprs.]
Wellesley index	W. E. Houghton, ed., *The Wellesley index to Victorian periodicals, 1824–1900*, 5 vols. (1966–89); new edn (1999) [CD-ROM]
Wing, *STC*	D. Wing, ed., *Short-title catalogue of . . . English books . . . 1641–1700*, 3 vols. (1945–51); 2nd edn (1972–88); rev. and enl. edn, ed. J. J. Morrison, C. W. Nelson, and M. Seccombe, 4 vols. (1994–8) [see also *STC, 1475–1640*]
Wisden	*John Wisden's Cricketer's Almanack*
Wood, *Ath. Oxon.*	A. Wood, *Athenae Oxonienses . . . to which are added the Fasti*, 2 vols. (1691–2); 2nd edn (1721); new edn, 4 vols., ed. P. Bliss (1813–20); repr. (1967) and (1969)
Wood, *Vic. painters*	C. Wood, *Dictionary of Victorian painters* (1971); 2nd edn (1978); 3rd edn as *Victorian painters*, 2 vols. (1995), vol. 4 of *Dictionary of British art*
WW	*Who's who* (1849–)
WWBMP	M. Stenton and S. Lees, eds., *Who's who of British members of parliament*, 4 vols. (1976–81)
WWW	*Who was who* (1929–)

Patel, Vallabhbhai Jhaverbhai (1875/6–1950), politician in India, was born in the town of Nadiad, Gujarat, some time between October 1875 and May 1876, the arbitrary date of 31 October 1875 being the officially accepted one. Fourth of six children of Jhaverbhai, a 10 acre farmer of Patidar caste, and his wife, Ladba, of Karamsad village, Kaira district, Gujarat, Vallabhbhai spent his youth in the village with his four brothers and a sister. As he was a middle child, his elder brothers were favoured over him both in family matters and in such life opportunities as early schooling. Although Vallabhbhai accepted his secondary position in the family and later in political life out of a sense of propriety and duty, initially to family then to his country, he also developed self-reliance, determination, toughness of spirit and character, mental balance, and a sardonic sense of humour that became his hallmark in life. He married Jhaverba, daughter of Desaibhai Punjabhai Patel, from the nearby village of Gana, in 1893 when he was seventeen or eighteen and she twelve or thirteen. Jhaverba died in January 1909, having borne two children, Manibehn and Dahyabhai, after which Vallabhbhai, thirty-three years of age at the time of his wife's death, never married nor had any known or suspected liaison with another woman.

Vallabhbhai was a relatively short man, 5 feet 5½ inches in height, dour and homely in appearance especially as he aged, whose demeanour exuded far more strength than his height and whose eyes emitted a penetrating glance which gave pause to all who did not know him well. Although he sometimes sacrificed his personal interests to those of his family, particularly his elder brother Vithalbhai Jhaverbhai *Patel, and fulfilled his formal parental duties after his wife's death, there is little evidence in his family relations with wife, children, or siblings of displays of affection, very little of personal attention, and some indication of neglect of his children. His daughter, Manibehn, who never married, nevertheless remained devoted to him, became his personal secretary, and looked after him in later life until his death. Vallabhbhai's close personal relations and affective ties were with a very small number of friends and supporters from the business community, with his closest comrades in the nationalist movement, and most of all with Mahatma Gandhi in his years of maturity and political struggle.

Education and early career Vallabhbhai Patel was a self-made man in all respects, including his education. He began his elementary schooling at the age of seven or eight, entered an English-medium school in his village at the age of fourteen, transferred to another English-medium school in the town of Petlad at the age of seventeen, and finally passed his matriculation exam in Nadiad in 1897, by which time he was already twenty-two years old. He then studied on his own for three years to pass the pleaders' examination, in which he succeeded at the age of twenty-five and after which he set up a practice in criminal law first in the town of Godhra, then in Borsad town. Prospering in his practice, he had saved enough money by 1905 to go to England to train as a barrister. However, at his elder brother Vithalbhai's request, he gave place to him to go in his stead and postponed his own departure for England for five years until 1910, when he entered the Middle Temple. He completed his training within two years, passing his examinations in the first class. During his two years in England he did little but grind, winning the respect of his teachers, but developing no lifelong friendships or new interests.

Back in India in 1913 Patel set up practice in Ahmadabad, Gujarat's principal city, where he soon had enough income to take care of all his family obligations and live the comfortable life of an outwardly Anglicized upper-class Indian, wearing English clothes, playing bridge, and spending his evenings at the Gujarat Club. Respect for his achievements and personal character also earned him a place in the developing political life of Ahmadabad, where he was elected unopposed to the municipal board in 1917, became chairman of its sanitary committee, in which capacity he displayed extraordinary devotion to duty and personal courage in fighting an outbreak of plague, and led a successful agitation for the removal of an unpopular British municipal commissioner. At first cynical towards, and holding aloof from, Mahatma Gandhi, who had recently returned from South Africa, he soon became impressed by the latter's defiance of British authority and began to play a more active part in the political life of the province: addressing political meetings in support of Gandhi's demand for *swaraj* (freedom, independence), intervening along with Gandhi on behalf of textile mill labourers in Ahmadabad, organizing with him a no-tax campaign in Kaira district, and helping Gandhi's recruitment drive on behalf of the British Indian army's participation in the First World War. For his part, Gandhi began to place responsibilities on Patel, appointing him in 1917 secretary of the executive committee of the Gujarat Sabha (association), the precursor of the Gujarat Provincial Congress Committee. In 1921 Patel became the first president of the latter body, a position which he retained until 1946.

Vallabhbhai's participation with Gandhi in the Kaira no-tax campaign was the decisive moment in his life, a turning point after which nothing remained the same. From this point on, in January 1918, Vallabhbhai devoted virtually all his time and energies to political activities and nationalist agitation in which, strong man though he was, he subordinated himself to the authority of Gandhi for the next thirty years to such an extent that he was sometimes described as the latter's 'blind follower', accepting with faith rather than reason his every twist and turn of policy and tactics. Like other nationalist leaders and followers of Gandhi, he abandoned Western clothes in favour of Indian dress, and took up spinning in his moments of relaxation.

Even so, Patel also made a name for himself separate from that of Gandhi. He continued until 1928 to play a dominant role, from 1924 to 1928 as president, in the Ahmadabad municipality. He also acquired a reputation as a man who could be counted upon to organize people and money in times of crisis, as when he took the leadership in famine relief in 1918 and flood and famine relief in 1927–8 in Ahmadabad district.

In 1923 Patel acquired country-wide recognition for his leadership of the flag *satyagraha* in Nagpur, in the Central Provinces, where he led a prolonged agitation against the prohibition by the British district commissioner there of the flying of the Congress-designed national flag of India. At the end of the same year, he also led in his home locality of rural Borsad a successful *satyagraha* campaign demanding the removal of a government-imposed tax upon all the residents of the Borsad *taluka* (administrative subdivision of a district) for their alleged complicity with local dacoits (criminal gangs). Vallabhbhai's most famous campaign was in Bardoli in 1928 when he led a long, hotly contested, but ultimately mostly successful campaign against an increase in the land revenue paid by the peasants in this area of Surat district. It was after this campaign that Vallabhbhai was given the popular title sardar (chief).

Although he adopted with great skill and success Gandhi's methods of non-violent resistance to unjust authority, his organizing abilities and his personal style were his own. In the latter respect, especially, his manner was different from that of Gandhi, for he was as apt to threaten and intimidate his opponents as to persuade them through gentle reason and self-sacrifice. He was known especially in his mature years for his 'iron will', 'nerves of steel', fearlessness, personal courage, bluntness of speech, and 'fighting capacity'. No doubt was ever cast, even by his enemies and political opponents, on his personal integrity, devotion to his country, and his ideals, especially for the independence, self-sufficiency, and unity of India.

Congress leader After the Bardoli campaign, Sardar Patel, as Vallabhbhai was also known, remained one of the best known and respected Congress leaders of the country, but most of his activities from then on until the transfer of power were either as Gandhi's chief lieutenant in national campaigns against British rule or as the principal party and electoral organizer and fund-raiser for the Indian National Congress. Throughout the remainder of his political career, though he was considered one of the four or five topmost Congress leaders of the country, he remained subordinate first to Gandhi and, after Gandhi's death, to Nehru as prime minister. Although he was proposed for president of the Indian National Congress after the Bardoli *satyagraha*, he gave place in 1929 to Jawaharlal Nehru, and did not receive this high honour until 1931. During the nationalist movement, beginning with his first arrest during Gandhi's salt *satyagraha* of 1930, Patel spent many years in gaol. The longest periods were for sixteen months, which he spent with Gandhi, in 1932–4; nine months in 1940–41; and nearly three years from 1942 to 1945.

Patel's importance in the highest councils of the Indian National Congress derived principally from the critical role he played from 1934 onwards within the party organization. Adopting his son's flat in Bombay as his home base from this time forward, he was the principal fund-raiser and played the critical role in the selection of Congress candidates to contest the 1934 elections for the central legislative assembly; again, as chairman of the central parliamentary board, in the selection and financing of candidates for the 1936 provincial elections; and in the constituent assembly elections of 1946 as well, where he came into frequent conflict with the then Congress president, Maulana Abul Kalam Azad, over the selection of Congress candidates. His responsibilities as party/election organizer also included exercising supervision and imposing discipline over the Congress members of provincial legislatures, including their selection of legislative party leaders and consequently the premiers in Congress-controlled provinces. Although his will did not always prevail, he firmly established the principle that the provincial party organizations and the legislative assemblies were subject to the ultimate authority of the national organization and leadership of the Indian National Congress.

By the time of independence Patel was supreme in the party organization in the country, though he was second to Nehru in the government. Although Nehru was the more popular figure in the country and Gandhi's choice for prime minister, Patel demonstrated his ability to checkmate Nehru in the party on several occasions after independence, the most notable being the selection of Rajendra Prasad as India's first president and the victory of his candidate for president of the Indian National Congress in 1950, Purushottam Das Tandon—in both cases against the wishes of Nehru. Nehru was not able, in fact, to assert his primacy over the party organization as well as the government until after Patel's death.

Patel's influence was not, however, by any means confined to the party organization. He was a critical figure as well in the final negotiations with the British concerning the transfer of power, in the deliberations of the constituent assembly, and in the first government of independent India.

On the executive council Patel became home member of the executive council on 3 September 1946. In this capacity he shared authority with Nehru and the Congress president, Azad, in formulating strategy for dealing with the Muslim League demands for Pakistan and with the viceroy in attempting to control the developing violence which surrounded the decision finally to partition India. Although hostile to Jinnah and the Muslim League's demands, Patel was among the earliest of the Congress leaders to accept the impossibility of Congress–League co-operation in an independent India and hence to accept the inevitability of partition. As the violence and mass transfer of populations began between India and Pakistan, Patel pressed Wavell, Colville, and Mountbatten in succession for sterner measures to be taken to control the violence, including the imposition of martial law. However, neither the British rulers nor Patel as home minister after independence proved able to act effectively to stem the violence, which reached terrible proportions during and after the transfer of power. He failed even to bring under control massive rioting in Delhi before extensive violence and murder had taken place. He was blamed also for failing to prevent the murder of Gandhi in Delhi, though he was prevented by Gandhi himself from imposing stricter security measures to protect his life.

Patel also left his imprint upon the constitution of India through his participation as chairman on important committees. His most important interventions involved support for measures to strengthen the central government in relation to the states and governmental authority in relation to society, protect private property against government expropriation without adequate compensation, and promote the unity of the Indian peoples. He supported a clause in the constitution, article 356, empowering the central government to take over the administration of any state under certain circumstances, the right of dispossessed landlords to adequate compensation for their land, the payment of privy purses in perpetuity to the former Indian princes in compensation for the loss of their kingdoms, the maintenance of the status and importance in government of the élite British Indian Civil Service, renamed the Indian administrative service, and the abolition of the system of separate electorates for Hindus, Muslims, and Sikhs.

Deputy prime minister Although there were many occasions of sharp conflict between Patel and Nehru during the period from independence until the former's death, including several when each offered to resign from government because of their differences, the two men nevertheless comprised a duumvirate in which Nehru relied heavily on Patel's advice on many matters of state. As deputy prime minister Patel held three portfolios: home, information and broadcasting, and states. Patel also served as acting prime minister on four occasions. However, the balance in the relationship gradually shifted in favour of Nehru after the death of Gandhi in 1948 and Patel's weakened condition after his first heart attack in March of the same year.

Nevertheless, in his capacity as minister for states, Patel had virtually complete control over one of the most critical matters faced by the government of India during and after the transfer of power from Britain, namely, the integration into the Indian Union of the now formally independent princely states. With the able assistance of his principal secretary, V. P. Menon, Patel bargained with, cajoled, and threatened when necessary the 562 rajas and maharajas into giving up their rule and acceding to the Indian Union. When even threats failed, Patel did not shrink from the use of armed force, as in the case of both the tiny state of Junagarh, and the much larger state of Hyderabad. In the case of Kashmir, however, Patel played a strongly supportive, but secondary role to Nehru, who took the integration of that state into the Indian Union as his personal responsibility.

Assessment and death Although Patel never developed a systematic set of ideas for India's political development, economic policies, or foreign relations, he had strong views on many matters, which were expressed in his actions and statements. He stood for the transformation of India into a major industrial power, which he thought could be achieved only by a strong, centralized state. Although not averse to a governmental role in industrial development and agrarian transformation, he did not support assaults against private industrial and commercial enterprises. He was sharply critical of and opposed politically the communist and socialist parties and their leaders, whose ideas he considered unrealistic and irrelevant to Indian society and economy. In agriculture he supported the rights of peasant proprietors against both the former landlords and the state. He opposed the demands for the reorganization of the internal boundaries of the Indian states on linguistic grounds as a potential threat to Indian unity, and favoured the adoption of Hindi as the official language of the country. As home minister he used his powers of arrest to stave off militant Sikh demands in Delhi for a special status for the Sikhs in Punjab. Although he declared his belief in the secular ideology of the Indian state, he adopted a patronizing attitude towards the Muslims who remained in India after partition, while on the other hand accepting as patriotic Indians the members of the militant Hindu organization, the Rashtriya Swayamsevak Sangh (RSS). He disputed the complicity of this organization in the murder of Mahatma Gandhi and urged an early removal of the ban imposed on it after Gandhi's assassination. However, Patel took a much stronger stand against communists: he successfully piloted the Preventive Detention Act through parliament in February 1950; it was intended to strengthen the government's ability to detain communists in gaol for longer periods without trial than the courts were willing to allow.

In foreign relations Patel took such a strong stand in favour of sanctions against Pakistan after partition that he earned the displeasure of Gandhi. He took a position opposite to that of Nehru in relation to Tibet and China, adopting an attitude of distrust towards China in general, condemnation of the Chinese invasion of Tibet in particular, and a willingness to provide Indian diplomatic support to Tibet. He favoured strong condemnation of North Korea's aggression against South Korea in June 1950. Nor did he share the mistrust of Nehru and others on the left in Indian politics of the United States and their reluctance to accept US aid. Patel also supported strongly the maintenance of India's membership in the Commonwealth.

Patel had his second heart attack on 15 November 1950 in New Delhi; it left him unable to function effectively. He returned to his flat in Bombay on 12 December and died there on 15 December. He was cremated the same day at the public cremation ground in Sonepur, Bombay. Although he had made money in his early career as a lawyer and had many friends among the industrial and commercial magnates of Ahmadabad and Bombay, Patel always lived simply in modest accommodation in Ahmadabad and Bombay, and left no substantial property to his descendants.

PAUL R. BRASS

Sources R. Gandhi, *Patel: a life* (1991) · D. Das, ed., *Sardar Patel's correspondence, 1945–50*, 10 vols. (1971) · P. N. Chopra, ed., *The collected*

works of Sardar Vallabhbhai Patel, 10 vols. (1990) · N. D. Parikh, *Sardar Vallabhbhai Patel*, 2 vols. (1953–6) · D. Hardiman, *Peasant nationalists of Gujarat: Kheda district, 1917–1934* (1981) · R. D. Shankardass, *Vallabhbhai Patel: power and organization in Indian politics* (1988) · R. Kumar, ed., *Life and work of Sardar Vallabhbhai Patel* (1991) · V. P. Menon, *The transfer of power in India* (1957)
Archives Maharashtra State Archives, Bombay, India · Navajivan Trust, Ahmadabad, India · National Archives of India, New Delhi · Sardar Vallabhbhai Patel Memorial Society, Ahmadabad, India | FILM BFI NFTVA, news footage
Likenesses statue on monument, Patel Chowk, Parliament Street, New Delhi, India

Patel, Vithalbhai Jhaverbhai (1873–1933), Indian nationalist and politician, the son of Jhaverbhai, a 10 acre farmer, and his wife, Ladba, was born on 27 September 1873 at his mother's home town of Nadiad and brought up in his father's village of Karamsad. Both of these places were in the rich farming tract of the Charotar, located in Kaira district, in central Gujarat (then in the Bombay presidency). He was the third of five brothers, the fourth brother being Vallabhbhai *Patel (1875/6–1950), the future deputy prime minister of India. He was of the Patidar caste, the dominant agricultural community of the area and an important force in the political life of the region. His own family was of high status in the caste, but not affluent. He was married at the age of nine to Diwaliben (d. 1910) who came from nearby Sojitra. They had no children.

Vithalbhai broke with family tradition, studied English and became a pleader in local courts in Gujarat. He and Vallabhbhai, who followed in his footsteps, specialized in criminal law, gaining a reputation for being able to secure acquittals in even the toughest of cases. After a few years' practice they had earned sufficient money to be able to finance further legal studies in England, Vithalbhai going first and being called to the bar by Lincoln's Inn in 1908. On his return to India he practised as a barrister in Bombay. He became involved in nationalist politics, and in 1911 he gave up his practice to become a full-time politician. He was elected to the Bombay legislative council in 1913, rising rapidly to prominence as a tireless opponent of British officialdom. He made vigorous attempts to secure for Indians a wider scope in public life. In 1918 he was elected to the central legislative council which sat in Delhi and Simla.

At this time the Indian nationalist movement was moving in a more radical direction under the leadership of M. K. Gandhi, and Patel, disappointed by the limited reach of the Montagu–Chelmsford constitutional reforms and the shameless reaction in right-wing circles in Britain to the Amritsar massacre of 1919, threw his support behind Gandhi, resigned his council seat, and became a leading figure in the non-co-operation movement of 1920–22. Although he worked closely with Gandhi at this time, he was never a 'Gandhian' in the sense of believing in non-violence as an absolute principle. After Gandhi called off the movement suddenly in 1922, he decided to return to legislative politics, even though this flouted the then Congress line. He was elected to the Indian legislative assembly in 1923, becoming its first Indian president (equivalent of speaker) in 1925.

Of this phase in his career it has been said that his venerable white-bearded appearance concealed a considerable fund of sheer *gaminerie*. His position allowed him to devise numerous means of harassing leading officials in the assembly and making the government of India look ridiculous. He was also instrumental in preventing the government from implementing repressive legislation designed to curb nationalist activity. In 1929 moves by supporters of the government to have him removed as president were thwarted only by the intervention of the viceroy, Lord Irwin, who was at the time trying to win over the radical nationalists to his side.

This Irwin failed to do, leading to Gandhi's launching of the civil disobedience movement in 1930. Patel resigned from the assembly in sympathy with this protest and was subsequently imprisoned. His health was deteriorating, and on his release in 1931 he went to Europe to seek medical aid. After stays in London and Vienna, he died in Geneva on 22 October 1933 and was cremated in Bombay on 10 November. In recognition of his great contribution to the Indian nationalist cause, a statue of him was erected in Bombay, the city which he had adopted as his home and represented in the legislative assembly. Being located on Chowpatty beach, the premier gathering place of the city, it has become a familiar landmark of modern Bombay.

DAVID HARDIMAN

Sources G. Patel, *Vithalbhai Patel: life and times* (1951) · D. Hardiman, *Peasant nationalists of Gujarat: Kheda district, 1917–1934* (1981) · *The Times* (23 Oct 1933)
Archives SOUND BL NSA, oral history interview
Likenesses photograph, repro. in Patel, *Vithalbhai Patel* · photograph, Nehru Memorial Museum and Library, New Delhi · statue, Chowpatty Beach, Bombay

Pater, Clara Ann (bap. 1841, d. 1910), tutor and promoter of the higher education of women, was baptized at St Thomas's, Stepney, on 5 September 1841. She was the youngest of four children of Maria Hill Pater (bap. 1803, d. 1854) and Richard Glode Pater (1797?–1842), surgeon, of Honduras Terrace, Commercial Road, Stepney, London, and the sister of William, Hester, and Walter *Pater. Deprived by death of her father almost immediately and of her mother in 1854, Clara was an orphan by the age of thirteen. She was among the last generation of middle-class women whose entire education was privately at home. Early in 1853 the family moved from Enfield, Middlesex, to Harbledown, Kent, to accommodate Walter's attendance at the King's School, Canterbury; and when in 1858 Walter left for Oxford, the sisters, accompanied by their aunt, departed for Germany to complete their education. Their aunt's death and Walter's degree coinciding almost precisely, Clara and Hester returned to London in early 1863 to live with another relative, Foster Pater. It is probable that in these London years, Clara first tutored students privately, initially in German, an occupation which she continued in Oxford where, in 1869, the two sisters joined their brother.

Having learned both Latin and Greek after her return

from Germany, Clara Pater was coaching pupils in classics in Oxford by 1879. While there is no record of her attending any of the London colleges which offered classical languages to occasional students, in 1874–5 she, along with Mary Ward and Louise Creighton, attended a Latin class in Oxford, offered by Henry Nettleship. Mary Ward suggests that at twenty-four or twenty-five Clara was 'intelligent, alive, sympathetic, with a delightful humour and a strong judgment, but without much positive acquirement. Then after some years, she began to learn Latin and Greek with a view to teaching' (H. Ward, 124). Another view of these years is that of Mark Pattison, the rector of Lincoln College, who writes in his diary of Clara's 'unhappy nihilistic state of mind' (25 June 1877) and of having her to dine with a suffrage speaker (12 April 1878). From 1879 Clara Pater served women students as coach in classics and German, and as resident tutor in classics at Somerville from 1885, when the Paters left their north Oxford house and moved to Kensington. Later she taught Virginia Woolf and others at the ladies' department, King's College, London, where she was lecturer in Greek and Latin from 1898 to 1900. While Clara's acquisition of competence in classics, a key, gendered subject, was informal and scrappy compared with Walter's, she eventually shared with her brother the vocation of classics don, she at Somerville and King's and he at Brasenose.

Clara Pater's contribution to the higher education of women at Oxford was not confined to teaching. An early member of Louise Creighton's Committee of Oxford Lectures for Ladies (c.1873), she was also an active participant and committee member of the Association for Promoting the Higher Education of Women in Oxford, founded in 1878, which became responsible for the academic arrangements and teaching for Lady Margaret Hall and Somerville. In the absence of Madeleine Shaw Lefevre, the first principal of Somerville, Clara Pater served as acting principal in the autumn of 1880, and again in Shaw Lefevre's absence on leave in the Lent and summer terms of 1885. She resigned as resident tutor after nine years in June 1894, before Walter's death in July, after which she decided, at fifty-three, to leave Somerville and Oxford altogether, and to return to Kensington. There is other evidence that Clara Pater found her work uncongenial: references to her health as 'not strong', to her low tolerance of fools, and to her strong opinions are reinforced by the impression of a distinct coolness on the part of Miss Lefevre toward her deputy. Moreover, as a tutor to students whose formal qualifications soon outstripped hers, Clara Pater's position as a teacher became anomalous. It is possible also that her position was not made easier by her association with her brother at Brasenose, in a period when the success of the women's colleges was felt to depend very heavily on their respectability.

In London, Walter Pater's renown was likely to recommend Clara Pater rather than endanger her, as Virginia Woolf's choice of Clara as her classics tutor shows. Woolf's impressions of Clara are recorded in her correspondence (1900–05), and there are two fictional traces, Julia Craye in 'Slater's Pins Have No Points' in *Moments of Being*, and Lucy Craddock in *The Pargiters*. The implications in Woolf's fiction regarding Clara Pater's homosexual orientation are anticipated by Vernon Lee who situates her among the Souls (*Vernon Lee's Letters*, 348). However, apart from Woolf's letters, and records at King's College, London, which show Clara Pater left owing to ill health, and despite A. C. Benson's diary and extant correspondence of Thomas Wright, Edmund Gosse, the Macmillans, and of Clara Pater herself, little is known of her London life. Unlike her Oxford friends, Charlotte Green, Louise Creighton, and Mary Ward, she did not sign Ward's 'Appeal against suffrage' in the *Nineteenth Century* (June 1889), nor does it seem that she joined the latter's Anti-Suffrage League in 1908. Clara Pater probably never published, although she is mentioned by Oscar Wilde and others as a prospective contributor to contemporary journals. She died, unmarried, of cancer at her home, 6 Canning Place, Kensington, on 9 August 1910, and was buried the same day in Holywell cemetery, Oxford, in Walter Pater's tomb, inscribed only as 'sister'.

LAUREL BRAKE

Sources Somerville College, Oxford, Somerville College MSS · calendars and minutes of management, King's Lond., Ladies' Department · M. Pattison, diary, Bodl. Oxf., MS Pattison 130 · *Vernon Lee's letters*, ed. I. C. Willis (privately printed, London, 1937) · *Memoir of a Victorian woman: reflections of Louise Creighton, 1850–1936*, ed. J. T. Covert (1994) · Mrs H. Ward, *A writer's recollections* (1918) · J. Courtney, *An Oxford portrait gallery* (1931) · T. H. Ward MSS, UCL · d. cert. · *CGPLA Eng. & Wales* (1910) · *IGI* · D. Ward, journal, UCL
Archives Brasenose College, Oxford | BL, Macmillan MSS · Indiana University, Bloomington, Lilly Library, Wright MSS
Likenesses T. B. Wirgman, watercolour drawing, 1870, Somerville College, Oxford · photographs, 1885–94, Somerville College, Oxford · L. Dickinson, oils, 1896, Somerville College, Oxford
Wealth at death £50 1s. 8d.: probate, 15 Oct 1910, *CGPLA Eng. & Wales*

Pater, John Edward (1911–1989), civil servant, was born on 15 March 1911 at 9 The Square, East Retford, Nottinghamshire, the son of Edward Rhodes Pater (1866–1942), pharmaceutical chemist, and his wife, Lilian, née Oswald, (b. 1866). He was educated at Retford high school, and then King Edward VI School, Retford, before becoming a foundation scholar at Queens' College, Cambridge, where he graduated with first-class honours in French (1932) and German (1933) in part one of the medieval and modern languages tripos. On 16 July 1938 he married Margaret Anderson Furtado (b. 1911), daughter of Montague Cornwell Furtado, retired civil servant; they had two sons and a daughter.

Pater entered the civil service in 1933 in the Ministry of Health. At a time when prospects for early promotion were bleak his worth was recognized early. He was appointed private secretary to the chief medical officer, and in 1936 to the permanent secretary. In 1941 he was introduced to the work which was to dominate his career—the future organization of hospital services—when he accompanied the surveyors and wrote much of the Gray–Topping report on London hospitals. From 1943 to 1946 he had a leading part in the formulation of plans for a new health service and in the tortuous negotiations and frequent modifications leading to the proposals eventually put before parliament. He was responsible for preparing the instructions for parliamentary counsel for the 1946 legislation.

As under-secretary from 1946 Pater had the task of ensuring that the terms of the legislation were made clear to the new hospital authorities. Most of the advice and guidance to them was written by him personally. The orderly transfer of hospitals from their former owners and the establishment of a coherent practice were achieved without major problems, a tribute to his skill in interpreting and explaining government policy. He remained in charge of the ministry's hospitals division until 1960, being appointed CB in 1953.

This long period in which Pater rendered invaluable service to the National Health Service impressed his reputation on those with whom he dealt, but possibly did not favour his career prospects. He became regarded as something of a specialist. This—and a strong sense of what was right and had to be fought for, sometimes expressed in opposition to policy proposals which he felt were being subordinated to the image of policy (though he was always loyal to decisions made)—did not help his advancement. He remained an under-secretary. He was director of establishments from 1960 to 1965 and from then until he retired in October 1973 took charge of the ministry's division dealing with local authority services, demonstrating his great interest in social services and his support for the recommendations of the Seebohm committee.

Both John Pater's grandfathers had been Wesleyan Methodist ministers, and work for the Methodist church formed a prominent part of his life. He held numerous offices in the Croydon circuit and then nationally. From 1959 to 1973 he was treasurer of the Methodist church department of connexional funds and finance board.

After retirement Pater was persuaded to write an account of the events surrounding the creation of the National Health Service. His book *The Making of the National Health Service* was published by King Edward's Hospital Fund in 1981. Although in a unique position to comment on the controversial negotiations which preceded the 1946 act, he eschewed anecdotes and personal reminiscences and drew his material entirely from sources in the Public Record Office and elsewhere. He was a great believer in the anonymity of civil servants. As a result of this work he was awarded a PhD in 1988 by the University of Cambridge.

Hill walking had always been a favourite pursuit but participation in this and an early interest in archaeology were severely limited by the burden of official and church work, by recurrent asthma and, in later years, by near blindness. Pater died in Croydon on 27 October 1989, and was cremated at Croydon crematorium. His wife survived him.   RAYMOND GEDLING

Sources private information (2004) [widow] • family records • personal knowledge (2004) • *WWW* • b. cert. • m. cert. • F. Honigsbaum, *Health, happiness and security: the creation of the national health service* (1989) • *CGPLA Eng. & Wales* (1990)
Archives CAC Cam., papers
Wealth at death £15,535: probate, 12 Jan 1990, *CGPLA Eng. & Wales*

Pater, Walter Horatio (1839–1894), author and aesthete, was born on 4 August 1839 at 1 Honduras Terrace, Commercial Road, Stepney, London, the third of the four children of Richard Glode Pater (1797?–1842), surgeon, and Maria Hill (*bap.* 1803, *d.* 1854). Ancestors of the Paters had come to England from the Netherlands in the seventeenth century and settled in Buckinghamshire. Pater's siblings comprised the eldest, William (1835–1887), who qualified as a surgeon and ultimately directed the Staffordshire county hospital for the mentally ill; Hester (Totty; 1837–1922), an accomplished embroiderer and friend of Mrs Humphry Ward and Virginia Woolf; and Clara Ann *Pater (*bap.* 1841, *d.* 1910), a founder and tutor of Somerville College, Oxford. The children's father died in 1842 when Walter was two, and the remaining extended family, including his widow, the four children, a paternal grandmother, and an aunt, left Stepney later that year for Grove Street near Victoria Park. This move to a more salubrious setting in suburban South Hackney brought them into the parish of the Revd Henry Handley Norris, influential leader of the high Anglican Hackney Phalanx. By 1847 the family had moved even further north of the conurbation, to rural Enfield in Middlesex. In both Hackney and Enfield the children were tutored privately at home until, from 1851, the boys peeled away: by that year William was at work, and in 1852–3, at twelve, Walter attended Enfield grammar school for a year, where he was known as Parson Pater.

Youth and friendships By early 1853 the family had moved to Harbledown, Kent, a county in which Pater's cousins resided, in order for Walter to attend the King's School, Canterbury, as a day boy. A year later, in February 1854, his mother died. Orphaned at fourteen and forced to confront the reality of death, he may have been particularly open to two aspects of his school life: the relationship between the King's School and the great cathedral at Canterbury on whose precincts the school buildings border, and the forging of close male friendships. If the cathedral reinforced the young man's imaginative involvement with religious experience in its widest sense, his close friendships with Henry Dombrain (from 1854) and John Rainier McQueen (from 1855), with whom he made up 'the triumvirate', established a pattern of shared studies, country rambles, and an enthusiasm for church services which is echoed in subsequent friendships with, for example, his student and colleague C. L. Shadwell at the beginning of his career and F. W. Bussell, the chaplain of Brasenose College, at its end. Certainly, diverse forms of Christianity and other systems of belief were to retain importance to him through periods of commitment to religion, repudiation of it, and ambivalence.

While at school Pater read works by contemporaries such as Tennyson, Ruskin (*Modern Painters*), and Dickens

Walter Horatio Pater (1839–1894), by Elliott & Fry, 1890s

(*Little Dorrit*), and wrote poetry of his own, some of which juvenilia is preserved in archives and biographies. According to McQueen (Wright, *Life* and *Autobiography*) Pater suffered a difficult period of religious doubt in 1857–8 and broke up the triumvirate as he prepared to leave for university. Having matriculated at Queen's College, Oxford, in June 1858, he left the King's School in August with prizes for Latin and ecclesiastical history, and an exhibition supplemented by an additional sum, probably from the McQueens. The tenuous income of the Pater family is also signalled at this moment of financial pressure by the abandonment of the Harbledown house and the departure of Hester, Clara, and their aunt for Heidelberg, where the girls could live cheaply chaperoned by their aunt, learn German with a view to teach, and perhaps take pupils in English.

At Queen's, Pater read classics; his tutor was W. W. Capes, a young non-clerical fellow whose special interest was ancient history and whose lectures stimulated students to read widely and so critically that when he took orders in 1862, many were surprised. In the wake of the Oxford Movement, Matthew Arnold's displacement of religion by culture, and the claims of science, debates within and about Anglicanism permeated all aspects of university culture in the late 1850s: by 1860, when Benjamin Jowett, a fellow of Balliol College and one of the 'seven against Christ' who contributed to *Essays and Reviews* (1860), offered to tutor Pater and his close friend Ingram Bywater, their association with Jowett located them among the renegades.

During the summer and autumn of 1860 McQueen angrily ended his friendship with Pater, for reasons he was never prepared to clarify, but his denunciation of Pater's apostasy to the bishop of London in 1862—when Pater was considering ordination—suggests that Pater's contact with Jowett did indeed signify an alliance with scepticism and the 'higher criticism' of the Bible as practised by German critics. Further understanding of the unspeakable reasons for McQueen's break with Pater may lie in Bywater's claim that, contrary to Edmund Gosse's account in the 1895 volume of the *Dictionary of National Biography*, in these early Oxford years Pater and Bywater shared 'a certain sympathy with a certain aspect of Greek life' (Jackson, 79). Pater's earliest published review essays, 'Coleridge's writings' (1866) and 'Winckelmann' (1867), respectively articulate these two alleged positions, on religion and sexual orientation, as do two unpublished essays of 1864, 'Diaphaneite', and the lost 'Subjective immortality' on Fichte written for the university essay society, Old Mortality, to which Pater and Bywater were elected in that year. So theologically objectionable was the Fichte essay in its denial of a Christian afterlife, that on hearing of it Canon Liddon, an active defender of the high-church party at Oxford, and Gerard Manley Hopkins, then an undergraduate, started a rival, Christian, society, the Hexameron. In 1864 too, Pater burnt his poetry, much of which had been religious, signalling his break with Christianity at this time.

Fellow of Brasenose In December 1862, disappointed with his (second-class) degree results in *literae humaniores*, Pater left Queen's; he moved to rooms in the High Street, Oxford, and began coaching, and attempted first to gain a curacy and then, stymied by McQueen's opposition, to seek fellowships, the first two unsuccessfully, perhaps *because* they were clerical. In February 1864 he was elected as a probationer to the first non-clerical fellowship at Brasenose College in classics; he tutored from the outset, and opted to lecture from 1867. Having installed his sisters in London just after he took his degree (his aunt, their chaperone, had died in Dresden), he was free in 1865 to vacate his High Street rooms for the unattached, male community at Brasenose, where he resided between 1865 and 1869. Among his tutorial students was Gerard Manley Hopkins; among his close friends in Oxford, Mary Arnold, Ingram Bywater, Mark and Emilia Pattison, C. L. Shadwell, T. H. Ward, and T. H. Warren; at Eton was Oscar Browning.

It was during this period of bachelor existence as a young fellow that Pater wrote three outspoken but anonymous review essays for the *Westminster Review* which were to set the tone, in their various assaults on orthodoxy, for his subsequent reputation and work. In the first, 'Coleridge's writings', he decries theological and philosophical absolutism; in 'Winckelmann' he explores a more corporeal aesthetic, unmistakably portraying Winckelmann's advocacy of the Hellenic and the homoerotic; in 'The poetry of William Morris' (1868), a substantial critique which makes explicit the links between Pater and his Pre-Raphaelite contemporaries, Pater is among the early advocates and definers of 'aesthetic poetry'. Culminating in a conclusion which reflects Morris's Pre-Raphaelite poetry of the 1850s and 1860s, the review recommends the cultivation of a life of 'highest' moments, free from dogma, to which aim—'to burn always with this hard, gem-like flame'—art and poetry lead most directly but not exclusively: allowance is made 'for the face of one's friend', continuing the homosexual motif of 'Winckelmann'. These earliest published pieces, written for the 'wicked *Westminster*', continued to attract controversy throughout Pater's career, and the 'Conclusion' from the Morris essay, denounced from pulpits and adopted by aesthetes, was to remain the keynote of Pater's reputation as a 'Protestant Verlaine' (Moore, 529) even while it swelled to include art history, the novel, the short story, classical philosophy, and archaeology.

In 1869 Pater and his sisters took a house at 2 Bradmore Road in north Oxford, joining a community which had as its typical resident a new kind of Oxford academic, the married fellow, whose existence gradually leavened the male, homosocial, and clerical community of the university which Pater and his contemporaries had entered. At Bradmore Road, Pater's social life expanded through entertaining and living with his sisters, the younger of whom, Clara, learned Latin with other female neighbours and helped to organize the Association for Promoting the Education of Women and to create Somerville College. From 1869 Pater began to dress like a dandy, wearing a top hat, apple-green tie, and pigskin gloves, and in that year he began a signed series of four articles in the *Fortnightly Review* on Renaissance subjects. The first, on Leonardo da Vinci (1869), included the now famous invocation of the Mona Lisa which begins 'She is as old as the rocks upon which she sits', the influence of which Yeats articulated and perpetuated late into the twentieth century when he printed this passage as the first poem in his *Oxford Book of English Verse* (1939). This first *Fortnightly* article of 1869 was the début of the association between Pater's name and literary style, for which his work came to be well known. Pieces on Botticelli, Pico della Mirandola, and Michelangelo followed, and in 1872 he collected these and 'Winckelmann', combined them with new essays produced expressly for his book, including a 'Preface' which drew on existing material (from 'Diaphaneite' and 'Coleridge's writings'), and appended the 'Conclusion' from the Morris essay, to form *Studies in the History of the Renaissance* (1873). This process of cultural production—accreting work over time and reproducing, reordering, and cutting and pasting it to form a shaped sequence—was to characterize, in various permutations, all of his subsequent books except *Marius the Epicurean*, which alone did not benefit from the system of pre-book serialization. However, truncated from its origins in the *Westminster Review*, the anonymous addendum to the review of Morris's work, recirculated and relocated as the famous 'Conclusion' to the signed volume of 1873, proved troublesome in its new context, being withdrawn in 1877 and reinstated in 1888. The same controversy attached to the body of the Morris review when, after twenty years, it was reintroduced in

1889 in *Appreciations* as 'Aesthetic poetry', only to be removed from the second edition of 1890.

In *Studies* Pater drew on current scholarship, extending the period and location of the Renaissance from sixteenth- and seventeenth-century Italy to fifteenth-century provincial France and eighteenth-century Germany, and the term 'Renaissance' from its historical manifestation in specific periods and locations to an idea which is transhistorical. He was to do likewise with the terms Romantic and classical in 1876 in his essay on Romanticism. Moreover, the 'Preface' of *Studies* directly addressed Matthew Arnold, deftly turning his emphasis on the quiddity of the object 'as it really is' to the subjective: 'What does it mean to me?' The volume was also notable for its admixture of genres—history, criticism, biography, portraiture—and its adherence to gendered discourse, in which homosocial histories and aesthetics were pursued and delineated. *Studies* attracted attention, in the press where its claim as 'history' was denied, in the pulpits of the university where the hedonism of the 'Conclusion' was rejected and its danger for students proclaimed by W. W. Capes and others, and at Brasenose where John Wordsworth, a colleague, objected privately by letter. Oscar Wilde's repeated designation of *Studies* as his 'golden book' from the late 1870s promulgated its notoriety to a wider public and for a longer period than it might otherwise have penetrated. It was twelve years before Pater dared to publish his next book.

A leading aesthete Through *Studies*, Pater was now publicly linked by reputation with the aesthetic school and the unorthodox sexualities associated with it through the work and lives of A. C. Swinburne and D. G. Rossetti. For those in a position to know, this was confirmed by knowledge of Pater's intimacy with the painter Simeon Solomon and Swinburne between the late 1860s and February 1873, the month in which *Studies* appeared, and Solomon was charged with gross indecency and imprisoned. A year later it was Pater's turn: in February 1874 letters signed 'yours lovingly', from Pater to a Balliol undergraduate, William Money Hardinge, were passed to the master of Balliol and resulted in the temporary suspension of Hardinge and a threat of exposure for Pater; interviewed by Jowett, Pater was warned to avoid application for any university post, and soon after he was passed over for the post of university proctor. Without much independent income, and helping to support both his sisters at that time, he was economically vulnerable; he needed to retain the salary attached to his fellowship, tutoring, and lecturing.

The danger of expulsion was real enough, as the ousting of J. A. Symonds from Oxford (1862) and Oscar Browning from Eton (1875) exemplified. Public and often homophobic hostility to aestheticism in the press, such as the Revd R. Tyrwhitt's article 'The Greek spirit in modern literature' (1877), and the verdict in the *Ruskin v. Whistler* libel case (1878), articulated and influenced public morality. If the portrayal of Pater as the aesthete Mr Rose in W. H. Mallock's satire *The New Republic* (June–December 1876) was more playful and benign, it nevertheless served to circulate Pater's reputation for hedonism, and to feed suspicion of his moral and sexual orthodoxy. The combination of this external pressure and his vulnerability at the university moved him to suppress the 'Conclusion' in the second edition of *Studies* (published as *The Renaissance: Studies in Art and Poetry*) in 1877, and in 1878 contributed in part to his decision not to publish a second book, *Dionysus and other Studies*, though type was set and the volume advertised. He also withdrew his applications for two university posts vacated by Matthew Arnold and John Ruskin respectively, the professorship of poetry in 1877 and the Slade professorship of fine art in 1885.

However, in parallel with these strategic acts of self-censorship after *Studies*, Pater continued to publish signed articles at regular intervals in the *Fortnightly Review* and *Macmillan's Magazine*, first on English literature, then more boldly, again, on Renaissance art ('Giorgione'). In 1876 he lectured and published three articles on ancient Greek texts and myths (Demeter and Persephone, and Dionysus) which permitted him to reiterate and explore moments of 'high passion', sexuality, and violence. In 1879, following the cancellation of his book, he published nothing, but in 1880 three more Greek studies appeared, and an essay on Coleridge, the first of two he was to contribute to T. H. Ward's Macmillan anthology *The English Poets*, the second being on D. G. Rossetti (1883). Besides bringing together his teaching (of classics) and his writing in this period, he developed the portrait/biographies of *Studies* into a hybrid genre of fiction and history which he called the 'imaginary portrait'. In 1878 the first, an autobiographical short story called 'The Child in the House', appeared in *Macmillan's Magazine*, and with the aim of writing a novel, he published very little between 1881 and 1884; in 1882 he travelled to Rome to research it, and in 1883 resigned his tutorship.

Marius the Epicurean, Pater's only finished novel, appeared in March 1885 in two volumes. Set in a period of transition between decadent classicism and new Christianity, in the Rome of Marcus Aurelius, *Marius* deals with questions of morality, Christianity, and gender in a structure which resolutely extends the boundaries of fiction to history and criticism, in a style which is elaborately literary. In the third edition of *The Renaissance* in 1888, Pater restored the 'Conclusion' excluded from the 1877 edition and, in a note of explanation, linked the critique it provoked with *Marius*; situating that novel as a response to the 'Conclusion', he claims that *Marius* dealt 'more fully … with the thoughts suggested by it'. An extended imaginary portrait, *Marius the Epicurean* reproduces too the gendered discourse of *Studies*, echoing its succession of male protagonists and pairs, and barely acknowledging the heterosexual exigencies of English fiction in this respect.

Marius seemed to liberate Pater at last from the shadow of controversy, a liberation which may have been enhanced by the transfer of the household from Oxford to 12 Earl's Terrace, Kensington, London, soon after *Marius* appeared, in August 1885. Under the new arrangement

Clara and Walter spent term-time in their respective college rooms in Oxford, and vacations and occasional weekends in the London house which Hester ran. A contemporary impression of the effect on Pater may be judged by perusing a pair of drawings by Charles Holmes, one of Pater unkempt in Oxford and the other of the dapper man of town in London. But it was probably liberating for Pater at both ends, from his sisters and domestic life in Oxford and from his colleagues in London.

Later works The second half of the 1880s proved one of Pater's most prolific periods; he published two books which rapidly went into second editions, a number of articles and reviews, and an unfinished serialized novel. *Imaginary Portraits* (1887) consisted of four short stories about four young men defined historically and geographically, but distant from the present and each other; all die young. 'A Prince of Court Painters' takes as its subject a student of Watteau, the Flemish painter Jean Baptiste Pater, whom the author regarded as his ancestor. 'Gaston de Latour', six chapters of which appeared between June 1888 and August 1889, similarly blends history and fiction and conforms to the pattern of the imaginary portrait; Pater described it in an undated letter as 'a sort of Marius in France, in the 16th Century' (*Letters*, 126).

Appreciations: with an Essay on 'Style' (1889) is Pater's only volume of literary criticism and his sole treatment of English literature, though contemporary reviewers noted the French origins of its title and its title-essay which is based on an earlier anonymous review of Flaubert. 'Greek as Mr. Pater is in soul, his models of style are all French', noted *Blackwood's Edinburgh Magazine* (Oliphant, 144). Pater dug deep to construct this eclectic book, which included articles originating in the 1860s, 1870s, and 1880s. Two theoretical pieces, 'Style' and 'Postscript', which frame the collection take issue with Matthew Arnold, 'Style' promulgating 'imaginative prose' rather than poetry as 'the special art of the modern world', and 'Postscript' Romanticism over the classical. Although *Appreciations* devotes no single essay to the English novel, its foregrounding in 'Style' of formal stylistic elements as the basis of good literature and the quality of the matter as the mark of great literature may be read as a tacit support of contemporary efforts by George Moore and others to free the novel from censorship. As a literary critic Pater wrote sparingly on contemporary or even modern writing; dividing his attention between French and English, he favoured English poetry and French prose, though he did review English prose by friends, such as Wilde's *Dorian Gray*, Mary (Mrs Humphry) Ward's *Robert Elsmere*, and Vernon Lee's *Juvenilia*. Close friends of the 1870s and 1880s, from Oxford and London, included Charlotte Symonds Green, Edmund Gosse, George Moore, Violet Paget (Vernon Lee), Mark-André Raffalovich, William Sharp, Arthur Symons, Mary Robinson, and Oscar Wilde, all of whom are characterized, notably, by their association with the violation in some respect of sexual conventions of the period.

In 1893 Pater published *Plato and Platonism*, which related closely to his teaching. Evolving characteristically serially, sections of it developed from lectures to chapters, and parts were serialized as magazine articles. Jowett, translator and popularizer of Plato, approved, and the two men made their peace almost twenty years after their confrontation in 1874. Pater's other work of the 1890s reflects the assimilation of French culture into English decadence of the period. Whereas after *Studies* Pater expunged references to Baudelaire from his published work, he now wrote preponderantly on French culture—on Prosper Mérimée and Pascal, and on churches at Amiens and Vézelay. He published too a last imaginary portrait, 'Emerald Uthwart' (1892), which, unusually, like 'A Child in the House', is set in England, invites reading as autobiography, and invokes in its title his youthful metaphor of the 'gem-like flame'.

There is no agreement among critics about Pater's degree of faith, if any, in the 1890s. Contemporary sources are almost all blighted by bias. His most intimate companion at Brasenose from 1891 was its dandified, multifaceted, and youthful chaplain, F. W. Bussell, with whom Pater used to dine, walk, attend chapel and diverse church services, and visit in the country and in London. It was Bussell with whom Pater chose to be paired in Will Rothenstein's lithographs of *Oxford Characters* (1895), and Bussell whose 'character' Pater contributed to that work. Bussell, in his memorial sermon, and Edmund Gosse in the *Dictionary of National Biography* attest to Pater's intensification of faith in his later life, whereas the first act of tribute by C. L. Shadwell, fellow of Oriel and Pater's literary executor and old friend, was to collect and publish a posthumous volume of *Greek Studies*. In a remarkable and frank testament to his friendship with Pater which Gosse published in the *Contemporary Review* in December 1894, and from which he extracted his more decorous *Dictionary of National Biography* life, Gosse, echoing Pater in 'Botticelli', surmised the following: 'He was not all for Apollo, nor all for Christ, but each deity swayed in him, and neither had that perfect homage that brings peace behind it' (Gosse, 810).

Between 1873 and 1894 Macmillan published five Pater titles, four in more than one edition, and three new titles appeared posthumously soon after his death. Contributing to a wide range of Victorian serials, from popular daily papers to high-culture quarterlies, topical monthlies, and weeklies, Pater steadily circulated his distilled prose and considered views on questions of his day. Henry James characterized Pater's alleged inscrutability as 'the mask without the face' (*Selected Letters*, 120), but, writing in the comparative safety of the period before the trials of Oscar Wilde and in the space 'classics' permitted, Pater's politics, and inscriptions of homosexual and homosocial histories, art, and culture, are pervasive, there for the reading, in journals as diverse as the *Westminster Review* and *Harper's*. Repeatedly invoked by younger decadents of the 1890s such as Yeats, Symons, Herbert Horne, Gleeson White, Le Gallienne, and Lionel Johnson, and honoured by discerning men and fewer women of his own generation, Pater was seldom accorded more general recognition in his lifetime; an honorary LLD from the University of Glasgow in April 1894 proved a singular exception. It

remained for biographers, critics, historians, and novelists in the twentieth century to piece together the elusive traces of his life, much of which had been withheld or destroyed by his family and friends, and to claim him variously as an important early modernist, and writer of gay discourse. In July 1893 the Paters left London to return to Oxford, possibly owing to Pater's gout, and on 30 July 1894, at his home at 64 St Giles', he died suddenly of a heart attack at the age of fifty-four. He was buried at Holywell cemetery, Oxford, on 2 August.　　LAUREL BRAKE

Sources T. Wright, *The life of Walter Pater*, 2 vols. (1907) · T. Wright, *Thomas Wright of Olney: an autobiography* (1936) · M. Levey, *The case of Walter Pater* (1978) · S. Wright, *Walter Pater: a bibliography* (1975) · E. Gosse, *Contemporary Review*, 66 (1894), 795–810 · *DNB* · B. A. Inman, 'Estrangement and connection: Walter Pater, Benjamin Jowett and William Money Hardinge', *Pater in the 1990s*, ed. L. Brake and I. Small (1991) · *The letters of Walter Pater*, ed. L. Evans (1970) · L. Brake, *Subjugated knowledges* (1994) · L. Brake, *Walter Pater* (1994) · T. Hinchcliffe, *North Oxford* (1992) · W. W. Jackson, *Ingram Bywater* (1917) · G. Moore, 'Avowals. vi: Walter Pater', *Pall Mall Magazine*, 33 (1904), 527–33 · *Selected letters*, ed. R. Moore (1988) · [M. Oliphant], 'The old saloon', *Blackwood*, 147 (1890), 131–51 · L. Dowling, *Hellenism and homosexuality in Victorian Oxford* (1994) · I. Fletcher, *Walter Pater* (1959) · R. M. Seiler, *Walter Pater: a life remembered* (1987) · *IGI* · grave, Holywell cemetery, Oxford, Oxfordshire · tithe book for South Hackney, 1843, Hackney Local History Library · *Kelly's Post Office London directory* (1845–6) · *Post Office directory of London and nine counties* [1846]

Archives All Souls Oxf., letters and unpublished chapters of *Gaston de Latour* · Bodl. Oxf., autobiographical notes, corresp., and MSS · Brasenose College, Oxford, corresp. and MSS · Colby College, Waterville, Maine, papers · Cornell University, Ithaca, New York, papers · Harvard U., Houghton L., corresp. and papers | BL, letters to E. Gosse, Ashley 5739 & A. 3733 · BL, corresp. with Macmillans, Add. MS 55030 · Colby College, Waterville, Maine, Vernon Lee MSS, letters · King's Cam., letters to Oscar Browning · King's School, Canterbury, Hugh Walpole collection · Morgan L., Gordon Ray bequest · NYPL, Berg collection, letters to Violet Paget (also known as Vernon Lee) and chapters of *Gaston de Latour* · U. Leeds, Brotherton L., letters to E. Gosse · University of Indiana, Bloomington, Lilly Library, Thomas Wright MSS, letters

Likenesses W. S. Wright, oils, 1870–1879?, repro. in Wright, *Life of Walter Pater*, 246 · S. Solomon, drawing, 1872, Uffizi Gallery, Florence, Italy · photograph, 1880–1889?, repro. in E. Gosse, *History of English literature* (1903) · C. Holmes, sketch, 1887, repro. in *Self and partners* (1936), following p. 102 · Elliott & Fry, photograph, 1889, Brasenose College, Oxford · C. Holmes, sketch, 1890–91, repro. in *Self and partners* (1936), following p. 102 · Elliott & Fry, photograph, 1890–94, NPG [*see illus.*] · Spider [J. Hearn], cartoon, Indian ink, 1890–94, repro. in T. Wright, *Autobiography* (1936), 212 · W. Rothenstein, drawing?, 1894, BM; repro. in *Oxford characters* (1896) · marble bust relief, memorial plaque, 1895, Brasenose College, Oxford · A. A. McEvoy, oils, 1906 (after sketches and photographs), Brasenose College, Oxford · R. Lasley, print, 1991, repro. in Brake and Small, eds., *Pater in the 1990s* · caricature, Queen's College, Oxford · group portrait, photograph, King's School, Canterbury · photogravure, BM; repro. in W. Pater, *Greek studies* (1895)

Wealth at death £2599 4*s*. 3*d*.: administration, 19 Sept 1894, *CGPLA Eng. & Wales*

Paterson. *See also* Patterson, Pattison.

Paterson, Alexander (1766–1831), Roman Catholic bishop and vicar apostolic of the eastern district of Scotland, was born at Pathhead in the Enzie, Banffshire, in March 1766. He entered the seminary at Scalan at the age of twelve, and was sent in the following year to the Scots College at

Douai, where he remained until 1793, when the institution was dissolved as a result of the French Revolution. On his return he was stationed successively at Tombae in Glenlivet (1793–1812) and Paisley (1812–16), and on 18 August 1816 he was consecrated bishop of Cybistra *in partibus*, and appointed coadjutor to Bishop Alexander Cameron (1747–1828). Between 1821 and 1830 he visited Paris, conducting ultimately successful negotiations to secure the property of the Scottish colleges in France that had not been sold under the revolutionary governments. He also performed a similar service for the Irish establishment. Rather than reopen the college in Paris, the decision was taken to retain the recovered funds in France to provide bursaries for the education of clerical students.

On the resignation of Bishop Cameron in 1825, Paterson succeeded him as vicar apostolic of the lowland district. In 1826 he visited Rome to secure the appointment of a third bishop for the Scottish mission. In this he also succeeded, for in February 1827 Leo XII decreed the division of Scotland into three districts or vicariates (the eastern, western, and northern), and Paterson became the first vicar apostolic of the newly created eastern district. Soon after his return he united the two seminaries of Aquhorties and Lismore into one college, established at Blairs, Kincardineshire, on a property transferred to him for that purpose by John Menzies (1756–1843) of Pitfodels. Blairs College continued training clerical students until its closure in 1986.

The last three years of Paterson's life were spent mainly at Edinburgh. He died at Dundee on 30 October 1831, and was buried in his church, St Mary's, Edinburgh, on 8 November 1831. His successor in the vicariate was Andrew Carruthers. Paterson's achievements were overshadowed by those of his distinguished predecessor, Alexander Cameron, but his principled and tactful character made him a significant figure in early nineteenth-century Scottish Catholicism.

THOMPSON COOPER, *rev.* MARY MCHUGH

Sources *The Scotsman* (2 Nov 1831) · *Dundee Advertiser* (3 Nov 1831) · *Catholic Directory for Scotland* (1832), 230–41 · *Caledonian Mercury* (10 Nov 1831) · papers on Scots College, Paris, Edinburgh, Scottish Catholic Archives
Archives Scottish Catholic Archives, Edinburgh, accounts, corresp., papers, and sermons
Wealth at death £481 19s. 7d.: inventory, 1832, Scotland

Paterson, Sir Alexander Henry (1884–1947), penal reformer and prison commissioner, was born on 20 November 1884 at Bowdon, Cheshire, the youngest child of Alexander Edgar Paterson, a solicitor, and his wife, Katherine Esther Dixon, a voluntary worker. The family background was Unitarian, although Paterson later became a member of the Church of England. He was educated at Bowdon College and at University College, Oxford, where he was secretary of the union. He graduated in 1906 with a third-class degree in *literae humaniores*. Much later, in 1944, he was elected an honorary fellow. He married Frances Margaret Baker in 1927 and the couple had one daughter.

Social work At Oxford, Paterson developed an enduring concern about poverty in London and became increasingly involved in voluntary social work with the Oxford Medical Mission in Bermondsey, later known as the Oxford and Bermondsey Club. He took a leading role in the development of the social club and following graduation went to live in Bermondsey, where he also worked as an unpaid elementary school teacher. Paterson devoted his attention to the plight of young people living in poverty, and in particular he involved himself in social work activities with boys. In 1911 he wrote *Across the Bridges*, in which he vividly described the extent of deprivation and material disadvantage in this part of London at that time. He urged the need for 'knowledge and understanding' of social problems and his ideals for change were based upon a faith which emphasized religion as an instrument of reform.

Paterson's social work activities in Bermondsey almost inevitably led to concerns about crime and about the treatment of offenders. In 1908 he became assistant director of the Borstal Association, which was responsible for the supervision and aftercare of borstal boys, and in 1909 he was asked to organize the first experiment in aftercare for adult prisoners. In 1911, when the Central Association for the Aid of Discharged Prisoners was formed under the instruction of the home secretary, Winston Churchill, Paterson became assistant director and made regular visits to convict prisons to discuss the needs of prisoners due for release.

In the First World War Paterson served in France with the Bermondsey battalion as a private and later as captain. His fellow soldiers, many of whom were young men from his social club, are said to have appreciated his courage and daring but also his good nature and sense of humour in what must have been grim circumstances. He was badly wounded in action and later received the Military Cross. Back home he became a founding member of Toc H, the society of (originally ex-service) men and women for Christian fellowship and social service, and was made the first chairman of its central executive when it received its charter in 1922.

Penal reformer Paterson was a major driving force behind penal reform as well as many of the more general reforms of the inter-war years. Following a period of attachment to the Ministry of Labour, in 1922 he became a member of the Prison Commission (later dissolved when the prison department of the Home Office was established in 1963). Unlike other prison commissioners Paterson had no official connection with the prison service or Home Office before his appointment and, while never chairman of the Prison Commission, he was its most dominant figure and spent nearly a quarter of a century working for reform of the prison system. This was a period of significant optimism in penal reform. A mood of scepticism about the efficacy of prison, which originated before the First World War and which was carried over into the inter-war period, was replaced by a new mood in which prisons were increasingly seen as positive institutions that could act as agencies for human change.

Paterson's vision for penal reform was very much influenced by his earlier work, which had shown him many of the social harms of imprisonment. He was well aware of the 'pains of imprisonment' and of the dehumanizing effects of confinement on the individual offender as well as the impact on their families. He highlighted the ways in which prisoners deteriorate, mentally and morally, throughout the duration of a prison sentence and argued that prisons should primarily be concerned with treatment and reform. Thus, in his evidence to the 1931 persistent offenders' committee he argued that imprisonment was a 'clumsy piece of social surgery' and advocated the abolition of all prisons, and their replacement with institutions dedicated to reform and training.

Paterson's evidence to the committee also shows the growing influence of the medical model of crime control, and how changing notions about penal purpose legitimated a treatment approach and the increased intervention of the medical profession. The role of the courts, he argued, was not 'to weigh out a dose of punishment', but rather 'to diagnose ... and to prescribe the right form of training or treatment for the condition' (*Departmental Committee on Persistent Offenders*, 3.669).

While Paterson's ambition of abolitionism was not achieved, the impact of the rehabilitative approach was swiftly felt. Among the many significant changes in penal measures was the removal of the more dehumanizing practices that destroyed self-identity and self-respect. Thus, the 'convict crop' and the broad arrows marking prisoners' clothing were abolished, facilities were made available for men to shave for the first time, and the rule of silence was greatly relaxed, allowing prisoners to associate for meals and recreation. Educational and training facilities were extended, and provision was made for prisoners to receive visits from voluntary prison visitors. Efforts were made to improve the work available to prisoners. Unproductive labour and the treadmill were abolished and a seven-hour working day was introduced. During this period also experiments with open prisons for adults were started at Wakefield prison, where certain prisoners were allowed to sleep in non-secure accommodation.

Borstals Of all his inspiring ideals for penal reform Paterson is perhaps chiefly remembered for his impact on the borstal system. Indeed, he has been described as 'the man whose conviction and initiative were to change the very spirit of borstal training in its golden age' (Hood, 104). He was largely responsible for refashioning the regime during this period. He intended borstals to be run according to English public school principles with the aim of reforming and training younger offenders. In contrast to previous regimes characterized by enforced discipline, Paterson introduced a system designed around notions of personal responsibility, self-discipline, and decision making. Thus, in his 1932 book, *The Principles of the Borstal System*, Paterson stated that his aim was 'Not to break or knead [the offender] into shape', but instead to 'stimulate some power within to regulate conduct aright' (Ruck, 97).

It was only through making their own decisions, Paterson believed, that people could change.

Paterson organized the borstals around the public school model of the house system, where institutional loyalty was fostered through inter-house sports and recreational activities. He appointed housemasters who were expected to take a close interest in their charges and introduced the post of matron to oversee housekeeping and to provide a maternal influence. In keeping with the emphasis on personal relationships, in 1924 uniform for borstal officers was abolished and all staff were encouraged to involve themselves with the boys in a wide variety of activities.

The growing influence of rehabilitationist arguments and the innovative optimism inherent in the borstal formula led to further experiments in the care of younger offenders. In 1924 cross-country marches and camping were introduced with apparent success (as measured by a lack of absconding). This success was self-propelling. In 1929 the prison commissioners' annual report foreshadowed the building of a new borstal at Lowdham Grange in Nottinghamshire to cope with the demand for places. This new establishment was inaugurated by a long march in 1930 by a group of staff and boys from Feltham borstal to Lowdham Grange. Led by the Feltham governor, W. W. Llewellin, this famous march is considered to be one of the high points of borstal history. In 1935 Llewellin led a second march from Stafford to Freiston, Lincolnshire, where another borstal, North Sea Camp, was established.

With a certain showmanship, and what has been described as 'that special blend of compassion and arrogance so long the hallmark of English public service' (King and Elliott, 5), Paterson promoted the borstal as a form of social service. In so doing he won support from the public and politicians alike. There were approving visits from senior politicians, and it is perhaps to Paterson's credit that developments in the borstal system received no serious criticism from the communities in which the institutions were located.

The goal of rehabilitation became foremost in the penal approach more generally and the borstal formula—emphasizing personal relationships, responsibility, and trust—gradually had an impact on the prison system as a whole. The need for a variety of security settings was increasingly recognized and an emphasis on casework, through care, and preparation for release and resettlement was paramount. Paterson became influential across the whole range of penal measures and his values were evident in penal documents and legislation on punishment throughout the 1920s and 1930s. Moreover, as a rehabilitationist who believed that crime, like other social problems, could be studied scientifically to establish its causes, Paterson, along with some senior government officials, strongly advocated the need to establish criminology as an academic discipline.

International influence An ardent traveller throughout the inter-war period, Paterson also drew upon the ideas and experiences of other countries. Like John Howard before him, he travelled abroad examining the various forms of confinement and reporting in graphic detail on prison conditions. On one such visit to Europe, he reviewed the conditions in a women's prison. He noted that while the prison was 'staffed by a splendid body of nuns', adherence to the silent system had a dehumanizing effect on the women prisoners. In an article in *The Times*, on 5 August 1925, he advocated that women prisoners should live and work together in small units in non-secure establishments, preferably in rural settings. In the early 1930s Paterson spent time visiting penal and reformatory establishments in the United States, and his findings were published in two articles, as 'U.S. way with crime', in *The Times*, on 10 and 11 July 1931.

As the English borstal system gained success and public esteem Paterson was invited to advise other countries on penal measures and his influence spread at an international level. In 1925, for example, he visited Burma where he demonstrated that younger offenders could be kept in non-secure settings, irrespective of the nature of their crime. His expertise on penal administration also formed the basis of advice to the Colonial Office, and throughout the 1930s he visited a number of British colonies. As a result of one visit to a penal settlement in Cayenne, Paterson was influential in the later decision to discontinue transportation to British Guiana.

Paterson became an active member of the international penal and penitentiary commission and was elected vice-president in 1938 and later acting president in 1943. At a congress meeting held in Berlin in 1935 Paterson fiercely opposed the reactionary penal doctrines advocated by members of the National Socialist Party in Germany. In keeping with his earlier work he argued that the purpose of imprisonment should be the 'protection of society by the social readaptation of the prisoners' and his proposals found support among delegates from a number of nations, including the United States, Belgium, Holland, and the Scandinavian countries.

During the Second World War, Paterson acted as director of the Czechoslovakia Refugee Trust, devoting his attention in particular to the social welfare of children and young people, many of whom were orphaned or otherwise separated from their parents. In other ways he was also involved in the war effort and in 1940 he was asked by senior politicians to visit internment camps in Canada to explore the extent of national sympathy.

The spirit of the Paterson era of penal reform faltered after 1945 as rehabilitative approaches fell out of favour. There was an unprecedented increase in recorded crime which, together with the growing post-war affluence, challenged reformers' claims that crime would be reduced through the growth of social welfare. The medical model, advocated by Paterson, began to come under considerable criticism, not least because it was becoming apparent that it could be used to legitimate a whole range of interventions in the lives of captive audiences that seemed far from humane. In addition, rehabilitative policies resulted in an increase in the length of prison sentences. Paterson himself, while advocating the abolition of prisons, had earlier acknowledged that if offenders were to go to prison, then the sentence needed to be sufficiently long for treatment and training to take effect. Thus in a 1927 *Report of the Commissioners of Prisons*, Paterson commented, 'if we are concerned to train [the offender], a few weeks in prison will be an idle pretence' (xiii). The longer sentences that resulted from rehabilitative policies, together with the individualization of sentences, made such approaches seem harsh and raised fundamental questions about justice and about the rights of offenders to receive proportionate sentences.

Significance In the early post-war years, the lack of any well defined objectives or indicators for judging the success or otherwise of the penal system became clearly evident. It has been argued that despite the 'well-meaning and paternalistic' efforts on the part of the prison commissioners to a process of penal reform, a lack of clarity of purpose dominated a system 'peopled at the top by gentlemen and amateurs' (King and Elliott, 5).

Paterson died in London on 7 November 1947, the same year in which he received a knighthood. He was survived by his wife. While many ardent supporters remained, the reformist tradition that was associated with Paterson did not last long. Within a few years of the end of the war penal priorities became increasingly driven by the sharp increases in crime and prison numbers and by the justice model of crime control.

Alexander Paterson has been described as a man with charismatic determination. In his advocacy of penal reform he proved to be one of a select group who might be considered as genuine innovators. He influenced a real change of penal perspective generally while also showing that imprisonment in England, and elsewhere, was deeply flawed. In addition to his public labour his social work values were evident in his personal work with individuals. He regularly corresponded and socialized with ex-prisoners and maintained his early commitment to principles of social welfare. He was physically depicted as a powerful man with broad shoulders, deep chest, and a 'contemplative face'; his contemporaries appreciated his capacity for enjoyment as well as his turn of phrase. Indeed, in addition to the real changes to the penal system he expressed many fine and subsequently oft quoted dictums. One such aphorism revealed his fundamental belief that 'men are sent to prison as a punishment, not for punishment'. In addition, his famous paradox of training people for freedom in an 'atmosphere of captivity and repression' has continued to haunt the prison system ever since it was first uttered. CATRIN SMITH

Sources S. K. Ruck, ed., *Paterson on prisons* (1951) · R. Hood, *Borstal re-assessed* (1965) · D. King and K. Elliott, *Albany: birth of a prison—end of an era* (1977) · N. Morris and D. Rotham, eds., *The Oxford history of the prison* (1995) · A. Edwards and R. Hurley, 'Prisons over two centuries', www.homeoffice.gov.uk/prishist.htm [extract from *Home office, 1782–1982*], 31 Oct 1998 · D. Garland, 'Of crimes and criminals: the development of criminology in Britain', *The Oxford handbook of criminology*, ed. M. Maguire and others (1997) · *WWW* · *Departmental committee on persistent offenders*, 3 (1931), 675, 669 · *CGPLA Eng. & Wales* (1948)

Likenesses E. I. Halliday, drawing, University College, Oxford

Wealth at death £2719 0s. 2d.: probate, 4 Feb 1948, *CGPLA Eng. & Wales*

Paterson, Andrew Barton [*pseud.* Banjo] (1864–1941), poet and journalist, was born on 17 February 1864 at Nyrambla station near Orange, New South Wales, Australia, the first of seven children of Scottish-born grazier Andrew Bogle Paterson (1833–1889) and his Australian-born wife, Rose Isabella Barton (1844–1893). Bartie, as he was known to family and friends, spent his early years with his family at Buckinbah sheep station near Yeoval, New South Wales, and then at Illalong, where he lived from 1870 to 1874. He rode a horse 4 miles to and from the school at Binalong.

At twelve Bartie went to live with his widowed maternal grandmother, Emily Mary Barton (*née* Darvall), at her house, Rockend, in Gladesville, Sydney, where he resided until he was twenty. Emily had lived in Yorkshire, Brussels, and Boulogne before migrating with her family to Australia and marrying Robert Johnston Barton, whom she had met on the ship from England. Emily, who wrote poetry herself, had a formative influence on her grandson's literary interests and skills. Paterson attended Sydney grammar school from 1875 to early 1881, when, after a severe bout of typhoid, he withdrew from the pursuit of university matriculation and sought entry to the legal profession. He commenced as an articled clerk in the Sydney office of Herbert Salwey in 1881 and in 1886 he was admitted as a solicitor to the supreme court of New South Wales. In 1888 he went into partnership with John William Street at 85 Pitt Street, Sydney.

Paterson's first published poem, 'El Mahdi to the Australian troops', which appeared anonymously in the Sydney *Bulletin* on 28 February 1885, signalled a young 'radical' prepared to criticize the British campaign in the Sudan and Australian involvement in it. In 1889 he published at his own expense his pamphlet *Australia for the Australians*, which argued the necessity for land reform combined with protection. In the 1880s and 1890s Paterson's poems were published in the *Bulletin*, the *Sydney Mail*, the *Lone Hand*, the *Australian Town and Country Journal*, and elsewhere. His first and most famous book of poems, *The Man from Snowy River and other Verses*, was published by Angus and Robertson in 1895, and 7000 copies were sold in a few months. Banjo, his pen-name, was borrowed from the name of a station racehorse. Reviews were positive in Australia, and in Britain the *Times* reviewer compared its author to Kipling. The book's title ballad became Paterson's signature poem, though another ballad, 'Clancy of the Overflow', provided two of his most quoted lines:

> And he sees the vision splendid of the sunlit plains extended
> And at night the wondrous glory of the everlasting stars.
> (*Complete Works*, 1.105)

A manufactured 'debate' in verse between Paterson and Henry Lawson in the *Bulletin* in 1892 accentuated differences between the two best-known Australian writers of their generation. Lawson presented himself as the realist, observing the harsh terrain of his homeland from on foot;

Andrew Barton Paterson (1864–1941), by unknown photographer, *c.*1890

Paterson offered a more romantic and adventurous landscape as if from horseback.

There has been some dispute about the origins of 'Waltzing Matilda', but most evidence points to Paterson writing the words to the tune of the march 'Craigielea' (adapted from the Scottish song 'Thou bonnie wood of Craigielea'), when he visited Winton in north-west Queensland with his fiancée Sarah Riley (whom he did not marry) in 1895. The song was popularized in its modern form by Marie Cowan's adaptation of Paterson's words to her tune in 1903, and by its use as an advertising jingle for Billy Tea for the tea-distributing firm Inglis & Co. 'Waltzing Matilda' tells of a swagman who evades the law by drowning himself in a billabong; its anti-authoritarian sentiments have appealed to subsequent generations of Australians. A national poll in 1977 placed 'Waltzing Matilda' second behind 'Advance Australia Fair', which became the national anthem in 1984.

Paterson was fascinated with war, but his crooked right arm, broken several times in childhood accidents, probably prevented any front-line action. On 28 October 1899 he set sail for the Second South African War on the *Kent* with the first contingent of the New South Wales lancers and their horses as special correspondent for the *Sydney Morning Herald*. In South Africa he was attached to General French's column and witnessed the surrender of Bloemfontein, the capture of Pretoria, and the relief of Kimberley. He was appointed as a correspondent for Reuters. He wrote twenty-two poems over this period, which are included in the posthumously published *Boer War Dispatches* (1983). These writings reveal a developing sympathy for the Boers, but largely ignore the black South Africans and never question Britain's right to be in South Africa. In dispatches, articles, and memoirs Paterson wrote vivid pen-portraits of Olive Schreiner, lords Kitchener and Roberts, Sir Alfred Milner, Cecil Rhodes, and fellow journalist Winston Churchill ('the most curious combination of ability and swagger'). When Paterson heard of Harry (the Breaker) *Morant's court martial and execution by firing squad in Pretoria in 1902, he could not at first believe the guilt of the carefree, theatrical young man he had met in Sydney in 1893, but as further evidence came his way from Morant's defence counsel in South Africa, he reluctantly acceded that justice had been done.

Paterson returned to Australia in September 1900 and sailed for China in July 1901 to cover the Boxer uprising for the *Sydney Morning Herald*. He met and interviewed there a fellow Australian, G. E. (Chinese) Morrison, the *Times* correspondent for China. Paterson went on to England, where he was a guest of Kipling at his home in Sussex in the winter of 1901–2, and returned to Australia in time for the publication of his second book of poems, *Rio Grande's Last Race and other Poems* (1902).

Paterson married Alice Emily Walker (1877–1963) of Tenterfield station on 8 April 1903 and they settled into their first home at West Hall, Queen Street, Woollahra, in Sydney. A daughter, Grace, was born in 1904 and a son, Hugh, in 1906. Paterson had left his legal practice, and in 1903 accepted an invitation to edit the Sydney *Evening News*, where he remained until 1908, when he became resident part owner of a 40,000 acre property at Coodra Vale, near Wee Jasper, in the southern highlands of New South Wales. In 1911 the family moved to a wheat farm south of Grenfell called Glen Esk. He collected and edited an influential book of folk ballads, *Old Bush Songs* (1905), and saw publication of his novel, *An Outback Marriage* (1906), which had been serialized in the Melbourne *Leader* in 1900. A treatise, *Racehorses and Racing*, was not published until 1983.

When Britain declared war on Germany in August 1914 Paterson gained authorization to travel as 'special commissioner' for the *Sydney Morning Herald* and honorary veterinarian on a ship of men and horses bound for Europe. He drove an ambulance for the Australian Voluntary Hospital in Wimereux before returning to Sydney in July 1915 and enlisting at the age of fifty-one in the remount service. As a lieutenant in the Australian military forces he travelled to the Middle East, where he served for three and a half years behind the lines, gaining promotion to major. Paterson returned to Australia in 1919, and he and Alice Emily (who had worked on voluntary hospital service in Egypt) moved back to Woollahra. He resumed journalism for Sydney newspapers, became a regular visitor to the Australian Club, and contributed occasional talks to the Australian Broadcasting Commission (founded 1932). He sat for a portrait by John Longstaff, which won the 1935 Archibald prize and hangs in the Art Gallery of New South Wales. He wrote a five-part series of reminiscences for the *Sydney Morning Herald* in 1939 and was appointed a CBE in the same year. After signs of heart trouble he was admitted to hospital and died in Sydney on 5 February 1941. He was cremated at the Northern Suburbs crematorium after a brief Presbyterian service.

Paterson's younger contemporary Norman Lindsay described him as an 'aristocrat' in body and spirit who took life as 'a high adventure in action, even to the risk of a broken neck' (Lindsay, 77, 82). Clement Semmler's study *Banjo of the Bush* (1966; 2nd edn, 1974) explored his contribution to a legend of Australian identity forged in the bush. Colin Roderick's biography, *Banjo Paterson: Poet by Accident* (1993), emphasized his abiding interests in sport and war and their interrelatedness. In a late essay, 'Looking backward' (1938), Paterson himself judiciously described his role in literary history as having provided 'footprints preserved for posterity' in 'a new country' (*Complete Works*, 2.759).   BRUCE BENNETT

Sources A. B. 'Banjo' Paterson: complete works, ed. R. Campbell and P. Harvie, 2 vols. (Sydney, Australia, 1983) • C. Roderick, *Banjo Paterson: poet by accident* (1993) • C. Semmler, *The Banjo of the bush: the work, life and times of A. B. Paterson*, 2nd edn (1974) • C. Semmler, 'Paterson, Andrew Barton', *AusDB*, vol. 11 • A. B. Paterson, '"Banjo" Paterson tells his own story', *Sydney Morning Herald* (4 Feb–4 March 1939) • R. Magoffin, *'Waltzing Matilda': the story behind the legend*, 2nd edn (1987) • N. Lindsay, 'Banjo Paterson', in N. Lindsay, *Bohemians of the Bulletin* (1965)
Archives Mitchell L., NSW, MSS • NL Aus., MSS
Likenesses photogravure, c.1890, NL Aus. [*see illus.*] • J. Longstaff, oils, 1935, Art Gallery of New South Wales, Sydney, Australia; repro. in *A. B. 'Banjo' Paterson*, ed. Campbell and Harvie, vol. 2, facing p. 711 • portrait, repro. in A$10 note, 1993 • portraits, repro. in *A. B. 'Banjo' Paterson*, ed. Campbell and Harvie
Wealth at death £1873 9s. 5d.: probate, 13 Oct 1941, *CGPLA Eng. & Wales*

Paterson, Charles William (1756–1841), naval officer, son of James Paterson, an army officer of the 69th regiment, was born at Berwick. In 1765 his name was put on the books of the *Shannon* at Portsmouth, and in 1768 on those of the *St Antonio*. His first voyage was probably in 1769, when he joined the *Phoenix* going out to the Guinea coast, with the broad pennant of his maternal uncle, Commodore George Anthony Tonyn. He afterwards served on the home and Newfoundland stations as able seaman and midshipman in the *Flora*, *Rose*, *Ardent*, and *Ramillies*, before passing his lieutenant's examination on 4 October 1775.

In 1776 Paterson was in Howe's flagship, the *Eagle*, in North America, and on 3 February 1777 Howe promoted him lieutenant of the fireship *Strombolo*. In Howe's engagement with d'Estaing on 11 August 1778 Paterson commanded the galley *Philadelphia*. In June 1779 he joined the *Ardent* (64 guns), which, on 17 August, was captured off Plymouth by the combined Franco-Spanish fleet. In April 1780 he was appointed to the *Alcide* (74 guns), which joined Lord Rodney in the West Indies in May; Paterson went to New York with him during the summer, returned to the West Indies in November, and in the following January was present at the capture of St Eustatius and the other Dutch islands.

In February 1781 Paterson joined the *Sandwich*, Rodney's flagship; he went home with the admiral in the *Gibraltar*, and returned to the West Indies with him in the *Formidable*. He was appointed acting captain of the armed ship *St Eustatius* in February 1782 and on 8 April was promoted to command the fireship *Blast*, in which he returned to England on the conclusion of the peace.

In 1793 Paterson was appointed to the storeship *Gorgon*, in which he served under Hood at Toulon, and on 20 January 1794 he was made captain of the *Ariadne* (20 guns). On the surrender of Corsica he was moved into the frigate *Melpomène*, before returning to England in 1795. In 1797 he was inspecting captain of the quota men in Kirkcudbright and Wigtownshire, and in 1798 superintended the fitting of the *Admiral de Vries*, until she was turned over to the transport board. He commanded the *Montagu* in the channel in 1800, and from 1801 to 1802 he commanded the *San Fiorenzo*. In March 1801 he married Jane Ellen Yeats, daughter of his first cousin, David Yeats, formerly registrar of East Florida.

Paterson had charge of the French prisoners of war in Rochester Castle in 1810, and from 1811 to 1812 he commanded the guardship *Puissant* at Spithead. He was promoted rear-admiral on 12 August 1812, vice-admiral on 12 August 1819, and admiral of the white on 10 January 1837, but had no further service, and died on 10 March 1841, presumably at his home, East Cosham Cottage, near Portsmouth. J. K. LAUGHTON, rev. RANDOLPH COCK

Sources commission and warrant books, PRO, ADM 6/21, 22 · lieutenant's passing certificates, PRO, ADM 107/6, fol. 346 · J. Marshall, *Royal naval biography*, 1 (1823), 518–28 · W. L. Clowes, *The Royal Navy: a history from the earliest times to the present*, 7 vols. (1897–1903) **Archives** PRO, commission and warrant books, ADM 6/21, 22 · PRO, lieutenant's passing certificates, ADM 107/6, fol. 346

Paterson, Daniel (1738–1825), compiler of road books and cartographer, was born on 11 or 17 December 1738, calculated from his age at death according to whether the reform of the calendar is taken into account. He was gazetted ensign in the 30th foot on 13 December 1765 and promoted lieutenant on 8 May 1772, captain in the 55th foot on 18 December 1782, captain in the 36th foot on 11 July 1783, major on 1 March 1794, and lieutenant-colonel on 1 January 1798. By 1771 and until at least 1791 he was an assistant to the quartermaster-general of HM forces at the Horse Guards, London. On 31 December 1812 he was made lieutenant-governor of Quebec, and held the appointment until his death. This appointment was a sinecure and it seems unlikely that Paterson ever went to Canada.

In 1776 Paterson published *A Scale of Distances of the Principal Cities and Towns of England*, a single-sheet publication with distances displayed in a triangle after the manner of John Norden. In 1771 he published *A New and Accurate Description of All the Direct and Principal Cross Roads in Great Britain*. The *Description* 'on a Plan far preferable to any work of the Kind Extant' in the words of the title-page, went through eighteen editions, including the twelfth (1799) which made extensive and unauthorized use of John Cary's survey as published in the latter's *New Itinerary* (1798), and the sixteenth (1822) which was extensively revised by Edward Mogg. *Paterson's Roads*, an epitome of the thirteenth edition, appeared in 1804. Though the

Description continued to bear his name it seems that he had withdrawn from its compilation by 1785. Paterson published a *Travelling Dictionary* which went through eight editions between 1772 and 1799 and included information in the manner of *A Scale of Distances*; and the *British Itinerary*, which included strip maps after the manner of John Ogilby (1785). In addition he produced several maps: to some, such as 'Bowles's new pocket map of England and Wales' (1773), his main contribution was to improve the information on roads. Others show his training as a land and military surveyor. He may have had some connection with Grenada, of which he produced a *Topographical Description* (1780) with a cadastral map, based on a survey by a M. Pinel.

Paterson died at the house of his friend Colonel Dare, on Clewer Green, near Windsor, on 14 April 1825, and was buried in the north aisle of Clewer church on 21 April.

Interest in road books and itineraries was kindled largely through the work of Herbert George Fordham in the early part of the twentieth century and Fordham's work on and collection of Paterson's road books show that Paterson made no significant innovations in the field, relying on the advances of Norden, Ogilby, and others. He made improvements in style and presentation, however, and added factual detail—so much so that his name was for many years an indicator of reliability in road books, and was attached to them long after he had stopped compiling them. ELIZABETH BAIGENT

Sources H. E. Fordham, 'The roadbooks and itineraries of Great Britain, 1570–1850', *Transactions of the Bibliographical Society*, 4th ser., 5/4 (1924) · H. E. Fordham, *Paterson's roads: Daniel Paterson, his maps and itineraries, 1738–1825* (1925) · H. E. Fordham, 'Paterson, Daniel', in *Corrections and additions to the Dictionary of National Biography*, Institute of Historical Research (1966) · A. S. Bendall, *Dictionary of landsurveyors and local mapmakers*, 2 vols. (1997) · M. J. Freeman and J. Longbotham, 'The Fordham collection: a catalogue', *Historical Geography Research, Series 5* (1981)

Paterson, Edith Isabel Myfanwy (1900–1995). *See under* Paterson, (James) Ralston Kennedy (1897–1981).

Paterson [*née* Smith], **Emma Anne** (1848–1886), trade unionist, was born on 5 April 1848 at St Peter's national school house, Belgrave Street, London, the daughter of Henry Smith (*d.* 1864) and his wife, Emma Dockerill. Her father was headmaster of St George's Hanover Square parish school and, largely educated by him, Emma for a time assisted with teaching there. However, at the age of eighteen she began work as an assistant to a lady clerk of the Working Men's Club and Institute Union; and by July 1867 she had become assistant secretary. Through her work she met the so-called 'Junta' of trade union leaders (George Howell, Robert Applegarth, Edwin Coulson, Daniel Guile, and George Odger). She also met Thomas Paterson (*b.* 1834), a cabinet-maker and self-educated positivist, whom she married on 24 July 1873. The marriage was childless and was brought to an end by Thomas Paterson's death on 14 October 1882. Thomas Paterson's opinions influenced Emma and she never became a socialist or militant foe of capitalism.

After five years with the Working Men's Club, Emma

Paterson resigned to become secretary of the Society for the Promotion of Women's Suffrage in February 1872, but was dismissed because 'her physique was too weak and her speech contemptible' (Dilke, 'Benefit societies', 852–6). Her face was oval with small features and was framed with short dark hair parted in the middle and combed back from her forehead. Yet, in spite of a supposedly weak physique, Emma Paterson was able to spend the remaining fourteen years of her life working for a variety of causes. While working for the suffrage association she also assisted Emily Faithfull's efforts to aid unemployed women bookbinders. These efforts were temporarily interrupted by a honeymoon trip to America where she was inspired by the successful Women's Typographical Society and the Female Umbrella Makers' Union.

After returning to England, Emma Paterson wrote an article for the April 1874 *Labour News* calling for women to form a central association to which local branches of different trades might affiliate. She cited the fact that women were paid half of male wages, for instance: unskilled men received 18s. a week, while most skilled women were paid from 11 to 17s. Emma Paterson urged women to erase this inequality through trade unionism rather than by government interference. She argued that trade unions should also provide sickness insurance, unemployment benefits, educational programmes, emigration clubs, and a job register. She urged men either to aid women in forming similar unions or to admit women to their unions on equal terms which would include full payment of dues (women union members in the cotton industry, for instance, were unable to make their weight felt because they were charged only half of the dues paid by men).

On 8 July 1874 a conference, chaired by Hodgson Pratt, a leading co-operator, was held to discuss Mrs Paterson's ideas. Attended by women's rights, trade unionist, positivist, and Christian socialist groups, it led to the formation of the Women's Protective and Provident League (WPPL). The WPPL's next meeting, held on 12 September 1874, saw the formation of the Society of Women Employed in Bookbinding with 300 members. This effort was aided by the secretary of the London Consolidated Society of Journeymen Bookbinders, H. R. King, and also by Edith Simcox and Emilia Frances Pattison (later Lady Dilke). Within the next year four other societies were founded, in the upholstery, dressmaking, shirt and collar making, and hat making trades.

In February 1876 Emma Paterson founded her own press, the Women's Printing Society Ltd, employing women as compositors and printers. She also edited the WPPL's monthly, the *Women's Union Journal*. During this period the WPPL organized a number of single-sex trade unions, although it favoured forming mixed societies. It did succeed in getting women admitted to the National Union of Operative Boot Riveters and Finishers in Leicester, the London Compositors, the London Cigar Makers, the Chain Workers, and the Sheffield Hand File Cutters. Nevertheless, the WPPL was financially weak, and over two-thirds of its funds came from the Revd Stopford

Brooke, a Christian socialist, and Mrs Brassey, daughter-in-law of Thomas Brassey, the famous railroad contractor. The WPPL offered its members a variety of benefits ranging from a halfpenny bank in 1878 to a reading-room, a circulating library, a Women's Union swimming club at St Pancras, and an unemployment register. In 1879 it succeeded in launching the first parliamentary inquiry directly initiated by women workers, into the government's discharge of 1500 royal army clothing workers at Pimlico. Although Emma Paterson succeeded in founding the London Tailoresses' Union with 171 members the WPPL failed to alter government policy as a result of economic circumstances, Liberal political chicanery, and bureaucratic red tape.

In 1875 the WPPL sent the first women delegates, Emma Paterson and Edith Simcox (1844–1901), to the annual TUC conference. Emma Paterson told delegates that any legislation that singled out women for special treatment would only lessen their chance of employment and that reduction in hours should come by pressure from women in trade unions. Henry Broadhurst, TUC parliamentary secretary, however, insisted that ameliorative legislation was a viable course of action and, more importantly, that factories were not suitable places for women as their proper place was in the home (Drake, 11).

At the 1877 TUC congress a separate women's meeting was held to discuss problems of special interest to women. Reflecting Emma Paterson's views, it opposed efforts to prohibit women from working in the chain and nail industry. Between 1879 and 1886 Emma Paterson attended every TUC annual conference except that of 1882, when her husband died. In 1886 she just missed election to the executive committee of the TUC by seven votes.

After her husband's death Emma Paterson was forced to live on a budget of 6d. a day and accept a small salary from the Women's Printing Society. She rejected an offer of £100 a year from the WPPL to serve as a paid organizer. As a widow and working woman, she proved an able figure at the Industrial Remuneration Conference of 1885 where she disputed the findings of Sir Robert Giffen, showing that his computations failed to include over 3.8 million working women whose average weekly wage was 13s. 8d. During this time she continued to support the cause of women's suffrage, especially after deputations of working women seeking the appointment of women factory inspectors were refused by the home secretaries of both political parties.

In 1886, the year Emma Paterson died, the WPPL held a meeting to assess the league's accomplishments. Of the societies in London, four had failed, one was struggling, and five were thriving; however, their total membership was only between 600 and 700. In the provinces, twenty-one societies were founded, but only nine survived with a total membership of 1800; by contrast, there were 30,000 women in the male-dominated textile unions. With over 3 million women in industry, why were the WPPL's efforts so lacklustre? The reason was in part the difficulty of creating all-female or mixed unions from potential members who lacked sufficient time, education, or money to participate in union affairs. To appreciate the WPPL's modest accomplishments it must be understood that it was founded during an economic climate when even the male TUC membership declined by 50 per cent. In addition, while the league received some financial aid and moral support from labour and middle-class supporters, it lacked sufficient funds to carry on a dynamic organizing campaign during Mrs Paterson's stewardship (its budget averaged only £110 a year and its three organizers were unpaid).

Despite the fact that Emma Paterson possessed little physical attraction or charm, Frederick Rogers believed that this quiet, shrewd little woman exercised an enormous influence on the labour movement. Her secret lay in her entire sincerity and absence of pose. Beatrice and Sidney Webb in their *History of Trade Unionism* (1894) called her 'the real pioneer of modern women's trade unions' (S. Webb and B. Webb, 336–7).

In 1885 Emma Paterson was diagnosed by Mrs Garrett Anderson MD as having diabetes. She died on 1 December 1886 at her home, 23 Great College Street, Westminster. The Revd Stewart D. Headlam, a long-time friend whose more radical views on league policy clashed with hers, officiated at her burial at Paddington cemetery.

NORBERT C. SOLDON

Sources 'Continuity of employment and rates of wages', *Industrial Remuneration Conference* (1885), 199–207; repr. with introduction by J. Saville (1968) · *Women's Union Journal* (1876–86) · WPPL, *Annual Reports*, 1–13 (1875–87) · E. F. S. Dilke, 'Benefit societies and trade unions for women', *Fortnightly Review*, 51 (June 1889), 852–6 · E. F. S. Dilke, 'Trades unionism among women', *Fortnightly Review*, 55 (May 1891) · H. Goldman, *Emma Paterson* (1974) · N. Soldon, *Women in British trade unions, 1874–1976* (1978) · B. Drake, *Women in trade unions* (1920) · C. J. Bundock, *The story of the National Union of Printing, Bookbinding and Paper Workers* (1959) · S. Lewenhak, *Women and trade unions: an outline history of women in the British trade union movement* (1977) · T. Olcott, 'Dead centre: the women's trade union movement in London, 1874–1914', *London Journal*, 2 (1976), 33–60 · J. Bellamy and J. Schmiechen, 'Paterson, Emma', *DLB*, vol. 5 · S. Boston, *Women workers and the trade union movement* (1980) · *Women's Union Journal* (Nov 1886) · *Women's Union Journal* (Dec 1886) · *Women's Union Journal* (Feb 1887) · *The Times* (6 Dec 1886) · *Englishman's Review* (15 Dec 1886) · *Club and Institute Union Journal* (18 Dec 1886) · S. J. Webb, B. P. Webb, and R. A. Peddie, *The history of trade unionism* (1894), 336–7
Likenesses photograph, Trades Union Congress, London · portrait, repro. in Lewenhak, *Women and trade unions*, 6

Paterson, James (1805–1876), journalist and writer, was born on 18 March 1805 at Struthers, Ayrshire. He was the son of James Paterson, farmer at Struthers, and his wife, the granddaughter of William Jamieson. Although Paterson's father was compelled by pecuniary difficulties to give up his farm, experiencing various vicissitudes, the son received a fairly good education, including one year in a local school run by Thomas McClelland. Ultimately he was apprenticed to a printer at the office of the *Kilmarnock Mirror*, and in his thirteenth year began to contribute to Thomson's *Miscellany*. Subsequently he was transferred to the *Ayr and Wigtownshire Courier* office in Ayr, and on completing his apprenticeship went to Glasgow, where he

joined the *Scots Times*. In 1826 he returned to Kilmarnock, and, having taken a shop as stationer and printer, he went into partnership and started the *Kilmarnock Chronicle*, the first number appearing on 4 May 1831, in the midst of the reform agitation, and the paper expiring in May 1832.

In 1835 Paterson left Kilmarnock for Dublin, where for some time he acted as Dublin correspondent of the *Glasgow Liberator*. From there he went to Edinburgh, and found employment at a small salary in writing the letterpress for Kay's *Edinburgh Portraits*, 1837–9, the majority of the biographies being contributed by him. Failing to find further employment in Edinburgh, he accepted in 1839 the editorship of the *Ayr Observer*. In 1840 he published *Contemporaries of Burns and the More Recent Poets of Ayrshire*, and in 1847 a *History of the County of Ayr*. Disappointed with his prospects on the *Ayr Observer*, he again returned to Edinburgh, where he supported himself chiefly by writing, his more notable productions being *Origin of the Scots and of the Scottish Language* (1855), *The Life and Poems of William Dunbar* (1860), and *The History of the Counties of Ayr and Wigton* (1863). In 1871 he published his *Autobiographical Reminiscences*. Shortly after this he was attacked by paralysis, and died in Edinburgh on 6 May 1876. His works, not characterized by much literary merit, were popular rather than scholarly. T. F. HENDERSON, *rev.* NILANJANA BANERJI

Sources J. Paterson, *Autobiographical reminiscences* (1871) · Irving, *Scots.* · catalogue [BM] · Boase, *Mod. Eng. biog.*

Paterson, James (1854–1932). *See under* Glasgow Boys (*act.* 1875–1895).

Paterson, John (1604–1679), bishop of Ross, was the son of Alexander Paterson, minister of Logie Dunro. He graduated MA from King's College, Aberdeen, in 1624 and was admitted to his first charge as minister of Foveran parish church in Aberdeenshire on 29 November 1632. An apparent supporter of Erastian episcopacy, Paterson refused to sign the national covenant in 1639 and like many of his co-religionists consequently fled Scotland to seek the king's protection. However, by July 1640 he had publicly recanted before the general assembly, was censured, and was restored to his previous incumbency of Foveran. Reconciled to the new regime he took an active role in the deliberations of the church and was a member of the commission of assembly in 1644, 1645, 1648, and 1649. He was appointed by parliament to conduct a visitation of the University of Aberdeen on 27 March 1647 and again on 31 July 1649. On 9 September 1649 Paterson was translated to Ellon, where he remained for the space of ten years before accepting a call, on 16 August 1659, to minister in Aberdeen. He was among the benefactors who contributed to the erection of a new building at King's College, Aberdeen, in 1658.

After the restoration of the monarchy and the re-establishment of episcopacy Paterson was promoted to the bishopric of Ross in January 1662 and received consecration in Holyroodhouse on 7 May that same year. In addition to being a noted poet, his *Tandem bona causa triumphat, or, Scotlands late misery bewailed, and the honour …*

of this antient kingdom asserted, a sermon preached to parliament in Edinburgh, was published in Edinburgh and London in 1661. His marriage to Elizabeth Ramsay produced six sons and one daughter: John *Paterson (1632–1708), later archbishop of Glasgow; George Paterson of Seafield (MA from Marischal College, 1656), commissary; Sir William Paterson (*d.* 1709) of Granton (MA from Marischal College, 1663), barrister and clerk to the privy council; Thomas Paterson (MA from Marischal College, 1658), regent; Robert Paterson, principal of Marischal College, Aberdeen; James Paterson (MA from Marischal College, 1671); and Isabella Paterson, who married Major Kenneth Mackenzie of Suddie. Paterson died in January 1679, and was buried on the 24th.   A. S. WAYNE PEARCE

Sources *Fasti Scot.*, new edn, 7.356 · *The memoirs of Henry Guthry, late bishop*, 2nd edn (1747), 77–8 · *The letters and journals of Robert Baillie*, ed. D. Laing, 3 (1842), 486 · *The diary of Alexander Brodie of Brodie … and of his son James Brodie*, ed. D. Laing, Spalding Club, 33 (1863) · *DNB*

Paterson, John (1632–1708), archbishop of Glasgow, was the eldest son of John *Paterson (1604–1679), minister of Foveran and later bishop of Ross, and Elizabeth Ramsay, his wife. Admitted to Marischal College, Aberdeen, in 1648, on 13 March 1655 he was admitted to study theology at St Andrews. Having taught for a year, on 3 February 1658 he was entered as a regent in St Leonard's College there. On 28 October 1658 he married Margaret (*d. c.*1685), daughter of Henry Wemyss, brother of the principal, George Wemyss of Conland. In April 1659, after the first child of their large family was born, Paterson publicly acknowledged his antenuptial fornication, the first of several scandals alleged during his lifetime.

On 6 November 1659 Paterson was called, against some opposition, to succeed his father at Ellon, Aberdeenshire, where he was admitted in June 1660. On 24 October 1662 Edinburgh town council chose him for the Tron Kirk, to which he was admitted on 4 January 1663. Appointed a royal chaplain on 6 May 1668, in 1671 he was considered for the archdeaconry of St Andrews, but on 12 July 1672 became dean of Edinburgh, and on 13 November 1673 a burgess there. Both Archbishop James Sharp and the duke of Lauderdale, for whom he acted as eyes and ears, appreciated his abilities and strong opposition to the agitation for a national synod during 1674, rewarding him with an appointment to the see of Galloway on 20 October 1674.

After his consecration in May 1675 Bishop Paterson mainly administered his diocese from Edinburgh, where he had licence to live on the grounds there was no sufficient dwelling in Galloway. He opposed further indulgence of presbyterians in 1676–7, zealously supporting Lauderdale's later policy of intolerance. His reward on 27 September 1678 was a seat on the privy council, which he very diligently attended. His brother William was council clerk. On 29 March 1679, at the duchess of Lauderdale's behest, he was translated to the bishopric of Edinburgh, which was vacated by the humiliating translation to Ross of Bishop Young to succeed Paterson's father, who had died in January. In 1681 Paterson was called upon to

John Paterson (1632–1708), circle of Sir John Baptiste de Medina, 1700

explain the Test Act to persuade refusers to comply. At this period he endured mockery as 'Bishop Band-Strings' in Gordon's *Reformed Bishop*, 1679 (p. 5), and attracted considerable odium as the only bishop on the privy council's committee for the security of the kingdom. In May 1684 the earl of Aberdeen stood accused of, among other wrongs, siding with those such as Paterson who were 'odious to the country' (Lauder, *Historical Observes*, 131). Caught in the struggle between Aberdeen, the marquess of Queensberry, and the earl of Perth, Paterson was omitted from the council on 15 July 1684, and stripped of his pension of £100 (granted on 9 July 1680), apparently because his claims for it were false. In April 1685 he was excluded from the new council appointed by James VII. That July he was granted 20,000 merks annually from the town of Edinburgh in lieu of an episcopal residence. About 1686 he married Mary Foulis (*d.* 1691) of the Colinton family.

In February 1686 Paterson accompanied Archbishop Arthur Ross to court to discuss church affairs and assure the king of their personal support for his proposed repeal of the sanguinary element of the penal laws against Catholics. On his return Paterson was reappointed to the council and granted a pension of £150 and other gifts, including the chancellorship of the University of Edinburgh, although the latter was not carried through. In May he helped to draft a bill for repeal, but it failed, partly because other bishops opposed it. He blamed the earl of Tweeddale and Viscount Tarbat, even boasting that he would have voted against the act. Fountainhall noted his 'craft and suttlety' (*Historical Notices*, 2.738). As Archbishop Alexander Cairncross of Glasgow fell from favour during 1686 Paterson and Ross were empowered to receive nonconformist clergy in his diocese. The council's records show that, despite his enduringly unpleasant reputation and political shrewdness, Paterson could also exercise clemency. James added him to the secret committee on 17 December 1686, and nominated him archbishop of Glasgow on 21 January 1687 in place of Cairncross, whom he deprived. On 8 March Paterson was translated to Glasgow. He sought unsuccessfully to hold Edinburgh *in commendam*, proposing the alienation of its revenues to the Chapel Royal at Holyrood, which prolonged the vacancy. On 29 January 1688 he preached a thanksgiving sermon for the queen's pregnancy. On 23 May he was reappointed to the privy council, and was consulted on measures against conventiclers.

On 3 November, in response to William of Orange's declarations, Paterson subscribed the bishops' declaration of loyalty, and in December he and his brethren commissioned bishops Bruce and Alexander Rose to consult the English hierarchy in London. He sought Archbishop William Sancroft's advice about representing the church's predicament, and excused his and the primate's compliance in 1686, which he ascribed to the bishops' vulnerability to the king's wide prerogative. On about 17 January he sent an address to Prince William for a proclamation to protect the parish clergy in the south and west subject to ejections. He recommended his dean, Robert Scott, who journeyed south for redress of their grievances, and was probably in London himself, returning in March for the sitting of the estates. He claimed that the bishops showed especial fortitude in upholding James's rights and interest in the intimidating presence of armed Cameronians, and under the temptation to comply with William and Mary's regime to secure themselves in office. In the committee of elections he vainly protested against the election of former traitors. He failed to persuade the convention to represent grievances to James before proceeding further, nor to prevent the forfaulture vote on 4 April by a strong speech in which he asserted James's rights, warned of civil war, and in the bishops' name dissented from the vote. The bishops withdrew from the convention and were absent when parliament abolished episcopacy on 22 July 1689.

As a result of his plotting with the earl of Arran and others, on 18 April 1691 the privy council ordered Paterson's imprisonment and the seizure of his papers. While in Edinburgh Castle, from which he was released once in July 1691 to visit his sick wife at Colinton, he persisted in Jacobite intrigue. Armed with evidence of a plot to coincide with a French invasion, the government persuaded him to accept voluntary banishment in January 1693. Next year, while at Leiden, where his son John was studying law, he attempted to gain the earl of Portland's favour by forwarding an invitation to St Germain that he had received from King James. He next lived in Hamburg. All his efforts to gain a remission failed until he was allowed to live under surveillance in London, where he arrived on 29 September 1695. He received an offer of marriage from a Lady Warner, which came to nothing. From June 1696 he sojourned at Norwich, then at Great Yarmouth, where

sympathizers 'much caress'd' him (*Letters of Humphrey Prideaux*, 181).

On his return to Scotland in early 1697 Paterson was obliged to live in or near Cupar, Fife. His complaints about confinement contrary to a subject's rights led to his release in 1701. At Queen Anne's accession he argued that episcopalians could now own Anne's title, because the Roman Catholic James Stuart was in effect a French prisoner, morally and physically incapable of the crown. At an episcopal meeting Archbishop Ross and Bishop Rose believed that they had secured an agreement not to adopt this legitimist position, but in January 1703 Paterson, aided by bishops George Haliburton and Ramsay, sponsored an address for toleration by about a hundred clergy. The Toleration Bill of 1703 failed, but Paterson tried to capitalize on his new found loyalty by unscrupulously highlighting his brethren's Jacobitism and portraying the duke of Queensberry, who had blocked the toleration measure, as the episcopalians' friend, much to the queen's bemusement. Nevertheless, besides stressing his role in fostering the former nonjurors' loyalty Paterson sought help for the clergy and his brother bishops at court during the winter of 1703–4. At the same time he wanted more for himself and his eleven children than the £300 sterling allowed to each archbishop in 1702. He secured a grant of £200 for their support after his death. His numerous begging letters during the years 1702–7 bear out the Jacobite George Lockhart of Carnwath's judgement that although possessed of 'extraordinary parts and great learning', Paterson above all indulged an 'avaricious worldly temper' (Lockhart, 1.84–5). Bishop Rose reckoned him the wealthiest churchman since the Reformation. Although the senior bishop from 1704, he was less active in church affairs than Rose, with whom in December 1704 he accredited Robert Scott as agent for the clergy charity. On 25 January 1705, in his private chapel, he, Rose, and Bishop Douglas consecrated John Sage and John Fullarton as bishops. He suffered increasing ill health, and after revoking parts of his peevish will, on 9 December 1708 he died at his house in Edinburgh, and was buried on 23 December in the Chapel Royal at Holyrood.

TRISTRAM CLARKE

Sources *Fasti Scot.*, new edn, vol. 7 · *DNB* · *Historical notices of Scotish affairs, selected from the manuscripts of Sir John Lauder of Fountainhall*, ed. D. Laing, 2 vols., Bannatyne Club, 87 (1848) · J. Lauder, *Historical observes of memorable occurrents in church and state, from October 1680 to April 1686*, ed. A. Urquhart and D. Laing, Bannatyne Club, 66 (1840) · *The Lauderdale papers*, ed. O. Airy, 3 vols., CS, new ser., 34, 36, 38 (1884–5) · *Report on the manuscripts of Allan George Finch*, 5 vols., HMC, 71 (1913–2003), vol. 3 · W. N. Clarke, ed., *A collection of letters addressed by prelates and individuals of high rank in Scotland ... to Sancroft, archbishop of Canterbury* (1848) · *Reg. PCS*, 3rd ser., vols. 5–16 · *Letters of Humphrey Prideaux ... to John Ellis*, ed. E. M. Thompson, CS, new ser., 15 (1875) · G. Lockhart, *The Lockhart papers*, 1 (1817) · P. Hopkins, *Glencoe and the end of the highland war* (1986) · J. Paterson, letters to Bishop Compton, 1698–1707, Bodl. Oxf., MS Rawl. C. 985 · P. J. Anderson and J. F. K. Johnstone, eds., *Fasti academiae Mariscallanae Aberdonensis: selections from the records of the Marischal College and University, MDXCIII–MDCCCLX*, 3 vols., New Spalding Club, 4, 18–19 (1889–98) · *The diary of Mr John Lamont of Newton, 1649–1671*, ed. G. R. Kinloch, Maitland Club, 7 (1830) · J. H. McMaster and M. Wood, eds., *Supplementary report on the manuscripts of his grace the* *duke of Hamilton*, HMC, 21 (1932) · D. Laing, notes on authors, U. Edin. L., MS La.IV.19, box P–R · J. Kirkton, *A history of the Church of Scotland, 1660–1679*, ed. R. Stewart (1992) · E. B. Fryde and others, eds., *Handbook of British chronology*, 3rd edn, Royal Historical Society Guides and Handbooks, 2 (1986) · J. Hunter, *The diocese and presbytery of Dunkeld, 1660–1689*, 2 vols. [1915], vol. 1 · testament and inventory, NA Scot., CC8/8/84, fols. 146v–157r · *The account book of Sir John Foulis of Ravelston, 1671–1707*, ed. A. W. C. Hallen, Scottish History Society, 16 (1894), 140 · NA Scot., CH12/12/1785; RD2/66, fols. 983–4 **Archives** Bodl. Oxf., papers relating to the Test Act · NA Scot., letters and MSS in the episcopal chest | BL, letters to duke of Lauderdale, Charles II, etc., Add. MSS 23135–23138, 23242–23249 · Bodl. Oxf., letters to Bishop Compton, Rawl. C. 985 · Buckminster Park, Grantham, corresp. with duke and duchess of Lauderdale · Glos. RO, letters to J. Sharp · LPL, letters to Archbishop Tenison · NA Scot., letters to earl of Mar · NL Scot., letters to earl of Balcarres **Likenesses** circle of J. B. de Medina, oils, 1700; Christies, Edinburgh, 8 June 1995, lot 825 [*see illus.*] **Wealth at death** £125,490 9s. 10d. Scots: will and inventory, NA Scot., CC 8/8/84, fols. 146v–157r

Paterson, John (1776–1855), missionary, third child of George Paterson of Duntocher in the parish of Old Kilpatrick, near Glasgow, was born at Duntocher on 26 February 1776, and became a student at the University of Glasgow in 1798. He was attracted by the religious revival which sprang out of the preaching of James Alexander Haldane, and applied for admission into a class formed by the Congregationalists to train young men for the ministry. He was sent to Dundee, and spent the greater part of 1800 there under the care of the Revd W. Innes. After moving to Glasgow, he on 5 July 1803 became the minister of a church which he had formed at Cambuslang, but relinquished it on 17 June 1804, with the intention of going out as a missionary to India. Accordingly, on 27 August, accompanied by his friend Ebenezer Henderson, he sailed for Denmark, but finding it impossible to continue from there to India he remained in northern Europe, where he became an effective missionary.

Gradually Paterson's connection with the churches in Scotland was dissolved, and he was left to his own resources. He remained in Denmark until after the bombardment of Copenhagen in 1807, when he settled in Stockholm. Here during the next five years he continued his labours among the Scandinavians. The British and Foreign Bible Society helped him to carry out his plans (though he was at no time the society's salaried agent). In 1812 he moved to St Petersburg, and on 1 November 1817 he received the degree of doctor of theology from the University of Abo in Finland. In 1822 he withdrew from the British and Foreign Bible Society, and Prince Galitzin and other friends in St Petersburg requested him to conduct the affairs of the Russian Bible Society. the emperor Alexander granted him an annual salary of 6000 roubles. On the death of the emperor the party in power raised objections to the circulation of the scriptures. Ultimately, in 1825, the emperor Nicholas issued ukases suspending the operations of the Bible Society and placing the society under the control of the Greek church. Thereupon Paterson left Russia; but the emperor treated him with great kindness, and continued to him his pension for life. During his residence in northern Europe he was connected with the work of translating and printing portions of the scriptures into Finnish, Georgian, Icelandic, Sami, Latvian, Moldavian, Russian, Samogitian, and Swedish.

On returning home Paterson settled in Edinburgh, and served for many years as secretary for Scotland of the London Missionary Society, also acting as chairman of the committee of the Congregational Union. In 1850 he moved to Dundee, where he occasionally preached.

Paterson married, first, at Stockholm, on 31 August 1809, Katrine Magarate Hollinder, who died on 7 March 1813, leaving two children, one of whom, Dr George Paterson (*b*. 18 March 1811), became Congregational minister at Tiverton. He married, second, on 19 April 1817, Jane, daughter of Admiral Samuel Greig of the Russian navy; she was born in Russia (26 October 1783), and from her knowledge of Russian and Russian dialects was of much help to her husband in his work at St Petersburg. She died on 19 January 1820, leaving a daughter, who became the wife of Edward Baxter of Kincaldrum. Paterson died at Kincaldrum, Forfarshire, on 6 July 1855.

G. C. BOASE, rev. H. C. G. MATTHEW

Sources W. Norrie, *Dundee celebrities of the nineteenth century* (1873) · *Memoir of the late Mrs Paterson … containing extracts from her diary and correspondence*, ed. W. Swan, 2nd edn (1823) · W. Canton, *A history of the British and Foreign Bible Society*, 5 vols. (1904–10) **Archives** CUL, corresp. and journals · SOAS **Likenesses** Jenkins, stipple (after Jarvis), NPG

Paterson, Mary Muirhead (1864–1941), factory inspector and philanthropist, was born in Glasgow on 23 June 1864, the daughter of Gavin and Annie Paterson. Her father was an affluent businessman; her mother came from a well-known Glasgow family, the Muirheads. Mary Paterson was described as having a gracious personality and great charm. She received her early education at Glasgow Ladies' College; later she was one of the first women students at Queen Margaret College, Glasgow, although the college did not at that time award degrees to women. She had an early and long-standing interest in industrial employment, informing herself of conditions in Scotland, Canada, and the United States of America. While undertaking charitable work in Scotland she gained much knowledge of working-class women's working conditions.

In 1893 Mary Paterson was appointed one of the first two female factory inspectors, together with May Tennant, and she was, therefore, one of the first women to exercise any real authority in industry or power over employers. Her appointment was the direct result of a recommendation of the royal commission on labour (1891–3) for the appointment of women factory inspectors; it was indirectly the result of years of campaigning among trade unionists for the appointment of (working-class) women inspectors, and by middle-class women for greater employment opportunities. In some ways Mary Paterson was pioneering a new kind of work for middle-class women, for—unlike many of the openings for women—factory inspection had no religious links, it was paid, it could not be seen as an extension of domestic work, and it did not fit in with Victorian notions of feminine respectability. There was, however, a link with women's philanthropic interest in the industrial working class. From the outset she drew attention in her reports, extracts of which were published annually, to the appalling conditions and long hours she unearthed in her investigations. Enormous praise was heaped on Paterson and the other early women inspectors, although what they were able to achieve in practice was severely limited; they dealt with the working conditions of all women and girls who came under the Factory and Workshop Acts. At first she was based in Glasgow and travelled around Scotland and the north of England undertaking inspections. In 1903 she was promoted to senior lady inspector and in 1908 to deputy principal lady inspector, with a transfer to London.

In 1912, as a result of the 1911 National Insurance Act, Paterson became one of the first national health insurance commissioners for Scotland, a post she held until 1919. Just as she had played a pioneering role in women's entry into the factory inspectorate, so too she now took on a newly created administrative role. Based in Edinburgh, she became widely known throughout Scotland as a progressively minded official, who was especially keen to bring women, most of whom were excluded from national health insurance, into the scheme. National health insurance commissioners formed a chain linking central government with local insurance committees and approved societies, to which they distributed money to meet insurance claims. Mary Paterson was well placed to play this bridging role: she was well known in influential London policy-making circles and she made a point of developing close contacts across Scotland. In 1920 she was appointed a CBE.

After her retirement Mary Paterson was heavily involved in philanthropic and civic activities. She again acted as a bridge, this time a symbolic one, between those women active in associational life, who in the nineteenth century and early twentieth century had been largely preoccupied with philanthropic work and local civic life, and a growing body of middle-class professional women, many of whose occupations grew out of this earlier voluntary tradition; the two now continued alongside one another. In the course of the 1920s and 1930s Paterson was variously a JP in Edinburgh, vice-chair of the Scottish Justices and Magistrates Association, chair of the District Nursing Association, honorary member of the British Federation of University Women, and a member of both the League of Nations Union and the Edinburgh Citizens' Association. In her later years she was interested in hospital work and became honorary secretary of the Edinburgh Hospital for Women and Children and a supporter of the Elsie Inglis Maternity Hospital in Edinburgh. She was a well-known speaker in various societies in Glasgow and Edinburgh. Mary Paterson died unmarried on 10 June 1941 at her home in Craufurd, Lasswade, Scotland.

HELEN JONES

Sources *Glasgow Herald* (11 June 1941) · *The Scotsman* (11 June 1941) · 'Chief inspector of factories and workshops', *Parl. papers* (1894–1912) [annual reports] · A. Anderson, *Women in the factory: an administrative adventure, 1893–1921* (1922), 5.56, 103, 115–16, 155–6, 201 · R. Squire, *Thirty years in the public service* (1927), 38 · *The Times* (31 March 1920) · H. Jones, 'Women health workers: the case of the first women factory inspectors in Britain', *Social History of Medicine*, 1 (1988), 165–81 · M. D. McFeely, *Lady inspectors: the campaign for a better workplace, 1893–1921* (1988), 15–17, 115, 122, 170 · *IGI* · census returns, 1901

Wealth at death £3588 1s. 10d.: probate, 15 Nov 1941, CGPLA Eng. & Wales

Paterson, Nathaniel (1787–1871), Free Church of Scotland minister and author, was born in the parish of Kells, Kirkcudbrightshire, on 3 July 1787, the eldest son of Walter Paterson (d. 1812), stone-engraver, and his wife, Mary Locke (d. 1819), and grandson of Robert *Paterson, the prototype of Sir Walter Scott's *Old Mortality*. He was educated at Balmaclellan parish school, where he gained a prize for cock-fighting, then a recognized school sport. He matriculated at Edinburgh University in 1804, where he studied for the ministry of the Church of Scotland, in which course he was soon followed by his brother Walter (1789–1850). Licensed by the presbytery of Linlithgow in April 1816, he occupied a number of positions as a tutor until ordained minister of Galashiels, Selkirkshire, in August 1821. His presentation to Galashiels was on the recommendation of David Monro Binning, the uncle of the patron, and to whose family at Auchenbowie, Stirlingshire, he had been tutor. Local opposition to his settlement was so strong that he was, in effect, intruded on the congregation. However, he overcame this, and grew in popularity in spite of his eccentric style of preaching: prone to nerves, he averted his eyes from his listeners, and his arms and hands took on a life of their own.

On 8 February 1825 Paterson married Margaret (1800–1864), daughter of Robert Laidlaw of Peel, with whom he had three daughters and six sons. His father-in-law was a friend and neighbour of Sir Walter Scott and Paterson also became friendly with the famous novelist. His wife's influence is credited for his growing earnestness as a minister and his 'conversion' from moderate views during this period. At the time of the Reform Bill he was assailed by a mob when he voted in the tory interest and he was spat upon in his own church. This may have influenced his decision to move soon after to St Andrew's parish, Glasgow, to which he was admitted in February 1834. In 1836 he published *The Manse Garden*, which had been written during a spell of illness at Galashiels and which displayed his extensive horticultural knowledge. Although it first appeared anonymously, its authorship was soon recognized and it passed through many subsequent editions. His other publications, lectures and sermons, were slight.

In 1837 Paterson was honoured with the degree of DD by Glasgow University. He left the established church at the Disruption of 1843 and ministered to the congregation of Free St Andrew's, Glasgow, thereafter. Although he fell ill during the cholera epidemic of 1848, he survived and served as moderator of the Free Church general assembly in 1850. He was also elected a member of the Royal Physical Society in that year. In 1856 his declining energies were acknowledged with the appointment of a colleague at Free St Andrew's. He moved to Helensburgh, Dunbartonshire, in 1868, where two of his daughters kept house for him until his death there, at Newark Villa, on 25 April 1871.

Of middle height, in later life Paterson presented a striking figure with a mass of white, curly hair reaching down to his shoulders, dark eyes, and a grave countenance; he was thus inevitably likened to an Old Testament prophet. Throughout his life he maintained a passionate interest in all aspects of nature, especially angling. Mechanical inventions likewise enthralled him and he was himself the designer of a lifeboat, a model of which he exhibited at the British Association meeting in Glasgow in 1840.

LIONEL ALEXANDER RITCHIE

Sources *Letters to his family by Nathaniel Paterson DD with brief memoir by Rev. Alexander Anderson* (1874) • *Fasti Scot.* • A. Trotter, *East Galloway sketches, or, Biographical, historical and descriptive notices of Kirkcudbrightshire, chiefly in the nineteenth century* (1901), 313–21 • R. Hall, *History of Galashiels* (1898), 212–15 • J. Smith, *Our Scottish clergy*, 2nd ser. (1849), 123–8 • *Border Magazine*, 9/101 (June 1904), 101–5
Likenesses J. J. Napier, portrait, exh. 1894 • photograph, repro. in *Letters to his family*, frontispiece • photograph (in later life), repro. in Trotter, *East Galloway sketches*, 313
Wealth at death £3010 0s. 9d.: confirmation, 2 Nov 1871, NA Scot., SC 65/34/17/196 • £669 9s. 10d.—funds invested in mortgage in America: further action, 2 Nov 1871, NA Scot., SC 65/34/17/196

Paterson, (James) Ralston Kennedy (1897–1981), radiotherapist, was born in Edinburgh on 21 May 1897, the eldest son of the Revd David Paterson (1862–1943) and his wife, Susannah Simpson Ralston Kennedy (1869–1951). He was a true son of the manse: as well as his father, four of his uncles and his maternal grandfather were ministers of the Free Church of Scotland and also his maternal grandfather. The young Paterson had outstanding intellectual and physical attributes. He left George Heriot's School in Edinburgh as gold medallist and dux (leader of his class). During the First World War he joined the army and fought as lieutenant with the Argyll and Sutherland Highlanders at Ypres and on the Somme. In 1918 he was awarded the Military Cross.

Upon demobilization Paterson entered the school of medicine of the University of Edinburgh. When he graduated MB ChB with first-class honours in 1923, he had already edged towards his vocation, having served an undergraduate attachment to Hope Fowler, senior radiologist of the Edinburgh Royal Infirmary. During the next six years Paterson acquired the experience and postgraduate diplomas which equipped him to fill most posts in radiology. He worked as a hospital radiologist in Aberdeen, Wales, and South Africa, and completed the six-month course in Cambridge for the university's diploma of medical radiology and electrology (DMRE). In 1925 he returned to Edinburgh to obtain the surgical fellowship (FRCS Edin.). The most decisive part of his training was a fellowship in 1926–7 in radiology at the Mayo Clinic, Rochester, Minnesota, which had divided its radiology department into three sections, each under the supervision of a dedicated radiologist. This opened Paterson's

(James) Ralston Kennedy Paterson (1897–1981), by Lafayette, 1950

eyes to the prospect of a career as a dedicated radiotherapist. Unlike most fellows he remained only three months in the diagnostic division before spending six months in therapeutics and three months in radium therapy. Then followed a further year of training in Chicago and two years of general radiological practice in Toronto.

In July 1930, in Manhattan, Paterson married his Edinburgh classmate Edith Isabel Myfanwy [**Edith Isabel Myfanwy Paterson** (1900–1995)], who was born at 221 Gorgie Road, Edinburgh, on 21 November 1900, the only daughter of Henry Irvine-Jones, medical practitioner, and his wife, Margaret Irvine. In 1926 she had sailed together with Paterson and his sister Susanne (also a doctor) to the USA to train as a paediatrician in San Francisco and at the Washington school of medicine in St Louis. The couple kept in touch, and after their marriage RP and EP (as everyone henceforth knew them) returned briefly to Toronto and packed their bags. Ralston Paterson had accepted an unexpected offer to be acting head of the radiology department of Edinburgh Royal Infirmary. But within months of starting work he discovered that the job combined administration with diagnosis and there was little scope for a dedicated radiotherapeutic practice.

In 1931 Paterson was offered the post of radium director for two facilities in Manchester; one of them was the Holt

Radium Institute, named after Sir Edward Holt, a local brewer and lord mayor of Manchester, who with his wife donated a store of radium to the community and a building to house it. The other was the Christie Hospital for Incurables, a hospice offering terminal nursing care for patients with inoperable cancer. Paterson foresaw the potential for creating a modern radiotherapy centre; he was the powerful catalyst that brought these institutions under one roof in 1933. His appointment as the director of the Holt Radium Institute at the Christie Hospital was the start of his major contributions. Paterson saw the need to centralize the costly diagnostic and treatment facilities under one roof, linked to small satellite clinics in the surrounding health region. This organizational concept became the blueprint for the United Kingdom when enshrined in the Cancer Act of 1939 and was widely copied abroad.

Paterson now set about reviewing the scientific fundamentals of radium and X-ray treatment, usually then seen as an adjunct to surgery or as a palliative option in patients with inoperable tumours. During visits to Paris, Stockholm, and other leading European centres, he was astonished to find widely discrepant views on important factors such as the strength of the radiation source, the duration and frequency of treatment, and the size of the dose delivered to the tumour. None of these variables had been tested scientifically; the success of treatment was judged by crude clinical impression. Paterson was encouraged by the knowledge that all humans respond to radiation in much the same way. By accumulating a body of clinical experience, including the meticulous follow-up of large numbers of patients, he believed that an optimum dose could be arrived at for a particular tumour. Paterson's approach was the basis of the Manchester system, which in the early 1930s aroused the curiosity of radiotherapists around the world and within a decade received their enthusiastic endorsement.

Novel aspects of the Manchester system were its emphasis on standardization, scientific measurement, and transferability; that is, treatments were so carefully planned and documented that a patient could transfer to another centre to complete the course. Paterson insisted upon sharing credit with his medical physicists, and notably with the young theoretician H. M. Parker (1910–1984). The Paterson–Parker dosimetry rules for applying radium to surface lesions (1934) and to internal tumours (1938) were immediately adopted by radiotherapists, and were to remain the basis of this treatment. All treatments at the Christie Hospital were standardized for the same type of tumour. Various 'gadgets' were devised to facilitate these aims, and they helped to give the Manchester system its style, which left a mark on countless radiotherapy departments around the world.

One of Paterson's Edinburgh referees described him as 'a young fellow full of brains and go … what we call a dour Scot', and these virtues were never more tested than during his early years in Manchester. Surgeons had to be weaned from implanting radium in their patients themselves and district hospital radiologists had to be won over

from using their X-ray apparatus to administer radiotherapy. Both of these groups had to be persuaded to refer cancer patients to the new professionals, the radiotherapists. Gradually Paterson's views prevailed, and by 1940 his dream had become a reality. Visitors arrived in droves to examine the details of Manchester's success, such as its peripheral clinics and ancillary departments—medical physics, clinical statistics, the central case registry, the plaster room, and notably the research department.

Edith Paterson exerted as intense a catalytic effect on basic cancer research as her husband had done on the clinical practice of radiotherapy. In 1933 she was allowed the free use of one room in the Holt Institute without equipment or salary, to elucidate clinical problems associated with the new radiation techniques being pioneered by her husband. She went to the Strangeways Research Laboratory, Cambridge, to learn about tissue culture, to enable her to utilize a technique using chick embryos in her own laboratory. The results of this early work led to her international recognition as an independent and respected researcher and one of the world's first radiobiologists; it heralded the start of serious research into cancer at the Christie Hospital. After some years Edith Paterson was elected to the hospital staff as a research radiobiologist and a consultant physician, and later she was appointed a university lecturer in radiobiology in the medical school. Using other tissue-culture techniques, she set out to explore whether X- and gamma-rays exert different effects on tissues, and she went on to discover important data of value in optimizing dose-fractionation regimens for tumours. Her early paediatric training reasserted itself, and she devised, with the physicists associated with Ralston Paterson's pioneering programmes, a radiotherapeutic technique for medulloblastomas and other malignant tumours of the child brain.

Ralston Paterson's papers appeared regularly in the medical press reporting promising results of cancer therapy or describing novel radiation techniques, which kept his name and his centre before a worldwide audience. In the early 1930s he was drawn into the political struggle of British radiologists with their hospital colleagues for equal medical status. It was widely recognized that this battle could be won only if the membership of their national body was restricted to radiologists, that is, specialist doctors. In 1934 the British Association of Radiologists was formed, and in the following year the Society of Radiotherapists of Great Britain and Ireland was created as an additional body for the therapists. In 1939 these two bodies merged to form the Faculty of Radiologists (the precursor of the present Royal College of Radiologists). Paterson was the key negotiator in all these arrangements and he was the only radiologist to serve as president of all three bodies—the association in 1936–7, the society in 1938–9, and the faculty in 1943–6.

During the Second World War, Paterson was invited by the Australian state governments to advise on the organization of regional radiotherapy centres. He and his wife travelled to Australia and consulted over plans to centralize cancer treatment in Sydney, Melbourne, Adelaide, and

Brisbane. This was a prelude to the visits Paterson made after the war to other parts of the old Commonwealth, and to Brazil, the Soviet Union, and elsewhere. The world-wide shortage of high-quality radiotherapy units immediately after the war prompted Paterson and others to offer a one-year course for prospective radiotherapists working towards the diploma of medical radiation therapy (DMRT). Similar courses were soon arranged in London, Edinburgh, and other cities, yet the Manchester course, on account of the strength of its physics content, was always the most popular. This venture had a rich reward. By 1950 there were already twelve directors of radiotherapy in the United Kingdom who had been Paterson's students. By the year of his death this number had risen to more than sixty in the United Kingdom and in sixteen other countries.

Arising directly out of his participation in the DMRT course, Paterson wrote a book, *The Treatment of Malignant Disease by Radium and X-Rays; being a Practice of Radiotherapy* (1947). He planned it as a *vade mecum* of irradiation methods rather than a clinical textbook, which disappointed some of his readers. But it found a niche in a post-war market hungering after authoritative texts, and sold well.

In 1949 the Royal College of Surgeons bestowed a rare honour on Paterson and elected him FRCS *honoris causa*. None of the many honours he received gave him greater pleasure. The following year he was appointed CBE, and in July 1950 he served as president of the Sixth Congress of Radiology in London, the first radiotherapist from any country to be so honoured. Gold medals from learned societies and academic honours followed.

In 1947 Paterson pioneered the concept of randomized clinical trials in cancer therapy, and he continued actively to promote the growth and scope of laboratory research. He was also much occupied with the central direction and planning of radiotherapy in the United Kingdom. In 1950 he served on four ministerial advisory committees, in addition to working for the British Empire Cancer Campaign and the Medical Research Council (MRC). A few years later the MRC sited their Betatron Research Unit at the Christie Hospital and appointed Paterson the honorary director. Immediately he devised a programme to test the comparative efficacy of 20 mv and 4 mv radiations using a wide range of modalities, such as radiation chemistry, tissue culture studies, and animal models in the laboratory, and a variety of clinical reactions. The Patersons published the results of this survey jointly in 1960; it was their final fundamental contribution to radiotherapy and radiobiology. In the same year the University of Manchester elected Ralston Paterson professor of radiotherapeutics. Two years later, on his retirement, he was made professor emeritus.

Edith Paterson retired in 1961 and Ralston Paterson in 1962. They made their home in the southern uplands of Scotland, at Stenrieshill Farm, near Moffat in Dumfries-shire. Both of them channelled their considerable energies into running their large holding, where they bred sheep and cattle. Ralston Paterson died there on 31 August 1981. He was cremated in Edinburgh, and his ashes were buried in the churchyard of Kirkpatrick Juxta church,

Beattock. He was survived by his wife, and their daughter and two sons. Edith Paterson, who was a keen birdwatcher and gardener, with a lively interest in music and painting, continued to run the farm until she was ninety-two. Ill health forced her to return to Edinburgh, where she died at 45 Canaan Lane on 27 September 1995. Her ashes were buried with her husband's.   E. H. BURROWS

Sources private information (2004) [Dr Elspeth Russell] • J. A. Del Regato, 'Ralston Paterson', *International Journal of Radiation Oncology and Biological Physics*, 13 (1987), 1081–91 • R. Paterson, 'Radiotherapy, 1929–59', *British Journal of Radiology*, 46 (1973), 768–70 • *BMJ* (16 Dec 1995), 1635 [obit. of Edith Paterson] • *Clinical Radiology*, 23 (1982), 119–20 • *British Journal of Radiology*, 54 (1981), 1122–3 • *BMJ* (26 Sept 1981), 868 • *Hospital Physicists' Association Bulletin* (7 Dec 1981) • *LondG* (16 Sept 1918) [suppl.; award of military cross] • letter from Miss K. H. Thomas, 24 April 1999, NAM • letter from Lieutenant-Colonel A. W. Scott, 5 May 1999, Regimental headquarters of the Argyll and Sutherland highlanders, Stirling Castle, Scotland • b. cert. [J. R. K. Paterson] • b. cert. [E. Paterson] • d. cert. [J. R. K. Paterson] • d. cert. [E. Paterson]
Likenesses Lafayette, photograph, 1950, priv. coll. [*see illus.*] • Topolski, cartoon • photographs, priv. coll.

Paterson, Rex Munro (1902–1978), agricultural innovator and farmer, was born on 15 February 1902 at 10 Oakhill Road, Wandsworth, London, the son of Claude Dunbar Paterson, clergyman, and Elsie Verdon Paterson, *née* Roe. His mother was the sister of Sir A. V. Roe, the famous aviation designer. Educated at Christ's Hospital school, in London, Paterson's early professional aspirations were divided between pursuing a career in engineering and farming in Canada. At the age of seventeen he emigrated to Canada, where he farmed until his return in 1925. On his return he initially took over a small farm in Hampshire, and then in 1929 he moved to a 400 acre farm in Wiltshire. In 1936 he became tenant of a 1000 acre farm in Sussex and in the following year he rented Hatch Warren Farm, Cliddesden, near Basingstoke, Hampshire; Hatch Warren became synonymous with the farming empire he helped to establish.

Paterson's success stemmed mainly from his adoption of a cheap, grass-based system of dairy production. This was founded on the outdoor 'bail' system pioneered initially by A. J. Hosier. His unorthodox yet highly profitable approach to outdoor milk production not only eliminated the need for traditional cowsheds but also led to a significant reduction in the amount of labour required. Herds of up to sixty milking cows were being managed by one man and an assistant. These contrasted starkly with the more usual herds, of fewer than twenty cows, which were milked in a cowshed. Paterson's successful system was not, however, widely adopted by other farmers. In part this was because it was only suited to lighter soils, but it also reflected farmers' attitudes to such pioneering systems.

The outbreak of the Second World War led to the continued expansion of Paterson's farming empire, which by 1942 amounted to more than 10,000 acres. By this time Paterson was the largest farmer in Hampshire. The wartime food production campaign, with its emphasis on arable rather than livestock farming, radically altered his farming system. It also, from 1943, led to a prolonged disagreement between Paterson and the administrators of the scheme, the Hampshire War Agricultural Executive Committee. This was only resolved following an official investigation during 1944 and 1945, which vindicated Paterson's claims that he was being victimized by the local officials.

After the war Paterson became county chairman of the National Farmers' Union and he served on a number of county and headquarters' committees, including the development and education committee. During this period he played an important role as an agricultural innovator in respect of mechanization. His major contribution in this respect was the development of the Paterson buckrake, a tractor-mounted machine designed to move grass more effectively than traditional methods. Paterson's first wife, Murial, with whom he had four children, died in April 1944 and a few years later he married Marjorie (née Davies), with whom he had two children.

In 1964 Paterson served as chairman of the Oxford farming conference; his services to agriculture were also recognized when he was appointed OBE. In the following year he received the Massey Ferguson award in recognition of his outstanding contribution to the advancement of agriculture in the United Kingdom. In 1967 he became the president of the British Grassland Society.

Paterson made a significant contribution to the development of British agriculture in the twentieth century. As a self-made man in the farming world he played a key role in devising a more efficient means of milk production, and also he helped to pioneer the development of mechanized large-scale farming. He died on 13 December 1978 at Basingstoke District Hospital and was buried at St Leonard's Church, Cliddesden, Basingstoke.

JOHN MARTIN

Sources 'The man who built a farming empire', *The Gazette* (22 Dec 1978), 2 · Q. Seldon, *The silent revolution* (1989) · 'Rex Paterson and the Hants WAEC', *Farmers' Weekly* (10 Nov 1944), 21 · 'Settlement in Paterson case', *Farmers' Weekly* (15 Dec 1944), 1 · 'Strong exception to minister's statement', *Farmers' Weekly* (5 Jan 1945), 12 · b. cert. · d. cert.
Archives SOUND U. Reading, Rural History Centre
Likenesses photograph, repro. in 'Rex Paterson and the Hants WAEC'
Wealth at death £374,042: probate, 14 June 1979, *CGPLA Eng. & Wales*

Paterson, Robert [nicknamed Old Mortality] (bap. **1716**, d. **1801**), stonemason, was born at Haggisha, in the parish of Hawick, and baptized on 25 April 1716, the youngest son of Walter Paterson, farmer, and his wife, Margaret Scott. In his thirteenth year he served an apprenticeship under his brother Francis at the Corncockle quarry, Lochmaben, and it was there that he 'mastered the stone-craft which was to carry his name wherever the English language is spoken' (Crockett, 171). Through his marriage about 1743 to Elizabeth, daughter of Robert Gray, gardener to Sir John Jardine, and for some considerable time cook-maid to Sir Thomas Kirkpatrick of Closeburn, Dumfriesshire, and with the assistance of Sir Thomas, Robert obtained from the duke of Queensberry a lease of a freestone quarry at Gatelowbrigg in the parish of Morton. There he built a house shortly before 1746, and it was soon thereafter that his house was plundered and he was arrested by the highlanders *en route* to Glasgow from England. One version has it that he had been so unwise as to curse the house of Stuart and to fulminate against the heresies of the Church of Rome. Another has it that he merely had to show the highlanders to the 'nearest smithy' (ibid., 172).

At some time after his release Paterson joined the sect of hillmen known as Cameronians, followers of the covenanting minister Richard Cameron (d. 1680). Paterson went frequently into Galloway to the Cameronian conventicles and made a more remarkable contribution to the sect by carrying gravestones from his quarry which he erected over the graves of martyred members of the sect. His religious piety may have degenerated into religious mania, and about 1758 he failed to return to his wife and five children from one of his journeys into Galloway. There is no evidence of marital discord, but when his twelve-year-old son, Walter, was sent to find him and persuade him to return home and failed in his attempts, Paterson's wife sent his daughters in quest of their father, who, when found, again refused to return home. His wife, after a period of some ten years, reconciled to his continued absence, moved to the little upland village of Balmaclellan in the Glenkins of Galloway, where she maintained her family by setting up a little school. She died in 1785.

Legend has it that for over forty years Paterson rode through the whole lowlands of Scotland on a white pony repairing Cameronian and other monuments without any fee or reward. Before being known as Old Mortality he was variously and affectionately called the Hewer or the Letterer or the Headstoneman. Indeed, there is documentary evidence that he was meticulous in paying for any food or lodging he was given, and when he died he was found to have but £1 7s. 6d. on his person. Paterson died at Bankhill, near Lockerbie, on 14 February 1801, leaving his three sons, John, Walter, and Robert, and, presumably, his two daughters, Margaret and Jane. He was buried in the churchyard of Caerlaverock in the same month. Sir Walter Scott's novel *Old Mortality* (1816) is based on Paterson's life, and Sir Walter's introduction to the novel is the basis for biographical accounts of Paterson's life. The two met in 1793, and the description of Old Mortality and his gaunt white pony in the novel is said to be from Scott's recollection of that meeting, a description that tallies with those of others of Paterson's contemporaries.

ARTHUR SHERBO

Sources W. Scott, *Old mortality*, ed. J. Stevenson and P. Davidson · W. S. Crockett, *The Scott original* (1932) · *DNB* · *The letters of Sir Walter Scott*, ed. H. J. C. Grierson and others, centenary edn, 12 vols. (1932–79), vols. 4, 10–11

Paterson, Samuel (1728–1802), bookseller and auctioneer, was born on 17 March 1728, probably in the parish of St Paul, Covent Garden, London, where his father was a woollen draper. On the death of his father in 1740 he was sent to France to be cared for by a guardian. He returned to London about 1748 and opened a bookshop specializing in foreign literature opposite Durham Yard in the Strand.

There is no record of his having received any formal education, but he obviously read widely and gained a reputation for great erudition. He had already married a Miss Hamilton (d. 1790), niece of the countess of Eglinton. They had three sons: Charles, John, and Samuel, whose godfather was Samuel Johnson and who gained some reputation as an artist. There was also at least one daughter, Margaret, who married James Pearson, a well-known glass-painter.

In 1747 Paterson published the *Poems on Several Occasions* by Charlotte Ramsay, who soon became Charlotte Lennox, the author of *The Female Quixote* (1752). He also introduced her to Johnson, who praised her work extravagantly and, in turn, introduced her to Richardson. Paterson was not, however, successful as a publisher and in 1753 established himself as a book auctioneer at Essex House in Essex Street, London. He there gained his great reputation as a cataloguer by issuing a series of classified catalogues with accurate, though brief, descriptions and by instituting the practice of selling books as individual lots. In 1757 he rescued the manuscripts of Sir Julius Caesar from a cheesemonger's shop to which they had been sold as waste paper, and auctioned them for £356. He continued to produce catalogues for notable sales, including the libraries of Sylvanus Morgan (1759), Robert Nelson (1760), James Parsons (1769), James West (1773), William Fletewode (1774), E. Rowe Mores (1779), Topham Beauclerk (1781), George Costard (1782), Thomas Crofts (1783), Maffeo Pinelli (1789), and John Strange (1801).

In 1771 Paterson issued a catalogue called *Bibliotheca Anglica curiosa*, an early contribution towards an English national bibliography, and, after several book-buying tours of the continent beginning in 1776, he produced *Bibliotheca universalis selecta*, according to the title-page a collection of 'almost every branch of science and polite literature', which he auctioned on Monday 8 May 1786 and over the following thirty-five days. His own original works of literature, however, did not increase his reputation; *Another Traveller*, issued under the pseudonym Coryat Junior between 1767 and 1769, followed a tour of the Netherlands in 1766. *Joineriana, or, The Book of Scraps* appeared anonymously in two volumes in 1772, and a sequel to part of it, *Speculations upon Law and Lawyers*, was published in 1788. In this latter work Paterson complains bitterly about the practice of English common law and demonstrates some real acquaintance with its machinations. At the end is announced, rather ominously, that shortly there will be published, by the same author, 'Letters written from the confines of the king's bench'. This work was never published, but the title is suggestive of what might have occupied some of his time between auction catalogues. From about 1788 until at least 1798 he was employed by the first marquess of Lansdowne as a librarian to arrange the famous collection of manuscripts which was sold to the British Museum in 1806. Paterson's last salesrooms were in King Street, Covent Garden. He died on 29 November 1802 at his house in Norton Street, from a wound caused by falling over a small dog-kennel which the landlady had left at the bottom of some stairs. He left £300 to his son John.

Samuel Paterson was remembered by his contemporaries, such as Joseph Nollekens, as a great cataloguer and auctioneer, and as a kind and amiable man with no head for business who would rather read his books than sell them. His series of catalogues, however, established him as a pioneer in the book auction trade. Each was arranged in a single alphabet by author and not broken down by book format, as was the usual custom. They were classified catalogues, the arrangement being set out at the beginning as an *ordo venditionis* ('order of sale'). Normally Paterson would begin with books on the history of language, and proceed through bibliography (an early use of the word, with its modern meaning, in an English context) and the history of libraries, theology, classical authors, modern languages, philosophy, science and medicine, history, geography and travel, and end with local topography. He would follow this with a *capita generalia*, which gave more detail for each class. The *Bibliotheca universalis selecta* also contained an index of authors and editors, possibly the first English auction catalogue to contain such a feature.   RICHARD LANDON

Sources *GM*, 1st ser., 72 (1802), 1074–5 · *European Magazine and London Review*, 41 (1802), 427 · A. Chalmers, ed., *The general biographical dictionary*, new edn, 24 (1815) · Nichols, *Lit. anecdotes*, 3.438–40; 8/483–4 · C. H. Timperley, *Encyclopaedia of literary and typographical anecdote*, 2nd edn (1842), 812–15 · J. T. Smith, *Nollekens and his times*, 2nd edn, 2 (1829), 279–84 · H. R. Plomer and others, *A dictionary of the printers and booksellers who were at work in England, Scotland, and Ireland from 1726 to 1775* (1932), 193 · S. Paterson, *Bibliotheca universalis selecta* (1786)
Wealth at death over £300: will

Paterson, Thomas (1780–1856), army officer, son of Robert Paterson of Plewlands, Ayrshire, entered the Royal Artillery as second lieutenant on 1 December 1795. After serving in Canada and the West Indies from 1796 to 1804, and becoming second captain on 19 July 1804, he took part in the expedition to Copenhagen under Lord Cathcart in 1807. He was attached to Baird's division, and after the army had landed he countered the Danish gunboats with his 9-pounders, while batteries were being prepared for the bombardment. He became captain on 1 February 1808, and in 1809 served in the disastrous Walcheren expedition.

Paterson was made brevet major on 4 June 1814; he became lieutenant-colonel in the regiment on 6 November 1827, and colonel on 10 January 1837. In 1836 he was made superintendent of the royal military repository, Woolwich. He was promoted major-general on 9 November 1846, and lieutenant-general on 30 June 1854, having become a colonel-commandant of the Royal Artillery on 15 August 1850. He died at Woolwich on 13 June 1856.

     E. M. LLOYD, *rev.* ROGER T. STEARN

Sources J. Philippart, ed., *The royal military calendar*, 3rd edn, 5 vols. (1820) · J. Kane, *List of officers of the royal regiment of artillery from 1716*, rev. edn (1869) · Irving, *Scots.* · *GM*, 3rd ser., 1 (1856) · Boase, *Mod. Eng. biog.*

Paterson, William (1658–1719), banking projector, was born in April 1658 in Skipmyre, Dumfriesshire, the son of John and Elizabeth Paterson. He had at least one sister. Paterson's early life is obscure, though Sir John Clerk of Penicuik later stated that he had been 'bred in England from his infancy' (*Memoirs*, 61). The first reliable record of his activities records his membership of the Merchant Taylors' Company on 16 November 1681; he was admitted to the livery of the company on 21 October 1689. In the years between, he had evidently been pursuing a precocious career as a merchant and projector in Europe, particularly in the Netherlands. His later career was spent promoting projects for an English bank on the Dutch model, for reform of the public revenues, and for a colony on the isthmus of Darien in Panama.

After the revolution of 1688, Paterson took advantage of the new fiscal and financial pressures created in England by the European wars entered into by William III and, along with other projectors, he throve off the inflated wartime economy. His projecting gained him a reputation for double-dealing and insincerity, as well earned as that for imagination and persuasiveness. Paterson first came to public notice in 1691, when he joined a group of London merchants who proposed that England should set up a bank of credit on the Dutch model. The proposal was initially rejected by a parliamentary committee in January 1692. In 1694 parliament approved a plan drawn up by Paterson, the merchant Michael Godfrey, and the Treasury commissioner Charles Montagu for a fund to support long-term public borrowing, a bank to administer it, and the mortgaging of future revenue for payment of interest to investors.

Paterson was thus among the first directors of the Bank of England when it was chartered on 27 July 1694. In a pattern typical of his career, he soon overreached himself and fell out with his colleagues. While still a director of the bank, he had proposed an interest-bearing fund to help City orphans, which his fellow directors saw only as competition to the bank in its search for capital. They pressed him to resign; he therefore sold his stock and left the board in high dudgeon on 27 February 1695. Thereafter, he turned to promote the longest-cherished of all his schemes, the plan for a colony on the isthmus of Darien. In 1702 he claimed that he had been promoting it since 1685; in 1687 he had been heard in the coffee houses of Amsterdam hawking his plan 'to Erect a Common Wealth and Free port in the Emperour of Dariens Countrey' (National Library of Scotland, MS Adv. 83.7.4, fols. 23v–24r); in 1690 he seems to have been the inspiration behind the foundation of the abortive Americaense Compagnie in Brandenburg. An act of the Scottish parliament of 26 June 1695 'for a Company Tradeing to Affrica and the Indies' named Paterson as one of ten London directors of the company. Opposition from the English East India Company forced Paterson to withdraw the original plan and propose a solely Scottish venture. Paterson subscribed for £3000 of company stock and in July 1696 was instrumental in persuading the company to create a free

William Paterson (1658–1719), by unknown artist, *c*.1708

port and colony in Darien. He travelled to Hamburg to encourage foreign subscriptions and organize the building of a fleet for the company. Paterson eventually accompanied the first, ill-fated, Scottish voyage to Darien in July 1698. After the collapse of a second expedition, and in the face of both Spanish and English opposition, the Scots abandoned the colony. Paterson married twice. His first wife was Elizabeth Turner, widow of Thomas Bridge, a minister of the gospel in New England, where she died. Paterson later married Hannah Kemp, widow of Samuel South; but his second wife and their child both died in Darien, where Paterson for a time lost his reason.

In 1701 Paterson proposed an interventionist council of trade to control Scotland's ailing economy in his *Proposals and Reasons for Constituting a Council of Trade*. The Scottish parliament did not take up his suggestion, and in London in 1701–2 he instead urged William III to revive the Darien Colony as a pan-British venture to counterbalance the Spanish-American empire in the face of the impending crisis over the Spanish succession; he also offered the king further plans for Anglo-Scottish union and the reform of public credit. In 1703 he proposed a public library of works on commerce and trade to encourage industry. By 1705 he was back in Edinburgh, this time as a pro-union propagandist for Robert Harley's government, as an observer of the Scottish parliamentary debates on union, and as one of the team that calculated the compensatory 'equivalent' for Scotland upon being subject to English customs and excise rates. The last session of the independent Scottish parliament in 1707 recommended Paterson to Queen Anne 'for his good service', and he was later returned as a member of the new parliament of the United Kingdom for Dumfriesshire in the election of 1708, though he was denied his seat on a technicality.

Paterson spent many of the remaining years of his life vexatiously petitioning the Westminster parliament for redress of the losses he incurred while a director of the Company of Scotland, though he finally received compensation only in 1715. He died in January 1719 (where is not known) and was buried in Sweetheart Abbey, Kirkcudbright. His will, proved at Doctors' Commons on 22 January 1719, left legacies to his step-children and to his sister Elizabeth. His lasting monument was the Bank of England. However, his attempt to supply London with water from reservoirs south of the Hampstead and Highgate hills in 1693, and his involvement with the Company of Scotland left behind more apt reminders of his erratic, ambitious, and controversial career: the Hampstead ponds and a handful of Scottish place names in Panama. Paterson was a classic example of the late seventeenth-century projector, more skilful at promoting his plans than at executing his projects, and more interested in his own self-advancement than in carrying through the consequences of his ideas. He was hardly the economic visionary hailed by his Victorian admirers; rather, he was a characteristic beneficiary of the novel economic conditions thrown up by the revolution of 1688, the beginnings of England's second hundred years of war against France, and the Anglo-Scottish union of 1707.

DAVID ARMITAGE

Sources *The writings of William Paterson*, ed. S. Bannister, 2nd edn, 3 vols. (1859) • W. Pagan, *The birthplace and parentage of William Paterson* (1865) • J. S. Barbour, *A history of William Paterson and the Darien Company* (1907) • T. J. Barratt, *The annals of Hampstead*, 3 vols. (1912) • *JHC* • Court Minute Book, 27/7/1694–20/3/1695, Bank of England Archives • J. Clapham, *The Bank of England: a history*, 2 vols. (1944) • Company of Scotland papers, NL Scot., MS Adv. • G. P. Insh, *The Company of Scotland trading to Africa and the Indies* (1932) • D. Armitage, 'The Scottish vision of empire: intellectual origins of the Darien Venture', *A union for empire*, ed. J. Robertson (1995), 97–118 • *Memoirs of the life of Sir John Clerk of Penicuik*, ed. J. M. Gray, Scottish History Society, 13 (1892) • *The manuscripts of his grace the duke of Portland*, 10 vols., HMC, 29 (1891–1931), vols. 4, 8 • D. Defoe, *History of the union* (1709) • *DNB* • will, proved, Doctors' Commons, 22 Jan 1719 **Archives** Glos. RO, letters | BL, Add. MSS and Harley MSS • Bodl. Oxf., Rawl. MSS • LUL, papers relating to Darien Co. • NL Scot., Advocates' MSS • NL Scot., letters relating to Darien Co. [copies] **Likenesses** pen-and-ink and wash drawing, *c.*1708, BL, Add. MS 10403, fol. iv [*see illus.*] • bust (after drawing in BL, Add. MS 10403), Bank of England, London • woodcut (after pen-and-ink and wash drawing in BL, Add. MS 10403), BM **Wealth at death** see will, proved at Doctors' Commons 22 Jan 1719, cited in *DNB*

Paterson, William (*fl.* **1716–1760**), colonial official and playwright, was born in Scotland. In February 1716 he

matriculated at the College of Edinburgh. After college he succeeded his brother James Paterson as master at Edinburgh grammar school before following his friend James Thomson to London. He became a member of the Society for the Encouragement of Learning in 1735, and a freemason in 1737.

Paterson's tragedy *Arminius*, whose hero and villain were thinly disguised portraits of, respectively, the prince of Wales and Walpole, was refused production by the lord chamberlain in 1740, but was printed in trade and subscription editions in that year. Patrick Murdoch, Thomson's biographer, claimed that Paterson was sometimes Thomson's amanuensis and that *Arminius* was banned unread because the submitted text was in the same hand as Thomson's already banned *Edward and Eleonora*. Thomson affectionately portrayed Paterson as a pensive, imaginative nature-lover in *The Castle of Indolence* (1748, I.lvii–lix).

By 1742 Paterson was in the service of Lord Tweeddale, secretary of state for Scotland. When the secretaryship was abolished Paterson became surveyor-general of customs for Barbados and the Leeward Islands, salary £400 p.a.; his warrant to start duty in Bridgetown, Barbados, is dated 29 May 1746. A letter by George Grenville, 3 September 1748, says that Paterson was appointed 'for Thomson's sake' (PRO Chatham MSS, 34). Murdoch claimed that Thomson was nominal holder of this post, procured for him by Lord Lyttelton.

Paterson's letters from Barbados to the board of customs advocate imperial expansion in the West Indies and, *inter alia*, offer shrewd economic analyses of the sugar and slave trades. He believed that prohibitions and high duties were 'the smugglers' harvest' (Bodl. Oxf., MS North A.6: 5 July 1751, 18 Dec 1758). His last reported visit to London was in April 1760. It is not known when he died.

JAMES SAMBROOK

Sources *James Thomson (1700–1748): letters and documents*, ed. A. D. McKillop (1958) • S. Johnson, *Lives of the English poets*, ed. G. B. Hill, [new edn], 3 (1905), 459–60 • P. Murdoch, 'Account of the life and writings of Thomson', in *The works of James Thomson*, ed. P. Murdoch, 1 (1762) • Bodl. Oxf., MS North a.6, fols. 173–83 • BL, Add. MS 6858, fol. 29 • BL, Add. MS 6861, fols. 118, 120, 124 • J. Sambrook, *James Thomson, 1700–1748: a life* (1991) • R. Pares, *War and trade in the West Indies, 1739–1763* (1936) • *Daily Gazetteer* (13 Sept 1737) • *European Magazine and London Review*, 24 (1793), 22–5, esp. 22–3 • A. H. Scouten, ed., *The London stage, 1660–1800*, pt 3: *1729–1747* (1961) • C. Atto, 'The Society for the Encouragement of Learning', *The Library*, 4th ser., 19 (1938–9), 263–88 • *Memoirs and correspondence of George, Lord Lyttelton, from 1734 to 1773*, ed. R. Phillimore, 1 (1845), 113 **Archives** Bodl. Oxf., papers • PRO, corresp., T1/329/62–71 | BL, Add. MSS 6858, fol. 29; 6861, fols. 118, 120, 124

Paterson, William (1745–1806), jurist and politician in the United States of America, was born on 24 December 1745 in co. Antrim, Ireland, the son of Richard Paterson, a tin-plate worker and shopkeeper, and his wife, Mary. In 1747 the Patersons moved to New Jersey, living near the College of New Jersey. William enrolled there at the age of thirteen, receiving a BA in 1763 and an MA in 1766. He then studied law under Richard Stockton, a prominent provincial attorney, and passed the bar in 1768. He then set up his own legal practice in nearby Somerset county. In 1779 he married Cornelia Bell (*d.* 1783), the daughter of a wealthy landowner and the sister of Andrew Bell, a fellow attorney and active loyalist during the American War of Independence. Cornelia died in childbirth and in 1785 Paterson married Eliphemia, the daughter of Anthony White, one of Paterson's wealthiest clients.

Although already well known as an up-and-coming attorney, Paterson's public career began in earnest in 1774 during the Anglo-American political crisis. In 1775 he became a delegate to the American patriot New Jersey provincial congress. Establishing his legal credentials in that body, he was appointed the attorney-general for the state's revolutionary government in 1776. In this post and as a member of several revolutionary committees, he tried to keep the legal system running in a state ravaged by marauding armies, both American and British, and subject to a violent internal civil war conducted along religious lines. He was thus forced to deal with issues such as prisoner treatment and the seizure of American loyalist property. Paterson handled all adeptly and won praise for his work.

Paterson left the service of New Jersey's government at the end of the war, declaring: 'It was with Reluctance that I consented to be put in Nomination the late time … I wish to wind up my official Course & return to private life.' But he remained interested in politics and became a critic of what he thought were destructive and inflationary state policies in regard to unsupported paper currency issues. These concerns encouraged him to participate in the convention for the federal constitution.

Paterson, along with David Brearly, William Churchill Houston, and John Neilson, was elected by the New Jersey legislature to go to the convention. Upon arriving in Philadelphia, Paterson quickly became a leading spokesman for the small states who had deep concerns over the consolidation of power proposed by James Madison known as the 'Virginia Plan'. Apparently without the kind of detailed preparation that underlay Madison's plan, Paterson put forward the so-called 'New Jersey Plan'. It would have assured small states, such as New Jersey, equal representation in the national legislature. When Madison and his supporters grafted this idea onto their own plan, giving smaller states equal representation in the legislature's upper house (the senate) but not the lower house, Paterson and the other small state representatives conceded, falling in behind the draft constitution. The New Jersey delegation became strong supporters of the document, and Paterson thereafter became an ardent 'federalist', or supporter of the constitution and the powers it granted to the federal government.

Paterson's role in defending the interests of the small states raised him to new heights of popularity in New Jersey, and in 1788 he was elected to the United States senate. In 1790 he became governor of his state, and in 1793 his legal career was capped with an appointment as an associate justice of the American supreme court, where he played an important role in the legal decisions that laid the foundation of the modern American judiciary. He sat as a justice until his death on 9 September 1806 in Albany, New York.

Although not recognized as part of the great pantheon of founding fathers, Paterson played a critical role in shaping the institutional parameters of both the legislative and the judicial branches of the United States government.   BRENDAN McCONVILLE

Sources *Selections from the correspondence of the executive of New Jersey from 1776 to 1786* (Newark, New Jersey, 1848) · R. P. McCormick, *Experiment in independence* (New Brunswick, 1950) · M. Marcus, 'Paterson, William', *ANB* · L. Gerlach, ed., *New Jersey in the American Revolution, 1763–1783: a documentary history* (Trenton, New Jersey, 1975) · W. A. Whitehead and others, eds., *Documents relating to the colonial, revolutionary and post-revolutionary history of the state of New Jersey*, 42 vols. (1880–1949)
Archives L. Cong., MSS · New Jersey Historical Society, Newark, MSS · Princeton University, New Jersey, MSS

Paterson, William (1755–1810), army officer and naturalist, was born on 17 August 1755 in Scotland of unknown parentage. There he developed a lifelong interest in botany. Supported by Mary Bowes, countess of Strathmore, he made four journeys from Cape Town into the interior of South Africa between 1777 and 1779, and ten years later published a *Narrative of Four Journeys into the Country of the Hottentots and Caffraria*, which he dedicated to Sir Joseph Banks.

On 7 October 1781 Paterson was gazetted an ensign in the 98th regiment and served in India, where he took part in the siege of Carour. He returned to England as a lieutenant in 1785 and was transferred to the 73rd regiment after the 98th was disbanded. Two years later, on 5 June 1789, he was gazetted a captain in the New South Wales Corps, which had been specially formed for garrison duty in the new Antipodean penal colony and which he had helped recruit. He reached Sydney in October 1791, accompanied by his devoted Scottish wife, Elizabeth Driver (1760x65–1825), whom he had married between 1785 and 1789. Described by the first fleet officer Ralph Clark as 'a good cosy Scotch lass and fit for a soldier's wife' (Heney, 89), Elizabeth was also thought of as 'very sharp' and someone who knew 'her own interest very well' (ibid., 208). Devoted to her husband, she formed part of the small coterie of officers' wives and, like them, took an interest in colonial affairs. Her particular concern was the plight of children, and she played an active role in the Orphans' School and the Female Orphans' Institution.

Soon after arriving at Sydney, Paterson was posted to Norfolk Island, which he commanded from November 1791 until March 1793. There he also found time to further his interests in natural history. Following his return to the mainland he took part in an attempt to cross the Blue Mountains which, though unsuccessful, resulted in the discovery and naming of the Grose River. He also discovered several new plants and imported others, which he planted on a 100 acre grant of land. After the departure of his commanding officer, Lieutenant-Governor Grose, in December 1794 he assumed charge of the settlement until Governor Hunter arrived some nine months later. He returned home on sick leave in 1796, following his promotion to major, and in 1798 became lieutenant-colonel and a fellow of the Royal Society. In March 1799 he was sent back to Sydney with orders to curb the trading activities of the New South Wales Corps, which had proved a thorn in Hunter's side. Little improvement occurred while Hunter was present, but the next governor, Philip Gidley King, was more energetic, and on his arrival in September 1800 he nominated Paterson lieutenant-governor, a nomination confirmed by the crown in June 1801. Throughout, Paterson maintained his contact with Banks and his scientific interests, but he was also involved in conflict with his quarrelsome subordinate John Macarthur, who was sent back to England after wounding Paterson in a duel in September 1801.

In May 1804 Paterson was given charge of a party of convicts and troops and sent to Van Diemen's Land to forestall a rumoured French occupation; he occupied Port Dalrymple and established a small outpost, part of which was located on the site of Launceston. He was made colonel by brevet on 25 April 1808, by which stage he had received news from the mainland that Governor Bligh had been overthrown the previous January. This dismayed him because, as the senior officer in the region, he was called upon to return to Sydney and take command. He was unwilling to become involved in the conflict between the governor and the corps, but after lengthy hesitation he left for Sydney on 1 January 1809. His refusal to reinstate Bligh caused friction between the two men, as did his insistence that Bligh and Colonel Johnston, who had led the march on Government House, return to England.

Paterson was assisted in his administration of New South Wales from April 1809 by his predecessor, Lieutenant-Colonel Joseph Foveaux. His second period in office aroused criticism similar to that directed against his first term. He was said on both occasions to have displayed an inability to control those under his command and to have allowed his officers to engross large areas of land as well as to profit from farming, grazing, and trade. It is true that he was by nature a weak and ineffective commander and also that he enjoyed poor health. However, the abuses that existed while he was in command should not be exaggerated. Much of the evidence, particularly during his second administration, was tainted by the fact that it derived from Bligh and his supporters, who had an interest in denigrating the New South Wales Corps. The settlement did not suffer under Paterson to the extent that has been suggested, and at no stage did he benefit from the malpractices that were evident.

On 31 December 1809 Governor Macquarie arrived with his own regiment to take command, and on 12 May 1810 Paterson departed with the New South Wales Corps. On 21 June his career came to an abrupt end when he died aboard the *Dromedary* off Cape Horn. Historians have rightly judged him more important as a natural scientist than as an administrator. He did little to affect the course of development in the settlements under his command, but he is still remembered for his explorations, his South African publications, and his botanical collections, which are located in the Natural History Museum, South Kensington.   Brian H. Fletcher

Sources F. M. Bladen, ed., *Historical records of New South Wales*, 7 vols. (1892–1901) · [F. Watson], ed., *Historical records of Australia*, 1st ser., 26 vols. (1914–25); 3rd ser., 6 vols. (1921–3) · Mitchell L., NSW, Banks MSS, vols. 3–4, 6–8, 15, 18–20, 22 · Mitchell L., NSW, P. G. King MSS, vol. 8 · Bonwick Transcripts Biography, Mitchell L., NSW, vol. 4 · L. Robson, *A history of Tasmania*, 1: *Van Diemen's Land from the earliest times to 1855* (1983) · B. H. Fletcher, *Landed enterprise and penal society: a history of farming and grazing in New South Wales before 1821* (1976) · *AusDB* · M. Bassett, *The governor's lady: Mrs Philip Gidley King*, 2nd edn (1956); repr. (1961) · M. H. Ellis, *John Macarthur* (1955) · H. Heney, *Australia's founding mothers* (1978)

Archives State Library of New South Wales, Sydney, Dixson Library, journals and letters | Mitchell L., NSW, Banks MSS · Mitchell L., NSW, P. G. King MSS · NHM, letters to Sir Joseph Banks

Paterson, Sir William (1874–1956), mechanical engineer, was born at Roslin, Midlothian, on 5 August 1874, the youngest of the five sons of James Paterson, a managing director, and his wife, Anne, *née* Hall. He was educated at George Heriot's School in Edinburgh, then at Heriot-Watt College, Edinburgh, where he took an engineering course. There followed a six-year apprenticeship (1891–6) in a firm of paper mill engineers, James Bertram & Sons, where he remained for a short period as a draughtsman. After a year in the drawing-office of D. and J. Tullis Ltd of Kilbowie, Glasgow, in 1898 he became assistant works manager with Masson, Scott & Co. Ltd of Wandsworth, London.

Early in his working life Paterson realized the importance of water treatment and between 1899 and 1904 he filed several patents. In 1902 he founded in Edinburgh, with just £700 capital and often working alone, the Paterson Engineering Company Ltd, chiefly concerned with the purification of water for all purposes. In 1904 he transferred his offices to Norfolk Street in London, and for some years shared lodgings with two other Scots destined to attain eminence in their professions, John Anderson (later Viscount Waverley) and Alexander Gray. (Both were present in 1952 at the celebration of the jubilee of Paterson's company.) On 16 April 1910 he married Dorothy Isabel (b. 1889/90), daughter of Herbert Frank Steedman, master tailor, of Bournemouth. They had one daughter.

Initially Paterson was particularly concerned with developing and patenting improved means of treating water for industrial use, a matter of great importance with the growing development of large manufacturing organizations. Within ten years he was addressing the need to improve the purification of drinking-water, which greatly widened his activities. An early installation was for the Weardale and Consett Water Company's pretreatment of 2.5 million gallons of water a day to improve its condition before passing through slow sand filters then in general use. Such pre-treatment greatly prolonged the life of the slow filters and obviated the need for large and costly extensions. In 1910 Paterson designed and installed a plant for the complete purification of 4 million gallons pumped daily from the River Severn for the drinking supply of Cheltenham. It was the first plant in Britain to use chlorine for the routine sterilization of a water supply to eliminate pathological bacteria. Paterson was always interested in the prevention of water-borne diseases, and he had extensive researches carried out on the use of chlorine gas for this purpose, either alone or in conjunction with ammonia to form chloramine. This led to important improvements in the method and equipment for applying these reagents for sterilization, and also in the use of ozone for the same purpose.

In 1913 Paterson was asked by the Indian army medical authorities to advise on the most suitable means of purifying the polluted water supplies in general use in India where outbreaks of dysentery and other water-borne diseases were common. A successful demonstration plant built at Poona led to the adoption of his process throughout India, and eventually to the formation of a Paterson company there.

During the First World War, Paterson set up a number of plants for munitions factories, including one with a capacity of 10 million gallons a day for the huge factory at Gretna in Dumfriesshire. The Second World War presented problems in the supply of reliable drinking-water to troops in the field, and a mobile filtration and sterilizing unit was designed which combined light weight and compactness with high capacity and great efficiency. This type of filter was widely adopted by British, American, and colonial forces and was responsible, to a large degree, for the extremely low incidence of fatal outbreaks of water-borne diseases among allied troops.

Paterson's activities resulted in many other important new developments in water treatment. These included the excess lime process of water softening and sterilization for public supplies in which he collaborated with Sir Alexander Houston, then director of water examination in the Metropolitan Water Board, and the use of chlorine gas for inhibiting algal accumulations in thermal electric power-station condenser systems. This method, originally applied in 1922, was adopted worldwide with important consequent fuel economies, estimated at perhaps half a million tons of coal a year in Britain alone.

As a result of his lifelong association with John Anderson, Paterson was asked privately by him in 1938, when, as lord privy seal, Anderson had special responsibility for manpower and civil defence, to devise a form of shelter which would not only be suitable for economical mass production and quick and easy to erect in individual homes, but which would also afford adequate protection against the blasts and flying debris caused by German bombing attacks. A simple sheet-steel air raid shelter, known as the Anderson shelter, was designed and patented by Paterson and Oscar C. Kerrison. The 1940 patent, taken out to prevent commercial exploitation, was immediately presented to the nation. The more than 3 million shelters supplied to the public saved many lives. Paterson was knighted in 1944 for this service.

In 1948 Paterson was elected an honorary member of the Institution of Water Engineers. He donated to them the Whitaker medal and the Alexander Houston medal, to be awarded to the presenters of outstanding papers on the treatment of water supplies. A member of the Royal Sanitary Institute since 1920, he was made an honorary member in 1949, and in 1952 a fellow after it had become the Society of Health. He was also elected an honorary fellow

of Heriot-Watt College, a vice-president of the Junior Institution of Engineers, and a life member of the American Water Works Association. He was also a long-standing member of the Institution of Mechanical Engineers, having joined in 1910 and served on its benevolent fund committee.

In January 1955 Paterson retired from the chairmanship of his company and active participation in the numerous companies comprising the Paterson group. During his career he had taken out more than seventy British patents, many of which presaged improvements only fully developed by the industry years later. 'The world history of water purification in the first half of the 20th century conforms closely to the pattern of the developments due to his foresight' (*Journal of the Institution of Water Engineers*, 496). Paterson died in Westminster Hospital, London, on 9 August 1956, a few days after his eighty-second birthday. His wife survived him.   ROBERT SHARP

Sources personal knowledge (1971) [*DNB*] · private information (1971) · *WWW* · *The Times* (10 Aug 1956), 11c · *The Times* (25 Aug 1956), 8b · *The Engineer* (17 Aug 1956), 220 · *Engineering* (17 Aug 1956), 196–7 · *Journal of the Institution of Water Engineers*, 10 (1956), 496 · *Royal Society of Health Journal*, 76 (1956), 648 · m. cert. · d. cert. · *CGPLA Eng. & Wales* (1956)
Likenesses W. Stoneman, photograph, 1949, NPG · P. Kaufmann, portrait, priv. coll. · photograph, repro. in *The Engineer*
Wealth at death £71,999 11s. 2d.: probate, 10 Sept 1956, *CGPLA Eng. & Wales*

Paterson, William Paterson (1860–1939), Church of Scotland minister and theologian, was born at Skirling Mains, Peeblesshire, on 25 October 1860, the eldest son of John Paterson (d. 1889), farmer, and his wife, Mary (d. 1899), daughter of John Waugh, laird of St John's Kirk. After Skirling school and three years at the Royal High School, Edinburgh, in 1876 Paterson matriculated at Edinburgh University, where he graduated MA with honours in classics (1880) and BD (1883). Two years (1883–5) of further study at the universities of Leipzig, Erlangen, and Berlin produced a lifelong interest in German culture.

After brief periods as assistant minister in Galashiels and at St Columba's Church of Scotland, London, Paterson was called in 1887 to the charge of St Michael's, Crieff. His seven years of ministry were punctuated by his marriage in 1888 to Jane Sanderson (d. 1928) and the birth of three of their eight children. In 1894 he was appointed by examination to the chair of systematic theology at Aberdeen University. Quickly establishing a reputation as a lecturer of clarity and preacher of eloquence, Paterson was awarded the degree of DD by his alma mater and subsequently appointed in 1903 to succeed his teacher Robert Flint as professor of divinity at Edinburgh University. He held the chair until his retirement in 1934 and served as dean of the faculty of divinity from 1912 to 1928. He was appointed a domestic chaplain to the king in 1916 and was awarded an LLD degree by Glasgow University in 1926.

Paterson's published work was marked by lucidity of exposition, wide-ranging scholarship in several languages, and an ability to harness philosophical argument to the defence of a broadly orthodox doctrinal stance. The alliance of liberal learning and evangelical piety in his thought was characteristic of Scottish theology in the late Victorian and Edwardian period. His two most notable works were *The Rule of Faith* (1912), which was the fruit of the Baird lectures (1905–6) after seven years of meticulous revision, and *The Nature of Religion* (1925), his Glasgow Gifford lectures of that year. *The Rule of Faith* is a careful examination of method and content in the leading doctrinal systems from the ancient church to the late nineteenth century. Although Paterson's own sympathies can be detected as ecumenical and reformed, he proves himself a patient and generally reliable expositor of different outlooks. *The Nature of Religion* is a bold attempt to argue from the empirical history of religions to a conception of the truthfulness and practical efficacy of theism, particularly its Christian variant. It is an outstanding example of the apologetic argument employed by successive Gifford lecturers in the early period of the twentieth century, and reveals the keen interest in the phenomena of world religion that had already been developed in Edinburgh in the time of Flint.

Paterson came to prominence as one of the leading church figures of the day through his popular preaching and involvement in ecclesiastical affairs. Widely respected within the United Free Church, he was one of the leading architects of its eventual union in 1929 with the established Church of Scotland, of which he was a minister. He was one of the drafters of new articles declaratory of the united Church of Scotland, and an influential supporter of the drive towards Presbyterian reunion.

At the outbreak of war in 1914, Paterson's life and career entered their most critical phase. Insight into this period is provided by the recent publication of diaries he kept from 1912 to 1928. A strong supporter of the war effort, Paterson argued that Britain and her allies had been subject to German aggression which required resistance by force. The struggle was typically cast in religious terms, by which the resurgent paganism within German culture faced the truer Christian spirit of the British empire. Paterson's expert advocacy of the allied cause was reflected in a series of sermons preached during a vacation in Newtonmore in the late summer of 1914, which were published as *In the Day of the Muster*. The ensuing carnage, however, brought the deaths of two of his own sons. On receiving news of the second loss he wrote in his diary:

> The last sermon he heard me preach was on providence: 'the hairs of your head are all numbered'. He thought I was rather too confident about the ways of providence. At the time he fell, I was conducting the evening service in St George's. We were singing 'Rock of Ages' about that time. I preached on, 'By grace ye are saved through faith', and in the morning I had preached on 'God is love'. It has been a terrible wrench to lose my darling boy. But at least he has been in the world twenty-one years, and it did not corrupt or injure him. And, as it was said in the prayer my father read to us many a time, 'The Lord gave and the Lord hath a sovereign right to take away'. (*Diaries*, 164–5)

Paterson continued his active involvement in church and social affairs throughout the war, his own personal tragedy doubtless enabling him to share in that of many others. Further wartime sermons were published as *In the Day of the Ordeal* (1917). Following the end of the war he was elected moderator of the general assembly in 1919. He continued to argue that the hand of providence overruled human history, which thus progressed towards the kingdom of God. In his moderatorial address he urged the League of Nations to reintegrate Germany within the international community. His later years were devoted to continuing, on a lower and more sombre key, his writing and academic commitments.

The task of unveiling war memorials around the country and the journey Paterson made to the scene of his sons' deaths were adjudged to have taken their toll. His wife died in 1928, and, though he did not retire until 1934, the theological culture of the post-war period was now rendering his work—generally liberal, optimistic, and orthodox—somewhat problematic. He died, as Europe was preparing for a further outbreak of war, on 10 January 1939 at Edinburgh, where he lived, and was buried at Skirling. Widely regarded for his charm, gravitas, and occasional eccentricities, Paterson was a tall and striking figure of imposing appearance. His earlier years were marked by sporting prowess, and something of his physical presence can be discerned in the portrait hung in the Rainy Hall, New College, Edinburgh. He was survived by six of his children, and his youngest son, Arthur, established a reputation in psychiatry as the founder of electroconvulsive therapy.

DAVID FERGUSSON

Sources *Fasti Scot.*, new edn, 7.385–6 · *DNB* · *The diaries of William P. Paterson*, ed. C. L. Rawlins (1987) · *CGPLA Eng. & Wales* (1939) **Archives** U. Edin., New Coll. L., MSS **Likenesses** H. W. Kerr, oils, 1903, U. Edin. · G. F. Watt, oils, U. Edin., New Coll. L. · photographs, repro. in Rawlins, ed., *Diaries of William P. Paterson* **Wealth at death** £2424 17s. 8d.: confirmation, 20 Feb 1939, *CCI*

Pates [Pate], **Richard** (1503/4–1565), bishop of Worcester, was probably born in Henley-on-Thames, Oxfordshire, the son of John Pates and his wife, Elinor, the sister of John Longland, bishop of Lincoln. He was admitted to Christ Church, Oxford, in June 1522 aged eighteen, graduating BA two years later. He was collated to the prebend of Centum Solidorum in Lincoln Cathedral on 4 June 1524, then to that of Cropredy on 25 September 1525. By 22 March 1527 he had exchanged that stall for the archdeaconry of Winchester, which he held until 31 December 1529. He became archdeacon of Lincoln on 22 June 1528, holding that benefice until 1542. During this period he travelled to Paris, where he took his MA. In a letter of 8 July 1524 to Pates's uncle, John Longland, the humanist Juan Luis de Vives described Pates as 'wonderfully studious' (*LP Henry VIII*, 4/1, no. 203). In 1531 he received a dispensation from attendance at university funerals and other formal occasions at Oxford on the basis that it would not be seemly for him to attend such acts in the academic dress of a bachelor of arts.

Pates was appointed ambassador to the court of the emperor Charles V in November 1533, perhaps through the influence of his uncle. It seems that he was a better scholar than politician. During his embassy, in a letter of

14 April 1536, he urged Henry VIII to restore his old alliance with the emperor, and to admit the authority of the pope in the hope that his marriage to Anne Boleyn might be recognized; he also pleaded for the legitimation of Princess Mary. Just eleven days later he received clear instructions from the king rejecting his proposals. In June 1536 he supplicated for the degree of BTh at Oxford. He was recalled from the imperial court in 1537, and replaced by Thomas Wyatt. Pates was back in England for the baptism of Prince Edward on 15 October. Although he does not seem to have been a great success in his diplomatic career—Henry VIII described him as 'trop inepte' in a letter to the imperial ambassador (*LP Henry VIII*, 15, no. 481)—he was appointed again in 1540. However, his opposition to the changes of religion in England led him to flee to Rome with his chaplain, Seth Holland, and on 8 July 1541 he was provided to the see of Worcester. The see was vacant by the death in Rome of Geronimo de'Ghinucci, who had been deprived by Henry VIII in 1535 and replaced (illegally, from the pope's point of view) by Hugh Latimer. Pates was consecrated bishop soon after, probably at Rome. An act of attainder against him for high treason was passed on 16 January 1542, as a result of which he was deprived of all his ecclesiastical benefices.

Pates remained in exile until after the accession of Queen Mary. As bishop of Worcester he attended a number of sessions of the Council of Trent between April 1546 and November 1551 (sessions 4, 5, 6, 7, 8, 13, and 14). In July 1552, during the prorogation of the council, Pates was at Bagnarea with Reginald Pole and the humanist Alvise Priuli. On the death of Edward VI, Pole wished Pates to precede him to England as his nuncio, but Queen Mary intervened to prevent this, considering it inopportune that he should enter the realm while Nicholas Heath, the bishop of Worcester according to English law, was still in possession of his see. In February 1554, when news arrived of disturbances in England over the expected arrival of Philip, Pates was sent to Brussels, to meet with the English ambassador, Thomas Thirlby, to learn if there was anything that Pole could do for the service and assistance of the queen. By November 1554 Pates was in England, and was sent by Pole from Canterbury to seek an audience with Philip and Mary. The situation of his bishopric was resolved by the translation of Heath to York, and Pates received the temporalities of the see of Worcester on 5 March 1555. Pates appears to have been active in the preaching drive by the Marian bishops, encouraged by Pole, for whom it was one of a bishop's most important tasks. The judgement of Anthony Wood, that he was 'a learned man, of a peaceable disposition, zealous in the faith he professed, yet always against inflicting corporal punishments on such that were opposed in religion to him' (Wood, *Ath. Oxon.*, 2.795), suggests a less aggressive approach to the prosecution of heresy than that of several of his fellow bishops. He was also active in attempting to secure the estates of his see, in 1555 proceeding in parliament against Sir Francis Jobson, the lessee of the valuable manor of Hartlebury Castle, both to establish his title and to secure payment of the full rent.

Pates was one of the co-consecrators of Pole as archbishop of Canterbury at the Greenwich Greyfriars on 22 March 1556, and according to Henry Machyn sang high mass three days later (the feast of the Annunciation) at Bow church, in the presence of Pole and other bishops and nobles. His long association with Pole caused Pates to be implicated in the suspicions held by Pope Paul IV and others in the curia, and when the pope acted to recall Pole as legate, Pates twice wrote to the queen on his behalf (16 August 1557 and 30 April 1558), beseeching her never to let the cardinal depart. Queen and cardinal died on 17 November 1558, and Pates was ordered to conduct Pole's funeral, along with Thomas Goldwell, bishop of St Asaph. He remained bishop of Worcester until 1559 when, along with almost all the surviving bishops of the English church, he was deprived of his see by Elizabeth I (Pates's deprivation taking place on 26 June) and on 20 May 1560 was committed to the Tower. On 12 February 1562 Pates made his will. It was mostly concerned with a bequest to Worcester Cathedral, which was only to take effect if England's schism from Rome was ended. But he also left 20 marks to endow four exhibitions for scholars to Gloucester College, Oxford. One of the executors was Thomas Goldwell, Marian bishop of St Asaph, who had fled to the continent in 1559.

Pates remained in the Tower until 1563, when on the intercession of the emperor Ferdinand he and the other confined bishops were released from prison and handed into the custody of Anglican bishops; Pates was lodged with John Jewel, bishop of Salisbury. Like the other deprived Catholic bishops he was kept in strict confinement; by order of the privy council, only protestant servants could approach him, he was required to take his meals alone rather than at the table of his custodian as was customary, had nothing but protestant books to read, and was forbidden to practise Catholic worship. He was released from Jewel's custody by the privy council on 30 January 1565, subject to the production of sufficient sureties, and though ordered to remain in or around London, immediately made his way abroad. He died in Louvain on 5 October 1565.   KENNETH CARLETON

Sources Emden, *Oxf.*, 4.435–6 · *Fasti Angl., 1300–1541*, [Lincoln] · *Fasti Angl., 1300–1541*, [Monastic cathedrals] · *Fasti Angl., 1300–1541*, [St Paul's, London] · *Fasti Angl., 1300–1541*, [York] · *Fasti Angl., 1300–1541*, [Bath and Wells] · *Fasti Angl., 1300–1541*, [Welsh dioceses] · *Fasti Angl., 1541–1857*, [Ely] · *LP Henry VIII*, vols. 4, 10, 12, 15–17 · Wood, *Ath. Oxon.*, new edn, 2.794 · *CSP Spain, 1553* · *VCH Worcestershire*, vol. 2 · C. Eubel and others, eds., *Hierarchia Catholica medii aevi*, 3, ed. W. van Gulik, C. Eubel, and L. Schmitz-Kallenberg (Münster, 1910) · *CPR, 1554–5* · *APC, 1558–70* · *CSP Venice, 1534–54* · *CSP dom., addenda, 1547–65* · Ludwig Freiherr von Pastor, *The history of the popes*, ed. and trans. R. F. Kerr, 12 (1912) [166]; 13 (1924) [284]; 16 (1928), 237; repr. 3rd edn (1951) · BL, Lansdowne MS 980, fol. 280 · F. Heal, *Of prelates and princes: a study of the economic and social position of the Tudor episcopate* (1980) · Herefs. RO, BA 2648/9 (iv) · W. M. Brady, *The episcopal succession in England, Scotland, and Ireland, AD 1400 to 1875*, 2 (1876), 2.283–9

Pateshull, Hugh de. *See* Pattishall, Hugh of (d. 1241).

Pateshull, Martin de. *See* Pattishall, Martin of (d. 1229).

Pateshull, Peter (*fl.* 1387), apostate Augustinian friar and religious controversialist, was at first a member of the Augustinian convent in London. According to John Bale he studied in Oxford, where he gained the degree of doctor of theology, but there is no contemporary confirmation for this. Thomas Walsingham, and chronicles dependent upon his work, describe how in 1387 Pateshull purchased from the Carmelite friar Walter Diss (*d.* 1404) a privilege from Pope Urban VI appointing him a papal chaplain, a post that released him from his order. Pateshull then proclaimed publicly in London the virtues of abandoning the religious life, and the vices and immorality of the fraternal orders. Pateshull incited a crowd of about a hundred Lollards gathered at the church of St Christopher Cornhill in London to destroy religious houses as centres of homicides, sodomites, and traitors to king and realm. Thomas Ashburne, another Augustinian, managed to placate the mob with the help of the sheriffs. Pateshull summarized his accusations, and posted them on the doors of St Paul's Cathedral in London; many knights read these charges, and made copies in sympathy. The order for the arrest of William Patishull, an apostate Augustinian friar, made by the king on 18 July 1387, probably refers to this same person. Walsingham linked Pateshull's actions to his sympathy with the Wycliffite cause, but there is no evidence for his views on matters other than the religious orders. Nothing further is known of his career.

Bale recounts this story, asserts that Pateshull fled to Bohemia (derived probably from Leland's confusion of Pateshull with Peter Payne), and lists fourteen works including five with incipits. Bale's extracts from one, a collection of scurrilous stories about the friars (chiefly the Dominicans), survives in one of his notebooks; Bale also owned a copy of some of Pateshull's works before he left Ireland. Four further texts, three of them with incipits, are identifiable with Latin poems (all with a final couplet introduced by the English phrase 'with an O and an I'), which survive but without ascription. Two (*Quis dabit meo capiti* and *Sedens super flumina*) refer to each other, and may reflect the anti-fraternal arguments of Richard Fitzralph's time (*c.*1357–60) rather than of Wyclif's period; a third (*Vox in Rama*) has signs of Benedictine authorship; the fourth (Bale's *De desolatione ecclesie* without incipit, but reasonably reflected by *Heu quanta desolacio*) comments on the events and personages of the Blackfriars Council of 1382. Pateshull's authorship of these has been generally, but perhaps too hastily, dismissed.　　　ANNE HUDSON

Sources *Thomae Walsingham, quondam monachi S. Albani, historia Anglicana*, ed. H. T. Riley, 2 vols., pt 1 of *Chronica monasterii S. Albani*, Rolls Series, 28 (1863–4), vol. 2, pp. 157–9 · Bale, *Cat.*, 1.509–10 · Bale, *Index*, 322–3 · *CPR, 1385–9*, 386 · A. G. Rigg, *A history of Anglo-Latin literature, 1066–1422* (1992), 270–71, 280–82 · Bale extracts, BL, Cotton MS Titus D.x, fols. 188–194*v* · H. McCusker, 'Books and manuscripts formerly in the possession of John Bale', *The Library*, 4th ser., 16 (1935–6), 144–65, esp. no. 50

Pateshull, Simon de. *See* Pattishall, Simon of (*d. c.*1217); Pattishall, Sir Simon of (*b.* in or before 1219, *d.* 1274).

Pateshull, Walter de. *See* Pattishall, Walter of (*d.* 1231/2).

Patey, Charles George Edward (1813–1881), naval officer and colonial official, was the son of Commander Charles Patey, one of five brothers who served in the navy during the Napoleonic wars, and whose sons and grandsons followed in their footsteps. He entered the navy in 1824. He was promoted lieutenant on 6 December 1836, and after serving in the *Caledonia* and *Princess Charlotte*, flagships in the Mediterranean, was, in 1840, first lieutenant of the frigate *Castor*, in which he took part in the operations on the coast of Syria, and in the bombardment of Acre. On the following day, 4 November 1840, he was promoted commander. He commanded the troopship *Resistance* (42 guns) from March 1842 until he was promoted captain on 18 May 1846. In 1851 he was appointed to organize the great rush of emigration from Liverpool to Australia, and was presented by the shipowners of Liverpool with a piece of plate. In December 1852 he commissioned the *Amphion*; but in the following year a severe injury, caused by a block falling from the mast head, compelled him to resign the command. He received a pension for the injury, and had no further service afloat.

In 1857 Patey was appointed superintendent of the packet service at Southampton. On 9 February 1864 he became a rear-admiral on the retired list, vice-admiral on 14 July 1871, and admiral on 1 August 1877. In 1866 he was appointed administrator at Lagos, whence he was removed, after a few months, to the Gambia. In 1869 he became governor of St Helena, and on the abolition of the office retired with a compensation grant in 1873. On 8 May 1874 he was created CMG. He died at Newton St Loe, near Bath, on 25 March 1881. He was survived by his wife, Caroline Emma (daughter of John Brendon of Treniffle, Cornwall), and a son in the civil service.

J. K. LAUGHTON, *rev.* ANDREW LAMBERT

Sources D. Syrett and R. L. DiNardo, *The commissioned sea officers of the Royal Navy, 1660–1815*, rev. edn, Occasional Publications of the Navy RS, 1 (1994) · P. H. Colomb, *Memoirs of Admiral the Right Honble. Sir Astley Cooper Key* (1898) · O'Byrne, *Naval biog. dict.* · *The Times* (29 March 1881) · *Navy List* · Kelly, *Handbk* · *CGPLA Eng. & Wales* (1881)
Archives Bodl. Oxf., corresp. with Lord Kimberley
Wealth at death under £7000: probate, 27 April 1881, *CGPLA Eng. & Wales*

Patey, David Howard (1899–1977), surgeon, was born on 25 October 1899 at 88 Tillery Street, Abertillery, Monmouthshire, the eldest of the three children of Frank Walter Patey (*c.*1877–1962/3), hotel furbisher, and his wife, Ann, *née* Davies (*d.* 1941). His father was English, from the west country, and his mother Welsh. He attended Llandovery School, where an iron regimen of the classics and rugby football prevailed, and having decided on a career in medicine he entered the Middlesex Hospital medical school in London with an entrance scholarship in classics in 1916.

Patey's studies (and rugby) were interrupted in 1918 by a period of combatant service in France and Belgium with the 2nd battalion of the Monmouthshire regiment. After returning to the Middlesex his brilliant student career culminated in 1923 in his being awarded the scholarship for the best student of the year at the Middlesex and the gold medal for the best medical student in the whole of the University of London. Patey became a fellow of the Royal College of Surgeons in 1924. His graduate training continued at the Middlesex, including two years in the pathology department that awakened what was to be a long-lasting interest in the morbid anatomical approach to disease. He became MS (London) in 1927. On 5 February of the same year he married Gladys Joyce (1898–1981), daughter of Gilbert Summers, of Hounslow; they had two sons and a daughter.

Between 1922 and 1932 Patey held surgical posts in London at the Middlesex Hospital, the Hampstead General Hospital, St Mark's Hospital, St Peter's Hospital, and Acton Hospital. He was appointed to the consultant staff of the Middlesex in 1930, the same year in which he was awarded the Jacksonian prize of the Royal College of Surgeons for an essay on tumours of the parotid salivary gland. In the following year he became Hunterian professor at the college. A sound clinician and operative surgeon, undoubtedly his major contributions lay in the fields of research and teaching. Particularly in his early years, his research ranged over a wide field, a conspicuous feature of his publications being that they have stood the test of time.

Without question Patey's most important work concerned the management of cancer of the breast and parotid tumours. The operation he described for removing the affected breast was as effective in removing cancerous tissue as its predecessors, but caused much less disfigurement. It was a seminal forerunner of the modern trend towards limited excision, relying on other means to deal with distant spread. By contrast his approach to the treatment of the apparently benign but potentially malignant tumours of the parotid was to insist on excision with wide margins, because they were thus eminently curable but likely to recur if the margin of clearance was compromised. The contrast between these two approaches to superficially similar situations demonstrates Patey's intellectual strength in stripping a problem down to its fundamentals. The quality of his research work was marked in 1964 by his election to an honorary fellowship of the American Surgical Association, a signal honour bestowed on few British surgeons. Patey was also president of the section of surgery at the Royal Society of Medicine (1951–2) and Colles lecturer at the Royal College of Surgeons in Ireland (1957), and he wrote more than a hundred learned publications.

Patey's bedside teaching was effective, but the full flowering of his educative role started in 1952 when he was appointed director of the department of surgical studies at the Middlesex Hospital medical school. He developed intellectually stimulating teaching methods. Apart from traditional bedside and outpatient teaching, he encouraged undergraduates to present cases at clinical demonstrations, organize co-operative seminars depending on literature searches, and undertake small research projects, some of which were published. These innovative techniques have been widely copied.

In 1952 the Society of University Surgeons in North America invited Patey to attend their annual meeting. Patey was impressed with the energy and enthusiasm of the young surgeons presenting their scientific work and returned to England determined to foster a similar development. He interested Professor Sir James Paterson-Ross, later president of the Royal College of Surgeons in London, in the concept, and they contacted the heads of all the university departments of surgery in the United Kingdom and Éire. Their suggestion that a surgical research society should be founded met with enthusiasm. When a subcommittee was set up to formulate the rules, Patey insisted on two of great importance, whose influence later spread widely beyond the society: namely, that papers should be spoken and not read, and that their delivery should take no longer than ten minutes. The first meeting of the Surgical Research Society was held at the Middlesex Hospital in 1954, with Sir James as the first president and Patey the first honorary secretary. Initially limited to fifty the membership later increased tenfold. Patey was the society's president from 1958 to 1960.

From its inception the Surgical Research Society had a profound influence on the development of surgical research in the British Isles because it coincided with the burgeoning of many new academic departments of surgery and provided a critical forum for young surgeons striving to apply new scientific methods to surgical problems. This influence spread to Australasia and South Africa, where similar societies were founded. Much of the reason for this success lay in Patey's characteristics: clarity of mind, scrupulous logic, transparent honesty, true humility, and the grace and charm with which he conducted himself, even when he was preventing a speaker from overstepping the ten minutes.

Of average height and powerful build and with a massive head, conservative in dress (the last at the Middlesex to wear spats), Patey's characteristic and frequently mimicked foibles of speech endeared him to staff and students. After he retired Patey continued to study philosophy and mathematics, and taught himself Russian to A level standard. He was a man of profound, though not unquestioning, religious faith and for many years acted as churchwarden at St Mary's, Bryanston Square, London. Proud of his Welsh roots, he was never happier than when holidaying in Wales, walking and fishing, or when playing the piano for family gatherings, concentrating on songs with a Welsh flavour. Patey died from cancer of the prostate on 27 March 1977, at his home, 2 Cannongate Close, Hythe, Kent. He was buried at Barham crematorium, near Canterbury, on 2 April.   MICHAEL HOBSLEY

Sources UCL, department of medicine, Patey collection · E. H. Cornelius and S. F. Taylor, *Lives of the fellows of the Royal College of Surgeons of England, 1974–1982* (1988) · L. P. Le Quesne, 'David Patey, surgeon and academic: lecture at the Middlesex Hospital, Dec 4 1995', *Journal of Medical Biography*, 5 (1997) · L. P. Le Quesne, 'David Patey, surgeon and academic: a memoir', *Journal of Medical Biography*, 5 (1997), 125–30 · *The Times* (16 April 1977) · *BMJ* (16 April 1977), 1035 · personal knowledge (2004) · private information (2004) · b. cert. · m. cert. · d. cert. · WWW

Archives Middlesex Hospital, London, memorabilia · Surgical Research Society · UCL, department of surgery

Likenesses H. Riley, pencil drawing, 1961, priv. coll. · photograph, c.1964, UCL, department of surgery

Patey [née Whytock], **Janet Monach** (1841–1894), singer, was born on 1 May 1841 at 13 Melton Place, Somers Town, London, the daughter of Andrew Whytock, a Scottish tinplate worker, and his wife, Charlotte, née Dunford. She received her first instruction in singing from John Wass, and in 1860 made her début at Birmingham under the name of Ellen Andrews; she had much success, but was so nervous that she lost her voice completely for six months afterwards. She then became a member of Henry Leslie's Choir, and at one of his concerts stood in for Charlotte Sainton-Dolby; the promise she exhibited was so marked that steps were taken immediately for furthering her musical education, and she became a pupil successively of Ciro Pinsuti and Emma Sims Reeves. In 1865 she made her first concert tour, travelling through the provinces with Helen Lemmens-Sherrington and others. On 23 April 1866 she married John George Patey (1835–1901), an operatic and oratorio singer of considerable reputation. In the same year she sang as principal contralto at the Worcester festival with conspicuous success, a success which was repeated at Birmingham in 1867 and at Norwich in 1869, when she was on tour with Sims Reeves's company. After the retirement of Charlotte Sainton-Dolby in 1870, Janet Patey was considered the leading British contralto. A successful tour of America in 1871 further enhanced her reputation.

In 1875 Janet Patey went to Paris, on the invitation of Charles Lamoureux, to take part in four performances of *Messiah* in French. Her success there led to an engagement to sing at a conservatoire concert in the same year, when her performance of 'O rest in the Lord' resulted in a contract for a second concert. A medal, struck in commemoration of the event, was presented to the singer, who was widely known as the 'English Alboni'.

In 1890 Janet Patey made a prolonged and triumphant tour of Australia, New Zealand, China, Japan, and other countries. On her return to England in 1891 she contemplated retirement, and at the end of 1893 she began a farewell tour through the English provinces, accompanied by her daughter. She appeared at Sheffield on 28 February 1894 and was so overcome by the enthusiastic reception she received that she had an apoplectic fit on the stage of the Albert Hall. She died at the Royal Victoria Hotel five and a half hours later and was buried at Brompton cemetery on 3 March.

Janet Patey's voice was a pure, sonorous and rich contralto, beautiful at its best in quality; she was celebrated both as a singer of opera and as a concert performer, and was associated particularly with the works of Handel.

R. H. LEGGE, rev. J. GILLILAND

Sources *The Times* (1 March 1894) · *The Times* (2 March 1894) · *New Grove* · b. cert. · m. cert. · d. cert. · J. D. Brown, *Biographical dictionary of musicians: with a bibliography of English writings on music* (1886) · *Baker's biographical dictionary of musicians*, rev. N. Slonimsky, 7th edn (1984) · Boase, *Mod. Eng. biog.* · L. C. Sanders, *Celebrities of the century: being a dictionary of men and women of the nineteenth century* (1887) · J. T. Lawrence, *A dictionary of musical biography* (1892) · D. Hyde, *Newfound voices: women in nineteenth-century English music* (1984)

Likenesses J. M. B., lithograph, 1888, NPG · portrait, repro. in *Biography* (Jan 1882), 36–8 · portrait, repro. in *London Sketch Book* (7 Aug 1875), 8–9 · portrait, repro. in *Illustrated Sporting and Dramatic News*, 12 (1876) · portrait, repro. in *Illustrated Sporting and Dramatic News*, 15 (1881), 217 · portrait, repro. in *Illustrated Sporting and Dramatic News* (3 March 1894), 885 · print, repro. in *ILN*, 104 (1894), 254 · three portraits, Harvard TC · wood-engraving (after photograph by Fradelle & Marshall), NPG; repro. in *ILN*, 66 (24 April 1875), 393
Wealth at death £4684 14s. 11d.: probate, 18 April 1894, *CGPLA Eng. & Wales*

Patey, Thomas Walton [Tom] (1932–1970), mountaineer, was born at the rectory, Ellon, Aberdeenshire, on 20 February 1932, the son of Thomas Maurice Patey, a minister of the Scottish Episcopal church, and his wife, Audrey Amy, née Walton. He was educated at Ellon Academy, Robert Gordon's College, Aberdeen, and the University of Aberdeen, where he studied medicine. His national service (1954–61) was spent as a surgeon lieutenant at the naval hospital in Gosport, and with the marine commando climbing unit. In 1961 he went into general practice at Ullapool. He married at St Andrew's Cathedral, Aberdeen, on 29 July 1957, Elizabeth Mary (Betty) Davidson (b. 1932/3), a shorthand typist, the daughter of William James Davidson, petroleum depot charge-hand. They had three children.

Patey was taken hill walking by his father, and continued with the Boy Scouts and friends from Gordon's College, where he began to collect 'Munros' (the Scottish peaks of over 3000 feet, listed by Sir Hugh Thomas Munro). His first contact with climbers came at the end of 1949, and he climbed his first major route in Scotland (Douglas-Gibson Gully) at Christmas 1950, shortly after entering university. He began a series of first ascents in the Cairngorms, and other parts of the highlands (many solo), and such was his reputation that he was considered for the Everest expedition of 1953, only to be rejected as too young. Also during the 1950s he initiated the exploration of Chudleigh Rocks in Devon, made some first British ascents in the Alps, several first ascents in Norway, and was a member of the successful Himalayan expeditions to Mustagh Tower in 1956 and Rakaposhi (with the Royal Marines) in 1958. During the 1960s he continued his major series of first ascents in Scotland, and made some important first ascents in the Alps (for example, the west face of the Aiguille du Plan). He was also involved in the well-known BBC television live broadcasts of rock climbs at South Stack in Anglesey (1966) and the Old Man of Hoy in Scotland (1967). The latter is significant since Patey is considered to have initiated sea stack climbing in Scotland, and was sometimes referred to as Dr Stack.

In addition to his prolific climbing achievements and his work as a physician, Patey was a talented musician and writer; he was often the life and soul of parties, where he played the accordion and sang songs, including comic parodies he had written such as 'Onward, Christian Bonington'. Bonington called him

the most unpredictable, sheer-fun-to-be-with, richest character I have ever come across in my climbing career and yet at the same time there was a very real depth to him, both in terms of the prolific number of new routes he achieved, and the range and quality of his writing. (Bonington, 11)

And Joe Brown noted, 'It was worth driving all the way up to the Highlands just to socialise with Tom' (Gray, 182–3).

Apart from his numerous first ascents, Patey's most enduring legacy is his writing, much of it collected in the posthumously published *One Man's Mountains* (1971). His work has won high praise from writers on the climbing scene: the American David Roberts considered that '*One Man's Mountains* may well be the most entertaining climbing book ever written' (Roberts, 90), while the British writer Jim Perrin described the essence of Patey's writing as 'a delicious and warm-hearted exaggeration of character, the art of comic deflation, a delicate sense of the inherent absurdity in all our actions' (Perrin, 129).

Tom Patey was awarded a queen's commendation for bravery during a mountain rescue; and was elected president of the élite Alpine Climbing Group in 1969. He died on 25 May 1970 of a fracture of the base of the skull sustained in an abseiling accident following an ascent of The Maiden, a sea stack off Whiten Head on the Sutherland coast. He was survived by his wife.   Peter Donnelly

Sources *The Times* (26 May 1970), 10 · C. Bonington, introduction, in T. Patey, *One man's mountains: essays and verses*, 2nd edn (1997), 11–13 · D. Gray, *Tight rope! The fun of climbing* (1993) · C. McNeish and R. Else, *The edge: one hundred years of Scottish mountaineering* (1994) · P. Nunn, 'Tom Patey is dead: a eulogy', *Mountain*, 10 (1970), 29 · P. Nunn, *At the sharp end* (1988) · T. Patey, *One man's mountains: essays and verses* (1971) · J. Perrin, 'The ice climbers: a literary discourse', *On and off the rocks: selected essays, 1968–1985* (1986) · D. Roberts, 'Patey Agonistes, or, A look at climbing autobiographies', *Ascent*, 2/2 (1974), 86–91 · W. Unsworth, *Encyclopaedia of mountaineering* (1992) · b. cert. · m. cert. · d. cert.

Likenesses photographs

Pathak, Laxmishanker Gopalji (1925–1997), businessman, was born on 5 March 1925 in Keshod, Gujarat, India, one of the six children of Gopalji Sunderji Pathak, farmer, and his wife, Harak Baa. Pathak's father supplemented his meagre income by making sweetmeats and savouries to sell to passers-by. Pathak was educated locally, but remained largely illiterate all his life. In 1938 he emigrated to Mombasa, Kenya, to join his eldest brother, who had moved there after their father's death and was running a shop, selling sweets and samosas to the growing Asian community; this was at a time when the British government was offering inducements to Indians to work in east Africa. Pathak married Shanta Gaury Pandit in 1945. They had four sons and two daughters.

In 1956, following the Mau Mau disturbances in Kenya, Pathak moved with his family to England, where he found it difficult to get a job, other than cleaning drains for Camden council, and decided to set up a business similar to the one he had had in Kenya, making sweets and savouries in the basement kitchen of his rented house in Kentish Town, and selling them to Indians in London. He supplied the Indian high commission with food for parties, and once provided snacks for a reception given by Lord Mountbatten, former viceroy of India. He opened a shop in Drummond Street, Euston, in 1958, and another in Bayswater in 1961, selling mainly to Indian restaurants,

many of which were staffed by recent immigrants with limited cooking skills. Although all the children were expected to work long hours after school for their father, Pathak, a devout Hindu, borrowed money in order to send his two oldest sons to a Dominican convent in Dublin, the only private education he could afford. He withdrew them when the oldest, Kirit, who had become an altar boy, announced his intention to become pope.

Pathak moved to Brackley, Northamptonshire, in 1962, to set up a factory in a converted mill. This enabled him to expand his range to include chutneys, pickles, pastes, and ready-made sauces, blending his spices according to old family recipes. It was he who invented the curry paste. Although he opened several new shops during the 1960s, Pathak suffered a setback because of mismanagement in the shops, and was almost bankrupted. He was saved by the arrival in England of thousands of Ugandan Asian refugees, expelled by Idi Amin in 1972. Pointing out that the refugees would want to eat Indian food, Pathak won the contract to supply the refugee transit camps, in return for printing and distributing leaflets in several Indian languages with information to help the refugees start a new life once they had been resettled. Not only did this revive business, but many of the new arrivals opened their own shops and restaurants, and used Pathak as their supplier.

Pathak handed over the business to his son Kirit on the latter's marriage to Meena, a graduate in food technology, in 1976. When the company moved to Wigan, Lancashire, in 1978, Pathak moved to Bolton in order to be close by, though he became involved in other business ventures while Kirit continued to expand the company. In his later years Pathak travelled frequently, mainly to India and Mexico, and in Mexico he rented a house for sanyasi, spiritual contemplation for the later stages of life. In 1988 he set up the Pathak Charitable Foundation, to improve health and education in India and other developing countries. His last years were occupied by a court case against the former prime minister of India, P. V. Narasimha Rao, whom he accused of fraud: Pathak claimed that he had paid a large sum of money in 1983 to Rao on the understanding that Rao, then foreign minister, would secure him a government contract to supply paper pulp, but that the contract had never materialized. He died before the trial ended.

By the time of Pathak's death, Patak's (in the brand name the 'h' was omitted) was supplying 95 per cent of the Indian restaurants in Britain, and all the main supermarket chains, and was one of the world's largest producers of authentic Indian curry sauces, pastes, and chutneys, exporting to over forty countries. It gave Pathak great pleasure to learn from one of his grandchildren that Patak's had been cited as a model company in a business studies textbook, alongside Coca-Cola and the Body Shop. When Pathak died, of a heart attack, on 31 March 1997, at his home, Orchard House, Victoria Road, Heaton, Bolton, Lancashire, the family's wealth was estimated to be about £60 million. Pathak was survived by his wife and six children.   Anne Pimlott Baker

Sources *The Times* (15 April 1997) · *Daily Telegraph* (7 April 1997) · *The Independent* (10 April 1997) · K. Pathak, 'Out of Africa', *Feedback* [published by the Food and Drink Federation], 25 (autumn 1997), 16–18 · private information (2004) [Kirit Pathak, son] · d. cert. **Likenesses** photograph, repro. in *Daily Telegraph* · photograph, repro. in *The Independent* · photograph, repro. in *The Times* **Wealth at death** wealthy

Patiala, Sir Bhupindra Singh. *See* Singh, Sir Bhupinder (1891–1938).

Patient, Thomas (*d.* 1666), Particular Baptist minister, spent years searching for 'the true way, which Christ would have his people to walk in' (Patient, sig. A4r) before concluding that episcopacy, the Book of Common Prayer, and mixed congregations of godly and profane people in parish churches were unscriptural. With other puritans he emigrated to New England, probably in the 1630s, and there became convinced that paedobaptism is based on folly and ignorance. When he refused to have his child baptized, a warrant for his arrest was issued in Massachusetts, but he was initially unconcerned, believing he 'walked up and down in the Woods in that Wilderness, about my businesse' (ibid., sig. B4r). He soon decided to return to England, having fled before he was charged at the quarterly court of Essex county on 27 June 1643.

Some time after arriving in England, Patient joined the Particular (Calvinist) Baptist congregation of William Kiffin, and in 1644 he signed the confession of faith issued by Particular Baptists in London. He was variously described as a glover, a tailor, and a bodice-maker. According to a letter dated 10 December 1645 which Thomas Edwards published in *Gangraena*, Patient and Kiffin anointed a female member of their church with oil to expedite her recovery from an illness. About this time the two men went to Kent in search of converts, only to lose them to the General (Arminian) Baptists. In 1646 Patient signed the second edition of the confession of faith. Patient, Kiffin, Hanserd Knollys, and Samuel Gorton were brought before the House of Commons' committee of examinations in February 1647 on charges of lay preaching, but Patient insisted he had been ordained in a house in Bell Alley, Coleman Street, London. When recruits were sought to serve with Philip Skippon in the summer of 1647, members of Kiffin and Patient's congregation were approached, suggesting that Patient supported the political independents. With other London Baptist leaders, on 2 April 1649 he dissociated himself from the Levellers in *The Humble Petition and Representation*, addressed to parliament, and the following year he and his colleagues warned Baptists against Quakers and Ranters in *Heart-Bleedings for Professors Abominations*. Patient, Kiffin, John Spilsbury, and John Pearson provided an epistle to the Baptist Daniel King's *A Way to Sion Sought Out* (1650), part of which denounced reputed Seekers.

By 15 April 1650 Patient was at Kilkenny, Ireland, from where he sent a letter to Oliver Cromwell exhorting him to remain faithful to his religious convictions. From 22 April 1650 to 23 February 1651 he served as chaplain to Henry Ireton's regiment of foot, and it was probably after

this that he went to Waterford, where he became the pastor of a Particular Baptist congregation. On 14 January 1652 this church sent a letter to John Rogers's congregation in Dublin denouncing its open-membership, open-communion principles. Taken to Dublin by two military officers, William Allen and John Vernon, the letter prompted some members of Rogers's congregation to secede. Rogers retorted by denouncing Patient and his supporters as 'uncharitable *Formalists*' (Rogers, 308). Among Patient's converts to the Baptists in Ireland were Daniel Axtell and Richard Lawrence, governors of Kilkenny and Waterford respectively, and Colonel Jerome Sankey. From 1 November 1652 until at least 27 November 1654 Patient was a paid chaplain to the general officers. Now in Dublin, he was one of five preachers assigned in December 1652 to take turns preaching in Christ Church Cathedral, and the same month he was one of seven ministers appointed by the government to consider how to improve preaching in Ireland and to identify qualified men for such work. He subsequently helped examine men for state-funded ministerial positions. The government provided him with a house and land for a garden.

Under Patient's leadership the first Baptist meeting-house in Ireland was built in Swift's Alley, Dublin, in 1653. His work was not without controversy, for the same year the council heard a complaint that dissolute people had cursed and stoned Patient and his followers. On 1 June 1653 he signed a letter from Baptists in Ireland to their counterparts in London, seeking greater fellowship among Baptist congregations throughout the islands.

Patient's only published work, *The Doctrine of Baptism, and the Distinction of the Covenants*, was issued by Henry Hills in London in 1654. A book of nearly 200 pages, it rehearsed the case for believers' baptism and argued against the automatic inclusion of believers' children in the covenant of grace. According to one of Secretary John Thurloe's correspondents, Patient's congregation was declining in the spring of 1654, but in July 1655 Charles Fleetwood and his council appointed him a Monday lecturer in Dublin. By 17 October 1655 Christopher Blackwood had succeeded him as pastor in Dublin, enabling him and Axtell to seek converts elsewhere in Ireland. On 19 December 1655 Patient preached the funeral sermon for William Allen's wife. In October 1656 he and others met with Henry Cromwell to express support for his policies and the religious liberty they enjoyed. The same year Major Edward Warren issued a response to Patient's *Doctrine of Baptism* entitled *Caleb's Inheritance in Canaan*, accusing him of shamefully perverting scripture. The saddler George Pressick also attacked Patient's views on baptism in 1656. After Oliver Cromwell rejected the crown, Patient and 118 others sent him an address expressing their loyalty. From 1657 to at least 8 July 1659 he was again a paid chaplain to the general officers.

About 1660 Patient returned to England. By December 1662 he was at Bristol, where he assisted Henry Hynam in ministering to the Particular Baptist church at the Pithay. For attending a conventicle he was incarcerated in Newgate on 4 October 1663; refusing to post bond for his good behaviour, he remained in prison until 1664. By 28 June 1666 he had returned to London as Kiffin's associate at the Devonshire Square Baptist Church. Hanserd Knollys and Edward Harrison participated in his ordination service. A victim of the plague, Patient died on 29 July 1666 and was buried in London the following day. His will, dated 29 September 1661 and proved on 2 August 1667, left his property and money, concerning which he provided no details, to his widow, Sara.   RICHARD L. GREAVES

Sources Thurloe, *State papers*, 1.731; 2.213; 4.90, 328; 5.710 · Bodl. Oxf., MS Rawl. A. 208 · T. Patient, *The doctrine of baptism, and the distinction of the covenants* (1654) · B. R. White, 'Thomas Patient in England and Ireland', *Irish Baptist Historical Society Journal*, 2 (1969–70), 36–48 · B. R. White, ed., *Association records of the Particular Baptists of England, Wales, and Ireland to 1660*, 4 vols. (1971–7), vol. 2, pp. 112–19 · M. Tolmie, *The triumph of the saints: the separate churches of London, 1616–1649* (1977) · St J. D. Seymour, *The puritans in Ireland, 1647–1661* (1912) · A. Laurence, *Parliamentary army chaplains, 1642–1651*, Royal Historical Society Studies in History, 59 (1990) · J. Rogers, *Challah, the heavenly nymph* (1653) · T. Edwards, *Gangraena, or, A catalogue and discovery of many of the errours, heresies, blasphemies and pernicious practices of the sectaries of this time*, 2nd edn, 3 vols. in 1 (1646), 88, 127–8 · will, PRO, PROB 11/321, sig. 132 · *CSP dom.*, 1659–60, 13 · R. Hayden, ed., *The records of a church in Christ in Bristol, 1640–1687*, Bristol RS, 27 (1974) · PRO, State Papers 28/74, 90–92, 94–6, 114–17 · W. Wilson, *The history and antiquities of the dissenting churches and meeting houses in London, Westminster and Southwark*, 4 vols. (1808–14), vol. 1, pp. 431–3
Archives Bodl. Oxf., MS Rawl. A. 208 · PRO, state papers, domestic, 28/74, 90–92, 94–6, 114–17
Wealth at death see will, PRO, PROB 11/321, sig. 132

Patmore, Coventry Kersey Deighton (1823–1896), poet and essayist, was born on 23 July 1823 at Woodford, Essex, and baptized on 11 June 1824, the eldest of the four children of the author Peter George *Patmore (*bap.* 1786, *d.* 1855), son of Peter Patmore and Maria Clarissa Stevens, and his wife, Eliza Robertson (1798–1851), of Scotland, who were married in 1822. Patmore distinguished himself as both a poet and an essayist.

Origins and early years Patmore was the grandson of prosperous London jewellers. His father was a friend of William Hazlitt's, to whom the notorious *Liber amoris* was addressed, and was also a regular contributor to the literary culture of the early nineteenth century. His life as a gentleman and man of letters was somewhat shadowed, however, not only by association with Hazlitt's sexual obsession but also by the unfortunate duelling death of John Scott, in which his probity as second had been questioned. He brought up his eldest son, in residences in London and the country (Highwood Hill, Middlesex), to occupy a similar gentlemanly position. Coventry Patmore was educated primarily at home with his father's indulgence, good literary counsel, and distinguished connections, and was given a half-year's finishing (1839) in Paris at a school at St Germain. It was at this time that he fell deeply in love with a Miss Gore, having visited her mother's Paris salon. She spurned him, however, and romantic obsession with lost love became incorporated in reflections on the nature of love which would have an

Coventry Kersey Deighton Patmore (1823–1896), by John Singer Sargent, 1894

important place in his later thinking about love and religion. He was subsequently recorded in his father's *Chatsworth, or, The Romance of a Week* (1844) as a type of the young man of Romantic poetic genius, being tall but of a delicate and sensitive appearance which would persist into middle age. A Romantic interest in feeling and its expression which led him early towards poetry and aesthetics was combined with a somewhat scientific bent, worked out in a youthful programme of scientific study.

The development of a model belated Romantic poet seemed to proceed without a flaw as, in his twenty-first year, Patmore brought out his first work, *Poems* (1844), with Edward Moxon, publisher of poets including Tennyson and Browning. The poems, which he progressively buried in radical revisions, including major omissions, show an interesting return, after the somewhat anti-Romantic work of Browning and Tennyson in the 1830s and early 1840s, to Romantic themes of intense emotion, passionate love, and medieval context or form. One appreciates them historically, not only for their echoes of Romantics, especially Coleridge and Wordsworth, but more positively as anticipations of the Pre-Raphaelite movement.

The early Victorian period offered few rewards for poetry; patronage and popularity for the Brownings and Tennyson were to come in the 1850s; meanwhile poets were self-financed, mainly by their families, sometimes by additional careers. Patmore, however, found the genteel supports of his dawning career suddenly pulled out from under him in 1845 as his father failed in a railway speculation. As a result the poet had to yield to the literary essayist. In his lifetime production of more than 200 essays he combined ease with precision, making them a pleasure to read. In the early Victorian period, where the prose which captured the public attention (such as that of Carlyle or Ruskin) was highly stylized and rhetorical, his was a quieter voice, a critical style with an authority based on argument and aesthetic theory rather than on class and tradition. He would continue in the later 1840s and 1850s, soon with less financial urgency, to write widely on subjects of canonical and contemporary English literature, German philosophy and aesthetics, architecture, and art.

Librarianship, marriage, and *The Angel in the House* Patmore's own financial difficulties were soon relieved, as through the intercession of a literary friend, Adelaide Ann Procter, he was recommended by Monckton Milnes, via the archbishop of Canterbury, to a position in the British Museum on 11 April 1846. He subsequently received the post of supernumerary assistant in the department of printed books on 24 November 1846 at 10s. 6d. a day. He retired on 31 October 1865, by then a first-class assistant (second 1851, first 1861) with a salary of £360 per annum. (His pension was almost £127.) This secure place and income, supplemented by a small inheritance in 1855, was the foundation on which he built a life and a poetic career. He was married in the Hampstead parish church of St John on 11 September 1847 to the talented and attractive Emily Augusta Andrews [see below]. They settled in a series of homes over the next fifteen years, all in north London, with a winter flat in Percy Street near the British Museum; and they proceeded to raise a family, ultimately of six children: Milnes, an active boy with whom Coventry had a good deal of conflict; Tennyson, who became a doctor; Emily Honoria Patmore (d. 1882), who became a nun; Gertrude; Bertha; and Henry John Patmore [see below].

Patmore's serious marriage to a clergyman's daughter mirrored his father's marriage to a serious Scotswoman, and he was himself more religious than his father and had even at one time considered taking orders. But his poetry continued in the Romantic and rather sexually explicit veins of 1844, issuing in two somewhat different versions of a volume, *Tamerton Church Tower and other Poems* (1853; 1854). The volume(s) confirm his closeness to the newly prominent Pre-Raphaelites, in whose periodical *The Germ* he had published a poem and an essay. There is a new and interesting psychologically penetrating awareness of the anxiety, leading even to angst, of love relations. This new awareness is repressed, however, in his more conformist, if none the less important, series of four poems: *The Espousals* (1854), *The Betrothal* (1856), *Faithful for Ever* (1860), and *The Victories of Love* (1862; 1863). The series is often referred to collectively by the joint title of the first two poems, *The Angel in the House*. As Tennyson had recently made his mark by a connected series of poems on death

and grief, Patmore determined to write *the* poetic series on that other Victorian obsession, married love. The passage of time has made it clear, however, that the result was far less positive for his career. He experienced good (not extravagant) sales during this period but was already encountering criticism from early feminist circles for his views on women and marriage. Later in his life, as Ian Anstruther has shown, the poem was reissued in a much more controversial context as an icon of traditional home values. As such it would be seized upon by Virginia Woolf as the ultimate symbol of the subordinated domestic woman; in a lecture, 'Professions for women' (1931), she forcefully expressed the need for the female writer to 'kill the Angel in the House' (Drabble, 29). There has been much twentieth-century critical vilification of Patmore's views as expressed in *The Angel in the House*, much of it uninformed and second-hand. As Alice Meynell early insisted, the 'angel' represents the love between the couple, rather than the wife herself, who in the poem is in any case an aristocrat, freed from all that is conventionally understood to have been 'angel' duties. Patmore's poem has formal brilliance and some interesting revival of metaphysical wit; but it is also in places Biedermeier glossy or plain saccharine, and is sometimes sadistic and sexually repressive. It is worth noting, however, that his wife was an intelligent, published author and his daughters were independent and remarkable, biographical information which should give pause to those who would consider him an uncomplicated advocate of some kind of absolute notion of repressive patriarchy. He does not deserve the misrepresentation and totemization he has polemically received for his voicing of what were common opinions of his time, misrepresentation which has made it difficult to judge his artistic ability fairly.

Loss, conversion, remarriage, more losses, the *Odes* The second set of poems in Patmore's series on married love is concerned with the process of love's loss and compromise rather than its fulfilment, and these poems reach a more profound level, with interesting reflections which anticipate the religious preoccupations of his best work. His personal life developed similarly, as, with the death of Emily on 5 July 1862, he was left a bereft father of six. That the seemingly patriarchal Patmore had been in fact the weaker half in his relation with Emily was made clear in his fulfilment, in Rome in 1864, of her prediction that he would convert to Roman Catholicism. From a central place among liberal protestant writers he now joined the growing number of converts to Rome who formed an intense other culture within Victorian literary society. On 18 July 1864 Patmore married Marianne Caroline Byles (1822–1880), a wealthy Catholic convert, and the daughter of James Hodge Byles of Gloucestershire and his wife, Judith. Able to depend upon her monetary resources as well as her religious convictions, in 1866 he could now settle as the gentleman poet that he had always considered himself to be; and he much improved an estate, Heron's Ghyll near Uckfield in Sussex. His architectural and financial successes and travails formed the subject of an engaging memoir in 1886, and his daughter Gertrude also produced a volume on local pets and animals.

However, Patmore's psychic life was preoccupied with absence and loss. Persistent rumours suggest that the marriage was unconsummated. Mary was in any case rather like a nun in residence, devoted to her translations (with Patmore) of St Bernard which were eventually published after her death (1891; 1894). Patmore was especially close to his poet son Henry, who died in 1883, and, above all, to his daughter Emily Honoria (Sister Mary Christina), a talented poet and mystic, who died on 15 July 1882 near her convent of the Society of the Holy Child Jesus at St Leonards, Sussex. When his second wife died on 12 April 1880, he memorialized her with a donation of £5300 to the construction of St Mary Star of the Sea Church at Hastings, Sussex, an ocean spot which he had admired since childhood and to which he had moved in 1875, setting up house in The Mansion in Hastings High Street. But the deeper loss, of his first wife, Emily, became the starting place of his major poetic work, the uneven but often masterful, sometimes sublime, elegiac odes of *The Unknown Eros*. Its publication history is characteristically complex; the majority of the work was first published in 1868 as *Odes* and was then revised and republished with additions under its later title in 1877, 1878, 1879, and 1886. In the final version, book I revisits the grief and restages the loss of his wife as a universal in particular, with powerful yet easily comprehensible odes such as 'The Azalea' treading close to emotional excess. Book II in the Dantesque/Petrarchan tradition moves from love of God's creation to the higher love of God. Yet in a more specific tradition of Catholic mysticism, Patmore counters the binary produced by this motion by insisting on the sensuous relation of man to God, thus making sexual love not a love which reaches but to dust but a step in a larger sexual relation to deity. Absence thus conjures presence out of its extreme lack. The poems are among the finest odes in English after the Romantics. Patmore's facility with the rapid rises and rapid turns of the Cowleyan irregular ode was doubtless enhanced by his theoretical work in the essay 'On English metrical law' (1857; 1878 in his *Poems*). This represented one of the central attempts at a new prosody in the nineteenth century responsive to the rediscovery of the older English oral rhythms based on natural stress rather than feet.

Patmore visited Lourdes, was received as lay brother Francis in the Franciscans, made retreats to monasteries, and planned a work on the nuptials of the Virgin ('Sponsa Dei') but was discouraged from this project by Gerard Manley Hopkins. Much of the thinking of that work probably found its way into the fine prose of Patmore's essays in *The Rod, the Root, and the Flower* (1895), a work which deserves a more major place in English mystical tradition.

Final years: marriage, devotion to 'ma dame', essays A year and a summer after the death of his second wife, Patmore married Harriet Georgina Robson (*bap.* 1841, *d.* 1925) on 13 September 1881. She was the daughter of George Robson, a civil engineer, and, somewhat controversially, had formerly acted as governess in his household. She was Catholic, had some literary talent, and had been his confidante for many years, particularly in helping him deal with the mental illness of his daughter Bertha. This third marriage was happy and full, and resulted in the birth of his seventh child, Francis Joseph Epiphanus (Piffie), who would write warmly of his affectionate relation with his ageing father and, like his deceased half-brother Henry, would eventually publish a small book of poems.

Two Patmores now seemed to exist simultaneously before the public eye: one the old-fashioned author of the increasingly popular mid-Victorian *Angel*, the other as austere and inaccessible as he appears in the famous portrait by John Singer Sargent appropriately reused for the figure of the prophet Ezekiel in Sargent's murals for the Boston Public Library. As a kind of prophet, he was honoured by a set of friends which centred on Wilfred and Alice Meynell. Here personal and public recognition oddly blended, as Patmore styled Alice *ma dame* in deliberate resuscitation of the courtly tradition and devoted poems and a good deal of personal attention to the Alicia he celebrated in his poems. There was resultant tension caused by his divided devotion to youngish wife and young *dame*. Meynell, who often expressed her admiration for Patmore in print, turned from him to George Meredith as the next figure in her series of platonic involvements with men. Clearly Patmore, who as a poet viewed all love, sexual and affective, as pointing to a greater consummation with God, had a startlingly modern multiplicity of mere mortal connections.

In his later years, Patmore was also courted and lionized by a friend, Frederick Greenwood, who published the *St James's Gazette* and for whom Patmore returned to the essay writing of his early maturity. He wrote mainly on cultural and religious issues, including more essays on architecture, Catholic religious history, and mystical tradition—essays which found a place in two collections: *Principle in Art* (1889; 1890) and *Religio poetae* (1893; 1898). He also wrote on English writers, dispraising Jane Austen in comparison to male novelists but also writing with sympathy on writers as different as Francis Thompson and Thomas Hardy. His attempts to define the mixture of male and female qualities in genius have generally not been positively received in the less clearly gendered twentieth century, though they could be seen as opening the possibility of androgyny or separation of gender from assigned sex.

Patmore moved in his lifetime from the role of engaging, slightly older Pre-Raphaelite half-brother, friend and co-host with his first wife to both that generation and to the slightly older generation of Tennyson, Browning, and Ruskin, through the period of religious withdrawal and preoccupation with estate and family, to the more distant friendship with a younger generation, including figures such as Edmund Gosse, Hopkins, and the Meynells. Against reductions of his complex life's work to stereotypes of wife-secreting patriarchy or sublime egotism we need to set the diversity of his interests, which make him both an important lyric poet of his age and also one of those Victorian sages whose minds ranged out so widely into history, religion, art, and architecture. Above all must be marked his openness to experiment, from early ventures in science, architecture, and sexual psychology, to the experimentalism in form and subject matter of the odes in *The Unknown Eros*, penetrating the mystic and sexual traditions of the Christian heritage, undigging, as he put it, the wells the prudish Philistines had filled with sand.

Patmore had been forced to leave his home in Hastings in the autumn of 1891; he moved to The Lodge at Walhampton, near Lymington, Hampshire, another situation on the coast, taking a lease on 1 September 1891. He died there of pulmonary congestion and cardiac failure on 26 November 1896 and was buried in the cemetery in nearby Lymington, in the Catholic section. He was survived by his third wife.

Patmore's first wife, **Emily Augusta Patmore** [*née* Andrews] (1824–1862), writer, was born on 29 February 1824, the daughter of Edward Andrews (1787–1841), a Congregational minister at Beresford Chapel, Walworth, south of London, who also acted as Greek tutor to Ruskin. Her mother, Elizabeth Honor Symons (1792–1831), died when she was still young and she took over household duties for her father. Probably under his tutorship she learned Greek, Latin, and French.

Emily Andrews married Coventry Patmore on 11 September 1847; her intelligence, serious 'man's' education, and attractive features made her popular and respected by Patmore's distinguished literary friends. While raising their six children on Coventry's modest middle-class librarian's salary, she managed to publish three books under the pseudonym of Mrs Motherly. One is a conduct book, *The servant's behaviour book, or, Hints on manners and dress for maid servants in small households* (1859), written in a direct, lucid style. The other two show more literary talent: *Nursery Poetry* (1859) contains lively verses on household matters, while *Nursery Tales* (1860) is improving and moralistic in tone. She also had an important part in developing her husband's anthology of excellent classic and contemporary poems, *The Children's Garland* (1862).

Emily became an icon of womanly distinction in her age. She was the subject of a medallion by Thomas Woolner, a painting by Millais, and a poem by Robert Browning, 'A Face'. Conversely, in the twentieth century, she became a negative icon as the supposed model for Patmore's 'angel'. Both stereotypes have effaced her individuality as a woman of her time who effected significant activity as a writer and independent thinker on literature and religion. To her dependent husband she suggested his central development from human love to divine. Emily died of tuberculosis on 5 July 1862 at home at Elm Cottage, North End, Hampstead, London, aged only thirty-eight, and only two years after the birth of her sixth child, Henry. She was buried at Hendon, London.

Henry John Patmore (1860–1883), poet, was born on 8 May 1860 in Muswell Hill, Middlesex, the youngest son of Coventry Patmore and Emily Augusta Patmore. He wrote some precocious poems before his untimely death from pulmonary tuberculosis and pleurisy at the age of twenty-two.

Henry Patmore had published at least three poems in magazines during his lifetime. In accordance with his deathbed wish, his father published in 1884, at Oxford with Henry Daniel, about forty pages of poems in a handsome edition with a memoir by his sister Gertrude. Some nine of these poems were published again as part of his father's collected *Poems* (1886) and in later editions. Four more, not in either of the above, were published by Gertrude in the *Ushaw Magazine*. His father rightly speaks of the poems as a 'very inadequate indication of the power and delicacy of the mind and heart which produced them' (C. Patmore in note to H. Patmore, *Poems*, 1884, vi). Most are brief lyrics, some expressions of love, some reflections on landscape, one a longer narration reminiscent of his father's early poems, but the most poignant is the 'Prologue to Poems Mostly Unwritten'. He died, unmarried, at his home, The Mansion, High Street, Hastings, Sussex, on 24 February 1883.   JOHN MAYNARD

Sources B. Champneys, *Memoirs and correspondence of Coventry Patmore*, 2 vols. (1900) · D. Patmore, *The life and times of Coventry Patmore* (1949) · J. C. Reid, *The mind and art of Coventry Patmore* (1949) [incl. appx with comprehensive bibliography] · I. Anstruther, *Coventry Patmore's Angel: a study of Coventry Patmore, his wife Emily, and 'The Angel in the House'* (1992) · J. Maynard, *Victorian discourses on sexuality and religion* (1993) · Sister M. A. Weinig, *Coventry Patmore* (1981) · P. Beal and others, *Index of English literary manuscripts*, ed. P. J. Croft and others, [4 vols. in 11 pts] (1980–), vol. 4, pp. 803–56 · G. Patmore, 'Biographical note', *Poems by Henry Patmore* (1884), i–iv [H. J. Patmore] · D. Patmore, 'Coventry Patmore's unhappy love for Alice Meynell', unpubd MS, Boston College, Massachusetts · E. Gosse, *Coventry Patmore* (1905) · J. M. Crook, 'Coventry Patmore and the aesthetics of architecture', *PBA*, 76 (1990), 171–201 · W. M[eynell], *The Academy* (5 Dec 1896), 496–7 · Father Anselm, *Franciscan annals* (1897), 7–10 · E. J. Oliver, *Coventry Patmore* (1956) · A Religious [L. Wheaton], *A daughter of Coventry Patmore: Sister Mary Christina, S. H. C. J.* (1924) · *A catalogue of the library of Coventry Patmore lately purchased by Everard Meynell* (1921) · *Victorian Poetry*, 34/4 (1996) [Coventry Patmore issue] · M. Drabble, ed., *The Oxford companion to English literature*, 5th edn (1985) · parish register (baptism), 11 June 1824 · d. cert. · b. cert. [H. J. Patmore] · register of deaths, 24 Feb 1883 [H. J. Patmore] · parish register (marriage), 11 Sept 1847, Hampstead, St John's [C. K. D. Patmore and E. A. Andrews] · parish register (marriage), 18 July 1864 [C. K. D. Patmore and M. C. Byles] · parish register (death), 5 July 1862 [E. A. Patmore] · parish register (death), 12 April 1880 [M. C. Patmore] · parish register (marriage), 13 Sept 1881 [H. R. Patmore] · *The Times* (13 Nov 1925) [H. G. Patmore]

Archives BL, corresp. and literary papers, Add. MSS 41737, 46145 · Boston College, Massachusetts, corresp., literary MSS and papers · Hants. RO, family corresp. · Knox College, Galesburg, Illinois, Seymour Library, letters and poem · Princeton University Library, New Jersey, corresp. and poems · U. Nott. L., corresp. and papers · U. Nott. L., notebook | BL, letters to J. D. Campbell, Add. MS 49525A · BL, letters to his daughter Gertrude, Add. MS 46145 · BL, corresp. with Macmillans, Add. MS 55008 · BL, letters to Royal Literary Fund, loan 96 · Bodl. Oxf., letters to Robert Bridges · Bodl. Oxf., letters to D. G. Rossetti · Bodl. Oxf., letters to F. G. Stephens · Bodl. Oxf., corresp. with H. H. Vaughan · CKS, letters to Lord Stanhope · Emory University, Atlanta, Georgia, Pitts Theology Library, corresp. with H. E. Manning · Lincoln Central Library, letters to Lord Tennyson · NL Scot., corresp. with Samuel Brown · NL Scot., letters to Alexander Campbell Fraser · Society of the Holy Child

Jesus, Mayfield, East Sussex, letters to his daughter Emily Honoria · Trinity Cam., letters to Lord Houghton · U. Durham L., corresp. with Gerard Manley Hopkins · U. Leeds, Brotherton L., letters to Sir Edmund Gosse · U. Reading L., letters to George Bell & Sons

Likenesses T. Woolner, medallion, 1849, repro. in Champneys, *Memoirs*, vol. 1 · T. Woolner, medallion, 1850? (Emily Augusta Patmore), priv. coll. · J. Millais, oils, 1851 (Emily Augusta Patmore), FM Cam. · J. Brett, wash drawing, 1854? (Emily Augusta Patmore), priv. coll. · J. Brett, pencil drawing, 1855, repro. in Champneys, *Memoirs*, vol. 1 · J. Brett, oils, 1859? (Emily Augusta Patmore), priv. coll. · J. Brett, pencil drawing, 1859 (Emily Augusta Patmore) · photograph, 1875 (Henry John Patmore), repro. in Champneys, *Memoirs*, vol. 2 · group portrait, photograph, 1880–89, repro. in Patmore, *Life and times* · G. Bradshaw, photograph, 1886, repro. in Champneys, *Memoirs*, vol. 1 · Barraud, photograph, 1891, NPG; repro. in Champneys, *Memoirs*, vol. 1, p. 11 · J. S. Sargent, oil sketch, 1894, repro. in Champneys, *Memoirs*, vol. 1 · J. S. Sargent, oils, 1894, NPG [*see illus.*] · J. S. Sargent, oils, 1894, Boston PL · M. Beerbohm, caricature, 1917, Tate collection; repro. in M. Beerbohm, *Rossetti and his circle* (1922) · J. Lavery, oils, 1938 (aged seventy-one; after Sargent), Boston College · R. Taylor & Co., group portrait, wood-engraving, NPG; repro. in *ILN* (15 Oct 1892) · photograph (Emily Augusta Patmore), priv. coll.

Wealth at death £9861 16s. 4d.: probate, 12 April 1897, *CGPLA Eng. & Wales*

Patmore, Emily Augusta (1824–1862). *See under* Patmore, Coventry Kersey Deighton (1823–1896).

Patmore, Henry John (1860–1883). *See under* Patmore, Coventry Kersey Deighton (1823–1896).

Patmore, Peter George (*bap.* 1786, *d.* 1855), writer and journalist, only child of Peter Patmore (*fl.* 1783–1821), silversmith and jeweller, and his wife, Clarissa Maria Stevens (*c.*1762–1853), was born in his father's house at 33 Ludgate Hill, London, and baptized at St Martin Ludgate on 10 September 1786. From his early twenties onwards he wrote for many of the best-known journals, was a friend of William Hazlitt and Charles Lamb and, later, a close acquaintance of Leigh Hunt.

In 1821 Patmore acted as second to the journalist John Scott in the duel in which Scott was killed. Charged with murder (though cleared at his trial), Patmore was shunned by many who held him responsible for Scott's death; the novelist Thackeray described him twenty-five years later as 'that murderer' (Gosse, 2). In 1822 he married Eliza Anne Bowring Robertson (1791/2–1851); they had four children, of whom the eldest was the poet Coventry *Patmore, whom Patmore attempted, to no lasting effect, to keep from all religious education and practices. His already notorious reputation was further sullied with the publication of Hazlitt's autobiographical *Liber amoris* (1823), in which Patmore was the 'C. P.' to whom Hazlitt confided an infatuated illicit relationship.

Patmore edited the *New Monthly Magazine* from 1841 to 1853. Much of his writing was published anonymously, and some pseudonymously, under the names Victoire de Soligny, and M. de Saint Foix. *My Friends and Acquaintance* (1854), however, appeared under his own name, and remains a work of some interest, although harshly condemned at the time for revelations, considered indiscreet,

regarding celebrities he had known. Patmore died at his home, 49 Whittlebury Street, Euston Square, London, on 25 December 1855, aged sixty-nine. S. V. SPILSBURY

Sources B. Champneys, *Memoirs and correspondence of Coventry Patmore*, 2 vols. (1900) · E. Gosse, *Coventry Patmore* (1905) · D. Patmore, *Portrait of my family* (1935) · *The Times* (3 March 1821) · *The Times* (14 April 1821) · letters to Leigh Hunt, BL, Add. MSS 38109, fol. 142; 38110, fol. 87; 38524, fol. 1 · *GM*, 2nd ser., 45 (1856), 206 · W. Hazlitt, *Liber amoris* (1823) · *Wellesley index* · *The letters of Charles Lamb*, ed. A. Ainger, 2 vols. (1888) · *The Post Office London directory* (1819); (1840); (1853) · *BL cat.* · *IGI*

Archives Princeton University Library, New Jersey, papers | Harvard U., Houghton L., letters to John Philippart · NL Scot., letters to Blackwoods

Likenesses P. G. Patmore, self-portrait, pen sketch, repro. in Patmore, *Portrait of my family*, facing p. 36

Paton, Alan Stewart (1903–1988), writer, educationist, and politician, was born on 11 January 1903 at 9 Greyling Street, Pietermaritzburg, Natal, the oldest of the four children, two boys and two girls, of James Paton (1872–1930), a Scottish shorthand writer who had emigrated to South Africa in 1895, and his wife, Eunice Warder James (1878?–1965), the daughter of a Bristol clerk and his South African-born wife, Edith. James Paton was a puritanical tyrant, from whom his oldest son learned an abiding hatred of violence and authoritarianism.

Alan Paton had a distinguished academic career at Maritzburg College (1914–18) and Natal University College (1919–24) before beginning work as a teacher at Ixopo, where he met his first wife, Doris (Dorrie) Lusted (1897–1967), daughter of a local solicitor, George Francis, and recently widowed. They married on 2 July 1928, and although the marriage was difficult from the start, it endured. Alan Paton in maturity was less than 5 feet 7 inches in height, very fair of complexion, and with piercing pale blue eyes.

Paton, who had not been happy as a teacher, made a momentous career change in 1935, taking on the post of director of a turbulent borstal for black youths, Diepkloof, near Johannesburg. It was at Diepkloof that he formed most of the important political ideas which were to shape his writing and his life. On his arrival he found that Diepkloof was run on prison camp lines, with armed guards, two high fences topped with barbed wire, a massive front gate and severe military discipline. In spite of these measures, or because of them, there were constant escapes. Paton saw that the gate, the guards, and the repressive discipline were part of the problem, and courageously decided to begin breaking them down. The youths would be controlled, not with counter-violence but with love and self-discipline. They were encouraged to spend their days in useful work, gardening, and education; the discipline was gradually made less severe; and after some months first the outer fence, then the huge gate, then the inner fence were removed. Critics such as H. F. Verwoerd, the architect of apartheid, predicted break-outs on a massive scale; in fact the number of escapees dropped sharply and remained low.

It was while he was principal of Diepkloof that Paton, in

1946–7, was sent on a government-sponsored tour of similar borstals in Scandinavia, Britain, and North America. While on this tour, beginning in Norway, he wrote *Cry, the Beloved Country: a Story of Comfort in Desolation*. He finished it in the United States, and it was immediately accepted by Scribners and published in 1948. Its success, both critical and popular, was great and lasting; it is widely recognized as one of the outstanding novels of the twentieth century.

Financial security and fame changed Alan Paton's life, as the experience at Diepkloof had done. Shortly before the Nationalist government came to power in the year of *Cry, the Beloved Country*'s publication, Paton resigned from Diepkloof and became a full-time writer, turning out a stream of poems and a succession of biographies and novels, including the haunting *Too Late the Phalarope* (1953), which focused attention on the tragedy of the Afrikaner, imprisoned and consumed by the apartheid he had created.

In pursuit of his non-racial ideals, Paton helped to found the South African Liberal Party in 1953, becoming its national chairman in 1956 and its president in 1958. From then on his career became increasingly political and dedicated to helping all racial groups in South Africa. Accordingly he was harassed by the Nationalist government, and only his international eminence saved him from imprisonment. He refused to be cowed or silenced, producing a steady stream of polemical articles which kept him in the public eye, and a constant flow of fine poems, many of them unpublished in his own lifetime, most of them having a political message and a satirical edge.

Paton also produced two important political biographies, of his political mentor J. H. Hofmeyr (*Hofmeyr*, 1965), and of the Anglican bishop Geoffrey Clayton (*Apartheid and the Archbishop*, 1974). He saw these two very different men as representative of the roots of South African liberalism, and his biographies, like his novels, poems, and other writings, are part of a consistent moral and political concern that actuated him all his life.

The same is true of his two volumes of autobiography, *Toward the Mountain* (1980) and *Journey Continued* (1988), in which there emerges clearly his view of human life as a moral and spiritual pilgrimage, in which our aim should be to live, not for ourselves, but for others. This aim he pursued all his life, though he felt it was an ideal of which he had often fallen short.

After the death of his wife, Dorrie, on 23 October 1967 Paton was sustained by the joy of a successful second marriage, on 30 January 1969, to his secretary, Anne Hopkins (*b.* 1927), an English-born divorcee. In his later years he found himself criticized both from the left and from the right, as political polarization produced greater extremism, but he stubbornly stood his ground, arguing that violence and repression were wrong no matter who was practising them. He died of cancer of the oesophagus on 12 April 1988 at his home near Durban, Lintrose, Botha's Hill. His ashes were scattered in the garden there in October of that year.   PETER F. ALEXANDER

Sources P. F. Alexander, *Alan Paton: a biography* (1995) · E. Callan, *Alan Paton* [1968]; rev. edn (1982) · A. Paton, *Some sort of a job: my life with Alan Paton* (1992) · M. Benson, *The African patriots* (1963); rev. as *South Africa: the struggle for a birthright* (1966) · M. Benson, *A far cry* (1989) · M. Black, 'Alan Paton and the rule of law', *African Affairs*, 91 (1992), 53–72 · R. M. Brown, 'Alan Paton: warrior and man of grace', *Christianity and Crisis*, 48 (June 1988), 204–6 · E. Callan, 'Alan Paton and the liberal party', in A. S. Paton, *The long view*, ed. E. Callan (1968), 3–44 · L. Chisholm, 'Education, punishment and the contradictions of penal reform: Alan Paton and the Diepkloof reformatory, 1934–1948', *Journal of Southern African Studies*, 17/1 (1991), 23–42 · E. Daniels, 'Salute to the memory', *Reality: a journal of liberal opinion*, 20 (1988), 6 · b. cert. · d. cert. · private information (2004) · E. Fuller, *Books with the men behind them* (1962), 83–101 · C. Gardner, 'Alan Paton: often admired, sometimes criticized, usually misunderstood', *Natalia*, 18 (Dec 1988), 19–28 · C. Gardner, 'Paton's literary achievement', *Reality*, 20/4 (1988), 8–11 · S. Haw and R. Frame, *For hearth and home: the story of Maritzburg College, 1863–1988* (1988) · M. Hooper, 'Paton and the silence of Stephanie', *English Studies in Africa*, 32 (1989), 53–62 · R. Italiaander, 'Das Engagement des Schriftstellers Alan Paton in Südafrika', *Profile und Perspecktiven* (Erlangen, 1970) · R. J. Linnemann, 'Alan Paton: anachronism or visionary', *Commonwealth Novel in English*, 3/1 (1984), 88–100 · T. Morphet, 'Alan Paton: the honour of meditation', *English in Africa*, 10/2 (1983), 1–10 · R. Moss, 'Alan Paton: bringing a sense of the sacred', *World Literature Today*, 57/2 (1983), 233–7 · N. Munger, *Touched by Africa* (1983), 29–43 · R. Rive, 'The liberal tradition in South African literature', *Contrast*, 14/3 (1983), 19–31 · A. Rutherford, 'Stone people in a stone country: Alan Paton's *Too late the phalarope*', *Literature and the art of creation*, ed. R. Welsh (1988), 140–52 · I. N. Stevens, 'Paton's narrator Sophie: justice and mercy in *Too late the phalarope*', *International Fiction Review*, 8/1 (1981), 68–70 · J. B. Thompson, 'Poetic truth in *Too late the phalarope*', *English Studies in Africa*, 24/1 (1981), 37–44 · S. Watson, '*Cry, the beloved country* and the failure of liberal vision', *English in Africa*, 9/1 (1982), 29–44 · N. H. Z. Watts, 'A study of Alan Paton's *Too late the phalarope*', *Durham University Journal*, 76 (1983–4), 249–54

Archives Kent School, Connecticut, MSS · L. Cong., MSS · Maritzburg College, MSS · NRA, priv. coll., MSS · Ransom HRC, MSS · University of Cape Town, MSS · University of Natal, Pietermaritzburg, Alan Paton Centre, MSS · Weill-Lenya Foundation, New York, MSS | Brenthurst Library, Johannesburg, Oppenheimer collection · University of Witwatersrand, Johannesburg, Hofmeyr collection | SOUND University of Natal, Pietermaritzburg, Alan Paton Centre

Likenesses photograph, 1938, Hult. Arch. · photographs, University of Natal, Pietermaritzburg, Alan Paton Centre

Wealth at death 788,989 rand

Paton, Alexander Allan (1874–1934), cotton merchant and broker, was the only son of the five children of Alexander Allan Paton (1837–1904) and his wife, Marie, the daughter of John Crowshaw of New York. His father was a successful Scottish-American cotton merchant who had emigrated to the United States about 1860 and during the American Civil War worked for the United States mail railroad, initially as a conductor. After the war he became general freight agent of the Memphis and Louisville railroad, but then in 1868 established a cotton marketing firm with branches in St Louis, Memphis, New Orleans, and Liverpool. R. G. Dun's Memphis agent reported in 1875 that Paton 'st[an]ds well with the Trade and Banks. Does an extensive business and is a shrewd and ever pushing man.'

These firms did well, and by the early 1880s they were worth in America somewhere between $150,000 and $200,000. The Liverpool branch was managed by Paton's

Alexander Allan Paton (1874–1934), by Lafayette, 1926

elder brother, Andrew Brown Paton (1833–1913), who, after private school and London University, had been a Congregational minister, but had retired from the ministry in 1869 on account of ill health. In 1889 Alexander Paton senior returned to Liverpool and established his own firm of Paton, Maclaren & Co. He managed the Liverpool branch, while George S. Maclaren took care of the Memphis branch. By 1900 this firm had become one of the largest cotton importers in Liverpool. A. B. Paton's firm also grew. After he retired in 1902, Andrew Vaughan Paton, A. A. Paton's nephew, succeeded, and in 1917 became president of the Liverpool cotton exchange. Alexander Paton junior therefore grew up in a rising Liverpool cotton marketing family.

When his father returned to England in 1889, Alexander Paton entered the Leys School, Cambridge. He joined his father's new Liverpool firm in 1892, and became a partner in 1898. In 1899, having learned the trade, he was sent out to manage the firm's purchasing operations in Memphis. He returned to Liverpool in 1903 and took over the business with a capital of about £20,000 from his father, who died in 1904. Barings' Liverpool branch reported: 'There is every reason to suppose the … firm will continue to be well and prudently conducted.' The firm indeed did well and in 1911 had branches in Liverpool and Memphis and also in Dallas, Hillsboro, and Sulphur Springs, Texas. Barings provided Paton Maclaren with credits. The firm purchased cotton in the southern USA, hedged it in New York, shipped it to Liverpool, and sold to a circle of Lancashire mills.

Paton quickly rose in the Liverpool cotton trade. He was a director of the Liverpool Cotton Association from 1907 to 1910 and was on the council of the British Cotton Growing Association. When the First World War broke out in August 1914, the Bank of Liverpool appointed him as one of two cotton directors to help restore confidence. The war ended normal peace-time operations, but Paton was able to use his commercial experience well. From 1915 to 1918 he worked in the contraband department of the ministry of blockade in the British embassy in Washington. In 1917 he advised the Balfour mission to the United States on the blockade. He declined an offer of an OBE for his work in 1918. He was at the Versailles peace conference in 1919 as adviser 'in charge of the Establishment at the Hotel Majestic', for which he was made a CB in 1920.

Paton re-entered the cotton trade after the war, but there is little information about the firm's activities. Generally Liverpool firms never recovered their pre-war position. Instead American firms such as Anderson Clayton dominated the trade, establishing buying agencies in the southern states and selling direct to continental European spinners. In Britain, however, the cotton trade was so large and varied that the Liverpool cotton exchange and Liverpool brokers remained vital intermediaries. Paton became vice-president of the cotton exchange in 1925 and president in 1926. He was also a member of the New York cotton exchange. He found additional new interests especially in the important financial institutions in Liverpool that had originally been created to service the cotton and other trades.

Paton continued to serve as director of the Bank of Liverpool and was deputy chairman from 1922 to 1929 and chairman from 1929 to 1934. While he was deputy chairman, the bank merged with Martins. When he became chairman he opened a new head office and reformed the bank's management. He also served on a bevy of insurance companies. He joined the board of the Royal Insurance Company in 1910 and became deputy chairman in 1924 and chairman in 1930. He was also chairman of the Liverpool and London and Globe, and a director of the Thames and Mersey, the Legal, and the British Foreign and Marine Insurance companies.

The cotton trade at that time provided many of the civic leaders in Liverpool. The elder Patons were strong believers in practical social reform. A. A. Paton senior served as a Liberal on the council, A. B. Paton was a generous philanthropist, and another brother, Dr John Brown Paton, was first principal of Nottingham Congregational college. The younger Paton also served as a Liberal on the Liverpool council, representing Sefton Park in 1911. On the council his main interests were as treasurer of the Unemployed Fund and president of the labour inquiry sub-committee which investigated unemployment. After the war he became an important supporter of the voluntary hospitals in Liverpool. He was president of the Royal Southern Hospital and on the board of the Liverpool Hospital for Consumption. He proposed that the Liverpool hospitals should merge to gain economies of scale. Then, as in America, high fees paid by the wealthy could subsidize services for the poor.

Paton never married, but found many other interests. Aside from public service he played cricket and golf and was a member of the Royal Clyde Yacht Club. In 1928 he purchased *Lulworth*, a fast racing cutter in which he was once able to defeat Sir Thomas Lipton's *Shamrock V* at Cowes. Paton died at his home, The Rocklands, Thornton Hough, Bebington, in the Wirral, on 27 June 1934, aged sixty, still holding many offices. All the managers of Martins Bank and the leaders of the insurance companies, the hospitals, and the cotton trade attended his funeral in Liverpool on 30 June. Paton was a quiet but effective man. Contemporary comments reveal that, despite a reserved and sardonic exterior, he privately earned affection for many generous acts. His estate in Britain passed largely to his sisters and their descendants. He also left assets in America.

J. R. KILLICK

Sources ING Barings, London, Barings archives · Harvard U., Baker Library, R. G. Dun & Co. Collection, Dun and Bradstreet credit registers · school records, Leys School, Cambridge · Liverpool City Libraries, Liverpool Cotton Association records · Liverpool worthies, newspaper cuttings files, Liverpool City Libraries · Memphis, Tennessee, Memphis Cotton Exchange records · G. Chandler, *Four centuries of banking*, 2 vols. (1964-8) · Liverpool trade directories · *The Times* (8 May 1917) · *The Times* (7 July 1934) · d. cert. · *Liverpool Daily Post and Mercury* (2 July 1934)
Likenesses Lafayette, photograph, 1926, NPG [*see illus.*] · portrait, repro. in *Liverpool Courier* (4 March 1908)
Wealth at death £428,688 10s. 6d.: probate, 14 Sept 1934, CGPLA Eng. & Wales

Paton, Amelia Robertson. *See* Hill, Amelia Robertson (1820-1904).

Paton, Andrew Archibald (1811-1874), diplomatist and author, son of Andrew Paton, saddler and government contractor, and Anne Gilchrist, his wife, was born at 75 Broughton Street, Edinburgh, on 19 March 1811. At the age of twenty-five he landed at Naples, and walked from there, with staff and knapsack, to Vienna. Thereafter travelling up and down among the eastern European states, and also in Syria and Egypt, he acquired an accurate and extensive insight into the manners, customs, and political life of the East. He published his observations, with descriptions of the countries themselves, in an interesting series of books.

In 1839-40 Paton acted as private secretary to Colonel George Hodges in Egypt, and was afterwards attached to the political department of the British staff in Syria under Colonel Hugh Henry Rose (afterwards Baron Strathnairn). He was given the rank of deputy assistant quartermaster-general. In 1843 he was appointed acting consul-general in Serbia, and in 1846 was unofficially employed by Sir Robert Gordon, then ambassador at Vienna, to examine and report upon the ports belonging to Austria in the Adriatic. In 1858 he became vice-consul at Missolonghi in Greece, but in the following year was transferred to Lübeck. On 12 May 1862 he was appointed consul at Ragusa and at Bocca di Cattaro.

Paton's works chiefly drew on his diplomatic experience, particularly *Servia* (1845), *Highlands and Islands of the Adriatic* (2 vols., 1849), *The Goth and the Hun* (1851), and *The Bulgarian, the Turk, and the German* (1855). He also wrote a history of the Egyptian revolution (2 vols., 1863), a romance, *The Mamelukes* (3 vols., 1851; republished as *Melusina*, 1861), *Sketches of the Ugly Side of Human Nature* (1867), and a biography of Stendhal (1874); he collected some of his writings in *Researches on the Danube and the Adriatic* (2 vols., 1862).

Paton was married to Eliza Calvert and they had at least one child. Paton died in post at Ragusa on 5 April 1874.

HENRY PATON, rev. H. C. G. MATTHEW

Sources FO List (1874) · FO List (1875)
Archives BL, letters to Sir Austen Layard, Add. MSS 38975-39001, 39101-39116
Wealth at death under £2000: probate, 20 June 1874, CGPLA Eng. & Wales

Paton, Sir (Thomas) Angus Lyall (1905-1999), civil engineer, was born on 10 May 1905 on the Channel Island of Jersey, the son of Thomas Lyall Paton and Janet (*née* Gibb). Angus (the name he preferred) spent the first years of his school life in France, transferring to the mainland to complete his education at Cheltenham College. At Cheltenham the combination of a first-class mathematics teacher, a good memory, and, he later confessed, being 'not much good at games' (*The Independent*, 14 April 1999) meant Paton excelled academically and at seventeen won a scholarship to University College, London; he graduated with a first-class BSc honours degree in civil engineering three years later.

Civil engineering was in Paton's blood. He spent the first three years of his career under the pupillage of his uncle Sir Alexander Gibb at his firm of consulting engineers. He worked on a variety of projects based in the UK and abroad, notably in Burma and Canada. He married Eleanor Joan Medora Delmé-Murray (1910/11-1964) on 7 June 1933, with whom he raised two sons and two daughters.

In 1934 Paton took on the biggest task of his career thus far by leading construction of the new Guinness brewery in Park Royal, north-west London. This £2 million project included seven large steel-framed buildings, a power station, storage silo, roads, and railway sidings. At the time of writing, beer still flows from these premises. The success of this work led to his being made a partner of the firm in 1938.

In the office Paton was renowned for his problem-solving skills; colleagues fully accepted he could do any job, quicker and better than anyone else. His interests did not stop at civil engineering, but extended from design and construction to financial and legal aspects of jobs. This knowledge, combined with his very direct manner and piercing gaze, put those around him from office junior through to senior clients on their guard. At the outbreak of the Second World War, Paton became a central figure in the British engineering war effort designing and constructing ordnance factories, underground aircraft assembly plants, and a new turbine factory for British Thomson-Houston Company.

Sir Alexander Gibb & Partners secured a huge number of government contracts, causing the workforce to leap by over 2000 in a couple of weeks in September 1939. Paton's work included supervising construction in the London docks of some of the massive concrete sections for one of the Mulberry harbours (a floating port built to assist in supplying allied forces in Normandy).

After the war Paton continued to work for Sir Alexander Gibb & Partners, now with Sir Alexander's son Alastair at the helm. He spent the next ten years developing the business overseas and upon Alastair's sudden death in a polo accident, took over as senior partner in 1955. At the same time he took charge of the vast and difficult Kariba Dam and hydroelectric power scheme on the River Zambezi in southern Africa. Paton described the project as the 'highlight of my professional career' (*The Independent*, 14 April 1999); it included a 420 foot high double curvature arch dam—the biggest ever constructed—and a 600 megawatt underground power station in a remote location 175 miles downstream from the Victoria Falls. Despite some of the worst flooding on record, the £75 million project was completed on time and to budget in 1960, an achievement for which Paton was appointed CMG. This acted as a springboard for Sir Alexander Gibb & Partners to win some of the biggest civil engineering contracts around the world. Paton continued to encourage the firm's expansion overseas and as the flow of work continued the size of the business grew. One of the biggest of these projects was to advise the World Bank during construction of the highly complex Tarbela Dam in Pakistan.

In addition to his engineering responsibilities, Paton took a very active interest in the profession as a whole—perhaps more so following the sudden death of his wife in 1964. He was elected a fellow of the Royal Society in 1969 and was president of the Institution of Civil Engineers in 1970/71. Besides many technical papers on civil engineering issues Paton published *Power from Water* (1960). He continually pressed the industry and its clients to spend more money on valuable research and development and was central to the formation of the government-backed Construction Industry Research and Information Association.

Paton was knighted in 1973 for his services to the construction profession and in 1976 was a founding fellow of the Fellowship of Engineering—later renamed the Royal Academy of Engineering. In 1977–8 he was one of the few practising engineers to serve as vice-president of the Royal Society. He retired from Sir Alexander Gibb & Partners in 1977. The last decade of his life was spent in Jersey from where he remained in close contact with the profession and his former colleagues, always retaining the sharp analytical mind and clear process of thought for which he was known throughout his career. Sir Angus died in St Helier, Jersey, on 7 April 1999, and was buried on 15 April at St Brelade church, Jersey.   ANTONY OLIVER

Sources Inst. CE · D. Anderson, T. A. L. Paton, and C. L. Blackburn, 'Zambezi hydro-electric development at Kariba, first stage', *PICE* (1960), 39–60 · presidential address, Nov 1970, Inst. CE · A. Oliver, *The Independent* (14 April 1999) · *The Times* (15 April 1999) · WWW · m. cert. · private information (2004)
Archives Inst. CE, contributions to *Proceedings* and other learned papers
Likenesses portrait, 1970, Inst. CE

Paton, Catherine Forrester- (1855–1914), philanthropist and a founder of women's missionary training in Scotland, was born on 1 June 1855 at Claremont Bank, Alloa; she was the second child and only daughter of Alexander Forrester (1823–1883), merchant and woollen manufacturer, and his wife, Mary (1813–1881), youngest daughter of John Paton of Kilncraigs, Alloa, founder of the woollen manufacturing business of John Paton & Son, and his wife, Catherine Kirk. Her father, by then partner and accountant in the family firm, assumed the name Paton in 1860. Her formal education, at Alloa Academy and then at Grange House School, Edinburgh, finished when she was fifteen, and she returned home to help ageing parents. Sharing their evangelical outlook and devotion to the United Presbyterian church she gained experience of social problems at home and knowledge of foreign mission work, and she learned to handle business affairs—it was said she had the efficiency of a commercial businessman. Following the deaths of her parents she inherited a considerable fortune. Unable because of uncertain health to fulfil her dream of becoming a missionary, she devoted herself to service for others.

The women's temperance movement was for Catherine a lifelong cause; from 1876, when the Alloa branch of the British Women's Temperance Association (BWTA) was formed and she, aged twenty-one, became secretary, to her death in 1914 she played an influential part, both locally and nationally. From 1906 she was president of the BWTA Scottish Christian Union. Her work for temperance was indicative of the growing independent activity by women for women in social, health, educational, and political fields.

In Alloa, besides the usual temperance meetings—the prayer meetings were for her the powerhouse of the work—she organized practical courses in cookery, laundry, and nursing of the sick, soup kitchens for the unemployed, and a centre for young people; she also ran refreshment tents at the local and national agricultural shows. Through the branch she started a district nursing service, one of the earliest in Scotland, which, with its emphasis on health education, became a model. Her interest in nursing and the needs uncovered by the district nursing service led her in 1899 to build and present to the people of Clackmannanshire, at a cost of over £10,000, the well-equipped County Accidents Hospital.

A natural affinity with young people led Catherine to help to found, about 1880, a YWCA branch, which met in her home, as did a Sunday afternoon class. Shortly before her death she planned an institute with meeting-rooms and tea room for the benefit of the townspeople, especially the young women. Throughout her life she continued church work, becoming well known nationally as a speaker at church and temperance meetings.

Her long-standing interest in foreign missions coincided with a growing demand for trained women for work among women abroad and at home—piety and good intentions were no longer enough—but there was in Scotland as yet no specific training. In 1891 she set up her own undenominational home, the Lady Missionaries' Training Home in Glasgow. Her courses were practical, equipping students with domestic, business, and nursing skills as well as biblical training and basic knowledge of the countries where they would work. The women came from Europe and America as well as from the British Isles. She knew them personally and continued to keep in touch by prodigious correspondence as well as by welcoming them to her home when they came on furlough. When the home closed, at Catherine's death, 220 women had passed through.

Catherine's portrait suggests the strength of character and serenity, based on her strong evangelical faith, that enabled her to accomplish so much. Cultured, widely read, and musical, she was also greatly loved and gentle, while formidable in her imaginative vision and practical abilities; bequests of over £53,000, from her estate of £117,855, reveal the breadth of her interests. Though not involved in the 'women's movement' she was still a leader; unusually, at her funeral, among the cord-holders customary at a Scottish graveside were two women. She died on 8 August 1914 at Grantown-on-Spey, where she had gone to convalesce from pleurisy. She was buried beside her parents in Greenside cemetery, Alloa, on 12 August.   ISABEL LUSK

Sources private information (2004) · *Glasgow Herald* (10 Aug 1914) · *Alloa Advertiser* (15 Aug 1914) · *Alloa Journal* (15 Aug 1914) · *Scottish Women's Temperance News* (Sept 1914) · Alloa British Women's Temperance Association, minute books, 1876–1914, Clackmannanshire Libraries · British Women's Temperance Association (Scottish Temperance Union), records, Edinburgh City Libraries, Huntly House Museum · Lady Missionaries Training Home, Glasgow, reports, –1908, Regent's Park College, Oxford · Lady Missionaries Training Home, reports, –1911, priv. coll. · Scottish Foreign Mission records, 1827–1929, NL Scot. · I. Lusk, *Catherine Forrester-Paton of Marshill House, Alloa, 1855–1914* (1997) · IGI
Likenesses oils, c.1906–1908, Huntly House Museum, Edinburgh
Wealth at death £117,855 12s. 5d.; bequests of £53,450: NA Scot., SC /64/40/3; *Alloa Advertiser* (22 Aug 1914)

Paton, David (d. in or after **1709**), portrait draughtsman and copyist, was a Scot, of whose origins very little is known. He specialized in making small monochrome drawings, both portraits and copies of old masters, in plumbago (lead point) as well as in pen and Indian ink on vellum. His earliest extant works are copies, signed and dated 1667. These are rectangular works drawn in plumbago on vellum after oil paintings by Giovanni Cariani and Titian, both of which were formerly in the collection of Charles I (both priv. coll.). At this date Paton was also copying miniatures by his older contemporary Samuel Cooper. There are two surviving copies by him of Cooper's famous large rectangular miniature of *Charles II* (priv. coll.), which is signed and dated 1665. One copy, signed and dated 1668, is at Ham House, Surrey; the other, signed and dated 1669,

is in the collection of the duke of Buccleuch. Paton also copied a large rectangular limning by John Hoskins, *Katherine Bruce, Mrs Dysart*, dated 1638; both the original and a copy are at Ham House. A copy by Paton after the miniature *William Murray, First Earl of Dysart*, attributed to David des Granges, is also at Ham House.

Paton's most important patron was the Dysarts' eldest daughter and heir, Elizabeth Murray, countess of Dysart, later countess and duchess of Lauderdale (1626–1698). Her first husband was Sir Lionel Tollemache, third baronet (1624–1669); in 1672 she married, second, John Maitland, second earl and first duke of Lauderdale (1616–1682). Of him Paton drew a small rectangular portrait, signed and dated 1669 (Ham House). Ham House, the Lauderdales' main residence, was Lady Lauderdale's own property, which they enlarged and extended, creating the famous Green Closet on the first floor for the display of miniatures and cabinet paintings. During the 1670s and early 1680s Paton accompanied the Hon. William Tollemache (1662–1694), the duchess of Lauderdale's youngest son, on a grand tour around Italy, visiting the court of Cosimo (III) de' Medici, grand duke of Tuscany, in Florence. A small oval portrait drawing on vellum, probably of the Hon. William Tollemache—also identified as his brother, General Thomas Tollemache, (c.1651–1694)—was drawn at Rome, as it is signed and dated on the verso: 'D. Paton fe. Romae. / 1674' (V&A). Paton was certainly in Padua during 1677, and he probably visited Rome that year. He must have visited Florence in 1683 because of the signature on one of two similar oval self-portrait drawings that are now in the Galleria degli Uffizi. The larger work is signed and dated on the front: 'David Paton / Scozzese Pict. / Flor. 1683'. This visit may be that referred to by Jacopo Giraldi, Tuscan envoy in London, in a letter of 16 March 1708, sent to Cosimo (III) de' Medici, in which he also refers to Paton's religious inclinations. (As a young man he was drawn to Roman Catholicism, but ultimately he remained a member of the Church of Scotland.)

After returning from the continent, Paton seems to have worked mainly in Edinburgh, making small portrait drawings of Scottish sitters. Edinburgh's poll tax records for 1694 note 'David Patton picttor drawer' as a lodger in the house of Robert Mylne (1633–1710), the king's master mason (NA Scot., E70/4/1). In addition, the city's annuity rolls twice mention 'David Paton Limner' (Edinburgh City Archives, 1697/8, fols. 24 and 65). Among Paton's drawings of Scottish sitters is the large octagonal double portrait, exquisitely drawn in lead pencil on vellum, *The Yester Lords* (late 1660s; NG Scot.). The sitters were formerly thought to represent members of the Hay family, who lived at Yester House, the seat of the Tweeddale family in Haddingtonshire. They are now more plausibly thought to represent John Maitland, second earl and first duke of Lauderdale, and his younger brother Charles Maitland (c.1620–1691).

Paton also drew in pen and ink on vellum an oval portrait of the Jacobite leader *John Graham of Claverhouse, Viscount ('Bonnie') Dundee* (c.1670; Scot. NPG). Four other oval portraits drawn in plumbago on vellum are *Charles II*; *James Scott, First Earl of Dalkeith*; *Sir John Dalrymple, Later First Earl of*

Stair; and *William III* (1695), all of which were sold at Sothebys, London, on 1 July 1920 (lots 602–5). A small plumbago on vellum, *Sir John Clerk of Penicuik, First Baronet*, also survives (priv. coll.), as does a pair of plumbagos, *Charles Stuart, Fourth Earl of Traquair* and *Mary Maxwell, Countess of Traquair* (both *c*.1694; priv. coll.), painted around the time of the couple's marriage.

In 1693 Paton completed an important commission of fifteen small family portraits, all drawn in pen and ink on vellum, for William Douglas, earl of Selkirk and third duke of Hamilton (priv. coll.). In 1698 he was paid £2 18s. for a picture for James Douglas, second duke of Queensberry, and in the following year he received £5 16s. from the same source (NA Scot., GD1/648/1).

In later life he moved from Edinburgh to London, a move recorded in a letter of 13 January 1708 from Jacopo Giraldi to Cosimo III. Giraldi also commented on his preference for Paton's earlier style of draughtsmanship. That same year Paton painted *Sir Isaac Newton*, which was sent by Giraldi to Cosimo III. An autograph oval drawing of *Sir Isaac Newton* also exists (ex Sothebys, London, 7 March 1983).

A small number of Paton's portraits were engraved. These prints were probably made mostly after drawings copied by the artist from oil paintings. They include P. Vanderbank's line-engraving, which is lettered 'D. Patton delin:', after an oil painting by an unknown artist, *General Thomas Dalyell* (now at the House of the Binns, Linlithgow). William Faithorne made a mezzotint engraving after Paton's portrait of Janet Smith, *née* Mylne (1663–1699), the wife of the Scottish architect James Smith (*c*.1645–1731), and Robert White made at least two line-engravings after drawings by Paton from oil paintings: of the Scottish judges *Sir Alexander Gibson of Durie* and *Sir John Nisbet, Lord Dirleton*. There is also John Smith's mezzotint engraving after Paton's *Robert Ker, Fourth Earl of Roxburghe*, which is lettered 'D. Pattin delin:'. In 1710 George Vertue's engraving *James Sharp, Archbishop of St Andrews* was published, taken from a drawing by Paton (lettered 'Da. Patton delin:') after the oil painting by Sir Peter Lely.

Paton's œuvre is generally of a very high quality and may be compared favourably with English masters working in the same medium during the late seventeenth and early eighteenth centuries, such as William Faithorne, David Loggan, Robert White, John Faber, George White, and Thomas Forster. STEPHEN LLOYD

Sources A. M. Crinò, 'Documents relating to some portraits in the Uffizi and to a portrait at Knole', *Burlington Magazine*, 102 (1960), 257–60 · *Catalogue of the well-known and valuable collection of plumbago, pen and ink, and coloured pencil drawings and miniatures … the property of Francis Wellesley, Esq.* (1920) [sale catalogue, Sothebys, London, 28 June – 2 July 1920] · M. Webster, *Firenze e l'Inghilterra: rapporti artistici e culturali dal XVI al XX secolo* (1971) [exhibition catalogue, Palazzo Pitti, Florence, 1971] · B. S. Long, *British miniaturists* (1929) · *The National Trust: Ham House* (1995) [guidebook] · D. Foskett, *Miniatures: dictionary and guide* (1987) · *Visual catalogue of miniature paintings in the Victoria and Albert Museum* (1981) [microfiche] · G. Burdon, 'Sir Thomas Isham: an English collector in Rome, 1677–78', *Italian Studies*, 15 (1960), 8–14 · J. Holloway, *Patrons and painters: art in Scotland, 1650–1760* (1989) [exhibition catalogue, Scot. NPG, 17 July – 8 Oct 1989] · *Engraved Brit. ports.* · J. Murdoch, *Seventeenth-century English miniatures* (1997) · M. R. Apted and S. Hannabuss, eds., *Painters in Scotland, 1301–1700*, Scottish RS, new ser., 7 (1978), 70

Archives Archivio di Stato, Florence, MSS Mediceo 4234 | NA Scot., Hamilton MSS · NA Scot., Wemyss Castle MSS

Likenesses D. Paton, self-portrait, miniature, 1683, Uffizi Gallery, Florence

Paton, David Macdonald (1913–1992). *See under* Paton, William (1886–1943).

Paton, Diarmid Noël (1859–1928), physiologist, was born on 19 March 1859 in Edinburgh, the eldest of the seven sons (there were four daughters) of Sir (Joseph) Noël *Paton (1821–1901), artist, and his wife, Margaret (*d.* 1900), daughter of Alexander Ferrier, of Bloomhill, Dunbartonshire. He was educated at Edinburgh Academy and Edinburgh University. He graduated BSc in 1880 and MB, CM, with first-class honours in 1882. In the same year he was elected Baxter scholar in natural science.

After a brief period of study in Vienna and Paris, Paton returned to Edinburgh, where he took up a house appointment at Edinburgh Royal Infirmary and later at the Royal Hospital for Sick Children. In 1883–4 he was awarded a biological fellowship in the Edinburgh physiological department under Professor William Rutherford. In 1886 Paton was elected lecturer in physiology at Surgeons' Hall (School of Medicine of Royal Colleges, Edinburgh), and in 1890 was appointed superintendent of the research laboratory of the Royal College of Physicians of Edinburgh. The output from the laboratory was remarkable for its quantity and diversity.

In 1898 Paton married Agatha Henrietta, daughter of Alexander Balfour, merchant, of Dawyck, Peeblesshire, and had one son and one daughter. He left Edinburgh in 1906 to take up the regius professorship of physiology in Glasgow University, a position which he held until his retirement in 1928. Paton was regarded as a stimulating teacher, a helpful colleague, and an enthusiastic researcher.

Attracted from the first by the chemical aspects of physiology, Paton was one of the earliest workers in Great Britain to take up the study of metabolism and nutrition. In 1901, with J. C. Dunlop and E. Inglis, he published *A Study of the Diet of the Labouring Classes of Edinburgh*, which was based on the methods of W. O. Atwater, the American pioneer of dietary surveys. Paton supervised a similar study of the working-class diet in Glasgow, published by D. E. Lindsay in 1913. During the First World War he served on the Royal Society's food (war) committee and represented the society on the Ministry of Food's rationing committee.

In 1913 Paton became responsible for supervising a large programme of research on rickets in Glasgow, for the newly formed Medical Research Committee (later Medical Research Council). This involved laboratory, clinical, and sociological investigations. The results of one of these projects were published as *Social and Economic Factors in the Causation of Rickets* by M. Ferguson in 1918. With Leonard Findlay, later professor of paediatrics at Glasgow, Paton opposed the vitamin theory of rickets of Edward Mellanby, arguing that the essential factors were not dietetic but hygienic, and that rickets was associated with lack of fresh air and exercise, poor housing, and inadequate maternal care.

As chair of the Medical Research Council's Scottish child life investigations committee, Paton was responsible for co-ordinating a wide range of studies on prenatal, infant, and childhood ill health. Paton and Findlay's report *Poverty, Nutrition and Growth* (1926) argued that the main factors influencing variation in the growth and nutrition of children were maternal efficiency and housing conditions rather than poverty *per se*.

Paton was also intensely interested in the endocrine glands, and in 1913 published his lectures on the subject as the *Nervous and Chemical Regulators of Metabolism*. In 1926 he also published *The Physiology of the Continuity of Life*, in which he vigorously attacked many of the orthodox views on the mechanisms of inheritance. In all he published some ninety papers, as well as textbooks for medical and veterinary students.

Paton was appointed a member of the royal commission on salmon fisheries (1900) and of the Medical Research Council (1918–23). Elected a fellow of the Royal Society in 1914, he was on its council from 1922 to 1924. He was also a fellow of the Royal Society of Edinburgh (1886), and a fellow of the Royal College of Physicians of Edinburgh (1886). He received an honorary LLD degree from Edinburgh University in 1919. He died suddenly, while walking to the River Tweed, near his home at Wester Dawyck, Stobo, Peeblesshire, on 30 September 1928. His wife survived him.　　　　E. P. CATHCART, *rev.* DAVID F. SMITH

Sources E. P. C. [E. P. Cathcart], *PRS*, 104B (1928–9), ix–xii · R. C. Garry, *Life in physiology*, ed. D. Smith (1992) · personal knowledge (1937) · *WWW* · *CGPLA Eng. & Wales* (1928)
Archives Medical Research Council, London, corresp. and papers | PRO, Medical Research Council MSS · RS, Food (War) Committee MSS
Likenesses T. and R. Annan & Sons Ltd, photograph, Wellcome L. · photograph, Wellcome L. · photographs, U. Glas.

Paton, Florence Beatrice (1891–1976). *See under* Paton, John (1886–1976).

Paton, George (1721–1807), antiquary and bibliographer, was born on 23 June 1721 in Edinburgh, the fifth of the eight children of John Paton (*bap.* 1677?, *d.* 1765), bookseller of Edinburgh, and Margaret (*bap.* 1683, *d.* 1771), daughter of George Mosman, printer and bookseller of Edinburgh, and Margaret Gibb. He thus came from an important background in the book trade: his father had acted as agent for the Advocates' Library and St Andrews University Library in demanding from Stationers' Hall books that they were entitled to claim under the Copyright Act of 1710, and his grandfather had supplied books to the Advocates' Library in the 1680s and printed its first catalogue in 1692. The Patons were also of good social standing, as seen from, for example, the presence of Robert Craigie, a future lord advocate, as a witness at George Paton's baptism.

Many generations of Patons had lived in the parishes of

George Paton (1721–1807), by John Brown

Muckhart in Perthshire and Dollar in Clackmannanshire, and George Paton attended grammar school in Perth. Details of the early part of his life are scarce, but in the absence of other indications the assumption is that as a youth he entered his father's bookselling business; imprints show that he was certainly a bookseller in the 1750s. About 1760 the Patons were unable to meet a debt and their business failed, and after 1760 George Paton earned a living as a clerk at the custom house in Edinburgh, a post secured through the influence of friends of his father. He continued to enjoy influential contacts and to move in good Edinburgh society, recognized more for his interest in antiquarianism than for his profession. He had money to spend on his library and other collections, but he seems never to have been a wealthy man. His salary was £60 per annum in 1767, and was never increased. Moreover, it is known from his letters that he lost savings in 1772, 1783, 1789, and 1793. On this last occasion the failure of the bank Bertram, Gardner & Co. cost him £200.

Paton is remembered chiefly for his support of the research and publications of others. For those outside Edinburgh this came about largely through correspondence, from which some selections have been edited by James Maidment, Robert Pitcairn, and A. F. Falconer. The names of over seventy correspondents are known. The list is headed—in terms of numbers, with over seven hundred letters in both directions—by the antiquary Richard

Gough: from his knowledge of Scottish antiquities and topographical works Paton made significant contributions to the 1780 revision of Gough's *Anecdotes of British Topography* (some surviving proofs with Paton's alterations help to demonstrate his role), enabling Gough 'to nearly double the article of Scottish topography' (Gough, *Anecdotes*, 2.554), and to Gough's 1789 edition of Camden's *Britannia*. Gough also acted as an intermediary between Paton and William Herbert, who, when he wrote on Scottish printing in his revision (1785–1790) of Joseph Ames's *Typographical Antiquities* (1749), acknowledged his debt to Paton, 'whose comprehensive mind takes in every branch of literature'. Paton provided information first on the volume of a number of small works from Scotland's earliest press (the 'Chepman & Myllar prints' of about 1508) that had come to light on being presented to the Advocates' Library in 1788; second, on the *Aberdeen Breviary* (1509–10), of which he donated the rare second volume to the Advocates' Library; and finally on the *Complaynt of Scotland* (c.1550), of which he owned one of the four copies now known. It was Paton's contribution that made Herbert's account of the history of the Scottish book the most important between Ames's original account (1749) and that of Robert Dickson and John Philip Edmond in the *Annals of Scottish Printing* (1890). The second largest group of letters are those from Thomas Pennant, which show Paton's interest in natural history. Letters received from George Low in Orkney reveal an exchange of information about the antiquities, natural history, and topography of Orkney and Shetland, but they are also of value for their testimony of the friendship and compassion with which Paton supported his friend, particularly at the time of the latter's wife's death.

Paton was a compulsive collector; according to the text accompanying John Kay's portrait, neither he nor his father would sell a volume that they desired to add to their collection. On the other hand, he lent his books out willingly and without discrimination, sometimes finding it difficult to secure their return. After his death, his books were auctioned off, the majority of them in February–March 1809 (2871 lots for a total of £1355 6s. 11d., as calculated by R. P. Doig from an interleaved copy of the catalogue) and the remainder (including books on coins) along with his manuscripts and other collections (coins, medals, shells, minerals, and so on) in December 1811. Doig's thesis has significantly altered our view of the man, which had formerly relied on the biographical sketch in Kay's *Portraits*. In contrast to earlier interpretations, Paton was not a scholarly recluse but a man with a wide circle of friends, many of them influential. His friendships were long-lasting and firmly based on helping others. This was the man who in 1780 helped the earl of Buchan in the founding of the Society of Antiquaries, and to whom in 1787 the earl wrote, when he was about to retire to Dryburgh Abbey, offering him a place there: 'You shall be my Rousseau and I will be your Mrs Fitzherbert.'

On 21 February 1762 Paton married Rosina (1717–1772), daughter of James Paton, a Church of Scotland minister;

he mentions her only once, to announce her death in a letter to Gough dated 24 June 1772. A supporter of the settlement that followed the revolution of 1688–9, he was strongly anti-Catholic and may be presumed to have belonged to the Church of Scotland, in which his wife's brother as well as her father were ministers. After his schooldays he seems to have lived all his life in Edinburgh, presumably at first in the family shop; later the evidence of city directories and occasional letters locates him in the Castlehill (1773–9), Liberton's Wynd (1779–90), the head of Forrester's Wynd (1790–91), and Lady Stair's Close (1791–1807). His health was generally poor, and after 1790, when he wrote to Gough that 'the load of years now bring on me many infirmities' (13 September), references to rheumatism and other problems become more frequent. He died, childless, aged eighty-five, on 6 March 1807 in Edinburgh and was buried three days later in the city's Greyfriars churchyard. BRIAN HILLYARD

Sources R. P. Doig, 'George Paton: a study of his life and correspondence', PhD diss., U. St Andr., 1955 · R. Gough to G. Paton, NL Scot., Adv. MS 29.5.6 · G. Paton to R. Gough, NL Scot., Adv. MS. 29.5.7 · R. G. [R. Gough], *British topography*, [new edn], 2 vols. (1780) · MS notes for 3rd edn of R. Gough, *Anecdotes of British topography*, Bodl. Oxf. · T. Pennant, letters to G. Paton, NL Scot., Adv. MS 29.5.5 · G. Low, letters to G. Paton, NL Scot., Adv. MS 29.5.8 · *The correspondence of Thomas Percy and George Paton*, ed. A. F. Falconer (1961), vol. 6 of *The Percy letters*, ed. C. Brooks, D. N. Smith, and A. F. Falconer (1944–88) · J. Kay, *A series of original portraits and caricature etchings … with biographical sketches and illustrative anecdotes*, ed. [H. Paton and others], 2 vols. in 4 (1837–8) · *Letters from Joseph Ritson, esq. to Mr. George Paton, to which is added, a critique by John Pinkerton, esq., upon Ritson's Scotish songs*, ed. J. Maidment (1829) · *Letters from Thomas Percy … John Callander … David Herd, and others, to George Paton*, ed. J. Maidment (1830) · J. Maidment and R. Pitcairn, eds., *Reliquiae Scoticae: Scottish remains, in prose and verse, from original MSS and scarce tracts* (1828) · R. P. Doig, 'George Paton's contributions to Herbert's *Typographical antiquities*', *Edinburgh Bibliographical Society Transactions*, 3 (1948–55), 215–19 · B. Hillyard, 'The formation of the Advocates' Library, 1682–1782', *For the encouragement of learning: Scotland's national library, 1689–1989*, ed. P. Cadell and A. Matheson (1989), 23–66 · B. Hillyard, 'Thomas Ruddiman and the Advocates' Library, 1728–1752', *Library History*, 8/6 (1991), 157–70 · parish register, Edinburgh, 25 July 1721 [baptism] · *Fasti Scot.* · record of interments, Greyfriars, Edinburgh, 9 March 1807

Archives Bodl. Oxf., *British topography*, 2nd edn (1780), with MS notes for a 3rd edn, MS 28065 | BL, letters to Thomas Percy, Add. MS 32332 · NL Scot., corresp. with Thomas Pennant, Richard Gough, and others · NL Scot., letters to Benjamin Waters · U. Edin. L., letters to James Cumming · Warks. CRO, letters to Thomas Pennant

Likenesses J. Brown, pencil drawing, National Museums of Scotland; on loan to Scot. NPG [*see illus.*] · J. Kay, caricature, etching, BM; repro. in Maidment and Paterson, eds., *A series of original portraits*

Wealth at death over £1355 6s. 11d.—value of auctioned books: Doig, 'George Paton: a study of his life and correspondence'

Paton, Herbert James [Hamish] (1887–1969), philosopher, was born in Abernethy, Perthshire, on 30 March 1887, one of twins born to William Macalister Paton, a Free Church minister, and Jean Robertson Millar. Both parents were Scottish. After the family moved to Glasgow, Hamish was educated at the high school and subsequently at the University of Glasgow, where he obtained a first-class honours degree in classics, but where he also learned philosophy in the idealist tradition taught by Sir Henry Jones.

He went to Balliol College, Oxford, in 1908 as a Snell exhibitioner; his tutor was J. A. Smith, who interested him in the idealism of Croce. After taking firsts in classical moderations in 1909 and *literae humaniores* in 1911 he was elected fellow and praelector in classics and philosophy at Queen's College, Oxford. In 1914 he joined the intelligence division of the Admiralty and became an expert on Polish affairs, in which capacity he attended the Versailles conference in 1919. He returned to Queen's and served as dean from 1917 to 1922.

A Laura Spelman Rockefeller research fellowship at the University of California in 1925–6 provided Paton with the opportunity to complete his first book, which was published in 1927. *The Good Will*, as its subtitle, 'A study in the coherence theory of goodness' suggests, is a work of idealist ethics. Paton himself thought he had written it too quickly and perhaps he did not know how far idealist claims in ethics were being challenged by leading philosophers such as Moore and Prichard. The book failed to engage with or provoke controversy.

In 1927 Paton was appointed to the chair of logic and rhetoric at Glasgow, and his ten years in this post turned out to be very fruitful. His own doubts about his previous philosophical position had been increasing and he became convinced that there was 'some flaw in the idealist doctrines, which could be corrected only by going back to the fountain-head', that is, to Kant ('Fifty years of philosophy' in *Contemporary British Philosophy: Personal Statements. Series III*, ed. H. D. Lewis, 1956, 348). Glasgow provided him with just the right opportunity, as tradition laid on the logic chair-holder the formidable obligation of lecturing on *The Critique of Pure Reason*. Thus began the work which was to culminate in Paton's major contribution to philosophical scholarship, his two-volume commentary on the first half of the *First Critique*, *Kant's Metaphysic of Experience* (1936). Against Kemp Smith he sought to show that the *First Critique* was no mere patchwork but a coherent set of doctrines; and against others, such as Caird and Prichard, he tried to show that Kant's position was philosophically defensible. Though some critics complained that Paton only expounded Kant in his own language and left the reader without sufficient external bearings, his book in its time raised the standard of exegesis and proved a valuable companion to those struggling with the often obscure sentences of Kant's great work.

In 1937 Paton was appointed as White's professor of moral philosophy at Oxford and became a fellow of Corpus Christi College. He was elected FBA in 1946. At Oxford, as at Glasgow, he lectured for some years on Kant, progressing through preliminary studies, until he produced *The Categorical Imperative* (1947), which (though primarily a commentary on the *Grundlegung*) was subtitled as a study of his moral philosophy. In his inaugural lecture, published as *Fashion and Philosophy* (1937), he set out to comment on contemporary philosophy, seeming to include himself among the fashionable by his suggestion that 'the modern tendency in philosophy is in some ways a recall to the eighteenth century, to the age of enlightenment which ... culminated in the Critical Philosophy of Kant' (p.

5). But it soon became clear that he was out of step with the then recent linguistic and analytical trends of Oxford philosophy. His *In Defence of Reason* (1951) opposed these trends with the contention that 'the main work ... of philosophy is to be synoptic ... to fit our different experiences and our different theories, as far as may be, into a consistent whole' (p. 13).

Paton took the opportunity of the Gifford lectures he gave at St Andrews to address the perceived conflict between science and religion. The resulting book, *The Philosophical Predicament* (1955) was to prove his most popular, though not his most profound. Philosophy, he suggested, can help to resolve this conflict by showing, in the manner of Kant's critical philosophy, that the world as science sees it does not include the whole of reality. He departed from Kant, however, in arguing, along with Otto and Buber, that the only ground for religious belief is religious experience. Paton's conclusions are theistic in sympathy but so cautiously expressed that they provoked no controversy among philosophers and can have provided little consolation for believers.

Paton's Perthshire roots remained important to him, and he kept a house near Bridge of Earn during the tenure of his Oxford chair. When he retired in 1952 he moved there, involving himself in Scottish affairs, both as crown assessor for the University of St Andrews and in his contribution to the debate on Scottish autonomy. In his *The Claim of Scotland* (1968) he proposed that 'under the Crown and within the framework of the United Kingdom, Scotland should have her own Parliament with genuine legislative authority in Scottish affairs' (p. 254). In these and in many other ways he showed his ability in reasoning about practical matters.

Paton was a man of distinguished and meticulous appearance, and in the opinion of some had a rather 'patrician' manner (Walsh, 295). But though he could be severe, he was often generous and was well liked by women and children (ibid.). He was married to (Mary) Sheila, daughter of Henry Paul Todd-Naylor of the Indian Civil Service, for twenty-three years, from 1936 until her death in 1959. His second wife, Sarah Irene, daughter of William Macneile Dixon, regius professor of English at Glasgow University, died, only two years after their marriage, in 1964. Paton had no children of his own though he had a number of close friendships and family attachments. He died at his Perthshire home, Nether Pitcaithly, Bridge of Earn, on 2 August 1969, and was cremated at Perth five days later.   STUART BROWN

Sources W. H. Walsh, 'Herbert James Paton, 1887–1969', *PBA*, 56 (1970), 293–308 · *WWW* · *Glasgow Herald* (Aug 1969)
Archives Bodl. Oxf., corresp. with Gilbert Murray · Bodl. Oxf., corresp. with H. A. Prichard
Likenesses photograph, repro. in Walsh, 'Herbert James Paton', pl. xx
Wealth at death £27,106 12s. 0d.: confirmation, 10 Nov 1969, NA Scot., SC 49/31/369/1251–5

Paton, James (*c.*1522–1596), bishop of Dunkeld, came from Middle Ballilisk, Kinross-shire. He studied at St Salvator's

College, St Andrews, when John Mair was provost, matriculating on 26 November 1540, presumably in his late teens, and determining in 1542. In 1567 he became minister of the parish of Muckhart, Kinross-shire, very probably obtaining the benefice through family connections. After Paton had bought the small farm of Muckartmill from the Douglas family, the fifth earl of Argyll is said to have persuaded him to convey it to himself in return for appointment to the see of Dunkeld, and also to promise him other episcopal revenues. At Dunkeld, Paton succeeded Robert Crichton, who had joined the queen's party and was forfeited on 30 August 1571. Paton was nominated bishop on 8 September 1571 and the chapter received licence to elect on 16 February 1572; crown confirmation and mandate to consecrate followed on 20 July and he was granted the temporalities on 27 April 1573, having taken the oath to James VI as the only true and lawful sovereign. He was obliged to pay the stipend of his successor at Muckhart for 1572, though there is no record of an appointment before that of Henry Colville in 1579.

Paton was under pressure throughout his episcopate, both from the newly reformed kirk and from members of the nobility. How far he involved himself in pastoral work in the parishes of his diocese cannot be ascertained, but it is significant that there is no record of his attendance at a general assembly until 1573, when he was delated at the first session for receiving the name of bishop but not exercising the office. He was also reproved for not proceeding against papists, notably John Stewart, fourth earl of Atholl, and was suspected of simony in his dealings with Argyll. Although the assembly subsequently appointed him to a commission set up to confer with the regent and the privy council, it also instructed him to visit his diocese and proceed against papists. In August 1574, however, Paton was instructed to excommunicate Atholl under pain of deprivation, and, though he promised to do so, he confessed at the following assembly to having failed to execute the sentence, whereupon he was commanded to confess his fault publicly at service time on a Lord's day in Dunkeld Cathedral.

Paton's relationship with Argyll did even more to undermine his episcopate. The earl had been granted the fruits of the then vacant diocese in September 1571 and custody of the temporalities in the following January. These revenues Argyll stood to lose when the see was filled, but at the time he was in a strong position to extract concessions from the incoming bishop, a position reinforced by the use of physical force. Having been charged with simony in 1573, a year later Paton admitted that he had been compelled to grant the earl 'certain pensions forth of the Bishoprick', but claimed he had done so out of 'a most just fear, which might fall on a most constant man, his house being besieged, and his son taken away' (Mullan, 41–2), and that in any case he had since revoked the grant. But he also owned to having granted Argyll a lease of tithes, exposing himself to accusations of dilapidating his benefice. His attempts to defend himself were overruled, and in 1576 he was deprived of his office. An appeal to Regent Morton proved unavailing.

Paton resisted his deprivation. Further decrees were passed against him in 1580 and 1582, but he defied them. On 2 December 1580 he was accused of giving treasonable assistance to George Gordon, sixth earl of Huntly, Colin Campbell, sixth earl of Argyll, and other opponents of Regent Morton. On 9 February 1581 the privy council decreed that as he had neither function nor charge in the reformed Scottish church he was consequently less worthy to enjoy the patrimony of the bishopric. He was therefore required to provide from it for the relief of his impoverished predecessor Robert Crichton, who was progressively restored to the see and received full restitution on 22 August 1584. Crichton died shortly before 26 March 1585 and was succeeded as bishop by Peter Rollock. Paton seems to have returned to Muckhart, though not as minister, and died there on 20 July 1596, a date recorded on his tombstone, which also describes him as formerly bishop of Dunkeld. With an unknown wife he had at least four sons, of whom the eldest, Archibald, on 20 May 1574 had a crown presentation to the altarage of St Peter, Dunkeld, for seven years, to enable him to study grammar in the school of Dunkeld.

T. F. HENDERSON, rev. DUNCAN SHAW

Sources *Fasti Scot.*, new edn, 7.339 · D. E. R. Watt, ed., *Fasti ecclesiae Scoticanae medii aevi ad annum 1638*, [2nd edn], Scottish RS, new ser., 1 (1969), 100 · C. H. Haws, *Scottish parish clergy at the Reformation, 1540–1574*, Scottish RS, new ser., 3 (1972), 187 · D. Calderwood, *The history of the Kirk of Scotland*, ed. T. Thomson and D. Laing, 8 vols., Wodrow Society, 7 (1842–9), vol. 3; vol. 4, p. 619; vol. 5, p. 727; vol. 6, p. 158 · *The autobiography and diary of Mr James Melvill*, ed. R. Pitcairn, Wodrow Society (1842), 32 · *Reg. PCS*, 1st ser., vols. 1–2 · T. Thomson, ed., *Acts and proceedings of the general assemblies of the Kirk of Scotland*, 3 pts, Bannatyne Club, 81 (1839–45) · D. Mullan, *Episcopacy in Scotland* (1986) · J. Kirk, *The Second Book of Discipline* (1980) · J. Kirk, *Patterns of reform: continuity and change in the Reformation kirk* (1989) · J. M. Anderson, ed., *Early records of the University of St Andrews*, Scottish History Society, 3rd ser., 8 (1926)

Paton, John (d. 1684), army officer, was born at Meadowhead in the parish of Fenwick, Ayrshire. Nothing is known about his parents. He spent his early years as a farmer but on reaching adulthood turned to military pursuits and served in Germany under Gustavus Adolphus. He fought in the Scottish army at the battle of Marston Moor (July 1644) and with the covenanter forces defeated by Montrose at Kilsyth in August 1645, escaping after the battle. After the execution of Charles I (30 January 1649) he adhered to the protester faction among the covenanters. He fought in Charles II's army at the battle of Worcester (3 September 1651), after which he returned to farming at Fenwick. He married his first wife, Janet Lindsay, about 1652, but she died soon afterwards. His second marriage, to Janet Millar (d. in or after 1684), took place about November 1666, and produced six children.

Paton was involved in the covenanter Pentland rising, holding command of a troop in November 1666. Although he was not at the battle of Drumclog (1 June 1679), in the subsequent uprising, he joined the covenanters' forces on 14 June and was described as being one of 'their best and greatest officers' (*Reg. PCS*, 6.241). Designated Captain Paton, he took part in the battle of Bothwell Bridge on 22

June, for which he was declared a rebel and a traitor. He evaded apprehension by living in fields and moors until early in 1684, when he was seized at the house of Robert Howie, a covenanter, in Floak, in the parish of Mearns. He was taken to Kilmarnock, Ayr, Glasgow, and, finally, Edinburgh, where he was tried before the lords of justiciary on 16 April 1684.

Paton was found guilty of open rebellion and high treason covering the years 1666 to 1684, though most of the emphasis at his trial was placed on his taking part in the battle of Bothwell Bridge. His goods were pronounced forfeit and he was condemned to be hanged at the Grassmarket in Edinburgh on 23 April. However, on 17 April, in response to his petition, an action which he appears to have later regretted, the privy council postponed his execution until 30 April, when he was further reprieved and granted 'a roume by himself that he may more conveniently prepare himself for death' (*Reg. PCS*, 8.503). He was executed on 9 May 1684 and was buried in Greyfriars churchyard, Edinburgh. His forfeitures were rescinded by act of parliament on 4 July 1690.   ALISON G. MUIR

Sources justiciary records, books of adjournal, NA Scot., JC2/16, 16/4/1684 · W. H. Carslaw, preface, in J. Howie, *The Scots worthies*, ed. W. H. Carslaw, [new edn] (1870), ix–xv, 479–94 · J. K. Hewison, *The covenanters: a history of the church in Scotland from the Reformation to the revolution*, 2 (1908), 200, 423–4 · R. Wodrow, *The history of the sufferings of the Church of Scotland from the Restoration to the revolution*, ed. R. Burns, 4 (1830), 64–5 · *Reg. PCS*, 3rd ser., vols. 6, 8 · *APS*, 1689–95, 164–6 · NL Scot., Wodrow MS Oct 28 · J. H. Thomson, ed., *A cloud of witnesses* (1871), 359–64 · J. H. Thomson, *The martyr graves of Scotland*, ed. M. Hutchinson (1903), 116–21
Archives NA Scot., 'Trial of John Paton of Meadowhead', justiciary papers · NL Scot., 'Last testimony of John Paton'
Likenesses T. Dick, engraving (after mezzotint by W. Macarthney), Scot. NPG
Wealth at death all goods declared forfeit: 'Trial of John Paton of Meadowhead', justiciary papers, NA Scot., 16 April 1684

Paton, John (1886–1976), politician, was born at 8 Gordon Street, Aberdeen, on 8 August 1886, the son of James Paton, a master baker, and his wife, Isabella Mitchell, formerly Bruce. His father soon left home, and Paton, his mother, and two brothers moved in with his maternal grandparents. He left St Luke's School, Aberdeen, before his thirteenth birthday. His principal work was in the hairdressing trade in Aberdeen and Glasgow. His experience included austere men's saloons in working-class districts and women's beauty parlours. During the 1914–18 war he ran his own hairdressing business in Aberdeen.

Paton joined the Independent Labour Party (ILP) in 1904. This became his established political home, apart from a brief involvement in Glasgow anarchist politics. He opposed British involvement in the 1914–18 war and became an increasingly prominent propagandist. The resulting publicity inevitably posed problems for his business. This was one factor which led to a change in career. In 1919 he became a full-time ILP organizer, initially for the north of Scotland, and a year later for the whole country. This was a demanding job; in many parts of Scotland the ILP was the Labour Party's most significant constituent. He also stood twice for parliament in North Ayrshire and Bute in 1922, and at South Aberdeen the following

year. A sympathetic Ayrshire observer saw him as: 'a young idealist with both feet on the ground' ('Onlooker', *Ardrossan & Saltcoats Herald*, 3 Nov 1922).

At the end of 1924 Paton became the London-based national organizer for the ILP. The party chairman, Clifford Allen, hoped that the ILP could formulate practical socialist politics for the broader Labour Party and develop a vibrant socialist culture. This agenda disintegrated in the face of personal tensions, political differences, and financial stringency. Gradually the ILP became the preserve of the left under James Maxton's leadership. Paton was involved heavily in these developments, becoming the party's general secretary in 1927 and editor of its newspaper, *New Leader*, in 1930. He was a strong advocate of the ILP's living wage doctrine, but wished to maintain the link with the Labour Party. Maxton's personality and leadership both attracted and exasperated him.

The relationship between the ILP and the Labour Party deteriorated as the 1929 Labour government demonstrated its economic orthodoxy. A small group of ILP MPs regularly voted against the government and cited ILP policy as their justification. The Labour Party leadership insisted that all Labour MPs must accept the standing orders of the Parliamentary Labour Party. Paton was involved heavily in attempts to broker a compromise but concluded that no agreement was possible. Reluctantly he decided that the ILP should break its link with the Labour Party.

The ILP's July 1932 decision to disaffiliate only led to further disagreements. Paton felt that the world economic crisis gave the ILP a credible chance of a vigorous future but he believed that success could only be at the expense of the Communist Party. His international contacts were with left socialists outside the Third International. This perspective was defeated at the ILP's 1933 conference. Despite a vigorous intervention by Paton, delegates voted narrowly to approach the Comintern. When the ILP's national administrative council endorsed this approach Paton announced his resignation as general secretary. This took effect at the end of 1933 and shortly afterwards he left the party.

A sense that this marked the end of a significant period in Paton's life was provided by the publication of two volumes of whimsical autobiography, *Proletarian Pilgrimage* (1935) and *Left Turn* (1936). He rejoined the Labour Party and was selected as parliamentary candidate for Norwich in December 1938. His organizational skills were expressed through the secretaryship of the National Council for the Abolition of the Death Penalty and as editor of the *Penal Reformer*. Elected for Norwich in 1945, he sat in the Commons until his retirement in 1964. He stayed apart from any faction, a conscientious constituency representative whose style articulated his traditional socialist commitment.

Paton was married twice, first in Glasgow to Jessie Macnab Thomson, before the First World War. They had one son. This marriage ended in divorce in the 1920s. Subsequently he married Florence Beatrice Widdowson [**Florence Beatrice Paton** (1891–1976)] on 5 April 1930. She was born at 50 Portman Street, Taunton, on 1 June 1891, the daughter of George Walker Widdowson, a railway guard, and his wife, Louisa Elizabeth Brown. In 1895 the family moved to Wolverhampton, where Florence Widdowson later became a schoolteacher. A prominent Methodist lay preacher and missionary from her mid-teens, her early politics were Liberal. These early commitments were at one with her family's nonconformity and political radicalism. She was active in the campaign to promote Lloyd George's pre-1914 proposals for land reform. However, Britain's entry into the First World War produced a political shift. She believed that the foreign policy of the pre-war Liberal government had been a significant cause of the hostilities. She moved to the ILP in 1917.

In the immediate post-war years Florence Widdowson travelled extensively in Europe, and was subsequently involved with the research department of the ILP. Adopted as Labour candidate for Cheltenham in 1926, she fought the party's first contest in that parliamentary seat at a by-election in 1928. This defeat was followed by two more in the Rushcliffe division of Nottinghamshire in 1929 and 1931 (she had by the time of the latter become Florence Paton). Initially she remained within the ILP after its disaffiliation from the Labour Party in July 1932, but in 1933 she quit the ILP in disagreement with its policy and tactics. By then, the Labour Party in Rushcliffe had selected another candidate to contest the seat, and it was only after this other candidate's defeat at a by-election in 1934 and again at the general election of 1935 that Florence Paton resumed as candidate.

Florence Paton's victory at Rushcliffe in the general election of 1945 led to a significant 'first'. In November 1946 she became the first woman MP to be appointed to the speaker's panel of temporary chairmen; in May 1948 she became the first woman to chair a session of the House of Commons. She was also a British delegate to the United Nations in 1947. An industrious backbencher, her defences of government policy demonstrated her background in the ILP. She saw government strategy as 'Revolution by consent—the democratic way' (Nottingham Journal, 4 Dec 1948). She contrasted this with communist suppression and violence; her underlying puritanism and ethical socialism led her to criticize the materialism of the United States as 'restless, vital almost hysterical activity, much of it pointless' (Nottingham Evening News, 13 Dec 1947). She expressed opposition to the government's decision, in spring 1947 and again late in 1948, to maintain peacetime conscription. Following electoral redistribution, she stood in the general election of 1950 for a new Nottinghamshire seat, Carlton. A narrow defeat was followed by further failures there in 1951 and 1955. Subsequently she was a member of the royal commission on common land, 1955–8. Florence and John Paton lived for several years in Welwyn Garden City, home to a number of politicians with ILP connections. She died in Wolverhampton on 12 October 1976. John Paton died at The Woodlands, 434 Penn Road, Wolverhampton, on 14 December 1976.

Within the post-1945 Parliamentary Labour Party, John and Florence Paton expressed an ethical socialism that was integral to the party's identity. Together they incorporated several ingredients central to this: for one there was her early involvement in religious nonconformity and the Liberal Party; for the other there was the influence of Scottish radicalism. Both had served their time as propagandists for their vision. They had remained active within the Independent Labour Party through its radicalization and disaffiliation, thereby highlighting the complex history of ethical socialism and its devotees' search for a principled and effective political strategy.

DAVID HOWELL

Sources J. Paton, *Proletarian pilgrimage* (1935) · J. Paton, *Left turn* (1936) · *New Leader*, esp. 1925–33 · *WWW* · b. cert. · m. cert. [2nd marriage] · d. cert. · b. cert. [Florence Beatrice Paton] · *CGPLA Eng. & Wales* (1976) [Florence Beatrice Paton] · *CGPLA Eng. & Wales* (1977) · press cuttings, People's History Museum, Manchester, Labour Party archive · *Labour Woman* (Aug 1928)
Archives NRA, priv. coll., corresp. | BLPES, corresp. with ILP | SOUND IWM SA, oral history interview
Likenesses photographs, repro. in *The Times guides to the House of Commons* (1950–59)
Wealth at death £6657: probate, 14 Feb 1977, *CGPLA Eng. & Wales* · £13,537—Florence Beatrice Paton: probate, 2 Dec 1976, *CGPLA Eng. & Wales*

Paton, John Brown (1830–1911), Congregational minister and philanthropist, the eldest of the eight children of Alexander Paton, a shopkeeper, and his wife, Mary, daughter of Andrew Brown of Newmilns, Ayrshire, was born on 17 December 1830 at Galston, Ayrshire. On his father's side he was descended from the covenanter John Paton (d. 1684). Both his parents, who were brought up in distinct seceding bodies (Burgher and Anti-Burgher), now belonged to the United Secession church at Newmilns. His father, on account of his sympathy with the more liberal theology of James Morison, joined the Congregationalists when the family moved to Glasgow in 1846. From Loudoun parish school Paton passed in 1838 to the tuition of his maternal uncle, Andrew Morton Brown, Congregational minister at Poole. In 1844 he worked for ten months in the printing office of the *Kilmarnock Herald*, of which Alexander Russel was editor. He then moved to Cheltenham where Andrew Brown was now minister, and there met the Congregational minister and writer Henry Rogers (1806–1877), who persuaded him to seek a career in the Christian ministry.

In October 1846 Paton was admitted to Spring Hill College, Birmingham, in which Rogers held the chair of literature and philosophy. With his fellow student, Robert William Dale (1829–1895), later of Carr's Lane, Birmingham, he formed a close and lifelong friendship. The pulsating civil, political, and cultural life of Birmingham left a lasting impression on the mind of young Paton. He became convinced that Christianity could not be divorced from the social and economic problems of the day. He also attended (from 1850) the ministry of Robert Alfred Vaughan, to whose 'intense spirituality' he owed much. During his college course he graduated BA from London University in 1849, gaining the Hebrew and New Testament prize in 1850 and a divinity scholarship in 1852 on

John Brown Paton (1830–1911), by Hugh Cameron, before 1884

the foundation of Daniel Williams (1643?–1716). In 1854 he won a double MA at London University in philosophy (with gold medal) and classics, the first to achieve such a distinction.

Paton left college in June 1854 and in October took charge of a mission in Wicker, a parish in the northern part of Sheffield. He was ordained there in July 1855. His ministry was eminently successful: the Wicker Congregational Church was built in 1855; in addition, the congregation in Garden Street Chapel, Sheffield, was revived. On 14 September 1859 Paton married Jessie, the daughter of William P. Paton of Glasgow. In 1861 Joseph Parker established Cavendish College, Manchester, for the training of candidates for the Congregational ministry; Paton travelled there weekly from Sheffield to teach theology and philosophy. In 1863 the institution was transferred to Nottingham as the Congregational Institute, and Paton was appointed its first principal on 10 September 1863. Temporary premises were exchanged for a permanent building in 1868, and the institute's reputation increased over the thirty-five years of Paton's headship. In his management of young men he was an ideal head; no feature of his teaching was more marked than the skill and judgement with which he conducted the work of sermon making and delivery.

Although a gifted teacher and a man of deep personal piety, Paton was above all a social crusader. He was a pioneer in seeking to embody Christian principles in practical schemes for social improvement. The Congregational Institute itself was created to enable men with no academic qualifications to be trained to serve rural churches, to be missionaries in the slums of the great cities, and to work aggressively among the poor. The lack of educational opportunities for workers led Paton in October 1873 to initiate lectures for working men, a scheme that contributed to the establishment of the University College of Nottingham in 1877 and provided the University of Cambridge with the inspiration to prepare courses of extension lectures. It was the need for effective technical education that influenced Paton to establish the Trades Council of Learning in 1880. In order to enrich people's literary culture he founded the National Home Reading Union on 13 April 1889. He evinced his concern for young people by creating the Boys' Life Brigade in 1900 and the Girls' Life Brigade in 1903, followed by the (unsuccessful) League of Honour in 1906.

In September 1873 Paton first expressed his conviction that the German Inner Mission, initiated in 1848 by J. H. Wichern of Hamburg, could provide a model for Christians of all persuasions in Britain to join together in applying the spirit of Christianity to the amelioration of social ills. This vision of Christian ecumenical co-operation provided the agenda for his subsequent career. He created social institutes to occupy the leisure time of workers and arranged holidays for them under the auspices of the Co-operative Holiday Association, established in 1892. In August 1893 he founded the English Land Colonisation Society, followed in 1894 by the Christian Social Union, which in 1895 established the first 'Colony of Mercy' at Lingfield, Surrey. The activities promoted by these organizations were intended to retrain the unemployed and to prove that those with acute physical disabilities had a creative role to play in industry.

Paton, in conjunction with Dale, edited the *Eclectic Review* during 1858–62. With his colleague F. S. Williams he edited the Home Mission and Tract Series in 1865, and he was a consulting editor during 1882–7 of the *Contemporary Review*. Paton was also a prolific author. His interest in promoting Christian brotherhood is evident in his *The Two-Fold Alternative* (1889), and his distaste for interpreting the ministry as a priesthood is expressed not only in this book but also in *The Origin of the Priesthood* (1877). His profound concern for social improvement may be seen in his six-volume collection, *Social Questions of the Day* (1906).

In 1882 Paton was made DD of Glasgow University. On his retirement his portrait, commissioned by a committee headed by Frederick Temple, archbishop of Canterbury, was presented on 26 October 1898 by John Percival, bishop of Hereford, to the city of Nottingham. Paton died at his home, 22 Forest Road, Nottingham, on 26 January 1911. The funeral service was held at Castle Gate church, and the burial service at the general cemetery was conducted by his friends John Percival and Henry R. Wakefield, dean of Norwich and later bishop of Birmingham. Paton was survived by three sons and two daughters. A son, William, was drowned at Barmouth on 1 August 1894, and an invalid daughter, Jessie Muriel, had died in May 1910. His son John Lewis *Paton (1863–1946) ended a distinguished career in education as president of Memorial College, St John's, Newfoundland, from 1925 to 1933.

Paton's activities had an intense and widespread influence on late Victorian life. His innumerable personal contacts crossed denominational divides and international boundaries (he was the first protestant in England to promote understanding with the Old Catholics after their exclusion from the Roman Catholic church). During his last years he was busily engaged in promoting evangelism in Scotland and in bringing practical help to Christians in China after the Boxer uprising. All in all Paton was one of the outstanding Christian leaders in Britain at the turn of the century.

ALEXANDER GORDON, *rev.* R. TUDUR JONES

Sources J. L. Paton, *John Brown Paton* (1914) · J. Marchant, *J. B. Paton* (1909) · A. Mansbridge, *The trodden road* (1940), 142–52 · A. Peel, *The Congregational two hundred, 1530–1948* (1948), 149–50 · *The Times* (27 Jan 1911) · *The Times* (30 Jan 1911) · *The Times* (1 Feb 1911)
Archives DWL, corresp. relating to *Contemporary Review* · JRL, Labour History Archive and Study Centre, letters to Ramsay MacDonald and others · LPL, corresp. with Archbishop Benson
Likenesses H. Cameron, painting, before 1884; Phillips, 25 April 1994, lot 84 [*see illus.*] · J. A. Brown, oils, 1898, Castle Museum, Nottingham · stipple, NPG · three photographs, repro. in Paton, *John Brown Paton* · three photographs, repro. in Marchant, *J. B. Paton*
Wealth at death £9061 14*s.* 5*d.*: resworn probate, 14 March 1911, *CGPLA Eng. & Wales*

Paton, John Gibson (1824–1907), missionary, was born on 24 May 1824 at Kirkmahoe, Dumfriesshire, Scotland. He was the eldest of the five sons and six daughters of James Paton, a stocking weaver, and his wife, Janet Jardine Rogerson. The family were members of the Reformed Presbyterian Church of Scotland, which upheld the ideals of the covenanters; James Paton was the dominant religious influence on his children. At Torthorwald, near Dumfries, where the family had settled about 1830, John Paton attended the parish school until the age of eleven; he then began work with his father, weaving stockings. In 1847 he went to Glasgow where he trained as a teacher at the Free Church Normal Seminary; he then taught briefly at several Free Church schools. He also attended classes at the University of Glasgow. In 1850 the Glasgow City Mission appointed Paton as a city missionary. For almost seven years he worked in Calton, one of the poorest parts of the city, where he met 'considerable opposition from Romanists and Infidels' (*Autobiography*, 43). He also undertook part-time study at the Reformed Presbyterian Divinity Hall at Paisley and, in preparation for work as a foreign missionary, attended lectures in the practice of medicine and midwifery at Anderson's University, Glasgow.

The Reformed Presbyterian church was already supporting a missionary, John Inglis, at Aneityum in the New Hebrides, in the south-west Pacific. The church's foreign missions committee was keen to extend its work in the region and in 1856 Paton offered his services. On 1 December 1857 he was licensed as a preacher and on 23 March 1858 he was ordained at Great Hamilton Street Reformed Presbyterian Church in Glasgow, where he was an elder. On 2 April 1858 he married Mary Ann Robson (1840–1859), daughter of Peter Robson of Coldstream. The couple

John Gibson Paton (1824–1907), by unknown photographer, 1884

sailed from Greenock on 16 April 1858 and reached the mission station at Aneityum on 30 August. Soon afterwards they moved to the adjacent island of Tanna, to open a new station at Port Resolution. Since 1839, when Samoan teachers of the London Missionary Society (LMS) were first sent to the island, there had been a series of attempts to convert the Tannese to Christianity, but without success. In February 1859 Mary Paton gave birth to a son; in March both she and the child died. In 1861 the introduction of measles, which killed many of the islanders, was followed by a series of hurricanes. Many of the Tannese opposed the mission, believing that the Christian God and his agents were responsible for their disasters. Their lives in danger, in February 1862 Paton and his followers fled to Aneityum. The other Presbyterian missionaries then sent Paton to the Australian colonies to promote their cause and to raise funds for a mission vessel.

Paton proved to be an effective preacher and speaker on behalf of the New Hebrides mission. Travelling around the colonies of New South Wales, Victoria, and South Australia, he addressed meetings almost every day, and three or four gatherings each Sunday. To arouse the interest of Sunday-school children he devised a scheme by which they could become sixpenny shareholders in the new mission ship, *Dayspring*, built in Nova Scotia in 1863. Among Australian Presbyterians support for the New Hebrides mission became a popular cause, and Paton raised £5000. Later in 1863 he returned to Scotland to continue his appeal and in 1864 he was elected moderator of the

Reformed Presbyterian church. On 17 June 1864 he married Margaret Whitecross [see below]. They had five surviving sons and one daughter. Two sons, Frederick and Francis (Frank), became missionaries in the New Hebrides and their daughter, Mary Ann (Minnie), married a missionary there.

Paton arrived back in the New Hebrides in June 1865 with his wife and two recruits for the Presbyterian mission. There he instigated an appeal by the missionaries to Commodore Sir William Wiseman of HMS *Curaçoa* to punish the Tannese for their killing of British subjects and their destruction of mission property. In August 1865 the *Curaçoa* shelled villages at Port Resolution and its sailors made an armed landing. This use of naval force to protect the mission was widely reported in the Australian colonial press and Paton was much criticized for his role. When he next arrived at Sydney he found himself, he recalled, 'probably the best-abused man in all Australia' (*Autobiography*, 298). The incident remains a controversial event in the history of Tanna.

In 1866 Paton was appointed by the Presbyterian Church of Victoria as its first missionary to the New Hebrides. After the events of 1865 it was not possible for him to return to his former field on Tanna, and he was therefore sent to the small island of Aniwa, where since 1840 LMS Polynesian teachers and Aneityumese teachers had attempted to introduce Christianity. This was to be Paton's base for the next fifteen years. For the first time his preaching was successful, so that the whole population of Aniwa, numbering about two hundred, eventually adopted Christianity.

In 1881, having been compelled by ill health to retire from missionary work in the islands, Paton and his family went to Melbourne, where he was appointed mission agent of the Presbyterian Church of Victoria. He had lost none of his skills as a publicist and fund-raiser. In total he raised about £83,000 for the New Hebrides mission, and the John G. Paton Mission Fund was founded in Britain in 1890 to support its work. Paton became moderator of the Presbyterian Church of Victoria in 1886. In the Australian and New Zealand colonies, and on his visits to the USA, Canada, and Britain, Paton was vocal on many issues concerning the New Hebrides. He opposed the growth there of French interests, he campaigned for British annexation, and he sought to prevent the sale of arms and alcoholic liquor to the islanders. In his addresses and writings he denounced as a slave trade the practice of recruiting island labour for the sugar plantations of Queensland and Fiji. His allegations were often exaggerated and he was unwilling to admit that the great majority of islanders entered labour contracts voluntarily, but politicians and government officials found him hard to ignore.

During a visit by Paton to Scotland in 1884, at the suggestion of his youngest brother, James, the missionary agreed to write his autobiography. James Paton, a Glasgow minister, shaped these notes into a book which, after the publication of the first two parts in 1889, played a large part in making the name of John G. Paton famous. In 1891 the University of Edinburgh conferred on him the honorary degree of doctor of divinity.

Margaret Paton (1841–1905), his second wife, was a founder of the Presbyterian Women's Missionary Union; she died on 16 May 1905, and the organization built a church at Vila in the New Hebrides and a hospital in Korea in her memory. John Paton died in Melbourne on 28 January 1907 and was buried near his wife in Boroondara cemetery, Kew, Melbourne.   DAVID HILLIARD

Sources *John G. Paton, missionary to the New Hebrides: an autobiography*, ed. J. Paton (1891) · A. K. Langridge and F. H. L. Paton, *John G. Paton: later years and farewell* (1910) · *Letters and sketches from the New Hebrides*, ed. J. Paton (1984) · R. Steel, *The New Hebrides and Christian missions* (1880) · R. Adams, *In the land of strangers: a century of European contact with Tanna, 1774–1874* (1984) · J. G. Miller, *Live: a history of church planting in the New Hebrides*, 2 vols. (1978–81) · *AusDB* · B. Dickey, ed., *The Australian dictionary of evangelical biography* (Sydney, 1994) · *The Age* [Melbourne] (18 May 1905) · H. R. Gillan, *Vanuatu victory* (1988)

Archives NLA | Australian National University, Pacific MSS Bureau, J. G. Paton (comp.), Newspaper cuttings relating to the labour trade between Queensland and the New Hebrides, 1890–95, microfilm · NLA, Ron Adams MSS

Likenesses photograph, 1884, NPG [see illus.] · T. Roberts, portrait, 1902, Synod of Victoria, Melbourne, Uniting the Church in Australia, archives

Paton, John Lewis Alexander (1863–1946), schoolmaster, was born at Brightside, Sheffield, on 13 August 1863, the second son of the Revd John Brown *Paton (1830–1911), a Congregational minister who moved to Nottingham in that year, and his wife, Jessie, *née* Paton. After early education in Germany, where he attended the Halle Gymnasium, and at Nottingham high school, Paton went to Shrewsbury School, where he became head of the school. Proceeding in 1882 to St John's College, Cambridge, where he was a scholar, he was placed in the first division of the first class in part one of the classical tripos in 1886 and in the first class of part two with special distinctions in the following year when he was also second chancellor's medallist. Elected a fellow of St John's in the same year, he immediately entered upon his life vocation by joining the staff of the Leys School in Cambridge.

In 1888 Paton became lower bench master at Rugby School, where his most famous pupil was William Temple. His friendly informality won the affection of his pupils at Rugby and especially among the day boys in Town House, whose tutor he became in 1891.

Paton's headmastership of University College School, 1898–1903, where he succeeded H. W. Eve, gave his genius for personal influence over his boys full scope. He never forgot a name or a face. Intolerant of insincerity or slackness, he inspired his boys with his own high standards of achievement and public service. By his ruthless opposition to obscurantism he incurred opposition, but it was usually dispelled by his obvious sincerity and abundant generosity of labour and money. Ultimately frustrated by the slow progress being made to separate the school from the college, and to move the school to a site out of central London, he accepted another appointment.

In 1903 Paton was appointed high master of Manchester grammar school. Every activity in the school felt the impact of his personality. He started holiday camps and visits abroad ranging from Norway to the Alps, and in particular Germany, with which, before 1914, he was keen to encourage friendship, and he helped to found the Old Mancunians Association. He brought distinguished men from home and abroad to lecture at the school and spent his money freely in helping the poorer boys and young masters. Often after morning prayers he would give short talks on domestic and foreign affairs; and his general-knowledge papers, which every boy had to take at the beginning of the school year, became famous. He revitalized the famous school and made it the exemplar of its kind.

Proud of his Scottish covenanting ancestry, Paton was strongly influenced by his nonconformist background, and he brought the puritan tradition with him to his teaching posts. He abstained from alcohol and tobacco, regarded sexual impurity and gambling with horror, and disregarded formal conventions in matters of dress and manners. He favoured an open-air, cold-bath regime (he slept in a tent in his garden during the summer months). Early morning bathing parties and cross-country runs, in which he took part even as headmaster, were a feature of the school camps which he instituted; he was an early supporter of the Boy Scout movement, and a keen cyclist. Unlike many headmasters of his period, he believed in the professional training of secondary teachers. He was president of the Teachers' Guild (1907) and of the Modern Languages Association (1911), and was a member of the consultative committee of the Board of Education (1907–15).

Paton's ideals, like those of his father, were strongly democratic and he encouraged pupils at his schools to perform acts of social service. At Rugby he organized classes for working men and led a troop of the Boys' Brigade; at University College School he helped to run the school mission, the Working Boys' Club at Clerkenwell; and at Manchester he was active in both the Hugh Oldham Lads' Club and the university settlement at Ancoats. As an early advocate of opening public schools to all classes he anticipated the recommendations of the 1944 Fleming report (which were, however, not implemented). His belief in the dignity of manual labour was strongly held: at University College School he joined the boys in painting the railings of the school grounds at Neasden; and at Manchester he took part in the physical work of levelling a patch of ground to form the playing field.

Paton retired from Manchester in 1924 and lectured for the Canadian National Council of Education; in 1925 he became the first president of the Memorial University College in St John's, Newfoundland, where he steadily improved the teaching until he retired to Kemsing, Kent, in 1933. He studied Newfoundland's economic conditions, made friends with its people, and pressed their cause in Newfoundland and England. During the Second World War, Paton worked in a preparatory school in England in which he continued almost to the day of his death.

Potentially one of the finest classical scholars of Europe, Paton gave himself entirely to his teaching, and his publications (apart from his life of his father, published in 1914) consist of no more than a number of papers on educational topics. His real memorials, resulting from his strenuous and selfless labours, were his influence on the development of the grammar school ideal in England, and in the achievements, in many spheres of national life, of those boys who came under his influence. The most unassuming of men, he would not sit for his portrait, and he destroyed his personal papers to ensure that no memoir of him would be written. It was said that he declined offers both of a knighthood and of the Companion of Honour. Paton had piercing blue eyes and was 'barely of middle height, sturdy of build, clean-shaven, strong-mouthed, with the fresh-complexioned, weather-beaten appearance of a sailor' (Barnard, 7). He died, unmarried, at his home, 10 Stanley Avenue, Beckenham, Kent, on 28 April 1946. J. COATMAN, *rev.* M. C. CURTHOYS

Sources *Manchester Guardian* (29 April 1946) · *The Times* (29 April 1946) · personal knowledge (1959) · private information (1959) · H. C. Barnard, 'A great headmaster: John Lewis Paton (1863–1946)', *British Journal of Educational Studies*, 11 (1962–3), 5–15 · J. A. Graham and B. A. Phythian, eds., *The Manchester grammar school, 1515–1965* (1965) · J. Bentley, *Dare to be wise: a history of the Manchester grammar school* (1990) · H. J. K. Usher and others, *An angel without wings: the history of University College School, 1830–1980* (1981) · *Lancashire: biographies, rolls of honour* (1917) · *CGPLA Eng. & Wales* (1946)

Archives BL, corresp. with Albert Mansbridge, Add. MS 65262 · Lancs. RO, letters to T. H. Floyd

Likenesses photograph, repro. in Usher and others, *Angel without wings*, 54 · photograph, repro. in Bentley, *Dare to be wise*, 89

Wealth at death £28,241 19s. 4d.: probate, 1 Aug 1946, *CGPLA Eng. & Wales*

Paton, John Stafford (1821–1889), army officer in the East India Company, born at Agra, India, on 3 March 1821, was the son of Captain John Forbes Paton (1796–1826), Bengal Engineers, and grandson of another Bengal officer, Colonel John Paton (d. 1824), who served for forty-one years in India, and whose *Tables of Routes and Stages in the Presidency of Fort William* (1821) went through several editions. John Stafford was educated at Addiscombe College, and in 1837 obtained a Bengal infantry cadetship.

On 3 October 1840 Paton was appointed lieutenant in the 14th Bengal native infantry, with which he served at the battle of Maharajpur in 1843, and in the First Anglo-Sikh War (1845–6), being present at Ferozeshahr and Sobraon, and in the expedition to Kot Kangra under Brigadier Alexander Jack. As a deputy assistant quartermaster-general he served in the Second Anglo-Sikh War (1848–9), and was present in the action at Ramnagar, and at the passage of the Chenab and the battles at Sadulapur and Chilianwala, where he was severely wounded.

In 1850 Paton served with the expedition under Sir Charles Napier against the Afridis, and was present at the forcing of the Kohat Pass, near Peshawar (medal). He became captain in his regiment on 8 February 1851, and received a brevet majority the day after for services in the Punjab in 1848–9. He married, in 1852, Wilhelmina Jane (d. 13 Aug 1859), daughter of Colonel Sir James Tennant KCB HEICS.

Paton served as brevet lieutenant-colonel and assistant quartermaster-general with the force sent to suppress the

Gogaira insurrection in 1857, where he commanded the field detachment from Lahore, which was three times engaged with the enemy. While Paton was thus employed, his regiment—the 14th native infantry—mutinied at Jhelum. He was appointed brevet colonel and deputy quartermaster-general in the Punjab in November 1857. He joined the Bengal staff corps on its formation, and became a major-general on 29 October 1866. He was quartermaster-general in Bengal in 1863–9, and was in temporary charge of a division of the Bengal army in 1870.

Paton, who during his active career had been thirty times mentioned in dispatches and orders, was made a CB in 1873. He became a general on the retired list on 1 October 1877. He died at his residence, 86 Oxford Terrace, Hyde Park, London, on 28 November 1889.

H. M. CHICHESTER, rev. JAMES LUNT

Sources *Hart's Army List* · *Broad Arrow* (7 Dec 1889) · H. M. Vibart, *Addiscombe: its heroes and men of note* (1894), 679 · H. C. B. Cook, *The Sikh wars: the British army in the Punjab, 1845–1849* (1975) · V. C. P. Hodson, *List of officers of the Bengal army, 1758–1834*, 4 vols. (1927–47) · C. E. Buckland, *Dictionary of Indian biography* (1906)
Wealth at death £10,643 6s. 1d.: probate, 23 Dec 1889, CGPLA Eng. & Wales

Paton, Margaret (1841–1905). *See under* Paton, John Gibson (1824–1907).

Paton, Mary Ann (1802–1864), singer, was born in Edinburgh in October 1802, the eldest daughter of George Paton, a writing-master and amateur violinist, and his wife, *née* Crawford, of Cameron Bank, also an amateur musician. As a child she studied the harp, the violin, and the piano, and made her first appearances in 1810 as a singer, also playing the harp and piano, and reciting. The family settled in London in 1811, and she sang at the Noblemen's Subscription Concerts, but then withdrew on health grounds. She continued to study, taking harp and piano lessons with Samuel Webbe the younger and resumed her career as a singer in Bath in 1820 and in Huntingdon the following year.

In 1822 Paton joined the Haymarket company, where her performances included Susanna in *The Marriage of Figaro* (3 August), the Countess in the same opera, Rosina in *The Barber of Seville*, Lydia in George Frederick Perry's *Morning, Noon, and Night*, and Polly in *The Beggar's Opera*. Among her roles at Covent Garden were Mandane in Arne's *Artaxerxes* and Clara in Linley's *The Duenna*. The critics of the day warned her against exaggerated ornamentation, but her success was undoubted. An article of 1823 commented,

> She was gifted with extraordinary powers, not only as relates to the physical organ, but with an enthusiasm, an intellectual vigour of no common kind. … Not yet twenty-one, yet her technical attainments, we are disposed to think, are nearly as great as those of any other vocalist in this country, with slight reservations and allowances … She is beautiful in her person and features … above the middle height, slender, and delicately formed; her dark hair and eyes give animation and contrast to a clear complexion, and sensibility illuminates every change of sentiment that she has to express. … Her compass is A to D or E.

At that time her voice was not evenly produced. Her technique was fluent:

> no difficulties appal or embarrass her. Even in Rossini's most rapid passages she multiplies the notes in a way few mature singers would attempt. … Her manner, exuberantly florid, is the fault of her age, and in some sort, of her attainment.

At her father's insistence Paton broke off her engagement to a young doctor named Blood, who acted for a short time under the name of Davis. Afterwards she became, on 7 May 1824, the wife of Lord William Pitt *Lennox (1799–1881). Her reputation was greatly enhanced when she sang Agathe in the first English version (by William Hawes) of Weber's *Der Freischütz* at the Lyceum on 22 July 1824. A still greater triumph followed with her creation of Reiza in the première of his *Oberon*, which he conducted on 12 April 1826. 'Miss Paton is a singer of the very first rank, and will sing Reiza divinely,' Weber wrote; but he later had difficulties with her in the rehearsals (which had to be interrupted when her child died) and, like others, found her a poor actress. He also deplored her ornamentation of his music. Fanny Kemble referred to 'the curious absence of dramatic congruity of gesture and action which she contrived to combine with the most brilliant and expressive rendering of the music', causing Charles Kemble to declare, 'That woman's an inspired idiot!' and Weber to wring his hands in despair. There was general agreement about her singing on this occasion, J. E. Cox describing her voice as 'sweet in tone, but also brilliant and powerful in strength, which study, practice and growth of years thoroughly mellowed and ripened'. Weber's last appearance was at her benefit on 29 May, a week before his death.

In 1831 Paton divorced her husband in the Scottish court of session, and in the same year she married the tenor Joseph Wood (1801–1890), with whom she had a son. In the same year she was engaged at the King's Theatre, where she sang in Rossini's *La Cenerentola* and other Italian operas. She then returned to Drury Lane, where she sang Alice in Henry Bishop's version of Meyerbeer's *Robert le diable*. She and her husband moved to Woolley Moor, Yorkshire, in 1833, though she later made three successful tours of America. She retired to a convent for a year, but reappeared at the Princess's Theatre and at concerts, in which her husband was also engaged. The couple finally settled at Bulcliffe Hall, near Chapelthorpe. She died there on 21 July 1864.

Paton's sisters were also singers. Isabella made her début at Mary Ann's benefit at Covent Garden in 1824, as Letitia Hardy; Eliza sang at the Haymarket in 1833.

L. M. MIDDLETON, rev. JOHN WARRACK

Sources *New Grove* · *The Harmonicon*, 1–4 (1823–6) · 'Miss Paton', *Quarterly Musical Magazine and Review*, 5 (1823), 191–7 · J. Wood, *Memoir of Mr and Mrs Wood* (1840) · E. C. Clayton, *Queens of song*, 2 vols. (1863) · W. T. Parke, *Musical memoirs*, 2 vols. (1830) · J. E. Cox, *Musical recollections of the last half-century*, 2 vols. (1872) · J. R. Planché, *The recollections and reflections of J. R. Planché*, 2 vols. (1872) · *Aus Moscheles' Leben: nach Briefen und Tagebüchern*, ed. [C. Moscheles], 2 vols. (Leipzig, 1872–3); trans. A. D. Coleridge, *Life of Moscheles: with selections from his diaries and correspondence* (1873) · F. A. Kemble, *Record of a* *girlhood*, 3 vols. (1878) · D. Reynolds, ed., *Weber in London, 1826* (1976) · J. Warrack, *Carl Maria von Weber* (1968) · d. cert.

Likenesses T. Woolnoth, stipples, pubd 1822 (after T. C. Wageman), BM, Harvard TC · R. Newton, line engraving, pubd 1823 (after W. J. Newton), BM · T. Woolnoth, stipple and line engraving, pubd 1823 (after T. C. Wageman), NPG · T. Sally, oils, 1836, Royal College of Music, London; study, NPG · J. Neagle, oils, 1848 (after his earlier portrait, 1836), Pennsylvania Academy of Fine Arts, Philadelphia · J. W. Childe, miniature, Guildhall Art Gallery, London · S. Chinn, oils, Guildhall Art Gallery, London · A. Easto, stipple (as Amazitli; after T. C. Wageman), BM, Harvard TC · J. Findlay, coloured etching (as Lydia in *Morning, noon, and night*), Harvard TC · C. Hunt, etching and aquatint (as Mandane in *Artaxerxes*), NPG · R. J. Lane, lithograph (as Reiza in Weber's *Oberon*; after F. Meyer), BM, Harvard TC · J. Stewart, watercolour drawing (as Susanna in *The marriage of Figaro*), Garr. Club · prints, BM, Harvard TC, NPG

Paton, Sir (Joseph) Noël (1821–1901), history painter, was born on 13 December 1821 at Wooer's Alley Cottage, Wooer's Alley, Dunfermline, the second of three children of Joseph Neil Paton (1797–1874), damask designer and manufacturer, and his wife, Catherine MacDiarmid (*d.* 1853). All three children followed their father into the business before pursuing artistic careers. Waller Hugh *Paton (1828–1895) became a landscape painter, and Amelia Robertson *Hill (1820–1904), a sculptor. Paton was educated at Dunfermline School and Dunfermline Art Academy, where his father was master from 1830 to 1833. In 1838 he accepted the post of director of the design department at W. Sharp & Co.'s sewed muslin factory at Paisley, where he remained for three years. In 1843 Paton left Dunfermline to become a student at the Royal Academy Schools in London. He stayed only a few months; indeed, throughout his life he seldom left Scotland, visiting Europe on only one occasion in 1863. However, though he spent only a little time at the Royal Academy Schools, throughout his career Paton remained faithful to the academic precept of heroic subject matter, particularly as expressed through the male nude.

During his stay in London, Paton made influential contacts. He met John Everett Millais, who was to become a lifelong friend, and entered the circle of Samuel Carter Hall, editor of the *Art-Union* and *Art Journal*, who commissioned illustrations for his *Book of British Ballads* (1842–4) and introduced him to the work of German illustrators such as Moritz Retzch, further confirming the linearity of Paton's style. Paton's first successes were in book illustration, with designs for Shelley's *Prometheus Unbound* (1844) and Shakespeare's *The Tempest* (1845), and he continued to produce illustrations throughout his career, most notably his designs for Coleridge's *Rime of the Ancient Mariner* (1863) and the collected volume of his illustrations to Shakespeare published in 1904.

In 1845 Paton submitted a cartoon for a large allegorical design, *The Spirit of Religion* (Dunfermline Corporation), to the Westminster Hall competition for designs to decorate the new houses of parliament, where it won a prize of 200 guineas. This design anticipated the religious and allegorical subject matter that dominated his work from the 1860s; however, his first successes as a painter came from literary and historical subjects. In 1847 *The Reconciliation of Oberon and Titania* won £300 at the second Westminster Hall competition, and was immediately bought by the Royal Scottish Academy. Two years later its pendant, *The Quarrel of Oberon and Titania*, was purchased by the Royal Association for the Promotion of Fine Arts in Scotland, and both works were given to the National Gallery of Scotland. These, together with *The Fairy Raid* (1867; Glasgow Art Gallery), are now his best-known works, and have come to be seen as principal examples of the genre of Victorian fairy painting. Yet at the time Paton was urged by his friend David Octavius Hill, president of the Royal Scottish Academy, to desist from fairy painting, lest the 'asinine multitude' think 'that you can do nothing else, and that you are raving mad' (Irwin and Irwin, 292).

During the 1850s Paton was influenced by the work of the Pre-Raphaelites, as can be seen in the minutely observed natural detail of *The Bluidie Tryste* (1855; Glasgow Museums and Art Gallery) and in the historical accuracy of *Dawn: Luther at Erfurt* (1861; NG Scot.). Perhaps their most striking influence was in stimulating Paton's short-lived interest in serious modern-life subjects: *Home from the Crimea: the Soldier's Return* (exh. RA, 1856; copy, 1859, Royal Collection) was an instantly popular, sentimental treatment of a topical theme. However, his second essay in a modern subject, *In Memoriam* (1858; priv. coll.) was widely criticized. This depicts a scene from the Indian mutiny, and shows frightened and cowering British women and children hiding in a cellar, with soldiers descending to their rescue. Originally the soldiers were sepoys, but were over-painted with a Highland regiment after intense public criticism. *The Athenaeum*, for example, thought it 'cruel and in woful [*sic*] bad taste. It should never have been hung' (8 May 1858).

On 17 June 1858 Paton married Margaret Gourlay (*d.* 1900), daughter of Alexander Ferrier of Bloomhill, Dunbartonshire, and moved to Edinburgh, in 1859 settling at 33 George Square, where the couple lived for the rest of their lives. They had seven sons and four daughters, who often served as models for their father; the eldest son, Diarmid Noël *Paton (1859–1928), was a noted physiologist. The need to provide for his family increasingly preoccupied Paton, significantly influencing his choice of subject matter in the direction of religious paintings, from which he could earn money from the sale of prints. However, Paton's view of his own vocation as that of a religious painter is implied by his poem 'A Confession':

Heart, mind, and soul, with reverent love confess
The Christian Painter, sent to purify and bless.
(*Poems by a Painter*, 1861, 56)

Paton's religious works were also influenced by his father's beliefs: originally a Methodist, Joseph Neil became first a Quaker and then a Swedenborgian. For example, the Swedenborgian belief in the equal reality of supernatural and material worlds found expression in allegorical works such as *Mors janua vitae* (1866; priv. coll.).

The popular taste for engravings of Paton's religious works formed the basis for his later success, much of which was due to the astute marketing of his work by his dealers, Henry Doig and McKenzie of George Street and Hugh Paton & Sons of Princes Street, Edinburgh, and

Haydon Hare of Scarborough. These firms bought both paintings and their copyright, publicized them in the press, displayed them in touring exhibitions with special gas lighting, and finally sold engravings of the pictures. The popularity of such works as *The Man of Sorrows* (1875; Laing Art Gallery, Newcastle upon Tyne) testifies to a widespread taste for monumental and didactic religious art diffused through engraved reproductions. The publication of several sermons using Paton's pictures as a 'text', such as the Revd Fergus Ferguson's *'The Choice': a Discourse Preached in Glasgow on Sir Noel Paton's Great Picture* (1888), shows how Paton's later work found an audience outside those who visited the annual exhibitions, and quite distinct in its preferences from the connoisseurs who formed the 'advanced' taste for aestheticism and classical subject pictures.

In 1863 Paton spent several weeks at Windsor working on sketches of the queen and her children for a memorial to Prince Albert, but this remained unfinished, owing partly to Paton's ill health and partly to his inaptitude for portraiture. Nevertheless, in 1867 he was knighted and appointed queen's limner for Scotland. In 1881 he was awarded an honorary degree of LLD by Edinburgh University. Paton was strikingly handsome with bright red hair; his prodigious work rate was made possible by great physical strength, 'almost Herculean in breadth of shoulder and depth of chest' (Story, 127). He died at his home on 26 December 1901, and was buried in the Dean cemetery, Edinburgh.   NICOLA BOWN

Sources M. H. Noel-Paton and J. P. Campbell, *Noel Paton, 1821–1901*, ed. F. Irwin (1990) · D. Irwin and F. Irwin, *Scottish painters at home and abroad, 1700–1900* (1975) · A. T. Story, 'Sir Noël-Paton: his life and work', *Art Journal*, new ser., 15 (1895), 97–128 · *The works of John Ruskin*, ed. E. T. Cook and A. Wedderburn, library edn, 39 vols. (1903–12), vol. 14 · *Fact and fancy: drawings and paintings by Sir Joseph Noel Paton, 1821–1901* (1967) · R. Schindler, 'Joseph Noel Paton's fairy paintings: fantasy art as Victorian narrative', *Scotia: an Interdisciplinary Journal of Scottish Studies*, 14 (1990), 13–29 · G. Halket, 'Sir Joseph Noel Paton', *Magazine of Art*, 3 (1879–80), 1–6 · J. M. Gray, 'Sir Joseph Noel Paton', *Art Journal* (1881), 78–80 · P. H. Bate, *The English Pre-Raphaelite painters, their associates and successors* (1899)
Archives NA Scot., letters · NL Scot., corresp.; diaries · Royal Scot. Acad., letters · U. Edin. L., letters | BL, letters to Macmillans, Add. MS 61894 · NL Scot., letters to J. S. Blackie · U. Edin. L., letters to David Laing
Likenesses J. Ballantyne, oils, 1867, Scot. NPG · A. R. Hill, marble bust, 1872, Scot. NPG · M. Klinkicht, woodcut print, 1880, NPG; repro. in *Magazine of Art* (1880) · G. Reid, oils, 1882, Aberdeen Art Gallery · R. N. Paton, pencil drawing, 1890, Scot. NPG · T. Annan, carte-de-visite, NPG · W. Graham Boss, pencil drawing, Scot. NPG · A. R. Hill, plaster medallion, Scot. NPG · A. R. Hill, wax medallion, Scot. NPG · Kingsbury & Notcutt, photogravure, NPG · McGlashon & Walker, carte-de-visite, NPG · photograph (with Waller Paton), repro. in Noel-Paton and Campbell, *Noel Paton* · photograph (in old age), repro. in Noel-Paton and Campbell, *Noel Paton* · photograph, NPG

Paton, Richard (1716/17–1791), marine painter, was born in London. He is said to have been of humble birth, and to have been found as a poor boy on Tower Hill by Admiral Sir Charles Knowles, who took him to sea. For many years he was employed in the Excise Office, and at the time of his death was one of the general accountants. How he acquired his art training is unknown. The earliest record of him as an artist is in 1762, when he exhibited with the Society of Artists two pictures, *The Action of Admiral Boscawen off Cape Lagos*, engraved by William Woollett, and *The Taking of the Foudroyant, in the Mediterranean, by the Monmouth*, which was etched by himself. These were followed from 1763 to 1770 by nineteen other works; but in 1771 he resigned his membership after a dispute over the hanging of his pictures of the battle of Finisterre.

George III gave Paton permission to paint the royal dockyards and in 1776 he exhibited views of Chatham and Deptford dockyards at the Royal Academy. These pictures are now in the Royal Collection. Paton's pedestrian compositions are enlivened by the figures which were painted by John Hamilton Mortimer ARA. Altogether he exhibited thirteen marine paintings at the Royal Academy between 1776 and 1780. Paton also painted four huge canvases for Catherine the Great depicting the Russian naval victory over the Turks at Chesma. These hung in the Hermitage until 1779, when they were transferred by the empress to another royal palace, Peterhof, on the Gulf of Finland. Paton was awarded a gold medal by Catherine which is now in the British Museum.

The National Maritime Museum at Greenwich has twelve of Paton's paintings, the majority being naval actions. The best of these is *Howe's Relief of Gibraltar, October 1782*, which is a vigorous and colourful work full of carefully observed detail. There is also a charming aerial view of Port Royal, Jamaica, which was probably painted from information supplied by naval officers. During his lifetime Paton was overshadowed by Dominic Serres RA, whose energy and personal charm secured him royal favour and numerous commissions. Paton is now considered a minor figure compared with the marine artists who were his contemporaries. He lacked the natural talent of Charles Brooking and the personal vision which gives a distinction to the best pictures by Samuel Scott and John Cleveley the elder.

Paton died in Wardour Street, Soho, London, after a long and painful illness, on 7 March 1791, aged seventy-four. Edwards states that he was a man of respectable character, but rather assuming in his manners (Edwards, 165).
     R. E. GRAVES, *rev.* DAVID CORDINGLY

Sources E. H. H. Archibald, *Dictionary of sea painters*, 2nd edn (1989) · E. Edwards, *Anecdotes of painters* (1808); facs. edn (1970) · Redgrave, *Artists* · *Concise catalogue of oil paintings in the National Maritime Museum* (1988) · *The exhibition of the Royal Academy* (1776–80) [exhibition catalogues] · A. G. Cross, 'Richard Paton and the battle of Chesme', *Study Group on Eighteenth-Century Russia Newsletter*, 14 (1986), 31–7
Archives RA, MSS relating to Society of Artists

Paton, Waller Hugh (1828–1895), landscape painter, was born in Wooers Alley, Dunfermline, Fife, on 27 July 1828, the younger son and the youngest of the three children of Joseph Neil Paton (1797–1874), damask designer, and his wife, Catherine MacDiarmid (d. 1853). He began his career designing damasks for his father and then studied water-colour painting briefly in Edinburgh with John Adam Houston (1813–1884), but was largely self-taught. On 3 June 1862 he married Margaret (Maggie) Kinloch (b. 1842), eldest daughter of A. J. Kinloch of Park, Aberdeenshire; they had four sons and three daughters. The family home was 14 George Square, Edinburgh, but during summer months school holidays were spent in a rented house, often in the highlands or on Arran where Paton could sketch and paint.

Paton was profoundly influenced by John Ruskin and the Pre-Raphaelite movement. John Everett Millais and Ruskin were lifelong friends of his elder brother, Sir Noël *Paton (1821–1901), and so both Paton brothers were likely to have been present at the famous Edinburgh lectures delivered by Ruskin in 1853 on the principles of Pre-Raphaelitism. Paton was extraordinarily prolific: he exhibited 384 pictures in the Royal Scottish Academy alone between 1851 and 1895, nearly all of which were painted in Scotland. He was equally at home in oil and watercolour. His watercolours, making extensive use of both body colour and stippling in order to build up a highly detailed finish, can look deceptively like oils and are often very large, while his oils can be quite small. He did paint buildings in a landscape setting, especially castles, but more often his landscapes were of mountains, lochs, and trees, with meticulously detailed rocks and plants. He was well known for his moonlit scenes and rather hectic sunsets. He did sometimes include people, but they are usually small and incidental. In this respect, he may have been influenced by J. M. W. Turner, whose landscapes he had copied in London in 1860, but Paton's figures appear more domestic: he painted people going about their daily lives rather than puny figures dwarfed by stupendous scenery.

Paton was elected to the Royal Scottish Academy in 1865 and to the Society of Watercolour Painters in 1878, and was an honorary member of the Liverpool Society of Watercolour Painters from 1872. His printed works include the illustrations for William Aytoun's Lays of the Scottish Cavaliers (1858) in collaboration with his brother Noël, and some landscapes which were engraved by W. Ballingall for The Shores of Fife, published in 1872.

Paton died on 8 March 1895 at his home, 14 George Square, Edinburgh, having been ill for some time with influenza and then having developed pleurisy. He was buried in the Grange cemetery, Edinburgh. His wife survived him. Throughout his career he had kept a series of notebooks in which he recorded details of his more important paintings. These notebooks contained small accurate watercolour sketches of each work, its medium, the circumstances under which it was painted (out of doors or in the studio), where it was exhibited, and, frequently, its sale price. These fascinating records constitute a remarkable and possibly unique insight into the practice of a Victorian landscape painter. The notebooks were sold in Edinburgh by Christies on 31 August 1995 and the pages of exquisitely painted miniatures were subsequently sold individually.

There are very few paintings by Paton in public collections. His diploma picture, Lamlash Bay, Isle of Arran, signed and dated 1865, is in the Royal Scottish Academy, and the National Trust for Scotland acquired the oil Outlet of Loch Achray (exh. Royal Scottish Academy, 1859) as part of the contents of Fyvie Castle, Aberdeenshire, in 1984, where it is now displayed. Paton was a successful painter and large sums were paid for his work in his lifetime, though his reputation declined with the reaction against Pre-Raphaelitism. It is only in recent years that people have begun to recognize his undeniable quality, the mastery of his technique, both in oil and watercolour, and his sympathetic interpretation of the Scottish countryside.

JUNE BAXTER

Sources J. Baxter, Waller Hugh Paton: a Scottish landscape painter (1992) [exhibition catalogue, Crawford Arts Centre, St Andrews, and Bourne Fine Art, Edinburgh] · P. de Montfort, The Patons: an artistic family (1993) [exhibition catalogue, Crawford Arts Centre, St Andrews] · M. H. Noel-Paton and J. P. Campbell, Noel Paton, 1821–1901, ed. F. Irwin (1990) · J. Halsby, Scottish watercolours, 1740–1940 (1986)
Likenesses D. O. Hill & A. MacGlashan, photograph, 1860–69, Scot. NPG · G. P. Chalmers, oils, 1867, Scot. NPG · W. H. Paton, self-portrait, pencil and watercolour with bodycolour, 1869, priv. coll. · Nesbitt & Lothian, carte-de-visite, NPG
Wealth at death £2128 11s. 8d.: confirmation, 28 May 1895, CCI

Paton, William (1886–1943), minister of the Presbyterian Church of England and missionary, was born on 13 November 1886 at Brixton, London, son of James Paton (d. 1943), sales manager of the Singer Sewing Machine Company, and his wife, Elizabeth Dunlop. The elder brother of five sisters, his family was of Scottish Presbyterian descent. He attended Whitgift School and Pembroke College, Oxford (1904–8), gaining a second class in Greats. At Oxford, he became an active member of the Student Christian Movement (SCM) in response to the preaching of Frank Lenwood. He studied theology at Westminster College, Cambridge (1908–11), and in July 1912 married Grace Mackenzie Macdonald, eldest daughter of the Revd David Macdonald, Presbyterian minister at Bexhill. At the time of their marriage she was secretary to Ramsay MacDonald (no relation). They had two daughters and four sons, the third of whom was the pharmacologist Sir William Drummond MacDonald *Paton. Paton was employed until 1921 as secretary to the SCM, and ordained as a Presbyterian minister in 1917.

Paton's work with the SCM, at a time when the watchword of its senior department, the Student Volunteer Missionary Union, was 'The evangelisation of the World in this generation', resulted in a strong sense of calling to missionary service. After a visit to India in 1917–18, Paton returned there in 1921 as secretary of the Indian Young Men's Christian Organisation. Soon afterwards, he was appointed first secretary of the National Christian Council of India, Burma, and Ceylon. While in India he gained direct experience of Hinduism and Islam, and his considerable literary output then and in later years was primarily devoted to asserting the superiority of Christianity while admitting the importance of presenting it with cultural sensitivity. He was convinced that 'The work of the missionary is always to prepare for a self-governing Church, and when it is beginning to appear, to subordinate himself to it' (Sinclair, 67). This emphasis on helping indigenous churches to autonomy was a hallmark of his missionary endeavours throughout his career. In addition to these activities he was instrumental in alerting the League of Nations to the extent of the opium trade, and a consistent advocate of Christian education, particularly of Indian women.

In 1927 Paton returned to England as a secretary of the International Missionary Council (IMC), the office which he held until his death. He was instrumental in the organization of the IMC's Jerusalem meeting in 1928 and the Tambarum meeting in 1938: large ecumenical gatherings for prayer and the discussion of missionary strategy. He travelled widely, undertaking several further trips to India and the United States, and a world tour in 1935–6. In 1938 he became general secretary of the provisional committee of the World Council of Churches at the invitation of William Temple, then archbishop of York, and despite his premature death in 1943 Paton has been aptly described as a 'selfless, highly efficient bureaucrat, administrator general of ecumenism' (Hastings, 304). Yet this bureaucratic efficiency was ever a means to an end; through it he sought to eliminate the institutional obstacles to the preaching of 'Christ crucified'. Paton's faith was simple, protestant, and orthodox. When Grace converted to Anglo-Catholicism in 1918, and again to Roman Catholicism in 1934, he supported her decision as 'God's will for you', but was unable to follow her: partly because of the Erastianism he detected in Anglicanism, partly because of his instinctive disinclination towards sacramentalism (Jackson, 26). Yet the ecumenical atmosphere of his own home, the zeal of his wife for social reform (see her own *The Child and the Nation*, 1915), and his enthusiastic role as father of six children were influences which complemented a public life in which immense labours were approached with apparently boundless energy and a boyish sense of humour.

A pacifist and member of the Fellowship of Reconciliation in the First World War, Paton moved towards 'political realism' (Jackson, 61–81) in the twenties and thirties. His first-hand experience of the exploitation of emperor worship for nationalistic purposes in Japan left him with no illusions about totalitarianism, and he was one of the few British churchmen to condemn the Munich agreement in 1938. However, he continued to uphold the rights of conscientious objectors during the Second World War, and campaigned against the banning of pacifist speakers on the BBC in wartime. In co-operation with Bishop George Bell of Chichester, Paton sought the release of German refugees who were imprisoned by the British government as 'enemy aliens'. He also negotiated with the Treasury for the transmission of funds to European foreign missions deprived by war of their normal means of support. A consistent advocate of Jewish mission, he also devoted himself to fund-raising for the victims of Nazi anti-semitism.

Paton was a prolific writer, his twenty-four books focusing primarily on Christian mission in the context of other world religions. His first book, *Jesus Christ and the World's Religions* (1916; rev. edn, 1926), was his most successful, selling more than 50,000 copies, and encapsulated his attitude to mission in the assertion that Christian scholars must 'treat other religions sympathetically but remain convinced of the supremacy of the revelation of God in Christ' (*World's Religions*, 1). Other works included his biography, *Alexander Duff* (1923), of the nineteenth-century missionary to India, the apologetic *A Faith for the World* (1928), and *The Faiths of Mankind* (1932). From 1927 onwards Paton was co-editor of the *International Review of Missions*.

Paton's sudden death on 21 August 1943, after an operation for an ulcer while on holiday in Kendal, was lamented by many beyond his own denomination; the archbishop of Canterbury, William Temple, testified at his memorial service at St Paul's that 'if any man … could be called indispensable for doing what seemed to many of us the most important tasks entrusted to the Christian people, it was he' (*DNB*). He was survived by his wife.

Paton's eldest son, **David Macdonald Paton** (1913–1992), Church of England clergyman, was born on 9 September 1913 in Hampstead, London. He was educated as a scholar at Repton School when Geoffrey Fisher, later archbishop of Canterbury, was headmaster, and at Brasenose College, Oxford, where he obtained a second in classical moderations in 1934 and a third in *literae humaniores* in 1936. From 1936 to 1939 he was midlands secretary of the SCM. He was ordained deacon in 1939 and priest in 1941. In 1940 he went to Hong Kong as curate of St Stephen's Church, and in 1941 he moved to China as a missionary, working mainly in the east Szechwan region. After leaving China (1944) he was chaplain and librarian of Westcott House, Cambridge (1945–6). In 1946 he married China-born Alison Georgina Stewart, with whom he had three sons. From 1947 to 1950 he was back in China as chaplain to the bishop of Fukien. He was then vicar of Yardley Wood, Birmingham (1952–6). His first book, *Christian Missions and the Judgement of God* (1953), criticized the colonial mentality of many missionaries and denounced 'rice Christianity'. From 1956 to 1959 Paton was a disappointing secretary of the SCM Press. He was more successful as secretary from 1959 to 1963 of the Council for Ecumenical Co-operation of the Church Assembly, and from 1964 to 1969 of its missionary and ecumenical council. He then served as rector of St Mary de Crypt and St John the Baptist, Gloucester, from 1970 to 1981, and as vicar of Christ Church, Gloucester, from 1979 to 1981. He attended the 1975 World Council of Churches assembly at Nairobi and edited its official report, *Breaking Barriers* (1976). He was honorary canon of Canterbury Cathedral from 1966 to 1980, then canon emeritus and a chaplain to the queen from 1972 to 1983. His numerous publications included *Anglicans and Unity* (1962) and *RO: the Life and Times of Bishop Ronald Hall of Hong Kong* (1985), and many book reviews. Although he was regarded by some as 'arguably the most farsighted English Anglican this century' (*The Guardian*), senior office eluded him. He died at Harpenden, Hertfordshire, on 18 July 1992 after a long illness, and was survived by his wife and three sons.   GILES C. WATSON

Sources E. Jackson, *Red tape and the gospel: a study of the significance of the ecumenical missionary struggle of William Paton (1866–1943)* (1980) · M. Sinclair, *William Paton* (1949) · R. Rouse and S. C. Neill, eds., *A history of the ecumenical movement, 1517–1948* (1954) · A. Hastings, *A history of English Christianity, 1920–1985* (1986) · *DNB* · *WWW* · *The Independent* (20 July 1992) · *The Independent* (21 July 1992) · *Daily Telegraph* (21 July 1992) · *The Times* (22 July 1992) · *The Guardian* (24 July 1992) · Crockford (1989–90) · *CGPLA Eng. & Wales* (1992) · *WW* · private information (2004) [Repton School]
Archives U. Birm. L., Orchard Learning Resources Centre, corresp. · World Council of Churches Archives, Geneva | BL OIOC, corresp. with S. K. Datta, MS Eur. F 178
Likenesses photograph, repro. in Jackson, *Red tape and the gospel*, frontispiece
Wealth at death under £125,000—David Macdonald Paton: probate, 1992, *CGPLA Eng. & Wales*

Paton, Sir William Drummond MacDonald (1917–1993), pharmacologist, was born on 5 May 1917 in Hendon, Middlesex, the third son in a family of four sons and two daughters of William *Paton (1886–1943), Presbyterian minister and secretary of the International Missionary Council, and his wife, Grace Mackenzie (1887–1967), daughter of the Revd David MacDonald, Presbyterian minister at Bexhill; she was private secretary to Ramsay MacDonald. Both parents were Scottish. The family moved to India in 1921, where William Paton was secretary of the Indian National Christian Council. Because of ill health young Bill returned to England in 1923 to live with his maternal grandmother and two elder brothers in St Albans. As a child he suffered a severe attack of pneumonia, which left him somewhat incapacitated and liable to recurrent chest infections throughout his life. He attended Miss Unwin's school in St Albans, then in 1927 he moved to Winchester House School in Brackley, and later won a scholarship to Repton School (1931–5), where he excelled. Against the advice of his headmaster, Geoffrey Fisher (later archbishop of Canterbury), Bill broke with the family tradition and chose a career in medical science rather than humanities, entering New College, Oxford, with a Theodore Williams scholarship in 1935. He gained a first-class degree in physiological sciences in 1938, completing his clinical training at University College Hospital, London, in 1942, winning the gold medal in clinical medicine and several other prizes. During his clinical studies he met Phoebe Margaret Rooke (*b.* 1916), a hospital almoner, and they married in 1942—a very happy and enduring marriage which lasted until Paton's death in 1993. They had no children.

Because of his poor health Paton was unfit for military service, or indeed for a full-time clinical career. Instead, he worked—somewhat frustratedly—as a pathologist for two years, before accepting an invitation to join the Medical Research Council's research institute in Hampstead, London, where he joined the physiological laboratory under the direction of G. L. Brown. After working as part

Sir William Drummond MacDonald Paton (1917–1993), by Walter Bird

of the war effort on applied physiological problems relating to diving and submarine escape, Paton began his first excursions into pharmacology, whence followed a highly productive decade of research leading to several important discoveries with which his name is associated. These included the discovery that many familiar drugs cause the release of histamine (a powerful endogenous chemical mediator) from tissues in the body—an effect which can give rise to unwanted side-effects when such drugs are used clinically. Also, with E. J. Zaimis, Paton discovered the important pharmacological effects of the homologous series of methonium compounds. These effects included the ability to block transmission through autonomic ganglia, and to paralyse muscles by blocking neuromuscular transmission by a mechanism known as depolarization block. Both discoveries led to new clinical applications. Ganglion blocking drugs, particularly hexamethonium, introduced in 1952, were the first effective agents for the treatment of high blood pressure, a disease which, in its severe form (malignant hypertension) had hitherto carried a very poor prognosis and a life expectancy of only a few months. The muscle paralysing action of another member of the series (decamethonium) quickly found applications in surgical anaesthesia, where paralysing agents are used to prevent unwanted movements. On the basis of these accomplishments Paton was elected a fellow of the Royal Society in 1956.

Soon after the Medical Research Council's laboratories moved to Mill Hill, Paton moved, in 1952, to a joint appointment between the medical unit at University College Hospital and the department of pharmacology at University College, London—an appointment which presaged the development of clinical pharmacology as an established discipline. After only two years he was invited by the Royal College of Surgeons to accept the first Vandervell chair of pharmacology, and to set up a new department of pharmacology. Under Paton's direction the department attracted several young research scientists who subsequently achieved eminence, including J. R. Vane, J. W. Thompson, and J. E. Gardiner. With a light teaching load, and good, if cramped, facilities, the department quickly established a reputation as an excellent research centre at a time when pharmacology as a discipline in many established medical schools was tending to become hidebound. During this time Paton became interested in the phenomenon of drug dependence, and developed a very simple *in vitro* laboratory preparation, based on an isolated segment of guinea-pig intestine, stimulated to contract by electrical pulses, which allowed many of the phenomena of opiate dependence to be reproduced and analysed in the laboratory. He also devised a new theoretical approach, known as the rate theory of drug action, published in 1961, which explained the way in which drug molecules, acting on specific receptors, can produce a range of stimulant or antagonistic effects, depending on the kinetics of the reaction between the drug and its receptors. Though this theory eventually proved incorrect it was influential in kindling interest in the molecular mechanisms involved in drug–receptor interactions—a topic which became one of the major themes of pharmacological research from 1970 onwards.

In 1959 the chair of pharmacology at Oxford became vacant through the retirement of J. H. Burn. Paton was the natural successor, and held this position, together with a fellowship at Balliol College, until his retirement in 1984. One of his major research initiatives on arriving in Oxford (apart from his insistence on carrying out an experiment on the first day of his appointment, somewhat to the consternation of the technical staff) was to set up a novel high-pressure laboratory, funded by the Wellcome Trust and the navy, in which to follow up his long-standing interests in diving, decompression sickness, mechanisms of anaesthesia, and related problems. This laboratory, with its gas cylinders, pressure chambers, copper tubing, and brass gauges, resembled a factory more than a conventional pharmacological laboratory, and caused a few raised eyebrows among Paton's colleagues. It proved highly successful, however, and the group made important discoveries relating to the narcotic effects of gases at high pressure, the formation of gas bubbles in the circulation during decompression regimes, and the ability of high pressure to reverse the effect of various anaesthetic gases. During the early 1970s Paton also built up a cannabis research group in Oxford, aiming to address the many unanswered questions about the biological effects of cannabis. This came at a time when activists were pressing for the legalization of cannabis in the United Kingdom; Paton was strongly opposed to this, on the basis that too little

was known about the drug to justify making it freely available. In the event, cannabis research rapidly gained momentum in many centres around the world, and the Oxford group, though it made significant discoveries, did not achieve pre-eminence.

Alongside his academic work Paton undertook many other advisory and executive tasks. He chaired the Medical Research Council decompression panel and the underwater physiology subcommittee of the Royal Naval personnel research committee—groups responsible for drafting civilian and naval diving regulations. He was secretary of the Physiological Society (1954–6) and chairman of the British Pharmacological Society (1978–82), Wellcome trustee (1978–87), Rhodes trustee (1968–87), and president of the Research Defence Society (1972–8). In his role as Wellcome trustee he was influential in strengthening the trust's support for the Wellcome Institute for the History of Medicine and the Wellcome Library, one outcome of which was the setting up of a contemporary medical archive collection, in which his own extensive collection of papers, together with those of many other distinguished medical scientists, were deposited. After his retirement from Oxford he agreed to serve as acting director of the Wellcome Institute, a post he held with distinction for five years, despite failing health. His many contributions to public affairs were recognized with a CBE in 1968 and a knighthood in 1979.

At a personal level Paton was a calm and thoughtful individual, who seldom showed anger or strong emotion, except when confronted by uninformed prejudice, which he detested. His advice, frequently sought, was given only after due consideration of the problem, and of its history. As a scientist he grew up in an atmosphere which supported individuals rather than organized research groups, and he ran his own laboratory accordingly, never fully adapting to the change in culture in the 1980s which favoured entrepreneurship and firm management of large groups as the formula for scientific success. In a distinguished career he achieved pre-eminence in several different fields—as an academic pharmacologist with a strong interest in the application of pharmacological knowledge to practical problems; as an expert on the physiological effects of working at high pressures, and the consequences for divers, caisson workers, and submariners; as an expert and activist on issues relating to drug dependence; as an active defender of the use of animals in medical research; and as a passionate bibliophile with a special interest in the history of science. He died of a stroke at his home, 13 Staverton Road, Oxford, on 17 October 1993, and was cremated at Oxford crematorium.

H. P. RANG

Sources H. P. Rang and Lord Perry of Walton, *Memoirs FRS*, 42 (1996), 289–314 · W. D. M. Paton, 'On becoming and being a pharmacologist', *Annual Review of Pharmacology*, 26 (1986), 1–22 · *The Times* (30 Oct 1993) · *The Independent* (6 Nov 1993) · A. R. Hall, 'Sir William Paton (1917–93)', *British Journal for the History of Science*, 27 (1994), 465–6 · *WWW* · personal knowledge (2004) · private information (2004) [family]

Archives Wellcome L., corresp. and papers incl. notes of experiments | FILM Oxford Brookes University, video interviews with distinguished scientists: 2 interviews with Sir William Paton | SOUND BL NSA, Bow dialogues, 17 Oct 1972, C812/33 C16 · BL NSA, performance recording

Likenesses W. Bird, photograph, RS [*see illus.*] · photograph, repro. in *The Times* · photograph, repro. in *The Independent* · seven photographs, repro. in *Memoirs FRS*

Wealth at death £483,483: probate, 19 Jan 1994, *CGPLA Eng. & Wales*

Paton, William Roger (1857–1921), epigraphist and classical scholar, was born on 9 February 1857 at 10 Chanonry, Old Aberdeen, the only son, and fourth of five children, of John Paton (1818–1879), a major, and later a colonel, in the Aberdeenshire militia and deputy lieutenant of Aberdeenshire, and his wife, Eliza Deborah (*d.* 1860), daughter of Thomas Burnett of Kepplestone, Aberdeenshire. He was educated, like his father, at Eton College (1871–3), apparently boarding in Edward Peake Rouse's house before transferring to Oscar Browning's. Paton matriculated in 1876 and read classics at University College, Oxford, obtaining a first in classical moderations (1877). He then decided to pursue a legal career and was admitted to the Middle Temple in January 1878. Paton returned to Oxford and obtained a third in *literae humaniores* (1880). This disappointing result may be explained in part by the death of his father in the summer before his final year in Oxford.

Although Paton was not called to the bar, he kept terms at the Middle Temple until 1884. He also seems to have served as a review editor for *The Academy* and he continued to maintain an interest in the classical world, joining in 1881 the newly formed Society for the Promotion of Hellenic Studies. His inheritance allowed him to travel to the islands of the Aegean to record previously unknown inscriptions. The search for new texts to supplement literary and historical works was characteristic of this period, exemplified by the travels through Anatolia of William Ramsay in 1881–2 and the American John R. Sitlington Sterrett in 1884, the work at Delphi through the 1880s of l'École Française d'Athènes under the direction of Paul Foucart, and the appearance of volumes of *Inscriptiones Graecae* under the auspices of the Berlin-based Akademie der Wissenschaften. During his epigraphic hunts, Paton fell in love with Irene (1869/70–1908), the daughter of Emanuel Olympitis, mayor of the island of Kalymnos, then part of the Ottoman empire. Irene's father did not approve of the match, and so Paton moved to the island of Kos where he made a study of the inscriptions of that island.

In 1885, while Irene was still in her mid-teens, her father gave permission for her marriage to Paton, which took place in the same year. The pair made their base at the farm Paton had acquired through his wife's dowry at Gumishlu, the site of ancient Myndus, on the mainland of Turkey: in the following year, George, the first of their five children, was born at Gumishlu. The married couple then returned to the Paton family home at Grandhome near Aberdeen. Paton, like his father, served as a justice of the peace and deputy lieutenant of the county of Aberdeen. The Patons eventually settled in Pothia, the main town of Kalymnos, which gave Paton an opportunity to investigate the archaeology of the island. A study of pottery from

graves on Kalymnos, and a report on an excavation at Assarlik on the Bodrum peninsula, appeared in the *Journal of Hellenic Studies* (1887); the finds were presented to the British Museum.

During the late 1880s Paton regularly sent details of new inscriptions to the epigraphist, later bishop of Lincoln, Edward Lee Hicks, then principal of Hulme Hall, Manchester. Drawing on Paton's knowledge of the island, and with the support of the German scholar Ulrich von Wilamowitz-Moellendorff, Hicks and Paton collaborated on *Inscriptions of Cos* (1891), described as 'a credit to British scholarship' (Tarbell, 278). Paton's knowledge of the islands led him to be invited, at the prompting of von Wilamowitz-Moellendorff, to contribute a fascicule on the inscriptions of Lesbos, Nesos, and Tenedos to the major series *Inscriptiones Graecae* (12/2, 1899). It is perhaps significant that the planned fourth fascicule of the same volume, which was to cover the islands of Kos and Kalymnos, was never published, possibly in the light of Paton's earlier work. Paton was made an associate of the German Imperial Archaeological Institute and in 1900 was awarded an honorary PhD from the University of Halle.

In 1893 Paton asked Ernest Gardner, then director of the British School at Athens, to help find a suitable student to make a topographical study of the Bodrum (Halikarnassos) peninsula in Karia. Gardner suggested that he be joined by John L. Myres who had been pursuing research on 'Oriental influences on prehistoric Greece'. Myres travelled to Kalymnos in May 1893, finding the Patons living above a café on the waterfront with Irene's family. Myres and Paton made the Myndus farm the base for their exploration. Myres later recalled the cosmopolitan nature of the establishment: 'Paton spoke Greek and French to his wife, German to the children's governess, English to me, Turkish to the servants, Latin and Gaelic to his children' (Myres, 10). The permit for Paton and Myres had indicated that they wished to visit the ancient city of Alinda (Muğla), but they decided to study the coast of Karia instead. During the survey, which continued until July, Paton and Myres were arrested on suspicion of being pirates. The survey was published jointly in the *Journal of Hellenic Studies* (1896) and the *Journal of the Royal Geographic Society* (1897).

Paton edited and translated several Greek texts alongside his epigraphic studies, including Plutarch's *Pythici dialogi tres* (1893) and *De cupiditate divitiarum* (1896), and a translation of Aeschylus's *Agamemnon* (1907). His interest in the Greek Anthology saw fruition in *Anthologiae Graecae erotica: the Love Epigrams, or, Book V of the Palatine Anthology* (1898). Along with Eugénie Sellers and others, he helped to translate Max H. Ohnefalsch-Richter's *Kypros, the Bible, and Homer: Oriental Civilization, Art and Religion in Ancient Times* (1893) into English.

The Patons continued to live on Kalymnos, and in 1907 Paton reported a newly discovered inscription on his farm at Myndus on the mainland relating to a cult of Zeus Askraios in *The Classical Review* (1907). Irene's death at Paris from typhoid in October 1908 seems to have precipitated a move to Ker-Anna, Perros Guirec, Côtes-du-Nord in

France. It seems that at this time Paton was offered a chair at Oxford, presumably the newly created Wykeham chair of ancient history filled by Myres in 1910, but he declined. His daughter Sevasti Augusta, in her unpublished memoirs, linked her father's decision to Paton's feelings about how Oscar Wilde had been treated; she recalled Paton 'could never work with a People who were capable of confusing the great Artist with the man'. In 1911 Paton married a widow, Klio, daughter of Ioannes Nomikos of Smyrna, and they settled in Vathy, the main town of the island of Samos. The following year, during the First Balkan War, the island was acquired by Greece.

During the First World War, in the aftermath of the Gallipoli campaign, there were increased attacks on the Turkish mainland by British naval units with the intention of tying down Turkish troops. During one of these raids Myres, serving as a naval officer, was forced to destroy the farm at Myndus: 'Mrs Paton's house on the beach … was occupied by a Turkish platoon and had to be destroyed, as were various other structures suspected of housing petrol dumps' (Myres, 14). In another major naval raid on the Turkish mainland at Asin (ancient Iassus) in late September 1916, Myres was forced to evacuate Mrs Paton's brother-in-law, Hadji Stephanos, to Samos. This led to the Patons making a complaint about Myres's activities which they claimed were damaging Greek interests in Anatolia; the raids were curtailed in early October. However, Compton Mackenzie, who served as an intelligence officer in the Aegean during the First World War, recalled in 1917 that

> the Greek wife of a distinguished English scholar in Samos used to scream at the top of her voice when from her balcony she perceived Myres walking along the street below, for she had an idea that Myres in the course of one foray had destroyed a family farm on the mainland opposite. (Mackenzie, *First Athenian Memories*, 253)

After moving to Samos Paton concentrated on his language interests. He prepared the five volumes of the Greek Anthology for the Loeb Classical Library (1916–19), and then started work on translating Polybius's *Histories* for the six volumes of the Loeb edition (1922–7). During the First World War Paton was asked, again at von Wilamowitz-Moellendorff's suggestion, to serve as an editor for the Teubner edition of Plutarch's *Moralia* (1925–9), published posthumously. Paton died suddenly, apparently from a heart attack while reading *The Pickwick Papers*, at Vathy, Samos, on 21 April 1921, and was buried on the island.

A glimpse into Paton's character is provided by Oscar Wilde. Paton had written to his old friend Wilde on his release from Pentonville in 1897, and Wilde responded, 'I have often heard from others of your sympathy and unabated friendship … I hope you are happy, and finding Greek things every day' (Hart-Davis, 629–30).

DAVID GILL

Sources *The Times* (2 June 1921), 12 · W. M. Calder III, 'Ambivalent loyalties: a letter of Ulrich von Wilamowitz-Moellendorff to W. R. Paton', *Text and tradition: studies in Greek history and historiography in honor of Mortimer Chambers*, ed. R. Mellor and L. Tritle (1999), 287–301 · J. N. L. Myres, *Commander J. L. Myres, RNVR: the Blackbeard of the Aegean* (1980) · C. Mackenzie, *First Athenian memories* (1931) · C. Mackenzie, *Aegean memories* (1940) · *The letters of Oscar Wilde*, ed. R. Hart-Davis (1962) · U. von Wilamowitz-Moellendorff, *My recollections, 1848–1914*, trans. G. C. Richards (1930) · F. B. Tarbell, review of W. R. Paton and E. L. Hicks, *Inscriptions of Cos* (1891), *Classical Review*, 6 (1892), 277–8 · Grandhome, Aberdeenshire, Paton papers · bap. reg. Scot. · Walford, *County families* · I. Anstruther, *Oscar Browning* (1983)

Archives BM, department of Greek and Roman antiquities, antiquities · V&A, Greek textiles · Grandhome, Aberdeenshire, family papers | Girton Cam., Sellers/Strong papers · priv. coll., Rouse papers

Wealth at death £3589 15s. 1d.: confirmation, 14 Feb 1922, CCI · £1: eik additional estate, 24 March 1933, CCI

Patrick [St Patrick, Pádraig] (*fl.* **5th cent.**), patron saint of Ireland, was the son of a deacon named Calpornius. Patrick was a Romano-Briton by birth, but subsequently became honoured as apostle to the Irish and Ireland's patron saint.

Sources Patrick is known primarily from two works of his which have survived, both of them written in Ireland after he had been there many years as a missionary. The earlier is an open letter, *Epistola*, directed against a British chieftain, Coroticus, and his armed followers, in which Patrick excoriates and excommunicates them for having slaughtered some and kidnapped and enslaved others of his newly baptized Irish converts to Christianity. The second work is Patrick's *Confession*. The shorter form of this in the Book of Armagh (807) is generally agreed to be a later abbreviation of the original text, which was probably made, at least in part, in order to omit passages showing Patrick's being reprimanded by British churchmen, and struggling—not always successfully—amid hostility in Ireland. The original, full text of the *Confession*, like that of *Epistola*, survived only on the continent.

Patrick originally wrote more than just these two works. *Epistola*, §3, refers to an earlier letter to Coroticus which is not extant. Bieler's edition, *Libri epistolarum* (1.103–5), includes some brief extracts which may be fragments of or references to other such letters. One, if genuine, would give the name of Patrick's mother as Concessa—although this information might have been interpolated from Muirchú (see below; Bieler, *Life*, 33). The fragmentary remains of a letter to two bishops in Mag nAí cannot be accepted as genuine (Binchy, 'Patrick', 43–5). Of the *Dicta Patricii*, or sayings of Patrick, the first is dubious; the second genuine, occurring in *Epistola*, §17; the third is spurious. As regards the so-called 'First synod of Patrick', which purports to be canonical decisions reached by bishops Patrick, Auxilius, and Iserninus, the general consensus would assign it to a later period, probably the sixth century, in its present form (Hughes, 44–50), although it is not impossible that some of its decisions could date from Patrick's own lifetime (cf. Dumville, *St Patrick*, 175–8). 'St Patrick's Breastplate', an Old Irish invocation of God's protection, is considerably later than Patrick's time (probably eighth century).

A reliable account of Patrick must be drawn primarily from what can be inferred from his two authentic works, but two other types of literary evidence deserve mention.

First, there are the Irish annal collections, which include some brief entries relating to Patrick. These entries were not being made contemporaneously; but it is possible that some of them are based on genuine information (Dumville, *St Patrick*, 33). Secondly, there are the hagiographical accounts of Patrick which were composed by Tírechán and Muirchú in the second half of the seventh century, together with some additional material contained in the Book of Armagh, a manuscript written in 807. Both Tírechán and Muirchú had a propagandist motive, and neither of them had access to reliable information about Patrick apart from what has come down independently. They should therefore be used as evidence for the cult of Patrick in the seventh century, not the historical Patrick of the fifth. None the less, three subjects dealt with in the lives require further comment. First, there is the question of Patrick's links with Auxerre. Muirchú ascribes to Patrick a period of training spent there with Germanus, and has him consecrated bishop by 'Amathorex', widely interpreted as a garbling of Amator, Germanus's predecessor as bishop of Auxerre in the early fifth century. These names, albeit in confused form, do suggest some genuine tradition and some link with Auxerre; but are these traditions correctly associated with Patrick? O'Rahilly has argued that the reason why there are no early Irish traditions about Palladius, Patrick's predecessor who was sent to Ireland in 431, is that traditions of his life were conflated with those of Patrick at an early date (O'Rahilly, 9–19). Although unprovable, this is plausible. Of course it is possible that Patrick, as well as—or because of—Palladius, could have had links with Auxerre; but the plausibility of confusion between the accounts of Palladius and Patrick means that Muirchú's narrative cannot be taken to contain genuine traditions about Patrick and Auxerre. Second, Tírechán ascribes four names to Patrick on the authority of 'a book of bishop Ultán' (*d. c.*657): Magonus, Succetus, Patricius, and Cothirthiacus. Whether this tradition has any authentic basis is unknown. Cothirthiacus is probably derived from Cothrige, a name attested elsewhere in Tírechán. This is generally regarded as a fifth-century Gaelicization of the name Patricius, although that view has been questioned. Finally, it should be noted that modern scholars draw on Muirchú and Tírechán in locating Patrick's missionary endeavours in the northern half of Ireland, rather than in Leinster or Munster.

In any case, the crucial text is Patrick's *Confession*. This is a complex work, combining the testimony of a dedicated Christian with apologetic elements. Patrick's intended readership and the circumstances that led him to write have both to be inferred from the text. Unfortunately its intended audience is far from clear. In some passages near the beginning Patrick seems to be gazing anxiously over his shoulder at well-educated Romano-Britons, themselves polished literary performers, who will look askance at his lack of literary skill. These, however, were not his primary readers, for Patrick shows greater concern to address a more sympathetic group (or groups): in §6 he

calls upon his 'brothers and kinsmen'; in his final paragraph 'those who trust in and fear God'. The crucial passage, however, is §§47–54, where he addresses his 'brothers and fellow servants' (§47) who have trusted him, and among whom he has lived from his youth; and he continues by defending his conduct in Ireland in such a way that it implies that this group was financing his mission. Confusingly, he then talks of how he spent freely 'on your behalf so that they might receive me, and I went amongst you and everywhere for your sake'. On this basis, Thompson has argued that Patrick's primary readership was educated Britons living in Ireland (Thompson, 113–24). A more traditional approach would point out that Patrick in any case addresses more than one group in his *Confession* and that he occasionally jumps from one thing to another in a most confusing manner (as in §21). It would see Patrick as addressing Christians in Britain in §§47–50, and then getting carried away by his subject matter to address those in Ireland directly (if rhetorically) in §§51–3 (Malaspina, 199–203, 223); one might compare the way his letter against Coroticus veers from one audience to another. Both views raise problems; the latter seems more plausible. It should be noted that 'brothers' need not carry monastic overtones in Patrick's writings.

From the tone of much of the *Confession*, it can be inferred that one important reason for its composition was that Patrick felt that his mission was misrepresented in Britain. Christians in the late Roman empire did not think in terms of having a missionary duty to take Christianity beyond its frontiers to the 'barbarians'. Some in Britain (perhaps the educated and aristocratic ecclesiastical hierarchy) were therefore highly dubious about Patrick's conviction that God had called him to go and preach to their Irish enemies. They regarded him as an improbable candidate for the job, given his rudimentary education; and they apparently felt that he must have an ulterior motive, a desire to make an economic profit. Other possible grounds for underlying tension might be their Pelagian leanings as opposed to Patrick's emphasis on grace, and conceivably their displeasure at Patrick's handling of Coroticus's raid (see below). Patrick, replying in his *Confession*, openly admits his educational deficiencies, but insists that it is God who has raised him up and called him to his task, and that he had no motive for returning to Ireland except to preach the gospel there. There is, then, much of autobiographical relevance in the *Confession*; but it is highly selective and told in terms of God's call to Patrick and Patrick's response, with few references to human or mundane agency, only two named places, and no dates.

Two literary antecedents can be suggested for the *Confession*. On the one hand, St Paul's letters in the New Testament were extremely influential on Patrick, primarily because he saw his calling to preach the gospel to the pagans in very similar terms to that of the apostle to the gentiles, and his mission placed him in comparable circumstances and laid him open to criticisms reminiscent of some that the Corinthians levelled at Paul (Nerney, 'Study'). Patrick frequently uses biblical quotations for expressing what he wishes to say and the number of citations from Romans and 1 and 2 Corinthians is particularly striking. A second possible inspiration may lie in Augustine's *Confessions*. True, some scholars regard Patrick's reading as limited to the Bible. He probably read more widely before he went to Ireland, however; and of this, something of the imprint may have remained, as Dronke has argued persuasively (Dronke, 24–34). The title of Patrick's work is obviously reminiscent of Augustine's, and his work, like Augustine's, is also a *confessio* in the threefold early Christian sense of that word: it contains and mingles elements of a confession of faith, an acknowledgement of sin, and praise of God. Again, the first part of Patrick's work is cast in the form of a spiritual autobiography, as with Augustine; but where Augustine presents his story chronologically, and controls his material so that the reader can follow a coherent and unfolding story, Patrick's style is very different. His mind works in terms of associations, rather than in terms of developing a single continuous line, whether a chronological line or a line of argument. This means that Patrick may jump from one event to another in what can seem a bewildering fashion.

A further difficulty is presented by Patrick's Latin. Patrick was presumably bilingual in British and Irish; but although he had learned Latin as a boy, he had consciously to translate what he wished to say into it (*Confession*, §9). His lack of a ready command of Latin is such that at times it is almost impossible to be sure what he is trying to say. Patrick, however, was no mindless babbler. There is a kind of coherence about the structure of his literary works and the concerns that animate them, even if the view that would see him carefully counting words and balancing themes is rejected. Patrick wrote out of what he had experienced and what he had given his life to, and he saw all of this as inspired by the loving purposes of God. For all their shortcomings, his works are powerful. Part of this is due to his use of visual images, but even more to the impressive integrity of this man who cares passionately about the mission to which, he feels, God has called him; and who abandons himself totally to God's will, something which leads him to go where none of his fellow countrymen would previously have ventured and to take risks, even to the extent of living in daily expectation of death—an outcome he readily accepts. All this comes across with a startling directness, which makes an undeniable impact on the reader.

Patrick's life Patricius, or Patrick, was born in the late fourth or first half of the fifth century in Roman Britain, that is, south of Hadrian's Wall. His father, Calpornius, was a deacon; his grandfather, Potitus, a priest. His mother may have been called Concessa. Patrick's family were of free birth and belonged to the local gentry. In addition to (or perhaps before) being a deacon, his father was a decurion, that is, a member of a 'city' council. Calpornius lived at the *vicus* ('small town') 'Bannauem Taburniae' (or 'Bannauem Taberniae'), owning a nearby country estate (*villula*) run by slaves, which was where Patrick was captured by Irish pirates (see below). Emendation to 'Bannaventa Berniae' produces a plausible place name, but it

still cannot be securely identified: Bannaventa near Daventry is too far from the coast for Irish raids; the Banna on Hadrian's Wall, now identified with Birdoswald, is on a military frontier with no appropriate villa sites nearby. The villa could well have been in south-west Britain, or perhaps somewhere not too far from the coast between Chester and the Solway Firth; Wales is unlikely.

It is possible that Patrick's father and grandfather sought ordination in order to escape the burdens which weighed heavily on decurions in the late Roman empire; but this is not necessarily so. True, Patrick proclaimed his youthful dereliction of God and imperviousness to the priests' teaching in his *Confession*. However, such behaviour can arise even when parents are devout; and in any case, Patrick's post-conversion confession of his pre-conversion sinfulness needs to be regarded somewhat sceptically. When he was about fifteen he did commit some kind of sin, perhaps sexual, which the church later regarded seriously. For the rest, the likelihood is that Patrick's 'sinful' youth was more a matter of enjoying himself and running a bit wild with companions of his own age. What he particularly regretted later was his lack of application to his studies, which left him unable to express himself elegantly. Patrick's mother tongue appears to have been British; but he would have had an education in Latin befitting his status, save that in his case it was interrupted before he reached the rhetor's school, where the art of expressing oneself eloquently was perfected. The combined effect of a non-studious childhood, an interrupted education, and decades spent in the Irish mission field, where he probably did not express himself creatively in Latin (other than in prayer, maybe)—all this left Patrick acutely conscious of his educational deficiencies.

Shortly before he was sixteen Patrick's life was turned upside down: his family's estate was raided, and he and many others were carried off and sold into slavery in Ireland. He probably ended up on a farm near Killala Bay, in co. Mayo (see below). Patrick was set to work as a herdsman, which involved his being out with the animals in all weathers; and there, in his isolation:

> the Lord opened my mind to an awareness of my unbelief so that … I might turn with my whole heart to the Lord my God, who … pitied my youth and ignorance … and comforted me as a father comforts a son.   (Patrick, *Confession*, §2)

He began to pray to God frequently, in the woods and mountains, by day and night, and in snow, ice, and rain. So assured was he that God spoke to him, that in accordance with a divine direction, 'Lo, your ship is ready', he ran away from his master after six years and made his way some 200 (Roman) miles across Ireland: no mean feat. After initial difficulties Patrick persuaded some sailors to take him aboard a ship leaving Ireland. Three days later they made land and then had to travel through a 'desert' for twenty-eight days, narrowly escaping starvation.

Much desirable information is excluded from Patrick's account, which focuses on what God has done for him, often in the way of supernatural help. So it is that Patrick's narrative casually jumps from his successfully reaching people after the journey through the 'desert' to a period a few years later, after he had been welcomed back home by his family:

> And again after a few years I was in Britain with my family … and there I saw in a vision of the night a man coming as from Ireland, whose name was Victoricus, with innumerable letters; and he gave me one of them and I read the beginning of the letter, which ran, 'the voice of the Irish'. And as I read the beginning of the letter, I thought that at that very moment I heard the voice of those who live by the wood of Foclut which is beside the western sea, and they cried out thus as if with one voice: 'We ask you, holy boy, to come and walk among us once more.'   (Patrick, *Confession*, §23)

Patrick took this dream as God's call to him to return to Ireland and preach the gospel there; and he thanks God that 'after many years' their call has been answered.

The natural interpretation of Patrick's dream and response is that Patrick was being recalled by those among whom he had lived as a slave for six years: the very specificity of 'the wood of Foclut' (Patrick, *Confession*, §23), which was not a famous place, indicates this, as does the wording 'once more'. Tírechán's account makes it possible to locate the wood of Foclut in the neighbourhood of the modern town of Killala, co. Mayo (O'Rahilly, 33–5, 60–64) and Tírechán's identification can be accepted. First, the name had survived from Patrick's time and was evidently still current in Tírechán's, and only one other place (in modern co. Westmeath) is recorded with this or a similar name (Hogan, 138–40). Second, Tírechán came from that area and was well informed about it. He did not, however, make any special claims for it based on its identification with the place named by Patrick; rather, he accepted the seventh-century Armagh view which placed Patrick's captivity at Slemish in co. Antrim. There is thus no obvious reason for him to have fabricated the identification (O'Rahilly, 62–3). Third, its location near Killala Bay fits with Patrick's description of it as 'beside the western sea' (Patrick, *Confession*, §23), a description which effectively rules out Slemish; and it can also be reconciled with Patrick's having to flee some 200 (Roman) miles before taking ship for Britain—which again seems implausible for Slemish.

Patrick's escape from Ireland at the age of twenty-one or twenty-two and the 'few years' which elapsed before he was with his family and had this dream, implies that the latter occurred when he was in his late twenties. From this point (apart from two accounts of experiences of the Holy Spirit when praying) Patrick's *Confession* appears to jump two decades or more; for the next incident he recounts, the attack on him by his seniors, came when he was forty-five on one interpretation and considerably older, perhaps in his late fifties, on another. What happened to him in the meantime? First, it was probably only after an inner struggle, perhaps a protracted one, that Patrick accepted the call (*Confession*, §46). Even when he had reached his own decision, people close to him, including his ecclesiastical 'seniors', tried to persuade him not to go. He quotes the revealing comment of 'many': 'Why does this man want to put himself in danger amongst enemies who do

not know God?' (*Confession*, §46). The very concept of a mission to pagan peoples outside the frontiers of the Roman empire was alien to the outlook of late Roman Christians. Patrick had, at the least, to get some ecclesiastical training, to find a bishop to ordain him, and to win the blessing of the church for his mission. These last were not readily forthcoming.

There remain two questions: did Patrick spend any time in Gaul between his escape from Ireland and his return as a missionary; and did he spend time in either country as a member of a monastic community? When writing from Ireland in his old age, Patrick expressed his longing to visit his native land and family, 'and also [to go] as far as Gaul to visit the brothers and that I might see the face of the saints of my Lord' (*Confession*, §43). In context, the implication is that Patrick would be revisiting people whom he already knew in Gaul, who were in sympathy with his mission to Ireland and encouragement of monasticism there; indeed, they may have been, or have included, monks. That Patrick lived for a period of a few months or even years in Gaul before he returned to Ireland is thus very likely; and he may well have lived in some kind of ascetic community either in Gaul or Britain (or both), though his language is too imprecise for certainty.

It is not known how long it was after his dream calling him back to Ireland that Patrick actually returned there as a missionary, but he may initially have gone as a priest. Even this, however, would not have happened very quickly; for in addition to training for ordination, Patrick had first to overcome the opposition of those who regarded his missionary vision as misguided (*Confession*, §§37, 46). What there is evidence for is a time when Patrick, now aged forty-five or more, was apparently being considered for promotion to the episcopate and came under attack from his 'seniors' for a sin committed long since. Whether these 'seniors' were senior members of a community or of the church hierarchy is unclear, but the context implies that Patrick was answerable to some in the British church. The account of their attack, which occurs in the *Confession* shortly after Patrick's vision of Victoricus, is difficult to interpret, but of great importance. For this reason, Patrick's own words will be given first, and then discussed:

> And when I was attacked by some of my seniors, who came, and [brought up] my sins against my onerous episcopate, on that day indeed I was hit hard so that I might have fallen here, and in eternity; but the Lord kindly spared the stranger and exile for his name, and came and strongly supported me in this trampling underfoot. … They found an occasion against me after thirty years, a word I had confessed before I was a deacon. Because of my worries I had confessed to my most close friend, with sorrowful mind, what I had done in my boyhood one day … I do not know, God knows, if I was then fifteen.   (*Confession*, §§26–7)

After a brief flashback, Patrick continues his story. He recounts a vision which he interprets as showing that God was angry with the seniors for their attack on him. His response was to thank God for upholding and strengthening him, with the result that 'he did not hinder me from the departure which I had decided on and also from my work which I had learnt of from Christ my Lord'. On the contrary, Patrick felt vindicated: 'my trust [or faith, *fides*] was proved right before God and man' (§§29–30). Patrick continued:

> But rather I grieve for my most close friend, because we deserved to hear such a response. To whom I had entrusted my very soul! And I learnt from some brothers before that defence—because I was not present, nor was I in Britain, nor did it come from me—that he too was pushing for me in my absence. Indeed, he had said to me with his own lips:'Look, you should be appointed to episcopal orders'—which I was not worthy of. ... I have said enough. But I ought not to hide the gift of God which he gave me in the land of my captivity, because then I vigorously sought him and there I found him. (*Confession*, §§32–3)

Much here is unclear. Should the thirty years' interval since his boyhood sin be counted from when Patrick committed the sin, in which case the attack on him would have come when he was aged forty-five; or from when Patrick confessed the sin before being ordained deacon, in which case it may be inferred that he was approximately fifty-five or more? Still more disconcerting is the difficulty of telling whether the attack was made on Patrick while he was already working as a bishop in Ireland (as *Confession*, §26 implies); or whether it came out of the process of deliberation as to whether Patrick should be promoted to the episcopate in the first place (as §32 implies). Scholars are divided on this issue.

The most plausible interpretation might be to take the events as falling at a time when Patrick was working as a *priest* in Ireland. That would allow the whole sequence of events recounted in §§26–32 to be viewed as a unity, as the text suggests, while still making sense of the implication that Patrick was then in Ireland, and that he was not yet a bishop. The starting point in the sequence of events would have been a debate about Patrick's suitability for promotion to the episcopate. That prompted his friend's disclosure of Patrick's sin, for there were canonical prohibitions against ordaining men who had at any time committed serious sins. This disclosure in turn led to the attack of the seniors against the plan to promote Patrick to the episcopate, followed by Patrick's devastation at what had happened—at his friend's breach of confidence, at the public disgrace, and at the setback to what he saw as his calling under God. In his hour of need Patrick had a dream which he interpreted as showing that God was on his side; and Patrick's already being in Ireland as a priest makes sense of the reference to God's kindness to 'a stranger and exile for his name', then living 'in the land of my captivity' (*Confession*, §§26, 33)—references which seem incompatible with the view that Patrick was in Britain or Gaul at the time. Support for the idea that the seniors' attack came while Patrick was already working in Ireland can also be found in a later passage of the *Confession*. Here, after mentioning the loss of his native land and family, Patrick tells how friendly attempts were made to dissuade him from going and how it was against the desire of some of his seniors (*Confession*, §§36–7, and cf. §46). The opposition of his seniors here sounds very different in spirit from that in *Confession* §§26–7; and that in turn would suggest that Patrick's original departure for Ireland occurred before the events just discussed, and has been omitted by Patrick, along with much else. The *Confession* does not reveal when Patrick was made a bishop; but at some point he was consecrated, though probably not to any fixed see (*Epistola*, §1).

After this it becomes impossible to continue with a chronological account. Patrick was active in Ireland for twenty years or more, spending the rest of his life there. In his *Confession*, written in his old age, he admits his longing to visit Britain and Gaul; but he refuses to do so lest it undo his missionary labours. Rather he talks of Christ's command to spend the rest of his life with his Irish converts: an injunction he willingly accepts, even if it should cost him his life. The last that is heard of him are the closing words of his *Confession*: 'And this is my confession before I die.' He should therefore be envisaged as dying in Ireland, possibly at Saul, in co. Down (see below). The year is not known, but the traditional date of 17 March, which is attested by Muirchú, may well be accurate.

Patrick's Irish mission The initiative for his return to Ireland as a missionary lay with Patrick, fired by his 'voice of the Irish' dream. Initially 'many' in Britain opposed the idea; but Patrick must have won a modicum of support there, for the British church appears to have been responsible for ordaining him (*Confession*, §§27, 32: though note that Bieler, 'St Patrick and the British church', 125–8, interprets the evidence differently). The defensive tone of much of the *Confession* suggests that Patrick was responding to criticisms from Britain. If it is correct to take *Confession* §§49–50 as addressed to Christians in Britain, the implication is that Patrick was being funded from there: perhaps he drew both human and financial resources from the Christian community where he had lived (*Confession*, §48) and from his own contacts, rather than being supported by the British church on an official basis. Alternatively, one group of bishops might have supported him. But the sense of isolation and of being held in contempt by many, which comes across from both Patrick's writings, implies that he did not receive full support from the British ecclesiastical hierarchy.

In addition to receiving some funding from Britain, Patrick almost certainly sold his family estates in order to help finance his mission (*Epistola*, §10; Thompson, 101). Considerable economic resources were essential to support his work, for although Patrick was of high standing in Britain, in Ireland he would have been a despised outsider, with no kin to protect him and no security against attack unless he were received under someone's protection. This meant that he would in practice have been dependent on the goodwill of the local king for any lengthy stay. Since Ireland was then divided into a multitude of petty kingdoms, travelling around would have been both complex and dangerous. In order to operate in these circumstances, Patrick gave gifts to kings, paid for a bodyguard of princes to accompany him, and expended very considerable sums on the judges in the areas which he visited most often. But for all this, he was frequently seized and kept captive, sometimes for weeks, or longer. Even towards the end of his life, he daily expected that he would be killed, or tricked, or enslaved.

Patrick, however, was a brave man, and a determined one. His readiness to carry on evangelizing, whatever the cost, led to many converts for Christianity. He talks about baptizing 'so many thousands', and of ordaining clergy 'all over the place' (*Confession*, §50). An aside mentions his success among Britons living in Ireland; but for the most part, his mission was aimed at the Irish themselves. Two types of convert are particularly mentioned: the sons and daughters of petty kings, who embraced the monastic life; and women who adopted the life of virginity against their family's will—and, in particular, slave women who opted for such a life despite much harassment. Patrick therefore made converts at both extremes of Irish society.

Patrick's missionary methods have to be inferred. He modelled himself on St Paul, and appears to have relied largely on preaching and teaching. Although he would certainly have visited kings, on whose support he depended, there is no indication that he concentrated his attention on them or saw them as instrumental in pressurizing people into conversion; on the contrary, he shows a particular concern for the most vulnerable. He refused to accept gifts from his converts, lest that should give hostile pagans a pretext for denigrating his work. He freely ordained native Irishmen, including one priest whom he had trained from childhood. He encouraged the monastic life: there are references to monks, virgins, widows, and the continent, and to Patrick's baptizing, confirming, and ordaining; but there are none to church buildings and nothing in Patrick's own writings indicates that he was in a position to organize his converts into regular dioceses. His *Confession* suggests rather that he spent his time travelling around; and his fear of losing his work if he left Ireland reveals the precarious position of Christianity and may imply that he was the only bishop, at least in that part of Ireland.

Patrick's letter against Coroticus provides some scanty details. Patrick had just baptized and confirmed a number of new Christians when Coroticus's men attacked: some were killed; others, male and female, were taken captive and shared out as booty or sold to the Picts and the *Scotti* (the latter probably, in this context, the pagan Irish of Scottish Dál Riata). Coroticus was a British ruler, presumably located in western Britain (Stancliffe, review-article, 128); he may plausibly be identified with Ceretic of Dumbarton, who ruled the British kingdom of Strathclyde (Binchy, 'Patrick', 106–9; Dumville, *St Patrick*, 114). Perhaps the most striking thing to come across from Patrick's anguished response is his helplessness and isolation: it was Patrick's own people who had launched the attack, but they had merely laughed at an earlier letter that he had sent. Did the British Christians, to whom Patrick now appealed, pay any more heed to his pleas to treat Coroticus and his men as excommunicate and to reject their gifts, unless they did penance? The sequel is unknown; but one conjecture is that the British might have regarded Coroticus as their protector and therefore winked at his

raid on Patrick's converts, seeking to deflect Patrick's outcry by querying his own credentials. On this hypothesis, it was to their criticisms that Patrick was responding in his *Confession* (Grosjean, 'Notes', 103–6; Malaspina, 194–9).

As regards the areas where he worked, Patrick is studiously vague: 'Established in Ireland, I profess myself a bishop', he declares (Patrick, *Epistola*, §1). His mission may well have reached the wood of Foclut (near Killala Bay): that is certainly one reading of Patrick's thankfulness that the cry of those from that area had been answered (see above), and it would tally with his words, 'the Gospel has been preached up to where there is no one beyond' (*Confession*, §34). Place-name evidence, such as it is, suggests a broadly northern sphere of authority for Patrick. Apart from Patrick's writings, there is no relevant literary evidence before the seventh-century propagandist documents produced by Armagh. The earliest of these, *Liber angeli* (probably *c*.650), proceeds on the assumption that Armagh was Patrick's chief church and assigns to Armagh's immediate jurisdiction a very extensive area in north-east Ireland, stretching from Slemish (in what is now co. Antrim) southwards almost as far as the Boyne. Tírechán omits most of this area and concentrates principally on southern Uí Néill areas and Connacht (though also including Dál Riata and the Cruithni areas of Ulster). He has only a glancing reference to Armagh, and omits most of the Airgiallan overkingdom in which it lay, as well as Dál Fiatach areas (now in eastern co. Down). Muirchú, however, focuses attention on the latter and on Armagh. He presents Patrick as dying in Saul, and being buried in Downpatrick, while assigning pre-eminence to Armagh. On the basis of these seventh-century texts, historians generally assume that Patrick's mission was based in north-east Ireland and probably extended westwards to Connacht. The evidence for Saul, and, in particular, Downpatrick, is not above suspicion: another tradition regarded the site of Patrick's burial as unknown! Patrick's association with Armagh can be questioned (Sharpe, 'St Patrick and … Armagh', 40–44); but it is taken for granted in *Liber angeli*, the oldest document, and was apparently widely accepted. It was perhaps one of the places which Patrick originally evangelized, only later assuming leadership of his churches (Doherty, 71–3). That Patrick's missionary area included north-east Ireland fits well with the few available pointers: with a raid by Coroticus; with Mauchteus, Patrick's disciple, who is traditionally associated with co. Louth; and with the general likelihood that a missionary coming from Britain would attempt to establish a bridgehead on the east of Ireland. It must, however, be recognized that the sources are late and capable of misinforming, as they do in placing Patrick's captivity at Slemish.

Chronology and relationship to Palladius's mission Patrick's writings give no dates and few allusions to datable occurrences. His references to his father as a decurion who owned a *villula*, and also to his own education (or its lack) all imply a Roman context, broadly speaking. But in some areas such a context might have lasted many decades after Britain formally ceased to be part of the Roman empire about 410—witness the sub-Roman inscriptions of Wales and the education which Gildas (*fl.* 6th cent.) received. The most useful *terminus a quo* for Patrick's *floruit* is therefore the evidence of the biblical texts he cites: his Old Testament was *vetus Latina*, but his text of Acts was a pure form of the Vulgate. This means that his theological training before he returned to Ireland as a missionary cannot have taken place before the early fifth century. Assigning a *terminus ad quem* for Patrick is more straightforward: in *Epistola*, §14 he implies that the Franks are pagans. Their formal conversion to Christianity can be dated to between 496 and 508.

Patrick's mission can thus be securely dated to the fifth century. The most significant question is whether it fell before, during, or after the mission of Palladius. The latter was sent by Pope Celestine as the first bishop 'to the Irish believing in Christ' in 431, according to the contemporary *Chronicle* of Prosper. The annals of Ulster date Palladius's arrival to 431, and Patrick's to 432. The latter entry, however, can probably be dismissed as erroneous: the work of a Patrician propagandist committed to bringing Patrick to Ireland as soon as possible in order to assign the glory of Ireland's conversion to him. None the less, it can be deduced that Patrick arrived after Palladius, because not only is the latter called the 'first bishop', but also Patrick's account, read carefully, implies that other missionaries had been in Ireland before him. He himself says that he had penetrated to areas which had hitherto not been reached by anyone to baptize, ordain, or confirm (*Confession*, §51), so implying that other areas had already received such episcopal ministrations.

Did Patrick's mission have any relation to that of Palladius? Muirchú's story of an Auxerre training for Patrick cannot be used (see above); but Patrick's strong theology of grace, and constant harping on how all that he had achieved was through God's gift, does suggest that his period of training fell at the time of the Pelagian controversy in Britain, perhaps some time between *c.*425 and *c.*445. In that case, he would at least have known of Palladius's mission. The latter's geographical focus was probably Leinster. Whether Patrick had any direct link with Palladius's mission (perhaps starting there as a priest before moving as bishop to the unevangelized north), or whether he went independently to a different, northerly, area of Ireland, is not known.

The Irish annals have obits for Patrick around the years 457 and 461 and also between the years 491 and 496. The latter are apparently more likely than the former to be based on authentic material (Dumville, *St Patrick*, 29–33); and the later dating would also fit more plausibly with the 535 annalistic obit of a disciple of Patrick, Mauchteus (assuming that he was a direct disciple). But the evidence is too inadequate for us to be certain that Patrick's mission should be dated to the later fifth century, rather than, say, *c.*440–*c.*465.

Patrick's achievement The conversion of Ireland was a long-drawn-out process, in which Patrick played but a part. It was, however, a significant part. Although Palladius preceded Patrick, he was originally sent to minister to an existing congregation, not to convert the pagan Irish. True, Palladius may have been encouraged to preach to the pagans as well; but even if he did, his mission was probably confined to a fairly restricted area of north-east Leinster. In any case, the main part of the work of conversion appears to have been undertaken by British clerics, not continental ones; this is the clear implication of the linguistic evidence.

This development should not be taken for granted. Certainly Britain is closer to Ireland than Gaul and this would have made it easier for the British to support missionary work there. Yet recalling the uncomprehending, negative British reaction to Patrick's desire to go and convert the pagan Irish and their failure to mount a full-scale mission to the Anglo-Saxons, leads to realization of how crucial his personal commitment was. Patrick was original in setting out with the primary goal of converting Irish pagans—normally seen by the British as their enemies; and he did this despite opposition from within Britain and persecution in Ireland. Indeed, the unpredictable, violent treatment he suffered there would have deterred one who lacked his personal conviction that God had entrusted him with that task. Patrick, however, persevered, and others came from Britain in his wake: Mauchteus is the only one who can be named; but the linguistic evidence implies a major British missionary contribution, and this lasted right through the sixth century and beyond. Thus Patrick's achievement should be thought of not only in terms of the direct contribution he made to converting the pagan Irish, but also of his indirect contribution: he paved the way for large-scale British involvement in Ireland's Christianization.

Patrick may also have contributed to various characteristics of early Irish Christianity: to its emphasis on rejecting the gifts of wrongdoers (*Epistola*, §8); to the development of its *peregrinatio* ('pilgrimage') ideal, as it is embodied by someone like Columbanus; and perhaps to the recognition that God could be worshipped anywhere, under the open sky as in a church building (cf. *Confession*, §16).

Armagh and the early cult Founder saints were of particular significance in early medieval Ireland. Here, written documents never superseded oral traditions as a legitimizing instrument, and as a result contemporary claims were frequently expressed in terms of stories about the founder saint and what he had done, or what grants had been made to him, or agreements reached between him and the ancestors of current leaders. So it was that in the seventh century the church of Armagh began using the figure of St Patrick in pursuit of its own far-reaching claims. Its success was partly due to the fact that there was already some recognition of Patrick's position elsewhere in Ireland: a hymn had been written in his honour, mentioning his 'apostolate from God', and likening him to St Peter and St Paul; again, he had been alluded to as *papa*, a term denoting considerable respect, by Cummian, writing in southern Ireland *c.*633; and clerics in the midlands had interested themselves in collecting stories about him.

Meanwhile his cult was spread by Fursa and his companions as far as northern Gaul (though Bede remained ignorant of him). But it was Armagh that capitalized upon this widespread respect to promote Patrick's claims as the apostle of the Irish.

Armagh's first extant document, the *Liber angeli* (probably *c.*650), portrays Patrick as the apostle of all the Irish, with his base in Armagh. In recompense for his ceaseless labour of evangelization, God sends an angel who extends Armagh's immediate control over a considerable area in north-east Ireland, while further announcing that God has given all the tribes of Ireland to Patrick and Armagh as a *paruchia*, or sphere of jurisdiction. Patrick's status as 'apostolic teacher and chief leader for all the tribes of the Irish' is emphasized and it is stated that 'he himself will judge all the Irish' on doomsday (*Liber angeli*, §§13, 23).

The germ of the idea of Patrick as the 'national apostle' for the whole of Ireland appears here; and much subsequent Patrician hagiography is simply a fleshing out of these audacious claims, here tersely expressed, with stories which (in early Irish terms) provide an evidential basis for them. So there is Tírechán's account, which portrays Patrick going round the kingdoms of the northern half of Ireland, and briefly into Leinster and Munster, founding churches as he goes. In this way, Tírechán is claiming that these churches should form part of Patrick's *paruchia*. Muirchú is equally concerned to vindicate Armagh's claims over all Ireland, but does it by focusing on Patrick's dramatic conversion of King Lóegaire mac Néill, here represented (unhistorically) as the king of all Ireland. Patrick with his paschal fire vanquishes the darkness of paganism and the king's druids, so symbolizing Ireland's conversion. In subsequent centuries Armagh continued adding to Patrician hagiography, weaving the accounts of Muirchú and Tírechán together, and greatly enlarging upon them. This gave rise to new Latin lives, which circulated widely abroad, while in Ireland itself it culminated in the related 'Tripartite life', written largely in Irish about the tenth century (see below). The fictional nature of Armagh's aetiological stories about Patrick is neatly illustrated by a poem (perhaps of the early twelfth century) which attributes the conversion of the Scandinavians of Dublin to Patrick, as a result of his miraculously restoring their king's son to life. The resultant tax due to Armagh is carefully detailed. Such propaganda led to widespread recognition of St Patrick's special status, accepted in one Munster text as early as *c.*680, and epitomized by the visit of Brian Bóruma to Armagh in 1005. Armagh's efforts were crowned in the twelfth-century reorganization of the Irish church, when it was assigned the primacy.

The growth of the legend and the cult The figure of St Patrick early developed a far wider aetiological role than functioning simply as a symbol of Armagh and its rights; for once Patrick became regarded as the bringer of the Christian dispensation to all Ireland, stories were told about him in the vernacular to demonstrate the accommodation reached between the church on the one hand, and pre-Christian traditions and their guardians on the other. Initially such stories cluster particularly around the story of Patrick's encounter with King Lóegaire. The ninth-century pseudo-historical prologue to the *Senchas Már* legal collection has a story of how Lóegaire urged one of his men to kill Patrick's charioteer in order to test Patrick in the matter of Christian forgiveness versus just retribution. This is followed by Patrick's conversion of the people of Ireland and his role in accommodating Christian requirements to Irish traditional law, expounded to him by Dubthach. A slightly later story, 'The Phantom Chariot of Cú Chulainn', tells how St Patrick resurrected Cú Chulainn from hell in order to try to convince Lóegaire to believe. Later still, in 'The colloquy of the ancients' (*c.*1200 for the original text, but with fresh recensions through to the modern period and W. B. Yeats), Patrick is found in company with the Fenian heroes Oisín and Caílte, asking them about their former life. Such stories illustrate the way in which the figure of Patrick was not restricted to Armagh or the ecclesiastical sphere, but could enter the world of traditional native learning and story-telling, and thus reach a wide lay audience throughout Ireland.

The longest and most extravagant telling of the Patrick legend, however, is found in the 'Tripartite life' already mentioned, which was produced at Armagh; and this vernacular presentation continued to provide the basis for Irish people's knowledge of Patrick right through the middle ages and beyond. Patrick is here represented as from the British kingdom of Dumbarton, but is made a close relative of St Martin of Tours on his mother's side. He works many childhood miracles, and his kidnapping is here attributed to marauding Britons, not Irishmen. After his release from slavery he spends a lengthy period in Gaul with St Germanus, and is tonsured by St Martin. At the age of sixty he is commissioned to preach to the Irish by God, on Mount Hermon. He insists on receiving the staff of Jesus (*bachall Ísu*) from God himself, from whom he obtains three boons: to sit on God's right hand in heaven; to judge the Irish on doomsday; and that as much gold and silver as his companions can carry should be given to the Irish for accepting Christianity. After ordination in Rome, he returns to Ireland where the narrative takes him the length and breadth of the country, converting kings, cursing enemies, founding churches, and working miracles. His prophecies of good fortune for those who welcome him, and misfortune for his opponents, are invariably fulfilled. Much here is founded on Muirchú and Tírechán, but Patrick's visits to Leinster and Munster are considerably expanded upon and much additional material is included. One version has him composing 'St Patrick's Breastplate' as he and his followers escape from the hostile King Lóegaire in the form of deer. Also interesting is Patrick's encounter with Cenn Crúaich, the chief idol of Ireland, which he overthrows with the *bachall Ísu*. Most rumbustious of all is the account of how Patrick fasted against God for the duration of Lent on top of Croagh Patrick, in order to wring concessions from him. Molested by black (demonic) birds, Patrick flings his bell at them to force them into flight, and is comforted by an angel who brings white birds to sing to him. Then Patrick bargains with

God, via an angel, to gain his demands. These include his bringing vast numbers of Irishmen out of hell, and 'that the English should not dwell in Ireland, by consent or force, so long as I abide in heaven' (Stokes, *Tripartite Life*, 1.116).

The emphasis of the 'Tripartite life' on St Patrick's looking after the Irish in exchange for their loyalty, but without making excessive demands, was well adapted to win popularity in Ireland, and alongside the ecclesiastically produced lives are found popular cult practices associated with St Patrick. Here, the saint may often have taken the place of previous deities (as at various holy wells). Particularly interesting is the annual pilgrimage up Croagh Patrick, which takes place on the last Sunday in July, the Sunday of Crom Dubh (probably to be identified with Cenn Crúaich). This appears to be a Christianization of an earlier celebration to mark the beginning of harvest on 1 August, the festival of Lughnasa (named from the god Lug). The pilgrimage is not directly attested until 1113—and then for St Patrick's day. But the legend of Patrick's forty-day sojourn there, together with God's injunction for holy men to climb thither, occurs already in Tírechán (§38), and is greatly expanded in the 'Tripartite life'. This may well imply a very early date for the pilgrimage's origin. Perhaps more remarkable is the fact that it survived the Reformation and is still flourishing. Pilgrims traditionally ascended barefoot and repeated a set number of Paters, Aves, and Credos while doing the rounds at various stations. Up to the mid-nineteenth century they used to kiss the 'black bell', which by tradition was the one that Patrick had thrown at the demons, and pass it sunwise three times round their bodies. Today the bell is in the National Museum of Ireland, Dublin, and most pilgrims go shod; but the pilgrimage still retains its popularity.

A second major pilgrimage associated with St Patrick, which again has lasted from the middle ages to the present, is the famous one at Lough Derg. The site is Station Island in Lough Derg, co. Donegal, which may only have become linked to the figure of St Patrick in the twelfth century. In the 1180s knowledge of it was brought to a wide public by brief accounts in Gerald of Wales's *Topographia Hibernica* and Jocelin's *Vita sancti Patricii*, and above all by H. (probably Henry) of Saltrey's *Tractatus de Purgatorio sancti Patricii*. The latter told the story of how the Irish had initially refused to believe Patrick's preaching, so Christ had revealed to Patrick a cave in a deserted place: whoever stayed in it for twenty-four hours would experience the torments of the wicked and the joys of the blessed. He might never return; but if he survived, he would be purged of his sins. This penance had been gladly undertaken by a knight, Owein, whose experiences were recounted in detail by 'H'. His work rapidly achieved widespread popularity, bringing pilgrims from all parts of Europe to Lough Derg. Meanwhile the Augustinian canons who controlled the Purgatory spread St Patrick's cult among their confrères abroad, where it flourished, particularly in Styria (now south-east Austria). Despite attempts to close down the Lough Derg pilgrimage at the Reformation, the practice persisted among the Irish.

Today it is said to draw some 30,000 pilgrims a year for a gruelling three-day penitential experience consisting of a round of stations with repeated set prayers; this is undertaken fasting, and with little sleep. Of the cave itself, no trace is known.

Even before St Patrick's Purgatory came to fame, Patrick was known on the continent and in Britain. Glastonbury even claimed that he had been its abbot and was buried there, and there is a tenth-century reference to Irish pilgrims frequenting his grave. In the early twelfth century William of Malmesbury wrote a life of Patrick for Glastonbury (surviving only in extracts), which is based on a Latin life known as *Vita iii*. The latter, which is closely related to the Irish 'Tripartite life', circulated widely outside Ireland and was incorporated in the great Austrian legendary compiled at Regensburg *c.*1160–1200.

A new phase of relations between Ireland and Britain began in 1169 with the Anglo-Norman invasion of Ireland. Eight years later John de Courcy conquered part of Ulster, including co. Down; and in 1185 he presided over the alleged discovery there of the remains of Ireland's foremost saints, Patrick, Brigit, and Columba, which he translated to the cathedral. He zealously promoted the cult of Patrick, issuing coins bearing the saint's name and commissioning a more serviceable life from an English Cistercian, Jocelin. Jocelin drew on a Latin life related to the Irish 'Tripartite' and rendered Patrick's story in a guise more appealing to the Anglo-Norman world. Patrick was recognized as 'the patron and apostle of Ireland', and his authorization from the pope was emphasized: the latter is represented as making Patrick his legate. Patrick's fast on Croagh Patrick is transformed into an occasion for divine contemplation, and this is linked with the story of his expelling all poisonous creatures from Ireland (Jocelin of Furness, §§148–9). This famous legend of Patrick's expulsion of the snakes makes its first appearance here and in a closely related fragmentary life (Bieler, *Studies on the Life*, no. 19, 228–9). Gerald of Wales refers to the story, but is sceptical of it. A late medieval depiction of St Patrick from Faughart, co. Louth, has an episcopal figure standing above a snake. Jocelin's *Vita sancti Patricii*, John de Courcy's promotion of Down as a pilgrimage site, together with Strongbow's seizure of the *bachall Ísu* and presentation of it to Holy Trinity Cathedral, Dublin, where it became the focus of a cult, were significant acts: they ensured that the cult of St Patrick would be promoted in those parts of Ireland held by the English, as well as within Irish-held areas. St Patrick would be a saint for all.

From the Reformation to the present The sixteenth and seventeenth centuries brought both Reformation and Counter-Reformation and the effective conquest and colonization of Ireland. In the conflicts thus engendered, the figure of St Patrick was called upon to exemplify opposing views. On the protestant side, Meredith Hanmer held that 'the onely doctrine Patricke read and expounded unto the people was the foure Evangelists conferred with the Old Testament' (Cunningham and Gillespie, 92), while Archbishop Ussher argued that the Church of Ireland was the legitimate descendant of the original church founded by

St Patrick, the latter having meantime been corrupted by subjection to Rome in the twelfth century. The Catholics, on the other hand, stressed the continuity of the faith in Ireland from St Patrick onwards, pointing to evidence of the mass, penance, relics, holy water, and so on in the lives of Patrick. Thus both sides pressed the figure of St Patrick into a predetermined mould; and these conflicting historiographical approaches beset all attempts to reach a soundly based interpretation of Patrick down to the twentieth century. The controversies did, however, lead Irish Franciscans on the continent to collect and publish original sources for Patrick and other native saints, while efforts were also put into retelling the life of Patrick in order to bring it into conformity with post-Tridentine models of sanctity. Jocelin's life was translated and abridged for this purpose, with the infancy miracles and cursing incidents omitted (1625). These efforts were rewarded when the feast of St Patrick was included in the Roman breviary (1631) and in the revised Roman calendar (1632). Meanwhile the scholarly Ussher, who was the first for many centuries to read Patrick's own writings and the lives of Tírechán and Muirchú, produced the first ever attempt at a historical (rather than hagiographical) account of Patrick in his *Antiquitates* (chap. 17). His pupil, Sir James Ware, published the first complete edition of Patrick's works in 1656.

In Catholic Ireland, however, the traditional image of St Patrick as depicted in the medieval lives still held sway. Edward Campion's history (1571) tells how 'a lewd prelate … was able to perswade his parish: that St Patricke in striving with S. Peter to let an Irish Gallowglass into heaven, had his head broken with the keyes' (Cunningham and Gillespie, 87): clearly St Patrick would fight for his own, at the highest level! Patrick, the protector of the Irish, was well suited to appeal to Catholics in this period. The rebels in Limerick in 1642 had a life of St Patrick which included prophecies by him and others to the effect that the English would be banished from Ireland: one recalls the pledge Patrick wrung from God in the 'Tripartite life'. Meanwhile, admiration for the Jacobite hero Patrick Sarsfield (*d.* 1693) led to the name Patrick attaining its remarkable popularity in Ireland.

The association of St Patrick with the shamrock first occurs on halfpennies issued in Dublin in the 1670s. These portray Patrick, attired as a bishop, holding up a shamrock in his right hand before which his audience kneels. The motto is 'ECCE GREX' ('behold the flock'). In 1681 an English traveller, Thomas Dinely, reported that on 17 March, St Patrick's day, 'ye Irish of all stations and condicions were crosses in their hatts, some of pins, some of green ribbon, and the vulgar superstitiously wear shamroges' (Shirley, 183). Explicit literary testimony to the 'tradition that by this three-leaved grass, [St Patrick] emblematically set forth to them the mystery of the Holy Trinity' comes only from Caleb Threlkeld, writing in 1727 (Hopkin, 109). The coin evidence, however, shows that the story was already current by *c.*1674. A further symbol, St Patrick's cross (a red diagonal cross on white ground), may also have had Patrician associations from at least the

seventeenth century. In the later eighteenth it was a device used by the knights of the Most Illustrious Order of Saint Patrick, instituted by George III in 1783, while the shamrock figured on their star. The red saltire's subsequent unpopularity in Ireland may stem from its incorporation into the union flag, accompanying Ireland's political unification with Britain in 1801. By the time of the popular ballad, 'The Wearin' o' the Green', St Patrick's green (perhaps shamrock green) is contrasted with 'England's cruel Red'.

The role of St Patrick in the development of Irish nationalism is a complex matter. In recent centuries St Patrick's day was customarily celebrated with just two distinctive customs: the wearing of crosses, coloured ribbons, or shamrock; and imbibing 'St Patrick's pot', with 'the drowning of the shamrock'. The wearing of special emblems and conviviality appear to have been common to all classes, and to both Catholics and protestants; but, initially, there was nothing to link the select celebrations of St Patrick's day involving the knights and other invited guests, which were held by the viceroy in Dublin Castle, with the general celebrations of the Catholic populace. In the early nineteenth-century aftermath of the foundation of the Orange order (1795), however, liberal Irish protestants sought to switch the main focus of Irish national celebrations from the Williamite anniversaries, which were now becoming seen as sectarian, to St Patrick's day. On 15 March 1825 a newspaper reflecting their views, the *Dublin Evening Post*, urged on 'the Orangemen of Ireland': 'however divided we may be in sentiments, in politics, in religion, let us never forget that we are *one nation*. … We shall all celebrate on Thursday next, the anniversary of our national saint' (Hill, 47). The Orangemen paid no heed, but from 1829 the viceroy made a formal appearance before the crowds in Dublin on St Patrick's day; and in subsequent years the playing of 'our Irish national anthem "St Patrick's Day"' alongside 'God Save the Queen' became a regular feature (*Freeman's Journal*, 18 March 1857; quoted in Hill, 48). Thus the viceroy, with shamrock in his hat, bridged the gulf between élite and popular celebrations and St Patrick's day became the major national anniversary recognized by the state in Ireland.

In the aftermath of the famine, however, St Patrick again became a figure of contention between protestant and Catholic ecclesiastics. J. H. Todd's *St Patrick, Apostle of Ireland* (1864), for all its virtues, sought 'to make St Patrick a precursor of the Established Church, of which he himself was a minister', in the manner of Ussher (Bieler, *Life*, 17). Catholic writers reverted to the Patrick of the medieval lives, or produced emotional sectarian hymns identifying the Catholics as St Patrick's children, the 'true Irish'. In the political sphere, the National Brotherhood of St Patrick, founded in Dublin in 1861 initially (after the model of the American Friendly Sons of St Patrick) to provide a common social organization for all nationalists, was immediately drawn into the Fenian penumbra. Within a few years it was effectively supplanted by the Irish Republican Brotherhood, which took over many of its British branches wholesale. At the same time 'God Save Ireland', written in honour of two Fenian heroes (the 'Manchester martyrs' of 1867), superseded 'St Patrick's Day' as the unofficial national anthem.

Meanwhile the celebration of St Patrick's day overseas had outstripped the relatively simple celebrations of his day in Ireland. Irish people abroad gathered together to celebrate their patron saint convivially, with many a toast; and the first St Patrick's day parade on record occurred in New York in 1762, when some Irish militiamen spontaneously decided to march behind their band with their regimental banners flying, *en route* to a St Patrick's day celebration. Thus began the tradition of St Patrick's day parades. Initially, celebrations were dominated by protestants of Ulster extraction who were loyal to Britain. It was only when America had won its independence, and after the suppression of the 1798 rising and subsequent Act of Union, that the ethos changed and toasts were drunk to Ireland's total emancipation from Britain. Boston initiated its St Patrick's day parade in 1812, and other American cities followed suit in the nineteenth and twentieth centuries. So too did Australia and other countries, although there, ambiguities of loyalty to Britain as well as Ireland were found. In America, the mid-nineteenth-century flood of Irish Catholic émigrés, reluctant exiles from their homeland, led to the St Patrick's day celebrations being charged with a nationalistic and nostalgic fervour. Today, the New York parade on St Patrick's day can see 100,000 people marching down Fifth Avenue, watched by a million onlookers, while bars offer green beer, and even Chinese restaurants serve green rice. Meanwhile, in distant Texas, the citizens of San Antonio dye the river green for the day!

In the twentieth century, the St Patrick's day parade was exported to Ireland itself. In Dublin, the taoiseach and the lord mayor review a parade of floats passing down O'Connell Street, while parades are found in many other towns, including Belfast in Northern Ireland. That has a nationalist, republican flavour. However, Church of Ireland protestants also celebrate the feast of Ireland's apostle in their own, less flamboyant way; and there is an ecumenical service at Downpatrick, the traditional site of Patrick's burial. Thus St Patrick continues to be recognized as the patron saint of Ireland by all Irish people, Catholic and protestant alike, although the different traditions still maintain their distinctive images of the national saint.

CLARE STANCLIFFE

Sources THE HISTORICAL PATRICK *Libri epistolarum Sancti Patricii episcopi*, ed. L. Bieler, 2 vols. in 1 (1993) [first pubd in *Classica and Mediaevalia*, 11 (1950), 1–150; 12 (1951), 79–215] · *Saint Patrick: Confession et lettre à Coroticus: introduction, texte critique, traduction et notes*, ed. R. P. C. Hanson, Sources Chrétiennes, 249 (1978) · *St Patrick: his writings and Muirchu's Life*, ed. and trans. A. B. E. Hood (1978) · *Gli scritti di san Patrizio: alle origini del cristianesimo irlandese*, ed. and trans. E. Malaspina (1985) [incl. discussion of dubious works; notes on Patrick's writings] · *Liber epistolarum Sancti Patricii episcopi: the book of letters of Saint Patrick the bishop*, ed. and trans. D. R. Howlett (1994) [incl. literal trans.] · *The works of St Patrick*, ed. and trans. L. Bieler (1953) · R. P. C. Hanson, ed. and trans., *The life and writings of the historical Saint Patrick* (1983) · L. Bieler, *The life and legend of St Patrick* (1949) · D. N. Dumville and others, *Saint Patrick, AD 493–1993* (1993) [incl. analysis of *Epistola* and annalistic evidence] · D. A.

Binchy, 'Patrick and his biographers: ancient and modern', *Studia Hibernica*, 2 (1962), 7–173 · T. F. O'Rahilly, *The two Patricks* (1942) · R. P. C. Hanson, *Saint Patrick: his origins and career* (1968) · E. Malaspina, *Patrizio e l'acculturazione latina dell'Irlanda* (1984) · E. A. Thompson, *Who was Saint Patrick?* (1985) · L. Bieler, *Studies on the life and legend of St Patrick*, ed. R. Sharpe (1986) · L. Bieler, *St Patrick and the coming of Christianity* (1967), vol. 1/1 of *A history of Irish Catholicism* · P. Dronke, 'St Patrick's reading', *Cambridge Medieval Celtic Studies*, 1 (1981), 21–38 · M. Herren, 'Mission and monasticism in the *Confessio* of Patrick', *Sages, saints and storytellers: Celtic studies in honour of Professor James Carney*, ed. D. Ó Corráin, L. Breatnach, and K. McCone (1989), 76–85 · D. S. Nerney, 'A study of St Patrick's sources', *Irish Ecclesiastical Record*, 71 (1949), 497–507 · D. S. Nerney, 'A study of St Patrick's sources', *Irish Ecclesiastical Record*, 72 (1950), 14–26, 97–110, 265–80 · C. Mohrmann, *The Latin of Saint Patrick* (1961) · C. E. Stancliffe, 'Kings and conversion: some comparisons between the Roman mission to England and Patrick's to Ireland', *Frühmittelalterliche Studien*, 14 (1980), 59–94 · C. E. Stancliffe, review-article of E. A. Thompson's *Who was Saint Patrick?*, *Nottingham Medieval Studies*, 31 (1987), 125–32 · R. Sharpe, 'Saint Mauchteus, *discipulus Patricii*', *Britain, 400–600: language and history*, ed. A. Bammesberger and A. Wollmann (1990), 85–93 · R. Sharpe, 'Some problems concerning the organization of the church in early medieval Ireland', *Peritia*, 3 (1984), 230–70 · H. Atsma, 'Klöster und Mönchtum im Bistum Auxerre bis zum Ende des 6. Jahrhunderts', *Francia*, 11 (1983), 1–96 · P. Grosjean, 'Notes d'hagiographie celtique, §10: quand fut composée la Confession de S. Patrice?', *Analecta Bollandiana*, 63 (1945), 100–11 · P. Grosjean, 'Dominicati rethorici', *Bulletin du Cange: Archivum Latinitatis Medii Aevi*, 25 (1955), 41–6 · L. Bieler, 'St Patrick and the British church', *Christianity in Britain, 300–700*, ed. M. W. Barley and R. P. C. Hanson (1968), 123–30 · C. Thomas, 'Saint Patrick and fifth-century Britain: an historical model explored', *The end of Roman Britain* [Durham 1978], ed. P. J. Casey (1979), 81–101 · C. Thomas, *Christianity in Roman Britain to AD 500* (1981) · T. M. Charles-Edwards, 'The social background to Irish *peregrinatio*', *Celtica*, 11 (1976), 43–59 · T. M. Charles-Edwards, 'Palladius, Prosper, and Leo the Great: mission and primatial authority', in D. N. Dumville and others, *Saint Patrick, AD 493–1993* (1993), 1–12 · D. Howlett, 'Ex saliva scripturae meae', *Sages and storytellers: Celtic studies in honour of Professor James Carney*, ed. D. Ó Corráin, L. Breatnach, and K. McCone (1989), 86–101 · K. Hughes, *The church in early Irish society* (1966) · D. Greene, 'Some linguistic evidence relating to the British church', *Christianity in Britain, 300–700*, ed. M. W. Barley and R. P. C. Hanson (1968), 75–86 · D. N. Dumville, 'Some British aspects of the earliest Irish Christianity', *Irland und Europa: die Kirche im Frühmittelalter*, ed. P. Ní Chatháin and M. Richter (1984), 16–24 · D. Flanagan, 'The Christian impact on early Ireland: place-names evidence', *Irland und Europa: die Kirche im Frühmittelalter*, ed. P. Ní Chatháin and M. Richter (1984), 25–51 · E. G. Bowen, *Saints, seaways and settlements in the Celtic lands* (1969) · J. Carney, *The problem of St Patrick* (1961) · J. B. Bury, *The life of St Patrick* (1905) [incl. discussion of sources] · A. L. F. Rivet and C. Smith, *The place-names of Roman Britain* (1979) · E. Hogan, *Onomasticon Goedelicum locorum et tribuum Hiberniae et Scotiae* (1910) · R. A. Markus, 'Chronicle and theology: Prosper of Aquitaine', *The inheritance of historiography, 350–900*, ed. C. Holdsworth and T. P. Wiseman (1986), 31–43 SUBSEQUENT CULT, LIVES, AND TRADITIONS L. Bieler, ed. and trans., *The Patrician texts in the Book of Armagh*, Scriptores Latini Hiberniae, 10 (1979) [text of *Liber angeli* and the lives by Muirchú and Tírechán] · W. Stokes, ed. and trans., *The tripartite life of Patrick, with other documents relating to that saint*, 2 vols., Rolls Series, 89 (1887) · K. Mulchrone, ed. and trans., *Bethu Phátraig: the tripartite life of Patrick* (1939) [Irish text only] · *Four Latin lives of St Patrick: Colgan's 'Vita secunda, quarta, tertia and quinta'*, ed. L. Bieler (1971) · Jocelin of Furness, 'Vita sancti Patricii', *Acta sanctorum: Martius*, 2 (Antwerp, 1688), 540–80 · *Gir. Camb. opera*, vol. 5 · D. Binchy, *Corpus iuris Hibernici* (1978) [incl. surviving remnants of the *Senchas Már*] · R. I. Best and O. Bergin, eds., *Lebor na hUidre / Book of the dun cow* (1929),

278–87 [The phantom chariot of Cú Chulainn] · W. Stokes, ed., *The colloquy of the ancients, Irische Texte*, ed. W. Stokes and E. Windisch, iv. 1 (1900) [see also S. H. O'Grady, *Silva Gadelica* (1892)] · C. Doherty, 'The cult of St Patrick and the politics of Armagh in the seventh century', *Ireland and northern France, AD 600–850*, ed. J.-M. Picard (1991), 53–94 · R. Sharpe, 'St Patrick and the see of Armagh', *Cambridge Medieval Celtic Studies*, 4 (1982), 33–59 · R. Sharpe, 'Armagh and Rome in the seventh century', *Irland und Europa: die Kirche im Frühmittelalter*, ed. P. Ní Catháin and M. Richter (1984), 58–72 · R. Sharpe, 'Palaeographical considerations in the study of the Patrician documents in the Book of Armagh', *Scriptorium*, 36 (1982), 3–28 · *Liber Ardmachanus: the Book of Armagh*, ed. J. Gwynn (1913) [diplomatic edn with introduction] · K. McCone, 'An introduction to early Irish saints' lives', *Maynooth Review*, 11 (1984), 26–59 · L. de Paor, 'The aggrandisement of Armagh', *Historical studies: papers read before the Irish conference of historians*, ed. T. D. Williams, 8 [1971], 95–110 · L. Bieler, *Codices Patriciani Latini: a descriptive catalogue of Latin manuscripts relating to St Patrick* (1942) · L. Gougaud, *Les saints irlandais hors d'Irlande: étudiés dans le culte et dans la dévotion traditionnelle* (1936) · M. MacNeill, *The festival of Lughnasa*, 2 vols. (1962) · M. Haren and Y. de Pontfarcy, eds., *The medieval pilgrimage to St Patrick's Purgatory: Lough Derg and the European tradition* (1988) · Y. de Pontfarcy, 'Le *Tractatus de purgatorio sancti Patricii* de H. de Saltrey: sa date et ses sources', *Peritia*, 3 (1984), 460–80 · P. Harbison, 'St Patrick's pilgrimages', *Pilgrimage in Ireland* (1991), 55–70 · C. Bourke, *Patrick: the archaeology of a saint* (1993) · B. Cunningham and R. Gillespie, '"The most adaptable of saints": the cult of St Patrick in the seventeenth century', *Archivium Hibernicum*, 49 (1995), 82–104 · J. R. Hill, 'National festivals, the state and "protestant ascendancy" in Ireland, 1790–1829', *Irish Historical Studies*, 24 (1984–5), 30–51 · A. Hopkin, *The living legend of St Patrick* (1989) · P. Seaby and P. F. Purvey, *Coins of Scotland, Ireland & the islands* (1984), vol. 2 of *Standard catalogue of British coins* · K. Danaher, *The year in Ireland* (1972) · E. P. Shirley, 'Extracts from the journal of Thomas Dineley, esquire, giving some account of his visit to Ireland in the reign of Charles II', *Journal of the Kilkenny and South-East of Ireland Archaeological Society*, new ser., 1 (1858), 143–6, 170–88 · E. MacNeill, *Saint Patrick* (1964) · H. Moisl, 'The church and the native tradition of learning in early medieval Ireland', *Irland und die Christenheit: Bibelstudien und Mission*, ed. P. Ní Catháin and M. Richter (1987), 258–71 · K. McCone, *Pagan past and Christian present in early Irish literature* (1990) [includes discussion of stories relating Patrick to native traditions] · L. Abrams, 'St Patrick and Glastonbury Abbey: *nihil ex nihilo fit?*', in D. N. Dumville and others, *Saint Patrick, AD 493–1993* (1993), 233–42 · R. Sharpe, *Medieval Irish saints' lives: an introduction to Vitae sanctorum Hiberniae* (1991) · A. Ford, '"Standing one's ground": religion, polemic and Irish history since the Reformation', *As by law established: the Church of Ireland since the Reformation*, ed. A. Ford, J. McGuire, and K. Milne (1995), 1–14, 223–7 · R. V. Comerford, *The Fenians in context: Irish politics and society, 1848–82* (1985) · L. J. Litvack, 'The psychology of song, the theology of hymn: songs and hymns of the Irish migration', *Religion and indentity*, ed. P. O'Sullivan, The Irish World Wide: History, Heritage, Identity, 5 (1996), 70–89 · O. MacDonagh, 'Irish culture and nationalism translated: St Patrick's day, 1888, in Australia', *Irish culture and nationalism, 1750–1950*, ed. O. MacDonagh, W. F. Mandle, and P. Travers (1983), 69–83 · P. Alter, 'Symbols of Irish nationalism', *Studia Hibernica*, 14 (1974), 104–23 · B. de Breffny, *In the steps of St Patrick* (1982) · J. F. Kenney, *The sources for the early history of Ireland* (1929), 165–9, 319–50 · C. Plummer, *Miscellanea hagiographica Hibernica* (1925), 219–22 · M. Lapidge and R. Sharpe, *A bibliography of Celtic-Latin literature, 400–1200* (1985), 9–11, 83–5, 103–8, 283–4, 317 · F. J. Byrne and P. Francis, 'Two lives of St Patrick: Vita Secunda and Vita Quarta', *Journal of the Royal Society of the Antiquaries of Ireland*, 124 (1994), 5–117 · D. N. Dumville, 'St Patrick in Cornwall? The origin and transmission of Vita Tertia S. Patricii', *A Celtic Florilegium: studies in memory of Brendan O Hehir*, ed. K. A. Klar, E. E. Sweetser, and C. Thomas (1996), 1–7 · B. McCormack, *Perceptions of St Patrick in eighteenth-century Ireland* (2000)

Patrick [Patricius, Gilla Pátraic] (d. **1084**), bishop of Dublin, was elected bishop in 1074, following the death of Dúnán (or Donatus), by the clergy and people of Dublin, who sent a letter to Lanfranc, archbishop of Canterbury, requesting his consecration. Lanfranc consecrated him in the fourth year of his pontificate, that is after 29 August 1074, in London. Patrick made a profession of obedience to Lanfranc as *Britanniarum primas* ('primate of the Britains') and was sent back to Ireland with letters to Guthric (Gofraid), king of Dublin, and Toirdelbach Ua Briain, king of Munster and overking of Dublin. Five poems and a prose tract in Latin, *De tribus habitaculis animae* ('On the three dwelling places of the soul'), are attributed to Patrick, from glosses on which it may be deduced that before his elevation to the see of Dublin he had been a monk of the Benedictine community at Worcester during the abbacy of Wulfstan. The name Patricius also occurs in a list of Worcester monks preserved in the Durham *Liber vitae*. Patrick was drowned, along with a number of companions, while crossing the Irish Sea (whether to or from Ireland is unknown) on 10 October 1084. His poem *Mirabilia Hiberniae* ('The wonders of Ireland') was based on an Irish vernacular text.

M. T. FLANAGAN

Sources *The writings of Bishop Patrick, 1074–1084*, ed. A. Gwynn, Scriptores Latini Hiberniae, 1 (1955) · M. Richter, ed., *Canterbury professions*, CYS, 67 (1973), no. 36 · *The letters of Lanfranc, archbishop of Canterbury*, ed. and trans. H. Clover and M. Gibson, OMT (1979), nos. 9, 10 · *The whole works of … James Ussher*, ed. C. R. Elrington and J. H. Todd, 17 vols. (1847–64), vol. 4, pp. 488–9, 564 · J. Earle, ed., *Two of the Saxon chronicles parallel: with supplementary extracts from the others*, rev. C. Plummer, 1 (1892), 289 · J. T. Gilbert, ed., *Chartularies of St Mary's Abbey, Dublin: with the register of its house at Dunbrody and annals of Ireland*, 2, Rolls Series, 80 (1884), 249–50 · *Ann. Ulster*, s.a. 1084 · [A. H. Thompson], ed., *Liber vitae ecclesiae Dunelmensis*, SurtS, 136 (1923), fol. 22r

Patrick, fourth earl of Dunbar (d. **1232**), magnate, was the son of *Waltheof, earl of Lothian (d. 1182), and his wife, Alina (d. 1179). The best documented of the early Dunbar earls, he makes his first appearance on the record about 1178, when he witnessed a royal charter as 'the son of Earl Waltheof'. When he succeeded, upon the death of his father, Patrick was the first to take the title 'earl of Dunbar', his predecessors having been styled 'of Lothian'. He also succeeded to the lordship of Beanley and other lands in Northumberland, which a document of 1212 reveals were held for the service of 'inborh and utborh', that is, the earls of Dunbar apparently had to regulate border disputes. These English lands engendered much litigation: in 1187 Patrick deprived a vassal of his lands of Dercester (modern Darnchester), in Berwickshire, and in 1226–7 he was involved in a dispute over tallage from the Middeltons.

Earl Patrick was among the most prominent of the Scottish magnates and was a frequent witness to the acts of *William the Lion between c.1178 and c.1210. When King William fell ill in 1195 and attempted to settle the succession upon Otto of Saxony, the proposed husband of the king's daughter Margaret, Patrick was in the forefront of the opposition to the scheme; but the king's recovery negated the need for immediate action. Earl Patrick was among those nobles from both England and Scotland present in November of 1200 when King William performed homage to King John at Lincoln. In 1221 he again accompanied a Scottish king to England: this time the monarch was *Alexander II, and Patrick was present at York for his marriage to Joan (Joanna), the sister of Henry III. The fact that at the end of John's reign he temporarily forfeited his lands in Northumberland suggests that Patrick had previously associated himself with Alexander's claims upon the northern counties of England. Roger of Howden, who described Earl Patrick's role in rebuilding the bridge at Berwick following its destruction in 1199, called him 'warden [*custos*] of Berwick and … chief Justiciar of the whole kingdom of the Scots' (Anderson, *Scottish Annals*, 322). Three royal charters, dating from 1195 to 1205 or 1206, style him *Justicia*, but since Earl Duncan (II) of Fife was chief justice at that time, Patrick was probably justice of Lothian, an office in existence by the late twelfth century. The reference to Patrick as *custos* of Berwick suggests that he held a prominent place in the community of the burgh and a position of responsibility on the Anglo-Scottish border. Like his ancestors, he endowed several monastic houses. He confirmed earlier grants and patronized the monks of Coldingham and Melrose as well as the canons of Dryburgh. But his relationship with the monasteries was often tempestuous, and led to a number of disputes. The best-known of these commenced in 1207, when Patrick had a falling-out with Melrose Abbey over a pasture on the Leader Water which was only resolved in 1208 with papal intervention.

In 1184 Patrick married Ada, the daughter of King William the Lion, providing a good indication of his high social status. Ada predeceased her husband in 1200, but the couple had several sons—Patrick, who succeeded as earl, William, Robert, and Fergus—and more than one daughter, for documents refer to all his sons and daughters. Some time after the death of his first wife, Patrick married Christina, the widow of William de Brus (*d.* 1211/12), but they are not known to have had any children. The chronicle of Melrose offers a touching portrayal of Patrick's death in 1232. It relates how, after celebrating Christmas with his children and kinsmen, Patrick was afflicted by a serious illness. He then:

> summoned Adam, the abbot of Melrose, his friend and kinsman; and he received from him the last unction, and the habit of religion. And bidding a last farewell to all, he closed his last day on the day of St Silvester [31 December], in the fiftieth year of his earldom. (Anderson, *Early Sources*, 2.486)

Patrick was buried in the Cistercian nunnery at Eccles and was succeeded by his son, Patrick, who had probably controlled the earldom for some years before his ageing father's death.   ANDREW MCDONALD

Sources A. O. Anderson, ed. and trans., *Early sources of Scottish history, AD 500 to 1286*, 2 vols. (1922); repr. with corrections (1990) · A. O. Anderson, ed., *Scottish annals from English chroniclers, AD 500 to 1286* (1908) · *CDS*, vol. 1 · G. W. S. Barrow, ed., *The acts of William I, king of Scots, 1165–1214* (1971) · A. A. M. Duncan, *Scotland: the making of the kingdom* (1975), vol. 1 of *The Edinburgh history of Scotland*, ed. G. Donaldson (1965–75) · J. Hodgson, *A history of Northumberland*, 3 pts in 7 vols. (1820–58), vol. 7 · *Scots peerage*, vol. 3 · W. P. Hedley, *Northumberland families*, 1, Society of Antiquaries of Newcastle upon Tyne, Record Series (1968) · W. W. Scott, 'The march laws reconsidered', *Medieval Scotland: crown, lordship and community*, ed. A. Grant and K. Stringer (1993), 114–30 · [C. Innes], ed., *Liber sancte Marie de Melros*, 2 vols., Bannatyne Club, 56 (1837) · *APS*, 1124–1423 · J. Raine, *The history and antiquities of north Durham* (1852) · G. W. S. Barrow, *The kingdom of the Scots* (1973), 83–138

Archives University of Guelph Archives, autotypes of charters, etc. collected by Sir Archibald Hamilton Dunbar

Patrick, fifth earl of Atholl (*c*.1222–1242). *See under* Thomas, earl of Atholl (*d.* 1231).

Patrick, James McIntosh (1907–1998), painter and etcher, was born on 4 February 1907 at 12 Muirfield Crescent, Dundee, the second son and youngest of four children of Andrew Graham Patrick (1864–1951), architect, and his wife, Helen Moncur McIntosh, *née* Anderson (1866–1953). He was educated at the Morgan Academy, Dundee (1912–24), where he began drawing seriously and experimenting with etching before going to Glasgow School of Art (1924–8). Owing to his precocity, he was admitted immediately into the second year of the four-year course, which he then followed with a year's postgraduate diploma study. He won many prizes at the college. These, coupled with work during the 1926 general strike, helped to finance a summer in Provence. The on-the-spot sketches made at this time became the source for an impressive group of etchings of Carcassonne, Avignon, Nîmes, and other medieval hilltowns: *Les Baux* was exhibited at the Royal Academy, London, in 1928. The assured design and strength of draughtsmanship displayed in these works attracted attention, and by the time he left Glasgow Patrick had signed a contract with Harold Dickins, one of London's leading print dealers and publishers. The Provençal etchings, strongly influenced by Patrick's admiration for the Italian Quattrocento, were followed by a series based on the Scottish landscape, most notably the dramatic scenery of Glencoe, in which nature is depicted with awesome grandeur.

The etching market collapsed in 1929 with the Wall Street crash, and did not revive for half a century, so Patrick, like other young etchers of his generation—such as Sutherland, Badmin, and Tunnicliffe—was forced to seek alternative sources of income. He found a ready market for drawings of local landmarks, which were published in the *Dundee Courier*, and in 1930 became a part-time teacher at Dundee College of Art. He also turned to oil painting, and recycled some of his earlier subject matter by exhibiting *The Church of St Francis, Assisi* (National Gallery of South Africa) at the Royal Academy in 1931, his most ambitious work to date. Three years later the academy inexplicably rejected one of his finest early works, *The Pass of Glencoe* (1933–4), as a result of which Harold Dickins introduced him to E. P. Dawbarn, managing director of the Fine Art Society in London's New Bond Street, who remained his principal dealers for the rest of his life. This first essay into Scottish landscape painting was followed by a successful series of the four seasons, each of which found a permanent home in a public gallery: *Winter in Angus*, painted in 1935, was purchased by the Chantrey Bequest for the Tate

Gallery, followed by *Springtime in Eskdale* (Walker Art Gallery, Liverpool), *Midsummer in East Fife* (Aberdeen Art Gallery) and *Autumn in Kinordy* (McManus Gallery, Dundee). Although *The Pass of Glencoe*, a snow-bound and desolate scene, is starved of human life, the landscapes which followed were of a more pastoral nature and celebrated the impact that man had had on nature: the influence of Breughel was now mixed with that of the earlier Italians.

On 4 July 1933, with his reputation increasing and his income underpinned by part-time teaching, Patrick married Janet Rosalind Winifred Watterston (1904–1983). They had two children: Andrew (b. 1935), who joined the Fine Art Society and later became its managing director and Ann (b. 1937), who became a painter. The steady flow of fine Scottish landscapes painted throughout the decade enabled Patrick in 1939 to purchase The Shrubbery, 67 Magdalen Yard Road, Dundee, a handsome Georgian house overlooking the Tay Bridge. The price was affordable because other potential buyers regarded the area as a prime target for German bombs. The house remained Patrick's home for the rest of his life, and from its windows he painted two of his most celebrated canvases: *A City Garden* (1939) and *The Tay Bridge from my Studio Window* (1948), both now in the McManus Gallery, Dundee. Called up in 1940, Patrick was trained initially as a tank driver before being commissioned in the camouflage corps, where his knowledge of the countryside was appreciated more than his artistic ability. He spent much time close to the fighting in north Africa and Italy, latterly at Capua, where he helped train other camouflage officers. Never employed as an official war artist, he was given no facilities for painting; sketchbook, pen, ink, and watercolour, rather than oils and canvas, became his constant companions, with the result that a new and direct naturalism superseded the studied studio painting of earlier years. One hundred of these watercolours—depicting views in north Africa, Italy, Scotland, and Yorkshire—were exhibited at the Fine Art Society in 1946, and well over half were sold.

In post-war Scotland Patrick resumed landscape painting, but his approach had changed dramatically; this, coupled with the visual stimulation of Glasgow's 1948 Van Gogh exhibition, confirmed his decision to paint out of doors. From then on, Patrick and his easel became a familiar sight in lanes and fields around Dundee. He was elected an associate of the Royal Scottish Academy in 1949, and a full member eight years later, but for much of the next thirty years he had to endure critical neglect, though Dundee University awarded him an honorary doctorate of laws in 1973. The public, however, remained sympathetic and in tune with his vision, as was handsomely borne out by his retrospective exhibition in 1987, mounted by Dundee Art Gallery to celebrate his eightieth birthday; this travelled to Aberdeen and Liverpool, attracting 100,000 visitors. Patrick's ninetieth birthday was marked by an equally popular exhibition, this time at the National Gallery of Modern Art in Edinburgh. He was awarded an honorary doctorate of arts by Abertay University in 1995 and created OBE in the 1997 new year honours list. He died at his home, The Shrubbery, on 7 April 1998 and was cremated eight days later: his ashes were scattered in the Carse of Gowrie, the subject of many of his paintings. He was survived by his son and daughter, his wife having predeceased him.

PEYTON SKIPWITH

Sources R. Billcliffe, *James McIntosh Patrick* (1987) • R. Thompson, *Easel in the field* (2000) • *The Scotsman* (9 April 1998) • *The Scotsman* (11 July 1998) • *The Times* (11 April 1998) • *Daily Telegraph* (16 April 1998) • *The Independent* (29 April 1998) • personal knowledge (2004) • private information (2004) [family]
Archives Scottish National Gallery of Modern Art, Edinburgh
Likenesses photograph, repro. in *The Scotsman* (9 April 1998) • photograph, repro. in *The Times* • photograph, repro. in *The Independent* • photograph, repro. in *The Scotsman* (11 July 1998)
Wealth at death £950,000: private information (2004) • £945,516.17: confirmation, 1998, Scotland, *CCI*

Patrick, Jane Hamilton [*known as* Jenny] (**1884–1971**), anarchist, was born on 11 February 1884 at 43 Dalhousie Street, Glasgow, the daughter of John Crawford Patrick, a 'ladies' costumier', and his wife, Elizabeth *née* Hamilton. Her father had a shop in Sauchiehall Street and the family lived in nearby Garnethill. Her mother died in childbirth, and her father immediately remarried. His family eventually numbered three girls and three boys; in worst stepmother tradition his second wife attired her own daughter in finery but Jane in cast-offs.

Jane Patrick attended Garnethill School. At fourteen she left and got a job as a copy-holder in a printer's in St Vincent Street, reading the copy while the printer corrected it. At sixteen she became a typesetter, arranging single letters into a composing stick and imposing them into a forme. Later she was employed as a printer by a footwear company.

Jane Patrick joined the Glasgow Anarchist Group in 1914, and became secretary in 1916, at a time when meetings required a lookout to warn of military patrols looking for deserters. In 1920 the group renamed itself the Glasgow Communist Group (GCG), hoping to unite with the growing communist movement on the basis of genuine (and, of necessity, anti-parliamentary) communism. However, in January 1921 much of the revolutionary left adopted the Comintern's pro-parliamentary strategy by uniting with the Communist Party of Great Britain (CPGB).

To revitalize the anti-parliamentary cause, the GCG published the *Red Commune* in February 1921, with Jenny Patrick (as she was usually known) chairing the anonymous five-person editorial board. Its uncompromising call was to 'work outside Parliament on the streets and in the workshops for the revolution' (*Red Commune*, vol. 1, no. 1), and to employ the 'Sinn Féin' or 'boycott of parliament' tactic. It was immediately seized by the Glasgow police, and Jenny Patrick, along with three others, was charged with sedition. She was sentenced to three months in gaol.

Despite the arrests Easter 1921 saw the formation of the Anti-Parliamentary Communist Federation (APCF). Jenny Patrick became its secretary. Throughout the 1920s she worked alongside its chief figure, Guy Aldred (1886–1963), to maintain a vigorous anarchist and anti-parliamentary presence in Glasgow. They entered a free union, at first living in a flat in Bakunin House (13 Burnbank Gardens), the headquarters of the APCF. Jenny ran the domestic side and supervised the printing operation in the basement. When in 1933 Aldred left the APCF to form the United Socialist Movement (USM), they took a room at 5 Balliol Street, Glasgow, where they stayed for the rest of their lives.

In 1936 Jenny Patrick went to Spain with Ethel MacDonald at the request of the CNT–FAI (the anarchist federations). Jenny served in Madrid with the CNT–FAI's Comité de Défense, editing the English section of their paper *Frente Libertario*, and experiencing the siege of Madrid. In 1937 she moved to Barcelona to take charge of the CNT's English radio and bulletin. With Ethel she experienced the momentous May days. Her eyewitness accounts of 'the murderous Communist Party counter-revolutionary conspiracy against the Anarchists' were rushed into print in Glasgow by Aldred in a special *Barcelona Bulletin* on 12 May 1937.

On her return Jenny Patrick joined with Aldred, Ethel MacDonald, and John Caldwell in setting up the Strickland Press in 1939 at 104–6 George Street. Here her experience as a printer was invaluable. For twenty-five years Jenny Patrick and the others worked long wageless hours, printing socialist and anarchist literature, notably the USM's *The Word*. In 1945, however, Jenny Patrick and Ethel MacDonald became involved in a dispute with the Scottish Typographical Association (STA). Although a time-served compositor, Jenny Patrick was not allowed to join the STA. As the Strickland Press refused to employ additional union labour, and Jenny Patrick and Ethel MacDonald insisted on their right to work for it, deadlock ensued. The STA imposed a boycott, whereupon, unable to contract it out, Jenny Patrick and Ethel MacDonald did the typesetting themselves.

Jenny Patrick outlived Ethel MacDonald and Guy Aldred, dying on 1 September 1971 at Drumchapel Hospital, Glasgow. She was cremated at Maryhill crematorium, Glasgow. A small woman, she was respected for her dynamic personality and resolute character. She never sought the limelight, but endured poverty and hardship for the sake of her anarchist principles.

JOHN T. CALDWELL and BOB JONES

Sources personal knowledge (2004) · J. T. Caldwell, *Come dungeons dark: the life and times of Guy Aldred* (1988) · G. A. Aldred, *Rex v. Aldred: London trial, 1909, Indian sedition, Glasgow sedition trial, 1921* (1948) · *Red Commune*, 1/No.1 (Feb 1921) · *News from Spain* [Glasgow] (1 May 1937) · *Barcelona Bulletin* [Glasgow] (12 May 1937) · *Barcelona Bulletin* [Glasgow] (15 May 1937) · *Regeneracion* [Glasgow] (29 July–7 Oct 1936), 1–19 · *Regeneracion* [Glasgow], new ser., 1/1–4 (21 Feb–14 March 1937) · J. McGovern, *Neither fear nor favour* (1960) · *Daily Express* [Scottish edn] (17 Oct 1963) · *Spur*, 1–7 (1914–21) · *The Word* [Glasgow], 1–25 (1938–65) · *Workers' Free Press* [Glasgow], 1–3/4 (Sept–Nov/Dec 1937) · *Frente Libertario* [Madrid] (1936–7) · *Boletin de Informacion CNT–FAI* [Barcelona] (March–May 1937) · b. cert.
Archives Mitchell L., Glas., Guy Aldred collection
Likenesses P. Miller, drawing, priv. coll. · photographs, repro. in *News from Spain* · photographs, repro. in *Daily Express*, 21
Wealth at death £460 gross, £327 net: solicitor's statement of her estate and disbursement

Patrick, John (*bap.* 1632, *d.* 1695), Church of England clergyman and religious controversialist, was baptized on 19 April 1632 at Gainsborough, Lincolnshire, the second son of Henry Patrick (*bap.* 1596, *d.* 1665), mercer, and his wife, Mary Naylor (*d.* in or after 1665), of Nottinghamshire. He was the younger brother of Simon *Patrick, bishop of Ely. The civil war disrupted Patrick's schooling, but the family found refuge at Brocklesby Park, the home of Sir William Pelham. Patrick matriculated from Queens' College, Cambridge, on 10 July 1647, graduated BA in 1651, and proceeded MA in 1654. He served as vicar of Battersea for his brother during 1662–71, where 'he never took institution, but held it in my right, and had entirely all the profits' ('Autobiography of Symon Patrick', *Works*, 9.455). While serving that cure he appears to have had a brush with the plague as on 3 September 1665 he was taken 'very ill and vomited forty or fifty times' (ibid., 9.444). In November 1671 he asked his brother to use his interest to procure him the post of preacher at Charterhouse, London, which he did successfully, Patrick being chosen on 8 December. He conducted his first marriage ceremony there on 22 December 1671.

At Charterhouse Patrick began to publish his works, beginning with his *Reflexions upon the Devotions of the Roman Church* (1674). He also took time to conduct his brother's marriage ceremony on 1 June 1675 in Gloucestershire. *A Century of Select Psalms and Portions of the Psalms of David* (1679) was for the use of Charterhouse, and ran to many subsequent editions. He also contributed to *Plutarch's Morals Translated from the Greek by Several Hands* (1684–94). On 30 June 1685 he was collated a canon of Peterborough. In 1687 he published *Religion of Protestants a Safe Way to Salvation*. Also in 1687 he published *Transubstantiation No Doctrine of the Primitive Fathers*, and in 1688 *A Full View of the Doctrines and Practices of the Ancient Church*, both of which works were part of the Anglican resistance to James II's religious policies.

After the Revolution of 1688, with his brother now bishop of Chichester, on 28 July 1690 Patrick was collated precentor of that diocese. Presumably because of his publications defending the Church of England, Archbishop Tillotson made him DD by Lambeth decree in 1691. He conducted his last marriage at Charterhouse on 10 September 1695. When Patrick wrote his will on 6 December 1695 he was 'labouring under some bodily infirmities' (PRO, PROB 11/429, fol. 313); he died at Charterhouse on 19 December, and was buried there the same day. His monument states that 'his works praise him' (Willis, 2.517). He left his brother 'a noble library, which cost him above £1000, and all he was worth, except some legacies to some particular friends' ('Autobiography of Symon Patrick', *Works*, 9.541–2). These legacies included a clock to Lady Sarah Cowper, wife of Sir William Cowper, second baronet, and £500 to his sister, Mary, the wife of Robert Middleton, of Cornfield, Suffolk, clerk.

STUART HANDLEY

Sources *The works of Symon Patrick, DD*, ed. A. Taylor, 9 vols. (1858), vol. 1, pp. cliv–clvi · 'The Autobiography of Symon Patrick', *The works of Symon Patrick*, ed. A. Taylor (1858), vol. 9, pp. 407–569 ·

Venn, *Alum. Cant.* • will, PRO, PROB 11/429, fols. 313r–313v • F. Collins, ed., *The registers and monumental inscriptions of Charterhouse chapel*, Harleian Society, Register Section, 18 (1892), 1, 7, 52, 87 • B. Willis, *A survey of the cathedrals*, 3 vols. (1742), vol. 2, p. 517 • *Fasti Angl., 1541–1857*, [Bristol], 125 • *Fasti Angl., 1541–1857*, [Chichester], 11 • B. Marsh and F. A. Crisp, eds., *Alumni Carthusiani* (1913), 285 • Wood, *Ath. Oxon.: Fasti* (1820), 292
Archives CUL, papers
Wealth at death see will, PRO, PROB 11/429, fols. 313r–313v

Patrick, Millar (1868–1951), hymnologist and liturgist, was born on 28 June 1868 at Ladybank, Fife, son of James Patrick, a railway locomotive fireman, and his wife, Jessie Millar. They belonged to the United Presbyterian church, a Victorian union of Secession traditions within Scottish Presbyterianism. From Dundee high school he went to St Andrews University, where he graduated MA (1890), but he made his greatest impact as editor, manager, and driving force of the immensely successful *Scottish Students' Song Book* (1891).

Patrick combined this venture in high-minded conviviality with preparation for the ministry at the Edinburgh United Presbyterian College (1890–93), and, after an assistantship at Claremont, Glasgow, was ordained at Moat Park, Biggar. He moved in 1899 to Trinity, Ayr, a year before the United Presbyterians merged with the main part of the Free Church of Scotland, heirs of the 1843 Disruption, in the United Free Church of Scotland. Patrick married Jessie Tod (d. 1940) on 5 September 1905, and they had a daughter, Lois, and a son, Denzil. He was minister at Perth North (1907–14) and Ferryhill, Aberdeen (1914–17), though seconded for war service with the YMCA in France. Until retirement in 1938 he was at Craigmillar Park, Edinburgh, a minister of the Church of Scotland after the 1929 Presbyterian union.

By then Patrick, a St Andrews DD from 1924, had edited a United Free Church Book of Common Order (1928) and contributed to reunion through liturgical consultations and as co-editor of the handbook which accompanied publication, for several Presbyterian churches, of the *Revised Church Hymnary* (1928). He was a key member of the committee responsible for the hymnary itself, compiled before some splendours of Victorian hymnody began to seem dated, but drawing widely on English-language sources and translations, especially from German. Patrick also had a leading part in producing a new musical edition of the psalter (1929).

Patrick's amiable disposition helped merge the publishing of the two Presbyterian traditions, to which he contributed vigorously himself, especially in writing for *Life and Work*. As convener of the reunited church's African foreign missions subcommittee he also helped maintain the missionary traditions of the United Free Church. But his prominence in Church of Scotland affairs was as joint public worship committee convener and (1934–45) first convener of its new advisory committee on artistic matters, with the artist D. Y. Cameron as deputy. He saw this as an opportunity to add greater concern for the beauty of church buildings and furnishings to traditional Presbyterian concern for dignity.

Patrick brought to twentieth-century Scotland something of the open-mindedness and capacity to blend innovation with tradition which the United Presbyterians had contributed to Victorian Scotland—not only in theology but in musical enthusiasm and in commissions to such architects as Alexander ('Greek') Thomson. In liturgy and hymnody Patrick's passion was also to reconcile cherished traditions and styles with wider influences. He became a major force in the liturgical, musical, and artistic life of Scottish Presbyterianism and an authority on the history of Presbyterian worship, especially the metrical psalms.

Patrick's most important work was *Four Centuries of Scottish Psalmody* (1949). He recognized that only the best metrical psalms remained usable, but maintained that they expressed two unchanging principles: the 'right of the people to bear the main part in the musical acts of public worship' and that 'materials used in Church worship should all be taken from the Word of God' (Patrick, 51–2). Scholarly enthusiasm, transmitted through lectures at the Scottish divinity colleges, also extended his influence beyond Scotland and Presbyterianism. He was the first editor of the Hymn Society's *Bulletin* and edited a supplement to John Julian's *Dictionary of Hymnology* (1st edn, 1892).

Faith and scholarship sustained Patrick in age and as a widower. His wife died in 1940. Patrick enjoyed tercentenary celebrations for the definitive Scottish psalter in 1950 and died at 32 Westgarth Avenue, Colinton, Edinburgh, on 2 August 1951; he was cremated on 4 August, at Warriston crematorium, Edinburgh.   R. D. KERNOHAN

Sources J. A. Lamb, ed., *The fasti of the United Free Church of Scotland, 1900–1929* (1956) • *Fasti Scot.*, new edn, vol. 9 • *Life and Work* (Sept 1951), 188 • *DSCHT* • *The Scotsman* (3 Aug 1951) • *Scottish biographies* (1938) • M. Patrick, 'The psalter', *Life and Work* (1938), 51–2 • b. cert.
Archives U. Edin., New Coll. L., hymnology notes
Likenesses bronze plaque, 1936, U. St Andr., students' union • photograph, repro. in *Life and Work*, 188
Wealth at death £2506 3s. 4d.: confirmation, 13 Sept 1951, CCI

Patrick, Richard (1769–1815), classical scholar and Church of England clergyman, was the son of Richard Patrick of Kingston upon Hull, Yorkshire, where he was born. He was educated in the public school there before entering Magdalene College, Cambridge, as a sizar on 26 October 1786. He graduated BA in 1791 and MA in 1808; in 1794 he became vicar of Sculcoates, Hull. He also acted as chaplain to Anne, widow of George, first Marquess Townshend from 1809 to 1815. Patrick published anonymously *The Adventures of a Hull Eighteenpenny Token* (1811) and *Geographical, Commercial, and Political Essays* (1812). He also contributed several articles to the *Classical Journal*, including 'Remarks on Sir George Staunton's penal code of China' (1810, 2.381); 'The Chinese world' (1811, 3.16); and 'A chart of ten numerals' (4.105ff.), followed by a descriptive essay. The latter was reprinted separately in 1812 as *A Chart of Ten Numerals in Two Hundred Tongues, with a Descriptive Essay*. It is an attempt, on a basis of comparative philology, at classifying the races of the earth. To E. H. Barker's edition of

Cicero's *De senectute* and *De amicitia* of 1811 Patrick contributed:

> an appendix, in which will be found remarks on the origin of the Latin conjunctions and prepositions; also some curious matter on the affinity of different languages, oriental and northern, to the Latin, including two essays on the origin and the extinction of the Latin tongue.

He died, unmarried, at his vicarage on 9 February 1815 and was buried in the churchyard at Sculcoates under a monument prepared by himself.

W. A. SHAW, rev. REBECCA MILLS

Sources Venn, *Alum. Cant.* · H. R. Luard, ed., *Graduati Cantabrigienses*, 7th edn (1884), 318 · L. Baillie and P. Sieveking, eds., *British biographical archive* (1984) [microfiche] · *GM*, 1st ser., 64 (1794), 1210 · *GM*, 1st ser., 82/2 (1812), 467–8 · *N&Q*, 8th ser., 8 (1895), 443–4 · J. Tickell, *History of the town and county of Kingston upon Hull* (1796), 902 · Watt, *Bibl. Brit.*, 2.737f. · private information (1895) [A. G. Peskett, master, Magd. Cam.]

Patrick, Robert William Cochran- (1842–1897), politician, the only son of William Charles Richard Patrick (afterwards Cochran-Patrick) of Waterside, Ayrshire, and Agnes, eldest daughter of William Cochran of Ladyland and Belltrees, was born at Ladyland, Ayrshire, on 5 February 1842. Having received his early education from private tutors, he matriculated at Edinburgh University in 1857, where he secured prizes in classics, logic, and moral philosophy, graduating BA in 1861, and passing first in metaphysics and logic. In 1861 he entered Trinity Hall, Cambridge, where his friends included Henry Fawcett, Leslie Stephen, and Robert Romer. He became captain of one of the boats of the hall, and carried off the university challenge cup for walking and other athletic prizes. As a volunteer he shot in a winning four with Edward Ross, the first queen's prizeman, and was a member of the amateur dramatic club, then under the management of F. C. Burnand. In 1864 he graduated LLB. On leaving Cambridge, he returned to Edinburgh for a year, with a view to qualifying for the Scottish bar, an idea he soon abandoned.

On 31 October 1866 Cochran-Patrick married Eleanora, younger daughter of Robert Hunter of Hunterston, Ayrshire. She died in 1884 having borne a son, William Arthur (*d.* 1891) and a daughter, Eleanor Agnes, who married in 1895 Neil James Kennedy, advocate. On his marriage, Cochran-Patrick settled at Woodside in Ayrshire, a property left him by his great-uncle. With a strong bent for sport and natural history, he was in his element as a country gentleman, also throwing himself with vigour into local and county business. He became a captain in the militia, chairman of the parish school and parochial boards, served as convener of the finance committee of the county, and occupied other public posts.

Taking up the study of archaeology, Cochran-Patrick became a fellow of the Society of Antiquaries of Scotland, and contributed many papers to the *Proceedings* of the society. In 1871 he was elected a fellow of the Society of Antiquaries of London, and in 1874 he was sent to Stockholm to represent Great Britain at the International Congress of Archaeology. In 1874 he was one of the founders of the Ayrshire and Wigtownshire Archaeological Association.

Robert William Cochran-Patrick (1842–1897), by W. Graham Boss

To the collections of this society he contributed numerous articles. But it is as a numismatist that Cochran-Patrick is best known, and his collection of Scottish coins was well-nigh unrivalled. On this subject in 1876 he published his first book, entitled *Records of the Coinage of Scotland from the Earliest Period to the Union* (2 vols.). This he followed up in 1878 with *Early Records Relating to Mining in Scotland*, in which he gave an account of the discovery of gold in Scotland, and descriptions of the lead and silver mines. In 1884 he published his third work, *Catalogue of the Medals of Scotland*, containing a learned account of Scottish medals, of which he preserved the best collection then extant. He published several other works on Scottish coins, and *Medieval Scotland* (1892), a reprint of newspaper articles.

In 1880 Cochran-Patrick contested North Ayrshire as a Conservative, and defeated J. B. Balfour (afterwards first Baron Kinross) by fifty-five votes. He was a frequent speaker in parliament, especially on education matters. In 1885 he was defeated for North Ayrshire by H. F. Elliot. In 1886 he became assessor to St Andrews University, and in 1887 a commissioner to inquire into the working of the Scottish Education Act. Shortly afterwards he joined the fishery board of Scotland, and was granted the degree of LLD from Glasgow University for his scholarly attainments. In December 1887 he was appointed permanent under-secretary for Scotland, an office in which he rendered most valuable assistance in the promotion of Scottish business, notably the Local Government (Scotl.) Act, 1889. On 15 June 1892 he resigned his appointment owing to failing health, and retired to Woodside. In 1894 he acted as a commissioner to inquire into the Tweed and Solway salmon fisheries, visiting the border towns, taking evidence, and inspecting the rivers. In 1896 he became vice-chairman of the Scottish Fishery Board. As a freemason he was for many years provincial grand master of

Ayrshire. On 15 March 1897, after returning from a meeting of the fishery board in Edinburgh, he died suddenly of heart disease at Woodside. His son-in-law assumed the name of Cochran-Patrick in terms of the entail of the property. GEORGE STRONACH, *rev.* H. C. G. MATTHEW

Sources *The Scotsman* (16 March 1897) · *Glasgow Herald* (16 March 1897) · *Scottish Review* (Jan 1898)
Archives NRA Scotland, priv. coll., corresp. and papers | NA Scot., corresp. with Lord Lothian
Likenesses W. Graham Boss, drawing, Scot. NPG [*see illus.*]
Wealth at death £14,539 os. 4d.: confirmation, 29 Oct 1897

Patrick, Samuel (1684–1748), classical scholar, was for some years usher (that is, second master) at Charterhouse School. Patrick appears to have been a figure like Scott's Dominie Sampson, deeply read in the classics and ignorant and oblivious of most other matters. He established some reputation as a scholar by his translation of Terence's *Comedies* (1745) and his edition of Robert Ainsworth's *Latin Dictionary* (1746). He also edited *M. B. Hederici lexicon manuale Graecum* (1727), *C. Cellarii geographia antiqua* (6th edn, 1731), and collaborated with George Thompson in the preparation of his *Apparatus ad linguam Graecam ordine novo digestus* (1732). Late in life Patrick was apparently granted the degree of LLD from St Andrews University. He also took holy orders, but received no preferment. He was married, though nothing is known of his wife. He died at Kentish Town, Middlesex, on 20 March 1748. Recensions of the *Clavis Homerica* (1771) and the *Colloquia* of Erasmus (1773) also purport to be by him.

J. M. RIGG, *rev.* PHILIP CARTER

Sources Nichols, *Lit. anecdotes* · *Scots Magazine*, 10 (1748), 153 · *London Magazine*, 17 (1748), 141 · *GM*, 1st ser., 18 (1748), 139 · *N&Q*, 8th ser., 8 (1895), 444 · PRO, PROB 11/760, fol. 379r–v [will]

Patrick, Simon (d. 1613/14), translator, matriculated as a pensioner at Peterhouse, Cambridge, on 21 May 1561 and was a member of that college at the time of Queen Elizabeth's visit to the university in 1564. Nothing is known of Patrick's parents or family background, but in his will he describes himself as 'of Castor' (that is, Caistor, Lincolnshire) and he is known to have had connections with Grimsby and Gainsborough. In his will Patrick mentions a 'sister Thompson', as well as a brother, Richard, who also lived in Lincolnshire.

Patrick married three times. With his first wife, Mary Phesant, he had two sons, Simon and Vincent. Mary died in 1587 and was buried at Caistor on 4 December. Patrick and his second wife, Dorothea Cartwright, had nine children: William and Francis (both of whom died young), Edward, John, Henry (later the father of two distinguished churchmen, Simon Patrick, bishop of Ely, and John Patrick), Bridget (who died young), Thomas, Jane, and Mary. Dorothea died in September 1601 and was buried at Caistor. Patrick's third wife was Susan Moigne, sister of Thomas Moigne, later bishop of Kilmore and Ardagh; they had three children: Faith, Elizabeth, and Francis.

In 1602 Patrick published two translations, both from French originals. *The Estate of the Church, with the Discourse of Times, from the Apostles untill this Present*, dedicated to Sir William Wray of Glentworth, Lincolnshire, translates Jean de

Hainault's *L'état de l'église* (originally published in Calvinist Geneva), including the preface by Jean Crespin. Patrick's version follows the 1581 edition of *L'état de l'église*, with additions from other sources (for example, Conestaggio, Chytraeus, Génébrard) to supplement Hainault's brief account of the years 1577–9, and continues the history as far as 1600. Some of Patrick's material in this continuation derives from named sources, mostly works of history by continental scholars, but also English writers including John Hooker, alias Vowell, John Stow, and Richard Hakluyt. Some passages of English history in the continuation may be Patrick's own work. *A Discourse upon the Meanes of Wel Governing a Kingdome … Against Nicholas Machiavell* is a translation of the *Anti-Machiavel* of Innocent Gentillet. Patrick's version of the treatise follows the French edition of the *Anti-Machiavel*, published in Geneva in 1576, but his dedicatory epistle, dated August 1577 and addressed 'To the most famous yong gentlemen, as well for religion, modestie, and other vertues, as also for kinred, Francis Hastings and Edward Bacon', follows the preface to the 1578 Latin edition. The Latin translation of Gentillet had gone through three editions before the two editions of Patrick's translation (the second edition was published in 1608). Although ideas from Machiavelli's *The Prince* had begun to filter through before Gentillet and his refutation which reprinted so much of the original, the different versions of Gentillet were primarily responsible for giving these ideas so wide a circulation. It has been suggested that Patrick's translation of Gentillet may also have circulated in manuscript before print-publication. The apparent echoing of some passages from Patrick's translation in Anne Dowriche's *The French Historie* (1589) provides some evidence to support this theory. Patrick's religious interests are also apparent in his will where, leaving his books to be divided equally between his two eldest sons, he specifies only that Simon shall have his complete and Vincent his incomplete copy of the book of martyrs.

Patrick's will, dated 12 September 1613, was proved on 28 May 1614, by his son Vincent, at the prerogative court of Canterbury. It makes provision for his widow and leaves portions to all his surviving children. Vincent, his residual legatee, inherited his father's windmill.

GILLIAN WRIGHT

Sources *The works of Simon Patrick, including his autobiography*, ed. A. Taylor, 1, 9 (1858) · Cooper, *Ath. Cantab.*, vol. 2 · A. D'Andrea, 'Machiavelli, Satan and the gospel', *Yearbook of Italian Studies*, 1 (1971), 156–77 · A. D'Andrea, 'Geneva 1576–78: the Italian community and the myth of Italy', in J. McLelland, *Peter Martyr Vermigli and Italian reform* (1980), 53–63 · H. Cotton, *Fasti ecclesiae Hibernicae*, 2 (1848) · *Associated Architectural Societies' Reports and Papers*, 8/2 (1866) · D. Chytraeus, *Saxonia, ab anno Christi 1500 usque ad MDXCIX* (Leipzig, 1599) · I. Conestaggio, *Dell'unione del regno di Portogallo alla corona di Castiglia* (Venice, 1592) · G. Génébrard, *Chronographiae libri quatuor* (Paris, 1600) · parish register, Caistor, 4 Dec 1587 [burial, Mary Phesant] · parish register, Caistor, 20 Sept 1601 [burial, Dorothea Cartwright] · parish register, Caistor, 19 Dec 1602 [baptism, Faith Patrick] · R. Martin, 'Anne Dowriche's *The French historie* and Innocent Gentillet's *Contre-Machiavel*', *N&Q*, 242 (1997), 40–41
Wealth at death at least £1000; £100 bequeathed to each of eight children; plus household goods; silver; also land and a windmill:

will, proved at the consistory court of Canterbury, 28 May 1613–1614

Patrick, Simon

Patrick, Simon [Symon] (**1626–1707**), bishop of Ely, was born on 8 September 1626 at Gainsborough, Lincolnshire, the eldest son of Henry Patrick (*bap.* 1596, *d.* 1665), a prosperous mercer and merchant, and his wife, Mary, the daughter of a Nottinghamshire minister named Naylor.

Early life and education, 1626–1655 The religious education provided by Patrick's parents combined practical protestant piety with the traditional Calvinist theology of the Church of England. Mary Patrick passed on the fruits of her own education by instructing her son with Lewis Bayly's *Practice of Pietie* (1611), while Henry Patrick, whose strict religious observance gained him a reputation for puritanism, was nevertheless an admirer of Robert Sanderson's sermons (1632). Henry was keen to foster Simon's scholarly ambitions and sent him to school under John Merryweather, the translator of Browne's *Religio medici* into Latin. At the outbreak of civil war in 1642 neutral Gainsborough was occupied by royalist troops. Patrick's schoolmaster fled and his father was forced to leave the town after refusing to take an oath. While the rest of the family took refuge at Sir William Pelham's house at Brocklesby, Simon went with his father to Boston and then to Hull, lodging with a family friend while he completed his education with a schoolmaster in Hull and possibly also at a school in Beverley.

Patrick's progress to university at Cambridge was now compromised by his father's dire financial straits (his goods at Brocklesby had been looted by parliamentarian troops) and the disorder caused by the war. At some risk to their personal safety, Henry and Simon travelled through Boston and King's Lynn in order to get to Cambridge. Patrick's father had letters of recommendation to Benjamin Whichcote and Ralph Cudworth, of Emmanuel College, where Henry hoped that they would accept Simon as a sizar. Although neither could take Patrick they recommended that they should try Queens' College, where he was duly admitted on 25 June 1644 in the care of John Wells. Patrick dutifully attempted to take the covenant but was excused when the authorities learned that he was just seventeen. Patrick soon improved on his position at Queens', acting as scribe to the master, Dr Herbert Palmer. He was rewarded with better scholarships and the status of pensioner. Patrick graduated BA on 21 January 1648 and was elected fellow of Queens' on 1 March 1649, proceeding MA on 18 January 1651. During his years at Queens' Patrick made the acquaintance of the Cambridge Platonist John Smith, an encounter that would shape his intellectual development. Smith confirmed Patrick in his doubts about absolute predestination and 'made me take the liberty to read such authors (which were before forbidden me) as settled me in the belief that God would really have all men to be saved' (*Works*, 9.419). Smith died in August 1652, and Patrick preached his funeral sermon (later printed by John Worthington before his edition of Smith's *Select Discourses*, 1662). Patrick served his college in the early 1650s as an administrator and a teacher. In 1653–4 he

Simon Patrick (1626–1707), by Sir Peter Lely, *c.*1668

was senior bursar and in 1654–5 dean of chapel. He lectured in philosophy, arithmetic, and Hebrew, but took particular care to instruct his students in scripture. In his teaching he made use of Henry Hammond's *Practical Catechism* and this earned him a public reputation as an Arminian, a position which he now espoused as a self-evident truth. Patrick was obliged to take orders two years after his MA and submitted to presbyterian ordination on 8 April 1653 in London. However, he subsequently read Hammond's treatment of Ignatius's epistles and Herbert Thorndike's *Primitive Government of the Church*, and these works convinced him of the necessity of episcopal ordination. On 5 April 1654 Patrick was ordained by Bishop Joseph Hall at his house at Potter Heigham in Norfolk.

Parish priest and early writings, 1655–1672 In 1655, at the recommendation of Samuel Jacombe, a London minister and Patrick's former colleague at Queens', Patrick became chaplain to Sir Walter St John at Battersea. Patrick proceeded BD on 18 January 1658 and about the same time St John, pleased with his chaplain, offered him the vacant vicarage of St Mary's, Battersea. Patrick was at first reluctant because he would have to undergo examination by presbyterian triers, but his inquisitors avoided any hard questions which might have disqualified him. Patrick held the vicarage at Battersea until 1675. Although at first overwhelmed by a punishing schedule, he grew to love his parochial work. It is from this period that his earliest printed work appears, most importantly his sacramental treatises *Aqua genitalis* (1659) and *Mensa mystica* (1660; for discussion of these see 'Devotional writings and preaching', below).

At the Restoration Patrick went to some trouble to prepare his parishioners for the return of Anglican forms of worship, convinced as he was of the necessity of a formal regime of prayer and public worship. On 29 April 1662 he heard of the death of the president of Queens' College and that the majority of the fellows wished to elect him. He set out for Cambridge but on 5 May discovered *en route* that although he had been formally elected, the ejected royalist nominee Anthony Sparrow had been installed on the king's mandamus. Patrick appealed to the court of king's bench, but to no avail. The case dragged on into the autumn term when it came before a commission which included the lord chancellor and the bishops of London, Winchester, and Ely, but nothing was resolved and the earl of Clarendon resorted to demanding that Patrick and his supporters drop the case or be noted as 'a company of factious fellows' (*Works*, 9.441). Patrick's legal adviser also mysteriously withdrew. Patrick pursued the issue until 1665, but with no result.

It may have been because of this shoddy treatment by the court that Patrick received an unexpected offer from the former parliamentarian William Russell, earl of Bedford. Thomas Manton, the presbyterian divine and rector of St Paul's, Covent Garden, had failed to conform in August 1662, leaving the rich benefice vacant and in the earl's gift. Patrick took up his new position on 23 September 1662 and held it until 1689, earning a reputation as an exemplary parish priest, not least because of his decision to stay with his parishioners during the plague of 1665. His correspondence with Lady Elizabeth Gauden dates from this period and provides a fascinating account of his experiences and thoughts during the plague. Patrick was diligent in improving the facilities offered by the church and later deployed the plentiful financial resources of his parish to endow additional services and lecturers—by the end of his tenure St Paul's was able to offer four services a day.

In April 1666 Patrick testified to the efficacy of Valentine Greatrakes, the famous 'stroker', after he was cured of illness by him. In June of the same year Patrick decided to take his DD, but at Oxford rather than Cambridge, probably as a result of his problems at Queens'. On the advice of his friend Dr Thomas Willis, he incorporated his BD into Christ Church on 27 June and was admitted DD on 5 July.

In 1668 Patrick, opposed to the schemes promoted by some of his latitudinarian colleagues for the comprehension of dissenters, produced the first of his popular *Friendly Debate* dialogues, denigrating nonconformist practices and calling upon dissenters to conform (see 'Polemical writings', below). He published the work anonymously but an appreciative archbishop of Canterbury discovered his identity, thus restoring Patrick to Sheldon's favours after the affair at Queens'. Offers of preferment soon followed. In 1669 the bishop of Lincoln offered Patrick the archdeaconry of Huntingdon, which he declined, typically 'not thinking himself worthy of it' (*Works*, 9.451). In 1671 he was made a royal chaplain 'whether I would or no' (ibid., 9.455) and on 13 July he received a prebend at Westminster, where he was installed four days later.

Dean of Peterborough and defender of Anglicanism, 1672–1689

In 1665 Patrick had met Penelope Jephson (1646–1725) briefly, but in 1666, having read Patrick's *Parable of the Pilgrim* (1664), she sought him out to advise her over an ill-considered vow of celibacy made in her younger years. Getting to know her better, Patrick fell in love with her and after his promotion to Westminster resolved to ask her to marry him. She rejected him initially, saying that she preferred to remain single. Their friendship continued until Penelope finally accepted his suit; they were married on 1 June 1675 at Miserden in Gloucestershire. They had three children, William (*b*. 1 July 1678), Simon (*b*. 2 Oct 1680), and Penelope (*b*. 1 Dec 1685), of whom only Simon survived infancy. Penelope outlived her husband: she died on 10 April 1725.

In 1674 Patrick became involved in measures designed to encourage religious teaching in Wales. These included the supply of bibles and religious literature in Welsh and led to Welsh-language editions of the Bible and the liturgy. In 1675 Patrick, now well established as a defender of Anglicanism, wrote a book (now lost) designed to persuade James, duke of York (later James II), to continue as an Anglican. 1679 saw Patrick publish his commentary on the book of Job, the first of his famous Old Testament commentaries, a major and lasting corpus of scholarship that he would continue to produce for the rest of his life.

Upon learning of the death of the dean of Peterborough, Patrick broke with habit and sought out patronage to secure the vacant deanery. He was successful, and was installed on 1 August 1679, holding the office together with the rectory of St Paul's. At Peterborough Patrick took the initiative in restoring the weekly communion. He also edited, extended, and published Simon Gunton's manuscript history of the church there, which was published in 1686. In 1680 the lord chancellor, Sir Heneage Finch, offered Patrick the rectory of St Martin-in-the-Fields, then reputed to be the best living in England, but Patrick was reluctant to leave his parishioners at St Paul's and was doubtful of his ability to carry out the work necessary. In his place he recommended his friend Thomas Tenison, who was appointed. An additional lecturer at St Paul's allowed Patrick to concentrate upon his biblical scholarship, but this soon gave way to works targeting the dangers of Roman Catholicism.

Patrick was one of the London clergymen who met soon after James II's accession to co-ordinate the production of anti-Catholic writings. James, who had retained Patrick as one of his royal chaplains, did not take kindly to reports of his sermons and in January 1686 complained to the archbishop of Canterbury, William Sancroft, about the London clergy who preached too much against popery, naming Patrick in particular. Patrick met James to emphasize that he remained loyal and a reconciliation was effected. However, in the autumn of the same year Patrick found himself in the front line of the controversy over James's religion when he and William Jane were summoned to participate in a debate with Catholic priests before the king. James wished his priests to convert the lord treasurer, the earl of Rochester, but the latter had insisted on hearing the Anglican cause defended. The king rejected Rochester's suggestions of John Tillotson and Edward Stillingfleet, but approved Patrick and Jane, then acting as the duty chaplains. On 29 November Patrick and Jane went to Whitehall to debate with Bonaventura Gifford and Thomas Godden. The conference dragged on into the night but eventually Rochester curtailed proceedings. The following day Rochester indicated that he remained convinced by Anglicanism, complimenting Patrick and Jane on their performance. James was apparently not so pleased, reportedly commenting that he 'never saw a bad cause so well, or a good one so ill maintained' (*Works*, 9.497n.). Patrick continued to campaign against popery from the pulpit, in print, and in more practical ways. In 1687, together with Tenison, he helped to establish a school adjoining St Martin's library, designed to confront the Catholic institution established at the Savoy. Patrick was the first to put his name to the resolution of the London clergy not to read the declaration of indulgence in May 1688.

Bishop of Chichester and of Ely, 1689–1707 In January 1689 Patrick was involved in Sancroft's proposed scheme for the comprehension of dissenters and was among those who drew up the proposals. The events of the 1680s had by then convinced Patrick that some form of accommodation with dissent was essential. In September 1689 he heard of the death of the bishop of Chichester, John Lake, and on 8 September, Patrick's birthday, he heard that the king and queen had elevated him to that see. Gilbert Burnet had recommended Patrick to the king as 'a man of an eminently shining life, who would be a great ornament to the episcopal order' (*Correspondence of … Clarendon*, 2.281). Patrick was confirmed as bishop of Chichester on 12 October and consecrated at Fulham the following day alongside Edward Stillingfleet and Gilbert Ironside.

From the beginning of October 1689 Patrick served on the ecclesiastical commission designed to revise the prayer book. At the end of November, regarded as something of an expert in the composition of prayers, he was instructed to revise the collects with a view to bringing them more into line with the epistles and the gospels. At the end of May 1690 Patrick settled in Chichester, beginning a visitation of the diocese. He stayed at Chichester for only a year. On 22 April 1691 he was translated to Ely to replace the nonjuror Francis Turner, being elected on 10 June and confirmed on 2 July. Patrick immediately got to work improving the material fortunes of the diocese, resolving a long-running dispute between the bishops of Ely and Lord Hatton's family over a contested lease, agreeing to a settlement which brought £100 per annum to the bishop and his successors in perpetuity. Acts of parliament in 1691 and 1698 restored and developed various rights for the bishopric. Patrick moved to Cambridgeshire in May 1692, reconstructing the bishop's palace at Ely and energetically pursuing pastoral and intellectual activities, particularly his growing series of Old Testament commentaries. He donated a large collection of valuable books to the cathedral library. At the same time he also played a role in establishing the Society for the Propagation of Christian Knowledge (SPCK). He not only acted as a trustee but established the charter of 1702 so that it constituted all bishops of Ely members of the society *ex officio*.

Patrick's change of heart over dissent led him in November 1702 to vote against the Occasional Conformity Bill. He is reported to have commented that although he had been known to write against dissent in his early years 'he had lived long enough to see reason to alter his opinion of that people and that way of writing' (*Works*, 9.554n.). In December 1702 Patrick purchased an estate at Dalham in Suffolk and began to rebuild the house there for his wife and family. He continued to exercise his many activities right up until the end of his life, in spite of growing infirmity. He composed his 'Autobiography' from the details of his now lost diaries in 1706 and continued to keep a diary until the last day of his life. Patrick died suddenly on 31 May 1707, aged eighty, at the bishop's palace, Ely. He was buried on 7 June on the north side of the presbytery of Ely Cathedral. A monument was soon erected, together with an epitaph by his successor, John Moore.

Works: the latitude-man Patrick is best known as a latitudinarian and is often assumed to be the author of what might be considered to be a manifesto of latitudinarianism, *A Brief Account of the New Sect of Latitude-Men* (1662), published under the initials S. P. Unusually, Patrick does not claim the pamphlet in his 'Autobiography' (where he owns to several anonymous works), but textual and circumstantial evidence suggests that even if he did not write the *Brief Account*, the work refers to him and may be related to the controversy aroused by the contested presidency at Queens'. 'Latitude-man' was a term of abuse aimed by high-churchmen at divines like Patrick who had been educated and promoted during the civil war period. The *Brief Account* seeks to clear those so labelled from allegations of disloyalty and expedient conformity by laying out their beliefs, and in these can be seen a fair reflection of Patrick's own positions. Theologically the latitude-man is portrayed as a moderate, rationalist Anglican with a strong Arminian bias. Free will is celebrated, as is the universal intent of Christ's death and the sufficiency of God's grace. There is a greater emphasis upon holy living than the external features of ritualized religion. Scripture, reason, and the primitive apostolic tradition offer complementary routes to establishing true religion, which is embodied in the established church. The latitude-man approves 'that vertuous mediocrity which our Church observes between the meretricious gaudiness of the Church of Rome, and the squalid sluttery of Fanatick conventicles' (S.P., *Brief Account*, 7). The *Brief Account* is famous for its rejection of scholastic Aristotelianism and support for the new natural philosophy on the grounds that 'True Philosophy can never hurt sound Divinity' (ibid., 24).

Much of this is consistent with Patrick's ideas as expressed elsewhere in his writings. His confirmation in his Arminian beliefs has been noted and he consistently favoured the Greek fathers and early Christian writers along with modern authorities such as Episcopius, Grotius, and Hammond. The influence of John Smith's Platonism is clear in Patrick's rationalism, in his emphasis upon a living faith rather than abstract doctrine, and in his conviction that a properly cultivated spirituality could offer a form of mystical reunion with God. At the same time, however, revolted by enthusiasm, Patrick was strongly drawn to the practical order and discipline within the Anglican tradition. His understanding of this was shaped by his early education but amplified through his reading Henry Hammond and Jeremy Taylor, influences which would direct the shape of his subsequent work.

Devotional writings and preaching In his lifetime Patrick was probably most famous for his devotional works, particularly those on the sacraments and his treatises concerning prayer. It was of course only fitting that he should have a particular interest in reconciling individual spirituality with an appropriate form of religiosity. After exploring sacramental issues in sermons, Smith's friend and editor John Worthington encouraged Patrick to publish extended treatments. The first of these was *Aqua genitalis* (1659) in which Patrick described baptism in terms of a federal rite acting as a seal upon the covenant between God and man in general. In his *Mensa mystica* of 1660 he extended his use of the covenant metaphor in the first of his extensive and popular series of writings on the eucharist which included *A Book for Beginners* (1662) and *The Christian Sacrifice* (1671). The eucharist took a central place in Patrick's theology, representing as it did the occasion for communicants not only to commemorate Christ's death but in doing so also to plead for God's grace. Patrick would remain a strong advocate of increasing the frequency of communion, and he encouraged the practice of a weekly eucharist at Peterborough and a monthly celebration at Ely.

Patrick's books of prayer were also phenomenally successful and his reputation in this area made him a natural choice to revise the collects in 1689. *The Devout Christian Instructed how to Pray* (1672), which had gone through nine editions by 1694, built upon the Book of Common Prayer in offering devotions for each day of the week. *The Christian Sacrifice* (fifteen editions by 1720) also provided suitable prayers and meditations for every month of the year and the principal religious ceremonies. Patrick's recurring concern is the proper focus of individual religious experience upon God as the source of all redemption. To that end, as he comments in *The Devout Christian*, Patrick avoids all 'affected expressions, fantastical allusions, insignificant allegories, pretended wit, elegant conversions of sentences and rash applications of holy scripture' (Patrick, *Devout Christian*, sig. A4r). He saw the directive form of prayer as essential, amplifying its spiritual effect. His recurrent concern was to foster spirituality, but in a directed and appropriate manner. In the words of one commentator, Patrick's devotions were 'sublime and not enthusiastical' (Knight, 132).

Known as the 'preaching bishop' (Overton, 250), Patrick earned a considerable reputation for his sermons during his lifetime and this figured prominently in Gilbert Burnet's recommendation that Patrick be elevated to Chichester. His earliest sermons bear the imprint of Smith's Platonism whereas his later style attracts adjectives from critics such as 'grave', 'earnest', 'plain', and 'perspicuous'—as his Victorian editor Alexander Taylor puts it, 'solid and serious rather than specious and brilliant' (*Works*, 1.cxx). The stylistic effect was of course no accident but connected to Patrick's deep anxiety over the disturbing effects of uncontrolled rhetoric which he always associated with the antinomian excess and against which he had campaigned in the Friendly debate pamphlets (1668–70). Preferring instead to elevate the message over the messenger, Patrick made a particular point of defending Anglican plain preaching against nonconformist criticism in *A Discourse of Profiting by Sermons* (1683). With the removal of the political imperatives that motivated Patrick's particular style, his sermons fell out of favour with subsequent literary critics and have largely been neglected.

Moral and consolatory writings Some of Patrick's most popular works were those designed to deal with moral and religious crises, and he specialized in spiritual counselling designed to reconcile the afflicted individual to the will of God. As a result they are characterized by an emphasis upon quietism and contemplative piety. His writings were often the product of specific cases. In 1660 Patrick produced *The Heart's Ease, or, A Remedy Against Trouble* for the wife of his patron, Lady St John, and he went on to produce a similar work combining sermons, maxims, and prayers in the 1670s (but published posthumously) under the title *Advice to a Friend* for his future wife, Penelope Jephson. However, Jephson was first attracted to Patrick as a counsellor after reading perhaps his best-known work in this genre, *The Parable of the Pilgrim*, written in 1663 but published in 1664. As Patrick made clear, *The Parable* was designed to provide moral guidance for an unnamed friend. The allegorical pilgrimage tradition of writing lent itself naturally to his aim of reconciling individual spirituality with an appropriate form of religiosity. He freely admits borrowing the model from the Benedictine Augustin Baker's *Sancta Sophia* (1657), which in turn had its roots in Walter Hilton's fourteenth-century work *The Scale of Perfection*. In the course of his journey to Jerusalem, Patrick's pilgrim Philotheus is encouraged to recognize the importance of his dependence upon his spiritual director who will guide him through life's trials in order to avoid spiritual trouble. The trouble stems from antinomian beliefs on the one hand and the temptations of Roman Catholicism on the other. *The Parable*'s grave message of conformity to the established church seems designed to reassure those whose consciences were too tender to endorse the Act of Uniformity in 1662. Patrick seeks not to negate spirituality, but rather to harness it within the traditions of Anglicanism. The work proved to be immensely popular and passed through six editions before 1687. Bunyan's rejection of *The Parable*'s conformist message in *Pilgrim's Progress* is perhaps the most famous response to Patrick's work.

Polemical writings As *The Parable of the Pilgrim* demonstrates, a polemical edge is rarely missing from Patrick's work, but some of his productions stand out in this respect. The targets were those whose extremism threatened to distort the fabric of the true church as Patrick conceived it, antinomianism on the one side and Roman Catholicism on the other. He had produced sermons against what he saw as the Pharisaism of puritans in Cambridge in the 1650s, and he expanded this into a work titled *The Jewish Hypocrisy* (1660), which compared puritan precisionism with Jewish formalism. During the 1660s Patrick remained hostile to nonconformists who campaigned for comprehension or toleration. The abortive comprehension scheme of 1668–9, involving more liberal latitudinarians such as John Wilkins and John Tillotson, moved him to publish his *Friendly Debate between a Conformist and a Non-Conformist* in 1669. In a change of tone which shocked dissenters and friends alike, Patrick poured out page after page of invective against nonconformists in this largely one-sided dialogue, accusing the dissenters of glorying in the theology and rhetoric of antinomianism and portraying both as the fuel of sedition and social disruption. Patrick's response was to preach an uncompromising conformist message. The pamphlet was immediately a bestseller, running through five impressions in the year of publication. It was followed by two continuations in 1669 and an appendix in 1670 which defended his claims against his nonconformist critics. Patrick's last word came in 1671, when he restated his injunction to conformity in *A Letter to the Author of a Discourse of Ecclesiastical Polity*. Although the works brought reconciliation with Archbishop Sheldon, Matthew Hale accused Patrick of careerism and Richard Baxter and Gilbert Burnet were concerned that it encouraged prejudice against dissenters in general. Patrick defended himself and restated his position as late as 1683 in the preface to the sixth edition of the *Friendly Debate*. His change of heart, at least over the toleration and comprehension of moderate nonconformists, seems to have been related to a greater awareness of the importance of protestant unity in the face of the threat of popery.

Patrick had roundly condemned popery in his earliest writings, but the anti-Roman theme in his polemical works comes to the fore from the late 1670s. In 1680 he produced a revised translation of Grotius's *De veritate religionis Christianae*, to which he added a seventh book summarizing the general arguments against the Roman abuse of the Catholic tradition, thus inoculating Grotius against charges of ambiguity towards Rome. Patrick's contributions in the 1680s defended Anglicanism more aggressively, for example upholding the primitive apostolic tradition and the rule of faith in *A Discourse about Tradition* (1683). In *The Pillar and Ground of Truth* (1687), his most systematic anti-Roman work, he demonstrated the full range of misinterpretation and innovation that characterized what he saw as Rome's deviation from the primitive apostolic church.

Exegetical work Patrick's Old Testament commentaries constitute one of his most enduring legacies. He published his annotations on the book of Job in 1679. The book of Psalms followed in 1680, Proverbs in 1683, Ecclesiastes and the Song of Solomon in 1685. Subsequently the complete paraphrase of and commentary upon all the books of the Old Testament were published in ten volumes between 1695 and 1710. Patrick deployed his considerable knowledge in a range of fields from ancient languages, the classics, and patristic writers through to natural philosophy. In his introduction to his commentary on Genesis he comments that he was motivated through a desire to demonstrate the truth of the scripture 'without forsaking literal sense, and betaking to I know not what allegorical interpretations' (Patrick, *Commentary*, sig. A1r). In this as in all his works, he is motivated by the desire to act as a guide to the interpretation of scripture, disproving sceptics and setting the bounds to the nature of the interpretation made. Patrick's work was widely praised and read well into the nineteenth century; it constituted a major part of the collection titled *A Critical Commentary and Paraphrase of the Old and New Testaments* (1727–60), better known by the names of the contributors: Simon Patrick, William Lowth, Daniel Whitby, and Richard Arnald.

Conclusion Patrick, so often taken to be the archetype of the latitudinarian clergyman, nevertheless stands out among his latitudinarian colleagues. Arguably the closest to the Cambridge Platonists in philosophy, he sought to harness their sense of spirituality within a traditional Anglican framework of scripture, tradition, and reason, keenly aware of the fragility of the boundary separating adoration from enthusiasm. This project is evident in his indefatigable practical ministry and throughout the devotional works for which he was famed. It also motivated his polemical works against those who rejected what he felt to be the most appropriate means of effecting a reconciliation with God. Although he would not achieve the same fame as his friends Tillotson and Stillingfleet, Patrick's long-term achievement lay in his ability to transpose what was distinctive about latitudinarianism into a working model of practical churchmanship which would prove to be influential long after his death.   JON PARKIN

Sources *DNB* · *The works of Symon Patrick, D.D.*, ed. A. Taylor, 9 vols. (1858) · S. Patrick, *The devout Christian instructed how to pray* (1672) · S. Patrick, *A commentary upon the historical books of the Old Testament*, 2 vols. (1738) · S. P., *A brief account of a new sect of latitude-men*, ed. T. A. Birrell (1963) · S. Knight, 'Life of Symon Patrick', CUL, Add. MS 20 · *The correspondence of Henry Hyde, earl of Clarendon, and of his brother Lawrence Hyde, earl of Rochester*, ed. S. W. Singer, 2 (1828) · *Works*, ed. T. Birch, 3 vols. (1752), vol. 1 · J. H. Overton, *Life in the English church (1660–1714)* (1885) · *Reliquiae Baxterianae, or, Mr Richard Baxter's narrative of the most memorable passages of his life and times*, ed. M. Sylvester, 1 vol. in 3 pts (1696), pt 3 · *Bishop Burnet's History of his own time: with the suppressed passages of the first volume*, ed. M. J. Routh, 6 vols. (1823), vol. 1 · J. van den Berg, 'Between Platonism and Enlightenment: Simon Patrick (1625–1707) and his place in the latitudinarian movement', *Nederlands Archief voor Kerkesgeschiedenis*, 68 (1988), 164–79 · H. R. McAdoo, *The spirit of Anglicanism* (1965) · *Fasti Angl.* (Hardy), vols. 1–3 · S. Patrick, *The parable of the pilgrim*, ed. T. Chamberlain (1839) · Venn, *Alum. Cant.* · Wood, *Ath. Oxon.*, new edn, vol. 4 · K. Stevenson, 'Ely episcopal theologians in the seventeenth century', www.ely.anglican.org/history/talk19990209/patrick. html, 25 Nov 2002 · S. Sim, '"Vertuous Mediocrity" and "Fanatick Conventicle": pilgrimage styles in John Bunyan and Bishop Simon Patrick', *English Studies*, 4 (1987), 316–24 · J. Spurr, *The Restoration Church of England, 1646–1689* (1991) · W. M. Spellman, *The latitudinarians and the Church of England (c.1993)* · G. R. Cragg, *From puritanism to* the age of reason (1950) • R. L. Colie, *Light and enlightenment: a study of the Cambridge Platonists and the Dutch Arminians* (1957) • I. Rivers, *Reason, grace, and sentiment: a study of the language of religion and ethics in England, 1660–1780*, 1 (1991) • J. Gascoigne, *Cambridge in the age of the Enlightenment* (1989) • J. Gascoigne, 'Isaac Barrow's academic milieu: interregnum and Restoration Cambridge', *Before Newton: the life and times of Isaac Barrow*, ed. M. Feingold (1990), 250–90 • J. Twigg, *A history of Queens' College, Cambridge, 1448–1986* (1987) • J. Twigg, *The University of Cambridge and the English Revolution, 1625–1688* (1990) • J. Tulloch, *Rational theology and Christian philosophy in England in the seventeenth century*, 2 vols. (1874) • J. Bentham, *The history and antiquities of the conventual and cathedral church of Ely*, ed. J. Bentham, 2nd edn (1812), vol. 1 • T. R. Preston, 'Biblical criticism, literature, and the eighteenth-century reader', *Books and their readers in eighteenth-century England*, ed. I. Rivers (1982), 97–126 • *Biographia Britannica, or, The lives of the most eminent persons who have flourished in Great Britain and Ireland*, 7 vols. (1747–66), vol. 5 • C. J. Abbey, *The English church and its bishops, 1700–1800*, 2 vols. (1887), vol. 1 • M. Jacob, *The Newtonians and the English revolution* (1976) • J. Parkin, *Science, religion and politics in Restoration England: Richard Cumberland's De legibus naturae* (1999) • *IGI* • will, PRO, PROB 11/497, sig. 226

Archives BL, private prayer for use in difficult times, Add. MS 40160, fol. 13 • CUL, corresp. and papers, Add. MSS 19–20, 24, 36, 40, 51, 53, 56, 61–66, 70–71, 78, 81–84, 103, 150 • CUL, MS Mm 1.40 • CUL, MS Dd. III.72 | BL, letters to Lord Hatton, Add. MSS 29565, 29584 • BL, letters to J. Edwards and J. Humfrey, Add. MS 4274

Likenesses P. Lely, oils, *c*.1668, NPG [*see illus.*] • oils, *c*.1691, LPL • R. White, line engraving, 1700 (after Kneller), BM, NPG • G. Vandergucht, line engraving, 1727 (after G. Kneller), NPG • Kneller, oils, Ely Cathedral; copy, Queen's College, Cambridge

Patridge, Dorothy (*fl.* 1694), midwife and student in astrology, is a shadowy and perhaps fictitious person known only from *The Woman's Almanack, for the Year 1694*. The title page, illustrated with a crude woodcut of the author, explained that the work contained 'many choice, useful, pleasant, and most necessary Observations; adapted to the Capacity of the Female Sex, and not to be found in other Almanacks'. Despite the title it contained no calendar or astronomical data, offering instead monthly advice on health and husbandry, with tips on how to predict the weather, harvest, and the healthiness of the season. These included predictions based on the day on which new year's day fell, critical days in diseases, and weather lore based on the behaviour of birds and animals. Many of the monthly observations concerned sexual matters, such as the note for April: 'This Month Venus is very rampant; get a lusty Husband, least worse befal the' (Patridge, sig. A2). Much of the other information was also titillating in character, or frankly mischievous, such as a device to test a young woman's virginity by administering a herbal potion containing pepper and observing whether or not she sneezed. Patridge also offered simple notes on palmistry, some of it again prurient in nature. One line near the thumb, she explained, showed if a woman would be unfaithful, 'kiss in a Corner, or beat her Puff-past with her Neighbour's Rowling-pin' (ibid., sig. B2). The almanac contained advice on cosmetics too, how to 'take out the furrow'd Rinkles as smooth as a Girl of Sixteen' (ibid.), and 'How to make Hair as red as a Fox, a lovely Brown' (ibid.), using an alarming compound of lead calcined with sulphur and quicklime. Patridge's almanac contained a table of expenses for housewives, calculated by the week,

month, and year, but in general it offered diversion rather than useful instruction.

Nothing further is known of the author. The work provides no evidence of knowledge of either midwifery or astrology, and it is quite likely that it was penned by a pamphleteer attempting to capitalize on the fame of the celebrated astrologer John Partridge (1644–1715). In 1710 and 1711 the rogue publisher Benjamin Harris issued spurious editions of John Partridge's almanacs, also using the name 'Patridge' as a stratagem to avoid prosecution, while in 1712 another bogus pamphlet, *The Right and True Predictions of Dr Patridge*, included a section headed 'Mrs Dorothy Patridge's Speculum of 1712' and listing 'good' and 'evil' days. BERNARD CAPP

Sources D. Patridge, *The woman's almanack for the year 1694* (1694) • B. S. Capp, *Astrology and the popular press: English almanacs, 1500–1800* (1979) • R. P. Bond, 'John Partridge and the Company of Stationers', *Studies in Bibliography*, 16 (1963), 61–80

Likenesses woodcut, repro. in Patridge, *Woman's almanack*, title page

Patrington, Stephen (*d.* 1417), Carmelite friar, theologian, and bishop of St David's, came from Yorkshire and presumably joined the Carmelite order there; he was ordained acolyte in the diocese of York on 19 December 1366, and priest on 8 June 1370. By that time, or not long afterwards, he must have begun to study in Oxford, as he was already prior of the Oxford house by 1373, bachelor of theology by 1382, and doctor by 1390. In 1382, when his confrère Peter Stokes (*d.* 1399) was active in confronting the powerful body of John Wyclif's followers in the university, Patrington co-operated with him, taking a letter of complaint from all the Oxford friaries to John of Gaunt, duke of Lancaster (*d.* 1399); he was one of the masters whom the chancellor of the university was prohibited from molesting for these activities. He was present at the Blackfriars Council of that year, where the teaching of Wyclif was condemned, and evidently wrote the connecting narrative to the Carmelite collection of documents in which the masters' condemnation was recorded; this collection, later expanded, became known as *Fasciculi zizaniorum* and attributed to another Carmelite, Thomas Netter of Walden (*d.* 1430). About the same time he was making a comprehensive collection of theological questions debated in the Oxford schools, his *Reportorium*, which had some circulation. Patrington played an active part in the diocesan work of preaching and hearing confessions. He was licensed to hear confessions in Canterbury diocese on 24 November 1373, and to preach and lecture in Lincoln Cathedral as the chancellor's deputy on 14 January 1390. By 1397 he was receiving the favour of John of Gaunt, from whom he received an annuity on 26 January 1397, confirmed by the duke's heir on 24 December, for good services to the duchess and himself, perhaps as confessor. His papal dispensation to hold a benefice with or without cure of souls (25 September 1397) was probably owed to Gaunt. He also preached before Henry IV (25 December 1401), and was confessor to Henry V; the fees and allowances paid to him and his attendants amounted to £69 10*s.* 6*d.* in 1413.

Patrington was elected prior provincial of his order in 1399, and was evidently re-elected in 1411, but ceased to hold office in 1413. There seems no documentary proof of his supposed election as prior provincial of Lombardy in 1405. But as royal confessor, he was an obvious choice for promotion to the bench of bishops, and Henry V had him provided to St David's, in succession to Henry Chichele (d. 1443), on 1 February 1415. He was consecrated at All Saints' Church, Maidstone, on 19 June, and there is some evidence of his activity in the fragment of his register that survives in Oxford, New College, MS 360, fols. 14r–17v. However, he must almost immediately have been nominated by the king for Chichester, which fell vacant in June 1415. The temporalities of that see were restored to him on 25 August 1416, but the vacancy in the papacy must have delayed his bull of translation, which was issued posthumously on 15 December 1417. These changes strongly suggest that Patrington generally remained with the king, presumably as confessor, and letters of protection, also issued posthumously, show that he was to accompany Henry V to France. He died, however, on 22 September 1417; his will was proved on 29 December.

Patrington was credited with lectures on the *Sentences*, questions, commentaries on the epistle to Titus, Aesop's fables, and the *Eclogues* of Theodulus, and a treatise on the office of priesthood, all on the authority of Bale, who as a Carmelite may have had some knowledge of them, but none of them is extant. His part in *Fasciculi zizaniorum* is attested by the formula *per Patrington* which follows some of the narrative sections in that collection. His *Reportorium*, which is extant in Cambridge, St John's College, MS 103, Venice, Biblioteca Nazionale Marciana, MS Z. Lat. 280, Florence, Biblioteca Medicea Laurenziana, MS Plut. XVII. sin. 10, and Dublin, Trinity College, MS 255, is firmly attributed, and clearly had some circulation among Oxford students of theology, but contains nothing, evidently, of Patrington himself.   JEREMY CATTO

Sources reportorium, St John Cam., MS 103 · Episcopal register, New College, Oxford, MS 360 · Lincoln Cathedral chapter acts, Lincs. Arch., A.2.27, fols. 35v–36 · [T. Netter], *Fasciculi zizaniorum magistri Johannis Wyclif cum tritico*, ed. W. W. Shirley, Rolls Series, 5 (1858) · Bale, *Index*, 418–19 · G. Wessels, ed., *Acta capitulorum generalium ordinis fratrum B. V. Mariae de Monte Carmelo*, 1 (Rome, 1912), 129, 130 · H. D. Emanuel, 'A fragment of the register of Stephen Patryngton, bishop of St David's', *Journal of the Historical Society of the Church in Wales*, 2 (1950), 31–45 · J. Crompton, 'Fasciculi zizaniorum [pts 1–2]', *Journal of Ecclesiastical History*, 12 (1961), 35–45, 155–66 · L. A. Kennedy, 'Late fourteenth-century philosophical scepticism at Oxford', *Vivarium*, 23 (1985), 124–51 · L. A. Kennedy, 'A Carmelite fourteenth-century theological notebook', *Carmelus*, 33 (1986), 70–102 · Emden, *Oxf.*, 3.1435–6 · J. H. Wylie and W. T. Waugh, eds., *The reign of Henry the Fifth*, 3 vols. (1914–29)
Archives Biblioteca Medicea Laurenziana, Florence, MS Plut.XVII.sin.10 · Biblioteca Nazionale Marciana, Venice, MS Z.Lat.280 · New College, Oxford, register, MS 360 · St John Cam., MS 103 · TCD, MS 255

Patten, George (1801–1865), portrait and history painter, was born on 29 June 1801, the son of William Patten, a miniature painter, whose works were exhibited at the Royal Academy between 1791 and 1844, and who died on 22 August 1843. George received his early training in art from his father, and in 1816 became a student at the Royal Academy, where he first exhibited a miniature of his father in 1819. In 1828 he took the unusual course of again entering the schools of the academy, in order to study oil painting, which he adopted in 1830 in preference to miniature painting.

In 1837 Patten went to Italy, visiting Rome, Venice, and Parma; later that year, on his return to England, he was elected an associate of the Royal Academy. Early in 1840 he went to Germany to paint a portrait of Prince Albert, which was exhibited at the Royal Academy, and engraved by Charles Eden Wagstaff. He was afterwards appointed portrait painter in ordinary to the prince consort, and obtained a considerable amount of patronage in the painting of presentation portraits, many of which appeared in the exhibitions of the Royal Academy. Among these were portraits of Richard Cobden; Lord Francis Egerton, (later earl of Ellesmere); and Paganini, exhibited in 1833, remarkable as being one of the very few portraits ever painted of the famous violinist. Patten exhibited a self-portrait in 1858, as well as a number of mythological and fancy, and a few biblical subjects, among which were *A Nymph and Child*, exhibited at the Royal Academy in 1831; *Cymon and Iphigenia* in 1834; *The Passions*, suggested by the ode by Collins, in 1838; *Dante's Descent with Virgil to the Inferno* in 1843; *Susannah and the Elders* and *Bacchus Discovering the Use of the Grape* in 1850; *Apollo and Clytie* in 1857; and *The Youthful Apollo Preparing to Engage in a Musical Contest with Paris*, the last of his exhibited works, in 1864. Several of these appeared also at the British Institution, together with some other works in the same styles. Unfortunately, his later works did not fulfil his earlier promise.

During the latter part of his life Patten resided at Goodrich Cross, Ross, Herefordshire, but before his death he returned to Winchmore Hill, Middlesex, where he died suddenly at Hill House, his residence there, on 11 March 1865, aged sixty-three. He left a widow, Lucy, and a son, Alfred Fowler Patten.

R. E. GRAVES, *rev.* PATRICIA MORALES

Sources *Art Journal*, 27 (1865), 139 · W. Sandby, *The history of the Royal Academy of Arts*, 2 vols. (1862) · Bénézit, *Dict.* · Thieme & Becker, *Allgemeines Lexikon* · *The exhibition of the Royal Academy* (1819–64) [exhibition catalogues] · *Catalogue of the works of British artists in the gallery of the British Institution* (1832–43) [exhibition catalogues] · CGPLA Eng. & Wales (1865)
Likenesses G. Patten, self-portrait, exh. 1858
Wealth at death under £5000: probate, 21 June 1865, CGPLA Eng. & Wales

Patten, (Alfred) Hope (1885–1958), Church of England clergyman and restorer of the shrine of Our Lady of Walsingham, was born at the Town Brewery, Sidmouth, Devon, on 17 November 1885, the only child of Alfred Patten, an indigent gentleman, and Mary Sadler, his wife. Pat to his friends, he was known after his ordination in the Church of England as Father Hope Patten. A highly strung, introspective, rather solitary boy, he embraced Anglo-Catholicism when a teenager in Brighton, and acquired a romantic view of the medieval church from his avid reading. He was drawn to the religious life, and in 1906 visited the Anglican Benedictines at Painsthorpe in Yorkshire, where he first met the abbot, Aelred Carlyle, who profoundly influenced him. In spite of his irregular and rather sketchy education, he eventually entered Lichfield Theological College, and although he never passed any examination he was ordained deacon in 1913 to serve at Holy Cross, St Pancras. After three other short curacies, he became vicar of Great and Little Walsingham with St Giles Houghton in 1921.

Patten quickly won over the villagers by his charm and sense of fun and his assiduous visiting. His life's work became the restoration of the shrine of Our Lady of Walsingham, destroyed at the Reformation. Within months he had set up in St Mary's a statue of Our Lady of Walsingham, modelled on the seal of the medieval priory, and instituted daily devotions to her. With the help of the League of Our Lady, later the Society of Mary, he organized the first pilgrimages from London. Faced with opposition from his bishop, he agreed to move the statue, and in 1931 used the opportunity to rebuild the Holy House of Nazareth, a copy of which had been at the centre of the original shrine, within a small church. This church was enlarged in 1938 to accommodate the growing number of pilgrims.

Establishing the shrine and fostering pilgrimage to it depended almost entirely on the drive and direction of Hope Patten. As Derrick Lingwood, who took charge of the financial side of the enterprise, said of him: 'In working out what he believed to be his vocation, he was ruthless with himself ... and others' (reminiscences of Derrick Lingwood). He imparted his vision to others and inspired them to do things of which they did not think themselves capable. He had an inimitable genius, according to Sir William Milner, for adapting the surrounding medieval cottages to house the pilgrims and the community which he founded. Patten also produced a stream of literature of high quality to promote and facilitate the pilgrimage and to record the development of the shrine, notably the *Pilgrims' Manual* (1928), *England's National Shrine of Our Lady Past and Present* (1939), and *Mary's Shrine of the Holy House, Walsingham* (1954). He started a quarterly paper, *Our Lady's Mirror*, in 1926 for the members of the Society of Our Lady of Walsingham, which he edited and largely wrote until his death. He had a remarkable gift, too, of making an occasion of events: the setting up of the statue, its translation to the Holy House, the blessing of the extension of the church, the jubilee of the shrine, and so on.

Patten's health was never robust. He suffered from bad eyesight and heart trouble and frequently collapsed from nervous exhaustion and had to take long holidays. He was credited with psychic powers: 'When he was exhausted he would go into a deep sleep from which it was very difficult to wake him and then he would seem to live in the past and describe things in great detail' (reminiscences of Derrick Lingwood). He could seem stern and aloof and behave very autocratically, especially with the college of guardians whom he had appointed to help him with his work and to continue it after his death, and yet he showed 'an almost feminine tenderness' (Stephenson, 235) to those

who were in trouble. Patten died on 11 August 1958 at The College, Little Walsingham, and was buried three days later in the churchyard of St Mary's.   PETER G. COBB

Sources C. Stephenson, *Walsingham Way* (1970) · P. G. Cobb, ed., *Walsingham* (1990) · *Our Lady's Mirror* [quarterly publication of the Anglican shrine of Our Lady of Walsingham] (1926–58) · reminiscences of Derrick Lingwood and Patrick Lauderdale, Walsingham College archives · private information (2004)

Archives Walsingham College, Norfolk, archive of shrine of our Lady at Walsingham, MSS

Likenesses Perera, oils, 1947, Walsingham College, Norfolk · photographs, repro. in Stephenson, *Walsingham Way*

Wealth at death £3616 4s. 5d.: probate, 5 Jan 1959, CGPLA Eng. & Wales

Patten, John Wilson-, Baron Winmarleigh (1802–1892), politician, was born John Wilson on 26 April 1802, the second of the two sons of Thomas Wilson of Bank Hall, Warrington, Lancashire. His father, whose original name was Patten, had in 1800 assumed the sole surname of Wilson in accordance with the will of Thomas Wilson, son of Thomas Wilson (1663–1755), bishop of Sodor and Man, to whose estates Thomas Patten succeeded. The family altered the surname to Wilson-Patten in 1823. John's mother, Elizabeth, was the eldest daughter of Nathan Hyde of Ardwick. His elder brother Thomas died at Naples on 28 October 1819, aged eighteen. He was educated at Eton College and at Magdalen College, Oxford, matriculating on 14 February 1821. E. G. G. S. Stanley, later fourteenth earl of Derby, was a contemporary and friend.

After leaving Oxford Wilson-Patten travelled for some years on the continent. On 15 April 1828 he married, in London, his cousin, Anna Maria, fourth daughter and coheiress of his paternal uncle, Peter Patten-Bold of Bold and his wife, Mary. Anna Maria died on 4 August 1846 having borne him a son, Arthur (1841–1866) and four daughters.

In 1830 Wilson-Patten entered the Commons as one of the members for Lancashire, Stanley being the other. He voted against the second reading of the Reform Bill, but did not stand in 1831 (giving way to Benjamin Heywood). In the reformed parliament of 1832 he was co-member for North Lancashire with Stanley, and he represented that constituency until 1874. Throughout this period, Wilson-Patten was a strong but on the whole constructive Conservative. He organized opposition to the Anti-Corn Law League in Lancashire but voted for repeal in 1846. For a time he worked with the Peelites but found his way back to the tories, being chairman of committees in the Commons, 1852–3, chancellor of the duchy of Lancaster, 1867–8, and chief secretary for Ireland, September–December 1868. Throughout his public life he retained good relations with Gladstone, who sometimes asked his advice. He was 'a sensible, moderate politician, unbiased either by passion or by ambition' (Vincent, 349).

Wilson-Patten's distinctive contribution was, however, in the field of industrial relations and factory law. He supported an early bill to remedy the truck system and helped to remove the tax on printed calicoes, so liberating trade in south Lancashire. In 1833 he carried by a majority of one a motion for a royal commission on the employment of women and children in factories, thus delaying Lord Shaftesbury's proposed bill. In the 1850s he was parliamentary spokesman of the National Association of Factory Occupiers, the textile employers' anti-factory act lobby. He was a member of the royal commission on the labour laws, 1874–5, and signed its majority report. He was active in alleviating distress during the 'cotton famine' in Lancashire in the early 1860s, and (in co-operation with Richard Cobden) persuaded the government to allow poor-law guardians to raise loans on the security of the rates. Wilson-Patten was also an active militiaman, commanding his regiment at Gibraltar during the Crimean War and being militia aide-de-camp to the queen from 1857 until his death.

On 16 March 1874 Wilson-Patten was created Baron Winmarleigh and from 1879 he was constable of Lancaster Castle. He developed his properties in the Wirral and Warrington and built Winmarleigh House at Garstang in 1871. There he died on 11 July 1892 and was buried at Warrington. He left no living male issue and the peerage became extinct.   H. C. G. MATTHEW

Sources GEC, *Peerage* · Boase, *Mod. Eng. biog.* · Gladstone, *Diaries* · Disraeli, *Derby and the conservative party: journals and memoirs of Edward Henry, Lord Stanley, 1849–1869*, ed. J. R. Vincent (1978) · P. Smith, *Disraelian Conservatism and social reform* (1967) · P. Joyce, *Work, society and politics* (1980)
Archives Lancs. RO, corresp. and papers mainly relating to family trusts | BL, corresp. with W. E. Gladstone, Add. MSS 44365–44786, *passim* · BL, letters to Lord Hardwicke, Add. MSS 35788–35808, *passim* · BL, corresp. with Sir Robert Peel, Add. MSS 40522–40600, *passim* · Bodl. Oxf., letters to Benjamin Disraeli
Likenesses G. B. Adams, marble bust; formerly at Warrington Museum · marble sculpture, Warrington parish church · oils; formerly at Royal Albert Museum, Lancaster · photograph, repro. in T. Cooper, *Men of mark: a gallery of contemporary portraits*, 2 (1877), pl. 6
Wealth at death £56,226 10s.: resworn probate, Sept 1893, *CGPLA Eng. & Wales* (1892)

Patten, Robert (*fl.* 1715–1718), Jacobite chaplain and writer, is of unknown parentage and upbringing. He had served as a curate at Penrith in Cumberland, and was occupying a similar position at Allendale in Northumberland when the 1715 Jacobite rising began. He led a party of keelmen from there to join the rebels, and on meeting a number of Scots on their way home to join the Jacobite forces persuaded them to join him. At Wooler he joined up with General Thomas Forster, the leader of the Northumberland Jacobites, and the earl of Derwentwater, who appointed him chaplain to their forces, which then marched to join the main Jacobite army at Kelso. As chaplain Patten preached many sermons on Jacobite themes such as the inviolability of hereditary right. He tried to persuade clergymen in the towns visited by the army to pray for James III—the Stuart pretender to the throne—but most declined. Among the sermons attributed to him was one calling for the complete extirpation of the enemy, including their wives and children, and this gave him a particularly bad reputation among the opposition.

Patten also took an active military role and sometimes functioned as a spy. At the battle of Preston, where the Jacobites were defeated on 13 November 1715, he served as an

aide-de-camp until his horse was shot under him. He was among the prisoners taken at Preston and was sent to London. In prison there he began to think of his future and appealed to the secretary of state, Lord Hardwicke, for a clergyman to be allowed to visit him. The Revd Dr Cannon was sent. Announcing that Cannon had convinced him of his wrongdoing, Patten offered to turn king's evidence. The offer was accepted, whereupon Patten became vociferously and publicly anti-Jacobite. On 22 July 1716 he preached an anti-Jacobite sermon at the parish church of St Mildred in Bread Street, London. This was soon published under the title *Christian Liberty Asserted*. In 1717 he published his *History of the Late Rebellion*, which appeared in two editions, the second much enlarged. Third and fourth editions were published in 1745, when Britain faced another Jacobite upheaval. In 1718 Patten produced a pamphlet entitled *The Rebel Convinc'd and Liberty Maintain'd*, in which he set out the arguments that were supposed to have changed his political outlook. Nothing more is known about him after this date.

ALEXANDER DU TOIT

Sources Dr Doran, *London in the Jacobite times*, 1 (1877), 106, 118–20, 286–7 · R. Patten, *The history of the late rebellion* (1717), preface · C. S. Terry, ed., *The Jacobites and the union* (1922)
Archives NL Scot., Walter Blaikie collection

Patten, Thomas (1714–1790), Church of England clergyman, the son of Thomas Patten, a Manchester grocer, was born on 5 October 1714; he was educated at Manchester grammar school, and afterwards at Oxford (Brasenose College, *c.*1729–1730; Corpus Christi College, 1730–33). He graduated BA in 1733, MA on 17 February 1737, BD in 1744, and DD in 1754; for a time he was fellow and tutor of Corpus, and later he became rector of Childrey, Berkshire. He married Elizabeth, daughter of Peter Brooke of Mere, high sheriff of Cheshire, at Rostherne, Cheshire, on 25 April 1765.

Patten, who was a friend of both Dr Johnson and Thomas Wilson, master of Clitheroe grammar school, probably influenced the latter's decision to dedicate his *Archaeological Dictionary* (1783) to Johnson. He was esteemed as 'a sound and excellent churchman', a poet and scholar, and an exemplary parish priest. A number of his sermons defending the Christian faith were published, including his university sermon at Oxford, *The Christian Apology* (1755). He was attacked in 1755 as a Hutchinsonian or follower of the high-church John Hutchinson by the Revd Ralph Heathcote and both later issued pamphlets dealing with the primary issue raised: the role of reason in matters of religion. In another sermon, published in 1759, Patten emphasized the importance of the gospel of Jesus Christ as against 'what is called the Religion of Nature'. He later wrote *A Letter to Lord North Concerning Subscription to the Thirty-Nine Articles* (1773). Patten died at Childrey on 20 February 1790; he was buried in Lancashire.   C. W. SUTTON, *rev.* ROBERT BROWN

Sources Foster, *Alum. Oxon.* · F. R. Raines, *The vicars of Rochdale*, ed. H. H. Howorth, 2 vols., Chetham Society, new ser., 1–2 (1883) · Boswell, *Life* · T. Wilson, *Miscellanies; being a selection from the poems and correspondence of T. Wilson* (1858) · J. Foster, ed., *Pedigrees of the county*

families of England, 1: *Lancashire* (1873) · *The private journal and literary remains of John Byrom*, ed. R. Parkinson, 2 vols. in 4 pts, Chetham Society, 32, 34, 40, 44 (1854–7) · T. Fowler, *The history of Corpus Christi College*, OHS, 25 (1893)
Archives BL, letters to Charles Poyntz · JRL, letters to Peter Legh the younger

Patten, William (*d.* in or after **1598**), author, was born in London, the son of Richard Patten (*d.* 1536), a city clothworker, and his wife, Grace, daughter of John Baskerville. His grandfather, Richard Patten of Boslow, Derbyshire, was a brother of William Waynflete (alias Patten), bishop of Winchester. Patten received some education at Gonville Hall, Cambridge. Although apparently not in full holy orders, from 1528 he was conduct (minor chaplain) and from 1533 parish clerk of St Mary-at-Hill, Billingsgate, London. In 1544 he was in France in the service of the sixteenth earl of Arundel. In 1547 he participated in and published an account of *The expedicion into Scotla[n]de of the most woorthely fortunate prince Edward, duke of Soomerset* (1548). This book, which recalls Patten's appointment during the venture as 'one of the judges of the Marshelsey' by the earl of Warwick, was compiled from his notes and those of William Cecil. Strongly anti-Catholic in tone it is none the less lively and detailed, the more so for being illustrated with crude woodcuts. It was used extensively by Holinshed in his chronicles, and also launched Patten's career as a minor official, for in July 1548 he was appointed collector of customs in London. Patten was married by this time. His first wife died at Billingsgate in 1549, and he subsequently married Anne, daughter of an heiress of Richard Johnson of Boston, Lincolnshire; the first of their seven children was born in 1560.

In 1550 Patten had leased the manor of Stoke Newington from Thomas Penrey, a lease renewed in 1565 for ninety-nine years commencing in 1576. In 1563 Patten completed extensive repairs on the manor house, and also on the church of St Mary, Stoke Newington, adding a vestry, aisle, private chapel, and schoolhouse. He became a JP for Middlesex, and in 1558 was appointed receiver-general of Yorkshire revenues. On 23 June 1562, at the height of his career, he was appointed a teller of the exchequer for life. Disaster struck in Michaelmas term of the year 1567/8, however, when the auditor of the receipt discovered that £7928 was missing from Patten's account. Patten was suspended on 13 January 1568 and, the barons of the exchequer having adjudged that he had forfeited his position, he was replaced on 13 July. The lease of Stoke Newington was given up, and he lost all his public offices. On 16 November 1572 he presented the queen with his 'Supplicatio Patteni' (BL, Lansdowne MS 739), an extended petition in pedestrian Latin verse copied out by his ten-year-old son Thomas, in which he eulogized Elizabeth and recounted his misfortunes—he had had to sell all his lands and belongings to the value of £500 per annum. Blaming one of his servants (characterized as a venomous snake) for the treasury's loss, he begged that the matter be investigated, but there is no evidence of a response.

Deprived of an income, Patten sought scholarly patronage. In April 1570 he produced a vocabulary and alphabet to accompany an Armenian psalter owned by Archbishop Parker, thus becoming the first scholar of that language in England. Similar interests were reflected in his next work, *The calendar of scripture. Whearin the Hebru, Challdian, Arabian, Phenician, Syrian, Persian, Greek and Latin names … in the holly Byble … ar set, and turned into oour English toong* (1575), in which he describes himself as 'unfortunate Patten … the sorrowing father of seven children'. Patten was obsessed with biblical numerology, which shapes two surviving metrical translations of psalms that he published as broadsides entitled *The Sallm by the Olld Translation called Deus Judicium* (1583) and *Anno foelicissimi regni augustae reginae nostrae Elizabeth quadragesimo primo fauste iam incepto Psal. terseptimus: domine in virtute tua* (1598). He also worked in commemorative genres. His broadside *A Moorning Diti* (1580) followed the death of his sometime patron Arundel. Another early patron was eulogized in *In mortem W. Wynter equitis aurati: monumentum diutinae mutuaeq. amicitiae ergao* (1589). Patten describes himself as a client of Sir Christopher Hatton in his *Luctus consolatorius: super morte nuper D. Cancellarij Angliae* (1591).

Patten was almost certainly the author of the anonymous satire in Warwickshire dialect suppressed by Cecil in 1575 but later printed as *A letter: whearin, part of the entertainment untoo the queenz majesty, at Killingwoorth Castl, in Warwick shear, in this soomerz progress 1575 iz signified* (1585). He was an early member of the Society of Antiquaries, for which he wrote 'Of sterling money' (T. Hearne, *Curious Discourses*, 1771, 1.317). John Stow describes Patten as 'a learned Gentleman and grave cittzen', recalling that he 'exhibited a Booke to the Mayor and communalitie' of London protesting against the increase of 'purprestures' (J. Stow, *Survey of London*, ed. C. Kingsford, 1908, 1.83). The translator Thomas Newton lauded him in verse as a celebrated historian.

Patten is remembered in Stoke Newington by the William Patten School in Church Street. It is not known when he died. Francis Thynne said he was 'now living' in 1587 (R. Holinshed, *Chronicles*, 1807, 4.949), and he was still publishing eleven years later. His eldest son Mercury matriculated to Trinity College, Cambridge, in 1567, and was Bluemantle pursuivant from 1597 to 1611.

PETER SHERLOCK

Sources B. Hill, 'Trinity College Cambridge MS B.14.52, and William Patten', *Transactions of the Cambridge Bibliographical Society*, 4 (1964–8), 192–200 · B. O'Kill, 'The printed works of William Patten (*c.*1510–*c.*1590)', *Transactions of the Cambridge Bibliographical Society*, 7 (1977), 28–45 · *VCH Middlesex*, 8.177–8, 205–8 · W. Robinson, *The history and antiquities of the parish of Stoke Newington* (1820) · Lansdowne MS, BL, 739 · J. C. Sainty, ed., *Officers of the exchequer: a list* (1983) · M. Merriman, *The rough wooings: Mary queen of Scots, 1542–1551* (2000) · *DNB*
Archives Harvard U., Baker Library, account book | BL, Add. MS 24127 · BL, Lansdowne MS 739 · CCC Cam., MS Small Parker 281 · CUL, MS Dd. 11. 40 · Trinity Cam., MS B.14.52
Likenesses J. Mills, engraving, repro. in Robinson, *History and antiquities*

Pattenson, Matthew (*fl.* 1623), Roman Catholic controversialist, was the author of *The Image of Bothe Churches, Hierusalem and Babel* (1623). Of his life very little is certainly known. It used to be believed, on the authority of Charles Dodd, that he was a physician-in-ordinary to Charles I, but no one of that name was admitted to the Royal College of Physicians during the period and the claim must be rejected. It is possible that the author was the man of that name who matriculated as a pensioner from Peterhouse, Cambridge, at Easter 1575, graduated BA in 1578–9 (84th in order of seniority), proceeded MA in 1582, and was incorporated at Oxford on 10 July 1593. It seems unlikely that this mature graduate would enrol, as a gentleman of that name did, as a student at Gray's Inn on 9 August 1599. But the common lawyer may have been the author. A Matthew Pattenson sat as the member of parliament for West Looe in 1588 and 1589, and for Heydon in 1601; this person may have been an official under Sir John Stanhope and a servant of Robert Cecil in 1603. The MP may have been the graduate, but seems rather too old to be identified with the controversialist, though this cannot be completely excluded. Of the author all we can say with any confidence is that in 1623 he was reported to be 'now in London', and that *The Image of Bothe Churches*, 'a bitter and seditious book' according to Gee, was indeed issued in that year at Tournai and can be attributed to him (Gee, 94).

In his preface the author explains that his book was issued in response to the public hostility aroused by the proposed marriage of Prince Charles to the infanta; aiming 'to stop the mouth of Polypragmus', the writer defends 'the benefits which the realm may reap by this match'. Addressing his work to 'the high and mighty prince Charles, Prince of Wales' Pattenson signs himself 'Your highness most humble orator and servant', which may be taken to imply that he was a royal chaplain (Pattenson, *Image*, preface and p. 2). There is no known record of this, and the possibility must be regarded with suspicion. The book defends the Jesuits' special vow of obedience to all commands bearing on the salvation of souls, widely held to include orders to murder or depose excommunicated princes; neither king nor prince could possibly have approved it. The period was one in which James had made concessions to Catholicism at court, and there was a deal of overheated speculation over the prospects for religion should the Spanish marriage be agreed. Whether Pattenson became over-enthusiastic, in the belief that the Roman religion was about to receive official state sanction, or whether the issue of the work at Tournai, near the French border of the Spanish Netherlands, signals that political mischief making was involved, is unclear.

Pattenson's death is as mysterious as his life. He appears in notes handwritten in a book issued in 1632: 'Judicious Mathew Patteson dead three years ago at Brussels though the last yet not the least admirer of nobility and forwarder of Herauldry and all Sem'inary acts and Jesuiticall projects' (Bailey, 327). This report is clearly a reference to the controversialist. If it is to be relied on, Pattenson died in Brussels no earlier than 1629.   STEPHEN WRIGHT

Sources M. Pattenson, *The image of bothe churches, Hierusalem and Babel* (1623) • J. Gee, *The foot out of the snare* (1623) • Venn, *Alum. Cant.* • T. A. Walker, *A biographical register of Peterhouse men*, 2 (1930) • Wood, *Ath. Oxon.*, new edn • J. Foster, *The register of admissions to Gray's Inn, 1521–1889, together with the register of marriages in Gray's Inn chapel, 1695–1754* (privately printed, London, 1889) • J. E. Bailey, 'Matthew Patteson', *N&Q*, 7th ser., 1 (1886), 327

Patterson, Colin (1933–1998), vertebrate palaeontologist, was born on 13 October 1933 at Hammersmith, London, the only child of Maurice William Patterson (1908–1991), bank manager, and Norah Joan (*née* Elliott) (1907–1984), secretary. He spent his childhood in Sheen but his early London education was disrupted by wartime evacuation to attend Hill Place boarding-school, Stow on the Wold, in 1942. He returned to London in 1947 and entered Tonbridge School, Kent. He left in 1952 for national service in the Royal Engineers. At Imperial College, London (1954–7), he gained first-class honours in zoology and was awarded the Forbes medal. His undergraduate notebooks demonstrate the clarity of expression, attention to detail, and competence in scientific drawing which typify all his later work.

In 1951 Patterson met Rachel Caridwen Richards (*b.* 1932), artist and elder daughter of Ceri Giraldus *Richards (1903–1971) and Frances Clayton (1901–1985), both of whom were well-known artists. They married on 9 April 1955 and had two daughters, Sarah (*b.* 1959) and Jane (*b.* 1963). Patterson was appointed assistant lecturer in biology at Guy's Hospital medical school in 1957, and at the same time began work on his PhD research under the supervision of K. A. Kermack at University College, London. His research concerned the anatomy and evolution of fossil acanthopterygians (spiny-rayed fishes related to modern-day perch, plaice, and mackerel) found in the English Chalk, a deposit laid down in seas about 95 million years ago. These fishes had previously been studied by A. S. Woodward in the late nineteenth century, but new techniques using acetic acid had recently been developed to dissolve the enclosing rock, leaving a fossil skeleton that could be studied in as minute detail as its modern counterpart. Patterson therefore became equally expert in the comparative anatomy of the skeleton of modern as well as fossil fishes. He gained his PhD from London University in 1961.

In July 1962 Patterson was appointed senior scientific officer in the department of palaeontology at the Natural History Museum (then called British Museum (Natural History)—a name that he continued to use until his official retirement in October 1993), where he became successor to E. I. White as researcher, and responsible for the national collection of fossil fishes. Throughout his life he continued to describe the anatomy of fossil fishes comparing them to their modern relatives. In 1975 he published 'A review of Mesozoic acanthopterygian fishes, with special reference to those of the English Chalk', a lengthy paper concerning the evolution of the braincase of actinopterygian fishes. This work, like his earlier thesis, was published in the *Philosophical Transactions of the Royal Society of London* and drew on his deep understanding of comparative anatomy; it has become the authoritative work to which other ichthyologists constantly refer.

In 1967 Patterson read the work of Willi Hennig, a German entomologist, who proposed a new method of biological systematics (the science of discovering genealogical relationships between organisms) later known as cladistics. To Patterson this was a revelation. He wrote many papers developing further the theory and methodology, and through his lucid prose and lecturing style he was one of the most influential proponents making cladistics the current systematic paradigm. In 'Morphological characters and homology' (*Problems of Phylogenetic Reconstruction*, ed. K. A. Joysey, 1982) he gave an insightful history into the recognition of biological homology and offered a modern formulation in which he argued that homology is a theory derived from observation. For Patterson empirical study of specimens led to the formulation of theory.

Patterson always kept up to date in his research interests, and when molecular biology began to produce amino acid and nucleotide sequences he quickly integrated these into his systematic work and clarified the relationship between morphological and molecular homology, editing in 1987 *Molecules and Morphology in Evolution: Conflict or Compromise?*.

As an undergraduate Patterson had attended lectures on evolution given by the entomologist O. W. Richards FRS. This remained a lifelong interest. In 1978 he published an eloquent account—*Evolution*—and with his characteristic candour pointed out the weaknesses as well as the strengths of the theory. He delivered the typescript of the second edition three days before his death.

The merit of Patterson's researches was recognized in rapid promotion to principal scientific officer in 1969, and then through individual merit promotion to senior principal scientific officer in 1974. He was elected to the Royal Society of London in March 1993. Throughout his career he was awarded many honours and awards including foreign honorary memberships of the Society of Vertebrate Paleontology, the Society of Ichthyologists and Herpetologists, and the Willi Hennig Society. He received the scientific medal of the Zoological Society of London (1972), the Romer/Simpson medal of the Society of Vertebrate Paleontology (1997) and, posthumously, the gold medal of the Linnean Society, which he had served as council member (1970–73, 1979–85), vice-president (1980–82), zoological editor (1978–81), and editorial secretary (1982–5).

Patterson was tall, imposing, and gentle, measured in speech with a remarkable memory and socially diverse circle of friends. Recollections of his character as well as his influence on colleagues were given in a special issue of *The Linnean* in 2000. For all but the first few years of his marriage Patterson lived in Barnes, London. He died on 9 March 1998 at Chelsea and Westminster Hospital after suffering a heart attack while bicycling to the Natural History Museum; he was cremated at Mortlake cemetery ten days later. He was survived by his wife.   PETER L. FOREY

Sources R. A. Fortey, *Memoirs FRS*, 45 (1999), 365–77 · P. L. Forey, B. G. Gardiner, and C. J. Humphries, eds., *The Linnean* [C. Patterson issue] (2000) · P. L. Forey, 'In Darwin's footsteps', *The Guardian* (26 March 1998) · personal knowledge (2004) · B. Gardiner, 'Colin Patterson', *The Independent* (24 March 1998), 22 a–b · private information (2004) [widow] · *The Times* (8 April 1998), 19 · d. cert.
Likenesses photograph, repro. in *The Guardian* · photograph, repro. in *The Times* · photograph, repro. in *The Independent*
Wealth at death £36,930—gross; £34,835—net: probate, 7 Oct 1998, *CGPLA Eng. & Wales*

Patterson [*née* Burr], **Gabrielle Ruth Millicent** (1905–1968), aviator, was born on 6 July 1905 at 23 Blomfield Court, Maida Vale, London, the eldest of four daughters of Malcolm Burr and his wife, Clara Millicent Goode. A mining engineer by profession but an entomologist by inclination, her father followed an explorer's life of prospecting and researching. His wife travelled with him, and Gabrielle and her sisters were educated in various European cities, including Paris, Berlin, Budapest, and Vienna. Having completed her education she was employed by her mother's family firm, Thos Goode & Sons, of South Audley Street, London, purveyors of china and glass to five generations of the royal family, and eventually became its company secretary. But a Mayfair showroom, however grand, was not exciting enough for her, and she took up the new sport of flying. At this time—the 1920s—flying clubs were being established and staffed in the main by ex-RAF pilots flying First World War aircraft.

Having gained a pilot's licence Gabrielle went on to become, in 1931, the first woman to hold an instructor's certificate. About this time she met her future husband, Arthur (Pat) Patterson (*d.* 1986), and was instrumental in teaching him to fly. They married on 26 June 1931 and their only child, Ian, was born in 1932. Pat qualified as an aviation engineer, and the couple moved around airfields as work opportunities arose. By 1933 they owned a Miles Hawk aircraft and Gabrielle Patterson had gained a B licence at the Cinque Ports Flying Club. This allowed her to fly as a commercial pilot for Silvertown Lubricants Ltd while continuing to instruct for the club. For a short time she was sales manager for the Miles Aircraft Company. The most prestigious aerial sporting event at this time was the King's Cup air race, and competition between the early aircraft builders to design an aeroplane capable of winning the cup became intense. Gabrielle entered in 1934, flying a Miles Hawk G-ACTZ designed by 'Blossom' Miles, wife of Fred Miles.

In the late 1930s Gabrielle Patterson was a leading figure in women's aviation and gained a lot of publicity. She started her own small flying school at Romford, Kent, in a barn with one Puss Moth. With the formation of the Civil Air Guard in 1938 she became chief instructor (and head of the women's corps of the Civil Air Guard) at Romford. She was joined there by other qualified women instructors who built up their flying hours in the months before the Second World War by training the influx of volunteers keen to take advantage of the cheap subsidized flying in the Civil Air Guard.

In 1939 the Pattersons' marriage failed, and they subsequently divorced. Pat was called up into the Fleet Air Arm and Gabrielle eventually joined the Air Transport Auxiliary (ATA). Created only in 1939, the ATA was composed mainly of pilots too old or unfit for the RAF. Referred to as the 'ancient and tattered airmen' they released RAF pilots from ferrying duties into active service. Initially there was official disapproval of women pilots, but after ceaseless lobbying Pauline Gower was allowed to form a women's section of the ATA. With 1530 flying hours Gabrielle Patterson was one of the first eight chosen to report for duty at Hatfield on 1 January 1940. At first the women were allowed to fly only training aircraft from the factories to the maintenance units but by the summer they were cleared to fly light operational aircraft. Patterson served as a first officer until the spring of 1943, when after contracting bronchitis she was grounded and subsequently left the ATA.

Gabrielle Patterson was a gifted teacher, always ready to encourage young flyers. Involved from the outset with the Women's Junior Air Corps, from 1946 to 1950 she served as commandant, and as chairman of its aviation committee she wrote the syllabus for the course work. Her outstanding ability was recognized when she became the first woman to be appointed to the Guild of Air Pilots and Air Navigators' panel of examiners. With the resumption of civilian flying after the war she moved to Barton in 1950 to become chief flying instructor of the Lancashire Aero Club, and shortly afterwards went to Ringway airport, Manchester, as chief flying instructor of the British European Airways staff flying club. After several years in this role she was forced to give up aviation for medical reasons, and subsequently read for a degree at Manchester University from 1954 to 1956.

Having won a scholarship in 1956 to the Sorbonne (University of Paris), Patterson, who was a lifelong Francophile, thereafter made her home in France. She taught English for the Otis Elevator Company. In later years she became concerned with the difficulty faced by pilots of non-British nationality in expressing themselves intelligibly in English over the radio-telephone, and gave time and effort to teaching them. After falling ill in 1968 she went to live with her sister Elizabeth at Little Missenden, in Buckinghamshire. She died, of cancer, in Wycombe General Hospital, High Wycombe, on 31 October 1968, and was cremated at Amersham. Her ashes were scattered from the air over White Waltham airfield in March 1969.

ENID DEBOIS

Sources private information (2004) [Ian Patterson, son] · b. cert. · d. cert. · L. Curtis, *The forgotten pilots: a study of the air transport auxiliary, 1939–45* (1971) · British Women Pilots Archive, Brooklands, Surrey · 'Girl pilots', *Picture Post* (22 Oct 1938)
Archives priv. coll.
Likenesses photograph, repro. in 'Girl pilots', *Picture Post*

Patterson, Sir James Brown (1833–1895), businessman and politician in Australia, born at Alnwick, Northumberland, on 18 November 1833, was the youngest son of James Patterson, a district road inspector, and his wife, Agnes, *née* Brown. He received an elementary education at Alnwick, and emigrated to Victoria in 1852 on the discovery of gold. After mining unsuccessfully at the Forest Creek goldfields, in 1856 he began farming on the River Loddon at Glenlyon, near Daylesford. In 1857 he married Anna Merrick Walton at Glenlyon, and in 1858 the couple moved to Castlemaine district, where Patterson ran a cattle-slaughtering business at Chewton. His business prospered, and though his methods were questioned he served as a local councillor and mayor. In 1870 they moved to Melbourne, where Patterson became a real estate auctioneer.

Patterson's ambition was for politics, and on 5 December 1870, after two unsuccessful candidatures, he was returned to the legislative assembly for Castlemaine, a seat which he retained until his death. He was a strong advocate of protection in trade, but for seven years supported various factions in the constantly changing scene of Victorian politics. He was in office for three months in Berry's radical ministry in 1875. When the latter was returned with an immense majority in May 1877, Patterson was put in charge of public works, as he had been in 1875, but was also a member of the ministry's inner cabinet; here he was very active and carried great weight in the government, winning a rather unwarranted reputation for extreme radicalism. After a short period in opposition Berry regained office after the elections in July 1880 and appointed Patterson minister of railways. He proved an efficient administrator and sought to reduce political patronage in the department, but, more importantly, profiting from previous experience, he was extremely moderate in his counsels and helped to bring about the compromise with the legislative council on its reform of the constitution. By this the property qualification for its members and electors was reduced, but its powers were unaltered, and there remained no provision for dealing with deadlocks.

On the defeat of the ministry in July 1881 Patterson went into opposition, where he remained for most of the decade, apparently still too radical for the coalition governments in office. He filled in his time by opposing, as an Orangeman, Irish home rule and in 1884–5 visiting England, where he spoke on the importance of the empire; on his return, however, he opposed imperial federation. In April 1889 he accepted the portfolio of minister of customs in the ministry of Duncan Gillies, whom he had until then opposed, and incidentally banned the import of novels by Zola, de Maupassant, and others as being immoral. He also introduced new or increased duties, though this he came to regret. In 1890 he firmly supported his colleagues in calling out the troops in Melbourne during the great maritime strike of 1890, an action which hastened the downfall of the ministry. After another visit to England in 1891 he became the virtual leader of the opposition, and in January 1893 was able to defeat the administration of William Shiels and become premier.

Patterson's arrival at the peak of his political career coincided with the depths of the 1890s depression, and was soon followed by a succession of business and building society failures which shattered public credit. He resisted incitements to grant relief to particular institutions, but he consented to the doubtful expedient of declaring a five-day bank holiday; this was intended to give the banks time to collect their resources but was too late to save most and, by undermining confidence, threatened those surviving, in some cases fatally. His government's policy of deep financial retrenchment caused a further loss of support, and in August 1894 Patterson was defeated on the budget and then in the election that followed. In opposition he supported Australian federation and continued to uphold the empire. A run-of-the-mill politician, self-made as in his business, he gained his success by energy and adaptability. He was created KCMG in 1894, but died suddenly of influenza at Murrumbeena, near Melbourne, on 30 October 1895. He was buried in Melbourne cemetery with Anglican rites on 1 November. His wife had died on 2 December 1894. Their only child, Rose, inherited his estate of £11,727. DON GARDEN

Sources AusDB · G. Serle, *The rush to be rich* (1971) · A. Deakin, *The crisis in Victorian politics, 1879–1881*, ed. J. A. La Nauze and R. M. Crawford (1957) · *The Argus* [Melbourne] (31 Oct 1895) · *The Age* [Melbourne] (31 Oct 1895) · *The Australasian* (2 Nov 1895) · *The Australasian* (14 Dec 1895) · *DNB*
Wealth at death £11,727—in Australia: AusDB

Patterson, John Brown (1804–1835), Church of Scotland minister, was born at Croft House, Alnwick, Northumberland, on 29 January 1804, the son of Robert Patterson of Croft House, Alnwick, and his wife, Janet Brown, the daughter of the Revd John *Brown (1722–1787) of Haddington, editor of the *Self-Interpreting Bible*. His father died when he was a child and his mother moved to Edinburgh with John, his younger brother, and his sister; there he attended the classical academy run by Benjamin Mackay (1810–15). In 1815 the family moved to Haddington, where John attended the grammar school, then returned to Edinburgh in 1818, where he joined the rector's class at the high school. Under the influence of James Pillans, he distinguished himself as a classical scholar, without his conspicuous ability ever estranging him from his boyhood friends. In 1820, he went on to arts and divinity courses at Edinburgh University, where he established a close friendship with William Cunningham (1805–1861). At that time Patterson was described as 'a little, dark, curly lad in spectacles, most gentle and loveable, and of rare promise' (Rainy and Mackenzie, 21). In 1827 he won the prize of 100 guineas, offered by the commissioners for visiting the universities and colleges of Scotland, for the best essay submitted under the title 'On the national character of the Athenians'.

In the spring of 1828 Patterson accepted a place as tutor to James Edward, tenth Baron Cranstoun, whom he accompanied to Oxford. Licensed by the presbytery of Kirkcudbright in January 1829, he had already attracted the interest of Sir Robert Peel, who was disposed to present him to a crown living. There was correspondence between the two men about the parish of Daviot, Aberdeenshire, but Patterson's friends opposed his translation to a rural backwater. He declined without injury to his prospects and was duly presented to the populous manufacturing parish of Falkirk, where he was ordained on 26 February 1830. As befitted a man with his ancestry, Patterson enjoyed good relations with dissenters, including his distinguished neighbour, Henry Belfrage. His views were strongly anti-patronage and he co-operated with Cunningham in mounting a series of lectures in Edinburgh on church establishments.

Patterson married, on 23 April 1833, Sarah Elizabeth (d. 1882), only daughter of the Revd George Atkin of Morpeth. The couple had two children, one of whom died shortly after birth. The other, a son, survived his father. Patterson looked after his parish with vigour but his health broke down while he was attending the general assembly in Edinburgh. He was taken to his mother's house, in Meadow Place, Edinburgh, where he died on 29 June 1835. He was interred in the burial-ground of his own church on 3 July. LIONEL ALEXANDER RITCHIE

Sources J. B. Patterson, *Discourses* (1837) · *Fasti Scot.* · *Edinburgh Christian Instructor*, 4 (1835), 503, 644–5 · R. Rainy and J. Mackenzie, *Life of William Cunningham D.D.* (1871) · J. McKerrow and J. Macfarlane, *Life and correspondence of the late Rev Henry Belfrage DD of Falkirk* (1837), 311–14 · *DNB*
Archives NL Scot., letters to J. J. Bonar
Likenesses W. Howison, portrait, repro. in Patterson, *Discourses*

Patterson, Robert (1802–1872), naturalist, was born on 18 April 1802 at Belfast, the eldest son of Robert Patterson, a Belfast merchant, and his wife, Catharine, daughter of David Jonathan Clarke KC, of Dublin and Portarlington, and widow of a Mr Keine of Dublin. He received his education chiefly at the Belfast Academy and at the Belfast Academical Institution. In 1818 he was apprenticed to his father's business. In 1833 he married Mary Elizabeth, youngest daughter of William Hugh Ferrar, stipendiary magistrate of Belfast. The couple had six daughters and five sons including Sir Robert Lloyd Patterson (1836–1906), president of the Belfast chamber of commerce and of the Belfast Natural History and Philosophical Society.

Patterson's leisure was devoted to the study of natural history, and especially to the investigation of the fauna and flora of the country around Belfast. In 1821 he was a co-founder (with seven others) of the Natural History Society of Belfast (later the Belfast Natural History and Philosophical Society). He delivered numerous lectures in connection with the society, a number of which were published. He was its president for many years, and took a foremost part in the erection of its museum in 1830–31. His efforts for the society were recognized in 1871, when he was presented with an illuminated address in recognition of his labours 'in popularising the general study of natural history and in advancing it to its rightful place as a recognised branch of school education'.

Patterson's first work, *Letters on the Natural History of the Insects Mentioned in Shakespere's Plays*, the substance of which had been given in a series of lectures before the Belfast Natural History Society, appeared in 1838. In 1846 he published what was probably his most important work, *Introduction to Zoology for the Use of Schools, First Part*, which was followed in 1848 by the second part, and later on by two small volumes, *First Steps to Zoology: Part i. Invertebrate Animals; Part ii. Vertebrate Animals*. His next work, in 1853, was his large coloured *Zoological Diagrams*. All these works had a very wide circulation, and gave a valuable stimulus to the study of zoology in schools.

Patterson was also a frequent contributor to several scientific journals. In the *Zoologist* (1843) he published 'The reptiles mentioned by Shakespere'. He wrote for the *Magazine of Natural History*, and contributed papers to the Royal Irish Academy, several of which were issued in its *Transactions*.

Patterson was one of the earliest and most zealous members of the British Association for the Advancement of Science, and in 1839 was appointed one of the secretaries of the section on natural history, an office which he held until 1844. When the association met in Belfast in 1852, he acted as local treasurer. In 1856 he was elected a member of the Royal Irish Academy, and on 9 June 1859 he was elected a fellow of the Royal Society. He belonged to several other learned bodies.

In Belfast, where he enjoyed universal respect, Patterson played an active part in the working of various local institutions. In 1844 he joined the committee of the Ulster Society for the Prevention of Cruelty to Animals, and he was a zealous promoter of the interests of the Belfast Society for Promoting Knowledge, of the Royal Botanic Gardens, and of his old school, the Royal Belfast Academical Institution. For twelve years, between 1858 and 1870, he was one of the Belfast harbour commissioners. In 1865 he retired from business. He died on 14 February 1872 at his residence, 6 College Square, north Belfast; he was survived by his wife. He was buried in the city cemetery, where a handsome granite monument marked his grave. In the First Presbyterian (Unitarian) Church, of which he was an attached member, a mural tablet was also erected to his memory by his sons.

THOMAS HAMILTON, *rev.* YOLANDA FOOTE

Sources private information (1895) [Richard Patterson; R. L. Patterson] · *Northern Whig* (15 Feb 1872) · personal knowledge (1895) · *Nature*, 5 (1871–2), 332 · Boase, *Mod. Eng. biog.* · *WWW* · *The tree: the centenary book of the Ulster Society for the Prevention of Cruelty to Animals, 1836–1936* (1936) · *CGPLA Ire.* (1872)
Likenesses T. H. Maguire, lithograph, 1851, BM, NPG; repro. in T. H. Maguire, *Portraits of honorary members of the Ipswich Museum* (1852) · engraving, 1859, repro. in *FRS* (9 June 1859)
Wealth at death under £20,000: probate, 20 March 1872, *CGPLA Ire.*

Patterson, Robert Hogarth (1821–1886), journalist and writer, was born in December 1821 at Edinburgh, where he was educated for civil engineering at the high school. When quite young he entered the printing office of his cousin, John Ballantyne, as a press corrector. He married at St Cuthbert's Church in Edinburgh, on 8 July 1848, Georgina, daughter of the late George Thompson, wine merchant in Edinburgh; they had a son, Robert Hogarth Patterson.

In 1852 Patterson left the printing business to become editor of the *Edinburgh Advertiser*. In 1858 he moved to London as editor of the Conservative weekly *The Press*, which had been launched by Disraeli in 1853. When later Disraeli sold his holding, Patterson became its proprietor. In 1865 he was appointed editor of *The Globe*, a London evening newspaper; he changed it to pink paper and in 1866

reduced its price from 6*d.* to 1*d.* He resigned in 1869 to join the board of referees appointed by parliament to investigate and report on the best means of purification of coal gas in London. Chemistry had always been one of his favourite studies, and his scientific knowledge enabled him to take a leading part in the proceedings of the referees, which resulted in the discovery of the process long used for the elimination of sulphur and ammonia impurities from gas.

In 1872 Patterson went to Glasgow as editor of the *Glasgow News*, but his health broke down and he returned to London in 1874, where he resumed his writing, contributing articles on politics, finance, science, and history to various magazines. In early life he contributed articles to *Chambers's Edinburgh Journal*, and later to the *Quarterly*, *Blackwood's*, *Bentley*, and the *Dublin University Magazine*.

Patterson gained a reputation as a financial expert, and was consulted by the Bank of England and the Bank of France on financial and currency questions. He was elected a fellow, and afterwards a member of council, of the Statistical Society. He published *The New Revolution, or, The Napoleonic Policy in Europe* (1860), which attracted considerable attention, owing to the fulfilment, soon after publication, of several of its predictions, books on economics, finance, the Irish question, and gas, and pamphlets on India, gas, and other subjects. Patterson died at his home, 22 Wingate Road, Hammersmith, London, on 13 December 1886.

GEORGE STRONACH, *rev.* ROGER T. STEARN

Sources Irving, *Scots.* · *The Athenaeum* (25 Dec 1886), 863 · *The Times* (14 Dec 1886) · private information (1895) · S. E. Koss, *The rise and fall of the political press in Britain*, 1 (1981) · D. Griffiths, ed., *The encyclopedia of the British press, 1422–1992* (1992) · *CGPLA Eng. & Wales* (1887) · m. cert.
Archives NHM, autobiographical notes | NL Scot., corresp. with Blackwoods and poems
Wealth at death £1170 17*s.* 9*d.*: probate, 7 Jan 1887, *CGPLA Eng. & Wales*

Patterson [*née* Caffyn], **Sheila** (1918–1998), social anthropologist, was born on 30 March 1918 at 64 Bower Mount Road, Maidstone, Kent, the daughter of Thomas Percy Caffyn (1871/2–1920), master draper, and his wife, Edith, daughter of Jason Saville, engineer. Her father had been ill for several years before her birth, and died when she was two. On 19 September 1928 her mother married Malcolm Kenneth Pridmore, solicitor, of Cromers Close, Kenilworth Road, Coventry. Sheila Pridmore, as she became, was educated at Roedean School and at St Hugh's College, Oxford, where she obtained a third class in classical moderations in 1938 and a third class in *literae humaniores* in 1940. She joined the War Office as a temporary civil servant in October 1940, but in 1941 became assistant secretary at Polish House, London, which came under the direction of the British Council. On 6 May 1944 she married Captain Zdzislaw Gadomski (*b.* 1909/10), an officer with the general staff of the Polish army. The marriage ended shortly thereafter, but she retained a keen interest in Poland and its émigré communities.

In 1947 Sheila Gadomski enrolled for a postgraduate diploma in social anthropology at the London School of Economics, and undertook research in South Africa. She was awarded the diploma in 1950 for her thesis, 'The status of the Cape Coloured people within the South African social structure'. Her research in South Africa led to two books, *Colour and Culture in South Africa* (1953) and a history of the Afrikaners, *The Last Trek* (1957), and to a lasting friendship with Ellen Hellman, a founder of the South African Institute of Race Relations. On 23 January 1948 she married Captain Bruce Tyrrell Patterson (*d.* 2000), with whom she had one daughter, (Anne) Clarissa (1953–1973). The marriage was again short-lived, and she returned to Britain in 1954, after two years' research among the Polish community in Canada. On 7 May 1955 she married, lastly, Tadeusz Horko, a Polish journalist, but she retained the name Sheila Patterson for professional purposes.

Between 1955 and 1959 Patterson undertook the research among West Indian settlers in Brixton, south London, which led to her best-known book, *Dark Strangers* (1959). This was a descriptive study based on the assumption that the settlers would eventually be assimilated into the general population. It was followed by a volume that earned her a London PhD in social anthropology, *Immigrants in Industry* (1968), which derived from research conducted in Croydon in 1959–60. In 1958 she had begun working for the Institute of Race Relations in London, a recent offshoot of the Royal Institute of International Affairs. From 1960 she edited the institute's newsletter, a factual record of events that included an occasional commentary. This work was later built into a book-length chronicle under her authorship, *Immigration and Race Relations in Britain, 1960–1967* (1969). Following a break in 1968–70 for research in Barbados and St Vincent, she was from 1971 for sixteen years editor of *New Community*, the quarterly journal of the Community Relations Commission (a body which later became the Commission for Racial Equality).

From the mid-1950s to the end of the 1960s public discussion of the issues posed by new Commonwealth immigration into Britain was led by a group disparaged by one critic as 'the lords and ladies of race relations'. Patterson might have been one of them. She had returned to Britain as a strikingly attractive and elegant woman with a cut-glass accent. Her sometimes imperious manner concealed a basic shyness: someone who worked closely with her in the 1970s testified that 'she declined more public speaking invitations than anyone I have ever known' (private information). The end of the era of the lords and ladies was foretold in 1967, when a very successful white-led pressure group, the Campaign against Racial Discrimination, was taken over by black militants. In 1972 the Institute of Race Relations was the subject of a take-over that gave it a radically leftist character. The Community Relations Commission, established under the Race Relations Act 1968 to promote harmonious community relations, occupied a central position in a very contested field. *New Community* set out to bridge the gaps between academics, those working in the applied field, and policy-makers, by publishing a wide range of research findings in a jargon-free style. Patterson was an excellent choice as editor, for she observed strict standards of accuracy in reporting, in the selection of appropriate names for groups and social processes, and in political impartiality. Though many of those around her were left-wingers, she was ready to tell them that she herself was a Conservative with a capital C. She and her husband had a flat in Nerja, Andalusia, Spain, where everything appealed to her: the warmth, the way of life, the food, and above all the people.

The 1970s were also a decade of change in social anthropology, with the passing of a generation of scholars who had conducted field research in the colonial era and had focused on the study of social structure. Interest switched to new fields and new theories. Patterson did not contribute to the change of direction, or, indeed, follow it very closely. She had by this time come to concentrate upon the study of race relations within the Commonwealth and to develop an approach that had more in common with that of a historian than of a social theorist.

Patterson retired as editor of *New Community* in 1987, though she maintained contact with her former colleagues in Britain and elsewhere. Her last years were spent at the Victoria Highgrove Nursing Home, 59 Dyke Road Avenue, Hove, Sussex, and she died there on 21 June 1998, following a stroke. Her husband Tadeusz Horko predeceased her.

MICHAEL BANTON

Sources *The Guardian* (1 July 1998) · *The Independent* (29 July 1998) · private information (2004) [Krystyna Horko; Nadine Peppard; Guida Crowley; St Hugh's College, Oxford] · personal knowledge (2004) · b. cert. · m. cert. [Zdzislaw Gadomski] · m. cert. [Bruce Patterson] · m. cert. [Tadeusz Horko] · d. cert.
Likenesses photograph, repro. in *The Guardian* · photograph, repro. in *The Independent*

Patteson, Sir John (1790–1861), judge, was born on 11 February 1790 at Coney Weston, Suffolk, the second son of the Revd Henry Patteson of Drinkstone, Suffolk, and his wife, Sophia, daughter of Richard Ayton Lee, a London banker. He was educated at a school kept by his father's curate, Mr Merest, before going on to Eton College, where his name appeared in the school lists in 1802 and he was elected a scholar in 1808. He was taught by John Bird Sumner, afterwards archbishop of Canterbury, and showed himself to be one of the best swimmers, scullers, and cricketers in the school. In 1809 he matriculated at King's College, Cambridge, as a scholar, which entitled him to graduate without having to sit the normal examinations. He was duly awarded a BA degree in 1813 and an MA in 1816. He won the Davies university classics scholarship in 1810, the first year in which it was offered, and was elected a fellow of King's in 1812.

Patteson was unsure whether to study medicine, law, or divinity, but chose in the end to pursue a career in law and joined the Middle Temple in London. In 1815 he went on the midland circuit as marshal to Mr Justice Chambre, and read in the chambers of Godfrey Sykes, an eminent pleader, and Joseph Littledale, afterwards a judge. On 23 February 1818 he married his cousin Elizabeth, daughter of George Lee of Dickleburgh, Norfolk; before her death on 3 April 1820 they had one daughter. In the following year, 1821, he began practice as a special pleader, and was called to the bar. He joined the northern circuit, and began to attract attention through his skill in pleading.

On 22 April 1824 he married Frances Duke (*d.* 1842), daughter of Captain James Coleridge of Ottery St Mary, Devon, and sister of the famous judge Sir John Taylor *Coleridge. In the same year he published an edition of Serjeant Williams' *Notes on Saunders's Reports*, which was well regarded in legal circles. One of the children of Patteson's second marriage was John Coleridge *Patteson (1827–1871), bishop of Melanesia.

Patteson became assistant to Littledale as counsel to the Treasury and his career began to take off; his argument in *Rennell* v. *Bishop of Lincoln* (reported in 7 Barnewell and Cresswell, 113) was well regarded. He was one of the legal commissioners on the reform of the Welsh judicature, whose report led to the act of 1830, by which three additional judges were appointed—one each in the king's bench, common pleas, and exchequer.

Although Patteson had never been king's counsel, in November 1830 Lord Lyndhurst appointed him to the new judgeship in the court of king's bench, and he was knighted. For over twenty years he was thought to be one of the most practical and learned judges in that court and was praised for his memory, clarity of expression, courtesy, and erudition. According to his contemporary, Sir Joseph Arnould, 'Take him altogether', he was 'one of the very best and ablest judges that ever sat in Westminster Hall' (Arnould, 1.419).

Deafness forced Patteson to resign at the end of January 1852. On 2 February 1852 he was sworn of the privy council, and served for some years on the judicial committee. He also acted as a commissioner to examine into the state of the City of London in 1853. He was frequently chosen as arbitrator in government questions, over disputes such as those which emerged between the crown and duchy of Cornwall or between the Post Office and the Great Western Railway. One award terminated a long-standing rating dispute between the city and university of Cambridge. Patteson died of throat cancer on 28 June 1861 at Feniton Court, Honiton, Devon, which he had bought in 1841, and was buried on 5 July in Feniton churchyard.

J. A. HAMILTON, rev. HUGH MOONEY

Sources Foss, *Judges* · *Solicitors' Journal*, 5 (1860–61), 620–21 · *Law Magazine*, new ser., 12 (1861–2), 197–224 · *Law Times* (6 July 1861), 434; (13 July 1861), 446–7 · C. M. Yonge, *Life of John Coleridge Patteson*, 2 vols. (1874) · J. Arnould, *Life of Lord Chief Justice Denman of England*, 2 vols. (1873) · *CGPLA Eng. & Wales* (1861)
Archives Glamorgan RO, Cardiff, opinion on the Criminal Law Consolidation Bill
Likenesses M. Carpenter, oils, King's Cam. · S. Cousins, mezzotint (after M. Carpenter), BM, NPG
Wealth at death £25,000: probate, 9 July 1861, *CGPLA Eng. & Wales*

Patteson, John Coleridge (1827–1871), bishop of Melanesia, was born in London on 1 April 1827, the elder son of Sir John *Patteson (1790–1861), judge, and his second wife, Frances Duke Coleridge (*d.* 1842). He was brought up at Feniton Court, Devon, where his family resided, so as to be

John Coleridge Patteson (1827–1871), by unknown photographer

near the home of his mother's relatives at Ottery St Mary. After three years at a school at Ottery, 'Coley' Patteson was placed in 1838 at Eton College, in the house of his uncle, the Revd E. Coleridge, son-in-law of Dr Keate, the former headmaster. Patteson remained at Eton until 1845; he was an undistinguished scholar, but he was captain of the cricket eleven and showed much strength of character. From 1845 to 1848 he was a commoner of Balliol College, Oxford, under Dr Richard Jenkyns. He was not particularly interested in academic studies, and obtained a second-class degree in *literae humaniores*, but he came into contact with Benjamin Jowett, afterwards master of Balliol, Professor Max Müller, John Campbell Shairp, Edwin Palmer, afterwards archdeacon of Oxford, James Riddell, John James Hornby, afterwards provost of Eton, and Charles Savile Roundell, all of whom became lifelong friends.

After taking his degree in October 1849 Patteson left to travel in Switzerland and Italy; he also learned German at Dresden and began the study of Hebrew and Arabic, discovering a remarkable gift for languages. After returning to Oxford in 1852, he became a fellow of Merton College, and there spent the year 1852–3. He was ordained in September 1853 to the curacy of Alfington, part of the parish of Ottery St Mary, of which he was practically in sole charge. His influence was beginning to be strongly felt, when the visit of George Augustus Selwyn, bishop of New Zealand, in the summer of 1854, determined his choice of a missionary career. He left England with the bishop in March 1855, and landed at Auckland in July.

In May 1856 Patteson sailed for the first time to Melanesia, as Bishop Selwyn's missionary chaplain. The scheme of the Melanesian mission, which had been begun by Selwyn in 1849, was to take boys, with their parents' consent, from the islands of the south-west Pacific, to instruct them during the summer at the mission school in New Zealand, and to bring them back the next year to their homes. The school was at first at St John's, some 6 miles from Auckland; then at Kohimarama, on the harbour; and later at Norfolk Island. This island had the advantage of a warmer climate and proximity to the Melanesian Islands. Patteson made annual missionary voyages to Melanesia, and almost every year from 1858 he lived for a few months on one of the islands of the Loyalty, Banks, or Solomon groups. At the mission's central school he devoted himself to his Melanesian pupils, teaching them the rudiments of Western knowledge and the Christian religion, which they were expected to impart to their families and friends on their return. Patteson refused to regard the Melanesians as an inferior race. His pupils appreciated his attitude, and his remarkable linguistic powers greatly aided him. Because of the great number of languages in Melanesia, he selected the language of the island of Mota in the Banks group as most typical in point of idiom, and employed it in the school. It became the common teaching language of the mission.

On 24 February 1861 Patteson was consecrated missionary bishop of the western islands of the south Pacific Ocean. He became the sole director of the mission, which was supported partly from his own funds—he retained his fellowship at Merton to the end, and he made over to the mission the money left him by his father in 1861. Patteson was joined in 1863 by Robert Henry Codrington, fellow of Wadham College, Oxford, and by other missionary recruits from England and New Zealand. At his headquarters at Norfolk Island Patteson worked incessantly from dawn until night, teaching, organizing, and conducting divine worship. Absorbed in his work, he refused to consider marriage. He deprecated all haste in making conversions. At the same time his labours as a linguist were not neglected. Eventually he spoke or had some knowledge of more than twenty Melanesian languages.

Patteson compiled and printed general vocabularies in three local languages, and lists of interrogatives, prepositions, and conjunctions in eleven; he translated into the Mota language the third and fourth gospels and other parts of scripture. He stopped, however, deliberately short in the academic part of the work, mainly because his time was absorbed by the mission. Instead he used languages for the purpose of teaching; Melanesian languages, he wrote, were

> very poor in respect of words belonging to civilised and literary and religious life, but exceedingly rich in all that pertains to the needs and habits of men circumstanced as

they are. I draw naturally this inference, 'Don't be in any hurry to translate, and don't attempt to use words as (assumed) equivalents of abstract ideas. Don't devise modes of expression unknown to the language as at present in use. They can't understand, and therefore don't use words to express definitions.' (Yonge, 2.128)

Missionary work in Melanesia was unusually difficult and during his lifetime Patteson's mission gained few converts. He was not disappointed for he believed he was laying foundations that would be lasting. He gave much thought to the ways in which Christianity should be adapted to Melanesian culture and social life. He believed that it should be possible for missionaries to distinguish between the fundamentals of Christian doctrine and practice—'all men must receive that'—and secondary matters of doctrine and practice which should be adapted to the circumstances of their hearers: 'We seek to denationalise these races, as far as I can see; whereas we ought surely to change as little as possible—only what is clearly incompatible with the simplest form of Christian teaching and practice' (Yonge, 2.112). Patteson recognized the importance of an indigenous clergy, whose qualifications should be adapted to the work they would be doing in their own society. In 1868 he ordained the first Melanesian clergyman, George Sarawia, who was in charge of the mission school at Mota. Patteson's missionary philosophy greatly influenced the later development of the Melanesian mission.

Patteson's interest in all that was going on in Britain was vividly maintained. He wrote regularly to his father until the latter's death in 1861, and to his two sisters and brother; he read widely; he kept up communication with many of his old friends; and he corresponded with Professor Max Müller about the Melanesian languages. He embraced enthusiastically Bishop Selwyn's plan of colonial church government, which led to the formation of a self-governing church in New Zealand in 1857. In theological matters his sympathies were enlarged by his experience. Though sympathizing with Pusey and Keble, and owing much to the latter, he criticized their tendencies and dissented from their views on the Lord's supper.

Patteson's life was often in danger. At Santa Cruz in 1864 he was attacked as he left the shore, and though he escaped, two of his companions, Edwin Nobbs and Fisher Young, were struck by the arrows and died of tetanus. The work of the mission was increasingly disrupted by a rival European influence—the labour trade in the south-west Pacific. The sugar planters of Fiji and Queensland required labourers, and many Melanesian islanders were willing to go to the plantations for a few years. Although abuses were common, Patteson was cautious in his criticism of labour recruiting. He never condemned the trade, believing that it might be carried on honestly and with benefit to all parties; but he desired that it should be subjected, as it was after his death, to regulation by the British government.

Patteson visited the island of Nukapu in the Santa Cruz group on 20 September 1871. He had been there before at least three times, and so landed alone and unarmed. His friends, who were waiting for him in the ship's boat at the reef outside the island, found themselves attacked by a flight of arrows, which wounded three of them; and soon after a canoe floated out from the shore, in which was the dead body of the bishop, with a frond of palm tied in five knots. This was believed to imply that he had been killed to avenge five of the islanders who had been abducted by a labour recruiter. Although this theory was almost universally accepted, other explanations are possible. Patteson was buried at sea. Two of his companions, Joseph Atkin and Stephen Taroaniara, who was from the Solomon Islands, died of tetanus a few days later.

After the bishop's death the members of the mission urged that there be no retaliation. However, in November 1871 Lieutenant A. H. Markham of the British warship *Rosario*, who had gone to Nukapu to investigate the incident, received a hostile reception. In retaliation he ordered the bombardment of the island. Patteson's friends were scandalized. In the Australian and New Zealand colonies the news of Patteson's death caused a 'profound sensation' and inspired a wave of public opposition to the unregulated labour trade. The British government had already drafted a bill to regulate labour recruiting by British subjects in the south Pacific. The news of the death of a well-connected missionary bishop hastened the introduction of the bill into parliament and in June 1871 it became law as the Pacific Islanders Protection Act. Relatives, friends, and admirers of Patteson raised money for memorials. These included a wall tablet in the chapel of Merton College, Oxford, a pulpit in Exeter Cathedral, and the richly furnished chapel of St Barnabas at the mission headquarters at Norfolk Island. A memorial cross was erected at Nukapu in 1884.

Through his violent death, and its association with the labour trade, Patteson achieved fame. Among Anglicans, especially those of high-church sympathies, he was honoured as a bishop who had died in the performance of his duty as a Christian missionary. In 1872 the Society for the Propagation of the Gospel, inspired by the news of Patteson's death, requested the archbishop of Canterbury to approve a day of intercession for missions; this became an annual observance in the Church of England. As the 'martyr bishop of Melanesia', Patteson has been the subject of numerous popular biographies. In the Melanesian mission, the day of his death—20 September—was subsequently observed as a holy day, and he became widely commemorated in Anglican church calendars.

W. H. FREMANTLE, *rev.* DAVID HILLIARD

Sources C. M. Yonge, *Life of John Coleridge Patteson*, 2 vols. (1874) · D. Hilliard, 'John Coleridge Patteson: missionary bishop of Melanesia', *Pacific island portraits*, ed. J. W. Davidson and D. Scarr (1970), 177–200 · D. Hilliard, *God's gentlemen: a history of the Melanesian mission, 1849–1942* (1978) · D. Hilliard, 'The making of an Anglican martyr: Bishop John Coleridge Patteson of Melanesia', *Martyrs and martyrologies*, ed. D. Wood, SCH, 30 (1993), 333–45 · R. M. Ross, *Melanesians at Mission Bay: a history of the Melanesian mission in Auckland* (1983) · J. Gutch, *Martyr of the islands: the life and death of John Coleridge Patteson* (1971) · [W. E. Gladstone], review, *QR*, 137 (1874), 458–92

Archives Bodl. RH, papers · NL NZ, Turnbull L. · Selwyn College, Cambridge, diaries · SOAS, corresp. | BL, W. E. Gladstone MSS · Mitchell L., NSW, corresp. with Lady Stephen

Likenesses T. Woolner, marble relief tablet, 1875, Merton Oxf. · C. H. Jeens, stipple (after G. Richmond), BM, NPG; repro. in Yonge, *Life of John Coleridge Patteson* · photograph, NPG [*see illus.*]

Patti, Adelina (1843–1919), singer, was born at Fuencarral 6, Madrid, on 19 February 1843, the last child of Caterina Barili-Patti (*d.* 1870) and Salvatore Patti (1800–1869), Italian singers with, between them, eight musical children including Carlotta *Patti. She was trained chiefly by her stepbrother Ettore Barili. From 1847 Salvatore managed a New York opera house, and his failure precipitated Adelina's concert début at the age of eight (22 November 1851). Success brought lucrative tours of North America and Cuba, in which she took up 'Home Sweet Home' and 'Comin' thro' the Rye', which were always to be her concert standbys. In her operatic début when she was sixteen at the New York Academy of Music, on 24 November 1859 (as Lucia), her 'brilliant execution … rank[ed] with that where the best singers end' (*New York Tribune*). After seasons in New York, New Orleans, and Havana, she sailed to England, where Frederick Gye, the manager of Covent Garden, engaged the unknown singer. Her début in *La sonnambula* (14 May 1861) established a 'phenomenon' peerless for over thirty years, as did her début in Paris (16 November 1862). She divided the 1860s between the two cities, with excursions to Vienna, Berlin, and Madrid; St Petersburg and Moscow followed.

In lighter parts (Lucia, Amina, Violetta, Linda) Patti displayed limpid high notes (reaching to f‴) and a nightingale-like trill; in time the high notes lost their ease and the lower ones strengthened, though she was never a mezzo (her Carmen in 1885 was a rare failure). She had a 'scale … of absolute accuracy and evenness, a tone of perfect purity … faultless phrasing … wonderful economy of breath' (E. Eames, 30). In dramatic parts—Leonora (*Il trovatore*), Valentine, Aida—Verdi thought her an excellent actress; but she performed them seldom, and never sang Wagner (other than one song and one aria in concert) as a part of her intense professional care for her health and doll-like face and figure. She would not attend rehearsals, was exacting about fellow singers and billing, and never sang more than three times a week—scarcely at all when not quite well. Bernard Shaw, who admired her voice and technique, noted that 'after two bars of really dramatic music' she would 'drop back into purely decorative roulade' (*Our Theatres*, 3.193).

Patti's letters show self-possession and an inflexible will demurely expressed. On 29 July 1868 she married the French Marquis Henri de Caux (1825–1889). The marriage soon collapsed; both had affairs, she with the married French tenor Ernest Nicolini (Nicolas; 1834–1898). Legal separation (granted to Caux in Paris on 3 August 1877) and divorce (15 July 1885) cost her half her fortune. At Craig-y-nos Castle, Ystradgynlais, Brecknockshire, which she bought in 1878, she and Nicolini led an extravagant late Victorian country life, with a staff of forty and a private theatre where she acted mimed plays; they married on 10

Adelina Patti (1843–1919), by James Sant, exh. RA 1886

June 1886. After Nicolini's death (18 January 1898) she married on 25 January 1899 Rolf Cederström (1870–1947), a Swedish baron twenty-seven years her junior; both had become British subjects. Cederström cut down the staff (to eighteen) and the social life, and gave her the devotion and flattery she needed.

Patti's brother-in-law and agent, Maurice Strakosch, had negotiated an early Covent Garden salary of £150 (rising to £400) a month, followed in 1863–7 by a fee per performance of £80, rising to £120. Caux pushed this up in 1872 to an ostensible £200, of which £60 was returned, supposedly without Patti's knowledge. With concerts, her average London income by 1869 was over £1000 a month. In the 1880s her tours of the Americas earned her about $5000 per performance ($8000 in Buenos Aires): she brought in more money than any other performer. In real terms (collocating easy travel, a wide middle-class audience, low theatre wages, and low taxes) she was the highest paid singer ever. In Britain she kept to concert tours from 1886, the last taking place in 1906–07. That her voice was past its best was shown in a failed 1903 American tour and in recordings of 1905–6. She suffered from heart trouble and died at Craig-y-nos on 27 September 1919. She had always kept in touch with her family; she was buried on 29 May 1920 near her father in the Père Lachaise cemetery, Paris.

JOHN ROSSELLI

Sources J. F. Cone, *Adelina Patti, queen of hearts* (1994) · H. Klein, *The reign of Patti* (1920) · letters of Adelina Patti, Metropolitan Opera Archives, New York · A. Patti, letters, NYPL for the Performing Arts · M. Ringel, 'Opera in "The Donizettian dark ages": management, competition and artistic policy in London, 1861–71', PhD diss., U. Lond., 1996 · M. Strakosch, *Souvenirs d'un imprésario* (1886) · H. Rosenthal, *Two centuries of opera at Covent Garden* (1958) · G. B. Shaw, *Music in London, 1890–94*, 3 vols. (1932) · G. B. Shaw, *London music as heard in 1888–89 by Corno di Bassetto* (1937) · *The Mapleson memoirs: the career of an operatic impresario, 1858–1888*, ed. H. Rosenthal (1966) · J. Rosselli, *Singers of Italian opera* (1992) · D. Brinn, *Adelina Patti* (1988) · E. Eames, *Some memories and reflections* (1927) · G. B. Shaw, *Our theatres in the nineties*, rev. edn, 3 vols. (1932), vol. 3

Archives Cardiff Central Library, corresp. · Georgia Department of Archives and History, Atlanta, Georgia, Barili-Patti collection · Metropolitan Opera, New York, archives · NRA, priv. coll. · NRA, priv. coll. · NYPL for the Performing Arts · Royal Opera House, London · West Glamorgan Archive Service, letters | BL, Gladstone MSS | SOUND La Cañada Memorial Library, La Cañada, California, W. R. Moran Collection

Likenesses Winterhalter, oils, in or after 1860–1869, Harewood House, West Yorkshire · Winterhalter, oils, 1862, Brita Cederström Elmes Collection, Newbury, Berkshire · G. Doré, oils, 1867, Glynn Vivian Art Gallery, Swansea · G. Doré, oils, 1867 · J. Sant, oils, exh. RA 1886, NPG [*see illus.*] · H. Schadow, oils, 1895, Guildhall, Brecon · Barraud, photograph, NPG; repro. in *Men and women of the day*, 2 (1889) · L. Durand, marble bust, Royal Opera House, Covent Garden · JMB, lithograph, BM; repro. in *The Magazine of Music* (1887) · London Stereoscopic Co., cabinet photograph, NPG · G. Pilotell, etching, BM · Sargent, oils, Lincoln Centre, New York, Library of Performing Arts, Billy Rose Theatre Collection · Steinhardt, oils (as Desdemona), NMG Wales · cartes-de-visite, NPG · coloured lithograph (after unknown artist), NPG · photographs, repro. in J. F. Cone, *Adelina Patti* · photographs, repro. in Klein, *Reign of Patti* · photographs, Saltykov-Shchedrin State Public Library, St Petersburg, Russia · photographs, Lincoln Centre, New York, Library of Performing Arts, Billy Rose Theatre Collection · photographs, priv. coll. · photographs, La Cañada College, La Cañada, California, W. R. Moran Collection · photographs, Theatre Museum, London · prints, BM, Harvard TC, NPG

Wealth at death £116,337 18s. 9d.: probate, 21 Nov 1919, *CGPLA Eng. & Wales*

Patti [*married name* de Munck], **Carlotta** (1835–1889), singer, born at Florence on 30 October 1835, was the daughter of Salvatore Patti (1800–1869), a tenor, and his wife, Caterina Barili-Patti, *née* Chiesa (d. 1870), a soprano. Eight years senior to her more famous sister, Adelina *Patti, Carlotta studied the piano under Heinrich Herz (1806–1888), but gave up that instrument to devote herself entirely to singing.

The family moved to the United States and Carlotta Patti made her début in 1861 at the Academy of Music in New York with pronounced success. An appearance there in opera the following year was to be almost her sole experiment in that field. She went on to join Max Strakosch's Concert Party, which was then touring in North America. She next travelled to England, where she made her début on 16 April 1863 at a concert at Covent Garden after the opera and attracted considerable attention; on 9 May she created almost a furore at the Crystal Palace. After taking part in some fifty concerts, as well as singing before the court, she spent a large part of the next six years in various continental tours; she sang at Vienna in 1865, and again in 1867 at the Carl Theatre.

In 1869 Patti returned to America, and became the leading attraction of Strakosch's company, gaining special praise for her singing of the Queen of Night in concert performances of *The Magic Flute*. In the spring of 1870 she was in Argentina, where, at Buenos Aires, she made a rare

Carlotta Patti (1835–1889), by Bassano

appearance on the stage, singing in Rossini's *The Barber of Seville* and in *Don Pasquale*. A concert she later gave in the same country for the benefit of the sufferers in the Franco-Prussian War realized a profit of 60,000 francs. In 1872 she was singing with Mario in the United States, but from time to time she reappeared in Europe, and sang at the London Philharmonic and other concerts. She was much incensed at being billed as 'the sister of Adelina Patti' for a concert in Birmingham in 1874, and at first refused to appear.

On 3 September 1879 Carlotta Patti married Ernest de Munck, a Belgian cellist, and retired from the concert platform. Thereafter she taught singing in Paris until her death, from cancer, at her house in the rue Pierre-Charron on 27 June 1889.

Carlotta Patti possessed a voice of great brilliancy and extensive compass: it was said to have extended to G in altissimo. Her style and execution were excellent and finished, and it was due almost entirely to lameness, the result of an accident, that she never attempted to take a more prominent place among operatic singers.

R. H. LEGGE, *rev.* J. GILLILAND

Sources *New Grove* · *Enciclopaedia delio Spectacolo* (1954) · J. F. Cone, *Adelina Patti* (1993) · F. Hays, *Women of the day: a biographical dictionary of notable contemporaries* (1885) · *Baker's biographical dictionary of musicians*, rev. N. Slonimsky, 7th edn (1984) · G. A. Dalmazzo, *Adelina Patti's life* (1877) · Boase, *Mod. Eng. biog.* · *The Times* (29 June 1889) · *Musical World* [various] · J. D. Brown, *Dictionary of musicians* (1886)
Likenesses Bassano, photograph, NPG [*see illus.*] · C. Reutlinger, carte-de-visite, NPG · photographs, NPG · portrait, repro. in *London sketch book* (Nov 1874), 1–2 · portrait, repro. in *Illustrated News of the World*, 11 (1862), 221 · portrait, repro. in *Illustrated Sporting News*, 4 (1865), 441 · portrait, repro. in *Illustrated Sporting News*, 5 (1866), 529 · portrait, repro. in *Illustrated Times* (13 June 1863), 405 · prints, Harvard TC

Pattinson, Hugh Lee (1796–1858), metallurgical chemist, was born on 25 December 1796, at Alston, Cumberland, the son of Thomas Pattinson, a shopkeeper of that town, and his wife, Margaret Lee. Both his parents were members of the Society of Friends. Hugh was educated at small private schools, but from an early age assisted his father, who died on 19 May 1812. He succeeded in acquiring a knowledge of electricity, and when only seventeen constructed some electrical apparatus; he also studied chemistry, especially in connection with metallurgy. On 25 December 1815 he married Phoebe, daughter of John Walton of The Nest, Alston, having two days before been baptized into the Church of England at The Angel inn, when he took the additional Christian name of Lee in honour of his mother.

About 1821 Pattinson became clerk and assistant to Anthony Clapham, a soap boiler in Newcastle. In 1825 he obtained the post of lead assay master to the lords of the manor at Alston (the Greenwich Hospital commissioners) and returned to his native place. In January 1829 he first discovered an easy and economic method of separating the silver from lead ore, but owing to want of funds was not then able to complete his researches. In 1831 he was appointed manager to the lead works of Wentworth Beaumont where, after further experiments, he perfected his process for desilverizing lead, and finally patented it in 1833. The following year he resigned his post of manager, and, in partnership with John Lee and George Burnett, established chemical works at Felling and afterwards at Washington, near Gateshead.

Pattinson's process for the desilverization of lead was a most valuable discovery, and permitted of the successful working of previously neglected lead mines. Before this invention the silver found in lead ore could be separated only by converting the ore into lead oxide, isolating the silver, then reconverting the oxide to metal; by Pattinson's process silver can profitably be extracted from lead when present only in the proportion of 2 or 3 ounces to the ton of lead. The technique gave rise to the German verb 'pattinsoniren' and the French noun 'pattinsonage' for the process. It brought him £16,000 in royalties. He made two other important discoveries, both patented in 1841: a simple method for obtaining white lead by a process which gave rise to the formation of the then new compound, oxychloride of lead; and a new process for manufacturing 'magnesia alba'. Pattinson also first announced the discovery, from observations which had been made at a neighbouring colliery in 1840, that steam issuing from an orifice becomes electrical, a phenomenon subsequently turned to account by William George Armstrong in his hydroelectrical machine.

Pattinson had joined in 1822 the Literary and Philosophical Society of Newcastle. He was vice-president of the chemical section of the British Association in 1838, a fellow of the Geological Society and of the Royal Astronomical Society, and was elected a fellow of the Royal Society in June 1852.

Pattinson visited America in 1839–40 to investigate a proffered mining speculation, which, however, turned out worthless, and he, with his party, had to decamp by night to escape the threatened violence of the disappointed proprietors. Before returning to England he went to Canada where he took the first photograph of Niagara Falls, using the daguerreotype process. One of his prints was sent to Paris where an engraving of the image was published in 1841.

On retiring from business Pattinson was able to indulge his interest in astronomy, to which end he devoted himself to the study of mathematics and physics. He had purchased in 1851 a refracting telescope with a 7½ inch lens by Thomas Cooke of York, one of the largest then made, which he erected at his home, Scotch House Boldon, co. Durham. Pattinson died at Scotch House on 11 November 1858. 	B. B. WOODWARD, rev. ANITA MCCONNELL

Sources J. Percy, *The metallurgy of lead* (1870), 121–40 · H. Lonsdale, *The worthies of Cumberland*, 4 (1873), 273–320 · C. Knight, ed., *The English cyclopaedia: biography*, 6 (1858), 979 · G. W. Garrett, 'Canada's first daguerrian image', *History of Photography*, 20 (1996), 101–3 · d. cert.
Archives Wellcome L., corresp. and papers
Likenesses portrait, repro. in Lonsdale, *Worthies of Cumberland*
Wealth at death under £35,000: probate, 15 June 1859, *CGPLA Eng. & Wales*

Pattishall [Pateshull], **Hugh of** (*d.* 1241), bishop of Coventry and Lichfield, was the son, and apparently heir, of Simon of *Pattishall (*d. c.*1217), the celebrated justice, and his wife, Amice. He began his career in the royal exchequer, having succeeded to his father's lands in 1218. He held the exchequer seal, and with it the office later called the chancellorship of the exchequer. On 1 June 1234 he was made treasurer, in place of Peter de Rivallis (*d.* 1258). As far as his ecclesiastical career is concerned, as well as receiving the benefices of Church Stowe, Ettingdon, and Cottingham in Northamptonshire, presumably his native county, he was also made prebendary of Nesden in St Paul's in 1238–9.

Pattishall was the first bishop to be elected to his see under the agreement of 1228 by which elections were to be held alternately at Coventry and Lichfield, with the prior of the former voting first and the dean of the latter second. His election, following the death of Alexander of Stainsby in 1238, was not the simple affair portayed by Lichfield sources, with monks and canons in full agreement, but a long-drawn-out process, with the canons originally preferring their own dean, William of Mancetter, and the monks favouring Nicholas of Farnham (*d.* 1257). Matthew Paris reports that Pattishall took a moving farewell of the barons of the exchequer, telling them that he left because he had been called by God to the cure of souls. He was consecrated at Newark, near Guildford in Surrey, on 1 July 1240. Because his episcopate lasted only sixteen

months, and his recorded acts are so few—the practice of recording them in a register had yet to take root in the diocese—it is hard to make any appraisal. However, it is clear that he took steps to redress the chronic shortage of funds suffered by his predecessors. He appropriated the church of Wybunbury in Cheshire in 1240, first for his own personal use, and then later formally to the episcopal *mensa*, and in the following year the important church of St Michael, Coventry, for the same purpose. This later became the Coventry Cathedral that was destroyed in the Second World War. In the same year he went on pilgrimage to the shrine of St Edmund in Suffolk, and elsewhere, attending a council of bishops in Oxford on 30 November on the way back. He died on the return journey at Potterspury in Northamptonshire on 8 December 1241 and was buried in the cathedral of Lichfield. 	M. J. FRANKLIN

Sources H. E. Savage, ed., *The great register of Lichfield Cathedral known as Magnum registrum album*, William Salt Archaeological Society, 3rd ser. (1924, [1926]) · Dugdale, *Monasticon*, new edn · Paris, *Chron.* · *Ann. mon.* · F. M. Powicke and C. R. Cheney, eds., *Councils and synods with other documents relating to the English church, 1205–1313*, 2 vols. (1964) · *CEPR letters* · *Les registres de Grégoire IX*, ed. L. Auvray, 4 vols. (Paris, 1896–1955) · *VCH* · *Fasti Angl., 1066–1300*, [St Paul's, London] · J. Bridges, *The history and antiquities of Northamptonshire*, ed. P. Whalley, 2 vols. (1791)

Pattishall, John (*c.*1293–1349). *See under* Pattishall, Sir Simon of (*b.* in or before 1219, *d.* 1274).

Pattishall [Pateshull], **Martin of** (*d.* 1229), justice, took his name from Pattishall, Northamptonshire, and learnt his profession as the clerk of Simon of Pattishall, King John's most experienced justice (the two were apparently unrelated). Already in 1201 'Martin the clerk of the lord Simon of Pattishall' was collecting the plea rolls made up by the clerks of the other justices of the bench on eyre. Martin the clerk was keeping another record at Westminster in Trinity term 1206, 'the book of death', containing the names of persons to be arrested as accessories to felonies; and Martin of Pattishall was the last witness, behind a series of royal justices, of a deed of King John at Clarendon in 1208, no doubt as the clerk who drew up the document. After the civil war which accompanied the accession of Henry III, Pattishall emerged as the chief of the king's professional legal servants and the leader in the re-establishment of the courts. Between November 1218 and April 1219 he was a justice on eyre in Yorkshire and Northumberland; in 1220–21 in Hertfordshire, at the Tower of London, and in the west midlands; in March and April 1226 again at the Tower of London; from September 1226 to February 1227 in Lincolnshire, Yorkshire, Lancashire, and Westmorland; and between September 1227 and October 1228 in Kent, Essex, Hertfordshire, Norfolk, and Suffolk. One of his clerks wrote in October 1226 that 'The said M. is energetic, and so conscientious and thorough in his work that he has overwhelmed all his fellows, especially W. of Ralege and myself, with the most exacting labour … Everyday he starts work at sunrise and does not stop till night' (Meekings, 5.492). Yet he took care not to hold sessions at harvest time, when poor men were too busy to serve on juries.

Almost thirty years after Pattishall's death, Henry of Bracton was instructed to bring his rolls to the exchequer, Bracton probably having received them as clerk of William of Raleigh, who had in his turn been Pattishall's clerk. Though he could serve on only a minority of eyre circuits between 1218 and 1228, it is overwhelmingly cases from Pattishall's sessions which are cited by name in the great treatise *On the Laws and Customs of England*, which was long regarded as the work of Bracton and of about the year 1250, but is now argued to have been started in Pattishall's lifetime. The account in the treatise of the opening of an eyre gives the 'words said by Martin of Pattishall' to the greater men of the county about 'the purpose of the eyre and the advantage to be derived from keeping the peace'. Both the law book and the collection of cases known as *Bracton's Note Book* register the influence of Pattishall's cases on the fast-developing common law, from the definition of the tenurial rights of villeins to the prescription of punishments for those found guilty by jury of the breach of the king's peace.

In 1224 Pattishall was involved in the curbing of a particular threat to the peace by Falkes de Bréauté, formerly King John's mercenary captain, who had retained castles and power in the midlands. In June 1224 Bréauté was provoked to open rebellion by justices of assize who were hearing a series of cases of disseisin against him at Dunstable. Dispatching a certain Master Thomas to help cure the wounds of those engaged in capturing Bréauté's men in Bedford Castle, Pattishall went to treat with their leader at Northampton; then as Bréauté was forced into exile, he resumed the hearings at Dunstable, apparently without requiring chancery writs to initiate cases. These proceedings are recorded on a plea roll of the court which normally sat at Westminster. Although the sessions of the justices on eyre and of assize in the county towns satisfied the requirement of chapter 17 of Magna Carta that common pleas should no longer follow the king but be heard in some fixed place, a central court separate from the exchequer was also needed as a focus for the system, and under Martin of Pattishall such a court, that of common pleas, began to take shape. When courts resumed in 1217, the justiciar, Hubert de Burgh, left Pattishall to preside at hearings of legal cases, to attest writs calling in assizes from the counties when mistakes were alleged, and to advise the chancellor on making new writs. The discretion he seems to have enjoyed in devising new remedies for complaints was particularly important at a period when the first registers of writs were being compiled.

An ordained clerk, Pattishall was rewarded with the deanery of Wimborne in Dorset, the archdeaconry of Norfolk, and finally, about August 1228, the deanery of St Paul's. He was already ill in 1227, retired from the bench in Hilary term 1229, and some time that year succumbed to a stroke. Proceedings after his death revealed that he had also held the living of Dilwyn in Herefordshire from the king and the livings of Brampton in Northamptonshire, Westleton in Suffolk, and Wigginton in Hertfordshire by the gift of others. A few years later William of Raleigh, who had been promoted to the bench as Pattishall retired, and who proceeded to much richer rewards, is recorded as parson of King's Somborne in Hampshire, previously held by 'Martin of Pateshull of good memory my sometime lord' (Meekings, 12.229).   ALAN HARDING

Sources *Chancery records* · D. M. Stenton, ed., *Rolls of the justices in eyre … Lincolnshire, 1218–1219, and Worcestershire, 1221*, SeldS, 53 (1934), xvi–xviii · *Curia regis rolls preserved in the Public Record Office* (1922–) · D. Crook, *Records of the general eyre*, Public Record Office Handbooks, 20 (1982) · H. de Bracton, *On the laws and customs of England*, ed. G. E. Woodbine, trans. S. E. Thorne, 4 vols. (1968–77) · C. A. F. Meekings, *Studies in 13th century justice and administration* (1981) · *Ann. mon.*, 3.66, 87, 115 · H. G. Richardson and G. O. Sayles, eds., *Select cases of proceedure without writ under Henry III*, SeldS, 60 (1941), xvii–xix, 49ff. · E. de Haas and G. D. G. Hall, eds., *Early registers of writs*, SeldS, 87 (1970), lxxvii–lxxx · *Bracton's note book*, ed. F. W. Maitland, 3 vols. (1887)

Pattishall [Pateshull], **Simon of** (*d. c.*1217), justice, was a native of Pattishall, Northamptonshire, where his family held a fee of the honour of Wahull. Pattishall first appears in the records in 1190, when he served as custodian of escheats in Northamptonshire, and as a justice at Westminster and on eyre. The next year he became custodian of Northampton Castle. He probably owed his entry into the administration to an early association with Geoffrey fitz Peter, sheriff of Northamptonshire, 1190–94, and later chief justiciar. Pattishall was sheriff of Essex and Hertfordshire, 1193–4, and then, as part of Richard I's reshuffling of sheriffs following his release from captivity, he was sheriff of Northamptonshire from 1194 to 1203. He served as an itinerant justice on all the general eyres of Richard I's and John's reigns, as well as serving continuously in the court of common pleas at Westminster, 1190–1207. He joined the court following the king on John's early visits to England, and again in 1204–5 and 1207; after the summer of 1207, he was with the court *coram rege* continuously until John's departure for Poitou early in 1214. He returned to the court at Westminster in 1214–15, until the baronial rebellion disrupted it.

The separation between the judiciary and the exchequer was not yet complete, and Pattishall often performed financial tasks. He was a collector of the carucage in 1198 and 1200, one of the keepers of the Jews in 1198, and in 1213 a commissioner assessing damage done during the interdict to churches in the diocese of Canterbury. Under King John Pattishall ranked as senior justice; the plea rolls reveal his special responsibilities, and his clerk's roll was the authoritative one. He accompanied John on his expedition of 1210 to Ireland to help in introducing English law and custom there. He was the most respected of a core of fifteen royal justices serving regularly under John, and Matthew Paris remembered him as one 'who at one time guided the reins of the justices of the whole kingdom' (Paris, 3.296). Even he ran foul of the king, however, and in 1207 he and a colleague on the bench were assessed for an amercement of 100 marks for allowing a compromise settlement of a criminal case, although they were later pardoned. At the outset of the baronial rebellion in 1215, King John ordered that Pattishall's lands be seized. Perhaps this was due less to his active disloyalty than to the location of his lands in a county under rebel control. Whatever the reason, on 20 May the king was persuaded by the abbot of Woburn to 'relax all our wrath and indignation which we had against you' (*Rotuli litterarum patentium*, 138). By December 1215 Pattishall had recovered his property, and by March 1216 he was back at judicial work in his native Northamptonshire, taking an assize there.

Pattishall greatly increased his landholdings during his career, accumulating almost six knight's fees as well as scattered smaller holdings centred mainly near Pattishall in Northamptonshire, but stretching into neighbouring shires. He held lands of religious houses that may have been retainers for his legal services, for example, half a knight's fee in Suffolk held of the abbey of Bury St Edmunds. He also held urban property in Northampton and in Stamford, Lincolnshire. King John granted him the manor of Rothersthorpe, Northamptonshire, part of the honour of Chocques. Other signs of royal favour were grants of temporary custodies, including Fotheringhay Castle in 1212. Pattishall was married to Amice, of unknown parentage. They had two sons who followed their father into the royal government: Walter of *Pattishall (*d.* 1231/2), who served Henry III as sheriff and justice, and Hugh of *Pattishall (*d.* 1241), a cleric who became canon of St Paul's and bishop of Coventry and Lichfield (1240–41), and who served as exchequer clerk, treasurer (1234–40), and royal justice. Simon of Pattishall also founded a judicial dynasty, for his clerk Martin of Pattishall moved on to the bench, as in turn did the latter's clerk, William of Raleigh. Simon made gifts to Pipewell Abbey, Northamptonshire, before his death in that county about 1217.   RALPH V. TURNER

Sources R. V. Turner, 'Simon of Pattishall, Northamptonshire man, early common law judge', *Northamptonshire Past and Present*, 6 (1978–83), 5–14 • GEC, *Peerage* • D. M. Stenton, 'Development of the judiciary, 1100–1216', *Pleas before the king or his justices, 1198–1212*, ed. D. M. Stenton, 3, SeldS, 83 (1967), xlvii–ccxliv • D. Crook, *Records of the general eyre*, Public Record Office Handbooks, 20 (1982) • *Pipe rolls* • *Chancery records* • *Curia regis rolls preserved in the Public Record Office* (1922–) • W. Farrer, *Honors and knights' fees … from the eleventh to the fourteenth century*, 3 vols. (1923–5) • Paris, *Chron.* • A. Hughes, *List of sheriffs for England and Wales: from the earliest times to AD 1831*, PRO (1898) • T. D. Hardy, ed., *Rotuli litterarum patentium*, RC (1835) • T. D. Hardy, ed., *Rotuli litterarum clausarum*, 2 vols., RC (1833–4)

Pattishall [Pateshull], **Sir Simon of** (*b.* in or before **1219**, *d.* **1274**), soldier and administrator, was the son of Walter of *Pattishall (*d.* 1231/2), who had been an itinerant justice in 1218 and the sheriff of Bedfordshire and Buckinghamshire between 1224 and 1228, and his wife, Margery, the daughter and heir of Richard d'Argentan. He was the grandson of Simon of *Pattishall, a prominent royal justice during the reign of King John, and the nephew of Hugh of *Pattishall, whose career as an exchequer clerk culminated in his appointment as treasurer (1234–40) and his election as bishop of Coventry and Lichfield (1240–41). It

was formerly believed that in 1257 Simon acted as one of the justices of the Jews, but this is erroneous. He seems never to have been a figure of much more than local significance. He married Margery, the daughter of Henry of Braybrooke.

In August 1258 Pattishall was one of the four knights appointed at the beginning of the period of baronial reform to inquire into official wrongdoing in Bedfordshire, and in October 1258 he was appointed sheriff of Bedfordshire and Buckinghamshire. In October 1259 he became sheriff of Northamptonshire and remained in office until July 1261, when he was one of the baronial appointees removed by the king. Pattishall evidently remained loyal to the baronial opposition. He was in Northampton with Simon de Montfort the younger when the town was besieged by the king in the spring of 1264, and became sheriff of Bedfordshire and Buckinghamshire again in June after the Montfortian victory at Lewes. It is unclear whether he fought at Evesham in 1265, but he was with the other Montfortians who held out in Kenilworth Castle after the Evesham débâcle. His lands were given to the royalist John Giffard and he was subsequently among the disinherited who joined up with Gilbert de Clare, earl of Gloucester. In June 1267 he received a pardon of the king's anger as one of Gilbert's bachelors, probably for his part in the earl's march on London, and by 1268 he had reached an agreement with John Giffard for the redemption of his lands. Pattishall fell very ill in 1273. He clearly remained a covert Montfortian at heart for it was apparently with the aid of a relic of the dead earl of Leicester that he recovered the power of speech, subsequently travelling to Evesham to give thanks. He died about Easter the following year.

With his wife, Margery, Simon of Pattishall was the father of John of Pattishall, who succeeded to most of his father's lands, and his younger brother, Robert, who was given family lands in Essex. John was elected knight of the shire for Bedfordshire in July 1290 but died later that year and was succeeded by his son and heir, another Simon. Simon married Isabel, the daughter and heir of John of Stonegrave. He died shortly before 2 December 1295, leaving as his heir his infant son, **John Pattishall** (*c.*1293–1349). By 1316 John Pattishall was in service with the earl of Hereford in Wales and later the same year, and subsequently, was summoned for military service against the Scots, and fought on the king's side at the battle of Boroughbridge in 1322. He received individual summonses to attend meetings of the king's council in 1324, 1335, 1338, and 1342, but never received an individual summons to parliament. As a prominent member of the local gentry he also received numerous judicial and other commissions to act in the counties of Bedfordshire, Buckinghamshire, and Northamptonshire, and in June 1327 he received a licence to crenellate his house in Bletsoe. In or before 1312 he married Mabel, the eldest sister of Otto Grandson. When he died in July or August 1349 he was succeeded by his son and heir, William. When William died childless in September 1359 he was in turn succeeded by his sisters, Sibyl, the wife of Roger de Beauchamp of Bletsoe, Maud, the wife of Walter Fauconberg, Alice, the wife of Thomas Wake of Blisworth, and Katherine, the wife of Robert of Tuddenham.   PAUL BRAND

Sources Chancery records · GEC, Peerage · Ann. mon., vol. 3 · G. H. Fowler and J. Godber, eds., The cartulary of Bushmead Priory, Bedfordshire Historical RS, 22 (1945)

Pattishall [Pateshull], Walter of (d. 1231/2), justice and administrator, was the elder son and heir of Simon of *Pattishall (d. c.1217), an important royal justice under Richard I and John, and of Amice, whose parentage is unknown. He inherited from his father lands in Northamptonshire, Buckinghamshire, Lincolnshire, Yorkshire, and perhaps elsewhere; by his marriage to Margery, daughter and heir of Richard d'Argentan, he acquired lands at Bletsoe, Crawley, and elsewhere in Bedfordshire. In 1222 he bought land at Deighton in Yorkshire. He was a subtenant of the honours of Wahull (Odell) and Bedford; and a benefactor, for his mother's soul, of Pipewell Abbey, Northamptonshire, where his father was buried.

Pattishall followed in his father's judicial footsteps, though with much less distinction. He first appears in royal service as a justice itinerant in the south midlands in 1218–19. Thereafter he was occasionally appointed as a royal justice, sitting for the last time in June 1231. But he came closest to the centre of political events when, following Falkes de Bréauté's dismissal as sheriff of Bedfordshire, he was appointed sheriff of Bedfordshire and Buckinghamshire on 18 January 1224. He thereby found himself at the spearhead of the royal government's developing confrontation with Bréauté. This reached a climax in the siege by royal forces of Bedford Castle, held on Bréauté's behalf by his brother William, between June and August 1224. After its fall Pattishall and Henry of Braybrooke (d. 1234) were ordered in the king's name to demolish it. This led to a minor conflict of loyalties, as each of them was 'a vassal and knight' of William de Beauchamp (Shirley, no. 206), lord of the honour of Bedford, who claimed the hereditary constableship of the castle, and had been seeking to recover it from Bréauté under the terms of the peace of 1217. Unsurprisingly Beauchamp was strongly opposed to the castle's destruction; but the pull of loyalty to the king proved stronger, and the castle was demolished. Pattishall was replaced as sheriff on 5 September 1228.

Pattishall was certainly dead by 20 August 1232, and may already have died by 25 August 1231. It seems likely that he was buried at Pipewell Abbey. He was survived by his wife, who made a gift for his soul to the hospital of Holy Trinity, Northampton, and by his son and heir, Simon of *Pattishall, who had come of age by 1236.

GEORGE GARNETT

Sources GEC, Peerage · W. Farrer, Honors and knights' fees … from the eleventh to the fourteenth century, 3 vols. (1923–5) · T. D. Hardy, ed., Rotuli litterarum clausarum, 2 vols., RC (1833–4) · CPR, 1216–32 · W. W. Shirley, ed., Royal and other historical letters illustrative of the reign of Henry III, 1, Rolls Series, 27 (1862), p. 236, no. 206 · C. Roberts, ed., Excerpta è rotulis finium in Turri Londinensi asservatis, Henrico Tertio rege, AD 1216–1272, 2 vols., RC, 32 (1835–6) · Curia regis rolls preserved in the Public Record Office (1922–) · Close rolls of the reign of Henry III, 14 vols., PRO (1902–38) · Calendar of the charter rolls, 6 vols., PRO (1903–27) · R. V. Turner, 'Simon of Pattishall, Northamptonshire man, early common law judge', Northamptonshire Past and Present, 6 (1978–83), 5–14

Pattison, Andrew Seth Pringle- (1856–1931), philosopher, was born Andrew Seth on 20 December 1856 at 1 West Claremont Street, Edinburgh, the second of seven children of Smith Kinmont Seth, bank clerk, and his wife, Margaret (1830–1911), daughter of Andrew Little, farmer, of Middle Blainslie, Berwickshire. He added Pringle-Pattison to his name in 1898 as a condition of receiving a bequest. He was educated at the Royal High School in Edinburgh and at Edinburgh University (1873–8), where he graduated with firsts in classics and philosophy.

After graduation Seth studied at Berlin, Jena, and Göttingen (1878–80), hoping to learn more of German idealist philosophy, which was becoming fashionable in Britain. In Germany, however, scientific materialism was in fashion, and he learned more of German idealism from reading the idealists than from attending German universities. At Göttingen he met Lotze, but was disappointed to find he was giving only introductory lectures. The results of his studies appeared in his first book, The Development from Kant to Hegel (1882).

On returning to Edinburgh, Seth became the assistant to his former teacher Campbell Fraser. During the three years he held this not very lucrative position he supplemented his income writing leaders and reviews for The Scotsman. He also achieved philosophical prominence by compiling, with R. B. Haldane, Essays in Philosophical Criticism (1883), the manifesto of the emerging neo-Hegelian movement that dominated British philosophy for the next twenty years. On the strength of this he was appointed professor of logic and philosophy at University College, Cardiff, a post which he held from 1883 to 1887. In 1884 he married Eva Stropp, whom he had met in Berlin, daughter of Albrecht Stropp, of Bogislavitz, Silesia. They had four sons (the youngest was killed in action in 1916) and three daughters (the eldest died in infancy). His wife died in 1928.

From Cardiff Seth visited Edinburgh to give two lecture series sponsored by A. J. Balfour specifically to give Seth 'an opportunity of producing original work' (Capper, 454). Two of his most important books resulted: Scottish Philosophy (1885) and Hegelianism and Personality (1887). A third series, on realism, was given in 1891 (published in the Philosophical Review, 1892–3; repr. as The Balfour Lectures on Realism, 1933). Seth meanwhile had moved in 1887 to St Andrews as professor of logic, rhetoric, and metaphysics, and in 1891 back to Edinburgh, where he replaced Fraser as professor of logic and metaphysics, a post he held until 1919. (From 1898 to 1924 the Edinburgh chair in moral philosophy was held by his younger brother James.)

In 1898 Seth inherited, from the widow of a very distant relative, a country estate, The Haining, near Selkirk, together with 7000 acres. He took his duties as a landowner seriously, which caused a long interruption in his career as an author. By mid-life he looked the part of a laird. He was a tall man, 'not very lithe' John Laird reported tactfully (*DNB*), with a magnificent white beard. Shyness prevented him from being a great debater: 'unready of speech he hugged the shelter of his manuscript, reading it beautifully to large classes which sometimes were almost openly restive' (ibid.).

Apart from a collection of essays (*Philosophical Radicals*, 1907, and *Two Lectures on Theism*, 1902) delivered at Princeton in 1896, Pringle-Pattison's subsequent books arose from his giving two double series of Gifford lectures: the first (1912–13) resulted in *The Idea of God in the Light of Recent Philosophy* (1917); the second (1921–3) gave rise to *The Idea of Immortality* (1922) and *Studies in the Philosophy of Religion* (1930)—the last more historical than philosophical.

Pringle-Pattison's earliest writings seemed to place him in the vanguard of the British Hegelian movement. His contribution to *Essays in Philosophical Criticism* attacked Kant for assuming that the mind was distinct from the things acting upon it, thereby admitting an unbridgeable gap between phenomena and noumena. He claimed that Hegel had shown how self-consciousness closed the gap by giving rise to ethical experience through which access to noumena was possible.

In *Hegelianism and Personality*, however, Pringle-Pattison broke ranks with the Hegelians, not on the fundamental role of self-consciousness, but on Hegel's locating self-consciousness in the Absolute rather than in individual persons. This he condemned as excessive abstraction at the expense of concrete particularity. His philosophy was thus a form of personal idealism, in contrast to the absolute idealism of Hegel and Bradley. In his essay on Kant he wrote: 'The individual is individualised only by his relations to the totality of the intelligible world' (*Essays in Philosophical Criticism*, 34). In *Hegelianism and Personality*, however, he wrote of selves in terms reminiscent of Leibniz's monads: 'Each self is a unique existence, which is perfectly *impervious* … to other selves' (*Hegelianism and Personality*, 216).

The reasons for this change are found partly in the influence of Lotze, another idealist inclined to monadology, but more importantly in his intervening book *Scottish Philosophy*, revealingly subtitled *A Comparison of the Scottish and German Answers to Hume*. In it he investigated the Scottish common-sense philosophy of Thomas Reid and took from it the view, *contra* Hume, that philosophy could never challenge our 'natural beliefs' in the external world, personal identity, and God. Having admitted all three, Pringle-Pattison faced the problem of explaining their interactions: the very problem Kant had been castigated for shirking. He attempted a solution in the *Balfour Lectures on Realism*, where he added a realist element to his already doubtfully consistent collection of beliefs. This never satisfied him: he was as unable to deny idealism as he was the external world. Idealist critics complained that, by insisting both that the external world was mind-independent and that our access to it was by means of ideas, he had reverted to the then universally discredited representational realism of Locke. Ironically, it was the unresolved tensions in his work that enhanced its appeal to many late Victorian thinkers, who—moved on the one

side by the scientific materialism of the 1860s and on the other by older religious lines of thought as well as newer idealist ones—were anxious to reconcile these. Although the *Lectures on Realism* did not achieve the hoped-for reconciliation, they do contain some of his more interesting claims. For example, he argued that only by presupposing realism could idealism or any other philosophy be stated. 'Idealism', he says (*Balfour Lectures on Realism*, 192), 'exists only as a criticism of Realism'. This anticipates, though for somewhat different reasons, a position taken by many ordinary language philosophers half a century later, for example P. F. Strawson, who argued that the existence of publicly identifiable material bodies was a necessary precondition for language.

Pringle-Pattison's later attempts to solve the problem are less interesting. In *The Idea of God* he blurs many of his earlier distinctions. He repents of describing selves as 'impervious' and claims that, while nature exists independently of man, it none the less exists *for* man. Quite how the system works is 'incomprehensible' to finite minds, but that it does so is a 'primary certainty' which 'no speculative difficulties could over-ride' (*The Idea of God in the Light of Recent Philosophy*, 391).

Pringle-Pattison's philosophy 'had a distinct attraction for philosophers of a not too rigorous cast of mind, in search of a philosophy that would tread a comfortable *via media* between naturalism and Absolutism, science and religion, the rights of personality and the demands of the community' (Passmore, 74). He was elected to the British Academy in 1904. He died at The Haining on 1 September 1931, and was buried at Morningside cemetery, Edinburgh, three days later.   NICHOLAS GRIFFIN

Sources G. F. Barbour, 'Memoir', in A. S. Pringle-Pattison, *The Balfour lectures on realism* (1933), 3–159 · J. Passmore, *A hundred years of philosophy*, 2nd edn (1966), 72–5, 279–80; repr. (1968) · J. B. Capper, 'Andrew Seth Pringle-Pattison', *PBA*, 17 (1931), 447–61 · J. B. Baillie, 'Pringle-Pattison as philosopher', *PBA*, 17 (1931), 461–89 · *DNB* · *The Times* (2 Sept 1931)

Archives U. Edin. L., lecture notes | BL, corresp. with Arthur James Balfour, Add. MS 47978, *passim* · NL Scot., corresp. with Lord Haldane

Likenesses A. E. Borthwick, portrait; presented to Pattison in 1925; in possession of his son in 1949 · E. R. Yerbury, photograph, repro. in Pringle-Pattison, *Balfour lectures on realism*, frontispiece · photograph, repro. in Pringle-Pattison, *Balfour lectures on realism*, 84

Wealth at death £12,531 8s. 9d.: Scottish confirmation sealed in London, 11 Nov 1931, *CGPLA Eng. & Wales*

Pattison, Dorothy Wyndlow [*known as* Sister Dora] (1832–1878), Anglican nun and nurse, was born on 16 January 1832 at the rectory, Hauxwell, near Richmond, Yorkshire, the eleventh of the twelve children of the Revd Mark James Pattison (1788–1865), rector of Hauxwell, and Jane Winn (1793–1860), daughter of a former mayor of Richmond. Her parents were evangelical and the children were brought up to fear God. Her father, who was mentally unstable, was obsessed with enforcing his authority over his wife and daughters. He forbade Dorothy and her sisters to carry out works of charity and would not consent to any of their marriages. While their two brothers

Dorothy Wyndlow Pattison [Sister Dora] (1832–1878), by
Charles Henry Jeens, pubd 1880 (after Mrs Williams)

were educated by their father and went to Oxford University, the ten sisters received no formal education. Mark *Pattison (1813–1884), the eldest child, became involved in the Oxford Movement and through his influence the sisters embraced this new teaching, causing further family anguish. Mark made himself responsible for Dorothy's education and under his guidance she developed an independent mind.

Tall and pretty, Dorothy Pattison was in love with several men during her life, both before and after she took religious vows; however, she consistently chose work rather than marriage. In 1860 she became the schoolmistress in Little Woolston, Buckinghamshire. She visited Coatham, near Middlesbrough, for holidays; there she observed the work of one of the first Anglican sisterhoods, the Christ Church sisterhood, which ran a convalescent home at Coatham. In September 1864 she joined the sisterhood, taking the name Sister Dora.

The sisterhood provided nurses for the cottage hospital in Walsall, and it was there that Sister Dora was sent in January 1865. The cottage hospital had been established to nurse the victims of industrial accidents in the town: she came to love both the work and the people. She received little nursing training from the sisters but was influenced by the spirit in which they cared for their patients: she learned to show personal kindness to each individual and the power of making patients cheerful. In addition to the in-patients she saw hundreds of out-patients every day, and said 'the more I have to do, the stronger and happier I feel'. By 1868, as acting matron of the hospital, she was regarded as indispensable. She developed great skill as a surgical nurse, attending post-mortems and dissections to increase her knowledge, and could set fractures and perform minor operations. One of the surgeons with whom she worked tried to persuade her to train as a doctor but she was not interested, recognizing that her inspiration was religious, not medical.

Tolerant of all beliefs, Sister Dora cared as much for the spiritual well-being of her patients as she did for their health, and on occasion undertook mission work. She told her patients that the hospital was their home, to which they could always return, and the people of Walsall regarded her as next to a saint, her presence itself appearing to bring them relief from suffering. In 1872 there was a fatal colliery disaster in the area and, although there was nothing she could do as a nurse, Sister Dora stayed at the pithead with the families of the victims, distributing blankets and food.

There had been differences between Sister Dora and the sisterhood concerning her work, and she had ignored recalls to Coatham. The final severance came in 1875, when Walsall was threatened with a smallpox epidemic and, without reference to the sisterhood, Sister Dora left the cottage hospital and went to the epidemic hospital for six months to nurse the victims. Several years later she was told that she had breast cancer. She decided to carry on working as long as possible: the foundation-stone for a new hospital had been laid some months earlier, in April 1877, and, having been one of the key persons behind the project, she was determined to live to see it completed. In the summer of 1878, six months before her death, she took a holiday and visited Paris and London. While in London she had an opportunity of observing Joseph Lister's pioneering work in antiseptic surgery. She completely accepted his theory, and ordered the necessary equipment for an antiseptic operating theatre for the new hospital in Walsall.

Sister Dora died in Walsall on 24 December 1878, six weeks after the new hospital opened. Her funeral took place on 28 December; eighteen railway workers carried her coffin and the whole town turned out for the occasion. She was buried in Walsall cemetery. None of her immediate family attended the funeral: they had never understood her choice of profession, and when two of her sisters visited her at the end of her life she sent them away, preferring to be nursed by 'her people' of Walsall. She had been estranged from her brother Mark, who regarded her work as menial and insignificant, for over twelve years.

Memorials took the form of a fund for sending convalescents to the seaside (1880), a stained-glass window in St Matthew's Church (1882–3), and a public statue, subscribed by the working people of the town and sculpted by Francis Williamson (1886). To nurses her name became identified with the style of cap which she always wore, known as Sister Dora caps. From necessity she had accepted lady-pupils to train at the old cottage hospital but she preferred to nurse 'her men' herself. Her career inspired other women to dedicate their lives to nursing;

her own inspiration came from Matthew 25: 40 'Inasmuch as ye have done it to the least of these my brethren, ye have done it unto me.'   SUSAN McGANN

Sources J. Manton, *Sister Dora: the life of Dorothy Pattison* (1971) · M. Lonsdale, *Sister Dora: a biography* (1880) · C. S. Latimer, *Sister Dora* (1988) · E. M. M. Ridsdale, *Sister Dora: personal reminiscences of her later years, with some of her letters* (1880) · M. Price, 'Inasmuch as ... ': the story of Sister Dora of Walsall (1952) · R. M. Hallowes, 'Sister Dora Pattison', *Nursing Mirror* (13 Jan 1956), iv–v, 1001

Archives Bodl. Oxf., Pattison MSS · Convent of the Holy Rood archives, Middlesborough · Walsall Local History Centre, letters to Kenyon Jones · Walsall Local History Centre, Walsall General (Sister Dora) Hospital archives

Likenesses H. Munns, oils, 1880 · F. Williamson, bronze statue, 1886, The Bridge, Walsall · F. Williamson, marble statue, 1886, Walsall council · C. H. Jeens, engraving (after Mrs Williams), repro. in Lonsdale, *Sister Dora* [see illus.] · photographs, Walsall Local History Centre · watercolour (after H. Munns), Walsall Hospital Trust; colour photograph, Walsall Local History Centre

Wealth at death under £5000: probate, 16 Sept 1879, *CGPLA Eng. & Wales*

Pattison, Emilia Francis. *See* Dilke, Emilia Francis (1840–1904).

Pattison, Granville Sharp (1791–1851), anatomist and surgeon, was born in the Barony parish of Glasgow on 23 January 1791. He was the fifth and youngest son of the eight children of John Pattison (1747–1807), a prosperous Glasgow merchant and muslin manufacturer, and his wife, Hope Margaret Moncrieff (1755–1833), the daughter of the Revd Matthew Moncrieff of Culfargie. Until the collapse of his father's business in 1806 Pattison's family lived in Kelvingrove House, an impressive mansion, but thereafter they lived in relative poverty. Pattison was brought up in a mainstream Church of Scotland household under a father with liberal / reform political leanings. He attended Glasgow grammar school from 1802 to 1804, and took medical courses at Glasgow University from 1806 to 1812 (including those of James Jeffray and Richard Millar), though, like many contemporaries, he did not take a degree. In 1809 Pattison became demonstrator (which also meant procurer of corpses) to Allan Burns at the private College Street medical school. On 4 October 1813 Pattison was admitted (after examination) a surgical member of the Faculty of Physicians and Surgeons of Glasgow (FPSG). Pattison succeeded Burns as lecturer in anatomy, physiology, and the principles of operative surgery and, in 1814, acquired Burns's extensive collection of anatomical and pathological specimens. At the same time Pattison was also working (under John Burns) as one of the surgeons at Glasgow Town's Hospital, a poorhouse hospital at which members of the FPSG worked part time.

Pattison's troubles began during 1813–14 when he was accused, but ultimately acquitted, of illegal exhumation, even though it was well known that he was the leader of Glasgow's student resurrectionists. On 27 October 1814 Pattison was a co-founder of the Glasgow Medical and Surgical Society. In the spring of 1816 he resigned as Town's Hospital surgeon, after having been found by the directors to be neglecting his duties, to take up the post of junior first-year surgeon at the Royal Infirmary, Glasgow. After only a few months he was accused of professional incompetence by a senior surgical colleague, Hugh Miller. Pattison was found guilty of professional misconduct in ignoring the recommendations of the surgical consultation in a case involving amputation, and performing instead his own preferred operation. He was censured by the infirmary's managers, and left office there in late 1817. The professional community in Glasgow believed he had been treated very harshly. However, on 14 March 1818 he was appointed professor of anatomy and surgery in the private medical school of Anderson's Institution (he also continued to lecture at College Street). Pattison immediately travelled to Paris, where he stayed until October, in an attempt to gather fashionable modern ideas from the Paris hospitals and medical schools for use in his new lectures. However, in January 1819 Pattison was named as co-respondent in the divorce of Dr Andrew Ure, professor of natural philosophy at Anderson's. Pattison was thereafter shunned by professional and polite society in Glasgow, and, faced with the prospect of censure by the managers of Anderson's, he resigned his chair on 8 May 1819. In the same month he went to London and was elected a member of both the Medical and Chirurgical Society of London (later the Royal Society of Medicine), and (after examination) of the Royal College of Surgeons of London.

Pattison then left for Philadelphia, where he had relatives, and set himself up as a private anatomy lecturer. He was soon in a very public professional wrangle with Nathaniel Chapman, professor of the theory and practice of medicine at the University of Pennsylvania, who resented the competition from Pattison as it threatened to diminish his own income from class fees. A pamphlet war ensued, Pattison challenged Chapman to a duel, and, in October 1820, he was arrested for publicly posting Chapman as a coward. In August 1820 Pattison had moved to take up the chair of surgery at the University of Maryland, in Baltimore. He quickly became engaged in another dispute, this time with William Gibson, professor of surgery at the University of Pennsylvania, over the legitimacy of Pattison's claim to have identified a new fascia of the perineum, which in fact turned out to be the same one discovered previously by Abraham Colles (*American Medical Recorder*, 3, 1820, 1–24). Pattison was co-editor of the *Recorder* during 1820 and this may have facilitated the publication of his controversial piece. In 1821 Pattison switched chairs to become professor of anatomy, and also dean of the medical faculty. During 1823 he edited Allan Burns's *Observations on the Surgical Anatomy of the Head and Neck*, adding a life of the author and additional cases. In April of that year Pattison severely wounded General Thomas Cadwalader in a pistol duel. A leading Philadelphia citizen and brother-in-law of Nathaniel Chapman, Cadwalader had tried to exclude Pattison from a society ball to spare Chapman's friends such unappealing company. Also in 1823 the 160-bed Baltimore Infirmary opened after Pattison had persuaded the medical faculty to establish the first modern residential teaching hospital in the country, so that students might learn about disease firsthand.

After resigning his chair in spring 1826 Pattison left for London, where, in 1827, he succeeded in obtaining the chair of anatomy and morbid anatomy at the new University of London (later University College, London) from 1828. He was also appointed professor of surgery in September 1830. During the summer of 1828 Pattison gave evidence to the House of Commons committee investigating the teaching of anatomy in which he supported the greater legal availability of cadavers. In September 1828 he was appointed surgeon to the University of London Dispensary (later University College Hospital). However, during the heightened atmosphere of summer 1830, with revolution in France, he became the victim of sustained student protest—both in his lectures (which were completely disrupted) and in the columns of *The Lancet*— which called into question his competence and the extent and currency of his knowledge. The university was founded and attended by middle-class radicals keen to gain power in a reformed British society and this dispute was part of the painful birth of its distinctive intellectual outlook. In medicine this meant opposing the social and intellectual domination of Oxford and Cambridge universities and London's royal colleges with new French ideas that already had a materialist, republican gloss. By his own admission Pattison taught nothing but traditional descriptive anatomy. Pattison's rival for student affections (and fees), the demonstrator, James R. Bennett, taught the new French general anatomy. Bennett's star waxed as Pattison's waned. In September 1830 Bennett was made adjunct professor of anatomy, encroaching near Pattison's professional sphere of influence. The new anatomy had two aspects: comparative and pathological. In the former, it followed the Lamarckian Étienne Geoffroy St Hilaire in using comparative anatomy to search for the universal scientific laws that underlay the development of all animals, including man. In the latter, it followed Marie François Xavier Bichat, in using the tissue type, not the organ, as the basic unit of analysis, and was linked with the French clinico-pathological method of understanding disease, which correlated signs and symptoms observed in the living patient with post-mortem findings. On 23 July 1831, after a tortuous debate, the university's council asked Pattison to retire, though they were careful to state that neither his general character nor his professional skill and knowledge was impeached. Rather, his old fashioned, conservative approach was not in tune (epistemologically or socially) with the new institution.

In July 1832 Pattison took up the position of professor of anatomy at Jefferson Medical College in Philadelphia. He appears to have used his new authority to award himself the degree of MD from the college. On 1 June 1833 he married a Scotswoman, Mary Sharpe; there were no children. Between 1833 and 1836 he edited the *Register and Library of Medical and Chirurgical Science*, a medical newspaper. He resigned from Jefferson in 1841 and took up his final appointment as professor of anatomy at the University of New York. In 1844 he edited an edition of J. Cruveilhier's *The Anatomy of the Human Body*. After repeated attacks of cholecystitis Pattison died on 12 November 1851, in New York, of obstruction of the common bile duct either from ulceration due to gallstones, or cancer of the head of the pancreas. He was buried in New York's Greenwood cemetery, but in 1852 his body was moved to the Pattison family grave in the western necropolis, Glasgow, where it remains. His wife survived him.

Pattison's colourful professional life testifies both to his own perseverance and to some of the typical trajectories, trials, and tribulations of an early nineteenth-century academic medical career. In both Britain and the USA intense competition for limited (and badly or barely paid) university and hospital posts governed by patronage, and between private lecturers, whose livings depended on attracting students in the medical marketplace, exacerbated professional politics and back-stabbing. Pattison often transgressed professional etiquette and was never at the cutting edge of his discipline, but his flamboyant, headstrong, and tenaciously quarrelsome nature made him particularly inept at the gentle art of academic politics, and this weakness made his setbacks more severe. He was described by one late nineteenth-century Glasgow writer as 'a man of brilliant abilities as an expounder of anatomy … [whose] life throughout was greatly marred by his rare genius for getting himself into trouble' (Duncan, 181). He published no original medical work of note.

ANDREW HULL

Sources F. L. M. Pattison, *Granville Sharp Pattison: anatomist and antagonist, 1791–1851* (1987) • H. H. Bellot, *University College, London, 1826–1926* (1929) • A. Desmond, *The politics of evolution: morphology, medicine and reform in radical London* (1989) • A. L. Goodall, 'Granville Sharp Pattison: the argumentative anatomist', *Proceedings of the Scottish Society of the History of Medicine* (1959), 20–23 • A. Duncan, *Memorials of the Faculty of Physicians and Surgeons of Glasgow, 1599–1850* (1896) • J. Coutts, *A history of the University of Glasgow* (1909) • Royal College of Physicians and Surgeons of Glasgow, William Mackenzie MSS, RCPSG 24 • 'Select committee on anatomy', *Parl. papers* (1828), 7.67–70, 83–5, no. 568
Archives NA Scot. • UCL, case MSS • UCL, letters | Mitchell L., Glas., GGHB archives
Likenesses J. Sartain, engraving, 1826 (after C. Harding), RCP Lond.; repro. in Pattison, *Granville Sharp Pattison*, xvi • portrait, c.1846, New York University Medical Center; repro. in Pattison, *Granville Sharp Pattison*, 203
Wealth at death $11,000: Pattison, *Granville Sharp Pattison*, 217–18

Pattison, Mark (1813–1884), college head and scholar, was born on 10 October 1813 at Hornby in the North Riding of Yorkshire, the first of two sons and twelve children of Mark James Pattison (1788–1865), subsequently rector of Hauxwell, near Catterick, and his wife, Jane (d. 1860), daughter and heir of Francis Winn, banker, sometime mayor of Richmond. He had an isolated upbringing in rural Wensleydale, where he developed his lifelong and solitary passions for books and for such rural pursuits as ornithology and trout fishing. He was not sent to school, but was educated by his father, a graduate of Brasenose College, Oxford, and acquired a good grounding in Latin, Greek, and mathematics, as well as a taste for literature

Mark Pattison (1813–1884), by unknown engraver, pubd 1884

and scholarship. His father, a devoted Oxonian, intended his son from the first to proceed to his old university and to win a fellowship. Pattison duly matriculated from Oriel College on 5 April 1832, and, following a somewhat solitary boyhood in a remote part of the country, he found himself shy and awkward in the face of Oxford society.

Pattison entered the pre-eminent college of the time, but when he matriculated Oriel had imperceptibly passed its zenith. Provost Hawkins, recently elected to the headship in preference to Keble, had ousted a remarkable group of tutors, J. H. Newman, J. A. Froude, and R. I. Wilberforce, and had replaced them with lesser men whom Pattison, in a brilliantly acerbic account in his memoirs, denounced for their pedagogical and scholarly incompetence. In June 1836 Pattison missed the first class on which his and his father's eyes had been set; by his own account the main reason was that his reading ranged too widely, and did not focus sufficiently closely on the narrow range of set books. 'I had strongly the desire of knowledge', he recalled, 'but not at all the desire of that particular knowledge which the examination test prescribes' (Pattison, 133). It was during his undergraduate career that he laid the foundations for his future mastery of eighteenth-century English literature and thought; and it was at the same time that he began to formulate systematic plans of study, recorded in a 'student's diary' which he was to keep up, with a few interruptions, for the rest of his life.

The 'whirlpool of Tractarianism' Up to and beyond his graduation, Pattison's religious opinions were on the liberal side of orthodoxy. It was in 1838, as a young graduate remaining in residence for the purpose of preparing for fellowship elections, that he was 'drawn into the whirlpool of Tractarianism' (Pattison, 171). He had been acquainted with Newman since the latter became dean in 1834, but relations between the two men did not become close until April 1838, when Pattison stood unsuccessfully for a fellowship at his own college. In 1838–9, at Newman's instigation, Pattison accepted an invitation to share a communal life with a number of other young graduates in a house taken by Dr Pusey in St Aldates.

Pattison was inclined, in retrospect, to depict his Tractarian phase (which lasted a decade) as an aberration. To the mature Pattison, learning stood opposed to ecclesiastical authority, but in fact Tractarianism played an important part in launching his scholarly career. Newman was the nearest thing to a mentor Pattison ever had, excepting only his father. If he ever had what would now be called a research training, it was during that period of residence in Pusey's house, when he collaborated on Newman's edition of Aquinas's *Catena Aurea*. His literary career was launched with contributions to the high-church periodicals, the *British Critic* and the *Christian Remembrancer*. He composed lives of two thirteenth-century churchmen, Stephen Langton and Edmund Rich, for Newman's *Lives of the British Saints*, and told one of his sisters that, 'it is a long time since I have felt so eager in any subject of study as I do at this present in this' (Montague, 166–7). In a later phase of his career, he conceived the idea of a series of Lives of the Scholars—surely a secularized version of Newman's project. Pattison, who afterwards became an acerbic anticlerical, was never heard to speak of his former master with disrespect, and acknowledged to Newman that, 'I can still truly say that I have learnt more from you than from any one else with whom I have ever been in contact' (Sparrow, 60). Certainly the two men were very close in 1845, and Newman, who perhaps did not fully appreciate the tendency of Pattison's later thought, never quite gave up hope that his former protégé might convert.

Tractarianism cast its shadow, too, over Pattison's relationship with his family. He was deeply marked by the experience of his cousin and childhood friend, Philippa Meadows. A young woman of great intellectual powers and learning, she took to Tractarianism under her cousin's influence, and after living for a time in Keble's parish of Hursley, was received into the Roman church in 1845, shortly before Newman himself. Pattison's mother and sisters too came under the influence of the Oxford Movement; his younger sister, Dorothy Wyndlow *Pattison, entered an Anglican sisterhood. They eagerly corresponded with him about ecclesiastical questions, and about the contents of the latest issue of the *British Critic*. Pattison's father, who had had a mental breakdown in 1834 and had spent some months in a lunatic asylum near York, deeply resented what he perceived as his family's perfidy, and this fed his subsequently erratic and tyrannical behaviour. He forbade any of his daughters to marry in his lifetime, and only two of them defied him to do so. When Eleanor did so, in 1853, he tried to block the marriage by telling her prospective father-in-law that there was insanity in the family; as if to prove it, he locked himself in the hay-loft in protest. He practically broke off relations with his son, who returned home only very occasionally. These family traumas had an incalculable impact on Pattison's psychological and emotional development.

Tutor and scholar It was fortunate for Pattison that he had left Pusey's house when Lincoln College advertised its intention to elect to a fellowship restricted to natives of Yorkshire; for had his churchmanship been notorious, his election would have been impossible at a college which was both staunchly anti-Puseyite and a stagnant back-water. It was his election to the fellowship (November 1839) that was to prove the making of Pattison. It was the fulfilment of the destiny prescribed for him by his father, and it provided the outward recognition which, as a man of little inward self-reliance, Pattison desperately needed. Although his Tractarianism was to deepen during his early years at Lincoln, his election to a fellowship effectively immunized him against the charms of Rome.

Pattison was ordained deacon in 1841 and priest in 1843, and won the Denyer theological prize in 1841 and again in 1842. But the decisive turning points were his appointment as tutor in 1843 and his nomination as public examiner in 1848. He held the office of tutor at Lincoln from 1843 until 1855; and this period of office, by providing a focus for his work, further contributed to keeping him from the Roman 'perversion'. He made himself one of the most notable tutors of his day and, prior to the rectorship election of 1851, the effective power in his college, whose reputation in the university rose through his efforts. In his college lectures, especially those on Aristotle's *Ethics*, he sought to provide fundamental tuition in place of the elementary and formulaic instruction that was then the norm. Convinced at this stage of the vital importance of the personal relationship of pupil and tutor, he began the practice of taking small reading parties to Bowness and Inveraray, and it was through these experiments that he established close and lasting friendships with a number of his pupils. They regarded him with awe, but also with genuine and heartfelt affection; they were aware of being in the presence of a remarkable man, and at the time of the rectorship election of 1851 he received strong backing from the undergraduates of Lincoln. Shortly before that election, he submitted notable evidence to the royal commission of inquiry into Oxford University: among liberal reformers, he was the one who most vigorously argued for the maintenance of the system of college teaching and against the extension of the professorial system.

In some ways this period may have been the happiest of Pattison's life. Even so, he considered alternatives. When the new Queen's University of Ireland was founded at Belfast, Pattison (in 1848) applied unsuccessfully for the chair of modern history. 'I feel symptoms of becoming weary of tuition, or rather a desire for literary occupation such as I used to delight in … I have always felt that literature was my proper vocation' (Montague, 175). He felt the call of what he termed (significantly) 'the spiritual life': a life free of administrative or tutorial burdens, and devoted wholly to research and writing.

Events were shortly to conspire to make him rethink his priorities; for in October 1851 the headship of his college became vacant upon the death of the elderly rector, Dr Radford. Pattison recognized the drawbacks of the post, given his lack of business or management skills: he acknowledged that the criticism levelled at him—'defect of judgment and temper'—contained a 'great proportion of truth' (Bodl. Oxf., MS Pattison 64). But the contest became a trial of strength between the progressive and the reactionary forces in college, and Pattison was the

obvious representative of the former. The election was one of the most notorious contests in Victorian Oxford, and was memorably and bitterly recounted in Pattison's *Memoirs*. For a time he seemed to be in sure possession of the five votes he needed for a majority, but the machinations of a former fellow, the evangelical tory Richard Michell (by now vice-principal of Magdalen Hall), persuaded one of the five, a non-resident fellow, to withdraw his support from Pattison and to transfer it to his rival. Pattison's party, seeing that their cause was lost, realized that their only hope was to block their opponents' candidate, whom they regarded as Michell's puppet, and by this means they secured the election of the obscure James Thompson, whom Pattison regarded as 'nothing better than a satyr' (Pattison, 290).

Pattison's relations with the new rector were poor. Thompson asserted his right to superintend tutorial arrangements in college, and this interference led Pattison to resign his tutorship in 1855 and live on his fellowship stipend alone, at that time worth £200 a year. It was at the same time that he launched his literary career in earnest with regular contributions to the periodical press; after the failure of his rectorship ambitions he needed a new field in which to achieve recognition. He served as an editor on the *Westminster Review*, and at one time hoped to transform that periodical into a vehicle for his brand of radical theology. He was also a frequent contributor to the newly founded *Saturday Review*. But in the meantime he was also formulating, in the broadest of terms, the scholarly projects that were to dominate the rest of his life, the large theme of which was 'the laws of progress of thought in modern Europe' (Pattison, 310–11). The first dimension of this theme he began to tackle was the history of universities, a subject which had obvious appeal and practical relevance at a period when university reform was in the air; and Pattison was (arguably) the first serious student of the subject in England. This interest was to bear fruit in a contribution to a volume of *Oxford Essays* in 1855, and infused his *Suggestions on Academical Organisation* in 1868.

The second identifiable branch of his literary pursuits was the investigation of 'the movement of theological sentiment in modern Europe'; within this field, it was the religious thought of eighteenth-century England that Pattison made his subject. His contribution to *Essays and Reviews* (1860), on 'Tendencies of religious thought in England, 1688–1750', stands out as the one essay in that controversial volume which was truly original in conception. An essay in the history of ideas, rather than in dogmatic theology, Pattison's contribution is at first sight set apart from the other essays, though even its dispassionate tone did not exempt its author from the controversies excited by the volume as a whole. An investigation of the rise and decline of deism, Pattison's essay had the more fundamental purpose of asserting the validity of a purely historical investigation of religious ideas:

> We have not yet learnt, in this country, to write our ecclesiastical history on any better footing than that of praising up the party, in or out of the Church, to which we happen to belong. Still further are we from any attempt to

apply the laws of thought, and of the succession of opinion, to the course of English theology.   (M. Pattison, 'Tendencies of religious thought in England, 1688–1750' in *Essays and Reviews*, 1860, 254–329)

In its way, this essay was as subversive as the more obviously controversial contributions to the volume, for it showed that religious ideas had a history, and that they were subject to laws of development; it thus seemed to banish the appeal to antiquity as an authority for current religious orthodoxy. It was of fundamental importance, too, in the particular field of eighteenth-century intellectual and religious history, the acknowledged inspiration of Leslie Stephen's *History of English Thought in the Eighteenth Century* (2 vols., 1876), and influential upon later work in its field.

At the same time it marked something of a dead end, or at least a crossroads, in Pattison's scholarly career. In his aim of writing 'a scientific history of the self-development of opinion' he was 'singularly unsuccessful', for there was, he concluded, 'no public in this country for the scientific treatment of theology'. Ecclesiastical partisanship always got in the way; and he resolved 'to wash my hands of theology and even of Church history' (Pattison, 314–17). The essay on 'Learning in the Church of England' which he contributed to the *National Review* in 1863 should be read in this light, for it constituted an extended critique of the 'partisan style of theology' he found in England. He asked, despairingly, whether it might be possible 'that religious truth, instead of the degraded instrument of clerical animosities, shall be reinstated as the "mater scientiarum", embracing in one compact hierarchy of science all the natural and historical knowledge now open to us' (M. Pattison, *Essays*, ed. H. Nettleship, 2 vols., 1889, 279–80).

In the meantime, another scholarly interest was forming in Pattison's mind: the history of classical learning from the Renaissance onwards. The key event here was the publication by Clarendon Press, in 1851, of an edition of the *Ephemerides* of the French philological scholar Isaac Casaubon. Pattison published an article on Casaubon for the *Quarterly Review*, and, nearly a quarter of a century later, the same man was the subject of his most significant scholarly monograph. He also published shorter studies of a number of other French scholars of the sixteenth and seventeenth centuries: Estienne and Huet, for instance. But the subject who appealed to him above all was Scaliger, whom Pattison revered as 'the most richly stored intellect that ever spent itself in acquiring knowledge'. When the German scholar Jacob Bernays published his *Joseph Justus Scaliger* in 1855, Pattison for a time renounced his intention of writing Scaliger's life and contented himself with essays in review of Bernays's work. But the Prussian diplomat and churchman Bunsen persuaded him that there was scope for a portrait of Scaliger as protestant hero; this appealed to Pattison's vigorously anti-Catholic sentiments but meant little to the devout Jew Bernays. It was a project which occupied much of the rest of Pattison's life, but which he never brought to fruition.

The Oxford at which Pattison had been educated was characterized by an involuted intellectual outlook and an obsession with narrowly Anglican theological quarrels. It was during his period in the wilderness in the 1850s that Pattison took the lead in developing extensive international scholarly connections. He undertook a number of study visits to German universities, including Heidelberg in 1856, and became something of an authority on German life and education. In 1858 he spent three months as Berlin correspondent for *The Times*, and in 1859 he was appointed one of the assistant commissioners to report on continental education in connection with the royal commission on popular education: his report on elementary education in Germany paralleled Matthew Arnold's better-known account of French schooling. Whereas he had been, in 1851, a tenacious opponent of the professorial model of university education, his contact with German universities in the 1850s helped transform him into the most enthusiastic of Germanizers.

Rector of Lincoln The death of Dr Thompson in 1861 led at last to Pattison's election to the rectorship, but he was by no means as active in that office as he might have been had he secured it a decade previously. He left much college business in the hands of the sub-rector, Thomas Fowler, for whom he had a great dislike. He had come to feel that his time could be better spent in scholarly work. In any case, he had little talent for administration; he was, for instance, a notoriously indecisive and ineffective chairman. He served as delegate to the university press and as curator of the Bodleian Library and of the Taylor Institution, and in 1870 he served, for the third time, as a public examiner; but otherwise he took little part in university affairs. He never sat on the hebdomadal council, and declined the vice-chancellorship when his turn came round in 1878. He did, however, use his position as a base from which to play a national role of some significance. He examined for the Indian Civil Service and for the University of London, and he served on the council of Bedford College. He gave evidence to the Devonshire commission on scientific instruction in 1872, and was elected member of the Athenaeum in 1862 under the rule allowing the committee to elect distinguished persons, and he served on the club's committee, and that of the London Library. He attended meetings of the Metaphysical Society, that celebrated assembly of the intellectuals of the age, and he twice presented papers. He was also active in the Social Science Association, and at its Liverpool meeting in 1876 he served as president of its education section. But he felt ambivalent about his assumption of a national role, concluding that 'this life of excitement and variety is not for me' (Bodl. Oxf., MS Pattison 130). He was happier when pursuing his literary work, the fruits of which included two editions of Pope (1869 and 1872), an edition of Milton's sonnets (1883), and a life of Milton for the English Men of Letters series. He also contributed seven terse but illuminating biographical articles to the ninth edition of the *Encyclopaedia Britannica*.

Marriage and personal relationships On election to the rectorship Pattison was freed from the requirement of celibacy that conditioned a fellowship, and in September of the same year he married Emilia Francis (1840–1904), daughter of Major Henry Strong, the manager of the Oxfordshire branch of the London and County Bank [see Dilke, Emilia Francis]. They had no children. Mrs Pattison achieved considerable distinction in her own right as a student of French art history. She was a beautiful, fashionable, and vivacious woman, and under her influence the rector's lodgings occupied a prominent place in Oxford society, though the rector himself frequently resented the need to entertain. The Pattisons' marriage was not a success. They had some intellectual interests in common, and both delighted to shock; but the rector did not adjust easily to married life, and though a man of considerable means he was pettily resentful of his wife's expenditure. From the first Mrs Pattison seems to have disliked sexual intercourse with her husband, and she broke off sexual relations altogether in 1876, by which time she was in any case spending stretches of time abroad, ostensibly on account of her rheumatic gout. She lived mostly in a villa near Nice, where she pursued her work in art history. In 1875 she renewed her acquaintance with Sir Charles Dilke MP, whom she had known before her marriage; and the friendship soon ripened. In 1885, following Pattison's death, they married.

Pattison developed few close friendships with his peers; perhaps his closest friend in that category was the philosopher J. M. Wilson, president of Corpus Christi College. On the other hand he evidently had, at his best, something of a genius for close friendship with the young, which clearly contributed to his success as a tutor. He was, effectively, the patron of a group of young university liberals of scholarly interests, some of whom he successfully steered towards distinguished research careers: these men included Ingram Bywater, A. H. Sayce, and Henry Nettleship. To exercise a personal authority of this kind he must have had an affectionate and generous side to his character. One former pupil, Richard Copley Christie, wrote of his 'magnetic influence' (DNB).

Pattison also attracted an admiring circle of young women with intellectual pretensions. These included Mary Arnold, later Mrs Humphry Ward, who used Pattison as the model for Squire Roger Wendover in her novel Robert Elsmere. (Pattison has also been identified as Professor Forth in Rhoda Broughton's Belinda, and, more tenuously, as Edward Casaubon in George Eliot's Middlemarch.) The most notable of his friendships was with Margaret (Meta) Bradley (b. c.1850), niece of the master of University College; she and Pattison formed an intimate or even passionate relationship which lasted from 1879 until his death. Unlike Mrs Pattison, Miss Bradley was neither particularly intelligent nor particularly attractive. She did, however, revere Pattison, and their relationship, though it probably did not involve sexual relations, was certainly amorous and verged on the scandalous in the small-scale Oxford society of the time. Mrs Pattison, for her own reasons, saw to it that the nature of the relationship became known in Oxford, and she spoke colourfully to her friends of 'the David and Abishag difficulty' (Sparrow, 52). In 1880 Pattison revoked the codicil to his will by which he had intended to leave £1000 to his college, determining to leave it to Miss Bradley instead. He also planned to make her his literary executor, though in the event the role was undertaken by his widow.

Death and appraisal Pattison returned to Oxford for the Michaelmas term of 1883 determined to bring his life of Scaliger to completion within twelve months; but it soon became clear that he was dying of cancer. He thereupon abandoned his magnum opus and, with the help of his extensive diaries, dictated his Memoirs, which his widow brought to publication in 1885. They were to be his most durable literary monument, though a volume of his college and university sermons appeared in the same year, and Henry Nettleship published an important two-volume edition of his Essays in 1889. In June 1884 he was moved to Harrogate, in his native county; he died there on 30 July 1884, and was buried, according to his request, in the neighbouring churchyard of Harlow Hill.

In appearance, Pattison was likened by one contemporary to a bird of prey; by another, to a Rembrandt etching. He had a long hooked nose, a sparse and reddish beard, and from middle age he looked old beyond his years. His face was harsh and pale, his skin withered; and observers commented upon the expressive sarcasm of his eyes and upon his cackling laugh. Friends and acquaintances commonly thought him a hypochondriac; and this judgment is amply borne out by his diaries and letters, in which he repeatedly complains that headaches or eye strain prevent him from working for more than three hours a day. He was, however, no recluse; he enjoyed playing rackets, and was close to being a national champion at croquet.

In spite of his Tractarian background and his role in Essays and Reviews, Pattison was not a dominating presence in the religious history of the Victorian age, and in the last two decades of his life he devoted no serious intellectual attention to theology. The university sermons he preached were intellectually substantial, but they read as educational rather than theological treatises. He esteemed the church when it acted as a patron of learning, but not when it set its face against the freedom of the intellect and rested its claims on authority. The reception of his contribution to Essays and Reviews convinced him that in England the hold of partisan churchmanship was so all-pervasive that the claims of theology and science were, for practical purposes, incompatible. That conviction hastened his gradual separation from the church. It seems beyond reasonable doubt that he died an agnostic. If not holding fast to God, however, he did hold fast to the clerical status that secured his office as rector. His growing unbelief did not prevent him from fulfilling his duties in attending college chapel, where he punctiliously took his turn in presiding at the eucharist. Likewise, on his visits to Yorkshire he assisted his brother-in-law, the rector of Richmond. 'Priests', he observed, 'are generally professional quacks trading in beliefs they don't share' (Sparrow, 58).

It is as a scholar that Pattison himself would have wished to be appraised. He had the reputation of being the most learned man in England, but though he wrote extensively for a variety of periodicals, his published works did not do full justice to the depth and extent of his learning. 'Mark Pattison is undoubtedly a researcher, so are we all,' wrote Mandell Creighton in 1872, 'but one Essay and Review and one edition of Pope's "Essay on Man" scarcely justify to the Philistine a large endowment' (L. Creighton, *Life and Letters of Mandell Creighton*, 1904, 1.135). Thus, while Pattison achieved a mastery of eighteenth-century literature and philosophy, it was a younger man, Leslie Stephen, who produced an authoritative and comprehensive work on the subject. Pattison's writings exhibit a literary style that is terse and lacks elegance, but possesses lucidity and force. But it did not come easily. He suffered from the perfectionism of one who lacked self-reliance and was acutely sensitive to the opinions of others. 'It takes me six weeks to write a sermon,' he once complained, 'and then I don't finish' (A. H. Sayce, *Reminiscences*, 1923, 36). Fortunately he preached little. Arguably his research ethic was inherently sterile. His typical advice to an aspiring scholar—to choose a subject and then devote half a lifetime to reading all relevant sources—was daunting and often offputting.

Pattison's most notable scholarly work, his *Isaac Casaubon*, has been criticized by later historians for devoting little attention to an appraisal of Casaubon's achievements as a scholar. This was, indeed, the substance of the criticism that Bernays made to Pattison himself. This was characteristic of Pattison. He was curiously indifferent to the outcome of scholarly and scientific inquiry. What interested him was scholarship as a way of life; a life lived in disinterested pursuit of universal knowledge. 'The scholar', he wrote, 'is greater than his books'; for 'the many thousand pages which Isaac Casaubon wrote may be all merged in the undistinguished mass of classical commentary, and yet there would remain to us as a cherished inheritance, the record of a life devoted to learning' (M. Pattison, *Isaac Casaubon*, 1875, 488–90). Pattison's model of the scholarly life was, perhaps, a secularized analogue of the Tractarian ideal of holiness; but he believed that Newman and his fellow converts had betrayed it in their submission to ecclesiastical authority. Newman's *Apologia* was, he thought, a 'most pathetic story! of a soul wholly detached from worldly interests, and seeking only its future interests—*not* truth … It has not the interest of a search for speculative truth, as in the Confessions of Augustine, or the Diary of Blanco White' (Bodl. Oxf., MS Pattison 130).

Pattison's writings on university reform should be read in the light of this conception of the life of learning. Although he urged the redirection of endowments from 'education' to 'science', he was no exponent of twentieth-century conceptions of academic research. The function of the professoriate, as he conceived it, was not to generate new knowledge, but to 'maintain, cultivate, and diffuse extant knowledge' (M. Pattison, *Suggestions on Academical Organisation, with Especial Reference to Oxford*, 1868, 171).

Pattison's idea of the university flowed from an intensely spiritual—and in its way deeply Victorian—vision of the character of the scholar. His chief monument is not to be found in any reforms accomplished, nor in his published works, nor even in his *Memoirs*; but in the numerous volumes of working notes and diary entries which he deposited in the Bodleian Library. It is in them that the character of the man and the scholar finds its fullest expression.

H. S. JONES

Sources M. Pattison, *Memoirs of an Oxford don*, ed. V. H. H. Green, pbk edn (1988) · *DNB* · J. Sparrow, *Mark Pattison and the idea of a university* (1967) · V. H. H. Green, *Oxford common room: a study of Lincoln College and Mark Pattison* (1957) · V. Green, *Love in a cool climate: the letters of Mark Pattison and Meta Bradley, 1879–1884* (1985) · F. C. Montague, 'Some early letters of Mark Pattison', *Bulletin of the John Rylands University Library*, 18 (1934), 156–76 · D. Nimmo, 'Mark Pattison and the dilemma of university examinations', *Days of judgement: science, examinations, and the organization of knowledge in late Victorian England*, ed. R. MacLeod (1982), 153–67 · D. Nimmo, 'Learning against religion, learning as religion: Mark Pattison and the "Victorian crisis of faith"', *Religion and humanism*, ed. K. Robbins, SCH, 17 (1981), 311–24 · M. Francis, 'The origins of *Essays and Reviews*: an interpretation of Mark Pattison in the 1850s', *HJ*, 17 (1974), 797–812 · D. Nimmo, 'Towards and away from Newman's theory of doctrinal development: pointers from Mark Pattison in 1838 and 1846', *Journal of Theological Studies*, new ser., 29 (1978), 160–62 · J. Morley, 'On Pattison's memoirs', *Critical miscellanies*, 3 (1886), 133–73; repr. (1888) · L. A. Tollemache, 'Recollections of Pattison', in L. A. Tollemache, *Stones of stumbling* (1885) · A. Momigliano, 'Jacob Bernays', *Koninklijke Nederlandse Akademie van Wetenschappen*, 32 (1969), 149–78 · A. Grafton, 'Mark Pattison', *American Scholar*, 52 (spring 1983), 229–36 · *CGPLA Eng. & Wales* (1884) · J. Sutherland, *Mrs Humphry Ward: eminent Victorian, pre-eminent Edwardian* (1990) · Bodl. Oxf., MSS Pattison

Archives Bodl. Oxf., corresp., papers, diaries, and accounts · Lincoln College, Oxford, family corresp., mainly letters to his sister Eleanor | Birmingham Oratory, letters to J. H. Newman · BL, letters to Gertrude Tuckwell, Add. MS 44886 · Bodl. Oxf., letters to Ingram Bywater · NL Wales, letters to T. C. Edwards

Likenesses photographs, *c*.1880, Lincoln College, Oxford · A. Macdonald, oils, after 1900, Lincoln College, Oxford · caricature, Lincoln College, Oxford · wood-engraving, NPG; repro. in *ILN* (23 Aug 1884) [*see illus.*]

Wealth at death £46,141 3*s*. 1*d*.: resworn probate, Nov 1885, *CGPLA Eng. & Wales* (1884)

Pattison, William (1706–1727), poet, was born at Peasemarsh, near Rye, Sussex, where his father, William Pattison, held a small farm from the earl of Thanet, who arranged for the young boy to attend the free school at Appleby, Westmorland. At school he was a promising scholar and began to write poetry, earning money to pay book bills by composing dedicatory odes to landowners. On 6 July 1724 he was admitted as a sizar at Sidney Sussex College, Cambridge; but he preferred fishing and poetry writing to serious study, and in the summer of 1726 he cut his name out of the college books, in order, apparently, to avoid being recorded as expelled.

Pattison went from Cambridge to London, where he mixed with such writers as Laurence Eusden, Walter Harte, and Matthew Concanen. His first letters from London were optimistic (*Poetical Works*) but he was soon reduced to poverty. In a poem addressed to Lord Burlington, 'Effigies authoris', he describes how he has spent nights on a bench in St James's Park. He was transcribing his poems for publication by Edmund Curll (1675–1747) when he died of smallpox on 10 July 1727. He had been taken in by Curll, and died in his London house (giving rise to the rumour, circulated by Pope, that Curll had starved him). He was buried at St Clement Danes, London.

Pattison's poems were published in two volumes by Curll in 1728, *The Poetical Works of Mr William Pattison*, and *Cupid's Metamorphoses*. Pope was included in the subscribers' list for the former, which consists of satires, odes, and love poems in contemporary, neo-classical style. The poem which has attracted scholarly interest subsequently is an imitation of Pope's 'Abelard to Eloisa'. Selections from Pattison's verse, particularly those with similarities to Waller, Pope, and Gay, continued to appear in anthologies of the early nineteenth century.

THOMAS SECCOMBE, *rev.* JOHN WYATT

Sources *The poetical works of Mr William Pattison late of Sidney College, Cambridge*, ed. E. Curll (1728) · 'The rape of the lock': and other poems, ed. G. Tillotson (1940), vol. 2 of *The Twickenham edition of the poems of Alexander Pope*, ed. J. Butt (1939–69), appx V, 415 · *Minor poems*, ed. N. Ault (1954), vol. 6 of *The Twickenham edition of the poems of Alexander Pope*, ed. J. Butt (1939–69), 441n. · *The prose works of Alexander Pope*, 2, ed. R. Cowler (1986) · *The works of Alexander Pope*, ed. W. Elwin and W. J. Courthope, 10 vols. (1871–89), vol. 1, p. 133 · L. S. Wright, '18th century replies to Pope's *Eloisa*', *Studies in Philology*, 31 (1934), 522–3

Likenesses Fourdrinière, engraving (after J. Saunders), repro. in W. Pattison, *Cupid's metamorphoses* (1728)

Pattle, Marmaduke Thomas St John [Pat] (1914–1941), air force officer, was born at Butterworth, Cape Province, on 23 July 1914, the younger of the two sons of Jack Pattle (*b.* 1884) of Butterworth and his wife, Edith *née* Brailsford, a nurse originally from Bishop Auckland, co. Durham. Pattle, known as Tom to his family, grew up in Keetmanshoop, formerly South-West Africa, where his father held a commission in the local police force and later bought a small farm. At Keetmanshoop Pattle learned to stalk and shoot, became a strong swimmer, a boxer, and a scout, and was greatly attracted to things mechanical. He attended the local secondary school and was later a boarder at Victoria Boys' High School in Grahamstown.

After matriculating in 1931 Pattle worked as a garage assistant. An early application to join the South African Air Force in March 1933 was rejected and he later became an assayer at the Sheba goldmine in Barberton. Physical fitness became a constant, along with the family motto, 'perseverance'. At the beginning of 1936 he joined the Special Service battalion, which gave cadet training to school leavers. This offered him a route into the South African armed services but he decided instead to apply to the Royal Air Force, responding to a recruitment campaign in the South African press. After passing a preliminary interview he was told that he would have to travel to England at his own expense for a selection-board interview and medical. Undeterred by the cost he wrote to his mother: 'I'm going to the RAF even if I haven't a penny in my pocket. I'm going to put the Pattles in the limelight again' (Lucas, 126).

Pattle's family paid for his passage and he left South Africa for England on 30 April 1936. After passing the

Marmaduke Thomas St John Pattle (1914–1941), by unknown photographer, 1941 [left, with his adjutant, Flight Lieutenant George Rumsey, at Larissa in April 1941]

necessary tests in London he was offered a four-year short-service commission and began flying training at the civil flying school at Prestwick. Determined to become a regular, he worked extremely hard, completing his flying training at Ternhill, in Shropshire, where he was rated an exceptional pilot. In May 1937 he was posted to 80 (fighter) squadron at Henlow and in October 1937 he became squadron adjutant. He remained with the unit until shortly before his death in 1941.

To his service colleagues Pattle was known as Pat. He was of medium height and spare frame, with striking grey-green eyes. Slightly older than his peers, he shared in their enthusiasms, but with 'reserve, thoughtfulness, and a hint of introspection' (Lucas, 128). In April 1938 the squadron moved to Egypt, initially to Isma'iliyyah. As a flight commander he proved adept at devising techniques to get the best out of the squadron's Gloster Gladiator biplanes, which by the outbreak of war trailed in performance behind the new breed of monoplane fighter. In this unequal contest, Pattle proved the ablest of all. He had perfect vision and what amounted to a sixth sense about the movement of the enemy. He also allied to remarkable flying skills a scientific approach to aerial combat, studying the characteristics of every enemy plane and devising different tactics to deal with each. He made best use of the sun and of cloud cover and shot with remarkable accuracy, on two occasions managing three victories in a single sortie. A strict disciplinarian on the ground and in the air, he was aggressive but neither reckless nor bloodthirsty.

Pattle first engaged in combat on 4 August 1940, shortly after 80 squadron had moved up to the Libyan border. His flight was attacked by a force of Italian air force CR 42s and Breda Ba65s, and although he claimed two victories three of the four Gladiators were shot down, including his own, and the fourth was badly damaged. He baled out over Italian territory but walked towards his own lines and was discovered exhausted by a long-range desert patrol the next day. His squadron moved to Greece in November 1940 to support Greek forces on the Albanian front. In this new theatre Pattle again achieved outstanding results and by December he was acting commanding officer. The combination of administrative duties, long two-hour patrols in freezing weather, and heavy combat, though, left him fatigued and in January 1941 he had ten days' leave in Cairo. He returned fit, and the next month was awarded the DFC—one of the first decorations to be won by the RAF in the Greek campaign.

Early in February 1941 the squadron was at last re-equipped with the 350 m.p.h. Hurricane, making Pattle's combat skills even more deadly. He scored his first victory in the new fighter on 20 February 1941, shooting down a Fiat G50, and thereafter he quickly accumulated a remarkable tally. When a bar to his DFC was gazetted early in March his total stood at twenty-three. During the appalling conditions in Greece that winter he was an inspirational figure in a unit that contained no fewer than nine future squadron commanders. On 12 March he was promoted to acting squadron leader and given the command of 33 squadron. Weeks later, following the German invasion of Greece on 6 April, the aerial war there turned decisively against the RAF. Outnumbered in the air by the Luftwaffe and bombed on the ground, the RAF units 'were engaged in increasingly chaotic conditions' (Shores and Williams, 486).

On 20 April 1941 Pattle led the combined remnants of 33 and 80 squadrons from Eleusis airfield near Athens. Though fatigued and suffering from influenza he flew three sorties that day, the last in the early evening when he led fifteen Hurricanes to intercept a large formation of Junkers 88 bombers, which were protected by almost a hundred Messerschmitt Bf109s and Bf110s. He was last seen shooting down a Bf110 from the tail of the Hurricane of Flight Lieutenant William Joseph 'Timber' Woods. Woods's plane also fell in flames and, moments later, so did Pattle's: in the act of firing he had been attacked by two Bf110s. His Hurricane crashed into Eleusis Bay. His body was never recovered and he is commemorated on column 239 of the memorial in the El Alamein war cemetery.

Many of Pattle's April claims did not receive official confirmation because squadron records were destroyed during the withdrawal from Greece. An 'official' estimate credits him with twenty-eight victories overall. This, though, is certainly an underestimate. One detailed source has concluded that by the time of his death 'his score had reached at least 50, making him the RAF's top-scoring pilot of the war', ahead of two aces of greater renown, James Edgar 'Johnnie' Johnson and Adolph Gysbert 'Sailor' Malan (Shores and Williams, 486). In all Pattle may have destroyed or damaged as many as sixty-nine enemy planes. It is an astonishing record, achieved in just nine months, most of which were spent in an obsolete biplane facing heavy odds. Because he fought in what was regarded as a sideshow to the main theatres of the war his achievements have been consistently underrated. But those who fought alongside him remembered 'an exceptional fighter leader and brilliant fighter pilot', and a man who was 'self-effacing, kind, and unselfish to the end' (ibid., 128, 129).   ROBIN HIGHAM

Sources E. C. R. Baker, 'The unknown ace', *The fighter aces of the RAF, 1939–1945* (1962) · L. Lucas, ed., *Wings of war: airmen of all nations tell their stories, 1939–1945* (1983) · C. Shores and C. Williams, *Aces high* (1994) · E. C. R. Baker, *Ace of aces: M. St. J. Pattle; top scoring allied fighter pilot of World War II* (1992) · J. D. R. Rawlings, *Fighter squadrons of the RAF and their aircraft* (1976) · *The Times* (22 Jan 1942), 7d · PRO, AIR 27/669
Likenesses photograph, 1941, IWM [*see illus.*] · photographs, repro. in Baker, *Ace of aces*

Patton, Charles (1741–1837). *See under* Patton, Philip (1739–1815).

Patton, George, Lord Glenalmond (1803–1869), judge and politician, was born at the Cairnies, Perthshire, in 1803, and baptized on 15 December that year, the third son of James Patton of the Cairnies, sheriff-clerk of Perthshire, and his wife, Ann Marshall. He received his early education at Perth. He matriculated at Trinity College, Cambridge, in 1822, and took his BA in 1826. On returning to Scotland he began his legal studies at Edinburgh University, and was admitted advocate in 1828. He was an ardent tory in politics, and it was not until Lord Derby's second government came into power in 1859 that Patton received official recognition, becoming solicitor-general for Scotland for a few weeks. In the spring of 1866 he entered the House of Commons as Conservative member for Bridgewater, and a few weeks later, when Lord Derby's third administration was formed, he was made lord advocate. The appointment necessitated a new election at Bridgewater, and Patton was defeated. Allegations were made that gross bribery had been practised at both these elections, and a commission was appointed to inquire into these charges. Patton was relieved of the necessity of taking any part in the inquiry by becoming, in 1867, lord justice clerk: the choice of this appointment lay with the lord advocate, and Patton thus conferred the office on himself, taking the title of Lord Glenalmond.

In August 1869 he succeeded to the estate and mansion at Glenalmond on the death of his elder brother, Thomas Patton, a solicitor. By some journalistic mistake, this was announced as the 'demise of the lord justice clerk'. It was variously contended that this error, or the controversy surrounding his self-appointment as lord president, affected the balance of Lord Glenalmond's mind. On Thursday 16 September 1869 he presided at the Ayr circuit, and on the following day he returned to Edinburgh, proceeding from there to Glenalmond. On the morning of Monday 20 September he committed suicide by cutting his throat and throwing himself into the River Almond on his estate. After its recovery his body was interred in the family burying-ground of Monzie, Perthshire. He left a widow, but no family. The contemporary view was that Glenalmond possessed considerable legal talents, but had insufficient opportunity for displaying administrative ability. In the management of his own small estate of the Cairnies he made many valuable experiments in arboriculture: he introduced *Cupressus Lawsoniana* and *Abies Pattoniana*, and had projected elaborate trials of various conifers at Glenalmond.

A. H. MILLAR, *rev.* ROBERT SHIELS

Sources W. Marshall, *Historic scenes in Perthshire* (1880), 299 · T. Hunter, *Woods, forests and estates of Perthshire* (1883) · *North British Daily Mail* (23 Sept 1869) · *Dundee Advertiser* (25 Sept 1869) · Boase, *Mod. Eng. biog.* · Venn, *Alum. Cant.* · J. Britten and G. S. Boulger, eds., *A biographical index of British and Irish botanists* (1893) · Irving, *Scots.* · *CGPLA Eng. & Wales* (1869)

Likenesses J. Steell, marble bust, NL Scot.

Wealth at death £108,121 16s. 3d.: confirmation, 9 Dec 1869, NA Scot., SC 49/31/88/1014–1040

Patton, Philip (1739–1815), naval officer, the eldest of five children of Philip Patton (d. 1792?), collector of customs at Kirkcaldy, Fife, and Agnes, *née* Loch, his wife, was born at Anstruther on 27 October 1739 and educated at the grammar school there. He entered the merchant service through his uncle, one of the largest shipowners in east Scotland. After some years in merchant ships, during which he made voyages to the Mediterranean and the Baltic, Patton entered the navy early in 1755 on the *Torbay* (90 guns), under the patronage of Vice-Admiral Edward Boscawen. He followed Boscawen to the *Invincible* (74 guns), the *Royal George* (100 guns), and the *Namur* (90 guns) and was present at the taking of Louisbourg in 1758 and the defeat of de la Clue in 1759. In the *Namur*, under Captain Mathew Buckle, he was present at the battle of Quiberon Bay. Still in the *Namur*, carrying the flag of Sir George Pocock, Patton went to the West Indies in 1762, and took part in the capture of Havana. On 3 July 1763 he was promoted lieutenant of the bomb-vessel *Grenada*, in which he returned to England that summer.

On 29 June 1765 Patton became second lieutenant of the *Emerald* (32 guns), stationed at Leith, and in her he served in the North Sea until 1767 and again from 6 June 1770 to 1772. During this time Patton's vigilance and skill twice saved the ship: once when, as lieutenant of the watch, he prevented her running on the rock of Gibraltar; and again when she ran aground on the Gunfleet Sand, sticking fast for several days and only getting off through the exertions of Patton, who was in charge of the pilot and now the ship's first lieutenant. The *Emerald* was so damaged that she was paid off and Patton returned to Scotland. He remained there until 1776 when he was appointed fifth lieutenant to the *Prince George* (98 guns, Captain Charles Middleton). At Middleton's request Patton followed him to the *Royal Oak* (74 guns) as first lieutenant, and this began a lifelong friendship which influenced Patton's later career.

When Sir Hyde Parker (1714–1782/3) hoisted his flag on the *Royal Oak*, Middleton was replaced by Parker's captain and Patton waited to be superseded by Parker's first lieutenant. But during George III's review of the fleet at Portsmouth in the spring of 1778 Patton, with other first lieutenants, was promoted commander and moved to the bomb-vessel *Etna* on 9 May. He was ordered to the Guinea coast, but, detained at Spithead, was appointed acting captain of the *Prince George*, whose captain, Sir John Lindsay, was needed as a witness in the Keppel court martial.

The *Prince George* was then sent to sea in Admiral Shuldham's squadron. Thoroughly dissatisfied, the crew mutinied on 19 January 1779, when Patton ordered them to bring up their hammocks from the middle and lower decks to allow for essential ventilation, prevented for some days by bad weather. On his return to Spithead Patton assumed command of the sloop *Thorn* but two months later, on 22 March 1779, he was posted to the *Namur*, the flagship of Rear-Admiral Robert Digby, and he moved with Digby to the *Prince George*. He thus took part in Admiral Rodney's defeat of Langara on 16 January 1780 at the Moonlight battle, when the *Prince George* took the Spanish *San Julian* (74 guns), later wrecked near Cadiz. Patton remained in the *Prince George* on her return to England until the autumn, when he was appointed to command the *Milford*, cruising as part of the Channel Fleet, first under admirals Hardy and Geary and then under Vice-Admiral George Darby. The *Milford* proved very leaky and the gale of 9 October, which damaged the Channel Fleet, so increased her defects that she was decommissioned in December 1780.

Patton immediately asked for another command and in February 1781 was appointed to the *Belle Poule* (36 guns), a French prize. At the particular request of Commodore Keith Stewart, who had long held a high opinion of Patton's seamanship, he accompanied Stewart, in the *Berwick* (74 guns), to Leith, capturing a troublesome Dunkirk privateer, the *Calonne* (32 guns, 240 men) commanded by the notorious Luke Ryan, on 17 April at the entrance to the Firth of Forth. Patton then joined Sir Hyde Parker's squadron in convoying a large merchant fleet from the Baltic. He was thus in the action on the Dogger Bank on 5 August 1781, a hard fought though indecisive battle; and on the following day, sent in chase of Dutch ships, he found the *Holland* (64 guns) which had sunk after the action, her mast heads still above water, flying her pennant. This Patton removed and brought to Parker as a victory trophy. Probably as a result of battle damage Patton reported the *Belle Poule* in danger of foundering in heavy weather and she was sent to Sheerness for repairs which occupied most of September. Once repaired she was sent to the Elbe, with two other frigates under Patton's command, to protect British trade, and then to Cork to escort troop transports, to Bristol, and Plymouth. She was paid off at the end of 1782. In the following year Patton married Elizabeth Dixon, only daughter of John Dixon of Fareham, Hampshire, and returned to Scotland.

Dividing his time between Hampshire and Kirkcaldy, Patton spent the next ten years unemployed but actively working on a book of naval signals which would be clear and simple to use and acceptable to the service. His other studies focused on the practical ways to defend trade through the allocation of adequate blockading forces, and on improvements to shipbuilding. In this Patton was encouraged by Middleton, now comptroller of the navy, but despite the latter's interest Patton's system of signals was not given a trial probably because Admiral Lord Howe's system carried greater influence. Patton's hopes of employment during the Spanish and Russian armaments (1790 and 1791) were also disappointed. When war broke out he wrote to Lord Chatham, the first lord of the Admiralty, on 13 February 1793, asking for employment and told Middleton he thought himself entitled to a

74-gun ship, though he did not want to be sent on a distant station during a war he expected to be short. Yet it was not until May 1794 that he was made one of the commissioners of the transport board, the creation of Middleton, now a member of the Admiralty.

Here Patton was undoubtedly useful; his experience and his reflective but practical nature were what such a newly created office needed. But the story that Chatham tried to persuade him to continue there, threatening that if Patton insisted on taking his flag he should not be employed, appears unlikely. Patton was promoted rear-admiral of the blue on 1 June 1795 but there was no change of transport board commissioners until September 1795, nine months after Chatham had been succeeded at the Admiralty by Earl Spencer. Any difference with Chatham could have been caused by Patton's growing unease over the likelihood of a general naval mutiny and his insistence, from 1794, on its real possibility. In 1790 Patton drew up fifty pages of observations on naval affairs, concerned with the conditions, pay, and promotion of seamen and warrant officers. In 1795 he revised his original ideas under the title *Observations on Naval Mutiny*, adding suggestions on prevention and asking that it be presented to the first lord of the Admiralty, and though Lord Spencer received it in April 1795 and copies were also sent to William Pitt, Henry Dundas, and William Wilberforce, no notice was taken. Conceivably it was this indifference to his warnings which caused Patton to retire from public life in 1795, to Fareham, Hampshire.

The mutiny did break out at Spithead and the Admiralty came to Portsmouth in April 1797. Patton waited on Lord Spencer on 19 April, reminded him of the *Observations* (which Spencer had forgotten), and presented him with another copy. Patton was in a despairing mood and deeply disturbed by the mutiny and suggestions that flag-officers should have their officers chosen for them.

> Nothing can make me believe that an Admiral can do his duty to his Country without the Captain and all the Officers of his own Ship being of his own chusing. No man upon whom the command of a considerable Squadron may devolve can rely upon Men put upon him indiscriminately. (Patton to Middleton, 21 April 1797)

Patton thought the only way to restore discipline and prevent future mutinies was to improve the pay of the warrant and petty officers and increase their numbers, giving due weight and promotion to experience and steady obedience and attaching the very best, skilled men to the service by these means. The considerable expense was justified. 'If we must have a Navy, there is a necessity for being at the requisite expence. Men will not now defend the State by compulsion' (Patton to Middleton, 20 April 1797). In this sombre mood Patton told Middleton he was unwilling to accept employment or any public situation and this is doubtless the reason why he remained in retirement.

On 14 February 1799 Patton was promoted rear-admiral of the red and on 1 January 1801 vice-admiral of the blue. War again broke out in 1803 and he was appointed second in command in the Downs to Admiral Lord Keith on 13 December. Despite some ill health he was active and vigilant, and Keith found him 'a sensible and honourable man' (St Vincent, *The Letters of Admiral of the Fleet the Earl of St Vincent*, ed. D. Bonner Smith, vol. 2, Navy Records Society, 61, 1927, 387). Patton, in turn, was grateful to Keith for his attention and confidence and expressed his surprise at his unexpected appointment to the Admiralty on 15 May 1804. He had had no previous acquaintance with Lord Melville, the first lord, and was modestly hesitant about his qualifications. He had already been created vice-admiral of the red on 23 April and was promoted admiral of the blue on 9 November 1805. He served at the Admiralty until 10 February 1806, when the change of ministry led, at the age of sixty-seven, to his retirement.

For the rest of his life Patton lived either at his house at Fareham or at Fleetland Farm, Alverstoke, Hampshire. Despite being troubled with cataracts Patton spent his time reading and writing, chiefly on naval themes, but he had a taste for poetry and translated Horace's *Odes* and *Epistles* for amusement. He was promoted admiral of the white on 31 July 1810 and of the red on 4 June 1814.

Patton died at Fareham on 31 December 1815, aged seventy-six. He was buried in the churchyard of St Peter and St Paul, Fareham. Numbers of men, many of them warrant officers, walked from Portsmouth to attend his funeral out of respect for Patton's attempts to improve their conditions. However, his publications are his real memorial; these include, in addition to those already mentioned, an *Account of the Mutinies at Spithead and St Helen's in April and May 1797* (1797), *Sketch of a Plan for Attaching Real Seamen to the Navy* (1802), and *The Natural Defence of an Insular Empire* (1810).

The first of Patton's younger brothers, **Charles Patton** (1741–1837), naval officer, entered the navy in May 1758 on the *Ripon* (54 guns). He was present at the capture of Guadeloupe in 1759 and the blockade of Brest in 1761. He was promoted lieutenant on 17 February 1780 and commander on 25 September 1781. He commanded the cutter *Rattlesnake*, designated a sloop in 1779, and was appointed lieutenant to the storeship *Camel* in the spring of 1791 during the Russian armament because he knew the Baltic and North Sea well. During this period he collaborated with Philip Patton in his work on signals, but he was particularly interested in problems of shipbuilding. Patton became post captain on 30 May 1795 and served as agent for transports at Portsmouth until 1815. The appointment was probably due to the influence of both Sir Charles Middleton and Philip Patton, the latter having become one of the commissioners for transports in 1794, but Charles Patton's exertions and efficiency in this post, particularly during the difficulties of the Peninsular War, were highly satisfactory to the Admiralty. Superannuated in 1816, he retired to Fareham, Hampshire, where he died on 16 January 1837, aged ninety-six. He was probably buried at Holy Trinity Church, Fareham, Hampshire. He wrote *A Sketch of the Life, Services and Character of the Late Admiral Philip Patton* (1818).

Robert Patton (1742–1812), army officer in the East

India Company, younger brother of Philip and Charles Patton, entered the army of the East India Company. He was a friend and admirer of Warren Hastings. Between 1776 and 1779 he lived in Thistle Street, Edinburgh, at Grange near Burntisland, or at Pitliven near Dunfermline; and in September 1797 he was based at Edinburgh Castle. He became governor of St Helena and died at Wallington, Hampshire, on 14 January 1812, aged sixty-eight, a fortnight after the death of his wife, Constantia Adriana, aged fifty-five, on 31 December 1811. Patton was buried with her at the parish church of St Peter and St Paul, Fareham, Hampshire.

Robert Patton published *An Historical Review of the Monarchy and Republic of Rome* (1797), which was prefaced by his brother Charles's work, and *Principles of Asiatic Monarchies Politically and Historically Investigated* (1803).

P. K. Crimmin

Sources DNB · J. Ralfe, *The naval biography of Great Britain*, 3 (1828), 387–400 · J. Marshall, *Royal naval biography*, 2 (1824), 93 · D. Syrett and R. L. DiNardo, *The commissioned sea officers of the Royal Navy, 1660–1815*, rev. edn, Occasional Publications of the Navy RS, 1 (1994) · captain's letters, PRO, ADM/6/20, 21; ADM1/2306, P. 1780–81 · P. Patton, letter to Middleton, 1779–97, NMM, Middleton papers, MID/1/140 · P. Patton, letters, NMM, Keith MSS, KEI/28/28–33 · will, 30 Sept 1809, Hants. RO, 10/M64/93; will, 8 May 1812, Hants. RO, 186/M86/6/2 · Hants. RO, 686/M86/3–5, 7 · Hants. RO, 64/M76/DL70 · monumental inscriptions, St Peter and St Paul, Fareham; Holy Trinity, Fareham, Hants. RO · B. Lavery, ed., *Shipboard life and organisation, 1731–1815*, Navy RS, 138 (1998), 613–15, 622–34 · BL, Hardwicke MSS, Add. MS 35651, vol. 303 · B. Tunstall, *Naval warfare in the age of sail: the evolution of fighting tactics, 1650–1815*, ed. N. Tracy (1990)

Archives NA Scot., documents relating to the Nore mutiny of 1805; letters to Lord Melville · NMM, book of signals | NMM, letters to Sir Charles Middleton · NMM, letters to Lord Keith

Likenesses portrait; in possession of Patton family, 1895

Wealth at death moderately wealthy: will, 1816, Hants. RO, 186M86/6/2

Patton, Robert (1742–1812). *See under* Patton, Philip (1739–1815).

Pattrick, George (1746–1800), Church of England clergyman, was born on 9 August 1746 at Marks Tey, near Colchester, Essex, the fourth son of Thomas Patrick, a wealthy farmer; his father and grandfather had both farmed the same land there for over a century. Pattrick went to St Paul's School, London, on 4 February 1756 and left about 1762 to become a law clerk in Colchester, and subsequently an attorney in London. Two years later he moved to Dedham in Essex, where he 'dissipated a considerable part of a moderate fortune left him by his father', largely by giving 'genteel and expensive entertainments' (Pattrick, 2). Finding the practice of law tedious he decided to seek holy orders. He was ordained deacon by Richard Terrick, bishop of London, on 23 December 1770, and took up a curacy at St Michael, Mile End, Colchester; on 29 December he was admitted a fellow-commoner at Sidney Sussex College, Cambridge. He graduated LLB in 1777.

Terrick ordained Pattrick priest on 22 September 1771, when Thomas Barrett-Lennard, seventeenth Baron Dacre, secured his presentation to the rectory of Aveley in Essex. In March 1773 he gained the post of curate of Wennington

George Pattrick (1746–1800), by Joseph Collyer the younger (after John Russell)

in Essex, which he held in addition to his benefice. In December 1775 he was appointed chaplain to Lord Dacre; his noble patron took advantage of his legal experience and degree in law to make him examine old deeds and draw up genealogies, so that 'he found that almost the whole week was frittered away among old parchments and that preparation for the duties of the Sunday was driven into a corner'. He was, indeed, not pastorally inclined and 'much of his time was taken up at the harpsichord and in electrical and other experiments' (Pattrick, 6).

It was said by Pattrick's biographer that 'The early part of his ministerial career was dissipated in the pursuits of a gentleman rather than occupied in those of the divine' (*Life of the Rev. George Pattrick*, 68) and indeed the nature of his ministry was not entirely unusual among incumbents at that time. The great change in his life came from about 1780, when he was gradually converted to evangelicalism after a woman in his parish persuaded him to listen to the evangelical preachers in London. In the later part of 1781 he introduced himself by letter to Dr Richard Conyers, vicar of Deptford, and joined the many who sought spiritual guidance from him. In 1782 he took lodgings in Deptford so as to be able to make numerous visits to his adviser. After travelling in France and Italy for his health, from June 1783 to June 1784, he resigned from Aveley and Wennington on 10 October 1787, when chosen to be chaplain of a charitable institution for the elderly, Morden College, Blackheath, Kent, through the influence of Charles Trevor Roper, eighteenth Baron Dacre, who had succeeded his uncle in the peerage in 1786 and had maintained Pattrick in the post of chaplain. Pattrick married, on 8 September 1789, Mary Ferriday of Madeley in Shropshire, where the vicar was the saintly evangelical John William Fletcher.

Pattrick's eloquent preaching was attractive to many who came to hear him in the chapel of Morden College but a number of the pensioners disliked him because he did 'treat almost solely of faith and grace and such like controversial points' (*Life of the Rev. George Pattrick*, 32), and the trustees were persuaded to dismiss him on 22 June 1790. He was appointed curate to William Rose, rector of Carshalton in Surrey, on 17 April 1791.

Though they were gaining support from the laity, clerical opposition made it difficult for the early evangelicals to get much in the way of ecclesiastical preferment. One method of making themselves heard was to seek election to the lectureships established, mainly by the seventeenth-century puritans, in order to secure regular weekly preaching in the parishes. Pattrick did this with varying success. On 12 January 1792 he was elected to a lectureship at Woolwich parish church but the rector at once dismissed him. He moved to London in the summer of 1793 and, despite having steadily refused to canvass, he was elected lecturer at St Leonard, Shoreditch, on 19 March 1796; he had stood against five other candidates, and polled 947 votes to his nearest opponent's 357. The churchwardens alleged that his supporters 'refuse the communion of the Church of England' (Ellis, 48) and 'endeavour to impose upon them a partizan of their own' (ibid., 49), but the vicar secured his acceptance as joint lecturer with the runner-up. Pattrick's first sermon at St Leonard's was preached on 4 December 1796 and subsequently published. In December 1797 he was chosen to be Sunday evening lecturer at St Bride's, Fleet Street; both St Bride's and St Leonard's were packed to the doors as he drew an average congregation of 1500, larger than in any other London church at that time. He had also a third share in an evening lectureship at St Margaret's, Lothbury. His other activities included assisting in the foundation of the evangelical Church Missionary Society in 1799 and taking an active part in its proceedings. At a meeting of the Eclectic Society, the evangelical organization founded by Richard Cecil and others in 1783, on 17 March 1800 he supported eight other evangelical clergymen in asserting that theatrical amusements were totally evil and should be opposed by all Christians. His rapid rise to importance was unexpectedly ended by a brief and fatal feverish illness. He died at Madeley on 14 September 1800 and was buried there on 17 September; his wife and two children survived him.

Pattrick was a moderate Calvinist, like most early evangelicals, who believed in justification by faith and final perseverance, while repudiating predestined reprobation. Declared to be 'more of a Barnabas then a Boanerges' (*Evangelical Magazine*, 492)—that is to say, more of 'a son of comfort' than 'a son of thunder'—he was an effective, persuasive preacher with a strong voice, clear enunciation, and widespread popularity. Early evangelicals wished to have their sermons printed for distribution, and Pattrick's *Sermons, with a Help to Prayer* were published posthumously in London in 1801. LEONARD W. COWIE

Sources G. Pattrick, *Sermons, with a help to prayer* (1801) · *Life of the Rev. George Pattrick* (1833) · 'Memoir of the Rev. Geo. Patrick', *Evangelical Magazine*, 8 (1800), 485–94 · D. M. Lewis, ed., *The Blackwell dictionary of evangelical biography, 1730–1860*, 2 vols. (1995) · L. E. Elliott-Binns, *The early evangelicals: a religious and social study* (1953) · G. R. Balleine, *A history of the evangelical party in the Church of England*, new edn (1933) · H. Ellis, *The history and antiquities of the parish of St Leonard, Shoreditch, and liberty of Norton Folgate* (1798) · F. K. Brown, *Fathers of the Victorians: the age of Wilberforce* (1961) · D. W. Bebbington, *Evangelicalism in modern Britain: a history from the 1730s to the 1980s* (1989) · C. Hole, *The early history of the Church Missionary Society for Africa and the East to the end of AD 1814* (1896) · E. Elbourne, 'The foundation of the Church Missionary Society: the Anglican missionary impulse', *The Church of England, c.1689–c.1833*, ed. J. Walsh and others (1993), 247–64

Archives NRA, priv. coll., diaries

Likenesses J. Collyer the younger, line engraving (after J. Russell), BM, NPG [*see illus.*]

Wealth at death see will, PRO, PROB 11/1351, sig. 888

Paul [St Paul, Paulus Aurelianus, Paulinus] (*fl.* **6th cent.**), bishop of St Pol-de-Léon, Brittany, was allegedly the son of Perphirius, a count in south-eastern Wales, and was supposed to have been born at Penn Ohen, near Llandovery. In his life and in place names his name is Paul, but in some early sources it is Paulinus; he may be identifiable with either of two obscure Carmarthenshire saints, Poul Penychen or Paulinus. The surname 'Aurelianus' may be genuine, or reflect the fact that his relics and life were later preserved at Orléans.

There can be little doubt that Paul existed, but his life, composed in 884 in elaborate Latin by Wrmonoc, a pupil of Abbot Wrdisten of Landévennec, Cornouaille, Brittany, contains little precise information. Paul is presented as an ascetic seeking solitude with a few followers, performing miracles and shunning worldly honours; a typically Brittonic detail is his miraculous bell. Like St Samson of Dol, from whose life certain episodes in Paul's are probably borrowed, he is supposed to have begun his career in Wales and visited south-west Britain *en route* for Brittany. The apparently Cornish sections of the life have attracted the most scholarly interest. When Wrmonoc wrote that Paul preached in the realm of 'King Marcus, whom they called by another name Quonomorius', he may have had access to some genuine information about the evangelization of Cornwall (Olson, 27).

Wrmonoc's account of the desolation prevailing at the site of St Pol-de-Léon on Paul's arrival there should be taken as allegory rather than as evidence for the depopulation of sixth-century Armorica, as has sometimes been done. Nor is there reason to assume that Paul was a leader and mediator for large numbers of British immigrants. The statement that he was ordained bishop at the court of the Frankish king Childebert may be a borrowing from the life of St Samson. Of more value is Wrmonoc's description of the landed endowment of the abbey bishopric of St Pol, which contains echoes of the terminology of early Celtic charters.

Paul was commemorated in liturgy throughout Brittany

and in Maine, Poitou, Anjou, and Saintonge, but not else-where. He is alleged to have died on the Île de Batz and his relics were preserved at St Pol and, from c.960, partly at Orléans, together with an early manuscript of his life. His feast, originally on 12 March (the day of his death), was later more often celebrated on 10 October, through confu-sion with that of St Paulinus of York. Many place names in Léon, some in Côtes-du-Nord and Morbihan, and one in Cornwall (Paul parish, near Penzance), testify to his cult.

CAROLINE BRETT

Sources 'Vita Sancti Pauli episcopi Leonensis in Britannia Minore auctore Wormonoco', ed. F. B. Plaine, *Analecta Bollandiana*, 1 (1882), 208–58 · C. Cuissard, ed., 'Vie de S. Paul de Léon en Bretagne d'après un manuscrit de Fleury-sur-Loire', *Revue Celtique*, 5 (1881–3), 413–60 · G. Doble, *Saint Paul of Léon*, 3rd edn, Cornish Saints Series, 46 (1941) · L. Olson, *Early monasteries in Cornwall* (1989) · W. Davies, 'The Latin charter-tradition in western Britain, Brittany and Ire-land in the early mediaeval period', *Ireland in early mediaeval Europe*, ed. D. Whitelock, R. McKitterick, and D. Dumville (1982), 258–80 · M. Lapidge and R. Sharpe, *A bibliography of Celtic-Latin literature, 400–1200* (1985) · *Acta sanctorum: Martius*, 2 (Antwerp, 1668), 111–20 · Aimoinus Floriac, 'De miraculis S. Benedicti', *Patrologia Latina*, 139 (1853), 801–52, esp. 841–3 · Wormonocus, *Vita Sancti Pauli*, ed. F. Plaine (1882)

Paul (d. 1093), abbot of St Albans, was outstanding among the monks from Normandy who, after the Norman con-quest, became abbots of English monasteries. His reputa-tion as an abbot who rebuilt extensively, ruled zealously, and augmented endowments is well established by brief comments written during the Norman period by Eadmer and William of Malmesbury. But the only extensive account of him is in the *Gesta abbatum*, which was the work of Matthew Paris, c.1250, although he apparently used an 'ancient roll' of Bartholomew the clerk, servant to the twelfth-century Adam the Cellarer; the *Gesta's* date and authorship must be remembered.

Paul was a nephew of Lanfranc of Pavia, archbishop of Canterbury (1070–89); one of his parents was apparently Norman, and he was himself born in Normandy. His hum-ble birth was noted; a rumour that he was Lanfranc's son is uncorroborated and almost certainly an unwarranted inference from Lanfranc's bounty. He was perhaps a monk at Bec in Normandy; he was certainly so at St Étienne at Caen, of which Lanfranc was the first abbot. In 1077 Lan-franc procured Paul's succession as abbot of St Albans, which, although in the diocese of Lincoln, was effectively independent and under Lanfranc's ultimate control. Lan-franc was no doubt glad to consolidate his own influence in a region where his predecessor Stigand (1052–70) had been strong.

Paul took office on 28 June 1077 and almost at once began to rebuild the abbey church on a grand scale, using stone and tiles from nearby Roman Verulamium and tim-ber gathered by earlier abbots, as well as baluster shafts from the Anglo-Saxon church. He also reconstructed almost all of the monastic buildings except the bakehouse and the kneading-room. He received generous financial support from Lanfranc, reportedly some 1000 marks. His building work was completed by 1088, though the church was consecrated only in 1115.

Paul left a reputation of strictness in his own religious life and of being well educated. At St Albans he took ener-getic steps to improve regular discipline and observance. He adopted the collection of monastic customs that Lan-franc compiled for Christ Church, Canterbury, with a smaller addendum. He was particularly concerned to enforce silence in the church, cloister, refectory, infirm-ary, and, above all, dormitory. He curbed the eating of meat by monks who had been bled or who otherwise lacked good reason. He provided for a lantern to be carried in church to arouse the somnolent during the night office; a large lantern was also to be carried before themselves by monks under penance. Paul tempered his strictness by introducing his measures gradually, thus avoiding dis-cord, especially among older monks; but he also con-structed a dark and strong monastic prison for the contu-macious. He regulated the life of nuns who served in the almonry. The scriptorium was an especial concern: a liter-ate Norman knight, Robert, provided an income so that professional scribes might be employed.

Paul successfully built up the abbey's endowments and wealth. He recovered lands lost under his predecessors, notably from bishops Odo of Bayeux and Remigius of Lin-coln. He acquired many new possessions, including chur-ches in London and Cambridge. He secured presents for his church: for example, two bells for its tower, the gift of an English thegn, Liulf, and his wife. Other gifts made by or through Paul included twenty-eight fine books, as well as numerous other liturgical books and relics, vestments, pieces of plate, and ornaments.

Paul established dependent cells, ruled by priors from St Albans, at Wallingford in Berkshire, Tynemouth in North-umberland, Belvoir in Leicestershire, Hertford, and Binham in Norfolk. In 1093 he was in dispute over Tyne-mouth with the monks of Durham Cathedral, who claimed that Earl Waltheof of Northumbria (d. 1076) had given it to them, and that they had been expelled by the then earl, Robert de Mowbray, from hatred for the bishop of Durham, William of St Calais.

Paul enjoyed excellent relations with Archbishop Anselm of Canterbury (1093–1109) as well as with Lan-franc. In 1077, at Paul's own request, Anselm had sent from Bec a letter of good wishes on his succession at St Albans; Anselm wrote that, although set over *barbari*, the good example of Paul's life would supply what the differ-ence of language would hinder (*Anselmi opera omnia*, 3.203–4). Paul aided Anselm upon his arrival as archbishop and was requited by Anselm's favour. Anselm approved and confirmed the monastic customs that Lanfranc had sent.

The *Gesta abbatum* gives a surprisingly long list of Paul's 'negligences' as abbot. He lost a number of the abbey's properties. He destroyed the tombs of former abbots, 'whom he was wont to call *rudes et idiotas*' (*Gesta abbatum*, 1.62), allegedly either despising them because they were English or envying their royal or noble blood. Following his predecessors, he failed to bring the bones of the founder, King Offa of Mercia (d. 796), into his rebuilt church. He practised nepotism in rashly and secretly mak-ing gifts to his Norman kinsfolk despite their base origins and unworthy characters. However, it was concluded that the good things which he did far outweighed the damage to his church.

Paul died on 11 November 1093 at Settrington, near York, while returning from Tynemouth. He was probably first buried in the apsidal east end of his new chapter house at St Albans, but in its enlargement of 1154–6 his body was removed to the east of the lectern. In 1979, after excavations, his remains were buried with those of later abbots before the high altar. H. E. J. COWDREY

Sources *Eadmeri Historia novorum in Anglia*, ed. M. Rule, Rolls Series, 81 (1884) · *Willelmi Malmesbiriensis monachi de gestis pontificum Anglorum libri quinque*, ed. N. E. S. A. Hamilton, Rolls Series, 52 (1870) · *Gesta abbatum monasterii Sancti Albani, a Thoma Walsingham*, ed. H. T. Riley, 3 vols., pt 4 of *Chronica monasterii S. Albani*, Rolls Series, 28 (1867–9), vol. 1, pp. 51–65 · *Symeon of Durham, Opera* · *S. Anselmi Cantuariensis archiepiscopi opera omnia*, ed. F. S. Schmitt, 6 vols. (1938–61) · L. F. R. Williams, *History of the abbey of St Alban* (1917) · R. Vaughan, *Matthew Paris*, Cambridge Studies in Medieval Life and Thought, new ser., 6 (1958) · *Matthaei Paris ... Historia major ... huic primum ed. accesserunt duorum Offarum Merciorum regum, et viginti trium abbatum S. Albani vitae*, ed. W. Wats, 2 vols. (1639–40) · Symeon of Durham, *Libellus de exordio atque procursu istius, hoc est Dunhelmensis, ecclesie / Tract on the origins and progress of this the church of Durham*, ed. and trans. D. W. Rollason, OMT (2000)

Paul [Páll þorfinnsson] (*d.* **1098/9**), earl of Orkney, succeeded to the earldom conjointly with his younger brother, **Erlend** [Erlendr þorfinnsson] (*d.* 1098/9), earl of Orkney, on the death of their father, Earl *Thorfinn (II) Sigurdson, *c.*1065. They were closely related to the ruling dynasties of Norway and Scotland, their mother, Ingebjorg (*d. c.*1070) (daughter of Finn Árnason), being cousin to Thora, wife of *Harald Hardrada, king of Norway, and their paternal grandmother being a daughter of *Malcolm II, king of Scots. Moreover, Ingebjorg is said in *Orkneyinga Saga* to have married *Malcolm III Canmore after the death of Earl Thorfinn. Paul, the first earl to have been given a Christian baptismal name, and Erlend are said to have been 'tall, handsome men, shrewd and gentle' (*Orkneyinga Saga*, chap. 31) and taking rather more after their mother's side of the family. They did not divide the earldom initially, being 'for the most part on friendly terms' (ibid., chap. 33), but Paul is specifically said to have been the one who was very much in charge. There is no mention of them having authority or raiding in any of the Scottish or Hebridean or Irish territories controlled by their father, suggesting that—as the saga says—these areas came under local rule and broke away from earldom control after Thorfinn's death.

Paul and Erlend had indeed to cope with a much more energetic exercise of authority by their Norwegian overlords in the earldom than their father had had to face, and soon after his death they were drawn into the ambitious campaign of Harald Hardrada to win the throne of England after the death of Edward the Confessor and the seizure of power by Harold Godwineson. The Norwegian king sailed to Orkney in the summer of 1066 with his fleet of over 200 ships and stayed there for a while gathering more forces; the earls would have been under an obligation to join him with their following of manned ships from their own territories. When the king and the earls sailed south, Harald's queen and his daughter remained behind in the Orkneys. Having raided the coastal parts of Northumbria *en route* for York, the Norwegian and Orcadian fleet then anchored at Riccall on the River Wharfe and launched an attack against Earl Morcar at the gates of York on 20 September. Four days later Harald and his Norwegian forces went to York to receive the submission of the city, leaving Paul and Erlend, along with the young Óláf Haraldsson, in charge of the ships. At Stamford Bridge the invading force was confronted by the English army, which had marched north with King Harold II (Harold Godwineson), and was defeated in the ensuing battle, in which the Norwegian king was killed. Somewhat surprisingly, as the Anglo-Saxon Chronicle tells, quarter was given 'to Olaf, the son of the king of the Norwegians, to their bishop, to the earl of Orkney, and to all those who were left aboard the ships' (*ASC*, s.a. 1066, text D). They had, however, to go to meet King Harold to swear oaths that they would maintain peace and friendship, and 'the king let them sail home with twenty-four ships' (ibid.). Óláf spent that winter in Orkney 'on the friendliest terms with the earls' (*Orkneyinga Saga*, chaps. 33, 34) before returning to take power jointly with his brother Magnús in Norway.

Paul's support for the episcopal structures established in the earldom by his father can be seen from a letter written (before 1073) by Thomas, archbishop of York, in which the earl is named (the first earl to be named in a non-Norse source) as having sent a bishop to him for consecration. This letter leaves no doubt about the earl's control over episcopal appointments, and shows that he concurred with York's claim over the Orkney diocese (although this may have been because the alternative archbishopric, Hamburg, was vacant at this time). It is unlikely that the two earls were supporting rival candidates, although that appears to have been the situation in the twelfth century.

Earl Paul married a daughter of the powerful Norwegian *jarl*, Hákon Ívarsson, and of Ragnhild, daughter of King Magnús the Good. Paul and his wife had one son and four daughters. The son, *Hákon [see under Magnús Erlendsson (1075/6–1116?)], named after his maternal grandfather, wanted to be foremost among all the cousins, considering himself 'more highly-born than the others'. Earl Erlend, however, 'wasn't going to see his sons back down to anyone there in the islands' (*Orkneyinga Saga*, chap. 34): so differences arose between the cousins and although their fathers tried to keep the peace they eventually parted on hostile terms. At a peace meeting held on the mainland of Orkney (perhaps at Tingwall) they agreed to divide Orkney into two parts—as in the time of earls Thorfinn (II) and Brúsi. It seems clear that Erlend and his sons, *Magnús and Erling, commanded more support at this time, for Hákon was induced to leave the islands and he went first to Norway where he visited King Óláf towards the end of his life (1091–2), and then to Sweden. *Orkneyinga Saga* also says that while Hákon was in exile Erlend and his sons had control of everything and Paul 'took little part in governing the earldom' (chap. 37).

Hákon Paulsson is represented in the saga as being the

instigator of the first expedition west undertaken by King Magnús Barelegs of Norway, in 1098, primarily to assert royal authority in Orkney and the Hebrides. Once more Paul and Erlend had to face the arrival of their Norwegian overlord in their earldom, but on this occasion there was direct action to bring the islands under royal control. The highly unusual step was taken of sending the two earls to Norway—under duress—and the young royal prince Sigurd was made overlord of the islands 'with regents to govern the earldom' (*Orkneyinga Saga*, chap. 39). Magnús continued west on his successful raiding expedition and took Hákon Paulsson and the Erlendssons in his retinue, clearly to tie them into his own military following as a preliminary to tightening royal control over the earldom. Authority was also asserted over the Hebrides, where the Norwegian entourage spent the winter. When King Magnús sailed north to Orkney the next spring he heard that Erlend had died and been buried at Trondheim, while 'Earl Paul was buried at Bergen' (ibid., chap. 42). According to *Magnus Barelegs' Saga* Erlend died of disease.

BARBARA E. CRAWFORD

Sources H. Pálsson and P. Edwards, eds. and trans., *The Orkneyinga saga: the history of the earls of Orkney* (1978); repr. (1981) • *ASC*, s.a. 1066 [text D] • B. E. Crawford, 'Bishops of Orkney in the eleventh and twelfth centuries: bibliography and biographical list', *Innes Review*, 47 (1996), 1–13

Paul Anglicus. *See* Paulus Anglicus (*fl.* 1404/5).

Paul of St Francis. *See* Atkinson, Matthew (1656–1729).

Paul of St Magdalen. *See* Heath, Henry (*bap.* 1599, *d.* 1643).

Paul the Silent [Páll inn Ómálgi], **earl of Orkney** (*d. c.*1137). *See under* Magnús Erlendsson, earl of Orkney (1075/6–1116?).

Paul, Brenda Irene Isabelle Frances Theresa Dean (1907–1959), actress and drug addict, was born on 10 June 1907 at 2 Kensington House, Kensington Court, London, the youngest of three children of Sir Aubrey Edward Henry Dean Paul, fifth baronet (1869–1961), captain in the Northumberland Fusiliers, and Irene Regina (1882/3–1932), singer, pianist, and composer, daughter of Henry Wieniawski of Warsaw and his wife, Madame Powdowska. On her own admission she was 'a curiously purposeful child' (Paul, 15) with a reputation for naughtiness, and attended seven different convent schools (the family converted to Roman Catholicism in 1914). She was close to her mother, Irene, and was influenced by her Bohemian lifestyle. Her parents separated in 1922. She and her mother moved to Ebury Street in 1923, becoming neighbours to Noël Coward; Paul, who was taking acting lessons, claimed Coward promised to write a play for her. She toured in repertory in 1924 and again in 1925, when she began a two-year relationship with an artist, 'W', ten years her senior.

The relationship ended in 1927, and Brenda left for Berlin, where she had been promised a film test with United Film Artists. In her three weeks there she experienced the night life of Weimar Berlin and was 'vastly amused' by its 'sexually complex Bohemians' (Paul, 81). Back in England, she resolved to go to Paris, 'being seized with a desire to witness for myself the intriguing, highly coloured underworld as described in cheap literature' (ibid., 85). Paris would, fatally, introduce her to drugs. But Paul differentiated between the 'drug addict' and the 'drug victim': 'I never "dabbled" in it for pleasure as a mirage or barrier for a dissipation warped soul. The laws regarding drugs have been made by fools, and it is from them that conclusions of the kind are derived' (ibid., 86). 'Leo', a heroin addict, taught her how drug assignations were made in theatres and music halls, and Paul tried cocaine for the first time: 'The result was hardly what I expected [:] no exhilaration was mine, no re-born vitality, just a feeling that the top of my head had been suddenly and neatly decapitated like that of a boiled egg' (ibid., 93).

On returning to London, Paul resumed her place among the 'illuminati' of the 'bright young things'. A figure more Hollywood than Mayfair with her sequins, satin, and platinum hair, she was famous, or notorious, enough for Evelyn Waugh to observe that, at a party for which guests were asked to dress as 'living celebrities', Olivia Plunket-Greene 'had had her hair dyed and curled and was dressed to look like Brenda Dean Paul' (*Diaries*, 286). Cecil Beaton admired her 'energetic and hilarious Charleston' (Beaton, 140); Peter Quennell was reminded of 'a Lely portrait of Nell Gwynne, *very like* … a nice, affectionate, drunken, amorous girl' (Luke, 63); and Hermione Baddeley described her as 'a voluptuous girl who has plenty of sex appeal and lets every man within eye-catching distance get the message' (Baddeley, 66). Among her lovers, Paul counted Baddeley's own partner, David Tennant, who took Paul with him to Canada in March 1929, only to send her back when she proved too trying (Luke, 71). On her return to London she fell in love with a man whom she referred to only as 'the romantic interest' (Paul, 157).

As one of the 'real original pioneers' of the 'bright young things', Paul had become a real-life Coward heroine, a poor little rich girl: 'For years I never went to bed before four or five in the morning' (Paul, 104). But she regarded the 'scene' as spoilt by its own publicity, incomers, and what she called 'social blood-poisoning' (ibid., 97) and in 1930 Paul left for Tahiti, 'without doubt … the only place for me … I come to life and bloom in the sun' (ibid., 130). After three months' tropical idyll, she returned to Britain and in January 1931 announced to the press that she was 'weary of modern social life' and was 'leaving England in March to live on Tahiti' (*Daily Express*, 17 Jan 1931). A month later, on 13 February, she appeared in court, accused of bouncing a cheque.

Meanwhile 'the romantic interest' had abandoned her, pregnant. Paul escaped to Paris with Anthea Carew, 'one of the staunchest friends I've ever had' (Paul, 166), and there fell ill with a suspected haemorrhage, possibly the after-effects of a miscarriage or an abortion. She was treated with morphine, and quickly became addicted to the drug. Paul underwent successive but unsuccessful cures, during the second of which she attempted suicide, cutting at her wrists with a broken glass. When she applied to her then seriously ill mother's doctor for a second prescription, Paul was arrested for seven offences against the Dangerous Drugs Act; it is evident that she was already under surveillance by the police. Tried at Marlborough Street on 5 December 1931 (Clive Bell stood bail for her), she was bound over in the sum of £50 and sent for another cure: punitive hyoscine 'knock-out' treatment.

In her memoirs Paul portrayed herself as a prisoner both of an unfair judicial system and of the drugs to which she was addicted. On 15 August 1932 she made a dash for Paris, with little money and no passport, and had to be rescued by a new fiancé. Her plight was followed all the while by the press, whose attentions she appeared to relish, casting herself as the actress she had not become: 'The scene resembled more the arrival and excitement of Greta Garbo, or Marlene Dietrich, instead of my humble self' (Paul, 218). She had become Britain's first (surviving) drug celebrity. Arrested again in January 1933 for illegally obtaining morphine, she was remanded for a week in Holloway before being freed under the care of Frederick Stuart (the Knightsbridge physician who had treated Billie Carleton). But her insistence on another hyoscine cure left her incapable of attending court as required, with the result that she was gaoled for six months.

As Prisoner 54086, Paul was subject to the pain of 'forced awareness' in the prison ward while she longed to 'lie in a trance, just living in one's own world of memories' (Paul, 244). Continually vomiting her food, she appears to have suffered from an eating disorder; freed on appeal and sent to a nursing home in Chobham, near Woking, her weight had dropped from 7 to 5 stone. Press reports declared her to be 'an absolutely incurable case', needing increasing doses of morphine merely to stay alive (Barrow, 65). Her response was to put herself through 'cold turkey'. When she was finally allowed to leave the home, a Sunday newspaper financed her ghosted memoirs, published in 1935 as My First Life. Publicity photographs show a ravaged face, sunken eyes, and lined cheeks, her limbs skeletally thin. The book ends with the declaration 'now that I can never hope for the fulfilment I desired, I should strive to become an actress, perhaps a great actress' (Paul, 286).

At the end of January 1935 Paul left Britain for America, to lecture on the evils of drugs to young people, although she continued to take them herself. Later in the 1930s the artist Michael Wishart, then a young boy, watched Paul in the King's Road, 'with her silver mane and slacks, scarlet mouth and man's overcoat to match, tottering with her friend Miss Baird to refill her hypodermic syringe' (Wishart, 7). In 1950 Wishart invited Paul to his wedding party at Francis Bacon's studio in Kensington. Dancing in high silver heels, scarlet trouser suit, and dark glasses, Paul 'wilted habitually at the approach of midnight when she and her friend Jean would disappear … to return … with … a simple white powder, which they dispensed generously with a thimble to our wearier guests' (ibid., 68). Later

Wishart watched as Paul, seated in a restaurant, 'produced from her handbag a hypodermic syringe of heroin, which she filled from a vase of flowers on the table, so urgent was her desire' (ibid., 124).

In November 1951 Paul was back in court, charged with possession of 100 milligrams of pethidine, and remanded on £100 bail. She habitually carried a lapdog with painted nails, and her notoriety was such that when Isabelle Strachey boarded a London bus, the conductor pointed out a figure with platinum blonde hair and said, 'That's Brenda Dean Paul' (private information).

In the late 1950s Wishart visited Paul in the Cromwell Hotel, where she was living. 'Brenda's enduring beauty was a good advertisement for drug abuse', wrote Wishart. 'The habit had apparently mummified her in her prime' (Wishart, 165). Paul was then ('unusually for her') working, 'making a rather sensational come-back' as the lead in Firbank's The Princess Zoubaroff at the Irving Theatre Club. In exchange for hearing her lines, Wishart was given

> anchovy toast and dangerous drugs … Brenda never got her complicated lines right; nor, on stage, could she act, but this is seldom a drawback to stardom, and if, in her very special way, Brenda was a star, no role, least of all life, was made for her.   (ibid., 165)

On 26 July 1959 Paul was found dead in her flat at 151 Kensington High Street and was widely thought to have died from an overdose, although her death certificate cited 'coronary occlusion due to atheroma'. She was fifty-two. Jean Baird, loyal to the end, told the newspapers, 'She really was one of the sweetest people you could ever have known' (Barrow, 208).   PHILIP HOARE

Sources B. D. Paul, My first life (1935) • M. Wishart, High diver (1977) • A. Barrow, Gossip, 1920–1970 (1978) • Daily Express (17 Jan 1931) • H. Baddeley, The unsinkable Hermione Baddeley (1984) • The diaries of Evelyn Waugh, ed. M. Davie (1976) • C. Beaton, The wandering years (1961) • M. Luke, David Tennant and the Gargoyle years (1991) • M. Kohn, Dope girls: the birth of the British drug underground (1992) • N. Coward, Present indicative (1937) • CGPLA Eng. & Wales (1960) • b. cert. • d. cert. • d. cert. [Irene Regina Dean Paul] • London, Express Newspapers photographic files; Keystone Picture Agency caption, 22/11/1951 • private information (2004)
Likenesses C. Harris, photograph, 1931, Express Newspapers, London, archives, L363-31L/col.P.1 • Barratts, Photo Press, photograph, 1932, Express Newspapers, London, archives, 15 July 1932 • Pictorial Press, photograph, 1935, Express Newspapers, London, archives, 6 Feb 1935 • J. V. Brown, photograph, 1953, NPG • photograph, repro. in Barrow, Gossip, 209 • photographic plates, repro. in Paul, My first life
Wealth at death £1926 13s. 5d.: administration, 29 March 1960, CGPLA Eng. & Wales

Paul, Sir George Onesiphorus, second baronet (1746–1820), prison reformer and philanthropist, was born on 9 February 1746 at Woodchester, Gloucestershire, the son of Sir Onesiphorus *Paul, first baronet (bap. 1706, d. 1774), a successful woollen manufacturer, and his first wife, Jane (c.1707–1748), daughter of Francis Blackburn of Richmond, Yorkshire. Paul, who was baptized Onesiphorus but used the additional forename George from about

Sir George Onesiphorus Paul, second baronet (1746–1820), by Robert William Sievier, 1825

1780, went to St John's College, Oxford, in 1763, graduating in 1766. His father's wealth enabled him to spend two full years between 1767 and 1769 travelling in the German states, Austria, and Italy. On his return to Gloucestershire he adopted at first a leisured life, entering his horses at local race meetings, visiting London, Bath, and Weymouth, and frequenting gaming clubs. After his father's death in September 1774 he inherited the family business and property, including Hill House, at Rodborough, near Woodchester. The cloth mill was let, and Paul lived on the rent of a modest-sized estate, which included farms adjoining Hill House, and others in Somerset, Shropshire, and Durham; with mortgage interest and other investments, that gave him an income of around £1600 a year in the last twenty years of his life.

In 1780 Paul began his role in Gloucestershire's public affairs, which, though one of the county's lesser gentry by birth and property, he came to dominate through his administrative ability and tireless energy. He was high sheriff for the year beginning Michaelmas 1780, and earlier that year he was chairman of the Gloucestershire Association formed in support of Wyvill's programme of economical and parliamentary reform. Like many moderates, he later distanced himself from the cause of reform, refusing indignantly in 1809, when approached, to lend his name to the agitation at the time of the army commissions scandal. He recalled then how he had entered public

life as a reformer 'until reformation was urged in the language and stalked in the guise of revolution' and turned instead to 'the school of a political philanthropy which best accorded with my creed of civil government' (G. O. Paul to Sir B. W. Guise, 30 April 1809, Clark and Smith MSS D 589). On at least two occasions, however, he contemplated standing for election as an MP for the county.

Paul's adoption of the cause of prison reform was prompted specifically by the state of Gloucestershire's county gaol, then housed in the remains of the keep of Gloucester Castle, and generally by the writings of John Howard. Howard visited the gaol in 1777 and 1784 and found the inhuman and insanitary conditions typical of the period. Paul, who probably corresponded with Howard though may never have met him, had studied the subject in depth by 1783 when he opened his campaign among his fellow magistrates of the Gloucestershire bench. At the March assizes at Gloucester, evidently at his prompting, they passed a series of resolutions committing themselves to reform the county prisons, and at the following assizes in August and at a general meeting of the county a few months later, Paul presented his ideas in detail.

Paul's address to the county magistrates in August 1783 (which began with a warm tribute to Howard's work) encapsulates most cogently the principles of the system he was to introduce in Gloucestershire: separation of the different classes of prisoners, confinement in separate cells, hard labour for convicts, provision of medical care, facilities for exercise and religious instruction, and the strict regulation of gaolers' fees. In 1785 a committee under his direction secured an act of parliament for building a new gaol at Gloucester and four houses of correction in other parts of the county, the sites chosen being Littledean for the Forest of Dean; Northleach for the central Cotswolds; Horsley for the populous clothmaking valleys of the west Cotswolds; and Lawfords Gate, Bristol, for south Gloucestershire. Work began in 1788 and the five new buildings were completed in 1792 at a total cost of £46,438, raised mainly by loans on the credit of the county rate. They were designed by William Blackburn, the specialist prison architect favoured by Howard, but Paul himself undertook much of the detailed planning and supervision, his labour made more intense by Blackburn's illness and death in 1790. That very personal involvement continued after the opening of the prisons: until almost the end of his life he paid close attention to all aspects of their administration.

Paul's scheme, having been brought to a successful conclusion, provided a model for the magistrates of other counties, who were able to benefit from his printed addresses on the subject and from his detailed rules and regulations for the Gloucestershire prisons, published in the first of several editions in 1790. In 1810 Sir Samuel Romilly cited the new Gloucestershire prisons, with that at Southwell, as the most remarkable of recent improvements, and Paul was called to give evidence to the select committee of the Commons considering the matter in 1811. He had won a national reputation in his field. Sir Walter Scott, who met him on holiday in the Hebrides in 1810, epitomized him as 'Sir George Paul, for prison-house renowned' and recorded their light-hearted surmise as to the relative comforts of a primitive dwelling on Inchkenneth (where the local laird had entertained Samuel Johnson in 1773) and a cell in Gloucester gaol (Lockhart, 2.315–16, 319).

Having demonstrated a talent for analysing and planning complex matters, Paul found himself consulted by colleagues in various fields. For his fellow governors of the county infirmary at Gloucester he reported in 1794 in his customary exhaustive detail on the possibility of admitting lunatics; a letter on the treatment of criminal and pauper lunatics he wrote to the home secretary in 1806 influenced the drafting of an act on the subject in 1808. Another careful report for the county infirmary in 1796 analysed its finances and management, and for his fellow JPs in 1803 he drew up a scheme for building a new shire hall.

As the leading magistrate in his home area of the county, the Stroud valleys, Paul brought the same meticulous attention to petty sessional business, to very minor matters of the government of Rodborough parish, to local charity schools, where he set himself to improve the quality of masters and introduce Andrew Bell's monitorial system, and to Stroud's pauper dispensary. During a severe slump in the cloth industry in 1784 Paul headed efforts to combat distress among the weavers and was the leading subscriber to their relief. He was also, in 1783, a promoter of a new Gloucester to Bath turnpike road made along the Woodchester valley below his house, building for it at his own cost a substantial coaching inn. When George III (then staying at Cheltenham) visited the area in 1788 it was Paul who organized the visit, entertaining the royal party at Hill House, and took pains to ensure that people turned out in suitable numbers to line the route.

Paul's humanity is clear from his descriptions of the sufferings of the debtors and remand prisoners in the unreformed county gaol, but equally important motivations were an unusually developed sense of public duty and a near obsessional preoccupation with improving the efficiency of any institution he encountered; the pursuit of such tasks, he admitted, gave him 'a personal gratification ... perhaps as great as the fox-hunter ... enjoyed in pursuing his fox' (Moir, 'Sir G. O. Paul', 223). He was not, though, a priggish or unduly austere man: his horse-racing, card playing, and visits to London and Bath continued for some years alongside his more serious pursuits; he spent over £6000 in the late 1780s on enlarging Hill House, and at his death he left an extensive wine cellar and a library with an eclectic range of works. While he sometimes betrayed a harmless conceit in his unique position within the county and in his wider reputation, he was quite prepared to devote time and attention to tasks which brought him little prominence or credit. He can best be characterized as one who came close to the ideal for a county JP in Georgian England.

Paul died at Hill House on 16 December 1820 and was buried on 23 December at Woodchester church. He never married and left as his heir a nephew, Robert Snow, who took the name and arms of Paul. The baronetcy was extinguished at his death but a new one was created in 1821 for a cousin, John Dean Paul. A monument, a bust of Sir George in Roman dress atop a sarcophagus, was commissioned by the Gloucestershire gentry, sculpted by Robert Sievier, and placed in a prominent site in Gloucester Cathedral in 1825. The inscription records that he 'first reduced to practice the principles that have immortalized the memory of Howard' and made his county

the example and model of the best system of criminal discipline, in which provident regulation has banished the use of fetters and health has been substituted for contagion, thus happily reconciling humanity with punishment and the prevention of crime with individual reform.

NICHOLAS HERBERT

Sources E. A. L. Moir, 'Sir G. O. Paul', *Gloucestershire studies*, ed. H. P. R. Finberg (1957), 195–224 · Glos. RO, Clark and Smith papers, D589 · printed addresses and reports by Sir G. O. Paul, Gloucester Library, Gloucestershire Collection · F. Hyett, 'Sir G. O. Paul', *Transactions of the Bristol and Gloucestershire Archaeological Society*, 51 (1929), 143–68 · E. A. L. Moir, 'Gloucestershire association for parliamentary reform, 1780', *Transactions of the Bristol and Gloucestershire Archaeological Society*, 75 (1956), 171–92 · M. Ignatieff, *A just measure of pain: the penitentiary in the industrial revolution, 1750–1850* (1978), 98–109 · C. R. Hudleston, *Transactions of the Bristol and Gloucestershire Archaeological Society*, 55 (1933), 384–6 · N. Herbert, '"The only resource for honest poverty": charity schoolmasters of the Stroud region', *Transactions of the Bristol and Gloucestershire Archaeological Society*, 111 (1993), 183–4 · *VCH Gloucestershire*, 11.221, 223, 300 · *Gloucester Journal* (26 Jan 1784) · *Gloucester Journal* (2 Feb 1784) · *Gloucester Journal* (1 March 1784) · *Gloucester Journal* (8 March 1784) · *Gloucester Journal* (16 June 1794) · *Gloucester Journal* (20 Sept 1819) · *Gloucester Journal* (25 Dec 1820) · J. G. Lockhart, *Memoirs of the life of Sir Walter Scott*, 2 (1837), 312, 315–16, 319–20 · J. Burke and J. B. Burke, *A genealogical and heraldic history of the extinct and dormant baronetcies of England, Ireland, and Scotland* (1838), 403 · parish register, Woodchester, 20 Feb 1746, Glos. RO, P375/IN1/1 [baptism] · parish register, Woodchester, 23 Dec 1820, Glos. RO, P375/IN1/2 [burial] · Foster, *Alum. Oxon.*

Archives Glos. RO, letters, accounts, executorship papers, etc.; family and estate papers | N. Yorks. CRO, corresp. with Christopher Wyvill

Likenesses R. W. Sievier, bust on monument, 1825, Gloucester Cathedral [*see illus.*]

Wealth at death £3770 estate in 1821; lands of annual value £1220; plus house: Glos. RO, D589, executors' calculation of estate, 22 Jan 1821

Paul, Hamilton (1773–1854), poet and writer, was born on 10 April 1773 in the parish of Dailly, Ayrshire, the son of John Paul. He attended the parish school, and went on to Glasgow University, where he took classes with the poet Thomas Campbell; the two men were to remain in correspondence for many years. At Glasgow, Paul acquired a reputation for improvising light verse.

On leaving university Paul became tutor in an Argyll family, but his literary inclinations led him to become a partner in a printing firm in Ayr, and for three years he edited the *Ayr Advertiser*. On being licensed to preach by the presbytery of Ayr on 16 July 1800, he became assistant at Coylton in that year, and held several similar positions until 1813, when he was appointed minister to Broughton, Kilbucho, and Glenholm, in Peeblesshire.

In 1800 a volume of verse entitled *Paul's first and second epistles to the dearly beloved the female disciples or female students of natural philosophy in Anderson's Institution, Glasgow* appeared, and in 1805 Paul published a rhymed pamphlet in support of vaccination (*Vaccination, or, Beauty Preserved*). In 1819 he edited the works of Robert Burns, with a memoir and ode in memory of the poet. 'As a broadminded member of the "New Licht" clergy, he defended Burns's attitude to religion, and his religious satire' (Lindsay, 281). He was also an enthusiastic supporter of the early Burns clubs, and wrote a poetic appeal for the preservation of the Auld Brig o' Doon, made famous by 'Tam o' Shanter'. Much of his work was published in newspapers and magazines, and went uncollected; among his circle he was valued less as a poet than as a humorist and raconteur, and even his sermons tended towards jocularity. He died, unmarried, at Broughton, Peeblesshire, on 28 February 1854.   J. R. MacDonald, *rev.* Douglas Brown

Sources Irving, *Scots.* · Boase, *Mod. Eng. biog.* · *Fasti Scot.* · J. G. Wilson, ed., *The poets and poetry of Scotland*, 1 (1876), 1.498 · M. Lindsay, *The Burns encyclopedia*, 2nd edn (1970) · bap. reg. Scot.
Archives NL Scot., corresp., literary MSS | Mitchell L., Glas., reminiscences and letters to William Beattie
Likenesses ink silhouette, Scot. NPG

Paul, Herbert Woodfield (1853–1935), author and politician, was born at Finedon, Northamptonshire, on 16 January 1853, the eldest son of George Woodfield Paul, vicar of Finedon and honorary canon of Peterborough Cathedral, and his wife, Jessie Philippa, daughter of Lieutenant Herbert Mackworth RN. From Eton College he won a scholarship at Corpus Christi College, Oxford, where he was president of the Union (1875), and obtained a first class in *literae humaniores* (1875). Called to the bar by Lincoln's Inn in 1878, he never practised, though he could be imagined as a formidable cross-examiner; but he devoted himself to literary work, largely in the political field, soon becoming a skilled leader writer for the *Daily News*.

In 1883 Paul married Elinor Budworth, daughter of William Ritchie, legal member of the viceroy's council in India, and sister of Sir Richmond T. W. *Ritchie. She was a lady of great charm. They had a son and a daughter.

From 1892 until 1895 Paul sat as member for South Edinburgh. A devoted follower of Gladstone, he was a strong party man and in particular a convinced free-trader, but although a capable debater, did not win in parliament the reputation merited by his exceptional talents.

Besides *Men and Letters* (1901) and a competent appreciation of Gladstone's career (*Life of W. E. Gladstone*, 1901)—an expansion of his memoir in the *Dictionary of National Biography*—Paul published in 1902 *Matthew Arnold*, with whom he had many literary sympathies, as he had with a very different figure, Lord Acton, whose letters to Mary Gladstone he edited in 1904. In 1905 came a defence of Froude as a historian (*Life of Froude*). His most solid and important work was the *History of Modern England* (5 vols., 1904–6), which was justly described as the *Annual Register*

Herbert Woodfield Paul (1853–1935), by unknown photographer, pubd 1907–9

tempered by epigrams. *Stray Leaves*, a collection of essays, was published in 1906. This book was followed by a study of the age of *Queen Anne* (a period in which he felt completely at home) for Goupil's illustrated monographs (1906; revised without illustrations, 1912), and by *Famous Speeches* (1910).

Meanwhile the Liberal triumph of 1906 had returned Paul for Northampton; but in 1907 a nervous collapse foreshadowed his retirement in 1909. By 1910 he had sufficiently recovered to undertake the office of second civil service commissioner (to which he had been appointed the previous year), and for which he was perfectly suited by his gifts and attainments, and which he held until 1918. The rest of his life was spent in retirement at Cherry Orchard, Forest Row, Sussex, where he died on 4 August 1935; he was survived by his wife.

Paul never sought or obtained popularity in the conventional sense; his comments, often sharp, but never captious or unfair, aroused the animosity of one or two fellow writers; but he was less contemptuous than he appeared to be, and recognized all work which was not slipshod or marred by prejudice. He ignored gossip and scandal, and despised those who found pleasure in discussing the weaknesses of men whom he deemed to be essentially great. He was no lettered recluse, but a pleasant companion in leisure hours. Nurtured in a county for which fox-hunting was a religious exercise, he could appreciate the points of a well-bred horse; and he thoroughly enjoyed good cheer and a glass of choice wine. He had some enemies, but was the most loyal of friends, and it is sad that he left a slighter mark on his age than some who could not claim a tithe of his ability or his acquirements.

CREWE, *rev.* H. C. G. MATTHEW

Sources *The Times* (7 Aug 1935) · personal knowledge (1949) · *CGPLA Eng. & Wales* (1935)
Archives BL, letters to Mary Gladstone, Add. MS 46252 · NL Scot., corresp. with Lord Rosebery
Likenesses B. Stone, photographs, 1906, NPG · photograph, pubd 1907–9, NPG [*see illus.*]
Wealth at death £7334 17s. 5d.: administration with will, 28 Oct 1935, *CGPLA Eng. & Wales*

Paul [*formerly* Featherstone], **Isabella** [*known as* Mrs Howard Paul] (1833?–1879), actress and singer, was born at Dartford, Kent; nothing is known of her early life. She made her first appearance on the London stage at the Strand in March 1853, under the name Isabella Featherstone, as Captain Macheath in *The Beggar's Opera*. With her great vivacity and spirit, distinct vocal gifts, and considerable stage talent, she made an immediate mark, and was engaged at Drury Lane and subsequently at the Haymarket, where she played Macheath on 24 April 1854. In that year she also acted in Howard Paul's *Locked out*. She married Paul (1830–1905) in 1857, and the following year she took part with him in *Patchwork*, described as 'a clatter of fun, frolic, song, and impersonation'. On 3 July 1858 she was Sir Launcelot de Lake in *The Lancashire Witches, or, The Knight and the Giants*, a burlesque included in an entertainment with which George Webster opened the Lyceum. In entertainments given by herself and her husband in London and the provinces in 1860 and successive years, Mrs Paul's share consisted largely of imitations of Henry Russell, Sims Reeves, and other well-known singers, in which she was very successful. On 2 September 1867 she was at the Strand playing Mrs Dove in her husband's *Ripples on the Lake*.

Mrs Paul's most ambitious appearance was at Drury Lane in February 1869, as Lady Macbeth to the Macbeth of Samuel Phelps and Charles Dillon on alternate nights. Foreshadowing later actresses, she softened the character of Lady Macbeth, making conjugal love her dominant trait. With this performance, which was not lacking in intensity, she doubled that of Hecate. She was also seen in Paris in comic opera. On 29 August 1872 she played Mistigris in Boucicault's *Babil and Bijou*, with music by Hervé and Frederick Clay, at Covent Garden. At the Olympic she appeared in *The Grand Duchess*, and she took a company of her own round the provinces, playing a species of drawing-room entertainment. In November 1877 she appeared at the Opera Comique as Lady Sangazure in Gilbert and Sullivan's *The Sorcerer*. This proved to be her last London engagement. While performing at Sheffield in *The Crisis* in 1879 she was taken ill suddenly; she was taken home to London, and on 6 June 1879 died at her residence, 17 The Avenue, Bedford Park, Turnham Green. She was buried at Brompton cemetery. Isabella Paul was a woman of ability whose talents were often frittered away in parts and occupations unworthy of them.

JOSEPH KNIGHT, *rev.* J. GILLILAND

Sources Ward, *Men of the reign* · D. Baptie, *A handbook of musical biography*, 2nd edn (1887) · *The Athenaeum* (24 April 1868) · *The life and reminiscences of E. L. Blanchard, with notes from the diary of Wm. Blanchard*, ed. C. W. Scott and C. Howard, 2 vols. (1891) · Brown & Stratton, *Brit. mus.* · *The Era* (15 May 1879) · Hall, *Dramatic ports.* · personal knowledge (1895) · d. cert.
Archives Theatre Museum, London, letters
Likenesses Southwell Bros., two cartes-de-visite, NPG · prints, BM, Harvard TC, NPG · woodburytype photograph, NPG
Wealth at death under £300: administration, 21 June 1879, *CGPLA Eng. & Wales*

Paul, Sir James Balfour (1846–1931), herald and genealogist, was born in Edinburgh on 16 November 1846, the younger of two sons of the Revd John Paul (1796–1873), minister of St Cuthbert's, Edinburgh, and moderator of the general assembly of the Church of Scotland in 1847–8, and Margaret (*d.* 1860), daughter of James Balfour of Pilrig, writer to the signet. He was educated at Edinburgh high school and at the University of Edinburgh, and was called to the Scottish bar in 1870. He was editor of the *Journal of Jurisprudence* and later served as treasurer of the Faculty of Advocates (1883–1902). Married on 18 June 1872, he and his wife, Helen Margaret (*d.* 20 Dec 1929), daughter of John Wairne Forman of Staffa, had three sons and a daughter.

Paul was appointed lord Lyon king of arms in March 1890 and held that office until 1926; he was also secretary of the Order of the Thistle in a period which saw the erection of the order's chapel at St Giles, Edinburgh. He was knighted in 1900 and appointed KCVO in the year of his retirement. He had the advantage of serving as Lyon at a time of renewed and well-informed enthusiasm for heraldry in Scotland. For many years the Lyon office had slumbered, and the court of the lord Lyon had exercised little more than a nominal jurisdiction. The little work that was expected of Lyon was performed, with greater or lesser skill, by an official called the Lyon-depute, who received a fraction of Lyon's sinecure. Reforms came, and Paul's immediate predecessor was George Burnett, a scholar and a gentleman, who had compiled the first good book on Scottish heraldry to be written for many years. Paul was determined to follow in this tradition.

Paul's chief and most lasting contribution to Scottish heraldry is his masterly edition of *The Scots Peerage* (1909–14) in nine finely printed and beautifully illustrated volumes. It was fortunate that a work of this magnitude was completed on the eve of the First World War. It effectively replaced all former Scottish peerage reference works and, on the whole, was comprehensive and accurate in the information it contained. Unlike *The Complete Peerage* it was not limited to successors to titles of honour and their immediate heirs. Amateurs of quaint and curious footnotes are likely to be disappointed. *The Scots Peerage*, as Paul acknowledged, was not his work alone—he received much assistance from a well-chosen body of able and learned persons—but there can be no doubt that he inspired the work and deserves most of the credit for it.

In the Lyon office Paul was best-remembered for his first two editions of a useful and almost essential guide to the contents of the Lyon register, valuable at a time when the number of grants and matriculations was rapidly increasing. His other important contribution to Scottish heraldic literature was his *Heraldry in Relation to Scottish History and Art* (1900), the publication of his Rhind lectures on archaeology delivered to the Society of Antiquaries of Scotland. To some extent this work represented a new and possibly enlightened view of heraldry. It was certainly a departure from the days of crudely painted armorials and dubious family histories, and it helped to introduce heraldry to the reader as an art form in itself. Additionally, Paul often contributed to journals on history and antiquities, and he was responsible for much of the work involved in preparing the Record series volumes of *Registrum magni sigilli* and *Accounts of the Lord Treasurer of Scotland.*

Paul was an enthusiastic and greatly appreciated member of the Royal Company of Archers (HM bodyguard for Scotland), which he joined in 1871; he published the history of the company in 1875. He took an active interest in the work of the Scottish History Society, the Scottish Record Society, and the Scottish Ecclesiological Society. In 1908 he was awarded an honorary LLD degree by his old university, in view of his public and scholarly achievements. He died on 15 September 1931.   DAVID BOGIE

Sources Burke, *Gen. GB* (1965) · J. B. Paul, 'A Lyon's tale', *Blackwood*, 316–17 (1974), 430–39, 502–10; 317 (1974), 27–35, 228–34 · *The Times* (16 Sept 1931)
Archives NRA, priv. coll., 'A Lyon's tale' MS autobiography | Lyon Office Library, notes for title claim of Sir N. W. Elphinstone
Likenesses P. Sturdee, oils, 1901, Scot. NPG

Paul, John (1707–1787), legal writer, was born at Highgrove, Tetbury, Gloucestershire, son of Josiah Paul of Tetbury and his wife, Hester, daughter of Giles Pike. He married Sarah Wight of Wotton under Edge, and succeeded to the estate of Highgrove when his father died on 2 October 1744.

Paul wrote popular legal manuals including *Every landlord or tenant his own lawyer, or, The whole law respecting landlords, tenants, and lodgers* (1775), which went to nine editions by 1806, *The parish officer's complete guide: containing the duty of the churchwarden, overseer, constable, and surveyor of the highways* (3rd edn, 1776), *A System of the Laws Relative to Bankruptcy* (1776), *The Law of Tythes* (1781), and *The Compleat Constable* (1785). Paul died childless on 2 September 1787.

J. M. RIGG, *rev.* ANNE PIMLOTT BAKER

Sources *European Magazine and London Review*, 12 (1787), 247 · J. G. Marvin, *Legal bibliography, or, A thesaurus of American, English, Irish and Scotch law books* (1847) · A. T. Lee, *The history of the town and parish of Tetbury, in the county of Gloucester* (1857) · W. Musgrave, *Obituary prior to 1800*, ed. G. J. Armytage, 1, Harleian Society, 44 (1899)

Paul, John (1777–1848), Reformed Presbyterian church minister and religious controversialist, was born in January 1777 at Tobernaveen, near Antrim, where his father, John Paul, was a farmer. Having determined to become a minister of the Reformed Presbyterian body, to which his parents belonged, he entered the University of Glasgow in 1796, and was licensed to preach at Garvagh on 16 November 1803. He became minister at Loughmourne, near Carrickfergus, co. Antrim, on 11 September 1805, and held the office until his death, residing mainly in Carrickfergus,

where he conducted a classical school. Paul married, in 1807, Rachel Smith (*d.* 6 Oct 1861) of Ballyearl, co. Antrim. They had several children and one of their daughters married the Revd Dr Stewart Bates, who produced an edition of some of Paul's works in 1855.

Paul played a prominent part in the Arian controversy which raged in the north of Ireland during the earlier part of the nineteenth century. In 1819 he published *Creeds and confessions defended in a series of letters addressed to the anonymous author of 'The battle of the two dialogues'.* The motto on the title page runs: 'Paul, thou art permitted to speak for thyself.' In 1826 he struck another strong blow in the controversy with *A Refutation of Arianism and Defence of Calvinism.* This work has been regarded as one of the masterpieces of Ulster Presbyterian literature produced by the debate. It was a reply to the *Sermons on the Study of the Bible and on the Doctrines of Christianity* (1824) of the Revd Dr William Bruce (1757–1841). A speech delivered by Henry Montgomery in 1827, at the annual meeting of the synod of Ulster in Strabane, produced a third work from Paul in 1828, *A review of a speech by the Rev. Dr. Montgomery of Belfast, and the doctrines of Unitarians proved to be unfavourable to the right of private judgment, to liberality, and charity, to the investigation of truth and the practise of virtue.* These three publications gained a very large circulation. Their incisive logic and vigorous style gave them a powerful role in the debate about orthodoxy and Arianism within the Presbyterian church.

Paul became involved in another controversy with a brother minister of the Reformed Presbyterian body, the Revd Dr Thomas Houston of Knockbracken, near Belfast, the point in dispute being the province of 'the civil magistrate'. He published several pamphlets on the question, the chief being *A review of the Rev. Thomas Houston's 'Christian magistrate', and a defence of the principles of civil and religious liberty* (1833). Eventually the controversy reached the synod of the Reformed Presbyterian church, and divided it into two bodies: one, the Reformed Presbyterian Synod of Ireland, adhering to the views of Houston; and the other, the Eastern Reformed Presbyterian Synod of Ireland, holding by those of Paul. But, though a keen polemicist, he was respected by those holding different opinions for his constant principles and his gift of expressing them so clearly and powerfully. He died at Carrickfergus on 16 March 1848.

THOMAS HAMILTON, *rev.* DAVID HUDDLESTON

Sources S. Bates, 'Memoir', in *Works of the Rev. John Paul* (1855) · W. T. Latimer, *A history of the Irish Presbyterians*, 2nd edn (1902) · Loughmorne Presbyterian church, *Graveyard and surrounding district, 1804–1994* (1994) · private information (1895) · J. S. Reid and W. D. Killen, *History of the Presbyterian church in Ireland*, new edn, 3 (1867) · P. Brooke, *Ulster Presbyterianism* (1987) · *A history of congregations in the Presbyterian Church in Ireland, 1610–1982*, Presbyterian Church in Ireland (1982)
Archives U. Edin., New Coll. L., letters to Thomas Chalmers
Likenesses woodcut, repro. in Loughmorne Presbyterian church, *Graveyard and surrounding district*

Paul, Sir John Dean, second baronet (1802–1868), banker and fraudster, was born on 27 October 1802, at 218 Strand, Westminster (adjacent to his father's bank), the eldest of three sons (there were four daughters) of Sir John Dean

Paul, first baronet (1775–1852), and his wife, Frances Eleanor Simpson (d. 1833). He was educated at Westminster School from 1811 and Eton College from 1817. John Dean Paul senior was a partner in the firm of Snow, Paul, and Paul which, originating as a firm of pawnbrokers in the second half of the seventeenth century, had been turned to banking by his maternal grandfather, Robert Snow; a baronetcy was revived in his father's favour in 1821 shortly after the extinction of an earlier creation held by his cousin Sir George Onesiphorus Paul.

In 1823 Paul junior became a partner in the bank, but took no share in its profits until he succeeded to his father's baronetcy in January 1852. The firm became known as Strahan, Paul, and Bates after Paul's kinsman and partner William Snow changed his surname to Strahan on inheriting £180,000 in 1831 and their managing clerk Robert Makin Bates joined the partnership in 1841. They traded as bankers at 217 Strand and conducted a profitable navy agency under the name of Halford & Co. in Norfolk Street. As early as 1816 the bank's partners had tampered with customers' money, and by 1849 it was insolvent. This decline was aggravated by their loans from 1848 to the first Baron Mostyn to develop his Flintshire coalmines. In 1850 Mostyn leased his colliery to the bank to secure debts then standing at £67,541. The bank then spent over £45,000 attempting to bring the colliery to productive order and this outlay, coupled with arrears of interest, brought the bank's involvement to £139,940 by June 1855. Already, in December 1851, a month before Paul inherited the chief partnership from his father, the bank was trading at a loss with its accounts showing a deficiency of £71,990. In a desperate gamble to retrieve the position, its partners in 1852 embarked upon a risky association with J. H. and E. F. Gandrell, who had contracted to build a railway from Lucca to Pistoia in Tuscany and to drain Lake Capestang in southern France. Although the bank held no tangible security, it continued advances to the Gandrells to over £300,000 in a vain attempt to avoid impending ruin. Financiers suspected that the bank had been imprudent, though not fraudulent (the sums involved in the Mostyn and Gandrell transactions totalled £483,000). A run on the bank, starting on 8 June 1855, resulted in the gazetting of its bankruptcy on 12 June (with debts of £750,000).

On the advice of Paul's solicitor James Graham Lewis the partners during bankruptcy proceedings provided a list of securities worth £113,625 belonging to their customers, which they had fraudulently sold or used to improve the bank's liquidity. Paul's paternal estate at Rodborough, near Stroud, having been sold to Lord John Russell, he was then living at Nutfield, where he was apprehended by police officers on 19 June 1855. He escaped from custody on the railway journey from Reigate to London, probably intending to bolt, but afterwards surrendered at Bow Street police station. Paul sat in despondent apathy during the trial of the partners at the central criminal court on a specimen charge of converting to their own use Danish bonds worth £5000 belonging to John Griffith, canon of Rochester (26–7 October 1855). He, Strahan, and Bates

were each sentenced to transportation for fourteen years, but Paul apparently never reached the Western Australian penal settlement, and was released with Strahan from Woking prison on 23 October 1859. His nephew, Augustus Hare, thought Paul 'rather mad. After he had done his best to ruin all his family, and had totally ruined hundreds of other people, he said very complacently, "This is the Lord's doing, and it is marvellous in our eyes"' (Hare, 1.494).

Paul professed high religious principles, and published *Harmonies of Scripture, and Short Lessons for Young Christians* (1846). He was treasurer, trustee, or committee member of numerous societies allied to the evangelical section of the Church of England and supported incumbents in poor parishes. At the time of his trial he was widely and heavily censured for 'his vile cant' (*ILN*, 3 Nov 1855, 515). Hare gives as an example of Paul's righteousness how in 1852 he wrote 'in the cruellest and harshest terms' to his sister (a Roman Catholic convert) in Rome, saying, 'Your eldest son is dying. It is quite impossible that you can arrive in time to see him alive. Your second son is also in a rapid decline, though if you set off at once and travel to England without stopping, you may still be in time to receive his last words' (Hare, 1.373).

Paul married first, in 1826, Georgina (d. 1847), daughter of Charles George Beauclerk, with whom he had one son. He accused Georgina of adultery in 1831 and obtained a deed of separation in 1832. He married second, in 1849, Susan (d. 1854), daughter of John Ewens; and third, in 1861, Jane Constance (d. 1877), daughter of Thomas Bridgen. The two later marriages were childless. After 1859 Sir John lived in a retired manner at Lower Lancing, Shoreham, on the Sussex coast. He became a wine merchant at Wheathampstead in Hertfordshire after the railway reached nearby Harpenden in 1867. Possibly this occupation contributed to his death from heart disease, liver complaint, and dropsy on 7 September 1868 at London Road, St Albans, Hertfordshire.   RICHARD DAVENPORT-HINES

Sources D. M. Evans, *Facts, failures, and frauds: revelations financial, mercantile, criminal* (1859), 106–53 • A. J. C. Hare, *The story of my life*, 1 (1896) • *The Times* (11 June–29 Oct 1855) • *ILN* (3 Nov 1855) • Boase, *Mod. Eng. biog.* • d. cert. • P. Feldman and D. Scott Kilvert, eds., *The journals of Mary Shelley*, 2 vols. (1987)

Likenesses L. Haghe, lithograph, BM • portraits, Mary Evans Picture Library, London?

Paul, (Charles) Kegan (1828–1902), publisher and author, was born on 8 March 1828 at White Lackington, near Ilminster, Somerset, the eldest of the ten children of the Revd Charles Paul (1802–1861) and his wife, Frances Kegan Horne (1802–1848) of Bath. His father's family was Scottish and his mother's of Dutch and Irish descent; both had West Indies connections. Paul was educated first at Ilminster grammar school (1836–9), and later at Eton College, where he entered Dr Hawtrey's house in 1841. He matriculated at Exeter College, Oxford, in January 1846. At this stage he regarded himself as 'a very broad High Churchman, broad that is in doctrine, but with a strong feeling for pomp of ritual, for music in church, paintings

(Charles) Kegan Paul (1828–1902), by unknown photographer

and symbolism of all kinds' (Paul, *Memories*, 166). He hoped to model his own life's work on that of Charles Kingsley, whom he met in 1849, by combining the Anglican priesthood with social reform and literature. He graduated BA in October 1849, was ordained deacon in the Lent of 1851, and spent a year as curate of Tew, in the diocese of Oxford, and a further six months—having been ordained priest in 1852—as curate of Bloxham, near Banbury, Oxfordshire. A sermon on the communion of saints was his first published work, in 1853. He developed a reputation for holding radical political opinions, and was associated with Frederick Dennison Maurice, J. M. Ludlow, and other co-operative and Christian socialist leaders.

After a stint as tutor to pupils travelling in Germany, Paul was appointed, in November 1853, to a chaplain's post at Eton, where he remained until 1862, having discovered a vocation for teaching. On 11 December 1856 he married Margaret Agnes Colvile (1829–1905), daughter of Andrew Colvile and his wife, the Hon. Louisa Mary Eden; Margaret had just published her first two novels, *Dorothy: a Tale* and *DeCressy*. The first three of their five children were born at Eton. Paul contributed to *Tracts for Priests and People*, brought out by Maurice and Hughes, a piece called 'The boundaries of the church' (1861), in which he stated that the very minimum of dogma was required from lay members of the Church of England. Partly because of a controversy over this view, he left Eton in 1862 to become vicar of an Eton living at Sturminster Marshall, Dorset. As the endowment was small, he took pupils. During these years he embraced a policy of total abstinence from alcohol and also experimented with vegetarianism. He contributed twenty-three articles to the *Theological Review*

between 1865 and 1876. In 1870 he joined a unitarian society called the Free Christian Union, and in 1872 he associated himself with Joseph Arch's movement on behalf of the agricultural labourers in Dorset. He gradually found himself out of sympathy with the teaching of the Church of England, and in 1874 abandoned his living and moved to London.

For some years Paul had been reading manuscripts for Henry Samuel King, the publisher in Cornhill who had brought out several of his books, as well as those of his wife; he now became King's manager and editor, and in 1877 he purchased the publishing business at 1 Paternoster Square, which became C. Kegan Paul & Co. and continued King's general publishing programme of theological, literary, and scientific works. Ideologically he now associated himself with Comtist positivism, and he took great pleasure in friendships with George Eliot and Thomas Hardy. He judged Hardy, Walter Pater, Cardinal Newman, and Hesba Stretton to be those living stylists who showed 'the perfection to which, in this age, our language can be wrought' (Paul, *Faith and Unfaith*, 225). He edited and published the *New Quarterly Magazine* from January 1879 to April 1880. Alfred Chenevix Trench (1849–1938) joined the firm about 1878, and from 1881 it was styled Kegan Paul, Trench & Co. Among the publications it inherited from King were Tennyson's works (until 1883) and the International Scientific series. Other important series were the Parchment Library of English Classics and the Pulpit Commentary, both dating from 1880, as well as works by Hardy, George Meredith, and Robert Louis Stevenson. After various vicissitudes, including a fire in 1883, the firm was amalgamated as a limited company in 1889 with two others, George Redway and the heirs of Nicholas Trübner. It moved into large new premises, Paternoster House in Charing Cross Road, in 1891. Kegan Paul, Trench, Trübner & Co. Ltd, as the firm was now styled, flourished until 1895, when the profits fell with alarming abruptness, the directors resigned, and the capital was reduced. Paul at the same time lost money as director of the Hansard Printing and Publishing Company, and other enterprises. The traffic accident that occasioned his disability and retirement also occurred in that year. The business survived until 1911 when it was incorporated into George Routledge & Sons Ltd, who operated it as a separate enterprise until 1946, after which date the old name survived in the Routledge and Kegan Paul imprint until 1985.

Paul's own literary work included translations of Goethe's *Faust* in 1873, Blaise Pascal's *Pensées* (as *Thoughts*, 1885), and Joris-Karl Huysmans's *En Route* in 1896; he edited William Godwin's essays in 1873 and Mary Wollstonecraft's letters in 1879. *William Godwin: his Friends and Contemporaries* appeared in 1876, *Biographical Sketches* in 1883, *Faith and Unfaith, and other Essays* in 1891, and in 1899 his collection of verse, *On the Way Side*.

From 1888 Paul began to attend mass, and in 1890, during a visit to France, he decided to enter the Roman Catholic church, and he made his submission at the church of the Servites at Fulham, London, on 12 August 1890. A volume, *Memories* (1899), which is largely made up of stories of his early life at school and Eton, ends with his conversion. His new views were displayed in tracts issued by the Catholic Truth Society and in *Confessio viatoris* (1891). Paul's friend Wilfrid Meynell recorded in an obituary that he:

always remained in general society a great favourite: a grave man, with serenity of discretion; a general lover of his race, but with a shrewdly sharp tongue for individual weaknesses; a man indeed of prejudices as well as of more agreeable prepossessions; seemingly aloof and independent, yet possessed ... by the overmastering personalities of two men [Kingsley and Newman] whose 'acolyte' he was. (*The Academy*, 115)

Kegan Paul died at his home, 9 Avonmore Road, West Kensington, London, on 19 July 1902 and was buried at Kensal Green in London. LESLIE HOWSAM

Sources L. Howsam, *Kegan Paul, a Victorian imprint: publishers, books and cultural history* (1998) · C. K. Paul, *Memories* (1899) · [W. Meynell], 'Charles Kegan Paul: by one who knew him', *The Academy* (26 July 1902), 113–16 · L. Howsam, 'Sustained literary ventures: the series in Victorian book publishing', *Publishing History*, 31 (1992), 5–26 · L. Howsam, 'Forgotten Victorians: contracts with authors in the publication books of Henry S. King and Kegan Paul, Trench, 1871–1889', *Publishing History*, 34 (1993), 51–70 · 'Publishers of today: Messrs Kegan Paul, Trench, Trübner & Co., Limited', *Publisher's Circular* (10 Oct 1891), 424–6 · F. A. Mumby, *The house of Routledge, 1834–1934, with a history of Kegan Paul, Trench, Trübner and other associated firms* (1934) · C. K. Paul, *Faith and unfaith, and other essays* (1891) · *CGPLA Eng. & Wales* (1902) · m. cert.

Archives King's AC Cam., letters to Oscar Browning · Trinity Cam., letters to Henry Sidgwick

Likenesses photograph, repro. in Mumby, *The house of Routledge* · photograph, repro. in *Publishers' Circular* (26 July 1902) · photograph, UCL, Routledge & Kegan Paul Archives [*see illus.*]

Wealth at death £2897 9s. 10d.: probate, 15 Oct 1902, *CGPLA Eng. & Wales*

Paul, Leslie Allen (1905–1985), author and college teacher, was born on 30 April 1905 in Dublin, the second son and second child in the family of three sons and two daughters of Frederick Paul, an advertising manager for a chain of provincial newspapers, who lived for most of his working life at Honor Oak in south-east London, and his wife, Lottie Burton, a state qualified nurse. He was educated at a London central school during and immediately after the First World War. Following his father's footsteps in the world of journalism he entered Fleet Street, and, after editing a newspaper which failed, earned his livelihood as a freelance journalist.

As a boy Paul had been a keen boy scout, and this enthusiasm led him to an interest in youth movements. In 1925, after some time with the Kibbo Kift (a pacifist movement with an emphasis on family and tribal ritual, begun by John Hargrave) he founded his own movement, the Woodcraft Folk. This included among its aims 'the communal ownership of the means of production'. Six years later he led a delegation to the USSR and published his findings in a book, *Co-Operation in the U.S.S.R.* (1934). This was not the first of his large and immensely varied list of publications, which poured from his pen almost to the end of his life. His first book was a volume of poems, *Pipes of Pan*, published in 1927.

During the 1930s Paul was occupied in educational and social work, mainly in London, but for a time on the continent with refugees; he was a tutor for the London county council and the Workers' Educational Association. In 1936 he published a novel, *Men in May*, about the general strike. The rise of fascism was abhorrent to him, and he outgrew his earlier pacifism. When war broke out he was called up and served in the Army Educational Corps, mainly in the Middle East, and also as a staff tutor at Mount Carmel College. It was during his war service that Paul returned to his boyhood Christian faith, as recorded in his *Annihilation of Man* (1944), for which he received the Atlantic award in literature (1946).

The post-war period was filled with writing and teaching. Two books were autobiographical—*The Living Hedge* (1946) and *Angry Young Man* (1951), the latter being perhaps his best-known work. Two years later, *The English Philosophers* and a life of Sir Thomas More appeared. A short spell of teaching at the Ashridge College of Citizenship (1947–8) was followed by a longer, more fruitful period (1953–7) as director of studies at Brasted Place, near Sevenoaks, a college for pre-theological training of non-graduate Church of England ordinands. More public recognition was shown by his appointments as a member of the departmental committee on the youth service (1958–60) and as a research fellow of King George's Jubilee Trust (1960–61).

In July 1960 the church assembly resolved to appoint a commission to consider, in the light of changing circumstances, the system of the payment and deployment of the clergy, and to make recommendations. The purpose was to examine the interrelated problems of clergy stipends, pensions, and appointments, and the task was given to the central advisory council for the ministry, which decided that a single person should be appointed so that the totality of the problem could be grasped by one mind. The person chosen was Leslie Paul. He began work in February 1962 and submitted his massive report in November 1963; it was published in 1964 as *The Deployment and Payment of the Clergy*. It was a remarkable achievement: the 135,000-word report, with sixty-two recommendations, was written virtually single-handedly by Paul, aided by one omni-competent secretary, Jean Henderson. The report was considered at three successive sessions of the church assembly, which appointed a commission under W. Fenton Morley (then vicar of Leeds) to consider the implementation of its main recommendations about the parson's freehold, patronage, and a fairer system of remuneration. Radical changes were made. The Church of England as an institution is not easy to change, but the Paul report was a landmark in its rationalization.

This was the peak of Paul's achievement, and he received widespread recognition, including a fellowship of the Royal Society of Literature and an American degree of DLitt. From 1965 to 1970 he was lecturer in ethics and social studies at Queen's College, Birmingham, a post followed by five years (1970–75) as a member of the general synod. During that decade and the ensuing five years he continued to write extensively—poems, a novel, and works of theology and philosophy. His last teaching post was an *ad hoc* appointment as writer in residence at the teachers' training college of St Paul and St Mary, Cheltenham. During the closing years of his life he lived in the village of Madley, outside Hereford, where he could indulge his recreation of bird-watching. He died there on 8 July 1985, just two months after his eightieth birthday. He was unmarried. W. H. SAUMAREZ SMITH, *rev.*

Sources L. Paul, *Angry young man* (1951) • personal knowledge (1990) • *CGPLA Eng. & Wales* (1985) • *The Times* (12 July 1985) **Archives** BLPES, corresp. and papers relating to the Woodcraft Folk • IWM, journals recording his experiences during the blitz and time in the army training corps, corresp. • King's AC Cam., memoir of T. S. Eliot • LPL, papers relating to the Paul report • NRA, papers **Wealth at death** £64,987: probate, 20 Dec 1985, *CGPLA Eng. & Wales*

Paul, Lewis (*d.* 1759), textile innovator, was the son of a Dr Paul, reputedly a druggist in St Paul's Churchyard and of French Huguenot extraction. Little is known of his early life, except that he was left an orphan under the guardianship of Lord Shaftesbury as a young child. His first marriage, said to have taken place in February 1728, may not have been properly contracted, although when his wife, Sarah Meade, *née* Bull, the widow of a solicitor, died in September 1729, he inherited a valuable estate.

During the 1730s Paul made considerable profit by designing a machine for pinking crapes to make shrouds. As well as working the machine, he sold licences for its use and also took pupils to train. About 1732 Paul moved to Birmingham, where he met John Wyatt, a carpenter with mechanical talents. Together they developed a file-cutting machine. Wyatt had also been experimenting in cotton spinning 'without the intervention of the human fingers'. Credit for discovering the principle of roller spinning, upon which Arkwright's later system was founded, was claimed for Wyatt by his son many years later, but it was Paul, in whose name a patent 'for the spinning of wool and cotton in a manner entirely new' was taken out in 1738, who was responsible for the original concept. Wyatt's contribution was nevertheless important, for he built the machine and overcame many practical difficulties, as well as investing money to help Paul with expenses and the patent. At one time Paul owed Wyatt over £800 in loans and unpaid wages, and he borrowed extensively from others, including Edward Cave, editor of the *Gentleman's Magazine*, Thomas Warren, a Birmingham bookseller, and Dr Robert James of Lichfield. Like Paul and Wyatt, these men were from Dr Johnson's circle of acquaintance.

Financial problems continued to plague Paul. His and Wyatt's spinning factory at Upper Priory, Birmingham, was not a success and had closed by 1745. Paul settled some debts with licences to use the patent: Edward Cave accepted a licence to use 500 spindles for £300, and set up a factory in Northampton which ultimately failed. The first spinning machine proved far from satisfactory, and Paul and Wyatt sought further improvements. Believing that fibre preparation was the key to successful mechanized spinning, by 1740 they had turned their attention to carding. Their carding innovations, a flat table with strips of card, and a version which substituted a cylinder for the table, were not patented until 1748, perhaps because of Paul's lack of funds. However, the carding patent proved to be less significant than the spinning innovations. Paul's final patent was in 1758, for an improved spinning machine.

Paul claimed in 1757 to have made £20,000 from one of his patents, presumably referring to the first spinning patent, in which case the claim must have been exaggerated. He tried to have his spinning machine adopted by the Foundling Hospital, perhaps in an effort to gain a pension. Although he spent a great deal of the money he had made, he was evidently in comfortable circumstances when he made his will in 1758. He was then living at Kensington Gravel Pits and kept a number of servants. The main beneficiary was a solicitor, Thomas Yeo, who was required to take Paul's name in order to inherit. Paul died at Brook Green, Kensington, and was buried at Paddington on 30 April 1759. Yeo duly assumed the name of Paul, but soon fled England, deep in debt, and most of Paul's machinery was distrained and subsequently lost. Within ten years of his death, Paul's principle of spinning by rollers had been successfully introduced to industrial use by Richard Arkwright.

R. B. PROSSER, *rev.* GILLIAN COOKSON

Sources R. Cole, 'Account of Lewis Paul at the British Association for the Advancement of Science, September 1858', in G. J. French, *The life and times of Samuel Crompton* (1859) • A. P. Wadsworth and J. de Lacy Mann, *The cotton trade and industrial Lancashire, 1600–1780* (1931), 415–83, 514–16 • S. Smiles, *The Huguenots: their settlements, churches and industries in England and Ireland* (1867), 416–25 • E. Baines, *History of the cotton manufacture in Great Britain* (1835), 113–46, 153, 171–5 • R. L. Hills, *Power in the industrial revolution* (1970) • P. Mathias, 'Dr Johnson and the business world', *The transformation of England: essays in the economic and social history of England in the eighteenth century* (1979), 307–9 **Archives** Birm. CL, Wyatt MSS **Wealth at death** bequests: indentures and probate of will, BL, Add. Ch. 5972–5974

Paul, Sir Onesiphorus, first baronet (*bap.* 1706, *d.* 1774), clothier, the son of Nicholas Paul, a clothier of Woodchester, Gloucestershire, and his wife, Elizabeth, the daughter of Thomas Dean, was born in Woodchester, and baptized at Rodborough on 2 March 1706. The family claimed to be of Huguenot descent. His grandfather and great-grandfather had both been clergymen, the former an Oxford MA, but his father was clearly a clothier of some substance. Paul followed his father into the cloth trade, and established himself as one of the leading gentlemen clothiers in the county.

Paul was married three times, first to Jane Blackburn (*c.*1707–1748), with whom he had two daughters and a son. After her death he married Catherine Freeman, who died in 1766. They had one child who died in infancy. Paul then married a widow, Sarah Turner, *née* Peach, who outlived him by twenty-seven years.

The Gloucestershire woollen industry in the eighteenth century produced some of the finest cloth in the country. Organized on the 'putting-out' system, it was dominated by large-scale capitalists called 'gentlemen clothiers' who, according to Josiah Tucker, dean of Gloucester, in 1757 were 'placed so high above the condition of the Journeymen [that] their conditions approach much nearer to that of a Planter and a Slave in our American colonies' (Tucker, 25). Clothiers in Gloucestershire purchased the raw wool, sorted and prepared it, and then put it out to specialist workers and master craftsmen—spinners, weavers, fullers, and shearmen—to work up in their own homes or workshops into the finished cloth. At all stages the material was returned to the clothier for inspection and payment prior to final marketing.

While trading conditions in the early eighteenth century were difficult, the industry remained very profitable for the largest clothiers, many of whom, upon making their fortune, established themselves on small estates in the Stroudwater area and joined the landed élite. This was a pattern noted by Defoe in 1724:

> it was no extraordinary thing to have clothiers in that country worth from £10,000 to £40,000 a man, and many of the great families who now pass for gentry ... have been originally raised from and built up by this truly noble manufacture. (Defoe, 1.281)

The larger clothiers were courted by the politically active aristocracy such as Lord Hardwicke, since their votes constituted a valuable bloc at elections. Throughout the eighteenth century many larger clothiers were invited on to the bench, a fact reflecting both their status and also the need to have an active magistracy in a district where the woollen workers had a notorious tradition of vigorous direct action and riot whenever provoked. This pattern, from counting house to court house to gentleman, was well portrayed in the career of Onesiphorus Paul.

Paul seems to have thrown himself energetically into the cloth trade. Around 1730 his firm built a new mill at Southfields, just south of Woodchester. Business prospered, and Paul acquired a reputation as an innovator, much interested in improving the finish of the woollen cloth. Since finishing could have a major influence upon the final value of the cloth, this was a stage where many clothiers preferred to exert more direct control over the production process, but Paul appears to have been unusual in that he was more conscious than most of the needs of fashion. He is credited with inventing in 1743 the knapping engine, a device, probably based upon the proscribed gig mill, which raised a lateral nap or ridge of small knots at regular intervals along the length of a cloth to produce a ribbed appearance.

Paul's most famous contribution to improving the reputation of Gloucestershire cloth, however, was his patent, granted in 1748, for 'A method of preparing cloths intended to be dyed scarlet, so as more effectually to ground the said colors and preserve their beauty'. While cloths from many rival regions were dyed in the wool, that is, the wool was dyed prior to spinning, Stroudwater was famous for its piece-dyed cloths, that is, cloths which were dyed a single colour after being fulled. The water quality in the many streams of the valley system converging at the town of Stroud was deemed particularly suited to such dyeing, and red cloth was very much the local speciality, a fact noted by Defoe and others.

Small clothiers utilized the services of public dyers, but larger clothiers could afford to erect their own dye shops and employ their own dyers. Paul took a keen interest in the dye works at his mill, and his method involved both a new mordant mixture and, unusually, two dyeings, one before the cloth was milled or fulled and one after. 'The principal art is in preparing or dying in part before milled which was never known to be practicable before' (patent no. 630, 1748). The consequence of both mixture and method was to produce cloths of very bright red colour and of uniform shade, highly valued by the market.

Paul's fame spread and his industrial success opened the way to social success. In 1750 the prince and princess of Wales visited Gloucestershire and, while staying with Lord Bathurst, made two excursions to the woollen districts. On the second, the royal couple accorded Paul the signal honour of taking breakfast with him, after which he 'demonstrated to [the prince] the several operations of the woollen manufacture, with which his Royal Highness seemed highly delighted, and expressed a very great regard for the same' (GM, 1st ser., 20, 1750, 331).

It is clear that Paul had by now sufficient fortune and connections to be able to establish himself in county circles. In 1757 he bought the Hill House estate at Rodborough, where he built a 'beautiful villa situated on an eminence, with a pleasant prospect of the river' (S. Rudder, New History of Gloucestershire, 1779, 629). Not all were inclined to view the rise of the clothier with pleasure. One account of Paul and his wife at Bath mocked him as a parvenu social climber acting above his station. Nevertheless, by 1760 Paul had risen to become the high sheriff of the county, a post which was several times in the century held by leading gentlemen clothiers, often at the point where they moved out of the trade. The prince of Wales, who had enjoyed his visit to Paul's mill ten years previously, was now king. Paul, who presented an address from the county upon George's accession, was knighted in December 1760. Two years later, in September 1762, the king made Paul a baronet of Great Britain. This honour was said to have been awarded for 'aid in supplying and maintaining a military force in Ireland in connection with the "plantation of Ulster"' (Gloucester Library, RF 300.12). Quite why Paul was involved in such an expensive undertaking so far from the usual domain of the Gloucestershire clothiers is by no means clear, though it may have been in connection with attempts to enforce the legal prohibition of Irish woollen exports, an issue which periodically agitated the English cloth makers.

When Paul finally gave up business is not known, but his son, George Onesiphorus *Paul, born in February 1746, was clearly not brought up to the trade of clothier. Rather, he was sent to St John's College, Oxford, in keeping with the family's new social status, and thence set out on the grand tour. He became famous as a prison reformer.

Onesiphorus Paul died on 21 September 1774 at Hill House, and was buried in Woodchester churchyard. The title passed to his son.   ADRIAN RANDALL

Sources H. P. R. Finberg, *Gloucestershire studies* (1957) · *VCH Gloucestershire*, vol. 2 · J. de L. Mann, *The cloth industry in the west of England from 1660 to 1880* (1971) · A. J. Randall, *Before the Luddites* (1991) · J. Tann, *Gloucestershire woollen mills* (1967) · J. Tucker, *Instructions for travellers* (1757) · *Gloucestershire Notes and Queries*, 1 (1881), 353–5 · J. Burke and J. B. Burke, *A genealogical and heraldic history of the extinct and dormant baronetcies of England, Ireland and Scotland*, 2nd edn (1841); repr. (1844) · [D. Defoe], *A tour thro' the whole island of Great Britain*, 3 vols. (1724–7); repr. in 2 vols. as D. Defoe, *A tour through England and Wales* (1928) · Glos. RO, D67/Z50 · Gloucester Library, RF 300.12 · PRO, SP 44/376, fol. 144

Paul, Robert Bateman

Paul, Robert Bateman (1798–1877), Church of England clergyman and writer, eldest son of the Revd Richard Paul, rector of Mawgan in Pydar, Cornwall (1763–1805), and his wife, Frances (1768?–1819), daughter of the Revd Robert Bateman, rector of Mawgan and St Columb-Major, Cornwall, was born at St Columb-Major on 21 March 1798. He was educated at Truro grammar school and at Exeter College, Oxford, where he matriculated in 1815 as an Eliot exhibitioner from his school. Elected a fellow of his college in 1817, he took a second class in classics in 1819, and graduated BA in 1820 and MA in 1822.

After having been ordained, Paul held the curacy of Probus in Cornwall until January 1824, and was chaplain to the earl of Probus, 1824–6. He returned to Oxford and in 1825 was appointed bursar and tutor of his college. During 1826–7 he served as public examiner in classics, publishing guides for undergraduates on Aristotle's *Ethics* (1829), Herodotus (1831), and the four gospels (1829). He vacated his fellowship on 11 January 1827 by his marriage to Rosa Mira (d. 1882), daughter of the Revd Richard Twopenny, rector of Little Casterton, near Stamford. They had four daughters, Margaret, Rosa, Harriet, and Fanny.

From 30 June 1825 to 1 August 1829 Paul held the college living of Long Wittenham, Berkshire, and from 1829 to 1835 he was vicar of Llantwit Major with Llyswyrny in Glamorgan. He remained without preferment for some time, travelling widely (he published an account of a journey to Moscow in 1836). In 1845 he was licensed to the incumbency of St John, Kentish Town, London. He retained this benefice until 1848, and from that year to 1851 he held the vicarage of St Augustine, Bristol. He was an energetic textbook compiler, producing a *History of Germany on the Plan of Mrs Markham's Histories for the Use of Young Persons* (1847; new edn, 1882) and contributing a number of translations of the works of German scholars on classical subjects to T. K. Arnold's series of educational books between 1847 and 1851.

Early in 1851 Paul emigrated to New Zealand where, at the time of the Canterbury settlement, he settled near Lyttelton, acting for a time as commissary of the bishop, as vicar of Canterbury, and from 1855 to 1860 as archdeacon of Waimea and afterwards of Nelson. He published *Some Account of the Canterbury Settlement* in 1854 and *Letters from Canterbury* in 1857.

Shortly after 1860 Paul returned to England, and in February 1864 was appointed to the rectory of St Mary, Stamford, which he resigned on account of old age in 1872. In 1867 he became a prebendary of Lincoln, and in the next year he obtained the confratership of Browne's Hospital at Stamford, which he held until his death. When an old man he wrote, under the pseudonym of 'the late James Hamley Tregenna', a novel in two volumes called *The Autobiography of a Cornish Rector* (1872), in which he recalled stories from local history and folklore from his youth in north Cornwall. Paul died at Barnhill, Stamford, on 6 June 1877, and was buried on 9 June in Little Casterton churchyard. W. P. COURTNEY, *rev.* ELLIE CLEWLOW

Sources Boase & Courtney, *Bibl. Corn.*, vols. 1, 3 · C. W. Boase, ed., *Registrum Collegii Exoniensis*, new edn, OHS, 27 (1894) · Foster, *Alum. Oxon.* · A. J. Jewers, ed., *Registers of the parish of St Columb Major, Cornwall, from the year 1539 to 1780* (1881) · *Lincoln, Rutland, and Stamford Mercury* (8 June 1877) · *Stamford and Rutland Guardian* (8 June 1877) · *Stamford and Rutland Guardian* (15 June 1877) · *CGPLA Eng. & Wales* (1877)

Wealth at death under £6000: probate, 17 July 1877, *CGPLA Eng. & Wales*

Paul, Robert William

Paul, Robert William (1869–1943), maker of scientific instruments and cinematographer, was born at 3 Albion Road, Holloway, London, on 3 October 1869, the son of George Butler Paul, a London shipowner, and his wife, Elizabeth Jane Lyon. He was educated at the City of London School and at the Finsbury Technical College of the City and Guilds of London Institute at Cowper Street, off City Road. There he received an elementary education in electrical instrument making, electric lighting, and general physics. He worked first in the workshops of Elliott Brothers, scientific instrument makers, then in a draughtsman's office. After a short spell in the factory of the Bell Telephone Company in Antwerp he started his own business in 1891 as an instrument designer and maker in Hatton Garden.

Paul maintained links with the college, where Professor W. E. Ayrton and his colleagues, John Perry, Thomas Mather, and others were engaged in designing electrical measuring instruments. Their ideas for instruments often helped Paul to find new products, which were sold under the inventor's name but succeeded thanks to Paul's manufacturing craftsmanship. In just three years his business expanded to include a four-storey factory in nearby Saffron Hill.

Paul became interested in the new art of cinematography; in 1894 two Greek showmen, who had brought some Edison and Dickson kinetoscopes to London, asked him to make another six. In fact he made sixty; Edison had not patented it in Britain, and Paul improved the design. When film from America became unavailable he collaborated with photographer Birt Acres to design a camera. This partnership was short-lived so Paul began to make his own films, designing a mechanical arrangement, a Maltese cross ('Geneva escapement'), to advance the film frame by frame. His projector, patented in March 1896, was called the theatrograph. He demonstrated it at Finsbury Technical College and the Royal Institution and was soon recognized as an expert in cinematography. A famous exploit was to film the prince of Wales's horse, Persimmon, winning the Derby in 1896; he showed the film several times to rapturous applause the following evening at the Alhambra, Leicester Square.

In the same year Paul began to make short films, initially using sets built on the Alhambra's roof. Such was their success that in 1897 he could afford not only to build a proper studio in Muswell Hill, but also, on 3 August, to marry his leading lady, Ellen Dawn; born Ellen Daws about 1867, she was the daughter of Augustus Daws, cabinet-maker, and also had some theatrical background.

Both the cinema side and the instrument making side of Paul's business flourished; in 1902 for the latter he added a purpose-built factory to the Muswell Hill site, where standard products were efficiently manufactured in large numbers. Of particular note was Paul's 1903 invention, the highly sensitive yet robust 'Unipivot' galvanometer which 'played an important role in taking instruments out of the laboratory and into industrial applications' (Cattermole and Wolfe, 165). Other Unipivot instruments followed: 126 pages of Paul's 1914 catalogue were devoted to them, and Unipivot was the telegraphic address for his works in New Southgate. His instruments were recognized internationally, winning gold medals at the 1904 St Louis Exposition and the 1910 Brussels Exhibition. By 1910, though, he had become disillusioned with 'show business' and concentrated on instrument work. He burnt his stocks of film and sold his film-making equipment. Despite the highly lucrative nature of this work, Paul had always considered it as a sideline, although in 1936, with Hepworth and Barker, he gave an interesting address to a meeting of the British Kinematograph Society entitled 'Before 1910: kinematograph experiences'.

Paul often made specialized instruments for friends to help their research. In 1911 he opened a branch in New York to where instruments were sent from Muswell Hill for American distribution. On the outbreak of war in 1914 his works were involved in providing signalling equipment for the army and navy, including wireless equipment for use in the trenches. This continued his association with Finsbury Technical College where W. H. Eccles was working on short-wave equipment for the signals experimental establishment at the War Office. Of particular note was the Paterson–Walsh auto-aircraft height-finder, manufactured by Paul once it was adopted by the War Office. He was also interested in submarine warfare and the problems of acoustic and magnetic mines and the detection of mines and submarines.

In early 1918 his Muswell Hill factory was bought by the War Office (signals department); Paul continued his experimental work in temporary premises in nearby Fortis Green with thirty of his best workmen from the factory. He bought the works back the following March and immediately negotiated to sell them to the Cambridge Scientific Instrument Company; this was completed in November to form the Cambridge and Paul Instrument Company. From February 1920 Paul sat on the new company's board but began to withdraw from instrument design, concentrating on financial affairs. In his own workshop, though, he did work on projects of particular interest to him. One such, in 1933, was the Bragg–Paul pulsator, a forerunner of the iron lung, for which he designed and built a small hydraulic machine which pressed and released rubber bellows on the chest of a man (a friend of Bragg's) suffering from muscular atrophy, thus greatly assisting his breathing.

Paul died on 28 March 1943 at The Priory, Roehampton, following a cerebral thrombosis. His will established the R. W. Paul Instrument Fund which was to help those whose research was hampered by the lack of funds for developing a particular instrument. He had also endowed the apprentices' prizes at the Physical Society's annual exhibition of apparatus. He had been loyally supportive of the society for many years, serving as a vice-president in 1928–31 and 1939–42, and as treasurer in 1935–9. He was awarded the Duddell medal in 1938. He was also founder fellow of the Institute of Physics and vice-president in 1927–31. He was a council member of the Institution of Electrical Engineers and served as a manager and vice-president of the Royal Institution, where he played an important role in the success of the Faraday Centenary Exhibition at the Royal Albert Hall in 1931.

ROBERT SHARP

Sources R. Whipple, *Proceedings of the Physical Society*, 55 (1943), 502–5 · W. H. Eccles, *Electronic Engineering*, 16 (Aug 1943), 99–102 · *The Times* (29 March 1943) · W. G. Barker, C. M. Hepworth, and R. W. Paul, 'Before 1910: kinematograph experiences', *Proceedings of the British Kinematograph Society*, 38 (1936) · M. J. G. Cattermole and A. F. Wolfe, *Horace Darwin's shop: a history of the Cambridge Scientific Instrument Company, 1878–1968* (1987) · b. cert. · m. cert. · d. cert.
Wealth at death £215,456 19s. 11d.: probate, 5 June 1943, *CGPLA Eng. & Wales*

Paul [Pagula], **William** (d. 1349), bishop of Meath, was born at or near York and joined the Carmelites there. He studied at Oxford where he incepted as a doctor in theology. By 1322 he was prior of the Carmelites in York, and on 16 February 1327 he was provided to the diocese of Meath. After his consecration in Avignon he returned to England, and on 19 August 1327 he was commissioned to reconcile the churchyard of the Carmelite house, Nottingham, after blood had been spilt there. He died in July 1349. Bale recounts that he was a learned man (Robert Walsingham, another Carmelite theologian of the early fourteenth century, quotes him in his *Questiones theologie*), a great preacher, and that he wrote one work, *De ente rationis formaliter*. Paul is confused by Bale and many later writers with William Pagham of Hanborough, an earlier Carmelite provincial, and with Master William Pagula, or Paull, the author of *Oculus sacerdotis*. RICHARD COPSEY

Sources J. Bale, Bodl. Oxf., MS Bodley 73 (SC 27635), fols. 118v, 137, 217 · Emden, *Oxf.* · C. Eubel, ed., *Hierarchia Catholica medii et recentioris aevi*, 2nd edn, 1 (Münster, 1913); repr. (Münster, 1960), 338 · E. Monsignano, ed., *Bullarium Carmelitanum plures complectens summorum pontificum constitutiones ad ordinem fratrum beatissimae*, 1 (Rome, 1715), 553–4 [incl. text of the bull for his appointment] · C. de S. E. de Villiers, *Bibliotheca Carmelitana*, 2 vols. (Orléans, 1752); facs. edn, ed. P. G. Wessels (Rome, 1927), vol. 1, pp. 605–6; vol. 2, p. 918 · J. Bale, BL, Harley MS 3838, fol. 6or–v · J. Bale, Bodl. Oxf., MS Selden supra 41, fol. 164 · *Commentarii de scriptoribus Britannicis, auctore Joanne Lelando*, ed. A. Hall, 2 (1709), 361 · J. Pits, *Relationum historicarum de rebus Anglicis*, ed. [W. Bishop] (Paris, 1619), 363–4 · Tanner, *Bibl. Brit.-Hib.*, 581–2 · *The whole works of Sir James Ware concerning Ireland*, ed. and trans. W. Harris, rev. edn, 1 (1764), 146; 2 (1764), 321

Paul, William. *See* Paule, William (1599–1665).

Paul, William (*bap.* **1679**, *d.* **1716**), Jacobite sympathizer and nonjuring Church of England clergyman, was baptized on 23 August 1679 at Ashby Parva, Leicestershire. The eldest of five children, he was born to John Paul, grazier, and Sarah Barfoot. Educated at Rugby, Warwickshire, he matriculated at St John's College, Cambridge, on 25 May 1698, graduating BA in 1702 and MA in 1705. A lifelong bachelor, he was ordained deacon on 20 September 1702 and priest on 23 September 1705. He served as curate at Caulton Curlieu, near Harborough, Leicestershire, and as chaplain to Sir Geoffrey Palmer, followed by service as curate and usher at the free school, Tamworth, Staffordshire, and then as curate at Nuneaton, Warwickshire. He was presented to the vicarage of Orton on the Hills, Leicestershire, on 5 May 1709, when he took the oaths to Queen Anne and abjured the Pretender.

Paul gave little evidence of either Jacobite or nonjuror sympathies before autumn 1715, when he joined the Jacobite forces, dressed in lay clothing, at Lancaster. He brought to the Jacobite leaders news of General Carpenter's forces, which were then at Barnard's Castle in the diocese of Durham. The Jacobite chaplain, Robert Patten, reluctantly acceded to Paul's request to serve as a chaplain. In that capacity he reportedly offered prayers for James III (James Francis Edward Stuart) as king. Leaving Preston before the battle, he went to Leicestershire and then London, where Thomas Bird, justice of the peace for Leicestershire, spotted him dressed 'in colour'd cloaths, lace hat, and long wig, and a sword by his side' (Patten, 98–9). Paul was arrested on 12 December 1715, taken to the duke of Devonshire, and then sent to Newgate prison on 26 December. Arraigned at Westminster on 31 May 1716, he pleaded not guilty, but withdrew the plea on 15 June in the hopes of gaining a pardon. Following his trial on 5 July, Paul, having no desire to die for the Jacobite cause, sent letters to the archbishop of Canterbury, William Wake, and Lord Townshend pleading for clemency and denying his guilt.

Paul and fellow prisoner, John Hall, upon their failure to gain the mercy of George I before he left for Hanover on 7 July 1716, were executed by being hanged, drawn, and quartered at Tyburn on 13 July, though twenty-two other prisoners were spared. Before their execution both men gave spirited Jacobite speeches, which were written by Paul and a young nonjuror clergyman, Thomas Deacon. Dressed in priestly habit, Paul repented for taking the oaths of allegiance to a usurping power and claimed to die a member of the nonjuring Church of England. Proclaiming James III to be the 'only rightful sovereign', he called for James to be restored to his throne. In his final words, he claimed that he wished he had enough quarters to send to each parish in the kingdom 'to testify, that a clergyman of the Church of England, was martyred for being loyal to his king' (*True Copy*, 4–5). Respondents to the speeches questioned Paul's character, consistency, and his claim to be a martyr. A. A. Sykes doubted his commitment to the nonjuror cause, as Paul had been ordained by 'a schismatical bishop' and then 'presented to his living by a schismatical bishop', while taking the oaths to Anne (Sykes, 4–5). An anonymous piece attributed to Daniel Defoe charged that Paul had been used by other Jacobites as a tool to foment rebellion. He claimed that despite the efforts made by the two prisoners to gain a pardon, the speechwriters attempted to 'delude the unthinking populace, and to make those men pass for valiant and glorious martyrs' (Defoe, 3–4).   ROBERT D. CORNWALL

Sources R. Patten, *The history of the late rebellion*, 2nd edn (1717) · *True copy of the papers delivered to the sheriffs of London, by William Paul, a clergyman, and John Hall, esq., late justice of the peace in Northumberland* (1716) · Venn, *Alum. Cant.* · S. Hibbert Ware, *Lancashire memorials of the rebellion*, 2 pts in 1, Chetham Society, 5 (1845); repr. (1968) · [A. A. Sykes], *The thanks of an honest clergyman for Mr. Paul's speech at Tybourn, July the 13th, 1716*, 2nd edn (1716) · [D. Defoe], *Remarks on the speeches of William Paul, Clerk, and John Hall of Otterburn, esq.* (1716) · *A collection of the several papers deliver'd by Mr J. Gordon, the earl of Derwentwater, Vt. Kenmure, Col. Oxburgh, R. Gascoigne, the Rd. Mr Paul, J. Hall, esq., Capt. J. Bruce, J. Knox …* (1717) · J. Baynes, *The Jacobite rising of 1715* (1970) · Dr Doran, *London in the Jacobite times*, 2 vols. (1877) · *A biographical history of England, from the revolution to the end of George I's reign: being a continuation of the Rev. J. Granger's work*, ed. M. Noble, 3 vols. (1806) · H. Broxap, *A biography of Thomas Deacon* (1911) · P. Rae, *The history of the late rebellion* (1718) · D. Szechi, 'The Jacobite theatre of death', *The Jacobite challenge*, ed. E. Cruickshanks and J. Black (1988), 57–73 · R. Halley, *Lancashire: its puritanism and nonconformity*, 2 vols. (1869) · *IGI*

Likenesses R. Grave, line engraving, BM, NPG; repro. in J. Caulfield, *Portraits, memoirs and characters of remarkable persons*, 4 vols. (1819–20) · Vertue?, portrait (with John Hall), NPG · line engraving, NPG

Paul, William (**1822–1905**), horticulturist, was born at Churchgate, Cheshunt, Hertfordshire, on 16 June 1822, the second son of Adam Paul (*d.* 1847), a nurseryman of Huguenot descent, originally from Aberdeenshire, who purchased the Cheshunt nursery in 1806. He was educated at a private school at Waltham Cross before joining his father's business. Following his father's death he and his elder brother, George, continued the business as A. Paul & Son. In 1860 this partnership was dissolved and his brother established the firm of Paul & Son at Cheshunt, while Paul himself concentrated on the Waltham Cross nursery, William Paul & Son, which he had founded in 1859.

Paul's earliest literary work was for John Claudius Loudon (1783–1843). Following Loudon's death he wrote articles for John Lindley; his series of articles entitled 'Roses in pots', which appeared in 1843 in the *Gardeners' Chronicle*, were issued separately in the same year, and reached a ninth edition in 1908. Paul's book, *The Rose Garden* (1848), was also immensely popular, reaching a tenth edition by 1903 and being reprinted as late as 1978. It is a practical treatise to which Paul's wide reading gave a literary character. Coloured illustrations initially made the book expensive; later editions were issued in two forms, with and without these plates.

Paul served on the committee of the National Floricultural Society from 1851 until it was dissolved in 1858. In July 1858 he joined the newly founded National Rose Society, and in 1866 he was one of the executive committee of twenty-one members for the great International Horticultural Exhibition. He also acted as a commissioner for the Paris Exhibition of 1867. He was elected a fellow of the Linnean Society in 1875, and received the Victoria medal of horticulture when it was first instituted in 1897.

Although best known as a rosarian, Paul also devoted attention to the improvement of other types of plants, such as hollyhocks, asters, hyacinths, phloxes, camellias, zonal pelargoniums, hollies, ivies, shrubs, fruit trees, and Brussels sprouts. He dealt with these subjects in *American Plants, their History and Culture* (1858), *Lecture on the Hyacinth* (1864), and papers on hollyhocks (1851) and 'Tree scenery' (1870–72). He contributed papers on the varieties of yew and holly to the *Proceedings of the Royal Horticultural Society* (1861, 1863). In addition to the *Rose Annual*, which he issued from 1858 to 1881, Paul was associated with his friends Dr Robert Hogg and Thomas Moore in the editorship of the *Florist and Pomologist* from 1868 to 1874. Clear and fluent as a speaker, he proved an acceptable lecturer. One of his best lectures, 'Improvements in plants', at Manchester in 1869, was included in his *Contributions to Horticultural Literature, 1843–1892* (1892).

Paul died at Waltham Cross of a paralytic seizure on 31 March 1905, and was buried in the family vault at Cheshunt cemetery. His wife, Amelia Jane Harding, predeceased him. His business was carried on by his son, Arthur William Paul. His rich library of old gardening books and general literature was sold at Sothebys after his death, but many volumes were bought by his son.

G. S. BOULGER, *rev.* PETER OSBORNE

Sources Desmond, *Botanists*, rev. edn, 540 · *The Garden*, 57 (1900), 166 · *The Garden*, 63 (1903) · *The Garden*, 67 (1905), 213 · *Journal of Horticulture*, 1 (1905), 305 · *Gardeners' Chronicle*, 3rd ser., 37 (1905), 216–7 · B. D. J. [B. D. Jackson], *Proceedings of the Linnean Society of London*, 117th session (1904–5), 46–7
Wealth at death £41,337 11s.: resworn probate, 12 Aug 1905, CGPLA Eng. & Wales

Paul, William Francis (1850–1928), grain importer and maltster, was born on 11 February 1850 at 39 Bank Street, Ipswich, the youngest of the seven children of Robert Paul (*c*.1806–1864), maltster and wharfinger, and his wife, Elizabeth, daughter of James Woods, ironmonger, of Stowmarket. For several generations, the Pauls had been prominent members of the Independent church in Suffolk, and William's early years were shaped by his close involvement in the thriving chapel at Tacket Street. After a private education he joined his brother Robert (1844–1909) in the small family firm, then administered by their father's trustees. In 1874 the brothers inherited the business and, under William's leadership, the partnership prospered. They acquired several local competitors and were soon numbered among Britain's leading maltsters; they became major importers of barley and maize; they built up their own fleet of steamships and barges and successfully diversified into the manufacture of animal feedstuffs. In 1893 R. and W. Paul was registered as a limited liability company with assets in excess of £200,000.

Paul was uncompromising and hasty. Typically, he resolved a dispute over the repair of barges by purchasing

William Francis Paul (1850–1928), by unknown photographer

his own shipyard. An opportunist, he was determined to remain at the forefront of progress. In 1899, accompanied by his son, Stuart, he undertook an extensive tour of the major grain-producing regions of America. They gained valuable trading links and firsthand knowledge of the latest developments in the handling and storage of grain. Three years later, Gillman and Spencer Limited, manufacturers of flaked maize and brewers' chemicals, was acquired, and their London wharf rebuilt as an American-style grain terminal. At Rotherhithe, the company also pioneered the production of animal feedstuffs from cooked, flaked maize. In Ipswich five large, modern maltings, designed by the brothers, were completed by 1912. A financial interest was taken in the Grantham maltsters Lee and Grinling, and further acquisitions (the Hull Malt Company in 1918, and the Cereals Company seven years later), laid the foundations of the twentieth-century enterprise.

William Paul's business acumen spilled over into other spheres. He began the family's deep involvement in farming, purchasing 1000 acres at Kirton, Suffolk. Active in civic life, Paul was a JP, a member of the Ipswich dock commission, the museum and library committee, and a trustee of Ipswich municipal charities. A staunch Liberal, he served as town councillor, 1890–1908, alderman, 1909–28, and mayor, 1900–01. An accomplished speaker, he was said to dominate the council chamber. He preached the virtues of self-help but, maintaining a lifelong commitment to his nonconformist faith, worked tirelessly to improve the welfare of the town's citizens. For many years chairman of the public health committee, he instigated the town's tuberculosis sanatorium and public refuse system. As a memorial to his brother Robert, to whom he was deeply attached, he established the William Paul Housing Trust, which in 1914 built its first tenements for the poor and elderly. And in 1927 he created Bourne Park in one of the most densely populated districts of the town. For his work at the auxiliary hospital for wounded servicemen there, Broadwater, which he donated, and administered throughout the First World War, he was appointed OBE and awarded the order of St John.

Paul was married on 27 August 1874 to Jessie Eliza Mary (1853–1887), daughter of James Springall, grocer, of Norwich; they had three sons and two daughters. The eldest son, Bernard, a personable playboy, was banished to an estate in Argentina and never reconciled with his father. His two brothers, Hugh and Stuart, followed their father into the family business. Stuart extended his father's estates, ultimately farming 6000 acres and becoming a noted breeder of Suffolk horses and redpoll cattle. In 1889, William married Ida Florence Lankester (1866–1965), of Stowmarket. The couple had one son, Cyril, and two daughters. Paul remained as managing director and chairman of R. and W. Paul until March 1927, when he resigned because of failing health. He died at his home, Orwell Lodge, Belstead Road, Ipswich, on 4 April 1928, following a heart attack, and was buried six days later at Ipswich borough cemetery.   CHRISTINE CLARK

Sources Pauls Malt Limited archives, Ipswich · *Suffolk Chronicle* (13 April 1928) · Tacket Street Chapel records, Suffolk RO, FK 3/1 · 'Ipswich men of note', *Ipswich Observer and Felixstowe Times* (23 March 1907) · R. Finch, *A cross in the topsail* (1979) · J. Freestone, 'A parish at war', *Suffolk Review*, new ser., 17 (1991), 1–17, esp. 10–12 · W. F. Paul, diary, 22 March–17 May 1899, priv. coll. · private information (2004) · *East Anglian Daily Times* (25 June 1965)
Likenesses photograph, 1900, Ipswich town hall · photograph, BOCM Pauls, Ipswich [*see illus.*]
Wealth at death £715,744: will, 16 May 1928, PRO

Paula, Frederic Rudolph Mackley de (1882–1954), writer on accountancy and industrialist, was born on 23 July 1882 at Avenue House, Tenterden Grove, Hendon, London, one of the five children of Friedrich Mortiz Alphonse Felix de Paula, a partner in the City solicitors' practice of Carey, Warburton, and de Paula, and his wife Ellen Harriet, *née* Mackley. Frederic, whose grandmother was of German origin, had one brother (who became a City stockbroker) and three sisters. Following his father's death in 1902, the family lived for a time in North Finchley, and later at Netherdale, Nether Street, Church End, Finchley. De Paula attended Mill Hill School before going to work in the City of London in 1901, when he became articled to the chartered accountant Charles F. Cape at 12 Coleman Street; he qualified in 1905 and set up in practice in 1909. A year later he was joined by Edgar John Turner, and practised as De Paula, Turner & Co. until 1913, when a further partnership change resulted in the creation of De Paula, Turner, Lake & Co.

De Paula's main contribution to accountancy was not as a practitioner but as a teacher and writer, industrialist, and champion of regulatory requirements concerning financial reporting practice. Soon after qualifying he presented auditing lectures to the finals students of the Chartered Accountants Students' Society of London. Increasingly dissatisfied with the literature available for students, he published in 1914 *The Principles of Auditing*, a successful text which ran to eleven editions during his lifetime. In 1920 he joined Lawrence R. Dicksee at the London School of Economics as a part-time lecturer on the new commerce degree. De Paula continued his involvement, part time, as a reader from 1924, and as professor of accountancy and business methods (in succession to Dicksee) in 1926. This was the year he presented arguably his most important public lecture, entitled 'The place of accountancy in commerce'. The lecture aimed to raise the status of the accounts department within companies by identifying its principal functions and making businessmen fully aware of the way it could contribute to the practical management of business organizations. It was a timely intervention. Accountants were beginning to move from the profession in growing numbers, sometimes at top level (with Francis D'Arcy Cooper's move to Lever Brothers the most celebrated example), but more often in a specifically accounting capacity. There was a need for greater recognition of the contributions they could make beyond keeping the records straight and assisting in the preparation of the published accounts. The opportunity for de Paula to put his ideas into practice was not long in coming. In 1929 he resigned his chair and his partnership in order to give full attention to his new appointment as chief accountant at the Dunlop Rubber Company, where he soon became controller of finance.

At Dunlop de Paula renewed personal links developed during the First World War, when he had joined the Ministry of Munitions and worked for Sir Eric Geddes. His immediate superior was George Beharrell, and in due course he succeeded Beharrell as director of the statistical section of the gun ammunition filling department. In 1917 he followed Geddes to France, and became the latter's assistant director-general of transportation at general headquarters, with the rank of lieutenant-colonel. With Dunlop suffering from financial problems in the late 1920s, it was perhaps natural that the company's chairman, Geddes, and managing director, Beharrell, should turn to de Paula to see what contribution an accountant could make to the resolution of their difficulties.

It is de Paula's contribution towards the improvement of Dunlop's financial reporting practices which has perhaps received most attention. The year 1931 saw the prosecution of the chairman (Lord Kylsant) and auditor (Harold Moreland, of Price, Waterhouse & Co.) of the Royal Mail Shipping Company for publishing a balance sheet which was false and fraudulent. Although resulting in acquittal, the prosecution served to demonstrate the lamentable state of financial reporting practice among many of Britain's largest companies. The prestige of the profession slumped to an unprecedented depth. De Paula had already persuaded Dunlop to make a number of innovations in the accounts for 1929, and these were taken further in 1931, and again in 1933, drawing acclaim from the financial press and being described by the *Daily Telegraph* as 'a joy to its own shareholders and the envy of all others'. In the aftermath of the Royal Mail case, Dunlop undoubtedly blazed a trail for other companies to follow.

Turning to the company's management information system, de Paula placed particular emphasis on the need to develop an integrated system of budgetary planning and control covering the company's entire financial affairs. Such ideas were not unknown in the literature, but British industry had been slow to give them practical effect. De Paula provided leadership, both in terms of the reforms introduced in Dunlop, which were copied by other companies (for example, Pilkington), and in important lectures delivered in the mid-1930s, which attracted widespread attention. A serious illness then led to his retirement in 1941. Later, however, he moved on to Harding, Tilton, and Hartley Ltd, a firm of shirt manufacturers at Taunton, as vice-chairman and joint managing director. He served as chairman of this company (renamed British Van Heusen Company) and on the board of other leading public companies.

De Paula's final major achievement was to help raise the awareness of the Institute of Chartered Accountants in England and Wales (ICAEW) concerning the need to cater for chartered accountants who had moved to industry. By the outbreak of the Second World War, about 50 per cent of all chartered accountants were working in business, but there was a tendency for the institute's leaders (drawn from public practice) to regard them as, at best, second-class citizens. Pressure from younger members in industry in the early 1940s, together with criticism in the press, helped to contribute to the establishment of the taxation and financial relations committee of the ICAEW, which dealt with the relationship of the business community with the Inland Revenue and other government departments. Also, for the first time, arrangements were made for the election of non-practising members to the institute's council.

De Paula was the first non-practising member appointed to council, and he was also elected vice-chairman of the new committee, which is today best remembered for the twenty-nine recommendations on accounting principles issued between 1942 and 1969. These forerunners of today's financial reporting standards were guidelines on best practice, which companies were encouraged to adopt, and it is generally agreed that they succeeded in raising significantly the general standard of financial reporting. De Paula was the committee's chairman between 1943 and 1945, during which time recommendations 6 to 10 laid out the main valuation bases for published accounts. The topics covered correspond fairly closely to the list of subjects requiring attention identified by de Paula in the preface to *The Principles of Auditing* (6th edn, 1933). De Paula was appointed CBE in the new year's honours list of 1951, partly in recognition of his work on a government committee appointed to review the organization and administrative methods of the Inland Revenue.

De Paula married, in 1912, Agnes Smithson, the daughter of Frances Joseph Clark, of the Quaker shoemaking family of Street, Somerset. They lived for many years in Radlett, Hertfordshire, where they served, respectively, as captain and lady captain of the Porters Park Golf Club. There were two sons from the marriage, Hugh Francis Mackley and Frederic Clive. The latter edited issues of *The Principles of Auditing* published after his father's death. De Paula died at his London home, 55 Park Mansions, Knightsbridge, on 13 December 1954. The Quaker influence was evidenced by his express wish that no mourning should be worn. His wife survived him.

John Richard Edwards

Sources J. Kitchen and R. H. Parker, 'Frederic Rudoph Mackey de Paula (1882–1954)', *Twentieth-century accounting thinkers*, ed. J. R. Edwards (1994), 225–51 · T. C. Barker, *The glass makers, Pilkington: the rise of an international company, 1826–1976* (1976) · *The Accountant* (18 Dec 1954), 669–70 · *The Accountant* (25 Dec 1954), 705–6 · S. A. Zeff, *Forging accounting principles in five countries: a history and an analysis of trends* (1972) · d. cert. · *CGPLA Eng. & Wales* (1955) · J. Kitchen, 'De Paula, Frederic Rudolph Mackley', *DBB*

Wealth at death £48,499 16s. 7d.: probate, 24 March 1955, *CGPLA Eng. & Wales*

Paulden, Thomas (1625–1702x10), royalist army officer, was born at the George and Crown inn, Silver Street, Wakefield, West Riding of Yorkshire, and baptized at Wakefield on 25 January 1626, the third son of William Paulden (*d*. in or after 1649) of Wakefield, a chapman, and his wife, Susannah, daughter of Edward Binns of nearby Horbury. He was admitted as a sizar to Clare College, Cambridge, on 18 June 1641, but did not proceed to a degree.

Paulden sided with the royalists during the civil wars and was possibly the Captain Paulden captured at Naseby on 14 June 1645. On the eve of the second civil war, hearing of the duke of Hamilton's plans to invade, Paulden was among those Yorkshire royalists encouraged by Lady Savile to meet in the woods around Brearley, Frickley, and Kirkby. He privately enlisted 300 foot and 50 horse from among disbanded comrades. Along with his brothers William (1618–1648) and Timothy (1622–1648) he was a confidant of Colonel John Morris, with whom he hatched a plot to seize Pontefract Castle, a plan frustrated on 18 May 1648 by the drunkenness of their agent in the garrison. However, on 3 June, disguised as countrymen delivering beds, Morris and William Paulden led nine men into the castle, where they overpowered the gatehouse, admitted their confederates, and captured the governor. On 6 June Thomas Paulden arrived in the castle with thirty cavalry reinforcements. The garrison's number eventually grew to 500 men and in July, Thomas was sent to garrison Thornhill Hall as an outpost, where he replied to Colonel Fairfax's summons to surrender on 16 July: 'You may not expect anything here, but what you can win by your sword' (Fox, 107). Two days later he agreed to parley with Sir Henry Cholmley, having returned to Pontefract Castle by 20 July when he led a nocturnal raid which rustled 300 cattle.

In October 1648 parliament sent Colonel Thomas Rainborowe to reinforce the besiegers, and he established his headquarters at Doncaster, 12 miles from Pontefract. At midnight on 27 October, Thomas Paulden accompanied his brother William and twenty-one others on a night ride to surprise Rainborowe in his quarters. They aimed to capture him unharmed and exchange him for their general, Sir Marmaduke Langdale, then imprisoned by parliament and under threat of execution. Arriving early in the morning, pretending to bear letters from Cromwell, they disarmed the guard and four of them entered Rainborowe's chamber, roused him from his bed and claimed him as their prisoner. Unarmed, Rainborowe acquiesced, but when downstairs and nearing his captors' horses in the street, he was killed in a scuffle while trying to raise the alarm. The party escaped back to Pontefract, soon after which Paulden's eldest brother, William, died of fever. Meanwhile London newsbooks reported Rainborowe's death as a deliberate murder.

Cromwell himself arrived to direct the siege in November 1648 and part of Pontefract Castle was blown up. On 30 November, Cromwell returned south, leaving Major-General John Lambert in command. Hearing news of the king's execution, the garrison proclaimed Prince Charles king; but in late February 1649 a message from him reached them excusing them from further resistance. Paulden later claimed that the garrison had been reduced through sallies, desertion, and disease to about 100 men. On 3 March six commissioners, including Thomas Paulden, attempted to negotiate surrender without success. The parley was renewed on 10 March, but Paulden objected to parliamentarian demands that six unnamed royalists in the garrison be exempted from the terms. Consequently he refused to act as a commissioner for the castle's surrender and terms were agreed without his participation on 17 March. Having withstood siege for nine months, the castle was finally surrendered on 24 March 1649.

Paulden joined Prince Charles in exile, secretly visiting England several times in the 1650s. Once he was betrayed and brought before Cromwell, but on his denying his name nothing was proved against him. Imprisoned in the Gatehouse, Westminster, Paulden escaped by throwing salt and pepper into the keeper's eyes. Having received payments from Prince Charles in 1652 and 1654, he procured Edward Hyde intelligence of the strength of Sir William Lockhart's English forces in Flanders in May 1657.

Paulden returned to England in 1660, and received some financial aid from the duke of Buckingham. In April 1668 the king requested Paulden's appointment as commissioner of excise upon the first vacancy. In February 1692 Paulden begged Lord Hatton to employ him as a servant to save him from debtors' prison. On 31 March 1702 he wrote a narrative of the siege of Pontefract and the attempted abduction of Rainborowe. No will has survived and Paulden died in poverty some time between 1702 and 1710. Ralph Thoresby recorded his visit to Paulden's sisters, who told him of their memorable brothers on 18 July 1710.   ANDREW J. HOPPER

Sources T. Paulden, *Pontefract Castle: an account of how it was taken: and how General Rainsborough was surprised in his quarters at Doncaster, anno 1648* (1702) [repr. 1983] · G. Fox, *The three sieges of Pontefract Castle from the manuscript compiled and illustrated by George Fox* (1987) · Venn, *Alum. Cant.* · 'A journal of the first and second sieges of Pontefract Castle, 1644–5, by Nathan Drake', ed. W. H. D. Longstaffe, *Miscellanea*, SurtS, 37 (1861) · R. Thoresby, *Ducatus Leodiensis, or, The topography of … Leedes*, ed. T. D. Whitaker, 2nd edn (1816) · *CSP dom.*, *1667–8* · M. A. E. Green, ed., *Calendar of the proceedings of the committee for compounding … 1643–1660*, 5 vols., PRO (1889–92) · *DNB* · J. W. Walker, *Wakefield: its history and people*, 3rd edn, 2 (1966) · *The diary of Ralph Thoresby*, ed. J. Hunter, 2 (1830)

Archives BL, account of the taking of Pontefract Castle, Lansdowne MS 896 | BL, Add. MSS 21417, 29551, 29565, 36996

Paule, Sir George (1563–1635), administrator and biographer, was the second son of Richard Paule of Norfolk and of Bridgnorth, Shropshire, and Dorothy, daughter of Fulk Lee of Langley, Shropshire. He was married twice, first to Joan (d. before 1635), daughter of Nicholas Oldman of Berkshire. Of his second wife, Rachel, we know only that she was still living on 8 October 1645, ten years after her husband's death, and that a child of their marriage, George, was not then of age. The boy must have been born when his father was quite old. Paule was a servant of John Whitgift by the time of his translation to Canterbury in 1584. From 1586 he leased the parsonage of Graveney which was owned by successive archbishops; on its renewal in 1596 the rent was £7 6s. 8d. On 21 November 1588 he acquired from Anthony Calton the post of registrar of the diocese of Ely, an appointment held jointly with Richard Massinger, but both men sold their interest in 1600. By 1599 he was the comptroller of the archbishop's household and was present at the dedication of Whitgift's hospital at Croydon on 10 July of that year. Probably on the initiative of Whitgift, and through the patronage of Bishop Bilson of Winchester, he was returned as MP for Downton in Wiltshire in 1597; in 1601, as member for Hindon, Wiltshire, he sat on two committees.

In March 1604 Paule's employer and patron, Archbishop Whitgift, was taken ill. He attended the archbishop through his sickness and at his death on 29 February 1604. It is for his biography of Whitgift that he is best remembered. The work contains inaccuracies, such as postdating Whitgift's doctorate by two years to 1569, and it appears that 'the suggestion that Grindal proposed to resign in favour of a named individual, Whitgift … must be dismissed as Paule's invention' (Collinson, *Grindal*, 278). But the book's chief defects can be seen from its preface dedicated to the new archbishop, George Abbot: 'I see it incident to personages of high place and deserving, to win by their living favours many obsequious followers; who after their decease prove but cold remembrancers of their bounty, or other virtues.' Paule, by contrast, was eager to 'show my own obligation to his memory, and to make known his worthy parts to future ages'. Such an approach led to a further promise, well kept, 'rather to imitate my master in his mild and moderate carriage, than willingly to be offensive or displeasing to any' (Wordsworth, 314). In 1612 the church hierarchy was anxious to put behind it the contentions caused, in part, by the combative Whitgift (and more recently by his pugnacious successor Bancroft): as Paule well knew, 'mild and moderate' was what they wanted to remember. Nevertheless the work is an invaluable source for the archbishop's tenure by an 'insider'. In several cases, when official papers show only grey, it is Paule who provides the colour of personal recollection: on Whitgift's 'first journey into Kent he rode to Dover, being attended with an hundred of his own servants, at least, in livery, whereof there were forty gentlemen in chains of gold' (ibid., 388).

Paule's fortunes did not decline after Whitgift's death. On 16 May 1603 he was appointed joint registrar and clerk of the acts; he was knighted on 5 July 1607 at Whitehall. Appointed to the commission of the peace in Surrey by 1610, he also served the state through his membership of two commissions, in 1609 and 1620, to investigate the regulation of starch production. On 30 March 1621, together with Sir Robert Heath, solicitor-general, he was granted the office of chief clerk in the king's bench; this position was held in trust for George Villiers, duke of Buckingham; control over the enrolment of pleas made it 'an office of exceptional value, the object of aristocratic and court rivalries' (Aylmer, 305–6). It may be assumed that the actual work involved was carried out by deputies. In 1621 he quarrelled with Cranfield, writing to Buckingham on 12 July, begging to be allowed to proceed in the house against his opponent, who would 'be found more corrupt than the late Lord Chancellor [Bacon] and there will be an uproar, when the House meets, against him' (CSP dom., 1619–23, 275). More than once, he tried to steer his powerful patron, and the government, to more moderate courses. On 25 March 1622 he wrote to Buckingham urging that 'the benevolence cannot go on well without a parliament' and suggesting 'that a tax of a 1d or 2d in the shilling on necessary commodities is likely to be much more cheerfully paid' (ibid., 362). Similarly, in a letter to Lord Conway, the king's principal secretary, dated 24 October 1625 from Twickenham, he reported 'great discontentment especially in these parts adjacent to London', and expressed 'astonishment' at the raising of new loans while the subsidy granted by parliament in 1625 was still being collected (Bidwell and Jansson, 4.225–6). He himself had sat for Bridgnorth in 1625, alongside George Vernon, his rival for the contested seat, in what appears to have been a double return, but which was not challenged in the house. He was not a member in 1626, but was returned once more for Bridgnorth in 1628.

Paule had been among those who wrote to Buckingham on 29 July 1623 with the news that the latter's debts, which had amounted to £24,000 before his departure for Spain, had ballooned to £29,000, and that it had become necessary to sell lands to the value of £17,000. In 1626–7, as Buckingham's financial position spiralled downwards, Paule and Sir Robert Heath acted as trustees jointly for the duke and four of his principal creditors, London magnates who were also customs farmers. In 1628, when Buckingham was killed, Paule and Heath became trustees for his seven executors, his administrator, and these four creditors. But Paule was soon ousted; in July 1629 he relinquished to Robert Henley the trusteeship both of the estate and of the office, by agreement of the executors,

the administrator, and the creditors. On 17 March 1631, then aged about sixty-eight years, he petitioned that upon surrendering the office he had been promised that, in respect of his age and infirmity, he would not be required to act as sheriff or to shoulder other burdens; on 27 March the request was granted and the attorney-general instructed accordingly. From 1625 he had been registrar of the court of high commission, holding this post until his death before 16 April 1635.   STEPHEN WRIGHT

Sources CSP dom., 1599–1635 · C. Wordsworth, Ecclesiastical biography, 6 vols. (1818) [incl. Paule's life of Whitgift] · R. C. Gabriel, 'Paule, Sir George', HoP, Commons, 1558–1603 · G. E. Aylmer, The king's servants: the civil service of Charles I, 1625–1642, rev. edn (1974) · P. Collinson, Godly people: essays on English protestantism and puritanism (1983) · P. Collinson, Archbishop Grindal, 1519–1583: the struggle for a reformed church (1979) · J. Strype, The life and acts of John Whitgift, new edn, 3 vols. (1822) · M. Prestwich, Cranfield: politics and profits under the early Stuarts (1966) · M. Jansson and W. B. Bidwell, eds., Proceedings in parliament, 1625 (1987) · VCH Shropshire, vol. 3 · W. Notestein, F. H. Relf, and H. Simpson, eds., Commons debates, 1621, 7 (1935), appx B · W. C. Metcalfe, A book of knights banneret, knights of the Bath and knights bachelor (1885), 158 · Sixth report, HMC, 5 (1877–8) · DNB

Paule [Paul], **William** (1599–1665), bishop of Oxford, was baptized at St Leonard Eastcheap, London, on 14 October 1599, a younger son and one of sixteen children of William Paul, butcher and citizen, and his wife, Joane, daughter of John Harrison, beadle of the Butchers' Company. He matriculated from All Souls College, Oxford, on 15 November 1616, aged seventeen, and graduated BA on 9 June 1618, having become a fellow of the college the previous year. He proceeded MA on 1 June 1621. Having been ordained, he became a frequent preacher in Oxford, and for two years from 1626 held part of the rectory of Patshull, Staffordshire. He proceeded BD on 13 March 1629 and DD on 10 March 1632, gaining notice for his participation in theological debate. David Lloyd remembered him as 'an accute scholar' (Lloyd, 611), while Anthony Wood, in an assessment that partially echoed Lloyd's, found him 'a person of good parts, and well vers'd in ecclesiastical and civil laws' (Wood, Ath. Oxon., 4.828), but he published nothing.

On 10 October 1632 Paule was instituted to the rectory of Brightwell Baldwin, Oxfordshire. That year he resigned his fellowship and made the first of the three socially advantageous marriages that, together with his continuing close ties to the City of London, may provide some explanation for his subsequent wealth and preferments. By licence dated 12 November 1632 he married Mary, daughter of Sir Henry Glemham of Glemham, Suffolk, and Anne, daughter of Thomas Sackville, first earl of Dorset. Mary's sister was the recently widowed second wife of Dudley Carleton, first Viscount Dorchester and secretary of state, whose family came from Brightwell Baldwin. Following Mary's death in 1633 a dispute between Paule and his sister-in-law, Lady Dorchester, over the latter's promise to pay £600 into a trust for Paule and his wife, was referred to Archbishop Laud and Lord Keeper Thomas

Coventry, who reported in February 1634 that the viscountess offered to pay £250. The outcome of this is unknown, but on 22 January 1635 Paule married, at St Giles-in-the-Fields, Alice, daughter of Thomas Cutler of Ipswich and Anne Dandy. This marriage too was brief: Alice died on 19 November the same year, and was buried the following day in Westminster Abbey. 'Almost immediately' (Chester, 131) Paule married Rachel (1617–1691), daughter of the leading Levant and East India merchant Christopher *Clitherow (1577/8–1641), lord mayor of London from November 1635, knighted in January 1636, who was 'probably part of a … London group of Arminian sympathisers' (Tyacke, 221).

By 1635 Paule had become a chaplain to the king, taking the November turn. In that year, according to Wood, he preached a sermon, evidently on the subject of superstition, at the visitation of John Bancroft, bishop of Oxford. In October 1637 he became a canon residentiary of Chichester, holding the prebend of Seaford. The outbreak of war in 1642 may have seen Paule in London, for on 5 October both the Lords and the Commons granted him a safe conduct to the king to fulfil his obligation as royal chaplain. He was listed in this capacity in 1643 and 1644, but the exact nature and extent of his subsequent contact with Charles and with the royalist cause is unclear. He was sequestered, but on compounding had been discharged, before November 1648; he was still in Brightwell Baldwin parish in 1652. Sir Edward Walker recorded in 1661 that Paule had 'in the late unhappy time of Distraction faithfully and actively assisted' Charles II (Rylands, 192–3), but David Lloyd suggested in 1668 that he had also possessed qualities permitting him to accommodate himself, more easily than other sequestered clergy, to the new regime. With a good grasp of law and 'admirably well seen in the Intrigues and Interest of State', this 'shrewd man in business, whether of Trade, Husbandry, Buying and Improving of Land, Disposing of Money' used his wealth and the respect it commanded to 'lend to advantages, to the most considerable men of that party' (Lloyd, 611).

At the Restoration, Paule recovered his Chichester prebend and the Brightwell Baldwin rectory, and once again became a royal chaplain. On 26 January 1661 he was presented by the king to the deanery of Lichfield, in which capacity he presided over the election of John Hacket as bishop. On 18 February that year he was granted a coat of arms in recognition of his loyalty during the 1650s. Through the influence of Gilbert Sheldon, his former warden at All Souls, and 'being esteemed wealthy, and knowing in secular affairs' (Wood, *Ath Oxon.*, 4.829), Paule was in the autumn of 1663 elected bishop of Oxford. Consecrated at Lambeth on 20 December 1663, he was enthroned by proxy on 7 January 1664. He was permitted to retain *in commendam* both Brightwell Baldwin and the rich rectory of Chinnor, which he had also acquired, because Sheldon hoped that he would use his ample means to rebuild the episcopal palace at Cuddesdon. However, Paule did not live long enough to make an impact, architectural or otherwise, on his diocese. Although in good health when

he drew up his will on 14 November 1664, he died at Chinnor on 24 August 1665; he was buried at Brightwell Baldwin, where a monument was erected.

Paule's will reveals that he had already bought timber: this he left to his successor at Oxford 'toward the building of the episcopall house'. The dean and chapter of Chichester and of Lichfield each received £100, respectively towards the 'building up of the north west end of their cathedrall long since fallen downe' and the 'building up of the steeple', while the poor of Brightwell, Chinnor, and Cuddesdon were also remembered (PRO, PROB 11/319, fols. 201r–202v). Paule's wealth is reflected in the portions totalling £5800 designated for his three daughters Mary, Bridget, and Johanna; his eldest daughter, Judith, who had married Alban Pigott of Marcham, Berkshire, in 1663, is not mentioned (although her husband was a witness and beneficiary), so may already have died. While Paule's younger son, James, was to have £500, the elder, Christopher, was left two manors in Oxfordshire and the profits of a share in customs on wines entering London and other ports. Paule's brothers-in-law John and James Clitherow were made guardians of all the children, and, with his nephew William Paule of London and friend Richard Stevens of Henley, were confirmed in running his business and landed affairs. The will was proved by Rachel Paule, the executor, on 21 February 1666. Christopher Paule, who had matriculated from Trinity College, Oxford, in June 1662, aged sixteen, graduated BA in 1668, and was called to the bar at the Inner Temple the following year. His younger brother James may have become a linen draper in the parish of St Michael Cornhill, London. It seems to have been their cousin William, rather than, as Wood and others assert, another son of the bishop, who as William Paul of Bray, Berkshire, was knighted at Windsor on 6 July 1671.   VIVIENNE LARMINIE

Sources J. L. Chester, ed., *The marriage, baptismal, and burial registers of the collegiate church or abbey of St Peter, Westminster*, Harleian Society, 10 (1876), 131–2 • Foster, *Alum. Oxon.* • Wood, *Ath. Oxon.*, new edn, 4.828–9 • *Walker rev.* • D. Lloyd, *Memoires of the lives … of those … personages that suffered … for the protestant religion* (1668) • PRO, PROB 11/319, fols. 201–3 [will] • W. J. Oldfield, 'Index to the clergy whose ordination, institution, resignation, licence or death is recorded in the diocesan registers of the diocese of Oxford … 1542–1908', 1915, Bodl. Oxf., MS Top. Oxon. c. 250 • N. W. S. Cranfield, 'Chaplains in ordinary at the early Stuart court: the purple road', *Patronage and recruitment in the Tudor and early Stuart church*, ed. C. Cross (1996), 120–47 • *Fasti Angl., 1541–1857*, [Chichester], 48 • *Fasti Angl.* (Hardy), 1.563 • *Fasti Angl., 1541–1857*, [Bristol], 76 • *CSP dom., 1631–3*, 376; *1660–61*, 476; *1661–2*, 171 • *The manuscripts of the Earl Cowper*, 3 vols., HMC, 23 (1888–9), vol. 2, p. 46 • M. A. E. Green, ed., *Calendar of the proceedings of the committee for compounding … 1643–1660*, 5 vols., PRO (1889–92) • *JHL*, 5 (1642–3), 386 • *JHC*, 2 (1640–42), 795 • W. H. Rylands, ed., *The four visitations of Berkshire*, 2, Harleian Society, 57 (1908), 192–3 • J. B. Whitmore and A. W. Hughes Clarke, eds., *London visitation pedigrees, 1664*, Harleian Society, 92 (1940), 43 • *Le Neve's Pedigrees of the knights*, ed. G. W. Marshall, Harleian Society, 8 (1873), 279 • N. Tyacke, *Anti-Calvinists: the rise of English Arminianism, c.1590–1640* (1987)

Wealth at death considerable: will, PRO, PROB 11/319, fols. 201–3

Paulet, Sir Amias (*c.*1457–1538), landowner and soldier, was the only son of Sir William Paulet (*c.*1404–1488) of

Hinton St George and Elizabeth, daughter of John Deneland of Hinton St George. Paulet was brought up to support the Lancastrian cause. He was attainted after Buckingham's rebellion in 1483, and restored in 1485. He was knighted in June 1487 after the battle of Stoke. He was a country gentleman of standing who was one of the greatest landowners in his native county of Somerset. His influence in Somerset was confirmed by his active role in county government, and underpinned by his procurement of important offices in the gift of the crown and by his service to the church. He was married twice: to Margaret, daughter of John Paulet of Basing in Hampshire, and, after 1504, to Laura, daughter of William Keilway of Rockborne, Hampshire. He had four children, all from his second marriage: Sir Hugh *Paulet, who succeeded him, Sir John Paulet, Henry, and a daughter, Elizabeth.

Paulet was given his first formal appointment in local government in 1485 when for the first of three occasions he was appointed sheriff for Somerset and Dorset. The following year he was appointed JP for Somerset and thereafter, until the mid-1510s, he was regularly placed on the Somerset commission of the peace, and was briefly also JP for Devon. In 1497, he was appointed to collect fines from men and women in the west country implicated in the Perkin Warbeck rebellion against Henry VII. In 1493 he secured the highly influential post of steward of the estates of the bishop of Bath and Wells. In 1501 he was chosen as one of the gentlemen to meet Katherine of Aragon at Crewkerne as she travelled from Plymouth on her way to her marriage with Prince Arthur in London. In 1504 he was appointed by the crown as steward of the duchy manors of Stoke-sub-Hamdon and Curry Malet in Somerset. He was initially excluded from the general pardon of April 1509, perhaps as a result of debt to the crown, but was duly pardoned by Henry VIII in August. In 1513 he took part in Henry's campaign against France, commanding twenty-five men. At about this time he was called to the bar and entered the Middle Temple. He was appointed treasurer of the Middle Temple in 1520 and 1521.

From about 1514 Paulet's involvement in the government of his county declined. He was removed from the commission of the peace for Somerset and was not again appointed to a local commission until 1523–4, when he was appointed to collect the subsidy in Somerset and Bath. Perhaps Paulet was now out of favour. George Cavendish, gentleman usher to Thomas Wolsey, notes in his biography of the cardinal that during his first period of office as sheriff Paulet ordered a then young Thomas Wolsey to be placed in the stocks in Lymington, Hampshire, as punishment for disorderly conduct at a local fair. Then, with his career much advanced and in a position of power, Wolsey took his revenge on the Somerset man by accusing Paulet of encouraging heretical teaching in the Middle Temple and by confining him to live in London for five or six years. Cavendish continues that it was only by placing Wolsey's badges prominently over the door of a new gateway built in the Middle Temple that Paulet sufficiently appeased the king's minister to be allowed to return home.

Paulet died on 1 April 1538 at Hinton St George, and was buried there.

Sir John Paulet (1453/4–1525), soldier, was the brother-in-law of Amias Paulet. He was possibly the son of John Paulet of Nunney, Somerset, and Eleanor, daughter of Robert Roos of Gedney and Irton, Lincolnshire. He married Alice, daughter of Sir William Paulet of Hinton St George, and sister of Sir Amias Paulet. William *Paulet, first marquess of Winchester, was John's son. John Paulet was a commander at the battle of Blackheath in 1497 and was made KB at the marriage of Prince Arthur to Katherine of Aragon in November 1501. He died on 5 January 1525. D. J. ASHTON

Sources G. Cavendish, *The life of Thomas Wolsey* (1893) · *CPR, 1485–1509* · *The Middle Temple: its history and associations* (1879) · C. G. Winn, *The Pouletts of Hinton St George* (1976) · A. R. Ingpen, *The Middle Temple bench book* (1912) · PRO, PROB 11/27, sig. 18r · F. W. Weaver, ed., *Somerset medieval wills*, 2–3; Somerset RS, 19, 21 (1903–5) · *Calendar of the manuscripts of the dean and chapter of Wells*, 2, HMC, 12 (1914) · *The registers of Robert Stillington, bishop of Bath and Wells, 1466–1491, and Richard Fox, bishop of Bath and Wells, 1492–1494*, ed. H. C. Maxwell-Lyte, Somerset RS, 52 (1937) · J. Collinson, *The history and antiquities of the county of Somerset*, 3 vols. (1791) · *LP Henry VIII*, vols. 1–5 · *The itinerary of John Leland in or about the years 1535–1543*, ed. L. Toulmin Smith, 5 vols. (1906–10); repr. with introduction by T. Kendrick (1964) · D. A. Luckett, 'Crown patronage and local administration in Berkshire, Dorset, Hampshire, Oxfordshire, Somerset and Wiltshire, 1485–1509', DPhil diss., U. Oxf., 1992 · D. J. Ashton, 'The Tudor state and the politics of the county: the greater gentry of Somerset, c.1509–c.1558', DPhil diss., U. Oxf., 1998 · W. Phelips, *The history and antiquities of Somersetshire*, 4 vols. (1836) · PRO, C 142/61/14 · *DNB*

Archives Som. ARS, DD/PT Poulett MSS, family MSS

Likenesses tomb effigy, St George's Church, Hinton St George, Somerset

Paulet, Sir Amias (c.1532–1588), administrator and landowner, was the eldest of three sons and two daughters of Sir Hugh *Paulet (b. before 1510, d. 1573), administrator and landowner, of Hinton St George, Somerset, and his first wife, Philippa (d. in or before 1560), daughter and heir of Sir Lewis Pollard of King's Nympton, Devon, and his wife, Agnes. The Paulet family was one of the oldest and wealthiest in the county. Little is known about Paulet's education, but he married well about 1557: his wife was Margaret (c.1536–1593), daughter and heir of Anthony Harvey of St Columb St John, Devon, with whom he had six children.

For fifteen years, from 1556 to 1571, Paulet deputized for his father as lieutenant-governor of Jersey, residing there almost continuously, except in 1567. He became joint governor with Sir Hugh in 1571 and then sole governor in 1572. His sojourn in Jersey offered exceptional opportunities for administrative and diplomatic experience at a young age. Following his father-in-law's death in 1564, Paulet succeeded to his wife's inheritance and in 1569 became JP for Devon. In 1571 he was elected MP for the only time for Somerset. He succeeded on his father's death in 1573 to most of the family estates in Somerset (though his stepmother survived until 1593), which enhanced his local consequence further. He was appointed JP for Somerset in 1573 and *custos rotulorum* in 1575, the year when he was knighted. While remaining governor of Jersey, increasingly he delegated his responsibilities to his brother George Paulet, bailiff of Jersey from 1583, and his son Anthony Paulet.

The governor of Jersey ruled a predominantly French-speaking population and defended it, principally against France, which at this time was undergoing wars of religion. As an outsider, Paulet had little sympathy for the islanders' aspirations and frequently clashed with their leader Sir Philip Carteret; he was, however, less rigorous and autocratic than his subsequent deputies, whose excesses he vainly sought to moderate. As a stern and committed protestant, he regarded it as his duty to repress Catholicism and to advance protestantism, which was already well-established there. In 1562 he appointed to the town church in St Helier Guillaume Morise, seigneur de la Ripandière, who instituted elders, deacons, a consistory, and, with Elizabeth I's approval, the Huguenot rite. Paulet attended the first communion celebration and subsequently, despite the queen's express prohibition, allowed French rites to be extended everywhere. Naturally sympathetic to the Huguenot cause in France, he received and harboured exiles despite the risk, which his father feared, of provoking French intervention.

The governorship was thus an appropriate apprenticeship to be resident ambassador in France. Paulet was appointed in succession to Dr Valentine Dale in September 1576. One of the main reasons for his posting was his fluency in French. He served for three years. It was a difficult position: French affairs, he complained towards the end, 'are so fickle and uncertain that nothing comes sooner to pass than what was least expected' (Read, *Walsingham*, 2.12). His embassy can be studied in depth both through his letter-books, which survive from May 1577 to August 1578, and through numerous lengthy dispatches. He sympathized with the Huguenots and distrusted Henri III and Catherine de' Medici, whom he suspected of making a secret alliance with the Spanish. He also distrusted François, duc d'Alençon, and his lack of enthusiasm for marriage between Elizabeth and the former was widely known in 1579. He had little to do with the negotiations, which were primarily conducted in England. Paulet strove to thwart the agents of Mary, queen of Scots. He was not content in Paris, where his eldest son, Hugh, was killed in 1579, a daughter died, and he started suffering from gallstones. He repeatedly begged to be recalled; yet he was able to live within his income, finding the cost of living lower than in England, and he made his reputation. He associated with the protestant élite. His secretary, Richard Lloyd, was a servant of Robert Dudley, earl of Leicester, and he impressed Sir Francis Walsingham, principal secretary, William Cecil, Lord Burghley, and the queen. It was rumoured in the early 1580s that he might be promoted to the privy council, but this did not happen owing to his absence in Jersey and his ill health. However, Elizabeth was uncharacteristically generous towards him. He received forty-year leases in 1582 on twenty-one properties in thirteen counties, in return for remission of £969 due for his father's fortifications at Jersey.

Paulet's nomination in January 1585 to be the next keeper of Mary, queen of Scots, was backed by Walsingham, Burghley, and the queen. He replaced Sir Ralph Sadler, who was considered too conciliatory towards Mary, the first choice, John St John, Baron St John of Bletso, having declined the appointment. His French was undoubtedly a consideration too. Paulet was required to be much tougher. Not surprisingly, Mary herself objected: he was not of sufficient rank and had acted against her interests when in Paris. Elizabeth replied that, if not a nobleman, he was of noble birth and that as ambassador he had done his duty. Thomas Morgan, Mary's French agent, penned a more balanced assessment:

> He is a gentleman of an honourable family, a Puritan in religion and very ambitious … He is courteous and I hope will know his duty to your majesty. But he will be very curious and watchful about your majesty and your people. (*CSP Spain*, 1584–5, 606)

Paulet's ambition, he suggested, might be exploited by promises about the governorship or even independent sovereignty of Jersey, proposals which Paulet firmly rebuffed. His ambition was satisfied by his appointment to the privy council about mid-1585. He was careful to send Burghley duplicates of all his dispatches to Walsingham. His instructions evidently required him to inspect all Mary's correspondence, to confine her more strictly, and to deny her some of the trappings of a royal court. He was further qualified for the post by his substantial wealth.

Paulet took up office on 17 April 1585, first at Tutbury Castle, then from December at Chartley, both in Staffordshire, and latterly, from September 1586, at Fotheringhay Castle, Northamptonshire, for her trial. Details of his custody are illuminated by his many letters. As a firm protestant and loyal subject, he had little sympathy for Elizabeth's Catholic rival who frequently bested him in debate and whom, he once revealed, he would kill rather than permit to escape. While always courteous, he was firm and unyielding to Mary's frequent complaints. His office was expensive to him. He had to maintain two households numbering a total of 127 and his salary and diet were invariably in arrears. He took great pains to keep her secure, to stop any secret correspondence, and to read all her incoming and outgoing letters. That done, Mary was allowed to establish communication with the plotter Anthony Babington, which both parties thought secret but which was perfectly well-known to Paulet and the government. Mary was allowed to move elsewhere temporarily in August 1586, thus enabling him to search her rooms for evidence for her trial. This took place at Fotheringhay in September, Paulet himself being a commissioner. Still her gaoler (from November with Sir Drew Drury), he treated her with less consideration and pressed repeatedly for her execution, which was delayed by Elizabeth's exasperating reluctance to sign Mary's death warrant. William Davison, principal secretary, suggested on 1 February 1587 that Paulet could safely circumvent this difficulty by murdering Mary privately, 'an act which God and the law forbiddeth' and which Paulet firmly declined. 'My goods and life are at her Majesty's disposition', he wrote, 'but God forbid I should make so foul a shipwreck of my conscience, or leave so great a blot on my poor posterity' (HoP, *Commons, 1558–1603*, 3.188). Elizabeth eventually signed the warrant and Paulet's employment ended with Mary's execution at Fotheringhay on 8 February. He was appointed to the prestigious office of chancellor of the Order of the Garter in reward.

This was Paulet's greatest service to Elizabeth and should have led directly to further advancement. Indeed she was highly satisfied with his performance of a difficult assignment. The moment he was free again, he was one of four commissioners on a mission to the states general of the United Provinces. He was Leicester's candidate for the chancellorship of the duchy of Lancaster, to which however Burghley secured Walsingham's appointment. He was appointed to the commission to treat with Alessandro Farnese, duke of Parma, in November 1587, despite objections concerning the inclusion of Mary's gaoler. However, he did not leave with the other commissioners early in 1588, presumably owing to ill health. He was also one of the greater gentry listed by Burghley in early 1588 as eligible for a peerage, which his grandson actually attained.

Although at most in his mid-fifties, Paulet was ailing. Probably he retired at first to Somerset, but was back in London by 4 January 1588, the date of his only recorded attendance at the privy council. It was also the date of his last will, in which he named his son Anthony Paulet as sole executor and as overseers his friends John Coles and Sir John Popham, attorney-general. His testamentary dispositions suggest extreme affluence; he held fourteen manors in Somerset and four in Devon. He provided for his widow, his sons Anthony and George, and his remaining unmarried daughter, Sarah, not yet fifteen years old or betrothed, whose portion he set at the substantial sum of £2000. He was 'very weak in body' when he added a brief oral codicil at London on 26 September 1588, the date of his death. Initially buried in the church of St Martin-in-the-Fields, Westminster, his body and monument were removed when it was rebuilt in the eighteenth century to the Powlett chapel at Hinton St George.

MICHAEL HICKS

Sources DNB · GEC, *Peerage* · HoP, *Commons, 1558–1603* · *The letter-books of Sir Amias Poulet*, ed. J. Morris (1874) · *Copy-book of Sir Amias Poulet's letters*, ed. O. Ogle, Roxburghe Club, 86 (1866) · G. R. Balleine, *A biographical dictionary of Jersey*, [1] [1948] · A. Fraser, *Mary, queen of Scots* (1969) · P. Falle, *Caesarea, or, An account of Jersey, the greatest of the islands remaining to the crown of England of the ancient Dutchy of Normandy*, 2nd edn (1734) · A. C. Sarre, 'The Paulet family, governors of Jersey, 1550–1600', *Annual Bulletin* [Société Jersiaise], 12/2 (1948), 141–52 · C. Read, *Mr Secretary Walsingham and the policy of Queen Elizabeth*, 3 vols. (1925) · C. Read, *Mr Secretary Cecil and Queen Elizabeth* (1955) · CPR, 1563–6 · will, PRO, PROB 11/23, sig. 27 · C. Read, *Lord Burghley and Queen Elizabeth* (1960)
Archives Bodl. Oxf., letter-books, MS Rawl. A. 331, Add. MSS c81–2 | BL, Cotton MSS, instructions and corresp. as ambassador in France
Likenesses G. P. Harding, double portrait, watercolour drawing (with Garter George; after type, c.1575), NPG · alabaster tomb effigy, St George's Church, Hinton St George, Somerset · engraving (after portrait), Société Jersiaise Museum, Jersey; repro. in A. C. Saunders, *Jersey in the 15th and 16th centuries* (1933)

Paulet [Powlett], **Charles**, first duke of Bolton (1630/31–1699), politician, was the eldest son of John *Paulet, fifth marquess of Winchester (1598?–1675), and his first wife, Jane (d. 1631), eldest daughter of Thomas, first Viscount Savage. Styled Lord St John he was brought up as a protestant despite the fact that his father converted to Catholicism and, indeed, the two had a distant and difficult relationship. He was apparently privately educated and travelled abroad to Italy. St John married Christian (1633–1653), eldest daughter and coheir of John, Lord Frescheville of Staveley, on 28 February 1652. She died in childbirth along with their infant son on 22 May 1653. On 12 February 1655 St John married Mary (d. 1680), widow of Henry Carey, styled Lord Leppington, and illegitimate daughter of Emmanuel Scrope, earl of Sunderland, and heir to his sizeable Yorkshire estates. Two sons, William and Charles *Paulet, and three daughters were born to this marriage.

A cautious young man St John steered clear of serious involvement in the political machinations of the interregnum, although he was briefly imprisoned in 1655 as a suspected cavalier activist presumably because of his father's staunch royalism. He subsequently represented Winchester in the Convention Parliament of 1660 and Hampshire in the Cavalier Parliament of 1661. He also served as lord lieutenant of the county from 1667 to 1676, warden of the New Forest from 1668 to 1676, and *custos rotulorum* from 1670 to 1676. Despite these and other appointments reflecting the prominence of the family St John did not cut a distinguished figure in the Commons. Like many new members he began the reign of Charles II as a supporter of the court, in principle if not in every particular, but by the early 1670s he had gravitated into the ranks of the opposition. Eventually he became a sufficient irritant on the political landscape to warrant removal from many of the positions he held at royal pleasure, but nevertheless remained steady in his support of the nascent whig party when he moved to the upper chamber as the sixth marquess of Winchester upon the death of his father in 1675. There he participated in the investigation of the Popish Plot as a member of the joint parliamentary committee on examinations; advocated impeachment of the earl of Danby; and exercised the considerable influence which his territorial and mining interests gave him in Hampshire, Yorkshire, and Cornwall to secure the return of whig candidates in 1679 to what became the first Exclusion Parliament.

On 22 April 1679 Winchester was one of several moderate whigs named to the privy council when it was reconstituted in an attempt to bridge the gap between the court and a hostile majority in the Commons. It was a scheme that failed, but the curious fact is that he retained his position on the council throughout the remainder of his life, bridging the reigns of Charles II, James II, and William and Mary. A man for whom self-interest seems to have become the guiding principle he accomplished this feat of survival by withdrawing almost immediately from active participation in the political arena. There is no evidence that he played any part in either the second or third Exclusion

Parliaments and, indeed, an entry for 30 October 1680 in the *Lords Journals* notes that he had gone abroad. A few years later Winchester again came to notice because of his support for court approved candidates in the election to the first and only parliament of James II's reign, although he himself subsequently attended neither session. By early 1688, however, he had entered into active correspondence with William of Orange, and later that spring his son Charles, Lord Wiltshire, went over to the Netherlands and joined William's service. Whether Wiltshire was acting independently or in concert with his father is unclear, and whether Winchester himself was at all involved in the preparations for the possibility of a northern descent on London given his base of influence in Yorkshire is unknown. The most that can be said with certainty is that he was one of the peers working in the prince of Orange's interest during the Convention Parliament of 1689.

Winchester was created duke of Bolton two days before William and Mary's coronation in 1689, and was restored as both lord lieutenant and *custos rotulorum* of Hampshire and as warden of the New Forest, positions he retained until his death. In the same year he was also appointed colonel of two regiments of foot, one of which was dispatched to the West Indies in October of that year and whose command was transferred to a military professional in 1692, and the other of which saw service in Ireland in 1690 but then remained based in England until being disbanded in 1698. During the Convention Parliament Bolton supported the whig agenda on issues ranging from comprehension to the Corporations Bill. The only time he took the lead in sponsoring legislation in the postrevolutionary period was in 1690 when he promoted a bill of recognition calling for confirmation of the acts of the Convention Parliament as *de jure* rather than *de facto*. It was a difficult pill for some tories to swallow, but the earl of Danby's flexibility on the point finally allowed passage of a measure some thought 'as to niceness, exceed[ed] the philosophicall distinctions of the schollmen' (Thompson, 2.146–7). For the remainder of the decade Bolton, generally classed a court whig, was invisible except when matters arose that touched on his personal interest.

Bolton was somewhat of an eccentric, given the sobriquet the Mad Marquess of Winchester by some chroniclers of the period. As Bishop Burnet recalled:

> He had the spleen to a high degree, and affected an extravagant behaviour. For many weeks he would take a conceit not to speak one word, and at other times he would not open his mouth till such an hour of the day when he thought the air was pure. He changed the day into night and often hunted by torchlight, and took all sorts of liberties to himself, many of which were very disagreeable to those about him. (Helms and Watson, 3.278)

Bolton, however, attempted to explain away his strange lifestyle as no more than a protective cover adopted to stay out of harm's way during dangerous times. Burnet conceded that the duke was a 'very knowing and a very crafty, politic man' (ibid.), judging him overall a 'strange mixture' (ibid.), 'in all respects the great riddle of the age'

(ibid.). Bolton died suddenly at Amport House, his Hampshire residence, on 27 February 1699, aged sixty-eight, and was buried at Basing on 23 March. He was predeceased by his wife and three of their children. His eldest surviving son, Charles, succeeded him as second duke, and his daughter Elizabeth (*d.* 1716) married John Egerton, fourth earl of Bridgewater.   DAVID HOSFORD

Sources *Bishop Burnet's History of his own time*, new edn, 2 vols. (1838) · J. Dalrymple, *Memoirs of Great Britain and Ireland*, 2 (1778) · N. Luttrell, *A brief historical relation of state affairs from September 1678 to April 1714*, 1–4 (1857) · *JHL*, 12–16 (1666–1701) · *CSP dom.*, 1689–1700 · J. E. Thorold Rogers, ed., *A complete collection of the protests of the Lords*, 1 (1875) · *Memoirs of Sir John Reresby*, ed. A. Browning (1936) · A. Browning, *Thomas Osborne, earl of Danby and duke of Leeds, 1632–1712*, 3 vols. (1944–51) · J. R. Jones, *Country and court* (1978) · R. H. George, 'Parliamentary elections and electioneering in 1685', *TRHS*, 4th ser., 19 (1936), 167–95 · S. Hall, *BIHR*, 19 (1941–3) · E. M. Thompson, ed., *Correspondence of the family of Hatton*, 2 vols., CS, new ser., 22–3 (1878) · *DNB* · GEC, *Peerage* · M. W. Helms and P. Watson, 'Powlett (Paulet), Charles', *HoP, Commons, 1660–90*, 3.276–9 · B. B. Woodward, *A general history of Hampshire*, 3 vols. (1861–9)
Archives Hants. RO, memoranda book and papers · N. Yorks. CRO, corresp. and papers | Bodl. Oxf., letters to officers of the ordnance and Sir Henry Goodricke · Hunt. L., letters mainly to Lord Bridgewater · N. Yorks. CRO, letters to Sir W. Chaytor · NRA, priv. coll., letters to Sir Robert Atkyns
Likenesses R. White, line engraving, 1679, BM, NPG; repro. in J. Guillim, *A display of heraldry* (1679)

Paulet [Powlett], **Charles**, **second duke of Bolton** (*c.*1661–1722), politician, was born about 1661, the second and eldest surviving son of Charles *Paulet, first duke of Bolton (1630/31–1699), and his second wife, Mary (*d.* 1680), the widow of Henry Carey, Lord Leppington, and the illegitimate daughter of and heir to the Yorkshire estates of Emmanuel Scrope, earl of Sunderland. He entered Gray's Inn on 10 March 1674 and was enrolled at Winchester College in 1675, but spent the next few years travelling in France. In 1675, following his father's accession to the marquessate of Winchester, he became known as earl of Wiltshire. On 10 July 1679 he married Margaret Coventry (1657–1682), the daughter of George, third Baron Coventry, at St Giles-in-the-Fields, London. Following her death, without children, he married Frances Ramsden (*d.* 1696), the daughter of William Ramsden of Byrom, Yorkshire, on 8 February 1683 at Duke Place, St James's, London. The couple had two sons and two daughters.

Wiltshire was elected to parliament in 1681 as member for Hampshire and represented the county until 1698. He supported the exclusion of the duke of York from the succession, and opposed his policies as James II. In April 1688 Wiltshire travelled to the Netherlands accompanied by his brother Lord William Paulet. He returned with William, prince of Orange, and was one of the advance guard who entered Exeter with the prince in November 1688. He spoke several times in parliament in favour of William's invasion and proposed the motion that William and Mary assume the crown. Shortly before the coronation his father was created duke of Bolton; Wiltshire then became known as marquess of Winchester. He was the bearer of the orb at the coronation on 11 April 1689 and held the office of lord chamberlain to the queen from 1689 to 1694.

During this period he was also sworn a privy councillor (3 June 1690), and during summer 1691 he fought with the campaign in Flanders as a volunteer. In the Commons, Winchester was a supporter of the government and occasionally acted on its behalf. In November 1692 he proposed the motion for a committee of the whole house to vote a supply to allow William III to continue the war. He was rewarded for his service with the profits of a prize ship in November 1693, and with some forfeited estates in Staffordshire in April 1694. Following the death of Mary II in December 1694, he organized her funeral, and he retained the £1200 per annum pension he had enjoyed as her lord chamberlain. In the parliament elected in 1695, he was one of the first to sign the Association following the discovery of the Assassination plot.

Winchester, a follower of the junto whigs, was anxious to gain office and was appointed a lord justice of Ireland in April 1697 on the recommendation of Sir John Somers, despite the reservations of William III. He promised to allow his colleagues, Henri de Massue de Ruvigny, earl of Galway, and Edward Villiers, Viscount Villiers, to take the lead in affairs, but drifted into alliance with the administration's opponents. In August 1697 it was rumoured he had married Henrietta Crofts (d. 1730), the illegitimate daughter of James *Scott, duke of Monmouth, and Eleanor Needham, a match opposed by the duke of Bolton; Winchester admitted the fact of the matter in October. The duke forgave Winchester at the king's insistence, but relations between father and son were already strained (Bolton's will, written in 1694, made barely any provision for Winchester) and during the election campaign of 1698 the duke lost faith in his son's candidacy for Hampshire, with the result that he was not returned to the Commons. Winchester succeeded his father as duke of Bolton on 27 February 1699, but remained a lord justice of Ireland until 1700, when a lord lieutenant was appointed; he had, unrealistically, hoped to gain the post himself.

Bolton became lord lieutenant of Hampshire and Dorset and warden of the New Forest following his father's death. He entertained William on more than one occasion at the family house, Winton, and despite his incompetence as a lord justice in Ireland, seems to have been on good terms with the king. His dislike for Princess Anne was intensified by jealousy of John Churchill, earl of Marlborough, and he is said to have conspired with John Holles, duke of Newcastle, with the intention of passing over Anne in the interests of Sophia, dowager electress of Hanover. He retained his offices under Anne, but continued to support his old junto friends while avoiding offending the queen and her ministers. In April 1705 he waited on the queen at Cambridge and was made doctor of laws by the university. In the following September he entertained Anne and her husband, Prince George of Denmark, with great pomp at Winton.

In 1706 Bolton was appointed a commissioner to negotiate the union between England and Scotland, and he was also a member of the special committee selected by the commissioners in May 1706. In February 1707 he was appointed governor of the Isle of Wight, a mark of the administration's increasingly whig complexion. Much annoyed by the elevation of John Campbell, second duke of Argyll, to the Order of the Garter, he was pacified by Marlborough, with whom he had gradually become reconciled, and continued his support for the war party. Following the formation of Harley's administration, in September 1710 he lost his governorship of the Isle of Wight, his lord lieutenancy, and the wardenship of the New Forest, as well as the vice-admiralship of Hampshire and Dorset, which last post he had held since 1692. In June 1710 he took what was generally considered to be the unwise step of requesting the House of Lords to examine the status of their privileges in the light of recent royal action. In April 1714 he again attracted attention in the Lords by seconding the motion putting a price upon the head of James Stuart, the Old Pretender; a few weeks afterwards he signed the protest against the Schism Act.

After the proclamation of George I in 1714 Bolton was named one of the lords justices. The king restored him to the lord lieutenancy of Dorset and Hampshire and the wardenship of the New Forest, and he was installed KG on 8 December 1714. His return to favour was marked by his wife's place as lady of the bedchamber to the princess of Wales and his own appointment as lord chamberlain (8 July 1715) and lord lieutenant of Ireland (16 April 1717). He was at Dublin for the opening of the Irish parliament on 1 July 1719, and is said to have made an excellent speech; he gave up the office in November of that year.

Contemporaries appear as to have regarded Bolton as incapable of undertaking serious political business. He is apparently one of the objects of Dr Joseph Brown's satire in *Country Parsons Advice to the Lord Keeper* (1706); Lady Cowper, in her diary, described him as generally to be seen with his tongue lolling out of his mouth; while Swift, in a note on Macky's character, believed that Bolton did not make a figure 'at court or anywhere else. A great booby' (*Prose Works of Jonathan Swift*, 5.258). It is debatable, however, whether Swift knew much of him; in the *Journal to Stella* he seems to confuse him with his brother Lord William.

Bolton died on 21 January 1722 at his house in Dover Street, London, and was buried on 1 February at Basing, Hampshire. The title passed in turn to his two sons from his second marriage, Charles *Powlett or Paulet and Harry. He was also survived by his third wife, who died on 27 February 1730, and his son from this marriage, Lord Nassau Powlett, MP for the borough of Lymington (1714–34), auditor-general of Ireland (9 Oct 1723), KB (May 1725), who died on 24 August 1741.   MATTHEW KILBURN

Sources P. Watson, 'Powlett, Charles I', HoP, *Commons, 1690–1715* · GEC, *Peerage*, new edn · M. W. Helms and P. Watson, 'Powlett (Paulet), Charles I', HoP, *Commons, 1660–90* · *Diary of Mary, Countess Cowper*, ed. [S. Cowper] (1864) · J. Swift, *Journal to Stella*, ed. H. Williams, 2 vols. (1948) · *The prose works of Jonathan Swift*, ed. H. Davis, 5: *Miscellaneous and autobiographical pieces, fragments, and marginalia* (1962) [258] · DNB · P. Watson, 'Powlett, Charles I', HoP, *Commons, 1690–1715*
Archives Hants. RO · Hunt. L. · N. Yorks. CRO · PRO NIre. · TCD
Wealth at death Bolton Abbey estate, North Yorkshire; interests in Hampshire: GEC

Paulet, Charles. *See* Powlett, Charles, third duke of Bolton (1685–1754).

Paulet, Sir George (1553–1608), administrator, was the son of Sir George Paulet (*d.* 1558) of Crondall, Hampshire, brother of the first marquess of Winchester, and his third wife, Elizabeth, daughter of William Windsor, second Baron Windsor. He was educated at Eton College, in 1564–72, and at King's College, Cambridge, 1572–5. He married, before 1586, Joan (*d.* in or after 1610), daughter and coheir of Richard Kyme of Lewes, Sussex, and had one son and one daughter. He appears to have been the person of that name who was MP for Bridport in 1589. He was a justice of the peace for Hampshire between 1593 and 1601, co-colonel of the musters there in 1600 (and may have gained some further military experience), and was one of a number of Hampshiremen to focus attention on Ireland where he acquired property at Derry in 1606.

The importance of Derry from an English perspective was that it had been garrisoned in 1600 under Sir Henry Docwra, in a crucial stage in the Nine Years' War. Docwra also secured possession, with the end of war in 1603, of an area of contiguous land of former ecclesiastical character, which supported a small settler town then becoming established there and itself something entirely new to Gaelic west Ulster. In July 1604 he procured this town's incorporation, begun 'by his valour, industry and charge' (Erck, 114), with himself its first provost and Sir Cahir O'Doherty of Inishowen one of its aldermen. But with the post-war settlement of Ulster, which favoured the earl of Tyrone at the expense of Donnell O'Cahan, making him unpopular and perhaps even putting his settlement's future in doubt, and with army reductions too, Docwra, who had sought a reward of a larger grant of forfeited land, had left Derry by 1606. Gaining no special munificence from the earl of Devonshire (the former Lord Deputy Mountjoy) in London early that year, and having told the earl that he had made contact with Paulet, 'a gentleman of Hampshire' whom Devonshire knew, with a view to selling Paulet his property, Docwra was not dissuaded by Devonshire, who asserted that 'there was no longer use for a man of war in that place' (Docwra, 282). In mid-July Lord Deputy Chichester, expecting Docwra not to return, hoped none the less that the Derry settlement, already 'declining', would be 'cherished and countenanced' in its 'infancy' (*CSP Ire.*, 1603–6, 524). Docwra's sale of his house and lands there to Paulet and his wife had in fact been formalized on 30 May, and on 23 July Paulet, commended as 'of good sufficiency and of service in the wars' (ibid., 529), was given royal instructions to Chichester and the Irish chancellor setting out the agreement: he should be governor of Derry, receive Docwra's foot company, and be allowed a patent of the purchased lands.

In Dublin in October 1606, and paid as captain of 50 foot from 1 July, Paulet arrived in Derry late in 1606, but his career there was to be a short one, terminated by O'Doherty's rising in 1608. By February 1607, when incidents had arisen in Donegal, Chichester thought him an ill exchange for Docwra there: he was not fit for the command and dissensions were taking place also. By March, one of these had surfaced in a complaint against him, probably about episcopal property at Derry and, if so, a long-recurrent issue, from the newly arrived Church of Ireland bishop, George Montgomery. After the flight of the earls in September, open mistrust arose between Paulet and Sir Cahir O'Doherty, whose movements he monitored with a suspicion apparently misjudged. However, when O'Doherty embarked on what he said was a tree-felling operation in Kilmacrenan late in October, Sir Richard Hansard of Lifford stated on 1 November that O'Doherty had in fact placed armed men on Tory Island, as a move in expectation of a rumoured new army from Spain. Paulet then on 4 November sought to take O'Doherty's Burt Castle, O'Doherty having withdrawn to Carrickbracky, and accused him by letter of plotting treason. O'Doherty appealed to Chichester in Dublin for vindication, who, when he went there, procured a recognizance (2 December) to contain him—he should not leave the realm and should appear before the lord deputy when summoned—but allowed him to return. Paulet, knighted on 26 June 1607, was given a small sum by concordatum to strengthen the Derry Fort.

O'Doherty's eventual rising, which gained additional supporters, is commonly interpreted in personal terms as revenge against Paulet for ongoing ill feeling. To the Irish annalists, indeed, it was precipitated by a recent incident between Paulet and himself. O'Doherty may, however, also have expected that, once overthrown, the fort and settlement would not be restored, though the possibility that he saw his actions—coinciding as they did with the assemblage of a Spanish fleet the purpose of which was causing speculation—as the necessary stimulus to the return of Hugh O'Neill is much less certain. On the night of 18–19 April 1608 he seized the outpost fort at Culmore and surprised Derry before daybreak. Paulet was killed in the attack, and the infant settlement sacked and burnt. Administration of Paulet's estate was granted to his widow in London on 27 August. The revolt, furthermore, was quickly suppressed, giving incentive to plans for plantation on the lands of the departed earls, now extended to take in O'Doherty's country. Derry and its environs became part of the land granted to the City of London, Paulet's widow being awarded £1400 on 25 May 1610 for surrendering the lands acquired in 1606, and it built a town there—Londonderry—of much greater substance. The deceased Paulet came in for much criticism, but a pamphlet published in London later in 1608 placed O'Doherty's rising in series, here with overtones of Catholicism, as one of many rebellions, in England, Ireland, and elsewhere, against the duty of obedience, and so Paulet got a memorial in print. **R. J. HUNTER**

Sources H. Docwra, 'A narration of the services done by the army imployed to Lough-Foyle', *Miscellany of the Celtic Society*, ed. J. O'Donovan (1849), 233–86 · *CSP Ire.*, 1603–10 · J. C. Erck, ed., *A repertory of the inrolments on the patent rolls of chancery in Ireland, commencing with the reign of James I*, 1/1 (1846), 114–16 · *Newes from Lough-Foyle* *in Ireland* (1608) • HoP, *Commons, 1558–1603* • J. S. Brewer and W. Bullen, eds., *Calendar of the Carew manuscripts*, 5: *1603–1623*, PRO (1871), 384 • T. W. Moody and J. G. Simms, eds., *The bishopric of Derry and the Irish Society of London, 1602–1705*, 2 vols., IMC (1968–83), vol. 1, pp. 40–42 • F. J. Baigent, *A collection of records and documents relating to the hundred and manor of Crondal in the county of Southampton* (1891), 1.469–76 • *VCH Hampshire and the Isle of Wight*, 4.6–7 • PRO, AO 1/289/1087–/290/1088 • PRO, PROB 6/7, fol. 124 • Hants. RO, MS 44M69/G5/20/82

Wealth at death probably not very wealthy; Derry lands surrendered for £1400, 1610: Moody and Simms, eds., *Bishopric of Derry* • Crondall lands probably not very large, with small rents; military salary in Ireland: *VCH Hampshire*, vol. 4, pp. 6–7

Paulet, Harry. *See* Powlett, Harry, sixth duke of Bolton (1720–1794).

Paulet, Harry (*d.* 1804), supposed seaman and benefactor, details of whose birth and parentage are unknown, is said to have been the master of a small vessel trading to North America before his capture by the French in 1758. Paulet's knowledge of the St Lawrence River made him a valuable prisoner; for this reason he was not exchanged but detained at Quebec and then sent to France. When the ship in which he sailed put into Vigo he was able to obtain a packet of dispatches, carelessly left within his reach, and escape overboard. There were two British men-of-war in the river, and Paulet swam to these and was taken on board. The dispatches proved of great value, and Paulet was sent with a copy of them to Lisbon, and from there to England.

In London, Paulet was examined by the authorities. On the information which he gave and that which was contained in the dispatches, General James Wolfe's expedition against Quebec was organized in 1759. Paulet himself received 'the pay of a lieutenant for life' (*GM*, 74.691). This annuity of £90 a year enabled him, it is said, to purchase a vessel, in which he ran cargoes of brandy from the French coast. On one voyage he fell in with the French fleet which had escaped out of Brest while Admiral Hawke 'lay concealed behind the rocks of Ushant' (ibid.). Paulet ran to find the British fleet, and demanded to speak with the admiral. The fleet then got under way, and Paulet, at his special request, was permitted to stay on board. In the battle which followed he behaved with the utmost gallantry, and was sent home 'rewarded in such a manner as enabled him to live happily the remainder of his life' (ibid.).

Such is Paulet's own story, which in J. K. Laughton's opinion he very probably brought himself, in his old age, to believe. The validity of Paulet's claims are impossible to verify and easy to call into question. As Laughton states, if at the end of 1758 the Admiralty had had a first-rate pilot for the St Lawrence at their disposal, that pilot would have been sent to the St Lawrence, and, if he had been examined either by the Admiralty or the secretary of state, there would be some record of the examination; but there is no such record. Furthermore had Paulet been granted the pay of a lieutenant for life, the amount would be charged somewhere; but it does not appear. In some way or

other Paulet certainly made money, and in his old age he was generous to the poor of his neighbourhood. He is said to have been an admirable narrator of his own adventures or of Hawke's battle. Paulet died, and was buried, in Lambeth in May 1804.

J. K. LAUGHTON, *rev.* RANDOLPH COCK

Sources *GM*, 1st ser., 74 (1804), 691–2

Paulet, Sir Hugh (*b.* before **1510**, *d.* **1573**), soldier and administrator, was the eldest son of Sir Amias *Paulet (*c.*1457–1538), and his second wife, Laura Keilway. Any relationship to the Hampshire Paulets, notably William, ultimately lord treasurer, was extremely distant, and does not seem to have affected his career. He entered the Middle Temple, of which his father was treasurer (1520–21), at an unknown date. He married, about 1530, Philippa, daughter of Sir Lewis Pollard of King's Nympton, Devon.

Paulet was appointed to the Somerset commission of the peace as early as 1532, and in 1534 succeeded his father as steward to the bishop of Bath and Wells, retaining that post until his death, and passing it to his descendants. He was a commissioner for the *valor ecclesiasticus* for Somerset in 1535. He was knighted on 18 July 1536, the day of the dissolution of the short parliament of that year, along with Thomas Cromwell. This has led to the supposition that he was a member of that parliament (and possibly also of the Reformation Parliament in its final phase), but there is no direct evidence. He led 300 men against the Pilgrimage of Grace in 1536. He became sheriff of Somerset and Dorset for 1536–7. This early rise to prominence may be due to the intimacy of his brother-in-law, Richard *Pollard, with Cromwell. Paulet succeeded his father in April 1538, and in November of the same year purchased the manor of Sampford Peverell in Devon from the crown for £1000. He was picked to inspect Somerset's coastal defences in 1539, and probably as a result became a member of the short-lived council of the west in 1539–40. He was also the senior knight of the shire for Somerset in the parliament of 1539–40. He was sheriff of Devon in 1541–2, and of Somerset and Dorset again in 1542–3 and 1547–8. He distinguished himself at the siege of Boulogne by capturing the 'braye', a necessary preliminary to the assault on the castle, on 1 September 1544, and became treasurer of Boulogne for the first two years of the English occupation (October 1544 – October 1546). His administrative duties did not preclude his leading a raid to destroy the nearby small town of Desvres in June 1545.

In 1547, on Henry VIII's death, Paulet was commissioned to put the west country in order against a possible invasion, and also, with Sir John Harington, to survey Calais and Boulogne. From 1547 he was on the Devon commission of the peace. In January 1549 he was sent to take charge of Thomas Seymour's house at Bromham, Wiltshire, when Seymour was accused of treason. He served as knight marshal in Lord Russell's army against the western rebels in the summer of 1549, and with Sir Peter Carew crushed the last remnant of the uprising. Curiously, in spite of the local connection, there seems no evidence that he was ever close to Protector Somerset.

Somerset was governor of Jersey, and on his fall Paulet was sent in November 1549 to investigate the state of the island. He dismissed Somerset's lieutenant Henry Cornish, and reported on the fortifications. No doubt it was the privy council, grateful for his services, that persuaded the bishop of Bath and Wells to grant him a ninety-nine year lease of the manor of Chard on very favourable terms in February 1550. Paulet was appointed governor of Jersey for life on 20 March 1550. As governor he continued the policy initiated by Somerset of using church revenues to modernize the fortifications. He also attempted to enforce the Reformation, and pressed for the translation of the Book of Common Prayer into French. That was not achieved until 1553, too late to take effect before the restoration of Catholicism under Queen Mary. Paulet seems to have adapted without difficulty to the new regime, and indeed appointed his conservative brother John as dean of Jersey in 1554. In contrast to Guernsey, Jersey saw no burning of heretics, although Dean Paulet tried, unsuccessfully, to assert clerical immunities against the secular authorities. Hugh Paulet did not spend all his time in Jersey. He was commissioned to settle the immigrant weavers at Glastonbury in 1551. He was recalled from Jersey urgently in 1556 as 'a man of great experience and credit in the west' on rumours of a possible conspiracy (*CSP dom.*, 1553–8, 473). While in England he advised on the fortifications of Scilly, and stood by for a possible landfall by Charles V on his last voyage from the Netherlands to Spain. Outbreak of war with France sent him urgently back to Jersey in July 1557.

From 1559 Paulet was an absentee governor, and day-to-day responsibility passed to his son Amias *Paulet (c.1532–1588) as lieutenant. Hugh Paulet distrusted the French Calvinists who had taken refuge on the island, whereas Amias sympathized with them and helped them surreptitiously to introduce a presbyterian system of church government. Hugh became, briefly, vice-president of the council of Wales in April 1559 with his usual troubleshooting brief, resulting in far-reaching proposals for reform. In June 1562 he was nominated for a commission to investigate Irish revenues, but a more urgent matter intervened, the ill-fated English occupation of Le Havre. In December 1562 he was sent to join the commander, the earl of Warwick, as his special adviser, in effect, it would seem, to try to prevent looming disaster. But in July 1563 Paulet helped negotiate the surrender, when, as he had forecast, desertion by the queen's Huguenot allies, coupled with an outbreak of plague, made the situation untenable.

Paulet spent his remaining years largely at Hinton St George, Somerset. His first wife, Philippa, died at an unascertained date. He had with her three sons, Amias, George, and Nicholas, and two daughters, Jane (who married Christopher Copplestone), and Anne. About the end of 1560 he married Elizabeth Blount, the rich widow of Sir Thomas Pope, designated after Pope's death as founder of Trinity College, Oxford. There were no children of this marriage. In 1562 Paulet added the Dorset commission of

the peace to those for Somerset and Devon, and was also appointed *custos rotulorum* for the Somerset bench. In 1571 he and Sir Maurice Berkeley were instructed by the privy council to see that suitable MPs were returned for Somerset. He was returned as a member for the county for the parliament of 1572 in which he served on several committees, most notably that on Mary, queen of Scots. He died on 6 December 1573, at Hinton St George, and was buried in the tomb he had already erected for himself and his first wife in the parish church (along with an almost identical tomb for his parents). His will, drawn up five days before his death, was largely concerned with seeing that his widow's marriage settlement was properly carried out, and with disclaiming any liability on his estate for the debts of Sir Thomas Pope or for debts arising from his service in Jersey; he claimed, indeed, to be still £1000 out of pocket over the Jersey fortifications. After his death his widow was to reveal herself a committed Catholic. She died on 27 October 1593 at Tittenhanger in Staffordshire, and was buried with Pope in Trinity College chapel.

C. S. L. DAVIES

Sources LP Henry VIII · CSP dom. · APC · HoP, Commons, 1509–58 · HoP, Commons, 1558–1603 · G. R. Balleine, *A biographical dictionary of Jersey*, [1] [1948] · C. S. L. Davies, 'International politics and the establishment of presbyterianism in the Channel Islands', *Journal of Ecclesiastical History*, 50 (1999), 498–522 · P. Williams, *The council in the marches of Wales under Elizabeth I* (1958) · C. A. H. Franklyn, *A genealogical history of the families of Paulet (or Pawlett), Berewe (or Barrow), Lawrence, and Parker: ... from Ealhmund, born circa 750, great-grandfather of Aelfred the Great through four Plantagenet descents to 1963* (1963) · J. L. Vivian, ed., *The visitations of the county of Devon, comprising the herald's visitations of 1531, 1564, and 1620* (privately printed, Exeter, [1895]) · F. W. Weaver, ed., *The visitations of the county of Somerset* (1885)

Likenesses tomb effigy (with his wife), St George's Church, Hinton St George, Somerset; repro. in *Proceedings of the Somerset Archaeological and Natural History Society*, 72 (1926), 33–4

Paulet, Sir John (1453/4–1525). *See under* Paulet, Sir Amias (c.1457–1538).

Paulet, John, fifth marquess of Winchester (1598?–1675), royalist nobleman, was the third but eldest surviving son of William, the fourth marquess (d. 1629), and Lucy Cecil (1568–1614), second daughter of Sir Thomas Cecil, afterwards second Baron Burghley and first earl of Exeter.

Early career Paulet was probably born at the family seat of Basing House, Hampshire, and nothing is known of his early life except that he was educated at home and then kept terms, without matriculating, at Exeter College, Oxford. He enters national history with his election to the 1621 parliament for the Cornish borough of St Ives, under his courtesy title of Lord St John. He obviously pleased James I, for he was called to the Lords on 10 February 1624, in his father's barony of St John. Charles I also favoured him, appointing him to the captaincy of the royal fort of Netley Castle in 1626 and to the keepership of the royal forest of Pamber when he succeeded to the marquessate on his father's death on 4 February 1629. These offices were both in Hampshire, and reinforced his position as

Iohn Pawlet, Marqueſſe of Wincheſter, Earle of Wiltſhire and Lord St. Iohn of Baſing

John Paulet, fifth marquess of Winchester (1598?–1675), by Wenceslaus Hollar, 1640s

one of the county's wealthiest landowners; but his Catholicism, coupled with the burden of debt inherited from his father, barred him from further employment.

Winchester passed the 1630s quietly at his seat, devoting his time to rebuilding the family fortunes. He had married his first wife, Jane Savage, in December 1622; she was the daughter of another Catholic nobleman, Thomas, first Viscount Savage, and her beauty and goodness won tributes from Milton and from James Howell, who had taught her Spanish. She died of a throat infection in April 1631, having given him his eldest son and heir, Charles *Paulet. In October 1633 he remarried into a grander Catholic house, by wedding Lady Honora De Burgh (b. 19 Aug 1610), daughter of Richard, first earl of Clanricarde and of St Albans. They had four sons, two of whom—John and Francis—survived to adulthood, three daughters, and the pleasures of a mutually affectionate and supportive partnership.

The siege of Basing House The blessings of strong family support were to be needed as the English civil war broke out, finding the Winchesters still living in seclusion at Basing. They took no apparent part in the opening stages of the crisis, and their loyalties only became active in the summer of 1643, a year after the outbreak of hostilities. In March complaints had reached parliament that royalist soldiers had been given shelter and refreshment at Basing House, and in late July the marquess heard that a parliamentarian force was planning to visit, disarm, and plunder it. He attended the king and asked to have soldiers

from the royal army sent to protect the mansion. Charles selected the recently raised foot regiment of the Yorkshireman Marmaduke Rawdon, and dispatched a hundred musketeers of it from Oxford, under the command of Lieutenant-Colonel Robert Peake, with an escort of horse. These arrived in the nick of time on 31 July, as the parliamentarians, led by the local activist Richard Norton, had reached the house and were being resisted by the marquess with just his servants and six gentlemen armed with muskets. The enemy withdrew, and Basing was now fortified with 14½ acres of earthworks, strong enough to resist all but a massive battery. Rawdon became the governor with Peake as his lieutenant.

This transformed Winchester's seat into the principal royalist fortress of northern Hampshire, covering the roads between London and the west country and thus of vital strategic importance. It was accordingly attacked as soon as parliament could bring a regional army to bear upon it, that of Sir William Waller, which assaulted it repeatedly between 6 and 13 November 1643. The garrison now numbered about four hundred; the marchioness and her ladies cast fresh shot for them out of lead stripped from the mansion, and the defences held out. By April 1644 the motto 'Love loyalty' was engraved on every window pane. It was tested in that month when Winchester's younger brother was discovered to be plotting to betray the house; he was turned out of it after being forced to hang his accomplices. The coming of summer made a sustained siege viable, and Norton opened one with the local parliamentarian forces on 11 June. It relied upon starvation, reinforced by desultory bombardment, but was broken by a relief force from Oxford on 11 September. Norton renewed it, only giving up when a detachment of the royal army approached on 20 November. The Winchesters had survived unharmed although a cannon-ball had once passed through the marquess's chamber while he lay in bed.

The garrison was now at peace, and in May 1645, at Winchester's insistence, was turned into a wholly Catholic body. Rawdon was removed to other commands, and Peake took over a force reduced to three hundred. On 23 August it was again besieged by local forces, this time under a Dutch professional, Colonel Dalbier. He slowly weakened the defences with bombardment until 8 October, when Oliver Cromwell arrived with an exceptionally powerful train of siege guns and reinforcements which brought the besieging army to about seven thousand. The odds were now too great; Cromwell's guns blew several breaches in the outworks and walls, which were stormed before dawn on 14 October. Religious rancour gave the action a brutality unusual in this war, and between one and two hundred of the defenders were slaughtered. Winchester himself was taken unhurt, together with his most distinguished guests: Peake, the artist Wenceslaus Hollar, and the architect Inigo Jones. They were, however, stripped of their clothes by the soldiers, and the house was accidentally set on fire after it had been looted bare. The victors estimated the total value of the plunder at £200,000.

Defeat and Restoration On 15 October 1645 the House of Commons resolved that the ruins of Basing House should be demolished, and on 20 October the Lords concurred with a further resolution that the marquess of Winchester be committed to the Tower of London and his lands confiscated. The marchioness had been at the royal court at Oxford since early 1644, and was allowed to go to London to assist him, at his request, in January 1646. On 15 January the Commons allowed him a pittance from his estates, as he had now no means of income at all and was nearing starvation. On 31 January some of his lands were granted to Cromwell; £15 per week was allowed from the residue to support the marchioness and the children, on condition that the latter were educated as protestants. The sale of the rest of the estate was ordered on 25 September, although the process was still not complete by 1660.

The marquess of Winchester apparently remained in the Tower until 7 September 1647, when he had become so ill that both houses allowed him to settle at Epsom and take the waters there. He was taken back into custody in the following spring, with the approach of the second civil war, and the Lords urged the Commons to allow him bail upon 30 June 1648, as he was again in serious bad health. The request seems to have been rejected, and in the propositions sent by both houses to the captive king on 13 October, Winchester was one of the royalists excepted from pardon. On 14 March 1649 the newly established republican House of Commons considered trying him for his life in the wake of the execution of the king and other royalist peers, and magnanimously decided to leave him in prison. This sustained animosity on the part of the MPs, especially marked in view of his utter lack of activism since 1645, may be ascribed primarily to his religion.

He was eventually released at some point in the early 1650s and retired to an estate at Englefield, Berkshire, which had been part of his wife's marriage portion. While in captivity he had commenced the translation of French works, mostly devotional, to which he added pious introductions: Jacques Hugues Quarre's *Devout Entertainment of a Christian Soul* (1648), Pierre Le Moyne's *Gallery of Heroic Women* (1652), and Nicholas Talon's *The Holy History* (1653). He continued to be vexed by financial troubles following the loss of most of his fortune, and in January 1656 petitioned Cromwell for relief after being imprisoned for non-payment of debts totalling £2000.

At the Restoration, Winchester was restored to his estates but not compensated for his losses, although the Convention Parliament discussed an award of £19,000 on 3 August 1660 and the Cavalier Parliament resolved upon, but never implemented, one of £10,000 on 2 July 1661. This was also the year in which he was recalled to his place in the House of Lords, but on 10 March 1662 he suffered a further loss of a different kind in the death of his wife, Honora. She was buried in the church at Englefield, and a striking example of personal continuities during the period, despite political and religious divisions, is that

Milton provided the epitaph for her tomb, saluting her virtues, just as he had written one for the first marchioness.

Winchester married for the third time before April 1669; his new wife was Isabella Theresa Lucy Howard (*b.* 1644), daughter of another Catholic dignitary, William *Howard, first Viscount Stafford. The union was childless, and she outlived him to die on 2 September 1691. Winchester took no further part in national affairs, save in attendance of the House of Lords, and returned to the quiet provincial life which had been interrupted by civil war. He made no attempt to rebuild Basing, but continued to live at Englefield House and to beautify and enlarge it as a new seat. His main interests were in agricultural improvement and in literature. The greatest vexation of his later years was probably his estrangement from Charles, his son and heir, who became opposed to him both in politics and religion, and was to make his own dramatic career in both. In 1663 a quarrel between them over the disposition of the family estates had already become so intransigent that it was only settled by an act of the Cavalier Parliament. The marquess died at Englefield, of unknown causes, on 5 March 1675, and was buried near his wife in the church. Another first-rank poet provided his tomb epitaph, John Dryden, who extolled the two obvious aspects of his career: loyalty and suffering.

Winchester's portraits show a neat and handsome man with gentle and rather melancholy eyes. In his fidelity to his monarchy and his church—at times, as in the dismissal of Rawdon, verging upon fanaticism—he reflected a nature which was always both serious and pious. His career, however, was in the main that of a man inclined to private and provincial life, whose enthusiasms were for letters, learning, and the improvement of his property. It was his tragedy that the centre of that retired existence, his country seat, should itself have been the cause of his propulsion to the forefront of national affairs, in especially traumatic, and disastrous, circumstances.

RONALD HUTTON

Sources *A description of the siege of Basing Castle* (1644) · *The full and last relation of all things concerning Basing-House* (1645) · *Lieutenant-General Cromwell's letter … concerning the storming and taking of Basing House* (1645) · *The souldiers report concerning Sir William Wallers fight* (1643) · *JHC*, 4–8 (1644–67) · *JHL*, 8–9 (1645–7) · Clarendon, *Hist. rebellion*, 3.408–15, 440–41 · *Mercurius Aulicus* (1643–4) · E. Archer, *A true relation of the marchings of the red trained bonds …* (1643) · *The Weekly Account, Containing Certain Speciall and Remarkable Passages* (June–Nov 1644) · *CSP dom.*, 1656, 105, 351 · *The manuscripts of his grace the duke of Rutland*, 4 vols., HMC, 24 (1888–1905), vol. 1, p. 440 · GEC, *Peerage*

Likenesses W. Hollar, engraving, 1640–49, NPG [*see illus.*] · line engravings, pubd 1798 (after W. Hollar), NPG · J. Adam, stipple (after unknown artist), BM, NPG · S. Cooper, engraving (after P. Oliver) · W. Hollar, etchings, BM, NPG · P. Oliver, miniature, repro. in G. N. Godwin, *The civil war in Hampshire* (1904), 88 · etching, BM, NPG

Paulet, Lavinia. *See* Fenton, Lavinia (1710–1760).

Paulet, William, first marquess of Winchester (1474/5?–1572), administrator and nobleman, was born at Fisherton-Delamare in Wiltshire, the eldest of four sons of

William Paulet, first marquess of Winchester (1474/5?–1572), by unknown artist, 1560s?

Sir John *Paulet (1453/4–1525), soldier, of Basing in Hampshire and Nunney in Somerset [see under Paulet, Sir Amias (c.1457–1538)], and his wife, Alice, daughter of Sir William Paulet of Hinton St George in Somerset and his wife, Elizabeth. He also had two sisters, Eleanor and Katherine Paulet. William Camden and Sir Richard Baker stated that Paulet was ninety-seven at the time of his death in 1572. Other years of birth have been suggested, including 1483 and 1488. The Somerset property is said to have come to Paulet's family through the marriage of his great-great-grandfather, William Paulet (d. 1435) to the heiress Eleanor de la Mere. The family held the estate from Edward IV as parcel of the duchy of Lancaster by 1461 and the manor and advowson, formerly the property of Glastonbury Abbey, was alienated to Paulet and his wife on 1 October 1543. According to a memorial poem written shortly after Paulet's death, he was born at another of the houses that were inherited through Eleanor de la Mere, Fisherton-Delamare. His main primary residence of Basing House was acquired through the marriage of Paulet's great-grandfather Sir John Paulet (d. 1437) to Constance (d. in or before 1428), daughter and coheir of Sir Hugh Poynings, eldest son and heir of Thomas Poynings, fifth Baron St John of Basing. Though a cousin, John Bonville, sued for title to Basing House, the Paulets appear to have sustained their claim, as in January 1531 Paulet was granted a licence to fortify the manor and create a park, and in 1537 was able to produce legitimate title to the lands.

Early years, 1474/5–1532 Details of Paulet's early life are sketchy. Rowland Broughton's poem states that Paulet went at an unknown date from school to Thavies Inn, and then to the Inner Temple, where he eventually became an utter barrister. Though there are no records of his legal education, in an order for division of matters to be 'treated' by Henry VIII's council in February 1526, Paulet is among those given responsibilities for dealing with legal matters. By 1509 he was married to Elizabeth (d. 1558), daughter of Sir William Capell, lord mayor of London in 1503, and his wife, Margaret. They had at least four sons, including John Paulet, future second marquess of Winchester (c.1510–1576), Chidiock Paulet (b. in or before 1521, d. 1574), and Giles (b. after 1521, d. 1580), and four daughters.

Paulet appears to have made little impression on local and central politics until the accession of Henry VIII. He was named sheriff in Hampshire on 8 November 1511, after being nominated, but not chosen, in each of the previous two years. He was again appointed to the post in 1518 and 1522. He was named to a commission on 2 May 1512 in Southampton to review, muster, and certify numbers of troops going to France, and named JP for Hampshire for the first time in January 1514. He was again on commissions of muster in Wiltshire in March 1539. Lucrative and important offices began to fall his way during the 1520s, but there is no clear evidence for how, or through whom, he came to the notice of the king. He appears to have been a protégé of Richard Fox, bishop of Winchester, who in 1517 wrote to Cardinal Thomas Wolsey, requesting the inclusion of Paulet in a commission for Southampton on unlawful assemblies. This is perhaps the first time Paulet was brought to Wolsey's notice. He also served as an executor of Fox's will, and his stewardship of the bishopric of Winchester probably dates from Fox's tenure. Certainly he served in this capacity from 1529 to 1530, when Wolsey was bishop of Winchester *in commendam*, and his local influence can be seen in Ralph Sadler's assurance that Paulet could secure a borough seat in parliament on Thomas Cromwell's behalf within the diocese. Paulet was knighted between 1523 and 1525 and was a member of the council from at least February 1526. The date of his knighthood remains obscure. He was styled 'Sir William Paulet' of Southampton on the subsidy roll of 2 November 1523, but subsequent use of the title is inconsistent until late 1525. His brother George Paulet named him Sir William Paulet on accounts dated December of that year (*LP Henry VIII*, 3, pt 2, 3504, p. 1458).

Paulet succeeded his father on 5 January 1525. On 3 November 1526 he was appointed, with Thomas Englefield, master of the king's wards, with power to keep lands, sell them, and appoint feudaries and officers (except in the duchy of Lancaster, the palatinate jurisdiction of Chester, and in Wales). This was the beginning of a 28-year tenure over wards, with increasing responsibilities over time. In January 1531 he was appointed surveyor-general of the possessions of royal wards, and of widows and idiots in England, Wales, and Calais. On 21 December 1534 he gained sole occupancy of the office of master, and when the court of wards was created on 26 July 1540, and later expanded to the court of wards and liveries (18 November 1542), he was appointed master for life. Such an office offered the incumbent splendid opportunities for the acquisition of rich wardships, and he acquired several during his years in office. He was returned as knight of the shire for Hampshire in 1529 and sat throughout the Reformation parliament.

Councillor, courtier, and nobleman, 1532–1547 In addition to the mastership of wards, Paulet gained the office of comptroller of the royal household in May 1532, giving it up in October 1537 for the post of treasurer of the household, in which he remained until 9 March 1539. He was promoted to lord great chamberlain about 16 May 1543 and was named great master of the household about November 1545, as well as lord president of the privy council. He relinquished these latter two offices on 3 February 1550, when he became lord treasurer. Further offices granted to Paulet, which broadened his range of responsibilities, were master of woods in England and the marches of Wales in June 1541, and warden of the forests south of the Trent in December 1545. He was also one of a small coterie of men given commissions in March 1544 to sell crown lands and confiscated goods, and settle fines and leases, and also given leave to temporarily endorse bills of sale with the king's stamp, part of an effort to facilitate crown business. In May 1546 he was on a renewed commission to sell crown lands.

Paulet spent much of his life at court. This was the making of him, according to the Elizabethan memorialist Sir Robert Naunton, who wrote that both Paulet and William Herbert, first earl of Pembroke, ran through their meagre inheritances and came to court 'where upon the bare stock of their Wits they began to traffick for themselves and prospered so well, that they got, spent and left more than any Subjects from the Norman Conquest' (Naunton, 25). Paulet was in regular attendance on Henry and still frequently present when the court was reduced in size. In a letter of 1534 to Cromwell he said that he would join the king shortly, 'as all other officers are absent' (*LP Henry VIII*, 7.527). As comptroller and then treasurer of the household, his frequent attendance was necessary, but his letters reinforce the impression that Henry valued his continued presence, and that he was included in the intimate counsels of the king. Letters to Cromwell in September 1534 indicate that Paulet travelled with the court to Langley and Woodstock in Oxfordshire. He was among those who discussed commissioning ships for Ireland and sent the king's orders in the matter to Cromwell. In a letter of 9 October 1535 he informed Cromwell of Henry's wishes regarding Princess Mary. Another letter between them of 20 October passed on the king's message that Cromwell should come to court only if he had matters needing urgent attention. Paulet was among those first named by Henry as part of his 'pryvey counsell' in 1536, or the 'emergency council' named during the crisis of the Pilgrimage of Grace (1536–7). Though he was not named to the privy council that was formalized in August 1540, he still sat as

judge in the Star Chamber between 1540 and 19 November 1542, on which date he was named a privy councillor.

Paulet and other members of his family were present at many of the important ceremonial events of the Tudor dynasty. He attended the baptism of Elizabeth I on 10 September 1533 and, with his son and heir, John Paulet, was present at the baptism of Edward, prince of Wales, on 15 October 1537. His wife was among the ladies in the funeral procession of Jane Seymour on 12 November 1537, and in a book listing the late queen's jewels is the notation of a gift to her of a 'border' (*LP Henry VIII*, 12, pt 2, 973/4). Paulet, along with Thomas Howard, third duke of Norfolk, made all the arrangements for Jane's funeral. Both his wife and he were appointed in 1539 to take part in the reception of Anne of Cleves. Chidiock and Giles Paulet were among several men who accompanied the body of Henry from Whitehall Palace to Windsor Castle in 1547. Paulet served as the escort for the French envoy at Edward's coronation on 20 February 1547 and was chief mourner at his funeral on 8 August 1553. On 30 September 1553 he walked in the ceremonial procession that escorted Mary from the Tower of London to Westminster Abbey, while his wife rode with the ladies accompanying Elizabeth and Anne of Cleves. The next day he carried the orb in the coronation ceremonies.

Beginning in April 1537 Paulet was put forward several times for nomination to the Order of the Garter. On 9 March 1539 he was created Baron St John in a ceremony that also elevated Sir John Russell and Sir William Parr to baronies. A description of the ceremony recounts how it took place at Whitehall Palace after communion at the king's mass. Paulet's robes were carried by Edward Fiennes de Clinton, ninth Baron Clinton, while George Brooke, ninth Baron Cobham, and Thomas Fiennes, ninth Baron Dacre of the South, led him in to the presence chamber, where he was invested with his robes and then led to Henry to receive his patent. Sir William Kingston was granted St John's office of treasurer of the household on the same day. St John was finally nominated to the Order of the Garter on 23 April and installed on 6 May 1543. Land acquisitions, either through purchase or through royal grant, made him one of the wealthiest men in the kingdom. By 1545/6 his landed estate alone was valued as worth at least £1000 per annum.

St John's appointment to the privy council reflects the strength of his personal relationship with Henry. In a deposition taken relative to the Pilgrimage of Grace he was named as one of a small group of councillors 'about the king', apparently those most constantly with, and trusted by, Henry, which concurs with his subsequent inclusion on the privy council (*LP Henry VIII*, 12, pt 1, 1013). His intimacy, and possible influence, with Henry was certainly assumed by those outside the court. In 1546 St John was, along with Katherine Parr, Thomas Wriothesley, first Baron Wriothesley, Russell, and Sir William Paget, petitioned by Oxford University to persuade the king not to reorganize the colleges.

With Wriothesley and Stephen Gardiner, bishop of Winchester, St John formed a triumvirate in the last years of Henry's reign which, as the nucleus of 'Council in London', was entrusted with entertaining various ambassadors, and ascertaining their opinions or transmitting their messages regarding specific issues of interest to the privy council and king. It also presented Henry's responses, messages, or instructions to the ambassadors. He was appointed to the commission of 17 June 1543 to treat for the marriage of Edward and Mary, queen of Scots. In 1546 Paget and he were entrusted with interrogating Norfolk concerning his alleged treason. St John was among those witnesses who signed Norfolk's confession in January 1547 and he sat as a judge at the trial of Henry Howard, earl of Surrey, on 13 January. St John was one of the privy councillors who were most frequently present at court and at council meetings in Henry's final years, and the king's will named him as one of the sixteen members of the regency council appointed guardians of Edward. He received a bequest of £500 in Henry's will.

Under Edward VI and Mary I, 1547–1558 St John bore the second sword at the coronation of Edward VI. He continued to enjoy favour under the regime of his kinsman Edward *Seymour (c.1500–1552), duke of Somerset and lord protector, and was reappointed to the privy council on 12 March 1547. On 26 May he was named to the quorum of the peace for every English county and *custos rotulorum* for Hampshire. In the unfulfilled gift clause it was initially proposed by Henry that St John be promoted earl of Winchester and receive an additional land grant worth £200 per annum. This was changed to a land grant of £100 per annum instead but St John was certainly among the close circle of privy councillors and often conducted royal administration with Somerset alone. However, seeing what way things were going, when Wriothesley (now first earl of Southampton) and John Dudley, earl of Warwick, initiated the coup against Somerset, he was instrumental in toppling his kinsman on 11 October 1549. He also warned Warwick that Southampton and Henry Fitzalan, twelfth earl of Arundel, were plotting to overthrow him. St John was rewarded with promotion to earl of Wiltshire on 19 January 1550, received large land grants on 26 January, and was named lord treasurer on 3 February (having relinquished his offices of lord president and great master to Warwick the previous day). Finally on 11 October 1551 he was created marquess of Winchester in a grand ceremony in the presence of the king. At his investiture he was led into Edward's presence by Lord Parr (now marquess of Northampton) and Russell (now first earl of Bedford), with his coronet borne by Henry Manners, second earl of Rutland, his sword by Cobham, and his patent by Sir Gilbert Dethick, Garter king of arms. At the dinner following, he sat at the highest bench with Henry Brandon, second duke of Suffolk, Warwick (now duke of Northumberland), and Pembroke. Winchester was named lord steward to oversee Somerset's trial for treason on 1 December 1551 but did attempt to help the duke's heir get some of his inheritance back in 1552. He replaced Somerset as lord lieutenant of Hampshire and the Isle of Wight on 16 May 1552. He was reappointed on 24 May 1553.

Thomas Fuller commented that Mary I and Elizabeth

'owed their crowns to [Winchester's] counsel: his policy being the principal defeater of Duke Dudley's design to disinherit them' (Fuller, 13). Certainly the imperial ambassador, Jehan Scheyve, reported that Winchester, despite his reputation for changing with the wind, was one of those who objected to the device to alter the succession, though he did sign the letters patent for the limitation of the crown on 21 June 1553. On 16 July he attempted to leave the Tower, where the privy council was gathered with Lady Jane Grey, but was forced to go back. Three days later he joined several other privy councillors in proclaiming Mary as the rightful queen.

Winchester's career under Mary was difficult and frustrating, despite his continuing as a privy councillor and lord treasurer. Mary may have retained his services primarily due to a desire for continuity and stability. She forced him to resign as master of wards on 30 April 1554, and it has been suggested that his attempts to reorganize the exchequer, after the courts of augmentation and first fruits and tenths had been reincorporated into exchequer finance in 1554, were undertaken as much to increase his own influence over fiscal policy and administration as to reform the fiscal apparatus. He attempted to force through the reinstatement of medieval exchequer practices. He hoped this would prevent more cases of corruption. However, Mary prevented him from restoring the 'ancient course', and effectively silenced him on fiscal policy by turning his attention to the financial administration of the navy in 1557, and by appointing him 'lieutenant about our person and of shires adjoining London' on 12 April 1558, charged with mustering the queen's forces for any event.

Restoration to favour and final years, 1558–1572 Under Elizabeth, who also confirmed him as lord treasurer, Winchester revived his project of reinstating ancient exchequer practice. He is credited with helping to turn the office of lord treasurer from the relatively unimportant sinecure of the early sixteenth century into the central post in royal finance of the late sixteenth and seventeenth centuries, with wide powers of patronage and control over leases, commissions, wood sales, and other revenue matters, as well as acting as adviser to the privy council on fiscal policy. Unfortunately the reforms that Winchester instituted established a dangerously loose system of accounting in which he had untrammelled control over cash flow. A sudden rush of defaults by exchequer tellers in 1571 revealed a system of personal borrowing from royal accounts in which Winchester was involved heavily. Death saved the lord treasurer from complete disgrace, but left his heir with debts of £46,000. Despite this, the second marquess was still one of the wealthiest peers, with an income of between £2000 and £3000 per annum. In the kindest view, his incompetence in this particular episode can be put down to great age and encroaching infirmity. In 1566 Elizabeth had dismissed him from performing the duties of speaker of the House of Lords, 'considering the Decay of his Memory and Hearing, Griefs accompanying hoary Hairs and old Age' (*JHL*, 1.558, 629–37). The marchioness of Winchester died at Basing House on 25 December 1558 and was buried at Basing church on 5 February 1559. By summer 1570 Winchester retired to Basing House, never to return to court. He died there intestate on 10 March 1572 and was buried in Basing on 28 April. Administration of his estate was first granted to his heir on 14 June. Winchester's altar tomb is in the north chapel of Basing church, along with that of his son, John Paulet, second marquess of Winchester.

Although Winchester was the most successful of the brothers, he was not the only one to gain fame or infamy. George Paulet of Crondall (*d.* 1558) appears to have acted as his eyes and ears in Hampshire while Winchester was pursuing his fortunes at court. A letter to Cromwell in 1535 states that George Paulet was passing information on issues in Hampshire to his older brother. On 31 July 1537 George Paulet was appointed a commissioner for the establishment of affairs in Ireland in the aftermath of the rebellion of Thomas Fitzgerald, tenth earl of Kildare. However, in 1538 he was accused of slandering Cromwell by speaking ill of him to others, claiming the principal secretary's high place was partly due to William Paulet's influence. George Paulet was imprisoned in the Tower and his brother wrote to Cromwell asking for mercy towards him. In the following year George Paulet was accused of forming a secret confederation in Ireland, with the lord deputy, Leonard Grey, Viscount Graney, who stood accused of treason. Anthony Budgegood, a servant of Cromwell, wrote a testimonial defending George Paulet's faithfulness to the king. He claimed that Grey spoke more with George Paulet than with anybody else because he received from him 'counsel without dissimulation' (*LP Henry VIII*, 13, pt 2, 43; *LP Henry VIII*, 14, pt 1, 1, p. 3). No long-term consequence came of it but George Paulet's sphere of influence retracted to the county. By 1541 he was auditor for St Swithin's, Winchester, after its conversion into a cathedral chapter, with his older brother as its steward, and in 1543 the privy council recruited him to handle matters of local business. Another brother, Richard Paulet, was a servant of Henry Courtenay, second earl of Devon and marquess of Exeter, and later became a receiver in the court of augmentations.

Assessment　Wallace MacCaffrey classed Winchester among the bureaucrats rather than the great peers of the privy council. Certainly during the French campaign of 1545 he seems to have been the efficient and indefatigable worker, caught up in the minutiae of victualling, rather than the glory of war. Despite his continued employment by the Tudors in fiscal matters, he does not appear to have been a brilliant financial manager, but rather a good administrator, one whose continuing importance was due to hard work, a willingness to address administrative issues, and the need for continuity. His correspondence with Sir William Cecil, early in Elizabeth's reign, shows a marked obsession with expense and careful husbandry, and his desire for exchequer reform apparently rose partly from his concern over better record keeping and the potential for corruption. His years as lord treasurer for Edward show that he was the expert on the day-to-day running of the exchequer rather than the policy-maker on

finance. His lack of understanding of the potentially negative effects of his style of exchequer administration was largely responsible for the ignominious end of his career.

The longevity of Winchester's career at court is even more remarkable considering his involuntary participation in some of the unhappier moments of his royal mistresses' early lives. He was one of the principals in reducing the status of Katherine of Aragon and Mary, being among those commissioned on 2 December 1533 for 'diminishing the house and order of the Princess Dowager' (*LP Henry VIII*, 6.1486). In January 1536 Henry commanded him to assume the duties of organizing Katherine's interment at Peterborough in Lincolnshire, and ordered all others to obey his directions in the matter of dispersing her possessions. According to Eustache Chapuys, the imperial ambassador, Winchester was the only non-ecclesiastical 'man of mark' who attended Katherine's funeral on 29 January (*LP Henry VIII*, 10, 282). Along with his heir, the earl of Wiltshire was given the unhappy task of overseeing Mary's change in circumstances, and of trying to convince her to accept such a change, which brought him into strong disfavour with the determined princess. Chapuys wrote that after one such visit in July 1534, the two men threatened 'to shut her up in her chamber' (*LP Henry VIII*, 7.980). However, Winchester appears to have offered her as much sympathy as he could, as in a letter of 29 August 1534 Chapuys states that he spared Mary from following Elizabeth's litter as she travelled with her, and in fact told her that she could choose to follow or lead. He appears to have been equally kind to Anne Boleyn during her fall from power, and in Kingston's account of her meandering statements in the Tower she 'named Mr. Controler [Winchester] to be a very gentleman', unlike others who she called cruel (*LP Henry VIII*, 10.797). Winchester's early involvement in Elizabeth's affairs was no less fraught. Southampton and he examined a servant of Thomas *Seymour, Baron Seymour of Sudeley (*b.* in or before 1509, *d.* 1549), after the lord admiral's arrest, and Winchester was also appointed, along with Thomas Radcliffe, third earl of Sussex, to escort Elizabeth to the Tower on 18 March 1554 for alleged complicity in the rebellion of Sir Thomas Wyatt the younger. Though it was Sussex, not Winchester, who was willing to permit Elizabeth the time to write a letter to Mary begging forgiveness, she does not seem to have held that against the marquess.

Winchester's religious views are obscure. He is generally believed to have been a Henrician Catholic, and sympathetic to Catholic interests, and he was certainly moderate in religious matters. He benefited from the dissolution of the monasteries, though Mary returned three of his manors to the bishopric of Winchester. Under successive monarchs he exhibited a willingness to adhere to religious changes without demur. He was on a commission of March 1540 'to repair to Calais, and make inquiry touching the state of religion and observance of the laws there', which the French ambassador, Charles de Marillac, bishop of Vienne, commented was due to the disruption caused by Anabaptists in that town (*LP Henry VIII*, 15.316,

370). He was also among the judges who passed sentence on Anne Askew and her supporters. Pro-Catholic leanings are attributed to him, due to his lack of support for either Katherine Seymour (*née* Grey), countess of Hertford, or Henry Hastings, third earl of Huntingdon, in the succession crisis of 1562, and his wish to await the decision of the judges. Similarly, he voted against the Supremacy Bill 1559. However, he allegedly dealt the death blow to the conservatives' chances in the power struggle of 1549 by siding with Warwick, helping to end any hopes of a return to Catholicism. Additionally, his role in begging Edward to permit his sister Mary to hear mass at Charles V's request presents him not as a defender of liberty of conscience but a willing mouthpiece for Warwick, who no longer wanted to antagonize the emperor. Winchester appears to have been primarily an extremely cautious man, whose politics and sense of survival influenced his religious scruples. He did not come out on the side of the reforming party until after Henry's death, nor did he speak up for a protestant succession at Edward's death; yet his greatest gains were made in the reign of the most reformist of the Tudor monarchs. He did have a positive genius for choosing the winning side. Sir Richard Morison, Edward's ambassador to the emperor, said Winchester 'hath a tongue fit for all tymes, with an obedience redie for as many newe masteres as can happen in his dayes', a cruel comment, but one that presumably reflects the views of some of his contemporaries (*Literary Remains*, ed. Jordan, 1.ccxxvii).

Winchester was an accomplished courtier, if not as able an administrator, though his final years as lord chancellor taint the estimation of his earlier fiscal capabilities. His greatest achievements were his rise from obscurity to great status, his magnificent building, Basing House, which was the largest private residence in Britain, and his ability to thrive under successive regime changes; his career served as an inspiration for ambitious men rather than idealistic ones. Naunton's *Fragmenta regalia* gives Winchester's character as that of a man who 'served then four Princes in as various and changeable season' by his complacency. Indeed Naunton claimed that Winchester's reply to a friend who asked the secret of his political longevity in turbulent times was '*ortus sum ex falice, non ex quercu*' ('I was made of the plyable willow, not of the stubborn oak'; Naunton, 25).   L. L. FORD

Sources HoP, *Commons, 1509–58*, 3.70–72 • GEC, *Peerage*, 12/2.757–64 • *LP Henry VIII*, vols. 3/2–3, 4/1, 5, 8/2, 9–10, 12–18 • *CSP dom., 1547–58* • *VCH Hampshire and the Isle of Wight* • R. Broughton, *A brief discourse of the life and death of the late right high and honorable Sir William Pawlet, knt., Lord St. John, earl of Wiltshire, marquis of Winchester* (1572) • Fuller, *Worthies* (1840) • G. W. Kitchin and F. T. Madge, eds., *Documents relating to the foundation of the chapter of Winchester*, Hampshire RS, 1 (1889) • R. Naunton, *Fragmenta regalia, or, Observations on the late Queen Elizabeth, her times and favorits* (1870) • F. A. Inderwick, *The Inner Temple: its early history, as illustrated by its records, 1505–1603* (1896) • W. C. Richardson, *History of the court of augmentations, 1536–1554* (Baton Rouge, Los Angeles, 1961) • D. E. Hoak, *The king's council in the reign of Edward VI* (1976) • G. Redmond, *In defense of the church Catholic: the life of Stephen Gardiner* (1990) • J. D. Mackie, *The earlier Tudors, 1458–1558* (1962) • *Literary remains of King Edward the Sixth*, ed.
J. G. Nichols, 2 vols., Roxburghe Club, 75 (1857) • P. Johnson, *Elizabeth I* (1974) • J. Loach, *Edward VI* (1999) • W. T. MacCaffrey, *The shaping of the Elizabethan regime: Elizabethan politics, 1558–1572* (1968) • C. Coleman, 'Artifice or accident? The reorganization of the exchequer of receipt, *c*.1554–1572', *Revolution reassessed: revisions in the history of Tudor government and administration*, ed. C. Coleman and D. Starkey (1986), 163–95 • A. J. Slavin, *Politics and profit: a study of Sir Ralph Sadler, 1507–1547* (1966) • J. A. Guy, *Tudor England* (1988)
Archives Hants. RO, corresp. and papers relating to Hampshire coastal defence
Likenesses oils, 1560–1569?, NPG [*see illus.*] • group portrait, oils on panel, *c*.1570 (Edward VI and the pope), NPG • portrait, exh. 1890, priv. coll. • portrait, exh. 1890 • portrait, repro. in Naunton, *Fragmenta regalia*

Paulet, William, third marquess of Winchester (*c*.1532–1598), nobleman and author, was the son of John Paulet, second marquess (*c*.1510–1576), and his first wife, Elizabeth (*d*. in or before 1552), daughter of Robert, second Lord Willoughby de Broke. Paulet entered the Inner Temple in 1546, and by 1548 had married Agnes or Anne (*d*. 1601), daughter of William, first Baron Howard of Effingham. The marriage was unsuccessful and broke down. In addition to a son and three daughters by his wife, he had at least four sons by his mistress Jane Lambert. Attempts were made by the queen in 1578 to reconcile Paulet with his wife: she was supported by Sir Amias Paulet, he by his relative Francis Russell, second earl of Bedford. Paulet made the Lamberts executors and chief beneficiaries of his will, which his family contested amid great acrimony.

Paulet was created knight of the Bath at the coronation of Queen Mary in 1553, served as high sheriff for Hampshire in 1560–61, as commissioner for musters and as joint lord lieutenant for Dorset in 1569, and sat as knight of the shire for Dorset in the parliament of 1571. In 1572 he was summoned to the House of Lords as Baron St John, and on 4 November 1576 he succeeded his father as third marquess of Winchester. Not satisfied with his father's will, he complained of the disposal of the family property due to the influence of his father's widow and third wife, Winifred (*d*. 1586), daughter of Sir John Brugge, lord mayor of London. He was joint lord lieutenant of Hampshire in 1585 and in 1586 became lord lieutenant of Dorset; in October of that year he was one of the commissioners appointed to try Mary, queen of Scots.

Paulet was a quarrelsome man, frequently embroiled in public and private disputes: he received several reprimands for his conduct from the privy council. His only literary work, *The Lord Marques Idlenes*, was printed in 1586 and reprinted in 1587: Thomas Nashe refers to it in his letter written about September 1596 to William Cotton (*The Works of Thomas Nashe*, ed. R. B. McKerrow, rev. F. P. Wilson, 5 vols., 1958, 5.194–5). Dedicated to Queen Elizabeth, Paulet's book takes the form of 'sage sentences, prudent precepts, morall examples, sweete similitudes, proper comparisons, and other remembrances of speciall choise' (sig. *2r). These are gathered in brief paragraphs under headings relating to such subjects as children and youth, death, justice and justicers, knowledge, and love, to form a sort of commonplace book. Written in the author's later years in 'mine olde plaine fashion' while unwell and 'under the phisitians hands' (sig. A3r), the brief aphoristic pieces exhibit a concern with the well-being of the commonwealth and a neo-Stoic outlook.

Paulet played a part in the defence of the south coast against the Armada and took part in the trial of Philip Howard, earl of Arundel, in 1589. In 1596 he was lord lieutenant for Hampshire, and in 1597 first commissioner for ecclesiastical causes in the diocese of Winchester. He died on 24 November 1598 at Basing, Hampshire, where he was buried.   H. R. WOUDHUYSEN

Sources HoP, *Commons, 1558–1603* · GEC, *Peerage,* new edn · *DNB* · PRO, SP 12/110/31, 12/125/41

Paulet, Lord William (1804–1893), army officer, fourth son of Charles Ingoldsby Paulet, thirteenth marquess of Winchester (1764–1843), and his wife, Anne (1773–1841), second daughter of John Andrews of Shotney Hall, Northumberland, was born at Amport House, Andover, Hampshire, on 7 July 1804. After attending Eton College (his name appears in the school lists of 1820), he was appointed ensign in the 85th (Duke of York's Own) light infantry on 1 February 1821. On 23 August 1822 he was made lieutenant in the 7th Royal Fusiliers; he purchased an unattached company on 12 February 1825 and exchanged to the 21st Royal North British Fusiliers. On 10 September 1830 he became major 68th (Durham) regiment of light infantry, and lieutenant-colonel on 21 April 1843, serving with the regiment at Gibraltar, in the West Indies, North America, and at home until 31 December 1848, when he exchanged to half pay unattached. He became brevet colonel on 20 June 1854, went to the Crimea as assistant adjutant-general of the cavalry division, under Lord Lucan, and was present at the Alma, Balaklava (where his hat was carried off by roundshot), Inkerman, and Sevastopol. On 23 November 1854 Lord Raglan appointed him to command 'on the Bosporus, at Gallipoli, and the Dardanelles', where the overcrowded hospitals, in which Florence Nightingale and her nurses had begun work three weeks before, needed an experienced officer in overall command. This post he held until after the fall of Sevastopol, when he succeeded to the command of the light division in the Crimea, which he retained until the allied evacuation. He was created CB (July 1855), the Légion d'honneur, and the order of the Mejidiye (third class).

Paulet was one of the first officers appointed to a command at Aldershot camp, where he commanded the 1st brigade from 1856 to 1860, becoming a major-general on 13 June 1858. He commanded the south-western district, with headquarters at Portsmouth, from 1860 to 1865. He was made KCB in 1865, and a lieutenant-general on 8 December 1867; he was adjutant-general of the forces from 1865 to 1870, and was made GCB in 1870, general on 7 October 1874, and field marshal on 10 July 1886. After a short period as colonel 87th Royal Irish Fusiliers, Paulet was appointed, on 9 April 1864, colonel of his former regiment, the 68th, in the interest of which he never ceased to exert his influence. He died, unmarried, at his London residence, 18 St James's Square, Westminster, on 9 May 1893.   H. M. CHICHESTER, *rev.* JAMES FALKNER

Sources Army List · Hart's Army List · The Times (10 May 1893) · Broad Arrow (13 May 1893), 590 · Boase, Mod. Eng. biog. · A. W. Kinglake, The invasion of the Crimea, [new edn], 9 vols. (1877–88) · GEC, Peerage · Burke, Peerage
Archives NAM, corresp. with Lord Raglan
Likenesses D. Cunliffe, group portrait, oils, 1846 (with the light infantry) · J. Barret, oils, 1857, NPG · engraving?, repro. in Daily Graphic (10 May 1893), 8 · wood-engraving, NPG; repro. in ILN (20 May 1893)
Wealth at death £173,124 6s. 8d.: probate, 3 June 1893, CGPLA Eng. & Wales

Pauling, George Craig Sanders (1854–1919), civil engineer and railway promoter, was born on 6 September 1854 at 4 Park Terrace, South Street, Lorrimore Road, Walworth, Surrey, the eldest child of the two boys and two girls born to Richard Clark Pauling (1833–1894), civil engineer, and his wife, Jane Sanders Bone (1834–1915). His father, grandfather, and great-uncle were all railway contractors. Pauling's father, having spent several years in India, intended him for service in that country, but George's schooling ended when the family income was reduced by his father's illness and irregular employment.

After casual work, Pauling was taken on as a pupil in 1870 by Joseph Firbank, a major railway contractor. In 1874 his father was appointed engineer to the Cape Government Railways, and first his younger brother Harold and then George himself joined him there in 1875; he soon became a contractor on his own account, forming Firbank, Pauling & Co. with his former employer. They won the contract for a tunnel on the Grahamstown line, then under construction, and made a respectable £15,000 profit. Thus financially secure Pauling married in 1878 Annie Ayton; they had two sons.

Throughout his life Pauling could not resist the lure of speculating in a variety of schemes and business ventures; he invested in a saddlery, and in an ostrich and cattle ranch started by friends, and having become a freemason he undertook to build the masonic temple in Grahamstown. He then departed for England, in 1879, with his wife and baby son, intending to find work there, but was forced to return in haste on learning that his investments in Grahamstown were at risk. Everything was going against him: a drought had reduced yields on the ranch, part of the masonic temple had collapsed, and one of his loans was unlikely to be repaid. In some desperation, Pauling called in his creditors in 1880. He later invested in gold mining at Witwatersrand, but left before the astonishing richness of that field was appreciated.

During the 1880s Firbank, Pauling & Co. undertook a number of major railway projects. The line between Port Alfred and Grahamstown was completed in 1884, and the firm was also responsible for Kimberley Railway. This 'brought to completion the railway construction scheme, which had been initiated in 1874 to connect the harbours of the Cape Colony with Kimberley' (Heydenrych, 535). In June 1885 Pauling's wife died, and Pauling sent his two sons to England to be cared for by his mother. In the succeeding years he operated on an international scale, travelling extensively through the Turkish dominions, where a railway was planned from Alexandretta (Iskenderun), through Persia, to Karachi. Pauling subsequently built railways in Greece and Puerto Rico. He constructed the line from Haifa to Damascus and undertook a number of other major civil engineering works, including the Tata and Shirawata dams in India. On 1 November 1887 Pauling married Edith Kate Halliwell in the UK; they had one daughter.

In 1889 Pauling was in Johannesburg having discussions with the financier Baron Emile D'Erlanger regarding investment in mines, when tenders were invited for the first railway in the Transvaal. This was the 'Rand tram', a railway from Johannesburg to Boksburg. Pauling, in partnership with James Butler, secured the contract; work began in 1890, and later additional lines were laid from Johannesburg to Krugersdorp and from Boksburg to Springs. Pauling and Butler also constructed part of the Delagoa Bay Railway at Krokodilpoort.

Through President Kruger, a friend of the family, and also through Cecil Rhodes, other railway projects materialized. These included the line from Vryburg to Mafeking, which Pauling completed in 1891, at Rhodes's request. His firm also constructed the line from Beira to Umtali, and on to Salisbury. Other major lines included the railway from Mafeking to Bulawayo, the line across Sir Lowry's Pass to Caledon, and also the railway from Ashton, via Swellendam and Riversdale, to Mossel Bay.

During these turbulent years, Pauling, a strong and sturdy man, always apt to respond with his fists rather than with words, resisted epidemics of cholera and conflicts with native peoples and with animals, mostly lions. He also undertook civil engineering projects in England, as one of the partners of Pauling and Elliott, until the partnership was dissolved in 1894. The contracting work was then undertaken by Pauling & Co.

Pauling was appointed commissioner of public works to the first legislative assembly in Rhodesia in 1895. At a later date he also served as vice-chairman of the Rhodesian chamber of mines. Pauling in 1903 established another firm, the Transvaal Engineering and Contracting Company, which built further railways in Natal and elsewhere.

More than anyone else, Pauling was the architect of the railway system in southern and central Africa. Between 1900 and 1918 he built several hundred miles of railway in Rhodesia, including an extension to the Katanga copper mines at Elizabethville (Lubumbashi) in partnership with Belgian interests. He was also responsible for part of the Benguela railway across Angola, as well as the railway from Port Herald to Blantyre in Nyasaland.

It is not known what became of his second wife but on 17 November 1906 Pauling married Dolores (Lola) Guibara and the marriage produced another daughter. Having abandoned freemasonry in his early years, Pauling subsequently became a staunch Roman Catholic. He generously funded the building of a Catholic church at Effingham, Surrey, where his last years were spent. Pauling died at his home, The Lodge, Effingham, on 10 February 1919, and was survived by his third wife.

ROBERT BROWN and ANITA McCONNELL

Sources *The chronicles of a contractor: being the autobiography of the late George Pauling*, ed. D. Buchan (1926); repr. (1969) · *The Times* (15 Feb 1919) · *The Times* (17 Feb 1919) · *WWW* · b. cert. · d. cert. · *CGPLA Eng. & Wales* (1919) · D. H. Heydenrych, 'Pauling, George Craig Sanders', *DSAB* · P. Duignan and L. H. Gann, *The economics of colonialism* (1975), vol. 4 of P. Duignan and L. H. Gann, *Colonialism in Africa, 1870–1960*, 390–92 · m. certs.
Likenesses portraits, repro. in Buchan, ed., *The chronicles of a contractor*
Wealth at death £530,000: probate, 28 May 1919, *CGPLA Eng. & Wales*

Paulinus. *See* Peulan (*fl.* 6th cent.).

Paulinus [St Paulinus] (*d.* **644**), bishop of York and of Rochester, was almost certainly an Italian by birth. He was one of the Roman monks sent by Pope Gregory the Great (*r.* 590–604) to England in 601 to support Augustine's mission. Gregory provided the party with a series of commendatory letters to the Frankish kings Theuderic II of Burgundy and Theudebert II of Austrasia, to their powerful grandmother Brunechildis, to King Chlothar II of Neustria, and to a number of Frankish bishops. From these, it can be deduced that the monks travelled, with possible diversions, through Toulon, Marseilles, Arles, Gap, Vienne, Lyons, Châlon-sur-Saône, Metz, Paris, and Angers. Reaching Kent by 604, they brought letters from Gregory to Augustine, to King Æthelberht, and to his wife, Bertha, together with ecclesiastical furniture, relics, and many books. In his letter to Augustine, Gregory expressed his desire that metropolitan sees be established at London and York.

Mission to Northumbria Paulinus's activities in the mission are entirely obscure until he was called upon to accompany to Northumbria Æthelburh, the sister of King Eadbald of Kent and daughter of King Æthelberht, following her betrothal to the Northumbrian king Eadwine. Bede, whose *Historia ecclesiastica gentis Anglorum* is the principal source for Paulinus's life, reports that Eadwine had promised to allow Æthelburh and her party the freedom to practise Christian worship. Paulinus, who must by this time have become a fluent speaker of English, was sent with Æthelburh to ensure that she and her companions 'were not polluted by contact with the heathen', whom, in addition, he earnestly desired to convert to Christianity (Bede, *Hist. eccl.*, 2.9). Before they left Kent, Paulinus was consecrated bishop by Justus, archbishop of Canterbury, an event which Bede dates to 21 July 625. This date is very likely to be accurate: the argument that it is six or seven years too late because Bede made mistakes in his calculation of seventh-century dates is inconclusive at best.

Conversion of the Northumbrians had to begin with their king, but winning Eadwine wholeheartedly round to a new faith was not straightforward. Bede drew on three stories of Eadwine's conversion, probably derived from Canterbury and perhaps ultimately from Paulinus himself, which he linked together into a continuous narrative. In the first episode, which he dates to Easter 626, Bede tells how an attempt to assassinate the king, inspired by the West Saxons, was foiled, and, on the same night,

Æthelburh gave birth to a daughter, Eanflæd. When Paulinus claimed that God had granted the child in response to his prayers, Eadwine promised that he would convert to Christianity, provided that God granted him victory over those who had tried to assassinate him; as a pledge of his word, he gave Eanflæd to Paulinus to be consecrated to Christ. She and eleven other members of Eadwine's household were the first Northumbrians to be baptized, at Pentecost 626.

Although, in due course, Eadwine was victorious over his West Saxon enemies, he would not accept Christianity 'at once and without consideration' (Bede, *Hist. eccl.*, 2.9). He no longer worshipped idols, sought to learn the faith systematically from Paulinus, and he and Æthelburh received exhortatory letters from Pope Boniface V (r. 619–25). But Eadwine still found it necessary 'to consult with the counsellors whom he considered the wisest' (Bede, *Hist. eccl.*, 2.9). Bede relates that, during these deliberations, Paulinus came to the king and, inspired by God, placed his right hand on the king's head, and asked him if he recognized this sign. Paulinus thus referred to a vision that Eadwine had had before he became king, when he was in exile at the court of Rædwald, king of the East Angles. Then, at a moment when Rædwald was considering handing him over to his Northumbrian enemies, Eadwine had encountered a stranger who knew his difficulty and offered him deliverance from his enemies, a kingship of unsurpassed power, and counsel as to his salvation, in return for a promise of obedience, to be claimed in the future by the laying of a hand on his head. As Bede tells the story, the stranger was a 'spirit', but the anonymous Whitby life of Pope Gregory the Great (written between 680 and 704) identifies him as Paulinus, although there is no independent evidence for Paulinus's having been active in East Anglia.

In reality, Paulinus, even in the guise of a divinely inspired agent, may have had less influence on Eadwine's decision than the attitude of the Northumbian aristocracy. While Eadwine declared to Paulinus his personal willingness to accept Christianity, Bede depicts, in a vivid tableau, a meeting of the Northumbrian council in the king's hall. Paulinus was asked to speak there, his task of promoting Christianity doubtless made easier by the immediate and frank admission of the pagan high priest, Coifi, that 'the religion which we have hitherto held has no virtue nor profit in it' (Bede, *Hist. eccl.*, 2.13), and by another counsellor's characterization of the ephemerality of earthly life. Paulinus's words were sufficient to persuade the high priest to convert to Christianity, and Eadwine skilfully led him to offer to destroy his own idols.

Bishop at York On Easter day, 12 April, 627, Eadwine was baptized at York in a hastily constructed church dedicated to St Peter, 'with all the nobles of his race and a vast number of the common people' (Bede, *Hist. eccl.*, 2.14). Paulinus's see was established at York and Eadwine set about building a stone church there, of which no trace has yet been discovered. A British tradition extant in the early ninth-century *Historia Brittonum* claims that Eadwine was baptized by Rhun, son of Urien. This statement is hard to accept as it stands, but if Rhun's father was Urien, king of Rheged (*fl.* 560–580), then his presence at Eadwine's court is at least chronologically plausible: the tradition may preserve the memory of preparatory British efforts at conversion in Northumbria.

For Bede, Northumbria owed its conversion chiefly to Paulinus. He recounts the numerous baptisms that the bishop performed, including Eadwine's sons from an earlier liaison, Osfrith and Eadfrith, one of Osfrith's sons, the children of Eadwine and Æthelburh, and 'not a few others of noble and royal stock' (Bede, *Hist. eccl.*, 2.14). At the royal palace at Yeavering, in the northern Northumbrian kingdom of Bernicia, Paulinus spent thirty-six days instructing converts and baptizing them in the River Glen. In the southern kingdom of Deira he baptized in the Swale, near Catterick. He also built a church in the royal vill at 'Campodunum' (possibly near Dewsbury, Yorkshire) which, however, afterwards burnt down. On one occasion he is said to have responded to a crow's ill-omened croaking by having the bird shot, and then using its death as an illustration of the futility of paganism.

Paulinus also preached in Eadwine's satellite kingdom of Lindsey. His first convert there, according to Bede, was the *praefectus* of Lincoln, a certain Blæcca. It was presumably through his influence that Paulinus was able to build a stone church in the city, the walls of which were still standing in Bede's day, which has been tentatively identified with the earliest phase of the church of St Paul in the Bail. Here Paulinus's status in the English mission reached its apogee. Some time between 628 and 631, as the only Roman bishop in England, he consecrated Honorius as archbishop of Canterbury after the death of Archbishop Justus.

Flight to Kent The Northumbrian mission came to an abrupt halt with the death of Eadwine at the battle of Hatfield Chase on 12 October 633. His realm disintegrated into its constituent parts, Deira and Bernicia, and there seems to have been a pagan reaction against the Christianity that Eadwine had promoted. For Paulinus and Æthelburh, Bede declares, 'there seemed no safety except in flight' (Bede, *Hist. eccl.*, 2.20). They set sail for Kent in the charge of one of Eadwine's loyal retainers, Bass, and together with Eanflæd, Eadwine and Æthelburh's son Uscfrea, and Eadwine's grandson Yffi. The two boys were sent for protection to King Dagobert I in Francia. Bede has a reliable report from Canterbury that the golden cross and chalice that Paulinus had brought with him were still preserved in Kent in his own day. At the invitation of Archbishop Honorius and King Eadbald, Paulinus took charge of the see of Rochester, whose previous bishop, Romanus, had died at least six years earlier. It was probably here that he received the pallium that Pope Honorius (r. 625–38), not then having heard of Eadwine's death, had sent, along with a letter to the king.

Paulinus's influence and appearance Although Bede, concerned to emphasize the role of the Augustinian mission in bringing the new faith to northern England, put a positive gloss on Paulinus's activities, it seems unlikely that Christianity struck deep roots in Northumbria during his episcopate. Its fragility is adequately attested by the pagan reaction on Eadwine's death. Although his immediate successors, Osric in Deira and Eanfrith in Bernicia, had been converted (the former by Paulinus, the latter in Ireland), both soon apostacized. Nevertheless, Paulinus did convert Hild, the future abbess of Whitby, and one of his companions, a deacon named James, remained behind in the church at York. James provided some continuity with the period in which Christianity truly flowered in Northumbria, from the time of King Oswald (d. 642), for he lived into Bede's own lifetime, teaching church music at York 'after the manner of Rome and the Kentish people' (Bede, *Hist. eccl.*, 2.20).

Bede's description of Paulinus's appearance, though it includes topoi from other sources, may contain some authentic elements. It was relayed to him by Deda, abbot of Partney, from an account of baptisms that Paulinus had performed at Littleborough (in modern Nottinghamshire) in the presence of Eadwine. The bishop 'was tall, with a slight stoop, black hair, a thin face, a slender aquiline nose, and at the same time he was both venerable and awe-inspiring in appearance' (Bede, *Hist. eccl.*, 2.16).

Death and sainthood Paulinus died on 10 October 644, his feast, under which day his name appears in pre-conquest calendars. His soul was reported to have been seen ascending to heaven 'in the form of an exceedingly beautiful great white bird, like a swan' (Colgrave, 101). He was buried in the sanctuary of the cathedral church of St Andrew in Rochester, where he was succeeded by a Kentishman, Ithamar. His body was translated into a silver shrine by Archbishop Lanfranc of Canterbury when the church was rebuilt in the 1080s. MARIOS COSTAMBEYS

Sources Bede, *Hist. eccl.*, 2.9–20; 3.14 · J. M. Wallace-Hadrill, *Bede's Ecclesiastical history of the English people: a historical commentary*, OMT (1988) · H. Mayr-Harting, *The coming of Christianity to Anglo-Saxon England* (1972) · B. Colgrave, ed. and trans., *The earliest life of Gregory the Great ... by an anonymous monk of Whitby* (1968); repr. (1985)

Paull, James (1770–1808), trader and politician, was the son of Alexander Paul, a tailor in Perth, and his wife, Elizabeth Adam. He was educated at the University of St Andrews and then briefly trained for the law with a writer to the signet in Edinburgh before leaving, at the age of eighteen, for India to seek his fortune. By 1790 he had established himself in Lucknow as a private trader, a role in which he prospered. In 1801 he returned to England with a fortune but spectacular losses at the gaming table forced him to return to India in 1802 in order to rebuild his finances. Initially he had received the assistance of the governor-general, Marquess Wellesley, in resuming his residence in Lucknow in the face of the objections of the nawab of Oudh but Wellesley soon changed his policy and sought to have all the private traders dispersed. This change of mind by Wellesley instilled a deep-seated sense of grievance in Paull who would, after once more returning to England in 1805, spend the next phase of his life pursuing a vendetta against Wellesley.

In May 1805 Paull purchased a seat in parliament for Newtown, Isle of Wight, largely out of a desire to further his campaign against Wellesley, and his first significant act upon being returned was to move for papers relating to Wellesley's conduct in India. From the outset Paull seems to have seen his campaign as a rerun of the impeachment of Warren Hastings in the 1780s with himself cast in the role of an avenging Burke and Wellesley as the hapless Hastings. It was an unrealistic hope. Paull was no Burke and the hopes he had of support from his contacts among the whigs and the supporters of the prince of Wales were to be disappointed. The whigs and Carlton House had initially appeared to be sympathetic to Paull's campaign against Wellesley, seeing it as a useful stick with which to beat the Pitt ministry. In some respects Paull's campaign does seem to have caused Wellesley some political and personal discomfort. Wellesley referred to 'the miserable attack of this obscure and low man' and to Paull as his 'assassin' (*Fortescue MSS*, 7.337; 8.204), and expended some £30,000 on his defence but William Pitt's death in January 1806 and the formation of the 'ministry of all the talents', combining Grenvillites, whigs, and supporters of the prince of Wales in a coalition ministry, robbed Paull's attack of any chance of ultimate success, despite the fact that it dragged on in parliament until 1808. The new first lord of the Treasury, Lord Grenville, was a close friend of Wellesley and this, together with the fact that the political benefits to be had from pursuing Wellesley were diminished given that the whigs were now in government, led them to pull back from their support for Paull's campaign. This betrayal, as Paull saw it, would help to push him towards alliance with radical politicians such as Sir Francis Burdett, John Horne Tooke, William Cobbett, and Major John Cartwright, who themselves had come, for various reasons, to be disappointed in the whigs.

It was through his friendship with William Windham that Paull had first met Cobbett in 1805 and it was through Cobbett that Paull would be introduced to such luminaries as Burdett and Horne Tooke, becoming a regular figure at the dinners Horne Tooke held at his home in Wimbledon, at which many of the leading lights of London radicalism regularly gathered. It was his involvement with these radical politicians and in particular his role in the politics of the constituency of Westminster which were to provide the most significant episodes in Paull's public life. The constituency of Westminster was something of a peculiarity in the unreformed electoral system owing to its electorate, which was both large (about 12,000) and socially diverse, encompassing the metropolitan élite as well as the tradesmen, artisans, and shopkeepers who formed the most numerous social grouping among the electorate. The death of the foreign secretary, Charles James Fox, in September 1806, who had been one of the constituency's two MPs since 1780, opened up the possibility for the independents and radicals in Westminster to exploit the peculiarities of the constituency and to try to break the aristocratic hold over the representation of Westminster. Paull was to be a central figure in this attempt.

At the by-election which followed Fox's death the ministry put forward Lord Percy, the son of the duke of Northumberland, as its candidate. Initially it looked as though Richard Brinsley Sheridan might also stand, but the embarrassment of two government candidates for one seat was avoided by Sheridan's withdrawal. Paull was a leading figure in the attempt by certain of the radicals to find a candidate to oppose Percy, angered by what they regarded as a typical aristocratic 'job'. This attempt failed and Percy was returned unopposed in October 1806 but his success was short-lived as the 'ministry of all the talents', desirous of shoring up its parliamentary position in the wake of Fox's death, dissolved parliament in late October 1806 and called a general election. In this election the radicals would mount a much more effective challenge at Westminster in the person of Paull himself.

Paull's opponents at Westminster in the general election of 1806 were Sheridan for the whigs and Sir Samuel Hood for the tories. Of the two it was Sheridan who had the most to fear from a challenge by Paull and it was from him and his supporters that the most sustained campaign against Paull came. In particular Sheridan, somewhat hypocritically given his own background, chose to focus on Paull's humble social origins as the son of a tailor: 'a stage from Drury Lane was brought to the hustings at Covent Garden with four tailors at work, a live goose (symbol of the tailor), and several cabbages (symbol of the tailor's meagre diet)' (Spater, 1.181). Also, a large pole with a cabbage and a smoothing iron on it and a man dressed as an ape carrying all the tools of a tailor were paraded in the constituency. This kind of vilification was repeated in some of Gillray's cartoons of the campaign, with Burdett portrayed as a goose and Paull being shown holding a giant pair of tailor's shears. Nevertheless Paull, standing as an opponent of 'oppression and corruption' (Fisher, 2.270), did well in the early days of the poll and Sheridan was able to pull ahead of him into second place only by coalescing with Hood. In the end, after fifteen days of polling Paull was beaten into third place, but by less than 300 votes: Hood polled 5478 votes, Sheridan 4758, and Paull 4481. Paull's narrow defeat by a whig–tory coalition was interpreted by his supporters as a moral victory for Paull but attempts to turn this moral victory into an actual one by petitioning against Sheridan's return were cut short by the dissolution of April 1807 which signalled another general election hard on the heels of the one of November 1806. Paull, given his showing in 1806, should have been in a strong position to take the seat but by early 1807 his relations with the other leading radicals had deteriorated. In truth, Paull's relations with the other radicals had never been easy or without their tensions: even before the 1806 election Cobbett, while approving of Paull's 'activity and zeal', had worried that he was 'too fond of the Bond Street set—has too great a desire to live amongst the great, to aim at the only objects that can save the throne and the liberties of the people' (Smith, 2.15–16).

The crucial breach in Paull's relations with the other radicals occurred when Paull tried, through a series of newspaper advertisements, to manoeuvre Burdett into standing as a joint candidate with himself at Westminster, possibly motivated by a belief that Burdett would pay his electoral expenses. The intricacies of the quarrel that ensued may never be fully known but Sir Francis Burdett, via a letter read out to a meeting of radicals held at the Crown and Anchor on 1 May 1807 by his brother, Jones Burdett, repudiated Paull's actions. Feeling himself ill-served by Burdett's behaviour Paull demanded satisfaction. Paull was known for his temper and had already fought a duel while in India which had left him unable to use his right arm fully. The duel with Burdett occurred on 2 May 1807 at Coombe Wood, Kingston, and on the second shot, which took place at Paull's insistence after the first shots missed, Burdett was hit in the thigh and Paull in the legbone. According to Francis Place, the leading figure on the radical electoral committee, many of Paull's supporters, in the light of his recent behaviour, had decided to abandon him even before the duel, but the duel certainly completed this process of alienation. At a meeting of radicals on 4 May 1807 at the Crown and Anchor pro-Burdett speakers were shouted down by the remaining Paull supporters but the Burdettites simply retired to another room and under Place formed a committee to return Burdett. Paull himself vacillated: two days before the poll at Westminster he withdrew but eventually allowed himself to be nominated only to withdraw again before the end of polling, in which he finished a distant last with only 269 votes, while Burdett, without any active participation on his part, topped the poll with 5134 votes, thanks to the activities of Place's Westminster committee. This crushing blow, brought on in part by his own impatience and scheming, was to mark the end of Paull's political career. The following year, after another large loss at the gaming tables and racked by pain from his various duelling wounds, Paull committed suicide on 15 April by cutting his own throat at his house, 2 Charles Street, Westminster. According to a contemporary obituary, Paull had recently been given to requesting that 'when he died, which would be soon, he trusted that his body would be conveyed back to the East Indies and blown up' (GM, 78, 1.373). This last wish was not granted and James Paull, who despite his faults was a key figure in opening up the Westminster constituency, was interred on 21 April 1808 at St James's, Piccadilly.

STEPHEN M. LEE

Sources J. W. Anderson and R. G. Thorne, 'Paull, James', HoP, Commons, 1790–1820, 4.733–5 · D. R. Fisher, 'Westminster', HoP, Commons, 1790–1820, 2.266–83 · M. W. Patterson, Sir Francis Burdett and his times (1770–1844), 2 vols. (1931) · G. Spater, William Cobbett: the poor man's friend, 2 vols. (1982) · GM, 1st ser., 78 (1808), 373–4 · C. Bewley and D. Bewley, Gentleman radical: a life of John Horne Tooke, 1736–1812 (1998) · E. Smith, William Cobbett: a biography, 2 vols. (1878) · J. A. Hove, For the cause of truth: radicalism in London, 1796–1821 (1982) · The correspondence of George, prince of Wales, 1770–1812, ed. A. Aspinall, 8 vols. (1963–71) · The manuscripts of J. B. Fortescue, 10 vols., HMC, 30 (1892–1927), vols. 7–8 · I. Butler, The eldest brother: the Marquess Wellesley, the duke of Wellington's eldest brother (1973) · J. M. Main, 'Radical Westminster, 1807–1820', Historical Studies: Australia and New Zealand, 12 (1965–7), 186–204 · DNB

Likenesses J. Gillray, caricature, 1806, repro. in Spater, William Cobbett · J. Gillray, caricature, etching, pubd 1806, BM, NPG; repro. in Patterson, Sir Francis Burdett and his times · J. Gillray, caricature, pubd 1807, BM, NPG; repro. in Patterson, *Sir Francis Burdett*, facing p. 202 · J. Gillray, caricature, 1807, repro. in Spater, *William Cobbett* · Hopwood, stipple, pubd 1808, BM, NPG · J. Gillray, caricatures, BM · J. Gillray, pencil drawing, BM

Paulton, Abraham Walter (1812–1876), politician and journalist, was the son of Walter Paulton of Bolton, Lancashire, where he was born. His family were Roman Catholics, and he was sent to Stonyhurst College to be educated for the priesthood as a Jesuit. There his views underwent a change, and on leaving college at the age of sixteen or seventeen he was apprenticed to a surgeon named Rainforth at Bolton. His thirst for general knowledge was strong, and he began to take a deep interest in current political questions, especially that of the controversial corn laws. He began to address public meetings, and soon became a good speaker.

Deeper involvement in the anti-cornlaw movement, in particular a brilliantly successful speech at the Bolton theatre in July 1838, induced Paulton to abandon the medical profession and take up politics. The Bolton speech was a milestone for him. Taking over from the ineffective Dr Birnie, he spoke fluently and convincingly for fifteen minutes to revive interest in the meeting and was asked to return to deliver a fuller lecture. He was soon afterwards introduced to Cobden, and at the behest of Archibald Prentice became the first lecturer for the Anti-Corn Law League. He spoke at the Manchester corn exchange and Birmingham town hall in October and November 1838 and, between December 1838 and January 1839, spoke before a total of 80,000 people on a missionary tour in Lancashire. However, his suspected Chartist sympathies and frequent desire to address a wider radical agenda meant this and subsequent lecture tours (in London and Scotland) were frequently counter-productive to the league. He was removed from his lecturing post in April 1839 to edit the fortnightly *Anti-Corn-Law Circular* (*Anti-Bread-Tax Circular* from April 1841), the earliest organ of the league and published in Manchester. This was succeeded in September 1843 by *The League*, which had its headquarters in London.

When the repeal of the corn laws made the league redundant, Paulton returned to Manchester. In conjunction with Henry Rawson he purchased the *Manchester Times*, a newspaper representing the views of the more 'advanced section' of the Liberal Party. This paper (later amalgamated with the *Manchester Examiner*) was managed by Paulton from 1848 to 1854.

In 1854 Paulton married Martha, daughter of James Mellor of Liverpool, and from that time he lived in London or at his country house, Boughton Hall, Surrey. In his retirement he remained interested in politics and current affairs and remained friendly with Cobden, John Bright, and other old associates. He was a man of great ability, deeply versed in political questions and the philosophy of politics, and in later years was keenly interested in physical science. His reputation was as a conversationalist of the first order. His writings, consisting mainly of newspaper articles, were not collected.

Paulton died at Boughton Hall on 6 June 1876, leaving his widow, a son, and a daughter. He was buried at Kensal Green cemetery. C. W. SUTTON, rev. MATTHEW LEE

Sources N. McCord, *The Anti-Corn Law League, 1838–1846* (1958) · D. T. W. Price, 'Paulton, Abraham Walter', *BDMBR*, vol. 2 · *Manchester Examiner and Times* (12 June 1876) · A. Prentice, *History of the Anti-Corn-Law League*, 2 vols. (1853) · J. Morley, *Life of Cobden*, 2 vols. (1881) · H. Ashworth, *Recollections of Richard Cobden … and the Anti-Corn-Law League*, new edn (1877) · A. Somerville, *Free trade and the league* (1852–3) · Boase, *Mod. Eng. biog.* · *CGPLA Eng. & Wales* (1876) **Archives** BL, corresp. with Richard Cobden, Add. MS 43662 · Man. CL, J. B. Smith's corn law MSS · Man. CL, Wilson MSS · W. Sussex RO, corresp. with Richard Cobden **Wealth at death** £8000: administration with will, 20 Oct 1876, *CGPLA Eng. & Wales*

Paulus Anglicus (*fl.* 1404/5), ecclesiastical controversialist, is the name which has long been given to the author of *Speculum aureum de titulis beneficiorum* (1404/5), a dialogue between Petrus and Paulus which advocates reform of the church, and attacks the abuses of the pontificate of Boniface IX, the second Roman pope of the great schism. Melchior Goldast, who published the work in his *Monarchia* (1621; 3.1527–58) was the first person to identify the author as English and to give him the name Paulus Anglicus. Others have endorsed this view, largely because the work attacks annates as a form of simony, and because there is a reference to *personatus* as meaning 'parsonage' (an English usage), an allusion to Thomas Becket, and a gratuitous reference to Canterbury as a metropolitan see. However, there are no English manuscripts of the work, all the early ones being Polish or Bohemian, and during the twentieth century it came to be accepted that the tract emanated from the circle of non-Gallican writers subsequently influential in the German nation at the Council of Constance (1414–18).

The identity of the author of the *Speculum aureum* seems unlikely to be definitively settled. The strongest candidate is Petrus (or Piotr) Wysz (*d.* 1414), a Padua-trained lawyer, who was a notable figure in the political and ecclesiastical life of Poland in the years on either side of 1400. Having become master of the faculty of arts at Prague University, he played an important part in the establishment of the University of Cracow, of which he was the first chancellor. Bishop of Cracow and Posen, he was also a councillor to Queen Jadwig and her husband King Władysław II, serving the latter as ambassador to the Council of Pisa in 1409. Another, less likely, possibility is Paulus Wladimiri (*d.* 1435x40), a native of northern Poland, who studied law at Prague, and who was later sent by Petrus Wysz to continue his studies at Padua. He subsequently taught at Cracow, where he was elected rector of the university in 1415. Like Wysz, he was also engaged in secular affairs, in 1419 acting as his country's proctor before the emperor Sigismund in a dispute between Poland and Prussia. Neither Wysz nor Wladimiri can be shown to have a connection of any kind with England, and in that respect, at least, the authorship of the *Speculum aureum* has unquestionably been misattributed. MARGARET HARVEY

Sources C. G. F. Walch, *Monimenta medii aevi*, 2, pt 1 (1761), 69–216 · H. Heimpel, *Studien zur Kirchen- und Reichsreform des 15. Jahrhunderts*,

2: *Zu zwei Kirchenreform-Traktaten des beginnenden 15. Jahrhunderts* (Heidelberg, 1974), pt 1 · P. H. Stump, *The reforms of the council of Constance, 1414–1418* (1994), 13–14, 173–205 · M. Goldast, *Monarchia sancti Romani imperii*, 3 (Frankfurt am Main, 1621), 1527–58

Paulus a Sancto Spiritu. *See* King, Paul (*d.* 1655).

Pauncefote, Julian, Baron Pauncefote (1828–1902), lawyer and diplomatist, was born on 13 September 1828 at Munich, Bavaria, the third and youngest son of Robert Pauncefote (formerly Smith; 1788–1843) of Preston Court, Preston, Gloucestershire, and his wife, Emma Smith (*d.* 1853), daughter of John Raphael *Smith, artist and engraver. His father, who had inherited Preston Court from Sir George Pauncefote of Stoke Hall, had sufficient means for the family to spend much of their time abroad, and the young Pauncefote grew up fluent in French and able to understand both German (which he did not speak) and Italian. His first school was in Passy, France, where instruction was entirely in French; his second was the Pensionnat Janin, Geneva. However, after 1840 the family spent more time in England and in 1843 his father died. In August 1843, when he was nearly fifteen, Pauncefote was one of the first 218 pupils enrolled at Marlborough College, Marlborough, Wiltshire, the decidedly robust environment of which, in his biographer's words, 'helped to fortify his solid English character and sound common sense' (Mowat, 6). Appointed a prefect in 1844, he left in the summer of 1845, intended, like his brother Bernard, for a career in the Indian army. He was commissioned in the Madras light infantry but did not serve; the death of his eldest brother, Robert, in 1847 caused him instead to stay in London and to read for the bar at the Inner Temple.

Legal practice in Britain and abroad Pauncefote was called to the bar on 4 May 1852 and practised for some ten years, interrupted, with important consequences for his future, by three months as private secretary to Sir William Molesworth, a position which reflected his membership at that time of a circle as noted for its artistic interests as for its Benthamite reforming zeal. It was thus that he met and later married, on 19 September 1859, Selina Fitzgerald (*d.* 1926), daughter of Major William Cubitt of Catfield Hall, Norfolk. They took up residence at 18 Chapel Street, Bedford Square, London. On 11 July 1860 a son was born, but lived for only three weeks. Almost at the same time Pauncefote lost almost all his private fortune by the collapse of a bank. He determined to repair his fortune by legal practice abroad and in 1862 sailed for Hong Kong accompanied by his wife and newborn daughter, the first of four daughters who were to survive him.

Hong Kong in 1862 was a turbulent place, and crime and piracy were rife. In May 1866 Pauncefote was appointed acting attorney-general of the colony, and on 22 July attorney-general, a post which left him free to continue his private practice and accumulate a moderate fortune (which, however, he lost in a second crash in 1874). Over the next seven years he worked with Governor Sir Richard Graves MacDonnell to reform the police and improve the administration of justice, being himself responsible for

Julian Pauncefote, Baron Pauncefote (1828–1902), by Elliott & Fry, pubd 1900

preparation of the colony's code of civil procedure. As attorney-general Pauncefote also deputized for the chief justice of the supreme court while the latter was on leave. During his own two periods of leave, in 1867 and 1871, he visited Shanghai. On leaving Hong Kong in December 1873 he was knighted for his services.

Pauncefote had left Hong Kong to take up the new post of chief justice of the Leeward Islands. After eighteen months at home he went out to Antigua in January 1874, leaving his family in London. His brief mission was successful though he did not enjoy it and missed his family. Fortunately he was soon able to return to the UK where he took a house for his growing family on The Green at Richmond. Lord Carnarvon, the colonial secretary, had noted his high legal reputation and wished him to succeed Sir Henry Holland as legal assistant under-secretary in the Colonial Office, which he did in September 1874. In this capacity Pauncefote helped facilitate the Disraeli ministry's purchase of the Khedive's Suez Canal Company shares.

At the Foreign Office In 1876 a similar post was created in the Foreign Office and Pauncefote was appointed to it by the foreign secretary, Lord Derby. In January 1880 he was created KCMG and three months later CB. In 1882, in a striking breach with precedent, the foreign secretary, Lord Granville, insisted he be appointed permanent under-secretary of state in succession to Lord Tenterden, many of whose duties Pauncefote was already discharging. On 1 October 1882 Granville wrote to Gladstone about Pauncefote: 'I have the highest opinion of his abilities, character and industry. He is popular in the office and with the Corps Diplomatique, an excellent Frenchman and his knowledge of law is constantly of use' (Fitzmaurice, 2.446).

Pauncefote's seven years as permanent under-secretary confirmed this high opinion. He had come to enjoy sunshine and found his return to London a real hardship. However, he was wholly dedicated to his work, which he enjoyed immensely; his principal and almost sole recreation being to enjoy a quiet Sunday with his family. Otherwise, according to his daughter Sibyl, he never liked being more than a brief drive from a railway station from which he could get back to work. Every working day he received the day's dispatch boxes in the morning at his home at 14 Cromwell Place and minuted the incoming correspondence, then some 60,000 items a year, for the secretary of state. He would then lunch and set off for the office at a quarter to two, remaining at his desk until seven o'clock or later. He was a member of Arthur's Club and the Wellington, but seldom went to either.

Though the Eastern question had been temporarily resolved in 1878, many tensions remained, and it fell to Pauncefote to deal with the thorny problem of navigation of the Danube. Dilke said 'that Pauncefote was the only man in England who understood it' (Mowat, 38). The European commission which he proposed to oversee the dredging of the mouth of the Danube was to survive even the First World War. It was Pauncefote, too, who proposed the plan which resolved tension with Germany over the settlement of New Guinea (Fitzmaurice, 2.430). But the free navigation of waterways was to be a continuing theme of his diplomatic career. In 1885, together with Sir Charles Rivers Wilson, he was appointed a delegate to the international commission in Paris on the free navigation of the Suez Canal, negotiating the draft settlement on which was based the convention of Constantinople (29 October 1888) which established the right of free passage in both peace and war. He was created GCMG in the new year honours list of 1886 and KCB in 1888.

Ambassador to the United States On 2 April 1889 Lord Salisbury appointed Pauncefote minister to the United States. The post had been left vacant for some months following the recall of Sir Lionel Sackville-West, Lord Sackville, until the new president, Benjamin Harrison, had taken office. Salisbury needed to appoint someone of sufficient seniority to soothe ruffled feelings, who had not previously served as ambassador. He sounded out Pauncefote, who enthusiastically agreed, believing as he did in the prime importance to Britain of the unity of the English-speaking peoples. In 1893, congress having decided to make it possible, Britain became the first country to raise diplomatic relations with the USA to ambassadorial level.

As a diplomatist Pauncefote showed 'solid rather than showy qualities' (*The Times*, 16 May 1902). His legal training was of inestimable value, since he had to deal with men who were also lawyers, and from the beginning he recognized the need to cultivate not only the members of the administration but leading members of the senate. Though he was perhaps less sensitive to the need to cultivate public opinion, and may have missed opportunities, more importantly he never put a foot wrong. To his success his warm personality and generous nature undoubtedly contributed much; Cecil Spring Rice commented in June 1891: 'I like old Pauncefote, who is kindness itself' (*Letters and Friendships*, 1.113). Pauncefote himself generously said that 'his success in Washington' (in a career lasting from 1889 to 1902) 'was due to two of his secretaries, Michael Herbert and Cecil Spring Rice', neither of whom

served with him, however, after 1895 (*Letters and Friendships*, 1.177). On other occasions he expressed equal appreciation of the support of his wife and eldest daughter, Maud, hostesses at the embassy on Connecticut Avenue.

Early negotiations The first major issue with which Pauncefote had to deal was the pelagic seals dispute. In 1881, on behalf of the American government, Secretary Blaine, whose hostility to Canada was notorious, claimed jurisdiction over the whole Bering Sea. British policy had to steer a fine line between letting the Canadian sealers down on the one hand and arousing American demands for annexation on the other. The importance of conservation was recognized by both sides and a *modus vivendi* established. Finally in February 1892 the issue was referred to the decision of an international commission of arbitration at Paris which in August 1893 rejected the American claim that the Bering Sea was territorial waters but confirmed the *modus vivendi*.

A much more serious challenge was posed by the Venezuelan boundary dispute. The dispute itself was of long standing and reflected the uncertainties of map making in the early nineteenth century, when Britain had been awarded Guiana. It erupted into public notice when on 20 July 1895 Secretary of State Robert Olney sent an intemperate note to London asserting the right of the United States to intervene in the dispute and citing the Monroe doctrine in support of his view. Unwisely as it turned out, Lord Salisbury believed that the matter was not urgent and could wait. Four months later he replied with a cool note denying the applicability of the doctrine. President Cleveland was incensed, and on 17 December sent a special message to congress. In it he stated that repeated American attempts to resolve the dispute had failed through British obduracy and that if necessary the United States should intervene to determine the correct line. 'Even Pauncefote, shrewd and experienced, very much *persona grata* in American political and government circles, and intimate enough with Olney to have an excellent basis for judgment, underestimated the moral content of the American stand' (Campbell, 25). Fortunately, though he did not hurry to do so, in February 1896 Salisbury agreed to arbitration, effectively conceding the Americans' right to intervene while denying them the opportunity to do so. In the event the arbitral award followed the existing line of demarcation (the Schomburgk line) with only two significant deviations in favour of Venezuela: a complete vindication both of British contentions and Pauncefote's skill as a negotiator.

In January 1897, therefore, the queen was able to announce to parliament the conclusion both of the Venezuelan arbitration agreement and of a general treaty of arbitration with the United States (the Olney–Pauncefote treaty). The latter, which reflected Pauncefote's personal commitment to the rule of law and the ideal of arbitration as a method of settling international disputes, was the first of its kind and in scope was much broader than those agreed upon later under presidents Roosevelt and Taft. The McKinley administration gave it its full support in the senate, but in the only major disappointment of

Pauncefote's career it failed of ratification by forty-three votes to twenty-six, three votes short of the necessary two-thirds, on 5 May 1897.

The Cuban War The explosion of the USS *Maine* in Havana harbour on 15 February 1898 raised passions which President McKinley, who was anxious to avoid war if at all possible, worked skilfully to restrain. Secretary of State William R. Day indicated that he would be prepared to listen to a European initiative. As dean of the diplomatic corps it fell to Pauncefote to lead the group of six who presented a prearranged joint message to the president on 5 or 6 April urging restraint. Neither the message nor the reply, which claimed that the situation in Cuba had become 'insufferable', nor the statement of Spain's position composed, at Pauncefote's suggestion, by the Spanish minister in Washington, had much effect, however (Offner, 167–8).

When McKinley finally sent his message to congress to obtain congressional authority for military intervention in Cuba, Pauncefote was deeply upset at his suggestion that the 'civilized world' approved of the American position. Given that the Spanish had agreed to all the demands presented up to that time, he believed that military force was an unjustified act of aggression and that a peaceful settlement was still possible. He was also concerned about the dangerous precedent that American seizure of Cuba would have for other European colonies in the Caribbean. Hence on 14 April he held a meeting at the embassy to urge a second European démarche, urging the American government to accept the Spanish minister's memorandum as the basis for peace, but for a variety of reasons none of the European governments concerned accepted the suggestion. During the war Pauncefote continued his efforts to bring about an early peace. The administration, however, was unwilling to take any action until both Cuba and the Philippines had been secured. Meanwhile British opinion had tended to side with the United States. A particularly enthusiastic speech by Joseph Chamberlain created problems for British diplomatists in Europe, but the overall effect of this support was further to improve the growing understanding between London and Washington.

At the end of the war John Hay was recalled from his post as ambassador to London and replaced Day as secretary of state in September 1898. As his biographer writes:

> He had, fortunately, a warm coadjutor in the British Ambassador, Sir Julian … Pauncefote, a diplomatist, conciliatory, open-minded, very sensitive to questions of honor, ready to assume, until he had proved to the contrary, that his colleagues' intentions were as honest as his own. During nearly four years he and Secretary Hay worked together to harmonise the interests of their respective countries. (Thayer, 2.202–3)

Pauncefote was in fact due to retire in September 1898, having reached the age of seventy. However, in view of the need for continuity he was asked to stay on—as it turned out, indefinitely.

Panama Canal negotiations The main issue with which Hay and Pauncefote had to deal was that of Britain's attitude towards an isthmian canal. The voyage of the USS *Oregon* round Cape Horn from San Francisco to Santiago de Cuba made the need for one obvious. The United States, however, by the Clayton–Bulwer treaty of 1850, had first to get Britain's agreement. To forestall the danger that congress might act unilaterally, at Hay's request in December 1898 the possibility of revising the treaty was put to Lord Salisbury by the American chargé d'affaires, Henry White. Salisbury agreed, stipulating only that tolls levied should be the same for all users, and suggested that, given his special knowledge of the question, Pauncefote should conduct the negotiations with Hay in Washington.

Negotiations were held up by the concurrent dispute about the Alaskan boundary, which after some moments of tension was resolved by treaty in 1902. Meanwhile Pauncefote was appointed senior British delegate to the first Hague conference (1899). He could not persuade the other countries to accept the principle of binding arbitration but they did agree to establish a permanent tribunal to which nations might have recourse, in recognition of which Pauncefote was appointed Britain's first member of the Permanent Court of Arbitration and raised to the peerage on 18 August 1899. On his return to Washington the Panama Canal negotiations were resumed. Britain's three main proposals—that the new treaty merely amend that of 1850, that the canal should not be fortified (on the analogy of the Suez Canal), and that the same tolls should be charged to all nations—were accepted and on 2 February 1900 Pauncefote was authorized to sign the resulting treaty, known in the USA as the first Hay–Pauncefote treaty. Three days later it was sent to the senate, where it immediately ran into trouble. The main bone of contention was the provision that the canal should not be fortified, and an amendment making this possible was one of three attached to the treaty when it eventually was passed in December 1900 with five votes to spare.

Britain therefore rejected the first treaty in February 1901. Pauncefote again returned to London for instructions and on his return he and Hay drew up a draft which, while maintaining the principle of equal tolls, abrogated the Clayton–Bulwer treaty rather than amending it and allowed the United States to fortify the canal provided that free passage was allowed to the ships of neutral nations in time of war, as at Suez. This draft Hay sent to the American ambassador in London, Joseph Choate, and it was he who with Lord Lansdowne, the new foreign secretary, was mainly responsible for shaping the final form of the new agreement. This, the second Hay–Pauncefote treaty, was signed on 18 November and approved by the senate by seventy-two votes to six on 16 December 1901.

By this time Theodore Roosevelt had succeeded McKinley as president, and Pauncefote, like his immediate successor Sir Michael Herbert, was one of those who belonged to Roosevelt's inner circle. 'He admired, liked, and trusted them, and they understood America and in turn were beloved by Americans that knew them' (Beale, 132). Pauncefote had been made an honorary doctor of laws of both Harvard and Columbia universities in 1900. He was suffering increasingly badly, however, from gout, and in April 1902 he sustained a major heart attack, believed at the time to have been precipitated by the German ambassador's allegation that in 1898 Pauncefote had been secretly working against the United States. After a short rally he died in his sleep in the embassy residence on the morning of 24 May 1902. The measure of the success of his unique mission was that there followed, in his daughter's words, a 'wonderful expression of sorrow, of esteem and even affection' (Mowat, xv). President Roosevelt broke with precedent by flying the American flag at half-mast on the White House and personally attended the official funeral ceremony organized by the American government on 28 May at St John's Episcopal Church, Washington, where Pauncefote had regularly worshipped. As a further courtesy the ambassador's body was conveyed to Southampton on the USS *Brooklyn* for interment in the family graveyard at St Oswald's Church, Stoke, near Newark-on-Trent, Nottinghamshire, on 15 August 1902.

PETER CALVERT

Sources *The Times* (26–30 May 1902) · *The Times* (3 June 1902) · *The Times* (2 July 1902) · *The Times* (15 July 1902) · *The Times* (16 July 1902) · *The Times* (2 Aug 1902) · *FO List* (1902–3) · R. B. Mowat, *The life of Lord Pauncefote, first ambassador to the United States* (1929) · *British and foreign state papers*, 89 (1896–7) · *British and foreign state papers*, 91 (1898–9) · *Papers relating to the foreign relations of the United States*, 1902 (1903) · H. K. Beale, *Theodore Roosevelt and the rise of America to world power* (1956) · A. E. Campbell, *Great Britain and the United States, 1895–1903* (1960) · *The letters and friendships of Sir Cecil Spring Rice: a record*, ed. S. Gwynn, 2 vols. (1929) · D. McCullough, *The path between the seas: the creation of the Panama Canal, 1870–1914* (1977) · J. L. Offner, *An unwanted war: the diplomacy of the United States and Spain over Cuba, 1895–1898* (1992) · W. R. Thayer, *The life and letters of John Hay*, 2 vols. (1915) · E. G. Petty-Fitzmaurice, *The life of Granville George Leveson Gower, second Earl Granville*, 2nd edn, 2 vols. (1905) · A. G. Gardiner, *The life of Sir William Harcourt*, 2 vols. (1923) · A. L. Kennedy, *Salisbury, 1830–1903: portrait of a statesman* (1953) · D. S. Murray, *James G. Blaine: a political idol of other days* (1963) · Lord Newton [T. W. Legh], *Lord Lansdowne: a biography* (1929) · GEC, *Peerage*
Archives Balliol Oxf., corresp. with Sir Robert Morier · BL, corresp. with Sir Charles Wentworth Dilke, Add. MS 43882 · Bodl. Oxf., corresp. with Lord Kimberley · CAC Cam., corresp. with Sir Cecil Spring-Rice · CCC Cam., corresp. with sixteenth earl of Derby · CUL, letters to Lord Hardinge · PRO, corresp. with Sir Evelyn Baring, FO 633 · PRO, Foreign Office records · PRO, corresp. with Earl Granville, PRO 30/29
Likenesses B. Constant, oils, 1894, priv. coll.; copy, Marlborough College, Wiltshire · Elliott & Fry, photograph, pubd 1900, NPG [*see illus.*] · T [T. Chartran], caricature, chromolithograph, NPG; repro. in *VF* (7 April 1883) · oils (after B. Constant, *c*.1896), Marlborough College, Wiltshire · photograph, repro. in Mowat, *Life of Lord Pauncefote*, frontispiece
Wealth at death £63,685 4*s*. 1*d*.: probate, 30 July 1902, *CGPLA Eng. & Wales*

Paveley, Sir Walter (1319–1375), soldier, was the son of Sir Walter Paveley (*d*. 1327) and Maud (1304–*c*.1366), daughter and heir of Sir Stephen Burghersh (*d*. 1310). As the only son of a Kentish gentleman, Paveley could have exercised some discretion in his choice of career, but his family connections left him well placed to find long and distinguished employment in Edward III's campaigns against the French. Though the existence of at least two separate branches of the Paveley family, one based in Wiltshire and the other in Kent, has caused some confusion, it is clear that Sir Walter belonged to the latter branch. Paveley's father was of Northamptonshire stock, but his wife's inheritance left him firmly established among the Kentish gentry. The family holdings were further increased by the death of his kinsman Henry *Burghersh, bishop of Lincoln, in 1340. Following the death of his father in January 1327, and the subsequent marriage of his mother to Sir Thomas Aledon (or Aldon), a family friend and fellow stalwart of the Burghersh circle, little is heard of Paveley until his military career began to flower in the opening exchanges of the Hundred Years' War, though he was precociously a knight by 1335.

Despite the problems of identification, Paveley's presence can be detected in a remarkable series of campaigns. His first recorded service was at the age of nineteen during the fitful Cambrésis campaign of autumn 1338. He then served in Brittany with Bartholomew Burghersh in 1342–3 and 1345. Froissart places him (as Guillaumes Penniel) with Sir Walter Mauny at the siege of Rennes in 1342, and in Gascony the following year. Paveley subsequently enlisted in most of the French expeditions mounted before the war was brought to a halt by the treaty of Bretigny in 1360, including the crucial Crécy–Calais campaign of 1346–7, and the Poitiers campaign of 1356.

Although Paveley was evidently an extremely experienced soldier, it is also clear that he owed his later prominence, at least in part, to a close friendship with the Burghersh family, above and beyond any kinship ties. Not only were most of Paveley's early campaigns conducted in the company either of Bartholomew *Burghersh, Lord Burghersh, or of the latter's son, also Bartholomew *Burghersh, but Paveley also enjoyed sufficient esteem with his baronial cousins to be involved in their personal affairs. For example, in June 1354 Paveley obtained letters of protection to travel to the Holy Land with the younger Bartholomew, who in May 1365, now Lord Burghersh, nominated Paveley as one of his attorneys as he prepared for a trip to Flanders; more significantly, in 1369 Paveley was named as one of Burghersh's executors and was left a gilt cup, a suit of armour, and some Kentish estates in the latter's will.

In itself useful, this connection may also have brought Paveley to the attention of Edward, the Black Prince—it can hardly be coincidental that both Bartholomew Burghersh junior and Walter Paveley appear frequently in the prince's household records, the former as an official and confidant, and the latter as a 'bachelor' with an annuity of 40 marks. It is difficult to pinpoint Paveley's initial contact with Prince Edward, but he was certainly held in high regard by the time of the battle of Crécy, where he acted as one of the prince's advisers, for which he was later rewarded with generous new year's gifts while on campaign in Normandy. Paveley's inclusion in the late 1340s among the original knights of the Garter confirms his membership of the close-knit body of aristocratic soldiers who provided the backbone of Edward III's armies.

Paveley died on 28 June 1375, and was buried in the church of the Blackfriars, London. With his wife (perhaps Joan St Philibert), to whom he was certainly married by

1354, he had two sons: Sir Edward, who died on 7 December 1375, and Sir Walter, who was killed in the naval expedition of 1379. Neither left any children, and their estates descended to the Aledon family. Paveley's arms, azure a cross flory or, appear in the thirteenth stall on the prince's side at Windsor.   RICHARD GORSKI

Sources Chancery records • exchequer, queen's remembrancer accounts various, PRO, E 101 • chancery treaty rolls, PRO, C 76 • chancery warrants, PRO, C 81 • G. F. Beltz, *Memorials of the most noble order of the Garter* (1841); repr. (1973) • M. C. B. Dawes, ed., *Register of Edward, the Black Prince*, 4 vols., PRO (1930–33) • N. H. Nicolas, ed., *Testamenta vetusta: being illustrations from wills*, 2 vols. (1826) • *Œuvres*, ed. K. de Lettenhove and A. Scheler, 28 vols. (Brussels, 1867–77) • *Chronicon Galfridi le Baker de Swynebroke*, ed. E. M. Thompson (1889) • F. Palgrave, ed., *The parliamentary writs and writs of military summons*, 2 vols. in 4 (1827–34) • *CIPM*, 7, no. 3; 14, no. 184 • W. H. Bliss, ed., *Calendar of entries in the papal registers relating to Great Britain and Ireland: petitions to the pope* (1896), 262

Paver, William (1802–1871), genealogist, was born in 1802. Little is known of his life other than as a genealogist. He was an assiduous collector of genealogical material. In 1867 he acted as registrar of births and deaths at 4 Rougier Street, York. There was strong criticism by contemporary genealogists of Paver's method of genealogical construction. It is even suggested that some of his evidence was forged. He sought to attract attention to his collections in a pamphlet called *Pedigrees of families of the city of York, from a manuscript entitled 'The heraldic visitations of Yorkshire consolidated'* (1842), and by a list of Yorkshire pedigrees in his possession, furnished to the *New England Historical and Genealogical Register* for July 1857. He also issued part 1 of *Original genealogical abstracts of the wills of individuals of noble and ancient families now or formerly resident in the county of York, with notes* (1830), the contents of which were superseded by the four volumes of *Testamenta Eboracensia* printed by the Surtees Society.

In 1874 Paver's extensive collections relating to Yorkshire were acquired by the trustees of the British Museum, where they are catalogued as Add. MSS 29644–29703. By far the most valuable portion of the Paver manuscripts is the transcripts of marriage licences, beginning in 1567, formerly preserved in the registry of York, as the originals have disappeared. These transcripts were printed, with notes, by the Revd C. B. Norcliffe in the *Yorkshire Archaeological and Topographical Journal* beginning in volume 7 (1882); but regrettably Paver omitted to give the day of the month as well as the year. The licences are still in print and are essential for historians of Yorkshire. His consolidation of the Yorkshire 'Visitations' of 1584, 1612, and 1665, contains about 900 pedigrees, but is not considered an important work. Paver's son, Percy Woodroffe Paver, also an industrious antiquary, made 'Extracts from his father's Yorkshire collections', 1852 (Add. MS 29692, fol. 49); 'Extracts out of Torre's MSS at York', 1848 (Add. MS 29689); and a useful general 'Index to York collections' (Add. MS 29691).

Paver, whose wife, Jane, survived him, died at Rishworth Street, Wakefield, on 1 June 1871.

GORDON GOODWIN, *rev.* MYFANWY LLOYD

Sources W. White, *History, gazetteer and directory of the East and North Ridings of Yorkshire* (privately printed, Sheffield, 1840) • Boase, *Mod. Eng. biog.* • N. H. S., 'Paver's abstracts of Yorkshire wills', *N&Q*, 3rd ser., 2 (1862), 387 • *N&Q*, 5th ser., 1 (1874), 360 • *N&Q*, 5th ser., 10 (1878), 336 • census returns, 1881
Archives BL, Yorkshire collections, Add. MSS 29644–29703 • Coll. Arms, abstracts of York marriage licences • Leeds Leisure Services, pedigrees of principal Yorkshire families • W. Yorks. AS, Leeds, Yorkshire Archaeological Society, Yorkshire collections • York Minster Library, York Minster Archives, Yorkshire pedigrees and abstracts | Bodl. Oxf., additions to Dugdale's visitation of Yorkshire • Bodl. Oxf., corresp. with Sir T. Phillipps

Pavlova, Anna Pavlovna [*formerly* Anna Matveyevna Pavlova] (1881–1931), ballet dancer, was born in St Petersburg on 31 January/12 February 1881 according to an entry in the register of the St Petersburg military hospital; she later changed her second name to Pavlovna. Her mother, Lyubov Fyodorovna Pavlova, a laundry maid, was married to a reserve soldier, Matvey Pavlov; but Anna was most probably the illegitimate daughter from an earlier relationship with a reserve soldier or minor official. There is also the suggestion that she was partly Jewish, which would have reinforced the social stigma of her birth in imperial Russia. Pavlova spent her childhood with her grandmother at Ligovo, outside St Petersburg, but in 1890 she was taken to see *The Sleeping Beauty*, the newly created ballet by Marius Petipa and Pyotr Tchaikovsky, at the Maryinsky Theatre. The production, music, and dancing captured Pavlova's imagination, and from then on she was determined to become a ballerina, although she had to wait two years to qualify for Imperial Ballet School. Ironically, having wanted to be Princess Aurora (a role she first danced in 1908), she never found this a character to which she was totally suited.

Early success At the age of eleven Pavlova made her first recorded appearance at the Maryinsky in *The Magic Fairy Tale*, choreographed by Marius Petipa for pupils of the school. In 1898 she made her official début in the *pas de trois* from *Pharaoh's Daughter*, some six months before graduating in April 1899, when she danced in Aleksandr Gorsky's *Clorinda* and Pavel Gerdt's *Imaginary Dryads*. Her rise through the company was swift and measured. She began as a *coryphée* and was promoted annually so that in 1906 she had reached the rank of ballerina.

Apparently frail in physique, Pavlova looked different from other dancers of the day (who tended to be stockier and more muscular than later dancers). Almost immediately she was singled out from her contemporaries for being graceful, soft, and feminine. It was these qualities rather than an outstanding technique that attracted attention. She was not a virtuoso dancer in the popular Italian style of the day, but she could be dramatic, poetic, flirtatious, or comic as roles required. She also performed lively character dances. On stage she hid her technique, but her line was impeccable and her arabesque and *pas de bourrée* unsurpassed. Dance was her religion: she was totally dedicated to the art. Like most dancers she worked on her technique throughout her career. In 1903 she and the ballerina Vera Trefilova travelled to Milan to study with Caterina Beretta, and in 1906 she engaged Enrico

Anna Pavlovna Pavlova (1881–1931), by Sir John Lavery, 1911 [*La mort du cygne: Anna Pavlova*]

Cecchetti as her private teacher knowing that he had helped other dancers, most notably Olga Preobrazhenska, overcome their weaknesses.

Among Pavlova's first successes were her Zulme in *Giselle* in September 1899 and her first created role, Hoarfrost in *The Seasons* in February 1900. In 1902 she consolidated her success by dancing Nikiya, the temple dancer heroine of *La bayadère*, and in 1903 the title role in *Giselle*. These ballets suited her, and used both her dramatic ability and outstanding ethereal lightness. *Giselle* was a ballet she continued to dance throughout her career. Although she would have liked to dance Nikiya in the West, *La bayadère* seemed too quaintly old-fashioned for audiences in the 1920s. As Nikiya and Giselle, Pavlova caught the attention of the ageing Marius Petipa, whom she asked to coach her in his ballets. Although at the end of his career, Petipa was still willing to adapt roles to show off the talent of dancers he wanted to encourage, and for her début in the title role of *Paquita*, he created a new variation to music for the harp by Riccardo Drigo.

Pavlova also worked with the next generation of choreographers, particularly the reformers Aleksandr Gorsky and Michel Fokine, both of whom welcomed her ability to act through dance. Both introduced a new plasticity to their dances, and Pavlova was a noted exponent of this new free-flowing style. In Gorsky's revised versions of established ballets, which replaced balletic clichés with an attempt at dramatic logic, Pavlova was called on to perform at the imperial theatres in both St Petersburg and Moscow. For Gorsky, Pavlova danced Kitri in *Don Quixote* and Bint-Ana in *Pharaoh's Daughter*. For Michel Fokine (also one of her regular partners at the Maryinsky) Pavlova created Armida in *Le pavillon d'Armide*, the Sylph of the Waltz in his first *Chopiniana* (which inspired his subsequent *Les sylphides*), and several other roles. Fokine's solo *The Swan*, danced to an extract from Camille Saint-Saëns's *Carnival of the Animals*, became Pavlova's signature work from the time she first danced it at a gala in December 1907. This minute dance encapsulates a whole history. Although it is based on classical steps, a series of *pas de bourrée* broken by an occasional attitude, the dancer's arms are expressive rather than formally academic, and thus it has been seen as a synthesis of traditional and modern. This was a synthesis that was symbolic of Pavlova's approach to her career.

In St Petersburg, Pavlova surrounded herself with influential supporters, as was necessary for the advancement of a ballerina. Most significant among these men was the aristocratic balletomane Victor Dandré, who set her up in an apartment with a ballet studio on the Angliisky Prospekt. Dandré was a member of the St Petersburg city council, but in 1911 he was arrested on a charge of appropriating vast sums of government money. He forfeited bail when Pavlova returned from America, and went with her to London. Pavlova remained loyal to Dandré, who became her manager (there is no evidence that they were ever married—indeed, her private life remains something of an enigma), setting up her tours and encouraging her to dance popular, easily accessible ballets for new audiences rather than to create more avant-garde works.

International career Pavlova had embarked on her international career in 1908. After performing at Riga in Latvia in February, she undertook a tour of Scandinavia in May. It was in Stockholm, where she gave six performances, that she realized the value of her art. As she noted in her brief memoir, *Pages of my Life*, she was overwhelmed by crowds at her hotel after her performances and at the railway station to see her depart. She asked her maid, 'But what have I done to move them to so great an enthusiasm?' Her maid replied, 'Madam, you have made them happy by enabling them to forget for an hour the sadness of life.'

In 1909 Serge Diaghilev invited Pavlova to be ballerina of the group he was taking to Paris. She agreed, but having previously committed herself to a spring tour of central Europe—Berlin, Leipzig, Prague, and Vienna—arrived in Paris only in June, when the season was already under way. She nevertheless scored a great success with Vaslav Nijinsky in *Les sylphides* and with Michel Fokine in *Cléopâtre*. Although Diaghilev had plans to work with her the following year, it is said that her conservative outlook clashed with the impresario's thirst for modernity. She refused the title role in *The Firebird* because she found Igor Stravinsky's score ugly. She had anyway become too involved in her own tours, and returned to the Ballets Russes only for its second London season at the Royal Opera House, Covent Garden, in 1911. Here she had the chance to be seen with Nijinsky in *Giselle*, *Cléopâtre*, *Le pavillon d'Armide*, *Les sylphides*, and the *pas de deux L'oiseau d'or*.

This was the season in which audiences had the opportunity to compare two great ballerinas, Pavlova and Tamara Karsavina. Perhaps it was their fellow dancer Lubov Chernyshyova who explained most clearly the contrast between the two artists. Karsavina 'was the most beautiful woman, all warm, wonderful woman. But Pavlova, when she danced—not woman at all—spirit!'

By this time Pavlova was a star in London in her own right. In 1909 she had travelled from Paris to London, where, partnered by Michel Mordkin, she danced for the king and queen. On 18 April 1910 Pavlova opened at the Palace Theatre, London, in a programme of divertissements as part of a variety bill. The dancers' repertory included *pas de deux* and duets for Pavlova and Mordkin: the exuberant and frenzied *Bacchanale* to music from Glazounov's *The Seasons*, the flowing *Valse caprice* to music by Anton Rubinstein; and solos for Pavlova: *Le papillon*, *La rose mourante*, and of course *The Swan*, all of which were acclaimed by the public. Pavlova's season in London was sandwiched between trips to the United States of America. During the first of these she made her début there in *Coppélia* at the Metropolitan Opera House, New York, and made brief visits to Boston and Baltimore. In the autumn Pavlova and Mordkin embarked on a nationwide tour with a full *corps de ballet* for which Mordkin staged *Giselle* and an exotic new work, *The Legend of Aziade*.

For her initial overseas tours Pavlova received leave of absence from the imperial theatres, between which she would return to the Maryinsky stage. At the start of her second American tour she requested leave for two years, and when it was refused she paid a large forfeit to break her contract. Nevertheless she returned to St Petersburg to dance in 1911 and 1913 and became cut off from Russia only by the First World War and the revolution. From 1912 she made London her base, living at Ivy House, Golders Green (on the edge of Hampstead Heath), which she purchased in 1914. Having already used English children for her production of *Snowflakes* (a version of 'Land of snow' from *The Nutcracker*) at the Palace Theatre in 1911, she began to train English recruits. After teaching her pupils at Ivy House she started employing English dancers for her company, including Muriel Stuart and Hilda Butsova (Boot), both of whom took over some of her own roles.

Popularizing classical ballet Anna Pavlova played a major role in popularizing fine classical ballet, introducing much of the work of Petipa (sometimes in the form of later revisions) to audiences outside Russia. These, rather than the innovations of other contemporary companies, are the ballets that have stood the test of time and are now danced by classical companies throughout the world. Much has been made of Pavlova's alleged artistic conservatism. It is true that she was not at home with music by Stravinsky, and the designs for many of her productions were merely routine, but she had helped Michel Fokine establish his programme of reforms, employed Leon Bakst as designer when she could, and at the end of her career invited Georges Balanchine to choreograph for her company. She recognized the taste of her audiences and tailored her programmes accordingly, demonstrating to them Russia's rich choreographic heritage. Many of her productions were staged by her ballet masters or her partners, who had to adapt large, spectacular works to the resources of a relatively small touring company. Even when the resources of Charles Dillingham's New York Hippodrome were available to Pavlova in 1916, so that she could mount a production of *The Sleeping Beauty*, it was only as one turn in *The Big Show*, and this ballet seems to have been too sophisticated for American taste at that time.

For twenty-two years Pavlova toured unceasingly, dancing in major cities and smaller towns, sometimes in venues at which ballet was unknown. She danced in opera houses, on open-air stages, and in public spaces such as bullrings in Mexico. Conditions were often difficult, and although her partners and company sometimes complained, Pavlova's missionary zeal carried her on. Having sailed to the United States in 1914 at the outbreak of war, she performed in North America and Cuba until 1917, when she embarked on a two-year tour of South America and did not return to Europe until 1919. Pavlova's punishing itinerary for 1914-16 is reproduced in Keith Money's *Anna Pavlova: her Life and Art* (1982). In 1922-3 Pavlova took her company to east Asia; in 1926-7 to South Africa, Australia, and New Zealand (where the meringue-based dessert crammed with fruit and cream was created and named for her); in 1928-9 she went on what proved to be her last world tour. Over a period of eight months Pavlova travelled extensively, dancing in South America, Egypt, India, Burma, Malaya, Australia, and elsewhere.

Much of Pavlova's work had instant appeal, and she was ideal as a representative of ballet for inclusion at London's first 'Royal variety show' on 1 July 1912; but she also presented some considerably more sophisticated programmes for opera house stages. In the 1920s these included dances learned on the company's world tours, and introduced a serious multiculturalism not found in other companies. Although most of her ballets were arranged for her company by others, Pavlova created a number of her own solos to considerable effect. She also choreographed a one-act ballet, *Autumn Leaves*, to music by Chopin in 1920, in which she played a chrysanthemum buffeted by the north wind; it is eventually picked, but then tossed aside by a poet. The ballet reflected her use of images drawn from nature, which also featured in the solos she made for herself.

Pavlova was one of the first great theatre artists who appreciated the value of film. Although dissatisfied with most of the results, she persevered with the new medium, recording some of her divertissements as well as providing glimpses of some of the larger works she presented. These were made by professional cameramen in Hollywood or for newsreels, or as home movies, and a compilation (assembled by Dandré) was released as *The Immortal Swan* in 1935. Pavlova also appeared in the feature film *The Dumb Girl of Portici* (1916), which she made to fund her company's tours in the United States of America. This is, in some senses, the best record of her artistry. Her joyous tarantella on the seashore and her helplessness and horror when trapped in a rat-infested prison indicate her range as an artist.

Final years Off-stage Pavlova accepted her role as a public figure and was always immaculately turned out. Her image was frequently used for advertising purposes by companies wanting to sell, for example, shoes, pianos, or face creams. Pavlova expected members of her company to create a good impression. She demanded much of her dancers, but she was also concerned for their development and welfare, and the parties she gave her whole company each Christmas became legendary. Although in most photographs she is fashionably attired, when relaxing away from the public gaze she frequently wore trousers. Pavlova's life centred upon the stage, but she had outside interests. She was actively involved in charity work, establishing and funding an orphanage at St Cloud outside Paris for destitute Russian children, and she was passionately fond of animals and birds; her menagerie at Ivy House included dogs and swans. She was also a talented sculptor.

It seems that Pavlova could never have been happy without performing, and as a result of her constant work burnt herself out. Her autumn tour of Britain in 1930 ended with a final performance at Golders Green Hippodrome, in which she danced in *Amarilla*, *Gavotte*, and *The Swan* and performed the *grand pas* from *Paquita*. After a short break in the south of France she travelled to the Netherlands for the start of her next tour. On the journey she caught a chill; she contracted pneumonia, which turned to pleurisy, and died at the Hôtel des Indes in The Hague on 23 January 1931. She was cremated at Golders Green, London. Her partner, Victor Dandré, outlived her.

During her lifetime Anna Pavlova was the best-known ballerina in the world. She toured worldwide, and, internationally, her name and the key roles that she danced became synonymous with ballet. As an indefatigable ambassador for her art, she made it her greatest legacy to inspire a whole generation to study ballet, to dance, and to choreograph. Frederick Ashton, for example, repeatedly described how she 'injected him with the poison' that made him want to be a 'ballerina' and then to dance and choreograph. He drew inspiration from his recollections of her performances for many of his creations. Pavlova was slim and ideally proportioned, which gave the illusion that she was taller than her height of 5 feet 3 inches. With her small head on its slender neck and her dark hair drawn back, her physical appearance came to typify what the public expected of a ballerina. Her dancing had a stellar quality that convinced an uninitiated audience that they were in the presence of theatrical greatness.

JANE PRITCHARD

Sources H. Algeranoff, *My years with Pavlova* (1957) · V. Dandré, *Anna Pavlova in art and life* (1932) · M. O. Devine, 'The swan immortalized', *Ballet Review*, 21 (summer 1993), 67–80 · M. Fonteyn, *Pavlova: portrait of a dancer* (New York, 1984) · A. H. Franks, ed., *Pavlova: a biography* (1956) · W. Hyden, *Pavlova: the genius of the dance* (1931) · J. Lazzarini and R. Lazzarini, *Pavlova: repertoire of a legend* (New York, 1980) · K. Money, *Pavlova: her life and art* (1982) · T. Stier, *With Pavlova round the world* (1929) · V. Svetlov, *Anna Pavlova* (1931) · O. Verensky, *Anna Pavlova* (1973) · DNB

Archives Museum of London, costumes and other material | FILM BFI NFTVA, version of *The immortal swan* · Museum of Modern Art Film Archive, New York, *The dumb girl of Portici*, Universal Studios (1916) · Museum of Modern Art Film Archive, New York, *The immortal swan*, (1935) · Pathé archives, newsreel material **Likenesses** J. Lavery, portrait, 1911, Tate collection [*see illus.*] · V. Gross/Hugo, portrait · M. Hoffman, sculptures · Javovleff, portrait · J. Lavery, portrait · Legat, caricature · Schuster-Woldan, portrait · V. Serov, Russian Museum, St Petersburg · Sorine, portrait · Steinburg, portrait · A. Stevens, portraits · photographs **Wealth at death** £14,147 18s. 7d.: administration, 24 April 1931, *CGPLA Eng. & Wales*

Pavy, Frederick William (1829–1911), physician and physiologist, was born at Wroughton, Wiltshire, on 29 May 1829, the son of William Pavy, a maltster, and Mary, his wife. Educated at Merchant Taylors' School in Suffolk Lane, London, which he entered in January 1840, he experienced a spartan discipline under James Bellamy, the headmaster. He proceeded to Guy's Hospital in 1847, and matriculated at the University of London where he gained honours at the intermediate examination in medicine in 1850, and the scholarship and medal in materia medica and pharmaceutical chemistry. In 1852 he graduated MB with honours in physiology and comparative anatomy, obstetric medicine and surgery, and the medal in medicine.

Pavy then served as house surgeon and house physician at Guy's Hospital; in 1853 he graduated MD and went to Paris, where he joined the English Medical Society of Paris, of which he became a vice-president. The society met in a room near the Luxembourg Gardens and owned a small library. It was the rendezvous of the English medical students, where they met weekly to read papers and to report interesting cases. In Paris Pavy came under the influence of Claude Bernard, who was at this time giving a course of experimental lectures on the role and nature of glycogen and the phenomena of diabetes. Pavy made the study of diabetes the work of his life and imitated his master in the manner of his lectures.

On his return to England Pavy was appointed lecturer on anatomy at Guy's Hospital in 1854 and lecturer in physiology in 1856. He married Julia (1830?–1902), daughter of William Oliver, on 25 July 1855. There were two daughters, both of whom predeceased him. His elder daughter, Florence Julia (1856–1902), married in 1881 the Revd Sir Borradaile Savory, second baronet, son of Sir William Scovell Savory, first baronet.

Pavy lectured on comparative anatomy until 1864 and on physiology and microscopical anatomy until 1877; later he lectured on systematic medicine. He was elected assistant physician to the hospital in 1858, on the promotion of William Gull, and became full physician in 1871, when the number of physicians was increased from three to four. He was appointed consulting physician to the hospital in 1890, his tenure of office on the full staff having been prolonged for an additional year.

At the Royal College of Physicians, Pavy was elected a fellow in 1860; he served as an examiner in 1872–3 and in 1878–9; he was a councillor from 1875 to 1877 and again from 1888 to 1890; and a censor in 1882, 1883, and 1891. He delivered the Goulstonian lectures in 1862–3, the Croonian lectures in 1878 and 1894, and the Harveian oration in 1886. He was awarded the Baly medal in 1901.

Pavy also did good work at the medical societies of London. In 1860 he delivered the Lettsomian lectures at the Medical Society 'On certain points connected with diabetes'. He served as president of the Pathological Society from 1893 to 1895 and as president of the Royal Medical and Chirurgical Society from 1900 to 1902. He acted for some years as president of the Association for the Advancement of Medicine by Research, and from 1901 he served, after the death of Sir William MacCormac, as president of the national committee for Great Britain and Ireland of the International Congress of Medicine. The permanent committee of this congress, meeting at The Hague in 1909, appointed him the first chairman.

Pavy was elected FRS in 1863; the University of Glasgow conferred on him the honorary degree of LLD in 1888, and in 1909 he was crowned lauréat of the Académie de Médecine in Paris and received the Prix Godard for his physiological researches. On 26 June 1909, at a meeting held at Oxford of the Physiological Society of Great Britain and Ireland, he was presented with a silver bowl bearing an expression 'of affection and admiration'.

Pavy was the last survivor of a line of distinguished physician–chemists who did much to lay the foundations and advance the study of metabolic disorders; at the same time he ranks as a pioneer among nineteenth-century chemical pathologists. As a pupil of Claude Bernard, he recognized that all advances in the study of disease must rest on investigations into the normal processes of the body; but as his investigations proceeded, he found himself disagreeing with the views of his master. He soon discovered that Bernard's theory of the glycogenic function of the liver was based on faulty experiments and showed that the saccharine condition of the liver was due to postmortem changes and was absent in the living animal. He also found that arterial and venous blood contained the same proportion of dextrose, indicating that dextrose did not pass from the liver to the tissues in the free state. Pavy also suggested that the kidney acts as a filter, allowing diffusible compounds such as urea and dextrose to pass from the blood into the urine. Hence, if free dextrose passed into the blood from the liver, as Bernard's theory suggested, the urine would provide evidence of the fact. Although he later found that glycogen was broken down by enzymes into dextrose and conveyed by the blood to the tissues, he maintained that the dextrose must be combined with blood proteins. He tested his new working hypotheses by experiment, but his theories did not always meet with the approval of those who were working along similar lines; some never obtained general acceptance. He made the study of carbohydrate metabolism the work of his life, and he was the founder of the modern theory of diabetes. In this connection his name was associated with many improvements in clinical and practical medicine. 'Pavy's test', using an ammoniacal copper salt for the quantitative estimation of reducing sugars, and his use of sugar tests and albumen tests in the solid form, made his

name familiar to physicians and medical students throughout the world. As a practical physician, too, he was greatly interested in the control of diabetes through the diet. He introduced almonds and other protein-rich bread substitutes. His treatment of diabetes began with the elimination of dextrose from the blood by means of a carbohydrate-free diet. He was one of the first to recognize the importance of acetone and other ketones eliminated in acute stages of diabetes, and albuminaria, often associated with the disease, also interested him. He was the first to recognize cyclic, or physiological, albuminaria. He wrote a well-known book on dietetics, *A Treatise on Food and Dietetics Physiologically and Therapeutically Considered* (1873).

Throughout life Pavy remained a student, and even to the last week of his life he was at work in the laboratory which he had built at the back of his consulting room in Grosvenor Street. Quiet in bearing, gentle and courteous in speech, and with a somewhat old-fashioned formality of manner, he was generous in his benefactions. At Guy's medical school he built a well-equipped gymnasium and presented it to the students' union in 1890. He also left in his will an endowment for its upkeep.

Pavy died at his house, 35 Grosvenor Street, London, on 19 September 1911, and was buried at Highgate cemetery.

D'A. POWER, rev. N. G. COLEY

Sources *The Lancet* (30 Sept 1911), 976–80 · H. White, 'Frederick William Pavy', *BMJ* (30 Sept 1911), 777–8 · F. Taylor, 'Dr F. W. Pavy', *Nature*, 87 (1911), 421–2 · H. W. Bywaters, 'Frederick William Pavy', *Biochemical Journal*, 10 (1916), 1–4 · E. H. S., *Guy's Hospital Gazette*, [3rd ser.], 25 (1911), 393 · D. Adlersberg, 'Frederick William Pavy', *Diabetes*, 5 (1956), 491–2 · S. P. W. Chave, 'Frederick William Pavy', *BMJ* (3 Aug 1957), 300 · personal knowledge (1912) · m. cert.
Archives RS
Likenesses G. Jerrard, photograph, 1881, Wellcome L. · W. Strang, drawing, 1908, Royal Society of Medicine, London · W. Strang, drawing, 1908, Guy's Hospital Medical School, London · P. Bigland, oils, Guy's Hospital, London · photograph, Wellcome L. · photomechanical print (after Bassano), Wellcome L.
Wealth at death £27,769 2s. 1d.: probate, 9 Oct 1911, CGPLA Eng. & Wales

Pawson, John (1737–1806), Methodist minister, was born at Thorner, near Leeds, on 12 November 1737, the elder son of respectable, church-going parents who (from his later Methodist perspective) were nevertheless 'entire strangers to the power of godliness' (Jackson, 4.1). He was given such education as his father could afford, since he was intended for the building trade, and aged fifteen was sent to his brother-in-law in Hull to learn the business. Here he first encountered the Methodists, but as a good churchman avoided contact with them for several years. In 1756 he set up as a builder at Harewood, and two years later began to attend the Methodist preaching services, despite his father's strong disapproval. A sermon at Otley by the itinerant James Oddie, reinforced by 'the serious and devout behaviour of the people', made him resolve to seek the truth, which he did by reading such books as Joseph Alleine's *Alarm to the Unconverted*.

After a lengthy period of spiritual agonizing, characteristic of early Methodist converts, he eventually found 'peace with God' in 1760. 'In a moment', he wrote, 'I was perfectly delivered from all my guilty fears; my deep sorrow, my extreme distress, was entirely gone. The peace of God flowed into my conscience and the love of God was shed abroad in my heart abundantly; my whole soul was filled with serious, sacred, heavenly joy' (Jackson, 4.6). This freedom from the guilt of sin, he claimed, led immediately to the experience of sanctification, or 'perfect love', which was the essence of John Wesley's teaching on 'Christian perfection'. The deeply serious, but somewhat humourless, piety that marked his ministry was already in evidence. Other members of his family, and in due course even his father, were won over by the Methodist preaching.

In rapid succession Pawson became a prayer leader, class leader, exhorter, and local preacher among the Methodists. In 1762 the Methodist conference met in Leeds and he found himself recommended to Wesley as a candidate for the itinerancy. Despite misgivings about his adequacy for the work, he was accepted and appointed to the York circuit. During the next forty years his appointments included four periods in Bristol, three in Leeds, and three in London. On 23 July 1773 he married Grace Davies of Bristol, who died on 9 December 1783. His memoir of her was printed in the *Arminian Magazine* (1793). His second wife (whom he married on 12 August 1785) was Frances Wren (*née* Mortimer), a widow from York, who outlived him.

In 1785 Pawson was one of three preachers chosen by Wesley to be ordained for the work in Scotland. Wesley's main intention seems to have been to enable them to administer the sacrament, a role which he firmly denied his lay preachers in English circuits in deference to Anglican usage. Wesley may also have hoped, somewhat vainly, to accord them some status in the eyes of the Scottish presbyterians. But when they were recalled to serve in English circuits, they were forbidden to continue to exercise whatever powers or gifts their ordination was thought to have conferred on them. Pawson's perplexity and frustration amounted to a crisis of conscience and thrust him, unwillingly, into the heart of the controversies that followed Wesley's death in 1791. Though he accepted separation from the church as inevitable, and even desirable, he was deeply concerned by the threat to the internal unity of Methodism and by its lack of any effective central government between annual conferences. He attended the meeting of senior preachers at Lichfield in 1794 and supported their abortive proposals for settling the connexion's affairs. The following year he published his *Affectionate Address to the ... Methodist Societies*, in which he advocated a compromise between the two wings of Methodism. His continuing misgivings that the Methodists were moving away from their 'primitive' simplicity was expressed in his *Serious and Affectionate Address to the Junior Preachers* (1798) and in many of his letters, which provide intimate details of the state of Methodism in the decades before and after Wesley's death.

Pawson was twice president of the conference, in 1793 and 1801. A man of deep but simple piety, he has been remembered as the man who in 1797 burned Wesley's annotated copy of Shakespeare, as 'unedifying'. But above all he was a peacemaker at a time of turbulent change in British Methodism. He died at Wakefield on 19 March 1806.   JOHN A. VICKERS

Sources T. Jackson, ed., *The lives of early Methodist preachers, chiefly written by themselves*, 4th edn, 4 (1873) · *The letters of John Pawson*, ed. J. C. Bowmer and J. A. Vickers, 3 vols. (1994–5) · G. J. Stephenson, *Methodist worthies*, 6 vols. (1884–6)
Archives JRL, Methodist Archive and Research Centre, corresp. and papers
Likenesses portraits, repro. in *Wesleyan Methodist Magazine*

Paxton, George (1762–1837), Original Secession minister, born on 2 April 1762 at Dalgourie, a village in the parish of Bolton, Haddingtonshire, was the eldest son of William Paxton, a joiner or house carpenter, and his wife, Jean Milne. Soon after George's birth his parents moved to Melrose, and then to Makerstoun, near Kelso and the Tweed. The picturesqueness of the place Paxton portrays in his poem 'The Villager'. The neighbouring laird, Sir Hay McDougal, colonel of the Scots Greys, became interested in the family, and young Paxton was educated under his eye at the parish school of Makerstoun. He subsequently went to Kelso, learning Latin and Greek, and, after a short experience as a carpenter, entered Edinburgh University, but left without a degree; in 1784 he went to Alloa to study divinity under William Moncrieff, and 'became a firm seceder'. On 17 March 1788 he was licensed to preach by the Associate Presbytery of Edinburgh, and his eloquence was at once recognized. He received calls from three churches almost simultaneously—Greenlaw, Craigend, and the united congregations of Kilmaurs and Stewarton. By decision of the synod he was ordained to the last-named congregations on 12 August 1789, and took up residence at Stewarton. After a few years the two congregations, at the advice of Paxton, separated, and Kilmaurs was assigned to him.

Owing to a hepatic malady, Paxton was soon forced to resign pastoral duty for seven years, and on his recovery the General Associate Synod elected him professor of divinity in 1807. He moved to Edinburgh, but his opposition to the union between the Anti-Burgher and the Burgher synods led him to resign his professorship and to his withdrawal from the General Associate Synod in 1820. He then became pastor to a body of sympathizers, who seceded with him, in a vacant chapel adjacent to the Grassmarket under Castle Hill. A new church was built in Infirmary Street, which his preaching soon filled, and he and his congregation joined with the Constitutional Presbytery of Seceders to which Dr Thomas McCrie belonged, and thus formed a new connexion styled the Associate Synod of Original Seceders, also known as the Constitutional Associate Presbytery and the Old Light Anti-Burghers. Paxton became their professor of divinity as well as continuing to minister. Despite his membership of this small sect, he was a strong apologist for established churches. Paxton took part in the controversy over the Apocrypha, publishing *The Sin and Danger of Circulating the Apocrypha in Connection with the Holy Scriptures* (1828). He also published works on religious covenants (1801) and on church unity (1802), a volume of poetry entitled *The Villagers* (1813), and *Illustrations of the Holy Scriptures in Three Parts* (2 vols., 1819; 3rd edn, 4 vols., 1841–3). He was made honorary DD of St Andrews University shortly before his death on 9 April 1837. He was buried in the West Kirk burial-ground, Edinburgh. In 1790 Paxton had married Elizabeth Armstrong (*d.* 1800), a daughter of a manufacturer in Kelso. With her he had two sons and three daughters. Paxton's only surviving son, George, was a doctor in India. Paxton's second wife, Margaret Johnstone, daughter of a farmer in Berwick, survived him.   W. A. SHAW, *rev.* H. C. G. MATTHEW

Sources J. Mitchell, 'Brief memoir', in G. Paxton, *Illustrations of the holy scriptures in three parts*, 1 (1843) [prefix] · J. M'Kerrow, *History of the Secession church*, rev. edn (1841) · R. Small, *History of the congregations of the United Presbyterian church from 1733 to 1900*, 2 vols. (1904) · G. Paxton, *The villagers* (1813)
Likenesses oils; in possession of the Revd W. Macleod, Edinburgh, in 1895
Wealth at death £176 9s. od.: will, 1840

Paxton, James (1786–1860), surgeon, was born in London on 11 January 1786. He was admitted MRCS in London on 16 March 1810, and graduated MD at St Andrews in 1845.

For a time Paxton acted as an army surgeon, but in 1816 he began to practise at Long Buckley, Northamptonshire. From there he moved in 1821 to Oxford, where he had considerable success as a general practitioner. He was assistant surgeon to the Oxfordshire militia. In 1843 he moved to a practice at Rugby. A small estate was bequeathed to him for his life in 1858 by George North Robinson, surgeon of the Oxfordshire militia, at Ledwell, a hamlet in the parish of Sandford St Martin, 17 miles from Oxford. Paxton married Anna Griffin, who died in 1864, and one of his two daughters married the Revd Henry Highton, headmaster of Cheltenham College. Paxton died at his residence, Ledwell House, after a brief illness, on 12 March 1860, and was buried in the churchyard of St Martin's, Sandford.

Paxton was a man of strong religious feelings, and was highly esteemed by his friends and patients. His writings, largely on anatomy and practical medical advice, had much success. He also edited William Paley's *Natural Theology*, in 1826.   E. H. MARSHALL, *rev.* PATRICK WALLIS

Sources E. Marshall, *An account of the parish of Sandford* (1866) · *Rugby Advertiser* (March 1860) · W. T. Lowndes, *The bibliographer's manual of English literature*, ed. H. G. Bohn, [new edn], 6 vols. (1864)
Wealth at death under £4000: probate, 22 May 1860, CGPLA Eng. & Wales

Paxton, John (*c.*1740–1780), painter, was born in Edinburgh, the third child of John Paxton (*c.*1697–1787) of Berwickshire and his wife, Helen (*d.* 1783), daughter of William Adams, an Edinburgh printer. John Paxton senior was chief clerk to Archibald Stewart, a rich Edinburgh wine merchant of Berwick origin, MP, and lord provost of Edinburgh at the time of the Jacobite rising of 1745. Paxton was a student at Foulis art academy in Glasgow and subsequently studied in Rome. He was one of the original members of the Incorporated Society of Artists, and signed their declaration roll in 1766. In that year he sent to their exhibition from Rome *Samson in Distress*. In 1769 and

1770 he exhibited portraits at the Royal Academy, and in the latter year settled in Charlotte Street, Rathbone Place, London, where he had considerable practice as a portrait painter.

Paxton continued to exhibit with the Society of Artists, of which he was director in 1775, sending chiefly portraits, but also scriptural, classical, and historical subjects. His brother Sir William *Paxton, merchant and banker, must have convinced him that he would find ample and lucrative employ for his artistic talents in India. In March 1776 he asked the directors of the East India Company if he might go 'to the East Indies to provide for himself in the way of his profession' (BL OIOC). In 1777 the portraitist Catherine Read, then active in Madras, received a not very appreciative account of her colleague from one of her correspondents: 'We have now another [artist] nam'd Paxton, but he is a very indifferent hand and yet gets employment' (Archer, 471).

Paxton painted a portrait of Signorina Zamperini as Cechina. A portrait by him of his fellow pupil James Tassie is in the Scottish National Portrait Gallery at Edinburgh. Paxton is alluded to in the fable of 'The Bee-Flower' in John Langhorne's *The Fables of Flora* (1771). He died, unmarried, in Bombay on 19 February 1780. In *RA Exhibitors*, Graves lists further works exhibited between 1802 and 1807 by John Paxton, but these were presumably by a different artist of the same name.

L. H. CUST, *rev.* WILLEM G. J. KUITERS

Sources BL OIOC, B/91, fol. 519 · W. G. J. Kuiters, 'William Paxton, 1744–1824: the history of an East India fortune', *Bengal Past and Present*, 111 (1992), 1–22 · M. Archer, *India and British portraiture, 1770–1825* (1979), 471 · Graves, *RA exhibitors*
Archives Scot. NPG, works
Likenesses self-portrait, exh. RA 1802, priv. coll.

Paxton, Sir Joseph (1803–1865), landscape gardener and architect, was born on 3 August 1803 at Milton Bryan (or Bryant) in Bedfordshire, the youngest of the eight children of William Paxton (1758/9–1810), an agricultural labourer, and his wife, Ann Rooke (1760/61–1823), who is said to have come from Whaddon Chase, Buckinghamshire.

Early years and training Joseph Paxton attended the free school at Woburn, and is said to have been a garden boy to Sir Hugh Inglis at Milton Bryan Manor. At the age of about fourteen he was placed under his elder brother John, the gardener at Battlesden, the estate of Sir Gregory Page Turner, where his father had also probably worked. He was later apprenticed for two or three years to William Griffin, the gardener to Samuel Smith of Woodhall Park, Watton, Hertfordshire, who was famous for his skill in fruit growing. In 1821 he returned to Battlesden, where he helped construct an ornamental lake of 13 acres, again under the direction of his brother.

In 1823 Paxton's mother died and he went to work at Wimbledon House, Surrey, where the gardener was another brother, probably James Paxton. He was unsettled there and seems to have left for Lee and Henderson's nursery garden in Kensington. On 13 November that year,

Sir Joseph Paxton (1803–1865), by James Henry Lynch (after William Edward Kilburn, 1851)

recommended by Samuel Smith, he was formally admitted by the Horticultural Society of London as a student gardener at the new experimental garden at Chiswick. When giving the required specimen of his handwriting he wrote that he was born in 1801, an untruth which has caused confusion ever since. The following year he was promoted to foreman in charge of the arboretum, covering 33 acres, and his weekly wage was raised from 14 to 18s. In 1826, 'owing to some misunderstanding with the authorities of the Society' Paxton intended to go to America (*Journal of Horticulture*, 446), but the duke of Devonshire intervened. The sixth duke was the landlord of the society's grounds, and, liking to stroll there and talk to young Paxton, he asked him to be head gardener at Chatsworth, his country house in Derbyshire. The duke is said to have been impressed with Paxton's bearing and general intelligence, but the deciding factor was his good manners: the duke was quite deaf, and Paxton took trouble to speak so that he could hear.

Chatsworth, 1826–1850 Paxton arrived at Chatsworth on 9 May 1826 and started work on a salary of £70 per annum. Returning to his estate after an absence abroad of seven months, the duke noted in his journal: 'my new gardener Paxton has made a great change' (Cavendish, journal, 10 Dec 1826). Although hitherto hardly interested in gardening, the duke became enthusiastic. He visited nursery gardens with Paxton for the latest plants and took him on garden tours in England and Paris. In 1838 the duke became president of the Horticultural Society, and that year, accompanied by Paxton, he set off on a seven-month grand tour of Europe, visiting Switzerland, Italy, and Turkey. By degrees a close friendship arose between duke and gardener. In 1844 Paxton, by now his confidential adviser, found the means to release his employer from an accumulated debt of nearly £1 million by producing a ready buyer, the railway entrepreneur George Hudson, for two Yorkshire estates.

On 20 February 1827 Paxton married Sarah Bown (1800–1871), whose father was a small engineer and mill owner at Matlock, Derbyshire, and whose aunt Sarah Gregory was housekeeper at Chatsworth. They were a devoted couple, Sarah having a strong character and sensible conservative outlook. 'Without a good wife', Paxton remarked many years later at the *Punch* dinner table, 'a man can't well succeed' (Silver). Six of their eight children survived, but their only son, George, turned out feckless and unpredictable.

Paxton's responsibilities at Chatsworth steadily increased. He was in charge of the woods in 1830 and of the roads in 1837, and by 1849 he was agent for the Chatsworth estate at a salary of £500 per annum. From 1844 he was also agent for the duke's estate at Bolton Abbey, Yorkshire, while at other properties, particularly Chiswick House, Middlesex, and Lismore Castle, co. Cork, the duke seldom made any changes without consulting Paxton.

Under Paxton's care, Chatsworth became the most famous garden in England. Largely self-taught, Paxton always encouraged the young gardeners (who included John Gibson, Edward Milner, Edward Kemp, and George Eyles) to study and improve themselves. Among his works at Chatsworth were the pinetum (1829), the arboretum (1834–5, with plants classified according to the system of Jussieu), whose cost was entirely defrayed from the sale of timber cleared off the site, and the orchid collection. He also designed numerous greenhouses and hothouses, using for many of them his own version of the ridge-and-furrow roof. They culminated in the conservatory or great stove (1836–41), a vast glass building with a double-curved framework of laminated wood, measuring 227 by 123 feet and 67 feet high. No glasshouse on this scale had ever been built before, and the cautious duke brought in his architect Decimus Burton as consultant; however, the design and its execution were undoubtedly Paxton's alone. To make the 20 or so miles of moulded sash bar the building required he invented a steam-powered cutting machine, for which in 1840 the Royal Society of Arts awarded him their silver medal. He constructed the rock gardens (from 1843) and designed and built the emperor fountain (1844), so named after Emperor Nicholas I of Russia (who, however, failed to visit Chatsworth), which, with a jet more than 260 feet high, was the tallest in the world. No new task was ever begun without the approval of the duke, with whom in many cases the idea had originated. But when the duke saw the scale of the works necessary for the great stove and the fountain he was quite alarmed.

Paxton's gardening was based on the published works of the Scottish encyclopaedist John Claudius Loudon. In the *Gardener's Magazine* of July 1831 Loudon published a long criticism of the Chatsworth gardens to which Paxton replied two months later in his own paper, the *Horticultural Register*, giving Loudon a mild rebuke. But by 1835, their quarrel over, Paxton and the Scot remained close and mutually supportive friends. Paxton made other lasting friendships with the botanists John Lindley and Sir William Hooker. With the help of the latter he arranged plant collecting expeditions: to Mexico (1835), unsuccessfully, and to California (1838), which ended in disaster when a boat party including two young Chatsworth gardeners was drowned on the Columbia River. But in July 1837 his assistant John Gibson returned from Calcutta with many fine new orchids, and the greatly coveted *Amherstia nobilis*. This much famed temple tree was taken to Chatsworth but failed to flower there. Paxton achieved notable success, however, in 1849, when the duke persuaded Hooker to send a small plant of the Amazon lily *Victoria amazonica*, which was ailing at Kew. Within three months Paxton had it flowering. It grew so rapidly that the following year he designed for it a new lily house, a rectangular glass lanthorn with horizontal ridge-and-furrow roof. In this simple building was the basic design of the Crystal Palace.

Architecture and private works to 1850 Paxton's first work as architect was the rebuilding, from 1837, of most of the cottages in Edensor village. It seems irregular for the duke to have given this job to his gardener rather than the clerk of works, but evidently Paxton had impressed him with ideas for a model village in the ornamental and 'historic' styles illustrated in Loudon's *Encyclopaedia of Cottage, Farm and Villa Architecture* (1833). Paxton in fact obtained designs from Loudon's principal draughtsman, John Robertson, who by 1840 was working full-time in Paxton's office and, besides Edensor, designed many ornamental houses at Chatsworth and elsewhere.

Paxton's private work in the 1840s was in every case undertaken with the duke's permission. In 1838 he assisted John Lindley in a report on the royal gardens. In 1842 he laid out Prince's Park, Liverpool. For Sir William Jackson between 1843 and 1847 he created the much greater Birkenhead Park out of a low-lying swamp, together with designs for five ornamental lodges. In 1845–7 he laid out the cemetery at Coventry, with an Italianate lodge and chapels in the Norman and Greek styles. As landscapes these were all pioneering works that influenced public park design throughout the nineteenth century. When F. L. Olmstead designed Central Park, Manhattan, his principal example was Birkenhead Park. Paxton also received commissions from a number of private patrons, notable among which was Burton Closes, near Bakewell, Derbyshire, a gentleman's villa in early Tudor style, with conservatory, lodge, and grounds, which he built for his stockbroker John Allcard; the interior and decoration, carried out by John Gregory Crace, was partly designed by Pugin. All of the above buildings were designed by Robertson, who some time after 1847 was replaced in Paxton's office by George Henry Stokes (1826–1871), a young architect whose name appears first in connection with the Coventry cemetery.

Although his education had been meagre, Paxton developed remarkable fluency in writing and public speaking. His first essay in publishing was the *Horticultural Register*, a monthly magazine for practical gardeners, which at first he edited with Joseph Harrison (the gardener at Wortley Hall, near Sheffield). It ran for five volumes (July 1831 through 1836), the format and admittedly much of the content taken from Loudon's *Gardener's Magazine*. Being considerably cheaper and easier to read than the latter, it took away much of Loudon's readership. Paxton's next monthly magazine, *Paxton's Magazine of Botany*, ran for sixteen years (1833–48) and was very popular. In both magazines he described many of his plants and innovations at Chatsworth, though, curiously, he never wrote about the great stove. *Paxton's Flower Garden*, his last magazine, was edited with John Lindley for three years (1850–52). In 1838 he published a little book, *The Cultivation of the Dahlia*, a work he had actually begun in 1825; it was translated into French and German, with introductions by Jussieu and Alexander von Humboldt, and into Swedish. In 1840 he published *The Pocket Botanical Dictionary*, which he had compiled with Lindley.

Also in 1840 Paxton, with Lindley, Sir C. W. Dilke (1810–1869), and William Bradbury, founded a weekly newspaper, the *Gardener's Chronicle*. Paxton's actual part in it was small because the duke expressed a 'great objection to your being connected with a newspaper' (Paxton archive, letter 91). But apparently owing to the considerable success of the *Chronicle*, the duke made no objection in 1845 when Paxton and Bradbury founded the *Daily News*, a newspaper intended to be the Liberal rival to *The Times*. Paxton himself raised £25,000, half of the initial capital. Edited by Charles Dickens, the first issue appeared in 21 January 1846, but it was a disaster. Dickens quit after three weeks and was replaced by Dilke's father (1789–1864); the paper survived, but for many years any profit was small. The staff of *Punch* magazine (owned by Bradbury and Evans) helped with the opening issues: John Lemon, Douglas Jerrold, and John Leech were among his intimate friends. Paxton, a welcome guest at the legendary *Punch* dinners, was the only outsider allowed into their jovial, Bohemian circle. It has been said that he supported *Punch* financially.

From about 1842 Paxton became increasingly rich. This seems likely to have been the result of speculation in railways, in which he had been an early if modest investor. George Stephenson rented Tapton House, Chesterfield, in 1838, when working on the North Midland Railway, and being both a neighbour and a keen gardener he became Paxton's close friend and, through Stephenson, Paxton met George Hudson. At the height of the railway mania of 1845–6 frantic letters between Paxton and Sarah, his wife, were chiefly concerned with share prices. The *List of Subscribers* to the railways, which was published for 1845 and for 1846, shows Paxton to have subscribed £35,000 and £101,750 respectively. He was a director of certain railway companies, including the Furness Railway, the Midland Railway, and, where he was particularly active, the Matlock Railway, which passed just south of Chatsworth.

The Crystal Palace Paxton's involvement with Prince Albert's Great Exhibition came about almost by chance. The exhibition was due to open on 1 May 1851, but less than eleven months before that date the building committee had not yet completed their design for the building in Hyde Park. On 7 June 1850 Paxton, in London, happened to tell a friend, John Ellis, that he had an idea for it; the same day Henry Cole at the Board of Trade said that the committee might still consider a new design. Paxton's drawings, which were presented on 21 June, were based on the as yet uncompleted lily house at Chatsworth, but extended in three dimensions: the building was to cover 19 acres, the roofs rising in great steps to provide galleries at two levels. The posts and trusses of this huge greenhouse were to be of iron; the floors, window sashes, and roof structure were of wood. Paxton immediately opened negotiations with the contractors, Messrs Fox and Henderson of Smethwick, and with Chance Brothers, who had supplied glass for the great stove. His design, published in the *Illustrated London News* on 6 July, was reluctantly approved by the committee on 26 July, partly on its merits but also because the contractors had given the lowest of all the tenders. One of the many advantages of Paxton's design was rapid construction, on account of the use of dry components and the standardization and prefabrication of every part. Yet it was chiefly through Charles Fox's determined efforts that the building was handed over to the exhibitors by 1 February 1851.

Paxton's Crystal Palace (so named by Douglas Jerrold in *Punch*) instantly turned public hostility towards the exhibition into excited anticipation. The *Illustrated London News* followed its progress week by week. Paxton's ferro-vitreous building was a novelty both in functional design and in modular construction; aesthetically too it proved to be more interesting than was expected. It won two council prize medals, one for the design and one for the construction. Paxton and Fox were awarded knighthoods, and to Paxton, who in order to lower the tender had waived his fee, Prince Albert gave £5000 out of exhibition profits. But the architectural establishment, vociferous in *The Builder*, was indignant that a gardener had succeeded where they had failed, and pointed out that in choosing Paxton's late design the commission's action was altogether irregular; that although Paxton was the designer there was no architect, since the technical part, detailed drawings, and execution were left entirely to the contractor; and that the design breached the competition rules, which disallowed galleries and forbade the use of wood and other combustible materials.

Before the close of the exhibition Paxton was campaigning for the retention of the Crystal Palace as a winter garden. The public generally were in favour of keeping it in Hyde Park, but the prince wished the building moved, and on 29 April 1852 parliament voted for that. Immediately the directors of the London, Brighton and South Coast Railway floated a company to buy the materials and re-erect the building at Penge Park, near Sydenham, Kent, to be open for the recreation and instruction of the public. Although he was not actually a director of the company, Paxton was indispensable to the whole scheme. Assisted by the contractor John Henderson he redesigned the building, supervised the winter garden, and laid out the terraced garden and park. The initial capital was £500,000, and in anticipation of high dividends the enterprise was heavily oversubscribed. But after two years the estimate was greatly exceeded, partly owing to the expenses of the building but, more culpably, because of Paxton's ambitious water gardens, which were intended to excel those at Versailles. The whole extent was depicted in a panoramic drawing by James Duffield Harding, exhibited at the Royal Academy in 1854 (Royal Institute of British Architects, drawings collection, London). The final estimate was £1,300,000. Share prices fell disastrously, but at the turbulent shareholders' meetings it was not Paxton but the directors who were held to blame. The Crystal Palace Company never in fact recovered from his extravagance.

If the Crystal Palace was an investor's nightmare, it was a great success with visitors. Queen Victoria was enchanted and opened the building, with the winter garden, historic courts, and sculpture, on 10 June 1854; the water gardens she opened on 18 June 1856. In order to attract crowds, the gardens were bedded out with high colour, a scheme reviled by William Robinson and others of the 'natural' gardening school. But in spite of bankruptcies and other vicissitudes, until the fire of 30 November 1936 Paxton's creation at Sydenham filled the contemporary need for a vast concert hall, exhibition palace, and open-air theatre for every kind of great public show. In 1857, and then triennially from 1859, Handel festivals were held in the central transept.

In 1851 Paxton had expected to lead a ferro-vitreous revolution in building construction, but it did not happen. In 1851 he designed a modestly sized crystal palace for New York, and in 1862 a much larger one with three domed transepts for St Cloud, Paris, intended for the 1865 Paris Exhibition, but neither was built. From 1853 he occupied Rockhills, a Regency house at the north end of the Crystal Palace, which the company gave him free of rent for his lifetime.

1851–1865 Paxton continued his architectural career alongside work at the Crystal Palace, building Mentmore, Buckinghamshire (1850–55), a grand country house in the Elizabethan style of Wollaton Hall, Nottinghamshire, for Baron Mayer Amschel de Rothschild; and for Baron James de Rothschild the larger Château de Ferrières (1853–9) near Paris, which was generally acknowledged to be the finest of French nineteenth-century châteaux. From 1849 the duke of Devonshire took a renewed interest in his Irish property, Lismore Castle, co. Cork. In 1850 Paxton rebuilt the ruined hall (with decorations by Pugin and Crace) and later the buildings on three sides of the courtyard. Paxton's architectural assistant, G. H. Stokes, married his eldest daughter, Emily, in 1853, and became his architectural partner. They had London premises, and by 1859 had settled at 7 Pall Mall East.

Paxton had many interests, and at the select committee on metropolitan communications in June 1855 he submitted his solution to London's traffic congestion, which was a 'girdle', or ring road, to link up the stations City and Parliament, lined on either side by shops, residences, and an atmospheric railway, all covered by an iron and glass roof. This visionary idea, for which a perspective drawing known as *The Great Victorian Way* survives at the Victoria and Albert Museum, London, raised much interest, but the eventual solutions to the traffic problem were the Metropolitan Railway and the Victoria Embankment. During the Crimean War, Paxton organized thousands of the workmen who had finished at the Crystal Palace to go to the Crimea, to be an Army Works Corps and build roads.

A Liberal in politics and a member of the Reform Club since 1847, Paxton was returned unopposed in November 1854 as one of the two members of parliament for Coventry, a seat which he retained until his last illness. In the house he spoke only occasionally, but with effect, particularly in 1860, when he moved for and subsequently chaired the select committee on the Thames Embankment. It was largely owing to Paxton's exertions that the Embankment was built shortly afterwards, combining London's low level sewer, the Metropolitan Railway, and a new thoroughfare.

During Paxton's frequent and long absences business at Chatsworth continued, with Lady Paxton supervising the wages and estate books. After the duke's death in 1858 Paxton had to resign his position at Chatsworth, his place being taken by a cousin of his wife, John Gregory Cottingham. The gardener's house at Chatsworth, which had been enlarged several times, was kept by the Paxtons for their lifetime. With time now to spare, Paxton was increasingly involved with railway contracts, principally with his friends Thomas Brassey and George Wythes. He had interests in railways in Spain, Mauritius, India, and Argentina. In order to survey the Bilbao and Miranda Railway he went with Brassey to Spain in three consecutive autumns (1859–61).

Paxton was a fellow of the Linnean Society (1831); honorary fellow and vice-president of the Horticultural Society; member and vice-president of the Royal Society of Arts; associate of the Institution of Civil Engineers (1851); and a knight of the Russian order of St Vladimir (1845). In stature he was short and he became stout. A flattering engraving after Octavius Oakley, published by Paxton on 1 May 1851, shows him with characteristic long hair, quiff, and whiskers—still a dandy, with white trousers and hat. A marble bust by Edward Wyon (1864, Royal Horticultural Society, London) shows him, though only sixty, to have greatly aged.

Paxton's health had deteriorated because of the difficulties with the Sydenham Crystal Palace. Early in 1863 he collapsed, probably from a heart attack, and he never really recovered. His last professional work was to lay out the park at Dunfermline, Fife, which he and Stokes surveyed in September 1864. He died on 8 June 1865 at Rockhills, where Mr and Mrs Gladstone were among his last visitors. He was buried at Edensor on 15 June and left a personal estate valued at just under £180,000.

Paxton 'rose from the ranks to be the greatest gardener of his time, the founder of a new style of architecture, and a man of genius, who devoted it to objects in the highest and noblest sense popular' (*The Times*, 9 June 1865). Of his energy and enterprise there is no question. His skill with plants was equalled by a keen eye for the picturesque, which is evident at Edensor village, in the siting of great houses, and in his public parks. He was a natural engineer for whom no task seemed insuperable. His genius was evident while the great stove and the Crystal Palace were yet standing, but his glasshouse technique was short-lived. The ridge-and-furrow roof was virtually obsolete by 1870. The ferro-vitreous building, apart from winter gardens, had few successors until the twentieth century, when many architects found in the 1851 Crystal Palace a model of functional and modular structure. In architecture, again self-taught, Paxton was competent but unexciting, and his achievement depended largely on his relationship with the duke of Devonshire. He relished adulation, but his integrity has never been in doubt. Popular and universally respected, he had a strong gift for friendship, and for long afterwards many people recalled his kindness.

JOHN KENWORTHY-BROWNE

Sources G. F. Chadwick, *The works of Sir Joseph Paxton, 1803–1865* (1961) · V. R. Markham, *Paxton and the bachelor duke* (1935) · W. S. Cavendish, *Handbook of Chatsworth and Hardwick* (1845) · M. Girouard, 'Genius of Sir Joseph Paxton', *Country Life* (9 Dec 1965), 1605–8 · R. Thorne, 'Crystal exemplar', *ArchR*, 176 (1984), 49–53 · J. Lees-Milne, *The bachelor duke* (1991) · duchess of Devonshire, *The house* (1982) · B. Elliott, *Victorian gardens* (1986) · H. Conway, *People's parks* (1991) · Y. ffrench, *The Great Exhibition* (1951) · P. Prévost-Marcilhacy, *Les Rothschild: bâtisseurs et mécènes* (1995) · G. Godwin, *The Builder* (17 June 1865), 421–3; (24 June 1865), 442–4 · J. Lindley, *Gardeners' Chronicle* (17 June 1865), 554–5 · *Journal of Horticulture and Cottage Gardener* (13 June 1865), 446–9 · H. Silver, Punch diary, Punch Library, London · journal of W. S. Cavendish, sixth duke of Devonshire, Chatsworth House, Derbyshire · letters, Chatsworth House, Derbyshire, Paxton MSS · parish register, Milton Bryan, Bedfordshire, 3 Aug 1803 [birth] · parish register, Derbyshire, 20 Feb 1827 [marriage] · K. Colquhoun, *A thing in disguise: the visionary life of Joseph Paxton* (2003)

Archives Chatsworth House, Derbyshire, archive, incl. corresp. | Beds. & Luton ARS, parish records, Milton Bryan, etc. · Durham RO, letters to Lord Londonderry's agent · ICL, Royal Commission for the International Exhibition of 1851 · RBG Kew, letters to Sir W. J. Hooker · RBG Kew, Lindley corresp. · UCL, corresp. with Edwin Chadwick

Likenesses H. P. Briggs, oils, 1836, Chatsworth House, Derbyshire · T. Ellerby, oils, 1843, Chatsworth House, Derbyshire · J. Jenkins, stipple, 1851? (after photograph by Kilburn), BM, NPG · S. Reynolds, engraving, pubd 1851 (after O. Oakley), BM · H. W. Phillips, group portrait, oils, 1853 (*The royal commissioners for the Great Exhibition of 1851*), V&A · E. Wyon, marble bust, 1864, Royal Horticultural Society, London · J. G. Crace, photograph, V&A · J. H. Lynch, lithograph (after daguerreotype by W. E. Kilburn, 1851), Linn. Soc. [*see illus.*] · O. Oakley, watercolour drawing, NPG · photograph, NPG · wood-engraving, NPG; repro. in *ILN* (24 June 1865)

Wealth at death under £180,000: probate, 4 Sept 1865, *CGPLA Eng. & Wales*

Paxton, Peter (*d. c.*1711), physician and writer on politics, was admitted to the degree of MD *per literas regias* at Pembroke College, Cambridge, in 1687. His name does not appear in the admission-book of Pembroke College, and he may have come from Oxford for an *ad eundem* degree. In 1704 he was known to be living in Beaufort Street, London. Apart from his writings, nothing more is known of Paxton's life. In 1701 he published *An Essay Concerning the Body of Man*, which traced all diseases to the fluids in the body.

This was followed by *The Grounds of Physick Examined* in 1703. Paxton's next three works were on political topics. *Civil Polity* appeared in 1703, *A Discourse Concerning the Nature, Advantage, and Improvement of Trade* in 1704, and *A Scheme for Union between England and Scotland* in 1705. Paxton went on to produce two more medical works: *A Directory Physico-Medical* (1707) and *Specimen physico-medicum*, which was published posthumously in 1711.

W. A. Shaw, rev. Michael Bevan

Sources Venn, *Alum. Cant.* · private information (1895)

Paxton, Stephen (*bap.* **1734**, *d.* **1787**), musician and composer, was baptized on 27 December 1734 at St Oswald's, Durham, the son of Robert Paxton. He gained his early musical training as a cathedral chorister until his voice broke. He spent the greater part of his life in London, and the earliest reference to his activities as a cellist in the metropolis dates from 20 April 1756. On 5 June 1757 he was elected a member of the Royal Society of Musicians. He married Martha Hunt (*d.* 1808) at St James's, Piccadilly, on 4 July 1771. His first published work appeared about 1772; his seven opuses included cello and violin duets, cello solos, glees, and lessons for cello and bass. He is listed as one of the four principal cellists at the first Handel memorial festival in 1784 and also played in 1786 and 1787. He performed principal parts at oratorio meetings, and Charles Burney praised his 'full and sweet tone' (Burney, *Hist. mus.*, 4.677) on the cello, combined with his 'judicious manner in accompanying the voice' (ibid.). On 21 March 1780 Paxton was elected a 'privileged member' of the Noblemen's and Gentlemen's Catch Club. Four pieces by him gained gold medals: the serious glees 'How sweet! How fresh!' (1779), 'Round the hapless André's urn' (1781), and 'Blest pow'r, here see' (1784), and the catch 'Ye Muses, inspire me' (1783); 'Come, oh come, ethereal guest' (1785) won a 5 guinea prize. Many of Paxton's glees are included in *Ladies' Amusement* (1791, vols. 1 and 2) and in Warren's *Collection of Catches*. He also composed and performed religious music, and was associated with the Sardinian chapel. He sold his music from his house, 29 Titchfield Street, London, and in music shops. Paxton died at Brompton Row, London, on 18 August 1787, aged fifty-two, and was buried in St Pancras churchyard. A requiem mass was held in his honour at the Sardinian chapel on 2 September; it is possible that he was a convert to Roman Catholicism. In his will, dated 2 May 1785, he counselled his widow 'to do Charitable Acts to my more distant Relations and to the Poor in General'. It was noted in the *Gentleman's Magazine* for September 1787 that his 'exemplary virtues and universal charity are ornaments that will make his memory ever respected' (*GM*, 1st ser., 57/2, 1787, 837).

One of Paxton's brothers, **William Paxton** (1725–1778), born on 8 February 1725 at Durham, was based in Durham throughout his life and was chorister and then lay clerk at the cathedral. He too was a cellist and composer of glees, and to him has been ascribed the glee 'Breathe soft, ye winds', which appears in Stephen's collection. William's six entries in 1779 and two in 1780 to the Catch Club were put forward by Stephen; two of his canons gained prizes, 'O Lord in thee' (1779) and 'O Israel, trust in the Lord' (1780). He was buried at Durham on 7 May 1778.

L. M. Middleton, rev. Fiona M. Palmer

Sources B. Crosby, 'Stephen and other Paxtons: an investigation into the identities and careers of a family of eighteenth-century musicians', *Music and Letters*, 81 (2000), 41–64 · Burney, *Hist. mus.*, vol. 4 · Highfill, Burnim & Langhans, *BDA*, 11.239–40 · S. Sadie, 'Paxton, Stephen', *New Grove* · 'Danby-Paxton-Webbe', *MT*, 38 (1897), 605–6 · F. T. Cansick, *A collection of curious and interesting epitaphs*, 1 (1869), 64 · *The Mawhood diary: selections from the diary notebooks of William Mawhood, woollen-draper of London, for the years 1764–1770*, ed. E. E. Reynolds, Catholic RS, 50 (1956) · will, Family Records Centre, Myddelton Street, London [transcript] · treasurers' books and account books, Durham Cathedral, U. Durham L., archives and special collections · parish register, St James, Piccadilly, City Westm. AC [marriage] · *IGI* · *Newcastle Chronicle* (20 Oct 1787)

Wealth at death over £10,000: *Newcastle Chronicle*

Paxton, William (1725–1778). *See under* Paxton, Stephen (*bap.* 1734, *d.* 1787).

Paxton, Sir William (1743/4–1824), merchant and banker, was born in Edinburgh, the third son of John Paxton of Berwickshire and his wife, Helen, daughter of William Adams, an Edinburgh printer. John Paxton was chief clerk of Archibald Stewart, a rich Edinburgh wine merchant of Berwick origin, MP and lord provost of Edinburgh at the time of the Stuart rebellion of 1745. At first William Paxton pursued a naval career. He started as a captain's servant in 1755, was at sea during the Seven Years' War, and rated midshipman at the end of it. In 1764 Paxton visited Robert Clive, armed with a letter of recommendation by John Stewart, Archibald's son, asking to be permitted to proceed to Bengal to serve as a mate in one of Bengal's country ships. Having been a free mariner in Bengal for nearly seven years, Paxton returned to London, where he became an apprentice to Francis Spilsbury and learned the art of assaying gold and silver and other metals. In February 1774 he petitioned the court of directors of the East India Company to be appointed assay master at Fort William in Bengal. Shortly afterwards, he left for Bengal for the second time, now in the company's service.

During his second stay in Bengal, Paxton mainly concerned himself with his private business. He founded what was to be the most successful agency house of its time. The Europeans in Bengal seem to have had confidence in his commercial abilities and character, trusting large parts of their fortunes to him. His contemporary Joseph Fowke, however, described him as having 'some slyness in his Nature, which sometimes joined to Cunning and sometimes to Roguery' (letter to Francis Fowke, 25 June 1784, BL OIOC, MS Eur. E6, fol. 37). In 1784 he entered into a partnership in India with Charles Cockerell; later, the firm came to be known as Paxton, Cockerell, and Trail, then Cockerell, Trail, and Palmer, and finally as Palmer & Co. (which, by 1813, had become the largest agency house in Calcutta). After several skirmishes with the East India Company authorities concerning his private trade, Paxton left Bengal. Once in London, he founded a branch of the Calcutta concern as Paxton & Co. (later Paxton, Cockerell, Trail & Co.); while continuing its Indian interests, and representing the Calcutta company in London, Paxton & Co. was also active in banking, lending important sums to industrial concerns such as the Gas, Light and Coke Company, of which Paxton was a director from its establishment in 1812 until his death.

In 1786, shortly after his return from Calcutta, Paxton married Ann Dawney (1764/5–1846), daughter of Thomas Dawney, and twenty-two years his junior. With her he had eleven children. He brought back from Calcutta one natural child, Elizabeth. Paxton's stately London house was at 24 Piccadilly. About 1790 he bought a country house and estate, Middleton Hall, in the county of Carmarthen, which he greatly improved and extended by buying up neighbouring property. At his death the estate amounted to 2650 acres. Paxton had a new mansion built by Samuel Pepys Cockerell, his partner's brother. A memorial tower in honour of Nelson, by the same architect, was built on a rise of the estate, overlooking the Towy valley, and is now called 'Paxton's tower'.

Paxton tried to obtain a seat in parliament, contesting Newark in 1790 and 1796; but he failed in both attempts, and incurred considerable expenses. He contested the 1802 county election of Carmarthen, but after spending the prodigious amount of £15,690 on his campaign, he was again unsuccessful. In 1803, however, John George Phillips resigned his Carmarthen borough seat, probably for a financial inducement, in Paxton's favour. Paxton undoubtedly returned from India a very rich man, and could meet such expenditure without hardship. At his death his fortune was estimated at £276,532. He was knighted at St James's Palace on 16 March 1803, and remained an MP until 1807.

A number of Paxton's children also sought their fortunes overseas. Some of his sons pursued a military career, others tried their luck in India. His daughter Anne married Arthur Goodall Wavell, and became the grandmother of Sir Archibald Percival Wavell, viceroy of India from 1943 to 1947. Sir William Paxton died at his London home on 10 February 1824, aged eighty, and was buried eight days later in the crypt of St Martin-in-the-Fields.

WILLEM G. J. KUITERS

Sources W. G. J. Kuiters, 'William Paxton, 1744–1824, merchant and banker in Bengal and London', MA diss., Rijksuniversiteit Leiden (NL), 1992 • W. G. J. Kuiters, 'William Paxton, 1744–1824: the history of an East India fortune', *Bengal Past and Present*, 111 (1992), 1–22 • BL OIOC, Francis Fowke's business corresp. (with W. Paxton and C. Cockerell), MS Eur D12 • burials in the parish of St Martin-in-the-Fields, 1824, City Westm. AC, fol. 347

Archives BL OIOC, Fowke MSS

Likenesses effigy on monument, Llanarthne parish church (St David's), Llanarthne, Carmarthenshire, Wales

Wealth at death £276,532: administration

Pay [Paye], **Henry** [*called* Arripay] (*fl.* 1402–1414), shipmaster, of Poole, Dorset, acquired a considerable reputation in the early fifteenth century because of his exploits in the seas off the south and west coasts of England. His enemies, especially those from Castile, bluntly called him a corsair, but at times he may well have been acting on his understanding of royal policy which only resolutely condemned attacks on the goods and ships of friendly aliens.

Acting with a small squadron of balingers and barges, the swift manoeuvrable vessels used for this kind of action, Pay was involved in 1402 in the capture of a Bremen ship with a rich cargo of Mediterranean goods including Valencian saffron, dates, and some barrels of 'prime sack'. In the next two years he seemed to prey particularly on Spanish vessels from Bilbao laden with iron bars, though in 1404 a mule, two silver girdles, and rich robes worth a total of 5000 nobles were also in the cargo. He seems often to have scoured the seas in the company of ships from Dartmouth and Kingswear, being on one occasion, in March 1404, the master of a barge belonging to the redoubtable John Hawley from the same town. His exploits sometimes show an element of bold daring; there is a chronicler's story of how Pay himself was boarded at sea by some Norman seamen and overpowered. The English crew were tied up on deck and their captors went below to look for booty, having first removed their armour because it was a very hot day. Pay and his men managed to free themselves and in their turn overpowered and killed their erstwhile captors in the hold. With his own vessel and the Norman prize Pay then sailed up the Seine showing French flags and burnt several small ships before escaping safely to the open sea.

The Castilians were more in awe of Pay than any other English raider; the chronicler of the exploits of Don Pero Niño describes his master's expedition in the channel in 1406, when he raided English coastal towns. They were particularly keen to attack Poole because it was known to be the base of the fearsome Arripay who had carried off the crucifix from St Mary of Finistère. The Castilians landed outside the walls of Poole and managed to get into the town, burning much property including a warehouse full of naval stores. Pay's brother was killed in the confused fighting, but Pay himself was not there. In 1404 the king had commissioned him to go to sea to 'provide for the destruction of the king's enemies' (*CPR, 1401–5*, 457). In 1405 he was with Lord Berkeley off Milford Haven operating against a French squadron which was supporting Owain Glyn Dŵr's rebellion. They managed to take fifteen French vessels including that taking the seneschal of France to Wales. In 1406 Pay was again in the channel, this time with the ships of the Cinque Ports, and took a large number of French ships suspected of trying to get supplies to the Welsh. In view of the ambiguous attitude of the crown to these actions in the channel at this date it is not surprising that Pay seems to have ended his career with an appointment as water bailiff of Calais with a royal pension. The date of his death is unknown, though he appears to have lived in Poole until at least 1414.

SUSAN ROSE

Sources C. L. Kingsford, 'West country piracy: the school of English seamen', *Prejudice and promise in XVth century England* (1925), 78–106; repr. (1962) • C. J. Ford, 'Piracy or policy: crisis in the channel, 1400–1403', *TRHS*, 5th ser., 29 (1979), 63–78 • Thomae Walsingham, *quondam monachi S. Albani, historia Anglicana*, ed. H. T. Riley, 2 vols., pt 1 of *Chronica monasterii S. Albani*, Rolls Series, 28 (1863–4) • G. Díez de Games, *El victorial: crónica de don Pero Niño*, ed. J. de M. Carriazo

(Madrid, 1940) • *Chancery records* (RC) • J. H. Wylie, *History of England under Henry the Fourth*, 4 vols. (1884–98), vol. 1, pp. 443–4

Paycocke [Peycocke], **Thomas** (*d.* 1518), clothier, was a younger son of John Paycocke of Coggeshall (*d.* 1505) and his wife, Emma. His father was described as a butcher, though this must understate the range and interest of his activities. There were many families of Paycocke or Peycocke in Suffolk and Essex from at least the thirteenth century. It is likely that Thomas was born and died in the small Essex market town of Coggeshall, where his brothers John (*d.* 1533) and Robert (*d.* 1520) also lived. Thomas and Robert may have been first-generation clothiers. On his memorial brass (which recorded the day of his death as 4 September) Thomas was described as 'clothworker', and by his will (dated the same day) he made specified bequests to named textile workers—two shearmen and their families, a weaver, a fuller, and a former apprentice. The broader scale of his cloth-making operations is better suggested by some further provisions:

> Item, I bequeth to all my wevers, Fullers and shermen that be not afore rehersed by name xij d. apece, and will they that haue wrought me verey moch wark haue iij s. iiijd. apece.
> Item I bequethe to be distributed amonge my kembers, carders and spynners summa iiij li.   (Beaumont, 324)

Nothing is known more precisely about the number of people he employed. He instructed his executors to give a broadcloth to the abbot and convent of Coggeshall, which perhaps indicates something about the sort of cloth he produced. The principal axis of Paycocke's trade, to judge from his will, was between Clare to the north and London to the south.

Paycocke married first Margaret, daughter of Thomas Horrold of Clare, and second Anne, daughter of George Cotton. In 1505, under the terms of his father's will, he inherited a newly built house in West Street, Coggeshall, which survives in the custody of the National Trust and has been described as 'one of the most attractive half-timbered houses of England' (Pevsner, 200). The elaborate wood carving that decorates the house includes, as a repeated motif, the family's merchant mark, an ermine tail. The house must have been intended specifically for Thomas Paycocke and his second wife, since their initials (T. P. and A. P.) recur in the oak rafters of the hall; it was perhaps built for them when they married. Thus Paycocke's chief claim to fame is perhaps his father's generosity, though a similar benevolence towards family, friends, and dependants is evident in his own will. After the death of his second wife it would seem that for want of a direct heir, the house passed to his nephew, John Paycocke. Paycocke is not known to have owned land.

Thomas Paycocke was a brother of the Crutched Friars of Colchester, whom he remembered in his will. He made numerous other bequests to local churches, as well as 6*s*. 8*d*. to St Paul's in London—'to the old warke in Pawlis and to Powlis pardone' (Beaumont, 323). He also left the substantial sum of £80 for repairing roads in Coggeshall and northwards towards Clare. He willed to be buried near his father, grandfather, and great-uncle in Coggeshall parish church. His monumental brass is lost, though that of his elder brother John survives. But he had the good fortune to be one of the six men and women commemorated in Eileen Power's *Medieval People*, first published in 1924 and many times reprinted, which has brought him a fame that his unremarkable career would never otherwise have earned for him.   R. H. BRITNELL

Sources G. F. Beaumont, 'Paycocke's house, Coggeshall, with some notes on the families of Paycocke and Buxton', *Transactions of the Essex Archaeological Society*, new ser., 9 (1903–6), 311–24 • E. Power, *The Paycockes of Coggeshall* (1920) • E. E. Power, 'Thomas Paycocke of Coggeshall: an Essex clothier in the days of Henry VII', *Medieval people* [1924] • *An inventory of the historical monuments in Essex*, Royal Commission on Historical Monuments (England), 4 vols. (1916–23), vol. 3, 115–23 • *Essex*, Pevsner (1965), 200
Wealth at death bequests: will

Paye, Richard Morton (*bap.* 1750, *d.* 1821), artist, was baptized on 14 June 1750 at Botley, Hampshire, the son of John Paye and his wife, Elizabeth, *née* Morton. Virtually nothing is known of Paye's early life, though he worked as a chaser from youth, perhaps a family occupation. In 1773 he first appeared in London at lodgings in Leicester Fields, from where he sent his first exhibits to the Royal Academy—two oil paintings and four wax models. His small-scale models earned comparison with those of George Michael Moser, with Paye possessing more of the 'spirit of sculpture and less of the French flutter' (*Library of the Fine Arts*, 3, 1832, 96). Yet none of these works can be identified today. A two-year gap from 1775 to 1777 suggests some time away from the capital, but there is no record of travel to Italy, as one might expect of a young artist of this date. From *c*.1778 to 1783 Paye resided in London at 26 Swallow Street, then the main thoroughfare between Piccadilly Circus and Oxford Street.

Paye attracted the patronage of the younger son of the famous doctor Percival Pott, the Revd Joseph Holden Pott, who bought *A Girl Sewing* (possibly *A Fancy Head*; exh. RA, 1773). This early work exemplifies Paye's interest in 'fancy pictures', everyday scenes featuring children, treated in the manner of old masters such as Rembrandt and Murillo, much in fashion in the late eighteenth century. In 1783 in *An Engraver at Work* (exh. Society of Arts, 1783; Upton House, Warwickshire), Paye depicted himself engraving a portrait of Pott's father, after Nathaniel Dance. A candle-lit scene, it well illustrates his reputation as a painter of chiaroscuro effects in the manner of Joseph Wright of Derby. His greatest bid for critical attention came when he showed this painting and nine others at the Society of Arts in 1783. By 1784 Paye had moved to 37 Broad Street, Golden Square, London. It is not known when he married, but his wife's maiden name may have been Hayward and his expanding family acted as models for his child-focused subjects.

Another early patron was Dr John Wolcot, the satirist with the pen-name Peter Pindar, who, after falling out with John Opie in 1783, turned his attention to Paye. The two men associated for about a year, perhaps sharing lodgings and profits from picture sales, but the arrangement failed when Wolcot accused the artist of 'obstinacy,

Richard Morton Paye (*bap.* 1750, *d.* 1821), self-portrait, exh. Society of Artists 1783 [*An Engraver at Work*]

ingratitude [and] not following his advice in the pursuit of his studies' (D.). A complete break occurred when Paye exhibited *Portrait of a Sulky Boy* at the Royal Academy in 1785, arguably his masterpiece (Sothebys, 10 November 1982), but calculated to anger Wolcot as it was a public display of the writer's supposed illegitimate son.

Paye's skill and originality reputedly prompted Sir Joshua Reynolds to invite him to mix in Royal Academy circles, but his diffidence prevented him from doing so. It is hard to reconcile this shyness with the subtle irony and humour evident in the artist's chosen area of specialization, the behaviour of children engaged in a common activity. Paye's inventive compositions and subjects also often featured identifiable locations in London, as in *Boys Throwing Snowballs* (exh. RA, 1784; engraved 1785), set under the portico of St George's, Hanover Square, and *Boys Playing at Marbles* (engraved 1786) set in the environs of Westminster School. Most of Paye's child subjects were issued as engravings in pairs, tapping into the growing market for prints at home and in France.

Paye exhibited regularly at the Royal Academy and once at the Free Society in 1783 and at the Society for Promoting Art and Design in Liverpool in 1787, with later appearances at the Society of Arts and the British Institution, showing more than seventy-five paintings. Yet only a fraction are known, chiefly through engravings, and fewer still are located now. He also painted portraits (for example, Richard Brinsley Sheridan, exh. RA, 1789) and history paintings. Stylistically, Paye graduated from a tightly defined precision in early portraits (reminiscent of Henry Walton's works) to the dramatic lighting effects of *An Engraver at Work*, to a later broader style. As a stylistic chameleon, Paye produced works destined to be misattributed. In the 1820s one of his major paintings, *The Miraculous Increase of the Widow's Oil* (also known as *The Widow's Cruse*), appeared with an art dealer as a work of Velázquez, and it was acknowledged as such by leading painters of the day, until a friend of Paye recognized the artist's family as the models.

Critical favour eluded Paye, with the style of his works in the 1790s considered 'woolly', and 'his execution slovenly' (D.), as in *The Boy Exulting over his Golden Eggs* (exh. RA, 1795; engraved 1796). However, he intended these more quickly executed genre subjects primarily as designs for engravings, then his main source of income. Paye enjoyed close relations with many of the best engravers of the day, including J. R. Smith and John Young, his greatest friend and supporter. In 1795, his final bid for success at the Royal Academy resulted in a display of seven paintings, hurriedly finished, as reported by Joseph Farington (Farington, *Diary*, 2.327, 18 April 1795); later in the year he did not receive a single vote when seeking election as an associate member, at the age of forty-five. Paye's fortunes then declined, with only infrequent appearances in exhibitions. He produced a design for a competition for a monument to Lord Nelson in 1807 while suffering with rheumatic fever and later suffered a stroke. John Young appealed to the Royal Academy on behalf of Paye 'now labouring under a stroke of Palsey, and in very poor circumstances' (ibid., vol. 11, 26 Jan 1812), and with the support of the president, Benjamin West, Paye received 20 guineas as a charitable gift. He carried on as an artist until at least 1815 when, according to the catalogue of the British Institution's annual exhibition, he showed *The Gout, or, A Lecture on Patience* which 'he painted with his left hand, after losing the use of the right by a paralytic fit'.

Towards the end of his life Paye resided with his daughter, Elizabeth Anne Briane, a successful miniaturist, at Queen Anne Street, London. He never progressed as far in his career as his early talents promised due to a 'retired disposition' and 'almost total exclusion from contemporary intercourse' (D.), and died in obscurity in December 1821.

BARBARA COFFEY BRYANT

Sources D., 'Biography: R. M. Paye', *Literary Gazette* (26 Jan 1822), 60 • 'R. M. Paye', *New Monthly Magazine*, new ser., 1 (1822), 137–8 • 'The British school of design: neglected biography no. I: R. M. Paye', *Library of the Fine Arts*, 3 (1832), 95–101 • *Library of the Fine Arts*, 3 (1832), incl., self-portrait, stipple engraving by R. Dagley • A. Laing, *In trust for the nation: paintings from National Trust houses* (1995), no. 24 [exhibition catalogue, National Gallery, London] • D. Alexander, *Dictionary of British engravers, 1700–1830* [forthcoming] • Redgrave, *Artists* • Graves, *RA exhibitors* • E. W. Clayton, 'Richard Morton Paye', *The Connoisseur*, 37 (1913), 229–36 • D. Foskett, *A dictionary of British miniature painters*, 1 (1972), 180, 440 • M. Postle, *Angels and urchins: the fancy picture in 18th-century British art* (1998), 16, 70 (n. 29), 71 (n. 38) [exhibition catalogue, Djanogly Art Gallery, Nottingham, and Kenwood House, London, 28 March – 9 Aug 1998] • Farington, *Diary*, 2.327, 329, 397; 11.4070 • A. Davies and E. Kilmurray, *Dictionary of British portraiture*, 4 vols. (1979–81) • R. Walker, *National Portrait Gallery: Regency portraits*, 1 (1985), 452 • council minute books, RA, 4 (1807–12), 329 • *DNB*

Archives RA, MSS, council minute books, vol. 4 (1807–12), 329

Payn, James (1830–1898), novelist and journal editor, was born on 28 February 1830 at Rodney Lodge, Rodney Terrace, Cheltenham, the second son of William Payn (1774/5–1840) and his wife, Harriet. His father, who was clerk to the River Thames commissioners, a justice of the peace, and also sometime treasurer for the county of Berkshire, lived at Kidwells, near Maidenhead, Berkshire, and kept the Berkshire harriers. James Payn's elder brother was General Sir William Payn (1823–1893), who served in India. As a young boy James Payn was introduced to country pursuits by his father and had to go hunting twice a week, but he preferred to read. His father died in 1840 when Payn was ten, and his mother took charge of his upbringing, but little else is known of her.

Payn went to a preparatory school which he did not enjoy as he 'hated lessons of all kinds' (Payn, *Literary Recollections*, 6), preferring to read 'works of the imagination'. Despite this loathing of school, he was popular, as he invented stories for his contemporaries. He left and went, as his brother William had done before him, to Eton College, in the summer of 1842. He did not take kindly to the fagging system or the bullying and disliked Latin and Greek. The rejection of an article for the college magazine dented his enthusiasm for writing. His stay was short: Eton College archives record that he left at Christmas of the same year. Payn, however, recalls that he left 'after a year or so' when he had been nominated for the Royal Military Academy, Woolwich, and was sent to one of the academy preparatory schools at Woolwich. This was a 'crammer' and he resented the system that allowed him no time for reading. In his *Literary Recollections* he refers to the school as 'Messrs. Hurry and Crammem's' and some years later used this experience in his novel *The Foster Brothers* (1859). He passed third for the academy and entered Woolwich in September 1846. His stay here was also short and he left owing to ill health in August of the following year. It was decided that Payn was to go to a private tutor in Devon prior to going up to Cambridge, as his father had wished him to enter the church. His stay in Devon was more conducive to his literary and scholastic interests than had been any of his previous educational establishments.

Payn was admitted as a pensioner at Trinity College, Cambridge, on 27 June 1849, graduating in 1853. He had an eventful university career, being president of the union in 1852, and a member of various societies, but he still had no enthusiasm for formal education. He was on good terms with the scholar William George Clark, and George Brimley (1819–1857), the college librarian. While at Cambridge Payn published his first poem, 'The Poet's Death', in *Leigh Hunt's Journal* (15 March 1851). He also published at his own expense his first volume of poetry, *Stories from Boccaccio and other Poems* (1852), which was well reviewed by George Brimley in *The Spectator*. Payn's university education and his acceptance in print led him to turn to literature as a career. In 1853 he published an article based on his experiences at Woolwich ('Gentleman cadet', *Household Words*, 9 April 1853, 231), which later led to a lasting friendship with Charles Dickens. The article was not well received by the governor of the Royal Military Academy, who complained to Dickens, as editor of *Household Words*, that the writer could not possibly have been a cadet at Woolwich. Payn continued to contribute to *Household Words* for a number of years.

After leaving Cambridge, Payn married Louisa Adelaide Edlin (*b.* 1830/31) on 28 February 1854 and they moved to Rydal Cottage, Ambleside. Among their neighbours were Mary Russell Mitford and Harriet Martineau. Payn had been introduced to Miss Mitford by his father and she introduced Payn to Harriet Martineau. Both writers encouraged him to further his literary career and through them he met Matthew Arnold, William Allingham, Arthur Clough, and Thomas De Quincey. Payn's early works show the influence of Dickens in characterization and plot, his *Stories and Sketches* (1857) being a good example. He greatly admired Dickens—the three-volume *Mirk Abbey* (1866) is dedicated to him—but he soon branched out into his own style and range of subject matter. His experiences of living and walking in the Lake District resulted in *Leaves from Lakeland* (1858), *Furness Abbey and its Neighbourhood* (1862), and the illustrated two-volume *Lakes in Sunshine* (1867).

Payn had now begun to contribute to *Chambers's Journal* and was invited to become co-editor by the novelist Leitch Ritchie in 1858. This required a move to Edinburgh but the Payns did not take to the city nor the Scottish sabbath and in 1861 moved to London, where Payn continued as sole editor of *Chambers's Journal*, a position he had held since 1859. His first successful novel was the two-volume *Lost Sir Massingberd: a Romance of Real Life* (1864) which like so many of his works appeared first in serial form, in this case in *Chambers's Journal*. It is claimed that the journal's circulation was increased by 20,000 copies as a result. The story concerns the disappearance of an unsavoury uncle, Sir Massingberd, whose body is finally found trapped in the hollow of an oak tree. Payn was grateful to the novel as 'it attracted the attention of some of my masters … among them was my friend Wilkie Collins' (Payn, *Literary Recollections*, 242), to whom he dedicated *Gwendolyn's Harvest* (1870). Dickens, too, praised the book.

Despite being a close friend of Robert Chambers (1802–1871) Payn resigned the editorship of *Chambers's Journal* in 1874 (Leslie Stephen says he was dismissed) as he could not work with Robert's brother William (1800–1883). In 1874 he was invited by Leslie Stephen to become reader for the publishers Smith, Elder, a post he held for about twenty years.

Payn's greatest literary success was the two-volume *By Proxy* (1878), set in China, in which the hero, Captain Conway, gives himself as the proxy victim for execution in place of his convicted, thieving friend Pennicuik. Needless to say in such a sensation novel, Conway somehow escapes death and returns later to England to put matters right. This novel, together with *Lost Sir Massingberd*, established Payn as a popular, but minor, novelist. Although he was never to repeat the success of *By Proxy*, he continued to produce novels using exotic locations and plots, with good characterization. In the earlier two-volume *Murphy's Master* (1873) he removes some undesirable characters from the story by introducing a sinking island, a fanciful idea which later occurred in real life. He was also a good short story writer and in one of the stories, 'The Fateful Curiosity' in his three-volume collection *High Spirits* (1879), his predictions include air-conditioning, a twice daily postal service from Australia, and even the channel tunnel. He contributed to numerous journals, including the *Westminster Review*, *Longman's Magazine*, *Nineteenth Century*, and a weekly article in the *Illustrated London News*.

In January 1883 Payn succeeded Stephen as editor of the *Cornhill Magazine*, when Stephen resigned to edit the *Dictionary of National Biography*. Payn was to have a great influence as editor: he increased the amount of light fiction at the expense of literary essays, reduced the size of the journal, and the price from 1*s.* to 6*d.*, with the introduction of a new series in July 1883. During his editorship he was a great supporter of rising young writers and he published Conan Doyle (to whom he dedicated his mystery novel *The Disappearance of George Driffel*, 1896), Henry Seton Merriman, Stanley Weyman, Rider Haggard, and F. Anstey, among others. Payn was closely involved with the Society of Authors founded by Walter Besant in 1884 to promote the rights of authors, especially in relation to copyright and overseas contracts.

Payn's strength was that he knew his limitations as a writer and worked within those limits. He could tell a good story with many ingenious twists and turns, and sometimes with bizarre locations, and he had a good eye for detail and characterization. He was a prolific writer, producing forty-six novels and eight collections of short stories and many essays. His plots ranged from the Gothic to the melodramatic and included comic and adventure situations, some of the latter being in the vein of writers such as Rider Haggard and Kipling. He knew what the public liked and was successful in catering for their tastes, although this is not to say that he wrote for that reason. All his novels were serialized before publication in book form, the majority in *Chambers's Journal* and the *Cornhill Magazine*. He also produced two volumes of memoirs, *Some Literary Recollections* (1884) and *Gleams of Memory* (1894). Payn is probably now known more for his verse on buttered toast than his novels:

> I had never had a piece of toast
> Particularly long and wide,
> But fell upon the sanded floor,
> And always on the buttered side.
> (*Oxford Dictionary of Quotations*, 1992, 370)

Frank Anstey describes Payn as 'tall, thin, and rather angular, he had a sharp high voice, there was a kindly twinkle behind his spectacles, and he was a brilliant and amusing raconteur' (F. Anstey, *A Long Retrospect*, 1938, 111). Leslie Stephen, who had known Payn since Cambridge, described him as an unaffected person with 'a remarkable skill in constructing ingenious situations' (*DNB*). He seems to have had a happy marriage resulting in at least nine children, mainly girls. His third daughter, Alicia Isobel, became the first wife of George Earle Buckle, the editor of *The Times*, though she died the same year as her father.

Chronic rheumatism forced Payn to resign his editorship of the *Cornhill* in March 1896. He spent the last years of his life housebound, although his friends, with whom he used to play whist every afternoon at the Reform Club, would come to him for a game. But his health continued to fail and he died on 25 March 1898 at his home 43 Warrington Crescent, Maida Vale, London, and was buried on 30 March 1898 at Paddington old cemetery, Kilburn. His wife survived him.   DAMIAN ATKINSON

Sources R. C. Terry, 'High spirits: James Payn, best of journalists', *Victorian popular fiction, 1860–80* (1983) • L. Stephen, introduction, in J. Payn, *The backwater of life, or, Essays of a literary veteran* (1899) • L. Huxley, 'James Payn, 1830–98', *Cornhill Magazine*, [3rd] ser., 68 (1930) • J. Payn, *Some literary recollections* (1884) • J. Payn, *Gleams of memory with some recollections* (1894) • Venn, *Alum. Cant.* • E. Kilmurray, *Dictionary of British portraiture*, 3 (1981) • Boase, *Mod. Eng. biog.* • *The Times* (26 March 1898) • *New York Times* (26 March 1898) • *New York Times* (9 April 1898) • *The Athenaeum* (2 April 1898) • *The Critic* (2 April 1898) • *The Spectator* (2 April 1898) • m. cert.

Archives BL, Add. MSS 46618, fol. 268; 46654, fol. 99; 58789, fols. 75–8 • Bodl. Oxf., MS Eng. misc. d. 179, fol. 253; MS Eng. misc. d. 533, fol. 2; MS Eng. lett. d. 458, fols. 78–83; MS Dobell c. 40, fols. 28–30 • Morgan L., letters • NL Scot., MS 3713, fol. 322; dep. 341/140 • U. Texas, Authors' Syndicate archives, letters | BL, letters to Royal Literary Fund, loan 96 • JRL, De Tabley MSS • NL Scot., letters to *Blackwood's* • NL Scot., letters to Robert Chalmers • NYPL, Berg collection, letters to Macmillan & Co. • U. Texas, Ruskin MSS

Likenesses Ape [C. Pellegrini], caricature, chromolithograph, NPG; repro. in *VF* (8 Sept 1888) • Barraud, photograph, NPG; repro. in *Men and Women of the Day*, 3 (1890) • A. Bassano, photograph, NPG; repro. in *Harper's Magazine* (June 1888) • W. & D. Downey, photograph, woodburytype, NPG; repro. in W. Downey and D. Downey, *The cabinet portrait gallery* (1890) • R. Taylor and P. Naumann, group portrait, wood-engraving (*Our literary contributors—past and present*), BM; repro. in *ILN* (14 May 1892) • photograph, NPG

Wealth at death £8367 9s. 5d.: probate, 15 April 1898, *CGPLA Eng. & Wales*

Payne. *See also* Pain, Paine.

Payne, (George) Adney (1846–1907), music-hall manager, was born in the Curragh, Ireland, the son of Edward Payne, a licensed victualler. Unlike most music-hall entrepreneurs of his generation, Adney Payne (as he was generally referred to), was not born into the theatrical profession. Indeed, he frequently recalled that his parents had held a very low opinion of the value of popular entertainments.

It was while working as a wine merchant in Greenwich that Payne first became involved in the music-hall business. In 1878 he and Charles Spencer Crowder purchased Lusby's music-hall, Mile End Road, for £25,000. Crowder took responsibility for the theatrical aspects of the business, while Payne utilized his experience as a licensed victualler in overseeing the backstage activities, primarily the sale of refreshments. Lusby's had a chequered history under Crowder and Payne's control. It bore the brunt of

Frederick Charrington's religious crusade against London's music-halls and was burnt down in 1884, soon reopening as the Paragon. Meanwhile, in 1882 Crowder and Payne also purchased the Canterbury music-hall, Westminster Bridge Road, Lambeth. When Crowder retired in 1887, Payne became managing director of the newly formed Canterbury and Paragon Limited.

Payne rose to prominence within the music-hall business during the West End boom of the 1890s as a key figure in the emergence of Henry Newson-Smith's syndicate of theatres. After the retirement of the latter in 1896, Payne, as the managing director of the Tivoli and Oxford music-halls and the London Pavilion, enjoyed a virtual monopoly over the West End's music-halls. He was largely responsible for nurturing the talents of many of the greatest 'stars' of the variety stage who rose to fame during the 1890s and was closely associated with the much heralded 'improvement' in both the artistic merit and the moral tone of performances and in the behaviour of audiences at this time. After the turn of the century Payne, in collaboration with Henry Gros, turned his attention to the booming suburban music-hall market, becoming joint managing director of 'Palaces' in Chelsea, Walthamstow, Tottenham, and East Ham. His influence over the metropolitan music-hall business was further enhanced by the marriage of one of his daughters to Walter Gibbons, another leading manager.

Payne was twice married. His first wife was Marion Ford (d. 1897); they had six children, two of whom died in infancy. On 15 November 1898 he married Clara Agnes Proctor (whose stage name was Ethel Earle), a theatrical and music-hall performer. She was the daughter of Alfred Pavey, a builder and estate agent. Payne was a keen fruit grower and horticulturalist and a member of the Hertfordshire yeomanry for seventeen years. He took especial pride in his thirty prizes for best turned-out man and horse at local shows.

According to one obituary Payne played a significant role in 'the foundation of the variety theatres into a large commercial industry' (Daily Mail, 16 May 1907); and he was certainly renowned for his energy and perseverance. An imposing figure, he was 'a man of wonderful decision and dominating temperament' (Daily Telegraph, 16 May 1907) and 'when his mind was thoroughly made up as to a particular course, nothing would divert him from it' (ibid., 18 May 1907, 4). In spite of his 'marshal [sic] bearing, [and] strict disciplinarian methods in business' (Daily Mail, 16 May 1907) Payne cultivated a paternalistic relationship with his performers and was a trustee of the Music Hall Benevolent Fund. Notwithstanding this image, Payne's halls were boycotted by performers during the infamous music-hall strike of 1907.

George Adney Payne died of a blood clot at the Mount Ephraim Hotel, Tunbridge Wells, on 15 May 1907, ten days after a serious motor car accident in the town. He was buried in a family plot in St Pancras cemetery, East Finchley, on 18 May. He was survived by his wife.

ANDREW CROWHURST

Sources Daily Telegraph (16 May 1907) · The Era (18 May 1907) · Daily Mail (16 May 1907) · 'A chat with Mr Adney Payne', The Era (11 Aug 1894) · A. Crowhurst, 'The music hall, 1885–1922: the emergence of a national entertainment industry in Britain', PhD diss., U. Cam., 1992 · Daily Telegraph (18 May 1907) · m. cert. · d. cert. · CGPLA Eng. & Wales (1907)
Likenesses photograph, 1908, repro. in Era Annual (1908)
Wealth at death £48,286 3s. 6d.: administration, 3 Aug 1907, CGPLA Eng. & Wales

Payne, Antony [Anthony; *called* the Cornish Giant] (d. 1691?), giant, was reputedly 7 feet 2 inches tall at the age of twenty-one. No authentic records of his parentage, birth date, baptism, or marriage survive, but there were certainly Paynes living during the seventeenth century in Stratton, Cornwall. Antony Payne evidently died and was buried there on 13 July 1691, according to later accounts aged about eighty. However, as the parish registers do not begin until 1687 it is possible that the record of Payne's burial has been lost and that the entry is of a kinsman of the same name. Sibilla Payne, buried at Stratton on 9 July 1691, may have been his wife. Payne was, it seems, throughout his life a devoted and valued retainer in peace and war of the Grenvilles of Stowe, notably of John Grenville, first earl of Bath. Again, documentation is lacking, but a clearly contemporary painting, confidently ascribed to Sir Godfrey Kneller and dated 1680, depicting a military Payne against a background of Plymouth citadel, where Bath was governor, gives credence to claims for Payne as a yeoman of the guard and halberdier there. After many vicissitudes of ownership and treatment, the portrait came late in the nineteenth century into the possession of the Royal Institution of Cornwall.

An engraving of the painting had accompanied a circumstantial account of Payne in C. S. Gilbert's *Historical Survey of Cornwall* (1817). From this point on the legend of a gentle giant—the 'Falstaff of the West'—began to emerge, clinched by an article by R. S. Hawker, vicar of Morwenstow, Cornwall, in *All the Year Round* for 1866 (vol. 16), later incorporated into his *Footprints of Former Men in Far Cornwall* (1870). Inimical to the current processes of reform in church and state, and nostalgic for his own (but shared) brand of Stuart Anglican royalism, Hawker was more than a mere romancer. A purpose underlay all his writings in prose and verse. A slipshod researcher who 'never let facts, or the absence of them, stand in the way of his imagination' (Granville, vii) or his aspirations, Hawker presented Anthony (his spelling) as 'a true Stuart', 'a wonderful boy', plebeian but a leader, physically skilled, brave and bright, loyal to the end. No contemporary report puts Payne present at the battle of Lansdowne (5 July 1643), but Hawker prints a handsome consoling letter from him to Grace, widow of Sir Bevil Grenville, heroically killed in action there. Its style soon exposed it as a fabrication, but Hawker's vivid characterization, supported by dubious artefacts—Payne's 6 quart flask—and invented folk metaphors—'as long as Tony Payne's foot'—created an instant tradition which survived with advantages in Cornish popular history. Therein lies the true historical significance of Antony Payne: hardly in what he was or did in his own time, but for what was made of him from two centuries on, as a symbol of a continuing Cornish patriotism generally and for glimpses of the values of an arch-conservatism for which Hawker was in effect an enthusiastic literary agent.   IVAN ROOTS

Sources C. S. Gilbert, *An historical survey of the county of Cornwall*, 2 vols. (1817–20) • R. S. Hawker, *Footprints of former men in far Cornwall*, ed. C. E. Byles (1908) • R. Granville, 'Anthony Payne', in R. S. Hawker, *Footprints of former men in far Cornwall*, ed. C. E. Byles (1908), appx E, 287–94 • M. Stoyle, *West Britons: Cornish identities and the early modern British state* [forthcoming] • R. Harvey, *A short account of Anthony Payne … and the history of his portrait presented to the Museum of the Royal Institution of Cornwall* [n.d., *c*.1880] • W. Jago, notes of the portrait of Antony Payne, 1889, Royal Institution of Cornwall • J. Stucley, *Sir Bevill Grenvile and his times, 1596–1643* (1983) • M. Coate, *Cornwall in the great civil war and interregnum, 1642–1660* (1933)
Archives Royal Institution of Cornwall, Truro
Likenesses G. Kneller, portrait?, 1680 (of Anthony Payne?), Royal Institution of Cornwall, Truro

Payne, Ben Iden (1881–1976), theatre director and actor, was born at Newcastle upon Tyne on 5 September 1881, the youngest in the family of two sons and two daughters of the Revd Alfred Payne, a Unitarian minister, and his wife, Sarah Glover. He was educated privately and at Manchester grammar school. He went into the theatre, making a début in November 1899 with Frank Benson's company—regarded then as the university of the theatre—at Worcester as Diggory in *She Stoops to Conquer*. During the following spring he had a few small parts with Benson in a London season at the Lyceum. He acted in various minor tours, and while he was at Waterford, in his mid-twenties, he met somebody he would describe later as 'a tall, dark man who looked, in his coal black suit and the dim light behind the scenery, so like a priest that for a moment I thought he was one'. This personage was the poet W. B. Yeats; it appeared that the actor–director A. Granville-Barker, impressed by Payne after one short talk in an ABC teashop, had recommended the thoughtful and intelligent young man to Yeats as stage director of the Abbey Theatre, Dublin. Payne was out of key there, but presently he met the wealthy theatre-minded philanthropist Miss A. E. F. Horniman, who was dissatisfied with events in Dublin where, a critic said, she had been 'acting as fairy godmother to the singularly ungrateful Cinderella' of the Abbey; she and Lady Gregory had been antipathetic. Liking Payne, she engaged him to advise on her further theatrical activities; he told her that Manchester, civilized in the arts, should be her centre, and when he was twenty-six, wise beyond his years, he inaugurated the English repertory movement—at first, during the autumn of 1907, in an oblong ballroom known as the Midland Hotel Theatre.

Soon, at Easter 1908, the company moved to the old Gaiety Theatre, before long to be reconstructed without any concession to more flamboyant tastes: no gilt, no flock wallpaper, neither brass nor drums in the orchestra. Payne's tastes, which matched those of Miss Horniman, were for a quiet, gentle austerity that he would not lose during the rest of his long career. The first Gaiety production was *Measure for Measure*, directed by a single-minded puritan zealot, William Poel, whose work on Shakespeare, with its insistence on fluidity of action, influenced

Payne throughout his life. The Gaiety company was remarkable: it would include, at various times, Sybil Thorndike, Lewis Casson, Mona Limerick, Herbert Lomas, Ada King, and the young Basil Dean. After four years of tireless, unassuming endeavour, during which he encouraged a regional school of dramatists and gave to Manchester an uncommon run of major plays, Payne left to tour and to originate seasons elsewhere with his first wife, the actress Mona Limerick—a much more forceful figure than the calm idealist Payne, though he did have an idealist's persistence. In the autumn of 1913 he went to America where he directed at Chicago and at Philadelphia and where most of his later life would be spent.

As general producer to Charles Frohman's company in New York (1917–22) Payne directed a wide variety of plays; with his experience he was able to take on anything and face the frustrations of the commercial Broadway stage, but his heart was always with the intellectual drama and particularly with Shakespeare. Later he held a number of academic appointments and acted two or three times—Henry Straker in *Man and Superman* by G. B. Shaw in Newport, Rhode Island, in 1932, was the last—for he still thought of himself as primarily an actor. His special reputation was as visiting professor, 1919–28, at the Carnegie Institute of Technology in Pittsburgh (the Carnegie Tech), which had the first American university drama department.

Payne was particularly delighted when Sir Archibald Flower invited him to succeed W. Bridges-Adams as director of what was then the new Shakespeare Memorial Theatre in Stratford upon Avon, opened only three years before. He was there for eight years from 1935 (when he began with *Antony and Cleopatra*), a disappointing period in a theatre unkind to his methods and to his use of modified Elizabethan staging, with its penthouse, various acting areas, and 'curtain-boys'. Relinquishing his post in 1942, in 1943 he gratefully returned to the United States. He became head of drama at several American universities; his work, now largely Shakespearian, was almost entirely so from 1946. He was appointed guest professor of drama at the University of Texas; a new 500-seat theatre there was named after him in 1976, only a month before his death. One production, *Hobson's Choice* (1953), would be a wistful memory of the Manchester school.

As innovator and teacher—his great gift—Payne was always warmly respected, though his name, for he believed modesty to be the best policy, was never as potent as it should have been in the wider world of the theatre. E. Martin Browne, the English director who for some time in the late 1920s was his assistant at the Carnegie Tech, called him a professional to the bone, 'slight and smallish, very agile, with a mobile face of great charm'. He was 'quite without the grand manner that his record in the theatre would have justified'. He had many theatrical awards and became honorary LLD of the University of Alberta, Canada, in 1963.

Payne's first marriage, in 1906, to Mary Charlotte Louise Gadney (Mona Limerick) was dissolved in 1950. They had one son and two daughters, one of whom, Rosalind Iden, married Donald Wolfit. In 1950 he married, second, Barbara Rankin Chiaroni, who survived him. He died in Austin, Texas, on 6 April 1976. J. C. TREWIN, *rev.*

Sources B. I. Payne, *A life in a wooden O* (1977) · E. M. Browne and H. Browne, *Two in one* (1981) · S. Beauman, *The Royal Shakespeare Company: a history of ten decades* (1982) · *The Times* (8 April 1976) · *The Times* (9 May 1977) · *The Times* (2 April 1978) · personal knowledge (2004)

Payne, Christopher Russell (1874–1952), naval officer, was born on 17 September 1874 at 2 Molesworth Terrace, Stoke Damerel, Devon, the son of the Revd Samuel Ward Payne, then chaplain of HMS *Implacable*, and his wife, Julia Florence Delmage. Payne joined the Royal Naval College, Dartmouth, in 1888, passed as a midshipman in 1890, was promoted sub-lieutenant in 1893, and lieutenant in 1895. In 1897 he was in the *Devastation* at Devonport when Captain Henry Bradwardine Jackson (later Sir Henry) was experimenting with wireless telegraphy at the Torpedo School. Payne qualified as a torpedo lieutenant at *Vernon* in 1899, and was appointed to the torpedo depot ship *Vulcan*, under Jackson, on the Mediterranean station.

After returning to *Vernon* to requalify in torpedo duties Payne joined the staff in 1902 as lieutenant in charge of the wireless telegraphy department. In 1903 Payne, Jackson, and F. G. Loring inspected Marconi's new tuned system, recommending an immediate service trial and that all navy ships have three wireless telegraphy ratings in peace and an additional one in war, and emphasizing the role of wireless telegraphy training and practice. From 1903 to 1905 Payne served as torpedo officer in *Duncan*, again under Jackson, with special wireless telegraphy duties in the Mediterranean and channel. Jackson reported that Payne was 'Very zealous and capable in all respects. Has greatly assisted development of W/T. Strongly recommended for early promotion' (PRO, ADM 196/43, p. 502).

Promoted to commander on 31 December 1905 and appointed to *Exmouth* for wireless telegraphy duties in the channel, Payne returned yet again to *Vernon* and was commander in charge of the wireless telegraphy department from 1906 to 1908. He served on the committee on entry and training of operators for wireless telegraphy, which led to the formation of the wireless telegraphy branch in 1907. With Loring he gave evidence to the select committee on the 1906 Radio-Telegraphic Convention. In 1908 he served on the committee on wireless telegraphy codes and ciphers.

Their lordships at the Admiralty expressed their appreciation for good results in wireless telegraphy trials between *Vernon* and *Indomitable* and noted Payne's good work with high power stations at Horsea and Gibraltar as commander of *Furious* (1908–9). But when a court of inquiry into the collision between *Crusader* and *Rother* considered he had committed an error in judgement, their lordships expressed displeasure and cautioned him to be more careful. However, he redeemed himself as their lordships conveyed satisfaction with him for designing a mechanism for experiments with submarine A1.

Payne was recognized as a leading naval wireless expert. In 1912 he inspected the Poulsen system of wireless telegraphy between San Francisco and Honolulu, attended the House of Commons Marconi committee, and was recommended for service on the signal committee. Promoted captain on 31 December 1912 and appointed for special service, he visited the Universal Radio Syndicate works in Copenhagen, and was a member of the committee on wireless telegraphy under Sir Henry Jackson.

Payne commanded *Vindictive* (1913–15), which acted as a wireless relay station during the battle of the Falklands. After command of *Celtic*, he was appointed head of signal section of the Admiralty war staff in January 1916. When in command of *Suffolk* (1917–19) he acted as British senior naval officer at Vladivostok in the rank of commodore. He ensured co-operation between the various forces, gaining universal regard for dealing with the political situation.

Created a commander of the Légion d'honneur in 1918, Payne was appointed CBE and received the grand order of the Rising Sun in 1919. He was appointed to command *Vernon* in April 1920 and after two years he was made an aide-de-camp to the king. Payne married late in life at Holy Trinity Church, Brompton, on 2 June 1921 Amy Dorothy Perrot Whinney (*b.* 1894), daughter of Sir Arthur Whinney (1865–1927), assistant accountant-general of the navy, and Amy Elizabeth Golden. They had four daughters: Julia Elizabeth, Penelope Mary, Diana Rosemary, and Susanna Delmege.

Payne's last command was *Malaya* from 1922 until his promotion to rear-admiral in 1923; but he was then not further employed and was placed on the retired list in 1925. In 1926 the director of the signal department paid tribute to the work of Jackson and Payne:

> [they] carried the Navy from the beginning of Wireless Telegraphy through the darkest days to the efficiency of recent times. They never allowed the disheartening effect of failures, and there were many, to delay improvements and advances, and by their persistence and ready help and advice to all W/T enthusiasts under them they brought Naval W/T through the stages of wonder, ridicule, doubt and tolerance to almost its present state of reliability. (PRO, ADM 116/3403)

Promoted vice-admiral on the retired list in 1928, Payne did valuable work for the British Legion, the church, and charities. He died at his home, Copthorne, Dover House Road, Roehampton, of cerebral haemorrhage and arteriosclerosis on Friday 15 February 1952. He was survived by his wife. Gifted with a first-class brain, he proved to be a notable expert in the early days of wireless telegraphy. His exceptional knowledge was put to good use by the signal and torpedo schools and the Admiralty staff.

A. J. L. BLOND

Sources naval service record, PRO, ADM 196/43, p.502 · *WWW*, 1951–60 · *WWW*, 1916–28 [Sir Arthur Whinney] · b. cert. · m. cert. · d. cert. · *CGPLA Eng. & Wales* (1952) · *The Times* (16 Feb 1952), 10e · R. Burmester, *The Times* (5 March 1952), 6e · Captain R. Fitzmaurice, lecture, Dec 1926, PRO, ADM 116/3403 · A. J. L. Blond, 'Technology and tradition: wireless telegraphy and the Royal Navy, 1895–1920',

PhD diss., University of Lancaster, 1993 · Crockford (1854) · Crockford (1861) · Crockford (1869) · Crockford (1873)
Archives FILM BFI NFTVA, news footage
Wealth at death £5994 14s. 3d.: probate, 24 April 1952, *CGPLA Eng. & Wales*

Payne, Edward John (1844–1904), historian, was born of humble origins at Easton Street, High Wycombe, Buckinghamshire, on 22 July 1844; he was the son of Edward William Payne, a gardener, and his wife, Mary Welch. Payne owed his education largely to his own exertions. After receiving early training at the grammar school, High Wycombe, he was employed by a local architect and surveyor named Pontifex, and he studied architecture under William Burges. Interested in music from youth, he also acted as organist of the parish church. In 1867, at the age of twenty-three, he matriculated at Magdalen Hall, Oxford, whence he passed to Charsley's Hall. While an undergraduate he supported himself at first by pursuing his work as land surveyor and architect at High Wycombe, where he designed the Easton Street almshouses, and afterwards by coaching in classics at Oxford. In 1871 Payne graduated BA with a first class in the final classical school, and in 1872 he was elected to an open fellowship in University College. He remained a fellow until his marriage when he was re-elected to a research fellowship.

On 5 April 1899 Payne married Emma Leonora Helena, daughter of Major Pertz and granddaughter of the historian Georg Heinrich Pertz. They had one son, the archaeologist Humfry Gilbert Garth *Payne. Their life was mainly spent in London, but Payne was keenly interested in the management of the affairs of his college, and during the years of serious agricultural depression his good counsel and business aptitude proved of great service.

On 17 November 1874 Payne was called to the bar by Lincoln's Inn, and in 1883 was appointed honorary recorder of High Wycombe, holding the office until his death. But his mature years were mainly devoted to literary work. British colonial history and exploration were the main subjects of his study. In 1875 he contributed a *History of European Colonies* to E. A. Freeman's Historical Course for Schools. In 1883 he collaborated with J. S. Cotton in *Colonies and Dependencies* for the English Citizen series, and the section on colonies which fell to Payne he later developed into his *Colonies and Colonial Federation* (1904). He also edited Edmund Burke's *Select Works* (1876; new edn, 1912) and *The Voyages of Elizabethan Seamen to America* (1880; new edn, 1907). But these labours were preliminaries to a great design of a *History of the New World called America*. The first and second volumes (published respectively in 1892 and 1899) supplied a preliminary sketch of the geographical knowledge and exploration of the middle ages, an account of the discovery of America, and the beginning of an exhaustive summing up of all available knowledge as to the ethnology, language, religion, and social and economic condition of the indigenous peoples. Nothing more was published, and an original plan to extend the survey to Australasia was untouched. Payne contributed the first two chapters on 'The Age of Discovery' and 'The New World' to volume one of the Cambridge Modern History (1902).

At the same time Payne wrote much on music. He contributed many pieces to Grove's *Dictionary of Music and Musicians*, and in particular the article on Stradivari. The history of stringed instruments had a strong attraction for him, and he was himself an accomplished amateur performer on the violin and on various ancient instruments. He helped to found the Bar Musical Society, and was its first honorary secretary. He was also a golfer.

In his later years Payne lived at Holywell Lodge, Wendover, and suffered from heart weakness and fits of giddiness. On 26 December 1904 he was found drowned in the Wendover Canal, into which he had apparently fallen in a fit. He was survived by his wife, one son, and two daughters; his widow was given a civil-list pension of £120 in 1905.   DAVID HANNAY, *rev.* H. C. G. MATTHEW

Sources *The Times* (28 Dec 1904) · *Oxford Magazine* (25 Jan 1905) · *MT*, 46 (1905), 114–15 · *WWW* · *CGPLA Eng. & Wales* (1905) · private information (1912) · b. cert.
Likenesses A. S. Zibleri, portrait; in family possession in 1912
Wealth at death £755 2s. 4d.: probate, 11 March 1905, *CGPLA Eng. & Wales*

Payne, Ernest Alexander (1902–1980), Baptist minister and ecumenist, was born on 19 February 1902 at 38 Ickburgh Road, Upper Clapton, London, the eldest of the three children of Alexander Payne (1862–1941), partner in an accountancy firm bearing his name, and his wife, Catherine Griffiths (1863–1943). The family became deeply involved in the life of the Downs Baptist Church in Clapton. It was in this church that Ernest Payne was baptized as a believer in July 1917.

Two further children were born to Alexander and Catherine Payne, Margaret in 1903 and Philip in 1905. In September 1911 Ernest Payne became a pupil at Hackney Downs secondary school. In spite of the difficulties of the war years he achieved well academically, so much so that in October 1919 he entered King's College, London, to study for a general arts degree in Latin, English, history, and philosophy. He graduated after two years and spent the next year studying for an honours degree in philosophy, which he gained in June 1922.

Payne became convinced that his future lay in full-time service within the Baptist denomination—very possibly abroad with the Baptist Missionary Society. He applied successfully for entrance to Regent's Park College, a Baptist ministerial training college in London. Here he studied from October 1922 to July 1925, gaining the degree of bachelor of divinity of London University. In 1923 he attended the first of his many Student Christian Movement conferences at Swanwick. These experiences introduced him to the early development of the ecumenical movement.

Payne's college years were increasingly clouded by the health problems of his younger brother and sister. Both developed early symptoms of Friedrich's ataxia, a disease which was thought to run in families. This raised questions as to the wisdom of his serving overseas with the

Ernest Alexander Payne (1902–1980), by Elliott & Fry, 1958

Baptist Missionary Society. As an interim measure in October 1925 he took up a place at Mansfield College, Oxford. Here he studied Sanskrit and wrote a thesis on the Saka movement in Hinduism, for which he was awarded in 1927 the degree of bachelor of letters. He was granted a scholarship by Mansfield College which enabled him to spend a semester at Marburg University. On his return to England in March 1928 he decided to seek settlement as a Baptist minister.

On 23 October 1928 Payne was ordained to the ministry and inducted to the pastorate of Bugbrooke Baptist Church in Northamptonshire. Here he met and married, on 28 October 1930, Freda Davies (1905–1997). In 1932 he accepted an invitation to join the staff of the Baptist Missionary Society and in 1936 he became its editorial secretary. During his tenure of this office he developed his considerable talent for writing, including for the *Baptist Quarterly*, the journal of the Baptist Historical Society to which he contributed ultimately more than seventy articles. Late in 1939 he was invited to join the staff of Regent's Park College. The college had, in 1927, moved to Oxford, and since 1933 Ernest Payne had been acting as secretary to the college council. So in June 1940 he moved to Oxford, where he stayed for eleven years. At the college he taught Christian doctrine, comparative religion, and church history, becoming an acknowledged expert on the Anabaptists. For six years he was university lecturer in comparative religion and history of modern mission. He was a popular tutor, enjoying the stimulus of teaching and

discussion. He produced three significant books: *The Church Awakes* (1942), which is an outline history of the modern missionary movement, *The Free Church Tradition in the Life of England* (1944), and *The Fellowship of Believers: Baptist Thought and Practice Yesterday and Today* (1952). He became involved in the World Council of Churches, attending in 1948, as a Baptist Union delegate, the inaugural assembly of the World Council of Churches in Amsterdam.

In 1950 Payne was invited to succeed M. E. Aubrey as general secretary of the Baptist Union of Great Britain and Ireland. He left Oxford reluctantly. When he was asked by his students if they could congratulate him on his move his reply was typical 'You may not congratulate me, but you may wish me well'. From 1951 to 1967 he led the Baptist Union. It was a period of reconstruction. He continued and developed the policies of his predecessor in the reconstruction of bombed church buildings. He encouraged the development of new churches, particularly through special grants for initial pastorates in new areas of building development. He helped to enlarge the union's finances and brought into action a new Home Work Fund Scheme for support of ministers in smaller churches. He called the denomination to celebrate the ter-jubilee of the union in 1962, which included the raising of a £300,000 Ter-Jubilee Fund. In preparation for these celebrations he wrote *The Baptist Union: a Short History* (1959), which in spite of its title was a significant and substantial contribution to Baptist history.

Payne's Baptist interests were worldwide: he served the Baptist World Alliance as a vice-president; he helped to develop European federation; ecumenically he served the Free Church Federal Council, being its moderator in 1958–9. He was involved in the British Council of Churches from its inception in 1942, holding office from 1962 to 1971 as chairman of its executive committee, and finally as its honorary president.

For twenty-seven years Payne shared in the work of the World Council of Churches. He was a member of the faith and order commission from 1947 to 1962. He was elected to the central committee of the world council in 1954 and immediately to its vice-chairmanship. His contributions to its deliberations were considerable, most particularly because of his negotiating skills in difficult situations and his drafting ability in preparing complex resolutions on divisive issues. He believed in pragmatism, but never adopted it as a principle. He was elected a president of the world council on his resignation from the central committee in 1968 and held that office until he retired from the council itself in 1975.

When he retired in 1967 Payne was elected to honorary membership of the Baptist Union council, and in 1977 he was president of the Baptist Union. His retirement years were spent at Pitsford, in Northamptonshire, and then back in Oxford. In the new year's honours list of 1968 he was made a Companion of Honour to mark his services not only to Baptists but also to the wider Christian church. Payne died suddenly at the Bonnington Hotel in Southampton Row, London, of heart failure on 14 January 1980;

he was cremated in Oxford on 21 January and his ashes were interred in Bugbrooke parish church.

Ernest Payne was small in stature and somewhat shy in disposition. He never sought office, but accepted it when it came. He had an incisive mind and balanced judgement. Ecumenically, he was acknowledged as a leader of outstanding quality. On the initiative of the dean of Westminster a thanksgiving service for him was held in Westminster Abbey. On 27 February 1980 the abbey was filled to capacity by a congregation which was representative of the world church. All had come to honour the memory of one who was a faithful Baptist, a profound ecumenist, a learned scholar, and a humble man. W. M. S. WEST

Sources W. M. S. West, *To be a pilgrim: memoir of Ernest A. Payne* (1983) · *Baptist Union handbook* · *Baptist Times* · Regent's Park College, Oxford, Payne collection · R. E. Cooper, *From Stepney to St Giles: the story of Regent's Park College, 1810–1960* (1960) · *CGPLA Eng. & Wales* (1980)
Archives Regent's Park College, Oxford, Angus Library, papers incl. journal, letters, travel diaries
Likenesses Elliott & Fry, photograph, 1958, NPG [*see illus.*] · oils, 1974, Baptist House, 129 Broadway, Didcot, Oxfordshire · oils, Regent's Park College, Oxford · photographs, Regent's Park College, Oxford; repro. in West, *To be a pilgrim*, cover · twelve photographs, repro. in West, *To be a pilgrim*
Wealth at death £57,120: probate, 28 Feb 1980, *CGPLA Eng. & Wales*

Payne, George (1781–1848), Congregational minister, was born at Stow on the Wold, Gloucestershire, on 17 September 1781, the youngest son of Alexander Payne (1748?–1819), a cooper, and his wife, Mary Dyer (1742/3–1814) of Bampton. His father, who was initially an Anglican, became a Baptist after hearing the sermons of Law Butterworth of Bingworth, and in 1783 became the Baptist preacher to the church of Walgrave, Northamptonshire, where he served for thirty-three years. Two years later, in June 1785, he baptized his own wife, and he was ordained on 6 July. Along with Fuller and Carey he was a founder of the Baptist Missionary Society.

George Payne went to school at Walgrave, and subsequently at the Northampton Academy. He entered Hoxton Academy to study for the Congregational ministry in 1802, and on 13 April 1804 he was elected, with Joseph Fletcher, Glasgow scholar on the Dr Williams trust. The two proceeded to Glasgow University together. Payne graduated MA in the spring of 1807, and returned home, marrying, on 30 October 1807, a daughter of Alexander Gibbs, a corn factor, and member of the Scottish church in Hoxton. He acted for a year as assistant minister to Edward Parsons of Leeds. On 28 August 1808 he accepted an invitation to become George Lambert's permanent coadjutor at Fish Street, Hull. After ending his engagement at Hull on 14 June 1812, Payne was ordained at Edinburgh on the following 2 July, and took charge of a congregation of seceders who had divided from James Alexander Haldane in March 1808 after his rejection of infant baptism. This body met in Bernard's Rooms, Thistle Street, Edinburgh, until a new chapel was built in Albany Street. It was opened on 2 May 1817, and here Payne ministered until 1823. While in Edinburgh he contributed to Congregational literature and

assisted in the foundation of the Edinburgh Itinerant Society and the Congregational Union of Scotland, of which he was joint secretary from 1812 to 1816.

In April 1823 Payne left Scotland to become theological tutor of the Blackburn Independent Academy, the precursor of the Lancashire Independent college (later Northern College), Manchester; for his first two or three years in Blackburn, Payne also acted as pastor to a Congregational church which met in Mount Street. On 18 November 1829 he received the degree of honorary LLD from the University of Glasgow on the occasion of the publication of his *Elements of Mental and Moral Science*. In July 1829 he left Blackburn to become theological tutor to the Western Academy, which had just moved from Axminster to Exeter. In 1836 he was chosen as chairman of the Congregational Union of England and Wales. In 1844 he preached the eleventh series of the Congregational lectures initiated by the committee of the Congregational library in Bloomfield Street, Finsbury; his course of eight lectures was published in the following year. In January 1846 the Western College (as it was now known) was moved from Exeter to a site between Devonport and Plymouth. In April 1848 Payne visited Scotland as the delegate from the Congregational Union of England and Wales.

Payne's writings prove him to have had a genuine gift for metaphysical speculation. He wrote, apart from sermons and short tracts, eleven books, of which the most significant were *Elements of Mental and Moral Science* (1828), *Lectures on Divine Sovereignty, Election, the Atonement, Justification, and Regeneration* (1836), and *The Doctrine of Original Sin, or, The Nature, State, and Character of Man Unfolded* (1845). Payne died on 19 June 1848 at Devonport, after preaching at Mount Street Chapel there. He was buried on 27 June at Emma Place Chapel, Stonehouse, in the grave of his wife, who had died on 25 October 1847.

W. A. SHAW, rev. R. TUDUR JONES

Sources 'Memoir of the Rev. George Payne', *Evangelical Magazine and Missionary Chronicle*, new ser., 26 (1848), 393–8, 415–16 · J. Pyer, 'Memoir', in G. Payne, *Lectures on Christian theology*, ed. E. Davies (1850) · W. D. McNaughton, *The Scottish Congregational ministry, 1794–1993* (1993), 124 · *Christian Herald* [Edinburgh], new ser., 2 (1823), 103 · *Scottish Congregational Magazine* (1850), 289–96 · W. I. Addison, *A roll of graduates of the University of Glasgow from 31st December 1727 to 31st December 1897* (1898), 493 · *Congregational Magazine*, 12 (1829), 344 · R. W. Dale, *History of English congregationalism*, ed. A. W. W. Dale (1907), 560 · A. W. Sims, *The Western College Bristol: an outline history* (1952)
Archives DWL, letters
Likenesses Freeman, stipple, pubd 1822, NPG · J. Cochran, stipple and line print, NPG

Payne, George (1803–1878), racehorse owner and gambler, was born at Northampton on 3 April 1803, the elder son in the family of two sons and two daughters of George Payne of Sulby Hall, Northamptonshire, and his wife, Mary Eleanor, daughter of Ralph William Grey of Backworth House, Northumberland. Payne's father was fatally shot in a duel on Wimbledon Common on 6 September 1810 by a man named Clark, whose sister he had allegedly seduced. Payne was educated at Eton College from 1816 to 1822 and at Christ Church, Oxford, where he matriculated in 1823 but indulged his sporting tastes so freely that the college authorities, after much patient deliberation, requested him to leave the university. He came of age in 1824 and took possession of the family seat, Sulby Hall, and the Northampton estates, with a rent roll of £17,000 a year. In addition, he took up the sum accumulated during his minority, amounting to about £300,000. This income proved incapable of keeping pace with his extravagance, however, which was apparent when, as sheriff of Northamptonshire in 1826, he met the judges with an unparalleled display of opulence.

Payne's great sporting love was horse-racing. He owned horses from 1824 to 1878 and attended meetings throughout England, in later years dressed in a black frock coat and a checked gingham neckerchief. Although his black and white racing colours, the famous 'magpie jacket', were familiar sights on racecourses, his only victories of any importance were with the purchased filly Clementina, which won the One Thousand Guineas in 1847, and with Glauca, which won the Cesarewitch. His reckless gambling proved to be his undoing. He would sometimes back as many as twenty horses in a race for a big handicap, and still miss the winner. He also spent nights at the card table, and was among those who in the winter of 1836 accused Henry William, twenty-first baron de Ros, of being a card sharp. During the resulting libel action, on 10 February 1837, when Payne appeared as a witness, his character was attacked by Sir John Campbell, who described him as a 'professional gamester … [who] started as a dupe [but] soon crystallized into something worse', although Campbell subsequently made an apology (*The Times*, 11 and 13 Feb 1837). He squandered his patrimonial inheritance, and Sulby Hall also passed from his hands, together with two other large fortunes which he had subsequently inherited from relatives. From 1835 to 1838 and again from 1844 to 1848 he was master of the Pytchley hounds.

Payne lived a useless life but was honourable and without malice. After being seized with partial paralysis he died, unmarried, at his London home, 16 Queen Street, Mayfair, on 2 September 1878. The prince of Wales and many friends from the racing world were present at his burial, at Kensal Green, on 6 September.

WRAY VAMPLEW

Sources R. Mortimer, R. Onslow, and P. Willett, *Biographical encyclopedia of British flat racing* (1978) · Thormanby [W. W. Dixon], *Famous racing men* (1882) · *Daily Telegraph* (3 Sept 1878) · *The Field* (7 Sept 1878) · *The Times* (7 Sept 1878) · Nimrod [C. J. Apperley], *The turf*, new edn (1869) · Burke, *Gen. GB* · H. O. Nethercote, *The Pytchley hunt* (1888)

Likenesses Ape [C. Pellegrini], caricature, watercolour study, NPG; repro. in *VF* (18 Sept 1875) · G. Thompson, double portrait, oils (with Admiral Rous), NPG · T. C. Wilson, lithograph, BM; repro. in Wildrake, *Cracks of the day* (1841) · portrait, repro. in Thormanby, *Famous racing men* · portrait, repro. in *Baily's Magazine*, 1 (1860), 183–6 · portrait, repro. in *Westminster portraits*, 10 (1878), 139 · portrait, repro. in Nethercote, *Pytchley hunt* · portrait, repro. in Rice, *British turf* (1879) · portrait, repro. in *Sporting Times* (8 May 1875) · portrait, repro. in *Illustrated Sporting and Dramatic News*, 4 (1876), 496 · portrait, repro. in *ILN*, 5 (1844), 72 · portrait, repro. in *The Graphic*, 18 (1878), 276

Wealth at death under £35,000: resworn probate, March 1879, CGPLA Eng. & Wales (1878)

Payne, Henry [*alias* Henry Nevill] (*d.* **1705**?), writer and Jacobite conspirator, was a member of the Payne family of Medbourne, Leicestershire, but although he was born before the civil war he was not the Henry Payne baptized at Medbourne on 29 December 1636. Through his mother he was related to Jane Goodwin (*bap.* 1618, *d.* 1658), second wife of Philip Wharton, fourth Baron Wharton, and he had an elder (?) brother, William. Bred a protestant, he claimed to remember Gilbert Sheldon preaching absolutism before Charles I, probably in civil war Oxford. According to a hostile but well-informed 1680 biographer he received little formal education, was apprenticed to a dealer in female clothes, and spent time in Clerkenwell House of Correction for impregnating 'Lucrece', the maidservant. After becoming a servant with the Nevills of Holt, a recusant family owning lands in both Leicestershire (where they had largely supplanted the Medbourne Paynes) and Essex, he eloped with Alice Nevill (*d. c.*1681?), apparently daughter of Henry Nevill (*d.* 1665). Payne thereafter assumed his wife's name with or instead of his own; and for some years advantageously left it unclear whether he was Anglican or Catholic. He was and is therefore sometimes confused with the political philosopher Henry Neville (*d.* 1694) or the Jesuit Edward Scarisbrick alias Neville—or his own nephew by marriage. By 1681 Alice was 'miserably poor' (*Calendar of Treasury Books*, 7.387) and abandoned by her relations; the couple had a daughter.

In the 1660s Payne was a theatrical prompter. In 1670, when Lord Berkeley of Stratton became a pro-Catholic lord lieutenant of Ireland, Payne was secretary to his Catholic, and corrupt, private secretary, Sir Elisha Leighton. He played a leading and profitable part in the high-handed intrigues which alienated the city of Dublin, and had a faction appoint him its London agent. After returning to England, Payne furnished the duke's company with three fairly successful plays. *The Fatal Jealousie*, appearing before August 1672, and licensed on 22 November, was a domestic tragedy in bad blank verse, with echoes of Shakespeare and Hobbes and some skilful twists of plot. A swashbuckling comedy, *The Morning Ramble*, written in nine days, was acted in early 1673. *The Siege of Constantinople*, a tragedy acted in 1674 and published in 1675, depicts a Shaftesbury-like chancellor who sets two royal brothers disastrously at odds: Payne visibly admired James, duke of York. With its profits Payne financed a voyage to Jamaica to sell coffee, chocolate, and indentured female servants. He supported Sir Henry Morgan's faction, was arrested by the governor, Lord Vaughan, returned home, and in 1677 furnished Vaughan's successor, the earl of Carlisle, with a useful description of affairs there and suggestions, which included obtaining the slave trading contract for the Spanish Caribbean colonies.

Perhaps inspired by his friend Edward Coleman, Payne became involved in domestic political intrigues: the Green Ribbon Club's first surviving record is a resolution that 'Mr Nevil the Pretended Politician' was a papist

(Magd. Cam., Pepys Library, MS 2875, 465). He confidently bought and furnished a large house on credit; but the Popish Plot permanently ruined his finances. On 16 December 1678 Payne was arrested with his manuscript poem 'To the Glorious Martyr Edward Coleman Esq.'. Examined by the House of Lords and privy council, he claimed, despite the sentiments it expressed, to be a protestant. He was tried for treasonable practices and imprisoned in the king's bench. There he became deeply involved in the obscure Catholic intrigues which culminated in the Meal-Tub Plot. He worked for the countess of Powis, and with Mrs Elizabeth Cellier until they quarrelled. The perjurer Thomas Dangerfield claimed that Payne was the Catholic party's main propagandist, writing, among other pamphlets, *Some Reflections upon the Earl of Danby* accusing the latter of involvement in Sir Edmondbury Godfrey's murder, but that, when temporarily bailed, he preferred the theatre to writing polemics. He was presumably freed by June 1680, when he was one of the defence witnesses ready but not called at the trial of the earl of Castlemaine, who described him as a protestant.

In early 1680 the penny post was first established. Payne was perhaps the least likely of the four persons who claimed to have originated the idea, but Titus Oates denounced it as Payne's invention and therefore intended for papist plotting. His brother William Payne, a chancery clerk, was convicted and fined in June 1682 as part author of a pamphlet claiming that Godfrey had committed suicide.

By 1685 Payne had found a new patron, George Villiers, duke of Buckingham, who though a former exclusionist shared his concern for religious toleration and the theatre. Buckingham's 1685 pamphlet *A Short Discourse*, which started the campaign for toleration under James II, began as a 'letter' to Payne, who defended it against attackers in *The Persecutor Expos'd*, criticizing the Church of England as isolated among the protestant churches, yet claiming absolute right to persecute. He claimed that he had never cringed either to 'the Vain Applause of the Eternally mistaken Rabble' (preface) or to great men. The pamphlet, opposing current government policy, presumably provoked the warrants for treasonable practices issued against him on 16–17 June 1685. After Buckingham's retreat to Yorkshire, Payne supplied him with political newsletters, tried to get his last play staged, and used his yacht for smuggling, to relieve his own desperate finances. Ostentatious Catholic piety won him a receivership of fines in the court of common pleas in April 1686. He collaborated with William Penn in an effort to bring Buckingham back into politics to check the earl of Sunderland's dangerous policies. In March 1687 he accused Sunderland before James of treasonable correspondence with William of Orange, but could not produce sufficient proof.

Following Buckingham's death in April, that summer Payne's creditors (perhaps encouraged by Sunderland, though other courtiers assisted him) put him into the Fleet prison. He nevertheless replied to the marquess of Halifax's *Letter to a Dissenter* in *An Answer to a Scandalous Pamphlet*, and probably to Pensionary Fagel's *Letter*. This was now part of a government sponsored campaign, but Payne received little further reward. Aphra Behn dedicated a novel to him in 1688. Gilbert Burnet called Payne:

> the most active and dextrous of all King James's agents, who had indeed lost the reputation of an honest man entirely; and yet had such arts of management, that even those who knew what he was were willing to imploy him. (*Bishop Burnet's History*, 4.61)

On the revolution he made his Fleet prison chambers a centre of Jacobite and Catholic intrigue. A raid in October 1689 revealed that he was writing the most effective Jacobite pamphlets and corresponding with many important figures.

Payne's greatest success was in Scottish affairs. When Sir James Montgomery, a leader of the presbyterian 'club' parliamentary opposition, reached London in September 1689, disaffected and suspicious, Payne inserted between him and William's favourite the earl of Portland a double agent, who fermented Montgomery's suspicions that Portland was seeking to frame him on a false charge of treason, and drove him into genuine conspiracy. This brought him directly to Payne, who, 'so far imposed upon him as to pretend he could, with … [James] and the Court of France, dispose of money, forces and titles of honour as he pleased' (Balcarres, 51). The club and Scottish Jacobites were to restore James through parliament, with English support from both tories and whigs, which Payne would help organize. Another whig turned Jacobite, Robert Ferguson, became a close ally. Records of later interrogation reveal that the government suspected that Payne had effected a temporary escape or release from prison in order to travel to the Netherlands and encourage disaffected Dutch republicans.

In early 1690 Payne, who now faced prosecution for treason, did escape. Arriving in May on the Scottish borders disguised as a merchant he stayed in a house in Annandale of the earl of Annandale, Montgomery's fellow conspirator, and wrote asking both men if he should come to Edinburgh. In mid-May, however, local people, including Annandale's uninformed servants, seized him and sent him to Edinburgh, hastening the collapse of the Montgomery plot. On 4 August the council received an order to torture him and other captured agents, but initially Jacobite death threats prevented this. Annandale's confession later that month provided firm evidence against Payne, and in mid-November William again ordered rigorous torture. Its legality was dubious, since Payne was English and captured after only four days in Scotland; the interrogation was virtually all on his English activities. On 10 and 11 December 1690 he was tortured, ultimately with both the boot to one leg and thumbscrews until his life seemed in danger, without confessing anything. He begged afterwards to be exiled to the Netherlands or Germany, and the council urged William either to try him or to return him to England. William instead kept him close prisoner in Edinburgh Castle, though dysentery endangered his life, until the council in late July allowed him open prison. Jacobite propaganda in England used this as proof of William's tyrannical intentions, while Payne's steadfastness helped to discredit and prevent future use of judicial torture.

Somehow Payne from his cell organized a Jacobite network of agents and sympathizers (including his relative Philadelphia Wharton, widow of the lord president, Sir George Lockhart), which sent information and advice to James at St Germain, and even to the pope. During the April 1692 invasion scare an outside plot for his escape was exposed, which the government suspected to be a cover for seizing Edinburgh Castle. Payne expected death, but was merely transferred in May to Blackness Castle and in November as close prisoner to Stirling Castle.

In December 1692 Payne wrote to St Germain advocating a speedy invasion, and requesting James secretly to recommend Lord Stair's son for town clerk of Edinburgh. Secretary James Johnstone, head of the presbyterian faction in the government, intercepted this and exploited it to get endorsement of the presbyterians' recent gross rigging of Edinburgh burgh elections. Payne was caught drafting a reply to William King's famous propaganda book on the Irish protestants. When Johnstone's opponents in the 1693 parliament, assured by the Jacobites that Payne's letter and related intercepts were forged, imprudently challenged him, he proved them genuine, published them for members' information as *Nevil Payn's Letter*, and stampeded parliament into voting huge taxes for troops to oppose a non-existent invasion threat. On 13 May the lord advocate raised an indictment against Payne for high treason. Johnstone planned to end the session on 13 June 1693 by trying and making an example of him, since, although the letter's meaning was obvious, its use of code names invalidated it as evidence in the regular courts. Payne secretly warned leading peers, particularly the commissioner, the duke of Hamilton, that although 'he would accuse none … he was resolved he would not die, and he could discover enough to deserve his pardon' (*Bishop Burnet's History*, 4.212). Those not frightened for their own safety were, like Hamilton, alarmed for that of close relatives. On 15 June a majority voted to remit the prosecution to the justiciary court. 'In a word he owes his safety to the dimensions of his crime' wrote Johnstone (Thorp, 378).

On 28 June 1693 Payne was transported to close confinement in bleak Dumbarton Castle. His petitions for release, stressing his age, ill health, and ruinous debts incurred to subsist in prison, made to the council and the 1698 parliament, obtained only a transfer to Stirling Castle in July 1695, and a payment to support him from April 1696. In July 1699 he requested liberty to leave the castle for 'ane experiment for river navigation, whereby safer, larger and swifter vessels may be made … than any now in use' (Thorp, 379). He was allowed half a mile outside under guard. A letter mentions that the boat would go against wind and tide at a mile an hour, suggesting a primitive steamboat.

Finally, heeding advice that the issue of Payne's long imprisonment without trial might cause trouble in parliament and that anyway he was a liar unworthy of the government's notice, William included him in a general order for the release of prisoners which arrived on 4 February 1701. On presentation of his petition Payne was immediately discharged.

Payne crossed via England to St Germain, but too late. Following James II's death in September 1701 his son's established ministers soon curbed the unconventional supporters he had attracted. Within a fortnight a Quaker was in the Bastille for repeating an indiscreet, and inaccurate, remark by Payne. Payne presented a memorial to James III (James Stuart, the Old Pretender) in January 1702, urging a rising to exploit William's unique unpopularity and showing distrust of the French and Jacobite ministers, but this got him nowhere. Payne probably died at Paris in 1705.   PAUL HOPKINS

Sources W. Thorp, 'Henry Nevil Payne, dramatist and Jacobite conspirator', *Essays in dramatic literature: the Parrott presentation volume*, ed. R. Craig (1935), 347–81 • B. Elliott, 'A Leicestershire recusant family: the Nevills of Nevill Holt—I', *Recusant History*, 17 (1984–5), 173–80 • *CSP dom.*, 1670–1702 • W. H. L. Melville, ed., *Leven and Melville papers: letters and state papers chiefly addressed to George, earl of Melville … 1689–1691*, Bannatyne Club, 77 (1843) • papers on Payne, 1690, NA Scot., Leven and Melville papers, GD26/7/59 • *Bishop Burnet's History* • C. Lindsay [earl of Balcarres], *Memoirs touching the revolution in Scotland*, ed. A. W. C. Lindsay [earl of Crawford and Balcarres], Bannatyne Club (1841) • J. Macpherson, ed., *Original papers, containing the secret history of Great Britain*, 2 vols. (1775) • *State papers and letters addressed to William Carstares*, ed. J. M'Cormick (1774) • James Johnstone's letter-book, NA Scot., SP3/1 • *Nevil Payn's letter* (1693) • H. Nevill Payne, *The persecutor expos'd: in reflections by way of a reply to an ill-bred answer to the D. of B.'s paper* (1685) • privy council registers, NA Scot., PC1/48–50 • *Reg. PCS*, 3rd ser., vols. 15–16 • R. Morrice, 'Ent'ring Book', DWL, Morrice MS P–R [vols. 1–3, London] • P. A. Hopkins, *Glencoe and the end of the highland war*, rev. edn (1998) • Duke of Buckingham, letter to W. Penn, 4 March 1687, Hist. Soc. Penn., Penn–Forbes papers, 36 • W. A. Shaw, ed., *Calendar of treasury books*, 7, PRO (1916) • Lady Lockhart, letter to Lord Wharton, 10 June 1693, Bodl. Oxf., MS Carte 79, fol. 495 • H. Payne, letter, 23 Dec 1690, Bodl. Oxf., MS Eng. hist. c. 287, fol. 46 • H. Nevill Payne, *The morning ramble, or, The humours of the town* (1673) • intelligence letter, 13 Jan 1688, U. Nott. L., Portland MSS, PwA 2131 • H. Nevill Payne, 'The present state of Jamaica, in a letter from Mr Nevil to the earl of Carlisle', BL, Add. MS 12429 • *Report on the manuscripts of Allan George Finch*, 5 vols., HMC, 71 (1913–2003), vol. 3 • R. Clarke and G. Moore, *Appeals to the House of Lords, 1717–1721*, BL, 19.h.1 (67) • G. H. Jones, *Charles Middleton, portrait of a Restoration politician* (1967) • Payne to F. Burghill, 20 Dec 1699, T. Thorpe, *Catalogue of autograph letters for 1844* (1844), 309 • F. Staff, *The penny post, 1680–1918* (1964) • *The earl of Castlemain's manifesto* (1681) • W. H. Hart, *Index purgatorius anglicanus* (1871–8) • G. Agar-Ellis, ed., *The Ellis correspondence: letters written during the years 1686, 1687, 1688, and addressed to John Ellis*, 2 vols. (1829)

Wealth at death in debt after having had to support self for first six years in prison: NA Scot., PC1/50, 475

Payne, Humfry Gilbert Garth (1902–1936), archaeologist, was born at Wendover, Buckinghamshire, on 19 February 1902, the only son of the historian Edward John *Payne (1844–1904) and his wife, Emma Leonora Helena Pertz, granddaughter of Georg Heinrich Pertz (editor of the *Monumenta Germaniae Historica*) and of James John Garth Wilkinson, the Swedenborgian. He was educated at Westminster School and then at Christ Church, Oxford, where he held an open classical scholarship and gained firsts in classical moderations (1922) and in *literae humaniores* (1924). In his last year at Oxford, partly under the influence of J. D. Beazley and Alan Blakeway, he became seriously interested in Greek art and found his vocation as an archaeologist.

After taking his degree Payne continued his studies as university research scholar in Mediterranean archaeology (1924–6). In 1926 he married (Elizabeth) Dilys *Powell (1901–1995), daughter of Thomas Powell, a bank manager of Bridgnorth and Bournemouth; there were no children. She had read modern languages at Somerville College, Oxford (1920–24), and retained the name Dilys Powell in her career as journalist and film and television critic. In the same year Payne was appointed as assistant in the coin room (then part of the department of antiquities) of the Ashmolean Museum, a position he held until 1928. This gave him the opportunity to work with his former teacher, Beazley, and together they published a selection of Attic black-figured pottery from earlier excavations at Naucratis in the *Journal of Hellenic Studies* (1929). Payne was a senior scholar of Christ Church (1926–31). He was awarded the Conington prize for classical learning in 1927 based on his submission of his work on the painted pottery and other arts at Corinth. In 1931 this was to be published as *Necrocorinthia*, which placed Payne at once, as was widely acknowledged, in the front rank of classical archaeologists. It was supplemented in 1933 by *Protokorinthische Vasenmalerei*.

Payne was at this stage linked with excavations on Crete. He excavated in the vicinity of Knossos in 1927 and 1929, concentrating on the post-Bronze Age remains rather than the 'Minoan' period which had been the focus of the work by Sir Arthur Evans. Payne was to resume excavations in the Fortetsa cemetery in 1933, supported by funds raised in Oxford by Alan Blakeway. Excavations in the cemetery continued in 1935; the archaeological report, *Fortetsa: Early Greek Tombs Near Knossos*, was published by James Brock, one of the excavators, in 1957. Payne had been hoping to develop a major excavation of an archaic site on Crete. In June 1929 he started work at Eleutherna in central Crete, a site earlier surveyed by P. J. Dixon, but the finds were disappointing and the work abandoned.

In the autumn of 1929 Payne took up residence as the newly appointed director of the British School of Athens. He then initiated the excavation of Perachora, a small but rich archaic site opposite Corinth, over four seasons from 1930 to 1933. The first volume of *Perachora*, edited by Thomas James Dunbabin, was published in 1940; most of it is by Payne. The second volume was to follow in 1962. One of his chief works as director was the publication of *Archaic Marble Sculpture from the Acropolis* (1936: a volume of photographs by Gerard Mackworth Young with text by Payne). This continued the British School's involvement with the publication of material from the Athenian acropolis initiated during R. M. Dawkins's directorship. Payne's volume set many statues and fragments in fresh light: two notable identifications were the matching of the upper part of a female statue in Lyons with its base on the acropolis, and the association of a head in the Louvre with an equestrian statue also in Athens. His former teacher, Beazley, described the particular qualities of his work: 'A fine eye, deep respect for the individual object, great structural power, wealth of detail combined with breadth of vision, perfect clearness of thought and expression' (*DNB*). He died at the Evangelismos Hospital in Athens from a staphylococcic infection, which had suddenly become acute, on 9 May 1936. He was buried in the cemetery of Ayios Yeoryios at Mycenae, and his gravestone is inscribed, 'Weep not for Adonis'.

Payne was described as '6 feet 5 inches in height, straight, slender, square-shouldered, with a small head, and small features (except the mouth), fair hair, a fresh complexion, eyes of a strong blue, and something boyish, yet resolute, in the face' (*DNB*). His widow wrote a good account of him, especially of his life in Greece, in *The Traveller's Journey is done* (1943).   DAVID GILL

Sources *DNB* · D. Powell, *The traveller's journey is done* (1943) · *The Times* (11 May 1936) · *Annual Report of the British School at Athens* (1935–6), 7–8 · D. Powell, *The Villa Ariadne* (1973) · H. Waterhouse, *The British School at Athens: the first hundred years* (1986) · A. M. Woodward, 'Archaeology in Greece, 1926–1927', *Journal of Hellenic Studies*, 47 (1927), 234–63 · A. M. Woodward, 'Archaeology in Greece, 1928–1929', *Journal of Hellenic Studies*, 49 (1929), 220–39 · H. G. G. Payne, 'Archaeology in Greece, 1932–1933', *Journal of Hellenic Studies*, 53 (1933), 266–99 · T. J. Dunbabin, 'Humfry Payne's drawings of Corinthian vases', *Journal of Hellenic Studies*, 71 (1951), 63–9, pls. 28–30 · R. Hood, *Faces of archaeology in Greece: caricatures by Piet de Jong* (1998)

Archives AM Oxf., antiquities · British School at Athens, Greece, drawings, MSS, and photographs | Bodl. Oxf., corresp. with J. L. Myres

Likenesses I. Colquhoun, Indian ink and watercolour, 1934, NPG · I. Colquhoun, oils, 1935, NPG · P. de Jong, caricature, watercolour on cartridge paper, 1936, repro. in Hood, *Faces of archaeology in Greece*; priv. coll. · Mr & Mrs P. Megaw, photograph, repro. in Hood, *Faces of archaeology in Greece*

Wealth at death £400 0s. 5d.: administration, 26 Nov 1936, *CGPLA Eng. & Wales*

Payne, John (d. 1507), bishop of Meath, was educated in the Dominican convent, Oxford. He became a doctor of divinity, and professor of theology in the convent, and was subsequently elected prior provincial of the Dominicans in England. On 17 March 1483 he was provided to the bishopric of Meath, having originally been granted custody of the temporalities on 15 February, and he was consecrated on 4 August following. A close ally of Gerald Fitzgerald, eighth earl of Kildare, and, like most of the palesmen, a staunch Yorkist, Payne became a leading supporter of Lambert Simnel after he landed in Ireland in the winter of 1486–7. He preached the sermon at Simnel's coronation in Christ Church, Dublin, on Whitsunday (24 May) 1487, but after the battle of Stoke he was among the first to make his peace with Henry VII.

In July 1488 Payne escorted the king's commissioner, Sir Richard Edgcumbe, sent over to pacify Ireland, from Malahide to Dublin, where he acted as an intermediary between Edgcumbe and Kildare. At Edgcumbe's instance, he published in Christ Church the papal bull excommunicating all who took part in the revolt, with the pope's absolution and the king's pardon to all who returned to their allegiance. After Payne's pardon, dated 25 May 1488, had been delivered, he was sent by Kildare and the council on a mission to court, where he apparently accused his metropolitan, Octavian de Palatio, archbishop of Armagh, of complicity in the revolt. The king rewarded him, but he was unsuccessful in a bid to secure a grant of the chancellorship.

According to James Ware, Payne was noted for his hospitality and alms-giving. In 1489 he assisted at a provincial synod in St Mary's Church, Ardee, arbitrating between rival claims by Tomás Ó Brádaigh and Cormac Mag Shamhráin to the bishopric of Kilmore. At the provincial synod at Drogheda in July 1492, however, a violent scene occurred when Payne called Primate Octavian, who had summoned him to answer certain charges, a tyrant. Octavian formally protested against his suffragan's disobedience. Payne apparently remained loyal during the Warbeck conspiracy, but at the great council at Trim in September 1493 he was bound over in 200 marks to observe certain articles tending to peace and good rule. He attended the provincial synod at Drogheda in July 1495, and the text of the resultant pastoral letter which Payne issued to his clergy still survives.

By then, however, Payne's relations with Kildare had broken down. Probably in 1494, after a fray, the earl pursued the bishop into a church and took him prisoner, only releasing him on a peremptory command from the king. When the two were at court in 1496, Payne denounced Kildare's conduct to the king, reportedly saying, 'All Ireland cannot rule yonder gentleman'; to which Henry allegedly replied, 'Then he is meet to rule all Ireland' (Book of Howth, 180). Payne was nevertheless appointed keeper of the rolls after his return from England, on 3 October 1496. He died on 6 May 1507, and was buried in the Dominican church of St Saviour, Dublin.   STEVEN G. ELLIS

Sources A. Gwynn, *The medieval province of Armagh, 1470–1545* (1946) · W. Harris, ed., *Hibernica, or, Some antient pieces relating to Ireland*, 2 vols. (1747–50) · *The whole works of Sir James Ware concerning Ireland*, ed. and trans. W. Harris, rev. edn, 2 vols. in 3 (1764) · J. Gairdner, ed., *Letters and papers illustrative of the reigns of Richard III and Henry VII*, 2 vols., Rolls Series, 24 (1861–3) · A. Cogan, *The diocese of Meath ancient and modern*, 1 (1862) · CPR, 1476–1509 · D. B. Quinn, 'Guide to English financial records for Irish history, 1461–1558', *Analecta Hibernica*, 10 (1941), 1–69 · D. B. Quinn, 'The bills and statutes of the Irish parliaments of Henry VII and Henry VIII', *Analecta Hibernica*, 10 (1941), 70–169 · J. S. Brewer and W. Bullen, eds., *Calendar of the Carew manuscripts*, 5: 1603–1623, PRO (1871) · E. B. Fryde and others, eds., *Handbook of British chronology*, 3rd edn, Royal Historical Society Guides and Handbooks, 2 (1986)

Payne, John (*d.* in or before 1648), printmaker, was by far the finest native-born engraver working during the reign of Charles I. His earliest plates, the portraits of Hugh Broughton and William Whitaker of 1620, are very much in the manner of Simon de Passe, whose pupil he very probably was. Payne's fifty-three known plates, which bear dates between 1620 and 1639, and most of which are portrait frontispieces or title-plates to books, vary widely

in quality. The worst are no better than those of many contemporaries, but the best, such as the portrait of Sir Benjamin Rudyerd of 1632, are outstanding. His masterpiece is the two-plate profile view of the ship *Sovereign of the seas*, which measures nearly 3 feet across. It was made in 1637–8 to celebrate the ship's launch, and was commissioned by its builder, Peter Pett. The print was praised by John Evelyn and an impression was acquired by Samuel Pepys on 31 January 1663. It was accompanied by a pamphlet by Thomas Heywood, *A true description of his majesties royall and most stately ship called the Soveraign of the seas* (1638), the text of which praises Payne and reveals that he was then living by the postern gate near Tower Hill.

On the evidence of a fellow engraver, John Sturt, George Vertue recorded that Payne loved drinking and was careless of his affairs, and that his irregular way of life resulted in his early death. Charles I had intended to appoint him royal engraver (presumably in succession to Robert van Voerst, who had died in 1636), but Payne had neglected to take up the invitation. Thomas Rawlins printed an epitaph to him in an appendix, entitled 'Calanthe', to a volume of meditations, *Good-Friday* (1648), where Payne was described as 'lately deceased'. This serves as a *terminus ante quem* for his death.   ANTONY GRIFFITHS

Sources Vertue, *Note books*, 1.139; 2.29 · A. M. Hind, *Engraving in England in the sixteenth and seventeenth centuries*, 3, ed. M. Corbett and M. Norton (1964), 6–30 · A. Griffiths and R. A. Gerard, *The print in Stuart Britain, 1603–1689* (1998), 100–03 [exhibition catalogue, BM, 8 May – 20 Sept 1998]

Payne, John (*d.* 1787), bookseller, was established in Paternoster Row, London, at least by 1745, working first alone and then in partnership with Joseph Bouquet until early 1752. From 1753 to 1758 Payne gave his address as 'Pope's Head in Pater noster Row', then simply as 'Pater noster Row', and from about 1765 'The Feathers, Pater noster Row'. Payne was sufficiently known to Samuel Johnson to be invited to join a club formed by Johnson in winter 1749, meeting every Tuesday evening at the King's Head in Ivy Lane near St Paul's, and later known as the Ivy Lane Club. It was through his friendship with Johnson that Payne published William Lauder's *Essay on Milton's Use and Imitation of the Moderns in his 'Paradise Lost'* (1750), to which Johnson contributed. Lauder—Scottish Latin scholar, schoolmaster, and armchair Jacobite—had been working since at least 1745 to prove that Milton had plagiarized *Paradise Lost*, suggesting that the epic bore a strong resemblance to works of certain neo-Latin writers. When John Douglas discovered that portions of the passages of the neo-Latin writers quoted in the *Essay* were, in fact, passages from *Paradise Lost* translated into Latin, he exposed Lauder's forgeries in *Milton vindicated from the charge of plagiarism brought against him by Mr. Lauder and Lauder himself convicted of several forgeries and gross impositions on the public* (1751). It was clear to both Johnson and Payne that something had to be done to salvage their reputations. Payne and Bouquet placed an advertisement in the newspapers and wrote 'A new preface' apologizing for the imposition on the public and attempting to explain how they had been deceived. Johnson wrote a 'New postscript' in which further disclaimers were made, which, like the 'New preface', was printed separately to be inserted in unsold copies and to be distributed to those who had already bought copies. The friendship between Payne and Johnson does not appear to have been damaged by this episode and would continue to the end of Johnson's life. Early in September 1784, a few months before his own death, Johnson wrote to a mutual friend about Payne (who was then ill) remarking, 'poor Payne ... I should count his death a great loss' (*Letters of Samuel Johnson*, 389–90).

Payne published Johnson's *Rambler* essays (1750–52), as well as the *Adventurer* essays (1752–4) edited by John Hawksworth, another member of the Ivy Lane Club, with contributions by Johnson. Later Payne was responsible with others for starting the *Universal Chronicle, or, Weekly Gazette*. To the first number Johnson contributed a two-part essay explaining first what the paper hoped to accomplish and second the responsibilities of those who write for such publications. In the second number of 15 April 1758 appeared the first *Idler* essay, a series for which Johnson produced all but twelve of 104 essays published during the next two years. *The Life of Harriot Stuart* (1750), the first novel of Charlotte Lennox, a person whose career Johnson was eager to advance, was another publication of Payne's. Payne also published his own writings. In 1758 he wrote and published *New Tables of Interest*, with a preface by Johnson, followed by *A Letter Occasioned by the Lord Bishop of Gloucester's 'Doctrine of Grace'* (1763), *The Ground and Nature of Christian Redemption* (1769), *Letter to a Modern Defender of Christianity* (1771), and other works on religious topics.

Payne had been elected to the service of the Bank of England in 1744, and he became deputy accountant in 1773 and accountant-general in 1780, before retiring on 30 June 1785. Throughout the period when he worked for the bank he maintained involvement with various aspects of the book trade: his hours at the bank allowed it and the low salary necessitated it. Payne died unmarried at Lympstone, near Exeter, on 10 March 1787, where he had probably been living since 1785. He had a brother, Henry, who was a bookseller in Pall Mall, London.

Payne has been confused with another **John Payne** (*fl.* 1762–1800), author and compiler, who was admitted a freeman of the London Stationers' Company by redemption on 7 December 1762. He went into partnership with the bookseller Joseph Johnson about July 1768 but in early January 1770 a fire destroyed most of their business and the partnership dissolved. Payne moved to Marsham Street, Westminster, and turned author and compiler, often under assumed names, such as George Augustus Hervey and William Frederic Melmouth. Among his works are *The naval, commercial, and general history of Great Britain, from the earliest times to the rupture with Spain, in the year 1779* (1780–83), *Universal Geography* (1791), *An Epitome of History* (1794), *Geographical Extracts* (1796), and *A Concise History of Greece* (1800). He was noted as being resident in King Street, Cheapside, in 1782 and in Pentonville in 1800.

O. M. BRACK

Sources Boswell, *Life*, 1.243 · J. L. Clifford, *Dictionary Johnson* (1979), 29–45, 59–70, 107–16, 191–9 · *ESTC* · J. D. Fleeman, *A bibliography of the works of Samuel Johnson*, 1 (2000), 183–5, 320–21, 334–9, 727–38 · *The letters of Samuel Johnson*, ed. B. Redford, 4 (1994), 350, 380, 389–90, 410–11, 416, 435 · J. Hawkins, *The life of Samuel Johnson, LL.D.*, 2nd edn (1787), 219–59, 275–87 · D. F. McKenzie, ed., *Stationers' Company apprentices*, [3]: 1701–1800 (1978) · I. Maxted, *The London book trades, 1775–1800: a preliminary checklist of members* (1977) · Nichols, *Lit. anecdotes*, 3.223, 433, 660; 5.39, 620; 8.415; 9.502, 779 · H. R. Plomer and others, *A dictionary of the printers and booksellers who were at work in England, Scotland, and Ireland from 1726 to 1775* (1932) · [D. Rivers], *Literary memoirs of living authors of Great Britain*, 2 (1798), 117 · C. H. Temperley, *Encyclopaedia of literary and typographical anecdote* (1842), 678–9

Payne, John (*fl.* 1762–1800). *See under* Payne, John (*d.* 1787).

Payne, John Wesley Vivian [Jack] (1899–1969), band leader, was born in Leamington Spa, Warwickshire, on 22 August 1899, the only son of John Edwin Payne, music warehouse manager, and his wife, Sarah Vivian Clare Gunn, of 10 Church Street, Leamington Spa. Jack Payne, as he was always known, first became interested in dance music during his service with the Royal Flying Corps in 1918, playing the piano in various amateur bands in the service. After demobilization he took up dance music as a profession and formed a small band which secured a position in the Hotel Cecil in London in the summer of 1925. With this he made his first records for Zonophone and Aco. When the BBC began relaying dance music from the hotel, four extra musicians were added, increasing the number to ten. In February 1928 Payne was appointed director of dance music to the BBC, a position he held from 2 March 1928 until 14 March 1932. In that period he and the BBC Dance Orchestra recorded exclusively for Columbia, and made daily broadcasts of about an hour from Station 2LO, later known as the National Programme. He was the first band leader to introduce and close each broadcast with a signature tune, in this case Irving Berlin's 'Say it with Music', and was one of the first to announce his music and sing the vocal refrains himself. In April 1930 Jack Payne and the BBC Dance Orchestra appeared at the London Palladium, and they returned there in August 1931. The full strength of the band was then sixteen, and it remained so for many years.

On leaving the BBC Payne took his band on nationwide tours, recording for Imperial Records; the labels showed his portrait in place of the gold crown trademark, and a gold facsimile of his signature. He is the only dance-band leader in the UK to have been accorded this honour. Late in 1932 he and the band appeared as the central figures in a film called *Say it with Music*, for which his arranger, Ray Noble, wrote the score. Towards the end of 1933 the band was reorganized, and continued to record on Rex Records, which had replaced Imperial as the principal product of the Crystalate Gramophone Record Manufacturing Company. At the end of 1935 Payne and his band made another film, *Sunshine Ahead*, on completion of which they visited South Africa very successfully during the summer of 1936.

In May 1937 Payne gave the members of his band two weeks' notice, and retired to his Buckinghamshire farm to concentrate on stock breeding; but he returned to the popular-music business in January 1938, and resumed recording (for Decca) and touring. During the Second World War he and the band entertained the services extensively, but within a year of the end of the war Payne again withdrew from the scene and became a very popular disc jockey, a host on his own television show, an artists' manager, and, finally, the manager of a hotel in Tonbridge. The last venture was not a success, and failing health and financial difficulties contributed to his death at the age of seventy.

Payne was also a composer. In 1930 he published two waltz ballads which were very successful—'Blue Pacific Moonlight' and 'Underneath the Spanish Stars'—and in 1931 another waltz, 'Pagan Serenade', among other numbers. His band was versatile, and in the course of a single show would play all kinds of popular tunes of the day, mostly romantic but freely intermixed with rousing chorus songs in ⁶⁄₈ time, paso dobles, pieces with African-American rhythms, comedy songs involving cameo sketches in which Payne himself would play cockney, north country, American, and Oxford-English character parts, and sometimes concert arrangements of standard classics, one of the most popular being Ravel's Bolero. One of Payne's most spectacular pieces of showmanship was to simulate a huge engine, appearing to be running out of the stage backdrop into the stalls of the London Palladium, with the members of the band seated on various parts of the engine as they played a popular instrumental number of the time (1931) called Choo Choo.

Payne was a perfectionist, a disciplinarian, an obvious leader, frank and sincere to a fault. These characteristics did not always find favour with his associates, but he left an indelible mark on the pages of the history of British dance music. He was twice married: first in 1923 to Doris Aileen (d. 1939), the daughter of Colonel H. H. Pengree, Royal Field Artillery; and second in 1942 to Peggy, daughter of Thomas Andrew Cochrane LLB (Edinburgh). A daughter was adopted in the second marriage. Payne died at his home in Tonbridge, Kent, on 4 December 1969.

BRIAN RUST, rev.

Sources J. Payne, This is Jack Payne (1932) · J. Payne, Signature tune (1947) · P. Cochrane, We said it with music (1979) · The Times (5 Dec 1969)

Likenesses photographs, 1930–40, Hult. Arch. · Bond, cartoon sketch, repro. in Radio Times (17 March 1933), 656 · Kapp, cartoon sketch, repro. in Payne, Signature tune

Payne, John Willett (1752–1803), naval officer and royal official, was born on 23 April 1752 at St Kitts in the Leeward Islands, the second son of Ralph Payne (d. 1760), chief justice of the island, and his second wife, Margaret, née Gallwey, of St Kitts. His brother was Ralph *Payne, later Baron Lavington. He was educated at Dr Brackyn's academy in Greenwich, where he formed a lifelong friendship with Hugh Seymour Conway. In spring 1767 he entered the Royal Naval Academy, Portsmouth, where he spent two and a half years before joining the frigate Quebec (32 guns).

Early in 1770, in the West Indies, Payne moved to Rear-Admiral Man's flagship, Montague. He came home in the sloop Falcon (18 guns) in 1773 and, after five months as midshipman in the Egmont, sailed for the Guinea coast, Jamaica, and Antigua with Commodore Thomas Collingwood in the Rainbow (44 guns). After returning to England about January 1775 he was again on the books of the Egmont when he passed his lieutenant's examination on 10 May.

On 26 December 1775 he sailed with Sir Peter Parker in the Bristol (50 guns) to Charlestown, and took part in the attack on Sullivan's Island. At New York he became Vice-Admiral Lord Howe's aide-de-camp in the Eagle, until he gained his first commission on 9 March 1777 as second lieutenant of the frigate Brune (32 guns), under the eccentric Captain James Ferguson, who became Payne's firm friend. Early in 1778 he moved to the Phoenix (40 guns) and was with Howe's squadron at Sandy Hook in July and off Rhode Island in August.

After rejoining Howe's flagship for a while, and then, it seems, commanding the West Florida (14 guns), Payne returned to England in the Roebuck (40 guns), and on 19 April 1779 was appointed first lieutenant of the Romney (50 guns). He was rapidly promoted by Commodore George Johnstone, through the influence of his half-brother Ralph, to commander of the Cormorant sloop on 6 November 1779 and then on 8 July 1780 to captain of the Artois, a captured French frigate. The following month he was caught up in a minor diplomatic row between Britain and Portugal over allegations of his having pressed Portuguese subjects when lying in the Tagus.

In August 1781 Payne took command of the frigate Enterprize (28 guns), cruising on the Jamaica station. In December 1782 Admiral Hugh Pigot gave him the Leander (50 guns), and near Guadeloupe on the night of 18 January 1783, while escorting a convoy, he came across a hostile ship which he chased and fought a two-hour engagement with. The identity of the other ship was never established, but it appeared to be a 74. Out-gunned, the Leander was very heavily damaged, but repulsed attempts at boarding, and Payne was rewarded for his gallantry with command of the Princess Amelia (80 guns), in which he returned home at the end of the war.

Shortly after this Payne became acquainted with George, prince of Wales, and there began between them what the prince later described as 'an old and steady friendship of upwards of twenty years standing' (Correspondence of George, Prince of Wales, vol. 4, no. 1780). In August 1785 Payne accompanied Lord Northington on the grand tour, visiting Paris, Geneva, Turin, Rome, and Naples. On his return in March or April 1786 he became the prince of Wales's private secretary and keeper of the privy seal, and subsequently also comptroller of the prince's household. He was elected MP for Huntingdon from 9 May 1787 on the recommendation of Lord Sandwich, who owed him money; he held the seat until 1796. In October 1787 Payne was appointed captain of the Phoenix, but he does not appear to have got near the sea in that command.

Throughout the crisis of November 1788 to February 1789 caused by George III's porphyria, Payne was very active in dealing on the prince's behalf with the supporters of a regency, especially Richard Brinsley Sheridan and Lord Loughborough. As a close friend, Payne also joined in the prince's ribald entertainments: at one masquerade, for example, 'Jack Payne … was dressed as a young lady … [and] chaperoned by Mrs Fitzherbert [the prince's secret Catholic wife]' (Molloy, 2.209). On another occasion, a disrespectful reference to the queen is said to have drawn from Jane, duchess of Gordon, the reproach: 'You little, insignificant, good-for-nothing, upstart, pert chattering puppy, how dare you name your royal master's royal mother in that style!' (ibid., 2.240). During July and August 1791 he was in France on the prince's business, and in October he was appointed (in addition to his other duties) auditor and secretary of the duchy of Cornwall.

The outbreak of war in 1793 seems to have interrupted Payne's search for a little country 'cottage' with a few acres of paddock; and from May he commanded the *Russell* (74 guns) in Howe's fleet. Fourth in the line, the *Russell* played a distinguished part in the battle of the Glorious First of June (1794), boarding *L'Amerique*, and 'our brave Captain [Payne, who] had many narrow escapes' (*Naval Chronicle*, 33), was one of those awarded a gold medal. Naturally, it was 'little Jacko Payne' (*Correspondence of George, Prince of Wales*, vol. 2, no. 895) in the *Jupiter* (50 guns), who was entrusted with the flotilla sent to Cuxhaven to bring the prince's future bride, Princess Caroline, to England between February and April 1795. Lady Jersey's scheming, and Payne's disapproval of the prince's conduct towards the princess, however, caused a rift between the two men, and in July 1796 he was formally dismissed from all his posts in the prince's service.

That summer Payne took command of the *Impétueux* (80 guns) which, as *L'Amerique*, he had played a part in capturing two years before; and for three successive summers he led squadrons cruising the Western Approaches. In poor health for some years, this last command brought on a severe illness which compelled him to resign.

Reconciled with his old friend in January 1799, and a rear-admiral since 14 February, Payne became treasurer of Greenwich Hospital in August, following the prince of Wales's personal appeal to William Pitt on his behalf. In November, *The Times* reported that Payne was to live in a house which the prince had bought and furnished for that purpose, next door to his own, Carlton House. He died, however, probably at the Royal Naval Hospital, Greenwich, on 17 November 1803, and was buried at St Margaret's, Westminster, on 25 November.

RANDOLPH COCK

Sources DNB · *Naval Chronicle*, 3 (1800), 1–38 · *The correspondence of George, prince of Wales, 1770–1812*, ed. A. Aspinall, 8 vols. (1963–71), vols. 1–4 · W. L. Clowes, *The Royal Navy: a history from the earliest times to the present*, 7 vols. (1897–1903); repr. (1996–7), vol. 4 · J. F. Molloy, *Court life below stairs*, 2 vols. (1885) · PRO, ADM 107/6, fol. 331 [lieutenants' passing certificates] · PRO, ADM 6/21, fol. 521, 541; 6/22, fol. 63 [commission and warrant books] · NMM, Sandwich MSS · M. H. Port, 'Payne, John Willett', HoP, *Commons, 1754–90*
Archives University of British Columbia Library, letters received and papers | NMM, letters to Lord Sandwich · Warks. CRO, letters to Lord Hugh Seymour

Likenesses J. Hoppner, oils, *c*.1795–1806, Royal Collection; versions, Courtauld Inst. and Weston Park, Shropshire · Bartolozzi, Landseer, Ryder and Stow, group portrait, line engraving, pubd 1803 (*Naval Victories: Commemoration of the Victory of June 1st 1794*; after R. Smirke), BM, NPG · Orme junior, stipple, BM

Payne, Joseph (1808–1876), educationist, was born on 2 March 1808 at Bury St Edmunds. Details of his early life are obscure but his parents, Joseph Payne and Elizabeth, daughter of Thomas Leader, were not wealthy. On the occasion of his own marriage in 1837 Payne's father was described as a builder. About the age of fourteen Payne came under the influence of a teacher called Freeman; he became an ardent student of the classics and English literature and determined on teaching as a career. In 1830, while teaching at a private boys' school run by John Gowring in the New Kent Road, London, he wrote a 56-page pamphlet entitled *A compendious exposition of the principles and practice of Professor Jacotot's celebrated system of education*. This attracted considerable attention and he became tutor to the children of David and Elizabeth Fletcher who lived in Camberwell. The tutorial class became a school and early in 1838 Fletcher and Payne established the Denmark Hill grammar school in a substantial house reputedly built by Sir Christopher Wren for Prince George of Denmark. On 28 December 1837 Payne married Eliza Dyer (*d*. 1875), daughter of the Revd John Dyer, secretary of the Baptist Missionary Society. The ceremony took place at the parish church of St Giles, Camberwell. The Paynes lived at Grove Hill House in Camberwell, where Eliza, herself an accomplished teacher who had spent some years in Paris, continued to keep a girls' school. Two sons, John Burnell and Joseph Frank *Payne, and a daughter, Mary Eliza, were born while the Paynes were at Denmark Hill; another son, William, was born after their move to Leatherhead.

In January 1845 Payne opened a new boys' school, known as the Mansion grammar school, at Leatherhead in Surrey. Unlike Denmark Hill House, which was demolished in 1873, the Mansion still stood in the 1990s, housing the Leatherhead branch of the county library. Payne's new foundation was another private establishment, attended principally by boarders, with fees of between 40 and 60 guineas per year. In the 1851 census fifty-one resident pupils were listed: their ages ranged from eight to sixteen years. The success of the school was shown by the examination performances of its pupils, particularly in the Oxford local examinations, and in 1865 Payne was invited to give evidence to the Taunton commission, as was the then headmaster of the Denmark Hill School, Charles Mason. Payne's evidence indicates that the curriculum at the Mansion grammar school was wide-ranging: for example, there was a laboratory and lessons were given in practical chemistry. The discipline was mild, indeed Payne dispensed with corporal punishment. While at Leatherhead the Paynes worshipped at the Congregational church, where Payne was appointed to the lay office of deacon in 1846.

Payne's first advertisements for his Leatherhead school advised that 'he advocates no exclusive system, but aims

Joseph Payne (1808–1876), by Charles William Sherborn, 1880 (after unknown photographer)

to adopt the most valuable features of all, combining with the solid instruction of the Old Grammar School a liberal infusion of sound mathematical and scientific knowledge'. His continuing commitment to broad learning was shown by the curriculum plan for a middle-class school for boys aged between eight and sixteen which he produced in 1866. For the first two years pupils would study reading, spelling and writing, history and geography, French, word and object lessons, and arithmetic. For pupils aged ten to twelve, English grammar, botany, and physics would be added. Latin would be introduced at age twelve, together with German, mathematics, English literature, and physics. Chemistry would be added in the final two years.

In 1863, after some nineteen years of strenuous devotion to the school, Payne retired from Leatherhead and lived at 4 Kildare Gardens, Bayswater, London. His later years were spent in a flurry of activities. In 1868 his reputation as a writer of textbooks was enhanced by the publication of *Studies in English Prose*, and there were further editions of *Studies in English Poetry* (1845) and of his best-known work, *Select Poetry for Children* (1839). This collection of poems for children aged between six and twelve, and intended for both 'schools and families', received its final revision and enlargement in the eighteenth edition of 1874. Payne's standing as a scholar was confirmed by work in the field of philology, and he was chairman of the council of the Philological Society in 1873–4.

Payne was a fierce critic of many elements of English society and of education. His criticisms of boys' public schools centred upon their custom and corruption, their inefficient teaching and limited curricula, and received powerful expression in an article on Eton published in the *British Quarterly Review* in 1868. His attack on elementary schooling centred upon the ethos engendered by the revised code of 1862 which, he believed, cast a blight upon all who came under its aegis: children, teachers, and inspectors. In 1872, in two papers delivered to meetings of the Social Science Association, Payne deplored the low standards of pupil attainment, and attributed these to a system which was 'mechanical in conception, mechanical in means, mechanical in results'.

But, though a critic, Payne was essentially a reformer with a firm belief in the power of education to transform individual lives and society. His campaign to improve the quality and status of the teaching profession began in 1846 as a founder member of the College of Preceptors. In the following year he became an examiner for the college's teachers' examinations in the theory and practice of education. He was vice-president of the college between 1862 and 1868, and also served at this time as vice-president of the Scholastic Registration Association. In December 1872 the council of the College of Preceptors invited Payne to become its first professor of the science and art of education. An inaugural lecture was given on 30 January 1873 and during that year Payne delivered three courses: ten lectures on the science of education, twelve on the art of education, and ten on the history of education. Of the seventy students who attended the first course, sixty-four were women. A second series of lectures was given in 1874, and a third in 1875.

Payne believed that the principles of a science of education were still scattered across many fields of knowledge—ethics, history, logic, philosophy, physiology, psychology. One of his major aims, therefore, was to bring these into a more coherent whole. Much of his inspiration in this work came from his own experiences as an autodidact and from his observation of the natural learning processes of young children. Accordingly he argued that educators should not only be proficient in the subjects they had to teach, but should also be well informed about their pupils, and about pupils in general. They should understand the basic principles of learning and teaching. The art of the teacher was to make formal schooling a progression and refinement of natural education, and to equip learners with the desire and ability ultimately to teach themselves. Historical study was important for the good (and bad) examples it provided of the science and art of education of former times.

A second element in Payne's reforming zeal was his commitment to the development of educational opportunities for girls and women. He argued that 'The mind has properly no sex … and consequently there must be a similarity of instruction of both sexes' (*Transactions of the National Association for the Promotion of Social Science, 1865, 1866*, 362). He was a friend and collaborator of such pioneers as Beata Doreck and Frances Buss, both of whom became members of the council of the College of Preceptors. From 1872 Payne served as chairman of the

Women's Education Union, and he was also one of the original shareholders of the Girls' Public Day School Company and chaired its council in 1872. Other offices held by Payne in the 1870s included membership of the council of the Social Science Association, and of the committees of the Kindergarten Association and of the Froebel Society. In 1875 he chaired the foundation meeting of the Society for the Development of the Science of Education. His interest in kindergarten methods led him to Germany, and a report on his tour of German schools in the autumn of 1874 was published posthumously in 1876.

Payne was described by his contemporary and colleague, W. B. Hodgson, as 'a dark-looking, broad-browed man, of short stature' who spoke 'with unusual clearness, force and accuracy of expression' (*Journal of the Women's Education Union*, 4, 1876, 86). On 12 October 1875 Eliza Payne died of enteric fever and Payne, himself unwell, found it necessary to give up his lecture course. In December 1875 he resigned the professorship. On 30 April 1876 he died at 4 Kildare Gardens, Bayswater, of Bright's disease of the kidneys. The death certificate was signed by Joseph Frank Payne, who was to become one of the most famous medical men of his day. In his will Payne bequeathed £200 to the College of Preceptors for the endowment fund for a professor of education, and £50 to Thomas John Barnardo or the treasurer of the East End Juvenile Mission. A codicil gave Herbert Quick first choice of fifty books from his library, while others of his educational books were left to the College of Preceptors. The remainder of his estate was divided equally between his two surviving sons, Joseph Frank and William. The former produced two edited collections of his father's lectures and writings: the first, *Lectures on the Science and Art of Education*, was published in 1880; the second, *Lectures on the History of Education*, in 1892. Payne had been a great admirer of the society and education of the United States and several editions of the first of these volumes were produced there.   RICHARD ALDRICH

Sources R. Aldrich, *School and society in Victorian Britain: Joseph Payne and the new world of education* (1995) • M. G. Fitch, 'Joseph Payne, first professor of education in England', *Journal of Education*, 66 (1934), 96–7, 188–90, 268–72, 390–92 • *The Educational Times* (1847–76) • J. V. Chapman, *Professional roots: the College of Preceptors in British society* (1985) • d. cert. • *CGPLA Eng. & Wales* (1878)
Archives NRA, priv. coll. • U. Lond., Institute of Education, family and personal corresp. and papers
Likenesses C. W. Sherborn, etching, 1877, NPG • C. W. Sherborn, etching, 1880, NPG [*see illus.*] • C. W. Sherborn, etching (after photograph by Messrs Sawyer and Bird), NPG; repro. in J. Payne, *Lectures on the science and art of education, with other lectures and essays*, ed. J. F. Payne (1880)
Wealth at death £4000: probate, 19 May 1876, *CGPLA Eng. & Wales*

Payne, Joseph Frank (1840–1910), physician and medical historian, was born in the parish of St Giles, Camberwell, in Surrey, on 10 January 1840, son of Joseph *Payne (1808–1876), professor and a founder member of the College of Preceptors, where education was taught, and his wife, Eliza, née Dyer (d. 1875), also a teacher. After education by his father he went to University College, London. In 1858 he gained a demyship at Magdalen College, Oxford, where he graduated BA in 1862 with a first class in natural science. He obtained the Burdett-Coutts scholarship in geology (1863), the Radcliffe travelling fellowship (1865), which took him to Paris, Berlin, and Vienna, and a Magdalen fellowship, which he vacated on his marriage (he became an honorary fellow on 30 May 1906). He graduated BSc (London) in 1865. Payne studied medicine at St George's Hospital, London, and graduated BM at Oxford in 1867 and DM in 1880. He became a member of the Royal College of Physicians of London in 1868, and was elected a fellow in 1873. Payne settled in London and became assistant physician at the Hospital for Sick Children in Great Ormond Street, and demonstrator of morbid anatomy at St Mary's Hospital, Paddington, in 1869. He left St Mary's in 1871 to become assistant physician to St Thomas's Hospital, where he was appointed physician in 1887. He retired in 1900. He was also on the staff of the Hospital for Skin Diseases at Blackfriars. He married, on 1 September 1882, Helen, daughter of the Hon. John Macpherson of Melbourne, Victoria. They had one son and three daughters.

Although primarily a physician, Payne made substantial contributions to pathology, epidemiology, dermatology, and the history of medicine. As pathologist he came to public prominence as expert witness for the defence in the trial of Louis Staunton and others for the murder of Staunton's wife, Harriet, at Penge in 1877. Although the jury convicted, Payne's argument that death was caused by tuberculous meningitis was eventually accepted. The home secretary commuted the death sentences on Louis Staunton, his brother, and his sister-in-law to penal servitude for life. Payne edited in 1875 *Manual of Pathological Anatomy* by Jones and Sieveking, and in 1888 he published *A Manual of General Pathology*, which in its emphasis on function and aetiology, as well as morbid anatomy, exemplified the view expressed in his presidential address to the Pathological Society of London in 1897 that 'it would be a loss rather than a gain were pathology to live like a cloistered recluse, in laboratories and museums, not breathing the common air of the whole medical world'. Between 1868 and 1891 he presented many case reports to the society. In 1891 he gave the Lumleian lectures at the Royal College of Physicians, entitled 'On cancer, especially of the internal organs'. His career as a descriptive morbid anatomist with clinical practice epitomized that of the physician–pathologist dominant in English medicine during the nineteenth and early twentieth centuries. Sir James Goodhart in his 1912 Harveian oration ranked him with Matthew Baillie, Richard Bright, Thomas Addison, John Bristowe, Sir William Jenner, and Sir Samuel Wilks, as a great master of morbid anatomy.

As an epidemiologist and medical historian Payne had a particular interest in plague. In 1879 he was sent to Russia by the government with Surgeon-Major Colvill to report on the epidemic of plague at Vetlyanka. He wrote articles on plague and the sweating sickness in the *Encyclopaedia Britannica* (9th edn), *St Thomas's Hospital Reports*, *Quarterly Review* (October 1901), and Allbutt's *System of Medicine* (vol. 2, 1907). He was also the spokesman of the committee of the Royal College of Physicians in 1905, on the Indian epidemic of plague. He had printed in 1894, with an introduction on the history of the plague, the 'Loimographia' of William Boghurst, who witnessed the London plague of 1665, from the Sloane manuscript. In some of his writing on the transmission of infection, Payne pioneered a quantitative approach—well before this became a common feature of studies on this subject. His main dermatological contributions were his *Observations on some Rare Diseases of the Skin* (1889) and his presidency of the Dermatological Society (1892–3).

Payne was held in high regard as a medical historian. He wrote a life of Thomas Linacre which was prefixed to a facsimile of the 1521 Cambridge edition of Linacre's Latin version of Galen, *De temperamentis* (Cambridge, 1881). In 1896 he delivered the Harveian oration on the relation of Harvey to Galen, and in 1900 he wrote a still useful life of Thomas Sydenham. He wrote long articles on the history of medicine in the *Encyclopaedia Britannica*, and in Allbutt's *System of Medicine* (vol. 1, 1905), besides seventy-eight lives in the *Dictionary of National Biography*. In 1904 he delivered the first FitzPatrick lectures on the history of medicine at the Royal College of Physicians. His last historical work was entitled *History of the College Club*, an account of a select dining society of the college, of which he was a member. It was privately printed in 1909.

For the Royal College of Physicians, Payne was an examiner for the college licence, a censor in 1896–7, and senior censor in 1905. He became Harveian librarian in 1899, and had a great knowledge of bibliography and of the history of woodcuts. He gave many books to the college library. In 1896 he edited the 'Nomenclature of diseases'. He sat on the royal commission on tuberculosis (1890), on the General Medical Council representing the University of Oxford (1899–1904), and on the University of London senate (1899–1906). He was on the London Library committee, and was himself the possessor of a fine library. Except for small bequests to the college, it was sold at Sothebys after his death. The catalogues emphasize the early medical works, the numerous books and tracts on pestilence from the earliest times to the eighteenth century, the rare herbals, and a series of the first and later editions of John Milton's writings and Miltoniana.

Payne first met William Osler in 1873, when he took him to a meeting of the Medical Microscopical Society, at which Osler read his first scientific paper. Osler held Payne in high regard; a particular interest that linked them was book collecting, one that persisted after Payne's death when Osler tried to secure the medical section of his library for the Johns Hopkins Library. The works were bought instead by Henry Wellcome—the most dramatic example of the book-collecting rivalry between Osler and Wellcome.

Payne was said to be ineffective in committees because he gave an opinion only when asked. Although verging on the polymathic—he wrote an article on furniture for the *Encyclopaedia Britannica*—he did not flaunt his learning, as illustrated by an anecdote in the *British Medical Journal* obituary:

> One wet Sunday in Switzerland a young lady came into the salon of the hotel, and joined a semicircle around Payne, who was distributing his golden share of information to any who cared to listen. Her comment on the close was, 'To think that I sat next to him at *table d'hôte* for three nights, and all he said was "please pass the salt"'. (*BMJ*, 2 (1910))

Payne was below middle height and had a curious jerky manner of expressing emphasis both in public speaking and in private conversation. He died at Lyonsdown House, New Barnet, Hertfordshire, on 16 November 1910, and was buried at Bell's Hill cemetery, Barnet.

T. H. PENNINGTON

Sources DNB · *BMJ* (26 Nov 1910), 1749–54 · J. Symons, 'Illustrations from the Wellcome Institute Library: Wellcome and Osler', *Medical History*, 41 (1997), 213–55 · J. B. Atlay, *Trial of the Stauntons* (1911) · J. F. Payne, 'Specific diseases considered with reference to the laws of parasitism', *St Thomas's Hospital Reports*, new ser., 20 (1892), 59–106 · J. F. Payne, 'Recollections of the medical school of Vienna', *BMJ* (25 March 1871), 307–8; (15 April 1871), 394–5; (22 April 1871), 418–19 · J. F. Goodhart, 'The passing of morbid anatomy', *BMJ* (26 Oct 1912), 1089–93 [Harveian oration] · *Transactions of the Pathological Society of London* (1869–1910) · *Catalogues of books from Payne's library to be sold at auction* (1911) [sale catalogue, Sotheby, Wilkinson, and Hodge, 12 July 1911 and 30 Jan 1912]

Archives CUL, letters and MSS, incl. that of J. B. Payne · Wellcome L., MSS relating to plague in Astrakhan

Likenesses J. S. Sargent, charcoal drawing, RCP Lond. · photograph, repro. in *BMJ*

Wealth at death £15,285 9s. 5d.: probate, 27 Jan 1911, CGPLA Eng. & Wales

Payne, Peter [Peter Engliss] (d. **1455/6**?), Wycliffite and Hussite heretic, was born at Hough on the Hill, near Grantham, Lincolnshire. According to Thomas Gascoigne (d. 1458), he was the son of a Frenchman and his English wife. He is referred to variously in the sources as Clerk or Freyng, and in Bohemia often as Engliss (Engliš).

Academic career in England Peter Payne was first induced to read John Wyclif's books at Oxford, where he started to study shortly before 1400, by his fellow student Peter Partridge (d. 1451), later chancellor of Lincoln Cathedral and Payne's adversary at the Council of Basel. Partridge, in turn, claimed that Wycliffite ideas reached the notorious Sir John Oldcastle (d. 1417) through Payne, an assertion supported independently by Robert Holbech, Oldcastle's excommunicated chaplain. Thomas Netter (d. 1430) later claimed that Payne, the most outspoken Wycliffite at Oxford, had once cried off from an arranged public debate with himself about pilgrimages, the eucharist, and mendicancy. Payne had become MA by 5 October 1406. At that time he managed somehow to have the university seal affixed to a letter affirming that Wyclif was upright of life, outstanding in his exposition of scripture, and never condemned for heresy. Gascoigne was to claim later that Payne simply stole and misused the seal, so as to persuade the dissidents in Bohemia that all England, with the exception of mendicant friars, held the same beliefs as they did in Prague. This possibility cannot be excluded; at any rate, Payne met two Bohemian scholars, Mikuláš Faulfiš and Jiří of Knínice, who returned home with the letter in 1407. It was published in Prague in early January 1409 by Master Jeroným Pražský, whom Payne may have met in England. There are also good reasons to assume that Payne acted as intermediary in the correspondence between Jan Hus, Richard Wyche, and Sir John Oldcastle between 1408 and 1413.

From 1408 Payne rented White Hall, Oxford, for 28s. 4d. p.a. In 1428 the imprisoned Lollard Ralph Mungyn attested that, although Payne propagated Wyclif's ideas at Oxford, London, and elsewhere, he evaded official investigation for a long time. Indeed, he even managed to succeed the excommunicated Lollard William Taylor as principal of St Edmund Hall next door as late as 1410. There is a strong probability that either he or Taylor wrote the extensive treatise (in English, despite its title) *Tractatus de oblacione iugis sacrificii* (BL, MS Cotton Titus D.v). On the other hand, he had nothing to do with another text, *De versione Bibliorum* (Vienna, Österreichische Nationalbibliothek, MS 244). Payne was summoned before a commission dealing with persistent Wycliffites in the university in autumn 1410. Archbishop Thomas Arundel of Canterbury (d. 1414) showed some benevolence and accepted him as orthodox on 6 November. Belatedly Payne may have been ordained by Bishop Robert Hallum of Salisbury (d. 1417) as subdeacon and deacon in February and April 1412. His tenure of the White Hall was terminated against his will in October 1412, but he still paid his rent of 30s. for St Edmund Hall for that year. However, shortly afterwards—in August 1413 at latest—when Oldcastle was arrested, Payne left both Oxford and England, probably to avoid prosecution.

In Hussite Prague Before Payne finally settled in Bohemia, his travels took him first to the Rhineland and to Deutach in Alsace where a young Waldensian emissary, Friedrich Reiser, met him in the house of his father, Conrad. Though sources about Payne's stays in Germany and perhaps also in Switzerland are unreliable, they do show a web of close connections between nonconformist in religion and mostly undercover centres across much of Europe. It was hardly a coincidence that Payne reappeared in Germany in 1418 or 1419, living in the house of a Nuremberg merchant named Hans von Plauen. Payne did not meet Jan Hus, head of the Bohemian reform movement, personally. This suggests that he arrived in Prague only after Hus's fateful departure for the Council of Constance, that is, after 11 October 1414. Payne aroused the interest of Prague reform circles by his very first known intervention in Bohemia, when he demanded reception of the eucharist by the laity *sub utraque specie* (that is, the receiving of both bread and wine), as against the Catholic practice of withholding the chalice. He is likely to have written this polemic against the priest Havlík, Hus's successor in the Bethlehem Chapel, in February 1415 (Krmíčková, 148–64). He took part in current debates in the university with a series of minor contributions such as his treatises against oath taking, *De iuramento* (Bartoš, *Literární činnost*, 96, no. 2), and on Wyclif's orthodox veneration of images, *De ymaginibus* (Nechutová, 326–33); his defence of predestination, *Tractatus de predestinacione*; and perhaps also by his assertion of the inevitability of all that happened in this world, *De necessitate absoluta evenientium*. Payne's rejection of oath taking is close to the position of Lollards and Waldensians, and he does not differ substantially from mainstream reform opinion on other questions. The delay of his registration as a master of arts at Prague until 13 February 1417 may have been caused, among other reasons, by the fact that his main Prague contacts were with German nonconformists around Nikolaus von Dresden of the Black Rose Hall. His appointment as examiner in the winter semester of 1417 may have prompted him to compose a mnemonic device for his students, the so-called *Dicta* (Bartoš, *Literární činnost*, 98, no. 6).

Payne returned from a visit to Nuremberg just in time to witness the stormy onset of the Hussite revolution in Prague. His opponents had assumed that he was still abroad, but when Master Mikuláš Stojčí made a public attack upon his defence of Wyclif's realist philosophy, Payne surprised him by announcing a date when he would stand up for that position. The confrontation, arranged for late April 1420 (Sedlák, 'Drobné texty', 114–15) failed to take place, because Prague had to face the threat of the first Catholic crusade against Bohemian revolt. The authority of Payne, as an English Wycliffite and defender of utraquism (that is, of the administration of the eucharist in both kinds, bread and wine), was now so great that the city of Prague chose him as one of its ambassadors to King Sigismund (r. 1419–37) at the beginning of May 1420. Any optimism was dashed by the ultimatum delivered to them at Kutná Hora (Kuttenberg). Nevertheless, a path to talks with orthodox Catholic theologians was then opened by the victory of Hussite troops over the crusaders on 14 July 1420. Payne is very likely to have participated, but first he appeared in what would be his future role as a go-between and impartial adviser on 5 August 1420, when he deliberated with the representatives of the Old Town of Prague over the twelve articles submitted as an ultimatum by the radical Hussite Tabor brotherhood. Evidently he performed well as a diplomat, for the towns of Prague nominated him in the embassy that was to offer the crown of Bohemia to King Władysław of Poland. On his return Payne found himself in agreement with the leading Hussite theologian, Jakoubek of Stříbro, when both presented arguments against a radical Prague preacher, John Želivský, in a congregation held in the Caroline College on 11 November 1421. Three days later Payne was elected to the Hussite consistory in Prague, in which he may have remained active until 1434.

Payne is then out of sight for more than a year, until his reappearance as an adviser to the lay arbiters in controversies between Prague and Tabor clergy at Konopiště Castle in June 1423. It is doubtful whether he did then contribute, as has been suggested, the two polemical treatises, *De corpore Christi*, defending the eucharist theology of the Taborites against his Prague colleague, Jan of Příbram (Sedlák, *Táborské traktáty*, 21–7), but he may, by his text, *Tripes*, have defended three of Wyclif's theses on the eucharist against Příbram. The assumption that Payne went for a second time to Poland as an envoy from Prague in March 1424 is unfounded; he has been confused, as on other occasions, with Matěj of Hnátnice, also nicknamed 'Engliss'.

In 1425–6 the Prague Hussite alliance had to cede primacy of power to the radical brotherhoods of the Taborites in southern Bohemia and the 'Sirotci' ('Orphans') in eastern Bohemia. Payne remained in Prague, but he faced opposition from conservative masters, and especially from Jan of Příbram, who launched a wholesale attack on the Wycliffite foundations of Hussite doctrine in 1426. Příbram decided to play the nationalist card against Payne, with whom he disputed at Christmas 1426 and again during Lent from 5 March 1427. He and his partisans denigrated Payne for his English origin, a position also reflected in a contemporary verse-composition in which the Devil lets Payne slip into Bohemia, taking from his homeland 'rights unwholesome for the Czechs'. Wyclif's undoubtedly awkward theology of the eucharist, one that many Hussites rejected outright, surfaced time and again in the polemics, and even Payne, in his brief *Confessio* of April 1427, preferred not to take an unequivocal stance. However, not long afterwards a popular rebellion purged Prague of all university conservatives, including Příbram.

In the service of utraquism In August 1427 the retreat of a crusader army under the papal legate, Cardinal Henry Beaufort (d. 1447), from the west Bohemian castle of Tachov undermined the position of the local Catholic alliance, which agreed to hold a debate involving clergy from both sides. With Beaufort's consent the Catholics nominated Master Šimon of Tišnov, while the Hussite position was to be defended by Payne. The disputation began at Žebrák Castle on 29 December 1427, but swiftly collapsed for lack of agreement over rules of engagement. It was to be almost a year before those advocating a peaceful solution to the Bohemian crisis prevailed at King Sigismund's court, and then only because he faced war on two fronts. For the negotiations that followed Payne was elected principal speaker of the Hussite delegation, possibly at the diet at Český-Brod on 1 January 1429, notwithstanding the widely differing attitudes of some leaders in the Hussite alliance. The choice of Payne was a recognition not only of his abilities, but also of his prudent occupation of a place between the moderate and radical Hussite theologians.

After a minor clash the official meeting between the delegation and Sigismund was rescheduled from Moravský-Krumlov to Bratislava, and opened on 5 April 1429 with speeches by Sigismund and Prokop Holý ('Prokop the Shaven'), the head of the Bohemian embassy. Then came Payne's turn. He argued that the Hussites' struggle was against all tyrants and for the sake of the law of God, not for their own glory. Very little was required to end the conflict; it all depended on Sigismund. If he could but see his way towards changing his policy, he would receive that most famous kingdom of Bohemia, setting free the truth, and would secure the allegiance of both the communities of Prague and of Bohemia (*Petri Payne*, 88). But all too soon the talks fell into deadlock over the problem of establishing arbitration in the conflict concerning

the Hussites' four articles—administration of communion in both kinds; free preaching of God's word; ecclesiastical abandonment of secular property; abolition of public mortal sins. Attempts to make progress were blocked by powerful hardline groups on each side. Even a second meeting with Sigismund at Bratislava in July failed to achieve any significant results.

Payne is unlikely to have taken part in this second phase of talks because he was needed for the diets and other proceedings in Prague. Master Jan Rokycana, successor to Jakoubek of Stříbro (d. 1429), sought to reconcile his university colleagues who had been forced out of Prague two years before. Jan of Příbram, who had returned home, renewed his assault on the ideas of Wyclif and his chief local adherent, Payne. An intense and highly sensitive disputation between the two lasting several days in September and October 1429 was attended by large numbers of the public. In their verdict on 20 October the eight referees ordered both masters to submit their arguments in writing, stop denigrating each other, and hold their fire until 4 June 1430. Payne duly produced the texts of both his disputations (Bartoš, *Literární činnost*, 103–4, nos. 13, 14); Příbram refused and left Prague once more.

At the end of December 1429 Payne is recorded as participating in business concerning the Caroline College in Prague, where he had become one of the masters, with a prebend in the collegiate chapel of All Saints—a position he may well have secured much earlier. Between 1432 and 1434, however, he was living in the Slavonic abbey called Emmaus in the New Town, perhaps because of discord within the college. Payne, like Příbram, felt the need to prepare his polemics carefully, just as he later prepared for his public debates with the theologians of the Council of Basel. With three or possibly even more assistants he completed a list and index of all Wyclif's writings by 1432 or 1433 at the very latest. This enabled the compilation of thematically specific anthologies, facilitating the work of scholars down to the present day.

The Wycliffite Peter Engliss was rated highly by the Taborites and so, at their instigation, the Hussite diet at the beginning of 1431 elected Payne to take part in a new embassy to the Polish king. Negotiations opened at the royal castle of Wawel on 19 March, but failed as a result of the irreconcilable theological positions of the two sides. As soon as the embassy returned, a major Hussite synod assembled in the Caroline College on 30 April 1431 to try to harmonize the conflicting positions of the Prague and Taborite clergy before the forthcoming negotiations with envoys from Basel. This purpose was not achieved, but one consequence of the synod was to give a spur to the doctrinal merging of east Bohemian and Prague Hussitism. Payne himself drew closer to the centrist group of the utraquist consistory in Prague.

At the Council of Basel Hopes for swift reconciliation between Hussite Bohemia, the Catholic church, and King Sigismund blossomed after the failure of a fourth crusade against the Hussites in August 1431. At the end of September the Council of Basel agreed to a public hearing for a Hussite embassy, and sent its official invitation to Prague on 15 October. The provincial diet met in February 1432, agreed to accept, and nominated a large delegation for preliminary talks at Cheb (Eger). Although Payne was among the Prague clergy chosen, the young and vigorous Master Jan Rokycana was clearly establishing himself among the Hussite leaders. As well as pronouncing upon matters of protocol, the Cheb provisions declared that the law of God, the practice of the early church, and the doctrines of the church fathers were to be the impartial 'judge' over the imminent talks. (Payne, at least, would come to show his trust in these criteria as agreed.) A diet at Kutná Hora in August and September selected the embassy to Basel; Payne was of course among the representatives of Prague and its university.

The council's speakers had been marshalling their arguments for some time, whereas their Bohemian opponents looked more for a simple victory for holy truths. It is not clear whether the defendants of each of the four articles were actually selected at the Kutná Hora diet or perhaps shortly afterwards. But, whatever the arrangements, quarrels broke out as soon as the Bohemian embassy reached Basel. This did not directly affect Payne himself, to whom the defence of the fourth article, concerning poverty of the clergy, seems to have been assigned back in Prague. Payne made his first public appearance as a speaker for the Hussite delegation on 13 January 1433, when he demanded in vain the transfer of the debate into the cathedral, and the public announcement of dates for each individual presentation. Payne spoke quite often thereafter, both on behalf of the embassy and for himself. Contemporary witnesses attest to the lively response aroused by his ironic and sarcastic formulations, though a number of the council's participants claimed to have difficulties with his English pronunciation of Latin.

Payne's turn to defend his assigned article came on the morning of 26 January 1433 (*Petri Payne*, 1–40). After only a few introductory words he submitted an unequivocal formulation. Both human and divine law, and the precepts of the fathers (who deployed actual examples from the New Testament), prohibited Christ's true clergy from holding any secular possessions or worldly power. Putting forward four premises, Payne defined the notions of 'possession', 'domination', 'law', and 'clergy', quoting numerous extracts from the Old and New testaments and from the fathers, in evidence. The next morning, the 27th, Payne continued with more extracts from the fathers and from more recent theologians. In the final part of his speech, on the morning of Wednesday 28 January, he buttressed his interpretation by recourse both to resolutions by early church councils and to the *Decretum Gratiani*. In conclusion Payne summarized his arguments, criticizing the charges against Wyclif and Hus, and asked those present to agree to the worldly disendowment of the church in the interest of all. None the less, in the course of a subsequent debate within the Bohemian delegation, Payne yielded to strong pressure and accepted a compromise demanding only the divestment of superfluous possessions, and that only from clergy individually culpable. A paragraph on the evangelical poverty of the early church, which he added to his original text in its written version of 4 February 1433, thus acquired the character of a hardly enforceable moral appeal.

The whole of February was taken up by the responses of the council's speakers, with only brief respite. Payne followed them all intently and interjected frequent comments, attacks and questions on behalf of himself and his remaining friends. His own designated opponent, Juan Palomar, archdeacon of Barcelona and papal auditor, began his reply on 23 February and tried to turn Payne's own weapon, biblical citation, against him. A rumour also spread through Basel the following day that an English embassy, which had just arrived, had brought with it accusations by the crown against Payne. This threat may have been nullified by the council's safe conducts to the leaders of the Bohemian delegation; when Palomar resumed his reply to Payne on 27 and 28 February, he assumed a perceptibly more civil attitude towards him.

March was reserved for the counter-replies of the Bohemian advocates. The planned departure of the embassy induced some cardinals and bishops to offer these Hussite theologians incorporation into the council. The latter chose Payne to discuss the offer, but on 12 March as the climax to an embittered confrontation he declared why it was unacceptable. Returning to his formal task, in his replication to Palomar (31 March – 1 April) Payne refuted his opponent's objections painstakingly and step by step. However, with rumours against him still circulating, he asked Cardinal Giuliano Cesarini for an opportunity to defend himself publicly before the whole council. He was allowed to do so three days later, but was then accused formally both of heresy and of treason against Henry VI by John Keninghale (d. 1451), the Carmelite provincial of England, and Peter Partridge, chancellor of Lincoln and his sometime friend. Payne denied the charges calmly, and was defended strongly by others of the Bohemian embassy. The two English envoys made their accusations again on the following day, 7 April, just as Palomar was about to respond to Payne's theological refutation. None the less, the disputation went on, hotly debated, until 9 April, Palomar conceded elements of truth in his opponent's arguments but yielded nothing in his final rejection of Payne's reasoning. The council was still very eager to keep the Bohemians at Basel, but the delegates refused all blandishments and set off for home on 14 April.

The final years Payne naturally assumed a major role in continuing negotiations with the council, both at Prague and Basel. Besides other tasks Payne had to ask the councillors of the New Town of Prague on 27 May 1433 to suppress any activities offensive to the council's envoys, while during the June diet of the same year he was among a group of authoritative Hussite theologians including Rokycana and a Taborite bishop, Mikuláš of Pelhřimov, who held learned debates with the embassy. In the diet of November and December that year he even had to face threats from conservative Prague masters, and the Caroline College witnessed such uproar that the provincial governor had to summon armed guards. In a session on 18 November Payne called in vain for unity, for on another occasion he was to denounce the council's envoys openly, claiming that they would really prefer to throw all Hussite clergy of any sort into a sack. In its efforts to subvert the Hussite movement the council now received crucial assistance from the former's right wing, which, in alliance with the Catholic nobility, defeated the troops of the radical Hussite unions in the battle of Lipany on 30 May 1434. According to a later report Payne himself was captured; certainly, if no more reliably, rumours of his death or imprisonment soon circulated as far away as London. If he was imprisoned, it cannot have been for long, because at the end of October 1434 a provincial diet nominated him as sole referee in debates between Prague and the Taborite clergy.

Here Payne faced a dilemma. At heart he undoubtedly wanted the embryonic Taborite church to retain its Wycliffite character. On the other hand, he surely realized that the only way out of crisis was through the unity of the whole calixtine party, so called from its demand for access to the chalice—*calix*—at the eucharist. Small wonder, then, that he kept postponing his arbitration. He had moved some time earlier to the town of Žatec (Saaz) in western Bohemia, from where he visited Prague for official business. Not even in Žatec, however, could he escape the attentions of conservative forces, now gathering strength as they sought to restore the old order. King Sigismund dared not deliver him to the Council of Basel but he did try to bring him and the Taborite radical Václav Koranda to submit fully to the rule of the church. Payne refused on 15 April 1437 at the Caroline College, whereupon Bishop Philibert of Coutances pronounced him the source of all errors in Bohemia, and Sigismund (soon to die) expelled him formally as a foreigner from all his lands. Payne's long-standing clerk and companion, John Penning, was arrested a week later and interrogated on the 28th.

It is not known where Payne sought refuge before his return to the colony of German and other nonconformists in Žatec. It may have been in one of the towns of the Taborite union, perhaps Klatovy. It was among people from there that he was arrested by a Catholic noble, Burian of Gutštejn, in October 1438. A search of his personal possessions uncovered material concerning negotiations with Poland, which may indicate that Payne was now engaged in a campaign against Sigismund's successor as king of Bohemia, Albrecht II of Habsburg. Burian hoped for a very substantial reward from England for this capture, but Henry VI wanted to transfer any cost to the papacy, as his secretary, Bishop Thomas Beckington, informed Eugenius IV (r. 1431–47) on 18 May 1440. Oxford University, asked for its opinion by the king, sent a message of praise to Burian but assured him that the English crown had no intention of paying a ransom. Thus disappointed, Burian changed course completely, and later in 1440 accepted 12,000 Bohemian groschen from the Taborite towns for Payne's release from Rabštejn Castle.

In the early 1440s Payne challenged his old foe, Jan of Příbram, in a treatise in which he took up again the question of the eucharist. Příbram came back at him as

strongly as ever, complaining to the burgesses of Žatec of Payne's persistent adherence to errors of doctrine, and offering a wager of 6000 groschen on a disputation with him at any Christian university, or, failing that, at Prague before the masters and the land diet. In fact it was Příbram himself who evaded a disputation with Payne in the course of a synod at Kutná Hora in July 1443, perhaps because it had elected Payne, together with Master Václav of Dráchov, as its president and correspondent to the general synod that followed. The Taborites took Payne's side, protesting against Příbram's slurs and, later on, accused him of having deliberately spoken in Bohemian during the Prague synod of January 1444 so that Payne could not understand him. By a historic irony, the final verdict of the provincial court of justice, against the creed of the Taborite clergy, on 31 January 1444, relied heavily upon Payne's own assessments of 1427 and 1436.

Nothing further is heard of Payne for a full eight years. Although it is tempting to identify him with the 'Constantinus Anglicus' who was in Constantinople as an ambassador of the utraquist consistory in 1451, there is no convincing evidence. His last public appearance in his adopted homeland was in September 1452, when he had to pronounce a judgment against Taborite doctrines for a third time. Yet when the fortress at Tabor capitulated to the provincial governor, Jiří of Poděbrady, on 1 September 1452, one of its conditions was that Jiří should recognize as a religious authority a special commission of which Payne was a member. Now an old man, Payne may indeed have ended his days as an adviser to the calixtine archbishop, Jan Rokycana. A rather unconvincing report dates his death to 1455 or 1456; he is presumed to have died in Prague.

Master Peter Payne was among those nonconformist scholars of the later middle ages who strove to achieve tangible reforms in the practices of the church and of lay religion. From his student days in Oxford he stood firm to the doctrines of John Wyclif and spent his life in promoting and defending them in both his homelands. In Hussite Bohemia he offered himself many times over the years both as a brave and respected arbitrator in the severe doctrinal disputes within the domestic streams of reform, and also as an impressive envoy to the Catholic world and an advocate of those four articles of Prague that tried to bridge the internal chasms. His literary bequest, though relatively slim, is an honest reflection of the often dangerous life of this dedicated intellectual reformer; his defence at Basel of the Wycliffite and Hussite stance on clerical poverty is no mean epitaph.   F. ŠMAHEL

Sources F. M. Bartoš, 'Z bratislavské schůzky krále Zikmunda s husitskými vůdci r. 1949', *časopis Matice moravské*, 49 (1925), 171–95 · F. M. Bartoš, *Literární činnost M. Jana Rokycany, M. Jana Příbrama, M. Petra Payna* (1928) · F. M. Bartoš, *M. Petr Payne, diplomat husitské revoluce* (1956) · F. M. Bartoš, 'A delegate of the Hussite church to Constantinople in 1451–2', *Byzantinoslavica*, 24 (1963), 287–92 · F. M. Bartoš, 'A delegate of the Hussite church to Constantinople in 1451–2', *Byzantinoslavica*, 25 (1964), 69–74 · *Petri Payne Anglici positio, replica et propositio in concilio Basiliensi a. 1433 atque oratio ad Sigismundum regem a. 1429 Bratislaviae pronunciatae*, ed. F. M. Bartoš (1949) · R. R. Betts, 'Peter Payne in England', *Essays in Czech history*

(1969), 236–46 • W. R. Cook, 'Peter Payne, theologian and diplomat of the Hussite revolution', PhD diss., Cornell University, 1971 • Emden, *Oxf.* • A. B. Emden, *An Oxford hall in medieval times: being the early history of St Edmund Hall*, rev. edn (1968), 133–62 • A. Hudson, *The premature reformation: Wycliffite texts and Lollard history* (1988) • A. Hudson, 'The Hussite catalogues of Wyclif's works', *Husitství-Reformace-Renesance*, ed. J. Pánek, M. Polívka, and N. Rejchrtová, 1 (1994), 401–17 • E. F. Jacob, 'The Bohemians at the Council of Basel', *Prague essays*, ed. R. W. Seton-Watson (1949), 81–123 • A. Jung, 'Friedrich Reiser, eine Ketzergeschichte aus dem fünfzehnten Jahrhundert', *Timotheus, eine Zeitschrift zur Förderung der Religion und Humanität*, 2 (1822), 37–101, 137–77, 234–80 • H. Krmíčková, *Studie a texty k počátkům kalicha v Čechách* (1997) • J. Macek, 'Die Versammlung von Presburg 1429', *Folia diplomatica*, 1 (1971), 189–207 • E. Maleczyńska, 'Piotr Payne a Polska', *Universitas Carolina, Historica*, 3/1 (1957), 49–64 • J. Nechutová, 'Traktát "de ymaginibus", připisovaný Petru Paynovi', *Husitský Tábor*, 9 (1986–7), 325–34 • J. Sedlák, 'Drobné texty k dějinám husitství 8. Payne a Stojčín', *Studie a texty k náboženským dějinám českým*, 3/1 (1917), 113–15 • J. Sedlák, *Táborské traktáty eucharistické* (1918) • F. Šmahel, 'Curriculum vitae Magistri Petri Payne', in M. Polívka and F. Šmahel, *In memoriam Josefa Macka, 1922–1991* (Prague, 1996), 141–60 • F. Šmahel, 'Doctor evangelicus super omnes evangelistas: Wyclif's fortune in Hussite Bohemia', *BIHR*, 43 (1970), 16–34 • S. H. Thomson, 'A note on Peter Payne and Wyclyf', *Medievalia et Humanistica*, 16 (1964), 60–63

Archives Österreichische Nationalbibliothek, Vienna, MSS 4333, 4342, 4550, 4937 • BL, Cotton MS Titus D.v • Knihovna Metropolitní Kapituly, Prague, MSS D 47, D 109 • Národní Knihovna, Prague, MSS IV.G.25, V.F. 9, X.E. 11

Payne, Sir Peter, *de jure* third baronet (1763–1843), radical, was born at Blunham House, Bedfordshire, in February 1763, the third son of Sir Gillies Payne, second baronet, of Tempsford, Bedfordshire. His grandfather Sir Charles (*d.* 1746) had inherited from his wife a large property in St Kitts, West Indies, and had been created a baronet on 31 October 1737.

Sir Gillies Payne (*d.* 1801) was high sheriff of Bedfordshire in 1771. He formed in his youth a liaison with Maria Keeling, daughter of a farmer at Potton, Bedfordshire, but delayed marriage with her until the death of his mother in 1761. Peter was the first child born subsequently. Nevertheless on the death of his father in 1801 he allowed his elder brother, John, to succeed to the title, and, when John died two years later, acted as guardian to his young children. It was not until 1828 that Payne, having vainly offered to submit his claims and those of his brother's heir to a court of arbitration, was induced to allow the matter to be raised incidentally in the chancery suit *Glascott* v. *Bridges*. In the course of the trial Sir John's widow made affidavit that she and her sister had burned the marriage certificate of Sir Gillies, but evidence brought forward convinced the court of its existence, and Sir Peter was declared the eldest son born in wedlock. This decision was however reversed by the lord chancellor in January 1829, and an issue was directed to be tried as to the legitimacy of John and Peter Payne. The question never again came before the courts, but during his lifetime Sir Peter's claim to the baronetcy was acknowledged. He refused, however, to register himself as a baronet.

Payne was educated at Hackney and at Queens' College, Cambridge, where he graduated BA in 1784 and MA in 1787. A handsome youth, though delicate, he took an active part in field sports, was a captain in the Bedfordshire militia, and was a deputy lieutenant for the county for more than half a century. In politics he was a strong whig, and he exerted much political influence in the midlands. In 1810 he published two pamphlets, entitled respectively *England the Cause of Europe's subjugation, Addressed to the British Parliament*, and *The Character and Conduct of British Ministers in War and Negotiation Illustrated by Facts*. In 1812 he attacked Pitt and attempted to convict Wilberforce of inconsistency in *Mr. Pitt the grand political delinquent; with a dedication to the solemnisers of his birthday, and an address to Wm. Wilberforce, esq., M.P.* In the same year he issued at Birmingham, under the pseudonym 'Philagathos', *Seven short and plain letters to the inhabitants of Birmingham on the leading points connected with the orders in council.*

Payne was intimate with the political reformer Major John Cartwright, for whom he stood bail when Cartwright was charged with sedition in August 1819. Among other friends were Sir Herbert Taylor and Dr Samuel Parr. In 1819 Payne published at Birmingham a *Letter to Lord Erskine in Defence of the Whigs*. On 5 May 1831 he was returned, with Lord Tavistock, as a whig member for Bedfordshire, but he retired at the dissolution in December 1832. He printed at Bedford in 1832 a pamphlet advocating repeal of the corn laws. He was also a strong opponent of the slave trade, and an advocate of higher education for women. In favour of the latter cause he wrote a pamphlet, which was published in 1811, under the title *Trial between the governess of a ladies' boarding school and the mother of a pupil committed to her charge.*

Payne married, in August 1789, Elizabeth Sarah, the only daughter of Samuel Steward of Stourton Castle, Staffordshire; they had two sons and four daughters. She died on 12 April 1832. Their grandson, Charles Robert Salusbury Payne, claimed the baronetcy in 1893, but the claim was not recognized. Sir Bernard Burke, after giving particulars of the separate claims in the editions of his *Peerage and Baronetage* between 1868 and 1878, thenceforth ignored the title. Foster's *Baronetage* of 1882 relegates it to the appendix 'Chaos'. Payne died at Blunham House, Bedfordshire, on 23 January 1843.

G. LE G. NORGATE, rev. H. C. G. MATTHEW

Sources E. Lodge, *Peerage, baronetage, knightage and companionage of the British empire*, 81st edn, 3 vols. (1912) • E. Shore, *Journal* (1891) • private information (1895)

Archives Beds. & Luton ARS, letters to Samuel Whitbread

Payne, Ralph, Baron Lavington (1739–1807), politician, was born in the parish of St George, Basseterre, St Kitts, on 19 March 1739, the second and only surviving son of Ralph Payne (*d.* 1763), chief justice of that island, and his first wife, Alice, the daughter and heir of Francis Carlisle of Antigua. His father was descended from a wealthy St Kitts family which had originally come from Lavington in Wiltshire. After being educated in England at Christ's Hospital, Payne returned to his native island, where he was at once elected a member of the house of assembly and unanimously voted speaker.

In 1762 Payne was again in England, and he then made the grand tour of Europe. Like William Beckford he became a successful representative of the political and social prominence of the wealthy absentee West Indian planters in Britain. On 1 September 1767 he married, at St George's, Hanover Square, Frances Lambertine Christiana Charlotte Harriet Theresa (d. 1830), the daughter of Henry (sometimes called Frederick Maximillian), Baron Kolbel, of Saxony, a general in the service of the Holy Roman empire. She had arrived in England with the Princess Joseph Poniatowski, sister to the king of Poland, and was a friend of Queen Charlotte. Payne made useful contacts through his wife, but it was an unhappy marriage, for which he was blamed, not least in a satirical verse by Sheridan. Finding her mourning the death of a pet, he quipped:

Alas! poor Ned
My monkey's dead!
I had rather, by half,
It had been Sir Ralph.
(*Memoirs of … Wraxall*, 3.411)

After his marriage Payne entered politics, and was returned to parliament for the borough of Shaftesbury, a seat he held from 1768 until 1771. He was a political weathercock, always voting with the government and switching his party allegiances accordingly. He was a close friend of Lord Mansfield, whom he defended in his maiden speech as a seconder of Blackstone's motion against Wilkes (2 February 1769). His speeches and correspondence were absurdly verbose. His cultivation of refinement and his obsession with etiquette similarly verged on the ridiculous, even by the standards of the age. Horace Walpole speculated that this exaggerated style was developed during youthful appearances at amateur dramatics. It may also have reflected the ambition of a colonial outsider for acceptance in metropolitan society. Nevertheless, Payne possessed considerable charm and was one of the most celebrated hosts in London.

On 18 February 1771 Payne was created a knight of the Bath at St James's Palace and in the same year was appointed captain-general and governor-in-chief of the Leeward Islands, where he had inherited a considerable estate from his parents. The colony was not a particularly desirable post because its division among several islands made it expensive and difficult to administer. After a devastating hurricane in 1772 Payne became the first governor in over half a century to tour all the islands in the colony. He was a patron of the artist Thomas Hearne, who painted some of the few contemporary landscapes of the Caribbean. One of these (in the Victoria and Albert Museum) features the arrival of Payne at the capital town of St John's in a coach-and-six with a military honour guard against the background of the court house and guard house.

Payne was a successful governor, despite the fragility of colonial politics in the Caribbean on the eve of the American War of Independence. Although the *Virginia Gazette* claimed that his inaugural speech to the island legislatures was written by Lord North, the colonists petitioned for his continuance in office on his departure in 1775. He received a sword set in diamonds by the unanimous vote of the assembly of Antigua. His popularity was helped by his native origins and because he allowed himself to be co-opted by the planter élite, with whom he avoided any confrontation.

Payne returned to England, where he re-entered political life. He sat for Camelford in Cornwall from November 1776 to 1780, and for Plympton, Devon, from 1780 to 1784. His attendance in parliament became irregular, perhaps because of the disastrous economic consequences of the American revolutionary wars for the British Caribbean. From June 1777 until the suppression of the office in 1782 he was a clerk of the board of green cloth.

After the American war Payne became a supporter of Fox. His house in Grafton Street became known, through his love of hospitality and the personal attractions of his wife, as the favourite resort of the whig leaders. He joined Brooks's Club, sponsored by Fox, on 2 August 1784 and the Whig Club on 16 January 1787. His expectations of office were frustrated by the rise of Pitt, however, and he left England for an extended tour of the continent in 1788. With the support of the prince of Wales he contested the borough of Fowey in 1790, but there was a double return in which the decision went against him. After this disappointment he wavered in his attachment to the whigs and seceded from the Whig Club. On 15 August 1793 he gave a 'considerable dinner' at his house, at which Pitt was a guest. It was at one of his dinner parties that Henry Dundas and Lord Loughborough plotted the alliance of the duke of Portland and Pitt. His change of allegiance was induced by declining profits from his sugar estates in the Leeward Islands. He was well rewarded by his new political patrons: he was created Baron Lavington in the peerage of Ireland on 1 October 1795. The same month he was returned to parliament for New Woodstock, which he continued to represent until 1799. He made no speeches and did not vote on the abolition of the slave trade.

In February 1799 Lavington was reappointed governor of the Leeward Islands, and later the same year was sworn of the privy council. He arrived at Antigua on 12 August 1801 and remained there until his death, at Government House, on 3 August 1807. He was buried the following day on his plantation, Carlisles, and an elaborate marble monument was erected to his memory by the island legislature in the church of the parish of St John's in Antigua. He died childless and almost destitute, and the legislature voted £300 per annum to his widow, who died at Hampton Court Palace on 2 May 1830. His career mirrored the meteoric rise and downfall of absentee sugar planters in Britain.

W. P. COURTNEY, *rev.* ANDREW J. O'SHAUGHNESSY

Sources V. L. Oliver, ed., *Caribbeana*, 6 (1919), 97–8 · HoP, *Commons, 1754–90* · HoP, *Commons, 1790–1820* · *The historical and the posthumous memoirs of Sir Nathaniel William Wraxall, 1772–1784*, ed. H. B. Wheatley, 5 vols. (1884) · D. Morris, *Thomas Hearne and his landscape* (1989) · *Virginia Gazette* (30 July 1772) · *Virginia Gazette* (23 Dec 1775) · GEC, *Peerage* · PRO, CO 9/31, 152/57

Archives University of British Columbia, corresp. and papers | BL, corresp. with first earl of Liverpool, Add. MSS 38203–38204, 38230–38234, 38311, 38471–38472, 38580

Likenesses T. Hearne, portrait, V&A

Wealth at death almost destitute: GEC, *Peerage*

Payne, Robert (*d.* 1593), writer on agriculture and entrepreneur, probably came from Nottinghamshire. Nothing is known of his family or his early life. He was the author of a single folio containing miscellaneous information for farmers and landowners, *The Vale Mans Table: Herein is Taught … howe to Drain Moores*, dated 16 November 1583. Payne adopts a jovial tone, acknowledging that some might mock his efforts, but asserting that his methods are fail-safe, dispensing advice on how to measure woods from a distance, use a compass, drain bogs and wet moors, as well as providing a table of years from the reign of William the Conqueror onwards. There is also a poem which criticizes ineffective citizens who let ground lie fallow and fail to benefit their fellows, and a plea that the work be sold at 6*d.*, not 2*s.* 6*d.*, as Payne had discovered booksellers charging, indicating that there may have been an earlier edition. Payne gives his address as Paines End.

Payne was patronized by Sir Francis Willoughby in the late 1580s and was engaged in projects to grow woad and produce jersey wool for stockings in Nottinghamshire. It was probably through Willoughby's connections with Phane Becher, a London businessman who had settled in Cork, that Payne was sent over to Munster with a view to preparing the way for twenty-five of his neighbours to follow afterwards. Payne obtained a freehold of 600 acres on the Munster plantation and began to investigate the possibility of establishing an ironworks in Kinalmeaky, which would have been overseen by an English manager, and would have used the woods that Willoughby had bought in the area. Payne appears not to have been the most scrupulous of businessmen and there was friction between him and Willoughby over the stockings project.

Payne's most significant work, a treatise entitled *A brife description of Ireland, made in this yeere 1589, by Robert Payne, unto xxv of his partners, for whom he is undertaker there* (1589), may have been written to entice his fellow workers in Nottingham to join in a similar project in Ireland. Payne's short treatise is a piece of colonialist propaganda designed to persuade English men and women that life in Ireland was better than they could expect in England. It was perhaps modelled on the example of Thomas Harriot's *Briefe and True Report of the New Found Land of Virginia* (1588), which had served a similar purpose (Harriot was included in the census of the plantation on 12 May 1589). Nevertheless it contains many useful and probably accurate eyewitness observations of Irish life, schools, agriculture, diet, society, and town life. There is also an important reference to the influence of Bartolomé de las Casas's writings in the British Isles. The *Brife Description* was evidently popular enough to be reprinted with some additions in 1590. Payne gives his address as his house at 'Poynes-End'.

Payne was made agent for Becher in Kinalmeaky in 1590, but was dismissed in 1591 when faulty accounts and other financial irregularities were discovered. In 1592 he was imprisoned in London at the behest of Phane Becher, and died in 1593.   ANDREW HADFIELD

Sources R. Payne, *A brief description of Ireland*, ed. A. Smith (1841) • M. MacCarthy-Morrogh, *The Munster plantation: English migration to southern Ireland, 1583–1641* (1986) • R. S. Smith, 'A woad-growing project at Wollaton in the 1580s', *Transactions of the Thoroton Society*, 65 (1961), 27–46

Archives U. Nott., Middleton MSS

Payne, Robert (1596–1651), Church of England clergyman and natural philosopher, was born in Abingdon, Berkshire, the son of Robert Payne (*d.* 1628), a wealthy woollen draper and four times mayor of the town, and his wife, Martha, daughter of William Branch, also of Abingdon. After attending the local Roysse Grammar School, Robert matriculated a gentleman-commoner at Christ Church, Oxford, on 5 July 1611, graduating BA on 4 July 1614 and proceeding MA exactly three years later. In 1612 he contributed a poem to *Iusta Oxoniensium*, a university volume grieving the death of Henry, prince of Wales, and another poem in 1619 to *Funebria sacra*, lamenting the death of Queen Anne. His surviving notebooks from this period attest to his developing interest in natural philosophy, in particular the philosophy of Roger Bacon, as well as to his embarking on the study of Hebrew.

Like many other scientifically minded scholars of the time Payne was reluctant to take holy orders and proceed with a clerical career, and he thus migrated in 1624 to the newly created Pembroke College where he became second foundation fellow. Two years later he stood candidate for the Gresham professorship of astronomy, vacant following the death of Edmund Gunter, but lost to another Oxford hopeful, Henry Gellibrand. An unpublished facetious poem also suggests his being, in 1626, an unsuccessful candidate for a Christ Church proctorship. However, he achieved some financial security when, after the death of his father in February 1628, he inherited a sizeable property. By 1630 Payne's scientific accomplishments had recommended him to the mathematician Sir Charles Cavendish and his brother William, successively earl, marquess, and duke of Newcastle, and the latter conferred on him the rectorship of Tormarton, Gloucestershire, that was in his gift. The living was certainly intended to serve as a sinecure for Payne, who was employed as the earl's chaplain and secretary. Consequently, his absence from Tormarton nearly resulted in his suspension in 1632. One of the delicate tasks with which Payne was charged was negotiating Ben Jonson's gratuity for the two masques he wrote on the occasion of the visits of Charles I in 1633 and 1634 to Welbeck Abbey and Bolsover Castle respectively. Jonson was effusive in praising Payne, his 'beloved friend' further intimating to Newcastle his joy in 'the good friendship and fellowship of my right learned friend Mr Payne' (*Ben Jonson*, 1.212–13).

For almost a decade Payne served as a key figure in the intellectual and scientific circle around the Cavendish brothers that extended to include other practitioners, such as William Oughtred, Walter Warner, John Pell, and Thomas Hobbes. Indeed, Payne was an intimate friend of the philosopher of Malmesbury and appears to have played a significant role in the development of the latter's optical theories, as well as his mechanistic philosophy more generally. It is quite likely that 'Short tract on first principles', usually attributed to Hobbes, was actually written by Payne—certainly the manuscript is in his handwriting. On similar grounds, another short treatise traditionally attributed to Hobbes, 'Considerations touching the facility or difficulty of the motions of a horse', should likewise be credited to Payne. During the mid-1630s Payne translated, for the benefit of Sir Charles Cavendish, Galileo's *Della scienza mecanica* and Benedetto Castelli's 'Della misura dell'acque correnti', both from manuscripts communicated to Sir Charles by Mersenne. He was also engaged in a variety of chemical experiments with the earl of Newcastle.

In 1638 Newcastle was entrusted with the education of Charles, prince of Wales, and with his move to London the Welbeck group dispersed. Payne returned to Oxford as canon of Christ Church, retaining contacts with Sir Charles and Hobbes through correspondence. Thus, for example, Payne was among those who circulated copies of Hobbes's *Elements of Law*. With the outbreak of the civil war and the removal of the court to Oxford, Payne was appointed royal chaplain, and on 1 November 1642 the degree of DD was conferred on him. In 1646 Payne was deprived of his Tormarton living and two years later he was not only expelled by the parliamentary visitors from Christ Church (whose treasurer he then was) but briefly imprisoned in London while a search was made of his property. Following his release Payne retired to his sister's house in Abingdon, occasionally visiting Sir William Backhouse at Swallowfield, Sir George Stonehouse at Radley, Berkshire, and the third earl of Devonshire at Latimers, Buckinghamshire. Payne's surviving correspondence with Gilbert Sheldon attests not only to the modest role he played in keeping the royalist cause alive following the execution of Charles I, but also to his continued intellectual activity. He was instrumental in the diffusion of the ideas of Hobbes, Descartes, and Gassendi in Oxford and elsewhere in England, but his efforts to defend Hobbes in the face of the growing hostility towards him from the Anglican establishment—some members of whom Payne actually accused of provoking Hobbes to embrace a hostile attitude towards the church—ended in failure.

Payne drew up his will on 16 May 1649, apparently during a serious bout of sickness, making his sister Martha executor and chief beneficiary of his estate. Though Payne recovered his health remained frail. By summer 1651 he had moved to Swallowfield where he died, unmarried, in early November. George Morley's eulogy of his friend is indicative of the high esteem in which Payne was regarded by contemporaries. No one, Morley wrote to Sheldon, was

> better made for a friend at all parts and to all purposes than he was. His Moralls were as good as his Intellectualls, and his Intellectualls such as I knew noe man had better: and both accompanied with a modesty allmost to an excesse. (*Walker rev.*, 176)

MORDECHAI FEINGOLD

Sources Wood, *Ath. Oxon.: Fasti* (1820), 49 • E. Ashmole, *The antiquities of Berkshire*, 1 (1719), 118–19 • W. H. Rylands, ed., *The four visitations of Berkshire*, 1, Harleian Society, 56 (1907), 63 • S. A. Strong, ed., *A catalogue of letters and other historical documents exhibited in the library at Welbeck* (1903), 237–40 [exhibition catalogue] • J. O. Halliwell, ed., *A collection of letters illustrative of the progress of science in England from the reign of Queen Elizabeth to that of Charles the second* (1841), 65–9 • *Ben Jonson*, ed. C. H. Herford, P. Simpson, and E. M. Simpson, 11 vols. (1925–52), vol. 1, pp. 212–13 • *Theologian and Ecclesiastic*, 6 (1848), 165–74, 217–24 • J. Jacquot, 'Sir Charles Cavendish and his learned friends', *Annals of Science*, 8 (1952), 13–27, 175–91 • *The correspondence of Thomas Hobbes*, ed. N. Malcolm, 2 (1994), 872–7 • M. Feingold, 'An early translator of Galileo and a friend of Hobbes: Robert Payne of Oxford', *The light of nature*, ed. J. North and J. Roach (1985), 265–80 • *Walker rev.*, 176 • Bodl. Oxf., MS Savile 41, fols. 145–163v • BL, Harleian MS 6796, fols. 297–308, 310–16, 317–39 • BL, Harleian MS 6492 • BL, Lansdowne MS 93, fol. 179 • BL, Lansdowne MS 841, fol. 92 • BL, Lansdowne MS 842, fol. 21r–21v • PRO, PROB 11/219

Payne, Roger (bap. 1738, d. 1797), bookbinder, was born at Eton, where he was baptized on 8 December 1738, the second of the five children of Thomas Payne, bookbinder (d. 1759), and Elizabeth Godwin (d. 1762). Shortly after his birth the Paynes moved to Windsor, but they were back in Eton by November 1747.

Payne and his younger brother Thomas took over their father's binding business after his death in May 1759. They worked for Walter Bowman in whose account for 1759 and 1760 they are mentioned as bookbinders in Eton. In 1761 Bowman refers to 'Roger Payne of Windsor', but in the following year he is again mentioned as 'Roger Payne of Eton'. A 1757 Birmingham Virgil is signed 'Eton. Bound by R. Payne'. It was presented by Henry Sleech to his pupil P. Bouverie in 1764 and is now at Cambridge University Library. Only a few bindings of Payne's Eton period are known. Both Roger and his brother Thomas are still mentioned as bookbinders in Eton in 1765 and they occur in the *Nugae Etonenses* of c.1766. About this time Roger Payne went to London, where, according to Dibdin, he worked for a few years for Thomas Osborne, bookseller of Gray's Inn (d. 1767). Though Payne does not mention Osborne in his bills or letters, he does refer to another bookseller, Samuel Baker of York Street, for whom he bound a copy of Edmund Spenser's *Faerie Queene* in 1772. In the late 1760s and early 1770s Payne was probably working independently in Leicester Square, having been set up in business by his namesake (but no relation) Thomas Payne, bookseller in Castle Street, Mews Gate. It is clear from several files and letters that Payne worked for Thomas Payne, paying off (some of) his debts.

Payne was joined in London by his brother Thomas and the brothers worked together, probably most of the time and certainly up to 1796. They both worked for A. M. Storer MP (d. 1799) and there are several fairly plain bindings signed by Roger and Thomas, probably dating from the 1770s, in Storer's library (now at Eton College). Another patron of Roger Payne during the late seventies was Michael Wodhull (1740–1816). An early binding for him covers a copy of Giordano Bruno, *De progressu et lampade venatoria logicorum* (1587), bought by Wodhull in 1778 for 2s. 6d. and bound by Payne for 4s. 6d. (B. Quaritch, Catalogue 166, Jan 1897, 195).

Both David Wier and his wife appeared to have worked for Payne. Mrs Wier, who apparently was a capable mender and restorer as well as 'an excellent hand at ruling red … lines on prayer books' (Jaffray, 4.182), was, according to Dibdin, 'pretty constantly and most successfully employed' (Dibdin, 517) by him, probably before 1774, while her husband (according to the same source) worked for Payne from 1777. The partnership was not a happy one—'Wier happened to be as fond of "*barley broth*" as his associate … They were always quarrelling' (ibid., 515)—and they parted company.

The bookseller John MacKinlay (d. 1821) also provided Payne with work. Throughout the 1790s Payne worked for the Revd C. M. Cracherode (1730–1799), whose library, now in the British Library, contains well over thirty books bound by him between 1790 and 1798. A 1694 Cambridge Euripides, bought in 1794, has Payne's bill (BL, C19.e.3). Another of Payne's patrons whose library is also in the British Library was the Hon. Thomas Grenville (1755–1846). He served many distinguished book collectors of the time, such as Topham Beauclerck (1739–1780), the author William Beckford (1759–1844), John Dent MP (1750?–1826), Colonel Stanley (d. 1818), the topographical author Sir Richard Colt Hoare (1758–1838) for whom Payne worked from c.1795 to c.1797 and for whom several bindings with their bills survive, and, best known of all, Earl Spencer (1758–1834), whose library is now in the John Rylands University Library, Manchester. Payne worked for him both directly and through the bookseller Thomas Payne, and Lord Spencer's 1480 Lascaris (JRL 7319) was bound by 'The Book-binders Roger and Thomas Payne' in dark blue straight-grain morocco. Several of Payne's bindings for Lord Spencer have either manuscript notes or bills, and several more are mentioned in the bookseller Thomas Payne's book bills to Lord Spencer, preserved at Althorp.

Roger Payne's bills and letters frequently describe in some detail the work carried out, and their tone is on the whole one of self-satisfaction and pride in his craftsmanship, as well as a justification for his prices. From these it is clear that he himself did some repair work, as well as doing both the forwarding and the finishing, and that, contrary to popular belief, he did not cut his own tools. He did, however, pay some attention to matching the tool design with the subject of the book in question. He also worked according to a pattern which, at least in some cases, was either specified or approved by the future owner. His typical and best-known bindings were usually in brown russia; red, blue, or green straight-grain morocco; or smooth olive morocco, frequently with purple or brown end-leaves and tall green headbands. Many have leather joints and doublures consisting of a leather frame and a paper centre panel. He used mainly small, naturalistic tools and most of the typical bindings of the 1790s have very elaborately tooled spines, frequently with two or three panels lettered, and the date of printing nearly always in Roman numerals. He was an excellent craftsman and, notwithstanding his reputation for a fondness for strong drink and his self-confessed ill health, his finishing was first rate. He charged his physician, Dr Benjamin Moseley, a special price out of obligation for the latter's professional services and several letters and bills exist in which reference is made to his health and to the doctor's orders and 'Learned Advice'. Nevertheless, his health deteriorated and his last work, the binding of Homer's *Iliad* on vellum (Venice, 1504) for Lord Spencer, remained unfinished.

The original watercolour drawing of Payne in his workshop is preserved with R. Gough, *Account of a … Missal … for John Duke of Bedford* (London, J. Nichols for T. Payne, 1794) (Shawyer and Haywood, 2.2715); it was used by Sylvester Harding for his well-known etching made for Thomas Payne, a proof of which is in the British Museum, and a smaller engraving by William Angus illustrates Dibdin's *The Bibliographical Decameron* (1817). In these portraits he looks tall, thin, and unhealthy, with sunken cheeks and hollow eyes. His verse in praise of barley-wine accompanying the bill to Mr Evans for binding Barry's *Wines of the Ancients* (Dibdin, 509), his household accounts as quoted by Thomas Payne's son (ibid., 508), and other near-contemporary accounts suggest his intemperate habits, and in an undated letter to Dr Moseley, accompanying his copy of Fortunius Licetus, *De Monstris* (Amsterdam, 1665), he describes himself as 'at times having been hardly able to stand to work without very great pains nights & Days even 30 Years since & upwards'.

Payne died, unmarried, on 20 November 1797 at his home at Duke's Court, St Martin's Lane, and was buried six days later in the churchyard of St Martin-in-the-Fields at the expense of his old benefactor Thomas Payne who, according to J. Nichols, had supported him financially for the last eight years of his life (Nichols, 3.736–7).

MIRJAM M. FOOT

Sources account books, bills, and letters, JRL, Spencer Collection · M. M. Foot, *The Henry Davis gift, a collection of bookbindings*, 1 (1978), 96–114 · Nichols, *Lit. anecdotes*, 3.736–7; 8.485 · T. F. Dibdin, *The bibliographical decameron*, 2 (1817), 506–19 · *GM*, 1st ser., 67 (1797), 1070–71 · R. Birley, 'Roger and Thomas Payne: with some account of their earlier bindings', *The Library*, 5th ser., 15 (1960), 33–41 · J. Jaffray, 'A collection of manuscripts relating to the art and trade of bookbinding', 1864, BL [typescript], vol. 4, p. 185 · C. Davenport, *Roger Payne* (1929) · C. H. Timperley, *Encyclopaedia of literary and typographical anecdote*, 2nd edn (1842), 795–6 · H. M. Nixon, *Five centuries of English bookbinding* (1978), no. 72 · M. M. Foot, *Studies in the history of bookbinding* (1993), no. 33 · N. M. Shawyer and J. Hayward, *The Rothschild library: a catalogue of the collection of eighteenth-century printed books and manuscripts formed by Lord Rothschild*, 2 (1954), 2700, 2705, 2708, 2715–16 · R. Colt Hoare, account book, 1776–1835, Hornby Library, Liverpool, 2 vols. · bills and letters, Eton · 'Thomas Payne's bookbills', Althorp, Spencer Collection · bills and letters, BL, Grenville and Cratcherode libraries · bills and letters, Morgan L., Toovey collection · bills and letters, Harvard U., Houghton L. · bills and letters, Hunt. L. · bills and letters, Trinity Cam. · parish register (baptism), Eton · parish register (burial), 1775–1802, St Martin-in-the-Fields, fol. 443

Archives Harvard U., Houghton L., bills and letters · Hunt. L., bills and letters · JRL, bills for binding [some photocopies] · Trinity Cam., bills and letters | Althorp, Northamptonshire, Spencer collection, bills and letters in 'Thomas Payne's bookbills' · BL, Grenville and Cratcherode libraries, bills and letters · Eton, A. M. Storer's library, bills and letters · Hornby Library, Liverpool, Sir Richard Colt Hoare's account book, bills, and letters · JRL, Spencer

collection, bills and letters · Morgan L., Toovey collection, bills and letters
Likenesses watercolour drawing, c.1794, repro. in N. M. V. Baron Rothschild, *Two bindings by Roger Payne in the library of Lord Rothschild* (1947), pl. I · W. Angus, engraving (after watercolour drawing, c.1794), repro. in Dibdin, *Bibliographical decameron*, vol. 2, p. 510 · S. Harding, etching (after watercolour drawing, c.1794), BM; repro. in Nichols, *Lit. anecdotes*, vol. 3, p. 737
Wealth at death believed to have died penniless: Nichols, *Lit. anecdotes*, 3.736–7; *GM*, 1070–71

Payne, Thomas (1716x18–1799), bookseller and publisher, was baptized on 26 May 1719 in Brackley, Northamptonshire, the younger son of Olive or Oliver Payne, and his wife, Martha. His obituary and epitaph (*GM*, 1799) variously describe him as being in his eighty-second year and aged eighty-two at the time of his death suggesting that he was born between 1716 and 1718. From c.1732 he was an assistant to his elder brother Olive (sometimes Oliver) Payne, a bookseller at Horace's Head, Round Court, opposite York Buildings in the Strand, London, who is said to have begun the practice of publishing regular catalogues of his stock. Following his brother's bankruptcy in March 1739 Thomas took over the business and issued his own catalogue in February 1741. In 1745 he married Elizabeth Taylor (d. in or before 1775), the sister of T. Taylor, a bookseller in Castle Street near the Mews Gate, Leicester Fields. In 1750 Payne succeeded to the business and premises of his brother-in-law, which were rebuilt in an L-shape. Thereafter his shop became known as the Literary Coffee House, from the many notable authors and collectors who frequented his salerooms.

After 1755 Payne steadily prospered both as a publisher and as a bookseller, and his name is to be found, together with those of other booksellers, on the imprints of many hundreds of works in all subjects. He was particularly involved in the publication of Richard Gough's enlarged 1789 edition of Camden's *Britannia*, having financed all the engravings in return for the bulk of the copies of the new edition. However, he is primarily remembered as an antiquarian bookseller and for his part in disposing of the collections of many notable antiquaries and book collectors. Between 1755 and 1790 he issued annual (and on occasion semi-annual) catalogues of not fewer than 200 pages, most of which are listed by John Nichols in *Literary Anecdotes* (3.655–60). Among the many notable collections he sold were those of Francis Peck, Ralph Thoresby, Benjamin Kennicott, and Francis Grose. He also visited Palgrave, Suffolk, in 1768 where he purchased many of the most valuable works from the library of Thomas Martin. Payne's success appears to have been based upon his shrewd purchases, together with a growing reputation among his customers for fair dealing, resulting in his widely known sobriquet Honest Tom Payne.

Thomas and Elizabeth Payne had two sons and two daughters. The elder son, also named Thomas *Payne (1752–1831), was in partnership with his father from about 1776 and took over responsibility for the business when his father retired to Finchley in 1790. One daughter, Sally, married Admiral James *Burney on 6 September 1785, and

Thomas Payne (1716x18–1799), by Louis François Gérard van der Puyl

the other, Sarah, married John Payne (possibly her cousin or nephew), who worked for her brother Thomas.

Payne is also known for his charitable works, notably his support of the impoverished and unrelated bookbinder Roger Payne for the last eight years of Roger's life, and paying for his burial. Payne also supported other members of his family in financial difficulty.

Payne died on 2 February 1799 at Finchley, and was buried there on 9 February alongside his wife and brother. His obituary in the *Gentleman's Magazine* describes him as 'warm in his friendships as in his politicks, a convivial cheerful companion', and refers to his 'character of an honest man to the last' (*GM*, 1799). Dibdin describes him in his *Bibliographical decameron* as 'a sterling example of genuine British integrity. There was neither pomp, nor parade, nor knavery, nor vehemence, nor violence, in any thing he said or did' (Dibdin, 436). The poet William Hayley likewise presented Payne's son with an epitaph in verse which was subsequently published in the *Gentleman's Magazine*.

Payne should not be confused with his two contemporary London namesakes: the bookseller at 14 Duke Street and the bookbinder of 24 Charlotte Street.

DAVID STOKER

Sources *GM*, 1st ser., 69 (1799), 171–2 · *GM*, 1st ser., 101/1 (1831), 275–6 · T. F. Dibdin, *The bibliographical decameron*, 2 (1817), 435–7 · I. Maxted, *The London book trades, 1775–1800: a preliminary checklist of members* (1977) · H. R. Plomer and others, *A dictionary of the printers and booksellers who were at work in England, Scotland, and Ireland from 1668 to 1725* (1922) · Nichols, *Lit. anecdotes*, 3.655–60; 736–7 and 6.438–40 · W. Hayley, 'Epitaph in memory of Mr Thomas Payne', *GM*, 1st ser., 69 (1799), 236 · Nichols, *Illustrations*, 5.428, 435 · D. Stoker, 'The ill-gotten library of "Honest Tom" Martin', *Property* *of a gentleman: the formation, organisation and dispersal of the private library, 1620–1920*, St Paul's Bibliographies (1991), 90–112 · G. Baker, *The history and antiquities of the county of Northampton*, 1 (1822–30), 586 · DNB

Likenesses L. F. G. van der Puyl, portrait, New York Historical Society [*see illus.*] · engraving, repro. in Dibdin, *Bibliographical decameron*

Payne, Thomas (1752–1831), bookseller, was born in London on 10 October 1752, the eldest of the four children of Thomas *Payne (1716×18–1799), bookseller and publisher, and his wife, Elizabeth, *née* Taylor (*d.* in or before 1775). He was educated by M. Metayer in Charterhouse Square, London, and trained in modern and classical languages to equip him for the family business. He entered into partnership with his father in 1776, and succeeded him in 1790.

The original L-shaped premises at Mews Gate, Castle Street, London, acted as a coffee house and bookshop. It rapidly became too cramped for the many men of letters—including Charles Lamb—who visited and 88 Schomberg House, Pall Mall, was acquired. Schomberg House soon became widely recognized as a popular literary centre. Payne traded alone after his father's death in 1799 and then took into partnership his apprentice Henry Foss in 1813. The business was renamed Payne and Foss, though Charles Lamb playfully called it 'Pain & Fuss' (*Early Diary of Frances Burney*, 2.130–31).

In 1817 Payne became master of the Stationers' Company. By 1820 his poor health meant that he had to give up travelling in search of books. Previous successes had included large collections from the libraries of Dean Lloyd, the Revd Henry Homer, and the last keeper of the seals of France, M. Chrétien François de Lamoignon, as well as the Borromeo collection of novels and romances. Such acquisitions meant that moving to the larger 81 Pall Mall became necessary in 1821.

Payne retired in 1825 and was succeeded by his nephew John Payne, but Payne and Foss continued until 1850. John Payne and his wife, Sarah Burney, then retired to Rome, where they spent their remaining years in the company of such distinguished figures as Cardinal Antonelli.

Thomas Payne died at 81 Pall Mall on 15 March 1831, after an attack of apoplexy on the 8th. He was buried in St Martin-in-the-Fields on 24 March 1831. At the time of his death he was considered the father of the London booksellers.   J.-M. ALTER

Sources GM, 1st ser., 101/1 (1831), 275–6 · Nichols, *Lit. anecdotes*, vol. 8 · *The early diary of Frances Burney, 1768–1778*, 2 (1889) · P. A. H. Brown, *London publishers and printers, c.1800–1870* (1982) · I. Maxted, *The London book trades, 1775–1800: a preliminary checklist of members* (1977) · T. F. Dibdin, *The bibliographical decameron*, 3 vols. (1817), vol. 2, 172; vol. 3, pp. 149, 161–80
Archives BL, letters to Lord Spencer

Payne, William (1649/50–1697), Church of England clergyman, was the son of William Payne of Hutton, Essex. He attended Brentwood Free School, Essex, before being admitted sizar at Magdalene College, Cambridge, in May 1665, aged fifteen. He graduated BA in 1669, proceeding MA in 1672. On 6 July 1671 he became a fellow at Magdalene, and remained so until 1675 when he married Elisabeth Squire, daughter of the vicar of St Leonard, Shoreditch. He was ordained deacon at Ely on 19 March 1671 and priest at Peterborough on 22 September 1672. In 1673 Payne was appointed rector of Wormshill in Kent, to which he added the parish of Frinsted in the same county the following year. In June 1681 he became rector of St Mary, Whitechapel, and quickly established a reputation in London as a fine preacher. Owing to his interest in experimental philosophy he was also in that year admitted as a fellow of the Royal Society. He was granted a DD by Cambridge in 1689.

Payne's first works, published between 1685 and 1688, were a series of tracts against Catholic doctrines such as the adoration of the host, communion under one kind, and the celibacy of priests. All these tracts went through several editions and were subsequently collected in Edmund Gibson's *Preservative Against Popery* (1738). Following the revolution of 1688 Payne, a latitudinarian, strongly supported the so-called Comprehension Bill introduced into parliament in 1689. Thomas Long, however, was undoubtedly speaking for the majority of the clergy when he denounced the bill in his pamphlet *Vox cleri* (1690). In *An Answer to 'Vox cleri'* (1690), Payne replied that far from bringing schismatics into the church comprehension would make dissenters friends; that it was a good thing for the church to make alterations 'as she thinks fit, whether the Dissenters propose or agree in them or not' (p. 7); and that those high-churchmen who threatened to go to Rome were putting too much stock in things indifferent.

Payne also became engaged in the controversy surrounding the oath of allegiance to William and Mary imposed in 1689 upon all beneficed clergy. Those who refused and were deprived of their livings were scathing in their denunciations of those clergy, like Payne, who had been preachers of the doctrine of non-resistance under James II and who were now supporters of the new monarchs. Payne published a defence of himself in 1691 entitled *An answer to a printed letter to Dr William Payne, concerning non-resistance and other reasons for not taking the oath*. While admitting that he had indeed preached non-resistance, he had not considered 'if any unseen and extraordinary Case should ever happen to be an exception against it' (p. 18). In the extraordinary case of King James positive law had had to give way to the 'greater Law of Necessity' (p. 10).

Possibly in reward for his support for royal policy and legitimacy after the revolution, in 1689 Payne was appointed lecturer at St Mildred Poultry, London, and chaplain-in-ordinary to William and Mary. In 1690 he was given a commission under the great seal to be visitor-royal over all London churches that were exempt from the jurisdiction of the bishop of London. Its purpose was to suppress clandestine marriages, especially in the notorious centres of St James, Duke's Place, and Holy Trinity Minories. More profitably for Payne he was authorized to appoint his own registrar and issue marriage licences for these places.

However, in 1695 Archbishop Tenison and Bishop Compton of London complained of the threat that Payne's commission posed to episcopal jurisdiction and pointed out to the lords justices that he was abusing his position—and depriving the crown of the revenue due to it under the Marriage Duty Act—by issuing blank licences. The patent was revoked, and Payne failed in his attempts to bargain some compensation for his loss of income, which he estimated at £500 per annum. In 1694 Payne was installed as a prebendary of Westminster.

Payne was also the author of *Family Religion* (1691) and *A Discourse of Repentance* (1693). A collection of his sermons, *Discourses upon Several Practical Subjects* (1698), was published posthumously by Joseph Powell. During the last two years of his life Payne preached a series of sermons on the Trinity in defence of William Sherlock. These sermons were published in 1696 under the title *The Mystery of the Christian Faith and Oft-Blessed Trinity Vindicated*. Payne was working on a book on the subject when he died in London on 20 February 1697. He was buried in St Mary, Whitechapel, four days later. MARTIN GREIG

Sources Venn, *Alum. Cant.* · DNB · J. Powell, preface, in W. Payne, *Discourses upon several practical subjects* (1698) · *CSP dom.*, 1689–90; 1695 · P. Cunich and others, *A history of Magdalene College, 1428–1988* (1994) · *Fasti Angl., 1541–1857*, [Ely], 86

Payne, William (1717/18–1782), carpenter and constable, was probably born in London; details of his parents and background are unknown. He is now best remembered for his activities from the late 1750s in policing London streets and as an agitator against the capital's Roman Catholic community, but he worked first as a carpenter. He was apprenticed to a master in Bell Yard, north of Temple Bar, on the border between the City and Westminster; he became a journeyman about 1740 and in the 1750s set up in the same street, purchasing membership of the Carpenters' Company in 1755; he lived in Bell Yard for the remainder of his life. By about 1750 he had married Elizabeth (b. c.1722, d. in or after 1794); the first of their children, William, was born in 1754 or 1755, and was followed by at least four daughters. Details of Payne's carpentry activities are scant; however, reports in the *London Gazette* show that he was still in business in the early 1770s; in 1774 he applied unsuccessfully for the post of Middlesex county surveyor. In later life he reportedly neglected the business which, when inherited by his son, provided only a meagre living, leaving the family in a 'Distressed Situation'.

Payne's negligence owed much to his growing involvement in local government, and in particular in social control and policing. In 1759 he was elected headborough—junior partner to the constable—for the Rolls liberty; thereafter he became involved with the recently re-established Society for the Reformation of Manners, dedicated to ending local incidents of profanity, illegal trading, and sabbath-breaking. Though his precise religious affiliation is unknown, Payne's membership of a society popular among lower middle-class dissenters, Calvinistic Methodists, and Wesleyan Methodists, hints at his perspective: characterized by the condemnation of sin,

intense protestantism, and a concomitant hostility to Catholicism or 'popery', which he saw as a threat to English political and religious liberty. During his association with the reformation society Payne focused on prosecuting sexual misdemeanours, for which he gained support from local traders, but also criticism from a middling and upper class suspicious of the society's fervent puritanism. He was depicted as the 'Little Carpenter' in a 1763 cartoon 'Dr Squintum's Exaltation, or, The Reformation' in which the Calvinistic Methodist leader George Whitefield was shown addressing supporters of the society shortly before its collapse under the burden of debt incurred in fighting counter-litigation.

In the following year Payne was sworn in as an extra constable with city-wide powers of arrest. He proved notably assiduous as a 'peace officer': according to local residents, he 'discharged his office in so faithful manner as to become a Terror to all Persons keeping disorderly houses as well as Common prostitutes, Pickpockets etc.' (CLRO, January 1776, court of aldermen papers); his remarkable performance was still attracting reminiscent praise in the early nineteenth century. A study of city magistrates' records has documented his prowess: between 1775 and 1780 Payne was responsible for three-quarters of recorded arrests of streetwalkers for soliciting. He worked closely with the City marshals and their assistants in policing crowds and public meetings, and was also active in prosecuting breaches of building regulations. In the 1760s, a decade of high prices and labour troubles, he policed markets and prosecuted forestallers. A charge that he had colluded in prosecuting a butcher to obtain a promised reward was investigated by the Treasury solicitor in 1767, but not substantiated. Payne for his part strove to present himself as a watchdog for the public interest: in 1766 he wrote to the chairman of the Lords committee on high prices to expose the misdeeds of one unscrupulous carcase butcher; in 1772, he presented to the Lords a new scheme for reducing the price of all sorts of provisions.

At the same time that Payne was exerting himself against market offences, he was particularly diligent in policing the city's Roman Catholic community. The recent decision to tolerate Catholicism in Quebec had led many anti-Catholics to fear that religious toleration might be extended in Britain itself. In summer 1765 Payne began to explore the London Catholic devotional world, inspecting mass houses, such as that on Ropemaker's Alley, Moorfields; later that year he made his first related arrest, of two men accused of hearing mass. His campaign against Catholic teachers and priests continued for five years, during which time he brought at least thirty prosecutions; these included that of John Baptist Malony, convicted in 1767 at Surrey assizes and imprisoned for life for practising as a priest (Malony was pardoned in 1771). Though he worked in association with men like Thomas Gates, the city marshal, Payne's endeavours were largely self-motivated. He gained some financial reward for his efforts (£100 for the conviction of Malony), and was charged by his critics with seeking gain only, but his actions were more probably driven by obsessive religious conviction.

Payne's zeal brought him critical notice from prominent political figures. To Lord Shelburne, Payne was 'the lowest and most despicable of mankind' (Cobbett, *Parl. hist.* 19, col. 1145), while Lord Chief Justice William Mansfield denigrated him as a 'very illiterate man; [who] knows nothing of Latin, the language in which Mass is said' (Barnard, 176–7). In return Payne showed his contempt for what he regarded as a pusillanimous and potentially traitorous judiciary. His pamphlet, *Cry Aloud and Spare not, or, An Alarm to All the Protestants of Great Britain and Ireland*, published under the pseudonym of 'the Little English Carpenter', highlighted the paradox that a pro-Catholic judge should be employed by a state threatened by a Jacobite and popish conspiracy.

By the 1770s Payne was a notable if not notorious figure, frequently mentioned in the press. The extent of positive support for him is suggested by the fact that in autumn 1778 he topped the poll in a common council election for the post of marshalman, joining a team of six working under the city's two marshals. Not surprisingly, Payne was active in the immediate aftermath of this in attempts by Lord George Gordon's Protestant Association to repeal the Catholic Relief Act (1778). According to Gordon himself, at a crowded meeting in Coachmakers' Hall in 1780, 'Mr Payne and his son and connections were the most active People' in overriding objections on the part of a nervous committee and insisting on a plan to march *en masse* on the House of Commons with an anti-Catholic petition (BL, Add. MS 42129, fol. 8). Payne led the City of London division on this march, and was later identified by a magistrate as having incited the crowds outside parliament at the start of six days of rioting. Payne has—unusually—left no trace of his activities (on either side) in the records of the disturbances, and a contemporary verse suggests that prostitutes enjoyed unusually free rein at this time; however, on 27 June he wrote to the mayor with a scheme for the recapture of prisoners freed when the rioters stormed Newgate gaol.

Thereafter Payne returned to his official duties. He was still making arrests in September 1782, but died in London on 27 November; his death was noticed in the press and in the *Gentleman's Magazine*, which dubbed him the 'little Carpenter', and 'the scourge and terror of the city prostitutes' (52.552). Payne was survived by his wife, four daughters, and his son, William (*d.* 1833), who inherited his carpentry business. His descendants continued his connection with City government. According to an early twentieth-century report, they had included 'a judge, two coroners, clerk to the sitting magistrates, two principal clerks to the Chamberlain and a Police Receiver' (GL, Noble collection, C 36).

Payne's career is of interest because it provides a well-documented insight into the concerns of an atypical but not wholly unrepresentative member of the eighteenth-century London *petit bourgeoisie*. It illustrates the significance of a culture of clubs and associations and the workings of local democracy among a lower middle class who found themselves as much scorned by their social superiors for their activities as they were themselves contemptuous of illegal traders and prostitutes. Francis Place, who

himself served an apprenticeship in Bell Yard shortly before Payne's death, emphasized the immorality of this milieu—yet Payne's activities suggest rather a keenly if no doubt imperfectly regulated community characterized by a rigorous puritan strain. Payne's own extreme brand of zeal propelled him into a particularly prominent position in a struggle over the issues that concerned him most: not the conventional party political issues of the day, but the contest between (as he saw it) current protestant liberty and potential Catholic tyranny.   JOANNA INNES

Sources Old Bailey sessions papers · J. Oldham, *The Mansfield manuscripts and the growth of English law in the eighteenth century*, 2 vols. (1992) · T. Henderson, *Disorderly women in eighteenth-century London: prostitution and control in the metropolis 1730–1830* (1999) · J. Barnard, *Life of the Rt. Revd. Richard Challoner* (1784) · E. Burton, *Life and times of the Rt. Revd. Bishop Challoner*, 2 vols. (1909), vol. 1 · J. Lesourd, *Les catholiques dans la société anglaise, 1765–1865*, 2 vols. (Paris, 1978), vol. 1 · J. Innes, *Inferior politics: social problems and social policies in eighteenth-century Britain* [forthcoming]
Likenesses caricature, 1763, BM

Payne, William (1760–1830), watercolour painter, was born on 4 March 1760 in London, the son of William Payne (1730–1794), and his wife, Eleanor Vardon (*fl.* 1728–1796). His father was a hop and coal merchant residing in Westminster, but was originally from Burwash in Sussex. In 1778, two years after he had first exhibited at the Society of Artists of Great Britain, Payne obtained a post as a draughtsman in the Board of Ordnance at the Tower of London, where he was instructed by the chief drawing master, Henry Gilder, a protégé of Thomas Sandby. In 1783 he was sent to Plymouth to survey the defences of Plymouth Dock (now Devonport): he spent the next six years mapping the coastal redoubts and making watercolours of the area. By 1786 his technique had advanced far enough for him to send drawings to the Royal Academy. In Plymouth, on 5 February 1785, he married Jane Goodridge (*fl.* 1763–1818); three of their eight children were born there.

Although working initially with the reed pen in a manner close to Paul and Thomas Sandby, Payne invented a number of devices which he used throughout his career. These included dragging colour with the side of the brush, reinforced by striations (parallel lines), to denote broken ground, and vigorously drawn loops of foliage. He also used for his foregrounds a grey pigment—still known as Payne's grey—a compound of Prussian blue, lake, and yellow ochre, which he had first employed in 1783 for a map of redoubts on Maker heights. With neatly applied colours he recorded the local topography, enlivened by well observed figures, thus attracting the praise of Sir Joshua Reynolds for some quarry views (exh. RA, 1788–9; Stourhead, and priv. coll.). By 1790 he had decided to pursue a career as an artist and drawing-master in London. He now adopted a looser style, which pupils could more readily copy, working with brush outlines (sometimes split, for foliage) rather than the pen, and he made more use of Payne's grey, adding indigo (unfortunately a colour subject to fading) and reddish hues to his pictures. He created landscapes, usually in a small format, with rocks or trees as a framing device, in which peasants converse or sea-farers—some of them smugglers—haul on ropes or load contraband onto pack-horses.

Payne's work was highly admired and he soon became the most fashionable drawing-master of the day. He numbered some professional artists among his pupils, including his eldest son, William Robert (who achieved little success), and John Glover, but he was more sought after as a teacher by aristocratic amateurs. As a result, a craze for manufacturing Payne-like landscapes became a feature of the fashionable London scene. After 1790 he ceased to exhibit for nineteen years and travelled in search of picturesque material to the west country and south Wales (from 1791), and later to the Isle of Wight, the Lake District, and north Wales. Although his pictures still commanded high prices when he started exhibiting again, upon joining the Old Watercolour Society in 1809, within a decade his popularity had declined, as new artists emerged. He attracted one important commission in 1818 from John Trower, an amateur artist, to work up some of Trower's Italian views, but his use of heightened pigments in body colour in the 1820s was hardly successful. The large oil paintings of this period (including a self-portrait now in the Castle Museum, Nottingham, showing a somewhat stern, bespectacled figure) display the same mannered devices.

Payne's innovations, however, had advanced the boundaries of watercolour technique. His initial popularity and extensive teaching practice contributed greatly to the burgeoning interest in watercolour, both as a social accomplishment and as a serious field for collectors. He died in 1830 at his home, 49 Upper Baker Street, Marylebone, Middlesex, and was buried on 12 August at Marylebone parish church. Examples of his work are in the British Museum and the Victoria and Albert Museum in London, the City Museum and Art Gallery, Plymouth, the Royal Albert Memorial Museum and the West Country Studies Library in Exeter, and the Yale Center for British Art, New Haven, Connecticut.   DAVID JAPES

Sources D. Japes, *William Payne—a Plymouth experience* (1992) · M. Hardie, *Water-colour painting in Britain*, ed. D. Snelgrove, J. Mayne, and B. Taylor, 3: *The Victorian period* (1968), 237–9 · I. O. Williams, *Early English watercolours and some cognate drawings by artists born not later than 1785* (1952); repr. (1970), 93–4 · marriage licences, 1758, vicar-general's office, Westminster, London · parish records, St James's, Piccadilly, City Westm. AC [marriages, births, 1758, 1760] · parish register, Plymouth Dock, Stoke Damerel church, 1785, Plymouth and West Devon Record Office, Plymouth [marriages] · board of ordnance records, PRO, MPH 14, 15; WO 51/262–285; MR 1391 · wills and probate, August 1794, August 1830, PRO, Chancery Lane · parish register, Burwash, 1730, E. Sussex RO · parish records, Marylebone parish church, 1830, LMA · rate books, London, 1774–1830
Archives PRO, map of redoubts on Maker heights, MR 1391
Likenesses W. Payne, self-portrait, oils, *c*.1820, Castle Museum, Nottingham
Wealth at death £3300; leasehold house 49, Upper Baker Street: account no. 35052/2, ledger no. 5, Bank of England Corporate Services Department, Archive Section (1830); will, 1830, PRO

Payne, William Henry Schofield (1804–1878), actor and pantomimist, was born in the City of London and was apprenticed to Isaac Cowen, a stockbroker. When he was in his eighteenth year he ran away, and joined a travelling theatre company on the Warwickshire circuit, and rose to play small parts at the Theatre Royal, Birmingham. After returning to London he studied under Joseph Grimaldi and Jack Bologna at Sadler's Wells Theatre, and then obtained an engagement at an East End theatre. In the following year, 1825, he migrated to the Pavilion Theatre, where he remained until 1831, and established a reputation for his hilarious characterization of barons and villains, as well as clowns. He was particularly admired for his skill as a mime artist. At Christmas productions he represented the clown, with Miss Rountree, afterwards his wife, as Columbine. The couple had four children, Harriet Farrell, Annie, Harry (1833–1895), and Frederick (1841–1880), all of whom took to the stage. On 26 December 1831 Payne made his first appearance at Covent Garden Theatre in the pantomime *Hop o' my Thumb and his Brothers*, by Charles Farley, in which he played Madoc Mawr, the Welsh ogre. He and his family played at Covent Garden for several decades, and his son Harry merited the distinction of principal clown at the theatre after the death of Richard Flexmore in 1860. In 1832 Payne senior was still more successful in the pantomime *Puss in Boots*, in which his character was Tasnar, chief of the Long Heads and No Bodies.

During his long career Payne played many parts, ranging from pantomime to tragedy. He was harlequin to Joe Grimaldi's clown at Sadler's Wells in 1827, he was Dandy Lover to young Joe Grimaldi's clown, and made a capital clown himself. He acted in tragedy with Charles Young, Charles Kemble, James Wallack, and Edmund Kean, and on Kean's last appearance (as Othello, Covent Garden, 25 March 1833), it was Payne, then acting Ludovico, who carried him off the stage when he was unable through illness to finish the part. He also figured prominently in grand ballet with Pauline Leroux, Cerito, Carlotta Grisi, the Elsslers, and other dancers of note, and played in state before George IV, William IV, Victoria, Napoleon III, and the Empress Eugénie.

In 1841 Payne was still at Covent Garden, and filled the role of Guy, Earl of Warwick, in the pantomime produced at Christmas. On 31 March 1847 he opened at Vauxhall Gardens in a ballet with his wife and his sister Annie Payne. In 1848 he was engaged by John Knowles for the Theatre Royal, Manchester, and here he remained for seven years, increasing the annual run of the pantomime from its usual 24 nights to 100, and making *Robinson Crusoe* so attractive that it was given on 125 consecutive nights. After leaving Manchester he appeared with his sons at Sadler's Wells in the pantomime of *The Forty Thieves* at Christmas 1854. The Payne family was also frequently seen at the Standard Theatre, the Crystal Palace, and other places. Payne, who was widely regarded by colleagues as a respectable man, died at Calstock House, Beach Street, Dover, on 18 December 1878. A writer in *The Spectator* said: 'The last true mime has departed in the person of W. H. Payne'.   G. C. BOASE, *rev.* BRENDA ASSAEL

Sources D. Pickering, ed., *Encyclopaedia of pantomime* (1993), 152, 82 · Boase, *Mod. Eng. biog.* · Hall, *Dramatic ports.* · *The Era* (22 Dec 1878) · *The Spectator* (28 Dec 1878) · E. Stirling, *Old Drury Lane*, 2 (1881), 204–5 · E. Reid and H. Compton, eds., *The dramatic peerage* [1891], 185–6 · *The life and reminiscences of E. L. Blanchard, with notes from the diary of Wm. Blanchard*, ed. C. W. Scott and C. Howard, 2 vols. (1891) · *CGPLA Eng. & Wales* (1879) · d. cert.

Likenesses R. J. Lane, lithograph, pubd 1838 (with George J. Bennett and Drinkwater Meadows), NPG · lithographs, 1839 · four prints, Harvard TC · lithograph

Wealth at death under £4000: resworn probate, April 1879, *CGPLA Eng. & Wales*

Paynel family (*per. c.*1086–1244), gentry, whose original home may have been Les Moutiers-Hubert in Normandy, was first represented in England by **Ralph Paynel** (*d.* before 1124) whose tenancy-in-chief was valued at over £80 a year in 1086, and who also held a tenancy of Ilbert (I) de Lacy in Yorkshire valued at £9 10s. a year. The Lacy tenancy may have been acquired through a possible marriage to Ilbert's sister or daughter. After 1086 Ralph acquired further estates in Yorkshire and Lincolnshire, including a share of the lands held in 1086 by Richard de Surdeval of Robert, count of Mortain, which may have come to Ralph as a result of a second marriage to a certain Maud, with whom Ralph had four sons and a daughter. The eldest son, Jordan, was provided for with most of the Surdeval estates, married Gertrude, a member of the *Fossard family, and eventually died childless. His estates thus passed to his brother Alexander Paynel (*d.* in or before 1153), the ancestor of the Paynels of Hooton Pagnell. In 1088, when William II faced a baronial rebellion in England, Ralph Paynel served as sheriff of Yorkshire, attended the trial of William de St Calais, bishop of Durham, and was accused by the bishop of invading and seizing his lands. In the period *c.*1090–1100 Ralph refounded Holy Trinity, York, as a dependent priory of the abbey of Marmoutier, Tours. He was also a benefactor of St Mary's Abbey, York, St Peter's Hospital, York, and the abbey of Selby.

Ralph's lands in Drax, Yorkshire, and Middle Rasen, Lincolnshire, passed by 1124 to his eldest surviving son, **William (I) Paynel** (*d.* 1145×7), who may also have secured possession of Les Moutiers-Hubert and Hambye in Normandy through him, and added further holdings in Leicestershire and Nottinghamshire to the Paynel honour. In September 1136 William's castle of Les Moutiers-Hubert was attacked by Geoffrey of Anjou, who opposed King Stephen. William, continuing the Paynel tradition of religious patronage, founded the Augustinian priory of Drax (*c.*1130–39) and the Norman abbey of Hambye (*c.*1145–7), and endowed the monasteries of Selby, Holy Trinity Priory, York, and St Stephen, Caen. William married first a daughter of William, son of Wimund, and sister of Robert d'Avranches, with whom he had four sons and possibly a daughter, and second Avice de Rumilly (*d. c.*1176), daughter and coheir of William Meschin, lord of Egremont, and Cecily de Rumilly, lady of Skipton, and widow of William (II) de Curcy. With Avice William had a daughter, Alice, who married first Richard de Curcy in or before 1147, and second Robert de Gant, younger brother of Gilbert (II) de Gant, earl of Lincoln, in or before 1153. After William's

death the cross-channel Paynel honour was broken up, and William's English estates, which had initially passed with his daughter to Richard de Curcy and then to Robert de Gant, were divided after 1154 between William's eldest two sons from his first marriage, Hugh (I) Paynel (*d. c.*1179) and **Fulk (I) Paynel** (*d.* 1182/3), and Robert de Gant. Hugh's portion included West Rasen, Lincolnshire, that of Fulk included Drax, and that of Robert was scattered in Yorkshire, Lincolnshire, Somerset, and Leicestershire. William's Norman estates were divided between Hugh and Fulk, the former receiving Les Moutiers-Hubert, the latter acquiring Hambye.

Fulk (I) was more interested in French affairs than those in England. He married Lesceline de Grippon or de Subligny (*fl.* 1198) with whom he had five or six sons. At some time between 1151 and 1153 he made an agreement with his brother Hugh for the partition of their mother's inheritance. Fulk attested over thirty of Henry II's charters in France between 1156 and 1183, campaigned with Henry in Brittany in 1166, acted as one of the guarantors of an agreement between Henry and Humbert, count of Maurienne, in 1173, and served as custodian of Alençon and La Roche-Mabille in 1180. Like his predecessors Fulk patronized religious orders. He helped his father to found Hambye Abbey and endowed the priories of Drax and Holy Trinity, York, and the abbey of Mont-St Michel.

Fulk was succeeded in Drax and Hambye by his eldest son, **William (II) Paynel** (*d.* 1184). William married Eleanor de Vitré, who brought him additional lands in Normandy and Suffolk, and was a benefactor of the abbeys of Hambye and Longues. Some idea of the value of the Paynel honour in England in the 1180s is provided by the exchequer accounts of the royal custodians to whom the lands were granted after the deaths of William and Peter Paynel (*d.* 1184), son and heir of Hugh (I) Paynel of West Rasen, when their under-age heirs were in the king's custody. With regard to William Paynel's lands, at Michaelmas 1186, 1187, and 1188 William Vavassor rendered account of £108 6s. 11d. for the farm of the lands, which appear to have amounted to five and a half knights' fees, owing an additional 20 marks in 1186 for the stock of the manor of Broughton, Lincolnshire. As for Peter's lands in West Rasen, these were stated in 1185 to be worth £42 a year if fully stocked, but at Michaelmas 1185 the sheriff of Lincolnshire paid in £54 12s. of the issues of Rasen, and in the following three years rendered account of £43 6s. 8d. per year for the farm of Rasen.

William Paynel's heir appears to have died in infancy and his lands passed to his brother **Fulk (II) Paynel** (*d.* before 1230) about 1188 or 1189. Although Fulk was a benefactor of Drax Priory, he also appears to have given priority to his Norman interests. This is reflected by his patronage of Hambye Abbey and by his marriages. His first wife was Cecily, daughter of Jordan Tesson and Lettice, niece and heir of Roger, vicomte de St Sauveur, and his second, whom he married in 1187 or later, was Agatha, daughter of William du Hommet, constable of Normandy, and widow of William, the son of Ralph de Fougères. The second marriage appears to have brought Fulk land in

Northamptonshire and Normandy, as well as five children, the marriages of two of whom, William and Lucy, strengthened the Paynel links with the Tesson and Vitré families respectively. In 1199 and 1200 Fulk was present in King John's court in Normandy, and in 1202 received custody of the Norman castle of Pontorson. Between 1198 and 1203 he made an agreement with Roger de Lacy, constable of Chester, concerning the honour of 'Vallis Seye' in Normandy. His association with du Hommet and the lordship of Chester emerges again in 1203 when King John, whose control of Normandy was then threatened by Philip Augustus of France, heard that the earl of Chester and Fulk Paynel were planning to withdraw their fealty and service to him. John travelled to the earl's castle of Vire, and on the following day Fulk and the earl appeared before the king and reaffirmed their allegiance to him. Fulk delivered his son to the king as a hostage, and the earl named William du Hommet as his pledge for good service and Roger de Lacy as his hostage. After John lost Normandy to Philip in 1204, Fulk continued to hold his Norman lands as a fief of the king of France and forfeited his English estates. He was one of the Norman barons who on 13 November 1205 drew up a record of rights that Henry II, Richard I, and they had in matters affecting the church. The bulk of Fulk's Yorkshire estates, including Drax and its dependencies, passed to Hugh (II) Paynel of West Rasen (c.1181–1244), grandson of Hugh (I) Paynel and Hugh's wife, Nichole, and son and (c.1200) successor of Peter Paynel. Hugh (II) received them as compensation for the forfeiture of his Norman honour of Les Moutier-Hubert to Philip Augustus after his decision to remain loyal to John, and thereafter pursued his career in England and was a benefactor of Drax Priory. Between 1226 and 1228 the soke of Drax was worth yearly £52 12s. and 120 hens and 700 eggs. Fulk was received into King John's favour in June 1214 and was granted the lands he had held of the king in England and other estates in Normandy as he had them when the king last crossed to Normandy. However, in June 1217 the sheriffs of Yorkshire and Leicestershire and the chamberlain were commanded to give seisin of all of Fulk's land to his brother Hasculf, a royal clerk.

The Paynels of Hooton Pagnell, descendants of Alexander son of Ralph Paynel, were an important branch of the Paynel family whose *caput* was almost certainly Hooton in Yorkshire. In addition to acquiring the lands of his brother Jordan, Alexander had probably received from his father, as a younger son's portion, the manor of Broughton. His marriage to Agnes, daughter of Robert, son of Nigel Fossard, strengthened further the Paynel links with the Fossards and the honour of the count of Mortain, and brought Alexander three sons and a daughter and control of land in Bramham, Yorkshire. Together with his wife Alexander was a benefactor of Nostell Priory, and also favoured Holy Trinity Priory, York. Most of his lands passed not later than 1153 to his eldest son, **William Paynel of Hooton Pagnell** (d. 1202), and amounted in 1166 to sixteen knights' fees in Yorkshire. William was a benefactor of St Peter's, York, Kirkstall Abbey, Roche Abbey, Nostell Priory, Gokewell Priory, Hampole Priory, the

templars and the hospitallers. His wife, Frethesant, was possibly one of the two daughters of Agnes de Montecaniso, and with her he had a son, Alexander, who died in his own lifetime, and two daughters, Frethesant and Isabel. They married respectively Geoffrey *Luttrell [see under Luttrell family (*per. c.*1200–1428)] and William Bastard, and were his coheirs. William's younger brother **Adam Paynel** (*fl.* 1166–*c.*1205) was holding Broughton in 1187 by royal grant, and was probably the Adam Paynel who was a benefactor of Guisborough Priory. The Paynels of Broughton continued into and beyond the thirteenth century, and from one of their younger lines sprang the Paynels of Boothby Pagnell, Lincolnshire, who continued to 1595. The arms of the Paynels of West Rasen and Drax were argent, a bend sable. PAUL DALTON

Sources W. Farrer and others, eds., *Early Yorkshire charters*, 12 vols. (1914–65) · T. D. Hardy, ed., *Rotuli chartarum in Turri Londinensi asservati*, RC, 36 (1837) · T. D. Hardy, ed., *Rotuli litterarum patentium*, RC (1835) · T. D. Hardy, ed., *Rotuli Normanniae*, RC (1835) · T. D. Hardy, ed., *Rotuli litterarum clausarum*, RC, 1 (1833) · *Calendar of the charter rolls*, 6 vols., PRO (1903–27), vol. 1 · H. C. M. Lyte, ed., *Liber feodorum: the book of fees*, 1 (1920) · J. H. Round, ed., *Calendar of documents preserved in France, illustrative of the history of Great Britain and Ireland* (1899) · *Matthaei Parisiensis, monachi Sancti Albani, Historia Anglorum, sive ... Historia minor*, ed. F. Madden, 3 vols., Rolls Series, 44 (1886–9), vols. 2–3 · Dugdale, *Monasticon*, new edn, vol. 5 · *Pipe rolls* · *CPR, 1225–32* · *Curia regis rolls preserved in the Public Record Office* (1922–), vol. 3 · D. M. Stenton, ed., *The chancellor's roll for the eighth year of the reign of King Richard the First*, PRSoc., new ser., 7 (1930) · W. T. Lancaster and W. Paley Baildon, eds., *The coucher book of the Cistercian abbey of Kirkstall*, Thoresby Soc. (1904) · J. H. Round, ed., *Rotuli de dominabus et pueris et puellis de XII comitatibus* (1185), PRSoc., 35 (1913) · A. Farley, ed., *Domesday Book*, 2 vols. (1783) · *VCH Yorkshire*, vol. 2 · Symeon of Durham, *Opera*, vol. 1 · GEC, *Peerage*, new edn · Ordericus Vitalis, *Eccl. hist.*, vol. 6 · T. Stapleton, ed., *Magni rotuli scaccarii Normanniae sub regibus Angliae*, 2 vols., Society of Antiquaries of London Occasional Papers (1840–44) · R. Howlett, ed., *Chronicles of the reigns of Stephen, Henry II, and Richard I*, 4, Rolls Series, 82 (1889) · L. Delisle and others, eds., *Recueil des actes de Henri II, roi d'Angleterre et duc de Normandie, concernant les provinces françaises et les affaires de France*, 4 vols. (Paris, 1909–27) · J. C. Holt and R. Mortimer, eds., *Acta of Henry II and Richard I* (1986) · C. T. Clay and D. E. Greenway, eds., *Early Yorkshire families* (1973)

Archives Archives of La Manche, St Lô, MS H4311 [extract from cartulary of Hambye Abbey] · Archives of La Manche, St Lô, MS H4309 [extract from cartulary of Hambye Abbey] · BL, Add. MS 37771, fol. 1525 [cartulary of Selby Abbey] · BL, Cotton MS, Claudius D xi [Malton cartulary] · BL, Cotton MS, Vespasian E xix, fol. 25 [Nostell Abbey cartulary] · Bodl. Oxf., Topography Yorks. MS c. 72 [cartulary of Drax Priory] · Bodl. Oxf., Dodsworth MS xxvi, fol. 25 · Bodl. Oxf., Dodsworth MS xcv, fol. 60 · Bodl. Oxf., Yorkshire charters, no. 97 [original charter] · Bodl. Oxf., Dodsworth MS viii, fols. 51d, 81, 81d, 83d, 188d, 189, 189d, 190, 245, 282, 285d · Bodl. Oxf., Dodsworth MS vii, fol. 47d · LPL, MS 1212, p. 75 · PRO, Exchequer K. R. memoranda roll no. 178, communia, Trin. term 3 Henry IV, mm. 14, 14d [refoundation of Holy Trinity Priory, York] · PRO, R. C. transcripts, series ii, p. 47, no. 1 [cartulaire de la Basse-Normandie] · PRO, charter roll 4 Edward II, m. 3 · PRO, Ancient Deed L. 43 · Everingham Park deeds [original charter]

Paynel, Adam (*fl.* 1166–*c.*1205). *See under* Paynel family (*per.* c.1086–1244).

Paynel, Fulk (I) (d. 1182/3). *See under* Paynel family (*per.* c.1086–1244).

Paynel, Fulk (II) (*d.* before **1230**). *See under* Paynel family (*per. c.*1086–1244).

Paynel, Gervase (*d.* 1194), baron, was the grandson of Fulk Paynel who married Beatrice, daughter and heir of William fitz Ansculf, a Domesday tenant with land in eleven counties later known as the barony of Dudley. Fulk founded the Cluniac priory of Tickford in Buckinghamshire. His son, Ralph Paynel, was a supporter of the Empress Matilda. Gervase had succeeded by 1153. Respecting his father's intentions he founded the Cluniac priory of Dudley, for the salvation of himself, his wife, Isabella, and his son, Robert. In addition to the site of the priory itself, he endowed the house with the churches of St Edmund and St Thomas in Dudley, together with four other churches and land at Churchill. The monks received tithes, pasture, pannage, and seignorial rights, and were made subject to the prior of Much Wenlock. His wife was Countess Isabella, widow of Simon (II) de Senlis, earl of Northampton and of Huntingdon, and daughter of *Robert, earl of Leicester. They married some time after August 1153. Gervase Paynel was also a benefactor to his father-in-law's foundation of Kintbury in Berkshire, later moved to Nuneaton in Warwickshire, and gave the nuns the mill of Inkpen, Berkshire. The vill of Greenham, in the same county, was given to the hospitallers. In 1166 Paynel reported to the king that he held fifty knights' fees of the old enfeoffment and five and two-thirds of the new. In 1172 he owed the service of one knight in the bailiwick of Le Passeis in Normandy; he had four knights in his own service. He participated in the rising of Henry, the Young King, in 1173–4 and in consequence Dudley Castle was destroyed by Henry II in 1175. Paynel was restored to favour for the sum of 500 marks. However, his liberties at Newport Pagnell were taken from him and were not restored in his lifetime. None the less, he spent time with the king, witnessing charters at Tours and at Chinon. The latter was a grant to the abbey of Marmoutier, of which Tickford Priory had once been a cell. In 1187 Paynel confirmed his father's and grandfather's grants to Tickford and added others of his own. He was present at the coronation of Richard I on 13 September 1189. Paynel died in 1194, and since his son, Robert, had predeceased him, his heir was his sister, Hawise, who married first John de Somery and, second, Roger de Berkeley of Dursley. Hawise died *c.*1208; the barony of Dudley had passed to her son, Ralph de Somery, who had paid 300 marks for seisin in 1194.

PETER COSS

Sources *VCH Worcestershire*, 2.159; 3.90–91 · *VCH Warwickshire*, 2.66 · *VCH Buckinghamshire*, 4.412 · W. Farrer and others, eds., *Early Yorkshire charters*, 12 vols. (1914–65), vol. 6, pp. 48–50 · BL, Additional Charter 47424 · BL, Harley MS 3868, fol. 274 · H. Hall, ed., *The Red Book of the Exchequer*, 3 vols., Rolls Series, 99 (1896), vol. 1, pp. 269–70 · Dugdale, *Monasticon*, new edn, 5.83–4, 202–4; 6/2.1097 · *Pipe rolls*, 21 Henry II, 69; 6 Richard I, 74 · *Curia regis rolls preserved in the Public Record Office* (1922–), vol. 9, pp. 330–31 · *Radulfi de Diceto ... opera historica*, ed. W. Stubbs, 1: 1148–79, Rolls Series, 68 (1876), 404 · W. Stubbs, ed., *Gesta regis Henrici secundi Benedicti abbatis: the chronicle of the reigns of Henry II and Richard I, AD 1169–1192*, 2 vols., Rolls Series, 49 (1867), vol. 2, p. 80

Paynel, Ralph (*d.* before **1124**). *See under* Paynel family (*per. c.*1086–1244).

Paynel, William (I) (*d.* **1145x7**). *See under* Paynel family (*per. c.*1086–1244).

Paynel, William (II) (*d.* **1184**). *See under* Paynel family (*per. c.*1086–1244).

Paynel, William, of Hooton Pagnell (*d.* **1202**). *See under* Paynel family (*per. c.*1086–1244).

Paynell, Thomas (*d.* **1564?**), translator, was a canon of Merton Priory, Surrey. In April 1538 Merton Priory was surrendered to the crown and Paynell received a pension of £10. Wood says that Paynell, who was descended from an ancient Lincolnshire family, the Paynells or Paganells, was educated at St Mary's College, the Austin canons' college at Oxford, where Erasmus had been welcomed by Prior Richard Charnock in 1499. Paynell should probably be identified with Thomas Paynell, priest, born near Bothby Paynell in Lincolnshire, who in his will, dated 10 March 1559 and proved on 22 March 1564 (Emden, *Oxf.*, 438), in which he left his books to St John's College, Oxford, is described as rector of Cottingham, Yorkshire, a post to which he was presented on 24 October 1540. This Paynell in addition became rector of All Hallows, Honey Lane, London, on 31 August 1545. His predecessor there was Richard Benese, who like Thomas Paynell the translator was a canon of Merton. There is evidence that the rector of Cottingham had been educated in Paris (Stevenson and Salter, 135). One of the books in St John's is inscribed 'Sum Paynelli, Anthonii Belashezi et amicorum' (ibid.). This points to an identity with a Thomas Paynell who accompanied Christopher Mount on a mission directed by Thomas Cromwell to the protestant princes of Germany since there is a familiar letter from Henry Malet priest to Dr Bellises, Cromwell's servant, passing on a commendation from Paynell to Bellises. Paynell, the translator, was chaplain to Henry VIII and orator to queens Mary and Elizabeth. He was an Erasmian who was able to accommodate himself to the successive Tudor regimes. He remained however loyal to Thomas More, associated his arms with those of the Throckmortons, and requested a traditional Catholic burial.

John Bale said of Paynell that if monkish superstitions had not got in his way he was a man born to help those around him as can be deduced from his writings (Bale, *Cat.*, 754). In fact the most obviously useful of Paynell's works were written in the period when he was still an Austin canon. *The Regimen Sanitatis: this Boke Techynge al People to Governe them in Helthe* (1528) was a translation of the commentary of Arnald de Villanova on the poem of John de Mediolano which had been written for William of Normandy. A 'temperate and moderate diete prolongeth man's life' is the keynote for a survey of the properties of all foods and drink, of remedies as 'for parbraykynge on the sea' and of the psychology of illness. It has a clear analytical table of contents with careful instructions on how to locate a page. It was reprinted throughout the century and as late as 1634. The success of this book caused his publisher Thomas Berthelet to prompt Paynell to translate Ulrich von Hutten's *De morbo Gallico* (1533). The German religious reformer's book established *guaiacum* as the new cure for syphilis, attacked traditional religious remedies, such as pilgrimages, and professional doctors intent only on making money. It promoted simple cures and self-administered medicine. The core of the book is an onslaught on luxury. *A Muche Profitable Treatise Against the Pestilence* (1534) is a good general survey of the causes, preventions, and cures for plague. It includes affordable cures for the poor and readvertises Hutten's cure for syphilis. In his final year as a canon at Merton, Paynell wrote the preface for a work of his fellow canon Richard Benese. *This Boke Sheweth the Manner of Measurynge of All Manners of Lande* (1537?) was a timely book when so much land was changing hands, and an interesting one for a canon regular to write. Paynell in his preface argues that the mechanical arts such as carpentry and masonry are the basis of modern civilization; that God created the world 'by nombre, weyght and measure', and that geometry and astronomy are one.

Paynell's translation of Agapetus's advice to the emperor Justinian (*The Preceptes Teachyng a Prynce or a Noble Estate his Duetie*, 1532?) is addressed to William Blount, Lord Mountjoy, friend and tutor of King Henry and a man who helped bring Erasmus to England. The reader is told that 'he who knoweth himself shall knowe god, he that knoweth god shall be likened to god' (section 3); that the rich man suffers from his abundance as does the poor from his scarcity and so the rich must give to the poor (section 15). In 1533, while still an Austin canon, Paynell translated Erasmus's *De contemptu mundi* with its conclusion that the monastic life can be lived outside the monastery, and in 1559 at the beginning of Elizabeth's reign Erasmus's *Complaint of Peace* with its emphasis on the rights of the common man.

Paynell's translation of Constantinus Felicius Duratinus's *Conspiracy of Catiline* (1541) carried a more authoritarian message. The translation converted what had been an exercise in Ciceronian Latin into popular history with contemporary colouring. The destruction of Catiline is Henry's God-given justification for punishment of his own rebels. This translation was republished in 1557 during Mary's reign with Alexander Barclay's translation of Sallust's history of Jugurtha which Paynell claimed to have corrected (but see Bennett, 132). This part of the work was dedicated to Lord Montague 'who hathe at all tymes, and against all the rabblement of heretyke sustained … the catholyke faith'.

Traditional forms of religious text had been dedicated to Mary as princess by Paynell: *A Compendious and a Moche Fruytefull Treatyse of Well Livynge … written by S. Bernard*, published in 1545, and an anthology of carefully selected biblical passages, *The Piththy and most Notable Sayings of al Scripture*, published in 1550. In 1558 he offered her a translation of Cuthbert Tunstall's Latin prayers. Perhaps his most significant activity during Mary's reign was his indexing of the English works of Thomas More. The index reads like an attack on reformed religion: 'Apostles dyd institute to pray for the dead', 'Apostles sayd masse before any gospell was written', and approvingly 'Why the clergy doth not suffer the Bybel to be had in Englyshe'. Yet by 1561 Paynell had translated a work by Nicolas Harape as *The Ensamples of Vertue and Vice, Gathered Oute of Holye Scripture* and addressed it to Elizabeth. There the reader learns that 'we oughte to have great reverence unto holye scripture which God himself did wryte, deliver and teache' (chap. 26). However the recommendation of poverty and the ideals of the early church (chap. 74) underline a consistency in Paynell's social concerns, which are illustrated also by his translation of Vives's *The Office and Duetie of an Husband* (1553).

Besides other extant works of Paynell described by Pollard in the *Dictionary of National Biography* there are two works mentioned by Wood and twelve by Bale which are no longer extant. A list of the books, including manuscript notebooks, bequeathed by Paynell to St John's College, Oxford, can be found in Emden (728–30). Disappointingly they shed little light on the work of Paynell the translator.

Paynell's ability to straddle the religious divide is demonstrated by his manuscript commonplace book (Salisbury MSS, Cecil papers, 5.332) which contains among much else 'The exposytone upon the psalme 127 by the famus and lerned doctor Martyne Luther of Wyteberge translated owt of Latyne in to Englyshe by Thomas Paynell Esquyre' and twelve lines of poetry on Thomas More (McConica, 139–40).

The starting point for any reassessment of Thomas Paynell is a letter of A. F. Pollard in the *Times Literary Supplement* (26 Feb 1931, 156), replying to a provocative, but informative, letter of H. E. Salter which appeared in the same journal (12 Feb 1931, 116). In this letter Pollard virtually repudiated his article in the *Dictionary of National Biography* and called for a new edition of the dictionary. He now identified five or possibly six Thomas Paynells. Noteworthy are a father and son of this name who were respectively protector and pupil of Robert Barnes. Coincidentally Barnes's fellow martyr Thomas Gerrard was Benese's predecessor at All Hallows. Benese was the appointee of Henry VIII, but Gerrard was, like the translator Paynell, the appointee of the Grocers' Company. Another Thomas Paynell was a cousin of the translator and bailiff of Boston. Their family had founded the house of Austin canons at Drax. Pollard drew attention in this letter to his commonplace book at Hatfield as an important source for future investigations of Paynell.

Geoffrey Eatough

Sources Bale, *Cat.* · H. S. Bennett, *English books and readers, 1475 to 1557: being a study in the history of the book trade from Caxton to the incorporation of the Stationers' Company*, 2nd edn (1969) · E. J. Devereux, *A checklist of English translations of Erasmus to 1700* (1968) · Emden, *Oxf.* · *LP Henry VIII* · G. Hennessy, *Novum repertorium ecclesiasticum parochiale Londinense, or, London diocesan clergy succession from the earliest time to the year 1898* (1898) · J. K. McConica, *English humanists and Reformation politics under Henry VIII and Edward VI* (1965); repr. with corrections (1968) · C. E. Mallet, *A history of the University of Oxford*, 3 vols. (1924–7); repr. (1968) · R. Newcourt,

Repertorium ecclesiasticum parochiale Londinense, 1 (1708) · A. F. Pollard, 'Thomas Paynell', *TLS* (26 Feb 1931), 154 · *DNB* · H. E. Salter, *TLS* (12 Feb 1931), 116 · W. H. Stevenson and H. E. Salter, *The early history of St John's College, Oxford*, OHS, new ser., 1 (1939) · Wood, *Ath. Oxon.*, 2nd edn

Archives St John's College, Oxford, benefactor book · Salisbury MSS, Cecil papers, 5.332

Wealth at death see Emden, *Oxf.*

Paynter, David William (*bap.* 1791, *d.* 1823), writer, was baptized on 4 March 1791 in St Ann's parish, Manchester, the son of Richard Walter Paynter (*d.* 1811), attorney, and his wife, Sarah, *née* Wittmall. He was educated at the grammar school there, and was intended for the medical profession, but much preferred poetry and the drama. He became closely associated with James Watson, a local literary character, with whom he frequently figured in the magazines and newspapers as Corporal Trim, while Watson called himself Uncle Toby. In 1820 he edited Watson's literary remains, under the title of *The Spirit of the Doctor*, to which he appended some of his own fugitive pieces, including letters from Lancaster Castle, where he was for some time a prisoner for debt. Paynter's *The Muse in Idleness* (1819) was the subject of a sarcastic review, 'Manchester poetry', published by James Crossley in *Blackwood's Magazine*.

In the introduction to his best-known play *King Stephen, or, The Battle of Lincoln* (1822) Paynter describes his efforts to get his productions put on the stage. After they had been declined by several managers he collected a company of his own, and brought out *King Stephen* at the Minor Theatre, Manchester, on 5 December 1821. He died at Manchester on 14 March 1823 and was buried at Blackley, near that city. He had married in 1813, and left children. After his death his tragedy *The Wife of Florence* was staged as a benefit for his widow and children.

C. W. SUTTON, rev. MEGAN A. STEPHAN

Sources R. W. Procter, *Literary reminiscences and gleanings* (1860), 57–65 · J. F. Smith, ed., *The admission register of the Manchester School, with some notes of the more distinguished scholars*, 3 vols. in 4 pts, Chetham Society, 69, 73, 93, 94 (1866–74) · *IGI* · review, *Blackwood*, 9 (1821), 64–75

Paynter, Thomas William [Will] (1903–1984), trade unionist and communist, was born at Whitchurch, near Cardiff, Glamorgan, on 6 December 1903, the second of three children and younger of two sons of Daniel James Paynter, coalminer, and his wife, Florence Ethel. His father originated from the Welsh borders and his mother's family were from Somerset. Will Paynter's family was therefore very much part of that great population explosion which accompanied the massive expansion of the south Wales coalfield in the two decades before the First World War.

After attendance at Whitchurch and Porth elementary schools, Paynter started work at the age of thirteen as a farm labourer at a local colliery farm. A year later he began work as a collier at the Coedely colliery on the edge of the Rhondda. He later moved to Cymmer colliery where he was to listen to underground discussions about the possibilities of world revolution following the Bolsheviks' seizure of power in Russia. Above ground, he was greatly influenced by his family's religious piety, and as a young man was a regular attendant at chapel, going three times on Sunday as well as attending prayer meetings and the Young People's Guild during the week.

Although he was an interested member rather than a leading activist of the South Wales Miners' Federation (SWMF), the miners' lock-outs of 1921 and 1926 were formative experiences for the young Will Paynter. After the second defeat, he turned to reading widely at the Cymmer Workmen's Institute Library. As a result of his study and his industrial experiences he gravitated towards the Communist Party which he joined in 1929 during the general election campaign in Rhondda East. The Communist candidate was Arthur Horner who was to be Paynter's mentor, father figure, and political inspiration for the rest of his life. There was much family anguish when he renounced the chapel in 1926 although his subsequent life in the Communist Party and the miners' union was characterized by uncompromisingly high moral standards of behaviour. Paynter had in fact delayed joining the Communist Party out of respect for his mother's feelings.

In 1929 Paynter was elected checkweighman at Cymmer colliery but spent the period of four months from May 1929 in gaol as a result of his political activities. In April 1931 he was removed by court injunction as a result of his strike activities. This began a decade of revolutionary politics which irrevocably shaped Will Paynter's future. Following his dismissal in 1931 and until 1936 he was a 'full-time revolutionary' working for the Communist Party, mainly in the Rhondda, but also for a period in 1935–6 as the south Wales district secretary of the party. In 1932–3 he spent a period at the Lenin School, Moscow, and on his return journey entered Nazi Germany on behalf of the Comintern in order to assist the communist resistance.

Paynter was a leading organizer of the 1931, 1932, and 1936 hunger marches and was also a local activist in the Rhondda of the National Unemployed Workers' Movement. Although he was an unemployed miner, his reputation was such among employed miners that he was elected in 1936 onto the executive council of the SWMF and rapidly assumed a prominent leading role particularly in the campaigns against the 'company' union and on international questions.

In 1937 Paynter married Irene Francis, a fellow communist from Tonypandy, and a few weeks later he was asked by the Communist Party to be a political commissar with the British battalion of the International Brigades in the Spanish Civil War. He was the leading political figure with a large Welsh mining contingent and returned in September 1937. In 1939 he was elected a full-time miners' agent in the Rhymni valley, an area not noted for its communist outlook: his reputation as an agitator for the unemployed, a union negotiator and campaigner, and a public speaker, and his service in Spain, had gone before him.

On 16 May 1940 Paynter's wife died giving birth to their

twin boys, David and William, who survived. Despite offers from friends, Paynter decided to rear the children himself. On 30 June 1943 he married his second wife, Elizabeth Ann (Betty) Thomas (d. 1988), his former housekeeper who had nursed the twins; they had five sons.

With the creation of the National Union of Mineworkers (NUM) and the election of the Labour government, both in 1945, and the nationalization of the coal industry in 1947, the role of a communist miners' leader was transformed. Paynter was now to play a leading role in south Wales as president from 1951 to 1958, and then nationally as general secretary of the NUM. In south Wales, the union, under his leadership and that of his vice-president and fellow communist Dai Dan Evans, became a powerful political and cultural force with a gala, an eisteddfod, educational programmes, wide-ranging international links, and its own monthly journal. In this buoyant period Paynter's reputation was enhanced as 'the uncrowned king of the valleys', despite his discouragement of the cult of personality and his opposition to unofficial sectional strikes.

Paynter was elected general secretary of the NUM by a large majority in 1959, despite the cold war and his own personal ambivalence about leaving south Wales. His elevation coincided with the beginning of the rundown of the coal industry which continued for a decade. His period of office was therefore characterized by attempts to persuade successive Conservative and Labour governments through force of political argument, rather than industrial action, of the need for an integrated energy policy. He organized such broad conferences as Britain's Coal in 1960, and several parliamentary lobbies, but the growing importance of oil and nuclear power was unremitting.

Nevertheless Paynter's achievements in the 1960s were considerable, and the national advances of the 1970s can be traced directly back to them. The national power loading agreement of 1966 effectively achieved a national wages structure for the first time since 1926. Paynter also began the process of creating a national culture for the union by developing a national educational programme and a national newspaper, The Miner. He was briefly a member of the general council of the TUC in 1960–61 but the Electrical Trades Union ballot-rigging scandal helped to remove him.

On his retirement, Will Paynter decided he would also 'retire' from the Communist Party. At different times he gave personal and political reasons for this: a longstanding family agreement and differences over industrial policy. He became a member of the commission on industrial relations in 1969 but resigned in 1970 when it became more an arm of state policy.

After writing two books, British Trade Unions and the Problem of Change (1970) and My Generation (1972), he gradually moved back into the political arena. Initially he was active in the pensioners' movement as chairman of the London region of the National Federation of Pension Associations and secretary of the London Joint Council for Senior Citizens. He returned to his political roots of the 1930s by campaigning for democracy in Spain and attended, as an observer, the trial of the 'Carabanchel Ten' in Madrid. He re-established his links with Wales by lecturing at miners' union schools, and through his presidency of Llafur, the Welsh labour history society.

Following his renewed links with international leftwing causes, especially Spain and Chile, Paynter rejoined the Communist Party in 1978. He was particularly active in fund-raising and public speaking during the miners' strike of 1984–5, in the midst of which he died suddenly on 12 December 1984 at his home, 32 Glengall Road, in Edgware, London. It was his wish that there should be no 'preacher' at his funeral, that his coffin be carried by his seven sons, and that the only hymn sung be 'Cwm Rhondda'. HYWEL FRANCIS

Sources U. Wales, South Wales Miners' Library, South Wales Coalfield collection, Will Paynter MSS · H. Francis and W. Paynter, interviews, 1969–83, U. Wales, South Wales Miners' Library · personal information (2004) · Llafur, 4/2 (1985), 4–9 · H. Francis and D. Smith, The Fed: a history of the south Wales miners in the twentieth century (1980) · H. Francis, Miners against fascism: Wales and the Spanish Civil War (1984) · W. Paynter, British trade unions and the problem of change (1970) · W. Paynter, My generation (1972) · d. cert.

Archives U. Wales, Swansea, South Wales Miners' Library, South Wales Coalfield collection

Paynter [Cambourne], **William** (1637–1716), college head, was born at Trelissick in the parish of St Erth, Cornwall, and baptized on 7 December 1637, the son of William Paynter or Cambourne, from Antron in Sithney, and Jane, the sixth child of Richard Keigwin of Mousehole. He was thus a kinsman of John Keigwin, the Cornish scholar. He matriculated from Exeter College, Oxford, on 29 March 1656, having been admitted as a poor scholar in February of that year. On 3 July 1657 he was elected to a fellowship of the college. He graduated BA in 1660 and proceeded MA in 1663 (incorporated at Cambridge in 1664), BD in 1674, and DD in 1695.

In 1669, on the grounds that Paynter had been elected to one of the fellowships earmarked for candidates from Devon, Arthur Bury, the college rector and a devout Devonian, suspended Paynter's fellowship, together with those of several other Cornishmen. In spite of this rebuff, in 1685 Paynter gave £100 to Exeter College. The same year he faced scandal when a child was laid at his door in college and was claimed to be his; it was later revealed that a disaffected undergraduate, John Jago, expelled by Paynter for debauchery, had tried to wreak revenge. It was not until 1686, having been appointed to the college living of Wootton, Northamptonshire, that Paynter actually vacated his fellowship.

Paynter married twice. Although the date of his first marriage is uncertain, it was possibly about the time of his appointment to Wootton rectory; his wife was Mary (1657–1695), daughter of John *Conant who had been rector of Exeter College during the interregnum, and his wife, Elizabeth. She was the widow of Matthew Poole MD of St Giles', Northampton. When probate was granted on Poole's will, on 15 March 1690, Mary was already married to Paynter. Mary died on 7 May 1695 and was buried at Wootton near her children, William and Elizabeth. On 16

May 1695, at Preston in Northamptonshire, Paynter married Sarah, daughter of Francis Duncombe of Broughton in Buckinghamshire.

On 15 August 1690, on the deprivation of Arthur Bury, Paynter was elected by a depleted fellowship to the rectorship of Exeter College. Bury appealed to the court of the king's bench which granted him management of the college until a definite decision on the legality of Bury's dismissal was made. The decision of the bench divided the Exeter fellowship; both Bury's supporters and his opponents attempted to run the college. The 'great Exeter schism' resulted in double elections to fellowships and the disorder was not put right until 1694, when the House of Lords reversed the decision of the king's bench and confirmed Paynter as rector. He held the rectorship until his death, and, in 1698 and 1699, was vice-chancellor of the university.

Paynter retained the rectory of Wootton until his death there on 18 February 1716; he was buried there on 22 February. His will was proved through the court of the university chancellor on 2 April. His second wife, who survived him, died on 22 September 1725, and was buried at Ilsington, Devon. It is not certain whether they had any children but a Mary Paynter, probably their daughter, married Philip Nanson, the vicar of Ilsington, in Exeter Cathedral in 1723.   J. H. CURTHOYS

Sources W. K. Stride, *Exeter College* (1900) · C. W. Boase, ed., *Registrum Collegii Exoniensis*, new edn, OHS, 27 (1894) · D. Gilbert, *The parochial history of Cornwall: founded on the manuscript histories of Mr Hals and Mr Tonkin*, 1 (1838) · H. I. Longden, *Northamptonshire and Rutland clergy from 1500*, ed. P. I. King and others, 16 vols. in 6, Northamptonshire RS (1938–52) · J. Bridges, *The history and antiquities of Northamptonshire*, ed. P. Whalley, 2 vols. (1791) · Foster, *Alum. Oxon.* · Venn, *Alum. Cant.*

Archives BL, letters, Add. MSS 4055, fol. 50; 28886, fol. 37; Harley MSS

Peabody, George (1795–1869), merchant banker and philanthropist, was born on 18 February 1795 in South Danvers (later Peabody), Massachusetts, USA, the third child in a family of four sons and four daughters.

Origins and early life Thomas Peabody, George's father, was descended from a Leicestershire man, Francis Peboddy, a dissenter who had emigrated to Massachusetts on the sailing ship *Planter* in 1635. His mother, Judith Dodge, was descended from the Spofford family, a dissenting family from Yorkshire, who had likewise emigrated to Massachusetts in the mid-seventeenth century. Thomas Peabody was a casual leather-worker and small-scale farmer who died in 1811, and both before and after his death the family was poor. Peabody's village schooling was limited and irregular, and came to an end at the age of eleven, when he was apprenticed to John Proctor, the owner of a country general store in Danvers. It was from this man that Peabody learned to keep accounts in a clear handwriting and to organize and discipline his daily activities. Over the next several years he changed his occupation several times: he worked on his grandfather's farm in Thetford, Vermont; he rode on horseback through Virginia, hawking goods; he clerked in the store owned by his

George Peabody (1795–1869), by André Adolphe Eugène Disderi, 1860s

elder brother David in Newburyport, Massachusetts; and he worked with his uncle, John Peabody, in the District of Columbia.

Here in 1814 Peabody's luck changed. He impressed a successful merchant of dry goods in Georgetown, Elisha Riggs, and the two of them opened a wholesale warehouse for dry goods, Riggs supplying the money. The next year the partnership of Riggs, Peabody & Co. was formed in Baltimore, specializing in importing dry goods from Britain; in 1822 branches were opened in New York and Philadelphia; and in 1829, with Riggs's retirement, the firm became Peabody, Riggs & Co., with Peabody as senior partner. In 1827 Peabody had made his first business trip to Britain: ten years later, after several such visits, he settled permanently in England.

Merchant and merchant banker In August 1838 Peabody bought a supply of quill pens and ledgers and opened a counting-house. He had survived the panic of 1837, responding to the early signs of trouble by contracting operations and concentrating on collecting debts, and helping other firms who were in difficulties. By now a man of substance, with capital of over $300,000 (£70,000), he could employ others to purchase the goods and sell them in the United States. Peabody was able to concentrate on the financial side of the firm, and during the period 1837–45 gradually turned himself into a merchant banker. He continued to deal in dry goods, in corn for Ireland, in rails for the USA, and in trade with China, but at the same time he increasingly spent his time financing others' foreign trade and dealt especially in American securities, for which he seems to have been the major London specialist. In short, he followed the classic development of a merchant banker in Britain: he began as a merchant, financed his own and then others' trade, and eventually gave up trade in commodities to concentrate on banking and on securities.

By the late 1840s Peabody had decided that he wanted to build up his firm as the leading American house in London—the centre of the American trade and for Americans in that trade. He needed correspondents in America, firms with whom he could maintain close connections as sources both of information and business; new types of business were required, and the support of a partner was essential. Building up a network of correspondents, Peabody subsequently moved into railway financing and the export of rails to America, and in 1854 he took a new partner, the American J. S. Morgan, with whose help he would achieve his ambition. Morgan thus joined the premier American house in London, though not yet the premier house in the American trade, a position contested by Baring Brothers and Brown, Shipley & Co. Arranged in an American manner, with current American newspapers laid out on the table, the offices were intended to be a centre for Peabody's American friends while they were visiting England. Peabody was said to entertain every American who arrived at his office, supplying a letter of credit and introducing him around London, and perhaps providing a box at the opera, with a corsage for his wife; in July 1855 he remarked that he had entertained eighty Americans for dinner and thirty-five at the opera within a week.

Peabody also provided rather more lavish celebrations, and in the 1850s he became known for sumptuous Anglo-American dinners in honour of American diplomats and other notables. During the Great Exhibition at Crystal Palace in 1851, for which the US congress had refused to support the American section, the British press criticized the American exhibits; Peabody advanced £3000 to the embarrassed exhibitors to provide for arranging and decorating the section. He also decided that a bold gesture was necessary, and he gave the first of a regular series of Fourth of July dinners: the duke of Wellington was the guest of honour. Where the duke led others followed, and these dinners were a highly publicized feature of London political life for several years.

Meanwhile Peabody and Morgan began soliciting business belonging to other firms by charging lower commission, a very un-English activity. This substantially increased business, but the outcome was nearly disastrous, as the company was caught out by the panic of 1857:

most of its American correspondent houses contracted, and in some cases failed, owing Peabody substantial sums. Peabody had to ask the Bank of England for a loan of £800,000; the bank would accept American securities as collateral only if guaranteed by residents in England. During the week it took to find these guarantors, rivals tried to force the firm out of business and Peabody 'dared them to cause his failure' (Parker, 95); but far from crashing, the firm emerged from the crisis with its credit intact.

This favourable outcome was the signal for Peabody to withdraw from active business. He was now sixty-three, tired, and ill, troubled by gout and rheumatism, and he felt time was running out: he was increasingly preoccupied with the dispersal of his fortune. Although he had never married, Peabody had been engaged for some months in 1838 to a young American woman twenty-four years his junior, Esther Elizabeth Hoppin. He had no direct acknowledged heirs, though he had had a mistress in Brighton who had borne him a daughter, to whom he was very generous during his lifetime—he would regularly withdraw some of his own personal securities, as much as £2000 at a time, to be realized and sent to her. However, he left them nothing in his will. Instead, he devoted the bulk of his fortune to the public good.

Philanthropy Peabody's philanthropies were divided between America and England. Much of his work in America was devoted to the support of education at many levels. On his visit to the USA in 1852 he gave $30,000 to his home town to found an educational institute, and on his visit in 1857 he founded the Peabody Institute in Baltimore with a gift of $300,000; both sums were later increased. The Baltimore Institute was to provide a library, a gallery of art, an academy of music, and prizes to encourage private and public school pupils. At the same time he gave $1200 annually for gold medals to female high-school graduates in Baltimore, to encourage support for the education of women. On his visit in 1866 he gave Harvard $150,000 to found an institute of archaeology (later the Peabody Museum of Archaeology and Ethnology), and he presented Yale with a similar amount towards the teaching of physical science (used to found the Peabody Museum of Natural History). Between 1866 and 1869—after the civil war—he gave $2,000,000 to the Peabody Fund for Southern Education, set up in the first instance to provide for the education of newly emancipated slaves.

In Britain Peabody's major philanthropy was centred on housing. He wanted to leave London some token of his affection for the city. He thought first of an elaborate system of drinking fountains; then he considered helping Lord Shaftesbury's 'ragged schools' for the children of the very poor. In the end, Shaftesbury convinced Peabody that it was more important to provide better housing conditions for the working classes, and in March 1859 Peabody decided that his gift would be a number of model dwellings. By means of the Peabody Donation Fund he gave £500,000 towards building houses to be inhabited by poor Londoners who had good moral characters and were good members of society. The first block was opened in Spitalfields in 1864, and it was soon followed by buildings in Chelsea, Bermondsey, Islington, and Shadwell; by 1882 the fund owned 3500 dwellings and housed more than 14,600 people, and by 1939 there were more than 8000 dwellings. In 1962 the queen mother unveiled a plaque to Peabody at another new Peabody estate in Blackfriars. Peabody was made a freeman of the City of London, the first American to receive this honour, though he turned down the offer of a barony from Queen Victoria. In 1867 the US congress conferred a gold medal on him. Popular subscription raised the funds in England to provide the statue of Peabody in the royal exchange, which was unveiled by the prince of Wales in 1869.

In 1864 Peabody withdrew entirely from George Peabody & Co., taking much of his capital with him (his fortune amounted to something over $10 million—more than £2 million). J. S. Morgan succeeded to the senior partnership and the name of the firm was changed to J. S. Morgan & Co.; in 1910 it became Morgan, Grenfell & Co.

Personality and final years Peabody was an imposing man. He stood 6 feet 1 inch tall, was broad-shouldered, with a round face and large nose, and had blue eyes and very dark brown hair, which by his early forties he was dyeing with 'African balm'. He always liked very good clothes, and when money was no object never economized on quality. Jovial with his friends, he was formal and restrained with many members of his family, his feelings of responsibility sometimes overcoming his feelings of affection—not surprisingly, when several of his relatives were distinctly feckless.

The career of George Peabody is an exemplification of much that the nineteenth century found admirable. Beginning his working life honest but poor, Peabody always worked hard—there are hints throughout his career of long hours and endless days without breaks—and he did not spurn 'twopenny' business. He was always willing to take a risk, but by and large they were well-judged risks. Another element in his success was his knack of making useful friends, who tended to be wealthy and influential businessmen. His personal traits encouraged trust: he was personally austere while publicly generous. Although he had attended a Congregational church in his youth, he was not ostentatiously religious. Rather, he carried out the puritan doctrine of the stewardship of riches: it has been estimated that he gave away more than $8,600,000. He ended his life wealthy and respected.

Peabody died on 4 November 1869 at the house of his friend Sir Curtis Miranda Lampson, at 80 Eaton Square, London. His funeral was held in Westminster Abbey, and Queen Victoria and the prime minister, W. E. Gladstone, jointly requested the Royal Navy to provide HMS *Monarch*, the navy's newest ironclad, to take Peabody's body back home; on the orders of President U. S. Grant, it was escorted by the USS *Plymouth*. The American authorities received the body at Portland, Maine, and there were elaborate services there and in Peabody (as South Danvers had been renamed in 1868). The family tomb, built by Peabody for his parents and other members of his family, was situated in a thick walnut grove in Harmony Rest cemetery on the boundary between Peabody and Salem, Massachusetts. He was finally laid to rest there on 8 February 1870.

KATHLEEN BURK

Sources F. Parker, *George Peabody: a biography* (1976) · *DNB* · K. Burk, *Morgan Grenfell, 1838–1988: the biography of a merchant bank* (1989) · Essex Institute Library, Salem, Massachusetts, USA, George Peabody MSS · GL, Morgan Grenfell MSS
Archives Essex Institute, Salem, Massachusetts, business, estate, and personal papers · GL, private ledger | GL, Morgan Grenfell MSS · GL, letters to Morrison, Sons & Co.
Likenesses A. Healy, portrait, c.1854, Smithsonian Institution, Washington, DC, National Portrait Gallery · A. A. E. Disderi, carte-de-visite, 1860–69, NPG [*see illus.*] · H. W. Pickersgill, oils, exh. RA 1863, Corporation of London · T. L. Atkinson, mezzotint, pubd 1869 (after H. W. Pickersgill), NPG · J. C. Buttre, line engraving (after photograph by Brady), NPG · D. J. Pound, stipple and line print (after photograph by H. N. King), NPG · W. W. Story, bronze statue, Royal Exchange, Threadneedle Street, London · carte-de-visite, NPG · cartoon, repro. in *Punch* (24 Feb 1866) · gold medal, Peabody Institute Library, Danvers, Massachusetts
Wealth at death under £400,000 in England: probate, 26 Jan 1870, *CGPLA Eng. & Wales*

Peace, Charles Frederick (1832–1879), burglar and murderer, was born in Nursery Road, Sheffield, on 14 May 1832, the youngest of the four sons of John Peace, shoemaker, and his wife, the daughter of a naval surgeon. Semi-literate after a cursory schooling, he had a talent for music, being proficient enough with a violin to be billed in his teens at local places of entertainment as the 'modern Paganini'. Despite his artistic pretensions, he was apprenticed to a local steel mill, where two accidents left him with a permanent limp and the loss of three fingers of one hand.

Although he was to become Britain's most successful cat burglar, Peace showed no early aptitude, and was frequently arrested. By 1854 he had graduated to longer spells in prison—three sentences totalling twenty years, substantially reduced through remission. Meanwhile, at the age of twenty-seven he met, and is believed to have married, Hannah Ward, a widow with a small child. They had a daughter and a son who died in infancy. But he was learning from experience and moved from town to town to polish his burglary skills.

By 1872 accrued capital enabled Peace to return to Sheffield with his wife and stepson, setting up as a picture framer. His income was supplemented from the sale of musical instruments and small antiques. Success as a burglar was achieved through skill, daring, and an ability to change his appearance—a considerable feat considering his distinctive appearance. The limp accentuated a natural bandiness, and being very short he was compared to a monkey, an impression heightened by thick features and a heavy lower jaw.

Peace's unfortunate appearance and lack of education was offset by a compelling personality, and in 1876 he embarked on an affair with a neighbour, the much younger Katherine Dyson. However, when he attacked her husband, Arthur, she protested and, in front of witnesses, Peace threatened her with a gun. A warrant for his arrest forced him to flee, committing a trail of burglaries in northern cities. In Manchester he was intercepted by PC Nicholas Cock, who was shot and killed. The police arrested John and William Habron, and managed to produce 'eye-witnesses' at the trial, which Peace attended in disguise. William was sentenced to death—commuted to life imprisonment because he was only eighteen.

Meanwhile, having returned to Sheffield, Peace shot and killed Arthur Dyson after an argument. Accompanied by his wife and stepson, he headed south, leaving his mark as a burglar. In Nottingham he acquired a mistress, Susan Grey, an attractive and educated widow who accompanied the Wards (he was now using Hannah's name) to London, where they eventually settled in Peckham. Susan was used to complete the air of respectability—the couple called themselves Mr and Mrs Thompson, and Hannah lived in the basement, posing as their housekeeper. Quite affluent, the newcomers entertained, although Mr Thompson managed to get away at nights, robbing houses across London. However, after considerable success he was eventually caught in October 1878, breaking into a house in Blackheath. Ambushed by two policemen, Peace was overpowered by PC Edward Robinson despite a bullet through the arm. The following month 'John Ward' was given a life sentence for shooting with intent to murder. At that stage Susan Grey revealed his true identity for the £100 reward.

On the train to face trial in the north, Peace jumped through an open carriage window, and although a guard clung to his shoe he wriggled free, only to be found unconscious in the snow. At Leeds assizes, the evidence of Katherine Dyson was conclusive. Awaiting execution, Peace finally confessed to the murder of PC Cock, providing the detailed evidence to persuade the authorities of Habron's innocence. Peace was hanged by William Marwood at Armley Prison, Leeds, on 25 February 1879, having composed his own memorial card, ending with the words: 'For that I don [sic] but never intended.'   R. H. LEWIS, rev.

Sources R. H. Lewis, *Victorian murders* (1988) · W. T. Shore, ed., *Trials of Charles Frederick Peace* (1926)

Peach, Benjamin Neeve (1842–1926), geologist, was born on 6 September 1842 at Gorran Haven, Cornwall, the youngest child of Charles *Peach (1800–1886), coastguard, and his wife, Jemima (née Mabson). Following his father's posting to Scotland, Peach attended schools at Peterhead and Wick. His father's important discovery of fossils at Durness was noticed by metropolitan geologists, and Sir Roderick Murchison, when visiting northern Scotland, also remarked on the son's abilities. Accordingly, in 1859 he arranged for Peach to attend the Royal School of Mines, where in the years 1860–61 he studied under A. W. Hofmann, T. H. Huxley, and A. C. Ramsay.

In 1862 Peach joined the staff of the Geological Survey. After work among the fossils at the London headquarters, he was soon transferred to the Scottish field service. Five years later, he met, and to some extent trained in the field, John *Horne, and thus began their lifelong friendship and scientific co-operation. Their best-known work was concerned with the southern uplands and the north-west highlands. In both cases, the views of the structures held by the senior men of the survey, especially Archibald Geikie, were questioned by Charles Lapworth. As a result of this, the southern uplands work had to be revised, and a major effort was required to sort out the geology of the north-west highlands. This involved the recognition of overfolding and thrusting, and the complex imbricate structures produced by repeated faulting. In such investigations Peach proved himself a master at interpreting the internal structure of an area from examination of its external appearances. It was, however, Horne who, in 1883, first realized that the 'official' view of a regular ascending stratigraphic sequence at Durness was mistaken; the following year, after mapping the imbricate structures at Eriboll, Peach reached the same conclusion. After years of detailed fieldwork the results were published in two notable memoirs: *The Silurian Rocks of Britain, 1, Scotland* (1899) and *The Geological Structure of the North-West Highlands* (1907).

In addition to his work in tectonics, Peach was an accomplished palaeontologist, with a special interest in fossil crustaceans and arachnids. His investigations in this area culminated with the publication of *The Higher Crustacea of the Carboniferous Rocks of Scotland* (1908). For the southern uplands, he had to do much work in the identification of graptolites. In his later survey work, Peach was involved in the revisions to the maps of the Scottish coalfields. He also worked on glacial geology and on the Old Red Sandstone.

In 1871, Peach married Jeannie Bannantyne, a farmer's daughter; they had a son and two daughters. After her death, he married Margaret Ann McEwan, daughter of the schoolmaster at Assynt, where much of Peach's most important surveying was done. They had two sons.

Peach was elected FRS in 1892. He was awarded the Murchison and Wollaston medals of the Geological Society (1899 and 1921 respectively), both in conjunction with Horne, and received the Neill medal from the Royal Society of Edinburgh and an honorary LLD from Edinburgh University. He was admired by all who knew him for his physical strength, kindness, and youthful enthusiasms. He was a gifted artist, and explained his ideas by means of diagrams better than in words. He is said to have been a reluctant reader and writer, but there is ample evidence of his epistolary activity in various archives. On several occasions Peach was called on by his chief, Geikie, to accompany him into the field; and Geikie evidently relied on the counsel of his subordinate about controversial issues to a considerable degree. Peach retired from the survey in 1905 and lived in Edinburgh until his death, after an illness of several weeks, on 29 January 1926.

DAVID OLDROYD

Sources J. H. [J. Horne], *PRS*, 100B (1926), xi–xiii · E. Greenly, 'Benjamin Neeve Peach: a study', *Transactions of the Edinburgh Geological Society*, 12 (1928–32), 1–11 · [J. Horne], *Proceedings of the Royal Society of Edinburgh*, 46 (1925–6), 376–81 · 'Retirement of Dr B. N. Peach', *Geological Magazine*, new ser., 5th decade, 3 (1906) · E. Greenly, *A hand* *through time*, 2 (1938) • D. R. Oldroyd, *The highlands controversy: constructing geological knowledge through fieldwork in nineteenth-century Britain* (1990) • A. Anderson, *Ben Peach's Scotland: landscape sketches by a Victorian geologist* (1980) • J. S. Flett, *The first hundred years of the geological survey of Great Britain* (1937) • E. B. Bailey, *Geological survey of Great Britain* (1952) • *DNB*

Archives BGS, corresp. and papers

Likenesses group portrait, photograph, *c.*1885 (with seven other members of the north-west highlands surveying team), BGS • S. H. Reynolds, photograph (with J. Horne), repro. in Oldroyd, *Highlands controversy*, 272 • photograph, repro. in Greenly, *Hand through time*, facing p. 515 • photograph, repro. in Greenly, 'Benjamin Neeve Peach: a study', pl. 1 • photograph, repro. in Horne, *Proceedings of the Royal Society of Edinburgh* • photograph, repro. in Anderson, *Ben Peach's Scotland*, 1 • photograph (with other members of Scottish branch of geological survey), repro. in Oldroyd, *Highlands controversy*, 166 • photograph (with C. T. Clough and J. Horne), repro. in Bailey, *Geological survey*, pl. 3

Wealth at death £5115 12*s.* 3*d.*: confirmation, 6 March 1926, *CCI*

Peach, Charles William (1800–1886), naturalist, was born on 30 September 1800 at Wansford, Northamptonshire, the son of Charles William Peach, saddler, farmer, and innkeeper, and Elizabeth Vellum. He was educated to the age of fifteen, his last three years of schooling being at Folkingham, Lincolnshire. In his youth, he participated enthusiastically in field sports. He first worked for his father, but in 1824 entered the mounted coastguard, initially at several places in Norfolk, then in Dorset and Devon, and subsequently at Gorran Haven, Cornwall, in 1834. On occasion, he had to engage in hand-to-hand encounters with smugglers. With anonymous support from the geologist William Buckland he transferred to the customs at Fowey in 1845. In 1849 he was posted to Peterhead, Scotland. From 1853 he was comptroller at Wick. He married Jemima Mabson on 26 April 1829. They had seven sons and two daughters. One son, Benjamin Neeve *Peach, became a renowned member of the Scottish branch of the geological survey.

Without formal scientific training, but with ample opportunity for studying coastal marine life and coastal rocks, Peach rapidly established a reputation as an observer and a collector. He corresponded with leading British naturalists, attended meetings of the British Association, and became a member or associate of numerous natural history societies, notably the Polytechnic Society of Cornwall and the Physical Society of Edinburgh. Eighty-six publications by Peach are listed in the *Royal Society Catalogue of Scientific Papers*. Peach was visited in Cornwall by such notables as Alfred Tennyson. In north Scotland he became a friend and fellow worker of the naturalist Robert Dick, the 'baker of Thurso'.

In marine zoology, Peach discovered new mollusca, encrinites, sea urchins, starfish, polyzoa, fish, sponges, and so on, and a spectacular holothurian with twenty tentacles. In 1838 he discovered obscure fossil fish remains near Polruan, and in the years following he rapidly extended his knowledge of fossil forms in areas of Cornwall previously regarded as unfossiliferous 'primitive' terrain. In 1843 he identified remains from near Polperro as Pteraspidian fish-shields. Frederick McCoy

thought these were sponges but Peach was subsequently vindicated by E. Ray Lankester.

Peach's fossil localities were reported for the benefit of other investigators, and he was always keen to share his knowledge with metropolitan scientists. His Cornish and Devon fossils were referred either to the Silurian (now Ordovician) or to the Devonian systems. He donated his large collection of Cornish fossils to the Geological Society of Cornwall and arranged the materials for them. In Caithness he investigated fossil fish of the Old Red Sandstone together with Dick. In 1853 he made an important fossil discovery in limestone on the coast near Durness, with forms that were construed as Silurian by Sir Roderick Murchison, who used the formation as a stratigraphic marker to claim the rocks of much of northern Scotland as Silurian, though today the schists there are placed in the Precambrian and the limestone is regarded as Cambro-Ordovician. Murchison and Peach undertook joint fieldwork in north-west Scotland in 1858. On retirement to Edinburgh in 1861, Peach did work on glacial geology and palaeobotany. He died at his home, 30 Haddington Place, Edinburgh, on 28 February 1886.

Peach's work met with much approbation. He was awarded several grants, notably the Wollaston Fund of the Geological Society of London, together with medals from the Cornwall Polytechnic Society and the Neill medal from the Royal Society of Edinburgh. His work was described and praised by Samuel Smiles in his biography of Dick, and both men could be said to exemplify Smilesian ideals of self-help.   DAVID OLDROYD

Sources H. N. Dixon, 'Charles William Peach, A.L.S.', *Journal of the Northamptonshire Natural History Society and Field Club*, 4 (1886–7), 33–40 • A. Taylor, 'Obituary notice of Charles William Peach, A.L.S. &c, Associate', *Transactions of the Edinburgh Geological Society*, 5 (1888), 327–9 • S. Smiles, *Robert Dick, baker of Thurso: geologist and botanist* (1878), 238–58, 259–81 • *Transactions of the Plymouth Institution and Devon and Cornwall Natural History Society*, 9 (1884–7), 209–11 • *Report and Transactions of the Devonshire Association*, 18 (1886), 64–6 • D. R. Oldroyd, *The highlands controversy: constructing geological knowledge through fieldwork in nineteenth-century Britain* (1990), 48–9, 64–70 • *Journal of the Royal Institution of Cornwall*, 9 (1886–9), 2–3, 95–6 • *The Athenaeum* (13 March 1886), 362–3 • *Geological Magazine*, new ser., 3rd decade, 3 (1886), 190–92 • *The Zoologist*, 10 (1886), 177–8 • *Nature*, 33 (1885–6), 446–7 • d. cert.

Archives BGS, corresp. and papers • GS Lond., corresp. and MSS • U. Edin. L., corresp. | NHM, letters to Joshua Alder and Revd Alfred Merle Norman • NL Scot., personal papers, Acc. 10073/6

Likenesses engraving (after photograph?), repro. in Smiles, *Robert Dick*, facing p. 238

Wealth at death £603 10*s.* 5*d.*: confirmation, 19 April 1886, *CCI*

Peach, Lawrence Du Garde (1890–1974), playwright and author, was born at home at 32 Conduit Road, Nether Hallam, Sheffield, on 14 February 1890, the son of a Unitarian minister, Charles Peach (1862–1943), and his wife, Mary Ann, *née* Munns (1863–1940). He was educated at Manchester grammar school (1903–9), where his outstanding abilities as an actor were soon revealed; he went on to graduate at Manchester University in English language and literature (1912). He then obtained a post as Lektor at Göttingen University. During the First World War he served in the Manchester regiment and in military intelligence, reaching the rank of captain. His marriage to Emily Marianne Leeming (1889/90–1972), a fellow student, the daughter of Matthew Leeming, a dentist, took place at the Chorlton-cum-Hardy Unitarian Church on 25 September 1915.

After the war Peach resumed his academic career, proceeding to the degree of PhD at Sheffield University (1921); the title of his two-volume thesis was 'A study of the dramatic relations of France, Spain, and England in the XVII century'—no doubt inspired partly by the work of his Manchester professor, C. H. Herford. Its object was largely to illustrate by comparative analyses the manner in which dramatic themes and situations already exploited by leading European playwrights were adapted by English authors—Dryden, Wycherley, and others—utilizing different stage conventions and more familiar modes of thought. In 1922 he was appointed to a lectureship at the University College of the South West of England and from 1924 to 1926 acted as central organizer of an appeal in support of efforts to secure full university status for the college. While at Exeter he engaged in freelance journalism, submitting sketches to such journals as *London Opinion*, *The Humorist*, and, most notably, *Punch*. But finding authorship more lucrative than university teaching, he resigned his post at the university college in favour of full-time literary work. In 1925 Chatto and Windus published some of his *Punch* contributions under the title of *Angela and I*—'Angela' being the female participant in his imaginary dialogues. Two years later John Lane at the Bodley Head brought out an illustrated travel volume, *Unknown Devon*. Peach's penchant for satire and 'situation comedy' led him to believe that his talents might find a market in the expanding field of playwriting for the amateur stage, as well as the professional theatre. He therefore planned several series of dramas 'tailored' to meet the needs of specific groups (such as plays for boys or plays for women) with a bias towards historical themes. His one-act and two-act plays were especially acceptable to youth groups, women's institutes, and educational organizations.

From 1923 Peach was keen to exploit the potentialities of broadcasting, and he is chiefly remembered as one of the pioneers of radio drama. He realized that this new medium demanded from scriptwriters a readiness to experiment with conventions not appropriate to stage presentation. He aimed also to appeal to juvenile listeners, for whom—in the *Children's Hour* especially—he produced innumerable examples of dramatized history and biography. At a later stage he utilized similar material when putting together ambitious pageants for Sheffield, Manchester, and other cities. He also composed film scripts, but turned down offers of prestigious employment in Hollywood because he was reluctant to submit to the vagaries of producers and sub-editors.

In 1918 Peach's father ended his association with Chorlton in order to become official minister at Great Hucklow, a small Derbyshire village formerly of some importance in the leadmining industry. Soon afterwards Lawrence and his wife also settled in the Peak District.

This gave him an opportunity to form a company of thespians capable under his direction of performing plays from the established repertory along with pieces composed by himself. The members of this troupe were mostly local people co-opted on the strength of their natural talent for acting; but at the back of Peach's mind was the conviction that such an amateur group could be trained to achieve a standard of performance higher than was common among many 'rude mechanicals'. In their early days these 'village players' had to make do with a stage constructed in one of the larger recreational rooms of the local Unitarian holiday home. Later the need for improved amenities induced Peach to purchase a rectangular building deserted by leadminers, and convert it into a small theatre. Right from the start this venture proved successful and led to a novel form of co-operative enterprise in a somewhat backward area. This activity was part of a national 'village drama' movement which Peach warmly supported. He chaired the drama committee of the Derbyshire Rural Community Council (1924) and espoused the cause of amateur theatricals in the pages of the *Derbyshire Countryside*, a monthly he edited from 1931 to 1948. Eventually the doings of the village players came to be so widely appreciated that a minimum of publicity was all that was needed to ensure capacity audiences, and 'house full' notices were frequently in evidence. But the claims of authorship and theatrical involvements did not deter Peach from taking on civic and political responsibilities. In 1929 he stood as Liberal candidate in the general election—though with little hope of victory, since Derby had long been a Labour stronghold. Even so, Peach's intervention helped to increase the Liberal vote from 7083 in the 1924 election to 11,317 in 1929.

During the *entre-deux-guerres* period Peach's engagements were multifarious: his services as author, lecturer, and adjudicator were in constant demand. He maintained a long-standing connection with the Sheffield Repertory Company, and when the Sheffield Playhouse suspended productions in 1939, he assisted in the company's evacuation to Southport. At first his own players were downhearted at having to abandon their annual three-weekly 'seasons'; but Peach attempted to counter their despondency by writing plays which reflected aspects of life amid wartime frustrations. Those male members of the village players who were of military age were either called up or enrolled in the Home Guard, in which Peach became a major. Admittedly, petrol rationing kept many visitors away from Great Hucklow; but in spite of the temporary closure of their little theatre, the company never suffered total collapse until 1971, when a combination of difficult circumstances put an end to further activities.

From the mid-1950s Peach found time to undertake a substantial non-dramatic assignment for the Loughborough-based educational publishers Wills and Hepworth. He was commissioned to produce a number of short illustrated volumes on historical and archaeological subjects intended for young people of school age. Each item in this highly successful Ladybird series—over twenty titles in all—ran to fifty pages and dealt with such topics as Stone Age man, Roman Britain, William the Conqueror, Oliver Cromwell, Charles II, Florence Nightingale, Captain Cook, and Charles Dickens. Peach had no qualms about adding to the already considerable stock of what many would regard as merely 'potted' knowledge: his efforts were anything but run-of-the-mill regurgitations of standard textbook material. In spite of their concise format, the Ladybird books are factually irreproachable and presented in a lively prose style calculated to awaken interest in Britain's cultural and political history. Peach's Ladybird books were as influential as any professional historian's in shaping youthful minds' knowledge of the British past.

Peach's success as a literary man was the outcome of a modest ambition to augment 'the public stock of harmless pleasure' while maintaining a keen interest in social affairs. For his services to literature he was made an OBE in 1972; he had been made an honorary DLitt of Sheffield University in 1964. Sadly he left no autobiography, which would have been a significant addition to the annals of English provincial drama. But tantalizing snatches of reminiscence occur in his various prefaces. If his plays are no longer seen on the commercial stage, this is attributable to changes of taste among theatregoers witnessed over the last fifty or sixty years. But Peach's enduring literary monument is unquestionably the unique account of dramatic activities at Great Hucklow which he published in 1952, *Twenty-Five Years of Play Producing, 1927–1952*. He died at his home, The Bungalow, in the nearby village of Foolow, Derbyshire, on 31 December 1974, his wife having died two years previously.   E. D. MACKERNESS

Sources WWW, 1971–80 · Y. R. Miller, *The history of the old chapel, Great Hucklow, 1696–1996* (1995) · A. Nicoll, *English drama, 1900–1930* (1973) · J. A. Graham and B. A. Phythian, eds., *The Manchester grammar school, 1515–1965* (1965) · S. A. Moseley, ed., *Who's who in broadcasting* (1933) · B. W. Clapp, *The University of Exeter: a history* (1982) · A. Briggs, *The history of broadcasting in the United Kingdom*, 2 (1965), 154 · I. Rodger, *Radio drama* (1982) · N. Ratcliffe, *Rude mechanicals: a short review of village drama* (1938) · T. A. Seed, *The Sheffield repertory company* (1959) · *Ulula: The Manchester Grammar School Magazine* (1873) · *Derbyshire Countryside* (1931) · L. du G. Peach, *Twenty-five years of play producing* (1952) · C. Whitaker, ed., *Whitaker's Almanack* (1930), 182 · *Unitarian and Free Church Christian Year Book* (1944), 78–9 · *The new Cambridge bibliography of English literature*, [2nd edn], 4, ed. I. R. Willison (1972), 973–5 · b. cert. · m. cert. · d. cert.
Archives BL · Derbyshire Local Studies Library, literary MSS, film and radio scripts | U. Reading L., letters to Bodley Head Ltd | FILM BFI NFTVA, performance footage
Likenesses E. Harcourt, portrait, repro. in L. du G. Peach, *Collected plays*, 1 (1955), frontispiece · photographs, repro. in Peach, *Twenty-five years of play producing* · portrait, repro. in V. Gielgud, *British radio drama 1922–1956* (1957), 48
Wealth at death £23,808: probate, 20 Feb 1975, CGPLA Eng. & Wales

Peacham, Edmund (1553/4–1616), Church of England clergyman and traitor, was born in Barton, Northamptonshire. Nothing is known about his parents or early life. He matriculated at the age of twenty-one as a sizar at Christ's College, Cambridge, in June 1575. He was ordained deacon in London in 1580 and priest the following year. In 1581 he was appointed vicar of Ridge, Hertfordshire. On 15 July 1587 Peacham was presented by the noted puritan Sir Amias Paulet to the rectory of Hinton St George in Somerset; there he remained until his death in 1616.

Peacham married Katherine Ballie (*bap.* 1576), from Devon, at Hinton St George on 26 August 1607. He was her senior by twenty-two years and the couple remained childless. He shared the puritan convictions of his patron, and conducted his ministerial duties in Somerset without any known scandal or controversy. Somewhat surprisingly this provincial cleric became embroiled in direct opposition to the policies of the government of James VI and I. Indeed, his actions and the views he expressed from the pulpit transcended the spiritual sphere of his ministerial calling. Peacham's activities brought him into conflict with the civil authorities. His intentions may have been treasonable, as he began to express more extreme ideas, or imprudent, perhaps both. As early as 1603 he was accused of preaching against the new king, the privy council, episcopate, and judiciary. On this occasion no action was taken against him, but his hostility towards the king's religious policies, including James's support for the bishops, coolness towards puritans and presbyterians, and demand for greater uniformity of worship, meant that he began to speak out against the ecclesiastical polity again in 1608. This reaction was triggered by the appointment of James Montagu as bishop of Bath and Wells. Peacham openly attacked Montagu from the pulpit, resulting in a reprimand in the consistory court. This failed to dissuade him from attacking the bishop and he continued to do so intermittently over the next six years.

In 1614 Peacham further estranged himself from the ecclesiastical authorities by refusing to subscribe to the required benevolence, claiming insufficient means but promising to pray for the king. Meanwhile, resenting the reprimand suffered at the hands of Montagu, he circulated in private a manuscript seriously questioning the bishop's character. In December 1614 Peacham was arrested by the court of high commission on a complaint brought against him by Montagu; he was convicted of libel and deprived of his clerical orders. A search for further evidence of his writings against Montagu revealed a sermon in Peacham's hand, in which he denounced the king, and foretold his death as divine judgment for the actions of the privy council and episcopate. He also wrote that rebellion would probably ensue. James was understandably alarmed when news reached him of the sermon, which though it was never preached seemed to trigger fears of a treasonous plot. The turn of events for Peacham was certainly unforeseen, but worse awaited him, when the king attempted to secure evidence of his treason. On 19 January 1615 Sir Francis Bacon, attorney-general, Henry Montagu (brother of James Montagu), king's serjeant, and the officers of the Tower of London had Peacham tortured. During this interrogation Peacham remained silent. The recourse to torture in such a case of suspected treason was defended by Bacon, setting the legal maxim that torture could be used 'for discovery and not for evidence' (*Works of Francis Bacon*, 3.114). The opposition of the Somerset gentry towards the benevolence in 1614 fuelled fears of a wider plot and the apparently ruthless interrogation of the suspect was intended to detect the extent of the threat to James.

The critical legal issue was whether Peacham should be tried for high treason. In an attempt to clarify this matter Bacon separately consulted the judges before the indictment was made against Peacham. His words were deemed to convey treasonable intent. Sir Edward Coke, chief justice of the king's bench, dissented from this position by asserting that a written attack on the king must 'disable his title' in order to be treasonable. Coke also protested against the canvassing of the judges in the matter. The deciding factor was the king's personal desire to pursue the case, based on his continued animosity towards Peacham.

Peacham desperately sought to stall the case against him. First he implicated Paulet, and then his patron's brother-in-law, Sir John Sydenham, who were both cleared of complicity after being summoned to appear before the privy council. Finally he suggested that the controversial sermon notes had been the work of his namesake, a contemporary writer, Henry Peacham. In July Edmund Peacham stood trial in Taunton, Somerset, charged with high treason. He was arraigned before Sir Christopher Tanfield and Henry Montagu. James sent Sir Henry Yelverton, solicitor-general, and Sir Randolph Crewe, lord chief justice of the king's bench, to conduct the case for the crown. Peacham was duly found guilty and condemned to death. On 31 August he apparently admitted writing the sermon. No evidence was ever found to substantiate a wider conspiracy against the king. The sentence against him was never carried out because it was not considered politically expedient.

Peacham died of natural causes in gaol in Taunton on 27 March 1616. The writer John Chamberlain alleged that he left behind an even worse sermon than he had previously written; the story may be apocryphal, but it conveys a sense of the contempt shown towards him. He was certainly guilty of treason. In his disagreement with the ecclesiastical policies of James he became dangerously politicized, hardened as he was by many years of personal opposition to James Montagu. No contemporary puritan tried to defend Peacham's actions, nor did any later question the legitimacy of the proceedings against him. None of his writings have been preserved. His infamy is based on other accounts of his political views as expressed in sermons. These views crossed the boundary between church and state, and the finest legal minds of the day were called upon to protect the person of the king. Their zeal in doing so, involving the use of torture and ignoring the objections of Coke, reveal something about the climate of political fear in Jacobean England as well as highlighting the wasted and blighted clerical career of Peacham.   ROGER N. McDERMOTT

Sources J. Peile, *Biographical register of Christ's College, 1505–1905, and of the earlier foundation, God's House, 1448–1505*, ed. [J. A. Venn], 1 (1910), 133 · Venn, *Alum. Cant.*, 1/3.325 · *The works of Francis Bacon*, ed. J. Spedding, R. L. Ellis, and D. D. Heath, 14 vols. (1857–74), 5.90–128 · *CSP dom.*, 1603–6 · *DNB* · E. Dwelly, ed., *Somerset parish registers*, 15 vols. (1913–) · *IGI*

Peacham, Henry (*b.* 1578, *d.* in or after 1644), writer and illustrator, was born in the parish of North Mimms, Hertfordshire, the second son of Henry Peacham (1547–1634) and his wife, Anne (*née* Fairclough).

Family and education At the time of his son's birth, the elder Henry Peacham was the minister of North Mimms, but in 1578 he also obtained the living of Leverton in Lincolnshire. He does not appear to have left North Mimms for Leverton until 1595, but he then served there until his death in 1634. Before leaving North Mimms, the elder Peacham had created what was to be his enduring monument by writing *The Garden of Eloquence* (1577), a book of rhetoric that was to become celebrated.

The younger Henry Peacham went to school near St Albans and then in London. In 1592 he matriculated as a sizar of Trinity College, Cambridge, where he took his BA degree in 1595, proceeding MA in 1598. About this time it appears that he may have visited Modena to study music under the direction of the distinguished composer of madrigals, Orazio Vecchi (1550–1605), whom he later described as 'mine owne Master' (H. Peacham, *Complete Gentleman*, 1622, 102). From about 1600 until 1607 Henry Peacham was teaching at Kimbolton School, Huntingdonshire. He was a reluctant schoolmaster, considering such teaching unrewarding and 'one of the most laborious callings in the World' (H. Peacham, *The Truth of our Times*, 1638, 19). Nevertheless, he had grudging recourse to the profession throughout his life.

While still at Cambridge, and at the age of seventeen, Peacham produced a work that reflected what was to be his lifelong interest in the graphic arts. This was his drawing of a scene from *Titus Andronicus* done about 1595, commonly accepted as the earliest illustration of a Shakespeare play. In subsequent years Peacham was to produce numerous portraits and emblem plates, as well as write instructional works in the graphic arts. His *Art of Drawing* (1606), a treatise on drawing and watercolours, was reissued in 1607, and expanded as *Graphice* (1612). *Graphice* was further expanded and published again in 1634 and 1661 as *The Gentleman's Exercise*, one of Peacham's most widely read works.

About 1603 Peacham turned to another of the arts and composed the words and music of a four-part madrigal, 'Awake softly with singing, Oriana sleeping'. This was not published, but is found at the end of the third manuscript version of his emblem book based on *Basilikon Doron* (1603).

Early emblem books Peacham had begun to explore the emblem convention in the early 1600s, and his contribution to emblem literature was ultimately to be both substantial and significant. His career as an emblem writer began in 1603 when he presented a few emblems of his own composition to James I in Huntingdon on 27–9 April as the new king was making his way south. This occasion was probably the beginning of Peacham's efforts to obtain preferment at court. Between 1603 and 1610 he composed three emblem books, each of them surviving only in undated manuscript form. They are each based on *Basilikon Doron* (1599), the king's own book of advice to his young son. The earliest, composed in 1603–4, is dedicated to Prince Henry, the two later manuscripts, probably written about 1604–5 and in 1610, are dedicated respectively to the king himself and again to Prince Henry.

The earliest of Peacham's manuscript emblem books contains fifty-six pen-and-ink pictures (Bodl. Oxf., MS Rawl. poet. 146), the second book has sixty-five such plates (BL, Harleian MS 6855, art. 13), and the third has seventy-eight (BL, Royal MS 12, A. lxvi). The last differs from the other two in having the plates completed in watercolour. Peacham's work as an emblem writer shows him to have been keenly aware of the symbolism of colour. The plan that he generally follows with each emblem is to base it on a quotation that he has selected from the 1603 edition of *Basilikon Doron*, interpret the picture in four lines of Latin, and add a motto, sometimes in Greek.

Towards the end of 1607 Peacham appears to have moved to London, where his first known address was Fetter Lane. Some time before 1612 he moved again, this time to the parish of St Martin-in-the-Fields, Westminster, where Sara, one of his two daughters, was baptized in the parish church on 27 April. Neither the name of Peacham's wife nor the dates of his marriage and the birth of his other daughter have been established.

While at St Martin-in-the-Fields Peacham produced his most serious work to date, the emblem book *Minerva Britanna, or, A Garden of Heroical Devises* (1612). Of its 204 emblems some sixty-two are derived from those of his three *Basilikon Doron* emblem-book manuscripts. But *Minerva Britanna* departs in important respects from his previous emblem works. The interpretative verse is in English, and many of the repeated plates differ in detail. Like the manuscript emblems those of *Minerva Britanna* are generally of the kind that has been labelled 'diagrammatic'. That is, the pictures present a number of different symbols assembled together to represent a single idea.

Minerva Britanna may properly be regarded as belonging to the earliest group of English emblem books. Its emblematic woodcuts are believed to be Peacham's own work. If so, his ability to conceive and execute his own designs meant that he had no need of the sometimes massive borrowing of plates to which other emblem writers perforce resorted. Although the pictures used in *Minerva Britanna* are of no great distinction they are, for the most part, simple, direct, and wholly relevant to Peacham's needs. The accompanying verse interpreting each plate is, similarly, competent rather than graceful. Although the range of Peacham's topics is wide, very many of them are familiar. He acknowledges numerous sources and it is easy to identify others. For example, like so many of his contemporaries, he draws heavily upon Cesare Ripa's *Iconologia* (1593) and to a lesser extent upon Spenser's *The Faerie Queene* (1596).

In 1612, shortly after Peacham moved to St Martin-in-the-Fields, Prince Henry, whose patronage he had so carefully sought, died. Although he was only eighteen years of age at the time of his death, the prince's accomplishments and his exciting promise were so universally respected as to make his passing a national disaster. From the flood of literary tributes to him a new kind of elegiac writing emerged. It was a genre at which Peacham was to excel and he began in this kind with *The Period of Mourning* (1613), lamenting the prince.

European travel and *The Complete Gentleman* Not long after the death of Prince Henry, and perhaps in some measure as a consequence, Peacham left England in order to travel, principally in France, Germany, and the Low Countries. On this tour he clearly sought every opportunity of enlarging his already wide interests and of acquiring a substantial part of his ultimately considerable learning.

Peacham's progress through Europe terminated at Utrecht where he 'lived at the table of that Honourable Gentleman, Sir *John Ogle*, Lord Governor of the town' (*Complete Gentleman*, 195). Ogle was a man of learning, and it was said that the company which assembled at his house effectively constituted an academy. Greatly to Peacham's advantage, he and Ogle became friends. While in Utrecht with Ogle, Peacham completed *Prince Henrie Revived* (1615), a lofty poem in honour of the birth in 1614 of Prince Henry Frederick, the son of Princess Elizabeth and the count palatine.

It was through Ogle that Peacham gained some knowledge of military affairs. In writing of his experiences Peacham does not make it clear whether he was, himself, a fighting member of the protestant forces in the Netherlands, but he was certainly with the section of Colonel Ogle's regiment that served under the command of Prince Maurice of Nassau in the autumn of 1614. Peacham's account of events was published as *A most True Relation of the Affaires of Cleve and Gulick* (1615). By the time this appeared Peacham was back in England, and had returned to teaching. He took up a post at the free grammar school in Wymondham, Norfolk, about 1615 and remained there until 1620.

Peacham's sojourn in Norfolk is noteworthy for the friends and acquaintances he made and for the publication of his next substantial work, *Thalia's Banquet* (1620), a book of epigrams. Many of the 127 epigrams are dedicated to his recent acquaintances. The composition of epigrams was not a new departure for Peacham since his first publication after his removal to London in 1607 had also been a collection of epigrams, *The More the Merrier* (1608). Among those persons of some consequence that Peacham came to know while living in Norfolk were William Howard, the young son of the earl of Arundel, and Richard Sackville, third earl of Dorset. He was to honour both of them in print.

By 1621 Peacham had returned to London and was teaching in St Martin-in-the-Fields. At this time he completed his *Emblemata varia*, the last of his four emblem books to survive only in manuscript. It is a much shorter work than any of the others, having only twenty emblems, none of them being used for the second time, and all of them presented with uncharacteristic economy. There is a striking absence of the marginal annotations found in Peacham's previous emblem books. The following year Peacham was living at Hoxton.

The Complete Gentleman (1622), which Peacham finished after his return to London, is probably his best-known work, and it occupies a significant place in the history of courtesy literature. Its immediate inspiration was Peacham's conviction, arising from his continental tour, that the education of young English gentlemen was markedly inferior to that afforded to European gentry. By now the courtesy book was being addressed to an audience less markedly aristocratic, and although *The Complete Gentleman* was for the use of William Howard it is clear that Peacham sought popular appeal. *The Complete Gentleman* offers advice over a wide range of topics with humour and sagacity, and reflects many aspects of Peacham's experience. It is not surprising that he should attribute poor education to the remissness of parents, nor that he wrote with urgency about painting and drawing. Several chapters have become classic statements, like that 'Of poetry' which was to be frequently quoted as a summary of contemporary views. The learning displayed here offers ample justification for Peacham's claim 'By profession I am a Scholler' (*Graphice*, 1612, sig. A2v).

No later than 1624 Peacham had returned to East Anglia, and was working as a schoolmaster in Boston. At this time he produced *An Aprill Shower*, the elegy on Richard Sackville, earl of Dorset. Although Peacham had enjoyed Lord Dorset's benevolence it was apparently not for long, and, now, once more, an untimely death deprived him of a patron. It is not clear how long Peacham's teaching appointment in Boston extended, but in 1632 he was given a temporary post at Heighington Free School, Lincolnshire.

In 1629 Frances Rich, countess of Warwick, invited Peacham to design for her a monument to be erected on her death in Snarford church, Lincolnshire. It was a task for which Peacham's talents were admirably suited; but Lady Warwick changed her mind, and the plan remained unused. In his elegy for her, *Thestylis atrata* (1634), Peacham writes of the 'many favors' that he had received from her. If these words are more than conventional it appears that death had yet again robbed him of the patronage he so obviously desired. The ten years between 1624 and 1634 which Peacham spent in East Anglia were relatively unproductive. But to this period there does belong the appearance in 1627 and 1634 of the important second and third editions of *The Complete Gentleman* and the 1634 edition of *The Gentleman's Exercise*.

Final years After concluding his period of teaching at Heighington School in 1635 Peacham appears to have returned, once more, to London. The final years of his life are obscure. He has recorded that some time during this period he was 'exercised in another calling' (*Truth of our Times*, 1638, 41), though its nature is unknown. But there was a recrudescence of his creative energy, and between 1636 and 1642 he published ten prose works. Most of these might be described as pamphlets, and their variety—from comic to polemic—has led to the speculation that Peacham was existing in poverty and making a living with his pen.

As a comic writer Peacham began with *Coach and Sedan* (1636), an exuberant piece of humorous writing cast in the form of a dialogue in which various modes of transport are considered. In a more serious vein he produced *The Truth of our Times* (1638), fundamentally an unembittered recollection of a lifetime's disappointments. Stylistically, this is among the best books Peacham ever wrote in prose, and he appears to have had especial affection for the work. *The Worth of a Peny* (1641), essentially a simple exhortation to thrift, was one of Peacham's most popular pieces (ten editions appearing in the seventeenth century alone). With the approach of civil war Peacham, a man of royalist and Anglican sympathies, joined in the current religious controversy with a polemic, *The Duty of All True Subjects* (1639), that makes his position clear. He deplores the zeal of those who would reform the monarchy and the church, and continued this theme with three more pamphlets in 1641 and 1642.

One of the happiest aspects of Peacham's life in these final years was his collaboration with Wenceslaus Hollar, the great Dutch engraver. Hollar had been brought to England by the earl of Arundel in 1636 and employed in creating a pictorial record of various objects in Arundel's celebrated collection of works of art and antiquities. All told Hollar and Peacham collaborated in producing six pictorial engravings with accompanying text by Peacham. The first of these, done in 1637, was an engraving of Giulio Romano's 'Seleucus and Son' to which Peacham provided accompanying Latin verse. This was their only joint product that was based on an item in Arundel's collection. The others depict a view of Greenwich (1637), a diptych of Richard II and the Virgin Mary (1639), a broadside emblem *En surculus arbor* (1641), a satirical work (1641?), and the interior of the Royal Exchange (1644).

The precise date and place of Peacham's death have not been satisfactorily established. Although there are some contemporary references, the evidence they provide is conflicting. It seems most likely that he was still alive when Hollar's engraving of the Royal Exchange, to which he contributed Latin and English verse, was published in 1644.   JOHN HORDEN

Sources M. C. Pitman, 'Studies in the works of Henry Peacham', MA diss., U. Lond., 1933 [summaries of theses, 116, summarized in *BIHR*, 11 (1933), 189–92] · A. R. Young, *Henry Peacham* (1979) · A. R. Young, 'Henry Peacham, author of *The garden of eloquence* (1577): a biographical note', *N&Q*, 222 (1977), 503–7 · A. R. Young, 'A biographical note on Henry Peacham', *N&Q*, 222 (1977), 214–17 · H. Peacham, *Minerva Britanna*, ed. J. Horden (1969) · H. Peacham, *Emblemata varia* (1976), introd. A. R. Young · R. C. Strong, 'Queen Elizabeth I as Oriana', *Studies in the Renaissance*, 6, 251–60 · STC, 1475–1640 · Wing, STC

Peache, Alfred (1818–1900), Church of England clergyman and benefactor, was born on 30 August 1818 at Belvedere House, Lambeth, London. His father, James Courthope Peache (1782–1858), was a wealthy timber merchant, barge builder, and barge owner—a man of property who became the chairman of the Lambeth Waterworks Company and a deputy lieutenant of Surrey. James Peache married Alice Coventry (1784–1859) and they had a family of eight boys and four girls, only three of whom survived beyond the age of twenty-four—the second child, Clement, the ninth, Alfred, and the tenth, Kezia [see below]. In 1834 the surviving family moved from Lambeth to Wimbledon.

Alfred was educated at the King's College School, London, and Wadham College, Oxford. He graduated BA in 1841 and MA in 1844 and, against his father's wishes, was ordained deacon in 1842 and priest in 1843. His first curacy was at Mangotsfield with Downend, near Bristol, and until his marriage Kezia lived there with him. In 1850 Peache married Julia Augusta (Gussie) Cox (1823–1890) and they had a family of four sons and three daughters. Peache moved to a further curacy at Heckfield-cum-Mattingley, Hampshire, in 1854.

In December 1857 Clement Peache died of a chill and within six weeks his father died without making a new will. The result was that Alfred and Kezia became the joint executors, and the considerable estate was equally divided between them. Kezia remained at Wimbledon and Alfred continued in parochial ministry until he was sixty. From 1859 he was the perpetual curate of Mangotsfield with Downend, and became the first vicar of Downend when it was made into a separate parish in 1874.

Kezia Peache (1820–1899), benefactor, was born at Belvedere House, Lambeth, in August 1820 and was educated at Prospect House School. She lived at the family home in Wimbledon, and then at Mangotsfield (1845–50); in 1845 she toured Europe with Clement. Kezia returned to Wimbledon in 1850, and was the organist of Wimbledon parish church (1854–69) and taught in the Sunday school. She gave the east window in memory of her father and supported numerous local charities and worthy causes. She was concerned about the housing of the poor and, as well as making donations to the Cottage Improvement Society, was responsible for the erection of nearly fifty artisans' cottages in Wimbledon. On 16 March 1899 she died unmarried at her home, 42 Church Road, Wimbledon, and was buried in Wimbledon cemetery.

Both Peache and his sister were devoted evangelicals and were determined to give away their fortune to worthy causes. In 1863 they put down an initial sum of £35,000 to establish the London College of Divinity (also known as St John's Hall). The college was opened in a former school in Kilburn, London, then moved to Highbury, in 1866, where it remained until 1940. In all Peache and his sister gave more than £100,000 to the college, and Alfred remained actively involved as a member of council and, for a few months before his death, as president. By 1900 well over 700 men had been trained for the Anglican ministry at the London College of Divinity. Also in 1863 Peache gave £5000 to endow the Peache chair of divinity at Huron College, London, Ontario, Canada, which, like the London college, had an evangelical foundation and similar trustees. The University of Western Ontario arose from the college and in 1881 Peache was awarded an honorary DD; in 1885 he became the second chancellor of the university.

Peache supported the schools in his parish and, with his sister, provided financial support for additional buildings of the Bristol Clergy Daughters' School. He was a council

member of Ridley Hall, Cambridge, and the largest subscriber to the Henry Martyn Hall, Cambridge, the memorial stone of which he laid in 1886. In 1875 Peache bought Monkton Combe School, near Bath, and sold it in 1877 for £3000. In 1869 he acquired land in Layer Marney, near Colchester, Essex, and ten years later he and Kezia became the lord and lady of the manor of Layer Marney.

To further the evangelical cause in the Church of England Peache acquired the right of presentation to appoint clergy to a number of livings. He had inherited the advowson of Mangotsfield with Downend from his father, and presented himself to the living in 1859. Over the years he purchased eleven other livings including that of Holy Trinity, Cambridge, where Charles Simeon had been the incumbent. These livings became the basis of the Peache Trust, established in 1877, which by the time of Peache's death held the patronage of twenty-three livings—one in Wales and the rest in England.

Peache died at his house, Danmore, Wimbledon, on 22 November 1900, and was buried at Downend next to his wife. In the funeral address he was well described as a 'simple-hearted, unassuming, courteous old gentleman'.

A. F. Munden

Sources *The Times* (24 Nov 1900) · *The Times* (27 Nov 1900) · *The Record* (7 Dec 1900) · *St John's Magazine*, 6/2 (autumn 1900), 35–45 · G. C. B. Davies, *Men for the ministry* (1963) · J. J. Talman, *Huron College, 1863–1963* (1963) · A. F. Munden, *The history of St John's College, Nottingham*, 1: *Mr Peache's college at Kilburn* (1995) · R. Milward, *Historic Wimbledon* (1989)
Likenesses J. E. Williams, portraits, 1872 (Alfred and Kezia Peache), St John's College, Nottingham · portrait (Kezia Peache), repro. in Milward, *Historic Wimbledon*, 109
Wealth at death £28,990 5s. 11d.: probate, 29 Dec 1900, *CGPLA Eng. & Wales* · £3,807 13s. 1d.—Kezia Peache: probate, 5 May 1899, *CGPLA Eng. & Wales*

Peache, Kezia (1820–1899). *See under* Peache, Alfred (1818–1900).

Peachell, John (1628/9–1690), college head, was the son of Robert Peachell of Fillingham, Lincolnshire. He was educated at Gainsborough School and on 1 August 1645, at the age of sixteen, was admitted a sizar of Magdalene College, Cambridge, where his tutor was John Dacres. Peachell's mother was aunt of the incumbent master, Edward Rainbow, and he undoubtedly came to the college by this connection. On 2 May 1646 he was admitted a scholar on Lady Warwick's foundation; he matriculated in that year and graduated BA in 1649. On 18 March 1650 he was elected and admitted a fellow on Smith's foundation, and on 3 January 1652 was elected to a Spendluffe fellowship. In 1653 he proceeded MA, and was incorporated at Oxford in the same year. On 3 November 1656 he was elected to a perpetual (founder's) fellowship, to which he was admitted on 6 November. On 20 September 1660 his fellowship was confirmed; he then temporarily resigned to allow the restoration of those ejected under the Commonwealth, on the understanding that he would recover his place and seniority when a vacancy occurred.

Peachell was a popular tutor, his pupils including his successor as master, Gabriel Quadring, and the Hon.

Clotworthy Skeffington, son of one of James II's most resolute opponents. Echoes of puritanism can be discerned in Peachell's letters, but he was drinking Charles II's health three months before the Restoration. Pepys (a Magdalene contemporary) records this and other meetings with Peachell, though he eventually felt ashamed to be seen with the red-nosed ('though otherwise … good-natured') don (Pepys, *Diary*, 8.199). In 1661 Peachell took the degree of BD. From 1663 to 1681, by the presentation of Sir John Cutts, he was rector of Childerley, Cambridgeshire. On 18 November 1667 his cousin Rainbow, now bishop of Carlisle, made him his archdeacon and a canon of his cathedral; these dignities were resigned by March 1669. Peachell also held the Cumberland livings of Great Salkeld (1667–8) and Stanwix. In 1679 he was appointed master of Magdalene by the earl of Suffolk, the hereditary visitor; his admission took place on 12 August. In the following year he took the degree of DD. In 1681 he exchanged his rectory of Childerley for that of Dry Drayton, Cambridgeshire.

In 1686 Peachell was elected vice-chancellor of Cambridge University, and in this capacity was faced with James II's command of 7 February 1687 that an MA be conferred on a Benedictine, Alban Francis, without the customary oath. When the king's letter was formally read on 21 February, the senate decided that the vice-chancellor should not confer the degree, and Peachell wrote to the duke of Albemarle (the chancellor) in the hope that the king would withdraw his contentious demand. Peachell also wrote anxiously to the bishop of Ely, Pepys, and others. On 11 March the senate advised the vice-chancellor to resist a further royal order, and unsurprisingly on 9 April the university authorities were summoned before the ecclesiastical commission. Peachell led the delegation, which made its first appearance on 21 April. He at once asked for time to submit a written deposition, which was allowed. On 27 April he was questioned by Lord Chancellor Jeffreys, and gave a convincing display of amentia. In this there may have been some artifice, for Peachell was well connected, and not so innocent of worldly affairs as he claimed. But his bumbling performance made easy work for the lord chancellor, who showed the Cambridge men's case to be unsound in law and precedent. Peachell was adjudged responsible for the university's flagrant disobedience, and on 7 May was dismissed from his vice-chancellorship and suspended as master (though the college quietly continued his emoluments). The Francis issue was forgotten as the larger controversy over Magdalen College, Oxford, developed. On 24 October 1688 Peachell was restored to his mastership by the king's order; his term as vice-chancellor would have by then in any case expired. A month earlier Pepys had offered him a naval chaplaincy; on 27 September Peachell replied that thirty years ago he had 'a little itch to such a service', but no longer (*Letters and the Second Diary*, 195).

Peachell died, unmarried, in 1690, supposedly after trying to keep sober for four days, and was buried in his college chapel. The college cook, Peter Betson, administered his estate. Peachell's most useful work was in soliciting funds for the new building which would form Magdalene's second court, and where Pepys's library would eventually be housed. C. S. KNIGHTON

Sources Magd. Cam., A/50/3/1–5; B/422, pp. 6, 60b, 63b, 66b, 69, reverse pp. 22, 23; B/423, p. 16 • Venn, *Alum. Cant.*, 1/3.325 • P. Cunich and others, *A history of Magdalene College, Cambridge, 1428–1988* (1994), 128, 135, 150–55 • Pepys, *Diary*, 1.68; 2.146; 8.199; 10.310 • *Letters and the second diary of Samuel Pepys*, ed. R. G. Howarth (1932); repr. (1933), 110, 176–7, 194–5 • *CSP dom.*, 1687–9, 329 • *Fasti Angl.* (Hardy), 3.150, 254 • C. H. Cooper, *Annals of Cambridge*, 3 (1845), 615–33 • *The autobiography of Symon Patrick, bishop of Ely* (1839), 229 • G. W. Keeton, *Lord Chancellor Jeffreys and the Stuart cause* (1965), 415–16 • *Gilbert Burnet: History of his own time*, ed. T. Stackhouse, abridged edn (1874); repr. (1986), 252–3

Peachie, John (*fl.* 1683). *See under* Pechey, John (*bap.* 1654, *d.* 1718).

Peacock, (Edward) Adrian Woodruffe- (1858–1922), ecologist, was born at Bottesford Manor, north Lincolnshire, on 23 July 1858, the son of Edward Peacock (1831–1915), farmer, antiquarian, historian, and author, and his wife, Lucy Ann Wetherell (1823–1887). Their seven children, Florence (1855–1900), Mabel (1856–1920), Edith (1857–1874), Edward, always known as Adrian, Max (1859–1903), Julian (1861–1944), and Ralph (*b.* 1863), were all baptized Woodruffe, but only Adrian used it as part of his surname from the late 1880s onwards.

Peacock's first schooling was with his brothers and sisters at home, supervised by their mother, and subsequently at Edinburgh Academy (1870–73) and St Peter's School, York (1873). He then received private tuition in Lincolnshire until April 1877, when he was admitted to St John's College, Cambridge, to study mathematics, classics, science, and natural history. Shortage of money, poor health, and the decision to become an Anglican clergyman cut short his stay there. In 1879 he transferred to Bishop Hatfield's Hall, Durham University. He sat for the degree examination at Easter 1881, but 'scratched', thinking that he had failed his Latin paper. However, he had obtained his licentiate of theology in December 1880, was ordained deacon in December 1881, and priest in December 1883. His curacies were at Long Benton, Northumberland (1881–4); Barkingside, Essex (1884–5); Long Benton (1885–6); and finally at Harrington, Northamptonshire (1886–90), where, on 10 July 1888, he married Ellen Mary, daughter of a London architect, George Adam Burn. In 1891 Woodruffe-Peacock accepted the living at Cadney, 10 miles from his birthplace. His son was born there, but his wife died in childbirth on 20 December 1891, aged thirty. On 8 October 1902 he married Charlotte Ann (1865–1935), only daughter of Thomas Warner of Leicester Abbey.

Woodruffe-Peacock was tall and broad in proportion, but his health did not match up to his stature: most of his life he suffered from chronic hay fever and rheumatism; his digestion was poor and on the advice of a specialist he gave up cycling. Nevertheless, he was a tremendous walker: 6 to 8 miles daily was quite usual since Cadney had a scattered parish community; his routes contained some of the best observed and documented habitats in the British Isles. The Cadney living was most conducive to his interests, providing him with the opportunity to make constant observations and recordings of natural changes over a limited area. Woodruffe-Peacock's bad memory prompted his custom of making notes on the spot and he maintained detailed diaries, composed on separate sheets of paper carried in an inner pocket of his jacket; further inner pockets designed to accommodate a pen and double safety inkwell allowed him to work continuously at his diary. After abstracting the natural history data he destroyed all his pre-1909 diaries, but those compiled from 1909 until his death in 1922 (2390 sheets) are housed in Scunthorpe Museum.

Not only was Woodruffe-Peacock's contribution to local biological knowledge considerable, but his varied interests made it possible for him to grasp ecological principles and readily understand the interrelationships between organisms. He was an early exponent of the ecological approach to natural history recording. His pioneering work was recognized by A. G. Tansley (1871–1955), the father of British ecology, but the originality of Woodruffe-Peacock's work has not received due credit. Tansley, impressed by the manuscript of his 'Rock-soil flora of Lincolnshire', offered to bear the cost of its publication; however, it is clear that the original text required major reduction. Woodruffe-Peacock worked at this for the rest of his life, but was never happy over the radical changes to his life's work. It remained unpublished, but the voluminous manuscripts, given to the botany school, Cambridge University, are a vast source of ecological information.

Woodruffe-Peacock compiled a *Critical Catalogue of Lincolnshire Plants* (1894–1900), superseded by his *Check-List of Lincolnshire Plants* (1909), allegedly based on an analysis of half a million observations. His section on the Lincolnshire flora for the Victoria county history was never published. The *Lincolnshire Place-Name and Dialect Dictionary* compiled by members of the Peacock family, with Woodruffe-Peacock as editor-in-chief, remained in manuscript until transcribed and published in 1997. At Cadney he found it necessary to augment his small clerical income by offering his services as a thoroughbred stud adviser and game specialist, being appointed additional field observer to the grouse commission. He published seventeen guides, mainly on animal and plant husbandry, under the title Rural Studies Series (1902–17). He further augmented his income through writing, including an unsuccessful novel, *Only a Sister?*, under the pen-name Walter Adam Wallace. His writing (often pseudonymous) for popular journals had better success, the income from it supporting his natural history pursuits.

Woodruffe-Peacock took a leading role in the foundation of the Lincolnshire Naturalists' Union in 1893, serving as organizing secretary in 1895 and president in 1905. He was the prime mover in establishing a museum for Lincolnshire, his extensive herbarium forming an integral part of its original collections and the foundation of the city and county museum's herbarium. He was elected a fellow of both the Linnean Society and the Geological Society in 1895.

In 1920 Woodruffe-Peacock was appointed rector of Grayingham, Lincolnshire, with a higher stipend, a smaller and less scattered population and a commodious rectory near his sister Mabel. Hardly had he begun to settle into a routine when his sister became ill; she died on 17 June 1920 and was buried at Grayingham. His sorrow, the pressure of the new appointment, and the disappointment over the radical changes needed for the publication of his 'Rock-soil flora' were too much for him. His health broke down and he died at the rectory at midnight on 3 February 1922; five days later he was buried in an unmarked grave beside his sister.   MARK SEAWARD

Sources M. R. D. Seaward, 'Biographical and bibliographical notes on the Rev. E. A. Woodruffe-Peacock, 1858–1922', *Lincolnshire History and Archaeology*, 6 (1971), 113–24 · M. R. D. Seaward, 'E. Adrian Woodruffe-Peacock (1858–1922): a pioneer ecologist', *Archives of Natural History*, 28 (2001), 59–70 · E. Elder, 'Edward Peacock and his family: an introduction to the Peacocks, collectors of north Lincolnshire dialect from 1850 to 1920', *Some historians of Lincolnshire*, ed. C. Sturman (1992), 70–81 · W. D. Roebuck, 'The presidents of the Lincolnshire Naturalists' Union: Edward Adrian Woodruffe-Peacock', *Transactions of the Lincolnshire Naturalists' Union*, 3 (1913), 71–80 · *The Peacock Lincolnshire word books, 1884–1920*, ed. E. Elder (1997) · E. Elder, 'The Peacocks of north-west Lincolnshire: collectors and recorders of Lincolnshire dialect from c.1850 to 1920', *Lincolnshire History and Archaeology*, 24 (1989), 29–39; 28 (1993), 44–57 · R. W. Goulding, 'E. A. Woodruffe-Peacock', *Report of the Botanical Society of the British Isles*, 6 (1922), 712–14 · E. J. Gibbons, *The flora of Lincolnshire* (1975) · J. Britten, 'Edward Adrian Woodruffe-Peacock', *Journal of Botany, British and Foreign*, 60 (1922), 161–2 · North Lincolnshire Museum, Scunthorpe, Peacock archive · b. cert. · d. cert.

Archives City and County Museum, Lincoln, Herbarium, MSS · North Lincolnshire Museum, corresp., diaries, and papers · NRA, priv. coll., MSS · U. Cam., department of plant sciences, corresp., journals, and papers | Lincs. Arch., letters to R. W. Goulding

Likenesses photographs, North Lincolnshire Museum, Scunthorpe, Peacock MSS · portrait, repro. in Seaward, 'Biographical and bibliographical notes' · portrait, repro. in Seaward, 'E. Adrian Woodruffe-Peacock' · portrait, repro. in Elder, 'The Peacocks of north-west Lincolnshire' · portrait, repro. in Elder, 'Edward Peacock and his family'

Wealth at death £3831: Peacock archive, North Lincolnshire Museum, Scunthorpe

Peacock, Sir Barnes (1810–1890), judge, was the third son of Lewis H. Peacock (*d.* 1839), a solicitor and messenger to the great seal, of 38 Lincoln's Inn Fields, London. On 29 January 1828 he was admitted at the Inner Temple, but postponed his call to the bar until he had practised for several years as a special pleader. He was called on 29 January 1836, joined the home circuit, and was soon considered a sound lawyer.

Peacock made his chief reputation as one of the counsel for Daniel O'Connell in his August 1844 appeal to the House of Lords, and a technical objection he suggested led the majority of the Lords to allow the appeal. He stated that the indictment contained numerous counts and several separate charges, and that some of the counts had been held bad in law. Yet on this indictment, and on good counts and bad counts indiscriminately, one general verdict and judgment had been given. This was in accordance with a practice which, however slovenly, was common and supposedly valid, but the House of Lords declared it a wrong practice, and that a judgment so given could not stand.

Despite this success Peacock did not become a QC until 28 February 1850; he was elected a bencher of the Inner Temple on 10 May the same year (reader, 1864). From April 1852 to April 1859 he was legal member of the supreme council of the viceroy at Calcutta, in succession to Drinkwater Bethune, and there, in the preparation of various codifying acts, he proved his quality as a jurist. Agreeing with 'the spirit of the age' (Ambirajan, 108) in 1853 he presented a bill, subsequently passed, to repeal usury legislation. He wrote an important minute on Oudh, advocating complete annexation. In 1859 he succeeded Sir James Colville in the chief justiceship of the supreme court in Calcutta, and was knighted by patent on 26 May. He held the post, the duties of which were modified in 1862 on the constitution of the high court, until 1870.

Peacock's belief in *laissez-faire*, property rights, and the classical economists was expressed in his 1862 key judgment on rents and Act X of 1859 in *James Hills* v. *Ishwar Ghose* when, citing Malthus, he ruled that the landowner should profit through rent from increased land value. He assumed zemindars were absolute proprietors and ryots only tenants at will. His judgment was a 'bombshell', a blow to the government policy of protecting the ryots, and was much criticized. Sir Henry Maine wrote of 'Peacock's principle of rackrent' (Ambirajan, 122) and a later historian has alleged that it was 'utterly devoid of any understanding of the sociological realities of the Bengal peasantry' (ibid.). However, Peacock's judgment was reversed by the 1865 verdict of the full bench in *Thakoorannee Dossee* v. *Kashi Prasad Mukherjea* (the 'Great rent case'), which ruled that rents could be increased by landlords only to the extent of the movement of the price level.

Peacock was indefatigable in moulding the practice of his court as an appellate tribunal, and for eighteen years, with remarkable vigour, worked in the plains of India with only one furlough. In 1870 he resigned and returned to England, where, in June 1872, he was appointed under the 1871 act a paid member (£5000 p.a.) of the judicial committee of the privy council. There his knowledge of Indian customs, his industry and accuracy made him especially useful. He was sitting to hear appeals only three days before his death.

Peacock married twice: first, in 1835, Elizabeth (*d*. 1865), daughter of William Fanning; and second, in 1870, Georgina, daughter of Major-General Charles Lionel Showers CB. He was slight and short, an indifferent speaker, but had exceptional memory and application. He died from heart failure at his home, 40 Cornwall Gardens, Kensington, London, on 3 December 1890. He was survived by his second wife.

Peacock's eldest son, **Frederick Barnes Peacock** (1836–1894), was educated at East India College, Haileybury, entered the Bengal civil service, and landed in India in February 1857. He was employed in the revenue and judicial department, became registrar of the high court in May 1864, was president of the committee on the affairs of the king of Oudh, officiating secretary to the board of revenue in 1871, a magistrate and collector in 1873, commissioner of the Dacca division in 1878 and of the Presidency division in 1881. He was admitted at the Inner Temple on 16 April 1866 and called to the bar on 9 June 1880. In 1883 he was appointed chief secretary to the government of Bengal for the judicial, political, and appointments departments, an acting member of the board of revenue in 1884, and an actual member in 1887, and in 1890 he was made a CSI (21 May) and retired. He died on board the *Britannia*, off Sicily, on 14 April 1894.

J. A. HAMILTON, *rev.* ROGER T. STEARN

Sources *The Times* (4 Dec 1890) · *The Times* (25 April 1894) · *Law Times* (20 Dec 1890) · J. Foster, *Men-at-the-bar: a biographical hand-list of the members of the various inns of court*, 2nd edn (1885) · Kelly, *Handbk* (1879) · Burke, *Peerage* (1889) · *Dod's Peerage* (1896) · Boase, *Mod. Eng. biog.* · S. Ambirajan, *Classical political economy and British policy in India* (1978) · H. E. A. Cotton, *Calcutta old and new: a historical and descriptive handbook to the city* (1907) · W. Menski, *Indian legal systems past and present* (1997) · E. Stokes, *The English utilitarians and India* (1959) · P. Spear, *The Oxford history of modern India, 1740–1947* (1965)

Archives Duke U., Perkins L., corresp. and papers

Likenesses wood-engraving (after photograph by Saxony and Co.), NPG; repro. in *ILN* (20 Dec 1890)

Wealth at death £23,325 12s. 2d.: resworn probate, July 1891 · £8182 10s. 4d. (in England) Frederick Barnes Peacock: administration with will, 29 Nov 1894, CGPLA Eng. & Wales

Peacock, Dmitri Rudolf (1842–1892), philologist, was born on 26 September 1842 at the village of Shakhmanovka, district of Kozlov, in the government of Tambov, Russia, the son of Charles Peacock, estate manager, and his wife, Concordia, *née* Schlegel. He was educated at a school in England, and afterwards at the University of Moscow. On 25 October 1881 he was appointed vice-consul at Batumi, which had become more important since its annexation by the Russians. He became consul on 27 January 1890. Travellers in the Caucasus found a warm welcome there.

Peacock probably owed his appointments to his familiarity with the Russian language: few foreigners were better acquainted with the languages and customs of the Caucasus mountain peoples, with whom he established such friendly relations that he was admitted into their remotest strongholds. His expeditions led to the publication of 'Original vocabularies of five west Caucasian languages'—Georgian, Mingrelian, Lazian, Svanetian, and Abkhazian (*Journal of the Royal Asiatic Society*, 1877, 145–56). Up to that time no contribution on these languages had appeared in English, and, unsurprisingly, it was not without errors. It was still considered an important enough work, however, to merit reprinting as a pamphlet in 1888, when the author's name was given as Demetrius R. Peacock.

On 14 October 1891 Peacock was appointed consul-general at Odessa, but had only been in residence a few weeks when he became ill, probably from Caucasian fever, the marshes which surrounded Batumi being very unhealthy. He died on 23 May 1892 at the Hotel de Londres, Odessa, and was buried in the British cemetery there. He left a widow, Tatyana, *née* Bakunin, and three sons and three daughters; they were living in 1894 at Dyadino in Russia. Peacock was a man of rare attainments, but left little that showed his abilities. According to the *Levantine Herald*, as quoted by *The Athenaeum*, he wrote a book on the Caucasus which was not approved by the Foreign Office. His widow promised to publish it, but it is not known whether it ever appeared.

W. R. MORFILL, *rev.* JOHN D. HAIGH

Sources personal knowledge (1895) · private information (1895) [Foreign Office] · *The Times* (17 June 1892), 8 · *The Athenaeum* (18 June 1892), 794 · *CGPLA Eng. & Wales* (1892)

Wealth at death £255 13*s.* 5*d.* in England: administration, 22 June 1892, *CGPLA Eng. & Wales*

Peacock, Sir Edward Robert (1871–1962), merchant banker, was born in the manse at Glengarry, Ontario, Canada, on 2 August 1871, the eldest son of the Revd William MacAllister Peacock (*d.* 1883), Presbyterian minister and third-generation Canadian, and his wife, Jane, *née* McDougall. When young he almost died of typhoid fever, and on doctor's advice he was prevented from attending school. In despair, at the age of ten he used the *Pilgrim's Progress* to teach himself to read and write; he always attributed his atrocious handwriting to his early lack of formal education.

Education, early career, and marriage Peacock's father died in 1883 and his mother, in straitened circumstances, took their daughter and three sons to Almonte where Edward attended the high school. In 1890 he entered the prestigious Queen's University, Kingston, where he read English and social sciences; he graduated *magna cum laude* in 1894, with prizes in philosophy and political economy. He then trained at the School of Pedagogy, Toronto, perhaps because teaching was commonly regarded as a stepping stone to other professions, and went on to attend Upper Canada College, a leading public school, as a teacher of English; he later became senior housemaster. Peacock's headmaster was Sir George Parkin who, along with G. M. Grant and Adam Shortt, both of Queen's University, was an apostle of imperial unity, and he strongly moulded Peacock's views.

In 1902 Peacock left teaching to join E. R. Wood, a leading Canadian financier, as his personal assistant. Wood had established the Dominion Securities Corporation in 1901, and on discovering that Peacock's work at Upper Canada College meant that he knew many wealthy people, he appointed him a bond salesman at Dominion; about 1905 he then made him 'manager' of what had become Canada's leading securities house. In 1907 Peacock went to London to open a European office and in 1909 he settled there permanently, at the same time as other Canadian financiers such as Max Aitken (Lord Beaverbrook) and Sir James Hamet Dunn (1874–1956) were also making London their home. In London, Dominion issued and placed Canadian industrial securities at a time when Britain's portfolio investment in Canada had peaked. Initially Dominion worked closely with Speyer Brothers. Peacock established himself surprisingly quickly, meeting Montagu Collet Norman (1871–1950) in 1907, with whom he became great friends, and leading figures such as Lord

Sir Edward Robert Peacock (1871–1962), by Sir James Gunn

Milner and Arthur Steel-Maitland. He was closely connected with the 'round table' movement, which was concerned with imperial affairs.

On 15 July 1912 Peacock was married in New York to Katherine (*d.* 1948), daughter of John Coates of Ottawa and widow of Frederick J. Campbell, and they brought up two adopted daughters. Coates was a civil engineer who in 1880 had formed John Coates & Co. in London and who later spent time in Canada and Australia, where he established local businesses connected with London. For some years Peacock was a director of John Coates & Co.

Growing reputation in finance By 1915 Peacock had achieved wide recognition within London's financial community. Dominion had financed the Brazilian Traction Light and Power Company Ltd, which controlled subsidiary companies in Barcelona and Mexico, and following the outbreak of war, when the Barcelona company experienced severe funding difficulties, Peacock negotiated a refinancing on behalf of its bondholders. However, when the company's president, Dr F. S. Pearson, perished in the *Lusitania* disaster of 1915, Peacock left Dominion to succeed him as president. He subsequently became president of the Mexican company, when it too ran into difficulties, and financial vice-president of the Brazilian company. For almost a decade Peacock nursed the Barcelona and Mexican companies back to good health, travelling widely and becoming well known in the business communities of Spain and Mexico, and of Paris and Brussels. Gaspard Farrer, a senior partner of Barings, the leading London merchant bankers, in 1922 urged a colleague 'to make tracks for him. He is well worth knowing. He took up Dr Pearson's interests … all in the same state of utter impecuniosity and brought them through in a wonderful way' (ING Baring Archives, DEP33.21). Peacock formalized his Barings' connection in 1920, when the firm underwrote a £1.05 million debenture issue for the Barcelona company.

The Bank of England and the Treasury In 1920 Peacock's old friend Montagu Norman became governor of the Bank of England, and in 1921 he 'exercised a good deal of influence' (ING Baring Archives, DEP200, 26) in arranging for Peacock's appointment to the bank's court. Norman, as well as wanting to introduce to the bank forward-thinking directors who understood the realities of Britain's postwar economy, also sought a representative from Dominion to encourage the introduction of central banking. As at other stages in his career the rise in Peacock's authority was meteoric. By 1922 he had joined the important committee of Treasury and had attended the Paris conference on Mexican debts and the International Economic Conference at Genoa.

On the Treasury committee Peacock worked closely with John Baring, second Baron Revelstoke, Barings' senior partner, who in 1923 invited him to join Barings as a partner. Initially Peacock declined, as it would have required him to leave the court, where tradition dictated that no one house could provide more than one director. However, he relented when the invitation was reissued a year later and joined Barings in early 1924. Revelstoke was now seeking a successor to his ageing deputy, Gaspard Farrer; he also sought his own successor, as he was now sixty years old and premature deaths had already removed potential successors from Barings' partners. The press described Peacock's as an 'interesting appointment' (*Morning Post*); certainly Revelstoke and Peacock were markedly different in both culture and temperament. It is hard to think that the hand of Norman was not at work, appointing a like-minded ally to an influential house, where Peacock could work at arm's length from the Bank of England but still take the lead in promoting Norman's ambitious plans for international monetary reconstruction and industrial reorganization. Farrer felt obliged to explain the appointment to Barings' correspondents: 'He is absolutely straight', he told Hopes of Amsterdam, 'and without any pretence to special brilliance, has one of the wisest heads I know' (ING Baring Archives, DEP33.22).

At that time Barings, a limited company, was controlled and largely owned by a partnership, and in this Peacock was given a 10/113ths interest. After Revelstoke's death in 1929 his interest was extended to 24/68ths, but by 1946 this had diminished to 14/68ths. Although not senior in name, his leadership was undisputed and he underlined it by taking over Revelstoke's suite of offices outside the partners' room at Barings and appointing his own expert team. He fitted well into the culture, but strains persisted. Cecil Baring dubbed him 'the paycock' (D. Pollen, 229), and Revelstoke's rather stilted correspondence with him betrayed the lack of intimacy which he enjoyed with Farrer.

Reforming staple industries Peacock's experience of Canadian industry, influenced by American technology and management practices, qualified him well to work with Norman for the rationalization and reconstruction of Britain's staple industries. In doing this he was responsible for the immensely successful transition of Barings from specialization in debt issues for foreign governments and businesses to the provision of corporate finance services to British industry. In this he differed greatly from Revelstoke, and in 1927 he seemingly over-stressed his viewpoint to this banker moulded by Edwardian international finance. Norman, Peacock's weekend guest, had stressed 'the importance of bringing about closer relationships and a much better understanding between the City of London and the great industries of England'. He told Revelstoke that on this point he found a sympathetic listener and felt that it was a matter of vital importance to Britain that there should be a 'much better understanding and more active intervention by the financial people, not merely the rather passive assistance afforded in the form of overdrafts by joint stock banks' (ING Baring Archives, 202040). His outlook was far removed from that of other pre-war London merchant bankers.

By this time Peacock had also had his skills tested by the great engineering company, Sir W. G. Armstrong Whitworth & Co. Ltd, which had run into severe difficulties following rapid yet unsustainable wartime expansion and poorly planned peacetime diversification. Armstrongs was heavily indebted to its bankers, the Bank of England, and its management was unequal to the task. Doubtless under pressure from Norman, the company appointed Barings its advisers in early 1924, and Peacock soon installed James Frater Taylor, a 'company doctor', who eventually took complete charge of its affairs. Peacock arranged a series of refinancings and reconstructions, and he backed Taylor in such measures as merging parts of the company with those of competitors, reorganizing the company structure, and introducing new management and controls. *The Economist* described the outcome as 'the greatest achievement of financial salvage ever attempted' though Armstrongs emerged as a shadow of its former self, with holders of shares and debentures having lost much of their capital through ruthless write-downs.

Norman and Peacock, with Taylor as their workhorse, became leading proponents of rationalization. 'Rationalisation means higher wages and a higher standard of living in spite of the fact that there may [be] short intervals of less employment', Peacock told Steel-Maitland in 1929 for the benefit of tory electioneering (ING Baring Archives, 202040). Its justification was that larger corporations, better managed and more able to afford capital expenditure, would achieve the economies of scale required in order to defeat foreign competition.

Whether correct or otherwise, Peacock's philosophy had a profound influence on the face of Britain's staple industries, and no more so than in Lancashire, where a large part of the cotton textile industry was reshaped. The industry was in severe difficulties due to foreign competition, and it risked dragging down those clearing banks which had over-lent to it. Peacock, again working closely with Norman, became involved in this area in 1928, and he devised a scheme to reorganize many of the industry's components into a single entity, the Lancashire Cotton Corporation. By 1933 the corporation had acquired more than 100 mills, and it closed down many—concentrating production at large plant with modern equipment. However, progress was not smooth, and it necessitated further schemes of reconstruction and the injection of new management, which eventually transformed the corporation into a viable unit.

Overseas issues at Barings Most of Barings' activities were far more conventional. In the 1920s its issuing business comprised largely the marketing of bonds of overseas sovereign entities, now frequently handled jointly with Rothschilds and Schroders, but with one house having management control. At Barings, Revelstoke played a leading part, but Peacock's role was increasingly important. One of his first initiatives was to create a large international bond issue in 1926 for the Belgium government; this was brought out simultaneously in London, New York, Amsterdam, Stockholm, and Switzerland. Its organization was centred upon Barings, and Peacock wrote that 'it gave me my first opportunity [at Barings] to show what I could do … as it fell to me to take on the supervision of the whole thing. … It all went very satisfactorily' (ING Baring Archives, DEP200, 27–8). Peacock's other major work in this area was the refinancing of large parts of Brazil's and Argentina's external debt in the late 1920s and 1930s, and he also was concerned with the London issuing houses' response to Germany's default in 1934. However, embargoes on the issue of foreign securities in London also meant the shifting of Barings' business to debt issues for British business.

Other activities with Barings In the 1920s and 1930s Peacock oversaw issues for, *inter alia*, the North Metropolitan Power Station Company, the Charing Cross Electricity Supply Company, the British Tanker Company, Goodyear Tyre and Rubber (Great Britain) Ltd, and the Southern Railway—modern industries forming the economy's dynamic sector. Of major importance were issues to finance the extension of the London Underground. In a notable break with practice, in 1926 Peacock joined as a preliminary the board of the Underground Electric Railway Company of London, his presence being insisted upon by Jimmy Speyer, an American investment banker and a major shareholder who would otherwise have blocked the underground's expansion plans. Another company to which Peacock led Barings was the Pressed Steel Company (Great Britain), established to use pioneering American technology and management to make motor-car bodies. Peacock, who was close to this business culture and whose passionate desire was for a buoyant and internationally competitive British motor industry (in part as a counterpoise to the declining staples), persuaded his fellow partners to join those of Schroders in subscribing for a major interest in the company's share and loan capital. He

placed Frater Taylor on its board to watch over this interest.

Peacock retired from Barings' partnership in 1946; his directorship continued until the end of 1954, but by then he had stayed for too long. Although increasingly detached from day-to-day leadership, however, his high status as the City's elder statesman meant that his advice was still eagerly sought outside Barings. Two issues much concerned him after 1945, namely the nationalization of industry under the Labour Party, which he strongly opposed, and the consolidation of family control of private businesses which were converted to public companies. Little could be done to hold back the tide of nationalization but Peacock's role was central in early discussions between industry leaders, the Bank of England, and the out-of-office tories, for iron and steel denationalization.

Peacock and the Bank of England Peacock's major interest outside Barings was unquestionably the Bank of England. He returned to the court in 1929, on Revelstoke's death, but in the interim he had been Norman's continuing confidant. Norman's initial idea of promoting central banking in Canada (and the other dominions) by taking in 'the best Canadian we can get … [so that] we are most likely to influence Canadian opinion without offending their susceptibilities' (Sayers, 203) in the short term came to nothing. But Peacock soon asserted himself in areas other than rationalization and became immensely powerful. 'Because I was the favourite of the Governor', he was later to write, 'it came to be recognised [by the court] that if things were to be got through with the Governor I had better make the approach and that happened very often' (ING Baring Archives, DEP200, 30).

Rationalization apart, until his retirement in 1946 Peacock had an important say in most vital matters, such as the conversion in 1932 of war loan stock as a step to cheaper money; the rescue from collapse of the Anglo-South American Bank at the time of the 1931 crisis, when it fell to him to plead for clearing bank support; and the chairmanship of a committee—the so-called Peacock committee—to review the administration of the bank, which made, in Peacock's words, 'revolutionary suggestions, all of which were accepted by our colleagues' (ING Baring Archives, DEP200, 40–41). In 1943 Norman sent him in secret to Canada to sound out Graham Towers, governor of the Bank of Canada, on his willingness to succeed Norman as governor of the Bank of England. As 'commander royal' Peacock travelled in the belly of a bomber aircraft, packed like a sardine alongside fellow passengers. In 1953, at the bank's behest, he was a somewhat reluctant midwife of the Commonwealth Development Finance Corporation, realizing that it would make little impact and that it would fail to attract high-quality proposals. However, he subsequently sat on the corporation's board.

Above all else, at the time of the 1931 economic crisis, which caused the government to fall and eventually drove the country from the gold standard, Peacock emerged alongside Sir Ernest Harvey, deputy governor, as the bank's natural leader in the prolonged absence of Norman due to sickness. From the end of July until about October, he and Harvey worked without a break, taking part in 'all the consultations that were almost continuous. We saw the Prime Minister and the Chancellor … every day, and with the permission of the Prime Minister we also kept the leaders of the two other parties informed' (ING Baring Archives, DEP200, 34).

On the evening of the government's fall and with the nation tottering on the precipice of economic collapse, Peacock was summoned to dine with George V (who knew him well) in order to brief the king on the impending crisis. As they dined the prime minister, Ramsay MacDonald, fled from a cabinet meeting in uproar and drove to Buckingham Palace to offer his resignation. There, after a telephone briefing from Harvey at Downing Street, Peacock found MacDonald 'dishevelled and wild' but ahead of him in his return to the king's presence. 'I rushed up one stairway as I saw MacDonald going up the other', Peacock later recounted, 'and managed to get in to see the King and tell that much and I added: "I am afraid, Sir, it is all up to you now"'. Counselled and placated by the king, who doubtless followed Peacock's advice, MacDonald returned to Downing Street with Peacock, and entered by the garden gate in order to avoid the press. There Peacock and Harvey spent the night encouraging MacDonald's acceptance of the king's wish for the formation of a government of national unity, as opposition party leaders arrived for discussions. They pointed to the prime minister's chief asset, namely his chancellor, Philip Snowden: he 'had been the sturdy, admirably courageous man throughout the trouble', wrote Peacock later, 'a realist who did not allow his theories to interfere with the facts' (ING Baring Archives, DEP200, 36–7).

Other public duties In 1929 Peacock took up the chairmanship of the channel tunnel committee at the request of prime minister, Stanley Baldwin, and in 1934 he was appointed a member of the royal commission on tithes. However, his most significant work in the service of the crown was as a Treasury representative, when he was charged in 1941 with the disposal of direct British investments in the United States. A powerful American lobby was then clamouring for Britain to do more to help itself in funding its war effort by selling direct investments at inevitable bargain prices. Over several months, by use of delaying tactics and calling upon the services of his old banking and political friends, Peacock staved off these emergency sales and eventually played a central role in negotiating loans totalling $425 million. However, it was not before the controversial sale of Britain's most valuable American asset, Courtaulds' American Viscose Corporation, was forced upon him so as not to imperil the passing of vital 'lend-lease' legislation.

Peacock's charitable interests were extensive. He succeeded Revelstoke as treasurer of the King Edward's Hospital Fund, the influential and wealthy London hospital charity, and he remained so until 1954. He was chairman of the trustees of the Imperial War Graves Commission; chairman of the board of management of the Royal Commission for the Exhibition of 1851; a trustee of the King George's Jubilee Fund from 1935; and, not least, a Rhodes trustee from 1925. At the behest of the prince of Wales he played a prominent part in the foundation of the National Council of Social Service, where he was important in ensuring the continuation and development of the Citizens' Advice Bureau service when its future was in doubt after the war.

Peacock succeeded Revelstoke as receiver-general of the duchy of Cornwall, and he also played a general role as financial adviser to many members of the royal family. At the time of the abdication crisis of 1936 he stood alongside Edward VIII and 'was more nearly in his confidence than anyone except Monckton and Allen' (Ziegler, 311). He offered advice well beyond financial matters and helped to thrash out the subsequent financial settlement, when his clarity of thought and directness of delivery again shone through. 'The discussions tended to become heated … so I intervened … and removed the technicalities', he later wrote, 'and stated directly and simply [to the King] what I thought would be his desire' (ibid., 328). His standing with other members of the king's family remained uncompromised and he served them until his death. For his services to the crown, George V appointed him GCVO in 1934.

Canada remained close to Peacock's heart throughout his life, and he had intended to live there in retirement. He was European director of the Canadian Pacific Railway Company from 1926 to 1961, and was on the board of the Hudson's Bay Company from 1931 to 1952. He continued as a director of Brazilian Traction, notably in the mid-1920s, dealing with the controversial Belgian financier Alfred Loewenstein, who had taken a large shareholding in the company; he subsequently took charge of Loewenstein's financial affairs when he ran into difficulties and disposed of this interest. He helped to supervise the finances of welfare agencies for Canadian forces abroad during the Second World War. In 1952 he took the initiative in Barings' formation, with Morgan Grenfell and Canadian interests, of the securities house Harris & Partners of Toronto, of which he was first chairman. He was a trustee of Queen's University from 1912 to 1947, and also a benefactor, in particular endowing two chairs.

Character, death, and reputation Contemporaries remember Peacock's immense presence and clear, penetrating eyes, his clarity of thought, his directness and decisiveness of approach, and his lack of affectation and pomposity. His capacity for, and speed of, work was immense and others had to maintain his pace. Fools were suffered with difficulty and mistakes not easily forgiven. His words were few and demanded brevity in others; his dictation went at a furious pace. 'The more difficult the matter, the faster he would dictate', his secretary later recalled. 'I sometimes wondered if I could get the page over in time to keep up'. His English and its construction would be 'faultless— short, clear, no superfluous words, simplicity in choice of words, never "pompous" or "clever". He was on top of the world when at his busiest' (ING Baring Archives, DEP237).

While he could become furiously angry with his staff, all of whom were devoted to him and he to them, no disaster or crisis ever shook his calm. For all his greatness, he was self-effacing and unassuming. He died in the Royal London Homoeopathic Hospital on 19 November 1962, and was cremated at Woking, Surrey, on 22 November.

Peacock was one of the City's most distinguished merchant bankers of the first half of the twentieth century. He dominated Barings in the 1930s and 1940s, and among other things he was responsible for the firm's immensely successful transition into a modern merchant bank focused on providing services, especially of corporate finance, to domestic industry. But his role at the Bank of England meant that, in the 1930s at least, his influence in the City was exceeded only by that of Norman. In particular he was an extremely important proponent of industrial rationalization, in which he called on his experience of large North American businesses. During the 1931 financial crisis, arguably the most serious to affect twentieth-century Britain, he outshone all his rivals in both the City and Whitehall. In reality there were few areas of British financial policy from the 1920s to the 1940s in which his contribution was not substantial. This achievement by Peacock, who was born far from the British establishment but who absorbed its values and won its acceptance without compromise to his Canadian culture and the humbleness of his origins, serves to underline the true remarkableness of his personal qualities.   JOHN ORBELL

Sources The Times (20 Nov 1962) • R. S. Sayers, The Bank of England, 1891–1944, 3 vols. (1976) • J. Orbell, Baring Brothers & Co. Limited: a history to 1939 (privately printed, London, 1985) • P. Ziegler, The sixth great power: Barings, 1762–1929 (1988) • H. P. Gundy, 'Sir Edward Peacock', Douglas Library notes, 12/1 (1963), 2–3, 3–7 • E. R. Peacock, Canada: a descriptive text book (1900) • D. McDowall, The light: Brazilian Traction, Light and Power Company Limited, 1899–1945 (1988) • K. Burk, The first privatisation: the politicians, the city and the denationalisation of steel (1988) • J. Fforde, The Bank of England and public policy, 1941–1958 (1992) • F. K. Procrasta, Philanthropy and the hospitals: the King's Fund, 1897–1990 (1992) • P. Ziegler, King Edward VIII: the official biography (1990) • J. Orbell, 'Peacock, Sir Edward Robert', DBB • DNB • J. Orbell, 'Taylor, James Frater', DBB • ING Barings, London, Barings archives, DEP 33.21, DEP 200, DEP 33.22 • D. Pollen, I remember, I remember (1983), 229 • Morning Post (1 Jan 1924) • The Economist (16 Feb 1929) • m. cert.

Archives ING Barings, London • Queen's University, Kingston, Ontario, papers | Bodl. Oxf., corresp. with L. G. Curtis • Bodl. Oxf., Round Table corresp.

Likenesses W. Stoneman, photograph, 1934, NPG • W. Stoneman, photograph, 1948, NPG • J. Gunn, oils, ING Barings, London [see illus.] • portraits, ING Barings, London

Wealth at death £166,077 11s. 2d.: probate, 21 March 1963, CGPLA Eng. & Wales

Peacock, Francis (1723/4–1807), dancing-master and musician, was possibly born in or near York, although precise details of his birthplace are unknown. He studied dancing under Desnoyer, later dancing master at George III's court. In 1747 he was recommended to Aberdeen as 'a capable master … of a discreet and moral character' (Aberdeen council register, 17 Jan 1747); he became 'sole dancing-master within the burgh during his good behaviour' (ibid., 14 Feb 1747), a monopoly that he held until 1790. In the year of his appointment he founded the Aberdeen Musical Society with the physician John Gregory, organist Andrew Tait, and music copyist David Young. Peacock acted as a director and occasional violinist for almost sixty years for the society, which gave private concerts, with profits going to charity.

On 15 February 1748 Peacock married Ellen Forbes (d. 1804) at St Nicholas's Church, Aberdeen. Their children, Elizabeth, Jannet, John, George, and Thomas, were baptized there or at St Paul's Scottish Episcopal Church; sponsors included James Beattie and John Gregory. From 1747 until 1766 Peacock lived in the Earl Marischal's house in Aberdeen's Castlegate. Later he built houses behind Skipper Scott's tavern, an area commemorated as Peacock's Close, where a wall of his granite house still stands. In the 1790s he moved to a new country house, Villa Franca (now the site of 156 Hamilton Place, Aberdeen). His last dancing premises were on Aberdeen's George Street.

Peacock arranged Fifty Favourite Scotch Airs (1762), influenced by Geminiani's The Art of Playing the Violin (1751), and composed a coronation anthem for George III (1761). He also studied painting with Francis Cotes, becoming a miniaturist (no examples are known). He championed the Aberdeenshire painter James Wales, commissioning a portrait which cannot now be traced. In 1805 Peacock published Sketches Relative to the History, Theory, but More Especially to the Practice of Dancing. His teaching favoured not country dances but minuets, 'a dance essential for children and young people … a foundation for the graces which distinguish people of fashion and breeding from others whose education has been neglected' (Peacock, 18). He dismissed technique ('as for the jigging part, and the figures of dances, I count that little or nothing'), instead emphasizing deportment and poise: 'A well-set head', 'A diversity of countenance', 'A graceful and dignified carriage' (ibid.). He charged 2 guineas a term. To Alexander Jaffray he was 'a really scientific professor … an excellent master but stern and severe when a dull pupil came under his hands' (Thom, 'Alexander Jaffray's recollections', 146). Gaelic dance-step names, such as kemshoole ('ceum-siubhal'), the gliding, travelling step of the reel, and kem Badenoch, which includes an entrechat, first appeared in Sketches. 'The greater part of [the highlanders] … excell [sic] in this dance [the reel] some … so superior … that I myself have thought them worthy of imitation' (Peacock, 86). The proceeds from Sketches, which was still influential in the 1880s, he intended for the newly built lunatic hospital to which, with other charities, he left over £1000. 'A useful citizen and a good man' (Aberdeen Journal, 7 July 1807), Peacock died in his eighty-fourth year in Aberdeen on 26 June 1807.   MARY ANNE ALBURGER

Sources I. Cramb, 'Francis Peacock, 1723–1807', Aberdeen University Review, 43 (1969–70), 251–61 • G. S. Emmerson, A social history of Scottish dance (1972) • R. Baxter, Peacock looks back (privately printed, Aberdeen, 1997) • F. Peacock, Sketches relative to the history, theory, but more especially to the practice of dancing (1805) • M. A. Alburger, Scottish fiddlers and their music (1983) • W. Thom, The history of Aberdeen, 2 vols. (1811) • W. Thom, 'Alexander Jaffray's recollections of Kingswells, 1755–1800', Miscellany of the Third Spalding Club, 1 (1935), 131–215 • Aberdeen Journal (7 July 1807) • will, Aberdeen City

Archives, PR 18/86 · Aberdeen council records, 1747 · Aberdeen Musical Society minute books, 2 vols., 1748–95, Aberdeen Public Library, Aberdeen, WW276 10632 (W 780.6 Ab3) · Aberdeen Family History Society Microfiches: records of marriages, births and christenings

Likenesses J. Wales, portrait

Wealth at death over £1000: will, Aberdeen City Archives, PR 18/86

Peacock, Frederick Barnes (1836–1894). *See under* Peacock, Sir Barnes (1810–1890).

Peacock, George (1791–1858), mathematician and university reformer, was born on 9 April 1791 at Thornton Hall, Denton, near Darlington, co. Durham, one of eight children and the youngest of five sons of Thomas Peacock, perpetual curate and schoolmaster at Denton. He attended Sedbergh School and then, at the age of seventeen, Richmond School under the mastership of James Tate, formerly a fellow of Sidney Sussex College, a moulder of numerous outstanding Cambridge students, and a staunch whig. Having stood at the head of his class at Richmond, in the summer of 1809 Peacock read with John Brass, a Trinity undergraduate who was to become the sixth wrangler of 1811. Peacock was admitted as a sizar at Trinity College, Cambridge, on 21 February 1809 and matriculated in the following Michaelmas Term. In 1810 he won one of the Bell scholarships dedicated to needy sons of clergymen, and in 1812 he was awarded a college scholarship. The following summer he read mathematics with Adam Sedgwick, later to become Woodwardian professor of geology. Like Peacock, Sedgwick was a whig in politics and a strong supporter of reform in the university, and the two were to enjoy a lifelong friendship. Peacock graduated as second wrangler and second Smith's prizeman in 1813, became a fellow of Trinity in 1814 and received his MA in 1816. He was elected a fellow of the Royal Society in 1818, and joined the Astronomical Society in 1820 and the Geological Society in 1822. He was also ordained priest (1822) and gained a DD (1839). He was a mathematics lecturer at Trinity from 1815, a tutor from 1823 to 1839, and Lowndean professor of astronomy and geometry from 1837 until his death.

As an undergraduate Peacock was a founding member of the Analytical Society (in 1812). The society dedicated itself to importing into Cambridge, and developing, continental pure analytics, mainly from France. Enamoured with the French, it denigrated the fluxional notation and the easily intuited fluxions and fluxional mixed (applied) mathematics derived from Isaac Newton, who was revered as the embodiment of Cambridge mathematics and English culture. In an era dominated by fear of the French Revolution and Napoleon, the clerics who ruled Cambridge, primarily the heads of colleges, were suspicious of French mathematics, and doubted the motives of the reformers. In this atmosphere the Analytical Society accomplished little. However, in 1816 Peacock joined two of its leaders, Charles Babbage and John Herschel, in translating a French calculus textbook by S. F. Lacroix. In 1820, the trio published a book of examples to illustrate

George Peacock (1791–1858), by Samuel Lane, exh. RA 1843

the theoretical calculus, in acquiescence to the Cambridge tradition of teaching by means of exemplification, as opposed to the French method of teaching via abstract principles that had earlier been advocated by the Analytical Society. This tactic of gaining influence through partial accommodation with the educational traditions of Cambridge was largely devised by Peacock. Supplemented by the collection of examples, the Lacroix translation, while updating Cambridge mathematics, also fitted into the Cambridge curriculum; consequently, the two publications had an immediate and long-lasting influence.

Peacock also ventured reform as moderator of the tripos. In the 1817 tripos, to the dismay of the Cambridge traditionalists, he stressed pure analytics. He also introduced the continental notation for differentiation. Even though he translated the foreign notation into the fluxional notation at the bottom of his papers, his employment of dy/dx raised an outcry against French mathematics from the university traditionalists to the point that Peacock feared some official proceedings against him. Peacock furthermore contrived to limit the *viva voce* portion of the tripos to allow more time for printed problem papers, in hopes of rewarding mathematical talent rather than memorization of standard bookwork. This endeavour failed when, under pressure from older members of the university, the other moderator and the examiners deserted Peacock. Likewise, they adhered to the traditional mathematics, much to the chagrin of Peacock who believed this vitiated any effect his own papers might have had. In the end, though historians almost universally point to Peacock's examination papers of 1817 as effecting the 'analytical revolution', Peacock himself concluded that they accomplished nothing.

In the tripos of 1819 Peacock and his fellow moderator, Richard Gwatkin, who had also been a member of the now defunct Analytical Society, again employed the continental notation, and from this point it became the norm at Cambridge. However, peeved by the students' lack of physical knowledge, Peacock decided to introduce a large dose of traditional mixed mathematics into the *viva voce* examination. He rationalized his retreat on the grounds that Gwatkin had forged ahead, and also on the grounds of political expediency: he hoped that his actions in 1819 would appease the powers that be whom he had alienated in 1817. He had been influenced by Jean-Baptiste Biot, the French physicist, who, while visiting Cambridge in 1818, had asserted that the French erred in neglecting Newton's *Principia*. In the same vein, Peacock pondered working Newton's optics into his college lectures. In mathematics education he was, from the start, a reformer who sought a middle ground between the traditionalists and the radical analysts, and he maintained this position of compromise: thus in the 1850s he argued for curricular emphasis on mixed mathematics, the maintenance of the older intuitive approach, and the suppression of excessive abstract analytics.

Peacock, like the French-based mathematician J. L. Lagrange, and like an older Cambridge reformer, Robert Woodhouse, urged founding the calculus by algebraically developing the successive derivatives of a function as the successive coefficients of the function's expansion in a Taylor series. He rejected limit theory-based calculus, be it that of Newton, of Lacroix in the textbook that he helped translate, or of Augustin Cauchy, the French mathematician who inspired the 'rigorous' foundations for the calculus as it would develop on the continent. He urged the Taylor series foundation, not because he thought it more rigorous—he thought all foundations could be made rigorous—but, rather, because he believed it to be more intuitively clear than limit-based formulations. In an 1833 report on analysis to the British Association for the Advancement of Science, Peacock noted Cauchy's insistence that only convergent series were legitimate and reviewed numerous convergency tests, but he rejected the necessity for these limit-based concerns in pure analysis. In his 1830 *Treatise on Algebra* (enlarged and revised edn, 1842–5), which he dedicated to Tate, Peacock provided his vision of analysis as formal algebra, a vision which reflected ideas of Woodhouse, Babbage, and other Cambridge mathematicians. Although this work earned Peacock renown as one of the founders of abstract algebra, here, as in his pedagogical predilections, he did not elude the intuitive, as recognized by his contemporaries and by modern historians.

Underlying Peacock's stake in intuitive mathematics was his interest in physical science. From 1816 to 1824, he was the primary mover in the building of the university observatory in opposition to some of the oligarchy. In 1819

he partook in the founding of the Cambridge Philosophical Society and became its vice-president (1831 and 1840) and president (1841–2). In 1830 he declined to sign a petition in support of John Herschel's candidacy for the presidency of the Royal Society during a campaign for the professionalization of British science organized by Charles Babbage. Moreover, as a member of the society's council, he worked closely with the duke of Sussex, the whig brother of the king, after the duke defeated Herschel in the presidential election.

In 1829 Peacock was the leading member of a syndicate charged with planning a university complex which included a substantial science centre. Although by February 1831 the senate had authorized financing for one half of the structure, including most of the science complex, a feud broke out between Peacock and another advocate for the structure, William Whewell. The feud lead to a scurrilous pamphlet war and caused the senate to question the proposals. The result was a decades-long delay in building the complex. None the less, upon being appointed to the Lowndean professorship by a whig government, Peacock gave well-attended lectures on practical astronomy in contrast to his predecessors in the chair who had given no lectures in the previous sixty-seven years. He also tendered lectures on pure mathematics, but these attracted no audience.

In 1843, five years into serving as a member of the commissions for restoring the standards of weight and measures which had been destroyed in the burning of the parliament building, and four years after having been appointed dean of Ely (1839) by a whig government, Peacock turned the astronomy lectures over to the Plumian professor of astronomy and experimental philosophy. He retained the Lowndean chair as a sinecure for the rest of his life. However, he sustained his interest in science, as witnessed by the fact that he continued writing a biography of Thomas Young, the natural philosopher who promoted the wave theory of light. Peacock published the biography and two volumes of Young's works in 1855.

In 1841 Peacock published *Observations on the Statutes of the University of Cambridge*, an advocacy of academic and political reform of the university and colleges based upon a whig interpretation of history. However, Peacock's ability to effect reform diminished when, later in 1841, a tory government appointed the Conservative Whewell to the mastership of Trinity, arguably the most powerful post in Cambridge and, not surprisingly, a position which Peacock, like Whewell, considered the summit of his ambition. Peacock gained the co-operation of Whewell in establishing a board of mathematical studies to rein in the anarchy of successive moderators and examiners expanding the tripos without approval of the senate, and he used his membership on the board, a consequence of his being Lowndean professor, to implement this restraint, but he had not the leverage within Cambridge to force political reform. However, whig governments appointed Peacock, Sedgwick, and Herschel to a royal commission of inquiry at Cambridge in 1850, and Peacock to a royal statutory commission for Cambridge in 1855. Although he died before the latter commission finished its work, through these commissions Peacock was able to initiate many reforms in the university and colleges, despite the vehement opposition of Whewell and other conservatives.

As dean of Ely, Peacock threw himself into the restoration of Ely Cathedral, both in directing the restoration and in raising funds. He was a prolocutor of the lower house of the convocation of Canterbury from 1841 to 1847 and from 1852 until 1857, when failing health prompted his resignation. He also brought about improvements in the city of Ely's drainage system and fostered the education of the middle and lower classes. In addition to his other ecclesiastical appointments, from 1847 onwards he was rector of Wentworth, near Ely.

In 1847 Peacock married Frances Elizabeth, daughter of William Selwyn, a QC and Cambridge graduate from Trinity. He suffered declining health over the ensuing decade, and he died, childless, on 8 November 1858 at 16 Suffolk Street, Pall Mall, London. He was buried in the Ely cemetery. In 1866, his widow married W. H. Thompson, whose tutor Peacock had been; Thompson had led the agitation for reform from within Trinity during the time of the parliamentary commissions, and a whig government, upon Whewell's death, appointed him master of Trinity shortly before the marriage.   HARVEY W. BECHER

Sources H. W. Becher, 'Radicals, whigs and conservatives: the middle and lower classes in the analytical revolution at Cambridge in the age of aristocracy', *British Journal for the History of Science*, 28 (1995), 405–26 · H. Becher, 'Woodhouse, Babbage, Peacock, and modern algebra', *Historia Mathematica*, 7 (1980), 389–400 · H. Becher, 'Voluntary science in nineteenth century Cambridge University to the 1850's', *British Journal for the History of Science*, 19 (1986), 57–87 · Trinity Cam., Peacock MSS · RS, Herschel papers · *PRS*, 9 (1857–9), 536–43 · Venn, *Alum. Cant.* · Trinity Cam., Whewell MSS · H. Becher, 'William Whewell and Cambridge mathematics', *Historical Studies in the Physical Sciences*, 11 (1980–81), 1–48 · G. Peacock, *Observations on the statutes of the University of Cambridge* (1841) · H. Pycior, 'George Peacock and the British origins of symbolical algebra', *Historia Mathematica*, 8 (1981), 23–45 · J. Richards, 'The art and science of British algebra: a study in the perception of mathematical truth', *Historia Mathematica*, 7 (1980), 342–65

Archives JRL, Methodist Archives and Research Centre, MS hymnbooks · JRL · Trinity Cam., corresp. | BL, letters to Charles Babbage, Add. MSS 37182–37201, *passim* · CUL, letters to Sir George Stokes · CUL, corresp. with Sir George Airy · Norfolk RO, letters relating to Ely Cathedral glass · Ransom HRC, letters to Sir John Herschel · RS, corresp. with Sir John Herschel · RS, letters to Sir John Lubbock · Trinity Cam., corresp. with William Whewell

Likenesses S. Lane, oils, exh. RA 1843; Christies, 12 July 1990, lot 123 [*see illus.*] · S. Lane, photograph, 1853 (after unknown portrait), Trinity Cam., Peacock MSS · D. Y. Blakiston, oils, RS · print (after D. Y. Blakiston), RS · woodcut, BM

Wealth at death under £10,000: probate, 15 Jan 1859, *CGPLA Eng. & Wales*

Peacock, George

Peacock, George (1805–1883), naval officer, was born at Navy House, Exmouth, Devon, on 9 June 1805, the second son of Richard George Peacock and his wife, Elizabeth Sanders. His father, a former master in the navy, then a merchant shipowner, took the boy from Dawlish grammar school, aged thirteen, to be his apprentice. Having served in the Mediterranean and Brazil, rising gradually to command a ship on a voyage to the Pacific, in 1828 Peacock joined the navy as second master on the *Echo*, the first

regularly commissioned steamship in the service, to survey the lower Thames. He was ordered to the West Indies in the *Winchester* in 1829, and was appointed acting master of the *Magnificent* in March 1831.

After exchanging to the *Hyacinth* he surveyed the harbour of San Juan de Nicaragua (San Juan del Norte) and suggested a route across the isthmus from San Juan to the Pacific. He also recommended Victor Cove (Colon) as the terminus of a railway across the isthmus of Panama. Fifty years later Comte Ferdinand de Lesseps acknowledged his debt to Peacock's survey in his own direction of the cutting of the Panama Canal (*Western Times*, 23 June 1882).

In 1835, as master of the *Medea* in the Mediterranean, he surveyed the isthmus of Corinth, marked the line of a possible canal, and presented his chart and plans to King Otho of Greece. In 1882, when work on the Corinth Canal began, King George of Greece honoured Peacock with the royal order of the Redeemer.

As master of the *Andromache*, Peacock surveyed, buoyed, and beaconed the harbours of Charlottetown and Three Rivers, Prince Edward Island, in 1838. After applying unsuccessfully to be appointed to a ship going to the First Opium War, he 'became disgusted with the Royal Naval service ... having been badly treated by the Admiralty generally *for want of influential political friends*' (his italics) and on 14 February 1840, 'reluctantly and respectfully' resigned his commission (Lpool RO, Pea 3/4).

Offered a post by the Pacific Steam Navigation Company, Peacock superintended the building and equipment of the *Peru* and the *Chile*. In overall command of the expedition, he took them, the first steamships ever to navigate the Strait of Magellan, to the Pacific coast. From 1840 to 1846 he was the company's marine superintendent there, during which time he

> laid down Buoys—erected Beacons—built a Lighthouse—surveyed Harbours—opened and worked Coal-mines—discovered new Guano-beds—suggested Railways—rendered valuable services occasionally to her Majesty's Cruisers—and ... in the face of a thousand unlooked for difficulties and perplexing annoyances, succeeded in establishing Steam Navigation under the Flag of England along the coast of Five Republics ... from Chiloe to Panama; and brought from Valparaiso to Panama ... the *first* regular Mails. (Peacock, 7)

In 1848 Peacock became dock master, subsequently superintendent, of Southampton docks. In the same year he formed a company, Peacock and Buchan, for the manufacture of his patented anti-fouling paint for iron ships. He was able proudly to claim that numerous iron sailing ships had returned from India and the west coast of South America 'after an absence of from TEN to FOURTEEN MONTHS with PERFECTLY CLEAN BOTTOMS' (pamphlet appended to G. Peacock, *A Treatise on Ships' Cables*).

Peacock was an indefatigable inventor. Aged seventeen he invented and fitted a screw propeller to the longboat of his father's brig *Fanny*. Between 1828 and 1876, he invented, among many other things, an invulnerable floating battery, a refuge buoy beacon, and Peacock's Synovia, a lubricating preparation for ships' engines. He devised a method of making fresh water from condensed sea water on steamships. Despite its successful use for many years on steamships he served in, the Admiralty scorned the idea. In 1839 someone pirated and patented the system with a few small changes, receiving praise and pecuniary reward from the government: 'Such are the Laws of Patent!' wrote Peacock in disgust (Lpool RO, Pea 3/32). His most charming invention was the Nautilus Bathing Dress of 1828, for 'Swimming in Safety with Decorum'. One of these garments, the top half inflatable by means of a nozzle, Captain Peacock carried always with him at sea, keeping it under his pillow at night. In 1879, it was put into manufacture, and he had himself photographed modelling both front and rear elevations. A sense of the ridiculous does not seem to have been among the captain's many estimable qualities.

In 1858, feeling 'desirous of ending his days … with some honourable acknowledgement of his services' (Peacock, 12), he petitioned the Admiralty to reinstate his name on the list of masters of 1835—but in vain. In 1860 he commanded an unsuccessful expedition, under the patronage of Napoleon III, to look for nitrates in the Sahara.

Peacock published several pamphlets, among them *Official Correspondence*, relating to his naval career (1859), *Handbook of Abyssinia* (1867), *A Treatise on Ships' Cables* (1873), *The Resources of Peru* (1874), and *Notes on the Isthmus of Panama and Darien* (1879). Peacock's wife, Jane, died in December 1878; his three sons also predeceased him. It was at Ashfield House, Holly Road, Fairfield, near Liverpool, the home of his only daughter, Jane Ash, wife of Henry Cookson, that he died on 6 June 1883. He was buried in the family vault at Starcross, Devon, three days later.

PETA RÉE

Sources Lpool RO, 387 Pea 1–9 · G. Peacock, *Official correspondence, certificates of service and testimonials* (privately printed, Exeter, 1859) · DNB · CGPLA Eng. & Wales (1883) · IGI
Archives Lpool RO, corresp. and papers · NMM, letter-book
Likenesses photographs, Lpool RO
Wealth at death £26,032 3s. 5d.: resworn probate, Feb 1884, CGPLA Eng. & Wales (1883)

Peacock, James (d. 1653), naval officer, was a native of Ipswich, and probably the son of James Peacock of that town, mariner, who was listed in 1617 and 1629 as a younger brother of Trinity House. The younger James Peacock appears to have begun his career as a merchant captain and is mentioned as captain and part owner of the *Dragon* collier which served parliament in 1642–5, but may then have been dropped, possibly because it had proved to be a 'heavy sailer' (*The Humble Remonstrance of Andrewes Burrell*, Thomason Tracts). He was commander of the 5th-rate *Warwick* in 1646 and in 1647 commanded a squadron of five ships in the North Sea. He was then promoted to the new 4th-rate frigate, the *Tiger*, which between October and December patrolled the waters around the Isle of Wight while the king was confined in Carisbrooke Castle.

During the second civil war in 1648, when much of the parliamentary fleet revolted to the king, Peacock remained loyal to parliament. He took an important part in the siege of Colchester, helping to capture Mersea Island Fort and defeating a sally aimed at recapturing

shipping in the river. He then joined the earl of Warwick in the Thames, was present at the confrontation with the royalist fleet and helped blockade it in Goree later in the year.

During 1649 Peacock again commanded the *Tiger* and a small squadron in the North Sea, capturing at least three prizes. He also had to suppress a mutiny over pay, for which a naval official held him partly to blame, accusing him of being 'too uxorious' and of 'lying ashore with his wife' (Worcester College, Oxford, Clarke MS 4/4/18). In 1650 the *Tiger* went with Blake to Portugal in pursuit of Prince Rupert. Peacock's predatory instincts were again in evidence when he captured a Portuguese man-of-war under the guns of Fort St Julian. The last mention of the *Tiger* was on 22 July, suggesting that Peacock had returned home with Badiley's squadron just before Rupert's escape. On 17 January 1651 he and his crew were paid a gratuity for their good service, which probably related to the capture of the privateer the *Crowned lion*, and he was also awarded a gold medal and chain to the value of £50. In February 1651 he sailed for the Mediterranean with the squadron under Captain Edward Hall. There are no direct references either to Peacock or the *Tiger* during the expedition and he was back in Tilbury Hope on 1 October. He then returned to his old beat in the North Sea, among other things convoying £80,000 to the army in Scotland.

Peacock was still in command of the *Tiger* when the First Anglo-Dutch War broke out. His ship was among those in the Downs on 7 June and he was commended by Blake for his capture of a Flemish privateer three days later. His assignment to North Sea convoy duties once more makes it unlikely that he was present at the battles of Kentish Knock and Dungeness but his capture of twenty prizes made a great impression and he was promised command of a squadron to be sent to the Mediterranean although, in the event, the expedition was abandoned. The respect with which he was by now held was demonstrated by his selection as one of six officers who drew up a revised fleet plan after Dungeness. In the subsequent reorganization he was assigned to the newly launched 3rd-rate frigate, the *Rainbow*, and made vice-admiral of the White squadron. On the first day of the battle of Portland, 16–18 February 1653, the White squadron was the last to engage and so Peacock missed the heaviest fighting. Shortly afterwards he was one of three officers chosen to present a petition for the adequate compensation of the widows and orphans of officers and seamen killed in battle, and the provision of proper facilities for the sick and wounded. After Portland he shifted his flag to the *Triumph* and fought in her at the battle of the Gabbard on 2–4 June 1653 where his casualties amounted to only one killed and two wounded. His luck ran out at the last battle off Scheveningen on 29–31 July, however, where he was mortally wounded, dying a few days later, about 4 August. He left a widow, Mary, and five children, to whom parliament voted £750 vested in Ipswich trustees and to be paid there.

MICHAEL BAUMBER

Sources S. R. Gardiner and C. T. Atkinson, eds., *Letters and papers relating to the First Dutch War, 1652–1654*, 6 vols., Navy RS, 13, 17, 30,

37, 41, 66 (1898–1930) · *CSP dom.*, 1648–53 · Bodl. Oxf., MSS Rawl. A. 220–222, A. 224–226 · Bodl. Oxf., MS Rawl. C. 416 · PRO, ADM 673, ADM 18/1–4 · J. R. Powell and E. K. Timings, eds., *Documents relating to the civil war, 1642–1648*, Navy RS, 105 (1963) · *JHC*, 4 (1644–6) · *Report on the manuscripts of F. W. Leyborne-Popham*, HMC, 51 (1899) · 'A few instances of English courage and conduct at sea', BL, Add. MS 11684 · G. Penn, *Memorials of Sir William Penn*, 2 vols. (1833) · B. Capp, *Cromwell's navy: the fleet and the English revolution, 1648–1660* (1989) · Bodl. Oxf., MS Tanner 56 · *To the right honourable, the high court of parliament, the humble remonstrance of Andrewes Burrell* [1646] [Thomason tract E 335(6)] · *A list of … ships … in this summers expedition* (1646) [Thomason tract E 669.f.9(58)] · [Robert, earl of Warwick], *A perfect remonstrance and narrative of all the proceedings of the Right Honourable Robert, earl of Warwick* [1649] · G. G. Harris, ed., *Trinity House of Deptford: transactions, 1609–35*, London RS, 19 (1983) · J. Matthews and G. F. Matthews, eds., *Abstracts of probate acts in the prerogative court of Canterbury*, 8 vols. (1902–28)

Peacock, James (1735/1738–1814), architect and surveyor, was for over forty years assistant clerk of works to the City of London. Nothing is known of his early life, although, according to Sir John Soane, Peacock became acquainted with George Dance the younger soon after Dance's return from Italy in December 1764. From then on the two formed a professional alliance which remained uninterrupted until Peacock's death; their abilities were complementary, with Peacock supplying the skills of surveying and estimating to Dance's abilities as a designer.

In December 1771 Peacock was appointed assistant to Dance, who had succeeded his father as clerk of works to the City of London in 1768, on Dance's recommendation and at his expense, although this arrangement was altered in 1776, when Peacock was given a salary by the corporation of £52 10s. He was also employed by Dance in his private practice. Peacock's only independent work of importance was the stock exchange in Capel Court, which was built to his designs in 1801–2 but reconstructed by Thomas Allason in 1853–4. He also carried out repairs to St Anne and St Agnes, Gresham Street, in 1781–2, and to St Stephen Walbrook in 1803–4.

More remarkable than his architectural works was Peacock's prolific output as an architectural theorist, an inventor, and a social reformer. His architectural publications have a radical, semi-satirical attitude to design and practice. The most important of these was *Oikidia, or, Nutshells*, published under the anagrammatic pseudonym of 'Jose Mac Packe, bricklayer's labourer' in 1785. At a time of a growing interest in the picturesque and increasingly elaborate exhibition drawings at the Royal Academy, Peacock recommended clients to commission strictly symmetrical plans for small villas with plain façades, and scale models complete with furniture instead of drawings and do-it-yourself estimates. These were the 'nutshells': 'the first and elementary principles of design' (p. 2). He repeated his mainly mathematical approach to architecture in his final publication, *Subordinates in Architecture* (1814). The anonymous *Essay on the Qualifications and Duties of an Architect*, published in 1773, may also have been by Peacock (Harris, 366–7). As an inventor he published *A Short Account of a New Method of Filtration by Ascent* in 1793, promising Londoners an inexhaustible supply of pure soft water from the Thames and neighbouring rivers.

Peacock was also interested in economic and social problems, and wrote a number of short treatises on these subjects. His *Outlines of a scheme for the general relief, instruction, employment, and maintenance of the poor* was published in 1777 and is described by him as 'an imperfect and crude performance' in another tract entitled *Proposals for a Magnificent and Interesting Establishment* (1790). In 1789 he published *Superior Politics* and in 1798 *The Outlines of a Plan for Establishing a United Company of British Manufacturers*. All of these tracts set forth, with various modifications, Peacock's main project of:

> giving protection and suitable incitement, encouragement, and employ to every class of the destitute, ignorant, and idle poor who shall be healthy, able to work, and willing to conform … to such … regulations as the company shall enact, and which are intended to be of mutual benefit and advantage to the company and the workpeople, and eventually so to society at large.

Peacock died on 22 February 1814 at 17 Finsbury Square, a house where he had lived for some years and 'which he apparently built for himself' (Papworth). His former residence was at Coleman Street Buildings. Little is known of his personality but in his edition of Chambers's *Treatise on Civil Architecture* (1875) Joseph Gwilt paid a tribute to Peacock's 'virtues and moral excellence', which 'will be honoured as long as the memory of his surviving friends remains sound' (Colvin, *Archs.*, 745). He was buried in the back cemetery of St Luke's, Old Street, where his headstone (now demolished) records that he died 'in the seventy-sixth year of his age' (Papworth), although according to the *Gentleman's Magazine*, he was in his seventy-ninth year.

LAURENCE BINYON, *rev.* MARGARET RICHARDSON

Sources Colvin, *Archs.* · D. Stroud, *George Dance, architect, 1741–1825* (1971) · E. Harris and N. Savage, *British architectural books and writers, 1556–1785* (1990) · P. de la Ruffinière du Prey, *John Soane: the making of an architect* (Chicago, 1982) · [W. Papworth], ed., *The dictionary of architecture*, 11 vols. (1853–92) · *GM*, 1st ser., 84/1 (1814), 411 · A. T. Bolton, ed., *The portrait of Sir John Soane* (1927), 3, 59, 95–8 **Archives** Sir John Soane's Museum, London, letters to J. Soane

Peacock, John Macleay (1817–1877), poet and Chartist, was born on 21 or 31 March 1817 at Kincardine, Perthshire, the seventh of eight children of William Peacock, seaman (his mother is unrecorded). While his family was young Peacock's father was lost at sea, and the struggle for existence became severe. No formal education is recorded, and Peacock was sent to work at the age of nine, first at a tobacco factory, and afterwards at some bleaching works. Ultimately he was apprenticed as a 'rivet laddie' on Clydeside, and boilermaking became his trade. Commercial fluctuations, and a strong natural disposition to travel, took him in the course of his lifetime to many parts of the world. As a young man he must have lived and worked in co. Cork, and the province of Cadiz in south-west Spain, as well as on Tyneside, Clydeside, and other shipbuilding centres in Scotland and England. Peacock was in the best sense self-taught, and his travels did much to broaden his knowledge and shape him as a clear and original thinker.

In both politics and religion Peacock was always radical. He was an active participant in the Chartist movement, and was sent as a delegate to the national convention in London (he published a 'Conventional Hymn' in the *Northern Star*, 2 March 1839). He was elected a commissioner of the movement in May 1848. Afterwards, for many years, until his death, he was an energetic secularist. Peacock married and settled in Birkenhead in the 1850s (his wife's name is unrecorded), and for many years he worked at Lairds iron shipbuilding works, Birkenhead, where the *Alabama* was built; but this did not prevent him from openly advocating the cause of the north in the American Civil War. Dismissed for his militancy, Peacock began publishing poetry in the 1860s as an alternative occupation. Physically he was delicate, and, his occupation being arduous, his health failed in middle life; thenceforward he only earned a precarious income, chiefly as a news vendor. He died in Glasgow, where he was then living, of heart disease on 4 May 1877; he was survived by his wife.

Peacock's poetry was highly valued by his friends and contemporaries. In Birkenhead, at the Shakespeare tercentenary (1864), he was considered the most fitting person in the town to plant the memorial oak tree. He wrote stirring and incisive political verse, as well as Scottish dialect material, contemplative verse, poems on topical events, and poems on shipbuilding and the industrial landscape. Three volumes of his poems were published in all: *Poems and Songs* (1864), *Hours of Reverie* (1867, which went into a second edition in the same year), and a selection of *Poems* (1880). The best of his work is in the 1867 and 1880 volumes (copies of which are held in Birkenhead and Manchester reference libraries). His work is also part of the Koehler collection of Minor British Poets in the University of California at Davis.

WALTER LEWIN, *rev.* JOHN GOODRIDGE

Sources W. Lewin, 'Introductory notice', *Poems by John Macleay Peacock* (1880) · D. H. Edwards, 'John Macleay Peacock', *Modern Scottish poets, with biographical and critical notices*, 4 (1882), 212–19 · J. M. Peacock, *Poems and songs* (1864) · J. M. Peacock, *Hours of reverie* (1867) · P. M. Ashraf, *An introduction to working class literature in Great Britain: poetry* (1978), 71–2, 100–01, 182 · J. T. Ward, *Chartism* (1973), 200, 210 · *Northern Star* (2 March 1839) [information from Stephen Roberts, University of Birmingham]
Likenesses photograph, repro. in Peacock, *Poems*
Wealth at death *Poems* (1880) was produced for benefit of widow

Peacock, Lucy (*fl.* 1785–1816), bookseller and children's writer, was probably born in London, where she kept a shop in Oxford Street. Although little is known of her life, it is likely that she was married, as the publisher's imprint on some of her works states that they were 'printed for R. and L. Peacock'. Her children's books were published for the most part anonymously. Among the earliest of these was *The adventures of the six princesses of Babylon in their travels to the temple of virtue: an allegory* (1785), of which five editions were printed, and which was 'dedicated, by permission to her Royal Highness the Princess Mary'. It was followed by *The Rambles of Fancy, or, Moral and Interesting Tales* and *Friendly Labours* in 1786. In the following years Peacock contributed similar moral tales to the *Juvenile Magazine*, and other periodicals. Among her publications were the allegorical narrative *The Knight of the Rose* (1793);

The Little Emigrant: a Tale (1799); and *Emily, or, The Test of Sincerity* (1816). *The Visit for a Week* (1794) was her most popular work, running into nine editions. Typically didactic, it deals with the visit of two children to their aunt, who teaches them that learning can be exciting, with her discourses on many varied topics. *The Visit* was translated into French in 1817 by J. E. Lefebvre.

Peacock also translated from the French *Ambrose and Eleanor, or, The Adventures of Two Children Deserted on an Uninhabited Island* (1796, 1812), an adaptation of *Fanfan et Lolotte*; Veyssière de La Croze's *Grammaire historique* (1800); and *Abrégé chronologique de l'histoire universelle* (1807). Many of her works were reprinted in America.

G. LE G. NORGATE, *rev.* M. CLARE LOUGHLIN-CHOW

Sources J. Todd, ed., *A dictionary of British and American women writers, 1660–1800* (1985) · [D. Rivers], *Literary memoirs of living authors of Great Britain*, 2 (1798), 118–19 · Allibone, *Dict.* · BL cat.
Archives BL, letters to Royal Literary Fund, loan 96

Peacock, Thomas (*d.* in or after **1581**), college head, was the son of Thomas Peacock, burgess of Cambridge (*d.* 1541), and his wife, Alice (*d.* 1546/7), and was born in Holy Trinity parish, Cambridge. He was elected to a fellowship at St John's College, Cambridge, in 1533/4, graduated BA that year, MA in 1537, and BTh in 1554. He should not be confused (as in the *Dictionary of National Biography*) with the Thomas Peacock who was active as a stipendiary priest in Ipswich in the 1530s and 1540s, as the Cambridge Peacock was active in college and university life throughout this time, and was not ordained until Mary's reign. Of conservative religious opinions, he was among the 'appellants' at St John's who unsuccessfully objected to the managerial regime of the college's evangelical master John Taylor in 1542. Peacock's mother died over the winter of 1546–7, and left him a house and two tenements in Cambridge. In 1547 he took up a fellowship at the newly founded Trinity College (joining several other refugees from St John's). Trinity, then under the mastership of John Redman (himself a former Johnian), was still loyal to the conservative traditions of the institutions it had swallowed up, King's Hall and Michaelhouse. During the royal visitation of the university in 1549, Peacock was identified by the protestant visitors as one of a group of hardline papists at Trinity, where there was 'such a nest of them as the like cannot be espied within the realm' (PRO, SP 10/7/10, fols. 39–40). Once Redman himself had been induced to subscribe to the Book of Common Prayer (apparently with some reservations), resistance collapsed. Peacock appears to have remained at Trinity throughout Edward VI's reign, notwithstanding the increasingly uncongenial doctrine and liturgy of the Church of England.

The accession of Queen Mary in 1553 must have come as a great relief to Peacock, and certainly did his career no harm. It was only now that he finally took his BTh and entered holy orders. He also found considerable preferment at the hands of the bishop of Norwich, Thomas Thirlby (himself a native of Cambridge, from the same parish as Peacock, namely Holy Trinity), who made him his chaplain and gave him a canonry at Norwich in 1554. When Thirlby was translated to Ely later that year, he took

Peacock with him, collating him to the rectory of Little Downham in 1555 and to a canonry at Ely in 1556 (in place of that at Norwich). In his capacity as Thirlby's chaplain, Peacock assisted at the trial for heresy of William Wolsey and Robert Pygot at Ely, preaching (on 1 Corinthians 5) at their burning on 16 October 1555. Peacock clearly had continuing links with Cambridge University: on 1 April 1555 he signed the articles which bound the university to Roman Catholic doctrine; and during Cardinal Pole's visitation of the university, he preached before the visitors at Great St Mary's on 11 January 1557, 'inveighing against heresies and heretics as Bilney, Cranmer, Latimer, Ridley, etc' (*Acts and Monuments*, 8.266). In January 1558 Thirlby presented him to the rectory of Barley (near Royston, Hertfordshire).

In the autumn of 1557, Peacock was elected president of Queens' College, Cambridge, where his tenure was brief and controversial. In March 1559 a dispute over fellowship elections became so embittered that both parties wrote to the university's chancellor, Sir William Cecil, in an attempt to have their position vindicated. Although the quarrel was over the implementation and interpretation of the statutes regarding elections, the underlying issues seem to have been both personal and religious. The minority appealing against Peacock suggested that the president and his supporters were rushing through improper elections in order to get people into the college ahead of the imminent restoration of protestantism. In a coda to this accusation, the dissidents charged him with paying £10 over the odds for a piece of land purchased for the college from a friend of his supporters among the fellowship, one Thomas Leete. Refusing to subscribe to the royal supremacy, which was restored by Queen Elizabeth in 1559, Peacock was stripped of his ecclesiastical preferments, although by resigning the presidency of Queens' in May he avoided the indignity of expulsion. Thereafter it might have been thought that he lived out his life obscurely in Cambridge, as in 1563 he made a grant of 20s. a year to the churchwardens of Holy Trinity parish, and in October 1581 he gave £20 to the city corporation to support a monthly dole for prisoners in the Tolbooth. However, he makes one remarkable appearance out of the shadows. A letter written in 1567 by none other than Nicholas Sander, a leading Catholic refugee on the continent, indicates that Thomas Peacock was one of four English priests who met the grand inquisitor in Rome in 1564 and personally received from him faculties to reconcile schismatics to the Roman Catholic church. Peacock certainly returned to Cambridge thereafter, but it is not known what use, if any, he made of these special powers. He left no will, so his donation to the city in 1581 may well have represented the disposal of his worldly goods, and he probably died soon afterwards.   RICHARD REX

Sources W. G. Searle, *The history of the Queens' College of St Margaret and St Bernard in the University of Cambridge*, 1, Cambridge Antiquarian RS, 9 (1867), 264–84 • PRO, SP 10/7/10, fols. 39–40 • *The acts and monuments of John Foxe*, ed. S. R. Cattley, 8 vols. (1837–41), vol. 7, p. 405; vol. 8, p. 266 • will, 4 March 1528, Cambs. AS, Cambridge, probate register, Archdeaconry of Ely, I, fols. 165-6 [proved 17 Oct. 1541]; will, 8 Oct 1546, Cambs. AS, Cambridge, Archdeaconry of Ely probate register, II, fol. 6or [Alice Peacock, widow, proved 24 May 1547] • M. Bateson, ed., *Grace book B*, 2 (1905), 186, 202 • W. G. Searle, ed., *Grace book Γ* (1908), 277, 314 • J. Venn, ed., *Grace book Δ* (1910), 97 • T. Baker, *History of the college of St John the Evangelist, Cambridge*, ed. J. E. B. Mayor, 2 vols. (1869) • A. O. Meyer, *England und die katholische Kirche unter Elisabeth* (1911), 412 • C. H. Cooper and J. W. Cooper, *Annals of Cambridge*, 5 vols. (1842–1908), vol. 2, p. 389 • Ely diocesan records, CUL, G/I/8, fols. 31-2 • W. W. Rouse Ball and J. A. Venn, eds., *Admissions to Trinity College, Cambridge*, 2 (1913), 10

Peacock, Thomas Bevill (1812–1882), physician, was born at York on 21 December 1812, son of Thomas Peacock and his wife, Sarah Bevill, who were members of the Society of Friends. When he was nine he was sent to the boarding-school of Samuel Marshall at Kendal, where he remained until apprenticed in 1828 to John Fothergill, a medical practitioner in Darlington. In 1833 he went to London to read medicine at University College; he also attended St George's Hospital. In 1835 he became a member of the College of Surgeons and a licentiate of the Society of Apothecaries. He then travelled to benefit his health, twice visiting Ceylon, and studying for a time in Paris. He spent 1838 as house-surgeon at the hospital at Chester, and in 1841 he went to Edinburgh, where he obtained an MD the following year. In 1844 he was admitted as a licentiate of the Royal College of Physicians of London, and in 1849 he was elected assistant physician to St Thomas's Hospital. In 1850 he married Cornelia Walduck (*d.* 1869); there were no children. In the same year he was elected a fellow of the College of Physicians, and in 1865 he delivered the Croonian lectures there, entitled 'Some of the causes and effects of valvular disease of the heart'. A dispensary which he began in Liverpool Street, London, eventually became the Victoria Park Hospital for diseases of the chest.

Peacock lectured at St Thomas's Hospital, first on materia medica and then on medicine. He was one of the founders of the Pathological Society of London in 1846, and a frequent contributor to its *Transactions*. He was its secretary in 1850, vice-president in 1852–6, and president in 1865 and 1866. In 1848 he published *On the Influenza or Epidemic Catarrh of 1847-8*, and in 1866 the treatise, *On Malformations of the Human Heart*. These, with his Croonian lectures of 1865 and his *Prognosis in Cases of Valvular Disease of the Heart* (1877), are his most important publications. Peacock was a candidate for the fellowship of the Royal Society in 1877 and 1878 but would not allow himself to be nominated again. However, the College of Surgeons gave him a gold medal in recognition of his valuable additions to their museum.

Peacock was fond of travelling, and visited North and South America as well as the Mediterranean. He lived at 20 Finsbury Circus, London, an area popular with many physicians in the second quarter of the nineteenth century. Peacock had an attack of left hemiplegia in 1877, but recovered from the paralysis, and saw patients and attended at the Pathological Society. In 1881 he had a mild attack of right hemiplegia, from which he also recovered. On 30 May 1882, while walking in St Thomas's Hospital, he collapsed and was carried into a ward where he died without having recovered consciousness. He was buried in the Quaker burial-ground at Tottenham, Middlesex.

NORMAN MOORE, *rev.* MARY E. GIBSON

Sources J. S. B., 'Thomas Bevill Peacock, MD FRCP', *St Thomas's Hospital Reports*, new ser., 11 (1882), 179–85 • *The Lancet* (17 June 1882), 1013–14 • *BMJ* (17 June 1882), 928 • I. H. Porter, 'The nineteenth-century physician and cardiologist Thomas Bevill Peacock (1812–82)', *Medical History*, 6 (1962), 240–54 • private information (1895) • d. cert.
Likenesses photograph, repro. in Porter, 'The nineteenth-century physician'
Wealth at death £17,510 15*s.* 2*d.*: resworn administration with will, Nov 1882, *CGPLA Eng. & Wales*

Peacock, Thomas Love (1785–1866), satirical novelist and poet, was born on 18 October 1785 at Weymouth, or Melcombe Regis, Dorset, the only child of Samuel Peacock (*c.*1742–*c.*1793), a London glass merchant, and his wife, Sarah, *née* Love (1754–1832), daughter of Thomas Love, a retired master in the Royal Navy. His parents, who were married at St Luke's, Chelsea, on 29 March 1780, both came from nonconformist families in the west of England: on his father's side Independents in Taunton, Somerset, on his mother's side Presbyterians in Topsham, Devon. Little is known of his father, who apparently lived apart from his wife and son, and died in reduced circumstances, leaving them three small annuities, all of which successively failed or expired. His mother was a strong-minded woman who encouraged her son in his literary pursuits. According to family tradition, 'he often said that, after his mother's death, he wrote with no interest, as his heart was not in the work' (Nicolls, xxvi).

Early life and poetry In 1791 Sarah Peacock took her son to live near her parents at Chertsey, and early in 1792 she sent him to a private school kept by John Harris Wicks at Englefield Green, where he remained for six and a half years and distinguished himself from his schoolfellows. 'The master was', he later recalled, 'not much of a scholar; but he had the art of inspiring his pupils with a love of learning, and he had excellent classical and French assistants' (*Letters*, 2.446). During his holidays at Chertsey the boy would listen to the reminiscences of his sailor grandfather, who had lost a leg in Rodney's great victory over De Grasse off Dominica on 12 April 1782. After being removed from school before his thirteenth birthday, presumably because his mother could no longer afford the expense, Peacock was entirely self-educated, eventually acquiring, by dint of steady application, a degree of erudition seldom found outside a university, including a thorough mastery of the Greek, Latin, Italian, and French languages. By February 1800 he was employed as a clerk for Ludlow, Fraser, & Co., merchants in the City of London, and in the same month he won an 'extra prize' from the *Monthly Preceptor, or, Juvenile Library* for his first publication, a verse 'Answer to the question: "Is history or biography the more improving study?"' While it is not clear how long his employment lasted, he apparently lived with his mother on the firm's premises at 4 Angel Court, Throgmorton Street, until about 1805. A miniature by Roger Jean shows him at this

Thomas Love Peacock (1785–1866), by Maull & Co., 1857

time as a handsome young man with dark blue eyes, a Roman nose, a high forehead, and a profusion of curly brown hair. Peacock continued to write occasional verse throughout his years in London, and his first volume, *Palmyra, and other Poems*, was printed by Thomas Bensley and published by W. J. and J. Richardson late in 1805, though postdated 1806. The rare octavo half-sheet containing his comic ballad *The Monks of St. Mark* was privately printed by Bensley in the same format, presumably about the same time (the date at the end of the poem, 'September, 1804', being that of composition, not of printing). Some time in the next year or so Peacock met Thomas Hookham junior and his brother Edward Thomas Hookham, who offered to become his publishers and to supply him with books from their father's extensive circulating library in Old Bond Street. Other close friends of his early years included William de St Croix of Homerton and Thomas (Ignatius Maria) Forster of Lower Clapton, another remarkable autodidact, with whom he sometimes corresponded in Latin.

For several years after the publication of *Palmyra*, Peacock's resources appear to have been just sufficient to enable him to live semi-independently as a poet and scholar. Always a sturdy pedestrian, he made a solitary walking tour of Scotland in autumn 1806, visiting many of the romantic scenes that had recently been popularized by Walter Scott. In the following summer, while living with his mother at Chertsey, he became engaged to a young woman named Fanny Falkner, but the engagement was broken off through the interference of one of her relations, and she died the following year, after marrying another man. His lasting memory of their love was later enshrined in his lines on 'Newark Abbey, August 1842, with a reminiscence of August 1807' (*Fraser's Magazine*, November 1860). In May 1808 he obtained an appointment as secretary to Sir Home Riggs Popham aboard HMS *Venerable* in the Downs. Although he regarded the ship as a 'floating Inferno', he remained in the position for almost a year to please some friends—probably his two maternal uncles in the navy—who thought there was a prospect of its 'conducing to advantage' (*Letters*, 1.25). After leaving the *Venerable* in April 1809, he decided to expand a poem on the Thames that he had written at sea into what eventually became *The Genius of the Thames*, published by the Hookhams in spring 1810. To gather material for the work, he traced the course of the river on foot from its source to Chertsey, stopping for a few days at Oxford. At the beginning of 1810 he went to north Wales, where he took lodgings for almost fifteen months at Tan-y-Bwlch, near Maentwrog, Merioneth, in the Vale of Ffestiniog, which he described as 'a terrestrial paradise' (ibid., 1.43). Here he developed a strong attachment to the Welsh landscape and a lasting interest in Welsh traditions. His letters to Edward Hookham and Thomas Forster provide glimpses of the young poet pursuing his course of solitary study, exploring the local scenery, and occasionally falling in or out of love. They also reveal that he had long since rejected Christianity as 'a grovelling, misanthropical, blood-thirsty superstition', and had more recently embraced philosophical scepticism as 'a complete Academic' (ibid., 1.57, 62). One of the two young women who interested him at this time was his future wife, Jane Gryffydh (1789–1851), daughter of the parson at Maentwrog, but he left north Wales in April 1811 without declaring his feelings, even though he thought her 'the most innocent, the most amiable, the most beautiful girl in existence' (ibid., 1.64).

Peacock may have been called home by an impending financial crisis, for within a few months his mother was forced by creditors to sell her furniture and leave Chertsey. With the assistance of friends, they were able to take up residence at a cottage in Wraysbury, where new creditors were soon clamouring for payment. Through the good offices of the Hookhams, Peacock's most pressing wants were relieved by grants from the Literary Fund in December 1811, May 1812, and June 1813. However, his despondency was serious enough to give Edward Hookham 'reason to dread that the fate of Chatterton might be that of Peacock' (*Letters*, 1.91). Peacock himself responded to the crisis by producing a new poem, *The Philosophy of Melancholy*, and a heavily revised 'second edition' of *The Genius of the Thames, Palmyra, and other Poems*, published in February and April 1812. With encouragement from James Grant Raymond, the acting manager of the Drury Lane Company, he also wrote three farces—'Mirth in the Mountains' (lost), 'The dilettanti', and 'The Three Doctors'—none of which was performed on the London stage.

Efforts to obtain pupils for a small educational establishment likewise failed. His only literary success during this period was a 'grammatico-allegorical ballad' for children entitled *Sir Hornbook, or, Childe Launcelot's Expedition*, which appeared late in 1813, with a title-page postdated 1814, and ran through five editions in as many years. Despite his financial difficulties, he continued his classical studies and translated a number of passages from Greek tragedies. His Aristophanic Greek anapests on Christ may also have been written at this time. In the early autumn of 1812 he visited Tunbridge Wells with Thomas Forster and made a two-week walking and sailing tour of the Isle of Wight with Joseph Gulston of Englefield Green, while in the following summer he paid a second visit to north Wales, returning to London by way of Bath. His cousin Harriet Love later described him as having been during this period of his life 'a sort of universal lover, making half-declarations to half the young women he knew' (*Works*, 1.civ).

The Shelley circle: satiric fiction It was in the hope of obtaining private assistance for his friend that Thomas Hookham junior introduced Peacock to Shelley in November 1812, and it was partly to relieve Peacock's distress that Shelley invited him to stay at Bracknell in September 1813 and then to join him and his wife Harriet and her sister Eliza on a journey to the Lake District and Edinburgh. 'At Bracknell' Peacock later recalled:

> Shelley was surrounded by a numerous society, all in a great measure of his own opinions in relation to religion and politics, and the larger portion of them in relation to vegetable diet. But they wore their rue with a difference. Every one of them adopting some of the articles of the faith of their general church, had each nevertheless some predominant crotchet of his or her own, which left a number of open questions for earnest and not always temperate discussion. I was sometimes irreverent enough to laugh at the fervour with which opinions utterly unconducive to any practical result were battled for as matters of the highest importance to the well-being of mankind; Harriet Shelley was always ready to laugh with me, and we thereby lost caste with some of the more hot-headed of the party. (*Works*, 8.70–71)

Peacock's attitude of amused detachment may have disturbed the Bracknell circle, but it did not prevent him from quickly becoming Shelley's closest friend and most trusted adviser. Shelley's marital crisis of July 1814 put him in an awkward position as a friend to whom both husband and wife turned for advice and consolation. Although Peacock was one of the few friends who remained loyal to Shelley after his elopement with Mary Godwin, his obvious partiality for Harriet made his relationship with Mary difficult. If Peacock's rationality and scepticism stood in sharp contrast to Shelley's impetuosity and enthusiasm, the two poets nevertheless shared many of the same ideals, and their mutual influence benefited both. Peacock's *Sir Proteus: a Satirical Ballad*, published under the pseudonym P. M. O'Donovan in March 1814, reveals a new interest in literary politics that may be one of the first signs of Shelleyan influence. On the other hand, his fragmentary romantic epic 'Ahrimanes'—written in Spenserian stanzas and originally projected as a twelve-canto narrative of two lovers involved in a struggle between the Zoroastrian principles of good and evil—clearly anticipates Shelley's *Laon and Cythna*. Meanwhile Peacock's personal fortunes reached their nadir in January 1815 when he was arrested for debt in Liverpool, after running off with a supposed heiress who turned out to have nothing. In the spring he considered emigrating to Canada and taking Marianne de St Croix, who was apparently willing to marry him despite her knowledge of his indiscretion with the heiress.

After Shelley reached a settlement with his father in May 1815 and began to receive an annuity of £1000, he allowed Peacock a regular income of £120 a year, until it was rendered superfluous by his India House appointment. In return, Peacock acted as Shelley's agent in business matters: paying bills, negotiating with creditors, and finding houses. It was presumably Shelley's allowance that enabled Peacock and his mother to settle at Marlow, where he could enjoy his lifelong passion for boating on the Thames. At the end of August he accompanied Shelley, Mary Godwin, and Charles Clairmont on a boating expedition up the Thames to Lechlade, and on the way up, at Oxford, he restored his vegetarian friend's health with his prescription of 'Three mutton chops, well peppered' (*Works*, 8.99). Peacock spent much of winter 1815–16 at Bishopsgate, near Windsor, reading Greek with Shelley and Thomas Jefferson Hogg, who became a lifelong friend. It was Peacock who proposed the often misconstrued title for Shelley's *Alastor, or, The Spirit of Solitude*. In the following summer Shelley wrote Peacock several long travel letters from Switzerland, two of which he published in revised form in *A History of a Six Weeks Tour* (1817). After Harriet's suicide in December 1816 Peacock was one of those who advised Shelley not to delay his marriage to Mary Godwin. In March 1817 Shelley moved into a house at Marlow that he took partly to be near Peacock, and for the next twelve months the two writers saw each other almost daily. During this period Peacock became acquainted with Leigh Hunt, John Keats, James and Horace Smith, and other liberal writers. In December he participated with Charles Ollier in the revision of Shelley's *Laon and Cythna* for reissue as *The Revolt of Islam*. Early in 1818 he unsuccessfully proposed marriage to Claire Clairmont, who was living with her daughter Allegra as a member of Shelley's household. After Shelley's departure for Italy in March, Peacock not only continued to act as his business agent but also read the proofs of the *Rosalind and Helen* and *Prometheus Unbound* volumes and tried to get *The Cenci* accepted for performance at Covent Garden. Shelley again chose Peacock as the recipient of his long descriptive travel letters from Italy, and their correspondence continued until Shelley's death in July 1822. As Shelley's executor Peacock was involved for several years in complex negotiations with Sir Timothy Shelley's solicitor, William Whitton, to secure financial support for Mary Shelley and her son Percy Florence. Shelley's will could not be proved until after Sir Timothy's death in 1844, when Peacock finally received two legacies totalling £2500.

Peacock's years at Marlow were the most productive period of his literary career as well as the period in which he discovered his true gift for satiric fiction. *Headlong Hall*, the first of his stylish and witty conversation novels, was an immediate success on its publication in December 1815, with a title-page postdated 1816. *Melincourt*—a more overtly political satire in which the civilized orang-utan Sir Oran Haut-ton is elected MP for the rotten borough of Onevote—also attracted a good deal of attention when it appeared in three volumes in March 1817. The fragmentary tale known as 'Calidore' was probably written in the spring or summer, along with *The Round Table, or, King Arthur's Feast*, a second children's book, published without date in the autumn. *Rhododaphne, or, The Thessalian Spell*, the last and best of Peacock's long poems, was finished in November and published in February 1818. Shelley immediately wrote an enthusiastic review of *Rhododaphne*, which was sent to *The Examiner* but never inserted. *Nightmare Abbey* was written in the spring and published in November 1818, in an attempt, Peacock told Shelley, 'to bring to a sort of philosophical focus a few of the morbidities of modern literature and to let in a little daylight on its atrabilarious complexion' (*Letters*, 1.152). Shelley may have been surprised to find himself caricatured in the book, along with Coleridge and Byron, but he nevertheless 'took to himself the character of Scythrop' (*Works*, 8.497). Peacock's Marlow journal for July–September 1818 records the writing of his unfinished 'Essay on fashionable literature' as well as the genesis of *Maid Marian*, which he intended to make 'the vehicle of much oblique satire on all the oppressions that are done under the sun' (*Letters*, 1.156). This satiric romance of the twelfth century, based on the popular ballads of Robin Hood, was nearly finished when it had to be laid aside at the end of the year. Unlike his early poetry, Peacock's first three novels found an appreciative audience. *Headlong Hall* reached a second edition in 1816, and a third in 1822; *Melincourt* was translated into French in 1818, and *Nightmare Abbey* into German in 1820; all three books were reprinted in America, along with *Rhododaphne*.

India House: the middle years About the beginning of January 1819 Peacock went to London to embark on his thirty-seven-year career in the examiner's office of the East India Company. His candidacy had been brought forward the previous autumn by his old friend Peter Auber, who was then assistant secretary of the company. Because he had no experience with Indian affairs, he was given several weeks to study for a special examination on systems of land revenue collection. The resulting paper, 'Ryotwar and Zemindarry settlements', is said to have been returned with the compliment 'Nothing superfluous and nothing wanting' (Nicolls, xxxvii). His provisional appointment as assistant to the examiner at an annual salary of £600 was approved by the court of directors in May 1819, as part of a larger experiment to open the higher posts in the examiner's office to outside talent. At the East India House he showed great skill in drafting dispatches, and his appointment was confirmed in April 1821 with a salary rise to £800. His subsequent career was one of steady advancement, at first in the shadow of James Mill, who was appointed at the same time, and who brought his son John Stuart Mill into the office in 1823. When James Mill became assistant examiner in April 1823, Peacock's salary was raised to £1000, and when Mill succeeded William McCulloch as examiner in December 1830, Peacock became a senior assistant to the examiner at £1200. In February 1836, with Mill seriously ill, Peacock became assistant examiner at £1500, and in July, a month after Mill's death, he was appointed examiner at £2000—a salary that remained unchanged until March 1856, when he retired on a pension of £1333 6s. 8d. and was in turn succeeded by John Stuart Mill. Through James Mill he became acquainted with almost all the leading philosophical radicals, including Bentham, with whom he is said to have been 'extremely intimate—dining with him *tête à tête*, once a week for years together' (Sir M. E. Grant Duff, *Notes from a Diary, 1851–72*, 1897, 1.60). He also influenced the careers of Henry Cole and John Arthur Roebuck by introducing them to John Stuart Mill.

With his prosperity virtually assured, Peacock took a house at 17 (later 18) Stamford Street, Blackfriars, in June 1819 and turned his thoughts to marriage. Despite his having had no contact with Jane Gryffydh for more than eight years, he proposed by letter in November 1819, and they were married at Eglwys-fach, Cardiganshire, on 22 March 1820. For the first few years the marriage seems to have been happy, and four children were born to the couple during the next eight years. But after the death of their second daughter, Margaret Love, in January 1826, Jane is said to have been 'inconsolable' and to have developed some kind of mental illness that left her 'a complete invalid', unable to 'attend to the care of their children, or undertake the troubles of housekeeping' (Nicolls, xxxix, xli). In 1823 Peacock had taken a cottage for his mother on the Thames at Lower Halliford, and in 1826 he took the adjoining cottage and turned the two into a comfortable country residence, where his mother looked after the children until her death in October 1832. To supply Margaret's place in the family, he informally adopted Mary Ann Rosewell, whose family lived in the neighbourhood, and who strikingly resembled the dead child. His epitaph for Margaret's tombstone in Shepperton churchyard caused a quarrel with the rector, who objected to the opening line: 'Long night succeeds thy little day'.

After his India House appointment and marriage, Peacock's literary work became more sporadic. His ironic essay 'The four ages of poetry', in the first and only number of *Olliers Literary Miscellany* (1820), provoked Shelley to write 'A Defence of Poetry'. *Maid Marian* appeared in March 1822, with a prefatory note explaining that all but the last three chapters had been written in the autumn of 1818—before Scott made Robin Hood a character in *Ivanhoe*. J. R. Planché's operatic adaptation, *Maid Marian, or, The Huntress of Arlingford*, with music by Henry Bishop, opened at Covent Garden on 3 December 1822 and enjoyed a successful run with Charles Kemble as Friar Tuck and Anna

Maria Tree as Maid Marian. Peacock's tale was translated into German in 1823 and into French in 1826 and again, more satisfactorily, in 1855. In 1823 Peacock met the Welsh antiquary and lexicographer William Owen Pughe, and in 1824 he joined the Cymmrodorion, or Metropolitan Cambrian Institution. During the financial panic of 1825–6, he wrote his *Paper Money Lyrics* but suppressed them to avoid offending James Mill. After Mill's death he permitted Henry Cole to publish some of them in *The Guide* and privately to print an edition of 100 copies, with a few other poems, in July 1837. His satiric romance *The Misfortunes of Elphin*, based on legends of sixth-century Wales, appeared in March 1829, and *Crotchet Castle*, containing a romantic interlude in Merioneth, followed in February 1831. *Elphin* includes, as 'the quintessence of all the war-songs that ever were written', the rollicking 'War-Song of Dinas Vawr', which begins:

The mountain sheep are sweeter,
But the Valley sheep are fatter;
We therefore deemed it meeter
To carry off the latter.
(*Works*, 4[1].89)

Crotchet Castle contains the Reverend Doctor Folliott's trenchant satire on the 'march of mind', as represented by the 'learned friend' (Lord Brougham) and the 'Steam Intellect Society' (the Society for the Diffusion of Useful Knowledge) (ibid., 4[2].13). But for all their satiric brilliance, neither of these new works seems to have enjoyed the same degree of success as the four earlier tales. Peacock was one of the original contributors to *Bentley's Miscellany*, edited by Dickens, and in April 1837 *Headlong Hall*, *Nightmare Abbey*, *Maid Marian*, and *Crotchet Castle* were reprinted, 'with corrections, and a preface, by the author', as no. 57 in Bentley's Standard Novels series. All Peacock's journalistic writing appeared in liberal or radical publications. He was induced to contribute four articles to the Benthamite *Westminster Review* under John Bowring's editorship, four more to John Stuart Mill's short-lived *London Review*, and one to the whig *Edinburgh Review*. Always a lover of opera, he also wrote opera criticism for the *Globe and Traveller*, edited by his friend Walter Coulson, and for *The Examiner*, owned and edited by Albany Fonblanque.

As one of the two highest permanent officials in the East India Company's home service, Peacock was an able administrator but never exerted the sort of powerful influence over Indian affairs that James Mill did. He had serious reservations about the utilitarians' programme of reforming Indian institutions along European lines, and the fundamental cast of his intelligence was practical rather than theoretical, sceptical rather than doctrinaire. It is entirely in keeping with his practicality that his most notable achievements as an India House official should have been in the burgeoning field of steam navigation. Peacock began to study all aspects of the subject in 1829 and quickly became the company's acknowledged expert in the field. From 1831 to 1833 he collaborated with James Henry Johnston in making arrangements for the steam navigation of the Ganges. His queries about Egyptian and Syrian routes to India stimulated Francis Rawdon

Chesney to explore both between 1830 and 1832, and he drew up the original plans and budget for the Euphrates expedition led by Chesney in 1835–6. Although he favoured the Euphrates route, he also advocated the employment of larger and more powerful steamers for the Red Sea route. To this end he supervised the design and construction of the *Atalanta* and the *Berenice*, the first vessels to steam the whole distance to India, and later the purchase and refitting of the *Semiramis*, then one of the most powerful vessels in the world. An early proponent of iron ships, he often worked closely with the Birkenhead shipbuilder John Laird and his brother the African explorer Macgregor Laird. As clerk to the company's secret committee, he not only procured river steamers for the Indus, the Euphrates, and the Tigris, but also supervised the design, construction, fitting, and trials of a new class of iron war-steamers with movable keels for both river and sea service. These were his 'iron chickens', whose names—*Nemesis*, *Phlegethon*, *Pluto*, *Proserpine*—and distinguished service in the First Opium War of 1839–42 led him to characterize them as 'the Infernal Flotilla dispatched against the Celestial Empire' (*Letters*, 2.269, 279). His visionary scheme of placing British steamers on the Aral Sea and the Oxus and Jaxartes rivers in central Asia prompted the fatal mission of Arthur Conolly to Khiva and Bukhara. While much of his evidence before parliamentary committees in the 1830s dealt with steam navigation, he also defended the company in 1834, when he resisted the claim of James Silk Buckingham to compensation for his expulsion from India, and in 1836, when he repelled the attack of Liverpool merchants on the Indian salt monopoly.

Later life and writings It was through his work as examiner and clerk to the secret committee that Peacock became an intimate friend of Sir John Cam Hobhouse, afterwards Lord Broughton, who was president of the Board of Control from 1835 to 1841 and from 1846 to 1852. From 1840 onward he spent many of his holidays at Erle Stoke Park, Hobhouse's country house in Wiltshire, where he met many distinguished Victorians, including Disraeli, Thackeray, and Macaulay. In the summer of 1843 he began to commute daily from Lower Halliford to the India House, reading Homer and Aeschylus in Greek in his corner of the railway carriage, and thereby confirming his opinion 'that the march of Mechanics is one way, and the march of Mind is another' (*Letters*, 2.279). Soon he gave up his house in Stamford Street, moving his London quarters first to 22 John Street, Adelphi, and afterwards to 1 Torrington Street, Russell Square. In 1841 his only son, Edward Gryffydh, went to India as a midshipman in the Indian navy but returned the following year on a medical furlough. Two years later Peacock obtained a clerkship for him in the examiner's office. In January 1844 Peacock's eldest daughter, Mary Ellen, married Lieutenant Edward Nicolls, who drowned two months later while in command of HMS *Dwarf* in Ireland. In August 1849, after five years of widowhood, she married George Meredith, then an ambitious young poet with no obvious prospects. Her sister Rosa Jane and her brother Edward also married before the end

of the year. While Peacock is said to have disapproved of all three of these 1849 marriages, he remained an indulgent father and tried to help the Merediths through years of financial struggle and emotional turmoil. He does not appear to have been particularly disturbed when Mary Ellen finally left Meredith in September 1857 for their painter friend Henry Wallis, who later acknowledged paternity of the son she bore the following spring. Wallis painted an informal portrait of Peacock in January 1858, but a photograph taken in the previous year by Maull & Co. provides a more satisfactory likeness of the writer in his old age.

Peacock's wife died on 23 December 1851 at Southend-on-Sea, and some time in the following year he proposed marriage to Claire Clairmont's twenty-seven-year-old niece Pauline, who 'looked daggers at the dear old man' (*Clairmont Correspondence*, 2.551). It was apparently through his connection with the Merediths that he returned to literary work in the early 1850s, after having published nothing new since 1838. George's first volume of *Poems* was published in 1851 by J. W. Parker & Son with a respectful dedication to Peacock, and Mary Ellen was commissioned by the Parkers to produce a revised edition of William Kitchener's *The Cook's Oracle*, a task in which she enlisted her husband and father as collaborators. Both of the Merediths occasionally contributed to *Fraser's Magazine*, edited by their friend John William Parker junior, and Peacock's hand is evident in an article entitled 'Gastronomy and civilization', published in December 1851 over the initials M. M. The following year Peacock's own scholarly series of *Horae dramaticae* began to appear in *Fraser's*. His Greek lines on an East India Company whitebait dinner were privately printed in 1851, and his little book of scatological Latin epigrams on a statue of Sir Robert Peel in 1854. About 1851 he undertook an edition of Aeschylus's *Supplices* that he worked at sporadically for many years but never finished. After his retirement from the India House, his contributions to *Fraser's* became more frequent. The most notable of these were his 'Memoirs of Percy Bysshe Shelley' (1858, 1860), which were followed by some 'Unpublished letters' (1860) and a 'Supplementary notice' (1862). Although often asked to write a life of Shelley, he had always refused because he did not want to revive old gossip by discussing his friend's marital affairs; but eventually he saw a need to correct the accounts published by others, especially those of Thomas Medwin and Thomas Jefferson Hogg. His insistence that Shelley was not separated from Harriet when he fell in love with Mary, as Lady Shelley implied in her *Shelley Memorials* (1859), led to a bitter quarrel with Sir Percy and Lady Shelley, in which Richard Garnett publicly took up their cause. The last of Peacock's novels, *Gryll Grange*, was serialized in *Fraser's* in 1860 and reprinted as a book in February 1861. In comparison with his earlier tales, the characters are more lifelike while the satire is at once more mellow and more idiosyncratic. His last published work was a translation, *Gl'inganati, the Deceived: a Comedy Performed at Siena in 1531, and Aelia Laelia Crispis*, which appeared in August 1862. Of the later works that remained in manuscript, the most characteristic are a reminiscence of 'The Last Day of Windsor Forest', possibly intended for *Fraser's*, and 'A Dialogue on Idealities', apparently written for Lord Broughton's daughter Charlotte Carleton.

After his retirement, Peacock rarely left Halliford except for his visits to Lord Broughton, which continued until 1860. For most of his adult life he had espoused the philosophical doctrines of Epicurus, but if he hoped to find tranquillity in his old age, he was doomed to disappointment. His wife's death had thrown him into a profound depression, and his spirits were even more severely shaken by the deaths of his two surviving daughters—Rosa Jane in October 1857 and Mary Ellen in October 1861. Even after the last and bitterest of these losses, he struggled to regain his equanimity and managed to find solace for a time in educating the sixteen-year-old Clari Leigh Hunt, who came to live with him shortly after Mary Ellen's death. Early in 1863 his health and spirits declined markedly, and for the next three years he saw few visitors except Thomas James Arnold. His death was apparently hastened by the shock of a fire that broke out in his house toward the end of 1865. In this crisis he retreated to his library and exclaimed to the local curate, who was urging him to take refuge elsewhere, 'By the immortal gods, I will not move!' (Nicolls, li). The fire was extinguished, but his already fragile health was badly shaken. He died in his sleep at Lower Halliford, Middlesex, on 23 January 1866 and was buried six days later in the new cemetery at Shepperton. The cause of death was certified as 'climacteric'. In a brief will dated 22 October 1864, he left his entire estate, valued at under £1500, to his adopted daughter 'May' Rosewell, who remained to nurse and comfort him to the end. His son, who was sufficiently provided for by an East India Company pension, survived him by less than a year. Peacock's library was sold at Sothebys on 11–12 June 1866.

Character, opinions, and reputation Peacock's friend Thomas Taylor the Platonist always called him 'Greeky Peeky' (Nicolls, xxxviii), and it would be hard to find any prominent contemporary figure, other than Taylor himself, who identified as completely as Peacock did with the life and ideals of the ancient world. He embraced the teachings of Epicurus as 'the noblest philosophy of antiquity' and considered the Epicurean doctrine of pleasures and pains to be the ultimate source of Bentham's principle of general utility, or 'the greatest happiness of the greatest number' ('Moore's *Epicurean*', *Works*, 9.67, 46–9). In true Epicurean fashion, Peacock's tastes and pleasures were simple, like those of the Reverend Doctor Opimian in *Gryll Grange*: 'a good library, a good dinner, a pleasant garden, and rural walks' (*Works*, 5.19). Although many of his friends were writers, he disliked literary society, despised literary gossip, and tried hard to avoid notoriety—all the more so on account of the scandals involving Shelley and Byron. Even within his own family he was extremely reticent about his private affairs, and his reserve led some of his acquaintance to suspect him of coldness. Yet he was by all accounts a delightful companion, with a ready wit, a powerful memory, and a large fund of amusing anecdotes. In the words of Sir Edward Strachey, he was 'a kind-hearted, genial, friendly man, who loved to share his enjoyment of life with all around him', and was 'self-indulgent without being selfish' (Strachey, 22). Hobhouse found him, both in his private life and in his official capacity, 'a man of most scrupulous probity—and generous & just in all his dealings' (MS journal, 8 Jan 1847).

Peacock was remarkable not only for his acquirements as a self-educated scholar but for his range and versatility as a writer. Most of his early verse tends to confirm Shelley's observation that his friend was 'a nursling of the exact & superficial school in poetry' (*Letters of Percy Bysshe Shelley*, 2.126). However, his genuine poetic gifts are evident in a few personal lyrics, in the best of the songs scattered through his novels, and in *Rhododaphne*, which influenced Keats and won praise from Shelley, Byron, and Poe. Peacock's satiric tales fall naturally into two types—the conversation novels and the satiric romances—both of which stand well outside the main traditions of the English novel, offering little to the ordinary reader in the way of plot or character development. With their curious mixture of poetry and prose, fantasy and reality, abstract theory and common sense, they have clear affinities with the ancient genre of Menippean satire and evidently belong to the class of satiric fiction in which 'the characters are abstractions or embodied classifications, and the implied or embodied opinions the main matter of the work'—a class in which he placed 'the fictions of Aristophanes, Petronius Arbiter, Rabelais, Swift, and Voltaire' ('French comic romances', *Works*, 9.258).

It is not easy to deduce Peacock's own opinions from his fictional dialogues, in which he told an admirer he had 'endeavoured to be impartial, and to say what could be said on both sides' (*Letters*, 2.425). Nowhere is the difficulty more apparent than in the running contrast between past and present that provides the central theme of his fiction. Because he so often satirizes the present in contrast with an idealized past, he has sometimes been mistaken for a reactionary and a pessimist, especially in his later years. But if a man is known by his associates, it must surely be significant that Peacock's friends were, almost without exception, either advanced liberals or radicals, though some of them became considerably more conservative, as he did, after 1830. When he satirized reformers in *Crotchet Castle* and *Gryll Grange*, it was due in part to the fact that their views had become the new orthodoxy, for he was by nature a contrarian in politics, telling Henry Cole that the 'predominant opinions of a community' were 'always a lie and a Tyranny' (MS journal, 8 April 1831). The general tendency of his satire remained liberal and progressive, even if he could not resist ridiculing his contemporaries for their complacency and their willingness to measure progress by advances in technology rather than by real improvement in the quality of physical, mental, and moral life. Robert Williams Buchanan, who visited Peacock in summer 1862, recognized that his negative stance was fundamentally an ironic pose: 'The pessimism which appears everywhere in his books was the daily theme of his talk; but to understand it rightly we must remember it was purely *satiric*—that, in truth, Peacock abused human nature because he loved it' (Buchanan, 244).

Peacock's reputation rests mainly on his seven novels, which have never been popular but have always found numerous admirers among readers with serious interests in literature and ideas. After suffering a marked decline in the late nineteenth century, his literary stock rose steadily in the twentieth. In the early twenty-first century he is widely regarded as the most distinctive prose satirist of the Romantic period and one of the most perceptive commentators on English intellectual life in his time.

NICHOLAS A. JOUKOVSKY

Sources *The letters of Thomas Love Peacock*, ed. N. A. Joukovsky, 2 vols. (2001) [incl. detailed chronology] · *The works of Thomas Love Peacock*, ed. H. F. B. Brett-Smith and C. E. Jones, 10 vols. (1924–34) · N. A. Joukovsky, 'Peacock before *Headlong Hall*: a new look at his early years', *Keats-Shelley Memorial Bulletin*, 36 (1985), 1–40 · C. Van Doren, *The life of Thomas Love Peacock* (1911) · E. Nicolls, 'Biographical notice', in *The works of Thomas Love Peacock*, ed. H. Cole, 3 vols. (1875), 1.xxv–lii · [H. Cole], *Thomas Love Peacock: biographical notes, from 1785 to 1862* ('only ten copies printed', [1874]) · R. Buchanan, 'Thomas Love Peacock: a personal reminiscence', *New Quarterly Magazine*, 4 (1875), 238–55 · E. Strachey, 'Recollections of Thomas Love Peacock', in T. L. Peacock, *Calidore and miscellanea*, ed. R. Garnett (1891), 15–23 · K. N. Cameron, D. H. Reiman, and D. D. Fischer, eds., *Shelley and his circle, 1773–1822*, 10 vols. (1961–2002) · *The letters of Percy Bysshe Shelley*, ed. F. L. Jones, 2 vols. (1964) · *The letters of Mary Wollstonecraft Shelley*, ed. B. T. Bennett, 3 vols. (1980–88) · *The Clairmont correspondence: letters of Claire Clairmont, Charles Clairmont, and Fanny Imlay Godwin*, ed. M. K. Stocking, 2 vols. (1995) · *The journals of Mary Shelley, 1814–1844*, ed. P. R. Feldman and D. Scott-Kilvert, 2 vols. (1987) · *The journals of Claire Clairmont*, ed. M. K. Stocking and D. M. Stocking (1968) · H. Cole, journal, V&A NAL · J. C. Hobhouse, Baron Broughton, MS journal, BL · N. A. Joukovsky, 'Thomas Love Peacock's manuscript "Poems" of 1804', *Studies in Bibliography*, 47 (1994), 196–211 · N. A. Joukovsky, 'The lost Greek anapests of Thomas Love Peacock', *Modern Philology*, 89 (1992), 363–74 · N. A. Joukovsky, 'A new "Little book" by Thomas Love Peacock', *Modern Philology*, 85 (1988), 293–9 · N. A. Joukovsky, '"A dialogue on idealities": an unpublished manuscript of Thomas Love Peacock', *Yearbook of English Studies*, 7 (1977), 128–40 · L. Madden, '"Terrestrial paradise": the Welsh dimension in Peacock's life and work', *Keats-Shelley Memorial Bulletin*, 36 (1985), 41–56 · M. Butler, *Peacock displayed: a satirist in his context* (1979)
Archives BL, letters, journal, and literary papers, Add. MSS 36815–36816 · BL OIOC, steam navigation papers, L/MAR/C562–96 · Harvard U., Houghton L. · NYPL, Carl H. Pforzheimer Collection of Shelley and His Circle, papers | BL, literary MSS and corresp. with Lord Broughton, Add. MS 47225 · Bodl. Oxf., letters to Mary Shelley · Bodl. Oxf., letters to P. B. Shelley · Bodl. Oxf., letters to William Whitton · NYPL, Berg collection · Trinity Cam., letters to Miss Fotheringham
Likenesses R. Jean, miniature, watercolour, *c*.1805, NPG · photograph, *c*.1852, Wallis Estate; repro. in D. Johnson, *The true story of the first Mrs Meredith and other lesser lives* (New York, 1972) · Maull & Co., photograph, 1857, repro. in *The works of Thomas Love Peacock*, ed. H. Cole, 3 vols. (1875) [*see illus.*] · H. Wallis, oils, 1858, NPG · photograph, 1861, priv. coll.
Wealth at death under £1500: probate, 7 March 1866, *CGPLA Eng. & Wales*

Peacocke [*née* Marshall], **Emilie Hawkes** (1882–1964), journalist, was born at 2 Larchfield Street, Darlington, on 26 March 1882, the eldest of six children of John Marshall (*c*.1856–*c*.1903), then chief reporter and later editor and co-proprietor of the *Northern Echo*, a Liberal newspaper produced in Darlington. Her mother, Mildred Hawkes, was also the child of a newspaperman and the family home was filled with journalists and shop talk to which the young Emilie would listen, hidden under a table, absorbing it all. Her parents taught her at home and allowed her to read the review copies of the latest fiction, including the controversial 'new woman' novels of the period that collected around the house. Through her grandparents she knew and admired Jessie White Mario. At fifteen Emilie studied shorthand and became a proof-reader's assistant on the *Northern Echo*; at sixteen she became a trainee reporter, learning the trade through an apprenticeship her father had devised for her, a thorough technical training that gave her experience not only in reporting but in editing, business, and production as well. Her days ended at 3 a.m. and she bicycled home 'filled with pride in the thought that I was already in possession of the news of the day that the people still asleep in the dark, silent houses would not learn till breakfast time' (Sebba, 49). She was good at her job and was quickly promoted to sub-editor.

Emilie Marshall enjoyed the sensation caused by being the only 'girl reporter' in town and it was not until she began looking for work outside her father's paper that she discovered being a woman could be a drawback. In 1902, when only nineteen, she applied for the post of sub-editor on the *Yorkshire Daily Observer*, concealing her age but not her sex. The paper replied that notwithstanding her excellent qualifications, it did not wish to employ a lady in the position.

Marshall was still with the *Echo* when her father resigned his job over his refusal to support the Second South African War, and moved his family to London. It was a difficult time for the Marshalls—John Marshall died about 1903 and Emilie had to seek work to support her family. Despite her impressive qualifications, she was repeatedly turned down with the protest, 'but we already have our lady' (Sebba, 50). She eventually got a job with the *Church Family Newspaper* and was sent to cover the joint convocations of Canterbury and York, only to be told that women were not admitted to these meetings. When she protested that she was present as a member of the British press and suggested that her paper would cover the convocations only if she was allowed in, a hasty compromise was devised whereby she sat behind a red silken cord, which indicated that, though present, she was officially non-existent.

By 1904, bored and in need of a higher salary, Emilie approached W. T. Stead, who had been her father's predecessor as editor of the *Northern Echo*, and asked him for a reporting job on his new venture: the *Daily Paper*. The new paper closed after only five weeks, but Emilie quickly found another job as the first full-time woman reporter on the *Daily Express*. Despite that paper's initial reluctance to let her use the staff room, mixing with the male reporters, she soon established herself as one of them and received from them nothing but courteous assistance and camaraderie. She was generally asked to cover topics thought appropriate to women, such as food, children, and the weather, but she distinguished herself and won a pay rise when she obtained by deception a scarce proof copy of the revised *Hymns Ancient and Modern* which many male reporters had requested in vain.

In 1906 Emilie Marshall left to join *The Tribune*, a new Liberal daily paper that seemed to offer fresh and more exciting opportunities. She covered the activities of the women's suffrage movement and became friendly with many of its leaders. Women's stories enjoyed unprecedented popularity and importance and she was ideally placed to write them. Through her friendship with the trade unionists Margaret Bondfield and Mary Macarthur, she met Keir Hardie and through him obtained the greatest scoop of her career. At his suggestion, she was in the House of Commons on the night when he introduced a women's suffrage resolution. The debate was interrupted by a shower of leaflets thrown by women in the ladies' gallery, and Marshall was the only journalist present. Although she supported women's suffrage and covered the women's activities sympathetically, her friends never persuaded her to give up journalism to campaign for the cause. Journalism was her life and she wanted no other. Her *Tribune* colleague Philip Gibbs modelled the heroine of his novel *The Street of Adventure* (1909) on Emilie, a woman for whom Fleet Street embodied all adventure, excitement, and romance.

The Tribune closed in 1908 and Emilie Marshall was hired as the first woman reporter on the *Daily Mail*. She covered the activities of the increasingly violent militant suffrage movement and often stood outside the gates of Holloway gaol in the early morning when the hunger strikers were released. Known and trusted by both militants and editors, she was beginning to make her name when in 1909 she fell in love with a reporter on a rival paper, Herbert Peacocke (1881/2–1931), himself a distinguished journalist. He was the son of James Goslin Peacocke, sheriff's officer. They married in secret at Holborn register office on 12 June 1909 and settled in Chancery Lane. Emilie's desire for secrecy proved well-founded, for when the *Daily Mail* heard she was married, and to an employee of its rival the *Express* as well, she was dismissed.

Peacocke continued to write, often doing freelance work for *The Observer* and *The Times*. The birth of her daughter, Marguerite, in 1915 slowed her output but did not halt it. In 1918 she worked for the Ministry of Information, writing articles celebrating the courage and resourcefulness of British women. After the armistice the *Daily Express* hired her, perhaps mindful of her changed circumstances, for Herbert Peacocke had been gassed at Ypres and Emilie must have been the sole support of the family. She covered the general election of 1918 and Nancy Astor's political campaign before being placed in charge of the leader page. She became editor of the women's feature of the new *Sunday Express* in 1920. Despite her aversion to being confined to women's issues as a journalist, Peacocke enjoyed this job, perhaps because women's issues were now more broadly defined and she sensed the power

of the women's market. In 1928 the *Daily Telegraph* persuaded her to head its new women's department and she remained there until her retirement in 1940.

Peacocke wrote a book for young women considering journalism as a profession, *Writing for Women* (1936), in which she urged them to approach the calling as a vocation, to despise no aspect of women's journalism, not even the lowly gossip column, and to be ready to seize opportunities. If a big story broke and a woman reporter was the only one available, most editors would send her to cover it—'the rest is up to her' (Peacocke, 9). In the 1930s she was a member of the University of London's journalism course committee. She joined both the Institute of Journalists and the National Union of Journalists, and was one of the first women to be admitted to the Worshipful Company of Stationers and Newspaper Makers in 1933. She was interested in practical details such as the exclusion of women, in early years, from journalists' dinners, and wrote about clothing suitable for women reporters (she favoured basic black with a shorter skirt than was then fashionable, as long ones dragged in the mud).

Herbert Peacocke died in 1931 and Emilie lived with her daughter, who also became a journalist, for the rest of her life. Emilie Peacocke died at their home, 12 Hillsleigh Road, Kensington, London, on 25 January 1964. She is remembered as a pioneer woman journalist who, though she was not always able to overcome discrimination, was usually able to find a way round it. She made her largest contribution to journalism by transforming the woman's story and the woman's page into an essential part of the modern newspaper, by writing women's news in a way that appealed to men as well as women, and by upholding in those pages the highest standards of journalism.

ELIZABETH J. MORSE

Sources A. Sebba, *Battling for news: the rise of the woman reporter* (1994) • F. Goodall, 'Emilie Peacocke (1883–1964)', *A skirt through history* (1994) • *WWW*, 1961–70 • E. Peacocke, *Writing for women* (1936) • *The Times* (27 Jan 1964) • b. cert. • m. cert. • d. cert.
Archives priv. coll., unpublished autobiography
Likenesses photograph, repro. in Goodall, 'Emilie Peacocke'
Wealth at death £13,947: administration, 18 Sept 1964, *CGPLA Eng. & Wales*

Peacocke, Joseph Ferguson (1835–1916), archbishop of Dublin, was born at Abbeyleix, Queen's county, on 5 November 1835. He was the youngest son of George Peacocke MD of Longford and his wife, Catherine Ferguson. He was educated at Trinity College, Dublin, where he graduated as senior moderator in history and English literature in 1857, also gaining a first-class divinity *testimonium* and winning the political economy prize for his year. Ordained deacon in 1858 and priest in 1859, he held his first curacy at St Mary's, Kilkenny, where he served from 1858 until 1861. He then became secretary of the Hibernian Church Missionary Society, a position which he held for two years. A strong evangelical, he was a firm supporter of foreign missions and of the Church Missionary Society in particular. In 1863 he went to Monkstown, co. Dublin, as curate of the parish church. In 1865 he married Caroline Sophia (*née* Irvine); they had one daughter and four sons, the eldest of whom was bishop of Derry from 1916 until 1945. Peacocke stayed in Monkstown until 1873, when he was appointed rector of St George's, Dublin, an important city parish. In 1878 he was recalled to Monkstown, where he had made himself popular with the parishioners, and remained as rector there until he was raised to a bishopric. Along with his benefice he held for a few months in 1894 the professorship of pastoral theology in Trinity College, Dublin, a post to which he was well suited.

In 1894 Peacocke, who had proceeded DD in 1883, was elected to the diocese of Meath, succeeding Charles Parsons Reichel as bishop. In 1897 he was translated to the archbishopric of Dublin, a post which he took over from William Conyngham, fourth Baron Plunket. No archbishop of Dublin for 200 years had previously held a cure of souls in the diocese; and Peacocke's reputation among the clergy for tolerance, holiness, and varied pastoral experience had preceded him. He presided with dignity over the dioceses of Dublin, Glendalough, and Kildare, publishing some charges and occasional sermons, and serving as a select preacher at Dublin and Cambridge, until 1915, when he resigned his see owing to ill health. He died at Hastings, Blackrock, co. Dublin, on 26 May 1916; his memorial tablet in Kildare Cathedral declared him to have served faithfully, humbly and with holiness ('Pastor fidelis, humilis, et sanctus corde'). Peacocke was said to have been a man of fine presence, who commanded respectful attention in synod and at the pulpit. A portrait by P. A. de Lászlo, presented by the diocese, was later housed in the palace at Dublin.

J. H. Bernard, rev. David Huddleston

Sources WW (1915) · Crockford (1901) · H. E. Patton, *Fifty years of disestablishment* (1922) · J. B. Leslie, ed., *Clergy of Connor: from Patrician times to the present day* (1993) · *CGPLA Ire.* (1916) · *CGPLA Eng. & Wales* (1916)
Archives TCD
Likenesses P. A. de Laszlo, oils, bishop's palace, Dublin · photograph, repro. in Patton, *Fifty years of disestablishment* · print, NPG
Wealth at death £22,620 18s. 1d.: probate, 21 July 1916, *CGPLA Ire.* · £13,187 7s.: Irish probate sealed in London, 17 Aug 1916, *CGPLA Ire.*

Peada (*d.* 656), king of the Middle Angles, was the son of *Penda, king of the Mercians, and perhaps of Penda's queen, Cynewise. At some point, probably in the early 650s, his father created him *princeps* ('ruler') of the Middle Angles, who would seem to have been a collection of minor tribes living in the area of the east midlands which lay between the two powerful kingdoms of East Anglia and Mercia. Penda had been battling for control over this region for much of his reign, and the establishment of his son as ruler over the Middle Anglian peoples may mark a final triumph. It seems probable that Peada ruled as a sub-king under his father's authority. He applied to *Oswiu, king of the Northumbrians, for the hand of his daughter, Alhflæd, which was granted on condition that he and his people accepted Christianity. Partly swayed by the advice of his close friend and brother-in-law, Oswiu's son *Alchfrith (married to Peada's sister Cyneburh), and partly by

the preaching which he heard at Oswiu's court, Peada agreed to convert. In 653 he and the nobles accompanying him were baptized by Finan, bishop of Lindisfarne, on a Northumbrian royal estate named Ad Murum ('by the wall'), so called from its proximity to Hadrian's Wall and usually identified as Wallbottle in Northumberland. Returning to his kingdom, Peada brought with him four priests, Cedd, Adda, Betti, and Diuma, who began the conversion of the Middle Angles. At the battle of the River 'Winwæd' in 655 Oswiu routed the Mercian forces, killed Penda, and temporarily took control of his kingdom. As Oswiu's son-in-law, Peada was treated leniently and was established as king of the Mercians living south of the Trent, perhaps in an attempt to foster Mercian support for the new regime. But at Eastertide in the following year he was murdered, allegedly through the treachery of his wife.

S. E. Kelly

Sources Bede, *Hist. eccl.*, 3.21, 24; 4.24 · D. Dumville, 'Essex, Middle Anglia, and the expansion of Mercia in the south-east midlands', *The origins of Anglo-Saxon kingdoms*, ed. S. Bassett (1989), 123–40
Likenesses coin, BM

Peak, James (*c.*1730–*c.*1782). *See under* Boydell, John, engravers (*act.* 1760–1804).

Peake, Arthur Samuel (1865–1929), theologian and biblical scholar, was born at Leek, Staffordshire, on 24 November 1865, the second son and third child in a family of seven of the Revd Samuel Peake (1830–1914), a Primitive Methodist minister, and his wife, Rosabella Smith (*d.* 1875), the daughter of a Herefordshire farmer. In accordance with the custom of the Methodist ministry, his father moved frequently from one circuit to another, and Peake was educated at various day schools, including Ludlow grammar school (1874), and a school in Stratford upon Avon (1876). From 1877 he attended King Henry VIII Grammar School, Coventry, before going up to St John's College, Oxford, in 1883, with a classical scholarship. After classical honour moderations he read for the honour school of theology, with a view to ordination in the Church of England. He obtained a first class in 1887, and continued to reside after graduation, winning the Denyer and Johnson scholarship in 1889 and the Ellerton essay prize in 1890. He was not, however, ordained, remaining a Methodist layman for the rest of his life.

In 1890 Peake was elected to a theological fellowship at Merton College, a position which he held for seven years. Earlier in the same year he had begun teaching at Mansfield College, which had been established at Oxford in 1886 for the training of candidates for the ministry of the free churches. His work here was mainly in the field of the Old Testament, though he was also interested in the New Testament and in early church history, especially in the Gnostics, Manichaeans, and Montanists. His distinctive contribution to biblical studies was possible only to one who was a master of more than one field.

Peake's future career, however, was soon decided by a call from his own church. The Primitive Methodists had been slow to make provision for the theological training of their ministry. A group of reformers, with the financial backing of William Hartley, a wealthy manufacturer from Aintree, decided to turn the existing Theological Institute at Manchester into a college with a full and modern theological curriculum. On the foundation of Hartley Primitive Methodist College at Manchester, Peake was asked to take responsibility for the curriculum, with the position of tutor in the college. After some hesitation, and against the advice of some of his friends, he accepted the post. He went to Manchester in 1892, and for the remaining thirty-seven years of his life he was identified with Hartley College. Initially his theological position was regarded with suspicion as dangerously 'advanced': already as a student he had made himself familiar with German theological works and had been particularly influenced by the writings of W. Robertson Smith. But by the time of his death he held a position of almost unique authority in his church, and the higher intellectual standard of its ministry, and the broader outlook of its members in general, were largely the result of Peake's teaching and influence.

Peake's work at Manchester was not confined to a denominational college. In 1904 it was decided to form a faculty of theology in the University of Manchester. The first theological faculty to be established in any of the 'secular' universities, it had from the outset an inter-denominational character. Peake played a leading part in the establishment of the faculty, and became the first occupant of the Rylands chair of biblical criticism and exegesis, while retaining his appointment at Hartley College.

In addition to his academic work, Peake served as chairman of the council of the John Rylands Library, from its foundation in 1899 until his death. He edited the *Holborn Review* from 1919 until his death, and took an active part in the ecclesiastical affairs of his own church, and of the free churches in general, strongly supporting the movement for reunion, both among the Methodist bodies and outside them. These numerous activities were carried out under the handicap of uncertain health: in 1902, he underwent a serious operation for the removal of a cyst attached to his liver, which permanently affected his health. A severe breakdown from overwork followed in 1915, and his health was very poor from 1921.

Peake's knowledge of current literature, both British and foreign, in the field of biblical studies, was exhaustive. His original contributions to biblical learning were marked by accurate scholarship and balanced and cautious judgement. He saw the Bible as the record of God's progressive self-revelation in history and held that the Old Testament witnessed to a developing system of belief and practice. He was thus able to reconcile Christian faith with historical criticism and with the Victorian belief in progress. Such books as *The Bible: its Origin, its Significance, and its Abiding Worth* (1913), and *The Problem of Suffering in the Old Testament* (1904), together with a *Commentary on the Bible* (1919) which he planned and edited, had a wide circulation and very great influence, helping many conservative Christians to come to terms with the consequences of recent biblical criticism. He also did much to save the free

churches of Great Britain from the baneful effects of 'fundamentalist' controversies.

Peake married on 29 June 1892 Harriet Mary (*b.* 1867/8), daughter of John Sillman, of Oxford, who survived him together with their three sons. He received the honorary degree of DD from the University of Aberdeen in 1907, and from the University of Oxford in 1920. He died at the Royal Infirmary, Manchester, on 19 August 1929, and was buried in the southern cemetery, Manchester.

C. H. Dodd, *rev.* J. W. Rogerson

Sources L. S. Peake, *Arthur Samuel Peake: a memoir* (1930) · A. S. Peake, *Recollections and appreciations*, ed. W. F. Howard (1938) · J. T. Wilkinson, ed., *Arthur Samuel Peake, 1865–1929: essays in commemoration* (1958) · J. T. Wilkinson, *Arthur Samuel Peake* (1971) · *The Times* (20 Aug 1929) · *CGPLA Eng. & Wales* (1929) · m. cert.
Archives JRL, corresp. and papers; notebooks and papers | Bodl. Oxf., letters to Gilbert Murray · NL Scot., corresp. with publishers
Likenesses A. T. Nowell, portrait; formerly at Hartley Victoria College · portrait, JRL
Wealth at death £13,580 6s. 2d.: resworn probate, 19 Nov 1929, *CGPLA Eng. & Wales*

Peake, Sir Charles Brinsley Pemberton (1897–1958), diplomatist, was born on 2 January 1897 in Leicester, the third child and only son of Colonel William Pemberton Peake, surgeon and medical officer, of Hildenborough, Kent, and his wife, Alice Ambrosing Bucknell. Educated at Wyggeston School, Leicester, he took a commission as a captain in the Leicestershire regiment in 1914. During the war he was badly wounded in the leg and suffered from the effects for the remainder of his life. He was mentioned in dispatches and awarded the MC.

In 1919 Peake entered Magdalen College, Oxford, where he took a shortened course as a war service candidate, and emerged with a degree in French in 1921. He entered the diplomatic service as a third secretary in February 1922 and served in the British legation in Sofia from April 1922 to April 1924, when he returned to the Foreign Office in London. He was promoted second secretary in July 1925, and was briefly attached to the embassy in Constantinople, from October to December 1925. On 3 July 1926 he married Catherine Marie, daughter of William George Knight, of the Indian educational service. They had four sons.

In October 1926 Peake was transferred to the British embassy in Tokyo; he was granted an allowance for knowledge of Japanese in May 1928. From June 1929 until February 1933 he served in Bern, where at various points he acted as chargé d'affaires. He then served in Paris, where he was promoted first secretary in July 1934. He 'profited greatly from the opportunities offered by what was at that time the most important and stimulating post in the service' (*The Times*, 11 April 1958), but in October 1936, at his own request, he was transferred to the news department of the Foreign Office which was then headed by Rex Leeper. This combination became known affectionately as 'Leak and Peeper' and by the time Peake succeeded Leeper in 1939 it was not a secret that he had become deeply convinced of the unwisdom of appeasement and of the need to galvanize the nation to the task of confronting Nazism. Contemporaries record that his dislike of the then prime minister, Neville Chamberlain, was considerable, so it is ironic that his next appointment, in January 1941, should have been that of personal assistant to the new ambassador to Washington, Lord Halifax, who had maintained a faith in appeasement which rivalled Chamberlain's. However, both men shared a deep commitment to Anglo-Catholicism, and despite the brevity of the appointment this period cemented a personal and lifelong friendship. Peake was appointed CMG in January 1941 and promoted counsellor in October the same year. On his return from Washington in February 1942, he was appointed British representative with the French national committee, where his considerable skills at personal diplomacy were amply tested and admirably deployed in smoothing the often fractious and capricious General De Gaulle. Between October 1943 and May 1945 he was political adviser to the supreme commander, Allied Expeditionary Force, with the personal rank of minister. In May 1945 he was appointed consul-general in Tangier where, despite his post, he was largely engaged in political work.

By temperament and ability, Peake preferred dealing with people rather than official papers, and these skills proved invaluable during his posting as ambassador to Belgrade between August 1946 and October 1951. The Balkans provided a rich background for Peake's innate flamboyancy and he established good working relations with several of the region's politicians, most notably Anna Pauker, then Romania's foreign minister. Sensitive to the nuances of the Soviet Union's relations with its satellites, he was among the first western observers to grasp the significance of rising tension in Yugoslav–Soviet relations during the spring of 1948. Following Yugoslavia's expulsion from the Cominform, he capitalized on the opportunity to smooth the Anglo-Yugoslav relationship which had been strained since the war, and to establish closer relations with Marshal Tito than would otherwise have been possible. He was advanced to KCMG in June 1948. In October 1951 he was appointed ambassador to Athens where he was equally successful until Anglo-Greek relations became overshadowed by the bitterness of the dispute over Cyprus. Peake retired from the foreign service in April 1957 and acted for a time as special adviser to the Colonial Office on Cyprus.

Peake was gifted with an imaginative mind and an excellent memory which he cultivated through wide reading. These qualities combined with a sharp wit and dramatic sense to form a brilliant raconteur who was widely regarded as delightful company:

> He loved expounding the intricacies of a given problem, and he would do it always in a way that was both lucid and agreeably flattering to his hearer, as though there was nothing really new in it all, but a reminder of known facts might be useful. (*The Times*, 11 April 1958)

Openly and sincerely religious, he was fondly remembered as a generous host and a loyal friend. Throughout his career he was ably assisted by his wife. He died in London on 10 April 1958.   Ann Lane

Sources *The Times* (11 April 1958) • *The Times* (17 April 1958) • H. M. G. Jebb [Lord Gladwyn], *The memoirs of Lord Gladwyn* (1972) •

Earl of Halifax [E. F. L. Wood], *Fullness of days* (1957) • *The diplomatic diaries of Oliver Harvey, 1937–40*, ed. J. Harvey (1970) • *The war diaries of Oliver Harvey*, ed. J. Harvey (1978) • *DNB* • *FO List* (1958)
Archives NRA, priv. coll., diaries and corresp. | Bodl. Oxf., corresp. with Lord Monckton
Likenesses W. Stoneman, photograph, 1950, NPG

Peake, Frederick Gerard (1886–1970), army officer, was born on 12 June 1886 at Ashtead, Surrey, the only son of Lieutenant-Colonel Walter Ancell Peake DSO, of Burrough on the Hill, Leicestershire, and his wife, Grace Elizabeth Ann Fenwicke. Peake was educated first at Stubbington House, Fareham. Originally intended for the Royal Navy, he eventually entered the Royal Military College, Sandhurst, and in 1906 was commissioned in the Duke of Wellington's regiment. Later that year he was posted to India where he did not much enjoy the social life but studied the local languages and followed the local hunt.

First World War Early in 1914 Peake was seconded to the Egyptian army and posted to the 4th infantry battalion in the Sudan. On the outbreak of war he applied to rejoin his British regiment, but his request was ignored. When the Darfur rebellion broke out in 1916 he transferred to the camel company; he had been promoted captain in 1915. Though due for home leave Peake asked to go to Salonika for action against the Bulgarians. He was temporarily posted to 17 squadron, Royal Flying Corps. Although he outstayed his leave of absence he was saved from court martial by General Milne, who sent him back to Darfur with no more than a reprimand.

On the last lap of his journey south Peake was thrown from his camel and severely dislocated his neck. A specialist told him his case was incurable. Later, walking in the hospital gardens and unable to raise his head from his chest, Peake crashed blindly into a tree. The jolt restored his neck to normal and there were no subsequent ill effects. He had no sooner returned to his unit than he developed a liver abscess and was sent home on sick leave. On the return voyage his ship was torpedoed near Alexandria. Peake jumped overboard with a bottle of beer and a packet of sandwiches and was picked up none the worse.

Early in 1918 Peake was sent to Sinai to command a company of the Egyptian camel corps. In April they joined T. E. Lawrence and Sharif Feisal's Arab army at 'Aqaba. Lawrence's task in the final phase of the Palestine campaign was to cut off and contain the large numbers of Turks defending the Hejaz railway and garrisoning the towns from Medina to Damascus. The Egyptian camel corps provided great assistance to Lawrence's guerrilla campaign northwards. The camels' mobility over ground inaccessible to armoured cars proved invaluable on occasions. The camel corps also proved adept as sappers, developing the 'tulip' technique for blowing up stretches of railway. Their last task before the final decisive battle of Megiddo was to cut the Dera'a–Damascus railway in order to disrupt the Turkish communications and hinder their retreat. The Turkish surrender soon followed and Peake's camel company returned to Egypt.

Transjordan after the war Transjordan, as the land lying to the east of the River Jordan came to be called, was in chaos

Frederick Gerard Peake (1886–1970), by Walter Stoneman, 1951

as the Turks hastened for home. The area had formerly been part of the Turkish province of Syria, and such administration as the Turks had previously exercised there had completely collapsed. The Arab inhabitants were warlike and intensely tribal, both nomadic and settled. The British government, recently awarded League of Nations mandates for Iraq, Transjordan, and Palestine, was determined not to be landed with the administration of Transjordan, and was particularly opposed to the involvement of British troops. Here the politicians and the generals were as one, despite the urging to the contrary by the high commissioner for Palestine, Sir Herbert Samuel.

British involvement was limited to the provision of six 'representatives' located at Irbid, Salt, Jerash, Kerak, and Amman, their function being wholly advisory. Amman was then no more than a village populated mainly by Circassians, and Captain C. D. Brunton began work there at the end of August 1920. In the following month Peake, then a lieutenant-colonel, joined the Palestine administration officially as district commandant, Palestine police, Galilee, but seconded for duty in Transjordan as from 12 September 1920 as inspector of gendarmerie. In fact the previous Turkish gendarmerie had disintegrated but Brunton had begun to collect a 'reserve force' to reinforce the ordinary gendarmerie when necessary. They totalled no more than 70 to 80 men but the target was more ambitious. However, there was no money with which to pay anyone.

There were plenty of swords for hire, including a large number of Syrians taking refuge from the French. Although Sharif Feisal had been proclaimed king of Syria on 8 March 1920, the French, who had been given mandates in Syria and Lebanon, defeated Feisal at Maysalum on 24 July 1920 and drove him into exile. Many Syrians took refuge in Transjordan and the French complained of raids launched across the border from Transjordan.

To complicate matters even further, Sharif Abdullah, second son of Sharif al-Hussein of Mecca, who had proclaimed himself king of Hejaz, turned up in November 1920 at Ma'an, which was then in Hejaz. With him was a force of tribesmen and former soldiers from the Turkish army, who had the proclaimed intention of restoring his brother Feisal to the Syrian throne. On 28 February 1921 Abdullah left Ma'an and on 2 March he entered Amman to receive a rapturous welcome from high and low.

It happened that the newly appointed colonial secretary, Winston Churchill, had called a conference in Cairo on 12 March 1921 to consider Britain's role in the Middle East. Peake was one of those present. He was now commanding the reserve force because Brunton had abruptly resigned in December 1920. Peake was much senior to Brunton. He had the local rank of *quaim-aqam* (colonel) and the honorific *bey*. The future of Transjordan was among the matters discussed. Samuel, the high commissioner, wanted to link it with Palestine. The Arabs were bitterly opposed. This was principally on account of the Balfour declaration. They wanted no Jewish immigration east of the River Jordan. And there was also the problem of Sharif Abdullah, now located in Amman, his brother Feisal having been offered the throne in Iraq, which had been originally intended for Abdullah.

Churchill invited Abdullah to meet him in Jerusalem where he had a boisterous welcome. They met on 28, 29, and 30 March. Abdullah was persuaded to take on the governorship of Transjordan on the understanding that it would not be included in the Palestine administrative system. The Balfour declaration would not apply. The Transjordan government would not be expected to promote Jewish immigration and colonization. Churchill suggested a trial period of six months and Abdullah after some hesitation agreed. The reserve force was to be increased to one thousand men and British financial aid was promised.

Forming the Arab Legion Peake reorganized the gendarmerie from top to bottom. He soon found, however, that he had to serve two masters. First was the amir, with whom he got on well on the whole. Then there was the chief British representative (CBR)—H. St J. Philby (1921–4) and Lieutenant-Colonel H. H. F. Cox (1924–39)—who controlled the purse strings and much else besides. Philby was an erratic genius and Cox an administrator pure and simple. Cox did not get on well with Abdullah and neither man was easy to serve.

'One of the first acts of the Amir on his return [from London in 1923] was to amalgamate the Reserve Force and the police, and to call it the Arab legion', wrote Peake. 'The present writer was appointed to command the legion, and became responsible to the Amir for public security'. The

Arabic title was *al-jaysh al-Arabi* (the Arab army). This was inherited from the force of Arab regulars which fought under Feisal. It was Peake who suggested the change of English title from reserve mobile force to Arab Legion. This was readily agreed by Philby. 'The strange thing is that nobody noticed the change', commented Peake (Peake's autobiography).

There were not many British involved for many years. From 1923 to 1930 there were only two or three, including Peake, who not only founded the Arab Legion on sound lines but who also played an important part in establishing the Hashemite kingdom of Jordan. Peake was a typical British officer of the pre-1914 army, a stern disciplinarian and a stickler for military conventions. The amir promoted him major-general (*amir liwa*) in 1923 and later gave him the honorific title *pasha*. A bachelor until almost the end of his service in the Arab Legion, he followed an Edwardian lifestyle, never failing to change for dinner, which he normally ate in solitary state. He affected to believe that it behoved senior officers to appear angry, and as he flew round his extensive parish—having been taught to fly at the age of forty-four—he was preceded by the codewords 'thunder cloud'. Peake's rages were legendary but he was really a kind-hearted man.

Unpopularity and resistance Peake's deputy was an Arab—Brigadier Abdel Quadir al-Jundi. The fact that Peake was British undoubtedly led to criticism and he had some narrow escapes. Once he was kidnapped by Sheikh Mithqal al-Fayiz of the Bani Sakhr tribe and held in a barley store for two or three days before being released. Over the years, with patience and insistence on high standards, he made the Arab Legion into an effective force, but its recruits were from the villages and towns only. Peake had no use for the Bedouin who roamed the desert east of the Hejaz Railway. Nor was he under any illusion regarding his own position. In 1924, in a report to Cox, Peake wrote: 'It cannot be too well known that the Amir, the Government except the new Prime Minister, and the Istaqlal [Independence Party] hate the Arab Legion. Their hatred is caused by different reasons, but they all agree on one point and that is the presence of a British officer' (Ma'an Abu Nowar 1.128).

Peake's prejudice against the Bedouin, originating in his experience of Feisal's tribal warriors in the advance to Damascus in 1918, was, to say the least, unfortunate. Although the Arab Legion established law and order in the settled areas, it could do little in the desert where the tribes acknowledged no master. In the 1920s the desert was much plagued by raids by Ibn Sa'ud's fanatical wahabis (al-ikhwan, the brotherhood) who killed all males regardless of age. The Arab Legion was no match for these savage warriors although it did play some part in defeating a massive raid on 14 August 1924 which came as close as 10 miles to Amman. It was chiefly defeated by the Bani Sakhr and other tribes in co-operation with the RAF planes and armoured cars, but the Arab Legion was also involved and had 21 killed. In 1926 Lord Plumer, high commissioner in Palestine and Transjordan, disbanded the Palestine gendarmerie and reduced the British garrison in Palestine. At the same time he reduced the Arab Legion from 1472 officers and men to 855 and abolished the artillery troop, machine gun platoon, and wireless section of the signals platoon. The Arab Legion became a police force pure and simple.

The transformation of the Arab Legion and the TJFF In its place Plumer formed the Transjordan frontier force (TJFF), an 'imperial' force, recruited mostly in Palestine and commanded and led by British officers. The TJFF was to be responsible for the defence of Transjordan in co-operation with the RAF. This was strongly opposed by the Amir Abdullah who had hoped the Arab Legion would be transformed into a proper military force. However, it would appear that Peake welcomed the new arrangement, in which he had no place. 'The defences of the country were strengthened by the formation of the TJFF', he wrote. Transjordan was to find a sixth of the new force's cost, and its main base was to be Zarqa, not far from Amman. Peake's support for the TJFF neither brought about good relations with the amir, nor added to his popularity in the Arab Legion.

The TJFF proved to be extremely successful in preventing Transjordan Bedouin from raiding Saudi Arabia and recouping the camels lifted by the Saudis, but it was hopeless in preventing the Saudi raiders from raiding the Transjordan tribes—so much so that the Transjordan Bedouin assumed their government was operating against them. Conditions were so bad in 1927–30 that Captain John Bagot Glubb, who had been very successful in pacifying the southern desert in Iraq, was invited to Amman and subsequently offered the appointment of deputy to Peake pasha to pacify Transjordan's desert. The offer was made by the amir and Cox. Peake was on leave at the time and was not consulted. Peake's great fear was that the British officers should be withdrawn from the Arab Legion leaving the tribal sheikhs with a military force with which they could dominate the settled areas, the age old struggle between the desert and the town. However much he disliked the recruitment of Bedouin and the militarization of the Arab Legion, Peake left his deputy to get on with it in the desert—and Glubb was amazingly successful.

Gradually Glubb built up his Bedouin force. They were to become the strike force of the Arab Legion during the Second World War as the desert patrol. In a surprisingly short time the Bedouin raiding ceased and the Jordan desert became safer for the traveller (and tourist) than many a European city. This may not have been appreciated by Peake but it certainly was by Amir Abdullah who had a special empathy for the Bedouin. It was therefore no surprise, on Peake's retirement in March 1939, that Glubb was appointed to succeed him in command of the Arab Legion.

Retirement and assessment Peake had held the local rank of lieutenant-colonel since 1921; in the Arab Legion he held successively the ranks of brigadier (1920–2) and major-general (1922–39), and was made pasha in 1926. He was made CBE in 1926 and CMG in 1939. He also had Transjordanian decorations. On 12 January 1937 he married

Elspeth Maclean, younger daughter of Norman Ritchie, of St Boswell's, Roxburghshire; they had one daughter. The couple retired to Elspeth's home in Kelso, Roxburghshire, where Peake served in civil defence throughout the Second World War. Elspeth died in 1967. Peake died at the Cottage Hospital, Kelso, on 30 March 1970, and was buried in Kelso.

Peake and Glubb were very different in character. Peake was an archetypal British officer of his period—an excellent organizer, brave, determined and upright—but he lacked Glubb's imaginative approach. Glubb could think like a Bedouin. Peake was always British. Glubb's loyalty to Amir Abdullah was absolute. Peake's was more ambivalent. He shared Cox's view that Abdullah was financially irresponsible and had to be kept under strict control. Nevertheless he built the Arab Legion on firm foundations and established a tradition of loyalty and efficient discipline which withstood many shocks both within and without the kingdom.   JAMES LUNT

Sources F. G. Peake, autobiography, IWM, Peake papers, DS/misc. 16, reel 1 · C. S. Jarvis, *Arab command* (1942) · J. B. Glubb, *The story of the Arab legion* (1948) · J. B. Glubb, *A soldier with the Arabs* (1957) · F. G. Peake, *A history of Jordan and its tribes* (1958) · T. E. Lawrence, *Seven pillars of wisdom: a triumph* (privately printed, London, 1926) · *The Times* (1 April 1970) · *The Times* (6 April 1970) · J. D. Lunt, *Glubb Pasha: Lieutenant-General Sir John Bagot Glubb, commander of the Arab legion, 1939–1956* (1984) · T. Royle, *Glubb pasha* (1992) · P. J. Vatikiotis, *Politics and the military in Jordan* (1967) · J. Lunt, *Imperial sunset* (1981) · Ma'an Abu Nowar, *The history of the Hashemite kingdom of Jordan (1920–9)*, vol. 1 (1989) · Ma'an Abu Nowar, *The history of the Hashemite kingdom of Jordan (1920–9)*, vol. 2 (1997) · U. Dann, *Studies in the history of Transjordan, 1920–49* (1984) · m. cert. · d. cert. · CCI (1970)
Archives NRA, corresp. and papers | St Ant. Oxf., Middle East Centre, General Glubb's MSS · St Ant. Oxf., Middle East Centre, corresp. with H. St J. B. Philby
Likenesses W. Stoneman, photograph, 1951, NPG [*see illus.*] · M. Guyon, portrait, priv. coll. · portrait, repro. in Abu Nowar, *History*, vol. 1, p. 133
Wealth at death £6740.13: confirmation, 20 Aug 1970, CCI

Peake, Harold John Edward (1867–1946), archaeologist, was born on 27 September 1867 at Ellesmere, Shropshire, the son of John Peake, vicar of Ellesmere, and his wife, Matilda Ann Marshall. Early training in estate management at Leicester gave him insight into the historical significance of changes of land tenure and land use and led to a valuable article on prehistoric roads in Alice Dryden, ed., *Memorials of Old Leicestershire* (1911).

In 1897 Peake married Charlotte Mary Augusta (d. 1934), daughter of Captain Richard Lane Bayliff, of the Royal Marine light infantry. There were no children. For their honeymoon the couple went round the world, spending some time on a ranch in British Columbia, where Peake gained an understanding of prehistoric pastoralism. They also studied art and ceramics in Japan and China.

On their return to England the Peakes kept an open house, on modest means, at their home at Boxford, Berkshire. From 1899 Westbrook House became a centre of leadership in archaeological and artistic efforts, the latter the special concern of Charlotte Peake, or Carli, as she was known. Francis Toye, a frequent visitor at Westbrook, remembered her as being 'interested in everything around her':

> she was a big woman in every sense, in stature, emotion, and sympathy, thus forming a perfect complement to her thin, very precise, and wholly cerebral husband. A more happy union of the arts and the sciences it would be difficult to conceive. (Toye, 44)

Peake became the honorary curator of Newbury Museum, and developed a selected series of implements, pots, potsherds, and maps; in exhibiting these he allocated each century from 3000 BC equal space. The Newbury Museum became well known for its pottery and the series of exhibits were the basis of a published chronological work by Peake, issued soon after 1920.

In addition to serving on a number of local committees, Peake was the motive power behind the Newbury District Field Club and superintended its archaeological investigations. In a wider field he served as a member of the council, and from 1926 to 1928 as president, of the Royal Anthropological Institute, which awarded him its Huxley memorial medal in 1940. He also presided over the section on anthropology of the British Association in 1922, and from 1928 to 1930 he served as a member of the council of the Society of Antiquaries of London.

Peake studied intensely the distribution of evidences of the human past, always in relation to the environment of the place and the time, and the peoples concerned. In the opinion of O. G. S. Crawford, whose early career was strongly influenced by Peake, the latter had a 'rather too fertile' imagination and was prone to 'theorizing and wild-cat schemes' (O. G. S. Crawford, *Said and Done*, 1955, 39, 64). But Peake's approach to the ancient past was essentially multidisciplinary, and he 'persistently upheld the need for emphasis on the unity of the various studies of man' (*The Times*, 24 Sept 1946). His catalogue of British prehistoric bronze implements, including some 17,000 entries, with measured drawings and data of location and so on, is in the care of the British Museum. His Gregynog lectures, published in 1922 as *The Bronze Age and the Celtic World*, attempted to relate archaeology and linguistics. In the same year he published *The English Village*, a stimulating study of social evolution. With Professor H. J. Fleure he collaborated in a series of books entitled *The Corridors of Time* (1927–36, tenth and final volume, 1956), which attempted to synthesize approaches to the interpretation of archaeological data in terms of human evolution. In this study Peake pioneered research into the beginnings of cereal cultivation which, he held, occurred in Syria-Palestine and northern Mesopotamia. His papers in the *Journal of the Royal Anthropological Institute* have lasting value. He also made an important contribution to the medieval section of the Victoria county history of Berkshire. He died at his home, Westbrook House, on 22 September 1946.   H. J. FLEURE, *rev.* MARK POTTLE

Sources *The Times* (24 Sept 1946) · *The Times* (26 Sept 1946) · *The Times* (30 Sept 1946) · H. Peake and H. J. Fleure, *Apes and men* (1927), vol. 1 of *The corridors of time* · F. Toye, *For what we have received: an*

autobiography (1950) · personal knowledge (1959) · private information (1959)

Archives AM Oxf., drawings and notebooks | Shrops. RRC, corresp. with L. F. Chitty

Likenesses Lafayette, photograph, *c*.1926–1928, Royal Anthropological Institute, London · A. Walker, portrait (as a young man)

Wealth at death £27,520 6*s*. 5*d*.: probate, 3 Dec 1946, *CGPLA Eng. & Wales*

Peake, Mervyn Laurence (1911–1968), artist and writer, was born at Kuling (Guling), in the province of Kiang-Hsi, China, on 9 July 1911, the younger son of Ernest Cromwell Peake MD (1874–1949), Congregational missionary doctor, of Tientsin (Tianjin), and his wife, Amanda Elizabeth Powell (1875–1939), a missionary nurse. In 1899 Ernest Peake had travelled to China to establish the first European medical district in Kiang-Hsi province and he took over the Mackenzie Memorial Hospital in Tientsin in 1912, when an uprising against the Manchu dynasty forced the family to flee to Hengchow (Hengyang). Peake was educated at the grammar school in the British Concession in Tientsin. At ten he wrote and illustrated 'Ways of travelling', which was published in the London Missionary Society's magazine *News from Afar*.

The family returned to England in 1923 and Peake attended Eltham College, formerly the School for Sons of Missionaries, Kent, from 1923 to 1929, where despite poor academic progress he impressed with his artistic gifts, nurtured by his teacher Eric Drake. Peake attended Croydon School of Art for a few months and then the Royal Academy Schools, where he won the Hacker prize (1931) and had his still life *Cactus* accepted by the Royal Academy. During this period Peake collaborated with his friend Gordon Smith on illustrated books, became a stage set designer, and exhibited work with the Soho group and the Twenties group.

With Peake's lack of interest in formal study it was not surprising that in the summer of 1933 he failed his examinations. The Royal Academy terminated Peake's studentship and he was enticed to the isle of Sark by Eric Drake, who had set up an artists' colony there. The first exhibition of the Sark group, in August 1933, attracted much attention and Peake was well represented. During this period in Sark he wore his hair long, had his right ear pierced, and wore a cape, and became briefly engaged to Janice Thomson, an art student from Boston. On the strength of his work he was offered a position at the Westminster School of Art in 1935, where he taught life drawing until 1939. At Westminster, he met Maeve Patricia Mary Theresa Gilmore (1917–1983), artist, then a student, youngest of the six children of Owen Eugene Gilmore MD FRCS; they married on 1 December 1937, and had two sons and a daughter. A solo exhibition of Peake's work in March 1938, which included oils, sketches, and watercolours, and macabre drawings, attracted much attention. In 1939 both Peake and Maeve exhibited in London, and Peake published a book intended for children, *Captain Slaughterboard Drops Anchor* (1939), the illustrations for which, in their characteristic grotesqueness, the *Punch* critic considered 'unsuitable for sensitive children'. He was also writing poetry, notably 'Epstein's Adam' and

Mervyn Laurence Peake (1911–1968), self-portrait, 1932

'Rhondda Valley', the latter inspired by a visit to the coalmines of south Wales.

In the Second World War Peake served in England in the Royal Artillery (by all accounts he was a hopeless gunner), being later transferred to the Royal Engineers as a bomb expert (he was put on light duties after accidentally setting fire to his barracks). He was invalided out in 1943 after a nervous breakdown. During the early stages of the war Peake worked on *Titus Groan*, a book that 'grew under duress' (Gilmore), and Chatto and Windus published *Shapes and Sounds* (1941), a volume of his poetry. He also provided the much-admired illustrations for *Ride-a-Cock-Horse and other Nursery Rhymes* (1940), which drew out the darkest implications of the stories, and, on the strength of those, for Lewis Carroll's *The Hunting of the Snark* (1941), where Peake found an absurdist spirit to rival his own. Recovering from his breakdown, he illustrated *The Rime of the Ancient Mariner* (1943); this is considered to be his greatest achievement as an illustrator and he was praised for adding a new spiritual dimension to the work. Other notable illustrations of this period included those for *All This and Bevin Too* (1943) for Quentin Crisp. After a year which had been dominated by writing and illustrating Peake was painting again. He thought of himself primarily as a painter even though this is the medium in which he was probably the least visionary.

After the birth of their second son the Peakes settled in Chelsea, London, where they socialized with Dylan Thomas, and Peake was able to consult Graham Greene, then a working director of Eyre and Spottiswoode, over *Titus Groan*. Towards the end of the war Eyre and Spottiswoode published *Rhymes without Reason*, a small volume of Peake's nonsense verse. While working for the Ministry of

Information from 1943 to 1945 he was inspired by glass-blowers making cathode-ray tubes and produced a series of work which was exhibited at the National Gallery. But it was not until just after the end of the war that Peake, after several failed applications, was finally appointed war artist with the rank of captain. On the basis of a caricature of Hitler, and his connection with *Lilliput* magazine, for which he regularly illustrated, he was commissioned by *The Leader* magazine to tour western Europe with the journalist Tom Pocock. They witnessed the first war crimes trial at Bad Neuenahr in June 1945 and Peake sent back haunting drawings of Bergen-Belsen concentration camp and composed a poem, analysing his guilty intrusion on suffering, which was later published as 'The Consumptive, Belsen, 1945'. The memories of the two weeks spent in Germany had a profound effect upon Peake; his wife recalled that 'he was quieter, more inward-looking, as if he had lost … his confidence in life itself' (Watney, 127).

Titus Groan was published in 1946. It was the first in a projected series in which Titus, the seventy-seventh earl of Groan, rebels against his ancestral home Gormenghast Castle and its restrictive duties, and attempts to find a new identity for himself in another land. Although showing the influence of Dickens, Lewis Carroll, and Kafka, the Titus books defy ready classification. The term 'fantasy' is perhaps the least inadequate, although Peake's work has nothing of the lightweight or evasive commonly implied by the word: but it is fantasy in being the creation of a fully realized 'other' world, ontologically separate from our own. Peake, who was agnostic and apolitical, distanced himself from moral, religious, political, and psychoanalytic interpretations of his work; as Anthony Burgess has commented, Peake's novels 'nourish the private imagination' (Burgess). The strength of *Titus Groan* is the thoroughness with which it is imagined (he sometimes drew the characters before writing about them), and the dialectical play throughout of the static, unchanging nature of the castle against the dynamic of the enemies within it. In Gormenghast Peake found the perfect literary expression for his interests as an artist: the arcane diction, the slow, heavily descriptive method of the style, and the delight in the individualities of people and objects are paralleled in the unmoving character of the castle (which has been interpreted as a symbolization of the 'labyrinthine human mind'; Irwin)—the obsessive preoccupation with minutiae which epitomizes the ritual laws which govern it, and the eccentric personalities it produces (such as the bloated cook Swelter, the predatory Steerpike, the camp intellectual Prunesquallor, and the power-starved enantiomorphous sisters Cora and Clarice). Gormenghast Castle is the natural home of Peake's imagination, a home to which he was irresistibly drawn, even while as a man and an artist he wished to escape it and explore new worlds. The undertow of Gormenghast drains the life from the portrayal of Titus's rebellion, and the imaginative unity and power of *Titus Groan* is increasingly lost in the succeeding volumes. Yet, considered as a whole, the Titus books (which include *Boy in Darkness*, a disturbing novella full of menace), remain a massive achievement.

In 1946 Grimm's *Household Tales* and Lewis Carroll's Alice books (1946; 1954) were published with Peake's unsentimental illustrations. In the same year Peake returned to Sark with his family, where they spent three serenely happy years in a house that had been the former headquarters of the German occupation, and where Peake wrote a children's book, *Letters from a Lost Uncle from Polar Regions* (1948), illustrated *Treasure Island* (1949), a book close to his heart, and otherwise devoted himself to *Gormenghast* (1950), the second Titus book. But a retainer from his publisher and a few commissions could not continue to meet the needs of a growing family, and in 1949 they came back to England, where Peake secured a part-time teaching post in London at the Central School of Arts and Crafts, Holborn; this, together with commissioned paintings and illustrations for books, and to a lesser extent his writing, formed the often uneven ground on which he supported his family. *The Drawings of Mervyn Peake* (1949) revealed that Peake's primary concern as an artist was with the human figure, rather than with landscape: of Gormenghast he has left us scarcely a pictorial trace. One of the most frequent and powerful of his effects is the portrayal of the frail verticality of his figures struggling against a dense and crushing atmosphere, or else bent or deformed by it.

In 1951 *Gormenghast*, which confounded critics who described it as 'wonderfully weird' and the 'finest imaginative feat in the English novel since *Ulysses*' (*Punch*), and *The Glassblowers* (a collection of poetry based on Peake's war work) won the W. H. Heinemann Foundation prize of £100 and Peake was awarded an honorary fellowship of the Royal Society of Literature. Peake does not have a clearly defined place in the development of poetry, belonging to neither the Romantic tradition nor to the anti-Romantic. But it was arguably poetry that for Peake was the most moving form of human expression, and he is at his best when an experience and its significance for him are fused, as for instance in 'The Glassblowers' or the frightening 'Heads Float About Me', rather than when he reflects on or self-consciously tries to proportion his feelings to his experience. A recurrent motif in his poetry is the idea of a face or body as a building or city, and vice versa: this transference is also seen in the interrelations of Gormenghast and its inhabitants. Peake's poetic voice was, however, largely silent after *The Glassblowers*.

After the novel *Mr Pye* (1953), about a self-appointed missionary to Sark who grows angel's wings, was ignored or slighted by the critics, Peake developed further interest in the theatre during the 1950s; he wrote at least five plays of which only *The Wit to Woo* and *The Connoisseurs* were performed. In 1956 he wrote dramatic versions of *Titus Groan* and *Mr Pye* and a Christmas play for radio. *The Wit to Woo*, which was staged at the Arts Theatre Club in London in 1957 and starred Kenneth Williams as Kite, was supposed to solve Peake's financial problems (he had taken on an unmanageable mortgage for a house in Kent), but it was received lukewarmly by the critics (perceived as a light 'drawing-room' comedy, it suffered in the wake of the iconoclastic *Look Back in Anger* and *Waiting for Godot*) and was a commercial failure. The disappointment induced a nervous breakdown. From this point Peake became increasingly incapacitated by what was eventually diagnosed as a form of Parkinson's disease (it has been conjectured that as a child Peake may have contracted encephalitis lethargica during the 'sleeping sickness' epidemic of 1917). He underwent treatment in the Holloway Hospital at Virginia Water for six months in 1958, and was able to complete *Titus Alone* (1959). Some critics have read the pared-down and more diffuse style of this final work as a symptom of Peake's progressive degeneration (the novel was revised in 1970 by the science-fiction writer Langdon Jones). But by 1960 he was obliged to give up teaching. There were occasional bursts of creativity: he began *Titus Awakes*, the projected fourth volume of the series, and with the help of his wife painstakingly supplied illustrations for his poem *The Rhyme of the Flying Bomb*, which when broadcast on BBC radio was received with ecstatic reviews. This marked the beginning of a new spark of interest in Peake's work, in both Britain and America, after years of utter neglect, although by this time Peake was unable to appreciate it. After an operation at the end of 1960 to alleviate his tremors failed in the long term, Peake had spells in various hospitals and nursing homes, and was eventually admitted to The Priory in Roehampton in 1964. He was transferred to a home run by his wife's eldest brother, The Close, near Abingdon in Berkshire, and died there during the night of 16/17 November 1968. He was buried in Burpham churchyard, Sussex.

Tall, thin, dark, and cadaverous, even before the illness which dramatically aged him, Peake was a romantic figure, with a 'face that belonged to another age' (Gilmore, 53), whose passionate and intense nature exhausted him: he lived always on 'this desperate edge of now', and wrote to pour himself forth, to empty himself of all his 'golden gall'. In some ways shy and reserved, he was innocently open and generous to all who asked for his help and, despite occasional indiscretions, unremittingly uxorious. In his wife's memoir he emerges as gentle, gracious, prankish, unworldly, and unpractical. He lived in many ways outside convention, behaving in a gently whimsical fashion which puzzled the ordinary. He did not care for 'arrangements' in life: he would gather materials for drawings simply by walking the streets of central London and stopping interesting subjects for on-the-spot sketches; and he would write amid his family circle. It was in part Peake's very proximity to and delight in life which produced his fantasy, and his sense of the individual his art of exaggeration: 'Anything', he once said, 'seen without prejudice, is enormous.'

Peake left a massive amount of unpublished material and a great deal of work in need of republication. The Penguin editions of the Titus books began to sell immediately to a new, appreciative generation, and his short stories, war poems, radio plays, and nonsense verse were collected in *Peake's Progress* (1979). Peake became the subject of theses, a Titus Groan pop group was formed, and in 1975 a Mervyn Peake Society. *Mr Pye* was reissued and hailed as a 'witty debate about good and evil' (Watney, 243)

and was dramatized on television in 1986. A television series based on the first two Titus books was broadcast by the BBC as their prestige millennium drama in January 2000, and this in turn stimulated renewed interest in Peake as both artist and writer.

COLIN MANLOVE, rev. CLARE L. TAYLOR

Sources M. Yorke, *Mervyn Peake: my eyes mint gold, a life* (2000) · J. Watney, *Mervyn Peake* (1976) · J. Batchelor, *Mervyn Peake: a biographical and critical exploration* (1974) · M. Gilmore, *A world away: a memoir of Mervyn Peake* (1970); repr. (1992) · S. Peake, *A child of bliss: growing up with Mervyn Peake* (1989) · G. Peter Winnington, *Vast alchemies: the life and work of Mervyn Peake* (2000) · A. Burgess, introduction, in M. Peake, *Titus Groan* (1968) · R. Irwin, 'Mervyn Peake', *St James guide to fantasy writers*, ed. D. Pringle (1996) · www. mervynpeake.org, 12 Dec 2000 · *The Times* (5 Aug 1978)
Archives Bodl. Oxf., MSS · IWM, drawings · NYPL, Berg Collection · UCL, corresp. and literary MSS | Tate collection, corresp. with K. Clark · UCL, letters to G. Greene
Likenesses M. L. Peake, self-portrait, oils, 1932, NPG [*see illus.*] · photographs, 1946, Hult. Arch. · M. Gilmore, oils, repro. in Watney, *Mervyn Peake*
Wealth at death £3225: probate, 24 April 1969, *CGPLA Eng. & Wales*

Peake, Osbert, first Viscount Ingleby (1897–1966), politician, was born on 30 December 1897, the second son and one of the five children of George Herbert Peake (1859–1950), of Bawtry Hall, Yorkshire, and his wife, Evelyn Mary (d. 1945), eldest daughter of the Hon. John Charles Dundas MP. He was educated at Eton College and the Royal Military College, Sandhurst. He served as a lieutenant in the Coldstream Guards (1916–19) and was wounded at Cambrai. After the war he became a major in the Nottinghamshire (Sherwood Rangers) yeomanry. In 1919 he went up to Christ Church, Oxford, where he completed a shortened course in history in 1920, graduating BA in 1921. He married, on 19 June 1922, Lady Joan Rachel de Vere Capell (d. 1979), younger daughter of George Devereux de Vere Capell, seventh earl of Essex; they had a son and four daughters, one of whom died in childhood.

Peake was called to the bar at the Inner Temple in 1923, but made his career in politics. He contested Dewsbury unsuccessfully as a Conservative at the general election of 1922 and in 1929 won Leeds North with a comfortable majority. He held the seat at each subsequent general election until, in 1955, the constituency was divided. Thereafter he represented Leeds North East until his elevation to the peerage in January 1956.

Peake's early performances in the Commons were inhibited by a slight stammer. With time he overcame this and developed a quiet, deliberate style of address that lent weight to his speeches. 'Broad-minded and liberal in outlook' (*The Times*) he was well qualified for his first ministerial post of parliamentary under-secretary of state to the Home Office, to which he was appointed in April 1939. He was soon immersed in the internal security measures necessitated by the outbreak of war, and in particular, 'regulation 18B', which allowed for detention without trial. He was sworn of the privy council in 1943. In October 1944 he was appointed financial secretary at the Treasury, a post often regarded as a stepping-stone to the cabinet.

He retained this office during the brief caretaker government of 1945. At the general election in July his usually solid majority at Leeds North was cut to 128 votes and he was the only Conservative to be returned for the city. He served as chairman of the public accounts committee in the new parliament, 1945–8.

From his seat on the opposition front bench Peake emerged as a leading spokesman on implementing the Beveridge proposals for social reform. He was at pains to counter labour claims that the Conservative Party was opposed to the spirit of the legislation. In the debate on the National Insurance Bill in February 1946 he pointedly declared his party's whole-hearted support for the measure, observing, with some irony, that it had originated in a wartime consensus: 'It is part of a very much larger picture of a better Britain which was planned under that much-maligned and much-despised Coalition Government which brought this country through the war' (Hansard 5C, 419, 1946, 84). And far from quarrelling with the proposed levels of benefit, Peake expressed concern that they might fall unless the value of money was maintained. It was a prescient warning, since the increase in the cost of living under Labour greatly diminished the purchasing power of benefits by 1951. The Attlee government gave only partial redress with an increase in retirement pensions, leaving other benefits—sickness, unemployment, industrial injury, widow's benefit—at 1946 rates. Peake condemned this as being contrary to the Beveridge plan. Unlike most Treasury officials and economists he believed in the paramount importance of 'preserving the independence of the insurance concept from budgetary considerations' (Seldon, 291).

After the Conservative victory in the general election of 1951 Peake was appointed minister of national insurance. His experience as an industrial employer—he was a coal owner in the days before nationalization and chairman of Airedale Collieries Ltd—gave him a special understanding of his work. His immediate priority was to consolidate the running of this new ministry, which had undergone major changes since its creation in October 1944. But he was also determined to improve the position of benefit claimants, and in 1952 legislation was introduced giving on average a 20 per cent increase. Peake took special interest in the position of the seriously disabled and those with industrial injuries. As an employer he had enjoyed good relations with the National Union of Mineworkers, and this helped in his ministerial dealings with the trade unions. Officials within the ministry credited Peake with playing an important role in gaining the confidence of the trade-union movement after 1951. In September 1953 he became head of the new combined Ministry of Pensions and National Insurance. In the following year intense political pressure built up for an increase in the level of retirement pensions. The issue was complex and Peake took a realistic view of the state's ability to meet its commitments. He sought to strengthen the contributory element of social insurance and in the longer term favoured raising the retirement age from sixty-five to sixty-seven. But

with an election in view, old-age pensions became an issue that demanded short-term solutions.

In August 1954 Peake travelled to Chartwell for an afternoon of intensive discussion with Churchill, who planned to make pensions the dominant feature of the coming year's legislative programme. In a letter to Clementine Churchill he observed: 'Peake hates Old people (as such) living too long and cast a critical eye on me … I felt vy guilty'. As a riposte he showed Peake proofs of the English Speaking Peoples, which brought a substantial revenue in dollars into Britain each year, telling him: 'You don't keep me, I keep you' (Gilbert, 1044). Peake was 'rather taken aback', but the exchange was good-natured. Churchill had full confidence in his minister's ability to carry out the important task assigned to him, and elevated him to the cabinet on 18 October. The pension increases were announced in the queen's speech on 30 November 1954. The ensuing national insurance act increased benefits by 23 per cent, while contributions rose by only 17 per cent: 6 million people were affected, three-quarters of them retirement pensioners. With this act Peake achieved his goal of restoring to benefits the purchasing power that had been intended in 1946.

During the cabinet debate on the higher retirement age Churchill had asked 'Not compulsory, I suppose?', to which Peake had replied, perhaps remembering their exchange at Chartwell: 'Well, no man is really fit for work after sixty-seven or sixty-eight'. The prime minister's face, recalled Harold Macmillan, 'was a masterpiece of acting' (Macmillan, 548). When Churchill did retire, in April 1955, Peake found it difficult coming to terms with his successor, Anthony Eden. In August 1945 the latter had privately dismissed as 'silly' Peake's suggestion that Samuel Hoare be included in the shadow cabinet, noting: 'There is no hope for the Tory party unless we can clear these disastrous old men out, & some of the middle-aged ones too!' (Rhodes James, 311). When it became clear to Peake that he would not advance under Eden—he had hoped at one time to be made home secretary—he offered his resignation and left the government in December 1955. In January 1956 he was created first Viscount Ingleby of Snilesworth, in the North Riding of Yorkshire. That month he was appointed chairman of the board of governors of St George's Hospital, London, and in October he chaired the Home Office departmental committee (the Ingleby committee) relating to the treatment and punishment of young offenders.

Peake remained outwardly loyal to the government, even though he was increasingly alienated from it. He kept silent during the Suez crisis and delayed making his maiden speech in the House of Lords until October 1957, when he explained that 'throughout the unhappy events of 1956 any speech of mine could only have been critical of my former colleagues, and unhelpful in its effects' (Hansard 5C, 205, 1957, 614). The proposed reform of the upper chamber, then being debated, was the first occasion on which he felt he could give the government whole-hearted support. He died on 11 October 1966 at Snilesworth Lodge, Osmotherley, Northallerton, Yorkshire, and was succeeded by his son, Martin Raymond Peake (*b.* 1926).

Peake's colleagues were divided over whether he was undervalued and never properly given his chance; this was the opinion of Lord Butler. Others saw him as simply lacking in drive and political acumen, the view of the chief whip Patrick Buchan-Hepburn. Peake was perhaps less assertive and ambitious than his colleagues, who found him 'something of an enigma, of indeterminate political views' (Seldon, 96). But he had an agile mind, 'a great fund of common sense' (ibid., 287), and a belief in the importance of social insurance that transcended party politics. He was given little scope for innovation but played 'an invaluable—and underestimated—role in consolidating the social security system' in the years after the Second World War (ibid., 294).   MARK POTTLE

Sources *The Times* (12 Oct 1966) · WWW · WWBMP · Burke, *Peerage* (1959) · Burke, *Peerage* (2000) · A. Seldon, *Churchill's Indian summer: the conservative government, 1951–1955* (1981) · M. Gilbert, *Winston S. Churchill, 8: Never despair, 1945–1965* (1988) · R. R. James, *Anthony Eden* (1986) · H. Macmillan, *Tides of fortune, 1945–1955* (1969) [vol. 3 of autobiography] · N. Timmins, *The five giants: a biography of the welfare state* (1995) · F. W. S. Craig, *British parliamentary election results, 1918–1949*, rev. edn (1977) · F. W. S. Craig, *British parliamentary election results, 1950–1970* (1971) · J. Ramsden, *The age of Churchill and Eden, 1940–1957* (1995)

Likenesses photograph, repro. in *The Times*

Wealth at death £287,762: probate, 19 Dec 1966, CGPLA Eng. & Wales

Peake, Richard Brinsley (1792–1847), playwright, was born in Gerard Street, Soho, London, on 19 February 1792, the eldest son of Richard Peake, a native of Staffordshire, and his wife, Ann. His father being under-treasurer and (from 1811 to 1815) treasurer of Drury Lane, the theatre was in Peake's blood from the very beginning. His middle name arose from his father's long professional association and friendship with Richard Brinsley Sheridan. Although Peake was apprenticed to the engraver James Heath from 1809 to 1817, he appears to have spent some time, certainly between 1812 and 1813 (and probably longer), assisting his father in his financial duties at the theatre. His first published piece was an illustrated work on French costume (1816), but the following year he began writing for the English Opera House, with the sketch *The Bridge that Carries us Safe over* and a neatly turned farce, *Wanted, a Governess*. Slowly Peake began to make his name as a writer of farces with two further pieces at the same theatre—*Amateurs and Actors* (1818) and *A Walk for a Wager, or, A Bailiff's Bet* (1819)—but his graduation to Covent Garden with *The Duel, or, My Two Nephews* (1823) and a melodrama, *Presumption, or, The Fate of Frankenstein* (1824), partly based on Mary Shelley's novel, opened up further opportunities, including commissions for Drury Lane. He continued to write for the minors (particularly the English Opera House and the more prestigious Adelphi), but he also became a regular writer at the patent theatres, where he was valued for his dependability. At Covent Garden he almost rivalled Planché in the number of new pieces written. About 1825 he married Susannah Snell; and in January 1826 Anna, the first of at least six children, was baptized at St Martin-in-the-Fields, London.

Like many of his colleagues, Peake tended to work best when he had in mind one particular performer for the principal role. John Liston, for example, who was probably the best low comedian of the period, was much acclaimed in the part of Sir Hippington Miff in Peake's farce *Comfortable Lodgings, or, Paris in 1750* (Drury Lane, 1827). Similarly, at the English Opera House in the mid-1820s Peake wrote for Charles Mathews senior, culminating in *Before Breakfast* (1826), which was one of the author's most successful plays, performed no fewer than thirty nights in its first season. Indeed Peake later blamed Mathews's subsequent absence from the company for the decline in his success rate at that theatre. He seems however to have resumed his partnership with Mathews at the Adelphi from 1829 onwards: he is said to have written most of Mathews's famous one-man shows, known as 'at homes'.

In the early 1830s Peake was a fairly prominent flag-waver for the dramatic profession in the movement for changes in the law relating to dramatic copyright and was one of the first members of the newly formed Dramatic Authors' Society in 1833. But he was in a minority among playwrights giving evidence at the 1832 committee in believing that he was '[u]pon the average' fairly remunerated for his work ('Select committee on dramatic literature', 193). At best a five-act comedy such as *The Chancery Suit* (Covent Garden, 1830) made him £200, but £100 was more usual for a shorter piece. He also wrote regularly for Madame Vestris at the Olympic in the early 1830s, including the drama *The Climbing Boy, or, The Little Sweep* (1832) and the farce *In the Wrong Box* (1834). Soon after the Lyceum (formerly English Opera House) reopened after a fire in 1834, Peake, while continuing his dramatic writing, took on the treasurership, thus filling for over a decade, until his death, the self-same position which his father had had at Drury Lane.

In the late 1830s and 1840s Peake also began to publish in the periodicals, beginning with a piece entitled 'The Toledo Rapier' for *Bentley's Miscellany* in November 1839. Almost all his work in this respect, apart from a very few pieces for the *New Monthly* and *Ainsworth's Magazine*, was for Richard Bentley's journal. It provided vital extra cash, even if Bentley was a slave-driver. In August 1840 Peake wrote to confirm that he was 'now fully employed in [Bentley's] service; I have written nowhere else' (BL, Add. MS 46650, fol. 106). His alliance was predicated on the somewhat misplaced confidence that Bentley would secure him a regular income. In fact, Peake was often reduced to special pleading for his fees. In the following month, after the transmission of another batch of material for *Bentley's Miscellany* and the final chapters of the Colman family *Memoirs*, Peake wrote: 'I have not been idle—but I am poor—if my mind is to be at ease, for the exercise of my imagination and pen, I must have my pocket comfortable' (ibid., fol. 126). His *Memoirs of the Colman family, including their correspondence with the most distinguished personages of their time* (2 vols., 1841), probably

Peake's most substantial achievement, combined theatrical knowledge with a personal note stemming from his friendship with George Colman junior. Although occasionally lacking in connecting material—partly because Bentley continually harried him into producing copy before he was entirely ready—it is still an important source of reference for theatrical historians.

Peake also wrote a light-hearted history of cockney sports under the title *Snobson's 'Seasons'* [1838] and a three-volume novel *Cartouche, the Celebrated French Robber* (1844). A comedy entitled *The Title Deeds*, one of several pieces written for the Adelphi in 1846–7, produced in June 1847, was probably his last play. His unexpected death on 4 October 1847 left his widow and their large family, according to *The Times*, 'in very difficult circumstances'. Peake was a popular and respected figure in theatrical circles and his untimely demise evoked much sympathy and concern, resulting in the launch of a public subscription and a benefit performance to alleviate the immediate financial distress of the family. JOHN RUSSELL STEPHENS

Sources *The Times* (7 Oct 1847) · *The Era* (10 Oct 1847) · BL, Add. MS 46650, fols. 106, 126, 129 · Genest, *Eng. stage* · 'Select committee on dramatic literature', *Parl. papers* (1831–2), 7.1–252, no. 679 · A. Nicoll, *Early nineteenth century drama, 1800–1850*, 2nd edn (1955), vol. 4 of *A history of English drama, 1660–1900* (1952–9) [bibliography of plays] · J. R. Stephens, *The profession of the playwright: British theatre, 1800–1900* (1992) · *The letters of Richard Brinsley Sheridan*, ed. C. Price, 3 vols. (1966) · *IGI* [parish records of St Anne's Soho, St Pancras Old Church, St Martin-in-the-Fields, London]

Archives Harvard U., Houghton L., corresp. · Shakespeare Birthplace Trust, Stratford upon Avon, English Opera House account books · University of Chicago Library, corresp. | BL, accounts with and letters to Richard Bentley, Add. MSS 46650–46651 · BL, letters to George Colman, Charles Kemble, and J. M. Kemble, Add. MSS 42891–42972, *passim* · BL, letters to Royal Literary Fund, loan 96

Wealth at death family left in very difficult circumstances: *The Times*

Peake, Robert (*c*.1551–1619), portrait and decorative painter, was born into a Lincolnshire gentry family. The son of William Peake, he was first recorded on 30 April 1565, upon his apprenticeship to the London goldsmith Laurence Woodham. If this took place at the customary age of fourteen, Peake must have been born about 1551. On 21 May 1576 he became a freeman of the London Goldsmiths' Company, which seems to indicate an unusually protracted apprenticeship, but in that and the following year he was working as a 'paynter' for the office of revels, preparing for the Elizabethan court festivities from Christmas through to Candlemas (2 February). He was paid for similar work in 1578 and 1579. From 1585/6 until about 1599 he rented a tenement in Green Dragon Court, in the Holborn Cross precinct of St Sepulchre's in the city of London.

The back of a portrait, *Unknown Military Commander* (1593; Yale U. CBA) is inscribed: 'M.BY.RO./PEAKE'. This work has been used as a touchstone to attribute other works to Peake, notably ones that bear a similar form of lettering to that employed for the date and sitter's age on the front of this portrait. The diverse nature of the handling of these portraits suggests, however, that more than

one hand was involved. Moreover, the script in question has been found on works painted after Robert Peake's death, such as the portrait of two children, *Lady Margaret and Lord John Russell*, dated 1623 (priv. coll.). It is possible that these works are attributable to Peake's son William *Peake (*c*.1580–1639) [*see under* Peake, Sir Robert (*c*.1605–1667)]. In 1598 Peake was among the artists working in Britain listed by Francis Meres in his book *Palladis tamia*. His earliest known portrait of Henry, prince of Wales (Metropolitan Museum of Art, New York), is dated 1603, the year in which Henry's father ascended the English throne as James I. The prince is portrayed as if on the deer-hunting field with a young companion, Sir John Harington. This image was probably originally paired with a portrait of Henry's sister, *Princess Elizabeth* (NMM), which bears the same date. As no payments for either portrait are recorded in the royal accounts, they may have been commissioned by Harington's father, John, first Baron Harington of Exton, who with his wife was entrusted from 1603 onwards with the full-time care and education of the princess. A similar but later portrait of the prince with the young Robert Devereux, third earl of Essex, also by Peake, is in the Royal Collection.

About 1605, as a churchwarden of St Sepulchre's, Peake was one of eighteen signatories of a petition to the earl of Salisbury (Hatfield House, Cecil Papers 197/88). Jointly with John de Critz the elder, he was appointed serjeant-painter to James I in June 1607, being paid £12 for 'sundry pictures by him made' for James's queen, Anne of Denmark, in 1606/7. Throughout this decade Peake seems to have produced a number of portraits of Prince Henry, which suggests that he acted as the prince's official portraitist. Between Easter and Michaelmas 1610, with the painter–stainer Paul Isaacson, Peake worked at Woolwich on the decoration of Henry's warship the *Prince royal*; his tasks included painting 'diverse histories' (presumably narrative pictures) in the cabins. In 1611 Peake published an English edition of Sebastiano Serlio's *The Firste Booke of Architecture*, which he dedicated to the prince. This had been translated from a Dutch version made after the original Italian, and the title-page stated that it was to be sold at Peake's 'shop neere Holborne conduit, next to the *Sunne Taverne*'. In 1612 he was paid for 'twoe great Pictures of the Prince in Armes at length sent beyond the seas' (Strong, *Henry, Prince of Wales*, 114), and it must have been at about this date he painted what can be considered his masterpiece, the immense, idiosyncratic *Henry, Prince of Wales, on Horseback* accompanied by the naked, elderly, winged figure of Time (priv. coll.) which reflects the great hopes invested in the energetic, art-loving prince, who was to die of typhoid in late 1612. For his funeral 'Mr Peake thelder Paynter' was allocated mourning cloth (Auerbach, 133). Also in 1612, Peake was paid £20 for three 'pictures' for Henry's younger brother, the future Charles I, and was mentioned by Henry Peacham in his book on painting and drawing *The Gentleman's Exercise*. The following year Peake was paid £13 6*s*. 8*d*. for a fine full-length portrait of Prince Charles, commissioned to mark the young heir's visit to Cambridge, and still in the possession of the university. In

1616, a warrant was issued to pay Peake £35 for three further portraits of Charles.

At the end of his life Peake seems to have moved to the Old Bailey precinct, London. He died there in 1619 and his will of 10 October was proved six days later. Peake's wife was Elizabeth, daughter of William Beckwith, prebendary of St Paul's Cathedral. Two sons are mentioned: William Peake whose son was Sir Robert *Peake (c.1605–1667), and Luke Peake, described in the will as 'ungoverned' and who is thought to have died before 1634. Peake's grandson, Sir Robert Peake, became a print publisher and a devoted royalist, knighted by Charles I at Oxford in 1645, and died vice-president of the Honourable Artillery Company.   KAREN HEARN

Sources A. J. Finberg, 'An authentic portrait by Robert Peake', *Walpole Society*, 9 (1920–21), 89–95 • E. Auerbach, *Tudor artists* (1954), 148–9 • E. Waterhouse, *Painting in Britain, 1530–1790*, 5th edn (1994), 41–3 • R. C. Strong, 'Elizabethan painting: an approach through inscriptions', *The Tudor and Stuart monarchy: pageantry, painting, iconography*, 2 (1995), 260–67 [repr., with a little updating, of *Burlington Magazine* article, 1963] • M. Edmond, 'New light on Jacobean painters', *Burlington Magazine*, 118 (1976), 74–83 • M. Edmond, 'Limners and picturemakers', *Walpole Society*, 47 (1978–80), 60–242, esp. 129–31, 145, 170 • R. Woudhuysen-Keller, S. Thirkettle, and I. MacClure, 'The examination and restoration of *Henry prince of Wales on horseback* by Robert Peake', *Bulletin of the Hamilton Kerr Institute*, 1 (1988), 15–39, 117 • E. Chirelstein, 'Lady Elizabeth Pope: the heraldic body', *Renaissance bodies*, ed. L. Gent and N. Llewellyn (1990), 36–59 • K. Hearn, ed., *Dynasties: painting in Tudor and Jacobean England, 1530–1630* (1995), 185–9, nos. 126–8 [exhibition catalogue, Tate Gallery, London, 12 Oct 1995 – 7 Jan 1996] • K. Baetjer, 'British portraits in the Metropolitan Museum of Art', *Metropolitan Museum of Art Bulletin* (summer 1999), 9–13 • T. V. Wilks, 'The court culture of Prince Henry and his circle, 1603–1613', DPhil diss., U. Oxf., 1987, 86–92, 97–8 • C. Bertana, 'Il ritratto di uno Stuart alla corte dei Savoia', *Studi Piemontesi*, 22/2 (Nov 1983), 423–6 • will, commissary court of London, GL, MS 9171/23, fol. 320r • R. C. Strong, *Henry, prince of Wales, and England's lost Renaissance* (1986)
Archives PRO, E 351/2249
Wealth at death see will, commissary court of London, GL, MS 9171/23, fol. 320r

Peake, Sir Robert (c.1605–1667), printseller and royalist army officer, was the grandson of Robert *Peake (c.1551–1619), principal painter to Henry, prince of Wales, son of James I, who in 1607 granted him the office of serjeant-painter which he held jointly with John De Critz. In 1611 the elder Robert Peake published a translation of Serlio's first book of architecture from his shop at Holborn Conduit where he evidently conducted a business in importing books and prints. On his death in 1619 the shop passed to his son **William Peake** (c.1580–1639), also a painter and a freeman of the Goldsmiths' Company, who expanded the operation into print publishing from 1626 onwards. 'Mr Peake the younger Paynter', like his father, was allocated mourning cloth for the funeral of Henry, prince of Wales, in December 1612 (Wilks, 281). In the accounts he was credited with fashioning a gilded staff for the prince's effigy. Although some paintings, such as the *Portrait of a Boy of the Howard Family with a Bow* (Ranger's House, Blackheath), have been attributed to the younger Peake, his actual *œuvre* remains unclear. He married first, on 2 February 1604, Ann Acton and second, at an unknown date,

Mary Dennis, and fathered at least five children. William Peake took over a large number of plates from William Humble, and also issued new plates engraved for him by George Glover, Thomas Cecil, and others. The engraver William Faithorne was apprenticed to him in 1635; another apprentice was the painter William Dobson.

On William's death in 1639 his son Robert—the subject of this article—inherited and continued the business. He published most of the finest British prints of the early 1640s, among them sixteen by Faithorne, Edward Pierce's set of friezes of 1640 (the earliest English ornament prints), and Wenceslaus Hollar's three-quarters-length *Seasons* in 1641. In a letter to Samuel Pepys written in 1690, John Evelyn remembered that Peake was the dealer 'who had the most choice' of prints in London (H. C. Levis, *Extracts from the Diaries and Correspondence of John Evelyn and Samuel Pepys Relating to Engraving*, 1915, 84).

At the outbreak of civil war in 1642 Peake joined the royalist army. In July 1643 he arrived at Basing House as lieutenant-colonel under the marquess of Winchester, and served with distinction during the long siege, being knighted by Charles I at Oxford on 27 March 1645. A 'box of brasse graven plates' was found among his possessions when the house fell in October that year (*Mercurius Britannicus*, no. 101). He was first imprisoned at Winchester House, and then in Aldersgate, before being exiled for refusing to take the oath of loyalty to Cromwell. His associate Thomas Rowlett restarted the print business. Most of their plates were subsequently acquired by the publisher Thomas Hinde, and later by Peter Stent.

It is not known where Peake went abroad or when he returned to England. After the Restoration he became vice-president and leader of the Honourable Artillery Company, and was so well known that a broadside panegyric was published after his death in London in 1667. He was buried in St Sepulchre's on 2 August. His will shows that he was a wealthy man who had wished to spend £500 on his funeral, but that the great fire of 1666 had consumed his houses and tenements on Holborn Conduit so that he had had to reduce the sum to £200.

                                                          ANTONY GRIFFITHS

Sources M. Edmond, 'Limners and picturemakers', *Walpole Society*, 47 (1978–80), 60–242, esp. 129–33 • A. Griffiths and R. A. Gerard, *The print in Stuart Britain, 1603–1689* (1998), 105–6, 125–8 [exhibition catalogue, BM, 8 May – 20 Sept 1998] • M. Edmond, 'New light on Jacobean painters', *Burlington Magazine*, 118 (1976), 74–83 • T. V. Wilks, 'The court culture of Prince Henry and his circle, 1603–1613', DPhil diss., U. Oxf., 1987 • private information (2004) [K. Hearn] • will, commissary court of London, 1619, GL, 9171/23 [Robert Peake], fol. 320 • will, 1667, PRO, PROB 11/324/96
Likenesses E. Harding, stipple, BM, NPG; repro. in F. G. Waldron, *The biographical mirrour*, 3 vols. (1795–1810)
Wealth at death wealthy: will, commissary court of London, Guildhall MS 9171/23, fol. 320; will, PRO, PROB 11/324/96

Peake, Thomas (1771?–1837), barrister and law reporter, was the only son of Thomas Peake of Lleweni, Denbighshire, and his wife, Martha, daughter of Robert Coventry. His father, who practised as an attorney at Lincoln's Inn, held office as a side-clerk in the exchequer office of pleas between 1792 and about 1801. Peake was admitted to Lincoln's Inn as a student on 13 February 1788 and was called to the bar on 6 February 1796. His practice included work as a special pleader. He was a member of the Oxford circuit and of Worcester and Stafford sessions.

In 1795 Peake published a collection of annotated reports of *nisi prius* cases in the court of king's bench covering the period 1790–94. Three editions of this popular work were produced, the last in 1820. The chief justice, Lord Tenterden, commended Peake's reports as being 'remarkably correct'. He added, 'I went the same circuit and was in the habit of taking notes. On many occasions I have compared the cases, and I know his to be particularly accurate' (Manning).

In 1801 Peake published *A Compendium of the Law of Evidence*. His aim, declared in the preface, was to produce a book 'which should be a companion on the circuit; always at hand, and ready for immediate reference'. Five editions in all appeared between 1801 and 1822. The popularity of the *Compendium* was not confined to practitioners. It won praise even from Jeremy Bentham, the radical critic of English law, who applauded the clear dividing line drawn between principles of evidence on the one hand and, on the other, rules of law governing proof in relation to particular causes of action. With characteristic robustness Bentham declared that existing works dealing with evidence by Lord Chief Baron Gilbert and Sir Francis Buller were, in comparison with Peake's work, 'like the drivelings [*sic*] of an old woman in her dotage' (Bentham, 7.341). The *Compendium* was also popular in America, where several editions appeared in the early decades of the nineteenth century.

On 21 January 1800 Peake married Eleanor (1773–1866), daughter and heir of James Budgen, an alderman of the City of London. There were five sons and three daughters of the marriage. The eldest son, Hugh Budgen Peake (*b.* 1803), was called to the bar by the Middle Temple and practised at Worcester. The second son, Thomas Peake jun. (1805–1837), was called to the bar by Lincoln's Inn. He produced in 1829 a compilation, with his own annotations, of additional cases recorded by his father between 1795 and 1812.

In February 1820 Peake was created a serjeant-at-law. He died of heart disease on 17 November 1837 at Chalfont St Peter, Buckinghamshire, and was buried at Kensal Green cemetery. An armorial window and a brass to his memory were placed at Henllan church, Denbighshire.

C. J. W. ALLEN

Sources W. P. Baildon, ed., *The records of the Honorable Society of Lincoln's Inn: the black books*, 1–2, 4 (1897–1902), vols. 1,2 (1896), 4 (1902). · J. Manning, *A digest of the nisi prius reports*, 2nd edn (1820), advertisement · J. Bentham, *An introductory view of the rationale of evidence* (1836–43), vol. 6 of J. Bentham, *The works of Jeremy Bentham*, ed. J. Bowring, vols. 6–7 · T. Peake, *A compendium of the law of evidence* (1801); 2nd edn (1804); 3rd edn (1808); 4th edn (1813); 5th edn (1822) · Walford, *County families* · d. cert. · *IGI* · *GM*, 1st ser., 70 (1800), 587

Likenesses portrait, priv. coll.

Peake, William (*c.*1580–1639). *See under* Peake, Sir Robert (*c.*1605–1667).

Pearce. *See also* Pearse, Peirce, Pierce, Piers.

Pearce, Alfred James (1840–1923), physician and astrologer, the son of Charles Thomas Pearce (1815–1883), and his wife, Elizabeth, *née* Eagles, was born at 9.20 a.m. on 10 November 1840, in his parents' home at 13 King William Street, London; there were two other children. The details of his birth were carefully recorded by his father, a member of the Royal College of Surgeons, who was a homoeopath with an interest in medical astrology. In 1849 a jury acquitted Charles Pearce of manslaughter, after a patient of his died of cholera; the charge had been brought by the reformer Thomas Wakley.

The young Pearce absorbed his father's medical values—including those of homoeopathy, hostility to vivisection and to compulsory vaccination—but developed medical astrology as his own lifelong preoccupation. He began studying astrology in May 1860 and joined R. J. Morrison's Astro-Meteorological Society in 1861; he contributed to Morrison's *Zadkiel's Almanac* the following year. In 1863, he published a precocious but robust *Defence and Exposition of the Principles of Astrology*, and followed it up the next year with a *Weather Guide-Book*. Pearce had begun a medical degree at University College, London, about 1861 but was forced to abandon it because of lack of funds. Instead, in 1869, he followed his father's general practice to Sutherland, where he acted as medical assistant, gaining valuable clinical experience. They worked closely together, comparing the son's prior astrological diagnosis with the father's medical one, whenever possible. On 31 January 1869 Pearce married Marie Léonie Riéder (1848–1930), daughter of Léon Eugène Riéder, a physician. They had eight children, five of whom survived into adulthood (two died in infancy and one was stillborn).

In February 1874 Zadkiel (Morrison) died, and so too, just over a year later, did his successor as editor of *Zadkiel's Almanac*. The Morrison family asked Pearce to become editor. He accepted, returned to London in May 1875, and settled in Wandsworth. In 1911 he and his family moved to Streatham; his last address there was at 10 Mount Ephraim Lane.

By the time he died, Pearce had edited *Zadkiel's Almanac* for forty-seven years, five more than its founder. He changed its character somewhat, in keeping with his guiding principles, demonstrating a combination of moral integrity and seriousness, unmistakably high-Victorian in tone, with an absolute conviction that astrology was a mathematical science of corresponding probity. 'We draw the line', he stated in 1880, 'at magic and spiritualism' (*Urania*, September 1880)—a line the first Zadkiel had conspicuously never drawn. Instead, readers were presented with fare such as a summary of Francis Galton's *Hereditary Genius*, in the issue for 1887. Yet Pearce does not seem to have lost the interest or loyalty of his readers thereby: circulation throughout the 1880s (the last decade for which there are figures) remained at about 150,000 a year.

Pearce produced several other astrological and astrometeorological journals, all of them short-lived: *Urania* (9 issues, January–September 1880); *The Future* (26 issues, February 1892–July 1894); and *Star Lore and Future Events* (January 1897–March 1903). He also wrote the last great Victorian work on the subject, *The Text-Book of Astrology* (2 vols., 1879 and 1889; 2nd edn, 1911). These covered every branch of astrology, including the dauntingly difficult method of Placidean 'primary directions' for predictions that had probably already been abandoned by most astrologers for the simplified method of 'secondary directions'. Between volumes one and two there appeared *The Science of the Stars* (1881). In February 1879, just after the publication of the first volume of his *Text-Book*, Pearce was working in the round reading-room in the British Museum. Richard Garnett, the superintendent, called him over to the centre desk and warmly congratulated him. Garnett, who as an astrologer wrote under the name of A. G. Trent, was one of his admirers and allies.

An indefatigable defender of astrology as an ancient and honourable science, Pearce felt himself to be fighting on two fronts. The internal enemies were the magical and latterly Theosophical astrologers led by Alan Leo (1860–1917), whose ideas (and their popularity), beginning in the 1880s, Pearce accused of 'misleading students … and bringing astrology into disrepute' with 'superstitious nonsense' (*Star Lore*, August 1897). His own work, by contrast, was expressly intended for 'the intelligent and highly educated portion of the community' (*The Science of the Stars*, 1881, 149). Unfortunately, just that portion of the community also supplied Pearce's external opponents, who condemned the whole subject. Representative figures, with whom he sparred in his almanac, were R. A. Proctor and Sir David Brewster. He also had correspondence defending astrology published in *The Lancet* in 1913–14. Unsurprisingly, however, Pearce made no headway in these circles. At best he won some faint praise from *The Athenaeum*, reviewing his *Text-Book*, for showing that astrology 'requires some degree of education and of labour', and that it was at least 'a more respectable science than Spiritualism' (*The Athenaeum*, 14 June 1879). Apart from that the reviewer asked for both a more convincing theory and better empirical evidence—something that Pearce's own claims for astrology as a mathematical and predictive science made rather easier to demand.

Ironically, Pearce almost met one of his reviewer's requests, namely 'a chronology or almanac of the future, not the past, life of the Prince of Wales'; in *Zadkiel's Almanac* for 1910 he warned that 'If the King's physicians would pay attention to astrological science, they would not advise His Majesty to travel abroad either this spring or summer'. On 7 March Edward VII caught a chill on his way to Biarritz; complications set in and he died two months later. This convinced no one who was not already convinced, and it underlined the impossibility of the task of changing educated opinion that Pearce had set himself. When the first Zadkiel had predicted the death of Albert the prince consort, he was fiercely denounced in the press; Pearce's effort was simply ignored—astrology was evidently no longer worth even outrage.

Pearce died at his home in Mount Ephraim Lane, Streatham, London, on 25 April 1923, and was buried in Wandsworth cemetery. The last eminent Victorian astrologer and astrological physician, he had survived into a very different time. *Zadkiel's Almanac* survived only until 1931, and it was overtaken by a greatly simplified psycho-spiritual astrology, whose popularity would have dismayed Pearce almost as much as astrology's continuing academic disrepute.   PATRICK CURRY

Sources P. Curry, *A confusion of prophets: Victorian and Edwardian astrology* (1992), chap. 4 · E. Howe, *Urania's children* (1967) [rev. edn as *Astrology and the third Reich*, 1984] · *Occult Review*, 37:5 (May 1923), 339–44 · C. Sherburn, 'Zadkiel', *Old Moore's Monthly Messenger*, 7 (1914), 170–72 · T. Whitehead, 'Looking at astrological themes in families in a personal account', *Astrological Journal*, 31:2 (1989), 77–83 · b. cert. · m. cert. · d. cert.

Archives priv. coll., workbooks

Likenesses photograph, repro. in A. J. Pearce, *The science of the stars*, 2nd edn (1898), frontispiece · photograph, repro. in *Occult Review*, 341

Wealth at death £575 3s. 8d.: probate, 19 Nov 1923, CGPLA Eng. & Wales

Pearce, Dorothy Norman. *See* Spicer, Dorothy Norman (1908–1946).

Pearce, Edward (c.1635–1695), architect and sculptor, was the son of Edward Pearce (d. 1658), a painter and member of the Painter–Stainers' Company who was employed on the interiors at Somerset House and St Paul's, Covent Garden, in London and at Belvoir Castle, Leicestershire. His father's work was accorded a favourable mention in George Vertue's *Note Books*, but most of it has been destroyed by fire. A volume of his designs for friezes, first published in 1640 and reprinted several times, was a likely source of ornament for his son's carved work, such as the staircase at Sudbury Hall, Derbyshire.

The *Dictionary of National Biography* refers to Edward Pearce junior's apprenticeship with Edward Bird 'the sculptor'; this was possibly the Edward Bird who became upper warden of the Painter–Stainers' Company in September 1656 or the William Bird who was master when Pearce was chosen of the livery in 1688. An Edward Bird appears to have had a near-monopoly of painting and gilding balls and vanes for Wren's churches, and Pearce made the models for the vanes of a number of these. In August 1680 he was paid £4 'for a carving of a wooden dragon for a moddell for the Vane of Copper upon the top of the Steeple and for cutting a relive in board to be proffered up to dycerne the right bignesse' for the church of St Mary-le-Bow (Bodl. Oxf., MS Rawl. B.387, fol. 125; and B.388, fol. 134v). 'Edward Pearse sonne of Mr Edward Pearse' was 'made free by patrimony' of the Painter–Stainers on 16 January 1656 and 'chosen of the livery' on 20 February 1668 (court minute book, fols. 46, 96, 285, and 333, GL, MS 5667/2/Part 1). He became a warden of the company in October 1683 and thereafter appeared intermittently as a member of the court until, on lord mayor's day 1693, he became master. This position he held for only a year, resigning perhaps through ill health on 24 October 1694. A licence was granted on 22 October 1661 to Pearce 'of St Botolph, Aldersgate' and Anne Smith (d. 1703) 'of St

Bride's, London, widow' to be married at St Michael Bassishaw. In 1678 Pearce was living in the parish of St Andrew, Holborn, though in the 1680s he moved west to the redevelopment of Arundel House, south of the Strand, on which he had been engaged, and he is recorded in the rate returns for St Clement Danes' duchy liberty as resident in Arundel Street.

The picture that emerges from a host of references in contemporary financial records is of Pearce's thriving and wide-ranging business practice in the building boom that followed the Restoration and the great fire of London. It encompassed to an unusual degree both architectural design for ecclesiastical and domestic patronage and building contracting, with the execution of ornament in both wood and stone. Richard Crutcher (c.1660–1725), William Beard, and William Kidwell (c.1664–1736), who later worked in Ireland, were his apprentices. Pearce worked with the leading architects of the day. Early records of his work are a copy of his letter to Sir Roger Pratt dated 24 April 1665 concerning 'the Molds of ye Great & lesser scroles' (Gunther, 130) and a bill for masons' work at Horseheath, Pratt's house for Lord Alington, completed in 1666. In relation to Wren, Pearce is referred to merely as the executor of the portrait bust of the latter (AM Oxf.), whereas the relationship was more complex and may have centred on a mutual regard for draughtsmanship. Pearce was one of the signatories endorsing the costs for the Monument, 'The Great Column of London', on the demise of the main contractor, Joshua Marshall, on 31 March 1679 (Bodl. Oxf., MS Rawl. B.363, fols. 7–8 and 13). He worked with Wren on the chapel at Emmanuel College, Cambridge, supplying drawings for the ground plan, wainscot, and seats, and in July 1676 was paid £2 for '5 several draughts', though the work was done by Cornelius Austin (Willis and Willis Clark, 2.707). Although not the contractor, Pearce similarly provided drawings for the front elevation of St Edmund the King, Lombard Street (1670).

In London Pearce was the master mason, or main building contractor, for four of Wren's churches and for parts of St Paul's Cathedral. He was sole contractor at St Lawrence Jewry from January 1670 and was paid £11,870 1s. 9d. Here he was responsible for pulling down the fire-wrecked old church and steeple, clearing the site, and laying the foundations, as well as for the overall building programme, providing labour and all the materials. He was also responsible for the detail of carved ornament. On the death of Joshua Marshall in 1679, he became joint master mason with John Shorthose to complete the rebuilding of St Clement Danes. From 1682 to 1685 he was the site contractor at St Matthew's, Friday Street, and at St Andrew's, Holborn, he was the joint contractor with William Stanton from August 1684. At St Paul's he was one of thirteen master masons, and his was one of six teams of masons. In 1678 he had the contract to build the south portico of the cathedral. On the death of Marshall construction work was divided between Pearce, Latham, and Strong, none of whom had the capital to undertake the whole programme: Pearce was responsible for the cornice in the choir. Rivalry between him and other contractors meant that he was not awarded the contract for the west end. Lang has suggested that Pearce quitted in dissatisfaction at the rates of pay, and that an unhappy relationship with Wren had developed when Pearce supported William Talman over a building disagreement at Hampton Court.

Correspondence for the year 1683 between William Craven and William Winde relating to the rebuilding of Combe Abbey, Warwickshire, for the earl of Craven refers to 'Edward Pearce the Stone Carver' and his involvement in the preparations for carving the Craven coat of arms and a rebus on the site (Bodl. Oxf., MS Gough Warwick 1, fol. 31). Drawings signed by Pearce and endorsed by Winde suggest he was responsible for both the design of the dining-room ceiling at Hampstead Marshall, Berkshire, dated 1686, and the chimney-piece of the parlour chamber at Combe Abbey. Other designs in the series, which may be attributed on stylistic grounds, indicate a greater involvement in the design of interior decoration at Combe Abbey than Pearce has hitherto been credited with. At Winchester College he appears to have been working independently on designs for the refitting of the chapel. The only complete building known to have been designed by Pearce is the former bishop's palace at Lichfield (1686–7). Correspondence concerning the deanery business from Dean Addison to Archbishop Sancroft refers to the taking down of war-damaged buildings and their replacement by a house according to 'the model drawn by Mr Pierce', for which the ground plan and elevation survive (Bodl. Oxf., MS Tanner 131, fol. 185v).

The full extent of Pearce's involvement with William Talman has yet to be established, but it seems to have been more extensive than scholarship has hitherto allowed. He worked with Talman at Chatsworth, Derbyshire, being named as a mason contractor in Wren's report of 1692 to the fifth earl of Devonshire on the costs of the south and east fronts, and at Hampton Court, where he was paid £250 for 'a great Vauze of white Marble, all the figures enricht with leaves and festoons of shells, and Pedestal of Portland, likewise all members enriched', and £745 10s. for 'a white great marble Urne with diverse figures and other ornaments'. For the reassembling of the Diana or Arethusa fountain in the privy garden at Hampton Court he was paid £1,262 3s. (declared accounts, 1 May 1689 to 24 March 1696, pipe roll 4, Wren Society, 4, 1927, 32–3). The two men clearly held each other in high esteem, and when Talman's son, John, entertained in Rome in 1711, he included Pearce in a painted pantheon, as a sculptor to vie with Glycon and 'Bonarota'.

Numerous drawings, formerly attributed to William Talman and others, have been reattributed to Pearce (AM Oxf., BM, V&A, and Sir John Soane's Museum, London), and a volume from the Talman series sold at Sothebys, London, on 24 April 1989 (lot 737, photographs, Courtauld Inst., Conway Library) provides an important corpus of work by him. He always signed himself Pearce, although contemporary and later documentation by others often gives his name as Pierce.

As with other master masons of the period, the production of church ornaments was a significant aspect of Pearce's work. While there are no known monuments signed by him, some, such as that to Margaret Vernon (1676; Sudbury, Derbyshire), are documented, while others, such as those to Viscount Irwin (d. 1688; Whitkirk, Yorkshire, completed by John Nost), John Withers (d. 1692; Arkesden, Essex), and Lady Warburton (d. 1693/4; St John's, Chester), have been attributed from designs in Pearce's hand.

Pearce's reputation as a sculptor survives on the basis of a number of individual works: a series of full-length kings and queens for the royal exchange and the Skinners', Goldsmiths' and Fishmongers' halls, the figure of William Walworth in wood (1684; Fishmongers' Hall, London), and documented busts of Dr Hamey (1675; RCP Lond.) and Thomas Evans, master of the Painter–Stainers' Company (1688). The marble bust of Christopher Wren in the Ashmolean Museum is regarded as the most outstanding portrait bust in England in the second half of the seventeenth century. It was presented in 1737 to the University of Oxford by the sitter's son, who, in a letter to George Vertue in 1742, gave it a date of 1673 and an attribution to Pearce. A marble bust of Oliver Cromwell (AM Oxf.), while inscribed 'E. Pierce Fecit', has had a convincing case made against its being by Pearce, and it is likely to have been made later in the next century. A clay head of Milton (Christ's College, Cambridge) has all the veracity of a contemporary portrait, but the attribution to Pearce is late and hopeful.

Pearce died in Arundel Street, Strand, London, in March 1695 and was buried at St Clement Danes. He was survived by one son, John, and a daughter, who married John Killingworth; both were beneficiaries, with his widow, of his will, dated 2 July 1694. Probate was granted on 20 April 1695. It is clear that Pearce was a man of substance. His portrait and that of his wife were, according to his son, 'of Mr Fuller's Painting', and he collected works of art. In his will Pearce stated that 'Mr William Tallman Comptroller of their Majesties works my very good friend to whom I have ben much oblidged' was 'to have ye Choise & picking of what therin shall seeme to make up ye worthy Collection he intends' (will, LMA, x001/160). The drawings Talman chose became part of the distinguished collection amassed by John Talman, which subsequently lost their provenance and with it their attribution, to the detriment of Pearce's reputation. The 'sirpluss of my Clositt', a collection 'of Books, Drawings, Prints, models & Plaster Figures', was sold with that of Mr Manby in January–February 1696 (Poole, 36).   KATHARINE EUSTACE

Sources R. Poole, 'Edward Pierce, the sculptor', *Walpole Society*, 11 (1922–3), 33–45; repr. (1969) • G. Beard and C. A. Knott, 'Edward Pearce's work at Sudbury', *Apollo* (April 2000), 43–8 • H. Potterton, 'A new pupil of Edward Pierce: William Kidwell', *Burlington Magazine*, 114 (1972), 864–7 • J. Seymour, 'Edward Pearce: baroque sculptor of London', *Guildhall Miscellany*, 1 (1952), 10–18 • Colvin, *Archs.* • K. Gibson, '"The kingdom's marble chronicle": the embellishment of the first and second buildings, 1600 to 1690', *The Royal Exchange*, ed. A. Saunders (1997), 138–73 • R. Gunnis, *Dictionary of British sculptors, 1660–1851* (1953); new edn (1968) • Wren Society, vol. 4, pp. 32–33; vol. 10, pp. 95, 98, 108; vol. 17, p. 80, pls.; vol. 19, pp. 9, 35, 133, pl. 56 • H. M. Colvin, ed., 'Letters and papers relating to the rebuilding of Combe Abbey, Warwickshire, 1681–1688', *Walpole Society*, 50 (1984), 248–309 • G. Parry, 'The John Talman letter-book', *Walpole Society*, 59 (1997), 3–179 • will, LMA, x074/009 and x001/160 • R. T. Gunther, *The architecture of Sir Roger Pratt* (1928) • G. Beard, *The work of Christopher Wren* (1982) • J. Lang, *Rebuilding St Paul's after the great fire of London* (1956), 128–9, 138–9 • S. Jervis, 'A seventeenth century book of engraved ornament', *Burlington Magazine*, 128 (1986), 893–903 • H. Colvin and H. Oswald, 'The bishop's palace, Lichfield', *Country Life* (30 Dec 1954), 2312–15 • R. Willis, *The architectural history of the University of Cambridge, and of the colleges of Cambridge and Eton*, ed. J. W. Clark, 2 (1886) • J. Cornforth, 'Seventeenth-century panelling in a school hall', *Country Life* (17 May 1961), 1102–4 • J. Cornforth, 'Winchester College's building warden: the achievements of John Nicholas', *Country Life* (26 May 1964) • K. Eustace, 'Post Reformation monuments', *A history of Canterbury Cathedral*, ed. J. Collinson, N. Ramsay, and M. Sparkes (1995), 511–52 • N. Penny, *Catalogue of European sculpture in the Ashmolean Museum, 1540 to the present day*, 3 vols. (1992) • J. Physick, *Designs for sculpture, 1680–1860* (1969), 46–7

Archives Bodl. Oxf., MS Gough Warwick I, fols. 13, 31, 41, 45, 47 • Bodl. Oxf., MSS Rawl. B. 363, fols. 7, 8, 13, B. 387, fols. 157–65, 305–8, B. 388, fol. 134v., 309v., 166v., B. 389, fol. 126 • Bodl. Oxf., MS Tanner 131, fols. 170–89 • City Westm. AC, church warden's accounts, St Clement Danes • GL, Painter–Stainers' Company, book of terriers • GL, Painter–Stainers' Company, court minute book, 2 vols.

Likenesses I. Fuller, oils (of Pearce senior?), Sudeley Castle, Gloucestershire • I. Fuller, oils, Yale U. CBA

Wealth at death £2516: will, LMA, x074/009 and x001/160

Pearce, Edward Holroyd, Baron Pearce (1901–1990), judge, was born on 9 February 1901 in Sidcup, Kent, the elder son (there were subsequently three daughters) of John William Ernest Pearce, headmaster of a preparatory school, and his wife Irene, daughter of Holroyd Chaplin. He was educated at Charterhouse School and Corpus Christi College, Oxford, of which he became an honorary fellow in 1950. He obtained a first in classical honour moderations (1921) and a third class in *literae humaniores* (1923). While at Oxford he showed great prowess on the games field. He was called to the bar in 1925 by Lincoln's Inn and the Middle Temple.

In the decade before the Second World War Pearce's promising career as a junior barrister was interrupted by tuberculosis. After a period in Switzerland he was sufficiently cured to enable him to resume his practice, but ever afterwards he had to be particularly careful about his health. Exempt from war service, he continued his practice throughout the Second World War. Pearce became deputy chairman of east Sussex quarter sessions in 1947 and was appointed a High Court judge in 1948, with the customary knighthood. He was first assigned to the Probate, Divorce, and Admiralty Division, moving to the Queen's Bench Division in 1954. In 1957 he was made a lord justice of appeal and a privy councillor. From 1962, when he was created a life peer, to 1969 he was a lord of appeal in ordinary. He was a popular and successful judge, with a clear and perceptive mind and friendly manner.

On his retirement in 1969 Pearce took over the chairmanship of the Press Council, which he held until 1974. He constantly emphasized the link between the freedom of the press and its responsibility. At the same time he became chairman of the appeals committee of the Takeover Panel (until 1976). He had also served on other important commissions and committees, notably (as chairman) the committee on shipbuilding costs (1947–9) and the royal commission on marriage and divorce (1951–5), of which he was an influential member. He was a leading figure in the committee of the four inns of court which set up a senate to iron out their differences (1971–3). He became a bencher of Lincoln's Inn in 1948 and treasurer in 1966. As past master and past member of the court of the Company of Skinners he was a governor of Charterhouse (1943–64), Tonbridge School (1945–78), and Sutton's Hospital in Charterhouse.

Pearce became a household name in 1971 when he became chairman of a commission set up to determine Rhodesia's reaction to a proposed constitutional settlement. The Pearce commission reported in May 1972 that the proposed terms were generally unacceptable and massively rejected by the Africans. The proposals were shelved and the status quo continued.

Pearce was exceptionally hard-working, cheerful, happy, and readily approachable. A distinctly attractive man, Pearce was ever smiling and good-humoured. About 5 feet 10 inches tall, he kept his light red hair to the end. He used plain language when unravelling problems at the bench and in the *Law Reports*. His simplicity of expression and manner made him an ideal chairman of committees. He was much in demand as a witty after dinner speaker. Both he and his wife were talented artists, who held shows together or separately, and he exhibited regularly at the Royal Academy. He was also an ardent collector of pictures and sometimes sculpture. He was president of the Artists League of Great Britain (1950–74) and a trustee of the Chantrey Bequest. At their home in Crowborough he and his wife made a lovely garden. In later years Pearce suffered with trouble to both his hips.

In 1927 Pearce married Erica (d. 1985), daughter of Bertram Priestman RA, artist. It was an extremely happy marriage and she did much to encourage his interest in art. They had two sons, both of whom became QCs, the elder of whom died in 1987 and the younger in 1985. Pearce was never a rich man—until the very end. His artistic eye had picked up a sculpture some thirty years beforehand for about £15. Just before his death this dancing faun turned out to be the work of a sixteenth-century Italian sculptor and was sold for £6.2 million in a London sale. Pearce died on 26 November 1990 in Crowborough, Sussex.

JAMES COMYN, rev.

Sources *The Times* (28 Nov 1990) · *The Times* (6 Dec 1990) · *The Independent* (28 Nov 1990) · *The Independent* (30 Nov 1990) · *WWW* · personal knowledge (1996) · *CGPLA Eng. & Wales* (1991)
Archives University of East Anglia, corresp. with J. E. B. Hill
Wealth at death £5406: probate, 5 June 1991, *CGPLA Eng. & Wales*

Pearce, Sir Edward Lovett (1699?–1733), architect, was born probably in 1699 or a little earlier, the son of Major-General Edward Pearce, first cousin to Sir John Vanbrugh. His mother was Frances, daughter of Christopher Lovett, lord mayor of Dublin in 1676–7, and his wife, Frances O'Moore, a descendant of Rory O'Moore of Laois. Almost nothing is known of his childhood, though a commission was purchased on his behalf in 1707. He is next heard of as a cornet in 1714 in the regiment of his father, and later, at the age of about sixteen or seventeen, in Morris's dragoons, a regiment with predominantly Irish connections which was disbanded in 1717. Both his father and his uncle General Thomas Pearce (later his father-in-law) were much involved in Irish affairs, and though the family had property at Witlingham, near Norwich, and perhaps elsewhere in England, Pearce probably spent some time in Ireland. Edward Pearce died in 1715, the year after his son's cornetcy. Direct evidence of his contact with his kinsman John Vanbrugh is still to seek. But the indirect evidence in the collection of architectural drawings formerly at Elton Hall, Huntingdonshire, is overwhelmingly strong, as are the Vanbrughian affinities in much of Pearce's own architectural work, in particular the use of corridors formed of chains of small domed compartments, chimney-stacks pierced by arches above the roof-line, and cylindrical corner-turrets.

In 1722–3 Pearce made the grand tour, perhaps as a protégé of the abortive New Junta for Architecture, a short-lived group associated with the third earl of Shaftesbury and comprising Robert, first Viscount Molesworth, and his son John, Sir George Markham, and the architects Thomas Hewitt and Alessandro Galilei. Like others, Pearce visited Nîmes, Florence, Bologna, Turin, Venice, and perhaps Rome. He made copious notes, on the spot, in his copy of Palladio's *Quattro libri* of 1601 (now in the library of the Royal Institute of British Architects), was in contact with Alessandro Galilei (also a protégé of the junta), and did commissions for William Conolly, the speaker of the Irish House of Commons. He returned to England, or perhaps Ireland in 1724. Two years later, on 26 March 1726, Vanbrugh died. Pearce himself is reported in 1726 as being 'at Death's door' with an 'Inveterate Cholick' but, by 1728, as having 'become a very healthy person' thanks to a 'milk and vegetable diet' (Perceval MSS, BL, Add. MS 47030). Although he is referred to as 'Captain Pearce', it seems likely that his military character was totally occluded by ill health and by the practice of architecture.

Pearce married, probably some time in the mid-1720s, his cousin Anne Pearce (d. 1749), with whom he had four daughters. For the next eight years until his premature death, he had so many architectural works in hand, mostly in Ireland but a few in England, that many—if not most—of them must have been proceeding simultaneously. Few of them are securely dated, although the south front of Drumcondra House, Dublin, for Marmaduke Coghill, his earliest recorded work on a private house, belongs to 1727. Certainly attributable to Pearce are: Bellamont Forest, co. Cavan, for Charles Coote, a compact Palladian villa with four formal elevations; Cashel Palace, co. Tipperary, for Archbishop Theophilus Bolton, with a brick entrance front and a plainer garden front in ashlar stone; 9 Henrietta Street, Dublin, for Thomas Carter, the master of the rolls, a close transcript of Mountrath House, Great Burlington Street, London; 10 Henrietta Street, for Luke Gardiner; and Christchurch deanery, Dublin (dem.), an ingenious block of three separate dwellings expressed as one. So is Summerhill, co. Meath (burnt 1921;

dem. *c.*1957), a vast house with a giant order, towered wings joined to the centre with two-storey links, and arcaded chimney-stacks in the Vanbrugh manner. Other highly probable attributions include: Woodlands, Santry, co. Dublin, a centrally planned square villa with central tower-lantern; Gloster, Shinrone, King's county; Cuba Court, Banagher, King's county (dem.); and the garden house at Kilmainham, co. Dublin. In a number of cases, the owners of the buildings were related to the architect. Some English concerns must be mentioned, notably a large scheme for a palace at Richmond for King George I, a long gallery at Ashley, Surrey, for Lord Shannon (now dispersed), and probably the saloon at 12 North Audley Street, London, for Colonel Ligonier.

Work had already begun on the great house of Castletown, co. Kildare, built for the speaker of the Irish House of Commons, William Conolly, when Pearce set out for Italy. There is reason to suppose that the elevations of the main house had been supplied by Galilei, and still better reason to credit the entrance-hall and the long gallery in its original form to Pearce, as well as the colonnades and wings. A drawing exists for the entrance-hall, while the colonnades show strong affinities with the parliament house and the style of the wings is subtly contrasted with that of the pre-existing façade of the main block. Purchased by Desmond Guinness in 1967, it became the headquarters of the Irish Georgian Society. This prior connection between Pearce and the speaker must surely account for the young architect's being chosen to design the new parliament house, over the head of Thomas Burgh, the sitting surveyor-general. Later, when Burgh died in December 1730, Pearce was appointed to succeed him in 1731; he was knighted in March 1732 and received the freedom of Dublin in April 1733. Pearce's design for the house was accepted in 1728 and the first stone was laid on 3 February 1729. Parliament sat in it in October 1731, and building was completed under Pearce's successor, Arthur Dobbs, before 1735. Before the building was finished, but when it was already in occupation, parliament paid public testimony on 13 December 1731 to the skill, diligence, and probity of the architect. Besides being the first building expressly designed for the housing of a bicameral legislature, it was a very original conception, embodying the most up-to-date architectural thought of the time. Though added to by James Gandon and others, it is externally intact and retains some notable interiors, especially Pearce's House of Lords chamber, and the domed corridors which surrounded the House of Commons.

Pearce was MP for Ratoath from 1727, and successfully promoted an act in 1729 to regulate the building industry and the size of bricks. A scheme to employ infantry to make a canal from Newry to Lough Neagh was instituted by him. A theatre which he designed was built in Aungier Street, Dublin, but was demolished soon afterwards. Pearce died on 16 November 1733, at his home at The Grove, a house on the estate of Lord and Lady Allen of Stillorgan, for whom he had prepared a grand scheme for the Palladianization of their house, and for the garden. The work on the house was not carried out, but that on the garden was, and the substantial grotto and other works survive, along with the large obelisk intended as a mausoleum for Lady Allen. He was buried in old Donnybrook graveyard, Dublin, on 10 December 1733.

Pearce was by far the most considerable architect to work in Ireland before the arrival of James Gandon: the parliament house alone would entitle him to this primacy. Richard Castle (or Cassels), whom he employed as his assistant and had perhaps also brought to Ireland, took over his practice after his death, especially with respect to country houses. The printing house in Trinity College, built by him in the year after Pearce's death, may well be Pearce's design. Through him a developed Palladian manner, with Vanbrughian overtones, was diffused throughout Ireland. His role in Ireland is closely analogous to that of the earl of Burlington in England, though there is little evidence of any direct connection. MAURICE CRAIG

Sources J. T. Gilbert, *An account of the parliament house, Dublin* (1896) · T. U. Sadleir, 'Sir Edward Lovett Pearce', *Journal of the County Kildare Archaeological Society*, 8 (1927), 231–44 · C. P. Curran, 'The architecture of the bank: the parliament house', in F. G. Hall, *The Bank of Ireland, 1783–1946*, ed. G. O'Brien (1949) · H. M. Colvin and M. J. Craig, *Architectural drawings in the library at Elton Hall by Sir John Vanbrugh & Sir Edward Lovett Pearce*, Roxburghe Club (1964) · M. Craig, 'Castletown, co. Kildare [pt 1]', *Country Life*, 145 (1969), 722–6 · M. Craig, 'Castletown, co. Kildare [pt 2]', *Country Life*, 145 (1969), 798–802 · E. McParland, 'Edward Lovett Pearce and the parliament house in Dublin', *Burlington Magazine*, 131 (1989), 91–100 · J. Harris, 'Ashley Park, Surrey', *Decantations: a tribute to Maurice Craig*, ed. A. Bernelle (1992), 78–87 · E. McParland, 'Edward Lovett Pearce and the deanery of Christchurch, Dublin', *Decantations*, ed. A. Bernelle (1992), 130–33 · Colvin, *Archs.* · M. Craig, 'The quest for Sir Edward Lovett Pearce', *Irish Arts Review Yearbook*, 12 (1996), 27–34 · E. McParland, 'Edward Lovett Pearce and the new junta for architecture', *Lord Burlington: architecture, art and life*, ed. T. Barnard and J. Clark (1995), 151–65 · *Journals of the House of Lords of the kingdom of Ireland*, 8 vols. (1783–1800) · *The journals of the House of Commons of the kingdom of Ireland*, 19 vols. (1796–1800)
Archives NL Ire., MS D20, 209

Pearce, Ernest Harold (1865–1930), bishop of Worcester, was born on 23 July 1865 at 48 Great Marlborough Street, London, the eldest son of James Pearce and his wife, Jane Courtenay Edmonds. His place of birth then housed the west branch of the Young Men's Christian Association, of which his father was the secretary. His mother was the eldest daughter of Walter Edmonds, of Penzance, and sister of the Revd Walter John Edmonds, chancellor of Exeter Cathedral. A severe attack of rheumatic fever at the age of seven seriously affected Pearce's heart and left him fearful of over-exertion for the rest of his life.

In 1874, on the presentation of the banker F. A. Bevan, Pearce was admitted to Christ's Hospital, and began a lifetime connection with the school: he was exhibitioner, assistant master, governor, almoner, chairman of the education committee, and vice-chairman of the council of almoners. He also became its historian in *The Annals of Christ's Hospital* (1901). In 1884 Pearce, who was a Grecian at Christ's Hospital, entered Peterhouse, Cambridge, as a classical scholar and choral exhibitioner, and obtained second classes in the first division of the classical tripos

(1887) and in the second part of the theological tripos (1888), graduating BA in 1887 and MA in 1891. He was ordained deacon in 1889 and priest in 1890 by Archbishop Benson, and went as an assistant master to the South Eastern College, Ramsgate. In 1891 he returned to Christ's Hospital as an assistant master, but in 1892 accepted the post of metropolitan district secretary of the British and Foreign Bible Society, of which he ultimately became a life governor, and vice-president in 1914.

In 1895 Pearce was appointed to the vacancy in the living of Christ Church Greyfriars, London, where the boys of Christ's Hospital attended the Sunday morning service: he soon re-seated the church and brought the boys down from uncomfortable galleries to the floor of the building. Pearce's appointment to the living led to his becoming chaplain in 1896–7 to the lord mayor of London, Sir George Faudel-Phillips, the alderman of his ward, and to a close association for many years with the Mansion House and the life of the City. During this time he became a freeman on the roll of the Musicians' Company and served as its chaplain; he was professor of biblical history at Queen's College, Harley Street (1899–1905); for four years he was secretary of the London Diocesan Church Reading Union; he was elected on to the court of Sion College, became treasurer and president, and in 1913 published its history, *Sion College and Library*; he was a member of the court of assistants of the Corporation of the Sons of the Clergy, was twenty-nine times a steward of its festival, and for ten years a treasurer, and wrote an account of the charity, *The Sons of the Clergy* (1904).

In 1899 Pearce joined the staff of *The Times* as its ecclesiastical correspondent and was in Printing House Square every night, except Saturday, in order to write up the news and to provide obituaries and editorials as appropriate. About this time he came into close contact with the prime minister's office and became an unofficial adviser in the allocation of ecclesiastical patronage, a position of influence he retained for much of the rest of his life. Interestingly, he was later criticized for his bias in the distribution of his own patronage as bishop and responded frankly: 'My business is to keep "advanced" men out of the diocese. You must look to my successor to redress the balance' (*The Times*, 29 Oct 1930, 16).

In 1911 Pearce was appointed by the prime minister, H. H. Asquith, to a canonry at Westminster Abbey, where he later became treasurer (1912–16), archdeacon (1916–18), and subdean (1918–19). Pearce spent a large amount of time in the abbey's archives and produced a significant work of ecclesiastical and monastic history, a register entitled *The Monks of Westminster* (1916). He also wrote two lives, *William de Colchester, Abbot of Westminster* (1915), and *Walter de Wenlok, Abbot of Westminster* (1920). Through this research he qualified for the Cambridge degrees of LittD (1917), BD (1920), and DD (1924).

In the First World War Pearce was appointed assistant chaplain-general (1915–19), with the substantive rank of brigadier, and greatly improved the organization and efficiency of the chaplain's department of the War Office. He

was a chaplain to George V in 1918 and 1919, and in 1919, at the close of the war, was made CBE.

In 1919 Pearce was nominated by Lloyd George to the bishopric of Worcester, and was consecrated in Westminster Abbey on 24 February. It was as an 'able and modest administrator' rather than as a 'profound thinker' or a great preacher that Pearce left an impression as bishop (*The Times*, 29 Oct 1930). Although often overly stubborn in his views, Pearce won respect for his business skills in running the diocese. But his ability not to take himself too seriously was shown in a disagreement with the theologian H. D. A. Major over whether a nominee for a particular post needed more parochial experience. Major provided a list of 'first-class bishops' who had little such experience. Pearce admitted the point and added, 'If you had made a list of bishops of the second or third class it might have included myself' (Stephenson, 139). In the controversies over the prayer book in 1927–8, Pearce always took the conservative side, and he spoke and voted in the House of Lords against the approval of the 'deposited book'.

His antiquarian interests (he was elected FSA in 1918) led Pearce to work upon the Worcester Cathedral archives and to edit for the Worcestershire Historical Society *The Register of Thomas de Cobham, 1317–1327* (1930); and from his knowledge of the register he had already published, *Thomas de Cobham, Bishop of Worcester* (1923). Other works included studies of early Christianity (1908) and the laws of the earliest gospel (1913).

Pearce's own college, Peterhouse, elected him an honorary fellow in 1919 and, after incorporating at Oxford and proceeding to the degree of DLitt in 1929, Worcester College, Oxford, paid him the same honour. Pearce never married. He served as a director of the London Life Association Ltd (which had absorbed the clergy mutual office). He was declared dead at Westminster Hospital, London, on 28 October 1930, after collapsing in Old Palace Yard, near St Margaret's Church, while on his way to attend the opening of parliament. He was cremated at Golders Green on 31 October and his ashes are buried in Worcester Cathedral at the foot of the monument of Bishop Hurd. Pearce's edition of the correspondence of Hurd with William Mason was published in 1930 posthumously.

E. C. PEARCE, rev. MARC BRODIE

Sources *The Times* (29 Oct 1930) · *The Times* (1 Nov 1930) · Venn, *Alum. Cant.* · *WWW* · A. M. G. Stephenson, *The rise and decline of English modernism* (1984) · personal knowledge (1937) · *DNB*
Likenesses W. Stoneman, photograph, 1919, NPG · S. J. Solomon, oils, *c.*1927, Hartlebury Castle, Worcestershire · A. Hyndman, oils, Christ's Hospital, Horsham, West Sussex · photograph, NPG
Wealth at death £29,321 1*s.* 0*d.*: probate, 15 Jan 1931, *CGPLA Eng. & Wales*

Pearce, Sir George Foster (1870–1952), politician, was born at Mount Barker, South Australia, on 13 January 1870, the fourth son of ten children of English emigrants James Pearce (*d.* 1919), blacksmith, born at Altarnun, Cornwall, and his wife, Jane Foster (*d.* 1880), born in London. He attended Redhill public school until the age of eleven, which provided him with his only formal education. When his father moved to Maitland on Yorke peninsula he worked for three years on a farm and then, after serving an apprenticeship as a carpenter, gained employment at Port Adelaide, where he witnessed at first hand the great national maritime strike of 1891. In the ensuing depression he was laid off and decided to try his luck in Western Australia. There, following a brief adventure on the Coolgardie goldfields, he became foreman at Whittaker Brothers' joinery at Subiaco. Simultaneously he had taken a key role in the burgeoning labour movement; by 1899 he was president of the Carpenters' Union and the Trades and Labour Council and was a leading figure in the newly established Labor Party. In all these activities the qualities which marked his subsequent political career were already apparent.

On 23 April 1897 Pearce married Eliza Maude (*d.* 1947), daughter of Richard Barnett, a french polisher, of Perth, Western Australia; they had two sons and two daughters. Neatly handsome, somewhat reserved and a lifelong teetotaller, Pearce was in public life conscientious, industrious, even-tempered, and pragmatic. He was a sound administrator and served four prime ministers in high cabinet office loyally and competently. He was brought up a Congregationalist, but in later life worshipped at Presbyterian churches.

A strong advocate of federation, Pearce was elected as a Western Australian senator to the first commonwealth parliament, a seat he held through various political vicissitudes until 1937. He initially supported free trade, favoured moderate social reform, opposed militarism and the Second South African War, and stood unequivocally for a 'white Australia'. Of all these the most important and enduring was the last. In speaking to the 1901 Immigration Restriction Bill he stated that his 'chief objection [to] coloured [peoples was] entirely racial' (*Commonwealth Parliamentary Debates*, 5, 7160, 13 Nov 1901). With Japan's defeat of Russia in 1905 Pearce, even more than most Australian political leaders, came to fear not only a migratory but also a military invasion from the north. Consequently, it was his view that Labor's ideals could only be attained if Australians were willing to fight for them: 'We have that danger to face. I allude to the rise of Japan, the possibility of aggression by that power, and of her expansion in the Pacific' (ibid., 31, 635, 22 June 1906). Neither the Anglo-Japanese alliance nor the British navy, anchored in the North Sea to ward off the German threat, could be depended upon. Thus as minister of defence in Andrew Fisher's Labor governments of 1908–9 and 1910–13 Pearce extended the compulsory military training of youths aged between fourteen and twenty-five, backed the move to establish an Australian navy, created a munitions industry, and founded an officer training college and a central flying school.

Pearce was minister of defence in Fisher's government elected to office in September 1914, in W. M. Hughes's Labor government of 1915–16, and in the successive Hughes National Party governments, 1917–21. While remaining anxious about Japan's intentions, he endorsed Australia's giving all aid to the mother country for both sentimental and national interests reasons: 'The White

Australia Act would not have been worth a snap of the finger but for the might of the British Navy … the shortest way to Australia's safety was to win this war as speedily as possible' (*West Australian*, 25 Oct 1916). Holding this view, Pearce backed Hughes's call in 1916 for conscription to reinforce the Australian Imperial Force on the western front, which resulted in Hughes and his followers, including Pearce, being forced out of the Labor Party and into government with the Liberals. Pearce represented Australia at the Washington conference in 1921–2 which encouraged him to believe that Japan was no longer a threat. It was in presiding over the raising, training, transporting, and demobilizing of the 350,000 strong Australian Imperial Force that Pearce made his greatest contribution to national life.

From 1923 to 1937, with the brief exception of 1929–31, when Labor was in office, Pearce held portfolios in conservative administrations, as minister for home and territories (1923–6) and vice-president of the executive council (1926–9) in S. M. Bruce's National-Country Party government and as minister of defence (1931–4) and minister for external affairs (1934–7) in J. B. Lyons's United Australia Party government. Following Japan's military seizure of Manchuria and the rise of the Nazis to power in Germany Pearce recognized that the British empire might have to fight a war on two fronts and in this case Australia would once again be vulnerable. To meet this crisis he made a rather muddled effort to build up Australia's defence forces, which had been greatly reduced in the previous decade, and he moved cautiously to prepare Australia for a more active role in foreign affairs. Amid the great depression Western Australia, disillusioned with a remote Canberra-based and eastern-dominated federal government, had in April 1933 voted overwhelmingly for secession from the commonwealth and in the 1937 election the secessionists urged voters to 'Put Pearce last' and he was defeated. On retirement he was appointed to directorships on the Commonwealth Grants Commission and during the Second World War on the Board of Business Administration, where both conservative and Labor governments drew upon his valuable experience.

Pearce was sworn of the privy council in 1921 and created KCVO in 1927. He died at his home in Elwood, Melbourne, on 24 June 1952 and was given a state funeral, the service for which was held at John Knox Presbyterian Church, Gardenvale.   NEVILLE MEANEY

Sources P. Heydon, *Quiet decision: a study of George Foster Pearce* (1965) · G. Pearce, *Carpenter to cabinet* (1951) · N. Meaney, *The search for security in the Pacific* (1976) · L. Fitzhardinge, *William Morris Hughes*, 2 vols. (1964–79) · J. Mordike, *An army for a nation: a history of Australian military developments, 1880–1914* (1992) · J. Merritt, 'George Foster Pearce: labour leader', MA diss., University of Western Australia, 1963 · J. Merritt, 'George Foster Pearce and the Western Australian labour movement, 1892–1901', *University Studies in History*, 4 (1965), 19–84 · J. Robertson, 'The conscription issue and the national movement in Western Australia', *University Studies in Western Australian History*, 3 (1959), 5–57 · G. Pearce, 'Democracy and defence', *Lone Hand*, 12 (March 1913), 366 · *The Argus* [Melbourne] (27 June 1952) · b. cert. · NL Aus., Pearce MSS · South Australian office for the registration of births, deaths and marriages, Adelaide

Archives Australian War Memorial, Canberra · NL Aus. | NL Aus., Heydon MSS · NL Aus., Hughes MSS · NL Aus., corresp. with Viscount Novar

Likenesses photograph, 1921–2, NL Aus. · W. A. Dargie, oils, 1941, Parliament House, Canberra · A. Mills, photograph, NL Aus. · Royal Warrant, photograph, NL Aus. · Swiss studio, Melbourne, photographs, NL Aus. · seven newspaper photographs, NL Aus.

Pearce, Sir (Standen) Leonard (1873–1947), electrical engineer, was born at Chapel House, Crewkerne, Somerset, on 28 September 1873, the only child of the Revd Standen Pearce, a Baptist minister, and his wife, Sarah Young. He was educated at Bishop's Stortford College and the Finsbury Technical College, subsequently serving his apprenticeship with the Electrical Engineering Corporation, of West Drayton, and with Thomas Richardson & Sons, of Hartlepool. After a year as an engineer at sea he returned to work for the Metropolitan Electric Supply Company. Two years later, in 1899, he joined the British Thomson-Houston Company, and took part in the construction of electrical equipment for the Central London Railway. In the following year he became assistant, then shortly afterwards superintendent engineer of the railway's Shepherd's Bush power station. In 1901 he returned to the electricity supply industry as deputy chief electrical engineer to the Manchester corporation. Also in 1901, on 18 July, he married Susannah (Susie) Kate (d. 1938), daughter of George R. Cockhead, of Crouch End, London, a dealer in rare books; they had one daughter. Three years later Pearce became chief electrical engineer, and then general manager of the electricity department and consulting electrical engineer to the corporation, a post which he held until 1925. During this period he was engaged in much development and constructional work, which culminated in the design and erection of Barton power station. In 1916, at the request of the Board of Trade, he formed a committee to consider the electrical supply resources of Lancashire and Cheshire, and in 1920 he played a leading part in the inception of the south-east Lancashire electricity scheme. The advisory board, of which he was chairman, was the first to function in any of the districts into which the country was divided under the Electricity (Supply) Act of 1919.

In 1924 Pearce spent six months in Australia at the invitation of the municipality of Sydney, to advise on various matters in connection with the electrical developments in that country. In the following year he was appointed an electricity commissioner, but in 1926 he became, and remained until his death, engineer-in-chief of the London Power Company, formed to co-ordinate and develop the generation of electricity in the metropolis. Of his valuable work in this capacity the most notable was the design and construction of the Deptford West and Battersea power stations. His association with Sir Giles Gilbert Scott in designing the latter marked the beginning of a close collaboration between engineers and architects in the building of power stations. At Battersea, Pearce also initiated, and successfully carried through, the design and construction of a flue-washing plant to eliminate fumes. For many years, power-stations of his design headed the list for efficiency, and his leadership in this field may be attributed not only to his own high standards but also to his emphasis on the importance of avoiding fixed ideas and of maintaining a breadth of view able to take account of progress in other spheres of knowledge.

Pearce was a valued member—in some cases an honorary member—of the institutions connected with his profession, which he served in various capacities. He was awarded the Constantine gold medal of the Manchester Association, the Watt gold medal of the Institution of Civil Engineers, and finally, in 1947, the Faraday medal of the Institution of Electrical Engineers. He was an honorary DSc of Manchester University (1926), was appointed CBE in 1919, and knighted in 1935. These honours he received with his customary reserved and modest attitude towards his own achievements, and a generous acknowledgement of the work of colleagues.

To his recreations, as to his profession, Pearce brought the same unassuming sincerity of purpose. He was a keen musician and, when living in Manchester, played the organ at the Baptist chapel which he attended. He was an enthusiastic mountain climber, in summer and winter, with more than 150 first-class ascents in the Alps to his credit. He planned methodically, was very safe, and always considerate of his guides. He regarded skiing as an aid to winter mountaineering, and he was also an expert skater. In his home and office were pictures of the mountains, which he loved and greatly missed during the war years of 1939–45, when he added the work of an electricity commissioner to his other tasks. In 1935 he had accompanied Sir William Ellis when he ascended the Jungfrau in celebration of his seventy-fifth birthday, but Pearce did not live, as he had hoped, to do the same, for he died aged seventy-four, on 20 October 1947, at his home, Crewkerne, 8 Park Hill, Bickley, Kent. C. E. H. VERITY, *rev.*

Sources C. E. H. Verity, *Institution of Mechanical Engineers: Proceedings*, 158 (1948), 256 · *The Engineer* (24 Oct 1947) · *Alpine Journal*, 55 (1948), 275–7 · private information (1959) · personal knowledge (1959) · b. cert. · m. cert. · d. cert. · *CGPLA Eng. & Wales* (1948)
Archives Inst. EE, papers, incl. photographs | Inst. EE, corresp. with Sir Henry Guy
Wealth at death £88,517 4s. 11d.: probate, 24 Feb 1948, *CGPLA Eng. & Wales*

Pearce [alias Clark], **Nathaniel** (1779–1820), traveller, was born on 14 February 1779 at East Acton, Middlesex. Incorrigibly unruly, he was sent to boarding-school at Thirsk, Yorkshire; twice apprenticed to London tradesmen, he twice ran away to sea, the second time joining a naval vessel. In May 1794 he was captured by the French, but eventually succeeded in escaping; he then served on various naval and merchant ships, meeting many adventures round the world. Having survived a shipwreck off Cape Town, he served some years in the *Lancaster*, under Admiral Sir Roger Curtis, going under the name of Clark, his mother's maiden name. While invalided in a hospital in Bombay, he accidentally fatally injured a guard, and, escaping, joined the *Antelope*, an East Indiaman under the orders of Viscount Valentia to map the African coast of the

Red Sea. To avoid a return to India he deserted at Mocha in 1804. He was obliged to profess Islam, but soon regretted it, and, on Valentia's return to Mocha, begged for rescue.

In June 1805, Valentia sent his secretary, Henry Salt, on a mission into Abyssinia, to establish friendly relations with Ras Welled Selassé of Tigré. Pearce, who accompanied Salt, was asked by the ras to enter his service. Several times, court intrigues and Pearce's own outspoken nature set the ras against him, but eventually his proven loyalty and courage made him a secure favourite. In 1808 he married Turinga, the half-Abyssinian daughter of a Greek, Sidee Paulus. In 1810 he escorted Salt's second mission into Abyssinia, acting as his interpreter. Another Englishman, William Coffin, remained to join the ras's service, and he and Pearce lived and fought side by side until the death of the ras in 1816 brought rival chiefs to battle over the succession.

In October 1818 Pearce and Turinga fled Abyssinia for Egypt, where Salt was now British consul-general. As servant to John Fuller and the Revd William Jowett, Pearce journeyed up the Nile, reaching Wadi Halfa. He became steward of Salt's consulate in Cairo, and was employed by Jowett to translate parts of the New Testament into Tigré, for the Church Missionary Society. Turinga died in May 1820 and Pearce was to return to England, the record of his naval desertion erased through the mediation of influential well-wishers. But, while awaiting a passage at Alexandria, he succumbed to a bilious fever and died on 12 August 1820. At his particular request, he was carried to his grave at the Greek convent in Alexandria by six English sailors.

Fuller wrote of Pearce:

> He was a man of superior intellectual powers, of great observation and able to communicate his thoughts in an original and vigorous style … He was altogether an extraordinary character. Great warmth of temper and an unbounded spirit of enterprise were the sources of all his errors. His good qualities were courage, activity, intelligence and zeal in the service of his employers. (Fuller, 259)

Salt wrote: 'His memory … will be forever held in respect by all who knew his sterling worth, and who admire an honest heart joined to a true English spirit' (Halls, 2.159). Pearce's journals were published in 1831 as *The Life of Nathaniel Pearce* (2 vols.). PETA RÉE

Sources The life of Nathaniel Pearce, ed. J. J. Halls, 2 vols. (1831) • J. J. Halls, *The life and correspondence of Henry Salt*, 2nd edn, 2 vols. (1834) • H. Salt, *A voyage to Abyssinia, and travels into the interior of that country … in the years 1809 and 1810* (1814) • J. Fuller, *Narrative of a tour through some parts of the Turkish empire* (1829) • G. Annesley [Viscount Valentia], *Voyages and travels to India, Ceylon, the Red Sea, Abyssinia and Egypt*, 2 (1809) • G. Finati, *Narrative of the life and adventures of Giovanni Finati*, ed. and trans. W. J. Bankes, 2 (1830)
Archives BM, Annesley MSS
Likenesses H. Salt, drawing, 1805, repro. in, *Voyages and travels to India*, vol. 2
Wealth at death approx. £150; various natural history specimens; MSS to Henry Salt for publication or editing: will, 1820, *Life*, ed. Halls

Pearce, Raphael (1599/1600–1651), headmaster, was born in Warwickshire; his parents are unknown. He matriculated at Balliol College, Oxford, on 20 November 1618

aged eighteen, graduated BA on 14 November 1622, and proceeded MA on 6 July 1626. From 1626 to 1642 he was vicar of Long Itchington, Warwickshire; there he acquired a wife, Joan, and numerous children.

In 1641 Pearce secured the headmastership of Rugby School on the ejection of Edward Clerke; his candidacy was promoted by Sir Roger Fielding, one of the trustees, despite the warnings of others that Pearce's poverty might prove an encumbrance. So it was. Pearce soon found that the trustees (especially, no doubt, those who had opposed his appointment) took no care for the school. In the course of the civil war the rent owing to the headmaster and the almsmen of the foundation became increasingly difficult to levy; tenants advanced plausible excuses for non-payment, but the overall impression is that Pearce had no head for business, and the tenants took every advantage of the fact. His problems were compounded by losing part of his house in a fire. He was said to have been reduced thereafter to chopping up the school beams and benches for firewood. Pearce seems to have given up his work altogether in the last months of his life. He died intestate in the summer of 1651—from 'want of sufficient dyet' according to his widow (Rouse, 404). Two years later letters of administration were granted to his widow, and a massively detailed petition of grievances on her behalf and that of the almsmen was addressed by the townspeople to the commission of charitable uses. The commission ordered payment of over £700 in withheld rents, from which the school was to be repaired and Mrs Pearce compensated. She was still receiving payments in February 1669.

Pearce's unhappy tenure brought Rugby to the point of extinction. His case highlights the precariousness of school foundations which did not have the associated administrative resources of a civic or ecclesiastical corporation. C. S. KNIGHTON

Sources Reg. Oxf., 2.372; 3.412 • Foster, *Alum. Oxon.* • W. H. D. Rouse, *A history of Rugby School* (1898), 64–9, 73–4, 391–406 • M. H. Bloxam, *Rugby: the school and the neighbourhood*, ed. W. H. Payne Smith (1889), 26–8, 37 • *VCH Warwickshire*, 6.46–7 • PRO, PROB 6/30, fol. 238v
Wealth at death none: administration, PRO, PROB 6/30, fol. 238v, 14 May 1653

Pearce, Samuel (1766–1799), Baptist minister, the son of William and Lydia Pearce, was born at Plymouth on 20 July 1766. His father was a silversmith; his mother died when he was a child, and he was brought up by his grandfather until he was seven or eight. He studied at the Baptist college, Bristol (1786–9), and in 1790 became minister of Cannon Street Baptist Church, Birmingham. There he laboured successfully until his death. On 2 February 1791 he married Sarah, daughter of Joshua Hopkins, a widower and a businessman of Alcester, Warwickshire. He wrote a number of affectionate love letters to his bride-to-be.

Pearce was one of the founder members of the Baptist Missionary Society, founded on 2 October 1792, which he passionately supported throughout his short life, assisting the society in various ways. He was disappointed to be turned down for missionary service, having studied Bengali for that purpose. He wrote several hymns which were included in nonconformist hymnals. He was a man of outstanding spirituality and wrote in a letter of 9 May 1791 to his friend William Steadman, 'I want to walk with God as Enoch walked' (Fuller, 8). Physically he was never very robust, and he died from tuberculosis on 10 October 1799 in Birmingham, where he was subsequently buried; his wife survived him by less than five years.

E. F. CLIPSHAM

Sources A. Fuller, *Memoirs of the late Rev. Samuel Pearce, AM* (1800) [repr with considerable additions by W. H. Pearce, 1831] · S. P. Carey, *Samuel Pearce, MA: the Baptist brainard* [n.d.] · E. A. Payne, 'Some Samuel Pearce documents', *Baptist Quarterly*, 18 (1959–60), 26–34 · S. P. Carey, 'Love letters of Samuel Pearce', *Baptist Quarterly*, 8 (1936–7), 96–102
Archives Bristol Baptist College, MS · Regent's Park College, Oxford, Angus Library, corresp.; family letters and sermons
Likenesses D. Orme, stipple, 1800 (after portrait by S. Medley), NPG; repro. in Fuller, *Memoirs of the late Rev. Samuel Pearce*, frontispiece

Pearce, Stephen (1819–1904), portrait and equestrian painter, was born on 16 November 1819 in London at the King's Mews, Charing Cross, to Stephen Pearce and his wife, Ann Whittington. Pearce's father was an official in the department of the master of the horse. In 1840 Pearce attended Henry Sass's academy in Charlotte Street and in the same year was admitted to the Royal Academy Schools. There he became a pupil of Sir Martin Shee in 1841. From 1842 to 1846 he acted as amanuensis to the novelist Charles Lever. After this employment, Pearce travelled to Italy, presumably as part of his artistic training.

Pearce exhibited his first work at the Royal Academy in 1839. The work, a portrait of one of his favourite horses (Tartar) in Queen Victoria's stables, set the tone for his career, and he became known for his equestrian portraits and groups, such as *Coursing at Ashdown Park* from 1869. Many of Pearce's early works were pictures of the queen's horses; as he recalled: 'Living at the Royal Mews, in the midst of the Queen's horses, I was always making sketches and paintings of them' (Pearce, 21). Colonel John Barrow, keeper of the Admiralty records and a friend of Pearce, brought him the commission for his painting *The Arctic Council Discussing a Plan of Search for Sir John Franklin*, a work that highlighted another important genre in Pearce's artistic output: portraiture. Completed in 1851, the work was exhibited at the Royal Academy in 1853 and sparked public interest in Franklin's fate. The work was sent to Buckingham Palace for viewing by Queen Victoria and Prince Albert and an engraving by James Scott after Pearce's canvas furthered its circulation and popularity. Lady Franklin commissioned Pearce to paint the portraits of other Arctic explorers. All of these portraits are now at the National Portrait Gallery, London. In the midst of these commissions, Pearce married Matilda Jane Cheswright on 13 April 1858, and they had five sons. Throughout his career, Pearce exhibited regularly at the Royal Academy, the British Institution, the Suffolk Street

Stephen Pearce (1819–1904), self-portrait

Gallery, and the Grosvenor Gallery. His works were regularly engraved and were praised at the time for being well-drawn, accurate likenesses.

Pearce retired from painting in 1885, and the contents of his studio were sold by Christies on 5 February 1886. In 1903 Pearce published his autobiographical *Memories of the Past*. He died on 31 January 1904 at his home, 44 Sussex Gardens, Bayswater, London, and was buried at the Old Town cemetery in Eastbourne, Sussex.

MORNA O'NEILL

Sources S. Pearce, *Memories of the past* (1903) · O. Millar, *The queen's pictures* (1977), 202 · Thieme & Becker, *Allgemeines Lexikon*, 330 · Wood, *Vic. painters*, 3rd edn · Graves, *Brit. Inst.*, 421 · J. Johnson, ed., *Works exhibited at the Royal Society of British Artists, 1824–1893, and the New English Art Club, 1888–1917*, 2 vols. (1975) · M. Hill, ed., *Concise catalogue, 1856–1969* (1970), 53, 114, 126, 143, 145 [National Portrait Gallery] · G. Chambers, *East Bourne: memories of the Victorian period, 1845–1901* (1910), 9 · m. cert. · d. cert.
Likenesses S. Pearce, self-portrait, NPG [see illus.] · carte-de-visite, NPG
Wealth at death £5853 14s. 5d.: resworn probate, 12 March 1904, *CGPLA Eng. & Wales*

Pearce, Thomas (*fl.* 1725–1756), legal writer and lawyer, is a figure about whom nothing is known apart from his publications. The earliest of these was *The Laws and Customs of the Stannaries in the Counties of Cornwall and Devon* (1725). Two other works were devoted to elucidating the office and duties of JPs (1754 and 1756). Another publication, *The Poor Man's Lawyer, or, Laws Relating to the Inferior Courts Laid Open*, appeared in 1755. Pearce has been confused with Thomas Pearse (d. 1743), MP for Weymouth and Melcombe Regis, but it is clear the two men were different.

J. M. RIGG, *rev.* ROBERT BROWN

Sources Boase & Courtney, *Bibl. Corn.* · J. Hutchins, *The history and antiquities of the county of Dorset*, 2 vols. (1774) · HoP, *Commons* · BL cat.

Pearce, Sir William, first baronet (1833–1888), engineer and shipbuilder, was born at Brompton near Chatham in Kent on 8 January 1833, the son of Joseph George Pearce. His early education is unknown, but he trained as a shipwright and naval architect at the Chatham Dockyard under Oliver Lang. His skill was recognized in 1861, when he was given responsibility for superintending the construction of HMS *Achilles*, the first iron-clad ship built in the naval dockyards. His experience in the new construction material brought him the position of Lloyd's surveyor on Clydeside in 1863, then the centre of the new iron shipbuilding industry.

Within twelve months Pearce was appointed manager of Robert Napier's shipyard to replace John Elder, who had set up in independent business with Charles Randolph. His influence on this great yard was immediate, designing pathbreaking, fast, transatlantic liners for the Compagnie Générale Transatlantique. His opportunity to become more than a manager came in 1869, when John Elder's early death set his widow and partners in search of a new associate. Pearce's proven skills in design and management were recognized as what was needed, and he joined John Ure, J. L. K. Jamieson, and Mrs Elder as partner and manager in the reconstructed enterprise now named John Elder & Co. The company had a fine reputation for its development work on the compound marine steam engine, and under Pearce this was enhanced further in 1874 when A. C. Kirk, working at the company, developed the triple expansion engine, which was to become the workhorse of the world's merchant navies for the next half century.

Pearce embarked on a rapid development of the markets served by John Elder and pushed out in three directions. In designing ships for the transatlantic route he emphasized speed, and to enhance his company's reputation he cultivated the idea of the Blue Riband for record crossings. He wagered his ships would break existing records, and they did, attracting for his company many new orders, especially from Nord Deutscher Lloyd and Cunard. He applied the same psychology to the fast, cross-channel steam packets, guaranteeing and achieving a crossing time of one hour each way between Dover and Calais. His third market direction was to establish the Govan shipyard as a naval builder, and he succeeded in attracting orders for hulls and engines in the 1870s as naval construction was extended to counter the expansion of Bismarck's new fleet.

Pearce's partners, Ure and Jamieson, retired in 1878 leaving him in command of what was then among the foremost shipbuilding concerns in the world, the Govan shipyard occupying over 70 acres, and employing as many as 5000 operatives. He built for the largest shipping lines, including the Pacific Steam Navigation Company, the New Zealand Shipping Company, and the British and Africa Steam Navigation Company. Pearce was a major shareholder in the first two of these, and was also chairman of the Guion Steamship Company, and of the Scottish Oriental Steamship Company.

As a leading Clydeside employer, Pearce became a commissioner for the Govan burgh, an honorary colonel of the second volunteer battalion of the Highland light infantry, and, as a mason, became provincial grand master of Glasgow. In politics he was a Conservative, and was elected as the first MP to represent the Govan division of Lanarkshire in 1885; he represented the constituency until his death. In 1886 he converted his company to limited liability status, taking the name of the Fairfield Shipbuilding and Engineering Company, of which he was chairman. In 1887, on Queen Victoria's jubilee, he was created a baronet, but enjoyed his new rank only briefly. He died suddenly at his home at 119 Piccadilly, London, on 18 December 1888, his heart weakened by the stress and high pressure of his work; he was survived by his wife, Dinah Elizabeth Socoter, and his only son, William George *Pearce, who succeeded to the baronetcy. He was buried on 22 December in Gillingham, Kent.

ANTHONY SLAVEN

Sources 'Men you know', *The Bailie* (2 July 1879) · J. Shields, *Clyde built: a history of ship-building on the River Clyde* (1949) · D. H. Pollock, *Modern shipbuilding and the men engaged in it* (1884) · *The Inquirer* (July–Dec 1888) · DSBB · Boase, *Mod. Eng. biog.* · CGPLA Eng. & Wales (1889)
Archives U. Glas., Fairfield MSS
Likenesses caricatures, repro. in *The Bailie* (24 March 1880) · lithograph, repro. in A. S. Boyd, *Twenty-six lithographs of Glasgow men* · photograph, Mitchell L., Glas.
Wealth at death £1,069,669 15s. 1d.: probate, 21 Feb 1889, CGPLA Eng. & Wales

Pearce, Sir William George, second baronet (1861–1907), shipbuilder and philanthropist, was born at Chatham, Kent, on 23 July 1861, the only child of Sir William *Pearce, first baronet (1833–1888), and his wife, Dinah Elizabeth, daughter of Robert Socoter of Gravesend, Kent. He was educated at Rugby School (1876–8) and went in 1881 to Trinity College, Cambridge, graduating BA and LLB in 1884. He was called to the bar at the Inner Temple in 1885.

On the death of his father in December 1888 Pearce succeeded him as chairman of the Fairfield Shipbuilding and Engineering Company of Glasgow, an undertaking the development of which had been the principal work of his father's life. Under Pearce's chairmanship, which lasted until his death, the company maintained its high reputation. He was also a chairman of the Scottish Oriental Steamship Company.

Pearce was returned to parliament in 1892 as Conservative member for Plymouth along with Sir Edward Clarke, but did not seek re-election in 1895. He was honorary colonel of the 2nd Devon volunteers Royal Garrison Artillery. He was a keen country sportsman, and his estate of Chilton Lodge, Hungerford, Berkshire, was noted for its shooting.

Pearce married Caroline Eva, daughter of Robert Coote, on 18 March 1905. They had no children. He died after a short illness on 2 November 1907 at his London home, 2

Deanery Street, Park Lane, and was buried at Chilton Foliat, near Hungerford. By his will he left the residue of his property, estimated at over £150,000, subject to his wife's life interest, to Trinity College, Cambridge, though he had had no close association with the college since his graduation. Lady Pearce survived her husband by only a few weeks, and the college thus acquired probably the most valuable of the many accessions which have been made to its endowments since its foundation by Henry VIII in 1546. H. M. INNES, *rev.* IAN ST JOHN

Sources *The Times* (4 Nov 1907) · *The Times* (8 Nov 1907) · F. Elgar, *History of the Fairfield works* (privately printed, [n.d.]) · *WWW* · *WWBMP* · *The Fairfield Ship-building and Engineering Works* (1909) · *CGPLA Eng. & Wales* (1907)
Likenesses photograph, repro. in *The Fairfield Ship-building and Engineering Works*, facing p. 12
Wealth at death £463,364 12s. 2d.: probate, 18 Dec 1907, *CGPLA Eng. & Wales*

Pearce, William Harvey (1920–1982), probation officer and prison inspector, was born on 8 April 1920 at 26 Lina Street, Walton, Liverpool, the son of William Charles Pearce, a dock labourer, and his wife, Agnes Jane Saunderson. His career in the Probation Service was extremely distinguished but almost did not begin. His early working life was in the merchant navy, and while serving on Atlantic convoys at the beginning of the war, he was torpedoed on 4 September 1939 and spent five days in an open boat. He managed to repeat this experience, being sunk once again. He was then transferred to special duties in preparation for the fall of Singapore. This also went wrong: he was captured, and was interrogated by the Japanese, but managed to escape. The illness he contracted during this period was followed by convalescence in South Africa and then by his medical discharge. His eventful war over, he returned to England and joined the Probation Service in 1944, aged twenty-four. His sense of adventure, survival instinct, and love of travel, however, were constant parts of his personality thereafter. On 14 December 1941 Pearce had married Agnes Teresa (1918–1994), a secretary, daughter of James Prescott, blacksmith.

Pearce served eight years as a probation officer in Southampton, London, and Berkshire until, uniquely, he jumped from a main grade post to the post of principal of the newly formed combined Durham Probation Service. This was a large service and represented a daunting responsibility for a man aged only thirty-two. He stayed in post for eighteen years, turning the service into one that was nationally admired at the time of his departure in 1970. During this time he held various teaching appointments at the University of Durham and was also a member of its council. He inspired a whole generation of probation officers, including many subsequent senior staff, by his outstanding leadership and commitment to the work.

During his time at Durham, Pearce was chairman from 1964 to 1967 of the conference of chief probation officers, and through his strong personality and powerful influence played a key role in the work of the Probation Advisory and Training Board. He was also a founder member of the Parole Board for England and Wales, a man much admired and appreciated by its first chairman Lord Hunt. During the 1950s and 1960s the Probation Service grew in size and reputation and became a key player in the criminal justice system. Its high reputation stemmed in large part from a tiny handful of individuals, of whom Bill Pearce was arguably the most prominent.

In 1970 Pearce became chief probation officer of the Inner London Probation Service, the largest in the country. Because of its location, it was critical to the health and well-being of the whole national service. It flourished under his leadership, which was not surprising given his imaginative gifts, and in many respects became a centre of excellence. His international influence also took off during this time. He had that rare gift of sharing with his staff the rewards and opportunities he won. Many probation officers had their horizons much widened by the opportunities he found for them in further study. He helped to pioneer the successful introduction of community service in Britain. More remarkably, Pearce held together a unique job-creation scheme called Bulldog, which he had seen operating in New York. Visitors from abroad flooded into the service to pick up ideas from him and tap into his innovative instinct.

Pearce was utterly unafraid, and this, allied to a sense of fun, made staff willing to take risks for him. He believed in the service and fought hard for its staff and its welfare during his time as its most significant leader. Abroad he was a visiting expert to the United Nations, and also for the Asia and Far East Institute for the Prevention of Crime and Treatment of Offenders. He undertook many international lecture tours, and his advice was constantly sought.

In 1980, after thirty-six years in the Probation Service, Pearce was appointed chief inspector of prisons. It was a new appointment, independent of the prison department and arising out of a key recommendation of the May committee. Sadly his time with the prison inspectorate was blighted by cancer, but he laid the foundations of that important body's future success.

Pearce was a giant of the Probation Service, both in Britain and abroad, who managed also to have enormous influence overall on the wider criminal justice system. With his lively and powerfully warm personality, he would have succeeded in whatever career he had chosen to follow. Pearce died of cancer on 4 January 1982 in the Royal South Hampshire Hospital, Southampton. His remains were cremated at the Stoneham Lane crematorium, Southampton, on 8 January. At his packed memorial service in St Margaret's Church, Westminster, on 12 March 1982, which was attended by the duke of Gloucester, those who celebrated his many achievements included the then home secretary, the recorder of London, the chief social work officer, and members of the Probation Service. GRAHAM SMITH

Sources Home Office, London, Inner London Probation Service staff records · personal knowledge (2004) · private information (2004) · *The Times* (6 Jan 1982) · service of thanksgiving, St Margaret's Church, Westminster, 12 March 1982 · *WW* · *CGPLA Eng. &*

Wales (1982) • b. cert. • m. cert. • d. cert. • T. Newburn, *Crime and criminal justice policy* (1995) • E. Stockdale and S. Casale, *Criminal justice under stress* (1992)

Likenesses photograph, 1981, Home Office prison inspectorate archive • photograph, 1981, Hult. Arch.

Wealth at death £32,729: probate, 17 March 1982, *CGPLA Eng. & Wales*

Pearce, Zachary (1690–1774), bishop of Rochester, was born on 8 September 1690 in the parish of St Giles, High Holborn, the son of Thomas Pearce (1666/7–1752), a wealthy distiller who retired at the age of forty to Little Ealing, Middlesex. Zachary was educated first at a private school in Great Ealing, then at Westminster School. He was elected a queen's scholar on 12 February 1704 and remained at Westminster until he was nineteen. The school liked to keep able boys as long as possible and Pearce attributed his linguistic and philological skills to this long initiation. He matriculated at Trinity College, Cambridge, on 8 June 1710, became a scholar in 1711, and graduated BA in 1713–14. In his early years at Cambridge he indulged himself in some humorous writing, contributing a fanciful account of a silent club to *The Guardian* in 1713 and an essay on quacks to *The Spectator* in 1714 under the pseudonym Ned Mum. In 1716 he published a scholarly edition of Cicero's *De oratore* which established his academic reputation. He dedicated this to the lord chief justice, Thomas Parker, who prevailed on Richard Bentley, master of Trinity, to award him a fellowship of the college that year.

Bentley agreed to this only on Parker's assurance that he would soon appoint Pearce to a benefice. Having proceeded MA that year, Pearce was made a deacon on 22 December 1717 and ordained priest on 8 June 1718 by William Fleetwood, bishop of Ely. On the appointment of Parker (by then Lord Macclesfield) as lord chancellor on 12 May 1718, Pearce became his household chaplain, and was instituted rector of Stapleford Abbots, Essex, in December 1719, and on 10 March 1720 rector of St Bartholomew by the Exchange, the most valuable living in the City of London in the lord chancellor's gift. Macclesfield also persuaded Thomas Pelham-Holles, duke of Newcastle, to make Pearce one of the king's chaplains after Newcastle had noticed Pearce saying grace at a dinner and remembered they had been at school together. Pearce was a royal chaplain from 1721 to 1739. He celebrated his progress and acknowledged his background by his marriage in February 1722 to Mary (1702/3–1773), daughter and heir of another wealthy Holborn distiller, Benjamin Adams. Pearce stated that they lived together happily for fifty-one years, although none of their children survived early infancy.

Meanwhile Pearce's career continued its advance. Macclesfield presented him to the living of St Martin-in-the-Fields on 10 January 1724, and the grateful Pearce dedicated his Greek edition of *De sublimitate* by Longinus to him later that year. 1724 also saw Pearce receive a Lambeth DD from William Wake, archbishop of Canterbury. When Macclesfield was impeached in 1725 Pearce lost a good patron, but remained faithful to the person, attending his

Zachary Pearce (1690–1774), by John Faber junior (after Thomas Hudson, 1754)

trial every day, and afterwards retained his friendship and dined regularly with this 'great and good man' (Pearce, *Commentary*, 1.xvi). He soon acquired new patrons: another old Westminster schoolboy, the politician William Pulteney, who became earl of Bath in 1742, remained a close friend and patron for forty years and left Pearce an emerald ring in his will; William Clayton, from 1735 Baron Sundon, MP for Westminster from 1727 to 1741, was a parishioner at St Martin-in-the-Fields and Clayton's wife, Charlotte, introduced Pearce to Queen Caroline who, shortly before her death in 1737 promised him the next deanery. When the deanery of Wells fell vacant in 1739 Pearce applied to Sir Robert Walpole, but Walpole needed to reward political allies in the borough of Wells and left the deanery unfilled until the death of the dean of Winchester. Pearce was then instituted dean of Winchester on 1 August 1739 and Wells received its necessary political appointment.

Pearce was a scholar who did not search out controversy, but engaged in it when required in his earlier years. When Francis Atterbury, bishop of Rochester, was committed to the Tower of London on a charge of high treason for his support of the Jacobite succession, Pearce published two letters *To the Clergy of the Church of England* (1722), in which he denounced the bishop as a man 'full of ambition' (*Letter*, 5) who sought to replace the present royal family with 'one grown up under the very Wing of the Papal See' (Pearce, *Letter*, 8); he defended the government action as 'reasonable and necessary' (*Second Letter*, 15). Echoing Swift's comments on Bolingbroke, Pearce denounced the tory ministers of Queen Anne during

1710–14 as 'Persons who retired from the Guidance of the Realm, to the loose and lascivious Pleasures of a Mistress's Bed; and rose in the Morning to a Council of State, from the jolly Noise of the Glass and Bottle' (*Second Letter*, 24). Soon, he moved from this vigorous support of whig orthodoxy to the defence of traditional Christian doctrine. In *The Miracles of Jesus Vindicated* (1729) Pearce attacked Thomas Woolston's series of discourses on the miracles, and in *A Reply to the Letter to Dr Waterland* (1731) he challenged Conyers Middleton's 1731 attack on Daniel Waterland's *Scripture Vindicated* (1730), accusing Middleton of seeking to weaken the authority of Moses. His attack in 1733 on Richard Bentley's new edition of *Milton's 'Paradise Lost'* (1732) was a strictly literary work in which he opposed Bentley's 'imaginary emendations' (*Commentary*, 1.xxxiii). He was an acquaintance of Sir Isaac Newton and discussed Newton's *Chronology of Ancient Kingdoms Amended* with the author shortly before Newton's death in 1727, and then attended his funeral.

Pearce's concern for orthodoxy and order within the church led him in 1756 to refuse George Whitefield permission to preach in Long Acre Chapel, but Whitefield ignored the prohibition and wrote a series of long letters of personal justification to Pearce suggesting 'France and Rome and Hell might be the common butt of our resentment' (Pearce papers, WAM 64773). Pearce was resolute in his opposition and soon a raucous mob outside the chapel regularly drowned Whitefield's words with the 'unhallowed noise' (Pearce papers, WAM 64775) of drums, copper furnaces, clappers, marrowbones, and cleavers. Whitefield threatened to publish the correspondence if this 'premeditated rioting' (Pearce papers, WAM 64777) continued and Pearce warned him it was illegal to publish the letters of a peer without permission. But the clamour ceased and Whitefield begged Pearce 'to accept my hearty thanking for stopping the noise that used to be made, since I hear it was owing to Your Lordship's admonitions' (Pearce papers, WAM 64778). However, despite this conciliatory act, Pearce remained hostile to the irregular activities of enthusiasts and evangelicals. In 1769 he reproved Sir Sidney Stafford Smythe for attending Selina Hastings, countess of Huntingdon's chapel in Tunbridge Wells and so encouraging 'great Irregularities with regards to the Discipline and good Order & Government of the Ch. of England' (Pearce papers, WAM 64547–8). Two years later, he described the design of the Feathers tavern petitioners as 'a wild, dangerous and impractical one … of a most mischievous nature' (Pearce papers, WAM 64474).

Although an anonymous critic in 1743 described Pearce as 'a Court-Clergyman, a Hunter of Preferments; a man who is for obtaining a Mitre, by Methods which ought in Justice to exclude him from a Curacy' (*A Letter to Dr Z. Pearce*, 18), in the memoir Pearce later wrote of his own life between 1710 and 1768 he portrays himself as a reluctant careerist who never sought high office. There is a degree of independent evidence to support this. In an age when most clerics' letters to their patrons are fulsome, Pearce's are concise and businesslike, at times almost terse. In 1746 he assured John Potter, archbishop of Canterbury, that he was financially secure and had no desire for a bishopric. Nevertheless he was offered Bangor in 1748. He declined and was summoned by Newcastle, who told him that although he could not hold the deanery of Winchester *in commendam* with Bangor, he could retain St Martin-in-the-Fields. Pearce declined again and was summoned to Lord Chancellor Hardwicke, who asked him 'If Clergymen of learning and merit will not accept of Bishopricks, how can the Ministers of State be blamed, if they are forced to fill them with others less deserving?' (*Commentary*, 1.xxiii), whereupon Pearce consented and was consecrated on 21 February 1748. Much of Pearce's reluctance was due to the remoteness of Bangor. On 26 January 1748, hearing of the death of Robert Butts, bishop of Ely, and presuming there would be a vacancy 'in one of the English Bishopricks now held by a Bishop educated at Cambridge', he had written to Newcastle begging 'that, instead of having my election to Bangor confirmed, I may be appointed to such English Bishoprick as shall become vacant' (BL, Add. MS 32714, fol. 111). In 1747 Thomas Secker claimed to be afraid to meet Mrs Pearce after his role in the Bangor appointment which forced her 'to quit the place [Winchester] she is so fond of' (Pearce papers, WAM 64681).

When Pearce's father died on 14 August 1752 he inherited his large fortune and three years later he told Archbishop Thomas Herring he wished to resign Bangor and enjoy a private life. With one exception, he had made annual visits to his remote diocese since his consecration, but now his health was poor. In a letter of 17 August 1752 Pearce complained to Herring: 'I went thro' many difficulties to get to this place, and many more have I undergone in my Visitation of my Diocese since my arrival here, by reason of bad roads and bad weather' (BL, Add. MS 32420, fol. 77). Herring, who had been at Bangor himself, sympathized about the remote country, dilapidated palace, and dangerous roads, and remembered experiencing 'on Horseback … the Terrors of those ugly stretches' (Pearce papers, WAM 67575). In his commonplace book, Pearce mocked both Welsh spelling and sobriety with the single word 'ddrrunnkq' (Pearce papers, WAM 64896, fol. 18). Herring had little difficulty persuading him to move from Bangor to Rochester, which see was traditionally held together with the deanery of Westminster. Pearce was duly installed as dean of Westminster on 15 April and bishop of Rochester on 9 July 1756. However, this was his final move; when the see of London became vacant in 1761 he resisted Lord Bath's urging to seek further promotion, and in 1763 he made a genuine effort to resign both his bishopric and his deanery. After a long correspondence with Thomas Secker, archbishop of Canterbury, about the legal precedents for a bishop resigning, both men agreed resignation should be made to the king, not the metropolitan. In an interview with the young king Pearce explained that, at seventy-three, he was too old for the job and wanted to devote his remaining years to devotion and study, wishing 'to have some interval between the fatigues of business and eternity' (Nichols, *Lit. anecdotes*,

3.109). The king agreed, but his ministers were anxious about the implications of such a precedent on their control of the system of preferment, and the royal permission was withdrawn. In 1764 Pearce's patron Lord Bath suggested he resign just the deanery and so 'get rid of the troublesome part of your preferment, & preserve the honourable part of it, which you may do with very little trouble' (Pearce papers, WAM 64724). The church hierarchy was anxious lest the link between Rochester and Westminster be broken. Thomas Newton, bishop of Bristol, begged him not to separate the bishopric and the deanery, pointing out how convenient the dean's house was for attending the House of Lords. However, five years later, the king did agree to his resignation of the deanery of Westminster.

On 1 October 1773, at Greenwich, Pearce confirmed around 700 of the laity, but the effort was too much for this 83-year-old man. The next day he was unable to speak and he never regained his former powers of easy articulation. His wife died on 23 October 1773. His paralysis increased; almost unable to swallow, he languished through months of lingering decay and died at his family home in Little Ealing, Middlesex, on 29 June 1774. His chaplain remembered him as tall of stature, venerable in appearance, and softly spoken. A sympathetic obituary claimed 'he was never puffed up with the general applauses of the world, but of a humble deportment' (*GM*, 1st ser., 45, 1775, 421), while another remembered his 'regularity of life, tranquillity of mind, and simplicity of diet' (*GM*, 1st ser., 46, 1776, 406). His extensive library contained the works of Rabelais and Rochester and two editions of Petronius's *Satyricon*, and his commonplace books reveal a man with a keen sense of humour, who was no prude; one holograph entry records that a

> Judge reprimanded a man who had ravish'd a Girl for picking sticks of his hedge, but was brought in not guilty at his trial; Sir, says he, you must leave off these practices, or you won't have a stick left in your hedge. (Pearce papers, WAM 64896, fol. 11)

Pearce was buried next to his wife in the church at Bromley, Kent, close to the palace of the bishops of Rochester. He left his library to the dean and chapter of Westminster and his manuscripts to his chaplain; he endowed an almshouse in Bromley, Westminster Hospital, and the Society for the Propagation of the Gospel, and built a registry for the records of the bishops of Rochester; his fortune was inherited by his brother, William Pearce of Abingdon Street, Westminster.   ROBERT HOLE

Sources Z. Pearce, *A commentary, with notes, on the four evangelists … to the whole is prefixed some account of his lordship's life and character*, 2 vols. (1777), vol. 1 · Pearce papers, Westminster Abbey Muniment Room, London, WAM 64300–64904 · Nichols, *Lit. anecdotes*, vol. 3 · *Old Westminsters*, vol. 2 · Venn, *Alum. Cant.*, 1/3 · [Z. Pearce], *A letter (A second letter) to the clergy of the Church of England: on occasion of the commitment of the … bishop of Rochester to the Tower of London, by a clergyman of the Church of England*, 2nd edn (1722) · Z. Pearce, *An account of what related to the publishing of Sir Isaac Newton's 'Chronology of antient kingdoms'* in 1728 [n.d.] · Z. Pearce, letters to C. Wetstein, BL, Add. MS 32420, fol. 77 · *GM*, 1st ser., 45 (1775), 421 · *GM*, 1st ser., 46 (1776), 406 · *A letter to Dr Z. Pearce* (1743)

Archives BL, absolution, Add. MS 38715, fol. 38b · BL, seals CLXII 50- · Bodl. Oxf., corresp. · Westminster Abbey | BL, letters to T. Birch, Add. MS 4316, fols. 177, 179–180; Add. MS 4326 B, fol. 1 · BL, letters to the first Lord Hardwicke, Add. MS 35589, fol. 327; Add. MS 35590, fols. 7, 85, 100, 342; Add. MS 35601, fol. 49 · BL, letters to Lord Macclesfield, Stowe MS 750, fols. 426, 441, 443 · BL, letters to the duke of Newcastle, Add. MS 32714, fol. 111; Add. MS 32886, fols. 358, 368, 393, 488, 533; Add. MS 32901, fol. 545; Add. MS 32954, fol. 150 · BL, letters to Sir T. Robinson, Add. MS 23810, fol. 404; Add. MS 23819, fol. 159; Add. MS 23821, fols. 102, 288 · BL, Stowe MS 810 · BL, letters to C. Wetstein, Add. MS 32419, fols. 256, 258, 379; Add. MS 32420, fols. 52, 77, 109, 120; Add. MS 32422, fol. 35 · BL, letters to C. Yorke, Add. MS 35635, fols. 67, 73 · NRA, priv. coll., letters to John Ellis

Likenesses T. Hudson, oils, 1754, LPL · T. Chambers, line engraving, 1768 (after E. Penny), NPG · W. Tyler, bust, 1774, Westminster Abbey · J. Faber junior, mezzotint (after T. Hudson, 1754), BM, NPG [*see illus.*] · E. Penny, oils, Trinity Cam. · oils, St Martin-in-the-Fields Church, London

Wealth at death £20,000 left to charitable causes; brother his heir: Nichols, *Lit. anecdotes*, 3.110

Peard, George (*bap.* 1594, *d.* 1644/5), politician, was baptized on 28 July 1594, eldest child of John Peard (*bap.* 1565, *d.* 1631), mayor of Barnstaple, and his wife, Julian (*d.* 1642), daughter of Roger Beaple, merchant of Barnstaple. He had four brothers and six sisters. He was admitted to the Middle Temple on 23 June 1613 and called to the bar on 30 June 1620. Barnstaple retained him as one of its counsel from 1628 and he practised in both Devon and London. He was unmarried and lived with his mother when he was in Barnstaple, where both of them refused to pay ship money in 1639.

Peard was appointed deputy recorder of Barnstaple in 1640 and represented the town in parliament. He attended almost daily in the Short Parliament and spoke frequently, especially against ship money, which he termed an abomination. He traced the historical background of the principle of no taxation without representation and argued that the judges overstepped their function in their decisions on it. In the Long Parliament he continued his attacks on ship money and the judges, especially Lord Keeper Finch, and was commissioned by the Commons to examine whether pressure had been put upon the judges by the crown. Over religious affairs he was outspoken against the recent canons, especially the etcetera oath, and was on the Commons committee to prepare the charges against Archbishop Laud. He was one of Pym's close supporters and moved to have the charges brought against Strafford, a motion Pym seconded. Later he was chairman of the grand committee of the house for the bill of attainder against Strafford when, with the doors locked, he reported on the result of the division. Peard was among the originators of the protestation and in December 1641 proposed the printing of the grand remonstrance.

With the outbreak of civil war Peard received the permission of the Commons to remain in Barnstaple, where he organized the fortifications and contributed to their cost. He was on the town's council of war, meeting daily in the guildhall, and had become the recorder by 30 May 1643. After the royalist success at Stratton some citizens of the besieged city of Exeter opened negotiations with the commissioners of the royal army and these were extended to include Barnstaple. Propositions were sent to the council of war at Barnstaple but suppressed on Peard's advice. When news of this leaked out thirty-six leading citizens wrote to the mayor and council of war to demand a town meeting to consider them. This was rejected on Peard's motion and the letter burned by the hangman. Now some members of the corporation sought terms and reassurances from Prince Maurice and only 'the petulancy of Master Peard (that prudent, learned and comely Gentleman)' (*Mercurius Aulicus*, 29 Aug 1643) delayed Barnstaple's surrender, which was agreed on 2 September. Peard still advised resistance and fomented opposition, which led to his arrest and imprisonment in Exeter. He became very ill and died in Barnstaple some time between 9 June 1644, when he added a codicil to his will, and 15 March 1645, when Richard Beaple's will was proved. He was buried in St Peter's, Barnstaple.   MARY WOLFFE

Sources parish registers, Barnstaple, St Peter's [birth, burial] · wills of George Peard, John Peard, Roger Beaple, Alice Beaple, and Richard Beaple, West Country Studies Library, Exeter · *The Short Parliament (1640) diary of Sir Thomas Aston*, ed. J. D. Maltby, CS, 4th ser., 35 (1988) · E. S. Cope and W. H. Coates, eds., *Proceedings of the Short Parliament of 1640*, CS, 4th ser., 19 (1977) · *The journal of Sir Simonds D'Ewes from the beginning of the Long Parliament to the opening of the trial of the earl of Strafford*, ed. W. Notestein (1923) · *A collection of speciall passages and certaine informations … from Munday Octob. 17 till Tuesday Novemb. 1* (1642) [Thomason tract E 242(2)] · *Mercurius Aulicus* (8 July 1643); (21 July 1643); (29 Aug 1643); (22 Oct 1643) [Thomason tracts E 60(18), E 63(2), E 67(7), E 75(13)] · R. W. Cotton, *Barnstaple and the northern part of Devonshire during the great civil war, 1642–1646* (1889) · J. F. Chanter, *Life of Martin Blake* (1920) · *The journal of Sir Simonds D'Ewes from the first recess of the Long Parliament to the withdrawal of King Charles from London*, ed. W. H. Coates (1942) · J. Rushworth, *Historical collections*, new edn, 8 vols. (1721–2) · *Notebook of Sir John Northcote*, ed. A. H. A. Hamilton (1877) · PRO, SP16/415/111, 442/100 · J. B. Gribble, *Memorials of Barnstaple* (1830) · W. H. Coates, A. Steele Young, and V. F. Snow, eds., *The private journals of the Long Parliament*, 1: 3 January to 5 March 1642 (1982) · C. Russell, *The fall of the British monarchies, 1637–1642* (1991) · H. A. C. Sturgess, ed., *Register of admissions to the Honourable Society of the Middle Temple, from the fifteenth century to the year 1944*, 3 vols. (1949) · J. F. Chanter and T. Warrington, eds., *Barnstaple records*, 2 vols. (1900) · *JHC*, 2 (1640–42) · D. Drake, 'Members of parliament for Barnstaple, 1492–1688', *Report and Transactions of the Devonshire Association*, 72 (1940), 251–64 · J. S. Cockburn, ed., *Western circuit assize orders, 1629–1648: a calendar*, CS, 4th ser., 17 (1976) · Keeler, *Long Parliament*
Likenesses bust on monument, St Peter's, Barnstaple
Wealth at death tenements of Horsewill and Little Pilland in Barnstaple: will, West Country Studies Library, Exeter

Peard, John Whitehead [called Garibaldi's Englishman] (1811–1880), army officer, born at Fowey, Cornwall, in July 1811, was the second son of Vice-Admiral Shuldham *Peard and his second wife, Matilda, daughter of William Fortescue of Penwarne. He was educated at the King's School, Ottery St Mary, Devon, and at Exeter College, Oxford (matriculated 4 March 1829, BA 2 May 1833, MA 17 November 1836). A youth of 'great stature and extraordinary muscular strength', who at nineteen years of age weighed 14 stone, he was described as possessing 'the shoulders of a bull'. As stroke of the college boat, he was famous on the river, and during the town-and-gown rows of his undergraduate days his height and skill in boxing

reputedly made him an object of terror to the roughs. In 1837 he became a barrister of the Inner Temple, being called on the same day with Sir F. H. Doyle, who described Peard's draining on a gaudy day in hall a loving-cup holding about 2 quarts of wine.

He married at East Teignmouth, Devon, on 7 June 1838, Catherine Augusta, daughter of the Revd Dr William Page Richards, formerly headmaster of Blundell's School, Tiverton; she survived him. For some time he went the western circuit, but life at the bar may have been too dull for him, and from 1853 to 1861 he was a captain in the Duke of Cornwall's rangers.

During his frequent visits to Italy Peard had been affronted by the brutality of Neapolitan officials and, largely as a result, he in 1860 joined the forces of Garibaldi, with whose aims he had become thoroughly sympathetic, enlisting as a volunteer in the Cacciatori delle Alpi volunteer corps. When Garibaldi made his expedition to Sicily he was joined by Peard, who distinguished himself by his gallantry and indifference to danger at the battle of Milazzo (20 July 1860), and at its conclusion was raised to the rank of colonel. He accompanied Garibaldi's forces on their advance to Naples, and was appointed to command the English legion. Despite his undeniable bravery he was a mediocre commander, and the legion gave much trouble before its eventual disbandment. For his services he received from Victor Emmanuel the cross of the order of Valour, and became known in England as Garibaldi's Englishman.

On the retirement of Garibaldi to Caprera Peard returned to England and lived quietly. When Garibaldi visited England he fondly paid a visit to his old comrade at his house at Penquite, on the Fowey River, on 25–27 April 1864, and there was a touching reunion between the two. Peard was a JP and deputy lieutenant for Cornwall, and he served the office of sheriff in 1869. He was also a prominent freemason, becoming past grand master of Cornwall on 26 August 1879. He died at Trenython, Par, on 21 November 1880, from the effects of a paralytic stroke, and was buried in Fowey cemetery on 24 November.

W. P. COURTNEY, *rev.* JAMES FALKNER

Sources G. M. Trevelyan, *Garibaldi* (1908) · A. Viotti, *Garibaldi* (1979) · G. M. Trevelyan, ed., 'The war journals of "Garibaldi's Englishman"', *Cornhill Magazine*, [3rd] ser., 24 (1908), 96–110, 812–30 · *Annual Register* (1880), pt 2, p. 217 · Boase, *Mod. Eng. biog.* · C. S. Forbes, *The campaign of Garibaldi in the Two Sicilies* (1861) · F. H. C. Doyle, *Reminiscences and opinions* (1886) · J. Pycroft, *Oxford memories* (1886)
Likenesses photograph, c.1860, repro. in Viotti, *Garibaldi*, 108 · H. Hering, carte-de-visite, NPG · T. Nast, wood-engraving, NPG; repro. in *ILN* (11 Aug 1860) · G. J. Sodart, stipple (after photograph), NPG
Wealth at death under £7000: probate, 12 Jan 1881, CGPLA Eng. & Wales

Peard, Shuldham (*bap.* 1761, *d.* 1832), naval officer, third son of Captain George Peard RN, was born at Penryn, Cornwall, and was baptized at the church of St Gluvias, Penryn, on 29 October 1761. At the age of ten he was entered on the books of the *Fly*, and afterwards on those of the *Racehorse*, as an able seaman. He probably first went afloat in 1776, in the *Worcester*, with Captain Mark Robinson; he was afterwards in the *Martin* with Captain (afterwards Sir William) Parker, and in the *Thetis* with Captain John Gell on the Newfoundland station. In 1779, having been sent away in command of a prize, he was taken prisoner and taken to Cadiz. After his return to England, he passed his examination on 6 April 1780, and on 26 April was promoted lieutenant. In June 1780 he was appointed to the *Edgar*, one of the Channel Fleet, and continued in her until February 1782, taking part in the relief of Gibraltar in April 1781. From 1785 to 1790 he was in the *Carnatic*, guardship at Plymouth; in 1790–91, during the Spanish armament, he was in the *Princess Royal*, flagship of Rear-Admiral Hotham, at Portsmouth, and was again in the *Carnatic* in 1791–2. In January 1793 he went on the *Britannia* to the Mediterranean with the flag of Hotham, and on 30 January 1795 was promoted to command the *Flèche*.

On 5 May 1795 Peard was posted to the *Censeur*, and in July was appointed to the *Britannia* as second captain. From her, in January 1796, he was moved into the *St George* (98 guns), which he still commanded on 18 January 1797, when, as the fleet was leaving Lisbon, she got on shore, had to cut away her masts, and was left behind disabled, while the fleet went on to fight the battle of Cape St Vincent. The ship afterwards rejoined the flag off Cadiz, and was still there in the beginning of July, when a violent mutiny broke out on board. Peard, with his own hands, assisted by the first lieutenant, seized two of the ringleaders, dragged them out of the crowd, and had them put in irons. His daring and resolute conduct cowed the rest, and they returned to their duty; but the two men were promptly tried, convicted, and hanged on 8–9 July. Of Peard's conduct on this occasion his commander-in-chief, St Vincent, thought very highly, and years afterwards wrote, 'his merit in facing the mutiny on board the St George ought never to be forgotten or unrewarded' (Tucker, 408).

In March 1799 Peard commissioned the frigate *Success* for the Mediterranean, and on his way out, when off Lisbon, met and was chased by the Brest fleet. He, however, escaped, and joined Lord Keith off Cadiz on 3 May, in time to warn him of the approaching danger. In the following February the *Success* formed part of the squadron blockading Malta, and on the 18th she had a large share in the capture of the *Généreux*, hampering her movements as she tried to escape, and raking her several times. On 9 February 1801 the *Success* was lying at Gibraltar, when a strong French squadron, under Rear-Admiral Ganteaume, passed through the straits. Peard conjectured—correctly—that they were bound for Egypt, and, thinking that Keith ought to be warned, he immediately followed, hoping to pass them on the way. He fell in with them off Cape Gata, but was prevented by calms and variable winds from passing, and, after a chase of three days, was overtaken and captured. From the prisoners Ganteaume learned that the route to Egypt might be full of danger to himself, and turned aside to Toulon, from where Peard and his men were at once sent to Port Mahon for an exchange of prisoners.

On Peard's return to England he was appointed, in June 1801, to the *Audacious* (74 guns), in which he joined the squadron at Gibraltar under Sir James Saumarez (afterwards Lord de Saumarez), and took part in the actions at Algeciras on 6 July, and in the straits on the night of the 12th. The *Audacious* was afterwards sent to the West Indies, and was paid off in October 1802. In 1803 and during the war Peard commanded the sea-fencibles on the coast of Cornwall. On 5 July 1814 he was superannuated as a rear-admiral, but was restored to the active list on 5 July 1827, and advanced to vice-admiral on 22 July 1830. He was twice married. His second wife was Matilda, daughter of William Fortescue of Penwarne, Cornwall; they had two sons. His elder son, Captain George Peard RN, died in 1837; the younger, John Whitehead *Peard (1811–1880) was 'Garibaldi's Englishman'. Peard died at Barton Place, near Exeter, on 27 December 1832.

J. K. LAUGHTON, *rev.* ANDREW LAMBERT

Sources *The Keith papers*, 2, ed. C. Lloyd, Navy RS, 90 (1950) · J. Marshall, *Royal naval biography*, 2/1 (1824), 23 · W. James, *The naval history of Great Britain, from the declaration of war by France, in February 1793, to the accession of George IV, in January 1820*, [2nd edn], 6 vols. (1826) · P. Mackesy, *The war in the Mediterranean, 1803–1810* (1957) · *GM*, 1st ser., 103/1 (1833), 270 · J. S. Tucker, *Memoirs of Admiral the Rt Hon. the earl of St Vincent*, 2 vols. (1844), vol. 2
Archives NMM, papers

Pearl, Cora [*real name* Emma Elizabeth Crouch] (**1835?–1886**), courtesan, was the second daughter of the six children of Frederick William Nicholls *Crouch (1808–1896), a composer, and his wife, Lydia Pearson, a singer. Her date and place of birth are disputed, as she is believed to have forged her birth certificate, giving the date as 23 February 1842, and the place as Caroline Place, East Stonehouse, Plymouth. It seems likely that she was actually born in London in 1835, the family moving to Plymouth about 1837. Her father, whose most successful composition was 'Kathleen Mavourneen', deserted his family in 1845 and emigrated to the United States in 1849. In 1847 she was sent to a convent school in Boulogne, where she acquired an imperfect command of French. Having returned to England in 1856, she claimed to have been seduced by a diamond merchant in London, and assumed the name Cora Pearl. By 1858 she had returned to France, and engaged in a series of liaisons with notable men in Paris, including Achille Murat, Victor Masséna, the prince of Orange, the duc de Mornay, and Gustave Doré. The longest of her *affaires* was with Prince Napoléon ('Plon-Plon'), who provided her with a house in the rue de Chaillot, known to her admirers as 'Les Petites Tuilleries'. She also entertained the prince of Wales on one of his many visits to Paris. Ostentatious and vulgar, she had neither modesty nor restraint; nor did she have any great liking for men, whom she exploited ruthlessly. For a time her taste in clothes and furnishings set the fashion in Paris, her horses and carriage being particularly admired. She was not considered beautiful, having red hair and a round face, from which she acquired her nickname, 'La Lune Rousse', but her figure was accounted exceptional. She had a reputation for offering adventuresome sex to her clients. She made her only stage appearance as Cupid in Offenbach's opera *Orphée aux enfers*; for her début the theatre, the Bouffes-Parisiennes, was filled with her admirers, including many members of the Jockey Club; but on the twelfth night she was hissed and never returned to the stage. She also had literary ambitions, a story appearing under her name in *Ficelles Littéraires* in 1868. She herself is recognizable in Ouida's novel *Puck* (1870).

On the outbreak of war in 1870, Cora Pearl left France for London, but, being refused admission to the Grosvenor Hotel, she returned to Paris where she converted her house into a hospital, tore up her sheets for bandages, and spent large sums of money on the care of the wounded which she hoped, vainly, to recoup from the commissioners. Her lover at this time was Alexandre Duval, the son and heir of a successful butcher and restaurateur, who was reputed to have spent his entire fortune, in the region of 17 million francs, on her. When his money was gone, she dismissed him, and he shot himself, although not fatally, in her house. The resulting scandal caused her to be expelled from France for a time. Despite the large amounts of money that passed through her hands, by 1873 she was in financial difficulties and was obliged to sell her house and its contents. Her last years were lived in increasing poverty, supported by regular but inadequate contributions from members of the Jockey Club. Virtually destitute, she began writing her memoirs, and, following the example of her professional predecessors, Harriette Wilson and Teresia Constantia (Con) Phillips, sent round advance notices to her former clients offering to omit their names in return for payment. The resulting narrative, which used false, but recognizable names, disappointed the prurient in its lack of detail. It was accepted for publication by Jules Lévy, and was issued four months before her death. She died from cancer, at 8 rue de Bassano, Paris, on 8 July 1886, and was buried in the Batignolles cemetery. K. D. REYNOLDS and J. GILLILAND

Sources W. H. Holden, *The Pearl from Plymouth* (1850) · C. Pearl, *Memoirs de Cora Pearl* (1886) · Baroness Hutten zum Stolzenberg, *The courtesan: Cora Pearl* (1933) · O. Leigh, *The queen of courtesans: Cora Pearl and la vie Parisienne* (1963) · B. Narran, *Cora Pearl: the lady of the pink eyes* (1919) · Ouida, *Puck* (1870) · J. Arnold, *Giants in dressing gowns* (1945) · H. Blyth, *Skittles: the last Victorian courtesan* (1970)
Likenesses De Gallois, statue and casts of hands, 1880 · F. E. de Lansac, portrait

Pearman, William (*b.* 1792, *d.* in or after 1825), singer, was born at Manchester of poor but respectable parents. He entered the navy as a cabin-boy, but, having been wounded in the leg at the battle of Copenhagen, retired with a pension from the service. He then made some unsuccessful attempts to become an actor, and appeared in London at Tooting and at the Sans Pareil Theatre (from October 1819 the Adelphi) in the Strand, and with W. C. Macready's company at Newcastle. He went on to achieve success as a singer of Charles Dibdin's nautical songs at Sadler's Wells Theatre in London. John Addison gave him lessons, which enabled him to take leading singing parts in provincial theatres, including those at Bath and Bristol,

and Macready engaged him once more at Newcastle as leading vocalist in musical drama.

On 7 July 1817 Pearman made his début at the English Opera House as Orlando in the comic opera *The Cabinet*, which was a great success. Other roles in light opera included Captain Macheath in *The Beggar's Opera*, which was judged to be the best on the stage. In 1819 Pearman was retained at Drury Lane for secondary parts (John Braham taking the leads), and in 1822 at Covent Garden; however, his voice and style seem to have been ineffective in a large house. His best effort there was said to be the imitative song 'Ne'er shall I forget the day', in the opera *Clari, or, The Maid of Milan*, composed for him by Sir Henry Bishop. In September 1824 he distinguished himself as Rodolph in one of several altered versions of Weber's *Der Freischütz* at the English Opera House, a role he repeated at Covent Garden.

Pearman's natural voice, soft or veiled in tone (Oxberry describes it as 'smothered'), did not reach beyond E, although he could force a G. His falsetto was sweet when audible, but it was not possible for him to sing many tenor songs in their original key. He was also unable to make use of the trill, and in 1825 he was taking lessons from an Italian singing teacher. He was a small man, about 5 feet 3 inches tall, but well proportioned. His complexion was 'sallow; his hair and eyes dark; and the *contour* of his countenance decidedly foreign' (*Oxberry*, 151). His manner was so graceful that his lameness (due to his injured leg) was scarcely evident. He was a good-humoured man whose talent as an actor was widely recognized. Oxberry hints at Pearman living beyond his means, and also mentions that he

> married, some years since, the daughter of a small innkeeper. The temper of our hero is not exactly of a nature to render the marriage state happy; and he who has been the victim of tyranny in his youth, too frequently becomes a tyrant in his turn. (*Oxberry*, 152)

Nothing is known of him after 1825.

L. M. MIDDLETON, *rev.* DAVID J. GOLBY

Sources *Oxberry's Dramatic Biography*, 1/9 (1825), 142–52 · *The Harmonicon*, 2 (1824), 192 · Brown & Stratton, *Brit. mus.*
Likenesses J. Rogers, engraving (after De Wilde), repro. in *Oxberry's Dramatic Biography*, 142 · prints, BM, NPG

Pears, Andrew (1766/7–1845). *See under* Pears, Andrew (1846–1909).

Pears, Andrew (1846–1909), soapmaker and perfumer, was born on 21 January 1846 at 55 Wells Street, near Oxford Street, London, one of several children of Francis Pears, soapmaker, and his wife, Mary Williams. He was the great-grandson of **Andrew Pears** (1766/7–1845), also a soapmaker and perfumer, who developed a soap formula in which ordinary soap was dissolved in alcohol, distilled, and shaped into individual bars. Born in Cornwall, Andrew Pears senior was apprenticed to a barber and went to London to establish his own barber's shop in Gerrard Street. It was there that he began making and selling his unique transparent soap in 1789. The popularity of the soap—and the eagerness with which enterprising competitors produced imitation soaps—led Pears to sign the wrapper of each bar as proof of its quality. In 1835 he established a partnership with his grandson Francis, centred on his unique formula, and founded the family business as A. and F. Pears. Andrew Pears senior resigned in 1838 and died on 24 April 1845 at his home, 55 Wells Street, London.

Andrew Pears junior was privately educated before being apprenticed to the family business. In 1862 at the age of sixteen he entered the soapworks at Isleworth, Middlesex, then newly built by his father, Francis. While still in his teens, Pears was placed in charge of the soapworks, retaining this responsibility throughout his forty-odd years with the firm. In 1865 Pears joined his father as a partner in the firm along with Thomas James Barratt, who had recently married Pears's oldest sister. Placed in charge of the London shop in Great Russell Street, Barratt began an ambitious programme of expansion which included increasing amounts of advertising. It was Barratt who paid £2000 for Sir John Millais's painting *Bubbles*, and turned it into one of the most famous brand advertisements of all time.

Francis Pears retired in the mid-1870s, perhaps out of a reluctance to participate in the firm's increased use of advertising, leaving the firm in the hands of his son and son-in-law. With Andrew Pears to direct the soapworks and Barratt in charge of sales, A. and F. Pears continued to expand, even briefly considering establishing a soapworks in America. Barratt's daring and innovation in advertising Pears soap outraged and delighted the British public by turns, making Pears a household name. Profit grew apace with advertising expenditure and in 1892 the firm went public with Pears as director and Barratt as chairman. During Pears's years of stewardship the firm expanded production and achieved a steady increase in sales, and Pears Soap became one of the first British soaps to reach a national and international market, and one of the most recognized products of the nineteenth century.

On 5 August 1869 Pears married Mary Ann Pearson, daughter of Edward Hollingham, confectioner; they had six sons and three daughters. Pears typified the successful industrialist of the day: a sportsman, active in public service, he still saw to the day-to-day running of the soapworks. He served as justice of the peace for Middlesex and as an alderman, and was an active member of the local Liberal Party. He was known and much loved for his charity and concern for his workers. Shortly before his death he donated several acres of ground to be used for playing fields.

Pears died on 10 February 1909 at Mevagissey, his home in St John's Road, Isleworth, and was buried at Isleworth cemetery three days later. He was survived by his wife. His place on the board was taken by Joseph Beecham, of Beecham's Pills, and Barratt continued to serve as chairman. With Pears's death A. and F. Pears ceased to be a family concern. His oldest surviving son, Thomas Pears, was rejected by Thomas Barratt at the annual meeting of the board in the spring of 1909, when *The Times* noted that 'The name Pears has nothing to do with father or son' (4 May 1909). In 1912 Tom Pears died in the sinking of the *Titanic*, and in 1914 A. and F. Pears was bought by its most important competitor, Lever Brothers.

KELLEY GRAHAM

Sources C. H. W. Jackson, 'The great persuader', *Blackwood*, 317 (1975), 204–19 · *The Times* (11 Feb 1909) · *The Times* (15 Feb 1909) [burial notice] · *The Times* (4 May 1909) [will] · *The Times* (28 Oct 1909) [annual meeting of A. and F. Pears] · 'Pears soap success', *The Times* (18 Oct 1913) · C. Wilson, *The history of Unilever: a study in economic growth and social change*, 1 (1954) · H. R. Edwards, *Competition and monopoly in the British soap industry* (1962) · C. K. Shorter, 'The romance of the house of Pears', *Pears Cyclopedia*, 19 (1915) · D. J. Jeremy, 'Pears, Andrew', *DBB* · will of Andrew Pears, senior, Bank of England, wills extracts (1845), 62 K–Z, no. 13022 · J. G. Millais, *The life and letters of Sir John Everett Millais*, 2 vols. (1899) · b. cert. · d. cert. · m. cert. · d. cert. [Andrew Pears]

Likenesses photograph, repro. in W. H. Beable, *The romance of great business* (1926)

Wealth at death £125,307 10s. 3d.: resworn probate, 30 April 1909, *CGPLA Eng. & Wales* · under £2000—Andrew Pears senior: Bank of England wills extracts, 1845, 62 K–Z, no. 13022

Pears, Sir Edwin (1835–1919), barrister, publicist, and historian, was born in York on 18 March 1835, the son of Robert Pears, a descendant of a younger branch of the Piers family of Piers Hall, Ingleton, Yorkshire, and his wife, Elizabeth, *née* Barnett. After being educated privately, he graduated from London University with distinction in Roman law and jurisprudence. On a voyage to Australasia in 1857 he married Mary, daughter of John Ritchie Hall, surgeon in the Royal Navy. They had four sons and three daughters.

In 1870 Pears was called to the bar at the Middle Temple, and began to practise as a barrister in London. In addition he undertook literary and administrative work and was for a time private secretary to Frederic Temple, then bishop of Exeter. He was also general secretary of the Social Science Association from 1868 to 1872 and of the International Prison Congress in 1872, and edited the journals of both organizations. In 1872 he became editor of the *Law Magazine*. Overwork began to tell on his health, and when, in January 1873, he heard that the practice of Sir Charles Parker Butt at the Constantinople bar was vacant, he decided to try his hand at the job. This decision was to determine his future career. Settling as a permanent resident in Turkey, he rose to become president of the European bar in Constantinople in 1881, and made a name for himself as a newspaper correspondent and historian of the city.

Pears's political attitudes and activities in the Levant were influenced by his arriving in the country in middle age, when he had already made political and personal connections in England. Although he rapidly rose to be one of the leaders of the British colony, he retained an independent and critical point of view with regard to local affairs and to the Eastern question. Holding, as he did, liberal convictions, he did not adopt the complacent attitude towards the Turks characteristic of many western Europeans living in the region. He had no illusions as to the intelligence and character of Sultan Abdul Hamid, and he expressed his views in the *Life of Abdul Hamid* (1917). He also wrote *Turkey and its People* (1911). Pears became interested in the more remote history of the Ottoman empire, and published two monographs which became standard texts, *The Fall of Constantinople* (1885) and *The Destruction of the Greek Empire* (1903).

Pears came to general prominence in 1876 through his reporting for the *Daily News* of the atrocities against Christian Bulgarians. His dispatches of 12 May, 23 June, and 7 August, particularly, played a major role in launching the subsequent 'Bulgarian agitation'. Pears's reports were confirmed by other observers and were taken up by the rest of the Liberal press; by September a full-scale campaign, led by W. E. Gladstone, was in progress. Despite this, Pears remained on fair terms with the Turks, though his role as a barrister required him to be cautious.

Pears was knighted in June 1909. He left Turkey in December 1914, as a result of the outbreak of war, but he returned in April 1919. He died after an accident at sea at the Zammit-Clapp Hospital, Malta, on 27 November 1919.

CHANDRIKA KAUL

Sources *DNB* · E. Pears, *Forty years in Constantinople* (1916) · R. T. Shannon, *Gladstone and the Bulgarian agitation, 1876* (1963) · *WWW* · *CGPLA Eng. & Wales* (1920)
Wealth at death £21,293 18s. 4d.: probate, 30 March 1920, *CGPLA Eng. & Wales*

Pears, Sir Peter Neville Luard (1910–1986), singer, was born on 22 June 1910 at Newark House, Searle Road, Farnham, Surrey, the youngest in the family of four daughters (one of whom died in infancy) and three sons of Arthur Grant Pears, a civil engineer and later a director of Burma Railways, and his wife, Jessie Elizabeth de Visme Luard. Pears's parents were married in Bombay in 1893. Much of his father's working life was spent overseas, which meant that Peter had little contact with him until 1923, when Arthur Pears retired to live in England. Pears's mother too was often absent, though it is clear from his letters that his relationship with her was a fond one and sustained throughout his young manhood. His brothers followed naval careers, continuing a family tradition in which there was a strong service element: his mother's father had been a general. But there was another, altogether different strand in Pears's ancestry, that of the church and, more particularly, the influence of Pears's great-great-grandmother Elizabeth Fry, the Quaker reformer. A bonding with Quakerism continued throughout Pears's life and was reflected in his pacifism, his sense of values, and his virtues. There was indeed something of the patrician Quaker in his looks, manners, and deeds. His habitual charm and courtesy rarely deserted him.

Pears's childhood, even though it may have lacked the continuity of a settled home, seems to have been happy, as indeed were his schooldays at Lancing College, Sussex, which he entered as a classical scholar in 1923. At Lancing he became aware of his homosexual nature, though it was some years before it found fulfilment. In this respect he lived at ease with himself throughout his life. It was at school, too, that his musical and theatrical gifts and inclinations showed themselves. He was a capable pianist, took part in operatic and dramatic productions, and

Sir Peter Neville Luard Pears (1910–1986), by Reg Wilson, 1967 [in the title role of *Peter Grimes* by Benjamin Britten]

involved himself in the school's cultural life. He was an accomplished cricketer. As his schooldays ended, his love of painting seems to have begun: his taste and judgement aided him in the acquisition over the years of a notable private collection which included many examples of work by the best British artists of the period.

In 1928 Pears went to Keble College, Oxford, to study music, but again without a very clear musical goal in mind. For a while he had a post at Hertford College as temporary organist. But his Oxford career was short-lived. He failed his pass moderations, left Oxford, and never returned. He went back to his preparatory school, The Grange, Crowborough, in 1929, this time as a teacher, and resumed his interest in cricket. At this point Pears's instinct for music finally located itself in his voice. This led to his undertaking, for the first time, professional vocal studies at the Royal College of Music in London, initially on a part-time basis and then, in 1934, as a full-time student (he was an operatic exhibitioner). Again, however, he failed to complete the course. He left after only two terms, during which he participated in college operatic productions, to begin his professional career as a singer, with the BBC Singers (1934–7) and, in 1936, the New English Singers, with whom he made his first visit to the USA. In finally making his commitment specifically to a singer's life, he was helped by Nell Burra. She was the twin sister of Peter Burra (1909–1937), a close friend of Pears at

Lancing and Oxford, whose life Pears briefly shared in 1936 and 1937. It was a friendship with a momentous consequence for Pears and indeed for the history of British music.

Burra, a gifted writer on the arts, had met the young composer Benjamin *Britten (1913–1976) in Barcelona in 1936, and the two men became friends. This was before Pears and Britten had met. It was Burra's untimely death in an air accident in 1937 that brought Pears and Britten together. Their remarkable partnership had its inception in April of that year when, as Burra's friends, they jointly sorted out his personal papers. Thus the end of one friendship was the beginning of another; and thereafter the careers of Pears and Britten were inextricably linked, as were their lives (they began to share a flat in 1938), though it was not until 1939 in Canada that the love of each for the other finally declared itself. It was sustained over thirty-six years. Pears had left England for North America with Britten in the same year and they did not return until 1942, when both men—convinced pacifists of long standing—sought and received exemption from military service, provided that they continued their wartime work as performing musicians.

Already in 1938 Pears had professional experience of opera as a member of the chorus at Glyndebourne, and in that year he was described by a fellow artist as 'tall, fair-haired, reserved and poetic-looking', most of which characteristics remained unchanged. Britten's phenomenal development as a composer for the opera house, which had begun in the USA, inevitably brought with it a comparable development in Pears, for whom Britten wrote an extraordinary number and variety of leading roles in almost all his principal operas, from *Peter Grimes* (1945) to *Death in Venice* (1973). It was in this last opera, dedicated to Pears, that Pears made his début at the Metropolitan Opera, New York, in 1974, at the age of sixty-four. But while it is true that Britten's operas shaped Pears's destiny as an opera singer, it must be remembered that Pears, on his return to England from America, had established himself independently as a notable member of the Sadler's Wells company, appearing in such roles as Alfredo in *La traviata*, Ferrando in *Così fan tutte*, the Duke in *Rigoletto*, Almaviva in *The Barber of Seville*, and Vašek in *The Bartered Bride*. His performances attracted critical attention for their exceptional musicality and intelligence, and admiration from Britten, who was often in the audience. It was his growing confidence in Pears's theatrical and vocal skills that enabled Britten to write the title role of *Peter Grimes* with Pears's voice in mind (he had at one time thought of Grimes as a baritone). The famous world première of the opera on 7 June 1945 placed the composer in the front rank of musical dramatists of his time and Pears as his principal interpreter.

It was not only as a singer that Pears and his unique voice had an influential role to play in Britten's operas. In one of them, *A Midsummer Night's Dream* (1960), he collaborated with the composer in converting Shakespeare's text into a libretto. He was also the inspiration of the long series of song sets and song cycles that Britten composed between 1940 (the *Seven Sonnets of Michelangelo*) and 1975 (*A Birthday Hansel*), a legacy of song perhaps without equal in the twentieth century. This rich fund of songs reflected the prowess of Pears and Britten as performers. They established themselves as one of the most celebrated and accomplished voice and piano duos of the post-war period, with an extensive repertory that included much of the work of Henry Purcell (when his songs were by no means the staple diet of recital programmes) and the great nineteenth-century classic song cycles—for example, Schubert's *Winterreise* and Schumann's *Dichterliebe*—in interpretations which themselves achieved classic status, and have been preserved on gramophone records. His partnership with the lute virtuoso Julian Bream became almost as celebrated, perhaps especially for performances of the Elizabethan master John Dowland, of incomparable sensitivity and skill from both singer and accompanist. Of equal note was Pears's Evangelist in the passions of Heinrich Schütz and J. S. Bach, roles to which he brought not only a predictable sensitivity but also an overwhelming sense of immediacy, as if he were a participant in the drama that was being unfolded. This was musical 'theatre' of an unusually exalted order.

Pears's life was inextricably interwoven with Britten's; until he suffered a slight stroke in 1973 as a result of his heart operation Britten was virtually the only pianist to accompany Pears. It involved strenuous recital tours at home and abroad, recording and broadcasting, and planning the policy of the English Opera Group (of which Pears was a co-founder, in 1947), and the programmes of the annual Aldeburgh festival (of which too he was a co-founder, in 1948). He played a leading role in both organizations as a performer and a stimulating, highly individual impresario.

Peter Pears was appointed CBE in 1957 and knighted in 1978. He received honorary degrees from several universities, and Keble College, Oxford, made him an honorary fellow in 1978. From 1957 he and Britten lived together in the Red House, Aldeburgh, Suffolk. After Britten's death in 1976 Pears continued to live in the house until his own death there on 3 April 1986. He was buried beside Britten in the churchyard of the parish church of St Peter and St Paul, Aldeburgh.

It was Britten's name, as opera and song composer and pianist, that was inevitably most closely associated with Pears's. But his distinctive interpretations of roles other than Britten roles will not be forgotten: his Tamino in *The Magic Flute*, Idomeneo (in Mozart's opera), David in *The Mastersingers*, and Pandarus in *Troilus and Cressida* by William Walton, were all marked by the exceptional musicality and intelligence that characterized him as a singer and, above all, by his exceptional response to, and articulation of, words. He was as sensitive to the sounds of words as he was to pitches. It was a gift that enabled him to bring even a 'dead' classical language to life, as in his masterly performance as Oedipus in Igor Stravinsky's opera–

oratorio, in which he collaborated with the composer. He was an enquiring and adventurous singer too, as the long list of first performances by living composers other than Britten amply demonstrates, among them commissions which he himself generously funded. His commitment to the singer's life and art, which had begun so tentatively in the 1930s, found further reflection in his later years when he was an active teacher in the Britten–Pears School for Advanced Musical Studies. This he had co-founded with Benjamin Britten in 1972, and, after the incapacitating stroke he suffered in 1980, which brought his career as a performer virtually to an end, he devoted more and more of his time to it. It was entirely appropriate that he should die at home at Aldeburgh, the focus of his personal and musical life for so many years, having completed, the day before, a full day's teaching at the school—a course, as it happened, on Bach's passions—passing on to future generations his own unique experience of music, of creative partnership, of the spectrum of the arts, and of life itself. It was the totality of all of these that coloured and informed Pears's voice and made it the unique instrument that it was. There were some who found it difficult to come to terms with its peculiar timbre. But his admirers worldwide rightly regarded it as a vehicle of civilization and sensibility without equal among English singers of his time.   DONALD MITCHELL, rev.

Sources C. Headington, *Peter Pears: a biography* (1992) · M. Thorpe, ed., *Peter Pears: a tribute on his 75th birthday* (1985) · *Letters from a life: selected letters and diaries of Benjamin Britten, 1913–1976*, ed. D. Mitchell and P. Reed, 2 vols. (1991) · personal knowledge (1996) · *The Times* (4 April 1986) · d. cert.
Archives Britten–Pears Library, Red House, Aldeburgh, Suffolk, papers | King's AC Cam., letters to G. H. W. Rylands
Likenesses K. Green, double portrait, oils, 1943 (with Benjamin Britten), NPG · photographs, 1945–67, Hult. Arch. · Fayer, photograph, 1950–59, NPG · G. Ehrlich, plaster cast for bronze head, 1963, NPG · R. Wilson, photograph, 1967, Rex Features Ltd, London [*see illus.*] · A. Newman, bromide print, *c*.1978, NPG
Wealth at death £641,777: probate, 30 Jan 1988, CGPLA Eng. & Wales

Pears, Steuart Adolphus (1815–1875), schoolmaster, was born at Pirbright, Surrey, on 20 November 1815, the seventh son of the Revd James Pears (1777/8–1853), headmaster of Bath grammar school, and brother of Sir Thomas Townsend *Pears. Pears was educated at Bath under his father, and was elected scholar of Corpus Christi College, Oxford, in 1832. After graduating BA in June 1836 with a second class in *literae humaniores*, he was elected fellow of Corpus, remaining in residence until 1838. He then became tutor to Lord Goderich (the first marquess of Ripon), of whom he took charge until 1842. In 1839 he gained the Ellerton theological prize for an essay entitled *The Conduct and Character of St Paul*, and in 1841 the Denyer theological prize for an essay entitled *The Divinity of Our Lord*. He was ordained deacon in 1839 and priest in 1842. In 1843 he was sent abroad by the Parker Society to search the libraries of Zürich and other places for correspondence relating to the English Reformation. In the course of his researches he discovered a number of original letters

in Latin from Sir Philip Sidney to his friend Hubert Languet, which he translated and published on his return (1845). During 1844 and 1845 he was in residence at Oxford as dean of Corpus Christi College. In 1846 he was appointed fellow and tutor of Durham University, and in 1847, at the age of thirty-two, assistant master at Harrow School under C. J. Vaughan. In December 1847 he married Catherine Temple (*d. c*.1866), the elder daughter of Temple *Chevallier, professor of mathematics and Hebrew in Durham University. He took the degrees of BD in 1846 and DD in 1851, when he published the sermons he delivered at Harrow, following these in 1852 with *Remarks on the Protestant Theory of Church Music*. He remained at Harrow until 1854, when he was elected headmaster of Repton School. At the time there were about fifty boys in the school, many of them village boys; the schoolhouse contained only two or three classrooms, and there were two boarding-houses.

Under Pears Repton achieved the standing of a leading public school. Influenced by the example of Rugby School during his period under Dr Vaughan, a pupil of Thomas Arnold, he instigated and helped to finance the building of a chapel following the celebration of the tercentenary of the school in 1857. At about the same time he built a boarding-house. Over the next few years, he built classrooms, fives-courts, and a library; and several other boarding-houses were erected during his headmastership. In 1862 the Repton School football rules were drawn up, and the first cricket fixture with Uppingham School was held in 1865. Pears published several school sermons, including *Short Sermons on the Elements of Christian Truth* (1861), *Sundays at School: Short Sermons Preached in Repton School Chapel* (1870), and various addresses, including *Mind and Body: and Moral Influence* (1855). He gave evidence in 1865 to the schools inquiry commission, chaired by Lord Taunton, when he indicated a commitment to the traditional curriculum and a scepticism towards the teaching of science. He attended the first Headmasters' Conference, held at Uppingham in 1869, and subsequently ensured that the new scheme for the constitution of Repton, agreed with the endowed schools' commissioners in 1874, secured its status as a first-grade school, catering for boys aged ten and over.

One of Pears's most distinguished pupils, William Sanday, recalled his 'spare rather tall figure' and 'his distinguished, somewhat worn and aquiline features'. He had a grave, almost austere, manner, and a natural dignity and authority, which did not need to be reinforced by corporal punishment (Macdonald, 174–5). The strain of seeing through the new constitution told on his health in the years following the death of his wife (*c*.1866), and he resigned the headmastership in 1874. On his retirement, pupil numbers had risen to nearly 300. Pears was shortly afterwards presented by the president and fellows of Corpus Christi College, Oxford, to the living of Childrey, Berkshire, where he died on 15 December 1875. A fine speech-room, named after him, was subsequently erected at Repton in his memory.   [ANON.], rev. M. C. CURTHOYS

Sources Boase, *Mod. Eng. biog.* · private information (1895) · A. Macdonald, *A short history of Repton* (1929) · *GM*, 2nd ser., 29 (1848), 304
Likenesses photograph, 1859, repro. in Macdonald, *Short history of Repton*, 177 · F. Grant, portrait · engraving (after F. Grant), repro. in Macdonald, *Short history of Repton*, 174
Wealth at death £18,000: resworn probate, Sept 1876, *CGPLA Eng. & Wales*

Pears, Sir Thomas Townsend (1809–1892), army officer in the East India Company, born on 9 May 1809, was the son of the Revd James Pears (1777/8–1853), headmaster of Bath grammar school, and the brother of Steuart Adolphus *Pears. He went to Addiscombe College in 1823, was commissioned lieutenant in the Madras engineers on 17 June 1825, and, after the usual Chatham course, sailed for India in late 1826. He was employed in the public works department, and became a superintending engineer as early as 1828.

Invalided to England in 1834, Pears returned to India overland through Persia in 1836, and was appointed commandant of the Madras sappers and miners. He was promoted second captain on 15 September 1838. In 1839, while still commanding his corps, he was appointed chief engineer with the field force employed in Karnal. After this expedition, which resulted in the capture of the fort and town of Karnal, and of the nawab, Pears was dispatched as field engineer with the force in China, and took part in the capture of the island of Chushan in 1840.

In 1841 Pears was appointed commanding engineer with the army in China under Sir Hugh Gough, and greatly distinguished himself. In Gough's dispatch of 3 October 1841, reporting the capture of the city of Tinghai (Dinghai), he stated that 'the scaling-ladders had been brought up in most difficult and rugged heights by the great exertions of the Madras sappers, and were gallantly planted under the direction of Captain Pears, who was the first to ascend'. After the capture of the fortified city and heights of Chapu (Zhapu), Pears was again mentioned for placing the powder bags which blew in the defences of a fort where a desperate resistance was offered. With the exception of the attack on Canton (Guangzhou) and the bombardment of Amoy (Xiamen), Pears was present as commanding engineer in every action of Gough's China campaign of 1841–2. He was repeatedly mentioned in dispatches, and at the close of the war was made brevet major on 23 December 1842, and CB.

On Pears's return to Madras he was employed in the public works department, as superintending engineer at Nagpur, and in various other responsible situations, chiefly in the inception and development of the railway system. From 1851 to 1857 he was the consulting engineer for railways to the government of Madras. He was then appointed chief engineer in the public works department for Mysore, and was the trusted adviser of Sir Mark Cubbon. He was promoted lieutenant-colonel on 1 August 1854, and colonel in the army on 1 August 1857. He retired on a pension on 8 February 1861 with the honorary rank of major-general, but, on his arrival in England, was offered, unsolicited, the appointment of military secretary at the India Office in succession to Sir William Baker.

When Pears took office under Sir Charles Wood (afterwards Lord Halifax) the duties were formidable and delicate, following the military reorganization after the abolition of the East India Company. Vested interests, often extravagantly asserted, had to be defended against often unreasonable attacks. Pears gained the trust of the ministers under whom he served—Sir Charles Wood, Sir Stafford Northcote, the duke of Argyll, and Lord Salisbury. The organization at home for the Abyssinian expedition of 1867 was entrusted to him, and Sir Stafford Northcote wrote to him expressing the highest appreciation. On 13 June 1871 he was appointed a civil KCB. He retired in 1877.

Pears had married, at Madras, on 31 December 1840, Bellina Marianne, daughter of Captain Charles Johnston of the Madras army. They had seven children, of whom six survived him. His eldest son, in the Bengal civil service, collector of Budaun, died at Allahabad in 1883. His second son, Major T. C. Pears, Bengal staff corps, became political agent at Alwar, Rajputana.

Pears's wife died at Putney on 17 January 1892. Pears died at his residence, Eton Lodge, Upper Richmond Road, Putney, on 7 October 1892, and was buried in Mortlake cemetery.
R. H. VETCH, *rev.* JAMES LUNT

Sources H. M. Vibart, *History of the Madras engineers* (1883) · H. M. Vibart, *Addiscombe: its heroes and men of note* (1894) · J. Ouchterlony, *The Chinese War* (1844) · BL OIOC · *Royal Engineers Journal* (Nov 1892) · V. C. P. Hodson, *List of officers of the Bengal army, 1758–1834*, 4 vols. (1927–47) · C. E. Buckland, *Dictionary of Indian biography* (1906) · Boase, *Mod. Eng. biog.* · Foster, *Alum. Oxon.*, 1715–1886 [James Pears, Steuart Adolphus Pears]
Archives BL OIOC, extract from overland journey to India, MS Eur. E 125 · BL OIOC, journal relating to Kurnool expedition and China War, MS Eur. B 368 | BL, letters to Sir Stafford Northcote, Add. MS 50030
Likenesses W. W. Ouless, portrait; in possession of Mrs Etherington-Smith in 1895 · portrait, repro. in *Daily Graphic* (12 Oct 1892)
Wealth at death £18,114 3s. 2d.: probate, 25 Nov 1892, *CGPLA Eng. & Wales*

Pearsall [*née* Gross], **Phyllis Isobel** (1906–1996), map publisher, was born on 25 September 1906 at Budapest, Court Lane Gardens, Dulwich, London. She was the younger of the two surviving children of Alexander Gross (formerly Grosz; 1880–1958), a Hungarian immigrant from Csurog, a village near Budapest, who was at that time selling oil lamps door to door, and his wife, Isabelle (1886–1937). Isabelle was a playwright and suffragette, and daughter of Arthur Crowley, a lapsed Irish Catholic priest and a dealer in second-hand pianos, of Peckham Rye, London, and his Italian wife. The artist (Imre) Anthony Sandor *Gross was Phyllis's brother.

After Alexander Gross had established Geographia—an initially successful map-publishing business—in 1907, the family began making annual visits to Hungary. Phyllis was sent to Roedean School in 1916 but when her father went bankrupt and fled to Chicago in 1920 her mother found her a job in France as a pupil teacher at the Collège des Jeunes Filles in Fécamp; she spent a year there before returning to England in 1922 to live with her grandparents in Worthing, where she attended the local convent school for two years. In 1924 she went to Paris and enrolled at the

Sorbonne, where she studied philosophy and Byzantine art for three years, supporting herself by writing for *John Bull*, an English-language magazine, translating, and giving English lessons. On 16 November 1927 she married Richard Montague Stack Pearsall, an artist fourteen years older than her and the son of William Booth Pearsall FRGS. For eight years they lived in Spain and travelled in Europe, before she left him in 1935; they were divorced in 1938. They published *Castilian Ochre: Travels with Brush and Pen*, an illustrated account of their travels in Spain, in 1935. Two of her etchings from this period, *The Cathedral, Toledo* and *Approach to Toledo* (both 1934) are in the permanent collection of the Victoria and Albert Museum.

Back in London in 1935 Phyllis Pearsall made a living painting portraits, but she was disillusioned by the pretentiousness of the art world and ready to take on a new challenge, and when she got lost one evening in the streets of London and subsequently realized that the most recent street map of London dated from 1919 she decided to produce her own. Starting with the Ordnance Survey sheets she walked the streets of London for eighteen hours a day, compiling a 23,000 card alphabetical index of streets, which she kept in shoeboxes under her bed, and produced the first *London A–Z Street Atlas* in 1936. After W. H. Smith had taken her first 250 copies the *A–Z* was in great demand, and she founded the Geographers' A to Z Map Co. Ltd in the same year. Her father had started a new map-publishing business in New York, producing street maps, and in order to help him re-establish himself as a map publisher in England she insisted, until his death in 1957, that all her publications carry the inscription 'produced under the direction of Alexander Gross', although he was not involved in the business in any way. She did all the research, printing, and distribution, and employed Mr Fountain, who had worked for her father, as her draughtsman. Her next publications included the *Premier Map of London*, *Thirty-Five Miles Round London*, and *London to the Sea*, as well as maps of England and Wales, and the world. As war became increasingly likely she turned her attention to war maps, producing maps of northern France, Norway and Denmark, the Netherlands and Belgium, and Finland. With government restrictions on the production of large-scale maps, in 1941 she joined the civil service, and worked in the home intelligence department of the Ministry of Information from 1942 to 1945, but at the end of the war she turned down the offer of a permanent senior civil service job at the Board of Trade and returned to the Geographers A to Z Map Co. Ltd.

Faced with paper shortages after the war Pearsall arranged to have a quarter of a million copies of the *A–Z* printed in Amsterdam, but on the return flight in November 1946 her plane crashed in the fog, and she fractured her skull and her spine. Her efforts to recover from her injuries and revive her business—with new titles including coloured premier maps of Birmingham, Manchester, and Leeds in 1950, and of Coventry and Glasgow in 1952—contributed to her suffering a severe stroke in 1952. It was during her slow recovery from this that she experienced

what she later described as a 'Damascene conversion' and became a 'born-again' Christian.

The company continued to bring out new titles—including quarter-inch maps of Wales (1957) and Scotland (1960) and a *Road Atlas of Great Britain* (1961)—and in 1962 moved from Gray's Inn Road to Sevenoaks, Kent. Chairman and managing director from 1957 and a multi-millionaire, Pearsall believed that a business should not be run solely for profit but also for the benefit of the employees, and in 1965 she set up the Geographers' Map Trust, transferring all her shares into it in order to safeguard the business against a takeover bid and to protect the jobs of her employees, some of whom worked for her for over forty years.

Pearsall continued to paint and write, especially from the late 1950s onwards, with regular exhibitions in London and elsewhere; her last exhibition, 'Alive with Joy', was in 1995 in the Little Gallery, Arundel. *Women, 1939–1940*, 'drawn and overheard by Phyllis Pearsall' (1985), and *Women at War* (1990) contained wartime drawings of women engaged in war work, with humorous captions; some of the originals are in the Museum of London. She published three autobiographical works: *Fleet Street, Tite Street, Queer Street* (1983), about her parents; *A–Z Maps: the Personal Story from Bedsitter to Household Name* (1990), a history of the company; and *An Artist's Pilgrimage in Business* (1993), which included her sketches of life in the office. She also published short stories, in the *New Yorker* and in a collection, *Only the Unexpected Happens* (1985).

Despite her bouts of ill health Pearsall, a tiny, frail-looking woman, remained chairman of the Geographers A to Z Map Co. Ltd until her death, though from the late 1950s she rarely visited the office, relying on her management team to run the business while she went on painting holidays in Europe. The fiftieth anniversary of the founding of the company, in 1986, was marked by an exhibition at the Royal Geographical Society; in that year she was appointed MBE. She died, of cancer, on 28 August 1996 at 5 Atlantic Court, Shoreham by Sea, Sussex, where she had lived since 1972. Her ashes were scattered in the garden of the A to Z office, at Borough Green, Sevenoaks, Kent.

ANNE PIMLOTT BAKER

Sources S. Hartley, *Mrs P's journey* (2001) · P. Pearsall, *Fleet Street, Tite Street, Queer Street* (1983) · P. Pearsall, *A–Z maps: the personal story from bedsitter to household name* (1990) · P. Pearsall, *An artist's pilgrimage in business* (1993) · *The Times* (29 Aug 1996) · *The Independent* (31 Aug 1996) · WWW · private information (2004) · m. cert. · d. cert.
Likenesses H. Turner, photograph, *c*.1940, repro. in Pearsall, *A–Z maps* · N. Syrett, photograph, 1988, repro. in Pearsall, *A–Z maps*, facing p. 199
Wealth at death £663,101: probate, 26 Nov 1996, *CGPLA Eng. & Wales*

Pearsall, Richard (1698–1762), Independent minister, was born and baptized at Kidderminster, Worcestershire, on 29 August 1698, the son of Nicholas and Anne Pearsall. Little is known of his early life, but it is said that his sisters Hannah and Phoebe encouraged him in faith. After Hannah married and became Hannah Housman, he published extracts of her diary in 1744 under the title *The Power and Pleasure of Divine Life*. Phoebe, who was married to Joseph

Williams of Kidderminster, was a correspondent of Philip Doddridge; her diary was published by the Society for Promoting Christian Knowledge. Richard grew up under the ministry of John Spilsbury and was educated at a dissenting academy at Tewkesbury under Samuel Jones. Joseph Butler and Thomas Secker were among his fellow students.

In a letter dated 18 December 1718 Pearsall wrote that he was setting out as a candidate for the ministry. He was ordained at Bromyard in Herefordshire in 1721, and succeeded Samuel Philips (d. 1721), whose daughter Anna he married at Avebury, Herefordshire, on 8 December 1724. They had two daughters. In 1731 he moved to Warminster in Wiltshire, where the church had divided after a dispute over charges of Arianism. From 1747 until 1762 he was minister of the Independent church at Taunton, Somerset. He conducted his last baptism in July 1762 and died at Taunton on 10 November 1762.

Pearsall was a keen correspondent, and wrote to Philip Doddridge, George Whitefield, and James Hervey among others. His friendship with Hervey may have encouraged him to attempt to write verse, and one of his poems was published in the *Gentleman's Magazine* (March 1736). After his death, under the title *Reliquiae sacrae* in 1765, Thomas Gibbons published a deathbed letter that Pearsall had written to his congregations, together with *Meditations on selected passages of scripture and sacred dialogues between a father and his children*. In addition to a few tracts, sermons, and letters Pearsall published contemplations on the ocean, harvest, sickness, and the last judgment (1753), which ran to several editions, and *Meditations on Butterflies: Philosophical and Devotional, in Two Letters to a Lady* (1758).

W. A. SHAW, rev. KAREN E. SMITH

Sources T. Gibbons, 'Memoir of the author', in R. Pearsall, *Reliquiae sacrae* (1765) [prefixed to] · *Evangelical Magazine*, 18 (1810), 377–81 · B. W. Kirk, *A history of Taunton United Reformed church* (1999) · *Calendar of the correspondence of Philip Doddridge*, ed. G. F. Nuttall, HMC, JP 26 (1979) · D. M. Lewis, ed., *The Blackwell dictionary of evangelical biography, 1730–1860*, 2 vols. (1995) · IGI
Archives DWL, letters, mainly to Doddridge
Likenesses W. Ridley, stipple, BM; repro. in *Evangelical Magazine*, 372

Pearsall, Robert Lucas (1795–1856), composer and antiquary, born at Clifton, Bristol, on 14 March 1795, was the son of Richard Pearsall, a former army officer and amateur musician, and his wife, Elizabeth Lucas, a descendant through her mother, Phillippa Still, of John Still, bishop of Bath and Wells. His mother had him privately educated with a view to a legal career. She also encouraged his musical talent; a cantata, *Saul and the Witch of Endor*, which he composed at about the age of thirteen, was privately published.

On 23 August 1817 Pearsall married Marie Henriette (or Harriet) Elizabeth Hobday, the daughter of William Armfield *Hobday and Elizabeth Dorothy, née Ivory; they had at least one son and two daughters. Pearsall was called to the bar in 1821, having kept terms at Lincoln's Inn, and was active as a barrister on the western circuit for four years, during which time he contributed regularly to a number of periodicals, including *Blackwood's Magazine*. In 1825, however, he went abroad, ostensibly for the sake of his health, and pursued his passions for music, history, heraldry, and genealogy. His earliest extant compositions date from this period: a minuet and trio in B♭ is dated 14 July 1825 at Willsbridge House, the family's seat near Bristol. At about the same time the well-known 'Duetto for [Two Cats]' (the last two words are represented on the title-page of the first edition by a drawing of two cats), which has sometimes been attributed to Rossini, was published by Ewer and Johanning under the pseudonym G. Berthold; the piece exists in Pearsall's autograph, and Edgar Hunt has persuasively argued that he was the composer of the work. For four years Pearsall studied music with Joseph Panny in Mainz, where he became interested in the Cecilian movement and composed a number of Latin motets in the 'strict style'.

In 1829 Pearsall revisited Willsbridge, leaving his family in Germany, but returned to the continent the following year and, for the sake of his children's education, settled in Karlsruhe, which remained his principal residence for the next twelve years. During this time, however, he travelled widely, pursuing his antiquarian and musical interests. In Munich in 1832 he met Caspar Ett (1788–1847), from whom he learned to transcribe early musical notation; in Vienna he formed a lasting friendship with the musicologist Raphael Georg Kiesewetter (1773–1850); and in Nuremberg he investigated a mode of torture known as 'the kiss of the virgin', which he described in *Archaeologia*, 27 (1838), 229–50. In these years he wrote a number of works with orchestra, including *Die Nacht eines Schwärmers* (1834), a 'ballet with songs', which was performed in the theatre he had built at his Karlsruhe residence, and the overture *Macbeth*, with witches' chorus (1839).

On the death of his mother in May 1836 Pearsall returned to England, where he remained until he sold Willsbridge a year later. In January 1837 he was a founder member of the Bristol Madrigal Society, by which many of his early madrigals, based on Thomas Morley's ballets, were performed. The success of these pieces encouraged him to write further madrigals and partsongs, some for many voices. 'The Hardy Norseman' and 'Sir Patrick Spens', in ten parts, and the eight-part settings of 'Great God of love' and 'Lay a garland on her hearse' were considered to be 'amongst the finest specimens of English part-writing' (*DNB*). His arrangement of the old melody *In dulci jubilo* (for eight solo voices and five-part chorus in his original version) is still a favourite Christmas song. It is on these compositions, though few are currently performed, that his significance as a composer principally rests; however, Pearsall himself considered his Requiem to be his finest work. Among his literary works at this time was a booklet, published anonymously in Karlsruhe, entitled *A few remarks on the position of the baronets of Great-Britain and the other branches of the British gentry, compared with that of the lesser nobility both at home and abroad, by a traveller*, of which a considerably enlarged version was published in London the following year. It was reissued several times. His other writings included an article in German on the origin and history of the English madrigal, which he contributed to the *Zeitschrift für Deutschlands Musik-Vereine* in 1842.

In that year Pearsall bought the castle of Wartensee on Lake Constance, Switzerland, which had previously belonged to his old teacher Schnyder von Wartensee, and at about the same time he separated from his wife. Apart from a short visit to England in 1847, he lived at Wartensee, restoring the castle and entertaining distinguished musicians, writers, and archaeologists until 1854, when he transferred ownership of the castle to his wife and son and took up residence in nearby St Gallen, Switzerland. During these years he continued to devote himself intensively to musical, literary, and artistic activities, making translations into English verse of Goethe's *Faust* and Schiller's *Wilhelm Tell*, writing several treatises on church music which he did not publish ('Observations on chanting', 'Musica sacra Gregoriana', 'Psalmodia: an essay on psalm tunes'), helping to edit the old St Gallen hymnbook, which was published in 1863 as *Katholisches Gesangbuch zum Gebrauch bei dem öffentlichen Gottesdienste*, and assisting in illustrating Hefter's *Geschichte der Geräthschaften des Mittelalters*. In 1856 he became ill and moved back to Wartensee, where his wife cared for him until he died, apparently of a stroke, on 5 August 1856. Three days before his death he was received into the Roman Catholic church by his friend the bishop of St Gallen. He was buried in the chapel of Wartensee Castle on 12 August.

CLIVE BROWN

Sources E. Hunt and H. W. Hunt, *Robert Lucas Pearsall, the 'compleat gentleman' and his music, 1795–1856* (1971) · E. Hunt, 'Robert Lucas Pearsall', *Proceedings of the Royal Musical Association*, 82 (1955–6), 75–88 · 'Robert Lucas Pearsall', *Musical Herald* (Aug 1906), 227–31 · E. de St Maurice Cabany, *Notice nécrologique sur R. L. de Pearsall* (1856) · H. W. Hunt, *Robert Lucas Pearsall and the Bristol Madrigal Society* (1916) · W. B. Squire, 'Letters of Robert Lucas Pearsall', *Musical Quarterly*, 5 (1919), 264–97 · *Musical Quarterly*, 6 (1920), 296 · W. B. Squire, 'Pearsall's letters', *MT*, 61 (1920), 662–5; 63 (1922), 318–19; 64 (1923), 359–60; 65 (1924), 24–8 · [J. S. Gassner], 'Pearsall, R. L.', *Encyclopaedie des gesammten musikalischen Wissenschaften*, ed. G. Schilling, 7 (1842), suppl. 96 · J. Marshall, 'Pearsall: a memoir', *MT*, 23 (1882), 376–6 · E. Hunt, ed., *Duetto for [two cats] by G. Berthold* (1973) · N. Temperley, 'Pearsall, Robert Lucas', *New Grove*
Archives BL, writings, corresp., MS music · NRA, priv. coll., MS music and corresp.
Likenesses P. S. Hughes, oils, 1849, NPG · watercolour drawing, Bristol City Museum and Art Gallery

Pearsall, William Harold (1891–1964), ecologist and botanist, was born at Stourbridge, Worcestershire, on 23 July 1891, the only son and second of the three children of William Harrison Pearsall, schoolmaster and Methodist lay preacher, and his wife, Mary Elizabeth Green, of Earl Shilton, Leicester. The family moved to Dalton in Furness when Pearsall was quite young; his father had been appointed headmaster of Broughton Road School in that town. Pearsall attended his father's school until 1905 and then went to Ulverston grammar school. In 1909 he was admitted to the University of Manchester to read chemistry. However, after his first year he changed to botany, graduating with first-class honours in 1913. From his earliest days he had accompanied his father, a keen amateur

William Harold Pearsall (1891–1964), by Elliott & Fry, 1948

naturalist with whom he later co-authored several scientific papers, on frequent excursions into the Lake District, where they had searched for water plants using a homemade boat launched dredger. A university graduate scholarship enabled him to devote himself to a systematic study of the distribution of aquatic plants in the English lakes. He was awarded his MSc in 1915 and in the following year he joined the Royal Garrison Artillery and saw active service in France, returning to civilian life in 1919 with troublesome hearing loss.

During the war, in 1917, Pearsall married Marjory Stewart, second child of Robert Peter George Williamson, director of education, of Stoke-on-Trent. She was herself a first-class honours graduate in botany of Manchester, where she was a fellow student of Pearsall's, and later lecturer in botany at Birmingham and then at Leeds. There were two sons, Alan William Harrison, a historian, and Ian Stewart, an engineer.

In 1919 Pearsall became an assistant lecturer under Professor J. H. Priestley at Leeds University. In the following year he was promoted to a full lectureship and was awarded a DSc by Manchester University for his researches on the English lakes. In 1922 he was made reader in botany at Leeds and in 1938 he was appointed professor of botany at Sheffield University. He was elected FRS in 1940 and in 1944 succeeded E. J. Salisbury in the Quain chair of botany at University College, London, retaining it until his retirement in 1957. He was well regarded at University College for both his teaching and his administrative flair, and many of his students acquired from his field excursions a lasting interest in the countryside.

Pearsall's earliest scientific publications (1917–21) related to his postgraduate studies of lakes and their vegetation. Consideration of the mode of erosion of wave exposed shores, and of the redeposition of the removed material, enabled him to explain the distribution of plant communities in and around Esthwaite Water. The shore vegetation at the north end of the lake was of special interest because it changed with distance from the mouth of the inflow stream which carried most of the incoming silt. Pearsall carefully mapped the plant communities, showing their relation to the water margin and to the fineness and chemical content of the accumulating sediments. When he remapped the area in 1929 all the zones had advanced into or towards the open water. The general interest aroused by this direct demonstration of plant succession led to the declaration of the North Fen as a national nature reserve in 1954 and to a further mapping in 1967–9 by a group from Lancaster University.

Pearsall next looked at the lakes as a whole in an attempt to account for differences between them. Since all occupy ice deepened rock basins which became ice free at much the same time, he argued that their present differences must have arisen from differing rates of subsequent change. The rocky lakes like Wastwater and Ennerdale must be relatively primitive, the much silted lakes like Windermere and Esthwaite must therefore be more advanced. The rocky lakes have very clear water, poor in dissolved substances, scanty vegetation, and trout as the most abundant fish. The silted lakes have water less clear but richer in plant nutrients, much more vegetation, and perch, pike, and eels as the typical fish. The publication in 1921 reporting these findings is typical of both the boldness of Pearsall's inferences from a large body of fieldwork and the simplicity of his resulting synthesis. Pearsall's work stimulated much further research, but doubts arose later when the analysis of deep lake sediments showed that there had in fact been great variations in rates of change and some reversals of direction. However, these ultimately proved explicable in the light of ideas largely suggested by Pearsall himself, resulting in a less simple, but more ecologically interesting, story.

From 1937 Pearsall's research included work on the ecological significance of the electric potentials of natural soils, which he interpreted as oxidation-reduction potentials. There were further valuable contributions on soils and studies on bogs. In his presidential address to section K of the British Association in 1954 he drew attention to the increasingly urgent problems of world food production. There followed a series of papers by himself and former pupils on production ecology which undoubtedly influenced the choice of biological productivity as one of two major topics for the International Biological Programme.

In 1950 Pearsall published *Mountains and Moorlands*, a work in which he drew on all his vast knowledge of Britain's highland zone and on his capacity for creative imagination and lucid writing. Although written primarily for the amateur naturalist, it nevertheless provided the university student with an unrivalled introduction to the scientific analysis of familiar ecological phenomena. His *Report on an Ecological Survey of Serengeti National Park, Tanganyika* (1956) was a classic of ecological literature.

Pearsall was one of three biologists principally involved in seeking to establish a British centre for lake research, efforts which led to the foundation of the Freshwater Biological Association in 1929. Pearsall was closely involved from the start in the development of the association's research, playing a very active role in guiding, encouraging, and inspiring the research workers until the end of his life.

Pearsall joined the British Ecological Society soon after its foundation and began his term as president in 1936. From 1937 to 1947 he edited the society's *Journal of Ecology*. His presidential address on 'The soil complex in relation to plant communities' was one of his most lauded achievements. He was editor of *Annals of Botany* from 1948 to 1961 and at the time of his death he was secretary of the Annals of Botany Company. He had a vision of the need for the conservation of nature long before it became fashionable and, with other prominent naturalists, played an important part in the creation of the Nature Conservancy, which was established in 1949, becoming a charter member. He was chairman of its scientific policy committee from 1953 to 1963. This enabled him to exert a powerful influence for the application of critical scientific thought to problems of nature conservation.

A number of academic and other honours came to Pearsall. He was honorary DSc of Durham (1958) and Birmingham (1963) universities and received the Linnean Society's gold medal for botany in 1963. He was made an honorary member of the British Ecological Society and the Society for Experimental Biology, and a foreign member of the Swedish Phytogeographical Society. He was a fellow of the Institute of Biology and its president in 1957–8.

Pearsall was of tall and slender but athletic build and, with a small close clipped moustache, had something of the military in his aspect. He was blue eyed, with fair hair and a pale skin. He always appeared vigorous and purposeful, most so, perhaps, when he was striding with obvious enjoyment across a moor or up a mountain, his companions trailing behind him. Those who met him for the first time were at once impressed by his wide knowledge and capacity for penetrating analysis, but they soon discovered his modesty and humanity and an endearing gaiety of spirit. He enjoyed fly-fishing, drawing in pen and ink or watercolour, and golf.

Pearsall died at the Victoria Hospital, Morecambe and Heysham, on 14 October 1964 of a brain tumour. His wife and sons survived him.

A. R. CLAPHAM, *rev.* GHILLEAN T. PRANCE

Sources A. R. Clapham, *Memoirs FRS*, 17 (1971), 511–40 · E. B. Worthington, *Proceedings of the Linnean Society of London*, 177 (1966), 121–2 · editorial, *The Naturalist* (Jan 1937), 1–2 · *Annals of Botany*, new ser., 29 (1965) · *CGPLA Eng. & Wales* (1965)

Archives Cumbria AS, Kendal, corresp. and MSS · Freshwater Biological Association Library, Ambleside, Cumbria, MSS | University of Sheffield, corresp. with Arthur Roy Clapham

Likenesses Elliott & Fry, photograph, 1948, NPG [see illus.] · D. Banner, pencil drawing, Freshwater Biological Association, Ambleside, Cumbria; repro. in Clapham, *Memoirs FRS*, 510 · photograph (in youth), repro. in *The Naturalist*, 3

Wealth at death £14,498: administration, 24 May 1965, *CGPLA Eng. & Wales*

Pearse, Edward (*c*.1633–1673), clergyman and ejected minister, matriculated as a servitor from St John's College, Oxford, on 10 April 1652 and graduated BA on 27 June 1654. Of his parents it is known only that his mother's name was Anne and that she survived her son. On 27 June 1657 Edward Pearse was appointed Sunday morning preacher in the parish of St Margaret's, Westminster, and on 31 December that year his salary was increased by 50s. a year; he was appointed lecturer at Westminster Abbey on 20 May 1658. After his ejection in 1660, Pearse's whereabouts are not certainly known. *A Beam of Divine Glory … whereunto is Added The Soul's Rest in God*, published posthumously in 1674, contained 'Mr Pearse's last letter To my dearly beloved friends, to whom, by the providence of God, I have some years last past preached the Everlasting gospel'. Perhaps his ministry was at or near Hampstead, for it was from there that the author signed his letter on 3 October 1672, during his last illness. He died, probably from tuberculosis, aged about forty according to Calamy, after the drafting of a codicil to his will on 21 March 1673, and before the grant of probate on 5 June following. In his will Pearse gave his wife's name as Grace and left provision for a daughter Sarah, aged less than ten years.

Pearse has previously sometimes been confused with Edward *Pierce (1630/31–1694), Church of England clergyman, but neither Edward Pearse nor Edward Pierce appears to have been related to **William Pearse** (*bap.* 1626, *d.* 1691), clergyman and ejected minister, who was born at Ermington, Devon, and baptized, probably at Ermington, on 26 January 1626, the son of Francis Pearse of Ermington. He attended school at Plympton St Mary and studied at Exeter College, Oxford, from 1649 to 1652. On 7 December 1655 he was admitted as vicar of the sequestered living of Dunsford, Devon, and he was ordained on 15 September 1659 by presbyters at Wolborough. After his ejection in 1660 Pearse returned to Ermington and rented Stretch-leigh Barten, 'being well skilled in Husbandry' (*Calamy rev.*). In 1669 Pearse succeeded as minister to the congregation which met at Tavistock Abbey, home of the earl of Bedford; he preached at the abbey for some nineteen years. At an unknown date he married. His wife's name was Mary, and they had at least two sons, Francis and William, and four daughters, Mary, Elizabeth, Agnes, and Damaris. In April 1672 he received a general presbyterian licence as of Dunsford, but he met with much official harassment: 'Six times a Year the Bailiff came to Stretch-leigh-house, to warn Mr. Pearse and his Wife, with his Son and Daughters, to appear at the Assizes at Exeter, to answer for Riots … and not obeying the Laws' (ibid.). Pearse moved to London, but found that it, too, was

dangerous for dissenters. On 21 January 1683 the authorities raided Stephen Lobb's meeting-place and 'seiz'd one Mr. Pearse and one Marmaduke Roberts both Preachers, who were both committed to New Prison' (ibid.). By 1690 Pearse had returned to Devon, where he acted as co-pastor with Thomas Palke at Ashburton. He was instrumental in building a meeting-house in the town and signed his will there on 2 April 1690. William Pearse died at Ashburton on 17 March 1691 and was buried in the town.

A. F. POLLARD, *rev.* STEPHEN WRIGHT

Sources *Calamy rev.* · Foster, *Alum. Oxon.* · E. Pearse, *A beam of divine glory … whereunto is added The soul's rest in God* (1674) · E. Calamy, ed., *An abridgement of Mr. Baxter's history of his life and times, with an account of the ministers, &c., who were ejected after the Restauration of King Charles II*, 2nd edn, 2 vols. (1713) · H. I. Longden, *Northamptonshire and Rutland clergy from 1500*, ed. P. I. King and others, 16 vols. in 6, Northamptonshire RS (1938–52) · Wood, *Ath. Oxon.*, new edn · J. T. Cliffe, *The puritan gentry besieged, 1650–1700* (1993) · C. Whiting, *Studies in English puritanism* (1931) · G. Cragg, *Puritanism in the period of the great persecution* (1957) · *Calendar of the correspondence of Richard Baxter*, ed. N. H. Keeble and G. F. Nuttall, 2 vols. (1991) · J. Bridges, *The history and antiquities of Northamptonshire*, ed. P. Whalley, 2 vols. (1791) · IGI · A. Gordon, ed., *Freedom after ejection: a review (1690–1692) of presbyterian and congregational nonconformity in England and Wales* (1917) · T. Kingdom, 'The cause of Independency in Tavistock', *Transactions of the Congregational Historical Society*, 4 (1909–10), 55–8 · will

Likenesses R. White, line engraving, 1673, NPG · engraving (in his early thirties), repro. in Pearse, *A beam of divine glory*

Pearse, John (*bap.* 1759, *d.* 1836), clothier and financier, was baptized at St Margaret's, Lothbury, London, on 19 December 1759, the eldest of the three sons of Nicholas Pearse (*d.* 1795), clothier, and his wife, Sarah (*d.* in or after 1770). Nicholas Pearse traded as Pearse and Bowden, Blackwell Hall factors, with premises at 41 Lothbury, City of London, and country houses at Woodford, Essex, and Heddington, Wiltshire. John Pearse was taken into partnership in Pearse and Bowden in 1780. He married, on 31 January 1787, Anne (*d.* in or after 1835), daughter and coheir of John Phillimore, silk merchant, of 15 New Broad Street, London; three sons and three daughters were born of the marriage. Phillimore died early in 1795, leaving £35,000 to Anne and £10,000 to John, who inherited another £30,000 when his own father died later that year.

Before this considerable increase in his material fortune Pearse had become involved with the Bank of England, where he served as a director (1790–91, 1793–8), as deputy governor (1799–1810), and as governor (1810–12), thereafter reverting to director until 1828. When the bank was confronted by the threat of invasion by Napoleon's troops in 1803, a 400-strong volunteer militia was raised from among the employees, which Pearse captained, and the important books and records were transferred to country houses for safe keeping; from 1806 to 1816 Pearse's home, Chilton Lodge, Chilton Foliat, Wiltshire (near Hungerford, Berkshire), was so used. From 1826 until his death in 1836 he was a governor of the Van Diemen's Land Company which traded with the colony of Van Diemen's Land.

Pearse and his family were also employed in the Sun Fire insurance office. His father was a manager from 1767 to

1795, he himself acted as one from 1785 until his death, and his brother Brice Pearse (1770–1842), of Monkhams in Essex, from 1803 to 1842. Brice's son and grandson continued the connection until 1875.

Pearse came into the public arena by signing the London merchants' declaration of loyalty to the administration of William Pitt the younger in 1795. Two years later he gave £10,000 through the bank and £1000 in a private capacity to the loyalty loan. His dealings as a clothier were denounced as corrupt profiteering in the House of Commons, where it was claimed that he had secured the contract to supply army greatcoats by undercutting his competitors with a bid of 16s., such garments being inevitably of inferior quality—'when he had signed the contract he ran off to Fenchurch Street, to a slopseller there, and agreed to pay him at the rate of 13s each' (*The Times*, 25 June 1808, 3b). Pearse's brothers, Nicholas and Brice, joined him in business, first at Lothbury and later at Long Acre, trading as J. and B. Pearse.

Chilton Foliat estate was acquired about 1806 and in 1807 Pearse bought the manor of Hidden to add to it. In 1835 he and his wife Anne settled both holdings on their son John, but are said to have sold them on later that year to the Revd Sir William Henry Cooper (*VCH Berkshire*, 4.193). Pearse also bought the manor of Hungerford Englefield in 1811.

Pearse's ambitions were not bounded by finance and commerce in the City of London. In 1818 he became MP for Devizes in Wiltshire, holding the seat until 1832 as a respected constituency figure and speaking regularly in the House of Commons where he was a recognized expert on financial matters. In 1819 he was consulted on the resumption of cash payments, and he supported post-war repressive measures in the autumn of that year. According to Thomas Moore he was 'a good hearty jolly man of the world; knows everybody; was intimate with Sheridan' (HoP, *Commons*). He died on 21 July 1836 at Craig's Court, Charing Cross, Westminster, London, leaving instructions that he was to be buried at Chilton Foliat.

PETER M. CLAUS

Sources R. G. Thorne, 'Pearse, John', HoP, *Commons* · *GM*, 2nd ser., 6 (1836), 220–31 · E. Bradby, *The book of Devizes* (1985) · W. M. Acres, 'Directors of the Bank of England', *N&Q*, 179 (1940), 131–4, esp. 133 · P. G. M. Dickson, *The Sun Insurance office, 1710–1860* (1960) · W. M. Acres, *The Bank of England from within, 1694–1900*, 1 (1931) · *VCH Berkshire* · *The Times* (25 June 1808), 3b · will, proved March 1795, PROB 11/1255 [John Phillimore] · will, proved December 1795, PROB 11/1269 [Nicholas Pearse] · J. Clapham, *The Bank of England: a history*, 2 vols. (1944) · parish register (baptism), London St Margaret's, Lothbury, 19 Dec 1759

Pearse, Patrick Henry (1879–1916), writer and Irish revolutionary, was born on 10 November 1879 at 27 Great Brunswick Street, Dublin, the elder son and second of the four children of James Pearse (1839–1900), stone carver, of London, Birmingham, and Dublin, and his second wife, Margaret, a shop assistant, one of two surviving daughters of Patrick Brady, coal factor, of Dublin.

Always exceptionally imaginative, young Pearse was greatly influenced by his maternal aunt Margaret, who stirred his romantic soul with patriotic ballads of death

Patrick Henry Pearse (1879–1916), by unknown photographer [detail]

and exile, tales of mythological Irish heroes, and hagiographical accounts of such doomed revolutionary leaders as Wolfe Tone and Robert Emmet. Like many children of his time he fantasized about becoming a hero, but his was a morbid preoccupation with suffering and dying for his country or his religion: his heroes had died painful deaths and his main religious devotion was to the crucified Christ.

Two Christian Brothers at his secondary school in Westland Row, Dublin, helped to spark in Pearse an uncritical passion for the Irish language and its literature: his view of Ireland past, present, and future was always to have mystical overtones. To him, the reputed feats of mythological heroes were real, and the dead whom he admired had mythological status.

At sixteen Pearse joined the Gaelic League, and henceforward took every opportunity to improve both his public speaking and his writing, in both English and Irish; before he was twenty he had published *Three Lectures on Gaelic Topics*. Able and industrious rather than brilliant, in 1901 he took a good second-class BA from University College, Dublin, in English, French, and Irish, won an exhibition, and was called to the bar, having studied for a BL at Trinity College, Dublin, and the King's Inns.

After his father's death in 1900 Pearse became head of his family, and with his brother, Willie—an artist and sculptor of slight talent—he tried and failed to keep the family firm prosperous until its final dissolution in 1910. None of the siblings married; Pearse himself seems to have been unconsciously homosexual. His mother, Willie, and his two sisters were all emotionally dependent on him, for though he was reserved and socially uneasy—especially with women—he had a strong personality and his passion for his causes was inspiring. Slightly above average height, of sturdy build, he was always self-conscious about an eye disfigurement; in maturity his was a solemn and imposing presence.

As a lecturer, committee man, writer, and teacher of Irish, Pearse was respected within the Gaelic League for his dedication, prodigious appetite for work, and high-mindedness, though his reserve precluded popularity. From 1903 to 1909 he was paid editor of the league organ, *An Claidheamh Soluis*. Although the league had to control his over-ambition and financial recklessness he was a success because of his enthusiasm and industry, and because of his innumerable thoughtful, passionate, and often provocative and courageous articles on such topics as education, history, literature, politics, religion, and theatre. Unlike many elements in Irish-Ireland, he was a modernizer who, for instance, put aside his youthful prejudices against Irish literature in the English language to welcome the contribution to literature of controversial figures like J. M. Synge and W. B. Yeats, and who embraced the Belgian model of bilingualism with enthusiasm. In his twenties the Irish language was his paramount concern: in its interests, although himself a nationalist, he praised certain measures of the British government, and, although a devout Catholic, on occasion fiercely criticized the Irish clergy.

During this period Pearse taught Irish extensively, and in 1908 founded St Enda's, a boys' bilingual secondary school (in 1910 he founded a girls' school, St Ita's, which collapsed two years later). He was a gifted, humane, and exciting—even mesmerizing—headmaster with a talented staff, and his selflessness and nobility were inspiring: the school was initially a triumph. In 1910, irresponsibly, he moved St Enda's to grand premises outside Dublin, where perforce it became a boarding-school. Henceforward he fought a constant battle to avoid bankruptcy. James Stephens wrote that 'when something had to be done he did it, and entirely disregarded logic or economics or force' (Dudley Edwards, 1990, edn, 343). As with teaching and journalism, so with literature: he developed what talent he had to the full, writing short stories, poems, and plays in Irish and English, which ranged from the mawkish to the genuinely moving.

Until 1910 Pearse's nationalist preoccupation was cultural: the school, like his other activities, was geared to spread the gospel of Gaelic-Ireland. But as he became disillusioned with the language movement and worn down by financial worries he increasingly developed his romantic and morbid fascination with people who had died in hopeless revolt; martyrdom became an important theme. In 1912 he called publicly for support for the Home Rule Bill, while threatening revolution if it were not passed. Yeats thought him 'a dangerous man; he has the vertigo of self-sacrifice' (Dudley Edwards, 1990, edn, 335).

The foundation in November 1912 of the anti-home rule Ulster Volunteers led a year later to the counter-balancing Irish Volunteers, of which Pearse was a co-founder and in which he was a highly enthusiastic participant at a senior level. Shortly afterwards he joined the Irish Republican Brotherhood (IRB) and went to America to raise funds for St Enda's. Mixing with hardline Irish-Americans who wanted only to hear that insurrection was nigh set him single-mindedly on a revolutionary course. Back home, valued by the IRB strategists as a fine and passionate orator and a highly persuasive political propagandist, in 1915

he was brought into their inner circle. In 1916 he published several political pamphlets justifying a military uprising, and on Easter Monday he and six IRB colleagues issued a proclamation declaring an Irish republic; Pearse was designated commandant-general and president of the provisional republic. A thousand Irish Volunteers and 120 members of the Irish Citizen Army formed by James Connolly took over major Dublin buildings. Pearse and Connolly were based in the General Post Office, with Connolly directing operations and Pearse producing morale-boosting propaganda. As a consequence of the fighting between the rebels and the British army about 250 uninvolved civilians were killed; on Saturday 29 April, Pearse surrendered to avoid further deaths. He was court-martialled and on 3 May 1916 executed by a firing squad in Kilmainham gaol, Dublin, as, on 4 May, was his brother, Willie, who had acted as his aide-de-camp. He was buried in the gaol. As the figurehead of the rising, and the author of memorable verse and prose in which militarism was equated with heroic self-sacrifice, Pearse became the most famous of the fifteen executed rebels and the centre of a powerful mythology: each generation of irredentist republicans has cited his uncompromising words in justification of their terror campaigns.

RUTH DUDLEY EDWARDS

Sources R. Dudley Edwards, *Patrick Pearse: the triumph of failure* (1977) · B. P. Murphy, *Patrick Pearse and the lost republican ideal* (1991) · *The letters of P. H. Pearse*, ed. S. O'Buachalla (1980) · D. Ryan, *Remembering Sion* (1934)

Archives NL Ire., corresp. with his family · Pearse Museum, St Enda's Park, Dublin, MSS · TCD, family papars | NL Ire., letters to John L. Burke · NL Ire., letters to J. J. Doyle · NL Ire., letters to Sean O'Kelly

Likenesses photograph, Hult. Arch. [*see illus.*] · portraits (posthumous), probably Pearse Museum, St Enda's Park, Dublin

Wealth at death virtually penniless

Pearse, Thomas Deane (1741/2–1789), army officer in the East India Company, was the son of Captain Thomas Pearse RN and his wife, Martha Purvis. After training at the Royal Military Academy, Woolwich, Pearse was appointed a fireworker in the Royal Artillery and saw service at St Malo and Cherbourg (1758), Martinique and Guadeloupe (1759), Belle Île (1761), and Havana (1762). He was appointed second lieutenant on 24 October 1761, and first lieutenant on 3 February 1766. In February 1768 he transferred to the East India Company service, becoming major in the Bengal artillery on 2 September 1768, lieutenant-colonel on 30 October 1769, and colonel on 22 January 1781. In 1775 he took command of the Bengal artillery, to which he introduced many reforms, confiding to a friend that he was 'astonished at the ignorance of all who composed [the corps]' (Buckle, 31). It had become clear from early campaign experience in India that British armies needed substantial field artillery in order to balance the invariably greater numbers of opposing Indian armies with greater firepower. In Pearse's time the Bengal artillery was expanded from five companies in 1770 to an independent brigade of a European regiment and three Indian battalions of over 3000 men by 1778.

Pearse was high in the favour of Warren Hastings, the

governor-general, and acted as Hastings's second in his duel with Philip Francis on 17 August 1780. In 1781, at the height of the Second Anglo-Mysore War, between Madras and Haidar Ali of Mysore in the Carnatic, Hastings decided to send a detachment of five regiments of sepoys and a detail of field artillery from Bengal to relieve the Madras presidency at Fort St George, and gave the command to Pearse. This provoked strong protests from infantry colleagues who believed that, as in the royal army, commands should not be given to artillerymen. The detachment proceeded south from Bengal near the coast on its march through Orissa and the Northern Circars and, having reached the vicinity of Madras in July 1781, it joined the Madras field army under the commander-in-chief, Sir Eyre Coote. During the ensuing arduous warfare in which they were engaged until the end of the war in June 1783, the Bengal corps, under Pearse, attained a lasting reputation for its actions in the battles of Polillur (27 August 1781) and Sholinghur (27 September 1781) against Haidar Ali, and in the attack on the French lines at Cuddalore near Fort St David (13 June 1783), the last being one of the first occasions on which European and Indian troops fought one another at bayonet point.

Some 2000 veterans of the original 5000 Bengal troops returned to Bengal with Pearse early in 1785, where they were congratulated for their services by Warren Hastings in person; Pearse was later awarded a sword of honour. He was made second in command of the Bengal army in July 1787. During his command of the Bengal artillery, Pearse had transformed an ill-equipped, poorly managed corps into a thoroughly professional force capable of filling the major role required of it. His wider interests were revealed by his foundation of a school to teach his men to read. In 1785 he contributed a paper entitled 'Two Hindu festivals and the Indian sphinx' to the Asiatic Society of Bengal; it was subsequently published in Dublin in *Dissertations and miscellaneous pieces relating to the history and antiquities … of Asia, by Sir W. Jones … and others* (1793). Pearse was married to an Indian, Panna Purree (*d.* 1820). He died on the River Ganges near Serampore, Bengal, on 15 June 1789.   B. H. SOULSBY, *rev.* G. J. BRYANT

Sources Madras and Bengal secret consultations, BL OIOC · E. Buckle, *Memoir of the services of the Bengal artillery from the formation of the corps to the present time with some account of its internal organization*, ed. J. W. Kaye (1852) · 'A memoir of Colonel Thomas Deane Pearse of the Bengal artillery, pt 1', *Bengal Past and Present*, 2 (1908), 305–23, 459–96 · 'A memoir of Colonel Thomas Deane Pearse of the Bengal artillery, pt 2', *Bengal Past and Present*, 4 (1909), 519–32 · 'A memoir of Colonel Thomas Deane Pearse of the Bengal artillery, pt 3', *Bengal Past and Present*, 5 (1910), 244–60, esp. 245, 251 · V. C. P. Hodson, *List of officers of the Bengal army, 1758–1834*, 4 vols. (1927–47) · J. Philippart, *East India military calendar*, 3 vols. (1823–6) · BL, Warren Hastings MSS, Add. MSS 29147–29193
Archives RS, meteorological journals | BL, corresp. with Warren Hastings, Add. MSS 29147–29193, *passim* · BL OIOC, Madras and Bengal secret consultations
Likenesses portrait, Royal Artillery Institution, Woolwich, London

Pearse, William (*bap.* 1626, *d.* 1691). See *under* Pearse, Edward (*c*.1633–1673).

Pearson. *See also* Peirson, Pierson.

Pearson, Alexander, Lord Southall (*d.* 1657), judge, was the son of Alexander Pearson, an Edinburgh merchant and bailie who represented the burgh at conventions of estates and parliament, and his wife, Bessie Eiston. He graduated from the University of Edinburgh in 1605 and was admitted advocate, acting as counsel for Lord Balmerino in his trial in 1634. He married Christian (*d.* 1659), daughter of William Rigg of Carberry, on 1 June 1615, the mother of his son and heir, William, also an advocate.

Pearson played a prominent role in public affairs during the covenanting era. He was one of the committee appointed to examine the authenticity of the registers of the kirk in 1638 and, in March 1649, was one of the eight lords of session nominated to replace those purged for their support of Charles I. He was also named one of the committee for the revision of the laws and acts of parliament, a commissioner for the plantation of kirks, and one of the visitors of the University of Edinburgh. He sat as lord of session until the supremacy of Cromwell in 1651, and in October 1653 he was appointed a commissioner of judicature by the English parliament. In 1654 he was conjoined, with Sir John Hope of Craighall, as judge of the high court; but, according to Nicoll, he was 'not comparable to Sir John nather in judgement nor actioun' (Nicoll, 122). In November 1655 Pearson was continued an extraordinary judge. He died at Edinburgh on 12 May 1657.

T. F. HENDERSON, *rev.* SHARON ADAMS

Sources *The historical works of Sir James Balfour*, ed. J. Haig, 2–3 (1824) · J. Nicoll, *A diary of public transactions and other occurrences, chiefly in Scotland, from January 1650 to June 1667*, ed. D. Laing, Bannatyne Club, 52 (1836) · *The letters and journals of Robert Baillie*, ed. D. Laing, 3 vols., Bannatyne Club, 73 (1841–2), vol. 1 · M. D. Young, ed., *The parliaments of Scotland: burgh and shire commissioners*, 2 (1993) · F. J. Grant, ed., *The Faculty of Advocates in Scotland, 1532–1943*, Scottish RS, 145 (1944) · D. Laing, ed., *A catalogue of the graduates … of the University of Edinburgh*, Bannatyne Club, 106 (1858) · H. Paton, ed., *The register of marriages for the parish of Edinburgh, 1595–1700*, Scottish RS, old ser., 27 (1905) · H. Paton, ed., *Register of interments in the Greyfriars burying-ground, Edinburgh, 1658–1700*, Scottish RS, 26 (1902) · *APS, 1643–60*

Pearson, Alfred Chilton (1861–1935), classical scholar, was born at 23 Campden Hill Square, London, on 8 October 1861, the only child of Robert Henry Pearson (*d.* 1893), merchant, of London, and his wife, Georgina Boswood, who died when Pearson was still a schoolboy. He was educated at Highgate and King's College schools, and at Christ's College, Cambridge, which he entered as a scholar in 1879. He was fortunate in being taught by John Peile, soon to be university reader in comparative philology, who introduced Pearson to Sanskrit and gave him 'a solid foundation for the linguistic studies of later life' (Richards, 3). After obtaining a first class in both parts of the classical tripos (1881 and 1883) he read for the bar and was called by Lincoln's Inn in 1885; in the same year he married Edith Maud, fourth daughter of Reuben Green, solicitor and town clerk, of Kensington, and they settled in London.

In 1890 Pearson became a schoolmaster: after two years at Bury St Edmunds and one at Ipswich he passed in 1893 to Dulwich College, which he left in 1900, in order to enter his late father's London business, moving at the same time to Warlingham in Surrey. He joined the National Liberal Club, which gave him a base in London, and maintained his links with teaching by examining, from 1900, for the Oxford and Cambridge schools examination board.

Pearson's publications began in 1887 with a note on the *Androtion* of Demosthenes in the *Classical Review*, which had just begun, and to which he continued to contribute articles and reviews on many Greek subjects: his first book was *The Fragments of Zeno and Cleanthes* (1891), an admirable work which had won him the Hare prize at Cambridge two years before. All his later books were editions of works of the Greek tragedians, although between 1908 and 1921 he contributed more than twenty articles to Hastings's *Encyclopaedia of Religion and Ethics*. He began with a series of school editions of Euripides (*Helena*, 1903; *Heraclidae*, 1907; *Phoenissae*, 1909) and with an abridgement (1907) of the *Ajax* of Sophocles edited by Sir Richard Jebb. Next, at the invitation of the syndics of the Cambridge University Press, he prepared for posthumous publication (1910) the verse translation and incomplete commentary on Aeschylus's *Agamemnon* left by W. G. Headlam, and also undertook the completion of the editing of the *Fragments* of Sophocles, a task begun by Jebb and continued by Headlam. Pearson spent several years on this difficult task, and in 1917 produced a masterly edition in three volumes, which established his reputation. The notes to this work ensure its lasting value to scholars.

In 1919 Pearson was elected Gladstone professor of Greek at Liverpool University, where he had the support of J. P. Postgate, professor of Latin. Pearson feigned surprise at his appointment: 'Rather a ridiculous adventure at my time of life! I did not even know the post was advertised' (Richards, 9). But he revitalized the department there and in 1921 succeeded Henry Jackson as regius professor of Greek at Cambridge, becoming thereupon a fellow of Trinity College. His chief remaining work was the Sophocles which he added to the Oxford Classical Texts series in 1924. Soon after this his health failed. He resigned his chair in 1928, and lived from 1932 to 1934 at Hunstanton before moving to London, where he died at his home, 61 Queen's Gate, Kensington, on 2 January 1935 after five years of total incapacity. His wife had died in 1930. They had a son and two daughters, the elder of whom predeceased her father.

Pearson was an active man, an oar and a cricketer in youth, and a keen golfer and walker in later life. Intensely loyal and generous, he combined deep modesty with strong opinions, carefully formed and not easily shaken. He did, though, resign his National Liberal Club membership and wrote in 1923 that, having ceased to be a Liberal, he expected 'to end as a crusted Tory' (Richards, 14). His scholarship was of a very high order, especially on the linguistic and grammatical side. All his books were models in their kind, and his masterpiece, *The Fragments of Sophocles*, shows a vast range of knowledge at the service of an acute

and sober judgement. He was elected an honorary fellow of Christ's College in 1922 and a fellow of the British Academy in 1924.   D. S. ROBERTSON, *rev.* MARK POTTLE

Sources The Times (3 Jan 1935) · G. C. Richards, 'Alfred Chilton Pearson, 1861–1935', *PBA*, 21 (1935), 449–63 [incl. bibliography] **Archives** Bodl. Oxf., letters to Gilbert Murray **Likenesses** A. Lawrence, chalk drawing, 1927, Trinity Cam. **Wealth at death** £53,385 18s. 2d.: resworn probate, 22 Feb 1935, *CGPLA Eng. & Wales*

Pearson, Anthony (*bap.* **1627**, *d.* **1666**), Quaker administrator, was baptized on 7 January 1627 at Cartmel Fell, Lancashire, the son of Edward Pearson. He may have studied law in London, though his name does not appear in the records of the inns of court. After becoming Sir Arthur Hesilrige's secretary in 1648, he was appointed judge advocate at Newcastle the following year to try officers and soldiers in northern garrisons for lesser offences, and clerk and registrar of the committee for compounding. He acquired the manors of Aspatria and Allerthwaite, Cumberland, in May 1650; Ramshaw Hall, near West Auckland, co. Durham, shortly thereafter; Marrowlee, Northumberland, in March 1653, and other estates seized from the marquess of Newcastle and Sir Thomas Riddell. He also managed Hesilrige's estates. On 10 February 1652 the committee for compounding appointed him sequestration commissioner for co. Durham, and the following month he became a JP for Cumberland and Westmorland. By 1652 he had married Grace, daughter of Thomas and Grace Lamplough of Ribton Hall, Cumberland.

George Fox described Pearson as 'a great persecutor of ffreindes' (*Journal of George Fox*, 1.108), but at the sessions in Appleby, Westmorland, in January 1653 he was moved by the testimony of James Nayler. On a visit to the home of Thomas and Margaret Fell, he met Fox, and he also received letters from Howgill and Margaret Fell urging him to become a Friend. In a missive to the latter dated 9 May 1653 he described his spiritual condition, seeking guidance from Fox and Nayler. Although he had considered himself a devout man, he now likened his state to that of a battered vessel, devoid of pilot or rudder. 'All my Religion was but the heareinge of the Eare, the beleeveinge and talkeinge of a god & christ in heaven or a place at a distance I knowe not where' (Swarthmore MSS, 1.87). He was probably convinced in the ensuing weeks, for Thomas Aldam and Richard Farnworth held meetings at his house in early June, and Nayler visited him in July, holding a meeting at which hundreds became Quakers. Pearson took his wife to meet Fox at Bootle, Cumberland, and subsequently travelled with Fox to Carlisle, where he and Gervase Benson defended Fox when the latter was imprisoned. On 3 October 1653 Pearson wrote an address *To the Parliament of the Common-Wealth of England*, placing responsibility for persecution on parliament, listing three dozen Quakers who had been persecuted in Yorkshire, Cumberland, and Westmorland, denouncing those responsible as tyrants, and disparaging 'the broken Cisterns of Universities and humane Studies' (p. 7).

Pearson may have been the 'A. Peirson' who was serving in Scotland as a commissioner for the administration of justice in December 1653, and he was still active as a sequestration commissioner in April 1654. In March 1654 he welcomed Fox to Ramshaw Hall, which became the base of Quaker operations in Durham, and in May he helped establish the first monthly meeting in Durham. Shortly thereafter he went to London, where he and Howgill were concerned about relations with Ranters. In *A Few Words to All Judges, Justices, and Ministers of the Law* (acquired by the bookseller George Thomason on 16 July 1654), he denounced the use of oaths, capital punishment, and compulsory tithing, adding that if tithes must be collected, they should be used to relieve the indigent and eradicate poverty. On 16 July he met with Oliver Cromwell, telling him that the civil wars had been for the benefit of the spiritual 'seed', that the protector had been chosen to overthrow oppression, and that the law prohibiting the disruption of church services was unjust. When he also attempted at the meeting to convert Cromwell's associates, Cromwell dismissed him, prompting Pearson to conclude that the lord protector was neither honest nor tender-hearted. When Pearson found Londoners difficult to convince, particularly 'rude savage apprentices and young people and Ranters', he advised Fox to send only mature Friends to London in search of converts (Barclay, 13). In September 1654 he met with John Wildman and other dissidents, but he apparently had no interest in opposing the protectorate. The following month he obtained an order for Aldam's release from York prison after meeting with the attorney-general, the treasury commissioners, the barons of the exchequer, and Cromwell.

Pearson and Aldam then mounted a concerted effort to obtain the release of other Friends. In April 1655 they wrote to Cheshire magistrates, protesting their treatment of Quakers, and in May, Pearson, Aldam, and Benson presented Cromwell with documents concerning imprisoned Friends. Pearson and Benson continued to collect information about Friends in northern England who had been prosecuted for refusing to remit tithes. During the ensuing months he travelled in Wales, Shropshire, Cheshire, Yorkshire, and Lancashire, where he was briefly incarcerated at Manchester. With Major-General Charles Worsley presiding, on 4 March 1656 he, Audland, Alexander Parker, Thomas Lawson, and others engaged in a debate with ministers at Preston. Tension with other Quakers, however, occurred as early as May, when William Caton chided Pearson for failing to assist Scottish Friends purchase a meeting-house in Edinburgh, and in July Lancelot Wardell accused him of preventing the publication of a document about the persecution of Durham Quakers. In a lengthy dispute with Wardell over finances, he had the support of Margaret Fell and George Taylor. He reported the notorious trial of Nayler, with whose convictions (though not actions) he concurred, to Fox in November. More controversy erupted in May 1657 when John Lilburne, now a Quaker, accused Pearson of conveying the title to some of Lilburne's property to Pearson's wife, Grace.

During the spring of 1657 Pearson supported the creation of a fund to support Friends who travelled in the ministry. He and Howgill nominated Quakers throughout England and Wales to serve as treasurers, a post he and George Adamson undertook for Durham. His principal work, *The Great Case of Tythes*, appeared in 1657 and reached a third edition two years later, with four more following in the eighteenth century. His examination of tithing among the biblical Jews and in the history of the church persuaded him that they were not required by divine law, equity, monarchical grants, parliamentary statute, or the rights of those who had purchased impropriated tithes, though he supported compensation for impropriators. The termination of tithing, he argued, would stop ceaseless lawsuits, provide incentives to raise more crops, and relieve the people of an oppressive burden. Immanuel Bourne offered a rebuttal in *A Defence and Justification of Ministers Maintenance by Tythes* (1659).

In the late 1650s Pearson helped establish Quaker business meetings in the north and was active on behalf of persecuted Friends, attracting the attention of George Monck in Scotland, who was concerned by his proselytizing. With Fox, Pearson conferred with the aldermen of Newcastle in 1657, and early the following year he arranged a meeting between Fox and Sir Henry Vane at Raby Castle, but the latter would have ousted Fox as 'a mad man' had Pearson not been present (*Journal of George Fox*, 1.314). On 24 June 1658 Pearson, Aldam, and forty-one others endorsed the establishment of a fund to support Quaker missions. The same year Pearson and nineteen others submitted a declaration to the council of state defending Quaker tenets, seeking the release of 115 imprisoned co-religionists, and protesting against high legal fees, lengthy delays, and attorneys' greed.

Amid the unsettled conditions in 1659, Pearson and fifteen others signed *A Declaration of the People of God*, including a list of potential JPs, among them Pearson, who had been removed from the commission of the peace by 1657. On 22 June he and Caton told Fell they were hopeful that parliament might undertake needed reform, and five days later Pearson and nineteen others presented parliament with a petition against tithes bearing 15,000 signatures. Because of Pearson's growing involvement in politics, once again as an associate of Hesilrige, Howgill shunned him in August. Although appointed a militia commissioner that month, he reportedly refused to wear a sword, yet he disarmed royalists and reputedly would have raised men to help John Lambert suppress Booth's rebellion had local JPs and commissioners not been reluctant. With other Durham Friends he signed a letter in October expressing concern about Fox's plan to establish quarterly sessions based on counties and proposing that funds raised by meetings be used to assist all needy Friends, not just those engaged in ministerial activities.

The government received a report in June 1660 that at least 100 Quakers met almost nightly at Ramshaw Hall, and that Pearson had recently received a substantial shipment of knives and daggers, but he was not arrested until

December 1661, when he went to London in supposed violation of a proclamation banning cashiered soldiers from within 20 miles of the city. Suspected of maintaining contacts with dissidents in Scotland, he denied the accusation and likewise insisted he had not commanded troops at the time of Booth's insurrection. On 9 January he renounced his self-described religious excesses ('the Chymericall Notion of those giddy tymes'), averred that he had always befriended the king's servants and sequestered clergy, and claimed that his change of heart had occurred many years earlier through the influence of Sir William Darcy when it was 'neither seasonable nor serviceable to discover it' (PRO, SP 29/49/27). As proof of his sincerity, he had voluntarily returned the estates of Newcastle and Riddell, surrendered his weapons, and pledged allegiance to the king. After his release on 16 January 1662, he offered advice to the government on 2 July 1663 concerning trade between England and Scotland. He was appointed under-sheriff of Durham by Bishop John Cosin on 2 March 1664, and in 1665 he was involved in a dispute over Cosin's appropriation of Vane's personal estate. After embracing the Anglican faith, Pearson died, probably in Durham and from the plague, on 23 January 1666, and was buried the next day at St Mary-the-Less, Durham. On 26 September 1673 his widow married the Quaker James Hall of Monk Hesleden, Durham.   RICHARD L. GREAVES

Sources RS Friends, Lond., Swarthmore MSS 1.84, 87, 146, 216, 308; 2.17; 3.14, 33–5, 61, 70, 78 · PRO, SP 29/45/42–43, 60; 29/49/27; 29/76/11; 29/127/33 · *The journal of George Fox*, ed. N. Penney, 2 vols. (1911) · A. R. Barclay, ed., *Letters, &c., of early Friends: illustrative of the history of the society* (1841) · M. A. E. Green, ed., *Calendar of the proceedings of the committee for compounding … 1643–1660*, 5 vols., PRO (1889–92), vol. 1, pp. 201, 541, 679, 812, 815, 821 · A. E. Wallis, 'Anthony Pearson (1626–1666): an early Friend in Bishoprick', *Journal of the Friends' Historical Society*, 51 (1965–7), 77–95 · A. E. Wallis, 'The establishment of a monthly meeting in Durham (1654) and a note on Anthony Pearson (d. 1666)', *Journal of the Friends' Historical Society*, 48 (1957), 119–22 · *The writings and speeches of Oliver Cromwell*, ed. W. C. Abbott and C. D. Crane, 4 vols. (1937–47), vol. 3, pp. 372–3, 504, 734 · *CSP dom.*, 1654, p. 126; 1658–9, p. 360; 1659–60, p. 127; 1661–2, p. 244 · *Seventh report*, HMC, 6 (1879), 93 · Thurloe, *State papers*, 6.811 · Greaves & Zaller, *BDBR*, 15–17 · W. C. Braithwaite, *The beginnings of Quakerism*, ed. H. J. Cadbury, 2nd edn (1955)
Archives Bodl. Oxf., Rawl. MSS A, Thurloe state MSS · RS Friends, Lond., Barclay MSS · RS Friends, Lond., Caton MSS · RS Friends, Lond., Swarthmore MSS

Pearson, Sir (Cyril) Arthur, first baronet (1866–1921), newspaper proprietor and philanthropist, was born on 24 February 1866 at Wookey near Wells, the eldest child and only son among the four children of the Revd Arthur Cyril Pearson (1838–1916) and his wife, Philippa Massingberd Maxwell Lyte (1846–1909). His great-grandfather was the hymnologist the Revd Henry Francis *Lyte. He was educated from the age of ten at Eagle House School, Wimbledon, going on after four years there to Winchester College. Straitened family circumstances forced his departure at the age of sixteen, and he returned home to be taught by his father. In 1884 he won a general knowledge quiz in Sir George Newnes's journal *Tit-Bits*; the prize was a clerkship at the *Tit-Bits* London office at a salary of £100 a

year. By the following year he had pushed himself into the position of manager.

When in 1890 Newnes and W. T. Stead devised the monthly digest *Review of Reviews* Pearson was made business manager, but finding his position now constrictive and unremunerative Pearson broke away in July 1890 to found his own journal. As the first number of *Pearson's Weekly* proclaimed on 26 July, it was intended 'to interest, to elevate, to amuse', and its amalgam of light instruction and entertainment ultimately proved extraordinarily attractive to an aspiring late Victorian middle- and respectable working-class readership. *Pearson's Weekly* struggled initially, however, until Pearson hit upon the key to his fortune, the 'Missing Word' competition. First announced in December 1891, its rapid popularity made him a rich man. Sales reached a peak of one and a quarter million in 1897, and *Pearson's Weekly* established a significant share of the popular magazine market. Wealth fuelled Pearson's philanthropy, and in 1892 he established the Fresh Air Fund in Britain, a means of sending children from city slums on annual trips to the countryside. Pearson also provided the initial funding for Robert Baden-Powell's Boy Scout movement.

Pearson subsequently founded the *Royal Magazine* and other titles and was able to go into semi-retirement in 1897. This soon palled with the energetic Pearson, and in 1899 he was teamed with Newnes once more on the board of the British Mutoscope and Biograph Company, the premier British film company of the period, with the bold but ultimately mistaken aim of providing illustrated journalism through motion picture devices for the home. He then turned to the launch of a daily newspaper. 24 April 1900 saw the first edition of the *Daily Express*, price halfpence, eight broadsheet pages with news innovatively featured on the outside. Pearson's main political passion at this time was tariff reform, and in 1903 he and Joseph Chamberlain formed the Tariff Reform League. During the period 1903–5 Pearson directed the operations of the Tariff Reform League as executive chairman and also served as vice-chairman of the tariff commission. His involvement undoubtedly led to his neglect of the *Daily Express*.

In 1905 Pearson acquired *The Standard* and *Evening Standard*, and made a failed bid for *The Times* in 1907–8, but he began to lose interest in his newspapers just as he lost interest in tariff reform after the general election of 1905. Partly this was Pearson's nature, always dropping an enthusiasm once the challenge was over, but the onset of blindness was no doubt the determining factor. He sold *The Standard*, along with the mildly profitable *Evening Standard*, in 1910, having despaired of 'a publication which showed no signs of becoming a genuine financial proposition' (Porter, 576).

Characteristically, Pearson did not dwell on his loss of sight, but set out to discover what was most positive about it. Having disposed of his newspaper holdings by 1912, he became president of the National Institute for the Blind. At the outbreak of war Pearson found fresh outlet for his energies by establishing a hostel for blinded soldiers, first in Bayswater in February 1915, but moving the following month to spacious accommodation at St Dunstan's in Regent's Park. Initially treating sixteen soldiers, by the end of the war St Dunstan's and other hostels had cared for over 1500. More than just treating blindness Pearson oversaw a whole policy of re-education and readjustment into society, doing remarkable work in the process to change public perception of blind people.

In recognition of these public services Pearson was created a baronet in 1916 and GBE in 1917. He was twice married: first, on 3 December 1887, to Isobel Sarah, daughter of the Revd F. Bennett, with whom he had three daughters; second, on 3 June 1897, to Ethel Maud (*d*. 1959), daughter of W. J. Fraser, with whom he had one son. Pearson died on 9 December 1921 at his Surrey home, Frensham Place, Farnham: he drowned after hitting his head on a bath tap. He was buried on 13 December in Hampstead cemetery. His only son, Neville Arthur Pearson, succeeded to the baronetcy.

Possessing an extraordinary enthusiasm for life, Sir Arthur Pearson revolutionized people's attitude towards blind people. His energy was intimidating to some, and Joseph Chamberlain paid him a double-edged compliment in calling him 'the greatest hustler I have ever known' (Dark, 104); but a man whose opinions were mostly caprice and whose thoughts were shallow could never be a great newspaperman. He was popularly mourned as the 'Blind leader of the blind'.

LUKE MCKERNAN

Sources S. Dark, *The life of Sir Arthur Pearson* [1922] · P. Broks, 'Science, press and empire: Pearson's publications, 1890–1914', *Imperialism and the natural world*, ed. J. M. Mackenzie (1990), 141–65 · A. Pearson, *Victory over blindness* (1919) · R. Allen, *Voice of Britain: the inside story of the Daily Express* (1983) · H. Herd, *The making of modern journalism* (1927) · A. Sullivan, ed., *British literary magazines*, [3]: *The Victorian and Edwardian age, 1837–1913* (1984) · R. Brown and B. Anthony, *A Victorian film enterprise: the history of the British Mutoscope and Biograph, 1897–1915* (1999) · *DNB* · *CGPLA Eng. & Wales* (1922) · D. Porter, 'Pearson, Sir Cyril Arthur', *DBB* · *WWW* · *The Times* (14 Dec 1921) · Burke, *Peerage*
Archives BL, corresp. with Lord Northcliffe, Add. MS 62172 · BLPES, letters to tariff commission · CAC Cam., letters to W. T. Stead · HLRO, corresp. with R. D. Blumenfeld
Likenesses Elliott & Fry, photograph, 1898, repro. in Dark, *Life of Sir Arthur Pearson* (1922) · Lafayette, photograph, 1900, repro. in Dark, *Life of Sir Arthur Pearson* · R. Haines, photograph, 1909, repro. in Dark, *Life of Sir Arthur Pearson* · J. Russell & Sons, photograph, 1918, St Dunstan's, London; repro. in Dark, *Life of Sir Arthur Pearson* · Spy [L. Ward], caricature, lithograph, NPG; repro. in *VF* (17 Nov 1904)
Wealth at death £93,926 14*s*. 8*d*.: probate, 21 Jan 1922, *CGPLA Eng. & Wales*

Pearson, Charles (1793–1862), lawyer and urban reformer, was born on 4 October 1793 at 25 Clement's Lane, London, son of Thomas Pearson, upholsterer and feather merchant, and his wife, Sarah. Educated at Eastbourne, Sussex, he was initially apprenticed to his father, but was admitted solicitor in 1816, and developed an extensive practice. He was made free of the Haberdashers' Company in 1817, and in the same year, on 20 March, married Mary Martha Dutton (*d*. 1871) of Brixton; their only child, Mary Dutton Pearson, was born in 1820.

Pearson began an active career in the City of London as common councilman for Bishopsgate ward, 1817–20 and 1830–36, becoming chairman of the City board of health in 1831–3, and under-sheriff in 1834–5. He was an active supporter of reform measures: the issues for which he campaigned included the freedom of Jews to hold public office, abolition of capital punishment, and reformatory treatment for juvenile offenders. He was opposed to the established church, and in favour of free trade, and similar 'progressive' causes. He protested against the practice of packing juries in political cases, and he is credited with the City's decision, taken in 1831, to erase the words in the inscription on the Monument which attributed the Great Fire of 1666 to 'the Popish faction'. He was a thorn in the flesh of the London gas companies. He 'felt passionately about whatever cause was for the moment uppermost in his mind' (Heap, 21–2).

In 1839 Pearson was appointed City solicitor and held the office until his death. In this position, and as MP for Lambeth from 1847 to 1850, he campaigned, by speech, pamphlet, and influence, for London improvements of many kinds: the embankment of the Thames, a new meat market, a central railway terminus in the Fleet valley (which happily did not come to anything), and improved transport by an underground railway. In this last he was successful. Pearson was associated, with the City's consent, with early versions of this project, and in 1857 he joined forces with the promoters of the Metropolitan Railway from Paddington to Farringdon Street, which was in financial doldrums with no work started; the City took £200,000 in shares in 1859 (which it later sold at a profit), and Pearson's skilful advice and lobbying were largely responsible for the work coming to fruition, four months after his death.

This was, however, only part of his vision, which also encompassed workers' housing in healthy suburban conditions away from the pent-up courts and alleys of the City, linked by railway communication with cheap workmen's fares. In this he was a visionary for his time; later generations took up the concept. Pearson died on 14 September 1862 at his home, Oxford Lodge, West Hill, Wandsworth, having suffered from dropsy, despite which he had continued to work up to a week before his death. He was buried in Norwood cemetery on 23 September. His wife survived him.

Without Pearson's constant advocacy—his gadfly conduct, which he managed to combine with holding high office in the City of London—the Metropolitan Railway, the first of its kind in the world, and the nucleus of London's underground system, could not have come into existence when it did.

MICHAEL ROBBINS

Sources *The Times* (16 Sept 1862) · *City Press* (20–27 Sept 1862) · *ILN* (20 Sept 1862), 303 · *ILN* (4 Oct 1862), 359 · T. C. Barker and M. Robbins, *A history of London Transport*, 1 (1963), 100–17 · D. Heap, 'The solicitor and the underground', *Law Society's Gazette*, 60 (1963), 21–2 · S. Everard, *The history of the Gas Light and Coke Company, 1812–1949* (1949), 154–5, 180 · notes on Pearson, 1951, 1980, 1993, CLRO · d. cert. · *CGPLA Eng. & Wales* (1862) · GL, MS 4783

Wealth at death under £20,000: administration, 8 Nov 1862, *CGPLA Eng. & Wales* · administration of goods unadministered, 1871, *CGPLA Eng. & Wales*

Pearson, Charles Buchanan (1807–1881). *See under* Pearson, Hugh Nicholas (1776–1856).

Pearson, Charles Henry (1830–1894), politician in Australia and writer, was born on 7 September 1830 in the principal's house, Church Missionary Institution, Islington, London, the fourth son and the tenth child of the Revd John Norman *Pearson (1787–1865) and his wife, Harriet, daughter of Richard Puller, a merchant banker. One of his brothers was the judge Sir John *Pearson. Until the age of twelve he was tutored at home by his exacting, ambitious, and puritanical father, then attended Rugby School from 1843 to May 1846. He was removed from the school after clashing with his form master G. E. L. Cotton, and was privately tutored for four months before in 1847 entering King's College, London. There he became a disciple of Frederick Denison Maurice and highly valued the teaching of Professor John Sherren Brewer. While acting as a special constable on 10 April 1848 at a Chartist demonstration, he contracted a chill, which had a bad and lasting effect on his health. He matriculated as a commoner from Oriel College, Oxford, in 1849, obtained a scholarship at Exeter College the following year, and was in the first class in the *literae humaniores* examination in 1852. He graduated BA in 1853 and proceeded MA in 1856. From boyhood he knew French, and while an undergraduate he studied German, Czech, Italian, and Swedish; he was a founder member of the Essay Society, a small society for intellectual discussion, and was president of the Oxford Union Debating Society in 1852–3. Intending to practise medicine, he read anatomy and physiology at Oxford for about two years after taking his degree, while also acting as a private tutor. In 1854 he was elected a fellow of Oriel, and soon after, being attacked by pleurisy, gave up his intention of becoming a physician, on the advice of his doctors. In the following year he was appointed lecturer in English literature, and shortly afterwards professor of modern history, at King's College, London. In 1861 he published *The Early and Middle Ages of England* and during the following two years edited the short-lived *National Review*; he also contributed to the *Saturday Review*. Believing that his broad-church religious opinions were not in harmony with those of the authorities at King's College, he proposed to the principal, the high-church Dr Richard William Jelf, that he resign his professorship, but was persuaded by Jelf to retain office, and did so until 1865.

For several years Pearson spent his vacations in Europe, studying foreign languages. In 1859, on the eve of the emancipation of Russia's serfs, he summarized the impressions of a long journey in *Russia: by a recent traveller: a series of letters, originally published in 'the Continental Review'* (reissued with a new introduction in 1970). In 1863 he risked his life to obtain first-hand knowledge of the Polish insurrection against Russian occupation. His account of 'The insurrection in Poland', which was sympathetic to the Poles, was published as a supplement to *The Spectator*

Charles Henry Pearson (1830–1894), by unknown engraver, pubd 1894 (after Foster & Martin)

on 12 September 1863, as a pamphlet under the pseudonym 'A Recent Traveller', and issued in Paris by the Polish diplomatic agency as *Un Anglais en Pologne*.

In 1864, after Britain had failed to act on Poland's behalf and Oxford had passed him over for the Chichele professorship of history, Pearson set off for South Australia, where he tried farming at Melrose, some 200 miles north of Adelaide. Although he thrived in the warm, dry climate and learned to respect the 'primitive democracy' of the local community, he was driven to England in 1866 by severe drought. In 1867 he defended the political stability of Australian democracy in *Essays on Reform*. The following year he brought out a revised two-volume edition of his history of England 'during the early and middle ages' and lectured on history for the new North of England Council for Promoting the Higher Education of Women. In 1869 the first edition of his pioneering *Historical Maps of England, during the First Thirteen Centuries* was published, and he contributed a historical essay to Josephine Butler's *Woman's Work and Woman's Culture* (1869).

In 1869, after visiting the United States and Sweden, Pearson began lecturing on modern history at Trinity College, Cambridge, but two years later, finding his eyesight suffering, and disappointed in the quality of his students, he returned to his South Australian farm via the United States and the Pacific, writing articles *en route* for the London *Spectator*. His health was again strengthened by his new mode of life. On 10 December 1872 he married, at Gawler, South Australia, Edith Lucille, daughter of Philip Butler of Tickford Abbey, Buckinghamshire, and Yattalunga, One Tree Hill, South Australia. Pearson was then forty-two, his bride twenty. At first the couple lived happily on his farm, where he worked at *English History in the Fourteenth Century* (1876). But his wife could not bear the very hot summers, and in 1874 they moved to Melbourne, where Pearson lectured on history at the university and founded a debating society whose members included Alfred Deakin, John Quick, and Henry Bournes Higgins. He resigned this post in 1875, and was appointed foundation headmaster of the Presbyterian Ladies' College, the first girls' school in Australia to match the leading boys' grammar schools in offering permanence, imposing buildings, and a large student body and boarding house. To inaugurate the college he gave a lecture on 'The higher culture of women', afterwards published as a pamphlet. He had not, however, given up his interest in politics. Fearing that most of the land of Victoria was falling into the possession of a few very wealthy proprietors, and aware that a newly formed Liberal Party was about to contest a forthcoming election, he proposed the progressive taxation of large estates at a 'monster meeting' held in Melbourne on 19 February 1877. He was thereupon asked to resign the headmastership, since his views on the land question were anathema to many of the college's supporters, who now saw him as a 'class traitor'. With a daughter aged two and a second child soon to be born, he now became, as Deakin wrote, 'a leading figure in one of the fiercest campaigns of party warfare waged within the Empire in this century' (*Daily Chronicle*, 28 May 1900).

Ironically, although the Liberals won a landslide victory on 11 May 1877, Pearson was allotted a virtually unwinnable seat by party managers, who were unhappy with his free-trade views. As compensation he was given a royal commission to report on public education in Victoria; his report of March 1878 covered all levels of education and provided a blueprint for many future developments. He was in the same year elected member of the legislative assembly for Castlemaine, a safe Liberal seat. In 1879 he accompanied Graham Berry on his unsuccessful mission to England to request the intervention of the home government to prevent future deadlocks between the houses of the legislature. He was re-elected for Castlemaine in 1880, and was minister without portfolio or salary in the Berry administration (1880–81), concerning himself with constitutional reform, with carrying an act 'to amend the law relating to the University of Melbourne', which, among other things, guaranteed equal rights for women, and with boarding out the 200 children housed in unhygienic state industrial schools.

When the Berry government was *in articulo mortis* Pearson was offered the agent-generalship of Victoria, but having previously criticized such appointments felt obliged to decline it. He did, however, accept an honorary trusteeship of the Melbourne Public Library, Museums and National Gallery, and in this capacity in 1882 worked effectively to secure the foundation of the Melbourne Working Men's College. He failed, however, to carry his proposal to open the Public Library, Museums and National Gallery on Sundays.

In 1883 Pearson was elected for the East Bourke boroughs, for which he sat until the general election in April 1892, when he did not contest the seat. On the formation of the Gillies–Deakin coalition government in February 1886 he became minister of education, a post he held until November 1890. From 1878 until taking ministerial office in 1886 his principal source of income came from writing leading articles and literary reviews for the Melbourne *Age* and its weekly, *The Leader*, both of which were owned by David Syme. Some 650 anonymous articles written by him from August 1880 to February 1884 had a wide influence on public opinion generally, and particularly in campaigns in which he was involved in his various public capacities.

As minister of education Pearson's greatest success lay in scientific and technical education. He led the government to more than double the grant for the teaching of science and technology, enabling not only the expansion of new technical colleges and established schools of mines, but the building of new chemical, biological, and mechanical laboratories in the university. He also established scholarships to enable 200 primary schoolchildren a year to proceed to independent secondary schools, expanded the state school curriculum to include more science and Australian history and geography, encouraged kindergarten teaching, and had built a fine new teachers' college near the university with residential accommodation for country teachers. In 1889 he successfully resisted a determined campaign by the National Scripture Education League to introduce Bible instruction into state schools during school hours, arguing that this would be offensive to large numbers of Roman Catholic parents and teachers. An honorary LLD from the University of St Andrews in 1889 recognized his work as an educationist.

An attack of influenza with pneumonia in 1892 led to Pearson's retirement from the assembly and to his return to England, where for a time his health was restored. Financial losses led him to accept in 1893 the post of permanent secretary to the agent-general. He contributed to some English journals, and in 1893 published *National Life and Character: a Forecast*, which attracted public attention in Britain, the United States, and Australia by its predictions first, that the so-called 'higher races of men, or those which are held to have attained the highest forms of civilization' (p. 30) would in a few decades find themselves 'elbowed and hustled and perhaps even thrust aside' (p. 85) by peoples whom they had assumed to be innately servile; and second, that in English-speaking and European countries the state would increasingly take over the traditional roles of family and church. Coming at the full tide of imperialist sentiment, this book produced the shock Pearson had expected. Theodore Roosevelt wrote to him: 'I don't suppose that any book recently, unless it is Mahan's "Influence of Sea Power", has excited anything like as much interest or has caused so many men to feel that they had to revise their mental estimates of facts' (T. Roosevelt to Pearson 11 May 1894, Bodl. Oxf., MSS Pearson). Like Sir M. E. Grant Duff, a former governor of Madras, Roosevelt took the view that the major powers of Europe and America would go to any military lengths to consolidate their dominance of the coloured races. In Australia the book was later quoted by Prime Minister Edmund Barton in defence of the exclusion of coloured migrants and taken up as a sophisticated warning against what Deakin would call 'the Yellow Peril to Caucasian civilization creeds and politics' (A. Deakin to Richard Jebb, 4 June 1908, NLA, MS 339). A second edition appeared in 1894, and a third, posthumously, in 1913.

Pearson died at the house of his sister-in-law, 75 Onslow Square, London, on 29 May 1894, survived by his wife and three teenage daughters. His personal estate was valued at only £511 14s. 4d., and in 1895 his widow was granted a civil-list pension of £100.

Widely travelled and read, with a large number of overseas correspondents, Pearson was the outstanding colonizer of ideas in Australia during the later nineteenth century. Popularly known as 'Professor Pearson', he combined a puritan determination with a gentle manner and a scrupulous respect for the traditional rules and courtesies of public debate. No one did more than he to prepare the way for what became known as the 'settled policies' of the new Australian commonwealth. 'I can candidly assure you', wrote Deakin, 'that on summing up your colonial experiences you would need to throw into the credit side of the scale an immense amount of other men's actions and words of which you have really been the parent' (A. Deakin to C. H. Pearson, 12 Aug 1892, State Library of Victoria, Pearson MSS).   JOHN M. TREGENZA

Sources J. Tregenza, *Professor of democracy: the life of Charles Henry Pearson* (1968) [incl. full bibliography of writings, descriptions of personal papers in Bodleian and La Trobe libraries, and sources of letters to others] · W. Stebbing, ed., *Charles Henry Pearson: fellow of Oriel and education minister in Victoria* (1900) · J. M. Tregenza, 'C. H. Pearson in Russia and his correspondence with Herzen, Ogarev, and others, 1858–1863', *Oxford Slavonic Papers*, 11 (1964), 69–82 · J. Tregenza, 'The Pearson papers', *La Trobe Library Journal*, 6 (1970), 45–50 · H. A. Strong, 'Memoir of Charles Henry Pearson', in C. H. Pearson, *Reviews and critical essays*, ed. H. A. Strong (1896) · S. Macintyre, *A colonial liberalism: the lost world of three Victorian visionaries* (1991) · J. M. Tregenza, 'Pearson, Charles Henry', *AusDB*, vol. 5 · G. C. Brodrick, *Memories and impressions, 1831–1900* (1900) · Bodl. Oxf., Pearson MSS · register (marriage), St George's, Gawler, South Australia

Archives Bodl. Oxf., corresp. and papers · State Library of Victoria, Melbourne, La Trobe manuscript collection | BL, Acland MSS · BL, Bryce MSS · Duke U., Field-Musgrave collection · Harvard U., Houghton L., Charles Eliot Norton MSS · NL Aus., letters to Alfred Deakin

Likenesses engraving (after photograph by Foster & Martin), NPG; repro. in *ILN* (9 June 1894) [see illus.] · photographs, Bodl. Oxf., Pearson MSS · portraits, State Library of Victoria, Melbourne, La Trobe picture collection

Wealth at death £511 14s. 4d.: probate, 18 July 1894, CGPLA Eng. & Wales

Pearson, Sir Charles John, Lord Pearson (1843–1910), judge, born at Edinburgh on 6 November 1843, was the second son of Charles Pearson, chartered accountant, of Edinburgh, and his wife, Margaret, daughter of John Dalziel, solicitor, of Earlston, Berwickshire. After attending Edinburgh Academy he proceeded to the University of St Andrews, and then to Corpus Christi College, Oxford, where he distinguished himself in classics, winning the Gaisford Greek prizes for prose (1862) and verse (1863). He graduated BA with a first class in the final classical school in 1865. He afterwards attended law lectures in Edinburgh and became a member of the Juridical Society, of which he was librarian in 1872–3, and of the Speculative Society. He was called to the English bar (from the Inner Temple) on 10 June 1870, and on 19 July 1870 he passed to the Scottish bar, where he rapidly obtained a large practice.

On 23 July 1873 he married Elizabeth, daughter of M. Grayhurst Hewat of St Cuthbert's, Norwood, with whom he had three sons.

Although Pearson was not one of the crown counsel for Scotland, he was specially retained for the prosecution at the trial of the directors of the City of Glasgow Bank in 1879. He became sheriff of Chancery in 1885, and procurator and cashier for the Church of Scotland in 1886. In 1887 he was knighted, and he was appointed sheriff of Renfrew and Bute in 1888, and of Perthshire in 1889. He was a Conservative in politics, and in 1890 he was appointed solicitor-general for Scotland in Lord Salisbury's second administration: concomitantly, he was elected unopposed as MP for Edinburgh and St Andrews universities, and in the same year he became a QC. In 1891 he succeeded James Patrick Bannerman Robertson, Lord Robertson, as lord advocate. At the general election of 1892 he was again returned unopposed for Edinburgh and St Andrews universities, but after the subsequent fall of Lord Salisbury's ministry he ceased to be lord advocate, and was chosen dean of the Faculty of Advocates.

Pearson received the honorary degree of LLD from Edinburgh University in 1894, and on the return of the Conservatives to power in the following year he became again lord advocate, and resigned the deanship. In 1896 he was appointed to the bench, from which he retired, owing to bad health, in 1909. He died at Edinburgh on 15 August 1910, and was buried in the Dean cemetery there. His wife survived him.   G. W. T. OMOND, rev. ROBERT SHIELS

Sources F. J. Grant, ed., *The Faculty of Advocates in Scotland, 1532–1943*, Scottish RS, 145 (1944) · [W. M. Watson], ed., *The history of the Speculative Society, 1764–1904* (1905), 156 · *Compendium of the acts of the general assembly of the Church of Scotland* (1886) · J. Foster, *Men-at-the-bar: a biographical hand-list of the members of the various inns of court*, 2nd edn (1885) · *The Times* (16 Aug 1910) · *The Scotsman* (16 Aug 1910) · *CGPLA Eng. & Wales* (1910)

Archives U. Edin. L., corresp.

Likenesses J. Irvine, portrait, priv. coll.

Wealth at death £27, 643 15s. 7d.: confirmation, 4 Oct 1910, CCI

Pearson, Colin Hargreaves, Baron Pearson (1899–1980), judge, was born in Minnedosa, Manitoba, Canada, on 28 July 1899, the younger son and youngest of three children of Ernest William Pearson (1861–1936), a lawyer, and his wife, Jessie Borland (d. 1948). The family moved to London when Pearson was seven. He was educated at St Paul's School. His sister died in childbirth and his brother was killed in the First World War. After military service in 1918 in the 5th Guards Machine-Gun regiment he went to Balliol College, Oxford, where he was a classical scholar and a Jenkyns exhibitioner. He obtained a first class in classical honour moderations (1920) and a second in *literae humaniores* (1922). He then turned to law. He was called to the bar in 1924 by the Inner Temple and held a Yarborough Anderson exhibition.

Pearson built up a sizeable common-law practice. In 1930 he was appointed junior counsel to the office of works. On 30 July 1931 he married Sophie Grace, eldest daughter of Arthur Hermann Thomas, an antiquarian and deputy keeper of records at the Guildhall; they had a son and a daughter. In 1937 Pearson was made recorder of

Hythe. During the Second World War he worked in the Treasury solicitor's office. He returned to the bar in 1945 and took silk in 1949. Only two years later, in 1951, although not well known as an advocate, he was appointed a judge of the King's Bench Division of the High Court. It was an inspired choice: he had now found his true role.

In 1960 Pearson was briefly president of the restrictive practices court, but in the following January he was promoted to be a lord justice of appeal. In 1965 he was further promoted to the House of Lords and sat as a lord of appeal-in-ordinary until 1974. After 1974 he occasionally spoke in debates.

Pearson never thought of himself as a great judicial intellectual, but he had a clear mind, profound legal knowledge, and unfailing courtesy. His judgments in some leading cases, if not couched in scintillating terms, have stood up well.

Pearson was a valuable committee man. He chaired a committee in 1958–9 about managing funds paid into court for widows and infants; served on the Supreme Court rule committee (1957–65); and chaired the Law Reform Committee (1963–73). But he did not restrict himself to the law. His name was increasingly brought before a wider public as he conducted inquiries into a whole series of industrial disputes—electricity supply (1964), shipping (1966–7), civil air transport (1967–8), steel (1968), and docks (1970). In 1971–2 he chaired the arbitral body on teachers' pay.

In 1973 Pearson was asked to head the royal commission on civil liability and compensation for personal injury. He regarded this assignment as the culmination of his career. The existing compensation arrangements, especially over the operation of tort in regard to work and road accidents, had been much criticized, and the review which he now undertook, lasting five years and involving the collection of much evidence at home and abroad, was the most thorough survey of its kind ever conducted. The commission had a widely drawn membership, but Pearson achieved a report which, on essentials, was unanimous. It concluded that social security and tort had developed as though they had little to do with each other, and proposed a new relationship, with tort having a junior topping-up role. Detailed recommendations included a 'no fault' scheme for road accidents and a regime of strict liability for defective products, including drugs, a proposal especially relevant to the thalidomide tragedy.

Pearson was greatly disappointed that there was so little response by government, and in his own profession, to the ideas so carefully argued in his monumental report. He admitted that he had underrated the strength of the forces opposed to change.

Pearson always took a close interest in education. He did much to help St Paul's School and Bedford College, London. He took particular pleasure in his appointment as visitor to Balliol College (1965–74). He was appointed CBE in 1946, knighted in 1951, and sworn of the privy council in 1961. He became a bencher of his inn in 1951, and was treasurer in 1974.

Pearson was a gentle, courteous, and patient man who inspired great affection. To the end, he remained remarkably receptive to new ideas. He made a notable contribution not just to the law but also to the wider concerns of society.

Pearson died in London on 31 January 1980. He was survived by his wife. ALLEN OF ABBEYDALE, *rev.*

Sources *The Times* (1 Feb 1980) · *The Times* (7 Feb 1980) · personal knowledge (1986) · private information (1986) · Burke, *Peerage* (1967)

Wealth at death £72,739: probate, 3 June 1980, *CGPLA Eng. & Wales*

Pearson, Sir (James) Denning (1908–1992), engineer and businessman, was born on 8 August 1908 in Bootle, Lancashire, the son of James Pearson, engineer, and his wife, Elizabeth, *née* Henderson. His father died when he was twelve and Pearson moved with his mother to Cardiff, where he was educated at Canton secondary school. Apprenticed at a local shipyard, C. H. Bailey, Graham, he studied part time at Cardiff Technical College, and was awarded a London University first-class honours degree in engineering. After a year of postgraduate research he was awarded a senior Whitworth scholarship, which he used for turbine research at Metropolitan Vickers. On 2 September 1932 he married Eluned (*d.* 1992), daughter of Edward Henry of Treherbert, Glamorgan. They had two daughters.

Pearson joined Rolls-Royce in 1932 to work in the aero-engine department, where Ernest Hives was in charge of the development of what became the Merlin engine. Because of the international situation Hives, general manager from 1936, accelerated work on the Merlin in order to ensure that there would be enough engines to supply the RAF when war broke out. The government built 'shadow factories' at Crewe, and Hillington, Glasgow, and leased them to Rolls-Royce for the production of Merlin engines, which were fitted into the Hurricanes and Spitfires that won the battle of Britain in 1940, and later into Lancaster bombers. Pearson was sent to Glasgow in 1941 as a technical production engineer, becoming chief technical production engineer later that year. As part of his job he made several visits to the United States to train the workforce at the Packard automobile factories to manufacture Merlin engines.

At the end of the war Hives sent Pearson to Canada for a year to open a technical office to service the modified Merlin engines that were being fitted into Douglas DC-4 airliners for sale to Trans-Canada Airlines, Canadian Pacific, and the Royal Canadian Air Force. In 1946 he returned to Derby as general manager for sales and service for the aero-engine division, becoming a director in 1949, general manager in 1950, and managing director in 1954. Remaining head of the aero-engine division until 1965, he became chief executive and deputy chairman of Rolls-Royce in 1957, when Hives retired as chairman. He was knighted in 1963. During his years as head of the division he concentrated on the civil aviation business, selling Rolls-Royce engines to airlines all over the world at a time when gas turbine engines were replacing piston engines. The Dart turbo-prop engine was fitted to the Viscount aircraft, the world's first turbo-prop airliner (which British European Airways brought into service in 1953 and which became Britain's most successful airliner), and the Avon jet engine was used in the Comet 2 and 4 jet airliners and in the French Caravelle. Rolls-Royce was involved in a number of new projects in the early 1960s, after the government announced that it would provide financial support for four new British airliners, including the VC10 and the Trident, all using Rolls-Royce engines. After Rolls-Royce took over its only British rival, Bristol Siddeley Engines, in 1966, it became the sole surviving British aero-engine manufacturing company, with a combined workforce of 80,000. In addition, in 1959 Pearson was responsible for setting up Rolls-Royce and Associates, a separate company, to supply submarine pressurized water reactors (PWR) for the Royal Navy's nuclear submarine programme. Rolls-Royce and Associates also took over the management of the nuclear reactor plant at Dounreay in 1965.

By the early 1960s it was becoming clear to Pearson that if Rolls-Royce was to survive as one of the three leading aero-engine manufacturers in the world it must develop a new large engine capable of powering the new wide-bodied jumbo jets which were being developed by the American aircraft manufacturers. As work began on the RB211 engine, Pearson sent teams to the United States in the belief that Rolls-Royce must secure a major order to supply a major American aircraft. Pratt and Whitney won the contract to build engines for the Boeing 747s, but in 1968, after fierce negotiations, the Rolls-Royce team beat off competition from General Electric and Pratt and Whitney to win the order to supply engines for ninety-four Lockheed airliners (later called TriStars). The British government agreed to provide a maximum of £47.1 million towards the development costs of the RB211 engine, which was 70 per cent of the estimated £65.5 million launching costs. In 1969, as the project was running into difficulties, Pearson succeeded Lord Kindersley as chairman of Rolls-Royce. Rolls-Royce, in its eagerness to win the Lockheed contract, had greatly underestimated the engineering problems and the timescale, and the estimated cost of launching the RB211 escalated. Despite a further £42 million from the government in 1969, in September 1970 Rolls-Royce reported to the minister of aviation that it could only continue in business if the government were to inject an additional £40 million over the next two years. After the government agreed in November 1970, on condition that there were changes in the top management, Pearson resigned. The Rolls-Royce board called in a receiver on 4 February 1971, and Rolls-Royce was taken into state ownership. The aero and marine divisions became Rolls-Royce Ltd, and the motor car division was floated as a separate company, Rolls-Royce Motors, in 1973. The RB211 was subsequently successfully developed, with sales to the end of 1991 amounting to some £11.5 billion in 1991 values.

Pearson was chairman of Gamma Associates, a consultancy firm, from 1972 to 1980. One of his most cherished beliefs was that a training in engineering was the best

training for management, and engineers were predominant on the board of Rolls-Royce. Pearson retained an interest in management training: he was a member of the universities/industry joint committee of the Confederation of British Industry, a governor of the London Graduate School of Business Studies, and a member of the council of Manchester Business School from 1962 to 1986. He died on 1 August 1992 at his home, Green Acres, Holbrook, Derbyshire. He was survived by his two daughters, his wife having died earlier in 1992.

ANNE PIMLOTT BAKER

Sources M. Donne, *Leader of the skies* (1981) · 'Rolls Royce Ltd and the RB211 aero-engine', *Parl. papers* (1971–2), 9.17, Cmnd 4860 · Francis, Lord Tombes of Brailes, *Rolls-Royce: a history of enterprise* (1992) · R. Gray, *Rolls on the rocks* (1971) · I. Lloyd, *Rolls-Royce*, 2: *The years of endeavour* (1978) · R. Harker, *The engines were Rolls-Royce* (1979) · D. Huddie, 'The launch of the RB 211', Rolls-Royce Heritage Trust lecture, 6 June 1992, Rolls-Royce Heritage Trust, Derby [video] · *The Times* (5 Aug 1992) · *The Independent* (15 Aug 1992) · *WWW*, 1991–5 · Burke, *Peerage*
Archives CAC Cam., papers
Likenesses double portrait, photograph, 1970 (with Leonard Griffiths), Hult. Arch. · J. Brewster-Beard, drawing, repro. in *Archive* [Rolls-Royce Heritage Trust magazine], 49, cover · photograph, repro. in *The Times* · photograph, repro. in *The Independent*
Wealth at death £259,868: probate, 4 Nov 1994, *CGPLA Eng. & Wales*

Pearson, Edward (1756–1811), Church of England clergyman and religious controversialist, was born at St George's Tombland, Norwich, on 25 October 1756, the eldest son of Edward Pearson (*d.* 1786), a wool-stapler at Norwich and later of Tattingstone, Suffolk, and a descendant of the family of Dr John Pearson (1613–1686), bishop of Chester. He was educated at home and then at Ipswich grammar school before matriculating from Sidney Sussex College, Cambridge, as a sizar, on 7 May 1778. He earned the favourable attention of the master, Dr William Elliston, and of the college tutor, the Revd John Hey, rector of Passenham, Northamptonshire, who appointed him his curate on 26 April 1781. Pearson was ordained deacon by the bishop of Peterborough in 1781 and priest in 1782. He graduated BA after coming out sixth senior optime in the mathematical tripos in the University of Cambridge for 1782. He was awarded MA in 1782 and BD in 1792, and was elected fellow of Sidney Sussex and college tutor in 1788. In 1786 he won the Norrisian prize in the University of Cambridge for his essay *The Goodness of God as Manifested in the Mission of Jesus Christ*. Pearson was appointed to curacies at Cosgrove and at Strutton and, in 1788, at Pampisford, near Cambridge. In 1797 he married Susan, daughter of Richard Johnson of Henrietta Street, Covent Garden, London. He left Cambridge in the same year and was presented by Elliston to the rectory of Rempstone, Nottinghamshire.

Pearson began to distinguish himself as a pulpit orator and religious controversialist, first in Cambridge and then on a wider stage. His credentials as a preacher were secured by the publication in 1798 of his *Thirteen Discourses to Academic Youth, Delivered at St. Mary's, Cambridge*. In 1807 he was appointed Warburtonian lecturer at Lincoln's Inn, and in 1810 he was elected Christian advocate in the University of Cambridge on the Hulsean foundation. His Warburton lectures were published in 1811 as *Twelve Lectures on the Subject of the Prophecies Relating to the Christian Church*. In 1808 he was elected master of his former college and in 1811 served as vice-chancellor of Cambridge University.

Pearson's staunchly orthodox Anglican churchmanship found expression in a prolific series of publications initially occasioned by a Cambridge academic context in which the influence of the moral philosophy of William Paley held sway. In 1800 Pearson subjected Paley's system to qualified criticism in his *Remarks on the Theory of Morals*, which he followed in 1801 with *Annotations on the Practical Part of Dr. Paley's Work*. As Pearson explained in this work his concern was to guard younger readers 'against the errors, into which that work notwithstanding its general excellence and usefulness, has a tendency to lead them' (pp. vi–vii). Pearson next turned his attention to the threat to the established church that he perceived to emanate from evangelicalism and especially Calvinism, characterizing it as a subversion 'from within, by the revival of certain gloomy, harsh, and revolting doctrines' (Pearson, x). He was the author of a series of polemical responses to Anglican evangelical apologetics from John Overton, author of *The True Churchman Ascertained* (1801), and the more moderate leader of the evangelical party in Cambridge, Charles Simeon. In his *Remarks on the controversy subsisting, or supposed to subsist, between the Arminian and the Calvinist ministers of the Church of England: in a second letter to the Rev. John Overton* (1802) Pearson not only repudiated Overton's Calvinist interpretation of Anglican formularies but objected to Simeon's use of the appellation 'evangelical' as the unwarranted 'assumption of a title which, by arrogating so much to yourselves, was directly calculated to derogate from the just claims of others' (p. 6). Pearson further repudiated Anglican evangelical doctrinal claims in *A letter addressed to the editor of the Orthodox Churchman's Magazine, containing remarks on the Rev. Mr. Simeon's sermon, entitled 'The churchman's confession'* (1806) and in his *Cautions to the hearers and readers of the Rev. Mr. Simeon's sermon entitled 'Evangelical and pharisaical righteousness compared'* (1810). He was also a frequent contributor, from 1801, to the *Orthodox Churchman's Magazine*, an orthodox Anglican and anti-evangelical as well as anti-Catholic periodical, one of his more significant contributions being an article in refutation of David Hume's argument against miracles (vol. 12, January 1807, 15–18).

Pearson was a firm advocate of the benefits of a national established church. His sensitivity to the threats to both the constitutional hegemony and the spiritual integrity and unity of the established church was illustrated by his published sermons and polemical treatises. Most of these writings were directly inspired by Pearson's parochial difficulties with protestant dissenters at Rempstone, especially his *Letters to a Young Man* (1801), in which he sought to persuade a candidate for the office of parish schoolmaster in Rempstone to abandon attendance at the local meeting-house as a prerequisite for appointment to that office. His sermon *The Sin of Schism* (1800) was published only on the insistence of William Gregory Williams, high sheriff of Nottinghamshire, that it would be beneficial because of 'the particular situation of our neighbourhood' (dedication). Pearson strove hard to persuade not only protestant dissenters but Roman Catholics to abandon what he regarded as their errors and to become reconciled with the Church of England. His anti-Calvinism and opposition to protestant dissent was matched by his anti-Catholicism, but in spite of the widely perceived threat from rational dissent and Paineite infidelity not all orthodox churchmen agreed with his argument 'that the established religion, so far as this part of the united kingdom is concerned, has less to fear from Catholics, than from almost any other sect', a view for which he was criticized in the *Orthodox Churchman's Magazine* (vol. 13, September 1807, 223).

While Pearson claimed to eschew party politics his defensive campaign in favour of the religious establishment involved close collaboration with Spencer Perceval, prime minister from 1807 until his assassination in 1812. It was Perceval who sought out Pearson's friendship, valuing him as 'a sincere and judicious adviser' (Pearson, viii–ix). An example of their collaboration came when Perceval, then chancellor of the exchequer, supported Pearson's proposal in the *Orthodox Churchman's Magazine* of May 1806 for the foundation of 'a ritual professorship in Divinity' at Cambridge. Perceval offered to guarantee the expenses for five years, but the scheme foundered on the refusal of the academic authorities to adopt it.

Pearson was scrupulous in the performance of his parochial duties at Rempstone. He instituted an evening lecture, in addition to double service, on Sundays, and also introduced weekday services for the purpose of reading portions of the liturgy. His biographer concluded that he 'seemed completely to realise the idea of a primitive pastor' (Pearson, xi). His devotional inclinations were well expressed in his *Prayers for Families* (1797), which went through four editions. He was assiduous as a catechist and wrote *Exhortations to the Duty of Catechising* (1805), though on his own admission the number of parishioners who presented themselves was very limited. However, his long-running feud with the evangelical party was reflected in his accusation that evangelical clergymen neglected catechizing their congregations. An indignant reviewer in the Anglican evangelical *Christian Observer* of 1805 condemned the work for its 'gross errors and calumnious representations' (p. 750).

Pearson, who had been of a playful, pleasant, and humorous disposition and manner, died of an apoplectic fit at his parsonage at Rempstone on 17 August 1811.

PETER B. NOCKLES

Sources E. Pearson, *Prayers for families … selected by the late Edward Pearson, prefixed with biographical memoir*, 4th edn (1819) · *Graduati Cantabrigienses* (1823), 362 · *GM*, 1st ser., 81/2 (1811), 198 · records, Sidney Sussex College, Cambridge · J. R. Tanner, *History of the University of Cambridge to 1910* (1917), 460 · Venn, *Alum. Cant.* · *Orthodox Churchman's Magazine* · Nichols, *Illustrations*, 5.86–91

Likenesses W. C. Edwards, line engraving (after W. M. Bennett), BM, NPG

Pearson, Eglington Margaret (*bap.* 1746, *d.* 1823). *See under* Pearson, James (*c*.1740–1838).

Pearson, Egon Sharpe (1895–1980), statistician, was born on 11 August 1895 at 7 Well Road, Hampstead, London, the only son and second of the three children of Karl *Pearson (1857–1936), mathematician and university teacher, and his wife, Maria (1853–1928), fifth daughter and sixth child of William Sharpe, solicitor, of Islington. He was educated at the Dragon School, Oxford, and Winchester College, and was then accepted in June 1914 as an entrance scholar to Trinity College, Cambridge. In spite of ill health, he obtained a first class in part one of the mathematical tripos. After a period of war service at the Admiralty and Ministry of Shipping, he returned to Cambridge where he graduated BA in 1920 (and MA in 1924).

After leaving Cambridge, Pearson joined his father's department at University College, London, as a statistics lecturer. He obtained his London DSc in 1926. He helped with the editing of the journal *Biometrika*, founded in 1901 by Karl Pearson and W. F. R. Weldon with the support of Sir Francis Galton, who had also on his death endowed the chair held by Karl Pearson at University College from 1911. By 1924 Pearson was assistant editor of *Biometrika* and he became managing editor in 1936 after his father's death. Three years earlier Karl Pearson had retired from the Galton chair, and his department was split into two, the eugenics (later human genetics) department with which the Galton chair was associated, and a statistics department, of which Pearson was made head with promotion to reader, becoming a professor in 1935.

An animosity between Karl Pearson and the new Galton professor, R. A. Fisher, neither of whom had approved the separation of the statistics department, did not augur well for its development. Moreover, Egon Sharpe Pearson was to have an important professional collaboration with Jerzy Neyman, a Polish mathematician whose interest in mathematical statistics had been stimulated both by his friendly association with Pearson while studying at University College, and indirectly by the work of Fisher, but whose theoretical approach appeared to Fisher to be of little relevance. Nevertheles, the Neyman–Pearson theory of testing statistical hypotheses, resulting from a collaboration extending over eight or nine years, secured a recognized place in textbooks on statistical inference, introducing such useful concepts as the 'power' of statistical tests against alternative hypotheses.

A less controversial development was Pearson's encouragement of statistical methods in industry in the United Kingdom, arising from a contact established with W. H. Shewhart of the Bell Telephone Laboratories during a visit to North America in 1931. This utilitarian approach to statistical methodology contributed also after 1939 to Pearson's war work, when he, with some of his staff, was seconded to the Ordnance board, where they were involved in such problems as assessing the effectiveness of patterns of fragmentation of anti-aircraft shells. After the war Pearson returned to University College, retiring in 1960 from his chair, but continuing with his editorial

work for *Biometrika*. Honours and awards included the Weldon prize and medal in 1935, appointment as CBE in 1946, and in 1955 the gold medal of the Royal Statistical Society, of which he was president in 1955–6. He was elected FRS in 1966.

On 31 August 1934 Pearson had married (Dorothy) Eileen (1901/2–1949), younger daughter of Russell Jolly, solicitor; they had two daughters. It was a great personal loss when his wife died from pneumonia in 1949, though he kept on their Hampstead house with the aid of a housekeeper, until 1967 when he moved to Cambridge after marrying (on 11 January) Margaret Theodosia (1896/7–1975), widow of Laurence Beddome Turner, reader emeritus in engineering, Cambridge, and second daughter of George Frederick Ebenezer Scott, architect, and Mrs Bernard Turner, of Godstowe School, High Wycombe. In 1975, after her death, he finally severed his remaining links with *Biometrika*, and moved to West Lavington, near Midhurst in Sussex.

Pearson had a quiet disposition, but his shy and rather diffident manner hid an independent and pertinacious spirit which had enabled him to surmount both the controversies surrounding his father and contemporaries such as Fisher and Neyman, and some health problems, such as his delicate health when an undergraduate, a heart condition of long standing, and occasional back trouble due to his considerable height. He died at the Pendean Home, West Lavington, on 12 June 1980.

M. S. BARTLETT, *rev.*

Sources M. S. Bartlett, *Memoirs FRS*, 27 (1981), 425–43 · *The Times* (20 June 1980), 16f · M. S. Bartlett, *Biometrika*, 68 (1981), 1–12 · N. L. Johnson, *Journal of the Royal Statistical Society: series A*, 144 (1981), 270–71 · private information (1986) · personal knowledge (1986) · b. cert. · m. certs. · d. cert.
Archives UCL, corresp. and papers | UCL, corresp. with David John Finney
Likenesses photograph, repro. in Bartlett, *Biometrika*
Wealth at death £26,066: probate, 29 Aug 1980, *CGPLA Eng. & Wales*

Pearson, George (*bap.* 1751, *d.* 1828), physician and chemist, the son of John Pearson, an apothecary, was baptized in Rotherham, Yorkshire, on 4 September 1751. After attending Doncaster grammar school he studied medicine at Edinburgh University from 1770 to 1774, graduating MD in 1773. He also studied chemistry under Joseph Black. After a short period at St Thomas's Hospital in London, he spent about two years in Europe. Pearson was married, and the father of at least two daughters. His eldest daughter, Frances Priscilla, married Sir John Dodson (1780–1858). Pearson became a licentiate of the Royal College of Physicians in 1784, and in 1787 was appointed chief physician at St George's Hospital, London, where he lectured on chemistry, materia medica, and therapeutics. He became a fellow of the Royal Society in 1791 and was for several years a member of the council. From 1792 Pearson lectured in chemistry in his laboratory at Wilcomb Street, London, and in physic at 9 Great George Street, Hanover Square, London.

During a visit to Europe in 1805–6 Benjamin Silliman, the American chemist and geologist, met Pearson and breakfasted with him and his family. However, he remarked that he felt 'out of place' in Pearson's company. Pearson was courteous, but apparently careless of his appearance. Silliman attended a lecture by Pearson which, he said, lasted two and a quarter hours without a break. 'There was no interval for breathing or for a gentle transition to a new subject. This mental repletion was not favourable to intellectual digestion.' He also commented on the paucity of apparatus in Pearson's lecture rooms, which he described as shabby and ill-furnished. Pearson's experiments, Silliman continued, were not well performed (G. P. Fisher, 1.144–5).

Notwithstanding this impression, Pearson seems to have been a competent chemist. His contributions to chemistry are not much mentioned in histories of the subject, but they were not trivial. On investigating James's Powder, a popular febrifuge which had made a fortune for Robert James, he found it to be a mixture of bone ash and antimony oxide ('Experiments and observations to investigate the composition of James's Powder', *PTRS*, 81, 1791, 317–67). Extending the work of Smithson Tennant, who had shown that carbon was obtained on strongly heating powdered marble (calcium carbonate) with phosphorus, Pearson found that sodium carbonate could be similarly decomposed. By heating quicklime (calcium oxide) with phosphorus he discovered calcium phosphide, and observed the spontaneous combustion in air of the gas (phosphine) that was generated when he added water to this compound. Phosphine had been first discovered by Gengembre, an almost unknown chemist, in 1783, but as yet was little known ('Experiments made with the view of decompounding fixed air, or carbonic acid', *PTRS*, 82, 1792, 289–308).

In 1789 Adriaan van Troostwijk and Jan Deiman had succeeded in decomposing water by frictional electricity. Pearson, in collaboration with John Cuthbertson, who had assisted the Dutch chemists and constructed their apparatus, improved on their results in being able to show more convincingly that the gases obtained were hydrogen and oxygen ('Experiments and observations made with the view of ascertaining the nature of the gas produced by passing electric discharges through water', *Journal of Natural Philosophy, Chemistry and the Arts*, 1, 1797, 241–8, 299–305, 349–55; abstract in *PTRS*, 87, 1797, 142–58).

Most of Pearson's other writings are on medical matters, several being devoted to investigating certain body fluids which occurred as a result of disease. Undoubtedly, in the history of chemistry, Pearson's most important work was his introduction into Britain of the new systematic nomenclature (the basis of the modern nomenclature in inorganic chemistry), devised by a group of French chemists, headed by Antoine Lavoisier, the man Pearson referred to as 'the immortal, and ever to be deplored Lavoisier' (Lawrence, 311). Pearson was one of the first British chemists to accept Lavoisier's oxygen theory of combustion, in place of the current theory of phlogiston. A feature of Lavoisier's *Méthode de nomenclature chimique* (1787) was a large folding sheet which listed in adjoining columns the current names of all known substances, and their proposed new names. Pearson published a translation of this, with additions and an explanatory text. He adopted the term 'nitrogen' (from 'nitrogène', suggested by J. A. Chaptal in 1790) in preference to 'azote' (*A Translation of the Table of Chemical Nomenclature*, 1794; 2nd edn with additions, 1799).

Pearson was one of the first physicians to express approval of the initiation by Edward Jenner of vaccination. Pearson collected a number of instances of an apparent immunity to smallpox of anyone who had contracted cowpox, and published them in his *An inquiry concerning the history of the cow pox, principally with a view to supersede and extinguish the small pox* (1798). In it he disclaimed any honour for the innovation, which he said belonged exclusively to Jenner.

Subsequently, however, it became clear that Pearson was intent on claiming undue credit for this historic step in preventive medicine. In December 1799, he opened, without informing Jenner of his intention, an institute for vaccination, which he was to head, at 5 Golden Square. Though Pearson shortly afterwards invited Jenner, in a rather offhand manner, to be a corresponding physician, the latter resolutely refused the offer. The ensuing quarrel culminated in 1802 with Pearson's intense opposition to Jenner's successful petition for government compensation for loss of earnings resulting from his preoccupation with promoting vaccination. At the hearing Pearson attempted in several ways to belittle Jenner's achievement. Pearson died on 9 November 1828 as a consequence of a fall at his house in Hanover Square, London, and was buried at St George's cemetery, Bayswater.

E. L. SCOTT

Sources *DNB* · G. P. Fisher, *Life of Benjamin Silliman* (1866) · R. B. Fisher, *Edward Jenner* (1991) · 'Memoir of George Pearson', *GM*, 1st ser., 99/1 (1829), 129–32 [with portrait] · S. C. Lawrence, *Charitable knowledge: hospital pupils and practitioners in eighteenth-century London* (1996) · parish register (marriage), 9 Dec 1778, Rotherham · J. Guest, *Historic notices of Rotherham* (1876), 522
Archives Wellcome L., notes on his lectures
Likenesses aquatint silhouette, 1801, Wellcome L. · T. West, etching, 1803, Wellcome L. · J. S., lithograph, pubd 1829 (after pen drawing), BM, NPG · etching, 1829, Wellcome L. · F. Chantrey, pencil drawing, NPG · drawing, RS · etching, Wellcome L. · line engraving, Wellcome L. · line engraving, NPG · portrait (after drawing), repro. in R. A. Hadfield, *Faraday and his metallurgical researches* · portrait, repro. in *Phil. Mag.*, 17 (1804) · silhouette, line engraving, BM

Pearson, Henry Hugh. *See* Pierson, Henry Hugo (1815–1873).

Pearson, (Edward) Hesketh Gibbons (1887–1964), actor and biographer, was born on 20 February 1887 in Hawford, Worcestershire, the second of the two sons and four children of Thomas Henry Gibbons Pearson (c.1853–1942), gentleman farmer, churchwarden, and amateur sportsman, and his second wife, Amy Mary Constance (c.1855–1934), eldest daughter of George Hesketh Biggs, vicar of Ettington. He attended Bedford grammar school.

As a man without qualifications Pearson drifted towards a commercial career but, after two and a half years in a City shipping office, he was rescued by a legacy of £1000 from an aunt. Having spent almost all this money on adventurous travelling in South America, the United States, and Canada, he returned in 1908 and was rescued this time by his brother, who employed him as manager of his motor-car showroom in Brighton. Pearson used these years to provide himself with an artistic education, listening to music, reading widely, and growing increasingly responsive to the beauties of the English countryside. He was particularly influenced by the works of Oscar Wilde and of Bernard Shaw, and by the Shakespearian productions of Herbert Beerbohm Tree: Wilde, Shaw, Shakespeare, and Tree, the four authors of what he called his 'revelations', were all to be subjects of his biographies. In 1911, despite his lack of training and regardless of parental disapproval, Pearson joined Tree's company and he subsequently acted also in the productions of Harley Granville-Barker and Sir George Alexander, whom he often understudied.

Though invalided out of the infantry in 1915 with tuberculosis, Pearson volunteered the following year for the Army Service Corps, and served for three years in Mesopotamia and Persia. He rose to the rank of captain and was awarded the MC. He almost died from a combination of dysentery, malaria, septic sores, and a head wound, and he attributed his unexpected recovery to reciting Shakespeare's plays, several of which he knew by heart.

In the 1920s Pearson resumed his acting career but he also began to publish short stories, essays, and journalism. His anonymous volume of pen portraits, *The Whispering Gallery being Leaves from the Diary of an ex-Diplomat* (1926), led to his arrest on a charge of 'obtaining or attempting to obtain money under false pretences', but under cross-examination his engaging candour appealed to the jury, which found him not guilty. In 1931 he left the stage to write biographies, beginning with a life of his maternal ancestor Erasmus Darwin, and he followed this with *The Smith of Smiths* (1934), a still popular biography of the Revd Sydney Smith, which carried an inviting introduction by G. K. Chesterton. Pearson's technique as a biographer derived from his career on the stage. To some extent he acted his subjects on the page. He did not take his readers back into history so much as bring Thomas Paine, William Hazlitt, Sir Arthur Conan Doyle, Sir Walter Scott, and others forward, as if they had suddenly walked in from the street. His treatment was informal and impressionistic, depending on entertaining anecdotes, skilful use of quotation, and the dextrous building up of incidents for its effect. Over the 1930s and 1940s he became the most popular biographer in Britain. Assessing his impact on the reading public, Graham Greene wrote that he had 'some of the qualities of Dr Johnson—a plainness, an honesty, a sense of ordinary life going on all the time'.

Pearson's work owed something to the influence of his Johnsonian friend Hugh Kingsmill. He was to pay tribute to Kingsmill after his death in an exchange of letters with Malcolm Muggeridge, published as *About Kingsmill* (1951), and he recalled what had been the deepest friendship of his life between the lines of *Johnson and Boswell* (1958), the last book written at the height of his powers.

Impetuous, opinionated, athletic, good-looking, and full of fun, Pearson was an attractive figure to many women. He felt no competitiveness with other writers and was encouraging to people younger than himself. His genial temperament was, however, punctuated by uncontrollable flashes of temper. These sudden rages, which he attributed to his head wound but which may have been connected with the suppression of inherited melancholy, always passed quickly and disappeared in late life. On 6 June 1912 Pearson married the actress Gladys Rosalind Bardili (1882/3–1951), daughter of Julius Carl Bardili, a German brewer, and his English wife, Emma Gardner, whose surname Gladys used on stage. They had one son who died in 1939. Shortly after his wife's death in 1951 he married on 14 June 1951 Dorothy Joyce Ryder (1912/13–1976), bank cashier, daughter of Frank Bonham Ryder, an electrical engineer. Pearson died on 9 April 1964 at his home, 14 Priory Road, Hampstead, London.

Pearson wrote two autobiographical books, *Thinking it Over* (1938) and *Hesketh Pearson by Himself* (published posthumously in 1965). After his death, from the 1970s into the new century, several of his biographies were reissued, including his lives of Shakespeare, Tree, Shaw, Wilde, and Whistler, with new prefaces by Anthony Burgess, Sir John Gielgud, Richard Ingrams, Peter Quennell, and Benny Green. These biographies and others have now been overtaken by recent scholarship, but they remain excellent introductions to their subjects' lives, and have begun to appear as audiobooks. MICHAEL HOLROYD

Sources R. Ingrams, *God's apology: a chronicle of three friends* (1977) · I. Hunter, *Nothing to repent: the life of Hesketh Pearson* (1987) · M. Holroyd, *Hugh Kingsmill* (1964) · *WWW, 1971–80* · H. Pearson, *Thinking it over* (1938) · *Hesketh Pearson by himself* (1965) · m. certs. · d. cert. · m. cert. [parents]
Archives U. Reading · University of Bristol Library, Penguin Book files, corresp. and literary papers | BL, letters to George Bernard Shaw, Add. MS 50547 · CUL, Royal Society of Literature archive
Likenesses photograph, repro. in Hunter, *Nothing to repent*, facing p. 117 · photographs, repro. in *Hesketh Pearson*, frontispiece and facing p. 38
Wealth at death £8434: probate, 7 Aug 1965, *CGPLA Eng. & Wales*

Pearson, Hugh (1817–1882). *See under* Pearson, Hugh Nicholas (1776–1856).

Pearson, Hugh Nicholas (1776–1856), dean of Salisbury, only son of Hugh Pearson, was born at Lymington, Hampshire, and matriculated from St John's College, Oxford, on 16 July 1796. He graduated BA in 1800, MA in 1803, and DD as 'grand compounder' in 1821. On 13 September 1803 he married Sarah Maria Elliott (1781–1858), eldest daughter of Charles and Sarah Ann Elliott of Clapham, Surrey. Pearson noted in his autobiography his attraction to her 'profile, shaded by a profusion of beautiful hair, inclining to auburn'. Both Pearson and his wife had connections with the Clapham sect of evangelicals.

In 1807 Pearson won the prize of £500 offered by Claudius Buchanan for the best essay on missions in Asia, and his work was printed at Oxford with the title *A Dissertation on the Propagation of Christianity in Asia* (1808). The interest thus aroused in Christian missionary enterprise in Asia prompted Pearson to undertake in 1817 his *Memoirs of the Life and Writings of the Rev. Claudius Buchanan* (2 vols.), dedicated to William Wilberforce; and in 1834 he produced a biography of greater interest, *Memoirs of the life and correspondence of the Rev. Christian Frederick Swartz, to which is prefixed a sketch of the history of Christianity in India*. This reached a third edition in 1839 and was translated into German by C. P. Blumhardt in Basel, in 1846.

After ordination Pearson was curate to the evangelicals Richard Cecil and John Venn. In 1822 he was appointed vicar of St Helen's, Abingdon, with Radley and Drayton chapelries, and in 1823 he was appointed dean of Salisbury and a domestic chaplain to George IV. He resigned his deanery in 1846 and died at Sonning in Berkshire on 17 November 1856. During the last years of his life he lived mainly with his fourth son, Hugh [see below].

The eldest son, **Charles Buchanan Pearson** (1807–1881), born at Elmdon, Warwickshire, graduated BA from Oriel College, Oxford, with a second class in *literae humaniores* in 1828. He took orders in 1830, and in November 1838 became rector of Knebworth, Hertfordshire, where he became friendly with the first Lord Lytton. Besides a paper entitled 'Hymns and hymn-writers', contributed to *Oxford Essays for 1858*, and *Latin Translations of English Hymns* (1862), he published *Sequences from the Sarum Missal, with English Translations* (1871), and *A Lost Chapter in the History of Bath* (1877). He was a competent hymnist. His wife was Harriet Elizabeth Pinkerton; they had two boys. He died at home, 2 Catharine Place, Bath, on 7 January 1881, survived by his wife.

The dean's second son, William Henley Pearson (1813–1883), assumed in 1865 the additional name of Jervis [see Jervis, William Henley Pearson-]. Another son, Henry Hugo, changed his surname to Pierson [see Pierson, Henry Hugo].

The fourth son, **Hugh Pearson** (1817–1882), was born on 25 June 1817, and graduated MA from Balliol College, Oxford, in 1841. He was in the same year appointed vicar of Sonning in Berkshire, a preferment which he held until his death. He was rural dean of Henley-on-Thames from 1864 to 1874, and of Sonning from 1874 to 1876; he was appointed chaplain to the bishop of Manchester in 1870, was created a canon of Windsor in 1876, and, on the death of his closest friend, A. P. Stanley, became deputy clerk of the closet to the queen.

By nature excessively retiring, and undogmatic to the extreme limits of latitudinarianism, Pearson was a notable figure within the church; while, outside it, his character endeared him to people of every rank in life. He was an excellent preacher, but would not allow his sermons to be printed; and though he had an extraordinary knowledge of literature, he never dreamed for a moment of becoming an author. Much of his emotional life centred on A. P. Stanley. He frequently accompanied Stanley abroad, and was with him in Italy just before Stanley's marriage and his decision to accept the deanery of Westminster in 1863;

he was present at Stanley's deathbed on 18 July 1881. He declined an invitation to succeed Stanley in the deanery at Westminster, on the ground that he wished to remain what he had always been—a private person. He died at Sonning, unmarried, on 13 April 1882, and was buried in Sonning churchyard, on 18 April. There is a memorial to him in that church.

THOMAS SECCOMBE, *rev.* H. C. G. MATTHEW

Sources W. H. Jones, *Fasti ecclesiae Sarisberiensis, or, A calendar … of the cathedral body at Salisbury* (1879) · *GM*, 3rd ser., 1 (1856), 775 · *Salisbury and Winchester Journal* (22 Nov 1856) · *The Times* (10 Jan 1881) · *The Times* (15 April 1882) · *The Times* (19 April 1882) · *The Times* (25 May 1882) · *The Guardian* (12 Jan 1881) · *The Guardian* (20 April 1882) · R. E. Prothero and G. G. Bradley, *The life and correspondence of Arthur Penrhyn Stanley*, 2 vols. (1893) · H. N. Pearson, 'Autobiography', Salisbury Cathedral Library · J. S. Reynolds, *The evangelicals at Oxford, 1735–1871: a record of an unchronicled movement*, [2nd edn] (1975) · *CGPLA Eng. & Wales* (1881) [Charles Buchanan Pearson] · *CGPLA Eng. & Wales* (1882) [Hugh Pearson jun.] · d. cert.
Archives Bodl. Oxf., S. Wilberforce MSS
Wealth at death under £14,000—Charles Buchanan Pearson: probate, 4 March 1881, *CGPLA Eng. & Wales* · £38,664 16s.—Hugh Pearson: probate, 25 May 1882, *CGPLA Eng. & Wales*

Pearson [*married name* Miller], **(Frances) Issette Jessie** (1861–1941), golfer, was born on 2 November 1861 at Gatcombe House, Littlehempston, near Totnes, Devon, the daughter of Thomas Pearson, 'gentleman with funded property' (b. cert.), and his wife, Mary Lucy, *née* Clover; her given name was Mable Frances but she always used the name Frances Issette Jessie and was known as Issette. She had two younger sisters. In 1864, after a bad investment brought him close to ruin, Thomas Pearson took his family to Birkenhead, where he began an insurance business. The success of this venture made possible a move to London and it was on Barnes Common, about 1887, that Issette (as she was always known) began to play golf.

Issette Pearson became a member of the ladies' section of the Royal Wimbledon Club and emerged as one of the best players of her era. She had 'few equals, and only one superior' (Stringer, 213): the remarkable Lady Margaret Scott, winner of the first three British ladies' open championships. Pearson met Scott on each occasion: she lost to her in the final at Lytham and St Anne's in 1893, again in the final at Littlestone in 1894, and in the third round at Royal Portrush in 1895. Pearson habitually suffered from match nerves and was said to be put off completely 'if faced with an opponent who could not take a beating cheerfully' (Cossey, 156). But her organizational responsibilities at the ladies' open championships must also have detracted from her game. She eventually retired from competition to concentrate full time on administration. After the championship of 1895 at Portrush she captained an England side in an impromptu match against Ireland, the first international, and throughout her career she was at the forefront of developments in the women's game.

Pearson was an influential honorary secretary of the Ladies' Golf Union (LGU) from its inception in 1893. The union originated with the determination of a group of Wimbledon players to start a ladies' championship. They sought advice from the leading Wimbledon player Laidlaw Purves, who advised them to make contact with other ladies' clubs, of which there were already more than fifty. Representatives of eleven of these met at the Grand Hotel, Trafalgar Square, London, on 19 April 1893, when they founded the LGU. It was to be a representative body in which all ladies' clubs would be invited to participate. Guided by Pearson's organizational drive, it quickly grew to become one of the foremost governing bodies in women's sport. By 1912 there were over 500 affiliated clubs. Initially the union was based at Pearson's home at 10 Northumberland Avenue, Putney. Assisted by golfing friends, principally but not exclusively female, Pearson was responsible for all of the initial organization. Single-minded and tough, she was reputedly 'as despotic as the Czar of Russia' (Cossey, 26). Of above average stature, Pearson was a dominant personality with strong views on, among other things, women's dress. She frowned on low-cut dresses and always, even at dinner, wore hers high to the neck. Her peremptory style attracted criticism, and spectators at competitions especially resented being ordered around by her when following a match. She was described by her nephew as 'a considerable hazard to all and sundry who happened to be enjoying a walk' (Mair, 18).

But Pearson's hard work on behalf of the union was widely recognized and she was the inspiration behind the handicap system that remains one of the greatest achievements of the LGU. In the early days of women's golf the vagaries of handicapping rendered the outcome of many inter-club and open contests meaningless. Pearson had personal experience of this when on one occasion she visited another club and received strokes from her opponent, when it was obvious after the first hole that she should have been giving them. Tackling this complex problem became one of the first priorities of the LGU. By 1896 the union had arrived at a standardized method of calculating, for any given course, 'par of the green': the score that a championship player would find great difficulty in lowering. A player's handicap then became the difference between this and the average of their three best scores. A handicap management committee at the LGU collated all the available information on courses and players and produced handicap lists. The widespread adoption of the system both reflected and ensured its success, and by 1906 Pearson could reflect on a battle won. It had involved a prodigious amount of work on the part of the union, and above all Pearson herself, 'the successful solver of the riddle of women's handicaps' (Stringer, 178).

With her close friend Mabel Stringer, Pearson also drew up the rules for county golf, in 1899, and edited the LGU handbook, issued annually from 1894, an important point of reference in the women's game. As well as encouraging new competitions she encouraged new competitors, and she was one of the first to recognize the great talent of Charlotte Cecilia ('Cecil') Leitch. Her involvement in the game, however, began to diminish after her marriage, on 6 September 1911, to Thomas Horrocks Miller, a wealthy widower of Singleton Park, Singleton, Lancashire. He was

himself a staunch supporter of women's golf, and was an early vice-president of the LGU (Stringer, 243). Marriage nevertheless entailed a change of direction for his new wife, who attempted to resign from the LGU in 1912. She cited as her reason the obligations arising from her husband's large household. She was, however, persuaded to stay on and was made a life member of the LGU just before the outbreak of war in 1914. The death of her husband in 1916 left to her the sole responsibilities of his large estate and it was to this that she now directed her energies. She lived increasingly in Lancashire and only rarely saw her old golfing friends. She eventually retired from the LGU in 1921, although she kept abreast of its affairs for some time afterwards.

Issette Pearson died at Singleton Park on 25 April 1941. It was a mark of the esteem in which she was held that for as long as the old telegraphic system prevailed the first line of the LGU's postal address was 'Issette'. Undeniably she had limitations, and she recognized them. Mabel Stringer described her as 'an autocrat of autocrats' (Stringer, 213). But Stringer also believed that this very quality was an important asset to ladies' golf in its pioneering days, when 'women had had little opportunity of combining for organised endeavour' (ibid.).   MARK POTTLE

Sources M. E. Stringer, *Golfing reminiscences* (1924) · E. Wilson, *A gallery of women golfers* (1961) · R. Milton, *A history of ladies' golf in Sussex* (1993) · R. Cossey, *Golfing ladies: five centuries of golf in Great Britain and Ireland* (1984) · L. Mair, *One hundred years of women's golf* (1992) · M. Hezlet, *Ladies' golf* (1907) · *The Times* (7 May 1941) · b. cert. · m. cert. · census returns, 1881
Wealth at death £39,842 17s. 8d.—save and except settled land: probate, 1941, *CGPLA Eng. & Wales* · £131,290 6s. 1d.—limited to settled land: probate, 1941, *CGPLA Eng. & Wales*

Pearson, James (c.1740–1838), glass painter, was born in Dublin but played a significant role in the revival of English enamel glass painting. He trained in the ceramics industry in Bristol but later moved to London and became a pupil of William Price the younger. His first documented commission was in 1769. His *Christ and the Four Evangelists* (1776), after designs by John Hamilton Mortimer, survives in Brasenose College chapel, Oxford. *Moses and the Brazen Serpent* (1781, after Mortimer) also survives in Salisbury Cathedral. Pearson produced a wide range of religious and secular works, heraldry, and ornament throughout his long career, and frequently exhibited from his own homes in London (21 Great Newport Street, Long Acre; 112 Great Russell Street) and in the Pantheon, Oxford Street. His speciality was large-scale copies of well-known paintings in which the supporting lead and iron work were skilfully concealed by complex technical means. A life-sized portrait of George III of 1793 (after Sir Joshua Reynolds) in the Stained Glass Museum in Ely Cathedral, and the east window of St Botolph, Aldersgate, of 1788—*The Agony in the Garden* (after Charles Le Brun)—are highly characteristic works. On 23 June 1768, at St Martin-in-the-Fields, Pearson married Eglington Margaret [**Eglington Margaret Pearson** (*bap.* 1746, *d.* 1823)], daughter of the auctioneer and bookseller Samuel Paterson (1724–1802) and his wife, whose maiden name was Hamilton. She had been baptized on 5 November 1746 at St Paul's, Covent Garden. She was also a talented glass painter specializing in small-scale, finely detailed panels—particularly flower and bird portraits—for the burgeoning domestic market. Her copies of the Raphael cartoons (one of which is in the orangery of Bowood House, Calne, Wiltshire) were much admired. The Pearsons both exhibited at the Society of Artists' exhibitions in 1775, 1776, and 1777 when they resided in Church Street, St John's, Westminster. Despite very different working styles they sometimes collaborated on individual pieces such as copies of *The Salutation* by Carlo Maratti and Guido's *Aurora*. A collection of their small paintings on glass was sold by auction in 1797. James Pearson was still exhibiting glass as late as 1821. He painted glass for the church of St Giles Cripplegate, and for the parish churches of Battersea and Wandsworth. Margaret Pearson died on 14 February 1823. In 1837 Pearson was forced to apply to the Royal Academy for financial assistance. He died in 1838.

L. H. CUST, rev. SARAH BAYLIS

Sources M. Wynne, 'Irish stained and painted glass in the eighteenth century', *Crown in glory: a celebration of craftsmanship*, ed. P. Moore (1982), 58–68 · S. F. Baylis, '"The most untractable of all Saxon uncouthness": eighteenth-century painted glass in Ely Cathedral and the removal of the choir', *Antiquaries Journal*, 68 (1988), 99–114 · Redgrave, *Artists* · J. Dallaway, *Observations on English architecture, military, ecclesiastical, and civil, compared with similar buildings on the continent* (1806), 287–8 · GM, 1st ser., 85/2 (1815), 28–9 · J. Pearson, 'Stained glass', *Literary Gazette* (26 Feb 1820), 138 · W. Warrington, *The history of stained glass from the earliest period of the art to the present time* (1848), 15–16 · Bryan, *Painters* (1849) · W. G. Strickland, *A dictionary of Irish artists*, 2 (1913), 224–5 · C. Hosken, 'An eighteenth-century woman glass-painter', *The Connoisseur*, 69 (1924), 133–4 · N&Q, 6th ser., 12 (1885), 187, 255 · IGI · sale catalogue [Christies]

Pearson, Sir James Reginald (1897–1984), motor vehicle manufacturer, was born on 17 November 1897 in Dudley, Worcestershire, the son of George Henry Pearson, a fender moulder, and his wife, Annie, *née* Stringer. He attended a local infant school after which he moved to Park demonstration school, and later to Dudley higher elementary school. When he was fifteen he took up a machining apprenticeship at Bullers Ltd of Tipton with attendance at evening classes. During the First World War he joined the Royal Flying Corps but was withdrawn to do essential war work, taking up a post at the national projectile factory in Dudley. He became unemployed after the war and in 1919 travelled to Luton to seek work, eventually finding a position at Vauxhall Motors. His first position was as a centre-lathe turner in the machine shop. He was to remain at Vauxhall for the next forty-three years, rising through the ranks to a seat on the board. In 1925 he married Nellie Rose Vittery (*d.* 1977), a draper's daughter; they had one daughter.

Pearson became a foreman in 1927, and two years later was again promoted, to area manager. He then progressed rapidly when his potential senior managerial qualities were recognized by the newly appointed managing director, Charles Bartlett, who in 1934 promoted him to

assistant production manager, beginning a working relationship which spanned the following twenty years and encompassed the enormous expansion of the company through peace and war.

In 1939 Pearson was promoted to the crucial position of production manager, and became a key figure in the wartime production changeover from cars to Bedford army trucks, Churchill tanks, and other war material. Both as assistant and as production manager Pearson was in close contact with production workers and, having risen from the shop floor himself, felt a close affinity with them. In his managerial philosophy he recognized that close involvement with the workforce to foster good industrial relations was essential for co-operation and high productivity. The implementation of these aims was embodied in the group bonus system, which had been introduced in the 1920s. His aim was to make time-and-motion measured operations comfortable for employees and to ensure a reasonable bonus for each group of workers. Such a system, he felt, encouraged team effort and a harmonious working atmosphere, and, together with the close working relationship between managers and the workforce, was, he believed, responsible for the comparatively untrammelled industrial relations at Vauxhall up to the 1950s.

In 1942 Pearson was made factory manager and became the supremo of wartime production at the Luton plant. Despite air raids and bombing, which frequently disrupted production, his capable management resulted in a smooth return to work and the fulfilment of ordnance contracts which often meant working under great pressure. In 1946 he was appointed a director of Vauxhall and in 1950 made OBE in recognition of his service to British industry in peace and war. In 1953 he was appointed executive assistant to the managing director, and in 1958 he became deputy chairman. He was knighted in the following year, and retired from Vauxhall in 1962.

Sir Reg, as he was known to his friends, led an active life in retirement, becoming lord lieutenant of Bedfordshire, chairman of Dawley New Town corporation (1963–8), and vice-president of the Royal Society for the Prevention of Accidents. The diversity of his other interests can be gauged by his membership of the Glyndebourne Festival Society and the English-Speaking Union, and his fellowship of the Royal Horticultural Society. He never lost his affection for Vauxhall and retained strong connections with it until his death. Living in nearby Harpenden he was called upon to act as guest speaker at numerous company functions, and was life president of its recreation club. He died at 220 Old Bedford Road, Luton, on 17 March 1984.

LEN HOLDEN

Sources J. R. Pearson, 'From group bonus to straight time pay', *Journal of Industrial Economics* (Oct 1960) · L. T. Holden, 'A history of Vauxhall Motors to 1950', MPhil diss., Open University, 1983 · L. T. Holden, 'Think of me simply as the skipper: industrial relations at Vauxhall, 1920–1950', *Oral history*, 9 (1981), 18–32 · M. Platt, *An addiction to automobiles* (1980) · P. W. Copelin, 'Development and organisation of Vauxhall Motors Limited', *Studies in business organisation*, ed. R. S. Edwards and H. Townsend (1961), 78–92 · K. Ullyett,

The Vauxhall companion (1971) • G. Turner, *The car makers* (1963) • W. J. Seymour, *An account of our stewardship: being a record of the wartime activities of Vauxhall Motors Ltd* (1946) • M. Sedgwick, *Vauxhall: a pictorial tribute* (National Motor Museum, Beaulieu, Hampshire, 1981) • L. C. Derbyshire, *The story of Vauxhall, 1857–1946* (1946) • L. Holden, 'Pearson, Sir James Reginald', *DBB* • *WW* • *Who's who in the motor industry* (1963) • d. cert.

Archives SOUND Beds. & Luton ARS, interview with Sir Reginald Pearson 1979 [by L. T. Holden (personal archive transcript)]
Likenesses photographs, Vauxhall Motors Ltd, Luton • photographs, repro. in L. Holden, 'Pearson, Sir James Reginald' • photographs, National Motor Museum, Beaulieu • photographs, Luton Central Library
Wealth at death £290,354: *The Times*; *Luton News* (17 March 1984)

Pearson [*née* Sibson], **Jane** (1735?–1816), Quaker minister and autobiographer, was born at Newtown, near Carlisle, one of the four children of Jonathan and Jane Sibson. Her posthumously assembled and published autobiography, *Sketches of piety, in the life and religious experiences of Jane Pearson extracted from her own memorandum* (1817), in which she recounts the 'Lord's dealings' with her 'backslidings' to assist 'some poor, tossed, afflicted, disconsolate, tempted, bewildered mind' (*Sketches of Piety*, 1), is the main source of information about her life. Born into a religious family, she loved to read the scriptures, and early in life experienced 'a godly sorrow' (ibid., 14). Following her father's death, when she was young, her mother hired a private schoolmaster to keep the children 'from associating with those of other persuasions' (ibid.).

Naturally timid and reticent, Jane Sibson struggled with her strong sense that she had a mission to convince 'the suffering seed' that she was 'compassionating their distress' (*Sketches of Piety*, 23). In 1757, at the age of twenty-one or twenty-two, she married John Pearson (d. 1774), a linen manufacturer of Greysouthen, Cumberland, who shared her religion. Although the marriage brought her happiness, within a year she was acutely aware of her 'undone condition' (ibid., 19), describing herself as 'a castaway' (ibid., 22). During this prolonged period of guilt-ridden temptation, marked by insomnia and inedia, she saw her mind as 'a place for dragons, for owls, and for screech owls, for cormorants and for bitterns' (ibid., 28–9). Divine intervention ultimately brought relief, yet she remained reluctant to speak about it for fear of being considered 'guilty of some gross thing' (ibid., 29).

Spiritual dilemmas and doubts are given much more space in Jane Pearson's memoirs than domestic details. She had seven children: four daughters and three sons. Two sons died young of smallpox, since she was 'not free to inoculate for it' (*Sketches of Piety*, 32), and the eldest son of a fever. The death of her husband in June 1774 elicited the moving testimony that she 'could have parted with her children to have had him spared' (ibid., 33). Following his death Jane Pearson embarked on her travels, with other Quaker women, through Lancashire and Yorkshire; she ministered at Quaker women's meetings for a total of forty-two years. The death of her youngest daughter, Hannah, at the age of nineteen, in 1784, prompted her to write some verses, which were printed in the *Sketches*. The death

of her only remaining daughter in 1806 led to the observation that 'the tree [was] wholly peeled' (ibid., 83). She died on 20 March 1816, aged 'about 81 years' (ibid., 95), and was interred in the Quaker burial-ground, Whitehaven, on 25 March.   PATRICIA DEMERS

Sources *Sketches of piety, in the life and religious experiences of Jane Pearson extracted from her own memorandum* (1817) • Blain, Clements & Grundy, *Feminist comp.*

Pearson, John (1613–1686), bishop of Chester, was born on 28 February 1613 at Great Snoring, Norfolk, and baptized there on 14 March. He was the eldest of the nine children of Robert Pearson (d. 1640) and his wife, Joanna, daughter of Richard *Vaughan, bishop of London. Robert Pearson, who came from Westmorland to Queens' College, Cambridge, as a sizar in 1587, became a fellow and MA in 1592 and DD in 1609. From 1607 to his death in 1640 he was rector of North Creake, near Walsingham, Norfolk, and from 1610 rector of Great Snoring nearby. Collated archdeacon of Suffolk in 1613, he appears from his *Articles to be Enquired of in the Ordinary Visitation* (1639) to have been a firm enforcer of Bishop Richard Montagu's church discipline. In 1626 John Davenant—bishop of Salisbury and formerly a fellow of Queens' with Pearson—gave to Pearson the prebend of Netherhaven, which he eventually resigned in 1639.

Student and chaplain John Pearson was a king's scholar at Eton College from 1623 to 1631. He was certainly a hard-working student: one story tells of his re-lighting his candle once the rest of the dormitory was asleep and, through these midnight studies, reading 'most of the Greek and Latin Fathers of the Church' before leaving school. Initially admitted to Cambridge at Queens' College on 10 June 1631, Pearson entered King's College as a scholar the following April, matriculating the same year. He contributed two Latin poems to *Anthologia Cantabrigiensis in exanthemate regia* (1632) on Charles I's recovery from smallpox and one to *Justa Edovardo King* (1638). Like other poems about Edward King, Pearson's fourteen lines—on the sea's protecting Britain and yet drowning this ornament to Cambridge—are overshadowed by Milton's 'Lycidas' at the volume's end. He contributed another poem to *Voces votivae* (1640) on the birth of Prince Henry. Pearson became a fellow of King's in 1635, graduating BA in 1636 and MA in 1639. Pearson's father's successor to the Salisbury prebend having died within a few weeks, Davenant chose Pearson to replace him on 30 December 1639, which obliged him to resign his fellowship on 2 August 1640. In June that year he became chaplain to Lord Keeper Finch; but Finch, implicated in Charles I's unpopular policies, was impeached in October and in December fled to The Hague.

Through these and the succeeding troubled times, Pearson was helped by a small inheritance from his father and much more substantially by the patronage of Sir Edward Coke's family. On 27 October 1640 Coke's son Henry presented Pearson to the rectory of Thorington, Suffolk; Pearson retained his predecessor's curate, John Freeman, and

John Pearson (1613–1686), by David Loggan

continued to spend at least some of his time at King's. Towards the middle of 1643 he preached a university sermon, 'The excellency of forms of prayer', a scathing attack on the extemporarians and on the impending Westminster assembly, to which, proclaims the last sentence, 'whosoever will not freely submit his judgement … deserves no better, than—to be counted a member of the catholic church!' (*Minor Theological Works*, 2.111). Like others embarking on the Church of England's defence, Pearson had to answer both sectaries' attacks on its traditions and Romanists' attacks on its authority: in *Christ's Birth Not Mistimed* (1649) he defended the celebration of the nativity, and in a preface to Lord Falkland's *Discourse of Infallibility* (1651 edn) he noted Hugh Cressy's uneasiness in adopting that doctrine.

In 1645 Pearson was in the west of England as chaplain to Goring's army, of which little remained after the battle of Langport on 10 July. He was obliged to give up the rectory of Thorington some time before 31 March 1646, at which time Henry Coke presented it to John Chunne. Henry's elder brother Robert reportedly made Pearson his chaplain, and Evelyn's diary for 1 August 1650 seems to corroborate this: 'after dinner at *Durdens* [Robert Coke's house at Epsom], meeting my former acquaintance *Mr. Pierson*, I had good Conversation' (Evelyn, 3.15). Subsequently Pearson is said to have been chaplain to Robert's brother-in-law George, Lord Berkeley, whose funeral sermon he preached in 1658, and to his son of the same name (who inherited Durdans in 1653). On 1 May 1658 Pearson delivered in London another funeral sermon, on his contemporary and fellow Cantabrigian the royalist poet John Cleveland. This sermon, which unfortunately does not survive, 'made his death glorious' (*Clievelandi vindiciae*, 1677, sig. A7v).

London preacher On 17 April 1652 Evelyn heard Pearson preach in Eastcheap—presumably at St Clement, where he heard him again on 9 March 1653. At that time, or certainly by August 1654, Pearson was one of the parishioners' voluntary lecturers, delivering the weekly sermons that led to the great book by which he is chiefly known, *An Exposition of the Creed* (1659). Written, as he explains, for both unlearned and learned readers, 'the body of it containeth fully what can be delivered and made intelligible in the English tongue', and in the margin

> is contained whatsoever is necessary for the illustration of any part of the Creed, as to them which have any knowledge of the Latin, Greek, and Oriental languages, of the writings of the ancient Fathers, the doctrines of the Jews, and the history of the Church.   (J. Pearson, 'To the reader', *An Exposition of the Creed*, 1659)

In the mid-1650s Pearson made extensive manuscript notes on the works of Aeschylus, which Thomas Stanley appropriated verbatim and without acknowledgement in his edition of 1663. The 'liveliness of perception and the keen interest in literary history' shown by Pearson's more general comments 'are no less noticeable … than his enormous learning' (Fraenkel, 1.80). His prolegomena to the Neoplatonist Hierocles's *De providentia* (1655) and his manuscript notes on the lexicographer Hesychius are also significant contributions to classical studies, and typical in their different ways of Pearson's scholarly interests.

In November 1652 Evelyn 'went to *Lond*: where was proposd to me the promoting of that greate Work (since accomplishd by *Dr. Walton* (*Bishop* of Chester) *Biblia polyglotta*), by *Mr. Pierson* that most learned divine' (Evelyn, 3.78). Pearson is not mentioned by Brian Walton among his collaborators; he helped, however, to assemble the commentaries and tracts of the substantial collection *Critici sacri* (1660), to which he also wrote the preface. In 1659 he wrote brief prefaces to David Stokes's *Explication of the Minor Prophets* and to the *Golden Remains* of 'the ever memorable' John Hales, a fellow of Eton in Pearson's schooldays. He was active once more in polemics: in 1657 he and Peter Gunning engaged 'two Disputants of the Roman Profession', and in 1660 he published two antipresbyterian tracts against reformation of the public doctrine of the Church of England.

Restoration churchman In 1660 Pearson petitioned Charles II for a mandamus to take his DD, from which he had been prevented because he 'could not submit to the late irregularities' (*CSP dom.*, 1660–61, 164); the degree was conferred the following year. Successive preferments now came to him: archdeacon of Surrey (presented by Charles II, 19 July 1660); rector of St Christopher-le-Stocks, Threadneedle Street, London (collated 17 August 1660); canon of Ely (collated fifth prebend 28 August 1660, first prebend 9 October 1661); master of Jesus College, Cambridge (admitted 4 December 1660). He owed the canonry and mastership to the patronage of Matthew Wren, bishop of Ely, whose funeral sermon he preached in 1667.

Pearson was a Lent preacher at court in 1661, and when the Savoy conference opened on 15 April he was one of the assistant commissioners on the episcopal side. He participated very actively and the bishops chose him, with Peter Gunning and Anthony Sparrow, to put their case in the formal disputation at the end. Their chief opponent, Richard Baxter, recalled

> Dr. *Pierson* was their true Logician and Disputant, without whom, as far as I could discern, we should have had nothing from them, but Dr. *Gunning*'s passionate Invectives mixd with some Argumentations: He disputed accurately, soberly and calmly (being but once in any passion) breeding in us a great respect for him, and a perswasion that if he had been independent, he would have been for Peace, and that if all were in his power, it would have gone well: He was the strength and honour of that Cause which we doubted whether he heartily maintained. (*Reliquiae Baxterianae*, ed. M. Sylvester, 1696, 2.364)

The doubt about Pearson's commitment sounds like wishful thinking.

When convocation met (initially in May 1661) Pearson among other duties took an active part in preparing a Latin version of the prayer book and, early in 1664, a standard Latin and Greek school grammar, an educational scheme that was not pursued. He and Gunning were 'the prime advisers' of the amplifications in the ordination formulae for priests and bishops (H. Prideaux, *Validity of the Orders of the Church of England*, 1688, 43). In June 1661, on the king's recommendation, Pearson succeeded Gunning as Lady Margaret's professor of divinity at Cambridge. He began his tenure with a series of scholastic lectures 'On the being and attributes of God'; the other lectures that survive, from the end of his professorship, are on the Acts of the Apostles. Related to these, as part of a larger projected work, are six 'Theological determinations' of specific questions. Pearson also left some learned Latin sermons from these Cambridge years and some more topical commencement orations. None of this Cambridge material was printed in his lifetime; in the 1660s the only substantial scholarly work he published was his preface to the Septuagint, 1665, defending the old translators against the censure of St Jerome.

Master of Trinity College, Cambridge On 14 April 1662 Pearson was translated by the king to the mastership of Trinity College, Cambridge, in place of Henry Ferne, promoted bishop of Chester. Writers on Pearson state that he never married and discount an octogenarian fellow's recollection of the master's wife at Trinity (Churton, 1.lxv, cxvi); however, a warrant for his presentation to the mastership was issued 'with dispensation for him to hold the said place, he being in a state of marriage' (*CSP dom.*, 1661–2, 173). So there is reason for uncertainty. Now, if not earlier, he resigned his Salisbury prebend and London benefice, to which his successors were chosen on 9 and 22 August 1662. At Trinity, Pearson proved an obliging and conscientious master, whose college business included the composition of eulogies later published in *Letters and Poems in Honour of the Incomparable Princess, Margaret, Duchess of Newcastle* (1676). He lived modestly and donated £250 (reckoned to be half his annual salary) to the rebuilding of St Paul's Cathedral; he also loaned the exchequer £100 'for his Majesty's service for the maintenance of the present war' (*Calendar Treasury Books*, 1667–8, 161–2). On 14 March 1667 he was elected to the Royal Society, proposed by Matthew Wren, Clarendon's secretary and son of the Matthew Wren, bishop of Ely. Although a barely active member, he was on the council in 1675 and he paid his subscription regularly through the 1670s.

In 1672 Pearson published his second great work, *Vindiciae epistolarum S. Ignatii*, written in Latin and directed primarily against the French protestant Jean Daillé. The point at issue was episcopacy, which after the Restoration became increasingly central to the Church of England's apologetics. Scripture uses the words *episcopos* and *presbyteros* interchangeably, but Ignatius makes bishops pre-eminent. As an apostolic father—the only one to express this view—protestants had to take account of Ignatius. The authenticity of his letters had been vigorously debated: some, and parts of others, looked to be spurious but there seemed no way to be certain. In 1645 James Ussher found the way with two manuscripts in which the text predated the medieval interpolations. This should have settled the matter, but anti-episcopalians could not give up, because the episcopal passages were still there in the genuine letters. French protestants, harassed by Louis XIV, felt especially vulnerable. Daillé, who had a considerable reputation as a learned and moderate writer, advanced sixty-six objections to Ignatius's authorship and dated the forgery about the year 300. Pearson demolishes first the external, then the internal, arguments of Daillé and other anti-episcopalians. His use of linguistic evidence is especially impressive, and his ability to come up with three or four refutations of an argument anticipates the treatment of Phalaris's letters by Richard Bentley, who memorably wrote of Pearson 'the very dust of his writings is gold' (R. Bentley, *Works*, ed. A. Dyce, 3 vols., 1836–8, 2.29). Pearson anticipates Bentley also in his sense of literary history and the character of particular ages. (On one important point he corrected Ussher, who was misled by the testimony of St Jerome into thinking there were six, not seven, genuine letters.)

Bishop of Chester According to a newsletter of January 1671 it was believed that Pearson would have one of the bishoprics then vacant; but his elevation did not occur until the end of the following year, when he was chosen for the see of Chester. As this was one of the poorer bishoprics, he was granted, like his predecessors, a dispensation to hold the rectory of Wigan, Lancashire, *in commendam*, and also to retain his archdeaconry of Surrey. Pearson was consecrated at Lambeth on 9 February 1673. For his first diocesan visitation he had printed *Articles of Inquiry* (1674); he held a second visitation in 1677. In 1675 he issued injunctions to the cathedral clergy, dealing among other things with the performance of the choir and the cathedral school. Initially he was lenient to nonconformists but later accepted the magistrates' increasing severity. On 25 September 1683 Secretary Jenkins complained about his administration: the Thanksgiving for

Charles's preservation from the Rye House plot was not performed in the archdeaconry of Richmond. Jenkins would have recalled the pro-Monmouth riots the previous September when the mob ransacked Chester Cathedral.

In the 1670s Pearson was often in London to attend parliament and also to preach his Lent sermon at court. In his first parliamentary session the Lords considered the Commons' bill for the toleration of dissenters, and other difficult questions of religion were to follow. On 31 October 1674 Secretary Williamson wrote to Pearson as one of the bishops 'particularly pitched upon' to meet and advise the king on 'the preservation and security of the Protestant religion'. Pearson was unwell, confined to his chamber by gout, but eventually left for London on 25 November. The bishops' advice, signed by Pearson and five others late in January 1675, called for firmer measures against Catholics (*CSP dom.*, 1673–5, 390, 403, 416, 437, 549–50). On 28 February 1675 Pearson ordained 'about 30 *Deacons & Priests*' at St Paul's, Covent Garden (Evelyn, 4.54). He described himself as 'infirme' in his will, dated 2 January 1678, but he was present at the opening of parliament on 15 January (PRO, PROB 11/384/116). He continued to be in London when parliament met and he attended the Lords fairly regularly, up to the dissolution in January 1681. He was at the third Exclusion Parliament, 21–8 March 1681, every day. But the following year he could no more make long journeys.

Pastor and scholar The notion that Pearson was a negligent valetudinary derives from Burnet's aspersion:

> He was not active in his diocese, but too much remiss and easy in his episcopal function; and was a much better divine than a bishop. He was a speaking instance of what a great man could fall to: for his memory went from him so entirely, that he became a child some years before he died. (*Bishop Burnet's History*, 3.134)

The image of senility is conveyed by Henry Dodwell's anecdote: the bishop, led into his library by an old nurse, 'held out his hands, and cried out, "O sad, whose books are all these?"' (E. Bridges, *Restituta*, 1, 1814, 53) This condition was shorter-lasting than Burnet's 'some years' implies: Pearson's detailed *Annales Cyprianici* introduced John Fell's 1682 edition of Cyprian, and in 1683 he was still composing his posthumously published dissertations on the succession of Roman bishops. He held an ordination service on 21 December 1684; he dictated the codicil to his will, although unable to sign it, on 18 June 1685; he performed his last institution in person on 3 September 1685; he appointed John Allen, his chaplain, archdeacon of Chester on 12 April 1686, and John Thane prebendary a week later. He died at Chester on 16 July 1686. In his will Pearson bequeathed his Norfolk property at Great Snoring and at 'Brownham' (Downham) to his brother Theophilus. He left money to other relatives and to the poor of Great Snoring and of St Oswald's parish, Chester. He had already helped his nephews, appointing Henry Dove archdeacon of Richmond, on 3 December 1678, and John Thane, who inherited most of his books and papers, Chester prebendary.

In Chester Cathedral Pearson's burial place, modestly unmarked and forgotten near the high altar, was discovered in 1841, and his body was moved to the north transept, where a very large tomb, designed by Sir Arthur Blomfield, was raised over it in 1863. Pearson's true glory was not a matter of marble and wrought iron: he belonged, in Pepys's phrase, among 'the great Cavalier parsons during the late troubles' (Pepys, *Diary*, 8.337); his friend Evelyn reckoned him 'the most learned Divine of our Nation' (Evelyn, 4.5–6), and Burnet acknowledged him 'in all respects the greatest divine of the age' (*Bishop Burnet's History*, 3.134). His *Exposition of the Creed*—clear, accurate, sensitive, and extraordinarily detailed—remains a standard work, unlikely to be surpassed. His *Vindiciae* effectively settled the authenticity of Ignatius's letters; indeed, when William Cureton argued in 1845 that the shorter, newly discovered Syriac version was the authentic core, one response was Edward Churton's new edition of the *Vindiciae* (1852). Moreover, as Fraenkel writes:

> Pearson, though primarily known as a theologian, was perhaps England's greatest classical scholar before Bentley (his only possible rival being Thomas Gataker); in range of learning and critical power he is probably inferior to no English scholar save Bentley. (Fraenkel, 1.40)

HUGH DE QUEHEN

Sources E. Churton, 'Memoir', in *Minor theological works of John Pearson*, 2 vols. (1844), 1.xiii–cxxxvi · *Fasti Angl., 1541–1857,* [Canterbury] · *Fasti Angl., 1541–1857,* [Salisbury] · *Fasti Angl., 1541–1857,* [Ely] · Evelyn, *Diary* · E. Fraenkel, *Prolegomena, Aeschylus: Agamemnon*, ed. E. Fraenkel, 1 (1950) · *CSP dom.*, 1660–86 · *JHL*, 11–14 (1660–91) · Venn, *Alum. Cant.* · *Walker rev.* · W. Sterry, ed., *The Eton College register, 1441–1698* (1943) · J. B. Lightfoot, *The apostolic fathers, part 2: S. Ignatius and S. Polycarp*, 2nd edn, 3 vols. (1889) · H. de Quehen, 'Politics and scholarship in the Ignatian controversy', *Seventeenth Century*, 13 (1998), 69–84 · *VCH Cheshire*, vol. 3 · *Bishop Burnet's History*, vol. 3 · M. Hunter, *The Royal Society and its fellows, 1660–1700: the morphology of an early scientific institution*, 2nd edn (1994) · Bénézit, *Dict.*, 4th edn · will, PRO, PROB 11/384, quire 116, fols. 201v–202r · R. V. H. Burne, *Chester Cathedral: from its founding by Henry VIII to the accession of Queen Victoria* (1958) · Bodl. Oxf., MS Tanner 35, fol. 162 **Archives** Brasenose College, Oxford, transcripts · Trinity Cam., MSS | Bodl. Oxf., Fell, Rawlinson, Smith, and Tanner MSS · CUL, *adversaria* **Likenesses** F. H. Van Hove, line engraving, 1675 (after W. Sonmans), NPG; repro. in J. Pearson, *An exposition of the creed*, 4th edn (1676) · I. Whood, oils, 1737, Trinity Cam. · W. Behnes?, bust, 1847, Eton · T. Earp, effigy on monument, marble, 1863, Chester Cathedral · W. Elder, engraving (after D. Loggan), repro. in J. Pearson, *An exposition of the creed*, 6th edn (1692) · D. Loggan, line engraving, BM, NPG, V&A [*see illus.*]

Pearson, John (1758–1826), surgeon, son of John Pearson of Coney Street, York, was born in Coney Street on 3 January 1758. He was apprenticed at the age of sixteen to a surgeon in Morpeth, Northumberland, from where he moved, in June 1777, to Leeds. There he lived for three years at the home of William Hey, the eminent surgeon to the Leeds Infirmary, whose biography he later wrote. Pearson travelled to London in 1780 and entered as a student at St George's Hospital to work under John Hunter. He appears to have been granted the diploma of the Company of Surgeons on 4 October 1781, when he was found qualified to act as surgeon to a regiment. In the same year he became house surgeon to the Lock Hospital at so critical a period in its fortunes that in 1782 he was appointed surgeon there, a post he held until 1818. He was also made surgeon, about this time, to the Public Dispensary, then newly founded, in Carey Street, an office which he resigned in 1809. He was elected a fellow of the Royal Society on 24 March 1803, and he afterwards became a fellow of the Linnean Society. In 1820 he was made an honorary member of the Royal College of Surgeons in Ireland, and he also became a member of the Royal Medical Society of Edinburgh. In 1785 he was living in Air Street, London, but he afterwards moved to Golden Square.

Pearson appears to have been a careful surgeon with a strong scientific bias. His writings, however, are neither numerous nor important. He wrote *Principles of Surgery* (part 1, 1788; the second part was never published). The principles are drawn up in a concise and aphoristical form for the use of students attending Pearson's lectures on surgery. His *Plain and Rational Account of the Nature … of Animal Magnetism* was published in 1790, *Practical Observations on Cancerous Complaints* in 1793, 'Some account of the two mummies of the Egyptian ibis' in the *Philosophical Transactions*, of 1805 (part 1, 264, and plates), and *Life of William Hey* in 1822. He married Sarah (1763?–1826), daughter and heir of Robert Norman of Lewisham. John Norman *Pearson (1787–1865) was their son. Pearson died on 12 May 1826. His wife survived him until September of that year.

D'A. POWER, rev. MICHAEL BEVAN

Sources GM, 1st ser., 96/1 (1826), 476 · GM, 1st ser., 96/2 (1826), 284 · *London Medical and Physical Journal*, 56 (1826), 51 **Archives** Royal College of Physicians of Edinburgh, casebook and lectures

Pearson, Sir John (1819–1886), judge, was born on 5 August 1819 at Tunbridge Wells, Kent, the son of the Church of England priest John Norman *Pearson (1787–1865) and his wife, Harriet Puller. He was the elder brother of Charles Henry *Pearson. He graduated BA at Gonville and Caius College, Cambridge, on 24 February 1841 and MA on 2 July 1844, having been called to the bar at Lincoln's Inn on 11 June that year. On 21 December 1854 he married Charlotte Augusta, daughter of William Short, rector of St George's, Bloomsbury.

A diligent lawyer, but without influential connections or conspicuous brilliance, Pearson rose slowly at the chancery bar, and did not secure queen's counsel until 13 December 1866. He was elected a bencher of Lincoln's Inn in 1867 and treasurer in 1884–5. On 24 October 1882, on the retirement of Vice-Chancellor Hall, Pearson was appointed to succeed him, but without the title of vice-chancellor; he was knighted at Windsor on 30 November.

During his brief judicial career Pearson proved a competent judge in land, patent, and company law. His decisions on the Settled Land Act of 1882 did much to decide the interpretation of that important statute. He was also a member of the councils of both legal education and law

reporting. Pearson died on 13 May 1886 at his residence, 75 Onslow Square, South Kensington, London, after a painful illness of some weeks' duration, and was buried in Brompton cemetery. He was survived by his wife.

J. M. RIGG, rev. HUGH MOONEY

Sources *The Times* (14 May 1886) · *Law Times* (22 May 1886), 69 · *Solicitors' Journal*, 30 (1885–6), 486–7 · *Law Journal* (22 May 1886), 297–8 · *Annual Register* (1886) · J. Haydn, *The book of dignities: containing rolls of the official personages of the British empire* (1851) · J. Foster, *Men-at-the-bar: a biographical hand-list of the members of the various inns of court*, 2nd edn (1885) · CGPLA Eng. & Wales (1886) **Archives** Bodl. Oxf., letters to Charles Pearson **Wealth at death** £49,986 6s. 4d.: probate, 22 June 1886, CGPLA Eng. & Wales

Pearson, John Loughborough (1817–1897), architect, was born on 5 July 1817 in Brussels, the youngest of the eleven children of William Pearson (1772–1849), topographical artist, etcher, and watercolourist, and his wife, Nancy (Ann), *née* Loughborough (1776–1869), who came from the Isle of Man. His grandfather Thomas Pearson, a solicitor, was a freeman of Durham.

Pearson grew up in Durham a sharp, clever boy, fond of acting and reciting. In 1831 he started his architectural training under Ignatius Bonomi at Durham, and he continued as Bonomi's principal assistant. His study of the great northern cathedrals and abbeys at this time inspired his future architectural style. Meanwhile he was influenced by George Townsend, a canon of Durham, in whose Sunday school he served.

Pearson left Bonomi at the end of 1841 and briefly worked for George Pickering before going to London early the next year. Here he lived for the rest of his life. He spent five months with his friend the architect Anthony Salvin, tracing from Salvin's library. In October he became Philip Hardwick's principal assistant, completing the drawings of the new hall and library of Lincoln's Inn, and executing these works.

In 1843 Canon Townsend asked Pearson to rebuild Ellerker Chapel, at Brantingham in the East Riding of Yorkshire, to a new, Decorated Gothic design. This work, consecrated in 1844, introduced Pearson to several of Townsend's friends, all, like Townsend, influential Tractarians. Impressed with Pearson's ability, they would commission from him over the next ten years several new churches in the Gothic style, as well as schools and houses. These commissions allowed him to leave Hardwick's employment, and formed the basis of an increasingly flourishing practice. Among them were new churches in the East Riding at Wauldby, North Ferriby, and Ellerton, and the restoration of Elloughton church, and also a new church at Weybridge, Surrey, and restorations at Stow on the Wold, Gloucestershire, and Lea, Lincolnshire; for the Raikes family (to become his oldest friends) he rebuilt Llangasty Tal-y-llyn church in Brecknockshire and built a new school and Treberfydd House (1848–52). In 1849 he started work on his first London church, Holy Trinity, Bessborough Gardens, Westminster (dem.), which was greatly praised for its correct interpretation of the English

John Loughborough Pearson (1817–1897), by Walter William Ouless, 1889

'middle pointed' (Decorated) Gothic style when completed in 1852. His restoration in 1850–52 of the Norman vault at Stow in Lindsay, Lincolnshire, which had collapsed in the later middle ages, was widely admired, and Pearson was consequently elected fellow of the Society of Antiquaries of London. Stone or brick vaults became an increasingly common feature of his new church designs thereafter.

Pearson had already undertaken a number of secular designs. Treberfydd House, completed in an attractively asymmetrical English Gothic style of the kind promoted by A. W. N. Pugin, was followed in 1856–9 by his second great house, Quar Wood, near Stow on the Wold, in a demonstratively French Gothic style (now extensively altered). This was prompted by foreign travel, an influence first evident following a visit to Amiens and Beauvais in 1853, inspired by the writing of John Ruskin and recorded in a small sketchbook (which, like many of his other surviving private papers, is in the possession of a great-grandson, whereabouts unknown). A second sketchbook records a journey later in the year through Belgium and up the Rhine from Cologne to Mainz. Quar Wood and the equally vigorous designs begun in 1857 for churches at Daylesford in Gloucestershire, Scorborough and Dalton Holme in the East Riding of Yorkshire, and Catherston Leweston, Dorset, are completely assured in their handling of French and Italian details, luxuriantly carved and decorated in multicoloured and patterned stone without prejudice to their underlying form.

The design of Titsey church in Surrey followed in 1859, the year of a visit to Normandy, recorded by another sketchbook. He found there what would inspire the last elements in his mature designs, namely rib-vaulting, tall turrets, and broached spires. Pearson's second London church, St Peter's, Vauxhall, Lambeth (1860–64), was immediately noticed for its brick vaulting: this was a constructional novelty, executed as cheaply as a conventional timber roof. The church's final cost of about £8000 was only two-thirds of the cost of Holy Trinity, Bessborough Gardens, and of other similar churches then being built. Pearson's application of the classical Golden Section (about 1 : 1.6) in this Gothic design, notably in the proportion of the width and height of the nave and chancel, remained unnoticed. The interior, lit by large clerestory windows, and vaulted in brick with stone ribs and arches, is truly monumental; a tall steeple and much of the proposed window tracery and rich carving were omitted to reduce costs, leaving a spare design, all the more effective for its strong massing and serene spaces. Beside the church a parsonage, an orphanage, and schools complete an impressive group of Gothic buildings, at once picturesque and original in their treatment.

With these London works adding to his laurels, Pearson's career steadily expanded: in the East Riding of Yorkshire he sensitively restored the Norman churches at Kirkburn and Garton in the Wolds and also Riccall church; in the North Riding, the ornate Christ Church at Appleton-le-Moors follows the design for Vauxhall on a small scale, but with a timber roof. Here he again provided a vicarage and school. His friendship with the Raikes family brought him a commission for a church, parsonage, and schools at Freeland in Oxfordshire, and this was followed by a church in 1865–8 and a school at Sutton Veny in Wiltshire, which show a more serene attitude to decoration, with less of the hectic vigour that characterized his previous decade.

Although registered as an architect with the newly founded Institute of British Architects in 1834, it was only in 1860 that Pearson was elected fellow of the now Royal Institute of British Architects, and within two years he started to play an active part as a member of its committees. At this time he met Jemima Christian (1829–1865), a native of the Isle of Man and sister of fellow architect Ewan Christian (1814–1895). They were married on 5 June 1862. Their only child, Frank Loughborough Pearson, was born on 14 January 1864. On 23 March 1865 Jemima died of typhoid fever. The young Frank was brought up on the Isle of Man with an aunt and educated at Winchester College before entering his father's office as an assistant.

While numerous restorations and other works followed in the 1860s, Pearson's first appointment as architect to a cathedral fabric came in 1870 with Lincoln. He restored the north transept vault and strengthened the south-west tower, works that left the cathedral looking hardly touched by what was increasingly seen elsewhere as the heavy hand of the Victorian restorer. Several more cathedrals came under his control: Bristol, Canterbury, Chichester, Exeter, Gloucester, Peterborough, Rochester, and also Westminster Abbey.

In 1870 Pearson designed the church of St Augustine's at Kilburn, which may claim to be his masterpiece. This is a wonderful amalgam of Gothic forms taken from all round Europe: a continuous nave and chancel are surrounded by aisles with a gallery set over them that supports internal buttressing, as found in Albi Cathedral, all lit by tall clerestory windows; beyond the aisles and galleries are mysterious transeptal spaces, the southern one opening into a morning chapel. Every part is linked by a great, uniting quadripartite rib-vault that adds a rationalizing element to the complex interior. Tall turrets and a magnificent steeple, inspired by examples in Normandy, are a prominent landmark.

The Kilburn church was acclaimed. Pearson's career came into late bloom with a great series of monumental town churches begun during the next dozen years: St John's, Red Lion Square, Holborn (dem.); St Michael's, Croydon; St John's, Upper Norwood, Croydon; St George's, Cullercoats, Northumberland; St Alban's, Bordesley, Birmingham; St Stephen's, Bournemouth; St Agnes's, Sefton Park, Liverpool; and St Michael's, Headingley, Leeds. These were mostly of brick with vaulted interiors, and several of them exploit the Golden Section in their proportions. Their lofty, plain naves and chancels are often entered by way of small narthexes, incorporating baptisteries, and contrast with small, intricately designed side chapels, themselves also vaulted and treated like tiny churches in their own right. Few of their proposed towers and spires were completed: enthusiasm and funds for church building were beginning to wane towards the end of the nineteenth century.

The earlier of these churches led to Pearson's being chosen in 1878 to design a new cathedral for the refounded see of Cornwall at Truro. Here, Pearson elected to retain the south aisle of the decayed medieval parish church as a link with the past and to serve parochial needs. This determined the layout of his cathedral and the rhythm of the bays of its choir, which rises dramatically beside it. The cathedral continues westwards as an idealized version of Lincoln augmented by many of the features developed after the tour of Normandy and now to be seen in the new town churches. Truro has the great advantage of a central tower and spire and a pair of similar west towers and spires, which dominate the city, rising above the houses at the bottom of the valley. Inside, the proportions of the Golden Section in the nave add a calm note before the vistas of columns and partly hidden spaces of the choir and the old church aisle. All these are vaulted, with quadripartite ribs to the east and sexpartite ribs to the nave, and, at a low level, an octagonal baptistery is linked into the vaulting system with a star vault of its own. The cathedral was begun in 1880, with the completed eastern parts being consecrated in 1887, the nave and crossing tower rising in 1897–1903, and the west towers being finished in 1910 under Frank Pearson's direction. The cathedral was criticized for not being Cornish enough, despite the use of local and not entirely suitable granite in its construction; it was thought too French and,

with more justification, too conservative and lacking the originality of Pearson's town churches. Yet, like Sir Christopher Wren, the last architect before him to design an English cathedral, Pearson was bound to follow the desires of the church, and the church was well satisfied. Largely in recognition of this work, Pearson was presented with the royal gold medal of the Royal Institute of British Architects in 1880. He also became a Royal Academician, having been an associate since 1874.

Pearson began a design for a new cathedral for Liverpool, which he abandoned on the grounds of ill health, and another for Brisbane, Queensland, which he completed in 1887–9 and then adapted for a new site shortly before his death. This again was entirely vaulted and had central and west towers; moreover, it had more of the originality found in his town churches, and made telling use of Spanish Gothic models, as these were appropriate to Brisbane's hot climate. Pearson's son Frank further modified and simplified the design before work started in 1901 on the east parts; these were finished in 1910, and the nave and aisles, started in 1955, are now largely finished, leaving just the west end to be completed.

These great ecclesiastical works overshadow Pearson's later houses, a varied group, ranging from the small, traditionally styled Roundwyck House at Kirdford, Sussex, Crowton vicarage (dem.) in Cheshire, and Whitwell parsonage in Derbyshire, to the Jacobean of the larger Lechlade Manor House, Berkshire, and the French Renaissance of Westwood House (dem.), Sydenham, London. In the 1890s he worked for William Waldorf Astor, designing a luxurious estate office in Tudor Gothic at Temple Place, Westminster.

All the while Pearson was increasingly involved in controversy surrounding his restorations. While his rebuilding of the north transept front of Westminster Abbey might have been more sympathetic to its former appearance, his urgent reconstruction of Peterborough's central tower, threatened with imminent collapse, was an unavoidably desperate remedy. The repair of Peterborough's west front in the last few years of his life caused bitter controversy, mainly through the intemperate objections of the Society for the Protection of Ancient Buildings, founded by William Morris in 1878, and the vociferous rejoinders of his supporters. Pearson avoided the clamour, but was branded a destroyer. Yet his work can now be seen as thoroughly competent. Unfortunately the problem of providing for continuing use—or even changes in use—while preserving the archaeological and historical record of a building, could not always be resolved, and his was the first generation to face this dilemma. His reputation suffered, despite the fertility of his art.

Advancing years reduced Pearson's output of new designs but not its quality. While his earlier works reached completion, he designed new churches at Hove in Sussex, Thurstaston in Cheshire, Friern Barnet in Middlesex, Port Talbot in Glamorgan, and Darlington, as well as the Catholic Apostolic Church in Paddington, a cemetery chapel at Ta Braxia, Malta, and convent chapels at Wantage, Berkshire, and Woking, Surrey. The latter was his last design, completed shortly before his death, and executed by his son, Frank. Several of these last works have early Christian elements in their design, influenced by a visit to Italy in 1874 and an increasingly liberal attitude to both style and the place of Gothic in a wider appreciation of medieval architecture. Nevertheless, the old intensity remained, together with a feeling for calm, contrasting spaces.

Pearson was short and stocky in stature. Two portraits in oil, by W. W. Ouless RA (1889; in the possession of the family) and by John Pettie RA (c.1880; Aberdeen Art Gallery), show his genial character and gentle, expressive eyes, smiling above a full beard and moustache. Sociable but modest, he never made his views public. His interests were few beyond architecture, to which he devoted great industry. Of over 250 major works, a third were new churches and nearly a half were restorations. Of his assistants, only W. D. Caröe achieved eminence. Pearson died at his home, 13 Mansfield Street, Marylebone, London, on 11 December 1897, and was buried in Westminster Abbey on 16 December. His son inherited his fortune of over £53,000 as well as his practice. He completed many of his father's works before his own retirement and death on 8 October 1947.

Pearson never gained a reputation for innovation or for the strenuous promotion of his own architectural principles. These were based on a conservative tradition, but they also married classical precepts of symmetry, proportion, and order with the structural methods of Gothic; above all he saw in Gothic its potential for picturesque sublimity. Through all the developing phases of the Gothic revival he managed to remain a leader. His works may sometimes seem a trifle cold, but they reveal a consistent architectural vision, and a rare capacity for synthesis and integration.

PAUL WATERHOUSE, rev. ANTHONY QUINEY

Sources A. P. Quiney, *John Loughborough Pearson* (1979) [incl. catalogue of works] · J. Lever, ed., *Catalogue of the drawings collection of the Royal Institute of British Architects: O–R* (1976) · A. P. Quiney, 'The church of St Augustine and its builders', *Transactions of the Ancient Monuments Society*, new ser., 36 (1992), 1–12 · J. E. Newberry, 'The work of John L. Pearson', *ArchR*, 1 (1896–7), 1–11, 69–82 · *RIBA Journal*, 5 (1897–8), 113–21 · W. C. Monkhouse, *Pall Mall Magazine*, 15 (1898), 92–110 · d. cert. · A. P. Quiney, 'The door marked "Pull": J. L. Pearson and his first clients in the East Riding of Yorkshire', *Architectural History*, 41 (1998), 208–19 · census returns, 1841, 1851, PRO, HO 107 · family bible · *The Times* (13 Dec 1897) · M. Tonkin, 'William and John Pearson, some mysteries solved', *Old Water-Colour Society's Club*, 58 (1983), 27–40 · *The Times* (17 Dec 1897) · *Church Times* (21 Nov 1997)
Archives English Heritage, Swindon, National Monuments Record, family MSS · RIBA, drawings collection · Truro Cathedral, archives | N. Yorks. CRO, corresp. relating to Clervaux Hall · Norfolk RO, reports, corresp., and notes relating to restoration of Norwich Cathedral
Likenesses J. Pettie, oils, 1880–84, Aberdeen Art Gallery · W. W. Ouless, oils, 1889, priv. coll.; repro. in Quiney, *John Loughborough Pearson* [see illus.] · W. W. Ouless, oils, 1889, NPG · A. Lewis, carte-de-visite, NPG · R. W. Robinson, photograph, NPG; repro. in *Members and associates of the Royal Academy of Arts* (1891) · photograph, repro.

in *The Graphic* (9 May 1874) · statue, Truro Cathedral · woodcut, NPG
Wealth at death £53,487 19s. 10d.: probate, 17 Jan 1898, CGPLA Eng. & Wales

Pearson, John Norman (1787–1865), Church of England clergyman, son of the surgeon John *Pearson (1758–1826) and his wife, Sarah, née Norman (1763?–1826), was born on 7 December 1787; he was educated at Trinity College, Cambridge (1805–9), where he gained the Hulsean prize in 1807. He then took orders, and acted as chaplain to Marquess Wellesley. He married on 11 September 1815 Harriet, daughter of Richard Puller of London and sister of Sir Christopher Puller; they had a large family. In 1826 the Church Missionary Society appointed him the first principal of its newly founded missionary college at Islington in London. In 1839 he was appointed vicar of Holy Trinity Church, Tunbridge Wells, a position which he resigned in 1853. He afterwards lived in retirement, performing occasional duties for the local clergy, at Bower Hall, near Steeple Bumpstead in Essex, until his death on 4 October 1865. His sons Sir John *Pearson and Charles Henry *Pearson are separately noticed. Pearson published various evangelical and anti-papal works, and in 1829 a biography of Archbishop Leighton.

D'A. POWER, rev. H. C. G. MATTHEW

Sources GM, 3rd ser., 19 (1865), 792 · Boase, *Mod. Eng. biog.* · Venn, *Alum. Cant.*
Likenesses oils; formerly at Missionary College, Upper Street, Islington, London in 1895
Wealth at death under £35,000: probate, 4 Nov 1865, CGPLA Eng. & Wales

Pearson, Karl [*formerly* Carl] (1857–1936), statistician and eugenicist, was born at 14 Albion Road, Holloway Road, Islington, London, on 27 March 1857, the second of three children of William Pearson (d. 1907), a barrister of the Inner Temple, and his wife, Fanny Smith (d. 1905), both of Yorkshire descent. He had an older brother, Arthur, and a younger sister, Amy, was born in 1859.

Education From 1863 to 1866 Karl and Arthur both boarded at William Penn's small school in Harrow. Then, for a short time in 1866, they received tuition from Penn at their family home, which allowed them to be closer to a mother who provided the emotional sustenance denied them by their stern and hard-working father. In the autumn of 1866 Karl was sent to University College School, London. He withdrew in 1873 owing to poor health and then went up to Cambridge to study with several private tutors. In April 1875 he obtained a scholarship at King's College, Cambridge, placing second on the list.

While at King's, Pearson gained notoriety when he rebelled against the required divinity lectures and chapel attendance, a campaign that resulted in the abolition of this system in March 1878. Although Pearson's rebellion was directed more against the requirements than against religion itself (after being released from compulsory chapel he shocked the tutors and deans by continuing to attend whenever the spirit moved him), it was nevertheless indicative of his early loss of Christian faith. He considered himself fortunate to have been raised by Quaker parents who did not encourage dogmatic belief in the biblical story of creation. By the time he was in his early twenties he had absorbed Darwinism and taken a special interest in Spinozism as an intellectual religion, thereafter identifying himself as a freethinker and an agnostic.

Pearson graduated BA in 1879 as third wrangler in the prestigious mathematical tripos. He was next awarded a King's College fellowship that allowed him financial independence for several years and an opportunity to travel to Heidelberg and Berlin, where he spent about eighteen months studying mathematics, physics, and philosophy. His first two publications (both anonymous) arose from his wide reading in philosophy, religious thought, and German history: *The New Werther* (1880) was a work of fiction written in the form of letters from a young man wandering in Germany seeking a creed of life, and *The Trinity: a Nineteenth Century Passion Play* (1882) attacked orthodox Christianity from the point of view of modern science and culture. Some of his essays and lectures dating from this period and covering a similarly broad range of topics were published in his *Ethic of Freethought* (1888).

Pearson's father had always intended that his sons follow him into the law, and so upon his return to London in November 1880 Karl entered Lincoln's Inn to prepare for a legal career and ensure himself a future livelihood. He was called to the bar at the end of 1881 but practised only a short time, apparently having been persuaded by the civil engineer Sir Alexander Kennedy to abandon law and return to mathematics, the subject at which he had excelled in his undergraduate studies.

Mathematics, mechanics, and *The Grammar of Science* Pearson next worked as a substitute lecturer in mathematics at both King's and University colleges in London, and published work on elasticity and the motions of bodies in fluid media. In June 1884 he received his first academic appointment as Goldsmid professor of applied mathematics and mechanics at University College. He was reported to have been an effective and charismatic teacher, devoting considerable time and energy to these duties while also producing an impressive output of original work in applied mathematics, including the laborious task of completing Isaac Todhunter's *History of the Theory of Elasticity* (2 vols., 1886–93).

Pearson's major accomplishment of this early period was his *Grammar of Science* (1892), later widely recognized as a significant contribution to positivist and phenomenalist philosophy of science. Pearson held that all knowledge was based on sense perceptions and that the task of science was to summarize the routines of experience by means of laws expressed in mathematical form. Theoretical terms such as 'atom' or 'gene' were allowable only when they served as instruments for economically describing phenomena, not when they were interpreted as referring to invisible entities. Thus for example he criticized certain evolutionists for seeking the hidden causes of biological variability rather than just trying to provide a quantitative description: 'the *why* of it is as much a mystery as the *why* of the law of gravitation' (Pearson, *The Grammar of Science*, 2nd edn, 1900, 451).

Pearson's phenomenalist stance was also articulated in a series of lectures he gave as holder of the Gresham College chair of geometry from 1891 to 1893. His Gresham lectures 'The geometry of statistics' and 'The laws of chance', in which audiences of as many as 300 students witnessed him use dice, roulette results, and 10,000 pennies scattered on the floor to demonstrate the laws of probability, marked a significant turning point in his career: they represented his earliest forays into statistical theory, the branch of mathematics in which he would soon make his scientific reputation. Pearson was responsible for almost

Karl Pearson (1857–1936), by unknown photographer, 1910

single-handedly establishing the modern discipline of mathematical statistics, including the invention of a number of essential statistical techniques, most notably the chi-square test for goodness of fit and the product moment method of calculating the correlation coefficient.

Pearson's interest in statistics was stimulated by Sir Francis Galton (1822–1911), the father of eugenics, and by W. F. R. Weldon, the zoologist who subsequently co-founded with Pearson the discipline called biometry, or the application of mathematical methods to the biological sciences. In the early 1890s Weldon sought out Pearson's assistance with the mathematical analysis of morphological variations in crab populations. His research involved determining whether a double humped frequency distribution for a given trait could be broken down into two normal curves representing a dimorphic population undergoing speciation. In the course of addressing such problems in evolutionary theory Pearson introduced powerful new statistical tools, especially his method of moments and system of frequency curves. Between 1894 and 1901 he communicated this work on curve fitting in a series of important papers in the *Philosophical Transactions of the Royal Society*. By 1906 he had already published over a hundred articles on statistical theory and applications.

Correlation theory and interest in eugenics Correlation theory constituted Pearson's other key line of research in mathematical statistics. The history of correlation began with Galton's work on inheritance, anthropometrics, and criminal identification carried out between 1876 and 1889. Thereafter the methods he invented for measuring variation and correlation were applied and extended mainly by his disciples Weldon and Pearson. Pearson recounted that Galton's *Natural Inheritance* (1889) had opened his eyes to the potential uses of statistical analysis for obtaining valid knowledge about living forms and human behaviour. After his initial success with speciation, Pearson went on to develop further statistical innovations particularly useful for the study of heredity and eugenics. For instance, in his very first correlation paper of 1896 he illustrated the practical value of these new tools by calculating regressions of offspring under selection pressures and by confirming the high degree of association between excessive fertility and undesirable traits. Later he utilized correlation coefficients and family pedigrees in his attempts to demonstrate that heredity was more important than environment in determining numerous human attributes and pathologies. Most of this material appeared in the multi-volume *Treasury of Human Inheritance* (1909–33). This research seemed to confirm the eugenic assumption that social reforms were powerless to remedy the crisis of racial degeneration: if health and ability were principally inborn traits, then only programmes for selective breeding could improve the biological fitness of the population.

Several of Pearson's essays dating from the 1880s and 1890s, published in his *Chances of Death, and other Studies in Evolution* (2 vols., 1897), show that he had already begun to explore scientific ideas that would become central components of his eugenic creed, such as Darwinism, the inheritance of physical and mental characteristics, and the differential fertility of fit and unfit stocks. His conversion to socialism during his year in Germany also influenced his thinking on the questions of national efficiency and racial health. Upon returning to London in 1881 he became associated with radical clubs where he lectured on Marx and Lassalle and wrote hymns for the socialist songbook. However, Pearson's version of socialism was reformist rather than revolutionary, defined in terms of ensuring a stable society and a strong state. His politics most closely resembled Fabian socialism, with its emphasis on replacing *laissez-faire* capitalism with state planning and technocratic management. He theorized that the way to regenerate the vitality of the British populace was by minimizing the struggle for existence between individuals through social welfare legislation and eugenics, while keeping up the intense competition between nations in the military and commercial realms.

Pearson's eugenics must also be considered in relation to his keen interest in the 'woman question'. In 1885 he had founded the Men and Women's Club as a forum for dispassionate discussion of questions pertaining to sexual relations. While the female members of the club were most concerned to voice their anxieties about such concrete problems as prostitution, coercive sex, and birth control, Pearson read papers on sexual passion and the eugenic significance of feminism. He considered himself a supporter of equal rights and opportunities for women (later in his capacity as a laboratory director he hired many female assistants), yet he also expressed a willingness to subordinate these ideals to the greater good of the race. Eugenic feminists such as Pearson still expected liberated women to sacrifice their individual development in order to fulfil their duties as race mothers. The Men and Women's Club further served as an opportunity for the rather shy Pearson to realize his courtship ambitions. After rebuffing the sexual overtures of the South African feminist Olive Schreiner, on 30 June 1890 he married another fellow club member, Maria Sharpe (1853–1928). They had one son and two daughters. After Maria's death Pearson married, on 22 March 1929, one of his long-time biometrical co-workers, Margaret Victoria Child.

By 1901 Pearson was devoting his full time to research and teaching in the new mathematical field of statistics, work for which he was awarded a grant from the Worshipful Company of Drapers that enabled him to establish a biometric laboratory at University College, London. He closely supervised all the projects undertaken by his staff and students, which ranged from further advances in statistical methodology to the analysis of data on heredity and physical anthropology. He also published on some non-biological topics such as astronomy and dam construction, thereby demonstrating the wide applicability of his new analytical techniques. He and Weldon founded the journal *Biometrika* in 1901 as a publication outlet for their original work in both mathematics and biology.

Eugenics Eugenics came to occupy an especially prominent place on Pearson's research agenda after the death of his close friend and collaborator Weldon in 1906. Pearson took over the directorship of the Eugenics Record Office at the behest of its benefactor Francis Galton in 1907, changing the name of this institution to the Galton Laboratory for National Eugenics. In this role he gave public lectures expounding the new science and with the help of a dedicated staff carried out painstaking statistical studies of various social ills. In 1911 he was appointed the first Galton professor of eugenics at University College. The eugenics and biometric laboratories were incorporated into a single department of applied statistics, which survived until Pearson's retirement in 1933 when separate departments of eugenics (later human genetics) and statistics were set up against his express wishes that the connection between these two sciences be maintained. R. A. Fisher subsequently held the chair in eugenics while Pearson's son Egon *Pearson became the new professor of statistics.

Over the course of three decades Karl Pearson published some fifty papers on eugenics, constituting almost 10 per cent of his remarkably prolific scientific output. His publications and joint laboratories laid the intellectual and institutional foundations of modern statistics. From the 1890s until the 1920s the biometrical school at University College represented the only place in Britain that offered advanced training in statistical methods. It attracted postgraduates and visitors from many disciplines and from around the world. The first generation of professional medical and biostatisticians were all Pearson's pupils, including Major Greenwood in Britain and Raymond Pearl in the United States. Statistics soon achieved recognition as a scientific speciality in its own right, with statistical workers in demand in academia, government, and industry. But Pearson's second goal, of establishing a eugenics laboratory in every British university, was never realized, since public interest in eugenics waned after the First World War and most of the biometricians he trained did not go on to help him spread the gospel of eugenics along with the new techniques of correlation.

Pearson disparaged old-school statisticians such as the members of the Royal Statistical Society (an organization he himself never joined) for employing a crude style of vital statistics that consisted simply of comparing percentages in order to make inferences about the causes of diseases and social problems. He insisted that only his biometricians were competent to analyse data collected in the laboratory, clinic, and social survey on such critical issues as alcoholism, tuberculosis, and infant mortality. His eugenics writings were marked by an extreme scepticism towards the investigations carried out by physicians and experimentalists, an attitude that on numerous occasions incited controversies with these reigning experts. The biometrical school is best known in the history of biology for its opposition to the Mendelian theory of heredity, which seemed to be inconsistent with Pearson's phenomenalism and evolutionary gradualism. Pearson similarly engaged in a fierce dispute with temperance

advocates and fellow eugenicists over the question of whether parental alcoholism produced degeneracy in offspring.

Personality In an autobiographical sketch written in 1934 Pearson accounted for his scientific achievements and success in founding a new academic discipline in terms of two purportedly inherited qualities: 'a capacity for hard work and a capacity for roving into other people's preserves' (quoted in Pearson, *Karl Pearson*, 2). He was an energetic teacher and researcher, as well as an inspirational if domineering leader of his research institute. Although always extremely generous with his co-workers, Pearson was also reportedly prone to angry outbursts. He engaged in intellectual disputes that often descended into personal bitterness, even with some of his former pupils and friends. He tended to be impatient and even insulting towards outsiders who were unable or unwilling to see his point of view, especially those who objected to his uncompromising hereditarianism. Pearson was sometimes labelled a proponent of the 'better-dead school' of eugenics, owing to his apparent lack of sympathy for the sick and the poor and his endorsement of brutal competition between nations or racial groups as the means of achieving evolutionary progress. He championed further statistical studies as the prerequisite for an effective programme of race regeneration, yet his own proposals for positive and negative eugenics were based more on social class prejudices than on sound scientific deductions.

For his fundamental contributions to statistics and evolutionary theory, Pearson was elected FRS in 1896 and awarded the society's Darwin medal in 1898. In 1903 he was awarded the Huxley medal of the Royal Anthropological Institute and in 1932 the Rudolf Virchow medal by the Anthropological Society of Berlin. He accepted the honorary degree of LLD from the University of St Andrews and of DSc from the University of London, and he was elected an honorary fellow of King's College, Cambridge, of the Royal Society of Edinburgh, and of University College, London. Pearson died suddenly while on holiday at his cottage, the Old School House, Coldharbour, Dorking, Surrey, on 27 April 1936. He was survived by his second wife.

JOANNE WOIAK

Sources E. S. Pearson, *Karl Pearson: an appreciation of some aspects of his life and work* (1938) · G. U. Yule, *Obits. FRS*, 2 (1936–8), 73–104 · *DNB* · D. MacKenzie, *Statistics in Britain, 1865–1930: the social construction of scientific knowledge* (1981) · T. M. Porter, *The rise of statistical thinking, 1820–1900* (1986) · B. Norton, 'Karl Pearson and statistics: the social origin of scientific innovation', *Social Studies of Science*, 8 (1978), 3–34 · D. J. Kevles, *In the name of eugenics* (1985), 20–40 · B. Norton, 'Biology and philosophy: the methodological foundations of biometry', *Journal of the History of Biology*, 8 (1975), 85–93 · J. R. Walkowitz, *City of dreadful delight: narratives of sexual danger in late-Victorian London* (1992), 135–69 · M. E. Magnello, 'Karl Pearson's Gresham lectures: W. F. R. Weldon, speciation and the origins of Pearsonian statistics', *British Journal for the History of Science*, 29 (1996), 43–63 · C. Eisenhart, 'Pearson, Karl', *DSB*, 10.447–73 · M. Merrington and others, *A list of the papers and correspondence of Karl Pearson (1857–1936) held in the Manuscripts Room, University College London Library* (1983) · K. Pearson, *The life, letters and labours of Francis Galton*, 3 vols. in 4 (1914–30) · M. E. Magnello, 'Karl Pearson', *The* *encyclopaedia of biostatistics*, ed. P. Armitage and J. Cotton (1998), 3308–15 · *CGPLA Eng. & Wales* (1936)

Archives RS, letters · UCL, corresp. and papers · Wellcome L., corresp. with Eugenics Society | King's AC Cam., letters to Henry Bradshaw · King's AC Cam., letters to Oscar Browning · Royal Anthropological Institute, London, corresp. with M. L. Tildesley · UCL, corresp. with Sir Francis Galton

Likenesses Elliott & Fry, two photographs, 1890, NPG · photograph, *c.*1897, NPG · two photogravures, 1910, NPG [*see illus.*] · F. A. de Biden Footner, pencil drawing, 1924, UCL · photograph, 1928, NPG · Crellin, carte photograph (as a child), NPG · H. R. Hope-Pinker, bust, UCL · photographs, repro. in Pearson, *Karl Pearson*

Wealth at death £37,576 5s. 7d.: resworn probate, 2 July 1936, *CGPLA Eng. & Wales*

Pearson, Lester Bowles

Pearson, Lester Bowles (1897–1972), diplomatist and prime minister of Canada, was born on 23 April 1897 at Newtonbrook (later North York), Ontario, the second of three children of the Revd Edwin Arthur Pearson, a Methodist minister, and his wife, Annie Sarah, the daughter of Thomas Bowles, sheriff of Dufferin county, Ontario. Both parents were Canadians of Irish protestant background who had emigrated to Ontario in the first half of the nineteenth century. The Bowles family came from Kilkenny and the Pearsons from Dublin. Although neither family had been notably religious in Ireland, their Methodism flourished in North America.

Methodism, education, and marriage Edwin Pearson was the son of a prominent Methodist minister, Marmaduke Pearson. Annie Bowles's father and uncles were lay Methodist preachers, and the minister who presided at the wedding of Annie and Edwin was Annie's cousin, the Revd R. P. Bowles, who later became the chancellor of the Methodist Victoria College at the University of Toronto. As the twentieth century began, the influence of the Methodist church in Ontario and in the rapidly developing west of Canada was at its height. The evangelism had become less fervent, but the church's sway had never been greater. Methodist farm-boys had become the financiers, industrialists, and retailers who dominated Ontario's economy, and they spun their economic and cultural web over the new Canadian settlements in the north and the west. The white clapboard churches of nineteenth-century rural Methodism often closed as young men and women left the farms; instead there were massive stone structures in city centres for them to continue their Methodist commitment.

In those days Methodist ministers accepted a 'call' after three or four years with a congregation and moved to a new town and church. Lester Pearson, therefore, changed schools regularly and never had a home town. His memories of youth nevertheless stress continuity because church life dominated the household, and the remarkable homogeneity of British Ontario in Edwardian times minimized disruption. When he left one British Ontario town for another, he found the same 'red Ontario readers' in the new classroom, and lessons were normally on the same schedule as those he had left.

When war came Pearson was a student at Victoria College where enthusiasm for the war was strong. Having turned eighteen on 23 April 1915 he enlisted immediately

Lester Bowles Pearson (1897–1972), by Yousuf Karsh, 1944

in the Canadian Army Medical Corps, knowing that the University of Toronto hospital unit would be going overseas presently. He crammed for his final examinations, accepted $25 from his father's Chatham congregation, and disembarked from Montreal on an old cattleship, the *Corinthian*, on 15 May 1915. After training in England, he served in Salonika with the no. 4 general hospital corps, but he yearned to join his brothers Marmaduke (known as Duke) and Vaughan on the western front. His father begged his fellow Methodist, minister of militia Sam Hughes, to let Lester do a 'bigger bit', and on 10 February 1917 Lester got his orders to return to England to qualify for the infantry. After training at Oxford, he elected to join the Royal Flying Corps. He crashed during training, however, and a few days later a bus hit him during a blackout. In the hospital, he suffered an emotional collapse; the medical diagnosis was neurasthenia.

After brief treatment Pearson returned in April 1918 to Toronto, where he became, with little training, an aeronautics trainer. Fortunately, the war ended soon afterwards. Pearson gradually regained emotional strength through participation in the Royal Air Force athletics teams, in which he excelled. He completed his university degree in 1919 and briefly studied law. He thought law dull and went to Chicago to join Armour & Co., the frequently vilified meat-packer. Thoroughly anglophile, Pearson resented the assertive American nationalism of the midwest and the anti-British rantings of Chicago politicians. He told his parents he wanted to return to Canada and become a professor at Toronto. With that goal in mind, he asked them to support his studies at Oxford. In the autumn of 1921 he entered St John's College, where he chose the honours school in modern history.

Pearson was a better athlete than scholar at Oxford, representing the university at lacrosse and ice hockey. After graduating with a second-class degree in 1923, he accepted a lecturer's position in history at the University of Toronto. One of his students was Maryon Elspeth Moody of Winnipeg, the daughter of Dr Arthur William Moody, a medical officer for the Canadian Pacific Railway. They quickly fell in love in the winter of 1923–4, and became secretly engaged in March 1924. Pearson gave his fiancée an 'A' two months later, and on 22 August 1925 they married. Their first child, Geoffrey, was born just before midnight on 24 December 1925, which an obliging doctor altered to read 25 December. A daughter, Patricia, was born on 9 March 1929.

Department of external affairs: London and Washington Between the birth of his children, Pearson successfully sat the examinations for Canada's small department of external affairs. He realized by 1928 that he would not excel as a scholar, and his colleagues at Toronto thought his future lay in coaching collegiate sports, especially baseball, rather than in the classroom and the archives. He came first place in the examinations, but it was his extraordinary charm and his quick wit that captured attention. An article on Canadian confederation written in 1927 suggests that Pearson's opinions were conventional. His enthusiasm for the British empire exceeded that of the prime minister, Mackenzie King, and of the under-secretary of state for external affairs, O. D. Skelton. He was also a stronger supporter of the League of Nations than they were. Those views would change, but his Canadian nationalism possessed neither a suspicion of Europe and the league nor a sense of North American exceptionalism.

After joining external affairs Pearson attended League of Nations' meetings, the London naval conference, and the Geneva disarmament conference, but his major work was in Ottawa, where his most significant efforts were on domestic matters. He served as secretary to the royal commission on grain futures in 1931 and to the royal commission on price spreads in 1934. For this work the prime minister, R. B. Bennett, recommended Pearson for an OBE in 1935, and in the same year he posted Pearson to the high commission in London as first secretary. Shortly after his arrival in London, Pearson went to Geneva for the historic league session dealing with the Italo-Ethiopian war. He advised the senior Canadian delegate, W. A. Riddell, to put forward a proposal calling for extensive sanctions against Italy. The proposal soon became known as the 'Canadian proposal', and Mackenzie King, who returned to office in October 1935, repudiated Riddell's action in December.

Pearson escaped blame, but the deteriorating European situation and the inattention of the new high commissioner, Vincent Massey, caused him to consider other positions. In the late 1930s, he frequently but anonymously commented on Canadian affairs for the British Broadcasting Corporation and he almost joined the newly created

Canadian Broadcasting Corporation. He tended to support early efforts at appeasement, but refused to cheer Munich and despaired for the future of Europe by early 1939. He came to believe that Canada should recognize that only Britain could lead the fight for democracy against the dictators, and began to urge his reluctant superiors in Ottawa to prepare for war.

Pearson fully supported the British declaration of war in September 1939 and worked to strengthen the ties between London and Ottawa. He thrived in the climate of danger of wartime London. He always treasured the memory of those tense days and the women and men who lived there with him. However, his marriage was increasingly difficult through long periods apart, and after 1941 public life came to fill his time and thoughts; his friends began to describe him as distant, and he socialized less. He returned to Ottawa in spring 1941, but Canada needed a stronger voice in Washington. Pearson therefore went to Washington as minister-counsellor in June 1942 where he served under the weak minister Leighton McCarthy.

At the time, the Washington posting disappointed Pearson, who very much wanted to become under-secretary; but Mackenzie King chose his colleague Norman Robertson on the death of Skelton. Pearson nevertheless made the best of the situation and emerged in Washington not only as the major Canadian personality but also as a principal figure in what his friend Dean Acheson called the creation of the post-war world. From his arrival Pearson represented Canada on myriad committees dealing with the war and reconstruction. He also developed a strong network of friends, who achieved later prominence in American public life. He even appeared on national quiz shows, where the extraordinary range of his general knowledge made him a winner. Among his American friends were James Reston, Dean Acheson, Walter Lippmann, Dean Rusk, Marquis Childs, and Jack Hickerson and Theodore Achilles of the state department. These relationships became invaluable assets for Pearson in later years.

The United Nations While arguing for a greater Canadian presence in wartime councils, Pearson took a strong interest in the development of strong international post-war institutions. He argued against the 'realism' of some of his colleagues in external affairs, a concept made fashionable by the writings of Hans Morgenthau, and committed himself and his government to active participation in the shaping of the new international institutions. Pearson realized by 1941 that the historic balance between Canada's British past and the North American present, which had sustained Canada's economy and polity, had tilted decisively towards North America. Strong international organizations, which would set rules, limit sovereignty, and mediate conflict, were essential for a country in Canada's position.

Pearson captured attention and won acclaim for his work as chairman of the United Nations Interim Commission on Food and Agriculture after July 1943. He declined to lead its successor, the Food and Agriculture Organization, but he did chair its founding conference in Quebec

City in October 1945. He became closely acquainted with the extent of European devastation through his work as chairman of the committee on supplies of the United Nations Relief and Rehabilitation Administration after November 1943. In January 1945, Mackenzie King appointed Pearson as Canada's first ambassador to the United States. His growing reputation in Washington gave Pearson a key role in shaping not only the Canadian but also the international response to the challenges of post-war reconstruction and allied disunity. Pearson also served as senior adviser to the Canadian delegation to the San Francisco conference in June 1945 and worked diligently to place Canadians on key committees shaping the United Nations Organization.

The new United Nations, however, disappointed Pearson. He deplored the great powers' insistence on the veto, the claims of the British, French, and Chinese for special recognition, and the weak enforcement provisions in the charter. The breakdown of the wartime alliance did not surprise him, and his experience with Soviet representatives in international forums made him suspicious of Soviet ambitions. As with many liberals his opposition to the Soviet Union derived from his belief that Soviet egalitarianism and revolutionary principles would vitiate the left's commitment to democratic and liberal principles. Nevertheless, he became a target for anti-communists because he refused to support purges of leftists in government and had personal links with some individuals whom American congressional investigators identified as spies.

In September 1946 Pearson returned to Ottawa as undersecretary, where he served the new minister of external affairs, Louis St Laurent. The partnership was effective domestically and internationally. The dominant cabinet minister from traditionally isolationist Quebec, St Laurent was a committed internationalist who offered invaluable support within the cabinet for Pearson's ambitious foreign policy. Although King became suspicious of Pearson's activist foreign policy, St Laurent's importance to King and the Liberal Party gave unusual freedom to Pearson, who used that freedom to commit Canada to UN activities such as the United Nations temporary commission on Korea, or, much more successfully, to the creation of the North Atlantic Treaty Organization. To his credit King recognized that St Laurent and Pearson were enormous political assets; and when he finally decided to retire in 1948 he used his decisive influence to ensure that St Laurent was his successor and that Pearson replaced St Laurent as secretary of state for external affairs, obtaining a seat in the Canadian House of Commons at a by-election in October 1948.

Secretary of state: NATO and Suez Pearson's accomplishments as minister remain the standard for his successors. The times favoured his ambitious activities: the cold war had brought consensus on foreign policy topics, St Laurent had complete confidence in his minister, and the Liberal government possessed a large majority in parliament. Freed from concern about domestic dissent and parliamentary votes, Pearson effectively furthered Canadian goals within the Atlantic alliance and the United Nations.

In the former, Pearson's strong support for the creation of a broad alliance reflected Canadian fears and hopes for NATO, espousing not merely the military defence of western Europe but also the cultural and economic linkage between NATO's Atlantic and European pillars. Pearson strongly promoted article 2 of the NATO charter, the so-called Canadian article, which called for an economic and cultural dimension for NATO. In the case of the UN, Pearson shared American doubts about the Soviet influence within the institution, but he firmly argued for the independence of the UN against American attempts to dominate, particularly during the Korean War.

Pearson tried to build coalitions with like-minded Western states and sought opportunities to draw in developing states such as India and Pakistan to the community of nations. His efforts brought him recognition, and he served as chairman of the first committee at the UN general assembly in April–May 1947. He chaired the NATO council in 1951–2 and was president of the general assembly for the seventh session in 1952–3. The latter task brought conflict with the Americans over the resolution of the Korean War. The American secretary of state, Dean Acheson, became annoyed with Pearson, and the American right became suspicious of Pearson's motives in pressing for conciliation. Elizabeth Bentley, a former communist, had told American investigators that Lester Pearson had given confidential information to friends that had been valuable to the Soviets. Moreover, Pearson had restricted American investigation of the loyalty of the Canadian diplomat Herbert Norman in the early 1950s and had also refused a request by congress to allow Igor Gouzenko, a Soviet defector, to testify in the United States. These actions created suspicions, and some American conservatives became strong critics of Pearson's international activities.

In 1956, however, Pearson co-operated very effectively with the Eisenhower administration in bringing an end to the British-French-Israeli attack on Egypt. The so-called Suez crisis created a profound schism between the French and British on the one hand, and the Americans and Soviets on the other. Pearson thought the situation threatened not only world peace but also the Western alliance. Working closely with the Americans and neutral nations, Pearson crafted a proposal for a UN peace-keeping force that cleverly prevented British and French landings on Egyptian soil. The creation of the United Nations emergency force on 4 November 1956 was an important moment for the UN and for Pearson. The concept of UN peace-keeping was strengthened, and the potential for a wider conflict ended. On 14 October 1957, Pearson won the Nobel peace prize in recognition of his peace-keeping efforts.

Leader of the Canadian Liberal Party Pearson particularly savoured the award after the Progressive Conservative Party unexpectedly won the federal election on 10 June 1957. The new prime minister, John Diefenbaker, lacked a majority, but he quickly gained credibility with imaginative programmes and parliamentary skill. St Laurent resigned in September after discussing the future leadership of the Liberal Party with Pearson. In the leadership contest that followed the resignation, Pearson's Nobel prize was a precious currency, as was his distance from the parliamentary quarrels of the mid-1950s. He had strong press support and significant financial help from Toronto business contacts, notably Walter Gordon. His victory on 16 January 1958 came on the first ballot.

Pearson was ill-prepared for the parliamentary challenges he faced and was no match for John Diefenbaker in the daily parliamentary jousting. He showed indecisiveness and even arrogance when he called on the new government to resign because of the failure of the Canadian economy, which was moving into recession. Diefenbaker denounced Pearson's motion and called an election on 1 February 1958 for 31 March.

Pearson performed badly in an election campaign that exposed the serious organizational and policy weaknesses of the Liberal Party. There were no debates between Diefenbaker and Pearson, but by election day Pearson knew that he had not convinced Canadians that the Liberals could form an effective government. Diefenbaker won the largest parliamentary majority in Canadian history up to that point, with 208 seats to the Liberals' 49. Watching the results, Maryon Pearson remarked to her husband: 'We've lost everything. We even won our own seat' (Pearson, *Mike*, 3.166).

Pearson shared his wife's ambivalence towards political life. He recognized that political office brought the satisfaction of influencing great events, but he resented the personal exposure and the countless demands for favour. He did consider other positions, but none offered the potential rewards of the prime minister's office. Moreover, the defeat of 1958 was embarrassing, particularly to one so ambitious, successful, and competitive. Pearson determined to remake his party, appeal to youth and new sectors, and, after 1960, identify with John Kennedy's 'new frontier' and Jean Lesage's progressive Liberal government in Quebec. He recruited candidates from his friends in business, the civil service, the academy, journalism, and even the hockey rink (Toronto Mapel Leaf star Red Kelly). With the assistance of Walter Gordon and journalist Tom Kent, he developed a programme that reflected the progressive Liberalism of the time, with its emphasis on health care, education, and poverty reduction.

Pearson's programme better defined the Liberal Party's identity, and John Diefenbaker's indecisiveness and inability to manage his cabinet were Pearson's greatest asset. Moreover, the Canadian economy weakened in 1961–2. When Diefenbaker called an election on 18 April 1962 for 18 June, the Liberals led in the polls. They could not maintain that lead, and on election night the Conservatives won 116 seats and the Liberals 100. Despite the disappointment, the Liberals knew that Diefenbaker's minority government was seriously troubled. Those troubles multiplied with the Cuban missile crisis of October 1962 when Diefenbaker hesitated to support the Americans in their confrontation with the Soviet Union and Cuba. Even though Pearson and President Kennedy had an excellent personal relationship, the American ambassador to Canada, Livingston Merchant, had been sharply critical of Pearson's opposition to nuclear weapons for Canadian forces. After the missile crisis, the Americans and the president in particular became bitterly antagonistic towards Diefenbaker. In January 1963 while Diefenbaker's cabinet argued about whether Canada should accept nuclear weapons, Pearson denounced Diefenbaker's indecisiveness and said that a Liberal government would honour the commitment Diefenbaker had made to arm new Canadian weapons with nuclear warheads. The Liberals would accept the weapons but would then negotiate a new role for Canada that did not require nuclear weapons.

Prime Minister of Canada, 1963–1968 Pearson's carefully crafted statement offended many on the left, especially in Quebec, but won strong support in English Canada. The Diefenbaker minority government fell on 5 February 1963. Diefenbaker's mishandling of Canada's all-important relationship with the United States was the main election issue, and Pearson found the issue well suited to him. Once again, however, the campaign failed to meet expectations. On 8 April the Liberals won most seats but not a majority. On 22 April 1963, one day before his sixty-sixth birthday, Pearson became prime minister and immediately promised 'sixty days of decision'.

Pearson stumbled badly during those sixty days, especially with the disastrous first budget of the finance minister, Walter Gordon. Nevertheless, he remained prime minister for almost five years even though he lacked a parliamentary majority, had low personal approval ratings, and seemed unable to lead his government away from crises and scandals. Moreover, the legislative record of his governments was remarkable, and later evaluations of his work have been most generous. There were four areas where Pearson's governments profoundly affected Canada's path: bilingualism and biculturalism; social welfare; national symbols; and immigration.

On 23 April 1963, the day before Pearson took office, a bomb placed by Quebec separatists killed a janitor in a Canadian Army recruiting office. The death confirmed that Quebec nationalism and separatism were the most dangerous issues facing Canada. Pearson spoke French poorly, but he recognized that his government had to respond to Quebec's demands and therefore appointed a royal commission on bilingualism and biculturalism. The commission recommended that the federal government be fully accessible to French Canadians and that federal institutions reflect more fully Canada's bilingual and bicultural character. Pearson began to implement these changes, which were completed under his successor, Pierre Trudeau. The effect on Canadian government in terms of language, personnel, and service was fundamental and controversial, especially in western Canada where some politicians accused the Liberal governments in Ottawa of 'tilting' towards Quebec.

When Pearson took office in 1963, the Quebec and Saskatchewan governments were pushing forward with, respectively, contributory pension legislation and state medical insurance. The Liberal election platform had promised action in the same areas, as well as the creation of a social safety-net for Canadians. With that platform and provincial initiatives already beginning, the Liberal governments transformed Canada's social system between 1963 and 1968. The flood of legislation was remarkable and included the Canada pension plan, a contributory social security scheme (1965); the Canada assistance plan, which supported provincial welfare programmes (1966); the guaranteed income supplement, an income-tested supplement for pensioners (1967); and the Medical Care Act, a national health-care programme (1966). Federal government support for higher education increased dramatically with the Canada student loans plan (1964) and additional funding for university research and post-secondary capital expenditures. Canada suddenly seemed less American and more European in its approach to social welfare.

Canada, however, became less tied to Europe through its symbols. After an angry parliamentary debate in 1964, a new national flag with a maple leaf at its centre was unfurled on 15 February 1965. Pearson personally pushed forward the legislation for a new flag despite strong opposition from many Canadians of British origin. He sought to strengthen Canadian national institutions and created a system of Canadian honours known as the order of Canada. The word 'royal' began to disappear from many federal institutions. Although a monarchist himself, Pearson believed that distinctly Canadian symbols were an important response to the challenge of Quebec separatism and Canadian diversity.

The diversity of Canada's population increased because of the 1966 decision to end all racial and geographical discrimination in the admission of immigrants to Canada. The traditional concern that immigrants be 'assimilable' ended, and the result was a dramatic increase in immigrants from the Caribbean, Asia, and Africa. By the 1980s the leading sources of immigration to Canada were non-European, and the impact on Canada's cities was visible. The city of Toronto at Pearson's birth in 1897 was more than four-fifths British and protestant, but a century later the British percentage was roughly one-fifth, and almost one-half of Toronto's residents were non-Caucasian.

The flood of legislation was interrupted by another election in 1965, which Pearson called in the hope of getting a majority. He failed, but he did bring in new representatives from Quebec, notably his successor, Pierre Trudeau. Pearson's first government sought to conciliate Quebec nationalism, but with Trudeau's arrival and the defeat of the Quebec Liberal government in 1966, the federal government challenged Quebec's demands for greater autonomy. No subject troubled Pearson more; and when he announced on 14 December 1967 that he intended to resign after a successor was chosen, he worked quietly to ensure that his successor came from Quebec. Trudeau succeeded Pearson, who resigned as prime minister on 19 April 1968. They were not close, and Pearson ceased to be consulted on policy matters.

Death and reputation Pearson developed cancer soon after his resignation. In retirement he gave the BBC's Reith lectures in 1968 ('Peace in the family of man'). He worked first on an important report on international development for the World Bank, *Partners in Development* (1969), and then, hurriedly, on his memoirs, *Mike*, which appeared in three volumes, two of them posthumous. He died in Ottawa on 27 December 1972 and was buried on 30 December in the nearby Gatineau Hills in Quebec beside his old diplomatic colleagues Norman Robertson and Hume Wrong.

By the century's end, historians and Canadians ranked Pearson highly as a prime minister (J. L. Granatstein and Norman Hillmer, *Canada's Prime Ministers*, 1999), and one poll that asked participants to identify Canadian heroes found Pearson the only politician among the top ten. His diplomatic achievements were remarkable, and so-called Pearsonian internationalism has become an identifying characteristic of Canada's sense of identity. Pearson's other work remains controversial. If Quebec separates, if the Canadian economy becomes weaker relative to the American economy, and if the Canadian experiment in multiculturalism ends in division, then Pearson's approaches to national unity, social welfare, and immigration may seem ill-conceived or even disastrous. At the time of writing, however, most Canadians disagree, and consider Pearson a highly successful architect of modern Canada.　　　　　　　　　　　　　　　　JOHN ENGLISH

Sources L. B. Pearson, *Mike: the memoirs of the Right Honourable Lester B. Pearson*, 3 vols. (1972–5) · L. B. Pearson, *Words and occasions* (1970) · L. B. Pearson, *Partners in development: report of the commission on international development* (1969) · J. English, *The life of Lester Pearson*, 2 vols. (1989–92) · J. L. Granatstein, *Canada, 1957–1967: the years of uncertainty and innovation* (1986) · P. Stursberg, *Lester Pearson and the dream of unity* (1978) · P. Stursberg, *Lester Pearson and the American dilemma* (Toronto, 1980) · D. Acheson, *Present at the creation: my years in the state department* (1969) · T. Kent, *A public purpose: an experience of liberal opposition and Canadian government* (1988) · S. Azzi, *Walter Gordon and the politics of nationalism* (1999) · J. L. Granatstein, *The Ottawa men: the civil service mandarins, 1935–1957* (1982) · Lester Pearson personnel file, Department of National Defence, Ottawa · NA Canada, Pearson collection · Pearson MSS [in family possession]
Archives NA Canada, papers, MG26N | NA Canada, department of external affairs, records | FILM BFI NFTVA, current affairs footage · Canadian Broadcasting Corporation Archives, Ottawa
Likenesses Y. Karsh, photograph, 1944, Karsh Camera Press [see illus.] · group portrait, photograph, 1949 (with Commonwealth premiers), Hult. Arch. · Karsh, portrait, NA Canada · H. MacKenzie, portrait, House of Commons, Ottawa

Pearson, Sir Richard (1731–1806), naval officer, was born in March 1731 at Langton Hall, near Appleby in Westmorland, the eldest son of Richard and Hannah Pearson, and baptized on 8 April 1731 at St Michael's Church, Appleby. After attending Appleby School (about 1740) he entered the navy in 1745 on the *Dover*, and joined in the Mediterranean the *Seaford*, commanded by his kinsman, Captain Wilson. Pearson remained in her for three years, and in 1749 joined the *Amazon* (Captain Arthur Gardiner). In 1750, seeing little prospect of promotion, he took service under the East India Company. He returned to the navy when war was imminent in 1755, passed his examination for lieutenant on 5 November, and on 16 December was promoted fourth lieutenant of the *Elizabeth*, which during 1756 was commanded by Captain John Montagu, and attached to the fleet employed on the coast of France and in the Bay of Biscay. In 1757 Montagu was superseded by Charles Steevens, who took the *Elizabeth* to the East Indies. Pearson was present in the actions of 29 April and 3 August 1758, and that of 10 September 1759. In one of these he was severely wounded. He was afterwards first lieutenant of the *Norfolk* with Steevens and Richard Kempenfelt, and was actually in command during a violent hurricane on 1 January 1761, owing to Kempenfelt's being disabled by an accident. It is said that Steevens was so well satisfied with his conduct that he promised him the first vacancy, and that his commission to command the *Tiger* (60 guns) was actually made out, but never took effect, as Steevens died before it was signed. At the capture of Manila in 1762 Pearson was first lieutenant of the *Lenox*; afterwards he returned to England in the *Seahorse*. On 28 January 1769 he married Margaret (*bap.* 1744), daughter of Francis Harrison of Appleby. They had two daughters, and four sons, one of whom, Richard Harrison Pearson, achieved the rank of vice-admiral in the navy.

Later in 1769 Pearson went out to Jamaica as first lieutenant of the *Dunkirk* with Commodore Arthur Forrest, who had promised him the first vacancy. Forrest, however, died before a vacancy occurred. In August 1770 Pearson received an acting order to command the *Phoenix*, but the appointment was disallowed by Captain Robert Carkett, on whom the command properly devolved. The Admiralty, however, took a favourable view of Pearson's claims, and promoted him on 29 October 1770 to command the sloop *Druid*. In January 1773 he was appointed to the *Speedwell*; and on 25 June, being at Spithead when the king reviewed the fleet, he was specially advanced to post rank. In 1776 Pearson was appointed to the *Garland*, in which he went out to Quebec in charge of convoy, and for the next two years was detained for service in the St Lawrence.

Pearson was appointed to command the *Serapis* (44 guns) in March 1778, and later he was sent to the Baltic with convoy. He was returning in company with the *Countess of Scarborough*, a hired ship, and the trade from the Baltic, when on the evening of 23 September 1779, off Flamborough Head, he met the American privateering squadron commanded by John Paul Jones. The *Pallas*, one of Jones's squadron, engaged and captured the *Countess of Scarborough*, while Jones's own ship, the *Bonhomme Richard*, grappled with the *Serapis*, and between the two one of the most obstinate fights on record took place. It was ended in favour of the *Richard* when the latter's consort, the *Alliance*, came under the stern of the *Serapis* and raked her, though the fire was not effective. Pearson felt unable to withstand a second enemy, and struck his colours. The *Richard* was on the point of sinking, and did sink a few hours after Jones had taken possession of the *Serapis*. Jones's cruise was necessarily brought to an end; and the defence of the *Serapis* against a nominally superior force

and his protection of the convoy won for Pearson a very general approval. He was honourably acquitted by a court martial held on 10 March 1780, and was afterwards knighted and presented with the freedom of Hull, Scarborough, Lancaster, and Appleby, and presented with handsome pieces of plate by the Russia Company and the Royal Exchange Assurance Company. Pearson was an honest, brave officer, and no blame was attributable to him for the loss of the *Serapis*. However, the *Serapis*'s part in the events of September 1779 did not merit an official reward, and should be regarded more as an encouragement to the numerous officers engaged in convoy duty. Jones's remark on hearing of the honour conferred on him was: 'Should I have the good fortune to fall in with him again, I'll make a lord of him.' In April 1780 Pearson was appointed to the *Alarm*, and afterwards he commanded the *Arethusa*. In 1790 he retired to the Royal Naval Hospital, Greenwich, where in 1800 he succeeded Captain William Locker as lieutenant-governor. He died there in January 1806 and was probably buried in the hospital's vault.

J. K. LAUGHTON, *rev.* A. W. H. PEARSALL

Sources J. K. Laughton, *Studies in naval history: biographies* (1887) · 'Memoir of the public services of the late Sir Richard Pearson', *Naval Chronicle*, 24 (1810), 353–6 · G. Atkinson, *The worthies of Westmorland*, 2 (1850), 254–66 · PRO, ADM MSS · Speedwell log, PRO, ADM 51/4350 · muster book, Seaford, PRO, ADM 36/3510 · letters to admiralty, PRO, ADM 1/2305 · parish registers, St Laurence and St Michael, Appleby, Cumbria AS, Kendal

Likenesses C. Grignion, oils, 1780, NMM · J. Watson, mezzotint, pubd 1780 (after C. Grignion), BM · Bromley, two portraits, engravings · H. R. Cook, stipple, BM, NPG; repro. in *Naval Chronicle* (1810)

Pearson, Richard (*bap.* 1764, *d.* 1836), physician, the son of Richard Pearson and Ann, possibly *née* Aris, was born in Birmingham, and baptized at St Philip's, Birmingham, on 9 June 1764. He was educated at Bishop Vesey's School, Sutton Coldfield, Warwickshire, from about the age of seven, and then at Dr Rose's school in Chiswick. His uncle was Thomas Aris (*d.* 1761), founder of the *Birmingham Gazette*. After the death of his parents he became, about 1779, a pupil of Thomas Tomlinson, a Birmingham surgeon and accoucheur; Tomlinson joined the staff of Birmingham General Hospital in January 1780. In 1782 Pearson was awarded the first gold medal of the Royal Humane Society for a dissertation on the clinical signs of death and suspended animation. His elder brother received the medal in London on his behalf; John Coakley Lettsom and John Fothergill were among the judges. Pearson entered the University of Edinburgh in the autumn of 1783 and gained the degree of MD on 24 June 1786. As a student he was president of the Royal Medical Society and of the Natural History Society at the university. His dissertation on scrofula was dedicated to Thomas Smith, a physician at Birmingham General Hospital and also an Edinburgh graduate, with whom he was later to work.

After qualifying Pearson travelled in Germany, Italy, France, and Austria, for two years, in the company of Thomas Knox (1753–1840), later first earl of Ranfurley. After returning to England he became a licentiate of the

Royal College of Physicians, on 22 December 1788. Pearson settled in Birmingham, living in New Street, and in June 1792 he was appointed *locum tenens* at the hospital in place of William Withering (1741–1799), who was already very ill; the appointment was confirmed on 17 September. Pearson's marriage to Mrs Elizabeth [?] Startin produced a son, Richard (1795–1853), later a cleric, and a daughter, Elizabeth Anne, who in 1834 married William Innes Pocock RN (1783–1836).

Pearson resigned from Birmingham General Hospital on 19 December 1800, as did Thomas Smith, and moved to London, where he lived in Keppel Street, Bloomsbury; however, from 1803 he subscribed £2 2s. a year to the hospital in Birmingham. On 3 February 1803 Pearson was elected FSA and became a member of the Medical Society of London, whose first paper he presented. He had moved to Reading by 1812, after which he lived briefly in Sutton Coldfield before returning in 1815 to Birmingham, where he spent the rest of his life.

Although retired, Pearson soon became involved in the preparations by William Sands Cox in 1825 for founding a medical school in Birmingham, of which Edward Johnstone was also a major supporter. Pearson gave the first introductory lecture, at its opening. He also published on a variety of topics: *Different Kinds of Airs* (1795), *Inflammatory Diathesis in Hydrophobia* (1789), in which he stressed his views against the contemporary practice of bleeding, and *The Bilious Fever of 1797, 1798 and 1799* (1799). In *The Epidemic Catarrhal Fever or Influenza of 1803* (1804) he incorporated the opinions of provincial practitioners treating the infection and noted the depression many patients suffered as a sequel to influenza. Pearson's other publications included *Materia medica* (1807), and works on salted fish (1812), on plague (1813), and on treatments for dropsy (1835).

Pearson had a considerable interest in natural history and botany and introduced *Lichen islandicus* to medicine for the alleviation of indigestion; he was an acknowledged authority on pharmacology. He was considered a sociable, convivial person, but some thought him eccentric. He died a widower at Birmingham on 11 January 1836 and was buried, at his own request, in the churchyard of St Paul's, Birmingham. In his will, made on 13 May 1834, as well as family bequests he left mourning rings to former medical school colleagues William Sands Cox and John Ingle; his medical books he gave to Dr John Eccles. JOAN LANE

Sources *Annual Biography and Obituary*, 21 (1837), 46–53 · Munk, *Roll* · F. L. Colvile, *The worthies of Warwickshire who lived between 1500 and 1800* [1870] · T. W. Peck and K. D. Wilkinson, *William Withering of Birmingham* (1950) · *Universal British Directory*, 2 (1793) · *Holden's Directory*, 3 (1811) · *Aris's Birmingham Gazette* (18 Jan 1836) · *Jopson's Coventry Mercury Extraordinary* (11 Nov 1782) · governors' minutes and annual reports, Birmingham General Hospital · papers, S. Antiquaries, Lond. · records, Royal Humane Society · U. Edin. L., special collections division, university archives · will, 13 May 1834, Lichfield Joint RO, ref. Pearson 1836 · parish register (baptisms), Birmingham, St Philip's, 9 June 1764 · parish register (death), Birmingham, St Paul's, 11 Jan 1836
Archives Birm. CA, General Hospital MSS
Likenesses A. Bracken, portrait; formerly priv. coll. · E. A. Pearson, pencil drawing; formerly priv. coll. · E. J. Posselwhite, stipple (after A. Bracken), BM, Wellcome L. · portrait, repro. in Peck and Wilkinson, *William Withering of Birmingham*, pl. xxviii · stipple (after A. Bracken), Wellcome L. · stipple, NPG; repro. in *GM* (1836)
Wealth at death see will, 1834, Lichfield Joint RO, ref. Pearson 1836

Pearson, Sir Thomas (1782–1847), army officer, was the son of the Revd Thomas Horner Pearson (1752–1832), rector of Podimore, Milton, and vicar of Queen Camel, Somerset, and his wife, Temperance. Two younger brothers, Charles (1789–1864) and George (1792–1816), distinguished themselves as officers in the Royal Navy. On 2 October 1796 Pearson was commissioned into the 23rd foot (Royal Welch Fusiliers), joining that élite but skeleton regiment at Chatham. He was present, but not landed, for the failed raid on the Ostend lock gates in May 1798.

Promoted first lieutenant on 25 April 1799, Pearson was first in hard infantry combat at the Netherlands (Helder) assault landings on 27 August, and twice more, at Egmont and Castricum, in that campaign. While on the Ferrol expedition, before landing against that Spanish naval base, he was promoted captain on 7 August 1800. The 23rd joined Sir Ralph Abercromby in the Mediterranean to expel the French from Egypt. After landing in Abu Qir Bay on 8 March 1801 Pearson was severely wounded in the thigh, but fought with his company for the whole campaign, and was awarded the sultan's gold order of the Crescent.

After nine months at Gibraltar, Pearson obtained his first home leave (six months) from the duke of Kent. He rejoined the 23rd in the Isle of Wight (1803–4). In December 1804 Pearson's recruiting earned him a majority in the newly formed 2nd battalion at Chester. Over 400 strong, it was inspected there under his command on 5 December 1806. Pearson and 257 men rejoined the 1st battalion at Colchester (February 1807). On 17 August Pearson led the 23rd's advance guard in the first skirmishing of the Copenhagen campaign and was almost daily in action until the city surrendered three weeks later.

The highlight of Pearson's 1808–10 posting to Nova Scotia was the expedition to capture Martinique. On 1 February 1809 he commanded the regiment's left wing in a seven-hour battle with the French. His 'spirited and judicious exertions' (Philippart, 2.35) were noted by Lieutenant-General Sir George Prevost on the 2nd, when Pearson took command of Prevost's division's light infantry battalion. Before Fort Desaix surrendered, Pearson was wounded by grapeshot in his leg. He was thanked for surprising a French picket. After returning to Nova Scotia, Pearson married Ann Eliza Coffin (1789–1859) the second daughter of the American loyalist Lieutenant-General John Coffin (c.1751–1838), on 28 June 1810, at Coffin's Alwington Manor, near Saint John, New Brunswick.

By November 1810 Pearson had sailed to Lisbon with the fusilier brigade (7th and 23rd foot) to enter the Peninsular War. Pearson led its light battalion in Wellington's March 1811 pursuit of the French from Portugal, then turned south as part of 4th division towards Badajoz. At Olivenza the fire of Pearson's fusiliers and riflemen kept the besiegers' losses to a minimum. On the bloody day of

Albuera (16 May 1811) Pearson commanded 4th division's ten light infantry companies as a right-flank hollow square against the French cavalry. This enabled the fusilier brigade to make its epic attack undisturbed. As the senior unwounded officer Pearson temporarily commanded that victorious but literally halved formation. A lieutenant-colonel from 30 May 1811, Pearson reverted to commanding the fusilier light companies. In a 27 September rearguard action at Aldea da Ponte, Spain, they twice helped retake the village, but their commander incurred a shattered thigh bone which caused his evacuation to Lisbon and England.

Recovered, Pearson became an inspecting field officer of militia in Canada on 28 February 1812. Bound for Quebec from Halifax in July or August aboard the schooner *Mary Ann* he, his wife and baby son were captured by the US Salem privateer *Buckskin* but were recaptured by the frigate HMS *Maidstone*. From late October he commanded at Prescott, a hamlet and battery (later Fort Wellington) on the vital St Lawrence River route to Kingston.

Surgeon William Dunlop recalled Pearson as 'as good a man, and as brave a soldier as ever drew a sword, but too much of a martinet to be favourite with the militia' (Dunlop, 27). Lieutenant Le Couteur relates how a militiaman seeking leave was told '"Go to Hell!"' The man persisted, '"Has your honour any orders for the Devil?" Pearson ... smiled: "What leave do you want?" "Six days!!!" He doubled his leave and gave him a pound to take home!' (*War of 1812 Journal*, 113).

On 9 November 1813 Pearson's 440 regulars, militia, and three 6-pounders at Prescott joined a 680-strong British-Canadian force pursuing over 7000 American troops advancing on Montreal. At the classic 'thin red line' victory of Crysler's Farm on 11 November, when Lieutenant-Colonel Joseph Morrison's second in command, he added a clasp to his army gold medal for Albuera and lost a horse. He was made a CB in January 1814.

At the request of Lieutenant-General Gordon Drummond, Pearson sailed to Fort George in April 1814 via Oswego to command a light brigade under Major-General Phineas Riall on the Niagara frontier. At the Chippawa River (3–5, 8 July), at Lundy's Lane near Niagara Falls (25 July, wounded in the arm), and in the siege of Fort Erie (until 17 September) Pearson displayed outstanding leadership of all-arms forces numbering up to 1100 regulars, militia, and Indians. By the time an American rifle bullet in the head put Pearson *hors de combat* (and destroyed the hearing of his right ear), Drummond's right division had fought the most formidable American army encountered to a tactical draw and a strategic victory.

After the wars Pearson briefly commanded 2nd battalion, 43rd light infantry, before disbandment. In July 1817 he took command of his former regiment, the 23rd, then in France, for thirteen years, serving in Ireland (1818–23) and Gibraltar (until 1827–8).

Pearson became major-general on 22 July 1830, leaving his beloved fusiliers. Knighted by William IV on 18 March 1835 he was made KCH that year. His son was Captain

Thomas Aylmer Pearson (also of the 43rd), aide-de-camp to the general officer commanding northern district of Ireland, in which command his father became lieutenant-general on 23 November 1841. Pearson received the colonelcy of the 85th light infantry on 21 November 1843. Following erysipelas for six days, he died at 1 Edgar Buildings, Lansdown, Bath, on 21 May 1847.   RANDAL GRAY

Sources R. G. Harris, 'Two military miniatures', *Journal of the Society for Army Historical Research*, 63 (1985), 99–103 · W. Wood, *Select British documents of the Canadian war of 1812*, 4 vols. (1920–28) [five 1813 letters in vol. 2] · A. D. L. Cary, S. McCance, and others, eds., *Regimental records of the Royal Welch Fusiliers* (late the 23rd foot), 7 vols. (1921–), vols. 1–2 · *The war of 1812 journal of Lieutenant John Le Couteur, 104th foot: merry hearts make light days*, ed. D. E. Graves (1993) · M. Glover, 'The royal Welch fusiliers at Albuera', *Journal of the Society for Army Historical Research*, 66 (1988), 146–54 · *Colburn's United Service Magazine*, 2 (1847), 479 · *Army List* · N. Holme and E. L. Kirby, eds., *Medal rolls: royal Welch fusiliers – Napoleonic period* (1978) · *Annual Register* (1847), 232 · *Dod's Peerage* (1841), 272–3 · *The Napoleonic war journal of Captain Thomas Henry Browne, 1807–1816*, ed. R. N. Buckley (1987) · R. G. A. Levinge, *Historical records of the forty-third regiment, Monmouthshire light infantry* (1868), 332 · W. A. Shaw, *The knights of England*, 1 (1906), 460; 2 (1906), 335; repr. (1971) · W. Dunlop, *Tiger Dunlop's Upper Canada* (Toronto, 1967), 27 · J. Philippart, ed., *The royal military calendar*, 3rd edn, 2 (1820), 35; 4 (1820), 339–41 · d. cert. · Foster, *Alum. Oxon.* · O'Byrne, *Naval biog. dict.* · *VCH Somerset*, 3.252 · A. L. Humphreys, *The Somerset roll* (1897), 78 · E. S. Maclay, *A history of American privateers* (1900), 410 · D. E. Graves, *Field of glory: the battle of Crysler's farm, 1813* (1999)

Likenesses C. Buncombe, miniature, c.1803–1804, NAM · pen-and-ink drawing, 1824, Royal Welch Fusiliers, Caernarfon, regimental museum · portrait, c.1841, Royal Welch Fusiliers, Caernarfon, regimental museum · portrait, Royal Welch Fusiliers, Caernarfon, regimental museum

Pearson, Thomas Hooke (1806–1892), army officer, the son of John Pearson, advocate-general of India, was born in June 1806. He was educated at Eton College, and entered the army as a cornet in the 11th light dragoons on 14 March 1825. In November 1825 he served at the siege of Bharatpur under Lord Combermere, where he volunteered for the assault, but was not used. The cavalry served well in preventing the escape of the usurping raja and his followers.

When Lord Amherst, the governor-general, visited Ranjit Singh, Pearson accompanied him as aide-de-camp, and received a sword from the maharaja for riding a horse that was believed to be unmanageable. He obtained a troop in the 16th lancers on 16 August 1831, and served with them at the battle of Maharajpur, where Sir Hugh Gough defeated the Marathas on 29 December 1843, and also in the First Anglo-Sikh War. At Aliwal (28 January 1846) Pearson commanded one of the squadrons which broke through an infantry square. During the latter part of that day, and at Sobraon (10 February), he was in command of the regiment; he was twice mentioned in dispatches, and received a brevet majority on 19 June 1846. In a letter written at Aliwal on 29 January 1846, Pearson said: 'I, of course led the charge, and was the first man over the enemy's entrenchments, and at no point of the whole affair had I a man in front of me' (Graham, 110). He became major in the regiment on 23 April 1847, but saw no further active service, and was placed on half pay on 7 April 1848. He became lieutenant-general on 1 October 1877, and was then retired with the honorary rank of general. He had been made a CB on 2 June 1869, and on 4 February 1879 was given the colonelcy of the 12th lancers. In 1867 he won the One Thousand Guineas, the Great Yorkshire Stakes, the St Leger, and the Doncaster Cup with his horse Achievement (d. 1872). He died at his home, The Hasells, Sandy, Bedfordshire, on 29 April 1892, leaving four sons and three daughters: his wife, Frances E. A. Pearson, had died in 1890.

E. M. LLOYD, rev. JAMES LUNT

Sources *The Times* (3 May 1892) · H. Graham, *History of the sixteenth, the queen's, light dragoons (lancers), 1759–1912* (privately printed, Devizes, 1912) · dispatches of Lord Hardinge, Lord Gough, Sir H. Smith · C. E. Buckland, *Dictionary of Indian biography* (1906) · Boase, *Mod. Eng. biog.*
Archives NAM, diaries in India
Wealth at death £36,938 17s. 3d.: resworn probate, Jan 1893, *CGPLA Eng. & Wales* (1892)

Pearson, Weetman Dickinson, first Viscount Cowdray (1856–1927), building contractor and oil producer, was born on 15 July 1856 at Woodfield House, Shelley, Kirkburton, near Huddersfield, eldest son among the eight children of George Pearson (d. 1899), of Brickendonbury, near Hertford, and his wife, Sarah (d. 1911), daughter of Weetman Dickinson, of High Hoyland, Yorkshire. Pearson attended a private school, Hallfield, in Bowling, Bradford, and at the age of thirteen went to Pannal College, near Harrogate. He left school at sixteen, and was apprenticed to the family firm of builders and contractors, S. Pearson & Son, founded by his grandfather, Samuel Pearson.

This marked the beginning of a remarkable and highly successful business career. In 1875, three years after joining the family business, Pearson was sent on a tour to the United States to seek new business, especially orders for the bricks, tiles, and piping whose manufacture was a major concern of the Bradford firm. He was very impressed by the energy and dynamism of the United States and, in turn, his visit was so successful that he was given growing responsibilities at S. Pearson & Son. In 1879 his grandfather retired from the business and gave him his share in it, making him his father's sole partner. Subsequently Pearson aggressively expanded the firm's business outside the north of England, especially in London, to which city he moved the headquarters in 1884. After the move to London, Pearson effectively ran the business, and in 1894 he became the sole partner. On 22 June 1881 he married Annie (1862–1932), daughter of Sir John Cass, of Bradford, Yorkshire; they had three sons, the youngest of whom was killed in action during the First World War, and one daughter, Gertrude Mary *Denman, Lady Denman.

Under Pearson's leadership the company rapidly emerged as one of Britain's leading contractors. During the 1880s the firm undertook major construction works in Britain and overseas. These included major dock construction projects at Milford Haven (1885–90), Southampton (1886–91), and Halifax in Nova Scotia (1886–9). In 1889 Pearson won two major contracts in the United States and Mexico which secured his leading role as a British contractor. The former was to build the Hudson River tunnel to connect New York with Jersey City, and the latter was construction of the Grand Canal designed to drain the swampy plateau on which stood Mexico City. The successful completion of these projects was followed by the construction of the Blackwall Tunnel under the Thames between 1891 and 1897, the building of the four East River tunnels connecting New York with Long Island for the Pennsylvania, New York, and Long Island Railroad Company in the 1900s, and a considerable number of railways, port and other infrastructure projects in Mexico.

Pearson's personality and business skills lay at the heart of his firm's success. He had immense personal magnetism, an urge to achieve and to succeed, and a capacity for hard work. He was motivated neither by money nor by social prestige, but rather by a restless search for new challenges. He had a notable ability to accept mistakes and to learn from failures which stood him in good stead, though in practice the number of failures were few, both because of good judgement and because he appeared to be unusually lucky. Contemporaries referred often to 'Pearson luck'.

Pearson possessed an unusual combination of entrepreneurial vision and the technical skills of an engineer. He had an extraordinary ability to perceive new opportunities and a willingness to take risks. Endowed with considerable technical knowledge and a profound understanding of both the engineering and strategic dimensions of the contracting business, Pearson was also noted for his considerable financial acumen. He costed many major contracts personally, or else relied on a trusted group of associates. He skilfully employed bank overdrafts, using his clients' securities as collateral, to finance large contracts, which made the work virtually self-financing.

Pearson's entrepreneurial spirit led him to become the pioneer of the Mexican oil industry. This remarkable development grew out of S. Pearson & Son's extensive construction work in Mexico, during which oil seepages had been discovered while looking for rock for harbour works. In April 1901 Pearson, because of a missed train connection, spent a night at Laredo on the Mexico–United States border, which was close to a large oil discovery in the Texan oilfields. Although entirely ignorant of the petroleum industry, he glimpsed the commercial opportunities if oil could also be discovered in Mexico, and began to acquire oil concessions, a process facilitated by his close relations with the Mexican dictator, Diaz. By 1907 the firm owned 600,000 acres of land in that country. There followed a considerable business drama and a vivid demonstration of 'Pearson luck'. Pearson invested heavily in refining facilities and shipping, but his drillers found comparatively little oil. He was forced to buy oil in Texas to meet his marketing commitments, and by 1908 things looked desperate as his personal fortune had been pledged to support the oil business. He also became embroiled in a vicious trade war with the American company which had formerly dominated the Mexican market. But in 1910 Pearson's drillers struck oil on an enormous scale. By 1914 Mexico had become the third largest oil producing country in the world, after the United States and Russia, and Pearson controlled about 60 per cent of this production. He created a large, vertically integrated business which controlled oil production, refining, distribution, and selling.

Pearson pursued a rather reluctant political career. He was elected a Liberal MP for Colchester in 1895, after failing to win the seat three years earlier, and retired in 1910. He appears never to have spoken in the House of Commons and he was so frequently absent that his critics called him the 'member for Mexico'. Nevertheless, he had strong political beliefs, advocating old-age pensions and other welfare measures, supporting the principle of home rule for Ireland, and—together with his wife—actively advocating female suffrage. For his various services Pearson was created baronet in 1894 and raised to the peerage in 1910 as Baron Cowdray, of Midhurst, Sussex. During the First World War Cowdray served as president of the Air Board in 1917. The output of aircraft increased significantly during his appointment, but he resigned in November of that year on learning that the prime minister, Lloyd George, had offered the newly created Air Ministry to Lord Northcliffe rather than to himself. Cowdray was created a viscount in 1917.

Cowdray maintained an active business career after the end of the war. Concerned about the deteriorating political situation in Mexico and anxious to pursue new business activities, in 1919 he sold the majority of his equity in the Mexican oil business to the Shell group. The deal was a further manifestation of 'Pearson luck', for by 1922 the most prolific Mexican oil well had been infiltrated by salt water, and in 1938 all foreign-owned oil properties in Mexico were nationalized. However, Cowdray continued to be involved in the oil business, and his drillers searched for oil in a range of countries, including Britain, where they had discovered oil in Derbyshire in 1917. The only long-term and commercially viable discoveries were made in the United States, where in 1919 Cowdray participated in the formation of the Amerada Petroleum Corporation. He also continued to be closely involved with contracting, especially the huge Sennar Dam project in the Sudan, designed to irrigate the Gezira plain which lay in the triangle between the Blue and White Niles to the south of Khartoum.

Cowdray was a generous benefactor to good causes. He gave £325,000 to establish the Royal Air Force Club after the end of the First World War, and made substantial donations to a number of universities, including Aberdeen, Birmingham, Cambridge, and University College, London. He owned extensive estates in Aberdeenshire and Kincardineshire, and made substantial donations to various causes in Aberdeen. In 1920 he was unanimously elected lord rector of Aberdeen University.

Cowdray was made GCVO in 1925. On 1 May 1927, two days before he was due to become a freeman of Aberdeen, he died in his sleep at his home, Dunecht House, Dunecht, Aberdeenshire, having suffered for some time from heart disease. He was buried at Echt on 3 May.   G. JONES

Sources J. A. Spender, *Weetman Pearson, first Viscount Cowdray, 1856–1927* (1930) · D. Young, *Member for Mexico: a biography of Weetman Pearson, first Viscount Cowdray* (1960) · R. K. Middlemas, *The master builders* (1963) · G. Jones, *The state and the emergence of the British oil industry* (1981) · D. J. Jeremy, 'Pearson, Weetman Dickinson', *DBB* · GEC, *Peerage* · d. cert. (Scotland)

Archives Sci. Mus., corresp. and papers | BL, corresp. with Lord Gladstone, Add. MSS 46476–46478 · Bodl. Oxf., letters to Herbert Asquith · CAC Cam., corresp. with Channel Tunnel Co.

Likenesses H. C. Grimwood, bronze bust, borough of Colchester · Vandyk, photograph, NPG · oils (after J. S. Sargent), Gov. Art Coll.

Wealth at death £4,000,000: administration with will, 3 July 1927, *CGPLA Eng. & Wales*

Pearson, Weetman John Churchill, third Viscount Cowdray

Pearson, Weetman John Churchill, third Viscount Cowdray (1910–1995), businessman and landowner, was born on 27 February 1910 at Midhurst, Sussex, the only son and third of six children of Weetman Harold Miller Pearson, second Viscount Cowdray (1882–1933), Liberal MP for Eye from 1906 to 1918, and his wife, Agnes Beryl (1881–1948), third and youngest daughter of Lord Edward Spencer Churchill (fifth son of George Spencer Churchill, sixth duke of Marlborough). Pearson was educated at Eton College and at Christ Church, Oxford, and became third Viscount Cowdray on his father's death on 5 October 1933. He married, on 19 July 1939, Lady Anne Pamela Bridgeman (b. 1913), third of the four daughters of Orlando Bridgeman, fifth earl of Bradford. There were three children of the marriage, Mary Teresa (b. 1940), Liza Jane (b. 1942), and Michael Orlando Weetman (b. 1944). The marriage ended in divorce in 1950, and on 4 March 1953 Cowdray married Elizabeth Georgiana Mather Mather-Jackson, second of the three daughters of Sir Anthony Henry Mather Mather-Jackson, sixth baronet. There were a further three children by this second marriage, Lucy (b. 1954), Charles Anthony (b. 1956), and Rosanna (b. 1959).

When succeeding to the title in 1933 Cowdray had taken over responsibility for two large estates—at Cowdray Park in west Sussex and Dunecht in Aberdeenshire—as well as a controlling interest in S. Pearson & Son, a diversified business group founded by his grandfather, Weetman Dickinson Pearson, first Viscount Cowdray, in the last quarter of the nineteenth century. S. Pearson was run at that time by his uncle, Clive Pearson, and Cowdray devoted much of his time to the management of the estates; he became a considerable authority on farming and forestry. He was also an active sportsman; in addition to the traditional country pursuits of hunting, shooting, and fishing he acquired a great enthusiasm for polo, reaching a handicap of four in 1939. In that year he joined the Sussex yeomanry as a captain. He was badly wounded at Dunkirk and lost his left arm. He made light of his disability and set about working out in practical ways how to minimize the damage—perfecting, with the help of his gunmakers, Purdey, and the Roehampton centre, an artificial arm with a safety release mechanism which would enable him to ride and play polo with great success for many years. For the rest of the war he worked in the Air Ministry, serving as under-secretary of state for air in 1941–2.

After the war Cowdray became increasingly involved in the affairs of S. Pearson, and took over as chairman when his uncle retired in 1954. The company, still wholly owned by the Pearson family, was in a difficult situation at that time. Its main aviation activities had been nationalized, as had its coal mines and electric utilities. It had a controlling interest in Lazards, the merchant bank, and a variety of other financial and industrial investments, including Westminster Press, a chain of provincial newspapers (of which Cowdray's twin sister, Angela, was chairman). Cowdray's achievement over the next twenty-three years was to transform the company, by acquisition, into a broadly based and highly profitable industrial group. Working closely with a group of talented colleagues, of whom Oliver Brian Sanderson Poole, later Baron Poole of Aldgate [see Poole, Oliver Brian Sanderson], was the most important, he looked for well-managed firms which had a strong position in niche markets and which were capable of being developed over the long term. One of his most astute purchases was that of the *Financial Times*, bought from the Eyre family in 1957; the *Financial Times* was then in the early stages of what proved to be a highly successful transition from City news sheet to major international newspaper.

Brendan Bracken, chairman of the *Financial Times* at the time of the takeover, had been greatly impressed by Cowdray's 'sound stewardship' of the Pearson business (Kynaston, 254), and this was an accurate description of his management style. While not afraid to take risks, he eschewed acquisitions which might overstrain Pearson's management resources. He was concerned, above all, with the quality of the businesses he was buying and the calibre of the managers in charge of them. A group that included newspaper and book publishing, Royal Doulton china and Madame Tussaud's, might not fit the fashionable concept of 'synergy', but the formula worked well. When Cowdray retired from the chairmanship in 1977 pre-tax profits were forty times the 1953 level, and gross earnings per share had increased twenty-eight fold. Meanwhile S. Pearson had become a public company; the shares were floated on the stock exchange in 1969.

Cowdray combined his business career with an active life as landowner and sportsman. Polo remained one of his greatest loves, and through his efforts Cowdray Park was central to the revival of the sport which took place in Britain after the war. In 1956 he introduced the Cowdray Park gold cup, which later acquired the additional title of the British Open Championship. Following in his father's footsteps, he also served the Hurlingham Polo Association, as steward and chairman from 1947 to 1967, and later as president.

Like Pilkington, the glass makers, S. Pearson was one of Britain's last great family business empires, and its durability owed a great deal to Cowdray's personal qualities. An old-fashioned sense of family pride and continuity was linked to a shrewd appreciation of modern management practices. He had a remarkable memory for facts and figures, and knew how to isolate what was important. Unassuming and unpompous in demeanour, he was receptive to new ideas, and listened carefully to all points of view before reaching a decision. When the decision was made, he let others get on with it without interference; if things went wrong, he was always supportive, and ready to work with the managers concerned to put matters right. Above all, he had a rocklike sense of values, and the standards which he set infused all the businesses which he controlled, even those which he rarely visited in person. At a time when family control in large businesses was giving way to professionalization, Cowdray represented an older ethos, but it is one which had a lasting impact on the character of the Pearson group.

Cowdray died at the King Edward VII Hospital, Easebourne, Midhurst, Sussex, on 19 January 1995, following a stroke. He was survived by his second wife and his six children; his son Michael succeeded him as fourth viscount. A memorial service was held at St Paul's, Knightsbridge, on 7 March 1995.   GEOFFREY OWEN

Sources *The Times* (20 Jan 1995) · *Daily Telegraph* (20 Jan 1995) · *The Independent* (21 Jan 1995) · *WWW* · Burke, *Peerage* · S. Pearson, annual reports · D. Kynaston, *The Financial Times: a centenary history* (1988) · d. cert. · private information (2004)
Archives FILM BFI NFTVA, current affairs footage
Likenesses two photographs, 1938–52, Hult. Arch. · photograph, repro. in *The Times* · photograph, repro. in *Daily Telegraph* · photograph, repro. in *The Independent*
Wealth at death £59,738,059: probate, 26 April 1995, *CGPLA Eng. & Wales*

Pearson, William (1767–1847), astronomer, was born at Whitbeck in Cumberland on 23 April 1767, the second son of William Pearson (*bap.* 1733, *d.* 1795), a yeoman, and his wife, Hannah Ponsonby (*bap.* 1739). Educated from 1785 at the grammar school of Hawkshead, near Windermere, in Lancashire, he became a teacher there before leaving to reside at Lincoln, where he taught at the free grammar school and became curate of St Martin's in 1794. His first scientific interest there was mechanical, for he constructed a curious astronomical clock and an orrery, described in 1797 a new electrical machine, and in 1798 devised a satellitian, for showing the phenomena of Jupiter's satellites. A copy of this last device is in the Museum of the History of Science at Oxford. In 1800 Pearson moved to London to become a partner in Elm House School, Parsons Green, Fulham; two papers on the minor planet Ceres were dated from there in 1802.

Pearson was one of the original proprietors of the Royal Institution, and in 1803 completed a planetarium for illustrating Dr Thomas Young's lectures. He designed and built, or had built, other planetary machines notable for their accuracy and also for being designed for use in large lecture halls. All his machines were described by him in his articles 'Orrery' and 'Planetarium' for Rees's *Cyclopaedia*. His final machine, an orrery built in 1813, survives, as original or as a copy, in the Science Museum, London. On 10 January 1810 he was presented to the rectory of Perivale, Middlesex, and, by Lord Chancellor Eldon on 15 March 1817, to that of South Kilworth, Leicestershire. In 1811 he became owner of a large and very successful private school at Temple Grove, East Sheen, Surrey, where, having established an observatory, he measured the diameters of the sun and moon during the partial solar eclipse of 7 September 1820 with one of Dollond's divided object-glass micrometers. These skills and researches gained him the award of an honorary LLD from the University of Glasgow in 1815 and election to fellowship of the Royal Society in 1819.

The foundation of the Astronomical Society of London was significantly due to Pearson's initiative. In 1812, and again in 1816, he made suggestions which were discussed at a meeting held at the Freemasons' Tavern on 12 January 1820. Pearson helped to draw up the rules, and acted as treasurer during the first ten years of the society's existence. On selling his school and quitting East Sheen in 1821 he moved to South Kilworth, where he lived for the rest of his life. There he erected his second observatory, first in a wing added to the rectory, later as a separate building. Among the fine instruments collected there were a 3 foot altazimuth, originally constructed by Troughton for the St Petersburg Academy of Sciences, an achromatic refracting telescope by Tulley, a transit by Simms, and a clock by Hardy. A piece of flint-glass by Guinand, nearly 7 inches across, purchased by him in 1823 for £250, was worked by Tulley into the largest object-glass then in England.

Pearson's first notable observations at South Kilworth were of the occultations of the Pleiades in July and October 1821. The two quarto volumes of his *Introduction to Practical Astronomy* were published in 1824 and 1829. The first was composed mainly of tables for facilitating the processes of reduction of astronomical observations, while the second gave elaborate descriptions of various astronomical instruments, accompanied by engravings of them and instructions for their use. For this publication, styled by Sir John Herschel 'one of the most important and extensive works on that subject which has ever issued from the press' (Herschel, 216), he received, on 13 February 1829, the gold medal of the Astronomical Society. To that body he bequeathed the stock and plates of the work. The second volume of *Practical Astronomy* drew heavily on some of the sixty-three articles which Pearson had previously contributed to Rees's *Cyclopaedia*. His articles on horology in that work were reprinted in 1970.

In 1831 Pearson was appointed to the new board of visitors to the Royal Greenwich Observatory, on which he served until his death. In 1830, assisted by a village mathematician named Ambrose Clarke, he began the reobservation and computation of 520 stars tabulated for occultations in his *Practical Astronomy*. The resulting catalogue was presented to the Royal Astronomical Society on 11 June 1841. On 29 October 1835 he observed Halley's comet, and in 1839 he deduced from his own determinations a value for the obliquity of the ecliptic. Some improvements effected by him in Rochon's doubly refracting micrometer were claimed by Arago, but the accusation of plagiarism was satisfactorily refuted.

On 22 February 1796, at Retford, Nottinghamshire, Pearson had married Frances Low (*b.* 1770), the second daughter of Robert Low of Lincoln, an ironmonger, with whom he had his only child, Frances, in 1797. They are depicted with Pearson and one of his planetary machines in an oil portrait by Thomas Phillips (*c.*1810). Following his wife's death in October 1831, about 1833, in Yorkshire, Pearson married Eliza Sarah, who appears to have been a widow many years his junior; she died in 1869.

Pearson died at South Kilworth on 6 September 1847 and was buried in the churchyard there on 13 September. A tablet inscribed to his memory in the church testifies to his example as a clergyman, a magistrate, and a benefactor. Pearson had become a wealthy man. He owned land in Leicestershire, Oxfordshire, Northamptonshire, Warwickshire, and Westmorland. He left his land to his nephew William Pearson, the eldest surviving son of his elder brother John, and £12,000 in cash went to other relatives. A. M. CLERKE, *rev.* DAVID PHILIP MILLER

Sources S. J. Gurman and S. R. Harratt, 'Revd Dr William Pearson (1767–1847): a founder of the Royal Astronomical Society', *Quarterly Journal of the Royal Astronomical Society*, 35 (1994), 271–92 · H. C. King, 'Some outstanding planetary machines of nineteenth-century Britain', *Geared to the stars: the evolution of planetariums, orreries, and astronomical clocks* (1978), 322–40 · R. Sheepshanks, *Memoirs of the Royal Astronomical Society*, 17 (1847–8), 128–33 · *History of the Royal Astronomical Society*, [1]: 1820–1920, ed. J. L. E. Dreyer and H. H. Turner (1923) · J. F. W. Herschel, 'An address … on February 13 1829, on presenting the honorary medals to the Rev. William Pearson, Professor Bessel, and Professor Schumacher', *Memoirs of the Astronomical Society of London*, 4 (1830), 215–24 · W. Pearson, 'The description of a new portable electrical machine', *Nicholson's Journal*, 1 (1797), 506–11 · W. Pearson, 'A model proposed for the construction of a satellitian', *Nicholson's Journal*, 2 (1799), 122–32 · W. Pearson, 'Concerning the new planet Ceres', *Nicholson's Journal*, new ser., 1 (1802), 284–7 · W. Pearson, 'On the new planet Ceres', *Nicholson's Journal*, new ser., 2 (1802), 48–55 · W. Pearson, 'A report on the properties and powers of a new three-feet altitude and azimuth instrument', *Memoirs of the Astronomical Society of London*, 2 (1826), 261–76 · W. Pearson, 'Observations of the occultations of the Pleiades by the moon', *Memoirs of the Astronomical Society of London*, 2 (1826), 289–90 · H. C. Plummer, 'William Pearson, 1767–1847', *Occasional Notes of the Royal Astronomical Society*, 6 (1939), 75–7 · parish registers (baptism), Whitbeck, Cumbd
Archives CUL, Airy MSS, Royal Greenwich Observatory MSS, RGO6 · RAS, RAS letters
Likenesses T. Phillips, group portrait, oils, 1800? (with wife and daughter), RAS · portrait, repro. in Dreyer and Turner, eds., *History of the Royal Astronomical Society*, frontispiece
Wealth at death approx. £2000 p.a. from land; also £12,000 cash legacies: Gurman and Harratt, 'Revd Dr William Pearson'; will, PRO, PROB 11/2066

Peart, Charles (1759–1798), sculptor and wax modeller, was born on 22 December 1759 at English Newton, Monmouth. In 1778 he exhibited three wax models at the Royal Academy, from Mr Abington's, Paulin Street, Hanover Square, and showed portraits, made exclusively in this medium until 1782. In 1781 he entered the Royal Academy Schools as a sculptor, where the following year he was awarded a gold medal for a model, *Hercules and Omphale*.

Some time after leaving the RA Schools, Peart went to work as an assistant to the sculptor John Charles Lochee (*b.* 1751), who was employed by Wedgwood. The great manufacturer employed Lochee to model plaques from the collection of gems at Stowe, Buckinghamshire, in

1787. Peart too was at Stowe in 1788, where he seems to have been employed, independent of his former master, by Wedgwood. In a letter written directly to Wedgwood's agent, Mr Bierly, Peart apologized for the delay in completing the modelling he had been commissioned to carry out, apparently in conjunction with the history and decorative painter Vincenzo Valdré (c.1742–1814), as an earlier assignment and the 'marquis's' desire to take Valdré to Ireland with him in August, necessitated that they 'work 14 Hours in a Day and which Sir, at present puts it quite out of my power to attend to anything else' (2 June 1788, Trustees of the Wedgwood Museum, Barlaston, Staffordshire). Peart, like Lochee, modelled a number of portraits for Wedgwood, including those of Lord Hillsborough and William Chambers.

Peart showed regularly at the Royal Academy throughout his life, from 1793 from a studio in New Road, close to the chief stoneyards. His exhibits from the late 1780s demonstrate a move towards larger scale, more monumental work and included designs for monuments, allegorical and classical friezes, and portrait busts. One of his first large commissions may have been obtained through the influence of his wife, Elizabeth (b. 1770/71), whose sister's husband, Mr Woodcock, worked for the East India Company. The monument to Lieutenant-Colonel John Campbell (d. 1784), erected in St Thomas's Cathedral, Bombay, is conventional in its design, with life-size figures of death and hope either side of an urn on a tall pedestal; the monument is signed, although the date and circumstances of the commission have yet to be established. In 1791 Peart received what was probably his most important commission, that of the monument to Joseph Moorhouse, a colonel in the company's coast artillery, who was killed at the storming of the Pettah Gate of Bangalore; his death was also commemorated in a painting by Robert Home of 1793. Commissioned by the court of directors of the East India Company, following a general order of the Madras government in 1791, the monument in St Mary's Church, Madras, comprises a sarcophagus set on lion's feet (signed and dated by the sculptor, 7 March 1791) above which a relief portrait bust of Moorhouse, set in a medallion, is raised up by a cherub to the figure of Britannia to be crowned with a laurel.

The only other recorded monument by Peart is that to John Finch at Dudley, Worcestershire. In 1792 he carved a statue of Henry V for his home town of Monmouth (above the shire hall) and in 1793 carved a marble chimney-piece for the marquess of Buckingham's house in Pall Mall. In spite of these larger scale commissions, Peart appears to have continued to work for Wedgwood. A letter dated 14 July 1794, again to Bierly, asks the agent to remit £20 on account, as 'at this time I have been laying in a large stock of stone to save the duty, which I am called on to pay of course immediately' (Trustees of the Wedgwood Museum, Barlaston, Staffordshire).

Peart died in 1798, leaving his widow with a young child. Farington records that in September 1799 Peart's affairs were not yet settled, but that Mrs Peart expected to receive little as he was 'much in arrears to the parish of St Pancrass having rec'd. money as Parish Officer' (Farington, *Diary*, 4.1281, 24 Sept 1799). She remarried in 1804.

DEBORAH GRAHAM-VERNON

Sources R. Gunnis, *Dictionary of British sculptors, 1660–1851*, new edn (1968) · Farington, *Diary* · B. Groseclose, *British sculpture and the company raj: church monuments and public statuary in Madras, Calcutta, and Bombay to 1858* (1995) · Graves, *RA exhibitors* · E. J. Pyke, *A biographical dictionary of wax modellers* (1973) · MS letters, Charles Peart, Trustees of the Wedgwood Museum, Barlaston, Staffordshire
Archives Trustees of the Wedgwood Museum, Barlaston, Staffordshire, MS letters

Peart, Edward (1755/6–1824), physician and writer on science and medicine, was an MD and a corresponding member of the London Medical Society. He practised for some time at Knightsbridge, but afterwards removed to Butterwick, near Gainsborough, Lincolnshire, where he wrote on numerous scientific topics. He was chiefly known for his works on physical and chemical theory, which involved him in polemics with the critical magazines. Although an acute critic of Lavoisier's chemical theories, he failed to grasp their theoretical scope or their experimental foundations, and hence his criticisms, though ingenious, ultimately proved unsound.

In his first work, *The Generation of Animal Heat* (1788), Peart explained all chemical and physical phenomena by assuming the existence of four elements—aether, phlogiston, the acid principle, and earth. In the following year these were reduced to three, two active principles, aether and phlogiston, and one fixed. As he explained in his next book, *On the Elementary Principles of Nature* (1789), when a fixed particle is surrounded by an atmosphere of particles of aether radiating from it in straight lines, it forms an earthy (alkaline) particle; a phlogiston atmosphere produces an acid particle. All actions 'at a distance', corresponding to the phenomena of electricity, magnetism, and gravitation, were explained by means of these 'atmospheres' in Peart's subsequent works, *On Electricity* (1791), *On the Properties of Matter* (1792), and *On Electric Atmospheres … [with] a Letter to Mr. Read of Knightsbridge* (1793). He used the same principles to criticize the theory of Lavoisier in *The antiphlogistic doctrine of M. Lavoisier critically examined … [with] strictures on Dr. Priestley's experiments* (1795) and *On the Composition and Properties of Water* (1796). Peart was also identified as the publisher of the anonymously authored anti-Lavoisian satire, *The Sceptic* (1800).

The least speculative of Peart's books were those on physiology and medicine, to which he turned later in his career: *Physiology* (1798), *Practical Information on Malignant Scarlet Fever* (1802), *Practical Information on St Anthony's Fire* (1802), *Practical Information on Rheumatism* (1802), *Practical Information on Inflammation of the Bowels* (1802), and *On the Consumption of the Lungs* (1803). In *Animal Heat* he had revived the idea of John Mayow that animal combustion takes place in the substance of the muscle and not in the lung, as Lavoisier thought. In the same book he saw clearly that the constant temperature of animals in exercise and at rest must be due to a correlation of various functions, and investigated the matter experimentally in a somewhat rough way. He expressed the view that 'excitability of the muscular fibres is the great characteristic of life in animals' (*Animal Heat*, 91). In his medical works he showed himself untrammelled by the prevailing doctrines of his day, using simple drugs, and ascribing their beneficial effects to direct action on the diseased matter. Peart declared (*On the Composition of Water*, 67), 'I write for amusement at my leisure hours', and, in the preface to *Physiology* (1798, xiii), 'I have no expectation of making converts to my peculiar views'. He seems to have made none. From his writings, and in spite of his controversies, Peart appears as a man of kindly though erratic tendencies. In *Physiology* and elsewhere he vigorously protested against the unnecessary vivisections of his time.

Peart died at Butterwick in 1824, probably in November. P. J. HARTOG, rev. JAN GOLINSKI

Sources GM, 1st ser., 94/2 (1824), 472 · T. Beddoes, 'E. Peart, *Antiphlogistic doctrine … critically examined*', *Monthly Review*, new ser., 19 (1796), 194–8 [review] · T. Beddoes, 'E. Peart, *On the composition and properties of water*', *Monthly Review*, new ser., 23 (1797), 139–42 [review] · private information (1895)

Peart, (Thomas) Frederick, Baron Peart (1914–1988), politician, was born in Durham on 30 April 1914, the elder son (there were no daughters) of Emerson Featherstone Peart, a Weardale schoolmaster, and his wife, Florence Maud Hopper. The harsh realities of life for the families whose children his father taught gave Peart a lifelong commitment to the labour movement. Starting his education at Crook council school, he went on to Wolsingham grammar school and Henry Smith's school in Hartlepool. He read science at the College of the Venerable Bede (Durham University), becoming president of the Labour Club and of the university union. Excelling at boxing, he also represented his university at rugby and football.

Unusually for a science graduate Peart began studying at the Inner Temple. He was not called to the bar, opting instead to return to his roots in Durham as a schoolteacher and a lecturer in economics, campaigning with characteristic vigour to improve educational opportunities in its mining communities. After serving from 1937 for three years on Easington rural district council he enlisted in the Royal Artillery as a gunner in 1940. After distinguished war service in north Africa and Italy he returned home as a captain in 1945 and was elected Labour MP for Workington, which he served for thirty-one years. In that year he married Sarah Elizabeth (Bette), daughter of Thomas Lewis, mining engineer in South America. They had one son. Welsh, articulate, highly principled, a history graduate and teacher, Bette shared her husband's passion for equality of educational opportunity. From 1945 to 1951 Peart was parliamentary private secretary to Thomas Williams, minister of agriculture in the newly elected Labour government. They worked in total harmony; indeed, so identified was he with Tom Williams that he was the natural choice for the Ministry of Agriculture after Labour's return to office in 1964 under the leadership of Harold Wilson. At the same time he was sworn of the privy council.

Cabinet pressure led Peart to reduce farm subsidies in his first (1965) farm price review, which provoked farmers to civil disobedience, but he emerged from this baptism of fire a widely respected minister. His reputation was further enhanced by courageous and decisive handling of Britain's worst ever epidemic of foot and mouth disease. In the countryside he was ever more warmly received by farmers and farmworkers alike.

Peart's reservations at that time about European Economic Community membership ran deep, echoing those in most farming communities. He opposed in cabinet the Labour government's 1967 application for EEC membership because he was convinced that the common agricultural policy would deprive British farmers of secure incomes and make consumers worse off by excluding cheap food imports from the traditional suppliers, and he was concerned also about harmful effects of the policy on the Commonwealth's poorer developing countries.

In 1968 he became leader of the Commons, first as lord privy seal (April–October) and then lord president of the council. His courtesy, friendliness, generosity, and good humour made him as popular as leader of the house as he had been as minister of agriculture. With Labour's defeat in 1970, he became opposition spokesman on parliamentary affairs (1970–71), agriculture (1971–2), and defence (1972–4). He also served as leader of Labour's delegation to the Council of Europe, of which he was vice-president in 1973–4. In February 1974, with Labour back in office, he became minister of agriculture again. By then, exploitation by Commonwealth beef and sugar producers of rising world prices for their products led him reluctantly to come to terms with Britain's EEC membership, to which British farmers were now more favourably inclined.

In 1976, with James Callaghan as prime minister, Peart received a life barony and, as lord privy seal, became leader of the House of Lords. Following Labour's defeat in 1979 he led the opposition peers until 1982. He was also chairman of the Advisory Council for Applied Research and Development (1976–80) and the Retail Consortium (1979–81). He was an honorary DSc of Cranfield Institute of Technology (1977), honorary FRCVS (1969), and a freeman of the City of London (1968).

Peart was one of the best-liked parliamentarians of his generation. Tall, gentlemanly, with patrician good looks and a naturally straightforward manner, he was always enjoyable company. In 1984 he was savagely attacked by two armed robbers who had broken into his home. His health was shattered and he never fully recovered. He died on 26 August 1988 in hospital in Tooting, London. He was survived by his wife. ALFRED MORRIS, rev.

Sources WWW · private information (1996) · personal knowledge (1996) · CGPLA Eng. & Wales (1989)
Wealth at death £440,855: probate, 24 Jan 1989, CGPLA Eng. & Wales

Pease, Sir Alfred Edward, second baronet (1857–1939), politician and sportsman, was born at Woodlands, Darlington, on 29 June 1857, the second of the eight children, and the eldest son, of Sir Joseph Whitwell *Pease, first baronet (1828–1903), businessman and Liberal MP for Barnard

Castle, co. Durham (1885–1903), and his wife, Mary Fox (*d.* 1892). He was born into an established Darlington Quaker family which figured prominently in the politics and economy of the region. His father, uncle, and grandfather were all Liberal members of parliament, and both he and his younger brother Joseph Albert (Jack) *Pease, who became Baron Gainford (1917), followed in this tradition. Pease was educated at Grove House, Tottenham, and entered Trinity College, Cambridge, in 1876, graduating BA in 1880 (MA, 1883). On 10 February 1880 he married Helen Ann (Nellie) Fowler (1858–1910), third daughter of Sir Robert Nicholas Fowler, first baronet, banker, and Conservative politician; they had two sons and a daughter. Pease entered business and became a director of the family firm, Pease & Partners Ltd, and of the National Provident Institution. He was an alderman of the North Riding from 1889 to 1937, and a deputy lieutenant for both the North Riding and London.

In 1885 Pease was elected Liberal MP for York, which he represented until his defeat at the 1892 general election; he was defeated there again in 1895. In January 1897, while travelling in Somaliland, he was elected for the Cleveland division of the North Riding and sat until 1902, when he accepted the Chiltern Hundreds. Though designated a Liberal, Pease preferred the appellation 'whig', and defended with gusto the principle of a ruling class whose members were born and bred in the traditions of government. At the same time he admired Gladstone and steadfastly supported Irish home rule, free trade, and temperance. Much happier in the Victorian political world than in the Edwardian, Pease opposed the 'people's budget' of 1909 as a 'socialist' measure. Believing that Asquith was 'out for the "Labour" vote' and had taken 'Lloyd George and Limehouse to his bosom', he severed links with the party of 'neo-Liberalism' (Pease, *Elections*, 301).

By this date, however, Pease's political career was over. During the 1890s the family textile business had gone into decline; when its failure became public in 1902 Pease resigned his seat. It was a humbling turn of fortune for one whose coming of age in 1878 had been celebrated with a party for 800 at his father's mansion, Hutton Hall, in Yorkshire. Although Pease avoided bankruptcy, only desperate measures enabled him to save Pinchinthorpe House, his Yorkshire home, from the creditors. In straitened circumstances he sought employment abroad and he was wryly amused when help eventually came from a political opponent and not from a political friend.

In 1903, the year that Pease succeeded to his father's baronetcy, Lord Milner, of whom he had been highly critical during the Second South African War, appointed him resident magistrate in the Barberton district of the Transvaal. After a period of service there in 1903–5, he pursued several speculative business ventures, including an ostrich farm in Africa, before settling again in England. Although none of his money-making schemes took off, Pease was able to live the remainder of his life as a gentleman of means. After the death of his first wife he married on 28 September 1912 Laure Marianne (1868–1922), daughter of Louis Philippe Sugnet de Montmagny. There were no children. During the 1914–18 war he served with the remount service and in September 1918, after his younger son had been killed in action, he joined the Church of England. His second wife died in January 1922 and on 1 August of that year, to the mild scandal of his friends and family, he married his nurse, Emily Elizabeth Smith (1897–1979), forty years his junior; they had three surviving children, two sons and a daughter.

In his memoir *Elections and Recollections* (1932) Pease has left a candid record of political life at the end of the nineteenth century. He had scant regard for the reputations of some famous contemporaries and wrote of John Morley: 'With all his historical and literary attainments, I never knew a distinguished man so destitute of any understanding of our race, or indeed any other' (Pease, *Elections*, 97). The book reveals Pease as an unflinching advocate of condign punishment: he was convinced of the deterrent value of heavy sentences—what he termed 'the mercy of severity'—and supported flogging.

A fine horseman and an ardent fox-hunter Pease wrote an entertaining history of the hunt to which he most commonly rode: *The Cleveland Hounds as a Trencher-Fed Pack* (1887). Hunting inspired some of his best writing, and his *Half a Century of Sport* (1932) recounts diverse exploits abroad, including the pursuit of lion in Africa, ibex in the Pyrenees, and Barbary sheep in Algeria—Pease rated the latter as one of the most difficult game to hunt. In England he found time to shoot, stalk, and follow otterhounds, and his *Hunting Reminiscences* (1898) has detailed chapters on hare, fox, cub, and badger hunting. Although Pease had no qualms about digging for badger, he denounced badger-baiting as 'a cruel and brutalizing sport'. He believed that 'all genuine sportsmen have something of the naturalist in their composition', and in parliament advocated an extension of the legislation to protect wild birds (Pease, *Hunting Reminiscences*, 236). Pease's attachment to the countryside of the North Riding is conveyed strongly in his *Dictionary of the Dialect of the North Riding of Yorkshire* (1928), an authoritative account on the subject. Pease died at his home at Pinchinthorpe in Guisborough, Yorkshire, on 27 April 1939.   MARK POTTLE

Sources Burke, *Peerage* (1999) · WWBMP, vol. 2 · *A wealth of happiness and many bitter trials: the journals of Sir Alfred Edward Pease, a restless man*, ed. J. G. Pease (1992) · A. E. Pease, *Elections and recollections* (1932) · A. E. Pease, *Hunting reminiscences* (1898) · A. E. Pease, *The Cleveland hounds as a trencher-fed pack* (1887) · *The Times* (28 April 1939) · Venn, *Alum. Cant.* · CGPLA Eng. & Wales (1939) · b. cert. · m. cert. [Emily Elizabeth Smith] · d. cert.
Archives McMaster University, Hamilton, Ontario, papers; letters to Major John Fairfax-Blakeborough · NL Scot., corresp. with Lord Rosebery and Lord Crewe
Likenesses photograph, repro. in Pease, *Elections*
Wealth at death £4664 18s. 6d.: probate, save and except settled land, 14 Aug 1939, CGPLA Eng. & Wales · £10,212: further grant, limited to settled grant, 23 Oct 1939, CGPLA Eng. & Wales

Pease, Sir Arthur Francis, first baronet (1866–1927), coal owner and industrialist, was born at Hummersknott, Darlington, on 11 March 1866, the eldest son of Arthur Pease, coal owner and MP, and his wife, Mary Lecky, daughter of Ebenezer Pike of Bessborough, co. Cork. He came from a

Quaker family which had long been associated with industrial development in Durham and Yorkshire. He was the great-grandson of Edward *Pease, railway projector; grandson of Joseph *Pease [see under Pease, Edward], also a railway projector, and the first Quaker to sit in parliament; and nephew of Sir Joseph Whitwell *Pease, first baronet, of Hutton Lowcross and Pinchinthorpe, who for nearly forty years represented a Durham constituency in the House of Commons. Pease was educated at Brighton College, and at Trinity College, Cambridge, and received a business training in Darlington with the family colliery concern, Pease & Partners.

Pease was fortunate to avoid the financial catastrophe which afflicted the family bank, J. and J. W. Pease, in 1902, when negotiations for a takeover by Barclay & Co. revealed the bank to be insolvent. Pease had earlier sold his interest in the business to his uncle, Sir Joseph Whitwell Pease, whose estate was forfeited to meet liabilities in excess of £400,000. A portion of this sum was owed to Pease & Partners and it was owing to Arthur Francis Pease's acknowledged non-involvement in the bank's collapse that he was able to become chairman and managing director of that concern in 1906. In the course of time Pease became associated as chairman or director with numerous coalmining and other industrial undertakings in the north of England; he was also a director of Lloyds Bank and of the London and North Eastern Railway Company. In 1889 he married Laura Matilda Ethelwyn, daughter of Charles Peter Allix, of Swaffham Prior House, Cambridgeshire, who survived him; they had a son and three daughters.

Pease became known to the public as a prominent negotiator when an organized demand arose among miners for a minimum wage. He was one of three representatives of the Durham owners who served on the committee of coal owners which was appointed in 1912 to meet the government and the Miners' Federation. Subsequently, when the joint district board for Durham was set up under the Minimum Wage Act of 1912, Pease was called upon to state the case for the owners. After the outbreak of the First World War in 1914, Pease's great experience of industrial affairs was at once available for the government, and during the years 1914–21 he was an active member of many government committees. He held office as second civil lord of the Admiralty from 1918 to 1919, and was created a baronet in 1920.

In the conduct of labour relations Pease departed from the principles of conciliation and arbitration which had informed Sir Joseph Whitwell Pease's stance as a negotiator in the Durham coal industry in the two decades before 1900. These were the years of 'Lib-Labism' when organized labour accepted a subordinate position in the hierarchy of liberal capitalism. As a unionist, Pease rejected this philosophy, especially in the years after 1906 when employers and trade unionists in the coal industry began to mobilize on a national basis in the face of declining productivity and profitability. In the great disputes of the 1920s Pease was a firm advocate of the view that, in the event of trade union opposition to wage reductions in response to trade depression, employers should resort to the tactics of the lock-out.

Pease devoted much time to the affairs of his native county. He was elected chairman of the Durham county council in 1922 and took an especial interest in education. He was a JP and a deputy lieutenant for the county of Durham, and in 1920 he served as high sheriff. During the First World War he helped to raise the 18th battalion of the Durham light infantry. Preoccupation with business affairs prevented him from seeking election to the House of Commons, but his strong political sympathies induced him to act as president of the Durham Unionist Association from the time of its formation in 1910. He was devoted to all forms of sport and was a regular follower of the Zetland hounds. Pease's health eventually became precarious as a result of overwork, and he died at his home, Middleton Lodge, Middleton Tyas, near Darlington, on 23 November 1927, after a cerebral haemorrhage during a meeting of directors. His son, Richard Arthur Pease, succeeded to the baronetcy. M. W. KIRBY

Sources M. W. Kirby, Men of business and politics: the rise and fall of the Quaker Pease dynasty of north-east England, 1700–1943 (1984) · M. W. Kirby, 'The failure of a Quaker business dynasty: the Peases of Darlington, 1830–1902', Business and religion in Britain, ed. D. J. Jeremy (1988), 142–63 · DNB · Venn, Alum. Cant. · The Times (24 Nov 1927) · d. cert.

Wealth at death £113,971 19s. 3d.: probate, 23 Jan 1928, CGPLA Eng. & Wales

Pease, Edward (1767–1858), woollen manufacturer and railway promoter, born at Darlington on 31 May 1767, was the eldest son of Joseph Pease, woollen manufacturer, and his wife, Mary Richardson. A brother, Joseph (1772–1846), was one of the founders of the Peace Society in 1817, and a supporter of the Anti-Slavery Society, for which he wrote tracts in 1841 and 1842. Edward was educated at Leeds under Joseph Tatham the elder, and at the age of fifteen was placed in the woollen manufacturing business carried on by his father at Darlington. Pease married, on 30 November 1796, a fellow Quaker, Rachel, daughter of John Whitwell, of Kendal. They had five sons and three daughters. Rachel Pease died at Manchester on 18 October 1833.

In 1809 Pease became interested in a scheme for improving navigation on the lower reaches of the River Tees, a project which eventually bore fruit as the Stockton and Darlington Railway linking collieries in south-west Durham with the London coastal trade in competition with established interests on the Tyne and the Wear. In 1818 preliminary steps were taken to obtain parliamentary sanction for the proposed railway, but the bill was thrown out owing to the opposition of the duke of Cleveland, near one of whose fox-covers the line was to run. In 1819 a new route was proposed, and the measure received royal assent on 19 April 1821.

Originally the railway was only intended to carry coal, and be drawn by horses; but in the spring of 1821 Pease recruited the Tyneside colliery engine-wright, George *Stephenson, as engineer to the line. Stephenson was the foremost locomotive engineer of the day and it was due to

Edward Pease (1767–1858), by William Miller

his advocacy that Pease was persuaded of the efficiency of steam locomotive haulage on the projected railway.

Pease's role as the driving force behind the Stockton and Darlington Railway project was facilitated by his status as a Quaker entrepreneur with extensive familial contacts within the Quaker banking community in Norwich and London. Following the opening of the railway in September 1825, intermarriage within the Quaker 'cousinhood', reinforced by intra-family share transfers, resulted in the Pease family's emergence as the leading stockholders in the railway. Thus, despite its status as a publicly quoted company the Stockton and Darlington Railway soon aspired to the standing of a family-run firm.

Pease's role as provider of capital is well illustrated in his contribution to the founding of Robert Stephenson & Co. of Newcastle upon Tyne in 1823 as a purpose-built locomotive building establishment. Of the modest initial capital of £4000, £1600 was advanced by Pease, but he also loaned Robert Stephenson £500 towards his own subscription.

Pease retired from active business life in 1833. He spent the remaining years of his life, as a notably 'plain' Quaker, consumed with guilt about his worldly riches and worrying incessantly about his sons' business speculations. He died of heart failure at his residence, Northgate, Darlington, on 31 July 1858. His relations with George Stephenson and his son Robert remained cordial to the end of his life.

In his *Lives of the Engineers*, Samuel Smiles described Pease as 'a thoughtful and sagacious man, ready in

resources, possessed of indomitable energy and perseverance'. His diaries were edited by his great-grandson Sir Alfred E. Pease in 1907. He was buried in the Quaker burial-ground, Skinnergate, Darlington.

The second son of Edward and Rachel Pease, **Joseph Pease** (1799–1872), Quaker railway company promoter and industrialist, was born at Darlington on 22 June 1799. Educated at Tatham's academy, Leeds, and Josiah Forster's academy, London, he subsequently aided his father in the projection of the Stockton and Darlington Railway, in 1819 and 1820 by preparing the company's first prospectus. He emerged as an influential voice in the management of the railway in 1828, when he took the lead in projecting an extension of the line from Stockton to the hamlet of Middlesbrough further down the Tees estuary. The effect of this development was twofold: first, to undermine the dominance of Tyne and Wear exporters in the London coastal market for coal; and, second, to lay the foundations for the emergence of Teesside as an outstanding centre for the production of iron. The latter was facilitated by Pease's in numerous railway projections in the north-east of England, all of them designed to open up the heavy mineral wealth of the region.

After the passing of the Reform Bill in 1832, Joseph Pease was elected MP for South Durham, and retained the seat until his retirement in 1841. He was the first Quaker member to sit in the House of Commons, and on presenting himself on 8 February 1833 he refused to take the usual oath. A select committee was appointed to inquire into precedents, and on 14 February he was allowed to affirm (*Hansard 3*, 15, 1833, 387, 639). As a 'worldly' Quaker, Joseph Pease was a frequent speaker on matters of social and political reform, always avoiding the use of titles when addressing the house, and retaining his Quaker dress.

Joseph Pease married, on 20 March 1826, Emma (*d.* 1860), daughter of Joseph Gurney of Norwich, and their surviving children comprised five sons and four daughters. Joseph Whitwell *Pease (1828–1903), the eldest son, who was created a baronet on 18 May 1882, was MP for South Durham from 1865 to 1885, and subsequently for Barnard Castle. Arthur Pease (*d.* 1898), the third son, was MP for Whitby from 1880 to 1885, and for Darlington from 1895.

In addition to commercial and industrial issues, Joseph Pease devoted himself to philanthropic and educational work, aiding Joseph Lancaster, and acting as president of the Peace Society from 1860. Before 1865 he became totally blind, but, with the aid of his secretary, republished and distributed many Friends' books; and in 1870 he had the *Essays on the Principles of Morality* of Jonathan Dymond translated into Spanish, for which service the government of Spain conferred on him (2 January 1872) the grand cross of Charles III.

Joseph Pease died on 8 February 1872 at his Darlington home, Southend, from heart disease. He was buried in the Quaker burial-ground in Darlington on 10 February. At the time of his death Pease's industrial concerns employed nearly ten thousand men in collieries, quarries, and ironstone mines. In addition he owned and directed woollen manufactories and was a leading shareholder in Robert Stephenson & Co., of Newcastle upon Tyne, numerous Teesside ironmaking concerns, and in the Middlesbrough estate.

Edward Pease's fifth son, **Henry Pease** (1807–1881), Quaker railway company promoter, was born at Darlington on 4 May 1807. He also entered with enthusiasm into the railway projects of his father. His principal achievement was the opening in 1861 of the line across Stainmoor, called 'the backbone of England', the summit of which was 1374 feet above sea level. It joined at Tebay the London and North Western Railway (LNWR), and was soon extended at its eastern limit to Saltburn-on-Sea. In January 1854 Pease was deputed by the meeting for sufferings, held on the 17th of that month, to accompany Joseph Sturge and Robert Charleton as a deputation from the Society of Friends to Russia. On 10 February they were received by the emperor Nicholas, and presented him with a powerful address, urging him to abstain from the then imminent Crimean War. He received them politely, but their efforts were unavailing, and Alexander William Kinglake ridiculed their action in his history of the campaign, *Invasion of the Crimea* (1863). Pease was MP for South Durham from 1857 to 1865. In 1867 he visited Napoleon III with a deputation from the Peace Society, but their request for permission to hold a peace congress during the Universal Exhibition in Paris was rejected.

Henry Pease married, on 25 February 1835, Anna, only daughter of Richard Fell of Uxbridge, who died on 27 October 1839, leaving a son, Henry Fell Pease, MP from 1885 for the Cleveland division of Yorkshire; second, on 19 January 1859, he married Mary, daughter of Samuel Lloyd of Wednesbury, with whom he had three sons and two daughters.

Henry Pease was chairman of the first Darlington school board in 1871, first mayor of the town, and president of the Peace Society from 1872. In the early 1860s, when negotiations were in hand for a takeover of the Stockton and Darlington Railway by the North Eastern Railway Company (NER), Pease declared his opposition to the merger, in spite of the generous terms on offer to his family as leading shareholders in the Stockton and Darlington Railway. Following the takeover, however, Pease's sensibilities were overcome by his appointment as vice-chairman of the NER board. It was in that capacity that he presided over the railway jubilee held at Darlington on 27 September 1875, at which eighty British and thirty foreign railways were represented. He was always a prominent member of the Religious Society of Friends. He died at 23 Finsbury Square, London, while attending the yearly meeting, on 30 May 1881, and was buried in the Quaker burial-ground at Darlington on 2 June.

Schools and a library were presented by members of the Pease family to Darlington, which benefited greatly from their benevolence until 1902, when the family fortunes were destroyed irrevocably as a result of the collapse of J. and J. W. Pease, the family counting house and banker to leading industrial enterprises in the north-east of England.

A. F. POLLARD and CHARLOTTE FELL-SMITH, rev. M. W. KIRBY

Sources *The diaries of Edward Pease: the father of English railways*, ed. A. E. Pease (1907) · M. W. Kirby, *Men of business and politics: the rise and fall of the Quaker Pease dynasty of north-east England, 1700–1943* (1984) · M. W. Kirby, *The origins of railway enterprise: the Stockton and Darlington Railway, 1821–1863* (1993) · M. W. Kirby, 'The failure of a Quaker business dynasty: the Peases of Darlington, 1830–1902', *Business and religion in Britain*, ed. D. J. Jeremy (1988), 142–63 · *A wealth of happiness and many bitter trials: the journals of Sir Alfred Edward Pease, a restless man*, ed. J. G. Pease (1992) · S. Smiles, *Lives of the engineers*, 3 (1862) · S. Smiles, *Lives of the engineers*, new edn, 5 (1874) · M. H. Pease, *Henry Pease: a short story of his life* (1897) · *Annual Monitor* (1859) · *Annual Monitor* (1873) · 'Joseph Pease: a memoir', *Northern Echo* (9 Feb 1872) · 'The Peases of Darlington', *British Workman*, new ser., 1 (1892), 127–14 · A. W. Kinglake, *The invasion of the Crimea*, 2 (1863) · *CGPLA Eng. & Wales* (1858) · *CGPLA Eng. & Wales* (1872) [Joseph Pease] · *CGPLA Eng. & Wales* (1881) [Henry Pease] · private information (2004)
Archives Durham RO, family and some personal papers | Edward Pease Public Library, Darlington, Pease–Stephenson MSS · Nuffield Oxf., Gainford MSS · priv. coll., Joseph Pease diary · PRO, Stockton and Darlington Railway MSS, Rail 667
Likenesses W. Miller, line engraving, NPG [*see illus.*] · portrait, repro. in Pease, ed., *Diaries of Edward Pease*, frontispiece · portrait, repro. in Kirby, *Men of business and politics*
Wealth at death under £120,000: probate, 15 Oct 1858, *CGPLA Eng. & Wales* · under £350,000—Joseph Pease: probate, 9 March 1872, *CGPLA Eng. & Wales* · £426,128 0s. 4d.—Henry Pease: probate, 21 July 1881, *CGPLA Eng. & Wales*

Pease, Edward Reynolds (1857–1955), secretary of the Fabian Society, was born on 23 December 1857 at Henbury Hill, near Bristol, the eldest son of Thomas Pease (*d.* 1884), retired wool-comber, and his third wife, Susanna Anne Fry, of the Quaker family of cocoa manufacturers. His father also came from a prominent Quaker family, being a son of the railway promoter and cousin of the more famous Peases of Darlington. Edward Pease was educated at home by two tutors, the latter of whom, Theodore Neild, held progressive views, being a teetotaller and supporter of women's suffrage. Aged seventeen, Pease went to London to work as a clerk in the firm of silk merchants in which his brother-in-law Sir Thomas Hanbury was senior partner. He also became secretary to a debating society at the Friends' Institute, thus, as he said, beginning his habit of becoming secretary of everything he became connected with. He relinquished his job rather than accept a posting to China, but a year later acquired, through Sir Thomas Hanbury, a partnership in a stockbroker's office. Pease never felt at home in the City and when his father died in 1884, leaving him £3000, he left.

Pease was raised as a Quaker but soon entered the realm of Victorian doubt. In London, his cousin Emily Ford took him to spiritualist séances, where he met Frank Podmore, who introduced him to the Society for Psychical Research. Pease became secretary of the haunted-houses committee, but his enthusiasm waned. In 1882 he attended meetings of the Democratic Federation, a socialist group run by the tory Marxist H. M. Hyndman. However, Pease favoured moral reform among the well-off leading to their abdicating wealth, rather than agitation among the workers leading to their seizing wealth. Hence he joined Percival Chubb in forming the Fellowship of the New Life around the wandering scholar Thomas Davidson. The fellowship advocated moral reform of the individual and society. Almost immediately a split developed between those who concentrated on personal regeneration and those who favoured social activism. On 4 January 1884 the latter group, led by Podmore, formed the Fabian Society.

The Fabians, who then numbered about twenty, met on alternate Friday evenings in Pease's lodgings at 17 Osnaburgh Street. They held diverse beliefs, including tory socialism, communal anarchism, and the ethical positivism of Pease and Podmore. For Pease, positivism solved various problems, religious and social, by stressing social duty. His socialism drew also on evangelical morality and biblical allusions, with socialism being defined as a practical economic expression of the injunction to 'love thy neighbour'. Pease argued that socialism was inevitable, so the main question was whether the upper and middle classes would oppose it, thereby causing bloodshed and confusion, or promote it, thereby ensuring peace and harmony. Hubert Bland, a fellow Fabian, satirized this ethical socialism in 'Something wrong' (*Weekly Dispatch*, 1886), a *roman-à-clef* in which Pease appears as the hero. Sydney Olivier, Graham Wallas, and Sidney Webb joined the Fabians in the mid-1880s, and although they started out as ethical positivists, they established, with George Bernard Shaw, a distinctive Fabian socialism committed to parliamentary gradualism, efficient administration, taxation, and collectivism.

We should not distinguish too sharply between the spiritualism, Marxism, personal regeneration, and ethical positivism that attracted Pease. London at that time was full of alternative bohemian schemes for the improvement of self and society, all of which looked forward to a time of fulfilment and harmony. William Morris, designer and socialist, occupied a prominent place in this bohemian world. Influenced by Morris, Pease decided, after his father's death, to become a craftsman. He trained as a cabinet-maker, and in 1886, having failed to get work in Morris's firm, joined a furnishing workshop in Newcastle upon Tyne. The workshop was nominally a co-operative, but in practice was privately owned and kept afloat by loans from Pease, amounting to half his capital, that were paid back only years later. While in Newcastle, Pease became engaged to a schoolteacher and Fabian, Mary Gammell (Marjory), the daughter of the Revd George Smyttan Davidson, minister of the parish of Kinfauns near Perth. The couple married in 1889, after Pease returned from a year's tour of the United States with Sidney Webb, and soon afterwards, they moved to Limpsfield on the North Downs, where they had two sons.

Olivier took over as secretary of the Fabian Society while Pease was in Newcastle. But when Pease returned to London, he had difficulty finding work, and the success of the *Fabian Essays in Socialism* (1889) enabled the Fabian Society to take on employed staff. So, in 1889, Pease was appointed as part-time secretary, becoming full-time a year later. Initially he was paid £50 a year and a similar sum nominally as secretary to Sidney Webb but really on Fabian duties. The post was an onerous one. In January 1891 alone he wrote over 600 letters, organized nine lecture courses as well as ordinary meetings, and managed the society's publishing business, including sales of the *Essays*. Soon after, the society set him up in its first formal office at 276 Strand. The staff still consisted solely of Pease, a typist, and an office boy—only in 1907 was a telephone installed as a labour-saving device. As secretary Pease sided with Sidney Webb, whom he admired greatly, through a series of disputes in the society. During the Second South African War, the quarrel with H. G. Wells, and debates with guild socialists, he defended the society's commitments to parliamentary politics and collectivism. Even antagonists admired his abilities: Wells observed that Pease 'did the work of a cabinet minister for the salary of a clerk' (*DNB*). Although Pease's principal contribution was administrative, he also updated Thomas Kirkup's *History of Socialism* (1913), and wrote *The Case for Municipal Drink Trade* (1904), several Fabian tracts, and various articles and reviews; most importantly, he wrote the official *History of the Fabian Society* (1916).

The Fabians played a vital role in establishing socialist ideas in Britain. Their role in establishing the Labour Party remains a matter of dispute, though it surely was not as great as they suggested. As secretary Pease acted as the main link between the Fabians and other socialist bodies. He was the society's delegate to the conference that formed the Labour Representation Committee and later its representative on the Labour Party's national executive committee (1900–13). He generally kept to his watching brief—benevolent but with no real involvement save the occasional attempt to promote more socialist policies. In 1916 he persuaded Sidney Webb to become the society's representative on the executive of the Labour Party, thereby bringing the two organizations closer.

In 1913 Pease retired as secretary of the Fabian Society after inheriting a capital sum from his uncle, Joseph Storrs Fry. The parting gift of the society was a set of the *Encyclopaedia Britannica*, appropriate, Shaw quipped, since Pease no longer had daily access to Sidney Webb. Pease took over as general secretary again from 1915 to 1918 while his successor, W. Stephen Sanders, was in the army. Otherwise he acted as honorary secretary and kept his seat on the executive committee until the society was reconstructed in 1939, though partial deafness restricted his involvement.

Pease was a shy man with a gruff manner but natural kindness who disliked ceremony. Retirement enabled him to give more time to his pleasures, including gardening and Norse sagas. His wife, a magistrate and local councillor, who stood unsuccessfully as Labour candidate for East Surrey in the 1922 general election, died in 1950. He died at his home, the Pendicle, Limpsfield, on 5 January 1955.   MARK BEVIR

Sources E. R. Pease, *The history of the Fabian Society* (1916) · N. Mackenzie and J. Mackenzie, *The first Fabians* (1977) · *Fabian Journal*

(March 1955) · B. Webb, *Our partnership* (1948) · *DNB* · *The Times* (7 Jan 1955) · N. Annan, 'The intellectual aristocracy', *Essays in social history*, ed. J. H. Plumb (1955) · R. Greenburg, 'Pease, Edward Reynolds', *BDMBR*, vol. 3 · *CGPLA Eng. & Wales* (1955)
Archives BLPES, corresp. and papers · Labour History Archive and Study Centre, Manchester, corresp. and papers · NRA, priv. coll., 'Recollections for my sons', 'Notes on my life', 'Reminiscences of E. R. Pease', and various letters · Nuffield Oxf., mimeographed 'Recollections for my sons' with MS annotations
Wealth at death £37,672 10s. 4d.: probate, 4 March 1955, *CGPLA Eng. & Wales*

Pease, Henry (1807–1881). *See under* Pease, Edward (1767–1858).

Pease, John William Beaumont, first Baron Wardington (1869–1950), banker, was born at Pendower, West Road, Newcastle upon Tyne, on 4 July 1869, the second son of the banker John William Pease (1836–1901) and his wife, Helen Mary Fox (1838–1928), both Quakers. He was educated at Marlborough School (1878–83) and then at New College, Oxford. A gifted sportsman, he was awarded a blue for both golf and lawn tennis.

Pease was a member of the leading business dynasty in the north-east of England responsible for the projection and management of the pioneering Stockton and Darlington Railway and the foundation of interlocking industrial interests embracing woollen textiles, coalmining, engineering, and metallurgical products. The Peases were related by marriage to other Quaker families with commercial interests, principally the Backhouses, Gurneys, and Foxes, and in that connection had founded a private banking partnership in the late eighteenth century which acted as the clearing house for the Peases' own concerns and also as a vehicle for the raising of capital. In this latter context the history of the Pease family is a testament to the strength of the Quaker credit network in mobilizing capital resources for industrial ventures.

Pease's father was a partner in the family bank in Darlington, but in 1859 he moved to Newcastle upon Tyne to become a partner in the banking firm of Hodgkin, Barnett, Pease, Spence & Co. This firm was founded in the wake of the collapse of the Northumberland and Durham District Bank in 1857, an event which precipitated the bankruptcy of the heavily indebted Derwent Iron Company located at Consett. As a major traffic-sender on the Stockton and Darlington Railway, there can be little doubt that Pease's father was propelled northwards to participate in the management of a new banking concern which was expected to play a leading role in the reconstruction of the iron company. This was achieved in 1864 with the foundation of the Consett Iron Company.

Pease himself became a partner in Hodgkin Barnett Pease Spence in the early 1890s, and as senior partner he was to play the leading role in negotiating a merger with Lloyds Bank in 1902. As a prosperous local bank possessing an extensive branch network in the north-east of England, Hodgkin Barnett Pease Spence had some claim to preferment within Lloyds' managerial structure and, after the formal amalgamation in 1903, Pease was elected to the London board of Lloyds. By 1910 he had risen to the position of deputy chairman and in 1922, following the death of Sir Richard Vassar-Smith, he succeeded to the chairmanship. He remained in office until December 1945, a period of service equalling the combined total of his three successors.

In the inter-war period Pease was perhaps better known as a talented amateur golfer than as a banker; he was invariably in contention for the UK amateur championship, and served latterly as chairman of the championship committee. On 6 April 1923 he married Dorothy Charlotte (*d.* 1993), the daughter of Lord Forster, governor-general of Australia, and the widow of the Hon. Harold Lubbock. They had two sons, Christopher Henry Beaumont (*b.* 1924) and William Simon (*b.* 1925). The elder son became a partner in the leading stockbroking firm of Hoare Govett.

Pease was notable for his conservative and orthodox policies while chairman of Lloyds, and during his tenure of office the bank developed a reputation for over-caution. Indeed, between the wars Lloyds' share of deposits and advances declined in relation to those of the other large clearing banks, indicating some loss of competitiveness. Presiding over the board with authority and dignity, Pease nevertheless discouraged discussion, so that board meetings tended to be rubber-stamp affairs. However, as a leading banker he owed his considerable reputation to his qualities of impeccable integrity and honesty. He was appointed chairman of the Committee of London Clearing Bankers and also served as president of the British Bankers' Association. In 1936 his services to banking were recognized in his elevation to the peerage as Baron Wardington, of Alnmouth, Northumberland. He died at Wardington Manor, Wardington, near Banbury, on 7 August 1950, and was cremated in Oxford on 14 August.

M. W. Kirby

Sources J. R. Winton, *Lloyds Bank, 1918–1969* (1982) · R. S. Sayers, *Lloyds Bank in the history of English banking* (1957) · M. Phillips, *A history of banks, bankers and banking in Northumberland, Durham, and North Yorkshire* (1894) · M. W. Kirby, *Men of business and politics: the rise and fall of the Quaker Pease dynasty of north-east England, 1700–1943* (1984) · *Pease of Darlington* (privately printed, *c.*1902) · private information (2004) · d. cert.
Archives Wellcome L., corresp. with National Birthday Trust Fund
Likenesses W. Nicholson, portrait, Lloyds Bank headquarters, London

Pease, Joseph (1799–1872). *See under* Pease, Edward (1767–1858).

Pease, Joseph Albert [Jack], first Baron Gainford (1860–1943), politician, was born at Woodlands, Darlington, on 17 January 1860, the younger son of Sir Joseph Whitwell *Pease, bt (1828–1903), industrialist and banker, and his wife, Mary Fox (*d.* 1892). Jack Pease, as he was known, enjoyed an early life of wealth and privilege in one of Britain's most prominent Quaker industrial and political dynasties. Like his older brother, Alfred Edward *Pease, he was educated at Grove House, Tottenham, a Quaker school. He was afterwards privately tutored by Mandell Creighton before following Alfred to Trinity College, Cambridge, in 1878. He took an undistinguished BA in 1882, but shone as secretary of the amateur dramatic club, was

Joseph Albert Pease, first Baron Gainford (1860–1943), by Lafayette, 1926

master of the university drag hounds, and represented the university at polo, rugby, and putting the weight. He captained the Trinity cricket eleven, was twelfth man for the university, and was then a founder member and captain of the Durham county side. *Wisden* records that he continued to play until, at the age of seventy-four, his inability to take quick singles persuaded him it was time to retire.

Cambridge friends such as J. M. (Harry) Paulton and Eddie Tennant (later Lord Glenconner) shared enduring interests in sport and politics. Tennant's sister Margot, whose passion for riding to hounds matched Pease's, was also to become a lifelong friend. Her marriage to H. H. Asquith drew Pease into the upper social circles of the Liberal Party. Comfortable berths in the family coal and banking enterprises had afforded him sufficient leisure to embark on a career in politics. A Durham county councillor from 1887 until 1902, Pease was mayor of Darlington during 1888–9 (Britain's youngest mayor). Elected MP for Tynemouth in 1892, he was parliamentary private secretary (1893–5) to John Morley as chief secretary for Ireland, a post to which he aspired himself in the latter years of Asquith's premiership.

Made a whip in 1897, Pease faithfully understudied Herbert Gladstone. In opposition he made well-publicized noises about not being a pro-Boer without ever aligning himself unequivocally with the Liberal Imperialists. A more serious impediment to his advancement when Campbell-Bannerman came to power was the collapse of the Pease fortunes (1902), a calamity largely attributable to his father's improvident management of the family businesses. Generous friends rescued him from the brink of bankruptcy, but Pease's reduced circumstances were to make personal financial concerns a continuing distraction thereafter.

Pease's formidable wife Ethel (Elsie; *d.* 1941), whom he had married on 18 October 1886, was particularly irked at the curb on her social ambitions. The daughter of Sir Henry Marshman Havelock-*Allan, bt, and granddaughter of the hero of Lucknow, Sir Henry Havelock, Elsie's hopes for her son and two daughters were as undisguised as her ambition for her husband. His elevation as Asquith's patronage secretary to the Treasury in 1908 brought limited satisfaction. Successful reorganization of the Liberal Party machinery and unobtrusively effective parliamentary management during the budget turbulence of 1909 impressed the prime minister. Asquith brought him into the cabinet as chancellor of the duchy of Lancaster notwithstanding the loss of his Saffron Walden seat in January 1910. A move to Rotherham gave him a constituency that was safe as long as the local miners did not unite behind a Labour candidate.

Pease's promotion to the cabinet mystified colleagues such as Walter Runciman, Edwin Montagu, and Lloyd George (who blamed him for the Liberals' poor showing in the January 1910 election). But Asquith, appreciating his loyalty, saw him as the man to carry forward the government's programme of franchise and electoral reform. When Pease's Franchise Bill foundered on the rocks of women's suffrage in January 1913, his dismay, like Asquith's, was tempered by relief that votes for women had been thwarted without splitting the government. A bigger disappointment was his failure as president of the Board of Education to enact major educational reforms. His appointment in October 1911 coincided with the departure of the permanent secretary, Sir Robert Morant. Pease reshuffled the senior staff of the ministry, choosing a team led by L. A. Selby-Bigge that responded well to a competent, congenial, and considerate chief. With George Newman, Pease greatly expanded school medical services. He strengthened the board's relations with teachers and improved professional training. When war came he encouraged his new parliamentary secretary, Christopher Addison, in mobilizing the nation's scientific and industrial research resources.

Remaining in the cabinet which made the decisions for war with Germany in 1914 was deeply troubling for Pease. He tried unavailingly to dissuade his son from enlisting, and was an early supporter of the Friends' Ambulance Unit. But he resigned from the presidency of the Peace Society and thenceforth publicly defended the government's position. Pushed to the margins of high policy making, he undertook relief co-ordination tasks and introduced educational and leisure activities in army training camps, overcoming ill-judged resistance from Lord Kitchener. A casualty of the May 1915 coalition, Pease served as an unpaid member of the War Claims Commission in France. He was embarrassed by the need to seek a political pension, but by late 1915 he had secured a £2000 a year consultancy by placing his coal industry expertise and political connections at the disposal of his old friend Christopher Furness.

An invitation to rejoin the government as postmaster-general (outside the cabinet), following Sir John Simon's resignation and Herbert Samuel's promotion in January 1916, delayed Pease's return to active business life. But revived hopes of political advancement were effectively extinguished by the formation of the Lloyd George coalition. Ennobled (3 January 1917) as Baron Gainford in the Asquith resignation honours, Pease became a leading figure in the post-war industrial world. He spoke for the Mining Association of Great Britain before the coal industry commission in 1919 and was elected president of the Federation of British Industries for 1927–8. As a 'prominent public man unconnected with any of the constituent companies' (Gainford MSS) he was asked to chair the infant British Broadcasting Company in 1922. He became a radio enthusiast, and was deputy chairman and a governor of the corporation from 1927 to 1932.

Well known in his retirement for his fishing (and a related concern for water conservation), hunting, shooting, and embroidery, Pease made faltering attempts to write his memoirs. His journals from 1908 to 1915, unknown to scholars for fifty years, are a revealing chronicle of Liberal politics. He died at his home, Headlam Hall, Gainford, co. Durham, on 15 February 1943.

CAMERON HAZLEHURST

Sources Nuffield Oxf., Gainford MSS · M. W. Kirby, *Men of business and politics: the rise and fall of the Quaker Pease dynasty of north-east England, 1700–1943* (1984) · M. W. Kirby, 'Pease, Joseph Albert', *DBB* · *A liberal chronicle: journals and papers of J. A. Pease*, ed. C. Hazlehurst and C. Woodland (1994) · GEC, *Peerage* · B. Green, ed., *The Wisden book of obituaries* (1986)
Archives Nuffield Oxf., corresp. and MSS | BL, letters to Herbert Gladstone, Add. MS 46022 · Bodl. Oxf., corresp. with H. H. Asquith · Bodl. Oxf., corresp. with Lord Kimberley · Bodl. Oxf., letters to Lewis Harcourt · Bodl. Oxf., corresp. with Arthur Ponsonby · HLRO, letters to David Lloyd George · U. Newcastle, corresp. with Walter Runciman
Likenesses J. Russell & Sons, photograph, c.1915, NPG · W. Stoneman, two photographs, 1917–38, NPG · Lafayette, photograph, 1926, NPG [*see illus.*]
Wealth at death £26,878 4s. 1d.: resworn probate, 25 May 1943, CGPLA Eng. & Wales

Pease, Sir Joseph Whitwell, first baronet (1828–1903), industrialist and banker, born at Darlington on 23 June 1828, was the elder son of Joseph *Pease (1799–1872), railway company promoter and industrialist [*see under* Pease, Edward], and his wife, Emma (d. 1860), daughter of Joseph Gurney of Norwich. Edward *Pease was his grandfather. In January 1839 he went to the Friends' school, York, under John Ford. Entering the Pease banking partnership at Darlington in 1845, he became largely engaged in the projection of railway enterprise and in the management of the woollen mills, collieries, and iron trade with which the firm was associated. He was soon either director or chairman of the Stockton and Darlington Railway, the

Owners of the Middlesbrough Estate Ltd, Robert Stephenson & Co. Ltd, Pease & Partners Ltd, and J. and J. W. Pease, bankers. In 1894 he was elected chairman of the North Eastern Railway, after serving as deputy chairman for many years. He also farmed extensively, having purchased a 3000 acre estate at Hutton Lowcross in the North Riding of Yorkshire in 1867. He read a paper, entitled 'The meat supply of Great Britain', at the South Durham and North Yorkshire chamber of agriculture, on 26 January 1878.

He married in 1854 Mary, daughter of Alfred Fox of Falmouth. She died on 3 August 1892. They had two sons and six daughters. The elder son, Sir Alfred Edward *Pease, second baronet, MP for York (1885–92), and for the Cleveland division of Yorkshire (1897–1902), was resident magistrate in the Transvaal in 1903. The second son was Joseph Albert *Pease, Lord Gainford, the Liberal cabinet minister.

In 1865 Pease was returned as Liberal MP for South Durham, which he represented for twenty years. After the Redistribution Act of 1885 he sat for the Barnard Castle division of Durham county, until his death. He strongly supported Gladstone on all questions, including Irish home rule, and rendered useful service to the House of Commons in matters of trade, particularly in regard to the coal and iron industries of the north of England. He was president of the Peace Society and of the Society for the Suppression of the Opium Traffic, and a champion of both interests in parliament. On 22 June 1881 he moved the second reading of a bill to abolish capital punishment, and his speech was separately printed. In 1882 Gladstone created him a baronet (18 May). No Quaker had previously accepted such a distinction, although Sir John Rodes (1693–1743) inherited one. In 1886 Pease unsuccessfully attempted to persuade Gladstone to defer his first government of Ireland act.

During the course of 1902 the family banking partnership, J. and J. W. Pease, became insolvent, the product in large measure of a court settlement against Pease in the matter of the administration of the estate of his niece (the countess of Portsmouth), for which he had acted as trustee for many years. Drained of capital, and dependent on secured and unsecured loans to meet the dividend payments of leading industrial concerns, including the Consett Iron Company, Pease & Partners Ltd, and the North Eastern Railway, the bank was absorbed by Barclay & Co. on disadvantageous terms. Although Pease and his sons were saved from bankruptcy proceedings by the receipt of generous financial support from business associates both in London and in the north-east of England, the settlement with Barclay & Co. entailed the forfeiture of the bulk of their estates. Pease died at Kerris Vean, his Falmouth home, of heart failure, on 23 June 1903, his seventy-fifth birthday, and was buried at Darlington.

CHARLOTTE FELL-SMITH, rev. M. W. KIRBY

Sources M. W. Kirby, *Men of business and politics: the rise and fall of the Quaker Pease dynasty of north-east England, 1700–1943* (1984) · M. W. Kirby, 'The failure of a Quaker business dynasty: the Peases of Darlington, 1830–1902', *Business and religion in Britain*, ed. D. J. Jeremy

(1988), 142–63 · *The Times* (24 June 1903) · *WWW* · *Hansard 3* (1881), 262.1037–48 · private information (1912)
Archives NRA, diary · Nuffield Oxf., corresp. and papers | Bodl. Oxf., letters to Lord Kimberley · Nuffield Oxf., Gainford MSS; Pease MSS
Likenesses Spy [L. Ward], chromolithograph caricature, NPG; repro. in *VF* (1 Oct 1887)
Wealth at death £2886 18*s.*: probate, 14 July 1903, *CGPLA Eng. & Wales*

Pease, Marian Fry (1859–1954), schoolteacher, was born on 3 April 1859 at Top Hill House, Westbury upon Trym, Gloucestershire, the second child of Thomas Pease (*d.* 1884), a Quaker industrialist, and Susanna Anne Fry, his third wife. Known as May to her friends, she was one of a large family of fifteen stepbrothers and stepsisters; Edward Reynolds *Pease, founder of the Fabian Society, was her elder brother. Her mother, who was active in temperance and peace groups, and president of the local branch of what became the National Council of Women, encouraged her interest in social issues. Both of her parents were supporters of education for girls. She was educated at home with her brother Edward. When she was a child the family moved to Cote Bank House in Westbury, her home for most of her life. In 1876 she was awarded a scholarship by the Clifton Association for the Higher Education of Women and attended undergraduate classes in mathematics, heat, light, sound, and political economy at University College, Bristol, where she was the first woman student.

Marian Pease left Bristol in 1880 with honours in all her subjects and became a schoolteacher. After a year of training at the Cambridge Training College for Women she spent two years (1890–92) as an assistant in the day training college at Mason College, Birmingham. In 1892 she returned to University College, Bristol, as mistress of method in the day training college, lecturing to women training to be elementary school teachers. She retired as reader in education in 1912, having been awarded the LLD of Bristol University in 1911, though she continued as a special lecturer in education until 1928. Marian Pease inspired her students: 'she was to us a new kind of person. Everything seemed turned upside down as there unfolded before our astonished eyes a newer and larger world of mind and spirit than we could have imagined' (Falk, 8).

Many girls were to benefit from Marian Pease and her lifelong Quaker belief in community service. She was an active social worker and with Hilda Cashmore co-founded in 1911 the Bristol University Settlement, where she taught on the two-year course for social workers. The settlement included a school, ante-natal clinic, and infant welfare services. It also served as the regional headquarters of the Workers' Educational Association, for which she lectured on literature. She also served as a governor of Sidcot School, a Quaker foundation, and of Red Maids' School, a Bristol school for girls. She funded the Bristol branch of the League of Nations Union, of which she was secretary and treasurer.

Of a fair and delicate complexion, Marian Pease was of medium height with neat hands and feet, a comely figure, and bright, blue, alert eyes. She was an attractive personality: discerning, tolerant, genial, and humorous, interested in fine art, but not musical or aesthetic. Her emphasis on treating girls as individuals, on community work, and on moral improvement was part of a missionary sense of vocation and of a belief in teaching as a force for good. Plagued with deafness in later life, she was mentally alert until her death, believing that she would be reunited with her mother, though 'I can't help believing that death will be something of a plunge' (Falk, 2). She died at Wraxhill Cottage, Street, in Somerset, on 25 September 1954, and was cremated at Bristol four days later. She never married, but was devoted to her family, of which she wrote an uncompleted history.

JOHN B. THOMAS

Sources M. M. Falk, 'Marian Fry Pease', MS, 1955 · J. B. Thomas, 'University College, Bristol: pioneering teacher training for women', *History of Education*, 17 (1988), 55–70 · M. F. Pease, 'Some reminiscences of University College Bristol', 1942, University of Bristol Library · D. W. Humphreys, *The University of Bristol and the education and training of teachers* (1976) · *Bristol Evening World* (28 Sept 1954) · b. cert. · *CGPLA Eng. & Wales* (1955) · d. cert.
Archives University of Bristol Library, notes on the Fry family of Sutton Benger and Bristol · University of Bristol Library, reminiscences of University College, Bristol
Wealth at death £22,010 15*s.* 1*d.*: probate, 6 Jan 1955, *CGPLA Eng. & Wales*

Peat, Stanley (1902–1969), chemist, was born at South Shields, co. Durham, on 23 August 1902, the eldest in the family of two sons and one daughter of John Peat, mining engineer of East Boldon, and his wife, Ada Bradford. He was a delicate infant, and was nursed through a serious illness (which left him with permanent curvature of the spine) by his maternal aunt, Alice Gibson. She was devoted to young Stanley, and for long periods she and her husband took care of the boy. Both the Gibsons were staunch Salvationists and it seems probable that Peat's ethics and lifelong love of music were a direct result of their influence. Peat's sickly childhood delayed his formal schooling until he was eight, when he attended Tyne Dock School and later Tyne Dock grammar school, but an active and fertile brain compensated for physical weaknesses and enabled him, in 1915, to win a scholarship to Rutherford College, Newcastle. There he was taught by several dedicated science teachers, including the chemistry master, William Carr, whose love of the subject fired Peat's imagination. In 1921 he won a state exhibition, an entrance exhibition, and an Earl Grey memorial scholarship to study at Armstrong College, Newcastle (later the University of Newcastle upon Tyne), where he read chemistry, and thus came under the influence of Professor W. N. Haworth. Peat graduated in 1924 with first-class honours, being awarded the Freire–Marreco medal and prize, and was invited to join Haworth's research school. At that time Haworth was carrying out fundamental studies on the structures of simple sugars, and Peat was soon involved in studies on the ring forms of glucose and on the structure of maltose. When Haworth moved to the Mason chair of chemistry at Birmingham in 1925, he took with

Stanley Peat (1902–1969), by Walter Stoneman

him an enthusiastic group of workers, including Peat as his personal assistant.

Peat, who was awarded his PhD in 1928, was appointed lecturer in biochemistry in the medical school at Birmingham but he returned to the chemistry department six years later. This brief excursion into biochemistry was to influence much of his later research. During the next fourteen years, and in spite of the advent of the war, Peat collaborated with Haworth to investigate the chemistry of sugars and important polysaccharides such as starch, cellulose, and agar, which resulted in the publication of over forty original papers in, mainly, the *Journal of the Chemical Society*.

In the summer of 1939 Peat married Elsie Florence, younger daughter of Henry H. V. Barnes, a dental surgeon who, with his family, had shared a house with Peat for some years. The couple had two daughters, Gillian (*b.* 1940) and Wendy (*b.* 1942). With the outbreak of hostilities Haworth turned his laboratories over to projects for the war effort, the start of an anxious period for Peat. He carried out work for the Admiralty and, for a time, worked on uranium compounds as part of the project leading ultimately to the atom bomb, but he was never happy in this work. He also served on the cellulose and cordite panel of the Ministry of Supply, and on a committee which was seeking alternatives to Japanese agar for microbiological work. During 1940 he became interested in work by C. S. Haines, which described the synthesis of starch using a plant enzyme. Haworth and Peat secured a sample of this

starch and from this initial study stemmed an interest in the biological synthesis and breakdown of starch which continued for the rest of Peat's life. At the end of the war Peat was awarded the DSc and promoted to a readership.

In 1948 Peat was elected a fellow of the Royal Society, and in the same year he was appointed to the chair of chemistry at the University College of North Wales, Bangor, where he quickly established a research school. With W. J. Whelan as his able collaborator, he began to publish widely on starch and a variety of other plant polysaccharides, gaining worldwide recognition for his work. In honour of his research achievements, the Chemical Society invited him to give the Hugo Müller lecture in 1959, but a serious illness prevented him from doing so.

In addition to his activities in research, Peat was a dedicated teacher, who took enormous pains over the teaching of organic chemistry to first-year students; he considered this the most important of the undergraduate courses. His clear and concise introduction to modern theories of chemical reactions was a revelation to generations of students. He also served in a wider sphere as dean of the faculty of science at Bangor, on the council and committees of the Chemical Society, and as a consultant to several research associations. From 1959 repeated illnesses prevented him from taking an active part in research, but he was always ready to give advice and encouragement to his colleagues until his death at Bangor on 22 February 1969, from a stroke. He was survived by his widow and daughters. J. R. TURVEY, *rev.*

Sources E. L. Hirst and J. R. Turvey, *Memoirs FRS*, 16 (1970), 441–62 · personal knowledge (1981) · private information (1981)
Likenesses W. Stoneman, photograph, RS [*see illus.*]
Wealth at death £16,978: probate, 23 April 1969, *CGPLA Eng. & Wales*

Peat, Thomas (1707/8–1780), lecturer on science and almanac editor, was born at Ashleyhay, near Wirksworth, Derbyshire, the son of a farmer. He soon showed an inclination for learning, which his father tried to repress. A brother, a joiner in Nottingham, to whom he became apprenticed, gave him no more encouragement. However, Cornelius Wildbore, a master dyer, who, like the Peats, regularly attended the Presbyterian High Pavement chapel, noticed him and enabled him to obtain books.

Peat became a writing master and teacher of mathematics, scientific lecturer, and land surveyor in Nottingham. In 1740 he was one of the principal projectors, with John Badder, William Whitehead, and others, of the *Gentleman's Diary, or, The Mathematical Repository*, an annual almanac with literary and mathematical sections on similar lines to the *Ladies' Diary*. Both Badder and Whitehead worked as surveyors with Peat. The first numbers, from 1741, were edited by Badder and had contributions from Peat; from 1749 to 1756 he was joint editor and on Badder's death in 1756 he became sole editor until his own death in 1780. His successor was the Revd Charles Wildbore, probably the son of his early patron. Subsequently Peat became anonymous editor of the *Poor Robin* almanac; his share in it ceased some time before his death.

Peat used the almanacs to advertise his services. About

1743 he projected a course of fourteen two-hour lectures at Nottingham on mechanics, hydrostatics, optics, pneumatics, astronomy, and the use of globes, possibly in association with William Griffis, who published a syllabus about 1746. Peat's undated syllabus was published at Nottingham, probably after 1753; the British Library copy has a manuscript note that the lectures were originally those of Griffis.

In 1768, when he was living at Thringstone, Leicestershire, Peat proposed to publish a map of the county from his own survey; in 1771 he removed to adjacent Swannington, and in 1779 he returned to Nottingham. He died in Nottingham, at his house in Greyfriars' Gate, on 21 February 1780, aged seventy-two.

A. F. POLLARD, *rev.* RUTH WALLIS

Sources R. C. Archibald, 'Notes on some minor English mathematical serials', *Mathematical Gazette*, 14 (1928–9), 379–400, esp. 382–3 · R. V. Wallis and P. J. Wallis, eds., *Biobibliography of British mathematics and its applications*, 2 (1986), 308–10 · E. G. R. Taylor, *The mathematical practitioners of Hanoverian England, 1714–1840* (1966), 164 · F. W. Steer and others, *Dictionary of land surveyors and local cartographers of Great Britain and Ireland, 1550–1850*, ed. P. Eden, [4 vols.] (1975–9); 2nd edn, ed. S. Bendall, 2 vols. (1997) · W. H. Wylie, *Old and new Nottingham* (1853), 158 · C. Brown, *Lives of Nottinghamshire worthies* (1882) · *Derbyshire Times* (10 Aug 1872)

Peat, Sir William Barclay (1852–1936), accountant, was born in Forebank St Cyrus, Kincardine, Scotland, on 15 February 1852, second son of James Peat, a farmer, and Margaret, *née* Barclay. Following his education at Montrose Academy, he became an indentured apprentice to a solicitor in Montrose. For reasons unknown, he abandoned the study of Scottish law and in 1870 moved to London where he was employed as a junior clerk by Robert Fletcher, a distinguished public accountant who had connections with railways, insurance companies, and also industrial undertakings, particularly in the iron industry. On 29 December 1873 Peat married Edith (*d.* 1929), daughter of Henry Roberts, a solicitor of Usk in Monmouthshire; they had six children. In 1876 Peat moved to the Middlesbrough office of Robert Fletcher & Co., and was admitted a partner of the firm in the following year. On Fletcher's death in 1883, the firm's name became R. Mackay & Co. In 1891 Roderick Mackay died in Monte Carlo, leaving behind substantial private debts. Peat immediately returned to London to take charge of the office there and to make sure that Mackay's debts were settled. The name of the partnership, comprising four members, was changed to W. B. Peat & Co. Three of Peat's children, Sir Harry, Roderick, and Charles, later became partners in the firm.

Under Peat's leadership the firm flourished, particularly through audit work. Peat or his firm acted as auditors for many banks and railway companies, and especially iron and steel organizations in the north of England. He was also appointed the auditor of the private accounts of the sovereign. In 1911, Peat met James Marwick, a Scottish chartered accountant practising in North America, while travelling to New York on the *Berengaria*. By the voyage's end, the two had agreed to a merger, the formal agreement for which was signed on 1 October 1911. The merged firm became Marwick, Mitchell, Peat & Co. in the USA, Canada, and France, while the UK firm remained as W. B. Peat & Co. until 1925 when the name Peat, Marwick, Mitchell & Co. was adopted for the UK, continental Europe, and North America. Peat retired in 1923 after thirty-two years as senior partner. During his active professional life, he engaged in insolvency work and also advised on many amalgamations in the iron and steel industry. He also served the industry as secretary of the National Federation of Iron and Steel Manufacturers during 1918–25.

Peat was a pioneer of the organized accountancy profession in Britain, and an important figure in its development. He joined the Institute of Accountants in 1879 as an associate. The following year he became a foundation member of the Institute of Chartered Accountants in England and Wales (ICAEW), joined its council in 1894, and served as president during 1906–8 in a total of thirty-seven years' service as a councillor. He was a most generous donor to the Chartered Accountants Benevolent Association, over which he presided for twenty years, and also gave generously in prizes awarded for ICAEW examinations.

Peat's public activities were many, including engagements on various government departmental committees. He was chairman of the royal commission on agriculture, 1919–20, sat on the royal commission on food prices, served as chairman of the subcommittee on night baking, and was a member of the Voluntary Hospitals Committee. He received a number of honours, including chevalier of the Légion d'honneur. He was knighted in 1912, and created CVO in 1921.

Sir William Barclay Peat died at his residence, Wykeham Rise, Totteridge, Hertfordshire, on 24 January 1936, and was buried at Totteridge church three days later. His obituary in *The Times* stated that Peat 'owed his success to a robust constitution, indefatigable energy, and a capacity to form shrewd and penetrating judgements'. The firm which Peat led continued to expand through internal growth and merger.

GARRY D. CARNEGIE

Sources *The Accountant* (1 Feb 1936) · *The Accountant* (15 Feb 1936) · *The Times* (25 Jan 1936) · T. A. Wise, *Peat, Marwick, Mitchell & Co.: 85 years* (1982) · R. H. Parker, ed., *British accountants: a biographical sourcebook* (1980) · S. A. Cypert, *Following the money: the inside story of accounting's first mega-merger* (1991) · H. Howitt and others, eds., *The history of the Institute of Chartered Accountants in England and Wales, 1880–1965, and of its founder accountancy bodies, 1870–1880* (1966) · 'Interim report', *Parl. papers* (1919), vol. 8, Cmd 345, 365, 391, 445, 473; 'Evidence' (1920), vol. 9, Cmd 665 [royal commission on agriculture] · 'Royal commission on food prices: first report', *Parl. papers* (1924–5), vol. 8, Cmd 2390 · *CGPLA Eng. & Wales* (1936) · d. cert. · General Register Office for Scotland, Edinburgh

Wealth at death £604,643 16s. 2d.: probate, 23 March 1936, *CGPLA Eng. & Wales*

Peate, Iorwerth Cyfeiliog (1901–1982), museum curator and scholar, was born on 27 February 1901 at Glan-llyn in the village of Pandy Rhiwsaeson in the parish of Llanbrynmair in Montgomeryshire, the younger son and third child of George Howard Peate (1869–1938), a craftsman-carpenter and teacher, and Elizabeth Peate (1872–1948), *née* Thomas, of Llanidloes in the same county. He attended the village's elementary school and, in 1912, entered the county school at Machynlleth, and lodged at nearby Cemmaes Road. As an undergraduate at the University College of Wales, Aberystwyth, he read history, geography, and Welsh, specializing in his last year in Celtic archaeology under the supervision of H. J. Fleure, one of the leading geographers of his generation, who held the Gregynog chair of geography and archaeology. Peate's first book, *Gyda'r wawr*, a survey of the prehistory of Wales, was written in association with a number of young Welsh scholars and published under Fleure's editorship in 1923. For his postgraduate degree he wrote 'The Dyfi basin: a study in physical anthropology and dialect distribution' in which he concluded that anthropometrical records and dialect distribution followed identical physical boundaries, a theory later incorporated in his book *Cymru a'i phobl* (1931). Peate learned the finer principles of dialectology from the Norwegian scholar of Celtic, Alf Sommerfelt. His education was completed during the four years he spent as lecturer in the extra-mural department at his old college, during which he had to pit his wits against those of his adult pupils, mainly countrymen and self-taught intellectuals, in wide-ranging discussion of cultural, linguistic, and theological subjects which was later to stand him in such good stead. In April 1927 he was appointed assistant keeper in the archaeology department of the National Museum of Wales in Cardiff, and so began his association with the institution with which his name was ever after synonymous. He married Anne (Nansi) Davies (1900–1986), his childhood sweetheart, on 9 September 1929, and they made their home at 29 Lon-y-dail in 'the workers' co-operative garden village' of Rhiwbeina, a suburb of north Cardiff.

The first fruits of Peate's work at the National Museum were *Guide to the Collection of Welsh Bygones* (1929) and a study of the craftsman in Wales, *Y crefftwr yng Nghymru*

(1933). In 1932 he joined the sub-department of folk culture and industries, which later developed into a department with Peate as its keeper. In this capacity he began to realize his dream of establishing in Wales a folk museum on the same lines as those of Scandinavia. In the decade between 1935 and 1945 Peate had been immensely productive as a pioneering writer on various aspects of folk life studies, and as a broadcaster and publicist for his chosen field of study. He produced, besides a large number of articles in learned and popular journals, three major works in English, namely *Guide to the Collection Illustrating Welsh Folk Crafts and Industries* (1935), *The Welsh House* (1940), and *Clock and Watch Makers in Wales* (1945), and one in Welsh, *Diwylliant gwerin Cymru* (1942). When, in 1948, the Welsh Folk Museum was opened at St Fagans, on the outskirts of Cardiff, in a castle and on land given by the earl of Plymouth, Peate became its first curator, a post which he held until his retirement in 1971. He continued to write prolifically on the material culture of Wales, especially on the rich heritage of its rural crafts; his last important book in this field was *Tradition and Folk Life: a Welsh View* (1972). A Festschrift in his honour was published as *Studies in Folk Life* (ed. J. Geraint Jenkins) in 1969.

During a long and distinguished career Peate was, *inter alia*, founder and first president of the Society for Folk Life Studies and a fellow of the Royal Anthropological Institute, the Museums Association, and the Royal Society of Arts. He also received honorary degrees from the National University of Ireland in 1960 and the University of Wales in 1970, and the medal of the Honourable Society of Cymmrodorion. By the time of his retirement the Folk Museum had acquired a European reputation comparable to that of the great Scandinavian open-air museums on which it had been modelled.

Throughout his life Iorwerth C. Peate engaged in scholarly and literary activity of a high order, mainly as an exponent of the sturdily nonconformist, radical folk-culture (now known in Wales, largely at his insistence, as 'the Llanbrynmair tradition'), represented by Samuel

Iorwerth Cyfeiliog Peate (1901–1982), by Geoff Charles, 1946 [opening the art and craft exhibition of the national eisteddfod, Mountain Ash]

Roberts (1800–1885), into which he had been born. He was a man of strong convictions and forthright manner, especially when expressing his views about the fate of the Welsh language: he did not believe that there could be a future for it in a bilingual society, contrasting what he saw as the barbarism of urban, English-speaking Wales with the stability of the culturally rich, monoglot, Welsh-speaking, rural society of his youth; more generally, he denounced 'the Age of Trash'. In religion he was not only nonconformist but Independent and opposed to ecumenism; he always gave his honest opinion even though it might cause offence and he was unable to accept dogma at second hand; his private manner, on the other hand, gave the impression of a much milder man. His views, which were based on principle rather than caprice or personal antipathy, are vigorously and sometimes caustically set forth in essay form in *Sylfeini* (1938), *Ym mhob pen* (1948), *Syniadau* (1969), and *Personau* (1982), and in his autobiography, *Rhwng dau fyd* (1976). The last-named book gives a precise but unbitter account of his suspension from his National Museum post in 1941 and his victimization on account of his registration on pacifist grounds as a conscientious objector to military service; he was reinstated eight months later after a good deal of public controversy and a stormy meeting of the museum court. He had joined the Peace Pledge Union and the Fellowship of Reconciliation in the 1930s. Although staunchly Welsh nationalist in politics and an early member of Plaid Cymru (but quickly disillusioned with the superficiality of Westminster politics), he was opposed to the famous act of arson carried out by Saunders Lewis and others at a bombing school being constructed at Penyberth on the Llŷn peninsula in September 1936, on the grounds that he could not condone violence of any kind whatsoever. One of his most moving essays describes the clearance of Welsh-speaking farming communities from the Epynt Mountain in Brecknockshire for the purposes of the British army.

In addition to his scholarly and prose writings, Peate published four volumes of poetry: *Y cawg aur* (1928), *Plu'r gweunydd* (1933), *Y deyrnas goll* (1947), and *Canu chwarter canrif* (1957); a fifth volume, *Cerddi diweddar* (1982), appeared shortly after his death. As a poet he was conservative, using traditional forms with great skill and sensitivity, although he did not write in the strict metres of Welsh prosody. His main theme was the inevitability of time's passing, but his love for his wife, for the natural world, and for the old rural way of life which he loved so passionately, were also sources of inspiration. Many of his poems have immense charm and some are among the most euphonious written in Welsh during the twentieth century.

Iorwerth C. Peate died suddenly on 19 October 1982 at his home, Maes-y-coed, St Nicholas, in the Vale of Glamorgan, and his remains were cremated at Coychurch crematorium six days later. His ashes were interred in the burial-ground of Capel Pen-rhiw, the small eighteenth-century Unitarian meeting-house which had been re-erected in the grounds of the Welsh Folk Museum in 1955; the spot was later marked by a stone which also commemorated his wife Nansi, and their only son, Dafydd, who predeceased them in 1980. A plaque was raised on Glan-llyn, the house near Llanbrynmair where Iowerth C. Peate was born. But his true monument is the museum itself (later renamed the Museum of Welsh Life and made part of the National Museums and Galleries of Wales), to the creation and work of which he dedicated his life.

MEIC STEPHENS

Sources C. Stevens, *Iorwerth C. Peate* (1986) • T. M. Owen, 'Iorwerth Cyfeiliog Peate, 1901–82', *Folk Life*, 21 (1982–3) • M. W. Roberts, *Barddoniaeth Iorwerth C. Peate* (1986) • I. C. Peate, *Rhwng Dau Fyd* (1976) • private information (2004) • M. Stephens, ed., *The new companion to the literature of Wales*, rev. edn (1998) • J. G. Jenkins, ed., *Studies in folk life* (1969) • T. M. Owen, *Welsh History Review / Cylchgrawn Hanes Cymru*, 11 (1982–3) • b. cert. • m. cert. • d. cert.
Archives Museum of Welsh Life, St Fagans, Cardiff, corresp. and papers • NL Wales, corresp. and papers | NL Wales, letters to Thomas Iorwerth Ellis • NL Wales, corresp. with G. E. Evans • NL Wales, letters to W. J. Gruffydd [in Welsh] • NL Wales, letters to J. W. Jones • NL Wales, letters to Sir Thomas Parry-Williams [in Welsh] | FILM BBC Wales | SOUND BBC Wales
Likenesses G. Charles, photograph, 1946, NL Wales [*see illus.*] • photographs, Museum of Welsh Life, St Fagans, Cardiff

Pebody, Charles (1839–1890), newspaper editor, was born at Queen Street, Leamington Spa, Warwickshire, on 3 February 1839, the son of Charles Pebody, a household servant, and his wife, Eliza, *née* Cory. His parents moved to Watford, Northamptonshire, from where the family had originated, and Pebody was sent to the village school, being taught privately by the schoolmaster afterwards. At the age of fourteen he went to London, where he joined a lawyer's office, but soon found work as a reporter, eventually joining the staff of the *Chelmsford Chronicle*. At the age of twenty-one he was appointed editor of the *Barnstaple Times* and at about the same time, on 22 August 1859, he married Mary Ann Martyn, the daughter of Henry Martyn, a bank clerk from Essex. They had one daughter.

From Barnstaple Pebody moved to Exeter as editor of the *Flying Post*, and from Exeter to Bristol as editor of the *Bristol Times and Mirror*. In 1875, when living in Bristol, Pebody won the prize of £50 offered by James Heywood for the best essay revision of the rubrics in the prayer book. His other works included *Authors at Work* (1872) and *English Journalism and the Men who have Made it* (1882).

In 1882 Pebody was appointed editor of the *Yorkshire Post*, a Conservative daily paper published at Leeds, a position he held from 1 October. During his time as editor the paper rapidly grew in circulation and influence, and by the year of his death had become one of the most important and influential local newspapers. An enthusiastic journalist, Pebody was a member of the board of directors of the Press Association and a member of the Yorkshire Newspaper Society, and was elected president of the West Riding district of the national Institute of Journalists by the working journalists of west Yorkshire at an annual meeting.

In 1888 Pebody suffered internal pain, supposedly from gout in the stomach, but after six months' rest he resumed work and organized a new evening paper. He died at his home, Towerhurst, 20 De Grey Terrace, Leeds, on 30 October 1890, survived by his wife; he was buried on 3 November in Lawnswood cemetery. Doctors diagnosed that he died from a malignant ulcer in the stomach.

A. R. BUCKLAND, *rev.* JOANNE POTIER

Sources *Leeds Mercury* (31 Oct 1890), 5 • Boase, *Mod. Eng. biog.* • *Yorkshire Post* (31 Oct 1890) • b. cert. • m. cert.

Wealth at death £6373 16s. 9d.: probate, 29 Nov 1890, CGPLA Eng. & Wales

Pecche, John (*d.* 1380), merchant and mayor of London, may have been the son of Bartholomew Pecche of London. Variously described as a fishmonger and draper, and dealing in wine and cloth, Pecche became very wealthy through his mercantile activities in London. He supplied drapery to the king's wardrobe, held the monopoly for sweet wine sales in London from 1373 to 1376, and had business dealings with the merchants of the Bardi family of Florence and the merchants of Lucca. He traded abroad, and also travelled overseas on pilgrimage in 1350 and again in 1367 to Rome. Pecche was a strong family man, who sought gentry status for his family in the countryside by purchasing property outside London from the 1350s onwards. The property which would become the family home for some 200 years was the manor of Lullingstone, Kent, which he purchased in 1360 from John Ruxley, grandson of Gregory of Ruxley, mayor of London during the reign of Edward I. At the time of his death he held land in Kent, Surrey, Middlesex, Cambridgeshire, Bedfordshire, Essex, Buckinghamshire, and London. His son and heir, William, was brought up as a member of the gentry, trained in the profession of arms, and lived at Lullingstone, not in London.

By the 1350s Pecche was an established member of the London merchant community and city patriciate. He was alderman of Walbrook ward from 1349 to 1376, sheriff in 1352, and mayor in 1361. In 1351 he was appointed by the city government to raise 20,000 marks from London for the French war. He advised the king at merchant assemblies in 1356 and 1358, represented the city in parliament in 1361, 1369, 1371, and 1372, and in 1370 was a city representative at a royal council. Pecche provided the crown with financial support by contributing to loans supplied by the city, as in 1340, 1346, and 1371; by making a number of personal loans to the exchequer in the 1350s, ranging from £20 to £100; and by acting with Richard Lyons in raising loans for the king from the London money market in the 1360s and 1370s. Pecche also held a number of royal appointments, notably as commissioner of the peace against a robber gang operating in the woods around London in 1353, while in 1358 he was appointed to inquire into the nature and value of the London property of the Augustinian friars, and in 1366 into that of Giovanni de la Mare, merchant of Genoa, who had fled from the realm in debt to the crown. He was commissioner of array in London, Kent, and Essex for men-at-arms and archers in 1358, and for mariners in 1360.

In 1376, however, Pecche was one of those Londoners impeached by the Good Parliament for financial corruption. This centred on his involvement with Richard Lyons

and Adam Bury, London merchants and citizens, in the sweet wine monopoly of the city granted him by the crown in November 1373. Under the monopoly only three London taverns were permitted to sell sweet wines, and all of these had been leased from the city by Lyons during Bury's mayoralty in 1365. And when Pecche obtained the monopoly in 1373, Bury was again mayor. This association of Pecche, Lyons, and Bury came under scrutiny in the Good Parliament and all three were found guilty on various corruption charges; Pecche was found guilty of exploiting the monopoly and deprived of his aldermanic rank and freedom of the city. The judgment was reversed in February 1377 and he was pardoned by the crown in April; but he was never restored either to office or to favour in London. However, the impeachment of Pecche, Lyons, and Bury caused divisions within the city which subsequently led to a brief period of constitutional experiment.

John Pecche married twice. His first wife was Ellen, with whom he had a son, William, and two daughters, Katherine and Philippa. There may also have been another son, John, who was dead by 1360. William Pecche, who became a member of the Grocers' Company, had been knighted by May 1380, and in September 1380 married Joan, daughter of John Hadley, a grocer and alderman of London. Katherine Pecche married Thomas Holbeche, a draper who was a business partner of her father's, some time before 1347; when she died in 1349, her children, Alice and William, were entrusted to the guardianship of their grandfather, but both were dead by 1365. Philippa Pecche married her father's ward, John Constantyn, but the marriage was annulled in 1371. When John Constantyn died in 1379, their son, another John, was also placed in John Pecche's guardianship. John Pecche made his will on his deathbed, on 27 May 1380, and was buried in the parish church at Lullingstone. He was survived by his second wife, Mary, who afterwards married Sir William Moigne, a Huntingdonshire landowner.

ROGER L. AXWORTHY

Sources R. R. Sharpe, ed., *Calendar of wills proved and enrolled in the court of husting, London, AD 1258 – AD 1688*, 2 vols. (1889–90) • R. R. Sharpe, ed., *Calendar of letter-books preserved in the archives of the corporation of the City of London*, [12 vols.] (1899–1912), vols. F–G • A. H. Thomas and P. E. Jones, eds., *Calendar of plea and memoranda rolls preserved among the archives of the corporation of the City of London at the Guildhall*, 6 vols. (1926–61) • *RotP*, vol. 2 • J. Stow, *A survey of London*, rev. edn (1603); repr. with introduction by C. L. Kingsford as *A survey of London*, 2 vols. (1908); repr. with addns (1971) • Chancery records • PRO, Exchequer documents • HoP, Commons • R. Bird, *The turbulent London of Richard II* (1949) • G. Holmes, *The Good Parliament* (1975) • *Registrum Simonis de Sudbiria, diocesis Londoniensis, AD 1362–1375*, ed. R. C. Fowler, 2 vols., CYS, 34, 38 (1927–38)

Pecche, Sir John (*c.*1360–1386). *See under* Lollard knights (*act. c.*1380–*c.*1414).

Pecham [Peckham], **John** (*c.*1230–1292), archbishop of Canterbury, presumably hailed from Patcham, Sussex, since he records that he grew up near the Cluniac monastery of Lewes, to which Patcham church had been appropriated, and was probably educated there. He was quite likely a member of the family who held land at Patcham in serjeanty from tenants of the honour of Warenne. The only certain members of the family are his brother Richard and nephew Walter, whom he made rector of Tarring and canon of his college at Wingham, and who seems to have inherited the family property. Others of the same name were prominent in the diocese of Chichester and in royal service during his archiepiscopate.

Studies in Paris and Oxford Pecham later told a cardinal that he had been educated in France 'from tender years' (Martin, 874), which, unless it is referring loosely to his late twenties, suggests that he was in the arts faculty at Paris in the 1240s; he later wrote treatises on optics (*Perspectiva communis*) and astronomy influenced by Roger Bacon, who was lecturing in Paris at that time, although the connection may have been made when both were in the Franciscan friary in the 1260s. It may have been the reputation for scientific and mathematical pursuits of the Oxford friary, where first Grosseteste and then Adam Marsh lectured, that drew Pecham back to England and into the Friars Minor about the early 1250s: Marsh tells of the conversion in a letter to a friend, in which he describes Pecham as *scholaris*, implying that he had not yet proceeded to his MA. Pecham's *Canticum pauperis* seems to be an autobiographical account of his own conversion, from the abandonment of bodily and worldly pleasures for learning, whose various branches he then tries in turn, before coming to rest on theology and its Franciscan exponents, with their complete renunciation of material things for the love of Christ. Marsh had gone down such a road before him, and may have been the old counsellor consulted by the *pauper* in the *Canticum*.

After spending his noviciate at Oxford, Pecham returned to Paris about 1257, and remained there until 1272, continuing his studies in theology to the doctorate under Bonaventure's pupils, and in 1269 becoming regent master in theology and lector at the friary. Pecham's reputation was high enough for him to be termed *doctor ingenuosus* in the next century, and he was heavily plagiarized by his pupil Roger Marston, through whom Duns Scotus drew on his work. His output, particularly his lectures and disputations (*quaestiones* and *quodlibeta*), and commentaries on Lombard's *Sentences* and some books of the Bible, covered the range of intellectual concerns of the later thirteenth-century university, in particular grappling with the question of how far Aristotle could be successfully integrated into a Christian theological scheme. Following Bonaventure, Pecham subordinated all learning to theology, just as he directed all human activity to the imitation of Christ through asceticism. For Pecham all thought had a typically Franciscan focus on the love of God, seen for instance in his adherence to the Augustinian doctrine of the direct divine illumination of the intellect.

Franciscan controversialist Pecham thus came to lead the conservative Augustinian theological position against not only the Averroists, but also Thomas Aquinas, who returned to Paris in 1269 for a second regency at the Dominican friary. Pecham was the Franciscan spokesman during the Averroist crisis which flared up in Paris in 1269–71, exposing the differences between the older theology and Aquinas's more thorough integration of Aristotle. In particular Pecham led the attack on Aquinas's doctrine of the unity of substantial form in man, which seemed to suggest that the body of Christ between death and resurrection, and in the eucharist, was wholly different from the live body, since it was activated by an entirely different form in each phase. Pecham put forward the pluralist view of forms, and his own view of the intellect, in disputation with Aquinas in early 1270, and he articulated his position in various *Quaestiones* and in his *Summa de esse et essentia* and *Tractatus de anima*. In the latter Pecham also asserted his typically Franciscan emphasis on the primacy of the will over the intellect (obedience being fundamental to Franciscan religious culture), through which he foreshadowed Duns Scotus.

Pecham was also in Paris at a time of acute tension between the seculars and mendicants, which broke out again in January 1269 in an attack by the seculars on the Franciscan theory of evangelical poverty. Bonaventure (now in Paris) and Pecham co-ordinated their response in two tracts which share material, though Pecham's *Tractatus de paupertate* is the more comprehensive. He set out to prove that Christ and the apostles practised strict poverty, and that the Franciscans were their closest imitators through physical asceticism which implanted obedience in the soul and sacrificial love in imitation of Christ crucified. Both developed arguments to justify the absolute poverty of their order, whose property was vested in the pope, as no mere legal fiction, which came to be crystallized into the *usus pauper* in later controversies by Pecham's pupil Peter Olivi. The seculars' claim of their higher vocation through the cure of souls was denied, on the grounds that mendicants practised both ministry and the scripturally approved contemplative vocation.

Pecham's return to Oxford by 1272 as Franciscan lector forced him to go over this ground again against the provincial of the Dominicans, Robert Kilwardby, on the eve of the latter's appointment to Canterbury. The *Contra Kilwardby*, however, couched the arguments in a caustic and bitter tone which matched the letter of Kilwardby's to which it was a reply, and thereby tended to reduce the argument to one of the relative perfection of the two orders, based on their intense competition for recruits within the university. He was presumably also in the thick of the continuing struggle against Averroism and Thomism, although none of his lectures or disputations survives from this period despite his reputation for having introduced the quodlibet to Oxford. This time Kilwardby was on his side, against his own order, although Pecham's summons to Rome to be lector at the papal university just prevented him from witnessing the archbishop's condemnation of thirty propositions, nearly half concerned with the unity of form, in March 1277.

Pecham's other works are connected with the specifically mendicant task of training friars for preaching and pastoral work in their houses all over Europe. His sermons offer a complete commentary on the gospels and epistles for every Sunday of the year, in pithy and memorable form. They reflect Pecham's emphasis on the generosity of God's love, and the response of the human soul in attempting to become reintegrated from its fallen state and ascend back to God. He also collected biblical texts under various headings for use in sermons, surveying a large range of theological themes and schemes, in the *Collectanea bibliorum*, printed several times in the sixteenth century. Pecham wrote an office for the Trinity which remained in use until the Council of Trent, and various other hymns and poems, particularly focused on Christ as suffering and eucharistic sacrifice (notably *Ave vivens hostia*). *Philomela* tells the story of salvation from the creation to the passion through the last day of a dying nightingale, an analogy for the soul which is also structured by the divine office for the day, by which Pecham set much store.

After Pecham had spent three years as lector at Oxford, his career moved rapidly: in 1275 he was elected prior of the Franciscan province in England, in which role he made his legendary walk barefoot to general chapter in Padua, a typically strict interpretation of the Franciscan prohibition of riding. His election brought him into closer contact with the king and magnates, while his appointment at Rome in 1277 additionally acquainted him with the machinery of papal administration, the four popes of his archiepiscopate, and many cardinals, to whom he lectured. It was while there that Nicholas III, having promoted Kilwardby to be cardinal of Porto, quashed the election of Edward I's chancellor Robert Burnell to Canterbury, and provided Pecham instead on 28 January 1279.

The reforming primate Pecham was consecrated on the first Sunday of Lent, 19 February, and set out for Amiens in order to meet Edward I. On 23 May he was received courteously by the king and had his temporalities restored immediately, in return sending an account to the pope of Edward's negotiations with Philippe III over Gascony that put the English case. Despite the king's friendship and generosity with grants then and later, Pecham was already encountering formidable financial problems: being a friar, with no property, he had had to borrow 4000 marks from the Riccardi while in Rome, and on arrival at Dover on 4 June he found that Kilwardby had sold to the king the corn and stock on his lands, which he had to buy back for 2000 marks, and had taken valuables to the tune of 5000 marks, as well as the records of the see. Debt dogged Pecham throughout his archiepiscopate, despite the increasingly efficient management of the estates by officials and the increased revenues thus procured; in 1290 the pope granted him the first fruits of vacated benefices for three years to apply to the debts of the see, but Winchelsey still found the archbishopric heavily burdened. As well as depressing Pecham's spirit and making it harder for him to give alms generously, this also weakened his negotiating position with the king, as the first episodes of his rule were to demonstrate.

Pecham had a clear idea of what he wanted to achieve at Canterbury, and immediately on landing at Dover he summoned the bishops of his province to a council at Reading for 29 June. There he surveyed the English ecclesiastical legislation of the thirteenth century (of archbishops Langton and Boniface, and the legates Otto and Ottobuono), which applied to England the great papal reforming programme of reviving, or creating, a Christian society throughout Europe, by ensuring that the ministers of the church were able to preach and minister effectively to the laity in every parish of the realm.

Pecham's initial emphasis was on abuses, which distracted the clergy from their fundamental task. In particular, he claimed at Reading that he had been sent by the pope to root out the evil of pluralism, since previous legislation had not been implemented. Its aim was to prevent clerks holding more than one benefice which involved cure of souls without papal dispensation; allied problems were non-residence without dispensation, and the failure of clerks to proceed to ordination as priests. Pecham therefore initiated a new campaign of enforcement, requiring clerks to vacate all but their last-received benefice, imposing deprivation on future recipients of plural benefices, and demanding that bishops systematically investigate and list the benefices in their sees and their rectors and vicars, and report back.

Pecham's other main addition to the previous legislation which was read out at the council concerned royal writs of prohibition, which ordered ecclesiastical judges to desist from hearing a particular case, a symptom of the tension between the two jurisdictions now more than a century old. The archbishop accepted that some prohibitions were legitimate, and therefore that some types of cases did fall to the secular forum; but overtly abusive prohibitions, interfering with spiritual jurisdiction, were to be rejected out of hand, as indeed were those that looked legitimate but which misrepresented the nature of the case. In either case, those whose intentions were malicious were to be excommunicated, and clerks were to be deprived. A further source of clerical grievance was the failure of royal ministers to co-operate in enforcing sanctions against excommunicates.

Relations with Edward I Pecham soon ran into opposition in these efforts; on 24 October he solemnly excommunicated those who were trying to resist in many different ways the statutes of Reading. His problem was that he had offended the king and his clerks, because, quite apart from their likely bias in favour of royal over ecclesiastical justice, the government depended upon pluralism and non-residence to pay and reward its clerks. A further difficulty for Pecham was that some of his bishops had been pluralists themselves, and some were still at the heart of government, notably Burnell. Pecham also compounded his offence by adding to the measures for the publication of the statutes of the council an order for Magna Carta to be posted in all cathedral and collegiate churches, and renewed annually.

Retaliation was swift: Pecham was obliged in parliament, about 10 November, publicly to withdraw the proposed publication of the charter, and three of the articles of excommunication, and to accept that none of the articles of Reading should lead to any prejudice to the king or realm. It is difficult, too, to deny entirely the possibility that the publication in this parliament of the Statute of Mortmain, apparently preventing the church from acquiring any more land, did not have some element of putting the archbishop in his place, although the statute had other substantial roots. Since Pecham's legislation on pluralism had the backing of a recent general council, the Second Council of Lyons, it is not surprising that Edward did not force Pecham to retract his measures in that field, but chose areas where the royal case was recognized to be stronger. But it is likely that pluralism was in the forefront of the royal ministers' minds, since they prepared at least one appeal to Rome against Pecham's strict approach, arguing the benefits to the realm of having pluralist royal clerks.

In the absence of much co-operation from his suffragans Pecham had to conduct the campaign against pluralism himself. He did so in his visitation of his entire province, which he completed in seven years, sending lists of pluralists to the bishops and demanding that action be taken against them. He was also able to demonstrate his strength of purpose by refusing to confirm the election of the archdeacon of Winchester to its bishopric because of his pluralism, and standing firm in his resolve for two years until Martin IV nominated John de Pontoise. This made its point since both the refusal and the grounds for it were noticed by the chroniclers. On the other hand, Pecham was unable to do anything about the notorious Bogo de Clare, brother of his friend and tenant, Gilbert de Clare, earl of Gloucester. Despite the success he had in individual cases, therefore, he failed to change attitudes to pluralism, except perhaps in prompting clerks to procure papal licences more carefully.

On prohibitions, and in defence of ecclesiastical jurisdiction in general, the clergy were more solidly behind their archbishop. During 1280, in response to the royal request for a subsidy, they drafted a list of twenty *gravamina*, to which Edward gave verbal replies in parliament on 3 November, the day Pecham issued orders for collection of a three-year fifteenth. The articles covered a wide range of jurisdictional issues, including those mentioned at Reading, and convey the sense that the royal courts were increasingly limiting the jurisdiction of the ecclesiastical, and royal officials were treating the clergy as the laity, spiritual property as temporal. After long discussions the king gave only unofficial answers, which offered reassurances of good intentions but few concrete concessions. Pecham continued to pressurize Edward by restoring virtually intact the excommunications withdrawn in 1279 to the articles of the Council of Lambeth in 1281, and afterwards he wrote to the king justifying his stance in the broadest terms. The centre of his argument was obedience to God, rather than man. It followed that ecclesiastical law was more binding than human, and secular law needed to be brought into conformity with the canons, its evil customs being abolished. The king was especially obliged to obey the church, since he derived his authority from it. A historical excursus proved that the natural condition of the church in England was immunity from the lay power, which still obtained in the Welsh church; it was

only in the reigns of Henry I and Henry II that the clergy had been prevented from obeying the law of the universal church, Becket preferring death to submission. Pecham's identification with his predecessor is seen in his use of the martyrdom for his counterseal.

It was not until the parliament of May–June 1285 that the clergy were able to force the crown to negotiate again over these issues. A list of seventeen grievances formed the basis for discussion, some covering old ground; but two developments worsened the atmosphere and put the clergy on the defensive. The Statute of Westminster II evoked a further nine protests from the clergy against clauses extending royal jurisdiction into areas which the clergy argued had always been ecclesiastical. Moreover, a royal edict had limited court Christian to testamentary and matrimonial jurisdiction and cases concerning sin. On 1 July Edward ordered the clergy of Norwich to desist from hearing a wide range of cases claimed for exclusive royal jurisdiction, and instructed his justices on eyre there to investigate all breaches since the beginning of the reign and to summon offending clergy. This naturally gave rise to a further barrage of complaints, which remained unanswered. The effect of the edict would have been to deprive ecclesiastical authorities of their power to discipline their own clergy in spiritual matters and to investigate and punish cases of sin among the laity, and also of their control over ecclesiastical property. The Dunstable annalist thought Pecham led the attempt to persuade the king to withdraw this comprehensive writ of prohibition; the ringing peroration of the petition, invoking Magna Carta, certainly bears his stamp.

In the middle of the following year the clergy finally won some satisfaction from the crown in the form of the writ *Circumspecte agatis*, which definitively and precisely listed the areas, beyond the testamentary and matrimonial, in which prohibition could not apply, and the processes and punishments which the church could freely use. The king's more accommodating attitude was confirmed in 1290 by the Statute of Consultation, which allowed ecclesiastical judges to consult the chancellor or chief justice as to whether a prohibition was valid, and to proceed if not. Pecham had won, through diplomacy rather than confrontation, significant recognition of the competence of ecclesiastical jurisdiction, and the issues at stake in 1285 had to some extent been resolved.

The problem of Wales Archbishop and king were bound by their offices to take opposing views in principle, and often in practice, as Edward's outright refusal to allow Pecham to visit royal chapels demonstrated forcibly. Nevertheless, personally they always remained on good terms, and could just as easily adopt similar stances, as in Wales during the renewed war of 1282–3. While Pecham desired peace, he consistently put the English case to the Welsh and demanded their submission. He subscribed wholly to the view that the Welsh were barbaric and would benefit from integration into English rule, and he equally desired the assimilation of the Welsh sees into his province. He was also instrumental in persuading his reluctant clergy to grant the king a two-year twentieth in October 1283, before the subsidy of 1280 had been completely collected. Nevertheless, he preferred a peaceful solution to violent conquest, with all its inevitable sacrilege to clerical persons and property, and he persuaded Edward to allow him to set out for Snowdon on 31 October 1282. His three days with Llywelyn attempting to mediate were doomed to failure since neither side wanted peace, and Pecham renewed his excommunication of the rebels on his return to Rhuddlan.

In the wake of the conquest, in summer 1284, Pecham visited all four Welsh dioceses, to provide an ecclesiastical parallel to Edward's settlement. He hoped to subject the dioceses entirely to his authority and to reorganize them along English lines, while also preserving their traditional immunity from lay power. He was unsuccessful in the latter aim, but successfully fought off the claim of the bishop of St David's to metropolitan status, and obtained some reparation from Edward for the spoliation and devastation of churches, in return for which he exhorted the Welsh to obedience to the English crown. But what mattered most to Pecham was a religious revival, to overcome the barbarism and ignorance of clergy and people. In attempting to realize this, he was applying his fundamental objectives for his whole province, as his more purely ecclesiastical activities demonstrate.

The archbishop and his suffragans Pecham applied himself to visiting all his eighteen dioceses with unremitting energy, in order to implement the programme announced publicly in councils and synods of eradicating abuses and bringing a higher quality ministry to the laity in every parish under his purview. This was most clearly announced in the canons of the Council of Lambeth, at which he laid down a detailed programme for improving the observance of the sacraments of the church by the parish clergy, especially the eucharist, baptism, and confession, and, most famously, the preaching of the clergy; in *Ignorantia sacerdotum* Pecham provided for quarterly recitation a schematized account of the essentials of the faith. Pecham's emphasis on the right use of the goods of the church (from which so much of his campaign against abuses stemmed) is equally seen in his insistence in his injunctions of 1287 for Canterbury on the clergy's keeping up alms to the poor, maintaining their churches, ornaments, vestments, and instruments in good repair, and their careful stewardship of revenues and rights, and recovery of those lost.

Such burning zeal, however, nurtured in the Franciscan culture of obedience and hierarchy, was bound to meet resistance from an acutely rights-conscious clergy. Another outbreak of the long-running saga between the two archbishops as to whether York could have his cross carried erect before him through the southern province was the forerunner of portentous events to come: in autumn 1279 this resulted in violence, the cross being smashed by armed men at Rochester. Nevertheless, it erupted again several times after 1285. Pecham could undoubtedly be high-handed, both in the tone of his communication and in his actions, and his suffragans were soon resisting the intrusiveness of his visitations, even if,

as both legate and metropolitan, Pecham was usually on firm legal ground. There were, however, genuine issues to be clarified as to the boundaries between diocesan and metropolitical jurisdiction, particularly with respect to the court of Canterbury. Apart from procedural inconveniences caused by its central jurisdiction, these centred on testamentary jurisdiction over those leaving goods in more than one diocese (in which the archbishops were ultimately to triumph), and the hearing of appeals from courts lower than that of the bishop. At the Easter council of 1282 the bishops presented twenty-one *gravamina* to the archbishop, who resisted their claims over visitations, but, having set up a commission to judge the jurisdictional issues, accepted many of the complaints and instructed his officials accordingly.

Ironically, it was zealous prelates, who were strong advocates of the rights of their sees, as canon law required them to be, who were most likely to resist the ministrations of an archbishop who was equally defending the rights of his position. Godfrey Giffard of Worcester confronted Pecham again in the years that followed, but his position had been immeasurably strengthened by the fate of the only other bishop who Pecham had initially thought would be an allied reformer, his former pupil Thomas Cantelupe of Hereford. Indeed it was Cantelupe's very zeal that made him enemies, and thus necessitated archiepiscopal involvement; his first appeal to Rome took him out of the country in May 1280, leaving an official, Robert le Wyse, determined to stir up trouble against Pecham. When Pecham and Cantelupe finally met again in autumn 1281, relations seemed amicable, but the legacy of le Wyse's resistance and Pecham's reaction soon undermined them, and Pecham finally excommunicated first le Wyse, and then Cantelupe when he refused to publish the sentence. Thomas Cantelupe's death at Rome in August 1282 when appealing again, the miracles that began at his tomb when the conflict between Pecham and the bishops was renewed in 1287, and his subsequent canonization, inevitably made him seem the victim of Pecham's implacable aggression, and concealed the essential issues under the personal story. Pecham fell victim to the same trap because of his strong sense of betrayal and encirclement by the intrigues of his suffragans in England at the curia.

Dealings with monks and friars The suffragans' determination to protect their rights against a Franciscan may have been stiffened by Martin IV's *Ad fructus uberes* of 1281, which allowed friars freedom to preach and confess without the consent of bishops and which led to intense conflict between the regular and secular clergy in France. Pecham certainly encouraged such freedom, seeing the friars as a vital supplement to the ministrations of the parish clergy. His position as conservator of the privileges of his order in England, and his willingness to support particular houses of Friars Minor, certainly antagonized monks, who were required to accept enlarged mendicant premises nearby, or who became involved in quarrels over freedom of burial, one of the staple issues of mendicant controversy. Pecham's interdict on Westminster, which may in part have caused his absence from Queen Eleanor's funeral on 17 December 1290, was the result of the abbey's harbouring a Franciscan apostate.

Pecham was thorough in including monasteries in his visitations, and he issued many sets of injunctions for correction, aimed at religious who neglected their offices and adopted secular lifestyles, so blurring the boundary between the cloister and the world through their frequent presence outside the convent, and the systematic intrusion of the laity within. As ever, he urged religious to keep their calling of worship at the centre of the picture, and to devote their resources as effectively as possible to that end: hence his opposition to the Benedictines' decision in 1277–9 to pare down accretions to the divine office, and his restoration of the full traditional *opus dei* at monasteries he visited; hence also his attempts to replace or supplement the rule of ineffective superiors, and especially to encourage financial stability, the latter no doubt informed by his personal experience of the deleterious effects of debt on the performance of duties. His own monastery at Christ Church, Canterbury, with its centralized treasury, provided the model that he successfully encouraged others to adopt.

Pecham's opposition to the foundation of a monastic house of study at Oxford was based on his deep suspicion of the growth of Thomism there. The Dominicans, led in Oxford by Richard Knapwell, had responded to the Franciscan corrections to Aquinas with their own *correctoria*, and were capturing the minds of the university; the reiteration of much of Pecham's old material by his pupil Roger Marston, Knapwell's Franciscan opponent, was hardly likely to stem the popularity of Thomism. Unity of form was once more the central issue, and Pecham highlighted the danger of its theological implications when he renewed Kilwardby's condemnations of 1277 on 29 October 1284, a procedure he adopted in part to fend off accusations that he was merely promoting rivalry between the orders. The Dominicans immediately reacted by appealing to Rome, and opened a campaign of propaganda which directed biting wit and furious invective at Pecham. Pecham's responses drew on his old polemical works but lacked their immediacy and fire, merely seeming uncomfortably extreme. Knapwell, in whose works eleven errors had been found, ignored citations and was excommunicated at Easter 1285, and his opinions, centring on unity of form, were condemned by Pecham and bishops Sutton of Lincoln, Swinfield of Hereford, and Giffard. Proceedings at Rome were, as ever, slow, and held up by the swift succession of popes, but the election of the Franciscan Nicholas IV in 1288 ensured that Knapwell would be silenced. In the longer run Thomism was irrepressible, but it was no mere obscurantism on the part of Pecham that prompted his deeply held opposition.

Last things Pecham's health was gradually failing in his later years, and the loss of various sections of his register makes it difficult to tell how far his activity was reduced; the flow of letters becomes very much sparser from the middle of 1285. He certainly only managed to visit a few dioceses for the second time, and latterly extreme moods and changes of mind, which began to alienate some of his previously loyal clerks, presaged his physical decline in the 1290s.

Pecham did have the opportunity to apply the strictures he had imposed on other churches, particularly in the financial field, to his own foundation, when in 1287 he brought to fruition Kilwardby's project for a secular college on the archiepiscopal manor at Wingham, near Canterbury. In his statutes Pecham was characteristically careful to prescribe how the property and income of the college was to be allocated and used, and insistent on proper observance of the hours. The provost and six canons were intended to expand the archbishop's resources of patronage for his clerks, although building work was still continuing at his death.

Pecham was able to exert himself to support the crusading project given renewed impetus by Nicholas IV, who imposed a six-year tithe on the clergy in 1290 on the basis of a new assessment, before the fall of Acre in May 1291 gave urgency to the process. Edward and other lords had taken the cross in the summer and autumn of 1290, and Pecham had started to grant crusading privileges to them. He personally presided at the council of his province of 13–16 February 1292, which the pope had ordered so that the whole church might be consulted as to how the Holy Land should be recovered and subsequently protected, and how popular enthusiasm and finance could be raised. Nicholas died on 4 April, before the council's proctors could reach him with their answers.

Pecham's last public appearance was at the consecration of the bishops of Salisbury and Exeter at Canterbury on 16 March, and thereafter his health overcame him in a long decline, at Otford and Mortlake, where he died on 8 December, in the presence of his long-serving clerical staff and two Friars Minor. Against his own preference for the London Franciscans, he was buried on the 19th at Canterbury in a wintry and ill-attended ceremony; but he insisted that his heart should be allowed to rest with the brothers of his own order. His Canterbury tomb, of grey Sussex marble, depicts him serenely, and perhaps accurately, in oak under a canopy with an early ogee arch, surrounded by his suffragans as weepers. Apparently the product of the Westminster workshop, this may have absorbed much of the £5306 he is said to have left, for the accounts of his executors, the Franciscans of Paris, revealed only 5*s*. 6*d*. after paying for his will (now lost), including also his debts, legacies to his clerks, and his funeral.

Successes and failures Pecham exhibits many of the faults and the virtues of the high-medieval churchman. At the centre of his being was devotion to Christ and the imitation of the apostles, filtered through the Franciscan tradition of complete material and spiritual poverty. He continued to style himself *frater Johannes humilis* as archbishop, wore a shabby habit, and was said to have fasted for seven Lents annually, taking up most of the year. Various chroniclers noted and even approved of the Franciscans' juxtaposition of Nicholas IV with him as the sun and moon of the order. Moreover, those who came into contact with him also noted his kindness, sincerity, and humility, and his writing and poetry testify to his capacity for deep and tender feeling. Trivet described him as 'a zealot for his order, a notable author of poetry, pompous in manner and speech, but tender of mind and liberal of soul' (*Nicholai Triveti Annales*, 300). On this basis, he rarely lost sight of his central religious objectives, whether he was realizing them through intellectual achievements as for so much of his life, or, latterly, in administering the English friars or the whole province of Canterbury itself. His archiepiscopate stands firmly in the tradition of the reforming church dating back to the mid-eleventh century, with its twin projects of transforming society through a transformed clergy.

Some of Pecham's failures in realizing these aims, however, can equally be attributed to the strength of his devotion and to his own conviction of being right. He found difficult the transition from an order where obedience and unity were fundamental, to a diverse secular church in which persuasion and tact were necessary. In pursuing reform through the dignity of his office he too often failed to have regard for the rights of others and their churches, so that his energy became overbearing and his zeal was seen as interference. His personal kindness was too often obscured by caustic rhetoric and a sharp tongue. Hence the—albeit partial—obituary of the monastic *Flores historiarum*: 'his wisdom was entirely spent before his death, and in his prosperity he scorned and despised many' (*Flores historiarum*, 3.81–2). While, therefore, his dedication and commitment shine out, his success seems more equivocal. If he failed on pluralism and partially over prohibitions, it is harder to measure the effect of his visitations and restoration of the Welsh church; and *Ignorantia sacerdotum* was a gift to posterity whose fruits in the thorough Christianization of later medieval society have only recently been re-evaluated. Indeed, the future was to lie not with high-church insistence on *libertas ecclesie* against the king, but with the patient groundwork of educating the clergy and improving the laity, those things to which Pecham quietly contributed. Now that high-medieval prelates seem to be less swimming against an inexorable tide of decline than part of a long-term process which only gradually came to fruition, representatives of their order such as Pecham may be seen in a new, and rather kinder, light.

BENJAMIN THOMPSON

Sources D. L. Douie, *Archbishop Pecham* (1952) · *Registrum epistolarum fratris Johannis Peckham, archiepiscopi Cantuariensis*, ed. C. T. Martin, 3 vols., Rolls Series, 77 (1882–5) · F. N. Davis and D. L. Douie, eds., *The register of John Pecham*, 2 vols., CYS, 64–5 (1908–69) · F. M. Powicke and C. R. Cheney, eds., *Councils and synods with other documents relating to the English church, 1205–1313*, 2 vols. (1964) · *Ann. mon.*, vols. 1–4 · *Chancery records* · *DNB* · J. S. Brewer, ed., *Monumenta Franciscana*, 1, Rolls Series, 4 (1858) · H. R. Luard, ed., *Flores historiarum*, 3 vols., Rolls Series, 95 (1890) · F. Nicholai Triveti, *de ordine frat. praedicatorum, annales sex regum Angliae*, ed. T. Hog, EHS, 6 (1845) · C. L. Kingsford, A. G. Little, and F. Tocco, eds., *Tractatus tres de paupertate*, British Society of Franciscan Studies, 2 (1910) · Emden, *Oxf.*, 3.1445–7
Archives LPL, registers
Likenesses oak on marble tomb, 1292–1300, Canterbury Cathedral · seal, Canterbury Cathedral, archives
Wealth at death left £5305 17s. 2¼d., all of which was probably spent on will, debts, and tomb, as 5s. 6d. was left when executors accounted: Matthew Parker, *De antiquitate Britannicae ecclesiae* (1572); *DNB*; *Registrum*, ed. Martin, 3. iv

Peche, Richard (d. 1182), bishop of Coventry, was almost certainly the son of Bishop Robert Peche, who occupied that see from 1121 to 1128. He was made archdeacon of Coventry, presumably the most lucrative of the archdeaconries of the see at that time, probably by his father, but there are no certain references to him as archdeacon before about 1140. There were obviously objections to his elevation in 1161, as the son of a priest, to the episcopate; indeed, in a famous passage concerning him, written near the end of the twelfth century, the chronicler Ralph de Diceto was moved to quote at length from Ivo of Chartres to justify the appointment of the son of a priest as a bishop. The fourteenth-century chronicle of Lichfield Cathedral, once attributed to Thomas Chesterfield, records a tradition that Bishop Richard's election met with universal acclaim. In reality this probably meant that neither the monks of Coventry nor the canons of Lichfield were actually opposed to his appointment (there had been disputes during and following the election of his predecessor, Bishop Walter Durdene). Whether Richard was a protégé of the king, or merely a local man too strong to be ignored, is uncertain, but the chronicler also claims that he was elected *voluntate regis Henrici mediante* ('by the intervention of King Henry's will') (Wharton, 1.435). The sources disagree as to whether he was consecrated, on 18 April 1161, by Archbishop Theobald, or by Walter, bishop of Rochester (d. 1182); it is clear, however, that the former was so near to death at that time that he might well have been too ill to perform the ceremony of consecration. Bishop Richard's place in the Becket dispute is by no means clear: David Knowles, vexed by Richard's apparent escapism in what he perceived as the church's time of peril, wrote icily of him as a man of no consequence. It seems, however, that he was a most active diocesan, and, although this may have been initially a papal initiative, he was concerned particularly to restore the finances of the church of Lichfield. The Lichfield Cathedral cartulary contains ten relevant charters of Bishop Richard's, some in favour of the common fund, some the precentorship, and some the deanery. Richard seems to have been a man of fairly conventional piety and was remembered, erroneously as it happens, as the founder of the Augustinian house in Stafford dedicated to the memory of St Thomas, to which he retired, having become a canon, shortly before his death on 6 or 7 October 1182.

M. J. FRANKLIN

Sources M. J. Franklin, 'The bishops of Coventry and Lichfield, c.1072–1208', *Coventry's first cathedral: the cathedral and priory of St Mary* [Coventry 1993], ed. G. Demidowicz (1994), 118–38 · D. Knowles, *The episcopal colleagues of Archbishop Thomas Becket*

(1951) • [H. Wharton], ed., *Anglia sacra*, 2 vols. (1691) • M. Richter, ed., *Canterbury professions*, CYS, 67 (1973) • *The historical works of Gervase of Canterbury*, ed. W. Stubbs, 2 vols., Rolls Series, 73 (1879–80) • *Radulfi de Diceto … opera historica*, ed. W. Stubbs, 2 vols., Rolls Series, 68 (1876) • M. J. Franklin, ed., *Coventry and Lichfield, 1160–1182*, English Episcopal Acta, 16 (1998)

Pechell, Sir **George Richard Brooke**, fourth baronet (1789–1860), naval officer, was born in London on 30 June 1789. He was the second son of Major-General Sir Thomas Brooke Pechell, second baronet (1753–1826), MP for Downton, Wiltshire, and his wife, Charlotte (*d.* 1841), second daughter of Lieutenant-General Sir John *Clavering. He was the younger brother of Sir Samuel John Brooke *Pechell. Pechell entered the navy in 1803, served in the *Triumph* in the fleet off Toulon under Nelson in 1804, and afterwards in the *Medusa*, at the capture of the Spanish treasureships off Cape St Mary on 5 October. In 1806 he was in the *Revenge* off Brest and Rochfort, and in 1809 in the *Barfleur* in the Tagus. On 25 June 1810 he was promoted lieutenant of the *Caesar*, from which he was moved in 1811 to the *Macedonian*, and in 1812 to the *San Domingo*, commanded by his brother, and flagship of his uncle, Sir John Borlase *Warren, on the North American station. By Warren he was appointed to the acting command of the brig *Colibri*, and afterwards of the *Recruit*, in both of which he cruised with some success on the coast of North America. On 30 May 1814 he was promoted commander, and in May 1818 commissioned the brig-sloop *Belette* (18 guns) for the Halifax station, where he enforced the treaty stipulations on the fisheries.

In October 1820 Pechell was appointed by Rear-Admiral Griffith to the command of the frigate *Tamar* which, being very sickly, had come north from Jamaica, and had lost her captain and a large proportion of her officers and men. The commander-in-chief on the Jamaica station, however, claimed the vacancy, and the matter being referred to the Admiralty, all the promotions were disallowed, and Pechell returned to the *Belette*. While in the *Tamar* he had obtained the authority of the Haitian government for stopping piracy by vessels claiming to be Haitian, and for searching all suspected vessels. He captured a large brigantine, with a crew of ninety-eight men, and forged commissions from different South American states. On 26 December 1822 Pechell was promoted captain.

Pechell married, on 1 August 1826, Katherine Annabella Bisshopp (*d.* 1871), daughter and coheir of the twelfth Lord de la Zouche; they had one son and two daughters. In July 1830 he was nominated gentleman usher of the privy chamber, and in April 1831 became equerry to Queen Adelaide. From January 1835 until his death he was whig MP for Brighton, taking an active part in public affairs, and especially in questions relating to the navy, mercantile marine, and fisheries. He favoured vote by ballot and a system of national education for all sects, and voted against church rates. On the death of his brother, on 3 November 1849, he succeeded to the baronetcy, and took the additional surname of Brooke. He became a rear-admiral on

the retired list on 17 December 1852, and vice-admiral on 5 January 1858. He died at his house, 27 Hill Street, Berkeley Square, London, on 29 June 1860. As his son had predeceased him, the baronetcy passed to his cousin, George Samuel Pechell.

J. K. LAUGHTON, rev. ANDREW LAMBERT

Sources O'Byrne, *Naval biog. dict.* • *The Times* (30 June 1860) • J. Vincent, *Pollbooks: how the Victorians voted* (1967) • Burke, *Peerage* • *CGPLA Eng. & Wales* (1860)
Archives W. Sussex RO, letters to duke of Richmond
Wealth at death under £30,000: probate, 1 Sept 1860, *CGPLA Eng. & Wales*

Pechell, Sir **Paul**, first baronet (1724–1800), army officer, the second son of Jacob Pechell (1679–1750), army officer, and his wife, Jane, daughter of John Boyd, was born at Owenstown, co. Kildare, on 12 November 1724. His father, Jacob, served in the British army and adopted the war office spelling Pechell. His grandfather, Samuel de Péchels (1644–1720), sieur de la Boissade, a native of Montauban, Languedoc, France, was ejected from his estate following Louis XIV's revocation of the edict of Nantes in October 1685. In a brief narrative (printed in *Sussex Archaeological Collections*, 26.116) he related how, after the 'missionary' dragoons entered Montauban, he was imprisoned at Cahors, and in 1687 taken to Montpellier, whence he was transported to the French West Indies. He escaped from St Domingo to Jamaica in 1688 and, after many hardships, reached England that autumn. His wife escaped separately, but his mother and youngest sister remained imprisoned in France. In August 1689 he accompanied William III to Ireland as a lieutenant in Schomberg's Huguenot regiment, and in January 1690 William—who valued Huguenot officers—granted him a pension. He subsequently acquired the estate of Owenstown, co. Kildare, died at Dublin in 1720, and was buried in St Anne's Church there.

Paul Pechell entered the army as cornet-en-second in the Royal regiment of dragoons (1st dragoons) on 17 March 1744. He was promoted captain in Brigadier-General Fleming's regiment (36th foot), later 2nd battalion, Worcestershire regiment, on 12 December 1746. At the beginning of 1747 the 36th embarked at Gravesend to join the army of the duke of Cumberland in Flanders. Pechell was at operations near the frontiers of Holland, which led to the battle of Lauffeld or Val, near Maastricht, on 2 July 1747. His regiment lost two officers, two sergeants, and twenty-two rank and file, and he was among the wounded. He received from the duke of Cumberland 'the greatest commendation' (*London Gazette*, 27 July 1747).

After the treaty of Aix-la-Chapelle on 7 October 1748, the establishment of the regiment was reduced on its return to England, and Pechell was gazetted captain in the 3rd dragoon guards on 31 May 1751. In the spring of 1752 the regiment escorted George II to Harwich, whence the king embarked for Hanover, and for the next three years the regiment was on coast duty suppressing smuggling in Suffolk, Essex, and Devon and patrolling against highway robbers. Pechell was gazetted guidon and captain in the second troop of the Horse Grenadier Guards (later the 2nd Life Guards) on 25 November 1754, lieutenant and captain on 5 July 1755, major on 7 February 1759, and lieutenant-colonel on 20 January 1762.

Pechell retired from the service on 24 June 1768, receiving a lump sum for his commission. He had married, on 11 February 1752, Mary (d. October 1800), only daughter and heir of Thomas Brooke, of Paglesham, Essex, and they had two sons and five daughters. He was created a baronet on 1 March 1797, and died, possibly at Paglesham, on 13 January 1800. His eldest son, Major-General Sir Thomas Brooke Pechell, second baronet (1753–1826), was father of Rear-Admiral Sir Samuel John Brooke *Pechell, third baronet (1785–1849), and of Admiral Sir George Richard Brooke *Pechell, fourth baronet (1789–1860).

B. H. SOULSBY, rev. ROGER T. STEARN

Sources Burke, *Peerage* (1956) · P. Butten, 'Castle Goring', *Sussex Archaeological Collections*, 26 (1875), 113–51 · E. Benoit, *Histoire de l'édit de Nantes*, 3 vols. (Delft, 1693–5) · D. C. A. Agnew, *Protestant exiles from France, chiefly in the reign of Louis XIV, or, The Huguenot refugees and their descendants in Great Britain and Ireland*, 3rd edn, 2 vols. (1886) · R. Cannon, ed., *Historical record of the first, or king's regiment of dragoon guards* (1837) · R. Cannon, ed., *Historical record of the third, or prince of Wales' regiment of dragoon guards* (1838) · *Army List* · *GM*, 1st ser., 70 (1800), 91 · R. D. Gwynn, *Huguenot heritage* (1985) · I. Scouloudi, ed., *Huguenots in Britain and their French background, 1550–1800* (1987) · Fortescue, *Brit. army*, vol. 2 · J. C. R. Childs, *The British army of William III, 1689–1702* (1987) · J. Philippart, ed., *The royal military calendar*, 3rd edn, 3 (1820), 342

Pechell, Sir **Samuel John Brooke**, third baronet (1785–1849), naval officer and politician, born on 1 September 1785 in Ireland, belonged to a French family which settled in Ireland after the revocation of the edict of Nantes. He was the eldest son of Major-General Sir Thomas Brooke Pechell, second baronet, and his wife, Charlotte, daughter of Lieutenant-General Sir John *Clavering; he was brother of Sir George Richard Brooke *Pechell, and nephew of Admiral Sir John Borlase Warren. Under Warren's care he entered the navy on board the *Pomone* in July 1796. In August 1797 he was moved into the *Phoebe*, with Captain Robert Barlow, and was present at the capture of the *Nereide* on 21 December 1797, and of the *Africaine* on 5 March 1800, two of the most brilliant frigate actions of the war. Barlow, who had been knighted, was next moved into the *Triumph*, and Pechell followed him, until in February 1803 he was appointed acting lieutenant of the *Active*, a promotion confirmed by the Admiralty on 1 April. In January 1806 he joined his uncle's flagship, the *Foudroyant*, and in her was present at the capture of the *Marengo* and *Belle Poule* on 13 March. On 23 March 1807 he was promoted to the command of the sloop *Ferret* on the Jamaica station, and on 16 June 1808 was posted to the frigate *Cleopatra* (38 guns), in which on 22 January 1809 he engaged the 40-gun French frigate *Topaze*, at anchor under a battery at Pointe-Noire in Guadeloupe. The battery had, however, only one effective gun, and the *Topaze*, having sustained great loss, struck her colours when, after forty minutes, the frigate

Jason and the sloop *Hazard* joined the *Cleopatra*. The disparity of force at the close of the action necessarily dimmed its brilliance, but Pechell's judgement in placing the *Cleopatra* so as to render the enemy's fire ineffective was deservedly commended. He afterwards took part in the reduction of Martinique. In October 1810 he was moved into the *Guerrière*, but returned to the *Cleopatra* in July 1811, and commanded her in the North Sea, on the coast of France, and at Gibraltar.

In December 1812 Pechell was appointed to the *San Domingo*, his uncle's flagship, as commander-in-chief on the coast of North America, and in her returned to England in June 1814. He was nominated a CB in June 1815, and in July 1823 commissioned the frigate *Sybille* for service in the Mediterranean, where, in 1824, she formed part of the squadron off Algiers, under Sir Harry Burrard Neale, and was afterwards employed in preventing piracy, or the semi-piratical attempts of the Greek provisional government, near the Morea.

The *Sybille* was paid off in November 1826, and Pechell, having, by the death of his father, succeeded to the baronetcy on 17 June 1826, took the additional surname of Brooke, in conformity with the will of his grandmother, the only daughter and heir of Thomas Brooke of Paglesham in Essex. He married, on 15 April 1833, Julia Maria (d. 6 Sept 1844), daughter of the ninth Baron Petre. They had no children. He had no further service afloat, but from 1830 to 1834, and again from 1839 to 1841, was a lord of the Admiralty. He was in parliament as member for Hallestone in 1830, and for Windsor in 1833. He attained the rank of rear-admiral on 9 November 1846, and died on 3 November 1849. The title passed to his brother, George Richard Brooke Pechell.

Pechell was one of the few officers of his time to recognize the immense importance of speed and precision in the aiming and firing of guns. Following the plan of Captain Philip Broke in the *Shannon*, he carried out, when in command of the *San Domingo*, systematic exercise and target practice, by which he obtained results then considered remarkable. In the *Sybille* he followed a similar method, again with results far superior to anything before known.

Pechell wrote a valuable pamphlet, *Observations upon the Defective Equipment of Ships' Guns*, first published in 1812 (3rd edn 1828). In combination with Sir Howard Douglas and Sir William Bowles he prepared the way for the establishment in 1830 of the *Excellent* gunnery training ship, under George Smith. Shortly afterwards he became a junior lord of the Admiralty at the insistence of William IV, another gunnery enthusiast, and was in a position to secure the permanence of the ship in 1832. He was also influential in the decision to appoint Sir William Symonds as surveyor of the navy. Recognizing that improved gunnery alone was of limited value, he supported larger and faster ships. A royal favourite and a wealthy man, Pechell was one of the architects of the professional navy of the later nineteenth century.

J. K. LAUGHTON, rev. ANDREW LAMBERT

Sources J. W. Wells, *The story of HMS Excellent, 1830–1980* (1980) · A. D. Lambert, *The last sailing battlefleet: maintaining naval mastery,*

1815–1850 (1991) • P. Padfield, *Broke and the Shannon* (1968) • C. J. Bartlett, *Great Britain and sea power, 1815–1853* (1963) • Burke, *Peerage*
Archives W. Yorks. AS, Leeds, letters to A. G. Stapleton

Pechey, John (*bap.* **1654**, *d.* **1718**), physician, the elder son of William Pechey (*d.* 1702), a practitioner of physic and surgery, was baptized on 11 December 1654 in Chichester, Sussex. Pechey matriculated at New Inn Hall, Oxford, on 22 March 1672, took his BA on 29 November 1675, and obtained his MA on 10 June 1678. An undated handbill of his, perhaps from the mid-1680s, advertised his move from 'Chequer-yard, near Dowgate, to Queen Street, near Cheapside', London, where he could be seen every day from nine to one o'clock, charging no more than 1*s.*, and offering free advice to the poor of his parish. From mid-October to mid-December 1684 he took the three-part examination of the Royal College of Physicians, and was awarded its licentiate on 22 December. On 12 August 1687 he signed a contract joining with four other licentiates of the college in a five-year lease on a property known as the Golden Angel and Crown in King's Street, London (the 'repository'), where they collected a stock of drugs and saw patients by turns. At the same time, each continued his private practice. They advertised by distributing handbills and by printing the jointly authored *Oracle for the Sick* (1687), which contained a series of medical questions with answers: the patient could circle or fill in the appropriate answers, send in the pamphlet, and get a diagnosis and medicines in the return post. Pechey also circulated handbills saying that 'the sick may have advice for nothing. And approved medicines at reasonable rates', and giving his address as the Angel and Crown in King's Street. When the lease on the repository practice ran out, about September 1692, Pechey moved to the Angel and Crown in Basing Lane, from where he circulated advertisements for pills to cure the French pox and scurvy: the pills could be taken at any time and 'hinder no business'. He also advertised in the *Athenian Mercury* in November 1693, and probably in other papers as well. From the start the censors of the Royal College of Physicians disliked the repository practice and its members, and from 15 November 1688 Pechey was personally named as needing to be disciplined for his advertising. The censors first warned him; when he continued to publish his announcements and refused to take down the sign over his door advertising his practice, he was fined £4. In the legal confusion following the revolution of 1688 Pechey simply refused to pay the fine. But from January 1690 to February 1694 Pechey and the censors engaged in battles, sometimes in court, over his behaviour, and unpaid dues and fines. His battles led to new attempts to discipline the members of the college generally.

About the time that Pechey had joined the college, he had begun to translate some of Thomas Sydenham's works into English. Since Sydenham, too, held the rank of licentiate, Pechey probably met him no later than 1684, during the process of joining the college. It is probable that Pechey had the tacit support of Sydenham in publishing, in the autumn of 1686, the first part of his *Collections of Acute Diseases*, which translated Sydenham's work on

smallpox and measles. The next two parts (1688) and parts four and five (1691) were also mainly translations from Sydenham; they were gathered together and issued by Henry Bonwick in 1691 with a single title page as *Collections of Acute Diseases, in Five Parts*. This was quickly followed by Pechey's *A Collection of Chronical Diseases* (1693), which, apart from the first chapter, was again from Sydenham. Pechey quickly followed with *Promptuarium praxeos medicae* (1693), with chapters on diseases and their cures listed alphabetically; *The London Dispensatory* (1694), a guide to useful medicines; and *The Compleat Herbal of Physical Plants* (1694), which contained directions for using simples and for making compounds. In these works, published during his disputes with the officers of the college, Pechey made plain his advocacy of clinical experience. In the preface to *The London Dispensatory*, he lambasted 'the vain fictions of a sort of men, whose business it is, to make every part of [medicine] obscure and misterious'; in *The Store-House of Physical Practice* (a rearranged translation of his *Promptuarium*, brought out in early 1695), he wrote that 'plain Practice must expect but cold Entertainment with the speculative Physician', and that 'Reason and Argument are not the true Tests of Physick, nor indeed of any thing else, when Experience, the great Baffler of Speculation, can determine the Matter'. He continued to promote the 'practical medicine' of Sydenham, and issued *The Whole Works* of Sydenham in English (drawing on his earlier translations and adding the rest) in 1696. He continued with five more English medical collections brought out between 1696 and 1698. Almost all Pechey's works ended with an advertisement for his pills.

In 1695 Pechey was listed as living in the parish of St Mary Aldermary, with his wife, Ann, a daughter, Ann, and two sons, Joseph and Whitlock. About Michaelmas of 1706 he moved to a corner of Robin Hood's Court, Bow Lane. He made out his will on 30 July 1718, naming a nephew, Francis, as well as the rest of the family, and was buried on 21 August 1718 in St Mary Aldermary. His eldest son later advertised that he was selling Pechey's pills from his house in Robin Hood's Court, carrying on his father's legacy.

In all likelihood, the **John Peachie** (*fl.* 1683), physician, who was an MD of Caen and extra licentiate of the Royal College of Physicians (26 July 1683), was not the same person as above. To this other Peachie has been ascribed, on slender evidence, a series of short tracts, published from 1672 to 1695, on various exotic botanicals, with titles of the form: *Some Observations Made upon the … Written by …*.

HAROLD J. COOK

Sources annals, RCP Lond. • J. Pechey, *Promptuarium praxeos medicae* (1693) • J. Pechey, *The store-house of physical practice* (1695) • Foster, *Alum. Oxon.* • Munk, *Roll* • H. J. Cook, *Trials of an ordinary doctor: Joannes Groenevelt in 17th-century London* (1994) • G. C. Peachey, 'The two John Peacheys, seventeenth-century physicians: their lives and times', *Janus*, 23 (1918), 121–41

Peck, Francis (**1692–1743**), antiquary, was born in the parish of St John the Baptist in Stamford, Lincolnshire, on 4 May 1692, the younger son of Robert Peck, merchant, and his wife, Elizabeth Jephson. Nothing else is known regarding his parents or his siblings. He was educated at Charterhouse School and then at St John's College, Cambridge, from where he graduated BA in 1716 and MA in 1727. His first publication, a 'hymn to the creator of the world'—a defence of the holy scripture—was published in 1716. He took holy orders and was ordained deacon (1715) and priest (1716) in the Church of England, becoming curate of King's Cliffe, Northamptonshire, in August 1719. In the same year he married Anne Curtis (d. c.1758), possibly the daughter of Edward Curtis, with whom he had three children, Francis (1720–1749), Thomas (who died in childhood), and Anne (1731–1793). In 1723 he purchased for £400 the living of Goadby Marwood in Leicestershire from Samuel Lowe MP, who was then lord of the manor and patron of the advowson. In 1736 he also obtained the prebendal stall of Marston St Lawrence in Lincoln Cathedral.

Peck lived at the rectory in Goadby Marwood for the rest of his life, and from there dedicated himself to his pastoral duties and his antiquarian and literary studies. His principal interests were in the history and antiquities of the local area—Lincolnshire, Leicestershire, and Rutland—and the political and literary history of seventeenth-century England. In 1721 he published his first proposals for printing the history and antiquities of the town of Stamford, which resulted in his first major publication, *Academia tertia Anglicana, or, The Antiquarian Annals of Stanford* (1727). As was not uncommon for such antiquarian works, Peck published all his books at his own expense. Dedicated to John Manners, duke of Rutland, it included a history of that family together with histories of the short-lived university, and the monasteries, guilds, churches, chapels, hospitals, and schools of the town. In the six years spent producing this work he ran into a vitriolic argument with **Francis Howgrave** (*fl.* 1724–1726), a young Stamford apothecary who in the year before Peck's volume appeared published *An Essay on the Ancient and Present State of Stamford*. The preface to this short history was highly critical of Peck's delays in publishing his book and of its projected expense. Peck in turn appears to have feared that Howgrave's book would steal his thunder. Either way, their argument illustrates the petty quarrels often arising between local antiquaries in this period. Peck described Howgrave (about whom little else is known other than that he wrote a short essay against smallpox inoculation published in 1724 as a letter to Dr James Jurin FRS) as 'such a Child in Antiquities' and threatened: 'I am yet only on the defensive: But if you begin the War, I thank God, I have both Money to sue, and Pen to answer him who bespatters' (Francis Peck to Francis Howgrave, 12 Aug 1726; Howgrave, preface, *An Essay on … Stamford*, iv). Nothing further is known of their argument, though Roger Gale remarked from London in 1728 that 'Mr. Peck's *voluminous work* is not much admired here; it is no hard matter, beside the labour, to compose such a great work, by writing everybodys life that has any relation to it' (Gale to Stukeley, 6 Feb 1728; *Family Memoirs*, 1.200). In 1729 Peck published a single sheet set of queries

seeking information on the natural history and antiquities of Leicestershire and Rutland, and in 1731 Thomas Hearne observed that Peck was in Cambridge collecting material for 'a fourth and fifth volume' of Sir William Dugdale's *Monasticon Anglicanum*, as well as for his history of Leicestershire. Hearne wrote that Peck's 'Collections are almost incredible for a man tyed down to a Country Cure' (*Remarks*, 10.475). Browne Willis, according to Hearne, described Peck as 'a Man of Parts, & no mean Scholar, tho' very conceited' (*Remarks*, 9.218). Peck met the antiquary William Stukeley in 1723, and when Stukeley moved to Stamford they became friends, establishing a couple of 'literary clubs' together. In 1744 Stukeley recalled that Peck 'had a good deal of pride, and after many attempts at London, finding he was not rewarded as he thought he ought to have been, he became recluse and angry with the world' (*Family Memoirs*, 2.248).

Peck was elected a member of the Society of Antiquaries on 9 March 1732, and he corresponded with some of the leading antiquaries of his day, including Hearne, Willis, Thomas Wotton, and Zachary Grey. In 1732 he published the first section of his illustrated *Desiderata curiosa, or, A collection of divers scarce and curious pieces, relating chiefly to matters of English history*, the work for which he became best known. A second volume appeared in 1735, and his complete catalogue of discourses 'written both for and against Popery' during the reign of James II also appeared in that year. William Cole wrote of Peck:

> Had he lived longer we might have had many more curious pieces of antiquity, which he seems to have been in possession of; but the chief and great failing of this gentleman seemed to be an eager desire to publish as little in one volume as he could, in order to eke out his collection. His 'Desiderata Curiosa' is full of curious things, but he has so disjointed, mangled, and new-sentenced all of them, and what with detached books, chapters, and heads of the chapters, that, in endeavouring to be more than ordinarily clear, he has become at many times quite the reverse. (BL, Add. MS 5833, fol. 176)

Peck's chaotic and verbose style was likewise criticized by a later historian of Stamford, William Harrod, who nevertheless relied upon Peck's diligent work in *The Antiquarian Annals of Stanford* for his own study. While Harrod considered Peck to be

> the only writer on this town who deserves the name of antiquary … I own it is the most unpleasant book of that kind I ever sat down to, merely through his ill chosen method, his abrupt departure from his subject, and his joining of long trifles, without any breaks to things of importance. (Harrod, 1.iii–iv)

In 1740 Peck published miscellaneous pieces on the lives of Oliver Cromwell and John Milton, as well as a catalogue of the several editions of Shakespeare's writings, and critical and explanatory notes. According to John Nichols, who had a more positive view of Peck's work than either Cole or Harrod, as these last were published

> at a period when that species of Criticism had not arrived to the perfection it has since attained by the united labours and genius of several successive and learned Commentators, [they] deserve particular commendation. He seems indeed to have first pointed out the mode [of criticism], which has

since been successfully pursued. (Nichols, *Lit. anecdotes*, 1.513)

Thomas Seccombe in the *Dictionary of National Biography* also described these critical notes as 'remarkable, as being perhaps the first attempts made to illustrate their writings by extracts from contemporary writers, in accordance with the method subsequently followed by Steevens and Malone'. However, Peck's off-hand attitude to historical veracity appears in an anecdote related by George Vertue, who informed Peck that the print of Milton he wished to use as the frontispiece to his book on the poet was very probably spurious. Vertue later recollected Peck's reply: '"I'll have a scraping from it however, and let posterity settle the matter"' (*Appendix to the Memoirs of Thomas Hollis*, 513). When Peck's last published work appeared he still had in completed manuscript form

> no less than nine different works, but whether he had not met with encouragement for those which he had already produced, or whether he was rendered incapable of executing them by reason of his declining health, is uncertain, none of them, however, ever were made public. (F. Peck, *Desiderata curiosa*, 1759, preface, x)

Peck died on 9 July 1743, of unknown cause; the only comment comes from Stukeley, who informed Roger Gale: 'Poor Peck is dead, and made a sad exit, being not quite *compos mentis*' (Stukeley to Gale, 6 Aug 1743; *Family Memoirs*, 80.431). He was buried in the choir of Goadby Marwood church. At his death Peck left unfinished his 'Natural history and antiquities of Leicestershire', the manuscript of which was bought by Sir Thomas Cave. It passed on to John Nichols, who made use of it in his *History and Antiquities of the County of Leicestershire* (4 vols., 1795–1815). The five quarto manuscript volumes of the 'Monasticon Anglicanum volumen quartum' to which Hearne had referred were also purchased by Cave. They were presented to the British Museum in 1779, where they were utilized by numerous antiquaries and county historians, and subsequent editors of Dugdale. Other numerous unfinished manuscripts included the history and antiquities of Rutland; the history and antiquities of Grantham; 'The annals of Stamford' continued; a third volume of 'Desiderata curiosa'; biographical notes on the life of the seventeenth-century politician and theologian Nicholas Ferrar of Little Gidding (which formed the bulk of Peter Peckard's *Memoirs of the Life of Mr Nicholas Ferrar*, 1790) and of William and Robert Burton (author of *The Anatomy of Melancholy*), and the lives of various other eminent local families and figures. Nichols reflected that Peck had lived 'a laborious, and, it may be affirmed, an useful life, wholly devoted to antiquarian pursuits' (Nichols, *Lit. anecdotes*, 1.520). **DAVID BOYD HAYCOCK**

Sources Nichols, *Lit. anecdotes*, 1.507–21 • R. Sweet, *The writing of urban histories in eighteenth-century England* (1997) • *Remarks and collections of Thomas Hearne*, ed. C. E. Doble and others, 11 vols., OHS, 2, 7, 13, 34, 42–3, 48, 50, 65, 67, 72 (1885–1921), vols. 9–10 • *The family memoirs of the Rev. William Stukeley*, ed. W. C. Lukis, 3 vols., SurtS, 73, 76, 80 (1882–7) • BL, Add. MS 5833, fol. 176 • W. Harrod, *The antiquities of Stamford and St Martin's*, 2 vols. (1785) • *Appendix to the memoirs of Thomas Hollis*, ed. F. Blackburne (1780) • DNB • GM, 1st ser., 61 (1791), 456 • Venn, *Alum. Cant.* • F. Howgrave, *An essay on the ancient and present state of Stamford* (1726)

Archives BL, monastic collections, Add. MSS 4934–4938 • BL, notes relating to history of St Leonard's priory, Stamford, Lansdowne MS 991 (40) • BL, poetic and antiquarian collections, Add. MSS 4934–4938, 28637–28638 • Leics. RO, papers • Leics. RO, corresp., topographical notes, and other papers • NRA, priv. coll., collections relating to Grantham, Lincolnshire, and Leicester • S. Antiquaries, Lond., discourse on money

Likenesses B. Collins, print, 1731, repro. in F. Peck, *Desiderata curiosa*, new edn, 2 vols. (1779), frontispiece • pen-and-ink drawing, 1731 (after B. Collins junior), NPG • etching, 1732 (after B. Collins junior), BM, NPG; repro. in F. Peck, *Desiderata curiosa*, 2 vols. (1732–5) • J. Faber junior, mezzotint, 1735 (after J. Highmore), BM; repro. in F. Peck, *Memoirs of the life and actions of Oliver Cromwell* (1740), frontispiece • line engraving (after B. Collins junior), NPG

Wealth at death left £400 to wife, £200 to son, £400 to daughter, and two freehold properties: Nichols, *Lit. anecdotes*, vol. 1, p. 520

Peck, James (*b.* 1773, *d.* in or after 1824), composer and music publisher, was born in London in 1773 and was perhaps (judging from several references in the *Gentleman's Magazine*) a member of a family of printers and booksellers residing at York and Hull. A musician named Peck, aged 100, died at Bath on 5 February 1784, but a connection with James cannot be established. Peck worked in London. His glee 'Kisses' was published by Preston about 1798; others, notably *Love and Sparkling Wine* (1796) and *Hail, Britannia*, were printed by himself at Westmorland Buildings, Aldersgate Street. From about 1802 he was based at 47 Lombard Street, from where he issued most of his publications, but by December 1824 he was at 52 Paternoster Row. Among his other works, many of which were for use by the Methodist church, were *Two Hundred and Fifty Psalm Tunes* (1798?), *Peck's Collection of Hymn Tunes, Fugues & Odes* (1799–1800), *Soft be the Gently Breathing Notes* (1803), *Peck's Miscellaneous Collection of Sacred Music* (1805–15), *The Vocal Preceptor, or, A Concise Introduction to Singing* (5th edn, *c*.1810), *The Flute Preceptor*, *Advice to a Young Composer, or, Short Essay on Vocal Harmony* (1811), *Sacred Gleanings, or, Hymn Tunes Adapted for Two Flutes*, and *Peck's Beauties of Sacred Harmony, or, Vocalist's Pocket Book* (1824?). *Peck's Pocket Arrangement, or, General Collection of Psalm and Hymn Tunes with Interludes* (3 vols., 1833?) was published by his son John Peck, the organist at St Faith's, in conjunction with another son, James Peck junior. John Peck's *The Union Tune Book, being a collection of psalm and hymn tunes, adapted for use in Sunday schools and congregations* appeared in 1837. In 1850 James Peck's business, which John Peck had taken over, was based at 44 Newgate Street. Peck's death has not been traced.

L. M. MIDDLETON, rev. DAVID J. GOLBY

Sources F.-J. Fétis, *Biographie universelle des musiciens, et bibliographie générale de la musique*, 2nd edn, 6 (Paris, 1864–5), 474 • F. Kidson, 'Peck, James', Grove, *Dict. mus.* • GM, 1st ser., 54 (1784), 152 • GM, 1st ser., 68 (1798), 1149 • GM, 1st ser., 71 (1801), 1210

Peckard [*née* Ferrar], **Martha** (1729–1805), poet, was the eldest daughter of Huntingdon attorney Edward Ferrar, a descendant of the Ferrar family of Little Gidding. Little is known of her early life and education. On 13 June 1755 she married the Revd Peter *Peckard (*bap.* 1717, *d.* 1797), later rector of Fletton, Huntingdonshire, and subsequently appointed dean of Peterborough and master of Magdalene College, Cambridge. Martha Peckard appears to have lived in the vicarage at the village of Fletton, from the appointment of her husband to the rectorship, for the rest of her married life. There she entertained friends and, perhaps, the poet Elizabeth Pennington. During a visit to London she met the novelist Samuel Richardson, who wrote to the Revd Peckard on 16 February 1756:

> I think it a very great felicity that I have been favoured with the sight, and (more than once in the short time of her being in town) with the conversation of a lady, whose genius and general character I very much admired before. I congratulate you both, kindred spirits (as you always were) on your happy union. (*Correspondence of Samuel Richardson*, 5.110)

Peckard's reputation as a poet is based upon two frequently anthologized works: 'Ode to Cynthia' and 'Ode to Spring'. John Duncombe praises both in his *Feminiad* (1754), calls the author Flavia, and writes:

> Haste, haste, ye Nine, and hear a sister sing
> The charms of Cynthia and the joys of Spring.
> (Duncombe, 11.275–6)

In Robert Dodsley's *Collection of Poems in Six Volumes, by Several Hands* (1748–58) the poems are attributed to 'Miss F.' (vol. 5, pp. 311–13). 'Ode to Spring' appears in the *Gentleman's Magazine* in January 1755 as 'By a Lady' (p. 37) and in May 1764 by 'J. F.' (p. 243); the first is accompanied by a note stating: 'A Copy of the following Ode, with several Faults, having stolen into another Magazine, we are desired, in justice to the ingenious author to present the reader with one more correct'. The only other published work known to have been written by Peckard is a seven-line epitaph composed for the gravestone of a Fletton parish clerk and submitted to the *Gentleman's Magazine* in 1789 (pt 2, p. 748) by an unidentified reader.

Peckard appears to have been left financially secure on her husband's death, which occurred on 8 December 1797. An obituary notice reports that the newly appointed rector of Fletton allowed her 'to reside in the house, and enjoy the gardens she had so much improved'; it adds, 'The Dean has left his fortune, after her decease, to augment the incomes of the master and fellows of Magdalen-college' (*GM*, 66). Her death occurred unexpectedly, at Fletton on 14 January 1805, for she is reported to have 'entertained a large party of friends at her house the preceeding day in apparent perfect health' (*GM*, 75).

JOYCE FULLARD

Sources *GM*, 1st ser., 25 (1755); 37; 34 (1764), 243; 59 (1789), 748; 62 (1797), 1076, 1126; 66 (1798), 440; 75 (1805), 92 · *The correspondence of Samuel Richardson*, ed. A. L. Barbauld, 6 vols. (1804), 5.110 · J. Duncombe, *The feminiad: a poem* (1754); Augustan Reprint Society, 207 (1981), 24–5 [introduction by J. Harris] · J. Todd, ed., *A dictionary of British and American women writers, 1660–1800* (1984) · E. Brydges, *Censura literaria*, 2nd edn, 10 vols. (1815), 7.333–4

Likenesses portraits (with her husband), Magd. Cam.

Wealth at death husband left his fortune, after her death, to Magdalene College: *GM* 66, 440

Peckard, Peter (bap. 1717, d. 1797), dean of Peterborough, was baptized on 2 November 1717 at St Margaret in the Close, Lincoln, the son of the Revd John Peckard (1689?–1765) of Welbourn, Lincolnshire, and his wife, Mary (d. 1786/7). In his youth he lost an arm in a shooting accident. He matriculated from Corpus Christi College, Oxford, on

20 July 1734, and proved to be a lively undergraduate: he was twice obliged to atone for misdemeanours by public penance on his knees in the college hall. Peckard graduated BA in 1738, proceeded MA in 1742, and became scholaris, or probationary fellow, in 1744. He was ordained deacon on 22 September 1745, and priested on 25 May 1746, by the bishop of Lincoln. On 26 February 1746 he had been instituted to the vicarage of St Martin's, Lincoln, which he held until 1750. From about 1752 to 1760 he was curate of King's Ripton, near Huntingdon.

On 13 June 1755 Peckard married Martha (1729–1805), accounted a local beauty, daughter of Edward Ferrar, a Huntingdon attorney and descendant of Nicholas Ferrar of the Little Gidding community. In 1760 Peckard was appointed rector of Fletton, near Peterborough, through the patronage of Lord Careysfort of the local Proby family, and to the vicarage of Yaxley nearby, a crown living. This pluralism required a dispensation from Thomas Secker, archbishop of Canterbury, who disapproved of Peckard's unorthodoxy as a 'mortalist' denying any intermediate state of consciousness between death and the Judgement. Before giving his assent Secker subjected him to rigorous examination in Latin and humiliatingly exacted his signature to four articles which constituted a partial retraction.

For a number of years Peckard combined his parochial responsibilities with those of army chaplaincy, and the *Army List* shows him on the strength of the 16th foot from 1755 to 1766, and of the Grenadier Guards from 1766 to 1782, though he evidently held leave of absence for much of the time. In the mess he was reckoned a convivial companion. He held prebends at Lincoln Cathedral from 1774 and Southwell Minster from 1777. In 1777 Peckard vacated Yaxley and was appointed to the rectory of Tansor, Northamptonshire, which he held until 1793. From 1781 until his death he was master of Magdalene College, Cambridge. He was appointed vice-chancellor of Cambridge University in 1784, created DD in 1785, and in 1792 was appointed dean of Peterborough. He was rector of Abbot's Ripton, Huntingdonshire, from 1793 to 1797.

While a Huntingdonshire curate Peckard incorporated in 1753 as a Cambridge MA, and became associated with the informal circle of liberal Anglican divines who helped make the university a citadel of mid-century latitudinarianism. Propagating his beliefs in a number of tracts and sermons, he covered some of his more heterodox views by a veil of prudent ambiguity or anonymity. Peckard was devout in his way, far from being a deist and bitterly critical of scoffers or sceptics like David Hume, yet his commitment to the principles of *sola scriptura* and private judgement led him to break with contemporary orthodoxy on several dogmas, including the Trinity, which he saw as a speculative opinion grafted onto the faith by subtle Platonizers. Like some of his friends, he demanded a 'further reformation' of the church to make its teachings and liturgy more consonant with the simple rule of life set out in scripture, and thus more defensible against sceptical attack. He strongly criticized the way in which assent to doctrinal confessions ('human impositions') was made a test of orthodoxy. In 1772, however, he did not sign the Feathers tavern petition to parliament demanding an end to obligatory subscription to the Thirty-Nine Articles, though he warmly endorsed the principle. He was keenly interested in the Last Judgement—which he believed might come in 2016—and in God's providential judgement of states and nations in this world. Though his theological views were never set out systematically, they can be pieced together from his various publications, particularly from *Subscription, or, Historical Extracts* (1776).

Peckard was strongly committed to whiggish principles of civil and religious liberty. He had a high view of natural rights, government by consent, liberty of conscience, and the need for the periodic review of human institutions. His earliest publication was a defence of the Jewish naturalization bill of 1753. By the early 1780s the focus of his political attention had moved to the anti-slavery cause, of which he became an eloquent supporter. Preaching the university sermon in Cambridge in 1784 he denounced the slave trade as a 'sin against the light of nature, and the accumulated evidence of divine Revelation' (Peckard, *Piety*, 6). As vice-chancellor in 1785 he set the legitimacy of slavery as the theme of the senior bachelors' Latin essay prize: it was won by Thomas Clarkson, who was thus set on his abolitionist career. Peckard's pamphlet demolishing notions of African inferiority, *Am I not a Man and a Brother?* (1788), may have launched the phrase as an anti-slavery slogan. He was a patron of Olaudah Equiano, the African-born abolitionist.

It was probably during his military service that he became a friend of Sir John Griffin Griffin, later Lord Howard de Walden, whose inheritance of Audley End gave him the right to appoint Peckard as master of Magdalene College. An advanced liberal, Peckard arrived in 1781 to head a college which had become an early haven for evangelicalism in the university. Yet the new master did not clash with the evangelical fellows. He saw eye to eye with them on the slavery issue and like them regarded the college 'not as a place of dissipation and expense but of economy and education' (Forbes, 246). Following the associationist psychology of John Locke and David Hartley, Peckard believed in the malleability of the human personality, and saw education as a vital means of social progress. Under his aegis Magdalene flourished, producing a stream of university prize-winners, missionaries, and evangelical leaders. A firm master, he stabilized the college finances, increased admissions, and maintained discipline. He was a major college benefactor, leaving lands and money to augment stipends and fund two open Ferrar scholarships in memory of his wife's family. Peckard compiled *Memoirs of Nicholas Ferrar* (1790).

In 1792 came Peckard's advancement to the deanery of Peterborough. His chapter grumbled at his refusal to provide them more than one annual dinner. In 1795, when old and infirm, he managed to deliver a sombre fast sermon in the cathedral, demanding peace with France and warning that the continuance of the slave trade would amplify God's present judgements on the nation. He died of cancer on 8 December 1797, having imprudently cut off a facial wen which hampered his shaving. He was buried in Peterborough Cathedral.   JOHN WALSH

Sources J. Walsh and R. Hyam, *Peter Peckard: liberal churchman and anti-slave trade campaigner* (1998) · Magd. Cam., Peckard MSS · master's private book, Magd. Cam. · *GM*, 1st ser., 67 (1797), 1076, 1126 · *GM*, 1st ser., 68 (1798), 440 · F. Blackburne, *Works*, 7 vols. (1804–5), 1.xlii–xliii, xciv–cvii · T. Kerrich, letters, CCC Cam., Hartshorne MSS, 77, 79, 81, 83, 111.5 · U. Aberdeen, Beattie MSS 30/1/292, 30/2/129, 30/2/585.6 · BL, Add. MSS 35642, fol. 238; 35682, fol. 243; 38219, fol. 85 · CUL, Add. MSS 4251 (B), 1085, 5805 (F), Mm 5 44 fol. 36 · Bodl. Oxf., MS Eng. poet. c. 51; MS Autogr. d.14 · register of absences and punishments, CCC Oxf. · *The literary correspondence of John Pinkerton*, ed. D. Turner, 2 vols. (1830), 1.44–9, 105–6 · *IGI* · P. Peckard, *Piety, benevolence and loyalty recommended* (1784), 6 · M. Forbes, *Beattie and his friends*, ed. M. Knight and M. Forbes (1904), 246

Archives Magd. Cam. | CCC Cam., Hartshorne MSS, Kerrich letters · U. Aberdeen, Beattie MSS

Likenesses Ralph, oils, Magd. Cam. · portraits, Magd. Cam.

Wealth at death £50,000—410 acres of land in Huntingdonshire; endowment for two open scholarships to Magdalene College, Cambridge: Peckard MSS, Magd. Cam.

Pecke, Thomas (*b.* 1637, *d.* in or after 1664), epigrammatist, was born at Wymondham, Norfolk, the son of James Pecke of Wymondham. His mother's maiden name was Talbot. He was educated at Norwich School, under Thomas Lovering, the recipient of one of his epigrams. He matriculated at Gonville and Caius College, Cambridge, on 3 October 1655; his tutor was William Naylor. He apparently left without a degree. He was admitted to the Inner Temple on 22 June 1657 and called to the bar on 12 February 1664. His uncle Thomas Pecke of Spixworth funded Thomas at university, but he withdrew his support when his nephew refused to travel to France; presumably his uncle wanted him to complete his education at a French academy (Pecke, *Parnassi*, 175).

Pecke was a friend of Francis Osborne, the author of *Advice to a Son*, and when Osborne was attacked by John Heydon, in his *Advice to a Daughter*, Pecke replied with a pamphlet entitled *Advice to Balaam's Ass, or, Momus Catechised* (1658). The second edition of *Advice to a Daughter* (1659) includes a vituperative attack on Pecke, who is accused of having written 'a Dialogue of Polygamy'. This is a reference to *A Dialogue of Polygamy*, published in 1657, translated from the work by Bernardino Ochino; it bears a dedicatory epistle to Francis Osborne, and there would seem to be little doubt that Pecke was indeed the translator.

Although Pecke was training as a lawyer, poetry was his preferred study; as he wrote in *Balaam's Ass*, 'I am none of the Greatest Stranger to Latin and English Poetry' (Pecke, *Balaam's Ass*, 12). In 1658 he published an elegy on John Cleveland, which was, according to his own account, received with plaudits (Pecke, *Parnassi*, sig. A3). In 1659 he published *Parnassi puerperium* ('The childbed of Parnassus'), a collection of English epigrams which includes translations of Latin epigrams from John Owen and Sir Thomas More, and also of Martial's epigrams, describing the rarities to be seen at Rome. It also includes original epigrams on the twelve Caesars, and another set of epigrams in which Pecke addresses friends and mentors, or draws himself to the attention of prospective patrons. The collection is prefaced by commendatory Latin verses by Payne Fisher. Some of the poems printed as Pecke's were, in fact, composed by the printer James Cottrell, such as the epigram addressed to James Howell, who is described as the poet's adopted uncle. Pecke held that 'if a poem be good, it consists of nothing else, but various Epigrams; cemented by a dexterous sagacity' (ibid., sig. A3). Pecke also wrote satires, but in spite of his promise to publish them, they were never to appear in print. The first of Pecke's epigrams is addressed to Richard Cromwell, the lord protector; he is compared to Augustus and his father to Julius Caesar, while Pecke hopes that he will prove his Maecenas. Pecke's last publication was a *Heroick Poem*, a pamphlet of fourteen pages, published the following year, in celebration of the Restoration. There is a portrait of Pecke facing the title-page of *Parnassi puerperium*, below which Latin verses assert optimistically that he is the greatest ornament of a distinguished family whose pen will win him eternal fame. IAN WILLIAM MᶜLELLAN

Sources T. Pecke, *Parnassi puerperium, or, Some well-wishes to ingenuity* (1659) · T. Pecke, *Advice to Balaam's ass, or, Momus catechised* (1658) · J. Venn and others, eds., *Biographical history of Gonville and Caius College*, 1: *1349–1713* (1897) · W. H. Cooke, ed., *Students admitted to the Inner Temple, 1547–1660* [1878] · *DNB*

Likenesses P. F., line engraving, repro. in Pecke, *Parnassi puerperium*

Peckham, Sir Edmund (*b.* in or before **1495**, *d.* **1564**), administrator, was the second son of Peter Peckham of London and his second wife, Elizabeth, daughter of Henry Eburton of London. His father also acquired property at Denham in Buckinghamshire, while by 1516 Edmund had married Anne (*d.* 1570), daughter of John Cheyne of Chesham Bois in the same county. He held a succession of offices related to government finance, beginning as a clerk in the counting house; in that capacity he accompanied Henry VIII to Gravelines in July 1520. In January 1524 he was promoted to be cofferer of the royal household, with joint responsibility for payment of household expenses and keeping its accounts. His further appointment in 1526 to the position of clerk of the green cloth brought additional responsibilities in the administration of household finances.

With promotion went rewards. Assessed in 1527 on lands valued at £126 per annum, in 1536 Peckham was granted the lease of the manors of Alford, Eccles, and Alderley, and the stewardship of Londondale, all in Cheshire, which had been forfeited that year by William Brereton. He also expanded his family's estates in Buckinghamshire when Biddlesden Abbey, dissolved in 1538, was sold to him on 1 November 1540 by Sir Thomas Wriothesley (his kinsman by marriage). His responsibilities away from court grew as well. A JP for Buckinghamshire from 1525 to 1543, and for Middlesex from 1537 to 1543, he was constable of Scarborough Castle between 1528 and 1537. On 18 May 1542 he was knighted.

Well known to the king and his advisers, and with over twenty years' experience in the management of royal finances, Peckham merited his appointment on 19 May 1544 as high treasurer of all the mints. His promotion to this newly created post came as part of a sweeping reform of the royal mint. Committed to a major continental campaign, and already heavily engaged in Scotland, Henry VIII was eager to generate further revenues and saw the production of more coinage as a means to this end. He adopted a two-pronged policy: by covertly ordering a debasement of the currency he could create more money out of less gold and silver bullion; and by opening new mints in Durham, York, and Bristol, as well as a second mint in the Tower, between 1544 and 1546, he could greatly expand the means of production. Peckham was not directly charged with either receiving bullion or striking coin, duties which were devolved to the under-treasurers of the individual mints. Even so he is likely to have been frequently stretched, as the man with overall responsibility for supervising the personnel and running the mints during a period of frenetic production: it was later estimated that between 1544 and 1551 the mints produced debased coin worth £1,323,281 14*s.* in gold and £3,015,895 2*s.* 6*d.* in silver. With the gradual abandonment of debasement in Edward VI's latter years, however, Peckham's workload at the mint is likely to have dwindled accordingly.

On 18 June 1546 Peckham was appointed to receive the proceeds of the 'loving contribution' granted that year to the king. In his will Henry VIII bequeathed Peckham £200 and appointed him both treasurer to the executors and an assistant executor. But his religious conservatism was doubtless largely responsible for his being effectively sidelined during Somerset's protectorate. He was replaced as cofferer of the royal household by John Ryther in March 1547, and although he was briefly appointed to the privy council at the time of the autumn coup of 1549, attending meetings between 6 and 30 October, he probably owed his brief membership to Wriothesley's sponsorship, consequently losing his position when his patron fell. He remained treasurer of the mint, however, where he seems to have won admiration for his integrity. In 1553 his honesty was favourably compared with the corruptibility of others—'he never robbed his grace when he had all the rule of his treasure, he used not to buy silver for 4*s.* an oz. and make the King pay 5*s.* 4*d.* as other false traitors did' (Brigden, 504–5).

Following the death of Edward VI, Peckham played a key role in securing the throne for Mary. On 16 July 1553 it was reported that he and others 'of the force of the shyres of Oxforde, Buckyngham, Berks, Myddlesex', in number an estimated 10,000, had resolved 'to mershe forth towards the Palaice of Westminster' (*APC, 1552–4*, 293). This threat from the west put pressure on an increasingly nervous council and prevented Northumberland from summoning reinforcements from London. On 29 July Peckham was sworn a councillor, a position he retained until the queen's death. In October 1553 and November 1554 he was returned to parliament as one of the knights of the shire for Buckinghamshire. His experience as a senior financial officer also brought him employment at the heart of Mary's government. At the end of 1553 a reorganization of government finance led to Peckham's being appointed on 5 December to receive and disburse all the revenues of the crown, an appointment which gave him effectively a treasurer's role until autumn 1555. In spring 1554 he was additionally commissioned to receive the issues of sales of crown lands. Not surprisingly, his involvement in the day-by-day working of the mint seems to have become increasingly nominal. For his services he was granted a life annuity of £60. He may have lost ground, however, as a result of the treason of his son Henry *Peckham, executed in July 1556 for his involvement in the Dudley conspiracy.

Following Mary's death Peckham ceased to be a privy councillor, but he again remained treasurer of the mint. In his will, drawn up on 12 May 1563, he made austere provision for 'my body and vile carcas which is but earthe and duste', but showed himself essentially Catholic by leaving 20 marks 'unto my poore neighbours of Denham to praye for my soule' (will). To 'my welbeloved wife Anne Peckham' he left £500 and a life interest in Denham manor and to his sons George *Peckham and Robert Peckham £100 apiece; George, who may have been specially favoured as the father of Sir Edmund's grandsons, was granted the reversion of Denham. There were also bequests to servants and friends, and £40 'to be bestowed in dedes of charitie'. Peckham died on 29 March 1564 and was buried in Denham church on 18 April.   LUKE MACMAHON

Sources LP Henry VIII, vols. 3–21 · HoP, Commons, 1509–58, 3.78–9 · C. E. Challis, The Tudor coinage (1978) · C. E. Challis, ed., A new history of the royal mint (1992) · G. R. Elton, The Tudor revolution in government (1953) · D. Loades, John Dudley, duke of Northumberland, 1504–1553 (1996) · C. E. Challis, 'Mint officials and moneyers of the Tudor period', British Numismatic Journal, 43 (1975), 51–76 · W. C. Richardson, Tudor chamber administration (1952) · W. H. Rylands, ed., The visitation of the county of Buckingham made in 1634, Harleian Society, 58 (1909) · D. Loades, The reign of Mary Tudor: politics, government and religion in England, 1553–58, 2nd edn (1991) · DNB · S. Brigden, London and the Reformation (1989) · will, PRO, PROB 11/47, fols. 215v–216v · APC, 1552–4
Wealth at death see will, PRO, PROB 11/47, fols. 215v–216v

Peckham, Sir George (d. 1608), colonial adventurer, was the third son of Sir Edmund *Peckham (d. 1564) of Denham, Buckinghamshire, former high treasurer of the mint, and his wife, Anne (d. 1570), daughter of John Cheyne of Chesham Bois. In 1554 he married Susan, daughter and heir of Henry Webbe; she died in childbirth, aged seventeen, on 11 December 1555. He had with his second wife two sons, Edmund and George. His Roman Catholic faith was not an impediment to early advancement. Knighted in 1570, he was sheriff of Buckinghamshire from 1572, and several orders in council relate to the duties he discharged in that office. The circumstances by which he came to be interested in colonial projects are obscure, but his name appeared with those of Sir Humphrey Gilbert, Sir Richard Grenville, Christopher Carleill, and eighteen others in a 'supplication of certen gentlemen in the west partes for a newe navigacon' of March 1574 (PRO, SP 12/95, 63). Although it was Gilbert alone who

in 1578 received letters patent 'to discover, settle and exploit such remote heathen and barbarous landes countries and territories not actually possessed of any Christian prince', Peckham was one of the adventurers who financed his first attempt to found an English colony in North America. He saw a potential solution to the plight of English Catholics in the establishment of settlements which, while remaining loyal to the English crown, would be sufficiently remote to avoid the crippling financial penalties imposed upon recusants. Gilbert's voyage of 1578 was entirely unsuccessful, although neither he nor Peckham was discouraged. But Peckham was diverted from the project for a time by his imprisonment in 1580 for harbouring Catholic priests.

Released in March 1581, Peckham immediately busied himself in assisting the preparations for Gilbert's second expedition, for which he secured the advice of the noted polymath John Dee and the colonial propagandist Richard Hakluyt. In April 1582 it was rumoured that he intended to sail in the voyage. In fact, as preparations proceeded, it was agreed that the Catholic group of investors, led by Peckham and Sir William Gerrard, would set out on their own expedition to claim and independently settle some 8.5 million acres of land assigned to them by Gilbert, half of which represented Peckham's personal investment. In June 1582 articles of intent regarding their expedition were drafted, for which Martin Frobisher and Sir Richard Bingham were named as potential commanders. The project was sufficiently attractive to interest a number of non-Catholic subscribers. In June 1583 Sir Philip Sidney, who had acquired from Gilbert assignments of 3 million acres on his own behalf, joined these to Peckham's.

Gilbert's death at sea in September 1583 was a severe blow to the Western planting movement. Furthermore, the Spanish crown and a number of powerful English Catholic exiles appear to have put pressure upon Peckham and others to abandon the project entirely: the former because it implicitly violated Spain's claims of exploitation of the New World, the latter because large-scale Catholic emigration from England would have represented de facto recognition of the Acts of Supremacy and Uniformity. Lacking Gilbert's reputation, Peckham had difficulty in securing further investment, though Sir Francis Walsingham assisted with a letter of recommendation. In a bid to spur interest in the project, Peckham published his True reporte, of the late discoveries ... by that valiant and worthy gentleman, Sir Humfrey Gilbert on 12 November 1583. Dedicated to Walsingham, it presented the arguments in favour of the project: in effect, presenting the voice of Gilbert from beyond the grave. It provided justifications for intercourse with 'savages' and justified the queen's right of title over them, examined the benefits arising to England from the establishment of colonies, and confirmed the vast profits to be had by any who might invest therein, concluding: 'Let us therefore with cheerefull mindes and couragious hearts, give the attempt, and leave the sequell to almightye God' (Hakluyt, 8.89–131).

Though a cogent plea for funds, the True Reporte failed to

excite sufficient interest, and once the queen had forbidden Sidney to sail upon the intended expedition its abandonment was inevitable, leaving future initiatives on American colonization to Adrian Gilbert and Walter Ralegh, who inherited Sir Humphrey's patent rights. Soon afterwards, in 1584, Peckham was in prison once more for some offence relating to his Catholicism. From a financial perspective he appears to have suffered severely from his commitment to the project, and from the penalties incurred by his continuing religious nonconformity. In 1595 at least part of his Denham estate was surrendered to the crown to meet his debts, but he retained possession of unspecified properties there. There is little information on his latter years. He died before 21 June 1608, probably in modest circumstances.

Although his career was marked by the failure of English Western planting, Peckham is regarded as one of the most active, if not innovative, proponents of Elizabethan expansionism. His *True Reporte* was the first published work specifically to address the prospects for, and requirements of, English colonies in the New World. He was survived by his son George, who co-invested with his father in Gilbert's scheme.   JAMES MCDERMOTT

Sources D. B. Quinn, ed., *The voyages and colonising enterprises of Sir Humphrey Gilbert*, 2 vols., Hakluyt Society, 2nd ser., 83–4 (1940) · R. Hakluyt, *The principal navigations, voyages, traffiques and discoveries of the English nation*, 8, Hakluyt Society, extra ser., 8 (1904) · APC, 1571–7, 1580–81 · G. Lipscomb, *The history and antiquities of the county of Buckingham*, 4 vols. (1831–47) · PRO, SP 12/95, 63 · PRO, C142/322/138 · J. Parker, *Books to build an empire: a bibliographical history of English overseas interests to 1620* (1965) · DNB

Peckham, Henry (*b.* in or before **1526**, *d.* **1556**), conspirator, was born by 1526, having been old enough to marry in 1547; he was the second of four sons and two daughters of Sir Edmund *Peckham (*d.* 1564), administrator, of Denham, Buckinghamshire, and his wife, Anne (*d.* 1570), daughter of John Cheyne of Chesham Bois, Buckinghamshire. Sir Edmund Peckham was a leading administrator in the exchequer and the royal household, and treasurer of the mint from 1544 to 1564. Henry Peckham's younger brother was Sir George *Peckham. Peckham's early life is poorly documented, but he probably received some education, like his elder brother, Sir Robert Peckham (*d.* 1569), who attended Gray's Inn in the 1530s. Peckham was described in 1550 as 'the king's servant'. He married Elizabeth (*c.*1530–1602), daughter of Robert Dacres of London and Cheshunt, Hertfordshire, and niece of Sir Anthony Denny and Sir John Gates, by a licence dated 6 November 1547. She and her uncles may have converted Peckham to protestantism. Apparently he lived at Denham or at his father's house at Blackfriars, London, though he acquired lands in Cornwall, Devon, Gloucestershire, Hertfordshire, and Sussex. Peckham was elected MP to Edward VI's last parliament in March 1553, sitting for the borough of Chipping Wycombe, Berkshire, perhaps with help from his father or from John Dudley, duke of Northumberland. He opposed Northumberland's attempt to place Lady Jane Grey on the throne in July 1553.

Peckham's career under Mary I is curious. His Catholic father and brother Robert became privy councillors, and both represented Buckinghamshire in parliament, Edmund in October 1553 and November 1554, Robert in April 1554. The protestant Henry was re-elected from Chipping Wycombe to the parliaments of October 1553, April 1554, and 1555. He supported 'true religion' against the restoration of Catholicism in Mary's first parliament. Yet, serving under his father during Wyatt's rebellion in February 1554, he defended Ludgate against the rebel advance on London, and Mary rewarded him with the manors of Wishanger, Gloucestershire, in 1554, and Tring, Hertfordshire, in 1555. However, he complained that she had 'given him but one hundred marks a yere and taken away four' (Loades, *Two Tudor Conspiracies*, 213). During the parliament of 1555 he was part of the opposition group, led by Sir Anthony Kingston, which met at Arundel's tavern in November–December and formulated a conspiracy against the crown.

Henry Dudley and his supporters were hostile to Mary's husband, Philip of Spain, her persecution of protestants, and the possible restoration of former ecclesiastical lands to the church. They sought backing from Henri II of France for a rising in southern England to oust Mary in favour of her sister, Princess Elizabeth, and they plotted to steal £50,000 in silver bullion from the exchequer to finance it. The conspirators met several times in Peckham's rooms at Blackfriars and considered storing stolen bullion there. Peckham involved his relatives Edmund and Francis Verney and John Bray, second Baron Bray, and boasted that he could raise a host in Buckinghamshire. He also persuaded Edward Lewkenor to obtain a copy of Henry VIII's will to prove that Mary was a usurper. However, Peckham was among the first group arrested and sent to the Tower of London on 18 March 1556. Indicted on 29 April, he was tried with John Danyell in the Guildhall on 7 May. According to the Venetian ambassador, Giovanni Michieli, it seemed at first that Peckham might be reprieved because of his father's influence and his own past service. His brother claimed that Henry had joined the conspirators only as a spy, and certainly his confessions of 9 May led to accusations that he had betrayed his fellow prisoners. However, Mary insisted that Peckham and Danyell suffer the full penalty of hanging, drawing, and quartering 'by reason of the small fruit derived from her past indulgence' (Loades, *Mary Tudor*, 336). Michieli claimed that they made 'a Godly and Catholic end'. Perhaps because there were demonstrations in favour of executed conspirators, Peckham and Danyell were the last to die, on 7 or 8 July. The value of the property Peckham forfeited as a traitor is unknown. Mary allowed his widow to keep Tring for life; subsequently she married John Blount of London.

WILLIAM B. ROBISON

Sources HoP, *Commons, 1509–58* · D. M. Loades, *Two Tudor conspiracies* (1965) · J. Bruce, ed., *Letters and papers of the Verney family down to the end of the year 1639*, CS, 56 (1853) · 'Peckham, Sir Edmund', *DNB* · *VCH Buckinghamshire* · *VCH Hertfordshire* · D. Loades, *Mary Tudor: a life* (1989) · CSP dom., *1547–58* · *The diary of Henry Machyn, citizen and merchant-taylor of London, from AD 1550 to AD 1563*, ed. J. G. Nichols, CS, 42 (1848) · J. G. Nichols, ed., *The chronicle of Queen Jane, and of two* years of Queen Mary*, CS, old ser., 48 (1850) • C. Wriothesley, *A chronicle of England during the reigns of the Tudors from AD 1485 to 1559*, ed. W. D. Hamilton, 1, CS, new ser., 11 (1875) • E. H. Harbison, *Rival ambassadors at the court of Queen Mary* (1940)

Peckham, John. See Pecham, John (c.1230–1292).

Peckham, Peter of (d. 1293). See under Fetcham, Peter of (fl. 1267–1276).

Peckham, Peter of. See Fetcham, Peter of (fl. 1267–1276).

Peckitt, William (bap. **1731**, d. **1795**), glass-painter, was born at Husthwaite, near Easingwold in the North Riding of Yorkshire, and baptized on 13 April 1731, the third of the six children of William Peckitt (1681/2–1776), fellmonger of Husthwaite and glove maker of York, and his wife, Ann (1690–1787), daughter of Thomas Hunt of Linton-on-Ouse. His grandfather and great-grandfather were also fellmongers from the North Riding, though he and his younger brother, Henry, claimed genteel origins from the medieval family of Picote of Yorkshire and assumed both a coat of arms and a crest. Peckitt appears to have helped in his father's business and to have moved with him to York before 1752 when his father had set up a glove-making business there. In the opening lines of his commission book he recorded that he began the art of painting and staining of glass at Michaelmas 1751. In 1752 he advertised in the *York Courant* that he had set up as a glass-painter in Colliergate, York.

Claims that Peckitt was taught by the glass-painter Henry Gyles (d. 1709) of Micklegate, York, are unfounded. Nor is there support for further claims that he was taught glass painting in London by William Price the younger (d. 1765), or that he was trained as a carver and gilder by his father-in-law, Charles Mitley of York. Mitley had died five years before Peckitt married his daughter Mary (1743–1826) on 3 April 1763, and twelve years after Peckitt declared himself a glass-painter. The declaration in Peckitt's trade notice that he had discovered the art 'by many experiments' was repeated in his letter to the Free Society of Artists of London in 1760. He continued to experiment throughout his fifty-five years as a glass-painter. In 1780 he patented an invention 'for blending Coloured and Stained Glass' (patents no. 1268), and by 1793 he had compiled a manuscript, intended for publication, entitled 'The principles of introduction into that rare but fine and elegant art of painting and staining of glass'.

Peckitt's first recorded commission, in October 1751, was for armorials for the deanery at York. John Fountayne, dean of York from 1747 to 1802, remained Peckitt's greatest single patron, and employed Peckitt throughout his working life in the repair and restoration of York Minster's medieval glass. Before he died Peckitt bequeathed three glass paintings to the minster to be inserted in the south transept, alongside his *St Peter* (1768). These were: *Moses* (c.1774), *Abraham* (1780), and *Solomon* (1780) (York Minster). Peckitt also painted the east windows of Lincoln (1762) and Ripon (1791) cathedrals and the west window of Exeter Cathedral (1767) (all subsequently removed and

fragmented in lesser windows in the respective churches). At the same time he adorned with armorial glass the deaneries and episcopal palaces of York, Exeter, Lincoln, Peterborough, and Armagh. Peckitt's early work chiefly comprised heraldic and genealogical subjects, historical scenes and portraits, dogs, horses, and animals for nursery windows. He also restored old glass. It was a secular subject for York Guildhall, *York's Car of Justice* after Elkaniah Settle, which earned him the freedom of the city of York in 1754. Peckitt's patrons steadily increased and his work was in demand throughout the British Isles. He even secured a commission in France, probably through his connection with Horace Walpole, who turned to Peckitt to embellish Strawberry Hill following the retirement of William Price in 1760. Under that *arbiter elegantiorum* the growth of gothick taste brought added encouragement to Peckitt and the handful of his contemporaries who practised as glass-painters.

Peckitt's portraits on glass, such as *William III* and *William, Duke of Cumberland* (York City Art Gallery), were much admired and in 1761 the earl of Bute commissioned a portrait of George III. Peckitt's accomplishment in this genre is best represented by his self-portrait from his portrait in oils (c.1760) by Johan Schuster of Saxony (both York City Art Gallery). By contrast, his *Presentation of Christ in the Temple* (1767) at Oriel College, Oxford, displays weak colours and poor draughtsmanship, the cartoons being executed by Dr John Wall of the Worcester porcelain factory. His west window for the chapel of New College, Oxford (1765), depicting *Christ, the Virgin and the Twelve Apostles*, was also criticized for the want of good cartoons and was subsequently removed to the side windows of the chapel and replaced in 1787 by Thomas Jervais's *Nativity and the Seven Virtues* from cartoons by Sir Joshua Reynolds. Peckitt eventually employed two Italian draughtsmen who were among the founders of the Royal Academy, Biagio Rebecca and Giovanni Battista Cipriani. The former drew the cartoons for *The Adoration of the Magi* (1772) and *The Last Supper* (1771), which Peckitt painted for the Gothic chapel at Audley End, Essex. Rebecca also provided the cartoons for the *Twenty-Four Patriarchs and Prophets* which were inserted in three windows of New College chapel, Oxford (1774). Cipriani's cartoon was used for the allegorical window of the *Muse Presenting Sir Isaac Newton and Sir Francis Bacon to George III* (1775) (Trinity College Library, Cambridge).

Peckitt was a modest, private person devoted to his wife, who described him as 'a kind and affectionate husband and a pious Christian' (Mary Peckitt, epitaph), and their four daughters. In his last years he began to write and in 1794 published in York a religious tract entitled *The Wonderful Love of God to Man, or, Heaven Opened in Earth*. He died at his house at Friars' Walls, York, on 14 October 1795. His wife's last tribute to him was the execution and erection of his memorial window (1796) in the church of St Martin-cum-Gregory, York, where he was buried.

Though much of Peckitt's work was derided and removed during the Victorian Gothic revival, he helped keep the art of glass painting alive during the eighteenth century, and contributed to the revival of an acceptable post-Reformation hagiography in the Church of England.

L. H. Cust, *rev.* Trevor Brighton

Sources J. T. Brighton, 'The enamel glasspainters of York, 1585–1795', DPhil diss., University of York, 1978, vols. 2–3 · J. T. Brighton, 'William Peckitt's commission book', *Walpole Society*, 54 (1988), 334–453 · J. T. Brighton, 'William Peckitt, greatest of the Georgian glass painters', *York Georgian Society Annual Report* (1967–8), 14–24 · J. T. Brighton, 'Cartoons for York glass: William Peckitt', *York Art Gallery Quarterly*, 19 (Jan 1969), 779–83 · J. T. Brighton, 'William Peckitt and portraiture on glass', *York Art Gallery Quarterly*, 34 (Jan 1984), 3–11 · J. T. Brighton and B. Sprakes, 'Medieval and Georgian stained glass in Oxford and Yorkshire', *Antiquaries Journal*, 70 (1990), 380–415 · J. T. Brighton and R. G. Newton, 'Peckitt's red glasses', *Stained Glass*, 81/3 (1986), 214–20 · J. T. Brighton and R. G. Newton, 'An interpretation of William Peckitt's 18th-century treatise on making glasses and the stains for them', *Glass Technology*, 30/1 (1989), 33–8 · J. T. Brighton, 'Reformation and post-Reformation stained glass in Britain', *The painter in glass*, ed. A. Lloyd (1992) · J. A. Knowles, 'William Peckitt: glass painter of York', *Walpole Society*, 17 (1928–9), 45–59 · J. A. Knowles, 'William Peckitt: glass painter', *Yorkshire Architectural and York Archaeological Society Annual Report* (1953–4), 99–114 · MS pedigree of Peckitt, York City Art Gallery · parish register, St Helen's, York, 3/4/1765 [marriage]

Archives BL · Essex RO, Southend, Audley End library · Exeter Cathedral · FM Cam. · Lincoln Castle · Lincoln Cathedral, fabric accounts · LMA · New College, Oxford, muniments · Patents Office, London, invention for blending coloured and stained glass, 1780, no. 1268 · Ripon Minster · RSA · U. Nott. · York City Archives, MSS, drawings, etc., E95/1696, B43/174, ACC/28/28 · York City Art Gallery, MSS, drawings, etc., Box D3 · York City Library, family Bible and books, Y927.48 · York Minster · Yorkshire Philosophical Museum, York, glass and corresp. with V&A | Bodl. Oxf., corresp. with John Charles Brooke

Likenesses W. Peckitt, self-portrait, glass, after 1760 (after J. Schuster, *c.*1760), York City Art Gallery · J. Schuster, oils, *c.*1760, York City Art Gallery · J. Stordy, miniature, *c.*1780, York City Art Gallery · miniature, *c.*1790, York City Art Gallery · J. R. Smith, engraving

Wealth at death approx. £3815—in houses, glass materials, books, MSS, etc.: will, Borth. Inst.

Peckover, Priscilla Hannah (1833–1931), peace campaigner, was born on 27 October 1833 in Wisbech, Cambridgeshire, third of the eight children of Algernon Peckover (1803–1893) and his wife, Priscilla (1803–1883). The Peckovers were a wealthy banking family, well established in the region; Priscilla's brother Alexander Peckover, first baronet (1830–1910), of Wisbech, was the first Quaker peer. Priscilla Peckover's education was predominantly private and included the mastering of several European languages. She devoted her youth and early middle age to raising the three daughters of the widowed Alexander, though she also worked among the poor, organized a Bible class for girls, and was active in the cause of temperance.

From a family who were long-time supporters of the Peace Society, Peckover began her own peace activities following the yearly meeting of the Society of Friends in 1875 when she discovered that the Quaker testimony against all war was to be addressed to women as well as men. She was put in touch with the Ladies' Auxiliary of the Peace Society and, finding that it had only two hundred members, went from door to door in her Bible district, adapting the technique developed from her temperance work to secure peace pledges from women. Her activism seems also to have been provoked by the Anglo-Afghan and Anglo-Zulu wars in which Britain was engaged in the late 1870s. The result was the founding by Peckover in 1879 of the Women's Local Peace Association (later renamed the Peace Union), which became the central association of a network of more than thirty local groups run mostly by Quaker women and which had affiliated groups in thirty-one foreign countries. In 1881 Peckover also founded the Wisbech Local Peace Association, the annual subscription of which was a penny so as to attract the widest possible membership. It has been cited as having 8000 members by 1914, though a large majority of these were associate members comprising all those involved in affiliated bodies such as chapels, Sunday schools, Primitive Methodist colleges, and railway missions. (The number of full members according to the 1900 report was 942, when the total membership was given as 6429.) As a means of communicating between branches of the Women's Local Peace Association, Peckover began in 1882 to edit and publish a quarterly journal, *Peace and Goodwill*, which combined her own Christian peace message with relevant excerpts from other publications.

Both the Peace Union and the Wisbech Local Peace Association were opposed to 'all war', as being 'contrary to the mind of Christ'. This stance was more explicit in its absolute pacifism than that of the Peace Society which, while reserving membership of its executive committee for absolute pacifists, asked its ordinary members simply to declare Christian opposition to war. Links between Peckover's organizations and the Peace Society—to which she was a generous contributor—were nevertheless strong.

Like other female Quaker peace activists of the period, including Ellen Robinson (1840–1912) and Mary Lamley Cooke (1841–1916), Peckover emphasized the importance of women to the peace cause, in particular their influence on children (for example, in her pamphlet *An Earnest Appeal to All Women, Everywhere*). The internationalism of the peace movement was also central to Peckover's activity: she financed continental peace groups, translated European peace literature into English (she learnt Danish for the specific purpose of translating peace pamphlets), and conducted correspondence with European peace activists. Peckover was also a regular attender at gatherings of the Universal Peace Congress, which took place most of the years between 1889 and 1913 having first been held in the mid-nineteenth century. She tended to view the familiar privileged social circle which met at these congresses as a microcosm of a wider internationalism, and was consequently convinced of the growing influence of the peace cause. Although she argued for international arbitration and disarmament, Peckover embodied an evangelical and educational rather than a political or pressure-group form of activism. Her greatest influence in the peace movement, alongside her financial input, was to represent Christian absolute pacifism at the Universal

Peace Congress, which was often dominated by continental, secular, and non-absolutist peace views. The First World War did nothing to shake Peckover's pacifism, though it reduced the membership of the Wisbech Local Peace Association by a half, and adherents continued to fall away during the 1920s.

Peckover was a minister and elder of her local Quaker meeting, known for her tolerance and her quiet sense of humour as well as for her thorough knowledge of the Bible. As president of the local Esperanto Society she was instrumental in having the Bible translated into Esperanto. She died a spinster at her home, Wistaria House, Wisbech, on 8 September 1931, while putting together what was to be the last edition of *Peace and Goodwill*.

PAUL LAITY

Sources Swarthmore College Peace Collection, Swarthmore, Pennsylvania, USA, Peckover MSS · 'Dictionary of Quaker biography', RS Friends, Lond. [card index] · P. H. Peckover, *Incidents in the rise and progress of the Wisbech Local Peace Association*, 2nd edn, 1925 (1906) · *Peace and Goodwill* (1882–1931) · *The Friend*, new ser., 71 (1931), 851–3 · *War Against War* (3 March 1899), 117 · P. H. Peckover, *An earnest appeal to all women, everywhere* [n.d.] · H. Josephson, ed., *Biographical dictionary of modern peace leaders* (1985), 736–8 · *CGPLA Eng. & Wales* (1931)
Archives Kongelige Bibliotek, Copenhagen, Bajer, Fredrik MSS · Swarthmore College Peace collection, Swarthmore, Pennsylvania, Peckover and Wisbech Local Peace Association MSS
Likenesses photograph, Friends House, London; repro. in *The Friend*, 851 · photograph, priv. coll.
Wealth at death £88,112 15s. 6d.: probate, 16 Oct 1931, *CGPLA Eng. & Wales*

Peckwell, Henry (*bap.* **1746**, *d.* **1787**), Church of England clergyman and Methodist preacher, was the son of Henry Peckwell (*d.* 1747) of Crane Street, Chichester, Sussex, of a Petworth family, variously described as a gentleman, victualler, innholder, and merchant, and Elizabeth, *née* Palmer (*d.* 1769), probably his second wife, and was baptized on 29 November 1746 at St Olave's Church, Chichester. About 1765 he entered the house of Samuel Lloyd, an Italian silk merchant in London, with the intention of representing the firm in Italy, but he became a regular attender at George Whitefield's Tabernacle and abandoned plans for a career in trade in favour of the ministry. He matriculated at St Edmund Hall, Oxford, on 17 May 1770, undeterred, like other evangelically minded young men, from going to the hall despite the expulsion of six students in February 1768 for their Methodist sympathies.

After ordination into the Church of England at Oxford in June 1772 Peckwell accepted the curacy of Winterbourne Gunner, Wiltshire, from the Revd Charles Coleman, but it was abruptly terminated after he had preached an evangelical sermon unacceptable to his patron. A curacy at St Martin's, Salisbury, lasted only slightly longer. Meanwhile Peckwell had attracted the notice of Selina, countess of Huntingdon, and soon gained a following as a popular itinerant preacher in south-eastern England within her connexion. Her influence on him was, for a while, paramount. On 23 February 1773 he married Isabella (Bella) Blosset (*d.* 1816) of co. Meath, from a minor gentry family of French Huguenot extraction, against her mother's initial opposition, because she had been recommended to him as a wife by Lady Huntingdon as 'an instrument to help you in your plan' (letter, 10 or 11 Feb 1772, Cheshunt collection, F1/1352). In April 1774 Peckwell assumed the leadership of the chapel in the New Way, Westminster, perhaps assuming much of the cost of repairing and opening the building himself. In the same year he also began a regular preaching schedule in the Mulberry Gardens, London, and was present at the opening of another chapel in his home town of Chichester. In August he preached the anniversary sermon at Lady Huntingdon's college at Trefeca, and he spoke in chapels as well as outdoors in Brighton, Maidstone, and Tunbridge Wells. His letters are full of fervent desires to serve: 'O that I could give up all for the Lord. I am a poor Disciple and all I can say is *I wish to follow Jesus*' (Seymour, 2.292).

Relations with Lady Huntingdon deteriorated in 1778 when Peckwell made it clear that he would rather leave the connexion than give up the Westminster chapel, that '… he would not be under the direction of any Committee or Person whatever, that he would, if employed in the connexion, go where he pleased & stay as long as he pleased' (Thomas Wills to Lady Huntingdon, 10 March 1778, Cheshunt collection, F1/1823). Although his ample patrimony meant he needed little patronage, he eventually accepted from Lord Robert Manners (whose wife was a regular correspondent of Lady Huntingdon) the rectory of Bloxholm-cum-Digby in Lincolnshire (presented 20 February 1782), which he retained until his death. He was also chaplain to the marchioness of Lothian.

About 1783 Peckwell travelled to Dublin. He delivered sermons at Lady Huntingdon's chapel in Plunket Street, Dublin, and other city churches and drew large congregations by dint of his electrifying preaching. Through the influence of Elizabeth Rawdon, countess of Moira, Lady Huntingdon's eldest daughter, he was permitted to preach in the chapel of the Magdalen Institution. However, his forthright sermons led to complaints from many members of this fashionable congregation. After an application was made requesting the archbishop of Dublin to curtail the spread of Methodism in the Church of Ireland, Peckwell crossed back to England.

Peckwell's last years, spent mainly in London, were distinguished as much for philanthropy as preaching. He was a member of the Humane Society and the Society for the Relief of Persons Imprisoned for Small Debts, and in 1784 he founded an institution called the Sick Man's Friend. It aimed to relieve the sick poor of all denominations, as well as supplying instruction. He studied medicine to make himself personally adept at this work, but died on 18 August 1787 at his house in Princes Street, Westminster, from the effects of pricking his hand while making a post-mortem examination of a consumptive. Mortification had spread too far to make amputation of the swollen limb possible, and his passing was 'regretted by thousands' (*GM*, 1787). He was buried in the church of St Peter the Great, Chichester, Sussex, on 23 August. Peckwell was well liked and respected for his combination of gifts. As one funeral eulogy put it: 'His heart was deeply impressed by, and had a powerful and sweet experience of those things of which his understanding had so clear a perception' (Townshend, 15). The sermons which he preached for the benefit of his charity produced as much as £400 p.a. for his widow, who died in her house in Wilmot Street, Brunswick Square, on 28 November 1816.

Peckwell published many sermons as well as *A Collection of Psalms and Hymns* (1774?). He had three children. His daughter, Selina Mary (named after her godmother, Lady Huntingdon), married George Grote the banker in 1793, and their son was George Grote the historian. His second son, **Sir Robert Henry Peckwell** [*later* Blosset] (*bap.* 1776, *d.* 1823), was baptized on 10 July 1776 at St Mary's Church, Marylebone. He matriculated at Christ Church, Oxford, on 23 October 1792, was awarded his BA in 1796 and MA in 1799, and became a barrister at Lincoln's Inn in 1801, and serjeant-at-law in 1809. He was deputy recorder of Cambridge, and a counsel on the Norfolk circuit. In 1822 he was knighted and appointed chief justice of Calcutta, where he died, unmarried, on 1 February 1823 after exercising his office for only two months. He took his mother's name of Blosset. He published *Cases of Controverted Elections in the Second Parliament of the United Kingdom*, 2 vols. (1804–6).

NIGEL ASTON

Sources *GM*, 1st ser., 57 (1787), 746, 834–5 · *GM*, 1st ser., 86/2 (1816), 568 · *GM*, 1st ser., 93/2 (1823), 83 · Foster, *Alum. Oxon.* · J. N. D. Kelly, *St Edmund Hall: almost seven hundred years* (1989), 62–6 · J. S. Reynolds, *The evangelicals at Oxford, 1735–1871: a record of an unchronicled movement* (1953) · *Copies of the letters which passed between the Rev. Mr Coleman and Mr Peckwell concerning the curacy of Winterbourn* [n.d., 1772?] · [A. C. H. Seymour], *The life and times of Selina, countess of Huntingdon*, 2 (1840), 77, 121, 169, 196–200, 293, 295, 303, 335, 339, 469 · H. Grote, *The personal life of George Grote* (1873), 5 · *A plain narrative of the much lamented death of the Rev. Henry Peckwell*, The Sick Man's Friend, 2nd edn (1790) · J. Townshend, *A sermon preached at Orange-Street Chapel, Leicester-Fields, on Sunday, 26 August 1787, occasion'd by the much lamented death of the Rev. Henry Peckwell, DD* (1787) · Westminster College, Cambridge, Cheshunt collection · presentation deeds, Lincs. Arch., Lincolnshire diocesan archives, PD138/13 · parish register, Sussex, Chichester, St Olave's, 29 Nov 1746 [baptism] · parish register, Sussex, Chichester, St Peter the Great, 23 Aug 1787 [burial] · C. H. Crookshank, *History of Methodism in Ireland*, 1 (1885), 266 · E. Welch, *Spiritual pilgrim: a reassessment of the life of the countess of Huntingdon* (1995) · private information (2004) [M. E. Chaney]

Archives Westminster College, Cambridge, Cheshunt Foundation, corresp. with Selina, countess of Huntingdon

Likenesses R. Houston, mezzotint, pubd 1774 (after J. Russell), BM · J. Fittler, line engraving, pubd 1787 (after R. Bowyer), BM, NPG · T. Trotter, line engraving, 1787, BM, NPG

Peckwell, Sir Robert Henry (*bap.* 1776, *d.* 1823). *See under* Peckwell, Henry (*bap.* 1746, *d.* 1787).

Pecock, Reginald (*b. c.*1392, *d.* in or after 1459), bishop of Chichester and religious author, was born in Wales, probably about 1392, and as a young man was associated with the diocese of St David's. There is, however, no evidence to support the tradition that he was born at Laugharne, Dyfed.

Early career in Oxford and London Pecock was a fellow of Oriel College, Oxford, by December 1414. He must have achieved the degree of BA by then, and so was almost certainly studying at Oxford during at least part of the period 1407–11 when Archbishop Thomas Arundel (*d.* 1414) attempted to inhibit free discussion of theological issues in the university. Arundel's action was part of a strategy designed to counter the spread of heretical doctrines associated with John Wyclif (*d.* 1384) and his Lollard followers. In 1411 fellows of Oriel were divided between support for and resistance to Arundel. In an election for provost in 1417 Pecock voted with Henry Kayll and John Martill, fellows who had supported Arundel. Also voting with this group was John Carpenter (*d.* 1476), later bishop of Worcester and an important future ally. In 1417–18 Pecock paid for the hire of schools from Stapledon Hall (Exeter College), Oxford, probably in connection with fulfilling academic requirements for the degree of master of arts. He was awarded the degrees of MA and BTh, and is last recorded at Oriel on 31 July 1424. He received from Oxford University the degree of DTh about 1445, apparently being exempted from the academic requirements for the degree, according to Thomas Gascoigne, a full but very hostile source. In his *Liber de veritatibus*, Gascoigne described him as having had a leprous appearance that reflected his 'mental leprosy', that is, his heresy.

While at Oriel, Pecock went rapidly through all the various stages of ordination between 21 December 1420 and 8 March 1421. His first benefice was the rectory of St Michael's Church, Gloucester, to which he was admitted on 25 October 1424 by the presentation of St Peter's Abbey, Gloucester. Possibly he resided in the rectory house in Eastgate Street. There is no evidence for the tradition in modern biography that Pecock secured the patronage of Humphrey, duke of Gloucester (*d.* 1447), on leaving Oxford. On the contrary, it may be significant that Pecock's first benefice was in the diocese of Philip Morgan, bishop of Worcester (*d.* 1435), who, like Pecock, was an Oxford graduate from St David's.

Pecock resigned the rectorship of St Michael's on 1 September 1431, in order to become master of Whittington College, a London college of priests founded in 1424 by the executors of Sir Richard Whittington, mercer and mayor of London. Thereby Pecock also became rector of the church of St Michael Paternoster Royal, which was served by the college. The appointment came when the college was still in the process of foundation. The college was supervised by Whittington's chief executor John Carpenter, common clerk of London, until his death in 1442, when governance passed to the Mercers' Company. Possibly Pecock had come to his notice through the agency of his Oriel College ally, also called John Carpenter. The two namesakes were certainly associates and may have been kinsmen. It must, however, have been the London John Carpenter who oversaw and approved Pecock's appointment.

By 1443 Pecock was a feoffee in a transaction of land associated with the foundation of a new chapel and hospital dedicated to the Virgin Mary and the Nine Orders of Angels at Isleworth, Middlesex. The instigator of this project was John Somerset (*d.* 1454), physician and chancellor of the exchequer to Henry VI. In 1446, moreover, Pecock became a founder member of an associated fraternity whose objective was to set up a perpetual chantry for Henry VI, Queen Margaret, and the founders. Pecock's associates in this venture were prominent in court, church, and city circles, and included the influential London clerics William Lichefield and Peter Hynford (probably Hyrford), Nicholas Ashby, bishop of Llandaff, John Somerset, and John Colop and Richard Hakeday, both of whom, like Pecock, were associates of John Carpenter, common clerk.

Early writings and controversies Despite Arundel's efforts to eradicate the Wycliffite heresy early in the century, Lollards were present in London when Pecock became master at Whittington. London may have been a centre for Lollard book production, particularly the area around St Paul's, close by Pecock's parish. Pecock was aware that the heretics circulated books among themselves, particularly the Bible and theological works in English. He studied Lollard doctrine in order to refute it. Grasping the importance Lollards placed on the written word, especially on vernacular writings, he decided to try to counter the heresy by composing and circulating vernacular books of his own. This was a different strategy from that of Arundel, who had prohibited the discussion of theological questions in the vernacular, and it made Pecock vulnerable to prosecution himself.

While he was at Whittington College, Pecock worked on some of the theological works which were to be examined at his heresy trial. He wrote part of *The Reule of Crysten Religioun* in 1443 (New York, Pierpont Morgan Library MS 519; ed. W. C. Greet, EETS, o.s. 171, 1927). He also wrote part of *The Repressor of Over Much Blaming of the Clergy* (CUL, MS Kk.4.26; ed. C. Babington, Rolls Series, 19, 1860) while at Whittington, and probably some or all of *The Donet* (Bodl. Oxf., MS Bodley 916; ed. E. V. Hitchcock, EETS, o.s. 156, 1921), an offshoot of *The Reule*. He records that he often worked on several books at once, and it is clear from the surviving texts that he was a habitual self-citer and cross-referencer. These aspects of his practice of composition make it difficult to date or even sequence his works.

In 1441 Pecock was nominated in the will of the London John Carpenter, together with William Lichefield, to choose books for the Guildhall Library (another of the Whittington charities) from the testator's private collection. His interest in providing books for those of limited financial means is attested by the survival of his *Poore Mennis Myrrour* (BL, Add. MS 37788; part edited in E. V. Hitchcock, *The Donet*), a digest of *The Donet* intended for those of modest means and education, though there is no evidence that it circulated widely. He shared these interests with John Colop, who developed a scheme for circulating books for 'common-profit'.

Pecock's interest in the circulation of theological writings, like his own prolific output, was motivated by his conviction that reasoned expositions of Christianity in English could counter the spread of heterodox ideas in Lollard books. He may have known some Lollards personally, and may have chosen to debate with them rather than to prosecute them. In his late work *The Book of Faith* (Cambridge, Trinity College, MS B.14.45; ed. J. L. Morison,

Reginald Pecock's Book of Faith, 1909), he claimed to have engaged in debate with important members of the sect. He also claimed that his writings had been read by some Lollards. In *The Repressor* he wrote that he had conducted an inquiry into personal and sexual morality among Lollards, in order to expose the hypocrisy of their claims to honest living.

Bishop of St Asaph and Chichester Pecock's tenure at Whittington College ended when he was provided to the see of St Asaph on 22 April 1444. The temporalities of the see were transferred to him on 8 June, and he was enthroned bishop at Croydon on 14 June 1444. Gascoigne wrote that he was promoted through the influence of secular lords. Pecock's involvement with John Somerset's foundation of a chapel under royal patronage, and his connection with John Carpenter of Oriel, also an associate of Somerset's and at one time clerk and chaplain to the king, may have provided an entry for Pecock into royal spheres of influence and thus made him a candidate for a see.

It appears that Pecock was largely an absentee bishop, continuing to reside in London. There is no firm evidence that he visited his diocese. The bishop's palace and houses, burned by Owen Glyn Dŵr in 1402, had still not been rebuilt. It appears that he continued to pursue his interests in London. These included mounting a defence of absentee bishops who (like himself) did not preach to their flocks in their dioceses. Probably in 1447, he delivered a sermon at Paul's Cross in London, arguing that prelates were not obliged to preach in their own dioceses, but that their duties did involve explicating complex points of doctrine. Afterwards he distributed his conclusions in English on this and the other contentious matter of bishops' payment of first-fruits.

Traditionally the butt of anti-clerical criticism, absentee bishops were a particularly sensitive issue during this period, when court prelates such as Adam Moleyns (d. 1450) were the targets of anti-Lancastrian action. By seeming to defend such bishops Pecock became vulnerable to popular anti-clericalism. Controversy ensued, including the charge that his conclusions were heretical, and as a consequence Pecock appeared before Archbishop John Stafford of Canterbury (d. 1452), threatening to sue his opponents for defamation. A record of the statement that Pecock made to Stafford has survived as the *Abrenunciacio Reginaldi Pecok* in the notebook of William Mede, monk at the Charterhouse at Sheen (Bodl. Oxf., MS Bodley 177, fols. 11–13r; part edited under the erroneous title *Abbreviatio Reginaldi Pecok* in C. Babington, *The Repressor*, 2.615–9).

Pecock explained that his motive had been to defend bishops against undue criticism. Gascoigne, keen to associate Pecock with unpopular court bishops, claimed that Pecock sent copies of his conclusions to Walter Lyhert, bishop of Norwich (d. 1472), Adam Moleyns, bishop of Chichester, and the papal subdeacon Vincent Clement. Pecock said that he believed he had the support of bishops, and if Gascoigne's testimony is correct, it is possible that Pecock expected Moleyns and Lyhert to use their influence at court, and the papal subdeacon to support his defence of bishops' payments of first-fruits to the pope.

Pecock said that he was only prepared to recognize opposition presented in academic form. Indeed, his opponents as named by Gascoigne were highly educated, graduate clerics: William Millington, Thomas Eborall, John Burbach, Hugh Damlett, Gilbert Worthington, William Lichefield, and Peter Hyrford. As well as sharing opposition to Pecock, several of them held powerful positions as rectors of London churches (Eborall was Pecock's successor at Whittington College), and some were involved with new educational and religious foundations. Pecock apparently preached on the issue again in 1449, and instigated a preaching campaign in his diocese.

While bishop of St Asaph, Pecock continued to be associated with a network of powerful courtiers and London citizens, particularly through transactions associated with the foundation dedicated to the Nine Orders of Angels. Such connections may be sufficient to explain his provision to the see of Chichester by a bull of Pope Nicholas V (r. 1447–55) dated 23 March 1450. When he was enthroned as bishop of Chichester on 31 May 1450, he became one of very few Welsh clerics to hold English sees in the fifteenth century. The vacancy had arisen because the previous incumbent, Adam Moleyns, the unpopular associate of the disgraced William de la Pole, duke of Suffolk, had just been murdered. The view that William de la Pole was one of Pecock's patrons at this time was retailed later by Pecock's enemies, Gascoigne in particular. There is no evidence to support it. However, this representation of Pecock as one of a corrupt circle against whom popular feeling was legitimately strong was an important element in his downfall.

No register survives either from Pecock's time as bishop of St Asaph or from his tenure of Chichester. The fact that the authorities later suspected that Pecock's writings might be circulating in the latter diocese suggests that Pecock may have been more involved in affairs in the diocese of Chichester than he had been in those of St Asaph. However, as bishop of Chichester, Pecock continued to write. He was at work on part of *The Folewer to the Donet*, a sequel to *The Donet* (BL, Royal MS 17 D.ix; ed. E. V. Hitchcock, EETS, o.s. 164, 1924) about 1453, when he wrote a passage that suggests that the controversy over non-preaching bishops was still not concluded. According to Gascoigne, Pecock was brought before John Kemp (archbishop of Canterbury, 1452–4) to defend his conclusions. Gascoigne also claimed that Pecock returned to the theme in a letter to the Franciscan friar William Goddard, in which Pecock called modern preachers 'pulpit-bawlers'.

Accusations of heresy As bishop of Chichester, Pecock attracted the suspicion of authorities outside the church, and his activities and opinions were brought to the attention of the crown. On one occasion, according to Gascoigne, an unnamed Oxford scholar, convicted of heresy, confessed to William, abbot of Abingdon, that he had learned all his heresies from Pecock, and Pecock's friends were obliged to protest his innocence to the king. In another incident, in 1456, Pecock reputedly wrote a letter to Thomas Canynges, mayor of London, that was forwarded to the king. Allegedly Pecock claimed that he and

his English books had adherents among the magnates of the kingdom. His letter was thought to manifest an undermining of the faith and insurrection in the kingdom, and Pecock was expelled from the council chamber.

John Beaumont, Viscount Beaumont (d. 1460), also wrote to Henry VI about Pecock, probably in 1457. In a letter that survives in the register of Richard Asshton, abbot of Peterborough, he said that it was rumoured that the bishop of Chichester was imprinting pernicious doctrines against the faith in men's hearts, and he urged the king to demand that the archbishop of Canterbury and his fellow prelates should commission university scholars to investigate Pecock's writings. Beaumont—appointed Queen Margaret's steward while Henry VI was suffering from a bout of insanity, Prince Edward was an infant, and the queen feared that Richard, duke of York (d. 1460), might seek to claim the throne—was probably acting in Margaret's interests. He may have thought that action against an unpopular prelate would help to restore royal authority. Pecock was an ideal target, both because he had himself attracted anti-clerical feeling, and also because he had tried to repress criticism of bishops in ways which appeared to compromise the authority and teachings of the church. In his letter to the king Beaumont represented the exceptional act of prosecuting a bishop for heresy as a measure that would devolve to the honour, authority, and long continuance of the Lancastrian dynasty. This suggests that an important motive behind Pecock's prosecution was the political one of bolstering the position of the Lancastrian dynasty.

Trial and conviction The process of examining Pecock's writings had begun by October 1457, by when Pecock had delivered certain of his English works to Archbishop Thomas Bourchier (d. 1486). The suspect texts were English and Latin writings which had been in circulation over the previous two decades or more. Pecock declined to stand by earlier, uncorrected works that had gone into circulation, guaranteeing only those written in the previous three years. He submitted for examination nine books which had evidently been recently revised. During this process Pecock complained to Bourchier that many were preaching and teaching that the views expressed in his books were heretical. Opposition had been expressed at Paul's Cross in London and throughout the province of Canterbury, even though the case was *sub judice*. On 22 October 1457 Bourchier issued a citation to all the clergy in his province, calling Pecock's accusers to make their case before himself, and to desist otherwise from public comment.

The most substantial survival from the examination of Pecock's writings is John Bury's *Gladius Salomonis*, a refutation of the first book of Pecock's *Repressor*. Bury addressed his work to Bourchier and marked it for the attention of John Lowe, bishop of Rochester (d. 1467), described as the archbishop's calm and stalwart companion in troubled times. On 11 November 1457 the masters of Oxford University requested the opportunity to examine Pecock's works, and asked for inspection copies. Pecock had allegedly asked for his works to be examined by his academic equals, but the masters' request need not be seen as the public support that he may have hoped for from the university, so much as a calculation of political self-interest on their own part. In a general procession in Oxford, on 17 December 1457, Pecock's books were denounced, and perhaps even burnt, before the chancellor, Thomas Chaundler (d. 1490).

The process of examining Pecock's writings concluded with the formulation of a list of heresies which Pecock was given the opportunity to abjure. In late November or early December 1457 he appeared before Bourchier and other bishops, and admitted to and revoked his heresies and errors in a signed statement. He then made a public recantation of his heresies in English at Paul's Cross and committed his books to a fire.

The details of the heresies vary in the sources. All copies of the recantation record two points of heresy concerning the authority of the church: that the church could err in matters of faith, and that Christians need not hold to the determinations of a general council of the church on matters of faith. Four other points, not attested in all sources, relate to the apostles' creed. These were that it was not necessary to believe in Christ's descent into hell; in the Holy Ghost; in the holy Catholic church; and in the communion of saints. A seventh point is attested in the *Registrum abbatiae Johannis Whethamstede* only, that it was not necessary to believe in any other sense of scripture than the literal sense. John Foxe cites a point not attested in the medieval sources, that it was not necessary to believe in the materiality of the body of Christ in the sacrament. The heresies listed have the appearance of travesties of some of Pecock's statements in *The Book of Faith*, rather than being genuine points of theological heterodoxy. There is no record that Pecock attempted to contest the charges.

Loss of episcopal see It is possible that Pecock thought it advisable to accept the offer of recantation, believing that once he had abjured he would be allowed to resume his bishopric. Bourchier may have indicated as much. Indeed, after Pecock's recantation the archbishop sent John Stokes, bishop of Ely, to absolve him and restore him to his see. This was ratified on 13 June 1458 in a bull of Pope Calixtus III (r. 1455–8). The evidence suggests that the crown opposed his reinstatement, supporting the view that Pecock's prosecution served Lancastrian political interests. A letter sent to Bourchier in the king's name, dated 17 September 1458, claimed that the bull was contrary to the Statute of Provisors and the royal prerogative. The archbishop was commanded to convene a meeting to consider the legal redress available to the crown. Thomas Bird, Pecock's successor in the see of St Asaph, Robert Stillington, a canon of Wells, Hugh Damlett, Pecock's long-standing opponent, and other doctors of divinity or law numbering about twenty in total, recommended that the king should request Pecock's removal from Chichester on the grounds that his translation to the see in 1450 had been void because he had been a heretic at that time. On 27 September 1458 the crown offered Pecock a pension on condition that he would renounce his claim to his see. If he did not, an appeal would be made to Rome. Probably Pecock refused. On 8 January 1459 Pope Pius II (r. 1458–64) provided John Arundel (d. 1477), the king's physician and chaplain, to the see of Chichester, which was considered vacant because Pecock had been a heretic when translated to the see.

Attempted destruction of writings Meanwhile the church authorities were seeking out any adherents of Pecock and copies of his works. Thomas Bourchier asked all bishops in the province of Canterbury to search for and seize any books by Pecock, and to note the names of their owners. Two of Pecock's alleged adherents, Thomas Lempster and John Harlowe, were casualties. In both cases the influence of the crown in the process against them is apparent.

After his recantation Pecock came under suspicion of hiding his writings for posterity. In response to the concerns expressed by the crown and certain nobles and prelates, Pius II issued a mandate on 7 April 1459 ordering an investigation into the alleged concealment of the books by Pecock and others. If Pecock was found to be concealing his works he should be sent to Rome for punishment or, if it was not possible to punish him in this way, he should be deprived of all the trappings of the episcopal order. It is clear from the pope's mandate that the authorities sought to extinguish Pecock's influence by taking his writings out of circulation.

Archbishop Bourchier issued a warning to adherents and put in hand, under the close eye of the crown, the final arrangements for depriving Pecock of the status of bishop. Pecock was sent to Thorney Abbey near Peterborough. On Bourchier's instructions he was to be assigned a private chamber and was to be allowed no visitors unless they were authorized by the king or archbishop. The only books he was to be allowed were service books, a psalter, a legendary, and a Bible. He was not permitted to have writing materials. In all likelihood he died at Thorney, in or shortly after 1459.

The attempts to eradicate Pecock's literary influence were evidently partially successful. From references in his extant writings and in the prosecution documents it appears that Pecock wrote many works that have not survived (a list of works presumed lost is provided by Green, 238–45). Apart from the six books mentioned above only a few fragments are extant: the material related to the preaching scandal in the *Abrenunciacio Reginaldi Pecok*, and extracts apparently from *The Boke of Sygnes* printed by John Foxe, *Commentarii rerum*, 1, fols. 199v–200r. Pecock's correspondence with William Goddard is last recorded in the seventeenth century. Nevertheless, one of the most remarkable achievements of Pecock's career is the sheer volume of what has survived. Despite the zealous campaign against him, his six surviving works comprise an extant *œuvre* larger than that of any other identified author of original Middle English prose.

Explanation for downfall Convicted of heresy on the evidence of his writings, Pecock became the only bishop before the Reformation to lose his see as a heretic. The explanation for Pecock's downfall has been a matter for debate. The tradition in modern historiography that he was a victim of a Yorkist plot because he was an associate of William de la Pole, duke of Suffolk, yielded to the view that the motive for his prosecution was theological rather than political. Both interpretations have been challenged in the light of Beaumont's letter and other prosecution documents (preserved in Bodl. Oxf., MS Ashmole 789), which reveal that the impetus came from the crown. In this interpretation the Lancastrian dynasty saw the prosecution of Pecock as an opportunity to restore its royal authority by directing powerful anti-clerical feeling to its own ends. WENDY SCASE

Sources W. Scase, 'Reginald Pecock', *Authors of the middle ages*, 3 (1996), 69–146 · E. F. Jacob, 'Reynold Pecock, bishop of Chichester', *PBA*, 37 (1951), 121–53 · T. Kelly, 'Reginald Pecock: a contribution to his biography', MA diss., Manchester, 1945 · T. Gascoigne, *Loci e libro veritatum*, ed. J. E. Thorold Rogers (1881) · H. T. Riley, ed., *Registra quorundam abbatum monasterii S. Albani*, 1, Rolls Series, 28/6 (1872) · J. Bury, 'Gladius Salomonis', in R. Pecock, *The repressor of over much blaming of the clergy*, ed. C. Babington, 2, Rolls Series, 19 (1860), 567–613 · J. Foxe, *Commentarii rerum in ecclesia gestarum* (1554) · register of Richard Asshton, abbot of Peterborough, CUL, Peterborough cathedral library, dean and chapter MS 2 · V. H. H. Green, *Bishop Reginald Pecock* (1945)

Archives BL, Add. MS 37788 · BL, Royal MS 17 D.ix · Bodl. Oxf., MS Ashmole 789 · Bodl. Oxf., MSS Bodley 916; 177, fols. 11–13*r* · CUL, MS Kk.4.26 · Morgan L., MS 519 · Trinity Cam., MS B.14.45

Pecthelm. *See* Pehthelm (*d*. 735).

Pectwin. *See* Pehtwine (*d*. 776/7).

Pedder, John (*c*.1520–1571), dean of Worcester, was born in Suffolk and educated at Cambridge, where he graduated BA in 1538, subsequently proceeding MA in 1542 and BTh in 1552. Having embraced protestantism, he went abroad on Queen Mary's accession in 1553. In 1554 he was at Strasbourg, and supported Grindal in his advocacy of the prayer book of the Church of England. But when, three years later, he was a member of the Frankfurt congregation, he took the side of the main body, the 'Knoxian' or Calvinistic church members, in the disputes as to discipline.

On his return to England at Elizabeth's accession, Pedder became chaplain to Sir Nicholas Bacon, lord keeper from 22 December 1558. In that position he was very influential in recommending candidates to Bacon for lesser crown patronage. On 27 December 1559 he was installed dean of Worcester, succeeding the Catholic Seth Holland, who was imprisoned. Pedder was already prebendary of the sixth stall at Norwich Cathedral and rector of Redgrave in Suffolk, positions he owed to Bacon. He resigned Redgrave on 24 February 1560. On 26 September 1561 he was collated to the vicarage of Snitterfield, Warwickshire, and on 15 May 1563 to a prebend at Hereford, which he retained until death. He resigned his Norwich prebend on 24 February. Cecil's memoranda show that Pedder was considered for appointment as a bishop, but he was never raised to the episcopacy.

Pedder attended the lower house of convocation in 1563 and subscribed the articles in February that year, although he also approved of and voted for the six articles propounding certain alterations in the rites and ceremonies (13 February 1563). In addition, he supported the twenty-one 'requests' in which the lower house of convocation petitioned for changes in the articles, liturgy, and discipline.

Pedder's stipend as dean was £133 6*s*. 8*d*. at a time when the cathedral's total receipts amounted to about £1200 a year. During an investigation of abuses in 1587 the sexton, Henry Hymbleton, said that at the beginning of Elizabeth's reign the plate and jewels remaining at the cathedral were removed by Pedder and the then prebendaries 'and devided amongst them, but to what use they did employ the same' he could not tell. 'And the Copes, Vestments, and suche ornamentes were converted, some of them to the making of Cushens, and to some suche other uses belonging to the Churche, and the rest thereof converted, he knoweth not to what uses' (articles of complaint concerning church estates, 1587, Worcester Cathedral Library, MS A.25).

Pedder died in 1571, between 7 April, when he drew up his will, and 4 May, when his successor was appointed, and was buried in the south transept of Worcester Cathedral, where a monument to his memory was later erected by Arthur Lake, dean of Worcester between 1608 and 1616. Its inscription recorded his exile under Mary and return under Elizabeth. His will shows him to have been a leaseholder of secular and ecclesiastical property on a modest scale in Gloucestershire and Worcestershire. His principal beneficiaries were his brother and sister; he also made bequests to the son and daughter of his (unnamed) deceased wife, in terms which show that she had been a widow when she married Pedder.

W. A. SHAW, *rev.* STANFORD LEHMBERG

Sources accounts, Worcester Cathedral Library · articles of complaint concerning church estates, 1587, Worcester Cathedral Library, MS A.25 · C. H. Garrett, *The Marian exiles: a study in the origins of Elizabethan puritanism* (1938) · W. P. Haugaard, *Elizabeth and the English Reformation: the struggle for a stable settlement of religion* (1968) · BL, Lansdowne MS 443 · will, PRO, PROB 11/53, fol. 226*r*–*v* · *Fasti Angl.*, 1541–1857, [Ely] · Cooper, *Ath. Cantab.*, vol. 1 · J. Strype, *Annals of the Reformation and establishment of religion … during Queen Elizabeth's happy reign*, new edn, 2 (1824) · W. Dugdale, *The antiquities of Warwickshire illustrated* (1656)

Likenesses monument, Worcester Cathedral

Wealth at death see will, PRO, PROB 11/53, fol. 226*r*–*v*

Peddie, James (1759–1845), minister of the Secession church, was born in Perth on 10 February 1759, the only surviving son of James Peddie, brewer, and his second wife, Ann Rattray. He was educated at the grammar school in Perth, spending some time with a private tutor before attending Perth Academy. At fifteen he joined a local religious society which met for prayer and scripture reading. In 1775 Peddie entered Edinburgh University, where he was influenced by the moral philosophers Adam Ferguson and Dugald Stewart. Two years later he left the university to attend the Secession Divinity Hall in Haddington where John Brown (1722–1787) had been appointed the theological tutor. Prompted by Locke's thinking on religious toleration Peddie began to question the statement from the Westminster confession of faith concerning the power of the civil magistrate in enforcing religion on society. Peddie was licensed as preacher of the gospel on 6 February 1782 and became minister of the Bristo Street meeting-house, Edinburgh, on 3 April the following year. His election came after a period of considerable controversy within the congregation which eventually divided, the minority building a second church in Rose Street in 1786. Peddie remained as minister of Bristo Street for the remainder of his life.

In May 1795 a proposal came before the synod permitting ministers to disagree with the Westminster confession's statement concerning the power of civil magistrates in religious matters. The Enlightenment ethos, with its encouragement of the right to freedom of enquiry and conscience, led many within the Secession movement to object to civil government's association with a single form of Christian faith. Peddie and other leading theologians of the New Light school advocated this liberal view. In 1799 the synod allowed ministers and elders to adopt divergent opinions on the issue at their ordination, although a minority of Old Light supporters broke away to form the Original Burgher Presbytery until it was united with the Church of Scotland in 1839.

In 1799 the Church of Scotland minister William Porteous accused the New Light Associate Synod of adopting principles of freedom and liberty that were influenced by the French Revolution. Peddie responded to Porteous in his *A Defence of the Associate Synod Against the Charge of Sedition*, which gained much praised from Dugald Stewart for its clarity and vigour, and as one of the 'most masterly pieces of classical sarcasm in our language' (J. Kay, *A Review of Original Portraits and Caricature Etchings*, ed. H. Paton, 2 vols., 1838, 2.352). Peddie also communicated his defence of the synod to the prime minister, William Pitt, with the effect that Henry Dundas expressed his confidence in the patriotism of these 'loyal citizens'. This defence of the synod followed several earlier publications for which Peddie had also been commended. In November 1788 he preached two sermons on the anniversary of the revolution of 1688 which praised the events of 1688–9 for delivering the nation from civil oppression, ecclesiastical tyranny, and 'popish superstition'. Both sermons were published a year later as *The Revolution the Work of God, and a Cause of Joy*. John Erskine, leader of the popular party of the Church of Scotland, claimed that of all the commentaries on the centenary of the revolution only Peddie's 'pleased my taste' (Erskine to Charles Nisbet, 21 April 1789, in S. Miller, *Memoir of the Rev. Charles Nisbet*, New York, 1840, 196). However, Peddie's stance also put him at odds with some Anti-Burgher seceders, such as Archibald Bruce, who believed that churches should not celebrate secular events. A prolific author, Peddie's other significant titles include *The Perpetuity, Advantages, and Universality of the Christian Religion* (1796), *Jehovah's Care to Perpetuate the Redeemer's Name* (1809), and *A Practical Exposition of the Book of Jonah* (1842). Between 1797 and 1802 Peddie was also an editor of the *Christian Magazine*, to which he was a regular contributor.

In a ministry spanning sixty years Peddie served as moderator of the Associate Synod in 1789 and, following the formation of the United Secession church (1820), once more in 1825. In line with the general expansion of the secession movement, the Bristo Street congregation increased in numbers and erected a larger building in 1804.

Although a member of a seceding denomination, Peddie was associated with many missionary, educational, and social enterprises. In 1791 he became treasurer of a fund to assist impoverished clergy in rural parishes, a position he held for forty-five years. In conjunction with Gavin Struthers, minister of the Relief church in Edinburgh, he formed the Edinburgh Subscription Library in November 1794. In the following year he supported the founding of the London Missionary Society, acting as a secretary to its Edinburgh auxiliary, as well as being a co-founder of the Scottish Missionary Society, established in February 1796. A year on he established a fund to provide for widows of dissenting ministers in Scotland. In 1818 he was awarded an honorary DD by Marischal College, Aberdeen.

Peddie was twice married: first, in 1787, to Margaret (*d.* 1792), the eldest daughter of the Revd George Coventry of Stichill, Roxburghshire, and second, in 1795, to Barbara, a daughter of Donald Smith, lord provost of Edinburgh, with whom he had nine children, including **William Peddie** (1805–1893), minister of the United Presbyterian church, who was born on 15 September 1805 in Edinburgh. William was educated at Crichton Street School, the high school in Edinburgh, and later at the university before entering the Secession Divinity Hall in Glasgow, where he was tutored by John Dick. He was licensed to preach the gospel in May 1827 and became his father's colleague at Bristo Street in October 1828.

James Peddie died in Edinburgh on 11 October 1845 and was buried at Warriston cemetery on 17 October. Thereafter William became the sole pastor of the congregation where, like his father, he remained for the rest of his life. In 1846 he published an edition of his father's *Discourses*, with a memoir, while himself serving as an editor of the *United Presbyterian Magazine*. A moderator of the United Presbyterian church in 1855, William Peddie had become an honorary DD from Jefferson College, Pennsylvania, in 1843. He died on 23 February 1893 and was buried in Edinburgh.   KENNETH B. E. ROXBURGH

Sources DNB · J. Thin, *Memorials of Bristo United Presbyterian church* (1888) · W. Peddie, 'Memoir', in *Discourses by the late Rev. James Peddie* (1846) · *United Presbyterian Magazine*, 10 (1893), 181

Likenesses J. Kay, caricatures, two etchings, 1791, BM, NPG · Ridley, stipple, pubd 1809 (after Branwhite), NPG · J. Kay, caricature, etching, 1810, BM, NPG · J. Ramage, line engraving (after G. Watson), NPG

Peddie, James Mortimer [Jim], **Baron Peddie** (1905–1978), co-operative movement activist and politician, was born on 4 April 1905 in Hull, one of the six sons of Crofton Peddie, a colour-works labourer, and his wife, Ethel, *née* Whisker. He was educated at St Paul's Church of England School and Hull Municipal College, and then studied at the London School of Economics, where he took day and evening classes on the general course in 1927–8, supporting himself by part-time night work. He returned to Hull to work as a lecturer in economics at Hull Technical College and then as a lecturer in economics and industrial administration at Hull College of Commerce until late 1939. In Hull Peddie was active in both the trading and the political sides of the local co-operative movement. In 1931 he married Hilda Mary Alice, daughter of J. E. Bull, a fish merchant; they had two daughters and a son, Ian James Crofton (b. 1945). Between 1940 and 1945 Peddie worked for the ministries of Food and Information and was appointed MBE in 1944.

Jim Peddie was a major co-op business figure between 1945 and 1965. He was a director of the Co-operative Wholesale Society (CWS) Ltd from 1945, and vice-chairman of its board from 1961 to 1965. For the same period he was a director of the Co-operative Permanent Building Society and also of the Co-operative Insurance Society, of which he was vice-chairman of the board. Writing in the Co-operative News on 19 April 1978, William Richardson, a lifelong friend and leading co-operator, recalled that Peddie 'never hesitated to initiate or take up a challenge. On the CWS board he was fertile of ideas and at times impatient that the federation was not making a great impact on the nation and the co-operative movement'.

Peddie's career as a co-operative businessman was closely linked with his involvement in co-operative and wider politics. He was the first person from the business side of the movement to become chairman of the Co-operative Party, a post he held from 1957 to 1965, a high point in its history. He firmly ensured that the Co-op movement's interests were safeguarded when the Labour Party sought in 1957 to limit the number of candidates sponsored by the Co-op. He was president of the Co-operative Union in 1958 when he chaired both the May annual congress and a special November congress to consider the report, largely written by Anthony Crosland, produced by the independent commission of inquiry into the effectiveness of co-operative production and marketing chaired by Hugh Gaitskell. Although Peddie spoke up vigorously for 'efficiency and progressive management', little was done.

During his years as chairman of the Co-operative Party, Peddie became a national figure and spoke at major labour movement meetings. He strongly supported Gaitskell's leadership of the Labour Party. While the Co-operative Party conferences supported unilateral disarmament Peddie bluntly told political audiences that he was 'a supporter of multilateral disarmament and could not support the unilateralist point of view'. He was created a life peer in 1961. After Gaitskell's death in 1963, Peddie became known as a supporter of George Brown— so much so that when Brown, as minister of economic affairs, set up the National Prices and Incomes Board in 1965, Peddie became one of its full-time members, resigning from his co-operative business positions as well

as the chair of the Co-operative Party. He succeeded Aubrey Jones as its chairman in October 1970 until its abolition on 31 March 1971. Under his chairmanship the board completed work on ten cases, including low pay, the prices, profits, and costs of food distribution, London Transport's fares, and solicitors' remuneration. He led joint parliamentary delegations to Sweden (1965) and Finland (1968) and in 1974 served on the Council of Europe.

Peddie had a reputation for being a tough negotiator and a very blunt Yorkshireman. A historian of the Co-operative Party wrote, 'Peddie is a character about whom few can be neutral—one either admires him considerably or dislikes him intensely' (Carbery, 53). Richardson, in his obituary in the Co-operative News, observed that he had been 'a bonny fighter for policies and principles that he believed in and he fought to win'. Peddie died on 13 April 1978 from bronchopneumonia and cancer at Epsom and Ewell Cottage Hospital. He was survived by his wife, son, and one daughter. Roy Hattersley, then secretary of state for prices and consumer protection, gave the address at his memorial service on 24 May 1978.

CHRIS WRIGLEY

Sources C. Wrigley, 'Peddie, James Mortimer', DBB · T. F. Carbery, Consumers in politics: a history and general review of the co-operative party (1969) · A. Bonner, British co-operation: the history, principles, and organisation of the British co-operative movement, rev. edn (1970) · A. Clinton, Post Office workers: a trade union and social history (1984) · W. Richardson, Co-operative News (19 April 1978) · The Times (14 April 1978) · W. R. Richardson, 'Jim Peddie: a profile', Co-operative Newsletter (April 1965) · d. cert. · Co-operative News (19 April 1978) · WW
Wealth at death £183,783—gross; probate, 24 Oct 1978, CGPLA Eng. & Wales

Peddie, Sir John (d. 1840), army officer, entered the army as an ensign in the 38th foot on 26 September 1805. He became lieutenant on 26 August 1807, and went with the 1st battalion to Portugal in 1808. He took part in the battle of Roliça, the battle of Vimeiro, Sir John Moore's advance into Spain, and the battle of Corunna. After serving in the Walcheren expedition he returned to Spain in 1812, and was present at the battle of Salamanca, losing his right arm. He was promoted captain on half pay on 23 September 1813, but was brought back to full pay in the 97th foot on 25 March 1824, and became a major in the 95th on 16 June 1825. After a further period on half pay, he became lieutenant-colonel of the 31st on 26 October 1830, and of the 72nd highlanders on 20 April 1832. In the same year he was made a KH.

At the beginning of 1835 the 72nd, then quartered in Cape Town, were ordered to Grahamstown to participate in the first of the Cape frontier wars. At the end of March the British troops, under Sir Benjamin D'Urban, entered Kaffraria, and on 8 April Peddie, leaving the camp at midnight with four companies of the 72nd and the 1st provisional battalion, ascended the Izolo Berg. Having divided his forces into two columns, he attacked and routed the Kaffirs. By September operations were at an end; the Gaika country was annexed as far as the Kei (though the annexation was not ratified until 1846), and the 72nd returned to Grahamstown. A town in the newly conquered territory was named after Peddie.

On 23 February 1838 Peddie exchanged into the 90th regiment, then stationed in Ceylon. There his health broke down, and he died at Newara Elija in August 1840.

E. M. LLOYD, rev. DAVID GATES

Sources Hart's Army List (1840) · A. M. Delavoye, The records of the 90th regiment (1880) · R. Muir, Britain and the defeat of Napoleon, 1807–1815 (1996) · D. Gates, The Spanish ulcer: a history of the Peninsular War (1986)

Peddie, William (1805–1893). See under Peddie, James (1759–1845).

Peden, Alexander (1626?–1686), preacher, was born probably in 1626, probably at Auchencloich, near Sorn, Ayrshire, the eldest son in a modestly propertied family on good terms with the Boswells of Auchinleck and other local gentry. Possibly after schooling at nearby Mauchline he attended Glasgow University between 1643 and 1648. Thereafter his movements are uncertain but he was most likely serving as schoolmaster or family tutor in different places. He was certainly schoolmaster, session clerk, and precentor at Tarbolton, 10 miles from his birthplace, during John Guthrie's ministry. In 1659 Peden passed his trials for licence in the presbytery of Biggar and Lanark, although Ayr presbytery may have been responsible for the actual licensing. It was while a probationer under the latter that a woman in Tarbolton accused him of fathering her child. The charge was exposed as false when the woman committed suicide, but Peden, who never married, may have been left scarred.

In 1659 Peden was ordained to New Luce in Wigtownshire, where he served until ejected in 1662 for refusing to conform to episcopacy. His parting sermon, on Acts 20: 31–2, lasted until midnight. He then symbolically barred the church door against an intruded successor; there was none, in fact, until after the revolution of 1688–9. Peden now took to field preaching over much of southern and central Scotland, becoming the most revered and romanticized of all the conventicle preachers. He exerted a profound hold over common folk by his oracular style, rich in vivid imagery and blunt aphorisms and elevated by a prophetic inspiration. Peden 'the prophet' combined a kind of second sight (insight and foresight together) with impassioned forewarning of imminent peril or unseen hope. His prophecies also assumed a denunciatory directness, decreeing by prediction death, or woe on specific godless individuals.

From early 1663 Peden was a marked man. Declared a rebel and forfeited on 25 January 1666, he was excluded from the pardon of 1 October 1667 after the Pentland rising. He retreated to Ireland between 1670 and 1673, but was apprehended in June 1673 in Knockdow, Ayrshire. After trial in Edinburgh before the privy council on 26 June he was imprisoned, with some forty covenanters, on the Bass Rock in the Firth of Forth until 9 October 1677, and thereafter in Edinburgh tolbooth. Refused release to move to Ireland, he was sentenced instead to transportation to Virginia and left Scotland in December 1678, but after the sea journey to London he and others were set free

when the outward bound captain refused to carry prisoners sentenced for religious convictions. After six months Peden returned to Scotland.

In the next few obscure years Peden paid at least two visits to Ireland. In 1685 he preached his last sermon, at Colinswood on the Water of Ayr. Prematurely aged and debilitated, he found shelter in a cave on the banks of the Ayr near Sorn. Sensing approaching death, he moved to his brother's house at Auchinleck, where he died on 28 January 1686. Buried at Auchinleck church, his remains were disinterred six weeks later by government troops. Failing to hang the corpse on the gallows at nearby Cumnock, they buried it at their foot. Out of reverence for Peden the community adopted the spot as their burial-ground. South and central Scotland is dotted with sites honouring Peden's memory—Peden's Pulpit, Peden's Stone—and some monuments were, even in the late twentieth century, still the scene of commemorative services. Patrick Walker assiduously assembled his experiences and prophecies, although only two sermons, preached when he revisited his old parish in 1682, survive; they were published as The Lord's Trumpet Sounding an Alarm (1720?). No other covenanter's name took such affectionate root among widespread localities. D. F. WRIGHT

Sources P. Walker, Some remarkable passages of the life and death of Mr Alexander Peden, 3rd edn (1728) · J. C. Johnston, Alexander Peden: the prophet of the covenant (1902) · K. Hewat, Peden the prophet (1911) · Fasti Scot., 2.345–6 · DSCHT · J. C. Johnston, Treasury of the Scottish covenant (1887)

Pedersen, Mikael (1855–1929), engineer and designer of bicycles, was born on 25 October 1855 at Marbjerg, near Roskilde in Denmark, the eldest of six children of Peder Hansen, farmer, and his wife, Karen Mathiasdatter. His parents were both Danish.

Pedersen was known in Marbjerg as an ingenious and musical child. After schooling in Fløng, he became apprenticed to the Maglekilde machinery factory in Roskilde where in 1878 he produced important improvements to cream separators. By 1878 he had moved to the Roskilde machinery factory where again he improved the separator design to create the famous Alexandra model. In 1889, Robert Lister of R. A. Lister & Co. Ltd, agricultural engineers of Dursley in Gloucestershire, acquired the selling rights of this model. However, the design was still imperfect, and after an accident in which the rotating bowl broke and killed a man, Lister invited Pedersen to Dursley to sort out the problem. Manufacture then began in Dursley itself. In 1893 Pedersen settled in Dursley.

At about this time Pedersen, who was a cycling enthusiast, invented a hammock saddle to make riding more comfortable and also designed a triangulated cycle frame to support it. In a small former woollen mill at the bottom of his garden in Dursley he refined his cycle design and attempted, unsuccessfully, to interest established cycle makers in manufacturing it. In consequence of this failure he opened his own factory in Dursley in 1899 under the name of the Dursley Pedersen Cycle Company.

Pedersen's talent as a designer flowered during this period. He built multi-seat cycles and produced new designs for many cycle parts and accessories. These latter included one of the first variable gears, a folding cycle which he vainly hoped would be of use in the Second South African War, and also a motor cycle. In 1905, because of financial problems, the company was taken over by R. A. Lister; cycle production continued until 1914. During the First World War Pedersen made thread gauges used in munitions production and is credited with the invention of the ML magneto which was used in most British aircraft of this time.

Like many inventors, Pedersen was obsessive and moody. He could be seen, lost in thought, striding the streets of Dursley, with his head down in his beard. At other times he was highly sociable, enjoying parties and holding musical evenings at which instruments of his own invention were played. He was said to be generous to his workforce and their families. Although involved with three women, it is not known whether he married any of them. With the last, Ingeborg, the relationship produced three boys and a girl.

In 1920 Pedersen returned penniless to Denmark where in 1928 he entered Den Gamle By, an old people's home in Copenhagen. There he died of old age on 22 October 1929. He was buried in Bispebjerg cemetery, Copenhagen. In 1995 the remains from his unmarked grave were brought to England and on 21 September re-interred in Dursley cemetery.

Although Pedersen's cycle had no real influence on the mass production cycle industry, his designs later became famed for their elegance and eccentricity. In the late 1970s interest in the Pedersen frame revived, when new machines to his designs were built, first in Denmark, then in England and Germany. DAVID E. EVANS

Sources *Dursley, Berkeley and Sharpness Gazette* (1889–1916) · private information (2004) · D. E. Evans, *The ingenious Mr Pedersen* (1978)

Likenesses photographs, priv. coll.; copies, Gloucester Folk Museum, Westgate Street, Gloucester

Pedler, Sir Alexander (1849–1918), chemist, was born on 21 May 1849, at 197 Fleet Street, London, the son of George Stanbury Pedler, a pharmacist of Fleet Street, and his wife, Hannah Rideal. He was educated privately and in the City of London School. From October 1866, with the assistance of a Bell scholarship, he studied in the laboratory of the Pharmaceutical Society of Great Britain in Bloomsbury Square, and won a certificate of honour in practical chemistry. Like many of his contemporaries, Pedler became fascinated by the use of the microscope and spectroscope as instruments of chemical analysis. In 1867 he was appointed chemical assistant at the Royal Institution, where he assisted Herbert McLeod in preparing the lecture demonstrations of Edward Frankland (professor of chemistry at the institution and at the Royal College of Chemistry) and Norman Lockyer. In 1868 Lockyer discovered terrestrial helium, and Pedler assisted his observations of solar prominences and spectral lines. The same year, at Frankland's direction, Pedler isolated the isomers of valeric acid, and published the first study of optically active compounds that followed Pasteur's pioneering work.

In 1868, at Lockyer's request, Pedler went to Sicily to observe the solar eclipse, and in 1869 visited America with the French Atlantic Cable Company. On his return he was enlisted as one of four chemical examiners at the Department of Science and Art, and signed on as a student in chemistry at the Royal College of Chemistry. In 1870 he was elected a fellow of the Chemical Society, and in 1871, when McLeod went to a chair at the newly founded Royal Indian Engineering College at Coopers Hill, Pedler succeeded him as assistant to Frankland and Lockyer. In 1873, on Frankland's recommendation, he was offered the inaugural chair of chemistry at the Presidency College of Bengal. His background in analytical and 'celestial' chemistry, his familiarity with laboratory methods, and his experience of examinations equipped him well for the passage to India.

At the age of only twenty-four Pedler arrived in Calcutta at an auspicious moment. Presidency College was affiliated with the University of Calcutta, which, in the previous year, had decided that its 400 students reading for the BA degree be required to take chemistry as a compulsory subject. Pedler's arrival coincided with the construction of a new building at Presidency College, which he duly fitted out for laboratory instruction and a modest research programme. In 1876, drawing on his experience of the British Association and the Royal Institution, Pedler helped establish the Indian Association for the Cultivation of Science, with its ambitious programme of research and classes for laymen. A model 'imperial scientist', he instituted a programme of work that mirrored the studies being done by colleagues in London, and produced analyses of coal gas and water supplies in the sprawling capital of Bengal. In 1878 Pedler married Elizabeth Margaret (*d.* 1896), daughter of C. K. Schmidt of Frankfurt.

In his Calcutta laboratory Pedler applied himself to the interests of his youth. Some early papers, such as that on the chemistry of cobra poison, took the form of letters home, while others were delivered as lectures to the Asiatic Society of Bengal. To England, he supplied accounts of the three solar eclipses observable in Calcutta during his lifetime (the last in 1898), and reports on imperial questions, including the corrosion of lead-lined Indian tea chests, and cyclonic activity in the Bay of Bengal. With a medical colleague, Charles Warden, he studied the toxicity of natural substances (for example, the arum plant), and pioneered the application of chemical methods to botanical analysis. The chemistry of light was a preoccupation in tropical India. In 1890 he reported to the Chemical Society photochemical observations on the effects of sunlight on chlorine in water; and to the Asiatic Society on the bleaching effects of sunlight on mercury compounds and organic colours. His contributions to environmental analysis were recognized by his election as a fellow of the Institute of Chemistry.

With missionary zeal Pedler instituted the first laboratory practicals in India. Nominated in 1887 by British colleagues, including Frankland, McLeod, and H. E. Armstrong, he was elected FRS in 1892, the first of four Presidency men to achieve this honour. Some criticized Pedler for failing to lead research into new avenues, but no one questioned his experimental skills. From 1894 his laboratory, fashioned along German lines, became a beacon for young Indian chemists. One, Prafulla Chandra Ray, was destined to succeed him, achieving international distinction as a chemist and historian of chemistry. Gradually Pedler acquired wider responsibilities—as meteorological reporter of the government of Bengal (1889–95), president of the Asiatic Society of Bengal (1896), and curator of the Bengal Museum. In 1896 he resigned his chair to become principal of Presidency College (1896–1904), and later vice-chancellor of the University of Calcutta (1904–6). Between 1899 and 1906, he was director of public instruction and a member of the legislative council of Bengal. In 1901 he was created companion in the Order of the Indian Empire, and on retirement in 1906 he was knighted.

Retirement brought a return to London, where Pedler began a second career of voluntary service to British science, working from his home in Stanhope Gardens, South Kensington. In 1907 he helped Lockyer inaugurate the British Science Guild, and served as honorary secretary of that 'ginger group' for the next eleven years. At that time he was described as a rational conservative. On the outbreak of war, he volunteered for work in the Ministry of Munitions, and was given an advisory position. He died at a committee meeting at the ministry, suddenly and without warning, on 13 May 1918. He was survived by his second wife, Mabel, daughter of William Warburton, of Dedham, Essex, whom he had married in 1905. He had no children from either marriage. He enjoyed lawn tennis and golf, and his membership of the Constitutional, Ranelagh, and Royal Automobile clubs. He was well remembered, especially by those sharing experience of science in the service of empire.   ROY M. MACLEOD

Sources RS · *Catalogue of scientific papers*, Royal Society, 8 (1879) · *Catalogue of scientific papers*, Royal Society, 10 (1894) · *Catalogue of scientific papers*, Royal Society, 17 (1921) · W. A. T. [W. A. Tilden], *JCS*, 115 (1919), 436–8 · *Journal of the Royal Institute of Chemistry* (1918), 27–8 · P. C. Ray, *Life and experiences of a Bengali chemist* (1932) · *Chemistry and theology in mid-Victorian London: the diary of Herbert McLeod, 1860–1870*, ed. F. A. J. L. James (1987) [microfiche] · F. V. Fernandes, 'The Indian school of chemistry: the researches of Professor Ray and his pupils at Presidency College', *Presidency College Magazine*, 1/3 (1915), 1–13 · U. R. Ghatak and others, *A century: the Indian Association for the Cultivation of Science* (1976) · H. E. Armstrong, 'The future of chemistry in India', *Acharya Ray commemoration volume*, ed. H. N. Datta and others (1932), 11–13 · CGPLA Eng. & Wales (1919)

Archives NRA, priv. coll., Sir Edward Frankland MSS, letters · Royal Institution of Great Britain, London, Herbert McLeod diaries

Wealth at death £71,407 10s. 10d.: administration with will, 30 Jan 1919, CGPLA Eng. & Wales

Pedler, Sir Frederick Johnson (1908–1991), colonial official and businessman, was born on 10 July 1908 at 27 Park Avenue South, Hornsey, London, the only child of Charles Henry Pedler (1865–1935), wholesale tea merchant, and his wife, Lucy Marian (May; 1878–1952), daughter of the Revd Simpson Johnson of Bishop Auckland. Both parents were Methodists. Pedler's earliest years were spent in Finsbury Park and Finchley, north of London, before the family moved to Watford in 1918, where Pedler attended Watford grammar school, becoming both head boy and captain of rugby. He won a scholarship to Gonville and Caius College, Cambridge, in 1927, becoming Goldsmith's exhibitioner in 1929, and graduating in 1930 with a starred first in history. He was awarded the Schuldham plate. In later years Pedler remained a staunch supporter of both institutions, twice serving as chair of the grammar school's Old Fullerians' Association, campaigning successfully to maintain the school's academic standards during a ten-year stint as chairman of the school governors in the 1960s and 1970s, and joining the Gonville and Caius investment committee.

On graduating, Pedler entered the administrative grade of the civil service, drawn by the opportunity for travel in the department of his choice, the Colonial Office. It was nevertheless only after some agitation on his part that he finally secured his dispatch to Tanganyika in 1934. As assistant secretary in Dar es Salaam he produced a paper (subsequently published by the Tanganyikan government) outlining the advantages of membership of the customs union with Kenya and Uganda, and (himself an enthusiastic boy scout) helped establish the scouting movement in the colony, before serving as an assistant district officer, first in Kwimba district and then in Moshi. On 11 June 1935 he married Esther Ruth Carling (b. 1908), teacher, and daughter of Henry Frank Carling (1873–1949) and Esther Lillie, *née* Colebrook (1870–1957), of Peppard Common, Oxfordshire. They had met in 1927 when both worked for an international holiday school. The couple had three children: Robin Henry (b. 1937), Esther Marian (b. 1940), and Martin Colebrook (b. 1943).

In September 1935 the Colonial Office cut short Pedler's Tanganyikan tour. In the following years he played a supporting role in some of the most significant episodes in the development of British African policy. In 1937 he was appointed secretary to the commission of higher education in east Africa and the Sudan, chaired by Lord De La Warr, to whom he was seconded as private secretary. The same year he was employed to edit the highly influential *African Survey* (1938) following Lord Hailey's breakdown, preparing some 'material that was scarcely in first draft' (MSS Afr. s. 1814, FP 9/79, survey chairman to De La Warr, 22 March 1938). At the Colonial Office's insistence, Pedler's substantial contribution went unacknowledged in the published version. His association with Hailey continued when the latter requested his appointment as secretary when asked to undertake a confidential survey of native administration in British Africa. The draft of the report (the basis for the Colonial Office's 1943 sketch for west African constitutional development, and a milestone in the evolution of official thinking towards native administration policy) was prepared by Pedler as the pair toured tropical Africa. Pedler also travelled to the Belgian Congo with Hailey when the latter was appointed head of the British economic mission to the colony in 1940–41, and on Hailey's departure he assumed control of the mission. The extent of Pedler's contribution to the final report is unknown (Pedler himself remained vague on this point), but the superior quality of this confidential report in comparison to a revised version Hailey published later led Hailey's biographer to speculate that it may have been considerable (Cell, *Hailey*, 296–7).

Pedler's experiences shaped his own relatively farsighted views on African political development. In 1942 (in contrast to Hailey) he supported the Gold Coast governor's proposals to admit Africans to the colony's executive council. While working on the *Survey*, he had privately recorded his own disagreement with Hailey's assessment of the native authorities (Pedler placing greater weight on the problems of investing traditional rather than educated African élites with powers of local government), and in 1946, when the Colonial Office debated their future, he wrote an influential memorandum stressing the extent of African politicization and recommending the democratization of African local government as essential to the maintenance of British African interests.

Pedler's next important assignment came in December 1942, when he served as chief British economic representative to French West Africa and Togoland, successfully handling the delicate negotiations between the free French, Americans, and British, to direct exports essential to the allied war effort and to handle the region's supply problems. Back in London he was promoted to head the department of finance and development, in 1944, before—to his dissatisfaction—he was assigned in January 1945 to assist Sir Ralph Furse in handling post-war colonial service recruitment. In January 1947, frustrated in this position, convinced (ironically in view of later developments) that, as he later recalled, Africa was 'a political backwater' in the Colonial Office, and keen to secure 'a position to influence policy in Africa' (MS Afr. s. 1718), he quit the Colonial Office and, drawing on contacts established particularly during his Dakar mission, opted for a more lucrative second career with the United Africa Company (UAC).

In various early managerial postings in Nigeria and the Gold Coast and as an area manager in London, Pedler became a leading player in framing UAC's response to the 1947–8 Gold Coast political developments. Thereafter, as UAC director (1951–68), managing director (1956–68), and deputy chairman (1965–68), as well as director of Unilever (1956–68), Pedler was a key figure in UAC's attempts via redeployment to adapt to the economic and political difficulties of operating in independent African states. During this period his friendships with various African nationalists led him into some unorthodox relationships (the future Ghanaian leader Kofi Busia corresponded with Pedler under a pseudonym during his exile), but could open doors for UAC: Pedler enjoyed famously easy access to Kwame Nkrumah. In Nigeria he was offered the vice-chancellorship of Ahmadu Bello University in October 1965, although the proposal lapsed with Sir Ahmadu Bello's murder. He retired from the United Africa Company in 1968.

Other activities testified to Pedler's continuing engagement with African affairs: he was chairman of the council for technical education and training for overseas countries, 1962–73, chairman of the East African and Mauritius Association, 1966–8, a member of the Inter-University Council, 1967–73, and treasurer of the School of Oriental and African Studies (SOAS), 1969–81. He was made an honorary fellow of SOAS in 1976. In 1969 he was knighted for 'services to technical education overseas'. Fluent in Swahili and Hausa, he also published many articles on Africa, and three west African historical and geographical surveys, *West Africa* (1951), *Economic Geography of West Africa* (1955), and *Main Currents of West African History, 1940–1978* (1979), which revealed disappointingly little of Pedler's own role in the region's affairs. More revealing was Pedler's personal memoir *Business and decolonization in West Africa, c.1940–1960* (1989). Pedler also published a business history, *The lion and the unicorn in Africa: a history of the origins of the United Africa Company, 1787–1931* (1974), as well as *A Pedler Family History* (1984) and *A Wider Pedler Family History* (1989).

As his career and active retirement demonstrated, Pedler was 'intelligent, hard-working and tough' (H. Macmillan, *War Diaries: Politics and War in the Mediterranean, January 1943–May 1945*, 1984, 422). He had also 'a capacity for making and keeping friends' and, although 'tough in pursuit of his objectives', possessed a 'strong sense of social justice and a concern for the individual' (*The Times*, 16 April 1991). After a long and happy marriage, Pedler died at Mount Vernon Hospital, Northwood, London, on 6 April 1991. He was survived by his wife and their three children.

SARAH STOCKWELL

Sources Bodl. RH, MSS Afr.s.1814 (FP 1–54) · interview, 1970, Bodl. RH, MS Afr.s.1718 · F. Pedler, *Business and decolonization in West Africa, c. 1940–1960: a personal memoir* (1989) · J. Pedler, *A Pedler family history* (1984) · *The Times* (16 April 1991) · *The Times* (7 May 1991) · J. W. Cell, *Hailey: a study in British imperialism, 1872–1969* (1992) · C. R. Nordman, 'The decision to admit unofficials to the executive councils of British West Africa', *Journal of Imperial and Commonwealth History*, 4 (1975–6), 194–205 · R. D. Pearce, *The turning point in Africa: British colonial policy, 1938–48* (1982) · D. K. Fieldhouse, *Merchant capital and economic decolonization: the United Africa Company, 1929–1987* (1994) · S. E. Stockwell, *The business of decolonization: British business strategies in the Gold Coast* (2000) · J. W. Cell, 'On the eve of decolonization: the colonial office's plans for the transfer of power in Africa, 1947', *Journal of Imperial and Commonwealth History*, 8 (1979–80), 235–57 · R. D. Pearce, 'The colonial office in 1947, and the transfer of power in Africa: an addendum to John Cell', *Journal of Imperial and Commonweath History*, 10/2 (1982), 211–15 · WWW, 1991–5 · d. cert. · A. H. M. Kirk-Greene, *A biographical dictionary of the British colonial service, 1939–1966* (1991)

Archives Bodl. RH, corresp. and papers · Bodl. RH, interview on career · United Africa Company, London, MSS | Bodl. RH, corresp. with Margery Perham and related papers · PRO, Colonial Office MSS

Likenesses photograph, repro. in *The Times* (16 April 1991)

Wealth at death £441,030: probate, 4 Sept 1991, CGPLA Eng. & Wales

Pedley, Robin [*formerly* Robert] (1914–1988), educationist, was born in Grinton, North Riding of Yorkshire, on 11 August 1914, the fourth in the family of four sons and one daughter of Edward Pedley, stonemason, of Grinton, and his wife, Martha Jane, postmistress, daughter of William Hird, farmer of a smallholding, also of Grinton. All the family attended Fremington School (the local Church of England elementary school), most leaving at fourteen, though Pedley's three brothers all later achieved distinction in their careers in education, the civil service, and the police force. Pedley was articled as a pupil teacher, but the system was abolished at that time (1928) and he went to Richmond School (North Riding of Yorkshire) for his secondary education (1928–32). He won an Ellerton scholarship to Durham University and obtained an upper second-class degree in history and economics in 1935. He joined the education department at Durham and acquired his teacher's certificate in 1936. Elected a fellow of Durham University (1936–8), he was awarded the Gladstone memorial prize in modern history in 1937 and, in the same year, the Gibson prize in archaeology. In 1939 Pedley gained his doctorate for a study of the political and economic history of the northern Pennines. In addition to these scholarly achievements Pedley proved himself an accomplished athlete at the university, excelling particularly in association football and cricket.

In 1938 Pedley was appointed to the Friends' school at Great Ayton. From 1943 to 1946 (Pedley was a conscientious objector) he was senior history master at the Crossley and Porter schools, Halifax, moving as a lecturer in education to the College of St Mark and St John, Chelsea, in 1946. In 1947 he was appointed as one of the founding members of the newly formed department of education at University College, Leicester.

It was at Leicester that Pedley fully developed his own outlook on educational policy and practice and soon made a national impact in his campaign for a comprehensive system of secondary education, based on what became known as the two-tier system. He believed in small schools as intimate communities and sought for a solution along these lines, rather than through the accepted policy of building large, 'all-through' schools catering for the entire eleven to nineteen age group.

The pattern Pedley favoured involved the division of secondary schooling at the age of fifteen. This had several advantages. First, comprehensive (or non-selective) education could be implemented in existing buildings, secondary modern schools taking in all local children at the age of eleven, and grammar schools those over fifteen. Secondly, both types of school, catering for local populations, could be developed as community schools, a project dear to Pedley's heart. Thirdly, both sets of schools could, in theory at least, be of reasonable size. Finally, senior pupils in upper schools could be treated as their increasing maturity required.

Pedley had already begun to develop his thinking along these lines in a set of articles published in the late 1940s. But the first breakthrough came in his *Comprehensive Schools Today* (1955), where articles on Pedley's proposed solution were commented on by leading educationists, especially those from local authorities. In 1956 his major book, *Comprehensive Education, a New Approach*, received wide publicity and was taken very seriously. At a meeting in that year with Sir David Eccles, minister of education, Pedley was left in no doubt about the ministry's readiness

to encourage experiment along the lines he suggested, and the county of Leicestershire announced its two-tier plan in 1957. In 1963 Pedley published what was to be his most influential book, the Pelican original entitled *The Comprehensive School*. This was immensely popular, going through five reprints or new editions by 1969, and is the book that brought the idea most closely to the attention of the general public during the 1960s and later.

It was at Leicester that Pedley made his main contribution to the movement for comprehensive education. Tall, handsome, and willowy in his prime, with an open, frank countenance, an accomplished sportsman and delightful colleague, he developed a persuasive style as a speaker and became adept in the presentation of his case to local authority representatives and others throughout the country.

Pedley remained at Leicester until 1963, when he accepted appointment as director of the Institute of Education at Exeter University. He was awarded a chair in 1970. In 1971 he was appointed professor of education and head of the school of education at Southampton University, where he acted as dean of the faculty for four years.

In 1951 Pedley married Jeanne Lesley, daughter of William Leslie Hitching, bank manager. They had one son and one daughter. Pedley died in Salisbury on 20 November 1988, officially of pneumonia but in reality of Alzheimer's disease, from which he had suffered for some years. He was survived by his wife.   B. SIMON, *rev.*

Sources D. Crook, 'The disputed origins of the Leicestershire two-tier comprehensive schools plan', *History of Education Society Bulletin*, 50 (1992), 55–8 · *The Times* (24 Nov 1988) · *The Independent* (24 Nov 1988) · private information (1996) · personal knowledge (1996) · CGPLA Eng. & Wales (1989) · WWW

Wealth at death £81,467: probate, 8 May 1989, CGPLA Eng. & Wales

Pedrog. See Petroc (*fl.* 6th cent.).

Peebles, David (*fl.* 1530–1576), composer, was a canon at the Augustinian priory of St Andrews until the Scottish Reformation of 1559–60. In 1571 Robart Stewart, commendator of St Andrews and a prominent reformer, granted Peebles and his spouse, Katherine Kynneir (d. 1592), a charter of land within the grounds of St Andrews, suggesting that he had remained in his former monastery. According to marginalia in the Wode partbooks, as 'ane of the cheiff musitians into this land' he was commissioned by James Stewart, former prior of St Andrews, natural son of James V and future earl of Moray and regent of Scotland, to 'set thrie pairts to the tenor' of certain of the psalms in a 'plane and dulce' style thereby forgoing 'the curiosity of musike'. Perhaps as a consequence of this stricture, Peebles 'wes not earnest' to complete what he may have regarded as a menial task, but the tenacity of the prior's agent Thomas Wode was eventually repaid with an extremely accomplished set of 105 psalm settings. These form the core of the Wode partbooks. Although Wode's manuscript remained unpublished, some of Peebles's psalms appeared in Edward Millar's psalter of 1635, where he is numbered among 'the primest musicians that ever this kingdome had'. The Wode partbooks also preserve two Latin motets by Peebles. According to Wode's marginalia, Peebles had composed his elegant four-part polyphonic setting of 'Si quis diligit me' about 1530 and presented it to James V, who 'being a musitian … did lyke it verray weill'. In 1576 Robart Stewart commissioned Peebles to set a protestant Latin version of Psalm 3, *Quam multi domine*. This dynamic work eloquently demonstrates Peebles's continuing acquaintance with contemporary compositional practices. He was dead by 1592, the date of his wife's will, which describes her as Peebles's 'relict' and also mentions two lawful sons, Andrew and Thomas.   D. JAMES ROSS

Sources D. J. Ross, *Musick fyne: Robert Carver and the art of music in 16th-century Scotland* (1993) · H. S. P. Hutchison, 'The St Andrews psalter: transcription and critical study of Thomas Wode's psalter', DMus diss., U. Edin., 1957 · K. Elliott, 'Music in Scotland, 1500–1700', PhD diss., U. Cam., 1960 · K. Elliott and H. M. Shire, eds., *Music of Scotland, 1500–1700*, 3rd edn, Musica Britannica, 15 (1975) · K. Elliott, 'Another of Thomas Wode's missing parts', *Innes Review*, 39 (1988), 151–5 · K. Elliott, *Fourteen psalm-settings of the early reformed church in Scotland* (1960)

Peebles, John (*d.* 1390/91), administrator and bishop of Dunkeld, is of unknown origins, though his name and early career suggest he was probably born and raised in the diocese of Glasgow. He attended the University of Paris from about 1351 to 1355, but did not obtain any formal legal degree before returning to serve in the court of, and as a legal official for, the bishop of Glasgow between 1355 and 1363. In 1363 he resumed his studies in France, and by June 1365 he had become a bachelor in both civil and canon law. By the time of his return to Scotland in 1368, moreover, he had obtained a doctorate in canon law. On his homecoming Peebles entered the service of David II and in 1369 he acted as the king's envoy to Rome, probably to represent the Scottish king in his divorce action against Queen Margaret. Peebles also enjoyed patronage from one of the most influential and powerful Scottish magnates of the time, William, first earl of Douglas; shortly before 13 March 1370 he was given charge of the church of Douglas, a benefice in the gift of the earl. After King David's death on 22 February 1371 Peebles passed into the service of his successor, Robert II. Peebles was identified as a royal clerk in the first parliament of Robert's reign and received a royal pension of 20 merks from November 1372 to early 1377. In September 1374 he was appointed to the archdeaconry of St Andrews previously held by William Grenlaw and in the following month succeeded Grenlaw as the collector of papal dues in Scotland. Between 11 February and 30 March 1377 Peebles was appointed chancellor of the kingdom, replacing John Carrick. He became bishop of Dunkeld in 1378 after first the death of Bishop Michael Monymusk in March 1377 and then the premature demise of Monymusk's elected successor, Andrew Umfray, at Rome between 1 July and 7 September 1377.

As chancellor, Peebles was a frequent witness to Robert II's charters and a regular auditor of the exchequer. He was also a very active diplomat, taking part in Anglo-

Scottish negotiations in the 1370s and 1380s, while in September 1384 he and Cardinal Walter Wardlaw, bishop of Glasgow, represented the Scottish crown at a conference at Leulinghen in France which arranged a general cessation in Anglo-Scottish and Anglo-French hostilities until May 1385. While in France, Peebles and Wardlaw seem to have concluded the agreement which saw Jean de Vienne, the French admiral, lead an expeditionary force to Scotland in the summer of 1385 as part of a combined Franco-Scottish assault on northern England on the expiry of the Leulinghen truce. On the whole, Peebles appears to have been a highly competent and respected administrator, employed by successive rulers because of his expertise and reliability.

Political changes in Scotland during 1388, however, may have reduced Peebles's influence in the royal administration. In a parliament on 2–7 April 1389 he was openly criticized for issuing letters of sasine in favour of Sir Malcolm Drummond, who was involved in a dispute with Archibald Douglas, lord of Galloway, over the inheritance of the second earl of Douglas, killed at the battle of Otterburn in August 1388. Archibald was an ally of Robert, earl of Fife, who had been appointed guardian of the kingdom on 1 December 1388. Peebles, on the other hand, may have been more sympathetic to the claims of Malcolm Drummond, the brother-in-law of the second earl and the son-in-law of the first earl of Douglas, one of Peebles's early patrons.

Peebles took part in another diplomatic mission in France in the final months of 1389, but had returned to Scotland by January 1390. On or about 18 March 1390 he demitted the office of chancellor, perhaps because of age or infirmity, and Alexander Cockburn appeared as custodian of the great seal. The last reference to Peebles suggests that he performed the coronation of Queen Annabella on 15 August 1390. He died before 1 February 1391, when Robert Sinclair, bishop of Orkney, was translated to the diocese of Dunkeld as his successor.

S. I. BOARDMAN

Sources G. Burnett and others, eds., *The exchequer rolls of Scotland*, 2–3 (1878–80) · J. M. Thomson and others, eds., *Registrum magni sigilli regum Scotorum / The register of the great seal of Scotland*, 2nd edn, 1, ed. T. Thomson (1912) · H. Denifle and A. Chatelain, eds., *Auctarium chartularii universitatis Parisiensis*, 1 (Paris, 1894) · The 'Original chronicle' of Andrew of Wyntoun, ed. F. J. Amours, 5, STS, 1st ser., 56 (1907); 6, STS, 1st ser., 57 (1908) · *CEPR letters*, vol. 4 · *APS*, 1124–1423 · *RotS*, vol. 2 · *CDS*, vol. 4 · T. Thomson, A. Macdonald, and C. Innes, eds., *Registrum honoris de Morton*, 2 vols., Bannatyne Club, 94 (1853), vol. 2 · W. Fraser, ed., *The Douglas book*, 4 vols. (1885), vol. 3 · Rymer, *Foedera*, 1st edn, vol. 7 · D. E. R. Watt, *A biographical dictionary of Scottish graduates to AD 1410* (1977), 440–43

Peek, Sir Cuthbert Edgar, second baronet (1855–1901), astronomer and meteorologist, born at Wimbledon, Surrey, on 30 January 1855, was the only child of Sir Henry William Peek (1825–1898), the first baronet (created 1874), of Wimbledon House, Wimbledon, a partner in the firm of Messrs Peek Brothers & Co., colonial merchants, of East Cheap, and MP for East Surrey from 1868 to 1884. His mother was Margaret Maria (*d.* 1884), the second daughter of William Edgar of Eagle House, Clapham Common. He was educated at Eton College and entered Pembroke College, Cambridge, in 1876; he graduated BA in 1879 and proceeded MA in 1884. After leaving Cambridge he went through a course of astronomy and surveying, and put his knowledge to practical use in two journeys, made in 1881, into unfrequented parts of Iceland, where he took regular observations of latitude and longitude and dip of the magnetic needle. On his return he set up a small observatory in the grounds of his father's house at Wimbledon, where he observed with a 3 inch equatorial. In 1882 Peek spent six weeks at Jimbour, Queensland, to observe the transit of Venus across the sun's disc in December of that year. With his principal instrument, an equatorially mounted telescope of 6.4 inches by Merz, he observed, in the days preceding the transit, double stars and star clusters. He paid special attention to the nebula in the constellation of Argus, one of the wonders of the southern sky, which he described in a memoir. Observations of the transit, however, were prevented by cloud. Peek travelled extensively in Australia and New Zealand, and brought back to England many items to add to a museum created by his father at Rousdon, Devon.

On 3 January 1884 Peek married Augusta Louisa, the eldest daughter of William Brodrick, eighth Viscount Midleton.

In 1883 he had established, on his father's estate at Rousdon, a meteorological station of the second order, and in 1884 he set up there an astronomical observatory to contain the Merz telescope and a transit instrument with other accessories. Assisted by Charles Grover, he began a systematic observation of the variation of brightness of long-period variable stars, by Argelander's method, and following the same plan as the Harvard College observatory. Annual reports were sent to the Royal Astronomical Society, which Peek joined on 11 January 1884, and short sets of observations were occasionally published in pamphlet form. The complete series of the observations of twenty-two stars extending over sixteen years was collected at Peek's request by Professor Herbert Hall Turner of Oxford and published by him after Peek's death in the *Memoirs of the Royal Astronomical Society*. The introduction to the volume contains a section written by Peek in 1896 explaining his astronomical methods. The regular observations of his meteorological instruments were also collected and published in annual volumes.

Peek succeeded to the baronetcy and to the estates that his father had bought in Surrey and Devon on the latter's death on 26 August 1898. He was elected FSA on 6 March 1890, was honorary secretary of the Anthropological Society, and often served on the council or as a vice-president of the Royal Meteorological Society from 1884 until his death. He endowed the Royal Geographical Society, of whose council he was a member, with a medal for the advancement of geographical knowledge. Interested in shooting, he presented a challenge cup and an annual prize to be shot for by members of the Cambridge University volunteer corps. He had been staying at Brighton for six months when he died, at 9 Eastern Terrace, Kemp Town, on 6 July 1901 of a brain tumour. He was buried at Rousdon. He was survived by his wife and their two sons and four daughters; his elder son, Wilfrid (1884–1927), succeeded to the baronetcy.

H. P. HOLLIS, *rev.* ANITA McCONNELL

Sources C. Grover, *The Observatory*, 24 (1901), 206–7 · *GJ*, 18 (1901), 222 · *Quarterly Journal of the Royal Meteorological Society*, 28 (1902), 194–5 · *Monthly Notices of the Royal Astronomical Society*, 62 (1901–2), 244–5 · C. E. Peek, 'Across Iceland by the Sprengisandr route', *Proceedings* [Royal Geographical Society], new ser., 4 (1882), 129–40 · d. cert.

Archives Devon RO, diaries and letters · Meteorological Office, Bracknell, Berkshire, National Meteorological Library and Archive, meteorological observations · Sci. Mus., papers, mainly relating to astronomical and meteorological observations

Wealth at death £240,476 6s. 11d.: resworn probate, April 1902, *CGPLA Eng. & Wales* (1901)

Peek, James (1800–1879), biscuit manufacturer, was born on 8 June 1800, the sixth and youngest son of John Peek, farm labourer of Loddiswell, Devon, and his wife, Susanna. He was educated locally and then joined his brothers Richard and William in a tea, coffee, and spice dealers' business in Coleman Street, London. The firm became Peek Bros. and Winch in 1895.

The brothers worked extremely hard. James Peek as a partner is said not to have taken even one day's holiday for many years, maintaining the books in the counting-house and keeping a weather eye on all sides of the firm. However, he found time to marry Elizabeth (d. 1867), only daughter of James Masters, a Londoner, in 1824; she was the last in line of the Lemaitre family, Huguenots who had emigrated from Dieppe after the edict of Nantes was revoked in 1685. They had three daughters and three sons; the eldest, Henry William (1825–1898), headed the tea firm, served as an MP, and was created a baronet in 1874.

By 1857 Peek had enough capital to consider setting up his younger sons in a separate business. That year he therefore established a biscuit manufactory, Peek Frean & Co., at Bermondsey in London, jointly with his nephew by marriage, George Hender Frean, a flour miller and engineer. Although both sons left the business, Peek stayed to become the driving force and main investor, exerting influence mainly from his nearby residence in Blackheath. His detailed instructions for managers show the bent of his mind. He insisted on the most thorough checks to avoid employee fraud. 'Suspicion is necessary in large establishments; *thousands are ruined for want of it*' (Davis, 1.23).

Peek's substantial investment of £30,000, plus the factory buildings he bought and leased to the firm, allowed it to start on a far more extensive scale than was usual; in 1858 it produced thirty-five different types of fancy biscuit. However, it incurred losses until mid-1861, partly through a decision to make under licence the aerated bread invented by Dr John Dauglish. This did not catch on; once it was discontinued, the firm moved into profit. John Carr, brother of Jonathan Dodgson Carr, was invited in 1860 to work for Peek Frean; in 1872 his son Arthur Carr joined the firm.

Peek Frean gained much publicity from its contract

with the French government to supply ship's biscuits during the Italian campaign of 1866, and again during the Franco-Prussian War of 1870–71; the latter contract also helped to relieve hunger during the siege of Paris. In mid-1871 the firm ceased producing ship's biscuits and concentrated on the fancy varieties; the Garibaldi, Pearl, and Marie biscuits were particularly popular. The original factory was destroyed by fire in 1873, and its successor's clock tower near London Bridge Station remained a landmark for many decades.

Frean ceased to be an active partner in 1875, and Peek brought in as partner his son-in-law Thomas Stone. The latter's two sons subsequently became partners, but the Stone trio were not very progressive. While turnover in 1879 totalled £475,000, net profit was only £20,000.

Peek was described as a little, dried-up man, clean-shaven and detesting beards; only the full beard sported by Frean was tolerated. Peek was invariably dressed in black, with an old-fashioned stock instead of a collar. Baptized in an independent chapel, throughout his life he held strong evangelical views, conducting business strictly but fairly, though somewhat over-anxious to chase the last halfpenny. In the year following his first wife's death in 1867, he married Jane, daughter of Sampson Trehane of Exeter, on 13 October 1868; they had no children. He died on 23 January 1879 at Watcombe Lodge, near Torquay, survived by his second wife, and bequeathing £50,000 to help poor people in Devon.

T. A. B. CORLEY

Sources F. C. Davis, 'Historical survey of Peek Frean & Co. Ltd, 1857–1957', typescript, 1957, U. Reading · *1857–1957: a hundred years of biscuit making by Peek, Frean, and Company Limited*, Peek, Frean, and Company [1957] · T. A. B. Corley, *Quaker enterprise in biscuits: Huntley and Palmer of Reading, 1822–1972* (1972) · Burke, *Peerage* · *Torquay Times and South Devon Advertiser* (25 Jan 1879) · *Torquay Times and South Devon Advertiser* (8 Feb 1879) · *Paignton and Newton Directory* (29 Jan 1879) · *Torbay Advertiser* (29 Jan 1879) · *CGPLA Eng. & Wales* (1879) · Boase, *Mod. Eng. biog.* · d. cert. · m. cert., 13 Oct 1868 · IGI
Archives U. Reading, Peek Frean MSS
Likenesses photograph, repro. in *1857–1957: a hundred years of biscuit making*, 5
Wealth at death under £180,000: probate, 1 March 1879, *CGPLA Eng. & Wales*

Peel. For this title name *see* individual entries under Peel; *see also* Lillie, Beatrice Gladys [Beatrice Gladys Peel, Lady Peel] (1894–1989).

Peel, Albert (1887–1949), Congregational minister and historian, was born on 20 March 1887 at Craven Lane, Gomersal, near Dewsbury, Yorkshire, the eldest of three children of Rawson Peel, a joiner journeyman, and his wife, Louisa, *née* Garnett. He attended Heckmondwike grammar school and, after working as a pupil teacher at Birstall, went in 1906 to the Yorkshire United Independent College, Bradford, to train for the Congregational ministry. Customarily Yorkshire College students took their degrees from Edinburgh University but Peel elected to take a BA from Leeds University, gaining first-class honours in history in 1909. He then spent two years at Oxford, acquiring a BLitt

and concurrently a Leeds MA and an intermediate BD from London University. He also attended lectures at Mansfield College, Oxford, in 1910–11, as the equivalent of his first theological year in Yorkshire. These exertions severely taxed his health. In 1915 Peel was awarded the LittD from Leeds, the first to receive this degree from the university. Peel appreciated his mentors, especially Sir Charles Firth, A. J. Grant of Leeds, W. B. Selbie of Mansfield College, and, in London, T. G. Crippen, the Congregational librarian.

Peel was ordained on 17 September 1913 at Great Harwood Congregational Church, Blackburn, Lancashire. He married in 1913 Ethel Constance Harrop (1888–1971), daughter of William Harrop, minister of Furthergate Congregational Church, Blackburn, and they had a daughter, Margaret. In 1922 Peel became minister of Clapton Park Congregational Church, London, where he proved both conscientious and innovative. He regularly worked between twelve and fourteen hours a day, including Sundays, writing, reading two books daily, and visiting, showing particular sympathy for the disadvantaged. In 1934 he resigned his pastorate but continued to preach his fluent, natural sermons on most Sundays.

In 1915 Peel's researches resulted in his editing the two volumes of *The Seconde Parte of a Register*, a calendar of sixteenth-century separatist manuscripts, to which Firth contributed the preface. In 1920 Peel published two important pamphlets, *The Brownists in Norwich and Norfolk about 1580* and *The first Congregational churches: new light on separatist congregations in London, 1567–1581*. In the latter he outlined his hope to write a detailed study of Elizabethan puritanism and separatism, a hope often renewed but sadly unrealized. Yet Peel became the English historian of sixteenth-century separatism.

In 1923 Peel founded the *Congregational Quarterly*, a serious theological journal, which he edited until 1945. In 1924 he was appointed editor of the *Transactions of the Congregational Historical Society* (founded 1901), a position he held at his death. Peel also became a director of the Independent Press at its founding in 1924 by the Congregational Union of England and Wales, and from 1929 he took charge of the Congregational Library. With so much activity historical research, although never abandoned, was given a low priority. In London, together with several minor publications, Peel produced a history of the Congregational Union, *These Hundred Years* (1931), and a significant study of the Elizabethan separatists in *Essays Congregational and Catholic* (1931), which he edited. In 1937 he wrote with Sir John Marriott the biography *Robert Forman Horton*. He was a fellow of the Royal Historical Society, publishing for it *The Note-Book of John Penry, 1593* (1944), and was transcribing a manuscript in the library of St John's College, Cambridge, which, after Peel's death, was prepared by Norman Sykes for publication as *Tracts Ascribed to Richard Bancroft* (1953). He often visited the United States of America, being awarded honorary doctorates from Carlton, Minnesota, and Rockford, Illinois.

In the late 1940s Peel developed a project to provide

definitive editions of the Elizabethan puritan and separatist writings, persuading his fellow trustees of the Sir Halley Stewart Trust to finance the scheme. When Peel died the first volume was in page proof and Leland H. Carlson agreed to continue this series. *Cartwrightiana* (1951) and *The Writings of Robert Harrison and Robert Browne* (1953) appeared under their joint editorship, while subsequent volumes were edited by Carlson alone. Peel's failure to write the history of Elizabethan puritanism and separatism marked a loss to scholarship and to his own fulfilment. He served as chairman of the Congregational Union in 1940–41. Increasingly isolated in later years, the uncompromising Peel continued to stress theological freedom when ministerial students were taught to value dogma, creeds, and written liturgies, especially by Nathaniel Micklem, then principal of Mansfield College.

Peel enjoyed cricket and was of medium height and build. Although outspoken and with few social graces, he was affable and clubbable. Relations with his wife in time became less easy. From 1926 to 1949 he lived at 97 Russell Road, Buckhurst Hill, Essex, although sometimes he stayed overnight at his office at Memorial Hall, Farringdon Street, London. Peel died from heart failure on 3 November 1949 at the McAlpin Nursing Home in Glasgow and was cremated in Glasgow. His ashes were taken to Bolton-le-Sands, Lancashire. ALAN ARGENT

Sources A. Argent, 'Albert Peel: the restless labourer', *Journal of the United Reformed Church History Society*, 4 (1987–92), 319–36 · R. Tudur Jones, *Congregationalism in England, 1662–1962* (1962) · private information (2004) · N. Sykes, 'Dr Albert Peel and historical studies', *Transactions of the Congregational Historical Society*, 17 (1952–5), 4–7 · *Congregational Year Book* (1950), 523–4 · L. H. Carlson, 'A corpus of Elizabethan nonconformist writings', *Papers read at the second winter and summer meetings of the Ecclesiastical History Society*, ed. G. J. Cuming, SCH, 2 (1965), 297–309 · A. J. Grieve, *Congregational Quarterly*, 28 (1950), 9–11 · P. Collinson, 'Towards a broader understanding of the early dissenting tradition', *Godly people: essays on English protestantism and puritanism* (1983), 527–62 · *Christian World* (10 Nov 1949) · *Manchester Guardian* (5 Nov 1949) · *The Times* (7 Nov 1949) · A. Peel, *These hundred years: a history of the Congregational Union of England and Wales, 1831–1931* (1931) · J. Creasey, *The Congregational Library* (1992) · b. cert. · *Congregational Year Book* (1853) · *Congregational Year Book* (1915) · *Congregational Year Book* (1922) · *Congregational Year Book* (1923) · *Congregational Year Book* (1925) · *Congregational Year Book* (1926) · *Congregational Year Book* (1947) · CGPLA Eng. & Wales (1950)

Archives JRL, Manchester Guardian Archives, letters to the *Manchester Guardian* · Norfolk RO, typescript article relating to the history of the church of Eccles-next-the-Sea

Likenesses Russell, photograph, 1931?, repro. in Peel, *These hundred years*, facing p. 400 · Russell, photograph, 1940, repro. in *Congregational Year Book* (1940), facing p. 1 · photograph, c.1943–1947, priv. coll.

Wealth at death £20,916 19s. 10d.: probate, 23 Feb 1950, CGPLA Eng. & Wales

Peel, Arthur Wellesley, first Viscount Peel (1829–1912),

speaker of the House of Commons, was born in London on 3 August 1829, the youngest of the five sons of Sir Robert *Peel, second baronet (1788–1850), prime minister, and his wife, Julia (1795–1859), daughter of General Sir John *Floyd, first baronet. He was named after his godfather,

Arthur Wellesley Peel, first Viscount Peel (1829–1912), by London Stereoscopic Co.

the first duke of Wellington. Among his brothers were Sir Robert *Peel, third baronet, Sir Frederick *Peel, and Sir William *Peel. Peel figures as a boy in *The Private Letters of Sir Robert Peel* (1920). His early years were spent at the family home, Drayton Manor, Tamworth, and he was educated at Hatfield, Eton College (1841–8), and Balliol College, Oxford, taking second-class honours in *literae humaniores* in 1852. His education was thus a departure from the Harrow–Christ Church tradition of the family.

In 1862 Peel married Adelaide (d. 1890), daughter of William Stratford Dugdale, of Merevale, Warwickshire, and his wife, Harriet Ella, née Portman. They had four sons, including the soldier and financier Sir Sidney Cornwallis *Peel, and three daughters. Peel followed his father politically, though they were not in personal terms particularly close, and Peel–Gladstone politics defined his early career, though he was always more a Peelite than a Gladstonian. In 1863 he stood as a Liberal at a by-election in Coventry but was defeated. In 1865 he was returned as one of the two members for Warwick, splitting the two tory candidates. In 1868 he held the seat comfortably, and in 1874 and 1880 marginally. In 1885, when Warwick was joined to Leamington, Peel held the seat; unopposed as speaker in 1886 and 1892, he was then described as a Liberal Unionist.

In Gladstone's first ministry, Peel was parliamentary

secretary to the poor-law board (1868–71) and then, from 1871 to 1873, secretary to the Board of Trade. From 1873 to 1874 he was Liberal chief whip, with the awkward task of reviving the party after its disintegration on the Irish universities question. He resigned as chief whip following the Liberal Party's defeat in the general election of 1874 and played no significant part in the crusades and campaigns of the opposition years. On his return to the premiership in April 1880, Gladstone made Peel undersecretary at the Home Office, but ill health required his resignation in December 1880. Peel was uneasy about the government's Irish policy and voted against its Crimes Bill in July 1882. In 1883 H. B. W. Brand told Gladstone, as prime minister, of his intention to retire as speaker. Gladstone invited Sir Francis Herschell and then G. J. Goshen, both of whom declined the invitation. Gladstone then turned to Peel (like Brand a former Liberal chief whip) despite his ill health and on the rather curious ground that he had never known a speaker 'whose health gave way under the pressure of his duties' (Gladstone, *Diaries*, 11.69). The Conservatives resented another former Liberal chief whip in the chair and on 26 February 1884 both Peel's nominators were Liberals (Northcote, as tory leader in the Commons, appearing to threaten opposition to Peel's subsequent re-election). He was elected unanimously, however, in 1884 (being also sworn of the privy council) and was re-elected unanimously on 12 January 1886, 5 August 1886, and 4 August 1892.

Despite the fact that he was hitherto well known for reticence in the Commons, Peel proved to be a formidable speaker, both physically and morally. He took office at a time of considerable animosity between the two main parties and held it during the years of Irish MPs' 'obstruction'. Peel's chief achievement was to maintain the dignity of the house despite these difficulties. His opening statement as speaker produced a memorable effect and his stern discipline was felt impartially by all members. He:

> removed the Speaker's office to a lofty and impregnable isolation. His appearance accorded with his demeanour. He was tall and lean, his face grave and unsmiling, the nose sharp, the lips thin, the austerity of the countenance emphasised by an iron-grey beard.   (Laundy, 323)

On 13 January 1884 he cut through the muddle which Speaker Brand had allowed to develop with respect to Charles Bradlaugh's oath of allegiance, by simply allowing Bradlaugh to take the oath and ruling Sir Michael Hicks Beach out of order in his objections as having not yet himself taken the oath. Peel's stern demeanour may, of course, have provoked as well as quietened Irish MPs, but his moral effect was famously seen on the night of 27 July 1893 when during the committee stage of the second Home Rule Bill a serious fight broke out on the floor of the house. The chairman of committees summoned the speaker, whose arrival in the house, like that of 'a parent, wise as well as fond', at once restored order.

The closure rule introduced in 1882 to speed the progress of government business depended on the speaker's initiative. Peel exercised it first on 24 February 1885, and again on 18 February 1887, after which the initiative was transferred from the speaker to the house, the speaker retaining, however, a veto on the introduction of the closure. Peel's willingness to allow the government to initiate closure was criticized on several occasions, and on 2 April 1887 Gladstone opposed what he saw as 'the mischievious Closure under the Speaker's authority' (Gladstone, *Diaries*, 12.22). The new standing orders of 1888, providing for an automatic interruption of business at midnight, were less contentious than the closure but the exceptions to the rule placed a burden on the speaker. Peel's authority helped the house through this period of adjustment. *The Times* noted in its obituary: 'Theoretically Peel was the servant of the House. There were occasions when a stranger might almost have regarded him as its master' (*The Times*, 25 Oct 1912).

Peel's wife died in 1890. In the autumn of 1894 he decided, for reasons of ill health, to retire as speaker. The Liberal government being in a minority, this posed problems for it and the retiral was several times delayed. At the end of February 1895 Peel declined to delay further, provoking a wrangle among the various candidates for his successor. On 4 April 1895 the cabinet agreed to the candidacy of W. C. Gully. Peel's resignation was announced on 8 April, leading to the first contest for the speakership since 1839. Peel was created Viscount Peel and accepted the speaker's pension.

Peel remained active in public life. He chaired the royal commission on the licensing laws (1896–9), leading the minority on the commission in producing a minority report opposing the creation of a perpetual interest in a terminable licence and favouring the rapid reduction of licences by a compensation fund levied on the drink trade.

Peel was visitor of Balliol College (1894–1912), chairman of the trustees of the National Portrait Gallery (1898–1908), and an active trustee of the British Museum from 1898 until 1908. He was also president of the Temperance Legislation League, first chairman of the State Children's Aid Association, chairman of the council of Toynbee Hall, a governor of Harrow School, and vice-chairman of the Bedfordshire county council. He received the honorary DCL at Oxford in 1887. Peel died on 24 October 1912 at Sandy, Bedfordshire, where he had lived for many years. He was succeeded as second viscount by his eldest son, William Robert Wellesley *Peel (1867–1937), also a politician.   H. C. G. MATTHEW

Sources *DNB* · GEC, *Peerage* · *The Times* (25 Oct 1912) · P. A. C. Laundy, *The office of speaker* (1964) · A. I. Dasent, *The speakers of the House of Commons* (1911) · Gladstone, *Diaries* · W. L. Arnstein, *The Bradlaugh case: a study in late Victorian opinion and politics* (1965) · T. A. Jenkins, *Gladstone, whiggery and the liberal party, 1874–1886* (1988)
Archives Beds. & Luton ARS, corresp. and papers, mainly relating to Eyeworth estate · Duke U., Perkins L., diary · priv. coll., corresp. and papers | BL, corresp. with W. E. Gladstone, Add. MS 44270 · BLPES, letters to Violet Markham · Bodl. Oxf., letters to H. W. Acland and S. A. Acland · CKS, letters to Edward Stanhope · Glos. RO, letters to Sir Michael Hicks Beach

Likenesses S. P. Hall, pencil drawing, 1886, NPG · Violet, lithograph, 1891, NPG · W. Q. Orchardson, oils, 1898, Palace of Westminster, London · L. Calkin, oils, NPG · W. Downey, woodburytype photograph, repro. in W. Downey and D. Downey, *The cabinet portrait gallery*, 3 (1892) · Elliott & Fry, cabinet photograph, NPG · H. Furniss, caricature, pen-and-ink sketch, NPG · F. C. Gould, caricatures, ink sketches, NPG · H. von Herkomer, oils, Balliol Oxf. · London Stereoscopic Co., cabinet photograph, NPG [*see illus.*] · W. Q. Orchardson, charcoal drawing, NG Scot. · Spy [L. Ward], caricature, watercolour study, NPG; repro. in *VF* (2 July 1887)

Wealth at death £128,175 17*s*.: probate, 18 Dec 1912, *CGPLA Eng. & Wales*

Peel, Beatrice Gladys. *See* Lillie, Beatrice Gladys (1894–1989).

Peel [*née* Bayliff], **Constance Dorothy Evelyn** (1868–1934), journalist and writer on household management, was born on 27 April 1868 at Ganarew, Herefordshire, the seventh of nine children (four of whom died in infancy) of Richard Lane Bayliff, captain in the 100th regiment and adjutant of the Monmouthshire Volunteers, and his wife, Henrietta, daughter of Robert Peel. Constance Bayliff's early childhood was spent in Wyesham, Monmouthshire, in straitened circumstances due to her father's poor health. Following a move to Bristol, she was mainly educated at home by her parents. Her education was constantly interrupted by asthmatic illness and she spent a considerable time convalescing with much wealthier relatives. She moved to Folkestone aged seventeen and came out at a military ball. She recalled that she and her sister 'lived what sensible people call an aimless life', visiting and party-going, which they could ill afford, struggling to 'freshen up' their few party dresses (Peel, 58). Her frugal upbringing, together with her parents' preoccupation with the poor and the extravagance she saw in the homes of her relatives, left a considerable impression on her.

Constance's journalistic career started after her family moved to Twickenham. Inspired by her sister, who was illustrating articles for *The Queen*, she won a competition for a dress article in *Woman*. Despite her poor education, she went on to write for most of the popular magazines and newspapers of her time, her earnings giving her an unusual amount of financial independence. Arnold Bennett, editor of *Woman*, told her that she did not know how to write and arranged for her to have grammar lessons from a board schoolteacher. She learned more, however, from Bennett's skilful editing.

On 6 December 1894 Constance married her second cousin Charles Steers Peel, the son of Francis William Peel, rector of Burghwallis, Yorkshire. Her husband was an electrical engineer and they moved to Dewsbury. Constance continued to work as a journalist in London, publishing as Mrs C. S. Peel. She inhabited three very different worlds: the artistic London world, the manufacturing town world, and the country house world (she was presented at court the year after she married), all of which influenced her writings. She drew on her experience of setting up home in her first book, *The new home: treating of the arrangement, decoration and furnishing of a house of medium size to be maintained by moderate income* (1898). Forced to run her own house when her maid left, she 'soon discovered how easily money could be wasted by bad kitchen management' (Peel, 111). She concentrated on work that she could do from home so that she could spend time with her young daughter. She was editor and managing director of *Hearth and Home*, *Woman*, and *Myra's Journal* from 1903 until 1906 and published a series of popular cookery books. She was also managing director of Beeton & Co. from 1903 to 1906.

Constance Peel took a break from work after the birth of her second child, Denise. A year and a half later she lost her third and last baby. She decided on a change of career and, fashionably, started a hat shop with her friend Ethel Kentish. The business met with some success, with famous clients such as Ellen Terry. However, she had doubts about the morality of fashion and eventually decided to close down the business owing to ill health. When she recovered in 1914 she wrote a novel, *The Hat Shop*, which met with critical acclaim, encouraging her to write three more.

By 1913 both children were at school and Constance Peel began to miss her former life as a journalist. She took up the post of editor of the household department of *The Queen*, a position she held for seventeen years, as well as working for *Hearth and Home* and *The Lady*. Her books such as *Marriage on Small Means* (1914) and *The Labour Saving House* (1917) instructed women in modern methods and technologies of household management. In 1918 Lord Northcliffe appointed her editor of the *Daily Mail* women's page. This was brought to an abrupt end when she was diagnosed with diabetes in 1920; her life was saved by the discovery of insulin later in the year.

During the First World War, Constance Peel organized a Soldiers' and Sailors' Wives Club in Lambeth, and was a speaker for the United Workers' Association and the National War Savings Association. In partnership with Maud Pember Reeves she worked as co-director of women's service for the Ministry of Food during the period of voluntary food rationing, March 1917–March 1918. She travelled round the country and delivered 176 addresses promoting the economical use of food. She was appointed OBE in 1919. After the war she worked for improvements in women's domestic lives. She served on two committees, under the Ministry of Reconstruction, on working-class housing and domestic service. She also was involved in committees of the Ministry of Health, the Town Planning and Garden Cities associations, Women's Pioneer Housing, and the Peckham Pioneer Health Centre. She was vice-president of the British Women Housewives' Association.

Constance Peel wrote five volumes of memoirs with vivid descriptions of interiors and a keen eye for social detail on the great social changes in her lifetime. In *Life's Enchanted Cup: an Autobiography, 1872–1933* (1933) she made it clear that she worked out of necessity as well as pleasure: to provide for her two children, to support an aunt, and to save for her old age. She died at 7 Knaresborough

Place, Kensington, London, on 7 August 1934 from complications induced by her long-standing myocarditis and diabetes. Her husband survived her. DEBORAH S. RYAN

Sources Mrs C. S. Peel [C. D. E. Peel], *Life's enchanted cup: an autobiography, 1872–1933* (1933) · *WWW* · b. cert. · m. cert. · d. cert. **Likenesses** photograph, 1917, repro. in Peel, *Life's enchanted cup* · photograph, repro. in Peel, *Life's enchanted cup* **Wealth at death** £8598 3s. 11d.: probate, 12 Oct 1934, *CGPLA Eng. & Wales*

Peel, Edwin Arthur (1911–1992), educational psychologist, was born on 11 March 1911 at 19 Copley Street, Everton, Liverpool, the son of Arthur Peel, a schoolmaster in an industrial school, and his wife, Mary Ann Miller. The family came from Yorkshire. Edwin was educated at Prince Henry's Grammar School at Otley, Yorkshire, and read chemistry at Leeds University (1930–33). As a student he competed in Cumberland wrestling.

Peel taught technical subjects at a number of London schools in the mid-1930s, juggling work with part-time study of psychology at the University of London. Obtaining an MA in 1938, he took a permanent post at the London County Council School of Building, before marrying (Nora) Kathleen Yeadon (d. 1988), a 25-year-old teacher, on 10 April 1939. From 1941 until 1945 Peel helped the war effort as an industrial chemist with the Ministry of Supply, while finishing a PhD thesis in educational psychology. It examined procedures for predicting the academic and technical ability of children, and used matrix algebra as a means of combining different measurements.

After lecturing at the London University Institute of Education in 1945 and at King's College, Newcastle upon Tyne, in 1946, Peel became reader in psychology (1946–8) and then professor of educational psychology (1948–50) at Durham University. Aptitude testing continued to interest him: he decided to replace pencil-and-paper tests with new exercises involving the arrangement of wooden blocks into various patterns. He was appointed professor of education at the University of Birmingham in 1950 and stayed there for the next twenty-eight years, overseeing the expansion of his department into several fresh areas of research (notably the special educational needs of children with disabilities).

While encouraging colleagues to pursue diverse lines of enquiry Peel concentrated on essential issues of teaching and learning, partly inspired by observing how his own two sons and two daughters came to understand their world. Learning to drive also furnished his lectures with many illustrative examples. He published *The Psychological Basis of Education* in 1956, a survey of existing theories of learning that was often used by students of the subject in the 1960s. A revised edition appeared in 1967.

E. A. Peel contributed numerous articles to the *British Journal of Educational Psychology*, the *British Journal of Mathematical and Statistical Psychology*, and the *Educational Review*. London University awarded him a DLitt in 1961, largely on the strength of his book *The Pupil's Thinking* (1960), which identified four kinds of thinking—the thematic, explanatory, productive, and integrative—and analysed development from early childhood to adolescence. Peel's ideas owed much to the theories of thought growth propounded by the Swiss psychologist Jean Piaget (1896–1980). His own empirical studies, based on Gestalt psychology, largely confirmed Piaget's models, once the mental age of the child was substituted for the chronological age.

Peel served as president of the British Psychological Society (1961–2) and chairman of his university's school of education (1965–70). In *The Nature of Adolescent Judgment* (1971), another specialist monograph, he categorized the intellectual processes whereby teenagers apprehend inconsistencies between the actual and the possible and reconcile the actuality of their existence with the possibilities that they envisage for themselves. Never tempted to offer grand recommendations, he yet wondered whether providing greater opportunities in school for early adolescents to discuss and evaluate problems with teachers and peers could lead to an earlier development of intellectual maturity. There might be a role here, he suggested, for the programmed techniques devised by behaviourists to teach learners how to think.

Edwin Peel, a craggy-faced Yorkshireman, much enjoyed gardening and cooking in his spare time. After his retirement in 1978, he continued to live in Birmingham at 47 Innage Road. He was proud to be elected a member of the Birmingham Society of Artists; his watercolours displayed considerable skill. Widowed in 1988, he moved into a rest home at High Callerton, Ponteland, Northumberland, not long before he died of bronchopneumonia at the Freeman Hospital, Newcastle upon Tyne, on 10 June 1992. JASON TOMES

Sources *The Times* (16 June 1992) · *The Independent* (18 June 1992) · b. cert. · m. cert. · d. cert. · *WW* **Likenesses** photograph, repro. in *The Times*

Peel, Sir Frederick (1823–1906), politician and railway commissioner, born in Stanhope Street, London, on 26 October 1823, was the second son of Sir Robert *Peel, second baronet (1788–1850), prime minister, and his wife, Julia (1795–1859), daughter of General Sir John *Floyd, first baronet. His elder brother was Sir Robert *Peel, third baronet; his younger brothers were Sir William *Peel, naval captain, and Arthur Wellesley (afterwards first Viscount) *Peel, speaker of the House of Commons.

Frederick Peel was educated at Harrow School (1836–41), and then at Trinity College, Cambridge (his father disapproving of the decline of discipline at Christ Church, Oxford, his own college). He graduated BA in 1845 as a junior optime and with a first class in the classical tripos, and proceeded MA in 1849. He was the ablest intellectually of the Peel children, and, from his father's viewpoint, the most dependable. On leaving Cambridge he became a student at the Inner Temple on 5 May 1845, and was called to the bar on 2 February 1849. In the same month he entered the House of Commons, being returned unopposed as Liberal member for Leominster; his choice of party was seen by many as confirmation of his father's inclinations. His maiden speech (11 May 1849) supported the removal of Jewish disabilities, and seemed to suggest a promising political career. Peel was a staunch supporter of free trade and of the extension of the franchise, but being distrustful of secret voting he was not in favour of the ballot. Despite his outspoken criticism of the Liberal government's Ecclesiastical Titles Bill (14 February 1851), Lord John Russell recognized his ability by appointing him under-secretary for the colonies. After the general election of 1852, when Peel successfully contested Bury, he resumed the post of under-secretary for the colonies in Lord Aberdeen's coalition ministry. On 15 February 1853 he introduced the Clergy Reserves Bill, designed to give the government of Canada effective control over the churches there and to end the use of Canadian land to subsidize the protestant clergy. Under Peel's auspices the bill passed the House of Commons, despite violent opposition from the Conservatives, and received the royal assent on 9 May 1853.

On the fall of the Aberdeen ministry in January 1855 Peel became Palmerston's under-secretary for war. In view of the popular outcry against the mismanagement of the Crimean War the post involved heavy responsibilities. Peel's chief, Lord Panmure, sat in the House of Lords, but Peel was responsible minister in the House of Commons. It was he who consequently bore the brunt of the criticism of the war and its inept handling. In 1857 he lost his seat at Bury and resigned office. In recognition of his services he was made a privy councillor. He was once more returned for Bury in 1859 and was appointed by Palmerston to the financial secretaryship of the Treasury, a post which he held until 1865, working with W. E. Gladstone, who was chancellor of the exchequer. In 1865 he was again defeated at Bury at the general election and lost his office. Peel then tired somewhat of the rough-and-tumble of political life. He unsuccessfully contested South-East Lancashire in 1868, and never re-entered the House of Commons. He was created KCMG in 1869, and turned to law and administration.

In 1873, on the passing of the Regulation of Railways Act, Peel was appointed a member of the railway and canal commission, on which he served until his death. The tribunal was constituted as a court of arbitration to settle disagreements between railways and their customers which lay beyond the scope of ordinary litigation. The commission rapidly developed in importance, and was reorganized by the Railway and Canal Act of 1888, a judge of the High Court being added to its members. Peel and his colleagues rendered useful service to the farming and commercial interests by reducing preferential rates on many railways. In *Ford & Co.* v. *London and South Western Railway* they decided that the existence of a favoured list of passengers constituted an undue preference (*The Times*, 3 Nov 1890). The decisions of the commissioners were seldom reversed on appeal. In the case of *Sowerby & Co.* v. *Great Northern Railway*, Peel dissented from the judgment of his colleagues, Mr Justice Wills and Mr Price, to the effect that the railway company was entitled to make charges in addition to the maximum in respect of station

accommodation and expenses, but the view of the majority was upheld by the Court of Appeal (21 March 1891). As senior commissioner, Peel became the most influential member of the tribunal. He had his father's judicial mind and cautious, equable temper, but his reticence, aloofness, and lack of ambition militated against his success in public life.

Peel married first, on 12 August 1857, Elizabeth Emily (*d.* 1865), daughter of John Shelley of Avington House, Hampshire, and niece of Percy Bysshe Shelley, the poet; and second, on 3 September 1879, Janet (*d.* 1925), daughter of Philip Pleydell Bouverie of Brymore, Somerset, who survived him. There were no children by either marriage. Peel lived at the manor house of Hampton in Arden, Warwickshire, which his father bought for him and bequeathed to him. He died at his London house, 32 Chesham Place, on 6 June 1906 and was buried at Hampton in Arden.   G. S. WOODS, *rev.* H. C. G. MATTHEW

Sources *The Times* (7 June 1906) · *Morning Post* (7 June 1906) · N. Gash, *Sir Robert Peel: the life of Sir Robert Peel after 1830* (1972) · C. S. Parker, ed., *Sir Robert Peel: from his private papers*, 2nd edn, 3 vols. (1899) · Gladstone, *Diaries*

Archives BL, corresp. with W. E. Gladstone and memoranda, Add. MSS 44118–44752

Likenesses W. & D. Downey, carte-de-visite, NPG · Spy [L. Ward], caricature, watercolour study, NPG; repro. in *VF* (17 Dec 1903)

Wealth at death £101,612 19*s.* 5*d.*: probate, 13 Dec 1906, *CGPLA Eng. & Wales*

Peel, James (1811–1906), landscape painter, born on 1 July 1811 in Westgate Road, Newcastle upon Tyne, was the son of Thomas Peel (*d.* 1822), a woollen draper and partner in the firm of Fenwick, Reid & Co., dealers in wine and woollen cloths. He was educated at Dr Bruce's school in Newcastle upon Tyne alongside Sir Charles Mark Palmer, later a shipbuilder, and John Collingwood Bruce, who became a noted antiquary. He then studied drawing with the painter Edward Dalziel, father of the wood-engravers the Dalziel brothers. In 1840 he went to London to paint portraits and continue his studies by making copies in the National Gallery.

Eventually Peel concentrated on painting landscapes, finding inspiration especially in Derbyshire, Yorkshire, and Wales. His pictures were remarkable for a truthful feeling for nature; he was praised for his treatment of running water and cloud-laden skies. Three of his paintings, *A Lane in Berwickshire*, *Cotherstone, Yorkshire*, and *Pont-y-Pant, Wales*, were acquired by the Laing Art Gallery in Newcastle upon Tyne, where a loan exhibition of his works was held in 1907. Others were bought by galleries in Glasgow, Leeds, and Sunderland, and for private collectors in Newcastle. On 30 May 1849, in Darlington, co. Durham, he married Sarah Martha Blyth, eldest daughter of Thomas Blyth; two sons and three daughters survived them. He lived in Darlington for a while, but in 1860 he returned to London with his family.

From 1843 to 1888 Peel exhibited regularly at the Royal Academy. He was also a leading supporter of the Society (later Royal Society) of British Artists, exhibiting there from 1845; he was elected as a member in 1871. With Ford

Madox Brown, William Bell Scott, and other artists he organized 'free' exhibitions, including ones at the Dudley Gallery and the ill-fated Portland Gallery in London. James Peel continued to work well into his nineties and died at his home, Western Elms Lodge, Oxford Road, Reading, Berkshire, on 28 January 1906.

F. W. GIBSON, *rev.* SUZANNE FAGENCE COOPER

Sources C. B. Stevenson, *Exhibition of works by James Peel RBA* (1907) · M. A. Wingfield, *A dictionary of sporting artists, 1650–1990* (1992) · M. H. Grant, *A dictionary of British landscape painters, from the 16th century to the early 20th century* (1952), 146 · *The Times* (5 Feb 1906) · *Newcastle Weekly Chronicle* (20 March 1897) · S. H. Pavière, *A dictionary of Victorian landscape painters* (1968), pl. 57 · J. Johnson, ed., *Works exhibited at the Royal Society of British Artists, 1824–1893, and the New English Art Club, 1888–1917*, 2 vols. (1975) · Wood, *Vic. painters*, 3rd edn · CGPLA Eng. & Wales (1906) · private information (1912) · Graves, *Brit. Inst.*

Archives Courtauld Inst., Witt Library

Likenesses photograph, repro. in *Newcastle Weekly Chronicle* · print, repro. in Stevenson, *Exhibition of works*

Wealth at death £1471 17s. 8d.: probate, 17 Feb 1906, CGPLA Eng. & Wales

Peel, John (1776–1854), huntsman, was born on 13 November 1776 at Park End Cottage, Caldbeck, Cumberland, the son of William Peel, a farmer and horse dealer, and Lettice Scott. In 1797 he eloped with Mary White of Uldale to Gretna in Scotland, where young couples could be married easily, quickly, and without parental consent; they were married on 18 December. It was a happy union, and of their thirteen children only one died young. Peel's love of hunting was remarkable. For fifty-five years he maintained, at his sole expense, a pack, usually of twelve couples, of hounds, and generally kept two horses. He had a faultless knowledge of the country and of hunting, and was long aided by his eldest son, 'Young John'. He was a coarse, heavy-drinking, rather selfish man, but could also be generous and passionate.

Peel's reputation was largely attributable to the song celebrating his prowess as a hunter by his friend John Woodcock Graves. This was written during the winter of 1829, when Peel and Graves were planning a hunting expedition in the parlour of the inn at Caldbeck. A casual question from Graves's daughter as to the words sung to an old Cumberland rant (tune), 'Bonnie Annie', caused Graves to write impromptu 'D'ye ken John Peel', the five verses of which he sang to the ancient air (William Metcalfe, the choirmaster of Carlisle Cathedral, set the verses to its actual music in 1869). Graves jokingly prophesied that Peel would 'be sung when we've both run to earth'. Few songs have so firmly established themselves in popular estimation and so significantly helped to create and diffuse an image of Cumberland.

Late in his life Peel's neighbours and friends, including Sir Wilfrid Lawson and George Moore the philanthropist, presented him with a sum of money in acknowledgement of his long services. Besides his patrimonial estate at Caldbeck, Peel acquired, through his wife, a property at Ruthwaite, on which his last years were spent. There he died on 13 November 1854, probably from a hunting injury. He

John Peel (1776–1854), by unknown photographer

was buried, and a headstone erected over his grave, ornamented with emblems of the chase, in the churchyard at Caldbeck.

Graves, who was born in a house next to the Market Hall in the High Street of Wigton in Cumberland on 9 February 1795, emigrated to Van Diemen's Land in 1833, and settled in Hobart Town, where he died on 17 August 1886, leaving a large family. He published *Songs and Ballads of Cumberland* and a *Monody on John Peel*.

ALBERT NICHOLSON, *rev.* S. R. J. BAUDRY

Sources *West Cumberland Times* (2 Oct 1886) · *West Cumberland Times* (9 Oct 1886) · Ferguson, *Cumberland fox hounds* · S. Smiles, *George Moore, merchant and philanthropist*, 4th edn (1879), 26 · The Druid [H. H. Dixon], *Saddle and sirloin, or, English farm and sporting worthies* (1870), 109 · *N&Q*, 7th ser., 10 (1890), 281, 369; 11 (1891), 9, 216 · H. Machell, *John Peel, famous in sport and song* (1926) · W. R. Mitchell, *The John Peel story* (1968) · 'John Peel, the man, the myth, and the song', *Cumbria Weekly Digest* (1976)

Likenesses C. Towne, oils, repro. in 'John Peel, the man, the myth, and the song', 12 · etching, repro. in 'John Peel, the man, the myth, and the song', 7 · oils, repro. in Machell, *John Peel* · oils, repro. in Mitchell, *The John Peel story*, 35 · photograph (aged seventy-eight), repro. in 'John Peel, the man, the myth, and the song', 16 · photograph, NPG [*see illus.*]

Peel, Jonathan (1799–1879), politician, soldier, and patron of the turf, the fifth son of Sir Robert *Peel, first baronet (1750–1830), cotton manufacturer, and his first wife, Ellen Yates (1766–1803), and brother of Sir Robert *Peel, second baronet, the politician, was born at Chamber Hall, near Bury, Lancashire, on 12 October 1799. He was sent to Rugby School in 1811, and on 15 June 1815, three days before the

Jonathan Peel (1799–1879), by Sir Francis Grant, exh. RA 1862

battle of Waterloo, he received a commission as a second lieutenant in the rifle brigade. The peace that followed prevented him from seeing service, and his subsequent steps were obtained by purchase. From 3 December 1818 to 13 December 1821 he served as a captain in the 71st highlanders, and from 7 November 1822 to 19 May 1825 as a major in the Grenadier Guards. He was a major of the 69th foot from 3 October 1826 to 7 June 1827, and a lieutenant-colonel of the 53rd foot from 7 June 1827 until he was placed on half pay on 9 August 1827. He became a brevet-colonel on 23 November 1841, a major-general on 20 June 1854, and a lieutenant-general on 7 December 1859, and sold out of the army on 4 August 1863. In 1854 he applied to Lord Panmure, the secretary for war, for permission to join the siege of Sevastopol in the Crimea; he was then a healthy man of fifty-five, but his application was refused on the grounds that he was too old.

On 19 March 1824 Peel married Lady Alicia Jane (d. 1887), the youngest daughter of Archibald Kennedy, first marquess of Ailsa, with whom he had five sons and three daughters. At the 1826 general election he entered parliament as a tory as one of the members for Norwich. He exchanged in 1831 for the more secure borough of Huntingdon, which he continued to represent until his retirement from parliamentary life at the dissolution of 1868. During his brother's second administration, in 1841–6,

Peel held the post of surveyor-general of the ordnance. He was not given office in Lord Derby's first administration in 1852; but when Derby again became premier in 1858, he appointed Peel as secretary for war and a member of the cabinet—a significant gesture towards the name of Sir Robert Peel, his former colleague and rival. Peel soon made his mark in official life, and became very popular. None knew better than he the wants of the army or more thoroughly mastered the details of the estimates. His letters to *The Times* on military expenditure showed a thorough grasp of the statistics of the subject. He again held the post of secretary of state for war in Derby's third administration during 1866–7, but he resigned office on 2 March 1867 with lords Carnarvon and Salisbury rather than support Disraeli's scheme of reform. Throughout his political career Peel preserved an irreproachable reputation, and, although a strong Conservative, showed himself when in office a strenuous supporter of inquiries into abuses in all matters of military organization.

Peel was noted for his devotion to horse racing and his deep knowledge of all things connected with the turf. His racing career began in 1821, when he was part owner of some horses with the duke of Richmond and Lord Stradbrooke. In 1824 his mare Phantom ran second for the Oaks to Lord Jersey's Cobweb. It was not until 1830 that Peel's name first appeared in the *Racing Calendar* when he raced in confederacy with his relative General Jonathan Yates. Two years later he enjoyed success when his horse Archibald won the Two Thousand Guineas, and his good fortune culminated with the triumph of his Orlando in the Derby of 1844. In that race, Ionian, another of his horses, came second. This was one of the most sensational races on record, and will always be associated with the exposure of a particularly serious fraud. A horse entered as Running Rein came in first but, after Peel's appeal, was disqualified as being a four-year-old, and the race was awarded to Orlando. Mr A. Wood, the owner of Running Rein, then brought an action against Peel, as a member of the Jockey Club, for recovery of the stakes. The case was heard before Baron Alderson on 1–2 July 1844, when, Wood not producing Running Rein, a verdict was returned for the defendant. On 18 August 1851 Peel sold his stud for 12,000 guineas; but on the death of the earl of Glasgow in 1869, having been left some horses, he resumed his connection with the turf. His favourite jockeys were Arthur Pavis and Nat Flatman. In the Newmarket second October meeting of 1878 Peel's purple jacket and orange cap, familiar on English racecourses for nearly sixty years, were borne to victory for the last time by a colt called Peter—so named after a nickname given to Lord Glasgow by his closest friends. At the time of his death, Peel's nominations for coming races numbered about fifty.

Peel died at his seat, Marble Hill, Twickenham, Middlesex, on 13 February 1879 and was buried in Twickenham new cemetery on the 19th.   EMMA EADIE

Sources F. Lawley, 'General Peel', *Baily's Magazine*, 54 (1890), 83–94 · Thormanby [W. W. Dixon], *Men of the turf: anecdotes of their career, and notes on many famous races* [1887], 120–24 · Thormanby [W. W. Dixon], *Kings of the turf: memoirs and anecdotes* (1898), 133–44 ·

New Sporting Magazine, 15 (1838), 371 · R. Mortimer, R. Onslow, and P. Willett, *Biographical encyclopedia of British flat racing* (1978), 449 · J. Kent, *Racing life of Lord George Cavendish Bentinck, and other reminiscences*, ed. F. Lawley (1892), 383–99 · Boase, *Mod. Eng. biog.* · Burke, *Peerage*

Archives Balliol Oxf., corresp. | BL, corresp. with Sir Robert Peel, Add. MSS 40245–40609 · Bodl. Oxf., letters to Benjamin Disraeli · Herts. ALS, corresp. with Lord Lytton · Lpool RO, letters to fourteenth earl of Derby · W. Sussex RO, letters to duke of Richmond **Likenesses** S. W. Reynolds, mezzotint, pubd 1825 (after Wilson), NPG · H. A. Frith, silhouette, 1850–75, Marble Hill, Twickenham · F. Grant, oils, exh. RA 1862, Huntingdon town hall [*see illus.*] · J. Brown, portrait (after J. Watkins), repro. in *Baily's Magazine*, 3 (1861), 273–8 · T. C. Wilson, lithograph (after pen sketch), BM, NPG; repro. in Wildrake [G. Tattersall], *Cracks of the day* (1841) · engraving, repro. in *Harper's Weekly*, 11 (1867), 168 · portrait, repro. in *New Sporting Magazine* · portrait, repro. in *Sporting Times* (13 Feb 1875) · portrait, repro. in *Illustrated Sporting and Dramatic News*, 1 (1874), 201–2 · portrait, repro. in *ILN*, 74 (1879), 2274 · portrait, repro. in Thormanby, *Kings of the turf* **Wealth at death** under £40,000: resworn probate, Sept 1879, *CGPLA Eng. & Wales*

Peel, Laurence (1801–1888). *See under* Peel, Sir Lawrence (1799–1884).

Peel, Sir Lawrence (1799–1884), judge in India, was born at Wandsworth, Surrey, on 10 August 1799, the third son of Joseph Peel (*d.* 1821), of Bowes Farm, Middlesex, and his wife, Anne, second daughter of Jonathan Haworth of Harcroft, Lancashire. His father was a younger brother of Sir Robert *Peel, first baronet (1750–1830), and so he was first cousin to Sir Robert *Peel, second baronet (1788–1850). He was educated at St John's College, Cambridge, matriculating in Lent 1817 and graduating BA in 1821 and MA in 1824. He was admitted at the Middle Temple on 31 October 1820 and called to the bar on 7 May 1824, went on the northern circuit, and attended the Lancaster, Preston, and Manchester sessions.

Peel was advocate-general at Calcutta from 1840 to 1842, and in 1842, on promotion to the chief-justiceship of the supreme court at Calcutta, was knighted by patent on 18 May. During 1854 and 1855 he was also vice-president of the legislative council at Calcutta. He resided in the suburbs, first at Cossipore and then at Garden Reach. He gave away in public charity his official income of £8000 per annum. He was consequently very popular and on his retirement in November 1855 a statue of him was erected in Calcutta.

After his return to England, Peel was sworn of the privy council and was made a paid member of the judicial committee on 4 April 1856. He was elected a bencher of the Middle Temple on 8 May 1856 and became treasurer of his inn on 3 December 1866. From 1857 he was a director of the East India Company, and on 16 June 1858 was made an Oxford DCL. In January 1864 he became president of Guy's Hospital, London. He was president of the East India Association (1874). He was for some years a correspondent of *The Times* on legal and general topics. He wrote *Horae nauseae* (1841), poems translated and original (the latter probably juvenile), and *A Sketch of the Life and Character of Sir*

R. Peel (1860). He died, unmarried, at his home, Garden Reach (named after the Calcutta suburb), Ventnor, Isle of Wight, on 22 July 1884.

Peel has sometimes been confused with his quasi-namesake **Laurence Peel** (1801–1888), sixth, youngest, and 'least distinguished' (Gash, 63) son of Sir Robert Peel, first baronet, who was born on 28 June 1801 and was educated at Rugby School from 1812 and at Christ Church, Oxford, where he matriculated in October 1819. Laurence Peel on 20 July 1822 married Lady Jane Lennox (*d.* 1861), daughter of the fourth duke of Richmond; they had several children. He was conservative MP for the Lowther family pocket borough of Cockermouth, Cumberland (1827–30), and a secretary of the India board. He died at 32 Sussex Square, Brighton, on 10 December 1888.

G. C. BOASE, *rev.* ROGER T. STEARN

Sources *The Times* (23 July 1884) · *The Times* (1 Aug 1884) · Venn, *Alum. Cant.* · Burke, *Peerage* (1999) · H. A. C. Sturgess, ed., *Register of admissions to the Honourable Society of the Middle Temple, from the fifteenth century to the year 1944*, 2 (1949) · Boase, *Mod. Eng. biog.* · H. E. A. Cotton, *Calcutta old and new: a historical and descriptive handbook to the city* (1907) · N. Gash, *Mr Secretary Peel: the life of Sir Robert Peel to 1830* (1961) · G. A. Solly, ed., *Rugby School register*, rev. edn, 1: *April 1675 – October 1857* (1933) · Foster, *Alum. Oxon.* · Kelly, *Handbk* (1879) · *CGPLA Eng. & Wales* (1884) **Archives** BL, corresp. with Sir Robert Peel, Add. MSS 40379–40874 **Wealth at death** £3129 3s. 11d.: administration, 8 Sept 1884, *CGPLA Eng. & Wales*

Peel, Paul (1860–1892), painter, was born on 7 November 1860 at London, Ontario, Canada, to English parents. His artistic ambitions were encouraged by his father, a marble cutter and drawing instructor, and he received his first formal training at the Pennsylvania Academy of Fine Arts in Philadelphia. He was elected a member of the Ontario Society of Artists in 1880, in which year he left for Europe. He studied for a time at the Royal Academy before moving to Pont-Aven in Brittany where, in the first part of 1881, he produced the religious work *Devotion*. Later that year he settled in Paris and in 1882 enrolled at the École des Beaux-Arts, studying under Jean-Leon Gérôme. He afterwards made only occasional short sojourns in his native country. His art was entirely French in character and he was a successful exhibitor at the salon of the Société des Artistes Français, gaining a third-class medal in 1891 for his large picture *After the Bath*. The previous year he had obtained honourable mention for *Life is Bitter*. Seven of his works were included in the Colonial and Indian Exhibition in London in 1886 and the prince of Wales was among his English patrons. Peel's favourite subjects were taken from the nursery, but during the summer months he used to work *en plein air* in the northern provinces of France. He was an excellent colourist and a master of delicate effects of light. He established a notable reputation in Europe during his brief lifetime and was elected to the Royal Canadian Academy in 1890. He died in Paris on 3 October 1892, leaving a widow and one son.

WALTER ARMSTRONG, *rev.* MARK POTTLE

Sources *The Times* (28 Oct 1892) · Thieme & Becker, *Allgemeines Lexikon*, vol. 26 · Bryan, *Painters* (1903–5), vol. 4 · private information (1895) · J. Turner, ed., *The dictionary of art*, 34 vols. (1996)

Peel, Sir Robert, first baronet (1750–1830), calico printer and politician, was born at Oswaldtwistle, Lancashire, on 25 April 1750, the third of the seven sons of Robert Peel (1723–1795), a dealer (or chapman) in the linen and cotton cloth known as 'Blackburn Greys', and his wife, Elizabeth, *née* Howarth. About 1760 the father went into partnership with his brother-in-law Jonathan Howarth, and four years later they began a small calico printing factory at Brookside, Oswaldtwistle; William Yates, the publican of the Black Bull inn, was brought in to provide warehouse space and additional capital. The earliest success of the enterprise was the production of a simple parsley leaf design from which Robert Peel senior earned his trade nickname, 'Parsley' Peel. Young Robert gained his early commercial and industrial experience in this small concern before attending Blackburn grammar school and undergoing an apprenticeship to one of the Yates family of Blackburn. He also had some brief commercial experience in London and on the continent.

Parsley Peel, according to his son Robert, 'possessed in an eminent degree a mechanical genius', and, seizing on a number of innovations in the 1760s, carried his firm into the forefront of development of the early English cotton industry. James Hargreaves, the inventor of the spinning jenny, was one of Howarth and Peel's weavers, so it was not long before Parsley Peel induced him to part with his secret. Arkwright was a close rival in the calico printing business, and his originality was vigorously contested by Peel and a group of other Lancashire manufacturers while they devoured what was most profitable in his new system of factory spinning, then quickly improved it. Robert Peel junior inherited his father's mechanical ability and enterprise, and had a similar way of assuming a leading role in successive innovations by means of acquisitions and partnerships. In particular, he was among the first group to buy an interest in Crompton's mule spinning technique (1780), and, through the Ainsworths of Haliwell, Bolton, he was in the vanguard of muslin making and chemical bleaching (1790). He was probably the first to apply steam power to mule spinning (1787).

Parsley Peel is said to have given Robert £500 to start business on his own account, very likely because his most able son was restless in the family fold. In 1772, at the age of twenty-two, he started a new enterprise on the Chamber Hall estate at Bury, 8 miles from Manchester, in partnership with William Yates and his uncle Howarth. The core of the business was a calico printing works, and there were also spinning mills in the vicinity and hundreds of handloom weavers employed in the Pennine villages and hamlets roundabout. The concern was established just as the cotton industry was taking off in Lancashire, and grew rapidly. On 8 July 1783 Peel married Ellen (1766–1803), the daughter of William Yates; they had nine surviving children, six sons and three daughters. By 1784 he was employing at least 6800 people directly or indirectly. Dr Aiken, writing in 1795, reported that the fabrics made and

Sir Robert Peel, first baronet (1750–1830), by Sir Thomas Lawrence, *c*.1825

printed were 'chiefly the finest kind of the cotton manufactory … in high request both in Manchester and London' (Aiken, 268). When the site became inadequate—bleaching fields took up many acres round all print works at this time—more land was acquired, then a second site was opened at Ramsbottom, just to the north of Bury. For most of the 1780s, Livesey, Hargreaves & Co. of Preston was the largest of the Lancashire calico printers, but the collapse of this leviathan of the trade in 1788 left Peel, Yates & Co. of Bury as undisputed leaders.

Not content with this spectacular achievement, Peel found further partners to start calico printing on other virgin sites. In the later 1780s, under the impetus of Crompton's mule spinning technique, Bolton was emerging as the centre of fine cotton spinning, and the possibility of imitating fine Indian cotton fabrics (muslin) challenged the Lancashire industry. Peel was the foremost partner in an integrated spinning, weaving, and finishing operation at three sites in Bolton, in 1787. The other partners were the Ainsworths, already noticed as pioneers of muslin manufacture and then of chemical bleaching in the area. Hand-loom weavers were in short supply, so Peels, Ainsworth & Co. employed them as far away as Warrington, Burnley, Chorley, Wigan, and even Paisley in Scotland.

The pinnacle of this tireless expansion was reached in the early 1790s, when Peel purchased an estate of 4000 acres at Fazeley, near Tamworth, Staffordshire, both to build another integrated cotton works and to satisfy his social and political ambitions. Tamworth is 70 miles from Manchester, well outside the area stimulated by the expansion of the cotton industry, and so lacked the internal economies of location, but this does not seem to have deterred Peel. The town had good communications by road and canal, adequate water power, cheap labour, and local capitalists willing to back him. Peel's net profits were said to be running at over £70,000 a year at this time, so there was no shortage of resources, at any rate for the time being. However, Peel's principal motive for this new venture was quickly revealed, for in 1790 he was elected member of parliament for Tamworth. There is some evidence of financial strain at points in the later 1790s—particularly the closure of Peel's Bank in Manchester in 1793—but by this time the entrepreneur was so rich that his position must have been virtually impregnable.

'Peel was to calico printing what Arkwright was to spinning: a man of iron frame and mind, possessing great mercantile talent and application' (Potter, 10), a quality much rarer in the industrial revolution than its early historians assumed. Like Arkwright, he 'introduced among his operatives that order, arrangement and subdivision of employment which form the marked characteristics of the factory system ... he insisted on a system of punctuality and regularity which approached the discipline of military drill' (Taylor, 1.6). But, perhaps most important of all, he had that keen sense of market opportunity that has been recognized as the common characteristic of all the outstanding entrepreneurs of the industrial revolution in Britain. English calico printing was established three-quarters of a century before Peel launched out in business, and was in high repute in Europe and America throughout the eighteenth century. Peel's policy was evidently the assiduous cultivation of the popular market, at first by copying London designs and undercutting the metropolitan prices, then by adoption of the new machinery and factory system which Lancashire pioneered.

In politics, as in industry, Peel learned much from his father, and drew on his family's status and authority in the cotton trade—Parsley Peel having appeared at the head of several Manchester-based agitations in the 1780s. Although Arkwright and his partners had secured the repeal of the Calico Act, the industry still laboured under a heavy excise duty, so the younger Robert Peel and his friends took up the cause of freedom from taxation. It was in this cause that he entered parliament and supported William Pitt, whom he regarded as an enlightened protector of industry.

However, Peel's political career is remembered principally for his promotion of the Health and Morals of Apprentices Act, effectively the first British factory legislation. By the end of the century Peel employed more than a thousand pauper apprentices, children sent from distant parts of England to work on routine tasks in the spinning factories. Having so many other matters to attend to, the partners delegated the supervision to overseers who were sometimes less than adequate; there were scandals at Radcliffe mill (1784) and following a report from the Birmingham overseers about children sent to Lancashire (1796). Peel had the candour to admit the excessive hours worked and his neglect of juvenile employees. The letter-books of

Edward Smith Stanley, MP for Preston, show the Lancashire manufacturers' angry opposition to Peel's act, so that his success displays his sincerity and determination as a reformer.

Peel was created a baronet in 1800 following his firm's £10,000 donation to the voluntary contribution against French invasion (1797) and his raising of six companies of militia soldiers at Bury (1798). The bankruptcy of the Howarths (former partners) in 1799 and of Peel, Wilkes, Dickinson and Goodall (the London branch of Peel's Bank) in 1806 evidently terminated any further expansion that Sir Robert had planned for his business. From this period he began to run down his industrial interests, mainly by sale (or gift) to competent managers and other connections. By the end of the Napoleonic War only a few peripheral members of the Peel family retained an interest in textiles. On 17 October 1805 Peel married Susanna, the daughter of Francis Clerke; there were no children of this union. She died in 1824. Peel had a serious illness that same year and a relapse in 1830. He died on 3 May 1830 at Drayton Manor, the house he had built near Tamworth, and was buried next to his first wife in the vault of Drayton Bassett church on 11 May. Of Sir Robert's nine surviving children, five, including William Yates *Peel and Jonathan *Peel, became MPs, two daughters married MPs, a son became a dean in the Church of England, and a daughter married a clergyman who later became a dean. His heir, Sir Robert *Peel, was prime minister in 1834–5 and from 1841 to 1846. His youngest son was Laurence *Peel [see under Peel, Sir Lawrence], MP for Cockermouth from 1827 to 1830.

S. D. CHAPMAN

Sources S. D. Chapman and S. Chassagne, *European textile printers in the eighteenth century: a study of Peel and Oberkampf* (1981) · A. G. E. Jones, 'The putrid fever at Robert Peel's Radcliffe mill', *N&Q*, 203 (1958), 26–35 · D. G. Stuart, 'The parliamentary history of the borough of Tamworth', MA diss., U. Lond., 1958 · J. Aiken, *Description of the country from 30 to 40 miles round Manchester* (1795) · E. Potter, *Calico printing as an art manufacture* (1852) · R. G. Thorne, 'Peel, Robert I (1750–1830)', HoP, *Commons* · W. C. Taylor, *Life and times of Sir Robert Peel*, 4 vols. (1846–51) · N. Gash, *Mr Secretary Peel: the life of Sir Robert Peel to 1830* (1961) · Burke, *Peerage*

Archives BL, corresp. with his son Robert and others | GL, Sun Fire Office policy registers · Lancs. RO, Stanley MSS · Warks. CRO, Birmingham overseers' records

Likenesses Hopwood, stipple, pubd 1815, NPG · W. Dickinson, mezzotint, pubd 1818 (after J. Northcote), BM · T. Lawrence, oils, c.1825, priv. coll. [*see illus.*] · H. Robinson, stipple and line engraving (after T. Lawrence), BM, NPG; repro. in W. Jerdan, *National portrait gallery of illustrious and eminent personages*, 5 vols. (1830–34), vol. 5

Peel, Sir Robert, second baronet (1788–1850), prime minister, was born on 5 February 1788 at Chamber Hall, Bury, the third child and the eldest boy among the eleven children of Sir Robert *Peel, first baronet (1750–1830), printed calico manufacturer, landowner, and MP, and his first wife, Ellen Yates (1766–1803), who was the daughter of one of his two partners, Haworth and Yates. Two sisters died in infancy. Three sisters and five brothers survived, and all married. Peel was only two when his father bought a property in Tamworth and entered parliament as the member for the borough in 1790.

Sir Robert Peel, second baronet (1788–1850), by Sir Thomas Lawrence, 1825

Education Peel showed an aptitude for his first lessons, taken with the rector of Bury, the Revd James Hargreaves, and may have preferred the schoolroom to the streets, where his red hair and curls exposed him to insult. Peel was eight when his father took possession of Drayton Manor, Tamworth, in 1796, and ten when the family moved in. He brought with him a Lancashire accent, traces of which could be detected in his speech throughout his life. At Drayton, he received his lessons from the Revd Francis Blick. Out of school, he had the run of the park. He learned to ride, but preferred to exercise on foot, with a gun, rambling and rough shooting. In 1800, when he was twelve, his father, a supporter of government, was made a baronet. In January 1801, when Peel was already beginning to grow tall, he was sent away from home to board at the Revd Mark Drury's house at Harrow School. He had been there two years, and was fifteen, when his mother died. Years later, he said that he had misspent his time at Harrow, and reminiscences tell of long excursions through the countryside with his guns, which he kept at a nearby cottage. But Latin and Greek came easily to him, and his schoolfellows ran to him for help with their translations and verses. In 1804 Byron and Peel declaimed together, Byron taking the part of the judicious Latinus, which allowed him—he was lame—to sit down, and Peel that of the impetuous Turnus. Peel left school at Christmas 1804, and resided for some months at his father's London house in Upper Grosvenor Street, attending lectures at the Royal Institution and listening to debates in the House of Commons. It is said that Pitt himself asked Sir

Robert who the young man was, and led him into the chamber.

Peel spent the summer of 1805 at Drayton studying mathematics with the Revd R. Bridge, a senior wrangler from Cambridge, before going up to Oxford in October. At Christ Church, Oxford, his first tutor was Thomas Gaisford and his second Charles Lloyd, the future bishop of Oxford, with whom Peel continued to correspond about church and state until Lloyd's death in 1829. Peel's closest friend was Henry Vane, son and heir of Lord Darlington, and later earl of Cleveland. Peel expanded at Christ Church. Cricket is mentioned, and rowing, and he dressed for effect. He entered his name for (oral) examination in both *literae humaniores* and mathematics in November 1808. In the weeks leading up to the examinations he overworked, could not sleep, and talked of withdrawing. The day before the exams he played tennis. Peel did not disappoint his examiners, or his audience. He was the first person ever to be placed in the first class in both schools, and his performance became legendary.

A young MP Peel did not follow his father and grandfather into the family business, and within a few weeks of his coming of age in February 1809, his father used his influence with the Portland ministry to secure him a seat in the House of Commons. There was a vacancy at Cashel, a corrupt borough with a couple of dozen voters. A deal was arranged by Sir Arthur Wellesley, and Peel was elected on 14 April. He took his seat straight away, but did not speak until 23 January 1810, when he was invited to second the reply to the king's speech. Acceptance signified allegiance to the ministry, and Peel took a patriotic line, urging resistance to Napoleon, support for Sir Arthur Wellesley's renewed campaign in the Peninsula, and confidence in British commerce. Four months later Lord Liverpool, the secretary of state for war and colonies (and another Christ Church man), offered Peel his first post as an undersecretary. Peel took charge of departmental correspondence with the colonies—everything, he said, from Botany Bay to Prince Edward Island. As his chief sat in the upper house, he was also called upon to answer questions in the House of Commons. His departmental and his parliamentary skills, his administrative abilities, and his authority as a speaker thus grew together. Lord Liverpool found Peel an official house, and here he began to entertain. It was in this period, rather than at school or university, that his enduring friendships were formed, with Henry Goulburn and John Wilson Croker.

Irish secretary In May 1812 Liverpool became prime minister and invited Peel to join the Irish administration as chief secretary. Peel held the post for six years—the longest tenure in the nineteenth century—and served three lord lieutenants, the duke of Richmond, Lord Whitworth, and Lord Talbot. Nothing in Peel's upbringing gave him the historical imagination to question the legitimacy of British rule in Ireland, and he cheerfully joined a regime which was locked into reliance upon penal laws and the protestant ascendancy. As chief secretary he was required to attend to business upon both sides of the water. In Ireland he stage-managed the election of sound protestants to parliament in 1812 and 1818, and persuaded Whitworth to dissolve the principal—and far from revolutionary—organization representing Catholics, the 'Catholic board', in 1814. In London, where politicians were, in the eyes of the administration in Dublin, embarrassingly soft about Catholic claims for political rights, he opposed every proposal for relief. Peel delivered an outspoken expression of the case against the Catholics in 1817 (*Hansard 1*, 36.404–23). Catholics owed allegiance to a foreign power, he was not prepared to erect the influence of the pope into 'a fourth estate', and he tied his belief in the future of the Union to his faith in the exclusive principle. What religion suggested was confirmed by political economy. Ireland was, in Peel's opinion, a primitive and backward land, and at this stage in his career Peel appears to have felt that in the long run the best hope for the country was that popery was something which a more prosperous people would grow out of. In the meantime Peel had to cope with the secret societies, the intimidation, and the crimes which resulted from the alienation of seven-eighths of the population. Like other chief secretaries he called for troop reinforcements, and renewed an Insurrection Act (in 1814, 1815, 1816, and 1817). More promisingly, he declared that he would always prefer an army of police to an army of soldiers, and established a new Peace Preservation Force, controlled by the government in Dublin. In 1817 he responded to a famine by the procurement of food and the distribution of money.

As chief secretary Peel proved his capacity to serve the lord lieutenant as 'his friend, his adviser, [and] his representative in parliament'. But the office had also begun to shape his life in other ways. His conduct in Ireland brought him the sobriquet Orange, bestowed by Daniel O'Connell, and led, in 1815, to a challenge to a duel, which did not take place, in Ostend. Peel was to carry with him for ever after a settled dislike for the great Irish patriot and all his ways. Peel's antagonism to Catholic claims for relief secured him the invitation, brought by Charles Lloyd, to stand, in preference to George Canning, for one of the two Oxford University seats in 1818. Peel was elected, but he had, perhaps, allowed himself to be miscast. His protestantism ran deep. But he acknowledged that Ireland had been misruled in the past. He had found the tools with which he was constrained to work—a jobbing aristocracy with a 'vortex of local patronage', and loyalist associations—distasteful, and he had spoken out in favour of the protestant ascendancy because he had been called upon to govern Ireland 'circumstanced as Ireland now is'.

The committee on cash payments For six years Peel took but one real holiday, in 1815, when he met Wellington in Paris, heard from his own lips how the battle of Waterloo had been fought, and went on to stay with the duke of Richmond in Brussels and view the ground where the victory had been won. Peel left Ireland in August 1818 (he never went back), and did not rejoin Lord Liverpool's administration until January 1822. In the meantime he chaired a committee considering the expediency of requiring the

Bank of England to resume paying gold, on demand, for its notes, and in due course he drafted the report and introduced the bill embodying the committee's proposals. The evidence taken before the bullion committee in 1811 had shown that the over-issue of paper currency since the suspension of cash payments in 1797 had resulted in a depreciation of the pound and a rise in the price of gold. The question was, did this matter? In 1811 the house had decided that the answer was yes, but not while there was a war on, and Peel himself had voted against resumption. Post-war experience persuaded him that over-issue also led to speculation, crises, unemployment, and political unrest. Now Peel thought the committee's first responsibility was to protect the public creditor, who was morally entitled to be repaid in the coin which he had lent and not in a depreciated one. The committee moved swiftly into a consideration of the when and how (Peel's favourite ground), the accumulation of a reserve of gold, and the successive steps by which, starting with the larger notes, paper was to be made convertible into gold bullion, at the current price of £4 1s. 0d. the ounce (1 February 1820), at £3 19s. 6d. (1 October 1820), and at the 'ancient and permanent standard of value' £3 17s. 10 ½d. (1 May 1821), until finally all notes, however small, were to be exchanged for £3 17s. 10 ½d. in specie (1 May 1823). In thus rounding up the theoretical complexities of an issue, and giving effect to the solution he favoured in the clauses of a durable act of parliament, Peel was to have no equal.

Marriage and family It is not clear whether, when he left Ireland, Peel had already fallen in love with Julia Floyd (1795–1859), the daughter of General Sir John Floyd, who was, when Peel arrived in Ireland in 1812, the second in command of the military forces, and his first wife, Rebecca Juliana, daughter of Charles Darke, a merchant in Madras. Julia had been born in India, and like Peel she had lost her mother (in 1802). She and her stepmother, Lady Denny, were entertained at the chief secretary's house in Phoenix Park. Peel, we are told, was unusually attentive to them when, in 1817, they left Dublin for London. When Peel himself returned to England in 1818 he wondered whether Julia 'would be able to abandon her gay fashionable world for the severer climate of a professional politician's wife. "You are my world", she replied disarmingly' (Gash, *Mr Secretary Peel*, 257). They became engaged in March 1820, and were married on 8 June. During the next twelve years, while Peel rose towards the top in politics, seven children were born: Julia (1821), Robert *Peel (1822), Frederick *Peel (1823), William *Peel (1824), John Floyd (1827), Arthur Wellesley *Peel (1829), and Eliza (1832). In London, they lived in a new house designed by Robert Smirke and built in 1824 at 4 Whitehall Gardens. Here, in a specially commissioned long gallery, Peel hung his collection of Dutch and Flemish paintings. These were purchased, with assistance from his father and advice from David Wilkie, in a period when the European salerooms were still busy following the upheavals of revolution and restoration, and included Hobbema's *The Avenue, Middelharnis* and Rubens's *Chapeau de paille*. Whenever Peel found himself alone in London he wrote to Julia every day, and no breath of scandal has ever attached to his name.

Home secretary In 1820 and 1821 Peel refused offers of a place in the cabinet as president of the Board of Control. But on 17 January 1822 he rejoined the administration as home secretary, a post he was to hold until Lord Liverpool suffered a stroke in 1827, and again, under the duke of Wellington, from 1828 to 1830. As home secretary Peel's primary responsibility was for law and order, and here he distinguished himself from other contemporary reformers by his ability to see the process whole and to attend to all aspects, from the formulation of the criminal law and the mechanics of policing, through indictment, trial, and sentencing, to punishment on the scaffold, in prison, and in penal colonies.

Contemporaries gave Peel credit for reducing the number of offences which carried the death penalty. But there was no fall in the number of executions, and the most striking achievement of his period at the Home Office, and perhaps of his whole career, was the consolidation of the criminal law. He began in 1823 where his predecessor, Lord Sidmouth, had left off, with the law relating to prisons. The following year he attended to the laws relating to transportation, and began to coax the Scottish judges towards a reform of Scottish criminal law. In 1825 he consolidated eighty-five laws relating to juries into a single act. In 1826 he proposed to consolidate the laws relating to theft. Out of 14,437 persons in England and Wales charged with various crimes in the course of the previous year, 12,500 (at least) had been accused of theft, which was the most important category of crime. Consolidation was needed because, year by year throughout the eighteenth century, specific acts (he cited the stealing of hollies, thorns, and quicksets) had been made into crimes instead of species of acts. There were now ninety-two statutes relating to theft, dating from the reign of Henry III, and Peel sought to unite them in a single statute of thirty pages. Upon this occasion his attempt to reduce the law to a single act proved to be too ambitious, and the bill emerged, finally, as four separate acts in 1827.

Peel's talents were never more apparent than in this labour of consolidation. In 1824 a select committee had recommended that consolidation and amendment should be kept distinct. Peel decided that they were not separable. He interpreted consolidation to mean the collection 'of dispersed statutes under one head' followed by the rejection of what was 'superfluous', the clearing up of what was 'obscure', the weighing of 'the precise force of each expression', and 'ascertaining the doubts that have arisen in practice and the solution which may have been given to those doubts by decisions of the courts of law' (*Hansard 2*, 14.1236). Where he found any gap 'through which notorious guilt escapes' (he instanced the theft of stock certificates in the funds which was not at that time an offence), he would remedy it (ibid., 14.1222–3). In Peel's hands, then, a consolidating act was a reforming act which incorporated case law and supplied omissions. As he turned from one aspect of the law to another, Peel circulated drafts of his consolidating bills among the judges,

and took pains to win their support, flattering Lord Eldon with a bag of game (which perhaps he had shot himself). He succeeded because nine-tenths of criminal law was statute law, which judges loved to criticize, and one-tenth, only, common law, the anomalies of which judges might seek to preserve.

On 9 March 1826 Peel's method of presenting a case came to maturity in his great speech on theft (*Hansard 2*, 14.1214–39). There was an apology (a preference really) for a topic which could 'borrow no excitement from political feelings' and might appear 'barren and uninviting'. There was a reference to a hypothetical fresh start ('if we were legislating de novo, without reference to previous customs and formed habits'). There was a glance at more radical proposals for 'rapid progress, which is inconsistent with mature deliberation', and a promise that, if he was allowed to have his way, there would be 'no rash subversion of ancient institutions' and 'no relinquishment of what is practically good, for the chance of speculative and uncertain improvement'. His own proposals were then presented as a middle way 'between the redundancy of our own legal enactments and the conciseness of the French code'. Finally he avowed his ambition to leave behind him 'some record of the trust I have held', and to connect his name with 'permanent improvements' to the institutions of the country.

The Catholic question, Liverpool, Canning, and Goderich So long as Lord Liverpool was prime minister Catholic emancipation remained an open question, and Peel, who as home secretary had overall responsibility for the administration in Ireland, continued to act as the protestant champion in the House of Commons. But the issue was beginning to pass out of control, both at Westminster and in Ireland. In 1825 the pro-Catholics won the annual vote in the House of Commons. Peel offered to resign, but was told that his resignation would bring Liverpool's government down. Understandably, he was unwilling to terminate the career of the statesman who had given him his first step up the ladder, and he allowed himself to be persuaded to continue. In 1826 there was a general election, and early in the following year Liverpool suffered a stroke. When the succession passed to George Canning, the leader, since 1822, of the Catholic party within Liverpool's administration, Peel (and others) did resign, and when Canning, too, died in August 1827 and was succeeded by Lord Goderich, Peel remained out of office. Early in 1828, when Goderich's administration collapsed and the king invited the duke of Wellington to form a government, Wellington asked Peel to return to the Home Office and to take the lead in the House of Commons.

Home secretary again At the Home Office, Peel resumed consolidating where he had left off. In 1828 he dealt with the law of offences against the person, reducing it from fifty-seven acts to one, and in 1830 he turned the twenty-seven acts relating to forgeries punishable with death into a single statute. Even more important in his eyes, he began at last to make progress with the police. In 1822 a committee had refused to recommend any reform. In 1828

Peel secured a new inquiry into the police of the metropolis, and the following year he was able to legislate. He had already given an indication of the way his mind was working when he praised the small force of full-time professional magistrates and constables established in London in 1793. But this efficient superstructure rested upon a complex of autonomous parochial and district watches. In St Pancras alone there were eighteen different night watches, many of which had no authority to intervene in a brawl on the other side of the street. Peel resolved to create a unified body under the control of the home secretary and paid for out of a general rate. The new force started patrolling the streets on 29 September 1829. They were not there to carry out sophisticated criminal detective work, but to restrain the thousands of vagrants, thieves, prostitutes, and drunks who tried to beg, steal, earn, or expend a living upon the streets of the capital, and to keep order. Peel's 'vigorous preventive police' carried truncheons but not firearms, and their secret (or innovatory) weapon was their military discipline. This 'unconstitutional' police force, as it was called in the Chartist petition, was bitterly resented, and there were many assaults upon policemen at first. But a force of just over 3000 men won control of the streets. The thin blue line penning vice back into the rookeries and shielding gentility from coarseness was a huge step up from the parish constables and night watchmen. In sterner times of supposedly revolutionary turmoil, it was also a reassuring step down from the use of soldiers and the risk of bloodshed. Like so many of Peel's reforms this one lasted. Fears of the police developing into a secret police on the continental model proved to have been exaggerated, and hostility to the very idea of an efficient police force ebbed away. By the mid-century the policeman's image was becoming a friendly, neighbourly one, and constables were being called 'bobbies' or 'Peelers' after their founder Robert Peel.

Catholic emancipation In the meantime, as leader of the House of Commons, Peel was obliged to grapple with the Catholic question. In 1827 the protestants had won the annual vote in the House of Commons. The following year, when the protestant dissenters and the Roman Catholics, in effect, came to terms, the government was heavily defeated on a motion for the repeal of the Test and Corporation Acts, and it was defeated again on a motion for Catholic emancipation. The first defeat was easy to deal with—Wellington and Peel gave way and brought in a bill of their own. The second was compounded by the rise of the Catholic Association and the defeat of Vesey Fitzgerald, a popular protestant landlord and government minister, by O'Connell, who was not eligible to take his seat, at a by-election in co. Clare. The protestant ascendancy had collapsed, and emancipation was now imperative. The only question was whether it should be undertaken by the king's present ministers or by a new political combination. Once again Peel offered to resign, and once again he was persuaded to stay. That decision taken, he offered to vacate his seat for Oxford University. His friends renominated him, but at the end of February he was defeated in a

poll by Sir Robert Inglis by 609 votes to 755, and the government had to ask Sir Manasseh Lopes to vacate his pocket borough at Westbury in Peel's favour. Peel was aware, then, when he rose on 5 March 1829 to introduce the cabinet's bill to emancipate the Catholics, that he would be asked why he saw 'a necessity for concession now, which was not evident before'. He answered that it was the condition of Ireland. '[The protestant] Reformation in Ireland' had hitherto 'made no advance', and after twenty years he was convinced that 'the evil' was 'not casual and temporary, but permanent and inveterate'. The time had come when less danger was to be apprehended from 'attempting to adjust the Catholic Question, than in allowing it to remain any longer in its present state'. 'I yield … unwilling to push resistance to a point which might endanger the Establishments that I wish to defend' (*Hansard 2*, 20.728–80). He ignored O'Connell, and saved face by announcing that the details of the measure had not been discussed with the Roman Catholics themselves. Catholics were to be allowed to enter both houses of parliament and to hold any office except regent, lord chancellor, and (more strangely) lord lieutenant of Ireland. In return Peel asked the Irish to accept the disfranchisement of the 40s. freeholders and a reduction of the electorate. The government did not ask for any control over the appointment of Roman Catholic bishops, because no British government, Peel said, could enter into negotiation with the court of Rome.

Coming to terms with parliamentary reform and whig government The bill passed, but it split the tory party, and politics were never to be the same again. Peel had spent his formative years in parliaments where ministers relied for their majority upon the sweetening effects of royal patronage, and where, for want of such influence, the opposition was weak. It was a situation in which a secretary of state could devote the greater part of his day to his department, and one in which, when he had framed a measure, he could come before the House of Commons with a reasonable expectation that he would prevail. Now, the ultra-tories began to mutter that a more popular parliament would never have passed an emancipation act. Their disaffection helped the whigs back into the mainstream of politics, and parliamentary reform became a practical issue. Between 1826 and 1830 Peel himself had been willing to transfer the two seats taken away from Penryn to Manchester. But he had acquiesced in the Lords' refusal to enfranchise any large town. Now, in 1830, reform motions were already being debated by the old parliament before George IV died in June, and new elections were held in July and August. The year was a watershed in Peel's personal as in his public life, for his father died on 3 May, and Peel became the second baronet, inherited the property at Drayton Manor (which, together with his dividends from the funds, brought him an income of £40,000 p.a.), and succeeded his father as the member for Tamworth, which he continued to represent until the end of his life. Wellington and Peel met the new parliament without any increase in strength. The ministry could not make overtures to the ultra-tories, and the followers of William Huskisson did not welcome the advances made to them. Peel felt that he was in a false position, and he was scarcely on speaking terms with the duke. When the ministry was defeated in a vote on the new civil list, on 15 November 1830, he was glad to go. He had been in office for fourteen of the past eighteen years, and he was wounded by charges of 'ratting' on the Catholic question.

In the course of the next two years—while a government headed by Lord Grey introduced a reform bill, called another general election, and sought to persuade William IV to create peers in order to carry their bill through the House of Lords—Peel was obliged to learn a new role, as leader of an opposition. He did not, at first, find it easy. In March 1831 he was appalled by the magnitude of the whig scheme, and on 9 April he was actually on his feet, and had lost his temper, when black rod arrived to summon the Commons to hear the announcement of the dissolution of parliament. During the election which followed, Peel's house in London had to be protected by the new Metropolitan Police, and Peel himself had to be stopped by his friends from becoming involved in a duel with Sir John Hobhouse. When the excitement over the bill moved on from the Commons to the Lords, Peel surprised Lord Harrowby and the waverers by saying that he would prefer the bill to pass by a creation of peers (whose effects, he believed, would be temporary, because the newly created peers would not remain radical for long) rather than a threat to create peers (which might establish a precedent for permanent revolution).

In May 1832, when ministers resigned, Peel declined the king's invitation either to form or to join a new administration. The bill, he thought, should be passed by the men who had introduced it. Once the bill became law, Peel accepted it as the settlement of a great question, and demonstrated confidence in the future by commissioning Robert Smirke to design him a new mansion, complete with every modern convenience of heating and plumbing, at Drayton. There it became a tradition for the family to lunch off silver and dine off gilt. Thither Peel transferred many of his British paintings. These included portraits, commissioned from Sir Thomas Lawrence, of his political colleagues Liverpool, Canning, Huskisson, Wellington, and Aberdeen—canvases to inspire him during the parliamentary recesses when he was considering how to block any further increase in popular power at the expense of the traditional institutions, crown, church, and aristocracy. At first the instruments to hand for this defensive warfare were weak. There were about 150 tories, only, of all kinds, returned at the general election in December 1832, and the party in the House of Lords was not his to control. Peel felt his way. Sitting for Tamworth, he had no experience of how respectable a contest in a newly enfranchised large borough might be, and he shared many of the ultra-tories' fears for the constitution. But he avoided making any premature attempt to reunite the party, and he waited for the tories to gather round him on his own terms. In the meantime he was fortunate. The

whigs began to fall out with their radical allies, and among themselves. This gave Peel the opportunity to step in and save the moderate whigs from the extremists, and in this way the new Conservatism was born.

Prime minister, 1834–1835 In July 1834, when Grey resigned, the king invited Peel to coalesce with Melbourne. But that was impracticable. Melbourne became prime minister, and when autumn came Peel took Julia and his elder daughter to Italy. They were in Rome when William IV dismissed Melbourne, and the duke of Wellington advised the king to send for Peel (and agreed to act as caretaker until Peel arrived). The king's messenger reached Rome on 25 November, and Peel was back in London on 9 December and kissed hands the same day. He never doubted that he must accept the commission—it had, in effect, been accepted for him, and refusal would injure the crown. The whig dissidents, Sir James Graham and Lord Stanley, were not yet ready to join Peel, whose cabinet could not then differ much from the duke of Wellington's cabinet in 1830. But Peel took the office of chancellor of the exchequer for himself, and he found new blood for junior offices—Gladstone, Sidney Herbert, and Praed. The ministry could not survive in the existing House of Commons, and Peel asked the king to dissolve parliament.

The Tamworth manifesto Next, Peel found an imaginative way of communicating with the electorate. The Tamworth manifesto was addressed to his own constituents, but it was distributed to the national newspapers and published on 19 December 1834. Peel appealed, in inspired words, 'to that great and intelligent class of society … which is far less interested in the contentions of party, than in the maintenance of order and the cause of good government'. He promised 'a careful review of institutions, both civil and ecclesiastical' and 'the correction of proved abuses and the redress of real grievances'. It did not take him long to show that this was no mere rhetoric. For his own part he found religiosity almost as distressing as impiety, and avoided religion as a topic of conversation. But he valued the church as an institution, and he persuaded the bishops to embrace an ecclesiastical commission, which would enable the church to reform itself and save it from its enemies. Hopefully this would atone, among the ultras, for his actions in 1829. Simultaneously, ministers let it be known that they were willing to consider the whole range of dissenters' grievances. In the elections which followed, early in 1835, Peel's supporters won 290 seats and became the largest single party in the House of Commons. It was not enough to give them a majority, and Peel was surprised by the skill with which Lord John Russell persuaded the whigs, the radicals, and the Irish to combine against him. First, they threw out the former speaker. Next they carried an amendment to the address. But the margin was small, Russell dared not take up Peel's challenge to move a motion of no confidence, and Peel gained time in which to introduce his Irish Tithe Bill. In the first week of April, Peel was defeated three times, and on 8 April he resigned. In the space of four months the king had elevated Peel into the leader of the party of resistance, and Peel had earned high praise. He had not been able to pass his own measure, but he had stayed in office long enough to get his opponents committed to the (unpopular) appropriation of the surplus revenues of the Irish church to the education of all classes of Christians. The contest thus begun, across the floor of the House of Commons, between Peel, with his tall stature, huge frame, and uneven, slightly wobbly legs (caught even better in *Political Sketches* by H. B. than in the portraits at age thirty-seven by Sir Thomas Lawrence, at fifty by John Linnell, and at fifty-six by F. X. Winterhalter), and the diminutive Russell, was to last, with many changes of fortune, to the end of his life.

An opposition leader For six years between 1835 and 1841 Peel showed a wonderful patience waiting for the whig ministry to perish, and for the premiership to return to him unencumbered by any debt to any man. At first he was extremely apprehensive. Party feeling reached a new peak in the summer and autumn of 1835. Inside parliament, Peel was afraid lest the tory peers, by challenging the government's Municipal Corporations Bill, bring about their own destruction. The reform was an inescapable postscript to the Reform Act, and he wanted it out of the way. He tried, as he expressed it in 1838, to 'diminish the risk and deaden the shock of collisions between the two deliberative branches of the legislature'. He lent his aid to see the bill safely through the House of Commons and onto the statute book, and then passed the recess reading Guizot's history of the French Revolution. The following year he continued to proclaim selective opposition. But he was happy to see the House of Lords block every whig measure for Ireland (tithe, corporations, poor law). Outside parliament he continued to develop the theme of the new Conservatism—in a speech in the City in May 1835, and in Glasgow (where he had been elected lord rector of the university) in January 1837.

Party and its organization was something Peel felt ambiguous about. He was not in love with parties, and he regretted the high profile of party warfare after 1830, which demanded more frequent attendance in parliament and took ministers away from their offices. But he did well what he had to do. He selected the chief whips, Sir George Clerk in 1835 and Sir Thomas Fremantle in 1837. He directed Lord Granville Somerset to operate—to the extent that the constituencies would allow it—a central clearing house for parliamentary candidates. He encouraged F. R. Bonham (a frequent visitor to Drayton) to brief him about the state of the electorate, and he reminded his supporters in the constituencies that 'the battle of the constitution must be fought in the registration courts'. At the general election of 1837, following the death of the king, the party won another twenty-three seats in the English counties. This left the whigs dependent for their majority upon O'Connell's Irish members. It was an inconsistency in Peel that, having sat for an Irish seat himself, he now thought it unconstitutional, almost, for the course of the United Kingdom to be determined by Irish

votes when they were not to his liking. But it was a prejudice shared by Graham and Stanley, who joined forces with Peel in 1838. Even after the whigs abandoned the appropriation clause in 1838, Peel denounced their plan for the state to construct the main lines of railway in Ireland (1839), and confined the Irish Municipal Corporations Act (1840) to almost the narrowest possible compass.

Whatever Peel gained in popular franchises in 1837 he lost, for the time being, with the accession of Queen Victoria. Melbourne had a hold upon her affections, and a partisan whig for a queen was a novelty. Peel kept Conservative spirits up with another speech in May 1838 at the Merchant Taylors' Hall. In 1839, when the whig majority fell to five upon a proposal to suspend the constitution of Jamaica, and the ministry resigned, Peel was unable to take Melbourne's place because the queen would not grant him the expression of confidence for which he asked—the dismissal of some (the queen thought he demanded all) of the whig ladies of the bedchamber. Peel could have forced the issue, but given his respect for royalty he preferred to yield and allow Melbourne to carry on. The ministry was weak, but Peel still lacked the means to topple it, and in the following year, when the Conservatives essayed a motion of no confidence, it was emphatically defeated. Peel did not exploit the ministry's difficulties over Canada.

The general election of 1841 In 1841 the whigs addressed themselves to the budget deficit. In trying to take politics onto new ground, they proposed to reduce the duties on sugar, timber, and corn. Peel made sport with them by drawing a picture of the chancellor of the exchequer 'seated on an empty chest, by the pool of bottomless deficiency, fishing for a budget', and defeated them upon sugar. He then moved a vote of no confidence which was carried by one vote on 4 June 1841. At the general election which followed, 'every Conservative candidate', J. W. Croker said, 'professed himself … to be Sir Robert Peel's man', and all turned on the name of Sir Robert Peel. The whigs campaigned upon a small fixed duty on corn. Peel skilfully avoided pledging himself to any particular course of action about the corn laws or anything else. The Conservatives won a majority of about 76. In the English and Welsh counties they won 137 out of the 159 seats. In the English and Welsh boroughs they took almost as many seats as the whigs, 165 to 176. In Scotland the Conservatives held 20 out of the 30 county seats, but two only of the 23 borough seats. In Ireland, where they made some gains, they held 43 out of 105 seats.

Prime minister, 1841–1846 The whigs met the new parliament towards the end of August and were ejected. The queen, who was now guided by Prince Albert, made no difficulty about the bedchamber, and on 30 August Peel at last became prime minister upon his own terms. Or so it seemed at the time. But in fact, for all his attempts to modernize the party and to broaden its appeal to the industrious middle classes, he was more dependent than ever upon the country squires. Analysis of the borough seats shows that Peel's success was concentrated in the small English boroughs, with fewer than 1000 electors, and that in the large English boroughs, with more than 2000 electors, he had actually won two fewer seats—15 to his opponents' 43—than in 1837. The triumph and the tragedy of the ministry of 1841–6 were written into the results.

Peel appointed Sir James Graham to the Home Office and Aberdeen to the Foreign Office. Goulburn became chancellor of the exchequer, and the earl of Ripon president of the Board of Trade (with Gladstone as his junior). Thus far, everything was under Peel's control. Graham acted as his lieutenant, Peel himself took responsibility for explaining Aberdeen's conciliatory conduct of foreign affairs to the House of Commons, and Goulburn and Ripon, survivors of the governments of the 1820s, both turned, by long habit, to Peel himself for advice. Stanley, who took the colonies, was more independent, and he was given early promotion to the House of Lords in 1844. Ellenborough became president of the Board of Control, and then, a month later, governor-general of India. The forward policy which he adopted towards Afghanistan and China, the annexation of Sind, and the conquest of Gwalior were not much to Peel's taste. Among the less-effectives, Knatchbull (paymaster-general) represented the ultras, as he had in 1835, and Buckingham was offered a place (lord privy seal) as a spokesman for the agricultural interest.

Peel's first objective was to restore the authority of government. Throughout the 1830s, the whigs (as he saw it) had allowed their policies to be suggested to them, and their measures to be amended, by their radical and Irish supporters. This was dangerous. Ministers should be seen to be in charge. It was imperative to put the political pyramid back the right way up again. Legislation should be prepared by ministers, with deliberation. Considered measures should then be respected as the work of professionals, and they should be seen to pass without amendment. Peel would exercise power upon his own 'conception of public duty', and he took pride in never having proposed anything which he had not carried.

The economy and the budget of 1842 Peel had now to grapple with the problem which had faced his predecessors, the recession, which had begun in 1838 and would not go away. He had come to power in the middle of structural changes in the economy, which led many to question whether the country had taken a wrong turning. Would manufacturing towns ever be loyal? Was poverty eating up capital? Was it safe to depend upon imports for food and raw materials? Could the fleet keep the seas open? Or should government encourage emigration and require those who remained behind to support themselves by spade husbandry? These were the 'condition of England' questions which Peel faced, together with the phenomena which rode upon them, Chartism and the agitation to repeal the corn laws. In accordance with Peel's governmental ethic, he did not introduce emergency measures in haste in the autumn of 1841. He and his cabinet spent the autumn and winter of 1841–2 taking stock, and then brought forward proposals fit for the hour.

Land, as Peel's supporters reminded him, was the historic basis of the constitution. It was a 'permanent' interest which appreciated in value with cultivation. Commercial capital, by contrast, put down no roots and might be taken to another country, while manufacturing capital depreciated with use. But commerce and manufactures had borne Britain to its pre-eminence in the world. Writing to J. W. Croker on 27 July 1842, Peel agreed that one might, if one 'had to constitute new Societies', 'prefer Corn fields to Cotton factories', but 'our lot' was cast (*Sir Robert Peel: from his Private Papers*, 2.529). The decision had already been taken in Peel's father's or in his grandfather's day, and there could be no turning back now. What was wrong with the economy was not that population had outrun capital, but that the power of production had overtaken the capacity to consume. The way to 'remove the burden which presses upon the springs of manufactures and commerce' was to make Britain a cheap country to live in (*Hansard 3*, 61.460).

In 1842, then, Peel was addressing himself through the fiscal system to the health of the economy and to the morale of the nation as a whole. He resolved to redistribute the tax burden by reducing duties upon articles of mass consumption and reintroducing the income tax which had been abolished after a back-bench revolt in 1815. Reducing duties would help to get the nation back to work and take the momentum out of the Chartist movement. Peel did not recognize the political aspirations of the Chartists, and (unlike his father) he would never himself propose statutory restrictions upon the hours of labour. But he understood hunger, and he wanted thoughts of 'sedition' to be forgotten 'in consequence of greater command over the necessaries and minor luxuries of life' (*Hansard 3*, 87.1048). Imposing a peacetime income tax would demonstrate that the British state was an equitable one, in which burdens were placed (despite the warnings of political economists who identified income as the source of savings and the route to capital formation) upon those best able to bear them.

These measures had to be sold to a party which was still solidly protectionist. Accordingly, in 1842, grain was singled out for separate treatment and dealt with first, and on 9 February Peel announced a thorough revision of the sliding scale of 1828—to make it more defensible. Then, on 11 March, when he introduced the budget—which he did himself (the complaisant Goulburn stepping aside)—he began by making much of the deficit. Having worked up a sense of urgency he explored and rejected alternative remedies (lower expenditure, increased duties, and the 'wretched expedient' of borrowing). Finally he came to his own plan. An income tax of 7*d*. in the pound on incomes over £150 p.a. was to be imposed for three years. This would turn the deficit into a surplus. With that surplus Peel proposed to undertake 'a complete review, on general principles, of all the articles of the tariff'. No duty should ever again be prohibitive. Imports were to be categorized (the word 'consolidated' was not mentioned but might not have been out of place) into raw materials, semi-finished articles, and manufactured products, which were not to pay more than 5 per cent, 12 per cent, and 20 per cent respectively. Duties were reduced on 750 out of the 1200 articles in the tariff (*Hansard* 3, 61.422–76). It was Peel's finest hour; the crisis of the century was met by the fiscal reform of all the centuries. The budget brought the resignation of the duke of Buckingham, and Peel recalled that 'these changes … were not effected without great murmuring and some open opposition to the Government on the part of many of its supporters' (*Memoirs*, 2.100–01). But in fact it was a wonderfully ambiguous measure. He had rationalized the tariff: he had taken a step towards free trade. He could still move in either direction.

The Canada Corn Act of 1843 In 1843 it appeared that the best way to save Canada from a future invasion by the United States was to try and interest the farmers in the American mid-west in selling their grain to Britain. The Canada Corn Act granted wheat shipped from Canada a privileged position in the British market (above other colonies), and nobody could doubt that the greater part of all the wheat which would come down the St Lawrence would have originated in the United States. In 1843 the protectionists in the party scarcely knew what to make of the Canada Corn Bill. They feared the consequences of opening the door to American grain, but they wanted to retain Canada, and the bill was introduced by Stanley who was known to sympathize with their own views.

The Bank Charter Act of 1844 The Bank Act of 1819 had imposed upon the Bank of England the duty of honouring its notes in gold if asked to do so. In normal times the bank's customers did not wish to exchange their notes for gold, and in 1819 Peel had believed that the bank could be trusted to decide how many more notes it would be prudent to put into circulation than it had gold to back. Upon several occasions since, when speculation was rife and sound management was called for, the bank had still been increasing its note issue when prices were rising and gold had already begun to leave the country. The Bank of England, then, paid too little attention to the state of the foreign exchanges, and the English country banks, which had about one-quarter of the circulation, paid none. The result was that the collapse, when it came, and the consequent business failures and distress were all the greater. Here was another factor bearing upon the condition of England question. Peel determined to end the discretion allowed to the bank. If gold was leaving the country, notes must be withdrawn from circulation until prices fell, British goods became attractive to foreign buyers, and gold returned to the country again to pay for them.

The bank's charter had been renewed in 1833. But there was a break clause, and Peel waited until he could move in and place note issue under statutory control. By the act of 1844 there were to be no new banks of issue. Existing country bank issues were frozen at their present levels, and no bank which gave up issuing its own notes would ever be allowed to resume. Note issue would imperceptibly become concentrated in the hands of the Bank of England. The bank itself was to be separated into a banking department and an issue department—the first free, the second regulated. Notes to the value of £14 million—the minimum amount needed if the business of the country was to continue—might be issued, backed by securities (the credit of the British government). Beyond that amount notes were only to be issued when there was gold in hand to back them, and the figures were to be published every week. The act had interesting overtones. It was a vindication of the right of the state to interfere with powerful interests, and, in a period when other monopolies were being swept aside, it established a new one. It has been criticized in detail for paying too little attention to other negotiable instruments such as cheques and bills of exchange and to the bank's role as lender of last resort, but it was a marvellous demonstration of Peel's command of an abstruse subject, and the act (which applied to England and Wales and was followed the next year by comparable measures for Scotland and Ireland) did help to reduce the severity of crises and lasted until 1914.

Gathering disaffection In other ways 1844 was not such a good year. There was a dispute with France over Tahiti which necessitated an increase in the defence estimates. The ministry was defeated by Lord Ashley, a tory paternalist, on the ten-hours issue, and by Philip Miles on its proposals to revise the sugar duties (with their complicated links to the issue of slavery). Both defeats were reversed by the threat of resignation. The tactic was sufficient unto the day, but it helped to accumulate resentment for the future. Then, in 1845, matters began to come to a head. The income tax was about to expire. But the economy was now in a position to benefit from another virtuous circle of tariff reductions, and Peel chose, once again, to introduce the budget himself, on 14 February. He renewed the income tax for another three years explicitly in order to enable him 'to make a great experiment' in reducing other taxes, 'the removal of which will give more scope to commercial enterprise, and occasion an increased demand for labour'. Customs duties were to be abolished on 430 articles which provided 'the raw materials of our manufactures'. The excise duty on glass was abolished too. Peel believed that the result of this 'extension of industry and encouragement of enterprise' would be 'the benefit of all classes of the community, whether they are directly or indirectly connected with commerce, manufactures, or agriculture' (*Hansard* 3, 77.455–97). But the distinguishing mark of this budget was abolition not rationalization. Peel had dropped the mask, and now appeared as a convinced free-trader. What, then, would happen to the corn laws? Nothing, perhaps, in that parliament, had it not been for Ireland.

Ireland lay athwart Britain's transoceanic trade routes. Peel dared not contemplate a repeal of the union, and in 1841 he invited an ultra-protestant, Earl De Grey, to become lord lieutenant. In thus signalling his determination to reverse the Irish policies of Lord Melbourne's administration Peel reignited the repeal movement. The government succeeded in banning a monster meeting at Clontarf in 1843, but an attempt to prosecute O'Connell failed. Realizing his mistake, Peel changed tack in 1843, and appointed the Devon commission to investigate the problems of Irish land tenure. The following year he began to send Ireland what Disraeli termed 'messages of peace', replacing De Grey with Heytesbury and passing a Charitable Bequests Act (to enable Catholics to bequeath money for the support of their clergy). In 1845 he passed a bill to establish three Queen's colleges, which would offer a university education to the Irish middle classes, and attended to the condition of the Roman Catholic college at Maynooth. Ireland could not be governed unless the priests preached obedience to the powers that be. If the British government did not see to the repair and upkeep of the seminary, then the priests would go abroad for their training, and who knew what they would preach then? Peel proposed to increase the existing grant to Maynooth, which had been paid for half a century, from £9000 to £26,000 p.a., to make a non-recurrent advance for new buildings, and to place the cost of repairs and maintenance upon the board of works. It was a small price to pay for the chance of peace in Ireland. But it led to Gladstone's resignation from the cabinet, it jarred nerves frayed by the 'betrayal' of 1829, and it roused protestants throughout the United Kingdom to a frenzy. The connections between protestants and protectionists in the Conservative Party were close: the bill was passed; but 148 Conservatives voted for the measure, 149 against. The government was saved by whig votes. So much for not consenting to hold office on sufferance. Peel's party was already in an ill humour, then, before the potato harvest failed in the wet summer of 1845, and Peel and his ministers met in the autumn to consider what to do about the corn laws.

Repeal of the corn laws Peel said later that 'in the interval between the passing of the Corn Bill in 1842, and the close of the Session of 1845' the opinions he had 'previously entertained on the subject of protection to agriculture had undergone a great change', and that 'many concurring proofs' had demonstrated to him that 'the wages of labour do not vary [he meant fall] with the price of corn' (*Memoirs*, 2.101). In 1844 he found himself unable to answer the arguments used by Cobden, and in 1845 he agreed with Graham, who said that, following the failure of the potato, 'the Anti-Corn Law pressure' would become 'the most formidable movement in modern times' (*Sir Robert Peel: from his Private Papers*, 3.224). Peel did not think it would be possible to suspend the corn laws and then reimpose them again afterwards; he did not think it would be wise to put the issue to the electorate, and on 15 October he wrote to inform Lord Heytesbury that he was considering 'the total and absolute repeal for ever of all duties on all articles of subsistence' (ibid.). His cabinet were not convinced of the necessity. Meeting followed meeting and still they could not agree whether to maintain, modify, suspend, or abolish the law of 1842. On 26 November the *Morning Chronicle* published Lord John Russell's 'Edinburgh letter', announcing his conversion to total and immediate repeal, and on 4 December Peel asked his cabinet to agree to a phased extinction of the corn laws over a period of eight years. Stanley warned him that this would break up the ministry, and on 5 December Peel decided to resign. In the ensuing two weeks, Stanley himself declined even to try and form a protectionist government, and Lord John Russell failed to form a whig one. Peel was not sorry to be required to carry on. He was always inclined to suppose that if a thing was good to be done it would be better done by himself. Now he believed that, with the elimination of the only possible alternatives, he would resume power 'with greater means of rendering public service' than he would have enjoyed had he 'not relinquished it' (*Memoirs*, 2.251). Others were more aware of the shame of abandoning their own law of 1842 and the likely effect upon the party. The ministry was recalled upon the understanding that it would propose a repeal of the corn laws. Wellington expressed the view that 'a good Government for the country' was 'more important than Corn Laws or any other consideration' (ibid., 2.200). Stanley and the duke of Buccleuch were the only members of the government who refused to return, and Peel brought Gladstone back into the cabinet as colonial secretary, though he had no seat in the Commons.

Peel introduced the bill to repeal the corn laws on 27 January 1846. In order to allow the landed interest time to prepare for the change the laws were to be abolished in three years' time, on 1 February 1849, after which all imported grains would pay only a 'nominal' registration duty of 1s. a quarter. In the meantime new scales of duty were to operate. Colonial grains were to be admitted at 1s., and foreign maize, too, was to be admitted at 1s. Other foreign grains were to pay duties ranging between 4s. and 10s. according to the price. Nobody got what they wanted. The Irish did not secure the suspension appropriate to their emergency, partly, perhaps, because Peel had already arranged for the government to buy maize on their behalf. The landowners lost their protection, and were offered cheap drainage loans by way of compensation. The Anti-Corn Law League did not win total and immediate repeal, but was, in effect, made an offer which it could not refuse. The Conservative Party split: Lord George Bentinck arose to lead the protectionists, and on 7 February the second reading found 112 Conservatives supporting Peel and no fewer than 231 following Bentinck in voting against the government's bill. The rancour was unbelievable, and from February to June the ministry was supported by whig and radical votes. The bill received the royal assent on 25 June, and the following day the whigs combined with the protectionists to defeat the government's Coercion Bill for Ireland. In his resignation speech on 28 June, Peel widened the breach with his former supporters by giving the whole credit for repeal to Richard Cobden, who was in their eyes no better than a demagogue. He ended with a prayer that he might

> leave a name sometimes remembered with expressions of goodwill in the abodes of those whose lot it is to labour, and to earn their daily bread by the sweat of their brow, when they shall recruit their exhausted strength with abundant and untaxed food, the sweeter because it is no longer leavened by a sense of injustice. (*Hansard 3*, 87.1055)

Death by accident Peel felt worn out. For twenty years he had been troubled by deafness following a mishap with a gun. In 1843 he had been the intended victim of an assassination which cost the life of his secretary, Edward Drummond. Above all there was the incessant work. There was so much more to do now than there had been in the 1820s, and Peel had shouldered responsibility for the operation of every department. He knew his backbenchers had found him cold, aloof, and unresponsive. He knew also that many tories, who had come to terms with Catholic emancipation and one betrayal, would never forgive him two. But he, too, felt let down. He had fought the battle for the squires stoutly until 1844. But he had received little support in the House of Commons from them, and being expected, for the sake of party, 'to adopt the opinions of men who have not access to your knowledge, and could not profit by it if they had, who spend their time in eating and drinking, and hunting, shooting, gambling, horse-racing, and so forth' was 'an odious servitude' to which he would not submit (Peel to Lord Hardinge, *Sir Robert Peel: from his Private Papers*, 3.474). He never wished to hold office again, and he showed little inclination to lead the ninety or so Peelites who were returned at the general election of 1847. He remained a favourite with the royal family, and, while still holding his distance, gave a general kind of support to Lord John Russell who succeeded him. In 1847 he was consulted about a possible suspension of the Bank Charter Act. In 1848 he laid a finger on the defects in the Encumbered Estates Act for Ireland. In 1849, when corn prices were low and Lord John was considering reverting to a fixed duty, Peel joined in a council at Woburn which stiffened the whigs' resolve to defend the free-trade policy. On 28 June 1850 he spoke against the government in the Don Pacifico debate. The following day, he was thrown by his horse at the top of Constitution Hill. He fell face downwards, and the horse then trampled on his back, causing internal injuries. He was carried home to Whitehall Gardens, and several long and very painful days later, on 2 July, he died. On 3 July the Commons adjourned on the motion of Joseph Hume and Gladstone, and on 4 July the house again adjourned after formal tributes had been paid. Lord John Russell, as prime minister, offered a public funeral, but Goulburn, on behalf of the Peel family, declined it, Peel having earlier in the year declared his wish to be buried in the churchyard of Drayton Bassett beside his mother and father. The interment took place in a private ceremony on 9 July. Upon that day, in an exceptional expression of national mourning, the mills in the great northern towns stopped work, shops closed, and in the ports ships' flags flew at half-mast. Peel had left firm instructions, Lord John Russell told the Commons on 12 July, that his wife and family were to accept no titles or rewards for his services. Julia Peel died on 27 October 1859 and was buried beside her husband.

Reputation The Peelite wing of the Conservative Party was gradually absorbed, between 1846 and 1859, into the Liberal Party. In his budget speeches of 1853–4 and 1860–66 Gladstone spoke of continuing and completing the free-trade policies of Sir Robert Peel. Within the family, Peel's second son, Frederick, entered parliament as a Liberal in 1849; his eldest son, the third Sir Robert, who succeeded to the representation of Tamworth, served for four years as Irish secretary in Palmerston's Liberal ministry of 1859–65; and his youngest son, Arthur Wellesley, began his political career as Liberal member for Warwick in 1865. It has therefore sometimes been suggested that Peel had all along been in the wrong party. But this is to ignore the fact that Peel himself, with his background, perceived no contradiction between manufacturing interests and tory principles. To portray him as a Liberal *manqué* overlooks his abhorrence of whig principles, and his contempt for the whigs' levity and carelessness in government. It overlooks, too, the extent to which Peel's supporters and the Peel dynasty did not so much choose to be Liberal as have Liberalism thrust upon them.

Historians have often professed to see continuity between the Conservatism of the Tamworth manifesto and the Conservatism of subsequent generations. Certainly, a reverential attitude to crown, church, and aristocracy may be said to link Peel with Lord Salisbury, and even with Stanley Baldwin. But Salisbury still referred unforgivingly to Peel as the man who had betrayed his party twice, and other Conservative leaders who conceded that one of Peel's two changes of course might have been a principled one did not agree which one. Catholic emancipation ceased, after a generation, to be an emotive issue, but protection and free trade continued, as Balfour and Baldwin found, to divide the Conservative Party. Far into the twentieth century, the party related more easily to the pragmatism and balance of the 1842 budget than it did to the capitulation of 1846. The shade of the supreme workman, who dominated the parliamentary debates of his age, found no assured resting place among succeeding generations of Conservatives.

In the *Dictionary of National Biography* Peel's grandson G. V. Peel wrote that in an age of revolutions Peel alone had had 'the foresight and the strength to form a conservative party, resting not on force or corruption, but on administrative capacity and the more stable portion of the public will'. Certainly Peel re-educated the party after the débâcle of 1831–2, and returned it to power in 1841. The case is strong, but the question then remains, why did Peel, in 1845–6, follow a course which led to the destruction of the party he himself had made? Peel explained that his 'earnest wish', during his tenure of power, had been 'to impress the people of this country with a belief that the legislature was animated with a sincere desire to frame its legislation upon the principles of equity and justice' (Gash, *Sir Robert Peel*, 590). When he perceived that 'it was impossible to reconcile the repeal of the Corn Laws by me with the keeping together of the Conservative party', he had 'no hesitation in sacrificing the subordinate object' (Peel to Aberdeen, 19 Aug 1847, *Memoirs*, 2.322). Here, he was not to be disappointed, and he rose in the affections of the people in proportion as he lost the favour of his party. While members of one sectional interest, tory landowners, draped their prints of Peel with crêpe or turned them to the wall, and those of another, at the heart of the Anglican university establishment, unforgivingly made sure that Peel's portrait never hung in his college dining hall, the nation's felicitous passage through the year of revolutions, 1848, showed that thoughts of the dissolution of our institutions were indeed being lost, as Peel had hoped they would be, amid the enjoyment of prosperity. Two years later, when Peel died, 400,000 working men contributed 1*d.* each to a memorial fund, used to buy books for working men's clubs and libraries.

Peel's *Speeches* were published in four volumes in 1853, an imperfect edition but one which has never been replaced. Peel's *Memoirs*, covering the three episodes he was most sensitive about—Catholic emancipation, the acceptance of the king's commission to form a ministry in 1834–5, and the disintegration of the Conservative Party during the corn law crisis in 1845–6—were published by Philip Stanhope (Lord Mahon) and Edward Cardwell in 1856–7. But plans for an 'official' biography hung fire. Peel's intimate, J. W. Croker, was the obvious choice. But he died in 1857 with nothing accomplished, and the commission passed first to Goldwin Smith and then to Edward Cardwell, both of whom gave up. In 1871 seventy-seven paintings from Peel's collection were sold to the National Gallery for £75,000, and Peel's reputation as a connoisseur was established. In 1891–9 C. S. Parker published three volumes of extracts from Peel's papers, which allowed Peel and his correspondents to speak for themselves, but offered little interpretation or evaluation. In the meantime various lives appeared—at least a dozen in the half century between 1850 and 1900. These were all based upon the readily available sources, and none was more authoritative than the article in the *Dictionary of National Biography*. No more could, perhaps, have been said, until Peel's papers were deposited in the British Museum in 1922. Even then many years passed before the first full-length case for the consistency of Peel's actions, the purity of his motives, and the scale of his achievement was at last made in Norman Gash's two-volume biography (1961, 1972), a portrait so favourable that it has already led to less flattering revisions—by Boyd Hilton and V. A. C. Gatrell especially. JOHN PREST

Sources L. W. Cowie, *Sir Robert Peel, 1788–1850: a bibliography* (1996) • N. Gash, *Mr Secretary Peel: the life of Sir Robert Peel to 1830* (1961) • N. Gash, *Sir Robert Peel: the life of Sir Robert Peel after 1830* (1972) • N. Gash, *Reaction and reconstruction in English politics, 1832–1852* (1965) • N. Gash, *Politics in the age of Peel* (1953) • 'Secret committee … on the state of the Bank of England', *Parl. papers* (1819), 3.363–798, no. 291 • 'Select committee on … the police of the metropolis', *Parl. papers* (1816), vol. 5, no. 510; (1822), 4.91, no. 440; (1828), vol. 6, no. 533 • *Speeches of the late Rt. Hon. Sir Robert Peel, delivered in the House of Commons*, 4 vols. (1853) [incl. index] • *Memoirs by the Rt. Hon. Sir Robert Peel*, ed. Lord Mahon [P. Stanhope] and E. Cardwell, 2 vols. (1856–7) • C. S. Parker, ed., *Sir Robert Peel: from his private papers*, 3 vols. (1891–9) • *Life and letters of Sir James Graham*, ed. C. S. Parker, 2 vols. (1907) • *The private letters of Sir Robert Peel*, ed. G. Peel (1920) • *Correspondence and diaries of J. W. Croker*, ed. L. J. Jennings, 3 vols. (1884) • *The Greville memoirs, 1814–1860*, ed. L. Strachey and R. Fulford, 8 vols. (1938) • A. R. Wellesley, second duke of Wellington, *Despatches, correspondence, and memoranda of Field Marshal Arthur, duke of Wellington, K.G.: in continuation of the former series*, 8 vols. (1867–80) • *The Creevey papers*, ed. H. Maxwell, 3rd edn (1905); repr. (1923) • *The letters of Queen Victoria*, ed. A. C. Benson, Lord Esher [R. B. Brett], and G. E. Buckle, 9 vols. (1907–32) • T. Martin, *The life of … the prince consort*, 5 vols. (1875–80), vols. 1–2 • B. Disraeli, 'Character of Sir Robert Peel', *Lord George Bentinck: a political biography*, 2nd edn (1852), 302–20 • W. Bagehot, 'The character of Sir Robert Peel', *Biographical studies*, ed. R. H. Hutton, 2nd edn (1889), 1–39 • F. P. G. Guizot, *Memoirs of Sir Robert Peel* (1857) [trans. from the Fr.] • G. J. Shaw-Lefevre, *Peel and O'Connell: a review of the Irish policy of parliament from the Act of Union to the death of Sir Robert Peel* (1887) • S. Buxton, *Finance and politics: an historical study, 1783–1885*, 2 vols. (1888) • G. S. R. K. Clark, *Peel and the conservative party, 1832–1841* (1929) • W. P. Morrell, *British colonial policy in the age of Peel and Russell* (1930) • J. B. Conacher, *The Peelites and the party system* (1972) • T. L. Crosby, *Sir Robert Peel's administration, 1841–1846* (1976) • R. Stewart, *The foundation of the conservative party, 1830–1867* (1978) • D. Read, *Peel and the Victorians* (1987) • D. E. D. Beales, 'Peel, Russell and reform', *HJ*, 17 (1974), 873–82 • D. R. Fisher, 'Peel and the conservative party: the sugar crisis of 1844 reconsidered', *HJ*, 18 (1975), 279–302 • B. Hilton, 'Peel: a re-appraisal', *HJ*, 22 (1979), 585–614 • I. D. C. Newbould, 'Sir Robert Peel and the conservative party, 1832–1841: a study in failure?', *EngHR*, 98 (1983), 529–57 • F. Herrmann, 'Peel and Solly: two nineteenth-century art collectors and their sources of supply', *Journal of the History of Collections*, 3 (1991), 89–96 • V. A. C. Gatrell, 'Mercy and Mr. Peel', *The hanging tree: execution and the English people, 1770–1868* (1994), chap. 21

Archives BL, official and private corresp. and papers, Add. MSS 40181–40615, 62939 • CKS, corresp. and papers • Duke U., Perkins L., letters • FM Cam., corresp. mainly with artists • NL Scot., corresp. • Staffs. RO, deeds, legal papers, and corresp. relating to Tamworth • Surrey HC, account, cheque, commonplace book, and notebooks • U. Mich., Clements L., letters | Alnwick Castle, Northumberland, letters to Henry Drummond • Beds. & Luton ARS, corresp. with second earl of Grey • BL, corresp. with fourth earl of Aberdeen, Add. MSS 43061–43065 • BL, corresp. with third Earl Bathurst, loan 57 • BL, corresp. with Sir James Graham, Dep. 9374 • BL, Gladstone papers • BL, corresp. with John Charles Herries, Add. MS 57402 • BL, Huskisson papers • BL, corresp. with Prince Lieven, Add. MSS 47291–47296 • BL, letters to earls of Liverpool, Add. MS 38195 • BL, letters to earls of Liverpool, loan 72 • BL, letters to Sidney Smirke on buildings at Drayton, Add. MS 59847 • BL, corresp. with Lord Wellesley, Add. MSS 37298–37313, *passim* • BL OIOC, letters to Lord Tweeddale, MS Eur. F 96 • Bodl. Oxf., corresp. with Benjamin Disraeli • Bodl. Oxf., corresp. with Sir Thomas Phillipps • Bodl. Oxf., corresp. with Samuel Wilberforce • Borth. Inst., letters to first Viscount Halifax • Bucks. RLSS, letters to first Baron Cottesloe • CKS, corresp. with first and second Marquesses Camden • CKS, letters to Sir Edward Knatchbull and Wyndham Knatchbull • CKS, letters to Lord Mahon • CKS, letters to Lord Whitworth • Cornwall RO, letters to third earl of St Germans • CUL, letters to A. W. Kinglake • Derbys. RO, corresp. with Sir R. J. Wilmot-Horton • Duke U., Perkins L., letters to Sir John Newport • Durham RO, letters to Lord Londonderry • Exeter Cathedral, letters to Henry Phillpotts • Glamorgan RO, Cardiff, corresp. mainly with Lord Lyndhurst • Harrowby Manuscript Trust, Sandon Hall, Staffordshire, corresp. with first and second earls of Harrowby, Lord Dudley Coutts Stuart, and William Collins • Hunt. L., letters to Grenville family • ICL, letters to William Buckland • ICL, letters to first Baron Playfair • Keele University Library, corresp. with second earl of Clare • LPL, corresp. with Christopher Wordsworth • Lpool RO, letters to Lord Stanley • Man. CL, Manchester Archives and Local Studies, letter to J. F. Foster, stipendiary magistrate, Manchester • McGill University, Montreal, McLennan Library, corresp. with first Viscount Hardinge • NA Scot., corresp. with Sir George Clerk • NA Scot., corresp. with Thomas, Lord Cochrane • NA Scot., corresp. with first marquess of Dalhousie • NA Scot., letters to G. W. Hope • NA Scot., letters to Sir Charles Augustus Murray • NA Scot., letters to R. A. Nisbet-Hamilton • NA Scot., letters among the Winton House papers • NL Ire., Richmond papers • NL Scot., corresp. with Sir Thomas Cochrane • NL Scot., corresp. with Edward Ellice • NL Scot., corresp. with Sir Walter Scott • Norfolk RO, letters to Sir Henry Bulwer • NRA, priv. coll., corresp. with Maurice FitzGerald • NRA, priv. coll., corresp. with earl of Haddington • NRA, priv. coll., corresp. with duke of Hamilton • NRA, priv. coll., letters to Sir John Sinclair and Sir George Sinclair • NRA, priv. coll., letters to John Swinton • PRO, Cardwell papers • PRO, corresp. with earl of Ellenborough, PRO 30/12 • PRO, corresp. with Sir George Murray, WO 80 • PRO, corresp. with Lord John Russell, PRO 30/22 • PRO NIre., corresp. with first marquess of Anglesey • PRO NIre., letters to J. L. Foster • PRO NIre., corresp. with John Foster • PRO NIre., corresp. with Sir G. F. Hill and G. R. Dawson • RA, letters to Sir Thomas Lawrence • Royal Arch., corresp. with Queen Victoria, Prince Albert, and G. Anson • Sheff. Arch., letters to first Baron Wharncliffe; letters to second Baron Wharncliffe • St Deiniol's Library, Hawarden, corresp. with W. E. Gladstone • St Deiniol's Library, Hawarden, corresp. with fifth duke of Newcastle • Staffs. RO, letters to William Dyott and Richard Dyott • Surrey HC, Goulburn papers • Trinity Cam., letters to Lord Houghton • U. Nott. L., corresp. with dukes of Newcastle • U. Southampton L., letters to duke of Wellington • UCL, corresp. with Sir Edwin Chadwick • UCL, letters to Josiah Parkes on drainage matters • W. Sussex RO, letters to fourth duke of Richmond and fifth duke of Richmond • W. Yorks. AS, Leeds, corresp. with first Earl Canning • W. Yorks. AS, Leeds, corresp. with fifth duke of Richmond • Wilts. & Swindon RO, corresp. with Sidney Herbert • Yale U., Beinecke L., letters to William Buckland

Likenesses T. Lawrence, oils, 1825, priv. coll. [*see illus.*] • P. C. Wonder, group portrait, oils, *c.*1826, NPG • W. Heath, coloured etching, pubd 1830, BM, NPG • F. Chantrey, two drawings, *c.*1833, NPG • F. Chantrey, marble bust, 1835, Royal Collection • A. R. Freebairn, line engraving, pubd 1837 (after J. de Veaux), NPG • J. Ottley, copper medal, 1837, Scot. NPG • D. Wilkie, group portrait, oils, 1837 (*The queen's first council*), Royal Collection • J. Linnell, mezzotint, pubd 1838, BM, NPG • J. Linnell, oils, 1838, NPG • W. J. Ward, mezzotint, pubd 1842 (after J. Wood), BM, NPG • W. Tell, caricature, wood-engraving, 1844, NG Ire. • J. Wedderburn, group portrait, pencil and watercolour drawing, 1844, NPG • F. X. Winterhalter, double portrait, oils, *c.*1844 (with the duke of Wellington), Royal Collection • A. Crowquill, lithograph, pubd 1850, NPG • J. Steell, plaster bust, *c.*1850 (after F. Chantrey), Scot. NPG • E. H. Baily, bronze statue, 1851, Bury, Lancashire • M. Noble, marble bust, 1851, NPG • J. Gibson, statue, 1852, Westminster Abbey • M. Noble, marble statue, 1852–4, St George's Hall, Liverpool • G. Baxter, print, 1853 (after T. Lawrence), BM, NPG • M. Noble, bronze statue, 1876–7, Parliament Square, London • J. Doyle, lithograph, NG Ire. • J. Doyle, political sketches, BM • H. B. [J. Doyle], cartoons, repro. in J. Doyle, *Political sketches* (1829) • G. Hayter, group portrait, oils (*The House of Commons, 1833*), NPG • J. Partridge, group portrait (*The fine arts commissioners, 1846*), NPG • H. W. Pickersgill, oils, NPG; version, Gov. Art Coll. • W. Tell, caricature, wood-engraving, NG Ire. • F. X. Winterhalter, group portrait, oils (*Queen Victoria receiving Louis Philippe at Windsor Castle, 1844*), Musée de Versailles • caricature, repro. in *Punch*

Wealth at death income of £40,000 p.a., which represents estate of over £1,000,000: Gash, *Sir Robert Peel*, 163–4

Peel, Sir Robert, third baronet (1822–1895), politician, eldest son of Sir Robert *Peel, second baronet (1788–1850), the prime minister, and his wife, Julia, *née* Floyd (1795–1859), was born in London on 4 May 1822. His brothers included Sir Frederick *Peel, Sir William *Peel, and Arthur Wellesley *Peel, first Viscount Peel. Peel was 'small, dark, almost foreign-looking, and volatile' (Gash, 176). Throughout his life he was blamed for lacking the *gravitas* which his father and the Peelites so especially

Sir Robert Peel, third baronet (1822–1895), by Camille Silvy

praised in public life. He went to Harrow School in February 1835 and matriculated from Christ Church, Oxford, on 26 May 1841, but did not take a degree (unlike his father, whose double first was legendary). Entering the diplomatic service, he became an attaché to the British legation at Madrid on 18 June 1844. He was promoted to be secretary of legation in Switzerland on 2 May 1846, and was chargé d'affaires there in November 1846. After succeeding his father to the baronetcy on 2 July 1850, he entered the Commons as Liberal Conservative member for his father's former constituency, Tamworth, on 19 July 1850 and held it until 1880.

On 24 April 1854 Peel was shipwrecked off the coast of Genoa in the steamboat *Ercolano*, and only saved his life by swimming ashore. From 29 March 1854 to 1859 he served as a captain in the Staffordshire yeomanry. In March 1855 Lord Palmerston, who had been foreign minister while Peel was in the diplomatic service, appointed him a junior lord of the Admiralty. Henceforth he was regarded as a Liberal, and his persistent advocacy of the liberation of Italy fully justified this view of his political opinions. Palmerston liked Peel's jaunty manner and became his chief political patron. In July 1856 Peel acted as secretary to Lord Granville's special mission to Russia at the coronation of Alexander II, but on 5 January 1857, during a lecture delivered at the opening of the new library at Adderley Park, near Birmingham, he spoke discourteously of the Russian court and the court officials. The lecture was severely commented on by the Russian and French press, was the subject of a parliamentary debate, and caused great annoyance to the English court. Nevertheless, on Palmerston's return to power, Peel became, on 26 July 1861, chief secretary to the lord lieutenant of Ireland and a privy councillor. Together with Thomas Larcom, he operated an effective system of active surveillance which curbed the early efforts of the Fenians. But this was accompanied by an over-genial public persona and an anti-Catholic stance which estranged Cardinal Cullen and the priesthood and led to the disaffection of Irish Roman Catholic MPs with Palmerston's government. Peel lacked the will or ability to develop a land policy of the sort increasingly expected by Irish Liberals. On Palmerston's death he was succeeded in the Irish secretaryship by Chichester Fortescue, and he did not again hold office. On 5 January 1866 he was created GCB.

Peel continued to sit for Tamworth as a Liberal, but was often a severe critic of Gladstone's government of 1868–74. In 1874 he for a second time christened himself a Liberal Conservative; and during the Eastern question debates of 1876–80 he supported the Conservative government's policies. He did not stand for Tamworth at the general election in 1880, but unsuccessfully contested Gravesend as a Conservative; after 1880 his voice was often heard on Conservative platforms, denouncing the action of the Liberal administration in Egypt and Ireland. *The Times* of 8 May 1880 published his letter recounting the offers from various governments of honours and offices which he had refused. On 21 March 1884 he was elected at a by-election as Conservative member for Huntingdon. When that borough was disfranchised, he was, in November 1885, returned for Blackburn. However, on the critical division on the second reading of the Home Rule Bill, on 7 June 1886, he abstained from voting, thus shocking his tory colleagues. He was the only Conservative MP who by supporting home rule balanced the flow of Liberals into Conservatism. At the general election in July 1886 he unsuccessfully contested the Inverness burghs against a Liberal Unionist. Subsequently, with characteristic impetuosity, he threw himself into the home-rule campaign as a supporter of the Irish demands, and at a by-election in 1889 came forward as a candidate for Brighton in the home-rule interest. He was hopelessly defeated, and his political career came to a disappointing close.

From about 1856 Peel was extensively engaged in racing under the name of Mr F. Robinson; and later on he had an establishment at Bonehill, near Tamworth, where he bred horses. He added to his father's fine collection of pictures and drawings, which included the well-known *Chapeau de paille* by Rubens, but his extravagance and declining financial position forced their sale to the National Gallery in March 1871 and, in June 1884, the sale of much of the Drayton estate, excluding the manor house, though he ceased to live there. Peel married, on 13 January 1856, Lady Emily Hay, seventh daughter of the eighth marquess of

Tweeddale. They had a son, Robert (the fourth baronet), and three daughters. Lady Emily left her husband and lived in Geneva (she later moved to Florence and died in April 1924). On 9 May 1895 Peel was found dead, from haemorrhage of the brain, in his bedroom at 12 Stratton Street, London. He was buried at Drayton Bassett parish church on 16 May.   G. C. BOASE, *rev.* H. C. G. MATTHEW

Sources *The Times* (10 May 1895) · *The Times* (13 May 1895) · N. Gash, *Sir Robert Peel: the life of Sir Robert Peel after 1830* (1972) · E. D. Steele, *Palmerston and liberalism, 1855–1865* (1991) · Gladstone, *Diaries* · *Sporting Times* (1 May 1875), 297, 300 · C. Smith, *Drayton Manor and village: home of the Peels* (1991)
Archives BL, letters to W. E. Gladstone, Add. MSS 44153–44783, *passim* · Bodl. Oxf., corresp. with Lord Beaconsfield · Bodl. Oxf., corresp. with Lord Kimberley · Glos. RO, corresp. with first earl of Redesdale · NRA Scotland, corresp. with Lord Wemyss · U. Oxf., Taylor Institution, letters to the Harding family · U. Southampton L., corresp. with Palmerston
Likenesses Ατη [A. Thompson], caricature, chromolithograph, NPG; repro. in *VF* (19 March 1870), pl. 44 · Disderi & Cie, carte-de-visite, NPG · John & Charles Watkins, carte-de-visite, NPG · C. Silvy, photograph, priv. coll. [*see illus.*] · portrait, repro. in *Sporting Times* · portrait, repro. in *ILN* (29 March 1851), 254 · portrait, repro. in *ILN* (18 May 1895), 606 · portrait, repro. in *St Stephen's Review* (9 May 1891), 13 · wood-engraving (after photograph), NPG; repro. in *ILN* (25 Feb 1860)
Wealth at death £9568 18s. 11d.: probate, 15 Jan 1896, *CGPLA Eng. & Wales*

Peel, Sir Sidney Cornwallis, first baronet (1870–1938), soldier and financier, was born on 3 June 1870, at 70 Eaton Place, Pimlico, London, the third son of Arthur Wellesley *Peel, first Viscount Peel (1829–1912), and his wife, Adelaide (d. 1890), daughter of William Stratford Dugdale. His father was the fifth son of the Rt Hon. Sir Robert *Peel, and was himself a politician, serving as a Liberal MP (1865–95), parliamentary secretary to the Poor Law Board (1865–71) and to the Board of Trade (1871–3), under-secretary at the Home Office (1880), and speaker of the House of Commons (1885–95). He was created viscount in 1895.

The younger Peel was educated at Eton College where he was a king's scholar and Newcastle scholar, and at New College, Oxford, where he was placed in the first class in honour moderations and Greats. He was elected a fellow of Trinity College, Oxford, in 1893. Shortly afterwards he became secretary to the licensing commission, of which his father was chairman. Based on this experience he wrote *Practical Licensing Reform* (1901). He was called to the bar at Lincoln's Inn in 1898.

Peel served in the Second South African War from 1900 as trooper in the Oxfordshire imperial yeomanry, for which he received the queen's medal with three clasps. He recounted his experience in his book *Troopship 8008: Experiences in the Boer War* (1901). Shortly after the war he went to Egypt as a newspaper correspondent and this led to a further book, *The Binding of the Nile and the New Sudan* (1904). At this time he began a business association with Sir Ernest Cassel, who was active in business and financial affairs in Egypt—an association which lasted until Cassel's death in 1921. This led to Peel's obtaining a number of important posts in the City of London, notably chairman of the London committee of the National Bank of Egypt (which had been founded by Cassel) and vice-president of the Morocco State Bank (also founded by Cassel). In 1901 he became an official in the National Discount Company, of which he became a director in 1911, and chairman in 1922. Also in 1911 he was appointed to the Oxford Chest at the invitation of the then chancellor of Oxford University, Lord Curzon.

In 1914 Peel married Lady Delia Spencer, daughter of the sixth Earl Spencer. There were no children. In the same year he became major of B squadron of the Bedfordshire yeomanry, of which he had been an officer since 1902. He became colonel in May 1915. In June 1915 he took the regiment to France, where it served as part of the 1st cavalry division. In this role, his brother later recalled, 'into the grisly outlook he infused a certain humour which appealed to all ranks ... a splendid regiment was the result' (The Times, 20 Dec 1938). For his services he was mentioned in dispatches and received the DSO. He recounted his war experiences in O. C. Beds. Yeomanry (1935). In November 1917 he was recalled to act as financial adviser to the Foreign Office. In December 1918 he was elected Conservative MP for the Uxbridge division of Middlesex, which he held until the general election of 1922. He did not stand for parliament again.

In his capacity as financial adviser to the Foreign Office, Peel attended the Versailles peace conference in 1919, at which he was especially concerned with the Bulgarian settlement. In 1919 he became chairman of the export credits guarantee department advisory committee, a position which he retained until his death and in which, according to his Times obituarist, 'he did some of the most original and successful administrative work of his life' (The Times, 20 Dec 1938). He became deputy steward of Oxford University in 1922, and a member of the Oxford University statutory commission on its formation in 1924, resigning when he was appointed British plenipotentiary to the tariff conference in China in 1925–6. In 1927 he went to India as a member of the special committee of inquiry into the relations of the Indian states with the British government, a duty which continued until 1929. He was a member of the municipal banks committee, in 1926–7, and of other government committees. For some years he was secretary of the National Trust. He was made CB in 1929 and first baronet (of Eyworth) in 1936.

Peel's brother wrote at his death:

In his youth my brother was reckoned to be as efficient in mathematics as in classics. In virtue of this two-fold capacity he could master any subject with an accuracy derived from the former and with a width derived from the latter of these branches of study. (The Times, 20 Dec 1938)

Peel died at his home, 26 Hill Street, off Berkeley Square, London, on 19 December 1938, after a lengthy and painful illness. His funeral service was held at St Michael, Cornhill. He was survived by his wife. PAT THANE

Sources The Times (20 Dec 1938) · WWW · b. cert. · d. cert.
Archives NRA, papers
Wealth at death £86,437 17s. 9d.: probate, 20 Feb 1939, CGPLA Eng. & Wales

Peel, Thomas (1793?–1865), settler in Australia, was the second son of Thomas Peel (1768–1843) of Peelfold, Lancashire, a calico manufacturer and landowner, and his wife, Dorothy, née Bolton (1769–1837), and the great-nephew of Sir Robert *Peel (1750–1830). He was educated at Harrow School (1806–11) and was then briefly put to an attorney's office, but apparently followed no occupation until his marriage in 1823 to Mary Charlotte Dorking Ayrton (1800–1857), the daughter of Mrs Bridget Ayrton (c.1758–1845) and possibly of Dr Edmund *Ayrton; they had two daughters and two sons. Another son by an unknown mother was born in 1819. The Peels resided at Carnourie, near Forglen, Banffshire, from 1825 to 1827 or 1828, when Peel decided to claim his share of the family estate (probably £20,000) and emigrate to Australia. In London he met Captain James Stirling, who was vigorously promoting a new colony at the Swan River in Western Australia. With three fellow members of the Windham Club, Peel formed an association to bring 10,000 settlers to Western Australia in return for a land grant of 4 million acres. They proposed cultivating tobacco, cotton, sugar, and flax; none of these crops has ever flourished subsequently in the region, and none of the partners had experience of them. In December 1828 the Colonial Office responded, offering no more than a million acres. The other partners withdrew, but in January 1829 Peel found a substitute in Solomon Levey, a prosperous ex-convict who had returned from New South Wales to his native London. With Levey as financier and Peel as front man they formed a partnership in April 1829 with the more realistic goal of bringing 400 settlers to Western Australia for a land grant of 250,000 acres. The scheme was unfairly attacked in the London press as a piece of political jobbery undertaken on his cousin's behalf by the home secretary, Robert *Peel (1788–1850).

Peel left Plymouth on the Gilmore in August 1829 with the first party of settlers, arriving at the Swan River on 15 December, too late for the deadline prescribed by the Colonial Office for selecting his first choice of land. His settlers were disembarked at Woodman's Point, 7 miles south of Fremantle, at a town site named Clarence, and Peel accepted a land grant 40 miles further south on the Murray River. Morale was poor at Clarence, scurvy and dysentery broke out, the arrival of more settlers strained resources further, and Peel injured his right hand by gunshot, either accidentally or through a duel. By the end of 1830 Clarence was abandoned and Peel settled permanently at Mandurah at the mouth of the Murray. In England and America (1833) E. G. Wakefield gave a highly coloured and inaccurate account of Peel's venture in support of his theory that cheap land led to labour shortages and an inefficient dispersal of settlement. Although refuted by writers with first-hand information, Wakefield's story influenced later writers such as Karl Marx, and discouraged investment and settlement in Western Australia.

In April 1834 Peel's wife landed in Perth with her mother and children, and in October he took part in the 'battle' of Pinjarra, when Governor Stirling led a punitive expedition against the local Aborigines (the Pindjarup Nyungar) to clear the Murray region for European settlement. In

1839 he was elected to the General Road Trust and nominated a justice of the peace, and the following January he was appointed to the legislative council, but he resigned these offices in 1841, a year after his wife and daughters returned to London. Because of his cantankerous temperament he never subsequently played a prominent role in Western Australian public life, though he accompanied Governor Charles Fitzgerald to the Champion Bay district in 1852. He died, reputedly after a surfeit of ripe figs, at Mandurah on 21 December 1865 and was buried at Mandurah, where an Anglican church was built as a memorial to him. He was a large man of imposing appearance, but his ambitions were disappointed and his friend Henry Lefroy wrote later that he 'never saw corroding care so strongly marked on any man's face as his'. The Peel estate passed to the Colonization Assurance Corporation, and was bought in 1920 by the Western Australian government for a highly unsuccessful soldier settlement scheme.   GEOFFREY BOLTON

Sources A. Hasluck, *Thomas Peel of Swan River* (1965) · R. Richards, *The Murray district of Western Australia: a history* (1978) · W. C. Smart, *Mandurah and Pinjarrah: history of Thomas Peel and the Peel estate* (1956) · E. G. Wakefield, *England and America* (1833) · R. T. Appleyard and T. Manford, *The beginning* (1979) · J. R. M. Cameron, *Ambition's fire* (1982) · H. Peel, *Our Cornish home and its people* (1909) · M. Bassett, *The Hentys* (1954) · [F. Watson], ed., *Historical records of Australia*, 3rd ser., 6 (1923), 588 · R. Erickson, ed., *Dictionary of Western Australians, 1829–1914*, 5 vols. (1979–86), vol. 3 · *AusDB*
Archives Land Titles Office, Perth | State Library of Western Australia, Perth, Colonial Secretary's Office · State Library of Western Australia, Perth, Swan River MSS
Likenesses cartoon, 1829, BM; repro. in Hasluck, *Thomas Peel*, 146 · E. Du Cane, double portrait, sketch, 1852 (with Governor Charles Fitzgerald), priv. coll.; repro. in Hasluck, *Thomas Peel*, frontispiece
Wealth at death £700: probate, Australia

Peel, Sir William (1824–1858), naval officer, third and favourite son of Sir Robert *Peel, second baronet (1788–1850), prime minister, and his wife, Julia, née Floyd (1795–1859), daughter of Sir John *Floyd, was born on 2 November 1824. His brothers included Sir Robert *Peel, third baronet, Sir Frederick *Peel, and Arthur Wellesley *Peel, first Viscount Peel. After private school and Harrow School, Peel entered the navy in April 1838 on board the *Princess Charlotte*, carrying the flag of Sir Robert Stopford as commander-in-chief in the Mediterranean, and was present at the operations on the coast of Syria in 1840. He was afterwards in the *Monarch*, and in the *Cambrian* in China with Captain Henry Ducie Chads, returning to England in the troopship *Belleisle* in September 1843. In November he joined the gunnery ship *Excellent* at Portsmouth, and in May 1844 passed his examination with the greatest credit.

On 13 May, Peel was promoted lieutenant and ordered to the *Winchester*, flagship of Rear-Admiral Josceline Percy at the Cape of Good Hope. In May, before he could join the *Winchester*, he was appointed to the *Cormorant* in the Pacific. From her he was moved to the *Thalia*, and afterwards to the *America*, from which he carried out a secret intelligence mission to report on the Columbia/Oregon

territory, then at the centre of an Anglo-American dispute. He then returned with dispatches overland from San Blas to Vera Cruz, and thence to England. In February 1846 he was appointed to the *Devastation* at Woolwich; in May to the *Constance* at Plymouth; and on 27 June 1846 he was promoted commander. In 1847–8 he commanded the *Daring* on the North American and West Indies station, and on 10 January 1849 was promoted captain.

Anticipating a period on half pay, Peel decided to explore the interior of Africa, with the hope of doing something to improve the condition of the inhabitants. In preparation he studied Arabic, under the tuition of Joseph Churi, a Maronite educated at Rome, and in September 1850 proposed to Churi that they should make a short tour to Egypt, Mount Sinai, Jerusalem, Nazareth, and Syria. They left England on 20 October, and were back by 20 February 1851. On 20 August following they left on the longer and more serious journey. They went up the Nile, across the desert to Khartoum, and on to al-ʿUbayd, where they suffered a severe attack of fever and ague. Peel returned to England early in January, and published an account of the journey, *A Ride through the Nubian Desert* (1852).

In October 1853 Peel commissioned the frigate *Diamond*, attached to the fleet in the Mediterranean, and afterwards in the Black Sea. He served with the naval brigade landed for the siege of Sevastopol, under the command of Captain Stephen Lushington, and repeatedly distinguished himself by his bravery. On 18 October 1854 he threw a live shell, the fuse still burning, over the parapet of his battery. On 5 November, in the battle of Inkerman, he joined the officers of the Grenadier Guards, and helped to defend their colours. On 18 June 1855 he led the ladder party at the assault on the Redan, himself carrying the first ladder, until severely wounded. For these services he was nominated a CB on 5 July, and on the institution of the Victoria Cross he was one of the first recipients.

On 13 September 1856 he commissioned the *Shannon*, a powerful 50-gun steam-frigate, for service in China. She did not sail until the following March. At Singapore she was met by the news of the Indian mutiny, and took Lord Elgin up to Hong Kong, arriving on 2 July. Admiral Sir Michael Seymour sent the *Shannon* back to Calcutta on July 16, with Elgin on board, together with a detachment of marines and soldiers. At Calcutta, Peel formed a naval brigade. On 14 August he left the ship with 450 men, six 24-pounder Bengal artillery guns, and two 8 inch howitzers. At Allahabad on 20 October he was reinforced by a party of 120 men, and from then on was present in all the principal operations. The coolness of his bravery was everywhere remarkable, and his formidable battery gave most efficient service: the huge guns were, under his orders, moved and worked as though they were light field pieces. On 21 January 1858 he was nominated a KCB and an aide-de-camp to the queen.

In 1858 Peel's brigade employed six naval 8 inch guns from the *Shannon*. Peel mounted these massive weapons, weighing 65 cwt each, on carriages locally constructed by the sailors. They provided the firepower to overcome the massive walls of Indian forts, and to keep down British casualties.

In the second relief of Lucknow on 9 March 1858 Peel was severely wounded in the thigh by a musket bullet, which was cut out from the opposite side of the leg. Still very weak, he reached Cawnpore on his way to England, and there, on 20 April, he contracted smallpox, of which he died on 27 April, aged thirty-three. He never married. His services in the field were the highlight of the Lucknow campaigns. His men achieved unparalleled feats of arms and endurance that broke the will of the enemy.

Peel was an officer distinguished alike for his bravery and his resourcefulness. He benefited from the rapid promotions provided for the son of a prime minister, although his father never actively solicited them; however, no one ever doubted that he was a worthy recipient. In creating a legendary Victorian hero, concentrating on his courage and tragic death, his hagiographers did scant justice to his professional skill and intellectual achievements. His death deprived the navy of one of its most brilliant officers; his career had only just begun.

J. K. LAUGHTON, rev. ANDREW LAMBERT

Sources N. Gash, *Mr Secretary Peel: the life of Sir Robert Peel to 1830* (1961) · N. Gash, *Sir Robert Peel: the life of Sir Robert Peel after 1830* (1972) · B. Gough, 'Lieutenant William Peel, British naval intelligence and the Oregon crisis', *Northern Mariner: Journal of the Canadian Nautical Research Society*, 4 (1994), 1–14 · A. C. Dewar, ed., *Russian war, 1855, Black Sea: official correspondence*, Navy RS, 85 (1945) · W. B. Rowbotham, ed., *The naval brigades in the Indian mutiny, 1857–58*, Navy RS, 87 (1947) · D. Bonner-Smith and E. W. R. Lumby, eds., *The Second China War, 1856–1860*, Navy RS, 95 (1954) · Burke, *Peerage* · CGPLA Eng. & Wales (1859)

Archives BL, Sir Robert Peel MSS

Likenesses T. J. Barker, oils, 1859, NPG · J. H. Lynch, lithograph, pubd 1859, BM; repro. in W. L. Clowes, *The Royal Navy*, 6 (1901) · J. J. Chant, mezzotint and stipple engraving, pubd 1860 (after J. Lucas), BM, NPG · W. Theed, statue, 1860, Greenwich · W. Theed, statue, 1861, St Swithun's Church, Sandy, Bedfordshire · W. Theed, statue, 1863, Calcutta, India · J. Lucas, oils (posthumous), NMM · marble statue, NMM

Wealth at death under £35,000: resworn probate, July 1859, CGPLA Eng. & Wales

Peel, William Robert Wellesley, first Earl Peel (1867–1937), politician, was born in London on 7 January 1867, the eldest of the four sons and three daughters of Arthur Wellesley *Peel, first Viscount Peel (1829–1912), and his wife, Adelaide (d. 1890), daughter of William Stratford Dugdale, of Merevale Hall, Warwickshire. His paternal grandfather was the prime minister Sir Robert Peel. His early years were spent in London and at The Lodge, Sandy, Bedfordshire; he was educated at Harrow School (1880?–1885) and at Balliol College, Oxford (1885–9). A contemporary recalled his youthful 'impression of high abilities, coupled with a relative indifference to school or university successes' (*The Times*, 30 Sept 1937, 14c). He gained second classes in classical moderations and *literae humaniores*, and was secretary of the Oxford Union and a member of the university dramatic society. In 1893 Peel was called to the bar by the Inner Temple and for the next few years went on circuit, sometimes acting as marshal to Roland Vaughan Williams. In 1897 he was a special correspondent

for the *Daily Telegraph* in the Graeco-Turkish war; this gave him his first experience of foreign affairs, which remained a lifelong interest. On 11 April 1899 he married the Hon. Eleanor (Ella), elder daughter of James *Williamson, first Baron Ashton. They had a son and a daughter.

Peel gained his first experience of public affairs as a member of the royal commission on the port of London, which reported in June 1902. In 1900 he began a long connection with London county council, sitting from 1900 to 1904 as a Municipal Reform Party member for Woolwich, from 1907 to 1910 for Westminster, and from 1913 to 1919 for Kennington. He was leader of the Municipal Reform Party from 1908 to 1910, and chairman of the county council from 1914 to 1916. Meanwhile he entered parliament as Liberal Unionist member for Manchester South following a by-election on 25 May 1900. In January 1906 he unsuccessfully contested Harrow, but he returned to parliament as member for Taunton following a by-election on 23 February 1909, and held his seat through both elections of 1910. He was elevated to the House of Lords following the death of his father on 24 October 1912.

Peel was appointed lieutenant-colonel of the Bedfordshire yeomanry in 1912. He served with his regiment in France in 1914–15 and was mentioned in dispatches, but he was obliged to relinquish this post in 1915 owing to ill health. He entered office as joint parliamentary secretary to Sir Auckland Geddes at the national service department, on 15 April 1918. On 10 October the following year he became under-secretary of state for war under Winston Churchill, and was sworn of the privy council. On 1 April 1921 he became chancellor of the duchy of Lancaster, to which post was added that of minister of transport on 7 November 1921.

On 19 March 1922 Peel entered the cabinet as secretary of state for India, a position he held until January 1924; he served initially under Lloyd George in his coalition government and then, having been one of those tories who in October 1922 had indicated a willingness to join a purely tory government, held office under Bonar Law and Baldwin. He owed his appointment to Austen Chamberlain's recommendation, and to the back-bench Conservative demand for a period of calm at the India Office, following the Montagu–Chelmsford reforms, the first non-co-operation movement, and Gandhi's imprisonment. One of Peel's first published dispatches set out his reasons for rejecting any further inquiry into constitutional reform. In other respects his tenure was characterized by a policy of 'safety first', although it was also noted for the appointment of the commission on the superior services in India under Lord Lee of Fareham, which led to a significant increase in the number of Indians employed in the Indian Civil Service.

Peel was appointed first commissioner of works in Baldwin's second government, on 10 November 1924, and served in that post for almost four years. During his years at that department he pursued established policies. On 10 October 1928 Peel again became secretary of state for India, following the resignation of Lord Birkenhead. His second term lasted only seven months, and was marked by a determination to maintain a steady course while the commission under Lord Simon was still in progress. In opposition after June 1929 he led an unsuccessful attempt to persuade Baldwin to oppose the declaration made by Lord Irwin on 31 October 1929, and as one of the Conservative delegates at the first Indian round-table conference in 1930–31 he fought a rearguard action in favour of the proposals of the Simon report. From 1931 to 1932 he was chairman of the more congenial Burma round-table conference, his skills as chairman bringing praise from all quarters. In 1933 he was to have chaired the joint select committee on Indian constitutional reforms, but illness prevented him, and he served only briefly as a member. Although he was increasingly out of favour with the Indian policy of the National Government, he dissociated himself from Churchill's campaign against the 1935 reforms.

Peel last held major office as lord privy seal, from 3 September to 5 November 1931. In May 1932 he was appointed chairman of the wheat commission, and in November 1934 he was appointed chairman of the royal commission on the dispatch of business at common law. His last public service was as chairman of the royal commission on Palestine, appointed in July 1936. After investigations on the spot, which put great strain on Peel's ailing health, the commission unanimously recommended cutting the Gordian knot of Arab–Jewish conflict by the drastic means of partition, leaving Jerusalem, the Holy Places, and Haifa as a buffer zone under British control. The commission's report, published in July 1937, met with a chorus of approval from the British press, but with hostility from both Arabs and Jews. Its recommendations were quietly dropped.

Although politics and public life were his overriding concerns, Peel also had extensive business interests. He succeeded as chairman of James Williamson & Co. on the death of his father-in-law in 1929; he was also a director of Barclays Bank and of the Great Northern Railway. He was created Earl Peel and Viscount Clanfield of Clanfield on 10 July 1929. For his services in the First World War he was awarded the American Distinguished Service Medal. He was appointed GBE in 1919 and GCSI in 1932. Peel was described as 'a big man, his most conspicuous features being his bright blue eyes and his thick moustache, which became the joy of the caricaturist' (*DNB*). His shrewdness, geniality, and sense of humour were appreciated by his contemporaries. Lord Lytton described him in 1925 as 'a good fellow with plenty of common sense' (Bridge, 12).

Peel died at his home, Leydene, East Meon, Petersfield, Hampshire, on 28 September 1937, and was buried on 2 October at East Meon church. His wife died in 1949. He was succeeded in his titles by his son.   ALEX MAY

Sources *DNB* · *Daily Telegraph* (30 Sept 1937) · *The Times* (30 Sept 1937) · *The Times* (1 Oct 1937) · *The Times* (4 Oct 1937) · *The Times* (6 Oct 1937) · *The Times* (22 Oct 1937) · A. Rumbold, *Watershed in India, 1914–22* (1979) · R. J. Moore, *The crisis of Indian unity, 1917–1940* (1974) · C. Bridge, *Holding India to the empire: the British conservative party and the 1935 constitution* (1986) · S. C. Ghosh, 'Decision-making and power in the British conservative party: a case study of the Indian problem, 1929–34', *Political Studies*, 12 (1965), 198–212 · A. M. Hyamson, *Palestine under the mandate* (1950) · R. Ovendale, *The origins of the Arab–Israeli wars* (1984) · G. Gibbon and R. W. Bell, *History of the London county council, 1889–1939* (1939) · *Dod's Parliamentary Companion*

Archives BL OIOC, papers relating to India, MS Eur. D 528 | BL OIOC, corresp. with Lord Goschen, MS Eur. D 595 · BL OIOC, corresp. with Lord Halifax, MS Eur. C 152 · BL OIOC, corresp. with second earl of Lytton, MS Eur. F 160 · BL OIOC, letters to Lord Reading, MSS Eur. E 238, F 118 · BL OIOC, corresp. with Sir Frederick Sykes, MS Eur. F 150 · BL OIOC, corresp. with Lord Willingdon, MS Eur. F 93 · Bodl. Oxf., Simon MSS · Bodl. Oxf., corresp. with Sir W. L. Worthington-Evans · CUL, corresp. with Lord Hardinge | FILM BFI NFTVA, 'Viscount Peel', Topical Budget, 23 March 1922; news footage

Likenesses W. Stoneman, two photographs, 1919–29, NPG · O. Edis, photograph, NPG · W. Nicholson, oils; formerly at County Hall, London · photograph, repro. in *The Times* (30 Sept 1937)

Wealth at death £82,711 3s. 1d.: probate, 11 Nov 1937, CGPLA Eng. & Wales

Peel, William Yates (1789–1858), politician, was born at Chamber Hall, Bury, Lancashire, on 3 August 1789, the second son of Sir Robert *Peel, first baronet (1750–1830), calico printer and MP, and his first wife, Ellen Yates (1766–1803). The future prime minister Sir Robert *Peel, second baronet (1788–1850), was his elder brother. He was educated at Harrow School and St John's College, Cambridge, graduating BA in 1812 and MA in 1815; he was admitted to Lincoln's Inn in 1812 and was called to the bar in 1816. He entered parliament in 1817 as MP for Bossiney. At the general election of 1818 he was elected one of the MPs for Tamworth, alongside his father, and retained the seat until 1830, when he made way for his brother. On 17 June 1819 he married Jane Elizabeth (d. 1847), daughter of Stephen Moore, second Earl Mountcashell, an Irish representative peer; they had four sons and nine daughters.

Peel did not share his brother's ambition, and after declining office early in his parliamentary career was reproached by his father for a lack of vigour. He subsequently held minor positions as commissioner of the Board of Control (1826–7) in Lord Liverpool's administration, and then as under-secretary of state at the Home Office (1828–30), under his elder brother, in the duke of Wellington's administration. He became a lord of the Treasury (1830), an office which he also held in his brother's first administration (1834–5). He sat briefly as MP for Yarmouth, Isle of Wight (1830–31), and Cambridge University (1831–2) before reverting to Tamworth (1835–7). To the embarrassment of his brother he unexpectedly stood again for Tamworth at the general election of 1847 and was elected. He vacated the seat later that year and retired from public life, having been badly affected by the death of his wife in September 1847. He died at his home, Baginton Hall, Warwickshire, on 1 June 1858.

GEORGE PEEL, rev. M. C. CURTHOYS

Sources *GM*, 3rd ser., 5 (1858), 191 · HoP, *Commons* · Venn, *Alum. Cant.* · Boase, *Mod. Eng. biog.* · N. Gash, *Politics in the age of Peel* (1953) · N. Gash, *Mr Secretary Peel* (1961) · N. Gash, *Sir Robert Peel: the life of Sir Robert Peel after 1830* (1972)

Archives BL, corresp. with Sir Robert Peel

Wealth at death under £300,000: probate, 9 July 1858, CGPLA Eng. & Wales

Peele, George (*bap.* 1556, *d.* 1596), poet and playwright, was baptized on 25 July 1556 in the parish of St James Garlick-hythe, London, probably the fourth of the five surviving children of James *Peele (*d.* 1585), clerk of Christ's Hospital, and his first wife, Anne (*d.* 1579). By 1562 the family had moved to St Olave Jewry. In its various forms, including Pile, Pill, Piel, and Pell, the Peele family name has been traced to Devon, the north country, Norfolk, Kent, Monaco, and Normandy. James Peele was the author of two works on double-entry bookkeeping, *The Maner and Fourme How to Kepe a Perfecte Reconyng* (1553) and *The Pathe Waye to Perfectnes* (1569). A respected citizen and salter of London, James was also responsible for city pageants, and he was the clerk of Christ's Hospital, the second in its history, from 1562 until his death.

Early years and education From 1556 until 1571 George Peele lived and was educated in the grounds of Christ's Hospital, a charitable institution for orphans, the elderly, and the poor. In 1571 he was living in Broadgates Hall, Oxford, across the street from Christ Church where he was residing by December 1574. He took his BA (1577) and MA (1579) from Christ Church, the latter degree one year before the normally required time. His earliest literary efforts and colleagues were Oxonian. The efforts included the no longer extant translation of Euripides' *Iphigenia*; the colleagues featured Thomas Watson (to whose verse collection, *Hekatompathia*, Peele addressed a commendatory poem in 1582) and William Gager, the Latin playwright who commended Peele's translation of Euripides in two Latin poems. Gager's poems praise Peele's classicism, as well as his mixture of sobriety and humour. They also offer a physical description of someone who might be Peele as 'strangely short of leg, dark of complexion, squint-eyed, and red-haired' (*Life and Works*, 1.45).

In 1579, the year of his mother's death, Peele was back in London at his father's house, for court documents dating from September of that year record his father's compliance with an order to have his son among other occupants removed from the premises of Christ's Hospital. Until recently, this document has been used as evidence that Peele lived a rowdy, immoral life; recent biographers prefer the explanation that James Peele was facing hard times (*Life and Works*, 1.47–9). Back in Oxford, George married a sixteen-year-old girl named Anne Cooke or Christian (*bap.* 1564, *d.* 1587?), the wedding taking place between early March and 18 October 1580. Her father's legacy produced legal disputes over property that would require the attention of the newly-weds for four years. Among the array of legal particulars assembled by David Horne (ibid., 1.50–57), one deposition given by George mentions the fact that he moved to London in 1581.

Poems and plays As Gager attests, Peele had commenced his literary work at Oxford. One of his first poems, *The Tale of Troy*, was probably written after his MA but in his last years of residence in Oxford, about 1580–81. First published in 1589, this poem in couplets was based on a variety of sources, especially Caxton, and it manifests Peele's continuing interest in antiquity. *The Tale of Troy* also inaugurates his tendency to mingle diverse genres or registers, in this case the chivalric and pastoral kinds so attractive to his contemporaries. Its focus on Trojan history would suit his audience as well, for Troy was imagined by the Elizabethans to have produced the origins of their own history.

In June 1583 Peele was consulted on the entertainment planned for the Oxford visit of Albertus Alasco, count palatine of Siradia, Poland. Peele was living in London, where he added plays to his poetic output. Of his five extant and complete plays, *The Arraignment of Paris* most reflects the influence of his university days. Performed before the queen by the children of the chapel between 1581 and 1584, it stages a mythological and pastoral treatment of one episode in the Trojan saga, the judgment of Paris. As in the case of his fellow Oxonian John Lyly, Peele's court drama was meant to please and praise Queen Elizabeth. It is possible that the fragmentary 'Hunting of Cupid' was another such attempt: it survives as excerpts in two miscellanies—*England's Helicon* (1600) and *England's Parnassus* (1600)—as well as in a 1609 transcription by William Drummond.

Like his father, Peele was enlisted to devise mayoral pageants for the city of London. Two of these are extant: *The Device of the Pageant Borne before Wolstan Dixi* (1585) and *Descensus Astraeae* (1591), the latter composed for the installation of William Webbe. In Peele's strange afterlife as a jest-book hero, he is remembered for his expertise in the composition of masques and pageants, and spectacle of one kind or another is a feature of his two main types of literary invention in the last years of his life: occasional poems in congratulation of various dignitaries, and dramas written for the professional theatre.

The occasions for Peele's verses included these: the departure of Sir John Norris and Sir Francis Drake on a naval mission against the Spanish (*A Farewell: Entituled to the Famous and Fortunate Generalls of our English Forces*, published with *The Tale of Troy* in 1589); the return of Robert, earl of Essex, from the Norris–Drake mission, for which Peele chooses Spenserian pastoral (*An Eclogue Gratulatorie: Entituled, To the Honorable Shepheard of Albions Arcadia*, 1589); two accession days for Elizabeth (*Polyhymnia Describing, the Honourable Triumph at Tylt*, 1590, and *Anglorum feriae*, 1595); and an induction ceremony into the Order of the Garter for Henry Percy, ninth earl of Northumberland, the famous 'wizard earl' (*The Honour of the Garter: Displaied in a Poeme Gratulatorie*, 1593). Like so many such occasions, these events presented Peele with challenges to the rhetoric of his praise. In celebrating the return of Essex from the Norris–Drake enterprise, Peele risked casting a negative light on the anti-Spanish mission that he had so recently lauded. The tilting ceremony behind *Polyhymnia* was the last for the master of the armoury, Sir Henry Lee; Peele faced the challenge of praising an old order and a new. Sometimes occasions skewed the balance of Peele's poetry of praise: in the mayoral show *Descensus Astraeae* he bestowed much more attention on the queen than he did on the lord mayor.

In the poems as in the plays, Peele develops a variety of English verse forms, not least the newly powerful and supple blank verse. Elizabethan anthologists commonly looked to him for selections to include in their miscellanies; for instance, his poem 'The Praise of Chastity' appeared in the 1593 miscellany entitled *The Phoenix Nest*. In quatrains rhyming *abab*, the poem seeks to prove 'by way of comparison, how great is the conquest over our affections' (*Life and Works*, 1.260). If Peele indeed wrote the 'sonet' appended to some copies of *Polyhymnia*, its three stanzas of six lines each, with a quatrain of alternating rhymes followed by a couplet, show his capacity for great lyric beauty.

Aside from some excellent lyric passages, Peele's occasional verse offers historical evidence about Elizabethan politics, patronage, and manners with little in the way of literary merit. His enduring monument was dramatic rather than panegyric. It is impossible to know with certainty when Peele's four professional plays were written or performed. But there is some consensus that *The Battle of Alcazar* was his first (*Life and Works*, 2.221–6). Acted by the Lord Admiral's Servants, it survives in its 1594 edition as well as in a handwritten plot outline indicative of a longer version of the play (BL, Add. MS 10449). But the play was probably written not long after the defeat of the Armada. Although its patriotic themes, exotic and homegrown character types, and theatrical devices are common enough in plays of his time, Peele's inventive combination of elements renders *The Battle of Alcazar* something of its own kind. So it is with much of Peele's theatrical work: what stands out is the combination of elements, not any one element in its own right.

The Battle of Alcazar divides its attention between three main groups. First there are the North African Moors whose custom of having brothers succeed one another to the throne has been transgressed by the son of one of the brothers. For English audiences, it would seem natural for a son to succeed a father according to the custom of primogeniture, and so the very premise of the play is as exotic as the setting. The transgressing son, Muly Mahamet or 'The Moor', is Peele's version of Christopher Marlowe's Tamburlaine, a passionately ambitious warrior whose fustian blank verse was lampooned by other playwrights of the time. Into the African contest for succession come two European groups of characters, each with its share of ambition if not spoken in the Moor's high-pitched pentameter. One group centres on King Sebastian of Portugal, the other on Thomas Stukeley, a renegade English Catholic whose plan to seize Ireland in rebellion against Elizabeth somehow did not prevent him from becoming a popular hero. It helps, no doubt, that he is distracted from rebellion by the prospect of glory in northern Africa. The play makes use of two spectacular stage devices: the commentary of a presenter and the foreshadowing of the dumb show. These devices are especially helpful in keeping the audience on top of a complicated plot with its strange notions of succession. But the themes of the play could not be more familiar to Elizabethan audiences: the perils of illegitimate succession, of rebellion,

and of ambition. Along the way, Peele makes sure that a character offers praise for Elizabeth and her protestant nation.

Of Peele's next two plays, *Edward I* and *The Old Wives Tale*, the former is a chronicle play with strong anti-Spanish sentiment. It is much harder to say what, generically or tonally, the latter play is. First published in 1593, *Edward I* was well received by Elizabethan audiences—hardly surprising, given its fervently anti-Catholic characterization of Queen Elinor. Between August 1595 and the next July, Henslowe recorded fourteen performances of a play called *Longshanks*, very likely an alias for Peele's chronicle play (*Life and Works*, 2.7–8). There was a second edition in 1599. The play's central theme of legitimate monarchy quashing rebellion in Wales and Scotland was sure to earn approval from Peele's audience. The playwright shows his liking for spectacular scenes when, as the title-page announces, he stages 'the sinking of Queene *Elinor*, who sunck *at Charingcrosse, and rose againe at Pottershith*, now named Queenehith' (ibid., 2.69). More inventively, if less marvellously, Peele also writes in a range of forms, from blank verse and tetrameter couplets to prose.

Peele's most famous and unusual play, *The Old Wives Tale*, leaves behind the lofty narrative region of the chronicle for the homely realm of the folk-tale. But with its elements of chivalric and fairy stories, the play's tone and genre are hard to measure, notwithstanding the 1595 title-page on which the play is dubbed 'A pleasant conceited Comedie, played by the Queenes Maiesties players' (*Life and Works*, 3.385). The play's simplicity is made all the more deceptive by its central device: rather than simply weave together strands of action in the manner of a history play, it interrelates zones of dramatic reality. At the outermost level, two pages with allegorical names (Frolicke and Fantasticke) spend a night listening to an old, amiable, and ingenuous housewife tell 'a merry winters tale' (ibid., 3.390). The tale itself sprawls from a beautiful princess captured by a sorcerer; to her brothers and a lover who seek her in the woods; to the young man transformed by the sorcerer into, alternately, an old man and a bear, together with the young man's wife driven mad by the sorcerer; to the opposite daughters of an unhappy father, both of whom—one ugly, the other beautiful—must seek their fortune in a special well. This summary omits the play's most notorious character, a braggart soldier named Huanebango whose foolish pomposity is arguably based on Peele's contemporary Gabriel Harvey (Frank Hook reviews the evidence and questions the Harvey parallels: ibid., 3.311–19). But the most extraordinary feature of the play is that as the old wife tells the two pages her story in all simplicity, the characters appear before the very eyes of the threesome. As the various strands and motifs of the tale unfold before them, Frolicke and Fantasticke persist in questioning the wife about the play within the narrative within the play that they witness.

If *The Old Wives Tale* testifies to Peele's belief in the power of even the simplest and most familiar stories, his fourth play for the professional theatre—*The Love of King David and Fair Bethsabe: with the Tragedie of Absalon*—ventures to dramatize the holy scriptures themselves. Published posthumously in 1599 but written between 1592 and 1594, *David and Bethsabe* takes as its focus the sins of David, Ammon, and Absalon as they are set forth in 2 Samuel, sins including adultery and treachery (David), rape and incest (Ammon), and rebellion (Absalon). Like his plays based on medieval and contemporary history, Peele's biblical drama explores the ways in which divine providence corrects human propositions, a more sober and conventional sense of diverse and interlocking realities than the lighthearted yet mysterious narrative device of *The Old Wives Tale*. Thrice excerpted in the miscellany *England's Parnassus*, *David and Bethsabe* also contains some of Peele's best verse.

Several other plays have been attributed to Peele, though most scholars now agree that only the fragmentary 'Hunting of Cupid' and the no longer extant *Turkish Mahomet and Hiren the Fair Greek* can safely be credited to him. Scholars have also divided on the question of whether Peele himself acted on the Elizabethan stage, with Peele's most exhaustive recent biographer, David Horne, deciding against the playwright's acting career (*Life and Works*, 1.83–7).

Last years and reputation It is possible that in the last decade of his life Peele was widowed in 1587 and married to one Mary Yates (or Gates) on 26 December 1591. But whatever his marital history, his financial and physical fortunes took a downward turn. On 17 January 1596 he sent via his elder daughter a presentation copy of *The Tale of Troy* to William Cecil, Lord Burghley. In the dedication, Peele complained of a long, enfeebling illness and attributed his boldness to necessity. Burghley responded by filing the request for patronage together with others made by those supplicants least worthy of any response. According to records for the parish of St James Clerkenwell, Peele died later that year—he was buried at St James's on 9 November 1596.

By the end of his life, Peele still retained some measure of his identity as a gentlemanly scholar with connections to the world of Oxford. But he was far more decisively identified as a professional playwright whose home was London. The author of *Greene's Groatsworth of Wit* (1592) placed Peele together with Marlowe and Thomas Nashe as fellow playwrights abused by the scapegrace players. In *A Knights Conjuring* (1607), Thomas Dekker located Peele in the Elysium of poets, a paradise dominated by Chaucer and Spenser but with Robert Greene, Nashe, Marlowe, and Peele in their own circle. Dekker's scene suggests that while the four are gentleman poets to be sure, they belong together as professional writers unable to rely on 'dry-fisted Patrons' (*Knight's Conjuring*, ed. Robbins, 156). But Peele's afterlife offered much more about his life than simply his beleaguered station as a professional playwright. In *Palladis tamia* (1598), Francis Meres not only ranked Peele among the best of England's poets and tragedians, but also claimed that the Oxford wit had died of the pox.

Meres's report of the playwright's syphilis, however, pales in comparison to the treatment of the protagonist in *The Merry Conceited Jests of George Peele* (1607). Some ten years after Peele's death, the biggest mystery of his life commenced, namely, how he came to be made into a jest-book hero whose decadence might explain his illness and whose prodigality might explain his poverty. This George is a witty, prodigal trickster who spends his time making merry in taverns; spending money and wit with a breathless velocity; devising exploits for fun and profit; wenching like a 'lecherous animal'; and idly wasting his dramatic talent on knavery and dodges. The jests trumpet George's scholarly and literary talents: he has 'all the oversight of the pageants' and is hired to translate a Greek book into English (*Works*, 2.391, 381). He is heralded as an 'excellent poet' and as a well-known playwright (ibid., 2.389). But these talents are miserably if humorously misspent with a prodigal wastefulness commonly attributed to the wittiest English writers of Peele's generation. George shows up as just such a wastrel in the character of George Pyeboard, featured in a 1607 play called *The Puritan* and written by W. S.

It is simply impossible to know for certain why, or how justly, Peele was chosen over, say, Thomas Nashe for the dubious honour of starring as a gentleman knave in a jest-book. For many years, at least until the twentieth-century scholarship of Thorleif Larsen and David Horne altered the case, Peele scholars tended to assume that the jest-book was essentially right about the poet. Had he not been removed from his father's house at Christ's Hospital? Had he not died of the pox? Was there not at least some fire where there was much smoke? Horne in particular, however, has retorted that the 'merry conceited jests' are virtually all conventional (*Life and Works*, 1.110–26). It might be noted, too, that Peele's writings (one thinks of such unimpeachable poems as 'The Praise of Chastity') never come close to the kind of erotic satire found, say, in Nashe's 'A Choice of Valentines' or in Marlowe's translation of Ovid's *Amores*. Whatever Peele's own proximity to the hero of the jest-book, he embodied for some of his contemporaries the perils of waste in an Elizabethan literary life begun in scholarship, offered out for patronage, and ended in the squalor of a professional playwright's meagre existence. But it is also typical of this character that he never loses the abundance and energy of his wit.

Nothing solidifies the contemporary choice of Peele to embody the brilliance yet peril of Elizabethan poets and playwrights more than the address to him in *Greene's Groatsworth of Wit*:

> And thou no lesse deserving than the other two, in some things rarer, in nothing inferiour; driven (as my selfe) to extreme shifts, a litle have I to say to thee: and were it not an idolatrous oth, I would sweare by sweet S. George, thou art unworthy better hap, sith thou dependest on so meane a stay. (*Greene's Groatsworth of Wit*, 83)

Whether or not Peele was loose in his living, it is certain that by the end of his life, his mainstay was 'so meane a stay', the actors of the Elizabethan stage. For however much praise Peele had bestowed on Drake and Norris, on Essex and Northumberland, on mayors and a queen, his appeal to Burghley demonstrates just how ignominiously a literary life in search of patronage often turned out, even for one with 'oversight of the pageants'. In 1604 Peele's old workhorse for patrons, *The Tale of Troy*, was published in a revised edition, and did him just as much good as it had done him in the presentation copy to Burghley. Thomas Nashe understood the burden of that poem: 'Others are so hardly bested for loading that they are faine to retaile the cinders of *Troy*, and the shivers of broken trunchions, to fill up their boate that else should goe empty' (*Life and Works*, 1.80).   REID BARBOUR

Sources *The life and works of George Peele*, ed. C. T. Prouty, 3 vols. (1952–70) · A. R. Braunmuller, *George Peele* (1983) · K. J. Donovan, 'Recent studies in George Peele (1969–1990)', *English Literary Renaissance*, 23 (1993), 212–20 · L. R. N. Ashley, *George Peele* (1970) · S. J. Kozikowski, 'George Peele', *Elizabethan dramatists*, ed. F. Bowers, DLitB, 62 (1987), 242–53 · *The works of George Peele*, ed. A. H. Bullen, 2 vols. (1888) · *Greene's groatsworth of wit*, ed. D. Allen Carroll (1994) · F. Meres, *Palladis tamia* (1598); facs. edn with introduction by D. C. Allen (1938) · *Thomas Dekker's 'A knights conjuring' (1607): a critical edition*, ed. L. M. Robbins (1974)

Archives BL, Add. MSS 10449, 21432 · St John Baptist College, Oxford, MS 216 | BL, Lansdowne MS 99, no. 54

Peele, James (*d.* 1585), writer on bookkeeping, whose origins are obscure, described himself in 1569 as 'Cittizen and Salter of London, Clercke of Christes Hospitall, practizer and teacher of the same' (that is, bookkeeping). He was appointed clerk of Christ's Hospital, London, in 1562, and continued working there until his death in 1585. His duties included those of bookkeeper. He introduced the double-entry system in the hospital's bookkeeping, and entries in several of the surviving ledgers are in his hand. There is indirect evidence that he was called in by merchants to settle disputes that involved accounts; and that he also taught bookkeeping.

Peele wrote two books on double-entry bookkeeping. The first, *The maner and fourme how to kepe a perfecte reconyng, after the order of the moste worthie and notable accompte, of debitour and creditour*, was published in London in 1553. It is a short book, dedicated to Sir William Densell, governor of the Company of Merchant Adventurers. Its treatment of the subject owes much to earlier published works, but includes some novelties. The second book, *The Pathe Waye to Perfectnes, in th'Accomptes of Debitour, and Creditour*, was published in London in 1569. It is a larger book than the earlier work, and is of much greater originality. The didactic part is presented in the form of a dialogue between a schoolmaster and a scholar, the latter a servant sent by a merchant to acquire a knowledge of double-entry bookkeeping. Peele displayed a thorough understanding of merchants' accounts, and he included a fully worked-out example of the division of the ledger between a secret or private ledger and the ordinary ledger for use in the ordinary course of business, on the lines proposed by John Weddington two years earlier.

Though some later authors, notably John Mellis in his *A Briefe Instruction* of 1588, borrowed from Peele's books, their influence seems to have been limited in spite of the high quality especially of his second book. However, Richard Dafforne recalled his name in 1635: 'Want of love to this Art [double-entry bookkeeping], is the cause why

James Peele, and others that have written in English upon this subject, are known by Name only, & not by Imitation' (*The Merchants Mirrour*, 1635, epistle dedicatory).

The title-page of Peele's second book includes an illustration of a man seated at a table; on the basis of the coat of arms displayed, this is said to be a representation of the author. His son George *Peele (*bap.* 1556, *d.* 1596), from his marriage to his first wife, Anne (*d.* 1579), became well known as a playwright and poet.   BASIL S. YAMEY

Sources B. S. Yamey, 'Peele's two treatises in context', *Further essays in the history of accounting* (1982)

Peend [de la Pend], **Thomas** (*fl.* 1565–1566), translator and poet, whose parentage is unknown, may have been related to Stephen de la Pyend of the Inner Temple, London, and Depden, Suffolk. He was educated at Oxford (according to Wood, *Ath. Oxon.*, 1.430) and was a London barrister with a 'chamber over agaynst Sergeants Inne in Chancery Lane' (Peend, *Fable*, 2). Peend is best known for *The Pleasant Fable of Hermaphroditus and Salmacis*, a translation of part of Ovid's *Metamorphoses* (IV.287–388), written in rhyming couplets in alternating lines of iambic octameter and hexameter. In the dedicatory epistle to Nicholas Sentleger of Eastwell, Kent, Peend dates the work to 1564 and claims to have translated additional sections of the *Metamorphoses*, but divulges that he will publish only this one tale because he has been pre-empted by another translator, doubtless a reference to Arthur Golding, whose English rendition of the *Metamorphoses* appeared in 1565. It is, however, unlikely that Peend executed his translation in 1564, and hence before reading Golding's, because (according to Taylor) the numerous parallels between the translations suggest that Peend knew Golding's work. Peend's text concludes with a glossary (in prose) of characters mentioned in the text so 'that the unlearned myght the better understande', from which we can infer his intended audience (Peend, *Fable*, 27). To educate his readers further, the fable is followed by a moralizing poem which casts Salmacis as 'eche vyce that moveth one to ill' (ibid., 16). This interpretation leads into the final part of the composition—a catalogue of evil, passionate women—which forms part of the anti-feminist side of the sixteenth-century debate on women. All the examples are drawn from classical sources, except for the stories of Romeo and Juliet (ibid., 22), Aleran and Adelasie (ibid., 21–2), and Gysmond and Guistardes (ibid., 22). This last allusion attests to Peend's knowledge of William Walter's text of the same name, dated 1532, and the others to his familiarity with Matteo Bandello's remarkably popular and influential *Novelle*. Indeed, Peend's second composition, *The Moste Notable Historie of John Lord Mandosse*, is a translation of one of Bandello's stories. Although Peend claims a Spanish source for *Mandosse*, he actually used Pierre Boaistuau's French translation (1559) of Bandello. Bandello and Boaistuau both allege a Spanish author for the tale (although Boaistuau's Spaniard purportedly wrote in Latin), and it is likely that Peend did the same to designate proximity to the original, thus lending more authority to his narrative (Bandello, 425; Boaistuau, 169).

Mandosse is dedicated to Sir Thomas Kemp, and is written in rhyming couplets in alternating lines of iambic hexameter and heptameter. Peend is also the author of a short poem prefixed to John Studley's *Agamemnon* (1566). Nothing is known of his later life. JOYCE BORO

Sources T. Peend, *The pleasant fable of Hermaphroditus and Salmacis* (1565) · T. Peend, 'To the reader', in J. Studley, *The eyght tragedie of Seneca: entituled Agamemnon* (1566), 11–12 · Wood, *Ath. Oxon.*, new edn, vol. 1 · M. Bandello, *La seconda parte de le novelle* (1993) · P. Boaistuau, *Histoires tragiques*, ed. R. A. Carr (1977) · A. B. Taylor, 'Thomas Peend and Arthur Golding', *N&Q*, 214 (1969), 16–20 · J. H. Runsdorf, 'Transforming Ovid in the 1560s: Thomas Peend's pleasant fable', *American Notes and Queries*, 5 (1992), 124–7 · E. Brydges and J. Haslewood, *The British bibliographer*, 2 (1812) · D. Bush, *Mythology and the Renaissance tradition in English poetry* (1932) · C. S. Lewis, *English literature in the sixteenth century excluding drama* (1954) · H. D. Smith, *Elizabethan poetry: a study in conventions, meaning, and expression* (1952) · R. Pruvost, *Matteo Bandello and Elizabethan fiction* (1937)

Peer, William (*d.* in or before **1713**), actor and property man, whose origins are obscure, served as a property man in London in 1659–60, according to *The Biographical Dictionary of Actors, Actresses … and other Stage Personnel in London*. His earliest known role was with the Duke's Company, Pecus in Ferdinando Parkhurst's *Ignoramus, or, The Academical Lawyer*, which was presented at court in November 1662. Peer seems to have moved to Dublin for several years following this initial engagement. William Smith Clark states that he played a servant in John Wilson's *Belphegor* in the Dublin playhouse, Smock Alley, though 'he moved [back] to Drury Lane about the fall of 1679 and eventually assumed the post of property man there' (Highfill, Burnim & Langhans, *BDA*, 82).

Perhaps because of his duties as props man Peer played only a few roles after he returned to London, as far as we know. He played Jasper in Thomas Shadwell's *The Scowrers* in December 1690 and then the Presbyterian parson in Thomas D'Urfey's *Love for Money* in January 1691. When Thomas Betterton and other performers left the United Company in London in winter 1694–5, Peer followed them and continued his career at the Lincoln's Inn Fields Theatre. He is listed as dresser at the Queen's Theatre in the Haymarket in March 1708, receiving a per diem wage of 4s. He played only one known role at this theatre, Second Ruffian in *King Lear* in October 1706.

Some contemporary writers believed that Peer was undeservedly relegated to small roles or kept off the stage altogether. Tom Brown's *Letters from the Dead to the Living* addresses Peer as:

> you, who must be honest, because your [*sic*] are so poor and a Man of Merit, because you never were promoted … For you, Sir … are one of the most ancient of his Majesty's Servants, under the denomination of a Player, and yet cannot advance above the delivering a scurvy Message, which the strutting Leaders of your House wou'd do much more aukardly. (Brown and others, 65)

In a letter written probably about 1707, *The Post-Man Robb'd of his Mail* calls this actor 'honest *Will Pierre*, who has stood the Shock of so many Turns of State, so many revolutions, and Transmigrations, without advancing beyond a Property-Man' (Gildon, 266).

Peer died at some time before 15 June 1713, since he appears on that date in an eulogistic article by Richard Steele in *The Guardian*. This piece offers us the most detailed information available on Peer, noting that Peer excelled in two small parts: the speaker of the prologue to the play within *Hamlet* and the Apothecary in Thomas Otway's version of *Romeo and Juliet*, entitled *The History and Fall of Caius Marius*. Steele states: 'It is no matter, say the Moralists, whether you act a Prince or a Beggar, the Business is to do your Part well' (Steele, 299). He further comments: 'It was an odd Excellence, and a very particular Circumstance this of *Peer's*, that his whole Action of Life depended upon speaking five Lines better than any Man else in the World' (ibid., 300). Unfortunately:

> in the Seventeenth Year of his Age he grew fat, which rendered his Figure unfit for the Utterance of the five Lines abovementioned: He had now unfortunately lost the wan Distress necessary for the Countenance of the Apothecary, and was too jolly to speak the Prologue with the proper Humility. (ibid., 301)

Steele writes that this loss of his parts contributed 'to the shortning his Days', though Peer had also been serving as a property man who was required to be 'always ready, in a Place appointed for him behind the Prompter, [with] all such Tools and Implements as are necessary in the Play … *Billetdoux*, Poison, false Mony, Thunderbolts, Daggers' (ibid., 300). Steele states that the theatre does not owe him any money except that for some miscellaneous props—'For Hire of six Case of Pistols', 'For Blood in *Macbeth*'—amounting to 11s. 1d. (ibid., 301). CHERYL WANKO

Sources Highfill, Burnim & Langhans, *BDA*, 11.248–9 · W. Van Lennep and others, eds., *The London stage, 1660–1800*, pts 1–2 (1960–65) · R. Steele and others, *The Guardian*, ed. J. C. Stephens (1982), 299–301 · [C. Gildon], *The post-man robb'd of his mail* (1719) · Thomas Brown and others, *Letters from the dead to the living*, 2nd edn (1702) · W. S. Clark, *The early Irish stage* (1955), 82

Peeris, William (*fl. c.*1520), chronicler, describes himself in the preamble to his only known work, a verse chronicle of the Percy family, as a clerk and priest who was secretary to Henry Percy, fifth earl of Northumberland. He has been plausibly identified with the William Pyers who in the year 1519–20 was paid 3s. 4d. by Beverley corporation for coming from Wressle to alter the text of the town's Corpus Christi play; another 7s. were disbursed 'to make an agreement with him for transposing' that play (Goldberg, 154–5). The earl of Northumberland was Beverley's patron, while Wressle, a few miles west of Hull, was one of his principal residences. Both there and at the earl's house at Leconfield there were walls and ceilings decorated with moralizing verses. The fact that Pyers is described in the Beverley records as a poet gives plausibility to suggestions that the same hand was responsible both for the verses and for Peeris's chronicle.

Described by Peeris as a new year's gift for the earl, the chronicle refers to the latter's daughter Margaret as married to Henry Clifford, the son and heir of the tenth Lord Clifford, and must therefore have been composed between Henry's marriage in 1513 and his father's death in 1523. It survives in a number of copies. Probably the earliest is Alnwick Castle, MS 79. Not only is this a roll whose ornamental margins (embellished with medallion busts of all the English kings between William I and a youthful and clean-shaven Henry VIII) suggest that it was prepared for presentation to its dedicatee, but it also differs from other versions in both its beginning and its conclusion. Of those later versions, British Library, Royal MS 18 D.ii, folios 186–95, forms part of a volume which belonged to the fifth earl, whose arms are illuminated on folio 162. Copies also survive in Alnwick Castle, MSS 521 (inexplicably ascribed to William Gamble) and 522, and in Bodleian Library, MS Dodsworth 50, folios 119–128v. The last, which suffers from a lacuna of nineteen stanzas, was published at Newcastle in 1847 in an edition by John Besley, vicar of Long Benton in Northumberland.

Peeris's chronicle is largely composed in seven-line rhyme royal stanzas, occasionally expanded to nine or eleven lines. In this it probably shows the influence of the fifteenth-century Northumbrian chronicler John Hardyng (a copy of whose chronicle was in the possession of the fifth earl, now Bodl. Oxf., MS Selden B. 10). Except in its earliest version, which postulates exploits 'in the lande of Perse' as the source of the family's name, Peeris's chronicle traces the fortunes of the Percys from the early tenth century down to the murder of the fourth earl in 1489. Peeris refers to a variety of written sources—deeds, charters, and tombstone inscriptions—as well as chronicles, but his purpose is not so much strictly historical as to celebrate the greatness of the Percy family and urge the fifth earl to maintain it. He takes a particular interest in religious foundations and donations, but is also careful to note royal and aristocratic associations. The sententious conclusion to the first version of the chronicle, urging the earl to 'liberalite' as the mean between 'prodegalite' and 'covetise', and advising him to 'Remember your progeny your excellent riall kyn', may have been excised from later copies as indiscreet, after debt and family discord brought disaster upon the Percys in the 1530s.

HENRY SUMMERSON

Sources Alnwick Castle, MSS 79, 521, 522 · BL, Royal MS 18 D.ii · Bodl. Oxf., MS Dodsworth 50 · *Reprints of rare tracts & imprints of antient manuscripts, etc.*, 1, *Biographical* (1847) · M. James, 'A Tudor magnate and the Tudor state: Henry, fifth earl of Northumberland', *Society, politics, and culture: studies in early modern England* (1986), 48–90 · P. T. P. Goldberg, 'Performing the word of God: Corpus Christi drama in the northern province', *Life and thought in the northern church, c1100 – c1700*, ed. D. Wood, SCH, Subsidia, 12 (1999), 145–70

Peers, Sir Charles Reed (1868–1952), architect and archaeologist, was born on 22 September 1868 at Westerham, Kent, the eldest son of the Revd William Henry Peers (1839–1921), then curate at Westerham and later vicar of Harrow Weald, Middlesex, and lord of the manor of Chiselhampton, Oxfordshire, and his wife, Dora Patience, daughter of William Carr of Dene Park, Tonbridge, Kent. Peers was educated at Charterhouse School and in 1887

Sir Charles Reed Peers (1868–1952), by Bassano

went to King's College, Cambridge, where he gained second classes in both parts of the classical tripos (1890, 1891), after which he studied briefly at Dresden and Berlin. In 1893 he became a pupil in the office of Thomas Graham Jackson, who encouraged his interest in medieval architecture. After three years with Jackson Peers spent a season in Egypt, working with George Somers Clarke at al-Qab and elsewhere before practising as an architect on his own account for six years, including a return visit to Egypt in 1902.

In 1903 Peers was appointed architectural editor to the recently founded Victoria History of the Counties of England and helped to develop its approach to the recording of historic buildings. Responsible for supervising a team of architects working on the topographical volumes, Peers produced phased period plans and concise descriptions of the buildings surveyed for the Victoria History of the Counties of England. These set the standard for the methodology adopted by the Royal Commission on Historical Monuments after its creation in 1908. For the Victoria History of the Counties of England Peers himself wrote the descriptions and drew the plans of a number of major buildings, including Winchester Cathedral and St Albans Abbey.

From 1900 to 1903 Peers was editor of the *Archaeological Journal* and in 1901 he was elected a fellow of the Society of Antiquaries. In 1908 he became its secretary, a position he held until becoming director in 1921. These honorary posts undoubtedly strengthened his candidacy for the post of inspector of ancient monuments in HM office (later Ministry) of Works, to which he was appointed in 1910, being promoted to the post of chief inspector following the Ancient Monuments Act of 1913. This act, in the preparation of which Peers played a leading role, consolidated those of 1882 and 1900 and was prompted in part by the threatened dismantling and export of Tattershall Castle, Lincolnshire, to the United States in 1911. Although still excluding from protection churches in use and private houses, the act reflected increasing public concern over the proper preservation of ancient monuments and was the first to introduce an element of legal compulsion, making it necessary for owners of a scheduled monument to apply for permission from the state before altering or demolishing their property. It also empowered the government to assume guardianship of nationally important monuments and to maintain them at public expense.

It was in this official capacity that Peers was able to develop his own approach to the physical preservation of ruined medieval buildings. Rejecting equally the highly speculative and extensive restorations associated with Viollet-le-Duc in France and the conservative repairs advocated by the Society for the Protection of Ancient Buildings (founded in 1877), he transformed 'the mouldering ivy-clad ruin(s) of the Romantic tradition' (Ralegh Radford, 365) into well-managed and informative, if often somewhat clinically presented, archaeological sites. While careful not to add new masonry unless necessary to support historic fabric, the scale of work undertaken was frequently vast, exemplified by the extensive 'clearance' during the 1920s of post-medieval building phases at monastic sites like Byland and Rievaulx in Yorkshire. Here fallen masonry was removed by labourers (many of them First World War veterans) along temporary light railway lines expressly constructed for the purpose. If many buildings were as a result robbed of their picturesque quality and much of their post-medieval construction history, the ministry's involvement ensured that still more was protected from further decay or deliberate vandalism. Indeed, the principles of repair and consolidation adopted by Peers and his colleagues remained largely unchallenged on guardianship sites until the late 1970s.

The stern puritanism with which Peers laid bare the ground plans and masonry footings of the abbeys and castles set in the manicured lawns, which became the hallmark of ministry sites, is matched in the many official guidebooks he wrote, their spare and economical texts recording the essential events in a site's history and concisely describing its architectural remains. These, along with his many excavation reports and earlier accounts of buildings for the Victoria History of the Counties of England, represent Peers's main written output, as he never wrote a major book.

Peers's retirement from the ministry in 1933 was preceded by the Ancient Monuments Act of 1931, which in the wake of quarrying immediately around Hadrian's Wall established the concept of protecting the setting of ancient monuments as well as their physical fabric. During his retirement, when according to his own assessment he was busier and better off than he had ever been as a civil servant, Peers was in much demand as a consultant architect, becoming surveyor to Westminster Abbey in 1935. He held similar posts at York and Durham, where as architect-in-charge he was responsible too for pinning the castle to the rock from which it was slipping. Seneschal of Canterbury Cathedral, he also advised the dean and chapter at Winchester, sat on the Oxford diocesan committee, and carried out work for New College.

Numerous honours were bestowed on Peers, both before and after his retirement: he was made CBE in 1924 and was knighted in 1931 during his presidency of the Society of Antiquaries, a position he held between 1929 and 1934, being awarded its gold medal in 1938. The holder of honorary doctorates from Leeds and London universities (1933 and 1936 respectively), he was a governor of Charterhouse and an honorary fellow of King's College, Cambridge. In 1930 he was made a trustee of the London Museum and from 1933 a trustee of the British Museum. Antiquary to the Royal Academy from 1933 to 1952, he was also a fellow of the British Academy from 1926 and of the Royal Institute of British Architects, receiving its gold medal in 1933. In 1932 he was elected president of the first session of the Congress of Prehistoric and Protohistoric Sciences and during its second session at Oslo in 1936 was made a knight commander of St Olaf. Of the many committees on which he sat he was a particularly active member of the Royal Commission on Historical Monuments, for which he was a commissioner from 1921.

On 13 April 1899 Peers married Gertrude Katherine (d. 1953), daughter of the late Francis Shepherd, vicar of Stoke-sub-Hamdon, Somerset, with whom he had three sons. Gertrude was an art historian and actively interested in his work. Inheriting the eighteenth-century Chiselhampton House in Oxfordshire from his father, Peers and Gertrude moved there in 1924 where in his spare time he tended the gardens and entertained his friends. Among these was George Hill, whom Peers had first met when they both applied for the same position at the British Museum in 1893; later Hill was to be director of the museum at the same time as Peers was one of its trustees. Peers got on well with many younger than himself and Mortimer Wheeler was among those he encouraged at an early stage of their careers.

A man of quick-witted charm, wide interests, and tremendous energy, Peers never suffered fools gladly but was usually prepared to listen to constructive criticism. Dogged by illness for the last seven years of his life, he maintained his antiquarian interests to the end, James Mann recalling that when he last visited him in the nursing home at Coulsdon, Surrey, he was reading the latest volume of the *Antiquaries Journal*. Peers died at Woodcote Grove House, Coulsdon, Surrey, on 16 November 1952 and at a funeral service conducted by the dean of Westminster on 21 November his ashes were placed in the abbey's Islip chapel.

Evaluations of Peers's contribution to the excavation

and public presentation of medieval military and monastic sites, the area of work for which he is best remembered, have altered significantly in the past half-century. At the time of his death it appears that for his own contemporaries and the two succeeding generations of archaeologists, many of whom he had directly influenced, the standards he established as chief inspector of ancient monuments were beyond dispute. To them the perceived benefits of the wholesale clearance of vegetation and post-medieval deposits and accretions from medieval fabric were irrefutable: as James Mann commented in one obituary notice, Peers 'founded a school of conservation which was a model to the world and one earnestly hopes will long survive him' (Mann, 149). Similarly, in another obituary, while acknowledging that Peers's approach and methods had aroused some controversy when first introduced, Ralegh Radford felt that this was 'now a matter of historical rather than practical interest' (Ralegh Radford, 365).

Today's archaeologists are, however, generally less sympathetic, several strongly criticizing the way in which the extensive clearance of monastic sites in particular destroyed much evidence for their post-medieval use. Others have lamented the way in which the sites in Peers's care, characterized by their ruthlessly mown lawns and herbaceous borders, were stripped of their former romanticism and recently there has been a conscious effort to reconcile the sometimes conflicting interests of nature and building conservation in the public presentation of state-owned archaeological sites and monuments. Academically, too, Peers has been attacked, appearing in one recent work merely as one of a long list of 'male historians of male monasticism [who] claimed that sources for religious women were simply not available or adequate' (R. Gilchrist, *Gender & Material Culture: the Archaeology of Religious Women*, 1994, 23). Others, though, such as Glyn Coppack, have been less severe and while regretting the damage caused by Peers's 'clearance' policy on many sites, have acknowledged the pivotal role played by him in the preservation of monastic and other ruins and in their display and interpretation to a wide public.

NICHOLAS DOGGETT

Sources C. A. Ralegh Radford, *PBA*, 39 (1953), 363–8 · J. G. Mann, *Antiquaries Journal*, 33 (1953), 149–50 · *The Times* (20 Nov 1952) · *The Times* (24 Nov 1952) · *DNB* · J. Evans, *A history of the Society of Antiquaries* (1956) · G. Coppack, *Abbeys and priories* (1990) · P. Fergusson and S. Harrison, *Rievaulx Abbey* (1999) · J. P. Greene, *Medieval monasteries* (1992), 37–40 · M. W. Thompson, *Ruins: their preservation and display* (1981) · *CGPLA Eng. & Wales* (1953)
Archives Oxon. RO, corresp. and papers | Bodl. Oxf., corresp. with J. L. Myres · Man. CL, Manchester Archives and Local Studies, letters to R. D. Radcliffe
Likenesses J. Russell & Sons, photograph, 1931, repro. in Ralegh Radford, *PBA* · F. Dodd, portrait, 1934, repro. in Evans, *History of the Society of Antiquaries* · F. Dodd, pencil drawing, c.1939, S. Antiquaries, Lond. · Bassano, photograph, NPG [*see illus.*]
Wealth at death £14,153 1s. 4d.: probate, 21 Jan 1953, *CGPLA Eng. & Wales*

Peers, Edgar Allison (1891–1952), Hispanic scholar and educationist, was born at Leighton Buzzard on 7 May 1891, the only son and elder child of John Thomas Peers (1860–

1944), civil servant, and his wife, Jessie Dale (1865–1951), daughter of Charles Allison. In the years 1892 to 1903 his father made frequent moves, and Edgar Allison attended several elementary schools, at the last of which he was drawn to the study of Spanish. At fourteen he went to Dartford grammar school, and after study abroad proceeded to Christ's College, Cambridge, of which he was a scholar and prizeman, his first interests being English and French literature. In 1910 he obtained an external BA degree at London, with second-class honours in English and French, and in 1912 at Cambridge a first class in the medieval and modern languages tripos. He shared the Winchester reading prize (1912), and won the Harness (1913) and the Members' English essay (1914) prizes. He obtained a first class with double distinction in the teacher's diploma at Cambridge in 1913. From 1913 to 1919 he taught successively at Mill Hill, Felsted, Essex (for five years), and Wellington as modern languages master. His first publications still concerned English and French literature (*Elizabethan Drama and its Mad Folk*, 1914, and *The Origins of French Romanticism*, with M. B. Finch, 1920), but his attraction to Spain deepened, and in 1920 he was appointed (despite internal opposition) to the Gilmour chair of Spanish at Liverpool, where he remained thereafter. On 19 March 1924 he married Marion (b. 1895/6), daughter of James Frederic Young, secretary to the Devon education committee. They had no children.

Peers was among the first to realize the importance and the potentialities of Spanish studies in Great Britain after the First World War. Through lectures, visits to schools, teachers' conferences, vacation courses in England and in Spain, and the editing of a steady stream of textbooks, anthologies, and study aids (notably *Spain, a Companion to Spanish Studies*, 1929; *A Handbook to the Study and Teaching of Spanish*, 1938; *A Critical Anthology of Spanish Verse*, 1948) he laboured indefatigably and with great effect to further them at both school and university level.

Peers was always keenly interested in the methods and aims not merely of modern language teaching but of higher studies in general, and he wrote under the pseudonym of Bruce Truscot three books: *Redbrick University* (1943), *Redbrick and these Vital Days* (1945), and *First Year at the University* (1946). Until his death their authorship was a well-kept secret. They popularized the terms 'Redbrick' and 'Oxbridge', urged the primacy of research, and made a major contribution to the discussion of university problems and policies at the close of the Second World War.

Peers's talent for organizing was expressed in many ways. He founded the Modern Humanities Research Association in 1918, and was its honorary secretary for eleven years and its president in 1931–2; founded in 1923 and edited until his death the quarterly *Bulletin of Spanish Studies* (from 1949 *Bulletin of Hispanic Studies*); founded in 1934 at Liverpool the Institute of Hispanic Studies; and was educational director from 1943 to 1946 of the Hispanic Council.

These manifold activities were matched by a record in scholarship impressive both in its scope and in its originality. Two fields in Spanish letters, nineteenth-century

Romanticism and the sixteenth-century mystics, Peers made particularly his own while they were still comparatively little known and studied, even in Spain. Especially ground-breaking was his *History of the Romantic Movement in Spain* (2 vols., 1940) and his *Studies of the Spanish Mystics* (2 vols., 1927–30). The latter, along with the masterly translations of the complete works of St John of the Cross (3 vols., 1934–5) and of St Teresa of Avila (3 vols., 1946, and her *Letters*, 2 vols., 1951), caused Spanish mysticism to be known and appreciated by English readers as never before. His achievement here, which received the imprimatur of the Roman Catholic church, was the more remarkable in one who was neither a Roman Catholic by persuasion nor a theologian by training. A number of his critical works on Romanticism and the mystics were republished in Spanish translation in Spain. Peers's other great enthusiasm was Catalonia and its medieval splendours: of Ramon Lull he translated much, including *Blanquerna* (1926), and wrote a full-scale biography (1929), while in *Catalonia infelix* (1937) he traced a sympathetic picture of the Catalan people and their history.

Peers's interest in Spain was always warm and personal. There over many years he spent some four months out of every twelve, and he produced a number of travel volumes, chief among them *Spain, a Companion to Spanish Travel* (1930) and *The Pyrenees, French and Spanish* (1932). A close student no less of contemporary events, he analysed these for nearly a quarter of a century in 'Spain week by week', a regular feature of the *Bulletin of Spanish Studies*. The outbreak of the Spanish Civil War in July 1936 thus found him admirably equipped to interpret to the English-speaking world its underlying causes. This he did in *The Spanish Tragedy* which, written with striking prescience, appeared within three months of the outbreak of the conflict, and was many times reprinted. *The Spanish Dilemma* (1940) and *Spain in Eclipse* (1943) provided a similarly penetrating guide to the war's aftermath. Himself an Anglican of deep religious conviction, he wrote in *Spain, the Church and the Orders* (1939) a warm defence of the record of the Roman Catholic church in Spain.

Peers received the honorary degree of LLD from Glasgow University in 1947. Foreign distinctions included visiting professorships of English literature at Madrid University (1928 and 1929), of modern comparative literature at Columbia University (1929–30), and of Spanish at the universities of New Mexico and California (1930). He was Rede lecturer at Cambridge (1932), Centennial lecturer at New York University (1932), and Taylorian lecturer at Oxford (1939), and was a member and medallist of the Hispanic Society of America, and honorary member of the American Academy of Arts and Sciences, and of the Institute d'Estudis Catalans.

Peers lived single-mindedly for his subject, and in part accomplished so much through meticulous planning and use of his time, down to the shortest train journey. Apart from a keen delight in music (in his early years he played the organ) he confessed to no recreations; he could seem brusque, though he was affable and a good mimic when with intimate friends. Peers died of congestive heart failure on 21 December 1952, at the Northern Hospital, Liverpool.   W. C. ATKINSON, *rev.* JOHN D. HAIGH

Sources *Bulletin of Hispanic Studies*, 30/117 (Jan–March 1953) [incl. sel. bibliography] · personal knowledge (1971) · private information (1971) · A. L. Mackenzie and C. Byrne, eds., *E. Allison Peers: Redbrick University revisited: the autobiography of 'Bruce Truscot'* (1996) · *WWW*, 1951–60 · *The Times* (24 Dec 1952) · m. cert. · d. cert. · *CGPLA Eng. & Wales* (1953)
Archives Modern Humanities Research Association, London, archives · U. Leeds, Brotherton L., corresp. and papers · U. Lpool L., papers, mainly relating to Spanish mystics
Likenesses photograph, repro. in Mackenzie and Byrne, eds., *E. Allison Peers*
Wealth at death £42,053 6s. 2d.: probate, 20 April 1953, *CGPLA Eng. & Wales*

Peers, Richard [Dic] (1645–1690), translator and author, was born in Lisburn, co. Antrim, the son of Richard Peers, a tanner. Young Richard became his father's apprentice, but 'being weary of that employment, gave his father the slip … obtaining a prosperous gale' to Bristol (Wood, *Ath. Oxon.*, 4.290), whence his uncle sent him to a school in Carmarthenshire. He then (possibly helped by the local schoolmaster, Jeremy Taylor) obtained a scholarship at Westminster School, which was, under Richard Busby, a centre of classical learning and versification. Peers proceeded to Christ Church, Oxford (matriculated 22 July 1664), and was elected a student in 1665, at the age of twenty ('over ripe for the university' according to Wood); he graduated BA in 1668 and MA in 1671. His limited income was supplemented by working for fellow undergraduates, 'for 'twas usual with him to make the exercises of idle scholars, either for money or something worth it from the buttery book' (ibid.); the practice was not uncommon, the exercises in question probably being Latin verse 'themes'. If his college superiors knew of this activity, they are unlikely to have had strong objections. Peers published Latin verses under his own name, including a page of elegiacs for the *Epicedia* (1670) lamenting the death of George Monck, duke of Albemarle.

Peers also wrote English poems as a student, published as *Four Small Copies of Verses on Sundry Occasions* (1667) and reissued, probably in the same year, as *Poems by R. P. Student of Ch[rist] Ch[urch] Oxon*. They probably failed to fulfil Peers's hopes for fame; his colleague Humphrey Prideaux later described them as 'musty ballads' producing 'little credit' (*Letters of Humphrey Prideaux*, 24). Peers addresses his academic patrons, Busby and John Fell, and offers an epitaph on a gentleman loyal to the king, who:

> Ne're followed a blind faith's fantastick guess,
> Ne're courted Faction in a *Modish* dress.
> (Peers, 8)

The most interesting poem in the collection is the fourth (pp. 11–20), 'To the Memory of Abraham Cowley', thirty-one stanzas in the form later used for Gray's *Elegy*, of which it is a not unworthy predecessor. Cowley's '*Pindarick* Muse so bravely soar'd'; even former opponents:

> Confess him now of Modern *Wits* the best,
> And next Immortal *Spencer* to be nam'd.

Cowley's situation is described with an impressive neatness of touch:

> He from the Noise and Injuries of Court,
> Does only so to silent Groves repair,
> As half-tir'd Passengers to *Shades* resort
> From the offensive fury of the Air.
> (stanza 27)

Peers was trusted by Dr Fell with a large share (together with Richard Reeves of Magdalen) in an important piece of work, the translation into Latin of Anthony Wood's *History and Antiquities* (begun 1670). He was to discover a disadvantage of translating living authors: they can hit back. According to Wood (whose account, written after Peers's death, may retain some personal bias) his initial work was poor, but gradually improved 'by great diligence and observation', so that he became 'a compleat master of the Latin tongue, and what he did was excellent' (Wood, *Ath. Oxon.*). The Latin edition appeared in 1674. Wood greatly resented changes that Fell and Peers had made to his text. Few translators can have endured worse relationships with their authors. Peers and Wood had fist fights in the printing house at the Sheldonian theatre, in a local cookshop, and elsewhere. Peers always lost, 'with a bloody nose or a black eye', and became afraid to meet Wood 'for fear of another drubbing'; when Peers became pro-proctor, they were both terrified to meet each other, according to Prideaux (*Letters of Humphrey Prideaux*, 8–12; Madan, 299). Peers did exercise his proctorial powers on others, and was reprimanded by the vice-chancellor for 'over hasty, and in his opinion imprudent' arrests (*Letters of Humphrey Prideaux*, 38).

In 1674 Peers proposed to publish 'some seaman's journall of the Streights of Magellan', which Prideaux thought 'a very ridiculous designe', beneath a scholar's dignity; that apart, 'Dic doeth nothing but drinke ale' (*Letters of Humphrey Prideaux*, 24–8). In 1675 Peers was cheated out of the living of Shrivenham, Berkshire, by Benjamin Woodruffe, who had promised to plead Peers's case while in London, and 'effectually doe his businesse for him; as accordingly he did in another sense, the next news we heard beeing that Woodruffe had it for himselfe' (ibid., 42–3). On 18 September 1675 Peers finally obtained preferment as a reward for his translation, being elected esquire bedell of arts; Wood rather churlishly claims that he would have prevented the appointment, if he had been present. Peers had previously been chosen as grammar lecturer for two years, a post his supporters exerted themselves to retain for him: their effort was wasted, when he 'indiscreetly, or rather knavishly' resigned it to a rival behind their backs, 'which hath soe much incensed the Dean that it is supposed he would turn him out at Xmas … none of us have ever since spake to him unlesse it be to obbraid him with his knavery' (ibid., 44–5). Peers created a precedent, a shocking academic sin. The bedell's post, however, proved profitable; he made 'above £200' in his first year, and eventually left his college studentship at the end of 1676 (ibid., 55).

Peers continued to be involved in various publication projects: in 1682 he compiled a large volume on the Netherlands for Moses Pitt's *English Atlas*, and in 1684 he contributed to a translation of Nepos. Peers married 'an Oxford lady' (since marriage would ordinarily have entailed the loss of his studentship, it must have depended upon his appointment as bedell): they had a son, Richard [*see below*]. Wood accuses Peers of neglecting his studies to marry and keep 'low, drunken company'; 'he enjoyed the comforts of the world', allegedly to excess, being too fat by 1687 to perform some of his ceremonial duties. Peers had been promoted to esquire bedell of physic, and on 6 July 1688 was licensed to practise medicine. According to Wood:

> in the latter end of the reign of king James II he applied his mind to the study of physic, having been secretly informed that his beneficial place was to be bestowed on a person more agreeable with the times; but fearing his bulk and fatness, which he had obtained by eating, drinking, and sleeping, would hinder his practice, he quitted that project … and was resolved, when turned out, to withdraw into the country, and teach a private school. (Wood, *Ath. Oxon.*, 4.290)

From that fate he was saved by the revolution of 1688. Towards the end of his life he compiled the first list of Oxford graduates, covering the years 1659–88 (published 1689; see *Hist. U. Oxf.* 4: *17th-cent. Oxf.*, 508n.). Peers died at Holywell, Oxford, on 11 August 1690, and was buried in St Aldate's Church.

Richard Peers (1685–1739), clergyman and author, was born in All Saints' parish, Oxford, on 15 July 1685, the son of Richard Peers and his wife. He attended Trinity College, Oxford (matriculated, 1701; scholar, 1702; BA, 1705; MA, 1708), and was vicar of Hartley-Wintney, Hampshire (1710–11), and of Faringdon, Berkshire (1711–39). The younger Peers wrote several popular religious works. His *Character of an Honest Dissenter* was the cause of some controversy, with replies from opponents in 1716, 1717, and 1718. *A Companion for the Aged* was reprinted many times, well into the nineteenth century. He died at Faringdon on 20 July 1739.   D. K. MONEY

Sources R. Peers, *Poems by R. P. student of Ch[rist] Ch[urch] Oxon.* (1667?) · *DNB* · Wood, *Ath. Oxon.*, new edn, vol. 4 · *Letters of Humphrey Prideaux … to John Ellis*, ed. E. M. Thompson, CS, new ser., 15 (1875) · D. K. Money, *The English Horace* (1998) · E. G. W. Bill, *Education at Christ Church, Oxford, 1660–1800* (1988) · *Epicedia*, Oxford University (1670) · *Hist. U. Oxf.* 4: *17th-cent. Oxf.* · F. Madan, *Oxford literature, 1651–1680* (1931), vol. 3 of *Oxford books: a bibliography of printed works* (1895–1931); repr. (1964), nos. 2780, 2781, 2996, 3021 · *Remarks and collections of Thomas Hearne*, ed. C. E. Doble and others, 2, OHS, 7 (1886)

Archives University College, Oxford, letters to A. Wood

Peers, Richard (1685–1739). *See under* Peers, Richard (1645–1690).

Peerson, Andrew (d. 1594), Church of England clergyman, graduated BA from Corpus Christi College, Cambridge, in 1542, subsequently proceeding MA in 1544 and BD in 1551. Soon after graduating BA he was elected a fellow of his college; for a time he was bursar, and laid out and planted with fruit trees the fellows' garden. In 1550–51 he served as proctor, and was also auditor of the Trinity chest. He vacated his fellowship about 1552 and seems to have accepted some cure in Cambridge, from which he was ejected on 3 October 1553, early in the reign of Mary Tudor, for continuing to administer the communion in the form used under Edward VI. Not known to have gone abroad, he was probably one of many protestants, like Matthew Parker, who lived in retirement during the later 1550s.

Following Elizabeth's accession, Archbishop Parker named Peerson his chaplain, almoner, and master of faculties, chose him to preach a sermon at the consecration on 21 January 1560 of four bishops, bestowed upon him the livings of Brasted, Wrotham, Chiddingstone in Kent, and, on the death of John Bale in 1563, secured his election to the eleventh prebendal stall in Canterbury Cathedral. Parker took a good deal of trouble to obtain this last preferment for his chaplain, and wrote to thank the queen once it had been achieved. He also recommended him for the provostship of Eton in 1561, but without success. In the convocation of 1563 Peerson sat as proctor for the clergy of the diocese of Llandaff, subscribed the articles then agreed upon, and voted against the six articles for abolishing certain rites and ceremonies. Peerson took part in preparing for press the Bishops' Bible of 1568, which Parker commissioned in the vain hope that it would supplant the popular Calvinist Geneva Bible published in 1560. Peerson was asked to revise the translation of Leviticus, Numbers, Job, and Proverbs. Tanner doubtfully attributes to him Ezra, Nehemiah, Esther, Job, and Proverbs.

In 1569 Peerson was one of two commissioners chosen to visit the diocese of Canterbury, and on 4 January 1571 had a licence for non-residence. In September 1573 he entertained Burghley at his 'fine house', as Parker called it, at Canterbury; in 1575 the archbishop named Peerson one of his executors and bequeathed him a gilt cup, the gift of Elizabeth. On 30 June 1580 he was presented to the living of Hardres, Kent, but resigned it in 1582. Peerson married twice. Nothing is known of his first wife, but on 16 April 1582 he married Sarah Sampson, widow, at Sheldwich, Kent. On 1 September 1589 he received the living of Harbledown, Kent. He died early in November 1594. In his will he mentions a son, Andrew Peerson, and daughter-in-law, Joan, and their children.

A. F. POLLARD, rev. STANFORD LEHMBERG

Sources W. P. Haugaard, *Elizabeth and the English Reformation: the struggle for a stable settlement of religion* (1968) • Cooper, *Ath. Cantab.*, 2.173 • R. Masters, *The history of the College of Corpus Christi and the B. Virgin Mary … in the University of Cambridge* (1753) • V. J. K. Brook, *A life of Archbishop Parker* (1962) • Tanner, *Bibl. Brit.-Hib.* • *Correspondence of Matthew Parker*, ed. J. Bruce and T. T. Perowne, Parker Society, 42 (1853) • E. Hasted, *The history and topographical survey of the county of Kent*, 2nd edn, 1 (1797); 3 (1797); 4 (1798) • R. Willis, *The architectural history of the University of Cambridge, and of the colleges of Cambridge and Eton*, ed. J. W. Clark, 1 (1886), 252, 261

Peerson, Martin (1571–1650/51), composer, was born at March, Cambridgeshire, the son of Thomas and Margaret Peerson. His father probably died shortly afterwards, since his mother remarried in 1573. Peerson came under the influence of the poet Fulke Greville at an early stage in his career, composing a setting of 'See, O see, who is heere

come a maying' which was performed at the Highgate home of Sir William Cornwallis as part of Ben Jonson's 'Private Entertainment of the King and Queene' on May day 1604. Evidently Peerson had Catholic sympathies, for in 1606 he was cited for recusancy. In 1609 he was living at Stoke Newington. In 1613 he graduated BMus at Lincoln College, Oxford. Possibly between 1623 and 1630 Peerson was sacrist at Westminster Abbey. Certainly at some point between June 1624 and June 1625 he became almoner and master of the choristers at St Paul's Cathedral; he lived in a dwelling nearby that was subsequently condemned to demolition before the repairing of the cathedral. Alternative accommodation large enough for Peerson and the choristers under his supervision was eventually found within the petty canons' college (perhaps he was made a petty canon before this removal).

Peerson's principal publications were *Private Musicke* (1620) and *Mottects, or, Grave Chamber Musique* (1630). The former, comprising secular vocal ayres (solos and duets) with viol accompaniment, is notable for its stylistic novelty, combining features of the madrigal, consort song, and anthem. The latter claims historical importance as the first known published musical collection in England to include a notated figured bass part, and is notable too for its largely melancholic idiom, in which the musical techniques (suggesting an awareness of declamatory possibilities imported from Italy) are devoted purely to the affective representation of rather sombre texts. Peerson also contributed three 'full' anthems to Sir William Leighton's *The Teares or Lamentations of a Sorrowfull Soule* (1613) and a psalm tune to Thomas Ravenscroft's *The Whole Booke of Psalmes* (1621). A significant number of English anthems (mainly 'verse' anthems, alternating soloists and full choir) survive in manuscript, principally in the British Library and the Bodleian Library, Oxford. They incorporate contemporary madrigalisms, including quite precisely crafted word-painting and affective use of chromatically inflected melody and harmony. Eleven Latin motets are preserved in a single manuscript (in the Bodleian Library), all lacking a treble part. Possibly Peerson's most famous compositions are the brief programmatic pieces for keyboard 'The Fall of the Leafe' and 'The Primerose' in the famous Fitzwilliam virginal book, compiled by Francis Tregian during the first two decades or so of the seventeenth century and containing music largely by Catholic composers (Peerson's keyboard music is found only in this source). There is also a small quantity of surviving music for consorts of viols, copied in manuscripts whose regional and chronological spread suggest that Peerson's work in this field enjoyed quite a wide currency during his lifetime and continued to be played after his death. These works are most impressive in their command of technical resource, featuring most prominently contrapuntal interplay between the different strands of the texture, regulated by canonic imitation.

Peerson, who was twice married, was buried in St Faith's under St Paul's on 15 January 1651. Among his legacies he left £100 to the poor of March for the purchase of freehold land of the yearly value of £4 or £5, the proceeds to be distributed every Sunday in twopenny loaves to eight, nine, ten, eleven, or twelve poor persons. He held property in the parishes of St Giles-in-the-Fields and Walthamstow, Essex.   JOHN IRVING

Sources A. Jones, 'The life and works of Martin Peerson', PhD diss., U. Cam., 1957 · M. Wailes, 'Martin Peerson', *Proceedings of the Royal Musical Association*, 80 (1953–4), 59–71 · *IGI* · *DNB*
Wealth at death at least £100, plus two properties: will, PRO, PROB 11/215, sig. 9, cited *DNB*

Peet, (Thomas) Eric (1882–1934), Egyptologist, was born in Liverpool on 12 August 1882, the eldest son of at least three children of Thomas Peet, corn merchant, of that city, and his wife, Salome Fowler. He was educated at Merchant Taylors' School, Liverpool, from 1893 and in 1901 obtained a Jodrell mathematics scholarship at the Queen's College, Oxford, where he was awarded a second class in classical and in mathematical moderations (both 1903) and in *literae humaniores* (1905). He then spent a term as a schoolteacher in Walsall. During his last year at Oxford David Randall-MacIver interested him in the then unexploited Italian prehistoric period; on a small grant from the Craven fund he made a brief reconnaissance in Italy, and in 1906 easily gained a Craven fellowship. During the next three years he explored early Italian and Maltese sites and wrote *The Stone and Bronze Ages in Italy and Sicily* (1909), which became the standard work on the subject. He was Pelham student at the British School of Archaeology in Rome in 1909. But, Italian archaeology offering no permanent livelihood, Peet turned to Egypt. In 1909 he excavated at Abydos, first under John Garstang for the Liverpool Institute of Archaeology, and afterwards for the Egypt Exploration Fund (later Society) from 1909 to 1913 under Edouard Naville and then independently; the results of his work for the fund are contained in *The Cemeteries of Abydos*, parts 1–3 (1913–14). He married in autumn 1910 Mary Florence, daughter of Richard Johnson Lawton, civil engineer, of Chiswick; they had a daughter, Patricia Mary.

From 1913 to 1928 Peet was lecturer in Egyptology at Manchester University. His next book was *The Inscriptions of Sinai*, part 1 (edited in collaboration with Alan Henderson Gardiner, 1917). In 1915 he obtained a commission in the Royal Army Service Corps, and showed great ability at Salonika, where he and one other man supervised the whole of the landing of supplies in 1916–17. By the summer of 1918 he was serving in France as a lieutenant in the 14th battalion of the King's Liverpool regiment.

Demobilized early in 1919, Peet was elected in the following year to the Brunner chair of Egyptology at Liverpool University, which Percy Edward Newberry had resigned in his favour. Early in 1921 he directed a season's excavations at Tell al-Amarna for the Egypt Exploration Society. In 1923 he became Laycock student of Egyptology at Worcester College, Oxford. At the outset of his Egyptological career Peet realized the importance of a good knowledge of the Egyptian language and writing, for which he had a remarkable gift, and these became his chief interest in later life; in several of his most important

works (for example, *The Mayer Papyri*, 1920; *The Rhind Mathematical Papyrus*, 1923; and *The Great Tomb-Robberies of the Twentieth Egyptian Dynasty*, 1930) he dealt with important texts in the often very difficult hieratic or cursive script, of which he had exceptional mastery. His *Egypt and the Old Testament* (1922) discussed with rare critical skill the biblical records of Egyptian contacts. In 1929 his Schweich lectures (published in 1931 as *A Comparative Study of the Literature of Egypt, Palestine and Mesopotamia*) broke fresh ground. Among his many activities he found time to edit the University of Liverpool's *Annals of Archaeology and Anthropology* from 1921 (from 1925 jointly), and the *Journal of Egyptian Archaeology* from 1923 until his death. He remained in the Brunner chair until 1933, when he was elected reader in Egyptology at Oxford and a fellow of Queen's. His tenure of these positions was short-lived, for shortly before the readership had been definitely converted into a chair he died unexpectedly on 22 February 1934 in the Acland Nursing Home, Oxford, after an operation to treat a throat condition. He was buried two days later in Wolvercote cemetery, Oxford. His wife survived him.

Peet's services to his science were many, and he was perhaps the best example that England has produced of an all-round Egyptologist, equally able in the field, the study, and the lecture theatre, in archaeology and philology, in the historic and prehistoric periods. Two areas in which he excelled were Egyptian history (he contributed largely to the *Cambridge Ancient History*) and mathematics. His other main interests were cricket (he captained for his school), tennis, swimming, walking, and music. In appearance he could be solemn or even glum until his interest was caught, but he nevertheless enjoyed the company of his friends; he was remembered for his modesty, kindness, and sense of responsibility.

BATTISCOMBE GUNN, *rev.* R. S. SIMPSON

Sources A. H. Gardiner, *Journal of Egyptian Archaeology*, 20 (1934), 66–70 · *The Times* (23 Feb 1934), 14, 19 · W. R. Dawson and E. P. Uphill, *Who was who in Egyptology*, 3rd edn, rev. M. L. Bierbrier (1995) · personal knowledge (1949) · private information (2004) [grandson] · H. W. Fairman, *Egyptian Religion*, 2 (1934), 155–60 [bibliography] · *Oxford Magazine* (1 March 1934), 531–3 · *CGPLA Eng. & Wales* (1934)
Archives U. Oxf., Griffith Institute, notebooks with copies and transcriptions, various indexes, drawings, notices, and MSS | Bodl. Oxf., corresp. with J. L. Myres · Egypt Exploration Society, London, corresp. with the Egypt Exploration Society
Likenesses Lafayette Ltd, photograph, repro. in Fairman, *Egyptian Religion*, 157 · caricature, Queen's College, Oxford
Wealth at death £2918 11s. 0d.: probate, 16 April 1934, *CGPLA Eng. & Wales*

Peeters, Gerard (*bap.* 1562?, *d.* 1598), author, was probably the child baptized on 20 September 1562 at Arundel, Sussex. His father may have been William Peeters of Arundel. Having been educated at Westminster School, where he was a queen's scholar, Peeters was elected in 1582, as an alumnus of that foundation, to a closed scholarship at Trinity College, Cambridge, from which he matriculated a member of Cambridge University on 13 October of that year. Despite the date of his election it was only in April

1583 that his formal admission as a scholar of Trinity College was recorded. He graduated BA in June 1586.

In October 1589 Peeters became a minor fellow of Trinity College, advancing to become a major fellow there in May 1590, in which year he proceeded MA. The senior bursar's accounts show him receiving his quarterly fellow's stipend from 1590 to 1593. His name does not feature in these accounts for either 1594 or 1595, suggesting that he had vacated his fellowship at the end of the fourth quarter in 1593. Peeters was incorporated MA at Oxford on 9 July 1594.

There is a long-standing tradition—at least as old as 1861—that Peeters was the author of two Latin works which challenged Alexander Dickson's ideas on artificial memory as being, in Eleanor Rosenberg's words, 'impious and vain' (Rosenberg, 38 n. 23). Prominently dedicated to Robert Dudley, earl of Leicester, Dickson's book was entitled *Alexandri Dicsoni arelii De umbrarationis & judicii, sive, De Memoriae virtute prosopopoeia* (1583). The works attributed to Peeters are: *Antidicsonus cuiusdam Cantabrigiensis G. P. accessit libellus, in quo dilucide explicatur impia Dicsoni artificiosa memoria* (1584) and *Libellus de memoria, verissimaque bene recordandi scientia* (1584). The *Antidicsonus* was answered by Heius Scepsius (a pseudonym for Dickson) in *Heii Scepsii defensio pro Alexandro Dicsono arelio adversus quendam G. P. Cantabrigien* (1584), which, like Dickson's earlier tract, was dedicated to Leicester. More definitely Peeters can be said to have contributed a Greek verse to the tribute to Sir Philip Sidney by Cambridge University: *Academiae Cantabrigiensis lachrymae tumulo nobilissimi equitis, D. Philippi Sidneii* (1587).

The date and location of Peeters's ordination (or ordinations) is obscure. His ecclesiastical preferments all seem to have lain within the diocese of Chichester, which was largely co-extensive with Sussex. In September 1591 he was instituted to the vicarage of Poling (near Arundel) on the presentation of William Day, provost of Eton College. The following February Peeters was presented by the crown to the Lewes rectory of St Peter in Westout and St Mary in Westout. Nevertheless it is not clear whether or not this presentation took effect, not least because, although the grant passed the signet office, a docket apparently remains among the state papers (domestic) and no notice of his institution has been found. What is known is that, described as vicar of Poling and rector of St John's sub Castro in Lewes, he was dispensed in January 1593 to hold two livings in plurality on the grounds that he was chaplain to Thomas Sackville, first Baron Buckhurst. In fact Peeters's institution to the latter benefice took place, following Buckhurst's presentation, in February 1593. In November the chaplain was further instituted to the rectory of Plumpton on the presentation of one Richard Leeche. By now Peeters had exceeded the terms of his dispensation, which probably explains why he resigned Poling vicarage by 22 April 1594. Even so he was both collated and installed in April 1596 to the prebend of Hampstead in Chichester Cathedral. This preferment was not Peeters's first link with the cathedral, for the dean and chapter had in May 1593 appointed him their attorney in

the matter of a livery of seisin concerning the rectory of Bedingham. His career as a prebendary began inauspiciously: failing to appear in June 1596 for the election of Anthony Watson as bishop, Peeters was declared contumacious. In May 1597 he protested for residence following the next vacancy among the residentiary canons, but died before that vacancy occurred.

Peeters wrote his will on 12 September 1598, and was dead by 22 November, when his successor was instituted to the rectory of Plumpton. Describing himself as of Lewes, yet mentioning only his Plumpton benefice, he asked that his body be buried at the discretion of his sole executor, his wife. He made generous provision for his mother; his son, Henry; his daughter, Joan; and the child with which his wife, Elizabeth, was then pregnant. If Henry died before reaching twenty-four then £20 of his £80 cash bequest was to be delivered, within one year of his death, to the mayor and four senior burgesses of Arundel to be employed, but without diminution, for the benefit of four poor folk there. Peeters's kindred were to be given preferential treatment in this charity should need arise. Having made various other provisions he devised the residue of his estate, which included land in Lewes, to his widow. Peeters's wife, Elizabeth (*b*. in or after 1567, *d*. in or after 1599), was one of the nine children of Dr Henry Blaxton or Blackstone (*d*. 1606) and his wife, Joan Nunn (*d*. 1607). Probate of Peeters's will was granted in the prerogative court of Canterbury in May 1599, when Elizabeth Peeters was still alive; her date of death is uncertain. It is not known where Peeters was buried, though it was not at Plumpton.

DAVID J. CRANKSHAW

Sources W. Sussex RO, MS PAR 8/1/1/1, p. 1 · will, PRO, PROB 11/93, sig. 36 · W. H. Challen, 'Henry Blaxton DD', *Sussex Notes and Queries*, 14 (1957), 221–5 · LPL, MS FI/B, fol. 166r · admissions and admonitions book, 1560–1759, Trinity Cam., pp. 12, 26, 235 · senior bursar's accounts, 1585–97, Trinity Cam., fols. 8v–9r, 37v–38r, 70v–71r, 106r, 123v–124r, 147v–148r, 173v–174r, 176r, 199v–200r, 209v, 223v–224r, 230v, 251v–253r, 260r–260v, 274v–276r, 283r–283v · H. M. Innes, *Fellows of Trinity College, Cambridge* (1941), 27–8 · CUL, department of manuscripts and university archives, MS Matr. 1, p. 328 · J. Venn, ed., *Grace book Δ* (1910), 406, 408 · Cooper, *Ath. Cantab.*, 2.178–9 · *Reg. Oxf.*, 2/1.354 · BL, Lansdowne MS 445, fols. 5v, 97r · PRO, SO 3/1, fol. 336v; E 334/12, fols. 3r, 53v · *CSP dom.*, 1591–4, 191 · W. Sussex RO, MSS Ep. I/1/7, fols. 51r, 53r, 54v, 56v; Ep. I/1/8, fols. 9v, 10r · W. D. Peckham, ed., *The acts of the dean and chapter of the cathedral church of Chichester, 1545–1642*, Sussex RS, 58 (1959), 136, 142, 144, 146, 166, 169 · *Old Westminsters*, 1.94, 2.728; suppl. [1938], 111 · J. S. Cockburn, ed., *Calendar of assize records: Sussex indictments Elizabeth I* (1975), 354 · E. Rosenberg, *Leicester: patron of letters* (New York, 1955), 38 n. 23

Archives Trinity Cam., Archives · W. Sussex RO, diocesan muniments

Peeters, John (1666/7?–1727?), painter, worked in England for about forty-two years, but almost all that is known of him comes from the notes of his contemporary and friend the writer George Vertue. Vertue recorded that Peeters, a relation of the marine painter Bonaventura Peeters (1614–1652), came from Antwerp, having studied under 'Eckhart an history painter a man of good esteem' (Vertue, *Note books*, 3.33). No history painter of this name is now known. Peeters came to England in 1685 at the age of eighteen and was recommended to Sir Godfrey Kneller, under whom he studied and then assisted, painting draperies until 1712. Peeters also worked for other painters, 'but chiefly employed himself in drawings and the mending or repairing of damaged or old pictures., in which he was very skilful having great knowledge in the hands of several famous Italian but especially Flemish masters' (ibid.); this was presumably after leaving Kneller's studio. From his success he earned the nickname of Doctor Peeters.

Socially and professionally Peeters seems to have been well connected with the London art world, as a member of the artists' Rose and Crown club in London. Peeters seems to have had an especially close relationship with Vertue, a fellow member of the club, who credited him with teaching him drawing, as well as giving him advice and helping him 'raise up my character' at the outset of the latter's career; Vertue even referred to Peeters as 'my grandmother' (Vertue, *Note books*, 6.32).

Peeters reportedly suffered from gout in his later years, did not produce much work, and became poor as a result. A 'lusty man of a free open temper a lover of good company and his bottle', a satirist who was fond of punch, Peeters remained single throughout his life (Vertue, *Note books*, 3.33). Vertue recorded his death in September 1727, but there is no record to corroborate his claim that Peeters was buried in 'St Martin's Church Yard Westminster' the same month, or indeed that year (ibid.).

NICHOLAS GRINDLE

Sources Vertue, *Note books*, vols. 1, 3–4, 6 · parish register, St Martin-in-the-Fields, London, City Westm. AC, vol. 12 [burial, microfilm] · I. Bignamini, 'George Vertue, art historian, and art institutions in London, 1689–1768', *Walpole Society*, 54 (1988), 1–148

Pegg, David (1935–1958). *See under* Busby Babes (*act.* 1953–1958).

Pegge, Sir Christopher (1764/5–1822), physician, was born at Westminster, London, the only son and one of the two children of Samuel *Pegge the younger (1733–1800), barrister, antiquary, poet, and musical composer, and his first wife, Martha (1732–1767), daughter of Henry Bourne, an eminent Derbyshire physician. He entered Christ Church, Oxford, as a commoner in April 1782. As an undergraduate he simultaneously held the Fell and Boulter exhibitions worth £10 and £8 respectively. He graduated BA on 23 February 1786 and was elected a fellow of Oriel College, Oxford, in 1788. In the following year he graduated MA and BM.

In 1789 Pegge began to practise medicine in Oxford. Opinion about his professional capabilities and achievements has varied. For example, Cox notes that while he had the ability and personality to have excelled in a fashionable part of London, he ran a 'hopeless race' in Oxford because he was in competition with two of the most popular physicians the city had ever seen, doctors Martin Wall and Robert Bourne (Cox, 132–3). On the other hand, Munk asserted that Pegge was 'for many years the leading physician' in Oxford, sharing with Bourne 'the medical emoluments of the university and neighbourhood' (Munk, *Roll*, 450). Later historians dismissed him as 'a physician of

dubious distinction' (Bill, 137), or maintained that his science was 'superficial' (Vassall, 340). Pegge resigned his Oriel fellowship in 1790 in order to return to Christ Church and take up the post of Lee's reader in anatomy. His duties as reader involved the delivery of two courses of lectures per year. His lecturing style has been described as both 'spirited' and 'easy and correct' (Tuckwell, 60–1; Cox, 132–3). At first his lectures were extremely popular, and it was 'not thought to be the thing to leave Oxford without attending one course' (Gibson, 107). Subsequently, however, Pegge came to be regarded as something of a bore. In 1790 he was elected a physician to the Radcliffe Infirmary, a position he held until 1808 when the asthma from which he long suffered obliged him to reduce his workload. On 29 March 1791 he married Amy, daughter of Kenton Couse of Whitehall in London. They had one daughter, Mary, born on 26 December 1791, who married the Revd R. M. Boultbee of Merton College, Oxford.

Pegge was awarded his DM in 1792. He became a fellow of the Royal Society in 1795 and a fellow of the Royal College of Physicians in 1796. He delivered the college's Harveian oration in 1805, and in 1817, having moved to London, he became a college censor. In 1799, soon after the duke of York had inspected the Oxford Loyal Volunteers, in which Pegge served as a major, George III conferred a knighthood on him. In 1801 he was appointed regius professor of physic, in which capacity he gave occasional lectures on aspects of animal economy and held the mastership of a charitable foundation, the Ewelme Hospital. Otherwise he had few duties. As for the authorship of papers and monographs, medical or otherwise, he appears to have written nothing whatsoever. Such reticence stands in contrast with the records of his father and paternal grandfather (Samuel Pegge the elder), both of whom achieved formidable literary outputs.

In his prime Pegge was 'a showy, handsome man' (Tuckwell, 60–61), with a 'fine portly figure and gentlemanly manners' (*Public Characters*, 261). As regius professor he cut a somewhat absurd figure for, notwithstanding his comparative youth, he affected the old-fashioned habit of cocked hat, wig, and massive gold-headed cane, all of which were spurned by his successor in the post, John Kidd. In 1816 an increased incidence and severity of asthmatic attack led Pegge to resign the Lee readership and to take up residence in George Street, Hanover Square, London in the hope of recovering his health. He engaged in medical practice in the capital but later moved to Hastings in Sussex, again for reasons of health. The modest obligations associated with the regius professorship enabled him to retain the post even after he had departed Oxford; he had merely to make occasional appearances at the university in accordance with its statutes. In the course of one of these visits, while occupying his lodgings in the High Street, he suffered an unusually severe asthmatic fit from which he died on 3 August 1822. He was interred in the south aisle of Ewelme church. His wife survived him.

P. W. J. BARTRIP

Sources *DNB* · A. G. Gibson, *The Radcliffe Infirmary* (1926) · Munk, *Roll* · W. Tuckwell, *Reminiscences of Oxford* (1900) · *A new biographical* *dictionary of 3000 cotemporary [sic] public characters, British and foreign, of all ranks and professions*, 2nd edn, 3 vols. in 6 pts (1825) • H. Rolleston, 'The personalities of the Oxford medical school, from 1700–1880', *Annals of Medical History*, new ser., 8 (1936), 277–87 • G. V. Cox, *Recollections of Oxford* (1868) • E. G. W. Bill, *Education at Christ Church, Oxford, 1660–1800* (1988) • *Public characters of the year* (1828) • *GM* [various] • H. R. V. Fox, third Lord Holland, *Further memoirs of the whig party, 1807–1821*, ed. Lord Stavordale (1905) • archives, Christ Church Oxf.

Archives Christ Church Oxf. | S. Antiquaries, Lond., letters to Richard Gough and John Nichols

Likenesses L. Agar, two coloured prints (wearing robes of Dr of Physic; after T. Uwins), Royal Society of Medicine, London • A. Plimer, miniature, V&A • T. Uwins, watercolour and pencil drawing, BM • engraving (after T. Uwins)

Pegge, Samuel (1704–1796), Church of England clergyman and antiquary, was born on 5 November 1704 in Chesterfield, Derbyshire, the only child of Christopher Pegge (*bap.* 1677, *d.* 1723/4), successively a cloth merchant in Derby and a lead merchant in Chesterfield, and three times mayor of Chesterfield, and his first wife, Gertrude (*d.* 1709), daughter of Francis Stephenson of Unstone in Dronfield. Samuel's parents were distant cousins. Of the four branches of the Pegge family in Derbyshire, Christopher belonged to that long established at Osmaston by Ashbourne, while Gertrude was descended from Edward Pegge of Beauchief. From another branch in Yeldersley came Katherine Pegge, mother of two of King Charles II's illegitimate children, including Charles FitzCharles (1647–1680), later earl of Plymouth.

Samuel Pegge was educated at Chesterfield and in 1722 became a scholar of St John's College, Cambridge. On the deaths of his father and the heir of his maternal grandfather, he inherited the Pegge estates in Osmaston by Ashbourne and half the Stephenson estates in Unstone. He graduated BA in 1725 and successfully applied in 1726 for a fellowship on the Beresford foundation at St John's, only to be removed in favour of Michael Burton, later vice-master, when the latter claimed founder's kin. Pegge was then regarded as an honorary fellow of the college until, on graduating MA in 1729, he was elected to a Platt fellowship. During his time at Cambridge, scholarly clubs modelled on the Society of Antiquaries were becoming fashionable. The Zodiac Club, founded in 1725, included Pegge as the original Mars among its twelve members from 1730 until he left the university in 1732. In 1730 he joined the Spalding Gentlemen's Society as a contributing member.

Pegge was ordained a priest in the Church of England in February 1730 and the following month became curate to the Revd Dr John Lynch, later dean of Canterbury, at Sundridge in Kent. Through Lynch, Pegge became vicar of Godmersham, also in Kent, in December 1731 and this preferment prompted him to marry, on 13 April 1732, Anne Clarke (*d.* 1746), the only daughter and heir of Benjamin Clarke of Stanley near Wakefield. Of their three children, the eldest, Samuel *Pegge (1733–1800), became a barrister and an antiquary himself, the second, Christopher (*d.* 1736), died in infancy, and the third, Anna Katherine (1735–1816), married the Revd John Bourne of Spital near Chesterfield, rector of Sutton cum Duckmanton.

Samuel Pegge (1704–1796), by James Basire, 1785 (after Arthur William Devis)

In Kent Pegge developed his antiquarian interests, collecting books and coins, corresponding with like-minded contemporaries, researching, and writing. After his wife's death in July 1746, he decided to move to his native Derbyshire and in 1747 he was nominated by the dean of Lincoln, patron of the living, to Brampton near Chesterfield. The parishioners disputed this right of patronage and repelled Pegge 'by violence' from entering the church for his induction in August 1748 (Nichols, *Lit. anecdotes*, 6.236). Despite proof later that year at Derby assizes that the Brampton parish records had been falsified to support his opponent's claim, Pegge did not take up the living. From 1749 to 1751 he was tutor to the son of Sir Edward Dering at Surrenden in Kent and did not return to Derbyshire until 11 November 1751 on his appointment as rector of Whittington near Chesterfield, where he lived until his death. Pegge exchanged Godmersham for the rectory of Brindle in Lancashire, which he held for seven years until he obtained the living of Heath near Whittington. In 1765 he acquired the perpetual curacy of Wingerworth, also near Whittington. Through Frederick Cornwallis, his diocesan bishop, Pegge became a prebendary of Lichfield Cathedral in 1757 and, additionally, in 1772 he was collated to the prebend of Louth in Lincoln Cathedral by his fellow collegian Bishop John Green.

On 14 February 1751 Pegge was elected a fellow of the Society of Antiquaries. To the classical and theological compositions of his youth, beginning in 1727 with the publication of a Latin ode on the death of King George I, he had added a body of predominantly antiquarian writings which increased substantially during his remaining forty-five years. Pegge was said to have been the most prolific of all contributors to the journal *Archaeologia* with more than fifty published articles and memoirs. His topics were as diverse as Anglo-Saxon jewels, the introduction of the vine into Britain, and the manner of King John's death, as well as more immediately local subjects such as bull-running at Tutbury in Staffordshire. The influence of the antiquary William Stukeley can be seen in Pegge's 'Illustration of some druidical remains in the Peak of Derbyshire' (*Archaeologia*, 7/2, 19) and 'Discoveries on opening a tumulus in Derbyshire' (*Archaeologia*, 9/18, 189). Between 1746 and 1795 Pegge often wrote for the *Gentleman's Magazine*, using anagrams of his name like 'Paul Gemsege' or the abbreviations 'T. Row' (the rector of Whittington) or 'L. E.', the last letters of his first and family names. He contributed seven articles to *Bibliotheca topographica Britannia*, including 'The history of Eccleshall manor' (1784), 'The Roman roads … discovered and investigated … through the … county of Derby' (1784), and 'The history of Bolsover and Peak Castle, Derbyshire' (1785). Among other major publications were his edition of Gustavus Brander's manuscript *The Forme of Cury: a Roll of Ancient English Cookery* (1780), *The Life of Robert Grossetete … Bishop of Lincoln* (1793), and the posthumously issued *Historical Account of Beauchief Abbey* (1801). Manuscript collections made by Pegge included two folio volumes on Kent entitled *Monasticon Cantianum*, an account of the antiquities of Wye in Kent, and a *Lexicon Xenophonticum*, together with eight folio volumes on Derbyshire history. The latter passed to his son, who gave them to John Nichols, the historian of Leicestershire, who in turn donated them in 1809 to the College of Arms where they remain.

On the centenary of the revolution of 1688, Pegge at the age of eighty-four preached a sermon on the history of Revolution House in Whittington where the aristocratic conspirators supporting William of Orange were said to have met. On 8 July 1791 he was created LLD by the University of Oxford while on a visit there to his grandson, Christopher Pegge, later regius professor of physic. Both a sociable companion and a conscientious pastor, Samuel Pegge died aged ninety-one on 14 February 1796 at Whittington rectory and was buried on 19 February in the church. A memorial tablet was erected to him but it did not survive the fire which destroyed the church in 1895. Although Gustavus Brander's portrait of Pegge at eighty-one was reproduced as a frontispiece to *The Forme of Cury*, Elias Needham's oil painting of him at the same age was said to have been a better likeness.

Samuel Pegge typifies Stuart Piggott's 'uncritical and omnivorous' eighteenth-century antiquary (Piggott,

Ancient Britons, 28), but his sometimes 'supremely ridiculous' conclusions, in the judgement of Sir John Evans, should not obscure the significance of some of his prodigious output (Evans, 7). He not only preserved historical information gathered by such earlier Derbyshire antiquaries as William Woolley, but was the first person to attempt to describe systematically the Roman road network in the county, and to publish inscriptions on lead pigs of the same era found in the Peak District. Pegge's pioneering work alerted contemporaries to the importance of topographical research, writing, and publishing and so laid the foundations for later field archaeologists and local historians, his son among them.

MARGARET O'SULLIVAN

Sources Nichols, *Lit. anecdotes*, 6.224–58 · T. W. Charlton, 'Some account of the family of Pegge of Shirley, Osmaston, Ashburne and Beauchief Abbey in the county of Derby', *Journal of the Derbyshire Archaeological and Natural History Society*, 2 (1880), 125–7 · *Collectanea Topographica et Genealogica*, 3 (1836), 240–49 · J. V. Colhoun, 'Osmaston juxta Ashbourne', *Derbyshire Miscellany*, 4 (1967), 30–36 · S. Piggott, *Ancient Britons and the antiquarian imagination* (1989) · S. Piggott, *William Stukeley: an eighteenth-century antiquary*, rev. edn (1985) · D. C. Douglas, *English scholars, 1660–1730*, 2nd edn (1951) · J. Evans, *Coins of the ancient Britons* (1864) · *DNB* · parish register, Chesterfield, St Mary's, 15 Nov 1704 [baptism] · parish register, Chesterfield, St Mary's, 31 May 1709, 6 Jan 1724 [burial] · parish register, Whittington, 19 Feb 1796 [burial]

Archives Bodl. Oxf., catalogue of coins and medals · Bodl. Oxf., collections relating to Kent · Bodl. Oxf., collections for a history of Lincolnshire and copies of works made by him · Bodl. Oxf., commonplace books · Bodl. Oxf., papers relating to English dialects · Coll. Arms, collections relating to Derbyshire, etc. · Derbys. RO, family MSS · Local Studies Library, Derby, dissertations on Anglo-Saxon remains · LUL, tables relating to English coinage · Sheff. Arch., book of Wingfield and Newton pedigrees | Bodl. Oxf., corresp. with John Charles Brooke · Bodl. Oxf., notes, some relating to Cambridge University · Derbys. RO, Gell family MSS · Derbys. RO, Pashley MSS · East Riding of Yorkshire Archives Service, Beverley, letters to Marmaduke Tunstall · S. Antiquaries, Lond., letters to Richard Gough and John Nichols · S. Antiquaries, Lond., letters to Hayman Rooke

Likenesses J. Basire, line engraving, 1785 (after A. W. Devis), BM, NPG [*see illus.*] · E. Needham, oils, *c*.1785 · P. Audinet, line engraving, pubd 1818 (after E. Needham), BM, NPG; repro. in Nichols, *Illustrations*

Pegge, Samuel (1733–1800), antiquary and writer, was born in Godmersham, Kent, on 21 February 1733, the only surviving son of Samuel *Pegge (1704–1796), antiquary, and his wife, Anne (*d*. 1746), daughter of Benjamin Clarke, of Stanley, near Wakefield. He went to school in Chesterfield, Derbyshire, and in 1751 matriculated at St John's College, Cambridge. In 1754 he was called to the bar at the Middle Temple. On 12 February 1759 he married Martha (1732–1767), daughter of Dr Henry Bourne, physician, of Chesterfield. They had a son, Sir Christopher *Pegge (1764/5–1822), and a daughter, Charlotte Anne (*d*. 1793). Through the patronage of the lord chamberlain, the duke of Devonshire, he was appointed a groom of the privy chamber to the king on 8 October 1762. He married second, on 1 May 1773 at St Martin-in-the-Fields, Goodeth Belt.

Pegge early acquired a considerable proficiency in music, writing many catches, glees, and songs. He was also the author of some theatrical prologues and epilogues, and of some pleasant tales and epigrammatic poems. His other publications included biographical memoirs, a memoir of his father, and several works of an antiquarian nature, including 'Illustrations of the churchwardens' accompts of St Michael Spurrier-Gate, York' in *Illustrations of the Manners and Expences of Antient Times* (1797) by John Nichols, and two works on the royal household, *Curialia, or, An Historical Account of some Branches of the Royal Household* (1782–1806) in five parts, the last two being edited by Nichols, and *Curialia miscellanea, or, Anecdotes of old times, regal, noble, gentilitian, and miscellaneous, including authentic anecdotes of the royal household* (1818), also edited by Nichols. On 2 June 1797 Pegge was elected a fellow of the Society of Antiquaries. He died on 22 May 1800 at Scotland Yard, Whitehall, London, and was buried on the west side of Kensington churchyard.

THOMPSON COOPER, *rev.* K. D. REYNOLDS

Sources GM, 1st ser., 70 (1800), 494 · Venn, *Alum. Cant.* · Nichols, *Illustrations* · IGI · J. C. Sainty and R. Bucholz, eds., *Officials of the royal household, 1660–1837*, 1: *Department of the lord chamberlain and associated offices* (1997)
Archives Derby Local Studies Library, collections for a new part of *Curialia* | Bodl. Oxf., letters to John Charles Brooke · S. Antiquaries, Lond., letters to Richard Gough and John Nichols · S. Antiquaries, Lond., letters to Hayman Rooke

Pegram, Henry Alfred (1862–1937), sculptor, was born at 72 King Street, Camden Town, London, on 27 July 1862, the son of Henry Pegram, a china shopman (and later a manufacturer of perambulators and rocking horses), and his wife, Matilda, *née* Spalding. He studied at the West London School of Art and won book prizes in national art competitions in 1881 and 1883. He entered the Royal Academy Schools in 1881, sponsored by Thomas Heatherley, founder of the Heatherley School of Fine Art. He was awarded prizes in 1882, 1884, and 1886 and was there for six years before working as the studio assistant of sculptor Sir (William) Hamo Thornycroft for four years. On 9 February 1884 he married, at Camden Town parish church, Alice Lambert (*b.* 1863/4) of 34 Ashmore Road, Paddington, daughter of the late Benjamin Lambert, a blacksmith. They had three sons and three daughters.

In 1889 Pegram received a medal for his *Death and the Prisoner* at the Paris Exhibition, later receiving a gold medal for *The Last Song* at Dresden in 1897 and a silver medal for *Labour* at the 1900 Paris Exhibition. He joined the Art Workers' Guild in 1890, was elected an associate of the Royal Academy in 1904, and became a Royal Academician in 1922.

Pegram's earlier work was influenced by Alfred Gilbert, and his greatest successes came earlier rather than later in his career. Two of his works, which perhaps he never equalled, show the influence of Gilbert's symbolist sculpture and were bought by the Tate Gallery, London, under the terms of the Chantrey bequest: a bronze relief *Ignis fatuus* (1889, a development of an earlier roundel by Gilbert)

and, in marble, a group *Sibylla fatidica* (1904), works which 'admirably illustrate the imaginative side of his art' (*The Times*, 29 March 1937). However, another early work, *Fortune*, a flamboyant nude (1900), showed little 'reflection of the new thought that characterises the work of Pegram's great contemporaries', perhaps an indication that he should be considered 'peripheral to the mainstream of the New Sculpture movement' (Beattie, 180).

Among Pegram's most notable 'ideal' works were the reliefs *Industry* and *Britannia* for the entrance to the Imperial Institute (1891–2); *The Bather* (1894); friezes at 20 Buckingham Gate, Westminster (1895), and at the United University Club, Suffolk Street (1906); a monument to Ninon, wife of Max Michaelis (1900); a relief *A Sea Idyll* (1902); *Into the Silent Land* (1905); a relief *By the Waters of Babylon* (1906); a group *Nereus and Galatea* (1911); a statuette *Chance* (1913); a group *Ophelia and the River Gods* (1914); a relief *Mater desolata* (1920); a group *Hylas* (1922, presented to the nation by the Royal Academy and placed, in 1933, in a pool of the rose garden at St John's Lodge, Regent's Park); and a group *Lux mundi* (1926). He also provided a large seated bronze statue, in Shakespearian pose, for the market place in Norwich, a monument to the seventeenth-century philosopher and physician Sir Thomas Browne (1905). There were also public statues of Sir John Campbell (at Auckland, New Zealand), Cecil Rhodes (at Cape Town, South Africa), and Sir Robert Hart (at Shanghai, China), as well as statues of Cardinal Newman (for Oriel College, Oxford) and of Prince Llewellyn (for Cardiff city hall), a monument to nurse Edith Cavell (at Norwich), and *Victory*, the Cunard war memorial (at Liverpool).

Pegram was also a long-standing member of the Society of British Sculptors. The society was split in 1914 over the Cardiff city hall commission when the president and council members allotted without competition the ten statues of famous Welshmen, sponsored by D. A. Thomas (later Lord Rhondda) to supplement the city hall's decoration. Pegram was one of the sculptors chosen.

Pegram's early career was characterized by decorative and ideal work, but perhaps he never fulfilled his promise as his 'work grew increasingly flamboyant in style and insensitive in execution, as shown, for example, in the deplorable bronze candelabra at St Paul's Cathedral' (Beattie, 248). He frequently exhibited at the Royal Academy, showing over 160 works between 1884 and 1936, not missing a year from 1888. He produced chiefly busts and reliefs, but there were also many groups, models, statuettes, and medallions. He usually worked in bronze but not infrequently in marble, and many of his works were of religious or classical themes. His exhibited busts included those of Cecil Rhodes (1903, a marble bust for the City of London), Edmond Halley (1904), William Herschel and Charles Dickens (both 1905), Rudyard Kipling (1909), Earl Jellicoe (1928), and Viscount Allenby (1930 and 1936). He exhibited two statuettes of golfer Harry Vardon (1908 and 1911); Pegram himself was a member of Mid-Surrey Golf Club. In July 1936 he was awarded a civil-list pension of £120 'in recognition of his services to art'. Following a cerebral haemorrhage, Pegram died at his home, 72 Belsize Park Gardens, Belsize Park, on 26 March 1937; he had been suffering from arteriosclerosis for two years. His wife and children survived him.   ROBERT SHARP

Sources WWW · *The Times* (29 March 1937), 12c · Graves, *RA exhibitors* · A. Jarman and others, eds., *Royal Academy exhibitors, 1905–1970: a dictionary of artists and their work in the summer exhibitions of the Royal Academy of Arts*, 5 (1981) · Thieme & Becker, *Allgemeines Lexikon* · b. cert. · m. cert. · d. cert. · S. Beattie, *The New Sculpture* (1983)
Wealth at death £2385 16s. 2d.: probate, 21 April 1937, *CGPLA Eng. & Wales*

Pegram [*née* Woods], **Lorna Gladys Hurst** (1926–1993), television producer and novelist, was born on 25 October 1926 at 386 Green Lane, Ilford, Essex, the only child of Reginald William James Woods and Sybil Hurst, both Salvation Army officers. Brought up in the East End of London, she was educated at Dagenham county high school and at King's College, London, from which she graduated with first-class honours, after writing a thesis on medieval mystery plays. On 25 October 1947 she married fellow student Roy William Pegram (*b.* 1922/3); they had two sons. The marriage ended in divorce and on 27 May 1961 she married Geoffrey Charles Newton Golden (*b.* 1933/4), an advertising executive, with whom she had a son, but retained the name Pegram.

In 1950 Pegram joined the production staff of BBC radio, working on *Listen with Mother* and *Woman's Hour*, where her voice became well known reading listeners' letters on air. She moved to BBC television in the late 1950s, again concentrating mainly on women's afternoon programmes such as *The Wednesday Magazine*, and *Look of the Week* with Robert Robinson. In the mid-1960s she moved to the arts features department and over the course of the next two decades she made a significant contribution to the corporation's coverage of the arts in general and fine art in particular, often in collaboration with the Australian art critic Robert Hughes, whom she first introduced to television in the late 1960s.

In the late 1960s Pegram was responsible for such series as *The Art Game*, a quiz chaired by Robert Hughes and featuring panellists ranging from Elisabeth Frink to George Melly, *Release*, a weekly arts magazine that succeeded Huw Wheldon's *Monitor*, and *Canvas*, a series of television essays on celebrated works of art. Her work for BBC2 in the 1970s included documentaries on Gunther Grass, Picasso, Jean-Louis Barrault, and Handel, three films written and narrated by Robert Hughes on Caravaggio, Rubens, and Bernini, and a series with the journalist Rene Cutforth examining the life and culture of the different decades of his life. In the early 1980s she worked with the distinguished architectural historian Vincent Scully on two films on American art.

However, Pegram is probably best remembered for her work on *The Shock of the New*, the eight-part television series on modern art, first broadcast in 1980, which she made with Robert Hughes. She produced the series and directed three of the eight programmes. To this series, as to all her work, she brought a strong sense of narrative, a direct and vivid visual style, and a down-to-earth approach that she used to curb her presenters' flights of theoretical fancy. Hughes's abiding memory was of her voice, cutting through the cigarette smoke that always accompanied her, 'It's a clever argument, Bob dear, but what are we supposed to be *looking at*?' He described her as 'Martinet, nag, *virtuosa*, fellow writer, and stubbornly tender friend … After fifteen years of working with her my admiration keeps growing' (Hughes, 7–8).

While working at the BBC, Pegram also pursued a career as a novelist, and she left the BBC in 1984 in order to write full-time. She published a total of seven novels between the 1950s and her death, including *Summer Fires* (1969), generally regarded as her best work, and *Another Island* (1989). None was a commercial success, but they received good reviews—*The Times*, for instance, hailed the proto-feminist *Summer Fires* as the product of 'a genuine, intriguing, sometimes baffling talent' (*The Times*, 24 May 1993). Her last novel, *Penelope's Web*, was completed shortly before her death.

Lorna Pegram died from lung cancer at home at 13 Silver Street, Deal, Kent, on 16 May 1993, aged sixty-six. She was survived by her three sons.   SIÂN NICHOLAS

Sources *The Times* (24 May 1993) · R. Hughes, *The shock of the new* (1980) · b. cert. · m. cert. [Roy William Pegram] · m. cert. [Geoffrey Charles Newton Golden] · d. cert.
Likenesses photograph, repro. in *The Times*
Wealth at death £313,681: probate, 13 Sept 1993, *CGPLA Eng. & Wales*

Pehthelm [Pecthelm] (*d.* 735), bishop of Whithorn, was for some time a monk or deacon with Aldhelm, probably at Malmesbury. It was from him that Bede heard the story of a vision seen in Mercia between 705 and 709, and Bede also cites him as an authority for facts connected with West Saxon history, especially for an account of events which occurred on the spot where Hœdde, bishop of Winchester, had died.

Pehthelm was consecrated as the first bishop of the see created by the Anglo-Saxons at Whithorn (known in Latin as Candida Casa) in Galloway, shortly before 731. He was learned in ecclesiastical law, and Boniface wrote to him in 735, asking whether a man may marry his godson's mother. Boniface had searched in vain through the papal decrees and canons for information, and asked both Nothhelm and Pehthelm if they could find the case mentioned. Boniface sent presents with his letter, including a corporal pallium. Pehthelm died in 735.

MARY BATESON, *rev.* MARIOS COSTAMBEYS

Sources Bede, *Hist. eccl.*, 5.13, 18, 23 · M. Tangl, ed., *Die Briefe des heiligen Bonifatius und Lullus*, MGH Epistolae Selectae, 1 (Berlin, 1916) · J. M. Wallace-Hadrill, *Bede's Ecclesiastical history of the English people: a historical commentary*, OMT (1988) · E. B. Fryde and others, eds., *Handbook of British chronology*, 3rd edn, Royal Historical Society Guides and Handbooks, 2 (1986)

Pehtwine [Pectwin] (*d.* **776/7**), bishop of Whithorn (known in Latin as Candida Casa), was consecrated by Archbishop Ecgberht at Elvet in Durham on 17 July 763 or 764. He died on 19 September 776 or 777.

MARY BATESON, *rev.* MARIOS COSTAMBEYS

Sources ASC, s.a. 763, 776 [texts D, E]

Peierls, Sir **Rudolf Ernst** (1907–1995), theoretical physicist, was born on 5 June 1907 in Oberschöneweide, a suburb in the south-east of Berlin, the youngest of the three children (Alfred (*b.* 1899); Annie (*b.* 1901); and Rudolf) of Heinrich Peierls (1867–1945), an electrical engineer from Breslau (Wroclaw) and managing director of a cable factory of the Allgemeine Elektrizitäts-Gesellschaft (AEG), and his first wife, Elisabeth (Elli; 1878–1921), daughter of Alfred Weigert (1848–1896) and his wife, Olga Hamburger, both of Breslau. Rudolf's parents were first cousins through the Weigert line. The Peierls families were assimilated Jews; Heinrich's children were baptized Lutheran. Rudolf's primary education was at a local preparatory school; his secondary education was at the local *Gymnasium*, later named the Humboldtschüle. In 1925 he passed the *Abiturium*, the high-school graduation examination, and then gained some practical experience in the AEG factory, which confirmed his inclination towards studies in theoretical physics. Rudolf's mother had died when he was fourteen years old; his father then married Else Hermann, about 1924. Rudolf and his stepmother had a good relationship but by this time he was mostly absent from the family home.

Study overseas In 1925 Peierls became a physics and mathematics student at Humboldt University, Berlin. He was critical of the physics professors' limited ability to interest students in their subjects. In 1926–7 he moved to Munich University, where Arnold Sommerfeld was enthusiastically applying the wave mechanics of Paul Dirac and Erwin Schrödinger. Peierls was especially attracted by the electron theory of metals and attended all the seminars and lectures which Sommerfeld arranged on this topic. He also met Hans Bethe, a year ahead of him, and they became lifelong friends. Since Sommerfeld was going abroad for 1927–8 Rudolf joined Werner Heisenberg at Leipzig and worked out there a hole theory to explain the negative Hall effect observed in metals having an almost full conduction band. Since Heisenberg went away for spring term 1929 Rudolf moved to work under Wolfgang Pauli, at the Eidgenössische Technische Hochschule in Zürich, where he developed his fundamental work on thermal conductivity. He was the first to recognize the importance of the Umklapp-processes on the phonon-phonon interactions at very low temperatures. It took about twenty years before techniques had developed sufficiently to test his prediction; even then it was verified only for materials which were pure, not only chemically but also isotopically. This theoretical work gained Peierls the DPhil degree from Leipzig University in 1929.

Peierls then became Pauli's research assistant for three years, an unusually long appointment. He developed there the first band theory of electrons in a one-dimensional metal, using a weak periodic interaction to represent its effect on the lattice. In 1930 Peierls was invited to attend the annual physics congress at Odessa in August. Here he met a young physics student, Eugenia Kannegiesser (1908–1986), from Leningrad, where she was

Sir Rudolf Ernst Peierls (1907–1995), by Bassano, 1947

a contemporary of Lev Landau, who was already known to Peierls. Their only shared language then was English, and Eugenia's English was quite limited. He went to Leningrad in spring 1931 to give a course of lectures. During his visit they married but she could not go to Zürich with him, since she needed a passport and an exit visa before she could leave Russia. Peierls went back to Leningrad in the summer, and they left for Zürich when her documents were ready. They had four children, Gaby Ellen (*b.* 1933), Ronald Frank (*b.* 1935), Catherine (Kitty; *b.* 1948), and Joanna (*b.* 1949).

Peierls was awarded a Rockefeller fellowship for 1932–3, six months at Rome and six months at Cambridge. While they were in England the Nazi party gained control of Germany and they could not return. Fortunately Peierls was given a two-year fellowship by the Academic Assistance Council of Manchester. Hans Bethe was there for one year as an assistant lecturer, living with them. When Peierls and Bethe visited Cambridge, James Chadwick challenged them to provide a theoretical model for the photodisintegration of a deuteron, whose rate he had just measured. On the train journey home they made a calculation of the process for him, assuming zero-range nuclear forces. This stimulated their interest in nuclear physics, which then became Bethe's main interest, Peierls following suit several years later. For 1935–7 Peierls accepted a two-year fellowship at the Mond Laboratory of Cambridge University, for solid state physics research. Just before they left for Cambridge, Manchester University awarded Peierls an honorary DSc degree, a remarkable testimonial.

In 1937 Peierls was appointed professor of applied mathematics in Birmingham University.

Nuclear weapons research When Otto Frisch visited Peierls from Copenhagen in 1939 Frisch was already uneasy about the Nazis, and he became stranded at Birmingham when Germany occupied Denmark. One day he asked Peierls how much U235 would be needed to make a U235 bomb. Peierls estimated this to be about 1 kg, a result which astonished them. The smallness of their value resulted from including *fast*-neutron fission of U235, which had not been considered by anyone else. They wrote an account of their calculations in March 1940, including a perceptive note about the human damage which would result if their superbomb were set off in a populated place, and sent it to higher authorities in Britain. The Peierlses took British nationality on 27 March 1940.

The MAUD committee (the British government committee set up to examine the civil and military uses of atomic science) discussed the Frisch–Peierls memoranda, commented on them, and sent a copy to the USA about 1 June 1941. No response came from there until Oliphant, visiting the USA for other reasons, managed to convince Ernest Lawrence of their importance late in September, just before he returned to Birmingham. Lawrence then persuaded the American authorities to take it very seriously. As it happened, the American government decided on 6 December 1941 to build an atomic bomb; this was the day before the surprise attack by Japan on Pearl Harbor, Hawaii.

Peierls and Francis Simon (another refugee from Germany, at Oxford University) saw that the separation of U235 from natural uranium (mostly U238) was vital for the success of the Frisch–Peierls proposal. Peierls kept on with a variety of calculations bearing on this separation problem, almost alone—pouring forth memoranda on uranium separation questions—until 28 May 1941, when he gained an assistant, Klaus Fuchs (naturalized British on 18 June 1941), who gave Peierls strong support, providing him with quick and accurate theoretical calculations when necessary. Both Peierls and Simon judged gaseous diffusion (of uranium hexafluoride) to be the most efficient process for separation, although it would require a large number of stages and therefore a large plant. It was realized early on that it was not feasible to build this plant in Britain under wartime conditions. Early in 1942 Peierls and three colleagues visited the USA briefly and were made welcome; they found that their American colleagues were making great progress without them. However, there was little further UK–USA contact—indeed it was forbidden by the US secret service—until Roosevelt and Churchill were each made aware of this situation; their discussions then led to the Quebec agreement of August 1943. A much larger group of senior UK scientists then moved to the USA and joined the Manhattan project. Peierls became the leader of the implosion dynamics group (needed for the plutonium bomb) within the theoretical physics division, headed by Bethe, of the Los Alamos Laboratory. Peierls had demanded that Fuchs should accompany him, as his indispensable assistant. Peierls attended the Trinity test (of a plutonium bomb) at Alamogordo on 17 July 1945. In 1946 he was appointed CBE.

Theoretical physics, at Birmingham After Hiroshima and Nagasaki, Peierls was free to return to England. After discussion he decided to return to Birmingham as professor of mathematical physics, where he had an independent department, strong on the research side, with some research fellowships attached. His department was housed in two wartime huts. Peierls soon put his stamp on the style of the department. The students were all placed under his supervision, generally working on problems suggested by him, but with some informal link to one of the postdoctoral members. Peierls was always a critical physicist; with new work he was well known for quickly asking searching questions. With the research students he was critical but in the end always encouraging, suggesting some new direction which could be tried, or some check which could be made, when the calculations made did not seem to accord with intuition. He was always positive and helpful in his remarks to them. Sometimes he would go to the blackboard and outline how the solution might be obtained, leaving the student to think it over, to fill in the details and to verify that the path proposed really did lead to the solution. No student was afraid of Peierls. He was very generous to many of them, not requiring his name on their published papers, even when he had proposed the topic and had made clear the method of the solution. All became conscious of being part of a common endeavour to push forward the frontiers of physics. There would often be discussion of tricky points around the daily lunch table. The atmosphere in the department was one of continual discussion—the offices of the students were all close to each other, as well as to Peierls's office—and the students learned of research as a way of life by following Peierls's example. Students who had gone through the department often developed their capabilities much more than they would have elsewhere. They had seen how theoretical physics could be done, following Peierls's style in the department. Peierls believed that theoretical physics was a co-operative venture in which interactions between physicists were crucial. This was the lesson he had learned in his years of wandering, going from one group to another for various reasons, to almost all the main centres of that time.

In summer 1947 Peierls held a national conference on nuclear physics, partly to place his department on the map. In 1948 he held an international conference, which was very successful, being perhaps the earliest such conference after the war. As a result of Peierls's personal connections with the major research centres, senior physicists came from widespread countries. From its beginning the department increased rapidly in both the number and the calibre of its students and staff.

Social links within the department were stimulated by parties organized by the Peierlses, inviting the entire department, together with their wives, at which group games were played, or there was dancing, or perhaps story-telling around the room. In the summer the parties were outdoors and the children would also take part. The atmosphere of the department was very happy, despite the crowding in it and the unavoidable noise from the corridor. One student there wrote in those early years: 'We are a happy family here and the Peierlses are father and mother to all' (private information). At Birmingham Peierls developed the major group in theoretical physics in Britain in his time. The times were anomalous, especially in the first ten years after the war. Many able students went to Birmingham because they were lacking proof of their ability in fundamental research, having worked in some rather narrow speciality during the war. Numerous older physicists chose Birmingham for their sabbatical year, and research students at other universities would choose to go to Birmingham for their final year, regarding it as a finishing school, after which they would write their PhD dissertations for their home universities.

One characteristic of Peierls's work was that he usually started from fundamentals, rather than from the work of others. This was the case for the Frisch–Peierls memoranda. His development of the dynamics of dislocations in crystalline solids was sparked off by a question from Egon Orowan. He demonstrated from first principles, using simple steps, that the Ising model in two dimensions *must* have a phase-transition, contrary to general opinion. His novel treatment and use of resonant states in nuclear systems also started from fundamentals. These cases and others illustrate how, in Peierls's hands, new areas of theoretical physics could grow out of simple questions and thoughts about them. That 'Peierls always starts from fundamentals' was the secret of his success and of his being one of the last of those wide-ranging universalists in physics—those physicists who could, for example, do research in both nuclear physics theory and condensed matter theory.

In 1950 Peierls was very shocked to learn that Fuchs had turned over to the Russians copies of almost all the calculations he had carried out during the war, and other secret documents which passed through his hands, despite his signing the Official Secrets Act. At first Peierls could not believe this, but Fuchs said that there was no mistake. In the cold war era Peierls chose to resign his consultancy with the Atomic Energy Research Establishment (AERE), Harwell, when he realized that as a result of Fuchs's treachery the US Security Service mistrusted him to such a degree that they were proposing not to permit AERE to receive US classified reports.

Wykeham professorship In 1963 the Wykeham professorship (theoretical physics) of Oxford University became free. When Peierls was asked to fill the chair he specified that there should be a department of theoretical physics to include all the theoretical physicists in Oxford, with a suitable building to house them all, and three adjoining houses were allocated to him.

The Oxford department of theoretical physics soon became larger than that at Birmingham and it was not possible for Peierls to work with all the students. It was divided into two large groups, elementary particle physics and condensed matter physics, and two smaller groups—astrophysics and nuclear physics. The first three were each placed under a senior researcher, while the last was under Peierls, who also took some students in solid state physics. There was much more administration to be done by Peierls in connection with the department than was the case in Birmingham. He had to serve on many internal university committees and continued on a number of external committees, on which he now represented Oxford instead of Birmingham. The Oxford department continued to grow in numbers and he had to work hard to secure more floor space to accommodate all of them. There was less departmental sociability than at Birmingham, since the colleges already generated links between students of differing subjects within the college. The parties happened less often, not all attended, and were held in the department building. Peierls kept an interest in all the work going on and attended a large fraction of the specialist seminars and most of the more general seminars and colloquia. As a result theoretical physics at Oxford gradually became more coherent, a great improvement on the past. This growth of coherence may perhaps be Peierls's greatest single contribution to Oxford in his period there. He was elected FRS in 1945, receiving the society's royal medal in 1959 and its Copley medal in 1986. He was knighted in 1968.

Although Peierls devoted much energy to improving accommodation for the increasing department numbers, space was not made available to him until 1974, when he was about to retire; the department moved from 12 Parks Road to 1 Keble Road three years later when the rebuilding work was complete. Peierls had spent a number of summer vacations working at the University of Washington at Seattle; for his retirement he accepted an appointment to that university as a half-time professor for 1974–7. After 1977 Peierls lectured at a number of summer schools. These lectures appeared in the proceedings volume for each school; he expanded his lectures at Les Houches (1953) to book length, publishing them under the title *Quantum Theory of Solids*.

Atomic Scientists' Association On his return to Birmingham in 1945 Peierls had played a leading role in forming an Atomic Scientists' Association, and was its first (acting) president. The association sought to inform the public about nuclear physics and nuclear energy, and especially the safeguards necessary in dealing with the decay properties of many nuclei. Their most effective means for this education was a travelling exhibition, known as the 'atomic train', which could stop at all towns served by railways. Later, by request, it also went abroad, and was very successful there. The association wound up in 1958 because it had achieved its purpose; also, the full members, those who had worked as professional nuclear scientists during the war, were diminishing in number. However, there was soon formed a British Pugwash Group, with Peierls as its first chairman until 1974, when he became an honorary (but active) member of its executive committee.

Peace movements Peierls attended his first International Pugwash conference in 1960, the sixth held and the first to be held in the USSR; he had met his Russian colleagues (for the first time after the war) at the Atoms for Peace conference at Geneva in 1955. He then attended the Pugwash conferences rather regularly; his ability with the Russian language was very helpful in discussions, for he could quickly clarify misunderstandings of technical translation. He became a member of its continuing committee (later named its council) in 1963, and its chairman in 1970, retiring from this post in 1974. In 1972 the twenty-second Pugwash conference was held in Oxford, when he was chairman of both International Pugwash and British Pugwash; the local arrangements were made by the latter group under his direction. In 1992 he attended the forty-second International Pugwash conference at Berlin—his twenty-fourth and last attendance.

Throughout this period Peierls was deeply involved in the anti-nuclear weapons movement in Britain. In 1983 the UK Coalition for a Nuclear Weapons Freeze began, which became known as FREEZE. It was unilateral, urging only that the UK should cease the production, testing, and deploying of nuclear weapons. In 1985 Peierls became a patron of FREEZE, taking part in the advertising of this drive, and in collecting signatures at Oxford, all leading up to the 'Giant Letter', which was presented to the government. Late in 1986 he was made a FREEZE director. In this FREEZE period Peierls adopted the slogan 'nuclear weapons are not battleships'; he felt that if people were able to understand this and its implications, they would give up the old 'numbers game' so frequently adopted. In the 1990s he collaborated with C. Hill, R. Pease, and J. Rotblat to produce an 80-page report from the British Pugwash Group entitled 'Does Britain Need Nuclear Weapons?', reaching the conclusion 'No', published in 1995.

Lady Peierls died at Oxford on 25 October 1986. Sir Rudolf then travelled the world, attending seven more Pugwash conferences, giving physics seminars at universities along his way, some of which bestowed honorary DScs on him. The Institute of Physics elected him honorary fellow in 1973, awarding him the Guthrie medal in 1968 and the Paul Dirac medal and prize in 1991. He was elected to numerous foreign societies, being especially gratified by his membership of the Deutsche Akademie Leopoldina, for German-born scientists, in 1981. However, in 1993 he was overtaken by pneumonia at Rome, which required his transport back to England by air on a stretcher bed. He sold his Oxford flat and moved into the country at Oakenholt, near Farmoor, Oxfordshire, where he could be independent, but with ready help near at hand. He was almost blind and unable to read, but was still able to communicate with others by voice, most often by telephone. Kidney trouble required regular dialysis sessions for him at the Churchill Hospital, Oxford, where he died on 19 September 1995.   R. H. DALITZ

Sources R. Peierls, *Bird of passage* (1985) • *The Guardian* (21 Sept 1995) • *The Times* (22 Sept 1995) • *The Independent* (22 Sept 1995) • *WWW* • personal knowledge (2004) • private information (2004) • naturalization certificate, PRO, HO 334/157/AZ 15795 • d. certs. [Rudolf Ernst Peierls, Eugenia Peierls] • *CGPLA Eng. & Wales* (1995)

Archives Bodl. Oxf., corresp. and papers | CAC Cam., corresp. with Sir James Chadwick • ICL, archives, corresp. with Dennis Gabor • University of Copenhagen, Niels Bohr Institute for Astronomy, Physics, and Geophysics, corresp. with Niels Bohr • University of Copenhagen, Niels Bohr Institute for Astronomy, Physics, and Geophysics, corresp. with H. A. Kramers

Likenesses Bassano, photograph, 1947, NPG [*see illus.*] • photograph, 1948, repro. in *The Guardian* • N. Sinclair, bromide print, 1993, NPG • photograph, repro. in *The Times* • photographs, repro. in *The Independent*

Wealth at death £331,170: probate, 14 Dec 1995, *CGPLA Eng. & Wales*

Peile, Sir James Braithwaite (1833–1906), administrator in India, born at Liverpool on 27 April 1833, was the second son of Thomas Williamson *Peile (1806–1882) and his wife, Mary (d. 1890), daughter of James Braithwaite. He was educated at Repton School, where his father was headmaster, winning a scholarship to Oriel College, Oxford, in 1852. In 1855 he received a first class in classics, and in the same year joined the Indian Civil Service.

Peile went out to India in 1856, beginning work in Bombay presidency as an assistant collector in the districts of Thana, Surat, and Ahmadabad. While in the latter two districts he mastered the Gujarati language, making good use of this skill in his subsequent career. He was in Ahmadabad during the revolt of 1857, and he described the events of the time in a graphic manner in private letters to friends, which were published in *The Times* on 3 December 1857. On 7 December 1859 he married, in Bombay, Louisa Elizabeth Bruce, daughter of General Sackville Hamilton Berkeley.

While in Ahmadabad district Peile became sympathetic to the problems of the *garasias* and *talukdars*, petty chiefs who had been granted landlord rights by the British. By the late 1850s they had fallen deep into debt to usurers, and the colonial civil courts were selling off their estates, often at very low prices, to repay these debts. Peile argued that if the British allowed this formerly warlike class to be ruined, they could cause difficulties in future. Largely as a result of his efforts, the Ahmedabad Talukdars Relief Act was passed in 1862, which enabled the state to take over and run badly indebted estates until the debts were paid off. Peile took an active role in implementing the legislation, in the process saving many of these landlords from destitution. As a class, however, they continued to be indebted, never becoming efficient estate managers. In April 1866 Peile was selected as commissioner for revising subordinate civil establishments throughout Bombay presidency, and then, during a wave of financial speculation, took an active part in compelling companies to furnish accounts. From 1869 to 1873 he served as director of public instruction in Bombay, being involved in extending primary education in the presidency. In 1872 he was appointed municipal commissioner of Bombay to sort out the financial problems of the city.

In 1873, and then from November 1874 to May 1878, Peile served as political agent in the peninsula of Kathiawar. This important agency covered 23,500 square miles, with a population of about 2½ million. The territorial sovereignty was divided between the Maharaja Gaikwar of Baroda and about 200 chiefs, some of whom, notably Bhaunagar, Jamnagar, and Junagarh, had extensive territories, while others ruled little more than a single village. There was little co-ordinated policing of the region, and Peile persuaded the chiefs to co-operate more in maintaining order, putting forward a scheme for reforming the system of village police which had considerable success. He helped improve the railways and roads of the region and gave his full support to educational reforms. He took an active role in organizing relief during the famine of 1877. With his knowledge of Gujarati and feel for local conditions, Peile won the respect of the chiefs of Kathiawar. In later years he asserted the rights of these chiefs to retain their salt and opium revenues and he encouraged them to send representatives to Bombay to discuss their problems with him and others.

Peile served a few months in Sind in 1878, but declined the offer of the commissionership there. He was a member of the famine commission in 1878–80, accompanying it on its tour of inquiry, and in the course of it was made CSI. In October 1879 he went to London to help in the writing of the famine report. From 1879 to 1882 he was secretary and acting chief secretary to the Bombay government. In December 1882 he became a member of council at Bombay and played a leading role in implementing Lord Ripon's policy of extending self-government at the provincial and local levels. Peile sought to dilute these reforms so as to prevent the emerging Indian middle class from gaining significant new powers. As a result of his insistence, considerable power in these bodies was retained in official hands. Peile was also active in educational affairs, being appointed vice-chancellor of Bombay University in 1864. In 1886 he was appointed to the supreme council by the new viceroy, Lord Dufferin.

In 1887 Peile left India on being nominated to the Council of India in London, and was made KCSI in 1888. He served for fifteen years, playing a very active role in the government of India. He became an advocate of greater devolution of power at provincial level, and sought to prevent Indian revenue being used too freely for overall imperial needs. He also objected to tariffs which discriminated against Indian cotton in favour of British cotton goods. Although he favoured a greater degree of Indianization of the civil service, he opposed the resolution of the House of Commons of 1893 for simultaneous examinations in Britain and India. He declined the offer of chairmanship of the second famine commission, but served on the royal commission on the administration of the expenditure of India in 1895, and recorded the reservations with which he assented to their report of 1900. He retired from the Council of India in 1902 and died suddenly on 25 April 1906 at his home, 28 Campden House Court, Kensington, London. He was buried at the Kensington Hanwell cemetery, Ealing. He was survived by his wife, a daughter, and two sons, one of whom, James Hamilton Francis, was archdeacon of Warwick.

DAVID HARDIMAN

Sources *The Times* (27 April 1906) · *DNB* · N. Charlesworth, *Peasants and imperial rule* (1985) · *CGPLA Eng. & Wales* (1906)
Archives BL OIOC, letters to Sir James Fergusson, MS Eur. E 214
Wealth at death £34,526 1s. 0d.: probate, 2 June 1906, *CGPLA Eng. & Wales*

Peile, John (1838–1910), college head and philologist, born at Whitehaven, Cumberland, on 24 April 1838, was the only son of Williamson Peile FGS and his wife, Elizabeth Hodgson. Sir James Braithwaite Peile was his first cousin. His father died when he was five, and in 1848 he was sent to Repton School, of which his uncle, Thomas Williamson *Peile, was then headmaster. He remained at Repton until his uncle's retirement in 1854. During the next two years he attended the school at St Bees, and in 1856 was entered at Christ's College, Cambridge. In 1859 he won the Craven scholarship, and in 1860 was bracketed with two others as senior classic, and with one of them as chancellor's medallist. He graduated BA in 1860 and proceeded MA in 1863. Having been elected a fellow of Christ's in 1860, and appointed assistant tutor and composition lecturer, he settled down to college and university work, which occupied him almost until his death. He took up the study of Sanskrit and comparative philology, and in 1865, and again in 1866, spent some time working with Professor Theodor Benfey at Göttingen. On 26 July 1866 he married Annette (1835–1920), daughter of William Cripps Kitchener and cousin of Lord Kitchener. He was obliged to vacate his fellowship on marriage but was re-elected in 1867.

Until the appointment of Professor Edward Byles Cowell in 1867, Peile was teacher of Sanskrit in the university; he had declined to stand for the chair so that another student of the subject might come to Cambridge. When Sanskrit became a subject in the classical tripos, he published a volume of *Notes on the Tale of Nala* (1881) to accompany the edition of the text by Professor Thomas Jarrett. He also corrected that edition, which in consequence of a difficult method of transliteration was very inaccurately printed. In 1869 appeared his book *An Introduction to Greek and Latin Etymology* of which there were two further editions. Later the point of view of comparative philologists changed to a marked degree, and Peile, who by this time was becoming more immersed in college and university business, allowed the book to go out of print. A little primer of *Philology* (1877) had for long a very wide circulation. To the ninth edition of the *Encyclopaedia Britannica* he contributed the article on the alphabet and also articles on the individual letters. He was for many years a contributor to *The Athenaeum*, reviewing classical and philological publications. In 1904 he was elected a member of the British Academy.

Peile was tutor of his college from 1870 to 1884, when, on his appointment to the newly constituted post of university reader in comparative philology, which was not tenable with a college tutorship, he resigned, but remained a college lecturer. On the death of Dr Swainson in 1887 he was elected the first lay master of Christ's; it is supposed that he would have been elected in 1881, had the statutes then allowed it. He continued to lecture for the university until his election as vice-chancellor in 1891.

Peile's two years' tenure of the vice-chancellorship (1891–3) was unusually eventful. The most important incident was the passing of an act of parliament, by which the perennial conflict of jurisdictions between 'town and gown' was brought to an end satisfactory to both parties, the university surrendering its jurisdiction over persons not belonging to its own body and receiving representation on the town council. The controversy had reached an acute stage over a case of proctorial discipline, and the new arrangement was mainly due to Peile's broadmindedness and statesmanship. Henceforward he became more prominent than ever in the affairs of the university. While he was vice-chancellor a new chancellor—Spencer Compton Cavendish, the eighth duke of Devonshire—was installed; and Peile visited Dublin on the occasion of the tercentenary of Trinity College, which conferred upon him the honorary degree of LittD in 1892 (he had been one of the early recipients of the degree of LittD on its establishment at Cambridge in 1884).

In 1874 Peile had been elected a member of the council of the senate, a position which he held uninterruptedly for thirty-two years. With Professor Henry Sidgwick and Coutts Trotter he represented in the university the liberalizing movement then perhaps at the zenith of its influence. He was long an active supporter of women's education and a member of the council of Newnham College, and in the university controversy of 1897 on the question of 'women's degrees' he advocated the opening to women of university degrees. 'His wisdom in giving advice in difficulties was equalled by his courage in defending the College in aspersions and attacks' (Gardner, 110). After the death of Professor Arthur Cayley in 1895 Peile became president of the council, and a new block of college buildings at Newnham was named after him. He was in favour of making Greek no longer compulsory on all candidates for admission to the university when the question was debated in 1891, and again in 1905 and 1906. He also took an active part in the university extension movement.

Although Peile never ceased to take an interest in comparative philology, and remained for many years an active and influential member of the special board for classics, most of his leisure, after he ceased to be vice-chancellor in 1893, was devoted to compiling a biographical register of the members of his college and of its forerunner, God's House, a work which entailed a great amount of research. In connection with this undertaking he wrote in 1900 a history of the college for Robinson's series of college histories. The first volume of his register (1448–1665) was completed before Peile's death, which took place at the college, after a long illness, on 9 October 1910. He was buried on 12 October in the churchyard of Trumpington, the parish in which he lived before becoming master of Christ's College. He had, besides two children who died in infancy, two sons (for whom see Venn), and a daughter, Hester Mary, who married, in 1890, John Augustine Kempthorne, afterwards bishop of Lichfield.

Peile was a man of moderate views who had the faculty of remaining on good terms with his most active opponents. He was an effective speaker and a good chairman. As a college officer he was very popular, and the college prospered under him. As a lecturer on classical subjects (most frequently on Theocritus, Homer, Plautus, and Lucretius), and on comparative philology, he was able to put his views clearly and interestingly, and, like Charles Lamb, he sometimes found the slight hesitation in his speech a help in emphasizing a point. To him as much as anyone was due the successful study of comparative philology in Cambridge for a generation.

PETER GILES, rev. JOHN D. PICKLES

Sources personal knowledge (1912) · private information (1912) · W. W. Skeat, 'John Peile, 1838–1910', *PBA*, [4] (1909–10), 379–83 · W. H. D. Rouse, *Christ's College Magazine* (1910) · *Cambridge Review* (13 Oct 1910), 8–10 · A. Gardner, *A short history of Newnham College* (1921) · J. Peile, *Biographical register of Christ's College, 1505–1905, and of the earlier foundation, God's House, 1448–1505*, ed. [J. A. Venn], 2 (1913), 545–6 · G. F. Browne, *Recollections of a bishop* (1915), 179–80 · *CGPLA Eng. & Wales* (1910) · *Cambridge Chronicle* (14 Oct 1910) · *IGI*
Archives King's AC Cam., letters to Oscar Browning
Likenesses G. Reid, oils, 1902, Christ's College, Cambridge; replica, Newnham College, Cambridge · Elliott & Fry, cabinet photograph, NPG · D. Smith, photograph, repro. in *The Gownsman* (4 Nov 1910), supplement · photograph, repro. in Rouse, *Christ's College Magazine* · photograph, British Academy, London
Wealth at death £21,648 18s. 4d.: probate, 25 Nov 1910, *CGPLA Eng. & Wales*

Peile, Thomas Williamson (1806–1882), Church of England clergyman and headmaster, eldest son of John Peile, a justice of the peace for Cumberland, was born at Whitehaven on 10 November 1806. He was educated at St Bees School and then under Dr Butler at Shrewsbury School, where he followed B. H. Kennedy as captain of the school, and in 1824 entered Trinity College, Cambridge. After gaining the Davies scholarship in his freshman's year, he graduated BA in 1828 as eighteenth wrangler and bracketed second in the first class of the classical tripos. He was also second chancellor's medallist. He proceeded MA in 1831, and held a fellowship of his college from 1829 until his marriage in 1831 to Mary (d. 1890), daughter of James Braithwaite of Whitehaven. Peile was an assistant master at Shrewsbury from 1828 to 1829. In 1829 he was appointed headmaster of the Liverpool Collegiate School, and in the same year was ordained by Bishop Sumner of Chester. He was chaplain to Lord Westmorland, and in 1831 became perpetual curate of St Catherine's, Liverpool. In 1834 he moved to Durham to hold one of the first tutorships in the newly constituted university. In 1836 he was appointed by the dean and chapter of Durham to the perpetual curacy of Croxdale, near Durham, which he held with his tutorship.

Peile was headmaster of Repton School from 1841 to 1854, when he was succeeded by Steuart Adolphus Pears. Peile began the transformation of Repton from a country grammar school into a boarding-school with the standing of a leading public school. Always known as the Doctor (having taken his DD degree in 1843), he was of 'precise and dignified appearance', disliking unconventional habits among boys and masters alike, his violent temper leading him into quarrels with the latter. He introduced the Shrewsbury practice of rewarding pupils, whose successes included ten fellowships at Oxford and Cambridge, with 'merit money'. Peile's policy was achieved at the cost of displacing local boys; a memorial to the governors on their behalf in 1844 was followed by an unsuccessful action in chancery, heard in January 1852, brought by Jeremiah Briggs, a Derby solicitor, alleging that the school was originally founded to provide a free education for the boys of Etwall and Repton. A breakdown in his health brought Peile's resignation in 1854.

Towards the close of 1857 Peile became vicar of Luton, Bedfordshire, a large and populous parish, which he began dividing into districts. But as the task proved too great for his strength, he moved in October 1860 to the newly formed parish of St Paul, South Hampstead. This he held until 1873, when he resigned. He lived in the district until his death at his home, 37 St John's Wood Park, London, on 29 November 1882. He was buried in Buckhurst Hill churchyard on 2 December. His widow and their large family survived him. The eldest son, Sir James Braithwaite *Peile (1833–1906), was an Indian civil servant; their eighth son, Clarence John Peile (1847–1900), was a barrister.

Peile was a sound scholar, and his knowledge of the classics, especially Thucydides and the Greek Testament, was remarkable. His principal works were editions of the *Agamemnon* (1839) and *Choephori* (1840) of Aeschylus, and *Annotations on the Apostolical Epistles* (4 vols., 1851–2). His *Sermons, Doctrinal and Didactic* was published in 1868. Peile's *The Church of England not High, not Low, but Broad as the Commandment of God: a Letter* (1850) was notable as one of the earliest usages of the term 'broad' in connection with the established church, though Peile himself was not an adherent of the so-called broad-church party.

J. H. LUPTON, rev. M. C. CURTHOYS

Sources *The Guardian* (6 Dec 1882), 1716 · Boase, *Mod. Eng. biog.* · Venn, *Alum. Cant.* · A. Macdonald, *A short history of Repton* (1929) **Archives** BL, letters to Bishop Butler, Add. MSS 34585–34592 **Likenesses** Mrs Burd, portrait (after Rippingdale), repro. in Macdonald, *Short history of Repton*, facing p. 152 · portrait, Repton School, Derbyshire **Wealth at death** £29,546 17s. 6d.: probate, 23 Dec 1882, *CGPLA Eng. & Wales*

Peirce, Sir Edmund (d. 1667), lawyer and politician, was born in Buckinghamshire and was admitted to Corpus Christi College, Cambridge, in 1629. On 16 August 1629 he married Jane (d. 1665), daughter of James Francklyn, subsequently recorder of Maidstone. They had two children, George Gilbert, named after his godfather George Gilbert of Colchester, Essex, and Margaret, who married Robert Hart of the Middle Temple. Peirce matriculated from Trinity Hall, Cambridge, in Easter term 1633, taking the LLB degree in 1635, and the LLD in 1639. In 1637 he became commissary of the archdeaconry of Suffolk, and judge of the vice-admiralty of Suffolk, in place of Henry Dade LLB. In 1639 Peirce examined and reported upon a cause in the court of high commission, and in 1640, after litigation in the court of arches resulting from his treatment of puritans, was the subject of a petition to parliament alleging

abuses in his court. There, it was said, fees had been wrongly exacted and puritans had been excommunicated for refusing to take communion at the altar rail. In 1640 Peirce was appointed a commissioner for piracy in Suffolk, and on 4 June 1641 was admitted to the Middle Temple. In 1642 'upon special trust and confidence' he was 'employed into the county of Kent' (Rylands, 195) by the king, and assisted in drafting the celebrated petition promoted at the Maidstone Lent assizes of 1642. Examined by the Commons concerning the petition, Peirce protested that he had been in Kent by chance 'to see his kindred' (*JHC*, 2, 1 April 1642), and that he had merely procured the insertion of a clause in favour of the civil lawyers.

After a brief imprisonment Peirce served in the Royal Life Guards before raising a regiment of horse, with which he served at Newbury, Cropredy Bridge, Cheriton, and Lostwithiel, combining his colonelcy with the offices of judge-marshal and advocate-general of the army, and master of requests. He was knighted at Raglan Castle on 10 July 1645. Petitioning to compound for his delinquency on 17 November 1646, he was assessed at one tenth, and fined £82. After the rising of 1655 he was again arrested, and imprisoned at Great Yarmouth, Norfolk. At this time he was living at Colchester, Essex, where he and his son had bought land from George Gilbert, who left them further property in Essex in his will. Between 1642 and 1660 Peirce issued at least nine tracts of a political or religious nature.

On 19 April 1660, with Sir Benjamin Ayloffe, Peirce presented the declaration of the Essex royalists to General Monck. In the same year he petitioned for a place as a master of requests, setting out his military service, his losses, and the pamphlets which he had written and published in support of the monarchy and the Church of England. In response he was appointed a master of requests extraordinary, to succeed on the next vacancy. In 1660 also came appointment as a master in chancery, as Admiralty judge in the Cinque Ports, as a justice of the peace in Essex, Kent, and Middlesex, and as vicar-general of spirituals in the diocese of Bath and Wells, the bishop, Dr William Piers, perhaps being a kinsman. From 1660 until his death Peirce was a commissioner for assessment in Kent, and from 1664 for Colchester and Essex. He was a commissioner under the Corporation Act in Kent in 1662–3, and for loyal and indigent officers in Essex, Kent, London, and Westminster in 1662. By 1664 he was also a justice of the peace in Somerset. In 1661 he was granted augmentations to his coat of arms in recognition of his service to the crown, and on 3 December 1661 was admitted to Doctor's Commons, where he had long had chambers, and as an advocate of the court of arches.

On 20 March 1661 Peirce was returned to parliament for the borough of Maidstone, probably being listed as one of Lord Wharton's friends in the Commons to be managed by Sir Richard Onslow. Very active as a member of the Cavalier Parliament, particularly in its earlier sessions, he sat on 221 committees, of which he chaired seven, and held five tellerships. In the session of May 1661 to May

1662 he was on the committee to consider the Corporations Bill, and took charge in committee of the bill for uniformity of public prayers and the bill to restore the temporal jurisdiction of the clergy. He was on the committee on the pains and penalties of those excepted from the Act of Indemnity, took the chair on a bill for the execution of those under attainder, and was among those nominated to manage a conference on that bill with the Lords. In February 1662 he was teller for those who found James Philipps, member for Cardigan Boroughs, guilty of sitting on a high court of justice which had condemned John Gerard to death for conspiring to assassinate Cromwell. He was chairman of the committee for the bill to repair Dover harbour, and was one of those appointed to prepare a bill to repeal the Triennial Act of 1641. Deputed with two others to ask the king for a rapid distribution of the money intended for loyal and indigent officers, he was a teller against imposing an oath on the contributors to the fund. He was among those who proof-read the text of the revised Book of Common Prayer, and opposed a debate on the amendments made by convocation. He remained active in the session of February to July 1663, and was named to the committee of elections and privileges for the Oxford session of 1665, but his wife's death, and her burial at St Aldates, Oxford, on 18 October 1665, prevented him from taking any further part in its proceedings. In the next session he was appointed to the committees to consider the public accounts bill and the bill against imports from France. He died intestate, and was buried on 10 August 1667 in the Temple Church, London.

N. G. JONES

Sources HoP, Commons, 1660–90 · B. P. Levack, The civil lawyers in England, 1603–1641 (1973) · P. R. Newman, Royalist officers in England and Wales, 1642–1660: a biographical dictionary (1981) · Venn, Alum. Cant. · CSP dom., 1636–41; 1650; 1655; 1660–61; 1667 · JHC, 2 (1640–42) · JHC, 8 (1660–67) · C. A. H. Franklyn, A short genealogical … history of the families of Frankelyn of Kent and Franklyn of Antigua and Jamaica … with … families of Bolton of Sanford and Gray of Billericay (privately printed, London, 1932) · The journals of Sir Simonds D'Ewes from the beginning of the Long Parliament to the opening of the trial of the earl of Strafford, ed. W. Notestein (1923) · Wing, STC · J. J. Howard, Miscellanea genealogica et heraldica, 3rd ser., 2 (1898) · G. D. Squibb, Doctors' Commons: a history of the College of Advocates and Doctors of Law (1977) · F. A. Inderwick and R. A. Roberts, eds., A calendar of the Inner Temple records, 3 (1901) · J. Foster and W. H. Rylands, eds., Grantees of arms named in docquets and patents to the end of the seventeenth century, Harleian Society, 66 (1915) · C. T. Martin, ed., Minutes of parliament of the Middle Temple, 4 vols. (1904–5), vol. 2 · Quarter sessions records for the county of Somerset, 4, Somerset RS, 34 (1919) · H. W. King, 'On the ancestry of Sir Denner Strutt … the cavalier', Transactions of the Essex Archaeological Society, 5 (1873), 147–53 · W. A. Shaw, The knights of England, 2 (1906) · J. L. Chester and G. J. Armytage, eds., Allegations for marriage licences issued from the faculty office of the archbishop of Canterbury at London, 1543 to 1869, Harleian Society, 24 (1886), 77

Peirce, James (1674–1726), Presbyterian minister and religious controversialist, was the younger son of John Peirce (d. c.1676) and his wife, Deborah (d. c.1681). His parents, 'who lived in good fashion', were both members of the Bull Lane Independent Church, Stepney, under Matthew Mead; Peirce was baptized at Bull Lane on 26 July 1674. His parents both died when he was young (Peirce, Second Letter, 29).

Early life After the death of his mother, when he was about seven, Peirce was placed with his older brother and sister under the guardianship of Mead, who took him into his own house and educated him with his sons. He received his grammar education from John Nesbitt and others. Peirce then studied at Utrecht from 1689 until 1692. His thesis, Exercitatio philosophica de homoeomeria anaxagorea (1692), was dedicated to Mead. At Utrecht he studied under Hermann Witsius, Melchior Leydekker, Joannes Georgius Graevius, Johannes Leusden, Gerard de Vries, and Jan Luyts. The celebrated orientalist Adrian Reland, a fellow student, was a friend until his death in 1718. He then studied at Leiden, where he attended the lectures of Jacobus Perizonius and Gerard Noodt, but he also heard Jacobus Gronovius, Johannes Marck, and Friedrich Spanheim. He was later to correspond with a number of these professors.

On returning to England in 1695, Peirce lived with his relations in London for a while, before studying privately at the Bodleian Library, Oxford. On returning to London he was admitted a member of Mead's church (11 February 1697). For two years he preached the evening lecture at Miles Lane Congregational Church, where Matthew Clarke (1664–1726) was minister. Avoiding denominational disputes, he became well regarded by the leading Presbyterian ministers in London. They persuaded him to become minister of the Green Street Meeting in Cambridge, a mixed congregation of Presbyterians and Independents, in succession to Thomas Taylor, who had died in November 1700. They themselves contributed 'liberally for my encouragement there' (Peirce, Second Letter, 31). He was ordained by four Presbyterian ministers, Matthew Sylvester, John Woodhouse, John Shower, and Christopher Taylor. He must still have ranked as an Independent, for he was made a trustee of the Hog Hill Meeting on 23 January 1702. At Cambridge his scholarship appears to have made him acceptable to members of the university, and he formed a close friendship with William Whiston, who thought him 'the most learned of all the dissenting teachers that I have known' (Memoirs of the Life and Writings, 121). During this period he read and studied much, often sitting in his study from nine at night until four or five the following morning.

Advocacy of dissent Peirce's removal to the major Presbyterian congregation at Toomer's Court, Newbury, Berkshire, probably coincided with the publication at the end of 1706 of his first major controversial work: his defence of the principles of dissent from the attack made by Edward Wells, rector of Cotesbach, Leicestershire, upon separation from the Church of England. Peirce's work Remarks on Dr Wells his Letter to Mr Peter Dowley, originally published anonymously, was well received by dissenters. Wells arranged for a copy of his reply to be sent to Peirce, 'for your Name and Abode, tho' Not Published by you in Print, yet is Sufficiently Published by your Friends and Acquaintance in Discourse' (Wells, 10). Peirce's Remarks on

Dr Wells his Letter, in answer to the doctor's *Letter from a Minister of the Church of England to Mr Peter Dowley* (1706) and *Theses Against the Validity of Presbyterian Ordination* (1707), appeared in eight parts between 1706 and 1707 (3rd edn., 1711). Peirce's growing reputation among dissenters was enhanced by his *Some Considerations on the Sixth Chapter* (1708) in answer to Thomas Bennet's *An Abridgment of the London Cases* (1700) on the lawfulness of imposed ceremonies, in particular the use of the sign of the cross in baptism. Wells was provoked to publish an *Answer to Mr Peirce's Post-Script at the End of his Considerations of the Sixth Chapter* (1708). It was the publication of the *Vindicae fratrum dissentientium* (1710) in reply to William Nicholls's *Defensio ecclesiae Anglicanae* (1707) that brought Peirce into national prominence as a writer in defence of the principles of dissent. Both works were published in Latin with the intention of influencing foreign protestants. After Nicholls published an English translation, *A Defence of the Doctrine and Discipline of the Church of England* (1715), Peirce translated his own work, with some major alterations, as *A Vindication of the Dissenters* (1718).

In 1713, 'without the least seeking on my part', Peirce was unanimously chosen as one of the ministers of James's Meeting, Exeter, in the place of George Trosse, who had died in January 1713 (Peirce, *Western Inquisition*, 10). Peirce had great difficulties with the invitation. His congregation at Newbury was very unwilling to release him, not least because they feared his removal would heighten the divisions among the dissenters in the town. Anxious to avoid any personal blame, Peirce resolved to accept the decision of others. Personally, he considered the state of his health to be the main factor, though he admitted that he had kept too many late hours studying. He also acknowledged that there were greater opportunities at Exeter. Although the Newbury congregation promised to subscribe for an assistant, he feared they would soon grow weary once the danger had passed. Nevertheless, in early March the Exeter dissenters believed that he had resolved to stay. They therefore appealed to the Exeter assembly of dissenting ministers in Devon and Cornwall for its support. Despite strong pleading by the Newbury congregation, the assembly, wishing to oblige the Exeter dissenters, eventually agreed to write to Peirce urging him to accept the invitation, for the sake of his health and because 'this post is of the utmost consequence to religion in these two counties' (Brockett, *Exeter Assembly*, 97). Dr Edmund Calamy, the nonconformist biographer and historian, witnessed the efforts of the Exeter dissenters to secure Peirce. 'Never before did I see such earnestness in any people for a minister's coming among them. They talked as if they were quite undone, if he did not accept their call. … They ran to such a height' he could not help thinking that their 'peculiar eagerness and impetuosity … boded very ill' (Calamy, 2.263–4).

At first Peirce found great acceptance and 'an extraordinary respect was paid him, … he was looked upon as the first man of the party' ('Memoirs of himself', 329). He soon displayed his ability as a controversialist. After Benjamin

Read, a ministerial candidate, conformed and was persuaded that his original baptism was invalid, Peirce derided his rebaptism in *A Caveat Against the New Sect of Anabaptists* (1714). At a time when dissent was under serious attack from high-churchmen, he published other works in defence of Presbyterian ordination. The controversy over the doctrine of the Trinity proved far more damaging to dissent. Peirce himself had held the orthodox position when he read William Whiston's *Essay on the Revelation of St John* (1706) in manuscript in 1706. On hearing of Whiston's change of views, he wrote to him from Newbury (10 July 1708) expressing amazement that he should 'fall in with the unitarians', and referring to the 'very melancholy instance' of Thomas Emlyn, who had been imprisoned for his Unitarian views. Peirce was, however, persuaded to study the writings of the early fathers of the church, after which he found himself unable to resolve the conflicting arguments over the Trinity. The difficulties of the question impressed him greatly. As a result of his studies, Peirce came to 'despair of getting clear notions of the Trinity' which 'render'd me more averse to the study of the controversy' (Peirce, *Western Inquisition*, 8). He therefore did not read Whiston's *Primitive Christianity Reviv'd* (1711–12) and more importantly Samuel Clarke's *Scripture Doctrine of the Trinity* (1712) until 1713, moved by Whiston's importuning. He came to realize that the theology in which he had been bred was really Sabellian. Nevertheless, he became convinced that error on this question was not fundamental, and that 'the safest way' was to keep closely to scripture. He had therefore already dropped the common form of the doxology before going to Exeter. Whiston claimed him as a Unitarian, but while he held (with Clarke) that the Son was subordinate, he denied holding Arian beliefs. His interpretation of scripture was critical to a fault rather than positively heterodox.

Controversy over doctrine The controversy which blasted Peirce's reputation and destroyed the doctrinal accord of Old Dissent began in November 1716, when the Arian opinions of a small group of younger ministers became public as a result of the indiscretion of Hubert Stogdon, who expressed his opinions freely in private conversation with the orthodox John Lavington. Lavington, Peirce's young colleague at Exeter, chose to publish the conversation, 'and the town presently rang of it'. On 17 May 1717 Henry Atkins of Puddington, when giving the lecture at James's Meeting for Peirce, who was in London, chose to preach on the Trinity, and thus brought the controversy into the open. According to Peirce, Atkins accused some of his hearers of 'damnable heresies'. Greatly offended, Peirce tried to persuade his colleagues to have Atkins excluded from their pulpit, but they refused. By request Peirce preached on 2 June on the atonement, but his attempts by scholarly means to reconcile the new teaching with orthodoxy failed to prevent the growing divisions. About a week later John Ball, the minister at Honiton, met Peirce and told him forcefully that 'people charg'd all the business upon me' and that he had the power to prevent Stogdon from spreading his opinions. Peirce denied that anyone had been 'influenc'd by me to alter his opinion about the Trinity' (Peirce, *Western Inquisition*, 13, 30–31).

Fearful of divisions at the next Exeter assembly, Peirce joined with Joseph Hallett (1656–1722) and John Withers on 15 July in giving Stogdon a testimonial as to his conversation and behaviour (but nothing about his opinions), and at the assembly in September he piloted John Fox, another of the younger heterodox ministers, through his examination for a licence to preach, refusing to require any 'explications' of doctrinal terms. The period of comparative calm which followed Stogdon's removal to Somerset ended as a result of Peirce's Christmas-week lecture which renewed doubts about his doctrinal soundness. In January 1718 the Committee of Thirteen, a body of thirteen lay trustees who managed the affairs of the Exeter dissenters, asked each of the four ministers to preach 'in defence of the eternal deity of Jesus Christ'. Peirce complied, and 'matters so much cooled' that the controversy was not mentioned at the May assembly. Lavington assured Peirce 'that we were now quiet' (Peirce, *Western Inquisition*, 65, 67–8). From early July Peirce was absent for six Sundays in London as was his custom, but on his return he found the controversy had been renewed.

Alarmed at news of Stogdon's ordination and the apparent falling away of the younger ministers from orthodoxy, John Walrond wrote to William Tong, one of the leading London ministers, who called an informal meeting of Presbyterian and Independent ministers on 25 August. Their advice was not to suspect anyone without good reason, but to warn the people against any minister who should be in error. Walrond announced his determination to call for a declaration of faith concerning the Trinity at the assembly to clear the ministers of the suspicion of Arianism. Attempts were made to avoid open disputes, and Peirce and Withers accepted Walrond's invitation to meet at his house with John Ball, but many country ministers were far less charitable. On the second day of the assembly, Ball proposed that the ministers present made a declaration on the Trinity. After a debate, where feelings ran high and which the moderator had difficulty controlling, a vote decided in favour of the declaration. There was further debate over the form of words. Hallett declared his beliefs in scriptural terms, Withers was scrupulously orthodox but refused the suggested form of words, but Peirce for the first time openly declared his belief in the subordination of Christ. Both sides issued a series of pamphlets. In November the Committee of Thirteen, though they had no authority to demand it, sought assurances from the four Exeter ministers on the disputed doctrine, but received satisfaction only from Lavington; Peirce expressly declared for the subordination of Christ. The committee wrote to the London ministers on 22 November seeking advice, but the latter were reluctant to become involved in so difficult an issue and delayed their answer until 6 January 1719, when they declined to 'interpose', advising the committee to consult with local ministers. Seven ministers in the neighbourhood, including Ball and Walrond, were invited to give advice, and they met in Exeter on 19 January, and the following day visited Peirce, Hallett, and Withers. The seven ministers agreed a resolution that there were errors of doctrine and congregations should withdraw from ministers who held them, but desired a fortnight in which to consult ministers in London, Devon, and Somerset. Peirce had in the meantime written to his friends in London, including John Shute Barrington, a fellow student at Leiden, who was managing the parliamentary campaign for the repeal of the Occasional Conformity and Schism acts. Because the dispute at Exeter was being used by opponents of repeal, Barrington sought to compose the differences and advised the Committee of Three Denominations (of Presbyterians, Independents, and Baptists) that any doctrinal test should be scriptural only. The three denominations decided to consult the London ministers, which by opening the dispute to public debate destroyed the doctrinal accord of Old Dissent. The London ministers met at Salters' Hall on 19 and 20 February and 3 March, and divided almost equally, one advising subscription to the Trinity, the other against subscription on principle.

Ejection In both cases the advice arrived too late to influence the outcome in Exeter. After waiting four weeks, the seven ministers met again on 4 March and sent their original resolution to the Committee of Thirteen. On 5 March the committee asked the Exeter ministers to subscribe to the Trinity. Peirce and Hallett refused. Withers's initial declaration was not accepted, but he subsequently subscribed and escaped ejection. Without giving notice, the trustees of James's Meeting locked the doors against Peirce on 6 March. A few days later the trustees of the three meeting-houses met and decided to close them to Peirce and Hallett. On the Sunday following his ejection, Peirce preached in a private house to an estimated 300 people on 'the evil and cure of divisions', which was later published. The following year his supporters built the Mint Meeting, appointing Hallett joint minister with him. In May 1719 the Exeter assembly called for a subscription from its members. Peirce with eighteen others declined and seceded, issuing a paper on 6 May denying the charge of Arianism and making a confession in scriptural terms.

According to Fox, Peirce never rose above the mortification inflicted upon him by his summary ejection, and he wrote numerous pamphlets in self-justification. Influential friends, such as Peter King, stood by him, but he felt deeply the loss of leadership. He moved to a country house at St Leonard's parish, in the suburbs of Exeter. The last four years of his life were the time of 'his greatest Usefulness' employed in the study of scriptures (Hallett, *Sermon*, 18). His paraphrases and notes on the epistles to the Colossians and Philippians after the manner of John Locke were published in 1725, and on that to the Hebrews—after Joseph (III) Hallett (1691–1744) had completed the final three chapters—in 1727 following his death. The latter was published in Latin in 1747 by J. D. Michaelis, the German biblical critic, who regarded Peirce's scholarship highly.

Death After a period of illness Peirce broke a blood-vessel in his lungs, lingered a few days in great composure, and died in St Leonard's parish, Exeter, on 10 March 1726. In his will he attested to his belief in 'one God, the God and Father of our Lord Jesus Christ' and declared that 'my Conscience reproaches me not for the part I have acted in the Controversy concerning the Trinity' (Hallett, *Sermon*, 17). He was buried in the churchyard of St Leonard's. Benjamin Avery published a long Latin inscription which was intended for Peirce's tombstone. The cutting of it was nearly finished when the rector, Richard Gay, intervened with a prohibition. Gay also objected to an alternative, 'Here lies the reverend, learned and pious Mr James Peirce': Peirce could not be reverend since he was not lawfully ordained, nor pious because he taught errors. The eventual inscription was 'Mr James Peirce's Tomb, 1726'. His funeral sermon was preached by Joseph (III) Hallett, who had followed his father as Peirce's colleague. Thomas Emlyn was invited to succeed him, but refused. Peirce seems to have been a reserved man with the manners of a gentleman, yet humorous and even jocose with friends. His preaching was scholarly rather than inspired. Yet 'he was, without doubt, a man of great parts and learning, and as such, made a much greater figure among the Dissenters than any among them for many years before him' ('Memoirs of himself', 329).   DAVID L. WYKES

Sources J. Peirce, *A second letter to Mr Eveleigh, in answer to his sober reply, &c. To which is added a confutation of a slanderous report* (1719), 29–32 · J. Peirce, *The western inquisition, or, A relation of the controversy … among the dissenters in the west of England* (1720) · A. Brockett, *Nonconformity in Exeter, 1650–1875* (1962), 74–95 · A. Brockett, ed., *The Exeter assembly: the minutes of the assemblies of the United Brethren of Devon and Cornwall, 1691–1717*, Devon and Cornwall RS, new ser., 6 (1963), 95–7, 97–8, 101–2 · 'Memoirs of himself, by John Fox … with biographical sketches of some of his contemporaries; and some unpublished letters [pts 2, 5]', *Monthly Repository*, 16 (1821), 193–200, esp. 197–9; 325–31, esp. 329–31 · 'Memoirs of himself, by Mr John Fox … with biographical sketches of some of his contemporaries; and some unpublished letters [pt 11]', *Monthly Repository*, 16 (1821), 721–7, esp. 723 · 'The Fox memoirs: worthies of Devon', *Devonshire Association*, 28 (1896), 144–7, 159–62 · J. Hallet, *A sermon preach'd in Exeter … upon … the death of the Reverend J. Peirce*, 2nd edn (1726) · B. Avery, 'Preface', in J. Peirce, *Fifteen sermons on several occasions, eight of which were never before printed, to which is added A scripture catechism, or, The principles of the Christian religion laid down in the words of the Bible* (1728) · J. Murch, *A history of the Presbyterian and General Baptist churches in the west of England* (1835), 421ff. · *Memoirs of the life and writings of William Whiston*, 2nd edn (1753), 121–2, 124–8 · [E. Wells], *Dr Wells's examination of the remarks on his letters to Mr Peter Dowley* (1706) · 'A booke for church affaires', Records of the Stepney Meeting House, London Borough of Tower Hamlets Archives, TH/8337/1, fol. 9v · J. Peirce, corresp., 1708–24, DWL, Congregational Library, MS I.b.13 · C. S. Kenny, 'A forgotten Cambridge meeting-house', *Transactions of the Congregational Historical Society*, 4 (1909–10), 225 · [J. Hallett], *The truth and importance of the scripture-doctrine of the Trinity … to which is added, a complete, chronological catalogue of Mr Peirce's writings* (1736) · E. Calamy, *An historical account of my own life, with some reflections on the times I have lived in, 1671–1731*, ed. J. T. Rutt, 2 vols. (1829) · will of John Peirce, 4 April 1674, PRO, PROB 11/351, sig. 70 · will of Deborah Peirce, 19 May 1681, PRO, PROB 11/367, sig. 97 · will of James Peirce, 22 Sept 1721, PROB 11/611, sig. 189 · register (baptism), Bull Lane Independent Church, Stepney, PRO, RG4/4414, 26 July 1674 · J. Peirce, pamphlets, 3 vols., JRL, Z632–34 [bound for presentation to Joseph (II) Hallett]

Archives DWL, Congregational Library, corresp., MS I.b.13 | BL, letters of scholars addressed to Professor John Ward, Gresham College, Add. MSS 6211, fols. 2r, 38r, 40r, 40v, 42r; 6212, fol. 4r; 6213, fol. 55r; 6224, fols. 47r, 49r, 51r; 6226, fol. 4v

Peirce [Pierce], **Robert** (*bap.* 1622, *d.* 1710), physician, the only son of the Revd Robert Pierce (1592–1641), rector of Combe Hay, Somerset, and his wife, Elizabeth (1597–1657), daughter of Chiddiock Tutt of Salisbury, was born at Combe Hay and baptized there on 6 March 1622. After attending King Edward's School, Bath, he was sent to Winchester College, and from there to Lincoln College, Oxford, where he matriculated on 26 October 1638. He graduated BA on 15 June 1642, MA and MB on 21 October 1650, and MD on 12 September 1661. His boyhood and youth were sickly: at ten he had general dropsy, at twelve smallpox, at fourteen tertian ague, and at twenty-one measles with profuse bleeding from the nose. In 1651 Peirce married Anna (1621–1688), daughter of David Trym (or Tryme) of Wookey, Somerset. They had two sons and two daughters. The first child, Elizabeth, died aged nineteen years. The second, Robert, died aged one year. The third, Mary, survived twenty-three years and produced for her parents a grandson, Pierce A'Court. Their fourth child, Charles, died aged four years.

After a short residence in Bristol Peirce settled in practice near the Somerset levels, where in 1652 he became ill again, this time with a 'quartan ague' (probably malaria, which was endemic in this area at that time). This weakened him so much that he decided to leave the district. His fellow collegian, Christopher Bennet, advised him to try London; but, though there were then three physicians in full practice at Bath, Peirce decided to settle there in 1653, and built up a 'riding practice', making visits to patients living between 10 and 30 miles from the city. On 15 April 1660 he was elected to the office of physician to poor strangers. As the older physicians died, Peirce established himself as a specialist in Bath mineral water treatment, taking patients of distinction to reside with him in the Abbey House, which he rented as a private lodging. Richard Talbot, earl of Tyrconnell, stayed with him for five weeks from April 1686, and was given Quercetanus's tartar pills for several nights, followed by two quarts of the King's Bath Water in the morning for several days, as severe measures were needed to get him fit within two or three months, so that he could take up his post in Ireland. The duke of Hamilton, the duchess of Ormond, the marchioness of Antrim, Lord Stafford, and General Talmash or Tollemache, were among Peirce's patients. He also cured Captain Harrison, son-in-law of Bishop Jeremy Taylor, of lead palsy. Sir Charles Scarborough, Sir William Wetherby, Sir John Micklethwaite, Phineas Fowke, Gideon Harvey, Richard Lower, Thomas Short, and many other famous physicians sent patients to him.

In 1689 Peirce visited London, and, having been nominated in James II's new charter to the Royal College of Physicians, was admitted a fellow on 19 March 1689. He had earned this honour by many original observations, which he eventually published in 1697 in his *Bath Memoirs*. He is probably the first English writer to note the now well-known occurrence of acute rheumatism as a sequel to scarlet fever; and his account of Major Arnot's case, in which muscular feebleness of the arm followed the constant carrying of a heavy falcon on one fist, is the first suggestion of the condition later described as 'repetitive strain syndrome'. He carried out post-mortem examinations on some patients, one of which was on the body of Sir Robert Craven, who had a mediastinal tumour; and another on a man with osteomyelitis of the hip. These original observations entitle him to a high place among English physicians. Peirce died in Bath in June 1710 and was buried in Bath Abbey.

NORMAN MOORE, rev. ROGER ROLLS

Sources Foster, *Alum. Oxon.* · E. Dwelly, ed., *Bishop's transcripts at Wells*, 1 (1913) · K. Symons, *The grammar school of King Edward VI, Bath* (1934) · F. Brown, ed., *Abstracts of Somersetshire wills*, 5 (privately printed, London, 1890), 45 · A. J. Jewers, ed., *The registers of the abbey church of SS Peter and Paul, Bath*, 2, Harleian Society, Register Section, 28 (1901) · R. Peirce, *Bath memoirs, or, Observations in three and forty years practice at the Bath* (1697) · R. Peirce, *History and memoirs of the Bath* (1713) · T. S. Holmes, *The history of the parish and manor of Wookey* (privately printed, Bristol, [1885]) · A. B. Connor, *Monumental brasses in Somerset* (1970)

Peirse, **Sir Richard Edmund Charles** (1892–1970), air force officer, was born at 57 Belvedere Road, Penge, Lewisham, London, on 30 September 1892, the only son (there were two daughters) of Admiral Sir Richard Henry Peirse (1860–1940) and his wife, Blanche Melville Wemyss-Whittaker. He was educated at Monkton Combe School and then HMS *Conway*, before attending King's College, London. During 1913 he learned to fly at Brooklands, and after gaining his pilot's certificate was commissioned as a sub-lieutenant in the Royal Naval Reserve, attached to the Royal Flying Corps's naval wing (later to become the Royal Naval Air Service).

During the First World War, Peirse served on the western front and took part in operations against German submarine bases at Ostend and Zeebrugge, for which he received the DSO; he was promoted flight commander in May 1915. On 18 August 1915, while on leave, he married Mary Joyce, the daughter of Armitage Ledgard, gentleman, of the Manor House, Thorner, Yorkshire. In June 1916 he was promoted to command a squadron, after which he returned to England for a tour of duty away from the front line. He was then sent to Dover to command the naval air units there, and completed his war service in Italy and the Adriatic. Once hostilities had ceased Peirse accepted, in August 1919, a permanent commission as squadron leader in the recently formed Royal Air Force.

Peirse's RAF career began well. After promotion to wing commander in January 1922, he was sent as a student on the first course at the RAF Staff College at Andover, where he studied alongside a number of colleagues who were to become prominent during the Second World War. After completing the course, in April 1923 he was posted to command the base at Gosport, then in 1926 he took up staff duties at the Air Ministry. He did not remain long at the Air Ministry, instead becoming a student once again, this time at the newly established Imperial Defence College from January 1927 until February 1928, when he was posted to the Middle East. There he spent three years on staff duties and commanding the station at Heliopolis. Promoted group captain in July 1929, he returned to Britain at the end of 1930 to serve as deputy director of operations and intelligence at the Air Ministry. In 1933 he was again in the Middle East, as air officer commanding Palestine and Transjordan. Promotions to air commodore (July 1933) and air vice-marshal (January 1936) followed, along with his creation as CB (1936). Appointment in January 1937 as director of operations and intelligence and deputy chief of the air staff took him back to Britain.

Peirse remained at the Air Ministry for the next three years. In October 1939 he became an additional member of the Air Council and was promoted to the rank of acting air marshal. The following year saw a change in the title and scope of his position, when in April 1940 he became vice-chief of the air staff. His tenure in this post ended six months later, when he was given the considerable challenge of taking over as air officer commanding-in-chief of Bomber Command.

Peirse took up his new post on 25 October 1940. Until September the RAF had concentrated upon the defence of the United Kingdom, with Bomber Command deployed in actions to repel any German invasion. On 30 September Churchill and the chiefs of staff decreed that the invasion threat had reduced, and Bomber Command turned its attentions to carrying the war to the German homeland. Peirse arrived as the new policy was being formulated, and found that his command was being asked to undertake roles that it was not, in his opinion, yet suited to fulfil. Priority was assigned to oil-related targets and then to the disruption of German transportation, but when weather conditions were unfavourable attacks were to be directed against Berlin or other central towns, in an attempt to target civilian morale in industrial centres. This latter requirement was to mark the move towards the controversial policy known as 'area bombing', although this was not articulated at the time.

Peirse was unlucky in that, although he took command during a period when bombing became the focus of British offensive operations, there were considerable demands upon resources. Bomber Command could not obtain all the equipment it required to meet expectations of what bombing could achieve. This was demonstrated most clearly in a report by D. M. Butt of the war cabinet secretariat, delivered to Peirse on 18 August 1941. Butt's studies revealed that only some 20 per cent of the bomber force was getting its bombs within 5 miles of the designated targets. Many other aircraft were failing to drop their bomb loads even within an area 75 square miles surrounding the intended targets. It was appreciated that these disappointing results could not be blamed upon Peirse's leadership; they were the consequence of inadequate training and navigation equipment. It also marked the end of Bomber Command's efforts at selective attacks on industry and completed the shift of emphasis to area bombing.

To achieve this it was suggested that the destruction of enemy cities could be achieved by dropping between

25,000 and 30,000 incendiary bombs, starting large con-flagrations which would be difficult for the German fire services to put out. This demanded sufficient concentration of the bombing force, so as to overwhelm the civil defences. Peirse expressed scepticism that his force could achieve this. His attitude seemed to be confirmed by events on 7 November 1941. During a series of attacks against Berlin, Mannheim, and targets in the Ruhr valley, casualties among the bombing force were heavy, causing concern at the highest level of government. This resulted in a directive on 13 November to conserve Bomber Command's forces, and had unfortunate consequences for Peirse. It initially appeared that poor weather forecasting had been the major cause of the losses, but further study appeared to suggest that the forecasts had been accurate and their significance not appreciated. Portal, the chief of air staff, considered that Pierse had made an error of judgement. Peirse disagreed, noting that many of the crews sent out were inexperienced, though this in itself could be interpreted as a failure by him to ensure that adequate training was provided. Confidence in him waned, which, coupled with the disappointing results of the bombing to date, led to the decision, taken after consultation between Portal and Churchill on 4 January 1942, to give Peirse a new command in the Far East. He was replaced at Bomber Command by Arthur Harris.

On 8 January 1942 Peirse left Bomber Command to prepare for his journey to the Far East. He arrived at a disastrous time, as the Japanese swept all before them in the opening phases of the Pacific war. Rather than becoming commander of allied air forces in the American-British-Dutch-Australian command, he found himself appointed in March 1942 air officer commanding-in-chief in India. RAF forces in the area were woefully under-equipped, and he began the process of building up a potent air force. He was promoted air chief marshal in August 1942, and from 1943 was an integral part of the new south-east Asia command headed by Lord Louis Mountbatten.

In November 1943 Peirse took command of all the allied air forces, much to the pleasure of Mountbatten, who found him an excellent subordinate, always ready to pursue confident policies. Mountbatten was aware of rumours concerning a developing relationship between Peirse and Jessie, Lady Auchinleck (b. 1899/1900), wife of Sir Claude Auchinleck, commander-in-chief, India. This did not at first affect Mountbatten's confidence in Peirse, who oversaw the successful transition of the RAF in south-east Asia from an under-equipped, ill-prepared force into a major factor in the offensive operations of 1944. But in April 1944 Portal referred to the risk of scandal when he asked Mountbatten whether he required a replacement for Peirse. Although Mountbatten was then content to retain him, by November the relationship was widely known and began to undermine Peirse's authority. It was time for him to be replaced. Even though his successor, Sir Trafford Leigh-Mallory, was killed in an air crash, Peirse's tenure was not extended. On 28 November 1944 he left for England, accompanied by Lady Auchinleck. He was quietly retired from service shortly afterwards, in May 1945.

Peirse divorced his first wife, with whom he had a daughter and a son (Air Vice-Marshal Sir Richard Peirse), and married Lady Auchinleck, who by then was also divorced and had changed her name by deed poll to Jessie Stewart Peirse, at Poole register office on 3 August 1946. He was appointed KCB in 1940. He died at Princess Mary's RAF Hospital, Wendover, Buckinghamshire, on 5 August 1970.   DAVID JORDAN

Sources *The Times* (6 Aug 1970) · C. Webster and N. Frankland, *The strategic air offensive against Germany*, 1 (1961) · H. Probert, *The forgotten air force: the Royal Air Force in the war against Japan, 1941–1945* (1995) · D. Richards, *The hardest victory: RAF bomber command in the Second World War* (1994) · P. Warner, *Auchinleck: the lonely soldier* (1981) · b. cert. · m. certs. · d. cert.
Archives Royal Air Force Museum, Hendon, papers
Likenesses photographs, repro. in Probert, *Forgotten air force*
Wealth at death £8953: probate, 8 Dec 1970, *CGPLA Eng. & Wales*

Peirson, Francis (1757–1781), army officer, was born in early January 1757, the eldest son of Francis Peirson of Mowthorpe Grange in the East Riding of Yorkshire. He was educated at Warrington Academy before entering the army, at the age of fifteen, on 16 July 1772. He rose to the rank of major in August 1779, when he was appointed to the 95th regiment, which in June 1780 sailed for Jersey. At this period the Channel Islands were subjected to the constant danger of attacks from the French, who made several unsuccessful attempts to gain possession. By far the most important of these raids was that of 6 January 1781, known as the battle of Jersey, when the French, under the baron de Rullecourt, landed under cover of night and took possession of the town of St Helier, making the lieutenant-governor, Major Moses Corbet, a prisoner in his bed. Under these circumstances, the colonel and lieutenant-colonel being absent from the island, command of the troops devolved upon the youthful Peirson. Rullecourt succeeded in inducing Corbet to sign a capitulation, and the island's Elizabeth Castle was summoned to surrender, but the officer in command refused to obey the order. Meanwhile the regular troops and the island militia, under the command of Major Peirson, advanced in two divisions towards St Helier's Royal Square, then the market place, where a vigorous engagement took place, resulting in heavy French casualties. Peirson's victory was complete but was gained at a heavy price, for at the moment of victory he was shot through the heart and fell dead in the arms of his grenadiers. Rullecourt himself was mortally wounded, and most of the French soldiers were taken prisoner. Peirson, who was then just twenty-four, was interred on 10 January in the parish church of St Helier with all the honours of war and in the presence of the states of the island, who erected a monument to his memory. The government provided Peirson's father with a pension of £250 per annum, while smaller sums were granted to his three remaining sisters. His gallantry was the subject of John Singleton Copley's painting *The Death of Major Peirson* and was commemorated by the naming of Peirson Place in St Helier.   E. T. NICOLLE, *rev.* PHILIP CARTER

Sources G. R. Balleine, *A biographical dictionary of Jersey*, [1] [1948] · R. Mayne, *The battle of Jersey* (1981)
Likenesses R. Marcurad, stipple, pubd 1781 (after Hays), NPG · J. S. Copley, drawing, *c*.1783, Tate collection · J. S. Copley, group portrait, oils, *c*.1783 (*The death of Major Peirson, 6 Jan 1781*), Tate collection

Peisley [*married name* Neale], **Mary** (1718–1757), Quaker minister, was born on 19 January 1718 at Ballymore, co. Kildare, the eldest of the three children of Peter Peisley (1694–1754), a farmer of nearby Baltiboys, co. Wicklow, and his first wife, Rachel Burton, a native of Mannin, co. Tipperary, who died when Mary was a child. The family moved in 1723 to the Queen's county and occupied a 300 acre farm at Paddock, near Mountrath, where Peter married in 1727, as his second wife, Anna Pim (1697–1768) of Lacka, with whom he had six further children. Their modest cottage home remained Mary's base for the rest of her life.

The Peisley family had strong links with the pioneering days of Quakerism. Mary's great-grandfather Peter Peisley (1624–1689), a native of Ascot under Wychwood in Oxfordshire, was involved in a dispute over tithe payments in 1649, even before Quakerism reached Ascot, and later moved to Ireland; he settled in co. Wicklow, first at Poolanarrick, where a Quaker meeting was established on his farm in 1668, and secondly at Baltiboys, where another early Quaker meeting was established. His descendants had maintained the Quaker testimonies in their original purity, and in Mary's day, when Irish Quakers were becoming more worldly, the Peisleys continued to live plainly and visitors to Paddock were delighted by the family's 'instructive conversation' (*Some Account*, 6).

Mary, who lacked 'the privilege of a liberal education', found employment in various affluent households (*Some Account*, 308). Aged twenty-six, and following a near fatal riding accident, she was converted to the religious life, and started to speak in Quaker meetings in 1744. Thereafter she embarked on a programme of self-denial and of purification through suffering, preaching against the dangers of wealth and the decline in Quaker spirituality, and seeing herself as a 'sharp threshing instrument' (ibid., 314), and as a 'pipe' through which God's message might be channelled (ibid., 314).

Following a short Irish tour in 1746 with the Limerick Quaker Elizabeth Tomey, Mary paid a long religious visit to England (1748–50), accompanied initially by Elizabeth Hutchinson, and later by Mary Weston and others. Guided and fortified by her faith she braved physical danger and hardship, covering 5000 miles on horseback in 29 months and attending 525 meetings. Her preaching was succinct and powerful, and her prophesyings remarkable when 'ministering to the state' (*Some Account*, 261) of individuals, whether in public or at private family opportunities. Mary's impact as a preacher, recorded in a verse 'To M.P. a Native of Ireland' (*GM*, 1st ser., 20, 1750, 86), was no doubt enhanced by her physical presence 'being near 6 foot' (ibid.). The rigours of this trip seriously affected her health. Another short Irish tour followed in 1751 and, while visiting Cork, her then companion, Catherine

Payton, was instrumental in converting Samuel *Neale (1729–1792), a paper manufacturer and Mary's future husband, to the religious life. He eventually became a Quaker minister.

Mary's final and most important religious journey, to America (1753–6), was again undertaken with Catherine Payton; before leaving England they had both been part of a group of six women who proposed to the London yearly meeting that a separate yearly meeting of women Friends should be established (this was not granted until 1784). Mary and Catherine landed at Charles Town, South Carolina, on 26 December 1753 and, travelling often through thinly inhabited country, braving dangerous creeks, swamps, and wild animals, they covered 8000 miles on horseback before they arrived back in Dublin on 19 July 1756. They laboured in the Carolinas, Virginia, Maryland, New England, and Pennsylvania. Everywhere they found 'the discipline sadly let fall' (*Some Account*, 343) and they were among the first to preach reform. Mary opposed Friends' ownership of slaves and pointedly held meetings with black people. She urged all Friends to avoid worldliness, particularly in politics, and complained about some Friends' deistical beliefs. She returned home with a certificate of approbation from American Friends, recording how 'acceptable and serviceable her labours had been amongst them'.

Aged thirty-nine, Mary married Samuel Neale at Mountrath on 17 March 1757, but she died unexpectedly, of 'cholic', three days later at Paddock; her body was interred locally, at the Quaker burial-ground, Mountrath, on 24 March.   PETER LAMB

Sources *Some account of the lives and religious labours of Samuel Neale and Mary Neale, formerly Mary Peisley, both of Ireland*, enlarged edn (1845) · *Memoirs of the life of Catherine Phillips* (1797) · T. Wight and J. Rutty, *A history of the rise and progress of the people called Quakers in Ireland* (1751) · A. J. Worrall, *Quakers in the colonial northeast* (1980) · M. H. Bacon, 'An international sisterhood: 18th century Quaker women in overseas ministry', *Friends Quarterly*, 28/5 (1995), 193–206 · R. M. Jones, *The later periods of Quakerism*, 2 vols. (1921) · R. S. Harrison, *A biographical dictionary of Irish Quakers* (1997) · H. Cairns, unpublished research on the Peisley family, priv. coll. · M. Grubb, *Quakers observed in prose and verse: an anthology, 1656–1986* (1999)

Pelagius (*fl. c*.390–418), theologian, is said by his contemporaries of the years about 400, such as Augustine of Hippo, Prosper of Aquitaine, Marius Mercator, and Paul Orosius, to have been of British origin. Beyond that there is no information, and attempts to interpret his name as a Hellenization of the Welsh 'Morgan' or the Irish 'Muirchu' represent philological wishful thinking. The dates of his birth and death are unknown. According to Augustine, Pelagius had long resided at Rome, before he emerged into disastrous prominence. He was a layman, and although sometimes called a monk is not known to have had any connection with a religious community. His concerns were theological, together with the spiritual direction of his patrons among the Christian Roman aristocracy. His interests included biblical commentary and theological doctrine as well as moral and ascetic theology. He was particularly concerned to vindicate Christian asceticism against any imputation of Manichaeism and to prove that a sinless life is possible for a practising Christian. Accordingly, he laid stress upon the freedom of will enjoyed by the baptized believer once the guilt of sin has been remitted in baptism. It was in this context that the denial of any transmission of original sin, a doctrine apparently learned from Rufinus the Syrian (not to be confused with Rufinus of Aquileia, the translator of Origen and Eusebius of Caesarea), who resided at Rome in the reign of Pope Anastasius (399–401), constituted an essential element in Pelagius's doctrine. With this view—a foundation article of belief for any Pelagian—went an understanding of grace (*gratia*) as being essentially a divine illumination which, following the remission of sins in baptism, enables the Christian to see what is right and then to do it by the power of his divinely created nature. Such a conception is utterly different from that of Pelagius's principal adversary, Augustine of Hippo, for whom grace was the divine aid necessary to perform every righteous action—a belief which seemed to Pelagius to remove any element of human initiative in good works. Hence his furious outburst at Rome about 405 when he heard Augustine's famous prayer from the *Confessions* quoted: 'Give what You command and command what You will' and declared that he could not endure such sentiments (Augustine, 'De dono perseverantiae', 20, 53).

Among Pelagius's Roman disciples was Caelestius, an aristocrat converted from a legal career to asceticism, a more forceful personality than Pelagius, and the real apostle of the so-called Pelagian movement. In 409, when Rome was menaced by Alaric the Goth, Pelagius and Caelestius abandoned the city and went to north Africa. Pelagius, having missed encountering Augustine, soon departed for Palestine, where many upper-class Romans had fled after the sack of Rome in 410. Caelestius remained behind, to proclaim Rufinus the Syrian's denial of the doctrine of original sin, for which he was excommunicated by a Carthaginian council in 411. He left Africa and went to Antioch, where he was subsequently ordained to the priesthood. However, Caelestius's theology remained influential and Augustine began to write and preach against it, though he had, as yet, avoided any breach with Pelagius, even sending him, in 413, a friendly letter, which Pelagius subsequently employed as proof of his own orthodoxy.

In Palestine, Pelagius was amicably received by Bishop John of Jerusalem and bitterly opposed by St Jerome, the biblical scholar and translator, then living at Bethlehem. In 415 Jerome was visited by a Spanish priest, Paul Orosius, entrusted by the African bishops with the task of making common cause with Jerome against Pelagius, to whom they imputed the doctrines condemned in Caelestius. At a diocesan synod at Jerusalem in late July 415 Orosius, when asked about Pelagius, denounced him and, in effect, invited John and his colleagues to condemn Pelagius and Caelestius because their doctrine differed from that of Augustine and Jerome. Pelagius was then invited to attend the synod and speak in his own defence. Orosius's domineering manner effectively turned the feelings of the synod

against himself, so that he was able to avoid a condemnation of his own position only by successfully proposing that the whole matter should be referred to Pope Innocent I. However, on 12 September Orosius was publicly accused by Bishop John of holding that human beings are so corrupted by the fall that they cannot avoid sinning even with the help of God's grace. Orosius indignantly denied the charge, composed an apologia, and returned to Africa in January 416, there to report the failure of his mission.

Meanwhile two Gallic bishops, Heros and Lazarus, political exiles in Palestine, brought an accusation of heresy against Pelagius which was heard at a council at Diospolis (Lod) in December 415. When it opened, however, neither of the accusers was present, and Pelagius was able to defend himself without cross-examination. Some of the charges he refuted; others, ascribed to Caelestius, he said were no concern of his. It is possible that he was disingenuous in his pleading, but the council was persuaded, and he was declared to be in communion with the faith of the Catholic church.

When the news of Pelagius's acquittal reached Africa, supplemented by the report of Orosius, the Catholic bishops were much alarmed, since it seemed to them that African theology, in which the transmission of original sin was an article of faith, had been repudiated by two oriental synods. Augustine was particularly concerned, for he had read Pelagius's treatise *De natura* and been shocked by its teaching. Two African councils, held in the middle of 416, denounced Pelagius and Caelestius and Pope Innocent I was persuaded to add his condemnation, which he did on 27 January 417, before dying on 27 March. His successor, Zosimus, when approached by Caelestius, decided to reopen the case, being persuaded that justice had not been done to the accused. His attempt, however, foundered on the implacable opposition of the Africans and the decision of the emperor Honorius (then residing at Ravenna) who, in a decree of 30 April 418, condemned anyone who denied the fall and ordered that Pelagius and Caelestius, both of whom he assumed to be at Rome, should be banished from Italy. Next day, 1 May, an African general council, held at Carthage, enacted a series of nine canons expressing the African doctrine of original sin in the most uncompromising terms. Under this pressure Zosimus then issued a decree, now lost, called the *Epistola tractoria*, which condemned and excommunicated both Pelagius and Caelestius.

For Pelagius, Zosimus's condemnation meant ruin. He endeavoured to effect a reconciliation with Augustine, whom he recognized as his principal opponent, but Augustine declined to accept his declaration of faith. He was subsequently expelled from Jerusalem and found refuge in Egypt, where St Cyril of Alexandria allowed him to settle. Thereafter he vanishes from history.

As a result of his condemnation Pelagius was, for centuries, regarded as a heresiarch of the deepest dye. Twentieth-century studies, initiated by Georges de Plinval's biography of 1943, see him rather as a would-be orthodox Christian thinker, whose system proved inadequate to meet the denunciation of Augustine and the

African episcopate. Judgement is not made easier by the difficulty of identifying his authentic writings from the mass of literature emanating from Pelagian circles. One thing however is clear: there was little capacity for leadership in Pelagius's character, such as appears in Caelestius, or any great controversial ability, such as that later revealed by the Pelagian apologist, Julian of Eclanum. The Pelagians were sometimes styled 'Caelestians', and this name seems more appropriate.

Despite his heretical reputation, Pelagius's Pauline commentaries remained popular in the middle ages, sometimes circulating under the name of his bitter enemy, St Jerome, as did his hortatory letter to the aristocratic virgin Demetrias, when she took the veil in 413.

Pelagianism is reported to have found considerable support in Britain, requiring visits by St Germanus of Auxerre in 429 and, less certainly, between about 436 and 444 to denounce it. It has been suggested by J. N. L. Myres, John Morris, and others that the alleged Pelagian denial of grace represented, in fifth-century Britain, an attack on political *gratia* (corrupt patronage and favour), thus understanding Pelagianism as a reforming movement in a society seeking to shake off Roman imperial decadence and to revive the traditional Roman virtues. The topic is too large to be fully discussed here. It may, however, be said that it has been powerfully criticized by J. H. W. G. Liebeschuetz (1963; 1967) and has failed to convince scholars who have studied Pelagianism as a theological system. As B. R. Rees has pointed out (*Pelagius: a Reluctant Heretic*, 1988, 112), far from being, as his opponents alleged, an *inimicus gratiae* (an enemy of *gratia*), Pelagius's principal defence of his orthodoxy was to claim that he accepted grace in the Augustinian sense, 'not for every hour or every moment, but for each individual action of our lives' (Augustine, *De gratia Christi*, 1,2,2). He deserved better than to be condemned as a heretic as a result of prejudice and a succession of unfortunate accidents which, with better luck, he might have escaped. GERALD BONNER

Sources Pelagius, *Commentary on St Paul's Epistle to the Romans*, trans. T. de Bruyn (1994) · 'Epistola Pelagii ad Demetriadem', *Patrologia Latina*, 30 (1846), 15A–46C · 'Epistola Pelagii ad Demetriadem', *Patrologia Latina*, 33 (1845), 1099–1120 · 'Dissertationes de historia Pelagiana', *Patrologia Latina*, 48 (1846), 598–606 · Augustine of Hippo, 'De gestis Pelagii', *Sancti Aurelii Augustini 'De perfectione justitiae hominis', 'De gestis Pelagii', 'De gratia Christi et de peccato originali libri duo', 'De nuptiis et concupiscenti ad Valerium comitem libri duo'*, ed. C. F. Urba and J. Zycha (Vienna, 1902), 51–122 · Augustine of Hippo, 'De dono perseverantiae', *Patrologia Latina*, 45 (1841), 993–1034 · Augustine of Hippo, *De gratia Christi et de peccato originali libri duo*, ed. C. F. Urba and J. Zycha, Corpus Scriptorum Ecclesiasticorum Latinorum, 42 (1902), 125–66 · F. Nuvolone and A. Solignac, 'Pélage et Pélagianisme', *Dictionnaire de spiritualité ascétique et mystique: doctrine et histoire*, ed. M. Viller and others (1937–95) · T. Bohlin, *Die Theologie des Pelagius und ihre Genesis* (1957) · R. F. Evans, *Pelagius: inquiries and reappraisals* (1968) · G. Bonner, *God's decree and man's destiny* (1987) · P. Brown, 'Pelagius and his supporters: aims and environment', *Journal of Theological Studies*, new ser., 19 (1968), 93–114 [repr. in P. Brown, *Religion and society in the age of St Augustine* (1972), 183–207] · P. Brown, 'The patrons of Pelagius', *Journal of Roman Studies*, 63 (1973), 56–72; repr. in *Religion and society in the age of Saint Augustine* (1972), 208–26 · J. N. L. Myres, 'Pelagius and the end of Roman rule in Britain', *Journal of Roman Studies*, 50 (1960), 21–36 · J. Morris, 'Pelagian literature', *Journal of Theological Studies*, new ser., 16 (1965), 26–60 · J. H. W. G. Liebeschuetz, 'Did the Pelagian movement have social aims?', *Historia*, 12 (1963), 227–41 · J. H. W. G. Liebeschuetz, 'Pelagian evidence on the last period of Roman Britain', *Latomus*, 26 (1967), 436–47 · R. A. Markus, 'Pelagianism: Britain and the continent', *Journal of Ecclesiastical History*, 37 (1986), 191–204 · R. A. Markus, 'The legacy of Pelagius', *The making of orthodoxy: essays in honour of Henry Chadwick*, ed. R. Williams (1989), 214–34 · G. Bonner, 'Pelagianism reconsidered', *Studia Patristica*, 27 (1993), 237–41 [repr. in *Church and faith in the patristic tradition* (1996)] · G. Bonner, 'Pelagianism and Augustine', *Augustinian Studies*, 23 (1992), 33–51 [repr. in *Church and faith in the patristic tradition* (1996)] · G. Bonner, 'Augustine and Pelagianism', *Augustinian Studies*, 24 (1993), 27–47 [repr. in *Church and faith in the patristic tradition* (1996)] · E. TeSelle, 'Pelagius, Pelagianism', *Augustine through the ages: an encyclopedia*, ed. A. D. Fitzgerald and others (1999), 633–40 · S. Thier, *Kirche bei Pelagius* (Berlin, 1999)

Pelgrim, Joyce (*d.* 1526?), publisher and bookseller, is first heard of when, with others in the book trade, he applied to have his appearance recorded, although nothing is known of their business. In 1504 an edition of the *Ortus vocabulorum* was printed for him in Paris. In 1506, in partnership with another stationer, Henry Jacobi, he issued a book of hours and a psalter according to the use of Sarum, and an edition of Lyndewode's *Provinciale*, at which time Jacobi lived at the sign of the Trinity, and Pelgrim at the sign of St Anne, both in St Paul's Churchyard. Under the patronage of William Bretton (*c.*1476–1526), an important merchant of the staple of Calais, who assisted them with money, they worked in partnership for a few years, having books printed for them both in the Low Countries and in France, and Pelgrim is recorded as importing several shipments of books in 1506–7. After 1508, when they had issued seven books, Pelgrim's name no longer appears in connection with the business, though Jacobi still continued at work. About 1513 the latter moved to Oxford, and opened a shop there under his old sign of the Trinity, but died in the following year. William Bretton, as a creditor, applied for letters of administration, and was represented at Oxford by his agent, Joyce Pelgrim.

In 1518–19 Pelgrim brought two chancery suits, the first against John Petyt, bookseller. He was living in the parish of St Faith under St Paul's Cathedral, when he was assessed for the subsidy of 1523 at £13 6*s*. The date of his death is not known. His will was proved in 1526, at which time he was described as of the parish of St Foster Vedast.

E. G. DUFF, rev. ANITA McCONNELL

Sources H. R. Plomer, 'Some notices of men connected with the English book trade from the plea rolls of Henry VII', *The Library*, 3rd ser., 1 (1910), 289–301 · will, London commissary court, GL, MS 9171/7, fol. 178 · PRO, E122/79/12; E122/80/4; E179/251/15B, fol. 25 · PRO, C 1/556/2

Pelham, Sir Edmund (*d.* 1606), judge, was the fifth son of Sir William Pelham (*d.* 1538) of Laughton, Sussex, and Mary, daughter of William *Sandys, first Baron Sandys. He was the brother of Sir William *Pelham (*d.* 1587), lord justice of Ireland in 1579–80. He entered Gray's Inn in 1563, was called to the bar in 1574, and was autumn reader in 1588. From about 1583 he was a justice of the peace for Sussex, and in October 1597 he became a member of parliament for Hastings. He acted again as reader in 1601 and in the same year was appointed serjeant-at-law. In September 1602 Pelham replaced Sir Robert Napier as chief baron of the exchequer in Ireland. The following year he acted as a justice of assize in Donegal, the first English judge to go on circuit to the north-west of Ireland. He recorded his impressions of the visit, commenting on the multitude of people, and how they welcomed him as if he had been 'a good angel sent from heaven' (HoP, *Commons, 1558–1603*, 3.193) and begged him to return and administer justice. Like many of his contemporaries in the administration he saw the power of Hugh O'Neill as oppressive and tyrannical and he commented that even the better sort were forced to defer to O'Neill before they would parley with him. Nevertheless he was confident that a parliament would remove these difficulties, and that a better acquaintance with English justice would ensure 'the greater number will grow human and civil and merit the name of a commonwealth' (*CSP Ire.*, 1603–6, 111).

In 1604 Pelham visited England and was knighted by James I at Greenwich on 3 July. He soon returned to Ireland, and in October was on a commission inquiring into the destruction of Sir Henry Harrington's lands during the recent war. In March 1605 he went on circuit, holding sessions in co. Meath, co. Westmeath, Longford, Queen's county, and King's county. But in 1606 he became ill and it was reported that he was unlikely to recover. He sailed to England and on the return journey died at Chester on 4 June 1606. On hearing of his death Sir Arthur Chichester said he was 'a very learned and worthy judge' (*CSP Ire.*, 1603–6, 522). Pelham was survived by his wife, Ellen, daughter of Thomas Darrell of Scotney. They had five sons—Herbert, George, Edmund, Henry, and Thomas—and three daughters—Elizabeth, Ellen, and Phillipa. His manor at Catsfield, Sussex, was left to his wife for her lifetime and thereafter to his son and heir, Herbert. Pelham's will was proved for his widow in 1609, at which time she was in trouble for her recusancy.

JUDITH HUDSON BARRY

Sources HoP, *Commons, 1558–1603*, 3.192–3 · *CSP Ire.*, 1601–6 · J. S. Brewer and W. Bullen, eds., *Calendar of the Carew manuscripts*, 4: 1601–1603, PRO (1870) · F. E. Ball, *The judges in Ireland, 1221–1921*, 1 (1926), 228 · E. Burke, ed., *Calendar of fiants, Elizabeth I* (1994), nos. 6677, 6698 · J. Morrin, ed., *Calendar of the patent and close rolls of chancery in Ireland, of the reigns of Henry VIII, Edward VI, Mary, and Elizabeth*, 2 (1862), 623 · J. Foster, *The register of admissions to Gray's Inn, 1521–1889, together with the register of marriages in Gray's Inn chapel, 1695–1754* (privately printed, London, 1889), 32 · W. A. Shaw, *The knights of England*, 2 (1906), 133 · R. Lascelles, ed., *Liber munerum publicorum Hiberniae … or, The establishments of Ireland*, later edn, 2 vols. in 7 pts (1852), vol. 2, p. 49 · will, PRO, PROB 11/114, sig. 103

Pelham, Edward (*fl.* 1630–1631), sailor, was a gunner's mate on board the *Salutation* of London in the service of the company of Muscovy merchants. On 1 May 1630 the *Salutation*, with two other vessels, under the command of Captain William Goodler, sailed for the north-west coast of Greenland on a whaling trip. On reaching the Foreland the *Salutation* was appointed to station there. When within four leagues of Black Point, Pelham and seven of her crew (William Fakeley, John Wise, Robert Goodfellow, Thomas Ayers, Henry Bett, John Dawes, and Richard Kellet) were dispatched in a shallop to Green harbour to meet the second ship. Missing both points, the shallop was given up as lost, and the Muscovy fleet returned home.

The eight men passed the winter in dire privation at Bell Sound. Having stocked up as best they could with meat, the men retreated to a 'tent', in fact a tiled, timber house used in season by coopers on whaling voyages, within which they erected another 'tent' and gathered wood for firing from the debris left by whalers. Pelham wrote:

> our greatest and chiefest feeding was the whale Frittars, and those mouldie too, the loathsomest meat in the world … 'twas a measuring cast which should be eaten first, Wee or the Beares, when we first saw one another … they had as good hopes to devoure us as wee, to kill them. (Pelham, 254–5)

Making good use of the materials left by the whalers and the knowledge of the region by at least two of the men, the party managed to stay in reasonable physical and mental health. On 25 May 1631 two ships from Hull came into the sound, followed on the 28th by the Muscovy fleet, again under the command of Captain William Goodler. The eight men were at once taken on board, and on 20 August departed for the Thames.

Pelham wrote an account of his privations in *Gods power and providence shewed in the marvellous preservation and deliverance of eight Englishmen, left by mischance in Greenland, anno 1630, nine moneths and twelve dayes, with a true relation of all their miseries, their shifts, and hardship … with a map of Greenland* (1631), which was later reprinted in 1855 for the Hakluyt Society by Adam White in volume 4 of the *Collection of Voyages and Travels* (1732, 1744, 1752) of A. Churchill and J. Churchill and in Edward Arber's *English Garner*, volume 8 (1896). The book is dedicated to Alderman Sir Hugh Hammersley, governor of the Muscovy Company, and to the company's assistants and adventurers. The work promises a description of the chief places and rarities of Greenland, but it is largely an account of the ingenious ways in which Pelham and the abandoned crew made shift to over-winter. This in no way detracts from their feat, but makes the book more of a curiosity than an influential geography or travel book.

W. A. SHAW, *rev.* ELIZABETH BAIGENT

Sources E. Pelham, 'Gods power and providence', *A collection of documents on Spitzbergen and Greenland*, ed. A. White, Hakluyt Society (1855), 254–83

Pelham, Frederick Thomas (1808–1861), naval officer, was born on 2 August 1808, the second son of Thomas *Pelham, second earl of Chichester (1756–1826), and his wife, Lady Mary Henrietta Juliana (1776–1862), daughter of Francis *Osborne, the fifth duke of Leeds. He entered the navy on 27 June 1823, and served as a midshipman aboard the *Sybille*, Captain Samuel John Brooke Pechell, in the Mediterranean. Here he was present at an attack on Greek pirates. In 1829 he passed his examination for lieutenant, and was promoted on 22 February 1830. He then served in the *Ferret* during 1831–2 and from May 1832 until his promotion to commander, on 21 September 1835, in the *Castor*, Captain Lord John Hay, on the north coast of Spain during the Carlist War. Between June 1837 and the autumn of 1838 he commanded the *Tweed* on the same station, and was awarded the Spanish cross of San Fernando on 9 August 1839 in recognition of his efforts.

Pelham was promoted captain on 3 July 1840. On 26 July 1841 he married Ellen Kate (*d.* 8 Jan 1900), daughter of Rowland Mitchell; they had four children. Between May 1847 and June 1850 he commanded the steam paddle frigate *Odin* in the Mediterranean. In March 1852 he was appointed private secretary to the first lord of the Admiralty, the duke of Northumberland, and he remained in the post until the end of the year. He was appointed at the suggestion of Admiral Sir Hyde Parker, the senior naval lord. This was a difficult post, when the ministers were anxious to keep down the estimates and reverse the strong tide of political support for the whigs in the dockyards. It was not rendered any easier by the politics of Pelham's brother, the third earl, and his close connections with Sir Francis Baring. Pelham was on particularly bad terms with Stafford O'Brien, the political secretary. His testimony on the 1853 select committee on dockyard appointments, which investigated Stafford's handling of patronage, was remarkably circumspect. On 14 August 1853 he was appointed to the *Blenheim*, to command the Portsmouth steam reserve, and aboard the same ship took a distinguished part in the Baltic campaign of 1854, notably at the capture of Bomarsund in August, where his initiative and skill in landing a heavy gun to support the attack were commended. In November 1854 he was appointed to the new battleship *Exmouth*, but in February 1855, before she was completed, he was selected by his friend Rear-Admiral Richard Saunders Dundas for the demanding position of captain of the fleet for the second Baltic campaign.

Pelham's experience proved invaluable to Dundas, and he directed the attack on Sveaborg (8–10 August), the major operation of the year. Others were less impressed, however. Captain Bartholomew James Sulivan, the brilliant surveying officer, attributed much of Dundas's caution to Pelham's influence. In June 1856 Pelham returned to the steam reserve. Ironically, given his experience in 1852, in December 1856 Sir Maurice Berkeley declined to have him at the Board of Admiralty, despite his ability and experience, claiming he was still connected with Northumberland and thus politically suspect. In November 1857 Berkeley retired and Pelham rejoined Dundas, now at the Admiralty under Sir Charles Wood. He left office with the ministry in March 1858. The place had been conditional on his being prepared to enter parliament, but he was not called upon to do so. On 3 March 1838 he was promoted rear-admiral. Pelham joined the new Liberal board in June 1859, now as second naval lord under the duke of Somerset and Dundas. He remained there until early June 1861, when he resigned on account of ill health. He died at 8 Waterloo Street, Hove, on 21 June 1861, and was buried at Highgate cemetery.

Pelham's career was made by his family and political connections, and his command appointments and critical promotions were all secured under whig/Liberal ministries. His efficient conduct of operations and administration demonstrated that he had considerable ability, but he was never tested in high command.

ANDREW LAMBERT

Sources Bodl. Oxf., Dep. Hughenden · BL, Wood MSS · O'Byrne, *Naval biog. dict.* · *Annual Register* (1861) · *Navy List* · A. D. Lambert, *The Crimean War: British grand strategy, 1853–56* (1990) · H. N. Sulivan, ed., *Life and letters of the late Admiral Sir Bartholomew James Sulivan, 1810–1890* (1896) · A. Phillimore, *The life of Admiral of the Fleet Sir William Parker*, 3 vols. (1876–80) · P. H. Colomb, *Memoirs of Admiral of the Right Honble. Sir Astley Cooper Key* (1898) · 'Select committee on dockyard appointments', *Parl. papers* (1852–3), vol. 25, no. 511 · Burke, *Peerage* (1959) · GEC, *Peerage* · Boase, *Mod. Eng. biog.* · *CGPLA Eng. & Wales* (1861)
Archives BL, Wood MSS
Wealth at death £14,000: probate, 22 July 1861, *CGPLA Eng. & Wales*

Pelham, George (1766–1827), bishop of Lincoln, born on 13 October 1766, was the third son and seventh and youngest child of Thomas *Pelham, first earl of Chichester (1728–1805), and his wife, Anne, *née* Frankland (1734/5–1813). Henry Thomas *Pelham, third earl of Chichester (1804–1886) was his nephew. He was at first in the English army, holding a commission in the guards, but soon changed his vocation to the church. After he had been trained by James Hurdis at the family seat of Stanmer, near Lewes, he was sent to Cambridge, matriculating from Clare College in 1784 and graduating MA in 1787. On 14 December 1792 he married Mary, third daughter of the Revd Sir Richard Nelson Rycroft (*d.* 1786) and his wife, Penelope, daughter of the Revd Richard Stonehewer. They had no children.

As the younger son of a leading whig family, Pelham was quickly promoted, and his political connections gratified a lust for lucrative office which quickly became notorious. He was ordained deacon and priest in 1789, and on 28 October 1790, when he was only twenty-four, was installed as prebendary of Middleton and canon residentiary in Chichester Cathedral; he held that preferment until his death. From 1790 to 1800 he was vicar of Laughton, Sussex. In 1792 the vicarage of Bexhill in Sussex was given to him by the bishop of the diocese; in 1800 he was appointed by his family to the vicarage of Hellingly. Both of these he also held until his death. From 17 November 1797 to 1803 he was prebendary of the eleventh stall at Winchester. Hurdis, who acknowledged many good qualities in his pupil, wrote to William Cowper, the poet, that young Pelham had 'just turned of five and twenty, and is already in possession of two livings' (Hurdis, xi).

Pelham was consecrated bishop of Bristol on 27 March 1803 in the chapel at Lambeth Palace, and at the same time received from the archbishop of Canterbury the degree of DCL. When the see of Norwich became vacant, he wrote (8 February 1805) from his house in Welbeck Street, London, to William Pitt, stating that he had heard 'from so many quarters' of his nomination for that bishopric, that he could 'no longer refrain expressing his gratitude', as it would be 'a lasting obligation'. A dry answer was immediately sent back by Pitt, that the report 'had arisen without his knowledge, and that he could not have the satisfaction of promoting his wishes' (P. H. Stanhope, *Life of … William Pitt*, 1861–2, 4.253–4). This was almost Pelham's only failure. In 1807 he was transferred to the diocese of Exeter, being installed on 28 September 1807, and holding with it the archdeaconry of Exeter and the treasurership of the cathedral, to which was annexed a residential stall. His desire for further preferment was realized in October 1820, when he was made bishop of Lincoln. Pelham was also clerk of the closet to the king. When raised to the episcopal bench he nearly went down on his knees to George III to be allowed to dispense with wearing his wig, but the king was unrelenting (A. Hayward, *Biographical and Critical Essays*, 2, 1873, 40). He was a friend of the prince regent and a regular diner and party-goer at the Brighton Pavilion in 1818.

Pelham was the author of two sermons and a charge. He is described as urbane in his manners, punctual in the discharge of business, and impartial in the distribution of patronage. He became a byword for much that was wrong with the established church of his day. However, when he confirmed the young W. E. Gladstone at Eton on 1 February 1827, the latter noted: 'Bishop not dignified in appearance—but went through the service apparently with great feeling and piety' (Gladstone, *Diaries*, 1 Feb 1827). Pelham had, on 19 January 1827, caught a cold at the duke of York's funeral. He died of pleurisy at Connaught Place, London, on 7 February 1827 and was buried in the family vaults at Laughton in Sussex on 15 February. Mary Pelham's poor health was, fancifully, given by her husband as a reason why he should be preferred. She was said to be haughty in style, and in the palace at Exeter never rose from her seat to receive visitors. She died on 30 March 1837.

W. P. COURTNEY, rev. H. C. G. MATTHEW

Sources GM, 1st ser., 97/1 (1827), 269 · GM, 2nd ser., 7 (1837), 553 · Venn, *Alum. Cant.* · G. Oliver, *Lives of the bishops of Exeter, and a history of the cathedral* (1861) · N&Q, 5th ser., 2 (1874), 213 · R. Polwhele, *Reminiscences in prose and verse*, 1 (1836), 137, 155 · Burke, *Peerage* · J. Hurdis, *The village curate* (1810) · Gladstone, *Diaries* · R. A. Soloway, *Prelates and people: ecclesiastical social thought in England, 1783–1852* (1969)

Archives BL, family corresp., Add. MSS 33093, 33126, 33130 | BL, Liverpool MSS · E. Sussex RO, letter to first earl of Sheffield
Likenesses I. W. Slater, lithograph (after J. Slater), BM, NPG

Pelham, Henry (1694–1754), prime minister, was born on 26 September 1694 in London, the eighth of the nine children of Thomas *Pelham, first Baron Pelham of Laughton (c.1653–1712), and his second wife, Lady Grace Holles (1668/9–1700), daughter of Gilbert Holles, third earl of Clare, and his wife, Grace Pierrepont. Throughout his life Pelham was deeply attached to his only surviving brother, Thomas Pelham *Holles, who was fourteen months his elder and who was created duke of Newcastle upon Tyne in 1715, after inheriting the great estate of their uncle John *Holles, duke of Newcastle upon Tyne. Pelham attended Westminster School, London, and was enrolled at Hart Hall, Oxford, on 6 September 1710. Upon his father's death in 1712 he inherited some annuities and £5000, at least part of which went to youthful extravagance. At this time his brother gave him an annuity of

Henry Pelham (1694–1754), by William Hoare, 1751?

£1000, and when he came of age in 1715 he inherited land in their home county of Sussex worth £1500 a year. During the Jacobite rising of 1715 Pelham commanded a troop of dragoons and took part in the battle of Preston (12–14 November). He then travelled on the continent, apparently to complete his education, and returned after his brother arranged his election on 28 February 1717 as member of parliament for Seaford, Sussex. The Pelham brothers were whigs, as their father had been since before the revolution of 1688. Their Pelham ancestors had held seats in the Commons since the reign of Elizabeth I.

On 5 April 1722 Pelham was elected to represent the county of Sussex, a seat he held until his death. While his brother Newcastle on 25 May 1720 secured him the court office of treasurer of the chamber, Pelham also became close to Sir Robert Walpole; in his first speech, on 6 May, he moved an address of thanks to the king which was seconded by Walpole. Pelham would never be known as an orator, for his speeches usually were plain and to the point, filled with facts and figures relevant to the subject under debate. On 3 April 1721 he was appointed a member of Walpole's Treasury board, a rapid rise for a young politician. The Pelhams' support of Walpole in his power struggle with John, Lord Carteret, was rewarded in 1724, when Pelham was appointed secretary at war (on 3 April) and Newcastle secretary of state for the southern department (on 14 April). Pelham acted as Walpole's lieutenant in the Commons and smoothed relations between his touchy brother and the chief minister. The fact that Newcastle quickly became the third most powerful man in the administration no doubt helped Pelham's career, for he was sworn of the privy council on 1 June 1725. Pelham supported Walpole's unpopular plan to reform the excise system in 1733 but voted in 1737, in opposition to his mentor, for a scheme to reduce the rate of interest on the national debt, a goal Pelham would later achieve himself.

Marriage and family On 29 October 1726 Pelham married Lady Katharine Manners (1700/01–1780) [see Pelham, Lady Katharine], daughter of John Manners, second duke of Rutland, and his wife, Catherine Russell. Newcastle marked the event with a gift of land in Sussex worth £800 a year and sold him some property worth £500 a year, giving him an annual income of £2800 plus his salary from office. The marriage portion was £10,000. The couple had two sons, who, to their parents' great grief, died on 27 and 28 November 1739 of a throat infection, and six daughters, two of whom also died in childhood. Illness in a friend's family was a painful reminder to Pelham of the loss of his boys and of his daughter Lucy little more than two months later: 'These incidents renew too much in me, what I ought and endeavor to forgett but I find I never shall' (Pelham to Newcastle, 1 July 1740, BL, Add. MS 33441, fol. 4). The eldest daughter, Catherine, her childless uncle's favourite, in 1744 married her first cousin Henry Clinton, ninth earl of Lincoln, who was made Newcastle's heir. Pelham was devoted to his wife and family and favoured spending his free time in privacy with them. In 1729 he purchased Esher Place, Surrey, close by his brother's estate at Claremont, and employed William Kent to renovate the house and gardens as a country retreat for his family. When Pelham was appointed paymaster-general on 8 May 1730, he found his official residence in Whitehall deficient and had it rebuilt, his first promotion of public architecture. In 1740 he bought a house in Arlington Street, London, which he had razed, and engaged Kent to design a fine Palladian structure, now no. 22. The family moved in on 25 May 1743. On Lady Katharine's appointment as ranger of Greenwich Park in 1745, Pelham arranged an expensive major restoration of the official residence, the Queen's House designed by Inigo Jones.

Accession to power Throughout the 1730s, both as Newcastle's brother and as Walpole's confidant, Pelham was privy to policy discussions of the inner cabinet, yet he was not in the public eye. This dual privity became a vice as Newcastle's ambition and differences with Walpole over policy towards Spain grew. Pelham, assisted by their close friend the lord chancellor, Philip Yorke, earl of Hardwicke, had to conciliate between the two and even softened the language of Newcastle's official letters to Spain to conform with Walpole's view. The grateful Newcastle said: 'My Brother has all the prudence, knowledge, experience, and good intention, that I can wish or hope in a man' (Coxe, 1.40). In the face of a public inflamed by accounts of Spanish depredations on British trade and sailors, Pelham helped Walpole to win passage of the convention of the Pardo on 8 March 1739. Spain's failure to meet the agreed terms forced the reluctant Walpole to accept the need for

war. Pelham continued his role of peacemaker as the ministers quarrelled over the conduct of the war, which Walpole called Newcastle's. When the expected quick victory failed to occur, the opposition, who had demanded war, began to mount damaging attacks on the chief minister in the Commons. On 13 February 1741 Pelham strongly opposed a motion for Walpole's removal, and, after Sir Robert was forced to resign, defended him in debate on 9 March 1742 over a motion for a committee of inquiry. Although he distrusted Newcastle, Walpole wanted Pelham to succeed him as chief minister. Even while he was Walpole's deputy, Pelham's affability and good character had gained him friends, and yet, despite Walpole's encouragement, he chose not to become chancellor of the exchequer in the new administration. However, in July 1742 he did become leader of the House of Commons. Pelham was a conciliator able to persuade discordant politicians to work together, his subtlety disguising his strength. When a death created vacancies in 1743, Pelham on 25 August became first lord of the Treasury and on 12 December chancellor. Walpole, now earl of Orford, congratulated him, saying:

> I do not load you with personal assurances; but I never knew a time when I thought it more incumbent upon me to exert myself in support of the government; and I rejoice, for your sake and my own, that affairs are put into your hands, where my private friendship, and my political opinion unite, in engaging me to do all I can, and call upon me to act in character. (Coxe, 1.92)

With power came great responsibility, for, in addition to the war with Spain, Britain was funding Austria's defence against Prussia and France, on which Britain declared war on 29 March 1744. Holding all the offices formerly Walpole's, and supported by Newcastle and Hardwicke, Pelham was chief minister in theory but not in fact: he lacked the approval of George II, who still favoured the German-speaking northern secretary, Carteret. The public and many members of the Commons, however, perceived a bias in Carteret towards Hanover over England, and disliked him accordingly, giving the Pelhams a lever to force his dismissal on 24 November 1744. The king was angry and unreconciled, rejecting men suggested for appointment and complaining 'he had been forced to part with those he liked' (Owen, 244). To counter the continuing influence at court of Carteret (now Earl Granville), Pelham had to strengthen his position in the Commons, where he did not yet have mastery over the newer members of his coalition. When the tory opposition in February 1745 demanded an inquiry into a failed naval operation, they were joined by some of the new allies Pelham had managed to place on the Admiralty board, who wanted to expose their predecessors as incompetent. Despite Pelham's efforts to keep the inquiry non-partisan, members chose for political reasons to support one or the other of the two admirals involved, Thomas Mathews and Richard Lestock. In order not to offend the king further, Pelham was forced to speak in support of Mathews, who was being attacked by his young allies.

The Jacobite rising of 1745 Pelham had little time to conciliate the king before the outbreak, on 25 July 1745, of the Jacobite rising. Although the secretaries of state had direction of policy in Scotland, the first lord of the Treasury controlled the subordinate revenue boards there and thus had considerable influence through patronage. Walpole had worked through the Scottish magnate Archibald Campbell, Lord Ilay, who became third duke of Argyll in 1743. Argyll's rival John Hay, fourth marquess of Tweeddale, a supporter of Granville, was appointed secretary of state for Scotland following Walpole's fall in 1742. After the cabinet had taken protective measures when rumours of invasion first circulated in 1743, Pelham in 1744 suggested arming Scottish loyalists and raising additional Highland regiments, but nothing was done by Tweeddale. Little more was heard until the regency board received warning of a possible French invasion in July 1745. Even after the landing of the Pretender became known, the public and Tweeddale dismissed the danger. Pelham said:

> I am not so apprehensive of the strength or zeal of the enemy, as I am fearful of the inability or languidness, of our friends … you would scarce, in common conversation, meet with one man who thinks there is any danger from, scarce truth in an invasion, at this time. (Coxe, 1.258)

With most of the British forces engaged on the continent, Pelham in alarm asked George II to return from Hanover but, because of on-going cool relations between king and first minister, gained no support. 'The conduct of a certain person is worse than ever. To speak of personal treatment is idle at this time, but we are not permitted either to give our advice or to act in consequence of any advice that is given', Pelham told a friend in September (Owen, 280). Granville and his allies told George II that the rebels could be crushed easily by the forces to hand and that Britain should maintain her European commitment. Despite the opposition of Tweeddale, the Pelhams finally convinced the king to recall his son, the duke of Cumberland, and ten battalions from the continent. The rebel success at Prestonpans on 21 September proved Tweeddale's incompetence, and he resigned in January 1746. Even before, Newcastle had begun organizing internal defences and naval operations to contain the rising. Pelham's correspondence makes clear how closely he studied the progress of the invasion and highland uprising. By the end of the year Cumberland's forces had regained the initiative and they finally destroyed the rebel army at the battle of Culloden on 16 April 1746. Scotland had specific rights under the Act of Union and could not be crushed, as Cumberland advocated. Pelham wanted to pacify Scotland and ensure its loyalty to the crown, but by moderate measures that would preserve the stability of his administration. Lord Hardwicke drafted bills that reflected public opinion and worked out final forms with Pelham and Newcastle. The act of attainder signed in June 1746 listed men declared guilty of treason, whose property could be confiscated, but only three peers were executed. The Disarming Act signed in August, which imposed fines for carrying or concealing arms, was difficult to enforce, and a ban on traditional highland dress was evaded or ignored.

To ensure passage of such bills, Pelham had to negotiate Argyll's assistance while reaching out to his rival Scottish lords. To Pelham, the most important measure was the Heritable Jurisdictions Act of 1747, which extended uniform royal jurisdiction throughout Scotland and so strengthened control by central government. Scottish lords who by tradition had inherited regalities were bought out, and their jurisdictions were returned to the crown. Pelham in consequence could influence the appointment of the most important officials in Scottish local government, the sheriff-deputes. By accepting recommendations for these posts from a number of Scottish lords, Pelham gained greater support for his pacification bills while preserving good relations with Argyll.

Chief minister Hard pressed to finance and conduct war on so many fronts, Pelham learned early in 1746 that George II wanted a new ministry headed by Granville, who still influenced the king's thinking on foreign policy. In consequence, Pelham, together with most of his administration, resigned on 11 February. Faced with a minority in parliament and the withdrawal of promised financial support for the government, George II was forced to recall Pelham and his colleagues within three days. Pelham could now turn to placating the king and strengthening his political position. Determined not to repeat Walpole's error of creating opposition by exclusion, Pelham had, after Granville's resignation, brought into his administration dissident whigs who had criticized the conduct of the war, such as the Bedford and Cobham factions, and thus gained some good speakers to support his proposals in the Commons. As a result some excellent political writers attached to these factions, Henry Fielding in particular, began to support the administration. When Pelham returned to office after his own resignation he brought in more new men—even the king's *bête noire*, William Pitt—to create a truly broad-bottom administration.

The only remaining serious opposition was the Leicester House faction headed by Frederick, prince of Wales. As early as 1737 Frederick had begun to gather a party loyal to him which was based on appointments to his household. These men, some of them peers, had votes in parliament and formed a shadow administration waiting to take office at what many thought to be the king's imminent death. Frederick allied himself with the Cobham and Bedford factions opposing Walpole but gave general support to the new administration after 1742. Late in 1746 he went back into opposition and began to create more salaried positions at his court in order to expand his party. The prince's substantial personal income made him the Pelhams' most dangerous opponent. Moreover, Frederick reached out to the tory country gentlemen in the Commons, men who had been marginalized by George II's distrust of them. Frederick and his friends challenged Pelham's control over elections by supporting their own candidates. To catch them off guard, Pelham called a snap general election on 20 June 1747 which brought him an increased majority. The resulting political calm and smooth passage of legislation contributed heavily to the recovery of royal favour. Pelham left little to chance in the

Commons, working out in advance the order in which legislation would be introduced in each session and selecting the speakers to support particular measures, always working to eliminate opportunities for opposition.

Conduct of foreign affairs Under the departmental form of government then used, formulation of foreign policy was the province of the secretaries of state. The monarch was arbiter of policy, and George II kept a close control over the army and relations with European states. When the king insisted on going to Hanover in 1743, a regency board made up of his ministers ran the government in London. Pelham became a member when he was appointed head of the Treasury and in consequence read most documents concerning foreign affairs. When Granville presented the treaty of Worms to the regency board, Pelham objected to the subsidies included and, with his allies, was able to reject it. While Granville had the king's ear over what part Britain should play in the War of the Austrian Succession, Pelham's influence was limited to supporting Newcastle's views and to the passage in the Commons of bills to pay troops and provide subsidies for allies. Defending measures over which he had no control was, as he told Newcastle, especially difficult in regard to the large subsidies: 'The Allys will take it [every sum of money we advance], and then act, as suits their own convenience and security best' (Owen, 227). Once Granville was finally ousted and Pelham had begun to win the king's confidence, he was able to exert more influence on foreign policy, but still primarily through his control of the Commons and government finance. His office determined his viewpoint. Each year he had to find the resources to pay for war, noting that 'when I came into the Treasury I found a vast arrear and the expenses have increased, and the revenue diminished ever since' (Wilkes, 105). Pelham corresponded with British diplomats and was well informed on the status of relations with other governments. When George II visited Hanover in 1748, 1750, and 1752, Pelham led the regency board and sent advice to Newcastle, who accompanied the king. When Pelham was out of London, Newcastle often sent him copies of diplomatic papers, although Pelham admitted difficulty with documents in French, 'which language I understand very imperfectly' (Coxe, 2.491). Since he also said 'I don't speak French', his ability to converse with foreign ambassadors must have been limited, although he did report meeting with several while Newcastle was at Hanover in 1750 (ibid., 1.168). As leader of the Commons, Pelham knew by 1746 that the public wanted an end to an expensive and unprofitable war. As head of the Treasury he was equally keen to end the financial drain on the country. As chief minister he wanted 'a good Peace', honourable and on terms acceptable to parliament: 'For God sake don't let us neglect the first opportunity that offers itself for that purpose' (Pelham to Hardwicke, 22 April 1748, BL, Add. MS 35423, fol. 28). Newcastle's rapid conversion to the king's strategy of deferring peace until more bargaining chips could be won put him at odds with Pelham, who believed further warfare would yield no better peace terms. When France's

desire for secret negotiations was rumoured in 1746, Pelham urged Newcastle to make contact, although it proved futile. From that time Pelham also supported measures to induce Frederick II to press France to negotiate, even though he knew George II distrusted his Prussian nephew. Pelham was outspoken, telling the Commons on 9 February 1748: 'it is my opinion that we ought to make peace but I have reason to believe that certain influences will prevail against my opinion' (copy of speech in Le Man to Huescar, 13 Feb 1748, BL, Add. MS 32811, fol. 155). Newcastle was certain a final blow could be launched against France with Dutch aid. Pelham believed the British envoy Lord Sandwich had misled Newcastle into thinking

> that Holland would bring such an Army into the field as would turn the ballance in our favor when he must know, if he knew anything at all, that they were no government, that they were a bankrupt people and could not pay the very small sums they owe to us for our advanced payments to them.   (Pelham to Hardwicke, 25 Sept 1748, BL, Add. MS 35423, fol. 64)

Dutch promises went unfulfilled, and Newcastle agreed to peace negotiations that led to the signing of a preliminary treaty in April 1748. Pelham told him:

> Peace is what I want, both for the sake of my king, my country, and myself. Peace will be had. I heartily wish it may be no worse, than what is represented in your paper. If so, I am sure it is to be defended; but if not so, it must be defended, and shall be, by me at least, if I have the honour to serve the king, at the time of trial.   (Coxe, 1.415)

The final terms, as Pelham predicted, proved no better than what might have been obtained in 1746.

Relations with Newcastle Britain was finally freed from the burden of war by the treaty of Aix-la-Chapelle, signed on 18 October 1748, but relations between the Pelham brothers had soured while Newcastle, now northern secretary, spent the summer with the king in Hanover. Newcastle had from the beginning been uncomfortable about his brother's power and, as early as 1743, had told Hardwicke:

> I do apprehend that my brother does think that his superior interest in the Closet, and situation in the House of Commons, gives him great advantage over everybody else. They are indeed great advantages, but may be counterbalanced, especially if it is considered over *whom* those advantages are given.   (Owen, 319)

After more disagreements in January 1745, Newcastle suggested a method of power-sharing:

> that every thing, as far as possible, should be first talked over by you and me, before it is either flung out in the closet, or communicated to *any* of our brethren; I always except the chancellor, who, I know, is a third brother; that we shall have no reserve, either *public* or *private* with each other; and, that in our transactions with the other ministers, and other persons, who may be negotiated with, we should always let it be understood, that we speak in the name of both, or in the name of neither. This conduct, once established, will grow easy and natural, and effectually prevent any jealousies, on one side, or disagreeable warmth, occasioned by them, on the other. In order to make this practicable, I will call every morning, as regularly at your house, as I once did at Sir Robert's. There the scheme of the day shall be settled, to be handed out to others afterwards, as shall be necessary; and a

frequent intercourse with ease, at each other's houses, and at all hours and times, will also make this very easy to us. (Coxe, 1.206)

Pelham willingly agreed. Yet, far away from London in 1748, the duke fell prey to his streak of jealousy and paranoia, in his letters accusing Pelham of imagined slights, a problem that would recur during later trips to Hanover. Ill and irritated by his brother's petulance, Pelham told Hardwicke:

> I must declare to your Lordship with all the coolness imaginable, it is not in my will, it is not in my power to undertake another sessions of Parliament upon the foot of expence we are now going into, and that only to preserve a bigotted notion of Old Systems and the House of Austria. (21 Aug 1748, BL, Add. MS 35423, fol. 54)

Newcastle was shaken and subdued upon learning that Pelham, whom he sincerely loved, had suffered a painful and debilitating attack of shingles in late August. The brothers' other occasional quarrels were over money, one cause being Newcastle's dismal personal finances. A settlement, made in 1741 after some acrimony, protected the rights of Pelham and his family as Newcastle's heirs. When the marriage in 1744 of Pelham's daughter Katherine to the earl of Lincoln necessitated new arrangements, Newcastle became enraged at the restrictions his brother demanded. Aside from his concerns for his daughters' rights, Pelham worried about how Newcastle's great debts might damage his public reputation and political credit. He warned his brother what a blow his loss of office would be because Newcastle's salary was an important part of his income. Because of their differences, the brothers did, on a few occasions, stop speaking to each other until Hardwicke interceded to heal the rift. Pelham usually made the first overture, perhaps because he was emotionally the stronger, and told his brother:

> We cannot change our natures nor add to our understanding; we must therefore be satisfied with each other and convinc'd that if we do differ, it is what we can't avoid, and endeavour that those differences shall have as little effect upon the Publick and be as little known as possible. (Pelham to Newcastle, 7 Sept 1750, BL, Add. MS 35411, fol. 122)

In national finance, Pelham intended to reduce government spending after the war, which would please the taxpaying landowners who made up his majority in the Commons and induce them to support his plan to reduce the interest on the national debt. Consequently, Pelham objected to Newcastle's promotion of subsidies in peacetime to cement foreign alliances for Britain, but could be persuaded to agree when he saw definite benefits would result. Hardwicke had his own view:

> When a Subsidiary Measure has been proposed which he has not been inclin'd to, & resolv'd not to yield to at first, or without difficulty, I have more than once known him to take up another Subsidiary Measure of much greater Extent & Expence, which has been talk'd of before, in order to shew the small importence & value of the one, & the preferableness of the other, tho' *that other* may not have been practicable. (Hardwicke to Newcastle, 28 July 1751, BL, Add. MS 32724, fol. 490)

Pelham reluctantly agreed to support Newcastle's plan to elect an heir to the throne of the Holy Roman empire, which involved paying large subsidies to German electors. Pelham presented the Bavarian subsidy to the committee of supply on 22 February 1751, saying that the election scheme was essential to hold France in check and to preserve the balance of power in Europe. At the time Pelham promised that no more subsidies were needed, and he quarrelled with his brother when Newcastle soon afterwards requested one for the elector of Saxony. Pelham was so angry that colleagues had to persuade him that a public rupture with his brother would destroy their party. Pelham finally agreed and presented the subsidy on 22 January 1752. Opposition was strong, but Pelham answered these objections 'finely, seriously, and pathetically; a manner in which he particularly shone' (Walpole, 1.167).

Pelham was also troubled by Newcastle's desire to monopolize the handling of foreign relations. In a letter to Pelham the duke claimed that the southern secretary, John Russell, fourth duke of Bedford, 'has just parts & understanding enough to confound you & business, and not to comprehend enough to forward either, tho he was never so well disposed to it' (Newcastle to Pelham, 2/13 Sept 1750, BL, Add. MS 35411, fol. 105). Pelham reminded him that:

> I have promised the king, and I will keep my word, that I would never enter into any cabal again, to prevent his Majesty from either removing, or bringing into his service, any person he had either a prejudice to, or a predilection for (Coxe, 2.389)

Even though Pelham was convinced Bedford neglected his duties, he did not want him replaced by someone completely subservient to Newcastle or by a member of parliament who might challenge Pelham's authority there. Moreover, Pelham did not want to lose the support of Bedford's friends in the Commons. Nevertheless, in June 1751 Pelham did finally assist Newcastle in gaining the king's consent to their manoeuvring Bedford into resignation. George II himself concluded that Bedford's slack work habits were not giving him value for his money and decided that he could also do without the services of his first lord of the Admiralty, Bedford's friend John Montagu, fourth earl of Sandwich, whom the king had always disliked. George II expected hard work and a suitable degree of deference from his ministers and never forgot which men, Bedford and Sandwich included, had denigrated the Hanoverian connection. Sandwich's dismissal forced Bedford to resign to protest. At the king's suggestion Robert Darcy, fourth earl of Holdernesse, an unambitious diplomat, replaced Bedford. Hardwicke's son-in-law George, Baron Anson, an admiral and member of the Admiralty board, was promoted to first lord. To please the king further, Granville was appointed president of the privy council, even though Pelham still distrusted the earl and doubted Newcastle's assurances that Granville was a changed man.

Achievements in office With the war ended, Pelham could implement some long-considered financial plans. In 1749 he approved designs for the rebuilding of the Horse

Guards, Whitehall, which would also provide accommodation for the secretary at war and other officials. On 20 December 1749 parliament enacted his plan to consolidate the national debt and reduce the rate of interest from 4 to 3 per cent by 1755. Pelham needed all his skills of persuasion to overcome the opposition of the great financial corporations to this plan. New Bank of England annuities at 3 per cent interest were offered for sale, while the rate on old debts was gradually reduced from 4 to 3 per cent and debts held by the East India and South Sea companies were transferred to the bank. The goal of the scheme was to convert all of the public debt into the new or consolidated bank annuities. The most threatening focus of political opposition to the administration was removed by the death of the king's unloved son Frederick, prince of Wales, on 20 March 1751. Just the year before, when the king fell seriously ill, Pelham had worried about the strength of this Leicester House organization and told Newcastle that the Commons 'is a great unwieldy body, and requires great Art and some Cordials to keep it loyal … [the Prince] has as much to give in present as we have and more in Reversion. This makes my task an hard one' (Newman, 75). The death of Frederick dispersed his party and eased Pelham's task immeasurably. Soon after, Pelham had

> an opportunity of talking thoroughly to the King, which I have done without reserve; he now knows upon what terms I can be his servant, and of *use* to him. Time must shew whether that is practicable or not … I am glad to be certain of the ground I stand upon. (Pelham to Henry Fox, 3 April 1751, BL, Add. MS 51379, fol. 93)

Pelham enhanced his position by reducing the king's spending on patronage and accomplishing another goal which: 'I have for some time despaired of, bringing his civil list finances into any order' (Pelham to Newcastle, 22 June 1750, BL, Add. MS 32721, fol. 144).

Soon after Frederick's death a message from the king to both houses of parliament proposed that his widow, Princess Augusta, be made regent if the king died before her eldest son came of age. This proposal, drawn up by the Pelhams and Hardwicke, angered the duke of Cumberland and his supporters because they felt he should be regent. When the Commons went into committee on the bill on 16 May, Pelham took the chair, a role he rarely filled because it barred him from taking part in the debate. He may have hoped thus to avoid further offending Cumberland or the new Leicester House faction, or he simply did not expect the heated opposition the bill provoked. Pelham's able lieutenants William Murray and Henry Fox spoke for the administration in the unexpectedly long and contentious debate, although Fox put some of his effort into defending Cumberland. Speaking for approval of the final bill, Pelham said that 'he was persuaded nobody would suspect him of any prospect of power for himself from this bill, as he should be too great a wretch to build views of grandeur on what he must regard as the greatest misfortune' (Walpole, 1.102).

Political stability was Pelham's goal in all his policies,

yet one of his highland pacification bills came under fierce attack in March 1752 by the two disgruntled dukes—Bedford, who hated the Pelhams, and Cumberland, who hated the Scots. A bill to annex to the crown some of the highland estates forfeited for treason had been produced after years of negotiation between Pelham, Hardwicke, Argyll, and other Scottish lords. Cumberland and Bedford claimed the bill rewarded the Scots for rebellion but could not stop its passage. Cumberland then accused Argyll of protecting Jacobites holding government office in Scotland, a charge Bedford repeated in the Lords while calling for an inquiry. The king was persuaded by his son to demand that Pelham investigate. Within a few months Pelham was able to gather sufficient evidence to exonerate Argyll and, by association, himself. In his report to the king Pelham said:

> Who can be responsible that no Jacobite shall ever, by any means, creep into the numberous employments of the revenue? As there are many rival connections in Scotland, all equally contending for power, interest and solicitations, may upon particular occasions, draw in a loyal subject to recommend a person whose character is not well known or misrepresented to him. (Jewell, 21)

At this same time, by chance, a genuine Jacobite plan, the Elibank plot, was being formed to seize George II and smuggle him out of the country. The Pelhams kept watch on the conspirators but also kept the plot a secret, probably because of the Argyll inquiry and possibly to prevent panic in the stock market, which would damage Pelham's reorganization of public finance.

Despite the competition for power at the highest level of politics, the peace and prosperity of the period allowed the Commons led by Pelham to give more time and thought to bills promoting public welfare, such as reform of poor laws, suppression of crime, construction of roads, and regulation of trade, all of which would contribute to social and hence political stability. Here Pelham's ability to gain co-operation from diverse groups was an important factor. While he and his lieutenants provided leadership and speeches to get bills through the Commons, much of the committee work on proposed legislation, the gathering of data, and the drafting of bills was done by back-bench members who held no office, and who included tories and independents as well as whigs. These men were more attuned to their constituents than to the court and could bring to Pelham's attention the needs and desires of the public. The felonies committee in 1751 investigated complaints that excessive consumption of gin was making workers idle and encouraging crime and as a remedy quickly produced the Gin Act regulating sale. When an epidemic of cattle distemper affected the whole country in the 1740s, the Commons supported privy council measures to contain the disease, even though they infringed property rights. After examining procedures for quarantining ships the Commons asked the king's ministers to find better means of keeping infectious disease out of the country and received a bill, enacted in 1753, that incorporated the members' suggestions. An adequate and wholesome supply of bread being essential to public order, the Commons in June 1749 passed a bill revising standards for the size and quality of bakers' loaves. A far more contentious aspect of the grain trade aroused debate and petitions to parliament after a nephew of Pelham, Charles Townshend, third Viscount Townshend, in 1751 published a pamphlet in which he urged abolition of the government bounty paid on grain exports. While popular with producers, the bounty was indeed a drain on the Treasury because exports had been exceptionally large since 1748. The issue caused so much worry and unrest among growers that Pelham, his health already failing, was forced to promise his Sussex constituents that the bounty would be retained. At a meeting held on 29 August 1753 to endorse his candidacy, Pelham said:

> as trade and particularly the corn trade is the chiefe concern of the County of Sussex, it shall be my constant care to encourage and support the same by encouraging our farmers in their agriculture and extending our commerce abroad[;] we have no reason to fear being what we ever have been, a rich and powerful people. (Connors, 275)

George II valued tranquillity in his subjects and any minister who could maintain it. 'Quiet', wrote Pelham, 'is what he loves better than all of us put together' (Coxe, 2.366). Three acts of parliament supported by Pelham did disturb both the public and the politicians, even though they effected necessary reforms. The Calendar Reform Act of 1752, which switched Britain to the Gregorian calendar used on the continent, caused some confusion and consternation. Hardwicke's Marriage Act of 1753, which prohibited clandestine and runaway marriages, divided the ministry and produced a vigorous pamphlet war between supporters and critics, who feared the elevation of the civil legislature over canon law and the granting of parental powers of veto for unattractive marriage proposals. The Jewish Naturalization Act of 1753 allowed Jews to take the oaths of supremacy and allegiance without using the word Christian. Pelham secured passage of the act because he thought it just and fair, but it may also have been in response to the Jewish community's help with the restructuring of the national debt. Replying on 7 May 1753 to expressions of the antisemitism common at that time, Pelham said, 'Surely, Sir, I am not to look upon every man as my enemy who differs from me in opinion upon any point of religion. This would be a most unchristian way of thinking' (Cobbett, *Parl. hist.*, 14.1414). Soon fierce public opposition was whipped up by propaganda misrepresenting the terms of the act, and by autumn Pelham began to fear that the controversy would affect the general election scheduled for April 1754. He therefore arranged repeal of the bill in December.

Hampered by his failing health and distracted by the uproar over the Naturalization Act, Pelham had to make time to deal with a gesture towards independence by the nominally subservient Irish parliament. The balance of domestic Irish politics had been disrupted by the intervention of the Anglican archbishop George Stone, whose faction was opposed by that of the speaker of the Irish

Commons, Henry Boyle. The ensuing disruptions in the parliament caused Newcastle, who was responsible for the political administration of Ireland, to doubt the ability of the lord lieutenant, Lionel Sackville, first duke of Dorset, to govern. After more than a year of conflict over how surplus money should be used, the Irish parliament in June 1753 petitioned the king to restore its right to dispose of that money as it wished. This was rejected as a threat to English supremacy, a move that provoked more turmoil in Dublin. When the Irish Commons in late December 1753 again presented its case, Pelham set the cabinet policy of completely rejecting Irish demands. He spent the next few months, the last of his life, preparing for the election.

Death Pelham died at his London house at about 6 a.m. on 6 March 1754. The previous July he had drunk the waters at Scarborough to treat a skin disorder. He fell ill about 15 December with fever, nausea, and skin eruptions that spread down his torso. His doctor drained a swelling then and another that developed in February. The few surviving descriptions of his symptoms are inadequate to suggest a diagnosis. Pelham returned to work on 7 January, telling Newcastle 'I am now, thank God, as well as ever I was in my life' (Coxe, 2.495), but he collapsed again with fever and skin eruptions on 3 March. He was buried in the family vault at Laughton, Sussex. After his death his brother was so overcome by grief that he secluded himself for several days. A contemporary said of Pelham:

> His abilities, integrity and candour gave him such confidence and trust as to enable him, by a proper and dexterous management of these qualities, to keep persons together and to give more Public quiet than I fear we shall see again for some time (J. Fowle to Henry Etough, 16 March 1754, BL, Add. MS 9201, fol. 103)

The tory Tobias Smollett wrote that Pelham's death was regretted by the nation 'to whose affection he had powerfully recommended himself by the candour and humanity of his conduct and character' (Wilkes, 214).

Pelham never used his offices for personal enrichment and never spared time to improve his estates, which brought in about £3000 a year at the time of his death. He owned his town house and country estate unencumbered. His total annual salary from both his offices was £11,600. He did try to put his affairs in order by drawing up a new will that took account of the marriage of his daughter Grace in 1752. On 25 November 1753 he wrote William Murray, Lord Mansfield, a letter containing the provisions, but he died before the final copy was ready, leaving a will dated 1748 with a codicil dated 1751. His executors found just under £10,500 in his account at Hoare's Bank, which was used to pay off a mortgage. The £10,000 marriage portion Pelham had agreed to in 1752 remained unpaid at his death. His personal estate was estimated at slightly over £15,000 and his debts and legacies at about £22,745, which forced his executors to sell land. Pelham profited from his long service to the crown little more than did his brother.

Portraits of Pelham in his chancellor's gown painted by William Hoare and John Shackleton about 1750 reveal his double chin and ample waistline but little of his character in the rather bland face shown. A more close-up portrait in plain dress, possibly by John Giles Eccardt, suggests strength and shrewdness, with a knowing look to the grey-blue eyes. When foreign relations were the predominant study of historians, Pelham seemed overshadowed by his brother Newcastle. His reputation as a statesman has risen, however, as economic historians have made clear that Britain's international power was built on the national system of finance. His restructuring of the national debt was Pelham's legacy to Britain and crucial to victory in the Seven Years' War. The stable government he provided during the brief mid-century peace inspired the renewed confidence the country needed after the uncertainties of the 1740s.   P. J. KULISHECK

Sources Pelham papers, U. Nott. L., Hallward Library, Newcastle (Clumber) MSS · BL, Newcastle MSS · BL, Hardwicke MSS · J. B. Owen, *The rise of the Pelhams* (1957) · J. W. Wilkes, *A whig in power: the political career of Henry Pelham* (1964) · W. Coxe, *Memoirs of the administration of the Right Honourable Henry Pelham*, 2 vols. (1829) · R. T. Connors, 'Pelham, parliament and public policy, 1746–1754', PhD diss., U. Cam., 1993 · B. F. Jewell, 'The legislation relating to Scotland after the forty-five', PhD diss., University of North Carolina, 1975 · J. L. McCracken, 'The conflict between the Irish administration and parliament, 1753–6', *Irish Historical Studies*, 3 (1942–3), 159–79 · A. N. Newman, 'The political patronage of Frederick Lewis, prince of Wales', *HJ*, 1 (1958), 68–75 · Cobbett, *Parl. hist.* · H. Walpole, *Memoirs of King George II*, ed. J. Brooke, 3 vols. (1985) · P. A. Luff, 'Mathews v. Lestock: parliament, politics and the navy in mid-eighteenth-century England', *Parliamentary History*, 10 (1991), 45–62 · P. C. Yorke, *The life and correspondence of Philip Yorke, earl of Hardwicke*, 3 vols. (1913) · R. Browning, *The duke of Newcastle* (1975) · R. Kelch, *Newcastle, a duke without money: Thomas Pelham-Holles, 1693–1768* (1974) · P. J. Kulisheck, *The duke of Newcastle, 1693–1768, and Henry Pelham, 1694–1754: a bibliography* (1997) · P. Campbell, ed., *A house in town: 22 Arlington Street, its owners and builders* (1984) · S. H. Nulle, *Thomas Pelham-Holles, duke of Newcastle: his early political career, 1693–1724* (1931) · P. J. Kulisheck, 'The "lost" Pelham papers', *Archives*, 24/101 (1999), 37–43 · baptismal register (1690–1719), St Giles-in-the-Fields, London · HoP, *Commons, 1690–1715* [draft] · L. B. Smith, 'The Pelham vault', *Sussex County Magazine*, 4 (1930), 370–72

Archives BL, biographical papers, Add. MSS 9202–9232 · Derbys. RO, corresp. relating to Ireland · RIBA, Arlington Street building accounts · Royal Institution of Cornwall, Truro, corresp. relating to parliamentary matters · U. Nott. L., corresp. and papers · Yale U., Beinecke L., corresp. | BL, corresp. with Lord Essex, Add. MSS 27732–27735 · BL, corresp. with earls of Hardwicke, etc., Add. MSS 35409–36137, *passim* · BL, corresp. with Lord Holdernesse, Egerton MSS 3413, 3437 · BL, corresp. with Lord Holland, Add. MS 51379 · BL, corresp. with duke of Newcastle, etc., Add. MSS 32686–33066, *passim* · Chatsworth House, Derbyshire, letters to dukes of Devonshire · Mount Stuart Trust Archive, Rothesay, corresp. with Lord Loudon · NMM, corresp. with Lord Sandwich · NRA, priv. coll., letters to first Earl Waldegrave · PRO, letters to Lord Stafford, PRO 30/29 · U. Cal., Berkeley, corresp. with earl of Chesterfield · U. Nott. L., letters to Richard Arundell

Likenesses attrib. J. G. Eccardt, oils, 1750?, Gov. Art Coll., London · W. Hoare, oils, 1751?, NPG [see illus.] · attrib. W. Hoare, oils, 1752?, Gov. Art Coll. · J. Shackleton, oils, c.1752, NPG; on loan to Gov. Art Coll. · J. Shackleton?, double portrait, oils, c.1752 (with his secretary), NPG; copy, Gov. Art Coll. · E. Harding, stipple, 1802, BM, NPG; repro. in W. Coxe, *Memoirs of Horatio, Lord Walpole* (1802) · W. Hoare, oils, replica, Palace of Westminster · R. Houston, mezzotint (after J. Shackleton), BM, NPG

Wealth at death personal estate approx. £15,000; landed estate c.£3000 p.a.; debts and legacies c.£22,745: U. Nott. L., Hallward Library, Newcastle (Clumber) papers, NeC 4297 and NeS 137

Pelham, Henry (1749–1806). *See under* Pelham, Peter (1695?–1751).

Pelham, Henry Francis (1846–1907), historian, was grandson of Thomas *Pelham, second earl of Chichester (1756–1826), and eldest of the five children of John Thomas *Pelham (1811–1894), bishop of Norwich, and his wife, Henrietta (d. 31 December 1893), second daughter of Thomas William Tatton of Wythenshawe Hall, Cheshire. Of his three brothers, John Barrington (1848–1941) was vicar of Thundridge, Hertfordshire (1908–14), and Sidney (1849–1926) was archdeacon of Norfolk (1901–16). Pelham was born on 19 September 1846 at Bergh Apton, Norfolk, then his father's parish. He attended Miss Hodgson's school, Brighton, and the Revd F. Storr's school in Kent. Entering Harrow School (Brooke Foss Westcott's house) in May 1860, he moved rapidly up the school, was three years in the sixth form, and left in December 1864. He was quiet, reserved, and apparently somewhat delicate in health. He was coached by a well-known scholar, the Revd North Pinder, rector of Rotherfield Greys, Oxfordshire, and formerly fellow of Trinity College, Oxford, in 1865. He won an open classical scholarship at Trinity College, Oxford (matriculating on 22 April 1865); he went into residence in October. At Oxford he was prominent in the Claret Club, played in the cricket eleven, and was a fine walker. He gained firsts in classical moderations and *literae humaniores* (BA, 1869; MA, 1872) and was elected fellow of Exeter College in 1869. In 1870 he won the chancellor's English essay prize with a dissertation on the reciprocal influence of national character and national language. He was classical tutor and lecturer at Exeter College from 1870 until 1889, and proctor in 1879. Losing his fellowship on his marriage in 1873, he was re-elected in 1882, under the statutes of the second university commission.

From school onwards Pelham's principal subject was ancient and especially Roman history. He published articles on this (first in the *Journal of Philology*, 1876), while his Exeter intercollegiate lectures attracted increasingly large audiences. He also planned, with the Clarendon Press, a detailed history of the Roman empire, which he was not destined to complete. In 1887 he succeeded William Wolfe Capes as common fund reader in ancient history, and in 1889 became Camden professor of ancient history in succession to George Rawlinson, a post to which a Brasenose fellowship was attached. As professor he attracted even larger audiences. His research was stopped by cataracts in both eyes (1890), and though an operation subsequently restored most of his eyesight, he had to limit his reading. A few specimen paragraphs of his 'History' were set up in type in 1888, but he completed in manuscript only three and a half chapters, on 35–15 BC, and never resumed the work after 1890; his other research, too, was thereafter limited to detached points in Roman imperial history. However, he joined actively in administration, for

Henry Francis Pelham (1846–1907), by Sir Hubert von Herkomer, 1893

which his strong personality and clear sense fitted him. He helped to found the school of geography: he served on many Oxford committees—including those of the Bodleian Library, Ashmolean Museum and geography school—and was a member of the hebdomadal council, with two brief intervals, from 1879 to 1905. A reformer, he urged the use of college revenues for university purposes. Pelham was a prominent Liberal, active as such in the university and in the city. One of the few academic Liberals to support home rule for Ireland, he helped to organize Gladstone's visit to Oxford in 1890.

Pelham supported women's education in Oxford. In 1879, with Professor T. H. Green, A. H. Acland, and other Liberal dons, he was a member of the committee for a non-denominational women's hall which that year founded Somerville Hall (later Somerville College), then a member of its council—fund-raising within the university—its vice-president (1886–93), and second president (1893–1907). A benefactor of its library and an occasional tutor to some of its best students, he was a familiar figure at Somerville (his contribution, minimized in the 1996 college history, was acknowledged in its predecessor of 1922). He pressed for women's admission to Oxford lectures, examinations, and degrees. In 1886, unlike most Oxford Liberal dons, he did not become Liberal Unionist, and he long presided over the Oxford City Liberal Association. When president of Trinity he was especially concerned with its mission at Stratford, east London. In 1897 he became president of Trinity. He was elected FSA in 1890, and honorary fellow of Exeter in 1895, was an original FBA

in 1902 and received an honorary LLD from Aberdeen in 1906. He was a governor of Harrow and other schools.

On 30 July 1873 Pelham married Laura Priscilla (d. 2 Nov 1918), third daughter of Sir Edward North Buxton, second baronet, and granddaughter of Sir Thomas Fowell *Buxton, first baronet (1786–1845). They had three sons and two daughters, of whom one son and one daughter died young.

Pelham was both a scholar and a practical man, forceful, direct, sometimes showing 'aristocratic impatience' (Haverfield, xxii), and overstating his case, he disliked opposition, but was also warm and sympathetic to undergraduates. An excellent teacher, lecturing at a time when Oxford was widening its outlook and Theodor Mommsen and his school were recreating Roman history, he helped to revolutionize the study of ancient history in Oxford, and so in England. Moreover, combining organizing skills with an understanding of the needs of learning and the character of scientific research, he did much to develop Oxford as a place of research, while conserving its educational role. He was prominent in providing endowments for higher study and research, in introducing archaeology and geography to Oxford's ancient historical work, and in founding the British Schools at Rome and Athens. He helped to put natural science, English, and foreign languages on a more adequate basis in Oxford, and to give women educational opportunities there.

Pelham wrote little. His chief publications were *Outlines of Roman History* (1893), enlarged from his article in *Encyclopaedia Britannica* (1887), and essays and articles on Roman history, of which the chief, with part of his unfinished 'History', were published in a posthumous volume of *Essays* (1911). Both books were considered to exhibit high historical powers. Pelham died in the president's lodgings at Trinity on 12 February 1907, and was buried in St Sepulchre's cemetery, Oxford. After his death his widow gave his library of works on Roman history and archaeology to Brasenose College, and his friends founded in his memory a Pelham studentship for Oxford men or women at the British School at Rome. His son, Sir Edward Henry Pelham (1876–1949), was permanent secretary of the Board of Education (1931–7).

F. J. HAVERFIELD, rev. ROGER T. STEARN

Sources *The Times* (13 Feb 1907) • F. J. Haverfield, 'Henry Francis Pelham, 1846–1907', *PBA*, [3] (1907–8), 365–70 • F. Haverfield, 'Biographical note', in *Essays by Henry Francis Pelham*, ed. F. Haverfield (1911) • private information (1912) • *WWW, 1897–1915* • Burke, *Peerage* (1999) • Foster, *Alum. Oxon.* • M. St. C. Byrne and C. H. Mansfield, *Somerville College, 1879–1921* [1922] • P. Adams, *Somerville for women: an Oxford college, 1879–1993* (1996) • H. Pelling, *Social geography of British elections, 1885–1910* (1967) • Gladstone, *Diaries*

Likenesses H. von Herkomer, oils, 1893, Trinity College, Oxford [see illus.]

Wealth at death £15,332 6s. 8d.: probate, 19 March 1907, *CGPLA Eng. & Wales*

Pelham, Henry Thomas, third earl of Chichester (1804–1886), ecclesiastical commissioner, the second, but eldest surviving, son of Thomas *Pelham, second earl (1756–1826), and Lady Mary Henrietta Juliana Osborne (1776–1862), daughter of the fifth duke of Leeds, was born in

Stratton Street, Piccadilly, London, on 25 August 1804, and was educated at Westminster School and Trinity College, Cambridge, which he entered as a nobleman in April 1822, taking no degree. On 24 April 1824 he entered the army as a cornet in the 6th dragoons, but, by the influence of the duke of Wellington, was able on 14 October of the same year to exchange into the Royal Horse Guards. He became lieutenant in 1827, captain (unattached) in January 1828, and major in the army in 1841. In 1844 he resigned his commission. He was afterwards an active supporter of the volunteer movement. In 1825 the duke of Newcastle invited him, without making any stipulation regarding Pelham's political principles, to accept his nomination for the parliamentary representation of the duke's borough of Newark, but Pelham succeeded to the earldom on 4 July 1826, before the election.

Chichester held whig opinions, but was not an ardent partisan. He was a strong evangelical who expressed his views temperately. He was deeply interested in religious, social, and educational questions. On 22 February 1841, just before the fall of the whig government, he was appointed an ecclesiastical commissioner, and on 30 January 1847 became a commissioner to report on the question of equalizing the pecuniary value of episcopal sees. When the church estates' committee was appointed in 1850 Chichester was made head of the board, with the title of first church estates' commissioner. He retained the position until October 1878, with a very heavy burden of work, and after his retirement from it continued to be an ecclesiastical commissioner. He was largely responsible for the important reforms carried out in the management and distribution of church revenues, and was the chief lay influence in the material reform and administration of the Church of England from the 1840s to the 1870s. Chichester was also for half a century president of the Church Missionary Society, and was connected with the Evangelical Alliance, the British and Foreign Bible Society, and the Church of England Temperance Society. He was president of the Royal Agricultural Society in 1849. He was also interested in the management of prisons, becoming in 1843 a commissioner of Pentonville prison, and editing in 1863 Sir Joshua Jebb's *Reports and Observations on the Discipline and Management of Convict Prisons*. In spite of his evangelical views, he spoke on 16 July 1845 in support of the grant to endow the Roman Catholic college of Maynooth in Ireland. He was a regular attendant, and not infrequent speaker, in the House of Lords.

Chichester was appointed lord lieutenant of Sussex on 21 November 1860, where he was very popular. He had married, on 18 August 1828, Lady Mary Brudenell, fifth daughter of the sixth earl of Cardigan, and his wife, Penelope Anne, *née* Cooke. She died on 22 May 1867, leaving four sons and three daughters. Chichester died at his seat, Stanmer Park, Sussex, on 15 March 1886. His eldest son, Walter John Pelham (1838–1902), MP for Lewes from 1865 to 1874, succeeded to the title.

G. Le G. Norgate, rev. H. C. G. Matthew

Sources GEC, *Peerage* · Venn, *Alum. Cant.* · *The Times* (17 March 1886) · *The Record* (19 March 1886) · *The Argus* [Brighton] (17 March 1886) · G. F. A. Best, *Temporal pillars: Queen Anne's bounty, the ecclesiastical commissioners, and the Church of England* (1964) · *CGPLA Eng. & Wales* (1886)

Archives BL, letters to W. E. Gladstone, Add. MSS 44351–44784 · BLPES, letters to Sir Joshua Jebb · Bodl. Oxf., letters to H. E. Manning · Bodl. Oxf., letters, incl. those of wife · LPL, corresp. with A. C. Tait · W. Sussex RO, letters to duke of Richmond

Likenesses F. Holl, oils, exh. RA 1886, County Hall, Lewes · J. Scott, mezzotint (after F. Holl), BM · portrait, repro. in *The Argus* · woodcut, NPG

Wealth at death £50,861 18s. 9d.: probate, 8 May 1886, *CGPLA Eng. & Wales*

Pelham, Herbert (c.1600–1674), colonist in America, was the son of Herbert Pelham (d. in or after 1629) of Boston, Lincolnshire, and his first wife, Penelope, daughter of Thomas West, second Baron De La Warr. Nothing is known of his early years or education but in 1626 he married, by licence dated 13 October, Jemima (d. c.1639), daughter of Thomas Waldegrave of Bures-ad-montem, Essex. The couple had seven children, including a daughter, Penelope, who married Josiah Winslow, governor of Plymouth Colony; Pelham's sister Penelope married Richard Bellingham, governor of Massachusetts Bay.

Along with his father and other members of his family Pelham became deeply involved in the work of the Massachusetts Bay Company in 1629, and was one of those engaged to 'frame the form of the oath for the Governor … also for his Deputy, & for the Counsell' (Shurtleff, 1.39). He had been preceded to New England by his younger brother William, who established himself at the new town of Sudbury and obtained grants of land there for his brother. When Herbert Pelham finally arrived in New England in late 1639 or early 1640, his first wife had recently died, and he married by 1640 Elizabeth Harlakenden, *née* Bosville (d. in or before 1659), widow of Roger Harlakenden of Cambridge, Massachusetts. The couple settled in Cambridge and had seven children; Pelham probably never resided on his lands in Sudbury.

During his residence in New England Pelham held a number of important offices. He was elected an assistant in 1645 and 1646, and also in 1646 was appointed commissioner from Massachusetts Bay to the United Colonies of New England. He was also appointed treasurer of Harvard College in 1643. Late in 1646 he returned to England, but was clearly expected for some time to go back to New England, as he was elected, *in absentia*, assistant in 1647, 1648, and 1649. By 1648 he had settled in Bures, Essex, at the manor of Ferrers, which had come to him through his first wife. In 1654 he sat in parliament for Essex. He resided at Bures for the remainder of his life, and was buried there on 1 July 1674.

Robert Charles Anderson

Sources M. B. Colket jun., 'The Pelhams of England and New England', *American Genealogist*, 16 (1939–40), 129–32, 201–5; 18 (1941–2), 137–46, 210–18; 19 (1942–3), 197–202; 20 (1943–4), 65–76 · P. P. Behrens, *Footnotes: a biography of Penelope Pelham, 1633–1703* (1998) · N. B. Shurtleff, ed., *Records of the governor and company of the Massachusetts Bay in New England*, 5 vols. in 6 (1853–4)

Wealth at death disposed of substantial landholdings in Essex, Lincoln, Ireland, and New England: will

Pelham, Sir John (d. 1429), landowner and administrator, was the son of Thomas Pelham of Warbleton, Sussex, and of Agnes, daughter of Robert Gensing and coheir of the manor of Gensing, Sussex. Probably of age by 1376, in September 1387 Pelham allegedly mounted a full-scale night assault in Cambridgeshire (a county in which he also had some family interests) on Sir John Shardlow's house at Fulbourn in order to abduct—and then marry—Margaret (1363–1390), widow of Shardlow's son, and heir in her own right of Sir Roger Grey of Cavendish, Suffolk. Margaret died in 1390; possibly in 1399 but certainly by May 1400 Pelham had married Joan (d. 1439), widow of Sir Hugh Zouche and daughter of John Bramshott. She brought to Pelham her first husband's lands in Cambridgeshire and Sussex. But Pelham's sole surviving child was apparently an illegitimate son, John, who was knighted in France in 1415, and to whom he left much of his property.

Pelham's administrative career began in the service of John of Gaunt, duke of Lancaster, on whose 1386 Spanish campaign he probably served and who in 1393 made him constable of Pevensey Castle for life. Posts in the archbishop of Canterbury's Sussex estates soon followed. He later served on royal commissions, including one seizing the goods of Richard (III) Fitzalan, earl of Arundel, after the earl's execution in 1397. Pelham's disappearance later that year makes it likely he followed Henry Bolingbroke into exile. On the latter's return Pelham regained control of Pevensey Castle and was besieged there by forces loyal to Richard II in July 1399, creating an important diversion from Bolingbroke's landing in Yorkshire.

The new Lancastrian regime soon displayed its confidence in one of its most dedicated southern partisans. Pelham was knighted on 13 October 1399 before Henry IV's coronation, then made royal sword-bearer and a knight of the household. His Pevensey constableship was confirmed, and buttressed with nearby lands. He represented Sussex in parliament continuously from 1399 to 1407, except in 1401–2 when he was sheriff of Sussex with Surrey instead. Henry IV found it increasingly convenient to employ him in neighbouring counties. He became a commissioner of array—and, more briefly, a justice of the peace—for Surrey and Hampshire as well as Sussex. After the death of William Wykeham in 1404 he was joint keeper of the bishopric of Winchester's temporalities for six months, and then took over keepership of the New forest, as well as becoming chief steward of the duchy of Lancaster estates south of the Trent. In 1409 Henry granted to him for life the duchy estates in Sussex, worth up to £270 a year—making him possibly the greatest landowner in Sussex, ahead of Thomas Fitzalan, earl of Arundel.

Pelham also had employments of more national significance. Entrusted with the removal of the deposed Richard II to Leeds Castle from the Tower of London late in October 1399, in 1405 he had Edward, duke of York (d. 1415), committed to his custody at Pevensey as suspected of treason, and from 1406 to 1409 Edmund and Roger Mortimer. He was a member of the royal council from 1404 until the restriction in membership in 1406, a period that coincided with his treasurership for war (11 November 1404 - 19 June

1406), jointly with Thomas Neville, Lord Furnival—a function that both incumbents sought to resign and finally induced parliament to support them in doing so.

Pelham was friendly with Prince Thomas (later duke of Clarence)—who named him as an executor in 1417—and with Archbishop Thomas Arundel (d. 1414), rather than with Prince Henry. When the latter took advantage of the king's illness in 1409, therefore, Pelham ceased to receive his usual commissions (even local ones) and patronage. The removal of the prince of Wales's friends in 1411 offered compensation: Pelham became treasurer (20 December 1411–20 March 1413) and was granted new Sussex lands which ultimately brought his landed income to over £870 a year, giving him a dominant position in the county after the death of the earl of Arundel in 1415.

Pelham's last service to Henry IV was to act as an executor of his will—a troublesome and protracted exercise in deficit finance. On Henry V's accession Pelham lost both the post of treasurer (to his local rival Arundel) and his Lancaster stewardship. Nevertheless, the new king was willing to employ Pelham on local commissions, and also on a powerful embassy to France (10 July–3 October 1414). Further important prisoners were sent to him at Pevensey, including James I of Scotland (for whose release he was one of the negotiators in 1423–4), and the dowager queen and alleged sorceress, Joan of Navarre (d. 1439).

Pelham returned to the royal council between Henry V's departure for France in July 1417 and the king's death in August 1422; he was a friend of Thomas Langley (d. 1437), chancellor from July 1417 to July 1424. He also again represented Sussex in the Commons in 1422 and 1427, perhaps largely in an attempt to facilitate the conclusion of Henry IV's troubled testamentary affairs. Pelham died on 12 February 1429, and was buried in the Cistercian abbey of Robertsbridge, Sussex. His monastic interests also involved the rebuilding of the collapsed Augustinian priory of Holy Trinity, Hastings, on his patrimony at Warbleton. Pelham's second wife, Joan, outlived him by ten years.

JULIAN LOCK

Sources L. S. Woodger and J. S. Roskell, 'Pelham, John', HoP, Commons · DNB · S. K. Walker, 'Letters to the dukes of Lancaster in 1381 and 1399', EngHR, 106 (1991), 68–79 · CPR · L. F. Salzman, 'The early heraldry of Pelham', Sussex Archaeological Collections, 69 (1928), 53–70 · B. Williams, ed., Chronicque de la traïson et mort de Richart Deux, roy Dengleterre, EHS, 9 (1846) · S. Walker, The Lancastrian affinity, 1361–1399 (1990)
Wealth at death wealthy; landed income over £870 p.a. in 1426: Woodger and Roskell, 'Pelham, John', 4.43

Pelham, John Thomas (1811–1894), bishop of Norwich, was born on 21 June 1811, the third son of Thomas *Pelham, the second earl of Chichester (1756–1826), and Lady Mary Henrietta Juliana Osborne (1776–1862), daughter of the fifth duke of Leeds. He attended Westminster School and proceeded to Christ Church, Oxford, where he matriculated in 1829. He graduated BA in 1832, and received his MA and DD in 1857. He was made deacon by Bishop Blomfield of London in 1834 and priested in 1835.

Pelham's first charge was the parish of Eastergate in the diocese of Chichester, where he entered into what became a lifelong friendship with Henry Manning. In May 1837 the earl of Abergavenny presented him to the rectory of Bergh Apton, a small village near Norwich. He married, on 6 November 1845, Henrietta (d. 1893), second daughter of Thomas William Tatton of Wythenshawe Hall, Cheshire. In 1847 he was made honorary canon of Norwich Cathedral and became chaplain-in-ordinary to the queen. In 1852 he moved to the north of London to become perpetual curate of Christ Church, Hampstead, whose patron was Sir Thomas Maryon Wilson. After only three years he received the important crown living of St Marylebone on the recommendation of Lord Palmerston, who had just become prime minister. His ministry here was destined to be short, as in 1857 Palmerston nominated him to the see of Norwich, which was vacant by the resignation of Samuel Hinds. Lord Shaftesbury had originally suggested that Pelham should be considered for London ('a fitter man could not be found in England') and that Tait should have Norwich, but other counsels prevailed. Palmerston accepted the advice that a forthright evangelical bishop of London would antagonize the Tractarians. Pelham was consecrated on 30 April 1857 by Archbishop J. B. Sumner and bishops A. C. Tait and C. R. Sumner. Pelham was bishop of Norwich for thirty-six years, which was longer than any of his predecessors except for Bishop Le Spencer, who held the see from 1370 to 1406.

As a bishop Pelham proved himself an able administrator and, though he rarely spoke in the House of Lords, unrivalled in the chairing of public meetings. He was a thoroughgoing pastoral bishop. In his first years of office he made rural deans the means of meeting with his clergy. In later times he visited them in a more systematic way. His custom was to spend a long weekend in each parish passing time with the clergyman's family, participating in the church services, and inspecting the Sunday and day schools. His constant activity even succeeded in stirring up the dormant energies of his senior clergy. Although of decidedly evangelical convictions he was conciliatory in his attitude to the high-church movement. In his diocesan charge of 1865 he dwelt on the current romanizing tendencies, but also referred to those of his clergy who undervalued the sacraments. He urged that holy communion services be held once a month and at festivals. Like other evangelicals of the period Pelham also advocated that baptism be held during public services. He pressed for the reform of convocation by consolidating the provinces of Canterbury and York and by extending the franchise to all licensed clergy in priests' orders. He urged the division of large dioceses, including his own, into smaller, more manageable units.

Pelham welcomed the 1870 Elementary Education Act, which he felt could bring great benefits to the church as a whole. Through a diocesan church association he provided the means for building and restoring churches, parsonages, and schools throughout the diocese. He also initiated a scheme to raise the stipend of the smaller benefices at the expense of part of his own income. Pelham was not given to the habit of writing and published little beyond his charges to the diocese. The text of a sermon he preached before the Church Missionary Society in May 1852 was printed in the same year. He also edited a small collection entitled *Hymns for Public Worship* in 1855.

Pelham resigned the see early in 1893. His wife died on 31 December 1893; he died at Thorpe, a suburb of Norwich, on 1 May 1894. He was a pastor of pronounced evangelical views which were coupled, according to the *Christian Remembrancer*, with 'some ability, entire earnestness, and the manners and feelings of a gentleman'. He left three sons and a daughter. The eldest son, Henry Francis *Pelham, became professor of ancient history at Oxford, and a fourth son, Herbert Pelham (1855–1881), died after a climbing accident in the Alps.　　　　NIGEL SCOTLAND

Sources *The Times* (2 May 1894) · *The Record* (18 May 1894) · Crockford (1893) · *Eastern Daily Press* (4 Feb 1893) · *Norwich Diocesan Calendar* (1894) · Boase, *Mod. Eng. biog.* · *Christian Remembrancer*, new ser., 36 (1858) · M. Hennel, *Sons of the prophets* (1979) · W. Benham and R. T. Davidson, *Life of Archibald Campbell Tait*, 2 vols. (1891) **Archives** LPL, letters to A. C. Tait **Likenesses** portrait, 1859, repro. in *The Church of England photographic portrait gallery* (1859) · portrait, repro. in *ILN*, 48 (1865), 365 · portrait, repro. in *Daily Graphic* (1 Feb 1893), 14 · portrait, repro. in *Norwich Diocesan Calendar* **Wealth at death** £13,605 0s. 5d.: probate, 4 June 1894, *CGPLA Eng. & Wales*

Pelham [née **Manners**], **Lady Katharine** (1700/01–1780), political wife, was the daughter of John Manners, second duke of Rutland (1676–1721), and his first wife, Catherine Russell (d. 31 Oct 1711), daughter of William *Russell, Lord Russell, and Rachel *Russell, née Wriothesley, and sister of Wriothesley Russell, second duke of Bedford. With such impeccable aristocratic whig credentials and connections, and a portion of £30,000 (also given as the marginally less spectacular £10,000), she was the ideal wife for any aspiring young whig politician, especially if he also happened to be a younger son. Henry *Pelham (1694–1754) was just such a man. The younger brother of Thomas Pelham-*Holles, first duke of Newcastle, Pelham was politically ambitious and was already secretary at war in Sir Robert Walpole's administration by the time of their marriage on 29 October 1726. In August 1743 Pelham would take up Walpole's mantle to become one of the eighteenth century's most successful first lords of the Treasury. While their marriage was a political success, linking two solidly whig families and providing Pelham with a secure place among the political élite, it was also remarkably happy despite personal tragedy. Of their eight children, two sons and six daughters, only four survived to adulthood. That one daughter died an infant was not unusual at the time, but losing both sons, Thomas and Henry, within two days of each other to an 'epidemic sore throat' (Walpole, *Corr.*, 17.398), probably diphtheria, in November 1739, and then another daughter, Louisa or Lucy, only two months later, was.

As the wife, later the widow, of one of Britain's leading politicians and the sister-in-law of his successor as prime minister, Lady Katharine lived and breathed politics until Newcastle's resignation in 1762. Given the centrality of patronage for anyone wanting social or political advancement in the eighteenth century and contemporary assumptions about the political influence that women were expected to have on their menfolk, as well as the wide assortment of useful connections that women in politically active families were presumed to form, it is not surprising that Lady Katharine's services as a patronage broker were continually in demand. A formidable woman who seldom minced words and did not suffer fools gladly, she used the patronage system astutely and successfully. She sought patronage not only for herself—she was appointed ranger of Greenwich Park in 1745—and her unmarried daughters, but also for a carefully chosen stream of applicants. Her correspondence reveals that she kept a close eye on what positions were available or likely to become available, and secured promises and reversions well in advance if possible. A well-chosen, acerbic reminder, especially to Newcastle who appears to have stood in awe of her, was enough to ensure that promises were not forgotten.

Lady Katharine achieved her greatest patronage success when she secured the parliamentary seat at Harwich for John Roberts over the king's chosen candidate. Roberts had managed government boroughs under Pelham and had taken advantage of the rivalry between the Treasury and the Post Office in Harwich to build up his own interest there. Pelham had suggested that he stand for election in 1754, but Roberts had refused. When William Ponsonby, Viscount Duncannon, succeeded his father as second earl of Bessborough and Baron Ponsonby of Sysonby, and the seat became vacant in 1758, Roberts was ready. He immediately enlisted Lady Katharine's support and she, in turn, immediately recommended Roberts to Newcastle. Newcastle agreed to bring him in at the next election. Problems arose, in 1761, however, when the new king, George III, decided that his candidate, Charles Townshend, should get Harwich. Newcastle was caught 'between the upper and nether millstone, the King and Lady Katherine Pelham, and he hardly knew which was the more formidable' (Namier, 372).

Lady Katharine was adamant. By February 1761 Newcastle was warding off her anger:

> I disputed it, combated [sic] it, and oppos'd it, as much as I could; I did not prevail; But yet I don't despair, but I shall at last be able to get Mr Roberts in at Harwich. But if I can't, It is not my Fault. (BL, Add. MS 32918, fol. 279v, Newcastle to Lady Katharine Pelham, 5 Feb 1761)

She was determined that Roberts should have both the seat at Harwich and the first vacancy at the Board of Trade. Her response to Newcastle's predicament was typical of their relationship: 'I am really sorry for the distresses you are in, and shall always wish to diminish, not increase them; but you must give me leave to say, that you bring them chiefly on your self' (ibid., fols. 471v–472, Lady Katharine Pelham to Newcastle, London, 12 Feb [1761]). In the end, she succeeded. Newcastle solved his problem elegantly: he installed both her candidate and the king's at Harwich and moved the other sitting member to a different seat.

Lady Katharine's frustration with Newcastle was due in part to personality differences and to the problematic relationship Newcastle had with his heir, Henry Fiennes Clinton, ninth earl of Lincoln [see Clinton, Henry Fiennes Pelham-, second duke of Newcastle under Lyme], who was also the husband of her favourite daughter Catherine (1727–1760). It was also exacerbated by her position as a political woman and an intermediary in the patronage system. While her personality, rank, and position in the political world due to birth, marriage, and widowhood gave her one of the most privileged political positions for a woman outside the inner circle of the royal family, and she was to use her influence successfully over an extended period of time, she was never a territorial political figure in the way that other élite women were; consequently, her political importance and involvement ended with Newcastle's resignation in 1762 and Henry Fox's subsequent purge of Pelhamites. Personally, however, she remained indomitable, putting her energy into social and familial affairs until her death at her home in Whitehall, London, on 18 February 1780, aged seventy-nine.

E. H. Chalus

Sources GEC, *Peerage*, new edn, 11.266–7 · A. Collins, *The peerage of England: containing a genealogical and historical account of all the peers of England*, vol. 5 · L. B. Namier, *The structure of politics at the accession of George III* (1960) · corresp. with duke of Newcastle, 1752–1765, BL, Add. MSS 32735–33072 · corresp. with earl of Hardwicke, 1756, 1760, BL, Add. MSS 35594, 35596 · case for counsel's opinion, 1758, Add. MSS 36189, 36224 · Lady Katherine Pelham v. Gregory, MS report, 1760, BL, Add. MS 36165, fol. 231 · letter to marchioness of Rockingham, 1768, BL, Add. MS 33082, fol. 6 · letters to earl of Chichester, 1765–1768, BL, Add. MS 33088, fols. 59, 96, 298 · letters to duchess of Newcastle, 1760–1778, BL, Add. MSS 33067, fol. 247; 33069, fol. 359; 33083, fols. 135, 149 · will, PRO, PROB 11/1063, sig. 155 · Walpole, *Corr.*, vols. 17, 21, 35, 43 · IGI

Archives BL, Newcastle papers · U. Nott., Newcastle collection

Wealth at death probably over £6000: will, 21 July 1775; codicil, 4 Feb 1780; proved 1780, PRO, PROB 11/1063, sig. 155

Pelham, Sir Nicholas (*d.* 1560), landowner and member of parliament, was the eldest son of Sir William Pelham (*d.* 1538/9) of Laughton, Sussex, and his first wife, Mary, daughter of Sir Richard Carew of Beddington. His maternal uncle Sir Nicholas Carew, after whom he was presumably named, was master of the horse to Henry VIII. Carew's attainder for treason in March 1539, accused of implication in the Courtenay conspiracy, cast a shadow over Pelham's succession as head of the family, though the damage done to his immediate prospects may have been offset by his links through his stepmother, Mary Sandys, to her father, the first Baron Sandys, who was lord chamberlain until December 1540. An illicit hunting party in the spring of 1541 at his recently enlarged family home at Laughton involved the killing of one of his gamekeepers by a servant of his near-contemporary and neighbour from Herstmonceux, Thomas Fiennes, ninth Lord Dacre of the South, for which Dacre was executed in June 1541. Pelham's marriage, by 1537, to Anne Sackville, the daughter of a rising Sussex gentleman, strengthened his family's ancient links with the Howard dukes of Norfolk and the Fitzalan earls of Arundel: with Anne he had eight surviving children. He pushed ahead with his father's scheme to drain Laughton marsh, and like his father invested in sheep. He also consolidated his estates in and around his home. Perhaps by inclination he eschewed attendance at court, answering only occasional summonses to major state occasions, for instance the reception of the admiral of France in 1546.

Named to the Sussex bench in 1544, Pelham became active in county administration, and he also distinguished himself in the region's defence against the French, in 1545 organizing the militia to repulse a landing between Newhaven and Brighton. He was twice returned to parliament, in 1547 for the borough of Arundel and in 1558 for the shire. Following the arrest of the duke of Somerset in the autumn of 1549 he was pricked sheriff of Surrey and Sussex, and on 17 November he was made a knight. The timing of these honours suggests that he had not rallied to Somerset against the earl of Warwick during the recent *coup d'état*. His political allegiance may not have been fixed, however, for two years later he was briefly imprisoned with Somerset and Arundel for plotting against Warwick, by now duke of Northumberland. While captive in the Tower, and evidently despairing of his life, he made a brief will in his own hand. Of his part in the succession crisis in 1553 nothing is known beyond his receipt of a letter dated 14 July from leading figures in Kent denouncing Lady Jane Grey's claim to the throne. Under Mary, Pelham's career continued apace, although his protestantism presumably made him an increasingly uncomfortable supporter of the regime. Early in 1554 his brother William supported Sir Thomas Wyatt in his rising against Queen Mary's plans to marry Philip of Spain, and his eldest son, John, fled abroad in 1556, travelling to Padua and Geneva. Pelham's refusal to provide men for the army in 1558 may have been a protest against the new regulations for musters, since after a spell in the Fleet prison he agreed to supply warhorses instead.

Pelham lived for almost two years after the accession of Elizabeth. On 6 February 1560 he made his second will, in which he expressed his confidence that he would be 'received amonge his [Christ's] electe'—a phrase which suggests Calvinist leanings (Manning, 264). He survived another eight months before he died on 15 September; he was buried in St Michael's Church, Lewes, where his funerary monument immortalizes his military prowess in 1545. His half-brother Sir Edmund *Pelham (d. 1606) was a lawyer who became chief baron of the Irish exchequer. Pelham's descendants remained a power in Sussex until in the eighteenth century their influence in the county became paramount under Thomas Pelham-Holles, duke of Newcastle.   ALASDAIR HAWKYARD

Sources HoP, *Commons, 1509–58*, 3.80–81 · HoP, *Commons, 1558–1603*, 3.192–5 · *LP Henry VIII*, vols. 15–21 · *APC, 1542–70* · *CPR, 1547–63* · W. A. Shaw, *The knights of England*, 2 vols. (1906) · C. H. Garrett, *The Marian exiles: a study in the origins of Elizabethan puritanism* (1938) · E. G. Pelham and D. McLean, *Some early Pelhams* (1931) · R. B. Manning, *Religion and society in Elizabethan Sussex* (1969) · *Sussex*, Pevsner (1965) · T. W. Horsfield, *The history, antiquities and topography of the county of Sussex*, 2 vols. (1835) · W. B. Bannerman, ed., *The visitations of the county of Sussex … 1530 … and 1633–4*, Harleian Society, 53 (1905) · wills, PRO, PROB 11/27, fols. 187v–188; 11/45, fol. 61

Archives Barbican House Museum, Lewes, Sussex, Laughton excavation reports · BL, Harley MS 249, fol. 43 · PRO, SP 1, 10, 11

Pelham, Peregrine (*bap.* 1602, *d.* 1650), politician and regicide, was baptized on 27 September 1602 at Bosham, Sussex, the eldest son of Peregrine Pelham of Wickham, Lincolnshire, and later of Hull, and his wife, Anne. His grandfather was the lord chief justice of Ireland, Sir William *Pelham (d. 1587), a descendant of the Pelhams of Laughton, Sussex. Pelham was apprenticed to the Hull merchant Thomas Aslaby and later admitted as a burgess of the town on 3 August 1626. He married his first wife, a sister of John Bowes, in or before 1628 when their son, John, was baptized in Hull. Presumably this wife died, as some time in or after 1630 Pelham married Jacoba Vanlore, the widow of Sir Peter *Vanlore (c.1547–1627), a wealthy merchant from Tilehurst, Berkshire. Pelham became prosperous in continental trade, importing French wines and exporting lead. He was elected chamberlain of Hull on 30 September 1630 and served as town sheriff in 1636. On Sir John Lister's death Pelham was elected MP for Hull on 18 January 1641. His commercial expertise was soon recognized and on 7 June 1641 he was named to the committee to regulate trade with Scotland.

Pelham was in Hull in April 1642 when the king appeared before the Beverley gate demanding entry. Pelham conferred with Hull's parliamentarian governor, Sir John Hotham, reputedly in the building now known as the White Hart inn, and refused the king admission, thereby preserving Hull's crucial arms magazine for parliament. On 18 May 1642 Pelham was appointed to a Commons committee sent north to assist Hotham on 24 May. Present in Hull during the siege of July 1642, he reported the town's successful defence in a letter to Speaker Lenthall on 13 July. However, Pelham soon clashed with Hotham over the town's government; by October Hotham was asking parliament to remove Pelham, whom he accused of spreading 'mutinous words' that 'disturbed the peace of the town' (*Portland MSS*, 1.66). Claiming that Pelham's anger was rooted in Hotham's refusal to admit into Hull Pelham's brother-in-law, Hotham added that Pelham had accused him of planning to plunder the town. Eventually, Hotham sequestered Pelham's property and sent him on a ship to answer charges in parliament.

Pelham cleared himself of Hotham's charges promptly; on 27 March 1643 he was named a sequestrator for Hull, and on 3 August as a commissioner for levying money. He became more prominent in parliament because of Hull's massive strategic importance and on 24 December 1644 commented on parliament's trial of Sir John Hotham and his son for treachery: 'They both deserve death' (Wildridge, 48). In 1884 a large cache of Pelham's letters was discovered; now held by Hull Record Office, forty-three of them appear in *The Hull Letters* edited by T. T. Wildridge. Pelham's correspondence with Hull's corporation reveals him to have been a conscientious and industrious MP. In June 1645 he defended the corporation in parliament; fearing the town's self-government would be threatened, he unsuccessfully opposed its inclusion in the northern association. In August 1647 the Commons accepted his petition for payment of money due to him, and ordered the Sussex sequestration committee to pay him out of the earl of Arundel's estate. In September he was appointed a commissioner for compounding with delinquents. On 30 May 1648 parliament instructed Pelham to travel to Hull to protect the port from the navy's revolted ships, and to confer with General Fairfax over the town's safety.

On 6 January 1649 Pelham was named to the high court of justice that was to try Charles I. Attending twenty-one sessions during the king's trial, he was among the most committed *Regicides. He finally became mayor of Hull in September 1649 with the special consent of parliament. He sat in the Rump and was alive in November 1650, but was dead by 27 December 1650. With more than £17,000 owed to him and ruined by the civil war he died, intestate, unable to pay his doctor's bill. Administration of his estate was granted to his son, John. Parliament granted £500 to pay for his funeral and his widow received the bounty of the Hull corporation.   ANDREW J. HOPPER

Sources Keeler, *Long Parliament* · M. J. Brown, 'Pelham, Peregrine', Greaves & Zaller, *BDBR* · W. L. F. Nuttall, 'The Yorkshire commissioners appointed for the trial of King Charles the First', *Yorkshire Archaeological Journal*, 43 (1971), 147–57 · T. T. Wildridge, ed., *The Hull letters: documents from the Hull records, 1625–46* (1886) · *DNB* · 'Papers relating to the civil war', City of Hull RO, BRS/7 · *JHC*, 2–5 (1640–48) · C. H. Firth and R. S. Rait, eds., *Acts and ordinances of the interregnum, 1642–1660*, 3 vols. (1911), vol. 1 · *CSP dom.*, 1628–9; addenda, 1625–49 · M. Noble, *The lives of the English regicides*, 2 (1798) · B. N. Reckitt, *Charles the First and Hull, 1639–1645* (1952) · A. R. Maddison, ed., *Lincolnshire pedigrees*, 3, Harleian Society, 52 (1904), 765 · *The manuscripts of his grace the duke of Portland*, 10 vols., HMC, 29 (1891–1931), vol. 1, p. 66
Archives BL, Stowe MS 184 · City of Hull RO, 'Papers relating to the civil war', BRS/7 · City of Hull RO, Hull corporation MSS, bench books
Wealth at death ruined and penniless; £17,000 owed to him: *DNB*

Pelham, Peter (1695?–1751), mezzotint engraver and painter in America, may have been the Peter Pelham born in 1695 in London, the son of Peter Pelham, gentleman, who died in Chichester, in 1756. He was apprenticed in 1713 to the mezzotint engraver John Simon and afterwards scraped good mezzotints for various printsellers, but chiefly Edward Cooper. He married Martha Guy on 29 February 1719 and three sons, George, Peter, and Charles, were baptized at St Paul's, Covent Garden, in 1720, 1721, and 1722 when the family was living in Long Acre. Pelham's portrait of Samuel Shute, governor of Massachusetts, was painted in London in 1724, and in 1727 the family emigrated to America. Later correspondence suggests that Pelham had quarrelled with his father and they remained estranged until 1739. The Pelham family settled first in Summer Street and then in Cornhill, Boston. Pelham launched his career in America with a memorial mezzotint of the Revd Cotton Mather, the celebrated witch-hunter. A subscription for this print was proposed in the Boston newspapers in February 1728. Its price at 5 shillings was three times that of an equivalent print published in London. Pelham also opened a school at which he taught dancing and arithmetic. A son, William, was born at Boston in 1729 and his first wife died soon after. On 15 October 1734 he married Margaret Lowrey and moved to Newport, Rhode Island. He was back in Boston by 1737

where he taught 'Dancing, Writing, Reading, painting upon Glass, and all kinds of needle work' (*Boston Gazette*, 6 Feb 1738). At this point Pelham contacted and was reconciled with his father and sisters in England, though his father was uneasy that Pelham had married a second woman with no fortune. On 22 May 1748, however, Pelham was married a third time, to the apparently slightly wealthier Mary Singleton, widow of Richard Copley, a tobacconist. Pelham moved in to her house in Lindall Street and added her tobacco shop to his other interests. He probably taught her son John Singleton Copley the rudiments of art before he himself died intestate in December 1751. Pelham was buried in Trinity Church, Boston, on 14 December 1751.

Henry Pelham (1749–1806), surveyor and artist, was born in Lindall Street, Boston, Massachusetts, on 14 February 1749, the son of Peter Pelham and his third wife, Mary. In 1770 he designed *The Fruits of Arbitrary Power, or, The Bloody Massacre*. His print was copied and hurriedly published by Paul Revere, an act of piracy that perhaps helped to push Pelham into the loyalist camp. Pelham left Boston for London in 1776, taking with him a fine *Plan of Boston in New England* that he published in 1777. He exhibited miniatures at the Royal Academy in 1777 and 1778 before settling in Ireland where he acted as agent to the Irish estates of the first marquess of Lansdowne. He also painted, engraved, and made maps including a twelve-sheet survey of co. Clare (1779). He married Caroline, daughter of William Butler of Castlecrine, possibly in 1778. He was drowned in 1806 while crossing the Kenmare River, co. Kerry.   TIMOTHY CLAYTON

Sources G. B. Banhill, 'Pelham, Peter', *ANB* · G. C. Groce and D. H. Wallace, *The New York Historical Society's dictionary of artists in America, 1564–1860* (1957) · corresp., *Collections of the Massachusetts Historical Society*, 71 (1914) · J. C. Smith, *British mezzotinto portraits*, 2 (1879), 532–99 · W. S. Baker, *American engravers and their works* (1875) · W. H. Whitmore, *Notes concerning Peter Pelham, the earliest artist resident in New England* (1867) · G. F. Dow, *The arts and crafts in New England, 1704–75* (1927) · W. G. Strickland, *A dictionary of Irish artists*, 2 vols. (1913) · J. D. Prown, *John Singleton Copley*, 2 vols. (1966) · *IGI* · *Boston Gazette* [Boston, MA] (6 Feb 1738) · *DNB*
Likenesses J. S. Copley, oils, c.1750 · J. S. Copley, portrait (Henry Pelham; *Boy with a squirrel*) · S. Hooper, portrait (Henry Pelham), Metropolitan Museum of Art, New York

Pelham, Thomas, first Baron Pelham (c.1653–1712), politician, was born at Halland Place, Laughton, Sussex, the eldest son of Sir John Pelham, third baronet (c.1623–1703), politician, and his wife, Lady Lucy (d. 1685), second daughter of Robert *Sidney, second earl of Leicester. He was educated at Tonbridge grammar school (1663–5) and by 1670 had entered Christ Church, Oxford, where he was one of the pupils of George Hooper, later bishop of Bath and Wells.

Pelham was returned to parliament for East Grinstead, Sussex, on 25 October 1678, and retained the seat until August 1679. In the election of October 1679 he was returned for Lewes—6 miles from Laughton—and continued to represent Lewes until July 1702, when, having been returned for Lewes and Sussex, he chose to sit for Sussex. In politics Pelham followed the family line and was a moderate whig. In 1679 the earl of Shaftesbury twice described him as 'worthy', although he made little mark on the parliaments of 1679–81 and abstained from voting on the first bill to exclude the duke of York from the throne. On 21 March 1680 Pelham married Elizabeth (c.1664–1681), daughter of the whig politician Sir William *Jones of Ramsbury, Wiltshire. Jones was said to have encouraged Pelham to remain a firm whig. The marriage licence of 26 November 1679 described Pelham as about twenty-six and Elizabeth as about fifteen. They had two daughters, one of whom was Elizabeth (d. 1711), who married Charles *Townshend, second Viscount Townshend. Elizabeth was buried at Laughton on 13 October 1681 and Pelham married, by a licence of 21 May 1686, Lady Grace (1668/9–1700), daughter of Gilbert *Holles, third earl of Clare. They had two sons, Thomas Pelham *Holles, duke of Newcastle upon Tyne and Newcastle under Lyme, and Henry *Pelham, and six daughters. Pelham's whiggish inclinations were presumably the reason he, along with his father and uncle, was dismissed as a JP for Sussex in 1687, following James II's remodelling of the commission of the peace.

After the revolution Pelham was appointed a commissioner of customs, from 20 April 1689 to 24 March 1691. He was also reappointed as a JP and was three times a lord commissioner of the Treasury (March 1690–March 1692; May 1697–June 1699; and March 1701–May 1702). Despite his periods in office, throughout the 1690s Pelham was a 'country' whig. He signed the Association promising to defend William III's life promptly in 1696 but he often took an independent line from the government, including opposing the impeachment of the Jacobite conspirator Sir John Fenwick in 1696 and the standing army in 1698.

After the accession of Anne in 1702, Pelham was once again out of office and remained true to his country whig principles. In 1704 he co-operated with secretary of state Robert *Harley in opposing the 'tack', an attempt by high tories to tack a bill against occasional conformity to a supply bill. He was appointed vice-admiral of the coast of Sussex on 21 May 1705. Having succeeded his father as fourth baronet in January 1703, in 1705 Pelham made his desire for a peerage known to the queen through his brother-in-law the duke of Newcastle and Robert Harley. He had to wait over a year but on 16 December 1706 he was created Baron Pelham of Laughton, and took his place in the House of Lords on 30 December. He died of apoplexy at Halland Place, Sussex, on 23 February 1712 and was buried in the chancel of Laughton parish church on 8 March. His friend the third earl of Shaftesbury remembered him as one of the 'honestest of men and most true to the interests of the public' (Life, ed. Rand, 487).

J. M. RIGG, rev. PETER LE FEVRE

Sources J. Comber, Sussex genealogies: Lewes centre (1933), 209–10 · P. Le Fevre, '"The workhorses of the county": the Sussex justices of the peace, 1660–1754', Sussex Archaeological Collections, 132 (1994), 129–42 · J. R. Jones, 'Shaftesbury's "worthy men": a whig view of the parliament of 1679', BIHR, 30 (1957), 232–41 · parish register, Laughton, E. Sussex RO [burial] · will, PRO, PROB 11/526, fols. 96–97v · will of Sir John Pelham, PRO, PROB 11/469, fols. 84–84v · W. G. Hart, ed., The register of Tonbridge School from 1553 to 1820 (1935), 35 · W. M. Marshall, George Hooper, 1640–1727, bishop of Bath and Wells (1986), 7, 17 · B. M. Crook, 'Pelham, Thomas', HoP, Commons, 1660–90 · H. Horwitz, Parliament, policy and politics in the reign of William III (1977) · The life, unpublished letters and philosophical remarks of Anthony, earl of Shaftesbury, ed. B. Rand (1900); repr. (1995)
Archives BL, papers, Add. MS
Wealth at death over £15,000: will, PRO, PROB 11/526, fols. 96–97v

Pelham, Thomas, first earl of Chichester (1728–1805), politician, born in Westminster, London, on 28 February 1728, was the only son of the two children of Thomas Pelham (c.1705–1737), of Stanmer, Sussex, and his wife, Annetta (d. 1733), the daughter of Thomas Bridges of Constantinople. His father was a first cousin of Thomas Pelham-Holles, duke of Newcastle, and after having been a merchant in Constantinople served as MP for Lewes from 1727 to 1737. He was educated at Westminster School and entered Clare College, Cambridge, in 1745 but left after a few months to embark on the grand tour. Between 1746 and 1750 he travelled with John Milbanke through France, the Netherlands, Switzerland, Italy, and Germany. In Florence he was entertained by Sir Horace Mann and also began a relationship with the Countess Acciajuoli, which delayed his return from Italy until August 1750. On 15 June 1754 he married, at Mortlake, Anne (1734/5–1813), the daughter and heir of Frederick Meinhart Frankland and his first wife, Elizabeth Cardonnel. They had four sons and four daughters.

While abroad, Pelham had been returned, on 13 December 1749 by the duke of Newcastle, as MP for Rye. Following Henry Pelham's death in 1754, he succeeded as knight of the shire, and he represented the county of Sussex from May 1754 until November 1768. In April 1754 Newcastle secured his appointment to the Board of Trade. Pelham was one of the leaders of Newcastle's 'young friends', and he co-ordinated the activities of Newcastle's Sussex supporters. In 1761 he was named a lord of the Admiralty. A year later, when Newcastle obtained for himself the barony of Pelham of Stanmer, its reversion was secured by the patent to Pelham. This attached Pelham firmly to Newcastle. After voting against the peace preliminaries on 10 December 1762 he was dismissed in the 'massacre of Pelhamite innocents'.

On the formation of the first Rockingham ministry in July 1765, Pelham became comptroller of the household and was sworn of the privy council. When Newcastle followed Rockingham out of office a year later, Pelham remained in government. Newcastle had called on his supporters to desert Chatham, but Pelham claimed that the welfare of his children had to take precedence over political loyalty. In government, however, he continued to be influenced by Newcastle. He voted for the reduction of the land tax on 22 February 1767, but the constraints of office persuaded him to vote with the government on the Nullum Tempus Bill. On the death, in November 1768, of

Newcastle, with whom he was in confidential correspondence until the last, Pelham became Baron Pelham of Stanmer and head of the family. He did not inherit Newcastle's political following, however. The boroughs of Rye and Seaford reverted to the Treasury, leaving Pelham with control over the solitary seat of Lewes. In 1773 he obtained the lucrative sinecure of the surveyor-generalship of the customs of London. From 1774 to 1775 he also held the nominal office of chief justice in eyre north of the Trent, which he gave up on his appointment as master of the great wardrobe. This office was abolished in 1782, and Pelham was its last holder.

In the Lords Pelham supported North until the fall of his ministry. He voted for Fox's East India Bill, and in 1788 his name was attached to the two protests drawn up against Pitt's provision for the expected regency. In spite of his consistent opposition to Pitt, which lasted until the French Revolution, Walpole ranked him among the 'court ciphers'. He was certainly intimate with Princess Amelia, and when she died in 1786 he acted as one of her executors. On 23 June 1801 he was created earl of Chichester. He died on 8 January 1805 at his country house of Stanmer, Sussex, and was buried at Laughton in the same county. His widow survived him, and died suddenly at Malling, Sussex, on 5 March 1813, aged seventy-eight. Only three of their children outlived their parents: the eldest son, Thomas *Pelham, second earl of Chichester (1756–1826), politician; George *Pelham (1766–1827), bishop of Lincoln; and Amelia, who died in 1847.

G. Le G. Norgate, rev. Martyn J. Powell

Sources J. Brooke, 'Pelham, Thomas', HoP, Commons · L. B. Namier, *England in the age of the American revolution*, 2nd edn (1961) · F. O'Gorman, *The rise of party in England: the Rockingham whigs, 1760–1782* (1975) · R. A. Kelch, *Newcastle, a duke without money: Thomas Pelham Holles, 1693–1768* (1974) · P. Langford, *The first Rockingham administration, 1765–1766* (1973) · J. Brooke, *The Chatham administration, 1766–1768* (1956) · H. Walpole, *Memoirs of the reign of King George the Third*, ed. G. F. R. Barker, 4 vols. (1894) · J. H. Jesse, *Memoirs of George III*, 3 vols. (1867) · J. E. T. Rogers, *Protests of the House of Lords*, 3 vols. (1875) · GEC, *Peerage*, new edn · *The last journals of Horace Walpole*, ed. Dr Doran, rev. A. F. Steuart, 2 vols. (1910) · J. Ingamells, ed., *A dictionary of British and Irish travellers in Italy, 1701–1800* (1997) · Venn, *Alum. Cant.* · R. Browning, *The duke of Newcastle* (1975)

Archives BL, corresp. and papers, Add. MSS 33085, 33087–33093, 33341–33343, 33623–33624, 64813 · E. Sussex RO, letters relating to militia and local affairs | E. Sussex RO, letters to John Holroyd, first earl of Sheffield · PRO NIre., corresp. with Robert Stewart, Viscount Castlereagh

Likenesses G. Hamilton, oils, 1750 · G. Hamilton, oils, 1777? · G. Stuart, oils, 1785, Saltram, Devon

Pelham, Thomas, **second earl of Chichester** (1756–1826), politician, was born in Spring Gardens, London, on 28 April 1756, the eldest of the three sons of Thomas *Pelham, first earl of Chichester (1728–1805), politician, and his wife, Anne Frankland (1734/5–1813), daughter of Frederick Meinhart Frankland. He was educated at Westminster School and at Clare College, Cambridge, and between 1775 and 1778 visited Spain (where he stayed with the ambassador, Lord Grantham), France, Italy, Germany, and Austria.

At the general election of 1780 Pelham was returned unopposed to parliament for Sussex on his family's interest. He sat undisturbed there for the duration of his Commons career. He had joined Brooks's Club four months before his return and became a member of the Whig Club in 1786. Accordingly he voted with the Rockingham whig opposition on economic reform on 26 February 1781, and against the American War of Independence on 12 December 1781, 22 and 27 February 1782, but, conscious of his father's financial dependence on his sinecure and household offices, he sided with the North ministry against the censure motions of 8 and 15 March 1782. On the formation of Lord Rockingham's administration the following month he was appointed surveyor-general of the ordnance under his Sussex neighbour and friend the third duke of Richmond. He remained in office when Lord Shelburne became prime minister after Rockingham's death and was privately critical of Fox for precipitately resigning. In August 1782 he declined the offer of a diplomatic post from Lord Grantham, Fox's successor as foreign secretary. On the formation of the Fox–North coalition in April 1783 he resigned. Four months later he somewhat reluctantly agreed to the request of the duke of Portland, the premier, that he become Irish secretary in the room of the ailing William Windham, who had recommended him as 'a man of engaging gentlemanlike manners and pleasant temper' (BL, Add. MS 33100, fol. 219). He sat for Carrick-on-Shannon in the Irish parliament. On the fall of the coalition in December 1783 he declined Pitt's offer to retain him in his office and resigned in January 1784, although he personally would have preferred a union of parties.

Pelham was an active member of the Foxite opposition to Pitt in the 1784 parliament. His personal charm and even temper won him the friendship of the leaders and his reputation for acuteness and reliability made him a significant figure in the second rank. He was, however, a nervous and lacklustre speaker, even though he moved the Furrukhabad charge against Hastings on 2 March 1787, and played a part in his trial; he was appointed a manager of the impeachment on 14 February 1791.

In June 1791 Pelham visited Paris, but he prudently destroyed the letters to Barnarve and Lafayette requesting guarantees for the safety of the French royal family with which Fox had entrusted him. He was at this point favourably disposed towards the new regime in France and was described by Burke as 'a runner to the French revolution', who was 'endeavouring everywhere by various rumours and idle speculations to reconcile the minds of people to it' (*Correspondence of Edmund Burke*, 7.30). The formation of the Association of the Friends of the People perturbed him, but he absolved Fox from blame for their excesses and, still deeply suspicious of Pitt and anxious to preserve the unity of the opposition, did not become an alarmist. From July 1792 to August 1793 he travelled in Europe, wintering in Italy with Elizabeth, Lady Webster, later Lady Holland, with whom he had an affair. Although he resisted pressure to go back to England at the turn of the year, when he was tentatively included in a list of Portland whigs, his political views had changed decisively. Dismayed by the violent progress of the revolution, he believed that Fox was taking a dangerous and misguided line, yet remained reluctant to break with him. On his return home he became one of the trustees of Fox's subscription fund, but he was now in political agreement with the Portland whigs, believing that for the moment it was better to support the war against France without taking office. He accordingly declined an offer of a diplomatic mission to Florence in December 1793 and, with Tom Grenville and William Windham, acted as one of the self-styled 'virtuous triumvirate' who refused to join the administration. He parted regretfully but amicably from Fox on 20 January 1794 and during the ensuing session worked with Windham to cultivate and encourage émigré leaders. He made little mark in the Commons, being undermined by illness and bouts of depression and self-loathing, partly on account of Lady Webster's continued absence in Italy. He confided to her in the spring of 1794 that while he approved the formal junction of the Portland whigs with the government he was unwilling to take any direct personal part in it. He turned down a ministerial proposal that he should take charge of affairs in the West Indies and resolved not to accept the Irish secretaryship, after having heard rumours that he would be appointed. In September 1794 he went with Windham, who was now the secretary at war, on a brief mission to the duke of York at army headquarters on the continent, but four months later he declined the duke's request to act as his parliamentary spokesman if he became commander-in-chief. Pelham hinted that he contemplated retiring from public life at the next dissolution.

On the recall of the Irish lord lieutenant Lord Fitzwilliam in early 1795, Pelham, however, allowed himself to be bullied by Portland, the home secretary, who made it clear that refusal of office would blight his future prospects, into going to Ireland as chief secretary to Lord Camden. He was duly returned to the Irish parliament for Clogher and spoke against Catholic relief on 4 May 1795, but his health was again poor and he returned to England in the summer of 1795. He was keen to step down and irritated by the government's distribution of revenue patronage to opponents of his family's electoral interest at Seaford. In September 1795 he refused the offer of a diplomatic mission to Vienna. Portland's persistent arm-twisting broke his resistance once again and in February 1796 he returned reluctantly to Dublin. Although he spent long periods in England, he dealt capably with the routine business of Irish administration and remained in Ireland during the difficult year of 1797. He got on well with Camden and became a popular secretary, even with the Irish opposition, but he was never in Pitt's confidence, had little influence on the general direction of Irish policy, and grew increasingly resentful of Portland's condescending and disdainful attitude towards him. When Abercromby, the commander-in-chief, publicly condemned the Irish military in February 1798, Pelham defended them in the Irish Commons, where he now represented Armagh. Soon afterwards he fell seriously and almost mortally ill. On his partial recovery he drafted, but never sent, a reproachful letter to Portland, in which he protested against the British cabinet's disowning of Abercromby's remarks and complained that he had been duped into resuming his office in 1796. He convalesced in England in the summer of 1798, intending to return to Ireland under Lord Cornwallis, but he eventually opted for retirement and was formally replaced by his locum, Lord Castlereagh, in November.

Pelham declined a diplomatic posting to Vienna in May 1799. A year later he was astonished by a report that Pitt believed that he did not want office and enraged by another report that Portland had suggested that he had given up his own pretensions for the sake of his relatives' claims. He made it clear to Pitt that he was still a contender for an office that would be financially beneficial. He mentioned the reversion of Lord Liverpool's Irish sinecure of clerk of the pells, but nothing came of this. When Addington replaced Pitt as prime minister early in 1801 Pelham, not wishing to be estranged from his closest associates, who were about to go out, refused two offers of a cabinet place, the second of which was coupled with a scheme to have him called to the Lords to take the lead there. Informed that the king, who had always had a soft spot for him, wanted him to join the new ministry, he acceded to another approach and anticipated becoming war secretary with the lead in the upper house. Yet Portland allowed Lord Hobart to be appointed instead and tried to persuade Pelham to become president of the Board of Control (of which he was a commissioner from May 1801 until July 1802). He refused this and asked Addington to postpone his elevation. It was eventually arranged that he should replace Portland as home secretary, and in the interim he chaired the secret committee on Irish disaffection, presented its report to the Commons on 13 April and 15 May, and introduced the Habeas Corpus Suspension Bill on 14 April. Determined to have the Home Office, he rejected Addington's offer of the Russian embassy. On 29 June 1801, six days after his father was created earl of Chichester, Pelham was called to the Lords in his barony of Pelham of Stanmer. He replaced Portland in July 1801 and on 16 July married Lady Mary Henrietta Juliana Osborne (1776–1862), daughter of Francis *Osborne, fifth duke of Leeds (1751–1799), and his first wife, Lady Amelia D'Arcy. They had four sons, the eldest of whom died in childhood, and four daughters.

Pelham's relations with Addington, with whom he clashed over foreign policy, Irish affairs, and patronage, were always strained. He became increasingly isolated in the cabinet and had little personal influence. In March 1802 he registered a protest against signing the definitive treaty of peace, which he was expected to defend in the Lords, in the same terms as the preliminaries, but he did not resign, to avoid upsetting the ministry. By 1803 Addington was eager to remove him from the Home Office, where he was said to be appallingly negligent, and in March Pelham played into his hands by expressing willingness to retire in order to facilitate a junction with Pitt.

This did not take place, but in August Addington unscrupulously replaced him with Charles Yorke, and offered the consolation of the chancellorship of the duchy of Lancaster and the presidency of the Board of Trade, with a seat in the cabinet, together with 'some patent office in reversion'. Pelham, who was seriously ill at this time, initially declined active cabinet office and wrote directly to the king asking to be restored to the head of the Sussex militia. Justifiably bitter towards Addington, he detailed his grievances in a further letter to the king on 13 September 1803. Later that month he applied for the duchy of Lancaster for life, to mark the king's approval of his conduct as home secretary and as insurance against dismissal if, as he thought likely, he found himself at odds with his colleagues on Irish policy. The king vetoed this, but it was indicated to Pelham that an alternative provision would be made for him when available, and in November 1803 he took the duchy, outside the cabinet, and 'subject ... to the contingencies to which other ofices held during pleasure are liable' (*Later Correspondence of George III*, 4.134n). Pitt discarded him on his return to power in May 1804, encouraging him to take a diplomatic post, which he declined, or the place of captain of the yeomen of the guard, which he also turned down after hesitating for two days. When he surrendered his seals the king, who was possibly unhinged, and without having consulted Pitt, physically forced the official stick of the captain of the yeomen on him. A distraught Pelham, believing that Pitt had tricked him into what he regarded as a degradation, resigned it almost immediately and in so doing angered the king, who to Pitt condemned his 'frequent political tergiversation' (ibid., 4.204).

On his father's death on 8 January 1805, Pelham succeeded as second earl of Chichester and to the family's Stanmer estate between Brighton and Lewes, where he initiated agricultural improvements. He refused an offer of the government of the Cape from the Grenville ministry in March 1806, but on the formation of Portland's second administration in the following year became joint postmaster-general, at £2500 a year. He retained the office in the ministries of Perceval and Liverpool and was sole postmaster from November 1823 until his death at his London house in Stratton Street on 4 July 1826. Lord Holland described him as 'somewhat timeserving', but 'a good-natured and prudent man' (Holland, 1.112). He was succeeded in the peerage by his eldest surviving son, Henry Thomas *Pelham (1804–1886), the future ecclesiastical commissioner. His other sons were John Thomas *Pelham (1811–1894), bishop of Norwich, and Frederick Thomas *Pelham (1808–1861), a naval officer.   D. R. FISHER

Sources M. M. Drummond, 'Pelham, Thomas', HoP, *Commons, 1754–90* · D. R. Fisher, 'Pelham, Thomas', HoP, *Commons, 1790–1820* · F. O'Gorman, *The whig party and the French Revolution* (1967) · *The later correspondence of George III*, ed. A. Aspinall, 5 vols. (1962–70), vol. 4 · *Diaries and correspondence of James Harris, first earl of Malmesbury*, ed. third earl of Malmesbury [J. H. Harris], 4 (1844), 284, 326–7 · H. R. Vassall, Lord Holland, *Memoirs of the whig party during my time*, ed. H. E. Vassall, Lord Holland, 2 vols. (1852–4), vol. 1, p. 112 · L. G. Mitchell, *Charles James Fox and the disintegration of the whig party, 1782–1794* (1971) · I. R. Christie, *The end of North's ministry, 1780–82*

(1958) · P. Zeigler, *Addington* (1965) · *The correspondence of Edmund Burke*, 7, ed. P. J. Marshall and J. A. Woods (1968), 30 · J. Ehrman, *The younger Pitt*, 2: *The reluctant transition* (1983) · J. Ehrman, *The younger Pitt*, 3: *The consuming struggle* (1996) · GEC, *Peerage* · DNB · L. Mitchell, *Holland House* (1980), 17 · PRO, IR26/1080/1052 · BL, Add. MS 33100, fol. 219

Archives BL, corresp. and papers, Add. MSS 33100–33103, 33629–33631, 64813 · E. Sussex RO, letters relating to 1812 election | Beds. & Luton ARS, corresp. with Frederick Robinson · BL, corresp. with Lord Hardwicke, Add. MSS 35647–35768, *passim* · BL, corresp. with Lady Holland, Add. MSS 51705, 51706 · BL, corresp. with first earl of Liverpool and second earl of Liverpool, Add. MSS 38250–38321, 38458, 38450, *passim* · BL, letters to Sir George Shee, Add. MSS 60337–60342 · CKS, corresp. with first marquess of Camden · E. Sussex RO, letters to first earl of Sheffield · NRA Scotland, corresp. with Lord Melville · PRO NIre., letters to Sir George Hill · Royal Arch., letters to George III · Sheff. Arch., corresp. with Earl Fitzwilliam · U. Nott., letters to duke of Portland

Likenesses S. W. Reynolds, mezzotint, pubd 1802 (after J. Hoppner), BM, NPG · N. Dance, portrait · Daniel, engraving (after Dance) · J. Hoppner, oils (as Irish secretary)

Wealth at death under £50,000: PRO, death duty registers, IR 26/1080/1052

Pelham, Sir William (d. 1587), lord justice of Ireland, was the third son of Sir William Pelham (d. 1538), a landowner of Laughton, Sussex, and his second wife, Mary, daughter of William Sandys, Lord Sandys. Pelham married, first, Lady Eleanor (d. 1574), daughter of Henry *Neville, fifth earl of Westmorland [see under Neville, Ralph]; their son Sir William Pelham succeeded him and married Ann, eldest daughter of Charles, Lord Willoughby of Parham. Pelham's second wife was Dorothy, daughter of Anthony Catesby of Whiston, Northamptonshire, and widow of Sir William Dormer; with her he had a son, Peregrine, and a daughter, Ann.

Pelham's father died in 1538, and he was probably thirty years old when appointed captain of the pioneers at the siege of Leith in 1560 where he was specially commended for valour. According to Humphrey Barwick's *Brief Discourse* (c.1594) it was Pelham's faulty engineering which was responsible for the wound inflicted on Arthur Grey, fourteenth Lord Grey of Wilton. Pelham commanded the pioneers at Le Havre under the earl of Warwick in November 1562, and in February 1563 he helped Admiral Coligny in the capture of Caen. In March he returned to Le Havre but in July he was wounded in a skirmish with the forces of the Rhinegrave. He then assisted in negotiations for the surrender of Le Havre, and became a pledge or hostage for the fulfilment of the surrender terms at the treaty of Troyes in April 1564.

On his return to England, Pelham was employed by Portinari and Concio in improving the fortifications at Berwick. The privy council was so impressed with his competency and good judgement that he was promoted lieutenant-general of the ordnance, and in that capacity was occupied for several years in strengthening the defences of the realm. In the summer of 1578 he accompanied William, Lord Cobham, and the chief secretary, Sir Francis Walsingham, on a diplomatic mission to the Netherlands. The following summer Pelham was sent to Ireland to organize the defences of the pale when the rebellion of James fitz Maurice Fitzgerald (d. 1579) threatened to spread from Munster; meanwhile, many of the sub-septs of the northern families united against the territorial ambitions of Turlough Luineach O'Neill. Pelham was knighted by Sir William Drury on 14 September 1579 and, on the latter's death on 3 October, was elected lord justice of Ireland.

In the aftermath of fitz Maurice's rebellion in Munster and the subsequent threats from Gerald Fitzgerald, fifteenth earl of Desmond, and his brothers Sir James and Sir John of Desmond, the disturbed state of the province drove Pelham to action. When his efforts at conciliation and those of the countess of Desmond proved futile he caused the earl of Desmond to be proclaimed a traitor on 2 November 1579. He wrote to the queen on 4 November: 'Ormond [Thomas Butler, tenth earl] has already drawn blood and kindled fire in the midst of Desmond's country. I have left the prosecution of the war to him' (Brewer and Bullen, 164). Pelham did not have sufficient cannon to attack Askeaton, the chief seat of the Desmonds on the Shannon, so he went with the governor of Connaught, Sir Nicholas Malby, on a tour of his province and thence back to Dublin. The queen, reluctant to engage in yet another costly campaign, was much displeased with Pelham's and Malby's harsh proceedings, and it became common knowledge by the end of November 1579 that she wanted Lord Grey of Wilton to be her lord deputy of Ireland. Pelham, smarting under the queen's displeasure, pleaded that the proclamation against Desmond was an absolute necessity, and 'because of your several causes of your disliking with me since I entered into this service', as he wrote to the queen on 15 December, he once again petitioned 'to be speedily discharged from this government' (ibid., 183).

When it became apparent that Ormond's resources were unequal to the task of quelling Desmond the queen ameliorated her severity towards Pelham and encouraged him to repair into Munster, where he signed a patent to permit Sir Warham St Leger the exercise of martial law (11 January 1580). Rumours of a further Spanish invasion drove him to entrust the coastal counties of Cork and Waterford to Sir William Morgan (d. 1584). Accompanied by the earl of Ormond's forces, he then marched towards the Dingle peninsula, 'to make as bare a country as ever Spaniard put his foot in, if he intend to make that his landing place', as he wrote to the privy council. In the same letter he expressed his admiration for his soldiers: 'if I have any judgment, all the soldiers of Christendom must give place to that of the soldier of Ireland' (Brewer and Bullen, 219–20). According to Irish reports, particularly that of the four masters, Pelham's Munster campaign was ruthless in 'killing blind and feeble men, women, boys and girls, sick persons, idiots and old people' (AFM). On 27 March 1580 he assaulted Carrigafoyle Castle, sparing neither man, woman, nor child. Desmond's main fortress of Askeaton then surrendered without resistance, and Newcastle, Rathkeale, Ballyduff, and Ballilogher fell into Pelham's hands at the same time.

During the campaign Sir Nicholas Malby had fallen out with Pelham, as had Pelham with the earl of Ormond. Pelham's aim of confining the war to co. Kerry meant containing Desmond by well-planted garrisons and co-operating with Admiral Winter's fleet to starve out Desmond's rebel support. He encountered many difficulties in getting victuals for his soldiers from the neighbouring gentry, and even among the better disposed Pelham found such a settled hatred of English government and lack of local co-operation that it became clear that only full-scale warfare would save Ireland for the crown. After delays both Pelham and Ormond entered co. Kerry together. At Castleisland they narrowly missed capturing Desmond and Nicholas Sander on 15 June 1580. Then they scoured the valley of the Maine and the Dingle peninsula and, with Admiral Winter's help, ransacked every cove and creek between there and Cork. Meanwhile Ormond harried the interior of co. Kerry, where he received the submission of many of Desmond's western chiefs before retiring in triumph to his own lands in Kilkenny. Pelham held a general meeting at Cork of all the lords and chiefs on 4 July 1580, receiving all to mercy except Lord Barrymore, and on the advice of Sir Warham St Leger took them all to his headquarters at Limerick.

To Desmond, now a fugitive in the Kerry mountains, unconditional surrender alone was offered. Although the war against Desmond was drawing to a close, Pelham was aware of the serious consequences of a Spanish invasion, particularly as the uprising of James Eustace, Viscount Baltinglass, in Leinster in July 1580 threw the general peace of Ireland into uncertainty. On 27 July he once again tendered his resignation to the queen: 'to be disburthened of this place is the greatest happiness that could light unto me' (Brewer and Bullen, 282). Pelham was preparing a fresh expedition into co. Kerry when he had news that Arthur, Lord Grey of Wilton had landed on 12 August 1580 as the new lord deputy, together with his secretary, Edmund Spenser. Sir Henry Wallop was to present the sword of state to Lord Grey. Pelham took offence at the lack of deference shown him by Secretary Spenser, and determined to go himself to Dublin. Nevertheless, he had expressed willingness to serve under Grey. He was delayed at Athlone by bad weather and it was not until 7 September 1580 that Pelham formally resigned the sword of state to the new deputy in St Patrick's, Dublin. There was a rumour that Pelham would be made president of Munster. He accompanied Grey to Drogheda to inspect the fortifications there; but being taken dangerously ill, he went back to Dublin and sought permission to return to England. He left Ireland early in October.

On 16 January 1581 Pelham was joined in commission with George Talbot, earl of Shrewsbury, and Sir Henry Neville to escort Mary, queen of Scots, from Sheffield to Ashby in Leicestershire. Though he was still lieutenant-general of the ordnance, by 1585 his expenses exceeded the profits of that office by £8000; and at the same time his personal debts were in excess of £5000. The queen refused to remit or even postpone that portion of his debts for which he was found personally responsible and made the payments of arrears an essential condition before allowing Pelham to serve under Leicester in the Netherlands. Pelham pleaded in vain: 'If you will not ease me of my debts, pray take my poor living into your possession, and give order for their payment, and imprest me some convenient sum to set me forward' (*DNB*). Both Lord Burghley and Leicester pressed the queen to relent; she went so far as to accept a mortgage on Pelham's properties, an arrangement which permitted him to accompany Leicester to the Netherlands in July 1586.

To the chagrin of the Norris brothers, Sir John and Sir Edward of Rycote, Oxfordshire, a prominent military family in Ireland and the Netherlands, Leicester made Pelham marshal of the army. At a drunken brawl in Count Hohenlohe's quarters at Gertruydenberg on 6 August 1586, Pelham nearly cost Sir Edward Norris his life, but Leicester put the blame on Norris. A few days later, inspecting the defences before Doesburg in Leicester's company, Pelham took a shot in the stomach while shielding his commander-in-chief. Thinking his wound to be fatal Pelham made 'comfortable and resolute speeches' and deemed himself fortunate to have saved Leicester. However, he was fated 'to carry a bullet in his belly', for he lived to participate in the celebrated siege of Zutphen in September 1586 where Sir Philip Sidney was mortally wounded. According to Fulke Greville, it was imitation of Pelham's chivalry that cost Sidney his life under the walls of Zutphen. When the garrison of Deventer under Sir William Stanley of Hooton in the Wirral betrayed the fortress and town to the Spaniards, Pelham had the task of quelling the mutiny, which he accomplished in summary and resolute fashion. In April 1587 Pelham returned to England with Leicester and took the waters at Bath to recover from his ailments. By autumn he was fit enough to go back to the Netherlands with reinforcements, but he died on 24 November 1587, shortly after landing at Flushing. His will requested his burial in England, and was puritan in tone.

Pelham's letter-book, which contains both a diary and his extensive official correspondence when lord justice of Ireland, is preserved among the Carew manuscripts in Lambeth Palace Library. The original compilation by Morgan Colman, Pelham's secretary, has an elaborately decorated title page, and consists of 455 folios. Pelham composed commendatory verses and these are prefixed to Sir George Peckham's *A True Reporte of the Late Discoveries ... of the Newfound Landes* of 1583. He also wrote a tract entitled 'A form or maner howe to have the exersyse of the harquebuse thorowe England for the better defence of the same' (PRO, SP 12/44/60). He collaborated in 1580 with Sir Henry Wallop and Sir Edward Waterhouse in writing a scheme for the government of Munster; although Pelham's contribution was mainly military, his plan also included ideas on taxation. The oil portrait of him in the earl of Yarborough's collection is attributed to Cornelius Ketel and seems to have been painted about 1580. Another portrait of Sir William Pelham, by an unknown artist, last appeared at Christies on 31 January 1968.

J. J. N. McGurk

Sources J. S. Brewer and W. Bullen, eds., *Calendar of the Carew manuscripts*, 2: 1575–1588, PRO (1868) · M. A. Lower, *Historical and genealogical notices of the Pelham family* (1849) · R. Bagwell, *Ireland under the Tudors*, 3 vols. (1885–90); repr. (1963) · T. W. Horsfield, *History of Lewes* (1835) · J. Hogan and N. McNeill O'Farrell, eds., *The Walsingham letter-book, or, Register of Ireland, May 1578 to December 1579*, IMC (1959) · *CSP Ire.*, 1509–85 · *CSP dom.*, 1547–80 · C. L. Falkiner, 'Spenser in Ireland', *Essays relating to Ireland, biographical, historical and topographical*, ed. F. E. Ball (1909), 3–31 · *Fulke Greville's life of Sir Philip Sidney*, ed. N. Smith (1907) · J. Bruce, ed., *Correspondence of Robert Dudley, earl of Leycester*, CS, 27 (1844) · P. Geyl, *The revolt of the Netherlands, 1555–1609* (1932) [repr. 1958] · J. R. Hale, *Renaissance war studies* (1983) · C. G. Cruickshank, *Elizabeth's army*, 2nd edn (1966) · J. Smythe, *Certain discourses military*, ed. J. R. Hale (1964) · J. L. Motley, *History of the United Netherlands*, 2 (1860) · C. Wilson, *Queen Elizabeth and the revolt of the Netherlands* (1970) · *AFM* · will, PRO, PROB 11/72, fols. 94v–96r · *DNB* · T. W. Moody and others, eds., *A new history of Ireland*, 9: *Maps, genealogies, lists* (1984)

Archives Lincs. Arch., ordnance accounts and estate survey · LPL, Carew MSS, letter-book | BL, corresp. with Privy Council, Egerton MS 3048

Likenesses attrib. C. Ketel, oils, *c.*1580, priv. coll.; repro. in R. Strong, *The English icon: Elizabethan and Jacobean portraiture* (1969), p. 156 · portrait; Christies, 31 Jan 1968, lot 10

Wealth at death left debts of £8807 14s. 5¾d. to be paid to Elizabeth I; £4000 to his daughter; manors in Lincolnshire to his son and heir William Pelham; £40 p.a. to Peregrine Pelham: will, PRO, PROB 11/72, fols. 94v–96r

Pélissier, Harry Gabriel

Pélissier, Harry Gabriel (1874–1913), comedian, composer, and producer, was born at Elm House, Church End, Finchley, Middlesex, on 27 April 1874, the second son of Frederic Antoine Pélissier (*d.* 1914), a French diamond merchant, and his wife, Jennie, *née* Kean. In 1894, after an unhappy six months in the family business in Berwick Street, Soho, London, he joined a small entertainment party run by the Baddeley brothers. They performed at charities and similar events around south London and were turned into a professional troupe by Sherrington Chinn. Pélissier bought him out and the renamed Follies opened as a pierrot show on Worthing pier on 7 August 1896.

While weak burlesques of Shakespeare and other serious dramas had been done before, Pélissier and his troupe broke new ground. Under his direction the Follies parodied not only the plots but the music of grand opera, musical comedy, the current rage for patriotic and sentimental songs, and every topic of the moment. Aspirants for a music-hall engagement were satirized in 'The Voice Trial', Germany's rearming produced the song 'Yes, I Don't Think', and Lloyd George's election promises were mocked in 'Back to the Land'. Pélissier's pastiches of patriotic songs and ballads were so accurate that it is difficult for modern readers to distinguish them from the originals. Making full use of his musical inventiveness, topicality, wit, and a carefully chosen cast of artistes, the Follies became known up and down the country and achieved success in London with a brilliant satire of the pantomime *Bill Bailey* at the Palace Theatre in 1904.

The following year Pélissier's reputation was confirmed with a command performance at Sandringham, especially when it became known that Edward VII had particularly enjoyed his brilliant parodies of Wagner's operas. In March 1907 he took the bold step of taking the Royalty

Theatre in London for a season, filling each evening with his own burlesques. The experiment proved a success and in 1908 he took the Apollo, where the Follies appeared for the next four years.

On 16 September 1911 Pélissier married Fay *Compton (1894–1978), a member of his troupe, daughter of the theatrical manager Edward *Compton, and sister of the author Compton Mackenzie, and the same year it became clear that he was ill. Seeking ever more extravagant stage effects, his last three Follies seasons were unsuccessful; he died at his father-in-law's home, 1 Nevern Square, Earls Court, London, on 25 September 1913 from cirrhosis of the liver, leaving an infant son. After cremation at Golders Green his ashes were placed in his mother's grave at Marylebone cemetery, on 29 September.

Generous and open-handed, Pélissier was a huge roly-poly of a man with a highly developed sense of the ridiculous. Although he gave an impression of utter irresponsibility he had an amazing capacity for work. When an injunction stopped his parody of *The Merry Widow*, then London's most popular musical comedy, Pélissier produced new music and words for *The Deceased Wife's Sister* in two hours in a style different enough to avoid legal problems but sufficiently similar to enrage the complainant and delight the public. Some of his sketches, published in 1913 as *Potted Pélissier*, give an indication of the wit and observation that made him the leading satirist of his time.   N. T. P. MURPHY

Sources F. Gardner, *Pure folly* (1909) · H. Finck, *My melodious memories* (1937) · *The Stage* (2 Oct 1913) · *Daily Telegraph* (27 Sept 1913) · J. B. Booth, *Pink parade* (1933) · *The Times* (27 Sept 1913) · d. cert. · m. cert.

Archives SOUND BL NSA, performance recording

Likenesses HANA, photograph, repro. in Gardner, *Pure folly*, 31 · photograph, repro. in Booth, *Pink parade*, 176 · photograph, Theatre Museum, London · two photographs, repro. in Finck, *My melodious memories*, 65

Wealth at death £13,098 0s. 6d.: probate, 23 Oct 1913, CGPLA Eng. & Wales

Pell, Albert (1820–1907), agriculturist and politician, was born on 12 March 1820, in Montagu Place, Bloomsbury, London, the eldest of the three sons of Sir Albert Pell (1768–1832), of Pinner Hill, Middlesex, and his wife, Margaret Letitia Matilda (1786–1868), third daughter and coheir of Henry Beauchamp St John, twelfth Lord St John of Bletso. Sir Albert Pell was serjeant-at-law in 1808. He retired in 1825 but in 1831 became a judge of the court of bankruptcy.

Albert Pell was brought up at his father's houses at Pinner Hill and in Harley Street, and he was educated at Rugby School under Thomas Arnold (1832–8). In 1839 he matriculated at Trinity College, Cambridge, where he described himself as 'idle and unstudious', though he helped to introduce Rugby football to Cambridge. He took the degree of MA in 1842, and was admitted to the Inner Temple in 1843, but he decided to abandon plans for reading for the bar, and took a farm in Harrow Vale, 12 miles from London.

In 1846 Pell married his cousin, Elizabeth Barbara, daughter of Sir Henry Halford, second baronet, MP for South Leicestershire, of Wistow Hall, Leicestershire. They had no children. In 1848 they settled at Hazelbeach, Northamptonshire, between Northampton and Market Harborough, in a house which Pell rented from his wife's relative Sir Charles Isham. He found his farm at Hazelbeach to be 'dreadfully out of order, foul, wet and exhausted', but he set to work on its improvement.

The outbreak of cattle plague in 1865 led Pell to campaign for the slaughter of animals to wipe out the disease, and he organized a meeting of agriculturists in London. One result of this was the establishment of the central chamber of agriculture, and Pell became its first chairman in 1866. He was chosen as Conservative candidate for the by-election for South Leicestershire in 1867 because of his work to eliminate the cattle plague, but he was beaten by a small majority. In 1868 he was returned, and he represented the constituency until his retirement in 1885. Although a tory, he always remained a radical at heart.

Pell was an authority on the poor law. He was guardian for his own parish of Hazelbeach as early as 1853. In 1873, at his own board of guardians (Brixworth), he moved for a committee to inquire into the methods of administration of outdoor relief, and following the committee's report outdoor relief was virtually abolished in the Brixworth union. In 1876 Pell carried an amendment on Lord Sandon's Education Bill, providing for the abolition of school boards in districts where there were only voluntary schools. From 1876 to 1889 Pell had a seat as a nominated guardian for St George-in-the-East, London, where he had property, and there he tried to enforce his views on outdoor relief. He failed to persuade the House of Commons to consider his proposals, but in 1884 he carried by 208 votes to 197 a motion against the government, which criticized the postponement of further measures of relief acknowledged to be due to ratepayers in counties and boroughs in respect of local charges imposed on them for national services. On this occasion he made his longest speech in the house, speaking for an hour and a half (*Hansard 3*, 286, 1884, 1023).

Pell was a prominent figure at poor-law conferences, and was chairman of the central conference from 1877 to 1898. He was also an active member of the Northamptonshire county council from its establishment in 1889. In June 1879 he and his friend Clare Sewell Read (1826–1905) went to America and Canada as assistant commissioners to the duke of Richmond's royal commission on agriculture to study agricultural questions. Pell was also a member of the royal commissions on the City guilds, the City parochial charities, and the aged poor.

In 1886, shortly after his retirement from parliament, Pell became a member of the council of the Royal Agricultural Society, and worked on its *Journal*, and on its chemical and education committees. He contributed to the *Journal* two significant articles, 'The making of the land in England' (1887 and 1889) and a biography of Arthur Young (1893), as well as other minor articles and notes. He was a member of the Farmers' Club, which he joined in February 1867; he became a member of its committee in 1881 and its chairman in 1888. He was one of the pioneers of the teaching of agriculture at the University of Cambridge, and was made honorary LLD there when the Royal Agricultural Society met at Cambridge in 1894.

At the end of his life poor health led Pell to spend the winters at Torquay, in Devon. He died on 7 April 1907 at Longwood, Torquay, and was buried at Hazelbeach in Northamptonshire.

ERNEST CLARKE, rev. ANNE PIMLOTT BAKER

Sources H. W. Woolrych, *Lives of eminent serjeants-at-law of the English bar*, 2 vols. (1869) · Burke, *Peerage* · Venn, *Alum. Cant.* · personal information (1912) · *Hansard 3* (1884), 286.1023 · *The reminiscences of Albert Pell*, ed. T. Mackay (1908) · *CGPLA Eng. & Wales* (1907) · d. cert.
Likenesses S. Stevens, portrait, 1886; at Wilburton Manor, Ely in 1912
Wealth at death £18,139 8s. 5d.: probate, 19 June 1907, *CGPLA Eng. & Wales*

Pell, John (1611–1685), mathematician, was born on 1 March 1611 at Southwick, Sussex, the second of two sons of John Pell (d. 1616), of Southwick, and his wife, Mary, née Holland (d. 1617), of Halden, Kent. Pell's father, reported by Aubrey to have been 'a kind of Non-conformist' (*Brief Lives*, 121) came of ancient Lincolnshire stock. Pell, to whom his father had left an excellent library, was educated at the newly founded free school at Steyning, Sussex, where he progressed rapidly. At the age of thirteen in 1624 he was sent to Trinity College, Cambridge. Though eminently skilled in Latin, Greek, and Hebrew, he never offered himself as candidate at the election of scholars or fellows at his college. He graduated BA in 1628 and MA in 1630, and in 1631 was incorporated in the University of Oxford. A few years later he was familiar with Arabic, Italian, Spanish, French, and Low and High 'Dutch' (German). He was celebrated for his immense knowledge and his unceasing industry. At the age of seventeen he corresponded with Henry Briggs about logarithms, but details of his study of mathematics (as well as of theology) do not seem to be known. From 1630 to 1638 he was assistant master at Collyer's School in Horsham and teacher at Samuel Hartlib's short-lived Chichester Academy in Sussex.

Pell was a striking figure, remarkably handsome, with strong, excellent posture, dark hair and eyes, and a good voice. His temperament was sanguine and melancholic. On 3 July 1632 he married Ithumaria Reginolles, the second daughter of Henry Reginolles (d. 1661) of London. They had four sons and four daughters. Pell's wife died on 11 September 1661, and he remarried before 1669.

Teaching mathematics In 1638 the group surrounding John Comenius, of which Pell was a leading member (in particular he had become a close friend of Theodore Haak), arranged his move to London, where apparently he taught mathematics. In worldly affairs he was very inexperienced; throughout his life he had need of friends to push him forward and recommend him to men of influence, but as a mathematician he soon won such a reputation, that—supported by a recommendation from Sir William Boswell, the English resident with the states general—in December 1643 he was chosen as successor to Martin Hortensius, the professor of mathematics at the *Gymnasium Illustre* in Amsterdam.

In June 1646 Pell was invited by the prince of Orange to become professor of philosophy and mathematics at Breda in the newly founded college (academy) with an annual salary of 1000 guilders. His duties were, however, restricted to those of a professor of mathematics. When the First English–Dutch War seemed imminent in 1652 Pell returned to London. From Cromwell's government he received an annual salary of £200 as 'Professor of Mathematics', but there is no evidence of any teaching. In 1654, on Haak's recommendation, Cromwell dispatched him to Switzerland on a diplomatic mission at an increased salary of £600, the object being to detach the protestant cantons from France, and to draw them into a continental protestant league headed by England. Interminable negotiations ensued. He returned to England only a few weeks before the Protector's death, and did not have the opportunity of an audience. During all the years of Pell's absence, Haak had taken care of his financial and family affairs.

After the Restoration, Pell accepted holy orders, being ordained deacon, and priest in 1661 when he was instituted to the rectory of Fobbing in Essex. In addition, in 1663 he was presented with the vicarage of Laindon and Basildon in Essex by Dr Gilbert Sheldon, bishop of London; he held both preferments until his death. Having been nominated domestic chaplain to Sheldon on his elevation to the see of Canterbury, Pell took the degree of DD in 1663, yet Anthony Wood noted in his diary:

> he was a shiftless man as to worldly affairs, and his tenants and relations dealt so unkindly to him, that they cozened him of the profits of his parsonage, and kept him so indigent, that he wanted necessaries, even ink and paper, to his dying day. (Wood, *Ath. Oxon.*, 1, cols. 461–4)

In fact he became so insolvent that twice he was thrown into the king's bench prison.

Pell was among the first elected fellows of the Royal Society, on 20 May 1663; on the same day, he was dispensed of the weekly payments. When the society formed several committees in 1664, Pell became a member of those in charge of mechanical and optical inventions as well as that responsible for reporting and conducting experiments on natural phenomena; later he was added to the committee on agriculture. In 1675 he was elected to the council, in the following year as one of its vice-presidents. In 1681 he reported at a meeting that he had translated most of Lazarus Ercker's famous book on minerals, *Beschreibung allerfürnemsten mineralischen Ertzt* (1574), into English.

Publications Pell's first mathematical publication was *An Idea of Mathematics*. To simplify the study of mathematics, Pell suggested in a few pages that all theorems and methods be collected in a kind of encyclopaedia of mathematics; it should make the study of all mathematical books published so far superfluous. This visionary plan (published in Latin of which a copy has recently been discovered in Hamburg, and English in 1638) was republished in English as an appendix to Dury's *Reformed Librarie-Keeper* (1650). In 1679 Hooke included the Latin version, together with comments from Mersenne and Descartes, in his *Philosophical Collections* (no. 5, 127).

Pell's fame was enhanced by his second mathematical publication, a refutation of Longomontanus's quadrature of the circle, initially published as a single sheet in 1644, reprinted in *A Refutation of Longomontanus's Pretended Quadrature of the Circle* (1646; Latin edn, 1647). In 1672 he published in London *Tabula numerorum quadratorum decies millium, or, A Table of Ten Thousand Square Numbers*. A table of antilogarithms (100,000 entries to eleven decimals)—the first of its kind—was computed by him and Walter Warner between 1630 and 1640 but has been lost or destroyed.

Pell was engaged for decades in preparing for the press editions or concise versions of several classical mathematical texts, though none appeared. He is reported to have 'done the second book of Euclid in one side of a large sheet of paper most clearly and ingeniously' (*Brief Lives*, 126), and Archimedes' *Sand-Reckoner* in a similar way. He also worked on Euclid, Book Ten of the *Elements*, and on Apollonius, Pappus, and Diophantus, without producing a result.

While in Zürich, Pell had privately instructed Johann Heinrich Rahn or Rhonius (1622–1676) in mathematics. Much of this instruction appeared in Rahn's *Teutsche Algebra, oder, Algebraische Rechenkunst* (1659). For an English translation prepared by Thomas Brancker or Branker (1633–1676), Pell's alterations and additions doubled the number of pages. It appeared as *An Introduction to Algebra, Translated out of the High-Dutch … much Altered and Augmented by D. P.* (1668); 'D. P.', or 'D. I. P.' in the preface, stood for Doctor (Iohn) Pell, as was generally known at the time of publication, indicating Pell's strong involvement. The book (in both the German and the English versions) contains some innovations in symbolism, and, as a novel feature, the addition of two parallel columns alongside the computations that amount to a programmed instruction for the single steps to be carried out—a novelty which Rahn expressly attributed to a high and very learned person who did not want his name to be made known. In spite of earlier doubts, this must be a reference to Pell's authorship; hence at least he deserves to be remembered in the history of programming.

It is often stated that the expression 'Pell's (or Pellian) equation', created by Leonhard Euler for an indeterminate equation of the second degree, is due to a confusion of Pell with Lord Brouncker. A special case of this type of equation appears in the Rahn–Pell *Algebra* but Pell contributed nothing to the methods of solution.

Closing years For some time Pell had boarded at John Collins's house, but in the summer of 1665 the plague forced him to leave London. For a number of years he lived at Brereton Hall in Cheshire as the guest of William Brereton, third Baron Brereton of Leighlin, who had been his

pupil in the Netherlands. In 1671 Pell's children were living in the same neighbourhood. From Aubrey's remark, 'Never was there greater love between master and scholar then between Dr. Pell and this scholar of his, whose death March 17, 1679/80 hath deprived this worthy doctor of an ingeniose companion and a useful friend', it may be inferred that Pell stayed with Brereton until 1680. Shortly afterwards, according to Aubrey, Pell lived 'in an obscure lodging, three stories high, in Jermyn Street, next to the sign of the Ship, wanting not only bookes but his proper MSS' (*Brief Lives*, 232).

After Pell's imprisonment, Dr Daniel Whistler provided the now totally impoverished mathematician an asylum in the College of Physicians in March 1682. Ill health, however, forced him to move to the house of one of his grandchildren in St Margaret's churchyard, Westminster, in June 1683. From there he was transferred to the lodging in Dyot Street, Westminster, of a Mr Cothorne, who was reader in the church of St Giles-in-the-Fields. Pell died in Dyot Street on 12 December 1685 and was buried in the rector's vault under that church.

Pell's reputation as a mathematician was mostly based on his impressive knowledge of mathematical literature and on his promise and did not outlast his lifetime. In his own peculiar way he was devoted to algebra (the solution of equations, in his days a much discussed subject), and the study of Diophantus, but he did not influence the future development of mathematics.

Christoph J. Scriba

Sources T. Birch, *The history of the Royal Society of London*, 4 vols. (1756–7), vol. 4, pp. 444–7 · S. P. Rigaud and S. J. Rigaud, eds., *Correspondence of scientific men of the seventeenth century*, 2 vols. (1841); repr. (1965) · J. O. Halliwell, ed., *A collection of letters illustrative of the progress of science in England from the reign of Queen Elizabeth to that of Charles the second* (1841) · Wood, *Ath. Oxon.* · *Brief lives, chiefly of contemporaries, set down by John Aubrey, between the years 1669 and 1696*, ed. A. Clark, 1 (1898), 121–31 · P. J. Wallis, 'Pell, John', *DSB* · C. de Waard, 'Pell, John', *Nieuw Nederlandsch biografisch woordenboek*, ed. P. C. Molhuysen and P. J. Blok, 3 (Leiden, 1914), cols. 961–5 · P. R. Barnett, *Theodore Haak, FRS, 1605–1690: the first German translator of 'Paradise lost'* (1962) · *DNB* · R. S. Westfall, *Catalogue of the scientific community of the 16th and 17th centuries* [web site: es.rice.edu/ES/humsoc/Galileo/Catalog/catalog.html] · J. A. van Maanen, 'The refutation of Longomontanus' quadrature by John Pell', *Annals of Science*, 43 (1986), 315–52 · C. J. Scriba, 'John Pell's English edition of J. H. Rahn's *Teutsche Algebra*', *For Dirk Struik: scientific, historical, and political essays in honor of Dirk J. Struik*, ed. R. S. Cohen, J. J. Stachel, and M. W. Wartofsky (1974), 261–74 · J. Bernhardt, 'Une lettre-programme pour 'l'avancement des mathématiques' au XVIIe siècle: l'*Idée générale des mathématiques* de John Pell', *Revue d'Histoire des Sciences*, 24 (1971), 309–16 · F. Cajori, 'Rahn's algebraic symbols', *American Mathematical Monthly*, 31 (1924), 65–71 · G. Wertheim, 'Die Algebra des Johann Heinrich Rahn, 1659, und die englische Übersetzung derselben', *Bibliotheca Mathematica*, 3rd ser., 3 (1902), 113–26 · N. Malcolm, 'The publications of John Pell F.R.S. (1611–1685): some new light and some old confusions', *Notes and Records of the Royal Society of London*, 54 (2000), 275–92 · J. A. Stedall, 'Moving the Alps: uncovering the mathematics of John Pell', *A discourse concerning algebra: English algebra to 1685* [forthcoming]

Archives BL, corresp. and papers, Add. MSS 4278–4474 · BL, diplomatic corresp. and papers, Lansdowne MSS 754–755 · BL, mathematical papers and notes, Add. MSS 4410–4431 · BL, proof sheets of the English edition of Rahn's *Teutsche algebra* and related papers,

Add. MS 4398 · BL, Sloane MS 4365 · Bodl. Oxf., letters to John Aubrey · priv. coll. (NRA) · RS, John Collins MSS · Worcester College, Oxford, cypher book

Pell, Sir Watkin Owen

Pell, Sir Watkin Owen (1788–1869), naval officer, was son of Samuel Pell of Sywell Hall, Wellingborough, Northamptonshire, and his wife, Mary, daughter of Owen Owen of Denbighshire. He entered the navy in April 1799 on board the *Loire*, and on 6 February 1800 lost his left leg in the capture of the French frigate *Pallas*, supported by a gun battery on one of the Seven Islands. He was consequently discharged, and remained on shore for the next two years, at the end of which time he rejoined the *Loire*. After serving in various ships on the home and West Indian stations, he was promoted, on 11 November 1806, lieutenant of the frigate *Mercury*, then on the Newfoundland station, and afterwards in the Mediterranean. Here, as first lieutenant in command of the *Mercury*'s boats, he repeatedly distinguished himself in capturing gunboats or small armed vessels on the coast of Spain or Italy, and on one occasion, on 1 April 1809, he was severely wounded in the right arm.

In August 1809 Pell was presented by the Patriotic Society with £80 for the purchase of a sword, and on 29 March 1810 he was promoted commander. In the following October he was appointed to the bomb-vessel *Thunder*, and was, during the next two years, mainly employed in the defence of Cadiz. On 9 October 1813, as he was returning to England to be paid off, he fell in with and, after a sharp engagement, captured the privateer *Neptune*, of much superior force, for which, and other good service, he was advanced to post rank, on 1 November 1813. From 1814 to 1817 he commanded the frigate *Menai* on the coast of North America. In May 1833 he commissioned the *Forte*, and in her acted as senior officer on the Jamaica station until March 1837. On his return to England he was knighted by the queen, and, in accordance with the intention of William IV, was nominated a KCH by the king of Hanover. In 1839 he was offered a seat at the Board of Admiralty, if he was prepared to stand the cost of an election, £100–£1500, by the political manager of the Admiralty, Admiral Sir J. W. D. Dundas. He declined. In 1840 he was appointed to the *Howe*, and in August 1841 to be superintendent of Deptford victualling yard, from which he was shortly afterwards moved to be superintendent of Sheerness Dockyard, and in December to be superintendent of Pembroke dockyard, where he remained until February 1845. In 1846 he was appointed a commissioner of the Royal Naval Hospital at Greenwich. In 1847 he married Sarah Dorothea, daughter of Edward Owen, of Maesmynan; she survived her husband.

Pell became a rear-admiral on 5 September 1848, and was offered, but did not accept, an active command in 1849 by Admiral Dundas. He became vice-admiral on 28 December 1855, and admiral on 11 February 1861. He died at his residence, the Queen's House, Greenwich, London, on 29 December 1869. A brave and resourceful junior officer who earned his promotions, and a favourite of William IV, Pell was independently wealthy and was patronized by his Northamptonshire neighbours, the Spencer family, to whom he was devoted. They secured his appointment to Deptford and Greenwich, the latter through Lord John Russell. He proved a competent administrator.

J. K. LAUGHTON, *rev.* ANDREW LAMBERT

Sources E. Fraser and L. G. Carr-Laughton, *The royal marine artillery, 1804–1923*, 1 (1930) · NMM, Pell MSS · PRO, Russell MSS · NMM, Minto MSS · O'Byrne, *Naval biog. dict.* · Walford, *County families* · *Dod's Peerage* (1858)
Archives NMM, corresp., diaries, and papers · NMM, letter-book
Likenesses J. Lucas, oils, *c.*1849–1850, NMM
Wealth at death under £30,000: probate, 12 Jan 1870, *CGPLA Eng. & Wales*

Pell, William

Pell, William (*bap.* 1634, *d.* 1698), clergyman and ejected minister, was born at Sheffield and baptized there on 1 February 1634, the son of William Pell. After attending the grammar school at Rotherham, Yorkshire, Pell was admitted as a sizar on 29 March 1651 at Magdalene College, Cambridge, where his tutor was Joseph Hill. He was elected scholar on 2 June 1654 and fellow 3 November 1656, having graduated BA in 1655. By a patent dated 15 May 1656 he was appointed as a tutor in the new college at Durham founded by Oliver Cromwell, and he was awarded his Cambridge MA in 1658. He was ordained by Ralph Brownrigg, bishop of Exeter, probably at Sonning, Berkshire, and on 13 April 1659 he was admitted to the sequestered rectory of Easington, Durham. At the Restoration the Durham college collapsed and Gabriel Clark, the sequestered rector of Easington, was restored.

On 11 February 1660 at Bishopwearmouth, Durham, Pell married Elizabeth (*bap.* 1638, *d.* 1707/8), daughter of George Lilburne of Sunderland; their daughter Elizabeth was born at Great Stainton, Durham, on 30 July 1662. Ten days earlier Pell had been presented to the rectory of that parish, but he was ejected within the month under the Act of Uniformity. He and his family remained in the county and his friends urged him to use his considerable scholarly talents, particularly as an orientalist, in a new and unofficial attempt to begin again the introduction of university learning in the north-east. But Pell refused, in the belief that he was bound by the terms of his Cambridge graduation oath, and it was Richard Frankland who shouldered the task of founding a northern academy. On 1 May 1672 Pell was granted a licence as a presbyterian teacher at his house in Durham or any other licensed place. Almost immediately Dr Isaac Basire, a prebendary of the cathedral and JP of the county, wrote to London complaining that Pell had preached at a conventicle at the house of a Mr Orton on 12 and 19 May, but had failed either to show his licence or to attend the justices for examination. Pell's continuing activities within sight of the cathedral spire provoked the fury of Archdeacon Denis Granville, who wrote from Durham on 5 July 1674 complaining against 'one Pell, a preacher in the times of rebellion, who hath the confidence to set up a congregation at our gates, and though excommunicated, dares to christen children, and ventures on other sacred offices'. Such practices, being 'extremely unusual in this place, are thereby extremely scandalous'; and Granville asked for official confirmation that he and other justices of the peace could 'proceed against schismatics according the last Act of Parliament' (*Ambrose Barnes*, 141).

It may have been soon after the archdeacon's request that Pell 'was imprisoned at Durham for his non-conformity: and removed himself to London by an Habeas Corpus; and was set at liberty by Judge Hales. He then lived in the northern parts of Yorkshire and practised physic' (Calamy, *Abridgement*, 2.289). Later he was reported to be preaching at Tattershall, Lincolnshire; perhaps this was after he gained employment as a domestic steward to Edward Clinton, fifth earl of Lincoln, which would have afforded some protection against arrest. Under King James's declaration of indulgence in 1687 Pell became minister to the nonconformists at Boston, Lincolnshire, where in 1690 there were reported to have been '2 or 300 auditors in the afternoone; they raise him about £60 per annum, but begin to be weary of soe much, since the death of some of the better sort' (Gordon, 70). In early 1691 Pell was canvassed to be minister of a congregation at Darlington, but did not take it up. In 1694, however, he did return to the north-east, becoming assistant to Richard Gilpin at Newcastle upon Tyne. There he died on 2 December 1698 and was buried on 6 December at St Nicholas's Church. His wife survived him by nearly ten years and was buried on 30 January 1708.   STEPHEN WRIGHT

Sources Calamy rev. · A. Gordon, ed., *Freedom after ejection: a review (1690–1692) of presbyterian and congregational nonconformity in England and Wales* (1917) · *Memoirs of the life of Mr Ambrose Barnes*, ed. [W. H. D. Longstaffe], SurtS, 50 (1867) · E. Calamy, ed., *An abridgement of Mr. Baxter's history of his life and times, with an account of the ministers, &c., who were ejected after the Restauration of King Charles II*, 2nd edn, 2 vols. (1713) · Venn, *Alum. Cant.* · CSP dom., 1672 · E. Calamy, *A continuation of the account of the ministers ... who were ejected and silenced after the Restoration in 1660*, 2 vols. (1727), vol. 1 · IGI

Pellatt, Apsley (1791–1863), glass manufacturer, was the eldest son of Apsley Pellatt (*d.* 1826) and Mary, daughter of Stephen Maberly of Reading. He was born on 27 November 1791, probably at 80 High Holborn, London, where his father kept a glass warehouse. Pellatt was educated by Dr Wanostrocht at Camberwell, and joined his father in business. He was twice married: first, in 1814, to Sophronia, daughter of George Kemp of Reading (she died in February 1815); second, in 1816, to Margaret Elizabeth, daughter of George Evans of Balham.

In 1819 Pellatt took out a patent for a process learned from a foreign source, 'crystallo-ceramie or glass incrustation', which consisted in enclosing medallions or ornaments of pottery ware, metal, or refractory material in glass, by which very beautiful ornamental effects were produced. The new process was described by the inventor with illustrations in his *Memoir on the Origin, Progress, and Improvement of Glass Manufactures* (1821). He took out a patent in 1831 for improvements in the manufacture of pressed glass articles, and another in 1845, with his brother, Frederick, for improvements in the composition of glass, and in the methods of blowing, pressing, and casting glass articles. In 1851 he discovered the Venetian secret art of making 'crackle-glass'. Under his care the products of the family's Falcon glassworks in Southwark attained a high reputation both for quality and artistic design. He devoted much time to the investigation of the principles of glass making both in ancient and modern times, and he became a high authority upon the subject. His book *Curiosities of Glass Making* (1849) comprised the text of his earlier memoir, his lectures on the manufacture of flint glass, delivered to the Royal Institution, and the fruits of his various researches. He was a commissioner for the Great Exhibition of 1851 and a juror for the 1862 exhibition, for which he wrote the report on the glass manufactures displayed. He travelled widely on business, visiting glassworks at Venice, Nievelt in Bohemia, Liège, and Baccarat, where he was welcomed by colleagues whom he had previously invited to tour his own factory. His knowledge of chemistry and art led to his serving on the council of the School of Design for seven years and he regularly attended its meetings.

Pellatt was elected an associate of the Institution of Civil Engineers in 1838, and in 1840 he became a member of the council. He contributed in 1838 and 1840 papers on the manufacture of glass, which were printed in volume 1 of the *Proceedings* (1838, 39; and 1840, 37–41), and he was a frequent speaker at meetings of the institution.

Besides his work as a glass maker, Pellatt took a great interest in public affairs. He was for several years a member of common council for the City of London, during which time he successfully campaigned for Jews to be admitted freemen of the City, which would entitle them to keep shops and enjoy other privileges from which they alone were excluded. His views were published in 1829 as *A Brief Memoir of the Jews in Relation to their Civil and Municipal Disabilities*. When he moved to Southwark, he was concerned with the improvement of drains and sewers in that district. He was actively involved in restricting Sunday trading, and gave evidence in favour of this to the House of Commons select committee on Sunday observance in 1832. His concern for social welfare manifested itself in his service and benefactions to the British Orphan School, the London Female Penitentiary, and many other institutions.

Pellatt represented Southwark in parliament as a Liberal from July 1852 until the general election in March 1857, but was unsuccessful in the elections of 1857 and 1859. He was a frequent speaker in the Commons, and he introduced a bill for facilitating dissenters' marriages in 1854, 1855, and 1856. In 1856 he brought in a bill to define the law as to crossed cheques, which was passed (19 & 20 Vict. 25). He was a prominent member of the Congregational body.

From 1843 Pellatt lived at Staines, where he established a model farm. He died of paralysis, on 17 April 1863, after little more than a week's illness, at the house of his brother-in-law at Balham. His wife and three daughters survived him, his only son having died about 1839.

       R. B. PROSSER, *rev.* ANITA MCCONNELL

Sources ILN (26 March 1853), 237–8 · PICE, 23 (1863–4), 511–12 · Boase, *Mod. Eng. biog.* · *Nonconformist* (22 April 1863), 309 · ILN (16 May 1863), 546 · *The Times* (20 April 1863), 12f · 'Select committee

on the observance of the sabbath day', *Parl. papers* (1831–2), 7.253, no. 679; pubd separately (1832)
Likenesses portrait, repro. in *ILN* · woodcut, NPG
Wealth at death under £40,000: probate, 10 July 1863, *CGPLA Eng. & Wales*

Pellegrini, Carlo [*pseud.* Ape] (**1839–1889**), caricaturist, was born in March 1839 in Capua, Campania, Italy, a scion of the Sedili Capuani, an aristocratic landowning family. His mother was said to be a descendant of the Medici. He was educated at the Collegio Barnibiti, and then at Sant' Antonio in Maddaloni, near Naples. Barely 5 feet 2 inches tall, with an unusually large head and ridiculously tiny feet, his winning personality attracted a variety of friends and patrons. By his twentieth year he was a 'pet' of fashionable Neapolitan society and he developed 'an extravagant taste for the pleasures of the high life' (E. Harris, 53). In return he humorously caricatured his friends, inspired no doubt by reproductions of Melchiorre Delfico's *portraits chargés* of Verdi and other prominent Neapolitan personalities. He apparently had no formal artistic training.

In the autumn of 1860 he joined Garibaldi's forces and fought in the last battles against the Bourbons at the Volturno and at Capua. He then returned to Neapolitan society. On 9 November 1862 he celebrated the coming-of-age of the visiting prince of Wales—an encounter which seems crucial to his career (E. Harris, 53–4). Less than two years later he unexpectedly left Italy, propelled, he asserted, by an unrequited love and the death of a sister. After travelling across Europe he arrived in London in November 1864. Poverty, he claimed, forced him to sleep on doorsteps in Piccadilly and Whitehall, and even in a hansom cab (Ward, 97). Nevertheless he swiftly became an ornament in bohemian society, and a court jester in the prince of Wales's set.

Pellegrini produced amusing caricatures of his royal companions; some are now in the Royal Library, Windsor. These came to the attention of the politician and newspaper proprietor Thomas Gibson Bowles, who commissioned him, as Singe, to produce coloured *portraits chargés* of Disraeli and Gladstone in January and February 1869 for *Vanity Fair*, Bowles's new society magazine. Reproduced as full-page illustrations by Vincent Brooks, then London's premier lithographer, they were an immediate success. Drawings by Ape (the *nom de crayon* Pellegrini used at *Vanity Fair*) shaped modern English caricature. They were styled after Delfico, Honoré Daumier, and the French school, which had itself been influenced in the 1830s by the Georgian caricaturists. 'Thus Pellegrini's coming to England and his subsequent triumphs in London closed the circle of European caricaturing' (Matthews and Mellini, 29). He inspired a raft of caricaturists: Spy (Sir Leslie Ward) was his grudging disciple, and Max Beerbohm idolized him, collected his work, and imitated him. Pellegrini was, Beerbohm wrote, 'by far the best caricaturist who lived within our time' (Beerbohm, 261). David Low called him:

a genius in his specialty. ... Ape's caricatures were maximum likenesses, that is to say they represented not only what he

Carlo Pellegrini [Ape] (**1839–1889**), by Jules Bastien-Lepage, 1879

saw but also what he knew. Most of them today look as though they were probably more like the persons they depict than were these persons themselves. (Low, 33)

Pelican, as Pellegrini was known to his bohemian friends, fell under Whistler's spell in the 1870s, with farcical results. He left *Vanity Fair* in 1871–2 and again in 1876 to caricature his society friends and to try to be a portraitist. His lithographs of twenty members of the Marlborough Club are now in the entrance hall to the royal enclosure at Ascot. His talent for portraiture did not equal his genius for caricature. His contemporaries agreed, as have more recent critics, that 'Being a good portrait painter is more than catching a likeness; and everyone would agree with Mrs. Jopling, "this essential 'more' Pellegrini did not possess"' (E. Harris, 57). Ape returned to *Vanity Fair* in early 1877. Until his death he shared the caricaturing with Spy and several other artists. Between 1869 and his death he caricatured 332 prominent Victorians for *Vanity Fair*; a number of his original drawings, most in gouache, are in the National Portrait Gallery, London; and the Royal Library, Windsor, also has a collection of his working drawings. His original drawings are highly prized by collectors because they reveal his incisive, affectionately witty eye.

Short and stout, Pellegrini was extremely fastidious, wore immaculate white spats and highly polished boots, and cultivated long Mandarin-like fingernails. He never walked when he could ride. He was kind, generous, and had a seemingly unending fund of charming tales and eccentricities. His fractured English, his flaunted homosexuality, his various whims which included bringing macaroni dishes to elegant dinner parties, his refusal of invitations to country houses for fear of strange beds, his habit of keeping a cigar in his mouth as he slept, his improvidence—all were tolerated (and sometimes relished) because he was such entertaining company. 'Whatever he did and wherever he went, he was the life and soul of the party' (E. Harris, 57). His dinners with the composer Paolo Tosti in the back parlour of Pagani's in Great Portland Street became a celebrated bohemian rendezvous in Victorian London. His caricatures, sketches, and the bars of music and other graffiti on the walls of Pagani's 'artist's room' survived the blitz and are now preserved by the BBC.

Generous to a fault, Pellegrini never lacked for friends. When debilitated by tuberculosis his fashionable friends raised the money for his care in a private hospital, settled all his debts, and provided the luxuries to which he was accustomed until he died at his home, 53 Mortimer Street, Cavendish Square, London, on 22 January 1889. The Fine Arts Society sold a proof from a destroyed plate of his much admired caricature of Whistler, with Whistler's signature, to pay for his gravestone in Kensal Green Roman Catholic cemetery, London.   PETER MELLINI

Sources L. Ward, *Forty years of Spy* (1915) · *Vanity Fair* albums, 1869–89 · E. Harris, 'Carlo Pellegrini: man and "Ape"', *Apollo*, 103 (1976), 53–7 · R. Ormond, *'Vanity Fair': an exhibition of original cartoons* (1976) [exhibition catalogue, NPG, 9 July – 30 Aug 1976] · R. T. Matthews and P. Mellini, *In 'Vanity Fair'* (1982) · *The Times* (23 Jan 1889) · *DNB* · D. Low, *British cartoonists, caricaturists and comic artists* (1942) · M. Beerbohm, *Caricatures of twenty-five gentlemen* (1896) · F. Harris, *My life and loves*, 4 vols. (privately printed, Paris, 1922–7) · L. Naylor, *The irrepressible Victorian: the story of Thomas Gibson Bowles* (1965) · J. J. Savory and others, *The 'Vanity Fair' gallery* (1979) · W. Feaver, *Masters of caricature: from Hogarth and Gillray to Scarfe and Levine*, ed. A. Green (1981) · M. Bryant and S. Heneage, eds., *Dictionary of British cartoonists and caricaturists, 1730–1980* (1994)

Archives John Franks collection of *Vanity Fair*, London, albums, originals for *Vanity Fair*, other works

Likenesses E. Degas, watercolour with oil and pastel on paper, *c*.1876–1877, Tate Collection · attrib. Ape [C. Pellegrini], self-portrait, watercolour drawing, 1877, NPG · J. Bastien-Lepage, 1879, NG Ire. [*see illus.*] · A. H. M. [A. H. Marks], lithograph, repro. in *VF* (29 April 1889) · H. Furniss, pen-and-ink sketches, NPG · A. J. Marks, caricature, chromolithograph, NPG; repro. in *VF* (27 April 1889) · H. Thompson, oils, NPG

Wealth at death £221 15*s*. 8*d*.: probate, 20 March 1889, CGPLA *Eng. & Wales*

Pellegrini, Giovanni Antonio (1675–1741). *See under* Venetian painters in Britain (*act*. 1708–*c*.1750).

Pellett, Thomas (*c*.1671–1744), physician, was born at Lewes, Sussex. He was a colleger at Eton College from 1687 to 1688, and was admitted at Queens' College, Cambridge, on 8 June 1689. He graduated MB in 1694, and in 1695 went to Italy with Richard Mead and studied at the University of Padua. In 1705 Pellett was created MD at Cambridge, and on 22 December 1707 was admitted a candidate at the Royal College of Physicians, London, where he began practice, and resided in Henrietta Street, Covent Garden. In 1712 he was elected a fellow of the Royal Society. On 9

Thomas Pellett (*c*.1671–1744), by Michael Dahl, 1737

April 1716 he became a fellow of the Royal College of Physicians, was censor in 1717, 1720, and 1727, and president in 1735–9. Pellett's only publication was the Harveian oration which he delivered on 19 October 1719. It is the only published Harveian oration which is partly in verse, and the only one in which a knight of the Garter (John, second duke of Montagu, a doctor of medicine of Cambridge) is congratulated on having become a fellow. The works of Thomas Linacre, Francis Glisson, Thomas Wharton, and William Harvey are described. Pellett edited Isaac Newton's *Chronology of Ancient Kingdoms* with Martin Folkes in 1728.

Pellett found it difficult to cope with private practice, and was inclined to give his time mainly to medical study and to general learning. He is listed as a subscriber to a number of books. He died in London on 4 July 1744, and was buried on 11 July at St Paul's, Covent Garden. A memorial inscription on a brass plate was erected in St Bride's Church, Fleet Street. He left at his death a widow, Ann, and a daughter, Jane. His will was proved on 17 August 1744, and his widow and daughter were the main beneficiaries.   NORMAN MOORE, *rev.* ANITA GUERRINI

Sources Munk, *Roll* · Venn, *Alum. Cant.* · P. J. Wallis and R. V. Wallis, *Eighteenth century medics*, 2nd edn (1988) · T. Pellett, *Oratio anniversaria habita in amphitheatro Collegii Regalis Medicorum Lond., in laudem benemeritorum & benemerentium de medicina, die XIX Octobris, anno 1719* · will, 17 Aug 1744, PRO, PROB 11/735, sig. 200

Likenesses W. Hogarth, oils, *c.*1735–1739, Tate collection · M. Dahl, oils, 1737, RCP Lond. [*see illus.*]

Wealth at death left wife and daughter 'plate and pictures'; left his 'Book and Jewells, also fifty pounds out of the arrears of my rent' to daughter; owed a servant seven years' wages: will, PRO, PROB 11/735, sig. 200

Pellew, Edward, first Viscount Exmouth (1757–1833),

naval officer, was born on 19 April 1757 at Dover, the second of the six children of Samuel Pellew (1713–1765), commander of a Dover Post Office packet, and his wife, Constance (*d.* 1812), daughter of Edward Langford of Penzance and his wife, Catherine. His younger brother Israel Pellew [*see* Pellew, Sir Isaac Israel] also achieved prominence in the navy.

Early years Following her husband's death Constance moved her family to Penzance, where Edward received an early education at the Revd James Parkins's school before attending Truro grammar school. In 1770 he ran away to sea to escape a flogging, securing a position aboard the *Juno* (Captain John Stott). Although the Pellew family had no great wealth they did have a distinguished Cornish pedigree and enjoyed the patronage and support of Lord Falmouth and the Boscawen family, the most powerful aristocrats in the area. Thanks to this influence Stott, Admiral Edward Boscawen's former boatswain, accepted the young Pellew as a captain's servant, a status frequently given to youngsters embarking on a career as a naval officer. Pellew joined the *Juno* in December 1770, sailing to the Falkland Islands and remaining aboard until she was paid off in January 1772. In the following August he rejoined Stott, now commanding the *Alarm*, and served in her in the Mediterranean until 1775. In that year, however, a disagreement with Stott resulted in Pellew and another midshipman being put ashore at Marseilles, whence the pair got a passage home in a merchant ship.

Pellew was fortunate that this escapade did no harm to his career, Boscawen influence not only securing him an immediate new position aboard the *Blonde*, but also the leadership and example of her captain, Philemon Pownoll, one of the most outstanding officers of the day. Pellew joined the *Blonde* in January 1776, she escorting a troop convoy to North America in the spring. After her arrival in the St Lawrence, Pellew joined a party of seamen sent to build and man a flotilla intended to wrest control of Lake Champlain from the American rebels. His boundless energy made Pellew a valued subordinate in the construction process, which was completed by October. In an action on the 11th he ended up commanding the schooner *Carleton* when both his senior officers were wounded, his gallantry helping to ensure that she was not captured at a moment of danger. Two days later the Americans were engaged again and their flotilla was destroyed. For his courage under fire Pellew was promised promotion to lieutenant, but this was to be delayed as he remained on Lake Champlain during the winter and was thereafter the commander of a group of sailors attached to General John Burgoyne's army. As such he endured the hardships of a campaign that ended with the surrender at Saratoga in October 1777, though not before he had again displayed

Edward Pellew, first Viscount Exmouth (1757–1833), by James Northcote, 1804

his courage when recapturing a barge loaded with vital provisions on the Hudson River. After the capitulation Burgoyne sent him home with his dispatches, Pellew finally receiving the promised promotion in January 1778.

As part of the Saratoga surrender Pellew was unable to serve in any active capacity until exchanged, this causing him much frustration as he had to spend much of 1778 serving on the *Princess Amelia*, a Spithead guardship. Not until October did he escape to become second lieutenant aboard the frigate *Licorne*, cruising first in the channel and then taking a convoy to Newfoundland in May 1779. She returned home with another convoy in November and in the following April his career took an important step forward when Captain Pownoll invited him to join his frigate, the *Apollo*, as first lieutenant. Pellew jumped at the chance and was aboard her on 15 June 1780 when she engaged a French frigate off Ostend. Pownoll was killed in the action and the command fell to Pellew, the enemy vessel suffering much the worse and fleeing into Ostend, then a neutral port. Although the engagement cost him an important service patron Pellew had the compensation of being promoted commander into the sloop *Hazard* for his endeavours. He served in the *Hazard* off the north-east coast until her paying off in January 1781, not receiving another vessel until March 1782, when he commissioned the sloop *Pelican* at Plymouth. In May 1782, having enjoyed some successes against French privateers, Pellew received the most important advance in a naval officer's career when he was promoted to post captain. With the whigs in power, though, his tory patron, Lord Falmouth, could not secure him a permanent command. Consequently he enjoyed only the temporary captaincy of the frigate *Artois* before the war came to an end.

Soon after this, on 28 May 1783, Pellew married Susan (1756–1837), daughter of James Frowde of Knowle, Wiltshire; the couple had two daughters and four sons including Fleetwood Broughton Reynolds *Pellew, naval officer, and George *Pellew, later dean of Norwich. Initially, with Pellew unemployed, the family lived in Truro, where he was a burgess supporting the interests of Lord Falmouth, moving shortly afterwards to Flushing, near Falmouth, when Pellew's elder brother Samuel became collector of the customs. He next went to sea in April 1786 when appointed to the frigate *Winchelsea* destined for the Newfoundland station, remaining in her until she was paid off in January 1789. He then moved to the *Salisbury*, continuing to serve off Newfoundland as she was the flagship of the station's commander, Vice-Admiral Milbank. After the *Salisbury* was paid off in December 1791 Pellew was again unemployed, trying his hand at agriculture by running a small family farm at Treverry, near Falmouth. In this venture he was singularly unsuccessful.

The famous frigate captain, 1793–1798 In early 1793 Pellew was rescued from the toils of agriculture by the coming war with revolutionary France. Indeed, Lord Falmouth's influence was such as to secure him command of the frigate *Nymphe* in mid-January before war had even been declared. For the next few months the *Nymphe* cruised the channel as well as taking a convoy to Cuxhaven, during which time Pellew was able to complete and train his crew, some of whom were former Cornish tin miners. This preparation was just as well, for on 18 June off Start Point the *Nymphe* fell in with the French frigate *Cléopâtre*, capturing her after a brief but bloody action that cost fifty British casualties out of 240 men present, the French losing sixty-three out of 320. This made Pellew's name, he not only having gallantly taken an enemy warship of equal force, but also having had the good fortune to score the first such success of the war. In the celebrations that followed he was knighted on 29 June.

Thereafter Pellew remained in the *Nymphe* before being transferred to the more powerful *Arethusa* in December 1793. The following year this vessel was part of the western squadron of frigates based at Falmouth under Sir John Borlase Warren, a force newly formed to counter the activities of several such enemy squadrons. On 23 April they engaged one of these to the south-west of Guernsey, the stronger British force quickly overpowering their opponents in an action where Pellew's *Arethusa* played the primary role in fighting the *Pomone*, at the time the largest frigate in service. After an engagement lasting under half an hour, during which she suffered between eighty and a hundred casualties, the *Pomone* surrendered, the *Arethusa* suffering only three dead and five wounded. Successful cruises continued for Pellew during the remainder of 1794 and in 1795, squadrons in which he either served or led destroying one frigate, capturing another, driving two corvettes ashore (at least one of which was later refloated after Pellew refused to burn them as they contained wounded men), and making many captures from French coastal convoys.

One event, however, underlined Pellew's reputation for heroism. On 26 January 1796 the *Dutton*, an East Indiaman hired by the government to transport troops to the West Indies, was driven into Plymouth by a gale. Losing her rudder on a shoal, the ship became unmanageable, went aground on some rocks under the citadel and lay broadside on to the waves, her rolling throwing all the masts overboard. She was, however, linked to the shore by a rope by which means all of her officers and some of her crew escaped, leaving about 500 men, women, and children still aboard to their fate. While a crowd milled around aimlessly on shore Pellew suddenly appeared. Having vainly offered financial inducements to get someone to go to their aid, he opted to do it himself, getting dragged aboard by a rope and receiving an injury to his back from one of the floating masts in the process. Once on the *Dutton*, sword in hand, he restored order amid the panic and oversaw the running of additional hawsers to the shore from which cradles were hung and some people pulled to safety. Others were placed in boats that had, with equal bravery, been brought alongside. By such means everyone was saved, Pellew being the last to leave. For his actions he was raised to the rank of baronet, also being given the freedom of the city of Plymouth and a service of plate from the Liverpool merchant community.

Service successes continued as well. Now in the powerful frigate *Indefatigable*, a 64-gun ship that had been cut down, Pellew commanded a squadron that in April 1796 captured the French frigates *Unité* and *Virginie*, the latter after a fifteen-hour chase extending over 168 miles. *Indefatigable* then became part of the force blockading Brest, Pellew spending freezing hours at the masthead observing the enemy's preparations for what turned out to be an abortive invasion of Ireland. When the French expedition finally sailed, on 16 November 1796, it was at nightfall in the hope of avoiding the British blockaders. The attempt, though, caused confusion among the poorly trained crews and Pellew gleefully added to the mayhem by closing with the *Indefatigable* and making a series of false signals by means of gunshots, rockets, and lights. After this the luckless French were buffeted by severe winter gales that scattered their vessels and ultimately wrecked the whole project. The British naval response, however, was slow and badly managed, being largely unable to take any advantage from the enemy's misfortune: Pellew was to provide the one exception.

On 13 January 1797 *Indefatigable*, with the frigate *Amazon* in company, spotted a sail some 150 miles south-west of Ushant. This proved to be the French 74-gun ship of the line *Droits de l'homme*, a class of vessel whose heavier armament normally made it impossible for a frigate to engage safely. However, in the rough seas pertaining at the time the larger warship could not open her lower gunports for fear of flooding, a weakness Pellew perceived and set about exploiting. The action began at 5.45 p.m. and continued, with brief pauses while the British repaired their rigging, for about eleven hours. The frigates hung on to the quarters of their larger opponent, constantly pouring fire into her and causing damage that made her more difficult to control. In the dark and stormy night all three vessels ended up in Audierne Bay on the coast of Brittany, the sudden sight of distant breakers just giving *Indefatigable*, with her masts damaged and 4 feet of water in her hold, time to alter course and escape—a difficult manoeuvre under the circumstances and one which was a great testimony to the crew Pellew had trained. The other ships were less fortunate. *Amazon* ran ashore, though the discipline of her crew meant that most were saved. The fate of the *Droits de l'homme* was infinitely worse. Grounding on a sandbank, dismasted, and lashed for days by a gale which prevented aid from reaching her, perhaps a thousand men from the soldiers and sailors packed aboard lost their lives. For Pellew the action was a triumph, Lord Spencer at the Admiralty acknowledging that for two frigates to destroy a ship of the line was 'an exploit which has not I believe ever before graced our naval Annals' (Parkinson, 181).

During the remainder of 1797 and through 1798 Pellew continued in command of a squadron watching Brest and operating against enemy cruisers, some fifteen of them being captured during the latter year.

Senior captain and admiral, 1799–1810 A more difficult period in Pellew's career opened in March 1799 when he was transferred to the *Impétueux*, a 74-gun ship of the line. Although in theory a promotion it was a step he vigorously resisted: commanding such a vessel virtually precluded the chances of large-scale captures (that is, of prize money), and also meant serving directly under the command of Lord Bridport, the commander of the Channel Fleet and a man for whom Pellew felt complete contempt. Worst of all it meant moving into a vessel whose crew was known to be mutinous. This discontent finally broke out at the end of May when the fleet put in to Bantry Bay after a cruise. Once again he proved equal to the occasion. When a large group of the crew surged on to the quarterdeck Pellew, who was a tall, athletic, and probably quite intimidating man, faced them down and, supported by his officers, brusquely seized the ringleaders. At that point the rebellion collapsed, three of the mutineers eventually being court martialled and hanged. Although the *Impétueux* would never be a happy ship, her crew had at least been brought to a state of obedience.

After a brief period in the Mediterranean in the summer of 1799 *Impétueux* served in the channel, and in May 1800 Pellew was made the commander of a squadron convoying troops and arms to support a French royalist revolt in the region around Quiberon Bay. However, the proposed uprising fizzled out and little was achieved. Similarly fruitless was a strike at Ferrol in August, *Impétueux* being one of the warships assigned to provide naval support for a venture that turned into a fiasco. Thereafter Pellew returned to the channel, being regarded by Lord St Vincent as one of the few officers he could rely on to perform the exhausting duty of blockading the French naval bases efficiently.

Impétueux was finally paid off in April 1802, the brief period of peace that followed seeing Pellew reinforce his political influence by becoming MP for Barnstaple in July. With the probability of hostilities resuming he was appointed to the 80-gun *Tonnant* in March 1803, and was sent in June with two other ships of the line to pursue a Dutch squadron said to be at Ferrol. In the event the Dutch evaded him, but Pellew ended up blockading the port as a French squadron returning from the Caribbean had sought shelter there. In the tedious months that followed Pellew's squadron was reinforced to six and then eight ships of the line.

On 15 March 1804 Pellew made his only significant foray into politics when he returned home to speak in support of Addington's ministry, then under severe pressure from Pitt and the opposition via attacks on St Vincent's efforts at naval reform. Pellew's speech made a considerable impact and certainly helped prop up the failing government. Pitt, it was said, never forgave him. The following month Pellew received his reward, being promoted to rear-admiral of the white and given the East Indies command, though his future prospects remained uncertain as Addington's administration finally collapsed in May, allowing Pitt back into office. Pellew was able initially to resist any urge the new ministers may have had to remove him from his new command by agreeing to resign his parliamentary seat in favour of a Pittite candidate, a step he took when, and not before, he boarded his flagship for the voyage to India in July 1804.

Such a bargain did not prevent the new first lord of the Admiralty, Lord Melville, from taking a more subtle revenge by dividing the East India station. Early in 1805 Rear-Admiral Thomas Troubridge was appointed to take command of the eastern, and more lucrative, half, while Pellew was left with the western section. Politically this was very clever, punishing one admiral who had opposed Pitt by appointing another, who was also a supporter of St Vincent, to a situation where conflict between the two was inevitable. Militarily, though, it was crass stupidity, not merely because a divided station denied the western commander access to the east Indian ports when the south-west monsoon made the western coast unsafe during the summer, but also because a divided command could easily lead to paralysis in the face of any enemy assault on British interests.

The two admirals finally met in August 1805 and, given that each was renowned for a fiery temper, the furious outcome was predictable, particularly when, on a technicality, Pellew refused to accept Troubridge's instructions. Pellew offered a compromise whereby Troubridge, as the junior admiral, would command the eastern region under Pellew's orders, but this was flatly refused. Within a week of the encounter the pair were not on speaking terms and were writing letters of protest to London. The whole mess was not resolved until January 1807 when news arrived that a new government in London had ruled in Pellew's favour, transferring Troubridge to the Cape.

Pellew retained the Indian command until February 1809, little of strategic significance occurring during the period. Pellew's naval attacks directed on Batavia Roads

(November 1806) and Griessie (December 1807) destroyed the moribund remains of Dutch naval power in the region, but financial stringency in India effectively prevented any occupation of those colonies or, more importantly, of the French islands of Mauritius and Bourbon. These remained the sources of constant attacks on British trade, a persistent worry for Pellew which embroiled him in a protracted feud with the merchant community of Calcutta. Their complaints respecting losses prompted an icy Admiralty demand for him to explain his seeming failure, though Pellew was able to counter that much of the trouble came not from any faulty employment of his warships, but from merchants who ignored convoys and rushed their vessels for markets. Certainly he enjoyed better relations with the Bombay business community who passed a vote of thanks for his efforts and pointed out that shipping insurance rates were lower in 1805–8 than they had been in 1798–1805.

In personal terms Pellew's time in India was more satisfactory. Two of his sons, Pownoll and Fleetwood, were naval officers and Pellew shamelessly took the opportunity to forward their careers, making both of them post captains and providing them with potentially lucrative cruising grounds. Pellew himself certainly increased his fortune: the capture of a Spanish treasure ship by one of his captains alone netted him £26,000 and doubled his personal wealth. Such riches enabled him, after he returned to Britain in July 1809, to purchase the estate of Canonteign near Teignmouth in Devon, as well as a large house, West Cliff, in Teignmouth itself.

High command, 1810–1833 Pellew, who had become a vice-admiral on 28 April 1808, was not re-employed until July 1810, when he became commander in the North Sea, his chief duty being to blockade the Scheldt. In April 1811 he was transferred to take command of the Mediterranean Fleet, a great compliment as, comprising some seventy to eighty warships, it was the largest naval force outside home waters and involved considerable responsibilities. These included the blockade of Toulon, by then the most important French naval arsenal; close co-operation with the various forces resisting Napoleon in eastern Spain; guarding the extensive British commerce in the region; patrolling the coasts of Napoleon's southern empire in Italy and the Adriatic; ensuring no further French adventures in Egypt; and maintaining the delicate diplomatic relations with the Ottoman empire and the Barbary powers. Pellew retained the command until Napoleon's abdication in 1814, being made Baron Exmouth on 14 May and promoted to admiral on 4 June. He returned the following year during the 'hundred days' when he provided naval support to forces assisting the royalists in southern France. On 2 January 1815 he had been made a KCB and shortly afterwards a GCB.

After Napoleon's second abdication Exmouth was directed to conclude treaties with the Barbary states for the abolition of Christian slavery, negotiations that took up the spring of 1816 and seemed to have been concluded successfully. On his return home, however, he discovered that troops of the dey of Algiers had massacred some 200 Christian fishermen, an act prompting fury in Britain and the desire for swift retribution. Exmouth was to be the instrument for this, for which purpose he immediately set about organizing and manning a squadron. This finally sailed in July 1816, reaching Gibraltar early in August, where it was joined by a squadron of Dutch frigates, the united force consisting of five ships of the line, one vessel of 50 guns, nine frigates, and various smaller warships, including four bomb ketches. Algiers was a formidable stronghold defended by approximately 450 cannon in well-protected batteries, but the attack which followed illustrated Exmouth's attention to detail. On the voyage out the British crews were subject to rigorous gunnery drills and had taken in massive stocks of ammunition. He had also ordered a reconnaissance of Algiers prior to the operation and when the ships finally reached the city on 27 August all the captains had been told what to do. At a little before 3 p.m. the action commenced and an intense bombardment was then sustained for over seven hours until the allies withdrew. By that time enormous damage had been inflicted on the defending batteries and most of their guns had been silenced. Furthermore the Algerine fleet of frigates and smaller warships in the harbour had been completely destroyed. On the next day the Algerines surrendered, agreeing to Exmouth's terms respecting their future behaviour and releasing more than 1200 Christian slaves. The battle had cost the allies 141 dead and 742 wounded, a higher proportion of those engaged than in any of Nelson's victories and indicative of its severity.

In the wake of the victory Exmouth was fêted as a hero: at home, in 1816, he was created Viscount Exmouth of Canonteign and received the thanks of parliament; decorations were also forthcoming from Spain, Naples, Sardinia, and the Netherlands. In 1817 he was given the position of port admiral at Plymouth and retained it until February 1821, then finally retiring from active service. He was made vice-admiral of the United Kingdom on 15 February 1832, but died at West Cliff House, Teignmouth, on 23 January 1833 and was buried on 6 February at Christow church. He was survived by his wife, who died on 29 October 1837.

In summing up Edward Pellew's career he may certainly be considered one of the foremost frigate captains of the age, combining qualities of seamanship, determination, and imagination that made him ideal for the sorts of responsibility that came with such a command. In action he was a fearless inspiration and was an officer who, even as an admiral, led by example. His real-life exploits were sufficiently dramatic for him to feature as Midshipman Hornblower's captain in C. S. Forester's famous novel. Yet Pellew was a short-tempered martinet who demanded the highest standards from both officers and men—in short, the type of leader who was respected rather than loved. Equally, his insistence after taking up the Indian command that all his captains submit regular monthly punishment reports to curb excesses indicate that he was no savage. His popular reputation lacks only the winning of a major naval engagement, but his leadership of the Mediterranean Fleet showed someone more than capable of shouldering the arduous burdens of an extremely important station, and was concluded by the reduction of a powerful fortress in an operation where the planning and execution were very much his own. In a time that produced a plethora of highly talented naval officers Pellew was one of the most outstanding.

CHRISTOPHER D. HALL

Sources DNB · C. N. Parkinson, *Edward Pellew, Viscount Exmouth, admiral of the red* (1934) · E. Osler, *The life of Admiral Viscount Exmouth* (1835) · J. Marshall, *Royal naval biography*, 1 (1823) · G. C. Boase, *Collectanea Cornubiensia: a collection of biographical and topographical notes relating to the county of Cornwall* (1890) · W. James, *The naval history of Great Britain, from the declaration of war by France in 1793, to the accession of George IV*, [3rd edn], 6 vols. (1837) · 'Admiral Viscount Exmouth', W. H. Tregellas, *Cornish worthies*, 1 (1884), 291–308 · L. Jewitt, *A history of Plymouth* (1873) · W. L. Clowes, *The Royal Navy: a history from the earliest times to the present*, 4–5 (1899–1900); repr. (1997) · C. N. Parkinson, *War in the eastern seas, 1793–1815* (1954) · *Naval Chronicle*, 18 (1807), 411–66 · U. Redwood, *The story of Flushing, Cornwall* (1967) · R. E. Davidson, *History of Truro Grammar and Cathedral School* (1970) · P. A. Symonds, 'Pellew, Edward', HoP, *Commons, 1790–1820*, 4.755–7 · will, PRO, PROB 11/1811, fols. 236r–247v

Archives Alnwick Castle, letter-book and corresp. · NMM, corresp. and papers · NMM, further papers · priv. coll., papers | Alnwick Castle, letters to duke of Northumberland · BL, corresp. with Sir William A'Court, Add. MS 41528 · BL, corresp. with Sir Hudson Lowe, Add. MSS 20114–20124, 20134, 20192 · BL, letters to second Earl Spencer · BL, corresp. with Lord Wellesley, Add. MS 13755 · BL, letters to William Windham, Add. MSS 37875–37879 · BL OIOC, letters to Sir George Barlow, MS Eur. F 176 · Hunt. L., letters to Grenville family · L. Cong., manuscript division, letters to Lord Melville · NL Scot., letters to Lord Melville · NL Scot., letters to first earl of Minto · NMM, corresp. with Sir Benjamin Carew · NMM, letters to Sir Richard Keats · NMM, letters to Sir Charles Yorke · NRA, priv. coll., letters to William Adam, etc. · NRA, priv. coll., letters to Henry Duncan · PRO, letters to second earl of Chatham, ADM 1 and 2, PRO 30/8 · U. Durham L., letters to second earl Grey · U. Nott. L., corresp. with Lord William Bentinck · Wilts. & Swindon RO, corresp. with Thomas Flindell

Likenesses J. Northcote, oils, 1804, NPG [*see illus.*] · C. Turner, mezzotint, pubd 1815 (after T. Lawrence), BM, NPG · W. Beechey, oils, exh. RA 1817, Ironmongers' Hall, London · C. Turner, mezzotint, pubd 1818 (after W. Beechey), BM, NPG · W. Owen, oils, 1819, NMM · G. Hayter, group portrait, oils, 1820 (*The trial of Queen Caroline, 1820*), NPG · P. Macdowell, statue, 1846, NMM · T. Lawrence, oils, repro. in Clowes, *Royal Navy*, vol. 5 · B. Thorvaldsen, plaster bust, Thorvaldsen Museum, Copenhagen

Wealth at death £60,000; plus Canonteign estate and West Cliff House, Teignmouth: Parkinson, *Edward Pellew*; will, PRO, PROB 11/1811, fols. 236r–247v

Pellew, Sir Fleetwood Broughton Reynolds (1789–1861), naval officer, second son of Edward *Pellew, first Viscount Exmouth (1757–1833), and his wife, Susan, *née* Frowde (1756–1837), was born on 13 December 1789. George *Pellew, Church of England priest, was his brother. In March 1799 he was entered on board the *Impétueux*, then commanded by his father, with whom he was afterwards in the *Tonnant*, and in 1805 in the *Culloden* on the East India station. On 8 September 1805 he was promoted lieutenant of the *Sceptre*, but, returning shortly afterwards to the *Culloden*, was successively appointed by his father to the command of the sloop *Rattlesnake*, and the frigates *Terpsichore* and *Psyche*, in which he was repeatedly engaged with Dutch vessels and Malay pirates. On 12 October 1807 he was confirmed in the rank of commander, but was meanwhile appointed by his father acting captain of the *Powerful* (74 guns) and, in the following year, of the *Cornwallis* (50 guns), and then of the *Phaeton* (38 guns). His commission as captain was confirmed on 14 October 1808, and, continuing in the *Phaeton*, he took part in the capture of Mauritius in 1810 and of Java in 1811. In August 1812 the *Phaeton* returned to England with a large convoy of Indiamen. Pellew received the thanks of the East India Company and a present of five hundred guineas.

Pellew then went out to the Mediterranean in the *Iphigenia* (36 guns), and from her was moved, in January 1813, to the *Resistance* (46 guns). In October she was part of a strong squadron which silenced the batteries at Port d'Anzo and captured a convoy of twenty-nine vessels that had taken refuge there. In February 1814 the *Resistance* was ordered home and paid off, apparently because of a mutiny, for which several men were condemned to death, and several to be flogged. The sentence was, however, quashed, on account of a technical error in the proceedings; and, though it did not appear officially, it was said that the men had been goaded to mutiny by Pellew's harshness. In June 1814 he was nominated a CB. In 1816 he married Harriet (d. 1849), only daughter of Sir Godfrey Webster, bt, and they had one daughter. From August 1818 to June 1822 he had command of the *Révolutionnaire* (46 guns), after which he was on half pay for thirty years.

In January 1836 the king made Pellew a KCH, and knighted him. On 9 November 1846 he was promoted rear-admiral. In 1851 he married Cécile, daughter of Count Edouard de Melfort, but was divorced from her in 1859. In December 1852 he was appointed commander-in-chief on the East Indies and China station, not without a strong expression of public opinion on the misguidedness of sending out a man of his age to conduct what might be a troublesome war in the pestilent climate of Burma. In April 1853 he hoisted his flag on board the *Winchester*, which returned to Hong Kong in the following September, when the men applied for leave. The question of leave there was then difficult, because of the heat, the poisonous spirits sold, and the filthy condition of the town. Pellew decided that the men should not have leave, at least until the weather was cooler; but he did not inform them of the reason. There was a mutinous expression of feeling; Pellew ordered the drum to beat to quarters, and as the men did not obey, the officers, with drawn swords, were sent to force them up. Some three or four were wounded, and the mutiny was quelled. On the news reaching England, *The Times*, in strong leading articles, pointed out the coincidence of mutinies on the *Winchester* and the *Resistance* within a short time of Pellew's assuming the command, and demanded his immediate recall. Even without this pressure, the Admiralty had decided that he had shown a lamentable want of judgement, and summarily recalled him. He had attained the rank of vice-admiral on 22 April 1853, and became admiral on 13 February 1858, but had no further service, and died at Marseilles on 28 July 1861.

Pellew's career was made by his father, who exploited

death vacancies and the impracticability of communicating with the Admiralty to promote him captain when he was only nineteen. This seems to have warped his character. Pellew was, like his father, a brave and resourceful seaman, but a harsh, overbearing, and insensitive disciplinarian. The two mutinies that defined his career were the result of his zeal, and his failure to take the men into his confidence. His selection for a command in 1852 reflected the scarcity of senior officers of suitable political persuasion, and was always regarded as doubtful, even by those who made it. A favourite of William IV, who shared many of his values, Pellew married for money, and possessed the independent means to survive his long years ashore in some style. J. K. LAUGHTON, rev. ANDREW LAMBERT

Sources C. N. Parkinson, *Lord Exmouth* (1934) · G. S. Graham, *The China station: war and diplomacy, 1830–1860* (1978) · M. Lewis, *The navy in transition, 1814–1864: a social history* (1965) · Cumbria AS, Carlisle, Graham MSS · *CGPLA Eng. & Wales* (1861)
Wealth at death £18,000: probate, 28 Oct 1861, *CGPLA Eng. & Wales*

Pellew, George (1793–1866), dean of Norwich, third son of Edward *Pellew, first Viscount Exmouth (1757–1833), and his wife, Susan, *née* Frowde (1756–1837), was born at Flushing, Cornwall, on 3 April 1793. Sir Fleetwood Broughton Reynolds *Pellew was his brother. He was educated at Eton College from 1808 to 1811, and admitted as gentleman commoner at Corpus Christi College, Oxford, on 20 March 1812, graduating BA in 1815, MA in 1818, and BD and DD in November 1828. In 1817 he was ordained in the Church of England, in which his family's connections made his preferment straightforward. In February 1819 he became, by the gift of the lord chancellor, vicar of Nazeing, Essex. In November 1820 he was advanced by the same patron to the vicarage of Sutton on the Forest, Yorkshire. He subsequently was appointed seventh canon in Canterbury Cathedral (14 November 1822 to 1828), rector of St George the Martyr, Canterbury (1827–8), prebendary of Osbaldwick at York (15 February 1824 to September 1828), prebendary of Wistow in the same cathedral (18 September 1828 to 1852), rector of St Dionis Backchurch, London (October 1828 to 1852), dean of Norwich 1828, and rector of Great Chart, Kent, 1852; he held the last two preferments until his death. Pellew was one of the last in the Church of England to accumulate pluralities on such a scale. As dean of Norwich he had a seat in convocation, where he took a very active part in the debates, which show him to have been a moderate churchman. He married, on 20 June 1820, Frances, second daughter of Henry *Addington, prime minister and first Viscount Sidmouth, and his first wife, Ursula Mary, *née* Hammond; they had one son and five daughters.

Pellew published many sermons and tracts, the most important of which was a *Letter to Sir Robert Peel on the Means of Rendering Cathedral Churches Most Conducive to the Efficiency of the Established Church* (1837). Many of his sermons were included in *Sermons on many of the Leading Doctrines and Duties Taught by the Church of England* (2 vols., 1848); they show him a strong defender of the Reformation. In 1847 he published *The Life and Correspondence of Addington,*

First Viscount Sidmouth; this biography of his father-in-law is still of use as a documentary source.

Pellew died at the rectory, Great Chart, on 13 October 1866, and the east window of the church was filled with stained glass in his memory. His widow died at Speen Hill House, Newbury, Berkshire, on 27 February 1870.

W. P. COURTNEY, rev. H. C. G. MATTHEW

Sources Burke, *Peerage* · Foster, *Alum. Oxon.* · *The Athenaeum* (20 Oct 1866), 499 · *GM*, 4th ser., 2 (1866), 705 · *Men of the time* (1865) · Crockford (1866)
Archives Norfolk RO, corresp. and papers, diary and notebooks | Devon RO, letters of, and MS of life of, Lord Sidmouth
Wealth at death under £30,000: resworn probate, Aug 1872, *CGPLA Eng. & Wales* (1866)

Pellew, Sir Isaac Israel (1758–1832), naval officer, was born on 25 August 1758 either at Flushing, near Falmouth, or at Dover, the third of the six children of Samuel Pellew (1713–1765), commander of a Dover Post Office packet, and his wife, Constance (d. 1812), daughter of Edward Langford of Penzance and his wife, Catherine. His elder brother was Edward *Pellew (later Viscount Exmouth). First going to sea in the sloop *Falcon* in 1771, he served for three years in the West Indies. After a short time on the *Albion* in 1775 he went to the North American station on the frigate *Flora* a year later. When she was scuttled to prevent her capture in 1778 he briefly served ashore and was commended for his conduct. On his return home Pellew was made lieutenant into the *Royal George* in April 1779 and then served on the frigates *Danaë* and *Apollo*. He was placed in command of the armed cutter *Resolution* in the North Sea in 1782, distinguishing himself on 20 January 1783 when she captured a Dutch privateer, and he retained command of her on the Irish station until 1787. In March 1789 he joined the *Salisbury*, and he was promoted commander on 22 November 1790, not being employed again during the peace.

In 1792 Pellew married Mary Helen Gilmore (1758–1844), and for a while they lived in Larne, co. Antrim, near her family: they had one son, Edward, an officer in the Life Guards who was killed in a duel in 1819. On the outbreak of war in 1793 Pellew served as a volunteer in his brother's frigate the *Nymphe*, being in charge of her aft guns when she captured the *Cléopâtre* on 18 June. For this he was presented to George III and made post captain into the *Squirrel*, being praised for his command of her off the Dutch coast. In April 1795 he was made captain of a larger frigate, the *Amphion*, commanding her off Newfoundland and in the North Sea. In September 1796, sailing to join his brother's squadron in the channel, Pellew took *Amphion* into Plymouth for repairs. At 4.30 p.m. on 22 September she suddenly exploded. The ship was packed with people, about 300 of whom were killed. Pellew, stunned and badly cut about the face—lacerations that scarred him for life—survived by throwing himself through an open stern gallery window on to the deck of an adjacent sheer hulk. An inquiry blamed the disaster on the *Amphion's* gunner, who was suspected of stealing gunpowder and carelessly leaving a trail that caught fire and led back to the fore magazine. However, it may also be significant that Pellew had already complained that the magazine was poorly constructed and unsafe.

In February 1797 Pellew was appointed to the *Greyhound* but, having been put ashore when her crew mutinied, and under pressure from his commander-in-chief, he resigned the command, being moved in July to the *Cleopatra*. He commanded her first in the channel, until November 1798, and then on the Halifax and Jamaica stations. He suffered a defeat in 1800 when sending boats from the *Cleopatra* and the *Andromache* to seize some Spanish vessels in Levita Bay, Cuba. The assault was anticipated and, though they captured a small galley, the attackers were driven off, suffering twelve dead and seventeen wounded. Later on Pellew also had the embarrassment of the *Cleopatra*'s running aground on Abaco, one of the Bahamas. She was stuck for three days and only escaped when her guns and part of her ballast had been thrown overboard. The *Cleopatra* returned to Britain in December 1801 and was paid off.

Pellew next went to sea in April 1804, commanding the ship of the line *Conqueror* in the channel before going to the Mediterranean in September. She fought at Trafalgar, being fourth ship in the van or weather column, and it was to her that the *Bucentaure*, Villeneuve's flagship, surrendered. She also engaged the *Santisima Trinidad* and attempted to block the escape of Dumanoir's squadron. Although *Conqueror*'s sails and rigging suffered considerable damage, she lost only three dead and nine wounded. One prize, however, was denied Pellew. He sent a marine captain and five men to secure the *Bucentaure*, that officer refusing to accept Villeneuve's sword and that of the commandant of her soldiers with the remark that the swords should go to Captain Pellew. In the heat of the action, though, they never reached him, ending up with Vice-Admiral Cuthbert Collingwood who, much to Pellew's disgust, kept them.

After Trafalgar the *Conqueror* helped blockade Cadiz and then, in 1807, was in the squadron sent to secure the Portuguese fleet and royal family. She remained off the Portuguese coast during much of 1808, eventually returning home after the surrender of Siniavin's Russian squadron in the Tagus. Pellew then left her and was appointed to superintend the payment of ships in the Medway.

On 31 July 1810 Pellew was promoted to the rank of rear-admiral and in the following year his brother, on receiving the command in the Mediterranean, made him captain of the fleet, a sort of naval chief of staff. He retained this position until 1816, taking a prominent part in the negotiations with the Barbary powers that year. This marked the end of his active service. Pellew, who had been made a KCB on 2 January 1815, advanced to the rank of vice-admiral on 12 August 1819 and admiral on 22 July 1830. He had moved to Plymouth and died there, after a long and painful illness, on 19 July 1832; he is buried at the town's Charles Church. He was survived by his wife, who died on 2 November 1844. CHRISTOPHER D. HALL

Sources DNB · E. Osler, *The life of Viscount Exmouth* (1835), appx A, 365–85 · *Annual Biography and Obituary*, 17 (1833), 300–06 · C. N. Parkinson, *Edward Pellew, Viscount Exmouth, admiral of the red* (1934) · J. Marshall, *Royal naval biography*, 1/2 (1823) · G. C. Boase, *Collectanea Cornubiensia: a collection of biographical and topographical notes relating to the county of Cornwall* (1890) · J. Ralfe, *The naval biography of Great Britain*, 4 vols. (1828) · Boase & Courtney, *Bibl. Corn.*, vols. 2–3 · *Naval Chronicle*, 3 (1800), 197–202 · W. James, *The naval history of Great Britain, from the declaration of war by France in 1793, to the accession of George IV*, [3rd edn], 6 vols. (1837) · W. L. Clowes, *The Royal Navy: a history from the earliest times to the present*, 7 vols. (1897–1903); repr. (1996–7), vols. 4–5 · G. Landmann, *Adventures and recollections of Colonel Landmann*, 2 vols. (1852) · B. Lavery, *Nelson's navy: the ships, men, and organisation, 1793–1815* (1989)

Wealth at death left £500 to a niece and remainder, incl. house in Plymouth, to wife: will, 1820, PRO, PROB 11/1805, sig. 595

Pellew, Thomas. *See* Pellow, Thomas (*b.* 1703/4).

Pellham, Edward. *See* Pelham, Edward (*fl.* 1630–1631).

Pelling, Edward (*bap.* 1640, *d.* 1718), Church of England clergyman, was the son of Thomas Pelling (*b.* 1599/1600) and his wife, Margaret Lovell. Edward was baptized on 21 June 1640 at Trowbridge, Wiltshire, where his father had been rector since 1621. Thomas Pelling refused to swear to the solemn league and covenant in 1643, but he managed to stay on as rector: as he and his family were quitting their house, a sympathetic parliamentary colonel gave him a copy and told him to put it in his pocket, and then proceeded to assure the authorities that upon his own knowledge Pelling had taken the covenant (Walker, 336). In 1655 the elder Pelling was still in place, though regarded as 'both ungodly & insufficient' (*Walker rev.*, 379). The younger Pelling may have been one of John Walker's correspondents for his account of the sufferings of the clergy.

Edward Pelling was a king's scholar at Westminster School and then was admitted to Trinity College, Cambridge, in 1658. His coming of age and early education, therefore, took place in the turbulent and confusing interregnum years, which undoubtedly influenced his outlook later in life. He was elected minor fellow of Trinity College in September 1664 and major fellow the following April. He graduated BA in 1662 and proceeded MA in 1665 and DD on the occasion of the visit of the new king, William III, in October 1689. He was vicar of St Helen, Bishopsgate, in London from May 1674, until he was collated to the rectory of St Martin Ludgate in October 1678. He became a prebendary of Westminster in 1683, but resigned both this and his living at St Martin Ludgate when he was presented to the rectory of Petworth, Sussex, in 1691 by Charles Seymour, duke of Somerset, whose chaplain he was. Pelling remained at Petworth until his death in March 1718. He also became chaplain in ordinary to William and Mary, then to Queen Anne, and was elected as the diocese of Chichester's proctor to convocation in 1710. He and his family were well connected to the clerical establishment in Sussex: his son, Thomas, became vicar of Rottingdean, and his two daughters married other clergymen in the county. It appears that the family made a particularly close alliance with the Bettesworth family, which was something of a high-church clerical dynasty in the county. His first wife's name is not recorded, but she is the one who bore his children. She must have died in or before 1710, because that is the year he married on 28 October Margaret Hill, a widow, who died less than four years later.

Pelling could be characterized as a high-churchman, though he was not a nonjuror. He entered the fray of political and religious debate in the late 1670s and early 1680s, first by preaching 30 January sermons that emphasized divine-right monarchy and absolute obedience. In 1680 he published his *magnum opus*, *The Good Old Way*, which argued that the Church of England's polity, doctrine, and rites (including high-church practices such as signing the cross and kneeling at communion) were apostolic and approved by God, and that dissenters were simply 'Seditious and Brain-sick People' (p. 7). In 1682 he defended divine-right monarchy, indefeasible hereditary right, and passive obedience. He wrote strongly in favour of Sir Robert Filmer (whose book *Patriarcha*, published in 1680, furnished tories with arguments for a generation) and George Hickes, the nonjuror, and maintained that republicanism was a 'Jesuitical Principal' (Pelling, *The Apostate Protestant*, 58). He was clearly frustrated by whig arguments for exclusion, and felt that 'true loyalty has been … reproached for a *Crime*, and esteemed a kind of *Treason* against the *People* to be Dutiful to the *king*' (Pelling, *Sermon Preached at St. Mary Le Bow*, 4). In 1685 he preached a thanksgiving sermon for James's victory over Monmouth, in which he likened James to the biblical King David. He had argued as early as 1679, however, that God sometimes allowed kings to be removed by violence and conquest (Pelling, *Sermon Preached on the Thirtieth of January 1678/9*, 20–24), and this enabled him to acknowledge William and Mary as his sovereigns. Whatever his feelings about the succession, by the early 1690s he was chaplain to their majesties. It is interesting to note that his sermons before the king and queen were markedly different in tone from most of his other printed works. There were none of the combative, defensive apologetics so common in his other works; these sermons were filled rather with platitudes on 'vertue', 'felicity', and 'happiness', and an emphasis on 'obedience to Divine Law' and a 'life of perfect Love and Peace' (Pelling, *Sermon Preach'd at White-Hall before the Queen*). It appears from this that he felt it necessary to moderate his rhetoric when preaching before the new king, and one wonders if he was entirely comfortable in this role. It is clear, however, that he had not lost all of his pre-revolution zeal: he continued in other contexts to preach in favour of a high view of episcopacy and against dissent and schism, and he voted for tory candidates for parliament in every election until his death.

Pelling died in March 1718 and was buried at Petworth. He was survived by his children: Thomas, vicar of Rottingdean; Martha, wife of Charles Bettesworth, rector of Kingston and Terwick (to whom Pelling gave £848 14s. 9d. worth of South Sea stock in the settling of his estate, which, one hopes, they sold off quickly); and Mary, wife of John Dunstall, rector of Newtimber and South Stoke.

J. S. CHAMBERLAIN

Sources Dunkin MSS on Sussex clergy, BL, Add. MS 32326, vol. 74:845 · will, 9 May 1717, PRO, PROB 11/563 · Venn, *Alum. Cant.* ·

E. Pelling, *A sermon preached on the thirtieth of January 1678/9* (1679) · E. Pelling, *The good old way, or, A discourse offer'd to all true-hearted protestants concerning the ancient way of the church and the conformity of the Church of England thereunto, as to its government, manner of worship, rites and customes* (1680) · E. Pelling, *The apostate protestant* (1682) · E. Pelling, *A sermon preached at St. Mary Le Bow, Novemb. 27, 1682* (1683) · E. Pelling, *A sermon preach'd at White-Hall before the queen, March the sixteenth, 1691* (1692) · E. Pelling, *A sermon preached Sept. 28, 1692 at a primary visitation held at Chichester* (1693) · J. S. Chamberlain, *Accommodating high churchmen: the clergy of Sussex, 1700–1745* (1997), 56–7 · Walker rev. · J. Walker, *An attempt towards recovering an account of the numbers and sufferings of the clergy of the Church of England*, 2 pts in 1 (1714), 336 · IGI

Archives BL, certification of Dr John Downes's conformity, Sloane MS 203, fol. 146 · W. Sussex RO, presentation to rectory of Petworth

Wealth at death £848 14s. 9d.—South Sea stock; also £20: will, PRO, PROB 11/563

Pelling, Henry Mathison (1920–1997), historian, was born on 27 August 1920 at 4 Curzon Road, Prenton, Wirral, Cheshire, one of the two sons of Douglas Langley Pelling, a stockbroker, and his wife, Maud Mary, née Mathison. He was educated at Birkenhead School (1926–39) and was elected to an open exhibition in classics at St John's College, Cambridge (1938). He matriculated in 1939 and was placed in the first class in part I of the classical tripos in 1941, whereupon his studies were interrupted by war service. The following year he was commissioned in the Royal Engineers. Having served in the Normandy campaign and the assault on Berlin (1944–5), he returned to Cambridge as an undergraduate (1946) and gained first-class honours with distinction (a 'starred' first) in part II of the historical tripos (1947). Under war conditions, he had qualified for the BA in 1942; he took his Cambridge MA in 1947 (incorporated as an Oxford MA in 1949), and was awarded the Cambridge PhD in 1950 and the LittD in 1975.

In abandoning classics in favour of modern history, Pelling found his vocation. He now began research on the early history of the Labour Party, a field where triumphalist myth making yielded to his exact scholarship. *The Origins of the Labour Party* (1954), reshaped from his PhD thesis, remains a classic pioneering study, built to last. From 1949 to 1965 he was fellow and praelector of the Queen's College, Oxford, living in college. His teaching covered both modern history and politics; a member of two faculties, he never agreed to become an examiner in either, preferring to put his research first. His move back to Cambridge in 1966, to the new post of director of research in the history faculty, acknowledged this priority. He had many graduate students and was a PhD examiner of formidable rigour, though he also showed real kindliness towards younger historians, many of whom became lifelong friends. While he was highly appreciative of female company, potentially uxorious, and fond of children, he remained unmarried.

Pelling's books represent a scholarly achievement in at least two fields. Having made himself the unrivalled authority on the history of the labour movement, he branched out in the 1960s into the new field of electoral history. *The Social Geography of British Elections* (1967) was the result—still an indispensable handbook to further research. Curiously, Pelling saved his most exciting ideas not for his big books, but for a series of trenchant essays, often originating as after-dinner talks or seminar papers. This was the origin of his influential volume *Popular Politics and Society in Late Victorian Britain* (1968). He became well known to generations of students through his *Short History of the Labour Party* (1961), which went through eleven editions in his lifetime. *The History of British Trade Unionism* (1963) was likewise updated many times; and Pelling published early books on American labour history which blazed a trail for later historians. His biography *Winston Churchill* (1974), though commercially successful (not least to the author), saw his talents less well matched to the subject. Accuracy always out-trumped rhetoric for Pelling. He liked to bet on election results, culminating in the general election of 1997, on which he made his usual healthy profit; and his shrewdness in managing money gratified him.

The pace slowed only with his serious stroke in 1971, which left him permanently scarred despite a resilient recovery; after this Pelling seemed older than his years. His achievement was recognized, perhaps belatedly, by his election as fellow of the British Academy in 1992. He had decided to retire early from his university post in 1980 (having been promoted to a readership at Cambridge in 1976) but he continued to live in St John's College, where he had held a fellowship since returning from Oxford, occupying a succession of book-lined, paper-strewn rooms. Pelling continued writing 'my last book' on *Churchill's Peacetime Ministry, 1951–55* (1997) which—tenaciously, triumphantly—he saw to publication in his final months. He had been admitted to the Midfield Lodge Nursing Home, Cambridge Road, Oakington, near Cambridge, and died there on 14 October 1997; the causes were given as congestive heart failure, ischaemic heart disease, hypertension, and myocardial infarction. A well-attended funeral in the chapel of St John's College on 22 October was followed by cremation at the Cambridge crematorium.

Pelling's career was his life, and his work won the kind of esteem that mattered to him: the respect of professional colleagues for his reputation as the foremost empirical labour historian of his generation. Many people were surprised at the value of his estate, over £1.8 million; but it was totally in character that it was divided equally between his college and the Save the Children Fund.

PETER CLARKE

Sources P. Clarke, *The Guardian* (21 Oct 1997) • P. Linehan, *The Independent* (21 Oct 1997) • G. Garnett, *Daily Telegraph* (29 Oct 1997) • *The Times* (31 Oct 1997) • Lord Morgan, 'Memoir of Henry Pelling at the Queen's College, Oxford', Queen's College Library, Oxford • will, 17 Feb 1981 • *WW* • b. cert. • d. cert. • passports • *WWW*

Wealth at death £1,864,656: probate, 4 Dec 1997, *CGPLA Eng. & Wales*

Pellow [Pellew], **Thomas** (*b.* 1703/4), writer of an account of Morocco, was born to parents of modest means but who were related to a family with numerous branches in Devon and Cornwall and which included Edward Pellew,

first Viscount Exmouth of Canonteign. Pellow attended Penryn School for some years and, though still only eleven years old, on the death of his father in 1715 he went to sea with his uncle John Pellew. He embarked at Falmouth in the spring of 1715 in the merchant ship *Francis*, but before the ship reached Genoa he had come to regret his decision to go to sea. Unfortunately on its return journey the *Francis* was captured off Cape Finisterre by a couple of Salé rovers, pirates operating from Salé on the Moroccan coast. The rovers were in turn surprised off the bar of Salé by an English cruiser commanded by Captain Delgarnoe, but the Moroccans saved themselves by running ashore. After getting to land as best they could the prisoners, consisting of twenty-five Englishmen and seventeen Frenchmen, were taken to a prison, and thence, after a brief delay, to Mesquinez or Meknes where the palace of the sultan, Mawlay Ismaʿil (1646–1727) (r. 1672–1727), was situated.

Being only a boy at the time Pellow was at first sent to clean arms in the armoury and was then given as a slave to the emperor's son, Mawlay Spha. His influence—reinforced by torture, according to Pellow's own account—caused Pellow to become a Muslim. Again according to Pellow's own testimony, however, he remained in his heart a Christian. Torture was commonly applied to Christian captives to induce them to renounce their faith, but it seems to have been especially severe in Pellow's case and he recounts how he was starved, beaten, and tortured by fire before he agreed to become a Muslim. Though the story rings true it would have been impossible for Pellow to say anything else in an account written for a British audience. As a Muslim, Pellow was excluded from the treaty negotiated by Commodore Charles Stewart in 1720, under which 296 Britons, mostly sailors, were released from slavery and allowed home. Pellow was thus left in Morocco a renegade, an object of suspicion to Muslim and Christian alike.

When he reached adulthood Pellow was given military training and about 1725 was put in command of a Moorish castle at Tannorah; he was subsequently employed by the sultan to put down an insurrection at Guzlan. Mawlay Ismaʿil died in 1727 and was succeeded by Mawlay Ahmad IV, during whose brief reign Pellow made an unsuccessful attempt to escape to Gibraltar, but was recaptured and narrowly escaped execution. He subsequently took part in the siege of Fez. In 1728 his wife, whom he had married under Mawlay Ismaʿil's order, and their daughter died. In his account he professed himself little upset by their deaths, but this was perhaps influenced by his need to support his claims that he had remained a true Christian at heart. With the death of Ahmad IV and the succession of Mawlay Abdullah V (1728–1757) his master changed, but his duties and way of life continued unaltered. During the next few years he was employed as a captain of horse helping to put down the frequent insurrections which characterized this unstable period of Moroccan history. Pellow's own fortunes waxed and waned as did those of his master. He was also, according to his own account, entrusted with a large caravan to Timbuktu looking for slaves and other merchandise. Pellow may be identified with Pilleau in

Braithwaite's *History of the Revolutions in the Empire of Morocco* (1729), which corroborates some of Pellow's claims in his own work. Pellow was occasionally employed as an interpreter at the embassy, but his staple employment—like that of a large number of renegades—was as a soldier, in which capacity he had to gain a precarious livelihood by plunder. Though he shared the prosperity of many renegades it was probably the strain of this hazardous way of life that decided him to plot his escape. It was not, however, until the beginning of 1738 that he was able to put his plan into action. The difficulty was to find a ship's captain bound for England who would take on board a Moroccan subject and conceal him until safe out of the sultan's dominions. To achieve this, after leaving Meknes he wandered the country for several months in disguise. After travelling with a party of conjurors, and as an itinerant quack, and after being several times attacked by brigands who robbed him of all his goods he arrived at Santa Cruz. There he lived for a long time in a cave in company with other outcasts, but failing to find a ship which would carry him he set out for El Waladia where he kept himself alive by stealing carrots. Finally he reached Salé where he managed without the knowledge of the Moroccan authorities to get a passage to Gibraltar in a small trading vessel, commanded by a Captain Toobin of Dublin. From Gibraltar, where a subscription was raised on his behalf, he sailed for London in the *Euphrates* (Captain Peacock) and, after a few days in London where the account of his long captivity drew some attention, he returned to Penryn on 15 October 1738.

The story of Pellow's experiences was published in 1739 under the title *The History of the Long Captivity and Adventures of Thomas Pellow in South Barbary; Giving an Account of his being Taken by Two Sallee Rovers and Carry'd a Slave to Mequinez at Eleven Years of Age*. A second edition appeared in 1740 and a third as *Adventures of Thomas Pellow of Penryn, Mariner* was edited by Dr Robert Brown for the Adventure Series (1890). Pellow's narrative, corroborated as it is by Braithwaite's book and the accounts of other captives in Morocco, appears to be based on personal experience accurately recorded but it was evidently edited rather liberally. As well as Pellow's own account it contains long extracts from John Windus's *Journey to Mequinez* (1725) and there is much stereotypical comment on the plight of Christians enslaved in Morocco. The most original and also the most graphic part is the account of Pellow's escape, which gives a picture of the turbulent state of the country under Mawlay Abdullah.

Nothing more is known of Pellow.

ELIZABETH BAIGENT

Sources T. Pellow, *The history of the long captivity* (1739) · N. Matar, *Turks, Moors and Englishmen in the age of discovery* (1999) · C. Lloyd, *English corsairs on the Barbary coast* (1981) · S. Clissold, *The Barbary slaves* (1977) · J. Braithwaite, *The history of the revolutions in the empire of Morocco* (1729)

Pelly, Sir Henry Bertram (1867–1942), naval officer, was born on 9 September 1867 in Upminster, Essex, the sixth of seven sons of Richard Wilson Pelly (1814–1890), captain, Royal Navy, and his wife, Katherine Jane (d. 1901), youngest daughter of John Gurney Fry of Hale End, Essex.

Pelly entered the navy as a cadet in the training ship HMS *Britannia* in January 1881 and during his early career spent long periods abroad on the China station and in the south Pacific, interspersed with service in the Channel Fleet. He departed from the usual career in 1897, when he declined the offer of command of a torpedo-boat destroyer and requested appointment to a larger ship because 'promotion would never come to me unless I could serve under a rising man rather than as my own head' (Pelly, 57). He was eventually able to put this into practice. After service in the royal yacht *Victoria and Albert* (1899–1901) and promotion to commander he was flag commander (1902–4) to the successive commanders of the Channel Fleet, admirals Sir A. K. Wilson and Lord Charles Beresford. On 14 December 1904 he married Lilian Katherine Hawkshaw (1883–1966), elder daughter of Sir William Vincent, twelfth baronet (1834–1914), of Stoke D'Abernon, Leatherhead, Surrey. The couple had two sons and two daughters.

Promoted captain on 1 January 1906, Pelly subsequently became flag captain to Rear-Admiral Sir Francis Bridgeman in the Mediterranean Fleet (1906–7) and flag captain to Admiral Beresford in the Channel Fleet (1907–9). He was inspector of contract-built ships (1909–12) and, just after the outbreak of the war in 1914, was given command of the battle cruiser *Tiger*, completing at Greenock. To date Pelly had enjoyed what was in appearance a charmed career, with a succession of posts as flag commander or flag captain to 'rising men', followed by command of the magnificent *Tiger*, whose arrival was eagerly awaited by Rear-Admiral Beatty, commander of the battle-cruiser force. However, this supposedly choice appointment had a host of problems. The ship was still unfinished and did not commission until 3 October, and even then did not land all civilian workers for another three months. There were numerous teething troubles, particularly with electrical systems and dynamos, and precious little time—only nine days according to Pelly—for her new and inexperienced crew to train before joining the fleet.

On 24 January 1915, acting on intelligence provided by wireless interception, Beatty engaged a German raiding force in the vicinity of Dogger Bank. A running battle followed in which Beatty, in the leading ship *Lion*, signalled: 'Engage the corresponding ship in the enemy's line'. *Tiger* was the second British ship and Beatty intended her to engage the second German ship, the *Moltke*. Pelly, however, considering that there were five British battle cruisers against three German battle cruisers and an armoured cruiser, interpreted this to mean that he should concentrate on the lead German ship, the *Seydlitz*, leaving the two rearmost British ships to concentrate on the last German ship, the armoured cruiser *Blücher*. This resulted in *Moltke*'s being left free to fire on the leading British ships; the errors were compounded after the *Lion* was damaged and fell behind. Beatty's signal 'Attack the rear of the enemy' was misinterpreted by the second-in-command, Rear-Admiral Sir Archibald Moore, to mean the now doomed *Blücher* instead of the escaping German battle cruisers. *Tiger*, though initially ahead of the other British ships, manoeuvred erratically, probably because of a shell that destroyed the intelligence office below the conning tower and damaged internal communications. Pelly chose not to continue the pursuit unsupported—had he done so other British ships might have followed—and the Germans escaped with the loss of *Blücher*. Pelly's post-battle explanation, that his conduct was based on the Grand Fleet battle orders pertaining to concentrating fire on the lead enemy ship as the best means of reducing the enemy's speed, was not accepted by Beatty, and Pelly was informed that Beatty's signals were for guidance not rigid adherence, and that the main objective had been the destruction of the enemy. Beatty made allowances for a newly commissioned ship and for the fact that Pelly's crew included a large number of recovered deserters, but he now regarded Pelly as 'a little bit of the nervous excited type' (Patterson, 145). Admiral J. A. Fisher, the first sea lord, was furious and referred to the captain of the *Tiger* as a 'poltroon' who 'ought to have gone on had he the slightest Nelsonic temperament in him, regardless of signals' (Marder, *Fear God*, 150–1). Fisher added: *'Any fool can obey orders!'* (ibid.). Pelly might very well have been relieved but for the intervention of the first lord, Winston Churchill, who possibly did not want to tarnish the British victory.

Pelly survived for the moment but there was a cloud over his future, and when *Tiger*'s gunnery did not improve his inclusion among the élite of the battle-cruiser squadron ended. In May 1916 Beatty reported the *Tiger*'s shooting 'as usual unsatisfactory' and, as there was a convenient opening ashore, Pelly was named commodore, Royal Navy barracks, Portsmouth. However, before the formal change of command the battle of Jutland took place, and Pelly received the CB for his conduct of *Tiger*. Promoted rear-admiral in 1917, he remained at Portsmouth for the rest of the war. He was subsequently rear-admiral, Egypt and Red Sea station (1919–20) and admiral superintendent of dockyard and senior naval officer of Gibraltar, 1920–3. He was promoted vice-admiral in 1922, and in 1925 was placed on the retired list, with promotion to admiral in 1926. In 1938 he published his memoirs, *300,000 Sea Miles: an Autobiography*. He died at Churchill, near Axminster, Devon, on 27 December 1942.

It was not only Pelly's mistake that permitted the bulk of the German force to escape at Dogger Bank—there were mistakes by others that contributed to this—and one cannot definitely say that, had it not happened, he would have risen to higher office in a reduced navy after the war. Nevertheless his questionable judgement at a crucial moment undoubtedly blighted a promising career and forever diminished his reputation in naval history.

PAUL G. HALPERN

Sources WWW · *The Times* (29 Dec 1942) · H. Pelly, *300,000 sea miles: an autobiography* (1938) · *The Beatty papers: selections from the private and official correspondence of Admiral of the Fleet Earl Beatty*, ed. B. Ranft, 1, Navy RS, 128 (1989) · *The Jellicoe papers*, ed. A. T. Patterson, 1, Navy RS, 108 (1966) · *Fear God and dread nought: the correspondence of Admiral of the Fleet Lord Fisher of Kilverstone*, ed. A. J. Marder, 3 (1959) · A. J. Marder, *From the Dreadnought to Scapa Flow: the Royal Navy in the Fisher era, 1904–1919*, 5 vols. (1961–70), vol. 2 · J. Goldrick, *The king's ships were at sea* (1984) · *The Royal Navy list, or, Who's who in the navy* (1917); repr. as *The naval who's who, 1917* (1981) · S. W. Roskill, *Admiral of the fleet Earl Beatty: the last naval hero, an intimate biography* (1980) · Burke, *Peerage* · Walford, *County families* · CGPLA Eng. & Wales (1943)
Archives IWM, papers | BL, Jellicoe MSS · CAC Cam., Fisher MSS · NMM, Beatty MSS
Likenesses photograph, repro. in Pelly, *300,000 sea miles*
Wealth at death £7991 3s. 0d.: probate, 25 Feb 1943, CGPLA Eng. & Wales

Pelly, Sir John Henry, first baronet (1777–1852), merchant, born on 31 March 1777, was the eldest son of Henry Hinde Pelly (1744/5–1818) of Upton House, Essex, a captain in the service of the East India Company, and Sally Hitchen, the daughter of John Blake. His grandfather John Pelly was also a captain in the company's service, and his grandmother was Elizabeth, the daughter and heir of Henry Hinde of Upton. John is said to have been in his youth in the navy. If so, he quitted it without obtaining a commission. It is more probable that he was with his father in the company's service; that he had nautical experience of some sort appears certain. Having settled in business in London, he became in 1806 a director of the Hudson's Bay Company, of which he was afterwards successively deputy governor and governor. On 13 July 1807 he married Emma (d. 1856), the sixth daughter of Henry Boulton of Thorncroft, Surrey, the governor of the Corporation of Working Mines and Metals in Scotland and a director of the Sun Fire Office. They had eight sons and two daughters who survived infancy. In 1823 Pelly was elected elder brother of Trinity House, and, some years later, deputy master. In 1840 he was a director of the Bank of England, and in 1841 governor.

As governor of the Hudson's Bay Company in 1835 Pelly is remembered for having sent out the exploring parties which, under Peter Warren Dease and Thomas Simpson (1808–1840), two of the company's agents, did so much for the discovery of the north-west passage and of the coastline of North America. His share in this work is commemorated by Cape Pelly which marks the eastern extremity of Dease and Simpson Strait. In August 1838 he and Simpson travelled to St Petersburg to negotiate with Baron von Wrangel of the Russian American Company. These talks led in 1839 to the Hudson's Bay Company's leasing the Alaskan peninsula from the Russians. On 6 July 1840 Pelly was created a baronet, on the recommendation of Lord Melbourne. The duke of Wellington was on friendly terms with him. He died at Upton House on 13 August 1852.

J. K. LAUGHTON, rev. ELIZABETH BAIGENT

Sources GM, 2nd ser., 38 (1852), 527 · *Annual Register* (1852), 300 · Burke, *Peerage* · T. Simpson, *Narrative of the discoveries on the north coast of America …, 1836–9* (1843) · DCB, vol. 8
Archives BL, corresp. with W. E. Gladstone, Add. MSS 44364–44368 · BL, corresp. with Sir Robert Peel, Add. MSS 40411–40592 · U. Southampton L., letters to first duke of Wellington
Likenesses H. P. Briggs, oils, Hudson's Bay Company, London

Pelly, Sir Lewis (1825–1892), army and political officer in India, was born at Hyde House, Minchinhampton, Stroud, Gloucestershire, on 14 November 1825, the youngest son of John Hinde Pelly (1786–1852) of Bristol and the Bombay civil service, and his wife, Elizabeth Lewis (1781/2–1852) of Brinscombe, Gloucestershire. His five brothers all had careers in India; he also had four sisters. He was educated at Rugby School, and in 1841 joined the East India Company's Bombay army as an ensign. He became lieutenant (1843), captain (1856), major (1861), lieutenant-colonel (1863), colonel (1871), major-general (1882), and lieutenant-general (1887). Early in his career he was seconded to the foreign department, and served in what came to be known as the Indian political service and was the machinery of British indirect rule over the princely states.

In 1851–2 Pelly was assistant to the British resident at the princely court of Baroda, and prosecuted the corruption (*khutpat*) inquiries before James Outram's commission. From 1852 to 1856 he was employed in a civil capacity in Sind, and in 1857 acted as aide-de-camp to General John Jacob, who was commanding the cavalry division of the Indian army in the Persian War (1856–7). In the following year he returned to Sind, where he joined Jacob again as brigade major of the irregular horse Sind frontier force. Pelly collected and published *Views and Opinions of General Jacob* on the reorganization of the Indian army, which reached a second edition in 1858.

In 1859 Pelly was appointed secretary of legation and subsequently chargé d'affaires at Tehran. He was inexperienced in the politics of the Persian Gulf and compromised the British government in discussions over the Persian claim to Bahrain, but was not reprimanded. He also came into conflict with J. Felix Jones, the British resident in the Persian Gulf. He returned to India in 1861, making the journey of 800 miles from Herat to Kandahar on horseback and without an escort. He spent a few months in Calcutta with Lord Canning, the viceroy, before joining a roving commission in east Africa; he was shipwrecked on the Comores archipelago in September 1861. At the end of that year he became political agent and consul at Zanzibar, where he confirmed earlier treaties with the sultan. In 1862 he replaced Jones as resident in the Persian Gulf, through the patronage of Sir Bartle Frere, by then governor of Bombay, and the official to whom the resident was answerable. A historian of the Persian Gulf observed that 'While Frere remained Governor of Bombay little that Pelly did was permitted to be criticized … However foolish Pelly's actions might be, Frere never failed to shield him from censure and rebuke' (Kelly, 575).

The nine years of Pelly's residency were marked 'not only by indecorous quarrels with other political officers, but also by ill-judged or inept acts of policy' (Kelly, 575), with long-term consequences for British involvement in the region. For example, when he was asked to mediate between the Wahabis under the leadership of the amir, Faisal, and Thuwaini, sultan of Muscat (through whose territory an important telegraph cable was to run), Pelly initially declined to become involved, but changed his mind and travelled to the interior to visit Faisal at Riyadh in February 1865. (He published both an official account and an article in the *Journal of the Royal Geographical Society*

describing his experiences there.) He was persuaded by his reception that Thuwaini should be supported against the threats of Faisal, particularly as Faisal appeared to be resisting British views on the slave trade in the gulf. His intervention served only to make the relationship between Faisal and Thuwaini worse, and the British sent gunboats to bombard Faisal into submission. When the bombardment failed (and despite news of Faisal's own, unrelated, death), Pelly bombarded the Wahabi adherents at Sur, in an alternative demonstration of British strength; in the meantime, Thuwaini was murdered by his son. Rash and even incompetent as Pelly's actions had been, he was sheltered by the support of Frere against the wrath of the viceroy of India, Lord Lawrence, who advised that Britain interfere henceforth as little as possible with the Arabs, whether on the coast or inland. He further entangled the British government in the affairs of Oman and Muscat during negotiations over the telegraph and attempts to suppress slavery in the gulf, and his vigorous but ill-informed support for various Arab leaders ultimately committed Britain to the financial and political support of particular rulers in the region. Excessively influenced in his advice to government by personal feelings towards his informants, whether British or Arabs, he was patently unsuited to the sensitivities of British interests in the gulf. He was nevertheless appointed CSI in 1868 and remained in post until 1873, when he joined Frere's anti-slavery mission to Zanzibar.

Later in 1873 Pelly returned to India, where he was appointed agent and chief commissioner to the states of Rajputana. He was appointed KCSI in May 1874, and later that year he was sent as special commissioner to Baroda, where the British resident, Colonel Robert Phayre, had apparently been poisoned. It was suggested that the Maharaja Gaikwar of Baroda himself had been responsible for the offence, owing to political differences with the resident. Pelly arrived in Baroda in November 1874, and in January 1875 arrested the Gaikwar, Malhar Rao, and had him tried by a special commission. Although the Gaikwar's guilt was not proved, the British government deposed him none the less, on grounds of incapacity to rule, and appointed a successor. Pelly's last important appointment in India was as envoy-extraordinary and plenipotentiary for Afghan affairs at Peshawar in 1877, where he held inconclusive talks with an Afghan representative, before being recalled in March; the Second Afghan War broke out the following year. In August 1877 he retired, was created KCB, and returned to England.

On 1 August 1878 Pelly married Amy Henrietta, only surviving daughter of the Revd John Lowder, British chaplain at Shanghai, and stepdaughter of Sir Rutherford Alcock; they had no children. He was offered, and declined, charge of the Congo Free State by the king of the Belgians in 1883, and spent the early years of his retirement assisting the Royal Geographic and Asiatic societies. He published *The Miracle Play of Hasan and Husain: Collected from Oral Tradition* in two volumes in 1879. In 1885 he was elected Conservative MP for North Hackney, was re-elected the following year, and continued to represent that constituency until his death. He rarely spoke in the House of Commons, confining himself largely to Indian affairs. He died at Rosemullion, Falmouth, Cornwall, on 22 April 1892; he was promoted full general the same day. A short, well-built man, he had his portrait painted by Louise Starr Canziani, and a portrait of Lady Pelly by the same artist was exhibited at the Royal Academy in 1884.

Pelly's elder brother, **Saville Marriott Pelly** (1818–1895), was born on 28 March 1818 and educated at Winchester College and Guy's Hospital, London, before joining the Indian Medical Service. He accompanied the Sind irregular horse during Sir Charles Napier's campaigns (1844–7), and subsequently on the Sind frontier under General John Jacob (with whom his brother was also serving). He served with the second regiment of light cavalry in Rajputana during the mutiny campaigns of 1857–8. He was principal medical officer of the Indian medical department throughout the Abyssinian campaign of 1867–8 under Lord Napier of Magdala, was appointed CB, and retired as inspector-general of hospitals in the Bombay presidency in 1870. He died at Woodstock Villa, Burnt Ash Hill, Lee, Kent, on 3 April 1895, leaving a widow, Jane Billing, *née* Morris, whom he had married in 1850, and two sons and two daughters.

WILLIAM BROADFOOT, rev. K. D. REYNOLDS

Sources P. Rich, *The invasions of the gulf* (1991) · J. B. Kelly, *Britain and the Persian Gulf, 1795–1880* (1968) · R. L. Bidwell, ed., *Arabian Gulf intelligence* (1985) · F. J. Goldsmid, *Proceedings* [Royal Geographical Society], new ser., 14 (1892) · W. Ballantine, *Some experiences of a barrister's life* (1882) · A. Forbes, *Afghan wars* (1896) · Burke, *Peerage* · m. cert. · d. cert.

Archives BL OIOC, corresp. and papers, MSS Eur. F 126 · PRO, corresp. and papers, FO 800/233-234 | SOAS, letters to William Mackinnon

Likenesses L. S. Canziani, portrait; in possession of Lady Pelly in 1895 · R. T., wood-engraving (after photograph by Russell & Sons), NPG; repro. in *ILN* (30 April 1892) · sketch, wood-engraving, NPG; repro. in *ILN* (3 April 1875)

Wealth at death £38,180 7s. 3d.: administration, 1892, *CGPLA Eng. & Wales* · £2927 19s. 8d.—Saville Marriott Pelly: probate, 1895, *CGPLA Eng. & Wales*

Pelly, Saville Marriott (1818–1895). *See under* Pelly, Sir Lewis (1825–1892).

Peltier, Jean-Gabriel (*bap.* 1760, *d.* 1825), journalist and political exile, was baptized on 21 October 1760 in the church of St Pierre, Gonnord, in the French province of Anjou, the eldest surviving son of Jean Peltier (*c.*1734–1803), a merchant and slave trader, and his first wife, Gabrielle Dudoyer (*b. c.*1735). He was educated at the Oratorian college in Nantes before embarking on a financial career in Paris, but by 1789 Peltier's banking house had collapsed. Police reports allege that Peltier was 'one of the most ardent agitators [*motionnaires*] of the Palais Royal', and among 'the first to hoist the colours of rebellion' and march on the Bastille on 14 July 1789 (Archives Nationales, F7 6330, dossier 6959). Nevertheless, when he fled to London in late September 1792, Peltier was already one of France's most celebrated counter-revolutionary journalists.

Although Peltier published a series of anti-aristocratic pamphlets between August and October 1789, his revolutionary zeal was tempered by concern at the transfer of the royal family to Paris, and a growing conviction that Mirabeau and the duke of Orléans were at the head of a conspiracy against the Bourbons. By the time he launched his celebrated right-wing satirical journal, *Les Actes des Apôtres*, on 2 November 1789, Peltier was firmly aligned with the *monarchiens* and other moderate counter-revolutionaries. From then until 10 August 1792, when he witnessed the overthrow of the monarchy, he edited a series of journals. Thereafter he went into hiding for several weeks before fleeing to London, where he lived until 1818, residing for a time in Duke Street.

In England Peltier conducted domiciliary visits to discover spies and revolutionaries among the émigrés, before launching his first exile periodical, *Le Dernier Tableau de Paris* (October 1792 to about July 1793). This paper, containing detailed eyewitness accounts of the overthrow of the monarchy and September massacres, was translated into English and ran through several editions, helping to harden British attitudes towards the revolution. It was followed, in rapid succession, by the optimistically titled *Histoire de la restauration de la monarchie française, ou, La campagne de 1793* (1793), *La Correspondance Politique* (1793–4), and *Le Tableau de l'Europe* (1794–5), before Peltier established his two longest-running periodicals, *Paris pendant l'Année* (1795–1802) and *L'Ambigu* (1802–18), which disseminated the black legend of Napoleon across Europe and the Americas. Recruited in 1798 by the count d'Artois to serve the Bourbons, Peltier became an uncompromising advocate of *pur* royalism and the scourge of his former *monarchien* associates, especially Mallet du Pan and Malouet.

After the peace of Amiens (1802), Peltier became a 'soft target' to test British resolve in Bonaparte's campaign against the London press and Bourbon supporters. Bonaparte demanded that Peltier be silenced or expelled from Britain, but eventually bowed reluctantly to the British insistence that a criminal libel trial was his only legitimate remedy. On 21 February 1803 Peltier was found guilty of criminal libel for inciting the assassination of the first consul, but escaped sentencing because of the renewal of hostilities (May 1803), and published an account of his trial which became a best-seller. Moreover, *L'Ambigu* was now hired as a propaganda journal by the Foreign Office, though it maintained an independent editorial line. According to several prominent contemporaries, including Talleyrand, Lord Whitworth, British ambassador to Paris, and Napoleon's secretary, Bourrienne, Peltier and his colleagues were a cause, as well as beneficiaries, of the war.

Peltier served several masters besides the exiled Bourbons. He was in the pay of Louis XVI from 1790 to 1792, the British Foreign Office from 1796, and the Portuguese legation in London in 1811, and he sought employment from the Swedish government, which in 1816 awarded him knightly status as a member of the order of the Polar Star. From 1807 to 1817 he was also the unofficial minister-plenipotentiary in London of the emperor, and thereafter king, of Haiti, Henri Christophe, and so simultaneously denigrated one revolutionary emperor while serving another.

In 1814 Peltier returned to Paris to solicit rewards for his service to the Bourbon cause, but his suit was rejected, a disappointment he blamed on his service of Christophe. He returned to England and resumed publishing *L'Ambigu*, offering a vociferous *pur* opposition to Louis XVIII's ministers until 1818, when he returned to Paris, where he lived until his death. Nevertheless, Peltier's services did not go unrewarded. From 1806 he was receiving a pension of £250 annually from secret service funds, which by 1822 was supplemented by a further 3000 francs per annum from the French foreign ministry, and 6000 more from the ministry of the interior.

Despite his income from pensions and the profits of his journalism and publishing ventures, Peltier consistently outlived his means, suffering a string of bankruptcies. He was a habitual womanizer and spendthrift, with a penchant for disastrous speculations and, as Chateaubriand recalls, a taste for champagne and extravagance. On 3 July 1799 Peltier married Anne Andoe, the refugee daughter of an Irish distillery owner from Bordeaux. They had no children, and were living separately, apparently without animosity, by 1818. Peltier died at his home,182 rue Montmartre, Paris, on 29 March 1825, probably of pneumonia, in obscurity and debt, his greatest legacy, after a quarter of a century in British exile, an illiberal and reactionary critique of the revolution and Bonapartism that had little to offer France and failed to provide any positive ideology for the Bourbons.   SIMON BURROWS

Sources H. Maspero-Clerc, *Un journaliste contre-révolutionnaire: Jean-Gabriel Peltier, 1760–1825* (1973) • S. Burrows, *French exile journalism and European politics, 1792–1814* (2000) • J-G. Peltier, *The trial of Jean Peltier* (1803) • genealogical records, archives départmentales, Nantes, France
Archives PRO, letters/corresp., FO 27, FO 95/630–32 | Archives Nationales, Paris, dossiers and Napoleonic police bulletins, F7; AF IV series • mémoires and documents, France, papers and corresp., vols. 615–642 • correspondance politique Angleterre, papers and corresp., 580–601
Likenesses print (after H. Villiers, 1807), Musée Carnavalet; repro. in Maspero-Clerc, *Un journaliste contre-révolutionnaire*
Wealth at death died heavily indebted, owing at least 13,000 francs (over £500): archives départmentales de la Seine, DQ 10 1429, dossier 1918

Pember, Edward Henry (1833–1911), barrister, the eldest son of John Edward Ross Pember of Clapham Park, Surrey, and his wife, Mary, daughter of Arthur Robson, was born at his parents' house on 28 May 1833. He was educated at Harrow School and briefly taught by T. Elwin, headmaster of Charterhouse School. He matriculated on 23 May 1850 at Christ Church, Oxford, where he was elected a student in 1854. He took a first class in classical moderations in 1852, and in 1854 he gained a first class in *literae humaniores*, and a third class in law and modern history. He entered Lincoln's Inn on 2 May 1855, reading in the chambers first of the conveyancer Joseph Burrell and then of George Markham Giffard. Called to the bar on 26 January 1858, he chose the midland circuit, and sought common

law practice. On 28 August 1861 he married Fanny, only daughter of William Richardson of Sydney, New South Wales, who survived him. His eldest and only surviving son, Francis William, became fellow of All Souls in 1884 and bursar in 1911.

Briefs were slow in coming when a fortunate accident introduced Pember to the parliamentary bar. For that class of work and tribunal Pember was well equipped. His presence, his command of English, together with his quickness of comprehension and his readiness in repartee, soon made him a prime favourite with the committees of both houses. Perhaps the most notable achievement in his career was his conduct of the bill for creating the Manchester Ship Canal, which was passed in July 1885 in the face of fierce opposition. His speeches were well prepared and literary. His treatment of witnesses was not always adroit, and he was over-prone to argument with experts. But his straightforwardness was admired. In April 1897 he appeared as counsel for Cecil Rhodes before the parliamentary committee appointed to investigate the origin and attendant circumstances of the Jameson raid. Pember took silk in 1874, was made a bencher of his inn in 1876, and served the office of treasurer in 1906–7. He retired from practice in 1903 in good health.

Pember was throughout his life a prominent figure in the social and literary life of London. He was an accomplished musician, having studied singing under Perugini, and possessed considerable technical theoretical knowledge. In 1910 he was elected perpetual secretary of the newly formed academic committee of the Royal Society of Literature. He was a constant contributor to the weekly press. He also produced a considerable amount of private writing, particularly classical translations from Greek and Latin and, later, classical plays in English produced for private audiences. He contributed 'Lives of early Italian musicians' to George Grove's *Dictionary of Music* (1878–90).

Pember died after a short illness on 5 April 1911, at his Hampshire home, Vicar's Hill, Lymington, and was buried at Boldre church, Brockenhurst.

J. B. ATLAY, *rev.* ERIC METCALFE

Sources *The Times* (6 April 1911) • Foster, *Alum. Oxon.* • *WWW* • J. Foster, *Men-at-the-bar: a biographical hand-list of the members of the various inns of court*, 2nd edn (1885) • W. J. Courthope, memoir, *Transactions of the Royal Society of Literature of the United Kingdom*, 2nd ser. (1911) • private information (1912) • *CGPLA Eng. & Wales* (1911)
Archives NRA, corresp. and literary papers | NL Wales, letters to George Stovin Venables • U. Leeds, Brotherton L., letter to E. Gosse
Likenesses E. Poynter, oils, 1909, Brooks's Club, London, Dilettanti Society • F. Holl, portrait, priv. coll.; in possession of his widow in 1912
Wealth at death £149,454 13s. 8d.: probate, 11 May 1911, *CGPLA Eng. & Wales*

Pember, Robert (d. 1560), classical scholar, went to Cambridge from the diocese of Hereford to take up a scholarship at St John's College, where he graduated BA in 1523. Following his election to a fellowship at St John's on 26 July 1524, he proceeded MA in 1527. In 1542 Pember was elected fellow of the King's Hall and on 19 December 1546 was appointed by the crown one of the founding fellows of Trinity College, Cambridge. At Trinity, founded by Henry VIII to be a centre of academic excellence, Pember worked as a tutor and reader in Greek.

A classical humanist trilingual scholar, Pember was proficient in Latin, Greek, and Hebrew. A later contemporary described him as 'a man of the most admirable competence in Greek' (Grant, *Oratio*). He taught Greek to Roger Ascham, who later became tutor to Queen Elizabeth I. He not only valued Ascham's pedagogic ideas greatly, but also became a close personal friend of his former student, advising him 'frequently to read Greek with the students; for it is more useful that you read them a fable by Aesop than to listen to the entire Iliad … expounded by a professor' (ibid.). Their friendship lasted beyond Ascham's time at Trinity. During his stay in Germany, for instance, Ascham sent coins to add to his former tutor's collection. In his will Pember left his extensive Greek library to Ascham.

Pember was respected throughout the university as a poet, but only left two Latin poems. Although he was asked to compose a funeral elegy on the death of the regius professor of divinity, Martin Bucer, in 1551, he was almost certainly no evangelical himself. While Pember maintained close ties with other evangelicals, such as Andrew Perne, master of Peterhouse, he also displayed a sharp sense for irony when he bequeathed him a copy of St John of Damascus's anti-iconoclastic tract *Of Images* in his will. His other Cambridge friends, Thomas Sedgwick, a later recusant priest, and George Bullock, the Marian master of St John's College, were both confirmed Catholics. Pember's subscription to the Catholic articles in 1555, therefore, was not only a shrewd move to retain his post but probably reflected his personal convictions as well. Pember died in Cambridge in 1560.

J. ANDREAS LÖWE

Sources CUL, department of manuscripts and university archives, vice-chancellor's court, MS UA VCC I.24, fols. 26v–27r · LP *Henry VIII*, 21/2, no. 648(43, 51); *addenda* 1/1, no. 357 · *Martini Buceri scripta Anglicana ferè omnia iis etiam, quæ hactenus vel nondum, vel sparsim, vel peregrino saltem idiomate edita fuêre, adiunctis* (1577), 903 · *Rogeri Aschami Angli, regiæ olim maiestati à Latinis epistolis, familiarium epistolarum libri III: magna orationis elegantiâ conscripti, nunc postremò emendati & aucti. Quibus adiunctus est commendatiarum petitoriarum, & aliarum huius generis similium epistolarum, aliorum nomine* (1578), 6–9, 11, 31, 228, 230 [to which is added E. Grant, ed., *Oratio E. G. de vita & obitu R. A.* (unpaginated)] · J. A. Giles, ed., *The whole works of Roger Ascham: now first collected and revised, with a life of the author* (1864–5), 1.2, 316; 3.308 · Cooper, *Ath. Cantab.*, 1.208 · Venn, *Alum. Cant.*, 1/3.338 · W. W. Rouse Ball and J. A. Venn, eds., *Admissions to Trinity College, Cambridge*, 1 (1916), 134; 2 (1913), 2 · T. Baker, *History of the college of St John the Evangelist, Cambridge*, ed. J. E. B. Mayor, 1 (1869), 282 · A. Katterfeld, *Roger Ascham* (1879), 14–16

Pemberton, Charles Reece (1790–1840), actor and public lecturer, was born at Pontypool, Monmouthshire, Wales, on 23 January 1790, and registered as Thomas Reece Pemberton. His father was from Warwickshire, his mother was Welsh, and he was the second of three children. When he was about four years old his parents moved to Birmingham, and he was sent to a Unitarian charity school under Daniel Wright. He was then apprenticed to his uncle, a brass-founder in Birmingham, but ran away in

1807 to Liverpool, where he was seized by a press-gang and sent to sea. He served for seven years, and saw some active service off Cadiz, Gibraltar, and Madeira. After the war he became an actor, and led a wandering life; he is said to have managed several theatres in the West Indies with some success. He made an unhappy marriage with a lady named Fanny Pritchard, and they soon separated.

By 1827 Pemberton was in England again, acting, lecturing, and reciting. On 19 February 1828 he played Macbeth at Bath. Genest reported: 'he acted tolerably, but nothing farther; he had an indifferent figure, and a bad face, with no expression in it; he had studied the part with great attention, and understood it thoroughly'. On 21 February he appeared as Shylock. During the same year he was acting at Hereford at the assizes; Serjeant (afterwards Sir Thomas) Talfourd was greatly impressed with his performances, and praised him highly in the *New Monthly Magazine* for September 1828, especially his rendering of Shylock and Virginius. Pemberton also played Hotspur, Sir Peter Teazle, and other characters, but was not successful in comic parts. On Talfourd's recommendation he was engaged at Covent Garden by Charles Kemble. He made his first appearance there in March 1829 as Virginius, and later played Shylock. There was much divergence among critics as to his merits, but Talfourd still eulogized him as a tragedian. Pemberton did not, however, reappear at Covent Garden, and, following an engagement at the Royal Theatre, Birmingham, he devoted himself to lecturing and reciting, principally at mechanics' institutes. His favourite subjects were the tragic characters of Shakespeare.

In 1833 Pemberton began writing for the *Monthly Repository*, then edited by William Johnson Fox, 'The Autobiography of Pel. Verjuice', in which he gave an account of his own experiences. He also wrote some songs and a few plays, notably two tragedies, *The Podesta* and *The Banner*, and the comedy *Two Catherines*, together with some pieces in prose and verse. In 1836 he played Macbeth and Shylock at Birmingham, and at the end of the year he visited the Mediterranean on account of his health. He recommenced lecturing in the summer of 1838 at the Sheffield Mechanics' Institute, but his powers were failing, and a subscription was taken up to enable him to spend the winter in Egypt. This visit brought about no improvement, and he died, not long after his return, on 3 March 1840, at the house of his younger brother, William Dobson Pemberton, on Ludgate Hill, Birmingham. He was buried in the Key Hill cemetery, and the Birmingham Mechanics' Institute, of which G. J. Holyoake was secretary, placed a memorial, with an epitaph by Fox, over his grave. Ebenezer Elliott, the corn-law rhymer, wrote some verses on him entitled 'Poor Charles'.

A. F. POLLARD, rev. NILANJANA BANERJI

Sources G. J. Holyoake, *Sixty years of an agitator's life*, 3rd edn, 1 (1893) · J. Fowler, ed., *The life and literary remains of Pemberton* (1843) · G. S. Phillips, ed., *The autobiography of Pel. Verjuice* (1853) · *Monthly Repository* (1833–4) · Genest, *Eng. stage* · A. Mathews, *The memoirs of Charles Mathews, comedian* (1839)
Likenesses C. E. Wagstaff, stipple, pubd 1840 (after O. Oakley), BM, NPG

Pemberton, Christopher Robert (1765–1822), physician, was born at Trumpington, Cambridgeshire, the fifth son of the Revd Jeremiah Pemberton (1714–1800) and his wife, Anne, daughter of Charles Barron. His grandfather was Sir Francis *Pemberton (*bap.* 1624, *d.* 1697), lord chief justice. After education at Bury St Edmunds he entered Gonville and Caius College, Cambridge, in 1784, where he graduated MB in 1789 and MD in 1794. In 1796 he was elected a fellow of the Royal Society and, on 25 June, of the Royal College of Physicians, where he was Goulstonian lecturer in 1797 and censor in 1796, 1804, and 1811, and delivered the Harveian oration in 1806. He was in that year physician-extraordinary to the prince of Wales and to the duke of Cumberland, and he afterwards became physician-extraordinary to the king. He was physician to St George's Hospital, London, from 25 April 1800 until 1808.

In 1806 Pemberton published *A Practical Treatise on Various Diseases of the Abdominal Viscera*. It consists of eleven chapters, which discuss the treatment of the peritoneum, the liver, the gall bladder, the pancreas, the spleen, the kidneys, the stomach, the intestines, and enteritis. His most original observations are that the disease known as waterbrash was a result rather of an imperfect diet than of excess alcohol consumption (p. 101); that cancer of some parts of the bowel may exist for a long time without grave constitutional symptoms (p. 186); and that the over-exertion of muscles may lead to a condition indistinguishable from palsy (p. 157). This last observation is one of the first contributions in English medical writings to the knowledge of the large group of diseases which became known as 'trade palsies'. Pemberton recommends the use of a splint supporting the hand in cases of bad palsy of the muscles of the back of the forearm. The book shows Pemberton to have been an excellent clinical observer, who had paid close attention to morbid anatomy.

Pemberton was married twice: first to Sarah, and second, from August 1794, to Eleanor (*d.* 1847), daughter of James Hamilton of Woodbrook, co. Tyrone. He suffered from intense facial neuralgia or tic douloureux, and the division of several branches of the trigeminal nerve by Sir Astley Cooper failed to give him any relief. He was obliged by his disease to give up practice and to leave London. Pemberton died of apoplexy at the home of his brother-in-law John Plumptre, at Fredville, Kent, on 31 July 1822.

NORMAN MOORE, rev. MICHAEL BEVAN

Sources Venn, *Alum. Cant.* · *The record of the Royal Society of London*, 4th edn (1940) · Munk, *Roll* · R. Bree, *Oratio Harveiana* (1826) · H. Halford, *Essays and orations*, 2nd edn (1833) · R. C. B. Pemberton, *Pemberton pedigrees* (1923) · IGI

Likenesses oils (after T. Lawrence, *c.*1810), RCP Lond.

Pemberton, Sir Francis (*bap.* 1624, *d.* 1697), judge, was baptized at St Albans on 18 July 1624, son of Ralph Pemberton, mayor of St Albans in 1627–8, and of Frances, daughter of Francis Kempe. Pemberton studied at St Albans grammar school before entering Emmanuel College, Cambridge, in August 1640; he graduated BA in 1644 and in November of that year moved to the Inner Temple. His father and brother supported parliament in the civil war

and served on county committees in Cambridgeshire and Hertfordshire, but Francis continued his studies, although he also spent some of this period in gaol for debt. Roger North suggested that incarceration was just what the young man needed to focus his mind on learning the law and that his fellow inmates provided him with his first opportunities to give legal counsel.

On 7 November 1654 Pemberton received his call to the bar. Little is known of his life in the decade following, though his practice grew sufficiently to permit his marriage on 12 October 1667 to Anne Whichcott (*d.* 1731), a London widow. Her father, Sir Jeremy Whichcott, settled the manor of Milton, Cambridgeshire, upon the couple. In the years following Pemberton bought Trumpington and other lands and manors in the area; in 1692 he extended this estate by buying up properties there from his recently bankrupted brother-in-law.

By the late 1660s Pemberton had earned a high professional reputation. In 1668 he assisted in the prosecution of the Bawdy House rioters for treason. Pepys described him as 'an able lawyer' in his handling of a prize case, and noted the 'heaps of money' on his table, though he later complained of Pemberton's sloppy work (Pepys, 9.61, 63). But Pemberton prospered: he was chosen a bencher of the Inner Temple in 1671 and Lent reader of his inn in 1674; he became a serjeant-at-law on 21 April 1675.

In May and June 1675 an angry House of Commons attacked Pemberton for a breach of privilege because he had appeared as counsel in the House of Lords in property litigation involving Thomas Dalmahoy, a member of the Commons. Sir Nicholas Crisp had asked Pemberton to serve as his counsel before the Lords; aware that Dalmahoy was an MP, Pemberton initially declined the request, but the Lords then ordered him to represent Crispe. When he did so, the Commons responded by voting by 154 to 146 to commit Pemberton and his co-counsel for a breach of the lower house's privilege. But the confinement order apparently meant little, for a few days later the speaker of the House of Commons encountered Pemberton in Westminster Hall where he neglected to doff his hat to the speaker. When Pemberton and his fellow counsel were imprisoned again, the Lords issued a writ of habeas corpus for their release. Pemberton, caught in a feud between the two houses, was trapped between contending claims about whose writs of habeas corpus or orders of commitment should be obeyed. Only parliament's prorogation on 9 June brought his release, though not a resolution to the question of precedence raised by the dispute. Later that year Pemberton nearly found himself in a similar contest between Lords and Commons when asked to provide counsel in the Lords for Dr Thomas Shirley against Sir John Fagg, another MP, though this time Pemberton appears to have avoided serving.

The remainder of 1675 looked brighter: on 12 August Pemberton became king's serjeant, and on 6 October he was knighted. On 1 May 1679, upon a general reformation of the bench in Westminster Hall, Pemberton was made a justice of king's bench. He thus was one of those presiding in the early Popish Plot trials, including that of Sir George

Wakeman. In the libel trial of the bookseller Benjamin Harris, only Pemberton's insistence prevented Chief Justice Sir William Scroggs from imposing a whipping as well as a heavy fine. By October 1679 rumours were already about that he would resign or be removed. On 16 February 1680 Pemberton was indeed removed for being 'too much opposite to the court interest' (Luttrell, 1.36), perhaps because he told the king there were limits to his power to continue collecting the excise.

In later years Gilbert Burnet suggested that Scroggs's dislike of Pemberton led to his removal from the bench. If so, Pemberton must have been delighted when Scroggs himself was removed and Pemberton replaced him as chief justice of king's bench on 11 April 1681. Despite the change, at least one observer thought that 'Pemberton is as great a rogue as his predecessor' (*CSP dom.*, 1680–81, 270). His first important task, in May, was to preside in the trial of Edward Fitzharris, which some believed Pemberton had been specially appointed to handle. Declaring Fitzharris's libel 'a piece of the art of the Jesuits' (*State trials*, 8.386) Pemberton sent him off to his execution.

At the same time Pemberton was called upon to release the earl of Danby from imprisonment according to a royal pardon. But Pemberton answered the earl's request by noting that as Danby had been committed on a charge in one court—parliament—the chief justice of another court—king's bench—could not take notice of a pardon delivered to him. When the attorney-general, Sir Robert Sawyer, again pleaded Danby's pardon, Pemberton answered that the king had declared he would rule according to law, and thus he would make the law his rule in this matter as in all others. Pemberton remanded the earl. After his return from the assize circuits, where he had energetically pursued alleged Catholics, Pemberton proved just as tough on the earl of Shaftesbury during his arraignment for treason. That autumn Pemberton provided a damning summation of the evidence against Lord Grey of Warke for his liaison with Lady Henrietta Berkeley, for which Grey was convicted, though the judgment against him was never entered.

Pemberton's star was rising at court, where he was reportedly a favourite of the queen. Some talked of his being made lord chancellor in the spring of 1682. Though this came to nothing, Pemberton took the oath of a privy councillor in December of that year and was made chief justice of common pleas the month following. While a more lucrative office, it is not clear that this move was a promotion. Having heard the initial pleadings in the *quo warranto* against London in king's bench, many thought Pemberton had been translated to common pleas for fear that he would rule against the crown after full arguments had been heard. As Roger North later opined, Pemberton 'never showed so much regard to the law as to his will' (*Lives*, 2.40), and thus was not trusted in so important a matter. None the less, Pemberton did preside over the trial of Lord Russell for treason, and though his summation of the evidence could not have helped Russell in the jurors' eyes, Pemberton was not thought vigorous enough against Russell. Pemberton was again removed from the

bench in September 1683; his exit from the privy council soon followed. There was little left for him but to return to his lucrative practice.

Pemberton continued his involvement in the leading legal actions of the day though he, like others, refused to serve as counsel to Arthur Godden when he sued Sir Edward Hales in a case testing the king's claim to have a power to dispense with statutory requirements meant to bar Catholics from office. Pemberton offered his strong opinion against the legality of the grant of a university degree to a Benedictine monk, Alban Francis, without the requisite oaths. And in June 1688 Pemberton declaimed against the dispensing power when he served as one of the counsel defending the seven bishops on the charge that they had libelled the king.

After the revolution of 1688 Pemberton found himself once again the target of parliamentary ire for a judgment he had given years earlier that allegedly breached the privileges of the house. He suffered another brief spell as the Commons' prisoner. But Pemberton soon continued his successful legal practice, arguing important matters in the House of Lords and elsewhere until June 1697, when, while attending hearings in Westminster Hall, he contracted a cold. Pemberton died on 10 June 1697 at his house in Highgate, survived by his wife and seven of their eleven children. He was buried at Highgate Chapel, from which his monument was removed to Trumpington when the chapel was demolished in 1833. In his typically priggish manner, Roger North declared Pemberton's morals 'debauched' (*Lives*, 2.38). But John Evelyn reports that at the time of his departure from the bench in 1683 Pemberton was considered 'the very learnedst of the judges and an honest man' (Evelyn, 3.342). Twice imprisoned by a zealous Commons and twice appointed to and removed from the judiciary in a period in which the bench was regularly broken up, Pemberton proved himself an able lawyer and a prudent judge, rarely pleasing and often offending people of all political persuasions.

PAUL D. HALLIDAY

Sources Bodl. Oxf., MS Eng. misc. 3.372 · Bodl. Oxf., MS Rawl. C. 201 · Foss, *Judges*, 7.149–55 · R. North, *The lives of … Francis North … Dudley North … and … John North*, new edn, 3 vols. (1826) · *State trials*, vols. 6–9 · *CSP dom.*, addenda, 1660–85; 1679–81; 1684–7; 1694–5; 1697 · *Report on the manuscripts of Allan George Finch*, 5 vols., HMC, 71 (1913–2003), vol. 2 · *Seventh report*, HMC, 6 (1879) · *Ninth report*, 2, HMC, 8 (1884) · *Calendar of the manuscripts of the marquess of Ormonde*, new ser., 8 vols., HMC, 36 (1902–20), vol. 6 · *Report on the manuscripts of the marquis of Downshire*, 6 vols. in 7, HMC, 75 (1924–95), vol. 1 · *The manuscripts of S. H. Le Fleming*, HMC, 25 (1890) · N. Luttrell, *A brief historical relation of state affairs from September 1678 to April 1714*, 6 vols. (1857) · E. Baines and W. R. Whatton, *The history of the county palatine and duchy of Lancaster*, 4 vols. (1836) · A. G. Davies, *Liberty, loyalty, property: the landed gentry of Hertfordshire from 1588 to 1688* (1988) · Venn, *Alum. Cant.* · Sainty, *Judges* · Pepys, *Diary*, vol. 9 · J. L. Chester and G. J. Armytage, eds., *Allegations for marriage licences issued by the dean and chapter of Westminster, 1558 to 1699; also, for those issued by the vicar-general of the archbishop of Canterbury, 1660 to 1679*, Harleian Society, 23 (1886) · *Burnet's History of my own time*, ed. O. Airy, new edn, 2 vols. (1897–1900) · *VCH Hertfordshire*, vols. 2–3 · *VCH Cambridgeshire and the Isle of Ely*, vols. 8–9 · Evelyn, *Diary* · *The diaries and papers of Sir Edward Dering, second baronet, 1644 to 1684*, ed. M. F. Bond (1976) · *JHC*, 9 (1667–87) · *The correspondence of Henry Hyde, earl of*

Clarendon, and of his brother Laurence Hyde, earl of Rochester, ed. S. W. Singer, 2 vols. (1828) • will, PRO, PROB 11/439, fols. 264*v*–266

Likenesses R. White, group portrait, mezzotint, 1688 (*Counsel for the seven bishops*), BM, NPG • T. Athow, watercolour, 1800–40, Harvard U., law school • monument, St Mary and St Michael's Church, Trumpington, Cambridgeshire • oils, Emmanuel College, Cambridge

Wealth at death extensive land holdings in Cambridgeshire and elsewhere: will, PRO, PROB, 11/439, fols. 264*v*–266

Pemberton, Henry (1694–1771), physician and mathematician, was born in London, the third son of Edward Pemberton and his wife, Elizabeth. Henry's father, a wealthy fruiterer, intended his son to become a physician; it was mathematics, though, which became his serious avocation. He also made contributions to the appreciation of contemporary poetry, and cultivated a degree of musical appreciation.

Pemberton's delicate health caused him to be sent to a country grammar school in Guildford, Surrey, where he first felt an attraction to mathematics. Having returned to London, he read classics with John Ward (later professor of rhetoric at Gresham College), but also devoted much time to the study of Apollonius of Perga's *Conics*. Despite these inclinations to antique studies, he was set to study medicine, and followed a common route of the day to Leiden, where he came under the influence of Herman Boerhaave. Pemberton next went to Paris to improve his knowledge of anatomy. James Wilson, Pemberton's contemporary biographer, maintained that Pemberton's mechanical dexterity helped him to become competent in dissection and surgery. While in Paris, Pemberton formed several scientific friendships, some of which led to his acquiring, at a sale there, a portion of the library of the mathematician Abbé Galois. After returning to London Pemberton attended St Thomas's Hospital to learn 'London physic', but never practised medicine regularly. In 1719 he again visited Leiden and graduated MD; by now he was a friend of Boerhaave, at whose house he lodged. In the same year Pemberton published *Dissertatio de facultate oculi* and *On the Power whence the Eye may Discern Objects Distinctly at Distances*; the latter was a work showing how certain results of Roger Cotes, hitherto found using ratios and logarithms, could be obtained using a circle and parabola. Pemberton became a fellow of the Royal Society in 1720.

About the same time Pemberton showed to John Keill certain new mathematical solutions he had obtained. Keill brought them to Sir Isaac Newton's attention, but the latter declined to take notice of them, believing that Pemberton was then connected with the circulation of untruths about him. However, Pemberton came to be on intimate terms with Richard Mead, Newton's physician; he helped Mead to write the eighth edition of his treatise on the plague, and, in 1724, to edit W. Cowper's *Myotomia reformata* (on muscles). At this time an Italian, M. Poleni, produced a paper about the force generated by a moving body on impact, which Pemberton refuted as erroneous. Pemberton's treatment of the problem was passed to Newton and this, together with Newton's own refutation

of Poleni's thesis, was published in the *Philosophical Transactions* in 1772. Intercourse between Newton and Pemberton thus became established and Pemberton was invited to superintend the editing of the third edition of the *Principia mathematica*, which appeared in 1726. Pemberton was then about thirty years old and was rightly flattered to get the opportunity to work so closely with the great eighty-year-old Newton. However, Newton often ignored Pemberton's editorial suggestions. Pemberton wrote *A View of Sir Isaac Newton's Philosophy* (1728), which he had partly read to the dying Newton. It made no great mark but could at least be recommended as being propaedeutic.

In 1728 Pemberton was elected Gresham professor of physic, and his *Scheme for a Course of Chymistry to be Performed at Gresham College* appeared in 1731. A set of lectures based on his course was published in 1771 and a second set on physiology in 1779; in both cases the editor was James Wilson.

Pemberton was said to have spent seven years (1739–46) preparing the fifth London Pharmacopoeia for the Royal College of Physicians, which edition proved he was well acquainted with pharmacy. It appeared in 1746 as *Translation and Improvement of the London Dispensary*, for which he was rewarded by 100 guineas and the gift of the volume's copyright.

Pemberton also encouraged a number of younger scholars. These included the young scientist–engineer Benjamin Robins, who was introduced to Pemberton on leaving school. Both Pemberton and Robins were also close friends of James Wilson. The poet Richard Glover also came under Pemberton's wing on leaving school. In 1738 he wrote *Leonidas*, an epic on which Pemberton made some acclaimed observations. Pemberton also wrote an *Account of the Ancient Ode* which prefaced Gilbert West's *Translations of Pindar* (1748).

Wilson's preface to Pemberton's *Course on Chemistry* (1771) is a substantial, detailed biography of Pemberton by one who knew him extremely well, describing in it his character as delicate, pleasant, and cultured.

Pemberton died in Cannon Street, London, on 9 March 1771, seemingly after a second attack of jaundice, and was buried in Bunhill Fields, London. He left a considerable fortune to Henry Mills, his niece's husband.

Many articles written by Pemberton remained unpublished at his death, notably 'A short history of trigonometry'.   W. JOHNSON

Sources J. Wilson, preface, in H. Pemberton, *A course of chemistry* (1771) • C. Hutton, *A philosophical and mathematical dictionary*, new edn, 2 vols. (1815) • A. R. Hall, *Newton and his editors* (1973) • *DNB* • *GM*, 1st ser., 41 (1771), 143 • R. V. Wallis and P. J. Wallis, eds., *Biobibliography of British mathematics and its applications*, 2 (1986) • *The record of the Royal Society of London*, 4th edn (1940)

Likenesses bust, Wedgwood medallion (after S. Bevan, 1778), Brooklyn Museum, New York, Emily Winthrop Miles Collection

---

Pemberton, Israel (1715–1779), merchant and politician in America, was born on 19 May 1715 in Philadelphia, the first son of Israel Pemberton and his wife, Rachel, daughter of Charles Read of Burlington, New Jersey. The elder Israel was a leading Philadelphia merchant, Pennsylvania legislator, and Quaker meeting clerk. Rachel Pemberton was active in the Philadelphia women's meeting. Israel junior's grandparents Phineas and Phoebe Pemberton were among the original Quaker founders of Pennsylvania.

Brought up to strict Quaker principles, Israel attended the Friends' school in Philadelphia and displayed aptitudes for learning and leadership at an early age. He also revealed an impetuous nature. In 1735 the tall, slender, dark-haired, blue-eyed youth went to England to represent his father's business. Pemberton engaged in some risky mercantile practices, and received his father's censure for buying too many goods on credit. Just as troubling to his family, Pemberton's rash courtship violated Quaker etiquette. Before leaving for England, Israel had become close to Sarah Kirkbride of Pennsbury in Bucks county. But when Israel left without making an official proposal, another Quaker, Anthony Morris, pursued Kirkbride's hand. Instead of waiting for Kirkbride officially to turn Morris down, Pemberton continued his own pursuit and caused a family feud that culminated in Morris's claim that he had been too 'free' with Kirkbride for her to be 'fit for anyone else' (Thayer, 8). Ultimately the controversy did not irreparably tarnish Israel's and Sarah's standing, for on 30 March 1737 the Philadelphia meeting approved and oversaw their marriage.

By 1745 Pemberton had become a leading Philadelphia merchant. His ships transported flour, rice, tobacco, sugar, molasses, rum, butter, other foodstuffs, lumber, other wood products, cloth, and even servants on transatlantic circuits that made stops in the British Isles, the Netherlands, Portugal, Spain, Italy, the Madeira Islands, the middle colonies, the Chesapeake, South Carolina, Georgia, and the West Indies. In his early days as a merchant, despite his Quaker commitment to pacifism, Pemberton supplied naval fleets and used military escorts. He also developed schemes to avoid or minimize insurance payments to British and Dutch bankers. Although Pemberton continued to trade, by the 1750s he had turned his attention away from transatlantic shipping and instead concentrated on land and the financial markets.

Pemberton lived in the most fashionable district in Philadelphia on the corner of Chestnut and Third streets, occupying a large brick building that was noted for its carefully manicured garden. He also owned several other estates near Philadelphia, including a country home in New Jersey called Bolton. His wife, Sarah, died in 1746, leaving him with seven children. Shortly thereafter, in 1747, Pemberton married the twice-widowed, older, and wealthy Mary Jordan, *née* Stanbury (d. 1778). Like his first marriage, this one caused some grumbling in the Quaker community when Samuel Jordan, Mary's brother-in-law, complained that the couple had been too hasty. But again, as with his first marriage, the Quaker meeting approved the wedding.

Pemberton was very active in Philadelphia's civic affairs and especially the Quaker church. He supported the Library Company, bringing in books, serving briefly as president, and revising the charter. Pemberton was appointed clerk of the Friends' public school in 1743 and managed its finances until his death. In 1752 Pemberton helped found the Pennsylvania Hospital and acted as a manager throughout his life. He also joined the Union Fire Company and made many contributions to private charity. His greatest influence came as a pilot of the Philadelphia Quaker meeting. In this capacity Pemberton corresponded with British Quakers and accompanied visiting ministers on their itinerant tours of America. Pemberton also served as an overseer of the press in 1743 and, most significantly, as the pre-eminent clerk of the Philadelphia yearly meeting from 1750 to 1759.

Pemberton was known as a powerful and contentious political leader. He briefly served as a Pennsylvania assemblyman in 1750, but was not re-elected. His political enemies in the colony derisively called him the 'King of the Quakers', and during the American War of Independence John Adams described him as an 'artful Jesuit' who would try to 'break up Congress' (Thayer, 233, 212). Pemberton's biographer, Theodore Thayer, wrote that Pemberton's 'leadership and prominence rest[ed] largely upon the fact that he lacked so many of the qualities of a good Quaker' (ibid., 233). Pemberton did indeed fight hard, and he did so to defend many Quaker principles and interests.

Most notably, during the French and Indian War Pemberton argued that instead of battling Indians, British Americans should attempt to pacify them through diplomatic agreements. To this end Pemberton protested military tax bills, petitioned government officials, invited Indians to his home, advised Delawares during treaty proceedings, and conferred with colonial governors, Indian agents, and even generals. He helped Delaware leader Teedyuscung accuse Pennsylvania's proprietors of defrauding them. When Pennsylvania's Governor Denny tried to curb Quaker participation at a treaty conference, Pemberton threatened to publish Lord Halifax's letter that referred to Indians as 'foreign princes & an Independent people' (Thayer, 139). Pemberton also founded the Friendly Association for Regaining and Preserving Peace with the Indians by Pacific Measures. This association appealed to Quakers and other pacifist groups to donate money, which was used to conduct Indian diplomacy, buy Indian gifts, support displaced Pennsylvanians, and ransom Pennsylvanian captives. Pemberton also wanted to use the contributions to stock a frontier post at Fort Pitt, which he hoped would enable him to trade fairly with Ohio valley Indians and eliminate French competition. But other trustees in the friendly association vetoed this profit-making venture, and Pemberton set up the business without them.

Pemberton was also a leader in the early abolitionist movement. In 1773 he unsuccessfully sued to free an enslaved Indian woman and her children. This incident led to the formation of Philadelphia's first abolition society, the Society for the Relief of Free Negroes unlawfully held in Bondage, in 1775. In addition, Pemberton paid visits to individual Quaker slave-owners to urge them to free their slaves.

During the 1760s and 1770s, Pemberton remained active in Quaker politics, though his brother James became the primary clerk of the Philadelphia meeting. In the 1760s he led a faction that opposed Benjamin Franklin's plan to remove the proprietary government and make Pennsylvania a royal colony. In the 1770s Pemberton urged Quakers to avoid all revolutionary associations, committees, and militias. In September 1777, as British armies closed in on Philadelphia during the revolutionary war, American authorities felt that the neutral Quakers might turn loyalist and exiled several of the most renowned leaders, including Israel Pemberton and his two brothers. The prisoners were escorted to and held in Winchester, Virginia, where three of the exiles died. Pemberton wrote many petitions arguing that they had not been duly charged. In addition he authored the pamphlet *An Address to the People of Pennsylvania* (1777), which recounted the Quaker side of the story. Pemberton asked his wife, Mary, secretly to distribute the pamphlet, which was also published in German. In April 1778 Mary (now seventy-five) and three other wives crossed to the American side, met George Washington, and petitioned the executive council to release their husbands. The council informed them that their husbands had been freed the previous day.

Pemberton returned to find his estates ransacked by British soldiers. Inflation and the gambling of his son Joseph further damaged his financial situation and he had to sell off much of his property. In October 1778 his wife died, and Pemberton's death followed soon after, in April 1779. His brother John said Israel had never recovered from the ordeal of exile. His funeral in Philadelphia was reportedly the largest in memory and attended by people of all denominations. Despite his losses during the war, Pemberton died a wealthy man. Anthony Benezet complained that he had willed his fortune of £60,000–70,000 to his profligate children and had left nothing to charity.

CARLA GERONA

Sources T. Thayer, *Israel Pemberton: King of the Quakers* (Philadelphia, 1943) · J. D. Marrietta, *The reformation of American Quakerism, 1748–1783* (Philadelphia, 1984) · F. Jennings, *Empire of fortune: crowns, colonies and tribes in the Seven Years' War in America* (1988) · S. V. James, *A people among peoples: Quaker benevolence in eighteenth-century America* (Cambridge, Mass., 1963) · J. R. Soderlund, *Quakers and slavery: a divided spirit* (1985)
Archives Hist. Soc. Penn., papers | Haverford College, Pennsylvania, Quaker Collection · Hist. Soc. Penn., Frank M. Etting collection, Pemberton family papers · Swarthmore College, Swarthmore, Pennsylvania, Balderston MSS
Likenesses caricature, 1764, Hist. Soc. Penn.
Wealth at death £60,000–£70,000

Pemberton [*married name* Rowe], **Muriel Alice** (1910–1993), painter and teacher of fashion, was born on 8 September 1910 in Tunstall, Staffordshire. Her father, Thomas Henry Pemberton, was a gifted amateur painter and innovative photographer who invented a one-camera

stereoscopic process; her mother, Alice, *née* Smith, gave up professional singing when she married, but was also a virtuoso needlewoman and skilled designer.

When Pemberton was ten some drawings she had made for her own amusement were entered without her knowledge in a competition for ceramic design, and won second prize. An impulsive and determined child, she happened when she was fourteen to be passing Burslem School of Art and noticed that there was an entrance examination that day, marched in, took the examination, and was offered a three-year full scholarship, with an additional £15 for materials. At fifteen she was by far the youngest student in the school. The main industry in the five towns being the potteries, it was expected that the majority of students (especially female) would find jobs as ceramic painters or designers. Even at eighteen Pemberton did not see this as her future. Determined to be a 'proper artist', she sat an entrance examination for the Royal College of Art and won a scholarship with free tuition and £100 a year for living in London and buying artist's materials.

When Pemberton entered the college in 1928 it was as a painter, in the supposedly élite school of painting. The most distinguished group of students at that time, including Edward Bawden, Eric Ravilious, Douglas Percy Bliss, and Helen Binyon, were nearly all in the school of design, and Bliss, the only one in the school of painting, regarded a move to design as degrading. So did Pemberton, but considering practicalities and the notice that her self-designed clothes seemed regularly to be exciting, she decided at the end of her first year that such a move might be desirable—though only if, once there, she could do a diploma in fashion. The trouble was that the school offered no such course. Nevertheless she asked the head of the design school, the distinguished medievalist Professor Ernest Tristram, if she could do something of the sort, and he answered that if she could make out an acceptable curriculum for herself he would authorize it. She could and he did. She proposed a combination of direct contact, sketching, and analysing with an actual couturier, learning the basic skills of cutting and sewing with a professional, and supplementing this with academic studies in the history of fashion and design at museums such as the Victoria and Albert. This curriculum she followed, all by herself, and was granted the first ever diploma in fashion at the Royal College in 1931.

After leaving college Pemberton immediately found employment teaching, along the lines she herself had laid down, at the St Martin's School of Art, supplementing her earnings by teaching also at the Katinka School of Cutting in Knightsbridge, and by drawing fashions for magazines and advertisements. At first she was teaching at St Martin's for only two days a week, within the graphics department, but as her courses attracted more and more pupils her work there became a full-time occupation and blossomed into a department in its own right.

Throughout the 1930s Pemberton continued to develop the department, as well as remaining a productive artist herself, mainly in watercolour, exhibiting regularly at the Royal Academy and designing cards for Fortnum and Mason, fabrics for Liberty, and stage costumes for C. B. Cochran. She also met at St Martin's John Hadley Rowe (1894/5–1975), head of the graphics department, whom she married on 17 October 1941. After the Second World War Pemberton entered her grandest and most prolific period. Not only was she covering fashion regularly for the *News Chronicle*, being the first visual correspondent to break in Britain the news of Dior's 'new look', but she was organizing her department completely as she wished, attracting the best students and turning out many of the best designers and fashion illustrators. Despite a degree of good-humoured eccentricity, she ran a very tight ship, possessing a highly organized mind and a brilliant intuitive grasp of human personality and potential, as well as boundless energy. The results of her teaching are evident in the careers of such designers as Bill Gibb, Bruce Oldfield, and Bjorn Lanberg, chief designer of the London house of Dior, among others.

Pemberton's revolutionary approach to the whole business of teaching fashion and its place in the art college curriculum was already noted internationally before the war, and was widely emulated, teachers coming from all over the world to study her methods. When she retired in 1975, the year of her husband's death, she immediately found herself teaching part-time in Brighton, and painting more enthusiastically than ever. She was made a fellow of the Royal Watercolour Society and of the Chartered Society of Designers, and in 1984 a senior fellow of the Royal College of Art. In 1993 she had a major retrospective of her paintings—mostly landscapes and flower pieces, with portraits and figure drawings and even a few abstracts—in a London gallery. This encouraged critics to wonder whether her importance in the field of fashion had not led to a radical underestimation of her qualities as a painter. Muriel Pemberton died at 56 Vale Road, St Leonards, Sussex, on 30 July 1993. JOHN RUSSELL TAYLOR

Sources J. R. Taylor, *Muriel Pemberton: art and fashion* (1993) · *The Times* (5 Aug 1993) · *The Independent* (3 Aug 1993) · *The Guardian* (7 Aug 1993) · *Daily Telegraph* (5 Aug 1993) · m. cert. · d. cert. · personal knowledge (2004) · private information (2004)
Likenesses photograph, 1931, repro. in Taylor, *Muriel Pemberton*, 31 · M. Pemberton, self-portrait, 1960–69, repro. in Taylor, *Muriel Pemberton*, 42 · photograph, repro. in *The Independent*

Pemberton, Thomas. *See* Leigh, Thomas Pemberton, Baron Kingsdown (1793–1867).

Pemberton, Thomas Edgar (1849–1905), theatre historian and playwright, born at Heath Green Cottage, Birmingham Heath, on 1 July 1849, was the eldest son of Thomas Pemberton, the head of an old-established firm of brass founders in Livery Street, Birmingham, and his wife, Lucy Johnston. The novelist Sir Max Pemberton was his younger brother. He was educated at the Edgbaston proprietary schools, and at the age of nineteen entered his father's counting-house. In due course he gained control of the business, with which he remained active until 1900.

Of literary taste from his youth, Pemberton began his career in writing with two indifferent novels, *Charles Lysaght* (1873) and *Under Pressure* (1874), but showed more promise in *A Very Old Question* (3 vols., 1877). *Born to Blush Unseen* (1879) was praised, and was followed by an allegorical fairy tale, *Fairbrass*, written for his children. He married, on 11 March 1873, Mary Elizabeth, the second daughter of Edward Richard Patie Townley of Edgbaston; they had two sons and three daughters.

In his youth at his father's house, Pemberton met E. A. Sothern, Madge Robertson (Mrs Kendal), and other actors on visits to Birmingham, and was inspired to write for the stage. His first comedietta, *Weeds*, was written for the Kendals, and produced at the Prince of Wales's Theatre, Birmingham, on 16 November 1874. Although his most popular farce, *Freezing-a-Mother-in-Law*, originally given at the Birmingham Theatre Royal, was later produced in New York by Sothern, most of his plays were rarely seen outside provincial theatres. He came to know the American author Bret Harte, and with his collaboration wrote the highly successful play *Sue*, produced in America in 1896 and at the Garrick in 1898. The partnership continued until Harte's death in 1902, upon which Pemberton wrote *Bret Harte: a Treatise and a Tribute*. Pemberton also dramatized novels, such as Thackeray's *The History of Henry Esmond* and Dickens's *A Tale of Two Cities*, adapted as *Sidney Carton*.

Pemberton succeeded his friend Sam Timmins as the drama critic of the *Birmingham Daily Post* in 1882. He retired to the country, at Broadway, Worcestershire, in 1900. He also contributed to the *Birmingham Daily Mail* a weekly column of dramatic gossip, entitled 'Flashes from the footlights'. But he made his widest reputation as a theatrical biographer, and wrote memoirs of Sothern (1889), the Kendals (1891), T. W. Robertson (1892), John Hare (1895), Ellen Terry and her sisters (1902), and Sir Charles Wyndham (1905). He frequently lectured on theatrical subjects, and was an excellent amateur actor. In 1889 he was elected a governor of the Shakespeare Memorial Theatre, Stratford upon Avon, and was for many years the honorary secretary of Our Shakespeare Club. He died after a long illness at his residence, Pye Corner, Broadway, on 28 September 1905, and was buried in the churchyard at Broadway.

W. J. LAWRENCE, *rev.* NILANJANA BANERJI

Sources *Birmingham Daily Post* (29 Sept 1905) · *Birmingham Daily Mail* (28 Sept 1905) · WWW · 'Notable Birmingham authors: Mr T. Edgar Pemberton', *Birmingham and Moseley Society Journal*, 7/75 (April 1900), 129–33 · *Edgbastonia*, 25/293 (1905) · P. Hartnoll, ed., *The Oxford companion to the theatre* (1951); 2nd edn (1957); 3rd edn (1967) · personal knowledge (1912) · private information (1912) · d. cert. · b. cert.
Likenesses portrait, repro. in 'Notable Birmingham authors'
Wealth at death £13,372 1s. 5d.: probate, 7 Dec 1905, CGPLA Eng. & Wales

Pemble, William (1591/2–1623), theologian and author, was born in Kent, possibly at Egerton. The son of a poor clergyman, he studied with John Barker at Mayfield, Sussex, before matriculating at Magdalen College, Oxford, on 18 June 1610, aged eighteen. A student of Richard Capel, who also taught some of John Dod's former pupils, he graduated BA on 3 March 1614 and proceeded MA on 9 June 1618. After receiving his bachelor's degree he became reader and tutor at Magdalen Hall, and, after his ordination, divinity reader. Although he criticized Henry Ainsworth for excessive reliance on the Talmud, he played an important role in encouraging Hebrew studies. Among the Hebraists he tutored were John Tombes and Edward Leigh, and possibly William Pincke and Thomas Coleman.

All of Pemble's works were published posthumously, mostly through the efforts of Capel. In *Vindiciae fidei* (1625), a series of lectures delivered at Magdalen Hall, he expounded on the doctrine of justification by Christ's imputed righteousness through the infusion of grace into the souls of the elect. In another series of lectures, *Vindiciae gratiae* (1627), he warned against excessive reliance on humane texts in the study of sacred subjects, espoused a supralapsarian view of predestination, contended that justification precedes faith, and averred that sanctifying grace operates without any assistance from its recipients because of their corrupt nature. Capel and George Walker published this book as a refutation of Arminianism. In *Tractatus de providentia Dei* (1631) Pemble explained providence as God's action in preserving, governing, and disposing everything, including their intermediate as well as ultimate ends. He called for the frequent observance of the Lord's supper in *An Introduction to the Worthy Receiving the Sacrament* (1628), yet warned that participation by the unreformed, the ignorant, and the superstitious was sinful.

Pemble's expository works included *Salomons Recantation and Repentance* (1627), a commentary on Ecclesiastes; *A Short and Sweet Exposition upon the First Nine Chapters of Zachary* (1629); and *The Period of the Persian Monarchie* (1631), an explanation of enigmatic passages in Ezra, Nehemiah, and Daniel, much of it derived from John Rainolds. He also borrowed extensively from William Gouge for his exposition of John 5 (1631). With an epistle by John Tombes, a collection of Pemble's pulpit oratory was published in 1628 as *Five Godly, and Profitable Sermons* on the subject of the slavery of sin (John 8: 34), the mischief of ignorance (Hosea 4: 6), the root of apostasy (Hebrews 3: 12–13), the benefit of serving God (Exodus 34: 23–4), and Christian love (Song of Solomon 2: 16). In *A Fruitfull Sermon* on 1 Corinthians 15: 19–20 (1629) he exhorted his audience to suffer for Christ, even to the point of martyrdom if necessary.

Among Pemble's philosophical works is *De formarum origine* (1629), which explored the origin of life and the soul, and reflected his interest in Aristotle and knowledge of Hebrew and Greek. He dedicated this work to the Calvinist Accepted Frewen, the future vice-chancellor of Oxford and archbishop of York. As his treatise *De sensibus internis* (1629) evinces, his reading extended from classical writings by Aristotle, Plutarch, and Aulus Gellius to the sixteenth-century Italian Aristotelian Jacobus Zabarella. In *A Summe of Morall Philosophy* (1630) he examined a wide variety of topics, ranging from ethics, passion, and pleasure to despair, fortitude, and the heroic spirit.

Pemble's *A Briefe Introduction to Geography* (1630) was a popular short textbook, which reached a fifth edition in 1675. He relied heavily on Ptolemy and was probably influenced by Bartholomew Keckerman's *System of Geography* (1611) or *Compendious System of All Mathematics* (1617). Pemble distinguished between topography, which described a small amount of land; chorography, which was concerned with a county or province; and geography, which was global or universal in scope, and which he explained through such traditional means as circles, horizons, and zones. He found the views of Copernicus improbable and irrational, not because they contradicted scriptural teachings but because they were contrary to experience, and in this limited respect he shared some affinity with the new scientists, yet he contributed nothing substantive to the study of geography or philosophy. However, his favourite student, Tombes, tutored John Wilkins, a prominent advocate of the new science.

As his health began to fail, Pemble retired to the house of Capel, who was now rector of Eastington, Gloucestershire. Here he died of a fever—according to Anthony Wood on 14 April 1623, although his will is marked 26 April in the probate register. He was buried in Eastington church's graveyard. Most of his estate went to his siblings Abel, Henry, and Mary Pemble; Abel, of Egerton, Kent, was granted probate on 12 June. Pemble's work attracted attention long after his death, helping to influence Richard Baxter against Arminianism and shape the high-Calvinist tenets of the eighteenth-century Baptists John Gill and John Brine. Baxter and Thomas Blake each cited Pemble in their dispute over the covenants and the role of scripture as an instrument of the Spirit. The Swiss minister Johann Zollikofer (1633–1692) published some of Pemble's work, and Humphrey Chambers thought Pemble and William Ames should not be criticized by name in print. In *The Divine Purity Defended* (1657) Thomas Pierce accused Pemble of antinomianism, but John Tombes cited him approvingly in his *Animadversions* (1676) against George Bull, and Thomas Danson, in *De causa Dei* (1678), accused John Howe of deviating from the true theological tenets of Pemble, Theodore Beza, and William Perkins.

RICHARD L. GREAVES

Sources W. Pemble, *The workes of that learned minister of Gods holy word, Mr William Pemble*, 3rd edn (1635) • Wood, *Ath. Oxon.*, new edn, 2.330–31 • Foster, *Alum. Oxon.*, *1500–1714*, 3.1140 • M. Feingold, 'The humanities', *Hist. U. Oxf.* 4: 17th-cent. Oxf., 211–358, esp. 314, 321 • M. Feingold, 'The mathematical sciences and new philosophies', *Hist. U. Oxf.* 4: 17th-cent. Oxf., 359–448, esp. 388, 451, 468–9 • D. D. Wallace, *Puritans and predestination: grace in English protestant theology, 1525–1695* (1982) • *Calendar of the correspondence of Richard Baxter*, ed. N. H. Keeble and G. F. Nuttall, 1 (1991), 132; 2 (1991), 38, 172 • R. Baxter, *Rich. Baxters apology* (1654), 32–3 • M. Bowen, *Empiricism and geographical thought: from Francis Bacon to Alexander von Humboldt* (1981), 69–70, 76 • P. Toon, *The emergence of hyper-Calvinism in English nonconformity, 1689–1765* (1967) • D. N. Livingstone, *The geographical tradition: episodes in the history of a contested enterprise* (1992), 88 • E. W. Gilbert, *British pioneers in geography* (1972), 53–4 • will, PRO, PROB 11/141, sig. 66

Likenesses J. Stow, line engraving, pubd 1817, NPG · G. Vertue, group portraits, line engravings, NPG; repro. in *Oxford Almanack* (1745)

Pembrey, Marcus Seymour (1868–1934), physiologist, was born at Oxford on 28 May 1868, the second son of John Crips Pembrey, a proof-reader in oriental languages at the Oxford University Press, and his wife, Annie Coster Tanner. He was educated at Oxford high school and from 1885 at Christ Church, Oxford, where he became a Fell exhibitioner in 1888 and graduated in natural science (physiology) in 1889. The award of the Radcliffe travelling fellowship in 1890 enabled him to visit the physiological laboratories at Kiel and Würzburg. However, Sir Henry Acland influenced Pembrey towards a career in medicine. After qualifying in medicine in 1892 from University College Hospital, London, he became a demonstrator in physiology at Oxford under J. S. Burdon-Sanderson. In 1895 he qualified MD and was appointed lecturer in physiology at Charing Cross Hospital medical school. He vacated this post in 1900 for a similar position at Guy's Hospital medical school, becoming professor in 1920. Pembrey was elected FRS in 1922.

Pembrey's first research on the respiratory exchange of mammals was soon coupled with an investigation of the regulation of body temperature, and experiments on the developing chick and newly born mammals did much to explain the characteristic difference between warm- and cold-blooded animals. This led him to investigate the respiratory process in hibernating mammals, which resemble cold-blooded animals during their winter sleep. After serving from 1906 to 1909 on a War Office committee which inquired into the physiological effects of food, training, and clothing on the soldier, he devoted much attention to the problem of general physical fitness and to the effects of muscular exercise on respiration, circulation, body temperature, and the kidneys. Pembrey himself took part in some of the long experimental marches, carrying full military equipment.

Working in co-operation with the physicians at Guy's Hospital, Pembrey showed how the physiologist could help the clinician and, with a quick appreciation of the significance of the discoveries of J. S. Haldane, he made important observations on clinical cases of periodic or Cheyne–Stokes breathing, on the respiratory phenomena associated with diabetes and cardiac disability, on changes of temperature resulting from lesions of the spinal cord, and on the elimination of water by the kidneys and skin. He contributed many papers to the *Journal of Physiology* and *Guy's Hospital Reports*; he edited *A Textbook on General Pathology* (1913) in collaboration with James Ritchie and was joint author of the textbooks *Physiological Action of Drugs* (1901) and *Practical Physiology* (1902). He was elected a member of the Physiological Society in 1893, and became treasurer in 1925.

Pembrey was a stimulating and original teacher, always ready to debate scientific problems, forthright in argument but never bitter. In 1895 he married Bessie Cecily Crake, daughter of Edward Ebenezer Crake, rector of Jevington, Sussex, and they had five sons and five daughters.

He enjoyed country life and farmed on a small scale at his home in Sussex while working at Guy's, and on his retirement moved to a farm at Ramsden in Oxfordshire. Pembrey died unexpectedly in the Acland Nursing Home, Oxford, on 23 July 1934. He was survived by his wife.

C. G. Douglas, *rev.* Caroline Overy

Sources C. G. Douglas, *Obits. FRS*, 1 (1932–5), 563–7 · *The Lancet* (4 Aug 1934) · *Guy's Hospital Reports*, 4th ser., 15 (1935) · personal knowledge (1949) · W. J. O'Connor, *British physiologists, 1885–1914* (1991) · *CGPLA Eng. & Wales* (1934) · Foster, *Alum. Oxon.* · WWW
Likenesses portrait, repro. in *Obits. FRS*
Wealth at death £12,709 7s. 5d.: probate, 19 Nov 1934, *CGPLA Eng. & Wales*

Pembridge, John [Christopher] (*fl.* 1347), chronicler, is probably to be identified with the John Pembridge, who, according to English exchequer records of the period, was the head of the Dominican order in Ireland between 1331 and 1343; no other evidence exists for a Pembridge in Ireland at that period and the strong Dominican slant in the chronicle supports this theory.

A mid-fifteenth-century manuscript copy of the *Annales Hiberniae ab anno Christi 1162 usque ad annum 1370*, preserved at Trinity College, Dublin, has at the conclusion of 1347 a note, with rubric, which states *Hic finitur cronica Pembrig*. These annals were printed in William Camden's *Britannia* in 1607, and in the *Chartularies of St Mary's Abbey, Dublin* published by the Rolls Series in 1884; both editions used the fifteenth-century Bodleian MS Laud 526, which carries no identification of author. Sir James Ware used the Dublin manuscript later in the seventeenth century to correct Camden's edition. The general acceptance of the name Christopher appears to originate in Walter Harris's edition of Ware's *De scriptoribus Hiberniae* (1746), which names Pembridge as Christopher; however Ware himself, in the first edition of *De scriptoribus*, published in 1639, only names the annalist as Pembridge. A letter from James Ussher to Richard Stanihurst states that he could never get sight of the chronicle by Christopher Pembridge. It may be that a note by Ware, 'C. [indicating *cronica*] Pembridge', was misinterpreted by Ussher and Harris as indicating that the chronicler's forename was Christopher.

As his initial source, Pembridge used the Cistercian annals of St Mary's, Dublin. The Cistercian interest is replaced by Dominican interest from the beginning of the fourteenth century; an entry in 1304 relates that Eustace le Poer laid the first stone of the choir of Friars Preachers on the feast of St Agatha (5 February). Further Dominican notices record donations to the building of St Saviour's in Dublin, and burials both there and in other Dominican priories. Pembridge covers the affairs of Dublin, religious and secular, recounting the foundation of Dublin University in 1320, and giving a graphic description of cooking on fires built on the frozen River Liffey in 1338. He records the panic in Dublin in 1317 occasioned by the Scottish invasion, and gives considerable detail of many other events of the period. The execution of Sir William Bermingham in 1332 elicits a personal lament, while the deaths of the justiciar of Ireland, Sir Ralph Ufford, and his wife in 1346 are greeted with joy.

Pembridge's annals are most informative on matters concerning the administration of Ireland, and contain material not found elsewhere; he evidently had access to firsthand information. His contribution to the annals ceases in 1347, before the black death, of which there is no mention. After the conclusion of the Pembridge chronicle in 1347 the entries indicate a continuing Dominican interest.   BERNADETTE A. WILLIAMS

Sources J. T. Gilbert, ed., *Chartularies of St Mary's Abbey, Dublin: with the register of its house at Dunbrody and annals of Ireland*, 2, Rolls Series, 80 (1884) · TCD, MS 584 · king's remembrancer, accounts various, PRO Exchequer, E 101 · J. Ware, *De scriptoribus Hiberniae, libri duo* (1639), bk 1, p. 68 · *The whole works of Sir James Ware concerning Ireland*, ed. and trans. W. Harris, 2/2 (1746), 83–4 · G. Camdeno [W. Camden], *Britannia, sive, Florentissimorum regnorum, Angliae, Scotiae, Hiberniae*, later edn (1607) · *The whole works of … James Ussher*, ed. C. R. Elrington and J. H. Todd, 17 vols. (1847–64), vol. 15, p. 15 · Bodl. Oxf., MS Laud 526
Archives Bodl. Oxf., MS Laud 526 · TCD, MS 584

Sir Richard Pembridge (*c*.1320–1375), tomb effigy

Pembridge, Sir Richard (*c*.1320–1375), soldier and administrator, was descended from one of the collateral branches of the Pembridge family, whose main line had been established in Herefordshire from the reign of Stephen. He rose from relative obscurity to become a Garter knight of Edward III. His success illustrates the social mobility associated with a career in arms during Edward III's French wars, while the serious reverse he encountered at the end of his life reflects the degree to which sustained success depended on the favour of the king.

Pembridge's father was Sir Richard Pembridge of Clehonger, who represented Herefordshire in the parliaments of September 1337 and February 1338 and died in 1345/6. His tomb, together with that of his wife, Petronilla, survives in the chantry chapel which he endowed at Clehonger church in April 1342. Like many young men of his class the young Richard found himself on the wrong side of the law, when in August 1345 he was included in a group of men whose arrest was ordered as a result of misdemeanours in the Forest of Dean. This boisterous disposition may have helped to secure him a prominent place in Edward III's French wars, a record of which is provided by frequent references in the chronicles of Froissart. He was present at the battle of Crécy in 1346 and also at Poitiers on 19 September 1356. By then he was high in royal favour. He was granted a pension of £30 a year from the exchequer in 1352, raised to £40 and assigned on the priory of Ware in September of that year. By 1353 he had been knighted and joined the royal household. From 1360 he was a member of Edward III's small group of chamber knights, a distinction which he retained until his fall from favour in 1372.

Pembridge's rising prestige is reflected in appointments to receive Pierre de Lusignan, king of Cyprus, in November 1363 and Jean, king of France, on 4 January 1364. He also accumulated substantial wealth. Some time after 1360 he made a profitable marriage to Elizabeth, formerly the wife of Lord St John and Gerard Lisle, who held the manors of Kingston Lisle in Berkshire and Chilton Foliat in Wiltshire. During the break in hostilities following the treaty of Brétigny in 1360 Pembridge was active in the land market, presumably investing the profits from his service in the war. In 1362–3 he bought the Berkshire manors of Wadley and Wicklesham from Stanley Abbey, and in 1362 the reversion to the manor of Orwell, Cambridgeshire, from Thomas Scalers, who had no heirs. To these he added a string of the lucrative royal grants habitually reserved to chamber knights. In 1361 the king made him lifetime grants of the custodianships of Southampton Castle, the park of Lyndhurst and the New Forest, and the hundred of Redbridge. In 1364 he received the manor of Burgate by Southampton, which had passed to the crown by right of escheat. On 15 August 1367 Pembridge was appointed keeper of Bamburgh Castle and entitled to retain all the profits for his own use including a farm of 26 marks provided he bore the costs of maintaining the fortifications. Since a commission of 20 October 1367 was appointed to survey the dilapidations to the castle during the keepership of Ralph Neville, and the crown later attempted to enforce compensation from Neville's executors, Pembridge may have faced costs well in excess of the expected profit. In 1368 his service and his increasing landed wealth were recognized by his election to the Order of the Garter, occupying the fourth stall on the prince's side, an advancement which may have been associated with Edward's plan for renewing the war. In 1370 Pembridge purchased the constableship of Dover Castle and the wardenship of the Cinque Ports from Ralph Spigurnell, paying in return an immediate lump sum of 400 marks and thereafter an annual pension of £100. This office carried an annual fee of £300 and gave him an important role in the organization of ordnance and supply which offered the chance of further profit. On 6 July 1370 he supervised the embarkation of Sir Robert Knolles's expedition and in the same year received £116 9*s.* 7*d.* for his expenses towards the war. In addition to his administrative responsibilities he continued active service and was present at the naval battle of Bourgneuf near Brittany in August 1371.

Pembridge's fall from favour was sudden and may have been related to the dismissal from the chancellorship of his associate William Wykeham, bishop of Winchester, in March 1371. Early in 1372 the king instructed Pembridge to take up office as lieutenant of Ireland. This was an awkward appointment and Pembridge refused it. The preceding years had been characterized by a shrinkage of the English crown's legal and territorial control there, and William Windsor's attempt to increase the Irish tax yield during his lieutenancy (1369–71) provoked such protest that Edward was forced to recall him. While Pembridge's recalcitrance is therefore understandable, the personal cost to him was high. He was deprived of his offices and ordered to leave the court. On 12 July 1372 a new commission was appointed to investigate the dilapidations at Bamburgh. But now special attention was paid to the peculation and maladministration of the deputies who had acted for Pembridge during his keepership. He died, still in disgrace, on 26 July 1375. His will is dated at London 31 May 1368, suggesting that it was prepared with the possible resumption of the war in mind. As well as making minor financial bequests to servants and associates Pembridge instructed that his body should be buried either in Hereford Cathedral or *in situ* if he died overseas. In either case a monument, enclosed with an iron railing and modelled on that of his fellow Garter knight William Beauchamp in St Paul's, was to be erected in Hereford Cathedral 'before the image of the blessed Mary on the south side' (Sharpe, 188–9). The monument, in alabaster and probably of London manufacture, was sited in accordance with his will. Before his wife, Elizabeth, died on 16 September 1362 she gave birth to one son, Henry. He died, still a minor, on 5 October, passing the inheritance to the children of Richard's sisters, Amice and Hawise.

ANTHONY GROSS

Sources C. Given-Wilson, *The royal household and the king's affinity: service, politics and finance in England, 1360–1413* (1986) • *Chancery records* • PRO, Exchequer records, E 101, 392/12, 397/5 • J. Duncumb and others, *Collections towards the history and antiquities of the county of Hereford*, 1 (1804), 540 • *Archaeological Journal*, 34 (1877), 410–11 • *A history of Northumberland*, Northumberland County History Committee, 15 vols. (1893–1940), vol. 1, pp. 41–2 • *CIPM*, 14, nos. 191–2 • R. R. Sharpe, ed., *Calendar of wills proved and enrolled in the court of husting, London, AD 1258 – AD 1688*, 2 (1890), 188–9 • G. M. Snewin, *All Saints Church, Clehonger: a short history* (1970), 9–10 • GEC, *Peerage*
Likenesses alabaster tomb effigy, Hereford Cathedral [*see illus.*]
Wealth at death four manors and one half in five counties: *CIPM* 14, no. 191

Pembroke. For this title name *see* Clare, Richard fitz Gilbert de, second earl of Pembroke (*c.*1130–1176); Marshal, William (I), fourth earl of Pembroke (*c.*1146–1219); Clare, Isabel de, *suo jure* countess of Pembroke (1171x6–1220); Marshal, William (II), fifth earl of Pembroke (*c.*1190–1231); Marshal, Richard, sixth earl of Pembroke (*d.* 1234); Marshal, Gilbert, seventh earl of Pembroke (*d.* 1241) [*see under* Marshal, William (II), fifth earl of Pembroke (*c.*1190–1231)]; Marshal, Walter, eighth earl of Pembroke (*d.* 1245) [*see under* Marshal, William (II), fifth earl of Pembroke (*c.*1190–1231)]; Eleanor, countess of Pembroke and Leicester (1215?–1275); Valence, William de, earl of Pembroke (*d.* 1296); Valence, Aymer de, eleventh earl of Pembroke (*d.* 1324); St Pol, Mary de, countess of Pembroke (*c.*1304–

1377); Hastings, Laurence, twelfth earl of Pembroke (1320–1348); Hastings, John, thirteenth earl of Pembroke (1347–1375); Herbert, William, first earl of Pembroke (*c.*1423–1469); Herbert, William, second earl of Pembroke (1455–1490) [*see under* Herbert, William, first earl of Pembroke (*c.*1423–1469)]; Herbert, William, first earl of Pembroke (1506/7–1570); Herbert, Henry, second earl of Pembroke (*b.* in or after 1538, *d.* 1601); Herbert, Mary, countess of Pembroke (1561–1621); Herbert, William, third earl of Pembroke (1580–1630); Herbert, Philip, first earl of Montgomery and fourth earl of Pembroke (1584–1650); Clifford, Anne, countess of Pembroke, Dorset, and Montgomery (1590–1676); Herbert, Thomas, eighth earl of Pembroke and fifth earl of Montgomery (1656/7–1733); Herbert, Henry, ninth earl of Pembroke and sixth earl of Montgomery (*c.*1689–1750); Herbert, Henry, tenth earl of Pembroke and seventh earl of Montgomery (1734–1794); Herbert, Elizabeth, countess of Pembroke and Montgomery (1737–1831); Herbert, George Augustus, eleventh earl of Pembroke and eighth earl of Montgomery (1759–1827); Herbert, George Robert Charles, thirteenth earl of Pembroke and tenth earl of Montgomery (1850–1895).

Pembrooke, Thomas (1658x62–*c.*1690), history and portrait painter, was possibly born near Canterbury, Kent. Of his parents, nothing is known. He was a pupil of Marcellus Laroon (whether the elder or the younger is uncertain) and executed several works for Charles Granville, earl of Bath, who became his patron. A picture by Pembrooke, *Hagar and Ishmael*, was engraved in mezzotint by John Raphael Smith. Pembrooke died young *c.*1690.

L. H. CUST, *rev.* SUSAN COOPER MORGAN

Sources R. de Piles, *The art of painting with the lives and characters of above 300 of the most eminent painters*, 3rd edn (1754) • H. Walpole, *Anecdotes of painting in England: with some account of the principal artists*, ed. R. N. Wornum, new edn, 3 vols. (1849); repr. (1862) • Bénézit, *Dict.*, 4th edn • E. K. Waterhouse, *The dictionary of British 16th and 17th century painters* (1988)
Archives Courtauld Inst., Witt Library, cuttings, MSS, photographs

Pemell, Robert (*d.* 1653), physician, seems to have spent most of his working life in the cloth town of Cranbrook in Kent. He may have been connected with the Pemyll family of Egerton. Nothing is known of his education except that he did not lay claim to any degree. He was probably the Robert Pemel who obtained an archiepiscopal licence to practise medicine about 1632. He may have shared in the puritan tendency of Cranbrook: his published works were all printed for the London theological bookseller Philemon Stephens, and produced in the early 1650s, at a time when publication in both the learned languages and the vernacular greatly increased.

Pemell's last work, on the diseases of children, was only the second monograph on the subject in English, the first being that of Thomas Phaer a hundred years earlier. General advice books directed at women, parents, or householders were, however, already a well-established genre. At various points Pemell's book on children directs the reader to fuller discussions contained in his earlier publications.

Pemell's publications were all in the vernacular, but showed some knowledge of Latin, and were derived from classical and contemporary learned authors, with a few references to his own experience. As R. P. he first published *De morbis capitis, or, Of the Chief Internall Diseases of the Head* (1650). A dedicatory Latin poem was contributed by John Elmeston, schoolmaster of Cranbrook. In the same year appeared *Ptōchoupharmakon, seu, Medicamen miseris, or, Pauperum pyxidicula salutifera. Help for the poor* (1650). This was aimed less at the poor themselves than at those able to help them and 'not able to make use of Physitians and Chirurgians'. A later edition (1653) included an appendix on whether to let blood in smallpox. Pemell's productivity continued with *Tractatus de simplicium medicamentorum facultatibus. A treatise of the nature … of such simples as are most frequently used* (1652). This was helpfully structured for 'the vulgar capacity' and young practitioners. A second part, *Tractatus de facultatibus simplicium*, followed in 1653. His final work, on children, he advertised as fulfilling his promise to follow up the *Tractatus*, but in 'more hast', because 'I see my glasse runs apace': *De morbis puerorum, or, A treatise of the diseases of children … very useful for all such as are housekeepers* (1653).

Pemell's will was dated 7 April 1652, he being then in 'good health'; he was buried in Cranbrook on 3 June 1653. He left a widow, Elizabeth, and three children, all under age. The eldest, Thomas, was to have 'all my books in case he betake himself to the study and practice of physic'.

MARGARET PELLING

Sources J. H. Raach, *A directory of English country physicians, 1603–1643* (1962) · G. F. Still, *The history of paediatrics* (1931) · C. Webster, *The great instauration: science, medicine and reform, 1626–1660* (1975) · will, PRO, PROB 11/241, sig. 442

Pemulwoy (*c.*1760–1802), Aboriginal warrior, was a member of the Bediagal band of the Dharug people, whose lands occupied the head of Botany Bay, 6 miles south of the Port Jackson convict settlement.

Within months of the first fleet's arrival in January 1788 wary Dharug–British relations degenerated into avoidance and violence. A thousand newcomers, equal to their own number, rent the Dharug's world. Competition for resources eased only momentarily in April 1789, when smallpox killed half the Dharug. On 10 December 1790 Pemulwoy, a young Dharug man with a blemish on his left eye and a shaven face indicating recent contact with the British, dramatically entered historical consciousness. Other Aborigines identified him as the man who, from ten paces, mortally speared John McIntyre, Governor Arthur Phillip's convict gamekeeper, whom Aborigines perceived, according to Captain Watkin Tench, with 'much dread and hatred' (Tench, 205). Phillip ordered the first punitive expedition against Aboriginal people to capture or kill six Dharug, but the expedition failed. In 1795 Pemulwoy speared a favoured Aboriginal man, 'Collins', who had accompanied the *Daedalus* to refresh Captain Vancouver at Nootka Sound in 1793.

By 1795 open deadly warfare erupted 30 miles away in the Hawkesbury district over corn, indicating Aboriginal hunger. Soldiers repulsed the Dharug by force and were ordered to gibbet any bodies recovered as a warning. Pemulwoy countered with a bold attack on a convict a mile from Sydney. In March 1797 vigilante action followed further Dharug raids and killings at farms. Pemulwoy's warriors boldly confronted the vigilantes in Parramatta as they rested. Violence erupted, the Dharug were routed, and Pemulwoy was hospitalized with shotgun head injuries, only to escape while wearing a leg iron. Pemulwoy again plundered and burnt crops. Constant reports of his death proved unfounded. Apparently Pemulwoy and the Dharug believed that he was impervious to guns, since he had survived numerous encounters with guns and gunshot wounds.

The Dharug's resistance campaign so alarmed the colony that in November 1801 Governor King ordered soldiers to patrol the farms on the George's River and shoot any Dharug on sight. It was feared that Pemulwoy was in league with convict escapees, and a price was placed on all their heads. After four more settlers were killed and some convict women 'cruelly used' (Governor King to Lord Hobart, 30 Oct 1802, *Historical Records of Australia*, 1st ser., 3.582), allegedly by Pemulwoy's band, he was ordered to be brought in dead or alive, and two settlers shot him dead on 2 June 1802. Reportedly some Aborigines unsympathetic to Pemulwoy's guerrilla war requested that his head be given to the governor and they be allowed to re-enter Parramatta. King dispatched Pemulwoy's severed head in spirits to Sir Joseph Banks, commenting: 'Altho' a terrible pest to the colony, he was a brave and independent character' (*Historical Records of New South Wales*, 4.784). Pemulwoy's son Tjedboro (Tedbury) raided farms between 1801 and 1805 and again in 1809 and consorted with bushrangers.

After instilling fear into the settlers for a decade, Pemulwoy was almost forgotten until historians rediscovered the Aboriginal resistance in the 1970s and the novel *Pemulwuy: the Rainbow Warrior* (1987) was written by one of the first Aboriginal academics, Eric Willmot. Sydney Aboriginal artists adopted Pemulwoy's name for their exhibition in 1990.

RICHARD BROOME

Sources D. Collins, *An account of the English colony in New South Wales*, 2 vols. (1798–1802); repr., ed. B. H. Fletcher (1975) · F. M. Bladen, ed., *Historical records of New South Wales*, 4 (1896) [repr. (1979)] · W. Tench, *Sydney's first four years: being a reprint of 'A narrative of the expedition to Botany Bay' and 'A complete account of the settlement at Port Jackson'*, ed. L. F. Fitzhardinge (1979) · J. Hunter, *An historical journal of events at Sydney and at sea, 1787–1792*, ed. J. Bach (1968) · K. Willey, *When the sky fell down: the destruction of the tribes of the Sydney region, 1788–1850* (1979) · J. L. Kohen and R. Lampert, 'Hunters and fishers in the Sydney region', *Australians to 1788*, ed. D. J. Mulvaney and J. P. White (1987), 343–65 · *The Pemulwoy dilemma: the voice of koori art in the Sydney region* (1990) · E. Willmot, *Pemulwuy: the rainbow warrior* (1987)

Pencester [Penchester, Penshurst], **Sir Stephen of** (*d.* 1298), administrator, is of obscure origins—surprisingly so, in the light of his prominence later. Evidence even for the names of his parents or his date of birth is lacking. Edward Hasted, the late-eighteenth-century historian of Kent, claimed that Pencester's family took their name from Penshurst soon after the time of William I, but this is conjectural. His manor of Penshurst was held at his death in portions from four different lords, so it is uncertain what he inherited there. Most of his other possessions were acquired in his own lifetime. He referred in a charter of 1282 to his uncle John Belemeyns, a canon of St Paul's, London, from at least 1216 to about 1252, who had endowed a chapel at Leigh near Penshurst.

Pencester first appears in royal records in June 1263, when, probably already a knight, he was made captain to repress disorder in Sussex and Kent. He must already have acquired administrative experience, perhaps in the service of the Clare lords of Tonbridge, 5 miles from Penshurst. If so, he changed his allegiance, once civil war began to divide local society, to the Lord Edward, who was henceforth his patron. He was certainly unsuccessful as captain: his powers were given to Roger of Leybourne in December 1263. Once royal authority was restored in 1265, however, Pencester's career revived. Keeper of Hastings, Winchelsea, and Rye from November 1265, he became constable of Dover Castle, initially as Edward's deputy, in December 1267, and sheriff of Kent from 1268 to 1271. In August 1271 he was first referred to as warden of the Cinque Ports; Leybourne's death in that year probably offers a partial explanation for his rise to local prominence. Thereafter Pencester served as both warden and constable until his own death. Deputies were often appointed, but royal mandates imply, and sometimes specify, that he exercised close personal control over his offices.

On Edward I's return to England in 1274, Pencester's appointments were confirmed, with an allowance of £274 13s. 4d. later raised to £300, to maintain Dover Castle and his staff. As warden, he enforced royal orders to regulate cross-channel travel and trade, such as the embargo on exports of wool to Flanders of 1270–74. He also supervised the government of the ports, exacting the services that they owed to the crown and intervening in their disputes, whether local, like those over rights in Minster and Fordwich, or with other towns, notably Yarmouth in Norfolk. These powers spilled over into more general peacekeeping in the south-east, orders to arrest malefactors in Kent and Sussex being accompanied by a stream of more specific oyer and terminer commissions, often joining Pencester with established royal judges. Some, like the inquiries into former rebels in Canterbury in 1275, or into royal rights usurped by Gilbert de Clare, earl of Gloucester, in 1279, reflected the inheritance of disputes from the civil wars of the 1260s. Responsibility for collecting revenues in the ports also led Pencester into a wider involvement with royal fiscal policy, joining a commission to prosecute coin-clippers, mostly Jews, and to regulate the workings of the royal exchanges in 1279. From 1281 he took a leading role in implementing Edward I's project to build the new town of Winchelsea. But Pencester's one diplomatic mission to Gascony, with Otto de Grandson in 1276, does not seem to have been repeated, though he was in Wales for part of 1277.

It seems therefore that the pattern of Pencester's regional responsibilities set in the 1270s lasted to the end of his life, though in the 1290s he had to cope with the additional demands of the French war: first the attempts to resolve maritime disputes in 1291–4, and then the war effort itself, culminating in the king's Flemish expedition of 1297. His career set important precedents in linking together responsibilities for the government of southeast England and its coastline under the wardenship of the Cinque Ports based at Dover. He showed an ability to work with other royal officials and with the leaders of local society, even in some measure to reconcile their interests; though the evidence for this is largely negative, in the relative paucity of complaints against him in Edwardian records. The chronicle of Dover Priory, championing the cause of Prior Richard de Wenchepe, who was faced with a revolt of his own monks in 1270–73, accused Pencester of hostility to the prior, and dramatized several conversations between them. But the events suggest rather that Pencester sought to avoid involvement in the dispute, until forced into action by royal command.

While the focus of his authority was in Dover, Pencester accumulated property near his original holdings in west Kent. A grant of free warren in his demesne lands at Penshurst, Tonbridge, Hever, and Chiddingstone in 1263 was augmented by another in 1280, for demesnes he now held at Allington, Boxley, and Aylesford. Licence to crenellate his house at Hever in 1271 was followed by another in 1281 for Allington, where he also held a market and fair. The flow of royal favours normal for an official in good standing was accompanied by occasional substantial grants, the largest that of £600 'for his long and praiseworthy service' in 1277 (*CClR, 1272–1279*, 379). Nevertheless, given the scale of that service over thirty years, his fortunes bear out the view that Edward I rewarded his agents sparingly.

Pencester married first Rose de Baseville, before 1268, then by 1281 Margaret, a member of the de Burgh family, though her exact parentage is unclear. On her death in 1308 her heir was John Orreby, her son from a previous marriage, while her dower lands reverted to Pencester's two daughters from his marriage to Rose: Joan 'aged forty and more' and Alice 'aged thirty and more'. Pencester himself died between 14 February and 14 April 1298, not 1299 as misreported in a later entry on the close roll for 1313. His failure to leave a male heir meant that his estates were broken up, and this has contributed to the obscurity of his family history. He is commemorated by the upper half of a Purbeck marble effigy in Penshurst church, where he was buried.   RICHARD EALES

Sources *Chancery records* · *CIPM*, 1, no. 737; 5, no. 134 · *The historical works of Gervase of Canterbury*, ed. W. Stubbs, 2: *The minor works comprising the Gesta regum with its continuation, the Actus pontificum and the Mappa mundi*, Rolls Series, 73 (1880) [incl. chronicle of Dover Priory] · K. M. E. Murray, *The constitutional history of the Cinque Ports* (1935) · J. Thorpe, ed., *Registrum Roffense, or, A collection of antient records, charters and instruments … illustrating the ecclesiastical history and antiquities of the diocese and cathedral church of Rochester* (1769) · A. J. Taylor, 'Stephen de Pencestre's account as constable of Dover Castle for the years Michaelmas 1272 – Michaelmas 1274', *Collectanea historica: essays in memory of Stuart Rigold*, ed. A. Detsicas (1981), 114–22

Likenesses marble tomb effigy, St John the Baptist, Penshurst, Kent
Wealth at death lands held: *CIPM*, 5, no. 134

Penda (d. 655), king of the Mercians, was the son of Pybba and (at least according to later genealogies) a scion of the Mercian royal dynasty which traced its origin back to Woden. The date at which Penda became king is far from certain. The Anglo-Saxon Chronicle puts his accession in 626 and notes that his reign lasted thirty years (this last detail is roughly consistent, for he died in 655); it also says that he was fifty years of age when he became king, which seems unlikely and is perhaps a mistake for his age at death. The chronicle goes on to mention a battle which took place at Cirencester in 628 between Penda on the one hand and the West Saxon rulers Cynegils and Cwichelm on the other, after which the combatants 'came to terms'; there is reason to think that these terms may have included an acknowledgement of Penda's overlordship over the southern part of the kingdom of the Hwicce (modern Gloucestershire), an area which would appear to have been under West Saxon control since 577. This picture of a flourishing start to Penda's reign is rather dashed by Bede's information about events in 633, when Penda allied with a (Christian) Welsh king, Cadwallon of Gwynedd, for a campaign against Northumbria. At the battle of Hatfield Chase on 12 October the Northumbrian army was routed and King Eadwine was killed, along with one of his sons; another son, Eadfrith, 'was compelled to desert to Penda' and later met his death at Penda's hands. It is a problem that Bede appears to date the beginning of Penda's reign to the year of this successful campaign: he states that he was 'a most vigorous man from the royal stock of the Mercians, who from that time ruled his people for twenty-two years with varying success' (*Hist. eccl.*, 2.20). To add to the complication, there is a third source that gives Penda a reign length of only ten years, starting apparently from 642, and which implies that his brother Eowa had been king of the Mercians before this point; this is the *Historia Brittonum*, which is a far less authoritative source than Bede and the Anglo-Saxon Chronicle. It has been sensibly suggested that the key to these seemingly contradictory details about Penda's accession and reign length may be Bede's observation that he ruled 'with varying success'; perhaps his reign was interrupted by reverses at various times, so that he had to re-establish his authority. There is also some possibility that Penda may have ruled jointly for some time with his brother Eowa, a situation which could have affected calculations of the length of his reign.

Nine years after dispatching King Eadwine, Penda returned to Northumbria and killed King Oswald at the battle of 'Maserfelth' (Bede, *Hist. eccl.*, 3.9); it would seem that it was during this battle that Eowa met his death. Again the Mercian forces appear to have had Welsh support; a Welsh poem which may be as early as the ninth century claims that a king of Powys fought in the battle on Penda's side. These military alliances with the British

kingdoms to the west of Mercia may provide some explanation for Penda's extraordinarily successful invasions of other Anglo-Saxon kingdoms. He seems to have made several incursions deep into Northumbria: on one occasion (perhaps in the aftermath of his victory at 'Maserfelth') his forces reached as far north as the Northumbrian citadel at Bamburgh, and were only prevented from capturing it by a fortunate miracle (Bede, *Hist. eccl.*, 3.10); and at a later date, some time between 651 and 655, the Mercian army destroyed a church not far from Bamburgh when Áedán had died (ibid., 3.17)). Yet Penda's relations with Northumbria were not always on a bellicose level. There is a possibility that he helped Oswald's son Æthelwald gain the throne of Deira; certainly Æthelwald was ranged on Penda's side against Oswiu of Northumbria during the Mercian king's final campaign against Northumbria in 655 (his last-minute withdrawal may have contributed to Penda's catastrophic defeat). At some point before 653 Penda married his daughter Cyneburh to Oswiu's son, *Alchfrith, and in 653 he allowed his eldest son, *Peada, to make a reciprocal match with Oswiu's daughter. In Bede's carefully wrought narrative Penda fulfils the role of an implacable pagan warrior-king, who makes apocalyptic descents on vulnerable Christian kingdoms to wreak God's mysterious will and provide opportunities for martyrdom and miracles. But these dramatic episodes were only a facet of his reign; it is clear that he also interacted with neighbouring dynasties and kingdoms in other ways.

Bede's brief notices of Penda's onslaughts on East Anglia give an impression of motiveless aggression. His armies invaded; the East Anglians feared that they would be defeated and so sought to enlist divine support by dragging their saintly former king Sigeberht from his monastery; but both Sigeberht and the current king, Ecgric, were killed. Later Penda also killed the succeeding East Anglian king, Anna. The chronology of East Anglian history in the seventh century is very difficult to establish, but there is reason to think that Anna died in 654. It has been suggested that there could be a connection between this (perhaps second) invasion of East Anglia and Penda's establishment of his son Peada as ruler of the Middle Angles in the early 650s. 'Middle Anglia' was a conglomeration of tribes and minor kingdoms located in the east midlands between Mercia proper and East Anglia. Overlordship of this region seems to have been contested between the Mercian and East Anglian rulers, so the appointment of Peada as king may mark Penda's final subjugation of Middle Anglia; certainly after this time the region remained firmly under Mercian control. It seems very likely that Penda's wars with the East Angles were prompted by strategic considerations.

There are some brief details about Penda's relations with the West Saxon rulers to the south. He married his sister to *Cenwalh, who ruled Wessex between 641 and 672; this alliance may perhaps have been arranged about 628, after Penda had fought against Cenwalh's father and brother at Cirencester, and may indeed have formed part of the 'terms' agreed by the antagonists. Shortly after Cenwalh's accession he repudiated his wife, prompting an angry Penda to invade and drive him from his kingdom, to take refuge with Anna of the East Angles; after three years' exile Cenwalh returned, apparently without opposition from the Mercian ruler (Bede, *Hist. eccl.*, 3.7). It seems very likely that both the initial repudiation and the insouciant return took place at times when Penda's power was on the wane, eclipsed by a Northumbrian resurgence or by internal difficulties within Mercia. Indeed, Penda's reign may have been punctuated by periods of domination over Southumbria alternating with periods when his influence was limited.

The last episode in Penda's career took place when his star was very much in the ascendant. Backed by a huge army he threatened Oswiu of Northumbria, who was forced to negotiate; at the time Oswiu's son Ecgfrith was a hostage at Penda's court. According to Bede, Oswiu offered the invader vast quantities of treasure if he agreed to return home and stop devastating Northumbria, but Penda refused, supposedly because he was determined to exterminate the whole Northumbrian people. The two forces met on the banks of the River 'Winwæd' (a tributary of the Humber), almost certainly on 15 November 655. Oswiu's army was (allegedly) tiny. Penda, on the other hand, commanded a force which is supposed to have consisted of thirty 'legions', each commanded by a 'royal ealdorman'. One of these allies was Æthelhere, king of the East Angles, and another was Æthelwald, sub-king of Deira: it seems that Penda's army included detachments from kingdoms which recognized his authority, and that the 'royal ealdormen' leading them would in some instances have been recognized as kings in their own right. Penda's ability to raise such forces under his command is a measure of his dominant position in 655; the clash with Oswiu can probably be understood as a campaign to challenge Northumbrian overlordship over Southumbria (hence Penda's refusal to compromise and his avowed intention of decisively defeating the Northumbrian people). But it was the Mercian king who was defeated and killed at the 'Winwæd', along with most of his followers. Oswiu occupied Mercia for three years, until a Mercian revolt established Penda's son *Wulfhere as king.

Of Penda's domestic policies in Mercia very little is known, although Bede provides an intriguing insight into his attitude to Christianity. He himself remained a committed pagan, but he allowed Christian missionaries to preach in Mercia, 'if anyone wished to listen' (Bede, *Hist. eccl.*, 3.21): it seems unlikely that the priests had much success with the Mercians in the face of their ruler's disapproval, and it was not until after Penda's death that an episcopal structure was established in the midlands. According to Bede, Penda reserved his contempt, not for Christians as such, but for those who had accepted the Christian faith but did not live according to its precepts. It is impossible to discover whether this was indeed Penda's own view, or whether it was Bede's decision to attribute this didactic sentiment to the most celebrated of Anglo-Saxon pagans.

Penda's queen at the time of his death was Cynewise, whose antecedents are unknown. Perhaps with her, or perhaps from an earlier alliance, Penda had at least three sons: Peada, who was ruler of the Middle Angles from 653 until 655, and then very briefly king of the South Mercians under Oswiu's authority; Wulfhere, king of the Mercians from 658 until 675; and *Æthelred (*d.* after 704), who succeeded Wulfhere. Later tradition also identifies Penda as the father of Merewalh, ruler of the Magonsæte (who lived in the area of modern Shropshire and Herefordshire). Opinions are divided on the validity of this suggestion; if correct, then it may be the case that Penda established Merewalh as sub-king of the western part of the Mercian confederation in the same way that he had made Peada his sub-king in Middle Anglia. One of Penda's daughters, Cyneburh, was married to Alchfrith, son of Oswiu and a Christian. She is supposed to have retired after her husband's death to a minster at Castor in Northamptonshire, where she was buried with her sister Cyneswith; their bodies are said to have been translated to the monastery at Peterborough in 963. A late hagiographical source states that Cyneswith had been married to Offa, king of the East Angles. Two further daughters of Penda are mentioned in hagiographical material connected with St Osgyth of Aylesbury: Wilburh (St Osgyth's mother) and Eadburh (probably the woman of that name associated with a minster at Bicester).

Penda was the last great pagan ruler of Anglo-Saxon England. He is remembered as a military leader of extraordinary effectiveness and a scourge of Christian kingdoms, responsible for the deaths in battle of two successive kings of Northumbria (Eadwine and Oswald), and of three East Anglian rulers (Ecgric, Anna, and the former king Sigeberht); but his greatest achievement seems to have been the establishment of a long-standing Mercian overlordship over the diverse tribes and kingdoms of the west midlands and Middle Anglia.   S. E. KELLY

Sources Bede, *Hist. eccl.*, 2.20; 3.7, 9–10, 17–18, 21, 24; 5.25 · *ASC*, s.a. 626, 628 [text A] · Nennius, 'British history' and 'The Welsh annals', ed. and trans. J. Morris (1980), 80 · N. Brooks, 'The formation of the Mercian kingdom', *The origins of Anglo-Saxon kingdoms*, ed. S. Bassett (1989), 159–70 · P. Sims-Williams, *Religion and literature in western England, 600–800* (1990), 25–9, 47–9, 77 · W. Davies, 'Annals and the origin of Mercia', *Mercian studies*, ed. A. Dornier (1977), 17–29 · D. Dumville, 'Essex, Middle Anglia, and the expansion of Mercia in the south-east midlands', *The origins of Anglo-Saxon kingdoms*, ed. S. Bassett (1989), 123–40 · D. W. Rollason, *The Mildrith legend: a study in early medieval hagiography in England* (1982) · F. M. Stenton, *Anglo-Saxon England*, 3rd edn (1971), 45, 47, 81–4 · J. Campbell, *Essays in Anglo-Saxon history* (1986), 13, 37, 76 · H. P. R. Finberg, 'The princes of the Magonsæte', *The early charters of the west midlands*, 2nd edn (1972), 217–24 · J. Blair, 'Frithuwold's kingdom and the origins of Surrey', *The origins of Anglo-Saxon kingdoms*, ed. S. Bassett (1989), 97–107 · D. Bethell, 'The lives of St Osyth of Essex and St Osyth of Aylesbury', *Analecta Bollandiana*, 88 (1970), 75–127

Pendarves, John (1622/3–1656), Particular Baptist minister, was born at Crowan, Cornwall, son of John Pendarves.

The Pendarves were county gentry but this branch seems not to have been prosperous, and at the age of fifteen John and an older brother, Ralph, entered Exeter College, Oxford, in 1638 as servitors. He graduated BA in 1642. Exeter College under John Prideaux was a stronghold of puritanism opposing the prevailing Laudian orientation of the university. According to Wood, Pendarves ran through the various forms of radical religion on offer before embracing Baptism in the later 1640s. In May 1644, when parliamentary forces took Abingdon (then in Berkshire) from the royalists, he became vicar of St Helen's, the larger, and traditionally the more radical, of the two churches in that town. He was also by 1649 minister of the nearby town of Wantage, but resigned both livings in or soon after 1650 and took on the formal leadership of the Particular (Calvinistic) Baptist congregation in Abingdon. In the rest of his short career, he became increasingly active and prominent in both local and national Baptist affairs.

By 1649 Pendarves was in contact with William Kiffin, the London Baptist leader, and was probably already engaged in preaching and organizing in the villages within reach of Abingdon and Wantage. Baptist churches were in being both in Abingdon and in Wantage before 1650, and drew their membership from a wide radius. Pendarves's slowness to resign from his parish cures even after he had become a convinced separatist, and his readiness to take the engagement in 1649, may have been a function of his financial needs. The incumbency of St Helen's was worth only £20 per annum but the committee for plundered ministers allocated him an additional £50 per annum, although the earlier payments fell heavily into arrears. Only after 1648 did a personal lectureship in Marcham and Abingdon guarantee him an independent income of £30 per annum. It was presumably in order to have central congregations of adequate size to support Pendarves and the Wantage minister, Robert Keate, with their voluntary contributions that no further Baptist churches were set up in the Vale of White Horse during Pendarves's lifetime, in spite of a general principle that such churches should be local. Soon after his death his congregation split, with ninety-nine members leaving to found new churches at Longworth and Faringdon to the west of Abingdon. Since the Abingdon church remained more significant than these, it probably numbered some hundreds of members at its peak.

Pendarves proved a talented organizer. To maintain co-ordination among Baptist congregations within a region which included, at its greatest extent, parts of Oxfordshire, Buckinghamshire, Bedfordshire, and Hampshire as well as Berkshire, he and Benjamin Cox had, in 1652, established the Abingdon Association, a forum at which 'messengers' would meet, usually three times a year for up to three days, at Tetsworth, Oxfordshire. This followed normal Baptist practice at this time. By the time of Pendarves's death, the number of individual churches represented was twelve. Discussion was limited to issues of local importance; questions of dogma and political strategy were referred up to the Baptist assembly at Petty France in London.

In spite of his sectarian position, Pendarves remained a figure of high local respectability. As late as 1653 he could still preach before the mayor of Abingdon and civic notables in St Helen's Church. He was not named to the Berkshire commission—the ejectors—which was dominated by Presbyterians, and declined to co-operate with them in 1654 in their prosecution of the Behmenist John Pordage of Bradfield; but one of the accusations made in the same year before the ejectors against the orientalist Edward Pococke, who had been banished from Oxford to his living at Childrey, was that he had refused Pendarves permission to preach from his pulpit.

Pendarves was known as a controversialist, always ready to engage in set-piece preaching contests with opponents. One such occasion was at Ilsley, Berkshire, in 1649, when Pordage's contribution led to his later heresy trial before the ejectors. Another was against the moderate Jasper Mayne at Watlington church in 1652, which seems to have been somewhat disturbed by Pendarves's rowdy followers. Mayne suggested that the standard appellations applied by radicals to the traditional Anglican church—'whore of Babylon', 'habitation of devils', and the like—were unnecessary and inappropriate. Pendarves was unimpressed, and in a major pamphlet, *Arrowes Against Babylon*, published in 1656, emphasized the radical view that the church, now dominated by presbyterians, was simply the same whore in attractive new clothes. He upheld the principle of the separation of the godly from the reprobate, and attacked the established clergy for allowing the latter into their churches. This provoked replies from John Tickell (*Church-Rules*, 1656) and William Ley (*Ueperaspistis*, 1656), Pendarves's successors at St Helen's and Wantage respectively, both of whom accused him of arrogance and authoritarianism.

Because of his west country origins, Pendarves was in close contact with the Baptist Western Association, and attended several of its meetings in the last years of his life. This association, under the influence of Thomas Collier and a group of Fifth Monarchist clergy, maintained a certain independence of the politically cautious line of the Particular Baptist leadership in London, and by 1655 was disillusioned with the protectorate and disappointed at the continued delay in the arrival of the millennium. Pendarves joined with the western millenarians in a pamphlet, *Sighs for Sion* (1656), warning the faithful against despair and enjoining them to increased spiritual effort by way of prayer and fasting. In the period of tension that followed the dissolution of the first protectorate parliament in early 1655, when Thomas Harrison and several other millenarians were effectively on trial before Cromwell and his council, Pendarves was one of a group brought in at their request to help them argue their case. Some of Pendarves's publications, perhaps most notably *Sighs*, can be read as subversive, but there is no evidence that he was ever personally involved in Fifth Monarchy plots.

Nevertheless, a proportion of Pendarves's historical importance is posthumous. As recounted by Wood and

William Hughes, following his death in London from dysentery in early September 1656, his body was returned to Abingdon and his funeral, on 30 September and the two days immediately following, was the occasion for a millenarian demonstration of force, with inflammatory preaching and provocation of the protectorate authorities. The proceedings were brought to an end, amid mutual recriminations, by cavalry units brought in from Wallingford under the command of Major-General Bridge. It was under cover of this gathering that plans were laid for Venner's first Fifth Monarchist rising, which duly took place in the following April and was speedily crushed. The prophetess Anna Trapnel celebrated Pendarves as a saint who had died so as to plead directly with God for the second coming of Christ.

Pendarves's writings also showed mainstream puritan preoccupations. He wrote against luxury in dress and personal adornments (*Endeavours for the Reformation in Saints Apparel*, 1656), which was a particularly strong concern of the Western Association. A tract against the Quakers (*Some Queries*, 1656) brought a turgid denunciation from James Nayler (*An Answer*, 1656) and an elliptical attack from Denys Hollister (*The Skirts of the Whore Discovered*, 1656), who claimed that it was a plagiarism. In spite of rigorism on believers' baptism, Pendarves was on friendly terms with the moderate Baptist and millenarian Henry Jessey and took an interest in his schemes for calendar reform.

Pendarves married before 1647 Thomasine Newcomen [**Thomasine Pendarves** (*bap.* 1618, *d.* in or after 1671)], daughter of Thomas Newcomen and his wife, Bathsabe (*née* Philpott), of St Petrox, Dartmouth. She was baptized at Dartmouth on 13 September 1618. The Newcomens were a prominent Devon family, with interests in tin mines and in the exploitation of Ireland. It seems that Thomasine Pendarves was influential among the Abingdon Baptists even before her husband had abandoned the established church. However, her religion was of a more mystical nature than his, and she caused him embarrassment on several occasions, most seriously in 1649. The ranter Abiezer Coppe dedicated to Thomasine his first major work *Some Sweet Sips of some Spiritual Wine*, and published in it an exchange of correspondence he had had with her; her identity was hidden by the use of Hebrew letters but would have been clear to those learned enough to read them and familiar with local personalities. The letters show her as aspiring to the type of visionary prophecy practised by Coppe, and might also suggest an improper relationship between them. Another of her letters was published in the same year by her friend the political prophetess Elizabeth Poole in *An Alarum of War*. Thomasine had intercepted a letter to her husband from William Kiffin, instructing him to anathematize Poole from the pulpit. Her reply to Kiffin argued against his policy and insisted that, as she could not trust her husband to take the right decision in the matter, further dealings should be with her and not with him. Kiffin does not seem to have responded.

Pendarves and his wife had six known children, of whom at least three died in infancy. Thomasine Pendarves was resident in Abingdon until at least 1671, paying occasional fines for attending conventicles, but then disappears from the record.   MANFRED BROD

Sources J. Atherton, *The pastor turn'd pope* (1654) · Wood, *Ath. Oxon.*, new edn, 3.419–21 · T. Pendarves, 'Letter to William Kiffin', in E. Poole, *An alarum of war* (1649) · A. Trapnell, *A voice for the king of saints* (1658), 52–3 · B. R. White, ed., *Association records of the Particular Baptists of England, Wales, and Ireland to 1660*, 4 vols. (1971–7), vol. 2, pp. 53–85; vol. 3, pp. 125–72 · B. R. White, 'John Pendarves, the Calvinistic Baptists and the Fifth Monarchy', *Baptist Quarterly*, 25 (1973–4), 251–71 [incl. bibliography] · A. Cheare and others, *Sighs for Sion, or, Faith and love* (1656) · *The Clarke Papers*, ed. C. H. Firth, 2, CS, new ser., 54 (1894), 242–6 · IGI [St Petrox, Dartmouth, registers] · G. F. Nuttall, 'Abingdon revisited, 1656–75', *Baptist Quarterly*, 36 (1995–6), 96–103 · W. A. Shaw, *A history of the English church during the civil wars and under the Commonwealth, 1640–1660*, 2 (1900), 561 · Bodl. Oxf., MS Rawl. D. 859, fol. 162 · *The complaining testimony of some … of Sion's children* (1656)

Pendarves, Mary. *See* Delany, Mary (1700–1788).

Pendarves, Thomasine (*bap.* 1618, *d.* in or after 1671). *See under* Pendarves, John (1622/3–1656).

Pender, Sir John (1816–1896), textile merchant and telegraph entrepreneur, was born on 10 September 1816, at Bonhill, Dunbartonshire, Scotland, the second child of James Pender, textile merchant of the Vale of Leven, Dunbartonshire, and his wife, Marion, *née* Mason. Pender had a sister, Margaret, born in 1814. He was educated at the village school, then at Glasgow high school, where he received a gold medal for design. He followed his father's trade, and by the age of twenty-one was the manager of a Glasgow textile firm, before embarking as a textile trader on his own account. He established himself in Glasgow, and then in Manchester, soon developing an extensive trade in fabrics to China, India, and the East, which brought him considerable wealth. In 1840 he married Marion (*d.* 1841), daughter of James Cairns of Glasgow. They had a son, James. In 1851 he married Emma (*d.* 1890), daughter of Henry Denison of Daybrook, Arnold, Nottinghamshire; they had two sons, Henry and John, and two daughters.

When a transatlantic cable was proposed, Pender was among those who invested in the new Atlantic Telegraph Company, formed on 20 October 1856. After various failures, a cable was successfully laid in the summer of 1858 but, although messages were passed, the link soon deteriorated. It failed after a few months, and never carried commercial traffic. Work continued, however, to improve both the cables and the associated telegraph apparatus, and Pender retained his interest in the affair. On 7 April 1864 he brought together the firms of Glass, Elliot, cable manufacturers, and the Gutta Percha Company, makers of insulated cable core, to found the Telegraph Construction and Maintenance Company (TCM), under his chairmanship. Pender and his co-director Daniel Gooch, who was also a director of the Great Western Railway Company and of the company that owned the ship *Great Eastern*, raised funds, and made an offer to the Atlantic Telegraph Company to make and lay a new transatlantic cable, chartering the *Great Eastern* as the only vessel large enough to carry the 2500 nautical miles of cable needed to span the ocean between Ireland and Newfoundland. Laying commenced in the summer of 1865, but was brought to a stop when the cable was lost in deep water. At this critical point, Pender offered his personal guarantee of £250,000, a new cable was manufactured, and in 1866 it was successfully laid. Much of the lost cable was recovered, and a second crossing completed.

In 1868 Gooch took over the chairmanship of TCM, leaving Pender to form the group of companies which were to link England with much of the rest of the world. Pender reorganized the four companies involved in the link to India: the British-Indian Submarine Telegraph Company, the Falmouth, Gibraltar, and Malta Telegraph Company, the Marseilles, Algiers, and Malta Telegraph Company, and the Anglo-Mediterranean Telegraph Company. When the line was completed, a grand celebration was held on 23 June 1870 at Pender's house, 18 Arlington Street, off Piccadilly, in London. The first messages were simply 'How are you?', to which came the reply 'All well'. The astonishing fact that this exchange took less than five minutes, when communication with India had previously taken several months, was truly a cause for celebration. Some 700 guests thronged Pender's house and the pavilion erected in his courtyard, ranging in status from the royalty of England and India through assorted European nobility and diplomats, naval officers, and other important persons. They were entertained by Cromwell Varley and Apps who performed various spectacular electrical and telegraphic demonstrations. Many messages were then passed to India; the *Liverpool Courier* reporting in awe, 'Sitting in the house of a commoner, the Prince of Wales sent a message to the Viceroy in India' (*Souvenir of the Inaugural Fete*, 53). This link with a distant colony was to change for ever the relationship of governor and governed.

Pender went on to form in 1872 the Eastern Telegraph Company, which absorbed numerous smaller companies and played an important role in the defence and prosperity of the United Kingdom. He came to preside over companies capitalized to nearly £15 million and operating over 73,000 nautical miles of cable. Eastern ultimately became the largest submarine telegraph company in the world.

In his later years Pender, as chairman of the Metropolitan Electric Supply Company, the largest undertaking of its kind, concerned himself with the electric lighting of London. He sat in parliament as Liberal member for Totnes in 1862–6, but was unseated on petition. In 1868 he unsuccessfully contested Linlithgowshire, but was returned for the Wick burghs, as a Liberal from 1872 to 1885 and as a Liberal Unionist from 1892 to 1896, when he resigned. He unsuccessfully contested the Wick burghs in 1885, the Stirling burghs and Wick burghs in 1886, and Govan in 1889. On the occasion of his being made a KCMG in 1888 the earl of Derby presided at a grand banquet in his honour, held in the Hotel Metropole, and presented to Lady Pender a portrait of Sir John by Hubert Herkomer RA. In 1892 he was promoted to GCMG. He held many foreign orders, among them the Légion d'honneur and the grand cordon of the Mejidiye. He was also a fellow of the Imperial Institute, of the Royal Society of Edinburgh, of the Royal Geographical Society, and of the Scottish Society of Antiquaries.

At one of his company meetings, Pender confessed to his shareholders that he had few outside interests, apart from yachting; nevertheless he held a very fine collection of porcelain, pictures, and fine art, which after his death took some eight days to pass under the hammer at Christies. A lavish privately published catalogue of 1894 detailed the oils, watercolours, drawings, and sculpture at Arlington Street and at Foots Cray Place, his country seat in Kent. Pender died at Foots Cray on 7 July 1896. He was buried in the parish churchyard. His son James sat as MP for Mid-Northamptonshire from 1895 to 1900, and was created a baronet in 1897; Henry died in 1881; and the youngest son, John Cuthbert Denison-Pender, followed in his father's footsteps, becoming manager, director, or chairman of numerous telegraph and cable companies. The younger daughter, Marion Denison, married Sir George William des Voeux, a colonial governor.

ANITA McCONNELL

Sources *The Electrician* (10 July 1896), 334–5; (17 July 1896), 379–80; (7 Aug 1896), 469 · *ILN* (21 Feb 1863), 205 · *ILN* (5 May 1888), 474 · *ILN* (11 July 1896), 38 · *Art Journal*, new ser., 12 (1892), 161–8 · *Souvenir of the inaugural fete held at the house of Sir John Pender … June 23 1870* (1870) · W. Agnew, ed., *Pictures, drawings and sculptures forming the collection of Sir John Pender* (1894) · K. R. Haigh, *Cableships and submarine cables* (1968) · b. cert. · m. cert. · d. cert. · *CGPLA Eng. & Wales* (1896)

Archives North Highland Archive, corresp. | Bodl. Oxf., corresp. with Lord Kimberley · North East Lincolnshire Archives, letters to John Wintringham

Likenesses H. von Herkomer, portrait, *c*.1888; in possession of Sir James Pender in 1901 · H. Adlard, stipple, NPG · H. J. Brooks, group portrait, oils (*Private view of the Old Masters Exhibition, Royal Academy, 1888*), NPG · PET, chromolithograph caricature, NPG; repro. in *Monetary Gazette and Mining News* (21 March 1877) · J. Rosey, stipple, NPG · J. J. Tissot, caricature, watercolour study, NPG; repro. in *VF* (28 Oct 1871) · wood-engraving, NPG; repro. in *ILN* (5 May 1888) · wood-engraving, NPG; repro. in *ILN* (21 Feb 1863)

Wealth at death £337,180: probate, 28 July 1896, *CGPLA Eng. & Wales*

Penderel, George (*d*. in or before **1684**). *See under* Penderel, Richard (*d*. 1672).

Penderel, Humphrey (*d*. **1687/8**). *See under* Penderel, Richard (*d*. 1672).

Penderel, John (*d*. *c*.**1683**). *See under* Penderel, Richard (*d*. 1672).

Penderel, Richard (*d*. **1672**), royalist sympathizer, was the third son of William Penderel (*d*. in or before 1651) and his wife, Jane (*d*. after 1662), of Hobbal Grange in Tong, Shropshire, where Richard was born. The family were Catholic and rented a 'little farm' (Broadley, 118) from another Catholic, Basil Fitzherbert of nearby Boscobel House. Richard was described by Thomas Blount as 'of honest parentage, but mean degree' (Blount, 40), while Father John Huddleston referred to him as a humble woodcutter and 'labouring' man (Matthews, 113). In an interview with Charles II in early June 1660 Richard allegedly called himself a 'raw and undisciplined rustic' (F. Grose, *Antiquarian Repertory*, 1780, 2.59). But, although illiterate, he was in fact of yeoman status, as appears by a letter of attorney which he authorized on 24 June 1663. By the time of Charles II's escape after the battle of Worcester in 1651 he had succeeded his father to the life tenancy of the Hobbal Grange property and it was from there that he was summoned to attend the king when the latter arrived at nearby White Ladies Priory in the small hours of 4 September 1651. The hapless monarch was placed under his care and protection. Penderel's first task was to disguise the king as 'William Jones', 'a la mode the woodman' (Fea, *Flight*, 1897, 204); this he did by cutting the king's hair 'with a pair of shears' and dressing him in a suit of his own clothes comprising 'a doe-skin leather doublet' and a pair of breeches made of 'green course cloth' (Matthews, 88). Fortunately for the king, Richard was a tall man like himself and thus his modest attire was a perfect fit. Richard next hid the king in an adjacent wood called Spring coppice and attended to his physical comforts as best he could, in the pouring rain, for the rest of the day, while maintaining a vigilant watch for the enemy. In the evening Penderel took the king to the family farm where his wife, Mary (*d.* in or after 1689), prepared supper while Charles held the couple's daughter, Nan, on his knee. From here the king and Penderel set out on foot for Wales. They had an unpleasant encounter at Evelith Mill when the angry occupant accosted them and gave chase as they fled down a muddy country lane, Charles being forced to listen to 'the rusling of Penderel's leathern Breeches' (Broadley, 122) to retain his sense of direction. By dawn the two men had reached Madeley and the king was not 'a little troubled' when Richard 'very indiscreetly and without any leave' aroused the household of Francis Wolfe and sought his protection (Matthews, 46). The king need not have feared, since Penderel knew Wolfe to be 'an honest man' (ibid., 44) from his previous acquaintance with him as a fellow Catholic. After hiding with the king in Wolfe's barn all next day, and discovering that the passage over the River Severn was blocked by Cromwell's troops, Penderel and his royal companion returned to Hobbal Grange early in the morning of Saturday 5 September, Charles at one point helping him over a stream because he could not swim. Charles immediately went on to Boscobel and the following Sunday Penderel served as one of Charles's bodyguard during the famous nocturnal journey from Boscobel House to Moseley Hall, near Wolverhampton.

Though much threatened by 'a peevish neighbour' (Blount, 42), who suspected his complicity in Charles's getaway, Penderel escaped detection until the Restoration, when he came into his own. 'Friend Richard' was warmly welcomed at court in June 1660 when the king urged all about him to 'respect this good man for my sake' (F. Grose, *Antiquarian Repertory*, 2.59). On 12 April 1662 Charles awarded Penderel £200 'to enable him to live in the quality of a farmer' (*CSP dom.*, 1661–2, 338), as well as subsequently settling upon him and his heirs forever an annual pension of £100. Penderel continued to live at Hobbal Grange but made regular visits to London to see the king and it was there, on 7 February 1672, while staying in the house of Henry Arundel in the Great Turnstile in

Lincoln's Inn Fields that he died of a fever. In his will, dated the same day, he proudly refers to himself as a 'gentleman' and was now clearly a man of substance, bequeathing his eldest son, Thomas, a newly built house at Statherton in Shropshire, an annuity to another son, Simon, and a tenement in Russell Street, Walsall, to a third, William. He was buried on 11 February in the churchyard of St Giles-in-the-Fields where his grave was marked by a special tomb-chest, reputedly commissioned by the king, which praised him as 'Unparaled Penderel' (*N&Q*, 1st ser., 11, 1855, 410). A portrait by Zoust depicts him as stockily built, with chubby cheeks, prominent nose, and long, flowing hair. He looks every inch 'an honest man' (Broadley, 60), and his likeness more than explains why his contemporaries dubbed him Trusty Dick (Matthews, 114).

Richard Penderel's four brothers were also instrumental in Charles II's escape. The eldest brother, **William Penderel** (*c.*1609–1700), was born at Hobbal Grange and was living with his wife, Joan (*d.* 1669), a sister of William Cope, husbandman of Tong, at Chillington in the neighbouring parish of Brewood, in 1641 when they were both indicted for recusancy. He was then described as a yeoman. By 1651 he was the caretaker of Boscobel House and on 29 August 1651 offered sanctuary to the royalist earl of Derby after his disastrous defeat at Wigan in Lancashire. Six days later he met the fugitive king in the inner parlour of White Ladies Priory and 'promised to do his utmost' (Broadley, 118) to assist him, a pledge he amply fulfilled on 6 and 7 September.

During the first day of the king's stay at Boscobel William and his wife furnished the wood ladder to enable Charles to climb into the boughs of the royal oak as well as providing two pillows for him to rest on, to say nothing of their diversionary tactic of 'peaking up and down' (Matthews, 92) in the adjoining wood to deflect the attention of the parliamentary cavalry, who were then combing the entire area. That evening and the following day the couple were equally solicitous about the king's welfare, plying him with food as well as ministering to his blistered feet and bleeding nose, hospitality which put Charles in a 'good humour' and prompted him to address William's spouse as 'My Dame Joan' (Blount, 39). After the king's departure husband and wife suffered considerable molestation, William being twice interrogated at Shrewsbury while Joan was 'much affrighted' (ibid., 39) by the frequent searches of Boscobel House.

Both William and his wife lived to see the Restoration. Joan died in 1669 and was interred in the graveyard of White Ladies Priory, while William continued to live at Boscobel. He was an extremely enterprising man, turning Boscobel into a tourist attraction and converting part of the house into an inn named, appropriately enough, the Royal Oak. He was also a recipient of the royal bounty, having a regular pension of £100 a year and other gifts of money. In his later years he was persecuted for his Catholicism, particularly during the Popish Plot, though he did receive the royal protection in January 1679. Like his brother Richard, William was a tall man; an engraving of him at the age of eighty-four suggests that he had an elongated face with a moustache and goatee beard. He died at Boscobel in August 1700.

According to Father Huddleston, the second eldest brother, **John Penderel** (*d. c.*1683), 'tooke the most pains of all the brothers' (Matthews, 113). During the civil war he fought for Charles I as a common soldier and probably served under Colonel William Careless in the royalist garrison at Tong Castle in his native parish. When Charles II took refuge at White Ladies on 4 September he was then living in the house, 'a kinde of woodward there' (ibid.). He was initially delegated the task of conveying the king's companion, Henry, Lord Wilmot, towards London; and after many narrow escapes finally left him with Thomas Whitgreave of Moseley Hall. He then trudged on foot back and forth between Moseley and White Ladies bearing messages from Wilmot to the king, who used him on 6 September to inform Squire Whitgreave of his intention to seek protection at Moseley. Along with his other four brothers, all armed, he escorted Charles at dead of night from Boscobel to his new sanctuary, and remained with him for the next few days serving as a royal messenger. At the Restoration he received an annuity of £100 and a number of other payments from the crown in recognition of his services. By the late 1660s he had migrated to Albrighton in Shropshire following his marriage to Jane Southall of Beamish Hall in that parish. At this time his social rank is given as that of a husbandman, suggesting that he did not prosper as well as the other Penderel brothers from the king's largesse, and significantly he left debts in excess of £100 at his death about 1683.

Humphrey Penderel (*d.* 1687/8), the fourth brother, was a miller at the time of the king's flight, running the mill next to White Ladies Priory. During Charles's concealment in Spring coppice on 4 September he acted as a scout and that evening at Hobbal Grange offered to reconnoitre in advance the king's route to Madeley, but his services were declined. On 6 September, while the king was hiding in the royal oak, he was sent to Shifnal to gather intelligence about the enemy troop movements, and there he was closely interrogated by a Cromwellian colonel who threatened him with dire punishment if he withheld information and promised a £1000 reward should he give it. But Humphrey 'pleaded ignorance and was dismissed' (Blount, 29). Unfortunately, on his return to Boscobel he rather tactlessly informed Charles of these proceedings, causing him some anxiety, and it took all of Humphrey's 'urgent asseverations' (ibid.) to set the king's mind at rest. It was during the famous night march from Boscobel to Moseley, however, that Humphrey Penderel made his most notable contribution to the royal escape. He provided his old mill horse for Charles to ride on, prompting the king to quip 'It was the heaviest dull jade' he had ever encountered, to which Humphrey supposedly replied 'Can you blame the horse … when he hath the weight of three kingdomes upon his back?' (Broadley, 67). This witty riposte is often regarded as apocryphal, but Penderel himself confirmed that he made it in a petition to Charles II in January 1673.

At the Restoration Penderel was rewarded with a pension, though his annuity of £66 13s. 4d. was less than the £100 assigned to his brothers. In May 1668 he was living at Little Bloxwich in Staffordshire and had now become a yeoman. He and his wife, Eleanor, had at least four children, which proved such a 'great charge' (*CSP dom.*, 1672–3, 496–7) that he was obliged to appeal to the king for a gift of £200 to satisfy his creditors. Charles not only furnished the money but secured Humphrey's son Edmund the position of footman to his wife, Queen Catherine. Humphrey died in 1687 or 1688 with a reputation for being a man of 'solid honesty' and 'resolved loyalty' (Broadley, 63).

George Penderel (*d.* in or before 1684) was the youngest of the five brothers. He too fought for Charles I in the first civil war and in 1651 was serving as a domestic in the White Ladies' household. He was the first man to welcome Charles at White Ladies on 4 September and spent most of that day in reconnaissance around Tong and Spring coppice to ensure that the king's pursuers remained at bay. He also shared a meal with the king and accompanied him to Hobbal Grange. His final assistance to the royal refugee was to guard him during the evening ride to Moseley. After the Restoration George settled at Hednesford in Staffordshire and thanks to royal favour rose in status, being described as a yeoman in May 1668 and a gentleman in February 1671. Such was his improved standing that he was appointed one of the three overseers of the poor in the parish of Cannock in 1670. During the Popish Plot hysteria he was regularly indicted for recusancy and had to be protected by the king, who exempted him from prosecution in January 1679. He married and had several children, and had died by June 1684. To the very end the king retained 'a gracious sense' (*CSP dom.*, 1684–5, 77) of his indebtedness to George and the rest of 'the five loyall and faithfull brothers' (Broadley, 101).   JOHN SUTTON

Sources T. Blount, *Boscobel, part 1* (1660), 18–19, 22–3, 25–7, 32, 40 · PRO, SP 29/50/38 · A. Fea, *The flight of the king* (1897); 2nd edn (1908), 333 · A. Fea, *After Worcester fight* (1904) · A. M. Broadley, *The royal miracle* (1912) · W. Matthews, ed., *Charles II's escape from Worcester* (1967) · J. Hughes, ed., *The Boscobel tracts*, 2nd edn (1857), 91–3, 369 · R. Ollard, *The escape of Charles II after the battle of Worcester* (1986), 26–8, 35–7 · 'Penderell's tomb in St Giles's in the Fields', *N&Q*, 11 (1855), 410 · J. T. Page, 'The Pendrell brothers', *N&Q*, 8th ser., 1 (1892), 107–8 · J. Penderel-Brodhurst, 'The Penderel brothers', *N&Q*, 8th ser., 1 (1892), 232 · will, PRO, PROB 11/338, sig. J20 [Richard Penderel] · will, PRO, PROB 11/395, sig. 53 [Mary Penderel]

Likenesses Zourt, oils, after 1660, NPG · I. Fuller, oils, *c.*1660–1670 (*Charles II at Whiteladies*), NPG · I. Fuller, oils, *c.*1660–1670 (*Charles II on Humphrey Penderel's mill horse*), NPG · R. Houston, mezzotint (after G. Soest), BM, NPG · print, repro. in A. Fea, *Flight* (1897), 217

Wealth at death see will, PRO, PROB 11/338, sig. J20

Penderel, William (*c.*1609–1700). *See under* Penderel, Richard (*d.* 1672).

Penderyn, Dic. *See* Lewis, Richard (1807/8–1831).

Pendle witches [Lancashire witches] (*act.* 1612) represented one of the larger groups of witches prosecuted in early modern England and one of the most famous. The mass of confessions and testimonies elicited before and during the trials at Lancaster in 1612 recalled events of up to eighteen years before and involved tensions between mothers and children, siblings, neighbours, and landlords and tenants.

At least nineteen alleged witches were charged at Lancaster assizes on 17 August 1612. Of these at least ten came from the Forest of Pendle and its adjacent townships, while one had already died in prison and a second had been hanged at York two or three weeks earlier. At the centre of the Pendle accusations were two elderly women and their families. **Elizabeth Sowthernes** [*alias* Demdike; *known as* Old Demdike] (*c.*1532–1612) was a widow, blind and poor, aged about eighty and living in Malkin Tower in the Forest of Pendle. She was accused of having been a witch for fifty years and bringing up her children and grandchildren in witchcraft—notably her daughter **Elizabeth Device** (*b.* before 1572, *d.* 1612), aged over forty, and Elizabeth's children **Alizon Device** (*d.* 1612), **James Device** (*d.* 1612), and **Jennet Device** (*b.* 1602/3), the last a witness rather than one of the accused. The other principal figure, **Anne Whittle** [*alias* Chattox] (*c.*1532–1612), allegedly both associate and enemy of Sowthernes, was accused with her daughter **Anne Redfearn** (*d.* 1612). Sowthernes never faced trial, having died in gaol between her commitment to prison on 2 April and the opening of the assizes. Her daughter Elizabeth Device, along with her children Alizon and James Device, and Anne Whittle and Anne Redfearn, were all hanged at Lancaster on 20 August. So also were a group who had been drawn into the trials through their reported presence at a feast at Malkin Tower on Good Friday 1612: **Alice Nutter** (*d.* 1612) of Pendle, Katherine Hewytte, alias Mould-Heels (*d.* 1612), wife of John Hewytte of Colne, John Bulcocke (*d.* 1612), and his mother, Jane Bulcocke (*d.* 1612), wife of Christopher Bulcocke, both of the Moss End near Newchurch in Pendle.

The relationship of two other witches condemned to the Pendle group is uncertain: they may have been victims of the local fears raised by news of Pendle rather than accused for any association with the group. Certainly there is no established connection with Isabel Robey (*d.* 1612) of Windle, near St Helens, who was also hanged. Margaret Pearson of Padiham was found guilty and punished by a year in prison and the pillory: this was her first conviction (though her third trial) and her victim had been an animal rather than a person. Anne Whittle testified against her but it is unclear whether she knew her before their shared confinement in Lancaster Castle. **Jennet Preston** [*née* Balderston] (*d.* 1612) of Gisburn in Craven, Yorkshire, had already been convicted at the York assizes of 27 July for the murder by witchcraft of Thomas Lister the elder and hanged two days later; she had allegedly been present at the Malkin Tower feast soliciting help in killing Lister's son Thomas. She continued to protest her innocence on the gallows, and her husband of twenty-five years, William (*bap.* 1564?), and her kin claimed that she was the victim of a malicious prosecution. She had been acquitted at the previous York assizes of killing a baby by witchcraft. Five of the accused at Lancaster—Elizabeth Astley, John Ramsden, Alice Gray of

Colne, Isabel Sidegraves, and Lawrence Hay—were found not guilty, although the judges clearly regarded at least some of them as guilty of witchcraft. The precise charges against them are not known, although Alice Gray had certainly been reported as present at the Good Friday feast. At the same assizes three other women were tried for witchcraft: Jennet Bierley, Ellen Bierley, and Jane Southworth, the so-called witches of Samlesbury. Their case was presented in the published account of the trials, *The Wonderfull Discoverie of Witches in the Countie of Lancaster* (1613), as a counterpoint to the Pendle witches. The Samlesbury women seem to have been the victims of false accusations instigated by Jesuit malice.

The Wonderfull Discoverie forms the main record of the trial. It was written by the man who had served as clerk of the court, **Thomas Potts** (*fl.* 1610–1614). He was brought up in the household of Sir Thomas Knyvett, later Baron Knyvett of Escrick. He served as clerk of the peace for the East Riding about 1610–11, and served as associate clerk on the northern assize circuit in the summer of 1612 (when the Pendle witches were tried) and in the summer of 1614. At the time he was writing the *Discoverie* he was in lodging in Chancery Lane, London. He published it at the instigation of the two assize judges, Sir Edward *Bromley and Sir James *Altham; the former revised and corrected the text.

The immediate events which led to the trials began on 18 March 1612, when Alizon Device asked a pedlar to sell her some pins and was refused. He accused her of bewitching him so that he was paralysed on one side. At the end of March the JP Roger Nowell questioned Alizon and her family on suspicion of witchcraft, and subsequently sent her for trial at the Lancaster assizes with her mother, her grandmother Elizabeth Sowthernes, alias Demdike, and Anne Whittle, alias Chattox, and Whittle's daughter Anne Redfearn. While they were there their children and friends held the meeting at Malkin Tower on Good Friday, where they plotted to release the prisoners, blow up the castle, and kill the gaoler. The accompanying feast of beef, bacon, and stolen roast mutton, at which (according to Jennet Device) only two men were present, was readily interpreted as a witches' sabbat. The plot prompted further interrogations (and the flight of a number of people to evade arrest), and at the end of April a series of examinations was obtained implicating the main members of the Device and Whittle families and several others, and telling of meetings with the devil, relations with familiars, charms that combined vernacular prayer and spells, and witchcraft worked on enemies.

Elizabeth Sowthernes confessed to having made a pact with the devil twenty years before, on her way home from begging, by which she promised him her soul in exchange for anything she wanted. After this she was visited regularly by a spirit named Tibb, who sucked her blood. With the aid of clay images she had used witchcraft to harm her enemies, including a local man who had refused to let her on his land. Sowthernes's widowed daughter Elizabeth Device was apparently marked out as a witch by having one eye lower than the other with a strange squint. She confessed to having a spirit named Ball, in the shape of a brown dog, which she had baptized. She was indicted for killing three men by witchcraft, one of whom, Henry Mitton, had allegedly refused her a penny. Elizabeth Device's son James Device, a labourer, confessed that although he had first resisted the persuasions of a hare-shaped spirit sent to him by his grandmother, he gave in when a spirit in the form of a dog showed him a way to revenge himself on a woman with whom he had fallen out. He bewitched her to death using a clay image and had the spirit, which he called Dandy, kill another man who refused him the gift of an old shirt. James's unmarried sister Alizon Device, with whom the trials had begun, confessed that she had been persuaded by her grandmother to allow a 'devil or familiar' in the shape of a black dog to come and suck on her breast, and that she had been present at many of her grandmother's acts of malice; her brother accused her of bewitching a child. Asked in court whether she could restore the pedlar she had stricken to health, she answered that only her grandmother, Elizabeth Sowthernes, could; but by then Sowthernes had died in prison. Elizabeth Sowthernes's son and daughter-in-law, Christopher and Elizabeth Howgate, were also accused of involvement in the Malkin Tower meeting. The key witness in these allegations was Elizabeth Device's nine-year-old daughter Jennet Device, who testified against her siblings, mother, and grandmother with 'modesty, government and understanding'; she claimed to have learned charms from her grandmother and to have seen the others plotting with their spirits (*Potts's Discovery of Witches*, sig. I). Confronted with her daughter's testimony her mother cursed and threatened her, but made a full confession.

The other principal accused, Anne Whittle, alias Chattox, was said to be an old enemy of Elizabeth Sowthernes. According to Alizon Device, about eleven years earlier Whittle had stolen clothes and oatmeal from them, and her daughter was seen wearing the clothes. She was also said to have threatened Alizon's father, Elizabeth Device's husband, into paying her a yearly dole of meal as protection from her witchcraft; when he failed to pay it he died. Whittle, too, was an elderly widow, living by carding wool and begging. Potts's description of her is particularly evocative of the contemporary misogyny that fuelled stereotypes of witches: 'a very old withered spent and decreped creature … Her lippes ever chattering and walking: but no man knew what' (*Potts's Discovery of Witches*, sig. D2). Anne Whittle said that she had been introduced to the devil about fourteen years earlier by Elizabeth Sowthernes. She allowed him to suck on her ribs and participated in a spirits' banquet, in which, as was customary, 'although they did eate, they were never the fuller, nor better for the same' (*Potts's Discovery of Witches*, sig. B4v). Her familiar appeared to her as 'Fancie'. He helped her drive cows mad and kill them but, she said, he had taken away most of her sight and he sometimes harassed and assaulted her. Like the Devices, Anne Whittle knew charms and spells, and was accused of bewitching adults and children to death, using clay images; firm evidence

was furnished by James Device, who dug up from his grandmother's house a set of teeth that Whittle had taken from skulls at a funeral twelve years earlier, and shared with Elizabeth Sowthernes.

Also central to the trials were the Nutter family, minor gentry in Pendle. Robert Nutter the elder owned the land the Whittles lived on. His son Christopher was said to have died of witchcraft about eighteen years before the trial. His grandson Robert was also said to have been bewitched to death about the same time: Anne Whittle confessed that she had been asked to kill him by his grandmother, so that two female cousins could inherit the land; she also said that his death was revenge for his threat to stop her daughter Anne Redfearn living on his property because Redfearn had refused his sexual propositions. A withered clay image of Anne Nutter was among the evidence produced by James Device from his grandmother's house. Another member of the Nutter family, Alice, was herself convicted of witchcraft on the grounds of conspiring with the Devices. While the Devices and Whittles were represented as bearing out contemporary beliefs that witches were most likely to be either poor and therefore easily tempted by the devil, or malicious and vengeful, Alice Nutter was elderly but married, the wife of Richard Nutter, wealthy and of good reputation locally, and she declared her innocence throughout. Nevertheless the evidence of Jennet Device and her siblings was enough to convict her of joining with Elizabeth Device in killing Henry Mitton for refusing Elizabeth a penny, and of conspiring with the rest at the Malkin Tower.

In 1634 the Device and Nutter families appeared again in a fresh series of trials which followed the fabrications of Edmund *Robinson. Jennet Device was found to have two witches' marks and was convicted of killing Isabel Nutter by witchcraft. She was not executed but, despite the discrediting of Robinson's story, she still lay a prisoner in Lancaster Castle in August 1636. Robinson was not born until ten years after the original Pendle trials, but in his account of a witches' feast drew on local memory of the Malkin Tower meeting. Among those he named as being present were Jennet's uncle, Christopher Howgate (Elizabeth Sowthernes's son) and his wife, Elizabeth, and Jennet Hargraves, all three of whom had been accused of attending the Malkin Tower feast.

Robinson's accusations formed the basis for Thomas Heywood's and Richard Brome's *The Late Lancashire Witches* (1634), which also included other echoes of the 1612 case, as did Thomas Shadwell's *The Lancashire Witches* (1681), which drew on both the 1612 and 1634 trials. The modern notoriety of the 1612 trials dates back to the 1840s, when the Manchester antiquary James *Crossley published his edition of Potts's book, and then encouraged his friend William Harrison Ainsworth to write his best-selling historical romance *The Lancashire Witches* (1848) around the case, the first of several fictional accounts of the events of 1612.

LAURA GOWING

Sources *Potts's discovery of witches in the countie of Lancaster*, ed. J. Crossley, Chetham Society, 6 (1844) · E. Peel and P. Southern, *The Lancashire witches* (1989) · collections relating to witchcraft and magic from sixteenth- and seventeenth-century manuscripts, BL, Add. MS 36674 · M. Gibson, ed., *Early modern witches: witchcraft cases in contemporary writing* (2000) · J. Lumby, *The Lancashire witch-craze: Jennet Preston and the Lancashire witches, 1612* (1995) · J. T. Swain, 'The Lancashire witch trials of 1612 and 1634', *Northern History*, 30 (1994), 64–85 · *CSP dom.*, 1634–5 · C. H. L. Ewen, *Witchcraft and demonianism* (1933) · J. S. Cockburn, *A history of English assizes, 1558–1714* (1972)

Pendlebury, Henry (1626–1695), clergyman and ejected minister, was born at Jowkin, Bury parish, Lancashire, on 6 May 1626. His father, Henry Pendlebury, a member of a family long established in West Houghton, Deane parish, Lancashire, may have been the vicar of Deane recorded as contributing towards a collection for the recovery of the palatinate in 1622, and may be the Henry Pendlebury who was interred in Bury in 1666. The name of his mother is uncertain, but she may be one of two wives of Henry Pendlebury recorded as buried in the parish: an unnamed woman in 1639 or Margaret in 1654. From Bury grammar school the younger Henry passed to Christ's College, Cambridge, where he was admitted sizar on 1 May 1645, graduating BA on 26 April 1648.

Pendlebury returned to Bury and came under the authority of the Bury presbyterian classis. In December 1648 he was preaching at Ashworth chapel, Middleton parish, to the east of Bury, but by 1650 the Commonwealth church survey noted that he was 'lately minister at Ashworth, but hath ceased to officiate for want of maintenance' (Fishwick, *Lancashire and Cheshire Church Surveys*, 1.26). For an individual who was to become one of the patriarchs of Lancashire dissent, his path to ordination was not smooth. On 11 July 1650 he appeared before the Bury classis to present his thesis and be examined; it was happy to proceed with his ordination upon the production of his university accreditation, a certificate of his having led an honest life at his last charge, and evidence that he had taken the covenant. He duly produced these at the meeting on 15 August, but by then he had fallen under the censure of the classis: 'in this interime Mr. Livesey had consumated a marriage betwixt the said Mr. Pendlebury and one Sarah Smith clandestinely irregularly' (Shaw, *Minutes of the Bury Presbyterian Classis*, 1.115). The irregularity seems to have lain in the lack of consent of either set of parents and that James Livesey was not at that point ordained. The two young men managed to placate the classis: parental consent was obtained and Pendlebury and Livesey were both ordained at Turton chapel, Bolton parish, on 23 October 1650.

If the classis minutes are literally true, then Pendlebury married Sarah Smith (d. 1714) in July or August 1650. But some confusion is caused by the record in Bury parish register of the marriage of a Henry Pendlebury to Sara Woolsenholm on 26 April 1648, who may or may not be the present subject (the marriage took place on the day recorded for his graduation from Cambridge). Possibly Sarah Smith was a second wife, or possibly Woolsenholm was an alias and the classis was misled as to when the marriage had actually taken place.

Pendlebury became minister of Horwich chapel in the parish of Deane. The classis minutes record repeated attempts to get him to proceed with the election of elders and have them approved by the classis. He had apparently not done so by the time he appeared before the classis on 9 February 1652 to explain why he had left the Horwich congregation and moved to Holcombe Chapel in Tottington township in the parish of Bury the preceding October. The remote townships served by Holcombe Chapel were to be made into a new parish in January 1659, but this augmentation was forced into abeyance by the Restoration. Pendlebury was removed from the chapel by sequestration. Though the Five Mile Act forced him for a while to live in Bolton with the father of the future presbyterian minister William Tong, he spent the rest of his life ministering to nonconformist communities in and around Bury and the Irwell valley. The Restoration and the Clarendon code provided only intermittent interruptions to this ministry. His biographer John Chorlton noted how:

> Before his exclusion from his Work in public, besides his constant Preaching Lord's-Day at Holcombe among his people, he preached much to other Congregations, both far and near, in the country, which had their monthly exercises; and after he was silenced, he continued as laborious in preaching as before. (Chorlton, xxxix)

During the Restoration period the chapelries of Manchester deanery were frequently host to nonconformist ministers, and in March 1670 Pendlebury was reported to the privy council for disturbing the reading of the service at Gorton chapel and proceeding to preach to the congregation. Under the declaration of indulgence he was licensed as a presbyterian preacher (when he is described as of Tottington) and he took out a licence for the court house at Holcombe as a meeting-house. Some time after 1672 a residence was built for him a mile or two away, at Bass House, Walmersley, also in Bury parish. After the Toleration Act Bass House was certified as a meeting-house, and at the quarter sessions held at Manchester in July 1691 Edmund Bury registered 'Some new building erected situate in Walmsley adjoining to Mr. Pendlebury's house rec. for a meeting pl. for an Assbly of Prot. Diss.' (Lancs. RO, QDV4) It is clear from Pendlebury's will of 1695, which describes this meeting-house as lately erected, that it was in the courtyard adjoining the house. He preached to the dissenting congregations at Rochdale and Holcombe on alternate Sundays, leaving money in his will to the poor of Rochdale and the poor of his congregation at Walmersley. Tottington, Holcombe, and Walmersley all lay within a few miles of each other on either side of the Irwell: though the exact location of Pendlebury's meetings changed over time, the congregation is likely to have been much the same.

The impression given of Pendlebury's ministry is of immense moral authority. He ventured into print in the controversies over popery in the 1680s (in the only work of his published in his lifetime, *A Plain Representation of Transubstantiation* in 1687), yet the sketch left of him by John Chorlton is of a man largely indifferent to politics but alive to the numinous and 'the sense of unseen things' (Chorlton, xliii). 'A man of great learning & strict godliness', as Matthew Henry described him, his other works were published posthumously (Chetham's Library, Manchester, Raines MSS, 1.291): sermons and other practical works, as well as an attack on the mass first published as late as 1768. Pendlebury was a spiritual father to many in the protestant dissenting ministry and, despite inducements to more lucrative ministries, he remained to minister in the semi-remote moorland townships of his youth. He avoided being dragged into the controversy around the alleged possession of the 'Surey Demoniack' Richard Dugdale and lived to participate in the founding of the Lancashire Provincial Assembly. This assembly of presbyterian and Independent ministers was established between 1691 and 1693; Pendlebury attended the general meeting in Manchester on 4 September 1694.

Pendlebury died at Bass House on 18 June 1695 and was buried two days later in Bury churchyard; his funeral sermon was preached at Holcombe Chapel by Robert Seddon. His remains were removed to a common receptacle when the new parish church was built in 1865. His widow, Sarah, died on 6 February 1714 and was also buried in Bury churchyard. Their marriage left no children: William Pendlebury, the protestant dissenting minister of Kendal (1701–6) and Leeds (1706–29), was a kinsman of Henry but not his son. He was the son of James and Ann Pendlebury of Turton, Bolton parish.   JONATHAN H. WESTAWAY

Sources J. Chorlton, 'A short account of the life of the author', in H. Pendlebury, *Invisible realities: the real Christian's greatest concernment, in several sermons on 2 Cor. Iv. 18* (1696) · W. A. Shaw, ed., *Minutes of the Bury presbyterian classis, 1647–1657*, 2 vols., Chetham Society, new ser., 36, 41 (1896–8) · E. Calamy, ed., *An abridgement of Mr. Baxter's history of his life and times, with an account of the ministers, &c., who were ejected after the Restauration of King Charles II*, 2nd edn, 2 vols. (1713), vol. 2, p. 400 · E. Calamy, *A continuation of the account of the ministers ... who were ejected and silenced after the Restoration in 1660*, 2 vols. (1727), vol. 2, pp. 562–3 · *Calamy rev.*, 386 · Chetham's Library, Manchester, Raines MSS, vol. 16 [abstract of Henry Pendlebury's will of 24 May 1695] · B. Nightingale, *Lancashire nonconformity*, 6 vols. [1890–93], vol. 1, pp. 214, 281; vol. 3, pp. 99, 154–8, 176, 241, 287; vol. 5, pp. 155–6 · F. Nicholson and E. Axon, *The older nonconformity in Kendal* (1915), 238–48 · *The registers of the parish church of Bury in the county of Lancaster: christenings, burials and weddings*, 2: *1617–1646*, ed. W. J. Lowenberg and H. Brierley, Lancashire Parish Register Society, 10 (1901), 322 · *The registers of the parish church of Bury in the county of Lancaster: christenings, burials and weddings*, 3: *1647–1698*, ed. A. Sparke, Lancashire Parish Register Society, 24 (1905), 129, 155, 232, 243 · register of dissenting meeting houses, 1689, Lancs. RO, LCRO MS QDV4 · G. T. O. Bridgeman, 'Contributions from the clergy of the diocese of Chester, 1622, towards the recovery of the palatinate', *Miscellanies, relating to Lancashire and Cheshire*, Lancashire and Cheshire RS, 12 (1885), 66, 80 · *DNB* · A. Gordon, ed., *Freedom after ejection: a review (1690–1692) of presbyterian and congregational nonconformity in England and Wales* (1917) · J. P. Earwaker, ed., *Local gleanings relating to Lancashire and Cheshire*, 2 vols. (1875–8), vol. 2, pp. 632, 740 · H. Fishwick, *The history of the parish of Rochdale in the county of Lancaster* (1889), 252 · H. Fishwick, ed., *Lancashire and Cheshire church surveys, 1649–1655*, Lancashire and Cheshire RS, 1 (1879), 26, 37 · H. Pendlebury, *Sermons by Henry Pendlebury of Rochdale*, 2nd edn (1711) [preface and dedication by John Chorlton and James Cunningham] · W. A. Shaw, ed., 'Minutes of the United Brethren, 1693–1700', *Minutes of the Manchester presbyterian classis*, 3, Chetham Society, new ser., 24 (1891), 349–65 · J. Westaway, 'Scottish influences upon the reformed churches in north west England, c.1689–1829: a study of the ministry within the congregational and presbyterian churches in Lancashire,

Cumberland and Westmorland', PhD diss., University of Lancaster, 1997
Archives Lancs. RO, register of dissenting meeting houses, MS QDV4
Wealth at death £87: will, Chetham's Library, Manchester, Raines MSS · £269 17s. 2(?)d.: inventory, *Calamy rev.*

Pendlebury, James (*d.* 1731), army officer and master gunner, first appears in the employment of the Ordnance office in 1695. It is probable that he served during the remainder of King William's war in Flanders until the peace of Ryswick in 1697, for he was appointed comptroller (at a salary of £45 per annum) of the first train of artillery in time of peace, established in May 1698. This regimental train was composed mainly of those who had served William faithfully in the Nine Years' War. The 'peace train' was disbanded in January 1699, to be replaced by a streamlined train (royal warrant, 14 February 1699), in which Pendlebury appears as a captain of fireworkers and petardiers (at a salary of £40) in January 1700.

In 1702 Pendlebury was made comptroller and lieutenant-colonel of the artillery train sent to the Netherlands, and he served continuously throughout Marlborough's campaigns, including Blenheim in 1704, for which he received a bounty of £60. He was appointed chief fire master (at a salary of £150) by the Board of Ordnance in May 1706 and was promoted 2nd colonel of artillery in the Netherlands in March 1708. He retained this rank and that of comptroller during the campaigns of 1709–11. His appointments as deputy governor of the Tower of London in June 1709 and master gunner of Great Britain in November 1710 (at a salary of £190) were assisted by the personal recommendation of the duke of Marlborough, in recognition of his long service with the train. He was placed on half pay in 1715.

Pendlebury's office as master gunner of Great Britain was made redundant by the creation of a new regimental establishment of four companies of gunners in 1716 (the origins of the Royal Regiment of Artillery). He continued to receive quarterly pay of £47 10s. until March 1731. Two final payments were made to his wife, Penelope Pendlebury; after 31 December 1731 all payments ceased. The presumption is that he was ill towards the end of his life and died in the second half of 1731: probate of his will was granted to his widow and executrix on 27 September 1731. Pendlebury was the last officer to bear the title master gunner of Great Britain and England, a line unbroken from 1485.   JONATHAN SPAIN

Sources C. Dalton, ed., *English army lists and commission registers, 1661–1714*, 6 vols. (1892–1904) · J. Kane, *List of officers of the royal regiment of artillery from the year 1716 to the year 1899*, rev. W. H. Askwith, 4th edn (1900), 171 · O. F. G. Hogg, *The Royal Arsenal: its background, origin, and subsequent history*, 2 vols. (1963) · O. F. G. Hogg, *English artillery, 1326–1716* (1963) · H. C. Tomlinson, *Guns and government: the ordnance office under the later Stuarts*, Royal Historical Society Studies in History, 15 (1979) · F. Duncan, ed., *History of the royal regiment of artillery*, 2 vols. (1872–3) · will, PRO, PROB 11/648
Archives BL, Blenheim MSS
Wealth at death all but £6 to wife: will, PRO, PROB 11/648

Pendleton, Edmund (1721–1803), revolutionary politician and judge in America, was born on 9 September 1721, probably in King and Queen county, Virginia, the youngest son of the planter Henry Pendleton (d. 1721) and Mary (1688–1770), the daughter of James Taylor and his second wife, Mary Gregory. On 21 January 1742 Edmund married Elizabeth, the daughter of John and Dorothy Roy; she died in November. In June 1743 he married Sarah (b. c.1725, d. in or after 1803), the daughter of Joseph Pollard and Priscilla Hoomes. Neither marriage produced any children.

After attending a local English school Pendleton was apprenticed in March 1735 to Benjamin Robinson, clerk of the Caroline county court and uncle of the powerful speaker of the house of burgesses, John Robinson. Pendleton then studied legal terminology at a Latin school. His first public appointments were as clerk to the vestry of St Mary's parish in 1737 and to the Caroline county courts martial in 1740. He was admitted to the Caroline county bar in 1741 and to the general court in 1745. In 1742 he began to acquire land near Bowling Green, Virginia, for Edmundsbury, a plantation eventually containing over 4200 acres. He became justice of the peace on the Caroline county court in 1751, and won election to the house of burgesses the next year. He joined the Loyal Land Company, aligning himself with the speaker's faction, from the middle and lower peninsulas, against the Ohio Company of Virginia, formed exclusively among residents of the Northern Neck. The line-up was a basic division in mid-eighteenth-century Virginia politics.

Pendleton soon appeared on key legislative committees, including one contesting Governor Robert Dinwiddie's imposition of a fee of one Spanish pistole for signing land grants. When the onset of the Seven Years' War forced Virginia for the first time to issue paper currency as legal tender, Pendleton vigorously defended the policy despite the unfavourable exchange rate with sterling. Robinson's death in 1766 revealed that the speaker in his dual post as the colony's treasurer had loaned favoured planters over £100,000 in currency that he should have retired. The scandal roiled the colony's politics for years. As principal executor, Pendleton committed himself to redeeming his mentor as best he could, and revealed his consummate negotiating skills by recovering enough to repay the treasury fully by 1781. The estate was not entirely settled until after Pendleton's death.

The constitutional crisis with Britain further uncovered Pendleton's political talents. From the beginning of the controversy he stood firmly against parliamentary taxation, but feared that mob violence and closing the courts would lead to anarchy. Although absent on the day, he doubtless would have opposed Patrick Henry's resolutions against the Stamp Act in 1765, for he declined to follow most other counties and did not close the Caroline court. Absent again in 1769 when the burgesses adopted a boycott of British imports to protest against the Townshend duties, he did help enforce the ban in Caroline county. His appointment by the burgesses to the committee of correspondence at its founding in 1773 inaugurated his rise to leadership in the resistance movement. His steadfast opposition to expansion of British authority in the colonies, coupled with a persistent search for accommodation, appealed to most Virginians. When Governor Dunmore dissolved the assembly in May 1774, Pendleton marched with the burgesses to the Ralegh tavern to adopt another boycott protesting at parliament's Coercive Acts against Boston. A few days later he was among a rump of legislators who called a convention in August to ban exports of tobacco in 1775 as well.

The convention elected Pendleton a delegate to the continental congress in Philadelphia and re-elected him the next spring. When Dunmore raided the Williamsburg magazine in April 1775, Pendleton helped deflect Patrick Henry's plan to march on the capital. At the second continental congress in May, he favoured another pledge of loyalty to the king while readying colonial defences. In August Pendleton returned for the third Virginia convention, which elected him president and head of a committee of safety to assume control of government and begin recruiting troops. The committee faced two major threats to the rebellion in Virginia. Before the new regiments were ready, Dunmore enjoyed a series of successes around Hampton Roads. Had he been sufficiently reinforced he might have created a second front, diverting the continental army from its siege of General Gage in Boston. Second, the convention elected Henry their commander-in-chief, despite his total lack of military experience. The committee's solution, for which Henry's friends were unforgiving, was to assign Henry to defend Williamsburg and send a veteran of the Seven Years' War, William Woodford, to Norfolk, where he succeeded in driving Dunmore to his ships in December 1775. Virginia's fourth convention that month and the fifth in May again elected Pendleton president. Despite dropping to fourth place on the ballot, he won re-election to the committee of safety and continued as its chairman. Hostilities resumed on 1 January when Dunmore bombarded Norfolk, and, though much more of the city was destroyed by American troops rampaging for three days, the British bore the blame. The burning turned Virginia public opinion overwhelmingly toward independence. The Henry affair erupted again in early spring, when congress offered the hero a colonelcy but promoted another veteran, Andrew Lewis, to brigadier. Henry resigned and barely kept his men from rioting. Most did not re-enlist.

At the May 1776 convention Pendleton offered the compromise that enabled the body to adopt, without dissent, Virginia's famous resolution calling on congress to declare independence. He supplied phrasing, too, that insured that the convention's ringing proclamation of human equality in the Virginia declaration of rights would not include slaves. Upon establishment of republican government, Pendleton became speaker of the first house of delegates. The legislature assigned him, Thomas Jefferson, and George Wythe to revise the colonial law code. Pendleton redrafted his share but resisted several of Jefferson's famous reforms: repeal of entail and primogeniture, disestablishment of the Anglican church, and land laws favouring smaller farmers. Jefferson considered him the most effective debater he knew, and his most formidable opponent.

When a crippling accident ended his legislative career in March 1777, the assembly elected Pendleton presiding justice of the high court of chancery and, in 1779, of the court of appeals, a post he held, though the court took different forms, for twenty-four years. His contributions to the formation of the state's judiciary, particularly his insistence on judicial independence, even review of the other branches, won from contemporaries the sobriquet 'the Mansfield of Virginia' (Mays, 2.280). In two centuries few of his opinions were reversed. Despite Pendleton's advocacy of the federal constitution, the Virginia ratifying convention in 1788, which initially appeared antifederalist in sentiment, unanimously elected him chair. The federalist leader, James Madison, credited him with a major share in winning ratification. George Washington considered him for the United States supreme court but concluded his disability would prevent him from accepting, and offered a district court appointment instead.

Pendleton preferred to remain leader of the state judiciary. He endorsed the Washington administration's belligerent American Indian policy and its neutralist foreign policy, but broke with it over Alexander Hamilton's economic programme. He and his protégé, John Taylor of Caroline, were in the forefront of the protests culminating in the Virginia resolutions against the Adams administration's Alien and Sedition Acts. Pendleton wrote essays endorsing Jefferson and the republicans in the 1800 and 1802 elections. After Gabriel's rebellion in 1801 Pendleton, who owned thirty-eight slaves, presided over the acquittal in Caroline county of four African-Americans and the execution of five others. His last judicial act was to prepare an opinion overturning the legislature's seizure of glebe lands, the final step in disestablishing the Anglican church. However, he died in Richmond on 26 October 1803 before delivering it. He was buried two days later at Edmundsbury.   JOHN E. SELBY

Sources D. J. Mays, *Edmund Pendleton, 1721–1803: a biography*, 2 vols. (1952) • D. T. Konig, 'Pendleton, Edmund', *ANB*
Likenesses attrib. T. Sully, portrait (after miniature by W. Mercer), Virginia Historical Society, Richmond, Virginia; repro. in Mays, *Edmund Pendleton*, frontispiece
Wealth at death Edmundsbury plantation comprising 2273 acres and with thirty-eight slaves: Mays, *Edmund Pendleton*, 2.344

Pendleton, Frederick Henry Snow (1818–1888), divine, born on 13 September 1818, was educated at the University of Ghent and at St Aidan's College, Birkenhead. After being ordained in the diocese of Winchester, he served as curate of St Martin's, Guernsey, from December 1849 to June 1851, and as senior curate of St Helier, Jersey, from August 1851 to July 1853. He was consular chaplain to the British residents at Montevideo in Uruguay from 6 May 1854 to 31 December 1858. During his residence there 150 natives of the Vaudois, driven by unemployment in Piedmont in northern Italy, left their native country and landed in Montevideo. They were followed in 1858 by about a hundred more, when the whole party settled at Florida, about 60 miles from the city. Jesuit opposition having arisen, the Vaudois settlers, under Pendleton's personal direction, removed to another locality known as the Rosario Oriental, where his influence obtained for them a church and a schoolroom. In 1857 yellow fever swept Montevideo, and Pendleton's services during the crisis were acknowledged by the French government, which granted him a gold medal. A similar recognition followed him from the Italian government. From 1863 to 31 December 1868 he was chaplain to the British residents at Florence. In 1862 and again in 1867 he revisited the Waldensian colony at Rosario Oriental. He resided at the Casa Fumi, Porta Romana, Florence, until 1876, when he moved to Sydenham, Kent. There he served as curate of St Bartholomew's Church until 1879. He was then curate of Ampthill, Bedfordshire, for two years, and finally he became rector of St Sampson's, Guernsey, in 1882. He died at St Sampson's rectory, Guernsey, on 13 September 1888. Pendleton wrote *Lettres pastorales* in 1851, and published various sermons in English and French between 1852 and 1868.   G. C. BOASE, rev. H. C. G. MATTHEW

Sources *The Times* (19 Sept 1888) • *The Guardian* (19 Sept 1888) • *FO List* (1887)

Pendleton, Henry (d. 1557), theologian, came from a Lancashire family. He entered Brasenose College, Oxford, about 1538, graduating BA on 16 November 1542, MA on 18 October 1544, BTh in 1552, and DTh on 18 July 1552. He was fellow of Brasenose from 1542 to 1554, vice-principal 1551–2, and senior bursar 1553–4. During Henry VIII's reign he preached against Lutheranism, but during Edward VI's reign he held protestant views, being one of the first itinerant preachers appointed by the earl of Derby to preach in the provinces. In 1552 he was appointed rector of Blymhill, Staffordshire, though the title was successfully disputed. Foxe records how, after the accession of Mary, Pendleton encouraged Laurence Saunders to stand firm in his protestant opinions, and boasted of his own steadfastness, declaring 'I will see the uttermost drop of this grease of mine molten away, and the last gobbet of this pampered flesh consumed to ashes, before I will forsake God and his truth' (*Acts and Monuments*, 6.629). Yet he soon converted, being rewarded with several preferments in 1554: he was made prebendary of Reculverland, canon of St Paul's (11 April), vicar of Todenham in Gloucestershire, and canon of Lichfield (15 June). He was also made prebendary of Ufton *ex parte decani*.

In 1555–6 Pendleton was made vicar of St Martin Outwich, London, which he resigned on 1 April 1556, being admitted to the living of St Stephen Walbrook. About this time he became chaplain to Bishop Bonner, and some of his disputations with those imprisoned for heresy were recorded by Foxe, including an encounter with John Bradford, in which Foxe portrayed him as somewhat confounded by Bradford's appeal to his former reformed convictions. Pendleton was famous as a preacher. A Spital sermon he preached on Easter Monday 1557, attended by mayor, alderman, and judges, had an audience allegedly 20,000 strong. During a Paul's Cross sermon on 10 June 1554 someone fired a gun at him, although Strype remarks that it was not clear 'whether it were done by some out of detestation of Pendleton's doctrine, or his person' (Strype, *Ecclesiastical Memorials*, 3.1.213). The shot missed.

Pendleton was one of the 'chapleynes, and frendes' with whom Bishop Bonner compiled the Book of Homilies in 1555. Pendleton's contributions were 'An homelye of the churche, what it is, and of the commoditie therof' and 'An homely of the authoritie of the Church declarynge what commoditie and profyt we have thereby'. The first of these emphasized how the true church was universal, visible, and united, 'not lurkynge in any corner, or anye one countrye' (Bonner, sig. H. ivv). The second explained that the two chief elements of the church's authority were the ability to identify and understand scripture, and the power to forgive the repentant and correct the obstinate sinner. This homily stressed the comfort which was to be found within the church and dwelt on the disasters that had befallen England since the schism, including the dissolution of abbeys and chantries and an increase in poverty. Pendleton died in September 1557. Foxe claimed he repented his conversion to Catholicism at the last, but references to a work now lost, entitled *A declaration of Hen. Pendleton DD in his sickness, of his faith in all points, as the Catholic church teachest, against sclanderous reports against him* (London, 1557), suggest that this was a matter of some debate. He was buried in St Stephen Walbrook, London, on 21 September 1557.   L. E. C. WOODING

Sources E. Bonner, *Homilies* (1555) · Wood, *Ath. Oxon.*, new edn, 1.325–6, 371 · *The diary of Henry Machyn, citizen and merchant-taylor of London, from AD 1550 to AD 1563*, ed. J. G. Nichols, CS, 42 (1848), 65, 74, 117, 131, 152 · J. Strype, *Ecclesiastical memorials*, 3 vols. (1822), vol. 3, pt 1, p. 213; vol. 3, pt 2, pp. 2–3, 18–19 · *The acts and monuments of John Foxe*, ed. S. R. Cattley, 8 vols. (1837–41), vol. 6, pp. 628–30; vol. 7, pp. 184–6; vol. 8, p. 635 · *Fasti Angl., 1541–1857*, [St Paul's, London], 54 · J. Strype, *Memorials of the most reverend father in God Thomas Cranmer*, new edn, 2 vols. (1812), vol. 1, p. 519 · BL, Lansdowne MS 981, fol. 7 · Emden, *Oxf.*, 4.440–41

Penelope. *See* Lankester, Phebe (1825–1900).

Penfold, Charles (1798–1864), surveyor and valuer, was born on 26 May 1798 in Croydon, Surrey, the third of ten children of Thomas Penfold (*b.* 1771), Croydon vestry clerk (1796–1834), and his wife, Edith. On 16 January 1822 he married Catherine Mary Chrees (*d.* 1866). His younger brother George, a solicitor, was vestry clerk from 1835 to his early death in 1852, by which time he was also clerk to the Croydon local board of health, established in 1849.

Penfold was an authority on rating and road making, whose evidence to the select committee on turnpike trusts and tolls (1836) was drawn upon by Sidney and Beatrice Webb for their famous book on the king's highway. In 1824 he and John Maberley, MP for Abingdon, of Shirley Park, Croydon, were elected surveyors of the parish roads. Only Penfold received a salary, and from 1828 his name appears alone. He held the office until Maberley left the parish because of bankruptcy in 1833. Penfold complained to the select committee that, after he had reduced the annual expenditure on roads from £1500 to £470, the vestry proposed halving his salary of 100 guineas before

taking up the offer of an amateur road maker, James Willoughby, to perform the work gratuitously. In 1837 Penfold was elected to the newly established board of highways, which employed Willoughby as surveyor, and continued as a member to Easter 1849, soon after which the board's functions were taken over by the local board of health. He was one of the surveyors of the Surrey and Sussex Turnpike Trust, responsible for about 100 miles of road, holding the post for thirty years, and was also surveyor of the Croydon and Reigate Trust.

Penfold first published his views on road making in 1834, eventually being published for the Society for the Diffusion of Useful Knowledge in the third volume, *Husbandry*, in 1840 as 'A practical treatise on the best mode of repairing roads'. He recommended county hundreds employing general surveyors to supervise parish surveyors, and advocated replacing statute duty by piece work, surfacing roads with a thin layer of hard, well-broken stones, and raking and watering the surface to keep it settled.

The board of highways made him responsible for examining the plans of the London and Brighton Railway Company, whose lines crossed the parish, to see how they affected the roads and footpaths, while his brother was employed in instigating litigation. In January 1842, just before Lord Denman's judgment about railway companies paying the poor rate in *R. v. London and South Western Railway Company*, Penfold wrote a letter to the *Railway Times* which attracted sufficient attention for him to write a series of letters on the rating of railways. He upheld Lord Denman's view that railways should be rated upon their total earnings, less expenses, not just upon tolls payable by any lessee. These letters were the start of a number of publications on the rating of railways, especially *The Principle and Law of Rating*, first published in 1847, which reached a fourth edition during his lifetime and, as *Penfold on Rating*, an eighth edition in 1893. Penfold believed in helping parishes benefit from the increased value of the land the railways occupied; as a valuer he assisted a number of parishes to make fresh valuations in the light of Lord Denman's judgment. The London, Brighton, and South Coast Company, later taken over by the South Eastern, appealed unsuccessfully against his valuation for the Croydon rate, by which the company paid a third of the total rates collected.

When the local board of health was being established Penfold had hopes of becoming its surveyor. He gave evidence to the public inquiry led by William Ranger, superintending inspector of the General Board of Health, presenting his own plan for supplying Croydon with water and sanitation. In *A letter to the Right Hon. the earl of Carlisle upon the drainage of the town of Croydon under the Health of Towns Act* (1849) he maintained he had been offered the post of surveyor and criticized the plans adopted by the board. His criticisms of the board may have been fuelled by the realization not only that his own standing in Croydon had been diminished—the board had not shortlisted him—but also that the dynastic rule of the Penfolds had been replaced by that of the Drummonds—John

Drummond being vestry clerk from 1852 to 1880, and his brother William chairman of the local board of health from 1853 to 1862. Penfold moved to Brunswick Square, near Holborn, about 1853, having had for some years an office in the City, first in Cornhill and then in St Helen's, Bishopsgate. He died on 23 May 1864.

BRIAN LANCASTER

Sources 'Select committee on turnpike trusts and tolls', *Parl. papers* (1836), 19.335, no. 547 · *Sussex Agricultural Express* (24 March 1849) · *Sussex Agricultural Express* (31 March 1849) · Board for repair of the highways in the parish of Croydon, minutes, vol. 1 (1836–42) · Board for repair of the highways in the parish of Croydon, minutes, vol. 2 (1842–9) · 'A proposed amendment in the highway laws of England addressed to the members of both houses of parliament, Croydon', 1834 · *Railway Times* (1842–4) · C. Penfold, *A letter to Lord Campbell … in reply to Mr Smirke's letter* (1851) · C. Penfold, *A letter to the Right Hon. the earl of Carlisle upon the drainage of the town of Croydon under the Health of Towns Act* (1849) · vestry minutes, St John the Baptist, Croydon, Surrey · parish register (birth), 26 May 1798, St John the Baptist, Croydon, Surrey · parish register (baptism), 17 July 1798, St John the Baptist, Croydon, Surrey · J. Comber, *Sussex genealogies*, 3 vols. (1931–3), vol. 1 · d. cert.
Archives UCL, letters to Society for the Diffusion of Useful Knowledge
Wealth at death under £2000: probate, 30 June 1864, *CGPLA Eng. & Wales*

Pengelly, Sir Thomas (1675–1730), judge, was the son of Thomas Pengelly, of Cheshunt, and his wife, Rachel (*fl.* *c.*1660–1715), daughter of Lieutenant-Colonel Jeremy Baines, a parliamentary officer during the civil war. His father was a wealthy merchant trading to the eastern Mediterranean and the Atlantic seaboard, with considerable property in London's East End and in Finchley, as well as in Hertfordshire. The future judge was certainly born at his house in Moorfields on 16 May 1675; but the family seat of Churchgate in Cheshunt subsequently provided a refuge for the former protector Richard Cromwell, who continued to board there with Mrs Pengelly after his host's death, and this association inspired a legend that the younger Pengelly was Richard's illegitimate son.

As a youth Thomas showed an aptitude for study. In 1691 he became clerk to a London attorney, and a year later, at the age of seventeen, he was admitted to the Inner Temple, where he was called to the bar on 24 November 1700. There is no evidence as to his early practice, but after only ten years at the bar he was created a serjeant-at-law. By 1720 he was certainly among the foremost advocates in Westminster Hall, being an acknowledged expert in the law of corporations, which in this period of party strife brought him much business in king's bench *quo warranto* proceedings about parliamentary boroughs, as well as a mass of cases for opinion. He does not seem to have appeared much in equity: many decades later a pamphlet alleged that he abandoned practice in chancery because of the partiality shown by the lord chancellor, Parker, towards the young Philip Yorke, afterwards Lord Chancellor Hardwicke. But although the story is plausible (Parker was inclined to favouritism), the author was hostile to Hardwicke, and his account is not corroborated by any contemporary witness. Indeed, Pengelly's counselling work was wide-ranging: his surviving correspondence

Sir Thomas Pengelly (1675–1730), by John Faber junior, 1730 (after James Worsdale)

shows that by 1717 he had become principal legal adviser to the duke of Somerset, and in the 1720s he was also counsel to the duchess of Marlborough, whom he represented in litigation arising out of the Blenheim estate. On 1 May 1719 he was knighted and chosen by Parker to succeed Sir Thomas Powys as the king's prime serjeant, and in that capacity he helped to conduct the trial of the Jacobite Christopher Layer for high treason during January and February 1722.

Upon Somerset's nomination in 1717 Pengelly was elected member of parliament for Cockermouth in Cumberland, defeating another lawyer and future judge, the former tory and government candidate Sir Robert Raymond. In parliament his activity tended to parallel his profession. He was most prominent in the aftermath of the South Sea crash and in pursuing other issues of corruption associated with commerce and law. He took a strong line against the delinquent South Sea directors, and was active in the subsequent committee of inquiry, while outside the Commons his reputation inspired a steady stream of cases from companies and projectors anxious to avoid the Bubble Act passed to inhibit speculative joint-stock ventures. In 1725, when it became clear that the financial ramifications of the crash had precipitated the failure of several masters in chancery who had invested suitors' money to recoup the high cost of purchasing their places from Lord Chancellor Macclesfield, Pengelly was active in promoting the chancellor's impeachment. He was subsequently one of the principal managers for the Commons at the trial: on the tenth day he replied to the legal points raised by the defence, arguing that sale of the offices violated common law and several statutes, and insisted that Macclesfield had consciously and corruptly used the power and authority of his office to extort money for his own benefit. One of his final acts in parliament, in February and May 1726, was to assist in the expulsion from the Commons of John Ward, a swindling businessman whom he had prosecuted for defrauding the duke of Buckingham.

As the leading common lawyer of his generation Pengelly had legitimate expectations of promotion to the top of his profession. But although he supported the government in parliament over major issues such as the repeal of the Occasional Conformity Act and the Schism Act, and spoke for the abortive Peerage Bill, it was difficult to navigate safely through the tortuous politics of the time. And after 1720, when Sir Robert Walpole and his allies began to fill the highest offices of state with their own creatures, his association with the independent Somerset was an impediment to his prospects of gaining the politically sensitive place of chief justice in king's bench. In 1723 he was earmarked for a second-rate judicial post: the duke of Newcastle wrote that if he would accept a vacant puisne judgeship 'he would be cheaply provided for, and the making him a Judge would be right ... that he may not do more hurt in another place' (Newcastle to Townsend, 1 Nov 1723, BL, Add. MS 32686, fol. 384). In the event the experience of being passed over for the chief justiceship in king's bench on the death of Sir John Pratt (in 1725) pushed him into association with Sir William Pulteney and the opposition whigs, but on 16 October 1726 he was appointed to succeed Sir Geoffrey Gilbert as lord chief baron of the exchequer—a post with no political influence. At the time both Somerset and Pulteney encouraged him to hope still for higher promotion, but after less than four years in the exchequer he succumbed to gaol fever, contracted from prisoners in court at the Lent assizes in Taunton. He died at Blandford in Dorset, on 14 April 1730, and was buried in the Temple Church on 29 April.

At a time when it was fashionable to condemn lawyers for self-serving avarice Pengelly was exceptional for attracting comments from people high and low about his honesty, independence, and altruism. Indeed, although he built himself a new mansion at Cheshunt, he died unmarried and childless, and there are hints of asceticism about his personality. A life published shortly after his death maintained that he sacrificed leisure hours and company to ensure that he was thoroughly prepared to represent his clients, and he certainly appeared gratis for poor suitors, or in deserving causes. The truth of this characterization is also supported by the evidence of his will, which bequeathed £2890 for the discharge of poor prisoners on the western circuit and in London. After setting aside other sums for the duke of Somerset and the duchess of Marlborough he left his estates in Hertfordshire and Hampshire and the remainder of his personal property to his clerk, John Webb.   DAVID LEMMINGS

Sources Bodl. Oxf., MS Eng. lett. c. 17 · BL, Add. MSS 6722–6727, 19773–19775, 22675, 32686 · *Some private passages of the life of Sir*

Thomas Pengelly, late chief baron of the exchequer (1733) · *Seventh report*, HMC, 6 (1879), 681–93 [Rev. T. W. Webb] · *State trials*, 16.1330–88 · HoP, *Commons, 1715–54*, 2.334–5 · A. B. Du Bois, *The English business company after the Bubble Act, 1720–1800* (1938) · D. Lemmings, *Gentlemen and barristers: the inns of court and the English bar, 1680–1730* (1990) · Foss, *Judges* · DNB

Archives BL, legal commonplace book, Add. MS 61942 · BL, legal papers, Add. MSS 19773–19775, 22675 · BL, papers, mainly law reports, Add. MSS 6722–6727 · Bodl. Oxf., corresp. and papers · Harvard U., law school, cases and opinions · PRO, inventory of goods and estate and family papers, C 103/197

Likenesses B. Ferrers, group portrait, oils, c.1725 (*The court of chancery*), NPG · J. Faber junior, mezzotint, 1730 (after J. Worsdale), NPG [*see illus.*]

Wealth at death estates in Hertfordshire and Hampshire; plus considerable personal property: *Some private passages*; *Seventh report*, HMC, appx, 693

Pengelly, William (1812–1894), geologist and archaeologist, was born on 12 January 1812 at East Looe, Cornwall, the first of ten children of Richard Pengelly (1787–1861), mariner, and his wife, Sarah (1787–1881), daughter of Abraham and Mary Prout of Millbrook, Cornwall. Pengelly attended two schools in East Looe before beginning work on his father's coasting vessel at the age of twelve. He left the ship's crew four years later, on the death of his younger brother, Richard, and devoted much time to reading and self-instruction in mathematics. About 1836, influenced by an aunt and uncle who lived there, he moved to Torquay and opened a school based on the Pestalozzian method, teaching mathematics. In 1846 he gave up the school to become a private tutor in mathematics and the natural sciences, and began a long career of lecturing around the country in subjects including astronomy, geology, palaeontology, and archaeology. Pengelly's desire to make education and learning more accessible led him to found the Torquay Young Men's Society in 1837 (in 1846 renamed the Torquay Mechanics' Institute); the Torquay Natural History Society in 1844; and the Devonshire Association for the Advancement of Literature, Science, and Art in 1862.

Pengelly married his cousin Mary Ann Mudge on 18 June 1838. The couple had six children, but all except their son Alfred died in infancy or childhood. Mary died in 1851, and on 28 June 1853 Pengelly married Lydia Spriggs, of a Quaker family of Worcester, with whom he had two daughters; the younger, Hester, became his biographer.

Pengelly's interests centred on the geology and palaeontology of Devon and Cornwall, and human prehistory, on which he published more than a hundred papers. He made significant contributions to the literature on the geology of Devon and Cornwall, and his collecting activities provided important primary material for other workers and students. In 1860 Miss Angela (later Baroness) Burdett-Coutts, a former pupil, provided Pengelly with funds to collect fossil plant material from the Tertiary lignite deposits of Bovey Tracey. Pengelly reviewed the geology of these deposits in an important paper read to the Royal Society in 1862, and in 1863 was elected a fellow of the society.

Pengelly's most lasting and original contributions to the

sciences remain his work on Devon caves and their associated human prehistory. On his arrival in Torquay he took an interest in Kent's Cavern, which had been excavated between 1825 and 1829 by the Revd John MacEnery, who claimed to have recovered flint artefacts together with bones from extinct animals. Pengelly's first excavations began in 1846 with the express purpose of attempting to demonstrate whether or not artefacts were contemporaneous with an extinct fauna, but his excavation controls were in their infancy and there was some disagreement with colleagues in interpreting the results. In 1858, however, an opportunity arose to investigate a newly discovered cave at Brixham, Devon, untouched by previous excavation. The Geological Society of London formed a committee for its investigation, with Pengelly in charge of supervising the excavations using an improved three-dimensional process of excavation and recording. Preliminary findings from Brixham were published in outline in Sir Charles Lyell's *Geological Evidence on the Antiquity of Man* (1863), and were central in the paradigm shift in accepting that humans had an ancient 'prehistory'. Pengelly returned to excavating Kent's Cavern with the support of the British Association for the Advancement of Science, and between 1865 and 1880 he refined his methods of excavation still further, providing geologists and archaeologists with vast collections of faunal and cultural remains with associated contextual data.

While Pengelly's motivation and application contributed greatly to his success, he was, in moving to Torquay, also in the right place at the right time. From the mid-nineteenth century Torquay became a highly fashionable resort for the middle and upper classes and thus Pengelly was able to meet influential people, and maintain important personal contacts over and above maintaining a voluminous correspondence. In addition, the geological and archaeological sites in the locality contained deposits in fields which were of central interest in the international scientific community of his time. Pengelly also found, in attending the British Association for the Advancement of Science meetings, an invaluable vehicle for communicating and maintaining contacts. He attended every meeting between 1856 and 1889, except for that in Montreal in 1884. He was president of the association's geological section in 1877, and the anthropological section in 1883. The Geological Society, of which he had been a fellow since 1850, presented him with the Lyell medal in 1886 for his contributions to geological science.

Pengelly had great energy and mental ability, and was an excellent communicator, especially as a lecturer, and meticulous in all he did. A benevolent man, he was noted by all that knew him for his charm and genial manner, and had a great sense of humour and ready wit—his habit of punning earned him the nickname of 'Pun-gelly' from friends at British Association meetings. Although baptized and brought up in the Church of England, Pengelly, who was teetotal, had become by the 1840s a convert to the tenets of the Society of Friends, whom he joined by the time of his second marriage. His firmly held nonconformist beliefs effectively disqualified him from applying for certain salaried appointments in which he was interested. Pengelly died at his home, Lamorna, Furze Hill Road, Torquay, on 16 March 1894, and was buried at the Torquay cemetery on 22 March.   MICHAEL J. BISHOP

Sources H. Pengelly, *A memoir of William Pengelly of Torquay, FRS, geologist* (1897) · Torquay Museum, Pengelly MSS · private information (2004) · *Torquay and South Devon Journal*, 55/2649 (1894), 3 · *Report and Transactions of the Devonshire Association*, 26 (1894), 44–9 · H. Woodward, *Journal of the Geological Society*, 51 (1895), liii–lvii · C. N. Warren and S. Rose, *William Pengelly's spits, yards and prisms* (1994), 40 · L. G. Wilson, 'Brixham cave and Sir Charles Lyell's *The Antiquity of Man*: the roots of Hugh Falconer's attack on Lyell', *Archives of Natural History*, 23 (1996), 79–97 · J. Thackray, 'William Pengelly: a west country geologist on the national scene', *Transactions and proceedings of the Torquay Natural History Society*, 22 (1996), 66–72
Archives BM, department of Greek and Roman antiquities · NHM, catalogue · Oxf. U. Mus. NH · RS, report · Torquay Museum, diaries, letters, and notebooks relating to excavation of Kent's Cavern | CUL, letters to Sir George Stokes · U. Edin. L., special collections division, corresp. with Sir Charles Lyell
Likenesses oils, c.1870–1879, Torquay Museum, Torquay · A. S. Cope, oils, 1881, Torquay Museum, Torquay · wood-engraving (after photograph by H. J. Whitlock), NPG; repro. in *ILN* (31 March 1894) · photographs, Torquay Museum, Torquay
Wealth at death £4601 18s. 0d.: probate, 13 April 1894, *CGPLA Eng. & Wales*

Penhafirme. For this title name *see* Sartorius, Euston Henry, count of Penhafirme in the Portuguese nobility (1844–1925) [*see under* Sartorius brothers (*act. c.*1857–1925)].

Penhaligon, David Charles (1944–1986), politician, was born on 6 June 1944 at Truro Nursing Home, the eldest son of Robert Charles Penhaligon (1903–1975), owner of a caravan park, and his wife, Sadie Jewell (*b.* 1913). Educated at Bosvigo primary school and Truro School, Penhaligon joined the Camborne engineering firm Holman Bros in 1962, studying towards a higher national diploma in engineering at Cornwall Technical College at the same time. As a chartered engineer he specialized in the research and development of rock-drilling equipment.

Although his parents were Conservatives, Penhaligon was inspired to join the Liberal Party after acting as a witness in a murder trial in 1963, in which his evidence failed to prevent both defendants from being hanged. Truro Liberal Association was then one of Cornwall's weakest, but Penhaligon's flair for organization and leadership fashioned the Young Liberals into a powerful force in the district. He swiftly assumed positions of prominence within the regional and national Young Liberal organizations, but his ambition to contest the Truro parliamentary seat in 1966 was thwarted. He was also rejected for the Falmouth and Camborne constituency in 1968, partly because of his youth but also because his thick Cornish burr was deemed unsuitable for a Westminster candidate.

Undaunted, Penhaligon was adopted as Liberal candidate for Totnes in 1970, finishing third in a disappointing election for the party. He was adopted, with little resistance, for Truro in 1971 and, inspired by the impact Wallace

Lawler had made in Birmingham, revolutionized electioneering in the constituency. Liberal candidates were encouraged to stand in local elections for the first time as Penhaligon worked tirelessly to promote the Liberal cause, appealing in particular to the staunchly Labour clay workers in the east of the constituency. Narrowing the Conservative majority to 2561 in February 1974, he bucked the national trend to win by 464 votes eight months later.

Penhaligon had married Annette Lidgey (*b.* 1946), a fellow Young Liberal, on 6 January 1968 and at the time of his election they ran the post office at Chacewater. They had a son and a daughter. His immediate impact in the House of Commons was as a champion of Cornish interests, often working across party lines with fellow MPs for the county. He cultivated the image of a political outsider, deploying humour and common sense to confound his opponents and to appeal to people, Liberal or otherwise, both within his constituency and beyond. He increased his majority substantially in the elections of 1979 and 1983.

Initially speaking for the Liberal Party on employment matters, Penhaligon was later spokesman for energy and industry, before becoming the party's Treasury spokesman in 1985. Throughout his political career he championed industrial profit-sharing schemes and worker participation in the management of companies. Decentralization of power was another consistent theme, and Penhaligon argued against the establishment of bodies representing the south-west of England but based in distant Bristol. He was a critic of the civil uses of nuclear power, but at the 1980 Liberal assembly told delegates that proponents of a non-nuclear defence policy were 'advocating surrender' (*The Times*, 23 Dec 86). No financial expert, he initially struggled with the high-profile Treasury brief, with which he was becoming more comfortable at the time of his death.

Behind his affable charm Penhaligon was a sharp political operator. Although not an enthusiastic supporter of the Lib–Lab pact, he worked well with Bill Rodgers on environmental matters, but less well with Tony Benn on energy. His speech to the special Liberal assembly of January 1978 made a significant contribution to the continuation of the pact. He played a key role in the allocation of constituencies to be fought by Liberal and Social Democrat candidates, before both 1983 and 1987 general elections, again working in tandem with Rodgers. He headed the Liberal by-election unit from 1983 to 1985.

A favourite of Liberal activists, he was the only sitting MP ever to be elected president of the party, in 1985. Above all, however, he was a politician who related to the lives of ordinary people, as was shown by the reaction to his death in a car crash at Truck Fork, near Probus, on the road between Truro and St Austell, on 22 December 1986. Thousands of people thronged the streets of Truro for a service of thanksgiving for his life at the city's cathedral on 10 January 1987 and supported a memorial fund set up in his name. David Steel described Penhaligon as 'an instinctive Liberal of the old school' (Penhaligon, 122) and his contribution to Liberalism was sorely missed in the years of turbulence which affected the Liberal Party and its successor

in the years after his death. Penhaligon was buried on 30 December 1986 at All Hallows Church, St Kea, Truro, and was survived by his wife. ROBERT INGHAM

Sources A. Penhaligon, *Penhaligon* (1989) · D. Brack and M. Baines, eds., *Dictionary of liberal biography* (1998) · *WWW* · *The Times* (23 Dec 1986), 14f · *West Briton and Royal Cornwall Gazette* (23 Dec 1986) · private information (2004) · *West Briton* (8 June 1944) · *West Briton and Royal Cornwall Gazette* (31 Dec 1986) · *West Briton and Royal Cornwall Gazette* (15 Jan 1987) · *West Briton and Royal Cornwall Gazette* (8 Jan 1968) · *West Briton and Royal Cornwall Gazette* (11 Jan 1968) · *West Briton and Royal Cornwall Gazette* (3 Oct 1974) · *West Briton and Royal Cornwall Gazette* (14 Oct 1974) · *West Briton and Royal Cornwall Gazette* (1 May 1975)
Archives Cornwall RO, constituency corresp., diaries, and surgery notebooks | FILM BFI NFTVA, current affairs footage · BFI NFTVA, news footage · ITN Archive, London, 'Lib–Lab pact' | SOUND BL NSA, current affairs recording · BL NSA, news recording
Likenesses photographs, repro. in Penhaligon, *Penhaligon* · photographs, repro. in *West Briton and Royal Cornwall Gazette* (23 Dec 1986), 1–2 · photographs, repro. in *West Briton and Royal Cornwall Gazette* (11 Jan 1968), 10f–g
Wealth at death £148,518: administration, 23 March 1987, *CGPLA Eng. & Wales*

Penhallow, Samuel (1665–1726), politician and historian in America, was born on 2 July 1665 at St Mabyn in Cornwall, a son of Chamond Penhallow, a gentleman farmer, and his wife, Ann Tamlyn. Nothing is known of Samuel's childhood, but in 1683, at the age of eighteen, his father enrolled him in Charles Morton's academy at Newington Green, Middlesex. After the closure of this dissenting school in 1685, Samuel decided to follow his mentor, Morton, to colonial Massachusetts in order to serve as a missionary to the Narragansett Indians. In 1686 he briefly attended Harvard College. By early 1687 Penhallow had abandoned his aim of becoming a missionary, and moved north to the frontier community of Portsmouth, New Hampshire. This decision proved momentous for Penhallow. On 1 July 1687 he married Mary Cutt (1666–1714), heir to the former president of New Hampshire, the late John Cutt, a fish-trading merchant who possessed the richest estate in the colony. Young Penhallow was thrust into a new world of trade and élitist politics where the chaos of the revolution of 1688, wars with the French and American Indians, and the Masonian proprietary controversy would soon dominate his life.

Penhallow, with wife Mary's help, learned the fishery business and became one of Portsmouth's leading exporters and retail merchants. His economic achievements led to his appointment in 1705 as commissary-general of the province in charge of provisioning the militia during the Indian wars. Two years later he transferred his Congregational church membership to Portsmouth, where he later served as a deacon. From 1713 to 1726 he was always among the top four taxpayers in the town. He and Mary had thirteen children, and after her death on 8 February 1714 he married, on 8 September 1714, the twice-widowed Abigail Oborne, *née* Atkinson (1672–1740); they had one child.

Politically ambitious, Penhallow at first allied himself with such leading pro-puritan landowners as the

Vaughans and Waldrons, who supported Massachusetts's resumption of jurisdiction over New Hampshire and opposed the Masonian proprietary claims to the colony. The Massachusetts government appointed him to the powerful position of treasurer of New Hampshire from 1690 to 1692, at which point English royal government was restored to the colony. For the next five years Penhallow opposed the new royal pro-proprietary officials, but when the earl of Bellomont was appointed royal governor in 1697 Penhallow appealed successfully to be restored as treasurer, an office he held from 1699 to 1722 and 1724 to 1726. He also received appointment as a justice of the peace in 1699, and then was elected to the New Hampshire assembly and was immediately elected its speaker. In 1702 the assembly chose him to be the province recorder, a post which he held between 1702 and 1704 and between 1719 and 1722. In 1702 a new royal governor, Thomas Dudley, appointed Penhallow to the New Hampshire council, where he served from 1702 to 1726. He now was an 'esquire', the highest status locally available. In 1714 Dudley appointed him judge of the superior court.

By 1714 Penhallow had clearly shifted his political ties away from the Vaughans and Waldrons to their opponents, the Wentworths and Atkinsons. In 1716, after the new governor Samuel Shute (a fellow graduate of Charles Morton's academy) arrived in New Hampshire and was residing at the Penhallow home, he dismissed six members of the council, including William Vaughan and Richard Waldron jun. As senior member Penhallow now became president of the council. Between 1717 and 1726 Penhallow, on Shute's appointment, served as chief justice of the superior court. In this position he gained a reputation as a strict, decisive, even harsh upholder of the law. Penhallow's political career had now reached its apex, while his house, located on Portsmouth's main pier, served as a centre of hospitality for the social élite.

As president of the council Penhallow helped execute a revolution in New Hampshire's politics which led to a long-term transformation of factionalism in the colony, with significant consequences in other areas of New Hampshire society. His roles in advising the dismissal of six members of the council and in helping replace George Vaughan with John Wentworth as lieutenant-governor created lasting enmity among the Vaughans, Waldrons, the old pro-puritan farmer–lumber-merchants, and their interior town allies. This faction obtained political revenge in 1730 after Jonathan Belcher, a Vaughan relative, was appointed governor and replaced Penhallow's allies with Richard Waldron (III), the son of Richard Waldron jun. Waldron's supporters dominated New Hampshire politics until 1741, when the Wentworth–Atkinson faction (mainly Portsmouth merchants) regained political power and held it until the American War of Independence. During the course of this factional strife, the Wentworth group created an Anglican church in the colony, obtained a huge increase in the province's boundaries, and became dominant in the colony's economy.

In the early 1720s Penhallow wrote his *History of the Wars of New England with the Eastern Indians* (1726), for which he is now best remembered. As treasurer and commissary-general Penhallow had financed and provided supplies to the militia during the Indian wars, and he used records, personal experiences, and interviews, and his son John's militia experiences, as sources for his *History*. He wrote it to record 'the bravery of these worthies who died … for the interest of their country'. The work detailed the ambushes, skirmishes, and battles among the French and American Indians and the New England colonists from 1703 to 1713 and from 1722 to 1725. Describing the Indians as 'bloody pagans', 'beasts of prey', and 'salvages', Penhallow saw them and the wars as 'a terrible scourge for the punishment of our sins', especially 'in neglecting the welfare of their souls' while seeking 'to advance a private trade' (*Penhallow's Indian Wars*, 18–19, 43, 45).

Penhallow died of unknown causes on 2 December 1726, in Portsmouth, where he was buried; he left about half his estate (which was inventoried at £1904) to his son John. He was one of a number of late seventeenth-century ambitious, intelligent Englishmen who took advantage of the numerous opportunities available in the colonies to marry into the local élite and to ally with local royal authorities in order to pursue his economic and political interests. He played a crucial role in administering New Hampshire's provincial government from the 1690s to the 1720s while influencing a transformation of political factionalism after 1715.   DAVID E. VAN DEVENTER

Sources D. E. Van Deventer, 'Penhallow, Samuel', *ANB* • N. Bouton and others, eds., *Provincial and state papers: documents and records relating to the province of New Hampshire*, 40 vols. (1867–1943), vols. 2–4, 17, 19, 32 • *Penhallow's Indian wars*, ed. E. Wheelock (1924) • Portsmouth town records, New Hampshire State Library, Concord, New Hampshire • *Collections of the New Hampshire Historical Society*, 1 (1824); 8 (1866) • J. R. Daniell, *Colonial New Hampshire: a history* (1981) • D. E. Van Deventer, *The emergence of provincial New Hampshire, 1623–1741* (1976) • *CSP col.*, vols. 1, 5, 7, 9–45 • S. Noyes, C. T. Libby, and W. G. Davis, *Genealogical dictionary of Maine and New Hampshire*, 5 vols. (Portland, ME, 1928–39); repr. (Baltimore, MA, 1972); repr. (Baltimore, MA, 1983)
Archives L. Cong., MSS | Mass. Hist. Soc., Belknap MSS • New Hampshire State Library, Concord, New Hampshire, Portsmouth town records, MSS
Wealth at death £1904 1s. 4d.: inventory, Bouton and others, eds., *Provincial and state papers*, vol. 32, p. 285

Penington, Edward (1667–1701). *See under* Penington, Isaac (1616–1679).

Penington, Isaac (*c.*1584–1661), local politician and regicide, was born in London, the eldest son of Robert Penington (1550–1627), a London merchant with estates in Norfolk and Suffolk, and Judith Shetterden (1559–1622), daughter of Isaac Shetterden of London. His grandfather William Penington (*d.* 1592), originally from Henham, Essex, had also become a London resident and was buried at St Benet Gracechurch.

Marriage, business and puritanism, 1613–1638 Gaining his freedom by patrimony in his father's company, the Fishmongers, Isaac Penington was admitted to the livery in 1613, joined its governing body in 1622, and was elected third warden in 1634–6; he was to become prime warden in 1640–42. On 7 February 1615 at Hackney he married his first wife, Abigail Allen (b. 1588), daughter of John Allen, a London merchant, with whom he had four sons and three daughters; three others died in infancy. His second wife, whom he married by licence dated 5 December 1629, was Mary Wilkinson (b. c.1587), widow of Roger Wilkinson of St Dunstan-in-the-West, haberdasher, and daughter of Matthew Young, a London brewer; there were no children from this marriage.

Penington began his commercial life as a substantial cloth trader in the Levant Company. He also had a moderate investment in the East India Company, which he had sold by the end of 1635, and an interest in the French wine trade. Yet he did not serve on any of the governing bodies of the great trading companies until the transformed circumstances of 1644, when he became governor of the Levant Company. Penington's second marriage extended his commercial interests to include a family partnership in a Whitefriars brewery. In addition, from 1626 he acted as a financial agent for his second cousin, Captain John *Penington, who was later knighted and became an admiral of the fleet and gentleman of the privy chamber. However, pursuit of his cousin's affairs brought problems, Penington's 'not having been used to dance attendance on great men's secretaries' (CSP dom., 1625–6, 305). Although he succeeded to his father's Norfolk and Suffolk estates in 1627, when he was sufficiently wealthy he chose to purchase a country residence, The Grange, at Chalfont St Peter in Buckinghamshire, some time before 1635. In London he was living in the parish of St Katharine Cree in 1629 but by 1633 had moved to St Stephen, Coleman Street, a parish with a strong puritan reputation. As a member of the general vestry in St Stephen's, he took part in the 1633 election of the future Independent leader, John Goodwin, as vicar. Penington also became a member of the committee for parish business in 1634, and served as collector for the poor in 1636 and an auditor for church-wardens' accounts in 1638, but he never held the office of churchwarden.

Penington's political and religious views and activities from the mid-1620s onwards bore most of the hallmarks of a puritan agenda. Writing to his cousin John in 1626, he expressed the view that there was 'little hope of any good unless the King and parliament agree' (CSP dom., 1625–6, 305). He favoured giving help to embattled protestants in continental Europe and waging war against Spain. Lodgings and a meeting-place in Whitefriars were also provided for puritan divines visiting London by Penington and his equally zealous second wife. In 1636 his attempt to establish a Sunday afternoon lectureship in his country parish of Chalfont St Peter led to a violent clash with the vicar during which Penington was said to have attacked Laud, claiming that 'since this same pragmatical bishop kept his visitation there is a great gap opened for the increase of popery and spreading of Arminianism' (CSP dom., 1635–6, 556–7). Penington complained to his cousin in 1637 that it was no longer safe for him to report the latest news from London and that same year his brewery was closed down by the authorities, ostensibly because of smoke pollution, but with a suspicion of vindictiveness.

Penington's election as a London sheriff in 1638, after several other nominees had refused to serve, was his first experience of senior City office and he had never been returned a common councillor. Although one contemporary claimed that Penington lived 'like a prince' during his shrievalty (CSP dom., 1638–9, 59), he himself later complained that the office had caused him considerable hardship. In January 1639 he was chosen alderman for Bridge Without, the only City ward denied the power to elect its own alderman or return common councillors. By 1640, therefore, he had had only recent experience of senior office and, although wealthy enough to be listed in May 1640 among the eight most prosperous citizens in his Coleman Street ward, he fell short of qualifying for membership of the City's mercantile élite.

The City and the Commons: MP and lord mayor Elected a London MP to the Short Parliament in March 1640, Penington combined a leading position among the City's godly citizens with entry into the counsels of the future parliamentarian leadership. He was also to develop close links with the Scottish commissioners sent down to London, with whom he shared a burning ambition to see an end of episcopacy in all three kingdoms. After the parliament's early dissolution Penington was one of seven London aldermen who refused to list inhabitants in their respective wards in preparation for a forced loan, yet seemingly he escaped punishment. Returned again a London MP in the Long Parliament, by the time of Pride's Purge he was to have served on 123 parliamentary committees, especially those concerned with religious reforms. Within the first week of the new parliament Penington joined Matthew Cradock, a fellow City MP, in backing a London petition condemning Laudian innovations and the fortification of the Tower. Shortly afterwards Penington could be seen playing a leading role in the organization and presentation of the first London root and branch petition (11 December 1640) and exactly one year later he was lending his support to the second London petition. His enthusiasm for godly reformation in the early 1640s put him at the forefront of the campaign to purge London pulpits of 'scandalous' and 'malignant' clergy to make way for godly and politically reliable divines, as in the case of Robert Chestlin, the rector of St Matthew's, Friday Street, and his replacement, Henry Burton, the puritan dissident. Penington's reforming zeal was also apparent in his introduction in February 1641 of a bill to abolish 'superstition and idolatry' from churches, including Laudian altars and rails, which finally received Commons sanction in their order of the following September. However, Penington's impatience to see the end of episcopacy and the full implementation of godly reformation sometimes caused problems for the more measured and circumspect parliamentary leadership.

During the early months of the Long Parliament Penington established himself as a vital intermediary between the Commons and City wealth in the negotiation of loans to pay for the English and Scottish armies, and he attempted to use this financial leverage to exert political pressure on parliament. The threat to withhold City loan money was deployed by Penington in January 1641, in an attempt (albeit an unsuccessful one) to reverse the reprieve of the Jesuit John Goodman, and in the following April to hasten Strafford's execution. Again Penington's militancy in deploying this tactic was probably unwelcome to the parliamentary leadership and may have been counter-productive. Furthermore, his ability to raise City money was not unqualified and he could find himself promising more than he could deliver, as in March 1641. Penington also forged a valuable political alliance with John Venn, a fellow City militant and, after a by-election in June 1641, MP. Both men were adept in drumming up popular support in London for radical causes in the early 1640s and were suspected (with more grounds in Venn's case) of orchestrating mass demonstrations outside parliament to intimidate MPs during the debate on the grand remonstrance. Penington also offered to provide the Commons with a guard of London citizens in November 1641 and the five members who fled the attempted coup in January 1642 may have taken refuge in his City home.

Lord mayor and after, 1642–1647 Penington was elected lord mayor in August 1642, despite his lack of seniority, after the removal of the royalist Mayor Gurney. He had already been appointed colonel of the White regiment of the London trained bands and in September 1642 he joined fellow radicals on the strategically important City militia committee. In the following July he was to be appointed lieutenant of the Tower of London in which capacity he was to accompany Laud to his execution in January 1645. As his grip on the City tightened he was able to deliver its resources for the parliamentarian cause, working closely with Pym and supported by a committed minority of citizens and clergy. Penington was responsible for several financial initiatives to support the war effort, such as the suggestion in June 1642 of weekly voluntary contributions in the City. His vigorous support for the war led him to clash in the initial stages with those Londoners working for an early peace and he made one of his rare appearances in the Commons since his election to the mayoralty to denounce the peace proposals as royalist-inspired. The king responded by condemning the 'pretended lord mayor' Penington as the 'principal author of those calamities' and grouping him with Venn and two other citizens as traitors who would never be pardoned (Rushworth, 5.111). His militancy undiminished, Penington and his equally committed wife rallied citizens to construct fortifications around London. He later became associated with the militant City remonstrance of Easter 1643, with its bold claims for parliamentary supremacy, and with radical initiatives, centred on the Salters' Hall sub-committee and the committee for the general rising, to raise independent military forces in London to intensify the war.

Penington continued to act as an intermediary between parliament and the City, and to assist in the raising of money and men for the war effort, after his replacement as lord mayor in October 1643 by the much more moderate Sir John Wollaston. The divisions that appeared in godly ranks after the decision to impose presbyterianism on England found Penington largely in the presbyterian camp. Having chosen the presbyterian Thomas Case to be his chaplain during his mayoralty, he took the covenant in November 1643 and was later to serve as an elder. Furthermore, in May 1645 he helped secure the removal of the Independent John Goodwin from St Stephen, Coleman Street, in favour of the presbyterian William Taylor and subsequently joined with other local zealots in assisting Taylor with the vetting of communicants. Yet Penington's preferred religious settlement was probably one which retained the parochial structure (which Goodwin was undermining) yet vested ultimate ecclesiastical authority in parliament and was content to tolerate gathered churches. In 1649 he was to assist in the reinstatement of Goodwin in St Stephen's.

Regicide and declining years, 1647–1661 Despite his moderate presbyterian inclinations Penington, like his ally Venn, became a leading political Independent. During the attempted counter-revolution of 1647 Penington was purged from the London militia committee, only to be restored to it after the army's intervention. Although no supporter of the Leveller party, after the defeat of the mutiny at Ware he expressed concern that parliament should not over-react or forget their record as faithful parliamentarians. After the second civil war he and Venn played a key role in ensuring that royalists and political presbyterians were not returned in the common-council elections of 1648. Penington was appointed to the high court of justice for the king's trial and attended eight of its twenty-two sittings. Although present when sentence was passed, he did not sign the death warrant, but he later assisted Mayor Andrews in proclaiming the abolition of kingship in the City [see also Regicides]. Penington served on the council of state in 1649–51 and 1651–2 and was nominated for one of the London seats in the first protectorate parliament but failed to attend the election. Personal economic difficulties increasingly claimed his attention after 1655. He had been involved in lengthy proceedings before the committee for advance of money since 1645 over a claim that he had retained at least £3000 from the estate of his cousin, the recently deceased Sir John Penington. After 1655, without his protection as an MP, his creditors were able to sue him and he was forced to appeal twice to the protector and his council to prevent his imprisonment and the confiscation of his lands. His financial difficulties were so severe by 1657 that he was forced to resign his aldermanry. Adding to his problems in the 1650s, his eldest son, Isaac *Penington junior (1616–1679) became a Quaker, as did two other children, while another son became a Catholic priest. At the Restoration Penington voluntarily surrendered himself, hoping to take advantage of the royal offer of indemnity in view of the fact that he had not signed Charles's death warrant. His remaining lands were seized and he was imprisoned for life in the Tower, where he died during the night of 16 December

1661. Penington's corpse was delivered over to his relatives on 19 December but there is no record of his burial place. His second wife survived him. KEITH LINDLEY

Sources HoP, Commons, 1640–60 [draft] · V. Pearl, London and the outbreak of the puritan revolution: city government and national politics, 1625–1643 (1961); repr. with corrections (1964), 176–84, 198–207, 210–17, 260–65 · CSP dom., 1625–6, 250, 281, 305; 1628–9, 156; 1635–6, 556–7; 1637, 249, 311–12, 559–60; 1637–8, 34, 498, 508; 1638–9, 59; 1661–2, 184 · vestry minutes, St Stephen Coleman Street, GL, MS 4458/1, pt 1, fols. 86, 89, 90, 91, 96, 101, 103, 104–5, 147, 161, 165 · A. B. Beaven, ed., The aldermen of the City of London, temp. Henry III–[1912], 2 (1913), 64 · J. Foster, Penningtoniana (1878), 66 · will of Robert Penington, PRO, PROB 11/151, sig. 36 · IGI · K. Lindley, Popular politics and religion in civil war London (1997) · The visitation of London, anno Domini 1633, 1634, and 1635, made by Sir Henry St George, 2, ed. J. J. Howard, Harleian Society, 17 (1883), 151 · marriage licence of Isaac Penington and Mary Wilkinson, 5 Dec 1629, GL, MS 10091/12 · J. Rushworth, Historical collections, new edn, 5 (1721), 111 · parish registers, St John's, Hackney, LMA, LMA, P79/JN1/022, 7 Feb 1615 [marriage, I. Penington to Abigail Allen] · W. J. Harvey, ed., List of the principal inhabitants of the City of London, 1640 (1886), 12 · VCH Buckinghamshire, 3.193

Likenesses line engraving, pubd 1800, BM, NPG · attrib. C. Jannsen, oils, Fishmongers' Company, London · engraving, repro. in A true declaration of the care of the Rt. Hon. Isaac Penington, Lord Mayor of London, in promoting the fortifications about the City and suburbs (1643) [Thomason Tracts, 27 April, E255/27]

Wealth at death estates seized for role in the regicide: HoP, Commons, 1640–60

Penington, Isaac (1616–1679), Quaker and writer, was born in London, the eldest son of Isaac *Penington (c.1584–1661), alderman, and his first wife, Abigail (b. 1588), daughter of the London merchant John Allen. He was admitted to the Inner Temple in November 1634 and called to the bar on 3 November 1639. In the meantime he matriculated from St Catharine's College, Cambridge, on 1 April 1637, though he apparently took no degree. Thomas Ellwood would later reflect that he had 'a sharp and excellent wit … well cultivated and polished with an ingenuous and liberal Education' (Works of … Isaac Penington, sig. c1v).

The pre-Quaker years Unsettled by the revolution Penington sought spiritual solace, the means to which he explored in A Touchstone or Tryall of Faith (1648). In addition to explaining how to discern genuine faith from that of the devil, 'that great cozouning merchant' (sig. A2r–v), he expounded on the practices of the primitive church. Unlike radicals who viewed the overthrow of monarchy with millenarian optimism, he was concerned about pervasive depravity, a theme he developed in The Great and Sole Troubler (1649). In A Word for the Common Weale (1650) he called on the Rump to enact sound laws to establish a salutary relationship between parliament and people. Having left the established church to become an Independent by 1649, he deplored the contentiousness over external forms that prevented England from attaining freedom of conscience. It was essential, he argued in A Voyce out of Thick Darkness (1650), to wait for the spirit's light, and in Light or Darknesse (1650) he recounted how he had been spiritually troubled and longed for 'somewhat more perfect' righteousness (p. 10). The struggle between the principles of light and darkness is also explored in Certain

Scripture Prophecies (1650), which reflects a knowledge of typology.

Apparently referring to reputed Ranters as well as apostates in general, in Severall Fresh Inward Openings (July 1650) and An Eccho from the Great Deep (1650) Penington addressed 'the Mad Folks' who had forsaken Christian beliefs and lived wickedly. Disillusioned, he resolved to 'retire into my secret corner, to lament and bewail that Misery and Desolation, which is seizing upon all things' (Penington, Openings, sig. A4r). Unless he was speaking figuratively, he embraced the unorthodox doctrine of the soul's sleep between death and resurrection.

During the spring of 1651 Penington addressed England's political problems. In The Fundamental Right, Safety and Liberty of the People (1651), directed to parliament and the people of 'this Sick Nation', he argued that parliament, like the Stuart monarchy, had exceeded its limits (sig. B1r). Proclaiming that people have the right to choose their polity and governors, he insisted they could alter them when the government becomes 'burdensome or inconvenient'. To keep parliamentary power from becoming arbitrary, elections must be free and frequent, MPs should not administer the laws, and parliaments should not engage in spiritual affairs. He was prepared to accept the return of monarchy if the prerogative were limited, people's rights were protected, and parliament had power to redress grievances. After the Rump's dissolution he wrote A Considerable Question (1653), averring that limited government, though less efficient, was preferable to absolute dominion. Rule by the saints—if they truly were—would be in the world's best interest, but otherwise not.

Penington continued to be dismayed by the emphasis on externals in religion at the expense of the inward substantial part—the divine seed implanted by the spirit as opposed to Satan's fleshly seed. Embodied in much of his writing, this concern received expression in The Life of a Christian (1653) and Divine Essays (1654). In pursuing the life of the spirit he found a kindred companion in Mary Springett (bap. 1623, d. 1682) [see Penington, Mary], daughter and heir of Sir John Proude of Goodnestone Court, Kent, and his second wife, Anne, daughter of Edward Fagge of Ewell, Kent; Mary's first husband, Sir William Springett, had died in 1644, and their daughter, Gulielma Maria, would later marry William Penn. On 13 May 1654, at St Margaret's, Westminster, Penington wed Mary, whose 'love was drawn towards him, because … he saw the deceit of all nations' (Experiences … of Mary Penington, 38). They had five children: John *Penington (1655–1710); Isaac (d. 1670); Mary (1657–1726), who married the London woollen draper Daniel Wharley in 1686; William (1665–1703), who became a druggist; and Edward [see below]. The Peningtons lived in London before moving in 1658 to the Grange, near Chalfont St Giles, Buckinghamshire, a wedding present from Penington's father. They also had estates at Causham (Caversham) Lodge near Reading, at Datchet, Buckinghamshire, at various places in eastern Kent, including Westbere, and, according to Ellwood, in Sussex.

Some time in the early 1650s Penington, feeling spiritually 'shattered' and 'broken', left the Independents in search of inner peace, a quest he shared with his wife. Typically described as Seekers, they belonged to no group. The Muggletonian John Reeve wrote to Penington about this time. In 1656 Penington published his lengthy *Expositions with Observations on Several Scriptures*.

Early Quaker years, 1658–1661 After reproving the Peningtons for their fashionable attire in 1657, an unidentified Quaker sent Thomas Curtis and William Simpson to visit them. Alexander Parker saw Penington at a Quaker meeting in Reading in February 1657, but not until May 1658 did Penington join the Friends after hearing George Fox speak at John Crook's home in Bedfordshire. The Grange soon became a hub of Quaker activity, and Fox held a meeting there in 1658. Reacting harshly to his son's convincement, the elder Penington threatened to disinherit him.

In his first Quaker publication, *The Way of Life and Death* (1658), Penington outlined his view of church history, according to which 'the true state of Christianity' was lost after the apostolic period, though God preserved a remnant of the faithful; Penington looked forward to the overthrow of the anti-Christian Babylon and the recovery of the true faith through life in the Spirit (p. 10). Anna Maria, Countess van Hoorn, translated the book into Dutch by 1661. Amplifying this theme in *Babylon the Great* (1659) he denounced Babylon, the spiritual fabric of evil and city of darkness, for its blasphemy, idolatry, spirit of witchcraft, and religious persecution. God, he proclaimed, is engaged in a controversy with England because of its adherence to Babylon. Where, he wondered in *The Scattered Sheep* (1659), were the praying people over whom a heathen spirit had descended? Distinguishing between human and divine faith in *The Axe Laid to the Root* (1659), he insisted that one must be guided by the light in one's soul, love simplicity, and live humbly to experience true religion. Those who ignore the inner light are like the ancient Jews, he contended in *The Jew Outward* (1659), for they commit the same errors, reject the doctrine of the new birth, and oppose Friends as the Jews rejected Christ.

Following the collapse of Richard Cromwell's government and the Rump's recall, on 18 May 1659 Penington wrote *To the Parliament, the Army, and All the Well-Affected*, accusing them of apostasy from the 'Good Old Cause' because they committed blasphemy, overthrew God's work, and failed to relieve the poor. Parliament, he argued, had one final opportunity to undertake God's work. In *To the Army* [1659] he reflected that God had accomplished great things by and for the military, yet it had betrayed his cause and brought global reproach on his name. After Monck's army had marched into England, Penington announced in a broadside dated 19 January 1660, *Some Considerations Proposed*, that the time of reformation had arrived, and he exhorted people to 'run not out into parties' but seek God. He published *A Question Propounded to the Rulers, Teachers, and People* on 14 February, asking how believers could belong to a church that still embodied the spirit of popery. In *Some Few Queries and Considerations Proposed to the Cavaliers* [1660] he pointedly enquired if their sufferings had been unjust in light of their previous persecution of the godly, their arbitrary rule, and the superfluity and evil ways of the court and gentry. Was not the cause of their opponents initially just?

Of the fourteen works he wrote in 1660, two—*Some Queries Concerning the Work of God* and *A Warning of Love*—were prophetic in tone, admonishing England for its adherence to false worship and religious persecution. Other publications were apologetic or controversial in nature. *A Brief Account of Some Reasons* explained the Friends' tenets to parliament, and *Where is the Wise?* explicated why the learned often opposed religious truth. Replying to Edmund Elys's defence of the Book of Common Prayer, Penington averred in *The Consideration of a Position* that genuine prayer comes only from the Spirit's 'breathings'. In *The New-Covenant* and *An Epistle to All such as Observe the Seventh Day* he rejected the sabbatarian claims of William Saller and others on the grounds that Jesus had dispensed with the old covenant. Keenly interested in the conversion of the Jews, he hoped they would once again become God's people, a point he made in *Some Considerations Propounded to the Jewes*. In *The Root of Popery* he contrasted the churches of Christ and Antichrist, repudiated Catholic claims to infallibility, and associated protestant governments that engaged in religious persecution with Catholicism. When the government in Boston, New England, threatened Quakers with banishment or death, Penington came to their defence in *An Examination of the Grounds*, insisting Friends did not teach destructive tenets or foment disturbances, and affirming their belief in the Trinity, though depicting Christ as the eternal light who assumed a bodily 'garment'. In *An Answer to that Common Objection* he offered to embrace all 'who suffered for the Testimony of a pure Conscience towards God', including John Hus and Martin Luther, but he insisted that God offers additional truth to each generation (p. 1).

By February 1661 Penington was in the Aylesbury gaol, having been arrested at a meeting in his house. His confinement lasted seventeen weeks, during which he refused to take an oath, a position he defended in *The Great Question* (1661). While in prison he was visited by Ellwood, whom he and his wife had convinced two years earlier. Ellwood reported that more than sixty Friends were incarcerated with Penington, who was ill with distemper. From his cell he issued *Somewhat Spoken to a Weighty Question* (1661), espousing religious freedom and pacifism, though recognizing that magistrates can legitimately use force to protect people. While visiting Friends in the same prison on 17 September he wrote to Charles II, warning him not to provoke God. He was referring in part to religious oppression, which he denounced in *Concerning Persecution* [1661] as contrary to righteous government. Undeterred by the state's repression of dissent, he continued to write, expounding on the 'breathings' of the spirit in *Some Directions to the Panting Soul* (1661) and *Concerning the Worship of the Living God* [1661], and using his experience to explain in

To All such as Complain (1661) that divine power often manifests itself gradually in individuals. His continuing interest in the conversion of the Jews was evinced in *Some Questions and Answers* (1661).

Trials and controversy, 1662–1671 Among Penington's works of 1662, *Three Queries Propounded to the King and Parliament* reminded readers that in the mid-century upheavals God had overturned the government and empowered men of low estate, and warned that he could do so again. No one, Penington insisted in *Some Observations* on Romans 14:20, has the right to destroy God's work. Each person must fear God and obey his commandments, he explained in *Some Questions and Answers Showing Man his Duty*, by responding to the divinely implanted 'principle of life' from which love, power, wisdom, and goodness spring. Nearly everything Penington wrote related to the spirit's workings and reflected his spiritual experience. 'I have had a very hard travel, and have felt [God's] power and cruelty beyond measure', he reflected in *Some of the Mysteries* (1663), 'yet the Lord my God hath helped me' (pp. 27–8). He believed he was the recipient of divine messages, including one recorded in *Concerning God's Seeking out his Israel* (1663) regarding God's search for the lost sheep who had experienced the spirit's warmth but not entered the new covenant.

In *A Weighty Question* (1663), addressed to king and parliament, Penington asked whether they had the right to enforce laws people could not conscientiously obey. Unpersuaded, magistrates imprisoned him at Aylesbury for seventeen or eighteen weeks in 1664 for having attended a conventicle. In prison he wrote *Some Queries Concerning the Order and Government of the Church*, explicating the role of ministers and extolling unity. The topic was timely, for the Friends were experiencing tension over the schismatic John Perrot. Penington had been moved by Perrot's suffering in Rome and had provided hospitality for him in 1662. Perrot's opposition to the removal of hats during prayer had prompted criticism from leading Quakers, and Penington, dismayed by the strife, warned in *Many Deep Considerations* [1664?] that God might permit church leaders to fall, thereby endangering ordinary believers. Concerned, William Smith and Francis Howgill wrote to Penington, and Richard Farnworth sent him a paper denouncing Perrot's innovations. Penington accepted their counsel, including Howgill's request that he write nothing else critical of Quaker leaders.

For attending a Quaker funeral Penington was fined and imprisoned for a month at Aylesbury in March 1665. About May he was arrested again, this time at the behest of the earl of Bridgewater, who was offended because Penington had refused to address him as 'My lord'. Released after nine months upon petition to the earl of Ancram, he was apprehended again about three weeks later and held in the Aylesbury gaol for a year and a half; he received his freedom about October 1667 after one of his wife's relatives obtained a writ of habeas corpus and had his case transferred to king's bench. These were difficult years,

partly because of what Ellwood, who tutored the Penington children between 1662 and 1669, called 'the Tenderness of his Constitution' (Ellwood, 164). During Penington's nine-month imprisonment in 1665 the crown seized the Grange, forcing Mary and her children to find other lodgings, primarily at Bottrels in Chalfont and then, the following year, at Berrie House in Amersham.

During his imprisonments Penington's pen remained active, partly with letters to his wife, magistrates, relatives, Quaker meetings, and even Bridgewater explaining why he could not use worldly titles. Someone sent him one of Richard Baxter's writings, which he returned with the comment that Baxter had not directed sinners to the principle of spiritual life and power. In *One More Tender Visitation* (1666) Penington appealed for an end to the persecution of Quakers, whose core belief in the contrast between the seeds of the spirit and the flesh he expounded in *Concerning the Sum or Substance of our Religion* [1666]. A companion piece, *Concerning the Church* (1666), defined the true church as a spiritual body gathered out of the world in contrast to the apostate churches of Catholics and most protestants. Members of the true church have the 'Principle of Life', the 'Seed of the Kingdom', he explained in *Some Things of Great Weight* (1667). In *A Question to the Professors of Christianity* (1667) he asserted that only those who feel the spirit have religious certainty. He also addressed internal tensions among Quakers, cautioning them in an epistle, *To Friends* [1666], to beware of the enemy's efforts to foment prejudice against God's ministers and not to impose spiritual criteria that contradict the spirit's manifestation in others.

Penington's first post-imprisonment writings included counsel to those seeking spiritual life (*To such as are not Satisfied*, [1668]), a fuller exposition of his view of history (*Of the Church*, 1668), and advice to the Royal Society on attaining religious certainty by heeding the light in their consciences (*Some Things Relating to Religion*, 1668). He engaged in controversy with an unnamed Congregationalist (*Reply to Queries and Animadversions*, 1668, published posthumously) and Lodowick Muggleton (*Observations on some Passages*, 1668); the latter responded in *An Answer to Isaac Penington* (1669). Penington apparently wrote nothing in 1669, perhaps because he and his wife, assisted by Ellwood, were planning the extensive renovation of Woodside (1669–*c*.1672), near Chalfont St Giles, which they acquired after selling the Westbere estate. About this time they sent their children to the Quaker school established by Fox at Waltham Abbey.

By May 1670 Penington was incarcerated at Reading, where he had gone to visit imprisoned Friends and had refused to take an oath. While in gaol he learned of the death of his son Isaac, lost at sea as he returned from Barbados. *A Salutation of Love* [1670], warning Buckinghamshire JPs of the imminent day of judgment, may have predated his incarceration, but at least seven works were composed during this twenty-one month confinement, including *Some Queries Concerning Compulsion in Religion* (1670), which reiterated the case for religious freedom. His account of the Friends was included in *Some Principles of the*

Elect People (1671), to which Fox and others contributed. *A Treatise Concerning God's Teachings* (*c*.1671) is noteworthy because of its autobiographical section, elements of which are echoed in *A Few Experiences* (early 1672, published posthumously). Also published posthumously but completed in May 1671, *Life and Immortality* discusses the covenants, the ability of everyone to respond to the inner light, and other Quaker tenets. *An Enquiry after Truth* [1672], finished in April, optimistically claimed that spiritual darkness is fading. In *The Holy Truth* (1672) he replied to Sir Henry Vane, repudiating both the doctrine that God justifies sinners without regarding their moral state and the doctrine of perseverance.

Last years, 1672–1679 Following Isaac's release in early 1672 the Peningtons witnessed the marriage of Penn and Gulielma Springett on 4 April. About this year, they moved into Woodside. Penington returned to his favourite theme of the inner light in *The Ancient Principle* (1672), and in *The Naked Truth* (1674) he asserted its primacy over scripture. In *Judas and the Jews* (1673) he expressed remorse for having criticized the Quaker leadership in 1664. With Penn, Ellwood, George Whitehead, and George Keith he engaged in a series of debates with Thomas Hicks and other Baptists between 1672 and 1674, and this led to his refutation of Hicks's *A Continuation of the Dialogue* (1673) in *The Flesh & Blood of Christ* (1675). During the 1670s he and other prominent Friends participated in the religious circle of Anne, Viscountess Conway, at Ragley Hall, Warwickshire, with Henry More and Francis van Helmont. When the Quakers were riven by the Story–Wilkinson dispute over the movement's institutionalization, Penington, siding with Fox, wrote to John Story on 21 September 1676, castigating him as stiff, exalted, and selfish, and he attempted, unsuccessfully, to persuade Curtis that something was 'deeply amiss inwardly' when he supported Story (Penington MSS, 4.141).

To the Jews Natural, and to the Jews Spiritual (1677) reiterated Penington's hope for the conversion of the Jewish people and depicted the saints as spiritual Jews. In September, while taking the waters at Astrop, Gloucestershire, he completed *The Everlasting Gospel* (1678), in which he professed not to dislike Catholics (his brother Arthur was a Catholic priest), Turks, and Jews, though he mourned their 'Mistakes' (p. 6). Two months later, in *Concerning the Dispensation of the Gospel* (1678), he expounded on the completion of the work of redemption, the translation of souls into the eternal kingdom, and their union with God. In July 1679 he explicated the doctrine of spirit-baptism in *A Reply to an Answer*, and at the month's end he reflected on his religious pilgrimage in *Some Experiences*, noting his feeling of certainty and sense of the spirit's infallibility. *Concerning the Times and Seasons*, composed in August at Meresborough, Kent, depicted history in terms of contrasting periods of joy (for example the creation and the promise of the blessed seed) and misery (the fall and the flood). While he and Mary were visiting their tenants in Kent Penington died at Goodnestone Court on 8 October, after a week's illness. He was interred later that month in the Quakers' burial-ground at Jordans, near Chalfont St

Giles, with hundreds of Friends and neighbours in attendance.

In her testimony Mary Penington remarked that no husband surpassed his kindness, tenderness, and love, and Fox recalled that Penington had undergone 'many Exercises, and Tryals, and Temptations, and Snares, both by them that were without, and False brethren' (*Works of … Isaac Penington*, sig. a2v). Fox was undoubtedly grateful that Penington had retracted his 1664 plea for broader toleration within the movement, and that in later years he had stood with the other leaders in deploring the divisions associated with Story and Curtis. According to Ellwood, Penington spent much of his time visiting Friends, ministering, reading the Bible, and waiting on the spirit, a key theme in his publications. He undoubtedly envisioned writing as a major part of his Quaker vocation, though his approximately ninety works (thirteen of them from his pre-Quaker period) are redundant and sometimes disjointed. His mystical approach to religion has led some commentators to suggest that he was influenced by Plotinus and Jacob Boehme, but there is no firm evidence of this. The leading proponent of a contemplative life among the Friends, he stressed the importance of meditation and self-denial. His Christology has sparked debate, for he downplayed the role of Christ's humanity while exalting that of the spirit. He suffered his imprisonments with equanimity, and apparently made no use of his legal training to obtain release. A number of his works were published posthumously for the first time, some of them in the two-volume folio edition of 1681. The most recent edition (1994–7), based on an 1863 American edition, is incomplete. His son John's transcriptions of his correspondence are preserved in the Friends' Library, London.

Penington's youngest son, **Edward Penington** (1667–1701), Quaker colonist, was born on 3 September 1667 at Amersham. He was tutored at home by Thomas Ellwood and others until 1680, after which he was educated at Edmonton. One of the first purchasers of land in Pennsylvania, he was appointed surveyor-general of the colony on 26 April 1698, and arrived in Philadelphia with Penn on 30 November of that year. On 16 November 1699 he married Sarah (*b*. 1679), daughter of Samuel Jennings, governor of New Jersey, and his wife, Ann (*née* Olliffe, or Olive); together they had one child, Isaac. The author of tracts defending the Friends against Keith and Thomas Crisp, Edward died, probably of smallpox, in Philadelphia on 11 November 1701.   RICHARD L. GREAVES

Sources *The works of the long-mournful and sorely-distressed Isaac Penington*, 2 vols. (1681) · T. Ellwood, *The history of the life of Thomas Ellwood*, ed. J. Wyeth, 4th edn (1775) [incl. suppl.] · Venn, *Alum. Cant.* · RS Friends, Lond., Penington papers · *Experiences in the life of Mary Penington* (*written by herself*), ed. N. Penney (1911); repr. (1992) · *The Conway letters: the correspondence of Anne, Viscountess Conway, Henry More, and their friends, 1642–1684*, ed. M. H. Nicolson, rev. edn, ed. S. Hutton (1992) · *Letters of Isaac Penington, an eminent minister of the gospel in the Society of Friends, which he joined about the year 1658*, ed. J. Barclay, 2nd edn (1828) · *CSP dom.*, 1660–85, 307–8 · J. Besse, *A collection of the sufferings of the people called Quakers*, 2 vols. (1753), vol. 1, pp. 31, 76–8 · M. W. Hess, ed., *The name is living: the life and teachings of Isaac Penington* (1936) · M. A. Creasey, 'Early Quaker Christology with special reference to the teaching and significance of Isaac

Penington, 1616–1679: an essay in interpretation', PhD diss., University of Leeds, 1956 [reissued in *Catholic and Quaker Studies*, 2 (1973)] · R. Moore, *The light in their consciences: early Quakers in Britain, 1646–1666* (2000) · W. C. Braithwaite, *The second period of Quakerism*, ed. H. J. Cadbury, 2nd edn (1961) · RS Friends, Lond., Swarthmore MSS 1.106; 3.144, 179 · *Papers of William Penn*, ed. M. M. Dunn and R. Dunn, 1–4 (1981–6) · *The short journal and itinerary journals of George Fox*, ed. N. Penney (1925) · T. I. Underwood, *Primitivism, radicalism, and the lamb's war: the Baptist–Quaker conflict in seventeenth-century England* (1997) · *DNB* · E. M. Bacon, 'Penington, Edward', *DAB* · A. Brink, 'The quietism of Isaac Penington: a study based on his pamphlets of 1648–1650', *Journal of the Friends' Historical Society*, 51 (1965–7), 30–53 · J. Punshon, 'The early writings of Isaac Penington', *Practiced in the presence: essays in honor of T. Canby Jones*, ed. D. N. Snarr and D. L. Smith-Christopher (1994), 60–67 · C. Kohler, *A quartet of Quakers* (1978)

Archives RS Friends, Lond., letters and MSS | PRO, SP 29/441/70 · RS Friends, Lond., Portfolio MSS, 3.83 · RS Friends, Lond., Swarthmore MSS, 3.144, 179; 1.106

Penington, Sir John (bap. 1584?, d. 1646), naval officer, was the son of Robert Penington (d. 1612) of Henham in Essex, described as a tanner. It has been suggested that his mother was Margaret, née Barfoot, and that he was baptized at Henham on 30 January 1568, but the circumstances of Penington's later career make it likely that he was born to Robert's second wife, Elizabeth, and that he was the John Penington who was baptized at Henham on 9 August 1584.

Early career Penington's early career is shrouded in obscurity. In June 1629 he recalled having captained ships for twenty years, although his naval service did not begin until 1621. He may have been the John Penington of Newhaven, Sussex, 'merchant', who embarked on a voyage to west Africa in 1612, and perhaps also the Captain Penington whose man-of-war was seized by the French off southern Italy in 1616. In 1617–18 he served as vice-admiral in Sir Walter Ralegh's ill-fated expedition to the Orinoco in search of a goldmine. Although Penington took no part in the attack on the Spanish settlement of St Thomas's, his ship, the *Star* of London (240 tons), was impounded at Kinsale on the way home in 1618 by order of the lord deputy, and in London Penington himself was thrown into prison. He subsequently helped to condemn Ralegh to the scaffold as, with another of the expedition's captains, he revealed that Ralegh had 'proposed the taking of the Mexico fleet if the mine failed' (Harlow, 300).

Penington claimed to have lost his entire fortune, amounting to £2500, in the Orinoco expedition, and on his release, which occurred some time before 6 October 1618, he sought gainful employment. He now enjoyed an enviable reputation for seamanship, Ralegh having described him in March 1618 as 'one of the sufficientest gentlemen for the sea England hath' (Bodl. Oxf., MS Tanner 290, fol. 4v). During the latter months of 1618 and through 1619 he repeatedly requested command of the next fleet to be set out by the East India Company. His applications were unsuccessful, but he attracted the attention of the new lord high admiral, George Villiers, marquess (subsequently duke) of Buckingham, who supported his applications to the company and then commissioned him as captain of an armed merchantman in the 1620–21 expedition against Algiers under Sir Robert Mansell. He evidently served with distinction, as on his return to England he was made flag captain to the earl of Oxford, who commanded a small squadron in the channel. However, he came out of pay on 18 May 1622 and received no further naval employment for three years. During this time he kept himself in readiness 'to do my King and country service when they shall call me unto it' (Centre for Kentish Studies, U269/1/OE1007). In August 1624 he obtained from the king a thirty-one-year lease of rents arriving from lands scattered though eleven counties, worth £150 per annum, thereby acquiring a regular income.

Wartime service, 1625–1629 In the spring of 1625 Penington commanded a squadron comprising a king's ship, the *Vanguard*, and seven armed merchantmen. These ships had been promised as loans to the French king, Louis XIII, to help quell the rebellion of the count of Soubise. However, neither Charles I nor Buckingham actually wanted them to be employed to suppress French protestantism. They hoped that by the time Penington's squadron reached France the Huguenots would have made peace with Louis, thereby allowing Penington's ships to be used in a combined Anglo-French military and naval operation against the Spanish satellite state of Genoa. He was accordingly given strict instructions to avoid involvement in France's civil wars. On his arrival at Dieppe in mid-June, however, he was ordered by the admiral of France to transport 1700 French troops to La Rochelle for service against the Huguenots. Penington was horrified, and returned to England, an action approved of by his superiors. He was nevertheless ordered back to Dieppe in mid-July, whereupon he asked to be relieved of his command. Buckingham feigned anger at this request, which he refused, but was secretly delighted by his subordinate's reluctance to co-operate with the French as there was as yet no confirmation of rumours that the Huguenots had agreed peace terms with Louis. Penington continued to give the duke secret cause for satisfaction, for at the end of July he connived at a mutiny by his crew which resulted in him returning to England for a second time. It was not until 5 August, when Buckingham and Charles were misled into thinking that Louis had made peace with the Huguenots, that Penington's ships (bar one) were transferred to French control.

Soon after he returned to England Penington was ordered to mount a blockade of Dunkirk, but a storm in mid-October scattered his ships and more than twenty Dunkirkers evaded his net. Buckingham did not blame Penington for this failure, and at the beginning of 1626 he ordered him to fit out thirty ships at Plymouth with the aim of assisting Soubise, who had been defeated in a naval engagement in September 1625 and was now regarded as England's ally. Over the next five months Penington strained his own finances to equip this fleet, but he was hampered by acute shortages of men, money, and victuals, and became despondent that he seldom heard from Buckingham, 'for I do not only honour my lord but love him as a young man doth his mistress, and am jealous of his favours, or the contrary' (PRO, SP 16/23/25). Buckingham was not indifferent to Penington's difficulties, however, but was distracted by parliament, where his enemies accused him, among other things, of contributing to the military problems of the Huguenots by lending warships to Louis XIII. On 6 May 1626 Penington, having played a key role in the loan of the ships, was summoned by Buckingham to Westminster to give evidence, during which absence part of his fleet mutinied for want of pay and clothing. By the time he returned to his station the mutiny had fizzled out. Charles and Buckingham now abandoned their planned assistance of Soubise and resolved instead that Penington's fleet should form the nucleus of a fresh expedition to Spain under Lord Willoughby, with Penington as its rear-admiral. Willoughby's fleet was no better prepared than Penington's had been, however, and by the time the expedition sailed from Falmouth on 7 October, Penington was predicting the overthrow of the voyage, 'the time of the year being so far spent and we being now victualled but for ten weeks' (PRO, SP 16/37/49). His pessimism proved well founded, for in the Bay of Biscay the fleet encountered storms which sent it hurrying back to England. The outcry which greeted Willoughby's premature return led to the creation of a commission of inquiry, of which Penington was a member, but he attended only one of its meetings (on 22 December) before he was ordered back to sea, this time as admiral of a fleet of twenty ships provided by the city of London. Relations with France were now at a low ebb and he was instructed to intercept several warships built in the Netherlands for the fledgeling French navy reported to be anchored off Havre de Grace. There he was to provoke a quarrel so as to capture or sink the French ships. However, on his arrival in the Downs he found only fifteen ships rather than the twenty he had been promised, and that none were suitable for use as men-of-war. After an unsuccessful attempt to cross the channel on 29 December, he dutifully scoured the French coast. By the time he learned of the whereabouts of the French, on 14 January 1627, the time allotted to his ships for their naval service had nearly expired and he was therefore unable to mount an attack.

Soon after the city ships were discharged, Penington was appointed (on 19 February) admiral of a squadron with orders to escort several detained French vessels from the western ports to the Thames and to sweep the channel clean of all enemy shipping. He carried out these instructions in spectacular fashion, taking twenty French prizes and bringing home goods and shipping valued at £128,600. Buckingham was delighted with this haul, which enabled him to complete his preparations for an assault on the Île de Ré in support of the Huguenots of La Rochelle. He accordingly ordered Penington to receive £1000 in recognition of his valuable service and bestowed on him the captaincy of Sandown Castle, at an annual salary of £20.

Shortly after the English landed at Ré, Penington, who commanded a squadron in Buckingham's fleet, offered to attempt to free the wine fleet which had been arrested at Bordeaux. However, Buckingham objected that he would

first need to secure the nearby island of Oleron, from where it was feared the French king would mount a counter-attack. In the event, Penington was merely detailed to 'guard' Oleron, but he proved powerless to prevent the French from building up their forces there, and as a result Buckingham's army was swept off Ré at the end of October. He returned to England ill and short of money, having received neither pay for the past eighteen months nor the promised £1000 reward. He was also thoroughly worn out, having been at sea almost continuously for the past two and a half years. In December he asked Buckingham to appoint him surveyor of the ordnance office, a position sufficiently remunerative to keep him from badgering Buckingham for money while still enabling him to 'be near and ready upon all occasions to attend your grace's commands' (PRO, SP 16/89/59). Buckingham was not yet ready to dispense with Penington's naval services, but he was willing to allow his subordinate a well-earned rest from sea service. Penington accordingly took no part in the earl of Denbigh's unsuccessful attempt to relieve La Rochelle in the spring of 1628, but instead was commissioned with the shipwright Phineas Pett to oversee the construction of ten small ships which were required both to row and sail. He discharged this role with his customary energy, and the new ships were launched later that year as the *Lion's Whelps*. Buckingham also ensured that he was paid the £1000 reward he was owed, and helped him to a royal grant of the Buckinghamshire manor of Hanslope, which Penington coveted owing to its proximity to one of the duke's residences.

By mid-July 1628 a refreshed Penington was back in harness, having been appointed to command a squadron in the fleet which Buckingham himself was preparing to lead to La Rochelle. In the event, he took no part in this expedition, which went ahead despite Buckingham's murder on 23 August. Penington had lionized Buckingham, and the duke's death must therefore have been a shattering blow to him. Buckingham's successors, the admiralty commissioners, enjoyed no such close relationship with Penington, and when in May 1629 they drew up a list of the captains for employment at sea that year they excluded him from it. His name was nevertheless inserted by the king, who placed him in command of a squadron to blockade the Elbe in support of the Danes. However, when news arrived that Denmark had concluded peace with the emperor his commission was revoked. His subsequent dispatches were ignored by the admiralty commissioners, much to his bemusement, as 'I am sure I have given no just cause of distaste to any either by neglecting my employment or otherwise' (PRO, SP 16/147/2).

The 1630s Once again Penington had found himself cast aside by the navy but in May 1631 he was unexpectedly appointed admiral of the narrow seas, the admiralty commissioners being disgruntled with the previous incumbent, Sir Henry Mervyn. Penington settled into his new role with his customary energy, and it was not long before the leading admiralty commissioner, Lord Treasurer Portland, expressed complete satisfaction with his performance. He remained admiral of the channel squadron for the next three years. By April 1632 he was also a gentleman-in-ordinary of the privy chamber, and two years later he was knighted aboard his flagship by the king.

As rear-admiral in 1635 Penington was disappointed by the failure of the first ship money fleet to confront the French. On learning that the king intended to set out another fleet the following year, Penington hoped that it would achieve more than the first, 'or the money were as well saved as spent' (*CSP dom.*, *1635*, 316). He served as admiral of the winter guard in 1635–6 and as vice-admiral of the second ship money fleet in 1636, when he also subscribed a series of criticisms of the navy's ships and provisions drawn up by the fleet's young commander, the earl of Northumberland. He retained the rank of vice-admiral in 1637 and again in 1638, when Northumberland's ill health caused Penington to be the senior officer at sea.

By 1638 Penington was in his mid-fifties and Northumberland, who was appointed lord high admiral in March, expected him to retire soon from sea service to make way for a younger man. When the surveyorship of the navy fell vacant in August, Northumberland therefore offered it to Penington, but the office was unprofitable and Penington apparently turned it down. Thereafter his relationship with the new lord admiral quickly deteriorated. In December, for instance, he was upbraided for taking his orders from one of the secretaries of state rather than from Northumberland, an offence he had committed in the previous year. Penington resented this admonition and privately complained to the former admiralty secretary Edward Nicholas that he could expect no better treatment 'so long as some are at the helm' (*CSP dom.*, *1638–9*, 188). His fears were justified, as Northumberland's response to the news that he had complained to the marquess of Hamilton about defects in some of his vessels in 1639 indicates. Penington, as admiral of a much reduced ship money fleet, had been ordered to transport Hamilton's army to Scotland to oppose the covenanters. Northumberland advised Hamilton 'not to give too much credit to what he tells you of this nature', being 'well acquainted with Sir John Penington's aptness to take up reports upon very slight information (which when they come to be examined never prove true)' (NA Scot., GD 406/1/1082).

Although held in low regard by Northumberland, Penington was an able and experienced seaman with a long record of loyal service, even if he was also a born grouser. His abilities were amply demonstrated in the following month when he reported that he had blocked up the Scottish forces in Leith harbour so 'that they cannot stir in or out with a boat but we snap them up, which does infinitely perplex and trouble them more than all the King's army' (*CSP dom.*, *1639*, 210). The simmering feud between Penington and Northumberland was exacerbated in the autumn of 1639, however, after a large Spanish fleet was chased into Dover Road by the Dutch navy. For some years England had attempted to exercise sovereignty over its adjoining seas by policing them with large fleets. English claims to sovereignty would be exposed as hollow if the

Spanish and Dutch came to blows in sight of the English fleet, yet there was nothing that Penington could do to prevent this as his force was too small. This was appreciated by Northumberland's admiralty secretary, Thomas Smith, who advised Penington to make a pretence of protecting the Spanish while not actually exposing his ships to any hazard.

Early on the morning of 11 October Penington consulted his captains after the Dutch admiral signalled to the rest of his fleet to engage the Spanish. They resolved to get to the windward of the Dutch, who, anticipating this manoeuvre, detached a portion of their fleet to maintain a watchful eye on the English. As the fight developed a Dutch captain remonstrated that the Spanish had fired first, but Penington retorted that the Dutch had provoked the battle by approaching so close with their fireships. In the ensuing confusion the English captured two Dutch vessels, but Penington, perhaps heeding Smith's sound advice, recommended to his captains that they should be released as 'they were no considerable satisfaction for his majesty for the affront done unto him' (P. White, *A Memorable Sea-Fight*, 1649, 46) and would merely provoke the Dutch, whose fleet was five times stronger than theirs. His captains took little persuading of the wisdom of this advice, and the two vessels were accordingly released. Penington was widely censured for this decision after the battle, and also for failing to ride close to the Dutch ships to prevent them from attacking the Spanish. Indeed, though roundly defended in public by Northumberland, privately the earl complained that 'Penington hath behaved himself basely' (BL, microfilm M285, fol. 235v), and soon after the battle tensions between the two men resurfaced, this time over the gathering-up of valuable wreckage to which Northumberland laid claim as lord admiral. On 30 October Penington was rebuked for making 'so much ado about a business wherein you had such punctual instructions' (*CSP dom.*, *1639–40*, 62).

King and parliament, 1640–1646 Penington was admiral of the last of the ship money fleets in 1640, and reverted to his former title as admiral of the narrow seas in 1641. In May 1641 the exchequer was ordered to allow him £3000 in recognition of his services, but a depleted treasury was unable to find the money. By 1642 Penington, finally tired of sea service, asked his friend Edward Nicholas to persuade the king to appoint him treasurer of the navy alongside the gouty and aged Sir William Russell. Penington was by now wealthy enough to serve in that office: in July 1640 he valued his estate for the purposes of his will at more than £13,732 in cash and loans. Much of this fortune had undoubtedly been derived from convoy money—the payments made by Spain in the later 1630s to the captains of the ship money fleets in return for the safe convoy of their treasure ships into Dunkirk harbour—but Penington had also profited from moneylending, a business carried on for him while he was at sea by his second cousin, the London alderman Isaac Penington. However, Charles resolved to maintain Russell as sole treasurer for the time being because Penington was more useful to him at sea. Indeed, it was Penington who spirited Lord Digby across the channel for him in January 1642, at which time Penington also secretly pledged to refer all his instructions to the king for his approval.

The part played by Penington in Digby's escape infuriated Northumberland, whose authority he had again bypassed. On 18 January the lord admiral sent Penington a curt letter requiring him to report to parliament, 'which is all I have to say at present' (PRO, SP 16/488/70). After consulting the king, Penington gave evidence to the Commons, whose speaker thanked him for an 'ingenuous confession' (Coates, Young, and Snow, 176). However, his explanation that he had been obliged to follow Charles's orders because he was employed by the king under the lord admiral was not well received. On 23 February Charles ordered Penington to accompany the queen to the Netherlands, where he was kept in her service until 23 March. His absence provided further proof that he was taking his orders directly from Charles, and therefore on 10 March the Commons resolved that the king should be asked to employ the earl of Warwick in his stead that summer. Charles refused to countenance their request, however, and later rebuffed a petition to the same effect from both houses.

Penington came out of pay on 5 April and subsequently joined the king at York. By the end of June the fleet was in Warwick's hands, but Charles was still determined to install Penington. However, Penington only hesitantly agreed to help oust Warwick. According to Clarendon, he feared capture and was in considerable 'perplexity' (Clarendon, *Hist. rebellion*, 2.225), while the royalist writer David Lloyd considered that he had been 'deluded by the faction' (Lloyd, 646), whose ranks included Isaac Penington. Whatever the reasons for his reluctance, Penington, instead of proceeding to the Downs himself, sent instructions to the aged comptroller of the navy, Sir Henry Palmer, a former seagoing officer who lived close by, to take command of the fleet on his behalf. Meanwhile, a royal courier required Warwick's captains to place themselves under Penington's orders. Clarendon relates that the captains received this message 'with great duty and submission' and stayed only to receive Penington's instructions. However none were forthcoming because Penington would not venture aboard ship until Palmer had signalled that it was safe to do so, and Palmer had not yet arrived, allegedly because he was unwell. Amid this confusion Warwick, who had been feasting ashore, learned of the king's message. Returning hastily to his flagship, the earl summoned his captains to him, and took prisoner those who refused to obey his commands. By the time Palmer arrived the game was up.

On the outbreak of civil war Penington was appointed an ordnance commissioner by the king. In August 1642 Charles finally agreed to appoint him joint treasurer of the navy, which was now largely in parliament's hands. Following the royalist capture of Bristol in July 1643 he was designated admiral of the fleet, with instructions to keep open the Bristol Channel and communications with south Wales and Ireland. By early August he had readied a force of eighteen ships at Bristol, where he remained until

at least April 1645. What became of him after Fairfax stormed the city in September is uncertain. According to Lloyd he died at Bristol in September 1646; he was certainly dead by 28 May 1648, when his will of 1645 was proved. In this he divided up his fortune of more than £13,500 in cash and £1000 in plate among various relatives and friends, having never married.

ANDREW THRUSH

Sources CSP dom., 1603–49 · PRO, SP 14, SP 16 · BL, Add. MS 37816 · V. T. Harlow, ed., *Ralegh's last voyage* (1932) · *CSP col.*, vol. 3 · J. Foster, *Pedigree of Sir Josslyn Pennington, fifth Baron Muncaster of Muncaster and ninth baronet* (1878) · *The manuscripts of the Earl Cowper*, 3 vols., HMC, 23 (1888–9), vols. 1–2 · NA Scot., GD 406/1/1082 · BL, Add. MS 9294, fols. 253–5 · BL, Egerton MS 2533, fols. 93–98v · *The autobiography of Phineas Pett*, ed. W. G. Perrin, Navy RS, 51 (1918) · PRO, E403/1740 · PRO, HCA 14/42/59 · navy treasurer's declared accounts, PRO, E351 · PRO, SO 3/8, SO 3/12 · W. H. Coates, A. Steele Young, and V. F. Snow, eds., *The private journals of the Long Parliament*, 1: 3 *January to 5 March 1642* (1982) · A. Steele Young and V. F. Snow, eds., *The private journals of the Long Parliament*, 2: 7 *March to 1 June 1642* (1987) · *JHC*, 2 (1640–42), 474 · J. R. Powell and E. K. Timings, eds., *Documents relating to the civil war, 1642–1648*, Navy RS, 105 (1963) · Clarendon, *Hist. rebellion* · D. Lloyd, *Memoires of the lives … of those … personages that suffered … for the protestant religion* (1668) · I. Roy, ed., *The royalist ordnance papers, 1642–1646*, 2 vols., Oxfordshire RS, 43, 49 (1964–75) · W. H. Black, ed., *Docquets of letters patent* (1837) · W. Lithgow, ed., *The totall discourse of the rare adventures* (1906) · W. A. Shaw, *The knights of England*, 2 (1906), 202

Archives NMM, naval journals

Likenesses C. Van Dalen, line engraving, c.1638, BM, NPG

Wealth at death over £14,500—incl. £13,500 cash and £1000 plate: will, Foster, *Pedigree of Sir Josslyn Pennington*, 64–5

Penington, John (1655–1710), Quaker apologist and controversialist, was born in London or at his mother's estate of Worminghurst, Sussex. His parents were Isaac *Penington (1616–1679), the friend of George Fox and William Penn, and his wife, Mary Springett, née Proude [see Penington, Mary (bap. 1623, d. 1682)], the spiritual autobiographer. John's childhood years must have been turbulent, since his father faced near continual persecution in the early Restoration period. Isaac was in prison for much of the decade of the 1660s, and during this period he lost his estate and suffered significant diminution of his wife's estates in Kent. Nevertheless, John received a good education, first of all as a student of Thomas Ellwood, who was employed as family tutor, then at the Quaker boarding-school at Waltham Abbey. In the early 1670s the family rebuilt Woodside House, near Amersham, Buckinghamshire, and settled there. John seems to have been a favourite of his father, at least after the death at sea of his brother Isaac, for he was often in his company during these years.

In 1679 Penington's father, who was much beloved by the Quaker community, died. Upon his death John inherited Woodside House as well as Goodnestone Court, his mother's estate in Kent. Isaac's Quaker mantle apparently fell to John, too, who seems to have taken a leadership role in the London community from this time on. He joined with other Quaker leaders (as well as his mother) in writing a tribute to Isaac. John's subsequent writings were largely directed to vindicating his father and other

Quaker authors. In 1681 he published *John Penington's complaint against William Rogers: relating to the abuse and injury done to the memory of his worthy father Isaac*, in which he accused Rogers of deliberately misrepresenting Isaac, who claimed that the latter had said that no 'outward Form of Government' was necessary in this life.

In the 1690s serious attacks were levelled at Quaker writings by the 'apostate' Quaker George Keith. Keith had been a prominent leader of the sect until he had a falling out with the Quakers of Pennsylvania in the early 1690s. In 1693 he returned to London and started writing against his erstwhile colleagues. Keith applied withering criticism to the writings of William Penn, George Whitehead, and Isaac Penington. John responded by pointing out Keith's own inconsistencies—in his past comments as well as his recent writings—and claimed to be able to quote 'Keith against Keith' (*Keith Against Keith, or, Some More of George Keith's Contradictions and Absurdities*, 1696). All told, Penington wrote five books or tracts against Keith, and debated with him publicly at Turner's Hall in June 1696. His most detailed and systematic attacks are *Keith Against Keith*, mentioned above, and *The fig-leaf covering discovered, or, George Keith's explications and retractions … proved insincere* (1697). Penington died at Goodnestone Court, Kent, on 8 May 1710 and was buried at the Quaker burial-ground at Jordans, Chalfont St Giles. He never married.

J. S. CHAMBERLAIN

Sources J. Penington, *John Penington's complaint against William Rogers: relating to the abuse and injury done to the memory of his worthy father Isaac Penington, in mis-representing and perverting some of his writings, in his book entitled, 'The Christian Quaker distinguished from the apostate and innovator, &etc.'* (1681) · J. Penington, *An apostate exposed, or, George Keith contradicting himself and his brother Bradford* (1695) · J. Penington, *Keith against Keith, or, Some more of George Keith's contradictions and absurdities* (1696) · J. Penington, *The fig-leaf covering discovered, or, Geo. Keith's explications and retractions of divers passages out of his former books, proved insincere, defective and evasive* (1697) · J. Penington, 'The testimony of John Penington, to his dear and deceased father Isaac Penington', *The works of Isaac Penington*, 4th edn (1861), 1.44–6 · M. Webb, *The Penns and Peningtons of the seventeenth century*, 2nd edn (1891) · Allibone, *Dict.* · *DNB* · 'Dictionary of Quaker biography', RS Friends, Lond. [card index]

Penington [*née* Proude], **Mary** [*other married name* Mary Springett, Lady Springett] (*bap.* 1623, *d.* 1682), Quaker and writer, was born at Goodnestone Court, near Faversham, Kent, and baptized on 13 December 1623 at Canterbury Cathedral. She was the only child and heir of Sir John Proude (*d.* 1628), an army officer, and his wife, Anne Fagge of Ewell, Kent (*d.* 1628). Sir John Proude fought for the United Provinces in the service of the prince of Orange and died in 1628 at the battle of Groll, in Guelderland, when Mary was about five. Her mother having died in the same year, Mary went to live with guardians whose identity remains unknown, but whose lack of religious rigour was distasteful to her.

From the age of nine until her marriage about the age of eighteen Mary Proude resided in Kent, in the home of Sir Edward Partridge and his extended family, including his recently widowed sister, Lady Katherine Springett, and

her three children, the oldest of whom, Sir William Springett (1621/2–1644), parliamentarian colonel, deputy lieutenant for the county of Kent, and devout puritan, became Mary's first husband in 1642. He was sympathetic with her attraction to puritanism, although both later rejected Independency. Married 'without a ring', they refused to have their only son, John (*d.* before 1647), baptized (*Experiences*, 78). Removed to London on account of the dangerous uprisings in the Vale of Kent, Mary Springett was heavily pregnant with her daughter, Gulielma Maria (1644–1693), when she undertook a harrowing winter journey to Arundel, Sussex, to visit her husband. Having successfully besieged Arundel Castle, he died from spotted fever in 1644. She refused to have her daughter, born after her husband's death, baptized.

During her widowhood, Mary Springett's spiritual life faltered. Experimenting with and then abandoning different religious 'notions', she also rejected her accustomed 'religious exercises' (*Experiences*, 28). Believing in 'the Lord and his truth', yet convinced 'that it was not made known to any upon earth' (ibid., 30), Mary Springett became part of fashionable and irreligious London society; she took up 'foolish mirth, carding, dancing, singing, and frequenting of music meetings', but with a 'heart … constantly sad, and pained beyond expression' (ibid., 30–31). Visited by vivid and prophetic dreams, she still could not pray nor 'call God father' (ibid., 34).

On 13 May 1654, 'being [long] wearied in seeking and not finding', Mary Springett married Isaac *Penington (1616–1679), Quaker convert and author of many spiritual tracts, who, like her, sought the 'truth' and 'refused to be comforted by any appearance of religion' (*Experiences*, 38). The couple lived in or near London, although they also had estates at Causham (Caversham) Lodge, near Reading, and at Datchet, in south Buckinghamshire. John *Penington, their eldest son and heir, was born in 1655 and before his death in 1710 he had produced a number of Quaker tracts and preserved the personal papers of his parents, including Mary Penington's spiritual autobiography. 'Convinced' about 1656 through the combined efforts of Thomas Curtis and William Simpson, they were publicly affiliated with the Quakers by 1658. Soon after, Mary and Isaac took up residence at The Grange, near Chalfont St Peter, Buckinghamshire, an estate which Isaac's father, Alderman Isaac *Penington (*c.*1584–1661), had given them at the time of their marriage. Their second son, Isaac, was born about 1656, and their only daughter, Mary, in 1657. The Grange was also the centre of the local Quaker community and a haven for the young Thomas Ellwood, who became the Peningtons' tutor in 1662, and whose father opposed his son's convincement. When The Grange was sequestered around 1665 because of Alderman Penington's involvement in Charles I's execution, Mary and her younger children settled near Isaac, imprisoned at Aylesbury (1665–8), while Gulielma Maria stayed with friends. Some time between 1666 and 1668 Mary and some of her children also boarded at Waltham Abbey School, Essex. About 1658–68 she began her spiritual autobiography, which she completed just before her death; it was published in 1821 as *Some account of circumstances in the life of Mary Penington. From her manuscript, left for her family.*

Ostracized on account of their Quakerism, Mary Penington and her husband faced lawsuits in chancery, brought by tenants and relations, all of whom took 'advantage' of their Quaker refusal to swear oaths (*Experiences*, 53). Judith Penington, Isaac's sister, used the terms of Mary Penington's marriage settlement in an at least partially successful action (*c.*1664–*c.*1667) to gain control over her sister-in-law's lands in Kent. Lawsuits led to the loss of at least one of Mary's estates and all of Isaac's. She retained at least one in Sussex (Worminghurst Hall) and several in Kent, including Westbeer, but sold the latter to purchase Woodside, a farm with a dilapidated house near Amersham, in 1669. Having given birth to William in 1665 and Edward in 1667, she renovated Woodside, which was ideally located so the family could remain part of the Chalfont St Peter Quaker community. She completed the work in 1672–3 (Penney, 13). In addition to raising her children during Isaac's imprisonments (1666–71), Mary Penington participated in Quaker controversies; her letters speak favourably of separate women's meetings, and address factionalism and backsliding. Isaac's death in 1679 prompted her publication of a testimony to his character, one of several which preface his collected works (1681). She also helped defend her own reputation as well as that of her husband against William Rogers's attacks in the *Christian Quaker* (1680). In *John Penington's Complaint Against William Rogers* (1681) she refutes the charge that she avoided the seizure of her property and thus shunned 'suffering' for truth (M. Penington, 'My mother's account', 11).

To Mary Penington's biographers she is the exemplary wife, mother, and 'helpmeet' to her famous husbands, although many also praise the literary skill evident in her manuscript biography of William Springett, *A Letter from me to my Dear Grandchild Springet Pen* (1680). Her works are also important 'social documents', which 'record the liberating effect that Quakerism had on … women' (Blecki, 20), offer an 'affecting evocation of a spiritual life lived in inviolable privacy even in the midst of a loving family' (Burns, 72), and present a record of a woman who embraced 'the Friends' imperative to break down the barriers between private spiritual conscience and public life' (Coleman, 93). Her works were first published in 1821, but fifteen extant manuscript copies (1680–*c.*1812) testify to the recognition of their spiritual and literary merits in England and America. The Victorian novelist Emma Marshall used a family copy of the manuscripts in her civil war romance *Memories of Troublous Times* (1880), which includes Mary Penington herself as a character.

Mary Penington's will, dated 18 July 1680, testifies to her successful stewardship of her estate in the face of the government's religious persecution. After giving enough to each of her younger sons 'to bind him to some trade', as well as an additional £400 when each turned twenty-two, she was able to leave gifts and annuities for friends, relatives, and her younger children totalling about £175. Mary's estates, which she had inherited from her mother

and father, went to John (M. Penington, 'Abstract of the will', 109–12). Mary Penington died of an illness, perhaps triggered by a serious fever in June 1680. A letter from Isaac Penington referring to Mary's journey to London to consult a physician suggests, however, that as early as 1667 she was suffering from some kind of painful internal complaint. She died on 18 September 1682 at Worminghurst Hall, Sussex, a property which was probably a gift from Mary to her daughter, Gulielma Maria, upon her marriage to William Penn. She is buried beside her husband, Isaac, in the Quaker burial-ground at Jordans, Buckinghamshire. **MARIE H. LOUGHLIN**

Sources N. Penney, introduction, in *Experiences in the life of Mary Penington*, ed. N. Penney (1911); repr. (1992), 7–16 [repr. 1992] • R. Hovenden, ed., *The register booke of christeninges, marriages, and burials within the precinct of the cathedrall and metropoliticall church of Christe of Canterburie*, Harleian Society, register section, 2 (1878), 5 • *Experiences in the life of Mary Penington*, ed. N. Penney (1911) [repr. 1992] • H. Penington, preface, in *Some account of circumstances in the life of Mary Penington, from her manuscript, left for her family* (1821) • T. Ellwood, *The history of the life of Thomas Ellwood*, ed. C. G. Crump (1900) • *Experiences in the life of Mary Penington*, ed. N. Penney (1911); repr. (1992), preface, pp. vii–xvii • 'Abstract of the will of Mary Penington, dated 18th July 1680', *Experiences in the life of Mary Penington*, ed. N. Penney (1911); repr. (1992), 109–12 [repr. 1992] • 'A testimony to the Lords power at the women's meeting at J. M.', RS Friends, Lond., Penington MS vol. iv, p. 159 • 'For those women friends that are dissatisfied at present with the women's meeting distinct from men …', RS Friends, Lond., Penington MS 4, 159–61 • 'M: P. concerning W: R's putting her in print', RS Friends, Lond., Penington MS 4, 162 • M. Penington, 'Mary Penington her testimony concerning her dear husband [Isaac Penington]', in *The works of the long-mournful and sorely-distressed Isaac Penington* (1681) • M. Penington, 'My mother's account is as followeth', in J. Penington, *John Penington's complaint against W. Rogers* (1681), 10–13 • M. Webb, *The Penns and Peningtons of the seventeenth century, in their religious and domestic life* (1867) • J. G. Bevan, *Memoirs of the life of Isaac Penington* (1807) • E. A. Benson, 'An account of the life of Gulielma Maria Springett Penn, 1644–1694', *Penn family recipes: cooking recipes of William Penn's wife, Gulielma* (1966) • Chancery records, 1 Feb 1664, PRO, C8, index vol. 10, bundle 319, no. 78 • C. La Courreye Blecki, 'Alice Hayes and Mary Penington: personal identity within the tradition of Quaker spiritual autobiography', *Quaker History*, 65 (1976), 19–31 • E. Marshall, *Memories of troublous times* (1880) • N. Burns, 'From seeker to finder: the singular experiences of Mary Penington', *The emergence of Quaker writing: dissenting literature in seventeenth-century England*, ed. T. N. Corns and D. Loewenstein (1995), 70–87 • L. Coleman, 'Gender, sect, and circumstance: Quaker Mary Penington's many voices', *Women's life-writing: finding voice, building communities*, ed. L. Coleman (1997), 93–107 • *Some account of circumstances in the life of Mary Penington, from her manuscript, left for her family* (1821) • T. N. Corns and D. Loewenstein, eds., *The emergence of Quaker writing: dissenting literature in seventeenth-century England* (1995)

Archives RS Friends, Lond., *Charles Lloyd extracts*, MS vol. 62 • RS Friends, Lond., MSS • RS Friends, Lond., MS box C2/10, MS K1/16, MS vol. 358 • W. Sussex RO, autobiography [photocopy and typescript] | Haverford College Library (PA), S. H. Shearman collection, 1995, *Commonplace book of Susanna Horsnaill Weston*, Quaker collection AM 1119, 975B; 975A • Hist. Soc. Penn., miscellaneous collection • RS Friends, Lond., Catchpool MSS, vol. 2 • RS Friends, Lond., Row MSS, vol. 6 • RS Friends, Lond., Swarthmore MSS, vol. 6, MS vol. 358 • RS Friends, Lond., Temp MSS, 904

Likenesses oils, *c.*1642–1644, Pennsbury Manor, 400 Pennsbury Memorial Road, Morrisville, Pennsylvania; repro. in Penney, ed., *Experiences in the life of Mary Penington*, frontispiece

Wealth at death probably over £2500 excl. landed property; 'suite of damask', 'great platt with the Springetts and my coat of arms upon it', 'silver two eared cup', 'silver chaffen dish', 'black straw basket', 'my dear husbands [Isaac Penington's] watch', 'violet velvet mantle, &c', 'green quilted satten mantle &c', various 'hoods scrafs [sic] gloves safe guard cloakes & such things'; approx. £2470 ready money; £55 annuities; 'land and house at Amersham Woodside', 'personal estate which I had before marriage', 'personal estate of my husband, Isaac Penington', 'lands and houses in Kent': 'Abstract of the will of Mary Penington, dated 18th July, 1680' RS Friends, Lond., repro. in Penney, ed., *Experiences in the life*, 109–112

Penketh, Thomas (*d.* 1487), Augustinian friar and theologian, describes himself in his theological notebook as of the Warrington convent in Lancashire, and evidently studied theology at Oxford before (probably immediately before) 1466; on the basis of his Oxford study he was granted leave to incept at Cambridge in the academic year 1466–7, and took the degree of DTh on 31 May 1468. He must have already had some repute within his order, since he was confirmed as prior provincial of England on 22 October 1469; but he evidently returned to Oxford, where he was permitted by his order to study and teach, until in 1474 he vacated the provincialship to study at Padua. He was appointed lector in metaphysics in the university there, almost certainly being the Master Thomas Anglicus confirmed in that post on 22 September 1475, and very probably holding it already in 1474, when he published in Venice his edition of the quodlibet questions of John Duns Scotus. By 1477, when he brought out an edition of Scotus's commentary on the *Sentences* of Peter Lombard, he was holding the post of lector in theology, which he still held in 1479 according to his confrère, Brother Iacopo Filippo da Bergamo. He was re-elected prior provincial in 1480 (confirmed 15 March 1481) and again on 1 April 1485, presumably until death. At Easter 1484 he preached a sermon in praise of Richard III, which, according to Sir Thomas More, was afterwards excoriated, but which brought him an annual pension of £10 from the king. He died in London on 20 May 1487.

Penketh's principal achievement was to be the first to publish scholarly but usable printed editions of the chief works of Duns Scotus and the Scotist theologian Antonius Andreae. His editorial work was crowded into the five or six years he spent at Padua, where he could be in touch with experienced printers; but it originated in the Scotist teaching of the Oxford and Cambridge theological faculties, as a surviving notebook in his hand shows (Oxford, Corpus Christi College, MS 126). It contains questions on universals by Brother William Russell, probably the Augustinian friar who incepted at Oxford in 1430, some unattributed questions on God and creatures, possibly Penketh's own, and a text of the commentary of Antonius Andreae on Aristotle's *Metaphysics* which he edited at Padua. All these texts are explicitly Scotist, one of the unascribed questions citing Scotus as *doctor noster subtilis*; together, they provide evidence of the theology taught at the Oxford Augustinian house from the 1430s to the 1470s, and of the Scotist learning that lay behind Penketh's editions of Scotus and Antonius Andreae. The editions ascribed to him are Scotus's *Quaestiones quodlibetales*, printed by Albert de Stendal (Padua, 1474), with the text

emended by Penketh, and printed again from Penketh's text for Johann of Cologne (Venice, 1477) and reissued both in Nuremberg and in Venice in 1481; Scotus's *Quaestiones super secundum librum sententiarum*, printed by Stendal and emended by Penketh (Padua, 1474); Antonius Andreae's *Quaestiones de tribus principiis rerum naturalium*, printed by Laurentius Canozius and emended by Penketh and Laurentius de Lendenaria (Padua, 1475); Scotus's *Quaestiones super libros sententiarum*, edited by Penketh with Bartolomeo Bellati and printed for Johann of Cologne and Nicholas Jenson (Venice, 1477, and reissued there in both folio and quarto editions in 1481); Antonius Andreae's *Quaestiones super 'Metaphysica'*, printed for Nicholas Petri of Haarlem and emended by Penketh (Vicenza, 1477, and reissued in London for William Wilcock in 1480). These editions, especially of Scotus, circulated widely and for some time were the standard texts; they were made more useful by the inclusion of the early *additamenta* of Scotus's pupils which some editors omitted.

Bale also ascribed to Penketh *Annotationes super Augustinum 'De civitate Dei'*, without incipit; and an *Ars sermocinandi* with an incipit which enables it to be identified with a tract surviving in Cambridge, Corpus Christi College, MS 423, and elsewhere. But this tract is found incompletely in Oxford, University College, MS 36, in a hand too early for Penketh's authorship.

JEREMY CATTO

Sources T. Penketh, notebook, CCC Oxf., MS 126 • Bale, *Index* • St Thomas More, *The history of King Richard III*, ed. R. S. Sylvester (1963), vol. 2 of *The Yale edition of the complete works of St Thomas More*, 58–9, 135, 234–5 • Emden, *Oxf.*, 3.1457 • Emden, *Cam.*, 448 • F. X. Roth, *The English Austin friars, 1249–1538*, 2 vols. (1961–6) • G. Brotto and G. Zonta, *La facoltà teologica dell'Università di Padova* (1922), 179–81 • *Ioannis Duns Scoti opera omnia*, ed. C. Balic and others, 1 (Vatican City, 1950) • R. Horrox and P. W. Hammond, eds., *British Library Harleian manuscript 433*, 1 (1979), 263 • T. M. Charland, *Artes praedicandi: contribution à l'histoire de la rhétorique au moyen âge* (Paris, 1936)
Archives CCC Oxf., MS 126

Penkethman, John (*fl.* 1623–1668), accountant, lived in the legal quarter of Chancery Lane, London, at one time at the Rolls, afterwards at chambers in Simond's Inn. He earned his living by casting accounts for chancery masters, and others, and by auditing accounts gratis, basing his charges on the number of errors which he uncovered. His earliest works, dating from 1623, were translations from the classical authors, and he advertised that he would undertake prose or verse translations from Latin. He also sold copies of his own commercial tables of subjects, such as interest or currency conversion; his last known book, *Accompts of Merchandise*, was published in 1668.

Penkethman's principal work was *Artachthos, or, A New Booke Declaring the Assise or Weight of Bread* (1638). Certificated by the lord mayor and aldermen of the City of London, it listed the prices which bakers could charge for their loaves, by troy or avoirdupois weight, according to the fluctuating price of corn. Penkethman was granted a privilege to print and publish this book for twenty-one years; certain sections were reprinted, probably during his lifetime, and a later edition was published in 1748.

Nothing is known of Penkethman's origins (the name is associated with Lancashire) or his personal life; the actor John Penkethman (d. 1740) may have been related to him.

W. A. S. HEWINS, rev. ANITA McCONNELL

Sources Wood, *Ath. Oxon.* • Rymer, *Foedera*, 1st edn, 20.278

Penkethman, William. *See* Pinkethman, William (c.1660x65–1725).

Penley, Aaron Edwin (1807–1870), painter and drawing-master, was the son of William Penley, a landowner; his brother William Henry Savley was also a drawing-master. Penley married Caroline Turner (d. 1889) of Sheffield on 10 March 1830, and the couple had eighteen children; one of the only two to survive into adulthood was the watercolour painter Charles Penley. Aaron Penley was self-taught and the first recorded event in his career came in 1834 with the award of the Heywood medal from the Manchester Institution for an oil of *Christ Granting the Petition of the Woman of Canaan*. He made his début at the Royal Academy a year later with three portraits and exhibited there sporadically until 1869; his exhibits included genre scenes and, latterly, landscapes in watercolour. Penley also showed at the British Institution and the Society of British Artists, but his main allegiance was to the New Society of Painters in Water Colours which he joined in 1838 and where he showed 309 works. He also received royal patronage. He was appointed painter in watercolour to Queen Adelaide, painted a miniature of Queen Victoria (1840; NPG) from an actual sitting, and taught her son Prince Arthur.

Penley also enjoyed success as a drawing-master. During the 1830s he built up a practice in the Southampton area and, between 1836 and 1842, at Devonport. In 1843 he moved to Bath to take up an appointment at Cheltenham College, and after a move to London in 1849 was appointed assistant professor of civil drawing at the East India Company's college at Addiscombe. Penley was an innovative teacher, introducing instruction in the art of photography, and was promoted to senior professor in 1855. When the college closed in 1861 he moved to the Royal Military Academy at Woolwich. His teaching experience informed a series of publications including *A System of Water-Colour Painting* (1850), *The Elements of Perspective* (1851), *Sketching from Nature in Water Colours* (1869), and, most impressively, *The English School of Painting in Water-Colours* with colour illustrations in chromolithography (1861). The last was notable for the use of new colours such as viridian and aureolin which Penley introduced into Britain.

Penley is best known today for the technically competent, but rather conventional, exhibition landscapes which he showed at the New Society of Painters in Water Colours. The *View of Ullswater from Gowbarrow Park, at Evening* (exh. 1854) typifies a strand of unadventurous mid-Victorian watercolour art which combined a well-known location, conventional composition, and an attractive effect. The artist travelled widely in Britain and his repertory included scenes from Scotland, Yorkshire, the west country, and Wales, as well as south-east England.

Although Penley's exhibited works could be overworked, his watercolour sketches retain a more attractive spontaneity. Penley died at his home, 5 Elliott Hill, Lewisham, on 15 January 1870 of heart disease. There are representative collections of his work in the British Museum and the Victoria and Albert Museum, London.   GREG SMITH

Sources J. Steegman, 'Aaron Penley: a forgotten water-colourist', *Apollo*, 57 (1958), 14–17 • J. Reynolds, 'Master of watercolour', *Antique Dealer and Collectors' Guide*, 50/7 (Feb 1997), 24–7 • D. Millar, *The Victorian watercolours and drawings in the collection of her majesty the queen*, 2 (1995), 688
Likenesses attrib. F. F. Cotton, double portrait, photograph, 1860 (with John Callow), NPG • photograph, repro. in H. M. Vibart, *Addiscombe: its heroes and men of note* (1894) • photograph, NPG
Wealth at death under £5000: probate, 5 Feb 1870, *CGPLA Eng. & Wales*

Penley, William Sydney (1852–1912), actor and theatre manager, born at St Peter's, Ramsgate, on 19 November 1852, was the only son of William George Robinson Penley, a schoolmaster, and his wife, Emily Ann Wootton, the widow of Walter Pilcher. His grandfather was Aaron Edwin *Penley, watercolour painter to William IV. The family had old theatrical associations; his great-uncles William, Sampson, and Belville Penley were all actor–managers, and his great-aunt Rosina Penley was an actress. Penley attended his father's school, Grove House Academy, initially at St Peter's, and later at Charles Street, Westminster, when his father moved there. In his youth he sang as a chorister at the Chapel Royal, St James's, Westminster Abbey, Bedford Chapel, Bloomsbury, and finally the Russian embassy chapel. After an apprenticeship with a City firm of milliners and fancy-goods manufacturers, he joined the staff of Copestake, Moore, Crampton & Co.

Through the introduction of William Terriss, Penley obtained an engagement at the old Court Theatre under the management of Marie Litton, and made his début on 26 December 1871 as Tim in the farce *My Wife's Second Floor* by John Maddison Morton. The following October he played in T. F. Plowman's *Zampa*, and later performed at the Holborn Theatre in *Doctor Faust*. In 1875 he appeared at the Royalty Theatre in his first successful role, as the Foreman in *Trial by Jury* by W. S. Gilbert and Arthur Sullivan. After touring in comic opera, he returned to London to appear at the Strand Theatre (October 1876) in the comic opera *Princess Toto* by W. S. Gilbert and Alfred Cellier. He remained at the Strand Theatre for three years under the management of Ada Swanborough, and appeared principally in burlesque. On 22 March 1879 Penley married Mary Ann, the daughter of James Ricketts, a cattle salesman; they had three sons and three daughters. In April 1879 he transferred to the Royalty, and later that year he toured the provinces as Sir Joseph Porter in Gilbert and Sullivan's *HMS Pinafore*. In March 1880 he appeared at the Gaiety as Popperton in *La voyage en Suisse* with the Hanlon-Lees, a well-known troupe of pantomimists, and accompanied them to the United States. He reappeared in London at the Globe Theatre (July 1882) in *The Vicar of Bray*, and at the Comedy Theatre (September 1882) in Robert Planquette's *Rip Van Winkle*.

Penley made the first notable advance in his profession when he appeared as Lay Brother Pelican in Chassaigne's *Falka* at the Comedy (October 1883), an exceedingly droll performance. A greater opportunity followed when he was chosen by Charles Hawtrey to succeed Herbert Beerbohm Tree in the title role of the Revd Robert Spalding in *The Private Secretary* when that play was transferred to the Globe Theatre in May 1884: he played this part for two years and firmly established his reputation. Penley remained with Hawtrey for some years at the Globe, at the Comedy, and at the Strand, appearing in many plays of varied merit. After this long engagement with Hawtrey had terminated he was seen at Terry's Theatre (1890) in Jerome K. Jerome's *New Lamps for Old* and Arthur Law's *The Judge*; the following January at Toole's Theatre in Henry Hamilton's *Our Regiment*, and later at the Savoy Theatre in the comic opera *The Nautch Girl*. In 1891 he returned to the Comedy Theatre for a short time.

In *Charley's Aunt* by Brandon Thomas—the famous farce first produced at the Royalty Theatre on 21 December 1892—Penley's remarkable impersonation of the part of Lord Fancourt Babberley became the talk of the town. The play, transferred to the Globe Theatre early in 1893, settled down to a record-breaking run for a farce, and was played continuously over a period of four years in 1466 consecutive performances. In 1898 Penley produced *A Little Ray of Sunshine*, by Mark Ambient and Wilton Heriot, first in the provinces and later at the Royalty Theatre (December 1898). He then acquired the lease of the Novelty Theatre, which he renamed the Great Queen Street Theatre, and opened on 24 May 1900 with the same play. At this house he also revived *The Private Secretary* and *Charley's Aunt*, but without much success, and his acting career ended with the run of the last-mentioned play in 1901. He retired to Woking, then to Farnham and St Leonards where he lived a quiet country life until his death, at 7 Grand Parade, St Leonards, on 11 November 1912. His funeral took place on the 13th, at the Hastings borough cemetery. Most of the large fortune which he had made from the success of *Charley's Aunt* was believed to have been lost in his later years, but he left more than £15,000 on his death.

Penley's face was his fortune. He had a great sense of humour; but it was the expression of his countenance and the dry, metallic quality of his voice which had such irresistible effect on his audience. He was keenly interested in charitable institutions, was an active churchman, one of the proprietors of the *Church Family Newspaper*, and also a prominent freemason. He was the author of *Penley on himself*, published in 1884.

J. PARKER, rev. NILANJANA BANERJI

Sources *Daily Telegraph* (12 Nov 1912) · *The Times* (12 Nov 1912) · E. Reid and H. Compton, eds., *The dramatic peerage* [1891]; rev. edn [1892] · B. Hunt, ed., *The green room book, or, Who's who on the stage* (1906) · J. Parker, ed., *The green room book, or, Who's who on the stage* (1907–9) · P. Hartnoll, ed., *The Oxford companion to the theatre* (1951); 2nd edn (1957); 3rd edn (1967) · P. Hartnoll, ed., *The concise Oxford companion to the theatre* (1972) · *WWW* · Hall, *Dramatic ports.* · m. cert. · d. cert.

Likenesses Spy [L. Ward], chromolithograph caricature, NPG; repro. in *VF* (22 June 1893) · photograph, repro. in *Daily Telegraph*
Wealth at death £15,642 13s. 1d.: probate, 5 April 1913, CGPLA Eng. & Wales

Penn, Granville (1761–1844), author, second surviving son of Thomas *Penn (1702–1775) and his wife, Lady Juliana Fermor (1729–1801), fourth daughter of Thomas, first earl of Pomfret, was born at 10 New Street, Spring Gardens, London, on 9 December 1761. He matriculated at Magdalen College, Oxford, on 11 November 1780, but took no degree. Subsequently he became an assistant clerk in the war department, and received a pension on retirement. On 24 June 1791 he married Isabella, eldest daughter of General Gordon Forbes, colonel of the 29th regiment of foot, and settled in London. They had three sons and four daughters. In 1834 he succeeded his brother, John *Penn (1760–1834), in the estates of Stoke Park, Buckinghamshire, and Pennsylvania Castle, Portland (later a hotel). He was a member of the Outinian Society, founded by his brother.

Penn published a number of competent translations from the Greek, and many theological and semi-scientific works. *A Comparative Estimate of the Mineral and Mosaical Geologies* (1822) was received with some approval in religious circles, but was severely censured elsewhere as an unscientific attempt to treat the book of Genesis as a manual of geology. A second edition, enlarged, and with answers to critics, appeared in two volumes in 1825. *The book of the new covenant of Our Lord; being a critical revision of the text and translation of the English version of the New Testament, with the aid of most ancient manuscripts* appeared in 1836. His life of his great-grandfather Admiral Sir William *Penn was published in 1833. He also produced a number of controversial works on biblical chronology and prophecy, geology, and classical literature. Penn died at Stoke Park on 28 September 1844.

CHARLOTTE FELL-SMITH, rev. RICHARD SMAIL

Sources *GM*, 2nd ser., 22 (1844), 545–6 · Foster, *Alum. Oxon.*
Archives BL, letters to Sir Alexander Ball, Add. MS 37268 · Magd. Oxf., letters to M. J. Routh
Likenesses C. Turner, group portrait, mezzotint, pubd 1819 (*Penn family*, 1764; after J. Reynolds), BM · portrait; Pennsylvania Castle, Portland, in 1895

Penn, James (bap. 1727, d. 1800), religious writer, son of John Penn, stationer, of St Bride's parish, London, was baptized at St Bride's on 9 June 1727. He was admitted a scholar of Christ's Hospital, London, from the parish of St Dunstan-in-the-West in April 1736, and in 1745, as a 'Grecian', obtained an exhibition at Balliol College, Oxford, where he matriculated on 4 July that year. He proceeded BA in 1749 and MA in 1752. He was elected under grammar master of Christ's Hospital in 1753, and in 1761 published a Latin grammar which was used in the school well into the nineteenth century. In 1756 he was curate of St Andrew Undershaft, Leadenhall Street, and the following year was curate of the united parishes of St Anne and St Agnes and St John Zachary in Aldersgate. In those two years he published the first two of his four volumes of miscellaneous tracts and sermons, some of which show 'far too large a portion of controversial spirit' (Orme, 345), but also considerable humour and satire.

In 1760 Penn was a candidate for the upper grammar, or headmastership, of Christ's Hospital but lost the election to Peter Whalley by one vote. He was appointed by the governors of the Hospital to the vicarage of Clavering-cum-Langley in Essex, which he held until his death. In 1762 the third volume of his works appeared. Penn continued at the school until 1767, when he was dismissed after a disagreement with the governors, and because 'his eccentricities were not less remarkable than his talents' (Trollope, 301). That year he published *The Farmer's Daughter of Essex* and, one of his most characteristic works, *By Way of Prevention: a Sleepy Sermon … for the Dog-Days*. The amusing *Reasonableness of Repentance*, which contains a dedication to the devil as 'Tremendous sir', appeared in 1768; in 1769 seven sermons were published together.

From about 1769 until 1779 Penn was domestic chaplain to Granville Leveson-Gower, second Earl Gower. In 1779 he published *The Surrey Cottage*, a novel, and in 1781 his *Remarks* on Martin Madan's *Thelyphthora*. He married twice and had a son and a daughter, John and Mary, from his first marriage. From March 1781 until his death on 15 August 1800 he lived at Clavering. He was buried in London and was survived by his second wife, Mary.

CHARLOTTE FELL-SMITH, *rev.* ADAM JACOB LEVIN

Sources W. Trollope, *A history of the royal foundation of Christ's Hospital* (1834), 301, 333–4 · will, PRO, PROB 11/1347, sig. 677 · W. Orme, *Bibliotheca biblica* (1824), 345 · W. J. Pinks, *The history of Clerkenwell*, ed. E. J. Wood (1865), 237 · Foster, *Alum. Oxon.*

Wealth at death £10 plus goods: will, 1 Sept 1800, PRO, PROB 11/1347, sig. 677 fol. 360

Penn, John (1729–1795), colonial governor, was born in London on 14 July 1729, one of four children and the eldest son of Richard Penn (1705/6–1771) and Hannah Lardner, and grandson of William *Penn (1644–1718), founder of Pennsylvania. At a secret service in 1747 he married a Miss Cox, daughter of his schoolmaster, James Cox, a union into which other family members believed he had been tricked. Then described as an indolent and corpulent young man, Penn was rescued from the marriage by his uncle Thomas *Penn (having been abandoned by his father) and was sent to the University of Geneva (1747–51) before travelling in Italy in October 1751. In the following year he moved to Philadelphia where he enjoyed a comfortable life as a member of the proprietor gentry and dabbled in politics and business. Penn was back in England from 1755 before returning to Pennsylvania as lieutenant-governor in November 1763.

These were difficult times for Pennsylvania's proprietary leadership, notwithstanding the initial support Penn received from the assembly. Border disputes with Virginia, Connecticut, and Maryland were exacerbated by assaults by Scots-Irish and German border settlers on members of the Conestoga nation, culminating in 1764 with the infamous attack by the Paxton Boys and subsequent American Indian reprisals. Because of this retaliatory action, Penn's early tolerance for the rights of Native Americans gave way to calls for a more aggressive response against the Delaware and Shawnee Indians which prompted the latter to sue for peace in September 1764, signed by the governor in December. During the summer of 1768 Penn organized the proprietor's case for a conference intended to end the territorial disputes between settlers and Native Americans through the Penns' purchase of contested land. The results of the Fort Stanwix treaty were mixed: while relations with American Indians stabilized, the settlement came at a considerable cost to the Penn family who, despite plans to sell on the land to loyal Pennsylvania officers, were unable to resist ongoing encroachments from Connecticut Yankees into the 1770s.

In October 1771, following his father's death earlier that year, Penn returned to England and was replaced by his younger brother Richard *Penn (1733/4–1811) as acting governor. Relations within the family were currently poor, with John held responsible for the high levels of compensation demanded from increasingly impoverished Pennsylvanian settlers. On the death of his father, Penn now became a minor proprietor of the colony with a one-quarter interest, with the remainder being held by his uncle. Through Thomas's influence John returned for a second term as Pennsylvania's governor in the autumn of 1773. Once more he entered a troubled political environment. Distracted by a renewed threat of border skirmishes from Native Americans, Penn was also involved in bitter exchanges with assembly members over Westminster's alleged challenge to colonial liberties in the wake of the Tea Act (1773). Penn adopted a conciliatory role as relations worsened between the colonial assemblies and Lord North's government, his aim being to weaken through compromise and negotiation the first continental congress which met in Philadelphia in September 1774. However, his proposals and work as an intermediary between North and the Pennsylvania assembly came to nothing and, in September 1776, the Penns' royal charter was annulled by constitutional convention.

In 1777 Philadelphia was occupied by the British under General William Howe, and Penn was arrested and forced into a year's exile in New Jersey. On his return to Pennsylvania he took a loyalty oath to the new revolutionary government and lived in his purpose-built residence, Lansdowne House on the Schuylkill River, with his second wife, Ann (*d.* 1830), daughter of Philadelphia's chief justice William Allan, whom he married on 31 May 1766; the couple had no children. In 1788 he travelled to England with his cousin, also John *Penn (1760–1834), to lobby parliament for additional compensation for lands confiscated during the war for which the family had received £130,000 from the new colonial administration and now obtained an annuity of £4000 from the British government. The last political link between the Penn family and the colony founded by his grandfather, John Penn died in Philadelphia on 9 February 1795 and was buried at the city's Anglican Christ Church burial-ground; his body was later removed to England.

PHILIP CARTER

Sources L. Treese, *The storm gathering: the Penn family and the American revolution* (1992) · DNB · H. J. Cadbury, 'Penn, John', *DAB*

Archives U. Mich., Clements L., corresp. with Thomas Gage

Penn, John (1760–1834), writer, was born in London on 22 February 1760, and baptized at St Martin-in-the-Fields on 21 March, the eldest surviving son of Thomas *Penn (1702–1775), landowner, and his wife, Lady Juliana (1729–1801), daughter of Thomas Fermor, first earl of Pomfret. William *Penn (1644–1718), founder of Pennsylvania, was his grandfather. On the death of his father in 1775 John succeeded to his property, which included the moiety of the last proprietorship of the province of Pennsylvania, with hereditary governorship, and Stoke Poges Park in Buckinghamshire, near Windsor, which his father had purchased in 1760. On the outbreak of the American War of Independence in 1775, John apparently accompanied his mother to Geneva. He went to Eton College and then entered Clare College, Cambridge, in 1776 as a nobleman (by virtue of his maternal descent). He matriculated in 1777 and was created MA in 1779 and LLD on 28 June 1811.

From 1782 to 1789 Penn lived in America, attending to his Pennsylvania property, and built the house called Solitude at Schuylkill. He and his cousin John *Penn (1729–1795) received from the assembly in 1786 the grant of £15,000 annually as payment for the estate vested in the commonwealth as by law passed on 18 January 1786. In 1789 he returned to England, and in the following year received his portion of the £4000 annuity granted by parliament in consideration of the losses in Pennsylvania. The house at Stoke Poges having fallen into decay, he commenced, in 1789, the erection of a new one in the centre of the park, from designs by Nasmith, which were completed by James Wyatt. He later published an anonymous *Historical and Descriptive Account of Stoke Park* (1813).

Penn drew on his American experiences to produce his drama *The Battle of Eddington, or, British Liberty* (1792), which was performed several times in the early nineteenth century. His *Letters on the Drama* (1796) appeared anonymously in London, and his *A Timely Appeal to the Common Sense of the People of Great Britain* was published there in 1798, followed by *Further Thoughts on the Present State of Public Opinion* (1800). Penn's primary literary interest was poetry, however, and in addition to a volume of *Poems* printed on his private press at Stoke Park in 1796, he also produced *Critical, Poetical and Dramatic Works* (1797), *Poems, Consisting of Original Works, Imitations, and Translations* (1801, 1802), and *Observations in Illustration of Virgil's Fourth Eclogue* (1810).

In 1798 Penn was sheriff of Buckinghamshire. He represented the borough of Helston, Cornwall, in the parliament of 1802 and continued to do so until 1805 when he was appointed governor of Portland Castle, Dorset, an office he held until his death. In 1800, he erected on Portland Island, from designs by Wyatt, a mansion which he styled Pennsylvania Castle. He was lieutenant-colonel of the 1st (Eton) troop of the 1st (South) regiment of the Royal Buckinghamshire yeomanry and commandant of the Royal Portland Legion.

The publication of an anonymous poem called 'Marriage', in the *Monthly Magazine* in the summer of 1815 led Penn to organize in 1817 a 'matrimonial society', which had for its object an improvement in the domestic life of married persons. Extending its aims to other schemes of domestic utility, the society changed its name in May to that of the Outinian Society. During the summer of 1818 meetings of the society took place at Penn's house, 10 New Street, Spring Gardens, London, and later at Stoke Park. Penn, who acted as president, edited the works of the society for publication from 1819 to 1823.

Penn died unmarried at Stoke Poges Park on 21 June 1834, and was succeeded in his estates there and at Portland by his brother Granville *Penn.

BERTHA PORTER, rev. REBECCA MILLS

Sources R. A. Austen-Leigh, ed., *The Eton College register, 1753–1790* (1921), 413 · Venn, *Alum. Cant.*, 2/5.84 · [J. Penn], *An historical and descriptive account of Stoke Park* (1813) · *GM*, 2nd ser., 2 (1834), 650–51 · J. Watson, *Annals of Philadelphia and Pennsylvania*, 3 vols. (1877–9), 1.125–6 · [J. Watkins and F. Shoberl], *A biographical dictionary of the living authors of Great Britain and Ireland* (1816), 269 · H. R. Luard, ed., *Graduati Cantabrigienses*, 6th edn (1873), 365 · H. R. Luard, ed., *Graduati Cantabrigienses*, 7th edn (1884), 404 · Watt, *Bibl. Brit.*, 2.744 · Genest, *Eng. stage*, 9.260 · Allibone, *Dict.* · J. Penn, *The seventh Outinian lecture* (1823)
Archives Hunt. L., letters | BL, corresp. with Walter Pollard, Add. MSS 35655–35656
Likenesses L. Schiavonetti, stipple, pubd 1802 (after J. Deare), BM, NPG · R. Dunkarton, mezzotint, pubd 1809 (after W. Beechey), BM · C. Turner, group portrait, mezzotint, pubd 1819 (after J. Reynolds), BM

Penn, John (1770–1843), engineer, was born near Taunton, Somerset, and apprenticed as a millwright (the name then given to mechanical engineers) at nearby Bridgwater. After a period working in Bristol he moved about 1793 to London. In 1800 he used his savings to open a workshop in Greenwich, specializing in milling machinery. He rapidly acquired a reputation for excellence of design and workmanship that was to remain a feature of the company he founded until its closure. His early speciality was in flour-milling machinery, where he improved and modernized the basic design, replacing the wooden framing with cast iron. His first major order was for machinery to equip the bakery at the Royal Navy's Deptford victualling yard. His work soon attracted the attention of prominent designers, leading William Cubitt to order his first treadmill from Penn in 1817; later examples were used in the London docks and in prisons. About 1824 Jacob Perkins employed him to build his ambitious and complex steam gun. The increasing use of steam for industrial power, together with his riverside location, led to Penn's becoming interested in marine steam engines. In 1822 the pioneer iron steamer *Aaron Manby* was assembled at Deptford by the Staffordshire engineer after whom she was named. Penn and his sixteen-year-old son John *Penn (1805–1878) took the opportunity to inspect her, and particularly her oscillating engines. Within three years Penn had built his first marine engine, for a coastal steamer on the London–Norwich route. The oscillating design was greatly improved from Manby's patent, and by 1838 he was supplying several prominent Thames shipbuilders, notably Ditchburn and Mare.

Penn, a friend of William Cobbett, was a political radical, and was a parliamentary candidate at Greenwich in

1832. His other interests included horticulture: he used his engineering abilities to improve the design and construction of greenhouses and conservatories. Having largely turned over the direction of the family business to his son John, he died suddenly at home in Lewisham on 6 June 1843. Penn played a vital part in the heroic age of steam engineering; what he lacked in vision and popularity he more than made up for by the quality of his work. He was one of the people who made the steam engine into the prime mover of British commercial, industrial, and strategic power.   ANDREW LAMBERT

Sources P. Banbury, *Shipbuilders of the Thames and Medway* (1971) · *DNB*

Penn, John (1805–1878), marine engineer, the son of the engineer John *Penn (1770–1843), was born at Greenwich, Kent, and was apprenticed to his father. At an early age he demonstrated remarkable aptitude for engineering—in practical workmanship, design, and management—and he soon joined his father in the management of the family business, later John Penn & Sons. From 1825 to 1840 the work of father and son is almost impossible to disentangle. About 1826 the younger Penn constructed the steam gun invented by Jacob Perkins, which was shown to Wellington and other officers, taken to Paris, and later exhibited at the Adelaide Gallery, London. He was elected an associate of the Institution of Civil Engineers in 1826, became a member in 1845, and served on the council from 1853 to 1856. In 1847 he married Ellen English, the daughter of another London engineer, William English of Enfield; they had four sons and two daughters.

The most lucrative source of marine engine orders in this period was the Royal Navy. It tended to be conservative, and restricted orders to known, approved contractors. In 1843 Penn approached the Admiralty with an unsolicited offer to install high-power oscillating engines in the Admiralty steam yacht *Black Eagle*. This was accepted, on the recommendation of Sir John Rennie. The success of these engines led to Penn's installing further examples in many of the last paddle-wheel warships down to 1852. A modified version was fitted to the pioneer iron screw steamer the *Great Britain* in 1852, when she was converted for service on the Australian route; the power and economy of Penn's engines opened this route to steamships.

For naval screw propeller vessels Penn developed the trunk engine, which combined laid-down (that is, horizontal) cylinders for safety below the waterline with the highest power yet achieved. For two decades they were the engines of choice for new, high-powered British warships. The first of the type, designed to run at what were then considered very high speeds to drive the screw propeller directly, rather than relying on bulky and noisy gearing, was installed in the pioneer screw frigate *Arrogant* of 1848; the type was enlarged and improved for the first steam battleship the *Agamemnon* in 1852, the first ironclad, the *Warrior* of 1861, and the first mastless battleship, the *Devastation* of 1871. During the Crimean War Penn's works were also employed in erecting 120 small

high-pressure engines for use in gunboats. They split this task with their major rivals, Maudslay, Son, and Field of Lambeth, leaving the casting of components to the smaller firms that shared the Thames riverside. These orders were secured by the excellent results that had been given by previous Penn engines, rather than by competitive tender, for it was widely recognized that the Royal Navy travelled first class and Penn's machinery was the best available. Penn engines, large and small, were noted for their high power, great reliability, and astonishing longevity. Those fitted to the early ironclads often served for more than thirty years, while the gunboat engines outlasted the craft in which they were first installed; many were reused in new vessels. Penn's own reputation was such that he was called in to arbitrate the quarrel between Isambard Kingdom Brunel and John Scott Russell over the *Great Eastern* in 1859.

Penn's works grew to meet the number and value of naval orders, leavened by a number of premium mercantile and liner contracts. By the time of his death it occupied 7 acres on Blackheath Hill, and there was a separate boiler works at Deptford. It was always considered the best-equipped marine engineering works, capable of meeting any demand. Penn was a model employer, one of the first to recognize the value of skilled employees through pensions, as well as the more typically paternalistic system of awarding Christmas gifts. His works also provided the education for a whole generation of marine engineers, and not a few naval officers, who took time to study there. In 1858–9, and again in 1867–8, Penn served as president of the Institution of Mechanical Engineers; he contributed several papers to their *Proceedings*. In June 1859 he was elected FRS, and in 1860 he helped to found the Institution of Naval Architects.

Penn developed, improved, and refined the ideas and engineering of others, and was among the first to employ the precision instruments and tools developed by his friend Joseph Whitworth. His approach was empirical, and he devoted much time and effort to solving fundamental problems. His most important contribution to marine engineering came in collaboration with Francis Pettit Smith: the two men developed the *lignum vitae* stern bearing, patented in 1854 and finally perfected in 1858. This enabled screw propeller ships to make oceanic voyages without wearing out their stern glands. It was typical of Penn that he should contribute the least obvious, but most important, step in the creation of the modern ship.

In 1875 Penn, by then very ill, retired from the management of the business, which passed to his two elder sons, who had been partners since 1872. He died at his home, The Cedars, Lee, Kent, on 23 September 1878, survived by his wife, and was buried at St Margaret's Church, Lee, on 29 September. By the time of his death the firm had built engines for 735 ships, ranging from river ferries to battleships. His eldest son, John (1848–1903), educated at Harrow School and Trinity College, Cambridge, managed the firm, but was not an engineer. He was Conservative MP for Lewisham from 1891 to 1903 and 'one of the best-known Parliamentary golfers' (Venn, *Alum. Cant.*, 5/2, 1953, 84).

The firm closed in 1914. John Penn was one of the giants of Victorian engineering, and was universally acknowledged as such in his lifetime. He deserves to be better known; his engines helped to maintain Britain's mastery of the seas for more than fifty years. As his friend John Bourne observed, he was an irreparable loss to the world of engineering: 'he produced engines such as no one else was able to equal or excel', while 'his merit was only excelled by his modesty' (*The Engineer*, 4 Oct 1878, 242).

ANDREW LAMBERT

Sources P. Banbury, *Shipbuilders of the Thames and Medway* (1971) · D. K. Brown, *Before the ironclad* (1990) · K. C. Barnaby, *The Institution of Naval Architects* (1960) · L. T. C. Rolt, *Isambard Kingdom Brunel* (1957) · R. Gardiner and B. Greenhill, eds., *The advent of steam: the merchant steamship before 1900* (1993) · A. Watts, *Pictorial history of the Royal Navy* (1970) · *The Engineer* (27 Sept 1878) · *The Engineer* (4 Oct 1878) · Venn, *Alum. Cant.* · *WWW* · *CGPLA Eng. & Wales* (1878) · Boase, *Mod. Eng. biog.*

Likenesses photograph, Hult. Arch.; repro. in Watts, *Pictorial history*, 135 · wood-engraving (after photograph), repro. in *ILN*, 73 (1878)

Wealth at death under £1,000,000: probate, 10 Oct 1878, *CGPLA Eng. & Wales*

Penn [*née* Arthur; *other married name* Hicks], **Julian** (*d.* 1592), moneylender, was apparently a daughter of William Arthur of 'Clapham' (Clapton in Gordano), Somerset, but nothing is known of her early life. She married Robert Hicks, whose family lived near her, in the Bristol area, but the date and place of the marriage are unknown.

After their marriage, Robert Hicks went on to keep the White Bear mercer's shop, on the southern side of Cheapside, London; he was assessed for subsidy in St Pancras parish in 1541. Robert and Julian Hicks had six sons, including Sir Michael *Hickes, who became prominent as secretary to Lord Burghley and Robert Cecil. By his will, made on 21 November 1557, Robert Hicks, by then an ironmonger, left lands in Bristol and elsewhere in Gloucestershire to his wife, who was to pay his mother £10 per annum; his property in St Katharine Coleman, London, was to go to his brother Richard, then to Julian.

Julian continued to manage her late husband's shop with the help of their sons, dealing with John and Gregory Isham, mercers; and she also became a prominent moneylender. Although her writing and spelling remained poor, even by the standards of the day, important clients usually treated her with respect. A letter written by William Cecil requests a loan of £50, for 'a great occasion I have to use it' (BL, Lansdowne MS 103, fol. 268): this was written after she had married Anthony Penn (probably in 1559) but perhaps was never sent.

By his will of 12 December 1570, Anthony Penn also bequeathed his goods to his wife. He was buried at St Mary Magdalen, Milk Street, on 16 July 1572, and probate was granted on the following day. In August 1573 Julian's prospective third marriage, to a Mr Twitty, did not materialize.

In an undated letter to a Mr Hardwick, Julian explained her financial situation: she was 'daily driven to pawn my plate to supply ordinary charges' (BL, Lansdowne MS 108, fol. 31*r–v*), but the debt remained unpaid. During 1576–7,

Mrs Penn listed her assets: 'I have in writings I think be good debts the sum of xviijC *li*[*bri*].' As well, she had plate, jewels, tapestry, linen, furniture, and:

> my lease of the White Bear in Cheapside and my house that I now dwell in [on St Peter's Hill, in the parish of St Peter, Paul's Wharf: purchased in 1559] … I have lost since that time by … ill debts and furniture of the White Bear … vjC *li*[*bri*] … I [ac]knowledge myself from the first day of my birth I never deserved penny or piece of bread … God hath done it all, giving and taking. (BL, Lansdowne MS 108, fol. 30)

In 1591 Edward de Vere, earl of Oxford, rented rooms in Mrs Penn's house at £100 per annum, but flitted without paying. Thomas Churchyard, who had stood surety for him, wrote to Mrs Penn that 'for fear of [ar]resting I lie in the sanctuary' (BL, Lansdowne MS 68, fol. 257). To Henry Fitzgerald, earl of Kildare, she wrote that 'But for the love I bear to my Lord Admiral [Charles, Lord Howard of Effingham] and my lady your wife [Effingham's daughter] I had ended my suit[,] for … the queen … hath promised me that I shall take no wrong at man's hand'. Kildare replied, on 23 June 1591, 'I desire you now to bear with me but till my man return with money out of Ireland which will be within this fortnight at which time I will pay you with great thanks' (BL, Lansdowne MS 68, fols. 207, 209).

Julian Penn died on 14 November 1592, and administration of her goods was granted to her son Michael on 22 December.

JOHN BENNELL

Sources A. G. R. Smith, *Servant of the Cecils: the life of Sir Michael Hickes, 1543–1612* (1977) · E. A. Fry, ed., *Abstracts of inquisitiones post mortem relating to the City of London*, 3: *1577–1603*, British RS, 36 (1908), 74, 268 · administration, 1592, GL, MS 9168/14, fol. 252 · A. Feuillerat, ed., *Documents relating to the office of the revels in the time of Queen Elizabeth* (1908), 99 · BL, Lansdowne MS 68, fols. 207, 209 · BL, Lansdowne MS 68, fol. 252*r, v* · BL, Lansdowne MS 68, fol. 257 · will, Robert Hicks, 1558, PRO, PROB 11.40/9 · will, Anthony Penn, 1572, PRO, PROB 11.52/24 · A. W. Hughes Clarke, ed., *The registers of St Mary Magdalen, Milk Street, 1558–1666, and St Michael Bassishaw, London, 1538–1625*, Harleian Society, register section, 72 (1942) · W. B. Bannerman, ed., *The registers of St Mary le Bow, Cheapside, All Hallows, Honey Lane, and of St Pancras, Soper Lane, London*, 2 vols., Harleian Society, register section, 44–5 (1914–15) · BL, Lansdowne MS 36, fol. 212 · BL, Lansdowne MS 103, fol. 268 · BL, Lansdowne MS 108, fol. 31*r, v* · BL, Lansdowne MS 108, fol. 30 · *Calendar of the manuscripts of the most hon. the marquis of Salisbury*, 13, HMC, 9 (1915), 476

Penn, Richard (1733/4–1811), colonial official and politician, was the second son of Richard Penn (*d.* 1771), and Hannah, daughter of Richard Lardner. William *Penn, the founder of Pennsylvania, was his grandfather, and John *Penn, lieutenant-governor of Pennsylvania, was his elder brother. He was educated at Eton College and matriculated at St John's College, Cambridge, in October 1752, aged eighteen, and went to the Inner Temple in the same year. In 1771 he was appointed by his uncle, Thomas *Penn, and his father, two of the first proprietaries of Pennsylvania, as deputy governor of the province during his brother's absence in England.

Penn arrived in Philadelphia on 16 October 1771, and occupied the post until John's return in August 1773. His care of the province's commercial interests made him popular with the white colonists. While in America he married Mary Masters on 21 May 1772; the couple had two daughters and two sons, William and Richard [*see below*]. He returned to England in 1775, carrying with him a petition from the first American congress to the king. Penn was examined before the House of Lords as to the support for independence in the colonies. In 1787 he and his family were granted considerable compensation from the United States for his loss of property there, and he visited America one last time shortly before his death.

On 9 April 1784 Penn was elected member of parliament for the borough of Appleby, Westmorland, which he represented until 20 December 1790, when he was returned for Haslemere, Surrey. From 1796 until 1802 he sat for the city of Lancaster, and in the latter year was again chosen for Haslemere. He supported Pitt, but was alone in not going over to the opposition during the regency. He died at his house at Richmond, Surrey, on 27 May 1811; he was survived by his wife.

Penn's elder son, **William Penn** (1776–1845), author, was educated at St John's College, Cambridge, but left without taking a degree. Aged seventeen he published, anonymously, *Vindiciae Britannicae: being Strictures on Gilbert Wakefield's 'Spirit of Christianity'* (1794); an appendix, in answer 'to the Calumnies of the *Analytical Review*', appeared later in the year. William Penn also wrote verse and prose for the *Anti-Jacobin Review* and the *Gentleman's Magazine*, in which he published under the pseudonym Rajah of Vaneplysia. Extravagance and conviviality ruined his prospects, and his drinking attracted comment from the prince of Wales. After spending much of his time in the debtors' prison, he died in Nelson Square, Southwark, on 17 September 1845. He was buried at St Mary Redcliffe, Bristol, beside his great-great-grandfather Admiral Sir William Penn.

William Penn's younger brother, **Richard Penn** (1784–1863), author, was employed at the Colonial Office. He was elected a fellow of the Royal Society on 18 November 1824. A cipher that he arranged for use in dispatches is illustrated in his pamphlet *On a New Mode of Secret Writing* (1829). He also wrote *Maxims and Hints for an Angler, and Miseries of Fishing* (1833), illustrated by Sir Francis Chantrey, to which was added *Maxims and Hints for a Chess Player*, with portrait-caricatures of the author and Sir Francis, by the latter. An enlarged edition was published in 1839, and another, containing *Maxims and Hints on Shooting*, appeared in 1855. Richard Penn died, unmarried, at Richmond, Surrey, on 21 April 1863.

CHARLOTTE FELL-SMITH, rev. TROY O. BICKHAM

Sources M. M. Drummond, 'Penn, Richard', HoP, *Commons, 1754–90* · *GM*, 1st ser., 81/2 (1811), 675 · *GM*, 3rd ser., 14 (1863), 800
Archives Hist. Soc. Penn., family MSS · Pennsylvania State Archives, Harrisburg · RS Friends, Lond., family MSS | Mass. Hist. Soc., letters to Richard Peters · PRO, Colonial Office MSS

Penn, Richard (1784–1863). *See under* Penn, Richard (1733/4–1811).

Penn, Thomas (1702–1775), landowner, was born at Kensington, London, on 8 March 1702, the second son of William *Penn (1644–1718), founder of Pennsylvania, and his

second wife, Hannah Callowhill (1670–1726). During his childhood the Penn family received little profit from the colony, and Thomas was apprenticed to a London mercer in order to provide an alternative financial security. Upon William's death in 1718 the children of his first wife disputed his will, which left the proprietorship of the colony to Thomas and his two brothers, John and Richard, by William's second wife. In 1727 Hannah won the upholding of her husband's will, which was further secured in 1731 when the descendants of William's first wife released their claims to the colony in exchange for a sum of money. In exchange for two beaver skins delivered annually to Windsor Castle the Penns were given absolute ownership of all lands and mining rights of Pennsylvania, but the proprietorship was still no guarantee of wealth. Rents had to be collected, payment for settled lands secured, and potential lands for settlement protected from French or American Indian attack.

Thomas Penn took the lead in the family's financial affairs, and in 1732 was the first family member to visit the colony since his father left in 1701. While in America Thomas devised new ways of categorizing the family's lands for rent and sale, as well as various ways to collect rents. He also renewed treaties with various American Indian communities and determined to strengthen his family's interests through strengthening the powers of an appointed governor. His success is perhaps best measured in the change from the warm welcome he received upon his arrival to the general colonial opinion of him as greedy and cold by the time of his departure in 1741. Upon his older brother's death in 1746 Thomas inherited his portion of proprietorship and thus held a three-quarters interest in the colony. On 22 August 1751 Thomas married Lady Juliana Fermor (1729–1801), daughter of the earl of Pomfret. They had four sons, including the writers John *Penn (1760–1834) and Granville *Penn (1761–1844), and three daughters. Although a Quaker by descent and association, Thomas had long since abandoned many of the denomination's practices, and his marriage in an Anglican church marked the end of his association with the Quaker faith. The Seven Years' War revealed the difficulties of managing the family's substantial American interests from England, and in 1763 John *Penn (1729–1795), Thomas's nephew, was appointed governor of Pennsylvania. John maintained a regular correspondence with Thomas and Juliana, who had assumed a role of increasing importance as Thomas's health worsened. He died on 21 March 1775 at his estate at Stoke Poges, Buckinghamshire, and was buried at the church there. He left his interests in Pennsylvania to his only surviving son, John, who was fifteen. Juliana and his son-in-law, William Baker, took the lead of the family's American affairs for the short time until the American War of Independence brought about the dissolution of the Penns' proprietorship in 1779. For their losses of about 24 million acres of land and £118,569 owed in rents, the Penns received £130,000 as compensation from the new government of Pennsylvania.

CHARLOTTE FELL-SMITH, rev. TROY O. BICKHAM

Sources L. Treese, *The storm gathering: the Penn family and the American Revolution* (1992) · J. E. Illick, *Colonial Pennsylvania: a history* (1976) · J. J. Kelley, *Pennsylvania: the colonial years, 1681–1776* (1980) · W. R. Shepherd, *The history of proprietary government in Pennsylvania* (1896) · *DNB* · 'Penn, William (1644–1718)', *DNB*
Archives Hist. Soc. Penn. | American Antiquarian Society, letters to Richard Peters · Mass. Hist. Soc., letters to Richard Peters
Likenesses D. Martin, mezzotint (after Davis), BM · C. Turner, portrait · P. Vandyck, portrait · portrait, repro. in Treese, *Storm gathering*, fig. 1
Wealth at death controlled three-quarters of Pennsylvania proprietaryship

Penn, Sir William (*bap.* 1621, *d.* 1670), naval officer, was baptized in St Thomas's Church, Bristol, on 23 April 1621, the son of Giles Penn, a seaman and merchant of the city, and his wife, Joan Gilbert of Somerset. The Penns had long been landowners in Buckinghamshire and Gloucestershire, but William, younger son of a younger son, with no expectation of inheritance, necessarily made his career in the sea and its commerce. About 1638 he began to serve under William Batten, his future colleague. Penn became a muster master or clerk of the cheque. He is said to have attained his first command at the age of twenty-one, though no specific record survives. On 6 January 1644 he married Margaret (*d.* 1682), daughter of Hans Jasper of Rotterdam and widow of Nicasius van der Schuren, a Dutchman living at Kilconry, co. Clare. Margaret had acquired an estate in Ireland from her first husband, to which Penn became entitled as her second, but it was far from lucrative, and the early years of their marriage were spent in a modest house on Tower Hill. Since the only account of these days is the later recollection of a spiteful neighbour, enthusiastically repeated by Pepys, it may be doubted if Penn was truly 'pitiful' or his wife 'a dirty slattern' (Pepys, *Diary*, 8.226–7). By the same dubious report Penn was at first disposed to drink the king's health, but later converted to the parliamentary cause.

Early naval campaigns Penn was certainly regarded as a reliable parliamentarian by 22 May 1644 when he was appointed to captain parliament's ship the *Fellowship*; on 31 December he was additionally commissioned rear-admiral of the Irish squadron. On 17 June he was designated to take the same ship into Scottish waters, but by early July he was transferred to the larger *Happy Entrance* with temporary rank of vice-admiral. He was instructed to assist at the siege of Youghal, where he arrived on 8 July. Although the siege was still proceeding when he left on 7 August, he had acquitted himself well and there was discontent among his crew when he was obliged to cede command to Crowther.

On 23 September Penn was returned to the *Fellowship*. On 21 February 1646 he was ordered to take charge of an operation in support of Bunratty Castle; this stronghold overlooking the Shannon estuary had been made available to parliament as a base from which to check royalist privateering out of Limerick. Penn arrived there on 20 March, and on 18 April was constituted rear-admiral. It proved impossible to sustain the castle by sea when the enemy were in occupation of the surrounding country, and no blame attached to Penn for the surrender of the

Sir William Penn (*bap.* 1621, *d.* 1670), by Sir Peter Lely, *c.*1666

garrison on 13 July. Indeed, on 4 August he was promoted to command the newly built *Assurance*, with orders to patrol between Land's End and southern Ireland. He was not enthusiastic for further minor operations on the Irish coast, and his election as freeman of Portsmouth indicates his wish to join the main fleet. But he was on the Irish station throughout 1647. In March 1648 he was ordered to act against the royalist rising in west Wales. Fears that he might have joined what he was sent to suppress prompted his summons to London on 14 April. Three days later the case against him was respited for want of information; on 2 May new operational orders were sent to him, and on 4 May he was informed that his loyalty was no longer in question. Early in 1649 he met Rupert off Castlehaven, but recognizing that he was outgunned, he withdrew without engaging. On 18 April he was reappointed vice-admiral of Ireland, with captaincy of the *Lion* (as which he was paid from 1 May that year to 25 June 1650). During this time he blockaded Waterford, Limerick, and Galway, and was commended for his 'more than ordinary care' (*CSP dom.*, 1650, 209).

On 26 August 1650 Penn was made captain of the *Fairfax*, at this point still attached to the Irish squadron. On 24 October he was instructed to bring her into Portsmouth to refit. Next day the admiralty committee decided to send him to Lisbon to relieve Blake and pursue Rupert. His instructions were approved by the council on 2 November, and he received them on the 25th. On 30 November he sailed from Spithead in the *Centurion*, as the *Fairfax* was not ready. On 21 January he was joined by Lawson in the *Fairfax*, to which he transferred; he now had his intended squadron of eight. His instructions were to go first to the

Azores and take any homebound Portuguese treasure ships he found, then to follow Rupert and attack him and the French as occasion served. He needed to avoid confrontation with the combined French and royalist forces, but would have superiority over the latter alone. Having found nothing in the Azores, he entered the Mediterranean on 29 March. He proceeded as far as Malta, where on 29 July he had reports of Rupert off Cadiz. He headed back at once, reaching Gibraltar on 9 September. On the 25th Rupert was reported in the Azores. Penn remained at the mouth of the straits, intending to intercept Rupert's return, never supposing that he would head in the opposite direction. Penn had neither instructions nor means to pursue the royalists to the Caribbean, and he returned to England by 18 March 1652. He had taken thirty-six French prizes and had significantly extended the range of English squadronal patrol in the Mediterranean, but he had never been close to Rupert or Maurice.

Dutch wars On 2 April 1652 in the Downs Penn was reunited with Blake, who on 5 May appointed him captain of the *Triumph*. On 19 May he was further advanced to be Blake's vice-admiral. He told Cromwell that many officers doubted the moral justification of the Dutch war now beginning, but Penn himself was assured it was God's will. At the first major engagement, Kentish Knock on 28 September, Blake and Penn ran aground while attacking the Dutch van. As the Dutch closed on them Penn was able to get free, and to turn on those who had seen him as easy prey: 'it fell out better … than we could have cast it ourselves' (Penn, *Memorials*, 1.447). His success here was blighted by the accusation that he had hidden in a coil of rope; this canard, apparently first circulated by Nehemiah Bourne, was given new life after Lowestoft in 1665, and would be enshrined in the satirical poem *Second Advice to a Painter* (lines 87–8). Penn was absent from the defeat at Dungeness (30 November) while engaged in convoying the Newcastle coal fleet. In January 1653 he was appointed captain of the *Speaker*, vice-admiral of the fleet, and admiral of the White squadron. He had to yield place to Monck, and it was as admiral of the blue that he fought at Portland on 18 February. His tacking through the Dutch line (commanded by the Dutch Admiral Evertsen) on this occasion brought praise for his courage and (perhaps inadvertently) innovative tactics.

In April 1653 Penn expressed his loyalty to the new regime established by Cromwell on his expulsion of the Rump. In this month he again convoyed the colliers. As captain of the *James* and admiral of the white he gained further honour in the battles of 2–3 June and 29–31 July. On 3 June Monck recommended to the admiralty commissioners that for his 'honesty and ability' Penn be appointed general-at-sea (Penn, *Memorials*, 1.492). On 6 August he was decorated with a gold chain worth £100, to which £30 would be added in January 1655. On 2 December he was formally nominated general and a commissioner of the admiralty, appointments confirmed the following day. Towards the end of the war he was anxious for peace, perhaps not least for time to settle his private affairs. On 1 September 1654 he petitioned the protector and council

for recompense of £8636 19*s*. 6*d*. said to have been lost to his wife's estate by the 'late horrid rebellion' (*CSP dom.*, *1654*, 351). He was immediately granted lands forfeited by the earl of Clancarty, with an annual value of £300.

Caribbean expedition Penn had already on 18 August been chosen to lead the protector's cherished expedition to the Caribbean, the 'western design' in which Cromwell hoped to find continuing use for his victorious navy by annihilating the Spanish empire in the West Indies. Penn would share command with Robert Venables (general of the land forces) and a body of civilian commissioners intended to supervise colonization once victory had been achieved. Instructions drawn up on 9 December spoke of 'getting ground' without naming any target (Firth, 109). The prime objective, it soon transpired, was Hispaniola, which had been the first European settlement in the Americas. The fleet sailed from Spithead on 25 December, Penn commanding from the *Swiftsure*, with thirty-seven other warships, support vessels, and 2500 to 3000 soldiers. On 29 January they came to Barbados where another 5500 men were engaged and 1200 of the seamen formed into a regiment to serve ashore. Penn seized a number of Dutch ships trading in contravention of parliament's orders and then sailed on 31 March, calling at Antigua and other islands already in English hands. On 13 April they came in sight of St Domingo on Hispaniola. Penn declined to risk a frontal assault, and the troops were landed next day some 25 miles west at Nizao. When they reached the capital they were easily repulsed. Penn offered his artillery in support of a further attempt, and was furious when this was rejected by Venables. There is no doubt that antagonism between Penn and Venables (which Cromwell had foreseen and attempted to defuse) contributed to lack of co-ordination at all levels. Penn was blamed by the military for the change of landing site, for denying them supplies, and for the unavailability of guides. For all these issues Penn advanced cogent operational reasons, and the failure of the assault was, as even Venables acknowledged, chiefly the fault of a 'rascally rabble of raw and unexercised men' and their inadequate provisions (Firth, 100).

The task force was, however, not crippled, and by 3 May when the troops re-embarked the 'general voice was for Jamaica' (Battick, 14). Penn confirmed this objective to his officers on the following day, and the island was sighted on the 9th. Penn personally led the landing on 10 May aboard the *Martin* galley, to which he transferred because of its shallow draught. At first the Spanish resisted, but their forts were abandoned before all the troops were ashore and the garrison surrendered next day. By 17 May the whole island was in English hands.

Penn subsequently sent two of his ships to reconnoitre the Spanish main, but made no further attempt to seize territory or shipping. After a month on Jamaica, increasingly ill, Penn decided to return home to report; he sailed on 25 June and made Spithead on 31 August. On 3 September the fleet was ordered into the Thames, and on the 12th Penn was interviewed in Whitehall. On the 20th he and Venables were sent to the Tower. Their arrest was gleefully reported by the royalists, who expected the commanders to be executed for failing to accomplish the 'design'. Clarendon would allege that both men were all along 'well affected to the King's service' and 'not fond of the enterprise they were to conduct' (Clarendon, *Hist. rebellion*, 6.5). As it happened the result had been as the royalists wished: Anglo-Spanish hostilities in Europe, which Cromwell had hoped to avoid, were provoked, while the protector was denied the great victory which would have buttressed his regime. But it is inconceivable that Penn and Venables, even had they been so minded, could have engineered just this outcome. Their imprisonment is adequately explained by their return without orders and Cromwell's pique at the frustration of his plans. On 25 October Penn apologized to the protector for his disobedience and begged to be freed for the sake of his family and his 'increasing distemper' (*CSP dom.*, 1655, 396). His release was ordered the same day on his relinquishing his commission. He was not to serve the protectorate again, and he declined to assist a long-running inquiry into unused slops. He retired to Ireland, and from his seat at Macroom, co. Cork, attended to his estates. He was not absolutely in disgrace, for in 1658 he received a knighthood from Henry Cromwell, and his wife was able to catch a lift to England aboard one of the state's ships.

Service ashore In 1659 Penn went to England, seeking to serve the republic but having already made contacts with royalists. While lodging in the Strand he received a friendly letter (dated 30 June) from Monck, offering to sponsor his return to naval service. In consequence Penn was restored to the admiralty commission on 24 March 1660. Monck was also responsible for securing Penn's election to the Convention Parliament as member for Weymouth. On 12 May Monck instructed him to prepare ships at Portsmouth and in the Thames to bring the king home, for which he would receive a special payment of £100. He sailed with the Restoration fleet, and on 9 June received an authentic knighthood. On 4 July he was nominated to the new Navy Board as an extra commissioner; his patent passed the seal on 17 August. He was a key adviser to the duke of York as lord high admiral, and it is likely that he helped draft the instructions issued in the duke's name, for which he collected a volume of precedents (BL, Sloane MS 3232).

At the Restoration Penn was also made governor of Kinsale, vice-admiral of Munster, and a member of the province's council. He commanded a company of foot in the Irish army and was *ex officio* JP for the counties in which the naval dockyards stood. He was re-elected for Weymouth in the Cavalier Parliament of 1661, retaining his seat until he died. He became an elder brother of Trinity House, of which he became master in 1667–8. Following the return of Lord Clancarty's lands under the Restoration settlement, Penn was on 28 October 1661 compensated with 12,000 other Irish acres, with an annual value of £423, but it would take until 1669 to secure his title against other interests.

Penn came into residence at the Navy Office in Seething Lane on 27 July 1660, thus becoming a neighbour of his junior colleague Pepys, in whose diary the last phases of Penn's career are sharply described. Pepys, although welcoming Penn as 'very sociable … and an able man' (Pepys, *Diary*, 1.241) soon fell out with him over contracts and appointments, and above all because he saw him as enemy to his own patron Sandwich. Penn was ever thereafter 'as false a fellow as ever was born' (ibid., 7.68) and Pepys took every opportunity to denigrate Penn's social address, service career, and administrative probity and competence. Yet he conceded he was the 'only fit man' to succeed the ineffectual Mennes as comptroller (ibid., 7.328). Mennes himself nominated Penn as his deputy when he went to sea in November 1661, but subsequently resisted all attempts to pass his duties to Penn in part or whole.

At the outset of the Second Anglo-Dutch War Penn served afloat again, initially (from 10 November 1664) aboard the *Royal James*, and after 18 November as chief of staff to the duke of York in the *Royal Charles*, with the unique rank of 'captain great commander'. In this capacity he served at the battle of Lowestoft on 3 June 1665, behaving 'so well that those who were most unsatisfied with him before are full of his commendations' (*CSP dom.*, 1664–5, 408). Penn retired exhausted after the day's action, unaware (he would claim) that a member of the duke's household took upon himself to give order to slacken sail, thinking to save his master from risk of another day's battle. There was some suggestion that Penn was involved in a cover-up: Burnet saw in it the origin of James's indulgence towards dissenters (Burnet, 78), but, malice apart, he may have confused Penn with the ship's captain, Harman. Penn's conduct on this occasion would not be significantly in question when he faced impeachment for the other great scandal of the year. On 2 July he had been made vice-admiral to Sandwich and admiral of the white. As such he was party to the breaking bulk of prizes taken at Bergen in September, and it emerged that he was the chief agent of this breach of maritime law (in some contrast to his strictures on the subject during his West Indies voyage).

Although briefly in command of the fleet in Sandwich's absence in November and December 1665, Penn's employment at sea for the rest of the war was prevented by Monck, who had accused him of recommending 'all these roguish fanatic captains' to the duke (Pepys, *Diary*, 6.291). Penn was, however, 'overwhelmed with a multiplicity of business' ashore in 1666 (*CSP dom.*, 1665–6, 445). It was as an armchair strategist that he offered his opinions on the conduct of the Four Days' Battle (1–4 June), stressing the importance of keeping line-ahead, and not allowing ships to withdraw for minor repairs.

On 16 January Penn was finally given an official responsibility for pursers' and victuallers' accounts, by way of devolving the duties of the comptroller. In July, as master of Trinity House, he had responsibility for the Thames defences in the face of the Dutch attack. Not uncharacteristically he failed to give the king a straight answer when asked about the advisability of clearing the river of blockships. On 21 October he faced the parliamentary inquiry into miscarriages of the war on the question of the failure to pursue the Dutch after Lowestoft; this issue was easily deflected. On 3 December he faced the more difficult accusation about the prize-goods affair. In March 1668 it was proposed that he should have a sea command; Penn was reluctant, but the king and duke insisted. MPs, however, were incensed that a new command should be given to one whom they had yet to examine fully about his last, and the prize-goods issue was subjected to intense scrutiny. Penn was called before the Commons on 14 April; a committee chaired by Sir Robert Howard reported on 21 April and articles of impeachment were read. The house decided to suspend Penn but not eject him. The matter then passed to the Lords, where Penn appeared on 27 April, calling himself a 'very unhappy man' (*JHL*, 12.235). He appeared again on the 29th, but there were no further proceedings. Penn had powerful friends, and the main purpose of the exercise—prevention of his command—had been achieved. This did not stop him from claiming the full allowance for six months' imaginary service.

Despite some enthusiasm for his new responsibilities at the Navy Board, Penn decided to resign his commissionership in 1668 on being offered a share in the new naval victualling contract; this was issued on 24 February 1669, and his patent was cancelled on 17 June. By 31 July he had also resigned the governorship of Kinsale to his kinsman Rooth. Penn's health had long been failing, and he died at Walthamstow, where he lived next to Batten, on 16 September 1670, On the 30th he was buried in the church of St Mary Redcliffe, Bristol, where his memorial stands. His wife survived him until 1682. In addition to his celebrated elder son, William *Penn (1644–1718), he had a son Richard and a daughter Margaret (who married Anthony Lowther in February 1667).

Penn was much distressed by his elder son's nonconformity, which led to his expulsion from Oxford and eventual imprisonment. Despite their arguments, mutual affection persisted. The younger William, though abhorring the profession of arms, defended his father's reputation in it and presented the king with a collection of Sir William's naval papers (Magdalene College, Cambridge, Pepys Library, no. 2611). When asked to return another document to the navy, he said he valued 'the smallest relic that may be deemed a badge of my father's trade' (*CSP dom.*, 1670, 562) and he named the colony he established in his father's honour.

Penn is said to have affected the puritan fashion to advance his career, but others have accepted his sincerity. He genuinely attempted to understand his son's beliefs, and was himself rumoured to have become a Quaker. At other times he was said to be an atheist, or hoping to 'live and die' an Anabaptist (*Samuel Pepys and the Second Dutch War*, 20). Yet he conformed to the religion and, it seems, the general morals of the Restoration. He has been judged too indecisive for supreme command, and his most important assignment was deemed a failure at the time. It has, however, since been recognized as a decisive moment in British imperial history, with continuing consequences for the present state of Jamaica.   C. S. KNIGHTON

Sources G. Penn, *Memorials of the professional life and times of Sir William Penn*, 2 vols. (1833) • *A collection of the works of William Penn*, 2 vols. (1726), 1.432–3 • M. R. Brailsford, *The making of William Penn* (1930) • J. R. Powell and E. K. Timings, eds., *Documents relating to the civil war, 1642–1648*, Navy RS, 105 (1963) • J. R. Powell, 'Penn's attempt to relieve Youghal, 1645', *Irish Sword*, 2 (1954–6), 83–7 • J. R. Powell, 'Penn's expedition to Bonratty in 1646', *Mariner's Mirror*, 40 (1954), 4–20 • H. M. Jenkins, 'The family of William Penn', *Pennsylvania Magazine of History and Biography*, 20 (1896), 1–29, 158–75 • *The manuscripts of his grace the duke of Portland*, 10 vols., HMC, 29 (1891–1931), vols. 1–4 • *CSP dom.*, 1644–70 • *CSP Ire.*, 1660–70 • *CSP col.*, vol. 1 • *JHC*, 6–9 (1648–87) • *JHL*, 12 (1666–75) • Clarendon, *Hist. rebellion* • *The narrative of General Venables*, ed. C. H. Firth, CS, new ser., 60 (1900) • J. F. Battick, ed., 'Richard Rooth's sea journal of the western design, 1654–55', *Jamaica Journal*, 5/4 (Dec 1971), 3–22 • HoP, *Commons*, 1660–90, 3.222–3 • will, PRO, PROB 11/334, fols. 9–10 • *The letters of John Paige, London merchant, 1648–1658*, ed. G. F. Steckley, London RS, 21 (1984), 118, 121, 123, 130–31 • Pepys, *Diary* • *Samuel Pepys and the Second Dutch War: Pepys's navy white book and Brooke House papers*, ed. R. Latham, Navy RS, 133 (1995) [transcribed by W. Matthews and C. Knighton] • J. S. Corbett, ed., *Fighting instructions, 1630–1816*, Navy RS, 29 (1905), 81, 92–3, 96, 98–104, 114, 120–22 • S. R. Gardiner and C. T. Atkinson, eds., *Letters and papers relating to the First Dutch War, 1652–1654*, 6 vols., Navy RS, 13, 17, 30, 37, 41, 66 (1898–1930) • *The journal of Edward Mountagu, first earl of Sandwich, admiral and general at sea, 1659–1665*, ed. R. C. Anderson, Navy RS, 64 (1929), 201, 236–8, 272 • *The Tangier papers of Samuel Pepys*, ed. E. Chappell, Navy RS, 73 (1935), 228 • *The letters of Robert Blake*, ed. J. R. Powell, Navy RS, 76 (1937) • *The journals of Sir Thomas Allin, 1660–1678*, ed. R. C. Anderson, Navy RS, 79 (1939), 239, 247 • J. R. Powell and E. K. Timings, eds., *The Rupert and Monck letter book, 1666*, Navy RS, 112 (1969), 44–5, 93, 111, 165, 209 • B. Capp, *Cromwell's navy: the fleet and the English revolution, 1648–1660* (1989), 24–5, 67, 87–90, 293–4 • *My Irish journal, 1669–1670, by William Penn*, ed. I. Grubb (1952) • J. M. Collinge, *Navy Board officials, 1660–1832* (1978), 129 • B. Pool, *Navy board contracts, 1660–1832* (1966), 2, 9 • J. D. Davies, *Gentlemen and tarpaulins: the officers and men of the Restoration navy* (1991), 123, 127, 135, 138, 146, 155–6 • R. Ollard, *Cromwell's earl: a life of Edward Mountagu, 1st earl of Sandwich* (1994), 25, 140–41, 143 • Evelyn, *Diary*, 3.508 • W. L. Clowes, *The Royal Navy: a history from the earliest times to the present*, 7 vols. (1897–1903); repr. (1996–7), vol. 2 • G. Burnet, *History of his own time*, ed. T. Stackhouse, abridged edn (1874); repr. (1979), 78 • *The poems and letters of Andrew Marvell*, ed. H. M. Margoliouth, 2nd edn, 2 (1952), 72–3 • F. Kitson, *Prince Rupert: admiral and general-at-sea* (1998), 54, 56, 61, 91–3, 223, 318 • *The diary of John Milward*, ed. C. Robbins (1938), 257, 259–60, 269 • C. H. Firth and R. S. Rait, eds., *Acts and ordinances of the interregnum, 1642–1660*, 2 (1911), 812, 1136 • *The Nicholas papers*, ed. G. F. Warner, 2, CS, new ser., 50 (1892), 178–80, 202, 309, 322, 332, 336, 338, 345 • R. L. Ollard, *Pepys: a biography* (1974), 63, 76–8, 205 • BL, Sloane MS 3232 • L. Street, *An uncommon sailor: a portrait of Admiral Sir William Penn* (1986)

Archives BL, letters, Egerton MS 928 • Hist. Soc. Penn., papers • NMM, corresp. and papers | BL, Sloane MS 3232 • Magd. Cam. • NMM, Wyn MSS

Likenesses P. Lely, oils, *c*.1666, NMM [*see illus.*] • R. Earlom, mezzotint, pubd 1811 (after P. Lely), NPG • W. Finden, stipple and line engraving, pubd 1833 (after unknown artist), NPG • G. P. Harding?, pen and ink, and wash drawing, NPG

Wealth at death left £4000 to younger son; £300 to wife; residue to elder son: will, PRO, PROB 11/334, fols. 9–10 • Irish estates said to be worth £1500 p.a.; £12,000 owing from crown: HoP, *Commons*, 1660–90

Penn, William (1644–1718), Quaker leader and founder of Pennsylvania, was born in the liberty of the Tower of London on 14 October 1644, the son of Sir William *Penn (*bap.* 1621, *d.* 1670), admiral in the English navy, and Margaret

William Penn (1644–1718), by Francis Place, c.1696

(1610?–1682), the daughter of John Jasper, a Dutch merchant of Rotterdam, and the widow of Nicasius van der Schuren.

Early years Penn's developmental years took a conventional route. His education was fairly typical of his social class, being schooled at home until the age of eleven. From eleven he began his formal training at Chigwell Academy, near Wanstead in Essex. Established in 1629, the academy comprised two schools within the same building. One school concerned itself with more practical applications such as reading, writing, and mathematics. The other was more classically orientated, teaching Latin and Greek. Given the political environment in which young Penn was being educated, it seems highly likely that he would be given instruction for more practical applications. Only after the fall of the protectorate, and the impending restoration of the monarchy, can we say for certain that Penn's education took a more classical turn.

Penn entered Christ Church, Oxford, in 1660 as a gentleman commoner. There, under the deanship of John Fell, he improved his knowledge of classical scholarship. Although he was to spend less than two years at Christ Church, he came into contact with men who would become political allies, such as Robert Spencer, later earl of Sunderland. Also at this time there were other men who influenced Penn's thinking in ways which would enhance his religious-political outlook. John Locke was then a lecturer at Christ Church and most probably instructed Penn in Greek. While it could not have been through any acquaintance with Locke that Penn would have developed a radical political philosophy at this time, since Locke was then still conservative in his thinking,

nevertheless Penn would have developed a rigorous style of debate that would serve the Quaker later in political and religious disputations. In later decades, however, the ideas of his former tutor may have influenced Penn's concept of colonization. Later in the 1690s Locke's influence would be seen in the development of colonial policy. Also during these early years Penn probably listened to the well-known puritan theologian Dr John Owen. Although this experience is usually seen as a turning point in Penn's religious leanings, it must be remembered that he came from a dissenting background. His father was a presbyterian, albeit one that conformed to the Church of England after 1660, and his mother was a Dutch Calvinist. Therefore, it would not have been unreasonable to be instructed by somebody sympathetic to dissent, in this case Owen, who had not yet been dismissed from the college.

By the winter of 1661 Penn left Oxford and went to the continent, ostensibly to escape the political controversy that was arising from the stringent enforcement of the Act of Uniformity on the university which even required students to wear surplices. While travelling through Europe with Robert Spencer, he spent time in Italy and visited the city of Turin, which was being rebuilt. The design of the city, along a grid pattern, may have influenced Penn's thoughts when, as proprietor of Pennsylvania, he developed Philadelphia in the same style. After his visit to the French court, where he made a dashing impression, Penn attended the protestant academy of Saumur under the tutelage of Moise Amyraut, one of the leading Calvinist theologians of the day. Although Penn's studentship was short, because Amyraut died in 1664, it was a watershed in his religious and political outlook. Amyraut's philosophy of non-resistance and the illumination of the mind and will, or the inner light, greatly influenced Penn's religious outlook. Amyraut also had entrée to the French court and supported the view on the divine right of kings; his position was probably influenced by the hiatus between the siege of La Rochelle, in 1628, and the revocation of the edict of Nantes, in 1685, when a window of toleration was opened. Amyraut's religious philosophy was tempered by political necessities. This philosophy not only helps to explain Penn's later attraction to the Quaker life, it also explains his political position particularly during the reign of James II. His recollection of the Frenchman's teachings might have influenced Penn's support of James II's toleration of Catholics, for which Penn was labelled as a papist.

Young adult years and Ireland A more mature Penn returned to England in 1664, ready to take on his responsibilities as heir. He spent some time in London learning law at Lincoln's Inn, a valuable foundation for anyone embarking on a life involving business, not least in pressing his father's Irish claims. He left there, possibly because of the plague, some time in the spring of 1665. Meanwhile, a second war had broken out between the Dutch and English, and in March Penn was actively involved in the effort, acting as messenger running between court and the flagship the *Royal Charles*. His position was no doubt due to the influence of his father, who was based at the Navy Office in London. By July Penn was cutting his teeth in the local politics of Buckinghamshire. As one of the commissioners for charitable uses, he determined cases brought on by complaints of abuse of charitable trusts. This position also gave him the experience of how government operated that he later applied so ably in his defence of religious toleration. Moreover, at this time he was establishing his influence in the locality which served him well in national politics during the period between 1679 and 1681.

In February 1666 Penn went to Ireland, where, as his father's agent, he settled the admiral's titles to the family estates in co. Cork. Subsequently the Irish years became a prelude and a training ground for William. His experiences there gave him the expertise for future business ventures, and it was the political arena in which he honed his disputatiousness. In May 1666 he travelled to northern Ireland, where he became involved in suppressing a mutiny in the English garrison at Carrickfergus in co. Antrim. The place erupted when the men, who had been unpaid for nine months, took over the castle. Penn impressed the duke of Ormond, who was lord lieutenant of Ireland, by assisting him and the earl of Arran in putting down the revolt. The grateful Ormond wrote to Sir William, recommending that his son take command of the garrison at Kinsale. Penn's father refused, not because he thought that his son could not handle the responsibility, but because of Sir William's plans to retire to his Irish estates in the near future and to live off the revenue from them together with the income from his post as commander of the garrison at Kinsale. As for young William, he was given the role of victualler at Kinsale, a position in keeping with his business responsibilities.

Though Penn made subsequent visits to Ireland in 1669 and 1698, his first marked a major turning point in his religious development. The time of his conversion to Quakerism is imprecise, but it is certain that in 1667 he attended a Quaker meeting in Cork and was subsequently brought before the magistrate for being part of what was termed a 'riotous and tumultuary assembly' (Penn to Orrery, November 1667, *Papers*, 1.51). Most likely, Penn's sympathy towards the Quakers was enhanced by the event.

Penn was increasingly being seen as the spokesman for a growing economic segment of society, in England as well as Ireland. By 1677 there were at least fourteen substantial Quaker merchants in London alone. These, together with Quaker merchants and tradesmen throughout England and Ireland, represented a sizeable contribution to the economic growth of the country. Therefore, his commercial connections were not limited to Quakers. It was his broader dissenting relationships which increased his political attraction, so much so that Penn was the leading spokesman for toleration when he presented evidence to a committee of the House of Commons debating the use of recusancy laws against Quakers.

On 4 April 1672 Penn married Gulielma Maria Springett (d. 1694), whom he had courted for the last three years. She was the daughter of Sir William Springett (d. 1643), of Brayle Place, a parliamentary officer who died at the siege

of Arundel Castle, and Mary Proude (*bap.* 1623, *d.* 1682), who married in 1654 Isaac Penington (1616–1679), a notable London merchant and Quaker [*see* Penington, Mary]. The pair had known each other since the 1660s and their marriage seems to have been a love match. One of their earliest known letters shows an affection that went beyond mere friendship. At the same time their relationship was based upon shared interests and background. Both were Quakers and both came from families of good standing—Gulielma held considerable lands in Kent and Sussex. They had three sons and four daughters; the youngest son, William, lived to adulthood, became a dissolute rake, and died in 1720; their only daughter to survive infancy, Letitia, married William Aubrey.

Quaker conversion Penn's conversion marked a crucial point in the path towards furtherance and consolidation in Quaker principles. Although the time of his conversion to Quakerism is not certain, it roughly coincides with his involvement at the Quaker meeting in Cork in 1667. By the time he returned to England that year, he had taken on the mantle of the Friends, ready to proselytize his beliefs. After a couple of spells in prison, in 1671 Penn embarked on an evangelical tour of Europe, making important contacts with Princess Elizabeth (1618–1680) of the Palatinate. He returned by the end of that year, by which time his father had died, leaving him heir to the family estates. Penn's position in society elevated him in the Quaker ranks as a force for the sect, for as an heir and gentleman of rank he had social clout. Paradoxically, his new status created tension between the unworldly philosophy of some Quakers and his involvement in the political world. Nevertheless, the radical tendencies of his youth were now tempered with his new responsibilities as head of the family.

By this time Penn had developed a close relationship with George Fox, whom he had met a couple of years earlier. This relationship resulted in a collaboration which created a coherent Quaker philosophy. Its beginnings can be traced to George Fox's decision to lay down the sword of violence and write the *Peace Testimony* at the time of Venner's rising in 1661. Through this document Fox hoped to show the restored monarchy the non-violent and non-threatening nature of the Friends. It went some way to distinguish a more pacific group from the radical elements in the society, but it also can be seen as the beginning of a move to regularize Quaker thought. Penn's relationship with Fox and his wife, Margaret Fell, can be traced to a mutual belief, not only in Quakerism, but in their similar pragmatic approach exhibited in the *Peace Testimony*. Whereas Fox's approach was unsystematic, Penn's input was to make it intellectually more rigorous. Penn added to this development in his own work, *No Cross, No Crown*, in 1669, which set out the rules for Quaker behaviour. Rejection of hat honour, titles, the vanity of apparel, and promotion of the use of 'thee' and 'thou' when addressing one another, regardless of title, were the outward hallmarks of a simpler approach to life. Penn listed scriptural reasons for the rejection of outward vanities, observing 'Honour was from the beginning, but hats, and most titles, here of late; therefore there was true Honour before hats or titles, and consequently true honour stands not therein'. Furthermore, he quoted James 2: 1–11, urging people to look further than man's outward appearance, not accepting any man just 'for his gay cloathing, rich attire, or outward appearance' (Barbour, 1.46, 47). As Penn became more involved in the politics of dissent, he found it increasingly difficult to maintain the standard he set in this work. Nevertheless, it was the first coherent guide on Quaker behaviour. Also, as he became more involved in court politics and when confronted with direct responsibility of running a colony marked by its religious tolerance, Penn found himself hard put to sustain these rules, particularly his support for eschewing oaths in favour of affirming. His apparent ambiguity was compared to that of the great courtier in the book of Esther and, as James II said of Penn, 'I suppose you take William Pen[n] for A Quaker, but I can assure you he is no more so than I am' (*Bishop Burnet's History*, 4.140).

Penn was, nevertheless, able to further the Quaker cause through his forceful polemics and by practical applications in parliamentary elections. His writings on dissent from his first exuberant tract, *Truth Exalted*, in 1668, to his final thoughts on life in general in *More Fruits of Solitude* in 1702, provide a map of his philosophical development. He wrote over forty works, most of which dealt with his ultimate goal of toleration in general. The only exception for toleration which Penn made was in the case of Roman Catholics as stated in his tract *A Seasonable Caveat Against Popery* (1670), but that is muted later under James II. Penn's first theological tracts, *Truth Exalted* and *The Guide Mistaken and Temporizing Rebuked*, published in 1668, reflect Amyrauldian influence. While the latter work is the more polemical in its reply to other dissenters, such as Jonathan Clapham, and his rationalization for conforming to the Act of Uniformity, both assert the inward light and the possibility for universal salvation. In *Truth Exalted* the young Penn challenged the doctrines of Catholics and protestants alike for not being based on the Bible. 'What Scripture ever made a Pope', and where do the scriptures 'own such persecutors', were some of the questions which Penn asked in order to illustrate how far professed Christians had moved away from their beginnings (Barbour, 1.29–30, 32). Penn argued that only by looking within one's self, or for the light within, could there be resolution and, ultimately, salvation. *The Guide Mistaken* furthers Penn's ideas on salvation by defending his stand against conformity, and comes ever closer to the issue of the Trinity, three persons in one God. 'The Scriptures do not warrant that division into, and appellation of three persons', Penn maintained, and queried whether or not we should take this on faith (Barbour, 1.195). Also written in the same year, *The Sandy Foundation Shaken* logically followed Penn's doubts on the Trinity and tested the grounds for the rejection of the divinity of Christ. If the Trinity was not valid, as he implied, was Christ of divine essence? 'If God, as the Scriptures testifie, hath never been declar'd or believ'd, but as the Holy ONE, then will it follow, that God is not a Holy THREE, nor doth subsist in THREE distinct and separate Holy ONES' (Barbour, 1.217). The immediate reaction to Penn was his being charged with Socinianism, which denied the doctrine of the Trinity. Although he quickly backed off this approach following a spell in the Tower, and published a new tract, *Innocency with her Open Face*, thereby mollifying the authorities by saying that he was misinterpreted over the issue of divinity, the label of deist stuck to him for much of his life.

Political career Although Penn's earlier writings included defences of the Quaker way, his first foray into political activism on behalf of dissent came with the onset of the new Conventicle Act in 1670. The new law prohibited sects such as Quakers from gathering for worship that was not in accordance with the liturgy and practice of the Anglican church. In response to this, and during another sojourn in Newgate prison, Penn wrote *The Great Case of Liberty of Conscience*, which was directed to the consideration of Charles II. The thrust of the tract was the immorality of persecution, which was against reason and nature. 'For my own part', he boldly proclaimed, 'I publickly confess my self to be a very hearty Dissenter from the establish'd religion of these nations' (Barbour, 2.419). Penn's protest against the Conventicle Act did not spare his being arrested under it for what the authorities claimed was sedition. Charged with addressing a tumultuous assembly at Gracechurch Street, he and a fellow Quaker, William Meade, were imprisoned at Newgate. But unlike his earlier imprisonments, where he modified his views, this time he was determined to defend them in court. Their arguments, based on the rights of Englishmen which were being threatened by the act, established an important precedent in English law. At the conclusion of the trial a verdict of not guilty was delivered, for which the jury was imprisoned by the mayor of London. The order was overturned by the chief justice, thereby establishing the future autonomy of juries. The action by the mayor, however, raised the spectre of arbitrary power that had not been seen since the reign of Charles I, and it heightened political tensions. It also brought Penn widespread respect for his able championing of dissent. From this point Penn was taken seriously by the crown as well as parliament as somebody who could influence the dissenting element in society.

Penn's networking certainly paid dividends, for he established valuable contacts with several prominent English politicians. One of the most useful of his friends was Robert Spencer, now second earl of Sunderland, with whom he shared a similar viewpoint on religious toleration; Sunderland was in a position of power, as privy councillor and secretary of state. Laurence Hyde, earl of Rochester, was another connection at court, perhaps even more useful to him than Sunderland. Rochester, together with his brother Henry, now second earl of Clarendon, and his father, had accompanied the king into exile, and had spent time in Europe as envoy; by the end of the decade he was first lord of the Treasury and a privy councillor. A third useful contact was Sidney Godolphin, whose career was intricately involved with that of Rochester. Both were employed as diplomats by Charles II in the late 1670s.

Godolphin purchased the post of master of the robes from Rochester and served under him as a commissioner of the Treasury. In 1680 these three men, all known to Penn, formed a ministry satirically dubbed the Chits on account of their youth and relative inexperience. It was Penn's relationship with such men, who were able to influence policy and act as brokers between the court and parliament, that gave him access to power. If he wanted a favour, it was accomplished through the mediation of these managers. They were men of broad experience, too broad to be hemmed in by a narrow view of the church. For this reason they were neither whig nor tory but court politicians. They took their lead from the king, not from party leaders.

Penn's political alignment with opponents of the crown such as the republican Algernon Sidney represented what was still a somewhat idealistic approach to politics. He supported Sidney's attempts to enter parliament at Guildford in the first election held that year, and at Amersham and Bramber in the second, and backed the son of a Cromwellian major-general at Bramber when Sidney withdrew. Penn had sufficient influence in the county of Sussex to support Sir John Fagg, another Cromwellian officer, against the dominant interest of the Pelhams, though Sir John Pelham topped the poll. His victory was commented on by his sister-in-law and mother to the earl of Sunderland; the dowager countess's contemptuous remark that 'Penn did what he could to help Fagg and hinder my brother, Pelham, who had not one gentleman against him' is more than socially revealing (Blencowe, 1.123). That Penn was worthy of mention illustrates the extent of his interest in Sussex, and his electoral activities displayed the natural interest of his gentry family more than the campaigning of a dissenting leader on behalf of whigs. Penn himself was never a whig. The electoral tract he wrote at that juncture, *England's Great Interest*, did not support exclusion. Rather it advocated country measures against the court. His disaffection with courtiers such as the earl of Danby arose from his frustrated efforts to petition for a colonial charter in those years. Where throughout Danby's ministry he had been knocking on a closed door, after the earl's fall the Chits opened it and beckoned him in. Penn's connections at court with managers like Sunderland and Rochester now began to pay off. He dropped his country acquaintances and became a court politician himself. He never looked back, always thereafter identifying his interests with those of the crown's managers. Although the politicians with whom Penn associated himself would change over time, their loyalty to the court rather than to a party would be the common denominator. Finally, in 1681, his tactics paid off in a land grant in the New World.

The Pennsylvania charter Penn claimed that the grant of a charter to colonize the large tract of land west of the Delaware River was in payment of debts owed by the crown to his father. This mundane motive has never been regarded as the main reason for his seeking a proprietary colony. Rather an explanation has been sought in Penn's Quaker commitment. Thus he has been regarded as desiring to obtain for the Friends a refuge where they could seek relief from persecution in England, and at the same time take part in a 'holy experiment' (*Papers*, 2.108). Penn's involvement in colonization stems from a 1673 letter to the duke of York in which Penn probably recommended somebody, possibly a relative, to a post in either Carolina or Virginia. The next and more significant involvement was as trustee for West New Jersey. In this capacity he mediated a dispute between two other Quakers involved in the initial sale of the colony. Ultimately the colony's shares were sold to resolve its financial difficulties, and a frame of government was drawn up, presumably by Penn. The West New Jersey concessions and agreements, which guaranteed the right to vote and hold office, as well as freedom of worship, provided a model for the future Pennsylvania government. Pennsylvania would test Penn's commitment to religious toleration and his conviction that it would generate economic growth. While the colony undoubtedly realized these hopes and expectations, such aspirations were not necessarily paramount in Penn's motivation throughout the 1670s while he was soliciting the government. Moreover, the Declaration of Indulgence of 1672, although the king revoked it the following year, did afford relief for dissenters, and particularly Quakers, for the rest of the decade. Whatever Penn's motives, the timing of the grant was dependent not upon him but upon Charles II. The king was persuaded to grant him a charter as part of a political strategy of dividing his opponents. Penn had support among the London merchant community, many of whom were dissenters who sided with the opposition in parliament. Charles was anxious to avoid pushing them into rebellion when his confrontation with the Exclusionists reached a crisis. The Pennsylvania charter, issued simultaneously with the dissolution of the Oxford parliament in March 1681, was one of the tactics employed by the crown to forestall civil war. Following his efforts in obtaining the colonial grant, Penn was nominated as a fellow of the Royal Society. That the grant had commercial as well as ideological appeal was shown when Penn insisted on also obtaining the three lower counties below Pennsylvania, which formed what was to become Delaware and were then part of the duke of York's proprietorship. James reluctantly yielded them, aware as Penn was of their economic value. They provided tobacco, a valuable export. They also were inhabited by Swedes, Finns, Dutch, and English, most of the latter being Anglicans rather than dissenters. Penn was particularly attached to this part of his grant and he was determined to keep it even when he later decided to sell Pennsylvania.

Having obtained his charter, Penn set out, in the company of fellow emigrants, to the new world. On arrival in October 1682, he received a piece of turf, a twig, and some river water from the Delaware inhabitants to symbolize his authority over the new land. After a brief stay at New Castle, he travelled up to Philadelphia, and for the next two years Penn proceeded to get the new government in working order.

Overall, Penn's philosophy of government was fashioned from the fires of political crisis in England on the issue of dissent. Pennsylvania would provide the political solution to the problem. The evolution of the colony's constitution from its first draft in 1681 to the final version of 1701 illustrates the priority put on inclusive political participation regardless of religion or ethnic background. Thus the colony's development as a holy experiment can be considered a success where trade, politics, and religion could coexist. Toleration of various religious groups percolated down to inclusive political participation. Oaths were not required for office holding, and there was no provision for an establishment church. Thus the make-up at one quarter sessions consisted of three Anglicans, six 'strong Foxonian Quakers, one Swede, and one sweet singer of Isreall' (Hunt. L., MS BL4, 'A brief narrative of the proceedings of William Penn'). Penn was no democrat and no republican, but he was anxious that there should be a consensus in the new society. Also, while he was not concerned primarily with the style of government, he was determined that it should rest on a firm basis of law. For those reasons, the government was run by elected freemen, yet the core of power rested in the proprietor's deputy lieutenant, who had final approval over elected office holders such as sheriffs, justices, and coroners, and his council, who held the legislative initiative until 1701. All these powers were subject to the proprietor's wishes. Penn's view of government was that, while it was to secure the people from the abuse of power, nevertheless he declared himself to be 'a palatine' and that his power was 'far greater than any kings governor in America' (ibid.).

Another concern was to try to implement a land policy which would settle the colony in line with his ideal of developing it so that it would be filled with inhabitants spread over the whole, with no empty spaces as had occurred in other colonies. To this end he hoped to allot land on the basis that every 5000 acres should have a minimum of ten families. Unfortunately for Penn such a tidy chequerboard scheme came into contact with economic realities. It would have proved impossible to cope with the tidal wave of settlers that moved into Pennsylvania in the opening years of the 1680s even if they had been content to conform to the proprietor's policy. But they wished to make their own arrangements, and more to the point were prepared to purchase plots from other buyers as well as Penn. In addition to internal squabbles over land, there were boundary disputes with Maryland which, in 1684, resulted in Penn returning to England, where he could lobby the court against Lord Baltimore's claims. The only solution to the land dispute for the time being was to set up a commission of proprietary to administer his policies in his absence.

Penn's relations with the indigenous people of the colony was, partly, an extension of crown policy, where peaceful coexistence through negotiations and treaties was the preference. Penn's attitude towards the native Americans can be gleaned through the colony's charter. Its instruction was to 'reduce the savage natives by gentle and just manners to the love of civil society and Christian religion'. To that end Penn took the trouble to learn the local language of the Lenne Lenape. He saw them as 'natural sons of Providence', and they returned the respect he paid them with the affectionate name of Miquon, or feather, to represent a quill pen (*Papers*, 2.448, 454). However, Penn's negotiations over land with the American Indians revealed a certain ignorance of the complicated ownership which had developed between the nations and settlers. Prior to Penn's grant the colony was under the jurisdiction of New York, whose governor had negotiated with the Iroquois Five Nations the 'covenant chain' in an effort to stabilize the area. The sectioning off of Pennsylvania for Penn did not necessarily invalidate the chain. However, he proceeded to set up another treaty, the 'friendship chain', in an effort to extend trading rights up to the New York border. The result was to threaten Anglo-Indian relations in general. Within his own colony, however, Penn was able to maintain good relations with the Indians through a presumption of fairness and goodwill.

Political years, 1685–1688 Between 1685 and 1688, during the reign of James II, Penn realized the highest point in his political career. He was cultivated by the king not only as a dissenter but also as a courtier. Thus he was groomed for high office in the customary way by being sent on an embassy. This was the route which such courtiers as Godolphin, Rochester, and Sunderland had taken when they were fledgeling politicians. Penn was sent as an unofficial envoy to The Hague in May 1686, to sound out the attitude of the prince and princess of Orange towards the repeal of the penal laws and Test Act. Ostensibly travelling through parts of Europe to visit Quakers and to proselytize, Penn was delegated by the king to travel to The Hague in order to find out how William and Mary viewed James's strategy for toleration. Penn had in 1680 gone to Holland to address the prince of Orange on behalf of fellow Quakers in the Netherlands who were being persecuted. This time, however, his hope that he could convince the pair on James's behalf was, alas, based upon sand.

Prince William assured Penn of his support for toleration, but he could not agree to abandoning the Test Act, because it was the only security for protestantism, especially when the king was of a different religion. He agreed with Penn that conscience was a private matter, but it was no good promising toleration without enacting it first into law. Otherwise it could be revoked on the king's whim just as the edict of Nantes had been by Louis XIV in 1685. Anyway, the number of dissenters in Britain was clearly in the minority; therefore, to ignore the primary base of support for the monarchy, the Anglican tories, was political suicide.

While William's view was more cynical, his wife's opposition came from her firm religious beliefs. As a staunch Anglican, she believed that as future protector of the established church, she would be responsible for the souls of her people. To open the door to what she considered nothing more than schismatic sects would weaken the pillar of religious belief and cause social instability. Only by James having a son would William and

Mary's claims be superseded. Paradoxically, the birth of a royal son in 1688 sealed James's fate and ensured their claim.

Penn also tried to persuade Burnet, who was also at the court in The Hague, to return to England and support James in his policies. In return, Burnet would be rewarded by preferential treatment from the king. James appreciated Burnet's role as an exiled whig confidant of Mary, and must have realized that, if he could persuade him, he would be able to sway his daughter. Burnet's description of Penn's visit was laced with venom. An egotistical man himself, Burnet recognized a like fellow in Penn. He depicted Penn's performance before William and Mary as one brimming with over-confidence with an address which was given in a 'tedious and luscious way', all of which would only succeed in boring the listener. None the less, Burnet declined Penn's invitation on the same grounds as that of the prince and princess, and probably because he had information that James had a contract out for his assassination. According to Burnet, Penn left him with a prediction passed on to himself by a man 'that pretended a commerce with angels'. According to this 'friend', in two years' time, 1688 to be exact, there would be momentous changes that would amaze all the world (*Bishop Burnet's History*, 4.139–41). The momentous event was not what Penn had envisioned. On his return from The Hague, Penn apparently satisfied Sunderland with the accomplishment of his mission. Although he was not entirely successful, since the prince and princess of Orange baulked at repealing the Test Act, they had expressed their toleration for all including Catholics. One sign of Penn's acceptance at court was his appointment as a deputy lieutenant in Buckinghamshire. This commission in the county militia, while perhaps curious for a Quaker, was quite fitting for a country gentleman.

A more significant sign of his arrival in power came in the spring of 1687, when Penn became involved with the writing of the declaration of indulgence. The declaration was seen as more than just a repeat of the attempt in 1672 by Charles II to carry through his promise at Breda to ensure the liberty of tender consciences. It was an edict of toleration, granting immunity from prosecution for breaches of the penal laws against religious dissent. In theory, it included not only Catholics and protestant non-Anglicans, but even non-Christians. The motives behind the declaration would fit in with Penn's aspirations. He certainly wanted religious and political liberties for his brethren even if it meant taking a softer line than before on the Roman Catholics. Furthermore, the declaration was preceded by a proclamation of toleration in Scotland, which specified groups such as the Quakers.

Penn's next step was to sell the declaration and promote the repeal of the penal laws and Test Act by writing tracts in support, organizing addresses thanking the king, and travelling throughout the country speaking for James's policies. However, the reasonableness of Penn's arguments did not convince opposition which existed on both sides of the religious divide. Dissenters as well as Anglicans feared the power of popery if Catholics were allowed political participation. In one embarrassing instance Penn was shouted down and forced to move on with 'the mob knocking the bulks as he passed' (*Westmorland MSS*, 376).

Penn became James's right-hand man, helping the king to regulate corporations, and acting as a commissioner into the regulation of recusancy fines, and as a mediator between the king and Magdalen College, Oxford. He became a general spokesman for James's policies and a door through which men had to pass to receive royal favours. Penn had, at last, the chance to use his unique position to further his aims for toleration. What emerged was the pairing of the king and the dissenter which created a possibility for a broader religious toleration that went beyond either one's expectation and beyond anything that England had experienced. At the same time Penn was fulfilling his father's ambitions for him. Towards the end of James's reign Penn held a position of influence which rivalled that of a minister. In May 1687 rumour had it that he would be named secretary of state, and shortly after he received a letter addressing him as Sir William (Sir Ralph Verney to John Verney, Middle Claydon, 15 May 1687, Claydon House, Verney Papers, microfilm 636, reel 41).

In summer 1687 the king dissolved parliament and set out to spearhead the campaign to convince people, either through reason or by browbeating them, to select amenable candidates for a new parliament. He had extended wholesale toleration to Catholics and dissenters alike, thus completely alienating the Anglican tories. Penn helped in the effort to fashion a pliable parliament by involving himself at the local level of politics. He was given the power to act as an intermediary regulating the corporations in Buckinghamshire and in Huntingdonshire. Writing from Kensington Palace to a friend and former Quaker, Robert Bridgeman of Huntingdon, Penn directed him to send a distinct account of all the representatives of that corporation and their political attitudes on the matter of the repeal of the penal laws and Test Acts. Penn was thus at the very heart of government in these months, and collaborated with the king over the packing of parliament. He later justified his involvement by saying that it was the only way to achieve his goal of toleration by an act of parliament even if it meant stacking the odds. 'I allwaies endeavoured an impartiall liberty of conscience to be established by law, that the Papists might never be able to null it, and this is all that can be charged upon me, and I count it no crime' (DWL, Morrice MS Q, pp. 353–4). In other words, the end sometimes justified the means and the language of denial by Penn was carefully chosen.

Penn was also on the road drumming up support for the king by organizing addresses of thanks starting with his own brethren. However, the number of addresses, of which there were only 197 over a period of a year, and the kinds of religious groups involved, qualified the success of the campaign. Indeed, the prospects for a compliant parliament were not auspicious. On the contrary, responses to a crude public opinion poll undertaken by the king were ominous. James asked the leading peers and gentry to answer three questions to ascertain their views on toleration. First, if elected to parliament, would they support the repeal of the penal laws and the Test Acts? Second, would they vote for candidates who supported the repeal? Finally, would they live peaceably with their neighbours no matter what their religious beliefs? By December 1687 the responses were largely negative. Penn, who had advised the king not to conduct the survey, concluded that an election must be postponed until March at the earliest. He was being much more realistic than the king, showing as much awareness of gentry as of dissenting opinion. Early in the new year he told James Johnstone that 'there would be a parliament at the end of May'. Johnstone replied that he 'would wager twenty to one against. He began to laugh, and said I imagined Sunderland had more credit than he actually possessed—he hadn't the power to prevent it, and he would be ruined if he did not allow it.' Johnstone replied 'that he had no need of power, he would use trickery instead. "That is what I fear myself", he said' (Kenyon, 187). Sunderland managed to put off the election until September, persuading James that his soundings in the constituencies did not augur well. By September, however, Sunderland and Penn were convinced that 'the Parliament will do what the king will have them' (ibid., 214). Confidence in the regime was such that Penn received the post of commissioner of the hearth and excise. This had a twofold effect in seeing to it that the king's much needed revenue would make him less reliant on parliament while making Penn a profit. Penn's increasing worldliness was also being noted by the Society of Friends, in their comparison of him to the great courtier in the book of Esther (Clarendon State Papers, 89, fols. 175–6, Dublin, September 1688). Unfortunately for Penn, his political career was put on hold when news arrived that William of Orange was preparing to invade.

Immediately James switched his allegiance back to the Anglicans and began the electoral process for a new parliament. However, upon hearing that William's fleet was blown back by a gale to Dutch harbours, James took it as a sign from above that providence had once again intervened, so the king ordered that the writs for elections be recalled. But, when he learned of William's landing at Torbay on 5 November, the king began backtracking by removing Catholic officials from their posts, and again issued writs for an election.

Serious doubts about the king's motives must have come surging forth in Penn's mind. He must have felt very insecure in the first instance when James stopped the issuance of writs, but his fears must have heightened on the second occasion when the king undid everything that he and Penn had accomplished in the past year. The only thing that Penn could do was clumsily to issue a tract, *Advice in the Choice of Parliament Men*, in which he once again attacked the Catholic element. He also tried to cobble a draft of confirmation of his authority over the three lower counties on the Delaware River, something which was never clarified, but it was too late. Only a partial draft was completed, dated 10 December 1688, the day before James made his first attempt to escape to France and the

very day the little prince of Wales and his mother were shipped off. James was caught at Faversham and brought back to London, but thirteen days later he succeeded in escaping from London and then to France. For the rest of Penn's life he was plagued with doubts over his hold on Delaware, doubts that people in the new regime seized upon. He had more immediate problems in the panic that ensued right after the king's departure.

In the vacuum between James's departure and the accession of William and Mary uncertainty and fear pervaded the country. Anybody suspected of having been part of James's inner circle was rounded up. Penn was looked upon with suspicion, and one of the first fruits of this suspicion was a hostile encounter, in December 1688, shortly after the king's escape. The council of peers of the realm ordered the safeguarding of the ports and seizure of anyone deemed to be a threat to the government at such a time. Penn had been walking past Scotland Yard in Whitehall when some officers of the guard seized him on suspicion and brought him before the peers at Whitehall. In fact, he had come from Lord Godolphin, who had just spoken to Prince William. Clearly, there was a lack of communication within the government brought about by the chaos, because Penn's abrupt arrival before the peers, many of whom were his personal friends, was somewhat embarrassing for both sides. Ultimately Penn was released on bail amounting to £5000, for which 'two gentlemen of great estates in his neighbourhood were his bayle' (R. Beddard, *A Kingdom without a King*, 1988, 175). The two gentlemen were Lord Philip Wharton and Charles Gerard, Lord Brandon, both whigs and no lovers of papists. Yet Penn was seen as a collaborator with James. In the whig view of the revolution, Penn and other dissenters who collaborated with the Catholic king were regarded as at best turncoats and at worst traitors. While many contemporary whigs and dissenters undoubtedly shared this view, there was a significant number who did not feel that co-operating with the king was a betrayal of their principles. They argued that the end of universal toleration justified the means whereby they sought to attain it through working with the monarch. Penn was one of these people, and his defence of his position was clearly accepted by most of the peers before whom he was brought.

Evidently the council was split over what to do in the interim between the flight of James and the acceptance of the government by William. At this point nobody had decided that William was to be king. The greater fear was for the safety of the realm against a Catholic insurrection or invasion. For that, Penn was looked upon as a Jesuit in Anglican quarters to the extent that he was referred to as Father Penn by his enemies. His opponents in the council were led by Sir Robert Sawyer, former attorney-general to James and virulent opponent of Catholic toleration, who resigned from office in 1687 over the issue. The combination of papist threats and the manner in which he pursued toleration put Penn squarely as one of the key collaborators with James and his policies. Therefore, Sawyer accused the Quaker as a dangerous invader of English laws and liberties. It was true that Penn took part in the strategy to pack parliament and could therefore be accused of subverting the liberties of Englishmen. He tried to justify his involvement by explaining his desire to secure toleration by means of a statute in law. That could only be accomplished through parliament. The process of selecting MPs was, perhaps, questionable, but Penn defended himself by saying that he had always endeavoured to secure liberty of conscience by law so that no papist could ever take it away. The explanation must have been particularly galling to the likes of Sawyer and incredible to the peers before whom Penn stood. No less than one of the greatest political minds of the period was part of that group: George Savile, marquess of Halifax, who had chastised Penn in print for his methods. At this point there was no hard evidence that Penn had ever subverted the freedoms of the people, so he was set free on bail. He had friends in high places including the council. Nevertheless, he found himself arrested time and again and in greater danger than he had ever been.

After the revolution Penn fell from favour. James had absconded to France, and the new regime of William and Mary looked upon him as a part of a larger threat to the country's security. He was accused of conspiring against the new regime. For this he was imprisoned and stripped of his right to govern Pennsylvania. The accusation that he was involved in Jacobite conspiracies to restore James II has generally been rejected by those who regard him as an icon and regard it as a stain on his character, but there is evidence of his being closely involved with Jacobite conspirators. Penn had to claw his way back to political influence by showing support for the new regime. His ability to sway dissent in England and his influence over his colonists in Pennsylvania were also factors in his return to power. His ability also to bring about a Quaker settlement with the new regime resulted in another milestone in his efforts to secure toleration for dissent through the enactment of the affirmation law. However, though he regained his colony and reinstated himself in the political environment, he never attained the pinnacle of influence in England that he enjoyed in the past, despite charges from some quarters that he 'hath greater interest at Court now than ever he had in King James's reign' (Hunt. L., Blathwayt MSS, box 4, BL 2). His second and last visit to Pennsylvania in 1699–1701 proved very disappointing for him. He had to make concessions to a strong anti-proprietary party by granting them the charter of privileges, thus annulling the right of the council to sit as a second legislative chamber, effectively making the Pennsylvania legislature unicameral. He also reluctantly conceded to the lower counties the right to secede, a right they exercised in 1704. In the last years of his life, during the reign of Queen Anne, Penn worked to put the Affirmation Act on a permanent basis. But, other than writing a tract against the Anglican effort to penalize occasional conformity at the outset of the reign, he seems to have distanced himself from any overt religious activity.

Last years and legacy On 5 March 1696 Penn married for the second time. His wife was Hannah Callowhill (1670–1726), daughter of Thomas Callowhill, an influential Bristol merchant. They had two daughters, one of whom, Margaret, lived into adulthood and married Thomas Freame of Philadelphia, and four sons, John, Thomas *Penn (1702–1775), Richard, and Dennis, all of whom became co-proprietors of Pennsylvania.

Penn's last years were overshadowed by illness and financial worries. He suffered two strokes in 1712 and left his wife to take care of his business. He died on 30 July 1718 at Ruscombe, Berkshire, and was buried at the Quaker burial-ground at Jordans, near Chalfont St Giles, Buckinghamshire.

By the time of his death Penn had become an inextricable part of the political life of England, connected with everyone who was anyone in politics and business. Among his contacts had been Godolphin, a central figure in English politics under the later Stuarts, the duke of Marlborough, Lord Somers, the leader of the whig junto, and the earl of Rochester, a prominent high-church tory. After the accession of George I he remained close to the powerful third earl of Sunderland and to the former tory prime minister, Robert Harley, earl of Oxford. Penn chose Harley to be one of the executors of his will. Even after his debilitating stroke in October 1712 Penn's influence was impressive enough to fend off creditors and political enemies. He influenced religious and political thought in an age of experimentation. Although he did not invent the concept of religious toleration, he brought it to its highest point in the governing principles of his colony. Such toleration became the touchstone of religious and ethnic plurality from which the American ethos grew. His political philosophy extended to Europe, where, in his efforts to resolve once and for all a continent in conflict, he showed his awareness of a changing world and an acumen for *realpolitik*. In his 1693 work *An Essay toward the Present and Future Peace of Europe*, Penn was able to assess astutely the realities of political diplomacy by recognizing Turkey in the great scheme of Europe rather than limiting his vision to a narrow view of Christendom.

MARY K. GEITER

Sources M. K. Geiter, *William Penn* (2000) · *Papers of William Penn*, ed. M. M. Dunn and R. Dunn, 1–4 (1981–6), vols. 1–4 · Hist. Soc. Penn., Penn papers · *CSP dom.*, 1690–91 · BL, Add. MSS 70015–70017 · *The manuscripts of S. H. Le Fleming*, HMC, 25 (1890), 280, 285, 314 · Bodl. Oxf., MS Rawl. C. 938, fol. 117 · *A collection of the works of William Penn*, ed. J. Besse (1726) · H. S. Barbour, *William Penn on religion and ethics: the emergence of liberal Quakerism*, 2 vols. (1991) · M. Amyraut, *A treatise concerning religion* (1660) · 'Ent'ring book', DWL, Morrice MS Q · *The manuscripts of the earl of Westmorland*, HMC, 13 (1885); repr. (1906) · *Bishop Burnet's History*, vol. 4 · *Diary of the times of Charles the Second by the Honourable Henry Sidney (afterwards earl of Romney)*, ed. R. W. Blencowe, 2 vols. (1843) · J. P. Kenyon, *Robert Spencer, earl of Sunderland* (1956) · Clarendon state papers, Bodl. Oxf., 89 · W. N. Hargreaves-Mawdsley, *Oxford in the age of John Locke* (1973) · Claydon House, Buckinghamshire, Verney papers · Hunt. L., Blathwayt papers · *DNB*

Archives American Philosophical Society, Phildaelphia, corresp. and MSS · Beds. & Luton ARS, papers · BL, papers, Egerton MS 2168 · Haverford College, Pennsylvania, letters and MSS · Hist. Soc. Penn., corresp. and MSS · Maryland Historical Society, Baltimore, papers | RS Friends, Lond., letters and other material · Surrey HC, letters to Lord Somers

Likenesses F. Place, drawing, c.1696, Hist. Soc. Penn. [*see illus.*] · B. West, portrait, 1773 · statue, 1893, Town Hall, Philadelphia · Prior?, etching, NPG · copy (of portrait, 1666), Hist. Soc. Penn. · copy (of portrait, 1666), Christ Church Oxf. · duplicate (of ivory bust by S. Bevan, 1727), Hist. Soc. Penn.

Wealth at death 12,000 acres in Pennsylvania and Shanagarry, Ireland; also Warminghurst Place, Sussex: Dunn and others, eds., *Papers of William Penn*

Penn, William (1776–1845). *See under* Penn, Richard (1733/4–1811).

Pennant, George Sholto Gordon Douglas-, second Baron Penrhyn (1836–1907), landowner and quarry owner, was born on 30 September 1836 at Linton Springs, Yorkshire, the elder son and third child of Edward Gordon Douglas (1800–1886), third son of John Douglas, second son of James Douglas, sixteenth earl of Morton. His mother (his father's first wife) was Juliana Isabella Mary (1808–1842), eldest daughter and coheir of George Hay Dawkins-Pennant of Penrhyn Castle. In 1841 Edward Gordon Douglas assumed the additional surname of Pennant by royal licence after his wife inherited a large estate in north Wales; he was raised to the peerage on 3 August 1866 as first Baron Penrhyn. Douglas-Pennant had a brother, four sisters, and five half-sisters. His stepmother was Maria Louisa Fitzroy (d. 1912), daughter of the fifth duke of Grafton.

Douglas-Pennant was educated at Eton College and at Christ Church, Oxford. In August 1860 he married Pamela Blanche (1839–1869), daughter of Sir Charles Rushout; they had a son, Edward Sholto (1864–1927), who succeeded as third Baron Penrhyn, and six daughters, the youngest of whom was Violet Douglas-*Pennant. Douglas-Pennant's second wife, whom he married in October 1875, was Gertrude Jessy (d. 1940), daughter of Henry Glynne and niece by marriage of W. E. Gladstone (who was called on to deal with several family disputes); they had two sons and six daughters. Penrhyn Castle was built by Thomas Hopper (1776–1856) over the years 1820 to 1837 in the revived Norman style. The Pennants' London house was Mortimer House, Halkin Street, Belgravia, and they had country houses at Wicken, Stony Stratford, at Betws-y-coed in Caernarvonshire, and at Cairnton in Banffshire. Master of the Grafton hounds from 1882 to 1891, Douglas-Pennant enjoyed horse-racing, shooting, and fishing.

In 1860 Douglas-Pennant became major commanding the Caernarvonshire rifle volunteers, which was affiliated in 1881 to the 4th (militia) battalion, Royal Welch Fusiliers; he later became its honorary colonel. He was a JP, a county councillor, and the deputy lieutenant of Caernarvonshire. In 1866 he was elected unopposed as Conservative MP for Caernarvonshire, but in 1868 he was defeated by the Liberal T. L. D. Jones-Parry. He regained the seat in 1874, but lost it in 1880 to the Liberal Watkin Williams.

Douglas-Pennant succeeded to the peerage in 1886 as second Baron Penrhyn; his inheritance included 41,348 acres in Caernarvonshire, and Penrhyn quarry, which, with 3000 men, was the largest slate quarry in the world. He was a controversial figure in north Wales. In his evidence to the Welsh land commissioners in 1893 he described the North Wales Property Association, which he had founded in 1886, as a 'mutual self-protection' society against the plans for land nationalization being promoted by sections of the Welsh press. He said the depression in agriculture had meant that for many years he had received from his land no income in excess of his expenditure upon it; and he indicated that in Wales land reform was linked to nationalism and to hatred of the 'alien' race.

Penrhyn quarry had a history of strikes, despite the wide-ranging paternalism of the Pennants. Many of the quarrymen lived in the nonconformist stronghold of Bethesda, 5 miles from Bangor, or in small quarrying communities. Increasingly, the Pennants were regarded as divided from the workers by class, language, politics, and religion. In 1901 half the workforce spoke Welsh only, but there were political and sectarian divisions as a minority were Conservatives and Anglicans. Unity was further reduced by disparity of earnings resulting from variations in the quality of the rock allocated to different groups, which encouraged favouritism. Lord Penrhyn's first action was to terminate the Pennant Lloyd agreement of 1874, which had allowed a workers' committee to control management, wages, and prices. The North Wales Quarrymen's Union (NWQU), established in 1874, was seen by him as a means of giving control to the workers, and he refused to accept collective bargaining. Arthur Wyatt, the inefficient manager, was discreetly dismissed, and was replaced in 1886 by E. A. Young (1860–1910), an energetic English businessman.

In August 1896 long-standing resentment over the employment of unskilled contractors flared up. On 29 September the men refused to accept their 'bargains' (allocations of rock), and they were locked out. Their grievances included strict discipline and lack of union recognition. They hoped for intervention by the Board of Trade, but under the Conciliation (Trades Disputes) Act of 1896 the board had voluntary powers only. In 1897 Lord Penrhyn and Young joined the National Free Labour Association, and three attempts to reopen the quarry failed. After complicated negotiations, which involved W. J. Parry, who had been secretary and president of the NWQU, the men accepted the terms of settlement in August 1897. Belatedly they realized that these terms contained no concessions. The net profit of the quarry for the year 1898 was £133,000, but uneasy labour relations prevailed.

The Penrhyn dispute (1900–03) began on 24 October 1900 with an outbreak of violence against two unpopular contractors, one of whom was seriously injured. On 1 November there was a further riot against another contractor, and the Bangor magistrates authorized the chief constable of Caernarvonshire to call in the troops. Six of the ringleaders were found guilty and fined. The men returned to the quarry on 22 November in resentful mood, and soon walked out again. Young closed the quarry, and Bethesda was besieged by London journalists. Many of the men took trains to south Wales in search of work. Relief for the suffering families came from the *Daily News* and *The*

Clarion, the Penrhyn Relief Fund, the General Federation of Trade Unions, the NWQU, and the Penrhyn choirs. Bethesda was improbably promoted as a holiday resort. On 11 June 1901 the quarry was reopened with about 600 men, whose individual applications had been vetted. Lord Penrhyn met the men and applauded their courage. Each was given a gold sovereign and a pay rise at the end of the day. At the mass meeting in the Bethesda market hall that night, a decision was taken to display notices in Welsh in the strikers' windows reading, 'There is no traitor in this house.'

In July 1901 W. J. Parry accused Lord Penrhyn of causing the death-rate to rise in Bethesda, although no rise had occurred. Penrhyn brought a successful libel action against Parry, and was awarded £500 damages in March 1903. Violence between the two sides erupted frequently, especially at holiday times when the strikers returned home, and on three occasions troops were brought in. Extra police were provided to escort the workers to and from the quarry. In March and April 1903 the Liberal Party and the Labour Party vied with each other in debates in the House of Commons in supporting the strikers and reviling Lord Penrhyn. The drying-up of funds finally forced the men to surrender, and on 14 November 1903 Henry Jones, chairman of the regular mass meetings, wrote to Lord Penrhyn that the struggle was at an end. Penrhyn acknowledged this letter briefly, and wrote to a friend that he had fought to deter 'socialist agitators' from 'deluding the working classes'. The steady decline in the slate industry reduced the number of jobs available, and many of the strikers were not re-employed. Union membership in the quarry almost collapsed, but Bethesda nursed its grievances and the divisions never completely healed.

A tall, spare, bearded figure, with a long, narrow face and melancholy eyes, Lord Penrhyn was slightly deaf. He died suddenly of influenza at Mortimer House on 10 March 1907, and was buried at St John's Church near Wicken. JEAN LINDSAY

Sources J. Lindsay, *The great strike: a history of the Penrhyn quarry dispute of 1900–1903* (1987) · J. Lindsay, *A history of the north Wales slate industry* (1974) · R. M. Jones, *The north Wales quarrymen, 1874–1922* (1981) · GEC, *Peerage* · 'Royal commission on land in Wales and Monmouthshire: first report', *Parl. papers* (1894), 36.1, C. 7439; 36.9, C. 7439-I; vol. 37, C. 7439-II · W. J. Parry, *The Penrhyn lock-out* (1901) · C. Parry, *The radical tradition in Welsh politics: a study of liberal and labour politics in Gwynedd, 1900–1920* (1970) · J. R. Williams, *Quarryman's champion: the life and activities of William John Parry of Coetmor* (1978) · B. Owen, *The history of the Welsh militia and volunteer corps, Anglesey and Caernarfonshire* (1989) · The National Trust, *Penrhyn Castle, Gwynedd* (1991) · Gladstone, *Diaries* · *Liverpool Courier* (12 March 1907)

Archives Gwynedd Archives, Caernarfon, Penrhyn quarry, Penrhyn quarry additional and unlisted · U. Wales, Bangor, political papers incl. diary | Clwyd RO, Glynne-Gladstone MSS

Likenesses group portrait, photograph, 1894 (the Pennant family and the prince and princess of Wales), Gwynedd Archives, Caernarfon · Faulkner & Co., photograph, 1902, repro. in *Candid Friend* (7 June 1902) · B. Leighton, oils, 1907, Penrhyn Castle, Caernarvonshire · G. J. Stodart, stipple (after photograph by R. Faulkner & Co.), NPG; repro. in *Baily's Magazine* (1888) · wood-engraving, NPG; repro. in *ILN* (23 Feb 1889)

Wealth at death £596,424 2s. 9d.: probate, 1 July 1907, CGPLA Eng. & Wales

Pennant, Richard, Baron Penrhyn (c.1737–1808), slate manufacturer and politician, was the second son of John Pennant (d. 1782), merchant, and his wife, Bonella Hodges (d. 1763), who were resident in Jamaica. His father was descended from Thomas Pennant, the fifteenth-century abbot of Basingwerk, and both parents had inherited substantial plantations in Jamaica, including those of Sir Samuel Pennant (d. 1750), who became lord mayor of London in 1749. John and Bonella Pennant went to London about 1737 and had a house in Savile Row, Hanover Square. Richard was probably born either there or at sea. He and his elder brother, John Lewis Pennant, attended Newcome's academy, Hackney, and were admitted as fellow commoners at Trinity College, Cambridge, at Easter 1754; John Pennant died later in the year. Richard did not graduate, but on 29 March 1758 he became a member of the Society for the Encouragement of Arts, Manufactures, and Commerce, founded in 1754.

By his marriage to Anne Susannah Warburton (1745–1816) on 6 December 1765 in Bath Abbey, Pennant acquired the Penrhyn estate in Caernarvonshire. Anne's maternal grandfather was Dr Edward Norris, MP for Liverpool from 1714 to 1722, and her family had influential connections in the borough, which aided her husband's political career. Her paternal grandmother, Anne, was the daughter of Sir Robert Williams (d. 1680), the last of the male heirs in line from John Williams, archbishop of York (d. 1650); Sir Robert had purchased the Penrhyn estate, which passed to Anne Williams conjointly with her sister, Gwen. Anne married Thomas Warburton of Winnington, Cheshire, and Gwen married Sir Walter Yonge of Escot, Devon. General Hugh Warburton (1695–1771) was the son of Anne and Thomas Warburton, and Anne Susannah was his only child and heir. In 1771, on the death of his father-in-law, General Warburton, Pennant took over Winnington Hall and the moiety of the Penrhyn estate. In 1785 he bought the remainder of the estate from Sir George Yonge, grandson of Gwen and Walter Yonge. The tenants at Cae Braich y Cafn, later the Penrhyn quarry, were paid a lump sum in 1783 in exchange for their right to take slates.

Richard's political career began in 1761, when as a whig he became MP for Petersfield, Hampshire. In 1767 he became one of the two MPs for Liverpool, the chief port of the slave trade. He was re-elected in 1768 and 1774, aided by his wife, whose talents as a canvasser were renowned. Richard spoke in the Commons to oppose the introduction of taxation in America, on 29 January 1769, and on 19 April 1774 he seconded the motion for the repeal of the tea duty; as the proprietor of extensive plantations in Jamaica he was well aware of the economic damage a war with America would bring. In 1780 he was defeated at Liverpool and in 1782 he became sheriff of Caernarvonshire. In 1783, on the recommendation of Charles Fox, he was created Baron Penrhyn in the peerage of Ireland. On 18 April 1785 he voted for the reform of parliament. In the election of 1784 he had narrowly defeated Colonel Tarleton, but in

1790 he withdrew as a candidate, expressing his unease at the election process.

In 1787 William Wilberforce promoted the campaign for the abolition of slavery, which Lord Penrhyn opposed. On 9 May 1788 Penrhyn spoke in a debate in the House of Commons in defence of both the slave-traders and the planters, and between 1789 and 1791 committees of inquiry were set up by parliament and by the assembly and council of Jamaica. Lord Penrhyn was an absentee landlord but he kept closely in touch by letter with his plantation attorneys. He failed to appreciate the degradation caused by slavery, but he did express concern about the condition of his slaves. In 1782 he sent out ploughs to ease conditions for the workers, and he frequently remarked that he did not wish 'the negroes and cattle to be overworked'. When the abolition of the slave trade became law in 1807, Lord Penrhyn regarded it as a dangerous experiment which would bring ruin to the Jamaican economy.

The profits from the Jamaican sugar and rum trade were used to expand the production and export of slates from Lord Penrhyn's quarry in Caernarvonshire. By 1790, having obtained a lease from the bishop of Bangor, Penrhyn had converted the mouth of the River Cegin into a harbour, called Port Penrhyn, from which slates were sent to London, Bristol, Liverpool, and Ireland. Framed writing-slates, manufactured at Port Penrhyn, were included in the ships' cargoes. Benjamin Wyatt (1745–1818), the Staffordshire architect, designed the port, and in 1782 his brother Samuel Wyatt remodelled the medieval Penrhyn Hall. In 1789 a cart road was built from Port Penrhyn to the quarry, and by 1800 this had been extended through Nant Ffrancon to Capel Curig. Such enterprises, together with his promotion of improvements in agriculture, earned Lord Penrhyn much praise as a benefactor to the community from contemporaries such as W. Bingley in *Excursions in North Wales* (1798) and from historians such as Richard Llwyd, who, in *The History of Wales* (1832), described the transformation as 'a new creation' of the neighbourhood.

In 1794 parliament imposed a tax of 20 per cent on all slate carried coastwise, and with falling profits from Jamaica, business survival became difficult. A tax was imposed on horses in 1797, and in 1800 work began on a horse-drawn railroad from Penrhyn quarry to Port Penrhyn, which gave employment to redundant quarrymen. The line was planned by Benjamin Wyatt on the basis of suggestions by Thomas Dadford; it was 6¼ miles long, had a gauge of 24½ inches, and was officially opened by Lord Penrhyn on 1 July 1801. William Williams (1738–1817) began the excavation of galleries at the quarry, and this work was continued after 1802 by James Greenfield (1774–1825). Having secured a grant from the crown in 1784, which enabled him to make enclosures on Llandygái Common, Lord Penrhyn built the 'model village' of Llandygái nearby. St Tegai's Church in the village contains a monument to Lord and Lady Penrhyn, sculpted by Richard Westmacott, for which Lady Penrhyn left £2000 in her will.

Lord Penrhyn died on 21 January 1808 at Winnington Hall, Cheshire, but was buried in a vault at St Tegai's Church. He was survived by his wife, but they had no children, and the title became extinct. By Penrhyn's will the estates passed to George Hay Dawkins, the second son of his cousin, Henry Dawkins, who added the surname Pennant to his own. Lord Penrhyn left debts of £150,000, to be paid, according to his will, out of the proceeds of the sale of the Jamaican properties. In 1808, however, these could not be sold for anything like the amount required. Winnington Hall was sold, a mortgage was raised on the Penrhyn estate, and the debts were paid off in October 1808. After the death of George Hay Dawkins-Pennant in 1840, the estates were inherited by his son-in-law, Edward Gordon Douglas (1800–1886), who added the name Pennant to his own in 1841, and was created Baron Penrhyn of Llandygái in 1866. JEAN LINDSAY

Sources B. Burke, *A genealogical history of the dormant, abeyant, forfeited, and extinct peerages of the British empire*, new edn (1883); repr. (1978) · J. E. Griffith, *Pedigrees of Anglesey and Carnarvonshire families* (privately printed, Horncastle, 1914) · J. Lindsay, *A history of the north Wales slate industry* (1974) · J. Lindsay, 'The Pennants and Jamaica, 1665–1808, pt 1', *Transactions of the Caernarvonshire Historical Society*, 43 (1982) · J. Lindsay, 'The Pennants and Jamaica, 1665–1808, pt 2', *Transactions of the Caernarvonshire Historical Society*, 44 (1983) · *GM*, 1st ser., 33 (1763) · *GM*, 1st ser., 35 (1765) · *GM*, 1st ser., 41 (1771) · *GM*, 1st ser., 78 (1808) · Cobbett, *Parl. hist.* · Venn, *Alum. Cant.* · J. I. C. Boyd, *The Penrhyn quarry railways* (1985), vol. 2 of *Narrow gauge railways in north Caernarvonshire* · E. H. D. Pennant, *The Pennants of Penrhyn: a genealogical history* (1982) · HoP, *Commons* · J. Evans, *A tour through part of north Wales in the year 1798, and at other times* (1800) · T. Pennant, *History of the parishes of Whiteford and Holywell* (1796) · *North Wales Gazette* (26 Jan 1808)

Archives Institute of Jamaica, Kingston, Jamaica · Jamaica Archives, Spanish Town, Jamaica · NL Wales, estate account · Royal Society for the Encouragement of Arts, Manufactures, and Commerce, London · U. Wales, Bangor, family papers

Likenesses attrib. J. Reynolds, oils, *c*.1760, Penrhyn Castle, Caernarvonshire · G. Romney, oils, 1789, Penrhyn Castle, Caernarvonshire · H. Thomson, oils, *c*.1790, Penrhyn Castle, Caernarvonshire

Wealth at death Jamaican properties to be sold to pay £150,000 debts: will, proved 4 May 1808, Penrhyn papers, U. Wales, Bangor · could not be sold for anything like real value 1808, so Winnington Hall sold and mortgage raised on Penrhyn estate; debts settled Oct 1808

Pennant, Thomas (1726–1798), naturalist, traveller, and writer, was born on 14 June 1726 at Downing in the parish of Whitford (sometimes Whiteford), near Holywell, Flintshire, the eldest son of David Pennant (*d.* 1763), landowner, and Arabella (*d.* 1744), third daughter of Richard Mytton of Halston, Shropshire. His parents, notably his father, were from long-standing families: the estate, centred upon the ancient house at Bychton, had been owned by Pennants since the Norman conquest although the first to take that name, from the Welsh 'Pen y Nant', was Daffyd ap Tudor in the fifteenth century.

Pennant tells us that he was delivered in 'the Yellow Room' by 'a Mrs Clayton of Shrewsbury', midwife, and, as was then customary among Welsh gentry, he was put out to foster parents nearby (Pennant, *History of the Parishes*, 2). At age seven he was sent to the Revd Lewis's Grammar School at Wrexham which, to judge by letters to his father, he enjoyed. At age fourteen Pennant was educated

Thomas Pennant (1726–1798), by John Keyse Sherwin, 1778 (after Thomas Gainsborough, 1776?)

at Fulham under the guidance of Thomas Croft. He was in poor health as a boy, and indeed suffered intermittently from depression for much of his life. When ill as a child he spent recuperative periods at Hadley, near Enfield Chase, at the home of his uncle, the Revd John Pennant, and at the Richmond home of James Mytton, a maternal uncle. On 7 March 1744 Pennant matriculated at Queen's College, Oxford, but, as the result of disciplinary matters stemming from a dispute between students and fellows, migrated to Oriel College in May 1748. He did not take a degree, but was made an honorary DCL by the university on 11 May 1771 in recognition of his zoological work.

Early publications Pennant's interest in natural history was first stimulated when he was aged about twelve by the present from his kinsman John Salisbury of a copy of Francis Willoughby's *Ornithology* (1678): [this] 'first gave me a taste for that study, and incidentally a love for that of natural history in general, which I have since pursued with my constitutional ardor' (Pennant, *Literary Life*, 1). In 1747 he toured Cornwall, where he met the naturalist and historian the Revd Dr William Borlase, who 'gave me a strong passion for minerals and fossils' (ibid.).

Pennant's first publication, an account of an earthquake felt in Flintshire on 2 April 1750, was published in volume forty-six of the Royal Society's *Philosophical Transactions*. He published five other articles there: on fossil corals, penguins, tortoises, the turkey, and a piece on 'several earthquakes felt in Wales in 1781' (*PTRS*, 71.193). During the early 1750s he participated in fossil-hunting expeditions in Wales, undertook a fifteen-week tour of Ireland

in 1754 where he collected mineralogical and natural specimens despite being distracted by 'the conviviality of the country' (Pennant, *Literary Life*, 2), and began a correspondence with scholars such as Benjamin Stillingfleet, John Ellis, Emanuel Mendes da Costa, and, notably, with Carl Linnaeus, through whose influence Pennant was elected a member of the Vetenskapsakademien at Uppsala in 1757. His network of correspondents included members of the Sicilian and Swedish nobility and the bishop of Bergen, with all of whom he exchanged mineralogical specimens: more than 800 of Pennant's specimens survive in the British Museum (Natural History). He was elected a fellow of the Society of Antiquaries on 21 November 1754, although he resigned in 1760, unable to pay the annual subscription fees.

To judge by a letter of June 1762 to Costa, Pennant had by then begun what he called his 'great Design of a British Natural History' (Warks. CRO, CR2017/TP408, fol. 165). The first volume of his *British Zoology* as it became was published in 1766. The delay between commencement, probably in 1761, and publication was most likely due to family circumstances. In April 1759 Pennant had married Elizabeth Falconer, daughter of James Falconer of Chester, a lieutenant in the Royal Navy. Their son, Thomas, was born in January 1760 but died in March; two further children, Arabella (*b.* 1761) and David (*b.* 1763), survived. Pennant's father, David, died in January 1763, at which point Pennant assumed the responsibilities of running the family estate (his mother had died of smallpox in April 1744). In June 1764 Elizabeth, his wife, died.

It has been surmised that Pennant's six-month tour of Europe in 1765 was undertaken to distance himself from these family affairs (Evans). That may be so, but it is clear that his 1765 tour provided Pennant with an important opportunity to meet fellow naturalists and inspect collections. During the tour he travelled through France, Switzerland, Germany, and the Netherlands and met, among others, the French naturalist the comte de Buffon, Voltaire, and the German naturalist Peter Pallas.

British zoology The first folio edition of Pennant's *British Zoology* was followed by a more successful and smaller second edition, and by additional volumes on reptiles, fish, and marine animals. The work was organized according to the classificatory systems of John Ray, whom Pennant much admired: in a letter of 19 July 1767 Pennant referred to Ray as 'the father of system especially of quadrupeds & birds' and considered that Linnaeus 'owes it all to our countryman tho he has horridly mangled & disjointed his excellent synopses' (NL Scot., MS 968, fol. 124). Five editions of *British Zoology* were published between 1766 and 1812. Its success prompted his election as a fellow of the Royal Society in 1767, the year in which he began that correspondence with Gilbert White, then curate at Farringdon in Hampshire, which, together with White's correspondence with Daines Barrington, formed the basis of White's *Natural History of Selborne* (1789).

Pennant's *British Zoology* was followed in 1769 by his *Indian Geology*, and in 1771 by *Synopsis of Quadrupeds* which, revised and enlarged, was published in 1781 as *A History of*

Quadrupeds. In 1773 he published *Genera of Birds*, and between 1784 and 1787 the three-volume *Arctic Zoology*. In the 'Advertisement' for this work Pennant acknowledged the influence of Francis Willoughby: 'Emulous of so illustrious an example, I took up the object of his pursuit'. *Arctic Zoology* was written as a series of excursions north from Britain and drew upon correspondents with local knowledge such as George Low who contributed information on the birds of Orkney as well as upon the researches of Pallas in Siberia and of Joseph Banks in Newfoundland. It was one of the first major studies of the zoology of the northern hemisphere and was widely acclaimed: French and German editions appeared in 1787 and 1789. Pennant was elected a member of the American Philosophical Society in 1791 for his contribution to American zoology.

Pennant's tour In 1769 Pennant undertook a tour of Scotland, chiefly of the highlands, a region then little known by outsiders yet of interest for its natural history. He again drew upon local specialist knowledge—men such as the Revd Dr John Walker, who had travelled extensively in the highlands and Hebrides in 1764 and 1766, and, in Aberdeen, the natural historian David Skene, who showed Pennant his cabinet of natural history and advised him on zoological and botanical specimens. Pennant's *A Tour in Scotland, 1769*, was published in 1771. It is of interest for its descriptions and for its method: Pennant circulated 'Queries, addressed to the Gentlemen and Clergy of North-Britain' [Scotland] with standard questions about natural history and the past and present state of the parish in order to allow locals to give 'a fuller and more satisfactory Account of their Country, than it is the Power of a Stranger and transient Visitant to give' (Pennant, *Tour in Scotland*, 287). In that regard Pennant has much in common with the earlier use of circulated queries by natural philosophers such as Robert Boyle and, in Scotland, by the natural historian and geographer Sir Robert Sibbald, and Pennant importantly prefigures the parish-based assessment of Scotland published by Sir John Sinclair in the 1790s.

Motivated by favourable critical reaction to his 1769 *Tour*, by the fact that his first Scottish work made no mention of the Hebrides, and, as he tells us, 'in order to render more complete, my preceding tour: and to allay that species of restlessness that infects many minds, on leaving any attempt unfinished', Pennant undertook a second tour of Scotland in 1772 (Pennant, *Tour in Scotland and Voyage to the Hebrides*, i). His 1772 tour was more meticulously organized than the 1769 tour, which had been a largely impromptu event, though both involved the use of pre-circulated queries and advance notices in the Scottish press of Pennant's intentions. In 1772 he was accompanied by travelling companions, each with particular skills: the Revd John Lightfoot, a botanist, and later author of *Flora Scotica* (1777), a study on Linnaean principles of Scotland's native flora; the Revd John Stuart, minister of Killin parish and a Gaelic scholar; and Moses Griffith, Pennant's personal draughtsman, whom Pennant referred to as 'My Treasure' and 'a good and faithful servant, and able artist' (Pennant, *Literary Life*, 10). Pennant used Joseph Banks's description of Staffa for his work and dedicated the book

to Banks. Stuart, together with other local ministers, assisted Pennant with Gaelic names of plants. Griffith and Pennant remained close: a bequest in Pennant's will provided for Griffith's children and Pennant's son, David, awarded Griffith a pension.

Pennant's 1772 *Tour in Scotland* (1774–6) was, like his 1769 tour, published by John Monk of Chester. It is best understood as a complement to his earlier Scottish work and the culmination of a longer enterprise designed to describe and understand Scotland. The aim of the Scottish tours was identical with that of geographies of more distant unknown lands such as the south sea islands.

Public reaction to Pennant's Scottish tours, as to his works of natural history, was generally favourable. The *Critical Review* considered his 1769 *Tour* 'the best itinerary which has hitherto been written on that country' (*Critical Review*, Jan 1772, 28). The first volume of Pennant's 1772 *Tour* influenced Samuel Johnson, then engaged in writing his own *Journey*, just as the 1769 work had been a prompt to Johnson's Hebridean travels with Boswell. Boswell recorded Johnson's defence of Pennant whose account of Alnwick and of the Percy estates in Northumberland was the subject of criticism by Bishop Percy who felt slighted that Pennant had called his garden 'trim'. Johnson termed Pennant 'A Whig, Sir; a sad dog', yet at the same moment remarked 'But he's the best traveller I ever read; he observes more things than anyone else does' (J. Boswell, *Journal of a Tour to the Hebrides*, 17 Sept 1773). Boswell thought this too high praise for someone:

> who traversed a wide extent of such currency in such haste, that he could put together only curt frittered fragments of his own … a writer, who at best treats merely of superficial objects, and shews no philosophical investigation of character and manners.   (Boswell, *Life*, 3.274, 12 April 1778)

Both Boswell and Horace Walpole thought Pennant's work further diminished by his reliance upon others' information.

More tours and travels Pennant undertook several other tours: of northern England in 1773, of Northamptonshire and of the Isle of Man in 1774, of Warwickshire in 1776, of Kent in 1776, and of Cornwall in 1787. Several tours throughout Wales in the early 1770s, where his Welsh-speaking friend and companion, the Revd John Lloyd of Caerwys, performed the same function as Stuart had in Gaelic Scotland, were brought together as *Tours in Wales* in three volumes (1778–83).

Pennant's second marriage, in Whitford in January 1777, was to Anne (d. 1802), elder daughter of Sir Thomas Mostyn, fourth baronet (d. 1758), and sister of Sir Roger Mostyn, fifth baronet (1758–1796), a prominent landowner in north Wales and friend to Pennant. Two children were born from this marriage: Sarah (1779–1794) and Thomas (1780–1845), a minister at Weston Turville, Buckinghamshire, who died childless.

Pennant's many travels to London were published as *A Journey from Chester to London* in 1782. Other tours were edited by his son David, and published posthumously: *A Journey from London to the Isle of Wight* (1801); *A Tour from Downing to Alston Moor* (1801); and *A Tour from Alston Moor to*

Harrowgate and Brimham Crags (1804). Other publications include his *Of the Patagonians*, taken from the testimony of a Jesuit missionary, Falkener, who had spent thirty-eight years in that region and whom Pennant visited in Worcester in 1771, and, in 1790, *An Account of London*, which took the form of a tour around the capital: Boswell rated it highly.

Last years Two of the three publications written towards the end of Pennant's life exemplify both his energy and the range of his writings. *The History of the Parishes of Whiteford and Holywell* (1796) offers a detailed local history and genealogical information on the Pennant family. His *Outlines of the Globe*, published in four volumes between 1798 and 1800 with volumes three and four being produced by his son David, was the only published outcome of twenty-two manuscript volumes of imaginary travels throughout the world. The first two volumes focused upon Hindustan and, although works of imagination, drew upon his knowledge of India and the writings of the explorer James Rennell. The title of the third, *The Literary Life of the Late Thomas Pennant Esq., by himself* (1793), hints at Pennant's sense of humour. It is signed only by dotted lines to indicate the death of the author: it is for that reason that his *History of the Parishes* is signed 'RESURGAM', with its implication of literary resurrection.

Pennant's *Literary Life*, which has several of his shorter works collected as appendices, makes clear his immense industry and the fact that his natural history writing and travelling were undertaken while fulfilling other responsibilities: he was high sheriff of Flintshire in 1761; author of pamphlets on road management and the militia laws; chairman in 1792 of the Flintshire Loyalist Association; and from 1763 improver of his own estates. Reflecting 'upon the multiplicity of my publications', he attributed his output to 'the riding exercise of my extensive tours, to my manner of living, and to my temperance' (Pennant, *Literary Life*, 35). He was much saddened by the death of his daughter, Sarah, in May 1794, and on 6 April 1795 he broke his kneecap which confined him to bed for six weeks. After prolonged breathing difficulties, he died at Downing on 16 December 1798.

Pennant's travels and natural history are distinguished by his personal energy, a keen observational sense, and by methodological organization and attention to facts. In such ways, and in his friendship and widespread correspondence with others of like interests throughout Britain and Europe, he may be said to exemplify those gentleman scholars of nature in the later eighteenth century whose interests in natural knowledge aimed at national improvement through intellectual enquiry. While he is perhaps better remembered for his Scottish tours, his *British Zoology* and *Arctic Zoology* in particular were important pioneering works and established him in the eyes of contemporaries as a leading European natural historian. For one modern scholar Pennant should be considered 'the leading British zoologist after Ray and before Darwin' (Beer, vi).   CHARLES W. J. WITHERS

Sources T. Pennant, *The literary life of the late Thomas Pennant esq., by himself* (1793) · T. Pennant, *The history of the parishes of Whiteford and Holywell* (1796) · R. P. Evans, 'A sketch of the life of Thomas Pennant, the literary squire of Downing', in T. Pennant, *The history of the parishes of Whiteford and Holywell* (1988) · T. Pennant, letter, 19 July 1767, NL Scot., MS 968, fol. 124 · T. Pennant, letter, June 1762, Warks. CRO, CR 2017/TP408, fol. 165 · T. Pennant, *A tour in Scotland, 1769* (1771) · T. Pennant, *A tour in Scotland and voyage to the Hebrides, 1772*, 2 vols. (1774–6) · Boswell, *Life*, vol. 3 · G. R. de Beer, ed., *Tour on the continent, 1765, by Thomas Pennant, esq.* (1948) · *Critical Review*, 33 (1772), 28 · Foster, *Alum. Oxon.* · *GM*, 1st ser., 68 (1798), 1144–6 · Burke, *Peerage* (1907) · *DNB* · *Report on the correspondence and papers of the Pennant family of Downing, Flintshire, 16th–20th century deposited in Warwick County Record Office by the earl of Denbigh*, HMC (1980) · *Report on deeds and papers of the Pennant family of Downing, Flintshire, 1299–1929*, HMC (1981) · *Report on additional deeds and papers of the Pennant family of Downing*, HMC (1983) · D. Pennant, *Outlines of the globe* (1798)

Archives AM Oxf., catalogue · AM Oxf., donations · American Philosophical Society, Philadelphia, papers · BL, autobiographical notes and letters · Bodl. Oxf., notes of journey in Scotland · Bodl. Oxf., topographical papers · Ches. & Chester ALSS, corresp. · Flintshire RO, Hawarden, corresp. and papers · NHM, copy of lists of questions and projects of Joseph Banks on his voyage to Newfoundland · NHM, zoological plates, author's annotated copy of his *Arctic zoology* · NL Scot., letters · NL Scot., corresp. and unfinished version of *Of the Patagonians* · NL Wales, corresp. and papers · NL Wales, Downing deeds, notebook, papers · NL Wales, treatises on Latin grammar · NMM, catalogues etc. · RS, papers and corresp. · Warks. CRO, corresp. and papers | BL, letters to Bishop Douglas, Egerton MSS 2180, 2185 · Bodl. Oxf., corresp. with Richard Gough and William Hutchison · Bodl. Oxf., letters to John Price · Divisional Library, Warrington, Johann Forster MSS, transcripts of letters [originals housed in Peabody Museum, Salem, Massachusetts] · Flintshire RO, Hawarden, corresp. with Feilding family · FM Cam., Perceval collection · JRL, letters to Henry Baker · JRL, letters to Hester Piozzi and others · Linn. Soc., letters to Carl Linnaeus · Linn. Soc., letters to Sir James Smith · Mitchell L., NSW, letters to Sir Joseph Banks · Morrab Library, Penzance, letters to William Borlase · NHM, zoological plates, author's annotated copy of his *Arctic zoology* · NL Scot., letters to John Mackenzie · NL Scot., letters to George Paton · NL Wales, corresp. with Edward Lhuyd · NL Wales, letters to John Lloyd · NL Wales, letters to William Owen-Pugh · NL Wales, letters to Paul Panton · NL Wales, letters to J. C. Potter · NMM, imaginary world tour · NRA, priv. coll., letters to Lord Kenyon · RBG Kew, corresp. with Sir Joseph Banks · Suffolk RO, Bury St Edmunds, letters to George Ashby · U. Aberdeen L., letters to David Skene · U. Edin., New Coll. L., MSS THO 2

Likenesses T. Gainsborough?, oils, 1776?, Downing, Flintshire · J. K. Sherwin, line engraving, 1778 (after T. Gainsborough, 1776?), NPG [*see illus.*] · Lizars?, engraving (after T. Gainsborough, 1776?), repro. in W. Jardine, *The naturalist's library*, 39 vols. (1833), vol. 15 · Stanier, engraving (after T. Gainsborough), repro. in *European Magazine* (1793) · C. A. Tomkins, mezzotint (after T. Gainsborough), BM, NPG · Wills?, oils, Downing, Flintshire · etching, NPG · line engraving, BM, NPG · plaster medallion (after Wedgwood), Scot. NPG · Wedgwood medallion, Wedgwood Museum, Stoke-on-Trent

Pennant, Violet Blanche Douglas- (1869–1945), air force officer, was born on 31 January 1869 at 23 Chapel Street, Belgrave Square, London, the sixth daughter of George Sholto Gordon Douglas-*Pennant, second Baron Penrhyn (1836–1907), JP and MP for Caernarvonshire, and his first wife, Pamela Blanche (1839–1869), who died five days after her daughter's birth, daughter of Sir Charles Rushout of Sezincote, Gloucestershire, and his wife, Cecilia Olivia Geraldine. Her father, a Welsh peer, was of Scottish descent, and her mother English. After a conventional upbringing Douglas-Pennant threw herself into philanthropy and local government. An interest in girls' youth clubs led to her becoming a volunteer worker with disabled children and the unemployed poor in London; she later acted as manager of various schools, and she served on Finsbury borough council's unemployment committee. Her interest in the Workers' Educational Association took her onto other local government committees in south London, some dealing with workers' pensions, and ultimately onto the London county council education committee. She also became a governor of the University College of South Wales, and was on its selection and executive committee for training women medical students. Though not a suffragette, she was on the council of the Conservative and Unionist Women's Franchise Association. In 1911 she was appointed national health insurance commissioner for south Wales. In the same year she became a lady-in-waiting to Princess Louise, the duchess of Argyll; during the early years of the First World War she accompanied Louise on visits to the British Red Cross hospitals in France. Douglas-Pennant had already raised money in 1914 to fund a 500-bed emergency hospital in Belgium, and she was a member of the South Wales Belgian Refugee Committee, and had chaired a selection committee on nursing staff for the Scottish Women's Hospital unit in Serbia. In 1917 she had been one of the moving spirits behind the Women's Army Auxiliary Corps (WAAC), and had later made recruiting speeches for the new Women's Royal Naval Service and the Women's Legion. Thus, although she had no direct experience of the new air force, she was a natural choice when the position of commandant of the Women's Royal Air Force (WRAF) became vacant.

The WRAF started with three different commandants in six months—a record that few organizations could survive. The reason was that near the end of the First World War, on 1 April 1918, the WRAF was created at the same time as the Royal Air Force, but the WRAF was a last-minute decision. Its nucleus was to be women formerly serving on air stations, who were to transfer from the army, the navy, and the British Legion, and the WRAF suffered from such a scrambled start. Its first commandant left after only a month, dismayed at its problems. Violet Douglas-Pennant was its second. She was the choice of Sir Godfrey Paine, director general of RAF manning. At forty-nine she was a handsome, dark-eyed woman of action, a fine public speaker with a silvery laugh and great charm. She later recalled, 'I was asked to take over the position on May 13 [1918]—unlucky day … and at first declined, but afterwards agreed to take a month's look around … I knew there had been serious difficulties before' (The Aeroplane, 15 Jan 1919, 308). Subsequently, on a week's tour, she found 14,000 WRAF supervised by only 75 officers scattered over 500 or so camps, many under inexperienced commanding officers. Some girls were without their promised uniforms and bonuses, in bad living and working conditions, and were undisciplined and prone to strike. Douglas-Pennant quickly saw that the root of the problem was a shortage of WRAF officers: existing provisions had trained only twenty-five in three weeks, while Berridge House, which was on loan to the RAF and had the capacity to train several hundred officers, stood empty. Her efforts to equip Berridge House met with endless bureaucratic delays, as she was expected to work through hidebound, often hostile, intermediaries. She wrote to Paine on 11 June, 'I am very sorry to be obliged to decline the appointment of Commandant … seeming to assume responsibilities to which I was not entitled, so I was blocked at every turn' (Mitchell, 231–2). Determined to keep her, Paine promised to have RAF orders defining her position published. Unfortunately this was not done until November, but her appointment was confirmed on 18 June.

Meanwhile nothing improved: necessary transport was rarely available; uniforms were still delayed; and, with no secretarial help, office work accumulated. The attitude of Douglas-Pennant's three deputies was casual and influenced by inter-service jealousies: five ladies who expected top jobs in the WRAF, but were offered lower ones, left in a huff, then Douglas-Pennant's deputies resigned en bloc. Douglas-Pennant brought in a clerk from her former staff and, with two RAF friends, she toiled late, dealing with neglected correspondence, ordering a chaotic filing system, and planning. She advised Lord Weir, secretary of state for air, to slow down WRAF recruiting, while through her London county council contacts she 'borrowed' Eltham Teacher Training College during the vacation, where she eventually trained 450 of her officers. Nevertheless, after three adverse parliamentary questions, on 3 August, Douglas-Pennant was overworked and frustrated, and she made two further attempts to resign, which Paine again rejected, assuring her of his approval and support.

Dissatisfaction with the WRAF was growing however. On 22 August the minister of national service wrote to Weir, 'I propose to embargo recruiting for the WRAF if things are not improved' (Reader, 78). To this Weir replied, 'I have made up my mind to supersede Miss Violet Pennant' (Mitchell, 234), and he delegated this task to Paine's replacement, General Sir Sefton Brancker. Brancker spent his first four days in post studying WRAF problems. His opinion that the commandant was meddlesome was reinforced when she refused certain WRAF accommodation as unsuitable and complained of immorality at Hurst Park, where his friend was commanding officer. On 27 August Douglas-Pennant was away settling a strike of 1000 women in Berkshire, but on the next day, summoned to Brancker's office, he told her brusquely, 'You have got to go, not because you are inefficient … [he thought she was efficient enough] but because you are so unpopular' (The Aeroplane, 15 Jan 1919, 308). When? 'Now! At once! Tomorrow morning!' (Izzard, 194). White and rigid with shock, she refused his outstretched hand and left, though she conscientiously remained in her office for five days to clear outstanding work.

The injudicious and callous dismissal of Violet Douglas-Pennant caused much publicity and public sympathy. A pamphlet war ensued, and her cause, somewhat exaggeratedly, became known as the British Dreyfus case. The two officers most involved with her dismissal were retired or demoted; there was a private inquiry by the prime minister's office; and there were debates in parliament, a select committee inquiry in the House of Lords, and libel suits, as well as Douglas-Pennant's own private crusade, which was ended only by her death on 12 October 1945. She never married.

An innocent in the military world, Violet Douglas-Pennant was too much of a lady to bully and she lacked the right contacts within the military's higher echelons to apply pressure in the right quarters. These qualities, however, were possessed in abundance by her successor, Mrs Helen Gwynne-Vaughan. This lady had been chief controller of the WAAC in France since March 1917 and, under the urgent persuasion of Major-General Brancker, had agreed to become the third commandant of the WRAF. She inherited the undeniable groundwork laid down so painfully by Violet Douglas-Pennant. It had blighted Douglas-Pennant's fruitful public career, her mental health, and the rest of her life.
BERYL E. ESCOTT

Sources *The Aeroplane* (15 Jan 1919), 308 · *The Aeroplane* (4 June 1919), 2273 · *The Aeroplane* (19 March 1919), 1206 · V. B. Douglas-Pennant, *Under the searchlight* (1922) · D. Mitchell, *Women on the warpath* (1965) · M. Izzard, *A heroine in her time* (1969) · N. Macmillan, *Sir Sefton Brancker* (1935) · W. J. Reader, *Architect of air power: the life of the first Viscount Weir of Eastwood* (1968) · A. Chauncey, *A woman of the Royal Air Force* (1922) · A. Boyle, *Trenchard* (1962) · B. E. Escott, *Women in airforce blue* (1989) · K. B. Beauman, *Partners in blue* (1971) · E. H. D. Pennant, *The Pennants of Penrhyn: a genealogical history* (1982) · J. E. Griffith, *Pedigrees of Anglesey and Carnarvonshire families* (privately printed, Horncastle, 1914) · Burke, *Peerage* (1939) · b. cert. · A. R. Orage, ed., *Politicians and the public service* (1934) · F. J. Milner, *Appeal for justice*, petition · pamphlets of the Douglas-Pennant League, 1935, BL · BL cat., vols. 242, 251
Archives Caernarfon Area RO, Gwynedd · Penrhyn Castle, Caernarvonshire · U. Wales, Bangor, family MSS | NL Wales, corresp. with Thomas Jones
Likenesses photograph, Penrhyn Castle, Caernarvonshire · photograph, U. Wales, Bangor · photograph, repro. in Douglas-Pennant, *Under the searchlight*, frontispiece · two portraits, repro. in Escott, *Women in airforce blue*, pp. 75, 79
Wealth at death £10,669 14s. 8d.: administration, 17 Jan 1946 [revoked 23 April 1947], CGPLA Eng. & Wales · £10,481 3s. 3d.: administration, 12 Sept 1947, CGPLA Eng. & Wales

Penne, Matilda (d. 1392/3). *See under* Women traders and artisans in London (*act. c.*1200–c.1500).

Penneck, Richard (1728–1803), librarian, was born on 14 April 1728 at Gwinear, Cornwall, the fifth son of Charles Penneck (b. 1683) and Lydia Borlace (b. 1693). The Pennecks had long been established in Cornwall, and Charles (a younger son) was steward to the second earl of Godolphin (1678–1766) of Godolphin House, Helston. After attending Mr White's school in Helston, Richard Penneck was admitted to Trinity College, Cambridge, in 1746 and graduated BA (1750) and MA (1753). He was ordained in 1752 or 1753, and incorporated at Oxford in 1754. In 1756 he became a chaplain in the Royal Navy, but cannot have served long in this capacity because he was chaplain to the second earl of Bristol when the earl became ambassador

in Madrid in 1758. He did not receive the patronage from the government which usually resulted from such employment, and he was said to be too diffident and delicate to press his claims. His only genuine patron was the second earl of Godolphin who obtained for him the rectory of Abinger, Surrey, in 1764, and that of St John Horselydown, Tooley Street, Bermondsey, in 1765. Both these benefices he held until his death, employing curates to care for them, for Godolphin had also secured him a post in the British Museum. In January 1761 he became keeper (superintendent) of the reading-room there, succeeding the first holder of this office, Peter Templeman, who had been keeper from 1758 to 1760.

Penneck remained in charge of the reading-room until 1803. He ranked as one of the four assistant librarians of the British Museum, and like the others was paid the small annual salary of £50 (plus free apartments). They, however, only worked for two or three days each week, while he was required to be present for five days. Despite ill health (he suffered from hereditary gout) he worked on for over forty years, despite the fact that his request in 1768 for an assistant was refused. His burden was, however, eased in 1778 when the trustees of the museum decided that he need only be present in the reading-room for two-thirds of the opening hours, with the other assistant librarians superintending for the remaining time. In the eighteenth century the reading-room was of course much less busy than it later became. Only about 100 admission tickets were issued each year, and as late as 1818 it was stated that no more than ten to thirty readers used the room each day. The basement room in use from 1758 only contained 870 square feet, and when as a result of Penneck's complaints about the damp there the reading-room was moved to the floor above, little more space was provided. Even so, at a time when few libraries were available in London, the services of the reading-room were much appreciated, and Penneck, described in the *Gentleman's Magazine* as 'a man of distinguished talents' (*GM*, 73/1.189), was a worthy predecessor of some of the better known reading-room superintendents of the late nineteenth and twentieth centuries. He was an eloquent preacher, but although he left many sermons in manuscript only one was printed (*A Sermon Preached on the General Fast Day, March the 12th, 1762*). This was preached at St Katharine Cree, Leadenhall Street, where Penneck was lecturer for many years. He was also one of the chaplains of Trinity College, Cambridge, from 1757 until 1802.

With three friends Penneck set up a club to assist persons known to them who were in need. Perhaps his charitable instincts account for the fact that his will shows that he left only a modest amount when he died unmarried at his residence in the British Museum on 29 January 1803. The cause of his death was given as 'age' by the searchers of the parish of St George's, Bloomsbury. He was buried on 2 February at St Giles-in-the-Fields.
P. R. HARRIS

Sources *GM*, 1st ser., 73 (1803), 189 · BM · Venn, *Alum. Cant.* · C. S. Gilbert, *An historical survey of the county of Cornwall*, 2 vols. (1817–20) · P. R. Harris, *A history of the British Museum Library, 1753–1973* (1998) · E. Miller, *That noble cabinet: a history of the British Museum* (1973) · St

George's Bloomsbury, searchers' reports, LMA, P82/GEO I/63 · parish register, St Giles-in-the-Fields, LMA, DL/T/36/6 [burials] · will, PRO, PROB 11/1391, sig. 361 · *IGI* · G. Taylor, *The sea chaplains* (1978) · *The Times* (31 Jan 1803), 4a

Archives BM, MSS

Wealth at death under £600: PRO, death duty registers, IR 26/74

Pennecuik, Alexander (1652–1722), physician and poet, was the elder son of Alexander Pennecuik (*d. c.*1693), an army surgeon under General Bannier in the Thirty Years' War and later surgeon-general to the auxiliary Scots army in England, and his wife, Margaret Murray, a descendant of the family of the Murrays of Philiphaugh. The elder Pennecuik, who claimed descent from the Pennecuiks of that ilk, bought in 1646 the estate of Newhall on the north Esk; by his wife's inheritance, he also acquired the estate of Romanno, within a few miles of his own and on the far side of West Linton in Tweeddale. The precise date of his death is not known, but his son's poem, 'Upon the Death of Alexander Pennecuik of New-Hall', which describes him as 'a gentleman by birth, and more by merit', testifies that he had lived to the age of ninety. He is said to have been buried in the churchyard of Newlands.

The elder son, Alexander Pennecuik, appears to have inherited both his father's estates and his commitment to the medical profession. Passages in his poems imply that, as a young man, he had travelled overseas, a normal practice for young Scotsmen of his time, but little is known of his professional education, beyond the fact that an Alexander Pennecuik graduated with the degree of MA from Edinburgh University on 18 July 1664. His life was peaceful and uneventful. According to A. D. Murray (*Transactions of the Hawick Archaeological Society*, August 1863), he practised 'in Edinburgh through the greater part of his life'; but it seems more likely that, though he may have begun there, his life from the age of thirty-three was spent in his native Peeblesshire, caring for his father in his declining years and pursuing his profession as a country doctor, in the course of which he became familiar with every corner of Tweeddale.

Pennecuik's devotion to the country and to country pursuits is revealed in his 'Answer to his brother J. P.'s many letters, dissuading him from staying longer in the country, and inviting him to come and settle his residence in Edinburgh'; the poem is addressed to his younger brother James, a member of the Faculty of Advocates, who had endeavoured to persuade him to move to Edinburgh. In it he maintains that he will not expose his old father to the dangers and unhealthiness of the city, 'to stifle him with smoke, though he be old', and describes lyrically the pleasures and comforts of the country life.

It was Pennecuik's devotion to his own neighbourhood and his close familiarity with the topography and botany of the area (he corresponded with James Sutherland, superintendent of the first botanic garden in Edinburgh) that caused Sir Robert Sibbald, who was preparing an account of the counties of Scotland, to invite Pennecuik to prepare a description of Tweeddale. He produced this with the assistance of the advocate John Forbes (who, by an ironic twist of fate, was later to inherit Pennecuik's

Newhall estate), but it was not published until 1715, when it appeared in a small quarto volume under the title, *A geographical, historical description of the shire of Tweeddale, with a miscelany and curious collection of select Scotish poems*, dedicated to William Douglas, earl of March (and lacking the promised map of Tweeddale, a circumstance attributed to 'Mr Adair's gout').

This volume contained the first published texts of Pennecuik's poems, introduced to the earl in the following words:

> To the following Treatise, My Lord, I have subjoined a few Pleasant and Select Poems, at the importunity of several Ingenious Gentlemen, my Friends; which were never before Published, or at least with my Consent and Knowledge; and if any of them has been Printed, it's owing to Surreptitious and False Coppies.

There is evidence that some of his poems did indeed circulate in broadside form earlier than this, and one of them, 'Lintoun address to his highness the prince of Orange' (1689), was included by James Watson in his *Choice Collection of Comic and Serious Scots Poems* (1706).

Pennecuik's total poetical output, which was small and undistinguished, was noticed briefly by Campbell in his *Introduction to the History of Poetry in Scotland* (1798): 'But of his poetry I am unwilling to say much to its dispraise, as I can in no wise qualify such with any commendation; therefore, I pass on, to notice another'. This judgement is corroborated more simply and briefly by an anonymous manuscript note on the flyleaf of a copy of the 1715 edition, 'Dr Pennecuik of Newhall, Romanno. A good sort of man tho' a very bad poet.'

It is not known whom Pennecuik married, but he had two daughters, the elder of whom married Mr Oliphant of Lanton, Edinburghshire, in 1702. The estate of Newhall was given to her on her marriage, but her husband, who was financially embarrassed, sold it in 1703 to Sir David Forbes, father of the John Forbes with whom Pennecuik collaborated over his description of Tweeddale, and who was the patron of Allan Ramsay. It was believed by John Pinkerton and later editors that Newhall inspired the setting for Ramsay's *The Gentle Shepherd*, but this theory has been discredited by the editors of the Scottish Text Society edition of Ramsay's *Works*. The estate of Romanno, where Pennecuik lived until his death, was bequeathed to his younger daughter, who had married Mr Farquharson of Kirktown of Boyne, Aberdeenshire. Pennecuik died there in 1722 and was buried beside his father in Newlands churchyard.

Dr Pennecuik is often confused with another minor poet, **Alexander Pennecuik** (*d.* 1730), often known as Mercator, assumed to be a relative, possibly a nephew. All that is known of him indicates that, though a man of education and some wit, his career was dissipated and impoverished. James Wilson (Claudero), in his 'Farewell to the Muses and Auld Reekie' (J. Wilson, *Miscellanies in Prose and Verse, on Several Occasions by Claudero*, 1766), promises

> To shun the fate of Pennycuik,
> Who starving died in turnpike-neuk;
> (Tho' sweet he sung with wit and sense,
> He like poor Claud, was short of pence).

He appears to have been involved in some way in the murder by Nicol Muschet, laird of Boghall, of Muschet's wife in 1721; Muschet's 'Last speech and confession' accuses a certain Alexander Pennycuik 'at present in the Abbey' (the abbey of Holyrood was the refuge of debtors) of having had a part in his criminal designs, a charge which Pennecuik refuted in *A Gentleman's Letter to the Laird of Boghall, the Day before his Execution* (1721).

Pennecuik contributed verses (signed by 'Al. P., Mercator Edinburgensis') 'To my honoured friend, Dr. P—k' which were prefixed to Dr Pennecuik's *Description of Tweeddale* (1715); these were reprinted in his *Streams from Helicon, or, Poems on various subjects, in three parts, by Alexander Pennecuik, gent.* (1720). The other publication by which he is best remembered is his prose *Historical Account of the Blue Blanket, or, Crafts-Mens Banner* by 'Alex. Pennecuik, burgess and guild-brother of Edinburgh' (1722). It is not known of which guild he was a brother.

Pennecuik's writing, though generally scurrilous, is more accomplished than that of his elder namesake and it frequently mimics the themes of his contemporary Allan Ramsay. All copies of his *Flowers from Parnassus*, which he apparently published in 1726, have disappeared. Numerous anonymous works are attributed to him, the most convincing attributions being *Groans from the grave, or, Complaints of the dead against the surgeons for raising their bodies out of the dust* (1725, see manuscript note on Maidment's copy in British Library). He died in 1730 and was buried in Greyfriars churchyard, Edinburgh, on 28 November. Collections of his poems published after his death include *A Collection of Poet Pennicuicke's Satires on Kirkmen* (1744); *A compleat collection of all the poems wrote by that famous and learned poet, Alexander Pennecuik*; and *A collection of Scots poems on several occasions, by the late Mr Alexander Pennecuik, gent., and others* (1787).　　　　　　　　HARRIET HARVEY WOOD

Sources A. Pennecuik, *A geographical, historical description of the shire of Tweeddale, with a miscelany and curious collection of Scottish poems* (1715) · *The works of Alexander Pennecuik esq., of New Hall, M.D., containing the description of Tweeddale, and miscellaneous poems, with copious notes; to which are prefixed memoirs of Dr Pennecuik* (1815) [memoirs by Robert Brown of Newhall] · W. Brown, 'Alexander Pennecuik MD and Alexander Pennecuik, merchant', *Publications of the Edinburgh Bibliographical Society*, 6 (1906) · A. Pennecuik, *A collection of curious Scots poems* (1762) · A. Pennycuik, 'Lintoun address to his highness the prince of Orange', in *James Watson's Choice collection of comic and serious Scots poems*, ed. H. H. Wood, 2 vols., STS, 4th ser., 10, 20 (1977–91), vol. 1, pp. 17–20; vol. 2, pp. 28–33 · 'Caledonia triumphans', *Various pieces of fugitive Scotch poetry; principally of the seventeenth century*, ed. D. Laing (1825) [broadside (1699)] · Chambers, *Scots.* (1835) · A. Campbell, *An introduction to the history of poetry in Scotland*, 2 pts in 1 (1798–9) · D. Irving, *The history of Scottish poetry*, ed. J. A. Carlyle (1861) · J. Veitch, *The history and poetry of the Scottish border*, new edn, 2 (1893), 241–3 · *The works of Allan Ramsay*, ed. B. Martin and J. W. Oliver, 1–2, STS, 3rd ser., 19–20 (1945–53) · *The works of Allan Ramsay*, ed. A. M. Kinghorn and A. Law, 3–6, STS, 3rd ser., 29; 4th ser., 6–8 (1961–74) · A. D. Murray, *Transactions of the Hawick Archaeological Society* (Aug 1863) · C. Rogers, *Monuments and monumental inscriptions in Scotland*, 1 (1871), 206 · A. Pennecuik, *Streams from Helicon, or, Poems on various subjects*, 2nd edn (1720) [Alexander Pennecuik (d. 1730)] · Claudero [J. Wilson], *Miscellanies in prose and verse* (1766) · *The works of Allan Ramsay*, 1 (1851), lvii–lviii · T. F. Henderson, *Scottish vernacular literature: a succinct history*, 2nd edn (1900) [Alexander Pennecuik (d. 1730)]

Pennecuik, Alexander (d. 1730). *See under* Pennecuik, Alexander (1652–1722).

Pennefather, Catherine (1818–1893). *See under* Pennefather, William (1816–1873).

Pennefather, Edward (1773–1847), judge, of Rathsellagh, Dunlavin, co. Wicklow, was born on 22 October 1773, the second son of Major William Pennefather (1732–1819), of Darling-Hill, co. Tipperary, MP for Cashel, and Ellen, eldest daughter of Edward Moore DD, archdeacon of Emly. He was the brother of Richard *Pennefather (1772–1859) and was educated with him at Portarlington and Clonmel schools; he graduated at Trinity College, Dublin, as BA in 1794, and MA in 1832. He had entered the Middle Temple, London, in 1792, and was called to the Irish bar three years later. On 6 January 1806 he married Susan (1785–1862), eldest daughter of John Darby of Markly, Sussex, and of Leah-Castle in King's county; they had four sons and six daughters.

The 'two Pennefathers' were leading practitioners at the court of chancery when Francis Blackburne (afterwards lord chancellor of Ireland) began to practise. Edward excelled his elder brother, Richard, as an advocate, and was without a rival as an equity lawyer.

Pennefather appears as king's counsel in 1816, and in the same year he was counsel for the plaintiff in the celebrated libel case, *Bruce v. Grady*, tried before Serjeant Johnson at the Limerick summer assizes of 1816, when O'Connell led for the defendant (*Authentic report of the interesting trial for a libel contained in the celebrated poem called The Nosegay*). The plaintiff, who claimed £20,000, obtained a verdict for £500.

Elected a bencher of King's Inns in 1829, Pennefather was appointed third serjeant in April of the following year, second serjeant in January 1831, and first serjeant in February 1832. On 27 January 1835 he became solicitor-general for Ireland in Sir Robert Peel's administration, and he was reappointed (in September 1841) on the return of Sir Robert Peel to power. In November he was appointed chief justice of the queen's bench and a privy councillor. In January and February 1844 he presided at the state trial of the O'Connells, Gavan Duffy, and their associates for conspiracy to effect the repeal of the Act of Union. The trial was the great legal event of the Peel administration, as memorable for its magnitude and longevity as for its political importance. John Mitchel says that 'the chief justice in his charge argued the case like one of the counsel for the prosecution' (J. Mitchel, *A History of Ireland from the Treaty of Limerick*, 1869, 194). Pennefather contended that neither secrecy nor treachery formed a necessary part of the legal definition of conspiracy. His charge was learned, lucid, and fair, although it was clear that in the opinion of the court the indictment had been in the main sustained. Sentence was pronounced on 30 May by Mr Justice Burton.

Pennefather retired from the bench in January 1846 and died at his house in Fitzwilliam Square, Dublin, after a long illness, on 6 September 1847. He was buried in the churchyard of Delgany church.

Although in his day Pennefather stood at the head of the Irish bar, he was nevertheless a man of unwavering modesty. A weighty advocate, in stature he was compared by James Whiteside to the great English lawyer, Lord Romilly. G. LE G. NORGATE, rev. NATHAN WELLS

Sources F. E. Ball, The judges in Ireland, 1221–1921, 2 (1926) · Law Times (11 Sept 1847) · E. Keane, P. Beryl Phair, and T. U. Sadleir, eds., King's Inns admission papers, 1607–1867, IMC (1982) · Shaw's Authenticated Reports of Irish State Trials (1844) · An authentic report of the interesting trial for a libel contained in the celebrated poem, called "The Nosegay"; wherein George Evans was plaintiff, and Thomas Grady, defendant [1816] · Burke, Gen. Ire.
Likenesses wood-engraving, NPG; repro. in ILN (1843–4)

Pennefather, Sir John Lysaght (1800–1872), army officer, was the third son of the Revd John Pennefather of New Park, co. Tipperary, and cousin of Richard *Pennefather, baron of the exchequer in Ireland. His mother was a daughter of Major Percival. He entered the army on 14 January 1818 as cornet in the 7th dragoon guards, becoming a lieutenant on 20 February 1823 and a captain on half pay on 5 November 1825. On 8 April 1826 he was appointed to the 22nd (the Cheshire regiment), in which he became major on 22 March 1831 and lieutenant-colonel on 18 October 1839. In 1834 he married Margaret, eldest daughter of John Carr of Mountrath, Queen's county; she survived him.

Pennefather had seen no active service, but in 1843 his was the one European regiment in the force with which Sir Charles Napier won the battle of Meanee (17 February), and it bore the brunt of that action, in which Napier defeated the more numerous army of Sher Mahomed. The battalion was about 500 strong, many Irishmen, like their commander. 'The noble soldier', as Napier described Pennefather, fell wounded—mortally, it was thought—on the top of the bank which bordered the river-bed and formed the crest of the Baluchis' position. He was made a CB (July 1843), and received the thanks of parliament. From June 1846 to June 1854 he was an aide-de-camp to the queen. In 1848 he gave up the command of the 22nd regiment, and was placed on half pay; in the following year he was appointed assistant quartermaster-general in the Cork district. In 1854 he was given command of the 1st brigade of the 2nd (Sir De Lacy Evans's) division in the army sent to the Crimea, and on 20 June he was made major-general. His brigade consisted of the 30th, 55th, and 95th regiments. He commanded with great credit at the battle of the Alma, and in the action of 26 October, when a sortie in force was made from Sevastopol against the heights held by the 2nd division on the extreme right of the allied position. Pennefather also distinguished himself at the battle of Inkerman on 5 November when, owing to Evans's illness, he was in command of the division. He had fewer than 3000 men under command, while more than 30,000 Russian infantry were converging upon him. On 26 October Evans had drawn up his force on the ridge immediately in front of the camp of the division, and allowed his pickets to be driven in rather than leave his chosen ground. Pennefather adopted a different course, and disputed every inch, kept only a few men in reserve on the ridge, but pushed forward all the men he could to support his pickets in resisting the massed assaults. The thickness of the weather favoured these tactics, and the result justified them. As reinforcements, English and French, came up, they were similarly pushed forward as soon as available. Lord Raglan arrived, and Sir De Lacy Evans came up from Balaklava during the course of the morning, but Pennefather was left to direct the fight, so far as any one person could direct it, and he encouraged and inspired his men. The battle lasted about six hours—from daybreak to 1 p.m.—when the Russians began their retreat, having lost very heavily.

Pennefather's 'admirable behaviour' was mentioned in Raglan's dispatch. A fortnight afterwards he was appointed to the colonelcy of the 46th regiment, and he succeeded to the command of the 2nd division when Evans returned to England in the latter part of November. He was invalided home from the Crimea in July 1855, and from 25 September 1855 until 1860 he commanded the troops in Malta, with the local rank of lieutenant-general. After brief service in the northern district he commanded at Aldershot from 1860 to 1865. He exchanged the colonelcy of the 46th for that of his former regiment, the 22nd, on 13 February 1860. On 12 November of that year he became lieutenant-general on the establishment, and on 9 May 1868 he became general. He had been made a KCB on 5 July 1855, and received the GCB on 13 May 1867. He was a commander of the Sardinian order of St Maurice and St Lazarus, a grand officer of the Légion d'honneur, and was awarded the order of the Mejidiye (second class). On 27 August 1870 he was appointed governor of Chelsea Hospital. A staunch, combative and respected soldier, he died at Chelsea Hospital on 9 May 1872, and was buried in Brompton cemetery.

E. M. LLOYD, rev. JAMES FALKNER

Sources Army List · W. F. P. Napier, The conquest of Scinde: with some introductory passages in the life of Major-General Sir Charles James Napier, 2 vols. (1845) · A. W. Kinglake, The invasion of the Crimea, [new edn], 9 vols. (1877–88) · Annual Register (1854) · Hart's Army List · W. H. Anderson, The history of the 22nd Cheshire regiment (1920) · B. Rigby, Ever glorious (story of 22nd regt), 1 (1982) · Boase, Mod. Eng. biog. · Dod's Peerage (1858)
Archives NAM, corresp. with William Codrington
Likenesses Maull & Fox, photograph, c.1870, priv. coll.
Wealth at death under £9000: probate, 7 June 1872, CGPLA Eng. & Wales

Pennefather, Richard (1772–1859), judge, was born into a well-known Irish protestant family at Knockevan, co. Tipperary, on 25 August 1772. He was the eldest son of Major William Pennefather (1732–1819), of Darling-Hill, co. Tipperary, MP for Cashel, and Ellen, eldest daughter of Edward Moore DD, archdeacon of Emly. Like his younger brother, Edward *Pennefather, he was educated at Portarlington and Clonmel schools, and he graduated BA at Trinity College, Dublin, in 1794, after a distinguished career there. He had entered the Middle Temple in London in 1792, and was called to the Irish bar in 1795.

About ten years later Pennefather enjoyed a reputation both on the Munster circuit and as a junior in the court of chancery. He appears as king's counsel in 1816, but was seldom employed as leading counsel, being overshadowed by William Plunket and William Saurin. In 1798 he married Jane, daughter of Mr Justice John Bennett of Dublin. They had eight children (of whom at least two predeceased their father); the civil servant Richard *Pennefather was one of the sons.

On 1 February 1821 Pennefather was appointed a baron of the Irish exchequer court, and he sat on the bench for thirty-eight years. He was a sound, able, and honourable judge, skilled in the digestion and elucidation of evidence, courteous in his bearing, and in criminal cases lenient. In his final years Pennefather lost his sight and this, coupled with his age (he being at the time over eighty) led to suggestions in the Commons that he be removed from the bench. Such suggestions were not favourably received, and the house united in paying tribute to the man: the Conservatives likened him to Lord Lyndhurst, and the Liberals admitted unreservedly his exceptional judicial gifts and undiminished popularity. So it was of his own accord that Pennefather retired, some three years later, in 1859. He died suddenly at his residence in Kiltegan, near Clonmel, co. Tipperary, on 7 August 1859, and was buried at Caher, co. Tipperary.

G. Le G. Norgate, rev. Nathan Wells

Sources F. E. Ball, *The judges in Ireland, 1221–1921*, 2 (1926) · E. Keane, P. Beryl Phair, and T. U. Sadleir, eds., *King's Inns admission papers, 1607–1867*, IMC (1982) · *Hansard 3* (1856), vol. 146 · Boase, *Mod. Eng. biog.*
Likenesses J. H. Lynch, lithograph (after P. W. Burton), NPG
Wealth at death under £10,000: resworn probate, May 1860, *CGPLA Ire.* (1859)

Pennefather, Richard (1806–1849), civil servant, born at Dublin on 3 September 1806, was the eldest son of Richard *Pennefather (1772–1859), judge, and his wife, Jane Bennett; William *Pennefather was his brother. Educated at Eton College, he matriculated at Balliol College, Oxford, in 1824, and graduated BA in 1828. In 1826 he was admitted at Lincoln's Inn. He married, on 26 July 1836, Lady Emily Arabel Butler, daughter of Richard, first earl of Glengall, who appointed him lieutenant-colonel of the Tipperary militia. On 21 August 1845 he was appointed undersecretary to the lord lieutenant of Ireland in Sir Robert Peel's administration. His promotion had been supported by Edward Eliot, chief secretary for Ireland, despite urgings that a Roman Catholic be placed in the position. Seated at Darling-Hill, co. Tipperary, he was high sheriff of the county in 1848, and in that capacity arranged for the state trials of William Smith O'Brien and other prisoners at Clonmel. Pennefather died of cholera on 26 July 1849, at Newtown-Anner, co. Tipperary, the seat of Ralph Bernal Osborne MP. In 1852 his widow married Colonel H. A. Hankey. He left a son and a daughter; the latter married Arthur, sixth Earl Stanhope. His younger brother, John Pennefather (1815–1855), also a graduate of Balliol College, became QC and a bencher of King's Inns, Dublin.

M. C. Curthoys

Sources *GM*, 2nd ser., 32 (1849), 424 · Foster, *Alum. Oxon.* · Burke, *Gen. Ire.* (1858) · C. S. Parker, ed., *Sir Robert Peel: from his private papers*, 3 (1899), 183–5

Pennefather, William (1816–1873), Church of England clergyman, the youngest of the eight children of Richard *Pennefather (1772–1859), baron of the Irish court of exchequer, and his wife, Jane, *née* Bennett, was born in Merrion Square, Dublin, on 5 February 1816; one of his elder brothers was Richard *Pennefather. He was educated first at a preparatory school in Dublin; then at Westbury College, near Bristol, where he was known as 'the saintly boy'; and finally, from 1832, he was privately tutored by the Revd William Stephens at Levens, near Kendal, Westmorland. He went to Trinity College, Dublin, in 1834, but suffered from consumption and did not graduate BA until 1840; he was drawn into the life of the evangelical community in the city. Ordained deacon in 1841 and priest in the following year, Pennefather was licensed to the curacy of Ballymacugh, co. Cavan, and then became incumbent of Mellifont, near Drogheda, in 1844. A keen supporter of Irish Church Missions, he was active during 1846 and 1847 in famine relief activities. On 16 September 1847 he married Catherine King [*see below*], eldest daughter of Rear-Admiral the Hon. James William King, youngest son of the second earl of Kingston, and his wife, Caroline Cleaver.

In 1848 Pennefather became perpetual curate of Holy Trinity, Walton, Aylesbury, Buckinghamshire, a recently created parochial district in the town. His successful ministry there led to his transfer, in 1852, to the perpetual curacy of Christ Church, Barnet, Hertfordshire. A few years later an extra aisle and gallery were added to his church. Pennefather and his wife, themselves childless, began the care of orphans in 1855. Annually from 1856 (except in 1857), he also organized a conference of Christian workers, concentrating on the themes of home and foreign missions, holiness, and the premillennial second advent. In 1860 he began the training of women workers as overseas missionaries, many of whom were to serve with the Church Missionary Society and Church of England Zenana Missionary Society.

In 1864 Pennefather left Barnet for the incumbency of St Jude's, Mildmay Park, Islington, in north London. His annual gathering, for which a purpose-built hall seating 3000 people was opened in 1870, became the Mildmay Conference. The training home evolved into an institution for deaconesses, primarily preparing women for work as uniformed domestic missionaries or, from 1866, as nurses. The strain of co-ordinating this growing evangelical empire led to a complete breakdown of Pennefather's health, which had always been delicate, early in 1873, and he died from apoplexy on 30 April at his home, Melford Lodge, Muswell Hill, Middlesex. He was buried at Ridge, near Barnet.

Dignified in bearing and courteous in manner, Pennefather impressed contemporaries by the depth of his devotional life and the warmth of his human sympathy. In his love of poetry he nurtured some skill as a hymn writer.

dictionary of hymnology (1892), 888–9 • D. W. Bebbington, *Evangelicalism in modern Britain: a history from the 1730s to the 1980s* (1989) • Burke, *Peerage*
Likenesses T. J. Hughes, sketch, repro. in Braithwaite, ed., *Life and letters*, frontispiece • engraving, NPG [*see illus.*] • portrait, repro. in *Christian portrait gallery*, 286
Wealth at death under £8000: administration, 9 June 1873, *CGPLA Eng. & Wales*

Pennell, Joseph (1857–1926), illustrator and writer, was born on 4 July 1857 in Philadelphia, Pennsylvania, the only child of Larkin Pennell, a teacher and shipping clerk, and his wife, Rebecca A. Barton. Following his graduation in 1876 from Germantown Friends' Select School, and against the wishes of his Quaker family, he studied first at night classes at the Pennsylvania School of Industrial Art and then at the Pennsylvania Academy of the Fine Arts. Headstrong and independent, he left both schools without graduating and, around 1880, opened his own studio. In July 1881 his first published work appeared in *Scribner's Monthly*, and thereafter he sold his work to a variety of American publishers of periodicals and books.

In 1883 Pennell accompanied the noted author William Dean Howells to Italy on a commission to illustrate a series of articles on Tuscany; on the way home he toured and drew in Italy, England, and Ireland. Back in Philadelphia in 1884 he married Elizabeth Robins (1855–1936), and they immediately left for London. His wife was a writer and became his lifelong collaborator, sharing the authorship of several books. In London the couple got to know many of the leading literary and artistic figures of the time, among them Robert Louis Stevenson, George Bernard Shaw, Edmund Gosse, and James Abbott McNeill Whistler.

Pennell first showed his etchings at the Society of Painter-Etchers in 1885. A decade later he became fascinated with lithography, partly through seeing the work of Henri de Toulouse-Lautrec, T.-A. Steinlen, and Odilon Redon in exhibitions in Paris, and partly through his association with Whistler. In his book *Lithography and Lithographers* (1898) he described the expressive possibilities of the technique and set forth his own working principles.

Pennell's style reflected his early enthusiasm for the work of Spanish artists, his admiration for French printmakers of his time, and his appreciation of Whistler. His work combines assured drawing with an ability to render architectural details accurately without being drily descriptive, and to evoke atmospheric effects on structures and on the landscape. Although he never lost his appreciation of French churches, Italian hill towns, or Venice, Pennell became a master at recording the industrial and urban scene; his lithographs of the construction of the Panama Canal, his etchings of steel mills, and scenes of shipyards set his work apart from much of the bucolic or anecdotal printmaking and illustration of his time.

Increasingly, Pennell turned to writing, frequently with his wife as co-author. His earliest book, *Canterbury Pilgrimage* (1885), was 'ridden, written, and illustrated' by both the Pennells. Several of their other titles were books of travels, but as early as 1889 Joseph Pennell published *Pen*

William Pennefather (1816–1873), by unknown engraver

Several of his compositions were published, though the only one which remained widely sung was 'Jesus, stand among us'. Pennefather's insistence that converted Christians of all denominations should co-operate is eloquently expressed in *The Church of the First-Born* (1865). He invited the American evangelist Dwight L. Moody to Britain, but died before the opening of his preaching tour. Pennefather's stress on holiness, like his inauguration of the Mildmay Conference, prepared the way for the Keswick Convention, which first took place two years after his death.

His wife, **Catherine Pennefather** (1818–1893), home mission worker, was active in parochial work throughout her married life. From 1858 she was president of the Association of Female Workers, connected first with Barnet and then with Mildmay. She relaunched her work among orphans in 1872 and, following her husband's death, she presided over the further development of the Mildmay institutions. By her own death on 12 January 1893 these included twenty missions in London staffed by some eighty deaconesses; a mission to the Jews (started in 1876); a medical mission at Bethnal Green (from 1877); and a cottage hospital (established in 1883). Catherine Pennefather edited the Mildmay monthly journal, *Service for the King*, and published several small volumes of verse and Bible class notes, including *Follow thou me* (2 vols., 1881).

D. W. BEBBINGTON

Sources *The life and letters of Rev. William Pennefather*, ed. R. Braithwaite (1878) • H. J. Cooke, *Mildmay, or, The story of the first deaconess institution*, 2nd edn (1893) • *The Record* (2 May 1873) • *The Record* (13 Jan 1893) • *The Christian portrait gallery* (1889), 286–9 • J. Julian, ed., *A*

Joseph Pennell (1857–1926), by James Abbott McNeill Whistler, 1896

Drawing and Pen Draughtsmen, which was followed by his book on lithography and other volumes on etching and illustration.

Their friendship and admiration for Whistler inspired Joseph and Elizabeth Pennell to undertake a major study of his life and art. Pennell and Whistler had much in common—in their combative personalities, their fascination with printmaking, and their shared admiration for such artists as Manet and Velázquez. The Pennells' study of Whistler was undertaken with the subject's cooperation, but Whistler died before the book could be completed. His executor, Rosalind Birnie Philip, tried to halt the publication of the book, but a court decision enabled the Pennells to publish *The Life of James McNeill Whistler* in 1908.

The Pennells returned to America in 1917 and settled in New York, where Pennell found new subjects and opportunities to teach and lecture. In 1921 they arranged an exhibition of their Whistler collection at the Library of Congress. They subsequently decided to bequeath their collection to the library, along with funds to support the acquisition of the work of contemporary printmakers. Joseph Pennell died in New York on 23 April 1926 and was buried at the Friends' meeting-house in Germantown, Pennsylvania. His wife lived on for another decade. In the 1928 edition of *The Art of Whistler* she saluted her late husband for his 'vigorous eloquence that came of his love for the truth and his strong convictions' (p. x). The Pennell fund at the Library of Congress continues to bring to the American public the work of talented graphic artists, fulfilling the Pennells' intentions. In addition to the prints, drawings, and pastels by Pennell in the Library of Congress, his work is held in several other public collections, including the Metropolitan Museum of Art, New York; the New York Public Library; and the National Museum of American History, Washington, DC.   ALAN M. FERN

Sources E. L. Tinker, 'Pennell, Joseph', *DAB* · J. Pennell and E. Robins Pennell, *The Joseph and Elizabeth Robins Pennell collection of Whistleriana* (Washington, DC, 1921) · *Joseph Pennell memorial exhibition* (1927) [exhibition catalogue, L. Cong.] · E. Robins Pennell, *The life and letters of Joseph Pennell*, 2 vols. (1929) · E. Robins Pennell and J. Pennell, *The life of James McNeill Whistler*, 2 vols. (1908) · J. Pennell and E. Robins Pennell, *Lithography and lithographers* (1898) · J. Pennell, *Pen drawing and pen draughtsmen* (1889) · J. Pennell and E. Robins Pennell, *A Canterbury pilgrimage* (1885) · E. Robins Pennell and J. Pennell, *The art of Whistler* (1928) · J. Pennell, *Adventures of an illustrator* (1925) · P. de Montfort, 'Pennell, Joseph', *ANB*

Archives L. Cong., MSS, photographs, and prints | BL, corresp. with Macmillans, Add. MSS 55226–55227 · Tate collection, letters to John Lavery

Likenesses J. A. M. Whistler, lithograph, 1896, L. Cong. · J. A. M. Whistler, lithograph, 1896, BM [*see illus.*] · C. Hassam, lithograph, 1917, L. Cong. · F. T. Morgan, etching, 1920, L. Cong.

Wealth at death £1471 19*s.* 5*d.*: resworn administration with will, 28 May 1930, *CGPLA Eng. & Wales*

Pennethorne, Sir James (1801–1871), architect, was born on 4 June 1801 in Worcester, the third of the seven children of Thomas Pennethorne (1762–1843), hop merchant, and his wife, Elizabeth, *née* Salt (*d.* 1849), who ran a school. The architect John *Pennethorne was his younger brother. He grew up in Worcester, and was educated in Dr Simpson's academy there, but in 1820 he took the place of his elder brother Thomas (1798–1819) as a clerk in the London office of the architect John Nash, whose second wife was his second cousin; the legend that he was an illegitimate son of the prince of Wales (later King George IV) by Mrs Nash cannot be substantiated.

Early training and travel abroad Nash's influence was crucial in shaping Pennethorne's career. It was Nash who arranged for him to be taught drawing by Augustus Charles Pugin in 1821–3, and he was involved in the preparation of the second volume of Pugin's *Specimens of Gothic Architecture* (1823). He also attended the Royal Academy Schools, and it was in Nash's magnificent new house at 14 Regent Street that he prepared his first architectural design, for a neo-classical monument to the battles of Waterloo and Trafalgar, exhibited at the Royal Academy in 1824 but never constructed. In October 1824 Pennethorne embarked on two years of foreign travel and study, financed by Nash and clearly intended to establish him as his successor. Most of the time was spent in Rome, where he carried out an intensive study of classical and Renaissance buildings, culminating in the preparation of two accomplished but fanciful perspective drawings of the restoration of the Roman forum, the second of which led in April 1826 to his election as a member of the Accademia di San Luca in Rome. He visited and illustrated the Greek temples of southern Italy and Sicily in the summer of 1826, and he also spent some time in Paris in the office of Augustus Pugin's brother-in-law Louis Lafitte before returning to Britain at the end of that year.

Early career and marriage Pennethorne corresponded regularly with Nash while abroad, and on his return he resumed his position in the older architect's office, becoming his chief assistant in 1828. In this capacity he supervised the last of the metropolitan improvements designed, under an act of parliament of 1826, to link the newly created Regent Street to Trafalgar Square and the Strand: notably Carlton House Terrace, the development of a block of crown property at the western end of the Strand, and the remodelling of St James's Park on picturesque lines. He was involved in the construction, and perhaps also to some extent in the internal design, of Nash's new state rooms at Buckingham Palace, and in 1830, when Nash retired to the Isle of Wight, he took charge of his London office. Here the quantity of work fell off drastically after the death of George IV and Nash's dismissal from his official appointments by the new whig government, and when Pennethorne took over full control in March 1834, a year before Nash's death, little remained beyond repairs and minor building work on the crown estate in London. One of the works in hand was the completion of Park Village West, one of Nash's speculations to the northeast of Regent's Park, and here Pennethorne supervised the building—and may have been involved in the design—of some of the houses. On 8 April 1834 he married Frances (d. c.1865), daughter of Deane John Parker, a Canterbury banker whose elder brother Henry, a tax official—the original 'Nosey Parker', according to family legend—had married Nash's sister-in-law Grace Bradley; the first of their eight children, Deane Parker Pennethorne, was born in 1835. Pennethorne moved out of 14 Regent Street when it was sold by Nash in 1834, and established his office first in Duke Street and then in Bury Street, St James's, before moving to Queen Anne's Gate, Westminster, where he was living in 1839.

Independent practice Pennethorne's independent career got off to a very slow start. His first building, delegated to him by Nash, was Crockford's Bazaar at 10 St James's Street (1831–2; subsequently remodelled), and during the rest of the 1830s he designed only a handful of country houses—notably Swithland Hall, Leicestershire (1834), and the rebuilding of Dillington House, Somerset (c.1837)—and two London churches: Christ Church, Albany Street (1836–7), an austere neo-classical building of some distinction, and Holy Trinity, Gray's Inn Road (1827–8; dem.). But he failed to win any of the competitions he entered, and, despite being recommended by Nash to the commissioners of woods and forests in 1834, he gained no official work until 1839, when he was appointed architect and surveyor to the commissioners for a new phase of metropolitan improvements designed to drive new streets through slum areas in or near the heart of London; the appointment was held jointly with Thomas Chawner, who retired in 1845. The most important of the new streets were New Oxford Street, cutting through the centre of the notorious St Giles Rookery, and Commercial Street, designed to divert traffic to and from the London docks away from the City and through the slums of Whitechapel. Though conceived in a spacious manner which owed much to Nash, they and the two other new streets

(Cranbourn Street and Endell Street) were drastically reduced in scale in 1840 as a result of political pressure and financial difficulties, and, as carried out in 1843–7, they made less of an impact on London than Pennethorne, who was solely responsible for their design, had intended. Meanwhile in 1841 he and Chawner were entrusted by the commissioners with the design of Victoria Park, the first park in the East End of London and the first park in any English city to be laid out with public funds for the benefit of the working classes. Here too there were savage cuts in funding before the park was completed in 1847, to Pennethorne's revised but still effective designs of 1845. A similar process occurred at Battersea Park, on the south bank of the River Thames, first designed by Pennethorne in 1845, but revised and reduced in scale in 1853–4 and not completed until 1863. Pennethorne's plans of 1851 for a third park, to be named Albert Park, in north London, never left the drawing board, and in 1855 responsibility for both new streets and parks passed from the government to the newly constituted Metropolitan Board of Works.

Major works For most of the 1840s Pennethorne's professional life was taken up with metropolitan improvements and the surveyorship of the crown estate in London, to which he was jointly appointed with Chawner in 1840. He took over as sole surveyor of the estate in 1845 and went on to redesign the Quadrant in Regent Street following the removal of Nash's arcade in 1848 and to lay out the street now called Buckingham Gate to the south of Buckingham Palace in 1853–8; he also supervised the realignment of the approaches to Windsor Castle in 1846–52. His official appointments brought him an office at 7 Whitehall Yard and a steady income which enabled him to settle in some comfort with his growing family at Elms Court, Highgate Hill, and when Chawner retired at the end of 1845 he gave up what remained of his private practice to work full-time for the government. He now began to be employed by successive first commissioners of woods and forests (from 1851 first commissioners of works) to design public and government buildings for which a competition was not deemed necessary, starting in 1846–51 with the Museum of Practical Geology in Piccadilly, a handsome structure (since demolished) with façades in the Italian Renaissance manner and an ambitious iron and glass roof lighting the main display area. The massive and austere Public Record Office in Chancery Lane followed in 1851–70, its Gothic exterior hiding a rigorously utilitarian fireproof interior (the west wing was built to the designs of Sir John Taylor in 1891–6), and in 1852–6 Pennethorne designed a new west wing at Somerset House for the Inland Revenue, externally echoing the main building by Sir William Chambers. He also added a new south range, including a lavishly decorated ballroom and supper room, to Buckingham Palace in 1852–6, and in 1854–7 new offices for the duchy of Cornwall were built to his designs at the eastern end of the newly opened Buckingham Gate, facing the palace.

Later career Pennethorne's later career is littered with the debris of abandoned projects for public buildings in London. In 1853 he was entrusted by the then first commissioner of works, Sir William Molesworth, with the design of a new block of government offices, including a new Foreign Office, on the western side of Whitehall, but in 1855 Molesworth was replaced by Sir Benjamin Hall, who abandoned Pennethorne's plans and announced a competition which eventually led, after many vicissitudes—including the temporary reinstatement of Pennethorne in 1857—to the erection of the present Foreign Office to the designs of Sir George Gilbert Scott in 1862–73. Designs for a new War Office in Pall Mall, conceived in 1856, also fell victim to Hall, and a succession of projects for enlarging the National Gallery in Trafalgar Square, the first of them dating from 1850, resulted only in the construction in 1860–61 of a new picture gallery which was demolished when the present main staircase was built to Sir John Taylor's designs in 1885. Elaborate designs for the layout of the South Kensington estate owned by the commissioners of the Great Exhibition also remained stillborn, and Pennethorne's only tangible contribution to the development of this district was the erection in 1856 of a temporary and short-lived lecture-room for the South Kensington Museum.

Pennethorne's ill-defined and ambiguous role as government architect was undermined by a series of reforms to the office of works carried out by Sir Benjamin Hall in 1856, and his official career was only rescued after he appealed directly to the Treasury, to which the office was subordinate. But, despite being viciously attacked in Beresford Hope's *Saturday Review*, he was awarded a special gold medal by the Royal Institute of British Architects in 1857 (for the completion of Somerset House), and when Hall stepped down as first commissioner of works after the fall of Palmerston's government in 1858 he recovered something of his former status in the office. Hall's successor, Lord John Manners, employed him to design the staff college at Camberley, Surrey (1859–61), in a plain classical style, and, as a result of a Treasury inquiry in the same year, he was given an annual salary of £1500 for 'general services', in addition to his existing salary of £850 as surveyor to the crown estate and the normal percentage fees for any new buildings he might be asked to design. His last major commissions were the completion of the Public Record Office, the internal remodelling of Marlborough House and the building of a new stable block there for the prince of Wales (1860–63), and, most important, the Senate House for the University of London (1867–70), an impressive and richly decorated classical building erected on ground to the north of Burlington House, acquired by the government on his recommendation in 1854 and for which he made several abortive proposals.

Pennethorne's post as 'salaried architect and surveyor' to the government was abolished following a further reorganization of the office of works by Gladstone's first commissioner of works, A. H. Layard, and he retired on 30 June 1870. He was given a royal gold medal by the Royal Institute of British Architects in 1865 and a knighthood in November 1870. His former assistant Arthur Cates, who succeeded him as surveyor to the crown estate in London, called him '[a] man of retired and studious habits, engrossed in the duties of his office, and mixing but little with society' (Cates, 60). His careful and refined style of classical architecture was not to the taste of the younger generation in the 1870s, and his immediate influence was slight: none of his pupils or assistants made a major impact on the late Victorian architectural world. His career was in some respects a frustrating one, plagued as it was by political interference and perhaps also by deep-seated failure to escape fully from the shadow of his mentor, John Nash. But Pennethorne's long-term legacy was greater than the relatively modest tally of his buildings might suggest. His former detractor, Beresford Hope, told the Royal Institute of British Architects in 1865 that he was responsible 'in no small degree [for] the revival of art-conscious on the part of our rulers' (*RIBA Transactions*, 1864–5, 1). He was one of the most accomplished classical architects of his age and, as a designer of new streets and parks, he played a crucial part in the shaping of mid-Victorian London.

Pennethorne moved to Worcester Park House, Long Ditton, Malden, Surrey, in 1865, and it was here that he died, from a heart condition, on 1 September 1871. He was buried in Highgate cemetery.   GEOFFREY TYACK

Sources G. C. Tyack, *Sir James Pennethorne and the making of Victorian London* (1992) · *The Builder*, 29 (1871), 717–18 · [Edward Hall], 'Pennethorne and public improvements: a retrospect', *Mechanics Magazine*, 26 (1871), 272–86 · A. Cates, 'A biographical notice of the late Sir James Pennethorne', *Sessional Papers of the Royal Institute of British Architects* (1871–2), 53–69 · C. Knight, ed., *The English cyclopaedia: biography*, 3 (1856) · J. M. Crook and M. H. Port, eds., *The history of the king's works*, 6 (1973) · J. Summerson, *The life and works of John Nash, architect* (1980) · G. H. Gater and E. P. Wheeler, *The parish of St Martin-in-the-Fields*, 1: *Charing Cross*, Survey of London, 16 (1935) · *The parish of St Anne, Soho*, 2 (1966) · *The parish of St James, Westminster*, 2/1, Survey of London, 31 (1963) · *The parish of St James, Westminster*, 1, Survey of London, 29–30 (1960) · P. A. Bezodis, *Spitalfields and Mile End new town*, Survey of London, 27 (1957) · W. H. Godfrey and W. M. Marcham, *The parish of St Pancras*, ed. J. R. H. Roberts, 3, Survey of London, 21 (1949) · G. H. Gater and F. R. Hiorns, *The parish of St Martin-in-the-Fields*, 3: *Trafalgar Square and neighbourhood*, Survey of London, 20 (1940) · letters and diary, 1832, RIBA BAL · *CGPLA Eng. & Wales* (1871) · d. cert.
Archives NRA, priv. coll., notebooks, etc. · NRA, priv. coll., genealogical and other MSS · RIBA, MS report relating to National Gallery · RIBA, travel journals, diaries, and letters home · Royal Arch. | Northumbd RO, Newcastle upon Tyne, letters to Sir Matthew Ridley · PRO, Work and Treasury
Likenesses photograph, c.1850, priv. coll. · photograph, c.1860, priv. coll. · engraving, repro. in *The Builder* (18 Sept 1869), 746
Wealth at death under £25,000: probate, 16 Sept 1871, *CGPLA Eng. & Wales*

Pennethorne, John (1808–1888), architect, was the youngest of the seven children of Thomas Pennethorne (1762–1843), a hop merchant, and his wife, Elizabeth, *née* Salt (d. 1849), a schoolmistress. He was born at Worcester on 4 January 1808 and in the late 1820s followed his older brother Sir James *Pennethorne into the office of John Nash in London. In 1830 he began a five-year tour of professional study in Europe and Egypt, visiting Paris, Milan,

Florence, Venice, Rome, Sicily, Athens, and Thebes, which determined his subsequent career. On his first visit to Athens in 1832 he became interested in the geometrical 'refinements' of the temples of the Acropolis, notably the introduction of subtle curvature for the horizontal lines—something alluded to by Vitruvius. While spending the winter of 1833 at Thebes he made careful studies of the mouldings and coloured decorations of the temples and tombs, and came to the conclusion that the colouring and ornamentation of Greek temples, as well as some aspects of their geometry, derived ultimately from Egypt. On returning to Athens in 1834, he renewed his study of the Parthenon, taking wax moulds of the mouldings and ornaments. He returned to England in 1835, but in 1837 he again visited Athens to make more complete observations and measurements of the curved lines of the steps, stylobate and entablature, and the inclination of the columns, of the Parthenon. He finally came to the conclusion that there was no foundation in fact for the conventional belief that the system of design in Greek architecture was absolutely rectilinear. The same conclusion had already been reached by Josef Hoffer, and Hoffer's research was published in C. F. L. Förster's *Allgemeine Bauzeitung* in 1838 (3.249) quoting measurements of the Parthenon which had been made independently of Pennethorne's investigations by Edward Schaubert, an architect working for the Greek government.

Ill health forced Pennethorne to return to England in 1837, and in 1844 he published, for private circulation, a pamphlet of sixty-four pages, *The elements and mathematical principles of the Greek architects and artists, recovered by an analysis and study of the remaining works of architecture designed and erected in the age of Pericles*, in which he drew upon passages in Plato, Aristotle, and Vitruvius, as well as his own discoveries, to set forth a theory of 'optical corrections'. His discoveries had already been noticed by W. M. Leake in his *Topography of Athens* (1841), and in 1845–7 they were pursued by F. C. Penrose, who in 1851 published his *Investigations of the Principles of Athenian Architecture*. The elaborate and exact measurements here given supplied Pennethorne with the mathematical data necessary to work out fully his theory of optical corrections.

In 1851 Pennethorne settled with his unmarried sister Anne at Hamstead, John Nash's farm on the Isle of Wight, and for several years he devoted himself to agriculture. He resumed his studies in 1860, and in 1878 he published, at his own expense, an impressive folio volume, *The geometry and optics of ancient architecture, illustrated by examples from Thebes, Athens, and Rome*, with fifty-six plates by John Robinson, a pupil of his brother James. His findings were summarized in a paper on 'The connection between ancient art and the ancient geometry, as illustrated by works of the age of Pericles', published in the *Transactions of the Royal Institute of British Architects* (1878–9). His argument was that the Greek architects, having first designed a building so that geometrically its proportions were harmonious, afterwards corrected those dimensions with reference to the visual angle under which it would be seen, and by

these methods of work produced a building which optically displayed the same harmony of proportion as characterized the merely geometrical projection. These optical corrections, he believed, contributed greatly to the superiority of Greek architecture over Roman. His conviction that Greek temples were designed to be seen only from certain points of view was challenged in his lifetime and was not accepted by later scholars. But his careful research, embodied in his book of 1878, made an important contribution to the understanding of the architecture of ancient Greece and of the importance of mathematics in determining architectural proportion.

Pennethorne died, unmarried, at Hamstead, Isle of Wight, on 20 January 1888.

ARTHUR CATES, *rev.* GEOFFREY TYACK

Sources J. Pennethorne, 'Preface', *The geometry and optics of ancient architecture* (1878) · W. H. Goodyear, *Greek refinements* (1911) · private information (2004) [Mrs Liddon Few, Isle of Wight] · J. Pennethorne, letters to his brother James, 1831–5, RIBA BAL, J. Pennethorne MSS · F. C. Penrose, *The Times* (25 Jan 1888) [letter] · 'Optical corrections', *The dictionary of architecture*, ed. [W. Papworth] (1853–92) · *CGPLA Eng. & Wales* (1888)
Archives RIBA, letters to his brother James
Likenesses photograph, priv. coll.
Wealth at death £53,630 16s. 11d.: resworn probate, Feb 1889, *CGPLA Eng. & Wales* (1888)

Penney, William, Lord Kinloch (1801–1872), judge, son of William Penney, merchant, of Glasgow, and Elizabeth, daughter of David Johnston DD, of North Leith, was born at Glasgow on 8 August 1801 and educated at the university there. On completing his education he entered the office of Alexander Morrison, solicitor, and afterwards spent some time in an accountant's office. In 1824 he was called to the Scottish bar, and he soon gained a large practice, principally in commercial cases. He was twice married: first, on 3 July 1828, to Janet (d. 1839), daughter of Charles Campbell of Argyll; and second, on 5 August 1842, to Louisa Jane, daughter of John Campbell of Kinloch, Perthshire. From the two marriages there were five sons and seven daughters.

In politics Penney was a Conservative, and he was raised to the bench on the recommendation of Lord Derby in May 1858, taking the courtesy title Lord Kinloch. In October 1868 he was appointed to the inner house, or first division, of the Court of Session. An obituarist noted that though 'not without some faults of judicial demeanour, he … was remarkable not only for the elegance of his judgments, but for their generally just practical sense and wisdom.' Penney was also the author of a number of devotional works, some in verse, that enjoyed a measure of contemporary popularity. He died at Hartrigge House, near Jedburgh, on 31 October 1872, and was survived by his wife.

A. H. MILLAR, *rev.* ROBERT SHIELS

Sources F. J. Grant, ed., *The Faculty of Advocates in Scotland, 1532–1943*, Scottish RS, 145 (1944) · *Journal of Jurisprudence*, 16 (1872), 650, 664 · *Law Magazine*, 3rd ser., 1 (1872), 1075 · Irving, *Scots.* · Boase, *Mod. Eng. biog.* · IGI · NA Scot., SC 70/1/160/120
Likenesses wood-engraving (after photograph by Claudet), NPG; repro. in *ILN* (9 Nov 1872)
Wealth at death £23,789 18s. 8d.: inventory, 27 Nov 1872, NA Scot., SC 70/1/160/120

Penney, William George, Baron Penney (1909–1991), mathematical physicist and public servant, was born at 4E Block, Naval Hospital Road, Gibraltar, on 24 June 1909, the only son and eldest of the three children of William Alfred Penney (*b.* 1881), sergeant-major in the Royal Army Ordnance Corps, and his wife, Blanche Evelyn, daughter of Henry Alfred Johnson. Penney's mother had been chief cashier in a Co-operative store before her marriage.

Education, early career, and marriage Penney's father served in a succession of postings in England and overseas, so his son attended a variety of schools in his early years. Young Penney was bright—he may have inherited his gift for numbers from his mother—but he often played truant because, he would say later, he found classes insufficiently demanding. Despite this, in due course he proved a good enough student to qualify for grammar school. It was not to be. His father, an authoritarian at home as at work, had little sympathy with his son's scholarly interests, besides which he knew he could not afford to maintain the boy as a boarder. So young Penney went to technical school, first in Colchester and then in his father's home town, Sheerness, Kent, where he lodged with an aunt. By good fortune, however, at Sheerness Junior Technical School he came under the influence of the principal, Albert Bell, a gifted teacher with a first-class degree in physics. Bell saw the boy's abilities, directed his interests, and helped him become a star student. Penney also flourished as a sportsman, distinguishing himself at boxing, athletics, cricket, and above all on the football field, where he played centre forward in a school team that included several future professional players.

Under Bell's guidance Penney won a Kent county scholarship and a royal scholarship to the Royal College of Science, part of Imperial College, London. This was the beginning of a whirlwind academic career. After just two years (he was granted exemption from the first year of the course) he graduated with a brilliant first in mathematics, in 1929, and after two more years, including a spell in the Netherlands at the University of Groningen, he was awarded his PhD. Thereafter he departed on a Commonwealth Fund fellowship to the University of Wisconsin, where he worked with, among others, the future Nobel prizewinner John Van Vleck, publishing a stream of papers and securing an MA. While in the United States he also toured the American west in a model A Ford he had bought, taking in such scientific landmarks as Carl Anderson's laboratory at the California Institute of Technology, Ernest Lawrence's new cyclotron at Berkeley, and the Oppenheimer brothers' ranch in the New Mexico mountains. It was not purely a scientific journey: he saw Babe Ruth play baseball and, the year being 1932, was able to watch track events at the Los Angeles Olympic games.

Penney returned to Britain in 1933 to take up an 1851 Exhibition senior studentship at Trinity College, Cambridge. Among his referees for this position was Van Vleck, who wrote:

> I regard him as an exceedingly promising research man. He has an unusual gift for absorbing new developments in theoretical physics very rapidly. Also he is a hard and

William George Penney, Baron Penney (1909–1991), by unknown photographer

persistent worker. This is evidenced by the fact that he has written several papers during the time that he has been at Wisconsin. His personality is good. In view of his diligence and especially his native ability in mathematical physics, it is my belief that he could very properly be awarded an 1851 studentship. (1851 Commission records, 2 Feb 1933)

Owen Richardson, another Nobel prizewinner, took a similar view, praising Penney as 'a mathematical physicist of great power and versatility' who had achieved 'a remarkable output for his years' (1851 Commission records, 7 April 1933).

By his mid-twenties, then, William Penney (known generally as Bill) had established an international reputation in a field that was one of the most exciting in science at the time. A mathematical physicist, he was engaged in applying and interpreting the new quantum mechanics with a view to improving the understanding of the structure and behaviour of particular metals and crystals. Of all his papers, mostly written with collaborators, it was the first, 'Quantum mechanics of electrons in crystal lattices' published in the *Proceedings of the Royal Society of London* in 1931 with the Dutchman R. de L. Kronig, that acquired the most lasting renown. Variants of the mathematical model it set out are still in use. Other papers in the early 1930s were pathfinding, such as those relating to the photoelectric effect in thin metallic films and to the polarization of light emitted from atoms excited by electron collision. At Wisconsin and Cambridge his interest turned further towards chemistry and he published a series of papers contributing to the development of the theory of bonds. While still at Cambridge he was invited to give a course of lectures on quantum mechanics to chemists at Imperial and this grew into a monograph, *The Quantum Theory of Valency* (1935), which proved to be his only book. (In chemistry valency relates to the power of atoms to combine.) He was awarded a PhD by the University of Cambridge in 1935 and a DSc by the University of London in 1936.

In 1936 Penney became for a short time Stokes student at Pembroke College, Cambridge, but later the same year he returned to Imperial College full time as assistant professor of mathematics, a post he held until 1945. He was twenty-seven years old and on 27 July the previous year had married Adele Minnie Elms (1913–1945), daughter of Percy Orrin Elms, of Queensborough, Kent. Penney and his wife had known each other since Sheerness days. They had two sons, Martin (*b*. 1938) and Christopher (*b*. 1941).

Many of the characteristics that were to determine Penney's future career were by this time already evident. He was a first-class mathematician, happiest when he had a problem and a pencil and paper to solve it, but he was also a natural interpreter and teacher with a gift for explaining his very complex subject to undergraduates and lay people. In this he was helped by a remarkably easy manner. Though his background was humble he had no chip on his shoulder; on the contrary, he enjoyed throughout his life a rare ability to deal as an equal with anybody he encountered, from prime ministers to private soldiers. Nor did he have what is known as 'side'. If he had a fault in his professional relationships it was a low boredom threshold; confronted with a problem that challenged nothing but his patience, he would allow his mind to wander. Subordinates found, later in his career, that the best way to engage his attention at such moments was to find some mathematical complication to the matter in hand.

War and the atom bomb On the outbreak of the Second World War, Penney registered as available for scientific war work, but heard nothing for several months. Then one day, he recalled later,

> I met Sir Geoffrey Taylor, a world authority on fluid mechanics, and he told me he was being asked by government departments lots of questions about explosions and that sort of thing. He could not deal with all the questions and therefore asked me to have a go at the pressure wave caused by an explosion under water. (Cathcart, 30)

It was a fateful meeting, for by joining Taylor's physics of explosives committee, known as Physex, Penney entered on a career of public service that was to dominate his life for twenty-seven years. For Physex he studied and interpreted the results of both laboratory experiments and real explosions, including bomb attacks in the field, and before long he was an authority on blast waves. This led to other war work. When in 1943 the D-day planners began to contemplate the possibility of improvising a harbour on the French coast—this became the Mulberry harbour—they turned to Penney for an analysis of the physics of sea waves. The result was the Bombardon breakwaters, long steel cylinders that floated on the surface and were weighted in such a way as to absorb wave energy. These

proved successful, but by then Penney was on his way to join the Manhattan Project.

In great secrecy work was under way in 1944 at a number of places in the United States to develop the nuclear fission bomb, with Britain involved as junior partner. Sir Geoffrey Taylor, acting as a consultant, had visited the laboratory at Los Alamos where the weapon was being designed and had seen a role for Penney. Once again this was to do with waves: the bomb would generate blast waves on an unprecedented scale and Penney had experience and knowledge in this field that no one in the United States could match. Though Imperial College, where he was still teaching, was reluctant to release him, Taylor was adamant and in June 1944 Penney travelled out to New Mexico.

At the Los Alamos laboratory, under the direction of J. Robert Oppenheimer, many of the world's leading physicists had been assembled to tackle the fundamental problems entailed in the design of a fission weapon. Among them were Enrico Fermi, Hans Bethe, Edward Teller, John von Neumann, and Emilio Segre, while the small British team included Otto Frisch, Rudolf Peierls, Klaus Fuchs, and for a short time Sir James Chadwick. One of Penney's first tasks there was to lecture on the science of bomb damage. Peierls described the occasion:

> His presentation was in a scientific, matter-of-fact style, with his usual brightly smiling face; many of the Americans had not been exposed to such a detailed and realistic discussion of casualties, and he was nicknamed, by Viktor Weisskopf, 'the smiling killer'. (C. R. Peierls, *Bird of Passage: Recollections of a Physicist*, 1985, 201)

The label did not stick, and Penney's new colleagues soon came to respect and like him.

By late 1944 the team was pursuing in parallel two designs for the fission weapon. The first, with the uranium isotope 235 as its fissionable material, would employ the gun method of detonation. The weapon dropped on Hiroshima, known as Thin Man, was of this kind. The second design used plutonium and would be detonated in a different way: by implosion. A quantity of plutonium alloy would be placed at the centre of a ball of conventional high explosive, which would then be detonated. The inward blast would crush the plutonium until it reached a supercritical state, unleashing the chain reaction. Fat Man (or Fat Boy), used at Nagasaki, was a plutonium bomb. Successful implosion required a uniform convergent wave, in itself a considerable scientific challenge, and Penney, as an expert in the mathematics of waves, was inevitably drawn into this work. Looking back later on his Los Alamos period, he wrote: 'I spent about half of my time working on some of the scientific phenomena going into the bomb and the other half on scientific phenomena going outwards' (Cathcart, 35).

As the actual use of the weapons drew closer, however, it was the outward matters that came to dominate for Penney and he became an important figure. General Leslie Groves, overall director of the Manhattan Project, wrote later of the final preparations for the atomic attacks on Japan:

Throughout the life of the project, vital decisions were reached only after the most careful consideration and discussion with the men I thought were able to offer the soundest advice. Generally, for this operation, they were Oppenheimer, Von Neumann, Penney, Parsons and Ramsey. (Cathcart, 37)

For a few weeks, then, Penney found himself in the innermost councils of the project, and indeed he was a member of the committee which chose the Japanese cities to be attacked. His calculations about the effects of the weapon were greatly assisted by the Trinity test of 16 July 1945, when an implosion-type weapon was detonated in the New Mexico desert. Though he designed some of the measuring equipment that was used (notable for its simplicity) he did not witness this first atomic explosion. He had been supposed to watch from an aeroplane but unfavourable weather left him stranded at the airbase.

On the eve of the attacks on Japan he was sent to the Pacific island of Tinian, from where the atomic raids were mounted, to be on hand for last-minute adjustments. The British government, meanwhile, had named him alongside Group Captain Leonard Cheshire VC as one of its official observers for the operation. In controversial circumstances they were excluded from the first flight but on 9 August they boarded a plane shadowing the mission to Nagasaki. Penney later described watching the city disappear in dust and smoke. 'All of us were in a state of emotional shock. We realized that a new age had begun and that possibly we had all made some contribution to raising a monster that would consume us all' (Cathcart, 38). Soon he was on the ground in Hiroshima and Nagasaki, conducting field studies with a view to calculating the yield of the two weapons. His method was characteristically simple: he made a large collection of bent poles, crushed cans, and dished metal panels and took them back with him to London (where customs officials were astonished at the contents of his luggage). From these he was able to deduce the force of the explosions, although the calculations were still approximate and he would return to the problem several times in later life to refine them.

With the war over, Penney's career stood for a time in flux. His wife, Adele, had died on 18 April 1945, having suffered from postnatal depression since the birth of their second son, and he had arranged for the two boys to be cared for in Wales. Now that he was back in London they rejoined him, but Penney had decisions to make. The United States government, it seems, wanted to recruit him permanently for Los Alamos, so valuable was his expertise to them. Imperial College wanted him, as did Oxford University, which offered him a chair in mathematics. So too did the British government. It was C. P. Snow, the novelist and civil service commissioner, who suggested to Penney that he should become chief superintendent of armament research, running a large guns-and-bombs empire based at Fort Halstead in Kent and embracing stations at Woolwich and a dozen other places around the country. Normally such a post would have no interest for an academic scientist, but Snow had an ulterior motive. Britain, he said, was likely to make an atomic bomb of its own and the government wanted Penney in this job, ready to play his part. Penney recalled later: 'Snow said, "Look, you must come into the Armament Research Department, just in case. Will you do it?"' (Cathcart, 40).

This invitation was a reflection of the stature Penney had acquired both as an atomic weapons scientist and as a guide to policy makers. In both capacities he was known for combining imagination with pragmatism, for seeking simple solutions to problems, and for plain talk. Of the dozen or so senior Britons who worked at Los Alamos he stood out as the best candidate for the post Snow envisaged, just as he was the one the Americans most wanted to keep. Penney, however, had qualms. He was aware of the moral implications of the weapon and like most of his Manhattan Project colleagues was uncomfortable with them. He had seen Nagasaki bombed and had walked the devastated streets afterwards. He knew what happened to people, houses, hospitals, and schools, and on what scale, and he viewed the possibility of future nuclear war with horror. But he was also loyal and patriotic. If the British government believed that this weapon was needed for the defence of the country and the empire, and that his help was necessary to make it, then he felt he had no choice. His appointment as chief superintendent of armament research was announced on 1 January 1946. He was appointed OBE and elected FRS later the same year.

The Attlee government's stance on the atom bomb was no less ambivalent. While it supported the efforts under way to establish UN control of all aspects of atomic energy, it felt at the same time that since such efforts had only a small chance of success it must proceed in secrecy with plans for a British weapon. As a first step, therefore, in December 1945 it commissioned the building of a large pile, or reactor, at Windscale; this would be at the heart of a complex of factories producing fissionable materials for bombs. The next step, authorizing the creation of the team and the facilities to design and build a working weapon, was deferred, which meant that Penney was left in limbo.

Penney was none the less extremely busy. For one thing he had married, on 3 November 1945, the nurse who had cared for his sons; she was (Eleanor) Joan Quennell (b. 1905), daughter of George Quennell, of Brentwood, Essex. It was to be a long and happy union. For another he was recruited by the American government as a consultant to advise on the first peacetime nuclear tests, at Bikini atoll in the Pacific Ocean in July 1946. The first of these tests gave Penney an opportunity to demonstrate his particular blend of intuition and inventiveness. Many elaborate arrangements had been made to measure the yield of the bomb, but he noticed that most of them required it to explode perfectly on target. As a precaution, therefore, he had 1000 jerrycans scattered over the test site. The bomb fell off target and many of the more sophisticated devices failed to function, but Penney, by measuring the effects on his cans, was able to provide adequate readings.

Until the spring of 1947 Penney worked mostly on the analysis of the Bikini tests for the Americans. This was seen as important by the British government, not least because almost all other aspects of atomic co-operation with the USA had ended when the McMahon Act was passed by congress in 1946. Thus Penney personally kept contact alive. In June 1947, however, having finally received the official go-ahead to begin work on a British atomic bomb, he set up a secret programme within his department under the cover name Basic High Explosive Research. While he employed a few other veterans of Los Alamos as consultants (notably Klaus Fuchs), the team he built was almost entirely drawn from the staff of the department or recruited through the civil service from industry and the university graduate stream. He proved a very shrewd judge of men. The work was initially shared between Fort Halstead and Woolwich, where it took place in buildings that were fenced off for additional security, while field tests of conventional explosives were carried out at Foulness on the Essex marshes. The chosen model for the bomb was the Nagasaki design, perceived to be more powerful and to have the greater potential for development.

For the first couple of years the team's priority was to develop the electronics and ordnance necessary for successful implosion. The bomb, a sphere 5 feet in diameter, would be simultaneously detonated at thirty-two points around its surface by a powerful electrical current. This would initiate inward blast waves in the sphere, which would be altered and shaped into a single, spherical convergent wave by the use of lenses of slow explosive, so that the plutonium core would be compressed in an even, symmetrical fashion. These tasks, undertaken without American assistance, took British weapons science into new territory.

Penney's role was primarily administrative, and he found the Whitehall battles about resources and recruitment wearisome, particularly as he was hamstrung by excessive secrecy (for a time not even the whole cabinet was allowed to know of the project's existence). His burdens grew when, in 1949, it was decided that his team should also be responsible for making the inner, radioactive components of the weapon. A complete new factory capable of handling these materials was required, and the result was the atomic weapons establishment at Aldermaston. While Penney disliked the bureaucratic side of management he had no problem with his other responsibilities of strategy and leadership. His command of the science enabled him to keep a clear-sighted view of the progress of the project, while his personal gifts of motivation were formidable. Even junior scientists on his staff found him popping up at their sides, wearing his genial smile, asking shrewd, helpful questions, and offering encouragement rather than criticism. A square-built man, 5 feet 10 inches tall, he had something about him—perhaps the boyish quiff of hair, perhaps the leather elbow patches and knitted sweaters—that suggested an eternal undergraduate, with all the enthusiasm and open-mindedness which that implied. His staff were in no

doubt about his scientific ability and they knew he was on their side. His popularity was enhanced by a readiness to swap jokes and talk about the latest sporting events, and he joined in the odd staff cricket game. These qualities did not dim, and became all the more vital, as time passed and timetables grew ever tighter.

The project had its set-backs. In 1950 the heart of the weapon had to be redesigned because of unforeseen problems in the arming process. Penney oversaw the changes, which substantially raised the stakes for his team: no longer a faithful copy of the Nagasaki weapon, their bomb had become an experimental design. In the same year Fuchs confessed to spying for the Soviet Union both at Los Alamos and in Britain. This was a blow to Penney, who had made considerable use of the German-born physicist, but more important was the damage the affair did to Anglo-American relations. It came at a moment when it seemed that atomic co-operation was about to resume, which would have lightened Penney's load considerably. The Fuchs affair put paid to that.

After a hectic final phase of preparation, the British bomb was tested in the Monte Bello Islands off north-west Australia on 2 October 1952. The trial, code-named operation Hurricane, was a fittingly torrid climax to five difficult years: the site was extremely remote and problematic; relations there between the scientists and the Royal Navy (which provided the necessary task force) were often poor, and the weather, which was all important, proved mercurial. Penney supervised the final phase and his good humour and confidence contributed significantly to a success that was somewhat against the odds. Within hours of the explosion he received a personal message of congratulation from Winston Churchill, the prime minister, and within days he was informed that he would be made KBE.

The Atomic Energy Authority After operation Hurricane the UK Atomic Energy Authority (UKAEA) was created, drawing nuclear energy, weapons, and research together in a single body, and Penney became member for weapons development. He and his wife settled in an official house close to the Aldermaston site and through the rest of the 1950s he oversaw an ambitious programme of work. Besides turning the prototype into a production bomb for the RAF his department also refined the design and developed alternative models, and from 1954 onwards turned its hand to creating a British hydrogen bomb. For this last task Penney had the assistance of William Cook, who ran the programme on a day-to-day basis. Up to 1956 Penney was heavily involved in further nuclear tests in Australia, which took place against a background of growing international anxiety about fall-out. Both behind the scenes and in presenting the issues to the Australian public his gift for straight talking proved invaluable, so much so that before one series in 1956 the high commissioner in Canberra begged for him to be allowed to come out early and give press interviews:

> Sir William Penney has established in Australia a reputation which is quite unique … His appearance, his obvious sincerity and honesty, and the general impression he gives that he would rather be digging his garden—and would be,

but for the essential nature of his work—have made him a public figure of some magnitude in Australian eyes.
(Arnold, *A Very Special Relationship*, 182–3)

If the British atom bomb had been a success against the odds for Penney and his team, the H-bomb was their triumph. Tests over the Pacific in 1957 and 1958, near Malden and Christmas islands, confirmed that Britain had developed a fusion weapon with a megaton-range explosive yield. Though the United States and the Soviet Union had got there first, Britain had achieved this at remarkable speed, at a fraction of the cost, and with far fewer test explosions. Soon afterwards the United States authorities finally agreed to resume co-operation in the nuclear weapons field, prompting Macmillan, the prime minister, to acknowledge the 'tremendous achievement' of the Aldermaston scientists and engineers, whose successes were a 'major factor' in persuading the Americans to heal the breach (Arnold, *A Very Special Relationship*, 230). Penney played an important part in the subsequent negotiations, which laid the foundations for a unique and enduring nuclear defence partnership.

For Macmillan, Penney became a trusted adviser, briefing the cabinet on nuclear matters and also attending summit meetings with presidents Eisenhower and Kennedy. He led a British delegation to the conference in Geneva in 1958 that first explored the possibility of a nuclear test ban and in the early 1960s he threw himself into the negotiations for a comprehensive test ban treaty. He believed passionately that such a treaty would be verifiable and that it would slow dramatically, if not halt completely, the East–West nuclear arms race. When, through lack of trust, the talks ended with only the partial test ban treaty of 1963, Penney was bitterly disappointed. Though it was a substantial achievement to have ended atmospheric testing by the big powers, the option of underground tests remained open, and was taken up.

In 1957 Penney was embroiled in the aftermath of the Windscale fire, the world's first serious reactor accident, which led to a release of radioactivity into the atmosphere. Three days after it took place he was appointed to lead an inquiry into what had gone wrong. The timing was awkward for him, since an important H-bomb test in the Pacific was imminent, but he was the only senior UKAEA member available. The case was urgent, so the panel conducted an intensive investigation at Windscale and produced a report in less than a fortnight. Though it placed no blame on individuals it was no whitewash; serious procedural and organizational faults were identified, and important reforms recommended. Macmillan wrote of the report's 'scrupulous honesty and even ruthlessness' (Arnold, *Windscale*, 83). Despite great public anxiety, however, and contrary to the wishes of the UKAEA, the report was not published. This decision, taken by Macmillan mainly for reasons of international diplomacy, rendered the report and Penney's role in it suspect; some thought he had been involved in a cover-up. Thirty years passed before the papers were made public and the doubts erased. Though he was no specialist in reactors, Penney had applied his customary scientific rigour to the task

and, given the limited time available, produced a verdict that was both clear-eyed and fair.

In 1959 Penney succeeded Sir John Cockcroft as UKAEA member for research; two years later he became deputy chairman of the authority and in 1964 he was made chairman, serving until 1967. This was a period of many difficult decisions, in which the shape and scale of Britain's nuclear energy programme were laid down. 'His was a voice of moderation', wrote Lord Sherfield, his predecessor as chairman, of their days together. 'Then, as later, he tried to avoid confrontation and controversy and to work for consensus' (Sherfield, 294–5).

Imperial College and retirement On his retirement from the UKAEA in 1967 Penney was created a life peer as Baron Penney of East Hendred, the village near Wantage, then in Berkshire but later in Oxfordshire, where he and Lady Penney had settled in 1963. No politician, he rarely attended the House of Lords and even more rarely cast a vote. In the same year, 1967, he accepted the position of rector of Imperial College, London, a job which proved considerably more demanding than he or anyone else anticipated. The late 1960s were turbulent times for the universities and before long Penney found his gifts of leadership and diplomacy taxed to the limit in keeping the college on an even keel. 'The students were sometimes uncontrollable', he wrote later, 'the heads of departments were bewildered and angry, the rest of the staff, including the technicians, wanted a say in how everything was run' (Sherfield, 296). He introduced significant reforms to make the administration more open and flexible, while at the same time directing an expansion of the college and keeping the finances in order. Despite the many trials he remained rector for six years instead of the planned five, bowing out in September 1973. The college's Penney Laboratory was named in his honour.

Penney received many academic honours and prizes, including honorary doctorates from the universities of Melbourne, Durham, Oxford, Bath, and Reading, and the City and Guilds of London Institute; honorary fellowships of St Catherine's College, Oxford, the Manchester College of Science and Technology, Trinity College, Cambridge, and Pembroke College, Cambridge; the Rumford medal of the Royal Society; the Glazebrook medal and prize; the James Alfred Ewing medal; and the Kelvin gold medal. He was made a member of the Order of Merit in 1969, and a freeman of the City of London in 1970. In retirement he played golf, fished, grew vegetables in his garden at East Hendred, and enjoyed the company of his grandchildren. He kept an office at Aldermaston for a time, returning occasionally to work on old problems that still fascinated him, notably the yields at Hiroshima and Nagasaki.

In 1985 Penney emerged from retirement to appear before an Australian royal commission into the nuclear weapons tests in Australia. The climate of opinion at the time was extremely hostile to all things nuclear. In Australia there were suspicions that the tests had been negligently conducted and had placed civilians, notably Aboriginal people, in danger, possibly causing deaths. In Britain there was concern that servicemen involved in the tests had been needlessly exposed to radiation and that some might have contracted illnesses and died as a result. Despite his advanced years Penney testified at hearings in London and because of his past seniority he in some respects bore the brunt of these public anxieties. The questioning was aggressive and the press coverage, both in Britain and Australia, was highly unsympathetic to his case, which was that due care was taken and that the tests conformed to the internationally accepted safety standards of the time. Alarming anecdotal evidence suggesting recklessness and incompetence was given much wider currency.

In its final report the commission broadly accepted Penney's view and reserved its principal criticisms for the Australian governments of the 1950s, but this brought little comfort to a man left crushed by what he felt had been an assault on his reputation and his integrity. Lady Penney believed that the experience prompted depression and possibly a nervous breakdown, and others close to him agreed that the affair took a toll on his health, possibly shortening his life. It was in this late and unhappy period that he burnt what personal papers he had. In January 1991 he was diagnosed as suffering from cancer and a few weeks later, on 3 March, he died at his home, Orchard House, Cat Street, East Hendred, Oxfordshire. He was cremated on 8 March and his ashes were taken to his home. A memorial service was held at St Augustine's, East Hendred, on 15 March.

Although Penney was an affable, often amusing man, held in great affection by those who knew him, he did not make close friends easily. His choice of a quiet retirement reflected a self-sufficiency and a preference for privacy which were present throughout his life. After the first British nuclear test in 1952 he had been lionized as a national hero and a genius, but he told a colleague at the time that he did not want to be remembered for making an atomic bomb. He knew better than most, after all, what this weapon could do. His instinct was sound, for the popularity soon evaporated and when he eventually returned to the limelight in 1985 it was in cruelly adverse circumstances. Under pressure before the royal commission he defended not just his record but the fundamental choice of his life:

> I thought we were going to have a nuclear war. The only hope I saw was that there should be a balance between East and West. That is why I did this job, not to make money. I did not make any money. What I really wanted to do was to be a professor. (Cathcart, 276)

At that time little was publicly known about his career, but more emerged in the 1990s and it showed what his close colleagues had always known. Penney was a public servant of consistent and high integrity—not perhaps a smooth man, but thoughtful, calm, and direct. Though he has been rightly described as a reluctant weaponeer, his gifts as a scientist and leader of men were indispensable to the success of the first British atomic bomb project, and he contributed enormously to subsequent weapons development (both in their time very high priorities in British government policy), while in later life at the UKAEA and at Imperial College he proved to have a wise head and a safe pair of hands. BRIAN CATHCART

Sources B. Cathcart, *Test of greatness: Britain's struggle for the atom bomb* (1994) · Lord Sherfield, *Memoirs FRS*, 39 (1994), 283–302 · M. Gowing and L. Arnold, *Independence and deterrence: Britain and atomic energy, 1945–1952*, 2 vols. (1974) · L. Arnold, *A very special relationship: British atomic weapon trials in Australia* (1987) · L. Arnold, *Windscale 1957: anatomy of a nuclear accident* (1992) · L. Arnold, *Britain and the H bomb* (2001) · F. M. Szasz, *British scientists and the Manhattan Project* (1992) · *The Times* (6 March 1991) · *The Independent* (6 March 1991) · Burke, *Peerage* · *WWW*, 1991–5 · private information (2004) · *CGPLA Eng. & Wales* (1991) · file on W. G. Penney, ICL, Archive of the Royal Commission for the Exhibition of 1851

Archives ICL, college archives, corresp. and papers | CAC Cam., corresp. with Sir Edward Bullard · CAC Cam., corresp. with Sir James Chadwick · ICL, Archive of the Royal Commission for the Exhibition of 1851, file on W. G. Penney · ICL, college archives, corresp. with Lord Jackson · Institution of Mechanical Engineers, London, corresp. with Lord Hinton · PRO, CAB 130, AB1, AB16, DEFE16, DEFE32, ADM 116, NRB | FILM BFI NFTVA | SOUND BBC sound archives

Likenesses two photographs, 1932–52, repro. in Cathcart, *Test of greatness* · photograph, *c*.1967, RS · photograph, *c*.1967, repro. in *The Times* · photograph, repro. in *The Independent* · photographs, Hult. Arch. [*see illus.*]

Wealth at death £183,026: probate, 7 May 1991, *CGPLA Eng. & Wales*

Pennie, John Fitzgerald (1782–1848), playwright and poet, was born on 25 March 1782 at the vicarage, East Lulworth, Dorset, the son of Robert Pennie and his wife Hannah, *née* Gould. In the sixteenth and seventeenth centuries the Pennie family had been socially important, but were ruined by their 'loyalty to the Stuart cause and the Roman Catholic religion' (Davies, 7). Pennie's parents were probably in service at the vicarage. He lacked a regular education, and, self-taught, at fifteen he wrote a tragedy, *The Unhappy Shepherdess*, based on a tale in Robert Greene's *History of Dorastus and Fawnia*. An appreciative neighbour, Captain Hay Forbes, directed him to London, but the manager of Covent Garden Theatre advised him to go home and write another tragedy.

After work as a solicitor's clerk in Bristol, and as an usher in a private school at Honiton, Pennie joined a travelling company of actors in the west of England. About 1810 he married Cordelia Elizabeth (1773/4–1848), orphan daughter of Jerome Whitfield, a London attorney, and presented a comedy in the theatre at Shaftesbury, with the mother and sister of Edmund Kean. The venture ruined him, and he suffered extreme poverty. In 1814 a company at Chepstow gave a benefit performance of his *Gonzanga*, published in October that year. Other theatrical engagements followed, but he quarrelled with all his managers. His tragedy *Ethelwolf*, published in 1821, was performed at Weymouth in 1826, and *The Varangian, or, Masonic Honor* was played with success at Southampton, but neither *Ethelred the Usurper*, written in 1817, nor *The Eve of St Bruce*, written in 1832, was performed.

Meanwhile Pennie had opened a school at Lulworth, and published in 1817 *The Royal Minstrel*. In the advertisement to this epic poem on the story of David, an impressive Miltonic pastiche, he describes himself as 'labouring under every possible disadvantage'. The school failed. In 1828 he moved to Kesworth Cottage, near Wareham, and began to write in the *Dorset County Chronicle* and in the *West of England Magazine*. Friends helped him to build a cottage at Stoborough, where he lived for the rest of his life. He named it Rogvald, after his second epic, published in 1823, an ambitious work with a west Mercian setting.

Pennie's autobiography, *The Tale of a Modern Genius*, published in 1827 under the pseudonym Sylvaticus, reveals a bitter sense of ill-usage and neglect. His other published works included *The Garland of Wild Roses*, poems for children (1822). To provide for his son and grandchildren he contracted debts, from which he had just cleared himself when he died at Rogvald on 13 July 1848. His wife had died two days previously. They were buried at East Lulworth.

BERTHA PORTER, rev. JOHN D. HAIGH

Sources Sylvaticus [J. F. Pennie], *The tale of a modern genius*, 3 vols. (1827), passim · G. J. Davies, 'John Fitzgerald Pennie: "Sylvaticus" (1782–1848)', *Proceedings of the Dorset Natural History and Archaeological Society*, 118 (1996), 7–12 · *GM*, 2nd ser., 31 (1849), 656–9 · *Dorset County Chronicle* (20 July 1848) · J. F. Pennie, *The royal minstrel, or, The witcheries of Endor* (1817)
Archives BL, letters to Royal Literary Fund, loan 96
Wealth at death not wealthy

Pennington. *See also* Penington.

Pennington, Anne Elizabeth (1934–1981), Slavonic philologist, was born on 31 March 1934 at Maarama, Pigeon Lane, Herne Bay, Kent, the second daughter of Alan Mather Pennington (1889–1955), manufacturer, and his wife, Janet Winifred, *née* Aitken (1894–1966), teacher. She was educated at Simon Langton Girls' Grammar School, Canterbury, and Lady Margaret Hall, Oxford. She gained first-class honours in French and Russian (1955), the diploma in Slavonic studies with distinction (1956), and completed a DPhil thesis entitled 'The language of Kotoshikhin' (1964). In 1959 she became a fellow of Lady Margaret Hall and in 1960 was appointed to a university lectureship in Russian. In 1980 she was elected to the chair of comparative Slavonic philology, which was combined with a professorial fellowship at St Hilda's College. In the same year Lady Margaret Hall made her an honorary fellow.

Anne Pennington's arrival in Oxford in 1952 happily coincided with the election of Boris Unbegaun to the newly created chair which she herself subsequently held. It was chiefly under his guidance that she developed her scholarly interests and skills. She was, like Unbegaun, a traditional philologist with a prime interest in establishing the history of language through the study of texts. Her major work was the comprehensive study of the Russian chancellery language of the seventeenth century based on Grigory Kotoshikhin's 1666 account of Russia in the reign of Tsar Alexis Mikhailovich (Kotošixin, *O Rossii v carstvovanie Alekseja Mixajloviča*, 1980). It admirably complements the work of Unbegaun (to whose memory it is dedicated) on the chancellery language of the preceding century (*La langue russe au 16e siècle*, 1935).

From the 1950s Anne Pennington developed wideranging interests in the languages and culture of the Slavs, with periods of study in Yugoslavia, Poland, Czechoslovakia, and Bulgaria. She was particularly drawn to the Balkan Slav countries, where she was a frequent visitor. She made an important contribution to the study of south Slavonic music manuscripts of the late medieval period. Her principal achievements in this field were the discovery of previously unknown works of Stefan the Serb, the attribution of a number of manuscripts to the scriptorium of the Putna monastery in Moldavia, and the establishment of the pronunciation norm of Serbian church singing in the fifteenth century. Her journal articles on the subject are collected in *Music in Moldavia, 16th Century* (ed. T. Moisescu, 1985).

Shortly before her death Pennington initiated a project to catalogue the Cyrillic manuscripts held in British collections and this was subsequently completed by one of her former students (R. Cleminson, compiler, *The Anne Pennington Catalogue: a Union Catalogue of Cyrillic Manuscripts in British and Irish Collections*, 1988).

Anne Pennington's concern with the culture of the Balkan Slavs was not only academic: she was a sensitive translator of contemporary Serbian and Macedonian poetry and made available in English the work of Vasko Popa (*Selected Poems*, 1969, and other volumes), Blaže Koneski, and others. She also translated, with Andrew Harvey, Macedonian folk-songs (*Songs from Macedonia*, 1978) and, with Peter Levi, Serbian folk-epic poems (*Marko the Prince: Serbo-Croat Heroic Songs*, 1984). On her travels she made field-recordings of Yugoslav folk music and collected Balkan costumes, jewellery, and musical instruments. She was also a skilled performer of Balkan dance. Though firm in her Anglican faith, she took an active interest in the Eastern Orthodox church, its liturgy and music, and sang regularly in the choir of the Greek and Russian Orthodox church in Oxford.

Apart from her teaching and writing, Pennington contributed to the advancement of Slavonic studies in other ways: she served on the international commission on Slavonic music manuscripts (from 1971) and the international committee of Slavists (from 1978), and was also an editor of *Oxford Slavonic Papers* (from 1979).

Modest and unassuming in manner, Anne Pennington had great fortitude and warmth of personality. She possessed a natural moral integrity and authority and had also the gift of sympathetic engagement with all kinds of people. Professionally, she was a dedicated scholar, an inspiring teacher, and a staunchly loyal upholder of the institutions she served. In her personal life she was genial, generous, and unstintingly hospitable to her wide and devoted circle of colleagues and friends in many countries. Anne Pennington died of cancer on 27 May 1981 in the John Radcliffe Hospital, Oxford. Her funeral took place in the chapel of Lady Margaret Hall on 2 June and, after cremation, her ashes were interred in Wolvercote cemetery, Oxford on 10 June.

I. P. FOOTE

Sources J. L. I. Fennell and I. P. Foote, 'Professor Anne Pennington', *Slavonic and East European Review*, 59 (1981), 565–71 [incl. bibliography of her publications] · M. O'Brien, 'Professor A. E. Pennington', *Brown Book* (1981), 24–8 · *The Times* (2 June 1981) · T. Moisescu, ed., *Music in Moldavia, 16th Century* (1985), afterword, 268–75 • personal knowledge (2004) • private information (2004) • *Oxford University Calendar*

Archives U. Oxf., Taylor Institution, MSS | SOUND U. Oxf., Taylor Institution, tape-recordings Yugoslav folk-music

Likenesses photograph, *c*.1975, repro. in R. Cleminson, ed., *The Anne Pennington catalogue: a union catalogue of Cyrillic manuscripts in British and Irish collections* (1988), frontispiece

Wealth at death £152,452: probate, 18 Aug 1981, CGPLA Eng. & Wales

Pennington, Elizabeth (1732–1759), poet, was born in the curate's house of the parish of St Mary and St Benedict, Huntingdon, in whose church she was baptized on 12 December 1732. Her father, the Revd John Pennington, who was curate, had married Mrs Elizabeth Torkington on 10 February 1732, and Elizabeth was their first child; her brother John was born on 17 March 1735. John Pennington ceased to be active as a curate in Huntingdon from 1751, and the family seems to have moved to London. Pennington's friendship with the poet Martha Ferrar, also born in Huntingdon, in 1729, outlasted this move and the two were commended in John Duncombe's *Feminead* (1754), which says that they both lived in 'H-nt-n' (Huntingdon). Ferrar was the main beneficiary of Pennington's will.

In London, Pennington became a friend of Frances Sheridan and Samuel Richardson. Her 'Ode to a Thrush' appeared in Robert Dodsley's *Collection*, and her 'Ode to Morning' in Alexander Dyce's *Specimens of British Poetesses*. Her most famous poem, 'The Copper Farthing', appeared in Francis Fawkes's and William Woty's *Poetical Calendar* (1763) and in the Dillys' *Repository* (1777); it was written in emulation of John Philips's 'Splendid Shilling' (as was Bramston's 'The Crooked Sixpence'). All are burlesque, but Pennington's ability to write in a learned and heroic style, despite her limited opportunity for education, is remarkable.

Pennington was found dead in her home in February 1759; her body was identified by an undertaker from the neighbourhood and by one 'John Duncombe clerk'—possibly the poet who was a clergyman. They testified on 26 February 1759 that she had been living in the area for six years, either in the parish of St Martin-in-the-Fields or of St Anne's, Westminster. The cause of death was not established but the date was estimated as 13 February.

JULIA GASPER

Sources parish register, Huntingdon, St Mary and St Benedict, Cambs. AS, Huntingdon [baptism] • J. Todd, ed., *A dictionary of British and American women writers, 1660–1800* (1984) • [R. Dodsley and I. Reed], eds., *A collection of poems by several hands*, new edn, 6 vols. (1782); facs. edn with introduction by M. F. Suarez (1997), vol. 5 • will, 4 March 1757, PRO, PROB 11/844, sig. 69

Wealth at death £200 and all clothes to Mrs Packard (*née* Martha Ferrar): will, 4 March 1757, PRO, PROB 11/844, sig. 69

Pennington, Sir Isaac (*bap.* 1745, *d.* 1817), physician and chemist, was born at Longmore in Furness Fell, Lancashire, the son of Paul Pennington, the captain of a merchant ship, and baptized at Colton, Lancashire, on 17 December 1745. He attended Sedbergh grammar school, and then entered St John's College, Cambridge, as a sizar, on 12 August 1762. He became a Lupton scholar on 4

November 1766. He went out as thirteenth wrangler in 1767, one of his examiners being Richard Watson, whom he succeeded as professor of chemistry. He was admitted as a fellow of St John's on 22 March 1768, and continued in this capacity until his death. He was admitted to the faculty fellowship in medicine on 18 October 1775, and thus retained his fellowship; he was president from 1787 to 1802. He graduated MA in 1770, and MD in 1777. He became the professor of chemistry in 1773, and in 1793 resigned, and was appointed regius professor of physic, a post he held until 1813. He was physician to Addenbrooke's Hospital from 1785 until 1817, and was knighted in 1796. He was elected a fellow of the Royal College of Physicians on 29 March 1779, and delivered the Harveian oration in 1783; this remained unpublished. Pennington made no attempt to introduce long overdue reforms to the teaching of medicine in Cambridge, and is perhaps mostly remembered for being challenged to a duel by a colleague, Busick Harwood. It appears that on the pair meeting one morning Pennington said 'Good morning, Sir, B. U. Sick?', to which Harwood is said to have replied 'Sir? I, Sick? I am never better in my life' (Towers, 74). Pennington died at his house in Bridge Street, Cambridge, on 3 February 1817, and is commemorated by a tablet in the chapel of St John's. He never married, and in his will, read on 11 March 1817, he appointed the Revd James Wood (master), the Revd Laurence Palk Baker (fellow), and the Revd Charles Blick (fellow and bursar), as his executors. He bequeathed his property in St Sepulchre's parish, Cambridge, to the master—this included his house in Bridge Street. He made a number of small legacies to servants and friends, but bequeathed the residue of his estate to the college; this included a small anatomical collection formed by the physician Thomas Lawrence. He also founded a number of exhibitions in the college, with a preference to candidates from Hawkshead and Colton near his birthplace in Lancashire.

NORMAN MOORE, *rev.* CLAIRE L. NUTT

Sources Munk, *Roll* • Venn, *Alum. Cant.* • T. Baker, *History of the college of St John the Evangelist, Cambridge*, ed. J. E. B. Mayor, 2 vols. (1869) • private information (1895) • H. Rolleston, 'Some worthies of the Cambridge medical school', *Annals of Medical History*, 8 (1926) • *IGI* • B. Towers, 'Anatomy and physiology in Cambridge before 1850', *Cambridge and its contribution to medicine* [Cambridge 1969], ed. A. Rook (1971), 65–77

Archives Suffolk RO, Bury St Edmunds, letters to Sir Thomas Cullum

Likenesses coloured pen drawing (after watercolour), Wellcome L. • oils, St John Cam. • stipple and line engraving, NPG • watercolour, Wellcome L.

Pennington, James (1777–1862), writer on currency and banking, born at Kendal, Westmorland, on 23 February 1777, was the son of William Pennington, a bookseller, and his wife, Agnes Wilson. Educated first at Kendal grammar school, he afterwards became a pupil of John Dalton (1766–1844) of Manchester. Subsequently Pennington worked in business in London. In 1811 he married Mary Anne, eldest daughter of John Harris of Clapham; they had four sons and three daughters.

At the end of 1831 Pennington was appointed to investigate the accounts of the East India Company, but the appointment was cancelled when the administration changed. Thrown out of employment Pennington devoted himself to the study of currency and finance, and attracted the favourable notice of William Huskisson, David Ricardo, and Thomas Tooke. On Tooke's recommendation he joined the Political Economy Club in 1828; he also contributed appendices to Tooke's *Letter to Lord Grenville* (1829), and to his *History of Prices* (2, appx C). When, on the emancipation of slaves in 1833, it became necessary to regulate the currency of the West Indies, Pennington was employed for that purpose by the Treasury, and framed the measures which were adopted. In 1848 he published *The Currency of the British Colonies*, which was printed for official use, and which contains much detail of historical interest.

As early as 1827 Pennington had urged, in a paper submitted to Huskisson, the desirability of some restriction on the issue of notes by the Bank of England. He had further explained his views in a pamphlet addressed to Kirkman Finlay (1840). During the preparation of the Bank Act (1844) he was confidentially consulted by Sir Robert Peel. Though he accepted the principle of that legislation, he was not in entire agreement with Peel, and disapproved of the separation of the banking and issue departments of the Bank of England. From this time until his death he was frequently consulted by the government on currency and finance, on which he was regarded as a leading authority. He died on 23 March 1862 at his home in Clapham Common. His son Arthur Robert became canon of Lincoln and rector of Utterby, Louth.

W. A. S. HEWINS, *rev.* H. C. G. MATTHEW

Sources *The Economist* (19 April 1862) · *The Times* (25 March 1862) · A. R. Pennington, *Recollections of persons and events* (1895) · J. R. McCulloch, *The literature of political economy: a classified catalogue* (1845)

Archives BL, corresp. with Sir Robert Peel, Add. MSS 40543–40610 · Derbys. RO, letters to Sir R. J. Wilmot-Horton

Wealth at death under £3000: probate, 1 July 1862, *CGPLA Eng. & Wales*

Pennington, Sir John (c.1394–1470). *See under* Pennington, John, first Baron Muncaster (*bap.* 1741, *d.* 1813).

Pennington, John, first Baron Muncaster (*bap.* **1741**, *d.* **1813**), army officer and politician, was born in Bath, Somerset, and was baptized in Bath Abbey on 22 May 1741; he was the eldest of the three sons and four daughters of Sir Joseph Pennington, fourth baronet (1718–1793), a landowner, of Muncaster Castle, Cumberland, and Warter Priory, Yorkshire, and his wife, Sarah (*d.* 1783), the daughter and heir of John Moore, an apothecary of Bath. She was long separated from her husband and died at Fulmer, Buckinghamshire, in August 1783. The Penningtons originated in Furness and had settled in Cumberland by the mid-thirteenth century, though they acquired property in Westmorland and Yorkshire by marriage. **Sir John Pennington** (c.1394–1470), soldier, the son and heir of Sir Alan Pennington (*d.* 1415) and his wife, Katherine, the daughter of Sir Richard Preston, fought as a young man at the battle of Agincourt in Lord Harrington's retinue. Later he was a commissioner of array and of the peace in Cumberland

(1427–59) and a warrior in Scotland under his Percy kinsman, the second earl of Northumberland. In 1448 he was captured by the Scots at the battle of the Sark. He sided with the Lancastrians in the Wars of the Roses, allegedly sheltering the fugitive Henry VI at Muncaster, and received from that king the cup preserved there as 'the luck of Muncaster'. In 1412 he married Katherine, the daughter of Sir Thomas Tunstall; they had a son and two daughters. He died on 6 July 1470 and was buried at Muncaster. The baronetcy dated from 1676, with Sir William, who married the heir of Warter. The second baronet, Sir Joseph, married into the Lowther family of Lonsdale, as did his daughter. His elder son, Sir John, who defended Carlisle against the Jacobites in 1745, died unmarried, and was succeeded by his brother Joseph, the father of the subject.

John Pennington was educated at Winchester School (1754–6), then entered the army as ensign in the 3rd foot guards. His military diary for 1758 survives among family papers now in the National Library of Scotland. He became lieutenant and captain in 1762 and transferred to the 2nd regiment as major in 1765. In 1771 he travelled to Spain. In 1773, as lieutenant-colonel of the 73rd foot stationed at Fort George, he met Dr Samuel Johnson and worsted him in a discussion about the respective military merits of Arab warriors and trained troops. In 1775 he left the army when his father moved to Warter and made over Muncaster to him. Relations between the two deteriorated following a dispute over the rental, and the arrangement was cancelled for a year until Pennington married, on 26 September 1778, Penelope (1744–1806), the daughter and heir of James Compton of New York. Their son, Gamel (1780–1788), named after a twelfth-century ancestor, and one of their two daughters predeceased him; the other became countess of Crawford and Balcarres.

Pennington had dabbled in politics before his marriage. He had intended to stand for Carlisle in 1774, and in 1780 he offered himself for Cumberland with government backing but declined a contest. His address suggested that his cousin Sir James Lowther had reneged on a promise of support for him. Instead he was returned for Milborne Port, on the Medlycott interest, on 4 December 1781. This cost him £3000, and was arranged by the prime minister, Lord North. When Rockingham succeeded North, Pennington was offered a place, which he declined, in exchange for giving up his seat. This was negotiated through the duke of Grafton, who had first offered Pennington his patronage in 1775 and threatened to resign office unless something was done for him. Grafton resigned, but, thanks to him, eight months later, on 21 October 1783, Pennington was created an Irish baron; an Irish peerage was thought appropriate as he expected to foreclose on a mortgage on an Irish estate, which was security for a loan, only partly repaid, made by the trustees of his marriage settlement.

An early adherent of Pitt the younger, Muncaster would have preferred to sit for his county, but Lowther continued to keep him out. He considered himself the government's best friend in Cumberland, and in 1789 erected a pyramid at Muncaster Castle to mark the king's recovery from his illness. In the Commons he seconded a successful motion on 20 March 1789 to commemorate the revolution of 1688 and on 14 December 1790 praised the convention with Spain. No later speech is known, but he found a new cause in William Wilberforce's campaign to abolish the slave trade: they had met in the Lake District in 1784. His *Historical Sketches of the Slave Trade and its Effects in Africa* (1792) proved a useful source book for abolitionists, and Wilberforce assured him that they were 'tuned in the same key' (Wilberforce and Wilberforce, 1.68). Muncaster was a teller for abolition in divisions of 1791, 1794, and 1796.

By 1796 Muncaster's constituency had succumbed to a rival interest and he turned to the government for a replacement seat. He was offered Colchester, which he could ill afford while engaged on a Gothic renovation of Muncaster, but he was returned, together with the well-to-do Robert Thornton, who headed the poll and was also linked with Wilberforce. His building activities, which included a choice octagonal library, soon prejudiced his parliamentary attendance, however, and he relied on Wilberforce and the press for political information. He raised 200 volunteer soldiers, or 'mountaineers', in 1798, and he backed Pitt's successor Addington, writing of his approval of peace preliminaries with France in November 1801. Realizing that his neglect would lose him Colchester in 1802, he offered himself at York, only to withdraw. In 1804 he revived his hopes of sitting for Cumberland at the next vacancy, but the Lowther interest withstood him. He lamented Pitt's death, which nevertheless led to his return to parliament for Westmorland, with Lowther's backing conditional on his support for the Grenville ministry. His wife died in an accident on 15 November 1806 while she was out canvassing on his behalf. In spite of his grief, Pennington travelled to Westminster to join Wilberforce in voting to abolish the slave trade in February 1807.

Muncaster's parliamentary seat proved to be secure with Lowther's support, but his interest in politics had waned, and he had to be importuned to attend in support of government. In January 1811 he voted for the regency restrictions only after ascertaining that a rumour of the Lowthers' desertion to opposition was false. His last political gesture was to vote against Catholic relief in the first session of the 1812 parliament. He died at Muncaster Castle on 8 October 1813 and was buried at Muncaster on 15 October. His age at death is incorrectly given as seventy-six on his memorial, one of several to members of his family that he designed himself. Muncaster Castle was his glory: he planted thousands of trees and stocked the demesne with cattle and Yorkshire wold sheep. He was an agricultural improver who imported new ideas or tried his own, such as summer fallows for wheat, feeding potatoes to cattle, growing cabbages and carrots, and using tidal mud and mussels as fertilizers and sea sand to check moss. He arranged for his daughter to have a twenty-one-year lease of Muncaster after his death.

Muncaster was succeeded in the barony by his surviving brother, **Lowther Pennington**, second Baron Muncaster

(1745–1818), army officer. Having been commissioned as an ensign in the Coldstream Guards in 1764, he was promoted lieutenant and captain in 1772, captain and lieutenant-colonel in 1778, colonel in 1783, major-general in 1793, lieutenant-general in 1799, and full general in 1808. His next brother had been killed in a duel, and he himself had killed a fellow officer in another duel at New York over the latter's humming of a tune in 1777. In 1793 he served in Flanders under the duke of York, who informed the king of his overzealous attack on a French battery, which cost his men heavily. The duke found that Pennington was unpopular with the Coldstreams, especially when he furiously insisted on the court-martialling of the regimental adjutant, who was acquitted. His personal bravery was not in question. The 131st foot, of which he was colonel in 1795, was called Pennington's regiment. He took half pay soon afterwards and became colonel of the 10th veteran battalion in 1806. He married, on 13 January 1802, Esther (*d.* 1827), the daughter of Thomas Barry of Clapham, Surrey, and the widow of Captain James Morrison, an infantry officer. Their only son inherited the barony on Pennington's death in London, on 29 July 1818, at his house in Grosvenor Place. He was buried at St George's, Hanover Square.   ROLAND THORNE

Sources J. R. E. Borron, 'John Pennington, 1st Lord Muncaster', *Transactions of the Cumberland and Westmorland Antiquarian and Archaeological Society*, new ser., 66 (1966), 347–68 · J. Brooke, 'Pennington, John', HoP, *Commons, 1754–90* · R. G. Thorne, 'Pennington, Sir John', HoP, *Commons, 1790–1820* · R. I. Wilberforce and S. Wilberforce, *Life of William Wilberforce*, 5 vols. (1838) · *GM*, 1st ser., 83/2 (1813), 405 · *DNB* · W. Whellan, ed., *The history and topography of the counties of Cumberland and Westmoreland* (1860), 490 · GEC, *Peerage* · *The later correspondence of George III*, ed. A. Aspinall, 5 vols. (1962–70), vol. 2, pp. 879, 905, 920, 923 · A. H. Burne, *The noble duke of York* (1949), 48, 59–60 · J. Foster, *Pedigree of Sir Josslyn Pennington, fifth Baron Muncaster of Muncaster and ninth baronet* (1878) · bound MSS repertory of Pennington references for the 15th century and later, Society of Genealogists

Archives Cumbria AS · NL Scot., corresp., diaries, and papers · U. Hull, Brynmor Jones L., Warter estate papers | Bodl. Oxf., corresp. with William Wilberforce

Likenesses oils, Muncaster Castle, Cumbria

Wealth at death £27,895: PRO, death duty registers, IR 26/590 · under £8000—Sir Lowther Pennington: will, 8 Aug 1818, PRO, death duty registers, IRC 26/752

Pennington, Lowther, second Baron Muncaster (1745–1818). *See under* Pennington, John, first Baron Muncaster (*bap.* 1741, *d.* 1813).

Pennington, Montagu (1762–1849), writer and literary editor, was born in December 1762 at Tunstall, Kent, the younger of the two sons of Thomas Pennington DD (1728–1802), rector of Tunstall, and Margaret, *née* Carter (1725–1798), the youngest child of Nicolas Carter DD (1688–1774) and sister of the classical scholar and author Elizabeth *Carter (1717–1806). Montagu Pennington was educated at home by his aunt Elizabeth. His baptismal name was derived from her friend the well-known bluestocking Elizabeth Montagu, whose many kindnesses to him included taking him on a four-month visit to Paris in 1776. On 23 October 1777 he matriculated at Trinity College, Oxford, and graduated BA in 1781 and MA in 1784.

Having taken holy orders Pennington was appointed in 1789 to the living of Sutton, near Dover. For nearly twenty years, beginning about 1788, he resided in Deal with his aunt in a house she later bequeathed to him. He was curate-in-charge of the adjoining parish of Walmer. Being fond of travel, he was visiting Lille in 1791 when, according to a letter from Elizabeth Carter to Elizabeth Montagu, the French Revolution drove him to the Netherlands (*Letters from Mrs. Elizabeth Carter*, 3.331).

Pennington became vicar of Westwell near Ashwell in Kent in December 1803, and of Northbourne and Sholden near Deal in 1806. Elizabeth Carter died in the same year, and Pennington was executor and residuary legatee of her estate. She left him all her papers, and he prepared for press the fourth edition of her translation of Epictetus (first published 1758), to which he added her last alterations and notes (2 vols., 1807). He also published the *Memoirs of the life of Mrs. Elizabeth Carter, with a new edition of her poems …, to which are added, some miscellaneous essays in prose* (1807; 2nd edn, 2 vols., 1808). The *Monthly Review* praised this work, noting that Pennington 'has executed his task with fidelity and general propriety' as well as 'unassuming modesty' (*Monthly Review*, 240). He edited *A series of letters between Elizabeth Carter and Catherine Talbot, 1741–1770, with letters from Elizabeth Carter to Mrs. Vesey* (2 vols., 1808; 4 vols., 1809); brought about the republication of the *Works of Miss Catherine Talbot*, 7th ed., first published by Elizabeth Carter and now republished (1809; 8th edn, 1812; 9th edn, 1819); and edited *Letters from Mrs. Elizabeth Carter, to Mrs. Montagu … between the years 1755 and 1800* (3 vols., 1817). In 1811 Pennington published *Redemption, or, A View of the Rise and Progress of the Christian Religion*. In 1814 Pennington became perpetual curate of St George's Chapel, Deal, a preferment he held until his death. He was also magistrate for Kent and the Cinque Ports. He married Mary Watts (1763–1830), widow of Captain Watts RN. She died at Deal on 24 March 1830, aged sixty-seven, without any children by Pennington.

In Kent, Pennington's friend and neighbour Sir Samuel Egerton Brydges, editor, author, and genealogist, valued him as his only literary ally among the 'stupid clanships' of the Kentish squires. Brydges described Pennington as a good classical scholar, with a 'great memory' and admirable judgement, but 'a little fastidious' (Brydges, *Autobiography*, 1.46). Brydges acknowledged Pennington's 'continual and various aid' in his ten-volume *Censura literaria* (10.v). Pennington was probably the author of a manuscript note in the British Museum's copy of *Censura literaria*, given to him by Brydges, which states that Pennington contributed all the articles in the section called 'The ruminator' signed '‡*‡', P. M., and Londinensis. Four of the essays signed P. M. are on the theological writings of Grotius. In a separate publication of *The Ruminator* (1813) essays on Jeanne d'Arc (no. 77) and on faith and natural religion (no. 85) signed P. M. are probably also by Pennington. Certainly, Brydges again acknowledged Pennington's 'valuable contributions' in the preface.

Montagu Pennington died on 15 April 1849 in Deal, where he was probably buried. Modern scholars will value

him most as Elizabeth Carter's first biographer and editor, as well as for assisting women's publications, most notably those of his aunt and her correspondents.

W. P. COURTNEY, rev. GRETCHEN M. FOSTER

Sources *GM*, 1st ser., 100/1 (1830), 283; 2nd ser., 32 (1849), 323 · Foster, *Alum. Oxon.* · E. Brydges, *The autobiography, times, opinions, and contemporaries of Sir Egerton Brydges*, 2 vols. (1834) · S. E. Brydges, *The ruminator*, 2 vols. (1813) · M. Pennington, *Memoirs of the life of Mrs. Elizabeth Carter, with a new edition of her poems, some of which have never appeared before, to which are added, some miscellaneous essays in prose, together with her notes on the Bible and answers to objections concerning the Christian religion* (1807) · *Letters from Mrs. Elizabeth Carter, to Mrs. Montagu, between the years 1755 and 1800*, 3 vols. (1817) · *Monthly Review*, new ser., 56 (1808), 225–40 · S. E. Brydges, *Censura literaria*, 10 vols. (1805–9), vols. 5, 8, 9 · M. Pennington, advertisement, in *The works of Epictetus*, ed. and trans. E. Carter, 4th edn, 2 vols. (1807) · C. R. S. Elvin, *Records of Walmer* (1890), 111 · S. E. Brydges, *Anglo-Genevan*, 2 pts (1831), pt 2, p. 460
Archives Harvard U., Houghton L., letters to S. E. Brydges · Yale U., Beinecke L., letters to S. E. Brydges

Pennington, Sarah, Lady Pennington (d. 1783), writer, is of unknown parentage. What little is known of her comes largely from her most famous work, *An Unfortunate Mother's Advice to her Absent Daughters, in a Letter to Miss Pennington*, a curious combination of conduct manual and scandalous memoir. In it she states that she was left motherless at nineteen and raised by a distant father who neglected her social education. She married Sir Joseph Pennington of Water Hall, Yorkshire, about 1746, and only when he formally separated from her about twelve years later was she made to realize the cost of social ignorance. Although the specific cause remains uncertain she herself attributed their marital discord to her own publicly coquettish behaviour. Sir Joseph, backed by eighteenth-century law, denied his wife access to her daughters and attempted to deprive her of a small inheritance.

Pennington was reduced to the expedient of communicating with her daughters through the highly public form of a published letter. It is therefore unsurprising that *An Unfortunate Mother's Advice*, published in 1761, serves both to defend her sexual purity and to advise her daughters to remain firmly within the boundaries of socially prescribed behaviour. She states:

> I would advise you always to remember, that, next to the consciousness of acting right, the public voice should be regarded; and to endeavour by a prudent behaviour, even in the most trifling instances, to secure it in your favour. (Pennington, 58)

Attributing her own misfortunes to the misguided belief that innocence alone is a defence against detraction, she laments:

> I was indeed early and wisely taught, that virtue was the one thing necessary … but, with this good principle, a mistaken one was at the same time inculcated, namely, that the self-approbation arising from conscious virtue was alone sufficient; and, that the censures of an ill-natured world, ever ready to calumniate, when not founded on truth, were beneath the concern of a person whose actions were guided by … obedience to the will of Heaven. (ibid.)

Her defensive tone and language of injured innocence

reflect that of scandal memoirists such as Laetitia Pilkington, and like her, Pennington attributes much of her misery to being privately virtuous but publicly coquettish, and thereby leaving herself open to wilful, malicious misconstruction.

Pennington's text is first used to defend her conduct and then develops into an advice manual similar to those produced by writers such as George Savile, marquess of Halifax (1633–1695), Anne-Thérèse, marquise de Lambert, Hester Chapone, and Hannah More. Worried about her daughters' social education she uses the remainder of *An Unfortunate Mother's Advice* to impart typical conduct-manual strictures regarding religion, modesty, and the importance of preserving an untarnished sexual reputation. What makes this work poignantly effective is that she speaks from the pain of personal experience: her text acts as a cautionary tale that presents an example to avoid, as well as a guide to social conduct that outlines a model to emulate.

Pennington's other texts included *Letters on different subjects, in four volumes; amongst which are interspers'd the adventures of Alphonso, after the destruction of Lisbon* (1766) and *The Child's Conductor* (1777); at least one of her works was written out of financial necessity. Following her separation she lived in Bath; she died in 1783, and was buried in Fulmer, Buckinghamshire. What is remarkable about her is that despite the social disgrace of her separation and the fact that, like the notorious memoirists Frances Vane (c.1713–1788) and Con Phillips (1709–1765), she published an account of this scandal, she died with a reputation for virtue and injured innocence. Her obituary in the *Gentleman's Magazine* noted her 'piety, charity, and benevolence' and spoke of her problems in terms of 'severe and uncommon afflictions' rather than the just deserts of a sexually fallen woman (*GM*).   EMMA PLASKITT

Sources S. Pennington, *An unfortunate mother's advice to her absent daughters, in a letter to Miss Pennington* (1761), in *The young lady's pocket library, or, Parental monitor* (1790); ed. V. Jones (1995) · J. Todd, ed., *A dictionary of British and American women writers, 1660–1800* (1984) · T. Bowers, 'Going public: the case of Lady Sarah Pennington', *The politics of motherhood: British writing and culture, 1680–1760* (1996), 225–33 · *GM*, 1st ser., 53 (1783), 918 · R. W. Uphaus and G. M. Foster, eds., *The other eighteenth century: English women of letters, 1660–1800* (Michigan, 1991), 269 · Blain, Clements & Grundy, *Feminist comp.*, 843–4 · E. Plaskitt, '"The Beauteous Frame": the treatment of female sexual reputation in selected prose by Eliza Haywood, Samuel Richardson, and Frances Burney', DPhil diss., U. Oxf., 1999, 36–9

Penny [*née* Hughes; *other married name* Christian], **Anne** (*bap.* 1729, *d.* 1780/1784), poet, was baptized on 6 January 1729, the daughter of the Revd Bulkeley Hughes (*d.* 1740?) and his wife, Mary, of Bangor, Wales. Her father was vicar of Bangor from 7 June 1713, and of Edern from 1723. Anne evidently was of Welsh descent, and her books show that she had a knowledge of the language. In 1746 she married Captain Thomas Christian (1716–1751), whose maritime career had enabled him to buy an estate in Oxfordshire. A year later she had her first child.

Having been widowed at the age of twenty-two Anne started to write, and in 1756 she published *Cambridge: a Poem*. Her second husband was Peter Penny (or Penné *d.* 1778/9), a Frenchman working in a customs house since the loss of a leg had ended his naval career. They moved to Bloomsbury Square, London, and in 1761 Anne Penny published her narrative poem *Anningait and Ajutt*, based on a romantic tale taken from *The Rambler* of December 1751; it was dedicated to Samuel Johnson, who is said to have 'much esteemed' her. Her *Poems, with a Dramatic Entertainment* (1771) contained translations such as 'Taliesin's Poem to Prince Elphin' and 'An Elegy on Neest', from Evans's *Specimens of Welch Poetry*. Subscribers included Dr Johnson, 'Mr. Walpole', the duchess of Bedford, and the duke and duchess of Marlborough; it was dedicated to Jonas Hanway, philanthropic founder of the Marine Society. The dramatic entertainment 'The Birth Day' is lightweight: a piece of sententious flummery teaching unswerving obedience to parents who turn out to be nothing of the kind.

Penny's most significant poem is *An Invocation to the Genius of Britain* (1778), a patriotic piece in rhyming couplets rousing England to war with France and glorifying the navy; it gives a foretaste of Victorian ideology in its stern imperialism and reproof of 'dissipation'. Her other works include the translation *Select Poems from Mr. Gesner's Pastorals* (1762) and, possibly, *A Pastoral Elegy on the Death of Lord Lyttleton* (1773).

At some time before May 1779 Penny was left a poor widow, and a new edition of her poetry came out, to raise money; the 300 subscribers included Horace Walpole, to whom she addressed verses. The Marine Society commissioned her to write a series of odes that were included in the volume. Her death, in London, has been dated variously 1780 (*DWB*) and 1784 (Lonsdale; Todd). Her son Sir Hugh Cloberry *Christian (*bap.* 1747, *d.* 1798) rose to the rank of rear-admiral.   JULIA GASPER

Sources A. Penny, *Poems, with a dramatic entertainment* (1771) · *DWB* · R. Lonsdale, ed., *Eighteenth-century women poets: an Oxford anthology* (1989), 294–6 · J. Todd, ed., *A dictionary of British and American women writers, 1660–1800* (1984) · J. R. de J. Jackson, *Romantic poetry by women: a bibliography* (1993), 253–4

Penny, Edward (1714–1791), portrait, historical, and genre painter, was born at Knutsford, Cheshire, on 1 August 1714, and was baptized on 15 August, one of the twin elder sons of Robert Penny (1687–1738), surgeon, and Clare (1683–1760), daughter of William Trafford of Swythamley, Staffordshire. Many in his family had pursued a career in the church or as a surgeon, as did his twin brother, Henry. Penny, however, pursued his interest in painting and was sent to London to study with Thomas Hudson, whose influence is clearly evident in his early portraits. He subsequently studied in Rome with the portrait painter Marco Benefiale. About 1748 he returned to England and began to execute portraits in all formats from oval to full-length, a practice he continued throughout his career. Penny married on 4 September 1755 at St Anne's, Soho, London, Elizabeth (1719–1790), daughter of John Simmons of Millbank, Westminster, and widow of Richard Fortnam of St George's, Hanover Square, London.

Just as his contemporary Sir Joshua Reynolds imbued portraiture with the grand manner, Penny developed a highly original amalgam of history painting and genre, infusing historical events with the quotidian and genre scenes with the gravitas of more elevated subjects. The first works he exhibited at the Society of Artists in 1762 were a small whole length of a lady and a scene from Nicholas Rowe's *Jane Shore*. Penny exhibited almost yearly at the Society of Artists until 1768, sending primarily subject paintings and history paintings. In 1764 he exhibited an innovative modern dress depiction of the death of Wolfe, signed and dated 1763 (Ashmolean Museum, Oxford). Another version without the subsidiary figures is at Petworth House, Sussex. Subsequent to the success of Benjamin West's version, Penny's was engraved by Richard Houston in 1772. He also displayed a scene from Swift's description of a city shower (engraved Thomas Chambers, 1775; Museum of London), one of several works by Penny that were favourably recognized by Walpole. The next year he exhibited *An Officer Relieving a Sick Soldier* (Ashmolean Museum, Oxford) which Walpole noted as depicting Lord Granby. The theme of charity would become one of the most prominent in his work. Penny became the vice-president of the Society of Artists in 1765, a position he held until his resignation from the society in 1768. He then became one of the founders of the Royal Academy and was appointed the first professor of painting.

At the first Royal Academy exhibition in 1769, Penny avoided the prohibition against quotation by exhibiting a painting with the following title: 'I saw a smith with his hammer thus,/The whilst his iron did on the anvil cool,/With open mouth swallow a taylor's news.' Shakespeare, *King John* (Tate collection, known as *The Gossiping Blacksmith*). Ostensibly a genre painting, the picture contained marked political overtones. It was engraved in 1771 by Richard Houston as *The English Politicians* and was quickly co-opted by the supporters of John Wilkes. A print based on Penny's painting was published in the *Oxford Magazine* in 1771 with the significant addition of a print of John Wilkes hanging on the back wall of the forge. Penny exhibited almost every year from 1769 to 1782. The India Office commissioned *Lord Clive explaining to the nabob the situation of the invalids in India; at the same time showing him a deed whereby he relinquishes Meer Jaffier's legacy, five lacke of rupees, to the honourable East India Company, for the support of the military fund* (Department of the Environment, Foreign and Commonwealth Office) which was sent to the Royal Academy in 1772. Throughout his career Penny executed a number of paired pictures. Two were sent to the Royal Academy in 1774, *The Profligate Punished by Neglect and Contempt* and *The Virtuous Comforted by Sympathy and Attention* (Yale U. CBA). His 1776 Royal Academy entry returned to the theme of Jane Shore. He exhibited *Jane Shore led to do penance at St. Pauls: the insolent in office, and pretenders to purity, by insulting the wretched, betray their own baseness* (Birmingham City Museum and Art Gallery). The flat bright colours of the painting and planar composition depart from Penny's usual style. Given the radical nature of the composition, it is not surprising that the painting remained in the possession of his family until the middle of the twentieth century. Penny's compositional experimentations are also evident in a pair of paintings exhibited in 1780, *A Boy Taken out of the Water, Drowned* and 'The boy by proper means recovered': vide Dr. Franklin's sermon to the Humane Society, humanie nihil a me alienum—Ter., in which the principal action described in the title takes place in the background of the painting and the foreground depicts the reaction to the main events. The pair was engraved as *Apparent Dissolution* and *Returning Animation* by William Sedgwick in 1784 and by J. Corner and P. Audinet (in smaller versions).

Penny resigned his professorship of painting owing to ill health on 31 December 1781. In the final year of his exhibition at the Royal Academy, 1782, among the pictures he submitted were *Widow Costard's cow and goods distrained for taxes, are redeemed by the generosity of Johnny Pearmain*. Penny died at Chiswick, Middlesex, on 16 November 1791, and was buried with his wife, who had died on 30 April the preceding year, at Chessington, Surrey. Penny's lectures were bequeathed by his will to his nephew, the Ven. George Buckley Bower, archdeacon of Richmond. There is no record remaining of the lectures, although they were praised by his successor as professor of painting, James Barry.   R. E. GRAVES, rev. T. J. EDELSTEIN

Sources private information (2004) [S. Harwood] · Graves, *Soc. Artists* · Graves, *RA exhibitors* · C. Mitchell, 'Benjamin West's *Death of Wolfe*; and the popular history piece', *Journal of the Warburg and Courtauld Institutes*, 7 (1944), 20–33 · E. Wind, 'Penny, West, and the death of Wolfe', *Journal of the Warburg and Courtauld Institutes*, 10 (1947), 159–62 · D. H. Solkin, 'Portraiture in motion: Edward Penny's *Marquis of Granby* and the creation of a public for English art', *Huntington Library Quarterly*, 49 (1986), 1–23

Likenesses E. Penny, self-portrait, oils, 1759, RA · J. Zoffany, group portrait, oils (*The Academicians of the Royal Academy*, 1771–2), Royal Collection

Penny, John (d. 1520), abbot of Leicester and bishop of Carlisle, was probably born at Leicester, where his father, John Penny (d. 1496), was a freeman of the borough c.1452 and mayor in 1481–2; his mother's name was Isabella Penny. His education is uncertain: he is said to have gone to Lincoln College, Oxford, and also to have become LLD of Cambridge, but neither claim can be substantiated. He was admitted a freeman of Leicester in 1475/6 as 'John Pene, pardoner' (that is, licensed to sell papal indulgences). In 1477 he was an Augustinian canon at the abbey of St Mary, Leicester, in 1493 prior, and on 25 June 1496 was elected abbot. Leland notes that Penny added to the abbey buildings: a long stretch of brick precinct wall he built, bearing his initials in darker bricks, survives. He was allowed to hold the Austin priory of Bradley, Leicestershire, in commendam from 14 September 1503. In 1505 he became bishop of Bangor, but because of the small revenues of that see retained his abbacy and priory until after he had been translated to the bishopric of Carlisle by a bull dated 22 September 1508. His register has not survived, and little can be said of his episcopate, but in 1513 Penny and the bishop of Durham pronounced the pope's censures against the Scots for their invasion of England. He was a man of active mind, and a letter which he wrote to Wolsey in 1519 from Melbourne in Derbyshire, a manor of the bishops of Carlisle, shows that he was ready to support the cardinal in his plans for ecclesiastical reform, but was prevented by illness from attending the council summoned by Wolsey to meet in London. Penny died at the abbey in Leicester in 1520 and was buried near his parents in St Margaret's Church, Leicester, where his well-preserved alabaster effigy (placed on a new tomb in 1846) may still be seen. He gave lands towards a free school in St Margaret's parish, but in 1552 it was found that they had been sold some years previously and the money embezzled by John Beaumont, master of the rolls and recorder of Leicester.   T. Y. COCKS

Sources *Fasti Angl., 1066–1300,* [York], 99 · *Fasti Angl., 1300–1541,* [Welsh dioceses], 5 · Foster, *Alum. Oxon.* · J. Nichols, *The history and antiquities of the county of Leicester,* 1/2 (1815), 268, 511; 2/2 (1798), 510 · J. Throsby, *The history and antiquities of the ancient town of Leicester* (1791), 277 · *LP Henry VIII,* 3/1.77 · C. Eubel and others, eds., *Hierarchia Catholica medii et recentioris aevi,* 2nd edn, 1 (Münster, 1913), 143, 168 · *The itinerary of John Leland in or about the years 1535–1543,* ed. L. Toulmin Smith, 11 pts in 5 vols. (1906–10), vol. 1, p. 17 · H. Hartopp, ed., *Register of the freemen of Leicester,* 1 (1927), xxxv, 52 · M. Bateson and others, eds., *Records of the borough of Leicester,* 3: *1509–1603* (1905), 69 · Emden, *Oxf.,* 3.1458 · *DNB*
Likenesses alabaster effigy, in or after 1520, St Margaret's Church, Leicester; repro. in A. Gardner, *Alabaster tombs of the pre-Reformation period in England* (1940)

Penny, John (1803–1885), journalist, born at Sherborne, Dorset, on 16 February 1803, was the third son of Elias Penny, bookseller and publisher of Sherborne, and was educated at the King's School there. In 1828 he became proprietor and editor of the old *Sherborne Journal.* In the columns of the paper he championed the cause of reform, and thus earned the gratitude of the whigs. In 1832 he published a pamphlet entitled *Dorsetshire Emancipated from Tory Dominion,* and was rewarded by Lord John Russell with the stamp-distributorship of Dorset. He then moved to Dorchester, but soon afterwards was promoted to a similar but more important post at Leeds. While there he wrote a drama, *Stephen, King of England* (1851), which was produced at the Leeds Theatre and favourably received. In 1858 he gave up the *Sherborne Journal,* and subsequently retired from official life. For a while he enjoyed his superannuation at the house he had built for himself at Harrogate, but in the early 1870s he developed acute asthma, for the relief of which he had to travel between Bath (for the beneficial waters of its pump room), Bournemouth (for its warm weather and sea air), and, occasionally, a villa in Chetnole, Dorset, which provided him with opportunities for regular walks and physical exercise. Penny died at Bath on 7 February 1885, and was buried on 12 February at Exeter with his wife and only son, who had predeceased him.

Penny's eldest brother, William Webb Penny (1799–1888), was proprietor and editor of the *Sherborne Mercury,* one of the oldest papers in the west of England, from 1829 until 1842. His youngest brother, Charles Penny (1809–1875), of Pembroke College, Oxford, was headmaster of Crewkerne grammar school from 1838 until 1875, and for many years rector of Chaffcombe, Somerset.

GORDON GOODWIN, rev. NILANJANA BANERJI

Sources *Sherborne Journal* (12 Feb 1885) · Allibone, *Dict.* · Crockford (1874) · C. H. Mayo, ed., *Bibliotheca Dorsetiensis: being a carefully compiled account of books and pamphlets relating to … Dorset* (1885)
Wealth at death £28,760 9s. 11d.: resworn probate, Nov 1885, CGPLA Eng. & Wales

Penny, Nicholas (1790–1858), army officer in the East India Company, was born in November 1790, fourth son of Robert Penny of Weymouth, Dorset, the descendant of a family long settled there. He was appointed to the Bengal army in 1806. He was gazetted ensign in the Bengal native infantry on 16 August 1807, and lieutenant on 19 December 1812, and, successively, brevet captain (5 March 1822), regimental captain (13 May 1825), brevet major (19 January 1826), regimental major (2 February 1842), brevet lieutenant-colonel (23 November 1841), regimental lieutenant-colonel (29 July 1848), brevet colonel (7 June 1849), regimental colonel (15 September 1851), and major-general (28 November 1854).

Penny served with distinction throughout the siege of Bharatpur, the First Anglo-Sikh War, and the Indian mutiny—from 1825 to 1858—and was repeatedly on active service. In November 1825 he accompanied the commander-in-chief, Lord Amherst, on service to Agra. He was present as deputy assistant quartermaster-general with the 2nd division of infantry at the siege of Bharatpur in December 1825 and January 1826, was thanked in divisional orders by Major-General Nicholls, and shared in the Bharatpur prize-money. He was brigade major on the establishment from 2 October 1826 to 19 May 1828. He was appointed to Mathura and Agra frontier on 4 October 1826, deputy assistant adjutant-general on the establishment on 19 May 1828, and assistant adjutant-general of a division on 9 July 1832. He married at Dinapore on 26 May 1830 Louisa Margaret, third and youngest daughter of John Gerrard.

Penny was granted the brevet rank of major for distinguished services in the field, and was appointed to command the Nusseree battalion (the first British Gurkha regiment) on 2 June 1841, and was reported as 'a most zealous officer'. He was appointed to command the 12th brigade of the 5th division of infantry of the army of the Sutlej on 1 January 1846, and on the breaking up of this brigade was appointed to command the 2nd infantry brigade (16 February 1846). He served at the battle of Aliwal, and was commended in dispatches. At the battle of Sobraon, in the First Anglo-Sikh War, Penny was slightly wounded; his services were commended in dispatches and he was made a CB on 27 June 1846. He was posted to the 69th Bengal native infantry, and ordered to Lahore on 27 September 1848. He was appointed to command of the 7th brigade of the 3rd infantry division of the army of the Punjab, with the rank of brigadier (13 October 1848).

Penny had ceased to command the Nusseree battalion on promotion to lieutenant-colonel (7 October 1848). He was transferred from the 69th to the 70th Bengal native infantry on 12 January 1849, and was present at Chilianwala in command of the reserve, and also at Gujrat. He was mentioned in dispatches, and received the thanks of the governor-general, Lord Dalhousie. He was transferred to the 2nd European regiment on 31 March 1849, and was appointed aide-de-camp to the queen, and promoted brevet colonel for his services in the Punjab.

In 1850 Penny was transferred from the 2nd European regiment to the 40th Bengal native infantry, was appointed second-class brigadier, and was posted to the district of Rohilkhand (14 July 1851). He was transferred to the command of the Jullundur field force on 2 February 1852, and on 28 August he was appointed to command the Sirhind division, and subsequently he was again transferred to the command of the Sind-Saugor district (22 November 1853), and to the Sialkot command (19 January 1854). In May 1855 he was appointed to the temporary divisional staff, and posted to the Cawnpore division, and on 30 June 1857 was appointed to the divisional staff of the army as major-general, and posted to the Meerut division. When the mutiny was at its height he was appointed to command the Delhi field force, in conjunction with that of the Meerut division, from 30 September 1857. This was after the capture of Delhi, as Sir Archdale Wilson kept command until the city was taken. Penny was killed by rebels at Budaun, while in command of the Meerut division, on 4 May 1858. He was buried at Meerut.

B. H. Soulsby, *rev.* James Lunt

Sources BL OIOC · T. R. E. Holmes, *India mutiny* (1883) · *Allen's Indian Mail* · *East-India Register* · H. C. B. Cook, *The Sikh wars: the British army in the Punjab, 1845–1849* (1975) · J. W. Kaye, *A history of the Sepoy War in India, 1857–1858*, 9th edn, 3 vols. (1880) · G. B. Malleson, *History of the Indian mutiny, 1857–1858: commencing from the close of the second volume of Sir John Kaye's History of the Sepoy War*, 3 vols. (1878–80) · Fortescue, *Brit. army*, 13.372 · V. C. P. Hodson, *List of officers of the Bengal army, 1758–1834*, 4 vols. (1927–47)

Archives BL OIOC, corresp. relating to Indian mutiny, MS Eur. C 738

Penny, Thomas (*c.*1530–1589), botanist and entomologist, was born at Gressingham, near Lancaster, one of two known sons of John Penny, a smallholder in the hamlet of Eskrigge in that parish. After perhaps attending the local grammar school he went up to Queens' College, Cambridge, as a pensioner in 1546, but on being awarded a sizarship at the larger Trinity College he transferred there in 1550, graduating BA in the following year. Elected a fellow in 1553 he stayed on to study, becoming senior bursar of Trinity in 1564.

Though not ordained until June 1561, Penny was already preaching, and on 2 March 1560 was collated to the prebend of Newington in St Paul's Cathedral. A strong supporter of the Reformation, his 1565 Spital sermon at Paul's Cross caused him to be censured by Archbishop Matthew Parker, as being ill-disposed towards the established church. With his clerical career in jeopardy, he imitated an earlier Cambridge divine and naturalist, William Turner, and went abroad to equip himself for medical practice instead. Already knowledgeable about butterflies and plants, he was warmly received in Zürich late in 1565 by Conrad Gesner, then engaged on his *Historia plantarum*. Penny presented Gesner with some choice plant specimens, and probably received some insect drawings by Gesner in exchange. Gesner's death a few months later, however, ended their collaboration, and led Penny to

Thomas Penny (*c.*1530–1589), by William Rogers [right, with: Thomas Moffet (bottom), Edward Wotton (left), and Conrad Gesner]

move to Geneva and spend the next summer exploring botanically the neighbouring mountains. He went next to Montpellier, where his friendship with Matthias de l'Obel, then a student there, doubtless originated, visited Majorca, and then seems to have travelled up through France to spend a period at Heidelberg. There he probably became acquainted with the elder Joachim Camerarius and collected plants and insects with two English medical students who were fellow naturalists. After a final tour of Prussia and the Baltic coast he returned to England, apparently in 1569, and set up in London in what proved to be a practice of some renown. No friend of established authority, however, he twice defied the College of Physicians by practising without its licence, even incurring imprisonment, before it eventually bowed to his reputation and admitted him a fellow (by 1582). Surprisingly, he retained his prebend until 1577, when he was deprived of it for nonconformity.

Anchored for the rest of his life in Leadenhall Street, Penny nevertheless travelled widely in England in pursuit of natural history, records credited to him in the works of de l'Obel, John Gerard, and others including several plants new to the British list. Though insects increasingly now became his dominant interest, he was still botanist enough to introduce Charles de l'Ecluse to several English rarities as late as 1581.

In November 1587 the death of his wife, Margaret, the

daughter of John Lucas, master of requests to Edward VI, seemingly hastened Penny's end. Asthmatic and suffering from symptoms diagnosed by his friend and colleague Thomas Moffet as due to abstinence from salt, he died in January 1589 in London and was buried in the churchyard of St Andrew Undershaft, his home parish. A puritan to the last, he stipulated in his will, dated 4 June 1588, that there should be no ceremony whatever at his interment, mourning apparel, ringing, and singing being all expressly prohibited. Papers he purportedly left to Turner's son Peter cannot now be traced; those he had been amassing for a major work on insects Penny left to Moffet. A book man where Penny had been a field man, Moffet went to much trouble in putting these into order and added so much that he felt justified in presenting the manuscript of 1200 folios he had ready for publication in March 1589 as having four authors. The first-hand observations and more detailed descriptions (including of nineteen British butterflies) were, however, probably Penny's. No copy appears to have survived of a German imprint of 1598, apparently the basis of Edward Topsell's plagiarism in an English translation under the title *A Historie of Foure-Footed Beasts* (1607), the earliest-known entomological work published in Britain. Moffet's Latin version, *Insectorum sive minimorum animalium theatrum*, repeatedly submerged by his many competing commitments, eventually appeared posthumously in 1634.

The Balearic St John's Wort now known as *Hypericum balearicum* was named *Myrtocistus pennaei* by de l'Ecluse in honour of its discoverer.   D. E. ALLEN

Sources W. Gardner, 'A Lancashire entomologist in the time of Queen Elizabeth', *Annual Report & Proceedings of Lancashire & Cheshire Entomological Society* (1928–30), 31–52 • C. E. Raven, *English naturalists from Neckam to Ray: a study of the making of the modern world* (1947), 153–91 • Munk, *Roll* • R. T. Gunther, *Early British botanists and their gardens* (1922), 234–5 • *DNB* • Thomas Penny's will, 4 June 1588
Likenesses W. Rogers, line engraving, NPG [*see illus.*]

Pennycuick, James Farrell (1829–1888), army officer, was born on 10 August 1829, second but eldest surviving son of Brigadier John *Pennycuick (1789–1849) and his wife, Sarah, daughter of the Revd James Farrell. After the Royal Military Academy (1844–7), he entered the Royal Artillery as second lieutenant on 2 May 1847. He became first lieutenant on 30 June 1848, and second captain on 21 September 1854. He served in the Crimea, and took part in the battle of Inkerman, his being one of the two 9-pounder batteries with the 2nd division, which were the first to engage the much more powerful Russian artillery. He received the brevet rank of major, and the fifth class of the Mejidiye. During the Indian mutiny he was engaged in the second relief of the Lucknow residency, the battle of Cawnpore (6 December 1857), and the siege and capture of Lucknow. He served in the 1860 China expedition, including the capture of the Taku (Dagu) forts, and was made brevet lieutenant-colonel (15 February 1861) and CB. He became a regimental lieutenant-colonel on 10 July 1871, regimental colonel on 1 May 1880, and on 8 November 1880 major-general. On 1 July 1885 he became lieutenant-general, and on 4 January 1886 general. He had married a

daughter of W. Rutledge of Victoria, Australia; they had sons and daughters. Pennycuick died at 50 Weymouth Street, Portland Place, London, on 6 July 1888, and was buried on 10 July at Bedford cemetery.

E. M. LLOYD, *rev.* JAMES LUNT

Sources *The Times* (12 July 1888) • J. Kane, *List of officers of the royal regiment of artillery from the year 1716 to the year 1899*, rev. W. H. Askwith, 4th edn (1900) • A. W. Kinglake, *The invasion of the Crimea*, [new edn], 9 vols. (1877–88) • J. W. Kaye and G. B. Malleson, *Kaye's and Malleson's History of the Indian mutiny of 1857-8*, new edn, 6 vols. (1897–8) • returns of officers' services, PRO, War Office, 25/794 • Boase, *Mod. Eng. biog.* • *CGPLA Eng. & Wales* (1888)
Wealth at death £1821 9s. 11d.: probate, 27 July 1888, *CGPLA Eng. & Wales*

Pennycuick, John (1789–1849), army officer, was born at Soilarzie, Perthshire, on 28 October 1789. He was appointed ensign in the Edinburgh militia on 17 February 1806, entered the army on 31 August 1807 as an ensign in the 78th (Highland) regiment, and became lieutenant on 15 January 1812. He served in the expedition to Java, and was wounded in the attack on the entrenched camp adjoining the fort of Meester-Cornelis on 26 August 1811. He married, at Lanesborough, co. Roscommon, on 21 March 1820, Sarah, daughter of James Farrell, vicar of Rathcline, and they had five sons and six daughters.

Pennycuick was promoted captain on 14 June 1821, and on 13 January 1825 he exchanged into the 47th regiment, with which he took part in the First Anglo-Burmese War in 1825–6. He became major, unattached, on 25 April 1834, and on 8 May 1835 obtained a majority in the 17th foot. With this regiment he took part in the campaign of 1839 in Afghanistan, including the capture of Ghazni, and was afterwards employed in Baluchistan under General Willshire, to subdue the khan of Kalat. He led the storming party in the capture of Kalat on 13 November 1839, and was made CB, having already obtained a brevet lieutenant-colonelcy for Ghazni. He had been made a KH in 1837.

Pennycuick became lieutenant-colonel on 12 June 1840, and in 1841 took and destroyed some Arab posts near Aden. In 1848 he exchanged from the 17th to the 24th regiment; at the end of that year he served in the Second Anglo-Sikh War, and commanded a brigade, which consisted of his own and two Indian regiments, in Thackwell's division (afterwards Sir Colin Campbell's). He was in the force under Thackwell which turned the Sikh position on the Chenab, by crossing at Wazirabad, and he was eager to attack at once; but others prevailed, and the Sikhs were allowed to retire. When Lord Gough decided to attack them near Chilianwala, on the afternoon of 13 January 1849, Pennycuick's brigade led the attack. They were told to advance without firing, as the 10th had done at Sobraon. The 24th carried the Sikh guns with a rush, but they had outstripped the two Indian regiments and found themselves exposed, with their own arms unloaded, to a heavy fire from the jungle round them. Pennycuick and Brooks, the other lieutenant-colonel of the 24th—'two officers not surpassed for sound judgment and military daring', as Gough wrote—were killed, and the brigade was driven back. The 24th lost twenty-two officers and 497 men. Among the officers killed was a younger son of Pennycuick, Alexander, a boy of seventeen, the junior ensign of the regiment:

> Young Pennycuick, [who] had been on the sick list, was brought to the field in a dooly—there he insisted on going with the Regt. into action—he retired with it, after the repulse, and at the village, heard of his father's fate. Immediately he went to the front in search of the body, and it would appear was killed by its side, for the two were found lying dead together. (Brereton, 122)

The two were buried alongside one another on the evening after the battle. Pennycuick's second son was James Farrell *Pennycuick.   E. M. LLOYD, *rev.* JAMES LUNT

Sources *Hart's Army List* · records of the 17th (royal Leicestershire) regiment · J. W. Kaye, *History of the war in Afghanistan*, 3rd edn, 3 vols. (1874) · E. J. Thackwell, *Narrative of the Second Seikh War, in 1848–49* (1851) · A. J. Macpherson, *Rambling reminiscences of the Punjab campaign* (1889) · G. Paton, F. Glennie, and W. P. Symons, eds., *Historical records of the 24th regiment, from its formation, in 1689* (1892) · H. C. B. Cook, *The Sikh wars: the British army in the Punjab, 1845–1849* (1975) · return of officers' services, PRO, War Office, 25/794 · W. S. Sampson, 'Lt Col. J. Pennycuick CB, KH', *Journal of the Society for Army Historical Research*, 52 (1974), 212 · J. M. Brereton, *History of the royal regiment of Wales/24th/41st foot* (1989) · C. T. Atkinson, *The south Wales borderers, 24th foot, 1689–1937* (1937)
Likenesses Campion, drawing; formerly in possession of the Parker Gallery, London · attrib. Green, portrait, repro. in *Journal of the Society for Army Historical Research*, vol. 52, 212, 246 · portrait, priv. coll.; formerly in possession of his grandson, Sir John Pennycuick · portrait, repro. in L. Cooper, *South Wales Borderers* volume, Famous Regiments series

Pennyman, John (1628–1706), Quaker schismatic, was born on 14 August 1628, the fourth son of Sir James Pennyman (d. 1655), of Ormesby, Yorkshire, and his second wife, Joan Smith (d. 1657), of London. His half-brother, Sir James Pennyman (1609–1679), was knighted by Charles I at Durham in 1642 and was later created a baronet by Charles II in February 1664. At fifteen John Pennyman went into the king's service and was made an ensign in the foot regiment of which Sir James was colonel. Following two years' service and the royalist defeat, he and two of his brothers took refuge abroad 'till his father and eldest brother had made their composition, and sent for them to come over' (Pennyman, *Life*, 1696, 1).

Early beliefs On 8 February 1647, aged eighteen, Pennyman was apprenticed to a Mr Fabian, a woollen draper and fervent royalist based in St Paul's Churchyard in London. In 1650 he experienced a 'conversion' while reading the epistles of St Paul and 'was fully convinced of the sad and woeful condition he was in by reason of his sins' so that 'he began to walk, not after the flesh, but after the spirit' (Pennyman, *Life*, 1696, 2–3). His parents greeted his new religious experiences with difficulty for they were 'very zealous for the king, and Church of England' (ibid., 5). In 1651 he heard the Fifth Monarchist Christopher Feake speak at Christ Church, Newgate Street, and joined the sect; he remained with them until Feake's committal to Windsor Castle about 1658.

In 1654 Pennyman married Elizabeth Heron (d. 1668); in his *Life* he states that they had three children, and Quaker

registers reveal that these included Anne (b. 1663), and Elizabeth who died in 1673 aged eight. At the time of his marriage Pennyman also notes that he had set up in business, and he evidently prospered as a woollen draper for he owned shops and houses at the west end of St Paul's.

Pennyman joined the Friends about 1658, 'finding the Quakers to preach up the power, and decry all forms', beliefs which 'seemed to come nearest to his sentiments'. He was also attracted to 'the simplicity of their doctrine, and their patience and constancy in their sufferings' (Pennyman, *Life*, 1696, 9). After some time, however, he came to believe that 'a great part of the Quakers' had 'degenerated into mere form', having '[set] up G.[eorge] Fox instead of the spirit of Christ, to be their Lord and law-giver' (ibid., 10). In 1660 Pennyman and others such as John Osgood and William Gosnell left the main body of the Friends, and held their own meetings in woods near Hanger's Green, but 'they still frequented their civil meetings … and stood by them in their sufferings' (ibid.). Pennyman's long-standing association with Thomas and Ann Mudd [see below], and John Perrot, also Friends, may have stemmed from this time.

In 1663 Pennyman is recorded as a woollen draper living in Paul's Yard, London. In his autobiography he also mentions a country house in Kentish Town, where he went each Saturday. During the plague Pennyman rejoiced that his family were left untouched; at the time he and his wife were in Yorkshire, but the rest of the family was in London. They also survived the great fire of London, the family and servants being sent to Mile End Green for their protection. Pennyman married again following his first wife's death from a fever on 24 February 1668, but he suffered further bereavement with the death of his second wife, Dinah (d. 1669), at the home of her father, Nicholas Bond, in Pall Mall, St James's, on 23 August 1669; like his first wife she was buried at Chequer Alley.

Separation from the Friends From about 1669 it appears that Pennyman began to have experiences more typical of the ecstatic behaviour found among some of the very early Quakers, and which consequently led eventually to his being disowned by the movement. In 1669 he recounted in his autobiography how he had gone to a meeting in White-Hart Court and, after standing up, had lost his breath and senses for a number of minutes, which seemed to provide him with spiritual refreshment. This same incident recurred at other meetings. In 1670 he related how he fasted for three days while confined to his bed and had a vision of the Lord. An incident with more serious repercussions occurred on 28 July 1670, when Pennyman began to find some Quaker books 'an oppression to him' (Pennyman, *Life*, 1696, 26) and asked two porters to carry a bag of Quaker books and two other bags to a Mr Bates in Cornhill; he then 'stopped on an impulse' at the exchange, where he asked for a candle and requested the porter to burn some of the books. This action caused a scandal in Quaker circles as rumour spread that he had burned the Bible, but in his autobiography he stresses that the books burnt were 'not the two bags where the Bible, Book of Martyrs, &c. were' (ibid., 27). He was committed to

Bishopsgate prison and later to Newgate. Pennyman defended himself in a letter to his brother which was printed and given away at the exchange. Nevertheless, on 10 August 1670, leading Friends disowned Pennyman for the public sacrificing of the scriptures and other books, declaring that they believed him to have been 'instigated by the Devil' and 'in some measure broken and discomposed in his mind and understanding' (*Testimony*). Pennyman had this broadside reprinted in red with a black border and had it widely distributed. He was soon released from prison through the influence of his brother and nephew.

A third marriage Pennyman's third wife, **Mary Pennyman** [*née* Heron; *other married name* Boreman] (1630–1701), was the sister of his first wife. She was born on 1 May 1630, the daughter of Edmund Heron, 'a gentleman of a good estate' and of 'great repute' who had incurred considerable losses following the execution of Charles I, and his wife, the daughter of Justice Wood of Woodborough (Pennyman, *Letters and Papers*, sig. A2v). She first married the Quaker Henry Boreman (d. 1662), who had been imprisoned in London at Newgate 'for selling religious books' and who died there on 17 October 1662 (Besse, 389) leaving her with three children and pregnant with a fourth. Mary had kept an oil shop in Leadenhall Street, but decided to give this up in 1670, after which she went to live with two other widows in Tottenham. It is possible that one of these was Jane Ward Lead or Leade (1623–1704), the central figure of the Philadelphians, a mystical sect who followed Jakob Boehme's theosophy. It is thought that Mary dissociated herself from the Friends for some time after Boreman's death and may have held views similar to the Philadelphians.

On 10 October 1671 Mary went to live with Pennyman in Aldersgate Street. He recounted that he requested Alderman Ashurst for the use of Merchant Taylors' Hall because the Friends refused him the meeting hall at White-Hart Court, and there 'by special motion, with great solemnity', published his marriage (Pennyman, *Life*, 1696, 50). Great provision was made for the celebration with meat and drink 'to be all of one sort', twenty-seven venison pasties, a hogshead of claret, 'and sufficient for about 250 persons' (ibid.). The union provoked yet another furore in Quaker circles, with William Penn writing:

> We countenance no clandestine marriages, as we have reason to believe John Pennyman's was: for he came not … to be married, but to declare he had taken Mary Boreman to be his wife … but when, how, and before whom he did it, is known to few, if any. (Penn, *Judas*, 62)

Clearly the union was not recognized by the Friends as a Quaker marriage as it had not followed 'those plain, public and orderly proceedings towards God, relatives and Friends, as which are owned and practised by us' (ibid.). In another tract Penn referred to Pennyman as 'that exalted J. Penniman' and criticized the Pennymans' 'costly clothes' and 'prodigal feast' (Penn, *Spirit*, 13). Mary in particular attracted Penn's opprobrium:

> [She] exchanged her cloth waist-coat for a silk farendine gown, her blue apron for one of fine holland, and her ordinary bodice for rich satin it self; to say little of her riding in fine coaches, and several other things (once accounted by her self righteous abominable things).   (ibid., 13–14)

The marriage was also the subject of a scurrilous ballad by Matthew Stevenson, entitled *The Quakers Wedding* (1671). Perhaps as a result of the mainstream Quaker reaction to the wedding, the Pennymans, along with William Mucklow and Ann and Thomas Mudd, for the first time openly rejected the Quaker leadership of George Fox.

In winter 1672–3 the Pennymans left London feeling called to visit Hertfordshire and Essex, which they did on foot. In a letter of 22 November 1673 William Penn wrote to Mary Pennyman, accusing her husband of being 'a reviler of our Friends behind their back & a Promoter of the Book Tyranny & Hypocrisie detected &c. by contributing to the Accusations therein mentioned' (Dunn and Dunn, 262). Penn also claimed that Mary had 'so puffd up the poor Man, that he is ever and anon ready to be cracked' and of having 'entered … & help'd to his being beguil'd, by swelling him beyond his place, as if he were some God on Earth' (ibid., 264). The book to which Penn referred, and which is thought to have been written by William Mucklow, was heavily critical of leading Friends and the central organization which was growing up in London. A number of Pennyman's letters to Mucklow, particularly in the early 1690s, were printed in his autobiography. In these Pennyman lamented the distance that had grown up between the two of them, which may have stemmed from a reluctance on Mucklow's part to continue his criticism of the Quaker leadership.

Pennyman appears to have lived at various places in the capital during the 1670s, including Hammersmith about 1672–3 and Hackney from 1674. He records how he was labelled 'a disturber' for interruptions to various Quaker meetings, apparently frequently (Pennyman, *Life*, 1696, 148). In 1689, seven years since he had been to a meeting, he related how he felt moved to go to White-Hart Court; there, before anyone else spoke, he exhorted the meeting to cleanse their hearts—for which he claimed he was violently pulled down by three or four Friends (ibid., 160). In 1692 Pennyman and his family went to live with his son-in-law John Barkstead at St Helen, Bishopsgate. After publishing his autobiography in 1696 as *A Short Account of the Life of Mr. John Pennyman*, he went to the country, 'supposing the time of my departure was then near', and stayed there for three months, during which time he examined the writings of Matthew Hale, extracts of which he had printed (Pennyman, *Life*, 1703, 188). It then appears that he lived in Hackney, about 1698, and in November and December 1700 visited all the Friends' public meetings, such as those at White-Hart Court, Devonshire House, the Bull, the Savoy, Westminster, Ratcliff, and others, where he was moved to warn Friends 'to hearken to truth and righteousness in your inward parts' for all hearing and preaching was 'in vain' (ibid., 203).

Writings Pennyman produced about thirty works, the majority aimed against the Friends, such as *The Quakers Unmasked* (1682). One of the few works which was not, written with Humphrey Woolrich and Thomas Coveney and published as *Some Grounds and Reasons Drawn from the Law of God* (1660), criticized the law of imprisonment for the refusal of hat honour. Pennyman also co-authored some works with his wife: for example, *The Ark is Begun to be Opened* (1671) and *John Pennyman's Instructions to his Children* (1674) in which he writes, 'beware of taking up your rest in any outward form of worship … for our eyes have seen the sad fruits and effects' (Pennyman, *Instructions*, 9–10). Mary also wrote *Something Formerly Writ* (1676). In 1700–01 John Pennyman published *Some of the Letters and Papers which were Written by Mrs. Mary Pennyman*, one of which included a letter to their friends Ann and Thomas Mudd in which she defended herself and her husband against their Quaker critics: 'they say we are turned into the world, but our desires truly are to get more and more out of the spirit of this world' (Pennyman, *Letters and Papers*, 10). Appendices to Pennyman's own autobiography were also published such as *An additional appendix to the book of Mr. Pennyman's life being a collection of some more of his writings* (1706).

Mary Pennyman died on 14 January 1701 aged seventy, following several years of ill health. The following testimony by her husband reveals the closeness of their relationship: 'she was one of the best of wives, and certainly one of the suitablest, serviceablest, and comfortablest companions, for many years, especially in divine matters, to me' (Pennyman, *Letters and Papers*, sig. A2r). John Pennyman died on 2 July 1706 and was buried at Bunhill Fields seven days later. Like many of the Quaker separatists, his life serves to highlight the changes in Quakerism in its first decades and the tensions which arose between the spiritual freedom which the early Friends appeared to offer and the constraints imposed following the establishment of the local and central meeting structure.

Ann Mudd (*b.* 1612/13, *d.* in or after 1693) was married to Thomas Mudd of Rickmansworth. Both became followers of John Pennyman and were either disowned by, or left, the Friends. Isaac Penington wrote to Ann and Thomas in 1672 with regard to forsaking meetings and criticism of ministers. In 1673 instances of Quaker violence in meetings were described in *Tyranny and Hypocrisy*, thought to be by William Mucklow, which also noted that the Friends 'would not spare that grave ancient gentlewoman Anne Mudd, who being moved to speak a few words among them, before their speakers began, Thomas Matthews, who guarded the stairs, pulled her away by violence' (Mucklow, 15). In 1678 Mudd wrote *A cry, a cry: a sensible cry for many months together hath been in my heart for the Quakers return out of that Egyptian darkness*, in which she accused the leading Friends in London of 'unworthy dealings' with John Pennyman, and criticized Quaker central organization, urging them to 'ponder well what your meetings are for: are they not to exalt yourselves, and to make you seem more holy than you are?' (A. Mudd, *A Cry*, 1678, 4). The exact date of Ann's death is uncertain; however, she did write to the Pennymans on 10 April 1693 from Wilscomb, describing herself as eighty years of age and advising them that her health had dwindled, and that she believed she was close to death.   CAROLINE L. LEACHMAN

Sources J. Pennyman, *A short account of the life of Mr. John Pennyman* (1696) · J. Pennyman, *A short account of the life of Mr. John Pennyman* (1703) · J. Pennyman, *Some of the letters and papers which were written by Mrs. Mary Pennyman* (1700–01) · *The papers of William Penn*, ed. M. M. Dunn, R. S. Dunn, and others, 1 (1981) · J. Smith, ed., *A descriptive catalogue of Friends' books*, 2 (1867) · Quaker digest registers, RS Friends, Lond. · J. Besse, *A collection of the sufferings of the people called Quakers*, 1 (1753) · 'Dictionary of Quaker biography', RS Friends, Lond. [card index] · *A testimony against John Pennyman's lyes, slanders, and false accusations of blasphemy* (1671) · J. Smith, ed., *A descriptive catalogue of Friends' books*, suppl. (1893), 266–7 · [W. Mucklow], *Tyranny and hypocrisy detected* (1673) · W. Penn, *Judas and the Jews* (1673) · J. Pennyman, *Instructions to his children* (1674) · W. Penn, *The spirit of Alexander Copper-Smith* (1673) · P. Mack, *Visionary women: ecstatic prophecy in seventeenth-century England* (1992) · L. H. Higgins, 'The apostatized apostle, John Pennyman: heresy and community in seventeenth century Quakerism', *Quaker History*, 69/1 (1980), 102–18 · *DNB*

Pennyman [*née* Angier], **Margaret** (*bap.* **1685**, *d.* **1733**), poet, was baptized at St Margaret's, Westminster, on 3 May 1685, the daughter of Barnet Angier of the City of Westminster, sometime carpenter to Charles II, and Jane Salter (or Slater). She is said to have been well educated and extraordinarily beautiful. In 1703 she eloped with Thomas Pennyman (*b. c.*1669), of a good Yorkshire family, and was married on 18 June at St Martin-in-the-Fields, Westminster. Around this time, Thomas Pennyman came into an inheritance on the death of an elder brother. His wife brought him a fortune of £2000, but the marriage was disastrous and the couple obtained a legal separation after only three months. She lost much of her fortune in the Mississippi scheme, having travelled to Paris to dispose of her stock in 1720. Her journey to Paris, undertaken with another young woman and two male relatives, is recorded in her journal, printed in the *Miscellanies in Prose and Verse, by the Honourable Lady Margaret Pennyman*, published posthumously in September 1739 (dated 1740 on title-page). The journal, which makes no direct mention of any financial transactions, is a pedestrian account of the logistics of travel and Parisian tourist sites. Pennyman does mention seeing Louis XV at mass, and shows an interest in Catholic rites and ceremonies. The preface to this volume, probably by her publisher, the scandalmonger Edmund Curll, states that after returning from France, Pennyman lived reclusively until her death.

The *Miscellanies*, a small octavo volume priced at a modest 3*s.*, gives some indication of Pennyman's life and ideas, as well as revealing an unconventional poetic talent. The most arresting poem, 'A Paradox Against Life' (dated 1713) provides a series of bitter philosophical reflections on the pointlessness of desire and hope, in fluent yet robust couplets:

> Life, the great Hinge, on which uneasy Man
> Does turn in Pain, and never quiet hang;
> Life, which from worldly Cares contracts each Day
> A Rust which eats our polish'd Joys away,
> Life is a strange and fatal Energy.

Among the more public poems, 'A Ballad on the Duke of Marlborough's Funeral' (dated 1722) adopts a similarly tough, sardonic tone in attacking the cruelty and greed of the man; it also implies that Pennyman may have been tory or Jacobite in her political opinions. A group of amorous lyrics, to 'Celia' and 'Chloe', are written in the persona of man, but hint at passionate friendships between the women. The pseudonym Celia is used again in the short series of Pennyman's private letters appended to the volume, where she appears as the younger friend of the principal correspondent 'Mrs. D. F.' (possibly the 'Mary Knight' of the acrostic poem in one of the letters). Pennyman's letters profess extravagant devotion to both 'Celia' and Mrs D. F. The friendship between Pennyman and Mrs D. F. cooled after the latter married in 1732 and thereafter Pennyman's letters become increasingly lonely and desperate: 'What can I say? What can I do? My Brain is strangely disordered'. Pennyman died soon after this great disappointment, on 16 June 1733, and was buried by her brother Burridge Angier in St Margaret's, Westminster. KAREN O'BRIEN

Sources E. Curll, 'Introduction', in M. Pennyman, *Miscellanies in prose and verse* (1740) · GEC, *Baronetage* · *IGI* · R. Strauss, *The unspeakable Curll* (1927) · J. L. Chester and G. J. Armytage, eds., *Allegations for marriage licences issued by the bishop of London*, 2, Harleian Society, 26 (1887) · *GM*, 1st ser., 9 (1739), 500

Pennyman, Mary (1630–1701). *See under* Pennyman, John (1628–1706).

Pennyman, Sir William, baronet (1606/7–1643), army officer and politician, was the eldest son of William Pennyman of St Albans, Hertfordshire (an illegitimate son of James Pennyman of Ormesby, Yorkshire), and of his wife, Anne (either *née* Tottle or *née* Aske). William Pennyman the elder was one of the six clerks in chancery, and on 28 June 1610 obtained a grant with George Evelyn of the office of comptroller and clerk of the hanaper. He died in 1628. William Pennyman the younger was educated at Westminster School, matriculated from Christ Church, Oxford, on 31 October 1623, aged sixteen, and was admitted a student of the Inner Temple in the same year. He was created a baronet on 6 May 1628, and was married to Anne Atherton (*c.*1609–1644) by January 1634. Pennyman succeeded to large estates in Yorkshire, acted as sheriff of the county in 1635–6, and was recommended by Strafford, in April 1637, for the post of *custos rotulorum* of the North Riding, on the ground of his integrity and good affection to the king's service 'which he hath given very good testimonies of in all the commissions he is employed on, as Deputy-Lieutenant, one of the Council of those parts, and as Justice of Oyer and Terminer and of the Peace'. He was an associate of Strafford in exploiting the Yorkshire alum mines in the 1630s. In December 1638 he purchased an office in the Star Chamber, worth £2000 per annum and became a bencher of Gray's Inn in 1639. During the two bishops' wars (1639, 1640) he commanded a regiment of the Yorkshire trained bands, and represented Richmond in the two parliaments called in 1640.

Pennyman was one of the witnesses called at Strafford's trial to testify to the earl's conduct concerning the Yorkshire petition, to the illegal levy of money to support the Yorkshire trained bands (for which Pennyman had been questioned in the Commons in December 1640), to Strafford's boast that he would make the little finger of the king heavier than the loins of the law, and to the crucial charge of planning to deploy the Irish army in England. He showed great reluctance to depose to anything against Strafford, and ultimately cast his vote against the bill for Strafford's attainder with fifty-eight other members.

Having lost office through parliament's abolition of Star Chamber, it was inaccurately reported in December 1641 that Pennyman would be appointed a treasurer of the navy. In April 1642 he accompanied Charles I in his bid to regain control of Hull and subsequently raised a troop of horse and a regiment of six hundred foot for the king, and joined him at Nottingham by 30 July 1642. He was disabled from sitting in the Commons on 11 August following.

Pennyman fought at Edgehill, and in April 1643 was appointed governor of Oxford in succession to Sir Jacob Astley. He fell a victim to the epidemic which prevailed in Oxford in the summer of 1643, died there on 22 August, and was buried in Christ Church Cathedral. His widow died on 13 July 1644, and was buried in the same grave as her husband; they left no children.

C. H. FIRTH, *rev.* R. M. ARMSTRONG

Sources J. T. Cliffe, *The Yorkshire gentry from the Reformation to the civil war* (1969) · GEC, *Peerage* · R. B. Turton, *The alum farm, together with a history of the origin, development and eventual decline of the alum trade in north-east Yorkshire* (1938) · J. Rushworth, *The tryal of Thomas earl of Strafford* (1680) · Foster, *Alum. Oxon.* · Keeler, *Long Parliament* · *CSP dom.*, 1603–10; 1641–3 · A. Steele Young and V. F. Snow, eds., *The private journals of the Long Parliament*, 2: 7 *March to* 1 *June* 1642 (1987) · M. Toynbee and P. Young, *Strangers in Oxford* (1973) · J. Foster, ed., *Pedigrees of the county families of Yorkshire*, 3 vols. (1874)
Archives Sheff. Arch., Strafford MSS · Sheff. Arch., Wentworth Woodhouse MSS · Teeside Archives, Middlesbrough, Pennyman of Ormesby Hall MSS

Penrhyn. For this title name *see* Pennant, Richard, Baron Penrhyn (*c.*1737–1808); Pennant, George Sholto Gordon Douglas-, second Baron Penrhyn (1836–1907).

Penrose, Sir Charles Vinicombe (1759–1830), naval officer, was born in the parish of St Gluvias near Penryn on 20 June 1759, the youngest of seven children of John *Penrose (1713–1776), vicar of St Gluvias and letter writer, and his wife, Elizabeth (1718–1782), daughter of the Revd John Vinicombe. In February 1772 he was admitted to the Royal Naval Academy, Portsmouth, and, after the full course of three years, he joined the frigate *Levant* (Captain the Hon. George Murray), in which he served for four years in the Mediterranean. In August 1779 he was promoted lieutenant and in November he joined the frigate *Cleopatra*, again under Murray. The vessel served in the North Sea for the remainder of the war, Penrose, by then her first lieutenant, suffering severely from hypothermia during the winter of 1780–81. He participated in the action off the Dogger Bank on 5 August 1781, and afterwards wrote a critical account of Sir Hyde Parker's conduct.

In January 1783 the *Cleopatra* was paid off and for the next seven years Penrose was ashore. Nevertheless he rejected an offer by some of the burgesses of Penryn to use their political influence to secure him promotion provided he became a voter in the borough. On 2 January 1787 he married Elizabeth Trevenen (1749/50–1832); the couple had three daughters, and during their early married life lived at Breage, near Helston. Penrose's refusal to advance his career through politics meant that he was still a lieutenant in 1790 when, again under Murray, he served in the *Defence* during the Spanish armament. In 1793 he joined the *Duke*, serving under Murray at the capture of Martinique in June, and later he followed his captain into the *Glory* and then the *Resolution*. In April 1794 Murray was promoted rear-admiral and given command of the North American station: Penrose too was promoted and followed his patron as commander of the *Lynx*. Further advancement was quickly forthcoming when he was posted into the *Cleopatra* in October; and he was briefly Murray's flag-captain in the *Resolution* in 1795 before returning to the *Cleopatra* the following year. Penrose returned home with Murray in June 1796 after the admiral had suffered a stroke. After extensive repairs the *Cleopatra* then served in the channel, though ill health obliged Penrose to leave her in July 1797. From 1799 he once again served in the West Indies, successively in the *Sans Pareil* and the *Carnatic*, before coming home with sunstroke in July 1802.

Between 1804 and 1810 Penrose commanded the seafencibles in the Padstow district. He was then appointed commodore for port duties at Gibraltar; in that responsible position he played an important role in helping Spanish forces fighting the French and also in the defence of Tarifa. In January 1813 his health again forced him home but he was able to participate in a small commission revising the establishment of stores in Plymouth Dockyard. On 4 December he was promoted to the rank of rear-admiral and placed in command of a small squadron operating off northern Spain and south-western France. This force distinguished itself in constructing a bridge across the Adour River in February 1814 and by clearing the Gironde of all French warships during March and April.

Upon Penrose's return to Plymouth in the autumn he was made commander of the Mediterranean Fleet, this lasting until May 1815 when Lord Exmouth, the fleet's former commander, resumed his position. Penrose remained as his second until again becoming overall commander when Exmouth went home in May 1816. In August Penrose was furious to learn of the expedition against Algiers, about which the Admiralty had sent him no word and of which he heard only by chance. He was even angrier to discover that a junior admiral, a stranger to the station, had been made the expedition's second-in-command. Exmouth was able to soothe Penrose's understandably hurt feelings and to persuade him to handle the concluding negotiations with the dey of Algiers. After this he resumed his sole command in the Mediterranean until returning home in 1819. On 19 July 1821 he was advanced to the rank of vice-admiral, having been made a KCB on 3 January 1816 and a KGCMG on 27 April 1818; he saw no further service.

Penrose retired to his home at Ethy, near Lostwithiel.

Between 1804 and 1810 he had contributed to the *Naval Chronicle* under the signatures A. F. Y. and E. F. G., and also to an account of Cornish agriculture published in 1811. He later wrote some pamphlets on naval matters and penned a memoir of his brother-in-law, Captain James Trevenen of the Russian navy, which was published by his nephew, the Revd John *Penrose. Charles Penrose died at Ethy, probably of a stroke, on 1 January 1830, and was buried in the churchyard at St Winnow. He was survived by his wife, who died on 3 April 1832.   CHRISTOPHER D. HALL

Sources J. Penrose, *Lives of Vice-Admiral Sir Charles Vinicombe Penrose KCB and Captain James Trevenen* (1850) · *Annual Biography and Obituary*, 15 (1831), 1–18 · Boase & Courtney, *Bibl. Corn.*, vols. 2–3 · G. C. Boase, *Collectanea Cornubiensia: a collection of biographical and topographical notes relating to the county of Cornwall* (1890) · PRO, ADM 1/421–2 · PRO, WO 1/402 · PRO, ADM 1/156 · S. Baring-Gould, *Cornish characters and strange events* (1909) · C. W. C. Oman, *A history of the Peninsular War*, 7 vols. (1902–30); repr. (1995–7) · *The dispatches of … the duke of Wellington … from 1799 to 1818*, ed. J. Gurwood, 13 vols. in 12 (1834–9) · *Supplementary despatches (correspondence) and memoranda of Field Marshal Arthur, duke of Wellington*, ed. A. R. Wellesley, second duke of Wellington, 15 vols. (1858–72) · W. James, *The naval history of Great Britain, from the declaration of war by France, in February 1793, to the accession of George IV in January 1820*, 5 vols. (1822–4) · E. P. Brenton, *The naval history of Great Britain, from the year 1783 to 1822*, 5 vols. (1823–5) · C. Redding, *Fifty years' recollections, literary and personal*, 2nd edn, 3 vols. (1858)

Archives NMM, letter-book · PRO, letters, WO 1/402 · Royal Naval Museum, Portsmouth, corresp. and papers | BL, corresp. with Sir William A'Court, Add. MSS 41534–41535 · NMM, letters to Lord Keith · NMM, papers relating to James Trevenen · NMM, letters to Charles Yorke · PRO, letters, channel fleet, ADM 1/156 · PRO, letters, Mediterranean fleet, ADM 1/421–2

Likenesses Allingham?, portrait, repro. in Penrose, *Lives* · R. J. Lane, lithograph, NPG · lithograph, NPG

Wealth at death £10,200: will, 1824, PRO, PROB 11/1765

Penrose, Edith Elura Tilton (1914–1996), economist, was born on 29 November 1914 at Sunset Boulevard, Los Angeles, California, the daughter of George Albert Tilton, a civil engineer involved in road construction, and his wife, Hazel Sparling, a descendant of a passenger on the *Mayflower*. She had two brothers, Harvey and Jack, both of whom were killed during military service, in 1952 and 1945 respectively. For a time she was brought up in road camps along the highway which her father surveyed, but the family eventually settled in the tiny Californian town of St Luis Obispo, where she went to school. She then studied at the University of California at Berkeley, graduating AB in economics in 1936. Her first job after graduating was in social work with an agency for depression relief. In 1934 she had married a lawyer, David Burton Denhardt, and in 1938 she was expecting their first child (a son) when Denhardt was killed in a mysterious hunting accident. In 1939 she began to work with Ernest Francis (Pen) Penrose (1896–1984), a distinguished economist who had been her professor at Berkeley, at the International Labour Organization in Geneva. She worked there as a researcher in the economics section of the organization, and her work on the food problems in wartime Britain gave rise to her first book, *Food Control in Great Britain* (1940). Fearing a German invasion, the organization moved to Montreal in mid-1940, but in March 1941 John Winant, the deputy director, who had initially brought Pen to Geneva, was appointed American ambassador to Britain. Pen joined him in London as economic adviser, and Edith joined his staff as a special assistant; they remained in London throughout the war, and married on 27 October 1944. They had three sons, one of whom died as a young child.

The Penroses followed Winant back to the United States in 1946 to serve under him on the US delegation to the newly formed United Nations. After Winant's death in 1947 they moved first to Princeton, and then to Johns Hopkins University in Baltimore, where Pen took a chair in human geography and Edith began her postgraduate studies in economics. Her doctoral thesis was supervised by the eminent neo-classical economist, Fritz Machlup, and was published as *The Economics of the International Patent System* (1951). This was the turning point in Edith Penrose's career. Through her doctoral research work and a subsequent research project involving fieldwork at the Hercules Powder Company, she became an industrial economist. Her major work, *The Theory of the Growth of the Firm* (1959), was the product of these endeavours. Her approach differed fundamentally from the prevailing microeconomic, neo-classical paradigm, in that it attached great importance to observing the world. Theory, she argued, was necessary to understand a complex reality, but should not be developed in isolation from that reality. For Penrose, the firm is a set of productive resources 'under administrative co-ordination for the production of goods and services for sale in the market for a profit' (Penrose and Pitelis, 9). The distinction between firm and market lies in the boundary: economic activity inside the firm is carried on within an administrative organization, while economic activity in the market is not. Growth is endogenous to the firm. The firm is defined in terms of resources (including managerial) which are not inputs but provide services which are themselves inputs, while neo-classical theory defines the firm in terms of outputs produced at the minimum point of the average cost curve. According to Penrose, the incentive to grow is attributed to the inevitable emergence of unused managerial resources after an expansion plan has been completed. 'Unused productive services are, for the enterprising firm, at the same time a challenge to innovate, an incentive to expand, and a source of competitive advantage' (ibid., 11). The book had a tremendous impact both on the theory of the firm, and, by extension, on issues of strategic management.

Throughout the 1950s Penrose was a lecturer and research associate at Johns Hopkins, but when she and Pen defended their colleague Owen Lattimore against Senator McCarthy's committee on unAmerican activities, they found it more congenial to leave the United States. Penrose then spent 1955–6 in Canberra as a visiting professor at the Australian National University, and 1957–9 as an associate professor at Baghdad University. At the latter she acquired the strong interest in the Middle East which bore fruit in her work on international oil companies. However, she never learned Arabic, and despite her affection

for the region she had no deep understanding of its peoples and their culture. In 1960 Pen had reached retirement age, and they both returned to England, where, on the strength of her recently published *Theory of the Growth of the Firm*, Edith Penrose was appointed to a readership in economics at the London School of Economics and the School of Oriental and African Studies. In 1964 the latter established a chair of economics with special reference to Asia, which she held until 1978, and she also chaired the newly established economics department for some years. Her major empirical work at this time was on oil companies, *The Large International Firm in Developing Countries: the International Petroleum Industry* (1968). In her work in this area she was among the first to discover the phenomenon of transfer pricing and its implications for tax optimization. To make the most of opportunities that reduce fiscal liabilities is a central feature of the multinational corporation's behaviour. The economic implications of this behaviour for oil markets and prices are wide-ranging; Penrose opened a field in which much research remained to be done.

On retiring from London University, Penrose moved to a different type of institution, INSEAD, the management school at Fontainebleau, France, where she was professor of political economy and associate dean for research and development. In a sense this took her back to the field where she had made her most significant and original intellectual contribution: the management of firms. At INSEAD she received belated and well-deserved recognition, whereas the time spent at the School of Oriental and African Studies and her work on economic development were perhaps a digression. Pen's death in 1984 had a profound impact on her, and she decided to retire to Waterbeach, Cambridge, to be near her son. She continued to lead an active professional life, sitting on boards and committees, acting as a consultant and expert witness, and contributing important articles to the economic literature. She died at her home, 30A Station Road, Waterbeach, from heart failure, on 11 October 1996.

Edith Penrose was petite, good-looking, extremely kind to those who needed her support, and very sharp with those she thought were able to take it. Not all were. She nevertheless won the affection and admiration of many who valued the independence of her mind and her indifference to social status and pretensions. She was a liberal in the substantive, not the romantic, meaning of the term. She was suspicious of any concentration of power, political or economic, and stood firm in defence of cherished values. She and Pen helped Jewish refugees in Switzerland in 1940, and their defence of Lattimore against McCarthy obliged them to leave the United States. She used to say, quoting John Winant, 'the important thing is to lose your illusions and not become disillusioned'. This was the motto of her life.   ROBERT MABRO

Sources P. Penrose and C. Pitelis, *Contributions to political economy* (1999), 18.3–21 • M. H. Best and E. Garnsey, *Economic Journal*, 109/453 (Feb 1999), pp. 187ss • *WWW* • *Daily Telegraph* (5 Nov 1996) • *The Independent* (19 Oct 1996) • *The Guardian* (19 Oct 1996) • m. cert. [Ernest Francis Penrose] • d. cert.

Penrose [*née* Cartwright], **Elizabeth** [*pseud.* Mrs Markham] (*c.*1779–1837), writer, was born at Goadby Marwood, Leicestershire, on 3 August 1780, the second daughter of Edmund *Cartwright (1743–1823), rector of Goadby Marwood, and his wife, Alice (*d.* 1785), the youngest daughter and coheir of Richard Whittaker of Doncaster. Her family were lively and intelligent: her father was a famous inventor of textile machinery, and her uncle, Major John *Cartwright (1740–1824), was a prominent radical reformer. Her brother Edmund (1773–1833), who took orders, was the author of a *Parochial Topography of the Rape of Bramber* (1830), and her youngest sister, Frances Dorothy *Cartwright (1780–1863), wrote a biography of their uncle (1826), and her elder sister, Mary, wrote one of their father (1843).

Alice Cartwright died on 12 September 1785, and on 5 June 1790 Edmund Cartwright married Susanna, daughter of the Revd John Kearney. His daughters lived almost entirely with paternal relatives after Cartwright's second marriage. The two eldest, Mary and Elizabeth, were sent to the Manor School in York; a former pupil, Eliza Fletcher, described the education offered at this boarding-school as 'artificial, flat and uninteresting', opining that 'nothing useful could be learned' (*Autobiography of Mrs Fletcher*, 17). Probably Elizabeth Cartwright developed her historical interests independently: her uncle, in a letter of 1796, recorded that 'Eliza, though a merry girl, devours folios of history with much more appetite than her meals' (*Life and Correspondence*, 1.411). Fair and slight, she became, according to Eliza Fletcher (162), 'a most delightful woman, with a lively, active, accomplished mind, and the most engaging sweetness and simplicity of manners'.

Elizabeth Cartwright spent much time with two unmarried aunts at Markham, in Nottinghamshire, where she met John *Penrose (1778–1859), a Cornish clergyman who was the elder brother of Mary Arnold, wife of the famous Rugby headmaster and historian. He became vicar of Bracebridge, Lincolnshire, in 1809, and married Elizabeth Cartwright on 6 May 1814. Their marriage, apparently a happy one, brought them three sons: John (1815–1888), who took holy orders and became an assistant master at Rugby; Charles Thomas (1816?–1868), who was later headmaster of Sherborne School; and Francis Cranmer *Penrose (1817–1903), an architect and astronomer. The daughter of the last, Emily *Penrose (1858–1942), became principal of Somerville College, Oxford.

In 1823 Elizabeth Penrose's first book, *A History of England from the First Invasion by the Romans to the End of the Reign of George III*, appeared under the pseudonym of Mrs Markham. It was first published by Archibald Constable of Edinburgh in 1823, but, after his notorious bankruptcy of 1826, John Murray purchased the remaining stock. In the same year a revised and enlarged edition appeared, with illustrations drawn from the antiquarian works of Joseph Strutt—a novel departure for an early nineteenth-century textbook. It was an immediate success and achieved 'a very large and regular circulation' (Smiles, 2.152).

According to the introduction Mrs Markham resolved to write the book, after her eldest son experienced difficulty reading Hume's *History of England*, as a didactic substitute for the usual bedtime story. The narrative is a domesticized version of English history, presenting historical figures as exempla of good and bad conduct in private life; the virtues advocated are familial duty, personal integrity, and social benevolence. But the *History* has wider implications: Elizabeth Penrose firmly supports the Anglican establishment and the social and political status quo. Her knowledge of the late eighteenth-century 'philosophical' historians was reflected in her determination to produce 'something more than a mere chronicle of events', hoping to trace 'the successive changes which have taken place in manners, arts and civilization'. These matters were covered in the conversations at the end of each chapter, where the author employed the question-answer technique common to the nineteenth-century textbook writer.

With her husband managing publication with John Murray and probably her other publishers, Elizabeth Penrose produced a succession of juvenile works, including *A History of France* (1828), which was republished by Murray in a revised edition in 1857 and 1882. Books of questions to accompany it were published in 1853, 1854, and 1860. Histories of Greece and Rome were announced, but never published. Elizabeth Penrose also published *A Visit to the Zoological Gardens* (1829), *Historical Conversations for Young Persons* (1836), *Sermons for Children* (1837), and *The New Children's Friend* (1832). The latter publication is a curious compound of didactic tales and conversations on matters as diverse as the history of the Isle of Man and the transmigration of the soul.

By 1834 Elizabeth Penrose was unwell; she and her family moved to the Minster Yard, Lincoln, which was considered a more healthy situation. Here she died on 24 January 1837 and was buried in the cloisters of Lincoln Cathedral.

A History of England proved more resilient than its author, and had reached its twelfth edition by 1846. It was republished in revised editions by Murray in 1853, 1859, and 1875. In 1865, when it was published by T. J. Allman, the editor, Mary Howitt, commented in her preface that the *History of England* was 'well-known to all mothers whose children, like mine, received their first lessons in English history from its pages'. The longevity of its reputation is confirmed by the appearance in 1926 of a parodic version by Hilaire Belloc. Books of questions to accompany the *History of England* were published in 1845, 1856, and 1858. With the possible exception of Maria Callcott's *Little Arthur's History of England* (1835), it was the most successful nineteenth-century history textbook: it is hardly an exaggeration to say that it 'held its place as almost the only textbook of English history used in schools and families for nearly forty years' (*DNB*).

ROSEMARY MITCHELL

Sources Boase & Courtney, *Bibl. Corn.*, 2.454–5, 457–8 · *DNB* · Burke, *Gen. GB* · H. Carpenter and M. Prichard, *The Oxford companion to children's literature*, pbk edn (1999), 338 · *Autobiography of Mrs*

Fletcher, of Edinburgh, ed. M. R. [M. Richardson] (1874), 17, 31–3, 162, 189 · *GM*, 2nd ser., 7 (1837), 332 · *The life and correspondence of Major Cartwright*, ed. F. D. Cartwright, 1 (1826), 407, 411 · V. E. Chancellor, *History for their masters: opinion in the English history textbook, 1800–1914* (1970) · John Murray, London, archives · R. A. Mitchell, 'Approaches to history in text and image in England, c.1830–1870', DPhil diss., U. Oxf., 1993, 1.55–89 · S. Smiles, *A publisher and his friends: memoir and correspondence of the late John Murray*, 2 (1891), 152 · *IGI*
Archives John Murray, London, archives

Penrose, Dame Emily (1858–1942), college head, was born in London on 18 September 1858, the second of five children and eldest of four daughters of Francis Cranmer *Penrose (1817–1903), architect and archaeologist, and his wife, Harriette Gibbes (*d.* 1903), and was baptized at Coleby, Lincolnshire, where her great-uncle, the Revd Thomas Trevenen Penrose, was vicar. Her paternal grandmother, Elizabeth *Penrose, was the writer Mrs Markham; she was related to the Arnolds by the marriage of her grandfather's sister, Mary Penrose, to Dr Thomas Arnold of Rugby. Her education at Conway House, Wimbledon, placed more stress on deportment than book learning, but was supplemented in the course of long family visits to the continent, which enabled her to study languages and the arts at Versailles, Paris, Dresden, and Berlin. In England, she borrowed books from friends, and was an enthusiastic attender of university extension lectures. She shared the scientific interests of her brother, Francis George Penrose (1857–1932), and was taught drawing and painting by her father, whom she accompanied to Athens in 1886 on his appointment as first director of the British School of Archaeology. While there, she took charge of the family business and learned modern Greek. The following year she returned to England and taught literature, languages, and drawing at Miss White's school in Brighton.

Her father's friendship with Henry Francis Pelham, professor of ancient history at Oxford and a leader of the Liberals in the university, determined the course of Emily Penrose's future career. At his suggestion she entered Somerville College, Oxford, as a scholar in 1889, at the age of thirty-one, to read *literae humaniores* (Greats). Starting with no Latin and only modern Greek, and choosing an archaeological special subject for which she could draw on her experience in Athens, she became in 1892 the first woman to be placed in the first class in Greats. Ineligible, as a woman, for an Oxford degree, she was to be one of the first to present herself for a Trinity College, Dublin, MA under the provisional *ad eundem* arrangements of 1904. She worked briefly as an extension lecturer in Oxford and London before being appointed in 1893 to the principalship of Bedford College, London, a post which she combined with that of professor in ancient history. In 1898 she moved to the Royal Holloway College, returning to Somerville, as principal, in 1907, at the invitation of the college council, on the death in office of Agnes Maitland.

To all three colleges, at different stages in their development, Emily Penrose brought a heightened sense of academic purpose and integration into a wider academic

Dame Emily Penrose (1858–1942), by C. W. Carey, 1890s

community. In London, she prepared the ground for Bedford and Holloway to be admitted in 1900 as schools of the university, and herself served as chairman of the classical board and as a member of the university senate. In Oxford, where in the early years of her principalship she also taught Somerville's Greats' students, she was immediately drawn into the negotiations which led to the establishment in 1910 of a university delegacy for women students, on which she served as an elected member, and ten years later to the admission of women to full membership of the university. During the First World War, when Somerville's buildings were requisitioned for use as a military hospital, she guided the college through an unsettling period of temporary accommodation in Oriel, while organizing—according to press reports, with unique efficiency—the national registration for Oxford, work for which the OBE was conferred on her in 1918.

Emily Penrose's standing in the university was enhanced by her experience of the larger world of academic politics and finance. She served in 1911 as a member of the advisory committee on university grants, and in 1916 as the only woman member of the royal commission on university education in Wales. In 1919 she was appointed to the royal commission on the universities of Oxford and Cambridge, becoming a statutory commissioner for Oxford in 1923. These public duties were combined with a heavy post-war burden of college business, as Somerville launched an appeal for funds, planned a new building (later named after her), and embarked on a series of major constitutional changes leading to its incorporation under royal charter in 1926.

Pressure of these various commitments obliged Emily Penrose to decline to serve in 1920 as one of the first women magistrates. It also told on her health, which had never been strong; and it was on her doctor's advice that in 1925 she tendered her resignation to the Somerville council. The university marked her retirement in 1926 by conferring on her the honorary degree of DCL—the first woman apart from Queen Mary to be so honoured. Sheffield followed with an honorary LLD, and in 1927 her work for education received national recognition when she was made a DBE. A modest person, she accepted these honours, as she said, 'for the college'. The large sum collected as a farewell present was used, at her request, to establish a students' loan fund. She retired to London, moving on the outbreak of war (by which time she was an almost complete invalid) to Bournemouth, where she died, unmarried, at 11 Dean Park Road on 26 January 1942.

Emily Penrose possessed a combination of scholarship with high administrative ability which was unusual at that date and which made her an important role model for the rising generation of women academics. The unexpectedly generous terms of the 1920 statute by which Oxford eventually conceded membership of the university to women owed much to her patient diplomacy, and hardly less to her personal example: in her presence it was not easy to make out a convincing case for the intellectual inferiority of women or their unfittedness for university business. A person of many accomplishments (a fine needlewoman, talented actress, and intrepid mountaineer), she was markedly lacking in certain social skills: stories abounded among undergraduates of her terrifying attempts at small talk. Her height, an embarrassment to her in adolescence, reinforced in later life a somewhat Olympian presence. Deeply reserved in all personal matters, she was a devout, but undemonstrative, Anglican, and a firm, but unmilitant, suffragist. She enjoyed the company of children, and was terrified of cats.

PAULINE ADAMS

Sources H. Darbishire, *Somerville College Report* (1942–3) • Somerville College Archives, Penrose MSS • M. J. Tuke, *A history of Bedford College for Women, 1849–1937* (1939) • C. Bingham, *The history of Royal Holloway College, 1886–1986* (1987) • P. Adams, *Somerville for women: an Oxford college, 1879–1993* (1996) • CGPLA Eng. & Wales (1942) • private information (1959)
Archives Royal Holloway College, Egham, Surrey, archives of Bedford College • Royal Holloway College, Egham, Surrey • Somerville College, Oxford, archives
Likenesses C. W. Carey, photograph, 1890–99, NPG [*see illus.*] • P. A. de Laszlo, oils, *c.*1907, Royal Holloway College, London • P. A. de Laszlo, oils, 1907, Somerville College, Oxford • F. Helps, oils, 1922, Somerville College, Oxford • photographs, Somerville College, Oxford • photographs, NPG
Wealth at death £26,445 9s. 8d.: probate, 18 Aug 1942, CGPLA Eng. & Wales

Penrose, Francis (1718–1798), medical writer, was a surgeon who practised for many years at Bicester, Oxfordshire. He bought property in the nearby village of Chesterton, and later bought Chesterton Lodge, which he greatly improved. The estate was sold after his death. Penrose was chiefly remembered in the area for his attempt to investigate the ruins of Alchester in Wendlebury, the Roman station at the junction of two roads adjoining Chesterton. There, in a wood on the west side of the castrum, he discovered in 1766 the remains of a large building, within which were a tesselated pavement and a hypocaust. This building he described as the Praetorium. Penrose left Bicester about 1782, and went to live in Stonehouse, Devon, but did not practise there.

Penrose was a prolific writer of pamphlets on scientific subjects related to medicine. His works do not, as a rule, repay perusal. He wrote *A Treatise on Electricity* (1752), and *An Essay on Magnetism* (1753). His *Physical Essay on the Animal Economy*, in which old physiological theories were revived, was published in 1754. His essay on the putrid sore throat and putrid fever, published in 1766, was a practical treatise, in which he recorded cases he had seen in his practice. His Newtonian *Letters Philosophical and Astronomical*, on 'the creation, the deluge, vegetation, the make and form of this terraqueous globe' was published in 1789. The letters were originally written to John Heaviside (1747/8–1828), and were dated from Stonehouse in 1783. The critical reviews in December 1788 said of them that 'the Mosaic account of the creation is here explained and defended, as well as the deluge, and gravity is accounted for by hot and cold ether'. Penrose's *Essays … Founded on the … Chemistry of Lavoisier, Fourcroy …* (1794) was severely handled in the first volume of the *Medical and Chirurgical Review* (1795). On the title-page he describes himself as MD for the first time; he is supposed to have obtained the degree at a German university.

Penrose's son, James Penrose (1750–1818), was appointed surgeon-extraordinary to George III in November 1793, in succession to John Hunter (1728–1793). Francis Penrose died in his son's house at Hatfield, Hertfordshire, on 17 January 1798. Both father and son were buried in the churchyard at Hatfield, but no trace of their tombstone exists.

D'A. POWER, rev. JEAN LOUDON

Sources private information (1895) • *GM*, 1st ser., 68 (1798), 88 • *Medical and Chirurgical Review*, 1 (1795), 158–63 • *GM*, 1st ser., 88/2 (1818), 641 [James Penrose]

Penrose, Francis Cranmer (1817–1903), architect, classical archaeologist, and astronomer, was born on 29 October 1817 at Bracebridge, near Lincoln, the youngest son of the Revd John *Penrose (1778–1859). His mother was Elizabeth *Penrose, *née* Cartwright (*c.*1779–1837), a children's writer under the pseudonym of Mrs Markham, and Francis was the original of the Mary in her *History of England*. Penrose's second name was a claim to direct descent through his mother from the sister of Archbishop Cranmer presaging his life-long protestant evangelical Anglican beliefs. His aunt Mary Penrose was the wife of Thomas Arnold, headmaster of Rugby School. He was educated at Bedford modern school (1825–9) and was a scholar at Winchester College (1829–35). His early drawing skills led him (1835–9) to the office of the architect Edward Blore. But instead of starting architectural practice, at the age of twenty-two he became an undergraduate at Magdalene College, Cambridge, graduating in mathematics as tenth

Francis Cranmer Penrose (1817–1903), by John Singer Sargent, 1898

senior optime in 1842. A noted athlete, he more than once walked in one day from Cambridge to London, and skated from Ely to the Wash. He rowed against Oxford, in 1840, 1841, and 1842, and was captain of the Cambridge University Boat Club in 1841. As captain of his college boat, he brought it to nearly head of the river. He was the inventor of the system of charts in the bumping races, which are still in use for registering the relative positions of crews. Among his friends while an undergraduate were the novelist and clergyman Charles Kingsley, almost a contemporary at Magdalene, through whom he came to know the theologian Frederick Denison Maurice, the chemist Charles Blachford Mansfield, the social activist John Malcolm Ludlow, and the astronomer John Couch Adams, who with George Peacock awakened an interest in astronomy. As a young man he saw much of his first cousin Matthew Arnold at Rugby, where his brother was a schoolmaster.

In 1842 Penrose was appointed travelling bachelor of the University of Cambridge and began an important European architectural tour (1842–5). Already a skilled draughtsman, he learnt the art of watercolour from Peter DeWint. He made his first prolonged halt at Paris, where he visited the observatory, as well as architectural scenes.

At Paris, and subsequently at Chartres, Fontainebleau, Sens, Auxerre, Bourges, Avignon, Nîmes, and Arles, he sketched and studied industriously. At Rome in 1843 his keen eye criticized the pitch of the pediment of the Pantheon as being 'steeper than I quite like', a comment subsequently justified by further research. Fifty-two years later M. Chedanne of Paris read a paper in London (at a meeting over which Penrose presided) and proved that the pitch of the pediment in fact had been altered. Penrose stayed six months at Rome, and thence wrote the stipulated Latin letter as travelling bachelor to the University of Cambridge. He chose as his theme the (Gothic) cathedral of Bourges.

Between June 1843 and spring 1844 Penrose visited the chief cities of Italy. He later started somewhat reluctantly for Greece, describing Athens as 'by far the most miserable town of its size I have ever seen' (9 January 1845). But he soon fell under the spell of the 'Pericleian Monuments', to which his initial enthusiasm for Gothic architecture quickly gave way. In August 1845 he made his way home through Switzerland, Augsburg, Munich, and Cologne.

Already Penrose realized the importance of exact mensuration to a critical study of Greek architecture. The pamphlet on the subject by John Pennethorne had already attracted his attention on its publication in 1844. On his arrival in England, the Society of Dilettanti had determined to test thoroughly Pennethorne's theories as to the measurements of Greek classical buildings, and they commissioned Penrose to undertake the task on their behalf. In 1846 Penrose was again at Athens. His principal collaborator in the work of measurement there was Thomas Willson of Lincoln. Their work was completed in May 1847. Despite corrections in detail Penrose confirmed in essentials Pennethorne's theories. When in 1878 Pennethorne brought out his *Geometry and Optics of Ancient Architecture* he adopted with due acknowledgement Penrose's mass of indisputable material.

Anomalies in the Construction of the Parthenon, which the Society of Dilettanti published in 1847, was the first result of Penrose's labours, but it was in 1851 that there appeared his monumental work, *Principles of Athenian Architecture*, of which a more complete edition was issued in 1888 on which his international reputation as a classical archaeologist is based. Penrose's exhaustive and minutely accurate measurements finally established that what is apparently parallel or straight in Greek architecture of the Periclean period is generally neither straight nor parallel but curved or inclined. He therefore solved the puzzle which all commentators on Vitruvius had found insoluble by identifying the 'scamilli impares' with those top and bottom blocks of the columns which, by virtue of the inclination of the column or the curvature of stylobate and architrave, are 'unequal' (i.e. they have their upper and lower faces out of parallel). Some important conclusions relating to the Roman temple of Jupiter Olympius at Athens, Penrose laid before the Institute of British Architects in 1888.

In 1852 Penrose succeeded C. R. Cockerell (who recommended him) as surveyor of St Paul's Cathedral. The appointment, technically with a view to the completion of the interior decoration in accordance with the intentions of Wren, was made impossible by the religious and artistic factionalism of the day, as shown in the attempts to restore the interior after various appeals. William Burges was even appointed as joint architect (1872–8) for one of these. As surveyor of St Paul's, Penrose was one of the few British architects to adhere to the classical style in the second half of the nineteenth century. He began to introduce Munich stained glass (des.), 'Roman' mosaic pavements, and furniture such as the large early Christian style pulpit (1860; dem. 1954). He demolished Wren's choir screen, divided the organ into two, and provided new choir stalls and desks. Of the two internal porches made from Wren's woodwork, only that at the south transept survives. Externally, he restored (1872) the square plan and divided layout of Wren's west-front steps and made the setting of the Queen Anne statue (1886). He defended the sculptor Alfred Stevens's proposal for the Wellington monument, for which he claimed 'general superintendence' (1858–79) finally erecting it in the nave (1893). Penrose had married in 1856 Harriette (d. 1903), daughter of Francis Gibbes, surgeon, of Harewood, Yorkshire.

Like Wren himself Penrose found relief from disappointment at St Paul's in astronomical study, which had already attracted him at Cambridge and in Paris. He was adept at mechanical inventions, and an instrument for drawing spirals won him a prize at the Great Exhibition of 1851. A theodolite which he had bought in 1852 primarily for use in measurement of buildings, he applied at the suggestion of Dr G. Boole to such astronomical purposes as accurate determination of orientation and time in connection, for example, with the fixing of sundials. In 1862 came the purchase of a small astronomical telescope which was soon superseded by a larger one with a 5½ inch object-glass (Steinheil), equatorially mounted by Troughton and Simms. In 1866 Penrose, finding the prediction of the time of an occultation of Saturn in the *Nautical Almanac* inadequate for his purpose, endeavoured with success 'to obtain by graphical construction a more exact correspondence suited to the site' of the observer. He published his results in 1869 in *The Prediction and Reduction of Occultations and Eclipses*, and the work reached a second edition in 1902.

In 1870 Penrose visited Jérez in the south of Spain to view the total eclipse of the sun with his smaller (2¼ inch) instrument. The observation was spoilt by a cloud, but Penrose made the acquaintance of Professor Charles A. Young of America, whom he met again at Denver in 1878. Penrose's observations on the eclipse of 29 July 1878 in Denver, when his principal object was to draw the corona, were published in the *Monthly Notices, Royal Astronomical Society*, 39 (1878–9), 48–51. He afterwards extended to comets the graphical method of prediction that he had applied to the moon (cf. his paper before the Royal Astronomical Society, December 1881, and chapter 6 in G. F. Chambers's *Handbook of Astronomy*, 4th edn, 3 vols., 1889).

Penrose's last astronomical work was a study of the orientation of temples, to which Sir Norman Lockyer directed his attention. Presuming that 'the object sought by the ancients in orienting their temples was to obtain from the stars at their rising or setting, as the case might be, a sufficient warning of the approach of dawn for preparation for the critical moment of sacrifice', he perceived the importance of calculating the places of certain stars at distant epochs, and the possibility of estimating the age of certain temples by assuming an orientation and calculating the period of variation or apparent movement in the stars due to the precession of the equinoxes. Penrose applied his theory to certain Greek temples (see *Proceedings* and *Philosophic Transactions of the Royal Society*), and with Lockyer he worked out a calculation on this basis in relation to Stonehenge (see also *Journal of Proceedings of the Royal Institute of British Architects*, 25 Jan 1902). He joined the Royal Astronomical Society in 1867, and in 1894 his astronomical researches were recognized by his election as a fellow of the Royal Society.

Penrose's practice as an architect was small, largely church-based. It did not reflect his obvious ability. At Magdalene College, Cambridge, he restored the west front (1873–4; unpicked 1954) and built the river court gate; he built a wing—the Penrose—at St John's College, Cambridge (1885–6); and at Rugby School he erected the sanatorium (1867). His many vicarages began with Burleigh, Somerset (1846); typically a vicarage might be related to a church restoration as at Escribe, Yorkshire (1849; church 1850). He designed a private house in Wimbledon to be shared by Thomas Hughes and Ian Ludlow (1852–3; dem.) and one in Colebyfield (1861–2) for himself. Alford House, Somerset (*c*.1877), was his only commission of country-house scale. His neo-baroque staircase projects (1860–88) for Ickworth House, Suffolk, were not executed; his garden terrace and stairs at Powerscourt House, co. Wicklow, Ireland (1874–5), are related. At Ickworth he was responsible finally for the Pompeian room (1878–9) painted by J. D. Grace. The town hall, Castle Cary, Somerset (1834–5), in a rationalist neo-Tudor Gothic, shows where his practice might have developed otherwise.

When in 1882 the foundation of the British School at Athens was projected, Penrose generously designed the building (a Graeco-Roman villa, 1855–6) without fee. It was completed in 1886, when Penrose accepted the directorate (1886–7 and 1890–91). At St Paul's, from where he practised, he designed the choir school (1873–5), Italianate, decorated externally in neo-Renaissance sgraffitto and polychromy. His surviving contribution is the massive Cornish porphyry sarcophagus on a granite plinth tomb of the duke of Wellington (1857) 'based on a small sketch by Cockerell, but I had complete charge of the detail and execution', he wrote. Also his are the Roman mosaic floor here and under the crossing around Nelson's tomb, the marble alterations, and wall tablet (1891) to Lord Napier of Magdala.

Penrose was an associate (1846), fellow (1848), and president (1894–6) of the Royal Institute of British Architects and he received the royal gold medal of the institute in

1883. Many of his office drawings and his own manuscript list of works were presented to RIBA in 1938. He became a fellow of the Society of Antiquaries in 1898, when he was elected antiquary to the Royal Academy, where he had often exhibited. He was made in 1884 one of the first honorary fellows of Magdalene College, Cambridge, and in 1898 he became a LittD of his university as well as an honorary DCL of Oxford. He was a knight of the order St Saviour of Greece. Penrose's portrait at the Royal Institute of British Architects is one of the most characteristic works of J. S. Sargent RA (a copy is at Magdalene College).

Penrose died at Colebyfield, Wimbledon, after forty years' residence on 15 February 1903. He was buried at Wimbledon. His wife predeceased him by twelve days. He left a son, Dr Francis G. Penrose, and four daughters, the eldest of whom, Emily *Penrose (1858–1942), became successively principal of Bedford College, Royal Holloway College, and Somerville College, Oxford. A lettered memorial tablet was placed in the crypt of St Paul's Cathedral by his architectural admirers.

PAUL WATERHOUSE, rev. RODERICK O'DONNELL

Sources RIBA BAL, F. C. Penrose MSS, PEF/1/3/711 • F. C. Penrose, *An investigation of the principles of Athenian architecture*, new edn (1888) • C. Plante, 'Francis Cranmer Penrose, 1817–1903', BA diss., U. Cam., 1987 • J. Lever, ed., *Catalogue of the drawings collection of the Royal Institute of British Architects: O–R* (1976), 46–8 • J. D. Crace, ed., 'Francis Cranmer Penrose', *RIBA Journal*, 10 (1902–3), 339–46 • R. Hyam, 'Unbuilt Magdalene: Penrose's plan for the second court (1872–3)', *Magdalene College Magazine and Record*, new ser., 30 (1985–6), 21–4 • N. Strachey, 'The Pompeian room at Ickworth: the work of F. C. Penrose and J. D. Crace', *Apollo*, 145 (April 1997), 8–12 • J. M. Crook, 'William Burges and the completion of Saint Paul's', *Antiquaries Journal*, 60 (1980), 154–69

Archives RAS, letters • RIBA, drawings and papers • RIBA, sketchbook of East Anglia, Lincolnshire, and Yorkshire churches • RIBA, corresp. and papers relating to Wellington monument, St Paul's Cathedral | CUL, travelling bachelor MSS • Magd. Cam., portfolio, vol. 6, MBC, 1 • St Paul's Cathedral, London, trophy room • Suffolk RO, Ipswich, Bristol family MSS, Penrose on Ickworth

Likenesses J. S. Sargent, oils, 1898, RIBA [*see illus.*] • portrait (after J. S. Sargent), Magd. Cam.

Wealth at death £25,584 4s. 8d.: probate, 13 March 1903, CGPLA Eng. & Wales

Penrose, Harald James (1904–1996), airman, was born at 103 Park Street, Hereford, on 12 April 1904, the son of James Penrose, an Inland Revenue clerk, and his wife, Elizabeth Alice, née Johnson. At the age of five he became enamoured with flight after his father showed him a picture of the monoplane in which Louis Blériot had just flown the channel. Two years later he was lifted a few feet aloft beneath a Cody-type kite. Several encounters with pioneer aeroplanes sustained his ambition to fly, not realized until 1919 in a war-surplus Avro 504K in which the former Royal Flying Corps pilot Alan Cobham was giving joyrides from a field in Reading. Failing to find employment with an aircraft manufacturer, Penrose pursued a four-year aeronautical course at the Northampton Engineering College of London University. All four students on the course gained diplomas, but Penrose was the only one to pass an early City and Guilds examination in aeronautics. In September 1926 he joined the Westland Aircraft Works

at Yeovil, Somerset, and by the new year he was overseeing the construction of the Widgeon III light sporting monoplane.

In 1927 Penrose obtained a commission in the Reserve of Air Force Officers (RAFO) and learned to fly in a Bristol type 73 trainer at the Bristol Flying School. After six hours' dual he went solo, progressing to a Jupiter-engined advanced trainer variant of the Bristol fighter. He then returned to Westland gazetted as a pilot officer RAFO, gained his private pilot's A licence in the same year, and made his first flights for Westland in the Widgeon. By March 1928, although he had less than 100 hours' total piloting experience, Penrose was authorized to fly a number of the company's new machines. He was also acting as a flight-test observer, and later that year was made manager of Westland's newly established civil aircraft department, overseeing development of the W.IV and Wessex tri-motor feeder liners. In October he qualified for his commercial pilot's B licence. On 23 March 1929, in Reading, he married Nora Sybil Bailey (1903/4–1986); they had a son and a daughter. That same year he also added responsibility for the technical side of civil sales to his company duties.

In 1930 Penrose began flying the Wapiti general-purpose military two-seater, and early in the following year he was entrusted with demonstrating a variant in South America in landplane and seaplane configurations. Shortly after his return, in May 1931, Westland's pilot in charge, Captain Louis Paget, suffered serious injuries in a crash, and Penrose was asked to fulfil Paget's duties—with no increase in pay, though his insurance coverage was increased. In his autobiography he recalled: 'It just seemed wonderful that Westland was letting me have extensive free flying which I would otherwise have been unable to afford'. When it transpired that Paget was permanently crippled, Penrose was appointed chief test pilot.

In the succeeding twenty-two years Penrose made the initial test flights of all of the Westland aircraft types, most notably the unconventional Pterodactyl series of tailless monoplanes designed by Captain Geoffrey Hill, the Houston-Westland PV3 which in April 1933 made the first flight over Everest, and the Lysander army co-operation aircraft used for flying agents into and out of enemy territory during the Second World War. On 24 August 1934 he became the first pilot to bale out of an enclosed-cockpit aeroplane when the Westland P7 general-purpose monoplane he was flying suffered a disastrous in-flight structural failure. When suction forces jammed the sliding roof, he was forced to make his exit through a side window. Production test-flying intensified with the outbreak of war. In October 1938 Penrose made the maiden flight of the new Whirlwind twin-engine fighter, which proved a disappointment. A one-off experiment was tried in the form of a tandem-wing version of the Lysander, which Penrose looped on its maiden flight in July 1944, but no development ensued. Penrose also carried out the production flight tests of other manufacturers' aircraft built under licence by Westland: Supermarine Spitfires and Seafires, Fairey Barracudas, and lend-lease

Curtiss Mohawk and Tomahawk fighters. The last war-time design to emanate from Westland, the Welkin high-altitude fighter, proved a troublesome mount for Penrose and his fellow pilots.

By far the most notorious aeroplane flown by Penrose, however, was the turboprop-powered Wyvern naval fighter, which suffered from being a new airframe married to new and under-developed engines. This large single-seater, first flown on 16 December 1946, cost the lives of three test pilots during its protracted development. Only his quick and instinctive reactions saved Penrose from becoming another victim when a Wyvern in which he was returning to Yeovil suffered a failed aileron linkage and turned over on its back.

In 1953 Penrose was appointed sales manager of Westland Aircraft Ltd, responsible for the Westland, Bristol, and Saunders-Roe helicopter group. By this time he had amassed some 5000 hours on no fewer than 250 different aircraft types, ranging from rotorcraft to jets. He continued flying for pleasure, acquiring a diminutive Currie Wot biplane after his retirement in 1967, and sampling other types whenever the opportunity arose. Penrose was also a keen ornithologist and a naval architect (he designed thirty-six boats and yachts), and he designed the house at Nether Compton, Dorset, in which he and his wife lived for fifty years.

Gifted with an elegant prose style rare in aviation writers, Penrose wrote a number of books. His outstanding autobiographical works were *I Flew with the Birds* (1949), *No Echo in the Sky* (1958), *Airymouse* (1982), *Cloud Cuckooland* (1981), and *Adventure with Fate* (1984). Other titles were *Architect of Wings* (1985), a biography of Avro designer Roy Chadwick; *Wings across the World*, a history of British Airways; and an impressive five-volume history of British aviation. Penrose was made a fellow of the Royal Aeronautical Society in 1936, and in 1993—when his tally had risen to 5500 hours on 309 types—he was presented with honorary fellowship of the American Society of Experimental Test Pilots. He died at his home, Broad Hill, Hardington Mandeville, Yeovil, on 31 August 1996.

PHILIP JARRETT

Sources H. Penrose, *Adventure with fate* (1984) · H. Penrose, *No echo in the sky* (1958) · *The Independent* (11 Sept 1996) · D. James, *Westland aircraft since 1915* (1991) · *The Times* (11 Sept 1996) · *The Guardian* (10 Sept 1996) · b. cert. · m. cert. · d. cert.
Archives Royal Aeronautical Society, London, papers | Westland Helicopters Ltd, Yeovil, Westland archive
Wealth at death £106,137: administration with will, 10 Dec 1996, CGPLA Eng. & Wales

Penrose, John (1713–1776), letter writer and Church of England clergyman, was born in Exeter on 22 September 1713, the younger of the two sons of Joseph Penrose (1688–1756), a tailor originally from Bodmin, and Frances, *née* Paul (d. 1756), from Exeter. John Penrose was educated at Exeter high school and at Exeter College, Oxford, where he matriculated on 16 October 1732. After graduating BA in 1736, he took holy orders and was successively curate at Malling in Kent, Shobrooke in Devon, and rector of Sowton, near Exeter. In 1737 he married Elizabeth (1712–

1782), daughter of the Revd John Vinicombe, of Exeter Cathedral; the couple had five daughters and two sons, John (1753–1829), later vicar of Thorney, near Newark, and Charles Vinicombe *Penrose, naval officer. Four years after his marriage John Penrose became vicar of the Cornish parish of St Gluvias (Penryn) with Budock where he remained for the rest of his life. He appears to have been a conscientious and well-respected clergyman. Local newspaper notices following his death spoke of his being 'assiduously watchful over the flock committed to his care' and eventually 'worn out by ... a regular Discharge of the Duties of an extensive and laborious Cure' (Penrose, 5). The ministry was also characterized by his efforts to protect the established church from what he saw as the threat of Methodism then being promoted in Cornwall by John Wesley and his followers.

However, Penrose is now better known for a series of letters he wrote to family members while taking the waters at Bath in the spring of 1766 and 1767. Though sometimes repetitive and prosaic, the correspondence provides an intimate and revealing insight into how one of Bath's many thousands of annual visitors perceived a resort that was for many contemporaries (and subsequent historians) the quintessence of eighteenth-century polite society.

Penrose's initial motive for visiting Bath with his wife was medical not social. Like many other middle-aged, middle-class gentlemen of the time, John was afflicted with gout for which he sought relief through a course of spa water. However, shortly after the start of his treatment in April 1766 he also began to engage in a number of the social entertainments available to male and female residents. To an extent Penrose's conduct at Bath closely followed the social ideal set out by the town's former master of ceremonies, Richard 'Beau' Nash, and subsequent commentators such as the historian John Wood. After breakfast Penrose and his wife visited the pump room or attended services at the abbey church; afternoon activities included walks, carriage rides, evening prayers, and, following dinner, tea with friends at their own or others' lodgings. Variations to this routine included several more formal encounters when Penrose met with his patron, Lord Edgcumbe, or attended a special breakfast reception held for Cornish visitors to Bath.

In many ways the correspondence charts an education in social conformity with a resulting sense of enhanced personal civility: 'I am grown vastly polite' wrote Penrose on 11 May 1766 (Penrose, 100). Yet, at the same time, the letters show his conscious rejection of aspects of Bath society that he found tiresome or disagreeable. Episodes of social conformity were therefore balanced by his refusal to bathe in the public baths or to attend the evening balls, despite their popularity with other clergymen. In part Penrose took these decisions to avoid what he considered the unnecessary and uncomfortable ceremonies demanded of would-be polite gentleman; several letters refer, for example, to his weariness at the need to dress up in public and his wish to 'unrig as soon as the Coast was clear' (ibid., 88). Penrose also grew increasingly critical of what he considered the triviality of many Bath fashions and modes of refined conduct. Targets of rebuke included the current master of ceremonies, Samuel Derrick ('an insignificant puppy' (ibid., 174), and the Methodist preacher, John William Fletcher, whom Penrose, in line with his long-term critique of religious enthusiasm, accused of fashionable affectation in the pulpit. In contrast to these vignettes of ridiculous folly, and indeed to the popular image of the relaxed polite gentleman, the correspondence also reveals a man often weighed down by the practicalities (and expense) of life at Bath. 'Between the Dearness of the Meat and Dressing we shall be ruined', bemoaned an anxious Penrose two weeks into his 1766 visit (ibid., 37).

Penrose's second visit to Bath in 1767 was to be his last. He died at the vicarage in Penryn on 25 June 1776 and was buried at St Gluvias, where he is commemorated by an epitaph composed by Hannah More. His correspondence was published in 1983 as *Letters from Bath*, with an introduction by his descendant Hubert Penrose. PHILIP CARTER

Sources J. Penrose, *Letters from Bath, 1766–1767*, ed. B. Mitchell and H. Penrose (1983) · P. Borsay, *The English urban renaissance: culture and society in the provincial town, 1660–1770* (1989) · Foster, *Alum. Oxon.*

Penrose, John (1778–1859), Church of England clergyman and theological writer, was born at Cardinham, Cornwall, on 15 December 1778, the eldest son of John Penrose (1753–1829), then vicar of that parish, and afterwards rector of Fledborough and vicar of Thorney, both near Newark, Nottinghamshire, and his wife, Jane (d. 1818), second daughter of the Revd John Trevenen.

Penrose was educated at home, and for a short time from 1794 to 1795 at Tiverton School. From there he went to Exeter College, Oxford, but stayed only three months before moving to Corpus Christi College, Oxford, to take up an exhibition. He graduated BA in 1799 and MA in 1802. After teaching for a few months, he was ordained at Exeter in 1801, and he officiated at the chapelry of Marazion in Cornwall until he left Penzance in 1802. Afterwards, he held the vicarage of Langton by Wragby, Lincolnshire, (1802–59) and that of Poundstock, Cornwall (1803–9). In 1805 he returned to Oxford to study, and was Bampton lecturer in 1808, in which capacity he wrote his *Attempt to Prove the Truth of Christianity*, published in that year. In 1809 he became vicar of Bracebridge, near Lincoln.

It was while living and teaching in Harefield, near Oxford, at this time that Penrose met and fell in love with Elizabeth (1780–1837), the daughter of Edmund *Cartwright (1743–1823) and Alice Whittaker. They were married on 6 May 1814 and settled in Bracebridge that summer. Elizabeth *Penrose was a children's historical author and teacher, writing under the pseudonym Mrs Markham. John (d. 1888), their first son, was born in 1815; his twin brother was stillborn. Two more boys followed: Charles Thomas (1816?–1868) and Francis Cranmer *Penrose (1817–1903), who was to become an architect and astronomer.

Over the next forty years Penrose published a large quantity of mainly religious works, notably *An Inquiry into the Nature of Human Motives* (1820) and *Of Christian Sincerity*

(1829). In 1837 his wife died. The same year, he was awarded the perpetual curacy of North Hykeham, Lincolnshire. In his later life, as well as sermons and treatises, he published the lives of his paternal and maternal uncles, Vice-Admiral Sir Charles Vinicombe Penrose and Captain James Trevenen, as well as, privately, a memoir of his father.

Penrose died at Langton by Wragby on 9 August 1859, and was buried in the churchyard there.

JESSICA HININGS

Sources A. B. Baldwin, ed., *The Penroses of Fledborough parsonage: lives, letters and diary* (1933) · G. C. Boase, *Collectanea Cornubiensia: a collection of biographical and topographical notes relating to the county of Cornwall* (1890) · J. Foster, ed., *Index ecclesiasticus, or, Alphabetical lists of all ecclesiastical dignitaries in England and Wales since the Reformation* (1890) · Foster, *Alum. Oxon.* · C. W. Boase, *An alphabetical register of the commoners of Exeter College, Oxford* (1894) · Boase & Courtney, *Bibl. Corn.* · *GM*, 3rd ser., 7 (1859) · J. Penrose, *The life of the Rev. J. Penrose, rector of Fledborough, Notts., 1783–1829* (1880) · *DNB*
Likenesses W. Sharp, lithograph, NPG
Wealth at death under £6000: resworn probate, Aug 1860, *CGPLA Eng. & Wales* (1859)

Penrose [née Miller], **(Elizabeth) Lee** [known as Lee Miller], **Lady Penrose** (1907–1977), fashion model and photographer, was born on 23 April 1907 at 40 South Clinton Street, Poughkeepsie, New York, USA, the only daughter and the second of the three children of Theodore Miller (1872–1971), an American mechanical engineer, and his Canadian wife, Florence Mary MacDonald (1881–1954), a nurse, the daughter of Scottish and Irish settlers from Ontario. The Miller family moved to a small farm on the outskirts of Poughkeepsie, where Lee grew up as an extreme tomboy. At the age of seven she was raped, which resulted in serious medical complications and a psychological trauma that almost certainly affected her for the rest of her life. At the time, as if in response, her daring and rebellious behaviour got her expelled from a great many schools in the Hudson valley.

Miller's further education consisted of a series of courses in lighting and design at the École Medgyès pour la Technique du Théâtre in Paris in 1925. The following year she enrolled in the Art Students League in New York, but her studies came to an end after a chance encounter with Condé Nast, the owner of *Vogue* and *Vanity Fair* magazines, who launched her career as a fashion model. Her short, silky blonde hair, piercing blue eyes, and athletic figure fitted the mode of the period perfectly and allowed her to model sportswear or the most sophisticated gowns with equal success. She was photographed by Edward Steichen, Arnold Genthe, and Nickolas Muray, and used the sessions to further her own knowledge of photography. Her modelling career ended in scandal when her image was used to endorse Kotex sanitary towels, so in May 1929 she departed for Paris.

Man Ray was the best-known modern photographer of his day, and in Paris Miller immediately became his lover, pupil, and model. Together they pioneered the use of the solarization process, and Miller became a photographer

(Elizabeth) **Lee Penrose** [Lee Miller], **Lady Penrose** (1907–1977), self-portrait, 1939

in her own right. She became part of the surrealist movement, starring in Jean Cocteau's film *Le sang d'un poète* in 1930. The surrealist way of seeing was to remain a detectable influence throughout her life's work, but it was at its strongest during this period. In the photograph entitled *Exploding Hand* (V&A) a woman's hand appears to emit a puff of smoke, which is in fact the sharply observed effect of countless scratches made by diamond rings on the glass of the door she is opening. Miller's first exhibition at Julien Levy's New York gallery in 1932 was favourably reviewed, as were further shows in New York and Paris.

By October 1932 Miller had left Man Ray and returned to New York to establish her own studio, and the following year she was listed by *Vanity Fair* as 'one of the seven most distinguished living photographers'. She abruptly abandoned her studio to marry, on 19 July 1934, Aziz Eloui Bey (*c*.1890–1976), an Egyptian businessman whom she had previously met in Paris.

During her first year in Cairo, Miller took few photographs, but then she became interested in long-range desert travel. Her pictures of rock formations, buildings, and oasis villages run to more than 2000 images, in which her surrealist vision is apparent. One of her best-known images, *Portrait of Space* (J. Paul Getty Museum, Los Angeles, California), allows the viewer to examine the sky and the desert, enigmatically framed through a hole torn in a fly screen door. Despite her renewed creative interest, Miller pined for the artistic life of Paris, and in 1937, when she returned there for a visit, she met and fell in love with Roland Algernon *Penrose (1900–1984), a British surrealist painter. They travelled together to Mougins in the south of France for a holiday with Paul and Nusch Eluard, Man Ray and Ady Fidelin, and Picasso, who was so fascinated by Miller's beauty that he painted four versions of her portrait. Her romance with Penrose continued with journeys made together in the Balkans and Egypt, and in 1939, shortly before the war broke out, she left Aziz Eloui Bey and joined Penrose in London.

Miller worked for *Vogue*, but during the blitz she photographed the often surreal effects of the bombing. Many of these images were published in 1941 by Lund Humphries in a book entitled *Grim Glory: Pictures of Britain under Fire*. A number of these contain jokes in their titling, such as *Eggceptional Achievement*, where a vast grounded barrage balloon appears as the egg of a proud pair of geese, or *Nonconformist Chapel*, where a pile of bricks become the nonconformists leaving the chapel. Miller's later work with the Women's Royal Naval Service (WRNS) was published by Hollis and Carter in 1945 as *Wrens in Camera*. But it was for her features in *Vogue* that she was best known, particularly after D-day when, as an accredited war correspondent, she followed the advance of the American army across Europe. During the liberation of Paris she photographed Picasso and many other figures of the art world, all friends from before the war. Contrary to army regulations she photographed combat on many occasions, being present at the siege of St Malo, and during the bitter fighting in the Vosges Mountains in the winter of 1944–5. She was also present at the liberation of four concentration camps, and most notably her images of Buchenwald and Dachau shocked the readers of *Vogue* in Britain and America.

After the war Miller continued travelling and photographing in Austria, Hungary, and Romania, from where she returned home to Penrose in 1946. She was accorded a heroine's welcome by the press in London and later in New York, which she visited with Penrose. She went back to work at *Vogue* but found it extremely difficult to come to terms with the disillusionment of peace as the cold war dashed hopes for international unity and the new and better forms of government that she had hoped would follow the war failed to materialize.

There followed a long period of depression and alcohol abuse, but by the late 1960s Miller reinvented herself as a gourmet cook and had the satisfaction of being featured in several magazines. She had married Penrose on 3 May 1947, a few months before their son Antony was born, and in 1949 they bought Farley Farm in Chiddingly, Sussex, which became their home. Miller undertook no further professional assignments after 1954, but during her visits with Penrose to the studios of their artist friends such as Picasso, Miró, Ernst, Man Ray, and Tàpies she photographed extensively. She died of cancer at Farley Farm on 21 July 1977, and her ashes were scattered in the garden at Farley on 26 July.   ANTONY PENROSE

Sources R. Penrose, *Scrap book, 1900–1981* (1981) · A. Penrose, *The lives of Lee Miller* (1985) · J. Livingstone, *Lee Miller: photographer* (1989) · A. Penrose, ed., *Lee Miller's war* (1992) · A. Penrose, *The legendary Lee Miller* (1998) · A. Penrose, *Roland Penrose: the friendly surrealist* (2001) · A. Penrose, *The home of the surrealists* (2001) · C. Burke, 'Lee Miller', 2000, priv. coll. · M. Ray, *Self-portrait* (New York, 1963); (1979) · N. Baldwin, *Man Ray, American artist* (1988) · W. Chadwick, *Women artists and the surrealist movement* (1985) · G. Colevile, *Scandaleusement d'elles* (Paris, 1999) · m. cert. [Roland Penrose] · R. Calvocoressi, *Lee Miller: portraits from a life* (2002) · *Roland Penrose, Lee Miller: the surrealist and the photographer* (2001) [exhibition catalogue, Dean Gallery, Edinburgh, and Scottish National Gallery of Modern Art, 19 May – 9 Sept 2001]

Archives Dean Gallery, Edinburgh, Roland Penrose archive · Lee Miller Archive, Chiddingly, East Sussex · priv. coll. | FILM BBC TV

archive · BFI, *Le sang d'un poète*, Jean Cocteau · Pathé News, two clips | SOUND BL NSA, interviews with Antony Penrose
Likenesses L. Miller, self-portrait, photograph, 1932, priv. coll., Lee Miller archives · R. Penrose, oils, 1937, priv. coll. · L. Miller, bromide print, 1939, NPG [*see illus.*] · D. E. Scherman, three photographs, 1943–5, priv. coll. · R. Penrose, portrait, 1946, Farley Farm House, Penrose collection · R. Penrose, photograph, *c*.1958, priv. coll.

Penrose, Lionel Sharples (1898–1972), physician, was born at 44 Finchley Road, London, on 11 June 1898 of Quaker stock, the second of the four sons (there were no daughters) of (James) Doyle Penrose (1862–1932), portrait painter, and his wife, Elizabeth Josephine (*d.* 1930), daughter of Alexander (later Baron) Peckover FSA, banker and collector. Sir Roland Algernon *Penrose (1900–1984) was his brother. Penrose was educated at the Downs School, Colwall, and Leighton Park School, Reading. On leaving school in 1916 he served in the Friends' ambulance train of the British Red Cross in France until the end of the First World War, when he went up to St John's College, Cambridge. His main interests were in mathematics and psychology. He eventually chose the moral sciences tripos, in which he gained a first in part two in 1921; he was also awarded the Newcombe prize. After a year's postgraduate work in psychology at Cambridge he repaired to Vienna, then a centre of psychiatric research, where he stayed for two years and became deeply interested in mental illness. He decided that for this work a medical qualification was desirable. He did his clinical work at St Thomas's Hospital, London, where he qualified MRCS LRCP in 1928 and gained the Bristowe medal (1929). On 17 October 1928 he married Margaret, daughter of John Beresford Leathes FRS, professor of physiology at Leeds; she was herself a physician. They had three sons and one daughter—Oliver became professor of mathematics at the Open University, Roger became Rouse Ball professor of mathematics at Oxford and FRS, Jonathan was British chess champion on ten occasions, and Shirley became a consultant paediatrician.

Penrose's first post was at the City Mental Hospital, Cardiff, where his study of schizophrenia formed the basis of a successful MD thesis (1930). In 1931 he moved to the Royal Eastern Counties Institution at Colchester, a mental hospital with a large number of mentally defective patients. He at once became interested in this hitherto neglected branch of medicine, not only because of the human aspects, but also because the 300,000 patients in the general population posed a serious social problem, and little thought had been given to the possibilities of the prevention of mental illness. Over seven years he made a detailed study of 1280 mentally defective patients and their 6629 siblings, plus their parents and other relatives. This was published in a Medical Research Council Special Report and later expanded in two books, *Mental Defect* (1933) and *The Biology of Mental Defect* (1949, 4th edn revised by J. M. Berg and H. Lang-Brown, 1972). This work not only shaped Penrose's own research career in mental defect and human genetics, but had a profound effect on the whole future of these subjects.

From 1939 to 1945 Penrose was director of psychiatric research in Ontario, Canada, where he made an important study on the efficacy of shock therapy. He was then appointed to the Galton chair of eugenics at University College, London. He reorganized the department and in 1963 had the name of the chair changed to the Galton chair of human genetics. He continued his work on mental defect, in particular on mongolism, which he renamed Down's anomaly (later Down's syndrome), and he wrote a notable monograph on the subject in 1966, the centenary of J. Langdon Down's first description of the condition.

In the 1950s methods were developed for isolating, counting, classifying, and examining chromosomes. Penrose's use of these methods made striking advances in the knowledge of human genetics. His *Outline of Human Genetics* (1960) had a third edition in 1973. He was apt at suggesting new and original lines of research. He was an authority on dermatoglyphs—the finger, palm, and sole prints which are of diagnostic value in mental disease. He made contributions to the diagnosis and treatment of phenylketonuria, an inherited metabolic anomaly, which, if not diagnosed and treated early in life, causes mental defect. He was one of the first to determine the mutation rate of harmful genes in man. He followed clues with unusual tenacity. One example was his reconstruction of the Lambert pedigree, dating from 1732. This family suffered from a peculiar skin disease, with an even more peculiar mode of inheritance, and was cited in most books on human genetics. With the aid of his wife, Penrose examined diocesan and parish records in Suffolk and showed that the pedigree abounded in errors and that the mode of inheritance was quite different from what had been claimed. When he retired from the Galton chair in 1965 he continued his work at the Kennedy-Galton Centre at Harperbury Hospital, near St Albans.

Penrose's work gained international recognition. He was awarded honorary degrees by McGill (1958), Edinburgh (1970), Newcastle (1968), and Göteborg (1966), the Weldon medal from Oxford (1950), the Albert Lasker award (1960), the international award of the Joseph P. Kennedy Foundation (1964), and the James Calvert Spence medal in paediatrics (1964). He was president of the Genetical Society of Great Britain (1955–8) and of the Third International Congress of Human Genetics in Chicago in 1966. He was elected to fellowship of the Royal Society in 1953, of the Royal College of Physicians of London in 1962, and of the Royal College of Psychiatrists in 1971.

Apart from Penrose's scientific work an enduring interest was his opposition to war, both on moral and practical grounds. He was one of the founders and for over ten years president of the Medical Association for the Prevention of War. He had many other interests, including music, painting, chess, and making ingenious puzzles both for children and adults, some of which were of scientific value in illustrating the biological principle of replication, as seen in the copying of genetic material. The combination of high intelligence, modesty, and a sense of humour made him an agreeable companion. He died at the General Hospital, Harlesden Road, Willesden, London, on 12 May 1972. He was survived by his wife.   A. M. COOKE, *rev.*

Sources H. Harris, *Memoirs FRS*, 19 (1973), 521–61 · Munk, *Roll*, vol. 6 · *The Times* (15 May 1972), 16g · *The Times* (22 May 1972), 16g · *The Times* (25 May 1972), 21g · *The Times* (29 May 1972), 10h · *The Times* (6 June 1972), 16g · *WWW* · D. C. Watt, 'Lionel Penrose, FRS (1898–1972), and eugenics', *Notes and Records of the Royal Society*, 52 (1998), 137–52, 339–54 · M. Smith, *Lionel Sharples Penrose: a biography* (1999) · private information (1986) · personal knowledge (1986) · b. cert. · m. cert. · d. cert.

Archives UCL, corresp. and papers
Likenesses photograph, repro. in Harris, *Memoirs FRS*
Wealth at death £85,794: probate, 10 July 1972, *CGPLA Eng. & Wales*

Penrose, Sir Roland Algernon (1900–1984), artist, writer, and exhibition organizer, was born at 44 Finchley Road, London, on 14 October 1900, into a Quaker family, the third of the four sons (there were no daughters) of (James) Doyle Penrose (1862–1932) and his wife, Elizabeth Josephine (*d.* 1930), daughter of Alexander Peckover, later Baron Peckover and lord lieutenant of Cambridgeshire; Roland's elder brother was the physician Lionel *Penrose. Penrose's Anglo-Irish father was a painter, a Royal Hibernian academician who disapproved of the modern art which would claim his son's passionate loyalty. But he stimulated Penrose's love of the arts, an interest reinforced by his maternal grandfather. The young Penrose gained a great deal from visits to his grandfather's Wisbech house where an extensive library and collection was available. After boarding at the Quaker Downs School, Colwall, until 1914, Penrose studied at Leighton Park School, Reading, where he decided to become a painter. In August 1918 he joined the Friends' Ambulance Unit (FAU) and in September that year was seconded to the 1st British Red Cross ambulance unit in Italy. He was demobbed in 1919, in which year he went up to Queens' College, Cambridge, to read history. However, in 1920 he switched to architecture, in which he graduated in 1922. At Cambridge he painted in his spare time, designed décor for and performed in plays by the Marlowe Society, and met in the rooms of J. Maynard Keynes such Bloomsbury figureheads as A. Clive H. Bell, Duncan Grant, and an especially encouraging Roger Fry. Soon after going down from Cambridge, Penrose set off for Paris to become a painter.

It was a profoundly liberating experience. Studying at André Lhôte's academy, Penrose quickly acquainted himself with the manifold pleasures of Parisian life in the early 1920s. He got to know Georges Braque, Man Ray, Max Ernst, and André Derain; close friendship with Ernst ensured that he became familiar with other surrealists, André Breton and Joan Miró prominent among them. In October 1925, in a civil ceremony in France, he married the beautiful young Gascon poet Valentine Andrée Boué (*d.* 1978), daughter of Maxime Boué, colonel, of Condom, France; a further marriage ceremony was conducted at Jordans meeting-house on 21 December. In 1928 he held his first one-man show at the Galerie Van Leer in the rue de Seine, Paris. But he also worked with other artists, organizing the publication of Ernst's *Une semaine de bonté* in 1934

and securing a small role in Luis Buñuel's film *L'âge d'or* (1930). Penrose met the young English poet David Gascoyne, who shared his enthusiasm for surrealism. The two men agreed that they would convert Britain to the surrealist faith, and in 1935 Penrose returned to England leaving his estranged wife to travel alone in India.

Wasting little time, Penrose organized the International Surrealist Exhibition at the New Burlington Galleries, London, in summer 1936. Aided by a committee which included Henry Moore, Paul Nash, and Herbert Read, he succeeded in assembling a major survey provocative enough to establish surrealism as a lively cultural force in England. The onset of the Spanish Civil War a fortnight after the exhibition closed did not prevent him from working with Christian Zervos in Spain on a book called *Catalan Art* (1937). Nor was he slow in raising money for Spain and putting pressure on the British government to back the republican cause. As for surrealism, he was tireless in its promotion. In 1937 he established the London Gallery in Cork Street under the directorship of the Belgian surrealist E. L. T. Mesens, and in the following year launched the *London Bulletin*, acting as assistant editor to Mesens.

While continuing to produce his own surrealist art, Penrose ensured that Picasso's *Guernica* toured several British cities after the Paris international exhibition had finished. He began to assemble a distinguished collection as well, including Picasso's great *Weeping Woman*, which was acquired by the Tate Gallery in 1987. In 1937 he met the American photographer Lee Miller (1907–1977) [*see* Penrose, (Elizabeth) Lee, Lady Penrose], daughter of Theodore Miller, of Poughkeepsie, New York, and divorced wife of Aziz Eloui Bey; she had been photographed memorably by Man Ray and starred in Jean Cocteau's film *Le sang d'un poète*. They toured the Balkans together by car in summer 1938, and Penrose dedicated his experimental book *The Road is Wider than Long* (1939) to her. Following his divorce from Boué on 19 June 1939, Miller moved into Penrose's house at Downshire Hill, Hampstead. They were finally married on 3 May 1947 and their only child, Antony, was born in September that year.

Although Penrose staged a one-man show in London at the Mayor Gallery in 1939, the war interrupted his art. He served as an air-raid warden in Hampstead and then as a camouflage instructor, but as soon as hostilities ceased he resumed all his old activities. In 1947 they bore ambitious fruit in the founding of the Institute of Contemporary Arts, of which Penrose became the first chairman. Dedicated to promoting the adventurous spirit of modern art on an international scale, but also extending a welcome to writers and musicians, it quickly established itself as an important meeting place for anyone with innovative ideas.

The post-war period also saw the emergence of Penrose as biographer and art historian. His biography of Picasso (*Picasso: his Life and Work*), published in 1958, was outstanding, and he followed it with studies of Miró (1970), Man Ray (1975), and Tapiès (1978). At the same time Penrose organized an impressive sequence of retrospectives at the

Tate Gallery. They commenced with a vast survey of Picasso's work in 1960, and continued with Ernst (1962), Miró (1964), and Picasso's sculpture (1967). His close friendship with each of these artists enabled him to select the shows with great authority, and his services to art in Britain were recognized by appointment as CBE in 1961 and a knighthood in 1966. In 1975 Penrose and Miller founded the Elephant Trust to support artists and writers who, because of the experimental nature of their ideas, might not gain funding elsewhere. The trust was funded by the sale from Penrose's own collection of Max Ernst's *Celebes* to the Tate Gallery and has continued to support artistic projects since Penrose's death.

To the end of his long life Penrose delighted in making inventive collages, and during his last years he produced some of his most exuberant images. He died at his home, Farley Farm, Chiddingly, Sussex, on 23 April 1984 of inflammation of the lungs. 'What matters to him is life, openness, receptivity, involvement, appetite, energy', wrote Norbert Lynton, who saluted Penrose 'as one whose very life has been an unconscious work of art performed to the benefit of all'. His art collection, which included works by Jean Arp, Georges Braque, Dalí, Paul Delvaux, Ernst, Alberto Giacometti, Barbara Hepworth, René Magritte, Man Ray, Miró, and Picasso, was dispersed, many items entering the collection of the Tate Gallery and the Scottish National Gallery of Modern Art. The latter gallery also houses the Roland Penrose archive.

RICHARD CORK, *rev.*

Sources R. Penrose, *Scrap book, 1900–1981* (1981) • R. Penrose, *Arts Council of Great Britain* (1980) [exhibition catalogue, Fermoy Arts Centre, King's Lynn, 25 July – 9 Aug 1980, and elsewhere] • R. Penrose, *Recent collages (a commemorative exhibition)* (1984) [exhibition catalogue, Gardner Centre Gallery, Brighton, May 1984] • A. Robertson and others, *Surrealism in Britain in the thirties: angels of anarchy and machines for making clouds* (1986) [exhibition catalogue, Leeds City Art Galleries, 10 Oct – 7 Dec 1986] • *Dada and surrealism reviewed* (1978) [exhibition catalogue, Hayward Gallery, London] • personal knowledge (1990) • private information (2004) • A. Penrose, *Roland Penrose: the friendly surrealist* (2001) • *Roland Penrose, Lee Miller: the surrealist and the photographer* (2001) [exhibition catalogue, Dean Gallery, Edinburgh, and Scottish National Gallery of Modern Art, 19 May – 9 Sept 2001] • b. cert. • m. cert. [Lee Miller] • d. cert.
Archives Institute of Contemporary Arts, London, papers • NRA, Roland Penrose collection, corresp. and papers • Scottish National Gallery of Modern Art, corresp. and papers
Likenesses group photograph, 1936, Hult. Arch.
Wealth at death £4,549,194: probate, 1 Nov 1984, *CGPLA Eng. & Wales*

Penrose, Thomas (1742–1779), poet, baptized at Newbury, Berkshire, on 9 September 1742, was the eldest son of Thomas Penrose (1715/16–1769), rector of that parish. He matriculated from Wadham College, Oxford, on 30 May 1759, aged sixteen. After 1762 he left the university and joined a private expedition, partly English and partly Portuguese, which was formed for the attack of Buenos Aires, under the command of an adventurer named Captain Macnamara. The party left the Tagus on 30 August 1762, and on its way attacked the settlement of Nova Colonia de Sacramento in the River Plate, which had been seized by the Spanish. Operations were at first successful; but the

chief ship, the *Lord Clive*, caught fire, and Macnamara was drowned, with most of the crew. The second vessel, the *Ambuscade*, in which Penrose served as a lieutenant of marines, escaped, and ultimately arrived at the Portuguese settlement of Rio de Janeiro. Penrose had been wounded in the fight and, although he recovered from his wounds, the hardships of the next month in a prize sloop undermined his constitution. Very soon afterwards he returned to England, and again settled at Oxford, graduating BA from Hertford College on 8 February 1766. In 1768 Penrose married Mary, eldest daughter of Samuel Slocock of Newbury.

Penrose is described as possessing learning, eloquence, and good social qualities. His principal writings are mainly imitative of Collins and Gray; but several of his poems deal in a natural vein with his disappointments in life. A poetical essay, 'On the Contrarieties of Public Virtue', shows powers of irony and satire. His chief works were *Flights of Fancy* (1775), *Address to the Genius of Britain* (1775), a poem in blank verse proposing a limit to our 'civil dissensions' and criticizing the conduct of the government towards America, and a posthumous volume of poems (1781) with a biographical introduction by James Pettit Andrews, who had married his sister Anne. His work was included in Anderson's *Complete Edition of the Poets* (vol. 11), Park's *British Poets* (vol. 33), Pratt's *Cabinet of Poetry* (vol. 5), and the Chiswick edition of *British Poets* (vol. 63); and several of his poems are in Bell's *Fugitive Poetry* (vols. 12 and 13). A poem by Penrose entitled 'Newberry Belles', signed 'P., Newbury, 8 May 1761', the characters in which are identified by Godwin, is in the *Gentleman's Magazine* of 1761 (pp. 231–2), and two more of his poetical pieces are in the same periodical for 1799 (pt 2, pp. 1177–8). Campbell included two of Penrose's pieces— 'The Helmets' and 'The Field of Battle'—in his *Specimens of the British Poets*.

Penrose took holy orders, and became curate to his father at Newbury. About 1777 he was appointed by a friend to the rectory of Beckington-cum-Standerwick, near Frome in Somerset; but his health failed. He died at Bristol on 20 April 1779, and was buried at Clifton, where a monument was erected in his memory.

Penrose's widow married at Newbury, in February 1786, the Revd Thomas Best, master of the free grammar school, and died about 1840, at the age of ninety-four. Penrose's only child, Thomas (d. 1851), was admitted on the foundation of Winchester College, became fellow of New College, Oxford, and vicar of Writtle-cum-Roxwell. He wrote *Sketch of the Lives and Writings of Dante and Petrarch* (1790).

W. P. COURTNEY, *rev.* MICHAEL BEVAN

Sources *Poems by the Rev. Thomas Penrose* (1781) [with biographical introduction by J. P. Andrews] • R. Anderson, *A complete edition of the poets of Great Britain*, 13 vols. (1792–5), vol. 11 • Foster, *Alum. Oxon.*
Likenesses W. Bromley, line engraving, 1823 (after N. Farrer), BM, NPG; repro. in B. W. Procter, *Effigies poeticae* (1824)

Penruddock, John (1619–1655), royalist conspirator, was the eldest son of Sir John Penruddock (d. 1648) of Compton Chamberlayne, Wiltshire. The Penruddocks had been established as a landed family in Wiltshire since the late sixteenth century and Sir John had served as sheriff of the county in 1635. John Penruddock was educated at Blandford School, Queen's College, Oxford, and Gray's Inn. In 1639 he married Arundel Freke, daughter of John Freke of Ewerne's Courtenay and Melcombe, Dorset. On the outbreak of the civil war the Penruddock family supported Charles I. John Penruddock rose to the rank of colonel and fought for the king until Easter 1645 when he resigned his commission and attempted to compound for his confiscated estates. Two of his younger brothers were killed fighting for the king. On his father's death in 1648 he inherited the family estate, but as a result of his inability to pay his composition fine, the lands remained sequestered for six years before he raised the £1300 required to regain them. He later estimated that he had amassed debts of about £1500 as a direct result of the war.

During the early 1650s Penruddock refused to become reconciled to the new English state and in 1655 he was heavily involved in an abortive rising mounted by the underground royalist organization, the Sealed Knot. The conspirators had intended to stage a series of co-ordinated armed insurrections in a number of locations throughout England, but on 8 March risings near Newcastle upon Tyne, York, and Nottingham were quickly suppressed and another in Cheshire failed to materialize at all. Penruddock and his supporters had originally planned to seize Winchester but they dropped the idea after the town's garrison was reinforced at the last minute. Instead, on the night of 11 March, several hundred cavalry led by Penruddock and Sir Joseph Wagstaffe rendezvoused at Clarendon Park in Wiltshire, and before dawn rode into Salisbury and arrested the sheriff of the county and the judges who were conducting the Wiltshire assizes sessions there. After proclaiming their support for Charles Stuart, they left Salisbury and rode westward through Blandford, Sherborne, and Yeovil in the hope that the royalists of Somerset and Dorset would come in to swell their numbers. Very few, however, joined them and several days later a small force of government troops from the garrison at Exeter commanded by Captain Unton Croke caught up with them at South Molton in north Devon. After a skirmish the royalists were defeated and Penruddock was captured.

In the aftermath of the rising Penruddock was put on trial for treason before a jury of local men at Exeter. According to his own account of his trial he argued that opposing Cromwell could not constitute treason as the protector's power had not been legally sanctioned, and declared to the judge: 'The law I am now tried by is no law, but what is cut out by the poynt of a rebellious sword' (Penruddock, 5). He told the jury: 'I observe treason in this age to be an *individuum vagum*, like the wind in the Gospel, which bloweth where it listeth; for that shall be treason in me today which shall be none in another tomorrow' (ibid., 6). He also argued that, on his surrender at South Molton, Croke had offered him security for his life and estates. These arguments were dismissed and he was sentenced to death.

At the end of the trial Penruddock expressed his hope that Cromwell would commute his sentence. His wife, Arundel, subsequently campaigned vigorously on his behalf, travelling to London to plead with Cromwell for his life. All her efforts were in vain, however, and he was beheaded at Exeter on 16 May 1655. Shortly afterwards an account of his last days and execution was circulated by his friend Seymour Bowman. This contained what the author claimed was the last correspondence between Penruddock and his wife. Penruddock was said to have written at one point: 'though the armies of men have been too hard for me, yet am I now lifting myself under the conduct of my Sovereign and an army of martyrs, that the gates of hell cannot prevail against' (Ravenhill, 15.3). No original manuscripts of this correspondence exist, and its authenticity must be doubted; none the less, its circulation along with the account of the trial did much to turn Penruddock into a martyr for the royalist cause. His estates were subsequently confiscated, but Cromwell later responded to a petition from his widow and granted a portion of them back to the family. The decision to send out major-generals to govern England in the autumn of 1655 was a direct response to Penruddock's rebellion.

CHRISTOPHER DURSTON

Sources W. W. Ravenhill, 'Records of the rising in the west, A.D.1655', *Wiltshire Archaeological and Natural History Magazine*, 13–15 (1872–5) • A. H. Woolrych, *Penruddock's rising, 1655* (1955) • J. Penruddock, *The trial of the honorable Colonel John Penruddock of Compton in Wiltshire* (1655) • D. Underdown, *Royalist conspiracy in England, 1649–1660* (1960) • *Memoirs of Edmund Ludlow*, ed. C. H. Firth, 2 vols. (1888) • M. A. E. Green, ed., *Calendar of the proceedings of the committee for compounding … 1643–1660*, 2, PRO (1890), 1054–5 • *DNB*
Archives Wilts. & Swindon RO, papers concerning his trial and execution | CKS, corresp. with wife on eve of execution
Likenesses G. Vertue, line engraving, 1735, BM, NPG; repro. in *Loyalists* • R. Earlom, mezzotint, pubd 1810, BM, NPG • G. Vertue, print, BM, NPG; repro. in E. Ward, *History of the rebellion* (1713)
Wealth at death confiscated to state

Penry, John (1562/3–1593), religious controversialist, was born in Brecknockshire, the son of Meredith Penry of Llangamarch. He may have attended the grammar school in Brecon before he entered Peterhouse, Cambridge, as a pensioner on 11 June 1580. He graduated BA in 1584 and then withdrew from his college for just over a year, spending part of this time in Wales. He went back to Cambridge in October 1585, but in the following June migrated to Oxford and took the degree of MA from St Alban Hall in July 1586. Probably already in close contact with the most forward protestants in Oxford, Penry refused to seek ordination in what he considered to be an insufficiently reformed church, though he preached in both universities and also in Northampton, where as early as 1587 Richard Bancroft believed he had become a member of the *classis*.

Immediately after he had obtained his master's degree Penry turned his attention to the state of the church in his native land, and in 1586 compiled *A treatise containing the aequity of an humble supplication which is to be exhibited unto hir gracious maiesty and this high court of parliament in the behalfe of the countrey of Wales, that some order may be taken for the preaching of the gospell among those people.* Having heard that parliament might be dissolved, early in 1587 Penry gained a licence for his tract, had 500 copies printed in Oxford, and brought them hurriedly to London. On 28 February he persuaded Edward Dounlee, the member for Carmarthen, to present *The Aequity* to the House of Commons, where it gained the enthusiastic support of the Warwickshire MP, Job Throckmorton. However, Archbishop Whitgift was indignant that parliament should be interfering in matters of religion, and even before the session had ended issued warrants for the seizure of the book and its author. Penry appeared before the high commission in March 1587 on a charge of having published treason and heresy, and was pronounced guilty and imprisoned in the Gatehouse for a month.

Determined not to abandon his mission to rescue his countrymen from their ignorance and blindness, Penry at once set to work on another publication. Since he now stood no chance of procuring an episcopal licence, he needed access to a secret press, and it seems that a Cambridge friend, John Udall, introduced him to the printer Robert Waldegrave, who in April 1588, at his printing house in the Strand, published *An exhortation unto the governours and people of her maiesties countrie of Wales, to labor earnestly to have the preaching of the gospell planted among them*. During the course of the year Waldegrave brought out two more editions of this much longer work, which denounced the bishops as soul murderers for their neglect of the people of Wales.

Penry had just taken the stock of his second book from Waldegrave's house when it was raided on 16 April 1588. The printer and his wife removed what type they could salvage to Elizabeth Crane's house in Aldermanbury and then, after Penry had procured a new press, resumed printing at Mrs Crane's country estate at East Molesey. The press was still in Surrey when in August 1588 Waldegrave published *A defence of that which hath bin written in the questions of the ignorant ministerie, and the communicating with them*, Penry's interim reply to *A Godly Treatise*, a vindication of the clergy of the English church by Robert Some.

At this period Penry seems to have been living intermittently in Northampton, and on 5 September 1588 he married Helen, the daughter of Henry Godly, a minor town official, in All Saints' Church. When Some brought out a rejoinder to *A Defence of that which hath bin Written*, Penry embarked on a second reply, but instead of printing this, in October 1588 Waldegrave gave precedence to *The Epistle*, the first of the Marprelate tracts.

Although there can be no doubt that by the summer of 1588 he had assumed the management of the secret press, most historians think that Penry took only a minor part, if any part at all, in the writing of the Marprelate tracts, and Leland Carlson has argued persuasively for Job Thockmorton's identification with Martin Marprelate. After the appearance of *The Epistle* and the ensuing publicity, Mrs Crane felt unable to shelter the press any longer, and in November Penry negotiated its removal to Sir Richard Knightley's house at Fawsley in Northamptonshire. Early in 1589 it was thought prudent to move the

press again, and Knightley arranged for it to go to his kinsman, John Hales, at the White Friars in Coventry. In between Marprelate tracts, Waldegrave published for Penry in February 1589 *A viewe of some part of such publike wants & disorderes as are in the service of God, within her maiesties countrie of Wales, togither with an humble petition, unto this high court of parliament for their speedy redresse*.

Increasingly uneasy over Marprelate's levity, Waldegrave left the press in March, sold his type to Throckmorton and withdrew to France, taking with him the manuscript of Penry's most autobiographical tract, *Th' appellation of John Penri, unto the highe court of parliament, from the bad and injurious dealing of th'archb. of Canterb. & other his colleagues of the high commission*. Here Penry bewailed yet again 'the lamentable misery of soules, wherein my countrymen the inhabitants of Wales live at this present', before going on to attack 'the unjust oppression of Gods church by ungodly and tiranical Lord Bishops' (Penry, *Th' Appellation*, 2, 16). Waldegrave printed *Th' Appellation* in La Rochelle in July 1589, returning secretly to England with copies of the work in the autumn.

On Waldegrave's departure Penry hired a new printer, John Hodgkins, and continued his association with the venture, which he next transferred to Wolston Priory at the invitation of Roger Wigston's wife. Government searchers, however, were making it impossible for the press to remain in the midlands, so Hodgkins attempted to move to the north of England, but the press was finally apprehended near Manchester towards the end of August 1589. Penry had not left Wolston when news of the seizure came, and for a time went from one hiding place to another. Then at the beginning of October, provided with money by Throckmorton, he fled to Scotland, where his wife joined him. Waldegrave also sought refuge in Scotland, finding work there as the king's printer.

Hospitably received by the Edinburgh ministers, in *A briefe discovery of the untruthes and slanders (against the true governement of the church of Christ)* Penry tried to repay their generosity by defending Scottish presbyterians against the aspersions of disloyalty made by Bancroft in his Paul's Cross sermon of February 1589. Waldegrave published this tract without attribution early in 1590, but when Penry next attempted to clear himself of treasonable activities, in *A treatise wherein is manifestlie proved, that reformation and those that sincerely favor the same, are unjustly charged to be enemies unto hir maiestie and the state*, he brought out the work as he normally did, under his own name.

Following protests from the English ambassador about Penry's activities, James VI had him proclaimed an outlaw in the summer of 1590, but apart from a clandestine visit to London at the time of the Hacket conspiracy in July 1591, Penry succeeded in remaining quietly in Scotland for a further two years, involving himself in the far less controversial task of translating a work by Theodore Beza, published as *Propositions and Principles* in Edinburgh in 1591. In Scotland he probably also began, but never lived to finish, *The Historie of Corah, Dathan and Abiram*, in which he attempted to make a complete separation between allegiance to the crown and membership of the English church. It was published posthumously in Middelburg in 1609.

Until he left England he was a firm believer in the presbyterian form of church government, but Penry, like Robert Browne before him, seems to have changed his opinions after experiencing a presbyterian church at first hand. When in September 1592 he decided to come south to make yet another attempt to procure the conversion of Wales, as soon as he reached London he attached himself to the separatist church of Barrow and Greenwood, then under the leadership of Francis Johnson. Although he accepted no formal office, he certainly preached to the church and drew up petitions for its freedom from arrest and for the release of its members from prison, in addition to composing an answer to *XV Slanderous Articles*, which had attacked the separatists.

After several months in flight from the authorities Penry was captured in Stepney on 22 March 1593. Subjected to a series of examinations, he admitted having published *Reformation No Enemie* and the *Propositions and Principles* while in Scotland. Desperate to prove his innocence of any crime, he next produced a 'Declaration of faith and allegiance', in which he protested his total loyalty to the queen while refusing to associate in public worship with the assemblies of the land. On 6 April Barrow and Greenwood were hanged for treason at Tyburn, and Penry realized that he might well suffer the same fate. On the day Barrow and Greenwood died he composed a farewell letter to his wife, on 10 April another letter to his daughters, and on 14 April one entitled *To the Distressed Faithfull Congregation of Christ in London*. His first trial took place in king's bench on 21 May, on a charge of intending to overthrow religion and inciting the queen's subjects to rebellion and insurrection. When the prosecution began using information from private papers taken from him in Scotland, Penry appealed to Burghley against the injustice of the procedure, and the trial was suspended. At a new trial which began on 25 May the prosecution employed *Reformation No Enemie* as evidence against him, and he was pronounced guilty of publishing scandalous writings against the church. Although the indictment had made no mention of the Marprelate tracts, the conviction that Penry was Martin Marprelate lay behind his condemnation. On 28 May Penry addressed a final plea to Burghley to procure a pardon from the queen, but Burghley could not help him. Early on 29 May 1593 Whitgift, Sir John Popham, and Sir John Puckering signed the death warrant, and later the same day Penry was hanged at St Thomas-a-Watering in Surrey.

Aged only thirty in 1593, in addition to his young wife Penry left four little daughters, Deliverance, Comfort, Safety, and Sure Hope, the eldest aged four, the youngest only a few weeks old at his death. Deliverance certainly lived to maturity. For a time a member of the household of Francis Johnson, the minister of the exiled separatist church, in May 1611 she married in Amsterdam an English bombazine worker, Samuel Whitaker.

CLAIRE CROSS

Sources J. Penry, *A treatise containing the aequity of an humble supplication which is to be exhibited unto hir gracious maiesty and this high court of parliament in the behalfe of the countrey of Wales, that some order may be taken for the preaching of the gospell among those people* (1587) • J. Penry, *An exhortation unto the governours and people of her maiesties countrie of Wales, to labor earnestly to have the preaching of the gospell planted among them* (1588) • J. Penry, *A defence of that which hath bin written in the questions of the ignorant ministerie, and the communicating with them* (1588) • J. Penry, *A viewe of some part of such publike wants & disorderes as are in the service of God, within her maiesties countrie of Wales, togither with an humble petition, unto this high court of parliament for their speedy redresse* (1589) • J. Penry, *Th' appellation of John Penri, unto the highe court of parliament, from the bad and injurious dealing of th'archb. of Canterb. & other his colleagues of the high commission* ... (1589) • J. Penry (?), *A briefe discovery of the untruthes and slanders (against the true governement of the church of Christ) contained in a sermon, preached the 8. of Februarie 1588. by D. Bancroft* ... (1590) • J. Penry, *A treatise wherein is manifestlie proved, that reformation and those that sincerely favor the same, are unjustly charged to be enemies unto hir maiestie and the state* (1590) • T. Beze [T. Beza] and A. Faius, *Propositions and principles of divinitie*, trans. J. Penry (1591) • J. Penry, *I John Penry doo heare sumarily set downe the whole truth ... which I hold ... in regard of my faith towards my God and dread souveraigne Queene Elizabeth* [1593] • J. Penry, *To my beloved wife Helener Penry, partaker with me in this life of the sufferings of the gospel* (1593) • J. Penry, *The historie of Corah, Dathan and Abiram etc. ... applied to the prelacy, ministerie and church assemblies of England* (1609) • A. Peel, ed., *The notebook of John Penry, 1593*, CS, 3rd ser., 67 (1944) • E. Arber, ed., *An introductory sketch to the Martin Marprelate controversy, 1588–1590* (1879) • *The writings of John Greenwood and Henry Barrow, 1591–1593*, ed. L. H. Carlson (1970), 314–15, 356–7, 386 • W. Pierce, *John Penry, his life, times and writings* (1923) • W. Pierce, *An historical introduction to the Marprelate tracts* (1908) • L. H. Carlson, *Martin Marprelate, gentleman: Master Job Throkmorton laid open in his colors* (1981) • C. Burrage, *The early English dissenters in the light of recent research (1550–1641)*, 2 vols. (1912) • Venn, *Alum. Cant.*, 1/3.342 • Foster, *Alum. Oxon.* • P. Collinson, *The Elizabethan puritan movement* (1967) • W. J. Sheils, *The puritans in the diocese of Peterborough, 1558–1610*, Northamptonshire RS, 30 (1979) • D. J. McGinn, *John Penry and the Marprelate controversy* (1966)

Archives Hunt. L., journal

Penson, Dame **Lillian Margery** (1896–1963), historian, was born in Islington, London, on 18 July 1896, the eldest daughter, but not the eldest child, of Arthur Austin Penson, wholesale dairy manager, and his wife, Lillian Alice Martha, *née* Brown. After private education she went to the University of London, first at Birkbeck College, then at University College. In 1917 she graduated BA with a first in history and in 1921 she became one of the earliest PhDs. She served as a junior administrative officer (1917–18) in the Ministry of National Service; then in 1918–19 worked in the war trade intelligence department. She taught as a lecturer at Birkbeck College from 1921 to 1930, and also part-time (1923–5) at East London (later Queen Mary) College.

In 1930 Lillian Penson was appointed to the chair of modern history held at Bedford College for Women. There she had as colleagues, besides some distinguished men, some remarkable women, who helped to give the college a distinctive quality, marked by a high degree of civilization. Among these were Susan Stebbing and Edna Purdie, who became her trusted friends. She opposed the introduction of male undergraduates to Bedford College, a proposal agitated during her later years, but not fulfilled until 1965.

Under the leadership of Lillian Penson the department of history flourished. Her lectures were immensely enjoyed. They were as carefully prepared as if they had been ceremonial performances for distinguished occasions: polished, lucid, not overloaded with detail, imaginative, at times witty or humorous, beautifully balanced, and economically worded, reflecting deep insight into issues and personalities. For many years her seminar at the Institute of Historical Research was a Mecca for diplomatic historians. In classes and seminars she had little patience with the shiftless; but for the serious she had generosity, patience, and helpfulness. A common epithet of disapproval, uttered in a certain tone of voice, was 'glib'. Eccentric but intelligent undergraduates, who seemed unusually incapable of a reasonable degree of conformity, she was inclined to defend, calling them 'my funnies'.

Lillian Penson's first researches were in colonial history, and bore fruit in *The Colonial Agents of the British West Indies* (1924) and other publications. Her commitment to diplomatic history seems to have begun with her appointment in 1918 as an editor of the peace handbooks prepared for the Paris peace conference. From this she went on to assist G. P. Gooch and H. W. V. Temperley on *British Documents on the Origins of the War, 1898–1914* (11 vols., 1926–38), being credited with assistant editorship on the title-pages of the later volumes. Temperley's influence on her was profound. He was for her what a historian should be. She stressed, as he did, the need for adequate linguistic equipment; the usefulness of knowing the folklores, literatures, and geography of the European countries; the need for careful study of private as well as public papers; and the value to the historian of some experience of affairs. With Temperley she produced *Foundations of British Foreign Policy* (1938) and *A Century of Diplomatic Blue Books* (1938). The planning of these projects and the business affairs connected with them provided excellent training for the administrator of later years. Had time allowed, she would have produced a magisterial work on Lord Salisbury's diplomacy. Papers in the *Cambridge Historical Journal* (1935), 'The new course in British foreign policy, 1892–1902' in the *Transactions of the Royal Historical Society* (1943)—a minor classic—and the Creighton lecture for 1960 (which by illness she could not deliver) give some idea of the directions the *magnum opus* would have taken.

Before war came in 1939 Lillian Penson was a person of importance in the university, not without hostile critics and anti-feminist opposition. Dean of the faculty of arts (1938–44), a member of the senate from 1940, in 1945 elected chairman of the academic council (a strategic position), and in 1946 a member of the court, she reached the peak of her career when in 1948 she became vice-chancellor, the first woman known to hold such an office. She had a unique knowledge of the university machine; she was clear-headed, generally tactful, and adept at conciliation, although some persons found her too trenchant for their liking. She was succeeded in 1951 by an old friend, H. Hale Bellot.

In two areas she took a special interest: the Fulbright scheme and colonial higher education. She was a founder member of the United States educational commission in the United Kingdom (1948) and acting chairman in 1953 and 1954. She did more than any other British academic to secure the co-operation of British scholars in this excellent scheme, so rewarding to British and Americans alike. The policy for higher education in the colonies, as worked out in 1943–5 by the commission under Sir Cyril Asquith, of which she was a member, involved the establishment of colonial university colleges, brought into 'special relationship' with the University of London, whereby curricula and examinations were conducted jointly by university and colleges. This was intended as a means whereby good standards would be established, preparatory to the colleges becoming independent universities. While ready to adjust London rules to meet colonial circumstances, she resisted in this, as in other connections, 'liberal' pressures for relaxation of standards. She made numerous laborious journeys to the colleges. She had a particular devotion to Khartoum. She became in 1955 a member of the council of the college at Salisbury, Southern Rhodesia. Her view of these developments she set forth, in historical perspective, in a Montague Burton lecture at Glasgow in 1954, *Educational Partnership in Africa and the West Indies*.

In 1951 Lillian Penson was appointed DBE. In 1949, the year following the admission of women to degrees there, Cambridge made her an honorary LLD, one of the first two women, after Queen Elizabeth, to be so honoured. Oxford made her an honorary DCL in 1956. Among the other seven honorary degrees which she received was the LLD of Southampton (1953), which had also enjoyed a special relationship with London. In 1959, in recognition of what she had done for medical studies, the Royal College of Surgeons made her an honorary fellow. She served three terms as a member of the council of the Royal Historical Society and as a vice-president, and was honorary vice-president from 1959 until her death.

Of middle height, as a younger woman Lillian Penson was slim, of a light and brisk step, and with black hair of rich texture, carefully groomed. In later years she was of heavier build, of heavier gait, and her hair touched with grey; her face fuller, of complexion somewhat more florid. Generally of kindly expression, she could, as she put it, 'look repressive'. Her eyes were singularly eloquent. She was not loquacious, but when she spoke, she spoke with authority. Early in her career she adopted, and maintained to the end, a professional costume of a two-piece dark suit, with white blouse, its front flounced, and over some thirty years of the same pattern. For social occasions, her dresses were of unobtrusive elegance. She held it important for herself and others to dress suitably to the occasion.

Marks of a puritanical upbringing were never effaced: a belief in work and duty, uneasiness with flippant talk about serious subjects, and integrity of a certain type. Moderately conservative in most ways, Lillian Penson hated the appeasement of the thirties, and admired Churchill. While many saw the public figure—*très autoritaire*, said a Frenchman—only a few saw the other

Penson, who believed that the last thing to do with your dignity was to stand on it; the compassionate person given to doing good by stealth; an excellent cook, judge of wines, and raconteur; a connoisseur of detective fiction; fond of country walks and fishing; excellent as hostess or guest; and a good listener. After two years in which she was gravely incapacitated, she died, unmarried, at her home, 54 Marine Parade, Brighton, on 17 April 1963.

ROBERT GREAVES, rev.

Sources J. D. Fair, *Harold Temperley: a scholar and Romantic in the public realm* (1992) · private information (1981) · personal knowledge (1981) · *CGPLA Eng. & Wales* (1963)
Archives PRO, corresp., BW 90 · Royal Holloway College, Egham, Surrey, papers
Likenesses photograph, U. Lond.
Wealth at death £24,380 14s.: probate, 16 July 1963, *CGPLA Eng. & Wales*

Penson, William (*d.* 1637), herald, was the son of William Penson (*d.* 1587), chancellor of Hereford Cathedral, and his wife, Alice Whittingham. His early life is obscure. In July 1603 he was made Rouge Croix pursuivant when the senior pursuivant, Thomas Knight, was promoted to be Chester herald. When Knight was prevented from obtaining his patent by an outbreak of plague, Penson obtained the patent as Chester herald for himself, possibly on the advice of Ralph Brooke, York herald. This inaugurated a decade-long conflict in which Penson maintained his irregular position against some of James I's most powerful courtiers.

Penson's case suggests the limitations of deference in Jacobean England. Allowed to wear a tabard at James's coronation, Penson was informed by Lord Henry Howard (later earl of Northampton and a commissioner for the office of earl marshal) and the earl of Worcester (acting earl marshal) that his service was for the day only and that he would have to bide the appointment of commissioners exercising the earl marshal's office. In February 1604 those commissioners ruled that Thomas Knight, not Penson, was rightfully Chester herald, whereupon Penson appealed to the court of common pleas. Beginning in April 1605 Penson spent twenty weeks in the Marshalsea by order of the commissioners. However, he was undeterred by his imprisonment, for upon his release he continued to stand on his patent, even suing Knight in the courts of common law, despite the commissioners' ruling.

Various legal actions, punctuated by Penson's imprisonments by the lords commissioner for contumacy, took place amid difficulties with other heralds as well. After eight years of contention Sir William Segar, Garter king of arms, tried to settle the impasse over Knight, who had been imprisoned for debt at Penson's suit over fees due to the Chester herald. At this point Segar intimated that the commissioners were effectively willing to cede the position of Chester herald to Penson if he would simply behave. For his pains Segar received a pungent letter purportedly from Penson's wife Elizabeth; the Harleian catalogue, terming it mildly 'somewhat bitter' (1.550), suggests it may have been written by Penson himself. In it Segar is accused of conspiring with other officers of arms, including Robert Treswell (also a subject of Penson's litigation), to ruin Penson. In fact Mrs Penson seems to have been quite capable of vituperation without assistance; years after the resolution of Penson's status as a herald, in June 1627, the earl of Arundel and Surrey as earl marshal evicted her family from the College of Arms for her 'u[n]ruly and troublesome behavior' (BL, Harley MS 1301, fol. 21) and for usurping the college's kitchen for the Pensons' private use. Their expulsion ended the practice of heralds' families living in the college.

At the end of 1613 Penson finally was given the post of Lancaster herald, with his first patent in that office following a year later. This ended his attempts to claim the position of Chester herald, which according to his own account cost him in the region of £1800. However unpleasant Penson was, and conceding that he suborned his patent as Chester, his career is still a remarkable example of obstinacy against authority. His pitting the courts of common law against the prerogative courts was both clever and effective, and he held on to his patent obdurately in the face of opposition from his fellow officers of arms and despite the fury of Northampton and the other commissioners for the office of earl marshal. He died on 20 April 1637 and was buried in the heralds' church of St Benet Paul's Wharf, London.

J. F. R. DAY

Sources Harley MS, 1, 107, 'Wm. Penson, Heraldic Collections', BL · 'The generall complaints of all the officers of armes against William Penson', BL, Cotton MS Faustina E.I, fol. 118 · 'On the office and privileges of heralds', BL, Harley MS 1301, fol. 21v · W. H. Godfrey, A. Wagner, and H. Stanford London, *The College of Arms, Queen Victoria Street* (1963) [officers of arms list by H. Stanford, London] · M. Noble, *A history of the College of Arms* (1805) · A. Wagner, *Heralds of England: a history of the office and College of Arms* (1967) · *A catalogue of the Harleian manuscripts in the British Museum*, 1 (1808) · Foster, *Alum. Oxon., 1500–1714*, 3.1144
Archives BL, MSS · Coll. Arms, MSS · PRO

Pentland. For this title name *see* Sinclair, John, first Baron Pentland (1860–1925).

Pentland, Joseph Barclay (1797–1873), naturalist and traveller, was born in Ballybofey, co. Donegal, Ireland, on 17 January 1797. Nothing is known of his early life save that he was educated at the Royal School, Armagh, and at the University of Paris. He became associated with Cuvier, vividly reporting day-to-day events in the Jardin des Plantes in a long series of letters to William Buckland and making percipient observations on the osteology of fossil marine reptiles (ichthyosaurs and plesiosaurs), which were to be drawn upon in W. D. Conybeare's descriptions. In addition to his work for Cuvier, Pentland studied fossil bones from India and Australia and collected them in Italy, an extinct pygmy hippopotamus from Sicily being named *Hippopotamus pentlandi* after him.

Appointed secretary to the British consul-generalship in Lima (1826–8), Pentland undertook extensive explorations in newly independent Bolivia. Using the most up-to-date barometers, he determined the heights of many Andean peaks, including Gualtieri (22,000 ft), Arequipa

Joseph Barclay Pentland (1797–1873), by Pierre Jean David D'Angers, 1832 [cast by Ecket Durand]

(later El Misti, 18,300 ft), Illimani (21,300 ft), and Chirquibamba (21,000 ft); the measurements, though since corrected, were of the right order of magnitude. Pentland recognized that most of these mountains were volcanoes, but also discovered Palaeozoic fossils at high altitudes (14,000 to 17,000 ft). He examined the antiquities of Cuzco and visited Lake Titicaca, perceiving that the Rio Desaguadero, hitherto thought to flow into the lake, was in fact its outlet. His *Report on Bolivia* to the Foreign Office, though the first substantial account of that country's geography, was not published until 1974, edited by J. V. Fifer (*Camden Miscellany*, 25).

After returning to Europe and preparing the posthumous catalogue of Cuvier's collection, Pentland was appointed consul-general in La Paz to the short-lived Peru–Bolivia Confederation (1836–9). He undertook further explorations, preparing a first map of Lake Titicaca (close to which he found fossil 'mastodon' bones) and disinterring human skulls from nearby tombs. He collected many plant and animal specimens, at least three plant species and a bird (the Andean tinamou) being consequently named after him.

Following his second return to Europe, Pentland remained interested in South America, supporting the work of explorers John Bowring and Hugh Weddell, encouraging the growing of Andean plants in Kew Gardens and the Jardin des Plantes and, in particular, being instrumental in arranging for the introduction of *Cinchona*—the quinine plant—to the West Indies. He helped Mary Somerville in the preparation for publication of maps of Peru and Bolivia for her *Physical Geography* (1848). A hitherto undescribed nickel–iron mineral he had obtained from Craigmure, Argyll, came to be named 'pentlandite'.

Pentland never married. From 1845 he made Rome his home, becoming so well acquainted with the antiquities

of Italy that he edited for John Murray three editions of *A Handbook of Rome and its Environs* (1860, 1871, and 1872); *A Handbook for Travellers in Southern Italy* (6th edn, 1868); and *A Handbook for Travellers in Northern Italy* (11th edn, 1869). During two visits by the prince of Wales to Rome, Pentland acted as his cicerone. He died at his home, 3 Motcomb Street, Belgrave Square, London, on 12 July 1873 and was buried in Brompton cemetery.

WILLIAM A. S. SARJEANT

Sources *The Athenaeum* (6 Sept 1873), 309 · J. B. Delair and W. A. S. Sarjeant, 'Joseph Pentland—a forgotten pioneer in the osteology of fossil marine reptiles', *Proceedings of the Dorset Natural History and Archaeological Society*, 97 (1975), 12–16 · W. A. S. Sarjeant and J. B. Delair, 'An Irish naturalist in Cuvier's laboratory: the letters of Joseph Pentland, 1820–1832', *Bulletin of the British Museum (Natural History)* [Historical Series], 6 (1977–80), 245–319 · J. V. Fifer, *Bolivia: land, location and politics since 1825* (1972) · J. B. Pentland, 'Report on Bolivia', ed. J. V. Fifer, *Camden miscellany, XXV*, CS, 4th ser., 13 (1974), 169–267 [see also Sp. trans. by J. A. Soux, *Informe sobre Bolivia* (Potosi, 1975)] · R. A. Humphreys, *Liberation in South America, 1806–1827: the career of James Paroissien* (1952) · W. A. S. Sarjeant, 'Joseph Pentland's geological and geographical work in Bolivia and Peru', *The XVII INHIGEO Congress* [Campinas, SP, Brazil], ed. S. Figueirôa and M. Lopez (1994), 11–27

Archives RBG Kew · RGS · U. Nott. | BL, letters to Sir Austen Layard, Add. MSS 38986–39120 · GS Lond., letters to Roderick Impey Murchison · NHM, corresp. with Sir Richard Owen and William Clift · NHM, corresp. with W. Parish and William Buckland relating to the fossil edentata of South America · NL NZ, Turnbull L., letters to Gideon Algernon Mantell · NMG Wales, De la Beche MSS · U. Nott. L., letters to William Buckland · U. St Andr. L., corresp. with James Forbes · Wellcome L., Hunterian Archives, Clift MSS

Likenesses P. J. D. D'Angers, bronze medallion, 1832, NPG [see illus.]

Wealth at death under £12,000: resworn probate, March 1874, *CGPLA Eng. & Wales* (1873)

Penton, Stephen (1639–1706), college head, the son of Stephen Penton, was born at Winchester on 30 March 1639 and baptized at St John's Church there on 9 April 1639. He was admitted as a scholar of Winchester College in 1653, matriculated from New College, Oxford, on 28 June 1659 and became a probationary fellow in the same year. From 1661 to 1672 he was a full fellow of the college. He graduated BA on 5 May 1663 and proceeded MA on 17 January 1667. From 1670 to 1676 he held the rectory of Tingewick in Buckinghamshire through the gift of his college. From at least 1671 he served as chaplain to Robert Bruce, earl of Ailesbury and Elgin, and as tutor to his son Thomas. On 15 February 1676 he was appointed principal of St Edmund Hall, Oxford, by the provost and fellows of Queen's College on the condition that he resign his living at Tingewick, to which his college, as part of this arrangement, later appointed a fellow of Queen's, Lancelot Bland.

Andrew Allum, Penton's vice-principal, considered him a less capable administrator than his predecessor, Thomas Tully. Certainly admissions declined during Penton's principalship from eleven in 1680 down to four in 1683. One reason for this downward trend, according to Allum, was Penton's marked preference for an 'inconsiderable set of gentlemen commoners, now his darling creatures' (Kelly,

46). As part of Penton's scheme to make the hall more attractive to the sons of the gentry he was responsible for building the college chapel and its adjoining library on a strip of land he obtained through his connections at New College. Money was raised out of Penton's own pocket and from the sale of plate given to the college by his predecessor. The chapel, built in the same Palladian style as neighbouring Queen's, was consecrated by John Fell, bishop of Oxford, on 7 April 1682. It was also a desire to attract more students from the gentry to Oxford that lay behind Penton's most famous literary work, *The Guardian's Instruction* (1688), which tried to demonstrate the value of an education at the university, particularly for those younger sons who would not inherit their father's estates. The aims of this work were expanded in Penton's *New Instructions to the Guardian* (1694), which covered the education of the sons of the gentry from the age of three to twenty-one and urged that the professions of law, medicine, and divinity were not beneath gentlemen. Aside from these works Penton also published, in 1682, a treatise asserting the lawfulness of bowing or kneeling at the altar.

The efforts to attract the gentry to St Edmund Hall were limited in their success. Penton resigned the principalship for reasons of health (he appears to have suffered from jaundice) on 7 March 1684 and on leaving made a present of twelve silver-handled knives and forks to the college. In 1684 he was nominated to the living of Glympton, Oxfordshire, by Frances Wheate, widow of Thomas Wheate, a position he held until 1693. Over the same period he was also lecturer in the neighbouring church at Churchill. On the nomination of his old pupil Thomas Bruce, now Lord Ailesbury, he was instituted on 27 September 1693 to the rectory of Wath by Ripon, in the North Riding of Yorkshire, and was collated on 28 May 1701 to the third prebendal stall at Ripon, holding both preferments until his death. He seems to have lived mainly in the north from 1693 onwards, though he still used his influence to get Robert Wood, the son of Thomas Wood, a fellowship at All Souls in 1694. A sermon given at Oxford in September 1705, praising the duke of Marlborough, is often attributed to Penton, as he had been a fellow of New College, but it was actually preached by his nephew Henry. Penton died a bachelor on 17 October 1706 at Wath by Ripon and was buried on 20 October in the chancel of Wath church, where an epitaph that he wrote himself was inscribed on a brass plate. This quaint inscription (it opened: 'Here lies what's left of Stephen Penton, Rector, who being dead, / Yet speaketh once for all: My beloved Parishioners. / Since any one of you may be the next, / Let every one prepare to do so') aroused some criticism from contemporaries (Whitaker, 187). He left most of his estate to the poor of the parish, having already given most of his books to the Bodleian and St Edmund Hall libraries.

EDWARD VALLANCE

Sources S. Penton, *The guardian's instruction, or, The gentleman's romance*, ed. H. H. Sturmer (1897) • [J. T. Fowler], ed., *Memorials of the church of SS Peter and Wilfrid, Ripon*, 2, SurtS, 78 (1886), 299–302 • J. N. D. Kelly, *St Edmund Hall: almost seven hundred years* (1989), 46–7 • E. Wood, 'Some Wood family letters', *Oxoniensia*, 51 (1986), 105–38 • DNB • *Remarks and collections of Thomas Hearne*, ed. C. E. Doble and others, 2, OHS, 7 (1886), 61, 67 • A. B. Emden, *An account of the church and library, St Edmund Hall Oxford* (1932), 40 • T. D. Whitaker, *A history of Richmondshire* (1823) • will, 8 Oct 1706, Borth. Inst. • probate, 10 April 1707, Borth. Inst.

Archives Winchester Cathedral | Bodl. Oxf., Tanner MSS • Bodl. Oxf., Rawlinson MSS • LMA, letters to Thomas Wood

Likenesses G. Vertue, portrait, repro. in *Oxford Almanack* (1747)

Wealth at death no debts, owned estates in Winchester; about £130 left in bequests and dole to poor; incl. £10 to choir at Ripon: will, Fowler, ed., *Memorials*, 301–2

Pentreath [*later* Jeffery], **Dorothy** [Dolly] (*bap.* 1692, *d.* 1777), native Cornish speaker, was born at Mousehole, Paul parish, Cornwall, and baptized on 16 May 1692. She was the second of six children of Nicholas Pentreath, a fisherman, and his second wife, Jone (for whom no maiden name is recorded). Her poverty as a fish-seller or 'jowster' may have been linked to the fact that she never married and in 1729 gave birth to an illegitimate son, John Pentreath (*d.* 1778). In an apparent attempt to establish some legitimacy, it seems that it was he who recorded her name at burial as Dolly Jeffery, the surname presumably of the putative father.

Although doubts have, on occasion, been cast on Pentreath's linguistic abilities and iconic status in Cornish studies, her claim to fame is as the last fluent native speaker of Cornish (as noted by Jago, Nance, and Pool), rather than as the last speaker of this Celtic language. Contemporary speakers who outlived her, including her friend William Bodinar (1711–1789), learned the language in their youth, whereas she claimed to have been a monoglot speaker until she was twenty. This claim seems exaggerated, but Cornish was certainly her first language.

Much of the information on Pentreath comes from Daines Barrington (1727–1800), who 'discovered' her in 1768, found out more about her from Walter Borlase in 1772, and published two papers about her and the other few remaining Cornish speakers in *Archaeologia* in 1776 and 1779. The historian Richard Polwhele (1760–1838) noted that in 1797 a Mousehole fisherman told him that William Bodinar 'used to talk with her for hours together in Cornish; that their conversation was understood by scarcely any one of the place; that both Dolly and himself could talk in English' (Polwhele, 5.19–20).

Towards the end of her life Pentreath became something of a celebrity for 'gabbling Cornish' (Barrington, 'Expiration', 283). About 1777 she was painted by John Opie (1761–1807), and an engraving possibly from life was published in 1781 by Robert Scaddan (1720–1802?). She died in Mousehole and was buried in Paul churchyard on 27 December 1777. Her epitaph in Cornish was written before December 1789 by an engineer named Tomson from Truro, an acquaintance of Polwhele, who published it in 1806. From this came the erroneous idea that she had died aged 102. In 1860 Prince Louis Lucien Bonaparte, the linguist, and the vicar of Paul, the Revd John Garrett, erected a handsome stone monument in the wall of the churchyard at Paul in her honour. In 1887 this was moved to her previously unmarked grave and her skeleton was exposed and examined. A lot of imaginative folklore

DOROTHY PENTREATH of MOUSEHOLE in CORNWALL,
the last Person who could converse in the Cornish Language?

Dorothy Pentreath (*bap.* 1692, *d.* 1777), by unknown engraver, pubd 1781 (after R. Scaddan)

Cornish painter', *Journal of the Royal Institution of Cornwall*, new ser., 7 (1973–7), 15–20 [with portrait] · M. Peter, 'John Opie RA, 1761–1807', *Journal of the Royal Institution of Cornwall*, new ser., 2 (1953–6), 47–62 · R. J. Pentreath, 'Dolly Pentreath', *Old Cornwall*, 11 (1991–7), 535–40 · M. Tangye, 'More about Dolly Pentreath', *Old Cornwall*, 12 (1997–2002), 33–5

Likenesses portrait, 1775?–1777?, repro. in *Western Antiquary* (1887); priv. coll. · J. Opie, portrait, *c.*1777, priv. coll.; repro. in Pool, *Death of Cornish* · R. Scaddan, engraving, in or before 1781, repro. in Staal, 'Robert Scaddan' · engraving, pubd 1781 (after R. Scaddan), NPG [*see illus.*]

Wealth at death poor; maintained partly by the parish: D. Barrington, *Archaeologia*, 3 (1776), 283

Penty, Arthur Joseph (1875–1937), architect and social thinker, was born at 16 Elmwood Street, St Laurence, York, on 17 March 1875, a son of Walter Green Penty (1852–1902), architect, and his wife, Emma Seller. After attending school in York he was apprenticed in 1888 to his father. Working in the leading architectural firm in late Victorian York, he attracted national and even international attention, including favourable notice in Herman Muthesius's *Das englische Haus* (1904).

While still in Yorkshire Penty worked to compensate for his short school career through membership of the Plato group and the Theosophical Society. He became politically active in the late 1890s, joining the Independent Labour Party and the Fabian Society. Through these organizations he began his intellectual partnership with A. R. Orage, with whom he collaborated in setting up the Leeds Arts Club, an eclectic lecture and discussion group. His professional and intellectual interests coalesced in his support for the arts and crafts movement.

When their father died in 1902, Penty's younger brother Frederick T. Penty (1879–1943) took over the business and Penty moved to London. Until the outbreak of war in 1914 he continued to make his living in architecture and furniture design, working for a year as a furniture restorer in New York from 1906 to 1907. He married Violet Leonard in 1910. Throughout this time he read extensively in the social sciences and wrote on contemporary issues, especially in the cultural journal *The New Age*. During the war Penty worked for the London Underground, London county council, and the Coal Commission. He then resumed his career as an architect, spending time with among others the architectural partnership of Parker and Unwin, with whom he worked on the Hampstead Garden Suburb.

Penty's social criticism developed through a total of thirteen books and a substantial corpus of articles and reviews in a wide variety of publications, including *The Guildsman*, the *Guild Socialist*, *G. K.'s Weekly*, *The Criterion*, *New Witness*, *The Crusader*, and the *American Review*. He elaborated a thoroughgoing critique of industrialism in its social, economic, and aesthetic aspects, and posited an alternative inspired by the agrarianism and craftsmanship of the middle ages. He acknowledged the influence of Ruskin, Carlyle, Matthew Arnold, and Edward Carpenter, and exchanged ideas with such like-minded associates as the Catholic intellectuals Hilaire Belloc and G. K. Chesterton, the Spanish conservative Ramiro de Maeztu, and the

about Dolly developed during the nineteenth century. The centenary of her burial was marked by a commemoration at the grave site, including readings in Cornish, and the event stirred an increasing interest in the language, leading to its revival at the beginning of the twentieth century. MATTHEW SPRIGGS

Sources D. Barrington, 'On the expiration of the Cornish language', *Archaeologia*, 3 (1776), 278–84 · D. Barrington, 'Mr Barrington on some additional information relative to the continuance of the Cornish language', *Archaeologia*, 5 (1779), 81–6 · parish register, Paul, Cornwall RO · R. Polwhele, *The history of Cornwall*, 7 vols. (1803–8), vol. 5, pp. 16–20, 43–4 · F. W. P. Jago, *The ancient language and the dialect of Cornwall* (1882), 8–12, 333–41 · W. T. Hoblyn, 'The probable parentage of Dorothy Pentreath', *Old Cornwall*, 3/11 (1936), 7–9 · W. E. Baily, 'The supposed remains of Dolly Pentreath', *Report and Transactions of the Penzance Natural History and Antiquarian Society* (1887–8), 365–7 · P. A. S. Pool and O. J. Padel, 'William Bodinar's letter, 1776', *Journal of the Royal Institution of Cornwall*, new ser., 7 (1973–7), 231–6 · Boase & Courtney, *Bibl. Corn.*, 1.271 · 'News from the societies', *Old Cornwall*, 8 (1973–9), 515–16 · R. M. Nance, 'Gwas Myghal and the Cornish revival', *Old Cornwall*, 2/8 (1931–6), 1–5 · R. M. Nance, 'Further note on Dolly Pentreath', *Old Cornwall*, 2/11 (1931–6), 9–11 · P. A. S. Pool, *The death of Cornish (1600–1800)* (1982), 25–8 [with portrait] · C. Staal, 'Robert Scaddan—a

Ceylonese art historian Ananda K. Coomaraswamy. He was also impressed by the anti-industrialism of Gandhi and the Indian independence movement. His *Old Worlds for New* (1917) was a reply to H. G. Wells's *New Worlds for Old* (1907). In *A Guildsman's Interpretation of History* (1920) he criticized the historical philosophy of linear progress and made the case for a reversion to simpler modes of social and economic organization. An Anglican, he set out the religious basis of his thought in *Towards a Christian Sociology* (1923).

For Penty a society's morality was expressed in its buildings. Consequently, his social theory was largely an extension of his architectural thinking. While earlier medievalists had supported the Victorian Gothic revival, Penty favoured the vernacular, or Queen Anne style, which he regarded as the legitimate successor to Gothic in the English architectural tradition. He published his ideas on the vernacular in *The Elements of Domestic Design* (1930).

This fusion of politics and aesthetics gradually separated Penty from his earlier political attachments. In 1902 he had an acrimonious exchange on architectural issues with the leading Fabian George Bernard Shaw. Later that year he clashed with Fabian Society secretary E. R. Pease over what he saw as the philistine architectural criteria for the design of the London School of Economics building. In 1907 Penty helped establish the Fabian Arts Group, but tensions between the group and the parent society led to its demise within four years.

As a result of such experiences Penty rejected mainstream collectivist socialism and sought alternatives that he considered to be more respectful of individualism, spirituality, and the arts. His first book, *The Restoration of the Gild System* (1906), did much to inspire the guild socialist movement that found expression in the National Guilds League after 1915. Following the Bolshevik revolution of 1917, Penty broke with the league over its increasingly Marxist ideology and its acceptance of industrial production methods.

The organizations to which Penty was subsequently affiliated included the Christian socialist Crusader League, which he helped to launch in 1923. In 1926 he contributed to the formation of the Rural Reconstruction Association, which championed agrarian revivalism as a programme of job creation and social reform. He was intrigued by the distributist ideas of Chesterton and Belloc, but criticized the Distributist League for its belief in unqualified private property rights. By the early 1930s Penty was attracted to the anti-modernism of the far right. He admired the corporatist economic organization of Mussolini's Italy, supported the nationalists in the Spanish Civil War, and interested himself in the ideas of Oswald Mosley. At the same time he denounced Italian imperialism in Abyssinia and rejected Nazism for its racial doctrines and its statism.

Penty died of heart disease at his home, 59 Church Street, Old Isleworth, Middlesex, on 19 January 1937; his wife survived him. In the academic literature he appears mainly as an original but ultimately marginal figure in the history of guild socialism. More positive assessments came from contemporaries outside the socialist fold. G. K. Chesterton in his preface to Penty's *Post-Industrialism* described him as 'one of the two or three truly original minds of the modern world' (1922, 7), and T. S. Eliot in *The Idea of a Christian Society* admiringly referred to him as a vigorous twentieth-century proponent of the Ruskinian tradition (Eliot, 31).   PETER C. GROSVENOR

Sources P. C. Grosvenor, 'A medieval future: the social, economic and aesthetic thought of A. J. Penty (1875–1937)', PhD diss., London School of Economics, 1997 • E. J. Kiernan, *Arthur J. Penty: his contribution to social thought* (1941) • A. D. Sokolow, *The political theory of Arthur J. Penty* (New Haven, Connecticut, 1940) • S. James, 'Arthur J. Penty: architect and sociologist', *American Review* (April 1937) • D. Thistlewood, 'A. J. Penty (1875–1937) and the legacy of 19th century English domestic architecture', *Journal of the Society of Architectural Historians*, 46 (1987), 327–41 • M. Swenarton, *Artisans and architects* (1989) • J. Vowles, 'From corporatism to workers' control: the formation of British guild socialism', PhD diss., University of British Columbia, 1980 • S. T. Glass, *The responsible society: the ideas of the English guild socialists* (1966) • N. Carpenter, *Guild socialism: a historical and critical analysis* (New York, 1922) • H. Muthesius, *The English house*, ed. D. Sharp, trans. J. Seligman (1979) • T. Steele, *Alfred Orage and the Leeds Arts Club, 1893–1923* (1990) • T. S. Eliot, *The idea of a Christian society* (1939) • b. cert. • *CGPLA Eng. & Wales* (1937) • d. cert.
Archives NRA, priv. coll., papers • U. Hull, collection of publications, cuttings, and corresp. [microfilm]
Likenesses photograph, priv. coll.; repro. in Swenarton, *Artisans and architects*
Wealth at death £266 13s. 5d.: probate, 9 Feb 1937, *CGPLA Eng. & Wales*

Penzance. For this title name *see* Wilde, James Plaisted, Baron Penzance (1816–1899).

Pepler, **Sir George Lionel** (1882–1959), town planner, was born at Croydon, Surrey, on 24 February 1882, the third child and second son of George Henry Pepler (1849–1884), brewer, and his wife, Emma Florence Mills (1853–1935); Harry Douglas Clarke *Pepler (known as Hilary) was his brother. Educated at Bootham School, York, and the Leys School, Cambridge, he was articled to Walter Hooker, a surveyor in Croydon. On 24 July 1903, at Clifton, he married Edith Amy (1877/8–1942), daughter of Alfred E. Bobbett, solicitor, of Bristol; the couple had two daughters and one son.

From 1905 until 1914, in partnership with Ernest G. Allen, Pepler carried on a practice in surveying and the then emerging vocation of town planning. The partners were awarded three gold medals at housing exhibitions in 1908 and 1910 and were among the first to specialize in laying out new villages and housing estates for landowners, among others at Fallings Park near Wolverhampton and at Knebworth, Hertfordshire. During that period Pepler became a member of the Garden City (later Town and Country Planning) Association, and was active in the advocacy of the garden city concept and of the operation by local authorities of their permissive planning powers under the first Town Planning Act, of 1909. In 1914 John Burns, president of the Local Government Board from 1905 to 1914 and the 'father' of the act, called Pepler into the planning administration of the board, where he succeeded Thomas Adams as chief technical planning officer,

Sir George Lionel Pepler (1882–1959), by Elliott & Fry, 1949

a position which he retained, through several changes of his designation and that of the department, until 1946.

Pepler's qualities proved admirably suited to the task of inducing local authorities to adopt town planning powers and guiding them in putting these into practice. Having a passionate belief in the necessity of planning, as well as persuasiveness, patience, and tact, he was allowed by successive ministers (or perhaps quietly assumed) exceptional freedom and scope in what was essentially propaganda. He was a major influence in the conversion of public and official opinion to acceptance of a new, contentious, and difficult governmental process. The experience and authority which he gained in this key position enabled him, just before his retirement, to make a weighty contribution to the formulation of the Town and Country Planning Act of 1947, which established the planning of all land as a normal function of central and local government.

Pepler's work and influence in planning extended far outside his official position. He was one of the founders in 1913 of the Town Planning Institute, its honorary secretary and treasurer until his death, twice president (1919–20, 1949–50), and first gold medallist (1953). Keenly interested in the training of planners, he was unfailingly helpful in encouragement and advice to students and young members of the profession, and was chairman (1930–59) of the Town Planning Joint Examination Board. He attended regularly the annual sessions of the town and country planning summer school from its foundation in 1933, and was its president in 1943–59. Pepler was also

active in the work of the International Federation for Housing and Town Planning, of which he was president in 1935–8 and 1947–52, and thereafter honorary president for life. The survival of the federation despite the disruption of the Second World War was due mainly to his devotion and that of the honorary secretary, Elizabeth Evelyn Halton, during the war years. On 31 January 1947 Elizabeth (1900/01–1998), the daughter of a merchant, Eldred Halton, became Pepler's second wife. She was a Conservative member of the London county council from 1946 to 1965 and deputy chairman of the council in 1956–7.

Pepler was a member of the regional survey committee for south Wales (1920), of the unhealthy areas committee over which Neville Chamberlain presided (1921), and of the royal commission on common land (1955–8); chairman of the Institution of Professional Civil Servants (1937–42), of the inter-allied committee for physical planning and reconstruction (1942–5), and for many years an active influence in the Council for the Preservation of Rural England and the National Playing Fields Association. With P. W. Macfarlane he prepared the outline plan for the north-east development area (1949) and in 1950–54 he was planning adviser to Singapore.

Pepler was elected an honorary associate of the Royal Institute of British Architects in 1937, appointed CB in 1944, and knighted in 1948. His recreations were mainly out of doors and included golf and other games, swimming, gardening, and bonfires. He had a cottage at Lulworth, Dorset, where, with his family, for nearly fifty years he spent happy holidays by the sea. He died at Moffatt House, Weymouth, on 13 April 1959 and was buried at West Lulworth church. In 1960 the headland previously known as East Point, Lulworth Cove, was renamed Pepler's Point. In 1963 the George Pepler international award was established to enable young people to travel abroad to study chosen aspects of town and country planning.

F. J. OSBORN, rev. CATHERINE GORDON

Sources The Builder, 196 (1959), 735 · The Builder, 196 (1959), 769 · W. G. Holford, ArchR, 125 (1959), 373 · Town and Country Planning, 27 (May 1959), 195 · Journal of the Town Planning Institute, 45 (1959), 154–5 · V. A. Coates, 'Sir George Pepler', RIBA Journal, 66 (1958–9), 333 · private information (1998) [archivist, Royal Town Planning Institute] · private information (2004) [Richard Pepler] · m. certs. · CGPLA Eng. & Wales (1959)

Archives Bodl. Oxf., notes relating to conservation and development of town and country planning · University of Strathclyde, Glasgow, corresp., papers and plans | King's School, Canterbury, letters relating to Sturry Court · Welwyn Garden City Library, corresp. with Sir Frederic Osborn

Likenesses Elliott & Fry, photograph, 1949, NPG [see illus.] · W. Stoneman, photograph, 1949, NPG · R. Darwin, oils, 1959, Royal Town Planning Institute, London

Wealth at death £48,739 5s.: probate, 5 Aug 1959, CGPLA Eng. & Wales

Pepler, Harry Douglas Clarke [Hilary] (1878–1951), printer and puppeteer, was born in Eastbourne, Sussex, on 14 January 1878, the elder son of George Henry (Harry) Pepler (1849–1884), a partner in Diplock Brewers, and his wife, Emma Florence (1853–1935), daughter of Robert Mills, a Spitalfields silk merchant, and his wife, Emma Gush. The designer Marian *Pepler (1904–1997) [see under

Russell, Richard Drew] was Pepler's niece. Harry's father disliked making his living from something that he thought made the poor poorer so he retired from his brewery post in the early 1880s. He then moved with his young family to Croydon with the intention of opening a school, but in 1884 he died before his dream was realized. For Harry the trauma of losing his father when he was six may in part explain why he took on his father's sense of responsibility for enriching the lives of the poor. In years to come, as an enthusiastic and earnest pioneer for social improvement, he argued that the family should be kept intact at all costs.

In 1889 Emma Pepler remarried; her second husband was a Quaker, Francis Thompson. In 1890 Harry and his younger brother, George *Pepler (1882–1959), later knighted for his work as a town planner, began studying at Bootham School in York, a Quaker establishment. There Harry made friends with the Meynell family and with Edmund Harvey, a lifelong worker for the peace movement. As a child he excelled at drawing maps, but when his art master suggested lettering as a career, Harry, thinking this plan unrealistic, did not mention it to his mother.

In 1894 Harry left school. He spent the next decade as—in his own words—'a rolling stone' (Sewell, 5). First he was apprenticed to Sir Reginald Hanson, a merchant tailor in the City of London; next he transferred to the tea trade; subsequently he ran his own business, casting pewter moulds for candle and ice-cream making. When the equipment became outmoded he sold up. In 1901 he was elected a liveryman of the Merchant Taylors' Company and was granted the freedom of the City of London. He was already interested in the theatre and once played Toby Belch in an amateur production of *Twelfth Night*.

Pepler suffered from an astigmatism in one eye. He was a tall, outspoken, and socially commanding character. In 1903 he met his wife, Clara Lilian Whiteman (1876–1960), whom he married in the following year. She was known as Clare, and called him Douglas; she was a painter and also a Quaker. In 1905 the Peplers moved to a five-storey house, 14 Hammersmith Terrace, beside the Thames, and their first son, David, was born. In the same year Pepler wrote *His Majesty*, which was illustrated by Clare. The pamphlet argued that the care of babies should be guided by the laws of nature: breast-feeding, fresh air, simple clothing, and the chance to discover the world for yourself within reasonable limits were recommended; babies should learn, for instance, that soap tastes unpleasant by biting it. The book warned against ill-coloured nursery rhyme illustrations, microbe-holding frills and drapery, and leaving babies in the care of anyone but the mother.

In 1907 Pepler became a social worker for London County Council. Among other ambitious tasks he organized free school meals in LCC schools. In the same year he co-founded the Hampshire House Club with his neighbours Fred Rowntree and Warwick Draper. The purpose of the club was to create a pleasant venue for workers in the district and to provide workshops where underprivileged men could learn a trade. Meanwhile at home, in Hammersmith, Pepler's immediate surroundings were strongly associated with arts and crafts history. Cobden-Sanderson's Dove Press had been located nearby, as had William Morris's Kelmscott House. The calligrapher Edward Johnston was a close friend and neighbour, but Eric Gill and his family had moved from Hammersmith to Ditchling in 1907, and Pepler did not meet Gill until about 1915. In 1908 a second son, John Stephen, was born (known first as Stephen he later published under the name Father Conrad Pepler when he became a Dominican monk), and in 1911 a third son, Mark.

Pepler attended meetings of the Fabian Society but it was the Christian cause known as 'distributism' that he

Harry Douglas Clarke [Hilary] **Pepler (1878–1951)**, by unknown photographer, 1921 [centre, with his family outside Fragbarrow Farm]

was to support in the long run. Hilaire Belloc and G. K. Chesterton were key figures in the movement, which argued for the redistribution of privately owned land to the poor so that they might be self-sufficient. Pepler distinguished between the two approaches to reform:

The Fabian proposing to remove all social ills by legislation, and the Christian hoping by precept example and charity to give every man his chance to attain and maintain an independence for his well-being.   (Pepler, 'Forty years back', 2/3, 78)

Pepler wrote about the ills of society in his vivid, prophetic style. His eldest daughter, Susan Falkner, remembers him as someone who was always writing; in every spare moment he had a pen and paper on his knee. *The Care Committee: the Child and the Parent* (1912) was a relatively tame volume explaining how care committees consisting of volunteers and paid officers could work with schools and families to ensure that poor children received appropriate clothing and food. *Justice and the Child* (1915) is a more radical study; its exasperated tone reflects Pepler's increasing dissatisfaction. The authorities saw their mission as 'saving' children from their parents rather than working with families to discourage young people from re-offending. Pepler argued for probation and aftercare rather than for Borstals and remand homes, which inevitably broke up the family.

Pepler was exempt from war service during the First World War because of his poor vision. In 1914 he had visited Venice, Vienna, and Budapest to study how juvenile crime was handled, but he found the penitentiaries 'dreary and unexpectant' (Pepler, 'Forty years back', 2/8, 250). Back in Hammersmith he took responsibility for refugee Belgian craftsmen and developed the Hampshire House Workshops, which operated as a company where the refugees could make hand-crafted furniture, embroidery, and shoes. Under the imprint of Hampshire House Workshops, London, Pepler also began to publish. His friend Gerard Meynell, of the Westminster Press, printed the first books. In 1915 Pepler wrote and published an anticapitalist satire, *Devil's Devices*. The Catholic convert Eric Gill, also exempt from war service while carving the stations of the cross at Westminster Cathedral, produced wood engravings for the book. This collaboration marked the beginning of nine years of close friendship between Gill and Pepler. The book fascinated the charismatic Dominican Father Vincent McNabb, and he invited Gill and Pepler to lecture at Hawksyard, where he was prior. After conversations with Father Vincent, Pepler converted to the Roman Catholic faith, and when he was baptized, in 1916, he officially took the name Hilary, by which he was thereafter known.

Pepler resigned from social work and moved his family to Sopers, a house in Ditchling village. There his first daughter, Susan, was born in 1916. Edward Johnston, never a Catholic but always a friend to Pepler, had already moved to Ditchling, and Pepler had been looking for a chance to follow him. Inspired by his first forays into publishing he started St Dominic's Press at Sopers in 1916 with a Stanhope handpress of 1790, two founts of Caslon old

face, and a supply of Batchelor's handmade paper. He was taught hand-printing by an aged printer known as Old Dawes. At the outset all activities were done by hand, even the making of ink. For Pepler, moving to the country meant the chance to put distributist theories into practice. At this time he believed passionately in the power of the book to reach a new audience and change people's thinking. The early books were planned by Pepler, with Gill providing most of the wood engravings. These publications sought to encourage rural, Catholic self-sufficiency; best-sellers such as Ethel Mairet's *Vegetable Dyes* (1916) were straightforward practical guides for craftsmen. The occasional magazine, *The Game* (1916–23), and the Welfare Handbooks series of publications offered more quirky propaganda: both derided birth control and custard powder because each interfered with nature.

For historians of the twentieth century private press movement St Dominic's Press is regarded as idiosyncratic: charming, casual, yet unpretentious. Pepler had a genuine gift for designing striking illustrated posters and beautifully balanced title-pages but he was never a perfectionist; he would correct errors by hand rather than reprint an edition. He was also a master of parody, able to conjure up a rhyme for all manner of events. His own writings appeared in *Concerning Dragons* (1916), *In Petra* (1923), and *Libellus lapidum* (1924)—poking fun in turn at nursemaids, suburbia, and Beatrice and Sidney Webb. Some of his poems, such as *The Dressmaker and the Milkmaid* (1926), were concerned with the fantasy of a resourceful Madonna who could weave gowns, make curtains, mill flour, and scrub floors as well as caring for the infant Jesus. Meanwhile life for the Pepler and Gill families at Ditchling eschewed all mod cons, and Clare Pepler was continually working in the home, unable to make time for her paintings.

Pepler's two youngest daughters, Janet and Margaret, were born in 1918 and 1920 respectively. In 1918 the Peplers moved onto Ditchling Common, 2 miles from Ditchling village, to a small farm known as Hallets. St Dominic's Press also moved to Ditchling Common. Later the family moved to a larger farm, Fragbarrow. The farmhouse was a little more modern than their other Ditchling residences, with running water and a bathroom, but still had no electricity. It was situated a field away from the Gills' home, at Hopkin's Crank. The Peplers' eldest son, David, took responsibility for farming at Fragbarrow.

A community of craftsmen continued to develop on Ditchling Common, but Johnston moved his family back to the village as the Roman Catholic agenda became more pronounced. In 1921 The Guild of St Joseph and St Dominic was formed to put the collaboration of Catholic craftsmen on a formal footing. The guild stood out against industrialism and promoted working with one's hands as a way of praising God. In 1923 Pepler was elected prefect of the guild, but there were disputes brewing between him and Gill over guild finances. Pepler came from an affluent background and favoured a pooling of resources between families, but Gill was more cautious. Further strain was caused by Gill's possessiveness as a father; he mistrusted the relationship of his eldest daughter, Elizabeth, with

David Pepler. Gill left Ditchling and the guild in 1924. Pepler was devastated by his departure and for many years sought a reconciliation. David and Elizabeth married, despite the breach. Pepler missed Gill, as a working companion and as a singing companion in chapel or at rowdy press suppers. Gill on the other hand referred to Pepler as 'Hilario Bottomlessfinance' and resisted all pleas for a reunion (E. Gill, MS letter, 8 Aug 1928, priv. coll.).

In 1924 Pepler and his family moved into Hopkin's Crank, the Gills' old home on Ditchling Common. Pepler lived there for the rest of his life. Visitors adored the lively, generous-spirited atmosphere of the new family home with its barn transformed into a puppet theatre. Puppets increasingly absorbed Pepler's attention. After Gill had left the guild St Dominic's Press published several plays for puppets. Pepler's own puppets were 'large, boisterous, clownish'—a far cry from elegant marionettes (Wall, 26). He was also developing an interest in mime, and in 1934 he toured the United States, lecturing on and performing mimes, with his daughter Susan accompanying him on pipes and cello.

Pepler also worked on mimes for early live BBC television broadcasts, including versions of *The Pilgrim's Progress*, *The Ancient Mariner*, and the story of Jacob and Esau. Reginald Jebb, later a colleague when Hilary worked for *G. K.'s Weekly*, summed up Hilary's interest in mime:

in art in general he favoured what was formal rather than the merely representational. This attitude was one of the many links he had with Eric Gill … This art-form of gesture and formalised movements appealed to him, I think, because he saw in it the groundwork of all stagecraft and one of the most fitting means of representing the climaxes of religion and life. (Jebb, 24)

St Dominic's Press continued until 1936. Pepler was voted out of the Guild of St Joseph and St Dominic for employing a non-Catholic apprentice and introducing a degree of mechanization. He made a big bonfire of St Dominic's Press material on Ditchling Common. Some locals with foresight retrieved David Jones's prints from the flames. The press was reformed as the Ditchling Press and moved back to Ditchling village. It used more modern machinery and was run by Pepler's son Mark.

For the Society of Typographic Arts, Chicago, Pepler wrote *The Hand Press* (St Dominic's Press, 1934), a book arguing in favour of hand printing and recommending that 'The hand printer should break away from the modern craze for outward uniformity and enjoy a freedom denied to the machinist' (p. 17). By the conclusion, however, Pepler let slip a more gloomy prognosis, that the book had been degraded. 'With its status gone as a thing to be cherished, its contents must deteriorate … good food is not put on dirty plates' (p. 72).

After G. K. Chesterton's death in 1936 Pepler was one of the group that took over *G. K.'s Weekly*, which was continued with Hilaire Belloc as editor and later became the *Weekly Review*; among other writings he contributed stage and film criticism. His publications in old age included *The Stations of the Cross in Mime: as Devised for Liturgical Presentation* (Blackfriars, Oxford, 1947).

On 20 September 1951 Hilary Pepler died of a severe heart attack while raking mown grass in his garden at Hopkin's Crank. The craftsmen still working in the Guild of St Joseph and St Dominic collaborated for his funeral; the woodworkers made a coffin and the weavers made the lining. Pepler was buried in the churchyard of St Margaret's, Ditchling, after a mass at the guild's Catholic chapel on Ditchling Common.   LOTTIE HOARE

Sources B. Sewell, 'Hilary Pepler: 1878–1951', *Aylesford Review*, 7/1 (spring 1965), 3–18 · M. Taylor, ed., *Saint Dominic's press: a bibliography, 1916–1937* (1995) · S. Falkner, *A Ditchling childhood, 1916–1936* (1994) · H. D. C. Pepler, *The hand press*, St Dominic's Press (1934); repr. Ditchling Press (1952) · *The Register* (1948–9) · F. MacCarthy, *Eric Gill* (1989) · H. D. C. Pepler, *His majesty* (1905) · H. D. C. Pepler, *A letter from Sussex* (Chicago, 1950) [about his friend Eric Gill] · H. D. C. Pepler, *The care committee: the child and the parent* (1912) · H. D. C. Pepler, *Justice and the child* (1915) · B. Wall, 'A note on Hilary', *Aylesford Review* (spring 1965), 26–7 · R. Jebb, 'Hilary Pepler, journalist', *Aylesford Review* (spring 1965), 18–26 · H. D. C. Pepler, 'Forty years back', *The Register*, 2/3 (1949), 78–9 · H. D. C. Pepler, 'Forty years back', *The Register*, 2/8 (1949), 250–51 · P. Johnston, *Edward Johnston* (1959) · *Eric Gill and the Guild of St Joseph and St Dominic* (1990) [exhibition catalogue, Hove Museum and Art Gallery] · b. cert. · b. cert. [G. H. Pepler; C. L. Whiteman] · d. cert. [G. H. Pepler; C. L. Pepler]
Archives Blackfriars, George Square, Edinburgh, Dominican Archives, records of the Guild of St Joseph and St Dominic
Likenesses photograph, 1921, priv. coll. [*see illus.*] · black and white photograph, c.1950, repro. in Falkner, *Ditchling childhood* · C. Pepler, *née* Whiteman, pencil sketch, repro. in Falkner, *Ditchling childhood*
Wealth at death £1589 15s. 8d.: probate, 7 Dec 1951, *CGPLA Eng. & Wales*

Pepler, Marian (1904–1997). *See under* Russell, Richard Drew (1903–1981).

Peploe, Hanmer William Webb- (1837–1923), Church of England clergyman and evangelical, was born on 1 October 1837 at Weobley, Herefordshire, the third son of the Revd John Birch Webb (d. 1869), vicar of Weobley and King's Pyon, and his wife, Annie (1805–1880), a well-known religious author. The family seat was at Garnstone Castle, also in Herefordshire. John Webb and his family assumed the additional name of Peploe in 1866. Hanmer was educated at Marlborough College, Cheltenham College, and Pembroke College, Cambridge, where he graduated in 1860. A serious accident in the gym at Cambridge forced him to spend prolonged periods lying on his back in bed. This did not entirely keep him from sporting activities, however, in which he excelled. An evangelical conversion changed Webb's course and he took orders in 1863. His early clerical career was centred on family livings: he was initially curate at Weobley (1863–8), taking over the vicarage of King's Pyon from his father in 1866. He married on 11 April 1863 Frances Emily, eldest daughter of Robert Lush QC. They had at least six children, of whom two sons and a daughter survived their father.

The death of an infant son in 1874 proved a turning point in Webb-Peploe's life. Burdened by a sense of inadequacy in the face of crisis, he felt the limitations of justification by faith alone at a time when many evangelical contemporaries were likewise searching for the means to

Hanmer William Webb-Peploe (1837–1923), by George Charles Beresford

greater moral and spiritual achievement in this life. Thus Webb-Peploe, until then an obscure country clergyman, rose to prominence in evangelical circles between 1874 and 1876 with the birth of the Holiness Movement. Though not present at the initial Oxford conference of 1874, Webb-Peploe participated extensively in subsequent developments including the first Keswick convention of 1875. Webb-Peploe became almost a fixture at Keswick until he became too ill to attend two years prior to his death. Like all advocates of the Holiness Movement, Webb-Peploe taught the possibility of freedom from the commission as well as the consequences of sin. His special contribution stressed the place of holiness in the larger picture of God's revelation 'from Genesis to Revelation'. This emphasis was no doubt due in part to his remarkable knowledge from memory of the Bible—the fruit of the long hours lying on his back in early manhood.

In 1876 Webb-Peploe was invited to become vicar of St Paul's, Onslow Square, an important evangelical parish in the West End. Thus began a remarkable 43-year incumbency in London, which fixed Webb-Peploe's reputation as a leading figure among Anglican evangelicals. He was undoubtedly at the height of his influence in the 1890s and was made a prebendary of St Paul's in 1893. In later years his congregations declined as his style of Anglicanism became less fashionable. Increasing age inevitably told on his powers and popularity also.

Webb-Peploe was a vigorous supporter of many causes dear to Anglican evangelicals in his day. He was vehement in his opposition to ritualism and was a founder of the National Protestant Church Union. He gave practical support to missionary work at home and overseas and was president of the Barbican Mission to the Jews. Like most Anglican evangelicals at that time he loathed socialism and was active in the Anti-Socialist Union of Churches. His influence was extensive through the training he gave to 110 candidates for the ministry.

A tall, strong man Webb-Peploe had a glass eye (the result of being attacked by a cat). He was the embodiment of a type of muscular Christianity popular with late Victorian evangelicals: he exuded physical vigour and was indefatigable in his work. Unfortunately he lacked tact and diplomacy, which may explain his lack of further preferment in the Church of England. His great achievement was his role as chief commender of Keswick ideas to a wider audience of Anglican evangelicals at the annual Islington clerical meeting and elsewhere. He died a revered figure in the evangelical party on 19 July 1923 at his home at 1 Evelyn Gardens, South Kensington, and was buried at Brompton cemetery.   I. T. FOSTER

Sources *The Times* (20 July 1923), 14 · *The Record* (26 July 1923), 483–6 · *The Record* (2 Aug 1923), 504 · Crockford · Venn, *Alum. Cant.* · J. C. Pollock, *The Keswick story: the authorized history of the Keswick convention* (1964)

Likenesses G. C. Beresford, photograph, NPG [*see illus.*] · photograph, repro. in H. W. Webb-Peploe, *The life of privilege: possession, peace and power* (1896), frontispiece

Wealth at death £52,067 8s. 6d.: probate, 17 Aug 1923, CGPLA Eng. & Wales

Peploe, Samuel (*bap.* 1667, *d.* 1752), bishop of Chester and religious controversialist, the son of Podmore Peploe, was baptized at Dawley Parva in Shropshire on 29 July 1667. Following attendance at Penkridge School in Staffordshire he matriculated as a batteler of Jesus College, Oxford, on 12 May 1687, graduating BA on 12 March 1691 and proceeding MA in 1693. After he had taken holy orders, his preferment was rapid: in 1695 he was presented to the rectory of Kedleston, near Derby, and in 1700 to the vicarage of Preston in Lancashire, where he quickly established a reputation as an outspoken enemy of a largely Roman Catholic population. His first wife, Ann Browne, with whom he had a son and four daughters, died on 25 November 1705; and on 8 January 1712 he married Ann Birch, a daughter of the previous incumbent at Preston. There were no surviving children from this second marriage.

Peploe's patrons at Preston, the Hoghtons of Hoghton Tower, were themselves staunch Presbyterians and it was undoubtedly Peploe's low-church sympathies in religion and strident whiggism in politics that recommended him to them. Lancashire in the first half of the eighteenth century was a county of religious and political extremes, where contemporary discourse portrayed the antagonism of a predominantly Roman Catholic, nonjuring, and Jacobite gentry to a palatine establishment well leavened with protestant dissenters. Conforming Anglicans like

Samuel Peploe (*bap.* 1667, *d.* 1752), by John Faber junior (after Hamlet Winstanley, 1733)

Peploe were obliged to pick their way between such rhetorical shoals with extreme care.

When the Jacobite forces entered Preston in November 1715 Peploe reportedly mounted his pulpit to preach a sermon exhorting his parishioners to abjure the pretender and manifest their loyalty to the house of Brunswick. But it was less this act of signal bravery than his well-publicized sermons against the dangers of popery and efforts on behalf of the forfeited estates commission that brought him to the attention of ministers. On 1 July 1717 he was nominated to the vacant wardenship of Manchester collegiate church; he was, however, subsequently refused induction by his diocesan, Francis Gastrell, on the grounds that the degree of bachelor of divinity conferred upon him by faculty at Lambeth was not a valid qualification. Years of litigation, pamphleteering, and personal enmity ensued, culminating in a determination in king's bench that, for such purposes at least, degrees conferred by the archbishop of Canterbury were of equal value to those granted by the universities.

When Bishop Gastrell died in 1725 the question of his successor at Chester was hotly disputed, with rival church dignitaries each pressing the merits of their clients upon the ministry. Peploe was almost certainly the candidate of Edmund Gibson, bishop of London, but he was assured by the duke of Newcastle that his advancement came as reward for his 'zeal and affection to the true interest of our king and country' (duke of Newcastle to S. Peploe, 15 Jan 1726, PRO, SP 35/61, fol. 15). He was consecrated on 12 April 1726 and, though obliged to resign his benefice at

Preston, was permitted to retain the wardenship at Manchester *in commendam*. Contention there, however, continued unabated, with bitter wrangles over the visitorship and appointment of a chaplain. Indeed in the absence of any county-wide election contests in Lancashire after 1722, Manchester College came to constitute a ritual forum in which local partisans could carry on their ideological battles by subtler means.

At first Peploe's situation at Chester was little better, with an episcopal bureaucracy appointed by his predecessors and his cathedral firmly under the control of a tory chapter. Over the course of the next twelve years, though, the new bishop worked diligently to build up the whig interest in his diocese, supplying men of proven whig loyalties to vacant benefices in his gift and using his credit with the government to make like-minded appointments to the chapter. By such methods was the tories' stranglehold on diocesan machinery eroded and eventually broken down: in 1738 Peploe resigned his wardenship at Manchester in favour of his son Samuel (1699–1781), and in the following year he saw a whig majority at last established in his cathedral.

From his earliest days at Preston, Peploe had identified himself with contemporary movements for the reformation of manners and the establishment of charity schools. He was a co-founder of the town's blue coat school in 1702 and of Cadley School five years later. Such institutions, he would assert in 1730, 'shewed the ways of piety, peace and temperance' (S. Peploe, *A Sermon Preach'd in the Parish Church of St Sepulchre, April the 2d 1730*, 1730, 20), made the rich mindful of their Christian obligations to the poor, and served as a bulwark against the moral depravity of society. Although frequently at odds with Anglican zealots, Peploe was nevertheless an assiduous defender of the church against its enemies. He understood the extent of popular prejudice against the clergy and strove to overcome it. 'They have represented us as Useless and Burdensome, as Idle and Superficial in our ministerial Performances,' he wrote in a charge to his diocesan clergy on the occasion of a visitation in 1747; 'which, however true it may be in regard to some particular Persons … yet surely, it is an unjust Imputation on the Body of the Clergy' (Green, 'Charity, morality, and social control', 21). During his episcopate he consecrated thirty-nine churches and chapels, largely with the aim of counteracting the influence of Roman Catholicism, and erected two new galleries in the choir of his cathedral; he was normally resident in his bishopric whenever parliament was not in session; and in general he carried out the pastoral duties of his episcopal office, including visitations and confirmations, with greater fervour and conscientiousness than was common among Hanoverian prelates.

A pugnacious temperament led Peploe into conflict with a succession of locally prominent figures and ensured that he would be remembered primarily as a protagonist in partisan causes. Perhaps his defining characteristic, though, was a virulent anti-Catholicism which, growing out of circumstances in his diocese, informed his theology as well as his politics. When the Jacobites threatened once more in 1745, he subscribed £200 towards local defences and delivered a sermon against 'Popish idolatry' in his cathedral. After years of failing health, which denied him translation to the see of Bath and Wells, he died on 21 February 1752; he was survived by his second wife. Peploe was buried in Chester Cathedral on 28 February.   STEPHEN W. BASKERVILLE

Sources P. G. Green, 'Samuel Peploe and the ideology of anti-Catholicism among the Anglican clergy in early Hanoverian England', *Transactions of the Historic Society of Lancashire and Cheshire*, 145 (1995), 75–94 • P. G. Green, 'Charity, morality, and social control: clerical attitudes in the diocese of Chester, 1715–1795', *Transactions of the Historic Society of Lancashire and Cheshire*, 141 (1991), 207–33 • S. W. Baskerville, 'The political behaviour of the Cheshire clergy, 1705–1752', *Northern History*, 23 (1987), 74–97 • C. M. Haydon, 'Samuel Peploe and Catholicism in Preston, 1714', *Recusant History*, 20 (1990–91), 76–80 • F. R. Raines, *The rectors of Manchester, and the wardens of the collegiate church of that town*, ed. [J. E. Bailey], 2 vols., Chetham Society, new ser., 5–6 (1885) • N. Sykes, *Edmund Gibson, bishop of London, 1669–1748: a study in politics & religion in the eighteenth century* (1926) • *N&Q*, 2nd ser., 1 (1856), 318–19 • Foster, *Alum. Oxon.* • IGI
Archives PRO, state papers domestic, SP 35 | Christ Church Oxf., Wake MSS, Arch W. Epist., 7–10
Likenesses H. Winstanley, oils, 1733, Bishop's House, Chester • J. Faber junior, mezzotint (after H. Winstanley, 1733), BM, NPG [*see illus.*]

Peploe, Samuel John (1871–1935). *See under* Scottish colourists (*act.* 1900–1935).

Pepper, John Henry (1821–1900), illusionist and educationist, was born at Great Queen Street, Westminster, on 17 June 1821, the son of Charles Bailey Pepper (*d.* 1854), a civil engineer. He was educated at Loughborough House, Brixton, and King's College School, in the Strand, London, and was then a pupil of the chemist John Thomas Cooper. In 1840 he was appointed assistant chemical lecturer at the Granger school of medicine. He married on 22 May 1845 Mary Ann Benwell; they had no children of their own but adopted a son.

In 1847 Pepper gave his first lecture at the Royal Polytechnic in Regent Street (founded in 1838), and in 1848 he was appointed analytical chemist and lecturer to that institution. Some four years later he became 'honorary' director of the polytechnic at a fixed salary, a post he held for twenty years. He lectured frequently at the polytechnic, and was invited to numerous schools, at which he delighted juvenile audiences by popular experiments, illusions, and magic-lantern displays. He also issued a series of unpretentious manuals of popular science, which had a wide circulation. Among the most popular was *The Boy's Playbook of Science* (1860), an extensively illustrated manual of experiments which could be carried out in the home to demonstrate the properties of matter. A revised edition appeared in 1912. On the title-pages of his books he described himself as fellow of the Chemical Society, and honorary associate of the Institution of Civil Engineers. His title of professor was conferred upon him 'by express minute of the Polytechnic board', and was not

therefore, he was careful to explain, that of a hairdresser or a dancing master (Pepper, 2).

Pepper ran educational classes in connection with the Department of Science and Art at South Kensington. These hardly covered the costs of his lease of the premises at the polytechnic, which was severely hit by declining attendances in the winter of 1862, following the success of the second Great Exhibition. His instincts as a showman succeeded in reviving the popularity of the institution and ensuring its future by means of presentations of an optical illusion, involving mirrors and a hidden stage, described by *The Times* as the most wonderful ever put before the public. In September 1858 Henry Dircks of Blackheath had communicated to the British Association the details of an apparatus for producing 'spectral optical illusions'. The idea was rejected by several entertainers, but Pepper recognized its potential and, after some not very important modifications in the machinery, exhibited the 'ghost' for the first time on 24 December 1862, in illustration of Dickens's *Haunted Man*. On 5 February 1863 the apparatus was patented in the joint names of Pepper and Dircks. The two men later fell out, Dircks complaining with some justification that his name as that of sole inventor was unduly obscured in the advertisements of the exhibition. Popularly known as 'Pepper's ghost', the illusion had an enormous vogue, was visited by the prince and princess of Wales (19 May 1863), commanded to Windsor, and transferred to the boards of many London theatres, to the Châtelet at Paris, to Wallack's Theatre, New York, and to the Crystal Palace.

In March 1872 Pepper temporarily transferred his exhibit to the Egyptian Hall, Piccadilly, but lost money on it. He travelled with his show in America and Canada during 1874–9, and took it to Australia in 1879–81. He settled in Brisbane as public analyst from 1881 to 1889, when he returned to England. He reintroduced his 'ghost' at the polytechnic, but the spectre failed to appeal to a sophisticated public, and its proprietor withdrew into private life. His first wife died in December 1889 and he married again. Later he entered the Church of Rome. The 'Professor' died at Ifield Villa, 55 Colworth Road, Leytonstone, Essex, on 25 March 1900, leaving a widow, Janet. He was buried in Norwood cemetery.

THOMAS SECCOMBE, *rev.* M. C. CURTHOYS

Sources *The Times* (30 March 1900) • *Daily Telegraph* (30 March 1900) • Boase, *Mod. Eng. biog.* • J. H. Pepper, *The true history of the ghost* (1890) • E. M. Wood, *A history of the polytechnic* (1965) • G. Speaight, 'Professor Pepper's ghost', *Theatre Notebook*, 43 (1989), 16–24 • Friends of West Norwood cemetery
Wealth at death £492 6s. 10d.: probate, 24 April 1900, CGPLA Eng. & Wales

Pepperrell, Sir William, first baronet (1696–1759), army officer and merchant, was born on 27 June 1696 at Kittery Point, Maine (then part of Massachusetts), the sixth of eight children of William Pepperell (1648–1734), merchant and shipowner, and his wife, Margery (1659–1741), daughter of John Bray. The son of a prosperous citizen

Sir William Pepperrell, first baronet (1696–1759), by John Smibert, 1746

who had emigrated from Devon or from Wales as a penniless fisherman, Pepperrell grew up in comfortable circumstances. He received some formal education from his father and private tutors, mostly in practical matters such as geography, surveying, and navigation. Taking a personal share in operating his father's store, he grew up affable, robust, and hardy. He was accustomed to Indian warfare, and was trained in the use of arms. He joined the Maine militia when he was sixteen and was a colonel by 1722. After becoming a partner in his father's business he rapidly improved it, building ships, trading in fish, and importing goods for sale in Boston. He and his father invested the profits from these ventures in real estate, and soon they were almost sole proprietors of the townships of Saco and Scarboro, with large properties in Portsmouth, Hampton, and elsewhere. Pepperrell was shortly one of the foremost men in the colony. On 21 February 1723 he married Mary Hirst (d. 1789), granddaughter of Samuel Sewall, chief justice of Massachusetts; they had four children, two of whom died in infancy.

In 1725 Pepperrell became a justice of the peace in York county. A year later he was elected to the Massachusetts general court and appointed commander of the Maine militia. He was elected to the Massachusetts council in 1727, and was thereafter annually re-elected until his death. He served for eighteen years as the council's president. Also in 1727 he attended his first Indian conference, afterwards becoming an expert in Indian affairs. He was appointed chief justice of the York county court of common pleas in 1730, and began studying law. When his father died in 1734 he inherited the bulk of the estate, thus becoming even richer and more powerful. Pepperrell underwent a religious conversion in 1734, was baptized, and subsequently evinced great and sincere piety. In 1744 his son Andrew joined him in business after graduation from Harvard College; Andrew died in 1751. Pepperrell's son-in-law, Nathaniel Sparhawk, who had married his daughter Elizabeth, also entered the business.

In 1745 Governor William Shirley of Massachusetts appointed Pepperrell to command an expedition against the French fortress of Louisbourg on Cape Breton Island. On 30 April Pepperrell landed an army of 4300 men near the fortress, and commenced a determined siege. He assaulted Louisbourg on 26 May, suffering huge casualties, and soon supplies ran short. His troops' morale flagged as half of them fell sick, but they were heartened in late May when the Americans captured a French frigate sent to resupply the fortress. On 16 June, one day before Pepperrell was to launch a second assault, the French garrison surrendered. Although he had not shown great martial skill, Pepperrell had held his forces together and retained the co-operation of the British fleet. For his services he was commissioned a colonel in the British army on 1 September 1745 and authorized to raise a regiment, which he did, the 51st regiment. Also, on 15 November 1746 he was created a baronet, the first such honour given a native-born American.

Pepperrell remained at Louisbourg until the spring of 1746, then returned home. In 1749, having retired from business, he visited London, where he was cordially received by George II and presented by the City with a service of plate. He helped negotiate a treaty with the Indians in 1753. On the renewal of war with France in 1755 he was commissioned a major-general and given command of the eastern frontier. He was acting governor of Massachusetts from March to August 1757. On 20 February 1759 he was promoted lieutenant-general, another first for an American-born Englishman. He died at his home at Kittery Point on 16 July 1759 after a 'lingering illness' (Fairchild, 195), leaving his vast estate to his grandson William Sparhawk, who took the surname Pepperrell.

PAUL DAVID NELSON

Sources *Collections of the Massachusetts Historical Society*, 6th ser., 10 (1899) [*The Pepperrell papers*] · 'The journal of Sir William Pepperrell kept during the expedition against Louisbourg, 24 March–22 August 1745', *Proceedings of the American Antiquarian Society*, new ser., 20 (1909–10) · U. Parsons, *The life of Sir William Pepperrell* (1856) · B. Fairchild, *Messrs William Pepperrell: merchants at Piscataqua* (1954) · R. P. Dufour, 'Pepperrell, Sir William', *ANB* · C. E. Clark, *The eastern frontier: the settlement of northern New England, 1610–1763* (1970) · D. E. Leach, *Arms for empire: a military history of the British colonies in North America, 1607–1763* (1973) · J. Ferling, *Struggle for a continent: the wars of early America* (1993) · C. H. C. Howard, *The Pepperrells in America*

(1906) · W. R. Nester, *The great frontier war: Britain, France, and the imperial struggle for North America, 1607–1755* (2000) · GEC, *Baronetage*, 5.93–4

Archives American Antiquarian Society, Worcester, Massachusetts, journal · Boston PL, MSS · Maine Historical Society, Portland, papers · Mass. Hist. Soc., papers · New England Historical and Genealogical Society, Boston, papers | Boston PL, Chamberlain papers

Likenesses J. Smibert, oils, 1746, Essex Institute, Salem, Massachusetts [*see illus.*]

Wealth at death left huge estate: will, 1759, Fairchild, *Messrs William Pepperrell*, 195–6, 199

Peppiatt, Sir Leslie Ernest (1891–1968), lawyer, was born on 7 November 1891 at West Hackney, London, the eldest son of William Robert Peppiatt, a railway clerk, and his wife, Emily Elizabeth Giles. He was educated, along with his two brothers, at Bancroft's School, Woodford, Essex. Emily Peppiatt was ambitious for her sons, but her husband's early death left the family struggling financially and Peppiatt left school at sixteen and took employment in a solicitors' office. He was, however, able to secure articles and, on his admission to the profession in July 1913, joined the firm of Ince, Colt, Ince, and Roscoe. On the outbreak of the First World War, Peppiatt joined the 7th London regiment, serving with distinction until 1918; he reached the rank of major, was twice mentioned in dispatches, and was awarded the MC and bar. Of his two brothers, both on active service, Kenneth Oswald Peppiatt (1893–1983), who was awarded the MC and bar, rejoined the Bank of England, where he had been a junior clerk before the war, in 1918, but the younger brother, Will, was killed.

Peppiatt returned to Ince, Colt, Ince, and Roscoe and in 1921 joined the British American Tobacco Company (BAT) as a legal adviser. On 16 June 1927 he married Cicely Mallyn, daughter of George Edward Howse, a director of the travel firm Thomas Cook. The Peppiatts bought a small house in Beaconsfield, moving later to a larger one they had built also in Beaconsfield. There were two sons of the marriage, Hugh and Martin. Both were educated, like their cousins (Kenneth's sons), who were of a similar age, at Winchester College; Martin became a clergyman and Hugh, after Oxford, joined Freshfields and became a City lawyer.

Peppiatt's work for BAT involved a great deal of travel and lengthy periods away from home, and in 1935 he accepted an invitation to become a partner with a City firm of solicitors, Freshfields. No doubt his brother Kenneth, who had risen rapidly in the Bank of England hierarchy, becoming in 1934 chief cashier, (and being knighted in 1941), effected the introduction.

Since early in the eighteenth century the firm, known in 1935 as Freshfields, Leese, and Munns—it became Freshfields in 1945—had held the appointment as solicitors to the Bank of England; it had other distinguished corporate clients as well as a large private client practice. Two years after Peppiatt joined Freshfields, the firm's senior partner, Sir William Leese, died suddenly. Peppiatt took over his role in managing the Bank of England's work, and although he did not become senior partner until 1953, he

was increasingly in control of the firm during the war and immediately afterwards. These were difficult times, particularly when the firm's offices in Old Jewry were completely destroyed by bombing in 1944. In the immediate post-war years the firm was smaller than its competitors such as Slaughter and May and Linklaters and Paines, while its image as solicitors to the establishment could sometimes discourage new clients as much as attract them.

As senior partner of Freshfields from 1953 to 1962, Peppiatt inaugurated a period of growth in the firm, necessary if it was to keep pace with the competition from other leading City law firms. The firm's connection with the Bank of England had always brought it other clients but had also led the firm sometimes to decline what it saw as unsuitable business. Peppiatt sought to redefine what might be seen as unsuitable in changing times as well as to extend the firm's financial and commercial practice at a time when the City's international financial business was expanding rapidly. A shrewd solicitor, he noted the growing importance of American investment in the sterling area and developed useful connections for the firm in the USA. At the same time he zealously protected the firm's connection with the bank and its reputation in the City. He represented the Bank's interests in the *cause célèbre* of the 1950s, the bank rate tribunal chaired by Sir Hubert Parker, charged with investigating whether information about a coming change in bank rate had been leaked.

Senior partners of City law firms were traditionally autocrats, but not all were, as Peppiatt was, also benevolent and charming. The strict formality within the office began to be relaxed in his time. Peppiatt's interest in people, combined with his personal belief that solicitors ought to play a part in public life, were both evidenced in his activities outside the firm. He served on a number of committees, including the Spens committee on the remuneration of medical specialists and dental practitioners in 1947 and the disciplinary committee of the Architects' Registration Council from 1949 to 1955. He chaired the departmental committee on betting on horse-racing in 1960. He helped to manage several charities, including the George VI Memorial Fund, the 1930 Fund for the Benefit of Trained District Nurses, the Solicitors' Benevolent Fund, and the Lord Mayor of London's Appeal Fund.

With his busy practice and public life Peppiatt had little time for his favourite leisure pursuit of fishing. Moreover he was from 1940 a member of the council of the Law Society, and president of the society in 1958–9. He was awarded the then customary knighthood in 1959. Peppiatt retired in 1962 and died on 15 November 1968 at his home, Cleve Cottage, Wisborough Green, Sussex, survived by his wife. Building on the post-war foundations he had laid, Freshfields continued to grow, not least when his son Hugh was senior partner (1982–90), becoming one of London's leading international law firms. JUDY SLINN

Sources J. Slinn, 'Peppiatt, Leslie Ernest', *DBB* · J. Slinn, *A history of Freshfields* (privately printed, 1984) · DNB · WWW · Burke, *Peerage* (1967)

Archives SOUND BL NSA, National Life Story Collection, interview with Hugh Peppiatt, 1992
Likenesses photograph, priv. coll.
Wealth at death £146,545: probate, 15 Jan 1969, *CGPLA Eng. & Wales*

Pepusch, John Christopher (1666/7–1752), composer and teacher of music, the son of a German protestant clergyman, was born at Berlin and baptized Johann Christoph Pepusch. Nothing more is known of his parents, nor is his date of birth certain, but according to the memorial tablet erected at the Charterhouse by his colleagues and pupils in 1767, he was eighty-five when he died. He studied theory under Martin Klingenberg, cantor of the Marienkirche in Berlin, and organ under Grosse, a Saxon otherwise unknown. At the age of fourteen Pepusch played the harpsichord at court and was soon afterwards appointed by Electress Sophie Charlotte of Brandenburg to be the teacher of the electoral prince (later Frederick William I of Prussia). He moved to London by way of Holland, supposedly after witnessing 'a terrible act of despotism' (Burney, 2.985) by the elector, arriving shortly after the treaty of Ryswick in September 1697.

Pepusch's first documented appearance in England was in April 1704, when he provided compositions for an ensemble of visiting musicians headed by his brother Heinrich Gottfried Pepusch (d. 1750), an oboist employed by the Prussian court from 1692 to about 1736. He may already have been a member of the band at the Drury Lane Theatre and he certainly moved from there in early 1708 to join the opera company operating from the new Queen's Theatre in the Haymarket. At the same time he took up residence in Hooker's (later Boswell) Court. For the next seven years he served the opera as violinist and harpsichordist, and prepared the pasticcio *Thomyris, Queen of Scythia* in April 1707, for which he composed the recitatives and added some additional songs.

Pepusch also served as the agent and accompanist for the soprano (Francesca) Margherita (also Marguerite or Margaretta) de *L'Epine (d. 1746) from about 1705, and as the organizer of public concerts at which many of his own works were performed. He was apparently already well known as a composer of instrumental works when he arrived in London, and he published a series of eight volumes in Amsterdam between 1705 and 1718, including five sets of violin sonatas, two of trio sonatas, and one each of recorder sonatas and concertos. A number of these works were also published in London, apparently without his permission. A number of concertos, solo and trio sonatas, and miscellaneous keyboard works remain in manuscript. The most interesting of these are seven sets of sonatas composed for various English violinists, each containing sixteen works in as many keys.

Pepusch was also active as a composer of vocal music. In 1710 he published *Six English Cantatas* to a set of texts by John Hughes. These, according to the poet, were written to demonstrate the desirability of setting English words to the newly imported Italian style of music. The most famous, *Alexis*, was sung well into the nineteenth century in a slightly adapted form with cello obbligato.

John Christopher Pepusch (1666/7–1752), by Thomas Hudson, *c.*1735

On 9 July 1713 Pepusch took his DMus degree from Oxford, matriculating from Magdalen College. The music to his academic ode in honour of Queen Anne, *Hail, Queen of Islands! Hail, Illustrious Fair*, does not survive, nor does that to his ode on the coronation of George I the following year.

In 1714 Pepusch transferred his allegiance to the Theatre Royal in Drury Lane, bringing with him singers and instrumentalists from the opera company at the Queen's Theatre. For this company he composed four masques with music in an Italianate style: *Venus and Adonis* (1715), *Myrtillo and Laura* (1715), *Apollo and Daphne* (1716), and *The Death of Dido* (1716). These works were generally well received and seem to have influenced Handel in his composition of *Acis and Galatea*.

For the 1716–17 season Pepusch joined John Rich's company at the theatre in Lincoln's Inn Fields, again bringing with him other performers. He remained until 1732 as director of the orchestra, while ceding most of the composing duties to John Ernest Galliard. Pepusch did continue to write cantatas, many of which were performed at public concerts or between the acts of plays. Some of these are included in his second book of *Six English Cantatas* published in 1720, and in other anthologies; perhaps a dozen more survive in manuscript or are lost. He also provided additional songs for a 1719 revival of *Thomyris, Queen of Scythia*.

Pepusch disappears from the London newspapers for the 1717–18 season, presumably because of his involvement with the musical establishment of James Brydges, second earl of Carnarvon and later first duke of Chandos.

He is recorded at Cannons, Chandos's estate near Edgware in Middlesex, as early as December 1717. He was again active at Lincoln's Inn Fields Theatre during the 1718–19 season, but seems to have been appointed musical director at Cannons in early 1719 with a salary of £25 per quarter. He held this position until mid-1723, after which he supplied musicians from London on an occasional basis.

At Cannons, Pepusch composed both sacred and secular music, in the earliest years as a colleague of Nicola Francesco Haym and George Frideric Handel, and was eventually responsible for an ensemble of some twenty-five singers and instrumentalists. The vast majority of Pepusch's fifteen known anthems, most for solo voices, chorus, and instruments, were written for services held in the parish church of St Lawrence, Little Stanmore, located adjacent to the estate. Pepusch also seems to have begun his career as a teacher of music about this time, and several of his students from Cannons, including Thomas Salway and Thomas Rawlings, became successful performers.

Some time during this period Pepusch married L'Epine, but the exact date has never been established. It may have been as early as 1718, when she first tentatively retired from the London stage, but it seems likely that Pepusch's appointment at Cannons in 1719 provided the financial security that permitted both their marriage and her official retirement from the stage after 28 May 1719. Their only child, a son, John, who died on 11 July 1739 after reputedly showing signs of considerable musical talent, was baptized at St Clement Danes on 9 January 1724. L'Epine remained active as a singing teacher, and Pepusch wrote cantatas during the 1720s for a number of her students.

Pepusch returned to Lincoln's Inn Fields Theatre for the 1723–4 season and provided a 'musical entertainment' for St Cecilia's day 1723 entitled *The Union of the Three Sister Arts*, the songs from which were published. He also provided new music (now lost) for a revival of Thomas Betterton's and John Dryden's *The Prophetess, or, The History of Dioclesian* the following year but composed relatively little after this date.

Pepusch was almost certainly in charge of the music for John Gay's *The Beggar's Opera*, which opened on 29 January 1728. He composed the overture and may have had a hand in arranging the airs; that the musically inept basses in the printed edition are a reflection of his work seems unlikely. Gay's sequel, *Polly*, was published in 1729 but not performed on stage until 1777; again the extent of Pepusch's involvement is unknown. Both Burney and Hawkins say that at about this time Pepusch set out for North America in support of Bishop George Berkeley's project for a college there, but was shipwrecked. However, Berkeley sailed (to Rhode Island) without misadventure and Pepusch is not mentioned among his travelling companions. He seems to have retired after the 1732–3 season when Rich decided to move the entire company to his Covent Garden Theatre, which was further away from Hooker's Court.

In 1726 Pepusch had been one of the founders of the Academy of Ancient Music, remaining its director until 1751, and from the 1730s it increasingly became a central focus of his activities. The singers were initially drawn from the choirs of St Paul's Cathedral and the Chapel Royal. In the early 1730s Maurice Greene left to establish a rival academy at the Apollo tavern, taking the St Paul's boys with him, and Bernard Gates also withdrew the Chapel Royal boys. After a year's struggle without trebles, it was arranged that Pepusch and at least one assistant would instruct boys in singing, accompanying on the harpsichord, and composition, as well as English grammar, writing, and arithmetic for a nominal fee. This may have been made easier by his move to a larger house in Fetter Lane in late 1734.

Pepusch also continued to teach privately, and his reputation grew. He was convinced of the perfection of Corelli's compositions, and published corrected and revised editions of the Italian composer's sonatas and concertos in score in 1732. According to Hawkins, Pepusch developed a 'musical code, consisting of rules extracted from the Works of his favourite Author, and the exercises which he enjoined his disciples were divisions on, and harmonies adapted to, basses selected from his works' (Hawkins, 'Life of Dr. Pepusch', 301). Among his pupils were William Boyce, James Nares, Samuel Howard, Benjamin Cooke, John Travers, William Babell, George Berg, William Savage, and John Christopher Smith jun.

In 1730 *A Treatise on Harmony: Containing the Chief Rules for Composing in Two, Three and Four Parts* was published anonymously. According to Hawkins, it was the work of Pepusch's student James Hamilton, Viscount Paisley and later seventh earl of Abercorn, and published without his permission. It probably illustrates elements of Pepusch's teaching, and the revised version which appeared the following year may have been done with Pepusch's assistance. Other reflections of Pepusch's teaching may be seen in the various 'Notes on harmony' compiled by Benjamin Cooke between 1745 and 1751 (manuscripts in the British Library and the Royal College of Music), but *A Short Account of the Twelve Modes of Compositions and their Progressions in every Octave* in a manuscript of 1751 mentioned by W. H. Husk in the first edition of *Grove's Dictionary of Music* cannot be traced.

In December 1737 Pepusch was appointed organist of the Charterhouse and moved to an apartment on the grounds. In the same year he offered William Oldys assistance in the preparation of a history of the art of music and its professors in England (Oldys, 15). His increasing interest in the music of the ancients led to his election as a fellow of the Royal Society in 1745 and the publication of his paper 'Of the various genera and species of music among the ancients' in the *Philosophical Transactions of the Royal Society* the following year.

His wife died on 8 August 1746 after which Pepusch increasingly retired from public life. He himself died in his rooms at the Charterhouse on 20 July 1752 and was buried three days later in the chapel there. According to his will, dated 9 July 1752 and proved in the prerogative court of Canterbury on 21 May 1753, his extensive library was to be divided between the Academy of Ancient Music, his colleague in the theatre Ephraim Kellner, and his student John Travers. Through a series of unfortunate circumstances it was scattered by the end of the eighteenth century and only a few pieces can now be identified. Pepusch's own compositions show great technical skill but little musical originality; they are well crafted but dull. His true legacy is to be found in the work of his students, both as composers and practical musicians and as collectors of the 'antient' music he so loved.

Graydon Beeks

Sources D. F. Cook, 'The life and works of Johann Christoph Pepusch, 1667–1752', PhD diss., U. Lond., 1982 · D. F. Cook, 'Venus and Adonis: an English masque "after the Italian manner"', MT, 121 (1980), 553–7 · G. Beeks, '"A club of composers": Handel, Pepusch and Arbuthnot at Cannons', Handel tercentenary collection, ed. A. Hicks and S. Sadie (1987), 209–21 · G. Beeks, 'The Chandos anthems of Haym, Handel and Pepusch', Göttinger Händel-Beiträge, 5 (1993), 161–93 · M. Boyd and G. Beeks, 'Pepusch, Johann Christoph', New Grove, 2nd edn [with D. F. Cook] · J. Hawkins, 'Life of Dr. Pepusch, the famous musical composer; with his portrait elegantly engraved', Universal Magazine of Knowledge and Pleasure, 63 (1778), 300–06 · R. Rawlinson, biographical notes on Oxford writers, c.1740–1755, Bodl. Oxf., MS Rawl. J 4⁰.6, fols. 319–20 · R. Rawlinson, continuation of Wood's Athenae Oxoniensis, c.1740–1755, Bodl. Oxf., MS Rawl. J., fols. 4, 202 · J. Hawkins, A general history of the science and practice of music, 5 vols. (1776) · Burney, Hist. mus. · Highfill, Burnim & Langhans, BDA · R. Fiske, English theatre music in the eighteenth century (1973) [rev. 1986] · J. G. Williams, 'The life, work and influence of J. C. Pepusch', PhD diss., University of York, 1976 · H. W. Fred, 'The instrumental music of Johann Christoph Pepusch', PhD diss., University of North Carolina, 1961 · C. W. Hughes, 'Johann Christopher Pepusch', Musical Quarterly, 31 (1945), 54–70 · G. Thewlis, 'Coronation of George I: a Bodleian song', MT, 78 (1937), 310–11 · B. Cooke, '[Notes on harmony]', 1745–51, BL, Add. MS 29429 · B. Cooke, '[Notes on harmony]', 1745–51, Royal College of Music, MS 806 · DNB · memorial, London, Charterhouse · poor rate books, Sherehone ward, Westminster Public Library, London · Charterhouse assembly orders, 1737, 373 · land tax assessment, parish of St Andrew, Holborn, ward of Faringdon Without, GL, MS 11316/10 · GM, 1st ser., 22 (1752) · W. Oldys, Memoir of William Oldys, ed. J. Yeowell (1862)
Likenesses M. Ricci, group portrait, oils, c.1708 (A rehearsal at the opera, three known versions), priv. colls.; repro. in Theatre Notebook, 14 (1959–60), pl. 1, 2, 3 · B. Arlaud, miniature, c.1710, Royal Collection · oils, c.1710, U. Oxf., faculty of music; repro. in Highfill, Burnim & Langhans, BDA · T. Hudson, oils, c.1735, NPG [see illus.] · portrait, Royal College of Music, London
Wealth at death see will, PRO, PROB 11/802, sig. 149; Highfill, Burnim & Langhans, BDA; Cook, 'Life and works'

Pepwell [Pepwall], **Henry** (d. 1539/40), printer, was born in Birmingham. His father was probably the John Pepwell of Birmingham who was sued by a mercer in 1520 for a debt on a bond signed in St Sepulchre's parish, London (PRO, CP 40/1029, rot. 323v). From 1518 his business was located at the sign of the Trinity in Paul's Cross Churchyard, London, formerly the house of the stationer Henry Jacobi, whose materials had passed to Pepwell. Jacobi's device, with the surname cut out, first appears on Pepwell's 1519 edition of Stanbridge's Accidence. Pepwell also employed

an assistant, Roger Shedmore. Pepwell was warden of the Company of Stationers in 1525–6.

Sixteen books survive that were printed by or for Pepwell between 1518 and 1539. Two are vernacular works of fiction: William Neville's Castell of Pleasure, with additions by Robert Copland, and the Boke of the Cyte of Ladyes, Brian Anslay's translation of the work by Christine de Pisan. There is a verse preface by the printer in the latter, describing the patronage of the third earl of Kent, Richard Grey. Pepwell was involved with printing of early English humanist texts, issuing a number of grammar books, including some by John Colet and William Lily for use at St Paul's School in London, and work by Erasmus. The remainder of the books that carry his imprint are legal or religious; they include an edition of Richard of St Victor with extracts from the writings of the English mystic Margery Kempe. Pepwell probably also printed indulgences and images of pity (see STC, 1475–1640, 14077c.11c).

In 1526 Pepwell was among those present when the bishop of London issued his second set of injunctions to the booksellers (Reed, 173–5). In 1531 he commissioned an edition of Eckius's Adversus Lutheranos from the Antwerp printer Michael Hillenius; John Bale states that Pepwell was employed by John Stokesley, bishop of London, to do so. In a letter of August 1533 from Stephen Vaughan to Thomas Cromwell about the recusant cardinal William Peto, Pepwell is identified for questioning about the business of Thomas Dockwray, a fellow stationer who was in Antwerp on behalf of Stokesley. In May 1538 Pepwell was one of six Londoners who each raised 500 marks bail for Stokesley following his arrest by Cromwell for the execution of a papal bull. In 1536 he was one of the syndicate of publishers involved with John Wayland in publishing Hilsey's primer.

Pepwell is often named in documents relating to the community of stationers at Paul's Cross in his parish of St Faith's. His business was valued at £40 for the 1523–4 lay subsidy for that parish, and he and Dockwray were appointed petty collectors of the king's subsidy in St Faith's in 1536. In 1538 he travelled to St Albans to accompany the monastery printer (probably John Herford) back to London, where the latter was questioned by the stationers William Bonham and Henry Tab on Cromwell's behalf. In September 1539 he was in arrears for his Paul's Cross property; the same document names Tab, Dockwray, Bonham, John Reynes, Thomas Petit, and Polydore Vergil as neighbours. Pepwell had been bequeathed £4 of books by Wynkyn de Worde in 1534 and he and Bonham are named in a fragment of a 1537 or 1539 account book from de Worde's shop, where Pepwell is charged for copies of a (probably 1536) edition of Adam Bell, Stanbridge's Accidence, and a Latin primer.

Pepwell died between 11 September 1539, when he made his will, and 8 February 1540, when it was proved by his widow, Ursula, his sole executor. This may or may not be the daughter of Paul Alexander mentioned as Pepwell's wife in a complaint to chancery of 1531/2 (PRO, C 1/608/29, C 1/609/39). He left instructions to be buried in the Pardon churchyard near St Paul's, and bequeathed a mass book and 5s. to his old parish church in Birmingham for prayers for his soul; Bonham is named as a supervisor. He divided his property among his widow and his children, none of whom is named in the will. Arthur Pepwell, who is mentioned in the Stationers' Company register after 1554, is probably a descendant. ALEXANDRA GILLESPIE

Sources STC, 1475–1640 · LP Henry VIII, 6.934; 13/1.1095; 14/2.241, 315 · DNB · E. G. Duff, A century of the English book trade (1905) · H. S. Bennett, English books and readers, 1475–1557 (1969), 34 n.3, 41, 61 · will, PRO, PROB 11/28, sig. 22 · common pleas suit, 1520, PRO, CP 40/1029, rot. 323v · chancery suit, 1531/2, PRO, C1/608/29, C1/609/39 · P. W. M. Blayney, The bookshops in Paul's Cross churchyard (1990) · E. G. Duff, 'Notes on stationers from the lay subsidy rolls of 1523–4', The Library, new ser., 9 (1908), 257–66 · G. Pollard and A. Ehrman, The distribution of books by catalogue from the invention of printing to AD 1800 (1965), 142–5 · R. B. McKerrow, Printers' and publishers' devices, 1485–1640 (1913) · Arber, Regs. Stationers, vol. 1 · M. C. Erler, 'Wynkyn de Worde's will: legatees and bequests', The Library, 6th ser., 10 (1988), 107–21 · A. W. Reed, Early Tudor drama (1926)
Wealth at death will, PRO, PROB 11/28, sig. 22 · valued £40 mid-career (1523–1524): Duff, 'Lay subsidy rolls'; Duff, English book trade

Pepys, Charles Christopher, first earl of Cottenham

(1781–1851), lord chancellor, was born on 29 April 1781 in Wimpole Street, Cavendish Square, London, the second of three sons (another was Henry *Pepys) of Sir William Weller Pepys, first baronet (1740–1825), a master in chancery (who was descended from John Pepys, great-grandfather of Samuel), and his wife, Elizabeth (d. 1830), eldest daughter of the Rt Hon. William Dowdeswell.

Early life and education Pepys was educated at Harrow School and at Trinity College, Cambridge, where he did not sit for the tripos but was content to graduate LLB in 1803. Contemporaries remembered him as a short,

> stout, sturdy, thickset boy, of blunt speech and cold disposition, aiming at no distinction, making few friends … None could say that he was clever; some of his schoolfellows pronounced him dull. His dark, searching eyes, massive forehead and expressive lips, refuted the charge.

He never lost his 'air of independence and determination which indicated an inward consciousness of superiority' (Le Marchant, 59–60).

Success at the bar and marriage Pepys was admitted a student of Lincoln's Inn on 26 January 1801 and was called to the bar on 23 November 1804, the same day as the future Viscount Melbourne. In 1837 he became treasurer of his inn. Like many of his distinguished contemporaries, he was a pupil of the famous special pleader, William Tidd. His fellow pupil, John Campbell, later Lord Campbell, described him as 'the greatest ornament of our [Tidd's] Bar' (Life of John, Lord Campbell, 1.138). He decided to practise at the emerging chancery bar (he was among the first generation of chancery lawyers who did not go circuit), so, having taken chambers in 16 Old Square, Lincoln's Inn, he began his study of equity with Sir Samuel Romilly. The fact that his father was a master in chancery must have helped his practice. Within five years of his call, his father wrote to Hannah More: 'The success of my second son at

Charles Christopher Pepys, first earl of Cottenham (1781–1851), by Charles Robert Leslie, exh. RA 1840

the Chancery Bar has been most rapid, and highly gratifying to me' (Gaussen, 2.295). His professional success came from his total dedication to his equity practice and his disdain for society; in later life his only recreation was foreign travel. A chancery advocate did not have to be an Erskine or a Scarlett. Pepys had a clear mind, reasoned cogently, was rarely repetitious, and 'never forgot that he was addressing a single judge and that judge a professional man' (Law Review, 14, 1853, 354).

Pepys's practice at the bar prospered, enabling him on 30 June 1821 to marry Caroline Elizabeth (1802–1868), the second daughter of William Wingfield KC, then chief justice of the Brecon circuit, and to become another master in chancery. On 24 August 1826 he received his silk gown from Lord Lyndhurst and became a bencher of his inn in November that year. Four years later he was appointed solicitor-general to Queen Adelaide, retaining that post until May 1832.

The unobtrusive politician Whiggism was in Pepys's blood; his maternal grandfather had been the chancellor of the exchequer in the Rockingham administration in 1765. Though he had shown little political ambition, in July 1831 he entered the House of Commons as the member for Higham Ferrers, a seat which he exchanged the following September for Lord Fitzwilliam's borough of Malton. In the house he rarely spoke, and then on purely legal questions; his first speech, on 31 October 1831, was on the Bankruptcy Bill. The whigs had a paucity of lawyers in the house, and their predicament became acute when Sir William Horne, who had become attorney-general on Sir

Thomas Denman's appointment as lord chief justice in November 1832, proved to be a disastrous choice. In 1834 he was pushed out of office. Campbell succeeded him and, to the surprise of the profession, Pepys became solicitor-general on 22 February 1834, receiving the customary knighthood. As solicitor-general Pepys was not active in the house. He piloted the bill to establish the central criminal court and spoke in favour of the new Poor Law Bill. But he had no taste for debate and his most successful intervention was his speech moving the appointment of a select committee to inquire into the law of libel.

In September 1834 the master of the rolls, Sir John Leach, suddenly died. Campbell, to his mortification, was passed over in favour of Pepys who, at the instigation of Brougham (whom Pepys had impressed), became master of the rolls on 29 September and a privy councillor a few days later. Brougham wrote that Pepys's elevation 'was his own best title to the gratitude of the profession' (Brougham, 3.430).

Lord chancellor The whigs returned to office in April 1835. The prime minister, Melbourne, resolved that Brougham should never again be his lord chancellor. The great seal was put into commission while the cabinet wrangled over an alternative to Brougham. The contest was between Henry Bickersteth and Pepys. On 17 January 1836 Pepys became lord chancellor of England, taking the title Baron Cottenham of Cottenham in the county of Cambridge. Greville described the promotion of this 'plain undistinguished man' as 'one of the most curious instances of elevation that ever occurred' (*Greville Memoirs*, 3.328). Pemberton Leigh, later Lord Kingsdown, recorded the comment that: 'Melbourne must have felt very much like a man who had parted with a brilliant capricious mistress and married his housekeeper' (Leigh, *Recollections*, 112; *Edinburgh Review*, 60). In 1841 the whigs were turned out of office. On their return in 1846 Cottenham became lord chancellor for the second time, again succeeding Lyndhurst.

Cottenham was unashamedly a party man, whose preference for whigs in his patronage appointments to the commissions of the peace and to the trusteeships of municipal charities infuriated the tories. But he failed his party in the Lords, as he had done in the Commons. A feeble debater, he was no match for Lyndhurst or Brougham. But Atlay thought that he 'was a much more useful member of the Cabinet than was generally suspected' (Atlay, 1.404), a judgement which Lord John Russell appeared to endorse, describing him as 'a direct man and a straightforward statesman' (Russell, 276).

A muted law reformer On 28 April 1836 Cottenham introduced a bill for dividing and distributing the duties performed by the lord chancellor. The bill left the jurisdiction and procedure of the court of chancery untouched, although the equity business of the court of exchequer was transferred to it. Its head was to be a permanent judge, the lord chief justice of the court of chancery, who was to devote himself solely to judicial business. The office of lord chancellor was to remain. Its holder would

keep the great seal and its traditional patronage, and preside over the House of Lords and the hearing of appeals to the House of Lords and the privy council.

It was predictable that the bill would be opposed by Lyndhurst, who depicted Cottenham's chancellor as a lawyer without a court. More disconcerting was the opposition of Bickersteth, now Lord Langdale and Cottenham's successor as master of the rolls, who strongly disapproved of its main provisions. Cottenham's defence of the bill was, in Campbell's words, 'tame, confused, and dissuasive' (*Life of John, Lord Campbell*, 2.82). The bill was handsomely defeated and with its defeat died any further attempt by Cottenham radically to reform the court of chancery.

The fifty-one new orders in chancery in 1841, although making detailed reforms, were quite inadequate attempts to remedy the defects of equity procedure. Equally unsuccessful was Cottenham's attempt to implement the recommendations of the commission of inquiry into the bankruptcy and insolvency laws. But he did have some minor successes. For example, in 1838 he secured the enactment of a statute abolishing imprisonment for debt on mesne process; thereafter a person could not be arrested on the mere affidavit of another that he was owed £20. In 1841 the statute which had prohibited the clergy from all dealings in trade was repealed; the earlier statute had been interpreted to mean that if a clergyman was a shareholder in a joint-stock company, the company was an illegal association and could not recover moneys due to it. And an act of 1847 enabled trustees who wished to be relieved of the responsibility of administering the trust to pay trust money into court.

Cottenham as judge Cottenham will not be remembered as a politician or as a law reformer. But as a judge he earned the praise, though not the love, of his contemporaries. Kingsdown said that he was 'one of the best judges I ever saw on the Bench' (Atlay, 1.402). Cottenham did not have Lyndhurst's brilliance of mind but his knowledge of equity was more profound. Among his decisions are *Tulk v. Moxhay* (1848), the corner-stone of the law of restrictive covenants, and *Saunders v. Vautier* (1841), which holds that all the beneficiaries of a trust, if of full age, may, if they so decide, determine the trust. The growth of the joint-stock company led to much litigation. Cottenham's decisions laid the foundations of modern company law. Prominent among them is *Foss v. Harbottle* (1843), which established that only the company, and not individual shareholders, can seek redress for the illegal acts of its directors.

Cottenham's judgments, which were meticulously prepared, are a model of what judgments should be. According to Le Marchant:

> The style of them, like the character of the man, was perfectly free from all affectation and display; whether written or spoken, they were always simple, terse and perspicuous; clear and condensed in their summary of the facts, and in their exposition of law, comprehensive and vigorous, but at the same time, cautious and precise. (Le Marchant, 64)

Cottenham, unlike Eldon, made up his mind quickly and

once made it was a Herculean task to persuade him to change it. 'His demeanour in Court was not without a certain dignity, but its prominent feature was an austerity, amounting sometimes to harshness, which maintained his authority rather than conciliated esteem' (ibid., 64). Impatient of empty and repetitious rhetoric, he listened patiently to cogent argument, rarely interrupting 'except for the purpose of bringing it to an issue, by showing that he had detected its weak point' (ibid., 65). However, during his second chancellorship he became increasingly inaudible, irritable, and intolerant.

Cottenham's relationship with his judicial colleagues was an uneasy one. Langdale's attack on his attempt to reform the court of chancery made a cool relationship even cooler. His dislike of the vice-chancellor, Sir James Knight Bruce, was long-standing. According to Lord Selborne, its source was their rivalry in Vice-Chancellor Shadwell's court, 'when that great lawyer, plain and dull of speech, had to endure what he regarded as daily affronts from his eloquent competitor' (Palmer, 1.375). Cottenham would not permit any deviation from the traditional practice of the court, even upholding one of the greater abuses of the master's office, 'hourly warrants', by which a fresh fee was payable every hour. In contrast, Knight Bruce was of a very different temper and had been allowed by an indulgent Lyndhurst to take procedural short cuts, freely granting amendments at the hearing of a cause. This practice infuriated Cottenham, who considered 'the system which he [had] to administer as the perfection of human wisdom' (Life of John, Lord Campbell, 2.207), and led to many bitter exchanges at the expense of hapless litigants. Knight Bruce was convinced that Cottenham approached his judgments with 'a disposition to reverse them' (Palmer, 1.375). Cottenham was on no better terms with the other vice-chancellor, Sir James Wigram.

To his contemporaries Cottenham was a man conscious of his dignity, touchy, aloof, self-centred. But he was a loving husband and devoted to his fifteen children, twelve of whom survived him. Unlike his father he had no interest in literature. His conversation with his few intimates, 'often enlivened by a vein of dry humour', was 'on the topics of the day' (Le Marchant, 67). Cottenham cared little for society. He was a private man.

Final years During his second chancellorship, which began in 1846 and lasted almost four years, Cottenham's powers deteriorated. The burdens of office, combined with his conscientious devotion to his judicial duties, led to longer and longer delays in giving judgments, standing important cases over to the long vacation, and issuing 'directions for enquiries' to the masters for further investigation of the facts. The arrears of the court built up. In November 1847 Cottenham broke a blood-vessel in his throat, and was thought to be dying. But in the new year he was back in the house and in court, though seldom appearing in the cabinet. A personal attack by a disgruntled attorney, William Dimes, clouded his last years. Dimes had unsuccessfully brought suit against the Grand

Junction Canal and had been committed by Cottenham for contempt for breach of an injunction. Dimes was a determined man and in 1849 brought an action to set aside Cottenham's judgment on the ground that Cottenham, a shareholder in the company, had an interest in the outcome of the proceedings. In June 1852 the House of Lords upheld that claim.

In the year following Dimes's action Cottenham was absent from court more frequently. On 27 May 1850 he abruptly resigned, to be granted in the following month the titles of Viscount Crowhurst and earl of Cottenham; in 1845 and 1849 he had succeeded to the baronetcies held by his older brother and uncle. He was advised to winter abroad and, in the spring of 1851, felt well enough to return home from Malta. But in Pietra Santa, near Lucca, in Italy, he was taken ill; he died on his seventieth birthday, 29 April 1851, and was buried in Totteridge in Hertfordshire. GARETH H. JONES

Sources J. B. Atlay, The Victorian chancellors, 1 (1906) · Holdsworth, Eng. law, vol. 16 · D. Le Marchant, Memoir of John Charles, Viscount Althorp, third Earl Spencer, ed. H. D. Le Marchant (1876) · The Times (3 Sept 1841) · The Times (8 May 1851) · W. M. Torrens, Memoirs of the Right Honourable William, second Viscount Melbourne, 2 vols. (1878) · R. Palmer, first earl of Selborne, Memorials. Part I: family and personal, 1766–1865, ed. S. M. Palmer, 2 vols. (1896) · EdinR, 129 (1869), 60 · Foss, Judges · J. Campbell, Lives of the lord chancellors, 8 vols. (1845–69) · Life of John, Lord Campbell, lord high chancellor of Great Britain, ed. Mrs Hardcastle, 2 vols. (1881) · The Greville memoirs, ed. H. Reeve, pt 1 in 3 vols. (1874) · A. C. C. Gaussen, A later Pepys: the correspondence of Sir William Weller Pepys ... master in chancery, 1758–1825, 2 vols. (1904) · [J. Russell], Recollections and suggestions, 1813–1873 (1875) · H. P. Brougham, The life and times of Henry, Lord Brougham, ed. W. Brougham, 3 vols. (1871)
Archives Lincoln's Inn, legal papers | PRO, corresp. with Lord Russell, PRO 30/22 · Sheff. Arch., corresp. with Earl Fitzwilliam · W. Sussex RO, letters to duke of Richmond
Likenesses C. R. Leslie, oils, exh. RA 1840, NPG [see illus.] · C. Marochetti, bust, 1852, Palace of Westminster, London · H. R. Briggs, oils, exh. South Kensington 1868 · S. F. Diez, drawing, Staatliche Kupferstichkabinett, Berlin, Germany · J. Doyle, caricature, pencil and pen drawing, BM · G. Hayter, group portrait, oils (The House of Commons, 1833), NPG · T. Lufton, engraving (after H. R. Briggs), repro. in Gaussen, ed., A later Pepys · Maclure, Macdonald & Macgregor, print, NPG · R. Stothard, lithograph, BM

Pepys [née de St Michel], **Elizabeth** (1640–1669), wife of Samuel Pepys, was born at Bideford, Devon, on 23 October 1640, the daughter of Alexandre le Marchant de St Michel (d. 1672), a descendant of a dignified Anjou family, and Dorothea (b. 1609, d. in or after 1674), widow of Thomas Fleetwood of co. Cork and daughter of Sir Francis Kingsmill, a prominent Hampshire landowner. According to an account by Elizabeth's brother Balthasar (known as Balty; b. 1640, d. after 1710), Alexandre de St Michel's had been a colourful life (letter to Samuel Pepys, 8 Feb 1674). Youthful conversion to protestantism (which cost him his inheritance) was followed by service in England with Charles I's queen, Henrietta Maria. Having lost his post at court, in 1639 Alexandre reappeared in Ireland, where he met and married Dorothea Fleetwood. The family then moved to Devon, where Dorothea had inherited land. The later loss of this property began a period of dislocation for the family, and they subsequently travelled between Germany, Flanders, and Ireland, where Alexandre is said to have fought in the Cromwellian army. From Ireland, Dorothea, along with Elizabeth and Balthasar, fled to Paris after their fortunes had been undermined by Alexandre's increasingly determined religious views. Her mother intending that she become a nun, Elizabeth was briefly placed in the city's Ursuline convent before she and Balty were removed to London by their father. At some point during this period she apparently also spent time with another family, the Palmers. Her peripatetic upbringing may have instilled in Elizabeth the independent, mature, and determined spirit, as well as the ambivalent opinion towards Catholicism, that characterized her adult life.

It was in London that Elizabeth de St Michel met Samuel *Pepys (1633–1703), then in the employ of Edward Mountagu, later first earl of Sandwich. Details of the circumstances of their meeting remain unknown, though it is evident, given that neither party stood to gain financially from the union, that theirs was a love match. The couple were married at a civil service at St Margaret's, Westminster, on 1 December 1655, when Elizabeth, described as being of St Martin-in-the-Fields, was aged fifteen and Samuel twenty-two. By the time of this service the couple had apparently already 'married' in an unrecorded religious ceremony which took place on 10 October, the date Pepys identified as their anniversary during his years of diary keeping.

The early months of their marriage were characterized by antagonism and argument. Certainly Elizabeth Pepys performed as was expected; writing over a decade later, Samuel recalled her diligence in making fires and washing 'my foul clothes with her own hands for me ... poor wretch! in my little room' (Pepys, *Diary*, 8.82, 25 Feb 1667). None the less, the cramped conditions of his attic apartment at Whitehall Palace exacerbated both Elizabeth's irritation at the prosaic nature of married life and Samuel's jealousy and sexual frustration which derived, in part, from his own and his wife's recurrent ill health. Within a year of their marriage Elizabeth followed her mother's example and left her husband to stay with her family at Charing Cross; she returned to Whitehall only in December 1657. In August of the following year the couple left for a house in Axe Yard, Westminster, where they stayed until July 1660 before moving to the Navy Office at Seething Lane.

By this date Pepys had begun a diary, which he maintained daily until six months before his wife's death. With no correspondence between the couple surviving, it remains the principal source of information on Elizabeth's life during the 1660s, and thus provides a subjective, though highly detailed, picture of a marriage and of 'my wife', whom Pepys never named in his journal. For her part Elizabeth appears to have been unaware that her husband was keeping a record: he wrote in a shorthand which she, despite her linguistic ability (she was a good French speaker), was unable to read.

During the early years of the diary Elizabeth's lifestyle continued much as it was at the start of her marriage. Pepys's opening reference to his wife, for example, is to her burning her hand while preparing food (1 January 1660); later that year he describes her killing a turkey and pigeons. She was also responsible for running the increasingly large household at Seething Lane and proved a considerate (in Pepys's opinion too considerate) mistress to her servants. Initially responsible for all domestic matters, Elizabeth gained additional leisure time as her husband's career, and salary, improved over the decade. She also enjoyed more freedom than many women of her status on account of the marriage remaining childless. Her response to this situation remains unclear but Pepys was certainly concerned and sought advice on several occasions, though after two false alarms in November 1663 and September 1664 (as well as a startling offer from Samuel's uncle to father a child with Elizabeth) the couple appear to have abandoned the idea of raising a family.

How Elizabeth Pepys spent her free time was not without its problems for her husband. An engraving after the portrait painted in 1666 by John Hayls shows an alluring woman (then aged twenty-five) with delicate, almost childlike features, dressed in a low-cut gown (the original painting was destroyed about 1830 by a servant who took exception to the revealing nature of the dress). Pepys had himself been attracted to Elizabeth by her beauty, and in addition to those from his uncle, she continued to receive compliments and approaches from a range of men, including the duke of York, Pepys's employer Lord Sandwich, and his personal servant Will Hewer. Alert to his wife's effect on other men, Pepys was careful in the opportunities he gave Elizabeth to enhance her charm either through dress—very interested in fashion, she was frequently denied the allowance she demanded—or through social accomplishments such as dancing. Having been encouraged to take lessons by another admirer, in March 1663 Elizabeth persuaded Samuel to pay for instruction with a Mr Pemberton, with whom she became intimate and whom the naturally jealous Pepys soon viewed as a rival. Such concerns were not unwarranted. Elizabeth knew of her attractiveness and enjoyed the attention, and instances of her flirtations are recorded throughout the diary. Moreover, when denied her own way she could display a sharp temper, as when she and Pepys quarrelled over Pemberton's increasingly frequent visits to the house. On other occasions, Samuel's outbursts over the limitations of her housekeeping or poor background were matched with equal abuse. Herself the victim of physical violence from her husband, she occasionally responded in kind, while threatening in November 1667 to slit the nose of their servant girl, and Samuel's mistress, Deb Willet. Pepys's relatives also complained to him of the encouragement she showed other men and of her rudeness when staying with them at the family home at Brampton near Huntingdon.

Elizabeth's temper was complemented by a strongly independent spirit, as displayed in events such as that of the evening of 13 January 1660 when Pepys decided to go out alone. Elizabeth's response was defiant, and, having followed him and been escorted home, she departed for friends with whom she stayed until after his return. During other quarrels she was prepared, much to her husband's embarrassment, to continue an argument in public or at his office. Such determination evidently unsettled Pepys and at times made him question his authority within the marriage. It may have been this concern, bolstered by memories of Elizabeth's departure in the mid-1650s, that prompted him to integrate her so closely within his own family, whatever their opinion of her conduct, and to maintain a distance from his in-laws' family with the exception of his wife's favourite, her brother Balty, whose career she encouraged Samuel to nurture. And yet, amid the quarrels, Elizabeth also provided support and reassurance to Pepys, expressing concern for his well-being and pleasure at his professional successes. Against points of conflict such as the dancing episode of 1663 should also be set the diversions—theatre trips, books, card games, home improvements, shopping, and gossip—shared and enjoyed by the couple. Unlike her husband, Elizabeth was also able to resist her many, often eligible, suitors and remained faithful to the marriage.

In June 1669 Elizabeth Pepys accompanied her husband and brother on a tour of northern France and the Netherlands. Here she contracted the fever, probably typhoid, which developed during their return journey and from which, aged twenty-nine, she died at Seething Lane on 10 November. At previous moments of crisis Elizabeth had expressed a desire to die in the Roman Catholic faith, though when the moment came Samuel chose an Anglican minister to offer the sacrament. Pepys had previously expressed concern about Elizabeth's possible Catholic sympathies (29 November and 6 December 1668), and in 1673 he was himself accused of Catholicism and of 'breaking his wife's heart, because she would not turn Papist' (*JHC*, 9.306). Following the accusation, Balty reassured his brother-in-law that, whatever 'thoughts, shee might in her more tender yeares have had of Popery', he was satisfied 'that you kept my Dear sister in the true protestant Religion till her Death'. Balty's letter also provides a rare if uncorroborated example of Elizabeth's own reported speech in a life otherwise recorded entirely in Pepys's voice. While admitting that she had been mistaken in her childhood, she is said to have told her brother, 'I have now a man to my husbande soe wise, and one to religious in the Protestant religion … to ever suffer my thought to bende that way any more' (Pepys, *Further Correspondence*, 44–5). Elizabeth Pepys was buried on 13 November in the chancel of St Olave's Church, Westminster, where a striking and expressive bust, probably by John Bushnell, was placed, and remains, high on the wall. Details of Pepys's response to his wife's death are hard to judge without the diary. However, his commissioning of a bust, together with a fulsome tribute on her epitaph, suggests that her sudden death was shocking and a source of considerable sadness. On his own death in 1703 Pepys's body was, as requested, interred alongside his wife's at St Olave's.

To Robert Latham the depiction of Elizabeth in the diary suggests a difficult marriage between an often temperamental woman and a man who was 'unfaithful, insensitive and overbearing' (Pepys, *Diary*, 10.317). Certainly Samuel's moods were at times exacerbated by her self-possession and independence, which found no check in the duties of motherhood. And yet Pepys was also 'genuinely affectionate' (ibid.) to his wife, and the diary provides many instances of intimacy and pleasant reminiscence: it was as though the idea of Elizabeth was often more pleasing to Pepys than a reality which saw him alternate between censure and remorseful compassion following his own unreasonable behaviour to her. In subsequent biographies of the diarist Elizabeth Pepys has often existed more as an appendage than as a personality: a necessary but intrinsically unimportant figure, valuable as the touchstone for Samuel's philandering and self-doubt. However, more recent biographers, notably Ollard (1974) and especially Tomalin (2002), have set Pepys in the context of his household and have paid closer attention to Elizabeth's character and influence. She has also been the subject of several works of fiction, including Vanessa Brooks's play *Poor Mrs Pepys* (1994) and Sara George's *Journal of Mrs Pepys* (2000). PHILIP CARTER

Sources The diary of Samuel Pepys, ed. R. C. Latham and W. Matthews, 11 vols. (1970–83) · C. Tomalin, Samuel Pepys: the unequalled self (2002) · Further correspondence of Samuel Pepys, ed. R. G. Howarth (1933) · A. Bryant, Samuel Pepys: the man in the making (1933) · R. Ollard, Pepys: a biography (1974)
Likenesses attrib. J. Bushnell, marble bust, 1669, St Olave's Church, Westminster; repro. in Tomalin, Samuel Pepys, facing p. 249 · T. Thomson, stipple, pubd 1828 (after J. Hayls, 1666), BM, NPG · plaster cast of bust (after marble bust attrib. J. Bushnell), NPG

Pepys, Henry (1783–1860), bishop of Worcester, was born in Wimpole Street, London, on 18 April 1783. He was the third son of Sir William Weller Pepys and his wife, Elizabeth, *née* Dowdeswell. Charles Christopher *Pepys, earl of Cottenham, was his brother. He was educated at Harrow School and at Trinity College, Cambridge, matriculating in 1800 and graduating BA in 1804; he then migrated as a fellow to St John's College, Cambridge, and proceeded MA in 1807, BD in 1814, and DD in 1840.

Pepys was ordained priest in 1808 and was curate of Swaffham Prior from 1808. He was rector of Aspeden, Hertfordshire, from 12 June 1818 to 28 April 1827, and held with it the college living of Moreton, Essex, from 16 August 1822 until 1840. On 3 February 1826 he was appointed a prebendary of Wells, and on 31 March 1827 rector of Westmill, Hertfordshire. In politics he was a Liberal. On 27 January 1840 he was, on Lord Melbourne's recommendation, elevated to the bishopric of Sodor and Man; he was consecrated at Whitehall on 1 March, arrived at Douglas, Isle of Man, on 27 April, was installed at St Mary's, Castleton, on 8 May 1840, and left the island on 4 May 1841, on his translation—also by the whig government—to the see of Worcester.

In the House of Lords, although Pepys voted in favour of

the chief Liberal measures, he spoke only twice, on ecclesiastical questions of small importance. He was one of the bishops who assisted at the controversial consecration of R. D. Hampden in 1847, and he publicly attacked the high-church bishop Henry Phillpotts. Personally Pepys was popular, and was conscientious in the discharge of his diocesan duties. He was a generous patron of the triennial festival of the Three Choirs.

Pepys married, on 27 January 1824, Maria, third daughter of the Rt Hon. John Sullivan, commissioner of the Board of Control. They had four children: Philip Henry, registrar of the London court of bankruptcy; Herbert George, honorary canon of Worcester; Maria Louisa, who married the Revd Edward Winnington Ingram; and Emily, who married the Revd William Henry Lyttelton, and died on 12 September 1877.

Pepys published *The Remains of the Late Lord Viscount Royston, with a Memoir of his Life* (1838), six charges, and two sermons. He died at Hartlebury Castle, Stourport, Worcestershire, on 13 November 1860. He was survived by his wife, who died aged eighty-nine, on 17 June 1885.

G. C. BOASE, *rev.* H. C. G. MATTHEW

Sources *The Times* (16 Nov 1860) · *Berrow's Worcester Journal* (17 Nov 1860) · *Guardian* (21 Nov 1860), 1006 · H. Phillpotts, *A charge delivered to the clergy of the diocese of Exeter* (1845)
Archives BL, letters to third earl of Hardwicke, Add. MSS 35645–35698
Likenesses oils, Hartlebury Castle, Worcestershire
Wealth at death £50,000: probate, 14 Dec 1860, *CGPLA Eng. & Wales*

Pepys, Sir Lucas, first baronet (1742–1830), physician, son of William Pepys (*bap.* 1698, *d.* 1743), a banker, and his wife Hannah (*d.* 1761), daughter of Dr Richard *Russell of Brighton and widow of Alexander Weller, was born in London on 24 May 1742. He was educated at Eton College and at Christ Church, Oxford, where he graduated BA on 9 May 1764. He then studied medicine at Edinburgh in 1765, and afterwards graduated at Oxford, MA on 13 May 1767, MB on 30 April 1770, and MD on 14 June 1774. Before his MB degree he obtained a licence to practise from the University of Oxford, took a house in London, and on 10 February 1769 was elected physician to the Middlesex Hospital, where he held office for seven years. In the summer months he practised in Brighton. On 30 October 1772 he married Jane Elizabeth Leslie (*d.* 1810), the widowed countess of Rothes, with whom he had two sons and a daughter.

Pepys was elected a fellow of the Royal College of Physicians on 30 September 1775, was censor in 1777, 1782, 1786, and 1796, treasurer from 1788 to 1798, and president from 1804 to 1810. In 1777 he was appointed physician-extraordinary to the king, and in 1792 physician-in-ordinary. He was created a baronet on 22 January 1784.

Pepys attended George III during his illness of 1788–9, and in that of 1804. He was examined on the subject of the king's health by a committee of the House of Commons on 7 January 1789. He then thought it likely that the king would recover in time, and stated that he had observed signs of improvement. He attended two days a week at Kew, where the king was, from four in the afternoon until eleven the next morning, having a consultation often with either Sir George Baker or Richard Warren.

In 1794 Pepys was made physician-general to the army, and was president of an army medical board, on which it was his duty to nominate all the army physicians. When so many soldiers fell ill of fever at Walcheren, he was ordered to go there and report. When he declined, the board was abolished; but he was granted a pension. Pepys had a large practice, and became an active supporter of the National Vaccine Institution. He was punctual and assiduous as president of the College of Physicians. His only published work was the Latin preface to the *London Pharmacopoeia* of 1809.

After the death of his first wife in 1810, Pepys married Deborah (*d.* 1848), daughter of Dr Anthony *Askew, on 29 June 1813. His house was in Park Street, Grosvenor Square, London, where he died on 17 June 1830. He was described by William Munk, as 'a person of great firmness and determination, somewhat dictatorial in his manner'.

NORMAN MOORE, *rev.* KAYE BAGSHAW

Sources B. Hill, 'Doctor among the blue-stockings: Sir Lucas Pepys, 1742–1830', *The Practitioner*, 213 (1974), 87–90 · Munk, *Roll* · *Authentic memoirs, biographical, critical, and literary, of the most eminent physicians and surgeons of Great Britain*, 2nd edn (1818) · Burke, *Peerage* · IGI
Archives JRL, letters to Mrs Thrale · NA Scot., documents concerning the dismissal of George Ernst from the king's service
Likenesses J. Godby, stipple (after Edridge), BM, NPG; repro. in *British gallery of contemporary portraits* (1809)

Pepys, Richard (*c.*1588–1659), judge, was born at Cottenham, Cambridgeshire, the second son of John Pepys (*d.* 1604) of the Middle Temple and of Impington, near Cottenham, and Elizabeth (*d.* 1642), daughter of John Bendish of Bower Hall, Bumpstead, Essex. Pepys joined the Middle Temple in 1609 and was called to the bar in 1617. He subsequently sat in the Short Parliament (March–May 1640) as member for Sudbury, Suffolk. In 1642 he was left heir to the estate of his elder brother, John, and in 1643–4 was elected treasurer of the Middle Temple, having previously served there as reader in 1640. In January 1654 he was appointed serjeant-at-law, and was immediately afterwards a member of the commission for the spring circuit through the midland counties. On 30 May in the same year he was appointed baron of the exchequer, in spite of scruples as to the protector's legal authority. In August, Pepys, by then over sixty, accepted appointment to Ireland, 'attracted (it seems) by the chance of improving his fortune' (Barnard, 284), though the move at his age could be viewed as foolhardy rather than wise. Made at the outset a member of the Irish lord deputy's council, he served under both Charles Fleetwood and Henry Cromwell and thus learned at first hand of the manner in which the council's work suffered from the 'lamentable rubbs and interruptions' of which Cromwell was to make complaint. When, in September 1657, Cromwell wrote privately to Secretary Thurloe on the subject of filling future vacancies on the Irish council, his list of qualifications was very likely based on his own assessment of Pepys's worth: councillors should possess sound judgment, be expert in draftsmanship ('conceiving and wordeing of orders') and prepared to 'take paines to observe and search into matters' (Thurloe, *State papers*, 6.505–6).

Pepys's principal duties were judicial. Named chief justice of the upper bench in 1654 he was associated with the revival of the Dublin four courts the following year. Until the appointment of William Steele as lord chancellor in August 1656 he was chief commissioner of the Irish great seal and in that capacity presided over a makeshift court which in a test case handed down a decision presaging a return to normality in Ireland's commercial life; he insisted on the payment of interest on debts contracted before 1641.

Pepys married, first, Judith, a daughter of Sir William Cutte of Arkesden, Essex, and second, Mary (d. 1660), daughter of Captain Gosnold. He left four sons and two daughters. His eldest son, Richard, married Mary, daughter of John Scott of Belchamp-Walter, Essex, and, with his wife and daughter, Mary, migrated to New England in 1634, but returned in 1650 and settled at Ashen Clare, Essex. A number of Pepys's letters to Richard have been printed (W. C. Pepys, *Genealogy of the Pepys Family, 1273–1887*, 1887). They possess great charm. Richard is urged to be careful about money, advised to decline the office of constable, something 'never before put uppon a judge's son' (Pepys, 60), and warned against false friends: 'Pray have a care to avoyd flattering companions and such as will if they can insinuate into you, pretending with love and intending theire owne advantage' (Pepys, 59).

Pepys died in Dublin on 2 January 1659. Henry Cromwell, in reporting the news, described Pepys as 'a good councellor, ... a good judge, and indeed a right honest man' (Thurloe, *State papers*, 7.590). Edward Worth, in his funeral sermon (*The Servant Doing and the Lord Blessing*, 1659), was even more effusive in his praise, drawing attention, in particular, to Pepys's fairness and to the fact that during his period of service in Ireland he did nothing to feather his own nest: 'As a magistrate, he might say with Samuel, "Whose ox or whose ass have I taken?"' (1 Samuel, 8: 16). Pepys was buried at Christchurch Cathedral, Dublin. He was a cousin once removed of the diarist Samuel Pepys. W. A. SHAW, *rev.* W. N. OSBOROUGH

Sources W. C. Pepys, *Genealogy of the Pepys family, 1273–1887* (1887) · Thurloe, *State papers* · R. Dunlop, ed., *Ireland under the Commonwealth*, 2 vols. (1913) · T. C. Barnard, *Cromwellian Ireland: English government and reform in Ireland, 1649–1660* (1975) · F. E. Ball, *The judges in Ireland, 1221–1921*, 2 vols. (1926) · E. Worth, *The servant doing and the Lord blessing: a sermon at the funeral of ... Richard Pepys* [1659] · Foss, *Judges* · R. Lascelles, ed., *Liber munerum publicorum Hiberniae ... or, The establishments of Ireland*, later edn, 2 vols. in 7 pts (1852) · T. Power, 'The "black book" of king's inns: an introduction with an abstract of contents', *Irish Jurist*, new ser., 20 (1985), 135–212 · R. Steele, ed., *Bibliotheca Lindesiana: a bibliography of royal proclamations of the Tudor and Stuart sovereigns*, 2 vols. (1910) · S. G. Drake, *Result of some researches among British archives* (1860) · J. Savage, *A genealogical dictionary of the first settlers of New England*, 4 vols. (1860–62) · *Report on the manuscripts of the earl of Egmont*, 2 vols. in 3, HMC, 63 (1905–9) **Archives** GL, family corresp. · priv. coll., corresp.

Pepys, Samuel (1633–1703), naval official and diarist, was born at the family home, Salisbury Court, Fleet Street, London, on 23 February 1633, the second son of John Pepys (1601–1680), tailor, and his wife, Margaret, *née* Kite (d. 1667), daughter of a Whitechapel butcher. He was the fifth of their eleven children, and the oldest to survive into adulthood. He was baptized on 3 March in St Bride's Church by James Palmer. Although his immediate background was urban and modest, Pepys's family came from Cottenham, Cambridgeshire, and he had landed connections there and in Huntingdonshire. Among these was his father's brother Robert, who owned an estate at Brampton, Huntingdonshire, which Pepys eventually inherited. Of more immediate importance was the marriage of John Pepys's aunt Paulina to Sir Sydney Montagu of Hinchingbrooke; their son Edward Mountagu (later earl of Sandwich), who was to have a large place in the Commonweath regime and a larger one in its overthrow, was the agent for Pepys's advancement into public service.

Pepys's childhood was only partially spent under his parents' roof. For a time he and his next brother, Tom, were sent to a nurse, Goody Lawrence, at Kingsland in the country just north of London. About 1644 he was living with his Huntingdonshire relations (probably at Brampton), because for a while he attended Huntingdon grammar school. He came away with an admiration for the school's favourite son, Oliver Cromwell, which he did not abandon despite his loyalty to the restored monarchy. His schooling was completed at St Paul's under its formidable high master John Langley. Pepys warmed more to the surmaster, Samuel Cromleholme, and was pained to see him degenerate into a comic drunk. From his schooldays Pepys kept a volume of Xenophon which he solemnly inscribed in Greek with his name and the date 1649—the year in which he was an approving spectator at the execution of Charles I.

St Paul's gave Pepys a leaving exhibition in 1650, and on 21 June he entered his name at Trinity Hall, Cambridge, where his uncle John Pepys LLD was a fellow. Several members of the family had distinguished themselves in the law, and Samuel seemed to be headed in the same direction. But it was at Magdalene that he was admitted a sizar on 1 October, and where he took up residence on 5 March 1651. On 3 April he was advanced to a scholarship on the foundation of John Spendluffe. Perhaps an invitation came from the new master, John Sadler, a neighbour of the Pepyses in Salisbury Court; another influence may have been Samuel Morland, who became Pepys's tutor, and who knew the Montagus. Whatever the circumstances, it was a move which Pepys and the college only once had occasion to regret (when he was reprimanded for drunkenness in hall on the night of 20 October 1653). Pepys retained fond memories of the college beer and the 'town tart'; he also made many lasting friendships. In the first year he kept with Robert Sawyer, a third-year man and a future attorney-general. Richard Cumberland, later bishop of Peterborough, had been a contemporary of Pepys at St Paul's, but it was at Magdalene that they became close friends. On 4 October 1653 Pepys was elected

Samuel Pepys (1633–1703), by John Hayls, 1666

to a Smith scholarship. He took his BA in March 1654, recording his new status in a book of cabalistic hokum which had taken his fancy. After he left Cambridge Pepys regularly visited his old college; he proceeded MA on 26 June 1660.

Soon after coming down Pepys was found employment in the London household of Edward Mountagu, now a councillor of state in Cromwell's protectorate. Pepys's duties were at first trivial, but as Mountagu's professional and family life took him increasingly away from London, he became effectively his master's secretary. Nevertheless he was scarcely well enough placed to marry, which at the end of 1655, when still living in one room of Mountagu's Whitehall lodgings, he did. He had fallen in love with Elizabeth [see Pepys, Elizabeth (1640–1669)], the fourteen-year-old daughter of Alexandre St Michel, an impoverished Frenchman who had briefly been gentleman carver to Henrietta Maria. Elizabeth brought the awkward legacy of a convent education, and a negative dowry of mendicant relatives, most notably her brother Balthasar (Balty). The marriage in St Margaret's, Westminster, on 1 December 1655 was a civil ceremony; they celebrated their anniversary on 10 October, probably the date of a preceding wedding according to prayer-book liturgy, which Pepys attended when he could. Before that anniversary had come for a second time, Pepys and Elizabeth had spent some time apart. This first crisis in their marriage was resolved; others would follow, but although childless they remained together until Elizabeth's death. On 26 March 1658 Pepys, who had long been in acute pain from a kidney stone, underwent a potentially lethal operation for its removal. The immediate problem was cured, but Pepys continued to suffer from genito-urinary disorders, which

may have prevented him from fathering children. By the end of August that year the Pepyses had moved into a house of their own, in Axe Yard, close to the present Downing Street. Coincidentally at about the same time (before Cromwell died in September), Pepys acquired a part-time place as teller in the exchequer under George Downing, after whom the street would be named. For Pepys it was a first foothold in the public domain, but he continued to serve his original master. Mountagu was now a general-at-sea; in May 1659 Pepys took dispatches to him in the Baltic, and so unwittingly began his own thirty years of service to the navy.

Opening his account It was certainly with some sense that his own life, as well as the nation's history, was at a pivotal point, that on 1 January 1660 Pepys began the diary which has made him famous. He opens with a self-conscious summary of his domestic circumstances and the political background; thereafter his writing takes on the structures and rhythms which are sustained for the nine and a half years which the diary fills. He had kept no previous journal, though his dispatches to Mountagu may have been his apprenticeship in reporting. A 'Romance' written at Cambridge (and destroyed along with other juvenilia in 1664) was the only previous literary effort he recalled (Pepys, *Diary*, 5.31). The extant manuscript of the diary is a fair copy, written up (in shorthand) every few days from a scribbled draft, collated with other private papers or printed sources to hand. Pepys undoubtedly improved on his text in this process, though without compromising the authenticity of the daily record. The result is properly acclaimed as an astonishingly vivid and disciplined exercise in self-analysis, a historical document of the first rank, and a literary classic. The diary is naturally the single most important source of knowledge about Pepys himself and his relationships, and his public reputation derives largely from the image he projects of himself during the diary years, 1660–69. As it happened these were all the years that remained of his married life, and the period in which his professional apprenticeship was completed.

Pepys had a rival for Sandwich's chief favour, John Creed, a man who shared many of Pepys's enthusiasms and with whom he maintained an uneasy friendship. Creed seemed more intellectually gifted, and had a larger social competence; but Pepys was the harder worker, and this was decisive. On 6 March Mountagu, who had been secretly negotiating for the return of Charles II, asked Pepys to go to sea with him as secretary. After a few days' thought Pepys accepted, and on 23 March, having put Elizabeth in a boarding house and bought some new clothes, he boarded the *Swiftsure*. With Mountagu he transferred to the *Naseby* when the fleet sailed to the Netherlands to bring back the king. Pepys contrived a place in the key documents of the Restoration by appending his counter-signature to the printed text of the king's declaration issued from Breda on 14 April. When the king came aboard the fleet on 23 May, Pepys heard him talk of his wartime escape; on the following day he was addressed by name by the duke of York.

Back home, Mountagu received the earldom of Sandwich and the Garter, and (on 2 June) promised Pepys that they would 'rise together' and he would in the mean time do him 'all the good Jobbs' he could (Pepys, *Diary*, 1.167). This pledge was promptly honoured with the post of clerk of the acts at the Navy Board, first mentioned by Sandwich on 18 June, and secured for Pepys by patent on 13 July. The board, which controlled most of the material needs and manpower of the navy, was reconstituted at the Restoration, and Pepys was obliged to settle a pension on his prewar predecessor. The clerk was secretary to the board, with a salary of £350, the prospect of much larger income from gratuities, and an official house. Pepys sensibly rejected an offered £1000 buy-out from another suitor, and moved from Westminster to the much larger accommodation in Seething Lane, where he entertained his friends for the first time on 18 July. He had resigned his post in the exchequer in 28 June, but on 23 July he was sworn in as a clerk of the privy seal, an extra little 'Jobb' Sandwich had found for him; this he relinquished two years later. On 24 September Pepys was sworn in as *ex officio* justice of the peace for Middlesex, Kent, Essex, and Hampshire (the counties where the royal dockyards lay).

Learning the business of the navy Pepys took up these responsibilities with only such knowledge of naval affairs as he had gathered from his two voyages in Mountagu's service; his principal colleagues at the Navy Board were men of incomparably greater experience: Sir George Carteret, the treasurer, who had held Jersey for the king; Sir John Mennes, the comptroller (from 1661), an unswerving servant of the crown on land and sea since the days of James I; Sir William Batten, the surveyor, whose loyalties had rather notably swerved during the civil war but whose seaworthiness was undoubted; and Sir William Penn, one of the heroes of the First Anglo-Dutch War and the conqueror of Jamaica. Carteret and Mennes had been 'gentlemen' captains, while Batten and Penn represented the alternative brand of 'tarpaulins', whose claim to naval command was based on experience rather than heredity and court connection. Pepys, who was neither a gentleman nor a tarpaulin, entered office with due deference to both sorts. He soon formed a prejudice (borrowed from Sandwich) against the 'gentlemen', and paradoxically perpetuated the notion of a division in the officer structure which in fact became blurred, not a little by his own efforts. Having been made welcome by his older colleagues, within a short time he came to despise most of them for what he considered their inefficiency and corruption. Batten, Penn, and Mennes would be the particular targets of venomous epithets which Pepys's most sympathetic biographers have found difficult to square with his pervading geniality. It is perfectly true that Mennes and the 'Sir Williams' were not well suited to the chores of bookkeeping and accountancy in which Pepys delighted, and he was soon able to outsmart them in points of detail. He made it his business very quickly to learn the multifaceted work which had fallen his way. He engaged a tutor to improve the arithmetic he needed to follow the international finance on which the naval supplies depended.

He made himself expert in the weights and measures of the goods themselves, talking to dockyard storekeepers, carpenters, and boatswains, getting to know all the wonderful wheezes and scams which could turn the king's shilling into a pretty penny. All this he carefully noted in a series of interrelating records, of which his personal diary was one. A contract with Sir William Warren for £3000-worth of Norway masts (concluded 3 September 1663), which Pepys had single-handedly negotiated, was the point at which he effectively outran his seniors at the board. Of these only Carteret and William Coventry, who sat without portfolio, retained his respect. But Coventry, who was also the duke of York's secretary, was hostile to Sandwich; an awkwardness for Pepys, who feared (wrongly, as it happens) that his own position would be threatened if his original patron lost favour at court.

While Pepys was mastering his core career, his concerns and contacts helpfully proliferated. In 1661 Robert Pepys had died, leaving a life interest in the Brampton estate to Pepys's father, who retired there; but Pepys himself had the reversionary interest and from now on managed the property. On 15 February 1662 he was admitted a younger brother of Trinity House, and on 30 April he received the freedom of Portsmouth. In August Sandwich nominated him for the committee which had been set up to run Tangier, a part of Queen Catherine's dowry. The financing of the garrison rapidly became a muddle, for which the solution was to appoint Pepys as treasurer (20 March 1665). He had been appointed to the commission of the royal fishery by its charter of 8 April 1664. On 21 February 1665 he was elected FRS; while never more than an interested observer, he became known in learned circles. The Second Anglo-Dutch War which began in the following week had been dreaded by Pepys, and it could indeed have brought his ruin; in fact it was his maturing. With Penn at sea, Batten dying, and Mennes never much help, the work of supplying the fleet at war lay almost wholly with Pepys; had become, as the duke of Albemarle told him in April 1665, 'the right hand of the Navy here' (that is, ashore), nobody else 'taking any care of anything' (Pepys, *Diary*, 6.89). At the outset of the war Pepys recommended a centralized victualling structure; his proposal was accepted and he was himself appointed surveyor-general of victualling, with a salary of £300 a year, on 27 October 1665. He adroitly disengaged himself from the scandal over prize-goods which disgraced Sandwich at the end of the year.

During the first months of the great plague which came in that same first year of the war, Pepys remained in London. On 18 August, following an order from the king, he and his staff were evacuated to Greenwich; Elizabeth was sent to the relative safety of Woolwich. During the great fire of September 1666, the first news of which he brought personally to the king, he evacuated what he could of his possessions (including the precious diary) to the country; in fact his house was saved. From its reporting of these two disasters to the metropolis in which he thrived, Pepys's diary has become a national monument. By 1667 the government had decided to abandon an unprofitable war, and Pepys approvingly helped to discharge the fleet.

Now that the English would not meet them on the high seas, the Dutch became a threat to the mainland. Although Pepys and his colleagues recognized this well enough—'all our care now being to fortify ourselfs against their invading us' (Pepys, *Diary*, 8.115)—the defences in the Medway proved inadequate against the superb seamanship of the Dutch. Early on 12 June Pepys recorded Albemarle's assurance that 'all is safe … the boom and Chaine being so fortified' (ibid., 8.260–61); but within hours he heard that the chain had been breached at Gillingham, and that the *Royal Charles* had been towed away.

Grace under pressure Pepys's immediate concern had been to get his wife, his father, and as much he could withdraw in gold coin, out of London. For as long as the Dutch remained in the river, he was virtually on active service. But it was already plain that the Navy Board, and its right-hand man, would face a formidable investigation unless the lynch mob got them first. Pepys came well enough through the first examination, held before a committee of the privy council on 19 June. As always he was armed with his files and letter-books, from which he could evidence the proper dispatch of orders and *matériel*. He sensed that the resident commissioner of Chatham, Peter Pett, was being targeted for blame, and was quick to follow the pack. Once the war ended in August, wider inquiries into its conduct were ordered by parliament. On 17 October the Commons appointed a committee of 'miscarriages'. The first Pepys heard from them (20 October) was a request for lists of ships and commanders at the time of the controversial division of the fleet in 1666; he was glad that they were 'after that business' (Pepys, *Diary*, 8.489): operational foul-ups were not the Navy Board's responsibility. So the news that the committee was much concerned with allegations of cowardice after the battle of Lowestoft was also welcome; indeed, the issue conveniently embarrassed Penn as commander without reflecting on him and his colleagues as commissioners. The board did face questioning on the Medway disaster, but from their first appearance (25 October) they insisted that 'Commissioner Pett was singly concerned in the executing of all orders at Chatham' (ibid., 8.501), and this convenient fudge was accepted by the committee when it reported in February 1668. Their one major criticism of the board was over the payment of seamen by tickets, promissory notes which could be cashed only at the navy treasury in London. The system was certainly bad, but it was not (as the parliamentarians suspected) a massive fraud run by the navy officers. The technicalities were explained and justified by Pepys in a lengthy speech at the bar of the Commons on 5 March. It was a virtuoso performance, capped by the personal congratulations of the king and the duke as they walked in the park next day.

However, another and more powerful tribunal, the commissioners of accounts, had already set to work in the premises at Brooke House, Holborn, from which they took their name. They asked much more searchingly about how the parliamentary vote for the war had been spent, and that took the investigation to the centre of Pepys's domain. For almost two years the commission gathered evidence, issuing occasional reports.

Pepys's anxieties were interwoven with domestic crises. His sexual misconduct, so relentlessly chronicled in the diary, touched its lowest point in October 1668 when Elizabeth found him indecently engaged with her maid. The resulting quarrel was contained chiefly by the mediation of Pepys's clerk and lifelong friend, Will Hewer. By the middle of the following year Pepys's eyesight had become so poor that he feared imminent blindness; and with this terrible expectation ('almost as much as to see myself go into my grave') he ended his diary on 31 May 1669, never to resume it (Pepys, *Diary*, 9.565). He had asked for three or four months' leave, which the king personally allowed. His eyesight improved, and so did his relations with Elizabeth; in June they went for a prolonged holiday in the Low Countries and France. Pepys was given a heavy sightseeing schedule by John Evelyn, who was becoming a good friend. They returned on 20 October, but Elizabeth developed a fever (perhaps typhoid) and died on 10 November.

Pepys had been unable to campaign personally for the Commons seat of Aldeburgh, sought for him by the duke of York and the local magnate, the duke of Norfolk's heir; the burghers were not minded to have an absentee and allegedly papist member foisted on them, and Pepys lost the election. Meanwhile the Brooke House commissioners had submitted eighteen 'Observations' on the conduct of the Navy Board during the war. By 27 November Pepys had completed a weighty response to each observation, which he followed on 6 January 1670 with a 'particular defence' of his own role. The issues were debated in a series of special meetings of the privy council chaired by the king, who had smartly manoeuvred the inquiry into a forum he could control (3 January–21 February). Pepys kept a journal which is the main record of these proceedings, in which he appears to confound his critics in every particular. Maybe it was not quite as easy as Pepys's carefully structured narrative suggests, and more than once the king helped him along. When the eighteenth observation had been disposed of, a final attempt was made to catch Pepys out by producing a seaman's ticket payable in his name. Pepys flatly denied receiving the sum stated, and the king dismissed the idea that 'one having so great trust … should descend to so poor a thing … in a matter of 7l. 10s.' (Latham, *Pepys and the Second Dutch War*, 431). In the end Brooke House proved to be a mare's nest, and Pepys emerged secure.

Off duty At about this time Pepys formed what became an enduring relationship with Mary, daughter of Daniel Skinner, a Mark Lane merchant whose business failed. Mary had been brought up by her aunt Elizabeth, wife of Sir Francis Boteler of Hatfield Woodhall, Hertfordshire, from whom in 1681 she received a handsome legacy. Although at first she maintained a separate establishment, she later became the accepted lady of Pepys's house. Why he did not make her his wife cannot be said; perhaps it was because her brother Daniel assisted Milton, and the family was therefore tainted with republicanism. She was nevertheless sometimes accorded the style of Mrs

Pepys. How faithful Pepys may have been to her is impossible to say. Since he was never denounced for immorality by his political opponents, it may be supposed that any additional passions were as furtively and fleetingly satisfied as those of the diary era.

'Music and women', Pepys had written in 1666, 'I cannot but give way to, whatever my business is' (Pepys, *Diary*, 7.69–70). His delight in music abounds in the pages of the diary, and is also evidenced by books and manuscripts he collected. It even surfaced in his public career, in making a point to a fellow 'understander of music' at the Brooke House hearings (Latham, *Pepys and the Second Dutch War*, 369). The diary gives valuable information about the reintroduction of Anglican church music at the Restoration, and the general development of musical culture in Charles II's London. Pepys knew many of the court and other professional musicians of the capital, and was competent enough to share in their impromptu music-making. He had evidently just mastered sight-reading in January 1660, and subsequently had lessons to improve his technique. He sang at home, in coffee-houses, and on one occasion as a deputy lay-vicar of Westminster Abbey. He could manage the lute (having his instrument upgraded as a theorbo in 1661), the viol, and the violin. In 1667 he acquired a flageolet and in the following year a recorder and a spinet. In learning to play these newly acquired instruments he was hampered by lack of knowledge of the gamut. It was only when, from 1673, he was able to employ a domestic musician (Cesare Morelli), that Pepys was provided with tablatures he could follow. Technical deficiency also impeded his aspirations to compose. He could sketch a melody well enough, but required professional help to supply the harmonization. When one of his distinguished teachers, William Child, was about to take the Oxford doctorate of music, Pepys had 'a great mind' to do the same (Pepys, *Diary*, 4.199); but the degree required an expertise which Pepys would never approach.

The theatre was Pepys's other great love. He had done some acting as a boy and in the 1660s he became an enthusiastic playgoer, though there remained on his conscience a puritan notion that all the stage was a vice. Naturally he enjoyed the spectacle and the social experience of the theatre, but he also had firm views on the linguistic and compositional requirements of a good play. He often found that a piece which read well played disappointingly. Yet on reading *Othello*, which he had admired on the stage, he found the structure much inferior to Samuel Tuke's *Adventures of Five Houres*, 'for the variety and the most excellent continuance of the plot' (Pepys, *Diary*, 4.8). In general he admired Shakespeare's tragedies and histories; his disparaging notices of the comedies (*Midsummer night's dream*: 'inspid'; *Twelfth Night*: 'silly'; ibid., 3.208; 4.6) have been smugly cited as evidence of poor judgement, but he probably saw them in adaptations which would horrify a modern audience.

The Admiralty and parliament On 24 January 1672 Pepys was admitted elder brother of Trinity House. War with the Dutch was resumed in March. Sandwich was a casualty at Sole Bay, and Pepys was a banner-bearer at the funeral in Westminster Abbey; they had ceased to be close, and Pepys's career now had its own momentum. In January 1673 a fire which destroyed the Navy Office obliged Pepys to take temporary lodgings in Winchester Lane. When the Test Act compelled the duke of York to resign as lord high admiral the king appointed an Admiralty commission, and by 19 June Pepys was promoted to be its secretary. This meant much more money (£500 per annum and a great deal more in legitimate fees) and enhanced status. However, while still clerk of the acts Pepys had extended his influence outside the strict remit of the Navy Board; his old place there could be shared between his undistinguished younger brother John and his former clerk Tom Hayter, while his own new post rather confirmed him in a larger place he already effectively held. More significant was his move in January 1674 to Derby House, which became the Admiralty's first dedicated premises. Pepys thereby inaugurated an institution which only the matching dynamism of Mountbatten could terminate. The king took a controlling interest in the new Admiralty administration, and the rapport he had established with Pepys during the Brooke House hearings was further developed. The king had helped him win election to the Commons as member for Castle Rising (Norfolk) on 4 November 1673; this time he was able to campaign with his own purse (to near £700). But the support he again received from the duke of York and the Howard interest prompted the opposition to denounce him as a crypto-papist, and to seek to have his election quashed. MPs were told of popish furnishings in Pepys's house; it emerged that the details were fabricated by Shaftesbury, who backed down when he could not substantiate them. In fact Pepys never inclined to Rome, but he courted suspicion by collecting Catholic books and pictures (which, when cornered, he denied) and by attending Catholic services. This activity is now recognized as the result of aesthetic and intellectual curiosity, but coupled with his adherence to the duke it raised in his contemporaries authentic fears, which the opposition were to reactivate.

For now Pepys kept his seat, but he never became a parliamentarian, having already developed the permanent secretary's disdain for part-time legislators. He regarded his political allies, the tory squires, as blockheads; they found him a painful reminder of the schoolroom. Pepys secretly admired the superior intellect and competence of the opposition; he was not himself really a party man, and he had (in the wider sense) no constituency except the navy. He entered the Commons for professional rather than personal reasons; in 1668 he had formed the 'great design, if I continue in the Navy … to be a Parliamentman' (Pepys, *Diary*, 9.385). He knew well enough that a fine speech from the bar was no substitute for the influence he could exercise from the dispatch box. A navy minister, as already existed in France and the United Provinces, might counteract 'the ignorance of our parliaments in matters marine' and command confidence for the supply on which the service depended (*Samuel Pepys's Naval Minutes*,

356). In due course Pepys came to fill that role, and so occupies a significant place in the developing balance between executive and legislature. Nevertheless, during the parliaments of Charles II he sat on few committees, and rarely spoke on non-naval matters. Other institutions claimed him: in February 1676 he was made a governor of Christ's Hospital, and would do much to foster the Royal Mathematical School there as an academy for seamen. On 22 May 1676 he was elected master of Trinity House, and on 8 August 1677 the Clothworkers' Company chose him as its master.

The years 1676–7 saw the principal achievements of Pepys's first secretaryship. He devised regulations for midshipmen and volunteers (4 May 1676), for men and guns (3 November 1677), and for naval chaplains (15 December 1677). The establishment of an examination for lieutenants (18 December 1677) was central to the professionalization of the officer corps. His political triumph was in persuading the Commons to vote £600,000 over two years for the thirty new ships needed to compete with the French (23 February 1677). When the Cavalier Parliament was dissolved in January 1679 Pepys had no need to risk the expense and uncertainty of a contested election, and was returned for Harwich on the Admiralty ticket. He had already been labelled 'vile' by the opposition, who rightly saw him as the duke of York's continuing agent, and they resolved to destroy him. There was a failed attempt to fit up his clerk Samuel Atkins for the murder of Sir Edmund Bury Godfrey: Pepys efficiently organized the defence, and Atkins was acquitted on 11 February. Pepys's position became precarious when the king was obliged to appoint a new and whig-dominated Admiralty commission on 21 April. A week later a Commons committee on naval miscarriages began to examine 'all enormities' and it was expected that Pepys was to be 'pulled into pieces' (*Ormonde MSS*, new ser., 4.507, 509).

On 20 May Pepys and the shipwright Sir Anthony Deane were charged with leaking naval secrets to the French; Pepys himself was again accused of popery. On the following day he resigned his secretaryship, and on the 22nd he and Deane were sent to the Tower. At once Pepys set his friends to gather evidence establishing his innocence and the unreliability of his accusers: these, it emerged, were his sacked butler, John James, and a footloose trickster, John Scott, whose previous dishonesties Pepys had exposed. In the event Pepys's defence dossier (ruefully called the 'Book of Mornamont' from Scott's imaginary castle) was not needed. Even in the prevailing anti-Catholic hysteria, the prosecution could not construct a case; Pepys and Deane, who had been bailed on 9 July, were eventually discharged on 30 June 1680.

In October Pepys attended the king at Newmarket, anticipating some reward for past service, if not a chance of future employment. What Charles II gave him was a dictated version of his great escape story (which Pepys took down in shorthand, and intended to publish) and two parts of the illuminated Anthony roll manuscript which had been presented to Henry VIII: magnificent but inedible. Pepys was in fact now unemployed; he had given up

his lucrative Tangier post in 1679 and had not stood for re-election to parliament that year. He was surprisingly still nominated to the bench, but for the present he had to live chiefly from his savings. Pepys's father had died in October 1680, and the small Brampton estate was now his. But having made his London house into an official residence he could not return to it; instead he lodged with Hewer at York Buildings, off the Strand. In 1685 he took the tenancy in his own name, and there his library achieved its maturity. In 1681, with his public life seemingly over, he had some hope of being nominated provost of King's College, Cambridge; but (probably correctly) he was doubtful of his credentials, and allowed his candidacy to lapse. He continued to show his face at court when he could, and he was duly invited to sail with the duke of York to Scotland in May 1682. He chose a comfortable cabin in the *Katherine* yacht rather than a place in the duke's ship the *Gloucester*, thereby avoiding the wreck of the latter in which many died. On reaching his destination he was displeased by the 'universal … rooted nastiness' of the inhabitants, though he was impressed by the beauty of Glasgow (*Letters*, ed. Howarth, 139).

Pepys's return to public service came in the following year when he was sent to Tangier in Lord Dartmouth's fleet. The mission, only disclosed after it left Portsmouth on 9 August, was the evacuation of a colony which had proved unsustainable. Pepys, as Dartmouth's secretary, had particular responsibility for assigning compensation for abandoned property; it was an uncongenial task, but accomplished with his customary efficiency, and giving him a pioneering place in the history of British imperial retreat. His duty done, he and Hewer took a holiday in Spain, reaching Seville on 3 February. Their travels were spoiled by foul weather, but Pepys did manage to collect a chestful of printed Spanish plays and ephemeral literature, now among the rarities of his library. He returned to England in March 1684. During the trip he had kept a journal, which has been called his second diary; it is indeed the most substantial of the various *ad rem* journals he wrote after 1669, and an important record, but it has little of the charm or the literary merit of the personal diary of 1660–69. For his final service to Tangier Pepys received almost £1000; more important was the reacquaintance it brought him with the navy and many of the personnel. He was confirmed in his view that the service was incompetently directed and negligently officered.

Recall of a former naval person On 19 May 1684 the king revoked the Admiralty commission of 1679, and for the remaining months of his life he was his own lord high admiral, assisted by the duke of York. On 10 June Pepys was returned to office by letters patent which named him secretary for the affairs of the Admiralty of England, a post created for him and of which he was the only holder. He began at once to take stock, and by the end of the year had presented the king with a detailed denunciation of the previous regime's record. On 1 December he was elected president of the Royal Society, as which he served for two years; in consequence Newton's *Principia* (1687), published by the society, carries Pepys's imprimatur. Following the accession of James II (6 February 1685) Pepys was confirmed in office; James, like his brother, was king and admiral, and by his own elevation Pepys became clear chief of the naval staff. At the coronation on 23 April he attended as a baron of the Cinque Ports, one of the bearers of the king's canopy. In the general election which followed he was returned for Sandwich and also for Harwich, choosing to sit again for the latter. In this parliament he served on nineteen committees, including some outside his departmental concern. On 30 May he was made deputy lieutenant for Huntingdonshire, and on 14 July was elected for a second term as master of Trinity House. Charles II had lacked opportunity to act on Pepys's recommendations on returning to the Admiralty; the new king, however, was ready to give his old servant free rein, but could do so only because his tory parliament was willing to vote ample supply. By the end of the year Pepys had (with especial prompting from Deane) concluded that the existing machinery of naval administration was incapable of the necessary reconstruction work.

On 1 January 1686 Pepys presented to the king a more detailed criticism of those who had run the navy in his absence, their dereliction of duty and the waste of *matériel* which had resulted. There is no doubt that here, and in his subsequent *Memoires of the Royal Navy*, he flagrantly misused statistics to besmirch his predecessors. He contrasted the strength of the fleet when he had left with that he had found on his return, without explaining that in 1679 ships were in pay which had been sent out to fight the French, whereas in 1684 a smaller fleet of less heavily armed ships was appropriate for the navy's current convoy and policing duties. His aspersions on the indolence and private trading of commanders were veiled criticisms of the king who patronized them. The solution offered in his 'Proposition' of 26 January 1686 was a three-year 'special commission' which would combine the functions of the Admiralty and the Navy Board; James agreed, and the commissioners (who included Deane, Hewer, St Michel, and others, all head-hunted by Pepys) began work on 22 March. The programme of refurbishment was so successful that the commission was prematurely dissolved on 12 October 1688; the threat of a Dutch invasion had additionally spurred its activities.

Pepys's thoughts on the approaching climacteric are never fully evident. Outwardly he supported James II's regime, and may indeed have believed it was 'very fitt … that the king should be at liberty to dispense with as well as make his own rules' (Magd. Cam., Pepys Library, MS 2860, p. 247), but he must have viewed James's headstrong Catholicizing with personal dismay and professional disdain. The failure of the fleet to repel, or even face, the Dutch when they came was no fault of his; he had sent Lord Dartmouth every resource except wind. James was sitting for a portrait for Pepys when he heard that William of Orange had invaded his kingdom. Pepys was among those who witnessed the king's will at Whitehall on 17 November, and in the afternoon he went with him to Windsor. He chose this moment to ask to be paid for his

past services; James wrote him what amounted to a dud blank cheque, which Pepys optimistically filled in for £28,007 2s. 1¼d. In the final days of the reign Pepys arranged for the escape of the queen and the prince of Wales; he had no involvement in the king's confused withdrawal. The provisional government which assembled on 11 December ordered an end to hostilities, and Pepys transmitted this instruction to Dartmouth; he may thereby be said to have signalled the end of the Fourth Anglo-Dutch War. Four days later Pepys attended the junta at Whitehall and advised on procedure for stopping the ports. On 19 December he was sent for by the prince of Orange and asked to stay in post, to which he agreed. At this point it was still possible to accept the prince as head of government without compromising allegiance to the head of state.

Pepys was confident of securing election for Harwich in the Convention Parliament summoned for 22 January 1689, but at the poll on the 16th he was defeated by the whig candidate. The accession of the Oranges on 13 February was followed by a comprehensive purge of officeholders; it is unlikely that Pepys would have been retained at the Admiralty even if (as was not the case) he had been prepared to swear allegiance to the new rulers. His last office business was done on 22 February, though he dated his resignation two days earlier. This time he managed to keep his house, York Buildings, by the simple tactic of not moving when the incoming Admiralty claimed it as an official residence. From 5 May to 15 June he was, along with Hewer and Deane, detained by a king's messenger on suspicion of treason against the new government. On 25 June 1690, when a French fleet stood menacingly in the channel, Pepys was imprisoned in the Westminster gatehouse; his release on medical grounds was ordered on 14 July. He did in fact suffer a return of his old kidney and eyesight troubles, but these did not impede an active retirement.

Last years, transcription of the diary, and reputation At first Pepys had some thought of ending his days as the country squire he had occasionally affected to be, but he decided he was not yet tired of London. The several institutions in which he was already well established—the Royal Society, Trinity House, Christ's Hospital, and the Clothworkers' Company—offered plentiful opportunities for social and intellectual pleasure. Above all he gave his time to his library and to scholarly enquiry. He was already a bibliophile in the diary years. Some books he acquired for their beauty or curiosity, or because they were the right thing to have, but for the most part what he bought he also read. Among contemporary authors Thomas Fuller was his favourite, and of the poets, Chaucer, while in a count of titles Robert Boyle has prime position. Pepys's lifelong enthusiasms for drama and music are well represented. He read French, Spanish, and Italian, and his library reflected this competence. He rarely wrote in his books, and the instances therefore invite attention: he bound Sternhold and Hopkins with Skelton to demonstrate that the metrical psalter compared well with 'the highest … secular poetry of that time' (Magd. Cam., Pepys Library, MS 228).

In 1666 Pepys had a dockyard joiner, Thomas Simpson, make the first of twelve glass-fronted book presses. Arranging the collection became a great hobby, and in his retirement he was able to employ library assistants, principally the translator Paul Lorrain. The books were shelved and numbered in order of ascending size; cataloguing and indexing the collection therefore became progressively more complex. Disappointingly as it now seems, Pepys often discarded older books as new ones were acquired, or as space in the presses determined. His nephew and eventual heir, John Jackson, helped to bring the collection to its target of 3000 volumes. Jackson was the younger son of Pepys's sister Paulina; the elder nephew, Samuel, all but wrote himself out of Pepys's will, but John proved an appreciative substitute. He was sent to Magdalene, and then to France and Italy—a trip which Pepys would have liked to make, but could now enjoy only vicariously. In particular Jackson was commissioned to bring back further treasures for the library.

Pepys's collection became well known, and was sought out by scholars. His manuscripts (then numbering 129) were listed in Edward Bernard's *Catalogi ... Angliae et Hiberniae* (1697), although Pepys had to be persuaded to allow the entry. He corresponded occasionally with some of the greatest men of his day (Newton, Dryden, Sloane), and prolifically with academics such as Humfrey Wanley, Arthur Charlett, and his kinsman Thomas Gale. While he kept in touch with Cambridge and Magdalene, and subscribed to the new building in his old college, most of his learned friends were now at Oxford. One such was the mathematician John Wallis, whose portrait Pepys commissioned from Kneller and gave to the university; in return he received a diploma from the public orator (29 October 1702). Chief among these elevated exchanges was his correspondence with Evelyn, which now literally fills a book. Their association, which had begun at a professional level during the 1660s, had developed into one of warm mutual regard. Evelyn came to represent the ideal gentleman-scholar which the retired Pepys aspired to be. Pepys had long intended to compile a naval history: the idea seems to have begun in 1664, when Coventry suggested he should write an account of the First Anglo-Dutch War. The scale of the proposed work gradually lengthened, and many books and notes were acquired with this distant prospect in view. Enforced leisure from 1679 to 1684 had allowed for further research, Evelyn providing much arcane knowledge from his own store. Pepys's renewed leisure, ample means, and reasonable health during the 1690s seemed likely to generate the great work, but it never came. The *Memoires* of 1690 were his only publication. The subsequently printed *Naval Minutes*, a commonplace book of matters historical and contemporary, gives some hint of the scope though not the arrangement of Pepys's intended survey.

In the last years of his life Pepys stayed frequently with Hewer at the grand house he now owned in Clapham. From 1701 he lived there permanently, and it was there that he died on 26 May 1703. On 4 June he was buried at St Olave, Hart Street; the archbishop of Canterbury and the bishop of London were present, but it was one of Pepys's circle, the nonjuring bishop of Thetford, George Hickes, who officiated.

Pepys left an annuity of £200, together with much plate, pictures, and other possessions, to Mary Skinner, acknowledging her 'steddy friendship and assistances' during the previous thirty-three years (Wheatley, *Pepysiana*, 262). Samuel Jackson received a token annuity of £40. The only property Pepys owned was the Brampton house with its 74 acres. Much of his will concerned investment of the hypothetical £28,007 which he still claimed from the crown, and which he fondly hoped would be settled on his heirs. John Jackson was the residuary legatee, and he inherited the library for his lifetime. Following Pepys's instructions, Jackson completed a few sets of volumes, and finished the catalogue. On Jackson's death in 1724, the collection passed to Magdalene where, as Pepys had stipulated, it was to be kept wholly apart from the college's other books. The convoy of wagons which took the 3000 books and their twelve presses to Cambridge was a sealed train carrying Pepys's reputation to posterity. His name was not forgotten in the navy, where many of his 'establishments' and administrative practices remained in use into Nelson's era and beyond; Barham in particular spoke highly of him. It was known that his library was rich in maritime history and other scholarly matters, but that it might contain more was unsuspected.

The seemingly impenetrable shorthand of the six volumes marked 'journal' discouraged examination until, it seems, the successful publication of Evelyn's diary (1818) prompted Magdalene to have Pepys's manuscript deciphered. An impecunious undergraduate of neighbouring St John's College, John Smith, was hired, and learned the characters by comparing Pepys's shorthand of Charles II's escape story with the longhand version. He did not know that the manual for the system, Thomas Shelton's *Tutor to Tachygraphy* (1642), was in the library. A first selection from the revealed text was published in 1825, edited by the third Lord Braybrooke, hereditary visitor of the college. The project was a great success, prompting progressively fuller editions. H. B. Wheatley's edition (1893–9) was complete save for what the *Dictionary of National Biography* confidently dismissed as 'passages which cannot possibly be printed'. The edition by Robert Latham and William Matthews (1970–83), based on a new transcription, at last provided the whole text, and corrected many other deficiencies in the previous versions. Meanwhile Pepys's professional achievements have become better known from the publication by the Navy Records Society of several of his other writings.

Pepys has thereby achieved something of a split reputation. Sometimes his professional career has not been taken seriously because of the hedonistic image perceived from the diary. Conversely those to whom the Pepys of the diary is sympathetic can be disappointed by all else that he wrote, and conclude that after 1669 his genius left him. However much his later life is examined, it is the diary which has made him famous, and from which he will be judged. Much has been made of the blemishes of character which the diary reveals, though the frankness of his confessions has generally brought absolution. Pepys is a persuasive companion, and because when he speaks directly to his reader he is so palpably honest, he can seem to have the right of every argument. There is a powerful personality at work here, but also great art. As a diarist he is simply the best there was, with the good fortune to be close to the centre of momentous events. He has the continuing compliment of countless imitators; he is commemorated in a good few hostelries, and in the activities of the club which bears his name. Not quite everyone has been seduced by his charm, but in the glass he holds up few can have found no reflection.   C. S. KNIGHTON

Sources Pepys, Diary · Private correspondence and miscellaneous papers of Samuel Pepys, 1679-1703, ed. J. R. Tanner, 2 vols. (1926) · Further correspondence of Samuel Pepys, 1662-1679, ed. J. R. Tanner (1929) · Letters and the second diary of Samuel Pepys, ed. R. G. Howarth (1933) · H. T. Heath, ed., The letters of Samuel Pepys and his family circle (1955) · The shorthand letters of Samuel Pepys, ed. E. Chappell (1933) · G. de la Bédoyère, ed., Particular friends: the correspondence of Samuel Pepys and John Evelyn (1997) · J. R. Tanner, ed., A descriptive catalogue of the naval manuscripts in the Pepysian library at Magdalene College, Cambridge, Navy Records Society, 26-7, 36, 57 (1903-23) · Samuel Pepys's naval minutes, ed. J. R. Tanner, Navy Records Society, 60 (1926) · The Tangier papers of Samuel Pepys, ed. E. Chappell, Navy RS, 73 (1935) · Samuel Pepys and the Second Dutch War: Pepys's navy white book and Brooke House papers, ed. R. Latham, Navy RS, 133 (1995) [transcribed by W. Matthews and C. Knighton] · R. C. Latham, ed., Catalogue of the Pepys Library at Magdalene College, Cambridge, 8 vols. (1978-94) · S. Pepys, Memoires of the Royal Navy, 1679-1688 (1690); repr. J. R. Tanner, ed. (1906) · A. Bryant, Samuel Pepys: the man in the making (1933) · A. Bryant, Samuel Pepys: the years of peril (1935) · A. Bryant, Samuel Pepys: the saviour of the navy (1947); concluding part reissued as Pepys and the revolution (1979) · R. Ollard, Pepys, a biography (1974) · HoP, Commons, 1660-90, 3.226-8 · B. McL. Raft, 'The significance of the political career of Samuel Pepys', Journal of Modern History, 24 (1952), 368-75 · J. D. Davies, 'Pepys and the admiralty commission of 1679-84', Historical Research, 62 (1989), 34-53 · J. R. Tanner, Samuel Pepys and the Royal Navy (1920) · J. R. Tanner, Mr Pepys: an introduction to the diary together with a sketch of his later life (1925) · E. Chappell, Samuel Pepys as a naval administrator (1933) · Calendar of the manuscripts of the marquess of Ormonde, new ser., 8 vols., HMC, 36 (1902-20), vol. 4, pp. 431, 507, 509, 515 · diaries and papers, Magd. Cam., Pepys Library · H. B. Wheatley, Pepysiana (1899), 251-70 · C. Tomalin, Samuel Pepys: the unequalled self (2002)

Archives BL, corresp. and papers, Add. MSS 38849, 39822; RP 555, 2903, 3910, 3918 · Bodl. Oxf., journal and papers · Bodl. Oxf., personal and official corresp. · GL, corresp. and papers relating to work at the Admiralty · Harvard U., Houghton L., letter-book and papers · Magd. Cam., diaries, political and naval papers, literary, historical, scientific and musical MSS, and printed books · NMM, letters and papers · NMM, corresp.; official letter-book · NRA, literary MSS and papers · NRA, corresp. and papers · NRA, priv. coll., papers relating to money owed for services to the Admiralty | BL, corresp. relating to Christ's Hospital, Add. MS 20732 · BL, letters to Sir Hans Sloane, Sloane MSS 4037-4039, 4060 · Bodl. Oxf., corresp. with Thomas Baker · Bodl. Oxf., letters to Martin Lister · Bodl. Oxf., letter-book relating to Captain Scott · Bodl. Oxf., letters to Thomas Smith · Christ Church Oxf., letters to John Evelyn · Hist. Soc. Penn., papers · Morgan L., papers · Princeton University Library, papers · PRO, state papers domestic, SP 29, 31, 46 · PRO, Admiralty papers, ADM 1, 2, 3, 106 etc. · Ransom HRC, papers · U. Cal., Los Angeles, William Andrews Clark Memorial Library, papers · Yale U., Beinecke L., letters to Lord Dartmouth

Likenesses J. Hayls, oils, 1666, NPG [see illus.] · attrib. J. Greenhill, oils, c.1673, Magd. Cam. · A. Verrio, group portrait, fresco, 1682

(James II and his court), Christ's Hospital, Horsham, Sussex · G. Kneller, oils, c.1682-1686, repro. in Ollard, Pepys, facing p. 144 · G. Kneller, oils, c.1682-1706, NMM; version, RS · oils, c.1685, Magd. Cam.; repro. in Mariner's Mirror, 86 (2000), 149 · J. Cavalier, ivory medallion, 1688, Worshipful Company of Clothworkers; repro. in G. Trease, Samuel Pepys and his world (1972), 106 · J. Closterman, oils, after 1689, NPG; repro. in Ollard, Pepys, facing p. 304 · attrib. J. Closterman, oils, c.1695, NPG · A. Blomfield, marble bust on monument, 1884, St Olave's, Hart Street, London; repro. in G. Trease, Samuel Pepys and his world (1972), 116 · R. White, engraving (after Kneller), repro. in Pepys, Memoires, frontispiece · oils, Magd. Cam.

Pepys, William Hasledine (1775-1856), surgical instrument maker and natural philosopher, was born on 23 March 1775, one of two surviving sons of William Hasledine Pepys (1748-1805), cutler and surgical instrument maker of the Poultry, London, and his wife, Letitia Weedon. The family claimed descent from Sir Richard Pepys (1588-1659), lord chief justice of Ireland. Nothing is known of Pepys's education, but he was among the group of young men interested in the new sciences who founded in 1796 the Askesian Society. He was a founder in 1805 and first secretary of the London Institution, and active in the British Mineralogical Society, founded in 1799, which in 1807 merged with the Askesian Society to form the Geological Society of London. Pepys was active and held office in all these groups; his skill in building apparatus for chemical and electrochemical investigations was important in advancing the sciences which underpinned the members' interests. An autobiographical note relates, 'The first experiments I made were in the early part of my life. I commenced with fermentations ... the methods required for their production brought me acquainted with gaseous fluids, and a great field was opened to me ... one experiment suggested another, and in the pursuit, discoveries were made that were not expected' (Royal Society, MS 155). When the new metal platinum was finding its way into scientific instrument workshops Pepys and his friends in the Mineralogical Society undertook electrical experiments with it. In May 1805 Pepys made up a platinum fruit knife which he presented to Sir Joseph Banks, and in June he presented two similar knives to George III.

Pepys succeeded to his father's business and extended it to scientific instrument making. He followed his father in the Cutlers' Company, becoming twice master during the 1820s, and he was in later years a benefactor to the Cutlers' charities. His work and interests brought him into contact with several Quaker scientists, notably William Allen and Luke Howard, though Pepys himself was a lifelong practising Anglican. With Allen he developed apparatus for researches into respiration in man, animals, and plants, which laid the basis for understanding the chemistry of that process. Mineralogy led him to the blowpipe for analysis of various minerals and of human teeth. In the new field of electrical technology Pepys investigated atmospheric electricity with Howard, delved into magnetism with Humphry Davy and others, and undertook the construction of several large batteries which he made available for electromagnetic researches.

Pepys married, on 21 September 1815 at Waltham Abbey, Lydia (*d.* 1851), an under-age daughter of Robert Walton. They had seven children: five daughters, of whom two died young, and two sons; William Hasledine Pepys (1817–1880) settled in Cologne and Robert Edmond (1819–1883) continued the business until 1863 when the Poultry shops were demolished for redevelopment.

Pepys enjoyed a long and influential relationship with the Royal Institution, from the time when Count Rumford proposed him as a proprietor in 1800 until 1846. Thereafter he served on the permanent committee set up to deal with chemical investigations undertaken in the institution's laboratory. In 1812 he directed John Newman, the institution's instrument maker, in a comprehensive overhaul of the institution's apparatus and the purchase of necessary new items. In 1814 he was elected as a visitor, in 1815 a manager, and in 1821 he became its secretary. In 1828 he joined the committee for regulating the discourses and lectures, and in 1830 the accounts committee. In February 1830 the institution awarded him the Fuller gold medal for his chemical researches and improvement of chemical apparatus. Pepys's experiments lacked originality but he was adept at devising and constructing apparatus. He was among the first to use mercury contacts for electrical apparatus, and to employ rubber-coated tubes for conveying gas. His eudiometer, air-holder, and mercury gasometer had proved useful for research into the constitution of air and gases, his researches into combustion of diamond, graphite, charcoal, and various metallic ores had commercial potential, and his work with Allen on respiration contributed to medical knowledge.

The London Institution, modelled on the Royal Institution, was established in 1805, its proprietors drawn from trade and industry. At first it offered members only a library, but in 1819 it moved into new purpose-built premises in Finsbury Circus, with a laboratory designed and equipped by Pepys, and he carried out many of his investigations there. He designed its great battery, built up from 2000 double plates. From 1819 until its plates finally corroded in 1835 it was used by other scientists, Davy and Brande among them, for experiments and demonstrations. In 1823 Pepys designed a huge single cell for the London Institution, each plate measuring 50 by 2 feet.

Pepys was elected FRS in 1808 and he published occasionally in the *Philosophical Transactions*, but the majority of his numerous articles appeared in Tilloch's *Philosophical Magazine*. He was elected to the Society of Arts in 1801, and served on its chemistry committee from 1850. He was a member of the Pitt Club from 1822, of the Royal Asiatic Society from 1823, and was also a member of the Athenaeum. Pepys died at his house in Earl's Terrace, Kensington, London, on 17 August 1856.   ANITA McCONNELL

Sources W. C. Pepys, *Genealogy of the Pepys family, 1273–1887* (1887) · RS, MS 155 · J. Golinski, *Science as public culture: chemistry and enlightenment in Britain, 1760–1820* (1992) · L. C. Ockenden, 'The great batteries of the London Institution', *Annals of Science*, 2 (1937), 183–4 · I. Inkster, 'Science and society in the metropolis: a preliminary examination of the social and institutional context of the Askesian Society of London, 1796–1807', *Annals of Science*, 34 (1977),

1–32 · managers' minutes, vols. 2–9 (1800–02, 1837–47), Royal Institution of Great Britain, London · Pepys correspondence, Royal Institution of Great Britain, London · will, PRO, PROB 11/2239, sig. 712 · C. Welch, *History of the Cutlers' Company of London*, 2 vols. (1923), vol. 2 · P. Weindling, 'The British Mineralogical Society: a case study in science and social improvement', *Metropolis and province: science in British culture, 1780–1850*, ed. I. Inkster and J. Morrell (1983), 120–50 · P. J. Weindling, 'A platinum gift to King George III: a gesture by William Hasledine Pepys, cutler and instrument maker', *Platinum Metals Review*, 26/1 (1982), 32–7 · F. Kurzer, 'William Hasledine Pepys FRS: a life in scientific research, learned societies and technical enterprise', *Annals of Science*, 60 (2003), 137–83 · *DNB*

Archives Royal Institution of Great Britain, London, corresp. and papers

Likenesses lithograph (after Walter), BM, NPG; repro. in *Athenaeum Portraits* (1836)

Pepys, Sir William Weller, first baronet (1740–1825), writer and literary scholar, was born on 11 January 1740, the elder son of William Pepys (*d.* 1743), banker, of Lombard Street, and his wife, Hannah Weller, *née* Russell (*d.* 1761). Pepys was taught at Eton College by Edward Barnard, and matriculated on 20 November 1758 from Christ Church, Oxford, where he became known as 'the Old Gentleman'. Despite ill health and eye trouble, for which he was treated at Bath, he took the degrees of BA in 1763 and MA in 1766. He had been admitted to Lincoln's Inn on 23 April 1760 and was called to the bar on 16 June 1766. In 1775 he became a master in chancery. He married Elizabeth (*c.*1748–1830), daughter of William Dowdeswell, on 21 June 1777. Their first son, William Weller, was born in 1778, followed by Maria Elizabeth (*b.* 1779), Charles Christopher (*b.* 1781), Henry (*b.* 1783), Isabella Sophia (*b.* 1785), and Anne Louisa (*b.* 1789). Their impeccable happiness as a family was remarked by observers such as Hester Chapone, Elizabeth Montagu, and Fanny Burney. Pepys describes a typical day of his summer residence at Tunbridge Wells in 1783:

> I rise at six, read or write till twelve. Get delightful rides. Come home very hungry. Walk out with Eliza and children to fly their kite till near dark. Take an hour of the best chat can get in the rooms, and home to bed soon after ten.   (*Later Pepys*, 2.236)

Pepys involved himself in charitable work and a ward in the Middlesex Hospital was named after him. He was a well-known member of the Streatham and Blue Stocking circles. In October 1776 he wrote some verses in praise of learned women to Henry Thrale on his wedding anniversary, which Hester Thrale copied into *Thraliana*. In June 1777 she wrote:

> Mr Pepys … is one of my great favourites … a Man of Virtue, a Man of Learning, a Man pious, frugal, charitable and kind: has a great many Anecdotes, to enliven his Talk, and dresses gayly to set off his Person.

She also thought 'his Person though is still mean, and his Talk artificial; his Struggles to gain Admiration are too apparent' (Piozzi, *Thraliana*, 56–7). Her journal shows a continuing struggle to assess her feelings about Pepys. She named him as one of the executors to Thrale's will, with a particular concern for the care of her daughters, but he declined. In one of the fictional dialogues on her death Mrs Thrale made Pepys converse with Johnson in a way which accentuated his vanity. In January 1782 she decided 'Pepys is a worthless Fellow at last' (ibid., 526). Dr Johnson resented Pepys's whig politics, his superficiality of manner, and his closeness to Mrs Thrale, who recorded Johnson's declaration after an argument about Ovid that 'I knew the dog was a scholar … but that he had so much taste and so much knowledge I did *not* believe.' She goes on: 'He did not however cordially love Mr. Pepys, though he respected his abilities' (Piozzi, *Anecdotes*, 108). Matters came to a head during the controversy over Johnson's disparaging *Life* of Lord Lyttleton, which was much resented by the Blue Stocking circle. Johnson found Pepys at Streatham and challenged him to argue his case in an 'unreasonably furious and grossly severe' manner, his resentment bursting forth 'with a vehemence and bitterness almost incredible'. Pepys, however, 'never appeared to so much advantage' and Johnson himself acknowledged that Pepys behaved nobly (*Diary … of Madame D'Arblay*, 2.31–2). Pepys records that subsequently Johnson 'did all in his power to show me that he was sorry for the former attack' (*Johnsonian Miscellanies*, 2.416). But in another dispute at Brighton in 1782 Pepys 'was so roughly confuted, and so severely ridiculed, that he was hurt and piqued beyond all power of disguise', and left the party abruptly (*Diary … of Madame D'Arblay*, 2.132).

Horace Walpole was on visiting terms with Pepys from 1789, when Pepys negotiated a lease on a manor house at Teddington; Walpole reports that during their move most of the family's belongings were stolen after the boatman cut them loose in a storm. But Pepys's most enduring friendships were with women, especially Hannah More and Fanny Burney, who was puzzled at his attempts to contrive meetings between her and George Owen Cambridge, but who forgave her 'old friend—& ci-devant persecutor' his 'tormenting tricks and watchings', choosing to regard them as well-intentioned (*Journals and Letters*, 4.180). In 1799 Mrs Chapone wrote to her to praise 'that excellent man … whose worthy heart you do not half know, & whom compassion has improved from a delightful companion & intimate old acquaintance to the most tender, attentive, and affectionate son to me' (ibid., 4.272n.).

On 23 June 1801 Pepys was created baronet. In 1805 he resigned from chancery, and in 1809 founded the Alfred Club. On 29 July 1813 he made out a long and elaborate will (PRO, PROB 11/1701/335) in which the paternal estate of Ridley Hall, Cheshire, was assigned to trustees for the use of his eldest son, who also received his papers, books, pictures, and a watch to commemorate 'the many happy hours it has pleased God to permit us to pass together'. He assigned funds for the purchase of land to support the other children, making several late codicils on their behalf. He wrote to Hannah More in 1820:

> Here am I, pass'd *fourscore*, in perfect health, with the same relish for books, conversation, and music, that I ever had; surrounded by children, who have turn'd out every thing that the fondest parent cou'd desire, with the very singular comfort of having my most intimate friend, in the person of my eldest son, who is my constant and most delightful companion! (*Later Pepys*, 2.338)

He contributed his Thrale verses (and some money) to *A Collection of Poems* (1823) edited by Joanna Baillie for charitable purposes; he was vice-president of the Literary Fund Society; he was involved in the first edition of Samuel Pepys's diary (1825). Burney recorded in 1821 that he 'has a constancy in his attachments as rare as it is honourable' (*Journals and Letters*, 11.207); her 'old Intimate Blue-Crony' continued to visit until three weeks before he died, on 2 June 1825, at his house in Gloucester Place. He was buried in the family vault in Totteridge churchyard, Hertfordshire. Selections from his correspondence were published in *A Later Pepys* (2 vols., 1904); the most interesting exchanges are those on literary and political subjects with Hannah More, who had included a portrait of him under the name 'Lelius' in her *Bas bleu* (1786). His portrait was painted by H. Thomson RA in 1808. PAUL BAINES

Sources A. C. C. Gaussen, *A later Pepys: the correspondence of Sir William Weller Pepys … master in chancery, 1758–1825*, 2 vols. (1904) • W. C. Pepys, *Genealogy of the Pepys family* (1952) • *Diary and letter of Madame D'Arblay*, ed. [C. Barrett], new edn, 7 vols. (1854), vol. 2 • *The journals and letters of Fanny Burney (Madame D'Arblay)*, ed. J. Hemlow and others, 12 vols. (1972–84) • *Thraliana: the diary of Mrs. Hester Lynch Thrale (later Mrs. Piozzi), 1776–1809*, ed. K. C. Balderston, 2nd edn, 2 vols. (1951) • H. L. Piozzi, *Anecdotes of the late Samuel Johnson*, ed. A. Sherbo (1974) • *Johnsonian miscellanies*, ed. G. B. Hill, 2 vols. (1897) • Walpole, *Corr.* • W. P. Baildon, ed., *The records of the Honorable Society of Lincoln's Inn: admissions*, 1 (1896) • W. P. Baildon, ed., *The records of the Honorable Society of Lincoln's Inn: the black books*, 3 (1899) • *Annual Register* (1826), 255 • *The letters of Samuel Johnson*, ed. B. Redford, 5 vols. (1992–4) • Foster, *Alum. Oxon.*

Archives BL, corresp., Stowe MS 754, fol. 131; Add. MSS 40862, fol. 87, 34412, fol. 315 | Herts. ALS, corresp. with William Franks • Hunt. L., letters to Elizabeth Montagu • JRL, Piozzi papers

Likenesses H. Thomson, oils, repro. in Gaussen, ed., *Later Pepys*; priv. coll.

Wealth at death bequeathed several thousand pounds in mourning gifts and other monetary gifts of stock, etc.; paternal estate (entailed) at Ridley Hall, Cheshire: will, PRO, PROB 11/1701, sig. 335

Perbroun [Perburn], **John** (d. 1342/3), merchant, was the son of Robert Perbroun of Great Yarmouth, Norfolk. The town was the centre of the internationally important herring trade in England and also a port that enjoyed a diversified trade with Bordeaux and other Atlantic and North Sea centres. John Perbroun became involved in all the trades underpinning the town's wealth. Between 1320 and 1324 his dealings in wine were worth at least £122 6s. 8d., and with those of his partners £696 11s. 2d. His purchase, with Herman Breton, a fellow burgess, of goods worth £340 4s. 6d. in 1323–4 for the purposes of trade indicates the scale of his activity at this time. His main involvement in the herring trade was as a host (surety) for foreign fishermen and as an owner of fishing boats, of which he had at least seven in 1337, and a fish house. He also dealt in wool, and owned at least four merchant ships.

Perbroun held many urban offices. At any one time Great Yarmouth had four bailiffs, and between 1312 and 1339 Perbroun served fifteen times as one of them. He was collector of murage in 1338–9, MP in 1322 and 1323, and represented the town at merchant assemblies, summoned by the crown for the negotiation of taxes on wool, in 1327 and 1340. Moreover, as a successful merchant and shipowner, he was an obvious choice for certain royal offices, including that of admiral, the official responsible for the impressment of shipping for the king's wars. Perbroun held this office north of the Thames at least eight times between 1317 and 1341. As admiral he received a regular income and, in 1334, a royal gift of £100. He was deputy to the king's butler at Yarmouth in 1323, collector of royal customs there in 1330–33 and 1334–41, and, with Thomas Drayton, a fellow burgess, farmer of the customs in 1333–4. It is difficult not to conclude that service as admiral gave him easier access to further offices.

Perbroun's career was not without its dangers and blemishes. In 1314, when he was town bailiff, hostility from the rival settlement of Little Yarmouth forced him to take refuge for a time at sea. In 1327 he supported Prince Edward against his father, and was subsequently pardoned for acquiescence in Mortimer's rule. In 1333 he defaulted on sums due from customs accounts, and the king was still seeking redress in 1343, after Perbroun's death. He was both a victim of piracy and a perpetrator of it. In general, however, he prospered, and in 1332 he was taxed at £3 for the subsidy on moveables, 50 per cent more than the next wealthiest burgess. In the next year his property in Yarmouth was valued at £8 0s. 7d. per annum. The sum points to a substantial but not unduly large investment in real property and suggests that much of his capital was tied up in his ships and merchandise. Perbroun had two brothers, and when he died, in 1342 or 1343, was succeeded by three sons and a daughter; his eldest son, Farman, who was taxed at 4s. in 1332, had three sons and four daughters. Farman, however, was impoverished in the late 1340s and died of the black death in 1348–9. No Perbroun is mentioned in Yarmouth after 1364, and with the exception of Roger Perbroun, who held church livings at Howe, Brandon, and Hemsby (all in Norfolk), and who may have been related to John, no member of the family can be traced after this time in rural Norfolk or Suffolk. Unlike some other influential families, such as the Elyses, Draytons, and Fastolfs, the Perbrouns failed to establish themselves as either an urban or a rural dynasty. The fortunes of the Perbrouns, bound up in shipping and the herring trade, provide a mirror of those of Great Yarmouth more generally. Prosperity in the late thirteenth century, and the early decades of the fourteenth, was followed by misfortune and decline, started by the Hundred Years' War and accentuated by the black death. A. SAUL

Sources A. Saul, 'Great Yarmouth in the fourteenth century: a study in trade, politics and society', DPhil diss., U. Oxf., 1975 · court rolls, Yarmouth, Norfolk RO · *Chancery records* · PRO, exchequer, king's remembrancer, E 101 [Accounts various] · PRO, exchequer, lord treasurer's remembrancer, E 356 [Enrolled customs accounts] · *RotP*, vols. 1–2 · *RotS*, vol. 1
Archives Norfolk RO, Yarmouth court rolls

Perceval, Alexander (1787–1858), politician and serjeant-at-arms of the House of Lords, was born on 10 February 1787 at Temple House, Ballymote, co. Sligo, the second son

and eventual heir of the Revd Philip Perceval, who succeeded his elder brother Guy Carleton Perceval in the family estates in 1792, and his wife, Anne, daughter of Alexander Carroll of Dublin. The first of the family to migrate from Somerset to Ireland had been Richard *Perceval (c.1558–1620), who as the confidential agent of Lord Burghley was credited with deciphering the communications which gave the first intelligence of the Armada. Philip Perceval had died by the time his son Alexander entered Trinity College, Dublin, on 7 November 1803 (Burtchaell & Sadleir, *Alum. Dubl.*, 662); the latter's landed inheritance in co. Sligo, where he largely resided, was a substantial one, and he later became an active justice of the peace. On 11 February 1808, the day after he came of age, Perceval married Jane Anne (d. 1847), eldest daughter of Colonel Henry Peisley L'Estrange of Moystown, King's county. They had a large family, of whom four sons and six daughters survived to adulthood.

Perceval was lieutenant-colonel of the Sligo militia from 1809 until 1851. At the general election of 1831 he was returned to parliament for co. Sligo after a contest. He was re-elected unopposed in 1832 and 1835, was again victorious in a contest in 1837, and came in without opposition in 1841. As 'an earnest and zealous Conservative' (*GM*, 3rd ser., 6, 1859, 209), he opposed the Grey ministry's reform bills, and as a member of the Orange Association of Ireland he was in the minority against the grant to the Catholic college of Maynooth of 26 September 1831. In January and February 1832 he was prominent in successful protests in the Commons against the practice whereby the Irish lord chancellor exacted fees from justices of the peace for the renewal of their commissions on a demise of the crown (*Hansard 3*, 9.794, 10.33–45). A founder member of the Carlton Club in March 1832 (*The Times*, 10 March 1832), he was treasurer of the ordnance in Sir Robert Peel's first administration from December 1834 until April 1835. The following year he acquiesced and aided in the dissolution of the Orange Association, of which he was by then treasurer, at the behest of the Melbourne ministry (BL, Add. MS 40424, fol. 267). During his ten-year Commons career he was a regular speaker, mostly on Irish subjects: some 500 interventions by him were reported. When Peel formed his second administration in September 1841 he appointed Perceval a lord of the Treasury, having been unable to effect a preferred arrangement to place him in the household (BL, Add. MS 40487, fol. 356). Perceval held the post for only twelve days before replacing Admiral Sir George Seymour as serjeant-at-arms of the House of Lords, which obliged him to relinquish his seat.

Perceval, who was created a DCL of the University of Oxford on 13 June 1834, served the upper house capably for more than seventeen years until his death, after 'two attacks of paralysis', at his home, 28 Chester Street, London, on 9 December 1858. He was described in an obituary as 'a highly educated gentleman, full of Irish humour and well-told anecdote', whose 'temper was one of deep unfeigned devotion' (*GM*, 3rd ser., 6, 1859, 209).

D. R. FISHER

Sources *GM*, 3rd ser., 6 (1859), 209 • Burke, *Gen. Ire.* (1976), 946–8 • Burke, *Gen. GB* (1886), 1448 • Burtchaell & Sadleir, *Alum. Dubl.*, 2nd edn, 662 • *Hansard 3* (1832), 9.794; 10.33–45 • *The Times* (10 March 1832) • BL, Add. MSS, 40424, fol. 267; 40487, fol. 356 • [H. T. Ryall], *Portraits of eminent conservatives and statesmen*, 2 [1846] • *DNB*
Archives BL, corresp. with Sir Robert Peel, Add. MSS 40239, fol. 122; 40424, fol. 207; 40487, fol. 356; 40515, fols. 149, 151
Likenesses G. Hayter, group portrait, oils (*The House of Commons, 1833*), NPG • Jenkinson, stipple, BM, NPG • portrait, repro. in Ryall, *Portraits of eminent conservatives*, xi
Wealth at death under £3000: probate, 1859, *CGPLA Ire.* • under £300—in England: probate, 20 Jan 1859, *CGPLA Eng. & Wales*

Perceval, Arthur Philip (1799–1853), Church of England clergyman and religious writer, was born on 22 November 1799, the fifth and youngest son of Charles George *Perceval, second Baron Arden (1756–1840), and his wife, Margaretta Elizabeth (1768–1851), eldest daughter of Sir Thomas Spencer Wilson, baronet. He entered Oriel College, Oxford, on 19 March 1817, graduating BA in 1820 and BCL in 1824; from 1821 to 1825 he was a fellow of All Souls College, Oxford. On 18 June 1824 he was appointed rector of East Horsley, Surrey, and on 15 December 1825 he married Charlotte Anne (*d.* 21 June 1856), eldest daughter of the Revd Augustus George Legge, fifth son of William, second earl of Dartmouth. They had three sons and two daughters.

In 1826 Perceval became chaplain to George IV, and continued as royal chaplain to William IV and Queen Victoria until October 1850, when he was deprived of his appointment for his opposition to the Gorham judgment. He was involved with the Oxford Movement from its beginnings in 1833 and was the author of numbers 23, 35, and 36 of *Tracts for the Times*. In 1841 he published a *Vindication of the Authors of the Tracts for the Times*, which particularly defended J. H. Newman against the attacks made on his Tract 90, and on 24 July 1838, when preaching as royal chaplain at the Chapel Royal, St James's, he advocated high-church principles before the queen, to her irritation. Bishop Blomfield of London, who was aware of Perceval's intention, was said to have preached for several Sundays in order to keep Perceval out of the pulpit; but when the bishop broke his collarbone Perceval found his opportunity (*Greville Memoirs*, 1.116).

Perceval was a prolific author, and his published works, though mainly composed of letters, sermons, and pamphlets, fill three pages in the British Library catalogue. Among the most characteristic are *The Roman Schism Illustrated from the Records of the Catholic Church* (1836), *Sermons Preached Chiefly at the Chapel Royal, St James's* (1839), *An Apology for the Doctrine of Apostolical Succession* (1839), and *A Collection of Papers Connected with the Theological Movement of 1833* (1842). Although a dedicated high-churchman, Perceval gradually distanced himself from the Oxford Movement. He died on 11 June 1853 at Little Bookham, Surrey, from an overdose of laudanum (*GM*, 208).

A. F. POLLARD, *rev.* DAVID HUDDLESTON

Sources Burke, *Peerage* (1970) • S. L. Ollard, *A short history of the Oxford Movement* (1915) • H. P. Liddon, *The life of Edward Bouverie Pusey*, ed. J. O. Johnston and others, 4 vols. (1893–7), vol. 1, p. 264; vol. 2, p. 178 • *GM*, 2nd ser., 40 (1853), 208 • *The Greville memoirs*, ed. H. Reeve, pt 2, vol. 2 (1885), 116–17 • Foster, *Alum. Oxon.* • Allibone, *Dict.* • J. Foster, ed., *Index ecclesiasticus, or, Alphabetical lists of all ecclesiastical dignitaries in England and Wales since the Reformation* (1890), 138 • E. G. K. Browne, *History of the Tractarian movement* (1856)
Archives BL, letters to Sir Robert Peel, Add. MSS 40417–40590 • Hants. RO, letters to William Heathcote, fifth baronet

Perceval, Charles George, second Baron Arden in the peerage of Ireland, and first Baron Arden in the peerage of the United Kingdom (1756–1840), politician, was born on 1 October 1756 at Charlton, Kent, the eldest son of John *Perceval, second earl of Egmont (1711–1770), landowner and politician, and his second wife, Catherine (1731–1784), the daughter of the Hon. Charles Compton. He had four sisters, and six brothers, the youngest of whom was Spencer *Perceval, the future prime minister. Their mother was created Baroness Arden in the Irish peerage in 1770, and following her death in 1784 Perceval succeeded as second Baron Arden; he took his seat in the Irish Lords in 1787. He was educated at Harrow School (1771–4), and at Trinity College, Cambridge (1774–7), whence he proceeded MA in 1777; he entered Lincoln's Inn in the same year.

Perceval was elected to the Commons on 28 November 1780 as MP for Launceston on the duke of Northumberland's interest. A supporter of North's administration, on 27 November 1781 he moved the address. He opposed North's successors until he was appointed a lord of the Admiralty by his friend Pitt, who became premier in December 1783. Despite having several times vocally opposed electoral reform, he voted for Pitt's proposals for parliamentary reform in 1785. On 1 March 1787 he married Margaretta Elizabeth (1768–1851), the daughter of General Sir Thomas Spencer Wilson, sixth baronet, of Uckfield, Sussex, and his wife, Jane Badger-Weller; they had six sons and three daughters. In 1790 he was returned for Warwick on Lord Warwick's interest and in 1796 for Totnes on the duke of Bolton's interest. In August 1790 he obtained the lucrative reversionary sinecure of registrar of the court of Admiralty, which had been granted to him in 1764, and he moved the navy estimates every year from 1792 to 1800 and spoke only on Admiralty questions. He remained a steadfast supporter of Pitt, who refused his resignation during the naval mutinies of 1797, and he contributed £10,000 to the loyalty loan. Rallying to Pitt's successor, Addington, in 1801, he was sworn of the privy council (20 February 1801) and served as master of the Royal Mint (March–July 1802) and an India board commissioner (May 1801–October 1803). At Addington's instigation he was made Baron Arden in the United Kingdom peerage on 28 July 1802. He was a fellow of the Royal Society and the Society of Antiquaries and a trustee of the Hunterian Museum.

On Pitt's return to power in May 1804, Arden became a lord of the bedchamber, and he transferred to Windsor from 1812 until George III's death in 1820. His Admiralty registrarship, to which his younger brother Spencer Perceval was reversionary heir, was attacked in the Commons in 1807, and Arden defended his family preserve in the Lords on 4 August by citing the royal prerogative. Brushing aside a government compromise, he further rebuffed his critics on 29 February 1808, 10 March 1808, and 20 February 1810. An act to suspend reversions temporarily was passed in 1812, but the attacks on Arden's sinecure continued in the Commons; in debate on 19 June 1812 Henry Martin alleged that Arden had profited by £30,000 in fees and £7000 annual interest on securities. The attack continued in 1813, and ministers agreed to the abolition of reversions, but not until after Arden's death, which took place at his home in St James's Place, London, on 5 July 1840. Caricatured as an arch sinecurist, Arden was then worth about £800,000 and had spent the last ten years of his life as lord lieutenant of Surrey. He was buried at Charlton, Kent, on 11 July 1840.   ROLAND THORNE

Sources M. M. Drummond, 'Perceval, Hon. Charles George', HoP, Commons, 1754–90 · R. G. Thorne, 'Perceval, Charles George', HoP, Commons, 1790–1820 · D. Gray, Spencer Perceval: the evangelical prime minister, 1762–1812 (1963), esp. 151–8 · GM, 2nd ser., 14 (1840), 320 · The later correspondence of George III, ed. A. Aspinall, 5 vols. (1962–70) · Cobbett, Parl. hist., vols. 21–3 · J. Debrett, ed., The parliamentary register, or, History of the proceedings and debates of the House of Commons, 45 vols. (1781–96), vols. 34–44 · J. Debrett, ed., The parliamentary register, or, History of the proceedings and debates of the House of Commons, 112 vols. (1775–1813), vols. 1–12 · Hansard 1 (1807), vol. 8; (1808), vol. 10; (1814), vol. 28; (1815), vols. 28, 30 · Hansard 2 (1820), 3.1619; (1830), 24.423 · GEC, Peerage · W. T. J. Gun, ed., The Harrow School register, 1571–1800 (1934) · Boyle's Court Guide

Archives BL, papers and family corresp., Add. MSS 47140–47143 · Bodl. Oxf., antiquarian collection incl. an armorial of the bondage of Ireland · Bodl. Oxf., corresp. mainly as lord lieutenant of Surrey | BL, corresp. with Spencer Perceval, Add. MS 49188 · CUL, corresp. with Spencer Perceval · Glos. RO, letters to Lord Redesdale · HLRO, Perceval (Holland) MSS · NRA, priv. coll., corresp. with Drummond family · PRO, corresp. with William Pitt, GD 30/8/108

Likenesses Facius, stipple and line engraving, 1806 (after J. W. Chandler), NPG · H. P. Briggs, portrait · J. W. Chandler, portrait · T. G. Lupton, mezzotint (after H. P. Briggs), BM, NPG

Wealth at death £800,000: GEC, Peerage, 1.191; Bank of England wills, Society of Genealogists, London, vol. 54, p. 11431

Perceval [Percival], **Jean** (d. 1561), Carthusian theologian, was a native of Paris who became a Carthusian monk there in 1522. In 1530 he published a theological work, Compendium divini amoris, also at Paris. According to John Bale, followed by later British biobibliographers, Perceval studied at English universities before making his profession; Anthony Wood inevitably claimed that he did so specifically at Oxford. No evidence survives to support these assertions, which probably stem from confusion with an older near-contemporary, the English Franciscan John Percival, who studied at both Oxford and Cambridge. Perceval's Compendium is based upon much theological learning, but he would not have needed to attend an English university in order to acquire this. His attacks on the heresies of the Beguines and Beghards, members of a movement of lay spirituality unrecorded in England, his admiring references to Jean Gerson, formerly chancellor of the University of Paris, and his anecdote of how a few years earlier he had himself been told by a woman of Paris of her son's defying his parents in order to become a Carthusian—all point to a continental and Parisian background.

Made prior of the Dijon Charterhouse in 1534, Perceval was appointed a co-visitor of the French Carthusian province in 1546 and sole visitor two years later. He died on 12 September 1561.   HENRY SUMMERSON

Sources A. Gruys, ed., Cartusiana: un instrument heuristique, 1 (Paris, 1976), 147 · Bale, Cat., 1.628 · Tanner, Bibl. Brit.-Hib. · Wood, Ath. Oxon., new edn, 1.6–7 · J. Perceval, Compendium divini amoris (1530)

Perceval, John, first earl of Egmont (1683–1748), politician and diarist, was born at Burton, co. Cork, on 12 July 1683, the second son of Sir John Perceval, third baronet (d. 1686), and his wife, Catherine (d. 1692), the fourth daughter of Sir Edward *Dering, second baronet, of Surrenden Dering, Kent. Following the death of their father in 1686 at the age of twenty-nine, John Perceval and his brothers Edward and Philip were placed in the care of a great-uncle, Sir Robert Southwell, of King's Weston in England. Their mother remarried in 1690 but two years later died in childbirth. Upon the death of his elder brother, Edward, at the age of nine, in November 1691, the eight-year-old John Perceval became the fifth baronet.

John Perceval and his younger brother, Philip, grew up in England under the guardianship of Sir Robert Southwell and, following his death in 1702, that of his son Sir Edward Southwell. After private tuition at home, and three years at Mr Demouere's academy in Westminster, Perceval matriculated at Magdalen College, Oxford, in November 1699. He left Oxford in 1701 without taking his degree but the following year, probably because of his great-uncle's influence, was elected a fellow of the Royal Society. Between 1704 and 1707 he travelled in England, Ireland, and continental Europe. He married on 10 June 1710 Catherine (1687/8–1749), the eldest daughter of Sir Philip Parker à Morley bt, of Erwarton, Suffolk. They had seven children, three sons and four daughters, of whom John *Perceval and his sisters Catherine and Helena reached adulthood. Perceval paid periodic visits to Ireland, and lived there between 1711 and 1714, but chose to make London his main residence.

In 1704, at the age of twenty-one, Perceval inherited the 22,000 acres of land in Cork and Tipperary which provided him with a healthy income for the rest of his life. In that same year he also embarked on his political career when he was returned to the Irish House of Commons as the member for County Cork. Later in 1704 he was sworn of the privy council in Ireland. In 1713 he was re-elected as the member for County Cork and two years later, after first refusing it on the grounds that it was inferior to its English equivalent, he accepted the Irish title of Baron Perceval of Burton in the county of Cork. He took his seat in the Irish House of Lords on 12 November 1715. Perceval had been led to believe by his friends in government and court circles that this Irish honour would shortly be followed by the English barony which he so craved, but this was not to be. However, in 1723 he was created Viscount Perceval of Kanturk, also in the county of Cork.

Although deeply disappointed by his failure to secure an English title, Perceval was immensely proud of the Irish

John Perceval, first earl of Egmont (1683–1748), by John Smith, 1708 (after Sir Godfrey Kneller, 1704)

Perceval was impressed by Berkeley's plan to found a colony in Bermuda for the training of Anglican missionaries and, although that plan came to nothing, Perceval retained his interest in the Americas. He was an early and an enthusiastic supporter of Oglethorpe's scheme to establish a new colony on the North American mainland, and he used his influential connections to secure support for the proposed colony of Georgia. In the royal charter of 9 June 1732 authorizing the founding of that colony he was named as the first president of the trustees. In the summer of the following year, partly because of his lobbying and partly because of his role in the Georgia project, he received another Irish honour when he was created earl of Egmont.

Between 1732 and the spring of 1742, when he resigned from the common council of the trustees because of his failing health, Egmont played a pivotal role in securing both the public and the private funding which were essential for the support and defence of Georgia. When the trustees' plan came under attack from the Georgia colonists and their allies in the House of Commons Egmont adroitly organized their defence. The survival of Georgia owed as much to Egmont's efforts in London as it did to Oglethorpe's activities in the colony. Egmont kept a personal diary for many years, and this, together with his accounts of the Georgia trustees' proceedings, provides a mine of information not only about his own life but also about many different facets of élite society in early Georgian London. Egmont's diaries, and the unreliable *Genealogical History of the House of Yvery*, published under his supervision in 1742, lend credence to the contemporary view of him as a pompous and conceited person. However, his diaries also reveal that he had a deep and abiding love of the arts and enjoyed a generally happy relationship with his wife. Egmont died in London on 1 May 1748 and was buried at Erwarton. He was survived by his wife, who died on 22 August the following year and by his son, John Perceval (1711–1770), who succeeded him as the second earl of Egmont. His name was often subsequently spelt Percival.

BETTY WOOD

Sources *The journal of the earl of Egmont*, ed. R. G. McPherson (1962) · *Manuscripts of the earl of Egmont: diary of Viscount Percival, afterwards first earl of Egmont*, 3 vols., HMC, 63 (1920–23) · *Berkeley and Percival: the correspondence of George Berkeley, afterwards bishop of Cloyne, and Sir John Percival, afterwards first earl of Egmont*, ed. B. Rand (1914) · R. Saye and A. Saye, 'John Percival, first earl of Egmont', *Georgians in profile: historical essays in honour of Ellis Merton Coulter*, ed. H. Montgomery (1958) · E. Wood, 'The earl of Egmont and the Georgia project', *Forty years of diversity: essays on colonial Georgia*, ed. H. H. Jackson and P. Spalding (1984) · Foster, *Alum. Oxon.*

Archives BL, corresp. and papers, Add. MSS 17720, 27980–27981, 27988–27989, 46964–47213 · Thomas Gilcrease Institute of American History and Art, Tulsa, Oklahoma, proceedings of the Trustees for the Establishment of Georgia · University of Georgia, Athens, papers relating to colony of Georgia

Likenesses V. Felici, marble bust, 1707, NPG · J. Smith, mezzotint, 1708 (after G. Kneller, 1704), BM, NPG [*see illus.*] · J. Faber junior, mezzotint, 1734 (after H. Hysing), BM, NPG · J. Faber junior, mezzotint, pubd 1742 (after H. Hysing), BM, NPG · portrait, 1744, repro. in McPherson, ed., *The journal of the earl of Egmont* · W. Verelst, group portrait, oils (*The Georgia Council of 1734*), Henry Francis du Pont Winterthur Museum, Winterthur, Delaware

honours bestowed on him. In 1719, and again in 1733, he was at the forefront of those Irish peers who tried to prevent either royal or parliamentary erosion of their authority. The stand taken by Perceval did not irreparably damage either his reputation or his career. He assiduously continued to cultivate the support of influential persons in the highest social and political circles, and he remained on the very best terms with the prince of Wales, later George II, Queen Caroline, and Sir Robert Walpole. Perceval became active in English politics during the 1720s. In 1727 he spent around £1000 to secure his election as MP for Harwich, but stood down in the election of 1734 in favour of his eldest son, John. Mainly because of the Walpole ministry's deep dislike of him, the young Perceval was defeated. Although his father never forgave Walpole for this affront, the prime minister remained relatively cordial towards Perceval.

In 1729 Perceval sat on the parliamentary gaols committee chaired by James Edward Oglethorpe, and the subsequent close collaboration between the two men was instrumental in the founding of the colony of Georgia. Perceval's interest in the Americas had been kindled in 1708 when, on a visit to Ireland, he met George Berkeley. They became firm friends and, when Perceval returned to England, they embarked on a lengthy correspondence.

Perceval, John, second earl of Egmont (1711–1770), politician, was born on 24 February 1711 at Westminster, the only surviving son of John *Perceval, first earl of Egmont (1683–1748), politician, and his wife, Catherine (1687/1688–1749), the eldest daughter of Sir Philip Parker, second baronet, of Erwarton, Suffolk, and Mary Forbrey.

Early political career Styled Viscount Perceval from 1733 to 1748, Perceval received a private education in which his father instructed him in history and antiquities. At the age of twenty he was returned for the seat of Dingle in the Irish parliament. In 1734 his father stood down at his parliamentary seat at Harwich in favour of his son, but Perceval was not returned, and both father and son blamed the defeat on Robert Walpole. Feeling slighted by both Walpole and the king, Perceval gave his support to the opposition and the use of his house in Pall Mall to Frederick, prince of Wales. The offer was refused, but the prince later took Perceval as his political adviser. At Kensington, on 15 February 1737, Perceval married Lady Catherine Cecil (1719–1752), the second daughter of James Cecil, fifth earl of Salisbury, and Anne Tufton. They had five sons and two daughters. Perceval tried twice more to gain a seat in the British House of Commons but was unsuccessful. He was then adopted as an opposition candidate for Westminster after 'intriguing' against two government candidates, and after the annulment of the election he was returned unopposed on 31 December 1741. His maiden speech in the Commons was in support of a motion to enquire into the conduct of the war, and was directed against Walpole. His pamphlet *Faction Detected by the Evidence of the Facts* (1743) earned the disapproval of the opposition and his constituents, resulting in the loss of his seat in 1747. Perceval was adept at making political enemies, for no sooner had he gained a new parliamentary seat at Weobley with the support of Henry Pelham than he went over to the opposition. He had been defeated at the poll but returned by petition, and demonstrated his loyalty to Pelham by calling him a treacherous servant of the king. After joining the Leicester House faction surrounding the prince of Wales, Perceval was made a lord of the bedchamber to the prince. According to Horace Walpole, both the old and new members of the ministry hated Perceval, and the tories could not forgive him for his conduct in the previous parliament. On 1 May 1748 Perceval succeeded his father as second earl of Egmont in the Irish peerage.

Egmont and Leicester House, 1749–1751 Egmont was now Frederick's chief political adviser, and between them they drew up detailed plans for Frederick's accession to the throne on the eventual death of his father George II. These plans included a distribution of offices and an analysis of the House of Commons to assist in the general election that would come about within six months of a new reign, the fixing of the civil list, matters concerned with foreign policy, and drafts of speeches to parliament. Egmont was now a prominent opposition speaker in the Commons, and his attack on the Mutiny Bill in 1749 caused Sir Hanbury Williams to pen an epigram in which he cast Egmont

John Perceval, second earl of Egmont (1711–1770), by Thomas Hudson, 1759

as someone who had mutinied for pay and twice deserted.

In 1749 Egmont published two political pamphlets critical of Henry Pelham and his brother the duke of Newcastle, and another concerning the 1743 treaty of Hanau. The following year he is supposed to have written *Constitutional Queries Earnestly Recommended to the Serious Consideration of every True Briton*, which was ordered to be burnt by the common hangman in 1751. The death in March 1751 of Frederick left Egmont's political ambitions in disarray. The princess of Wales summoned him and directed him to go to Carlton House to collect the prince's papers. The political papers concerned with the accession were burnt, though Egmont retained copies that have survived. Egmont then held a meeting at his house in Pall Mall of the main opposition members, and resolved to stand by the princess and her children. However, the princess found that it was in her best interest to abandon her husband's friends, and the bulk of the prince's faction dispersed, leaving Egmont in opposition for the remainder of the parliament. To his political misfortunes was added a personal one with the death of his wife on 16 August 1752.

Ambitions for a British peerage, 1754–1762 In the general election of April 1754 Egmont was returned for Bridgwater. The princess now persuaded him to accept office. He was sworn of the privy council on 9 January 1755, but refused to serve with Henry Fox, now leader of the house. He was also supplanted at Leicester House by Lord Bute. On 26 January 1756 he married Catherine (1731–

1784), the third daughter of the Hon. Charles Compton and Mary Berkeley. They had three sons and six daughters. Spencer *Perceval (1762–1812), his second son by this marriage, became prime minister in 1809 and was assassinated in 1812. In October 1756 the duke of Newcastle offered to make Egmont a secretary of state and leader of the House of Commons, but Egmont refused unless he was also made an English peer. This did not suit Newcastle, as he needed Egmont in the Commons. Egmont again refused office in May 1757. About this time, James Waldegrave, second Earl Waldegrave, described Egmont as a good speaker in parliament who was not easily intimidated and whose only amusements were business and politics, yet 'he respected himself rather more than the world respected him' (Namier, 3.267). Egmont continued in opposition during the remainder of the reign but was not politically active, even though he consistently opposed William Pitt, whom he detested.

The accession of George III in 1760 raised Egmont's hopes that his political fortunes might change. Returned once more for Bridgwater in March 1761, he became associated with Lord Bute. He had asked Bute the year before if he could be of service to the king, hoping that he would be made a British peer. This ambition was achieved on 7 May 1762 when he was created Baron Lovel and Holland of Enmore, Somerset. Three days later he took his seat in the House of Lords, and on 27 November 1762 he was made joint postmaster-general. A less controversial figure than in former times, Egmont now settled down to the work of government. He became associated with a political grouping that came to include Bute and Charles Jenkinson and was attached solely to the crown rather than to any political faction.

First lord of the Admiralty, 1763–1766 Egmont's capacity for business was finally realized when, on 10 September 1763, he was appointed to succeed the earl of Sandwich as first lord of the Admiralty, in George Grenville's ministry. First, however, he was able to make use of his position to provide for his numerous family. His third son, Philip, an officer in the navy, was appointed to the command of the *Ramilles*. Charles *Perceval and Spencer, sons from his second marriage, were made registrars of the Admiralty through reversionary grants by letters patent. But his achievement at the Admiralty has been unrecognized, largely as a result of Horace Walpole's unflattering portrayal of him as a wasteful eccentric who left the navy in a wretched condition, throwing away between £400,000 and £500,000 'on pompous additions to the dockyards' (Walpole, *Memoirs of … George III*, 4.136–7).

Egmont's delight in antiquities and his eccentric taste as well as a number of unusual schemes served to make contemporary observers such as Walpole portray him as a figure of ridicule. Egmont had produced two volumes of the *Genealogical History of the House of Yvery* in 1742, giving a fanciful account of the origins of his own family. His house at Enmore, near Bridgwater in Somerset, was rebuilt as a moated castle. His most unusual scheme, however, was to submit a memorial to the king in December 1763 asking for a grant of the island of St John in the Gulf of St Lawrence, to be settled on a feudal basis. He estimated that 800,000 acres could be held by military tenure and that, if the system should be extended to the newly acquired lands in Canada, a feudal levy of 724,000 men could be raised for the defence of America. In this venture he gained support from respected naval officers such as Keppel and Saunders, but after strenuous objections from General Conway the scheme was set aside.

There was nothing fanciful about Egmont's management of the navy between 1763 and 1766. By his predecessor's estimate, it would take over five years and more than £3 million to put the navy on a respectable footing after the hardships of the late war. The Admiralty's task was complicated by reduced parliamentary supplies, a navy debt of over £4½ million, and a programme of retrenchment. Egmont made a visit to the dockyards in the spring of 1764, the first such visitation since that of Sandwich and Anson in 1749. He noted a number of inadequacies in the infrastructure and organization of the yards, and he ordered that repair priorities be rearranged so that ships could be brought forward more quickly. All new ships were to be built on slips to free the docks to undertake repairs, and he requested detailed information on the regulation and economy of the yards. Turning his attention to the shipwrights and artificers in the yards, Egmont called for reports on the numbers and occupations of dockyard workers, the condition of the ships, and the length of time and number of men required to undertake specific tasks. He then made a number of productivity calculations. He increased the number of shipwrights by 400 and introduced a scheme of superannuation for deserving elderly shipwrights which allowed their places to be taken by able-bodied and more productive workers. By his efforts the dockyards were made more efficient and productive. It was also during Egmont's period at the Admiralty that Byron was sent on his voyage of discovery to the Pacific, and that a settlement was made in the Falkland Islands, named Port Egmont in honour of the first lord.

In 1765 Egmont's need for further naval expenditure was resisted by George Grenville, first lord of the Treasury and prime minister. Grenville had brought the navy's debt down to manageable proportions and was anxious that an increase in naval appropriation would cause alarm both at home and abroad. Egmont was particularly concerned that the Treasury had reduced the naval estimates and that money needed urgently for the expansion of the dockyards at Portsmouth and Plymouth had been cut entirely. He consulted in secret with the Navy Board, which produced detailed plans of expenditure that Egmont submitted to the king through the earl of Halifax on 30 May, along with accounts of the French and Spanish fleets. The Treasury, on learning of these accounts, attempted to undermine Egmont by dealing directly with the Navy Board on matters of expenditure. Egmont had already removed Grenville's power to cut appropriation for dockyard expansion by obtaining a privy council order directing a sum for this work to be included annually in the estimates. The Treasury's response was to interfere in the affairs of the Navy Board, and this was an affront to Egmont's authority. Grenville was already on bad terms with the king, and further aggravation was avoided by the dismissal of Grenville and his ministry.

Egmont had usually remained silent in Grenville's cabinet, but he emerged from the collapse of the ministry as the king's man. In much the same way that he had advised Prince Frederick in the composition of a new government, Egmont, along with the duke of Cumberland, the king's uncle, now assisted George III in the construction of a new administration to be led by the marquess of Rockingham. Egmont remained in the new ministry as first lord of the Admiralty. He was free from Treasury interference and by September 1765 could report that the fleet would muster sixty-two ships of the line of sixty guns or more, all in good condition, with a further twenty fit for service by the end of 1769. This achievement was in large measure due to Egmont's competent management of the navy's affairs.

The Rockingham administration collapsed in 1766 and a new ministry was formed under William Pitt, now ennobled as earl of Chatham. Despite his antipathy to Pitt, Egmont, with the support of the king, remained at the head of the Admiralty. However, he soon resigned (on 12 August), since he found Pitt's overbearing nature too much to tolerate. He explained to the king that he disapproved of Chatham's foreign policy, and feared that he would embarrass his majesty's affairs if they were debated in council: 'He could submit to the majority; but as he found one man was to have more weight than six, he begged to be unemployed' (Walpole, *Memoirs of … George III*, 2.155).

Death and character Egmont played no further part in government or politics. He had a clear aptitude for public business, though his political judgement did not always work to his advantage. His parliamentary notes, written in neat columns with tiny characters, display a methodical and highly organized mind. Dr Johnson wrote of him that he was 'a man whose mind was vigorous and active, whose knowledge was extensive and whose designs were magnificent, but who had somewhat vitiated his judgement by too much indulgence in romantic projects and speculations' (GEC, *Peerage*, 5.30). Horace Walpole has left an illustration of Egmont's personality:

> His heart rather wanted improvement than his head, though when his ambition and lust of Parliament were out of the question, he was humane, friendly and as good humoured as it is possible for a man to be who was never known to laugh; he was once indeed seen to smile, and that was at chess. He did not dislike mirth in others but he seemed to adjourn his attention till he could bring back the company to seriousness. (Walpole, *Memoirs of … George II*, 1.23)

Egmont died at his home in Pall Mall, London, on 4 December 1770 and was buried on the 11th at Charlton in Kent. He was survived by his wife, who had been created on 23 May 1770 Baroness Arden of Lohort Castle, and died at Langley, Buckinghamshire, on 11 June 1784.

CLIVE WILKINSON

Sources L. B. Namier, 'Perceval, John', HoP, *Commons, 1754–90* · R. R. Sedgwick, 'Perceval, John', HoP, *Commons, 1715–54* · C. Wilkinson, 'The earl of Egremont and the navy, 1763–6', *Mariner's Mirror*, 84 (1998), 418–33 · A. Newman, ed., 'Leicester House politics, 1750–60, from the papers of John, second earl of Egmont', *Camden miscellany, XXIII*, CS, 4th ser., 7 (1969), 85–228 · H. Walpole, *Memoirs of King George II*, ed. J. Brooke, 3 vols. (1985) · H. Walpole, *Memoirs of the reign of King George the Third*, ed. G. F. R. Barker, 4 vols. (1894) · admiralty board minute, 6 Oct 1763, PRO, ADM/3/71 · admiralty board minute, 30 June 1764, PRO, ADM/3/72 · BL, Egmont MSS, Add. MS 47053, 47092 · GEC, *Peerage* · DNB

Archives BL, corresp. and papers, Add. MSS 46982–47213 | BL, corresp. with duke of Newcastle, Add. MSS 32737–33070, *passim*

Likenesses J. Reynolds, oils, *c.*1756, Bradford City Art Gallery · T. Hudson, oils, 1759, NPG; on loan to Beningbrough Hall, Yorkshire [*see illus.*] · J. Macardell, engraving, 1764 (after T. Hudson), NMM · J. Faber junior, mezzotint (after F. Hayman), BM, NPG · J. Faber junior, mezzotint (after C. F. Zincke), BM; repro. in J. Anderson, *A genealogical history of the house of Yvery*, 2 vols. (1742) · R. Josey, double portrait, mezzotint (after J. Reynolds), NPG · marble bust, Castle Ashby, Northamptonshire

Perceval, Sir Philip (1605–1647), politician, was the younger of the two sons of Richard *Perceval (*c.*1558–1620) of Sydenham, Somerset, and his second wife, Alice, daughter of John Sherman of Ottery St Mary, Devon. He succeeded his father and brother as clerk and registrar to the commissioners of the Irish wards, a post which he held in sole right after 1624. In the late 1620s and 1630s Perceval became feodary and escheator in co. Limerick and clerk of the court of wards in Munster, and he used his position to lease wards' lands at low rates, lending the profits to local families in return for mortgages. His moneylending schemes were extremely lucrative, as Old English debtors, unable to pay the sums due, were forced to surrender their estates. The Barrys, MacCarthys, O'Callaghans, and Roches all fell victim to Perceval's designs, and by 1641 nearly 100,000 English acres in Munster—yielding rents in excess of £4000—had come into his possession. Financial success brought social acceptability, helped by his marriage on 16 October 1626 to Katherine, daughter of the well-connected Dublin official Arthur Ussher. He also became a friend of other acquisitive New Englishmen in Munster, including the first earl of Cork and Sir William St Leger.

In the 1630s Perceval's prospects improved still further with his successful attempt to court the favour of the new lord deputy, Viscount Wentworth. By early 1634 he had become friendly with two of Wentworth's closest advisers, Sir Philip Mainwaring and Sir George Radcliffe. In 1636 he was admitted to King's Inns, Dublin; in the same year he was knighted by the lord deputy at Dublin before accompanying him to England. In the later 1630s Perceval aided Wentworth's schemes to find royal title to lands, preparatory to plantation, in Connaught, Munster, and the Byrnes country in co. Wicklow, in which he and other government lackeys also benefited. With the fall of Wentworth in 1640–41, Perceval's part in these irregular land deals was exposed, and he narrowly avoided prosecution in England ('among those whose actions are re-examined and reflected upon'; *Egmont MSS*, 1.142) in September 1641.

The execution of Wentworth did not, however, leave

Perceval entirely without allies. A particularly useful patron was the twelfth earl of Ormond, whose business associations with Perceval dated back to 1631, and who had used him as guarantor of his debts in March 1641. After the outbreak of rebellion in Ireland in October 1641 Ormond repaid the favour by commissioning Perceval first as captain of firelocks in his own regiment, and then as commissary-general of the victuals. In turn Perceval, who had travelled to England in the winter of 1641–2, defended Ormond against accusations of colluding with the Catholic rebels, raised by parliamentarians suspicious of his Old English ethnicity.

In the meantime the Irish rising had spread to Munster, where resistance was mounted by Perceval's old friends the earl of Cork, Sir William St Leger, and St Leger's son-in-law, Lord Inchiquin. Perceval's lands were overrun, with his castles at Liscarroll and Annagh holding out until September 1642. It was the local crisis, and the fear that the onset of civil war in England would prevent any further aid to the protestants in Ireland, which encouraged him to support negotiations which led to a truce with the Catholic confederates in September 1643. In March 1644 he was chosen as one of four agents sent by Ormond to Oxford to turn the cessation into a permanent peace. Yet Perceval and his colleagues found that many prominent courtiers (including Prince Rupert) supported the demands of the confederates, and in reaction they were vociferous in their opposition to peace on easy terms. This brought condemnation from many at Oxford. As Radcliffe told Ormond in June 1644: 'Perceval … had gone here for a roundhead if your excellency had not recommended him as he did' (Bodl. Oxf., MS Carte 11, fol. 175). Perceval had left Oxford at the end of the month, but instead of returning to Dublin, he stayed with friends in Hertfordshire. In August, following the defection to parliament of the Munster forces led by Lord Inchiquin, Perceval went to London, where he too embraced the parliamentarian cause.

From 1645 until his death in 1647 Perceval was a crucial figure in Anglo-Irish politics. He was on good terms with Inchiquin in Munster, and at Westminster sided with those Irish protestant MPs aligned with the presbyterian party, especially Sir Robert King, Sir John Clotworthy, and William Jephson. Perceval also remained on good terms with Ormond, and was an important part of the network which kept open lines of communication between Dublin and London. The rival Independent party, who were suspicious of Ormond and Inchiquin, recognized Perceval as a threat, and from the autumn of 1645 mounted a vigorous campaign to discredit him, reminding the parliamentarians that he had supported the 1643 cessation, and hinting that he had come to Westminster 'with the king's leave, and acted for him here ever since', and stating that he was 'so engaged to Lord Ormond that he was not capable of public employment' (Egmont MSS, 1.279, 353–4). Such attacks did not deter Perceval from acting as intermediary between parliament and Ormond in their abortive peace talks in the autumn of 1646, or in defending Inchiquin against Independent attacks in the winter of 1646–7.

Perceval's stance on Irish affairs recommended him to the leaders of the presbyterian party, and as early as March 1647 there were moves to secure him a seat in parliament. His election on 19 May to the Cornish borough of Newport was probably on the interest of Thomas Gewen MP, who was recorder of the nearby town of Launceston. Perceval's arrival in the Commons caused a storm of protest from the Independents, who reminded the house on 2 June that he had supported the cessation and was a 'special confidant of the Lord of Ormond' (Egmont MSS, 1.411, 413). A further attack came on 5 July, when the Independents were narrowly defeated in an attempt to disable any member who had supported the 1643 cessation. This assault was interrupted by the 'forcing' of the houses in late July and early August, when a presbyterian mob invaded parliament. Perceval remained at Westminster during this period, and supported attempts to defend London against the New Model Army. The victory of the army and their Independent allies heightened the danger to Perceval, and by the end of August he had withdrawn from the Commons, staying with friends such as the earl of Suffolk and William Jephson outside London, and preparing his defence against any impeachment proceedings initiated by his enemies. Before he could vindicate himself, however, Perceval fell ill, and died in London on 10 November 1647. He was buried at St Martin-in-the-Fields, with a funeral sermon preached by his wife's kinsman Primate Ussher. Through his eldest son, John Perceval, he was the ancestor of the earls of Egmont.

PATRICK LITTLE

Sources 'Perceval, Sir Philip', HoP, Commons, 1640–60 [draft] · BL, Add. MSS 46929–46931 · BL, Add. MSS 46920–46931 · Report on the manuscripts of the earl of Egmont, 2 vols. in 3, HMC, 63 (1905–9) · J. Anderson, A genealogical history of the house of Yvery (1742) · The manuscripts of the marquis of Ormonde, [old ser.], 3 vols., HMC, 36 (1895–1909) · CSP Ire., 1625–60 · Bodl. Oxf., MSS Carte 10, 11, 19 · JHC, 5 (1646–8) · W. A. Shaw, The knights of England, 2 vols. (1906) · E. Keane, P. Beryl Phair, and T. U. Sadleir, eds., King's Inns admission papers, 1607–1867, IMC (1982)

Archives BL, corresp. and papers, Add. MSS 46920–46931 | BL, Egmont papers, Add. MSS 46929–46931

Likenesses J. Faber junior, mezzotint, 1743, BM, NPG; repro. in Anderson, A genealogical history

Perceval, Richard (c.1558–1620), administrator and lexicographer, was the eldest son of George Perceval (d. c.1600), a gentleman of Nailsea and Sydenham, Somerset, and Elizabeth, daughter of Sir Edward Bampfylde of Poltimore, Devon. His life was the focus of a family history commissioned by his descendant the first earl of Egmont, which confused many of the details of his career. Perceval was educated at Merchant Taylors' School, London, from 1571, and at Lincoln's Inn in 1576. He married as his first wife Joan (d. c.1585), daughter of Henry Yonge of Buckhorn Weston, Dorset, who was probably the widow of John Royall and brought him no dowry. His father, upset by the match, disinherited him, and he spent four years in Spain. He presumably returned to England at the outbreak of war in 1585, after which he taught for several years at his old school. He also drafted a Spanish-Latin-English dictionary and grammar with the assistance of some of the

Armada prisoners, whose ransom he helped to negotiate. His book *Bibliotheca Hispanica* (1591) was dedicated to Robert Devereux, second earl of Essex, presumably in hope of preferment; but about 1594 he joined the secretariat of the earl's rival Sir Robert Cecil upon a recommendation from his relative Roger Cave.

Despite his linguistic abilities, Perceval had little to do with Cecil's diplomatic activities, although he later boasted of his speedy translation of a captured Spanish dispatch in 1598 which proved that Henri IV of France was about to abandon his alliance with England. His chief role was the handling of petitions for leases of the estates of minors whose wardship fell to the crown, many of which crossed Cecil's desk both before and after he became master of the court of wards in 1599. Perceval's family claimed his post had been worth £2000 a year, probably an exaggeration, but he is known to have been offered generous gratuities by suitors, and he procured leases of several wardships for himself and his relatives. In addition to his main role, he occasionally supervised Cecil's building works.

Perceval was returned to parliament in 1604 as MP for Richmond, Yorkshire, probably through the intervention of the borough's recorder and former MP Cuthbert Pepper, surveyor of the wards. Cecil (newly elevated to the Lords) may have intended to use him as one of his unofficial spokesmen in the Commons: in April 1604 Perceval suggested a compromise over the king's proposal to retitle his realms 'Great Britain'. However, in the same speech he declared his opposition to 'an inundation, or deluge' of Scottish courtiers, a remark unlikely to endear him to the king. This may explain why Perceval was not subsequently used as a 'man of business', although he and Sir Walter Cope were sent to reassure the house when rumours of James's assassination circulated on 22 March 1606. Surprisingly, he played little part in the 1610 debate on the great contract, which proposed to abolish the court of wards.

Perceval lost his main income on his master's death in 1612, which may explain why he sold his Somerset estate in the following year. However, he continued as clerk registrar of the wards until 1614, when he was dismissed by the new master, William, Lord Knollys. Called to the bar at Lincoln's Inn in 1615, he may have intended to practise as a lawyer, but in 1616 he was sent to Dublin as clerk to the fledgeling Irish court of wards, a post he held until his death at Dublin on 4 September 1620. He was buried in St Audoen's Church, Dublin, where his monument stated he had died in his sixty-ninth year; he was probably somewhat younger, as he only entered Merchant Taylors' as a schoolboy in 1571. He had three sons (all of whom died young) and two daughters by his first marriage; his second, to Alice, daughter of John Sherman of Ottery St Mary, Devon, produced two sons and two daughters. His youngest son, Sir Philip *Perceval, inherited the estate at Liscarroll, co. Cork, which he had bought in the last years of his life, and founded an Anglo-Irish dynasty.

SIMON HEALY

Sources J. Anderson, *History of the house of Yvery* (1742) · *Report on the manuscripts of the earl of Egmont*, 2 vols. in 3, HMC, 63 (1905–9), vol. 1, pp. 487–8 · HoP, *Commons, 1604–29* [draft] · P. Martin, *Spanish Armada prisoners* (1988) · A. G. R. Smith, 'The secretariats of the Cecils, *c*.1580–1612', *EngHR*, 83 (1968), 481–504 · R. B. Wernham, *The return of the armadas: the last years of the Elizabethan war against Spain, 1595–1603* (1994), 220–26 · V. Treadwell, 'The Irish court of wards under James I', *Irish Historical Studies*, 12 (1960–61), 1–27 · *JHC*, 1 (1547–1628) · *Calendar of the manuscripts of the most hon. the marquis of Salisbury*, 24 vols., HMC, 9 (1883–1976) · *CSP dom.*, *1580–1618* · *APC*, *1613–23* · Hull RO, MS L. 160 · F. W. Weaver, ed., *The visitations of the county of Somerset* (1885), 61 · J. L. Vivian, ed., *The visitations of the county of Devon, comprising the herald's visitations of 1531, 1564, and 1620* (privately printed, Exeter, [1895]), 39
Archives Hatfield House, Hertfordshire, Cecil MSS
Likenesses J. Faber junior, mezzotint, 1743, BM, NPG; repro. in Anderson, *History*

Perceval, Robert (1756–1839), physician and chemist, the youngest son of William Perceval, barrister, and his second wife, Elizabeth Ward of Lisbane, co. Down, was born in Dublin on 30 September 1756. He was descended from Sir Philip Perceval (1605–1647), and hence related to the earls of Egmont. Perceval's early education was at Dr Darby's school in Ballygall in north co. Dublin. He entered Trinity College, Dublin, in April 1772, and graduated BA in 1777. He then went to Edinburgh, where he studied medicine, was taught chemistry by Joseph Black, and graduated MD on 24 June 1780, with a thesis on the physiology of the heart.

After studying for two years on the continent Perceval returned to Dublin via London in late 1782. In the following year he was appointed lecturer on chemistry in the university. On 24 November of the same year he was elected a licentiate of the King and Queen's College of Physicians; he subsequently became a fellow. In 1785 he was appointed first professor of chemistry in the University of Dublin, and remained in this post until 1805. Also in 1785 he took an active part in founding the Royal Irish Academy, his name appearing in the charter, and he served as secretary to the academy for a number of years. In the same year he helped to found the Dublin General Dispensary. His scientific papers all appear in the *Transactions of the Royal Irish Academy*.

In 1786 Perceval was appointed inspector of apothecaries, and while carrying out this work incurred some temporary unpopularity. He was one of the compilers of the Dublin *Pharmacopoeia* for the Irish college of physicians. He married, in 1786, Anne, daughter of W. Brereton of Rathgilbert. Perceval now began to devote much of his time and money to medical and other charities in Dublin. He was admitted MB and MD by Dublin University in 1793.

Largely because of pressure exerted by Perceval through the university, in April 1799 a committee of the Irish House of Lords was appointed to inquire into the application of the funds left by Sir Patrick Dun. Perceval was examined, and stated that he did not think the King and Queen's College of Physicians had properly fulfilled its obligations under Dun's will. Following the report of the Lords' committee, the School of Physic Act became law on 1 August 1800. In accordance with this act a hospital, called Sir Patrick Dun's Hospital, was built from the surplus funds of Dun's bequest, and was opened on 25 October 1808. Three professorships in medicine were also established. Although Perceval had been censured by the College of Physicians for his share in the promotion of the act, he was elected president of the college on 4 November 1799. However, at his own wish a special clause was inserted in the act, according to which no university or King's professor could remain a fellow of the college. Perceval therefore resigned his presidency and fellowship, but was elected honorary fellow on 18 October 1800. He subsequently became involved in a controversy with Dr E. Hill, who was obliged, under the provisions of the act, to resign the professorship of botany, which he had held simultaneously with the regius professorship of physic.

Perceval now became an active member of the Prison Discipline Society, which subsequently merged with the Howard Society, and he became known as 'the Irish Howard' for his concern with the welfare of prisoners. On 18 March 1819 he was appointed physician-general to the forces in Ireland. In 1821 he published an essay in which he sought to show from the texts of the New Testament that Christ, although a divine person, was distinct from the deity, a doctrine similar to that of Adam Clarke (1762–1832). After a lingering illness Perceval died in Dublin on 3 March 1839.

Perceval was a successful physician, but his claims to fame rest chiefly on his philanthropic efforts. His published contributions to chemistry were insubstantial; the notes for a medical treatise he intended to publish were handed to John Mason Good when Perceval heard that Good was contemplating a similar project.

P. J. HARTOG, rev. PATRICK WALLIS

Sources Burtchaell & Sadleir, *Alum. Dubl.* · J. D. H. Widdess, *A history of the Royal College of Physicians of Ireland, 1654–1963* (1963) · T. G. Moorhead, *A short history of Sir Patrick Dun's Hospital* (1942) · W. B. S. Taylor, *History of the University of Dublin* (1845) · T. Ó Raifeartaigh, *The Royal Irish Academy: a bicentennial history, 1785–1985* (1985) · C. A. Cameron, *History of the Royal College of Surgeons in Ireland* (1886) · private information (1895) · W. J. Davis, *Robert Perceval (1756–1839), first professor of chemistry at Trinity College, Dublin* (1997)
Archives PRO NIre., corresp. and family papers · TCD, lecture notes · Wellcome L., case notes · Wellcome L., lecture notes
Likenesses W. Gillard, portrait, Royal College of Physicians of Ireland, Dublin

Perceval, Spencer (1762–1812), prime minister, was born on 1 November 1762 in Audley Square, London, the second son of John *Perceval, second earl of Egmont (1711–1770), and his second wife, Catherine (1731–1784), third daughter of the Hon. Charles Compton and granddaughter of George, fourth earl of Northampton. Being the second son of a second marriage he had numerous close relatives (three stepbrothers and one stepsister at the time of his birth, as well as an elder brother, Charles George *Perceval, and, later, three sisters) but little prospect of an inheritance sufficient for a life of leisure.

Early years, education, and evangelicalism Perceval's earliest years were spent with his family in their manor house in Charlton, Kent, but in 1774 he was sent to Harrow School and in 1780 entered Trinity College, Cambridge,

Spencer Perceval (1762–1812), studio of Joseph Nollekens [original, c.1812]

taking an honorary MA in 1782. His education at both institutions was marked by two themes: academic success and a growing commitment to evangelical Anglicanism. At Harrow he won prizes and was remembered by one of his tutors for his avoidance of 'desultory reading' and for his 'intense perseverance' in pursuit of an accurate understanding of the set texts. At Cambridge, under the supervision of William Lort Mansel and Thomas Mathias, he won the college declamation prize for English and was noted for his studiousness.

The evangelicalism which was later to distinguish Perceval from the general run of professional politicians developed, it seems, as much from contact with others as from private contemplation. One of the closest and most enduring friendships he made at Harrow was with Dudley Ryder, the second earl of Harrowby, who became a noted evangelical; other contemporaries included two famous for that tendency, the Revd Thomas Gisborne and Thomas Bruce, the future seventh earl of Elgin. More significantly, he associated himself closely at Cambridge with a small but highly influential group of evangelicals, one of whom was the Revd Isaac Milner.

Legal practice, religious convictions, and marriage In the absence of any significant private means on leaving Cambridge, Perceval needed a profession and an income. He therefore entered Lincoln's Inn in 1783, was called to the bar three years later, and having practised with success on the midland circuit, began to accumulate posts through his connections. The first was the deputy recordership of Northampton, secured in 1790 through the influence of his mother's family, the Comptons of Castle Ashby. Others, in the form of a commissionership of bankrupts and the sinecure post of surveyor of the meltings and the clerk of the irons, followed by 1791 as a result of the influence of his elder brother, Lord Arden, who had become a lord of the Admiralty in Pitt's administration.

It was at this critical juncture that Perceval turned his attention to politics. In 1791 and 1792 he published two anonymous pamphlets, the first in favour of continuing the impeachment of Warren Hastings and the second offering advice for those who wished to resist radicalism. This readiness to contribute to public debate on the side of those who were alarmed by the impact of the French Revolution on British politics certainly did no harm to his prospects at the bar. He was appointed junior counsel for the crown at the trials of the two most influential radicals, Thomas Paine and John Horne Tooke, in 1792 and 1794, and in the latter year was made counsel to the Board of Admiralty through Lord Arden's influence. Two years later he was made a KC and became a bencher at Lincoln's Inn; at this time his private practice was worth about £1000 p.a.

By now Perceval's private life and convictions had characteristics that were to change little during the remainder of his career. Small of stature—Lord Eldon referred to him as 'Little P'—he magnified his naturally pale complexion by dressing usually in black, thereby exuding an air of zealousness. The impression created was not an illusion. Perceval's earlier contact with evangelicalism had led to a commitment to living the life of a Christian gentleman—to being in the words of one commentator, 'Christianity personified'. Throughout his life, for example, he was the most generous and charitable of men, giving away large sums of money to good causes. In addition, he was a stern sabbatarian, a pungent critic of gaming, drunkenness, hunting, and adultery, as well as a consistent supporter of the abolition of slavery. However, his evangelicalism was of the conservative brand. Unlike some evangelicals, he rejected the view that any gathering of believers constituted a church, and was a firm upholder of the Church of England. From this conviction flowed many of the public policies with which he was associated: reform of the established church in the shape of measures to reduce non-residence, to improve clerical stipends, and to build churches in industrial towns; and, most famously, his opposition to Catholic emancipation. This was based partly on the practical grounds that while failing to appease Catholic Ireland it would weaken the established church; and partly on a combination of millenarianism and bigotry. Thus in a pamphlet on biblical prophecy published in 1800 he wrote of the French Revolution as a divine instrument destined to destroy 'popish superstitions'.

Perceval's religiosity was matched by his commitment to family life. Never gregarious by nature, he was married on 10 August 1790 to Jane Wilson, the sister of his elder brother's wife and the daughter of Sir Thomas Wilson, a former soldier and MP who had bought the Percevals' manor house in Charlton. The marriage, of which Sir Thomas had disapproved in view of what he regarded as Perceval's poor financial prospects, proved an enduring love match and produced six sons and six daughters. Moreover his wife shared his devotion to religion and joined him wholeheartedly in daily prayers as, in due course, did the rest of his family.

Entry into politics It was characteristic of Perceval that his entry into politics was more the initiative of others than his own. Shortly before Perceval took silk in 1796, Pitt and the home secretary, the duke of Portland, considered him for the vacant chief secretaryship in Ireland and he was pressed to accept by both the lord lieutenant, Lord Camden, and the first lord of the Admiralty, Lord Spencer—the latter offering the inducement of a sinecure. Perceval declined the opportunity, pleading the disruption the appointment would cause to his family and his aversion (and presumably that of others) to sinecures. Moreover his return to parliament for Northampton at a by-election in May 1796 was in response to an invitation from his cousin, Lord Compton, who had succeeded to an earldom and wanted a locum tenens until his heir came of age. Elected without a contest then, Perceval stood again as a Compton candidate at the general election later in the year, retaining his seat in a contest in which he declined an alliance with a potential supporter of Pitt's administration in deference to the needs of the family interest.

However, it was also to be characteristic of Perceval that, once he had been drawn into a new field of endeavour, he devoted himself to it seriously if cautiously. In order to make a mark in the 1790s a great speech was required. Perceval was certainly aware of this and prepared drafts of speeches with great care but none that he delivered attracted notice until 4 January 1798 when he responded to Fox's and Burdett's criticisms of the war effort during a debate on the Assessed Taxes Bill. In his speech he justified the continuation of the war and castigated Fox for both his secession from parliament and his demand for reform at a time of national crisis. It was in effect, if not in fact, his maiden speech and received widespread praise. Granville Leveson-Gower thought it 'incomparable' and Pitt judged it 'one of the best I ever heard' (Gray, 41).

The speech established Perceval's reputation as a parliamentarian and as a possible future minister. Pitt evidently considered him an eligible heir and steps up the administration's legal ladder followed quickly. In August 1798 he was appointed solicitor to the ordnance and later, in 1799, solicitor-general to the queen. For his part, Perceval spoke more frequently in debate and often acted as a government teller. Besides continuing to argue the case for the war, in which he once identified Bonaparte as the woman in Revelation 17: 3–6, 'who [sits] upon a … beast … the mother of harlots … drunken with the blood of the saints', he endorsed the strategies of the controversial Dutch and Egyptian campaigns, defended the income tax, and supported the union with Ireland. In short, and with the exception of the resort to biblical prophecy, he was a thorough Pittite.

In the period between Pitt's resignation in February 1801 and Lord Grenville's six years later—a period characterized by unstable administrations and a proliferation of parliamentary factions—Perceval became one of the four leading contenders for the leadership of Pitt's friends, the others being Castlereagh, Canning, and Hawkesbury (later the second earl of Liverpool). He acquired rather than pursued that position. Declining to resign with Pitt over the Catholic question, he was appointed solicitor-general (1801) and attorney-general (1802) under Addington, retaining that position in Pitt's last administration, though only after stipulating political terms. He therefore became the Pittites' leading law officer in the Commons at a time when the cases in which he was involved against the radicals Despard, Peltier, and Cobbett (1803–4) and the minister Lord Melville (1805), and in favour of the princess of Wales, whom he defended (1806–7), were high-profile political issues. However, the principal reason for his elevation was his ability as a debater. He was the most powerful defender of the Addington ministry following the renewal of the war in 1803 and the most effective critic of Lord Grenville's, speaking then on more than seventy occasions and providing rallying points for an emerging Pittite opposition.

On the other hand, Perceval was more than a skilled advocate of a party brief. He developed his own idiosyncratic set of views, components of which appealed to various wings of Pitt's party: opposition to Catholic emancipation and parliamentary reform; support for the abolition of the slave trade and the regulation of child labour; and a determination to continue with the war. Moreover, although he acquired no personal following, he demonstrated a capacity for independent judgement and for leadership. During Grenville's ministry, for example, he often led for the opposition and rejected attempts to recruit him into government on the grounds of policy differences and loyalty to his colleagues.

Chancellor of the exchequer and leader of the house, 1807–1809 There was therefore no doubt that Perceval could command high office in the Pittite ministry formed in March 1807 by the infirm stop-gap prime minister, the duke of Portland, following the collapse of Grenville's government on the Catholic question. Indeed his claims were particularly strong as he was the only member of the quartet of future Pittite leaders whose degree of opposition to Catholic emancipation coincided with that of the king. Portland consequently offered Perceval the chancellorship of the exchequer with the 'lead' in the Commons, the latter, perhaps, because of the equal pretensions of the emerging rivals for the succession to Pitt, Castlereagh and Canning. However, much to the consternation of his colleagues and friends, Perceval initially declined the exchequer, pleading as his reasons his preference for the attorney-generalship (and the continuation of his private practice), the inadequacy of the income of £3700 p.a., and his distaste for the 'financial and other labours' which the

post would involve. It was only after several days of discussions that he was persuaded to change his mind, the pill being sweetened by the additional post of the duchy of Lancaster which raised the annual salary to £4000. Once again he had been drawn into a position rather than having marked it out for himself.

The Portland government of which Perceval thus became a part was confronted by two outstanding problems: Bonaparte's European hegemony and, in numbers at least, one of the strongest parliamentary oppositions since the early 1780s. Perceval's chief responsibility at the exchequer was to find the economic means to confront the threat from abroad. This he did by framing the orders in council which put under blockade all harbours from which British ships were excluded by Bonaparte's Berlin decrees of 1806; and by budgets in 1808 and 1809 which, while imposing no new taxes, made economies in expenditure and raised loans for the war effort at very favourable rates. None of these policies was novel: the orders drew heavily for argument on James Stephen's 1805 pamphlet on the subject; and Perceval's budgets were in line with the orthodox view of the time that the economy could not bear additional taxation.

The task of confronting the opposition as leader of the Commons proved much more demanding and contentious. Although by no means united in purpose, elements of the opposition harried the ministry on the issues of Catholic emancipation, the conduct of the war (including the related issue of the alleged peculation of the commander-in-chief, the duke of York), and, most persistently as a result of the inquiries and reports of a Commons finance committee, the allegedly excessive patronage available to ministers through places, pensions, sinecures, reversions, and the purchase of seats in parliament.

After a characteristically hesitant start Perceval responded with a successful resistance. His most uncompromising stand was taken on the Catholic question. In his address to the Northampton electors at the by-election following his appointment to office in March 1807 he nailed his colours firmly to the theme of 'No Popery'—a theme that became a popular anthem at the subsequent general election. Later he opposed the increase of the annual grant to Maynooth College and led the successful opposition to the Catholic petition of 1808. On other matters, however, he was prepared to compromise. In the case of the defence of the duke of York, for example, he performed brilliantly in the house as the duke's counsel but was realistic enough to recognize that the majority that he secured for a plea of innocence would evaporate unless the duke resigned. This was advice that the king and the duke accepted.

Perceval was equally realistic about ministerial patronage and power. The most radical proponents of reform sought full disclosure of all places and pensions held by MPs, the abolition of reversionary posts, and the outlawing of the purchase of parliamentary seats; these were hors-d'oeuvres to the main radical dish of 'parliamentary reform', shorthand for an extension of the franchise and a redistribution of seats. Perceval himself had no time for pensions and reversions but he recognized that the existing form of government could be sustained only by some measure of ministerial patronage and was conscious that his own brother, Arden, was one of the best-endowed sinecurists. He consequently sought to moderate rather than resist radical demands. With regard to the disclosure of places and pensions he successfully persuaded its sponsor to require the names of all holders rather than just those of MPs. This had the effect of delaying disclosure until 1810. In the case of a bill to bring to an end the appointment to reversionary posts—an issue which most closely touched Arden's interests—he manoeuvred its blockade in the Lords in 1807 and eventually came to an arrangement with its sponsor that limited its operation to one year. As for the sale of parliamentary seats, he successfully weakened Curwen's bill of 1809 which was designed to bring the practice to an end. There, however, his flexibility ceased for on the issue of parliamentary reform he expressed, once again, implacable opposition.

The premiership In the second week of August 1809 the duke of Portland suffered a stroke. With encouragement from the king, his colleagues immediately set about deciding on a successor. The portents for calm and rational deliberation could hardly have been more unpropitious. Earlier in the year Canning, the foreign secretary, had threatened to resign over what he regarded as an incompetence of Castlereagh, the secretary at war. As a result the king had concocted a plan to transfer responsibility for the war from Castlereagh to Canning. However, the plan depended on Castlereagh's being kept in the dark until the end of the parliamentary session, by which time the military expedition to Walcheren, which he had planned and on which war hopes were pinned, would have taken place. As details of the plan became known to a widening circle of cabinet members but not to the hapless Castlereagh, intrigue and recriminations flourished.

Perceval responded to these developments honourably and realistically. He deprecated the deception of Castlereagh and threatened to resign if it was carried through. As for the premiership, for which he was obviously a leading candidate, he wrote of it as an exceedingly unattractive proposition given the existence 'of so many ... of equal or nearly equal importance' within the cabinet (Perceval to Huskisson, 21 Aug 1809, Perceval MSS). Eschewing any eagerness for it for himself he recommended his friend Lord Harrowby to Canning at the end of August.

The choice of a successor took a further month of elaborate negotiation. Canning responded to the suggestion of Harrowby with the view that Portland's successor should be in the Commons and also indicated that he himself would not serve under Perceval. Perceval, for his part, considered whether his own dignity would enable him to serve under Canning but decided against once Liverpool and others had said that they would not do so. Canning subsequently withdrew from the contest and, fearing that he and his followers would vote against them, Perceval and his colleagues opened a negotiation for a coalition government with the opposition leaders, lords Grenville

and Grey, Perceval expressing a willingness to serve under either as home secretary. This too came to nothing, with the result that on 30 September the cabinet recommended Perceval to the king as Portland's successor. The king did not 'pause' in accepting their recommendation and Perceval responded on 2 October that although he would not be found 'wanting in exertion, in industry, in zeal & in duty ... in talent & power, he feels his great defects for such a station in such arduous times' (*Later Correspondence of George III*, 5.386). As these words and his previous conduct suggest, it was not an advancement he had engineered or sought.

Perceval nevertheless proved to be a remarkably resilient prime minister. His primary responsibility was to construct and maintain a strong administration at what was a critical juncture in the war. The falling-out of Pitt's friends and the numerical strength of the opposition groups made this an unusually difficult task. As a result of their differences over the succession to Portland, Canning declined to play a part and took with him three of his own followers. In addition, Perceval was unable to come to terms with three other Pittite alumni, lords Hardwicke, Sidmouth, and Melville, the last two of whom commanded significant parliamentary groupings of their own. A further set-back occurred when he was obliged to continue as chancellor of the exchequer, this time unsalaried, as a result of a succession of refusals to fill the post. His nine-man cabinet, which had only two members in the Commons, was therefore unable to command the firm allegiance of all the significant figures in his own party.

Furthermore the political problems Perceval confronted in his first year in office were exceptionally severe. In the 1810 parliamentary session the government was pressed hard, principally on what turned out to be a disastrous Walcheren expedition, but also on the composition of the finance committee: in fact it was defeated in six major divisions of the Commons, in some cases as a result of the opposition of Canning, Castlereagh, and even the small band of MPs who shared Perceval's evangelicalism—the 'Saints'. Moreover a potentially fatal blow was delivered in October when the king, the Perceval government's main prop among the neutrals in parliament, lost his sanity.

Perceval confronted these problems stoutly and with little disposition to trim—he was, as Whitbread put it on one occasion, 'as bold as brass'. He made some concessions on measures, most particularly on the inquiry into Walcheren, but otherwise steered his own course. Recognizing his weaknesses in parliament, for example, he made several attempts between the spring and summer of 1810 to recruit Sidmouth, Canning, and Castlereagh but declined opportunities to take them in individually, preferring as complete a reunion of Pitt's friends as possible. Moreover in response to the king's illness he did not hesitate to introduce (13 December 1810) Pitt's Regency Bill of 1788, albeit for a year only, which, by placing restrictions on the regent's powers, was bound to give the prince of Wales and his supposed friends, the whigs, a major opportunity to topple the government. That he survived these vicissitudes owed more to luck than to judgement. On the critical issue of the Walcheren inquiry, the government survived as a result of the resignation of the expedition's commander, Lord Chatham, and the fact that waverers and independents in the Commons preferred the government to the opposition. As for the Regency Bill, the opposition played its hand poorly with the result that the bill passed with paper-thin majorities in full houses. Moreover the run of good fortune continued when, despite rumours to the contrary, the prince abandoned the whigs in February 1811 and retained Perceval in office, largely from fear of what the king would do should he recover his sanity and find Lord Grenville or Lord Grey his prime minister.

The satisfactory outcome of the Regency Bill proved to be the turning point for the government. During the year of its operation, despite successfully resisting some of the prince's more extravagant claims upon the taxpayer, Perceval gradually earned his favour. When the restrictions came to an end in February 1812, the prince tried to persuade the whig leaders to join the government but was unsuccessful: thereafter the prince's political support, now as important as that of the king had once been, flowed in the government's direction. Perceval, for his part, adroitly manoeuvred the one loose cannon in his cabinet, the foreign secretary, Lord Wellesley, into resigning in February 1812 and introduced into it lords Castlereagh and Sidmouth. In the summer of 1811 Lord Liverpool had written of Perceval's having 'acquired an authority' in the House of Commons, 'beyond any minister in my recollection, except Mr Pitt' (Yonge, 1.372). By the spring of 1812 the ministry as a whole looked impregnable.

Perceval's policies also contributed to the improvement in the government's fortunes. His principal objective was to fund the offensive against Bonaparte that the Peninsular campaign had put into motion. To achieve this in his capacity as his own chancellor he pursued much the same policies as he had done when Portland's. He therefore continued with economies and rationalization in government departments. With regard to budgetary policy he did prepare a daring plan to 'raid' the hallowed sinking fund for supplies but, fearing the outcry, dropped it and adopted the traditional policy of raising money by loans as opposed to new taxes—the loans being based on rigorously scrutinized terms and funded in part by annual exchequer bills, thereby limiting long-term debt. Finally, he produced successful plans of his own to purchase at the best prices the specie necessary for the troops at the front. These were practical policies within an orthodox financial framework: they eschewed newfangled theories of debt redemption and set to one side the fears resulting from the depreciation of paper currency. In fact Perceval was so wedded to his particular recipe for an offensive war that he introduced a bill to make paper currency legal tender—thereby flying in the face of the growing army of bullionists; and only conceded with extreme reluctance the case for an inquiry into the orders in council (March 1812) on the grounds of its damaging impact on the economy. On the other hand, from the evidence of the Peninsular campaign Perceval could claim with justice that the war effort had prospered under his stewardship.

Perceval also ploughed a well-established furrow with regard to domestic issues. His principal objective remained resistance to any change in the balance of the constitution whether pressed by British radicals or Irish Catholics. The first test for this resolve came early in 1810 when London-based radicals, including Sir Francis Burdett, the MP for Westminster, construed a standing order that enabled the Commons to clear the gallery of strangers as an attack on the liberty of the press and called for a public debate on the issue. Despite the fact that Burdett had acquired a heroic stature among popular radicals in London, Perceval decided on the sternest possible response—Burdett's commitment to the Tower for accusing the house of the arbitrary use of its privileges—and engineered successful motions to this end by two backbench MPs. This led in early April to one of the most dangerous confrontations ever seen in Hanoverian London between radical and government forces, which nevertheless resulted in Perceval's standing firm and achieving Burdett's imprisonment. He thereby underlined his staunch support for the *status quo* and seemed to be vindicated in his judgement on the preponderance of conservative over radical forces when Burdett's release in June passed off without incident.

A similar line of resistance can be detected in his dealings with the Catholic question. The new factors here were the whigs' idea of a royal veto on episcopal appointments to make emancipation more palatable to traditionalists, and the supposed sympathy of the prince of Wales for Catholic claims—a sympathy which encouraged the Catholic leaders in Dublin to summon a convention to apply pressure when the regency came into effect. Perceval stood firm. In response to the idea of a royal veto he wrote an anonymous pamphlet, *Six Letters on the Subject of Dr. Milner's Explanation* (1809), which reaffirmed his opposition to emancipation. As for the proposed convention, he was anxious to prevent the ardently anti-Catholic lord lieutenant from acting too firmly against it but was saved any embarrassment when the prince himself effectively scuppered its prospects of success by discovering his obligations to the established church. As in the case of winning the parliamentary battle, Perceval's fortunes as prime minister were strongly affected by the whims of the prince of Wales.

Death by assassination, 1812 On 11 May 1812 and at the height of his power Perceval was shot dead in the lobby of the House of Commons by John *Bellingham, a merchant with an uncontrollable grudge against the British government, which he focused on the prime minister. Stunned, and fearful that the assassination signalled a popular uprising—as indeed it was seen to be by popular elements in London and the economically hard-pressed midlands—the Commons met the following day and voted Jane Perceval £2000 p.a. with remainder to her eldest son, a grant of £50,000 to his family, and a monument to her husband in

Westminster Abbey. On 16 May Perceval was given a private funeral at his wife's request and was buried in Lord Egmont's family vault at St Luke's, Charlton, near to his birthplace. In the meantime Bellingham was tried and condemned to death, his plea of insanity being rejected. On 18 May he was hanged.

Assessments Assessments of Perceval's personal qualities made at the time of his death have scarcely been altered by subsequent research. The consensus then was that he was the epitome of virtue: loyal and caring to his family and friends, a devout Anglican, incorruptible, hard-working, and straightforward in his dealings with others. Charles Herries, who knew him well, summed him up as 'the model of a high-minded, high-principled, truthful, generous gentleman, sans peur et sans reproche' (Herries, 1.20). Subsequent research has confirmed this judgement.

Much the same can be said about the fundamental reason why Perceval became the first acknowledged leader of Pitt's friends—his debating skill. He could not, of course, rival Pitt: as one contemporary (J. W. Ward) commented: 'He wanted Mr Pitt's splendid declamatory eloquence' (*Letters to Ivy*, 157). On the other hand he could deal fully with a subject in plain English and, as the same contemporary noted in comparing him with Pitt:

> in quickness and dexterity as a debater he was (I think) hardly inferior to him. On the whole he appeared to me the most powerful man (independently of his situation) that we had had in Parliament since the death of Mr Fox. (*Letters to Ivy*, 196)

These are also judgements that have stood the test of research.

On the other hand, assessments of Perceval's role as a minister have changed over time. Before the publication of Gray's biography (1963) he was generally judged a reactionary with insufficient ability for the office of prime minister. Since then Gray and others have put his thoughts and actions into context. Evangelicalism, for example, is now regarded as a much more influential and widespread body of ideas than was once thought, and although Perceval was undoubtedly a member of its most conservative wing, his desire to reform the Church of England and to resist Catholic emancipation was not unpopular. Perceval may have been the first evangelical prime minister but he was not unique in his evangelicalism nor in his belief that the confessional state would not survive Catholic emancipation. Moreover the priority he gave as a minister to winning the war is now seen as part of a continuous official and popular commitment which whig historians, following the contemporary apologists for a peace, conveniently ignored. Further, the financial policies he pursued for that purpose, though not in themselves novel, played an important part in the success of the Peninsular campaign and in the subsequent allied victory, as Wellington later acknowledged.

That said, Perceval's vision was too limited and his outlook too narrow for him to have had a lasting impact on politics. His philosophy was marooned in the alarmism of the 1790s. He knew little at first hand of the world outside London and is said to have travelled no further than Knutsford and then only once. Moreover, though he filled the highest offices he did so more out of a sense of duty than of ambition. This may be the reason why he was unable to meet the needs of his followers by replacing Pittism with a fresh body of ideas. Perhaps the most appropriate final judgement is that of his great adversary on the Catholic question, Henry Grattan: 'He is not a ship of the line, but he carries many guns, is tight-built, and is out in all weathers' (Gray, 468).   P. J. JUPP

Sources D. Gray, *Spencer Perceval: the evangelical prime minister, 1762–1812* (1963) · R. G. Thorne, 'Perceval, Spencer', HoP, *Commons* · DNB · S. Perceval, *A review of the arguments in favour of a continuance of impeachments notwithstanding a dissolution* (1791) · S. Perceval, *The duties and powers of public officers with respect to violations of the public peace* (1792) · S. Perceval, *Observations intended to point out an application of a prophecy in the eleventh chapter of the book of Daniel to the French power* (1800) · E. Herries, ed., *Memoir of the public life of the Rt. Hon. J. C. Herries*, 2 vols. (1880) · *Letters to Ivy by Lord Ward and Dudley*, ed. S. H. Romilly (1905) · S. Perceval, *A letter to the Rev. Dr. Mansel on the Curates' Bill* (1808) · A. B. [S. Perceval], *Six letters on the subject of Dr. Milner's explanation* (1809) · W. Cobbett, *The parliamentary debates* · B. Hilton, *The age of atonement: the influence of evangelicalism on social and economic thought, 1795–1865* (1988) · S. Walpole, *The life of the Rt. Hon. Spencer Perceval*, 2 vols. (1874) · J. C. Earle, 'Spencer Perceval', *English premiers from Sir Robert Walpole to Sir Robert Peel*, 2 (1871), 101–30 · P. Treherne, *The Rt. Hon. Spencer Perceval* (1911) · C. V. Williams, *The life and administration of the Rt. Hon. Spencer Perceval* (1812) · *The later correspondence of George III*, ed. A. Aspinall, 5 vols. (1962–70) · C. D. Yonge, *The life and administration of Robert Banks, second earl of Liverpool*, 3 vols. (1868)

Archives BL, corresp., Add. MSS 38191, 38243–38247 · BL, corresp. and papers, Add. MSS 49173–49195 · CUL · FM Cam., letters and papers · priv. coll., corresp. and papers | All Souls Oxf., letters to Charles Richard Vaughan · BL, letters to Lord Bathurst, loan 57 · BL, corresp. with Lord Wellesley, Add. MSS 37292–37296 · BL, corresp. with Sir James Willoughby Gordon, Add. MS 49476 · BL, corresp. with C. P. Yorke, Add. MS 45036 · Bodl. Oxf., corresp. with George Canning and Lord Portland [copies] · CKS, letters to William Pitt · Glos. RO, corresp. with Lord Redesdale · NA Scot., corresp. with Sir Alexander Hope · NA Scot., corresp. with Lord Melville · NL Wales, letters to first Baron Newborough · priv. coll., letters to William Adam · priv. coll., letters to A. B. Drummond · priv. coll., letters to Lord Eldon · priv. coll., corresp. with Lord Melville [copies] · PRO, letters to William Pitt and Lord Chatham, PRO 30/8 · PRO NIre., corresp. with Lord Castlereagh · PRO NIre., corresp. with John Foster · Royal Arch., letters to George III · Sandon Hall, Staffordshire, Harrowby Manuscript Trust, corresp. with Lord Harrowby · W. Yorks. AS, Leeds, letters to George Canning · Wilts. & Swindon RO, corresp. with eleventh earl of Pembroke

Likenesses W. Beechey, portrait, 1812, University College Hospital, London · A. Cardon, stipple, pubd 1812 (after Miles; after miniature), BM, NPG · Godby and Dubourg, lithograph, pubd 1812, BM, NPG · G. F. Joseph, oils, 1812 (after death mask by Nollekens), NPG · G. F. Joseph, oils, 1812 (after death mask by Nollekens), Trinity Cam. · G. F. Joseph, portrait, 1812, Royal Courts of Justice, London · J. Nollekens, marble bust, c.1812, NPG · J. Nollekens, marble bust, 1813, Wellington Museum, London · W. Skelton, line engraving, pubd 1813 (after W. Beechey), BM, NPG · G. F. Joseph, oils, 1816 (after death mask by Nollekens), Gov. Art Coll. · R. Westmacott, monument, 1816, Westminster Abbey · F. Chantrey, marble bust, 1817, probably Charlton church, Greenwich, London · F. Chantrey, statue, 1818, Northampton town hall · J. Nollekens, marble bust, 1818, Belton House, Lincolnshire · studio of J. Nollekens, marble bust (after original, c.1812), NPG [*see illus.*] · stipple, BM, NPG; repro. in *Trial between the duke of York and Col. Wardle*

Percival, Arthur Ernest (1887–1966), army officer, was born on 26 December 1887 at Aspenden Lodge, Aspenden, near Buntingford, north Hertfordshire, the younger of the two sons of Alfred Reginald Percival, from a well-known Northamptonshire family, land agent of the Hamels Park estate, and his wife, Edith, *née* Miller (*c*.1857–1941), from a Lancashire cotton family. From 1897 to 1901 he and his brother attended the private Bengeo School, Hertford. In 1901 they went to Rugby School, where they were in School House on the classical side. Percival excelled neither at school work—'not a good classic' (Kinvig, 5)—nor at games, but gained a higher school certificate. He was colour sergeant in the volunteer rifle corps. He left school in 1906 and in 1907 became a clerk in a City of London firm, Naylor, Benzon & Co., iron ore dealers, of Abchurch Lane. He ran cross-country, played games, and was a member of the Youngsbury rifle club and a skilled shot. But for the First World War he would not have become a professional soldier.

Early military career After the outbreak of war Percival enlisted in the Inns of Court Officers' Training Corps (OTC). After training, in September 1914 he received a temporary commission as second lieutenant, and was appointed to the new 7th (service) battalion, the Bedfordshire regiment, in Kitchener's volunteer 'New Army'. In December he was promoted lieutenant. In February 1915 his battalion was transferred to 54 brigade, 18th (Eastern) division, the latter commanded by Major-General Ivor Maxse (1862–1958), an old Rugbeian and an exceptional military trainer and commander. Percival remained with the same regiment, brigade, and division throughout the war. In July 1915 the 7th Bedfords went to France, and from August they served on the western front. They suffered heavy casualties on the first day of the Somme, 1 July 1916. Percival survived unscathed and was awarded an MC for his 'fine leadership and determination under heavy shell and machine gun fire … with absolute disregard of danger' (Kinvig, 30). In September 1916, during the attack on the Schwaben redoubt, he was wounded by shell fragments, then hospitalized in England. In October, while in hospital, he was gazetted a regular army captain in the Essex regiment, though he continued to serve with the Bedfords. During the German offensive in March 1918 the Bedfords were forced to retreat, but they successfully counter-attacked at Babœuf. Percival was awarded the DSO (September 1918) and the Croix de Guerre. In May he was temporary acting brigade commander, 54 brigade. In that month the 7th were incorporated into the 2nd battalion and Percival became its commander. In 1918 he was described as 'a slim, soft-spoken young man … with a proven reputation for bravery and organisation powers' (ibid., 47). At the end of the war his brigade commander reported that Percival was 'an excellent and most efficient officer, beloved by his officers, NCOs and men … a very brave and gallant officer … exceptionally gifted' (ibid., 48). He was lucky to have survived: of his OTC intake nearly a third died in the war.

In 1919 and 1920 Percival served as major and second-in-command of the 46th Royal Fusiliers in Brigadier-General Edmund Ironside's north Russian relief force, part of the allied anti-Bolshevik intervention in the former Russian empire. For his role in the successful August 1919 Gorodok operation, south-east of Archangel, he was awarded a bar to his DSO (January 1920). From 1920 to 1922 he served on counter-insurgency operations in co. Cork with the 1st battalion, the Essex regiment, surviving attempts to murder him. In 1921 he was awarded an OBE. In 1923–4 he attended the Staff College, Camberley, where he was taught by J. F. C. Fuller and played cricket and tennis. Ironside, the commandant, considered him 'an officer of exceptional ability and intelligence' (Kinvig, 92) and recommended him for accelerated promotion. In 1923 he was promoted major in the Cheshire regiment. From 1925 to 1929 he served as staff officer with the Nigerian regiment in Northern Nigeria. On home leave he married at Holy Trinity Church, West Brompton, London, on 27 July 1927, Margaret Elizabeth (Betty) MacGregor Greer (1897/8–1953), daughter of Thomas MacGregor Greer, a linen merchant, of Tullylagan Manor, Tyrone, Northern Ireland. They had one daughter, Dorinda Margery, later Lady Dunleath, and one son, James, later an officer in the Cheshire regiment.

After a brief period as a company commander in the 2nd Cheshires in England, Percival in 1930 attended the course at the Royal Naval College, Greenwich. In 1931–2 he was an instructor (general staff officer, 2nd grade) at the Staff College under Major-General John Dill, whom he liked and admired. Dill was impressed by Percival—'the best officer I have met for a long time' (Kinvig, 95)—became his patron, and for the next decade advanced his career. From 1932 to 1934 Percival commanded the 2nd battalion, the Cheshire regiment, in Malta. He attended the 1935 course at the Imperial Defence College.

Malaya, with its rubber and tin exports and the Singapore naval base—intermittently constructed since 1923—was most important to the British empire. To defend Malaya and other British imperial interests in the Far East and the Pacific against Japanese aggression, the 'Singapore strategy', flexible offensive and defensive plans, envisaged sending a large balanced fleet to Singapore. The scenario of a Japanese invasion of Malaya and attack on Singapore from the north was studied by British officers, including Percival, at the Staff College and the Imperial Defence College. Promoted colonel, Percival was, through Dill's influence, from 1936 to 1938 general staff officer, Malaya, effectively chief of staff to Major-General William Dobbie, GOC Malaya (1935–9). Percival travelled extensively and found the defence situation unsatisfactory, with inter-service disagreement and the civil authorities unco-operative. He was aware of Japanese espionage and amphibious capability, and warned against their trying to 'burgle Malaya by the back door' (Kinvig, 106), using bases in Siam. In 1937, with Dobbie's approval, he wrote an appreciation warning of Japanese use of Siam and Kelantan, emphasizing the importance of defending northern Malaya, and the need for air, sea, and land reinforcements; he submitted a copy to the War Office.

From 1938 to 1939 Percival was brigadier-general staff

(BGS), home command, at Aldershot under Dill, GOC-in-C home command, training for war. After its outbreak Dill commanded the 1st corps of the British expeditionary force (BEF) in France, with Percival his BGS, during the 'phoney war'. In February 1940 Percival was appointed to command the 43rd Wessex division in England. He was briefly an assistant chief of Imperial General Staff at the War Office, and from 1940 to 1941 GOC 44th (Home Counties) division.

Malayan tragedy, 1941–1942 In May 1941 Percival, selected by Dill over several more senior officers, was appointed GOC Malaya with the acting rank of lieutenant-general. He was a brave, hard-working, and outstanding staff officer, but he had a reputation as a 'staff wallah': from 1932 to 1941 he had spent nine years as a staff officer and less than a year as commander of a formation. He had had no combat experience since 1922, and no experience of higher command in war. Moreover, as the Malayan campaign showed, he lacked drive, aggression, ruthlessness, robustness, decisiveness, leadership, and the ability to inspire his troops. He was unwilling to take calculated risks and acted more as a staff officer than a commander. Duff Cooper told Churchill Pervical was no leader. Pownall thought him 'an uninspiring leader and rather gloomy' (Simpson, 269). Gordon Bennett thought him 'weak and hesitant though brainy' (ibid., 263). Ian Morrison, a journalist, wrote that he was 'a completely negative person, with no vigour, no colour, and no conviction' (ibid., 270). He was modest and self-effacing. Moreover, his appearance was unimpressive and uninspiring: 'a tall thin person, whose most conspicuous characteristics were two protruding rabbit teeth' (ibid., 269). An army veteran later stated, 'He just didn't look the part' (Elphick, 161).

Percival arrived at Singapore in May 1941. He knew that the Japanese might attack northern Malaya and thence Singapore, and the relative status of his command in British grand strategy. Yet he lacked vision, thoroughness, and flexible forward and contingency planning and preparation in the event of possible reverses. He requested reinforcements, including tanks, for which both his two predecessors had also asked. He ordered training based on the orthodox UK syllabus, not for local conditions, and failed to ensure that formations trained well: most did not. Before and during the campaign he failed, despite advice, to implement sufficiently early and on a sufficient scale, fixed defences on the mainland and Singapore Island. Nor did he order stay-behind guerrilla units of local Europeans and Chinese—who loathed the Japanese for their invasion of China and the atrocities they committed there—to attack the Japanese line of communication and rear. He also failed to ensure efficient destruction of abandoned airfields, military supplies, and other resources. Moreover, he failed to inspire his troops and to instil in them an ethos of competence and confidence.

As commander against the Japanese invasion Percival had a most difficult, arguably impossible, task. By 1940 the Singapore strategy had vanished, with no main fleet to send. Churchill's government gave priority to the Near East and Russia. The RAF in Malaya was understrength, with largely obsolete aircraft. The Hurricanes sent were too few and too late. There was no radar outside Singapore Island. Moreover, the RAF was betrayed by a traitor, Captain Patrick Heenan (1910–1941). The pre-war defences on Singapore Island, the misnamed 'Fortress Singapore', were against seaborne attack. Though it was a later myth that the heavy guns all pointed the wrong way, they had largely armour-piercing shells. Percival was subordinate to Air Chief Marshal Sir Robert Brooke-Popham (commander-in-chief Far East command) and to Wavell (the supreme commander of the American-British-Dutch-Australian command), and part of a cumbrous, top-heavy, civil-military command structure, lacked control over the unco-operative civil authorities, and had limited but undefined authority over the Australian Imperial Force. His staff was inadequate and some of his subordinates incompetent and querulous. His command was heterogeneous and polyglot, many units had only recently arrived, and both radio and telephone communications were inadequate. Though a few units—notably the Gurkhas and the 2nd battalion, Argyll and Sutherland Highlanders—were good, many of Percival's troops were raw, insufficiently trained, and inexperienced. Many Indian units had been 'milked' of experienced officers and NCOs, and some sepoys had never seen a tank. Percival lacked tanks and sufficient anti-tank and anti-aircraft guns. Moreover, British disadvantages were exacerbated by an almost incredible sequence of bungling and mischance. These included the *Automedon* episode—in 1940 crucial British data on the defence of Malaya, conveyed in the merchant ship *Automedon*, was captured by Germans and passed to the Japanese—and the destruction of force Z. The claim, later much repeated, that the British forces outnumbered the Japanese, was arguably irrelevant. The Japanese had decisive air, naval, tank, and intelligence superiority.

Percival saw his mission as defending the Singapore naval base and therefore all of Malaya, including the scattered RAF airfields. He chose to deploy by the beaches to repel invasion rather than concentrate inland for a counter-offensive, so his inadequate forces were widely dispersed. Assuming that the Japanese would attack from Thailand (Siam), Percival and Brooke-Popham planned a pre-emptive move thither, operation Matador. In August 1941 Brigadier Ivan Simson arrived in Singapore as chief engineer, Malaya command. He was efficient, energetic, and up to date on fixed defences, having worked on the UK anti-invasion defences. He proposed a system of defensive positions to complement mobile troops. Percival and his staff rejected it, alleging that it would harm the troops' morale and offensive spirit. The British government and Brooke-Popham delayed Matador until too late to start. The Japanese attacked Malaya from 8 December 1941. The RAF, obsolete and outnumbered, failed to inflict the promised losses (up to 40 per cent) on the invaders, but themselves suffered heavy losses. On 10 December force Z was destroyed. The Japanese Twenty-Fifth Army, commanded by Lieutenant-General Yamashita Tomoyuki (in

1946 hanged as a war criminal for atrocities in the Philippines), largely combat-experienced, with air superiority and over 200 tanks, repeatedly outfought the British forces tactically, using mobility, infiltration, and outflanking, driving them south and capturing airfields, supplies, and boats. Some British units fought well and had local successes, but repeatedly the failures of pre-war training, planning, and preparation showed. Japanese tactics were not countered, bridges not blown, airfields not cratered, and abandoned supplies and transport were not destroyed. Percival, leaving battles to subordinate field commanders, attempted to plan strategy and to respond to the fluid situation of defeats and withdrawals. Reinforcements continued to reach Singapore: not tanks, but raw, inexperienced, and unacclimatized troops. Percival tried to fight a lengthy delaying action in Perak, but unsuccessfully. He made avoidable mistakes and what were, with hindsight, wrong decisions. He dispersed his troops instead of concentrating against the main enemy thrust, enabling the Japanese to defeat the British piecemeal. He failed to construct defences in Johore and to counter-attack there when the Japanese were at the end of a long line of communications and running short of ammunition.

Surrender of Singapore On 31 January 1942 the British retreated onto Singapore Island. Despite its designation, Singapore was not a fortress with all-round fortifications. In December Simson had made a comprehensive proposal for improving defences. Percival rejected this, claiming that 'defences are bad for morale—for both troops and civilians' (Murfett and others, 221). Unwilling to take a calculated risk, he dispersed his troops to defend the entire coastline, over-garrisoning the south, which already had fixed heavy artillery, and failing to concentrate on the vulnerable north. Against evidence and advice, he assumed that the Japanese would attack from the north-east, not the north-west. Belatedly he changed his mind, but the damage was done. On 8 February the Japanese invaded Singapore Island. The defence was bungled and Percival decided against a general counter-attack. An RAF officer who saw him on 13 February described him as 'in such a state of dither. He appeared utterly broken' (Allen, 7). Wavell reported low morale among the defenders and their 'inferiority complex which bold and skilful Japanese tactics and their command of the air have caused' (Gilbert, *Road to Victory*, 54). With the situation further deteriorating, on the morning of Sunday 15 February 1942 Percival convened the decisive conference at Fort Canning. He and his subordinates agreed that a counter-attack would fail and that they should surrender. They were influenced by shortages of ammunition and other supplies, by belief that the water supply was about to collapse (an assumption later questioned), and by the massive desertion, notably of Australians, still an emotive and contentious issue, which for political reasons the British official history glossed over. Yet the desertion itself was 'the terrible end-result of many other factors' (Elphick, 364). With plummeting morale too few troops were still willing to fight.

Possibly, but for this, a counter-attack might have succeeded: 'Percival and his staff cannot escape a large share of the blame' (Murfett and others, 359). In his last cable to Wavell, reporting the surrender decision, Percival wrote 'All ranks have done their best' (Churchill, 94), a claim that historians have subsequently rejected. Later that day, in an event stage-managed, filmed, and photographed by the Japanese for their propaganda, Percival and three officers, one carrying a union flag and one a white flag, marched to the Ford factory at Bukit Timah. There Percival negotiated with Yamashita and agreed to almost unconditional surrender. He later claimed, 'There was not much chance of bargaining, but I did what I could' (Percival, 292). It was, Churchill wrote, 'the worst disaster and largest capitulation in British history' (Churchill, 81). It was followed by years of immense suffering and mortality among the prisoners of war, 10,000 of whom died in captivity. It was followed also by the Japanese massacre of Singapore Chinese, possibly over 50,000, 'ethnic cleansing … appalling genocide' (Murfett and others, 249–50). After the surrender some soldiers bitterly blamed Percival, but others claimed that he was the scapegoat.

Prisoner of war and the post-war period, 1942–1966 Maltreated and malnourished, Percival was held prisoner at Changi, then in Formosa and Manchuria. After the Japanese surrender, he was freed by American and Russian troops in August 1945. At MacArthur's invitation in September he attended the Japanese surrender ceremony on board USS *Missouri* in Tokyo Bay, and was placed immediately behind MacArthur. He also attended Yamashita's surrender at Manila. He flew back to England in September, and at the War Office wrote his Malaya dispatch. As a result of pressure from the Air Ministry and the Colonial Office it was modified, delayed, and not published until early 1948: 'something of a damp squib' (Kinvig, 242), it was suspected of being a cover-up. In 1946 Percival was retired with the honorary rank of lieutenant-general, but not with the knighthood customary for one of his rank. In 1949 he published *The War in Malaya*, a restrained and not entirely accurate account, favourably reviewed by J. F. C. Fuller. In it he exaggerated Japanese numbers, alleged that pre-war British soldiers had been 'pampered' and softened, and attributed the defeat to 'the lack of readiness in the British Commonwealth for war … failure to prepare for war' (Percival, 306), and to Japanese sea, air, and tank superiority. He read the draft of Major-General S. Woodburn Kirby's official history and disputed parts of it. After his release in 1945 he was shocked to learn of the barbaric Japanese treatment of prisoners of war: the mortality of prisoners of the Japanese was 27 per cent, compared to 4 per cent among those captured by the Germans. He became the active president of the Far East Prisoners of War Association (FEPOW), was instrumental in obtaining some, if very inadequate, compensation for ex-POWs from frozen Japanese assets, and became chairman of the FEPOW Welfare Trust. Expressing widely felt anger by former POWs at the film *The Bridge on the River Kwai* (1957), he helped to secure a screen statement that it was fiction. Percival resided at Bullards, Widford, Ware, Hertfordshire.

He was deputy lieutenant of Hertfordshire (1951), president of the Hertfordshire Red Cross, and from 1950 to 1955 colonel of the Cheshire regiment. He died on 31 January 1966 at King Edward VII's Hospital for Officers, Beaumont House, Beaumont Street, Westminster, and was buried in Hertfordshire.

Honourable, brave, combat-experienced, and a highly regarded army high flyer, Percival ultimately failed. He became internationally known and will be remembered as the general who surrendered at Singapore; the photograph of him marching to surrender was one of the best-known images from the war, repeatedly reproduced. He was not included in the *Dictionary of National Biography*. His friend Sir John Smyth VC wrote a eulogistic authorized biography, *Percival and the Tragedy of Singapore* (1971), emphasizing his qualities, especially his courage, and Clifford Kinvig wrote a fuller, sympathetic biography, *Scapegoat: General Percival of Singapore* (1996). There has also been a succession of books on the Malayan campaign and the fall of Singapore. A psychologist, Norman Dixon, in his controversial *On the Psychology of Military Incompetence* (1976), argued that military incompetence derived from psychological flaws, including 'ego-weakness', fear of failure, and authoritarianism. He cited Percival, alleging his passivity and rigidity, and claimed that Percival's dislike of 'effeminate' fixed defences resulted from unconscious doubts about his masculinity. Military historians were unconvinced. Nevertheless, most consider that in Malaya, although the odds were heavily against him, Percival was partly responsible for the speed of the British defeat, and should have done better.   ROGER T. STEARN

Sources C. Kinvig, *Scapegoat: General Percival of Singapore* (1996) · A. E. Percival, *The war in Malaya* (1949) · J. Smyth, *Percival and the tragedy of Singapore* (1971) · *The Times* (2 Feb 1966) · *WWW*, 1961–1970 · O'M. Creagh and E. M. Humphris, *The distinguished service order, 1886–1923* [1923]; repr. (1978) · b. cert. · m. cert. · d. cert. · Kelly, *Handbk* (1939) · M. H. Murfett and others, *Between two oceans: a military history of Singapore from first settlement to final British withdrawal* (1999) · W. D. McIntyre, *The rise and fall of the Singapore naval base, 1919–1942* (1979) · S. W. Kirby, *Singapore: the chain of disaster* (1971) · L. Allen, *Singapore, 1941–1942* (1977) · M. Shennan, *Out in the midday sun: the British in Malaya, 1880–1960* (2000) · N. Dixon, *On the psychology of military incompetence* (1994) · P. Elphick, *Singapore, the pregnable fortress: a study in deception, discord and desertion* (1995) · K. Simpson, 'Percival: Lieutenant-General Arthur Percival', *Churchill's generals*, ed. J. Keegan (1999), 256–76 · P. Elphick and M. Smith, *Odd man out: the story of the Singapore traitor* (1994) · M. Gilbert, *Winston S. Churchill*, 6: *Finest hour, 1939–1941* (1983) · M. Gilbert, *Winston S. Churchill*, 7: *Road to victory, 1941–1945* (1986) · C. M. Bell, 'The 'Singapore strategy' and the deterrence of Japan: Winston Churchill, the admiralty and the dispatch of Force Z', *EngHR*, 116 (2001), 604–34 · W. S. Churchill, *The Second World War*, 4 (1951) · B. Bond, *British military policy between the two world wars* (1980) · B. Bond, *The pursuit of victory: from Napoleon to Saddam Hussein* (1996) · *CGPLA Eng. & Wales* (1966) · A. Warren, *Singapore 1942: Britain's greatest defeat* (2002)
Archives IWM, papers | FILM IWM FVA, film of the 1942 surrender
Likenesses drawing, 1941, repro. in Kinvig, *Scapegoat* · group portrait, photograph, 1945 (*Japanese surrender*), Hult. Arch. · W. Stoneman, photograph, 1949, NPG · photograph, 1950, repro. in Kinvig, *Scapegoat*
Wealth at death £102,515: probate, 18 March 1966, *CGPLA Eng. & Wales*

Percival, John (*d.* 1505), Franciscan friar, appears to have been a native of the midlands, since by 1463 he had become a friar in the Franciscan convent at Lichfield, and between that year and 1465 took orders up to the diaconate in that diocese. He had moved to the Cambridge convent by 12 March 1467, when he was ordained priest in the diocese of Ely, and later transferred to Oxford, where in 1482/3 he paid £6 13s. 4d. on his becoming doctor of theology. Some time between 10 February 1490 and 4 February 1498 he was appointed forty-seventh provincial minister of the English Franciscans. He died, still in office, on 16 December 1505, and was buried in the choir of the Greyfriars Church, London.   HENRY SUMMERSON

Sources Emden, *Cam.*, 450 · H. E. Salter, ed., *Mediaeval archives of the University of Oxford*, 2, OHS, 73 (1921), 336 [for 1919] · C. L. Kingsford, *The Grey friars of London*, British Society of Franciscan Studies, 6 (1915), 67, 73, 195, 211 · A. G. Little, *Franciscan papers, lists, and documents* (1943), 205

Percival, John. *See* Perceval, Jean (*d.* 1561).

Percival, John (1834–1918), headmaster and bishop of Hereford, was born at Brough Sowerby, Westmorland, on 27 September 1834, the eldest son of William Percival, a 'statesman' (that is, a farmer who owned his own land), and his wife, Jane (*d.* 1838), daughter of William Longmire (also a farmer) of Bolton, Westmorland. His boyhood was tough. Following the death of his mother he was brought up by her relatives, helping his uncle on the farm. He attended village schools at Winton and Hackthorpe before going to Appleby grammar school (1846–54), trudging to and from school in his studded clogs with a blue linen bag over his shoulder. To the end of his life he retained his broad Westmorland accent.

In 1854 Percival won an open scholarship to Queen's College, Oxford, where his intellectual qualities were quickly recognized. He gained the university junior mathematical scholarship and took firsts in classics and mathematics before being elected a fellow of Queen's in 1858. Long periods of intense study led to a breakdown in his health, and he spent the winter of 1858–9 recuperating at Pau in the south of France. There he met Louisa, daughter of James Holland. They married in 1862 and subsequently had a family of six children. In 1860 he was ordained deacon and accepted Frederick Temple's offer of a mastership at Rugby School. This began a lifelong friendship with the Temple family, especially with William Temple, Percival's godson and later his biographer.

On Frederick Temple's recommendation Percival was appointed in 1862 as the first headmaster of the newly founded Clifton College, Bristol. A born leader and pioneer he made Clifton into one of the leading public schools, largely because of his shrewd choice of masters. His sermons at Clifton, *Some Helps for School Life*, were published in 1880. Bristol gave him the opportunity to engage in other educational developments. He promoted a ragged school in the city, gave active support to the ideals and implementation of the Elementary Education Act of 1870, and with his wife was one of the organizers in 1868 of a committee to promote the higher education of women. In

1877 he helped to found Clifton High School for Girls and subsequently became president of the girls' high school at Redland. In his influential pamphlet, *The Connection of the Universities and the Great Towns* (1873), he urged Oxford and Cambridge to provide university teaching in provincial towns and cities, and with Gilbert Elliot, dean of Bristol, he was a leader in the movement to establish University College, Bristol, which opened in 1877.

In January 1879 Percival left Clifton College to become president of Trinity College, Oxford, where he remained until 1886. His time at Trinity was not the happiest of his life, largely because his manner and temperament suited that of a headmaster of a school more than head of a college. However, his work outside the college gave him the greatest satisfaction and opportunity. He was chairman of the committee which in 1879 founded Somerville Hall, Oxford, the non-denominational college for women, and he was instrumental in recruiting Madeleine Shaw Lefevre as its first principal. He was also a vigorous promoter of the university adult education movement and played an influential part in Michael Sadler's appointment as secretary of the Oxford Extension Delegacy. From 1882 to 1887 he was a canon of Bristol Cathedral, residing there in university vacations, where he started Sunday evening services.

In May 1887 Percival became headmaster of Rugby School. There was a feeling that the school had slackened under his cultivated predecessor, Jex-Blake, and he set about a moral crusade with a relentless and puritanical fervour. He terrified new boys by his dour warning, 'There are many bad boys here, there is a lot of evil in the place. Eh, I shall be watching you every day of your lives' (Temple, 113). He attacked 'idleness' and 'loafing', while signifying his anxiety about 'impurity' by his insistence that boys' football shorts should be worn below the knee and secured by elastic (hence his nickname, 'Percival of the Knees'). Within a short time the prestige of the school rose under his stern moral, spiritual, and intellectual leadership.

In January 1895 Lord Rosebery, the Liberal prime minister, nominated Percival to the bishopric of Hereford. The queen attempted to resist the recommendation on the ground that Percival, a strong Liberal in politics, was a known supporter of disestablishment of the Welsh church (having written to *The Times* on the subject in May 1894). Rosebery prevailed, insisting that he could not appoint a supporter of the establishment to a diocese which included thirteen Welsh parishes. The Hereford years were lonely ones for Percival, who lost his wife in 1896. He missed the fellowship of school and university life, though his marriage in 1899 to an old family friend, Mary Georgina, daughter of Frederick Symonds, brought him solace and affection. He found the large sprawling rural diocese difficult to administer; nor was it easy to create a sense of fellowship within it. He appointed distinguished scholars to the cathedral canonries, but they were largely out of touch with the parishes. In an agricultural and predominantly Conservative region Percival's radical views on social and political issues did not always go down

well; he chaired the 1897 Lambeth conference's committee on industrial problems, supported the Liberal government's 1906 Education Bill, and attacked slum landlords in 1909. He was a broad-churchman, suspicious of ritualists. His invitation to nonconformists to join holy communion at Hereford Cathedral to mark the coronation of George V attracted strong protests from Lord Halifax and the English Church Union.

His successor, Hensley Henson, commented that Percival's 'interest and his influence were national rather than diocesan, educational rather than ecclesiastical' (H. H. Henson, *Retrospect of an Unimportant Life*, 1, 1942, 273). The early years of the twentieth century saw Percival once more involved in movements concerned with educational development and reform. He chaired the founding meeting of the Workers' Educational Association at Oxford in 1903 and gave its founder, Albert Mansbridge, unstinting help in its early years. He saw the development of working-class adult education as one of the great pioneering achievements of the time. In 1907 he spoke in the House of Lords in favour of Bishop Gore's motion for reforming the ancient universities, voicing the demand that Oxford should play a full part in the working-class educational movements then developing. His vision of education was to develop the faculties of all children as a matter of Christian love and social justice, believing that it was through education that men and women of all classes could rise and reach their fulfilment. This vision Percival shared with Albert Mansbridge, William Temple, R. H. Tawney (the two latter having been pupils under him at Rugby), and others who pioneered the course of national and adult education in the twentieth century.

Percival announced his retirement from Hereford in 1917. He retired to Oxford, where he died at his home, 64 Banbury Road, on 3 December 1918. He was buried in the crypt of the chapel of Clifton College, Bristol. Memorial services were held in Hereford Cathedral, at Trinity College, Oxford, and in St James's, Piccadilly, where William Temple, the rector, spoke of him as 'one of the pre-eminent figures of the nineteenth century, a century rich in educators'.

JOHN SADLER

Sources W. Temple, *Life of Bishop Percival* (1921) · O. F. Christie, *A history of Clifton College, 1860–1934* (1935) · D. Winterbottom, *John Percival: the great educator* (1993) · E. G. Sandford, ed., *Memoirs of Archbishop Temple, by seven friends*, 2 vols. (1906) · F. A. Iremonger, *William Temple, archbishop of Canterbury* (1948) · J. Roach, *Secondary education in England, 1870–1902* (1991) · P. Adams, *Somerville for women: an Oxford college, 1879–1993* (1996) · L. Goldman, *Dons and workers: Oxford and adult education since 1850* (1995) · J. Potter, *Headmaster: the life of John Percival, autocrat* (1997)

Archives U. Durham L., scheme for instruction of working men at Durham University | BL, Mansbridge MSS · Clifton College, archives · LPL, corresp. with Temple · Oxf. UA · Temple House, Bethnal Green, London, WEA MSS · University of Bristol

Likenesses Bassano, photographs, c.1898, NPG · H. G. Riviere, oils, exh. RA 1899, Trinity College, Oxford · A. H. Fry, photograph on postcard, NPG · H. von Herkomer, oils, Queen's College, Oxford · B. Johnson, portrait, Somerville College, Oxford · G. F. Watts, portrait, priv. coll. · marble relief, Hereford Cathedral · two photographs, NPG

Wealth at death £40,437 11s. 4d.: probate, 2 May 1919, CGPLA Eng. & Wales

Percival, Robert (1765–1826), army officer and writer, became a captain in the 18th Irish regiment and in 1795 sailed for the Cape of Good Hope, then held by the Dutch. Percival disembarked in Simon's Bay, and was entrusted by General Sir James Henry Craig with the tasks of attacking the Dutch in the defile of Muisenberg and in Wynberg. He was successful in both undertakings. Meanwhile a Dutch fleet under Admiral Lucas, which had been sent to save the colony, was captured. Percival was the first to enter Cape Town (16 September 1796), and there he remained until 1797.

On his return to Britain Percival published a narrative of his journey, *An account of the Cape of Good Hope, containing an historical view of its original settlement by the Dutch, and a sketch of its geography, productions, the manners and customs of its inhabitants* (1804). This work, though rather thin, was not uninteresting, and was warmly received. His criticisms of the Dutch settlers, especially of their cruelty to the natives, were severe. But he depicted the Cape climate as the finest in the world, and urged the British government, which had just restored the province to the Dutch under the treaty of Amiens, to reoccupy it.

In 1797 Percival travelled to Ceylon, where he seems to have remained for three years; afterwards he published *An account of … Ceylon … [with] the journal of an embassy to the court of Candy* (1803). In this he described the effects of Portuguese and Dutch rule, citing instances of Dutch cruelty and treachery, and discussing the population, economy and main towns of Ceylon. Sydney Smith declared the work to 'abound with curious and important information'. Percival died in 1826.

C. R. Beazley, *rev.* David Gates

Sources R. Percival, *An account of the Cape of Good Hope* (1804) · R. Percival, *An account of the island of Ceylon … to which is added the journal of an embassy to the court of Candy* (1803) · C. A. Walckenaer, *Histoire générale des voyages*, 17 (1831) · T. C. W. Blanning, *The French revolutionary wars, 1787–1802* (1996)

Percival, Thomas (1719–1762), antiquary, son of Richard Percival of Royton Hall, near Oldham, Lancashire, was born there on 1 September 1719. He was brought up a Presbyterian, but joined the Church of England; he was a whig in politics, and he welcomed the Hanoverian succession. On 14 March 1738 he married Martha (1714/15–1760), daughter of Major Benjamin Gregge of Chamber Hall, Oldham, at St Mary's, Oldham.

In 1748 Percival wrote two pamphlets opposing the high-church clergy and the nonjurors of Manchester. In 1758 he took part with some operative weavers in a dispute with their employers about wages; he subsequently published *A letter to a friend occasioned by the late dispute betwixt the check-makers of Manchester and their weavers; and the check-makers' ill-usage of the author* (1759). On 13 June 1751 Percival read his paper 'Observations on the Roman colonies and stations in Cheshire and Lancashire' to the Royal Society. This prompted William Stukeley to describe him as 'a learned person who lives in the north, and has taken a good deal of pains by travelling to search out the Roman roads and stations mentioned thereabouts' (*Family Memoirs*, 2.244); a shorter paper on the same subject was published in *Archaeologia*, volume 1. He discovered that Kinderton was the site of Roman Condate; and his paper entitled 'Account of a double child' was published in the *Philosophical Transactions* (68, 1752). Some of the plans in John Aikin's *A Description of the Country … Round Manchester* (1795) were drawn by Percival. He was elected FRS on 25 November 1756, and FSA on 12 June 1760.

Percival died in December 1762, and was buried in the vault of St Paul's Chapel, Royton, where his wife had been buried in March 1760; she had died aged forty-five. Their only child and heir, Katherine, married Joseph Pickford of Alt Hill, Lancashire. Her husband was later known as Sir Joseph Radcliffe of Milnesbridge, Yorkshire, into whose possession Percival's collection of manuscript pedigrees and other papers passed. Thomas Percival the antiquary should be distinguished from his namesake, Thomas *Percival (1740–1804), the physician, with whom he is often confused.

C. W. Sutton, *rev.* J. A. Marchand

Sources *N&Q*, 12 (1855), 373, 440 · *GM*, 1st ser., 93/1 (1823), 505–6 · IGI · *The private journal and literary remains of John Byrom*, ed. R. Parkinson, vol. 2, pt 2, Chetham Society, 44 (1857), 44, 461–2 · F. R. Raines, *The fellows of the collegiate church of Manchester*, ed. F. Renaud, 2, Chetham Society, new ser., 23 (1891), 255 · J. Butterworth, *An historical and descriptive account of the town and parochial chapelry of Oldham* (1817), xi · *The family memoirs of the Rev. William Stukeley*, ed. W. C. Lukis, 2, SurtS, 76 (1883), 244 · J. Hunter, *Familiae minorum gentium*, ed. J. W. Clay, 1, Harleian Society, 37 (1894), 119 · J. Whitaker, *The history of Manchester*, 2 books (1771–5), 1.94, 137 · *The works of John Collier, in prose and verse*, ed. H. Fishwick (1894), 117 · R. G. [R. Gough], *British topography*, [new edn], 1 (1780), 503 · E. Baines and W. R. Whatton, *The history of the county palatine and duchy of Lancaster*, 4 vols. (1836) · C. W. Sutton, *A list of Lancashire authors* (1876) · Chatham Library, Raines MSS

Percival, Thomas (1740–1804), physician, born at Sankey Street, Warrington, Lancashire, on 29 September 1740, was the son of Joseph Percival (1694–1744), a merchant in Warrington, and his wife, Margaret Orred (1704–1744). His grandfather Peter Percival, the younger son in an old Cheshire yeoman family farming an estate they had long held near Thelwall, Latchford, practised physic in Warrington. His parents died in March 1744, a few days apart, when Thomas, the only surviving son, was three; he was left to the care of an elder sister. In 1750, when he was ten, Thomas Percival MD, his father's eldest brother, a physician in the town and district around Warrington, died, and left him a valuable library and modest private means; Percival was educated first at a private seminary, and then at Boteler grammar school in Warrington, with a year at Manchester grammar school, and he resolved to enter the medical profession.

Percival was a dissenter, and was known in later life as a staunch Unitarian; in 1757 he is said to have been the first student enrolled at the newly established Warrington Academy, which was founded to give a collegiate education to dissenters. On the completion of his course at Warrington he proceeded to the University of Edinburgh, about 1761, where he formed lasting friendships with William Robertson, the historian, David Hume, and other distinguished men. While still a student at Edinburgh he spent a year in London, where he became known to many scientific men, and through the influence of its vice-president, Lord Willoughby de Parham, he was elected a fellow of the Royal Society on 7 March 1765. It is said that he was the youngest man at that time on whom that honour had been conferred. From Edinburgh he proceeded to Leiden, where he completed his medical studies, and he took his degree on 6 July 1765. For two years he practised his profession in his native town. On 24 March 1766 he married Elizabeth (1747–1822), the only surviving child of Nathaniel Bassnett, merchant, of London.

In 1767 Percival moved to Manchester, where he immediately made many friends; he abandoned his original intention of going to London, and lived in Manchester for the rest of his life. He soon made a reputation by contributing papers to the *Philosophical Transactions*, and various periodicals, and his essays, medical and experimental, published between 1767 and 1776, attracted wide attention. In 1775 he published the first of three parts of *A Father's Instructions*; the concluding part was not issued until 1800. This book for children achieved great popularity. In reply to Richard Price's *Observations on Reversionary Payments* (1771), Percival wrote his *Proposals for Establishing More Accurate and Comprehensive Bills of Mortality in Manchester*—a contribution to the growing interest in demography. This appeared in his *Essays Medical and Experimental* (1773).

Percival became a central figure in the cultural circles of Enlightenment Manchester. At his house the Manchester Literary and Philosophical Society was brought into being in 1781. He was elected a vice-president on its foundation, and, with the exception of one year, he occupied the presidential chair from 1782 until his death. In 1785 Percival aided the removal to Manchester of the Warrington Academy, and he took a great interest in its management. An endeavour on his part and that of his friends to found a college of arts and sciences proved unsuccessful, but the scheme was accomplished half a century later under the will of John Owens.

Percival served but briefly as a physician to the Manchester Infirmary, but he helped to lead the reformist faction which took over the governance of the infirmary in 1790 and greatly expanded its services. He helped to form a committee to enforce proper sanitation in Manchester, and advocated the establishment of public baths. He may also be considered as the earliest advocate of factory legislation. On 25 January 1796 he addressed the Manchester committee or board of health on certain evils which had arisen from the growth of the factory system, and he recommended legislative interference in the working conditions of those employed in factories. He helped to found the Manchester Fever Hospital in 1796, and his involvement with infirmary politics led to the publication of his *Medical Ethics* (1803), which was widely influential in Britain and the USA. Percival's charm of manner and wide learning gained him friends and correspondents among the most distinguished men and women of his time, in both Europe and North America.

Percival died at his house in Mosley Street, Manchester, on 30 August 1804, leaving a widow, three sons, and more than one daughter. He was buried in the church in which he had been baptized, Warrington parish church, on 3 September, where there is an epitaph by his friend Dr Samuel Parr. A memorial tablet was placed above the president's chair in the rooms of the Manchester Literary and Philosophical Society.

ALBERT NICHOLSON, rev. JOHN V. PICKSTONE

Sources *The works literary, moral and medical of Thomas Percival: to which are prefixed memoirs of his life and writings and a selection from his literary correspondence*, ed. E. C. Percival, 4 vols., new edn (1807) · R. B. Hope, 'Dr Thomas Percival, a medical pioneer and social reformer, 1740–1804', MA diss., University of Manchester, 1947 · J. V. Pickstone, 'Thomas Percival and the production of medical ethics', *Medical ethics and etiquette in the eighteenth century*, ed. R. Baker, D. Porter, and R. Porter (1993), vol. 1 of *The codification of medical morality*, 161–78 · J. V. Pickstone and S. V. F. Butler, 'The politics of medicine in Manchester, 1788–1792: hospital reform and public health services in the early industrial city', *Medical History*, 28 (1984), 227–49 · K. Webb, 'The development of the medical profession in Manchester, 1750–1860', PhD diss., University of Manchester Institute of Science and Technology, 1988 · R. W. Innes Smith, *English-speaking students of medicine at the University of Leyden* (1932), 180 · E. M. Brockbank, *Sketches of the lives and work of the honorary medical staff of the Manchester Infirmary: from its foundation in 1752 to 1830* (1904) · R. A. Smith, 'A centenary of science at Manchester', *Memoirs of the Literary and Philosophical Society of Manchester*, 3rd ser., 9 (1883) [whole issue] · F. Epinasse, *Lancashire worthies*, 2 (1877) · J. Kendrick, ed., *Profiles of Warrington worthies*, 2nd edn (1854) · J. Hunter, *Familiae minorum gentium*, ed. J. W. Clay, 1, Harleian Society, 37 (1894) · *The record of the Royal Society of London*, 4th edn (1940)

Archives American Philosophical Society, Philadelphia, Franklin MSS, letters to Benjamin Franklin · BL, corresp. with E. M. de Costa, Add. MS 28540, 193–6 · BL, letters to second Lord Hardwicke, Add. MSS 35607, fol. 45; 35163, fol. 243 · JRL, press cuttings and biographical notes

Likenesses miniature, priv. coll.; photograph, Manchester Medical collection, JRL · silhouette, repro. in Kendrick, *Profiles of Warrington worthies*

Wealth at death total under £7500; stamp duty paid £75; widow free to select 200 volumes; remaining books to son: will, probate (8 Nov 1814), and codicils, Lancs. RO

Percy, Alan (c.1480–1560), college head, was the third son of Henry *Percy, fourth earl of Northumberland (c.1449–1489), and Maud (d. in or before 1485), daughter of William *Herbert, first earl of Pembroke. He was ordained by 1 May 1513 when he received the prebend of Dunnington, York Minster, which he resigned before 1 November 1517, and on 6 May 1515 was presented to the rectory of St Anne, Aldersgate, in London, which he held until 1518. Percy was formally admitted as master of St John's College, Cambridge, on 29 July 1516, at the public opening of the college; but he received at John Fisher's behest a half-yearly instalment paid for the six months ending at Michaelmas 1516, which suggests that he took office earlier in the year. He was granted a university grace to incept in arts, graduating MA in 1518. During Percy's short mastership he took an active part in the process of annexing Ospringe Hospital, Kent, to St John's. His expenses between August 1516 and February 1517 included riding to supervise lands, reparations, and sound administration there, and for business in London.

Percy resigned his mastership by an undated document in the autumn of 1518: on 1 November according to Thomas Baker. On 21 November he was granted an annual pension of £10 and use of the master's low parlour and two inner chambers at St John's. This provision reflected his noble status as brother of the earl of Northumberland, Henry Algernon *Percy, to which Fisher had referred in the college statutes of 1516 when awarding him the large salary of £20 as master. This was actually no more than had been paid to Robert Shorton, but Shorton had supervised the building of the college. In a letter of 6 April (year uncertain), Nicholas Daryngton, fellow of St John's, reported to the master that he had sent Percy £5 which the latter had begged for several times, being in need. Percy resigned his pension and room rights on 4 February 1521, the king having on 2 April 1520 granted him a house and garden at Stepney, Middlesex.

On 25 October 1521 Percy became rector of St Mary-at-Hill, London, and in 1526 he was presented by the earl of Rochford to the rectory of Mulbarton-cum-Keningham, Norfolk. He became in 1539 warden of the College of the Holy Trinity at Arundel, Sussex, which he and two fellows surrendered to the king on 12 December 1545. In June 1527 he acted as a trustee for the estate of his brother the earl of Northumberland who had died on 19 May. In 1530 it appears that he owed Cardinal Wolsey's estate £9 for expediting a suit for the union of certain unspecified parishes. In 1547 he was presented by the dean and chapter of St Paul's, London, to the vicarage of Kensworth, Hertfordshire. Percy was a benefactor to Norwich, having given it a messuage in 1534, and his portrait dated 1549 hangs in the guildhall there. The duke of Norfolk presented him to the rectory of Earsham, Norfolk, in 1558. Percy died before 7 May in 1560 and is alleged to have been buried in St John's College chapel, but the site of his tomb has not been identified.   MALCOLM G. UNDERWOOD

Sources Cooper, *Ath. Cantab.*, vol. 1 · T. Baker, *History of the college of St John the Evangelist, Cambridge*, ed. J. E. B. Mayor, 2 vols. (1869) · R. F. S. [R. F. Scott], 'Notes from the college records', *The Eagle*, 32 (1910–11), 1–32 · M. Bateson, ed., *Grace book B*, 2 (1905) · Venn, *Alum. Cant.*, 1/3 · J. E. B. Mayor, ed., *Early statutes of St John's College, Cambridge* (1859) · annual accounts, 1511–19, St John Cam., Archives, D107.1–2 · documents relating to Alan Percy, St John Cam., D57.1–7 · letter, Daryngton to Metcalfe, 6 April [no year], St John Cam., D105.246 · E. B. Fryde and others, eds., *Handbook of British chronology*, 3rd edn, Royal Historical Society Guides and Handbooks, 2 (1986) · *LP Henry VIII*, 1/1.414; 4/2.3213; 4/3.6748 · *Associated Architectural Societies' Reports and Papers*, 25/1 (1900) · GEC, *Peerage*, new edn, 9.718

Likenesses oils, 1549, Norwich Guildhall, council chamber · C. E. Brock, oils, 1892 (after oil painting, 1549), St John Cam.

Percy, Alan Ian, eighth duke of Northumberland (1880–1930), politician and propagandist, was born on 17 April 1880 in London, the seventh of the thirteen children and fourth of the seven sons of Henry George Percy, Earl Percy (1846–1918), from 1899 seventh duke of Northumberland, and his wife, Lady Edith Campbell (d. 1913), eldest daughter of George *Campbell, eighth duke of Argyll. Although born into privilege and acquiring a great inheritance, his childhood was austere and his mature life one of relentless activity and commitment—products of a family tradition not just of public service but also the stern evangelistic faith of the Irvingite Catholic Apostolic church, a sect within the Church of England. He was educated at Eton College (1893–7) and at Christ Church, Oxford (1897–9), though with an aristocratic younger son's intention of making his career in the army. He joined the Grenadier Guards in 1900, saw active service in the Second South African War (1901–2), and was promoted to lieutenant in 1903. From 1907 to 1910 he served in the Egyptian army, in 1908 as captain of a company of Arab camel corps during the Kordofan campaign in the Sudan. After returning to the British army he was in 1910–11 an additional aide-de-camp to the fourth Earl Grey, governor-general of Canada, before retiring in 1912 with the rank of major and with his prospects transformed. His eldest brother, Henry, Earl Percy, MP, had died in 1909, and as his second and third brothers died in childhood he succeeded as heir to the dukedom, and to the courtesy title of Earl Percy. In 1911 he married Lady Helen Magdalen Gordon-Lennox (1886–1965), youngest daughter of Charles, seventh duke of Richmond and Gordon. They had four sons and two daughters.

Percy's military interests now found a new outlet, which gradually developed into an unusual career for one of his lineage and status: that of publicist, controversialist, and publisher. In essays and articles during 1911 and 1913 he forecast war with Germany, criticized the Haldane army reforms, argued that the proposed expeditionary force was far too small, and supported Lord Roberts's calls for military conscription. Events from 1914 no doubt confirmed the sense of prophetic power which so imbued his subsequent writings. On the outbreak of the First World War he rejoined his regiment and was for two years an official eye-witness, supplying battle-front descriptions to newspapers. The resulting journalistic experience and contacts with editors was put to less official uses after his appointment in 1916 to the directorate of military operations, attached as a lieutenant-colonel to the general staff in London. A vigorous partisan of the army command during the great debates from 1916 to 1918 with opposition politicians and government ministers over strategy and logistics, he supplied sympathetic journalists, particularly H. A. Gwynne, editor of the *Morning Post*, with inside information and counter-arguments to support the generals' cause. By 1918 he had a deep distrust of the political élite, and an especial loathing for Lloyd George.

On his father's death in May 1918, and after a second retirement from the army at the end of the war, Northumberland entered into the large possessions and numerous public, institutional, and social duties of the Northumberland dukedom. To these he added still further involvements. Rarely content with merely honorific status he became a man of many causes—agricultural, industrial, historical, archaeological, scientific, ecclesiastical. A long list of positions includes lord lieutenant of Northumberland, president of the Northumberland Territorial Army Association and the Newcastle Society of Antiquaries, master of the Percy hunt, chancellor of Durham University, and president of the Institution of Naval Architects. He was both president of the Royal Institution, in succession to his grandfather and father, and an active lay churchman, as chairman of the house of laymen of York diocese and from 1919 to 1923 vice-chairman of the national church assembly's house of laity. Two of his short stories were published posthumously: *The Shadow on the Moor* (1930) and *La salamandre* (1934).

Northumberland's kindly interest in the concerns of his tenants and organizational associates attracted affection, in striking contrast to the enmities he paraded and provoked in his politics. His inheritance included his father's diehard Conservatism, which he characteristically turned into yet more extravagantly reactionary opinions. The owner of three great houses and some 180,000 acres spread across Northumberland, Middlesex, and Surrey, there was nothing apologetic about his defence of property. A robust justification of his huge coal royalties in evidence to the Sankey coal commission of 1919, against the miners' union and socialist criticisms of Robert Smillie, Frank Hodges, Sidney Webb, and Richard Tawney, gave him a notoriety which encouraged him to offer a wider political lead. The *Times* obituarist described him as 'a strong Tory, militant and uncompromising' (*The Times*, 25 Aug 1930); less friendly commentators thought him either a dangerous fanatic or a useful example of reactionary absurdity. Yet in the tense post-war public atmosphere his views had real purchase among discontented Conservatives, and from 1920 he became important as a leader of the diehard movement against the Lloyd George coalition government. He joined the fourth marquess of Salisbury's Association of Independent Unionist Peers, and had a small following among Conservative back-bench MPs. But his main contribution lay in a rare talent for written invective, in numerous intemperate yet penetrating articles in the *Morning Post* and the *National Review*, and in his books, *International Revolutionary Propaganda* (1920), *Conspiracy Against the British Empire* (1921), *The Passing of Liberalism* (1925), and the posthumously published *The History of World Revolution* (1954). He created further outlets for this peculiarly ferocious style of propaganda in founding the Boswell Press (1921) and the *Patriot* (1922). His anti-Liberalism was nearly as strong as his anti-socialism, and his anti-communism was obsessive: for him Liberalism represented the start of a slippery descent into the atheistic and expropriatory horrors of bolshevism. No less obsessive were his British chauvinism, contempt for the League of Nations, hatred of anti-imperialist movements, and his antisemitism. Everywhere he saw danger, betrayal, and plots: wittingly or not Indian and Egyptian nationalists, Irish republicans, and the British Labour Party were all members of an international revolutionary movement against British power directed by Bolshevik-Jewish adventurers in Moscow. From such a perspective, a coalition government led by and including Liberal ministers was manifestly incapable of defending anything of value. In autumn 1921 he tried unsuccessfully to mount a party revolt against the Conservative leadership over the

government's treaty with Irish republicans; his alternative solution was the military reconquest of Ireland. In March 1922 he was a co-signatory to the diehard manifesto which announced a combined rebellion of various elements of the Conservative right, and in June he used the honours scandal for a particularly bitter attack on Lloyd George. For the rest of the decade he persistently sought to expose Lloyd George's political fund as a source of public corruption.

After the collapse of the coalition government in October 1922 Northumberland was reconciled to a Conservative leadership now formally freed of Liberal pollution, even, surprisingly, tolerating Stanley Baldwin's Conservatism. He was president of the Conservative National Union in 1924, and by the time he succeeded Lord Salisbury as chairman of the Association of Independent Unionist Peers this had mellowed from a group of rebels into the back-bench Conservative organization in the House of Lords. Also during 1924, under Conservative central office prompting, he led a consortium to buy the *Morning Post*, securing it from the unfriendly clutches of Lord Rothermere. After withdrawing from the Boswell Press and the *Patriot* he became an active newspaper proprietor, commenting regularly on editorial policy and continuing to publish articles on causes dear to the Conservative right. He thought the labour disputes of 1925–6 'a vast conspiracy to ruin the country, to starve the workers & destroy civilisation' (to Gwynne, 26 Sept 1925, H. A. Gwynne MSS), and again defended coal royalty owners during the Samuel coal commission hearings. However, his inflammatory brand of reactionary politics had now lost much of their force and following. He died on 23 August 1930 at his home, 17 Princes Gate, London.

PHILIP WILLIAMSON

Sources DNB · *The Times* (25 Aug 1930) · *The Times* (27 Aug 1930) · *The Times* (11 Oct 1930) · Burke, *Peerage* (1980) · Bodl. Oxf., H. A. Gwynne MSS · R. C. Bosanquet, 'Memoir of Alan Ian, eighth duke of Northumberland, K.G., president of the society', *Archaeologia Aeliana*, 4th ser., 8 (1931), 1–5 · M. Cowling, *The impact of labour, 1920–1924: the beginning of modern British politics* (1971) · [H. Begbie], 'A gentleman with a duster', *The conservative mind* (1924) · [J. G. Lockhart and Lady Craik], 'The janitor', *The feet of the young men* (1928) · G. C. Webber, *The ideology of the British right, 1918–1939* (1986) · S. E. Koss, *The rise and fall of the political press in Britain*, 2 (1984) · CGPLA Eng. & Wales (1930)

Archives Alnwick Castle, Northumberland, corresp. and diaries | Bodl. Oxf., Gwynne MSS · Hatfield House, Hertfordshire, Salisbury MSS · HLRO, corresp. with John St Loe Strachey | FILM BFI NFTVA, news footage

Likenesses P. A. de Laszlo, oils, 1927, Alnwick Castle, Northumberland

Wealth at death £2,000,000: probate, 8 Oct 1930, CGPLA Eng. & Wales

Percy, Algernon, tenth earl of Northumberland (1602–1668), politician, was born on 29 September 1602 at Essex House, London, and baptized on 13 October at St Clement Danes in the City, the third but eldest surviving son of Henry *Percy, ninth earl of Northumberland (1564–1632), and Lady Dorothy Perrott (d. 1619), widow of Sir Thomas Perrott, and daughter of Walter Devereux, first earl of

Algernon Percy, tenth earl of Northumberland (1602–1668), by Sir Anthony Van Dyck, c.1636–8

Essex. His parents married in 1594 and later quarrelled over the ninth earl's belief that his wife had not honoured the marriage contract. Moreover, the Devereux connection turned sour when Dorothy's brother Robert, the second earl of Essex, far from becoming an asset to the family, became a serious liability owing to his disobedience and later rebellion against Elizabeth I. The couple were eventually reconciled and Algernon had two sisters, Dorothy (1598–1659), who married Robert Sidney, second earl of Leicester, and Lucy, later countess of Carlisle (1599–1660) [see Hay, Lucy], and a brother, Henry *Percy, Baron Percy of Alnwick (c.1604–1659).

Early years and education The ninth earl, a domineering father, controlled the education of Algernon even while imprisoned in the Tower of London from 1605 to 1621 for suspected complicity in the Gunpowder Plot. Algernon, who was styled Lord Percy until 1632, frequently visited his father, remaining with him for four or five days consecutively, as the ninth earl strove to limit his wife's influence. His letter to the twelve-year-old's tutor before he went up to St John's College, Cambridge, is characteristic.

After explaining 'that many worthy spirits in this kingdom are lost by the neglect and ignorance of fathers', he proceeded to enumerate his son's defects, since his virtues soon would 'plead for themselves if he have any'. These defects fell under the general heading of a pale and sallow complexion and 'abundance of moisture'. He was a phlegmatic youth, more inclined to 'bashfulness' than to lively spirits; in fact, he was unlikely to be 'passionate of anything'. With this unpromising material, the tutor, Daniel Horsmanden, was to produce a sound Latin scholar with a little Greek who could use the terms of the arts, logic, and rhetoric. According to the ninth earl, Algernon would become an 'inward man' with the attributes of a judge (Syon MS P.I. 3x). In 1609 he had written an 'Advice' to his son, instructing him in personal, family, and estate management (Alnwick MS 322. 102). He had learned these lessons through bitter experience, and was at pains to ensure that his son, of whom he seemed not to have a high opinion, would be taught how to conduct his life.

In Easter term 1615 Algernon matriculated as a fellow-commoner from St John's College, Cambridge, and was admitted to the Middle Temple in London the following August. At Cambridge he was under the tuition of Edward Dowse and was created MA in 1616; in the same year he was created a knight of the Bath. He and Dowse embarked on a continental tour in 1618, and travelled in the Netherlands, Italy, and France. Algernon returned to England in 1624 and is said to have joined his father at court. In January 1629 he married Lady Anne (bap. 1612, d. 1637), the eldest daughter of William Cecil, second earl of Salisbury. The union was much against the wishes of his father, who blamed the first earl of Salisbury for his imprisonment in the Tower, declaring that the blood of Percy would not mix with the blood of Cecil 'if you poured it in a dish' (De Fonblanque, 2.370). The ninth earl did not, however, prevent the match, believing in his son's right to choose a wife. After his marriage Algernon visited the Percy estates in the north, the family having been prevented from living there since the time of the seventh earl in 1569. Anne died of smallpox on 6 December 1637, having had five daughters, of whom two survived into adulthood. Commenting on Algernon's loss, a friend said that passion had the least outward power on him of any man he knew.

Public life before the civil wars Percy sat as MP for Sussex in 1624–5 and as member for Chichester in 1625–6. He was summoned to the Lords in his father's barony as Lord Percy, taking his seat in March 1626, and was a leader of the anti-Buckingham faction within the house. In the following November he was appointed joint lord lieutenant of Cumberland, Northumberland, and Westmorland. Upon the death of his father in November 1632 he became the tenth earl of Northumberland.

The new earl felt the weight of Charles I's policy of 'thorough', having been obliged to pay off relief of £7000 on an estate valued at £12,750 at his accession. Nevertheless, he seized the opportunity to travel with Charles on his coronation trip to Scotland in 1633. Northumberland tried to attach himself to the court, but was fined in June 1634 for living in London against the king's general order of 1632. In fact his sister complained that he was so busy playing the courtier that he had little time left for his family. At the queen's urging, he was admitted to the Order of the Garter in 1635 after at least one earlier rejection. Clearly he was winning acceptance, finally to be rewarded with command of the ship money fleet in March 1636 and again in February 1637. As admiral of the ship money fleet, the king's most effective fighting force, he began to play a major role in Charles's government. Almost immediately he pressed for naval reforms, including 'girdling' leaks, lowering high galleries, replacing rotten cordage, proper victualling procedures, and improved recruitment. Northumberland ran foul of the lords of the admiralty, having submitted his reforms directly to the king and privy council. The man primarily responsible for his admiralty appointment, Thomas, Viscount Wentworth, chided him:

> A very small belief might be persuaded that Commissioners of the Admiralty would not be well pleased with the prosecuting of abuses in the Navy, especially where the complaint went immediately to his Majesty without calling in upon them by the way.   (Strafford, 2.43)

The new admiral did succeed in ousting three Catholic officers, having pressed the oath of supremacy on the fleet early in his tenure. Though almost certainly not a puritan, he displayed an anti-Catholic bias throughout his life.

Northumberland went to sea with the fleet in the summer of 1636. Its primary mission was to force the sale of licences on Dutch fishing boats in waters claimed by England. Surprised, many Dutch captains purchased the licences along with assurances of protection from Dunkirk pirates. If they refused, their nets were cut. Strongly pro-French, Northumberland was less enthusiastic about transporting Spanish money to the Netherlands in July. The summer campaign of 1637 was much less successful as the Dutch fished in convoys. Six ships of the fleet under the command of Captain Ramsborough did, however, succeed in avenging the raids of Salé pirates, by successfully attacking their stronghold and rescuing 271 English sailors.

Though Northumberland had begun to make influential enemies at court such as Cottington and Windebank, he also had powerful friends, particularly Thomas Wentworth and Archbishop William Laud. Yielding to their persistent urging, Charles made Northumberland lord admiral on 13 April 1638, the first appointed since the assassination of Buckingham in 1628. It was intended that Northumberland would hold the office until the duke of York's majority. In the event, he held it until his commission was revoked by Charles in late June 1642. The earl became gravely ill from mid-April to July 1638. Recurrent illness hindered his exercise of the many powers conferred on him by Charles. The possibility also exists that he may have claimed illness to avoid abhorrent responsibilities. With his recovery in July, Northumberland was appointed one of the eight members of the important privy council subcommittee for Scotland. This committee was created to determine England's response to the Scots' rebellion against the prayer book. Wentworth, who was in

Ireland, was not present for the initial meetings of the committee. However, in a letter of July 1639 he introduced his ideas through his close friend and client, Northumberland. This outlined the Straffordian policy that was to precipitate two wars with Scotland, necessitating the calling of the Long Parliament. Though he was the channel for Wentworth's ideas, Northumberland profoundly disagreed with his belligerent policy toward Scotland. The marcher lord heritage of the Percys had convinced him of the danger of war with the Scots, especially with an underfinanced and ill-disciplined army. Moreover, should the Scots invade England, many of his estates in the north would be occupied. Wentworth was convinced that the English people would rally to the king in a war with the Scots; Northumberland was not. This disagreement finally drove a wedge between the two friends, especially as Wentworth had saddled Northumberland with responsibility for prosecuting the second bishops' war, advising the king to appoint him general of the forces in the north in January 1640. Another of Northumberland's illnesses prevented him from joining the army, so he was not directly involved in its defeat. His attitude towards the campaign, however, was entirely defeatist. He was one of two in the committee for Scotland who opposed the dissolution of the Short Parliament on 5 May 1640, for which he earned the disfavour of the king, widening the breach with Wentworth, now earl of Strafford. His disillusionment was expressed after the utter defeat of the ragtag army at Newburn in August: 'Never man hath been so used, as the King our master, in all the counsels that have been given him concerning this war by those persons whose judgments he only trusted for governing of these affairs' (Collins, 2.691). Northumberland had not been an effective general, having been more concerned with the unconstitutional application of martial law than with preparing the army to fight; but he can be credited with clearsighted assessment of the folly of challenging the Scots with an unpaid army.

When the Long Parliament met in November 1640 Northumberland was one of the critics of royal policy. In fact he became the highest-ranked member of Charles's government to join parliament in the civil war. He refused the king's request to perjure himself in Strafford's trial, and his depositions both for the prosecution and the defence were damaging. He was ill when the Lords voted on the attainder, but there can be no doubt that he had rejected his friend and benefactor. In the hysteria of the time, he may even have feared prosecution as a Straffordian.

By the time of Strafford's trial Northumberland had shown signs of his intent to persevere with the king's opponents. In December 1640 he told his brother-in-law, the earl of Leicester, that he could secure from parliament the vacant lord lieutenancy of Ireland for him. He added that soon Charles would be obliged to listen to parliament. Shortly after Strafford's trial he persuaded his brother, Henry, to write a letter revealing a plot to use the army against parliament to rescue Strafford. Northumberland, urged by Pym, allowed Denzil Holles and John

Hampden to copy the letter for publication. Clarendon refers to this incident as the first sign of Northumberland's defection.

The civil wars In addition to his wealth and prestige as lord admiral, Northumberland's support was a key prize for parliament. In November 1641 he obeyed a parliamentary order to prepare four ships to take arms and ammunition to Ireland. In the same month he wrote that he favoured excluding bishops from the House of Lords, but would not commit himself on the grand remonstrance. In January 1642 he headed the list of lords who protested against the failure to censure the duke of Richmond for breach of privilege when he suggested that parliament be adjourned for six months. In February parliament made him lord lieutenant of Sussex, Northumberland, Pembrokeshire, and Anglesey; and in the same month he enthusiastically voted for the militia bill. Parliament's control of the navy was critical in the defeat of the royalists, and the lord admiral was the primary agent. Too late, on 28 June 1642, Charles revoked Northumberland's commission. Ever the man of honour, he laid it down on 1 July. Three days later, he was appointed to parliament's committee of safety.

Why did a man so favoured by Charles I rebel? According to Clarendon:

> Of those who were of the King's Council and who stayed and voted with the Parliament, the earl of Northumberland may well be reckoned the chief, in respect of the antiquity and splendor of his family, his great fortune and estate, and the general reputation he had amongst the greatest men, and his great interest by being High Admiral of England. (Clarendon, *Hist. rebellion*, 2.537)

He then enumerates all Northumberland's offices and honours, concluding 'which was such a quick succession of bounties and favours as had rarely befallen any man who had not been attended with the envy of favourite' (ibid., 538). Great men had to make lacerating decisions in the early 1640s and Northumberland's was based primarily on constitutional principle, mixed with family tradition, and fear of being labelled a Straffordian.

In the manuscripts of Alnwick Castle there is a document entitled: 'Questions made at the holding of a court between the Lord Algernon Percy and Mr. Francis Powlton' (Alnwick MS 521, fols. 41–77). This manuscript, intended for the instruction of the young Algernon, presents the constitutional position of the common lawyers. Asserting the antiquity of the balanced constitution, the dialogue argues strenuously against unfettered royal prerogative in favour of the rule of immemorial law and the requirement of parliament to represent the kingdom's interests. The subsequent behaviour of the earl of Northumberland before and during the civil wars certifies that he assimilated the lessons of this dialogue. Writing to his friend, the attorney-general John Bankes in June 1642, Northumberland said:

> we believe that those persons who are most powerful with the King do endeavour to bring Parliaments to such condition that they shall be instruments to execute the commands of the King, who were established for his greatest and most supreme council … but let us have our laws and liberties and privileges secured to us. (G. Bankes, *Story of Corfe Castle*, 1853, 122–3)

The Percy tradition of rebellion also had its effect. The sixth through to the eighth earls died violently in rebellion against the crown, and the ninth earl suffered a long imprisonment at the hands of James I. Furthermore, Northumberland was the nephew of the rebellious earl of Essex. Religion, on the other hand, was not a powerful factor in his decision. He was certainly anti-Catholic, but there is little evidence that religion had a powerful hold on him. Likewise, the Percy estates had prospered under the Stuarts once the ninth earl attended to their management. The tenth earl, having continued the tradition of sound management, had no reason to feel economically aggrieved under Charles's rule.

When the war went badly for parliament in 1642–3, however, Northumberland wavered. He hoped that parliament would reward him with reappointment to the admiralty, but its choice, driven by the radicals in the Commons, was the earl of Warwick. Appalled by the reality of war at Edgehill and Turnham Green (where he was probably in arms), he became a leader of the peace party. Never bold, his abhorrence of fratricidal bloodshed was compounded by parliamentary defeats. D'Ewes reports that Northumberland's shift to the peace party was definite in March 1643. The earl led the parliamentary delegation at the Oxford peace negotiations in the following April, where Charles, negotiating from strength, yielded little. On 18 April, the day of his return from Oxford, he struck Henry Marten with a cane because Marten had intercepted and opened a letter from Northumberland's young wife, Lady Elizabeth (c.1608–1705), second daughter of Theophilus Howard, second earl of Suffolk, whom he had married on 1 October 1642. This was but one episode in the looming confrontation between the war and peace parties that culminated in physical threats to some lords outside parliament on 5 August, orchestrated by Lord Mayor Pennington in the hope of arresting Northumberland and other leaders of the peace party.

In June 1643 Northumberland was accused of complicity in the Waller plot, but D'Ewes reports that although Henry Marten pushed to prosecute him, Waller could not substantiate the charges. After the tumult of 5 August, having been unable to persuade his cousin, the third earl of Essex, to support further peace efforts, Northumberland retired to his Sussex estate, Petworth, while other peace lords defected to the royalist headquarters at Oxford. It is clear that he was tempted to follow them, but his nature counselled caution. What he waited on was the outcome of negotiations between parliament and the Scots. Always ambivalent toward Scotland, Northumberland preferred not to invite the Scots into England's war, while recognizing that the best hope for parliamentary victory lay with an alliance. The solemn league and covenant, signed in late September, paved the way for his return to active involvement in parliament. In fact, despite this absence, he was the most regular attendee of Lords' committees from August 1642 until the end of 1644. He took the covenant on 30 October 1643, having already been appointed to the Westminster assembly the previous June. On 18 February 1644 he became the first chairman of the committee of both kingdoms, faithfully participating throughout its life. Baillie may have put his finger on the key to Northumberland's co-operation when he wrote that the earl would be a supporter of the Scots on the committee now that they had occupied his lands in the north.

Northumberland definitely moved towards the war party in 1644, though he continued to spearhead peace efforts. According to Clarendon:

> the repulse he had formerly received at Oxford upon his addresses thither, and the fair escape he had made afterwards from the jealousy of the Parliament, had wrought so far upon him, that he resolved no more to depend upon the one or to provoke the other, and was willing to see the King's power and authority so much restrained that he might not be able to do him any harm. (Clarendon, *Hist. rebellion*, 3.495)

In April 1645 he broke ranks with the peers, registering one of four Lords' votes for the self-denying ordinance. In the previous month he had signalled his intentions by protesting against the removal of forts and garrisons from Fairfax's command, as well as the inclusion of a clause in Fairfax's orders to protect the king's person. He was a strong supporter of the New Model Army, and in this he was no doubt influenced by his servant, Robert Scawen, who chaired parliament's army committee. On 18 March 1645 Northumberland was given charge of the king's two younger children, the duke of Gloucester and Princess Elizabeth; it was reported that the duke might be made king with the tenth earl as lord protector should Charles refuse further negotiations. This occurred after the failure of the treaty of Uxbridge in February, where Northumberland led the parliamentary delegation to a king whose position was weakening. The earl had managed the preparations for the treaty in both the Lords and the committee of both kingdoms. Failure at Uxbridge solidified Northumberland's alignment with the war party, now known as the Independents. His letters in 1645 and 1646 show an unusually high level of commitment to the parliamentary cause—though there were limits, as his refusal to vote for the attainder of Laud in January had signalled.

Northumberland was particularly active in parliament as the first civil war drew to a close. He attended an unusually large number of committees in summer 1646, including the committee to analyse the king's letters taken at Naseby. In October he was appointed to the committee to draw up the ordinance for the sale of bishops' lands, having earlier been added to the committee of the revenue as a reward for his support of the self-denying ordinance and the New Model. He also pursued personal business intensely at this time in an attempt to recover his northern rents. The Percys were not popular with their northern tenants as a result of their long enforced absence and the harsh administration of the ninth earl. Moreover, most of the tenants were royalists. Until February 1647 most of the northern estates were occupied and sometimes looted by the Scots. Northumberland drew his servant, Hugh Potter, from his parliamentary duties (as MP

for Plympton in Devon) in 1643 to look after his interests in the north. Two-thirds of the Percy revenues came from their northern estates, mostly in Yorkshire and Northumberland. However, with royalist and Scots occupation annual northern revenues of about £10,000 sank to under £3000 in 1643, recovering only slowly to £8800 by 1646. Discouraged by the difficulty of collecting his northern rents, the tenth earl sold £9000 worth of northern lands in 1647 and a further £7000 in 1648. Additional complications were created by parliament's efforts to collect subsidies once the north came within its orbit, whipsawing tenants between taxes and rents. County committees obviously favoured tax over rent collection.

Northumberland took advantage of his good standing with parliament to submit a bill for £42,000 in losses from the war, mostly arrears in rent; he was granted £10,000. He also pushed unsuccessfully to have the full allowances paid for his custody of the king's children. After the fall of Oxford in July 1646 the duke of York was added to his charge, and the expenses for all three children greatly exceeded his reimbursements. In February 1648 he asked to be relieved of the king's children, declining responsibility should they escape. In fact the duke of York escaped in April and, after an investigation, the tenth earl was absolved of blame. At his suggestion, in May 1649 the duke of Gloucester and Princess Elizabeth were handed over to Northumberland's sister, the countess of Leicester.

In January 1647 Northumberland combined with Manchester and the presbyterian peers to draw up proposals that might be acceptable to the king. These were sent to the queen through the French ambassador, Bellievre. In February the earl was nominated to the important committee of Irish affairs. However, as parliament and its army fell out over pay and power, Northumberland sided with the army. He was among the group of nine peers who left parliament for the army after riots in and around Westminster in July, signing an engagement with the army for the restoration of the freedom of both houses on 4 August. The meeting between army officers and lords was held at Northumberland's Syon House and his servant, Scawen, as chair of the army committee, moderated the meeting. This was the apex of the tenth earl's courtship of the army. As one of the commissioners for the four bills, he then made one more effort in December 1647 to treat with the king, but Charles rejected the proposals.

Regicide and the interregnum The general hardening of antagonism towards Charles following the second civil war pushed Northumberland in the opposite direction. He opposed the vote of no further addresses to the king in January 1648, and it was said that no man at the time was so hard to understand as Northumberland. In September and October he was one of fifteen parliamentary commissioners at the Newport treaty, making the opening speech to the king. He, along with Holles and Pierrepont, stayed into November in a desperate attempt to reach an acceptable accommodation with Charles, but their efforts proved fruitless. On 2 January 1649 Northumberland led the Lords' votes against the ordinance to try the king, as well as the proposition that it was treason for Charles to levy war against parliament. He had become a defender of the king against a Rump Parliament which desecrated his long-held commitment to a balanced constitution, declaring:

> The greatest part (at least twenty to one) of the People of England were not yet satisfied, whether the King levied war against the Houses, or the Houses against Him. And if the King did levy war first against the Houses, we have no Law to make it Treason in Him so to do. And for us to declare Treason by an Ordinance, when the matter of fact is not yet proved, nor any Law extant to judge it by, is very unreasonable. (C. Walker, *History of Independency*, 2, 1650, 55–6)

Northumberland withdrew from public life during the Commonwealth and protectorate. He took the engagement to be loyal to the Commonwealth, but he was not trusted by the military regime. Having been relieved of the charge of the king's children in May 1649, he no longer had official duties. His sister, the countess of Carlisle, had been examined and confined to the Tower in March for her involvement with the earl of Holland in the second civil war. One of Northumberland's prized possessions in the north, Wressel Castle, was destroyed in 1650, having earlier been protected from slighting. In the same year he successfully defended himself against an accusation of delinquency, preventing confiscation of his estates. Throughout the interregnum he was forced to defend himself against a claim from the City companies regarding a loan of £50,000 to Charles I in 1640 for which he and several lords stood surety. In spring and summer 1655 he was under house arrest. Thurloe, whose spies had already intercepted at least one letter to Northumberland, believed that the earl had instructed Hugh Potter to prepare his northern tenants to assist in Penruddock's rising. As a result the tenth earl was reported to have had a three-hour interview with Cromwell. Towards the end of the protectorate Northumberland declined the invitations of both Oliver and Richard Cromwell to sit in the upper house of their parliaments. Expressing once again his cherished constitutional views, he told Richard that, 'till the government was such as his predecessors have served under, he could not in honour do it' (*Clarendon State Papers*, 2.432).

The Restoration the restoration of Charles II brought fresh hope to Northumberland. He thrust himself into the fluid politics of early 1660 by organizing the Suffolk House cabal, named after the house that came to him through his marriage with Elizabeth in 1642. Meeting in April, the cabal included Manchester, Holles, St John, and Pierrepoint. Northumberland had an earlier meeting with Monck at which he believed he had secured Monck's support. The plan of the cabal was to have those who sat in 1648 constitute the House of Lords and then impose on Charles II the conditions offered to his father at Newport. In so doing Northumberland could realize his constitutional convictions while assuming considerable political power. However, the cabal collapsed when Monck supported the Convention Parliament at the end of April.

Charles II arrived in May and Northumberland rushed to secure his favour. He did, however, unsuccessfully support a general act of indemnity, opposing the questioning of those involved in the late king's execution, saying that

> though he had no part in the death of the King, he was against questioning those who had been concerned in that affair; that the example might be more useful to posterity and profitable to future kings, by deterring them from the like exorbitances. (*Ludlow's Memoirs*, ed. C. H. Firth, 2 1894, 267–68)

By again asserting his belief in limited monarchy, he did not endear himself to the new king and he was rewarded with mere trappings without any substance of power. Northumberland's condition was aggravated by a report that he attempted to have Hyde (later earl of Clarendon) excepted from an act of indemnity because he was thought to have recommended to Charles I that he should treat with Spain and not with parliament.

On 31 May 1660 Northumberland was sworn as a privy councillor and in August he was made lord lieutenant of Sussex, to be followed with the lord lieutenancy of Northumberland in September. He was diligent in his county responsibilities, organizing the militias, and in 1662 enforcing the Clarendon code. In April 1661 he was the lord high constable at the coronation of Charles II. However, the earl of Manchester was his only friend at court and, more importantly, Clarendon had good reason to oppose him. Northumberland requited him by voting for his impeachment in November 1667.

Having failed to secure power Northumberland spent most of his time at Petworth during the 1660s. He continued to discharge his lord lieutenancies, particularly in Sussex; for example, in January 1667 moving to disarm popish recusants while complaining that others were not equally diligent. In country retirement he retained his interest in the navy, compiling documents detailing its condition. He died on 13 October 1668 at Petworth, where he was buried in that month. He was succeeded by his only son of his second marriage, Jocelyn; who died aged twenty-six in 1670. The countess Elizabeth survived until March 1705. In the December following the tenth earl's death, Jocelyn received an impressive testimonial from a former royalist, Sir William Temple, describing Northumberland as a man of truly noble quality who acted with restraint, constancy, honesty, integrity, and compassion, but not familiarness; who did all this in spite of the disadvantage of living in a divided age. Jocelyn also received a touching letter from the duke of York praising the kindness that Northumberland had shown him during his period of custody.

Reputation Clarendon, who knew Northumberland well, but was not unbiased, called him 'the proudest man alive', continuing 'If he had thought the King as much above him as he thought himself above other considerable men, he would have been a good subject … He was in all his deportment a very great man'—a person who behaved with dignity and independence more characteristic of a feudal baron than a seventeenth-century lord (Clarendon, *Hist. rebellion*, 3.495; 2.538). He was not a man of great abilities, but he enjoyed the reputation and influence of such a person.

> Though his notions were not large or deep, yet his temper, and reservedness in discourse, and his unrashness in speaking, got him the reputation of an able and a wise man; which he made evident in the excellent government of his family, where no man was more absolutely obeyed; and no man had ever fewer idle words to answer for; and in debates of importance he always expressed himself very pertinently. (ibid., 2.538)

Clarendon's assessment in some ways echoes the ninth earl's characterization of young Algernon to his tutor, Daniel Horsmanden.

In the final analysis, the tenth earl was a man of high principle and dispassionate demeanour, more suited to lead in settled times than the tumult of civil war. As his older sister Dorothy remarked in 1637, he was cold to his friends, 'but there is more truth and fidelity in him than in 1000 Hollands and as many Henry Percys' (*De L'Isle and Dudley MSS*, 6.92).   GEORGE A. DRAKE

Sources Alnwick Castle and Syon House, duke of Northumberland papers [also microfilmed by the British MSS project; negative at L. Cong. and positive at BL] · Alnwick Castle and Syon House, duke of Northumberland papers [also microfilmed by the British MSS project; negative at L. Cong. and positive at BL] · E. B. De Fonblanque, ed., *Annals of the house of Percy*, 2 vols. (1887) · Clarendon, *Hist. rebellion* · W. Sussex RO, Petworth papers · *DNB* · *CSP dom.*, *1625–49* · JHL, 4–10 (1628–48) · draft journal of the House of Lords, HLRO, Braye papers · *Report on the manuscripts of Lord De L'Isle and Dudley*, 6, HMC, 77 (1966) · PRO, Ship money fleet records, Admiralty records, Records of the second bishops' war, SP 326, 338–339, 343, 349, 365, 372, 390, 410, 425, 447, 451, 453, 458, 460, 463, 469, 483, 485–486 [16 vols.] · A. Collins, ed., *Sydney state papers*, 2 (1746) · G. Radcliffe, *The earl of Strafforde's letters and dispatches, with an essay towards his life*, ed. W. Knowler, 2 vols. (1739) · Sheff. Arch., Wentworth Woodhouse muniments · *The journal of Sir Simonds D'Ewes*, BL, Harley MSS 163–165 · will, PRO, PROB 11/328, fols. 155r–159v · S. R. Gardiner, *History of the great civil war, 1642–1649*, new edn, 4 vols. (1893) · *JHC*, 2–5 (1640–48) · B. Whitelocke, *Memorials of English affairs*, new edn, 4 vols. (1853) · *Calendar of the manuscripts of the most hon. the marquess of Salisbury*, 22, HMC, 9 (1971) · GEC, *Peerage* · parish register of St Clement Dane, London · Venn, *Alum. Cant.* · *Calendar of the Clarendon state papers preserved in the Bodleian Library*, ed. O. Ogle and others, 5 vols. (1869–1970) · L. Stone, *The crisis of the aristocracy, 1558–1641* (1965)

Archives Alnwick Castle, MSS [microfilm negative at L. Cong.; microfilm positive at BL] · BL, orders for reform of the navy, Sloane MS 3232 · NMM, journal of voyages, etc. · priv. coll., household and personal aocounts, papers · Syon House, MSS [microfilm negative at L. Cong.; microfilm positive at BL] | BL, *The journal of Sir Simonds D'Ewes*, Harley MSS · Bodl. Oxf., Clarendon MSS, subcommittee for Scotland · Bodl. Oxf., Rawlinson MSS, privy council notes · Bodl. Oxf., Tanner MSS, naval papers · Central Library, Sheffield, Wentworth, Woodhouse MSS · CKS, letters to second earl of Leicester · HLRO, Braye MSS, draft journal of the House of Lords · PRO, ship money fleet records, Admiralty records, records of the second bishops' war, SP 326, 338–339, 343, 349, 365, 372, 390, 410, 425, 447, 451, 453, 458, 460, 463, 469, 483, 485–486 · W. Sussex RO, Petworth MSS

Likenesses A. Van Dyck, two oils, *c.*1636–1638, Alnwick Castle, Northumberland [*see illus.*] · S. Cooper, watercolour on vellum, before 1637 (after A. Van Dyck), V&A · A. Van Dyck, group portrait, oils, before 1637, Petworth House, West Sussex, duke of Northumberland's collection · R. Dunkarton, mezzotint, pubd 1814 (after A. Van Dyck), BM, NPG · W. Hollar, line engraving, BM, NPG · oils (after A. Van Dyck), Audley End House, Essex

Wealth at death one of the five wealthiest English peers; revenue from rents exceeded £15,000 p.a.; estates in Yorkshire, Northumberland, Cumberland, Somerset, Dorset, Sussex, Middlesex, Wales; plus house in London; son valued at £41,982 (1670): *MSS of the duke of Northumberland*; L. Stone, *Crisis of the aristocracy*, 161 · rental income: will, Petworth MSS, W. Sussex RO; *MSS of the duke of Northumberland* · fully recovered estates after civil wars; northern estates provided two thirds of income; practised demesne farming at Petworth: account rolls

Percy, Algernon, fourth duke of Northumberland (**1792–1865**), landowner and philanthropist, was born at Syon House, Middlesex, on 15 December 1792, the second son of Hugh *Percy, second duke of Northumberland (1742–1817), and his second wife, Frances Julia (1752–1820), third daughter of Peter Burrell of Beckenham, Kent. As a second son in wartime formal education was dispensed with, and he joined the navy at the age of twelve (3 May 1805), serving as midshipman in a succession of frigates in the Mediterranean in Admiral Collingwood's fleet and taking part in the bungled action off Toulon in 1808. Made lieutenant in 1811, he was promoted to commander in 1814, and in the last year of the war was acting captain of the *Caledonia*, Lord Exmouth's flagship. His naval career ended in 1815, when he was only twenty-three, and he went on half pay and did not see active service again; but on the reserve list he became rear-admiral in 1850, vice-admiral in 1857, and admiral in 1862. Although subsequently credited with a distinguished naval career (Burke, *Peerage*), it seems likely that this was a sycophantic piece of flattery, and that his elevation to the peerage as Baron Prudhoe in 1816 owed more to his father's wealth and position (he was one of the regent's set) than to his own achievements.

Prudhoe took his seat in the Lords but seldom spoke, and indeed was seldom in the country, his political career, such as it was, coming only some time after his succession to the dukedom in 1847. In the 1820s and 1830s he travelled extensively in Africa, being one of the early English aristocratic explorers of ancient Egypt, bringing back a collection of over 2000 objects, later housed in Alnwick Castle, while in 1834 he helped to finance, and accompanied, the astronomer Sir John Herschel's expedition to Cape Town to observe the southern constellations. This gained him an honorary DCL from Oxford in 1841, and his continuing interest in astronomy led him to meet the costs of the publication, in 1847, of the results of Herschel's Cape observations of double stars and nebulae. A larger commitment to scholarship grew out of his friendship with Edward William Lane, whom he first met in Cairo in 1826, and whose return to Egypt in 1842 to collect materials for his Arabic lexicon was both suggested by, and financed by, Prudhoe; he supported Lane and his work for the next twenty-three years, and the first volume of Lane's *Lexicon*, published in 1863, was dedicated to the duke, 'the originator of this work, and its constant and main supporter' (Lane, 1.ii). In recognition of the importance of his contributions as patron of science and learning he was elected FRS, FSA, and FRGS. After the duke's death his widow continued this patronage of the *Lexicon*, the final volume appearing in 1892, sixteen years after Lane's own death.

On 25 August 1842 Prudhoe married the 21-year-old Lady Eleanor Grosvenor (1820–1911), eldest daughter of Richard *Grosvenor, second marquess of Westminster, whom Peel described as 'homely enough looking, and very short' (GEC, *Peerage*). It might be thought that marriage into the Grosvenor family would have whiggish effects, but in the event Prudhoe's one venture into high politics was in the high tory interest when (as duke of Northumberland) he accepted office in Derby's 1852 'Who? Who?' ministry as first lord of the Admiralty, although the duke regarded himself as a non-party naval person, and Victoria had remarked of the previous year's abortive negotiations with Derby that 'The Duke of Northumberland was the only person not properly belonging to the Protection Party who had accepted office' (*Letters of Queen Victoria*, 2.369). He held office for only ten months and it was an unhappy experience, as he found himself falsely accused by his own parliamentary secretary, Augustus Stafford, of abusing Admiralty patronage by making a key appointment on merit and not on the customary party grounds, when in fact the duke had believed he was appointing 'a sure Tory—otherwise Captain Lushington is not an officer I should have appointed' (R. Blake, *Disraeli*, 1966, 321). Stafford was zealous in trying to mobilize as much government patronage as possible in the tory interest, and tried to revive party use of dockyard jobs, discontinued in 1849, and his 'electioneering imprudences compromised [the duke] to some extent: he thought his colleagues less forward than they might have been to take up his defence … and on the making up [*sic*; perhaps breaking up?] of Lord Derby's government he withdrew from practical politics' (*Disraeli, Derby and the Conservative Party*, 227). In the meantime, as a sailor intent on promoting the interests of the Royal Navy and in particular increasing its steam power, the duke had done his bit to bring down the Derby government by insisting on raising the Admiralty estimate by £800,000, thus blowing a hole in Disraeli's already rickety budget (ibid., 87).

As a young man Lord Prudhoe, it was said, 'was of a playful disposition … He was tall and fair and wore his hat just a little bit on one side' (Locker-Lampson, 84). If that was so he put childish things behind him on succeeding to the dukedom in February 1847, on his elder brother's death, and quickly assumed, at least in public, the solemn and earnest demeanour of one who took the moral and social responsibilities of his position as Northumberland's chief landowner very seriously. Already in 1852 ministerial colleagues called him the Doge, and although there was a touch of malice in this he was definitely conscious of his own dignity. The Percys were accustomed to being treated as the uncrowned kings of Northumberland, and Algernon the Good, as he came to be called, earned this position by his good works and not simply by his possessions and

lineage. He was in the happy position of having a large and growing income from coal royalties, as well as vast landed estates, and his 191,000 acres and income of over £150,000 placed him among the half dozen wealthiest aristocrats of the time. He and his wife had no children to provide for, and without any family constraints on his expenditure he was free to indulge his plans for improvements and embellishments of his inheritance. The detailed application of his ideas for improving the agricultural estate, chiefly by field drainage and by providing modern farm buildings, was the work of Hugh Taylor, previously the estate's colliery agent, whom the duke at once made into the chief commissioner in sole charge of managing the estate. The enabling force, which supplied well over £0.5 million for investment in these things and in cottage building, was the duke's own will, while the more bizarre manifestations of faith in new technologies, such as the creation of the post of his grace's manager of the steam plough and the experiments with raw sewage irrigation through a grid of cast iron pipes, were pure ducal whim. His personal contribution to the welfare of his tenants and workers was most directly expressed in his benefactions, which included ten new churches, as many new schools, half a dozen new vicarages, and a number of new model self-righting lifeboats, the design of which he sponsored. His liberality and hospitality at great dinners for his chief tenants, and even larger but less lavish dinners for their labourers, earned him the genuine affection of many Northumbrians, and at the national level his charitable activities made him president of the Royal National Lifeboat Institution, the Westminster and Middlesex hospitals, the Seamen's Hospital Society, the Westminster General Dispensary, the Royal Institution, and the Royal United Service Institution, and vice-president of the Royal Humane Society and the Royal Naval Benevolent Society.

Of all his works, however, the duke was proudest of the vastly expensive 'restoration' and embellishment of Alnwick Castle, carried out to the designs of Anthony Salvin, the foremost castle architect of the day, at a cost of £320,000. Completed in the last year of his life this enterprise recreated a romantic medieval border fortress which was habitable, tolerably comfortable, and supplied with modern hydraulically powered gadgetry in kitchens and dining rooms. Viewed in the long term this piece of feudal extravagance probably created the Percy family's most valuable and enduring asset. The duke and his duchess, although they gave convincing performances of their feudal role when at Alnwick, preferred living in the original Smithson family seat in the North Riding, Stanwick Hall, where they could keep 'less state', or better still staying in Kielder Castle on the north Tyne, 'where he and the Duchess pass a couple of months with never more than two friends, the house being so small that the dinner-room is also the sitting-room' (Ticknor, 307). It was, however, at Alnwick that the duke died on 12 February 1865, lying in state in the castle for two days while the tenantry and local notables filed past, then going by special train to London for another lying in state in Northumberland House, where admission was by ticket only for the 5000 who attended, before burial in the Percy chapel of Westminster Abbey on 25 February. He was succeeded by his first cousin, the second earl of Beverley. The dowager duchess, Eleanor, was provided with Stanwick Hall and its 5000 acre estate, and lived there until she died in 1911.

F. M. L. THOMPSON

Sources Alnwick Castle, Northumberland, Alnwick MSS · F. M. L. Thompson, 'The economic and social background of the English landed interest, 1840–70', DPhil diss., U. Oxf., 1956 · DNB · *Disraeli, Derby and the conservative party: journals and memoirs of Edward Henry, Lord Stanley, 1849–1869*, ed. J. R. Vincent (1978) · *The Times* (13 Feb 1865) · *The Times* (15 Feb 1865) · *The Times* (22 Feb 1865) · *The Times* (24 Feb 1865) · *The Times* (27 Feb 1865) · G. Ticknor, *Life of William Hickling Prescott* (1863) · Burke, *Peerage* · GEC, *Peerage* · *The letters of Queen Victoria*, ed. A. C. Benson, Lord Esher [R. B. Brett], and G. E. Buckle, 9 vols. (1907–32) · F. Locker-Lampson, *My confidences: an autobiographical sketch addressed to my descendants*, ed. A. Birrell, 2nd edn (1896) · E. W. Lane, *Lexicon*, 1 (1863)

Archives Alnwick Castle, Northumberland, corresp., journals, and papers | BL, corresp. with J. W. D. Dundas, Add MS 41370 · Bodl. Oxf., corresp. with Sir J. G. Wilkinson, papers · CUL, corresp. with Joseph Bonomi · Lpool RO, letters to fourteenth earl of Derby · NL Scot., letters to Sir George Brown

Likenesses S. Cousins, mezzotint (after F. Grant), BM · oils, Alnwick Castle, Northumberland · wood-engraving, NPG; repro. in *ILN* (1845–6) · wood-engraving, NPG; repro. in *ILN* (1865)

Wealth at death under £500,000: probate, 29 March 1865, CGPLA Eng. & Wales

Percy, Lady Elizabeth. *See* Seymour, Elizabeth, duchess of Somerset (1667–1722).

Percy, Elizabeth [*née* Lady Elizabeth Seymour], **duchess of Northumberland and** *suo jure* **Baroness Percy (1716–1776)**, courtier and diarist, was born on 26 November 1716, the daughter of Algernon *Seymour, earl of Hertford and later seventh duke of Somerset (1684–1750) [*see under* Seymour, Charles, sixth duke of Somerset], and his wife, Frances *Seymour (1699–1754), daughter of the Hon. Henry Thynne, eldest son of the first Viscount Weymouth. Her girlhood appears to have been a happy one in a devoted family. On 16 July 1740 she married Sir Hugh Smithson, fourth baronet [*see* Percy, Hugh, first duke of Northumberland (*bap*. 1712, *d*. 1786)], reputedly an unusually handsome and accomplished man, with whom she had two sons, Hugh *Percy, second duke of Northumberland (1742–1817), and Algernon, first earl of Beverley (1750–1830), and a daughter, Elizabeth.

On the death of her brother Lord Beauchamp in 1744 Elizabeth became heir to her father's barony of Percy and estates in Northumberland and Middlesex that had been part of the inheritance of her grandmother, Elizabeth *Seymour, duchess of Somerset. On her father's death in 1750 she inherited the barony of Percy while her husband succeeded to the earldom of Northumberland created for the seventh duke of Somerset in 1749. The earl and countess began the improvement of their estates and great houses, Alnwick Castle, Syon House, and Northumberland House. Elizabeth's entertainments at Northumberland House, at which the best musicians performed, were famous, and she was a patron of leading painters, cabinetmakers, and craftsmen. Her husband was closely attached

Elizabeth Percy, duchess of Northumberland and *suo jure* Baroness Percy (1716–1776), by Sir Joshua Reynolds, 1757–9

to Lord Bute, whose daughter married their son in 1764. While Bute was in power the Northumberlands were a significant political couple. James Boswell, who prided himself on being invited to her select Friday gatherings, attested to her influence as a political hostess and patronage broker by applying to her in 1762 to help him secure a commission in the guards, but though he reminded her of it frequently she proved either unwilling or unable to effect it. In 1763 the earl was appointed lord lieutenant of Ireland, where the couple entertained lavishly and were popular, but in 1765 he voluntarily resigned the office for reasons of political expediency. For his many services to the crown he was rewarded with the dukedom of Northumberland in 1766. In 1768–70 the duke and duchess played prominent parts in the Middlesex elections, seeking to defend their influence in the county in the face of Wilkesite radicalism. The threat spread to Westminster where the position of their son Hugh, Earl Percy, as MP was threatened.

Elizabeth became a lady of the bedchamber to Queen Charlotte and was a personal friend until she fell from favour, according to Horace Walpole, who considered her ostentatious and vulgar and given to excesses of patrician pride, because she kept more footmen than the queen.

According to her own diary for 4 February 1770 she resigned in 1770:

> long determin'd to quit the Court where I found I had no longer the Degree of favour I had before enjoy'd and my health being not so good as when I was younger and also the part my Lord had taken in Politics making it much eligible for me to be no longer a dependant, a State I ever detested. (*Diaries of a Duchess*, 97)

After retiring from the court she travelled extensively in France, Flanders, Holland, Germany, Switzerland, and the British Isles, undeterred by her gout or the several coaching accidents carefully detailed in her diary. She visited Voltaire at Fermy and Louis XVI at Versailles. She continued to play a role in politics such that Horace Walpole characterized her as 'a true *Joan* [of Arc] in spirit, style, and manners' (Walpole, *Corr.*, 24.51, 22 Oct 1774) for her performance to get her son Earl Percy (at the time absent in America) re-elected in the general election for Westminster; he was impressed by how 'she sits at a window in Covent Garden, harangues the mob, and is "Hail, fellow, well met!"' (Walpole, *Corr.*, 39.196, 16 Oct 1774). Walpole thought her a figure of contradictions, aristocratic but vulgar, willing to mix with all sorts and conditions of people but passionately fond of pomp and show. Louis Dutens, who knew her intimately, credited her with 'a good and compassionate heart, and above all, a strong attachment to her friends' (Dutens, 2.99–100).

The lively diary the duchess kept from 1752 to 1776, only substantial excerpts from which have been published, presents social and political events and travels rather than the diarist's inner life, faithful to her aim, as expressed on 2 November 1769, 'throughout these Anecdotes [to] scatter here & there forms, customs, rules &c of the Court to shew their variations at different periods & likewise the manners of the Times' (*Diaries of a Duchess*, 95). It reveals as well a personality fascinated not only by pomp and show—through its detailed descriptions of ceremonies, dress, and jewels—but also by exciting calamities like disastrous explosions, mob hysteria and rioting, and romantic elopements with social inferiors. She enjoyed shaping vignettes of country scenes and compiling lists of data, and could turn a phrase deftly, as when describing a Dutch theatre where 'All the men stand in the Pit there being no such thing as either a Woman or a Bench in it' (*Diaries of a Duchess*, 72, 17 Oct 1766), or of proceeding to 'Windsor to Dr. Biddle where he and his Niece were so fulsomely officious that they tired my heart out' (*Diaries of a Duchess*, 51, 21 Sept 1762). Her published writings do not include her copious descriptions of country house travels with their invaluable descriptions and attributions of interior decoration, furnishings, and architecture; these remain with the rest of her diaries at Alnwick Castle, as does the questionnaire she drew up in 1760 listing over 150 queries about what to observe on her visits, and several notebooks with records of ceremonies since ancient times. Her *Short Tour*, taken from her travel diaries and bearing neither her name nor a publisher's, may have been unauthorized. To *Poetical Amusements*, compiled by Lady Anna Miller at Bath,

an exercise in bouts-rimés (requiring the writer to incorporate given rhyme words), she contributed in 1775 a ten-line poem with a line ending 'butter'd muffin' (Percy, 'The pen') that aroused the ridicule of Walpole, though Samuel Johnson, while deploring the book, none the less opined that she 'may do as she pleases: nobody will say anything to a lady of her high rank' (Boswell, 1.513). She died at Northumberland House, Strand, London, on 5 December 1776, shortly after her sixtieth birthday, and was buried in the family vault in Westminster Abbey on 18 December. Boswell, with whom she had corresponded, praised her in 1778 as 'a lady not only of high dignity of spirit, such as became her noble blood, but of excellent understanding and lively talents' (ibid., 2.776).   HARRIET BLODGETT

Sources *The diaries of a duchess*, ed. J. Greig (New York, [1927]) · 'Percy, Hugh (1715–1786)', *DNB* · Walpole, *Corr.* · L. Dutens, *Memoirs of a traveller, now in retirement*, 5 vols. (1806) · E. S. Percy, 'The pen which I now take and brandish', in R. A. Hesselgrave, *Lady Miller and the Batheaston literary circle* (1927), 44 · J. Boswell, *The life of Samuel Johnson*, [new edn], ed. R. Ingpen, 2 vols. (1907) · *Boswell's London journal, 1762–63*, ed. F. A. Pottle (1950), vol. 1 of *The Yale editions of the private papers of James Boswell*, trade edn (1950–89) · V. Percy and G. Jackson-Stops, 'The travel journals of the first duchess of Northumberland', *Country Life*, 155 (1974), 192–5, 250–52, 308–10 · E. S. Percy, *A short tour made in the year one thousand seven hundred and seventy one* (1775) · P. Schlueter and J. Schlueter, eds., *An encyclopedia of British women writers* (1988) · GEC, *Peerage*, new edn, 9.742–4; 10.469; 12/1.80–81
Archives Alnwick Castle, MSS | BL, corresp. with Lady Luxborough, Add. MS 23728 · BL, corresp. with Thomas Percy, Add. MS 32334
Likenesses J. Reynolds, portrait, 1757–9, Syon House, Brentford, London [*see illus.*] · Bacon, photograph (after A. Ramsey), repro. in Greig, ed., *Diaries of a duchess* · Bacon, photograph (after J. Reynolds), repro. in Greig, ed., *Diaries of a duchess* · R. Houston, mezzotint (after J. Reynolds), BM, NPG · S. W. Reynolds, mezzotint (after J. Reynolds), BM, NPG

Percy, Eustace Sutherland Campbell, Baron Percy of Newcastle (1887–1958), politician and educationist, was born in London on 21 March 1887, the twelfth of the thirteen children and youngest of the seven sons of Henry George Percy, Earl Percy (1846–1918), from 1899 seventh duke of Northumberland, and his wife, Lady Edith Campbell (d. 1913), eldest daughter of George *Campbell, eighth duke of Argyll. From his family he derived a commitment to public service and an attachment to the evangelical Catholic Apostolic sect within the Church of England, which gave him an ascetic, even pious (some thought prim) temperament. He also retained his family's allegiance to the Conservative Party, although his education, early career, and foreign experience removed him from the diehard and chauvinist instincts of both his father and his elder brother, Alan *Percy, eighth duke of Northumberland. Lord Eustace Percy, as he was styled from 1899, was educated at Eton College and at Christ Church, Oxford (1904–7), where he took a fashionable interest in social reform issues, obtained a first class in modern history, and acquired an academic cast of mind.

After several months in Paris learning French, and brilliant success in the entrance examination, Percy joined the diplomatic service in 1909. From May 1910 to June 1914 he was a secretary at the British embassy in Washington, where the ambassador, James Bryce, became an intellectual mentor. He studied American institutions, travelled widely, and made influential friends, establishing an enduring reputation as an American expert. After the outbreak of the First World War he served successively in the Foreign Office's western, war, and contraband departments. He returned twice to Washington on official business, the second time in April 1917 as a member of the Balfour mission, prolonged to twelve months as representative of the ministry of blockade. Then, as an assistant to Lord Robert Cecil and from January to March 1919 a Foreign Office representative at the Versailles peace conference, he helped draft the League of Nations covenant and was a joint secretary of the inter-allied commission on the league.

On 4 December 1918 Percy married Stella Katherine (1895–1982), eldest daughter of Major-General Laurence Drummond; they had two daughters. A settled family life contributed to Percy's decision to leave the diplomatic service and enter domestic politics. He stood as Conservative candidate at the Kingston upon Hull by-election in March 1919, but was defeated by the Labour candidate. Subsequently elected to the London county council, he became vice-chairman of its housing committee and during 1920 supervised a novel housing bond campaign, an only partially successful scheme to raise funds by popular subscription for relieving the city's housing problems. Meanwhile he earned his living by part-time work for the Shell-Royal Dutch oil group, responsible for its Anglo-Egyptian oilfields and visiting Egypt, Sudan, and Palestine.

In May 1921 Percy won the parliamentary by-election at Hastings, a seat he held until 1937. He became an able critic of the coalition government, but from a quite different direction to that of his elder brother—as a sympathizer with Cecil's brand of Conservative social idealism and support for the League of Nations, having published *The Responsibilities of the League* (1920) and serving on the League of Nations union executive into the 1930s. After the coalition's collapse he received rapid political advancement. He was appointed parliamentary secretary at the Board of Education from March to May 1923 and the Board of Health from May 1923 to January 1924, then as a protégé of Baldwin became, in November 1924, an unusually young cabinet minister as president of the Board of Education. Yet, although he made important contributions to educational policy, this early political promise was largely dissipated. He retained the first Labour government's commitment to renovating elementary schools, reducing class sizes, and expanding secondary education. He presided over the separation of elementary schools into junior and secondary branches at age eleven, and the reorganization of secondary schools as recommended in the 1926 Hadow report. He was especially concerned to promote technical education, for this purpose abolishing the restrictive compulsory state curriculum. But he resisted the more radical reformers' desire to raise the school-leaving age, also recommended in the Hadow

report, and became a target for Conservatives who disliked his progressive views and wanted financial retrenchment. Under Treasury pressure in November 1925 he issued board circular 1371, which threatened to cut expenditure on schools and incurred the enduring wrath of teachers, educational administrators, and Labour politicians, even after its withdrawal in March 1926. Moreover, in the House of Commons and cabinet he seemed aloof, superior, portentous, and pedantic, always ready to magnify small differences. By 1928 Baldwin thought of removing him to the ambassadorship in Washington, a post Percy himself coveted but which the Conservative government's defeat at the 1929 election denied him. Nor did Baldwin recommend him for ministerial office in the 1931 National Government.

Out of office Percy continued to contribute to educational debates, publishing *Education and the Crossroads* (1930) and editing *The Yearbook of Education* from 1932 to 1935. He organized the formation of the Conservative Party's research department during the winter of 1929–30, and created a reputation as a progressive Conservative intellectual with a series of writings—most notably *Democracy on Trial* (1931) and *Government in Transition* (1934)—arguing for national modernization not just of policies but also of institutions, including a reorganization of government and parliament along corporatist lines. As a senior ex-minister he was appointed chairman of the Indian federal finance committee (involving investigations in India itself) from December 1931 to March 1932, and a member of the parliamentary joint select committee on Indian constitutional reform in 1933 and 1934, drafting the introduction to its report—an important restatement of the principles of imperial rule. Percy's prominent part in defending the National Government's Indian policy in the House of Commons against Churchill and other Conservative critics restored his claim to ministerial office, but not Baldwin's confidence in his capacity to head a department. Percy later considered his period as minister without portfolio from June 1935 to March 1936 as a 'suicidal ten months' (Percy, 152) because with a cabinet seat yet no staff and no clear responsibilities he could do little, and was widely criticized for doing nothing.

Disillusioned with political life, Percy spent a few months in 1936–7 as chairman of the British Council, negotiating its grant from the Treasury in October 1937. After fulfilling a religious interest by publishing *John Knox* (1937), he resigned his parliamentary seat in order to become the first rector of King's College, Newcastle. Here he thought he did his best, as well as personally most congenial, work. He turned a newly created amalgamation of colleges, formed as a division of the University of Durham, into an effective institution and planned a successful post-war expansion in scientific and technical departments; this gave it the impetus to become, after his death, the independent University of Newcastle. In 1944 he chaired the Ministry of Education's committee on higher technological education, recommending closer ties with industry. After retiring as rector in October 1952, he was created Baron Percy of Newcastle (on 12 February 1953).

He chaired the Burnham committee on teachers' salaries from 1953 to 1956 and the royal commission on the law relating to mental illness and mental deficiency from 1954 to 1957, the basis for the 1959 Mental Health Act. He also resumed his reflections on government in *The Heresy of Democracy* (1954), and published one of the most intelligent, interesting, and self-critical political autobiographies, *Some Memories* (1958). He died at his home, the Old Rectory, Etchingham, Sussex, on 3 April 1958, when his title became extinct.   PHILIP WILLIAMSON

Sources DNB · *The Times* (5 April 1958) · *The Times* (11 April 1958) · E. Percy, *Some memories* (1958) · H. Nicholson, 'Lord Percy of Newcastle', *Durham University Journal*, 51 (1958–9), 97–105 · D. T. Jack, 'Lord Percy as rector', *Durham University Journal*, 51 (1958–9), 110–13 · B. Simon, *The politics of educational reform, 1920–1940* (1974) · J. R. Brooks, 'Lord Eustace Percy and the abolition of the compulsory, elementary curriculum in 1926', *Contemporary Record*, 7 (1993), 86–102 · Burke, *Peerage* (1999) · WW (1933) · *Debrett's Peerage*
Archives BL, letters to Albert Mansbridge, Add. MSS 65257 B-8 · Bodl. Oxf., corresp. with Gilbert Murray · CUL, Stanley Baldwin MSS · NA Scot., corresp. with Lord Lothian · PRO, Board of Education MSS
Likenesses W. Stoneman, photograph, 1924, NPG · L. Gowing, oils, c.1953, U. Newcastle · oils, U. Newcastle
Wealth at death £14,190 18s. 11d.: probate, 21 May 1958, CGPLA Eng. & Wales

Percy, George (1580–1632/3), colonist in America, was the eighth and youngest son of Henry *Percy, eighth earl of Northumberland (c.1532–1585), and his countess, Katherine Neville (1545/6–1596). He was born at Petworth, Sussex, on 4 September 1580, and was educated at Eton College, Gloucester Hall, Oxford, and the Middle Temple. Georgy Percy was a sickly child, apparently troubled in his youth by epilepsy and other ailments. Current medical thinking held that patients in such cases often prospered in warmer climates. Accordingly he embarked in 1602 on a sea voyage to the West Indies. Little is known about this adventure, but he reappears visiting his brother Sir Richard Percy in Ireland in summer 1603. This early experience of the Americas must surely help to explain why a younger son of a prominent English nobleman is found, five years later, among the band of settlers which established the first enduring English colony in the New World, near the mouth of the James River, in what is today the state of Virginia.

There was another reason. After the discovery of the Gunpowder Plot in November 1605 George's brother Henry *Percy (1564–1632), the ninth earl, was arrested under suspicion of complicity. Although never shown to have been directly involved, the earl remained a prisoner in the Tower of London for nearly sixteen years, a grievous blow to the fortunes of his family. For a well-travelled younger brother, the prospect of distant horizons and new possibilities must have been welcome. George Percy was almost certainly encouraged in his plans by the earl himself, who collected an impressive geographical library while in the Tower, and retained an abiding interest in exploration.

At first Percy was carried away with the excitement of his new surroundings. The land appeared fertile, and the Virginian Indians seemed friendly. However, his dream rapidly turned sour. The settlers fell out among themselves, supply ships failed to appear, disease and starvation took hold. Treacherous acts on both sides blighted relations with the Native Americans, and a series of horrific slaughters ensued. On one occasion he writes movingly of his unsuccessful attempts to spare the lives of an American Indian 'queen' and her children in the face of his men's implacable determination that all should be put to the sword. In 1609, as a senior member of the colony's ruling council, he deputized as its president for six months between the departure of Captain John Smith and the arrival of Sir Thomas Gates, and he did so again for just over one month in 1611. But given the colony's continuing misfortunes and his own recurring ill health he then decided to return home, setting sail for England in April 1612.

Under the terms of a family settlement Percy enjoyed a small annuity derived from rents on lands within the Percy estates in Cumberland and Yorkshire. During his years in America, however, his brother the earl agreed to take this income in return for settling debts which George Percy incurred with London merchants. This was convenient at the time, but the earl was subsequently plagued by opportunists who came to him seeking payment for debts allegedly run up long before. Northumberland's patience with the ostensible creditors eventually wore thin. 'This', he wrote at the foot of one such petition, 'I granted not, for I have too many of this nature brought me every day' (Syon MS X II I, box 21, bundle g).

Percy, as has been noted, kept some form of journal in America. While the original has been lost, extracts were published by Samuel Purchas under the title 'Observations gathered out of a discourse of the plantation of the southerne colonie in Virginia by the English'. As it comes down to us, this account breaks off in 1608. In the mid-1620s, however, his former commander John Smith published a self-congratulatory memoir. Percy then wrote his own version of events between 1609 and 1612 to counter Smith's 'many untrewthes'. He had sided against Smith in the faction struggles that had engulfed their colony, and his 'Trewe relatyon', which survives in his own hand and remained unpublished for three centuries, is a valuable corrective to Smith's hugely popular book.

Later years are thinly documented. In 1615 he considered joining one Captain Bud on a voyage to the Amazon delta, not least because, as he put it in his letter seeking support from the earl, 'my fitts here in England are more often, more longe and more greevous, then I have felt them in other parts neerer the lyne [the equator]' (Alnwick MSS, letters and papers, vol. 10, fol. 220). Four years later he assumed the role of his family's champion when one Richard Plumleigh slandered the earl's recently deceased countess. He challenged Plumleigh to a duel, and the privy council was forced to compose the quarrel. Thereafter we are left with little more than family tradition, which has it that he commanded a company when war broke out again in the Low Countries in 1627. From the indirect evidence available, he was alive when the ninth earl died in November 1632, but died during the following winter.

In a family of eight brothers only the earl produced a male heir, and the young Lord Percy, later the tenth earl, was made much of by both his father and his numerous uncles, each man seeing the boy as the best hope of restoring their family's fortunes. George Percy named a fort on the Chesapeake Algernon's Fort, in the child's honour, and later dedicated the 'Trewe relatyon' to his nephew in very graceful terms.

There is no contemporary evidence to suggest that George Percy ever married. Again, however, family legend credits him with a wife in Virginia. When the genealogist T. C. Banks visited America in the early 1800s he met two brothers Percy—landowners in Virginia—who claimed descent from George. Banks declared that, if what they said was true, they would be 'the right male heirs of the earldom of Northumberland of the *de novo* creation, the ancient one being suspended in the crown' (Banks, 1.369). The claim was never pursued.   MARK NICHOLLS

Sources Alnwick Castle, Alnwick MSS · Alnwick Castle, Syon MSS · PRO, SP 14 · [G. Percy], *Observations gathered out of 'A discourse of the plantation of the southern colony in Virginia by the English, 1606'*, ed. D. B. Quinn (1967) · P. L. Barbour, ed., *The Jamestown voyages under the first charter, 1606–1609*, 1, Hakluyt Society, 2nd ser., 136 (1969), 129–46 · G. Percy, 'Trewe relatyon', *Tyler's Quarterly Historical and Genealogical Magazine*, 3 (1922), 259–82 [MS now in the Free Library, Philadelphia] · M. Nicholls, '"As happy a fortune as I desire": the pursuit of financial security by the younger brothers of Henry Percy, ninth earl of Northumberland', *Historical Research*, 65 (1992), 296–314 · J. W. Shirley, 'George Percy at Jamestown', *Virginia Magazine of History and Biography*, 57 (1949), 227–43 · P. L. Barbour, 'The honourable George Percy, premier chronicler of the first Virginia voyage', *Early American Literature*, 5 (1971), 7–17 · T. C. Banks, *Baronia Anglica concentrata*, 2 vols. (1844) · *APC, 1619–21*, 25 · W. Sterry, ed., *A list of Eton commensals, 1563–1647* (1904), 27 · W. Sterry, ed., *The Eton College register, 1441–1698* (1943), 264 · H. A. C. Sturgess, ed., *Register of admissions to the Honourable Society of the Middle Temple, from the fifteenth century to the year 1944*, 1 (1949), 71 · Foster, *Alum. Oxon.*

Archives Alnwick Castle, Northumberland, papers, MSS of duke of Northumberland (incl. the collections formerly at Syon House)

Likenesses portrait, 1615, Syon House, Brentford, London

Percy, Gilbert. See Macquoid, Katharine Sarah (1824–1917).

Percy, Sir Henry de (d. 1272), baron, was the eldest son of William de *Percy (1191×3–1245) and William's second wife, Elena, daughter of Ingram de Balliol. Early in 1249, while still under age, he made a proffer of £900 to gain control of his lands and marriage. He was knighted before June 1257, the year in which he served in Henry III's army in Wales. In 1259 Percy was listed among the friends and allies of the earl of Gloucester in an agreement with the Lord Edward, indicating that he initially supported the baronial reform movement. However, he afterwards sided with the king, and in 1263 was among those attesting Louis IX's attempted settlement of the dispute between Henry III and the barons in which the French king favoured his fellow monarch. Percy accompanied the king in the siege of Northampton in April 1264 and then helped defend Rochester Castle against Simon de Montfort. He was captured at the battle of Lewes on 14 May 1264 and

held prisoner until the battle of Evesham on 4 August 1265.

Percy married, in September 1268, Eleanor, elder daughter of John de Warenne, earl of Surrey (d. 1304), and Alice de Lusignan, half-sister of Henry III. According to later genealogies they had three sons, William, John, and Henry *Percy, but contemporary evidence can be found only for the last two. Henry died on 29 August 1272, and was buried at Sallay Abbey, Yorkshire, where his wife was later buried with him. He was eventually succeeded by his son Henry.   HUGH M. THOMAS

Sources [M. T. Martin], ed., *The Percy chartulary*, SurtS, 117 (1911) · *Chancery records* (RC) · GEC, *Peerage* · C. Roberts, ed., *Excerpta è rotulis finium in Turri Londinensi asservatis, Henrico Tertio rege*, AD 1216–1272, 2 vols., RC, 32 (1835–6) · [W. Rishanger], *The chronicle of William de Rishanger, of the barons' wars*, ed. J. O. Halliwell, CS, 15 (1840) · R. Howlett, ed., *Chronicles of the reigns of Stephen, Henry II, and Richard I*, 2, Rolls Series, 82 (1885) · *Report on the manuscripts of Lord Middleton*, HMC, 69 (1911) · R. F. Treharne and I. J. Sanders, eds., *Documents of the baronial movement of reform and rebellion, 1258–1267* (1973) · *Paris, Chron.* · J. McNulty, ed., *The chartulary of the Cistercian Abbey of St Mary of Sallay in Craven*, 2 vols., Yorkshire Archaeological Society, 87, 90 (1933–4) · *CIPM*, 3, no. 214

Percy, Henry, first Lord Percy (1273–1314), magnate, was the son of Sir Henry de *Percy (d. 1272) and his wife, Eleanor. Born after his father's death, at Petworth, Sussex, about 25 March 1273, he had succeeded his elder brother, John, as heir before 11 June 1294. He married Eleanor (d. 1328), sister of Sir Richard Arundel, with whom he had two sons, Henry *Percy and William (d. 1355).

After taking part in the Welsh expedition of 1294 Percy began a decade of active involvement in the Scottish wars of Edward I. He served during the siege of Berwick and on its capture was knighted by Edward I on 30 March 1296. He fought at the battle of Dunbar on 27 April 1296. From then on he was one of Edward I's leading commanders. In September 1296 he was made warden of Galloway and Ayrshire and justiciar in Dumfries, offices he was to hold during several periods in the years that followed. In July 1297 he was one of the English lords who received the submission of Scottish prelates and nobles. After the defeat of John de Warenne, earl of Surrey (d. 1304), at Stirling Bridge in September 1297, together with Robert, Lord Clifford, he raised forces for the invasion planned to restore the English position. In 1298 he was one of six English magnates who furnished 500 heavy cavalry for Scotland, his share being fifty. He took part in the siege of Caerlaverock in 1300. On 5 April 1306 he was appointed the king's lieutenant and captain of all men-at-arms, both horse and foot, in the counties of Lancaster, Westmorland, Cumberland, Ayr, Wigtown, Dumfries, and the whole of Galloway to repulse the rebellion of Robert I. He and his retinue were in the army that Edward I was leading when he died at Burgh-on-Sands on 7 July 1307.

The record of his services in the Scottish wars demonstrates that Percy was one of Edward I's principal commanders, second only to a few leading earls. His rewards were commensurate with the scale of his services. On 20 February 1299 he was granted all the estates in both England and Scotland that had belonged to Ingelram de

Balliol, a cousin, deceased, apparently because the heir was a rebel. Apart from two manors in England, this grant brought Percy the barony of Urr and Red Castle in Angus. In 1304 he received the earldom of Buchan. His tenure of this was short-lived, since the Scottish earl returned to the allegiance of Edward I. Recompense for the loss of Buchan, however, was handsome and also a testimony to the importance of his services. In, perhaps, April 1306 he was granted the earldom of Carrick forfeited by the rebellion of Robert I. According to the contemporary chronicler Walter of Guisborough in February 1307 (or thereabouts) Percy was besieged by Robert in Turnberry Castle until relieved by a force led by Edward I. For a time, therefore, he controlled at least part of his earldom of Carrick.

Both his status as a leading baron and his involvement in the Scottish ambitions of Edward I meant that Percy was bound to have an active role in the period of crisis that followed the accession of Edward II. At the beginning of the reign he appears to have been on good terms with the king and his favourite, Piers Gaveston. On 16 June 1308 he was one of the small group before whom a number of letters patent to Gaveston's advantage were read out and sealed by the king; these included the grant of the earldom of Cornwall. At some point thereafter he joined the opposition to the court. While not himself one of the lords ordainer, on 5 October 1311 he was one of the group of councillors who announced the ordinances of reform to the people in the churchyard of St Paul's. His motives for supporting the cause of reform can only be conjectured, but it is reasonable to assume that he saw the need for peace in the kingdom in the light of the collapse of the English position in Scotland, a matter in which he had a substantial vested interest. Indeed, unlike most of the magnates who were later allies, he had responded to the king's summons to meet him at Northampton the previous August in order to proceed against Robert I. However, from October 1311 onwards he was a trusted ally of the ordainers, as the grants he received during their period of control demonstrate. On 20 March 1311 he was granted the keepership of the temporalities of the bishopric of Durham. On 2 December 1311 he was made justice of the forests beyond Trent and on 18 December keeper of Bamburgh Castle.

Percy remained steadfast to the ordainers' cause after Edward II's revocation of the ordinances and his rehabilitation of Gaveston, events that led to his loss of the justiceship of the forests beyond Trent and his replacement by Gaveston. He played an important part in the plan to capture Gaveston, the northern of the four zones into which the kingdom was divided for this purpose being entrusted to him and Roger Clifford. Together with the earls of Pembroke and Surrey he besieged Gaveston in Scarborough Castle and received his surrender on 19 May 1312. He took no part in Gaveston's execution. Although his lands were then seized, he was a beneficiary of the eventual settlement between Edward II and his opponents, being pardoned on 16 October 1313.

From the point of view of Percy himself, and from that of his family's fortunes in succeeding decades and centuries, the most important event in his career was his acquisition of the castle and barony of Alnwick in Northumberland. This estate was conveyed to Percy by Antony (I) Bek, bishop of Durham (d. 1311), by a charter dated 19 November 1309; but the transaction must have been a more complicated one than this grant suggests, since in an agreement of 1 April 1310 the bishop had a right of repurchase until the following Michaelmas. According to a contemporary source Bek held the estate in trust for William, an illegitimate son of William de *Vesey (d. 1297), the last Vesey lord of Alnwick, but there is no convincing evidence in support of this story. And there is nothing to suggest that, if fraud did occur, Percy was a party to it. He apparently paid a market price, possibly assisted by a loan from Italian merchants (the Bellardi of Lucca). His acquisition of this estate laid the foundations of his family's position on the borders with Scotland. He himself became the leading landowner, lay or ecclesiastical, in Northumberland. Although there is no direct evidence of his motivation, it is a fair inference from the circumstances of his career that the acquisition of Alnwick resulted from his involvement in the Scottish wars (which must have led to close contacts with Antony Bek). In 1309 the hope of recovering his gains in Scotland must have been a real one. The castle and barony of Alnwick would provide both a staging post between Scotland and his estates in Yorkshire and a base for his involvement in further warfare in Scotland.

Percy died between 2 and 10 October 1314, within twelve months of the royal pardon for his part in the events that led to the death of Gaveston. It is reasonable to suppose that he was already ill when he received his summons to the campaign that was to end in the defeat at Bannockburn, since there is no evidence of his presence there. He was buried at Fountains Abbey, and was eventually succeeded by his eldest son, Henry.   J. M. W. BEAN

Sources *Chancery records* · *RotS* · *CDS*, vol. 1 · W. Stubbs, ed., *Chronicles of the reigns of Edward I and Edward II*, 2 vols., Rolls Series, 76 (1882–3) · *The chronicle of Walter of Guisborough*, ed. H. Rothwell, CS, 3rd ser., 89 (1957) · P. Chaplais, *Piers Gaveston: Edward II's adoptive brother* (1994) · J. R. Maddicott, *Thomas of Lancaster, 1307–1322: a study in the reign of Edward II* (1970) · [M. T. Martin], ed., *The Percy chartulary*, SurtS, 117 (1911) · W. Dickson, ed., 'Chronica monasterii de Alnewyke', *Archaeologia Aeliana*, 3 (1844), 33–45 · J. M. W. Bean, 'The Percies' acquisition of Alnwick', *Archaeologia Aeliana*, 4th ser., 32 (1954), 309–19 · E. B. De Fonblanque, *Annals of the house of Percy, from the conquest to the opening of the nineteenth century*, 2 vols. (privately printed, London, 1887) · GEC, *Peerage*
Archives Alnwick Castle, Northumberland · Syon House, Brentford, London

Percy, Henry, second Lord Percy (1301–1352), soldier and magnate, was born probably in February 1301, the elder son of Henry *Percy, first Lord Percy (1273–1314), and Eleanor Arundel (d. 1328). Percy was given custody of Alnwick Castle and all his father's lands (except those in Yorkshire) in October 1318. Despite his youth Percy attended the meeting of northern magnates held by Thomas, earl of Lancaster, in May 1321. But he stayed loyal to Edward II. He did homage and received livery of his inheritance on 26

December 1321. He married Idonea (*d.* 1365), daughter of Robert, Lord *Clifford.

Early service and lands in Scotland, 1322–1332 He was summoned for service against the Scots under the command of Andrew Harclay, earl of Carlisle, on 26 March 1322, in which year he was also knighted. The following September he was serving in Northumberland under David Strathbogie, earl of Atholl, being enjoined to give sufficient attention to the defence of Alnwick Castle. He was involved in relations with Scotland for the remainder of Edward II's reign; he was, for example, one of the English hostages for the safety of the earl of Moray in April 1323, and one of the commissioners appointed to keep the truce with the Scots in July 1325.

Percy supported Queen Isabella against the Despensers when she returned to England in October 1326. The change of regime, faced as it was with a raid into Northumberland a few weeks after the coronation of Edward III, led to an especially active involvement in relations with the Scots. On 14 February 1327 the king's council entrusted Percy with the general defence of the north of England. In return for a fee of 1000 marks (£666 13s. 4d.) he was to serve until the following Whitsunday with a force that included 100 men-at-arms and as many of his own men as he chose. This was joined two days later with the custody of the marches of Scotland for the same period. On 23 April 1327 he became one of the ambassadors appointed to negotiate with the Scots. On 5 September 1327 there followed an appointment as chief warden of the marches until the following Christmas, and on 9 October 1327 he was one of the two envoys appointed to negotiate a final peace with Scotland.

During his stay in Scotland Percy displayed a concern that was to dominate his career for the next six years—his territorial claims and the opportunities for further gains there. On 28 July 1326 King Robert confirmed to Percy the Scottish lands that had belonged to his father 'by hereditary right or in any just and legitimate manner whatsoever' (Nicholson, 57). The lands in question were the barony of Urr in Galloway and Red Castle in Angus. Percy was one of a number of 'disinherited' who had lost lands held, or claimed, in Scotland. There can be no doubt that he had used his role in the negotiations with the Scottish king to advance his personal interests. His claim was, in fact, legally dubious, since on 3 June 1331 he paid the rightful heir the sum of 200 marks for the surrender of his claims. This, however, suggests that at least for a short time he enjoyed his Scottish inheritance.

Support for Edward Balliol and further rewards, 1333–1334 A new turn in England's relations with Scotland occurred with the invasion of Edward Balliol, who was seeking to regain the Scottish throne lost by his father and assisted by some leading disinherited. At first Percy's own conduct was cautious. But, as soon as Edward III abandoned his policy of non-intervention, he became a leading supporter of Balliol. On 9 May 1333 he undertook to serve Balliol within Scotland for life, saving his allegiance to the king of England, with a contingent of either 100 men-at-arms or 30

knights. In return Balliol promised him lands in Scotland worth 2000 marks a year. In less than three months Percy had virtually gained his promised reward. The first instalment on 29 July 1333 occurred shortly after the surrender of Berwick—the peel of Lochmaben and the valleys of Annandale and Moffatdale. Another grant of 5 September 1333 gave him a collection of forfeited holdings in the Cause of Stirling to the value of £629 16s. 8d. On 20 September 1334 the Vale of Lochmaben grant was increased to 1000 marks a year, bringing the total of Percy's reward to just below the promised amount.

The importance of Percy's services, especially during the siege of Berwick, may have led Balliol to ignore the claims of another of the disinherited—Edward de Bohun, a younger son of Humphrey (VII) de Bohun, earl of Hereford, who had received Lochmaben and Annandale from Edward I in 1306. What made possible a settlement of the dispute that flared up between Bohun and Percy was the fact that these lands were within the area of southern Scotland ceded to Edward III in perpetuity by Balliol. On 20 September 1334 Percy surrendered his lands to the English crown. In return he and his heirs received from Edward III a grant worth 1000 marks a year—the castle, constabulary, and forest of Jedburgh, an annuity of 500 marks a year from the customs of Berwick, and the custody of the castle there.

Nor was this all that Percy gained from the Scottish wars of the early years of Edward III. At the king's accession he had entered into an indenture of war to serve for life with a company of men-at-arms in return for an annual fee of 500 marks. On 1 March 1328 the crown assigned to Percy, in return for the surrender of this fee, the rights to the reversion of the estates of the Clavering family in Northumberland, which included the castle and barony of Warkworth. When such indentures of war were declared illegal in parliament in 1331, the indenture was surrendered by Percy; but the king, with the assent of parliament, then regranted the estates to Percy. The last Clavering died in 1332; and the reversion of all his holdings in Northumberland to Percy was completed with Clavering's widow's death in 1345.

Victory and consolidation on the northern marches, 1334–1352 By the summer of 1334 rebellion had shattered Balliol's hold on his kingdom. For the next three years Edward was engaged in efforts in his support. His immediate response, made on 3 August 1334, was to appoint Percy and Ralph Neville chief wardens of the marches and of the king's lands in Scotland. In January 1335 Percy defeated a Scottish raid in Redesdale, and in July of the same year he played a leading role in a grand two-pronged offensive, being the leading English commander in a force that Balliol led from Berwick. He accompanied Edward III on expeditions into Scotland in 1336 and 1337. From then on, during years in which the Scottish conflict was absorbed into the wider one with France, Percy, whether or not holding a formal appointment, played an integral role in the defence of the north of England. His importance in this respect achieved recognition on 28 April 1340, when he was appointed one of the councillors who were to advise the young Prince Edward during Edward III's absence overseas.

Percy's main achievement in the years that followed was the part he played in the defence of the north against the grand invasion launched by David II in 1346. When the English king and his eldest son left for the campaign in France that was to culminate in their victory at Crécy, Percy was made one of the custodians of the kingdom. He was one of the leaders of the army collected to repel the Scots and led the first division in the victory at Nevilles Cross on 17 October 1346. According to the Lanercost chronicle he was too ill to take part in the invasion of Scotland that followed.

The capture of the Scottish king and the death or capture of leading Scottish magnates at Nevilles Cross created opportunities similar to those of 1333–4. On 26 January 1347 Percy entered into an indenture with Lionel of Antwerp, earl of Ulster, Edward III's second son, who was guardian of England during his father's absence in France, to serve in Scotland for a year with a contingent of 100 men-at-arms and 100 mounted archers. The invading army was under the command of Edward Balliol who led one contingent from Carlisle, Percy leading the other from Berwick. But, presumably because of the pressure of the siege of Calais on English resources, the expedition was not strong enough to effect the reconquest that was necessary if Balliol was to regain his throne. It did, however, regain English holdings in southern Scotland, thus strengthening Percy's control of his Jedburgh estate.

In the history of the Percy family and that of England the second Percy baron of Alnwick deserves at least an equal place with his father, the first baron. His father had begun the family's involvement in the Scottish wars and given it the leading position in Northumberland. The son did much more than consolidate his father's gains by acquiring the Warkworth estates close to Alnwick. The total failure of Balliol to keep his Scottish throne may have meant that Percy lost for ever the lands that he had been granted in the area of Stirling. But the dispute with Bohun over his other gains at Balliol's hands turned out to his territorial advantage. Added to his holdings in Northumberland, his compensation from the English crown locked him firmly into the defence of England against the Scots and into English ambitions in the northern kingdom, thus giving his heirs very great territorial power that made them an essential part of the English crown's policies towards Scotland.

Death and children Percy died at Warkworth Castle on 26 February 1352. His testament, dated 13 September 1349 (a date that suggests fear of death from plague), enjoined interment at Sawley Abbey; but he was buried at Alnwick Abbey. One of his bequests reveals that while pursuing his territorial ambitions in Scotland and military activity in the north of England he had contemplated going on crusade to the Holy Land. He left the sum of 1000 marks (in Florentine florins), which he had collected for this purpose, to his heir, with the wish that the latter go in his place.

With his wife, Idonea, he had six sons—Henry *Percy,

his heir, Richard, Roger, Robert, Thomas [see below], and William—and four daughters—Margaret, who married first Robert Umfraville, son and heir of Gilbert, earl of Angus, and second William *Ferrers, third Lord Ferrers of Groby (1333–1371) [see under Ferrers family (per. c.1240–1445)], Isabel, who married William, son and heir of Sir Gilbert Aton, Matilda, who married John, Lord Neville of Raby, and Eleanor, who married John, Lord Fitzwalter.

Thomas Percy (c.1332–1369), bishop of Norwich, was the fifth son of Henry Percy, second Lord Percy. A series of preferments followed rapidly on studies at Oxford, beginning with the canonry and prebend of Chester-le-Street in the diocese of Durham in June 1351. In his nineteenth year he received a papal dispensation to hold a benefice with cure, notwithstanding the canonry and prebend he already held, this being at the request of the queen, the queen mother, and the earls of Lancaster and Arundel, as well as of his father. On 4 February 1355 he was made bishop of Norwich by papal provision. He owed this remarkable appointment to his brother's brother-in-law, Henry, duke of Lancaster, who was present at the papal court in Avignon as the leading English envoy in negotiations there with an embassy from France. Duke Henry seized the opportunity created by the death of his fellow envoy William Bateman, bishop of Norwich, to petition the pope for his relative's promotion, though he was still in his twenty-third year. Thomas Percy received the temporalities on 14 April 1355 and was consecrated bishop on 3 January 1356. He died on 8 August 1369 (the date suggests that he fell victim to plague in that year).

Despite his privileged background and youth there is nothing to suggest that Thomas Percy was not a competent and conscientious diocesan by the standards of his time. His surviving register (consisting of formal administrative documents) contains no indications to the contrary, and he was benefactor to the fabric of his cathedral. His testament, apart from bequests to close relatives, is notable for the concern it displays for the poor and for the welfare of quite menial members of his household. He did not hold any secular offices, though the explanation may lie in his youth and early death. The available records reveal that he was a trier of petitions in all save one of the parliaments of the years 1363–9. On 1 February 1362 he was present at Westminster at Edward III's confirmation of his treaty with the king of Castile. The main interest of Bishop Percy's career must be seen in its testimony to the position and influence achieved by his father and grandfather, especially in the light of his appointment to a bishopric that lay totally outside the area of Percy power and influence.

J. M. W. BEAN

Sources Chancery records · RotS, vol. 1 · CDS, vol. 3 · W. Stubbs, ed., Chronicles of the reigns of Edward I and Edward II, 2 vols., Rolls Series, 76 (1882–3) · J. Stevenson, ed., Chronicon de Lanercost, 1201–1346, Bannatyne Club, 65 (1839) · Scalacronica, by Sir Thomas Gray of Heton, knight: a chronical of England and Scotland from AD MLXVI to AD MCCCLXII, ed. J. Stevenson, Maitland Club, 40 (1836) · [M. T. Martin], ed., The Percy chartulary, SurtS, 117 (1911) · W. Dickson, ed., 'Chronica monasterii de Alnewyke', Archaeologia Aeliana, 3 (1844), 33–45 · J. R. Maddicott, Thomas of Lancaster, 1307–1322: a study in the reign of Edward II (1970) · R. Nicholson, Edward III and the Scots: the *formative years of a military career, 1327–1335* (1965) · J. M. W. Bean, 'The Percies and their estates in Scotland', *Archaeologia Aeliana*, 4th ser., 35 (1957), 91–9 · J. M. W. Bean, *The estates of the Percy family, 1416–1537* (1958), introduction · E. B. De Fonblanque, *Annals of the house of Percy, from the conquest to the opening of the nineteenth century*, 2 vols. (privately printed, London, 1887) · [J. Raine], ed., *Testamenta Eboracensia*, 1, SurtS, 4 (1836) · Emden, *Oxf.*, 3.1462 · register of Thomas Percy, Norfolk RO, DN/Reg 2 book 5 · GEC, *Peerage*, new edn, 10.459–62

Archives Alnwick Castle, Northumberland · Syon House, Brentford, London | Norfolk RO, register, DN/Reg 2 book 5 [Thomas Percy]

Wealth at death see will, Raine, ed., *Testamenta*, 57–61

Percy, Henry, third Lord Percy (*c.*1321–1368), magnate, was the eldest son of Henry *Percy, second Lord Percy (1301–1352), and his wife, Idonea (*d.* 1365), daughter of Robert, Lord *Clifford. During his father's lifetime the younger Percy followed the sort of career in the king's wars expected of the son and heir of a leading baron. His father's constant involvement in the north meant that he could give his energies to campaigning in France. He served under the earl of Arundel in March 1344, and in August 1346 he was at Crécy. He then transferred to service under the earl of Lancaster both in June 1347 and in November 1349, in Gascony.

Entry into his inheritance in 1352 did not present a continuation of the sort of opportunities that had faced Percy's father. The character of relations between the English crown and Scotland had changed. By the time of the second Lord Percy's death Edward III was to all intents and purposes leaving Edward Balliol to his fate. Instead, he gave his attention to the exploitation of the captivity of David II, king of Scots, so as to secure a settlement that would detach the Scots from the French alliance. It was certainly a policy that made use of Percy, since it also required attention to the defence of the border.

In July 1352 Percy was joint warden of the marches, and in September 1355 he became keeper of Roxburgh Castle and sheriff of the county for two years. On 30 January 1356 he was one of the witnesses to Edward Balliol's surrender of the kingdom and crown of Scotland to Edward III; and he then took part in the invasion of Scotland that followed. In July 1356 he was once again joint warden of the marches and was then employed in the negotiations that led to the treaty of Berwick of October 1357. But the period of truce that ensued left no opportunity for martial exploits on the border. His role in the affairs of the region became essentially a diplomatic one, involving him in the protracted negotiations over the ransoming of David II and efforts to achieve a permanent settlement between England and Scotland.

The changed conditions on the border did permit Percy to participate in Edward III's military efforts in France. In September 1355 he was marshal of the royal army at Calais. In 1359–60 he took part in the English king's grand campaign aimed at the capture of Rheims and his coronation as king of France. Percy was one of the English magnates at Calais on 24 October 1360 who swore to observe the terms of the treaty of Brétigny. As in the case of Scotland, however, there were no further opportunities for a military career in France for the remainder of his life. As a leading magnate on 19 October 1364 he witnessed at Dover the treaty for the marriage of Edmund, earl of Cambridge, the king's youngest son, to Marguerite, duchess of Burgundy.

Percy's contemporary, the chronicler of Alnwick Abbey, summarized his place in his family's history with the judgement that, 'content with the lordship [dominio] left him by his father, he wished to obtain the lands or possessions of no one' (Dickson, 41). But these words contain an element of distortion since they ignore the nature of Anglo-Scottish relations in his time. What territorial gains might have come his way if he had been faced with the sort of opportunities available to his father and grandfather can only be the subject of speculation. Nor could he have been lacking in any kind of territorial ambition, since he chose as his second wife the sole heir to a baronial estate.

Percy had married first Mary (*d.* 1362), daughter of Henry, earl (later duke) of Lancaster, and second Joan (*d.* 1368), daughter and sole heir of John, Lord Orreby. With his first wife he had two sons: Henry *Percy, his heir, and Thomas *Percy. With his second wife he had a son who died in his father's lifetime and a daughter, Mary, aged two at her father's death. Percy died on about 18 May 1368, probably at his castle of Alnwick, and was buried in Alnwick Abbey. J. M. W. BEAN

Sources Chancery records · RotS, vol. 2 · CDS, vols. 1–2 · W. Dickson, ed., 'Chronica monasterii de Alnewyke', *Archaeologia Aeliana*, 3 (1844), 33–45 · E. B. De Fonblanque, *Annals of the house of Percy, from the conquest to the opening of the nineteenth century*, 2 vols. (privately printed, London, 1887) · GEC, *Peerage*, new edn, 10.462–3

Archives Alnwick Castle, Northumberland · Syon House, Brentford, London

Percy, Henry, first earl of Northumberland (1341–1408), magnate and rebel, was the elder son of Henry *Percy, third Lord Percy of Alnwick (*c.*1321–1368), and his first wife, Mary (*d.* 1362), the daughter of *Henry, duke of Lancaster (*d.* 1361).

Early life Born on 10 November 1341 Percy spent much of his youth in the royal household and in that of his uncle, Henry, duke of Lancaster. On 12 July 1358 he married Margaret (*d.* 1372), widow of William, Lord Ros of Helmsley, and daughter of Ralph *Neville, fourth Lord Neville of Raby. His involvement in the affairs of the Scottish border began in his father's lifetime. Despite his youth he was a warden of the marches in 1362, being appointed to negotiate with the Scottish government. In February 1367 he was entrusted with the supervision of all castles and fortified places in the Scottish marches. When he entered into his inheritance in 1368, however, it was France that provided the obvious outlet for martial ambitions: in August 1369 he took part in the *chevauchée* led by John of Gaunt, duke of Lancaster, and he joined Edward III's brief and abortive expedition in 1372, and Gaunt's expedition of 1373. He was made knight of the Garter on 29 January 1366.

During these years Percy showed every sign of following a policy of expanding his family's territorial power and influence in the north. In 1373 he bought from the crown

Henry Percy, first earl of Northumberland (1341–1408),
manuscript painting, c.1400–25 [standing at horse's head]

the wardship of lands of David Strathbogie, the last earl of
Atholl, together with the wardship and marriage of his
two daughters and heirs, who were in due course married
to Percy's two younger sons. It was also in these years that
he began the negotiations which, on the death of Gilbert
Umfraville, earl of Angus, in 1381, brought him a substantial share of the Umfraville inheritance. His gains
included the castle and lordship of Prudhoe, thus enlarging his wealth and power in Northumberland.

The Good Parliament and its aftermath, 1376–1377 The
events of the Good Parliament of 1376 propelled Percy
into the first rank of the kingdom's politicians. When the
Commons through their speaker sought the appointment
of a committee of lords to assist them in the discussion of
grievances, Percy was one of the four barons and ban-
nerets they requested. It may well be that the leaders of
the Commons were aware of a personal grievance on Percy's part against one of the court faction—Alice Perrers.
When Percy's father died in 1368, he left a two-year-old
daughter from his second marriage who, on her mother's
death in May of the same year, became sole heir to the baronial family of Orreby. As a close kinsman who could not
inherit, Percy would have had reasonable expectations of
a grant of the wardship of his half-sister's lands. Two decades later, indeed, the terms of her testament suggest a
close relationship between her and her half-brother. As it
was, in December 1369 her wardship and marriage were
granted to Sir Alan Buxhull, who by May of the following
year had sold them to Alice Perrers. There is certainly evidence that Percy was interested in his half-sister's wardship, since following Alice Perrers's condemnation in the
first parliament of the next reign he succeeded in securing the wardship of the bulk of her lands (20 May 1378),
with effect from the date of Perrers's forfeiture. In any
event, there can be no doubt that Percy played a leading
role in the campaign against the court faction waged by
the Good Parliament. According to Thomas Walsingham,
it was Percy who accused Lord Latimer of suppressing a
letter sent to the king and the imprisoning of its bearer.
When in due course the chancellor and treasurer were

replaced and Alice Perrers excluded from court, Percy was
one of the new council appointed.

When the Good Parliament's successor met in January
1377, Percy more than acquiesced in its reversal of its predecessor's reforms. He had become an active supporter of
the court, now openly led by John of Gaunt. His motives
can only be guessed. It may well be that he had hopes of
crown patronage, including his half-sister's wardship: it is
equally possible that he was concerned about hostile
activity on the part of the Scots in the summer and
autumn of 1376, and saw advantages to be gained from
active support of the government. In December 1376 he
had been appointed marshal. He was vigorous both in the
performance of his duties and in support of John of
Gaunt. He accompanied Gaunt, preceding him in procession, when he appeared in person in support of John Wyclif when the latter was summoned before the assembled
bishops at St Paul's on 19 February 1377. Percy's use of
force to clear a way for Gaunt and himself led to an angry
confrontation with the bishop of London, as also did his
request that Wyclif be seated.

The following day a mob of London citizens rioted in
defence of the city's privileges and released a prisoner
from the Marshalsea by force. Gaunt and Percy had to flee
the city and take refuge with the princess of Wales at her
manor of Kennington. These events, however, did not
ultimately interfere with the undoing of the work of the
Good Parliament. When its successor ended, Gaunt and
Percy were firmly in control. Percy's membership of the
group that held power in the kingdom was marked on St
George's day 1377, when his three sons were knighted in
company with the heir to the throne, the king's youngest
son, and Gaunt's son and heir. The accession of the new
king, Richard II, produced evidence of Percy's increased
importance. On 16 July 1377 he was created earl of Northumberland and officiated as marshal at the coronation.

The border and John of Gaunt, 1377–1385 The new earl's career soon took a change of direction. Northumberland had
on 8 May 1377 been appointed captain of Calais. But if this
indicated an interest in the French war it was quickly
dropped. He also gave up the office of marshal. It is quite
likely that he wished to avoid a prolonged dispute with
Margaret Brotherton over her family's hereditary claims
to the office. Certainly experience had shown him that the
office was a risky one in terms of the holder's popularity
in London if he decided to take his duties seriously. In any
case the truce with Scotland was no longer effective, and it
was necessary to attend to his interests on the border. He
responded to an attack on Roxburgh by the earl of Dunbar
with an invasion of Scotland, laying waste Dunbar itself.
In November 1378 a Scottish force seized Berwick and the
earl and his son Henry *Percy (Hotspur) retook it.

Shortly after this, however, a rift appears to have developed between Northumberland and the government,
dominated by John of Gaunt, over policy towards Scotland. When in the summer of 1380 the Scots invaded Cumberland, pillaging Penrith and threatening Carlisle, the
government forbade Northumberland to respond. When
he attended the council, despite an outwardly friendly

reception, he was told to take his complaints to the next marcher court. The government was following a deliberate policy of maintaining the truce with Scotland, being prepared to overlook the occasional provocation of a border raid. It was realized that the *ad hoc* arrangements hitherto employed on the border, involving either commissions of local landowners with powers lasting only a few months, or the appointment of individual magnates to raise retinues—Northumberland himself had been employed in this way in the summer of 1380—were inadequate to maintain the government's authority, especially if a truce was to be preserved. The result was the appointment of John of Gaunt as the king's lieutenant in the marches towards Scotland, with responsibility for the defence of the north and the power to make truces with the Scots.

This led to an open feud between Northumberland and Gaunt, which flared up in the course of the peasants' revolt of 1381. When the revolt broke out, Gaunt was on the border engaged in negotiations with the Scottish government. News of the rebels' deep hostility towards himself led him to take refuge in Scotland for a short time. When he returned and began his journey southwards, he expected to receive hospitality from the earl of Northumberland. Instead, he was refused admission to Alnwick Castle. The earl claimed he was acting in Gaunt's interest. In a letter delivered by two of his retinue to Gaunt within sight of the castle walls he gave advice (in which the bishop of Hereford and earl of Stafford concurred) that Gaunt return to Bamburgh Castle and wait there until he was 'well-informed about the estate of the King and the business of the Commons' (Goodman, 81–2). It may well be, however, that there was also some sort of oral message, since according to both Knighton and the Anonimalle chronicle the earl expressed doubts about the king's intentions towards Gaunt. After Gaunt had taken refuge a second time in Scotland, it became clear that there were no grounds for such doubts.

For Gaunt, a prince of royal blood, the wealthiest magnate in the realm, and the king's lieutenant, the episode was a public humiliation. On his return to England he refused the protection that Northumberland had been commanded by the king to give him. A very public quarrel ensued. It is possible that Gaunt did not throw down his gauntlet, as Froissart relates. But there can be no doubt that a confrontation occurred at a royal council at Berkhamsted on 19 October 1381, when the earl's language offended the king as well as adding further insult to Gaunt. He was temporarily arrested for *lèse-majesté* and had to appear to answer Gaunt's charges in parliament in November 1381. The upshot was his public apology.

Gaunt's behaviour in this episode can be explained simply in terms of his need to compel a leading earl to understand that he could not insult the foremost prince of royal blood with impunity. In contrast, Northumberland's motives were much more complicated than simple caution during the crisis of the peasants' revolt and a desire to avoid involvement in Gaunt's unpopularity. As the leading magnate in the border region he may well have resented Gaunt's supreme role as royal lieutenant there. It is, however, possible to detect a motive of potential territorial rivalry behind this concern over Gaunt's authority. Gaunt's son and heir had married one of the two daughters and heirs of the last Bohun earl of Hereford. The inheritance they had to share included the lordship of Annandale and Lochmaben Castle. Northumberland may thus have feared an extension of the territorial power of the house of Lancaster into an area he had come to regard as his sphere of influence.

Why, however, did the earl act so strongly in the summer of 1381? The explanation must lie in the greatly increased territorial power in the north that he achieved during this very time. Before 15 December 1381 he had married as his second wife Maud (*d.* 1398), the widow of Gilbert Umfraville, the last Umfraville earl of Angus, and daughter of Thomas, Lord Lucy. In addition to her dower in the Umfraville estates she held in her own right the inheritance of the baronial family of Lucy, which included the castle and honour of Cockermouth. How far Northumberland at the time of the marriage had expectations of adding this great estate to his own family's inheritance is not known; but during the life of his wife he was now the leading landowner in Cumberland. His achievement must have made the prospect of Gaunt's power and ambition on the border especially difficult to bear.

Northumberland's apology in November 1381 did not end tensions between him and Gaunt. On 16 December 1381 the Lancastrian retainer, John Neville, lord of Raby, was appointed sole warden of the east march, the earl receiving the sop of a middle march. The changes then made in this arrangement mirror the tensions between Northumberland and Gaunt. On 14 March 1382 both the earl and Neville were, with others, made wardens of both east and west marches. Within a few months, on 26 June 1382, with Gaunt once more as king's lieutenant, Northumberland's authority as a warden was limited to the middle march and the area of his lordships of Alnwick and Warkworth, an arrangement repeated the following year on 25 July 1383.

The end of the truce with Scotland, followed by an abortive invasion by Gaunt in April 1384, eventually led to a recognition of the realities of Northumberland's territorial power on both sides of the Pennines. On his return from Scotland, before returning south, Gaunt made an agreement with Northumberland, effectively handing over defence of the north to him from 1 May to 11 June 1384. It had become clear that the territorial power of the Percys was now firmly entrenched in Cumberland as well as Northumberland, since the Lucy inheritance was in the process of being entailed within the Percy family. Even so, the earl's authority in the marches was far from secure. In July 1384 he had to share the marches with lords Neville and Clifford.

Tensions between Northumberland and Gaunt had by no means disappeared. The latter took advantage of the embarrassing position in which Northumberland found himself when attending parliament in November–December 1384. A band of Scots seized Berwick, of which he held the custody, by bribing his deputy. Gaunt took the lead in accusing him of negligence. Judgment was given against him on 14 December 1384 that, in the event of his failure to recover the town, all his property was to be at the king's pleasure. He took prompt action. Deciding to avoid the risks of a long siege, he paid the Scots to leave. He received a royal pardon on 17 February 1385. When an army under the king's command invaded Scotland in August 1385, Northumberland led the rearguard.

Richard II and the border Northumberland's ambitions had to adjust to changed political circumstances when Gaunt left England to pursue his claims to the kingdom of Castile in July 1386. A source of conflicting ambitions and personal antagonism had been removed. Instead, the policies of the young king and the ambitions of his courtiers became the dominating influences in the kingdom's affairs. Northumberland was bound to play an important role in national politics as well as the affairs of the north. In the struggle between the king and the lords appellant in 1387–8 he followed a policy of caution. He was sent by Richard II to seize the earl of Arundel; but he withdrew when he saw that Reigate Castle was well defended. At a later stage he took on a mediator's role when he assured the king of the loyalty of the duke of Gloucester and his other opponents, urging him to hear their grievances. By doing nothing against the appellants he was protecting his interests on the border, since their policy of war with France was bound to create opportunities in the north.

The appellants responded to a threatened Scottish invasion in the summer of 1388 by making the earl's son Hotspur warden of the east march for three years and ordering his father and seven other lords to remain on their estates to defend the north. There then occurred one of the most famous episodes in the history of both the Percy family and English chivalry. Hotspur took the field against a diversionary raid into Redesdale by the earl of Douglas, while his father stayed at Alnwick Castle intending to bar the Scots' return home. At Otterburn Douglas was killed, but Hotspur was defeated, and he and his brother Ralph were captured.

The following year conditions in the kingdom changed with the return of Gaunt and the beginnings of a decline in the position of the appellants. Gaunt was no longer a threat to Northumberland. One of his first acts after his return was to comply with the king's request to renounce any enmity towards the earl; and, in any event, his interests moved to Aquitaine. But what had a decisive effect on the position of Northumberland was the change of direction in government policy that followed the failure of renewed efforts made against France during the regime of the appellants. A truce with France in 1389 was followed later that year by one with Scotland. At the same time the king began to assert his personal authority in the knowledge that more peaceful conditions on the border had reduced his government's need for the power of Northumberland.

In June 1389 Richard II appointed Thomas (I) Mowbray, earl of Nottingham, warden of the east march, inserting into border society a courtier who had no territorial interests there. There are clear indications of Northumberland's hostility, since when Mowbray requested an extension of his appointment for five years, in October 1389, the earl and other lords voiced strong opposition in the council. Although they failed to prevent the reappointment, a deal was put together: Hotspur became warden of the west march for five years, and his father became captain of Calais. It may well be that the king then concluded that his own interests required more recognition of Percy ambitions. Whatever the reasons, Northumberland and Nottingham switched offices. On 1 June 1391 Northumberland became warden of the east march for five years, his son retaining the west march.

Thus in 1391 the efforts to secure control of the defences of the border that Northumberland had made, at least since the beginning of Richard II's reign, had achieved success. But it was short-lived. Hotspur was replaced by Lord Beaumont in June 1395. On 1 June he in turn replaced his father in the east march. The family had controlled both marches for no more than four years, and those in a period of truce that offered no opportunities against the Scots.

From 1395 onwards Northumberland must have become increasingly dissatisfied with the policies of Richard II. Even during the years when he and his son held both wardenships, the king had pursued negotiations with the Scottish government intended to secure some form of permanent peace between the two kingdoms. When Richard II left for Ireland at the end of May 1399, there can be no doubt that Northumberland and his son were ready to rebel if a good opportunity arose. It is, however, difficult to chart in detail their disillusionment with the king. If any credence can be given to a story told by Froissart, there was an open rift when Richard II set sail for Ireland. He describes how the king came to hear of complaints about him on the part of the earl and Hotspur. Richard then sent the earl a special order to attend on him, in addition to the summons he had received for service in Ireland. His refusal to comply led to the banishment of Northumberland and his son. There is nothing to support the details of this story; and there is no record of a summons to service in Ireland. But the story itself, even if inaccurate, may mirror a situation of potential conflict between the king and the earl in the spring and early summer of 1399. Even so, in the preceding two years there had been no indications of open hostility. Northumberland appears to have accepted the king's coup of September 1397 and his revenge against the three leading appellants of a decade earlier. And he was a member of the committee appointed by the Shrewsbury parliament of February 1398 to deal with its remaining business.

It is possible that Northumberland had anxieties about the increase in the power of the Nevilles at the hands of the crown. In September 1397 Ralph, Lord Neville, was made earl of Westmorland. And on 7 October following he and his wife were granted in tail male Penrith and other lands in Cumberland together with £120 a year from the customs of Newcastle. But the Nevilles had played an important role, often in conjunction with the Percys, in the affairs of the Scottish border since the early years of Edward III; and Northumberland's first wife had been Neville's aunt. It is unlikely that Northumberland regarded Neville as a threat, at least not to the extent of prompting open hostility to the crown. Yet he seized the opportunity to rebel when it came. His main motive lay in the policies that Richard II was following in the north and towards Scotland. He sought to assert his authority by importing into the marcher wardenships courtiers who had no territorial interests in the region, a policy that was part of a larger one of seeking a permanent accommodation with the Scottish crown. The long truce with France made in 1396 was followed by negotiations with Scotland in which Northumberland and his son had no part. Richard II thus planned a future that had no place for the territorial ambitions that were part and parcel of the Percy family's interests and traditions.

The deposition of Richard II and the accession of Henry IV A new phase in Northumberland's career and the fortunes of his family began with the landing of Henry Bolingbroke in Yorkshire in July 1399. Northumberland and his son Hotspur were among the first, if not the first, leading magnates to join him. It is clear that Bolingbroke's successful progress through England, culminating in the seizure of Richard's person, would not have been possible without the Percys' active support. Northumberland seems to have acted as the commander of his forces, and it was Hotspur who quelled resistance in Cheshire. There is no reason not to believe that they were ready participants in those acts in which Bolingbroke acted as a *de facto* ruler of the kingdom, despite the adherence to his cause of the lieutenant appointed by Richard II, the duke of York. Indeed, one of these acts benefited Northumberland himself: on 2 August 1399 he was appointed warden of the west march under the seal of the duchy of Lancaster, and he and his son thus regained the control of the border which they had lost in 1396.

Beyond these basic facts, however, it is difficult to achieve certainty about the Percys' conduct and the motives underlying it. The reason lies partly in the weaknesses and contradictions of the narrative sources, but also in the difficulty of discovering the truth of claims made by Northumberland, his son, and his brother Thomas *Percy, earl of Worcester, at the time of their rebellion against Henry IV in 1403. In effect, they then denounced Henry IV as a perjured usurper. Shortly after landing in July 1399 he had sworn an oath at Doncaster that he sought only his rightful inheritance as duke of Lancaster, together with the estates that were his due as the husband of his late Bohun wife. It is not certain that this incident occurred, since John Hardyng, who in the second version of his chronicle provides the Percy manifesto of 1403, omits all mention of it in the earlier, 'Lancastrian', version. The origins of the story may simply lie in the Percys' propaganda (the sole other source differs in detail, and places the oath at Bridlington).

The important issue, however, is whether the Percys were aware, if an oath was sworn, of different intentions

on Bolingbroke's part. It is difficult to believe that a man with the earl's political experience—much more, in fact, than either Bolingbroke himself or his other leading supporter, the earl of Westmorland—would have played so active a role in the events that led to Bolingbroke's accession without a careful appreciation of the latter's intentions. It must have been obvious that a change of king was at least likely. And the capacity for revenge that Richard II had demonstrated, notably in 1397, made this especially so. When Northumberland accepted the wardenship of the west march under the duchy seal, he was co-operating in Bolingbroke's use of the royal prerogative. It is possible to argue that in so acting Bolingbroke was performing as steward of the kingdom; but there was no emergency that necessitated his performance of this particular duty.

The most important service that Northumberland performed on Bolingbroke's behalf occurred when he acted as his emissary to Richard II who, after his return from Ireland, had eventually taken refuge in Conwy Castle. There is now a consensus among historians that the most important and reliable account of this episode is that of the French metrical chronicler Jean Creton. Although he was not present at the meetings between the king and the earl, his informant, the earl of Salisbury, was. Northumberland probably arrived at Conwy on 11 August with a small entourage, having placed most of his men some miles away. On meeting the king he made a number of demands for reform on behalf of Bolingbroke. The king was in no position to refuse these. But according to Creton he secured an oath of loyalty from Northumberland, who at the same time gave an assurance about Bolingbroke's own intentions, by swearing that he had heard him swear at Chester that he did not seek the throne. After some hesitation the king agreed to leave the castle on 14 August, Northumberland riding ahead of him. He was then met by Northumberland's main force. According to Creton, Richard, despite his initial anger and distress, was persuaded to accept the escort the earl had planned without his knowledge. It is difficult to see what alternative he had. And it is impossible not to conclude that Northumberland had on Bolingbroke's behalf plotted to secure the person of the king.

This episode and Northumberland's involvement in it paved the way for the removal of Richard II from his throne. As in the case of earlier events, absolute certainty about the Percys' participation in the events that followed is difficult. According to the account given by Hardyng in the earlier, 'Yorkist', version of his chronicle, and also the manifesto published by the Percys when they rebelled in 1403, they pressed the claim of the boy earl of March who, by the rule of primogeniture, was the heir. In principle it would have been in their interests to do so, since Hotspur was married to March's father's sister, so that the Percys could in the event of his accession look forward to at least a period of dominance in the affairs of the kingdom. It is more than likely that, once the removal of Richard II had been determined, March's claims were debated in some way. In the sermon he preached after Bolingbroke had been accepted as king, Thomas Arundel, archbishop of

Canterbury, referred to the dangers that might face a kingdom ruled by a child. This, and the discussions to which it may have referred, may have given a degree of plausibility to the story in the Percys' manifesto. But there is nothing in Northumberland's conduct between July and September 1399 to give support to it. On the contrary, the earl acted openly as a supporter of the accession of Henry IV. He was one of the two earls on the deputation sent to the Tower of London to receive the abdication of Richard II as part of the procedures followed for his removal from the throne. It was Northumberland who presided over the Lords' discussion of what to do with the former King Richard. At the new king's coronation he stood by Henry's side, carrying Lancaster's sword which had been worn by Bolingbroke when he landed in Yorkshire three months earlier.

A series of royal grants and appointments then substantially strengthened the position of power that Northumberland had occupied in the preceding three months. On 30 September 1399 he became constable of England for life, the highest military office in the kingdom. His position on the Scottish border was recognized by a fresh appointment as warden of the west march, his son Hotspur retaining the east march, both appointments being for ten years. The most remarkable grant, however, occurred on 19 October 1399 when the earl and his heirs were granted the Isle of Man. The full importance of these gains can be appreciated only in the light of those also made by his son Hotspur and his brother, the earl of Worcester. Hotspur, in addition to the wardenship of the east march, received a number of offices in north Wales, including that of justice of Chester. Worcester became admiral of England for life. Taken together, the gains made by the Percys present two features. First, they now dominated the military and naval leadership of the kingdom. Second, they now extended their power and influence into fresh areas—Wales and the principality of Chester. In this connection their link by marriage with the house of Mortimer was also recognized. On 17 November 1399 the farm of the greater part of the Mortimer estates during the minority of the young earl of March was given to four persons, of whom Northumberland and his son were two. On 1 October 1401 the farm was transferred to the earl alone. The effect was to increase, if only temporarily, the Percys' new influence in Wales and the marches.

Henry IV and the rebellion of 1403 The Percys' position of dominance in the affairs of the realm was maintained to all appearances during the first three years of the new reign. Northumberland was the leading member of the council, and played an equally important role in the public events of royal diplomacy, being, for example, a joint commissioner to arrange the marriage of the king's daughter to the son of the king of the Romans. But tensions between the king and Northumberland and his family were growing. It is fair to assume that Ralph Neville, earl of Westmorland, felt inadequately rewarded in comparison with the Percys for his support of Henry in July–September 1399; and he was married to the king's half-sister Joan Beaufort, whose brothers were only too ready

to undertake roles in government. At the same time, once the immediate needs of the usurpation were over, the new king was bound to rely more and more on nobles and gentry who had risen in the service of his father.

At first the rise to power of a court faction consisting of these elements was hampered by the government's financial difficulties. In the parliament of 1401 the Commons regarded the earl of Northumberland as an ally in their struggle to restrain royal expenditure. The earl and his brother were members of a sworn and enlarged council, while the latter recovered the stewardship of the royal household which he had held under Richard II.

A number of developments then produced a rift between the king and the Percys. If any single event can be said to mark an open deterioration in their relations, it occurred in March 1402, when the captaincy of Roxburgh Castle was transferred from Hotspur to the earl of Westmorland, a change that dented the Percys' control of the Scottish border. The cause of the deterioration, however, was a growing realization on the part of the earl, his son, and his brother that they were being increasingly detached from the centre of power. Their dissatisfaction took the form of complaints about the crown's failure to finance adequately the duties they performed on its behalf. In a series of letters the earl and Hotspur complained of their treatment, the first known being from May 1401. Two written by Northumberland himself belong to 30 May and 26 June 1403, the second complaining of the dishonour inflicted on the kingdom and the Percys themselves by the king's unwillingness to meet their financial needs. The earl denied the rumour that he and his son had received £60,000 from the crown since the king's accession, and claimed that £20,000 was owing to them. An analysis of the actual treatment they received, based on the issue and receipt rolls of the exchequer, shows that they were not ill-treated in terms of the financial situation of the crown. They may well have felt some financial strain in performing their duties, but this was a risk implicit in the acceptance of offices that at the same time carried with them benefits in terms of patronage and territorial influence. It is quite clear that these financial disputes with the crown became known outside the immediate circles of government. One of the chroniclers describes a confrontation between Northumberland and the king in which the earl demanded money for the defence of the marches and the king angrily replied, 'Aurum non habeo, aurum non habebis' ('I have no gold, you will have no gold'; *Eulogium historiarum*, 306). It is difficult not to believe that in these disputes over money the earl and his son felt the need for special treatment, at least partly out of a sense that their influence in the kingdom's affairs was diminishing.

There were other sources of disagreement and tension. Northumberland and his son were not happy about the king's policies in Wales, apparently preferring a policy of negotiation with Owain Glyn Dŵr, probably because they wanted resources to be diverted to the war in the north. A more personal dispute occurred as a result of the capture of Hotspur's brother-in-law, Sir Edmund (IV) Mortimer, by the Welsh rebels. The king refused to permit the Percys to arrange his ransom, accusing Mortimer of treason. But the worst dispute occurred as a result of the crushing defeat that the earl and his son inflicted on a Scottish invading force at Homildon Hill on 14 September 1402. The king refused to allow any ransoming of captives without his leave. For the Percys it was a blatant royal interference within an area they controlled. Father and son responded defiantly. The earl in the end surrendered his captives; but Hotspur refused to part with his, the chief of whom was the earl of Douglas.

Beyond this pattern of events the sources do not provide any glimpse of the discussions that must have occurred between Northumberland, his son, and his brother. The financial records of the exchequer suggest that every effort was made to meet the financial needs of the earl and his son in the late autumn and winter of 1402–3. On 2 March 1403 Northumberland and his heirs were granted a great tract of territory, covering the greater part of the area of southern Scotland claimed by the English crown. This was a resounding recognition of the Percys' dominance of the Scottish border and of a tradition of family aggrandizement that was now a century old.

Despite this, in the summer of 1403 the Percys rebelled. On 21 July 1403 Hotspur and his uncle the earl of Worcester met Henry IV in battle at Shrewsbury. Their defeat and the death of Hotspur in the battle, followed by the execution of his uncle two days later, ended the rebellion. Even though Northumberland himself was not at the battle, there can be no doubt that he was a full participant in rebellion. He was named with his son and brother both in the manifesto in which, on the eve of the battle, they defied Henry IV. The chronicler Hardyng, who was present at the battle, regarded Northumberland as a fully involved conspirator, describing how he raised troops and began to move south. Equally there can be no doubt that the Percys' intention was the removal of Henry IV from the throne and his replacement by the young earl of March. By this means they intended to retain the gains they had already made and to control the kingdom, at least during the minority of the new king.

Beyond this, however, there are problems and difficulties arising out of the apparent timing and strategy of the rebellion. It is clear that the Percys were in collusion with the Welsh rebel Owain Glyn Dŵr, and also that Hotspur moved from the north via Cheshire, aiming at Shrewsbury, the headquarters of the prince of Wales for his operations against Glyn Dŵr. At first sight it is puzzling that the Percys rose in rebellion within a few months of a royal grant that greatly increased their power on the Scottish border. But it is more than likely that they were contemplating rebellion in the autumn of 1402 and deferred action until after the winter. The royal grant of March 1403 may well have upset their plans by presenting a test of their time-honoured territorial ambitions, impelling them to make a visible effort to assert their new rights. Indeed, Hotspur laid siege to the castle of Cocklaw in Teviotdale.

It is the role of Northumberland himself that presents the most serious difficulties. It is impossible to accept Hardyng's account as a basis for an understanding of events. He wrote in the 'Yorkist' version of his chronicle that:

His [Hotspur's] father came not out of Northumberland,
But failed hym foule without witte or rede.
(*Chronicle*, ed. Ellis, 361–2)

Northumberland, in fact, did move south, but found his way barred by the earl of Westmorland and the forces he had raised. At that point Northumberland did not know of his son's death. His moving south does suggest, however, that the Percys were following a two-pronged strategy, the intention being that their two armies would later unite. It is more than possible that their timing had gone awry. Hotspur may have been precipitate and moved towards Shrewsbury too fast. Or the earl's departure from Northumberland may have been delayed because of a threat of invasion by the Scots: Hotspur's attempt to exercise his family's rights under the grant of March 1403 had led to mobilization on the part of the Scottish government.

At any rate the royal victory at Shrewsbury and the earl's withdrawal back into Northumberland left him totally isolated. After some time at Warkworth Castle he went south again, this time to submit to the king at York, on 8 August 1403. He was imprisoned at Baginton (a castle between Kenilworth and Coventry). He had to agree to the placing of royal garrisons in his castles of Alnwick, Warkworth, Prudhoe, and Langley. When his constables refused to admit the royal appointees on the ground that they held their offices for life, the earl was compelled to issue his own commands to his men that they give up their posts (October 1403). But as late as 13 January 1404 his men still controlled Alnwick, Warkworth, and Berwick.

At this point, when a parliament was about to meet, it must have been clear to Henry IV and his advisers that it was going to be extremely difficult to dislodge Northumberland from the position of power and influence in the north that his family had built up over the preceding century. In any event it would have been impossible to charge him successfully with treason. He was able to deny that he had conspired with his son and brother; and there is no evidence that the crown had information to contradict this. In terms of the law of arms he had never unfurled his banners against the king. Some sort of rehabilitation for him was inevitable.

On 6 February 1404 Northumberland came before the king, Lords, and Commons in parliament, asking for pardon. The Lords then declared that he was not guilty of treason but of trespass and offences against the Statute of Liveries, offences that carried a fine and ransom at the king's pleasure. The earl then took an oath of allegiance and secured a royal pardon. An account of this business, apparently sent to Durham Cathedral priory at the time, indicates that the formal parliamentary record does not give the full facts, since the king had pardoned the earl two days earlier (probably to make it clear that this was a matter for the king, not the Lords).

Northumberland's rehabilitation was far from total. He was no longer constable of England. His family had lost the wardenships of the marches that it had achieved in 1399, his own west march going to the earl of Westmorland who had forestalled his march south. Apparently there was also a price to pay for his pardon. What pressures were brought to bear in the succeeding months is not known, but on 9 July 1404 Northumberland promised to deliver to royal commissioners between the following 20 July and 1 August the castle of Berwick, the annual revenue of 500 marks from the customs of the town, the castle of Jedburgh, and the Forest of Jedworth. He was promised in exchange lands for himself and his heirs; but he had lost a powerful body of interests in the affairs of the Scottish border secured by his grandfather seventy years before.

The rebellion of 1405 and its aftermath It is fair to assume that Northumberland's feelings were ones of humiliation rather than gratitude for escape from the total consequences of rebellion. Even so, he remained a magnate with considerable territorial power; and the difficulties encountered by the government in its efforts to secure control of his castles had demonstrated the depth of loyalty among leading retainers. He could have chosen to bide his time, seeking to safeguard the interests of his heir, Hotspur's son. Yet he chose to rebel again.

It is not certain when the planning of another rebellion began. It may have been under way by January 1405. Whether or not he was implicated in a plot to seize the young earl of March, he made excuses for not coming south to attend a meeting of the council that month. One result of his planning was an alliance with Owain Glyn Dŵr. Aside from circumstantial indications, this alliance is commemorated in the text of the tripartite indenture between Northumberland, Glyn Dŵr, and Sir Edmund Mortimer of February 1405. It is not certain that the details are trustworthy; but it divided England and Wales between the three allies, the earl's share being twelve counties, stretching from the north into the midlands. In terms of the history of Percy ambitions, this is not incredible. The conspiracy also stretched into England. Richard Scrope, archbishop of York, apparently had genuine concerns about the government of the kingdom which, if Hardyng can be trusted, may have involved sympathy with the rebellion of 1403. Thomas (II) Mowbray, earl marshal, nurtured grievances against Henry IV as his late father's enemy, though the motives of Thomas, Lord Bardolf, are not clear.

Both circumstantial evidence and the comments of the chroniclers leave no doubt that Northumberland was the leader of the rebellion that followed. However, he never brought the forces he had raised to join up with those led by his allies. For him the deciding event in the rebellion was one that resulted from an anxiety to avoid the mistakes of 1403. He attempted to remove the earl of Westmorland as a potential opponent. Early in May 1405 he marched at night with a force of retainers to seize Westmorland when the latter was staying with Sir Ralph Eure at Eure's manor in Durham. When Westmorland, forewarned, made his escape, Northumberland apparently decided that the rebellion was doomed and abandoned

the archbishop and the earl marshal to their fate. His decision to do nothing further did not save him. When the king advanced north from York, he and Bardolf fled to Scotland. His attainder and forfeiture followed in the next parliament.

The rest of Northumberland's career consisted of moves from refuge to refuge and futile efforts to launch further rebellion. His stay in Scotland lasted no more than a year. When he and Bardolf learned of the Scottish government's intention to hand them over to Henry IV, they fled to Owain Glyn Dŵr in Wales. A journey to the French court failed to secure the French king's help in replacing Henry IV with the earl of March. By the summer of 1407 the two fugitives were back in Scotland. There followed a desperate attempt at an invasion of England. In February 1408 they reached as far south as Tadcaster in Yorkshire, a Percy manor. At the nearby Bramham Moor they encountered a force raised by the local sheriff. Northumberland was killed in battle on 19 February, his body receiving the customary treatment for a traitor—decapitation and quartering. His head was set on London Bridge. His remains were eventually brought together and buried in York Minster.

With his first wife Northumberland had three sons: Henry Percy Hotspur, Thomas, and Ralph. Thomas died in 1387, while serving on John of Gaunt's expedition to Castile. His son and heir, Henry Percy of Athol (so-called because his mother was the elder coheir of the last Strathbogie earl of Atholl) died without male issue in 1432. Ralph Percy fought against the Turks in the battle of Nicopolis in 1396 and died abroad the following year, presumably on his journey home.

Assessment and legacy Northumberland's whole career can be divided into two main phases. In the first, ending with the Lancastrian usurpation of 1399, he achieved gains that alone would have secured him a leading position in the history of his family, at least equalling those of his grandfather and great-grandfather. As well as strengthening his territorial power in Northumberland, he secured, in the Lucy inheritance in Cumberland, the most substantial estate on the western side of England's border with Scotland. He played a role in national politics far greater than that of any earlier head of the house of Percy. But this period also revealed a concern, almost obsessive, with maintaining a dominant position on the Scottish border by exploiting the potential rewards of the wardenships of the marches. In the second period, following the accession of Henry IV, this came to the fore, as did an ambition to dominate the affairs of the whole kingdom. In these years it is difficult to avoid the conclusion that the Percys' very success had isolated them. In 1403 they had no help from other magnates. And in 1405, bereft of his son and brother, Northumberland showed lack of judgement in rebelling without substantial allies. Thereafter his efforts to avenge the failures of 1403 and 1405 were as futile as they were bitter.

The failure of the rebellions against Henry IV left a permanent mark on the fortunes of the Percy family. In November 1414 Northumberland's grandson and heir,

Hotspur's son, was restored to the entailed estates held by his father and grandfather. And in March 1416 he recovered the title of earl of Northumberland. His restoration to the Percy inheritance was, however, far from complete. The taint of the attainders of Henry IV's reign lay over the family until it was removed in 1484; and the recovery of some entailed estates was not immediate. More significant, however, was the permanent loss of two important territorial gains achieved in the course of the fourteenth century. The Isle of Man, granted by a grateful Henry IV in 1399, was lost for ever. Above all, the Jedburgh estate, the revenue from the customs of Berwick, and the hereditary captaincy there had been surrendered to the crown and the promised compensation was never received. Although their dominant territorial position in Northumberland remained, the Percys' claim to total primacy on the eastern march was permanently damaged.

J. M. W. BEAN

Sources Chancery records · RotS · CDS, vol. 3 · [T. Walsingham], *Chronicon Angliae, ab anno Domini 1328 usque ad annum 1388*, ed. E. M. Thompson, Rolls Series, 64 (1874) · *Thomae Walsingham, quondam monachi S. Albani, historia Anglicana*, ed. H. T. Riley, 2 vols., pt 1 of *Chronica monasterii S. Albani*, Rolls Series, 28 (1863–4), vol. 2 · V. H. Galbraith, ed., *The Anonimalle chronicle, 1333 to 1381* (1927); repr. with corrections (1970) · *Johannis de Trokelowe et Henrici De Blaneforde … chronica et annales*, ed. H. T. Riley, pt 3 of *Chronica monasterii S. Albani*, Rolls Series, 28 (1866) · F. S. Haydon, ed., *Eulogium historiarum sive temporis*, 3 vols., Rolls Series, 9 (1858), vol. 3 · *Knighton's chronicle, 1337–1396*, ed. and trans. G. H. Martin, OMT (1995) [Lat. orig., *Chronica de eventibus Angliae a tempore regis Edgari usque mortem regis Ricardi Secundi*, with parallel Eng. text] · L. C. Hector and B. F. Harvey, eds. and trans., *The Westminster chronicle, 1381–1394*, OMT (1982) · G. B. Stow, ed., *Historia vitae et regni Ricardi Secundi* (1977) · M. V. Clarke and V. H. Galbraith, eds., 'The deposition of Richard II', *Bulletin of the John Rylands University Library*, 14 (1930), 125–81, esp. 164–81 [chronicle of Dieulacres Abbey] · [J. Creton], 'Translation of a French metrical history of the deposition of King Richard the Second … with a copy of the original', ed. and trans. J. Webb, *Archaeologia*, 20 (1824), 1–423 · *The chronicle of John Hardyng*, ed. H. Ellis (1812) · *The chronicle of Adam Usk, 1377–1421*, ed. and trans. C. Given-Wilson, OMT (1997) · G. Holmes, *The Good Parliament* (1975) · A. Goodman, *John of Gaunt: the exercise of princely power in fourteenth-century Europe* (1992) · J. M. W. Bean, *The estates of the Percy family, 1416–1537* (1958) · J. A. Tuck, 'Richard II and the border magnates', *Northern History*, 3 (1968), 27–52 · J. M. W. Bean, 'Henry IV and the Percies', *History*, new ser., 44 (1959), 212–27 · J. Sherborne, 'Perjury and the Lancastrian revolution of 1399', *Welsh History Review / Cylchgrawn Hanes Cymru*, 14 (1988–9), 217–41 · P. McNiven, 'The Scottish policy of the Percies and the strategy of the rebellion of 1403', *Bulletin of the John Rylands University Library*, 62 (1979–80), 498–530 · C. M. Fraser, 'Some Durham documents relating to the Hilary parliament of 1404', *BIHR*, 34 (1961), 192–9 · P. McNiven, 'The betrayal of Archbishop Scrope', *Bulletin of the John Rylands University Library*, 54 (1971–2), 173–213 · J. H. Wylie, *History of England under Henry the Fourth*, 4 vols. (1884–98), vols. 1–2 · E. B. De Fonblanque, *Annals of the house of Percy, from the conquest to the opening of the nineteenth century*, 2 vols. (privately printed, London, 1887) · GEC, *Peerage*

Archives Alnwick Castle, Northumberland · Syon House, Brentford, London

Likenesses manuscript painting, c.1400–1425, BL, Harley MS 1319 [*see illus.*] · miniature, BL, Cotton MS Nero D.vii, fol. 111

Percy, Sir Henry [called Henry Hotspur] (1364–1403), soldier, was born on 20 May 1364 at Alnwick, the eldest son of Henry *Percy, first earl of Northumberland (1341–1408),

and his first wife, Margaret (d. 1372), daughter of Ralph *Neville, Lord Neville of Raby (d. 1367).

Growth of a chivalric reputation Knighted by Edward III in 1377, the young Henry Percy quickly began to make a name for himself as a successful war-captain, 'who above all else desired feats of arms, always the first in the skirmish at the barriers' (*Œuvres de Froissart*, 13.210). He was first armed in November 1378, when he assisted his father in recapturing Berwick Castle from a band of Scottish raiders. He married Elizabeth Mortimer (1371–1417), eldest daughter of Edmund (III) Mortimer, third earl of March (d. 1381), before December 1379. They had two children: Henry *Percy, created earl of Northumberland in 1416; and Elizabeth, who married John, Lord Clifford, and, second, Ralph Neville, second earl of Westmorland (d. 1484). Percy served in Ireland with the earl of March in 1380, then travelled and crusaded in Prussia and Asia Minor during 1383. It was on the Scottish border, however, that he made his reputation and acquired his nickname, Hotspur, bestowed on him by the Scots as a tribute to his speed in advance and readiness to attack. In May 1385 Percy was appointed warden of the east march and, in the following month, accompanied Richard II into Scotland with his own company of sixty men-at-arms and sixty archers. He subsequently played an important part in securing the line of the royal army's withdrawal, beating off a series of Scottish attacks. Hotspur relinquished the wardenship in April 1386 and was immediately sent to reinforce the Calais garrison, with a company of 100 men, in the face of a rumoured French attack; characteristically, he took the opportunity to lead several raids into Picardy. Between August and October 1387 he had command of a substantial naval force in the channel and attempted, without success, to relieve the siege of Brest. The appellant regime showed their gratitude for these military endeavours by nominating Percy as a knight of the Garter early in 1388 and reappointing him as warden of the east march for three years in June, at the substantial fee of £12,000 p.a. in time of war and £3000 p.a. in peace. Taken unawares by large-scale Scottish raids through the march the same summer, Hotspur caught up with the force of James, second earl of Douglas, at Otterburn in Redesdale. In the confused engagement that followed—'as hard an encounter and as well-fought a battle as there could ever be' (*Œuvres de Froissart*, 13.219)—Douglas was killed and Hotspur captured. It is an indication of the public esteem he already enjoyed that the bulk of his ransom, set at 7000 marks, was met by royal gift and parliamentary subscription.

At large again by July 1389 Henry Percy was appointed warden of the west march for five years in June 1390. Despite the cessation of open hostilities against the Scots and French, his chivalric reputation continued to grow, fostered by displays of prowess at the jousts of St Inglevert in March 1391 and at Smithfield, during the festivities that followed the king's marriage, in 1396. Hotspur was sent on a diplomatic mission to James, king of Cyprus, in June 1393 before taking up the sensitive post of lieutenant in the duchy of Aquitaine, then in a state of near rebellion against the king's grant of the duchy to his uncle, John of

Gaunt, duke of Lancaster. He returned to England in January 1395, joining Richard II's expedition against the Irish, before going back to Aquitaine in the following autumn in order to consult with the Gascon estates over their continued opposition to Lancastrian rule. In 1396 Hotspur spent the summer at Calais, moderating and resolving outstanding ransom disputes between the French and English. Such consistent military and diplomatic employment brought with it growing evidence of royal favour. Richard had retained Hotspur for life in January 1391, at a fee of £100 p.a., and he granted him the chief forestership of Inglewood, with power to nominate a deputy, in May 1393. Percy was appointed warden of the east march, in succession to his father, for the exceptionally long term of ten years, in June 1396 and granted wardship of the extensive Umfraville inheritance in Northumberland, free of rent, in January 1399.

Support for Henry IV and its rewards Despite such tokens of royal favour the Percy family viewed with suspicion Richard II's attempts to dilute their monopoly of border office; the town of Berwick was, for instance, removed from Hotspur's command in January 1399. This was one influence on the Percys' decision to support Henry of Lancaster on his return from exile in June. Joining forces at Doncaster, Hotspur and his father accompanied Lancaster on his march south. While the earl of Northumberland played a crucial role in negotiating Richard's surrender, Hotspur was prominent militarily, beating off an attack by dissident Cheshire forces as the Lancastrian army moved towards London in August. The Percys were lavishly rewarded for their support. Within a year of Henry IV's accession Hotspur had been reappointed as warden of the east march for a further term of ten years, with the garrisons of both Berwick and Roxburgh included within his command, nominated as sheriff of Northumberland, and granted the castle and lordship of Bamburgh. He was also made justiciar of north Wales and Chester, and his authority in the region further underwritten by an extensive series of grants, including the castles of Chester, Flint, Conwy, Caernarfon, and Beaumaris, the shrievalty of Flint, the county and lordship of Anglesey, and the custody of the valuable Mortimer lordship of Denbigh.

These grants gave Percy a virtual monopoly of civil and military authority on the east march and in north Wales, two areas vital to the security of the new Lancastrian regime. In the north Hotspur was able to translate his augmented powers into military success but, as the rebellion of Owain Glyn Dŵr gathered strength, his Welsh commands proved unexpectedly taxing. Early in 1400 he and George Dunbar, earl of March, raided through the Lothians; the following autumn he was stationed at Dunstanburgh in order to protect the east march from retaliatory raids in the wake of Henry IV's campaign in Scotland. At Easter 1401 Conwy, one of the Welsh castles under Hotspur's command, was captured by rebels. After conducting the siege to recapture it at his own expense, and successfully negotiating the rebels' surrender, he remained in north Wales for the rest of the summer,

co-ordinating the English forays against Glyn Dŵr's forces. The king's continuing confidence in Hotspur's military ability was underlined by his appointment as royal lieutenant in north Wales in March 1402 while, in September, he and Dunbar won a considerable victory over an invading Scottish force at Homildon Hill, capturing the earl of Douglas and many other nobles.

Rebellion and death Building on this success against the Scots, Percy and his father sought to make good a royal grant to themselves of the Douglas estates in southern Scotland by besieging the fortress of Cocklaw, near Hawick, in May 1403. In July, however, Hotspur moved south, 'with a small company, feigning peace' (Galbraith and Clarke, 177). Once in Cheshire he issued proclamations accusing Henry IV of oath breaking and tyrannical government, declared his continuing allegiance to Richard II, and, joined by his uncle, Thomas Percy, earl of Worcester, marched on Shrewsbury in order to engage the forces of Henry, prince of Wales. Arriving outside the town on 21 July, however, Hotspur found that the king was there before him and he was forced to give battle against the superior royal forces. The fighting was exceptionally intense, with heavy casualties sustained on both sides, but the Percy forces broke when Hotspur himself, driving his way towards the royal standard, was struck down and killed. His body was taken for burial at Whitchurch, Shropshire, by Thomas Neville, Lord Furnival, but, on hearing that rumours circulated that Hotspur was still alive, Henry IV had the corpse exhumed and displayed it, propped upright between two millstones, in the market place at Shrewsbury.

Hotspur's rebellion was the final result of the growing discontent felt by the Percys at their treatment by Henry IV. On the march they believed their legitimate territorial ambitions in southern Scotland were being hampered by the king's failure to pay the wages due to them for their war service sufficiently promptly, while their sense of grievance was further inflamed by the favour Henry showed towards George Dunbar. Hotspur and his father had already expressed the frustration they felt on this issue by refusing to hand over to the king the prisoners taken at Homildon. In Wales the continuing success of Owain Glyn Dŵr was an additional source of tension. Frustrated by the king's reluctance to contemplate the negotiated settlement with the Welsh he had sought to promote, Hotspur had been forced to accept a substantial reduction in his regional predominance when a unified military command in the principality was created in April 1403 and vested in Henry, prince of Wales. A further, more personal, grievance was Henry IV's continued refusal to ransom Sir Edmund Mortimer, Hotspur's brother-in-law, after his capture by the Welsh in June 1402. This connection by marriage with the Mortimer family, who possessed a plausible claim to the English crown, may have been the decisive consideration in Hotspur's decision to rebel. In the parley before Shrewsbury Henry accused him of ambitions to rule the kingdom in the right of his wife and, in the heat of the battle itself, Hotspur's soldiers set up the cry 'Henry Percy King'. It was a fittingly grandiose epitaph for the most famous soldier of his day, whose military talents, allied to the shrewd political opportunism of his father, briefly secured for the Percy family a pre-eminent position among the English nobility.

SIMON WALKER

Sources Chancery records · Enrolled Foreign Accounts, PRO · Œuvres de Froissart: chroniques, ed. K. de Lettenhove, 25 vols. (Brussels, 1867–77) · Thomae Walsingham, quondam monachi S. Albani, historia Anglicana, ed. H. T. Riley, 2 vols., pt 1 of Chronica monasterii S. Albani, Rolls Series, 28 (1863–4) · M. V. Clarke and V. H. Galbraith, eds., 'The deposition of Richard II', Bulletin of the John Rylands University Library, 14 (1930), 125–81, esp. 164–81 [chronicle of Dieulacres Abbey] · N. H. Nicolas, ed., Proceedings and ordinances of the privy council of England, 7 vols., RC, 26 (1834–7), vol. 1 · RotS · E. B. De Fonblanque, Annals of the house of Percy, from the conquest to the opening of the nineteenth century, 2 vols. (privately printed, London, 1887) · R. L. Storey, 'The wardens of the marches of England towards Scotland, 1377–1489', EngHR, 72 (1957), 593–615 · R. R. Davies, The revolt of Owain Glyn Dŵr (1995) · P. McNiven, 'The Scottish policy of the Percies and the strategy of the rebellion of 1403', Bulletin of the John Rylands University Library, 62 (1979–80), 498–530 · J. M. W. Bean, 'Henry IV and the Percies', History, new ser., 44 (1959), 212–27 · CPR, 1401–5 · W. Dickson, ed., 'Chronica monasterii de Alnewyke', Archaeologia Aeliana, 3 (1844), 33–45, esp. 42–4 · GEC, Peerage

Wealth at death 4000 marks, value of royal grant from forfeited goods: CPR, 384

Percy, Henry, second earl of Northumberland (1394–1455), magnate, was the son and heir of Henry *Percy (1364–1403), known as Henry Hotspur, who fell at Shrewsbury in 1403 in rebellion against Henry IV, and Elizabeth Mortimer (1371–1417), eldest daughter of Edmund (III) Mortimer, earl of March, and Philippa, granddaughter of *Edward III. He was born on 3 February 1394.

Recovering lost ground Percy's early years were blighted by the consequences of rebellion, for although his grandfather Henry *Percy, the first Percy earl of Northumberland, presented him to Henry IV at Doncaster in June 1404, when the earl fled to Scotland in 1405 young Henry followed him and was detained for ten years by the duke of Albany, who treated the boy honourably. After Henry V's accession Percy was eager to return to England to recover his title and family estates, predominantly in Yorkshire, Northumberland, and Cumberland, with others in the south (including Petworth, Sussex). His rehabilitation may have been encouraged by the king's aunt, Joan *Beaufort, countess of Westmorland, who in October 1414 arranged his betrothal to her daughter Eleanor Neville, the widow of Richard, Lord Despenser (d. 1414). They had a number of children including Sir Ralph *Percy. Percy petitioned Henry V for the reversal of his grandfather's attainder, and on 11 November 1414 he was restored in parliament to his entailed estates. Henry V welcomed reconciliation with the Percys, which would help to secure northern England and reduce a Scottish threat should the king embark on war with France.

The arrangements for Henry Percy's return were complicated. Henry V sought to exchange him for Murdoch Stewart, earl of Fife, the duke of Albany's eldest son and a prisoner in England; Percy agreed to pay the £10,000 ransom required for Stewart. About the same time, however, the Southampton plotters against Henry V, including Sir

Thomas Grey of Heaton, a north-country landowner, conceived the idea of seizing Stewart and themselves exchanging him for Percy, who could then bring a Scottish army to help the plotters overthrow Henry V. They seized Stewart on 31 May 1415 while he was being taken north to effect the king's exchange, but he was quickly recaptured, and the episode did not upset Henry V's arrangements to restore Percy, who was innocent of the plot, to a position in England. The final terms of this exchange were agreed on 1 July, and in February 1416 Percy crossed the border; on the way, at Berwick, he married Eleanor Neville. In parliament (April 1416) he did homage for his earldom, though as a new creation, thereby stressing the attainder of his grandfather and the king's act of clemency: Percy was then formally regranted his family's entailed estates and was knighted. In the years that followed, Northumberland tried to recover all the estates, though many had been granted away after their forfeiture. Most were eventually recovered, even if in some cases it took a long time, as with those granted to John, duke of Bedford (d. 1435), and his duchess; others were only recovered by his son, the third earl. Northumberland was therefore far from being the richest of English earls, and his additional grants from Henry V and Henry VI were modest. Yet the gross value of his estates at the time of his death in 1455 has been estimated at over £3100, perhaps double the value of twenty years earlier.

Border warden Northumberland's service to Henry V was largely confined to the defence of the Scottish border. Although in July 1416 he went to Normandy on the king's service, he provided only a small contingent for the expeditionary force of 1417. Rather more important was his commission of the wardenship of the east march towards Scotland, to which he was appointed on 11 April 1417, with responsibility for Berwick Castle (of which the duke of Bedford was custodian). During the next seventeen years he negotiated with the Scots, raided southern Scotland, and strove to resist incursions into northern England. His first negotiation was authorized on 7 June 1417: his earlier contacts with Scotland and its politicians were doubtless considered an asset. But on 31 July, just as Henry V was embarking for France, he wrote to the king from Warkworth, one of his castles, to warn that his erstwhile captor, the duke of Albany, was preparing to attack Berwick. Weeks later Albany and the earl of Douglas did invade, attacking Berwick and Roxburgh; Northumberland helped to raise a force, and when the Scots retreated he pursued them across the border. During the king's absence in France, Northumberland supported Bedford in other ways, not least (as in November–December 1417) in persuading parliament and convocation to grant subsidies for the war. When Henry V returned to England with his queen in 1421, Northumberland acted as steward at Catherine's coronation on 24 February, and he witnessed the king's new will at Dover on 10 June. But his most valuable service continued to be in the north. In June 1421 he was reappointed warden with the promise of £2500 per annum in peacetime and £5000 per annum in wartime to maintain his retinue; he had difficulty in securing regular payment from then until the end of his wardenship in 1434, when he surrendered his commission in exasperation.

Henry V's death meant that Northumberland was required to join the conciliar regime during Henry VI's minority. He was appointed a councillor on 16 November 1422, and frequently attended council meetings when his other responsibilities allowed. For much of the time he seems to have been in Bishop Henry Beaufort's circle, and Beaufort's loans were an important source of finance for the wardenship. A rare venture to the continent may have taken place after he was appointed in 1423 an envoy to the Council of Pavia; but his main preoccupation in the 1420s—albeit a frustrating one—was to negotiate with the Scots. He was involved in the discussions of 1423–4 about ransoming the Scottish king, James I, who had been in English custody since 1406, and he accompanied James across the border in March 1424. In the following decade he tried to control cross-border warfare, investigating breaches of truces in 1426 and 1433, and accompanying Bishop (and now Cardinal) Beaufort to Berwick in 1429 to negotiate a new truce with King James. The king's council granted him £50 for his efforts on the border on 18 February 1434; but the fact that in June 1434 he and his burgesses of Alnwick were authorized to build walls round the town after the Scots had burnt it demonstrates that the Scottish problem had not been solved. In 1434 he surrendered his warden's commission; two decades later he was still owed outstanding wages.

Northern politics In these years Northumberland's links with the Neville family were amicable enough, and together they shared responsibility for protecting the border. In 1426 Northumberland bought the marriage of the young Ralph Neville, earl of Westmorland (d. 1484), and married him to his widowed sister, Elizabeth Percy; by May 1429 he was receiving a life pension from Cardinal Beaufort, the brother of Joan, dowager countess of Westmorland. Richard Neville, earl of Salisbury, was equally exasperated at the level of support given to him as warden of the west march; after he surrendered the wardenship, Northumberland and the earl of Huntingdon were jointly appointed wardens of both marches in July 1435, though they served for only one year. Such instability on the English side of the border led to further Scottish incursions. Outright war was in prospect by 1436, encouraged by the Burgundian attack on Calais. Northumberland may have raided into Scotland with Sir Robert Ogle, who was defeated at Piperden in September. James I besieged Roxburgh in August, but he was forced to retire when Northumberland advanced. This time, the government rewarded him with an annual grant of £100 for life, and in 1438 truce negotiations were resumed.

After Henry VI came of age, Northumberland continued to serve as a royal councillor, and in July 1438 received an annuity of £100 for life for attending council meetings. In 1441 he was on the commission of inquiry into charges of sorcery against the duchess of Gloucester. However, in the 1440s he was much occupied with the claims and franchises of a fellow councillor, Archbishop John Kemp of York, which impinged on Percy lands and rights in Yorkshire. Kemp was a formidable opponent, with the result that the earl was drawn into outbreaks of violence. In 1442 Percy retainers raided the archiepiscopal estates at Ripon and Bishopthorpe, and attacked Kemp's officials. The king's council intervened: Kemp appears to have had Henry VI's sympathy, and on 20 May 1443 Northumberland was ordered to surrender himself at the Tower of London, where he agreed not to travel more than 7 miles from London, unless it were to his manor at Dagenham, Essex; the archbishop's franchises were confirmed in 1444. Northumberland seems to have largely withdrawn from the council in the later 1440s, though he kept in touch with the court and may have spent much time in southern England; from 1443 he was involved in plans for the king's new college at Cambridge.

By 1450 Northumberland may have sympathized with criticisms levelled at the king's government. After the duke of Suffolk's murder he was appointed constable of England (25 May 1450) when certain governmental changes were made; though his military experience also commended him at this juncture. He was soon embroiled in Cade's rebellion, as one of the king's intermediaries sent to negotiate with the rebels at Blackheath in mid-June. He may also have sympathized with the duke of York's desire for reform in the autumn of 1450; on 11 September he was replaced as constable by the duke of Somerset when the royal courtiers reasserted themselves. Yet there is no sign that Northumberland approved of York's persistent criticism of the regime in the years that followed; in any case, in June 1452 he was commissioned again to treat with the Scots.

The quarrel with the Nevilles Northumberland's relations with the Nevilles deteriorated sharply in the early 1450s, as a result of the behaviour of younger members of the two families (especially Thomas *Percy, Lord Egremont, who was Northumberland's second son, and Sir John Neville) and the deepening political divisions at Westminster. By this stage Northumberland was spending an increasing proportion of his estate income on his retinue, while his eldest son, Henry *Percy, Lord Poynings, was warden of the east march and Salisbury had returned to the west march. By July 1453 the king was ordering Northumberland and Salisbury to maintain the peace and keep their sons under control, but matters reached a serious pitch with the marriage of Thomas Neville, Salisbury's son, to one of Lord Cromwell's two heiresses at Tattershall Castle, Lincolnshire. Cromwell held two rich, former Percy manors—Wressle, Yorkshire, and Burwell, Lincolnshire—which might fall to the Nevilles as a result of this marriage. Such an eventuality would seriously hinder Northumberland's recovery of ancestral Percy lands and at the same time enrich his Neville rivals. A month later, on 24 August 1453, while the Nevilles were returning from the marriage, the younger Percys ambushed the wedding party, including Salisbury; a skirmish took place at Heworth, near York, between the earls' sons—and some of Northumberland's retinue were involved.

On 8 October Northumberland and Salisbury were summoned to appear before the council and told to end their warlike activities. This was ignored, and Northumberland himself joined the Percy force that converged on Topcliffe to confront Salisbury and the Nevilles in October, though conflict was avoided. This lawlessness was made more serious by the involvement of the duke of Exeter, who claimed some of Lord Cromwell's estates in Bedfordshire and had his own political ambitions. Exeter allied with the Percys, especially when the duke of York, with whom the Nevilles were associated by 1453, was appointed protector of the realm in March 1454 during the king's incapacity. In 1454 Exeter raised his banner against York in the north and made common cause with the Percys. On 10 May 1454 Salisbury and Northumberland were again ordered to attend the council (on 12 June) to implement measures to restore order. Despite efforts to calm matters (including suspending all judicial process against Northumberland in July), little was achieved before the king's recovery at the end of 1454 and the confrontation between Henry VI and York at the battle of St Albans on 22 May 1455. Indeed, the early months of 1455 saw Northumberland identify himself decisively with the king's interests and those of the duke of Somerset, the enemy of York and the Nevilles. The Percy–Neville feud in the north, along with the Somerset–Neville feud in Wales, had been critical in alienating the Nevilles from the Lancastrian regime. Accordingly, at St Albans the Nevilles joined forces with York, and Northumberland was slain in the king's company. This battle seems to have been an arena for settling personal, political, and north-country scores, as well as for attempting to reform the government. Northumberland was buried in the nearby abbey.   R. A. GRIFFITHS

Sources PRO · PRO, Chancery, inquisitions post mortem, C139/160 no. 37 · *Chancery records* · N. H. Nicolas, ed., *Proceedings and ordinances of the privy council of England*, 7 vols., RC, 26 (1834–7) · *RotP*, vols. 4–5 · J. M. W. Bean, *The estates of the Percy family, 1416–1537* (1958) · R. L. Storey, *The end of the house of Lancaster* (1966) · R. A. Griffiths, 'Local rivalries and national politics: the Percies, the Nevilles, and the duke of Exeter, 1452–55', *Speculum*, 43 (1968), 589–632 · *RotS*, vol. 2 · Rymer, *Foedera*, 3rd edn · *Reports … touching the dignity of a peer of the realm*, House of Lords, 5 vols. (1820–29) · J. A. Giles, ed., *Incerti scriptoris chronicon Angliae de regnis trium regum Lancastrensium* (1848) · A. J. Pollard, *North-eastern England during the Wars of the Roses: lay society, war and politics, 1450–1500* (1990) · T. B. Pugh and C. D. Ross, 'The English baronage and the income tax of 1436', *BIHR*, 26 (1953), 1–28 · C. J. Neville, *Violence, custom and law: the Anglo-Scottish border lands in the later middle ages* (1998)
Archives Alnwick Castle, Northumberland, ministers' accounts · Petworth House, West Sussex, ministers' accounts
Wealth at death approx. £3100 gross (at least £2600 for taxation purposes, 1436): PRO, C 139/160/37; Pugh and Ross, 'The English baronage', 8–9

Percy, Henry, third earl of Northumberland (1421–1461), magnate, was the son and heir of Henry *Percy, second earl of Northumberland (1394–1455), and Eleanor, daughter of Ralph *Neville, first earl of Westmorland (d. 1425). He was born on 25 July 1421 at the Percy manor of Leconfield, Yorkshire. With his father a member of Henry VI's minority council, he was knighted on 19 May 1426 along with the young king. The second earl and his kinsman,

Cardinal Beaufort, secured for him (c.1434) the marriage of Eleanor (1428–1484), granddaughter and heir of Robert Poynings, fourth Baron Poynings. When Poynings died in 1446 Percy acquired (16 November) the baronies of Poynings, Fitzpayn, and Brian, with estates in Kent, Sussex, East Anglia, and Somerset; henceforward he was known as Lord Poynings. On 1 April 1440 he assumed responsibility for the east march towards Scotland (which his father shouldered until 1434) and custody of Berwick, and his commission was periodically renewed until his death. He was assigned substantial fees and wages—£2500 per annum in peacetime and £5000 per annum in wartime, with an annual sum for Berwick's upkeep (100 marks in peacetime and £200 in wartime)—though securing payment was not easy. With his father he defended the north against Scottish incursions, and in May 1448 invaded Scotland with Sir Robert Ogle and burnt Dunbar; the Scots retaliated by burning his father's castles at Alnwick and Warkworth. Later that year Henry VI travelled to Durham and dispatched Poynings to Dumfriesshire, but he was forced to retreat and was taken prisoner near the River Sark. On regaining his freedom he was recompensed for his ransom with half the goods of Sir Robert Ogle, now an outlaw. In April and July 1451 he was commissioned to negotiate with the Scots and in August became one of the conservators of a truce. In July 1452 he was granted the fee farm (£80 per annum) of Carlisle for twenty years, but in August 1454 the grant was transferred to Richard Neville, earl of Salisbury. By then Poynings was embroiled in his family's violent dispute with the Nevilles in Yorkshire where, at Topcliffe on 20 October 1453, he and his father assembled a force to confront Salisbury and his family. This seems to have been Poynings's first overt participation in the feud. By February 1454 he was reported to be planning to attend parliament with a strong force, and on 10 May he and his father were summoned to the council probably in an effort to prevent further lawlessness and a rising in Yorkshire by the duke of Exeter and Poynings's younger brother, Thomas *Percy, Baron Egremont.

His father's death at the battle of St Albans in May 1455 meant that Poynings inherited the earldom of Northumberland and, in view of his loyal service to Henry VI, he was allowed to enter his lands without payment of relief. He returned to the north, and in July 1455 foiled James II's attack on Berwick. Indeed, his duties in northern England meant that, later in the year, he was excused from attending parliament. But in January 1456 the delicate political situation that led to the ending of the duke of York's protectorate required his presence in London. A year later he joined the king and his court at Coventry, where he was confirmed as warden of the east march. With a substantial force and accompanied by his brother, Egremont, he attended the great council that assembled in London in January 1458 to reconcile the leading magnates. The Londoners were reluctant to allow large Lancastrian retinues into the city and Northumberland's was refused entry. Nevertheless, he took part in the formal reconciliation on 25 March: the greatest concessions were made by the Nevilles and the duke of York; Northumberland and

Egremont concluded a bond with them for £8000. He attended the Coventry parliament in 1459 that accused York of causing the death of Northumberland's father at St Albans; Northumberland himself swore to uphold the Lancastrian dynasty. In the face of continued Scottish threats, efforts were made in the late 1450s to ensure that Northumberland was paid his fees and wages as warden, and as a Lancastrian stalwart he was more successful than Salisbury on the west march in securing payment, including part of his accumulated arrears of £17,000. He also recovered, in November 1459, the Carlisle fee farm after Salisbury was attainted, and received an annuity of 100 marks from York's forfeited lordship of Wakefield, Yorkshire. For his services against the rebels, presumably at Ludford Bridge, he was rewarded, on 22 December 1459, with a life appointment as chief forester north of the Trent and constable of Scarborough Castle. On 30 May 1460 he was nominated to a wide-ranging commission of oyer and terminer to deal with all treasons and insurrections in Northumberland; a few days later he secured a twelve-year lease of Salisbury's estates in Yorkshire, Derbyshire, and Cambridgeshire. In the last years of his reign Henry VI relied on Northumberland to defend and control northern England, at the expense of York's and the Nevilles' power. Nevertheless, it was costly loyalty, for the Percy estates, especially in the north, had been declining in value for decades, and although the debt to him as warden had been reduced, it still stood at about £12,000 in 1461.

The Yorkist regime established after Henry VI's capture at Northampton in July 1460 tried to wrest the grants of forfeited property from Northumberland; and in October he was ordered to appear in chancery accused of looting York's and Salisbury's estates; following a meeting with his allies, lords Clifford and Dacre, at York in November 1460, further plundering of these Yorkist lands took place. York himself marched north against Northumberland: at a skirmish near Wakefield on 30 December 1460 the duke and his second son, Rutland, were killed, and Salisbury was beheaded immediately after. Northumberland proceeded to help Queen Margaret to raise an army, and he marched south with her, plundering along the way. They defeated the earl of Warwick and recaptured Henry VI at St Albans on 17 February 1461; but then, having failed to gain immediate entry to London, they retired north to York. Northumberland seems to have been in joint command of the army that then turned to confront the new monarch, Edward IV, at Towton on 29 March. In the battle Northumberland commanded the van, but his archers were blinded by snowstorms. The Lancastrians were defeated and Northumberland was killed in close fighting. He was probably later buried in the church of St Denis, York. In Edward IV's first parliament he was posthumously attainted (4 November). By 1469 the Percys were striving to restore their honour and reassemble their estates, but it was only when his son Henry *Percy, fourth earl of Northumberland, petitioned the parliament of 1472 that Northumberland's attainder was reversed.

R. A. GRIFFITHS

Sources PRO · *Chancery records* · N. H. Nicolas, ed., *Proceedings and ordinances of the privy council of England*, 7 vols., RC, 26 (1834–7) · *The Paston letters, AD 1422–1509*, ed. J. Gairdner, new edn, 6 vols. (1904) · J. S. Davies, ed., *An English chronicle of the reigns of Richard II, Henry IV, Henry V, and Henry VI*, CS, 64 (1856) · J. M. W. Bean, *The estates of the Percy family, 1416–1537* (1958) · R. L. Storey, *The end of the house of Lancaster* (1966) · R. A. Griffiths, 'Local rivalries and national politics: the Percies, the Nevilles, and the duke of Exeter, 1452–55', *Speculum*, 43 (1968), 589–632 · 'John Benet's chronicle for the years 1400 to 1462', ed. G. L. Harriss, *Camden miscellany, XXIV*, CS, 4th ser., 9 (1972), 151–233 · R. L. Storey, 'The wardens of the marches of England towards Scotland, 1377–1489', *EngHR*, 72 (1957), 593–615 · F. P. Barnard, *Edward IV's French expedition of 1475: the leaders and their badges* (1925) · A. J. Pollard, *North-eastern England during the Wars of the Roses: lay society, war and politics, 1450–1500* (1990) · GEC, *Peerage*, new edn, 9.716–17

Percy, Henry, fourth earl of Northumberland (*c*.1449–1489), magnate, was the only son of Henry *Percy, third earl of Northumberland (1421–1461), and his wife, Eleanor, Baroness Poynings (1428–1484). Despite their reputation as the leading northern family, rivalled only by the Nevilles of Middleham, the Percys had still not entirely recovered from the reverses they suffered between 1403 and 1408, when in 1461 the third earl died fighting for the Lancastrians at Towton. He was attainted by the victorious Yorkists, and in 1464 the forfeited earldom and most of the Percy estates were conferred on the earl of Warwick's brother, John Neville, Lord Montagu, in reward for his recent victories over the Lancastrians. Lord Percy, as Henry was called, was then confined in the Fleet, attended by four servants; by 1468 he was the ward of William *Herbert, first earl of Pembroke (*d.* 1469), whose daughter Maud (*d.* in or before 1485) he later married (*c*.1476). Probably only the breach between Edward IV and the Nevilles allowed the future fourth earl to rebuild the fortunes of his family, though the difficulties facing any government that tried to rule the north of England without the Percys were also a significant factor in Henry Percy's recovery of his earldom. Following renewed disturbances in the north, which were accompanied by a demand for his restoration as earl, Henry Percy was released from the Tower of London on 27 October 1469 and did homage to Edward IV at Westminster. During March 1470 the Percy estates in Northumberland were restored to him following their surrender, with the earldom, by John Neville, who was promoted instead to be Marquess Montagu; and on the 25th, after Warwick's flight, Henry Percy was created earl of Northumberland, with custody of his father's estates elsewhere. On 24 June he was appointed to the wardenship of the east and middle marches, an office traditionally held by the Percys.

Percy retained his earldom during the readeption of Henry VI in 1470–71, though displaced from his warden's office by Montagu, and he played a crucial role in Edward's recovery of his crown. Challenged after his landing at Ravenspur, Edward replied 'that he came thedere by the Erle of Northumberlondes avyse, and schewede the Erles lettere y-send to hym' (Warkworth, 14). The earl then sat still, so doing Edward 'a notable good service', since 'grete partye of [the] noble men and comons in thos parties [which] were towards th'Erle of Northumberland, and would not stire with any [other] lorde' did likewise, despite their Lancastrian loyalties and bitter memories of kinsfolk killed at Towton. (*Historie of the Arrivall*, 6–7). The earl's reward, given on 12 June 1471, was restoration as march warden, initially for five years, and appointment as justice of the forests beyond Trent and constable of Bamburgh for life. His father's attainder was reversed in the parliament of 1472, and during 1474 he received life grants of other key border offices, as constable of Newcastle upon Tyne and sheriff of Northumberland, while his election as a knight of the Garter attested his favour at court. In 1475 he accompanied Edward IV to France, serving with 10 knights, 50 esquires, and 350 archers, and was present at Edward's interview with Louis XI at Picquigny. And in 1482 he raised 6000 men and commanded the van in Richard of Gloucester's invasion of Scotland.

Apart from a few months immediately after Henry Tudor's accession Northumberland controlled the wardenship of the east and middle marches for the rest of his life. The extent and strategic location of the Percy estates explain their central importance to the earl. The terms of his restoration had been generous, giving him a relatively compact lordship initially worth approximately £3200 a year gross, all but £400 coming from Yorkshire and the border counties of Northumberland and Cumberland. Yet border estates also needed defending against Scottish incursions and the depredations of the borderland's reiving clans. In the 1470s the earl appointed itinerant commissioners to tighten estate administration, and he also made intermittent efforts to exploit their mineral resources. The terms on which he held the wardenship gradually deteriorated, but new lands worth almost £800 per annum which he inherited in the south in 1484 and 1488 compensated for this financially, without much altering the geographical balance of his estates.

Throughout Edward's second reign, however, Northumberland was overshadowed in northern government by the king's younger brother, Richard, duke of Gloucester, warden of the west marches, and inheritor of the Neville interest and estates. Initially the earl attempted to compete by building up his connection, but the threat posed by the duke's superior resources was underlined by Gloucester's retaining of John Widdrington of Chipchase, the earl's master forester of Alnwick, and by his displacement of the earl as justice of the forests beyond Trent in 1472. An unsuccessful attempt at mediation by the king's council in 1473, and the well-known indenture between duke and earl in 1474, seeking to limit their rivalry and safeguard the peace, shows Northumberland on the defensive. In effect Northumberland was obliged in the indenture to become Gloucester's 'faithful servant' (de Fonblanque) in return for assurances that the duke should neither retain any of the earl's servants, nor claim any office or fee which Northumberland had of the king. The agreement was flexibly observed by both parties: the earl was unchallenged in Northumberland, where he continued to fee the leading gentry, and in north Durham too,

but in the west he granted no new fees. In Yorkshire the earl dominated the East Riding, where he had most land, while North Riding gentry mostly followed Gloucester. Relations between the two magnates were apparently amicable too, as was attested by their co-operation during the Scottish war of 1480–83. Although Gloucester was appointed king's lieutenant, and so given general precedence in the north, after the recovery of Berwick it was the earl who received command of this key outpost; and initially, too, he had the gift of 600 places in the garrison, at a cost of £438 per month.

Northumberland's support for Gloucester was crucial in providing the military muscle behind the latter's coup in June 1483. The earl raised troops in his own territory, particularly the East Riding, and had command of the northern army which backed Richard's claim to the throne. He bore the curtana, the blunt sword which was the emblem of royal mercy, at Richard III's coronation; and once Richard was established at Westminster, Northumberland no doubt hoped to take over his role as king's lieutenant in the north. He was to be disappointed. The earl was handsomely rewarded for his support, with the title of great chamberlain of England and probably the most valuable land grant (approximately £1500 per annum) of the reign. But a third of this land (by value) was the Brian estate in the south-west, which the earl claimed through his mother; and in political terms the forfeited Stafford lordship of Holderness merely complemented his existing East Riding possessions. In Northumberland he continued to act as warden, albeit from year to year, but any expansion of Percy influence in the region was checked by Richard's decision to retain direct control of the north through his ducal household and council there, headed successively by his son and his nephew. Moreover, the king's local knowledge, his continuing reliance on his northern affinity, and his more attractive lordship, probably meant that Northumberland's position was now even weaker. Several Percy associates entered the king's household, accounting for about one-eighth of his known knights.

As in 1471, therefore, circumstances again prompted Northumberland to place personal interests before the loyalties and expectations of his retainers. Perhaps calculating that an inexperienced king without other supporters in the north would allow him the regional hegemony Richard had withheld—and perhaps also in accordance with an earlier undertaking to Henry Tudor—Northumberland brought a large army to Bosworth but then once more sat still, so keeping his retainers, and probably many of Richard's northern supporters, out of the battle. In the short term this strategy proved successful. Richard III was defeated and killed, and although Northumberland was briefly imprisoned after Bosworth, lack of support in the north soon forced Henry VII to restore the earl—albeit, in effect, on probation. The earl lacked connections at the new king's court, but again built up his regional affinity: by 1489 he was retaining eighty-four lords, knights and esquires, and spending

£1708 a year (42 per cent of his income) on fees to officials and retainers. And over the next three years he repaid Henry's confidence in him with unswerving loyalty as king's lieutenant in a hostile north. In April 1486 he brought a powerful retinue, including thirty-three knights, to escort the king into York at the time of Lovell's rebellion. In June 1487 he reacted promptly to Lambert Simnel's invasion, organizing York's defence, and raising 6700 men to hold the north-east against the rebels. And in April 1489, upon news of a tax rising in Cleveland, he summoned his retainers to come with 'bowes & arrowes & pryvy harnest' (*Plumpton Letters*, no. 74) and set out to enforce collection.

Yet Northumberland's equivocal conduct at Bosworth was widely seen as treachery; many northerners suffered in the ensuing political reaction against the followers of Richard III; and subsequently the earl's energetic enforcement of Tudor policy in the region marked him as the leading instrument of an unpopular regime. These developments so undermined the earl's standing among his retainers that they failed to protect him, instead leaving him to be killed when he confronted a mob of protesters at South Kilvington, just outside Thirsk, on 28 April. In John Skelton's words:

Barons, knightis, squyers, one and alle,
… Turnd ther backis and let ther master fall,
… Alas his golde, his fee, his annuall rente,
Upon suche a sort was ille bestowde and spent.
(*John Skelton: the Complete English Poems*, 31–2)

Northumberland was buried as he had requested in Beverley Minster, after a lavish funeral costing £1037. His wife had died before 1485, but he was survived by their four sons and three daughters, of whom the eldest son, Henry Algernon *Percy, succeeded his father as fifth earl. Their third son, Alan *Percy, became master of St John's College, Cambridge. STEVEN G. ELLIS

Sources M. A. Hicks, *Richard III and his rivals: magnates and their motives in the Wars of the Roses* (1991) • A. J. Pollard, *North-eastern England during the Wars of the Roses: lay society, war and politics, 1450–1500* (1990) • R. Horrox, *Richard III, a study of service*, Cambridge Studies in Medieval Life and Thought, 4th ser., 11 (1989) • J. M. W. Bean, *The estates of the Percy family, 1416–1537* (1958) • M. J. Bennett, 'Henry VII and the northern rising of 1489', *EngHR*, 105 (1990), 34–59 • M. Weiss, 'A power in the north? The Percies in the fifteenth century', *HJ*, 19 (1976), 501–9 • E. B. De Fonblanque, *Annals of the house of Percy, from the conquest to the opening of the nineteenth century*, 2 vols. (privately printed, London, 1887) • [J. C. Hodgson], ed., *Percy bailiff's rolls of the fifteenth century*, SurtS, 134 (1921) • 'The Yorkshire rebellion in 1489', *GM*, 2nd ser., 36 (1851), 459–68 • F. P. Barnard, *Edward IV's French expedition of 1475: the leaders and their badges* (1925) • M. Bennett, *Lambert Simnel and the battle of Stoke* (1987) • K. Dockray, 'The political legacy of Richard III in northern England', *Kings and nobles in the later middle ages*, ed. R. A. Griffiths and J. Sherborne (1986), 205–27 • C. L. Scofield, *The life and reign of Edward the Fourth*, 2 vols. (1923) • J. Warkworth, *A chronicle of the first thirteen years of the reign of King Edward the Fourth*, ed. J. O. Halliwell, CS, old ser., 10 (1839) • J. Bruce, ed., *Historie of the arrivall of Edward IV in England, and the finall recoverye of his kingdomes from Henry VI*, CS, 1 (1838) • *The Plumpton letters and papers*, ed. J. Kirby, CS, 5th ser., 8 (1996) • *John Skelton: the complete English poems*, ed. J. Scattergood (1983) • GEC, *Peerage*, new edn, 9.717–19

Archives Alnwick Castle, Northumberland • BL, Royal MS D ii • Bodl. Oxf., MS 3356 • Syon House, Brentford, London | Cockermouth Castle, Lord Leconfield's MSS • Petworth House, West Sussex, Lord Leconfield's MSS
Likenesses tomb, Beverley Minster, Yorkshire
Wealth at death wealthy; incl. £4044 p.a. gross from lands: Bean, *Estates of the Percy family*, 129

Percy, Henry, eighth earl of Northumberland (c.1532–1585), magnate and conspirator, was born at Newburn Manor, Northumberland, the younger son of Sir Thomas Percy (d. 1537), landowner and rebel, of Prudhoe, Northumberland, and his wife, Eleanor (d. 1567), daughter and coheir of Sir Guischard Harbottle of Beamish, co. Durham; he was aged about five in 1537. He was the younger brother of Thomas *Percy, seventh earl of Northumberland (1528–1572), magnate and rebel. Their father was executed at Tyburn on 2 June 1537 for his role in the Pilgrimage of Grace. After this, they were removed from their mother's custody and placed under the care of Sir Thomas Tempest of Holmside, co. Durham.

Thomas and Henry Percy were restored in blood on 14 March 1549. Henry Percy was returned as MP for Morpeth, Northumberland, in 1554 and knighted on 30 April 1557. Thomas was restored to the earldom of Northumberland on 1 May 1557, with the tail male in remainder to Henry, who became deputy warden of the east and middle marches. Henry Percy purchased the captaincy of Norham Castle at the end of 1557. All this was intended to recover family power through acquisition of traditional Percy offices. Elizabeth I initially favoured him. He was appointed to the queen's council in the north in December 1558 and named of the quorum for co. Durham and for Northumberland in 1559. Percy was a commissioner to treat with the lords of the congregation and encouraged rebellion in Scotland, goading James Hamilton, duke of Châtelherault, in February 1559 to take action. The French ambassador in Scotland, Henri Cleutin, seigneur d'Oysel, complained about Percy's interference on 30 July. Percy participated in the Scottish campaign in 1560, commanding a band of horse pistoleers and distinguishing himself, and was appointed governor of Tynemouth Castle, Northumberland, in December as a reward.

Percy was appointed a commissioner to treat with the French on 25 May 1560. He reported on the newly adopted doctrines of the Scottish church and corresponded with John Knox, who was convinced of his protestantism. Châtelherault believed Percy was protestant in 1559, as did Francis Russell, second earl of Bedford, in 1565, but Sir Ralph Sadler was unconvinced. Percy was commissioned on 5 May 1561, along with Thomas Young, archbishop of York, to administer the oath of supremacy to the clergy of the northern province. By 25 January 1562 he married his cousin Katherine (1545/6–1596), first daughter and coheir of John Neville, fourth Baron Latimer, and his wife, Lucy. The couple had eight sons, Henry *Percy, ninth earl of Northumberland (1564–1632), Thomas (d. 1587), William *Percy (1574–1648), Sir Charles Percy (d. 1628), Sir Richard Percy (d. 1648), Sir Alan Percy (d. 1611), Sir Josceline Percy

(d. 1631), and George *Percy (1580–1632/3), and two daughters, Lucy and Eleanor (d. 1650). Percy ensured that his children were very well educated. Katherine Neville's younger sister, Dorothy, married Thomas *Cecil (1542–1623) on 27 November 1564. Percy was sheriff of Northumberland from 1562 to 1563. He was appointed a commissioner to suppress piracy on 8 November 1565 and to enforce the Acts of Uniformity and Supremacy in the archdiocese of York in 1568. The following year he was named of the quorum for Cumberland and for the North and East ridings of Yorkshire.

During the northern uprising of 1569–70, while Northumberland played a leading role in supporting Mary, queen of Scots, Percy remained loyal to Elizabeth. He joined the royal forces and held Tynemouth for the queen, who wrote to him in gratitude on 17 November. Although his motivations are unknown, Percy was proud and quarrelsome, yet displayed 'a cautious "loyalist"' attitude during the rebellion (James, 295). It is possible that the brothers took opposing sides in order to preserve the family estates. When Northumberland escaped to Scotland and was imprisoned there, Percy wrote urging him to confess and appeal to Elizabeth's mercy. Percy was rewarded with the stewardship of the crown property at Tynemouth in 1570. He was returned as MP for Northumberland in 1571, probably to ensure his inheritance. The act for confirmation of attainders of May 1571 contained a clause guaranteeing Percy's rights. He technically succeeded to the earldom when his brother was executed on 22 August 1572.

Despite his previous loyalty, Percy opened communication with John Leslie, bishop of Ross, at Easter 1571. Again, his motivation for offering to assist Mary to escape as part of the Ridolfi plot is unclear. It is possible that Roberto di Ridolfi's agents contacted Percy, as acting head of the family. Despite Percy's professing Catholicism, Thomas Howard, fourth duke of Norfolk, did not trust him. Percy was found out and while in the capital was arrested and lodged in the Tower of London on 15 November. He begged Elizabeth for mercy on 23 February 1572, which was granted, but was tried privately in November, having accepted a secret punishment rather than open trial. The queen was angry with him for his ingratitude and dissimulation, while William Cecil, Baron Burghley, was regarded as too partial towards him because of marital ties. In November she renewed her order to Robert Dudley, earl of Leicester, that Percy be kept in close confinement, his fault being 'as great as any Man's, though it be no hie Treason' (W. Murdin, ed., *A Collection of State Papers Relating to Affairs in the Reign of Queen Elizabeth, from … 1571 to 1596*, 1759, 229). Percy was fined £3333 6s. 8d., which he never paid, and told to stay at his house at Petworth, Sussex. He had been removed from the queen's council of the north in April 1571, and Francis Hastings, second earl of Huntingdon, did not want him restored. Huntingdon wrote to Leicester on 20 January 1573, requesting successfully that the eighth earl of Northumberland remain under house arrest at Petworth. Northumberland was permitted to go to London on 12 July 1573 and set at liberty shortly afterwards.

Northumberland was unpopular with his tenants, who accused him of being a cruel landlord. He attempted to improve his estates, building a forge and a double furnace in Petworth Great Park, which was probably what upset his tenants. However, Northumberland preferred the court to the country. Writing in the early seventeenth century, William Camden described him as 'a man of lively and active Spirit and Courage' (Camden, 193). Northumberland's exile from court was lifted, and he first took his seat in the House of Lords on 8 February 1576. He began rebuilding Petworth from 1576, and it was his principal residence during the last years of his life. In 1577 he was nominated to be a commissioner to promote the breeding of warhorses in Sussex. After his father-in-law died on 22 April 1577 the countess of Northumberland inherited a quarter of the Latimer estate, including Burton Latimer, Northamptonshire.

Northumberland continued to dabble in treasonous plots surrounding Mary. He had several of his sons educated in Paris by Charles Paget. Paget was an accomplice of the conspirator Francis Throckmorton, and visited Northumberland at Petworth in September 1583, perhaps hoping to make it the base for his invasion of England but more probably trying to apprise his associates of the current situation, advising them not to support any plots. Certainly Northumberland was sympathetic to Mary, enjoyed intrigue, and had a weakness for indiscreet comments. The government was convinced that he was seriously involved, and in December he was placed under house arrest for assisting Thomas Paget, third Baron Paget, and Charles Arundell to escape to France and for speaking with Charles Paget. He was removed from his governorship and his stewardship. Northumberland was sent to the Tower on 9 January 1584 for denying matters confirmed by witnesses. Sir Francis Walsingham was convinced that he was a Catholic.

In June 1585 the government considered bringing charges of treason against Northumberland but did not pursue it, although the reason why is unknown. He was found in bed in the Tower on the night of 20–21 June, dead from a shot through the heart inflicted with his own pistol, which was still in his hand. The Star Chamber inquest held on 23 June determined that his death was suicide. He was buried on the same day in the chapel of St Peter ad Vincula in the Tower. Some Catholics, however, were convinced that Sir Christopher Hatton, the vice-chamberlain, had the earl murdered on the government's orders. A Latin pamphlet published at Cologne made this claim; it was soon translated into German, Italian, Spanish, and English. If Northumberland had been shot three times in the chest, as some affirmed, this would indeed seem to rule out suicide, but if not, suicide does seem much more probable; it protected his family from confiscations. The popular belief in Hatton's guilt, however, was strong. In a letter of 1601 to Sir Robert Cecil, Sir Walter Ralegh casually referred to Hatton as Northumberland's murderer. The declaration by the crown after Northumberland's death stated that he conveyed Charles Paget and Arundell out of the country after Throckmorton's arrest, because they were the only real witnesses against him. The dowager countess of Northumberland remarried shortly after 5 December 1587, her second husband being Francis Fitton of Binfield in Berkshire, a kinsman of Northumberland who had long been her steward. She died on 28 October 1596 and was buried in Westminster Abbey.

CAROLE LEVIN

Sources L. Stone, *The crisis of the aristocracy, 1558–1641* (1965) • W. T. MacCaffrey, *Queen Elizabeth and the making of policy, 1572–1588* (1981) • W. T. MacCaffrey, *The shaping of the Elizabethan regime: Elizabethan politics, 1558–1572* (1968) • A. G. Vines, *Neither fire nor steel: Sir Christopher Halton* (Chicago, 1978) • B. W. Beckingsale, *Burghley: Tudor statesman, 1520–1598* (1967) • G. Bren and W. A. Lindsey, *A history of the house of Percy, from the earliest times down to the present century* (1902) • W. Camden, *The history of the most renowned and victorious Princess Elizabeth*, [new edn], ed. W. T. MacCaffrey (1970) • M. James, *Society, politics and culture: studies in early modern England* (1986) • R. Lomas, *A power in the land: the Percys* (1999) • *The works of Sir Walter Ralegh, kt*, ed. W. Oldys and T. Birch, 8 vols. (1829) [repr. 1964] • C. Sharp, ed., *Memorials of the rebellion of 1569* (1840); repr. with foreword by R. Wood as *The rising in the north: the 1569 rebellion* (1975) • 'A true and summarie reporte of the declaration of some part of the earle of Northumberland's treasons', *Elizabethan backgrounds: historical documents of the age of Elizabeth I*, ed. A. F. Kinney (Hamden, Conn., 1975) • HoP, *Commons, 1509–58*, 3.83–4 • HoP, *Commons, 1558–1603*, 3.203–4 • GEC, *Peerage* • *The household papers of Henry Percy, ninth earl of Northumberland, 1564–1632*, ed. G. R. Batho, CS, 3rd ser., 93 (1962)

Percy, Henry, ninth earl of Northumberland (1564–1632), nobleman, was born in April 1564 at Tynemouth Castle, the eldest son of Sir Henry *Percy (*c*.1532–1585), from 1572 eighth earl of Northumberland, and Katherine Neville (1545/6–1596), daughter and coheir of John Neville, Lord Latimer; he was the elder brother of George *Percy (1580–1632/3) and William *Percy (1574–1648) the playwright was another of his brothers. After early instruction in the protestant faith from the vicar of Egremont, Cumberland, Percy went abroad to complete his education. He was probably in Paris when, on 21 June 1585, he succeeded to the earldom upon the suicide of his father in the Tower of London. In later life the earl confessed that his youth had been profligate, but he outgrew these indiscretions. He embarked upon a series of initiatives to improve returns from his estates, which lay not only in the family's traditional heartland of Yorkshire, Northumberland, and Cumberland, but also scattered right across England and Wales. This process continued over the next forty years. William Camden claims that Northumberland served as a volunteer against the Armada (*The History of the … Princess Elizabeth*, 1688, 414). There is no further evidence for this, but the earl did visit the Low Countries in 1588, an experience which stimulated his lifelong interest in siege warfare and military tactics.

During the 1590s the earl enjoyed a measure of favour at the hands of Queen Elizabeth. Though hardly well disposed to the Percy family, Elizabeth liked to indulge the young men at her court. She restored Northumberland to the eighth earl's governorship of Tynemouth Castle in

Henry Percy, ninth earl of Northumberland (1564–1632), by Nicholas Hilliard, 1590–95

1591, and made him a knight of the Garter in 1593. Prudently, the earl avoided giving any offence in the exercise of religion: eschewing the attachment to Catholicism that had so blighted the careers of both his father and his uncle, he remained a lifelong member of the established church.

In 1594 Northumberland married Lady Dorothy Perrott (*d*. 1619), widow of Sir Thomas Perrott, son of Sir John Perrott, the late lord deputy in Ireland, and sister of Elizabeth's favourite, Robert *Devereux, second earl of Essex (1565–1601). Their marriage proved tempestuous, the Devereux connection turning sour as Essex's fortunes declined and Northumberland maintained his longstanding friendship with Devereux's adversary, Sir Walter Ralegh. In 1600 the earl again visited the Low Countries and, finding life there congenial, did not return until February 1601. He hurried home only after learning that his brother-in-law had staked and lost everything on rebellion.

The variety of Northumberland's interests is illustrated by his well-stocked library. Insofar as it can be reconstructed, it consisted principally of books on science, medicine and anatomy, military matters, architecture, travel, and classical texts. At various times the earl was a patron to and friend of some notable scholars, including Walter Warner, Robert Hues and, particularly, Thomas

Harriot, associated with the earl from the 1590s. Indeed, his patronage earned him notoriety, as an atheist and dabbler in forbidden knowledge, a 'wizard earl', a man 'who troubled not much himself' about religion (PRO, SP 14/216/116). In addition to three 'Advices' of 'Instructions' to his son, sections of which were variously later published, the earl drafted a substantial work on the art of war and composed two literary conceits, 'Love' and 'Friends and Friendship'. Yet, although he was long troubled by deafness, and was described by one admiring contemporary as 'civill, modest and quyett', both 'inward and reserved' (BL, Hargrave MS 226, fols. 241–3), Northumberland was never the detached scholar. Household accounts provide ample evidence that he lived court life to the full, ready to sit at the gaming table and happy to participate in the ceremonial.

Northumberland was rather easily led and incapable of keeping a secret, and there is, too, an occasional glimpse of ungovernable temper. In 1587 he was imprisoned for causing a disturbance at his mother's house, while in 1597 and 1602 he was only narrowly prevented from fighting duels with the earl of Southampton and Sir Francis Vere, an antagonist of long standing. In 1599, following the deaths of two infant sons in 1597 and the birth of a daughter, Dorothy (1598–1659), later married to Robert Sidney, earl of Leicester, the earl and his countess separated after a furious row. However, they were eventually reconciled, and further children followed: Lucy (1600–1660), later Lucy *Hay, countess of Carlisle, Algernon *Percy (1602–1668), later the tenth earl, and Henry *Percy (c.1604–1659), later Baron Percy of Alnwick.

Soon after Essex's downfall Northumberland, along with the queen's secretary, Sir Robert Cecil, Sir Walter Ralegh, and other leading courtiers, made secret overtures to James VI of Scotland against the time when Queen Elizabeth should die. As his go-between to Edinburgh the earl selected a trusted cousin and estate officer, Thomas Percy, and through the Catholic Percy he sought toleration for English Catholics. Giving vague assurances, James promised nothing. When, in March 1603, Elizabeth lay dying, Northumberland was among those invited to join the council in their deliberations, and there seems to have been a suggestion, perhaps from Cecil, that the earl should act as protector of the realm while James made his way south to London.

Nothing came of this, but Northumberland nevertheless reaped an immediate reward in James's new world. He was sworn a member of the privy council in April 1603, and was appointed captain of the gentleman pensioners, the official royal bodyguard, in May. Once again, however, he risked advocating some form of toleration, forwarding a petition from English Catholics at one of his first meetings with James. This did not immediately mar the cordial relations between king and earl, but during the summer that all-important bond began to weaken. The dispatches of the French ambassador, Christophe Harlay, comte de Beaumont, are full of assertions that the English are dissatisfied with their king, and while Beaumont never names his source, the earl, a carefully cultivated friend, is

an obvious suspect. Though each authority alone may be considered unreliable, the observations of Beaumont's compatriot, the marquis de Rosny, and the writings of various discontented Englishmen at Madrid and Brussels during the summer of 1603 together suggest that Northumberland was growing increasingly disillusioned with James and his Scottish entourage.

Just when the council was investigating two linked conspiracies against the king, Northumberland put a foot wrong. On either 12 or 13 July 1603, in front of king and court, he spat in the face of his old adversary, Vere. James was deeply offended. The earl was banished from court to cool his heels in the archbishop of Canterbury's summer palace at Croydon. Vague rumours, almost certainly without foundation despite his friendship with Ralegh, one of the principal conspirators, linked Northumberland's name to the so-called Bye and Main treasons. On this occasion he survived and gradually began to rebuild his position at court.

Two years later, he was not so fortunate. With the discovery of the Gunpowder Plot it was revealed that one of the ringleaders was none other than the trusty Thomas Percy. Northumberland, it transpired, had not only made Percy a gentleman pensioner, he had dispensed with the oath of supremacy which the king had ordered should be demanded from new members of the band. Still more damning, Percy had visited the earl for dinner on 4 November, the day before the projected destruction of the Lords. Northumberland always insisted that his private discussions with Percy that fateful day had touched on estate business—nothing more—but his arguments never quite convinced anyone else. Percy was killed soon afterwards in open rebellion: while he could never now accuse Northumberland of complicity in the Gunpowder Plot, he was equally unable to clear him. As the earl put it, 'noen but he can shew me clere as the day, or darke as the night' (PRO, SP 14/216/225).

James and his council struggled to identify a nobleman sufficiently eminent to serve as protector of the realm had the plot succeeded. That mastermind was never found. The surviving plotters claimed that any decision on the protectorate had been deferred until after the explosion, but, again, their assurances failed to convince. Suspicion against Northumberland grew accordingly; no one could quite credit that Percy would have let him die in the Lords. After a lengthy examination on 23 November Northumberland was dispatched to the Tower on the twenty-seventh.

Following months of government indecision, the earl was charged with contempt and on 27 June 1606 proceeded against in Star Chamber *ore tenus*, which could in theory only follow upon a confession of guilt by the accused. Northumberland's fellow councillors stripped him of all public offices, fined him £30,000 and condemned him to imprisonment during the king's pleasure. Some admitted that the penalties appeared harsh, but thought it appropriate that James should enjoy scope for clemency. The king, however, was disinclined to be generous. Northumberland remained in the Tower until June

1621, James's suspicions enduring long after the deaths of those councillors who in popular imagination and in the earl's increasingly mordant conceits had conspired to keep him under lock and key. His countess, a loyal and tireless visitor, died in August 1619 and Northumberland's grief at her passing was touchingly genuine.

Liberation eventually came as part of an amnesty to mark James's fifty-fifth birthday. The earl emerged into a world greatly altered. Determined to improve his son's prospects at court, he cultivated both his son-in-law James Hay and the duke of Buckingham, setting aside his distaste for the parvenu courtier. Northumberland lived on for eleven years of placid retirement, at Petworth, Bath, and London and with his daughter Dorothy Sidney and her husband at Penshurst. He died at Petworth, apparently of a malignant disease, not inappropriately on 5 November 1632, and was buried there within twenty-four hours. MARK NICHOLLS

Sources Alnwick Castle, Duke of Northumberland MSS [includes MSS formerly at Syon House] · PRO, SP 12 · PRO, SP 14 · Hatfield House, Hertfordshire, Salisbury–Cecil MSS · GEC, *Peerage* · M. Nicholls, *Investigating Gunpowder Plot* (1991) · G. R. Batho, 'The finances of an Elizabethan nobleman: Henry Percy, ninth earl of Northumberland (1564–1632)', *Economic History Review*, 2nd ser., 9 (1956–7), 433–50 · G. R. Batho, 'The education of a Stuart nobleman', *British Journal of Educational Studies*, 5 (1956–7), 131–43 · G. R. Batho, 'The payment and mitigation of a star chamber fine', *HJ*, 1 (1958), 40–51 · G. R. Batho, 'The library of the Wizard Earl: Henry Percy, ninth earl of Northumberland (1564–1632)', *The Library*, 5th ser., 15 (1960), 246–61 · M. E. James, ed., *Estate accounts of the earls of Northumberland, 1562–1637*, SurtS, 163 (1955) · G. B. Harrison, ed., *Advice to his son by Henry Percy, ninth earl of Northumberland (1609)* (1930) · M. Nicholls, ed., 'The wizard earl in star chamber', *HJ*, 30 (1987), 173–89 · M. Nicholls, '"As happy a fortune as I desire": the pursuit of financial security by the younger brothers of Henry Percy, ninth earl of Northumberland', *Historical Research*, 65 (1992), 296–314 · *The letters of John Chamberlain*, ed. N. E. McClure, 2 vols. (1939) · *The Wizard Earl's advices to his son*, ed. G. R. Batho and S. Clucas (2002)

Archives Hatfield House, Hertfordshire, letters and papers | Alnwick Castle, Northumberland, papers of duke of Northumberland at Alnwick Castle, incl. the collections formerly at Syon House · NRA, priv. coll., letters to earl of Essex · W. Yorks. AS, Leeds, Yorkshire Archaeological Society, rental of estates, certificate of enquiry regarding lands, and account of proceedings in star chamber

Likenesses N. Hilliard, miniature, 1590–95, Rijksmuseum, Amsterdam [see illus.] · F. Delaram, line engraving, 1619 (hl with hat), BM, NPG · F. Delaram, line engraving, BM, NPG · N. Hilliard, miniature, FM Cam. · A. Van Dyck, oils, Petworth House, Sussex · double portrait, oils (with Gater George), Petworth House, Sussex; version, Alnwick Castle, Northumberland

Percy, Henry, Baron Percy of Alnwick (*c*.1604–1659), royalist army officer, was a younger son of Henry *Percy, ninth earl of Northumberland (1564–1632), and his wife, Dorothy (*d*. 1619), daughter of Walter *Devereux, first earl of Essex, and widow of Sir John Perrot. Henry was educated at a school in Isleworth under Thomas Willis; he subscribed at Christ Church, Oxford, on 7 December 1624.

Percy entered politics by representing Marlborough in the parliament of 1628–9. When Charles I embarked upon his period of personal rule Percy naturally turned to the

Henry Percy, Baron Percy of Alnwick (*c*.1604–1659), by follower of Sir Anthony Van Dyck, 1640s

court for advancement. His early attempts to gain a 'place', first as secretary to the chancellor of the exchequer in March 1631 and afterwards to obtain the proprietorial command of a company in Thomas, Viscount Wentworth's, Irish army, both failed, but he did succeed in establishing himself within the circle of courtiers surrounding the queen, Henrietta Maria. As a royal favourite his career then prospered in a most gratifying manner, particularly as he was able to further the interests of his eldest brother, Algernon *Percy, now tenth earl of Northumberland, and his brother-in-law Robert *Sidney, second earl of Leicester.

In 1639 Percy was named a colonel in the army raised for the abortive war against the Scots. In October that year he also gained the extremely prestigious appointment of master of the horse to the prince of Wales, and in the following year he was appointed captain of the king's life guard. Returned as MP for the borough of Portsmouth in the Short Parliament, he rather more appropriately represented the county of Northumberland in the subsequent Long Parliament, until his progress was abruptly terminated by his involvement in the failed first army plot of March 1641. Unlike his late father James VI and I, Charles I was an enthusiastic but uniformly unsuccessful exponent of armed coups. In this particular case Percy, if not the originator, was certainly a chief conspirator in a scheme to bring the army down from the north into London in order to intimidate parliament, but upon the plot's being discovered he attempted to flee the country. Unfortunately he did not get very far, but was set upon by a mob in Sussex, beaten up, and forced into hiding. Badly frightened, he promptly presented his brother Northumberland with a detailed account of the conspiracy in return for his protection and immunity from prosecution. Percy claimed that he and his colleagues had merely been encouraging the army's officers to subscribe to an innocuous declaration of support for the king's policies. When at the king's instigation they had met Henry Jermyn and Sir John Suckling, whose parallel conspiracy did involve the use of armed force, Percy had opposed the more extreme plan and had reported back to the king who had vetoed it. This confession was enough to confirm parliament's suspicions and at the same time alienate Percy's erstwhile colleagues who unsurprisingly accused him of treachery. It was also, as he had hoped, sufficient to save him from impeachment and his only material punishment was his formal expulsion from the House of Commons on 9 December 1641.

However, now equally unpopular with both sides, Percy judged it expedient to retire to France. An inveterate schemer, he nevertheless began to make himself useful to the queen, who similarly found herself forced abroad as the political situation worsened, and in a complete reversal of fortune he returned to England as her agent. Rather ironically in the circumstances, the queen wrote 'I think him very faithful and that we may trust him' (*DNB*). Armed with that remarkable endorsement he was appointed general of the ordnance on 22 May 1643 and created Baron Percy of Alnwick on 28 June. He possessed no discernible military qualifications to justify this, apart from his vicarious employment as a colonel in 1639, but the post was actually an administrative one rather than a combat command. The ordnance department was primarily responsible for the procurement, manufacture, storage, transportation, and issue of a wide variety of military hardware including cannon, ammunition of all calibres, muskets, bandoliers, pikes, and even the more mundane items such as spades, pickaxes, duckboards, and buckets. Much of the credit for this onerous job generally goes to his indefatigable deputy, Sir John Heydon, but there is no doubt that Percy did in fact take his duties fairly seriously and once famously grumbled that the train of artillery was a sponge which sucked up money and could never be satisfied. Despite their best efforts Percy and Heydon never managed to keep up with the insatiable demand for ammunition and, on the night of 20 September 1643, Percy reported that the day's fighting in the first Battle of Newbury had consumed no fewer than an astounding eighty barrels of powder and that only ten remained for the artillery and none for the infantry. The royalist army had in effect run out of ammunition in the middle of the battle and thus forfeited the king's only realistic chance of winning the war.

In a more direct military role Percy had also become colonel of both a regiment of foot and a regiment of horse. The first had originally formed part of the escort to a large ammunition convoy, brought down from the north by Colonel Thomas Pinchbeck. Although most secondary sources state that these men came from Yorkshire, all the officers surviving in 1663 came from Northumberland so

it is perhaps unsurprising that Percy should have taken them on. The origins of his regiment of horse are, however, rather more obscure. In 1644 Percy accompanied the king on the campaign which culminated in the victory at Cropredy Bridge on 29 June, and afterwards went with him into the west country, but on 14 August was unexpectedly forced to resign his post as general of the ordnance after being implicated in Lord Wilmot's plot to seek an accommodation with parliament. Initially he appears to have retained his regiments, but finally he lost them when he was arrested on 11 January 1645 on a charge of corresponding with the enemy. There seems no reason to doubt the truth of these charges, for not only was the outlook becoming increasingly bleak for the royalists, but Percy was also subject to conflicting family loyalties. Although, as a courtier, he was himself firmly attached to the queen's party, both his elder brother, Northumberland, and his cousin, Robert *Devereux, third earl of Essex, were equally committed parliamentarians. It was perhaps in recognition of these difficult circumstances that Percy was released from custody a few weeks later, and having obtained a pass from his cousin, took ship for France where he once again rejoined the queen.

Despite being a favourite of the queen, he was, not surprisingly, distrusted by many of his fellow exiles. He was, perhaps rather hopefully, reported to have been wounded in a duel with Prince Rupert in March 1648, and was briefly arrested after a quarrel with Lord Colepeper in the following October. Nevertheless in time he mellowed and was appointed lord chamberlain and admitted to Charles II's émigré privy council in 1653. Although this initially aroused considerable resentment in certain quarters he was subsequently reconciled with Edward Hyde (later earl of Clarendon) who dissuaded him from making his peace with the lord protector, Oliver Cromwell. Destined never to see England again, Percy died unmarried in France, probably in Paris, on 26 March 1659. Although Clarendon recorded that during the war 'he was generally unloved as a proud and supercilious person' (Clarendon, *Hist. rebellion*, 3.393), he also praised his economical handling of the exiled king's household, and his tenure as general of the ordnance shows some genuine administrative ability.

STUART REID

Sources Clarendon, *Hist. rebellion* · I. Roy, ed., *The royalist ordnance papers, 1642–1646*, 1, Oxfordshire RS, 43 (1964) · I. Roy, ed., *The royalist ordnance papers, 1642–1646*, 2, Oxfordshire RS, 49 (1975) · P. R. Newman, *Royalist officers in England and Wales, 1642–1660: a biographical dictionary* (1981) · S. Reid, *All the king's armies* (1998) · P. Young, *Edgehill 1642* (1967) · Burke, *Peerage* (1999) · GEC, *Peerage* · C. Russell, 'The first army plot of 1641', *TRHS*, 5th ser., 38 (1988), 85–106 · *DNB* · *The Nicholas papers*, ed. G. F. Warner, 1–2, CS, new ser., 40, 50 (1886–92)
Archives Bodl. Oxf., ordnance corresp., MS Rawl. D. 395 · CKS, letters to second earl of Leicester
Likenesses A. Van Dyck, oils, c.1638, Petworth, West Sussex · follower of A. Van Dyck, portrait, 1640–49, Petworth, West Sussex [see illus.]

Percy, Henry (1785–1825), army officer, fifth son of Algernon Percy, second Baron Lovaine and (from 1790) first earl of Beverley (1750–1830), and his wife, Isabella Susannah

(1750–1812), *née* Burrell, was born on 14 September 1785; Algernon Percy was the brother of Hugh *Percy, bishop of Carlisle, and of Vice-Admiral Josceline *Percy. Educated at Eton College, on 16 August 1804 Henry Percy was appointed lieutenant in the 7th fusiliers. He became captain unattached on 9 October 1806 and captain 7th fusiliers on 6 November. He was aide-de-camp to Sir John Moore at Corunna. On 21 June 1810 he transferred as captain to the 14th light dragoons. He was taken prisoner during the retreat from Burgos in 1812, and was detained in France until the peace. He had at least two illegitimate sons, one of whom, with a Frenchwoman, Jeanne Durand, was Henry Marion *Durand.

In 1815 Percy was appointed aide-de-camp to the duke of Wellington. He brought home the Waterloo dispatches, arriving by post-chaise in London on the evening of 20 June with the dispatches and captured eagles, and was next day made CB, and a brevet lieutenant-colonel from 18 June 1815. He retired on half pay in 1821. From 1823 until his death he was MP for Bene Alston, Devon, a burgage borough controlled by his father. Once a dashing, handsome young man, Percy prematurely lost his health. He died at his father's house in Portman Square, London, on 15 April 1825, and was buried in St Marylebone cemetery.

H. M. CHICHESTER, *rev.* JAMES FALKNER

Sources *Army List* · *GM*, 1st ser., 95/1 (1825), 567 · *Hart's Army List* · E. Lodge, *Peerage, baronetage, knightage and companionage of the British empire*, 81st edn, 3 vols. (1912) · V. C. P. Hodson, *List of officers of the Bengal army, 1758–1834*, 2 (1928) · GEC, *Peerage* · HoP, *Commons*

Percy, Henry Algernon, fifth earl of Northumberland

(1478–1527), magnate, sometimes known as the Magnificent, was born on 14 January 1478, the eldest son of Henry *Percy, fourth earl of Northumberland (*c.*1449–1489), and Maud (*d.* in or before 1485), daughter of William *Herbert, first earl of Pembroke. Alan *Percy, who became master of St John's College, Cambridge, was his younger brother. Northumberland succeeded his father aged eleven when the latter was murdered at Cocklodge, near Thirsk, on 28 April 1489. The young earl was made a knight of the Bath on 21 November 1489 and a knight of the Garter in 1495. He received livery of his estates in 1498.

Youthful frustration Following the overthrow of Richard III, the fourth earl had raised the standing of his family to new heights, essentially through the holding of crown offices. Despite the views of some historians, there is no reason to believe that the fourth earl's death was either contrived by or welcome to Henry VII. The challenge for the fifth earl was to restore this standing after a decade's atrophy. The vacuum in northern government left by his father's death had been filled by a council under the earl of Surrey, acting as lieutenant first to Prince Arthur and then, after 1494, to Prince Henry. But whereas it might have been decided to wind up the northern council on the fifth earl's attaining his majority, the decision was taken to keep it in existence under Thomas Savage, archbishop of York, again as lieutenant to Prince Henry. The earl's frustration at his inability to recover his father's position was acknowledged in loose talk by some of his servants reported in 1509: 'that if their lord had not room in the north as his father had, it should not be long well' (*LP Henry VIII*, 1/1, no. 157).

His efforts to re-create a regional hegemony brought Northumberland into a series of conflicts with Savage and others, especially over Beverley, in his father's day a Percy town. The earl was indicted by Savage for retaining in 1502 and 1504. Then on 23 May 1504, as earl and archbishop were both leaving York with their retinues at about the same time, their parties became entangled at Fulford, south of the city, and a fracas took place in which Northumberland was assaulted. Depositions taken afterwards reveal the antipathy between the two men, and also show the deep hostility between their respective households. Both men were forced to enter bonds with the council in November for their future good conduct. It may be suggested that this unexpected conflict ruined the reputation of both men. Northumberland continued on a career of minor brigandage and was the subject of complaints laid before the council in Star Chamber. In 1505 he was fined £10,000—£5000 on a recognizance at the king's pleasure and £5000 to be paid at 1000 marks per annum—for abducting Elizabeth Hastings, the daughter and heir of Sir John Hastings of Fenwick in Yorkshire; her subsequent death in the earl's custody deprived the crown of her wardship. Northumberland assigned manors to feoffees for the payment of this fine. Edmund Dudley, when clearing his conscience after being arrested in 1509, recalled that the king had intended to demand only £2000, although Dudley thought that even this was excessive for the offence. In fact, £3000 had been paid by the time of the king's death: the outstanding balance was forgiven in 1510. The earl's servants were accused of violence against Sir John Hotham in 1506, and in 1516 he was himself imprisoned in the Fleet for contempt of the council's jurisdiction in private suits, although his exact offence is unrecorded.

An earl without power Not only did neither Henry VII nor Henry VIII show any inclination to concede ground to the earl in Yorkshire, they also went out of their way to deny him the border offices which an earl of Northumberland might expect to exercise and was best equipped to fulfil. When the earl was made warden-general of the marches in June 1503, it was merely as a ceremonial post to escort Margaret Tudor into Scotland. Thereafter he never held office on the borders, the middle and east marches falling under the control of Thomas, second Baron Dacre, from 1511 onwards. This was not for any lack of military capability on Northumberland's part. In 1497 he served in the royal army against the Cornish rebels and fought at Blackheath. He led his gentry and their tenants from Northumberland, Cumberland, and Yorkshire to France in 1513. In 1523 he served on the Scottish borders. By 1522 Dacre was urging that Northumberland's eldest son, Henry, be appointed warden in his place, a choice which perhaps recognized that the fifth earl was still unacceptable to Henry VIII. Hall, however, is the sole authority for the statement that Northumberland was offered and accepted the wardenship in the autumn of 1522, but that he subsequently lobbied the council to be discharged, resigning probably early in 1523 in favour of Thomas Howard, earl of Surrey. This cannot be verified, and some have thought it unlikely.

Perhaps because Northumberland lacked opportunities for military service, most of his public appearances were ceremonial in character. Thus he escorted Queen Margaret of Scotland from York to the border in 1517 (and subsequently complained of the cost). He was among those who attended the king at the Field of Cloth of Gold and was present when Henry met Charles V in 1522. In 1525 he assisted at the ceremony at which Henry Fitzroy was created duke of Richmond. Northumberland died at Wressle on 19 May 1527 and was buried in Beverley Minster, with little ceremony, probably on 6 June.

Resources Even if, as Hall says, Northumberland's rapid surrender of the wardenship in 1522/3 led to his not being 'regarded of his own tenants which disdained him and his blood and much lamented his folly, and all men esteemed him without heart or love of honour and chivalry' (Hall, 652), he still controlled a considerable force. In the 1530s the Percy estates in Northumberland could raise 1967 men under the command of the constable of Alnwick, the Yorkshire lands 2280 horse and 3953 foot, and the Cumberland estates 1030 horse and 2011 foot. It seems unlikely that a force on such a scale was ever deployed, however: for the earl's retinue drawn from Yorkshire, when it mustered at Newcastle in 1523, totalled 762 men, of whom 170 were drawn from stewardships under his control and not his estate.

As for his wealth, it is clear that the fifth earl of Northumberland was among the richest peers of his generation. Although he was assessed for the subsidy at £2920 in 1523, it has been suggested that his rental income would have been about £4700, and his clear income after the deduction of fees and other expenses about £3600. There is little compelling evidence that the earl was significantly in debt at the time of his death. While he may be thought to have deserved it, the sobriquet of the Magnificent which is sometimes applied to him dates only from the beginning of the nineteenth century, and probably arises from the impression created by the publication of his household book in 1770. This describes an opulent and well-organized household, which in 1511–12 was financed out of an assignment of £933 6s. 8d.; slightly later it was in receipt of £1000 yearly. In fact the long familiar household book is only the first of a pair—a second, a volume of chapel and other regulations, was purchased by the Bodleian Library in 1962 (now MS Eng. hist. b. 208). The books shed a little light on the earl's intellectual tastes, providing, for instance, that his almoner should be 'a maker of Interludys' (James, 83). Northumberland is also said to have endowed a teacher of grammar and philosophy at Alnwick Abbey, and, in a letter to his son-in-law the first earl of Cumberland, he justified the appointment of a chantry priest to keep a grammar school at Cockermouth as a 'marvelous good and meritorious deed' (Hoyle, 'Letters of the Cliffords', 94–5). The earl's secretary, William Peeris, wrote a verse chronicle of the family, which he presented to his master as a new year's gift. Leland described an impressive library at Wressle which has almost entirely disappeared.

The grounds of failure Northumberland may best be seen as a transitional figure. As a young man he attempted to dominate through the violent exercise of his power. Loose talk by his household servants revealed the scale of his ambitions. His imprisonment in 1516—for whatever reason—shows that he had not lost his capacity to challenge royal authority in the pursuit of his private objectives. Hence he was among those nobles—the duke of Buckingham being another—whom in a famously paranoid letter of 1519 or 1520 the king instructed Wolsey to keep watch over. Wolsey himself reassured Northumberland that he was not suspected of collusion with Buckingham after the latter's execution. This did not prevent the cardinal from interfering when the earl's son became emotionally involved with Anne Boleyn some time in the early 1520s. In any case royal suspicion of Northumberland, and the latter's tactless disregard for royal authority, seem to have led him to be excluded from office. Fears of the earl's latent power continued even after his death: Wolsey's interference in the arrangements for the earl's funeral have been read as an example of the cardinal's belief in the incompetence of the sixth earl, but it testifies equally to a determination that the funeral should be a low-key affair and not a demonstration of pro-Percy sentiment.

One of the few manuscripts known to survive from Northumberland's library contains an emblematic drawing of a Tudor rose representing the sun in which is framed a figure (probably the young Henry VIII). From this sun there fall drops of liquid onto an eye (itself weeping) contained within a crescent moon (a Percy badge). Under this lie verses, the first of which is 'I receyve noo lighte but of thy beames bright' (Dickens, 42): the Percy moon reflected only the rays of the Tudor sun and no longer emitted any light of its own. The proverbs painted in the high chamber at Leconfield also point to an essential pessimism about life and its stability: no hope should be placed in the world, riches, or honour, for all are uncertain or transitory: instead, hope should only be placed in God. 'Trust hym he is moste trewe' and 'is above fortunes fall' (James, 89–90). The weight of his family's history, the circumstances of his father's death, and his own failure to satisfy the expectations placed on him by others may have made Northumberland a melancholic in adverse times. It remains to be resolved why, having been brought up at court, he never established a relationship of trust with Henry VIII. Here it may be suggested that, as a young man, he strove too hard to recapture the authority which had been his father's but which the elder Tudor had determined to keep for himself. Recourse to violence destroyed the possibility of trust. Northumberland's response was to eschew royal office except for the ceremonial which he was required to dignify as a noble: in this there is a clear parallel with the duke of Buckingham, another senior noble who found no role in the inner circle of government.

Before 1502 Northumberland married Katherine, daughter of Sir Robert Spencer of Spencercombe in

Devon. She survived her husband, dying in 1542. They had three sons: Henry *Percy, sixth earl of Northumberland (*c*.1502–1537), Sir Thomas, executed 1537, and Sir Ingelram or Ingram (*d*. 1538); and two daughters, Margaret (*d*. *c*.1540), who married Henry, Baron Clifford, created earl of Cumberland in 1525, and Maud, who is alleged to have married William, first Baron Conyers (although she does not appear in the Conyers pedigrees).   R. W. HOYLE

Sources M. E. James, 'A Tudor magnate and the Tudor state', *Society, politics and culture: studies in early modern England* (1986), 48–90 · R. W. Hoyle, 'The earl, the archbishop and the council: the affray at Fulford, May 1504', *Rulers and ruled in late medieval England*, ed. R. E. Archer and S. Walker (1995), 239–56 · P. Gwyn, *The king's cardinal: the rise and fall of Thomas Wolsey* (1990) · J. M. W. Bean, *The estates of the Percy family, 1416–1537* (1958) · A. G. Dickens, 'The Percy royal emblem in Royal MS 180 D ii', *Reformation studies* (1982), 41–6 · T. Percy, ed., *The regulations and establishment of the household of Henry Algernon Percy, fifth earl of Northumberland, begun 1512* (1770), repr. (1827); and (1905); and in F. Grose, *Antiquarian repertory*, vol. 4 (1809) · D. M. Barratt, 'A second Northumberland household book', *Bodleian Library Record*, 8 (1967–72), 93–8 · R. W. Hoyle, ed., 'Letters of the Cliffords, lords Clifford and earls of Cumberland, *c*.1500–1565', *Camden miscellany, XXXI*, CS, 4th ser., 44 (1993), 1–189 · *LP Henry VIII*, vols. 1–4 · *Hall's chronicle*, ed. H. Ellis (1809) · GEC, *Peerage*

Percy, Henry Algernon, sixth earl of Northumberland

(*c*.1502–1537), magnate, known by the eighteenth century as 'the Unthrifty Earl', was the eldest son of Henry Algernon *Percy, fifth earl of Northumberland (1478–1527), and his wife, Katherine Spencer (*d*. 1542). He had two younger brothers, Thomas and Ingram, with whom his relations were never cordial. In this, and in several other respects, there is much that is enigmatic about his life.

Upbringing and marriage The young Lord Percy was educated in the household of Cardinal Wolsey, who is known to have had a low opinion of his charge, not least for his lack of financial sense. The cardinal continued to bully Percy even after he had become earl, for instance trying to ensure that all his contacts with the king and court were made through himself. He forbade Percy to attend his father's funeral and tried both to foist a household supervisor on him and to control his domestic expenditure. William Worme, the earl's auditor, seems to have been employed as an informant by Wolsey; some time after 1532 Worme submitted a petition to chancery claiming that he had been detained at Alnwick against his will for five years.

No later than 1516 there were proposals that Lord Percy should marry a daughter of George Talbot, fourth earl of Shrewsbury (1468–1538). The king gave his approval, but while he was still in Wolsey's household Percy formed a romantic attachment to Anne Boleyn after her return to England at the end of 1521, when she was one of Queen Katherine's maids of honour. The story that the couple entered into some commitment dogged Percy for the rest of his life. According to the cardinal's biographer George Cavendish, Wolsey stopped the courtship because the king had designs on Anne, but the dating makes this impossible. The likely reason for his intervention was the threat to existing plans to marry Percy to Mary Talbot and Anne to James Butler, son of Piers Butler, who was then claiming the earldom of Ormond against Anne's father, Sir Thomas Boleyn. Wolsey summoned Percy's father to court, and he admonished his son sharply for his recklessness. By the end of 1523 the affair was over; Percy married Mary Talbot between 14 January and 8 February 1524.

Governing the north Even before his father died, and despite Wolsey's misgivings concerning his capacity, Lord Percy was seen as a plausible candidate for the wardenship of the east march and other offices in the north of England which the king's suspicion had denied to the fifth earl. In 1522 he was made a member of the council of the north and in October deputy warden of the east march. Thomas, second Baron Dacre, the warden-general, canvassed Percy as his possible successor in the east. Nothing came of this, but when war threatened with Scotland that year, Percy and his father were both among the northern lords chosen to advise the king's lieutenant-general, the earl of Shrewsbury. Then on 2 December 1527, less than six months after the death of his father, the new earl of Northumberland was made warden of the east and middle marches. At once he faced the problem of dealing with Sir William Lisle of Felton, whose violence towards his neighbours had led to his being imprisoned at York after a star chamber action. Sir William broke out of prison and took refuge in Scotland, from where he and a band of gentry followers conducted a campaign of raids on the property of his English opponents and even on Wolsey's lordship of Hexham. After Northumberland's appointment as warden Lisle and his supporters surrendered themselves to him at Alnwick on 25 January 1528. Despite his close connections with the Percys—he had been constable of Alnwick Castle since 25 March 1525—the earl was unable to save Lisle from execution.

While this episode may have damaged Northumberland's reputation in the north-east, he appears to have been an efficient and trusted warden, though he may have taken some time to establish that reputation. On 2 November 1528 he told his friend the twelfth earl of Arundel of his wish to hold Wark and Dunstanburgh castles, as previous wardens had done, but perhaps thanks to Wolsey he was unable to obtain them. However, he was elected to the Order of the Garter in 1531, was considered perfectly competent to manage the war against Scotland which erupted briefly but fiercely at the end of 1532, was *de facto* president of the council in Yorkshire from 1533, and was granted the shrievalty of Northumberland for life in February 1534. All this implies that Wolsey's assessment of the earl and his persistent meddling in his affairs arose from either a personal dislike or a determined attempt to belittle his former charge; it did not reflect the earl's natural ability. Northumberland may well have enjoyed implementing the king's order to arrest Wolsey at Cawood on 4 November 1530, but even then the cardinal could not take the earl entirely seriously, patronizingly reminding him of 'my old preceptes & Instruccions w[che] I gave you whan ye ware abydyng w^t me in yor youthe' (Cavendish, 155).

Failure of marriage and health Northumberland is occasionally recorded at Westminster. Thus in October 1529 he was a trier of petitions in parliament and also attended the very full council session held immediately after Wolsey's resignation as chancellor. At almost exactly the same time he was confronting the collapse of his marriage. Countess Mary had given birth to a stillborn child in April that year, but on 3 September the earl wrote to the third duke of Norfolk reporting how he had ordered that she be 'entertained a great deal better than she hath deserved', and how he had told one of Shrewsbury's servants that he was willing to send her back to her father 'with a reasonable finding' (*LP Henry VIII*, 4/3, no. 5920). Subsequently they lived apart. In 1532 the countess stated that her husband had claimed that their marriage was invalid because he had been contracted to Anne Boleyn, now increasingly close to Henry VIII. Recognizing the damage that this did to her position (and perhaps also seeing this as a way to secure an annulment), Mary Talbot told her father, who wrote to the duke of Norfolk, Anne's uncle, who in turn broached the claims with his niece. Anne informed the king and insisted that the allegations be investigated. In July 1532 Northumberland was examined by the archbishops of Canterbury and York as to any undertakings between himself and Anne: he then swore that there had never been any contract between them. Nevertheless rumours to the contrary, and even that their relationship had been consummated, circulated throughout their lives. There was nothing uncertain about the earl's relationship with his wife, however: Northumberland clearly loathed her and took pleasure in leaving her unprovided for at his death.

Northumberland suffered from persisting ill health. In 1529 he reported the return of his 'old disease' and expected to die. He was ill in late 1532 and early 1533 and again in mid-1534. In February 1536 he wrote saying that he had not been outside his chamber at Topcliffe for a year (demonstrably untrue), but a protracted illness is indicated. In November 1536, when warned that he was in danger from the Pilgrimage of Grace, he said that 'he did not care, he should die but once. Let them strike off his head whereby they should rid him of much pain, ever saying he would be dead' (*LP Henry VIII*, 12/1, no. 380). The only account of his physical symptoms comes from immediately before his death, when he was reported to be barely able to speak and losing his sight; his stomach was distended and 'his whole body yellow as saffron', but his memory still unimpaired (*LP Henry VIII*, 12/2, no. 165). The symptoms suggest liver failure. It is no coincidence that both of Northumberland's doctors, Stephen Thomasson and Thomas Wendy, were rewarded handsomely by the earl, who sought to secure the grant of an abbey for Wendy.

In July 1534, despite his ill health in that year, Northumberland was able to attend the trial for treason at Westminster of William, third Baron Dacre, an enemy who was also the husband of one of Countess Mary's sisters. In May 1536 he was tangentially caught up in the fall of Queen Anne Boleyn. He was not spared attendance at her trial. Like the other peers he gave his verdict against her, then collapsed after sentence of death had been pronounced. Rumours of Anne's pre-contract to the earl were again rife, possibly circulated in the hope of justifying the king's annulment of his marriage to her, and Northumberland wrote to Cromwell reiterating the denial he had made on oath four years previously. Later that year he was too sick to play any role in the Pilgrimage of Grace. The pilgrims were determined to have his support, and following their first assembly at Doncaster the earl was visited at Wressell on 30 October 1536 by his former secretary Robert Aske, who tried to reconcile him to his brother Sir Thomas, but without success. A further visitor next day found Northumberland in bed, 'weeping, ever wishing himself out of the world' (Dodds, 1.284). On 1 November the earl allowed himself to be sworn to the insurgents, having asked the vicar of Brayton to send 'two gentlemen of worship to take him because he would be taken with no violence' (Hoyle, *Pilgrimage*, 446). He then put Wressell at the disposal of Aske (who made it his headquarters), subsequently justifying his action on the grounds that he had wanted to escape from the commons and secure his evidences on the king's behalf; he left first for York and later for Selby.

Dismembering an inheritance It is against the background of a failed marriage and continuous ill health that Northumberland's breaking up of his patrimony must be seen. In 1528–9 he made extensive grants of his west country manors to Thomas Arundell, who had been his contemporary in Wolsey's household. He made sales of other manors in 1531–2. At least some of these should be viewed as attempts to liquidate debts, probably contracted before he inherited his estates. But he also made grants to three young household intimates, apparently with the aim of raising their social status and military capacity, together with large numbers of disadvantageous leases to household servants, a practice which continued until the eve of his death. By the earl's gifts Thomas Johnson was raised from the status of household servant to gentleman (and may also have been knighted by Northumberland in the Scottish war of 1532–3). Sir Reynold Carnaby had grants of leases from 1530 onwards: the earl tried to obtain an abbey for him, and in 1538 he was granted Hexham. In October 1530 Sir Thomas Wharton (later first Baron Wharton) had the grant of the hereditary lieutenancy of Cockermouth, along with six manors in Cumberland and an annuity from the Percy estates, and he received other lands in Yorkshire in 1531. Johnson appears to have been advanced purely from personal friendship, but the grants to Carnaby and Wharton were probably also intended to enable them to perform military functions on the border which ill health prevented the earl's performing himself.

In 1532 Northumberland granted the Percy fee in Craven, Yorkshire, to Henry, Lord Clifford (his nephew and later second earl of Cumberland), although conditionally on his death without male issue and with the reservation of the rents to his heirs. These and other grants served to diminish the estate likely to be inherited by Sir Thomas Percy, the earl's next brother, and in particular some of the grants to Carnaby of lands previously assigned to Sir Thomas. The latter complained to Cromwell in July 1535 of the influence which his household servants had over the earl, saying that they had 'caused division between the Earl and his wife, his brethren, and nearest friends' (*LP Henry VIII*, 8, no. 1143). When Sir Thomas Clifford, the captain of Berwick and also the earl's brother-in-law, took Sir Thomas's side in an increasingly bitter family dispute in 1535, Northumberland turned against him too. It seems likely that by 1536 the earl was determined to disinherit his younger brothers, referring, in a letter to Cromwell, to the 'debility and unnaturalness of those of my name' (*LP Henry VIII*, 8, no. 166).

The question arises of the crown's attitude to Northumberland's protracted decline and progressive disinheritance of his brothers. By a statute of 1536 the earl's interest in the estates was limited to life and it was ordained that the king would inherit them on his death. There can be no doubt that just before his death the crown moved to seize the estates to prevent them from being further ruined by grants. Moreover, the crown had purchased the honour of Cockermouth from the earl in 1531 and then in 1535 annulled this grant and received the honour of Petworth, Sussex, the manor of Hackney, and other lands in its place. Superficially it would appear that it was always the crown's intention to annex the lands of the earldom and that it exploited the psychological weakness of the earl to do so, but on closer scrutiny the traditional account does not quite hold up.

First, the crown was interested in the estates because of the failure of an Italian merchant, Antonio Bonvisi, on whose behalf Northumberland had entered bonds. The transfer of Cockermouth in 1531 and, after its return, of the other lands, was for the settlement of Northumberland's exposure to Bonvisi's liabilities. Second, the crown compelled Northumberland to sign covenants in July 1532 whereby he was permitted to sell some further estates to redeem the honour of Cockermouth, but undertook to allow the estates in Northumberland, Yorkshire, Lincolnshire, Somerset, and Dorset to descend to 'one person bearing the name of Percy and the blood of the said Percys' (Hoyle, 'Henry Percy', 194). These covenants were not honoured by the earl. Third, it was the earl who, by letters of 2 February 1536, announced his intention of disinheriting his brother and making the king his heir, and had articles to this end notarized and sent to London. The statute of 1536 was prompted by the earl. By limiting his rights in the estate, it is likely that the crown hoped to ensure the survival of the earldom. If its lands were vested in the king, they could be transferred to Sir Thomas Percy at some later date. (The assumption that Sir Thomas would inherit the earldom was widespread during the pilgrimage, when he was sometimes—to his embarrassment—addressed as Lord Percy, the courtesy title held by the heir to the earldom.) By May 1537, with reports of the earl's continuing generosity to suitors circulating, the decision was made to seize the estates. On 3 June Northumberland offered to make an unconditional and immediate grant to the king, asking only for some income from the estates, but he died on 29 June.

The fall of the Percys However, Sir Thomas had himself been executed on 2 June 1537. It has sometimes been argued that the younger Percy brothers took part in the pilgrimage to try to recover the family estates. But although both were said to have expressed anti-Cromwellian sentiments, there is no reason to believe that either saw the pilgrimage as a vehicle for regaining their inheritance. There is no request for the restoration of the earldom in the Pontefract articles drawn up at the beginning of December 1536. Although Sir Thomas had been prominent in the pilgrimage, he was protected by the pardon granted by Norfolk at Doncaster on 4 December 1536. He was tried and executed for contrived offences postdating the pardon, primarily that about Christmas he had received a petition from the monks of Sawley Abbey who sought his advice after the Doncaster settlement. He advised them not to resist any commissioners who came to Sawley from the king, but this was read as aiding the abbey, whose convent had re-entered its lands after its dissolution. In a deposition made by George Lumley of Thwing, who had been caught up in Sir Francis Bigod's failed rising of early 1537 (of which Percy had been ignorant), Lumley referred to Percy as the 'lock, key and wards' of the venture (*LP Henry VIII*, 12/1, no. 369). By this he meant that without Sir Thomas the rising was bound to fail; but the implication that Percy could have led a successful rebellion may have prompted fears of a Percy revanche and so ensured his fate. Sir Thomas and his younger brother Sir Ingram were arrested in London in March 1537, and Sir Thomas was tried and then executed in York. He was posthumously attainted in the parliament of 1539. Sir Ingram died in the Tower. Thereafter the earldom went into abeyance until Sir Thomas's elder son, another Thomas Percy, was created seventh earl in 1557.

Northumberland died at Hackney on 29 June 1537, aged about thirty-five, and was buried on the same day in Hackney parish church, with proper dignity and ceremony. There was a monument, but this had disappeared by 1767. The earl made no provision for his widow. Early in 1536 the countess's father approached Henry VIII, asking him not to approve the bill then before parliament confirming the transfer of lands from Northumberland to the crown until his daughter's rights had been secured, and during the pilgrimage he sent directly to the earl to try to obtain provision for her. Northumberland responded that as Shrewsbury had never paid his daughter's promised dower, he could not himself be expected to pay her an allowance, and he died without doing anything for his wife. Negotiations with the crown continued after the earl's death, and the dowager countess petitioned the king in person in May 1542. Henry is reported to have observed that her father had brought her troubles upon her by failing to pay her portion to the Percys. Only in 1549 did she receive a royal grant in compensation for her jointure. Suspected of harbouring Catholics in 1571, she died between 16 April and 6 June 1572.

Northumberland made a will in which the king was named supervisor and Edward Fox, bishop of Hereford, and Thomas Cromwell his executors. It does not survive, and partly for that reason little is known of the earl's cultural or religious taste. He maintained a chantry at Topcliffe, where a priest was charged with praying for the souls of the earl's ancestors, and especially his father and mother, and in 1531 appointed another priest, George Lancaster, as chantrist at Warkworth, where he was to pray for 'the good estate of all such noble blood and other personages as be now living and the souls of such men as be departed to the mercy of God out of this present life' whose names were in a parchment delivered to him; Lancaster was also to say a requiem mass for them each week (PRO, E326/10479). In 1536, moreover, the earl gave an annuity to his father's chaplain, John Bell, to pray at Leconfield for the souls of the earlier Percys, including his parents. However, Fox was a known reformer, and given Northumberland's education in Wolsey's household, and perhaps also his association with Anne Boleyn, it would not be too surprising if Thomas, Baron Darcy, was correct in claiming (under cover of a hostile reference to Lutheranism) that the earl, like others of his generation, inclined towards reform.   R. W. HOYLE

Sources GEC, *Peerage*, 9.720–22 · E. B. de Fonblanque, *Annals of the house of Percy*, 2 vols. (1887) · R. W. Hoyle, 'Henry Percy, sixth earl of Northumberland, and the fall of the house of Percy, 1527–1537', *The Tudor nobility*, ed. G. W. Bernard (1992), 180–211 · R. W. Hoyle, *The Pilgrimage of Grace and the politics of the 1530s* (2001) · G. Broce and R. M. Wunderli, 'The funeral of Henry Percy, sixth earl of Northumberland', *Albion*, 22 (1990), 199–215 · M. E. James, *Society, politics and culture: studies in early modern England* (1986) · E. W. Ives, *Anne Boleyn* (1986) · M. H. Dodds and R. Dodds, *The Pilgrimage of Grace and the Exeter conspiracy*, 2 vols. (1915); repr. (1971) · H. Miller, *Henry VIII and the Tudor nobility* (1986) · G. Cavendish, *The life and death of Cardinal Wolsey*, ed. R. S. Sylvester, EETS, original ser., 243 (1959) · *LP Henry VIII*, 1–12/2 · R. W. Hoyle, ed., 'Letters of the Cliffords, lords Clifford and earls of Cumberland, c.1500–1565', *Camden miscellany, XXXI*, CS, 4th ser., 44 (1993), 1–189 · exchequer, augmentation office, ancient deeds series B, PRO, E 326/10479

Archives Alnwick Castle, estate archive · BL, political and military corresp. and papers, Cotton MSS

Percy, Henry Algernon George, Earl Percy (1871–1909),

politician and traveller, was born at 25 Grosvenor Square, London, on 21 January 1871, the eldest of the six sons of Henry George Percy, Earl Percy (1846–1918), who became the seventh duke of Northumberland, and his wife, Lady Edith Campbell (1849–1913), daughter of the eighth duke of Argyll. Until 1899 he was known as Lord Warkworth. From 1884 to 1889 he attended Eton College, where he won the prize for English verse, and then Christ Church, Oxford, obtaining first-class honours in classical moderations in 1891 and in *literae humaniores* in 1893. At Oxford he also won the Newdigate prize for English verse in 1892, writing on the subject of St Francis of Assisi.

In the 1895 general election Warkworth stood unsuccessfully as the Conservative candidate for Berwick upon Tweed. But later in that year he was successful at a by-election in South Kensington, and he represented this constituency until his death. In 1895 he also first visited

Turkey and the other areas of the Near East which were to form an abiding personal and political interest for him. He travelled to the area again in 1897, and wrote of his experiences in *Notes of a Diary in Asiatic Turkey* (1898), in which he stated that he had 'no desire to conceal my sympathy with the Turks' (p. xii). He visited again in 1899, subsequently writing *The Highlands of Asiatic Turkey* (1901), in which he began to expound more fully his views on the political situation in the region, concluding his work with the chapter 'Wanted, a policy'. Earl Percy (as he was known from 1899, when his father succeeded to the dukedom) promoted an alliance between Germany and Britain over Turkey to promote stability and stem Russian influence.

By the time Percy was invited, in July 1902, by the new prime minister, Balfour, to become parliamentary under-secretary for India, he was acknowledged as 'a well-known expert on Middle Eastern problems … [and] one of the leading Turcophiles on the conservative side' (Steiner, 59). He moved much more effectively into his area of interest when he was appointed under-secretary to the foreign secretary, Lord Lansdowne, the following year. In this role Percy was unusually independent of his chief, particularly in connection with issues related to the Near East. With his perhaps excessive sympathy for Turkey, Percy regarded the issue of Macedonia as 'one of the most important with which he had to deal' and he took a 'rather different' standpoint on this matter from that being promoted generally within government (*The Times*, 31 Dec 1909, 11).

Despite disagreements on policy, Percy's talents were well recognized by party leaders. He has been widely credited as the author of the proposal to renew and strengthen the Anglo-Japanese alliance, which resulted in this 'decisive step' being taken by the government in 1905 (Monger, 180). After losing office with the fall of the Conservative government in 1905, Percy contributed forcefully to the debates concerning Indian reform; he was particularly concerned to see that Muslims in India were not disadvantaged by proposed electoral arrangements. The committee of the London branch of the All-India Muslim League later expressed their thanks to Percy 'whose consistent friendship towards the Musulman subjects of his Majesty had won their grateful regard and esteem' (*The Times*, 13 Jan 1910, 11).

Percy's abilities and his political potential were highly respected both within the Conservative Party and more broadly across the parliament. Balfour said of his 'dear friend' that he was 'destined to play a very great and leading part in the history of his country' (*The Times*, 31 Dec 1909, 7), while the Liberal Asquith described Percy as 'one of the most distinguished of the younger men amongst our opponents … in the first rank as a public and parliamentary speaker. He had shown in office great administrative talents' (*The Times*, 4 Jan 1910, 5). Percy became a trustee of the National Gallery in 1901 and in 1907 received the degree of DCL from the University of Durham. While travelling through France he contracted pneumonia, and he died on 30 December 1909 at the Gare du Nord Hotel,

Paris. He was buried in the Lesbury churchyard, near Alnwick, Northumberland, on 4 January 1910. He was unmarried.　　　　　　　　　　　　MARC BRODIE

Sources The Times (31 Dec 1909) · The Times (3–4 Jan 1910) · The Times (13 Jan 1910) · Z. S. Steiner, The foreign office and foreign policy, 1898–1914 (1969) · G. W. Monger, The end of isolation: British foreign policy, 1900–1907 [1963] · M. N. Das, India under Morley and Minto: politics behind revolution, repression and reforms (1964) · M. Yusuf Abbasi, London Muslim League (1908–1928): an historical study (1988) · Burke, Peerage · GEC, Peerage · The Eton register, 5 (privately printed, Eton, 1908)
Wealth at death £212,617 2s. 10d.: administration, 11 Feb 1910, CGPLA Eng. & Wales

Percy, Lord **Henry Hugh Manvers** (1817–1877), army officer, third son of George Percy, fifth duke of Northumberland (1778–1867), and his wife, Louisa Harcourt (1781–1848), third daughter of the Hon. James Archibald Stuart-Wortley Mackenzie, was born at Burwood House, Cobham, Surrey, on 22 August 1817, and educated at Eton College (1832–5). He entered the army as ensign in the Grenadier Guards on 1 July 1836, and served during the insurrection in Canada in 1838. As captain and lieutenant-colonel of his regiment he served in the Crimean War, including the battles of the Alma, where he was wounded, Balaklava, Inkerman, where he was again wounded, and the siege of Sevastopol. At the battle of Inkerman, on 5 November 1854, he found himself, with many men of various regiments who had charged too far, nearly surrounded by the Russians, and without ammunition. By his knowledge of the ground, although wounded, he extricated these men, and, passing under a heavy fire from the Russians then in the Sandbag Battery, brought them safe to where ammunition was to be obtained. He thereby saved about fifty men and enabled them to renew the combat. For this act of bravery he was, on 5 May 1857, rewarded with the Victoria Cross. For a short period he held the local rank of brigadier-general in command of the British Italian Legion in the Crimea. From 29 June 1855 to 10 February 1865 he was an aide-de-camp to the queen. During the December 1861 *Trent* crisis he was sent to New Brunswick in command of the 1st battalion, Grenadier Guards. He had been promoted major in 1860 and retired from active service on 3 October 1862. He was Conservative MP for North Northumberland from 19 July 1865 to 11 November 1868. He was appointed colonel of the 89th regiment on 28 May 1874, and was made a general on 1 October 1877. On 24 May 1873 he was made a KCB. He was found dead in his bed at his residence, 40 Eaton Square, London, on 3 December 1877, and was buried in the Northumberland vault in Westminster Abbey on 7 December. He was unmarried.　　　G. C. BOASE, rev. ROGER T. STEARN

Sources The Times (5 Dec 1877) · Annual Register (1877) · R. W. O'Byrne, The Victoria cross (1880) · Burke, Peerage · M. Barthorp, Heroes of the Crimea: the battles of Balaclava and Inkerman (1991) · Dod's Peerage (1877) · Boase, Mod. Eng. biog. · WWBMP · GEC, Peerage · CGPLA Eng. & Wales (1881)
Archives Staffs. RO, corresp., diaries, and papers
Likenesses Notman, carte-de-visite, 1863, NPG · G. Pope, oils, 1878, Alnwick Castle, Northumberland
Wealth at death under £140,000: probate, March 1881, CGPLA Eng. & Wales

Percy [formerly Smithson]**, Hugh,** first duke of Northumberland (bap. **1712**, d. **1786**), politician, was the only son of Langdale Smithson (b. c.1682) and Philadelphia Reveley (bap. 1688, d. 1764), the daughter of William Reveley. He was baptized on 10 December 1712 at Kirby Wiske, near Northallerton, Yorkshire, and very close to Newby Wiske, which was the home of his mother, whose family had moved there from Northumberland. The Smithsons had made their money as haberdashers in Cheapside; they purchased Stanwick, near Catterick, in 1638, supported the king in the civil war, and obtained a baronetcy from Charles II in 1663. Brought up as a Catholic, Smithson conformed at the time of his father's death in the 1720s.

Smithson's genealogical luck was phenomenal. His father died early and he inherited the baronetcy from his grandfather Sir Hugh Smithson, third baronet, in 1729, at the age of seventeen. He was admitted to Christ Church, Oxford, in 1730. In 1734 his sister Dorothy died, leaving him £10,000. By 1738 he was sheriff of Yorkshire. In 1740, a cousin, Michael Godfrey Smithson, having died, he inherited estates in Middlesex and at Armin, near Goole, from Hugh Smithson MP, his grandfather's first cousin. In the same year he was elected MP for Middlesex (which Hugh Smithson had represented), defeating Henry Barker, a whig, with little difficulty. Meanwhile, in 1739 at Swillington, he had become acquainted with Elizabeth Seymour (1716–1776) [see Percy, Elizabeth], the daughter of Algernon *Seymour, seventh duke of Somerset (1684–1750) [see under Seymour, Charles, sixth duke of Somerset], and his wife, Frances *Seymour, née Thynne (1699–1754). Her grandmother, Elizabeth *Seymour (1667–1722), had been heir to all the Percy estates in Middlesex and Northumberland, being the only surviving child of Josceline Percy, eleventh earl of Northumberland, who died in 1670. Smithson's estate at this time was said to be worth £4000 per annum, with £3000 per annum more to come by inheritance. Despite opposition from Elizabeth's grandfather, Charles Seymour, sixth duke of Somerset ('the proud duke'), their marriage took place on 16 July 1740. They had two sons and one daughter. In 1744 Elizabeth's brother George Seymour died of smallpox on the grand tour, leaving her sole heir.

Smithson's political career began in opposition to Walpole, and he voted with the tories against the employment of Hanoverian troops in 1742 and 1744. The Jacobite rising of 1745, during which he displayed zeal for the Hanoverian succession, gave him the chance to transfer to the Pelhamite whigs. He spoke on the government side in April 1747 on the bill to abolish hereditable jursidictions in Scotland and at the general election of 1747 was once more returned for Middlesex, this time as a government candidate.

Smithson's first objective was to safeguard his wife's inheritance. In 1744 the duke of Somerset asked George II for the earldom of Northumberland, with a special remainder to his grandson Sir Charles Wyndham, thus cutting out his granddaughter. At an audience with the king, Smithson protested successfully on behalf of his father-in-law, Lord Hertford. On Somerset's death in 1748,

Hugh Percy, first duke of Northumberland (*bap.* 1712, *d.* 1786), by James Barry, *c.*1784–6

the seventh duke of Somerset persuaded the king to grant him the earldom of Northumberland, with a special remainder to Smithson and his heirs by Lady Elizabeth. The Wyndhams were bought off with the earldom of Egremont. Smithson succeeded to the title in February 1750 and assumed the name Percy by act of parliament. 'Earl Smithson' was a predictable sneer, yet honours now crowded upon him. He took his seat in the Lords on 1 March 1750 and in January 1751 moved the address to the throne. In January 1753 he was appointed a lord of the bedchamber, in March 1753 he was made lord lieutenant of Northumberland, and in 1756 he was given the Garter. He steered clear of party commitments. During the struggle between Fox, Pitt, and Newcastle in June 1757 he was reported to have said: 'Let who will resign; he would not, but would support whatever minister the king appointed' (*Eighth Report*, HMC, 1.225a).

Northumberland's next task was to build up his political base. The estates of the family, which had been neglected by the sixth duke of Somerset, were taken in hand, and an income of some £8000 per annum was raised to £50,000 per annum, largely by exploiting coal measures. He also bought up advowsons and by the end of his life

held more than a dozen. His electoral interest, which was little more than one seat for Northumberland in 1750, was increased to seven seats, mainly by the purchase in the 1770s of three boroughs in Cornwall and Devon with two seats apiece. He overreached himself at the general election of 1774 when an attempt to carry both seats in Northumberland failed, but by the 1780s he commanded one of the largest parliamentary groups.

Northumberland's progress continued in the next reign. George III at once appointed him a lord of the bedchamber in November 1760. He became lord chamberlain to Queen Charlotte in May 1762, was sworn of the privy council in November, and succeeded Newcastle as lord lieutenant of Middlesex in December 1762. He was on close terms with the king's minister Lord Bute, and his son married Bute's daughter in 1764. In the reorganization that followed Bute's decision to retire in 1763, Northumberland came up as a possible replacement: John Calcraft wrote to Shelburne in March 1763 that, 'with our hold on Lord Northumberland, is it possible to think of placing him as a great lord … at the head of the Treasury, either for some short time, or till you could take it?' (Fitzmaurice, 1.195–6). Fox's proposal was to make him lord privy seal, but in the end George Grenville became first minister and Northumberland went to Ireland as lord lieutenant, arriving on 21 September 1763.

Northumberland remained in that post from April 1763 until May 1765. His wealth enabled him to entertain lavishly, much to his wife's liking; Horace Walpole called her 'junketaceous' (Walpole, *Corr.*, 38.59). Halifax, the secretary of state, however, was not an easy man to work with, and Northumberland complained of his incivility. The political situation at Dublin was difficult, with Edmund Pery and the patriots pressing for constitutional concessions—habeas corpus, a septennial act, and restrictions on the Irish pensions list. Ministers at Westminster were irritated at the Irish address on the peace treaty, which was pointedly unenthusiastic. On 10 November, Northumberland wrote urgently for instructions whether he should punish unreliable placemen or 'temporize': Halifax, in reply, though exasperated, recommended mildness and offered some pension concessions. The award of a grand title, vice-admiral of all America, in December 1764 was a sop—'a mere feather' in Walpole's phrase (Walpole, *Corr.*, 38.492, 497).

As early as January 1765 Northumberland was indicating reluctance to continue, pleading ill health. Grenville's suspicions of his Bute connections were reinforced in April 1765 when the king asked him to sound out a change of government, bringing in Pitt and the Rockinghams. Northumberland approached Cumberland, who was to act as broker, at a meeting in the stables at Newmarket. The proposal that Northumberland might act as first lord of the Treasury was raised, but Lord Temple, Pitt's brother-in-law, angrily refused to serve under 'Bute's Lieutenant'. The negotiations broke down, Grenville stayed in office, and Northumberland was replaced as lord lieutenant by Lord Weymouth.

When Rockingham replaced Grenville in July 1765, the

king hoped that a place would be found for Northumberland. At one stage he was considered for the French embassy. But though he remained on friendly terms and voted for the repeal of the Stamp Act, the Bute connection held him back. In May 1766, when the king had tired of the Rockinghams, Northumberland was again involved in negotiations to change the ministry. This time he did not emerge empty handed. Pitt agreed to take office. When the lord chamberlainship and the mastership of the horse, which he had wanted, went elsewhere, Northumberland complained that he had received no mark of favour for his Irish exertions. Pitt suggested a step up in the peerage to a marquessate, but Northumberland held out for a dukedom, which the king, plainly disconcerted, granted with some reluctance rather than offend Pitt at the outset.

Although Northumberland had assured the king that he would not again solicit office, his political aspirations were by no means extinguished. In May 1767, with Chatham mysteriously ill, Walpole reported that opposition hoped Northumberland would be called upon to preside over a ministry of Lord Bute's friends. A year later, Burke told Rockingham that the Bedfords named the duke 'for a proper person for the Treasury' (*The Correspondence of Edmund Burke*, ed. T. W. Copeland and others, 10 vols., 1958–78, 2.5). In October 1769 Rockingham, in another conversation at Newmarket, found the duke 'very hostile to the present administration' (ibid., 2.91). When Grafton and Camden resigned in January 1770, Northumberland moved into opposition, joining in a number of protests over the Middlesex election issue. He fought hard to retain his position in Middlesex and Westminster. The first was lost to the Wilkite radicals, but Westminster, which his eldest son, Hugh *Percy, had represented since 1763, was retained in 1768 and 1774. In 1776 Northumberland was joined in the Lords by his son, who succeeded to his mother's barony, becoming Lord Percy. Each of them toyed with opposition, but in February 1778 Northumberland was once more employed by the king to discover whether Chatham would join North's ministry. The negotiation failed, but in December 1778 Northumberland resumed office as master of the horse, though Walpole wrote that he had gout and was too lame to ride, and even the king admitted that he was 'not capable of attending much' (*Correspondence of George III*, 4.209, letter no. 2436). He held the post until December 1780, when he retired on grounds of ill health.

It was no more than an indication of the king's desperation that he should mention Northumberland in March 1783 to head a ministry to save him from the Fox–North coalition. Nothing came of it, but later that year Northumberland had one more card to play. He voted in December against Fox's India Bill, as the king wished, and the following month, while Pitt's new ministry faced a hostile House of Commons, his seven votes were at a premium. The price of his 'zeal' was the barony of Lovaine, to descend to his second son, Lord Algernon, raised in 1790 to the earldom of Beverley. Northumberland died at Sion House,

Middlesex, on 6 June 1786 and was buried in Westminster Abbey on 21 June.

Northumberland's remarkable rise drew upon him envy and scorn. Walpole maintained a battery of sneers against his pretensions and 'Percy blood'. George III's impression of him was not, at first, very flattering: of the proposal to make him lord chamberlain to the Queen, he wrote to Bute in 1762: 'I think him quite cut out for the nothingness of the employment' (George III, *Letters … to Lord Bute, 1756–1766*, ed. R. Sedgwick, 1939, no. 229). But Northumberland was a handsome man of good presence, his property gave him a certain independence of mind, and he was far from foolish. His position as lord lieutenant of Middlesex brought him considerable unpopularity. During the Wilkite riots of 1769 he was accused of hiring an election mob and threatened with a prosecution. In 1780 the Gordon rioters remembered his family's Catholic origins: he was assaulted and had his pocket picked, and the windows of Northumberland House were broken. His great wealth meant that office was not essential to him and he seems soon to have tired of the routine of attendance and administration. He was FRS, a trustee of the new British Museum, a discerning patron of the arts, and courteous to Johnson, Goldsmith, Thomas Percy, and the botanist John Hill. Northumberland House and Sion House were greatly embellished, and he employed James Paine, Robert Adam, and Capability Brown on a massive rehabilitation of Alnwick Castle. In 1756 he was reported to be 'making fine things there', and in 1768 it was said that 'the old naked castle is now the noblest seat I think in the kingdom' (*Buckinghamshire MSS*, 261, 264–5).

Northumberland's eldest son, Lord Hugh, had a distinguished army career: his second son, Lord Algernon, represented Northumberland from 1774 until 1786 but was in poor health and of a retiring disposition. The duchess, regarded as a peeress in her own right, was prominent in society—'constantly wagging' (running around), in George Selwyn's phrase; parts of her journal were published in 1926 as *The Diaries of a Duchess*. She was a lady of the bedchamber to Queen Charlotte until 1770, when her husband's temporary move into opposition prompted her to resign. One of the duke's illegitimate children, James *Smithson (1764–1829), was a chemist and mineralogist and left money to found the Smithsonian Institution in Washington.

JOHN CANNON

Sources GEC, *Peerage* · G. Brenan, *A history of the house of Percy*, ed. W. A. Lindsay, 2 (1902) · *Additional Grenville papers, 1763–1765*, ed. J. R. G. Tomlinson (1962) · *The Grenville papers: being the correspondence of Richard Grenville … and … George Grenville*, ed. W. J. Smith, 4 vols. (1852–3) · G. Thomas, earl of Albemarle [G. T. Keppel], *Memoirs of the marquis of Rockingham and his contemporaries*, 2 vols. (1852) · *The correspondence of King George the Third from 1760 to December 1783*, ed. J. Fortescue, 6 vols. (1927–8) · *The diaries of a duchess: extracts from the diaries of the first duchess of Northumberland (1716–1776)*, ed. J. Greig (1926) · *CSP dom.*, 1760–65 · E. Cruickshanks, 'Smithson, Hugh', HoP, *Commons, 1715–54* · HoP, *Commons, 1754–90* · Walpole, *Corr.* · *Life of William, earl of Shelburne … with extracts from his papers and correspondence*, ed. E. G. P. Fitzmaurice, 3 vols. (1875–6) · *Eighth report*, 1, HMC, 7 (1907–9) · *GM*, 1st ser., 4 (1734), 275 · *GM*, 1st ser., 34 (1764), 603 · J. Cannon, *Aristocratic century: the peerage of eighteenth-century England* (1984), 68 · H. Walpole, *Memoirs of King George II*, ed.

J. Brooke, 3 vols. (1985) · A. G. Olson, 'The duke of Richmond's memorandum, 1–7 July 1766', *EngHR*, 75 (1960), 475–82 · parish register (baptisms), Kirby Wiske, 10 Dec 1712

Archives Alnwick Castle, Northumberland, corresp. and papers, incl. papers as lord-lieutenant of Ireland; corresp. · PRO NIre., papers as lord-lieutenant of Ireland | BL, corresp. with duke of Newcastle, Add. MSS 32724–33071 · BL, letters to Lord Hardwicke, Add. MSS 35610–35662, *passim* · NRA, priv. coll., letters to Lord Shelburne · PRO, letters to first earl of Chatham, PRO 30/8

Likenesses J. Reynolds, oils, *c*.1760, Alnwick Castle, Northumberland · attrib. J. Reynolds, oils, *c*.1760, Alnwick Castle, Northumberland · R. E. Pine, oils, 1761, Middlesex Hospital, London · J. Reynolds, oils, *c*.1762, The Mansion House, Dublin · J. Finlayson, mezzotint, pubd 1771 (after pastel drawing by H. D. Hamilton), BM · J. Tassie, paste medallion, 1780, NPG · T. Gainsborough, oils, exh. RA 1783, Middlesex Guildhall, London · T. Gainsborough, oils, *c*.1783, Albury Park, Surrey; version, NG Ire. · J. Barry, oils, *c*.1784–1786, Syon House, Brentford, London [*see illus.*] · T. Bewick, Indian ink miniature, BM · H. D. Hamilton, pastel drawing, Alnwick Castle, Northumberland · W. Hole, etchings, repro. in De Fonblanque, *Annals of the house of Percy* · D. Pariset, engraving (after P. Falconet) · attrib. Phillips, group portrait (*The Henry V Club*), Royal Collection · A. Ramsay, oils, Albury Park, Surrey · J. Zoffany, double portrait, oils (with Henry Selby), Albury Park, Surrey · marble bust, Syon House and Gardens, Syon Park, Brentford, London

Wealth at death large; approx. £50,000 p.a.: Brenan, *History of the house of Percy*

Hugh Percy, second duke of Northumberland (1742–1817), by Gilbert Stuart, 1785

Percy, Hugh, second duke of Northumberland (1742–1817), army officer and politician, was born in the parish of St George's, Hanover Square, London, on 14 August 1742. He was the eldest son of Sir Hugh Smithson (*bap.* 1712, *d.* 1786) [*see* Percy, Hugh, first duke of Northumberland] and Lady Elizabeth Smithson (1716–1776) [*see* Percy, Elizabeth], who in April 1750 adopted the name Percy in place of Smithson on Sir Hugh's inheriting the title of earl of Northumberland from his wife's father, Algernon Seymour, seventh duke of Somerset. From 1750 until his father became first duke of Northumberland in October 1766, Hugh Percy was styled Lord Warkworth. Thereafter, until he inherited his father's dukedom, he was generally known as Lord or Earl Percy.

Percy was educated at Eton College from 1753 to 1758, and then at St John's College, Cambridge, in 1760. On 1 May 1759, not yet aged seventeen, he was gazetted ensign in the 24th foot; four months later he exchanged to the 85th with the rank of captain. He may have served at the battle of Minden as a volunteer, and in 1762 he became lieutenant-colonel of the newly raised 111th foot and received a commission as a lieutenant-colonel in the Grenadier Guards.

In 1763 and again at the 1768 general election, Percy was elected, unopposed, an MP for Westminster. In the Commons he supported the Grenville ministry, and in February 1766 he voted against the repeal of the Stamp Act. He aligned himself with the Chatham administration, and in December 1768 became colonel of the 5th foot. In 1770 Percy and his father went into opposition to the new ministry led by Lord North. Nevertheless, George III threw his electoral weight behind Percy and Lord Thomas Clinton in the 1774 general election, mainly because the alternative candidates for Westminster were Wilkite radicals of

whom the king disapproved still more. The decisive factors in Percy's victory, however, were probably the local influence of his father and the direct involvement of his mother, who, according to Walpole (Walpole, 428), 'Sat daily at a window in Covent Garden making interest for her son'.

Percy himself took no part in the election campaign; he had departed with his regiment in May 1774 for service in North America. He watched with increasing dismay as the situation deteriorated in New England: 'this Country', he told his father on 12 September, 'is now in as open state of Rebellion as Scotland was in the year 45' (Percy papers, vol. L, pt A, fol. 16). When at length hostilities began at Lexington and Concord on 19 April 1775 Percy played a crucial role in saving Lieutenant-Colonel Smith's force from destruction as it retreated to Boston. Percy's brigade, together with two field pieces, met Smith's beleaguered column on the road between Menotomy and Lexington. Percy's troops held the enraged Massachusetts militiamen at bay while Smith's men regrouped, and then escorted Smith's battered command back to Boston under heavy fire. His coolness was widely praised, and he became the hero of the hour in besieged Boston. In July 1775 he was appointed major-general in America, and in September major-general in the army.

In 1776 Percy was involved in the campaign in and around New York. After the British victory on Long Island (27 August 1776) he wrote that the Americans 'will never again stand before us in the Field. Things seem to be over with Them & I flatter myself now that this Campaign will put a total End to the War' (*Letters*, 69)—a misjudgement, but one shared by many of his colleagues. He took part in the storming of Fort Washington on 16 November 1776, and at the beginning of December he went with General Clinton on the expedition to occupy Newport, Rhode Island. In January 1777 Clinton left Rhode Island for England, leaving Percy in charge of the garrison.

Over the next few weeks Percy's relationship with General Sir William Howe (1729–1814), the British commander-in-chief in America, rapidly deteriorated. Percy complained at Howe's decision to reduce the number of troops under his command in order to reinforce the army operating in New Jersey. He was further aggrieved when Howe pressed him to send a large quantity of forage to New York, which Percy believed could not be spared. When Howe criticized a civil appointment that Percy had made on Rhode Island, then reversed the decision of a court martial over which Percy had presided, and finally implied that he should have taken Providence as well as Newport in the preceding December, Percy decided that he would not allow himself to be 'subject to another such indignity' (Willcox, 127–8). Howe, for his part, regarded Percy as over-sensitive and too status-conscious: 'he thinks I have not treated him according to his rank as an Offr. & *Heir apparent* to ye Dukedom of Northumberland' (Howe to General James Grant, 18 March 1777, Macpherson Grant papers, bundle 252). Percy returned to England on 5 May, his departure lamented by both the army and the civilian population of Rhode Island, where his humanity and concern for the inhabitants earned him much popularity. Ostensibly, he left America to inherit the Percy barony from his mother, but the real reason for his return home was soon widely known.

Back in England, Percy was promoted in August 1777 lieutenant-general, but he played no further active part in military operations during the American war. In November 1784 he was appointed colonel of the second troop of Horse Grenadier Guards. He inherited his father's dukedom in June 1786, and was lord lieutenant and vice-admiral of Northumberland in 1786–99 and 1802–17. He was promoted general in October 1793, and was colonel of the Royal Horse Guards from December 1806 to 1812.

Percy married on 2 July 1764 Lady Anne Stuart (*b.* 1746), third daughter of John *Stuart, third earl of Bute (1713–1792); they had no children. The fashionable *Town and Country Magazine* of London alleged in 1772 that Percy was virtually impotent from masturbation at school and frequenting brothels in his youth, and that his wife was a 'notoriously promiscuous adulteress' (Stone, 258). He divorced her by act of parliament (16 March 1779) for criminal conversation with William Bird of Trinity College, Cambridge. Percy then married on 25 May 1779 his sister-in-law Frances Julia (1752–1820), third daughter of Peter Burrell of Langley Park, Beckenham, Kent; they had three sons, including Algernon *Percy, and two daughters. He was one of the richest men in England, his wealth increased by mines in Northumberland. According to the *Gentleman's Magazine* obituary his annual income was estimated at not less than £80,000. He was extravagant and generous. He paid fares home for widows of men of his

regiment killed in America. After 1815 when agricultural prices fell he reduced his rents by a quarter; his grateful tenants erected a memorial column in 1816.

In politics, although at first an admirer of Pitt, Percy veered towards the opposition, was a leader of the 'armed neutrality', during the 1789 regency crisis, and subsequently joined the prince of Wales's circle. When in 1797 he was approached by Lord Moira with a view to reviving the 'armed neutrality', he eventually withheld support, remarking that no ministry could last two whole sessions of parliament against both Pitt and Fox. In 1803 he declined joining on attack on Addington, on the grounds that it would make room for Pitt, whose principles he detested. That year, on the resumption of war with France, he resigned the lord lieutenancy of Northumberland in protest at the military arrangements then put in place. Nevertheless, in view of the threatened invasion he raised at his own expense a volunteer unit from his tenantry. He was also dissatisfied with the 1806 coalition of the Foxite whigs with his hated cousin Lord Grenville. Complaining he had not been consulted, he initially instructed his parliamentary interest (principally his Cornish boroughs) to withhold support from the ministry of all the talents. It took the prince of Wales's intervention to secure Percy's reconciliation with Fox. Percy was a competent soldier but very mediocre politician: his family pride militated against success in either field.

Percy died of rheumatic gout at Northumberland House, Strand, London, on 10 July 1817 and was buried on 19 July 1817 in the family vault (built in 1776 for his mother) in Westminster Abbey. He was succeeded by his eldest son, Hugh *Percy (1785–1847).

STEPHEN CONWAY

Sources Northumbd RO, Percy papers · Boston PL, Percy letters · Ballindalloch Castle, Macpherson Grant papers · U. Mich., Clements L., Sir Henry Clinton papers · *Letters of Hugh, Earl Percy, from Boston and New York, 1774–1776*, ed. G. K. Bolton (1902) · K. G. Davies, ed., *Documents of the American Revolution, 1770–1783*, 21 vols. (1972–81) · H. Walpole, *Journal of the reign of King George the Third*, ed. Dr Doran, 2 vols. (1859) · DNB · W. B. Willcox, *Portrait of a general: Sir Henry Clinton in the war of independence* (1964) · I. D. Gruber, *The Howe brothers and the American Revolution* (Chapel Hill, NC, 1972) · R. A. Bowler, *Logistics and the failure of the British army in America, 1775–1783* (1975) · E. B. De Fonblanque, *Annals of the house of Percy, from the conquest to the opening of the nineteenth century*, 2 vols. (privately printed, London, 1887) · *The later correspondence of George III*, ed. A. Aspinall, 5 vols. (1962–70) · *The correspondence of George, prince of Wales, 1770–1812*, ed. A. Aspinall, 8 vols. (1963–71) · GEC, *Peerage* · HoP, *Commons* · Burke, *Peerage* (1999) · L. Stone, *Road to divorce: England, 1530–1987* (1990) · *GM*, 1st ser., 87/2 (1817), 83–5, 182, 382 · Venn, *Alum. Cant.*

Archives Alnwick Castle, Northumberland, corresp. and papers | BL, letters to Lord Grenville, Add. MS 58992 · BL, corresp. with first earl of Liverpool, Add. MSS 3811–3815, 38304–38309 · BL, corresp. with George Rose, Add. MS 42774 · Hunt. L., letters to Hastings family, HU · N. Yorks. CRO, corresp. with Christopher Wyvill, ZFW · U. Durham L., Grey of Howick collection, letters to Earl Grey · Yale U., Beinecke L., letters to J. Davidson and T. Davidson, Percy short list

Likenesses N. Dance, double portrait, oils, 1762 (with Rev. J. Lippyatt), Syon House, Middlesex · J. Finlayson, mezzotint, pubd 1765 (after P. Batoni), BM, NPG · A. Van Rymsdyke, oils, 1776 (after P. Batoni), Syon House, Middlesex · G. Stuart, oils, 1785, Syon

House, Middlesex [see illus.] · T. Phillips, oils, 1801, Petworth House, West Sussex · L. S. Stadler, coloured lithograph, pubd 1814 (after C. Rosenberg & Son), NPG · P. Batoni, oils, Alnwick Castle, Northumberland · T. Phillips, oils (after Reynolds), Eton

Wealth at death under £700,000 personal property: GM, 2.382

Percy, Hugh (1784–1856), bishop of Carlisle, the third son of Algernon Percy, first earl of Beverley (1750–1830), and Isabella Susannah (1750–1812), second daughter of Peter Burrell and sister of Lord Gwydyr, was born in London on 29 January 1784. His mother was sister to Frances Julia Burrell, who married Hugh Percy, second duke of Northumberland. Henry *Percy and Josceline *Percy were his brothers. He was educated at Eton College and St John's College, Cambridge, where he was admitted in December 1802, graduating MA in 1805 and DD in 1825; he was admitted *ad eundem* at Oxford in 1834. Having taken holy orders, he married, on 19 May 1806, Mary, eldest daughter of Mary and Charles Manners *Sutton, archbishop of Canterbury, by whom in 1809 he was collated to the benefices of Bishopsbourne and Ivychurch, Kent. In 1810 he was appointed chancellor and prebendary of Exeter, which appointments he held until 1816. On 21 December 1812 he was installed chancellor of Salisbury Cathedral. In 1816 he was collated by his father-in-law to a prebendal stall at Canterbury Cathedral, and in the same year he received the enormously rich stall of Finsbury at St Paul's, which he held until his death. The income from these livings and stalls was over £6000 p.a. In 1822 he was made archdeacon of Canterbury, and in 1825, on the death of Gerrard Andrewes, he was raised to the deanery. Two years later (15 July 1827), on the death of Walker King, he was consecrated bishop of Rochester, from which see, after a few months' tenure, he was translated, on the death of Samuel Goodenough, to that of Carlisle. This was just before his father-in-law's death. This bishopric he held until his death.

While dean of Canterbury Percy promoted the repair of the interior of the cathedral, 'clearing off the whitewash and removing modern incongruities', personally superintending the work. As a bishop, he was an opponent of the ecclesiastical commission's attempts to reform the church. He became a public enemy of the commissioners when in 1846 they reduced his subsidy from £2000 to £1500 p.a. Despite pressure, he refused to resign his chancellorship or his prebend. Geoffrey Best sees him as one of the 'conspicuous episcopal survivals from the prehistoric Hanoverian church' (Best, 404). Within his diocese Percy was less reactionary, though he was not popular; during the Chartist period bricks were thrown at him in Carlisle and his effigy burned. In 1838 he established a clergy aid society, and in 1855 a diocesan education society. He built thirteen new churches or chapels and rebuilt eighteen. He was first president of the Cumberland Infirmary, on which he spent much effort (a ward in the infirmary was named after him). He found Rose Castle, the episcopal residence, much dilapidated and deformed with incongruous additions. Determined to make it worthy of the see, he called in the Quaker architect Thomas Rickman,

under whose directions the house was entirely remodelled without any detriment to its medieval character. The main cost was defrayed out of the episcopal revenues, but Percy is stated to have spent £40,000 of his own money on the gardens, grounds, and outbuildings. A rosary, in which he delighted, was laid out by Sir Joseph Paxton, who also formed the terraced gardens. Percy was a highchurchman, and disliked Tractarians and evangelicals. He 'set not his affection on mediaeval frippery' (*Carlisle Patriot*, 9 Feb 1856). He was, Ellen Goodwin recalled,

> a great farmer; he was reputed the best judge of a horse in all
> the district. … He used to drive his own four horses all the
> way to London and to say there was no such hill as 'Rose
> Brow' in all the distance. (Bouch, 387)

Dictatorial and distant from his clergy, he had by the end of his life become a noted local character.

Percy's first wife, with whom he had a large family of three sons and eight daughters, died in September 1831. He married, second, on 3 February 1840, Mary, the daughter of Sir William Hope Johnstone. His eldest son, Algernon, married Emily, daughter of Bishop Reginald *Heber and heir of her uncle, Richard *Heber, and assumed the name of Heber in addition to his own. Percy died at Rose Castle on 5 February 1856, and was buried in the parish churchyard of Dalston.

EDMUND VENABLES, *rev.* H. C. G. MATTHEW

Sources Venn, *Alum. Cant.* · GM, 2nd ser., 45 (1856), 421 · G. F. A. Best, *Temporal pillars: Queen Anne's bounty, the ecclesiastical commissioners, and the Church of England* (1964) · C. M. L. Bouch, *Prelates and people of the lake counties: a history of the diocese of Carlisle, 1133–1933* (1948)
Archives Cumbria AS, Carlisle, papers
Likenesses J. Opie, oils, Canterbury Cathedral, deanery · T. Phillips, oils, Eton

Percy, Hugh, third duke of Northumberland (1785–1847), politician and landowner, was born on 20 April 1785, the eldest son of Hugh *Percy, second duke (1742–1817), and his second wife, Frances Julia, *née* Burrell (1779–1820). He was educated at Eton College and at St John's College, Cambridge, obtaining an MA in 1805 and an LLD in 1809. A tory like his father, but of a more moderate variety, he was elected MP for Buckingham in August 1806 and for Westminster in October the same year, and in May 1807 won a contested election for the county of Northumberland and an uncontested election for Launceston, which he had represented since the previous November, and where the Percys exercised political patronage. He chose to sit for the former, and continued to do so until summoned to the Lords in 1812 as Baron Percy, during his father's lifetime. Percy rarely spoke: his most dramatic, and puzzling, Commons interventions came in 1807 when he first tried to turn the Slave Trade Abolition Bill into a Slavery Abolition Bill by moving an amendment to emancipate every black child born after 1 January 1810. After the Slave Trade Abolition Bill had been passed on 16 March 1807 he moved the next day to introduce a new bill for the gradual abolition of slavery itself through the freeing of all slave children born after a date to be fixed. He may have been an ardent, and impetuous, anti-slaver, as many supposed, but since his move was vehemently opposed by

Hugh Percy, third duke of Northumberland (1785–1847), by William Holl, pubd 1838 (after George Ward)

Wilberforce on the tactical grounds that the hostility provoked by pressing the larger measure of total abolition would endanger the chances in the Lords of the lesser measure of abolition of the slave trade, it is just as likely that Percy was indulging in a wrecking ploy. Certainly he was known as a high tory on the Catholic question, and there is no record that he ever spoke on slavery matters again after 1807. His subsequent parliamentary utterances were infrequent and illiberal. In 1819, as lord lieutenant of Northumberland, he strongly supported a bill to prohibit all drilling and training without a licence from a lord lieutenant, citing as fact an alarmist rumour that between the rivers Tyne and Wear there were 100,000 armed men ready to rise, including 16,000 armed colliers. In 1820 he took the government line in the Queen Caroline affair, denouncing her 'most indecent conduct' and the 'adulterous intercourse between her and Bergami' (*Hansard 1*, 6 Nov 1820, 1669); his next, and last, speech came in 1832, when he called for the protection of the rights of lords of manors in a bill intended to encourage the employment of agricultural labourers.

On 29 April 1817 at Northumberland House, London, Percy married Lady Charlotte Florentia Clive (*d.* 1866), second daughter of Edward *Clive, first earl of Powis, and granddaughter of Robert Clive, scarcely three months, as it turned out, before he succeeded to the dukedom. It was accounted a successful marriage. Greville thought the duke:

> a very good sort of man, with a very narrow understanding, an eternal talker, and a prodigious bore. The Duchess is a more sensible woman, and amiable and good humoured. He is supposed to be ruled in all things by her advice. (*Greville Memoirs*, 1.164)

Mrs Arbuthnot agreed that 'she is excessively good humoured and has very popular manners' and noted that

'he is as rich as Croesus, [and] fond of magnificence' (*Journal of Mrs Arbuthnot*, 2.231). He covered his wife with diamonds, but they had no children. An opportunity for public display of his opulence and extravagance came in 1825 when he went to Paris as special ambassador at the coronation of Charles X with a magnificent spread of costumes, liveries, and plate all provided at his own expense. Four years later this outfit came in handy when he was appointed lord lieutenant of Ireland with instructions to give Dublin a semi-regal performance: a caravan carrying £90,000 worth of the duke's plate from the Paris mission was seen passing through Staffordshire on its way to Dublin, escorted by a body of soldiers. The previous lord lieutenant, the marquess of Anglesey, was dismissed at the end of 1828 because he was deemed to have gone native in his warmth towards the Catholics, meeting both O'Connell and Lord Clancurry (who had been in the Tower for treason in 1798), and Northumberland was sent to be a firm and dignified governor, aloof from politics. Some contemporaries found it a surprising appointment, considering the duke's political inexperience, and his reputation as 'a stupid, prosing, man' and 'an amazing bore' (ibid., 2.231, 241), and his strong anti-Catholic views. Nevertheless it was, in Peel's view, an inspired choice: when Northumberland resigned along with the Wellington government in November 1830 he described him as 'the best chief Governor who ever presided over her [Ireland's] affairs' (Gash, 654). In its obituary in 1847, however, *The Times* was lukewarm about his viceroyalty, remarking that 'he possessed neither the talent nor the energy to make himself thoroughly hated' (13 Feb 1847). The duke was stolidly unimaginative, rather than stupid—a standing joke was that he gave a deputation of distressed weavers an order for a waistcoat—but unthinking stolidity and unquestioning faith in the duke (Wellington) were exactly what was required in Dublin in 1829–30 to see through the implementation of Catholic emancipation by its previous opponents without encouraging triumphalist behaviour on the part of the Catholic Association, which was suppressed.

No further public appointments came the duke's way after the Irish viceroyalty, and he retired to Northumberland, with seasonal visits to Northumberland House whose views onto the Thames he defended vigorously against various threats by railway speculators. He became a governor of King's College, London, in 1831, a trustee of the British Museum in 1834, high steward of Cambridge University also in 1834, and chancellor in 1840. He was not popular in Northumberland, where he was regarded as unfriendly, reactionary, and self-important, with some justification. He made continual encroachments on common rights, and he contrived the exclusion of the borough of Alnwick from the Municipal Reform Act of 1835. He persisted in regarding the coalminers, on whom a significant part of his wealth depended, as unruly, disaffected, and potentially rebellious, and was always ready to use force to break strikes; at the height of the 1844 miners' strike he warned the home secretary, Sir James Graham, that 'masses of people may be forwarded by Rail Road and

Steamer to a given spot, far beyond the controul [*sic*] of the Civil Power' (Alnwick MSS, third duke's letter-book, August 1844). He spent quite freely on improving the comforts of Alnwick Castle, and while he discussed agricultural improvements with his commissioners (land agents) he never got round to carrying them out, but he supported many local charities. He wrote to Wellington, as master of Trinity House, about Grace Darling's part in rescuing nine people from the wreck of the steamship *Forfarshire* on Starket Rock, Farne Islands, within days of its happening in September 1838, and was fully appreciative of her heroism.

On 12 February 1847 Northumberland was found dead in his bed at Alnwick. *The Times* observed that 'of the House of Lords he was by no means a distinguished member' and that 'he was a man whose intellect and attainments procured for him a very moderate degree of respect' (13 Feb 1847). Nevertheless, his death occasioned county-wide mourning, thousands went to his lying-in-state in Alnwick Castle, the road from Alnwick to Gateshead Station was lined almost throughout for his funeral procession, platforms of stations on the route to London were crowded with people to see the special funeral train pass, and he was buried in Westminster Abbey on 23 February with great pomp. He was succeeded by his brother Algernon, and his widow lived in the original Smithson family seat at Stanwick, Yorkshire, on a jointure of £12,500 a year until her death in 1866.   F. M. L. THOMPSON

Sources third duke's letter-book, Alnwick Castle, Northumberland, Alnwick MSS · *Hansard 1* · *DNB* · *The Times* (13 Feb 1847) · N. Gash, *Mr Secretary Peel: the life of Sir Robert Peel to 1830* (1961) · *The journal of Mrs Arbuthnot, 1820–1832*, ed. F. Bamford and the duke of Wellington [G. Wellesley], 2 vols. (1950) · Burke, *Peerage* · GEC, *Peerage* · *The Greville memoirs, 1814–1860*, ed. L. Strachey and R. Fulford, 8 vols. (1938) · *Mr Gregory's letter-box, 1813–30*, ed. I. A. Gregory (1898) · E. Law, Lord Ellenborough, *A political diary, 1828–1830*, ed. Lord Colchester, 2 vols. (1881) · *Newcastle Courant* (12 Feb 1847) · *Newcastle Courant* (26 Feb 1847)

Archives Alnwick Castle, Northumberland, corresp. and papers; bank books | BL, corresp. with Sir Robert Peel, Add. MS 40327 · RS, corresp. with Sir John Herschel · Trinity Cam., letters to W. Whewell · U. Durham, corresp. with second Earl Grey

Likenesses T. Phillips, oils, 1803, FM Cam. · J. Downman, chalk and watercolour drawing, 1811, Syon House, Middlesex · R. Graves, line engraving, pubd 1825 (after Mrs Robertson), BM, NPG · W. Holl, stipple, pubd 1838 (after G. Ward), BM, NPG; repro. in H. T. Ryall, *Portraits of eminent Conservatives and statesmen* [in pts, 1836–46] [*see illus.*] · J. G. Lough, bust, 1843, Alnwick Castle, Northumberland · M. Cregan, oils, Dublin Castle · G. Hayter, drawing, NPG · G. Hayter, group portrait, oils (*The trial of Queen Caroline, 1820*), NPG · T. Phillips, oils (as a young boy), Alnwick Castle, Northumberland · T. Phillips, oils, Eton · group portrait, oils (*The coronation of George IV*), Royal Collection

Percy, James (1619–*c*.1690), peerage claimant, was born at Harrowden, Northamptonshire, the eldest surviving son of Henry Percy, a servant in the household of Lord Chancellor Francis Bacon, and his wife, Lydia, daughter of Robert Cope of Horton, Northamptonshire. The elder Percy left Bacon's service following the chancellor's fall and moved to Dunnington, Lincolnshire, where in 1626 he deserted his family for London, taking with him a maidservant, with whom he had at least one son. The family, in

serious want, relocated to Ireland, where James's uncle, James Percy, had emigrated. The young James took up trunk-making in Dublin, and built up a successful business, eventually setting himself up as a merchant. At an unknown date he married Sarah Sayer (*d.* in or before 1670). Percy's efforts brought him a modest fortune and the self-confidence he needed to pursue his claim to noble blood. After his uncle's death in 1654 he travelled to England, where he presented himself to the tenth earl of Northumberland as the head of the Irish branch of the family. Percy later claimed that both the tenth earl and his son Josceline Percy, the eleventh earl, acknowledged his relationship.

The eleventh earl died with no male heir at Turin on 21 May 1670. His countess, pregnant at the time, later gave birth to a stillborn child. Shortly afterwards, in February 1671, Percy entered his claim to the title. His faith in his right to the earldom was strong: when it was disputed by the eleventh earl's mother and wife on behalf of the three-year-old heir, Lady Elizabeth Percy, he was at first taken aback, but afterwards determined to triumph over the 'high privilege, policy, and potency of his opponents' (*House of Lords MSS*, 1.213), and so he embarked upon a ruinous twenty-year struggle, the final result of which was complete failure.

Percy could prove his descent from his grandfather, Henry Percy of Pavenham, Buckinghamshire, but establishing his connection to the main line of the family proved far more difficult. Not surprisingly the countess refused to allow him access to the family papers, without which, Percy argued, he could not prove his right. In his first effort he claimed the title as the great-grandson of Sir Richard Percy, a soldier and fifth son of the eighth earl. Unfortunately there were no documents to prove the relationship and, moreover, for it to be true Sir Richard would have to have been a grandfather at sixteen and a great-grandfather at forty-four. But the House of Lords refused to dismiss Percy's case out of hand, and in February 1673 gave both sides a month to gather evidence. In March they appeared at the bar, where testimony regarding Sir Richard's age carried the day. At the motion of the earl of Suffolk, the dowager countess's brother, Percy's petition was rejected. Nothing daunted he continued his struggle against formidable odds. In succeeding years he petitioned the king, the Lords, the Commons, and the duke of York. Further research led him to modify his claim, and in 1677 he identified another younger son of the house of Percy as his great-grandfather: Sir Ingelgram, third son of the fifth earl. Once again there was no written evidence backing his assertion. In fact, Percy's case was a weak one: Sir Ingelgram had very probably died about 1540 leaving only a single illegitimate daughter. Nevertheless, the dowager countess was not prepared to leave the case to mere proofs of evidence. She and her allies exploited their parliamentary privileges, forcing repeated delays in court, and they launched vexatious suits, forcing Percy to defend himself at great expense for years. These set-backs put his claim ever farther out of reach, though they also won him some public sympathy. Further attempts to gain the title, accompanied by a barrage of genealogical charts and printed petitions, came in 1678, 1679, 1680, 1685, and, finally, 1689. In the last case the Lords acted decisively, declaring Percy's claim to be 'groundless, false, and scandalous' (Brenan, 2.366). They ordered a public humiliation of the old man, who would appear in Westminster Hall wearing a paper describing him as the 'False and Impudent Pretender to the Earldom of Northumberland' (ibid.), a sentence which seems never to have been carried out. In the end the weight of the interests ranged against him as well as his own stubborn refusal to admit defeat destroyed James Percy. His fortune lost, he seems to have died shortly after his final humiliation by the Lords.

VICTOR STATER

Sources G. Brenan, *A history of the house of Percy*, ed. W. A. Lindsay, 2 (1902), 310–69 · [J. Percy?], *A narrative of the proceedings of the petitioner* (c.1680) · [J. Percy?], *The case of James Percy, the true heir male and claimant to the earldom of Northumberland* [1680] · [J. Percy?], *The case of James Percy, claimant to the earldom of Northumberland* (1685) · *Ninth report*, 2, HMC, 8 (1884), esp. 21 [House of Lords] · *The manuscripts of the House of Lords*, 4 vols., HMC, 17 (1887–94), vol. 1, pp. 213, 306–8 · *CSP dom.*, 1673–5, 100–01; 1677–8, 67–8; 1682, 168
Archives HLRO, Main papers

Percy, Sir (John Samuel) Jocelyn (1871–1952), army officer, was born at Gibraltar on 9 March 1871, the seventh of the eleven children of Edward Joscelyn Baumgartner (1815–1899), a barrister and registrar of the supreme court of Gibraltar, and himself the fourth child in a family of thirteen, and his second wife, Sarah Woodlaid (d. 1886), about whom little is known. An uncle was General Thomas Mowbray Baumgartner; another was General Robert Julian Baumgartner. Though descended from eighteenth-century Swiss immigrants, at the height of the First World War the English Baumgartners changed their surname to Percy, after the Northumberland house of Percy to which they were also related.

Percy left Gibraltar for Britain only in September 1884, accompanying his father's sister, who had married into the Charrington family of brewers and paid for his education. In January 1890, after Queen Elizabeth's Grammar School in Sevenoaks, Percy entered the Royal Military College, Sandhurst. He passed out in December 1890, went to Switzerland to improve his French, then received his commission into the East Lancashire regiment in July 1891.

The earliest years of Percy's military career were spent in Ireland and later on active service on the north-west frontier, where he served in the 1894 Waziristan campaign, as assistant superintendent army signalling, and the following year as a transport officer in the Chiltral relief force. During the Second South African War he served in Robert's horse from 1899 to 1901, and for thirteen months in Colonel Byng's column, and for five in Colonel Garrat's. He rose to brevet major, received two mentions in dispatches, and survived the battle of Koorn Spruit, on 31 March 1900, when five VCs were won, and Percy, in his squadron alone, lost one officer, fourteen men, and thirty-five horses, including his own killed under him.

Before the outbreak of the First World War, Percy spent several more years in India, as a brigade major and deputy assistant adjutant-general, followed by a spell at home on the staff at Sandhurst. In December 1902 he was also married, after an engagement of nearly seven years; his wife was Inez d'Aguilar Jamieson (1874–1948), daughter of Colonel Alister William Jamieson (1847–1924) and Geraldine Alice, *née* d'Aguilar (1848–1932). They had a son and a daughter.

Percy's service during the First World War was varied and distinguished. In France he held posts on the general staff of the 27th and 48th divisions and was with the 31st division for its doomed attack north of the Ancre on 1 July 1916. Later he served as a brigadier-general on the staff of 11th corps and as a major-general with the Fifth Army and the Second Army, becoming chief of staff to General Gough and General Plumer. He was mentioned in dispatches on six occasions, received a DSO, and was created CMG and CB. Among many foreign awards, he was appointed commanders of the Légion d'honneur, the order of Leopold of Belgium, and the star of Romania, and received a Belgian Croix de Guerre and the order of the sacred treasure of Japan.

After the end of hostilities Percy served with the British army of the Rhine until 1919, first on the general staff, then as commander of the 3rd London brigade, before joining the British military mission fighting the Bolsheviks in southern Russia. There he worked closely with the White Russian general Denikin and Wrangel and in 1920 assumed command of the mission. In March 1920, when the Bolsheviks reached an armistice with Poland and forced Wrangel back into the Crimea, Percy played a central role in the successful evacuation of over 30,000 White Russian troops, and over 10,000 refugees, from Novorossiysk. He was twice mentioned in dispatches, received two Russian awards, and was appointed KBE. He retired from the army in August 1920.

Forty-nine years old and with a family to support, Percy did not find it easy to adjust to civilian life. He took the family to British Columbia, cleared land, and began to farm, but returned to Britain when Lady Percy found it too hard to adjust. By 1926 he was selling a convector system of central heating. So when approached, albeit from a strange and exotic quarter, with an offer of employment that promised responsibility, financial security, a certain degree of adventure, and a return to uniform and military life (of a sort), he found it difficult to resist. In September 1926, apparently recommended by Harry Eyres, a retired British consul for Albania, and after a quick look at the country, Percy took up the post of inspector-general of the Albanian gendarmerie.

Percy replaced Lieutenant-Colonel W. F. Stirling, formerly Lawrence of Arabia's staff officer and British governor of southern Palestine, whom Albania's new president, Ahmed Zogu (later King Zog), had engaged three years earlier to advise on internal administration. In 1925 Stirling was then asked to reorganize and train the gendarmerie, but the task proved beyond him in a country riddled with corruption and dogged by banditry and blood feud. Percy's long experience of staff work, however, stood him well for the post and he set about building and testing a fresh organization. He established a training school and ensured his gendarmes were better uniformed, armed, quartered, and paid. He assigned units to prefectures and sub-prefectures, and connected all posts with a telephone system that worked. And he employed a new inspectorate of around a dozen Britons, all former army officers, whom he mostly recruited in person on brief trips back to London. Between 1926 and 1928 he also spent many months in the unsettled mountains of northern Albania, where his presence as a kind of military commander-in-chief restored confidence and stability following a rising against the government. A British Foreign Office official observed in 1928: 'thanks to General Percy's personality, British prestige in the north stands at a truly Kiplingesque height' (Martin, 157).

By the 1930s the great affection and respect for Britain that existed throughout Albania owed much to Percy and the improvements he had made in enforcing law and order, suppressing extortion, investing the gendarmerie with an exceptional reputation for honesty, and generally making Albania a safer place in which to live. Crimes were detected more quickly, local influence on the gendarmerie was much reduced, and even the intensity of blood feuds began to lessen as it became evident that the gendarmes might be trusted to catch their man. And though Percy and his inspectors were strictly impartial and independent of the British government, their presence in Albania even went some way towards checking the territorial ambitions of both Yugoslavia and fascist Italy. In the judgement of one of his British inspectors, Percy's service to Albania was 'magnificent' (private information).

Lean and tall (at 6 feet 3 inches he towered over most Albanians), Jos Percy was a gentle, sensitive man whose charm, travels, and military adventures made him excellent company, and whose quiet and collected manner unfailingly commanded respect. Well-liked by his British inspectors, their dispersal around the country and his isolation in the capital sometimes depressed him. His wife did not follow him to Albania, but his son and niece would both visit, and for two years his daughter kept house for him in Tirana. In his first years in Albania he enjoyed walking and fly-fishing in the mountains; later he rented a hut on the picturesque Durres beach; always he would enjoy spending time in his workshop making furniture and fittings for his home.

In September 1938, under growing pressure from fascist Italy, King Zog was forced to terminate Percy's contract and those of his team of inspectors. After twelve years in Albania, Percy returned to Britain and a directorship of Charrington's brewery in Mile End, London. After the outbreak of war he took command of a Home Guard battalion, and his pre-war experiences also proved useful in encouraging guerrilla resistance to the occupying axis forces in Albania. He advised Britain's Special Operations Executive, made broadcasts to the Albanian people over the BBC, and agreed to chair a London committee of prominent Britons interested in Albania. He was convinced that the allies should promise the post-war independence of the country as an incentive to Albanians to resist. In May 1940 his son, Alister, who had served for a time as his aide in Albania, was killed in France flying Hurricanes with 501 squadron, RAF.

In 1945 Percy retired to Nether Stowey, Somerset. Three years later he and his wife flew out to east Africa to spend time with their daughter's family. There his wife died soon after their arrival. After returning to Britain in 1949, he went to live with two of his sisters in the Hotel Wellington at Crowthorne. Later he moved to Huntly, a home for retired officers at Bishopsteignton, Devon, where he died of heart failure, in his sleep, on 25 August 1952.

RODERICK BAILEY

Sources private information (2004) · S. Martin, 'The gendarmerie mission in Albania, 1925–38: a move on the English chess board?', *Contemporary European History*, 7/2 (1998), 143–59 · D. Oakley-Hill, 'The Albanian gendarmerie, 1925–1938, and its British organizers', *Albania*, ed. National Democratic Committee for a Free Albania (1962), 403–6 · *Daily Sketch* (15 March 1933) · *Sphere* (29 April 1933) · *Daily Mail* (14 Dec 1934) · d. cert. · *CGPLA Eng. & Wales* (1952) · WWW

Wealth at death £710 5s. 6d.: probate, 8 Nov 1952, *CGPLA Eng. & Wales*

Percy [*alias* Fisher], **John** (1569–1641), Jesuit, was born on 27 September 1569 in co. Durham, in the village of Holmside, the son of John Percy, yeoman, and Cecilia Lawson, both protestants. At the age of fourteen he was sent to live with a Roman Catholic woman and due to her influence and the persuasions of a local Catholic priest he converted to Catholicism and in 1586 crossed the channel and entered the English College at Rheims. In 1589 he matriculated at the Jesuit-run English College at Rome, and on 13 March 1593, by papal dispensation, was ordained a priest before the full canonical age. In May 1594 he was admitted into the Society of Jesus and began his noviciate at Tournai. In the following year, however, he became ill due to overwork, and was ordered to England to recuperate. Upon arrival in London he was arrested and committed to Bridewell prison, where after seven months he managed to escape with two other priests and seven laymen. After hiding for a short time in London he was sent to Yorkshire and in 1598, after reportedly reconciling his mother and sister to the Catholic faith, he joined John Gerard as a chaplain in the Vaux household at Harrowden. In carrying out his pastoral duties there Percy became confessor to Grace, the wife of Sir John Fortescue, son of the chancellor of the exchequer. The young Jesuit was also instrumental in the conversions of members of the Digby family, including Sir Everard Digby, his wife, Mary, and John Digby of Rutland. In 1599 he became the Digbys' household chaplain. Although not involved in the Gunpowder Plot of 1605 he was considered by government officials to be guilty by association with the Digby and Vaux families, and also because he had accompanied some of the conspirators on a pilgrimage to St Winifred's Well in Wales. Nevertheless, he was not apprehended and remained hidden at Harrowden until 1610.

In the years between 1605 and 1610 Percy emerged as an important apologist for the Roman faith. Although he used Fisher as an alias, in 1605 he published *The Treatise of*

Faith using the pseudonym A. D. The *Treatise* was primarily a *reductio ad absurdum* negation of protestantism. 'There must be one true faith which has existed visibly in all ages', Percy's argument went. Since Catholics could show a visible apostolic pedigree and protestants only a church since Luther, the Catholic faith must be true while protestantism was novel and therefore false. Answering Percy's question 'where was your church before Luther?' became a provocative challenge for protestants and both Anthony Wotton, lecturer at All Hallows Barking by the Tower in London, and John White, chaplain to the king, published replies in 1608.

In November 1610 Harrowden was raided and Percy, along with Elizabeth Vaux and Nicholas Hart SJ, was arrested. Percy and Hart were sent to the Gatehouse prison at Westminster while Mrs Vaux was thrown into Fleet prison. The affair was widely reported in news dispatches and Gilbert Pickering, the JP who arrested the trio, was knighted. Though the two Jesuits received death sentences, James I commuted them to exile and in 1612 Percy and Hart left for Flanders. Percy remained very active in exile. In 1613 he was appointed vice-regent of the English mission in Flanders as well as professor of holy scripture at the Jesuit noviciate house in Louvain. In 1612, from the secret press at St Omer, he published *A Reply to Mr. Anthony Wotton and Mr. John White, Ministers*. The appendix contained 'A Catalogue of Divers Visible Professors of the Catholike Faith', to which Percy added 'A Challenge to Protestants' to display their own historical pedigree. In 1614 John White replied again to Percy with his *Defense of the Way to the True Church*.

In 1615 Percy again travelled to England, only to be seized and thrown into the New prison. Since the king was now actively pursuing the favour of Spain, English Catholics were receiving numerous gestures of leniency. Along with other Jesuit prisoners Percy was allowed a daily furlough outside the prison and he regularly ministered in the homes of wealthy courtiers. He also became involved in the distribution of Catholic tracts. John Gee, a convert to protestantism, reported that Percy's secret London residence contained 'a greater store of books … than I ever beheld in any stationers ware-house' (Gee, 24). Even inside the prison Percy kept his personal library, celebrated mass, and actively engaged in debate with protestant churchmen, among whom were puritan ministers George Walker and Henry Burton.

The reputation of 'Fisher the Jesuit' grew in the years between 1622 and 1624. In 1622 the countess of Buckingham, mother of George Villiers, the duke of Buckingham and the king's favourite, announced her conversion to Catholicism. Several members of her family also converted and, according to William Laud, the duke was wavering in his religious commitments. Percy was directly involved as he was by this time the chaplain in the Buckingham household, and the countess's confessor. In the wake of growing protestant protests against the Spanish match the king needed to squelch the rumours of these conversions. Publicly, the countess and her female kindred were quickly confirmed by the bishop of London.

Privately, the king arranged a series of three debates with Percy, held before the Buckinghams on 24–6 May 1622. On the first day he was called to debate with the dean of Carlisle, Francis White, the brother of John White. On the second day he debated with the king himself, and on the third day with William Laud, then bishop of St David's. After the debates the king delivered a note to the Jesuit, containing 'the principal points which with-hold my joining unto the Church of Rome' (Percy, *Answere to the Nine Points*, title-page). In 1624 White wrote *A Replie to Jesuit Fishers Answere to Certain Questions* and Laud published the *Answere to Mr. Fishers Relation of a Third Conference*. Laud's work was attributed to his chaplain Robert Baillie, but in 1639 Laud admitted that he was the author and published an enlarged version. The *Relation of a Conference between William Laud and Fisher the Jesuit* became a celebrated text in Anglican theology and forms part of Laud's collected works. With the assistance of his fellow Jesuit John Floyd, Percy formally responded to the debates in 1625 with the *Answere unto the Nine Points of Controversy*.

In 1623 Francis White and Daniel Featley, chaplain to Archbishop Abbott, engaged Percy and his fellow Jesuit John Sweet in another debate held at the home of Sir Humphrey Linde before a large audience of London's élite society. This debate also resulted in numerous publications including Featley's *Fisher Catched in his Owne Net* (1623), Percy's *Answere to a Pamphlet* (1623), and Featley's response, *The Romish Fisher Catched and Held in his Owne Net* (1624). Featley's work prompted another reply by Percy in 1625 entitled *A Reply to D. White and D. Featley*. About 1625 Percy persuaded William Chillingworth, the well-known Oxford scholar and godson of William Laud, to become a Roman Catholic. Even though the conversion was widely celebrated by Catholics, Chillingworth renounced this new found faith by 1630. After Charles I married Henrietta Maria in 1625 Percy was granted a pardon. Nevertheless, in 1634 he was arrested and ordered to depart the realm. When he refused he was again confined in the Gatehouse until August 1635 when the queen interceded and he was released. Shortly after this he began to suffer from cancer and on 3 December 1641 he died in London.

TIMOTHY WADKINS

Sources T. Wadkins, 'Theological polemic and religious culture in early Stuart England: the Percy/"Fisher" controversies, 1605–1641', PhD diss., Graduate Theological Union, 1988 · T. Wadkins, 'The Percy–"Fisher" controversies and the ecclesiastical politics of Jacobean anti-Catholicism, 1622–1625', *Church History*, 57 (1988), 153–69 · T. H. Wadkins, 'King James I meets John Percy, SJ (26 May 1622)', *Recusant History*, 19 (1988–9), 146–54 · J. D. Hanlon, 'The effects of the Counter-Reformation upon English Catholics, 1603–1630', PhD diss., Columbia University, 1959 · P. Milward, *Religious controversies of the Jacobean age* (1978) · A. Milton, *Catholic and Reformed: the Roman and protestant churches in English protestant thought, 1600–1640* (1995) · J. Gee, *Foot out of the snare* (1624) · *The works of the most reverend father in God, William Laud*, ed. W. Scott, 2 (1849), ix · H. Foley, ed., *Records of the English province of the Society of Jesus*, 7 vols. in 8 (1875–83)
Archives Archives of Archbishop of Westminster, WA MSS 16, 18, 19, 21, 23, 29 · Archives of the British province of the Society of Jesus, Stonyhurst College, Lancashire, Anglia MSS vols. 1–7 · Archivum Romanum Societatis Iesu, Rome, Anglia MS 32 (1) · LPL,

Lambeth MS 1372 · PRO, state papers of the reign of James I and Charles I, SP 14, SP 16

Percy, John (1817–1889), metallurgist, was born at Nottingham on 23 March 1817, the third son of Henry Percy, a solicitor. He went to a private school at Southampton, and then returned to Nottingham, where he attended chemical lectures by a Mr Grisenthwaite at the local school of medicine. He wished to become a chemist, but yielded to his father's desire that he should graduate in medicine, and in April 1834 was taken by his brother Edmund to Paris to begin his medical studies. While in Paris he attended the lectures of Gay-Lussac and Thénard on chemistry, and of A. de Jussieu on botany. In 1836 he went on a tour in Switzerland and the south of France, and compiled a large collection of mineralogical and botanical specimens. In the same year he went to Edinburgh, where he became a pupil of Sir Charles Bell and a friend of Edward Forbes. In 1838 he graduated MD in the university, and obtained a gold medal for a thesis on the presence of alcohol in the brain after poisoning by that substance.

In June 1839 Percy married Grace Mary (d. 1880), daughter of J. E. Piercy, of Warley Hall, Birmingham. In the same year he was elected physician to the Queen's Hospital, Birmingham, but, having private means, did not practise. The metallurgical works in the neighbourhood excited his interest in metallurgy. In 1846 he worked with David Forbes and William Hallowes Miller on crystallized slags. In 1847 he became a fellow of the Royal Society, and served on the council from 1857 to 1859. In 1848 he contributed a paper to the *Chemist* on a mode of extracting silver from its ores (depending on the solubility of the chloride in sodium thiosulphate), which led to the Von Patera process, used at Joachimsthal, and the Russell process, employed in the western states of America. In 1851 he was elected fellow of the Geological Society, and was appointed lecturer on metallurgy and metallurgist to the museum at the newly founded Metropolitan School of Science in London, under Sir Henry Thomas De la Beche; the post was later made a professorship.

The influence exerted by Percy, while holding this position, on English metallurgy was of the utmost importance. As he said in his inaugural address, metallurgy was then looked on as an empirical art, and 'experience without scientific knowledge [was thought] more trustworthy than the like experience with it' (*Nature*, 206). He was an excellent lecturer and teacher, and most English metallurgists of his time were his pupils. Although the silver process was the only metallurgical one he actually invented, his work suggested many others; the important Thomas-Gilchrist process for making Bessemer steel from iron ores containing phosphorus was an outcome of his work and was discovered by his pupils. In 1851 he undertook to superintend the analysis of a large number of specimens of iron and steel collected by his friend, S. H. Blackwell, that were exhibited at the 1851 exhibition and later displayed at the geological museum in Jermyn Street. His results constituted the first serious attempt at a survey of

John Percy (1817–1889), by unknown engraver (after Sir John Gilbert, 1859)

iron ore deposits in Britain. They were included in the volume *Iron and Steel* (1864), part of his great *Treatise on Metallurgy*, of which the first volume was published in 1861. This treatise (1861–80), which remained uncompleted, contains over 3500 pages of terse and exact description of metallurgical processes, of minute and scientific discussion of the chemical problems they involve, often based on the author's careful original research, and of suggestions for future investigation. The drawings of plants are remarkably exact. The book, which was translated into French and German, and became a classic, involved an immense amount of labour.

Percy was appointed lecturer on metallurgy to the artillery officers at Woolwich about 1864, and he retained this post until his death. He was appointed superintendent of ventilation of the houses of parliament on 6 February 1865. He was also a member of the secretary for war's commissions on the application of iron for defensive purposes (1861) and on Gibraltar shields (1867), and of the royal commissions on coal (1871) and the spontaneous combustion of coal in ships (1875). In 1876 he was awarded the Bessemer medal of the Iron and Steel Institute, of which he was an honorary member, serving as president during 1885 and 1886. In December 1879 the government decided to complete the removal of the Royal School of Mines from the Museum of Practical Geology in Jermyn Street to South Kensington. Objecting strongly to this course, Percy twice offered to rebuild the metallurgical laboratory in Jermyn Street, but his offer was refused and he resigned in December 1879. He circulated a pamphlet containing his views on the subject. He received the freedom of the Turners' Company in 1883. He was an honorary member of the Institution of Civil Engineers and in 1887 he was awarded a Miller prize. He received the Albert gold medal of the Society of Arts on his deathbed in 1889. He died at his home, 1 Gloucester Crescent, Hyde Park, London, on 19 June 1889.

Percy was very tall and spare, and had a strong physique and a commanding presence. He frequented the Athenaeum and Garrick clubs, and was of a genial, though at times brusque, temper. He took an interest in social and political questions, on which he wrote many trenchant letters to *The Times* under the signature 'Y', and he could not refrain from denouncing the home rule movement in his presidential address to the Iron and Steel Institute in 1886. A fair artist himself, he made a valuable collection of watercolour drawings and engravings which were sold in 1890. The manuscript catalogue of the watercolour drawings was bought by the British Museum. Percy's collection of metallurgical specimens was deposited in the museum at South Kensington. The Royal Society's catalogue of scientific papers lists twenty-one papers published by Percy singly, one in conjunction with W. H. Miller, and one with R. Smith. P. J. HARTOG, rev. R. C. COX

Sources *Journal of the Iron and Steel Institute*, 1 (1889), 210 · *The Times* (11 Dec 1879) · *The Times* (1 Jan 1880) · *The Times* (11 Feb 1880) · *The Times* (13 Feb 1880) · *Men of the time* (1884), 879 · *Proceedings of the Geological Society* (1890), 45 · W. C. R. A., *PRS*, 46 (1889), xxxv-xl · *Nature*, 40 (1889), 206 · *CGPLA Eng. & Wales* (1889)
Archives BL, lecture notes, Add. MS 31199 · Sci. Mus., corresp. and papers | CUL, letters to Sir George Stokes · ICL, letters to Richard Smith · V&A NAL, corresp. with Sir Henry Cole
Likenesses engraving (after J. Gilbert, 1859), Sci. Mus. [*see illus.*]
Wealth at death £17,503 4s. 4d.: resworn probate, Sept 1890, *CGPLA Eng. & Wales*

Percy, Josceline (1784–1856), naval officer, was the fourth son of Algernon Percy, second Baron Lovaine of Alnwick (1750–1830), and afterwards (1790) first earl of Beverley, and grandson of Hugh *Percy, first duke of Northumberland. He was born in London on 29 January 1784. His mother was Isabella Susannah (1750–1812), second daughter of Peter Burrell of Beckenham, Kent, and sister of Peter, first Baron Gwydyr. Henry *Percy (1785–1825) and Hugh *Percy (1784–1856) were his younger and twin brothers respectively. Percy entered the navy in February 1797, on the *Sanspareil*, flagship of Lord Hugh Seymour. In 1801 he was moved into the *Amphion*, in which he went to the Mediterranean in 1803, when he followed Nelson and Hardy to the *Victory*; in August he was appointed acting lieutenant of the *Medusa* with Captain (afterwards Sir John) Gore. In her he assisted in the capture of the Spanish treasure ships on 5 October 1804. His commission was confirmed to 30 April 1804.

In 1806 Percy was in the *Diadem* with Sir Home Riggs Popham at the capture of Cape Town. He was promoted on 13 January to command the brig *Espoir*, and was posted the same day to the Dutch ship *Bato*, reported to be in Simon's Bay. The *Bato*, however, was found to have been effectually destroyed, and as the *Espoir* had meantime sailed for England, Percy had to return to the *Diadem* as a volunteer. On 4 March the French 46-gun frigate *Volontaire* came into Table Bay, ignorant of the capture of the Cape. She was seized, commissioned by Percy as a British warship, and sent to St Helena, whence she took charge of the convoy to England. Percy's two promotions were confirmed, dating respectively from 22 January and 25 September 1806.

From 1806 to 1820 Percy was tory MP for his father's pocket borough, Beer Alston, Devon. In 1807 in command of the *Comus* (22 guns), he assisted, under Sir Samuel Hood, in the occupation of Madeira; and in 1808, then captain of the *Nymphe* (36 guns), he carried the French commander, Junot, from Portugal to La Rochelle, according to the convention of Cintra, which stipulated that the beaten French forces be returned to France with all arms and equipment. In November 1810 he was appointed to the 36-gun frigate *Hotspur*, which he commanded on the coast of France, and afterwards at Rio de Janeiro and Buenos Aires, for five years, returning to England at the end of 1815. Percy married, on 9 December 1820, Sophia Elizabeth (*d.* 13 Dec 1875), daughter of Moreton Walhouse of Hatherton, Staffordshire; they had one son and three daughters. On 26 September 1831 he was made a CB, and was promoted rear-admiral on 23 November 1841. He commanded at the Cape of Good Hope from November 1841 until spring 1846. He became vice-admiral on 29 April 1851; and from June 1851 to June 1854 was commander-in-chief at Sheerness. He died at his country seat near Rickmansworth, Hertfordshire, on 19 October 1856.

Percy's younger brother **William Henry Percy** (1788–1855), sixth son of the first earl of Beverley, born on 24 March 1788, entered the navy in May 1801 on the *Lion* (64 guns), in which he went to China. On his return in November 1802 he joined the *Medusa*, of which his elder brother was shortly afterwards appointed acting lieutenant. He was promoted commander on 2 May 1810, and during 1811 commanded the *Mermaid*, transporting troops to the Iberian peninsula. He was posted on 21 March 1812. In 1814 he commanded the *Hermes* (20 guns) on the coast of North America; but, on 4 April, having lost fifty men killed and wounded in an unsuccessful attack on Fort Bowyer, Mobile, his ship was set on fire to prevent her falling into enemy hands. After the peace of 1815 he had no further service in the navy, but was for many years a commissioner of excise. From 1818 to 1826 he was tory MP for Stamford, Lincolnshire, returned through the influence of the second marquess of Exeter, stepson of his maternal aunt, the dowager duchess of Hamilton. He became a rear-admiral on the retired list on 1 October 1846, and died, unmarried, at the home of his brother, the second earl of Beverley, 8 Portman Square, London, on 5 October 1855. J. K. LAUGHTON, rev. ANDREW LAMBERT

Sources D. Syrett and R. L. DiNardo, *The commissioned sea officers of the Royal Navy, 1660–1815*, rev. edn, Occasional Publications of the Navy RS, 1 (1994) · statement of services, PRO, navy records · O'Byrne, *Naval biog. dict.* · *GM*, 3rd ser., 1 (1856), 782 · Burke, *Peerage* · J. Marshall, *Royal naval biography*, suppl. 1 (1827), 184 · Boase, *Mod. Eng. biog.* · HoP, *Commons*

Archives Alnwick Castle, Northumberland, duke of Northumberland MSS

Percy, Lady Mary (*c*.1570–1642), abbess of the Convent of the Assumption of Our Blessed Lady, Brussels, was one of the four daughters of Thomas *Percy, seventh earl of Northumberland (1528–1572), and his wife, Anne Somerset (*d*. 1591). After the earl's execution on 22 August 1572 as a result of his involvement in the 1569 rebellion of the northern earls, his widow fled abroad, leaving her children in England. Later Lady Mary Percy went to Flanders, although it is not clear whether she lived with her mother. She spent some time in Flemish Augustinian convents but the experience left her determined to establish a Benedictine house specifically for Englishwomen. Though not professed as a nun until 1600 she was persuaded by an English Jesuit, Father Hoult, to join with Dorothy and Gertrude Arundell and together they founded a Benedictine convent in Brussels dedicated to the Assumption of Our Blessed Lady. Mary Percy carried out the main practical work relating to the foundation. In April 1598 she bought a house in Hietgatts, Brussels, for 10,500 florins, and obtained permission for the convent from the pope and the local authorities. The new foundation required a sister with appropriate training and qualities to become the first abbess and Mary Percy invited Lady Joanna Berkeley from the Benedictine house at Rheims to take charge of the eight choir nuns and four lay sisters at Brussels. At its dedication on 21 November 1599 Archduke Albert and Archduchess Isabella, rulers of the Spanish Netherlands, laid on a lavish feast inviting the local notables to celebrate. Mary Percy had rejected the offer of a foundation from Archduchess Isabella in order to avoid external control over the choice of abbess. However, the archduchess maintained a personal interest in the welfare of the convent throughout its early years when the choice of a confessor caused bitter disputes.

The origin of the disputes, which split the convent, lay in Abbess Berkeley's decision to permit some nuns to have an English Jesuit as their spiritual director. Under its constitutions the convent was subject to the authority of the archbishop of Malines; he had appointed a secular priest to that position. Mary Percy was unanimously elected abbess in 1616 and seems, at some point, to have forbidden the Jesuits to act as confessors. The chief dissidents, under Lucy Knatchbull, left Brussels to found a convent in Ghent in 1624. A new confessor, Anthony Champney, vice-president of Douai, was appointed in 1628 but was unacceptable to the remaining nineteen dissidents who complained to the papal nuncio. Mary Percy took their lack of obedience as a challenge to her authority and a breach of monastic vows, and the dispute escalated with appeals to Rome. Peace was not finally restored until 1639 when she reported to Cardinal Barberini that the archbishop of Malines had intervened. In a letter written in 1634 she referred to the 'many unrests which afflicted and agitated our poor convent for many years which were like a fire enclosed in the precincts of our walls' (Arblaster, 519).

Despite the problems of its early years the reputation of the convent and the gentility of its sisters attracted a number of aristocratic recruits with substantial dowries. The account books show that until 1618 receipts were always higher than expenses, allowing part of the dowry income to be banked. New buildings were erected: 7000 florins were spent on a new house for scholars before 1616 and a new chapel was dedicated in 1618. From the start, high standards were established in the practice of the liturgy and the observance of monastic hours, and the vigour of the spirituality of the nuns was widely admired. Musicians taught Gregorian chant and after she became abbess Mary Percy sought out the service of the distinguished English organist and composer Richard Dering who described himself as organist to the English convent at Brussels.

An educated woman, Mary Percy was responsible for most of the work on the translation, from a French edition, of Achilles Galhardi's *Breve compendio intorno alla perfezione cristiana*, being assisted by Anthony Hoskins. It was published in 1612 but for some time her contribution was unknown due to the omission of her initials from the second printing. A measure of the respect in which she was held by contemporaries may be seen in the dedication to her of Miles Carr's 1632 translation of I. P. Camus's *La lutte spirituelle*, where he describes her as having a mind 'full of prime nobilitie, pure Religion, solide pietie, prudence, candor and native goodnesse' (Carr, 5r). She died in 1642, but her foundation, in spite of the problems that tore it apart, survived and continued to attract recruits, many of whom came from families persecuted for their religion in England. It was the spiritual source of the other English Benedictine communities founded for women in the first half of the seventeenth century and is an example of a successful pioneering venture carried out largely under female organization. The standards set in the Brussels house for contemplative life were widely admired and respected.

CAROLINE M. K. BOWDEN

Sources *Chronicle of the first monastery founded at Brussels for English Benedictine nuns* (1898) · P. Arblaster, 'The infanta and the English Benedictine nuns: Mary Percy's memories in 1634', *Recusant History*, 23 (1996–7), 508–27 · A. Pasture, ed., 'Documents concernant quelques monastères anglais aux Pays-Bas au 17e siècle', *Bulletin de l'Institut Historique Belge du Rome*, 10–12 (1930–32) · J. S. Hansom, ed., 'The register books of the professions, etc., of the English Benedictine nuns at Brussels and Winchester', *Miscellanea, IX*, Catholic RS, 14 (1914), 174–203 · D. Lunn, *The English Benedictines, 1540–1688* (1980) · A. F. Allison, 'New light on the early history of the *Breve compendio*: the background to the English translation of 1612', *Recusant History*, 4 (1957–8), 4–17 · P. Guilday, *The English Catholic refugees on the continent, 1558–1795* (1914) · C. Dodd [H. Tootell], *The church history of England, from the year 1500, to the year 1688*, 3 vols. (1737–42) · GEC, *Peerage*

Archives Downside Abbey, Bath, 'Ann account of all such monie as the first beginners of this Inglish monasteri of the Holie Order of S Benet in Brussells had in stock at the first erection of that Anno 1599' · Downside Abbey, Bath, 'An historical account of the first establishment of the convent of the English Dames of the Holy Order of St Benedict att Bruxells'

Likenesses marble effigy; formerly at East Bergholt convent, Suffolk

Percy, Matilda de, **countess of Warwick** (*d.* 1204), magnate, was the daughter of William de Percy (*d.* 1175) and his first wife, Alice of Tonbridge (d. 1148). She became the eventual coheir of her father after the death before 1175 of her brother Alan de Percy. Her sister and coheir was Agnes de Percy, who married Joscelin de Louvain, the brother of Adeliza, second wife of Henry I. Matilda was born at Catton, near Stamford Bridge, Yorkshire, and was married to William, earl of Warwick (d. 1184), as his second wife. In the partition of the Percy estates in 1175 Matilda's husband received the equivalent of twenty knights' fees, while Joscelin and Agnes received twenty-three. Some lands were held in common, but in general it seems that Matilda and Earl William may have received the less profitable upland areas in Yorkshire. During the lifetime of her husband Matilda was actively involved in the administration of her inheritance: on 28 December 1175 she confirmed various lands to Fountains, for example, and she and Warwick jointly granted other charters to that abbey. Between 1175 and 1181 they set about the restoration of her father's foundation of Sawley Abbey in Yorkshire by granting it the hospital of Tadcaster.

In 1185, after her husband's death, Matilda owed 700 marks to the king for inheritance of her father's land, her dower, and to have the freedom from marrying at the king's will. She continued to patronize religious houses after 1184, acquiring a seal to authenticate her documents. She made various benefactions to Fountains Abbey, Sawley Abbey, Kirkstead Abbey, Warter Priory, Stainfield Priory, Lincolnshire, the hospital of St Peter, York, and Tadcaster church. As a dowager she continued to work for the fortunes of Sawley, which had suffered severe depredations at the hands of the Scots, with a renewal of her former grant made with her husband, confirmation of which she sought from Henry II c.1181. As part of her role as a great lay landholder she administered her lands, rewarded servants, and enfeoffed vassals on her lands: for example, at some time between 1175 and 1194 she granted lands to the value of a quarter of a knight's fee to Henry de Puiset for which he gave her 15 silver marks and a palfrey. She had a female chamberlain, Juliana of Warwick, to whom she granted lands in Yorkshire which were subsequently given by Juliana to Fountains. In 1195 she accounted for 40 marks for scutage owing on fifteen knights. On her death, before 13 October in 1204, Matilda was buried at her favourite religious house of Fountains Abbey in Yorkshire.   SUSAN M. JOHNS

Sources W. Farrer and others, eds., *Early Yorkshire charters*, 12 vols. (1914–65) · *VCH Cheshire*, vol. 3 · GEC, *Peerage* · Pipe rolls, 5–34 Henry II

Percy, Peter (*fl.* 1486), alchemist, is known only from one tract preserved in two later transcripts in the Ashmole collection at the Bodleian Library. The earliest of these, in Bodl. Oxf., MS Ashmole 1423, was made in 1595 by Thomas Mountford, a London doctor, alchemist, and antiquary. The second, in MS Ashmole 1406, was made in 1600, probably by another physician, Simon Forman (d. 1611), who had read and written his name into Mountford's copy in 1598. Percy's tract, which bears the date 1486, is a record of alchemical practice, incorporating sixty-two recipes, three in English and the rest in Latin, all making frequent

use of the symbolic alphabet of the Hermetic vocabulary. It has none of the theoretical and literary content found in the works of better known fifteenth-century alchemists. The heading of the transcription made in 1600 states that Percy was a 'canon' of the college at Maidstone in Kent. Secular colleges often served as local centres of medical practice and were therefore likely to cultivate alchemy as a related discipline. It is unlikely that Peter Percy was a close relative of the Percy earls of Northumberland. There had been Percys settled in Kent from at least the thirteenth century and in 1456 Robert Percy, a tailor from Erith, led an insurrection against the crown.

ANTHONY GROSS

Sources Bodl. Oxf., MS Ashmole 1406, art IV, fols. 79ff. · Bodl. Oxf., MS Ashmole 1423, fols. 11–81 · L. M. Eldredge, *A handlist of manuscripts containing Middle English prose in the Ashmole collection, Bodleian Library, Oxford* (1992) · W. H. Black, *A descriptive, analytical and critical catalogue of the manuscripts bequeathed unto the University of Oxford by Elias Ashmole*, 2 vols. (1845–66) · I. M. W. Harvey, *Jack Cade's rebellion of 1450* (1991)
Archives Bodl. Oxf., MSS Ashmole 1406, art IV; 1423

Percy, Sir Ralph (1425–1464), soldier, was the son (probably the seventh) of Henry *Percy, second earl of Northumberland (1394–1455), and Eleanor (d. after 1465), widow of Richard Despenser, styled Lord Despenser, and daughter of Ralph *Neville, first earl of Westmorland, and Joan *Beaufort. He was born on 11 August 1425 at Leconfield in the East Riding of Yorkshire. He spent his life in support of his family and of the house of Lancaster. He was active on commissions in Northumberland, being on the commissions of the peace there in 1447, 1455, and 1460, and on various other commissions in the 1440s and 1450s, including the commission of array in December 1459. He was knighted between July 1448 and April 1449, and was steward of his father's court in Northumberland in 1450. He took a leading part with his brothers in the rivalry between the Nevilles and Percys and was commanded with his eldest brother, Lord Poynings, to appear before the king's council in May 1454 to answer for his part in disturbances in Yorkshire (although this letter was never sent: (*Proceedings ... of the Privy Council*, 6.179)). With his brother Richard he pledged himself in the sum of 2000 marks for offences against the duke of York and his associates in March 1458. Before this he fought at the first battle of St Albans in May 1455. He also fought at the battle of Wakefield and was afterwards named as one of those responsible for the death of the duke of York.

Sir Ralph married, before about 1452, Eleanor (d. after 1498), daughter of Lawrence Acton, of Acton, Northumberland, and his wife, Matilda. They had three sons, Sir Henry (d. 1486), Sir Ralph (d. after 1489), and George (d. 1500), and probably one daughter, Margaret.

In 1457 Percy was appointed constable of the castle of Dunstanburgh, although he had apparently been living there as deputy constable, possibly from 1451, and the last few years of his life were spent in and around the castles on the north-east coast. He does not appear to have fought at the battle of Towton, since he was not attainted afterwards. He surrendered Dunstanburgh at Michaelmas 1461 and was allowed to hold it for Edward IV. In October 1462, however, when Margaret of Anjou landed with a small army on the north-east coast, Sir Ralph Percy surrendered Dunstanburgh to her and with others was placed by her in command of Bamburgh Castle. By December, Bamburgh and Dunstanburgh were under siege by the earl of Warwick and on 27 December, Percy reversed his loyalties again and surrendered on condition that if he swore allegiance to Edward IV, he would be given back command of Bamburgh, as was done. To show his trust, on 17 March, Edward further granted Percy authority to receive unattainted repentant rebels into the king's grace, at Percy's discretion. At about the same time Percy reversed his allegiance for the last time and allowed the Scottish and French supporters of Margaret of Anjou to occupy the two castles of Bamburgh and Dunstanburgh.

By December 1463 Percy had been joined in Bamburgh by the duke of Somerset and Henry VI. In the early months of 1464 Percy and Somerset were raiding in Northumberland and further afield and, having learnt that Lord Montagu, with a small force, was travelling to the Scottish border to escort Scottish ambassadors, attempted to intercept him. Montagu was warned in time to avoid ambush but was attacked at Hedgeley Moor by Percy and his forces on or about 25 April 1464. Percy's force was routed and he himself killed. Traditionally, as he lay dying he cried out that he had 'saved the bird in his bosom' (Hall, 260), said to mean that he had kept his oath to Henry VI—a rather strange meaning if true, given his disloyalty to both sides. A column called Percy's Cross still stands on the traditional spot where Sir Ralph fell. He was attainted in parliament in 1465.

                                                    P. W. HAMMOND

Sources C. Ross, *Edward IV* (1974) · C. L. Scofield, *The life and reign of Edward the Fourth*, 1 (1923) · R. L. Storey, *The end of the house of Lancaster* (1966) · *Collins peerage of England: genealogical, biographical and historical*, ed. E. Brydges, 9 vols. (1812), vol. 2 · *Hall's chronicle*, ed. H. Ellis (1809), 260 · R. Somerville, *History of the duchy of Lancaster, 1265–1603* (1953), 538 · *CPR, 1446–52*, 183 · J. Stevenson, ed., *Letters and papers illustrative of the wars of the English in France during the reign of Henry VI, king of England*, 1, Rolls Series, 22 (1861), 491 · *RotP*, 5.511 · N. H. Nicolas, ed., *Proceedings and ordinances of the privy council of England*, 7 vols., RC, 26 (1834–7), vol. 6

Percy, Reuben. *See* Byerley, Thomas (1789–1826).

Percy, Richard de (*b.* before 1181, *d.* 1244), baron, was the second son of Agnes (*d. c.*1202), heir of the original Percy family, and Joscelin de *Louvain (*d.* 1180), a younger son of Godefroi, duke of Lower Lorraine, and brother of Queen *Adeliza, wife of Henry I. Besides his elder brother Richard de Percy had two brothers and four sisters. He first appears in the pipe rolls in 1181. Some time in or before 1198 Percy's elder brother, Henry, died, leaving a son, William de *Percy (1191x3–1245), to whom Joscelin de Louvain's lands passed, but when Agnes de Percy died *c.*1202, Richard, probably taking advantage of the fact that King John had inherited the kingdom in preference to the son of a dead older brother, was able to claim her lands. He also obtained a small part of the lands of his aunt Matilda, the other heir to the Percy lands, when she died *c.*1204, although in an apparent compromise between the claims

of uncle and nephew the bulk of Matilda's lands went to William de Percy, who in 1214, shortly after he came of age, claimed Richard's lands. This sparked an ongoing legal battle, punctuated by short-lived settlements, that lasted until 1234, when a more permanent settlement was made.

Richard de Percy served frequently on royal expeditions early in John's reign but he was one of the northern barons who began the struggle which ended in the signing of Magna Carta by refusing to accompany the king to France in 1214. On 7 May 1215 he and some others made an attempt to treat with the king; one of the twenty-five executors of Magna Carta, he was excommunicated by Innocent III by name on 26 December. In 1216 he and other northern barons reduced Yorkshire to the obedience of the dauphin, Louis of France. On 11 May 1217 Henry III granted Percy's lands to his nephew William, but they were restored by the king on Percy's submission on 2 November.

Percy helped to besiege Ralph de Gaugi in Newark Castle in 1218, and was one of three barons charged with the destruction of Skipton Castle in 1221; he served on campaign with the king in 1224 and 1230. In 1236 he appears among the witnesses of the confirmation of the charters. Percy generally maintained a low political profile in Henry III's reign, but in 1237, when in the parliament the barons prepared to deliberate apart on the king's demands, Gilbert Basset suggested to the king that he should send some of his friends to attend the conference. The words caught the ear of Richard de Percy, and he indignantly cried, 'What did you say, friend Gilbert? Are we foreigners then, and not friends of the king?' (Paris, 3.381–2).

Percy married first Alice, of unknown parentage; on her death he married Agnes de Neville. He had a son, Henry, who must have been illegitimate since Percy's heir was his nephew William. Percy died in 1244, before 18 August. During his lifetime, he made gifts to the priory of St Lô in Rouen, Sallay Abbey, and Fountains Abbey, to which he gave Litton and Littondale in return for £100 a year for life; if arrangements specified in a grant to Fountains were carried out, he was buried in that house.

                              W. E. RHODES, *rev.* HUGH M. THOMAS

Sources J. C. Holt, *The northerners: a study in the reign of King John*, new edn (1992) · W. Farrer and others, eds., *Early Yorkshire charters*, 12 vols. (1914–65), vol. 11 · [M. T. Martin], ed., *The Percy chartulary*, SurtS, 117 (1911) · *Chancery records* · Paris, *Chron.* · *Rogeri de Wendover liber qui dicitur flores historiarum*, ed. H. G. Hewlett, 3 vols., Rolls Series, [84] (1886–9) · *Pipe rolls* · W. T. Lancaster, *Abstracts of the charters and other documents contained in the chartulary of the Cistercian abbey of Fountains*, 2 vols. (1915) · *Curia regis rolls preserved in the Public Record Office* (1922–) · D. M. Stenton, ed., *Rolls of the justices in eyre ... Yorkshire in 3 Henry III, 1218–1219*, SeldS, 56 (1937) · J. Parker, ed., *Feet of fines for the county of York, 3: from 1218 to 1231*, Yorkshire Archaeological Society, 62 (1921) · C. Roberts, ed., *Excerpta è rotulis finium in Turri Londinensi asservatis, Henrico Tertio rege, AD 1216–1272*, 2 vols., RC, 32 (1835–6)

Percy, Sidney Richard (1821–1886), landscape painter, was born in Lambeth, London, the fifth son of the landscape painter Edward *Williams (1781–1855) and his wife,

Sidney Richard Percy (1821–1886), by unknown photographer [detail]

Ann Hildebrandt (*bap.* 1780, *d.* 1851); their six sons all became successful landscape painters, three of them working under other names to avoid confusion. Henry John *Boddington (1811–1865) adopted his wife's surname but Arthur Gilbert (1819–1895) and Percy used their last forename.

S. R. Percy, as he was known, trained with his father but soon evolved an individual style which was to establish him as one of the most popular landscape artists of the Victorian era. He was best-known for highly finished paintings of dramatic mountain scenes in Wales, Scotland, and the Lake District, executed with a fluent use of colour and a marked sense of design. A view of Llyn-y-Ddinas in north Wales, exhibited at the Royal Academy in 1853, was described in the *Art Journal* of that year as 'A work of very high character, everywhere powerful, leaving nothing to be desired'. His pictures in this manner, with gleaming lakes and watering cattle, achieved such a fashionable vogue that there is an inevitable similarity in many of these scenes. He exhibited over 300 works in London exhibitions, including the Society of British Artists, and also in the provinces and at the Paris Salon.

In 1846 Percy left central London to join his father at 32 Castelnau Villas (now 92 Castelnau) in the suburban district of Barnes. On 30 June 1857 he married Emily Charlotte Fairlam (1835/6–1904), daughter of a local jeweller, who had stipulated that she would not consider any suitor with less than £2000 a year, a condition which Percy was more than able to meet. After some years at Florence Villa, Inner Park Road, Wimbledon Park, Surrey, the couple moved in 1863 to Hill House, Great Missenden, Buckinghamshire, where they were neighbours of the watercolourist William Callow, who later remembered Percy as a clever landscape painter, with a gentle and retiring nature. Percy's only visit to the continent was with Callow in 1865.

The characteristic foreground figures which appear in many of Percy's paintings were directly based on his own photographs of Gypsy girls from the encampments on Barnes and Wimbledon commons; a series of these photographs is now in the Victoria and Albert Museum, London. His obituarist in *The Athenaeum* later described him as 'The well known and popular landscape painter, founder of the so-called School of Barnes'. There is no evidence for such a movement, which is now thought to have been a light-hearted term, which was subsequently given too much credence.

Percy returned to the London area in 1873, living at Bickley Lodge, Meadvale, Redhill, Surrey. His final home was at Woodseat, Mulgrave Road, Sutton, Surrey (dem. 1969), where he died, aged sixty-four, on 13 April 1886, following the amputation of a leg. He was buried at Beckenham, Kent. Percy and his wife had four children, but two died young. His surviving son, Herbert Sidney Percy (1863–c.1940), painted landscapes and portraits in a capable technique but with only minor success. His younger daughter wrote novels under the name of Mrs Fred Reynolds. Her elder son, Richard Frederic Reynolds, killed in action in 1918, was a pupil of Stanhope Forbes. The extravagances of his much younger wife had caused Percy to live up to his income and he was therefore only able to leave £712; a studio sale was held at Christies on 27 November 1886.

Many national and some international collections have landscapes by Percy. *In Snowdonia* (1853) is held in the Tate collection. *The Fern Gatherers* (1857), in the Castle Museum, Nottingham, includes the foreground figures typical of his work, as do examples in the Ferens Art Gallery, Hull. Among his works in the Museum and Art Gallery, Salford, is *Autumn in the Highlands*; and there are also examples in the Victoria Art Gallery, Bath; the National Museum and Gallery of Wales, Cardiff; Temple Newsam House, Leeds; the Leicestershire Museum and Art Gallery; the Mappin Art Gallery, Sheffield; the Sunderland Museum and Art Gallery; the City Art Gallery, York; and the Musée des Beaux-Arts, Montreal, Canada. *Llyn Dulyn, North Wales*, purchased by Prince Albert in 1854 as a present for Queen Victoria, is in the Royal Collection at Osborne House, Isle of Wight.   JAN REYNOLDS

Sources J. Reynolds, *The Williams family of painters* (1975) · *Art Journal*, 15 (1853), 150 · Graves, *RA exhibitors*, 6 (1906), 106 · Graves, *Brit. Inst.*, 423–4 · J. Johnson, ed., *Works exhibited at the Royal Society of British Artists, 1824–1893, and the New English Art Club, 1888–1917*, 2 vols. (1975) · W. Callow, *William Callow, RWS, FRGS: an autobiography*, ed. H. M. Cundall (1908) · J. Reynolds, *William Callow* (1980) · *Gazette des Beaux-Arts*, 15 (1863), 40, 42 · *The Athenaeum* (1 May 1886), 592 · private information (2004) · Wood, *Vic. painters*, 2nd edn · CGPLA Eng. & Wales (1886)

Likenesses daguerreotype, *c.*1845–1850, priv. coll.; copy, NPG · photograph (in later life), priv. coll.; copy, NPG · photograph, priv. coll. [*see illus.*]

Wealth at death £712 14s.: probate, 20 May 1886, CGPLA Eng. & Wales

Percy, Thomas (*c.*1332–1369). *See under* Percy, Henry, second Lord Percy (1301–1352).

Percy, Thomas, earl of Worcester (*c.*1343–1403), soldier and diplomat, was the younger son of Henry *Percy, third Lord Percy (*c.*1321–1368), and Mary (*d.* 1362), daughter of

*Henry of Lancaster, a grandson of Henry III recognized as earl of Lancaster in 1327. Mary's niece, Blanche, married John of Gaunt, duke of Lancaster, and he, Richard II, and Henry IV acknowledged the Percys as kinsmen. Thomas's brother, Henry *Percy (1341–1408), was created earl of Northumberland on 16 July 1377. Thomas Percy never married. His father granted him three manors in Yorkshire, Lincolnshire, and Leicestershire for life or term of years in 1364 and 1368, but he spent almost all his life serving as a soldier, commander, diplomat, household officer, and councillor.

War and capture Percy probably began his career as a soldier in Aquitaine in the early 1360s and was certainly in Gascony in 1367. He may have served with Edward, the Black Prince, and Gaunt in Spain and at the battle of Nájera in 1367. From 1369 he is frequently mentioned in Froissart's chronicles, and record sources often confirm the facts. Early in 1369 Percy was with the Black Prince in Bordeaux, and in the summer, now seneschal of La Rochelle, he served under Sir John Chandos in Sir Robert Knolles's campaign in the Dordogne and Quercy. He was with Chandos at the siege of the castle of La Roche-sur-Yon in Poitou, which was granted to Gaunt and leased by him to Percy and two others. He was serving under Chandos when the latter was killed at Mortemer on 31 December 1369 and succeeded him as seneschal of Poitou and governor of the Île d'Oléron. In 1370 and 1371 he served on a number of campaigns including the siege and sack of Limoges in September 1370 under the Black Prince—who granted him an annuity of £100 and considerable forfeited land in Aquitaine—and then under the prince's lieutenant, Gaunt. The English suffered a series of defeats in 1372 and in the late summer Percy was captured in a night engagement at Soubise by 'Houwel Flinc', a Welshman serving under Owen of Wales with the Castilian fleet which had defeated the earl of Pembroke's fleet at La Rochelle on 23–24 June. Percy was taken to Paris and on 10 January 1373 Houwel surrendered him to the king of France who permitted him to return to England until Easter to raise a ransom. He was still a prisoner in December, and was given his final release by Jean, duke of Berri, only on 2 October 1374.

Service and its rewards Percy's reputation as a knight was now high and, probably recommended by the Black Prince and Gaunt, he became a king's knight and by April 1376 a Garter knight. In December 1375 he brought a report to Edward III from Gaunt and others negotiating with the French at Bruges and in January 1377 was sent to Flanders to bring a report from Jean, duke of Brittany, who had asked for a council knight and specified Thomas Percy. On 5 November 1376 Edward III granted him an annuity of 100 marks at the exchequer and permitted his brother to grant him another of 100 marks from the 500 marks he received from the customs of Berwick. Richard II confirmed these grants on 1 February 1378, describing Percy as retained for life. Royal pardons were now granted at his request and he served in many ways. For example,

he attended his brother at Richard II's coronation; in October 1378 he and another royal knight brought John Wyclif before the Commons in parliament to attack the right of sanctuary; in June 1381 he was one of the group that accompanied Richard to meet the rebel peasants at Mile End, and he took part in the suppression of the revolt in Essex and St Albans.

Percy rarely served in north-east England and the border, the area of most Percy lands and interests. He was one of the joint keepers of the eastern marches for a few months in 1377 and from 1383 to 1384; a commissioner to negotiate with the Scots in 1378, 1384, and 1398; and keeper of the isolated castle of Roxburgh from 24 June 1377 to 1380 or 1381. He served in Richard II's army in Scotland in 1385 with sixty men-at-arms and sixty archers. He must have seen little of Roxburgh for he served at sea, with large forces of soldiers and sailors, as commander under the earl of Buckingham in 1377–8 and under Gaunt in 1378; as admiral of the north in 1379; and with Sir Baldwin Raddington in 1385. He and Sir Hugh Calveley were joint captains of Brest, leased from the duke of Brittany, from 20 May 1379 until 24 June 1381, when Percy became sole captain until 18 February 1386.

Percy was out of England during the political upheavals of 1386–8, for on 15 February 1386 he contracted to serve with 80 men-at-arms and 160 archers on Gaunt's expedition to Spain, and about this time he became Gaunt's feed retainer. He was admiral of Gaunt's fleet which sailed from Plymouth on 7 July and fought in the campaign in Galicia and beyond. But his more important role was as a diplomat. He accompanied Gaunt's daughter Philippa to Portugal for her marriage to King João and was commissioned on 10 June 1387, with Sir John Trailly, to negotiate a settlement of Gaunt's claims with Castilian envoys at Trancoso in Portugal. By July a draft treaty had been agreed and at the turn of the year Percy returned to England to report it to King Richard. He was back in Bayonne in June 1388 and the treaty—'whose sponsor and promoter was lord Thomas Percy' (Thompson, 369)—was ratified there on 8 July with Percy, styled Gaunt's chamberlain, the first witness.

Percy remained Gaunt's retainer and served with him on commissions; in February 1398 he was the first-named lay executor of Gaunt's will. But early in 1390 he began to receive commissions, grants, and appointments from Richard II, and became an important courtier. He was under-chamberlain of Richard's household from 22 February 1390 to 22 February 1393 and steward of his household from 24 March 1393 to late August 1399. He accompanied Richard to Ireland in 1395 and 1399. While under-chamberlain Percy often attended the king's council and as steward regularly witnessed royal charters. He served on missions to France (1391–3) and was justiciar of south Wales (1390–99). In the September parliament of 1397, where Richard took revenge on four lords for their part in restricting his authority in 1386–8, Percy was proctor for the clergy to approve the verdicts and sentences. He then shared in the rewards. On 29 September he was created earl of Worcester and received forfeited property valued at £400 a year. Further grants followed, and in October his brother granted him the castle, town, and forest of Jedburgh and now the full annuity of 500 marks that he himself received from Berwick. For the first time he was well endowed.

A change of loyalty Percy accompanied Richard to Ireland in June 1399, and, when Gaunt's son, Henry Bolingbroke, returned from exile and raised an army, returned in late July with the king to south-west Wales. Near Carmarthen, Richard, now aware of the collapse of support for him in England, abandoned his army and rode to Conwy with a few friends. Percy was not one of them, not surprisingly because his brother was Henry's principal supporter. Walsingham reports that Richard released Percy and his household and that Percy broke his steward's rod. In contrast to French writers English sources do not charge him with disloyalty. He joined Henry Bolingbroke at Chester but did not take a prominent part in the deposition of Richard or the accession of Henry IV. Very soon, however, he was active in Henry IV's service. By 12 October as 'our very dear and faithful cousin' he had been appointed to head the delicate negotiations with French envoys about the maintenance of the truce and the restoration of Richard II's queen, Isabella (PRO, E 404/15/33). These negotiations continued until 1401 and it was Percy himself who delivered Isabella to the count of St Pol on 31 July near Calais. Percy was an active member of the king's council from November 1399—a French envoy describes his leading role there in the absence of the king in October 1400. He was again steward of the household from 1 March 1401 until early March 1402; admiral of the north and west from November 1399 until April 1401; and one of those who conducted Joan of Navarre, duchess of Brittany (d. 1437), to England in January 1403 to marry Henry IV. In 1399 Percy had been obliged to surrender the forfeited property he had been granted in 1397, but he was compensated by an annuity of 500 marks and his other royal grants were confirmed.

Rebellion and death Percy had received life grants of the lordships and castles of Emelyn in 1390 and Haverfordwest in 1393, and an annuity of 100 marks in south Wales from 1396; although he was no longer justiciar, he retained these grants in 1399 and it was in Wales that he ended his career of service. On 21 October 1401 he was appointed king's lieutenant in south Wales, with particular responsibility for the castles of Cardigan and Aberystwyth, and in November he became governor of Henry, prince of Wales. He could now normally attend the council only in the early months of the year; much of the rest he spent in Wales. He and his nephew, Henry Percy (Hotspur), who had served in north Wales, were frustrated by royal policy in Wales and the failure to pay them on time. His last campaign was in June and July 1403 under Prince Henry in north Wales, for which he provided the largest retinue. In early July, Hotspur came to Chester to mount a rebellion and Thomas Percy joined him with many of his retinue. They were surprised when they reached Shrewsbury on 20 July to find that the king had already joined

Prince Henry there. The following morning the king offered negotiations in which Percy played a central role, and Walsingham accuses him of obstructing and misrepresenting them. If true, this was probably because Percy felt that it was too late to draw back. Whatever the case, a fierce battle followed in which Hotspur was killed and Thomas Percy was captured. He was summarily tried and beheaded two days later (23 July) and his head was displayed on London Bridge until December. His body was interred in the abbey church of St Peter in Shrewsbury. The January parliament of 1404 declared his actions to be treasonable but the parliament of 1484 reversed his attainder and forfeiture. Froissart describes Thomas Percy as a gentle, loyal, and valiant knight, and throughout his life others wrote about him in similar terms.

A. L. BROWN

Sources J. Froissart, Œuvres, ed. K. de Letterhove (1866–77) · M. D. Legge, ed., *Anglo-Norman letters and petitions from All Souls MS 182*, Anglo-Norman Texts, 3 (1941) · *Thomae Walsingham, quondam monachi S. Albani, historia Anglicana*, ed. H. T. Riley, 2 vols., pt 1 of *Chronica monasterii S. Albani*, Rolls Series, 28 (1863–4) · *Johannis de Trokelowe et Henrici de Blaneforde … chronica et annales*, ed. H. T. Riley, pt 3 of *Chronica monasterii S. Albani*, Rolls Series, 28 (1866) · [T. Walsingham], *Chronicon Angliae, ab anno Domini 1328 usque ad annum 1388*, ed. E. M. Thompson, Rolls Series, 64 (1874) · *Chancery records* · T. Carte, *Catalogue des rolles gascons, normands et françois, conservés dans les archives de la Tour de Londres*, 2 vols. (1743) · *RotS* · J. M. W. Bean, *The estates of the Percy family, 1416–1537* (1958) · J. W. Sherborne, 'The English navy: shipping and manpower, 1369–1389', *Past and Present*, 37 (1967), 163–75 · PRO, E 404/15/33 · PRO, E 404/17/234 · PRO, E 101/38/3 · PRO, E 101/178/20

Percy, Thomas, first Baron Egremont (1422–1460), nobleman, was the second surviving son of Henry *Percy, second earl of Northumberland (1394–1455), and Eleanor Neville, daughter of Ralph *Neville, first earl of Westmorland. Born on 29 November 1422 at the Percy manor of Leconfield, Yorkshire, he has been described as 'Quarrelsome, violent and contemptuous of all authority' (Storey, 125). As a young man he was embroiled in riots and disturbances which may have embarrassed his father and elder brother, Lord Poynings [see Percy, Henry, third earl of Northumberland]. In July 1447 he was involved in a skirmish at Stamford Bridge with tenants of the archbishop of York, with whom the Percys had been at odds; he was imprisoned at York as a result. Thereafter, Thomas concentrated on consolidating his family's power in Cumberland, where he held the Percy honour of Cockermouth. His father was doubtless instrumental in securing his creation, by royal patent, as Baron Egremont, a title derived from the Percy castle in Cumberland, on 20 November 1449, in expectation of his 'keping of the rest and pees of oure lande' (Proceedings … of the Privy Council, 6.159), together with a modest annual grant of £10 from Cumberland's revenue. His regime in Cumberland was turbulent: during 1449–53 he was involved in disorder, lawlessness, and attacks on royal officials, including the sheriff (1453). This intensified Percy rivalry with the Nevilles, which his brother's election as bishop of Carlisle in August 1452 doubtless accentuated. Nevertheless, on a visit to London in February 1452, he joined the king in confronting the duke of York at Dartford, Kent. By 1453 Egremont was recruiting followers on the Percy estates in Yorkshire and in the city of York, where he quarrelled with John Neville, the earl of Salisbury's younger son. In June both were summoned to the king's council; Egremont refused to respond and in July he was accordingly instructed to keep the peace and even to prepare to sail to Gascony. Towards the end of July an inquiry into disturbances in all the northern shires led to an order to Egremont and John Neville to keep the peace on pain of forfeiture; Northumberland and Salisbury were required to ensure their sons' good behaviour. But on 24 August Egremont, his brother Richard, and a large retinue of Yorkshiremen, with others from Cockermouth, attacked a Neville party returning from the wedding of Thomas Neville and Lord Cromwell's niece at Tattershall, Lincolnshire, to Sheriff Hutton, Yorkshire; at Heworth, near York, the ambush involved almost the entire Percy and Neville clans. The situation remained explosive, and in October another clash seemed likely between Percys and Nevilles at Topcliffe. When the duke of Exeter, for his own dynastic and territorial reasons, intervened on the Percys' side, the feud acquired a new dimension. Egremont met Exeter in January 1454 and at Tuxford, Nottinghamshire, 'ben sworne togider' (Gairdner, 2.296). After Egremont was reported to be raising forces in preparation for the forthcoming parliament, he was summoned to attend the council on 3 March and, following condemnation in parliament, another summons was issued on 10 May. That same month, the duke of York, as protector of the realm, decided to move in person against Egremont and Exeter and the men they were assembling at Spofforth and elsewhere in Yorkshire, Cumberland, and Westmorland; they were even negotiating with the Scots. Exeter, Egremont, and Richard Percy fled, but a commission at York in June investigated their activities: recruiting men and giving livery to those who were not their personal retainers, lawyers, or servants. Although Exeter was apprehended, Egremont eluded capture. At the end of October 1454, at Stamford Bridge, the Percys, led by Egremont and Richard, fought a battle with the Nevilles; the two Percys were captured and, in November, condemned by justices who ordered them to pay the Nevilles £11,200; both were consigned to Newgate prison. Two years later Egremont escaped, much to the Nevilles' anger.

By 1458 the Percys were valued allies of the Lancastrian monarch. At the formal reconciliation of leading nobles organized by Henry VI in March 1458, Egremont concluded a bond of 10,000 marks with York and the Nevilles; but the large fine previously imposed on him was reduced to a bond of 4000 marks to keep the peace for ten years towards Salisbury, his family, and retainers. Moreover, in June, Egremont was granted for life the castle and manor of Wressle, Yorkshire, the former Percy manor whose possession by Lord Cromwell had been at the heart of the disturbances of 1453. A fortnight later he received permission to leave the realm with twelve servants in order to go on pilgrimage, as he promised at the March reconciliation. Whether he did so or not is unclear. He had certainly returned to England by December 1459, when he was granted the constableship of the duke of York's forfeited castle of Conisbrough, along with a life annuity of £40. Egremont was at the battle of Northampton on 10 July 1460, fighting in support of Henry VI whom Warwick captured. He was probably beheaded after the battle: Warwick could be pardoned if he felt satisfaction that the bane of his family's fortunes in the north for a dozen years had been dispatched. Percy is not known to have married, but his son, Sir John *Egremont, was born c.1459.

R. A. GRIFFITHS

Sources PRO · *Chancery records* · N. H. Nicolas, ed., *Proceedings and ordinances of the privy council of England*, 7 vols., RC, 26 (1834–7) · *The Paston letters, AD 1422–1509*, ed. J. Gairdner, new edn, 6 vols. (1904) · *RotP*, vol. 5 · 'John Benet's chronicle for the years 1400 to 1462', ed. G. L. Harriss, *Camden miscellany, XXIV*, CS, 4th ser., 9 (1972) · R. L. Storey, *The end of the house of Lancaster* (1966) · H. Summerson, *Medieval Carlisle: the city and the borders from the late eleventh to the mid-sixteenth century*, 2, Cumberland and Westmorland Antiquarian and Archaeological Society, extra ser., 25 (1993) · A. J. Pollard, *North-eastern England during the Wars of the Roses: lay society, war and politics, 1450–1500* (1990) · R. A. Griffiths, 'Local rivalries and national politics: the Percies, the Nevilles, and the duke of Exeter, 1452–55', *Speculum*, 43 (1968), 589–632 · C. L. Kingsford, ed., *Chronicles of London* (1905)

Percy, Thomas, seventh earl of Northumberland (1528–1572), magnate and rebel, was born on 10 June 1528, the elder son of Sir Thomas Percy (*b.* after 1502, *d.* 1537), rebel, and his wife, Eleanor (or Alianore; *b.* in or before 1513, *d.* 1567), daughter of Guiscard Harbottal of Beamish, co. Durham. His younger brothers were Henry *Percy, eighth earl of Northumberland (*c.*1532–1585), magnate, and Guiscard Percy, who died in infancy. He had three sisters, Joan (*d.* 1572), Mary (*d.* 1598), and Katherine. Sir Thomas and his brother Ingram Percy were disaffected when they were disinherited by their childless elder brother Henry Algernon *Percy, sixth earl of Northumberland (*c.*1502–1537), magnate, who began alienating land to the crown and others some years before his death. Sir Thomas Percy headed 10,000 Richmondshire and North Riding men during the Pilgrimage of Grace from October 1536. Early the following year his name was invoked to try to start new revolts in the North and West Ridings of Yorkshire. As a result, he was executed at Tyburn on 2 June 1537. Ingram Percy apparently died naturally about the same time, probably in prison.

The Percy restoration, 1549–1558 The pilgrimage's suppressor, Thomas Howard, third duke of Norfolk, sent Thomas and Sir Thomas Percy's other sons to stay with a member of Henry VIII's council of the north. Initially, they stayed with their kinsman Sir Thomas *Tempest (*c.*1500–1545) [*see under* Tempest family (*per. c.*1500–1657)], at Holmside, co. Durham, and then at Tong Hall, Yorkshire. They are also said to have spent time at Liverpool, probably after their mother's second marriage in 1541 to Sir Richard Holland (*d.* 1548) of Denton, Lancashire. Thomas Percy was

Thomas Wharton, first Baron Wharton, for example, naturally hung on to the north-western lands he had given them. The seventh earl of Northumberland was restored to a landed revenue of £3077 per annum—only about three-quarters of his grandfather's patrimony, without considering inflation—and that derived from depreciated capital resources. The Percys' Northumberland seat of Alnwick—and presumably also more distant estates—had been substantially stripped since 1537. The stewardship of the royal honour of Richmond was, however, a valuable resource to the new earl.

The restoration was made in reward for Thomas Percy's action at Scarborough, but also in hope of useful activity on the Scottish border. Old Percy connections had been disinclined to assist Wharton, who was regarded as a newcomer who had unduly profited from the family's fall and was rewarded with appointment as warden of the middle and east marches as a result. Northumberland took these offices over on August 1557. The privy council expressed to Francis Talbot, fourth earl of Shrewsbury, the hope that thus 'the untowardnes of the Northumberlande men … will be partely reformed' (G. W. Bernard, *The Power of the Early Tudor Nobility*, 1985, 117). Northumberland and his brother Sir Henry Percy defended the border in 1557–8 with some success, assisted by the growing dissension between the Scots and the French. Shrewsbury complained, however, of Northumberland's alarmist reports and premature demands for expensive support.

Northumberland married on 12 June 1558 Anne (*b.* in or after 1526, *d.* 1591), third daughter of Henry Somerset, second earl of Worcester, and his second wife, Elizabeth. Their only son, Thomas Percy, died in 1560. Their daughters were Elizabeth (*b.* 1559, *d.* in or after 1604), Mary (*bap.* 1560, *d.* before 1564/5?), Lucy (*b.* before 1564/5, *d.* *c.*1601), Jane (*b.* after 1564/5?, *d.* after 1591), and Mary Percy (1570–1642).

Elizabethan eclipse, 1558–1569 Northumberland was told he could not be spared from the north to attend Elizabeth I's first parliament, and his proxy, Henry Fitzalan, twelfth earl of Arundel, proved inactive as a champion of Roman Catholicism. He was confirmed as warden of the east march on 18 January 1559. Officially in charge of Anglo-Scottish peace negotiations at Norham in February 1559, Northumberland delegated largely to his protestant brother Percy, who was quietly conferring with Scottish protestants on behalf of Sir William Cecil. Sir Ralph Sadler, on an inspection tour of the border in the autumn, recommended replacing both Percys, though Northumberland, as a 'rank papist' was the worse. An overheated dispute erupted when Northumberland tried to insist that his brother-in-law Slingsby, as keeper of Tynedale, be accommodated in Hexham Abbey by Lady Carnaby (probably the widow of Sir Reynold Carnaby, a counsellor of the sixth earl of Northumberland allegedly behind his disinheritance of his brothers). Northumberland would not 'beare the contempte and despite offred unto me'; but he, according to Sadler, wrote 'lettres … the lyke wherof I have not sene wrytten in such a case by any subject' (*State*

Thomas Percy, seventh earl of Northumberland (1528–1572), by unknown artist, 1566

restored in blood by the 1549 parliament. John Dudley, duke of Northumberland, who was acquiring Percy estates in the north from the early 1550s, made a token gesture by giving the two brothers £66 13s. 4d. per annum from former family property, and later granted Thomas Percy lands worth some £100 per annum around Langley, Northumberland.

The execution of the duke in 1553 freed the Northumberland title and lands, potentially to return to the Percys. However, Mary I showed little haste to do so until unrest in the north made it advisable. In November 1554 Thomas Percy served as knight of the shire for Westmorland. By 1555 he had secured his father's office of constable of Prudhoe Castle, Northumberland. In another centre of family influence, the North Riding, he distinguished himself in the recapture of Scarborough Castle from Thomas Stafford in April 1557. This led immediately to his knighthood and elevation as Baron Percy on 30 April and as earl of Northumberland the next day. He was then appointed high marshal of the army in the north (30 May) and member of the council of the north.

Although the Percy landed base had created 'enormous problems of government in the north-east', it was not in the crown's power to reverse fully the sixth earl of Northumberland's dissipation of it (Hoyle, 36). The Cliffords and

Papers and Letters, 1.426, 443). The outcome was the resignation first of Slingsby and, by the end of the year, of Northumberland. He managed to keep his successor, his wife's uncle, William Grey, thirteenth Baron Grey of Wilton, new warden of the east march, from using Alnwick Castle as his base. The earl's plea that it was unfurnished is confirmed elsewhere, but Grey of Wilton continued to complain of Northumberland's underhand influence and punished some of his men, such as George Clarkson, his deputy steward.

Despite Sadler's opinion of his religion, Northumberland's local influence had been recognized by making him a member of Elizabeth's ecclesiastical visitation for the northern province. Presumably he did nothing to enhance its efficiency in imposing a protestant settlement, but he had not as yet become an ostentatious recusant. Once free to go to parliament, he did take the opportunity to oppose new measures and attended some 60 per cent of sessions in 1563 and 75 per cent in 1566, acting as the queen's sword-bearer for the 1563 closure and the 1566 opening. However, he was habitually passed over for committees, except ones of inescapable local relevance or needing a muster of major peers (such as the 1566 succession delegations). In 1563 he was said to have warned against punitive enforcement of the oath of supremacy—'when they had beheaded the clergy they would claim to do the same to the lay nobles'—and in 1566 he was one of eleven opposing confirmation of episcopal consecrations (*CSP Spain, 1558–67*, 293).

Elizabeth's government made some minimal gestures of inclusion towards such a major peer, notably nomination to the Order of the Garter on 22 April and installation on 23 May 1563, but Northumberland's disconnection from the court was clear. The 1562 project for Mary, queen of Scots to meet Elizabeth was bound to involve Northumberland as an escort to Newcastle. He obtained assurances that he would not be expected to receive her at Alnwick, stressing his 'unabilitie … much the worse for the service I was lately in, in the northe partes, which as yet is far unrecovered' (Sharp, 337). He was removed from the quorum of the peace in Northumberland and the commissions of the peace in Yorkshire in 1564 in a purge of known Catholics.

Northumberland had some contact in Yorkshire with Margaret Stewart, countess of Lennox, and was regarded as a key player in her rather overblown reputation for political intrigue. Allegedly he was required at court at Christmas 1561 to keep him away from her: there was a project to marry one of his sisters to the Yorkist claimant Arthur Pole. At the height of English opposition to the marriage in 1565 of Margaret's son Henry Stewart, Lord Darnley, to Mary, queen of Scots, the latter's half-brother, James Stewart, earl of Moray, convinced Sir Nicholas Throckmorton in Edinburgh that Northumberland was part of a Lennox plot and should again be kept in London.

Northumberland's power in the north may have been regarded as a potential threat by the privy council, but he perhaps failed to cultivate and entrench his local power sufficiently during the 1560s. At best, he based himself at Topcliffe in the North Riding or Leconfield in the East Riding and neglected to exercise effective lordship in Northumberland. He never proceeded with his aim of 'continually lying' at Alnwick Castle (Batho, 'Percies and Alnwick', 50). Clarkson complained that the baronial court had also largely collapsed, leaving 'the lorde himselfe in his owne countrie not regarded' and 'tenants … not so much in feare of his lordshipe … as of other gentlemen ther neighbours' (James, *Society*, 296–7). If they wanted a Percy, Sir Henry Percy was close by to divert loyalties from the earl, much as their father and Ingram Percy had from the sixth earl of Northumberland, while Sir John Forster, leading the other gentlemen who had done well out of the Percy forfeiture, had established himself at Alnwick Abbey and had largely taken over even in the Percy heartland.

The government later presented Northumberland as a spendthrift, this being an aspect of his moral degeneration—at all events, financial problems were never far away. He was baulked by the crown in his most innovative attempted solution. Admittedly the initiative in starting to mine copper as well as coal on his estate at Newlands, Cumberland, came from crown patentees, but he thought he saw an opportunity to claim at least a share. By 1568 Northumberland's hopes 'to make more yearlye of the mynes of Newland then of all his inherytance' were dashed (PRO, SP 12/42/39). The exchequer ruled that traces of precious metal in copper made the latter crown property—a new precedent and, to landowners, a sinister one. By October 1568 Northumberland was sufficiently disgruntled to seek a licence to travel abroad, as he told Robert Dudley, earl of Leicester, still insisting that 'most of the best learned' favoured his case (*Pepys MSS*, 135).

When Francis Yaxley was shipwrecked off Northumberland in 1565 with money from Pius IV for Mary, queen of Scots, Northumberland annexed the salvage. Reportedly, though the queen got a share, the earl still acquired over £2000. Supposedly 'the seventh earl had no particular reason to make a grievance of his treatment by the law', but the defeat over mining copper probably rankled (James, *Society*, 302). The incident also showed that Northumberland was more interested in profit than in conciliating the pope or the queen of Scotland. The idea that he gave asylum to the latter's opponents, such as James Douglas, fourth earl of Morton, and that they subsequently betrayed him to Elizabeth is, however, over-artistic—their reception was a matter for the royal officers on the border.

Hereditary instinct made it difficult to favour Mary while queen of Scotland, but as a Catholic heir within England it was rather different. She landed in May 1568 at Workington, within Northumberland's liberty of Cockermouth. He obtained an order from the council of the north to take charge of her, which they later claimed presupposed he would be first on the scene. However, Sir Richard Lowther had already taken Mary to Carlisle and was unmoved by the earl, telling him he was 'too meane a man to have such charge' and a 'varlett' (Sharp, 340). Northumberland pleaded that 'my credyt be not so much impared in the face of my contrey, as she shuld be taken from me', but unsuccessfully (ibid., 318). Sir Francis Knollys went north on behalf of the privy council to tell him 'he had overshott himself verie muche to the discontentation of her highnes' (ibid., 341). This was the start of Northumberland's interest in alliance with Mary, contradicting his imputed closeness to the Lennox Stewarts, who believed the Scottish queen had murdered Darnley.

Northumberland flirted with various abortive projects to free Mary, one of which was based on his wife visiting and changing clothes with her. Having been called to Whitehall Palace at the end of 1568 for the hearings on charges against Mary (as spectator rather than commissioner), he took the opportunity to confer with the ambassadors of Philip II and Mary, Guerau de Spes and John Leslie, bishop-elect of Ross, on occasion 'disguised, at four o'clock in the morning' (*CSP Spain, 1568–79*, 96). Surreptitious proceedings did not, however, lead to any effective conclusions. By the time the court conspiracy based around Thomas Howard, fourth duke of Norfolk, had reached a crisis, Northumberland was in the north, communication delays leaving him behind events. Norfolk's submission left Northumberland dangerously implicated but 'out of all hope, of eyther ayd or mayntenance' (Sharp, 203).

Northumberland also moved towards a religious justification for resistance to Elizabeth. By 1572 at least he was well acquainted with two of Nicholas Sander's works of Catholic controversy, *The Supper of Our Lord* (1566) and *The Rock of the Church* (1567). He implied that such reading had cured him of any inclination to religious compromise and that he had been reconciled to the Catholic church about late 1567 or early 1568 by 'one Master Copley', and then started to discuss the legitimacy of rebellion, the general feeling being that it was justifiable only if the prince 'were lawfully excommunicated by the hed of the church' (Sharp, 204). On 8 November 1569 Northumberland and Charles Neville, sixth earl of Westmorland, on the point of rebellion, wrote to Pius V asking him to excommunicate Elizabeth, which elicited the bull *Regnans in excelsis* (May 1570).

The northern uprising, 1569 Northumberland's own account of how he came to rebel in November 1569 certainly contains self-serving elements, but it is broadly confirmed elsewhere. The prime movers were members of the gentry such as the Norton family—many related to Westmorland to some degree—while the two earls could not even agree on aims between themselves. Westmorland, Norfolk's brother-in-law, supported the project for the duke's marriage to Mary but demurred at a religious justification for revolt. Northumberland had little interest in supporting Norfolk's marriage, preferring that Mary marry a Catholic—though when he suggested 'the king, his master' to the Spanish ambassador, the latter merely 'wagged his hed' (Sharp, 190). It was only Westmorland whom Norfolk thought he could dissuade from revolt when he feared 'losing of his hed': Northumberland was to 'do what him list' (ibid., 196).

Relations with Thomas Radcliffe, third earl of Sussex,

the lord president of the north, remained cordial enough for the earls to hunt with him during the autumn and to confer gravely about the deplorable nature of all the rumours that they were about to revolt. Sussex's attitude changed in early November, when he advised Elizabeth that formally summoning Northumberland and Westmorland to appear at court would precipitate a crisis. She did so nevertheless, so uncharacteristic a piece of brinkmanship that she cannot have believed him. That the consequent revolt was as unco-ordinated and containable as it proved was not predictable. It was the outcome of desperation. Westmorland claimed on 6 November that he dare not appear for fear of enemies, while Northumberland still temporized at Topcliffe, convenient for York if he had been interested in a mooted project to capture Sussex and the council of the north. On 9 November he withdrew suddenly to Westmorland's castle of Brancepeth, co. Durham, after an alarm that Sir Oswald Wilstrop had come to arrest him, an alarm allegedly contrived by co-conspirators to frighten him into action. He and his wife claimed that the queen had ordered Sussex 'to take him and sende him upp moffeled' to court (Sharp, 22). Elizabeth subsequently affirmed, but regretted, that Sussex had not attempted this (Haynes, 553). Northumberland's own account naturally stressed his reluctance, that he 'could not get away', and even that 'some of the others meant me a displeasure' if he attempted it (Sharp, 199–200). Thomas Bishop added that Northumberland was threatened with dags.

The escalation and changing dynamic of the rebellion certainly neither betrayed Northumberland's influence nor was calculated to exploit it. Different accounts agree that he had only eight men with him at Brancepeth. His inclination, 'being forced to depart my house upon the soddaine of a false larum [alarm] … to have repayred to Anwick', and later to go 'into Northumberland and provide my force there' and join Westmorland 'about the Water of Tyne' were natural Percy instincts, but his fellows allegedly did not trust him to return (Sharp, 198–9). He could achieve little in co. Durham, though he was doubtless the prime mover in recruiting the 1241 rebels recorded in Richmondshire, where his opposition as steward of the liberty (from 26 July 1557) to new enclosures for which Elizabeth had reproved him might have stood him in good stead.

Whether thousands would still follow a Percy in Northumberland could not be fully tested because he did little to raise the county. Only eighty to a hundred horse were said to have joined the earl. Efficient recruiting at Westmorland's relatively small Northumberland estates made the Percy effort seem especially deficient. Even his brother-in-law Slingsby, beneficiary of Northumberland's efforts in 1560, preferred to secure his position with an access of loyalism. In Yorkshire, only a minority of Percy tenants turned out, and disproportionately from Topcliffe—hardly any came even from his other principal estate of Leconfield because he did not make a personal appearance. Cash was also wanted, and with only £130, plus £60 from pawning his Garter collar, Northumberland could not provide it. There was also a half-hearted attempt by Northumberland's men to hold Alnwick and Wark castles. Sir John Forster made the most of his own achievement in obtaining their surrender; with these added to the royal strongholds of Berwick and Newcastle, the rebels lost any chance of junction with Mary's partisans in the Scottish east march. Northumberland's rebellion indeed was a testimony to the decay of the Percy position and a desperate counter-measure against it.

If his recruiting successes were mixed, Northumberland was prominent in the restoration of mass at Durham and Ripon. It was alleged that he needed periodic encouragement by his wife lest he submit. Henry Carey, first Baron Hunsdon, wrote that 'the gray mare ys the better horse' (Sharp, 77); Elizabeth supposedly opined that the countess deserved to be burned for treason. None of the rebels, however, adopted a successful strategy. It took a week to move from Durham to the area of York: bypassing the city to the west suggested an incipient strike south to free Mary, but the opportunity for that had long gone. After increasingly aimless movements, the rebels went into Northumberland in the second week of December. This was retreat, not belated Percy enlistment, and on the 16th the earls left their followers to their own devices and fled from Hexham towards the border.

Scottish pawn, 1569–1572 Leonard Dacre, in a (bootless) attempt to dissociate himself from his former collaborators, turned them away from Naworth in Cumberland. They had to cross the border on 20 December and throw themselves on the mercy of the notorious Armstrongs of Liddesdale. Successive losses of horses and valuables caused Northumberland to leave his wife—pregnant, and probably tired—with 'Jock [Armstrong] of the Side' and continue himself to the house of Hector Armstrong of Harlaw in Liddesdale, who was supposed to owe him a favour but helped Martin Elliot capture him on behalf of Moray on Christmas eve. Thomas Kerr of Ferniehurst, however, rescued the countess, who was later accommodated by Alexander Hume, fifth Baron Hume.

Moray's first instinct was to offer his prisoner to Elizabeth in exchange for Mary; later he mentioned delivering him in conjunction with a request for subsidy, mooting the question of sale even if not as baldly as his successors did. The exchange option was also downgraded from Mary to John Leslie, the troublesome bishop-elect of Ross. Moray's committal of Northumberland to William Douglas at Lochleven Castle, when he found the suggestion of extradition unpopular in Scotland, was meant to buy time.

Obtaining Northumberland became a significant plank of Elizabethan policy towards a divided Scotland. Negotiations to restore Mary also presupposed delivering him. However, his wife believed she had as much chance as Elizabeth of buying him from Lochleven with funds from Philip and Pius. By the beginning of 1572 the countess had 7000 escudos (£2000) in hand. Unfortunately all funds had come through Fernando Álvarez de Toledo, duke of Alba,

governor of the Netherlands, whom she blamed for wasting the previous year—'the duke never gave me a flatt denyall, but with fayre words delayed me from tyme to tyme, and all upon a feare lest the money shuld be cast away' (Murdin, 188). It is true that he did not want to spend the pope's money on Northumberland. Greater speed might not have helped: the countess's offer of £2000 only brought an invitation to Elizabeth to match it. On 6 June 1572 Northumberland was sold to England, Scottish face scarcely saved by the pretence that the money was reimbursement for the expense of his imprisonment, which he promptly dismissed with complaints of the cheap food provided.

Morton, Douglas's cousin, attracted popular odium for Northumberland's surrender, although in fact he seemed to oppose it. It occurred on the authority of the current regent John Erskine, sixth earl of Mar, who extracted vague and noncommittal statements that Northumberland would be treated clemently. It was alleged that while still at Berwick, Northumberland was hopeful of obtaining leniency. Hunsdon followed the queen's instructions to encourage Northumberland to co-operate but to avoid making definite commitments in her name. Though finding little dignity in the proceedings, it was primarily for jurisdictional reasons that he insisted Forster take Northumberland to York. Prior attainder for treason made a trial redundant.

The day after Northumberland's old enemy brought him to York, 22 August 1572, the earl was beheaded in the Pavement. His body was buried the same day in the nearby St Crux Church and his head displayed on Micklegate Bar after a period in the Tolbooth on Ousebridge, during which William Tesimond cut off some hairs of the beard as a relic. Sir Thomas Gargrave reported Northumberland's last profession of Catholic faith and refusal to ask the queen's forgiveness: he made a remark variously reported as 'symple Tome must dye to sett up crewell Henry [Percy]' or 'crewell heresy' (Sharp, 335). Northumberland's attainder specifically reserved the rights of his brother Sir Henry Percy to allow him to inherit the title.

The martyr and his family Allegedly manipulated in his lifetime by the countess, who had the distinction of being attainted as a separate individual, Northumberland's posthumous reputation was enhanced by her long survival as a senior Catholic exile. From 1571 she was based at Malines. By about 1575 she was at Brussels, nearer the Spanish viceregal government, when English pressure induced it to expel her, but only to the adjacent episcopal territory of Liège. By 1577 she was back in (technically) Spanish territory at Luxembourg, encouraging Don John of Austria to intervene and marry Mary. Cecil (now Baron Burghley) and Robert Persons were in unusual agreement in saying that the frustrations of the dowager countess's position led to madness. She died of smallpox at a Namur convent on 8 or 9 September 1591. She had substantial financial support from Philip (though her monthly pension was said to have shrunk from perhaps £50 to £25) and

from other Catholic sources, so she had not only main-
tained a fair household but left enough for her daughter
Jane Percy to be advised to hurry from England to collect it
(PRO, SP 12/240/19).

Northumberland's daughters had been left at Topcliffe
during the rising—their uncle Sir Henry Percy found
them there 'in harde case' in January 1570 (Fonblanque,
2.73). It would seem likely that, after the younger Mary
Percy was born at Aberdeen on 11 June 1570, her mother
took her overseas. Mary Percy later went to England and
was maintained in family property in Blackfriars but
returned to the Low Countries after her mother's death,
was professed at Brussels in 1600, and became abbess in
1616. Elizabeth and Lucy Percy married into families that
showed some evidence of recusancy—their respective
spouses were Richard Woodruffe of Woolley, Yorkshire,
and Sir Edward Stanley of Eynsham, Oxfordshire. Jane
Percy, less predictably, married Lord Henry Seymour,
younger son of Edward Seymour, duke of Somerset, and
vice-admiral covering the Flemish coast during the
Armada campaign.

The dowager countess's friend Nicholas Sander wrote
an account of Northumberland's death, published in John
Bridgewater's *Concertatio ecclesiae Catholicae* (1589). 'The
good earle' was named specifically as a martyr in Richard
Bristow's *A Brief Treatise* (1574) (fol. 73r). William Allen,
after initial doubt, affirmed this in *A True, Sincere, and Modest Defense of English Catholics* (1584), 'for, what former quarrel or cause of his death soever there was … he was offered
his life if he would alter his religion' (Allen, *Defense*, ed.
R. M. Kingdon, 1965, 107–8). Such an equivocal figure was
not included among the fifty-four martyrs beatified by Leo
XIII in 1886. Thomas Percy did in fact appear in
Circignano's fresco cycle of martyrs but anonymously, as
a nobleman being beheaded. Northumberland was
among nine more candidates advanced by the English
Catholic bishops and beatified in 1895: his veneration by
the Benedictine nuns possibly helped. The grounds were
not just his Catholic declaration on the scaffold, but the
idea that he was offered a reprieve if he apostatized,
which lacks convincing proof. In fact Northumberland
performed far better as martyr than as politician or rebel.

JULIAN LOCK

Sources E. B. de Fonblanque, *Annals of the house of Percy*, 2 vols.
(1887) · C. Sharp, ed., *Memorials of the rebellion of 1569* (1840); repr.
with foreword by R. Wood as *The rising in the north: the 1569 rebellion*
(1975) · B. Camm, ed., *Lives of the English martyrs declared blessed by
Pope Leo XIII in 1886 and 1895*, 2 vols. (1904–5) · *The state papers and
letters of Sir Ralph Sadler*, ed. A. Clifford, 3 vols. (1809) · S. Haynes, ed.,
*Collection of state papers … 1542–70 … left by William Cecil, Lord Burgh-
ley … at Hatfield House* (1740) · W. Murdin, ed., *Collection of state
papers … left by William Cecil, Lord Burghley … 1572–96* (1759) · S. E.
Taylor, 'The crown and the north of England 1559–70: a study of
the rebellion of the northern earls, 1569–70, and its causes', PhD
diss., University of Manchester, 1981 · M. E. James, *Society, politics,
and culture in early modern England* (1986) · HoP, *Commons, 1509–58*,
3.84–5 · GEC, *Peerage* · M. E. James, ed., *Estate accounts of the earls of
Northumberland, 1562–1637*, SurtS, 163 (1955) · *The household papers of
Henry Percy, ninth earl of Northumberland, 1564–1632*, ed. G. R. Batho,
CS, 3rd ser., 93 (1962) · G. R. Batho, 'The Percies and Alnwick
Castle', *Archaeologia Aeliana*, 4th ser., 35 (1957), 48–63 · R. R. Reid,
'The rebellion of the earls, 1569', *TRHS*, new ser., 20 (1906), 171–
203 · J. K. Lowers, *Mirrors for rebels: a study of the polemical literature
relating to the northern rebellion of 1569*, University of California English Studies, 6 (1953) · 'The daughters of Thomas Percy, seventh
earl of Northumberland', *N&Q*, 169 (1935), 165–6, 231, 246–7 · state
papers domestic, Elizabeth, PRO, SP 12 · state papers additional,
Elizabeth, PRO, SP 15 · BL, Lansdowne MSS 8, 11–13, 15, 18, 109 ·
Report on the Pepys manuscripts, HMC, 70 (1911) · *CSP Spain, 1558–67,
1568–79* · *CSP Scot.* · *CPR, 1550–53; 1555–66* · *LJ*, vol. 1 · L. Stone, *The
crisis of the aristocracy, 1558–1641* (1965); rev. edn (1979) · R. W. Hoyle,
The pilgrimage of grace and the politics of the 1530s (2001) · W. T.
MacCaffrey, *The shaping of the Elizabethan regime, 1558–72* (1969)
Archives Alnwick Castle, Northumberland · BL, corresp. and
instructions as warden of the marches, Add. MSS 33591–33592 ·
Syon House, Middlesex, accounts | BL, Lansdowne MSS · LPL,
corresp. with Francis Talbot, earl of Shrewsbury · Magd. Cam., letters to Robert Dudley, earl of Leicester · PRO, SP 12, SP 15, SP 59
Likenesses oils, 1566, Petworth House, West Sussex [*see illus.*] ·
engraving, repro. in R. Verstegan, *Theatrum crudelitatum haereti-
corum* (1592), sig. K2 · oils, Alnwick Castle, Northumberland; repro.
in Fonblanque, *Annals*, vol. 2, frontispiece · portrait; in possession
of Charles Slingsby of Scriven in 1895
Wealth at death none; attainted traitor; had had considerable
landed income; assessed after forfeiture at £2418 9s. 10d., incl. £977
from Northumberland, £695 from Yorkshire, £338 from Cumberland, £160 from Sussex: BL, Lansdowne MS 12, fols. 198–9 · the £39
13s. 10d. in palatinate of Durham apparently Beamish manor; incl.
in Lansdowne MS under Northumberland: Sharp, *Memorials*,
138n. · some march lands near Wark seemingly excluded; restoration grant of 1557 supposed for £3077 p.a.: Loades, *Reign of Mary
Tudor*, 351 · Percy income over £4000, incl. lands of dowager countess which were assessed for subsidy at £200 and therefore might
typically have been worth c.£1000: BL, Lansdowne MS 13, fol. 62r;
Stone, *Crisis of the aristocracy*, 760

Percy, Thomas (1560–1605), conspirator, was a younger
son of Edward Percy (c.1524–1590) of Beverley and Elizabeth Waterton. His grandfather, Josceline Percy (d. 1532),
was fourth son of Henry Percy, fourth earl of Northumberland. Little is known of Percy's early life, following
matriculation from Peterhouse, Cambridge, in 1579. He
subsequently forged a career in the service of his cousin
the ninth earl of Northumberland. As Northumberland
came to trust him more and more, Percy was promoted to
the post of constable in the earl's northern stronghold,
Alnwick Castle. In 1601 he travelled with his master to the
Low Countries, receiving a gift of £200 shortly afterwards.
The date of Percy's marriage to Martha Wright, sister of
two future co-conspirators in the Gunpowder Plot, is now
unknown.

Percy was a pugnacious character. The Jesuit John Gerard noted that 'for the most part of his youth he had been
very wild more than ordinary, and much given to fighting'
(Morris, 57). In 1596, during a border affray, Percy killed
one James Burne, a Scot. By the 1590s both governments
were punishing such lawlessness, and Percy was committed to a London gaol. However, Northumberland's
brother-in-law the earl of Essex wrote mitigating the
offence, and the prisoner was released. Returning the
favour, perhaps, Percy participated enthusiastically in a
subsequent conspiracy engineered by Essex to entrap the
Scottish warden of the middle marches.

According to Gerard, conversion to Catholicism

Inscriptions on engraving: BRITANNIÆ MAGNI ANGLVS NOBILIS PERSI THOMAS REGIS STIPENDIARIVS ANNO 1605

Hæc est vera & prima originalis editio Thôæ Perci

Crispinus
Van de Pas
excudet

Thomas Percy (1560–1605), by Crispijn de Passe the elder, c.1605

reclaimed Percy from manifold vice to sober contemplation and religious virtue, and his comments are supported by those of another Jesuit father acquainted with the man, Oswald Tesimond (Edwards, 58). But the priests' claims were true only up to a point. Percy's enduring ruthlessness and lack of scruple, indeed, appear to have been precisely the traits which recommended him to Northumberland. In 1603 he was appointed receiver of the earl's rents in both Cumberland and Northumberland, a hard job, requiring energy and single-mindedness. Despite—or perhaps because of—the usual squabbling among estate officers, the earl's confidence in his capable servant remained unshaken (Nicholls, 150–52).

Northumberland's trust extended to matters of high politics, with the greatest prizes at stake. When, after Essex's downfall, the earl wanted to open a channel of communication with James VI, he turned to Percy, and it was the man whom Northumberland later called his 'ancient Mercury' who undertook three clandestine missions to the Scottish court (PRO, SP 14/4/85). James gave some unspecific assurances to requests from either the earl or his messenger that English Catholics might receive kinder treatment under a Stuart king—promises which Percy magnified for his own purposes after 1603. More immediately, these hugger-mugger services cemented the bond of trust between Northumberland and his officer. When the earl was appointed captain of the gentleman

pensioners, early in the new reign, he disregarded James's instructions and dispensed with the oath of supremacy when admitting Percy to this royal bodyguard. This may have been mere oversight or the convenient omission of an oath offensive to a Catholic, but, given Percy's subsequent career, dereliction of duty was held to be as bad as wilful disobedience.

The full story of Gunpowder Plot is told elsewhere [see Fawkes, Guy]. In conversation with friends, among them Robert Catesby, the conspiracy's organizing genius, Percy bemoaned the weaknesses and futility of Catholic resistance to the new regime: 'Shall wee alwais talk, gentelmen, and never doe any thing?' (Hatfield MS 113/54). Catesby quietly reassured him that drastic action was indeed being contemplated. Sworn into the plot in May 1604, Percy subleased a dwelling adjacent to the House of Lords from Henry Ferrers of Baddesley Clinton, who in turn had leased the property from John Whynniard, keeper of the Old Palace of Westminster. From here the plotters began to drive a tunnel under Parliament House. Early in 1605 it was again Percy who took the lease of a ground-floor vault under the Lords' chamber itself, and it was there that Fawkes, posing as Percy's servant, was eventually arrested, as he prepared to fire over 18 hundredweight of gunpowder. After spending the autumn of 1605 collecting Northumberland's rents, Percy was in London by the evening of 2 November. Pursuing his own scheme of kidnapping the king's younger son, despite the doubts of his colleagues, he studied Prince Charles's daily routine at court. He also bolstered the faltering spirits of fellow conspirators before visiting Northumberland for dinner on 4 November, apparently to check that the plot had not yet been discovered.

Early on 5 November word spread that Fawkes had been captured. In a proclamation for his arrest issued shortly afterwards Percy is described as a tall, florid man, with a broad beard—'the head more white then the beard'—and stooping shoulders, being also 'long footed, small legged' (Larkin and Hughes, 1.123). He joined in the rebellion which followed, and on the morning of 8 November, in a final stand at Holbeach House, Staffordshire, Percy and Catesby, fighting back to back, were shot and mortally wounded with a single bullet. Percy's body was stripped by what the sheriff of Worcestershire termed the 'baser sort' among his posse (Hatfield MS 113/4). His head was sent to London. A sword which he had commissioned but never collected from the Catholic London cutler John Cradock may survive in the Swiss National Museum, Zürich, as accession LM 3675.

Percy was apparently estranged from Martha Wright, who, along with their daughter, drew an annuity of £50 paid by Lord Monteagle. Another, unnamed, woman is also described as his wife at the time of Gunpowder Plot. In November 1605 Martha resided in the midlands, while the other 'spouse' lived 'very private' as a schoolteacher in Holborn (PRO, SP 14/216/15, 134). A son, Robert, married Emma Mead at Wiveliscombe, Somerset, on 22 October 1615. Of two known daughters, one is rumoured to have married Catesby's son Robert.

MARK NICHOLLS

Sources Alnwick Castle, archives of his grace the duke of Northumberland, Alnwick and Syon MSS • PRO, SP 14 • M. Nicholls, *Investigating Gunpowder Plot* (1991) • Hatfield House, Hertfordshire, Salisbury–Cecil MSS • *The condition of Catholics under James I: Father Gerard's narrative of the Gunpowder Plot*, ed. J. Morris, 2nd edn (1872) • *The Gunpowder Plot: the narrative of Oswald Tesimond alias Greenway*, ed. and trans. F. Edwards (1973) • J. F. Larkin and P. L. Hughes, eds., *Stuart royal proclamations*, 2 vols. (1973–80) • M. E. James, ed., *Estate accounts of the earls of Northumberland, 1562–1637*, SurtS, 163 (1955) • Venn, *Alum. Cant.* • C. Blair, 'A gunpowder plotter's sword', *Handbook to the Eleventh Park Lane Arms Fair* (1994), 1–6 • J. Bain, ed., *The border papers: calendar of letters and papers relating to the affairs of the borders of England and Scotland*, 2 vols. (1894–6), vol. 2, p. 279 • PRO, E 134 4 James I/Trinity/6
Archives Alnwick Castle, Northumberland, archives of duke of Northumberland, MSS • PRO
Likenesses C. de Passe the elder, engraving, *c.*1605, NPG [*see illus.*]

Percy, Thomas (1729–1811), writer and Church of Ireland bishop of Dromore, was born on 13 April 1729 at The Cartway, Bridgnorth, Shropshire, the son of Arthur Lowe Percy (*d.* 1764), wholesale grocer and tobacconist, and his wife, Jane, *née* Nott. The surname appears as Pearcy in the baptismal register at St Leonard's Church, Bridgnorth; Percy himself wrote Piercy until 1756, when he definitively opted for Percy.

Education and early career Percy was educated at Bridgnorth Free School (1737–41) and Newport School, Shropshire (1741–6). At the age of seventeen he went to Christ Church, Oxford, as a Careswell exhibitioner. His undergraduate studies were mainly classics, with some Hebrew. After taking his BA (1750) he continued with Hebrew as a part-time postgraduate, adding French and Italian. He obtained his MA in 1753.

Percy was ordained first as deacon (1751)—in which capacity he preached in several churches in his home area—and two years later as priest. Shortly after this Christ Church presented him with the living at Easton Maudit, Northamptonshire. He took up residence at Easton in 1756 and in the same year became rector of Wilby, some 6 miles away. He owed the latter appointment to the earl of Sussex, who also appointed Percy as his personal chaplain.

As a parson Percy was sincere, but perhaps somewhat worldly, with a liking for sightseeing, shooting, horseracing, card games, plays, operas, coffee houses, and pleasure gardens. Nevertheless he was a keen and wide-ranging reader. In the early 1750s he began to write verse, some of which shows the possible influence of the ballads in a manuscript collection he had discovered. While visiting Humphrey Pitt at Shifnal, 11 miles from Bridgnorth, probably in 1753, Percy noticed a battered volume 'lying dirty on the floor, under a bureau in the parlour … being used by the maids to light the fire' (Hales and Furnivall, 1.lxiv). It proved to be a seventeenth-century collection, which he persuaded Pitt to reprieve from the flames. In due course it provided the basis for Percy's anthology, *The Reliques of Ancient English Poetry* (1765), and for his enduring fame.

Marriage and maturity On 24 April 1758 Percy married Anne Gutteridge (*d.* 1806) of Desborough, Northamptonshire, who brought a dowry of £2000. Between 1760 and

Thomas Percy (1729–1811), by William Dickinson, pubd 1775 (after Sir Joshua Reynolds, 1773–4)

1772 their long-lasting union produced six children, of whom two died in infancy and two more, including their only son, Henry, predeceased them. Before these grievous losses, Percy in his sixteenth-century vicarage, with bees and fruit trees, wife and first child, pronounced himself (in 1760) the 'happiest of men' (Davis, 69).

Much though he relished the role of rural parson and patriarch, Percy looked to wider horizons. In 1765 he became chaplain and secretary to Lord Northumberland and tutor to his son, Algernon, in which capacities he often visited Northumberland House in London and also Alnwick Castle. His wife was signally honoured to be appointed (at a salary of £200 a year) wet-nurse to Queen Charlotte's baby son, Edward (the future father of Queen Victoria); she spent eighteen months at Kew and Buckingham House (1767–8), after which she received an annual pension of £100 for life. Percy himself became in 1769 one of the king's chaplains-in-ordinary, a post which required him to preach from time to time before George III. He received DD degrees from Cambridge in 1770 and from his own university twenty-three years later.

Percy took the opportunity of visiting London to mix in literary and artistic circles, where he made many friends, including Edmund Burke, David Garrick, Oliver Goldsmith, Thomas Gray, David Hume, Samuel Johnson (who made a lengthy visit to Easton in 1764), Elizabeth Montagu, and Joshua Reynolds (who painted his portrait). The first such friend, William Shenstone, Percy met at the Leasowes, the latter's home near Halesowen, Shropshire. The ability to make and retain such friendships reflects well on Percy, who kept up a relentless round of meetings, backed by copious correspondence.

Publications Percy's first published works were two sonnets printed in a periodical called the *Universal Visiter* (1756). A further poem of his, simply entitled 'Song' and beginning 'O Nancy, wilt thou go with me?' appeared in a collection of poems published by Robert Dodsley in 1758. This was later set to music by Joseph Baildon and famously described by Robert Burns (in 1792) as 'perhaps the most beautiful Ballad in the English language' (*Letters of Robert Burns*, ed. J. D. Ferguson, 1931, 2.126).

With the apparent gift of sensing a need for the new, while at the same time making use of his linguistic skills, Percy then turned away from his own light verses to translating the exotic, the primitive. He catered to the taste for chinoiserie by translating a Portuguese version of a Chinese novel, the argument of a play, some proverbs, and poems, under the title of *Hau Kiou Choaun, or, The Pleasing History* (4 vols., 1761), and by editing, the following year, two volumes of *Miscellaneous Pieces Relating to the Chinese*.

In 1763 Percy turned to the north, with *Five Pieces of Runic Poetry*, which he translated from the Icelandic with the acknowledged help of a clergyman neighbour, the Revd Edward Lye, a distinguished Anglo-Saxon scholar. Other translations were from Hebrew, French, Latin, and Spanish. His new version of the Song of Solomon appeared in 1764. *Northern Antiquities* (1770) consisted of Percy's translations both of Paul-Henri Mallet's *Introduction à l'histoire du Dannemarc* and of Goranson's Latin version of the *Prose Edda*. From the Spanish, Percy's *Ancient Songs Chiefly on Moorish Subjects* was ready for the press in 1775 but published only in 1932.

An original work, *A Key to the New Testament* (1766), quickly went through four editions. It shows, with *The Song of Solomon*, that Percy was not forgetting his clerical role. Nor did he neglect his patrons, the duke and duchess of Northumberland: in 1768 he published his edition of *The regulations and establishment of the household of Henry Algernon Percy, the fifth earl of Northumberland … begun anno domini MDXII*. It is possible that a similar motivation lay behind his ballad-style poem in 800 lines, *The Hermit of Warkworth*, begun in 1767 and published four years later. Despite such intense productivity, during the same eventful period Percy conceived, and in some cases started work on, a series of projects which either failed to come to fruition or did so at the hands of others: editions of *The Guardian*, *Spectator*, and *Tatler*; of Buckingham's *Rehearsal* and Tottel's *Miscellany*; and of his own favourite book, *Don Quixote*.

The *Reliques* Another product of the hectic literary activity at Easton Maudit turned out to be Percy's most important and influential work, the three-volume anthology of which the full title is *Reliques of ancient English poetry: consisting of old heroic ballads, songs, and other pieces of our earlier poets. (Chiefly of the lyric kind). Together with some few of later date* (1765, published by Robert and James Dodsley). If indeed Percy rescued the original folio manuscript in 1753 it was probably consigned to a cupboard in the Pitt household for several years before he was able to beg it. His mind may have been brought back to it when Shenstone, whom he was visiting in the summer of 1757, read him a version of the ballad 'Gil Morrice'. It was only in November of that year that he wrote to Shenstone that he had 'a very curious old MS. Collection of ancient Ballads' which Johnson had seen and urged him to publish (*Percy Letters*, 7.1–3).

Johnson, despite being somewhat contemptuous of ballads and prone to teasing Percy with parodies of them, had offered to help select and annotate the material, though he did not do so. The task fell to Shenstone, who greatly influenced both Percy's selection of ballads and his editorial policy. Until Shenstone's death in 1763 the two men engaged in sustained correspondence on ballad topics with frequent exchanges of ballad texts. In addition Percy travelled at least twice to Halesowen, taking with him the precious folio. At an early stage he decided not to publish the manuscript in its entirety but to supplement it from other sources. In the end only a quarter of the printed work came from the folio, though the original contents influenced Percy's selection of material: historical ballads, Robin Hood ballads, metrical romances, traditional items, and modern ballad imitations.

To request possible material and to discuss it Percy wrote to academics such as Thomas Warton of Oxford and Richard Farmer of Cambridge, antiquarians such as the Scots lawyers John McGowan and David Dalrymple (later Lord Hailes), and ballad scholars or collectors such as Evan Evans and David Herd. He went carefully through published anthologies of ballads and consulted unpublished collections held by such bodies as the Society of Antiquaries or preserved in libraries. He went to Magdalene College, Cambridge, to see the Pepys collection, and with the help of amanuenses took copies of a large number of black-letter broadsides. He contacted a contemporary printer, Cluer Dicey, who supplied him with over eighty street ballads issued by his father, William (characterized by Percy as 'the greatest printer of Ballads in the Kingdom'; *Percy Letters*, 7.109).

The ballad trade was, to say the least, not held in high esteem, and Percy 'could never quite satisfy himself that ballad editing was a suitable employment for a conscientious clergyman' (Davis, 104). Yet he persevered, commenting in 1761:

> I am content to perform the office of scavenger for the public, and as Virgil found *Gold* among the *Dung* of *Ennius*, from all this learned Lumber I hope to extract something that shall please the most delicate and correct Taste. (S. H. Harlowe, 'Letters from Dr Percy to T. Astle, esq.', *N&Q*, 4 ser., 3, 1869, 25–7)

To this end, Percy excluded bawdy, as well as almost all politics and protest. He saw himself including 'effusions of Nature' (Hales and Furnivall, 1.1), deriving from the unspoilt childhood of literature and the nation, yet he was happy to collate, patch, and rewrite whenever he deemed it necessary. He planned to dedicate the book to the memory of Shenstone but at a late stage offered the dedication to Elizabeth Percy, countess (later duchess) of Northumberland. When she accepted, Johnson, swallowing his dislike of patrons, agreed to Percy's request that he write a (suitably grovelling) dedication. Percy then went through the whole text again to ensure that the countess's sensibilities could not possibly be offended, excising and bowdlerizing as he did so. In addition the planned volume 3 was brought forward to be volume 1 so as to give prominence to ballads on the Northumberland Percys.

When the book came out, the *Gentleman's Magazine* reviewer commented that Percy 'has with great judgement selected such specimens [of ballads] as either shew the gradation of our language, exhibit the progress of popular opinion, display the peculiar manners and customs of former ages, or throw light on our early classical poets', and expressed the view that the work 'well deserves the encouragement of the public' (*GM*, 1st ser., 35, 1765, 179, 183). The public duly responded. Within five months 1100 sets of the three elegant volumes (out of 1500 printed) had sold, at half a guinea a time. Percy's editorial policy seemed to be vindicated, with some of the most doctored ballads securing the highest approval.

One critic, at least, remained unconvinced, the eccentric and choleric Joseph Ritson, who suggested that the 'learned collector has preferred his ingenuity to his fidelity' and alleged that the folio manuscript did not exist at all (J. Ritson, ed., *Ancient Songs and Ballads*, 1792, xix–xxi). He kept up the criticism for many years, accusing Percy of printing scarcely 'a single poem … fairly or honestly' and of practising 'every kind of forgery and imposture' (Ritson, *Romanceës*, 1802, cix, cxliii n.). A cartoon of 1803 by James Sayer shows Ritson trampling underfoot 'Dr Percy's ancient ballads', while penning from an inkpot marked 'Gall' a statement including 'Dr Percy a Liar Warton an infamous Liar a pipeër better than a parson' (BM satire 10171).

Ritson's criticisms, seen to be broadly justified in 1867–8 when the folio manuscript was published, have been largely endorsed by later scholars. But Percy did at least take ballads seriously, annotating them with great care. He treated them as literary phenomena, largely ignoring their music and their links with oral tradition, but a scholar in the late twentieth century made this assessment: 'Percy's work was brilliant and blundering, inspiring both the interest and standards which were later to condemn it. It was, however, a noble experiment and one as remarkable for its failures as for its triumphs' (Knapman, 213).

Most of Percy's contemporaries welcomed the *Reliques* as a powerful blast of fresh air. 'Poetry has been absolutely redeemed by it', wrote Wordsworth ('Essay supplementary to the preface', *Lyrical Ballads*, 1815, 3, 75). Several generations of poets felt its influence: Blake, Coleridge, Keats, Rossetti, Morris, Swinburne, and many lesser lights. Scott, both as novelist and ballad-editor, owed a debt to the book, as did figures such as Bürger, Herder, and the Grimm brothers in Germany, and by extension European Romanticism in general.

Late years After the early 1770s Percy wrote little, perhaps burnt out after a prolonged period of frenetic activity. There were verses on the death of Johnson (1785) and a memoir of Goldsmith (1801), together with editions of the works of Buckingham (2 vols., 1806?) and of Surrey and Wyatt (with George Steevens, 2 vols., 1807). A second edition of the *Reliques* appeared in 1767 and a third in 1775. When a fourth was called for Percy published it (1794) under the ostensible editorship of his nephew and namesake since he felt that the book was not consistent with his position as bishop.

Percy was appointed dean of Carlisle in 1778, thanks to the patronage of Northumberland. He did not sever his links with Northamptonshire until 1782, when he became bishop of Dromore in northern Ireland. He immersed himself in his pastoral duties in this small town some 60 miles west of Belfast, to the exclusion of much else. After forty-eight years of marriage his wife, Anne, died in December 1806 and was buried in her husband's cathedral. By this time Percy was losing his sight. He died at the bishop's residence, Dromore, more or less blind, on 30 September 1811 at the age of eighty-two, and was buried next to his wife. Several people in northern Ireland were moved to send valedictory poems to the *Gentleman's Magazine*, where an obituarist wrote that Percy:

constantly resided [at Dromore], promoting the instruction and comfort of the poor with unremitting attention, and superintending the sacred and civil interests of the diocese, with vigilance and assiduity; revered and loved for his piety, liberality, benevolence, and hospitality, by persons of every rank and religious denomination. (*GM*, 1st ser., 81, 1811, 483)

Reprints of some of Percy's books continued through the nineteenth century and into the twentieth. His *Key to the New Testament* was republished as late as 1842, *Northern Antiquities* in 1882, *The Hermit of Warkworth* in 1883, *Regulations and Establishment* in 1905, and *Life of Goldsmith* in 1976. These were far outstripped by the *Reliques*, of which well over a score of reprints or adaptations appeared in the nineteenth century alone. The Everyman edition of 1906 had at least five printings, and as late as 1996 a facsimile of the first edition of the *Reliques* came out.

Nine volumes of Percy's correspondence were published between 1944 and 1988. Percy material, published and otherwise, is widely scattered through private collections in Britain and America, New Zealand, and South Africa. The famous folio is in the British Library. Percy's work continues to attract the attention of scholars around the world. Percy not only travelled from grocer's warehouse to bishop's palace but in a parallel literary career produced at least one book, the *Reliques*, long recognized as 'a seminal work of English Romanticism' (Groom, 1.1) and considered a landmark in European literature.

ROY PALMER

Sources B. H. Davis, *Thomas Percy: a scholar-cleric in the age of Johnson* (1989) • T. Percy, ed., *Reliques of ancient English poetry*, rev. H. B. Wheatley, 3 vols. (1886); facs. edn (1966) [incl. new introduction by N. Groom] • J. W. Hales and F. J. Furnivall, eds., *Bishop Percy's folio manuscript: ballads and romances*, 3 vols. (1867–8) • A. Johnston, *Enchanted ground: the study of medieval romance in the eighteenth century* (1964) • A. B. Friedman, *The ballad revival: studies in the influence of popular on sophisticated poetry* (1961) • J. Ritson, ed., *Ancient songs and ballads* (1790) [marked 1790; in fact 1792] • J. Ritson, ed., *Ancient Engleish metrical romanceës* (1802) • Z. Knapman, 'A reappraisal of Percy's editing', *Folk Music Journal*, 5 (1985–9), 202–14 • *The Percy letters*, ed. D. N. Smith and C. Brooks, 1–6 (1944–61) • *The Percy letters*, ed.

C. Brooks and A. F. Falconer, 7–9 (1977–88) • L. Shepard, 'The finding of the Percy folio manuscript: a claim of prior discovery', *N&Q*, 212 (1967), 415–16 • W. J. Bate, 'Percy's use of his folio manuscript', *Journal of English and Germanic Philology*, 43 (1944), 337–48 • P. A. Harrison, 'Samuel Johnson's folkloristics', *Folklore*, 94 (1983), 57–65 • *GM*, 1st ser., 35 (1765), 179–83, 230–31 • *GM*, 1st ser., 81/2 (1811), 460–61, 483, 556–7 • J. F. A. Mason, 'Bishop Percy's account of his own education', *N&Q*, 204 (1959), 404–8

Archives Alnwick Castle, Northumberland, corresp. • BL, corresp., papers, and genealogical and ballad collections, Add. MSS 22592–22595, 27879, 32323–32339, 34756, 38728, 39547, 42515–42517; RP413, 1632, 2619, 3781 • BL, annotated collection of ballads • Bodl. Oxf., corresp. and papers • Bodl. Oxf., letters and accounts relating to the purchase of Scottish firs • Boston PL, letters and papers • GL, genealogical collections relating to the Percy family • Harvard U., Houghton L., corresp. and papers • Hunt. L., corresp. and literary MSS • NL Scot., corresp. and notes • Queen's University, Belfast, library with marginal notes, and papers • Shrewsbury School, sermons • TCD, notes relating to *Hudibras* • Yale U., Beinecke L., corresp., papers, and literary MSS | BL, letters to Thomas Birch, Add. MS 4316 • BL, corresp. with Richard Farmer, Add. MS 28222 • BL, letters to earls of Hardwicke, Add. MSS 35350, 35611, 35728–35763, *passim* • BL, corresp. with William Shenstone, Add. MS 28221 • BL, letters to Thomas Warton, incl. notes and transcripts of ballads, Add. MS 42560 • Bodl. Oxf., letters to Thomas Apperley [copies] • Bodl. Oxf., letters to Sir Robert Chambers • Bodl. Oxf., corresp. with Edmund Malone • Bodl. Oxf., letters to Samuel Pegge • Bodl. Oxf., corresp. with Jane West • FM Cam., letters to Joseph Cooper Walker • Hunt. L., letters and literary MSS • NL Scot., letters to Sir David Dalrymple • NL Scot., letters to Lord Hailes • NL Scot., corresp. with George Paton • NL Wales, letters to Evan Evans • Shrops. RRC, letters to J. B. Blakeway • W. Yorks. AS, Leeds, Yorkshire Archaeological Society, letters to John Watson • Yale U., Beinecke L., corresp. with James Boswell • Yale U., Beinecke L., letters

Likenesses oils, 1773 (after J. Reynolds), Art Institute of Chicago • W. Dickinson, mezzotint, pubd 1775 (after J. Reynolds, 1773–4), BM, NG Ire., NPG [*see illus.*] • attrib. T. Robinson, group portrait, oils, *c.*1801–1808, Castle Ward • stipple, pubd 1811 (after J. Reynolds, 1773), NG Ire. • Audinet, line engraving, NPG • J. Ogborne, line and stipple engraving (after L. F. Abbott), BM, NPG; repro. in F. G. Waldron, *The biographical mirror 2* (1802)

Percy, Thomas (1768–1808), Church of England clergyman, the eldest child of Anthony Percy (1731–1795), merchant, and his wife, Mary Mason (*d.* 1795), was born in Southwark on 13 September 1768. He was the nephew of Bishop Thomas *Percy (1729–1811), for whom he was named. He began to write poetry in his early years at Merchant Taylors' School, where he was a pupil from 1775 to 1785. Daines Barrington relates that by the age of nine Percy had composed not only a ballad which was set to music by the composer Samuel Wesley, but also the first canto of an epic poem on Caesar's invasion of Britain. In this work, says Barrington:

> there are strong marks of a most early genius for poetry, which he likewise recites admirably well upon the first stool you may place him. I asked this wonderful boy how many books he intended to divide his Epic Poem into; when he answered, that he could not well bring all his matter into less than twenty-four. (Barrington, 308)

Two short poems written by Percy at the age of nine or ten were published in the *Gentleman's Magazine* in the years 1778–9. Another of pamphlet length, *Verses on the Death of*

Dr. Samuel Johnson (1785), was printed anonymously at the expense of his uncle, Bishop Percy. His precocity showed itself not only in the private work of composition, but also in his leading role in the organization of a literary society, the 'Council of Parnassus', formed with the aim of reciting and criticizing its members' verses in public. This group's main achievement was the publication, supervised by the fifteen-year-old Percy, of a volume titled *Poems by a Literary Society* in 1784.

These juvenile exploits seem to have exhausted Percy's poetic energies: apart from some verses in the *Poetical Register*, this completes the list of his literary publications. He matriculated at St John's College, Oxford, on 27 June 1786, graduated BCL at Oxford in 1792, became a fellow of his college in the same year, and proceeded DCL in 1797, having previously in 1793 been presented to the vicarage of Grays Thurrock in Essex.

In 1795 Percy was the ostensible editor of the fourth edition of his uncle's *Reliques of Ancient English Poetry*. Though it is the only achievement for which he is remembered, this editorship was no more than a polite fiction arranged by his uncle, whose collection of ballads and other early English verse had become extremely popular since its first publication in 1764. Created bishop of Dromore in 1782, Percy's uncle felt himself unable to acknowledge his continuing interest in the frivolities of poetry, and unwilling to engage in public controversy over the authenticity of his manuscript texts, even if friends urged him to issue a new edition, and even if his detractors, notably Joseph Ritson, ought to be answered. Perhaps the bishop had also hoped that after the death of his son in 1783 he would find in his nephew a congenial spirit to take over the editing under his guidance. He was eventually disappointed, and the editorial work was evidently undertaken by the bishop himself, as was the composition of a prefatory advertisement for putting his name to which Percy received a share in the book's profits. This dissociated the bishop firmly from a work that, it claimed, 'the original editor had no desire to revive [because] more important pursuits had … engaged his attention' (Percy, 1.ix). The fourth edition was the definitive form of this highly influential collection for over fifty years, and hence the vehicle through which the younger Thomas Percy's name became widely known.

Although his uncle placed opportunities for other editorial projects in Percy's way around this time, nothing came of them, probably because his interest was lukewarm. Nevertheless, he was installed on 3 December 1796 as rector of one of the bishop's churches, at Magheralin in the diocese of Dromore, Down, and simultaneously as precentor of Dromore Cathedral, a sinecure paying £500 per annum. This appointment served to forestall legal action by his former parishioners at Grays Thurrock, who were about to bring a suit against him for his neglect of the church's fabric; but it prevented his free movement back to England, where he was liable to prosecution.

Little is known of Percy's last decade, which seems not to have been happy. He died, unmarried, at Ecton, near

Northampton, on 14 May 1808, of what the obituary written by his uncle describes as 'a fever, which baffled all medical skill' (*GM*).   STUART GILLESPIE

Sources DNB · D. Barrington, *Miscellanies* (1781) · *GM*, 1st ser., 78 (1808), 470 · [T. Percy], ed., *Reliques of ancient English poetry*, 4th edn, 3 vols. (1794) [1794 for 1795] · B. H. Davis, *Thomas Percy: a scholar-cleric in the age of Johnson* (1989) · B. H. Davis, *Thomas Percy* (1981) · Nichols, *Lit. anecdotes* · Nichols, *Illustrations*, vols. 7–8 · V. H. Ogburn, 'Thomas Percy's unfinished collection: ancient English and Scottish poems', *ELH: a Journal of English Literary History*, 3 (1936), 183–9 · C. J. Robinson, ed., *A register of the scholars admitted into Merchant Taylors' School, from AD 1562 to 1874*, 2 vols. (1882–3) · Foster, *Alum. Oxon.*

Percy, William de (d. 1096x9), baron and administrator, probably took his name from Percy-en-Auge, Calvados, Normandy. According to the cartulary of Whitby Abbey, he bore the nickname of Asgernuns or Ohtlesgernuns, which may have been in allusion to his moustaches. An untrustworthy late memorandum in the Whitby cartulary claims that William de Percy came to England with Hugh d'Avranches, earl of Chester, and William the Conqueror in 1067. This may have been an invention to support the charter which the Whitby monks had concocted in his name, supposedly giving them the churches of Whitby and Flamborough. It is unlikely that Percy was originally Hugh's man or that he came to England in his company, but in 1086 he was the tenant of Earl Hugh at Whitby and Sneaton, Yorkshire. In Percy's foundation charter for Whitby Abbey, Earl Hugh was described as Percy's lord.

William de Percy was with the Conqueror on his expedition to Scotland in August 1072, and after his return he superintended the rebuilding of the castle at York under the direction of Hugh fitz Baldric, the sheriff. Soon after 1077 Percy endowed the community of St Peter and St Hilda at Whitby, which had been newly re-established by the hermit Reinfrid, one time monk of Evesham. Shortly afterwards there was a schism within the community, the reasons for which are unknown. Abbot Stephen (d. c.1112) and the main body of the convent moved to Lastingham, part of the royal demesne. Prior Reinfrid and the remainder of the Whitby monks later moved to Hackness, with Percy's consent, in order to escape from the assaults of robbers and pirates. It appears that Percy attempted to recover his donations from Abbot Stephen and return them to Reinfrid, whom he had first sponsored at Whitby. The monks went back to Whitby, possibly by c.1090 and certainly before 1096 when Percy issued a charter confirming them in considerable possessions. William Rufus granted and confirmed various privileges and the church of Allsaints, Fishergate, York, to Prior Reinfrid and the monks at Whitby and later liberties, the church of Hackness, and various lands to Percy's brother, Prior Serlo de Percy.

In 1086 William de Percy was a tenant-in-chief in Yorkshire (where he held the bulk of his lands), in Lindsey, in Nottinghamshire, and in Hampshire. The lands he held as tenant-in-chief in Yorkshire were worth approximately £64 19*s*. Domesday Book also records that he was a tenant of the bishop of Durham at Scorbrough, Yorkshire, and in several other locations in the county. Percy's son Alan was

to come into conflict with the bishop over holdings at Lund, Holme on the Wold, and Welton in the reign of William Rufus. William de Percy also possessed property in the city of York and the church of St Mary, Castlegate. He was present when William the Conqueror heard a plea relating to the property of the abbey of Fécamp c.1086, and he later witnessed charters of William Rufus in the period 1091–5. He is known to have built castles at Topcliffe, Spofforth, Sneaton, and Hackness, in Yorkshire.

William de Percy married Emma de Port, a kinswoman of Hugh de Port of Basing, and the marriage brought Hambledon, Hampshire, to the Percy family. Emma herself was a benefactor of Whitby, granting to the abbey lands in Cambridgeshire which had formed part of her dowry; she survived her husband. William de Percy went on the first crusade, in 1096, and died in Palestine, where he was buried. He was succeeded by his son and heir, Alan de Percy (d. 1130x36). His other sons were: Walter; William, who may be identical with a certain William de Percy, canon of York; and Richard of Dunsley, who patronized the family foundation at Whitby with his eldest brother. In 1166 William de Percy's grandson and namesake, another William, answered for twenty-eight knights' fees of the old enfeoffment and just over eight fees of the new enfeoffment. Percy's brother Serlo was prior of Whitby Abbey and his nephew William de Percy was later the abbot of the house in the reign of Henry I. Picot de Percy, a Yorkshire tenant of William de Percy in 1086 who witnessed a number of Whitby charters, was probably closely related to William. Another likely kinsman was Ernald de Percy, a tenant of Robert de Brus, who witnessed William's charter for Whitby c.1090–96.

EMMA COWNIE

Sources J. C. Atkinson, ed., *Cartularium abbathiae de Whitby*, 1, SurtS, 69 (1879) · H. Hall, ed., *The Red Book of the Exchequer*, 1, Rolls Series, 99 (1896), 424–6 · J. H. Round, ed., *Calendar of documents preserved in France, illustrative of the history of Great Britain and Ireland* (1899) · *Reg. RAN*, vol. 1 · GEC, *Peerage*, new edn, 10.435–43 · W. Farrer and others, eds., *Early Yorkshire charters*, 12 vols. (1914–65), vol. 2, no. 13; vol. 11, nos.1–10, 20–23 · L. C. Loyd, *The origins of some Anglo-Norman families*, ed. C. T. Clay and D. C. Douglas, Harleian Society, 103 (1951), 69, 77 · I. J. Sanders, *English baronies: a study of their origin and descent, 1086–1327* (1960) · J. A. Green, *English sheriffs to 1154* (1990), 89 · J. Burton, 'The monastic revival in Yorkshire: Whitby and St Mary's, York', *Anglo-Norman Durham*, ed. D. Rollason, M. Harvey, and M. Prestwich (1994), 41–51 · C. P. Lewis, 'The formation of the honor of Chester, 1066–1100', *Journal of the Chester Archaeological Society*, 71 (1991), 37–68 [G. Barraclough issue, *The earldom of Chester and its charters*, ed. A. T. Thacker]

Percy, William de (1191x3–1245), baron, was the eldest son of Henry de Percy (d. c.1198) and Isabel de Brus, daughter of Adam de Brus and Juetta d'Arches. He had a younger brother, Henry. From at least 1200 his guardian was William *Brewer, a royal favourite. He came of age between 1212 and 1214, whereupon he gained control of the honour of Petworth, which his father, Henry, had inherited from his own father, Joscelin de *Louvain, the younger son of Godefroi, duke of Lower Lorraine, and brother of Henry I's second wife, Queen *Adeliza. He should also have inherited the Percy estates, which had been divided between his paternal grandmother, Agnes, and her sister

Matilda, who died without heirs, but because of a legal technicality he had to share these lands with his uncle Richard de *Percy until the latter's death in 1244; this division of lands created a large amount of litigation in the meantime.

In 1214 William de Percy participated in King John's expedition to Poitou. He was later listed by Matthew Paris as one of the followers of the twenty-five barons of Magna Carta, but there is no other evidence that he supported the rebel cause. He was certainly a supporter of the king in the civil war that broke out following the king's repudiation of Magna Carta, for in May 1216 King John granted him the lands of his uncle Richard, a prominent rebel and one of the twenty-five barons, and of other rebels, although these grants were revoked when peace was made early in Henry III's reign. Percy served Henry III in the campaign against William, count of Aumale, in 1221 and participated in later campaigns as well, although he paid £100 to avoid the Poitevin campaign of 1242. He was a generous benefactor to the church, for he gave the manor and forest of Gisburn to Sallay Abbey and made gifts to the hospital of Sandon, the nunnery at Stainfield, Coverham Abbey, Shulbrede Priory, and Healaugh Park Priory.

Percy married first Joan, one of the five daughters of his guardian, William Brewer. They had five daughters of their own who in 1233 (their mother having died) inherited one fifth of the Brewer estates after the death of William Brewer the younger. Percy's second wife, who survived him, was Elena, the daughter of Ingram de Balliol. They had at least six sons, Henry de *Percy, William, Walter, Ingram, Alan, and Joscelin; a seventh son, Geoffrey, is mentioned in later genealogies. Percy died not long before 28 July 1245. His body was buried at Sallay Abbey in Yorkshire but his heart was buried with his first wife, Joan, at the hospital of Sandon in Sussex.

Hugh M. Thomas

Sources C. T. Clay, ed., *The Percy fee* (1963), vol. 11 of *Early Yorkshire charters*, ed. W. Farrer (1914–65) · [M. T. Martin], ed., *The Percy chartulary*, SurtS, 117 (1911) · *Chancery records* · Paris, *Chron.* · *Curia regis rolls preserved in the Public Record Office* (1922–) · J. Parker, ed., *Feet of fines for the county of York*, 3: *from 1218 to 1231*, Yorkshire Archaeological Society, 62 (1921) · *Pipe rolls* · J. McNulty, ed., *The chartulary of the Cistercian Abbey of St Mary of Sallay in Craven*, 2 vols., Yorkshire Archaeological Society, 87, 90 (1933–4) · J. C. Atkinson, ed., *Cartularium abbathiae de Whitby*, 2 vols, SurtS, 69, 72 (1879–81) · W. Brown, ed., *Yorkshire inquisitions of the reigns of Henry III and Edward I*, 1, Yorkshire Archaeological Society, 12 (1892), 66–72 · *CClR, 1242–7*, 332

Percy, William (1574–1648), poet and playwright, probably born in Tynemouth, was the third son of Henry *Percy, eighth earl of Northumberland (c.1532–1585), and Katharine Neville (1545/6–1596). In mid-1583, with two of his brothers, he was sent to Paris where Robert Persons hoped that the children would be 'made firm in the Catholic religion' (*Miscellanea*, 99), but the earl insisted they return to England. On 13 June 1589 Percy matriculated from Gloucester Hall, Oxford, where he studied under Dr John Case, 'the great tutor for Roman Catholic scholars'

(Wood, MS top. Oxon. C.10.232, interleaf *v*). Percy studied Italian and Latin but his primary interest was contemporary literature, including the works of Peele, Dekker, Gabriel Harvey, Sidney, and Spenser.

At Oxford, Percy belonged to a Catholic literary coterie which included Barnaby Barnes, whose *Parthenophil and Parthenope: Sonnettes, Madrigals, Eligies, and Odes* (1593) was dedicated 'To the right noble and virtuous gentleman' William Percy 'his dearest friend'. Percy published his own collection *Sonnets to the Fairest Coelia* in 1594. In the preface he promises: 'ere long I will impart unto the world another Poem which shall be both more fruitfull and ponderous'. He includes a sonnet dedicated to Barnes (Parthenophil). Although Percy's sonnets show no real talent, he was favourably reviewed by William Clerke, in *Polimenteia* (1595), who describes the sweet singers of Oxford as 'Britten, Percie, Willobie, Fraunce, Lodge, Master Davies of L. I., Drayton, Learned M. Prat' (sig. Q3*v*). Percy's circle included Charles Fitzgeoffrey, author of *Sir Francis Drake* (1596), who, in his *Caroli Fitzgeoaffridi Affaniae* (1601), praises Percy as a poet. The coterie also included the Mychelbourne brothers, Edward, Lawrence, and Thomas, all of whom feature in Percy's poems. A later member was Thomas Campion, a Cambridge man, who praises Percy in his *Epigrammatum II* (1619) for his wit. One of Percy's six extant plays, *The Cuck-Queanes and Cuckolds Errants, or, The Bearing Down the Inn* concerns the adventures of two Oxford undergraduates, has a prologue spoken by Tarlton, and is set in the year of the Armada (1588); it concludes with a panegyric to Sir Francis Drake.

Percy had moved from Oxford to London by 1595 for on 25 January in that year he, along with the earl of Northumberland, acknowledged a debt to Arthur Medleycote, merchant taylor, for £2400. The debtors were required to repay £1226 by 29 February 1596; by 9 July 1600 Medleycote declared himself satisfied. There is no indication as to how Percy incurred such huge debts. In February 1596 he fought a duel with one Henry Denny, who was wounded 2 inches deep under the chin. Denny seemed to make a full recovery but sickened and died on 19 March. The inquest, however, declared Denny died 'by reason of … sickness and by the visitation of God' (Alnwick Castle, Percy papers, 5, fol. 108*v*). By August 1599 Percy was again in debt in the sum of £50 to one Valentine Browne of Crofte in Lincolnshire. By 5 July 1604, however, this debt was vacated.

Percy wrote six plays, which he continually revised. He may have produced a version of *The Faery Pastoral, or, Forest of Elves* for the visit of James I to Syon House on 8 June 1603, but he seems to have most especially aspired to have his plays performed by either or both of the Children of Paul's and the Children of the Revels. All three extant autographs of his plays have modifications to devise suitable variants for performance by children. *Arabia sitiens, or, A Dreame of a Drye Yeare: a Tragaecomodye* (1601), *A Country Tragaedye in Vacunium* (1602), and *The Aphrodysial, or, Sea Feast: a Marinall* (1602) are dedicated 'unto the children of the Revells and of Poules'. At the end of one autograph there is a note:

to the Master of the Children of Poules. Memorandum, that if any of … these Pastoralls and Comoedyes … shall but over reach in length (the children not to begin before foure, after prayers, and the gates of Pawles shutting at sixe) the tyme of supper, that then in tyme and place convenient, you do let passe some of the songs, and make the consort the shorter, for I suppose these plaies to be somewhat too long for that place.   (Reynolds, 259)

A version of these plays could possibly have been played at Paul's in the early phase of their revival (1599–1603). His last play, *Necromantes, or, The Two Supposed Heds: a Comicall Invention* (1632) is designated 'For Actors only' (Hillebrand, 401).

By late 1603 Percy may have been living near Bamber Rape, Sussex, for, at the end of *The Faery Pastoral* he writes 'Finis 1603 Wolves Hill my Parnassus which is in Sussex' (Hillebrand, 401); by 1611 he was in prison in Oxford for on 12 February 1612 the earl of Northumberland's accounts speak of 'Owing by Mr. Wm. Percy viz. To Mr. Bagwell the keeper of Oxford Castle for the charges of Mr. Percy's diet there £11. 19s.' (ibid., 399). In 1638 the Reverend Garrard describes Percy living obscurely in Oxford, where he 'drinks nothing but Ale' (G. Radcliffe, *The Earl of Strafforde's Letters and Dispatches*, ed. W. Knowler, 1739, 2.168) and eventually he died 'an aged Bachelor, in Penny Farthing St. … after he had lived a melancholy and retired life many years; and was buried in the Cathedral of Christ Church, near to the grave of Sir Henry Gage, the 28th of May 1648' (Wood, MS top. Oxon. F.4, fol. 83).   REAVLEY GAIR

Sources H. N. Hillebrand, 'William Percy: an Elizabethan amateur', *Huntington Library Quarterly*, 1 (1937–8), 391–416 · A. Wood, Bodl. Oxf., MS Top. Oxon. c. 10 · *Miscellanea, IV*, Catholic RS, 4 (1907) · G. F. Reynolds, 'William Percy and his plays, with a summary of the customs of Elizabethan staging', *Modern Philology*, 12 (1914–15), 241–60 · R. Gair, *The Children of Paul's: the story of a theatre company, 1553–1608* (1982) · Alnwick Castle, Northumberland, Percy papers, vol. 5 · B. Barnes, *Foure bookes of offices* (1606) · T. Campion, *Epigrammatum II* (1619) · W. Clerke, *Polimenteia* (1595) · M. H. Dodds, 'William Percy and Charles Fitzjeffrey', *N&Q*, 160 (1931), 420–21 · M. H. Dodds, 'William Percy and James I', *N&Q*, 161 (1931), 13 · C. Fitzgeoffrey, *Affaniae* (1601) · Foster, *Alum. Oxon.* · *The sonnets of William Percy*, ed. A. B. Grosart (1877) · Wood, *Ath. Oxon.*, new edn

Archives BM, papers (Alnwick Castle), vol. 5 [microfilm]

Percy, William Henry (1788–1855). *See under* Percy, Josceline (1784–1856).

Percyvale, Sir John (d. 1503). *See under* Percyvale, Thomasine (d. 1512).

Percyvale [*née* Bonaventure], **Thomasine** (d. 1512), trader and school founder, was born in Week St Mary, near Bude in Cornwall, daughter of John and Joan Bonaventure. She became the subject of a legend, recounted by Richard Carew in his *Survey of Cornwall* (1602), which described the visit of a London merchant to Week St Mary, where Thomasine, the daughter of a poor family, kept sheep on the moor. The merchant, admiring her beauty and virtues, rescued her from poverty and took her to London where she married three times, her last husband becoming mayor of the city, and founded a school in the parish of

her birth. Far from being poor, however, Thomasine's parents were in fact of gentry rank and were related by marriage to the Dinhams of Lifton. She may have gone to London about 1460, possibly as a servant to Richard Nordon, a wealthy London tailor with business links in Cornwall. He was an associate of one of her brothers, Richard, who from 1463 was rector of Chelsfield in Kent where their parents were eventually buried. Her first husband, whom she married before 1466, was Henry Galle, a London tailor who supplied clothes to Sir John Howard, later duke of Norfolk (d. 1485). Galle died probably in April 1466, leaving her his business, which she ran for a short while, before marrying Thomas Barnaby, another tailor and a fellow parishioner of St Dunstan-in-the-West. This marriage was even more short-lived, and Barnaby died in March 1467, leaving her a young but wealthy widow, capable of running a business and training apprentices.

Thomasine's third husband, whom she married *c.*1469, was **Sir John Percyvale** (d. 1503), merchant and mayor of London. Born probably *c.*1430 in Macclesfield, Cheshire, Percyvale began his career in London as a servant in the mayor's household, becoming serjeant-at-mace in 1457. By the late 1460s, perhaps because of his marriage to Thomasine, he was active as a tailor and cloth merchant, becoming a liveryman of the Tailors' Company in 1468/9. He was elected master of the craft in 1485, and became an alderman, first for Vintry ward (1485–96) and then for Langbourn (1496–1503), serving as sheriff in 1486–7. He acquired property in both wards as he expanded his business interests as a general merchant. Percyvale was knighted by Henry VII when the king arrived in London in 1485. His election to the mayoralty in 1498 was controversial: he had been an unsuccessful candidate on three previous occasions, primarily because of the rivalry which existed between the tailors and other companies, particularly the drapers. A chronicler also blamed the 'hote apetyte' which Percyvale himself was rumoured to have for the post. He died in May 1503, shortly after founding a free grammar school in Macclesfield with the assistance of two Cheshire men, Thomas Savage, archbishop of York (d. 1507), and Sir Richard Sutton. In his will, dated 4 March 1502, he made substantial bequests of goods and clothing to parish churches in London and Cheshire and left lands in London and Kent to his widow. In the absence of any children from his marriage to Thomasine, other lands in London were to revert to his nephew and heir, Richard Percyvale of Ipswich, after her death.

Thomasine continued to run the business and train apprentices, and she maintained a large household at their mansion in Lombard Street, London. In November 1508 her prominence and wealth made her a target for a 'forced loan' of £1000 levied by the crown. She shared her late husband's interest in education and after his death brought up and instructed several poor children. In 1506 she began to make arrangements for her own grammar school, in Week St Mary, and the foundation deed of 10 July mirrored that of her late husband's school in Macclesfield, in providing for board and education to be given free of charge by a graduate of Oxford or Cambridge. The endowment, comprising lands in Devon purchased by Thomasine from Sir John Lisle, was to be placed in the hands of nineteen feoffees on her death. These arrangements were largely complete by February 1508 when Thomasine made the first of her two wills, in which she gave property to the Merchant Taylors' Company to augment the chantry, founded by her late husband in St Mary Woolnoth, which was administered by the company. Later that year she acquired a royal licence enabling her to found a chantry in the church at Week St Mary, and soon afterwards the first master of the school was appointed. She died before October 1512 and left the final arrangements for the school in the hands of her cousin, John Dinham. Her will, dated 26 March 1512, included a large number of cash bequests to servants, friends, and her remaining family in Cornwall, as well as money for charitable works. She also established numerous post-obit arrangements in London and Cornwall through her bequests to churches and religious houses. In a codicil dated 10 April she made over more lands in Devon to the trustees of her school. She was buried alongside her third husband in the church of St Mary Woolnoth in London. MATTHEW DAVIES

Sources M. P. Davies, 'Dame Thomasine Percyvale "the maid of Week" (d. 1512)', *Medieval London widows, 1300–1500*, ed. C. M. Barron and A. F. Sutton (1994), 185–207 · N. Orme, *Education in the west of England, 1066–1548* (1976) · P. L. Hull, 'The endowment and foundation of a grammar school at Week St Mary by Dame Thomasine Percyvale', *Journal of the Royal Institution of Cornwall*, new ser., 7 (1973–7), 21–54 · R. Carew, *The survey of Cornwall* (1602) · CLRO · PRO · MS records, Merchant Taylors' Company, London

Pereira, George Edward (1865–1923), army officer and explorer, was born on 26 January 1865, at 4 Upper Portland Place, Marylebone, London. He was the second of four children and eldest son of Edward Pereira (1817–1872), gentleman, of 23 Grosvenor Square, and his wife, the Hon. Margaret Anne Stonor (1839–1894), eighth daughter of Thomas Stonor, third Baron Camoys, and his wife, Frances.

Educated at the Oratory School, Edgbaston (1876–83) under Cardinal Newman, and at the Royal Military College, Sandhurst (1883–4) where he was a contemporary of Leslie Napier Younghusband, brother of Sir Francis Younghusband, Pereira was commissioned in the 3rd battalion of the Grenadier Guards on 23 August 1884. A hunting accident in January 1885 left him with a permanent limp which threatened his two great ambitions—to see active service and to explore unknown lands. Hoping to be selected for the expeditionary force to the Sudan, he went to Cairo to learn Arabic, but his lameness was against him and he remained on home service until 1899.

In April 1899 Captain Pereira was seconded for service with the Chinese regiment of infantry recently formed at Weihaiwei. In 1900 he took part in the fighting at Tientsin (Tianjin) where he was slightly wounded and in the relief of the legations at Peking (Beijing). He was awarded the DSO 'in recognition of services during the recent operations in China'. After spending much of 1901 touring the provinces of north-east China, Major Pereira in May 1902 rejoined his battalion in South Africa for the campaigns in

the Transvaal and Cape Colony. Late in 1903 he went to Korea, and in January 1904 he was appointed temporary military attaché to the British minister at Seoul in Korea. In 1905, as military attaché with the Japanese army, he witnessed the Manchurian campaign, and at its close became military attaché at Peking, a post he held until 1910. He was made a CMG in March 1906.

As military attaché Pereira made a series of long journeys in every part of China during 1906–8, visiting various units of the Chinese army. His tact and understanding and his conversational ability enabled him to make many personal friends among high officials. The knowledge he gained of Chinese people from the soldiers of his Weihaiwei regiment to the highest levels of officialdom was of great value for his later travels. He came back to Europe in 1909, but peacetime soldiering held no attractions and he resigned his commission in July of that year.

In the following year Pereira returned to China and journeyed from Peking through Chihli (Zhili) and Shansi, across the Ordos to Ninghsia. In 1911 he spent nine months exploring and shooting in the Altai and T'ien Shan. In 1912 he visited the Kumbun and Labrang monasteries in south-western Kansu before moving south along the upper reaches of the Salween and Mekong rivers and crossing briefly into the Shan states in Burma. He then moved across country to Foochow (Fuzhou) and by steamer to Shanghai. During these years he travelled 11,000 miles on foot.

In September 1913 Pereira became a lieutenant-colonel in the reserve officers list, and being at home on the outbreak of war in 1914 he rejoined the service. He was posted to the staff of the 47th London division and went to France with them. In June 1915 he took command of the 4th Royal Welch Fusiliers and led them in the battle of Loos, where he was slightly wounded. From January 1916 until November 1917 he commanded the 47th brigade of the 16th division. In 1918 he commanded the 43rd brigade during the final advance of the allies. He was made CB in January 1917. He always won the absolute confidence of his troops by his complete disregard for danger. He retired at the end of the war with the rank of brigadier-general and in 1919 joined General Knox's mission to Admiral Kolchak in Siberia.

Pereira returned to China in 1920, over fifty-four years old, lame, in indifferent health, and with the goal of Lhasa in mind. As a schoolboy he had read the account by two French Lazarist missionaries, Evariste Huc and Joseph Gabet, of their journey to Lhasa in 1846, an achievement which had never been repeated by Europeans. He left Peking in January 1921 crossing the famine-stricken provinces of Chihli, Shensi (Shanxi), and Honan (Henan). He went to Honan Fu (Loyang) at the invitation of General Wu P'ei-fu in order to visit his model army. From July to October Pereira undertook three most arduous shooting trips in the wild mountainous district of Muping in Szechwan (Sichuan), hoping to shoot a giant panda, a rare animal that few Europeans had seen. He failed to get one but did shoot a pandar cat or red panda, equally rare, which was sent to the Natural History Museum at South Kensington.

Because of the constant need to ford streams and climb slippery surfaces he discarded his boots and tried native sandals, but these gave his feet little protection and he was laid up in one town for seven weeks with a poisoned foot. In his last camp at 10,000 feet the cold and wet forced him to return to town, walking 48 miles in sandals through deep snow. He was again laid up, suffering from frost-bitten feet.

Pereira left Tangar in Kansu in May 1922, and reached Jyekundo on 23 June, after crossing an area with little food or grazing, and waterless in places. During this journey he lost most of his transport animals, but was fortunate in obtaining assistance from passing caravans. Chamdo was reached on 28 July after eighteen days of difficult travelling. On 3 September he received permission to proceed to Lhasa. The next six weeks were spent in a succession of journeys following valleys and crossing numerous passes, varying in height from 14,500 to 16,800 feet, scrambling over tracks covered with large boulders where the height above sea level made every step an exertion. Pereira arrived at Lhasa on 17 October, completely exhausted and suffering from thrombosis in his left leg. There he was comfortably housed by the Tibetan commander-in-chief, and had an interview with Tubten Gyatso, the great thirteenth Dalai Lama. He returned through Gyantse and Darjeeling, reaching Calcutta early in December, where he was treated in hospital for thrombosis.

In January 1923 Pereira left Calcutta for Bhamo in Burma, crossing into Yunnan, visiting Lolo and Miao areas, and then travelling down the Yangtze (Yangzi) to Shanghai which he reached on 13 May. He returned through Indo-China to Yunnan where he was joined by Dr H. G. Thompson and together they made their way to Batang in Szechwan. On the next stage of their journey to Kantze, Pereira became seriously ill and died from gastric ulcers on 20 October 1923. He was buried in the Chinese cemetery in the shadow of the Great Kantze Lamasery about 30 miles from the Tibetan border. His remains were later transferred to consecrated ground in the Roman Catholic mission at Tatsienlu (Dajianlu).

Pereira kept detailed diaries recording his travels and the people whom he met. Some of this material appeared in his articles written for the *Geographical Journal*. These diaries are now in the Royal Geographical Society together with his photographs. An account of his journey from Peking to Lhasa was printed as an official report in 1923, but it was his friend Francis Younghusband who compiled *Peking to Lhasa: narrative of journeys in the Chinese empire made by the late Brigadier-General George Pereira* (1925).

Pereira was 5 feet 9 inches tall, lame, and not physically strong. He had, however, great energy, a genius for leadership, and an absolute determination to carry out his plans combined with an indifference to danger, discomfort, and fatigue. He was ready to talk about his journeys but in a purely impersonal manner. Although he had a very proper sense of self-respect, and was not a man to be trifled with, he had great charm and was modest with an innate courtesy and a dry sense of humour. 'It is lucky therefore that

the brigands are so utterly ignorant of brigandage as a fine art'. His experiences of brigands he described as 'a regular Gilbert and Sullivan opera'. He spoke Mandarin Chinese and had some knowledge of dialects which made him independent of interpreters for all but Tibetan conversations. He was deeply religious and a devout Catholic, but with a broad sympathy for people of all kinds. Army life coupled with a restless spirit made him disinclined to a settled life and he never married though he remained devoted to his family.

Pereira's journeys, mostly on foot, through areas of eastern Tibet and western China rarely if ever crossed by Europeans covered almost 45,000 miles. They were made in unsettled times, frequently verging on civil war, and produced much new topographical and ethnographical information, including the first accounts of Mount Amne Machin. His reports confirmed the belief that the Himalayas end in Assam and Burma rather than extending into China. Had he lived he would have been recommended for the gold medal of the Royal Geographical Society.

M. J. POLLOCK

Sources DNB · GJ, 63 (1924) · Nature, 112 (1923), 837 · F. Younghusband, ed., *Peking to Lhasa: narrative of journeys in the Chinese empire made by the late Brigadier-General George Pereira; compiled from notes and diaries* (1925) · G. E. Pereira, over 90 vols. of diaries and letters, and boxes of photographs, RGS · G. Pereira, 'A journey across the Ordos', GJ, 37 (1911) · G. Pereira, 'A visit to Labrang monastery, south-west Kan-Su, north-west China', GJ, 40 (1912) · G. Pereira, 'Brigadier-General George Pereira's journey to Lhasa', GJ, 61 (1923) · C. Pereira, 'Peking to Lhasa (from the diaries of the late Brig.-Gen. George Pereira)', GJ, 64 (1924) · H. G. Thompson, 'From Yunnan-Fu to Peking along the Tibetan and Mongolian borders including the last journey of Brig.-Gen. George E. Pereira', GJ, 67 (1926), 2–27 · LondG (25 July 1901) [suppl.; award of DSO] · LondG (1 Jan 1917) [suppl.; award of CB] · 'dispatches', LondG (1915–17), suppl. · *Journal of the West China Border Research Society* [Shanghai], 7 (1935), 29 · North China Daily News (19 Nov 1923), 5 · South China Morning Post [Hong Kong] (28 Nov 1923), 9 · b. cert. · d. cert.
Archives RGS, diaries and notebooks | BL, corresp. with F. M. Bailey, MS Eur. F 157
Likenesses W. Stoneman, photograph, 1918, NPG · photograph, repro. in Pereira, 'Peking to Lhasa', frontispiece
Wealth at death £32,487 12s. 8d.: probate, 3 Jan 1924, CGPLA Eng. & Wales

Pereira, Isaac (c.1658–1718), army contractor, was born in the Netherlands to Portuguese Jewish parents, being the third of four sons of **Jacob Pereira** (1629–1707), a jeweller, and his first wife, Ribca de Paiva (b. 1631), who married in Amsterdam in 1651 and then settled at The Hague. Isaac's grandfather Thomás Rodriguez (later Abraham Israel) Pereira had been a banker in Madrid who took refuge in Rotterdam in 1648 and converted to open Judaism.

In 1674 Jacob Pereira entered into partnership with Antonio (Moses) Alvares Machado, *providiteur generaal* to the army of William of Orange, who needed a man at The Hague to solicit payments for supplies from the Dutch government ahead of other creditors and to raise funds to finance his work in the field when payments were overdue. Jacob Pereira's sons, Abraham (b. 1651), Isaac, and Francisco (Aaron; b. 1660), worked as Machado's assistants in this army provisioning business. Machado accompanied William to England in 1688 and organized the feeding of Dutch troops, but then had to return to the Netherlands to serve their army in Europe. On Machado's recommendation, Isaac Pereira was engaged to provision William III's forces during the Irish campaign and held contracts for supplying bread, biscuits, horses, horseshoes, fodder, axle grease, and bread wagons. The duke of Schomberg wrote to the king of his relief at Pereira's appointment.

The sums of money involved in the contract were large. In June 1691 a warrant was issued to pay Isaac Pereira £125,468 for supplies and shipping he had provided. He discharged his duties to the satisfaction of Schomberg, General Godart de Ginkel, and the king. Like his father and Machado, he made a fortune as an army contractor far faster than did most merchants. While their religion was a political disadvantage, they won and held William III's patronage by sheer professional competence. Outliving his royal patron, Pereira died at The Hague on 8 June 1718 and was buried, like his father, in the Portuguese Jewish cemetery at Oudekerk in the Netherlands. His will, made on 30 August 1713, and translated out of Dutch before probate was granted in London to Francis Aaron Pereira on 28 October 1718, indicates that in the last years of his life Pereira had still been dividing his time between the Netherlands and England. EDGAR SAMUEL

Sources E. Samuel, 'A Kneller portrait discovered', *The Connoisseur* (Oct 1975), 108–11 · *Correspondentie van Willem III en van Hans Willem Bentinck*, ed. N. Japikse, 2 (The Hague, 1935), Deel 2 · W. A. Shaw, ed., *Calendar of treasury books*, 1, PRO (1904) · D. L. de Barrios, *Triumpho del govierno popular y de la antiquidad Holandesa* (Amsterdam, 1683) · will, PRO, PROB 11/566, sig. 222
Likenesses G. Kneller, oils, 1696, repro. in *The Connoisseur* · miniature (after G. Kneller), Holburne Museum of Art, Bath

Pereira, Jacob (1629–1707). *See under* Pereira, Isaac (c.1658–1718).

Pereira, Jonathan (1804–1853), pharmacologist and physician, was born on 22 May 1804 in Shoreditch, London, the son of Daniel Lopes Pereira, a Lloyd's underwriter of Portuguese-Jewish extraction. He acquired the rudiments of education at one of the small schools in Shoreditch and from the age of ten attended a 'classical academy' in Queen Street, Finsbury, where the master judged him to be a boy of considerable merit. At the age of sixteen Pereira was articled to an apothecary named Latham who had a general medical practice in the City Road but the indentures were cancelled when Latham became mentally ill. In 1821 Pereira became a student at the General Dispensary, Aldersgate Street, and attended courses in chemistry, materia medica, and practical medicine by Henry Clutterbuck, on natural philosophy by George Birkbeck, and on botany by William Lambe. Two months before his nineteenth birthday, on 6 March 1823, he qualified as licentiate of the Society of Apothecaries and was appointed apothecary to the Aldersgate dispensary. He began to study surgery at St Bartholomew's Hospital and qualified as a surgeon in 1825.

While acting as an apothecary at the dispensary Pereira discovered his vocation as a teacher. He gave private lessons to medical students and prepared texts to assist them

Jonathan Pereira (1804–1853), by D. J. Pound, pubd 1853 (after John Jabez Edwin Mayall)

in their studies. In 1823 he published *Synopsis of the Chemical Decomposition that takes place in the Preparations of the London Pharmacopoeia*. In 1824 he published his English translation of the newly revised *Pharmacopoeia Londinensis* and *Selectae e praescriptis*, a selection of medical prescriptions. There followed *A Manual for the Use of [Medical] Students* (1826) and *A General Table of Atomic Numbers with an Introduction to Atomic Theory* (1827). In 1826 he succeeded Clutterbuck as lecturer in chemistry at the Aldersgate dispensary and two years later began to teach the courses in materia medica. About this time he was made a fellow of the Linnean Society and was a member of the Phrenological Society and the Meteorological Society. In the years that followed he achieved considerable success as a teacher and was described as a man of commanding appearance, looking older than his years, who retained the interest of his audience by the novelty of his facts. Attendances at his courses generated a large income, sufficient to enable him to build a new lecture theatre at his own expense. His teaching and duties at the dispensary left him little time for original work and he published only one paper between 1827 and 1835.

In 1832 Pereira married Louisa Jane Lucas, resigned his office of apothecary at the dispensary and set up in medical practice in Aldersgate Street near his home in Finsbury Square. He was appointed professor of materia medica at the new medical school in Aldersgate Street and lecturer in chemistry at the London Hospital. He declined an invitation to become professor of chemistry and materia medica at St Bartholomew's Hospital because the by-laws required him to relinquish all other posts. His lectures in materia medica, published in the *Medical Gazette* between 1835 and 1837, were translated into German and republished in India. In 1838 he was elected a fellow of the Royal Society.

In 1840 Pereira resolved to leave London and graduate from one of the universities in Scotland but changed his mind when he was told of the prospect of a vacancy in the post of assistant physician to the London Hospital. At short notice he prepared for and passed the licentiate examination of the Royal College of Physicians. He also obtained an MD from Erlangen, and on 3 March 1841 was appointed to the post at the London Hospital. In 1845 he became a fellow of the Royal College of Physicians. He was made a member of the pharmacopoeial committee and curator of the museum. He became full physician at the London Hospital in 1851.

From 1842 Pereira devoted much of his time and energy to the completion of the third edition of *The Elements of Materia Medica and Therapeutics*, which was his major work. The first edition based on his published lectures appeared in 1839 and an enlarged second edition followed in 1842. The third revision attempted to resolve problems relating to the identification, action, and use of medicinal substances, and place the knowledge of the action of drugs on an organized and scientific basis. The first volume of this encyclopaedic work was published in 1849 and was devoted to general pharmacology and the inorganic bodies used in therapy. Pereira saw the first part of the second volume through the press in 1850 but the final part was incomplete at the time of his death. It was published in 1853, having been completed by Alfred Swaine Taylor and George Owen Rees. Pereira's treatise, published at a time when pharmacology was evolving into an experimental science, surpassed all other works on materia medica, introducing readers to a detailed scientific and clinical knowledge of each of the medicinal agents then in use.

At the time that he was revising his book on the materia medica Pereira was closely associated with the newly formed Pharmaceutical Society of Great Britain. He gave active support to Jacob Bell, whose objective was to raise the status of pharmacy in Britain and promote the advancement of pharmaceutical science. In 1842 Pereira had expressed his opinion that the low state of pharmacy in Britain was due to the want of a scientific education by practising chemists and druggists. His reputation and enthusiasm for the improvement of pharmacy were of great value to the founders of the Pharmaceutical Society in its early years when it was opposed by sections of the medical establishment and from within the trade itself. Pereira became a close friend of Bell and had considerable influence on the editorial policy of the *Pharmaceutical Journal*, contributing numerous articles on the materia medica. He became professor of materia medica at the School of Pharmacy and encouraged Bell to form a committee of leading scientists and pharmacists for the advancement of pharmacology. The object of the committee was to gather and sift information on the natural history and uses of substances employed in medicine. Pereira observed that no country possessed so many facilities for carrying out these enquiries as Great Britain, which governed colonies all over the world. When he resigned as professor of materia medica at the London Hospital in 1851 he presented his collection of specimens to the Pharmaceutical Society. His contributions to their evening meetings became the subjects of two books: *Lectures on Polarized Light* and *A Treatise on Food and Diet*, both published in 1843. Foodstuffs were discussed in the first editions of the *Elements of Materia Medica* but the publication of Justus von Liebig's *Animal Chemistry* in 1842 necessitated a revision, and Pereira, in his treatise, gave an account of the chemical elements of food in addition to the alimentary principles and dietetical treatments of disease.

Pereira's letters to Jacob Bell reveal him to have been a very hard-working good-humoured man, direct and frank in his manner, tolerant when the occasion demanded. He was charged by some with a want of originality but this had little effect on his widely held reputation which was built upon his qualities as a teacher and his ability to gather, organize, and record the numerous facts and disparate theories relating to the materia medica and the actions of medicines. His thirty-page 'Tabular view of the history and literature of the materia medica' in the third edition of the *Elements* is an indication of the range of his studies. He made it a rule, whenever possible, to have firsthand experience of the substance or species he was describing in his book. It was for this purpose that he was visiting the Hunterian Museum in December 1852 when he fell on the stairs and ruptured muscles and tendons in both legs. Disabled and in pain he continued to write until 20 January 1853 when he collapsed with severe chest pains and died that same day, at 47 Finsbury Square. He was buried in the cemetery at Kensal Green. He was survived by his wife.　　　　　　　　　　　　　　　　M. P. EARLES

Sources 'Memoir of the life of Jonathan Pereira', *Pharmaceutical Journal and Transactions*, 12 (1852–3), 409–16 · *The Lancet* (29 Jan 1853), 124 · *The Lancet* (5 Feb 1853), 139–40 · Munk, *Roll* · C. Cloughly, J. Burnby, and M. Earles, *My dear Mr Bell: letters from Dr Jonathan Pereira to Mr Jacob Bell, 1844–1853* (1987) · E. W. Morris, *A history of the London hospital*, 3rd edn (1926) · J. O'Hara-May, 'Foods and medicines', *Transactions of the British Society for the History of Pharmacy*, 1 (1970–77), 80–90 · J. Bell and T. Redwood, *Historical sketch of the progress of pharmacy in Britain* (1880) · *Association Medical Journal*, 1 (1853), 94 · *Annual Register* (1853) · d. cert. · DNB

Archives Wellcome L., annotated copy of *Elements of materia medica* | Royal Pharmaceutical Society, letters to Jacob Bell

Likenesses D. J. Pound, stipple and line engraving, pubd 1853 (after photograph by J. E. Mayall), NPG [*see illus.*] · Wyon, medal, 1853; struck by Royal Pharmaceutical Society in his memory · P. MacDowell, bust · J. E. Mayall, wood-engraving, Wellcome L. · D. J. Pound, stipple (after daguerreotype by J. E. Mayall), Wellcome L. · bust (after P. MacDowell, *c.*1854)

Perez, Miguel. *See* Philips, Miles (*b. c.*1554).

Perfect, William (1731/2–1809), physician specializing in the treatment of the insane, was the son of the Revd William Perfect (*d.* 1757), from 1745 vicar of East Malling, Kent, and his wife, Sarah (*d.* 1769). He was probably born in

Oxfordshire. In 1749 he was apprenticed to William Everred, a London surgeon. During his apprenticeship he attended lectures by Colin Mackenzie, a Scot specializing in obstetrics, and many years later published his correspondence with Mackenzie, relating to various difficult births at which he had assisted. Three editions of this, entitled *Cases in Midwifery*, appeared between 1781(?) and 1787.

In 1754 Perfect was working in Dartford, probably as assistant to a surgeon, having married the previous year Elizabeth Shrimpton (1730/31–1764), descended from a Penn, Buckinghamshire, family. The Perfects moved permanently to West Malling, Kent, in 1756, where William took over an established practice in the High Street. On his wife's early death in 1764 Perfect was left a widower with five children: Elizabeth, Sarah, William, Huntley, and George—a sixth, Daniel, had died shortly after his mother. One of his daughters married the artist Silvester *Harding (1745x51–1809); George Perfect *Harding was their son.

Grief at the loss of Elizabeth seems to have resulted in Perfect's becoming a freemason about 1765, and it was in freemasonry that he obtained his greatest social distinctions. He was promoted to the office of provincial grand orator in 1787, and eight years later became provincial grand master of the county of Kent, an office which he retained until his death.

During the 1760s Perfect threw himself into what was becoming virtually a crusade throughout the country to eliminate smallpox through the introduction of inoculation. Working with another local doctor he undertook the general inoculation of whole parishes in Kent and elsewhere, and appears to have travelled widely for this purpose until about 1769.

Perfect had already become interested in what was then termed lunacy, and now began to specialize in this, accommodating patients in his own house. Gentleness and common sense seem to have characterized his approach, whether dealing with women in childbirth or the insane. A keen believer in the value of advertising, he frequently publicized his medical services in the newspapers. An account of various mental afflictions which he had treated successfully, *Methods of Cure, in some Particular Cases of Insanity*, which was probably written originally for the purpose of advertisement and first published about 1778, was later expanded and, under various titles, including *Annals of Insanity*, had reached some seven editions by 1809. The book helped to establish his reputation in this field. Perfect obtained his MD from St Andrews University in 1783. Perfect's lunatic asylum remained the principal private asylum in Kent for many years, although it does not appear to have been very large. On Perfect's death his son George, who had worked alongside his father for some years, continued to run it, although with less success, becoming insolvent in 1815. As a result it was sold, the new owner, Robert Rix, soon transferring to the larger premises of Malling Place. The asylum begun by William Perfect remained in existence until the end of the twentieth century.

Perfect always enjoyed writing, both prose and verse: friends often received letters couched in rhyme. In the 1750s and 1760s he seems to have been one of a coterie of young scribblers who styled themselves Parnassians. These included William Woty, a Chatham friend Folly Streeter, and John Nichols, the future printer and writer, a few of whose poems appeared in Perfect's two-volume collection, *The Laurel Wreath* (1766). This was the second of his literary publications. The first was *A Bavin of Bays* (1763). Both books contained poems which had first appeared in one of several London magazines to which Perfect was a contributor, particularly the *General Magazine of Arts and Sciences*, the *Political Chronicle*, and the *Westminster Journal*. Perfect's work continued to appear in the London press for many years, most of it signed with one of his numerous pseudonyms. In September 1795 the *Freemasons' Magazine* carried the 'Memoirs of William Perfect, M.D., member of the London Medical Society', which are useful for extending our knowledge of Perfect's medical output, though one or two items are now no longer traceable, and others were never completed.

After his marriage about 1768 to a second wife, Henrietta (1745/6–1804), Perfect's family increased by four more children: Folliott Augusta, Lucy, Thomas, and Almeria. Following Henrietta's death, at the age of fifty-eight, Perfect married again, about 1805, his third wife being almost certainly Elizabeth Selby (1767–1851), of West Malling. He became ill in that year, however, and although able to officiate as provincial grand master in 1806, his health deteriorated from then on. Perfect died at home, in High Street, West Malling, on 5 June 1809, and was buried on 17 June with masonic rites in the vault in East Malling churchyard which he had had built some years earlier to commemorate his father and grandfather, both buried in East Malling church.   SHIRLEY BURGOYNE BLACK

Sources S. B. Black, *An eighteenth century mad-doctor: William Perfect of West Malling* (1995) · S. Pope, 'Freemasonry in Canterbury and provincial grand lodge, 1785–1809, and Dr Perfect, provincial grand master of Kent 1795–1809', *Ars Quatuor Coronatorum*, 52 (1939), 6–58 · 'Memoirs of William Perfect, M.D., member of the London Medical Society', *Freemasons' Magazine*, 5 (1795), 147–51 · Masonic Museum and Library, Canterbury, William Perfect MSS, 9 folio vols., 1754–1773 · P. J. Wallis and R. V. Wallis, *Eighteenth century medics*, 2nd edn (1988) · *General Magazine of Arts and Sciences: miscellaneous correspondence, 1755–1760*, 4 vols. (1759–64) · Vicar-general marriage allegations, LPL · *GM*, 1st ser., 79 (1809), 684 · *GM*, 1st ser., 74 (1804) [Henrietta Perfect]
Archives Masonic Museum and Library, Canterbury
Likenesses M. W. Sharp, oils, *c*.1796, Masonic Museum and Library, Canterbury · W. S. Leney, engraving, repro. in Black, *An eighteenth century mad-doctor* · W. Say, mezzotint (after M. W. Sharp, *c*.1796), BM

Perham, Dame **Margery Freda** (1895–1982), writer on African affairs and university teacher, was born at 219 Walmersley Road, Bury, Lancashire, on 6 September 1895, the youngest in the family of five sons and two daughters of Frederick Perham (1854–1924), wine and spirit merchant, and his wife, Marion Hodder Needell (1855–1929). Her grandmother was Mary Anna Needell, a novelist. All seven Perham children were sent to good northern public schools, four of them, including the two girls, attending

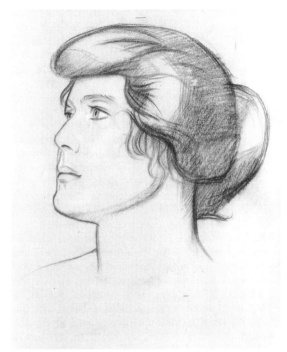

Dame Margery Freda Perham (1895–1982), by Sir William
Rothenstein, 1919

Oxford, Cambridge, and Leeds universities. From St
Anne's School, Abbots Bromley, Staffordshire, Margery
won an open scholarship to read history at St Hugh's College, Oxford, in 1914.

The death of her favourite brother, Edgar, in 1916, in the
First World War battle of Delville Wood, deeply wounded
Margery. At her time of greatest need she had no refuge
because her parents, never very affectionate, had closed
the family home to live in a hotel. The rest of the family
could offer her no home; even her sister, Ethel, who had
married Major Harry Rayne, a former big-game hunter
from New Zealand, then lived in Jubaland. Margery, firmly
dissuaded by her tutors from enlisting as a dispatch rider,
remained in Oxford, obtained the first-class degree
expected of her, and then, very reluctantly, became a history lecturer at Sheffield University, teaching former servicemen resuming their education. Vacations from
Oxford were spent partly with her parents in Harrogate
Spa or coastal guest houses, visiting school friends and her
old school, but for most of the time fending for herself in a
hotel near the British Museum.

In Sheffield, Margery was miserable as the only woman
teaching in the history faculty. Her students, many older
than she was, were a constant reminder of her dead
brother. Though her colleagues avidly produced academic
papers, she wrote none; her ambition had died with
Edgar. While writing *Aethelburga*, a play for the drama society about the introduction of Christianity to northern
Britain in the seventh century, she lost her own faith.
Hockey, tennis, golf, walking on the moors, riding her
motorbike, and giving occasional talks to the Workers'

Educational Association and the settlement in Sheffield
afforded some relief, but in the vacations she unwisely lectured on the origins of the war to the troops in France and
on Salisbury Plain. Among her few friends one or two
young men were attracted to the tall (almost 6 foot), handsome girl with brown hair and eyes and a stubborn jaw.
Behind a screen of constant activity she existed in a
slough of despond until she had a nervous breakdown
which forced her to take a year's leave in 1920.

Margery chose to convalesce with her sister's family in
Somaliland, where Rayne had been appointed district
commissioner at Hargeisa. The Perham sisters were thus
the first white women to live in the drought-ridden
Somali hinterland. Margery fell in love with Africa and the
life of the colonial officer administering justice, developing the district and caring for the people. She fulfilled a
childhood ambition to be a big-game hunter, shooting for
the pot and for sport, and rode on patrol with the camel
corps along the Ethiopian border.

Back in Sheffield, Margery added a course on imperial
history to her teaching curriculum, and gave some extramural lectures on Somaliland, but turned to novel writing
to resolve her personal problems rather than to academic
research. *Major Dane's Garden* (1925) was based on her African experience, *Josie Vine* (1927) on her family life, and
both analyse the difficulties of a young woman having to
make her own way in a predominantly man's world. She
consistently denied that these novels were autobiographical, yet parallels with her diaries are close.

In 1924 Margery returned to Oxford as tutor for modern
history, politics, philosophy, and economics at St Hugh's.
The reformed university curriculum allowed her to lecture on her particular interests, as the work of the League
of Nations permanent mandates commission encouraged
political scientists to study racial relations. In 1926 both
Oxford and Cambridge universities initiated courses for
postgraduate training of colonial service probationers.
Margery's knowledge of the duties and responsibilities of
colonial officers, though scant, was unique within the history faculty. Consequently, for five years she taught both
undergraduates and probationers, observed sessions of
the mandates commission in Geneva and began research
into the life of Sir William Johnson, an early administrator in New England.

In 1928–9 Margery successfully applied for a Rhodes
Trust travelling scholarship to study native administration in the United States and the British empire. The trustees' influence secured her assistance from influential men
in the university, Whitehall, Westminster, and the colonial administrations, and from journalists, philanthropists, and educationists. She received hospitality from governors and district officers, as well as from the indigenous
people. Secretariat and district files were opened for her
use and reports sent back to St Hugh's for later study. Governors detailed officers to take her on trek and opportunities for adventure cropped up everywhere. She walked
unaware and unscathed through a rebels' picket in Western Samoa, attended a riotous meeting of the black Industrial and Commercial Workers' Union in Durban, hunted

buffalo with Baron von Blixen and fell in love on trek with a married district commissioner. Frugal use of her funds, official generosity, and a renewal of her scholarship enabled her to travel from July 1929 until early 1932, visiting the United States, the Pacific islands, Australia, New Zealand, and much of Africa south of the Sahara. She wrote multitudinous notes, several articles on native administration for *The Times*, and sent home vivid diaries illustrated with photographs which, after copying and circulating among friends, were saved for her later use. They were eventually edited and published as *Pacific Prelude* (1988), *African Apprenticeship* (1974), *East African Journey* (1976), and *West African Passage* (1983). In 1930 two cables arrived in Tanganyika: one from Lord Lothian, secretary of the Rhodes Trust, offering an extension of travel, the other from her college asking her to return or resign her fellowship. Long afterwards she would tell how she dispatched two one-word replies: 'Accept' and 'Resign' (*DNB*).

The price paid was loss of her teaching post, though St Hugh's made Margery a non-stipendiary research fellow to maintain her connection with the university. With Ethel and Harry she invested her parents' legacies in a Surrey farm where, in a converted barn, she wrote *Native Administration in Nigeria* (1937), edited *Ten Africans* (1936), and, with Lionel Curtis, transformed their combative *Times* articles into *The Protectorates of South Africa* (1935). Later she produced a similar book with Elspeth Huxley, *Race and Politics in Kenya* (1944). Writing was punctuated by riding over to Little Parkhurst to discuss indirect rule with its originator, Lord Lugard.

Lugard and J. H. Oldham, promoting her reputation as an academic observer of colonial rule, nominated Margery to give evidence to the joint parliamentary committee on closer union in east Africa. Their International Institute of African Languages and Cultures gave her a grant to study anthropology at the London School of Economics and later a Rockefeller fellowship to travel in Sudan and east Africa to produce a companion book to the Nigerian one. Although she worked on it for a considerable time this book was never completed because of bouts of ill health, the outbreak of war, and the demands of her fast-developing academic and public life. Lord Lothian co-opted her to the committee advising Lord Hailey on the compilation of *An African Survey* (1938).

In 1935 Margery was appointed research lecturer in colonial administration, an Oxford post created after long pressure by General Smuts, the Rhodes trustees, and leading academics to make Rhodes House a centre of African research. This was the first step in transforming colonial studies from strictly historical observation of constitutional facts into examination of the duties and principles of colonial rule. When Lord Nuffield decided to endow a new Oxford college for postgraduate work in the social sciences, Margery was involved in its planning and, though the war postponed all building, she was appointed the first official and only woman fellow in 1939. As such she supervised research into imperial government and economics and edited the resulting series of Nuffield books (*Studies in Colonial Legislatures* and *Studies and Economics of a Tropical Dependency*) as well as *Colonial and Comparative Studies*), while G. D. H. Cole directed a parallel social survey of Britain. Both projects were designed to assist the post-war rehabilitation of Britain and the Commonwealth.

More direct government advisory service began in 1939 with Malcolm MacDonald's inclusion of Margery in his private conference on the principles of future colonial policy and the Colonial Office advisory committee on education in the colonies. This led to service on the Asquith commission on higher education in the colonies in 1943–5 and the West Indies higher education committee in 1944, the Irvine commission. During the war she also provided briefs for the committee of vice-chancellors advising the colonial secretary on reconstruction of the colonial service to prepare officers for the wider demands of the post-war dependencies. The resulting Devonshire courses embodied many of her recommendations, in particular the refresher courses for serving officers.

During a holiday in the Cotswolds spent reviewing family matters, the European political situation, difficulties with the Foreign Office over her book on Ethiopia, her own intellectual position in regard to the war, her achievements so far and the direction her life was taking, Margery heard by chance an instalment of Dorothy Sayers's radio play *The Man Born to be King*. Its vigorous vernacular treatment of the Christian story rekindled her faith so strongly that by 1965 she was prepared to preside over the merger of the Universities' Mission to Central Africa with the Society for the Propagation of the Gospel, for which an uncle had been a missionary in Borneo.

Margery's most compatible friends, Lugard and Sir Douglas Newbold, civil secretary to the Sudan government, both died in 1945. On visits to Sudan she would argue with Newbold into the early hours (and later by letter) about the way each wanted the political development of the dependent peoples to proceed. Lugard and his brother Edward had chosen Margery to write his official biography. For fifteen years she toiled at this major literary work which appeared in two volumes in 1956 and 1960. She published four volumes of Lugard's diaries (1959–63), and in 1965 the fifth edition of his magnum opus, *The Dual Mandate in British Tropical Africa*, first published in 1922. To do so, in 1948 she relinquished her university readership and resigned the directorship of the Institute of Commonwealth Studies which had evolved from her Nuffield College responsibilities, accepting in lieu a less demanding college fellowship in imperial administration. However, her public service, for which she had that year been appointed CBE, increased. She became a valued friend and adviser of Arthur Creech Jones, the Labour colonial secretary, and of his successors in both parties. Through membership of the Inter-University Council for Higher Education in the Colonies she designed curricula for the schools of public administration attached to the universities in Sudan and Uganda, in preparation for their achievement of independence. In

Oxford she befriended and assisted the education and political development of African students who were to become eminent in their own countries, among them Kofi Busia, Mekki Abbas, and Tom Mboya. As a founding member of the Africa Bureau she not only opposed the federation of British Central Africa but used her influence to help Tshekedi Khama, an old friend, and his nephew Seretse Khama to resolve their differences with the British government.

Letters from Margery appeared in *The Times* whenever an issue of imperial importance arose. These and her other ephemera were republished later in two volumes as *Colonial Sequence* (1967–70), presenting an account of the evolution of colonies into independent states, her own colonial policy development and occasional inconsistencies throughout four decades, and a reflection of the shifts in public opinion. She gave the Reith lectures, published as *The Colonial Reckoning*, in 1961 and two delightful series of travel reminiscences on the radio in 1963. Her status as an *éminence grise* was accepted in the universities as colonial studies grew and she was awarded many honorary degrees, but the one she most appreciated, because she felt that she had indeed earned it, was that of DLitt, Oxon., on her retirement in 1963.

Two years later Margery Perham's title changed on her appointment as dame commander in the Most Distinguished Order of St Michael and St George, on a par with many of her gubernatorial friends. They criticized her strongly in 1968 when she espoused the better publicized Biafra cause in the Nigerian civil war. To gain her support General Gowon, the Nigerian ruler, invited her to go to Nigeria to discover the true situation. She visited the battle lines and then appealed over the radio to the Biafran leader, Colonel Ojukwu, to cease fighting for his people's sake. On returning to England she recanted her earlier views in the most public way possible on the radio and BBC television. Her 'Reflections on the Nigerian civil war' were published eighteen months later in *International Affairs*.

Ever since the mid-1940s Margery's sister had lived with her and managed their domestic affairs. Margery now cared for Ethel while the health of both deteriorated. She relinquished all writing and membership of committees and learned bodies, even the chairmanship of the Rhodes House colonial records project, her cherished creation which made primary sources available to all investigators of colonial affairs. Margery's memory eventually became confused and so she entered a residential home, The Close, at Burcot, near Oxford, where she died on 19 February 1982. She was cremated and her ashes were scattered on the South Downs. Two memorial services were held: on 5 March by Nuffield College in the chapel she had helped to furbish, and on 1 May by the university in its own church of St Mary the Virgin. PATRICIA M. PUGH

Sources Bodl. RH [esp Lugard MSS; Oldham MSS, MS Afr.s.1829; Africa Bureau MSS, MS Afr.s.1681; Hailey MSS; Rhodes Trustees MSS; Jones MSS, MS Brit. Emp.s.332] · NA Scot., MSS of P. Kerr, eleventh earl of Lothian · Bodl. RH, MSS Brit. emp. S.30–90 · St Hugh's College, Oxford · Nuffield Oxf., archives · Nuffield Oxf., N. Chester MSS · records, Royal Institute of International Affairs, Chatham House, London · records, St Anne's School, Abbots Bromley, Rugely, Staffordshire · records, Harrogate Ladies College · records, St Stephen's College, formerly of Windsor · wine and spirit trade directories · directories, Bury, Lancashire, and Leeds and Harrogate, Yorkshire · records, University of Sheffield · P. Pugh, *Catalogue of the papers of Dame Margery Perham, 1895–1982* (1989) · *DNB* · J. W. Cell, *Hailey: a study in British imperialism, 1872–1969* (1992) · R. Coupland, *The empire in these days* (1935) · 'Joint committee on closer union in east Africa', *Parl. papers* (1930–31), vol. 7, no. 156 · J. H. Oldham, *White and black in Africa* (1930) · R. Symonds, *Oxford and empire: the last lost cause?* (1986) · A. Smith and M. Bull, eds., *Margery Perham and British rule in Africa* (1991) · *CGPLA Eng. & Wales* (1982)

Archives Bodl. RH, corresp. relating to her life of Lord Lugard · Bodl. RH, papers · PRO, corresp., BW 90 | Bodl. RH, corresp. with Lord Lugard · CUL, Royal Commonwealth Society collection, corresp. with H. B. Thomas · NA Scot., corresp. with Lord Lothian · U. Edin. L., letters to Reginald Davies

Likenesses W. Rothenstein, chalk drawing, 1919, NPG [*see illus.*] · P. Wardley, charcoal drawing, 1966, Bodl. RH

Wealth at death £145,989: probate, 25 May 1982, *CGPLA Eng. & Wales*

Peri, Peter Laszlo [*formerly* Ladislas Weisz] (1899–1967), sculptor and etcher, was born on 13 June 1899 in Budapest, Hungary, the eldest of the eight children of Emanuel (Mano) Weisz, tailor and railway porter, and Amalia Goldstein. Pre-1914 antisemitism in Hungary led the family to change its name to Peri. Educated at a grammar school in Budapest, Peri was articled as a lawyer's clerk but quickly developed passionate interests in art and communist politics. After attending evening classes in art, he became apprenticed to a stonemason in Budapest. Enthusiastic supporters of the communist revolution led by Béla Kun, Peri and his wife, Irma Mackassy, whom he had recently married, were touring with an agitprop theatre group in Czechoslovakia in 1919 when the Hungarian soviet fell. They fled to Vienna and Paris, and finally in 1920 settled in Berlin, where Peri worked with Der Sturm, a group of avant-garde artists, many of whom were Hungarian exiles. In the 1920s he acquired a reputation as a leading constructivist artist. His innovative Space Constructions, painted on shapes of wood and canvas, were first shown in a joint exhibition with László Moholy-Nagy in 1922. In keeping with the Bauhaus notion of 'socially useful' art, Peri turned to architecture and worked from 1924 to 1927 in the Berlin city architect's department.

In 1928 Peri returned to sculpture but in place of his earlier abstract constructions he made small bronze figures in a realist style. Later he rebuked suggestions that he had rejected his period of abstraction. Indeed, he viewed it as 'a historically essential cleansing process' (Kay and Lloyd, 7) which had provided the preliminary training for his realist sculpture. He believed that artists had a responsibility to reflect everyday life and should work in a way which could be understood by ordinary people. He always conveyed a warm optimistic vision of humanity which was never darkened by his later personal isolation.

After divorcing his first wife, in 1932 Peri married Mary Macnaghten (*b.* 1903), a British music student in Berlin, with whom he later had a daughter, and a son, William.

Peter Laszlo Peri (1899–1967), by Wolfgang Suschitzky

He drew cartoons for *Rote Fahne*, a communist daily, and for *Der Lautsprecher*, the monthly journal of the Siemens factory workers. In 1933, following his wife's arrest for the distribution of communist literature, the Peris sought political exile in England. In 1935 Peri moved to Hampstead, London, a haven for many émigré artists and writers. Having left most of his work in Germany, he was an unknown artist whose realist work attracted scant interest. However, his political sympathies drew him to other anti-fascist artists with whom, in 1933, he co-founded the Artists International Association. A regular exhibitor, he became one of the association's most dedicated figures. Peri had a lifelong interest in developing new sculptural techniques, such as the unusual method of modelling figures with wet concrete which he had initiated in Berlin. After successfully completing a commission for a wall relief for the Cement and Concrete Association, in 1938 he was invited to have a major exhibition of his work, 'London life in concrete', at 36 Soho Square. For Peri the new material of concrete was cheap, versatile, easy to colour, quick, and modern—a view not shared by some critics, who accused him of using a crude, inartistic medium.

In 1939, after six years as an émigré artist in England, Peri acquired naturalized British citizenship and used Peter as his first name. During the Second World War he took up etching and produced two of his finest series of prints, *Gulliver's Travels* and *Pilgrim's Progress* (impressions in the British Museum, London). He also made his *Little People*, a series of small concrete figures—some only a few inches high—which depicted ordinary people in everyday social situations and working activities such as sweeping up, reading, and playing football. After the war he perfected techniques using polyester resin, developing 'Pericrete'—a secret mixture of concrete and polyester resin with metallic powders. A series of public commissions, including work on South Lambeth estate for London county council, enabled him to use new materials and explore his interest in the relationship between sculpture and architecture. *The Sunbathers*, his sculptural mural for the Festival of Britain in 1951—a horizontal relief, so-called because it jutted out from the wall—was succeeded by numerous commissions for education authorities, notably in Leicestershire. Typical of these were three concrete reliefs of playing children for Langmoor primary school, Oadby, near Leicester, made in 1955.

Short, bearded, and rarely seen without his French-style beret, Peri retained a marked continental accent. In 1968 John Berger, an art critic, friend, and admirer, identified Peri's sense of isolation, describing him as an 'eternal exile' (Berger, 2). Peri was acutely aware of the indifference of the art world to his work, and his prolific output largely remained unsold in his Camden studio where he had lived since 1937. He was divorced a second time in 1958 and increasing artistic isolation added to his sense of exile. Suffering bouts of depression, he devoted himself wholly to his art. Although he never abandoned his socialist beliefs, he found solace and spiritual peace in the Quaker movement. Peri's third marriage, on 10 September 1966, to (Margaret) Heather Hall (*b.* 1944/5), an art student and daughter of John Hall, an engineer, briefly brought him contentment and gave him renewed enthusiasm for his work. After a heart attack, Peri died on 19 January 1967 in University College Hospital, St Pancras, London, and was cremated at Golders Green crematorium. A memorial exhibition was held at Swiss Cottage Library, London, in 1968. His work is represented in various collections in Great Britain and abroad, including the Tate collection, the Museum Bochum, Germany, and the Centre Georges Pompidou, Paris. Since his death, shifting art-historical focus has provided a more favourable reception for social realist sculpture. Peri's realist figures and reliefs offer both a poignant commentary on the human condition and a dynamic exploration of perspective and space. As such, they may eventually attract as much critical interest as his earlier abstract constructions.

GILLIAN WHITELEY

Sources J. Kay and J. Lloyd, *Peter Peri, 1899–1967* (1991) [exhibition catalogue, Leicestershire Museum and Art Gallery, 3 August – 29 Sept 1991] • *Peter Peri, 1899–1967*, The Minories Gallery, Colchester (1970) [exhibition catalogue, the Minories Gallery, Colchester, June–July 1970] • J. Berger, *Peter Peri, 1899–1967* (1968) [exhibition catalogue, Swiss Cottage Central Library, London, 8–21 May 1968] • R. Watkinson, *Peter Peri* (1973) [exhibition catalogue, Gardner Centre for the Arts, U. Sussex] • *Sculpture in concrete* (1938) [exhibition catalogue, 36 Soho Square, London] • *The Times* (25 Jan 1967) • C. King, 'Peter Peri', *The Studio*, 159 (1960), 208–9 • J. Lloyd, *Fighting spirits: Peter Peri, sculptures, and Cliff Rowe, paintings* (1987) [exhibition catalogue, Camden Arts Centre, London] • *Peter Peri—Peter Gabor Peri* (1995) • Peter Peri Archive, Tate collection, TGA 704 • drawings, catalogues, photographs, Henry Moore Centre for the Study of Sculpture, Leeds • CGPLA Eng. & Wales (1967) • m. cert. [P. L. Peri and M. Hall] • d. cert. • private information (2004)

Archives Henry Moore Institute, Leeds, Centre for the Study of Sculpture, drawings, catalogues, photographs • Tate collection

Likenesses W. Suschitzky, photograph, Henry Moore Institute, Leeds [*see illus.*] • photographs, Henry Moore Institute, Leeds

Wealth at death £39,409: administration, 18 Sept 1967, CGPLA Eng. & Wales

Peries, Ivan St Elmo Ignatius (1921–1988), painter, was born on 31 July 1921 in Dehiwela, near Colombo, Ceylon, the younger son of James Francis (Jim) Peries, medical practitioner, and his wife, Winifred. His elder brother was

Lester James Peries (*b.* 1919), film director. He was educated at St Peter's College, Colombo, where, under Harry Pieris's tutelage he studied painting and developed his sense of colour. His earliest landscape painting, produced at nineteen, was *Homage to El Greco* (1939–40). At this stage he was strongly influenced by Cézanne's colourful harmonies and compositions, which he emulated by distorting forms and perspectives. In *Homage to El Greco* the tension between the calm, flat, uncluttered middle area and the energetic movement of the sky, earth, and trees in the upper and lower spaces is striking.

In 1943 Peries was a founder member of the 43 Group, with W. J. G. Beling, George Claessen, Aubrey Collette, Justin Daraniyagala, Richard Gabriel, George Keyt, L. T. P. Manjusri, Harry Pieris, and Lionel Wendt. Peries's short-lived enthusiasm for Marxism and involvement with the Friends of the Soviet Union had a subtle political influence on the 43 Group. They were not political revolutionaries who wanted to change the hierarchical social status in Ceylon. Rather, the group aimed to challenge the imported and orientalized academicism of the Ceylon Society of Arts, which catered to the taste of a small, Westernized élite, and to make new national emblems of modern Asian art. They used Western modernist techniques and integrated them with symbols from their indigenous culture. The 43 Group had an international reputation and showed regularly outside Ceylon: in 1952 at the Imperial Institute, London; in 1953 at the Petit Palais, Paris; in 1956 and 1958 at the Venice Biennale; in 1960 at the South London Gallery; in 1964 at the Commonwealth Institute, London; and in 1987 at the Royal Festival Hall. Peries's work was included in each of these exhibitions.

In 1946 Peries won a government scholarship to study at the Anglo-French Arts Centre in London. There he continued to explore his interest in modern art. He returned to Ceylon in 1949 but found that the painting milieu had changed drastically. *The Beloved* (1949) was a formalistic painting, dominated by delineated figures and patches of colours. In 1953 he returned to London, where he lived for ten years. On 27 April 1955 he married (Nancy) Veronica Perry (*b.* 1928/9), hospital nurse, and daughter of William Perry, shipping engineer. They had three sons and a daughter. In the early 1960s Peries and his family moved to Southend-on-Sea.

Following his return to Britain, Peries had little contact with the other members of the 43 Group. Working in isolation, he continued to make paintings of the Ceylonese landscape. *The Arrival* (1959–60)—which took 'two years to plan, six months to execute, working 20 hours a day' (*Sunday Times* [Colombo], 30 March 1997), following which Peries suffered a nervous collapse—is about symbolic visions of suspended time and leisure. His style changed in this work: paint is thinly applied over a gesso surface, and the relationship between the grain and painted surface creates texture. This work and several brightly coloured semi-abstracts were included in a retrospective exhibition at St Catherine's College, Oxford, in 1965.

Peries's work changed again in the 1970s. He started to paint with rough brushstrokes or impasto applied with a palette knife. He toned down his colours until eventually in the 1980s he was producing black, grey, and white semi-abstract landscape paintings. These works were shown at the Newman Room, Oxford, in 1979, at the Galerie Abras Mont des Arts, Brussels, in 1981, and the Sapumal Foundation, Colombo, in 1983.

Peries died at his home, 7 Cromer Road, Southend-on-Sea, on 13 February 1988, and was survived by his wife and four children. His work was included in 'The Other Story' (Hayward Gallery, 1989) as an example of black art in Britain, and can be found in many permanent collections, including the Victoria and Albert Museum, London; the Petit Palais, Paris; Pembroke College, Oxford; and the Sapumal Foundation, Colombo.   PAULINE DE SOUZA

Sources S. Bandaranayake, 'Ivan Peries (painting 1939–1969): the predicament of the bourgeois artist in the societies of the Third World', *Third Text*, 2 (winter 1987/1988), 77–92 · S. Bandaranayake and M. Fonseka, *Ivan Peries paintings, 1938–88* (1996) · *The Times* (23 Feb 1988) · *Sunday Times* [Colombo] (30 March 1997) · m. cert. · d. cert.
Likenesses A. Collette, watercolour sketch, Sapumal Foundation, Colombo, Sri Lanka

Perigal, Arthur, the elder (1784–1847), painter, was born in London on 10 January 1784, one of the six sons and seven daughters of François Perigal (1731–1821) and his wife, Marie Ogier (1744–1824). On 21 January 1808 he entered the Royal Academy Schools, where he studied under Henry Fuseli. After winning a silver medal in 1809, and the gold medal for history painting in 1811 with *Themistocles Taking Refuge at the Court of King Admetus* (exh. RA, 1812), he embarked on a career as a painter of ambitious subjects from Shakespeare, Scott, Plutarch, English history, and the Bible. He showed nine of these at the Royal Academy and twelve at the British Institution but few found buyers and he turned increasingly to portraiture and landscape painting. On 1 September 1812 he married, in London, Louisa Susanna Pilleau (1780–1861), with whom he had four sons including Arthur Perigal the younger [*see below*] and one daughter. In 1821 he had an address in Sheep Street, Northampton, but in 1823 he lived at 48 George Street, Manchester. There he practised as a portrait painter and art teacher and was active in setting up the Royal Manchester Institution (since 1882, Manchester City Galleries). By 13 December 1828 Perigal had begun work on a large canvas, *The Manchester Fancy Dress Ball* (City of Salford Museum and Art Gallery), portraying the culminating event of the Manchester music festival of that year. Despite measuring 7 feet by 10 feet this painting is really a *tour de force* of the miniaturist's art. At a significant point in the growth of 'Cottonopolis', Robert Peel, home secretary, and 400 members of Manchester's merchant élite are portrayed at leisure, all dressed in exotic costumes of the most striking variety. A probable self-portrait is included on the right-hand side. Perigal attended in the costume of 'an old gentleman of George

II. d's time' (*Manchester Guardian*, 4 Oct 1828). Completed in eighteen months, the picture was praised in the *Manchester Guardian* (10 July 1830) as 'a faithful representation of the most brilliant scene ever witnessed in Manchester'. Yet it was not a significant popular success, and could not compete with the drama of John Martin's *Fall of Nineveh* shown in the city some months earlier. It was subsequently raffled and presented to Salford Art Gallery in 1852. Twenty-one related watercolour studies are in Manchester Public Library. Several of the likenesses, executed in tiny hatched strokes, are superior to those in the finished oil painting, but the handling of the drapery is cursory.

Perigal moved to Edinburgh in 1832 where, assisted by his sons, he set up a 'Drawing Institution', first at 19 Hill Street, then at 21 Hill Street. From 1833 until 1846 he exhibited landscapes, portraits, and miniatures at the Royal Scottish Academy. He also showed some of his early history paintings, which remained unsold after nearly thirty years. On 19 September 1847 he died at his home, 21 Hill Street.

Perigal's son **Arthur Perigal the younger** (1816–1884), landscape painter, was born in London on 17 August 1816 and baptized at St Mary, St Marylebone Road, on 9 October 1816. He first exhibited at the Royal Scottish Academy in 1837 and thereafter showed more than 300 landscapes. On 1 September 1847 he married Hannah Stevenson (*b.* 1827), with whom he had nine children. After 1861 he also exhibited at the Royal Academy and the British Institution in London. Working initially with his father, he mainly portrayed scenes in the Scottish highlands and the borders but occasionally also worked in the Lake District and north Wales. After an extended tour of Norway in 1870 and a later visit to Italy he also exhibited views of these countries together with some Swiss scenes. He worked in both oils and watercolours and was elected an associate of the Royal Scottish Academy in 1841 and a full member in 1868. From 1880 to 1884 he served as the academy's treasurer. He died suddenly at his home, 7 Oxford Terrace, Edinburgh, on 5 June 1884 and was buried in the Dean cemetery; his wife survived him. There are examples of his paintings in Glasgow Art Gallery and Museum, Dundee City Art Gallery, the National Gallery of Scotland, and other public collections.   EDWIN BOWES

Sources F. Perigal, *Some account of the Perigal family* (privately printed, 1887) · *Manchester Guardian* (1823–30), esp. 19 Jan 1828, 13 Dec 1828, 19 June 1830, 10 July 1830, 24 July 1830 · *DNB* · bound volume of watercolour sketches, Man. CL, BR f391.M8 · Graves, *RA exhibitors* · Graves, *Brit. Inst.* · S. C. Hutchison, 'The Royal Academy Schools, 1768–1830', *Walpole Society*, 38 (1960–62), 123–91, esp. 164 · A. Perigal, letters, Royal Scot. Acad. · T. Fawcett, *The rise of English provincial art: artist, patron and institution outside London, 1800–1830* (1974) · W. D. McKay and F. Rinder, *The Royal Scottish Academy, 1826–1916* (1917) · *IGI* · *CGPLA Eng. & Wales* (1884)

Archives Royal Scot. Acad., letters

Likenesses A. Perigal the elder, self-portrait?, oils, 1830, City of Salford Museum and Art Gallery · D. Macnee, oils, 1881 (A. Perigal the younger), Scot. NPG · A. Perigal the elder, oils (A. Perigal the younger), Royal Scot. Acad.

Wealth at death £6943 6s. 4d.—Arthur Perigal the younger: confirmation, 28 July 1884, *CCI*

Perigal, Arthur, the younger (1816–1884). *See under* Perigal, Arthur, the elder (1784–1847).

Peris, Ceridwen. *See* Jones, Alice Gray (1852–1943).

Perkin, Arthur George (1861–1937), organic chemist, was born on 13 December 1861 at Sudbury, Middlesex, the younger son of Sir William Henry *Perkin (1838–1907), manufacturing chemist, and his first wife, Jemima Harriet (*d.* 1862), youngest daughter of John Lissett. His elder brother, also William Henry *Perkin (1860–1929), became the leading British organic chemist of his generation, ending his career as Waynflete professor of chemistry, University of Oxford. Arthur's delicate health did not prevent his being sent in the late 1860s to a boarding-school at Margate. In 1872 he joined his brother at the City of London School, chosen by their father, himself an old boy, for its good science teaching. During the holidays the boys, who were dedicated to chemical research, experimented in a hut fitted as a laboratory in the garden of their home. They were also excellent musicians: Arthur played the flute in the nine-strong family orchestra.

In 1878 Perkin entered the Royal College of Chemistry, London, where he studied under Edward Frankland and Frederick Guthrie. Having spent the year 1880–81 working under E. J. Mills at Anderson's College, Glasgow, he won a Clothworkers' Company scholarship tenable in the newly opened colour chemistry and dyeing department of the Yorkshire College of Science, Leeds (later Leeds University), where he researched with J. J. Hummell from whom he derived a lifelong interest in natural dyes.

In 1882 Perkin became chemist and in 1888 manager at the alizarin works of Hardman and Holden in Manchester. In 1887 he married Annie Florence, daughter of James E. Bedford of Leeds; he had met her through an acquaintance with her brother, Charles Bedford, a fellow researcher at Leeds. Indeed, the centrality of Leeds in Perkin's life was confirmed in 1892 when he returned there as a lecturer and research assistant (retitled to research chemist in 1907) in the colour chemistry and dyeing department of Yorkshire College. Aided by a light teaching load and the Clothworkers' Research Laboratory, opened in 1900, he enjoyed twenty-two years of intense research and incessant publication on the structure and properties of natural dyes. Though he mainly left it to others to confirm by synthesis his postulated structures, he was so skilful in exploiting degradative methods that he was elected a fellow of the royal societies of Edinburgh (1893) and London (1903) and attracted research students from abroad, especially from India and Japan.

In 1916 Perkin succeeded A. G. Green as professor of colour chemistry and dyeing at Leeds. He contributed to the chemists' war by researching for the Ministry of Munitions and leading the Leeds colony of British Dyes' research chemists. With A. E. Everest he published in 1918 a classic text, *The Natural Organic Colouring Matters*; he received the accolade of the Royal Society's Davy medal in 1924, and retired officially in 1926 but continued to

Arthur George Perkin (1861–1937), by Richard Jack, 1927

research in his department until February 1937 when he was taken ill. He died at home, Grosvenor Lodge, Grosvenor Road, Headingley, Leeds, on 30 May 1937 and was buried at Adel, Leeds, on 2 June 1937. He was survived by his wife.

Both Perkin and his brother had childless marriages; both earned the nickname 'Pa Perkin' from their students, and, again like his brother, Perkin was a dab hand at the research bench where he thrived on noxious vapours. He maintained his interest in music, as first bassoon in amateur orchestras in Yorkshire. Unlike his brother, he was neither a discipline builder nor an activist in national scientific affairs. Gentle and unambitious, he was happy to spend thirty-four years at Leeds (which conferred an honorary DSc on him in 1927), enjoying research in his laboratory, where he chain-smoked, summer holidays always taken in the Isle of Man, and his domestic pets.

JACK MORRELL

Sources F. M. Rowe and R. Robinson, *JCS* (1938), 1738–54 · R. Robinson, *Obits. FRS*, 2 (1936–8), 445–50 · E. J. Cross and F. M. Rowe, *Journal of the Society of Dyers and Colourists*, 53 (1937), 349–56 · U. Leeds, central records office, Perkin papers · Annual reports of the department of colour chemistry and dyeing to the Clothworkers' Company, U. Leeds · *Yorkshire Post* (31 May 1937) · *Yorkshire Post* (3 June 1937) · G. G. Bradshaw, 'Recollections of dyeing department, 1915–21', U. Leeds · *CGPLA Eng. & Wales* (1937)
Likenesses R. Jack, oils, 1927, U. Leeds [*see illus.*] · W. Stoneman, photograph, 1932, NPG · group portrait, photograph (with staff and students), U. Leeds, archives · photograph, repro. in Robinson, *Obits. FRS*, 2 · photograph, repro. in Cross and Rowe, *Journal of the Society of Dyers and Colourists*, 350
Wealth at death £25,257 13s. 2d.: probate, 15 Oct 1937, *CGPLA Eng. & Wales*

Perkin, Sir William Henry (1838–1907), chemist, was born on 12 March 1838 at King David's Lane, Shadwell, London, youngest of the three sons of George Fowler Perkin (1802–1865), a builder and contractor, and his wife, Sarah Cuthbert. With his two brothers and three sisters he inherited a pronounced musical talent from his father. He also inherited a strong Anglican faith, and religion played an extremely important role in his life. After early education at a private school Perkin was sent in 1851 to the City of London School, where his aptitude for chemistry was encouraged by his teacher, Thomas Hall. In 1853 he entered the Royal College of Chemistry as a student under August Wilhelm Hofmann. By the end of the second year he had, under Hofmann's guidance, carried out his first piece of research, the results of which he announced in a paper read before the Chemical Society of London.

In 1854 Perkin fitted up a laboratory at his home, where he undertook independent research, sometimes collaborating with Arthur H. Church, and the next year he started work as Hofmann's assistant. During the Easter vacation of 1856 Perkin attempted, in his home laboratory, to synthesize quinine by oxidizing a salt of allyltoluidine with potassium dichromate. The experiment failed. On repeating the method with aniline instead of the toluidine derivative, he obtained on work-up a purple-coloured solution which proved to possess dyeing properties, especially on silk. This was the first aniline or coal-tar dye to be discovered. Encouraged by Pullars of Perth, he filed a patent for this process (patent no. 1984 of August 1856).

Perkin now resigned his position at the Royal College of Chemistry and embarked on a career in industrial chemistry. Assisted by his father and brother Thomas Dix Perkin he opened a chemical factory at Greenford Green, northwest of London, towards the end of 1858. The dye was first manufactured at the Perkins' works under the name of 'aniline purple' or 'Tyrian purple'. The name 'mauve', from the French word for the mallow flower, was given to the dye in England early in 1859 (chemists later called it mauveine). Perkin developed improved processes for manufacture of nitrobenzene from coal-tar benzene, and reduction of the nitro compound to aniline. He also undertook research into silk dyeing, and, of far greater commercial importance, the application of mauve to cotton dyeing and (calico) printing, for which mordants were required. Perkin's discovery and manufacture of the first aniline dye eventually led to the displacement of natural by artificial, or synthetic, dyestuffs, also made from various coal-tar products. In recognition of his invention of the mauve process, the *Société Industrielle de Mulhouse* awarded him, in 1859, a silver medal, and afterwards a gold medal.

On 13 September 1859 Perkin married Jemima Harriet Lissett (d. 1862), daughter of John Lissett, of Huguenot descent. There were two sons, William Henry *Perkin (1860–1929) and Arthur George *Perkin (1861–1937). Following Jemima's death Perkin married, on 8 February 1866, Alexandrine (Sascha) Caroline Mollwo, daughter of Ivan Herman Mollwo, of Russian descent. She was the mother of Perkin's third son, Frederick Mollwo Perkin, and four

Sir William Henry Perkin (1838–1907), by Sir Arthur Stockdale Cope, 1906

daughters, Helen, Mary, Lucie, and Annie. William Henry Perkin became professor of organic chemistry at Manchester University and later Oxford; Arthur George and Frederick Mollwo both distinguished themselves in the same branch of science as their father.

In 1868 the German chemists Carl Graebe and Carl Liebermann showed that alizarin, the important red dyestuff present in the root of the madder plant and widely used in calico printing and Turkey red dyeing on cotton, was a derivative of the coal-tar hydrocarbon anthracene (and not, as previously believed, of naphthalene). Although they patented a process for synthesis of alizarin the product was too costly to compete with the red dye from the madder plant. During 1869 Perkin, and, independently, the Hoechst dyeworks and Heinrich Caro at BASF, developed much more economical (and almost identical) processes for the manufacture of artificial alizarin via a sulphonic acid derivative of anthraquinone. Perkin also invented a process based on dichloroanthracene. This afforded an anthraquinone derivative similar to alizarin that found considerable use as a textile dye. During 1869–70 Perkin and BASF pooled their resources and agreed to divide up the European market in synthetic alizarin. Perkin, with his brother, designed and erected suitable manufacturing plant.

This branch of the coal-tar dye industry developed rapidly, and through the displacement of the madder dye and the application of formal knowledge to industrial problem-solving, foreshadowed the age of modern, science-based industry. The English market in alizarin was almost entirely held by the Perkins until the end of 1873, at which time intense competition and major technical advances by German manufacturers led the Perkins to sell their works to the firm of Brooke, Simpson, and Spiller. Following retirement after eighteen years in the synthetic dye industry, William Perkin thereafter devoted himself to pure chemical research at his home, The Chestnuts, in Sudbury, near Harrow. Perkin delivered before the Society of Arts in 1879 two lectures, which were published under the title *The History of Alizarin and Allied Colouring Matters, and their Production from Coal-Tar*. These described mainly Perkin's work on the manufacture of alizarin.

Even while actively engaged in industrial work Perkin had maintained a strong interest in pure chemistry, publishing many papers in *Transactions of the Chemical Society* (where his contributions finally numbered ninety). In 1867 he published a description of his method for synthesizing unsaturated organic acids, later known as the 'Perkin synthesis'. During the following year the synthesis of coumarin, the odorous substance contained in such plant products as the tonka bean, was announced, and the continuation of this work after his retirement from industry led to his discovery of the synthesis of cinnamic acid from benzaldehyde. Scientific papers on the chemistry of mauve were published between 1863 and 1879. In 1881 he first drew attention to the magnetic rotatory power of some of the compounds which he had prepared in his researches. It was mainly to the study of this property as applied to the investigation of the constitutions of various compounds that he devoted the rest of his life.

Perkin's services were widely recognized. He joined the Chemical Society of London in 1856, was its president from 1883 to 1885, and received its Longstaff medal in 1888. He was elected FRS in 1866 and received from the Royal Society a royal medal in 1879, and the Davy medal in 1889. He was president of the Society of Chemical Industry in 1884–5, receiving its gold medal in 1898, and at his death was president of the Society of Dyers and Colourists. The Society of Arts conferred on him its Albert medal in 1890, and the Institution of Gas Engineers its Birmingham medal in 1892. He also received honorary doctorates from the universities of Würzburg (1882), St Andrews (1891), and Manchester (1904).

In July 1906 the jubilee of Perkin's discovery of mauve was celebrated in Europe and North America. Perkin was knighted and received honorary doctorates from the universities of Oxford, Leeds, Heidelberg, Columbia, Johns Hopkins, and the Munich Technische Hochschule. He was presented with the Hofmann medal by the German Chemical Society, the Lavoisier medal by the French Chemical Society, and a special Perkin research medal by the New York section of the Society of Chemical Industry. After his death, a sum of £2000, subscribed by chemists of all countries, was handed to the Chemical Society as the Perkin memorial fund, to be applied to the encouragement of research in topics related to the coal-tar and allied industries. A Perkin medal was instituted by the Society of

Dyers and Colourists in recognition of contributions to the 'tinctorial industries'. The first recipients, in 1908, were Graebe and Liebermann. An American joint committee extended the Perkin research medal initiative with, from 1908, a Perkin medal for American chemists engaged in industry-related work.

Perkin attended Christ Church, South Harrow, and supported Anglican and Free Church places of worship with considerable generosity. He died at his home in Sudbury on 14 July 1907, and was buried at Christ Church; his second wife survived him.   ANTHONY S. TRAVIS

Sources R. Meldola, *JCS*, 93 (1908), 2214–57 · R. Meldola, A. G. Green, and J. C. Cain, eds., *Jubilee of the discovery of mauve and of the foundation of the coal-tar colour industry by Sir W. H. Perkin* (1906) · A. S. Travis, *The rainbow makers: the origins of the synthetic dyestuffs industry in western Europe* (1993) · S. M. Edelstein, 'Sir William Henry Perkin', *American Dyestuff Reporter*, 45 (1956), 598–609 · L. E. Morris, 'The genius of Perkin', *Dyer, Textile Printer and Finisher*, 115 (1956), 747–64 · F. M. Rowe, 'Perkin centenary lecture: the life and work of Sir William Henry Perkin', *Journal of the Society of Dyers and Colourists*, 54 (1938), 551–62 · *Perkin centenary London: 100 years of synthetic dyestuffs*, Tetrahedron, suppl. 1 (1958) · A. J. Greenaway, 'Personal', *The life and work of Professor William Henry Perkin* (1932), 7–38

Archives Museum of Science and Industry, Manchester, corresp. and items deposited by family · NRA, priv. coll., corresp. and papers | Deutsches Museum, Munich, Caro Nachlass, corresp. with Caro · Wellcome L., letters to John Spiller

Likenesses self-portrait, photograph, 1852, repro. in Meldola, Green, and Cain, eds., *Jubilee*, facing p. 20 · self-portrait, photograph, 1852, repro. in *Perkin centenary London*, pl. 3 · group portrait, photograph, c.1855 (with Hofmann and students at the Royal College of Chemistry), Manchester · photograph, 1860, repro. in Meldola, Green, and Cain, eds., *Jubilee*, facing p. 22 · group portrait, photograph, in or before 1873 (with William and Thomas Dix Perkin, and three other persons), repro. in W. H. Cliffe, *Journal of the Society of Dyers and Colourists*, 73 (July 1957), facing p. 316 · H. Grant, oils, 1898, Leathersellers' Hall, London; destroyed, 1941? · A. S. Cope, oils, 1906, NPG [*see illus.*] · group portrait, photograph, 1906, repro. in *Perkin centenary London*, pl. 8 · group portraits, photographs, 1906 · photographs, 1906, Deutsches Museum, Munich, Caro Nachlass · S. Perkin, charcoal drawing, priv. coll. · F. W. Pomeroy, marble bust, Royal Society of Chemistry, London · photograph (after painting by R. A. Cope), repro. in Meldola, Green, and Cain, eds., *Jubilee*, frontispiece · photograph, Manchester

Wealth at death £78,611 5s. 5d.: probate, 28 Aug 1907, *CGPLA Eng. & Wales*

Perkin, William Henry

Perkin, William Henry (1860–1929), organic chemist, was born on 17 June 1860 at 1 or 2 Chesham Villas, Sudbury, Middlesex, the elder son of Sir William Henry *Perkin (1838–1907), manufacturing chemist, and his first wife, Jemima Harriet (d. 1862), youngest daughter of John Lissett. Having attended two preparatory schools, in 1870 Perkin entered the City of London School where he was stimulated by good teaching in science and mathematics. Simultaneously he worked in his father's private laboratory. Though his father did not give him formal instruction, Perkin imbibed the idea of research as a supreme good. As a boy he followed his father in becoming an accomplished pianist and violinist. In 1877 he migrated to the Royal College of Chemistry, London, where he studied under Edward Frankland and W. R. E. Hodgkinson, head of the laboratories, who had worked under Johannes Wislicenus. After some hesitation by his father, who

regarded Germany as a dangerous centre of free thought, Perkin went in 1880 to Würzburg to work for a PhD under Wislicenus, a master of syntheses in organic chemistry and an undictatorial paternalist as a supervisor.

Having gained his doctorate in 1882, Perkin spent four years at the University of Munich with Adolf von Baeyer, mainly as a *privat Dozent* and personal research assistant. Baeyer soon became a chemical hero for Perkin, who was amazed by the excellent laboratories designed by him and impressed by the research productivity achieved by his steadfastness at the laboratory bench. A master of structural organic chemistry, Baeyer was generally indifferent to theory and to the then-new physical chemistry. Above all, Baeyer created by example an atmosphere in which research was the only thing that mattered, so that his research group was outstanding in size, productivity, and endurability. Perkin also saw that over half of Baeyer's researchers went into industry or commerce. In these ways Baeyer provided for Perkin an example to be followed or modified.

In 1886 Perkin accepted an invitation from Harold Dixon, professor of chemistry at Owens College, Manchester, to work in a vacant laboratory there. Next year he became the first professor of chemistry at the Heriot-Watt College, Edinburgh, where his assistant was Frederic Stanley Kipping, who had studied under him at Munich. They soon began the collaboration which produced three enduring textbooks, *Practical Chemistry* (1890), *Organic Chemistry* (1894–5), and *Inorganic Chemistry* (1909). On 31 December 1887 Perkin married Mina, the eldest daughter of William Thomas Holland, of Bridgwater. They had met in Manchester in Kipping's home where she was staying with a younger sister, Lily, Kipping's fiancée. Elected FRS in 1890 Perkin accepted in 1892 an invitation to succeed Carl Schorlemmer as professor of organic chemistry at Owens College.

At Manchester, Perkin created an internationally renowned school of organic chemistry in which two future Nobel prizewinners, Walter Norman Howarth and Robert Robinson, both Manchester graduates, and the first president of Israel, Chaim Weizmann, were trained. The Perkin group of organic chemists was accommodated in impressive new research laboratories, some of which Perkin designed. He had an enviable knack of being associated with such munificent external endowments as the Schorlemmer Laboratory (1895), the Levinstein Laboratory (1895), the Schunck Laboratory (1904), and the John Morley Laboratories (1909) paid for mainly by Andrew Carnegie. In this greatly expanded accommodation, chiefly devoted to organic chemistry and unrivalled in any British university, Perkin pursued research and consultancies, encouraged pure and technical organic chemistry, and launched his pupils on academic and industrial careers. For Perkin there was no divide between pure and applied chemistry. Though his forte lay in producing academic organic chemists, he was concerned about the British organic chemical industry, which in his view relied too much on rule-of-thumb methods and neglected research because it was obsessed with short-term commercial interests. His solution was to produce trained research chemists for industry and establish co-operation on the German model between industry and universities. He did lucrative commercial work in his university laboratories at Manchester, his final venture being the manufacture of synthetic rubber. The project was marred for Perkin by a fracas with Weizmann, whom he sacked from the rubber team.

In 1912 Perkin was invited by the University of Oxford to become Waynflete professor of chemistry, to rescue the subject from the parlous state to which it had sunk under William Odling. He accepted the chair on the understanding that his main role would be to build up research as rapidly as possible. Aware of Oxford's conservatism, collegiate structure, devotion to arts subjects, suspicion of specialized research, and hostility to industry, Perkin acted resolutely. He maintained his output of research and played a leading role in persuading the university, at a time of national emergency, to add a fourth year of research to the existing degree course in chemistry (1916) and to establish the research degree of DPhil (1917). Exploiting the dire contingency of war, he introduced into Oxford the notion and practice of industrial research, using chemists employed by the government-backed British Dyes and recruited mainly from outside Oxford. He persuaded Charles William Dyson Perrins, partner in the famous Worcestershire Sauce firm, to pay two-thirds of the cost of the first stage of a new chemical laboratory completed in 1916 and then, with an entrepreneurial wiliness bordering on deception, induced the university to pay for most of the second stage opened in 1922.

In this Indian summer of his career Perkin suffered some disappointments: he had to recruit staff from outside Oxford, very few of his protégés secured permanent posts at Oxford, and only a handful of Oxford graduates researched with him. Even so he put organic chemistry at

Oxford on the international map. His interests in music, horticulture, hospitality, and travel helped to make his aims and practices eventually acceptable in Oxford. At Manchester he was such an accomplished pianist that he played duets with the famous violinist Adolf Brodsky. At his Oxford home Perkin soon removed a partition wall to create a long room for chamber music. To the end of his life he practised at his piano every day before breakfast. For diversion on train journeys he used to read the score of a string quartet. He had green fingers with flowering plants, of which many were donated to the University Parks. He kept a good cellar and gave many parties at Magdalen, his college. In summer he regularly visited the Swiss and Italian lakes. Such connoisseurship, which made him an English version of the best sort of German professor, ended in 1929 when his robust health gave way. Perhaps weakened by strychnine, which he was studying, and by accidental poisoning by mercury vapour, he died at his home, 5 Charlbury Road, Oxford, on 17 September 1929 from pleurisy which affected his heart; he was buried at Wolvercote cemetery near Oxford on 19 September. His will showed his unfaltering commitment to research. His marriage being childless, the bulk of his estate reverted after his wife's death to Magdalen College for research studentships in organic chemistry.

A large, portly man, gruff-voiced and with a bushy moustache in his prime, Perkin was the leading British organic chemist of his generation, being awarded the Longstaff medal of the Chemical Society (1900), of which he was president 1913–15, and the Davy and royal medals of the Royal Society (1904, 1925). With his large hands and spatulate fingers he was a renowned experimentalist who could induce reactions to 'go' and gums to crystallize. He was a bench chemist who adored the laboratory and its ineffable art. His field of research was not new or wide: he worked on the determination of the structure of naturally

William Henry Perkin (1860–1929), by Lafayette, 1928

occurring organic substances, using the established techniques of degradation (breaking the substance down into identifiable fragments) and synthesis (making it from chemicals of known composition and structure by a series of controlled reactions whose course was indisputable). He exploited reagents and reactions devised by others, but in his time the Perkin triangle was a piece of apparatus widely used in collecting fractions during distillation under reduced pressure. All his life he suspected that physical chemistry was bogus so he did not use physical methods. Except in his research on synthesizing compounds containing rings composed of three, four, and five atoms of carbon, which confirmed Baeyer's strain theory, he avoided theoretical chemistry.

With a rare combination of ability, enthusiasm, stamina, and guile, Perkin managed to continue at Oxford his Mancunian roles of researcher, research school director, designer of new laboratories, and securer of external funding. His research students and associates regarded him with respect and affection. They had confidence in his fairness and judgement; they admired his honesty, sincerity, and his unaffected large-heartedness, and revered him as 'Pa Perkin'. His pupils filled many chairs in British universities, mainly in organic chemistry, the best known being Robinson, his successor at Oxford and closest collaborator, W. N. Haworth, J. L. Simonsen, Kipping, J. F. Thorpe, H. C. H. Carpenter, W. A. Bone, F. L. Pyman, W. O. Kermack, J. Kenyon, G. R. Clemo, J. M. Gulland, R. D. Haworth, and W. Baker. Through them the Perkin gospel dominated British organic chemistry as long as it was concerned with structure, not mechanism, and as long as physical techniques of investigation were not widely employed.   JACK MORRELL

Sources [A. J. Greenaway, J. F. Thorpe, and R. Robinson], *The life and work of Professor William Henry Perkin* (1932) · J. B. Morrell, 'W. H. Perkin, junior, at Manchester and Oxford: from Irwell to Isis', *Osiris*, 2nd ser., 8 (1993), 104–26 · R. Robinson, *Journal of the Society of Chemical Industry*, 48 (1929), 1008–12 · R. Robinson, 'The Perkin family of organic chemists', *Endeavour*, 15 (1956), 92–102 · W. N. Haworth, *Journal of the Society of Chemical Industry*, 49 (1930), 886–9 · H. E. Armstrong, *Nature*, 124 (1929), 623–7 · W. H. Perkin, 'Wislicenus memorial lecture', *Memorial lectures delivered before the Chemical Society*, 2 (1914), 59–92 [1905] · W. H. Perkin, 'Baeyer memorial lecture', *Memorial lectures delivered before the Chemical Society*, 3 (1933), 47–73 · *The Times* (20 Sept 1929)

Archives NRA, priv. coll., corresp. and papers | Wellcome L., letters to John Spiller

Likenesses three photographs, 1887–1929, repro. in Greenaway, Thorpe, and Robinson, *Life and work* · photograph, *c.*1910, Royal Society of Chemistry, London · photograph, 1926, MHS Oxf. · Lafayette, photograph, 1928, NPG [*see illus.*] · E. Gillick, bronze plaque, 1929?, University of Manchester · Elliott & Fry, photograph, repro. in Robinson, *Journal of the Society of Chemical Industry*, 1009 · Maull & Fox, photograph, RS

Wealth at death £45,015 6*s.* 6*d.*: resworn probate, July 1931, *CGPLA Eng. & Wales*

Perkins, Sir Aeneas (1834–1901), army officer, born at Lewisham, Kent, on 19 May 1834, was the sixth son in a family of thirteen children of Charles Perkins, merchant, of London, and his wife, Jane Homby, daughter of Charles William Barkley (*b.* 1759), after whom Barkley Sound and Island in the Pacific are named. His grandfather was John Perkins of Camberwell, a partner in Barclay and Perkins's brewery. A brother George, in the Bengal artillery, was killed at the battle of the Hindan before Delhi in 1857. Perkins was educated at Dr Prendergast's school at Lewisham and at Stoton and Mayor's school at Wimbledon, where Frederick Roberts, his lifelong friend, was his schoolfellow. He entered Addiscombe College on 1 February 1850, at the same time as Roberts. Perkins showed ability in mathematics, and was a leader in all sports. Commissioned second lieutenant, Bengal Engineers, on 12 December 1851, he, after professional instruction at Chatham, arrived at Fort William, Calcutta, on 16 January 1854.

As assistant engineer in the public works department Perkins was soon employed on irrigation work on the Bari Doab Canal in the Punjab. Promoted first lieutenant on 17 August 1856, he was transferred in November to the Ambala division, and in the following May, when the Indian mutiny began, joined the force under General George Anson, commander-in-chief in India, which marched to the relief of Delhi. Perkins was present at the battle of Badli-ki-sarai on 8 June, and at the seizure of the Delhi Ridge. He did much good work during the early part of the siege. On 11–12 June he was employed in the construction of a mortar battery—known as 'Perkins's battery'. On 17 June he took part in the destruction of a rebel battery and the capture of its guns, and on 14 July in the repulse of the sortie. He was wounded a few days later near the walls of Delhi, and sent to Ambala. Although he soon recovered from the wound, he was forced by broken health to remain there until March 1858, when he was invalided home.

After returning to India in 1859 Perkins held various offices in Bengal, including those of assistant principal of the Civil Engineering College at Calcutta, assistant consulting engineer for the railways, and executive engineer of the Berhampore division. On 12 March 1862 he was promoted second captain. He married in 1863 Janette Wilhelmina (who survived him), daughter of Werner Cathray, formerly 13th light dragoons, and they had two sons— Major Arthur Ernest John Perkins, and Major Aeneas Charles Perkins, 40th Pathans—and three daughters.

In the autumn of 1864 Perkins took part as field engineer in the Bhutan expedition, during which he was three times mentioned in dispatches for gallant conduct, and was recommended for a brevet majority. Towards the end of the expedition he was appointed chief engineer of the force. A Victoria Cross recommendation for gallantry in storming a stockade at the summit of the Baru Pass was rejected as too late. For his services in Bhutan, he received a brevet majority on 30 June 1865.

Perkins was executive engineer at Murshidabad, and from 1866 in the Darjeeling division. Promoted first captain in his corps on 31 October 1868, two years later he was sent to the North-Western Provinces as superintending engineer, and in April 1872 he was transferred in the same grade to the military works branch. He became regimental major on 5 July 1872, brevet lieutenant-colonel on 29 December 1874, and regimental lieutenant-colonel on 1 October 1877.

A year later, at Roberts's request, Perkins was selected for active service in Afghanistan, and was appointed commanding royal engineer of Roberts's Kurram field force. During the operations in front of the Paiwar Pass he skilfully reconnoitred the enemy's position, and selected a site from which the mountain battery could shell the Afghan camp. The works carried on under his orders in the Kurram valley greatly facilitated the subsequent advance on Kabul. He was mentioned in dispatches, and was made a CB in 1879. On the conclusion of peace with Sirdar Yakub Khan, Perkins remained in the Kurram valley, laying out a cantonment at Shalofzan, but on the news of the massacre of Sir Louis Cavagnari and his escort at Kabul an immediate advance was made by the Kurram column, and Perkins was present at the victory of Charasia on 6 October, and at the entry into Kabul (8 October 1879), and was mentioned in dispatches. The engineers' work was then very heavy. At Kabul the Sherpur cantonment and Bala Hissar had to be repaired, and a new line of communication with India via Jalalabad had to be opened out. The Sherpur cantonment was rendered defensible by the beginning of December, just in time. A few days later the Afghans assembled in such overwhelming numbers that Roberts had to concentrate his entire force within the walls of Sherpur. Under Perkins's direction emplacements and abatis were rapidly constructed, blockhouses were built on the Bemaru heights, walls and villages dangerously near the cantonment were blown up and levelled, and a second line of defence within the enclosure was improvised. On 23 December the enemy attacked in great numbers. They were repulsed, and dispersed by a counter-attack. Perkins was mentioned in dispatches and promoted brevet colonel on 29 December 1879.

Perkins attempted to make the position at Kabul secure. A fort and blockhouse were erected on the Siah Sang Ridge, the Bala Hissar and the Asmai heights were fortified, Sherpur was converted into a strongly entrenched camp, bridges were built across the Kabul River, the main roads were made passable for artillery, and many new roads were constructed. The works completed during the next seven months, mostly by unskilled Afghan labour, comprised ten forts, fifteen detached posts, three large and several small bridges, 4000 yards of loopholed parapet, 45 miles of road, and quarters for 8000 men. At the end of July 1880 the news of the Maiwand disaster reached Kabul. Perkins accompanied Roberts as commanding royal engineer with the force of 10,000 men in the famous march to Kandahar, and was at the battle of Kandahar on 1 September 1880. Soon afterwards he returned to India, and was made an aide-de-camp to the queen.

Perkins rejoined the military works department, was appointed superintending engineer at Rawalpindi, and from April to July 1881 officiated as inspector-general of military works. After two years' furlough he was appointed chief engineer of the Central Provinces, was transferred in the same capacity in April 1886 to the Punjab, and on 10 March 1887 was promoted major-general. In May 1889, on reaching fifty-five, he vacated his military works appointment, and in 1890 was selected by Roberts,

then commander-in-chief in India, to command the Oudh division, but this command was cut short by his promotion to lieutenant-general on 1 April 1891, and he returned to England. He was promoted general on 1 April 1895, made a colonel commandant, Royal Engineers, on the same date, and in 1897 was made KCB. He died at his home, 1 Bolton Street, Piccadilly, London, on 22 December 1901, and was buried at Brookwood cemetery, near Woking, Surrey. Roberts considered him 'an unusually intelligent, energetic gallant officer with considerable experience of war' (*Roberts in India*, 69) and publicly praised him as 'talented and indefatigable' (*Forty-one Years*, 373). However, Charles Metcalfe MacGregor described him as 'about the worst tempered fellow I know', and when he left the Oudh division it was described as 'the third relief of Lucknow' (Robson, 428).

R. H. VETCH, rev. ROGER T. STEARN

Sources *The Times* (23 Dec 1901) · *Royal Engineers Journal* (June 1903) · private information (1912) · H. M. Vibart, *Addiscombe: its heroes and men of note* (1894) · Lord Roberts [F. S. Roberts], *Forty-one years in India*, 31st edn (1900) · C. Hibbert, *The great mutiny, India, 1857* (1978) · B. Robson, *The road to Kabul: the Second Afghan War, 1878–1881* (1986) · *Roberts in India: the military papers of Field Marshal Lord Roberts, 1876–1893*, ed. B. Robson (1993) · E. W. C. Sandes, *The military engineer in India*, 2 vols. (1933–5) · *CGPLA Eng. & Wales* (1902)
Archives NAM, letters to Roberts
Wealth at death £24,947 14s. 4d.: resworn probate, April 1902, *CGPLA Eng. & Wales*

Perkins, Angier March (1799–1881), heating and steam engineer, was born on 21 August 1799, at Old Newburyport, Massachusetts, USA, the second son of the six children of **Jacob Perkins** (1766–1849) and his wife, Hannah, *née* Greenleaf (1770–1837). He was named after his father's brother-in-law and close friend, Angier March. Jacob Perkins, after a brief schooling, had been apprenticed to Edward Davis, a goldsmith, where he acquired his facility for fine metalwork and machinery. When Davis died in 1781, Jacob Perkins, aged fifteen, took charge of the business for his widow. Over the following years he embarked on a multitude of innovative projects, handing over the subsequent tedious business of production to family and friends. His most important lines were the manufacture of dies for coinage, and siderography: the technique of printing banknotes from a sequence of engraved steel plates, so as to defy counterfeiting. In 1809 he met Joseph Chessborough Dyer, a wealthy American who shortly afterwards went to England, where he acted as the patent agent for American inventors. Through this channel Jacob Perkins's siderographic plates became known in England.

In the course of his involvement with coins and banknotes, Jacob Perkins took his family to Philadelphia in 1817, then went to England in 1819 with his elder son, Ebenezer (1797–1842), in pursuit of a contract for engraving banknotes for the Bank of England. They won the contract; Dyer backed Jacob Perkins with £12,500, and machinery and men were brought over for the firm, known initially as Perkins, Fairman, and Heath, to commence printing. Angier Perkins later spoke of his own arrival in England:

> We embarked in the ship *Electra*, 500 tons, about November 1821 and arrived in England in thirty days where we found my father and brother and all our friends. I … went at once into the employment of my father and his partners and was engaged for the next eight years in manufacturing banknotes, dies and plates. During the latter part of the time I taught other parties to do the work I was engaged upon and my services in the firm became unnecessary and I found myself obliged to obtain other business.   (Bathe, 91)

The family resided in Fleet Street, in the City of London, above the business premises.

Jacob Perkins soon left his printing business in the hands of Angier, and then of his son-in-law Joshua Butters Bacon. In 1839 Perkins, Bacon, and Petch (as it was then known) was the firm chosen to print the first engraved adhesive stamps for the new penny post. Meanwhile Jacob Perkins's inventive mind turned to the advantages of high-pressure steam, as applied to locomotives, and to a 'steam-gun' (which the English military establishment spurned though the French were briefly tempted), to refrigeration plant, and to the creation of the Adelaide Gallery of Practical Sciences. This establishment, located at the western end of the Strand, opened in 1832 for the display and demonstration of new inventions and works of art. By the end of the 1840s, having ceased to draw the scientific and mechanically minded, it declined into a mere place of vulgar entertainment. In 1836 Hannah Perkins returned to Newburyport, where she died on 5 October 1837. Jacob Perkins continued to live with his son Angier, being now entirely dependent on him. On 15 July 1849 he took to his bed with what proved to be acute enteritis, and he died on 30 July. He was buried in the family vault at Kensal Green cemetery, which had been constructed for the interment of his daughter Louisa Jane in 1833.

Angier Perkins established his independent business as a heating and steam engineer in 1828, at Harpur Street, Holborn. In 1831 he married Julia Georgiana Brown and set up house, with his parents and sisters (his brother having returned to America), at 21 Great Coram Street, Bloomsbury. The same year he filed the first of many patents relating to heating apparatus. His first heating system was installed in 1832 at the villa of J. Horsley Palmer (1779–1858), governor of the Bank of England, at Fulham, where it was used for forcing grapes in wintertime. Another plant was erected in the Guardian Fire office in the City of London. At this time he took enlarged premises at Francis Street, off Gray's Inn Road, which he shared with his father, whose inventive mind remained as fertile as ever, despite his lack of business success.

Shortly after 1843 Perkins moved to 18 Regent Square, a more imposing dwelling, befitting his increasing prosperity. His involvement with steam engineering led him to propose improved methods of manufacturing and smelting iron, and designs for pipe couples and joints. His high-pressure steam heating systems were adapted to industrial use; his mobile baker's oven, exhibited at the Paris Exhibition of 1867, was earlier adopted by the British army.

Perkins's eldest son, Angier Greenleaf (1832–1871), also an engineer, died young; his second son, Loftus *Perkins, was apprenticed to his father, probably in 1848. He was taken into partnership in 1866, after which the firm traded as A. M. Perkins & Son. Angier Perkins was elected an associate of the Institution of Civil Engineers in May 1840, and was a fellow of the Royal Society of Arts from 1849. He died at his home, 140 Abbey Road, Hampstead, London, on 22 April 1881 and was interred in the family vault at Kensal Green cemetery.   ANITA McCONNELL

Sources G. Bathe and D. Bathe, *Jacob Perkins: his inventions, his times, and his contemporaries* (1943) • B. Hunnisett, *Steel engraved book illustration in England* (1980), 10–17 • 'The Paris exhibition: Perkins's portable oven', *The Engineer*, 23 (1867), 519 • E. M. Harris, 'Experimental graphic processes in England, 1800–1859', *Journal of the Printing Historical Society*, 4 (1968), 66–74 • *PICE*, 67 (1881–2), 417–19 • *Scientific American* (8 Sept 1849) [obituary of Jacob Perkins] • d. cert. • *IGI*
Likenesses portrait (Jacob Perkins), Franklin Institute, Philadelphia, Pennsylvania • silhouette, repro. in Bathe and Bathe, *Jacob Perkins*

Perkins [Parkins], **Sir Christopher** (1542/3–1622), diplomat, was born in Berkshire, most likely at Ufton Court. Little is known about his family background except that he described himself as a 'near kinsman' of Francis Parkins in his petition to acquire the latter's recusancy fines in 1599 (*Salisbury MSS*, 9.76). According to the Winchester College lists, he was twelve when he was admitted in 1555.

In 1596 Perkins explained to Sir Robert Cecil, principal secretary, that he had been educated first at Winchester and then at the University of Oxford. It is commonly believed that he attended New College because of its traditional connection with Winchester, but there is no evidence to support this. Perkins graduated BA on 7 April 1565. Presumably about this time he decided to leave England for religious reasons. He entered the Society of Jesus in Rome on 21 October 1566. After completion of his Jesuit noviceship in 1569, he studied philosophy at the Roman College. He was transferred to the Jesuit college in Dillingen in Germany to study theology in May 1572. He was ordained priest in Augsburg in April 1575. The Jesuit Henry More, the first historian of the order in England, claimed that Perkins 'heard theology at Dillingen with sufficient profit to get himself employed on occasion as assistant lecturer to James [Gregorio] of Valentia at Ingolstadt' (More, 33). In early 1579 Perkins was teaching philosophy at the University of Ingolstadt, but by November, then stationed at the Jesuit college in Innsbruck, he requested permission to work at the English College in Rome.

The Jesuit mission to England opened with great fanfare in April 1580. Years later, Robert Persons recalled that he and William Allen deemed Perkins fit for the mission. With the approval of the father-general of the order, Everard Mercurian, they wrote to Perkins about this assignment. To their astonishment, Perkins replied:

> that he would go willingly; but that if he went it would be advisable that he should have dispensation from the Pope for certain things, as, for example, to go to the Protestant churches and to take in a good sense the oath of the Queen's ecclesiastical supremacy and other like things.

Persons and Allen attributed the reply 'to the simplicity of the people with whom he [Perkins] lived, or to the little information he possessed about English affairs' and clung to the hope that he would eventually embark on the mission (*Memoirs*, 101). As late as 16 June 1581, Persons, now in London, still expected Perkins's imminent arrival.

The reasons for Perkins's departure from the Jesuits are unclear. In July 1580 Peter Canisius, father provincial of southern Germany, complained about his troublesome behaviour and made it clear that he would not welcome him back into his province if he left for Rome. Perkins set out for Italy none the less. On 30 September he was in Milan on his way back to Germany (whether he had already visited Rome is not known). In November he found the doors of the Jesuit community in Hall near Innsbruck closed to him: Canisius had carried out his threat. Over the next year Perkins wandered from college to college in the Jesuit province of the Rhineland. On 14 October 1581 he was dismissed from the society. According to the official register in the *Archivum Romanum Societatis Iesu*, he requested dismissal, but Persons contended Perkins was expelled because of 'bad conduct' (*Memoirs*, 101).

After leaving the Jesuits, Perkins resided in Venice and Rome. There is no evidence that he had abandoned either his priesthood or his allegiance to the Church of Rome. Indeed, his good standing is implicit in his successful intervention in the case of William Cecil, grandson of William Cecil, Lord Burghley, the lord treasurer. Most likely between July and November of 1585, Cecil visited Rome where he encountered problems with the Inquisition. A. F. Pollard blamed 'an indiscreet expression of protestant opinions', but Godfrey Goodman and Anthony Wood claimed that he was a victim of vindictive exiles at the English College seeking revenge for Burghley's role in the execution and imprisonment of Catholics (*DNB*). In some unexplained way, Perkins interceded, despite his later claim that he too was in peril in Rome because he professed himself the queen's 'faithful servant', and accompanied Cecil back to Padua and not to England as many suggest (Wernham, 2.449). Cecil, however, did carry with him a manuscript written by Perkins in Venice about the Jesuits. Unfortunately the pamphlet was never published and no extant copy has been identified. While he was on the continent, Perkins acquired a doctorate from an unknown university.

By October 1588 Dr Perkins was communicating with Sir Francis Walsingham, principal secretary, and serving as his informant. He was engaged on business 'in behalf of the Queen's subjects' and had been received, apparently at Elbing, 'as coming from the Queen of England'. He informed Walsingham that he was about to leave for Poland. In reply to the secretary's query about returning to England, Perkins considered his religion a hindrance: 'the laws as to it he cannot approve, though he admires the political institutions and would enjoy them, but will not be a judge or disturber of the laws of religion' (*Salisbury MSS*, 3.411). He abhorred the Spanish faction among English Catholics but had not abandoned Roman Catholicism. More likely he stressed his aversion to the Spanish faction because of suspicions generated about him by the alchemists Sir Edward Kelley and Dr John Dee.

Perkins met Kelley and Dee in Prague. In June 1589 Kelley accused him of being a papal emissary and of complicity in a plot to assassinate Elizabeth I. In his diary Dee recorded that on 5 August Edmond Hilton departed for England 'with my letters to disclose the treason of Perkins' (*Private Diary*, 31). By September Perkins had returned to England, perhaps to defend himself against their accusations. On 21 September the privy council instructed John Young, bishop of Rochester, to receive into his custody 'one——Perkins, a student heretofore in Oxford, a man learned and a Doctour of the Civill Lawe' (*APC*, 18.136). On 12 March 1590 Perkins wrote to Walsingham that he hoped that Kelley would 'deal sincerely' with him, a hope that lacked solid foundation if Kelley followed 'the counsel of his friends and ghostly fathers the Jesuits'. Moreover, Perkins produced in his defence a letter from Sigismund III Vasa, king of Poland (ironically a fervent supporter of the Society of Jesus and the Counter-Reformation), and anticipated that Burghley 'would lend his assistance to deliver the innocent from the malicious practice of common enemies' (*CSP dom.*, *1581–90*, 653). By 9 May he had been exonerated and was granted £300 for a journey to Poland and Prussia on the queen's service. Perhaps, at this time, he demonstrated his innocence by conforming to the Church of England.

Throughout the early 1590s Perkins served on numerous diplomatic missions: special ambassador to Poland, Denmark, and the Hanse cities (May 1590 – July 1591); to the empire and various German states (April–September 1593); and to Poland (December 1594 – June 1595). Periodically he begged for preferment 'to some living without cure', so that he could continue to serve the queen (*Salisbury MSS*, 4.583). However, such preferment was not offered. With no more income than the annual stipend of 100 marks promised in December 1591, Perkins suspected that the government discriminated against him, despite his years of service and loyalty, because of his foreign education and his former Catholicism. 'Some endeavour to insense that I am no great matter by birth, other that I am moved by the dregs of superstitious Papistical impressions' even though, as he claimed on 14 December 1597, he had renounced Catholicism 'as soon as he could judge thereof' (ibid., 7.516). Through the intercession of the Cecils, he secured the deanery of Carlisle in 1596. According to Goodman, Perkins anticipated a quiet life in the country but 'being all alone and having no employment, he became melancholy, for remedy whereof he did resolve to come up to London' (Goodman, 1.331).

On 20 February 1597 Perkins was admitted a member of Gray's Inn. On 16 September, presumably through the intercession of Cecil, he was elected MP for Ripon, West Riding of Yorkshire. He was returned from the same district in 1601. He continued to serve as special ambassador to Denmark (and made the journey three times in the final years of Elizabeth's reign: May–June 1598, September–December 1598, and March–July 1600) and as the government's principal adviser on mercantile matters with the

Baltic countries. Two aspirations were eventually achieved: he was appointed master of requests extraordinary in 1598 and Latin secretary on 21 August 1601.

James VI and I increased Perkins's annuity to £100 and, on 23 July 1603, knighted him in Whitehall. In James's first parliament in 1604 Perkins was returned as MP for Morpeth, Northumberland, again through the influence of Cecil. On 20 March 1605 he was admitted commoner of the College of Advocates. After years of acting as deputy to Sir Daniel Donne, Perkins succeeded him as master of requests in 1617.

Goodman, More, and Wood claimed that Perkins, on the basis of his friendship with Richard Bancroft, archbishop of Canterbury, helped formulate the oath of allegiance to 'determine' the loyalty of Catholics after the Gunpowder Plot of 1605, a concern that earlier lay behind his refusal to serve on the English mission unless he could take an oath to his queen. Despite Persons's accusation that Perkins exercised the 'office of Inquisitor against Catholics' (*Memoirs*, 101), the latter had little involvement in the persecution of his former co-religionists. He served on parliamentary committees concerned with penal laws, examined at least one Jesuit priest, William Wright, after his arrest in 1607, and discussed religion with Sir Tobie Matthew and Francis Walsingham (alias John Fennell), as they abandoned the Church of England in favour of the Church of Rome, but there is no record that he betrayed Catholics, lay or clergy. None the less, Catholics spread rumours that he was an 'atheist' and 'given wholly to gluttony and lechery, to feasting and women' (*Salisbury MSS*, 14.42), or, in the case of Matthew, that Perkins was homosexual: 'Now this Sir Christopher Perkins loved music very much, and had a boy whom he was yet suspected to love more' (Matthew, 70).

On 5 November 1617 Perkins married Anne, daughter of Anthony Beaumont of Glenmore, Leicestershire, and widow of James Brett of Hoby, Leicestershire. She was the sister of Mary Villiers, countess of Buckingham, the mother of George Villiers, duke of Buckingham. Goodman attributed this strange marriage to ambition. However, Perkins married her on the condition that he was not obliged to pay her debts. This clause so outraged Buckingham that he vowed that Perkins would rise no higher. Perkins did not—but whether that was because of Buckingham's intervention or Perkins's old age is not known. Suggestions that Anne was his second wife because of the mention of a 'Lady Parkins' in 1611-12 seem to be unfounded (*CSP dom., 1611-18*, 107). It is highly doubtful that the wife of Perkins would have sent a daughter to a Roman Catholic convent on the continent at that date.

Although not a rich man, Perkins was not penurious in his final years. Brian Levack evaluated his annual income to be at least £450, with two manors and investments in various mercantile operations. Perkins's will was dated 30 August 1620. According to Goodman, he left his wife as little as possible so that 'he might revenge himself on the kindred' (Goodman, 1.335). Anthony Bright was his heir and sole executor—and the recipient of a small estate. Other beneficiaries were Westminster Abbey and the poor

of the parish, Gray's Inn, Doctors' Commons, the Clothworkers' Company, and the University of Oxford. He mentioned no relatives but the children of his sister and his wife. Perkins died at the end of August 1622 and was buried on 1 September on the north side of the long aisle in Westminster Abbey. Commenting on his death, John Chamberlain wrote that Perkins 'was said to be a papist, or Jesuit, a doctor, a dean, a master of Requests, a knight, and what not' (Birch, 2.332).   THOMAS M. MCCOOG

Sources APC · G. M. Bell, *A handlist of British diplomatic representatives, 1509-1688*, Royal Historical Society Guides and Handbooks, 16 (1990) · T. Birch, *The court and times of James the First*, 2 vols. (1849) · O. Braunsberger, ed., *Beati Petri Canisii Societatis Iesu epistulae et acta* (Fribourg, 1922), vol. 7 · J. L. Chester, ed., *The marriage, baptismal, and burial registers of the collegiate church or abbey of St Peter, Westminster*, Harleian Society, 10 (1876) · *CSP dom., 1581-1623; addenda, 1580-1625* · R. Deacon, *John Dee: scientist, geographer, astrologer and secret agent to Elizabeth I* (1968) · C. Dodd [H. Tootell], *The church history of England, from the year 1500, to the year 1688*, 3 vols. (1737-42) · *Calendar of the manuscripts of the most hon. the marquis of Salisbury*, 24 vols., HMC, 9 (1883-1976), vols. 3-24 · G. Goodman, *The court of King James the First*, ed. J. S. Brewer, 2 vols. (1839) · *The private diary of Dr John Dee*, ed. J. O. Halliwell, CS, 19 (1842) · B. P. Levack, *The civil lawyers in England, 1603-1641* (1973) · T. M. McCoog, *The Society of Jesus in Ireland, Scotland, and England, 1641-1688: 'Our way of proceeding?'* (Leiden, 1996) · T. M. McCoog, *English and Welsh Jesuits, 1555-1650*, 2 vols., Catholic RS, 74-5 (1994-5) · A. H. Matthew, ed., *A true historical relation of the conversion of Sir Tobie Matthew* (1904) · *The Elizabethan Jesuits: Historia missionis Anglicanae Societatis Jesu* (1660) of Henry More, ed. and trans. F. Edwards (1981) · 'The memoirs of Father Robert Persons', ed. J. H. Pollen, *Miscellanea II*, Catholic RS, 2 (1906), 12-218; *Miscellanea IV*, Catholic RS, 4 (1907) · *DNB* · HoP, *Commons, 1558-1603* · R. B. Wernham, ed., *List and analysis of state papers, foreign series, Elizabeth I*, 7 vols. (1964-2000) · Wood, *Ath. Oxon.*, new edn, vol. 1 · will, PRO, PROB 11/140, fols. 175v-176v

Archives Archivum Romanum Societatis Iesu, Rome | BL, Cotton MSS · Hatfield House, Hertfordshire, Cecil MSS

Wealth at death bequeathed various annuities and gifts to the poor, University of Oxford, etc.; Anthony Bright was named heir and executor and received small estate: will, PRO, PROB 11/140, fols. 175v-176v

Perkins, Erasmus. *See* Cannon, George (1789-1854).

Perkins, Francis Arthur [Frank] (1889-1967), diesel engine manufacturer, was born on 26 February 1889 at Clifton Villa, Park Road, Peterborough, Northamptonshire, the second of the three sons of John Edward S. Perkins, who became managing director of Barford and Perkins Ltd, makers of agricultural machinery, and his wife, Margaret Charlotte, *née* Long. He was educated at Lindley Lodge preparatory school (1899-1902), Rugby School (1902-4), and Gresham's School, Holt (1904-7), and went up to Emmanuel College, Cambridge, in 1907, leaving with a pass degree in mechanical engineering in 1910.

A career in agriculture was always likely, given his background, and Perkins initially rented a farm in Hertfordshire. On the outbreak of the First World War he volunteered, and was commissioned in the army, serving in the 34th divisional company of the Royal Engineers in the Dardanelles, Palestine, and Egypt. In 1915 Perkins, who was commonly known as Frank, married Susan Gwynneth Gee, daughter of Hugh Roberts Williams, a government inspector. They had one son and three daughters. Perkins was demobilized in 1918 with the rank of major and worked for Lawes Chemicals Ltd before joining the family firm at the Queen Street ironworks in Peterborough.

Barford and Perkins was one of fourteen firms to join the Agricultural and General Engineers (AGE) group, a holding company formed in 1919 on the initiative of Thomas Aveling and Frank Garrett to enable leading British manufacturers of agricultural machinery to compete against American rivals in the world market by rationalizing production and centralizing sales. In the 1920s Barford and Perkins was developing roadrollers powered by petrol engines, and in 1928 Perkins moved to the leading British manufacturer of steamrollers and steam traction engines, Aveling and Porter Ltd of Rochester, another AGE member, as works director and vice-chairman; in the same year the two companies formed a joint roller manufacturing company. Perkins became involved in the development of a four-cylinder high-speed diesel engine to power agricultural tractors made by Garretts of Leiston, also a member of AGE. A Garrett tractor, with an Aveling and Porter Invicta diesel engine, was exhibited at the Smithfield Show and at the World Tractor Trials in Wallingford in 1930, and in 1931 it broke the world non-stop ploughing record in a ploughing marathon organized by the Oxford University Institute of Agricultural Engineering, ploughing for 977 hours. But the project was halted in 1932 when AGE went bankrupt and was disbanded and its companies were sold off individually.

Aveling and Porter and Barford and Perkins were sold together, and a new firm of Aveling and Barford Ltd began manufacturing at Grantham. Perkins bought the development and production rights on the Invicta engine and started his own company, F. Perkins Ltd, to continue the development of a lightweight high-speed diesel engine at the Queen Street works in Peterborough, which had closed at the end of 1931 but which still belonged to his father. With Charles Chapman, former head of engineering at Aveling and Porter, as chief engineer, and three former employees of Aveling and Porter, he was testing the first Perkins engine, the four-cylinder Vixen, by the end of 1932. This became the Wolf series, and was accepted by Commer Cars Ltd at the end of 1933 to power Commer trucks.

Perkins drove from Peterborough to Perth in a Hillman Wizard fitted with a Perkins Fox engine, at a fuel cost of one-eighth of a penny per mile, in 1933, and from Helsinki to Moscow in 1934, and in 1935 a racing car fitted with a Wolf engine broke or set six world records for diesel at the Brooklands circuit. However, the main demand for diesel engines at this point was for commercial vehicles. Diesel engines were not only cheaper to run, but they could cope with heavier loads than their petrol equivalents, and the firm converted many trucks and vans from petrol to diesel for its customers. It was five years before the company started to make a profit, following the success of the first six-cylinder diesel engine, the P6, which came on to the market in 1937, and could be used to power boats, trucks, vans, and industrial machinery. Sales rose from £7006 in

1933 to £206,320 in 1939. Shortly before the outbreak of the Second World War, the Air Ministry commissioned F. Perkins Ltd to provide engines for air–sea rescue launches, and during the war these made up the bulk of the company's production.

After the war the world demand for diesel tractors and commercial vehicles grew, and the Perkins P6 became the most popular engine, with customers including Ford UK and Massey-Harris of Canada. The company moved to a new factory at Eastfield, outside Peterborough, in 1947, and turnover grew from £1.25 million in 1946 to £9.35 million in 1951. In 1951 F. Perkins Ltd launched itself as a public company. Although it continued to expand during the 1950s, with overseas plants and sales and service outlets in France, Spain, India, and Brazil, and a turnover in 1956 of £21.5 million, problems were developing. Customers began to think about manufacturing their own engines rather than buying from Perkins, and at the same time competitors were producing lighter-weight, more economical engines.

Too late, Perkins put more money and time into research and development rather than being content with the success of the P6, but the new design, the R6, was developed too quickly and was not properly tested, leaving dissatisfied customers. Following the closure of the Suez Canal in 1956 and the subsequent loss of markets in India and the Far East, the value of sales fell by a third in 1957, and for the first time Perkins incurred losses, of £319,000. Following a report prepared by Perkins's deputy, Monty Prichard, which recommended amalgamation as the only way forward, a deal was made with Massey-Ferguson, one of its biggest customers, at the beginning of 1959. Massey-Ferguson bought all the shares in F. Perkins Ltd, which became a subsidiary and continued to produce engines in Peterborough. Production grew from 77,000 engines a year in 1959 to 250,000 in 1963. Perkins remained as chairman until 1962, when he was elected honorary president.

In 1961 Perkins's first wife died, and in 1965 he married a widow, Maud V. Dixon, daughter of Robert L. Andrews, a retired army captain. Perkins's interests—shooting, fishing, and sailing—were those of a country gentleman, and he owned and managed a small arable farm. He was president of the Society of Motor Manufacturers and Traders (1956–7), high sheriff of Cambridgeshire and Huntingdonshire (1956–7), and president of the Peterborough Agricultural Society from 1961, and was made an honorary freeman of the City of Peterborough in 1962. Perkins died on 15 October 1967 at his home, Alwalton Hall, near Peterborough.   ANNE PIMLOTT BAKER

Sources J. C. Thompson, 'Perkins, Francis Arthur', *DBB* · D. Porteus, *The Perkins story* (Perkins Engines Co., 1995) · E. P. Neufeld, *A global corporation: a history of the international development of Massey-Ferguson Limited* (1969), 319–29 · P. Cook, *Massey at the brink* (1981), 168–171 · M. Williams, *Massey-Ferguson tractors* (1987), 100–03 · J. M. Preston, *Aveling and Porter Ltd* (1987) · R. A. Whitehead, *Garrett diesel tractors* (1994) · *A hundred years of road rollers: a pictorial history*, Aveling-Barford Limited (privately printed, Lingfield, Surrey, 1965) · *The Times* (16 Oct 1967) · *The Engineer* (27 Oct 1967) · CUL,

department of manuscripts and university archives • Emmanuel College Archives, Cambridge • *CGPLA Eng. & Wales* (1968) • d. cert.
Likenesses photograph, *c.*1950, repro. in Thompson, 'Perkins, Francis Arthur'
Wealth at death £137,403: probate, 24 Jan 1968, *CGPLA Eng. & Wales*

Perkins, Frederick (1780–1860). *See under* Perkins, Henry (*bap.* 1777, *d.* 1855).

Perkins, Henry (*bap.* 1777, *d.* 1855), book collector and brewer, was baptized on 2 January 1777 at St Swithin London Stone, London, the son of John Perkins (1729/30–1812) and his wife, Amelia, widow of Timothy Bevan. John Perkins was the chief clerk of the Anchor Brewery in Southwark, which he was credited with having saved from demolition during the Gordon riots of 1780 by a judicious offer of porter to an angry mob. The following year, in partnership with his wife's Quaker relatives David Barclay, Robert Barclay, and Sylvanus Bevan, he bought the business for some £135,000. It was of this sale that Dr Johnson commented, 'we are not here to sell a parcel of boilers and vats, but the potentiality of growing rich beyond the dreams of avarice' (Cockes and Cook, 16). Johnson's friend Hester Thrale (later Piozzi), the wife of the brewery's late owner, Henry Thrale, gave assistance to Perkins with the purchase, and in 1790 she arranged for the celebrated Samuel Parr to tutor two of Perkins's sons—almost certainly Henry and his younger brother **Frederick Perkins** (1780–1860), who was baptized on 29 September 1780 at St Swithin London Stone. With apparent relish at taking down the *arrivistes*, Hester Thrale noted that they were 'sad mean boys … [their mother] fancied they would be scholars, but they prov'd poor creatures it seems' (Pudney, 73). Frederick was apprenticed at the brewery in February 1796, and received half of his father's quarter share in the concern by an indenture of September 1808; Henry received the other moiety, probably at the same time. Neither son appears to have taken a particularly forward role in the firm's management, though both served a term as master of the Brewers' Company—Henry in 1817 and Frederick in 1823.

The brewery continued to prosper and, as if in defiance of Hester Thrale's remark, the Perkins brothers spent much of their wealth on the accumulation of rare and valuable books. Henry, who was a fellow of the Linnean, Geological, and Horticultural societies, began collecting in the early 1820s, when he was resident at Springfield, near Tooting, Surrey; later, about 1836, he moved to Hanworth Park, Middlesex. His agents were John and Arthur Arch of 61 Cornhill, London, and his most significant bulk purchase was of items from the collection of John 'Dog' Dent (1750–1826). Perkins's library was not notably extensive, but it included two copies of the Gutenberg Bible (one paper, one vellum); a first edition of the Latin Bible (1462); a Coverdale Bible (1835); the first four Shakespeare folios; several works from the press of Caxton; and some fine illuminated manuscripts, among them John Lydgate's *Sege of Troy* (*c.*1425). Perkins had married Susannah Latham on 2 April 1803; they had one son and three daughters, and she apparently predeceased him. He died at

Dover on 15 April 1855, whereupon his eighth share in the brewery and his books passed to his son, Algernon (*bap.* 20 December 1808). After the latter's death in 1870, the library was dispersed; the 865 lots in the sale (held on 3–6 June 1873) raised nearly £25,000, the largest amount hitherto realized for a collection of its size. One commentator, writing in 1892, ventured that it was 'in certain respects the most valuable ever brought together' (Kearney).

Frederick Perkins's collection was larger but less distinguished: its chief ornaments were the first four Shakespeare folio editions (not to be outdone by his brother), and a number of separate plays in quarto, including six first editions. A fifteenth-century copy of Chaucer's *Canterbury Tales* and several illuminated manuscripts also featured. With his wife, also named Susannah, whom he had married before February 1803, he had at least one son, Frederick Oswald Perkins (*bap.* 8 May 1804), who succeeded to his interest in the brewery. Perkins died at his residence at Chipstead Place, Kent, on 10 October 1860; the subsequent book sale of 2086 lots, held on 10 July 1889, raised £8222 7*s.*   H. J. SPENCER

Sources W. Y. Fletcher, *English book collectors* (1902) • M. Kearney, 'Henry Perkins', *Contributions towards a dictionary of English book-collectors*, ed. B. Quaritch, 2 (1892) • B. W. Cockes and L. W. Cook, *Three centuries: the story of our ancient brewery, Barclay, Perkins and Company* (1951) • J. Pudney, *A draught of contentment: the story of the Courage group* (1971) • P. Mathias, *The brewing industry in England, 1700–1830* (1959) • J. L. Clifford, *Hester Lynch Piozzi* (1987) • PRO, PROB 11/2218/725 • *DNB* • *GM*, 1st ser., 73 (1803), 190, 380 • *GM*, 1st ser., 82/2 (1812), 592 • LMA, Barclay, Perkins & Co. archives, ac. 2305 • Boase, *Mod. Eng. biog.* • IGI
Archives LMA, Barclay, Perkins & Co. MSS, letters, MSS
Wealth at death £100,000: PRO, death duty registers, IR 26/2043/865

Perkins, Jacob (1766–1849). *See under* Perkins, Angier March (1799–1881).

Perkins, John (*d.* 1545?), legal writer, is said by Wood to have been 'born of genteel parents' and to have studied grammar and logic at Oxford (Wood, *Ath. Oxon.*, 1.147), though whether he had any direct evidence for these assertions is unclear. If the Master Walbeiff whom Perkins referred to as his old master may be identified as John Waldboeuf, an official in Brecknockshire, then an origin in south Wales seems likely. Perkins was admitted to the Inner Temple about 1518, when he was assigned a chamber in 'Le Lane Syde', and called to the bar in due course. There is nothing to suggest that he had much to do thereafter with the affairs of the inn, which in 1530 discharged him from all offices except those of steward and reader, and in 1539 sued him for outstanding dues. In fact he never did read and did not become a bencher (as stated in some sources), and no contemporary evidence has been found of the extensive practice claimed for him by Wood. Indeed, there was a rumour—which Perkins felt obliged to deny as a slander in 1537—that his 'heels was turned upward' in Westminster Hall twenty years earlier (PRO, SP 1/115, fol. 110*v*), a punishment meted out to dishonest attorneys rather than barristers.

Certainly by the later 1530s Perkins was residing and practising in Oxford, where he became a thorn in the side of the university and Osney Abbey. In his later years he became mentally unbalanced. He wrote a long letter to Cromwell in 1537 proposing a means of suppressing the northern rising by a combination of espionage and terror, such as killing women and children, and a scheme for dissolving and remodelling on secular lines the colleges at Oxford and Cambridge, each of which would be required to do away with academical dress and raise and maintain a contingent of archers and halberdiers. A flimsy accusation of treason and unmentionable vices which he simultaneously flung against two local abbots led to imprisonment, banishment from Oxford, and an end as obscure as his beginning. Bale said he died in 1545, and Wood conjectured (probably wrongly) that he was buried in Temple Church.

Despite his disturbed professional and personal life, Perkins was a household name for generations of law students by reason of his little book on land law, called *Perkins' Profitable Book*, which first appeared (in law French) in 1528 under the Latin title *Perutilis tractatus magistri Johannis Parkins interioris Templi socii*. A manuscript version in the British Library (Hargrave MS 244), fairly copied but lacking the last page or two, seems to be more or less coeval with the first printing. There were three further editions in French, and then an English translation in 1555 (*A Verie Profitable Booke Treating of the Lawes of this Realme*) which went through seventeen editions or reprintings before 1660, was again reprinted in 1757, enjoyed a Dublin edition in 1792, and reached its final form in a new edition (called the fifteenth), with notes by Richard J. Greening of the Inner Temple, in 1827. There is a different English translation by Gilbert Trobridge, admitted to the Middle Temple in 1594, in the British Library (Harley MS 5035). The English versions are divided into eleven chapters (dealing with grants, deeds, feoffments, exchanges, dower, curtesy, wills, devises, surrenders, reservations, and conditions) and 845 numbered sections. The *Profitable Book* was intended as a kind of supplement to Littleton's *Tenures*, dealing chiefly with points of conveyancing which were not to be found in Littleton, and it does not therefore have the coherence or elegance of Littleton's great work. It nevertheless has a thoughtful jurisprudential preface, is clearly written, and was considered authoritative. Coke praised it as witty and learned, though in 1600 William Fulbeck offered the more severe opinion that 'it might be wished that he had written with less sharpness of wit, so he had discoursed with more depth of judgment' (Fulbeck, 72). J. H. BAKER

Sources G. R. Elton, *Star chamber stories* (1958), 19–51 • PRO, SP 1/115, fols. 95–110 • Wood, *Ath. Oxon.*, new edn, 1.147 • F. A. Inderwick and R. A. Roberts, eds., *A calendar of the Inner Temple records*, 1 (1896) • Foster, *Alum. Oxon.* • PRO, CP 40/1100, m. 681d • BL, Hargrave MS 244, fols. 170–314 • BL, Harley MS 5035 • P. Winfield, *Sources of English legal history* (1925), 330 • W. Fulbeck, *Direction or preparative to the study of the law*, ed. T. H. Stirling, 2nd edn (1829), 72

Perkins, John [*nicknamed* Jack Punch] (*c*.1745–1812), naval officer and spy, was born in Jamaica. Nothing certain is known of his origin, but he is described as a 'mulatto', the child of a white father and a black mother, and if so it is highly probable that his mother was a slave. Under Jamaican law, this would have made the boy himself a slave, but the mixed-race sons of white men in positions of authority were often emancipated and educated to the level of clerks or overseers. Perkins must already have been an experienced mariner by the outbreak of the American War of Independence in November 1775, when he entered HMS *Antelope*, flagship at Jamaica, as a pilot, and he later claimed to have been 'from his youth ... engaged in the Sea Service' (PRO, CO 140/75, 30). He continued on the books of various ships on the station throughout the war, but in practice he seems to have been detached most of the time in various small tenders cruising against enemy privateers. In command of the schooner *Punch* in 1778 and 1779, Jack Punch, as he was nicknamed, won a remarkable reputation: his claim to have taken 315 prizes and captured over 3000 prisoners in the course of the war was officially endorsed by the Jamaican house of assembly. Perkins also scouted enemy preparations at Cap François and Havana, making clandestine visits to the shore. On 15 October 1781 he was commissioned by Sir Peter Parker as lieutenant commanding the schooner *Endeavour*. In her he continued his spectacular career, taking a prize much larger than his own vessel, and in July 1782 Rodney, in a characteristically irregular promotion, made him commander of the *Endeavour* with a lieutenant under him. This was disallowed, and he was still a lieutenant at the end of the war.

What Perkins did during the peace is unknown, but on the mobilization in 1790 he offered his services to Rear-Admiral Affleck, was sent on an espionage mission to Hispaniola, and was about to go on another to Cuba when the threat of war receded. In February 1792, probably engaged again on intelligence work, he was arrested and condemned to death by the French authorities at Jérémie in St Domingue, and only rescued at the last minute by the interposition of a British warship. In June 1795 he was at sea once more, in command of the schooner *Marie Antoinette*, from which in June 1797, 'an old and deserving officer' (PRO, ADM 1/250, P50), he was promoted by Sir Hyde Parker into the sloop *Drake*. This time the commission was confirmed, and in September 1800 Parker made Perkins post in the frigate *Meleager*, from which he soon transferred to the *Arab*, and in 1804 to the *Tartar* (32 guns). In the *Arab* he occupied the island of St Eustatia on its evacuation by the French in April 1801. In the *Tartar* he was much on the coast of St Domingo during the war between the French and the slaves, led by Dessalines. There he found himself caught between, on the one hand, Edward Corbett, 'extra minister' sent from England to assess the situation, who complained that Perkins was unduly friendly to the black population, and, on the other, his admiral, Sir John Duckworth, who firmly backed him, and Lieutenant-Governor Nugent, who sought his advice. By now Perkins was no longer young, and after several bouts of illness (described as asthma) he was forced towards the end of 1804 to resign his command. He retired to his home in Kingston, where he died on either 24 or 27

January 1812—probably the latter, as he was buried on the 28th.

Perkins was a remarkable character, whose rise from obscurity, if not slavery, to the rank of post captain, coupled with his extraordinary skill, daring, and success, made a great impression on contemporaries. Though of no great education, he was functionally literate and sufficiently polished to move in naval and colonial society. He was probably unique among naval officers in apparently never once having visited Britain.   N. A. M. Rodger

Sources Admiralty correspondence, ships musters, other documents, PRO, CO 140/75, 30; ADM 1/250, P50 · W. L. Clowes, *The Royal Navy: a history from the earliest times to the present*, 7 vols. (1897–1903), vol. 4, p. 471 · *Lady Nugent's journal: Jamaica one hundred and thirty years ago*, ed. F. Cundall, 3rd edn (1939) · *Naval Chronicle*, 458 · *Naval Chronicle*, 27 (1812), 351–2 · *Journals of the Jamaican house of assembly*, 8

Perkins, John Bryan Ward- (1912–1981), archaeologist, was born on 3 February 1912 at Bromley, Kent, the elder son (there were no daughters) of Bryan Ward-Perkins, of the Indian Civil Service, and his wife, Winifred Mary Hickman. He was educated at Winchester College and New College, Oxford, where he graduated with a first class in *literae humaniores* in 1934, going on to hold the university's Craven travelling fellowship at Magdalen College. The groundwork of his career in archaeology was laid at this time, with excavation and pottery studies in Britain and France. In 1936 he took up a post as assistant at the London Museum under the direction of Mortimer Wheeler, producing a notable catalogue of the museum's medieval collection, besides directing his own excavations at Oldbury hill fort, near Ightham, Kent and at Lockleys Roman villa, near Welwyn Garden City, Hertfordshire. His work was already remarkable for its range and for the fresh insights which it introduced; the publication of the Lockleys excavation remains a *locus classicus* for the use of archaeology to trace the history of a small Roman farm in southeast Britain.

In 1939 Ward-Perkins went to take up a chair in archaeology at the Royal University of Malta but had only been there six months when war broke out, and he returned to England to enlist in the Royal Artillery (Territorial Army). His war service took him to north Africa and ultimately to Italy, where, as a lieutenant-colonel, he participated in the allied invasion. His archaeological expertise and organizing ability were recognized in his appointment as director of the allied subcommission for monuments and fine arts in Italy, a post which involved the salvage of art works dispersed and damaged in the course of the war. In 1943 he married Margaret Sheilah, daughter of Henry William Long, lieutenant-colonel in the Royal Army Medical Corps, with whom he had three sons and a daughter.

In 1946 Ward-Perkins became the first post-war director of the British School at Rome, where he stayed until his retirement in 1974. His twenty-nine years at the helm of a small, ever-changing community of British artists and academics in Italy gave him the opportunity to produce much of his finest work. During the first decade he orchestrated programmes of survey and excavation in Cyrenaica and Tripolitania, writing seminal papers and books on the art and archaeology of a region whose richness in monuments had been revealed by Italian excavations in the 1920s and 1930s. At the same time his concern with Roman architecture, and especially with its technical and organizational aspects, led to important studies on the necropolis under the Vatican basilica (*The Shrine of St Peter and the Vatican Excavations*, with J. M. C. Toynbee, 1956) and on Roman brick construction in *The Great Palace of the Byzantine Emperors*, edited by D. Talbot Rice (1958). In the last two decades in Rome his major achievement was the organization of the south Etruria survey, a project for the recording and analysis of remains of all periods within a region where the archaeological evidence was rapidly being destroyed by modern development. This type of systematic field survey, which evolved from the earlier topographical studies of Thomas Ashby to the south and east of Rome, helped to confirm the prestige of the British School as the main centre for research into the historical landscape of Italy.

In his later years Ward-Perkins was involved in the organization of international projects such as the Tabula Imperii Romani, a scheme to produce detailed maps for all regions of the Roman empire; he promoted research into the identification and classification of Roman marbles, a vital prerequisite for the understanding of the building industry and of sarcophagus production; and he organized a major exhibition on Pompeii at the Royal Academy in 1976, which later travelled to various cities in America and Australia. His mature thoughts on Roman architecture were set out in his Pelican History of Art volume, originally issued in tandem with Axel Boethius's survey of the Etruscan and early Roman material, but later revised and published separately as *Roman Imperial Architecture* (1981).

Ward-Perkins towered above the Roman archaeologists of his generation. Many of his approaches, as in the use of field survey to study patterns of land use over the ages, and his emphasis on the importance of data on materials and techniques to the understanding of sculpture and architecture, have radically affected the thinking of researchers in the area. He was generous in his encouragement of younger scholars and particularly successful in his recognition of amateur talent. In most of those who knew him he inspired great loyalty and affection; he was a charismatic figure with an expansive personality, and his impatience with those who could not see issues as clearly as he did was readily forgiven. His personal interests—gardening, stamp-collecting, music—were pursued with the same dedication and attention to detail as his professional activities. His work was rewarded with election to fellowship of the British Academy (1951), honorary degrees from the universities of Birmingham (DLitt, 1961) and Alberta (LLD, 1969), and appointment as CBE (1955) and CMG (1975). His overseas honours included membership of various academies and election to the presidency of the International Association for Classical Archaeology (1974–9). He died in Cirencester, Gloucestershire, on 28 May 1981.   Roger Ling, *rev.*

Sources *The Times* (5 June 1981) · *Papers of the British School at Rome*, 1 (1982) · J. J. Wilkes, 'John Bryan Ward-Perkins, 1912–1981', *PBA*, 69 (1983), 631–55 · personal knowledge (1990) · private information (1990) · *CGPLA Eng. & Wales* (1981)
Archives British School at Rome, corresp. and papers while director of British School at Rome
Likenesses photograph, repro. in *PBA*, 69 (1983), facing 631
Wealth at death £109,095: probate, 31 July 1981, *CGPLA Eng. & Wales*

Perkins, Joseph (*bap.* 1657), poet, was baptized on 6 May 1657 at Slimbridge, Gloucestershire, the son of George Perkins. He matriculated from Oriel College, Oxford, on 16 July 1675, and graduated BA in 1679. After this his career must be reconstructed from his works.

Perkins became a chaplain in the navy, and sailed to the Mediterranean in the *Norfolk* under Admiral Edward Russell (afterwards earl of Orford). He was cashiered for having, it was alleged, brought a false accusation of theft against a naval officer, and his response was a series of publications in 1697. *Capellanus regiae cuiusdam navis* (1697) set out the terms of his grievances in verse, and he also published several Latin elegies, including the one he had written in 1694 for the death of Admiral Russell from illness, the occasion for which had been spoiled when Russell unexpectedly recovered. At the same time he published three texts with links to Tunbridge Wells: an open letter remonstrating with the church authorities, 'who denied him the use of the pulpit there', a poem composed extempore on a musical contest at Tunbridge Wells on 9 July 1697, and a Latin poem celebrating the ladies who accompanied Queen Anne on her visit there in the same year.

In the succeeding years Perkins printed various further sermons and elegies. In 1707 another burst of publications included a collection of poetry: *The Poet's Fancy, in a Love-Letter to Galatea, or any other Fair Lady, in English and Latin*. He also printed a sermon, on the title-page of which it is claimed that Perkins 'heard the voice of an angel or spirit speaking to him two several times, in one night'.

Perkins's last known work is an elegy on the death of Thomas Ken, published in Bristol in 1711. He styled himself the White Poet and the Latin Laureate, but seems to have been largely unsuccessful in his quests for patronage.   MATTHEW STEGGLE

Sources Foster, *Alum. Oxon.* · *IGI* · *DNB*

Perkins, Loftus (1834–1891), mechanical engineer, was born on 8 May 1834 in Great Coram Street, London, the son of Angier March *Perkins (1799–1881), engineer, and his wife, Julia Georgiana Brown. Probably apprenticed in 1848 to his father, in 1853–4 he went to New York to practise on his own account. (Jacob *Perkins [*see under* Perkins, Angier March], Loftus's grandfather, had come from New England and the Perkins family was still numerous in that area.) After returning to England he remained with his father until 1862, then spent four years in business at Hamburg and Berlin, designing and executing heating installations for buildings in various parts of the continent. He again returned to England in 1866 and entered into partnership with his father, trading as A. M. Perkins & Son, a style which continued until his father's death.

Perkins inherited his grandfather's inventive brilliance, plus a greater appreciation of the practical difficulties involved in high-pressure engineering. He took out a large number of patents, the first, in 1859, relating to a steam engine designed to operate at 600 lb per square inch. His 1872 patent for gunmetal piston rings was a most important advance for engineering. By 1874 the British army had fifty-six of Perkins's horse-drawn mobile steam ovens to feed troops on the march; these were known to the soldiers as 'Polly Perkins'. His commercial baking ovens based on his steam heating system, 'the stopped-end tube', were widely used in bakeries. In 1871–3 Perkins made successful trials with a tractor powered by high-pressure steam, and at the 1873 International Exhibition in London he demonstrated his noiseless road engine which travelled at 8 m.p.h. His 70 ton yacht *Anthracite*, driven by engines working with steam at 500 lb pressure, travelled across the Atlantic and back in 1880, consuming only 25 tons of coal. In 1883 Mrs Perkins launched the steamship *Express* on the Thames; 160 feet in length, with a Perkins 800 hp quadruple compound engine and speed of 14 knots, it was licensed to carry 677 passengers on the river and 345 at sea. Many engineers came to inspect it. *Express* was later sold for midnight sun cruises in Norway, proof that high-pressure steam was both safe and economical.

Perkins's experiments in refrigeration led him to design and patent in 1888 his Arktos cold chamber, suitable for preserving meat and other foodstuffs. It functioned entirely without moving parts or valves by what is now known as the automatic ammonia absorption system. This was his last major achievement, and the long hours through which he nursed it to perfection contributed to the breakdown of his health. Perkins became a member of the Institution of Mechanical Engineers in 1861 and of the Institution of Civil Engineers in 1881. His wife, Emily Patton (*b.* 1837/8), came from New York; their sons Loftus Patton Perkins (*b.* 1867) and Ludlow Patton Perkins (1872–1928) joined their father in business. The firm passed from family control after Perkins's death and subsequently amalgamated with Joseph Baker, Sons & Co., as Baker Perkins. Perkins died on 27 April 1891 at his home, 148 Abbey Road, Kilburn, London, and was buried at Kensal Green cemetery on 1 May. He was survived by his wife.

ANITA MCCONNELL

Sources G. Bathe and D. Bathe, *Jacob Perkins: his inventions, his times, and his contemporaries* (1943) · *PICE*, 105 (1890–91), 311–15 · *The Engineer* (1 May 1891), 349 · A. Muir, *The history of Baker Perkins* (1968) · *CGPLA Eng. & Wales* (1891)
Archives Sci. Mus., archives
Likenesses A. Edouart?, silhouette, repro. in Bathe and Bathe, *Jacob Perkins*, 162
Wealth at death £1829: probate, 28 May 1891, *CGPLA Eng. & Wales*

Perkins [Parkins], **Richard** (*c.*1579–1650), actor, gave his age in a legal deposition of 1623 as '44 yeares, or

Richard Perkins (c.1579–1650), by unknown artist, late 1640s

therabouts', so that he was about twenty-three when his name first was recorded in Henslowe's *Diary* (September 1602) as a member of the theatrical company Worcester's Men. He remained with the same troupe when they became Queen Anne's Men in 1603, emerging as a leading player within the next decade, and acting principally at the Red Bull playhouse. He probably played the role of Flamineo in the first performance of Webster's *The White Devil* in 1612. Webster's epigraph to the published play speaks of Perkins as 'my freind', and praises his acting. In the same year Perkins also claimed the dramatist and actor Thomas Heywood as '*my loving friend and fellow*' in prefatory verses he contributed to Heywood's *An Apology for Actors*. Heywood was also a member of Queen Anne's Men, as was Christopher Beeston, with whom Perkins was to have a long professional relationship. Perkins was an overseer of and witness to the will of his senior colleague Thomas Greene in July 1612; with his fellows he received a pair of gloves as a memorial gift, as well as considerable problems ensuing from the share in the company inherited by Greene's widow. The troupe was already in some financial difficulty by the time of the queen's death in 1619, when it disbanded. Perkins and a number of other actors returned to the Red Bull from the Cockpit playhouse in Drury Lane, to which Queen Anne's Men had moved in the final two years of their existence, and performed there as the Players of the Revels.

Perkins lived in Clerkenwell, near to the Red Bull in the parish of St James, until at least the 1620s—in 1623 at the northern end of St John's Street—and he was living there at the end of his life. By 1620 he was married to a woman named Elizabeth, who gave evidence in that year in a law case in which he was involved; in March of the following year she died, and Perkins may have remarried on 5

November 1621, if the Richard Perkins who married Philadelphia Kelly in All Hallows, Lombard Street, was the actor.

In 1623 Perkins became a member of the King's Men, but for a brief period only: by late 1625 he had joined Queen Henrietta's Company, led by Christopher Beeston, at the Cockpit playhouse in Drury Lane. As a leading performer with this company for eleven years his roles included Barabas in a revival of Marlowe's *The Jew of Malta*, Sir John Belfare in Shirley's *The Wedding*, Fitzwater in Davenport's *King John and Matilda*, Captain Goodlack in Heywood's *The Fair Maid of the West*, and Hanno in Nabbes's *Hannibal and Scipio*; he would have taken principal roles in other plays by Heywood, Shirley, and Ford, among other leading dramatists in the company's repertory. Perkins's playing of Barabas is praised by Heywood in a prologue and epilogue written for the revival of the play in 1633, in which the actor is favourably compared with his famous predecessor in the role, Edward Alleyn. Perkins was undoubtedly the star actor at the Cockpit, one of the two principal London theatres in the 1630s, and a rival to the player Joseph Taylor at the Blackfriars. During 1636–7 the company was disbanded, and Perkins was among a number of older actors who joined a new Queen Henrietta's Company, acting at the Salisbury Court playhouse from late 1637 until the cessation of playing five years later. With both generations of the company Perkins appeared frequently at court; he undoubtedly acted in the productions of Heywood's *Love's Mistress*, staged with scenery by Inigo Jones, presented before the king and queen at Somerset House in November 1634.

There was at least one Richard Perkins (or Parkins) living in the parish of St Giles-in-the-Fields from the mid-1620s until the mid-1640s, and it has been suggested that the actor may have moved to the district near the Cockpit playhouse. He appears to have married again, and buried children at St Giles. His presence there until the latter half of 1645 is further indicated by the bequest of a former colleague, the third player who remembered Perkins at his death. (In 1634 he was willed a mourning ring by his old fellow from Queen Anne's Men, Thomas Basse.) Michael Bowyer made his will in September 1645, leaving 'to my loveing frend mr Richard Perkins of St Giles in the feildes London fyftie poundes of currant English money to be payed unto him by fyve shillinges a week, yf he shall soe long lyve' (Bentley, *Jacobean and Caroline Stage*, 2.635). Bowyer and Perkins had been chief actors with Queen Henrietta's Men from 1625 to 1636, and Perkins had stood surety for Bowyer when he joined the King's Men in 1637; he may indeed have lent Bowyer money, of which the bequest was a repayment rather than a gift.

By the time of the outbreak of war in England, Perkins was sixty-three, and it seems unlikely that he would have joined the king's army, as so many of his professional colleagues did. According to James Wright in *Historia histrionica* (1699) he spent his last years in Clerkenwell, sharing a house with his old acting colleague John Sumner, suggesting rather straitened circumstances, and that neither man had a family at the end of his life: 'Susan wife of Richard Parkins' had been buried at St Giles-in-the-Fields in August 1645; Perkins himself was buried at St James's, Clerkenwell, on 20 April 1650.

Towards the end of his life Perkins's portrait was painted, an event which speaks of prosperity and a continuing position in the world rather than of hard times. The painting survives in the collection of the Dulwich Picture Gallery: it is a half-length on canvas (69.8cm x 61.9 cm), with the subject turned three-quarters to the left, his left hand resting on his breast. The painter belonged to the school of Gerard Soerst, who was active in London from the late 1640s, and who copied the style of Van Dyck. Perkins, in his late sixties, is shown in sober dress, with shoulder-length hair, and beard worn in a royalist style. He has a long, expressive face and commanding if rather mournful eyes. His hand is somewhat swollen with age, but is perhaps given prominence in the picture to demonstrate another chief medium of the sitter's art.

JOHN H. ASTINGTON

Sources G. E. Bentley, *The Jacobean and Caroline stage*, 7 vols. (1941–68) • C. J. Sisson, 'The Red Bull company and the importunate widow', *Shakespeare Survey*, 7 (1954), 57–68 • E. A. J. Honigmann and S. Brock, eds., *Playhouse wills, 1558–1642: an edition of wills by Shakespeare and his contemporaries in the London theatre* (1993) • *Mr Cartwright's pictures: a seventeenth century collection* [1987] [exhibition catalogue, Dulwich Picture Gallery, London, 25 Nov 1987–28 Feb 1988] • E. Nungezer, *A dictionary of actors* (1929) • G. E. Bentley, 'Players in the parish of St. Giles in the fields', *Review of English Studies*, 6 (1930), 149–66 • *The works of John Webster*, ed. D. Gunby, D. Carnegie, and A. Hammond, 1 (1995)

Likenesses portrait, 1646–9, Dulwich Picture Gallery [*see illus.*]

Perkins, Robert Cyril Layton (1866–1955), entomologist, was born on 15 November 1866 at Badminton, Gloucestershire, the second of the five children of the Revd Charles Mathew Perkins and his wife, Agnes Martha Beach, daughter of the Revd Percy Thomas. His grandfather, father, and uncle were all interested in natural history and Perkins himself showed an interest in the subject from a very early age. He was educated at Merchant Taylors' School (1877–85) and Jesus College, Oxford, where after two years he changed from classics to science, obtaining a fourth class in 1889. His first great interest in entomology was Lepidoptera, but contact with Edward Saunders during his last years at school fostered an interest in Aculeata (stinging wasps, ants, and bees), which he retained throughout his life.

Perkins briefly worked as a private tutor at Dartmouth, but in 1891 was selected by the Sandwich Islands committee (set up by the British Association and the Royal Society) to go as collector to the Hawaiian Islands. There he spent the greater part of the next ten years collecting all groups of terrestrial animals—returning to England periodically to work on the results. His expeditions into the islands' interiors were almost always made alone, since local porters refused to stay in the forest. As a result each trip was limited to about six weeks as, being short and spare in stature, he was unable to carry equipment for a longer stay.

In 1895 Perkins met Albert Koebele, and in the next few years helped him with the liberation of insect parasites which Koebele was sending to Honolulu for the control of pests. In 1897 they visited Mexico, where, from observations of the *Lantana* weed, they started the successful use of insects in controlling its spread in the Hawaiian Islands. In 1901 Perkins married Zoë Lucy Sherrard Alatau (*d.* 1940), daughter of A. T. Atkinson, sometime superintendent of public schools in the Hawaiian Islands, and granddaughter of Thomas Witlam Atkinson. Of their four sons, one died in infancy. From 1902 to 1904 Perkins worked for the board of agriculture of the Territory of Hawaii, organizing inspection of imported plants to prevent the introduction of pests.

In 1904 Perkins became director of the new division of entomology at the Hawaiian Sugar Planters' Association's experimental station. The most urgent problem was to prevent the havoc then being wrought by the sugar cane leafhopper. No suitable means could be found of applying insecticides in cane fields, and so Perkins and Koebele went to Australia to collect the parasites of leafhoppers in the cane fields there, where the insects appeared to cause little damage. After returning to the Hawaiian Islands they raised stocks of the parasites for liberation and dispersal in the cane fields, where their introduction proved of great benefit. This work occupied Perkins throughout the day. At night he spent long hours studying the classification of these insects, of which little was known. He was able to correlate various biological observations with taxonomy, particularly in the Dryinidae, and the results of this work were published by the Hawaiian Sugar Planters' Association in a series of bulletins.

Perkins retired to England from his post in 1912 on account of ill health and settled in Devon, but was retained on the staff as a consulting entomologist. From then on his work on Hawaiian insects was concerned mainly with taxonomy. He also resumed his study of the British Aculeata which led to a series of papers on the species of the larger and more difficult genera, greatly simplifying their recognition. Associated with this work, he studied the *Stylops* parasites of British bees. He had a large correspondence and often gave help to young students of Aculeata. He encouraged a continued interest in the group, which was consequently one of the best worked of the order in Britain, both systematically and biologically. In the early 1920s Perkins helped the Revd F. D. Morice in his contemplated revision of the group of British sawflies, work which led to preliminary revisions of some of the critical genera.

In addition to his entomological work, Perkins had interests in terrestrial zoology and he supplied information on the Hawaiian birds, many of which later became extinct. He had most acute vision and a remarkable visual memory, which aided both his field and his taxonomic work. In the latter he had a faculty for observing and selecting characters which vary little within a species, thus making identification simpler.

Although not robust, Perkins had a great interest in sport. In his young days he enjoyed skating, and at Dartmouth he used to run with the beagles. Above all else he preferred trout fishing, which he continued until his eyesight began to fail. He retained his great interest in classics throughout his life.

In 1906 Perkins was awarded an Oxford DSc and in 1912 he received the gold medal of the Linnean Society of London. He was elected FRS in 1920. Following the death of his first wife, he married, in 1942, Mrs Clara M. J. Senior (née Dowse); she died in 1949. In his last days Perkins went blind; he died at his home, Wotton, Newton Road, Bovey Tracey, on 29 September 1955.

J. F. PERKINS, *rev.* V. M. QUIRKE

Sources H. Scott, *Memoirs FRS*, 2 (1956), 215–36 · personal knowledge (1971) · *CGPLA Eng. & Wales* (1956)
Archives Oxf. U. Mus. NH, entomological corresp. and papers
Wealth at death £19,565 16s. 3d.: probate, 9 Jan 1956, *CGPLA Eng. & Wales*

Perkins [Maundeville], **William** [*alias* Jack Sharp of Wigmoreland] (*d.* **1431**), rebel and alleged Lollard, was the bailiff of Abingdon, whose name is recorded in official documents as William Perkins but given in some chronicles as Maundeville. His public appearance as a rebel under the name Jack Sharp covers only a few days in 1431, but he may have been a man accused by an approver in 1424, and was almost certainly identical with one whose arrest was ordered in 1427 to answer to 'divers transgressions'. In neither of these earlier cases, however, is there any suspicion that he was accused of heresy. The troubles of 1431 apparently began in London in March, but there were more widespread manifestations of discontent in the south midlands and as far north as Coventry. Plots were afoot at Abingdon in April, and on 9 May open disorder broke out at Salisbury. Perkins may have been present at the Salisbury riots, but his main share in the revolt was six days later, when he led a group of rebels from East Hendred to attack Abingdon Abbey. The troubles created considerable alarm in government circles, for the protector, Humphrey, duke of Gloucester (*d.* 1447), found it necessary to ride from Greenwich to Oxford to deal with the rising personally. After its failure Perkins took flight, but he was captured in Oxford, tried before Gloucester, condemned, and beheaded—an appropriate fate for a traitor—with seven others. His prominence in the rising, which is suggested by the chroniclers, is confirmed by the fact that his head was set on London Bridge as a deterrent to other rebels.

The nature of 'Sharp's revolt' is uncertain. It was strongly anti-clerical, because bills were circulated in the form of a petition to parliament, based on the Lollard disendowment bill of 1410, which in turn looked back to proposals voiced in 1395. There is however little evidence of doctrinal irregularity, and it is significant that Perkins was executed rather than burnt. Only one chronicle source refers to a case of eucharistic heresy during the upheaval, and there was nothing to connect Perkins with this. The pseudonym 'Jack Sharp of Wigmoreland', which he assumed, has both social and political overtones. The first half echoes such names as 'Jack Straw' with the implication of peasant discontent, while the second may well be

hinting at the Mortimer territorial base inherited by Richard, duke of York (*d.* 1460), who represented an alternative claim to the throne. It may well have been these latter elements, as much as the anti-clerical tone of the manifesto, that prompted the authorities to suppress it so ruthlessly.

JOHN A. F. THOMSON

Sources J. A. F. Thomson, *The later Lollards* (1965) · M. Aston, *Lollards and reformers* (1984) · PRO, Court of king's bench Coram rege rolls, KB 27/653, 663, 682, 683, 686 · N. H. Nicolas, ed., *Proceedings and ordinances of the privy council of England*, 7 vols., RC, 26 (1834–7) · *Annales monasterii S. Albani a Johanne Amundesham*, ed. H. T. Riley, 2 vols., pt 5 of *Chronica monasterii S. Albani*, Rolls Series, 28 (1870–71)

Perkins, William (1558–1602), theologian and Church of England clergyman, was born at Marston Jabbett in the parish of Bulkington, Warwickshire. His parents, Thomas and Anna, both outlived him. While his father's vocation is unknown, the family apparently had sufficient means to enrol William in June 1577 as a pensioner at Christ's College, Cambridge. He graduated BA there in 1581 and proceeded MA in 1584.

Youth and reformation Perkins's early adulthood at Cambridge was apparently marked by moral laxity and dissipation. Indeed, one possibly apocryphal story has it that he reformed his life after hearing a Cambridge woman say to her child, 'Hold your tongue, or I will give you to drunken Perkins yonder' (Haller, 64). Some have speculated that during his years of undergraduate debauchery Perkins may have fathered a daughter out of wedlock, but the rumour cannot be confirmed; there is also speculation regarding his youthful flirtation with astrology, an encounter which may explain his vehement opposition to astrology in his mature years. But although scholars disagree as to the nature of Perkins's reformation of life, it is generally acknowledged that probably between 1581 and 1584, and concurrently with his taking up of the study of theology, he made a religious decision which shaped his future vocation within the Church of England.

Perkins was recognized as an able and popular advocate of that Calvinist doctrine common among 'the group of moderate Puritans' in Cambridge, 'a spiritual brotherhood' which included his tutor and lifelong friend, Laurence Chaderton, and Richard Greenham. His particular version of Calvinism was similar to that of such second-generation continental Calvinist theologians as Theodore Beza, Girolamo Zanchi, and Zacharias Ursinus, who 'faced with a resurgent Rome, were concerned to weld the protestant case into a coherent and self-consistent whole' (Lake, *Moderate Puritans*, 218–19).

Employing a style which modern historians have described as 'denunciatory', Perkins preached first and briefly to the prisoners in Cambridge gaol, and soon after as lecturer at St Andrew's Church, where large numbers of scholars and laypeople assembled to hear him. Thomas Fuller reports that 'his sermons were not so plain but that the piously learned did admire them, nor so learned but that the plain did understand them' (Fuller, *Holy State*, 81). He also records how Perkins 'would pronounce the word *Damne* with such an emphasis as left a dolleful Echo in his auditours ears a good while after' (Merrill, xvi). The protestant polemicist Samuel Clarke describes Perkins's ministry in Cambridge as 'a burning and a shining light, the sparks whereof did fly abroad into all the corners of the kingdom' (Clarke, *Generall Martyrologie*, 23).

Godly luminary Perkins is frequently described as a 'puritan' or a 'moderate puritan'. Indeed, Collinson describes him as 'the prince of puritan theologians and the most eagerly read' (Collinson, *Elizabethan Puritan Movement*, 125). Yet the term 'puritan' should not be applied without some qualification. Perkins was perhaps the most significant English theologian of his age. And while his theology was generally representative of a Calvinist scholasticism or orthodoxy that elevated the doctrine of election and placed particular emphasis on the religious experience of the individual—doctrinal positions which have been equated with 'puritanism' by some scholars—it has also been demonstrated that 'between 1560 and 1625 the doctrine of predestination was accepted without question by virtually all of the most influential clergymen in England, puritan and nonpuritan alike' (Durston and Eales, 7). Although Perkins, along with other theologians who have been described as 'moderate puritans', raised a version of predestination common among Calvinist theologians to a central position, his thought transcends narrow doctrinal labels. It is more credible, following Peter Lake, to understand Perkins as a 'moderate puritan' in the light of his ecclesiology. Lake observes that 'the core of the moderate puritan position lay neither in the puritan critique of the liturgy and polity of the church nor in a formal doctrinal consensus', but 'in the capacity, which the godly claimed, of being able to recognize one another in the midst of a corrupt and unregenerate world' (Lake, *Moderate Puritans*, 282). Perkins's writings in such works as *A treatise tending unto a declaration whether a man be in the state of damnation or in the estate of grace* (c.1588) and *A Graine of Musterd-Seede* (1597), often reflect precisely such an understanding, though his ecclesiology also recognized the historical problem that the visible church consists of both elect and reprobate.

Relations with the Church of England As a fellow of Christ's College, where he taught from his election in 1584 until he resigned his fellowship at Michaelmas 1594, Perkins exercised considerable influence. Through lectures and writings he helped establish the boundaries for a moderate churchmanship that rejected the extremes of separatism and nonconformism, and especially the opinions of those sectarian branches of English protestantism which had Anabaptist, chiliastic, and millenarian tendencies. Yet he also became a powerful advocate for protestants whose theological convictions were in conflict with anti-puritans within the Church of England, as is apparent in his defence of Francis Johnson, a fellow of Christ's College who was imprisoned because he favoured a presbyterian form of church polity. Perkins's resentment over Archbishop John Whitgift's repression of puritanism—the primate used subscription in an attempt to enforce unity in the Church of England and strenuously resisted forms of

protestantism which encouraged presbyterian structures of ecclesiastical government—emerges clearly in the preface to *Armilla aurea* (1590).

Despite Perkins's criticism of what he termed 'corrupt' and 'idolatrous' Roman Catholic influences on its worship, he remained a devoted defender of the essential doctrines and liturgical practices of the Church of England. He raised critical objections to certain of these latter; for example, in a sermon preached at Christ's on 13 January 1587 he objected to such practices as kneeling at the reception of the eucharist, and had to answer to the vice-chancellor and other officials for his remarks. On the other hand, some historians have argued that Perkins 'was as powerful an apologist for the Anglican Church as Richard Hooker' (Merrill, xvii), even though Hooker directed his arguments against presbyterians while Perkins reserved his fiercest criticisms primarily for Catholicism. However, Perkins's attitude toward the Church of England was perhaps more complex than this comparison admits. Although he was undoubtedly cautious in public statements about the latter's liturgy and discipline, especially in light of the criticism he received after his confrontation with the vice-chancellor over the eucharist, he remained tenaciously supportive of the puritan movement within the church, and was deliberately less helpful than the prosecution seems to have wished when he was called as a witness in the 1590–91 trial of puritan ministers. When asked about meetings of puritans to discuss the Book of Discipline, he recalled clearly that those present had discussed whether the Book of Discipline was consistent with the word of God, but he said he had no recollection of the identity of anyone who was actually present at the discussion.

Theological doctrine Although Perkins was conversant with the thought of John Calvin, Martin Luther, Philip Melanchthon, and William Tyndale, his theology was more profoundly indebted to the Calvinist scholasticism of Pietro Martire Vermigli, Theodore Beza, Girolamo Zanchi, and Caspar Olevianus. His theological method also reveals a considerable reliance on Peter Ramus, whose approach to logic was characterized by an intentional bifurcation of subjects. The influence of Ramus on Perkins is given vivid visual expression in charts like the one appended to *A Golden Chain, or, Description of Theology* (1591), illustrating the main points of religion and their interconnection, although it must be added that such charts also reveal a marked similarity to the approach of Theodore Beza who, while he ardently opposed Ramus, nevertheless represented the broad outlines of his theology in the form of a similar chart in his own *Summa totius theologicae*.

Perkins's moral theology, as expounded in *A Discourse of Conscience* (1596), addresses both the puritan preoccupation with the individual Christian's need to gain an assurance of election and the writer's concern for the social as well as individual aspects of Christian morality. Rejecting the notion that the human conscience is interior to the individual, Perkins instead places it between God and the individual, thus showing that he understands the conscience as that place where God strives with human beings in order to give them an apprehension of his judgement upon their actions. Perkins followed the *Discourse* with a fuller treatment of moral theology, *The Whole Treatise of the Cases of Conscience*, published posthumously in 1606, in which he returns to a scholastic approach to casuistry, distinguishing, for instance, between mortal and venial sins, and providing tools to determine the degree of one's moral culpability. Porter, indeed, maintains that Perkins's reputation rests primarily on his casuistry; he is:

> at one with the medieval moralists and with such godly pastors as Lancelot Andrewes, George Herbert and Jeremy Taylor in the resolve 'to educate the individual conscience in the way of holiness and to educate the social conscience in the way of justice'. (Porter, 288)

Commenting upon Perkins's *Cases of Conscience*, Louis Wright observes that Max Weber could have found in Perkins evidence that 'Calvinism produced a hospitable milieu for the development of the capitalistic spirit' generations earlier than the examples Weber drew from English puritans such as Richard Baxter (Wright, 182).

The genius of Perkins's work did not lie in its originality—his theology represents a conventional recital of Calvinist scholasticism in virtually every respect. His gift lay rather in bringing to a broad audience a variety of theological and moral issues, popularizing essentially technical discussions, and therefore, as Fuller observed, humbling 'the towering speculations of philosophers into practice and morality' (Fuller, *Holy State*, 81). In Perkins's own words, 'Theology is the science of living blessedly for ever' (*Works*, 177); for him, theology was in every respect a practical study.

Contemporary and posthumous influence In 1597 Perkins's polemical influence spread throughout Europe following the publication of *A Reformed Catholike*. Perkins argues in this treatise that the term 'reformed Catholic' properly conveys the posture of the protestant. His purpose, he writes, 'is to show how near we may come to the present Church of Rome in sundry points of religion and wherein we must ever dissent' (*Works*, 521). Although his arguments are unrelentingly anti-Roman, they led William Bishop, titular bishop of Chalcedon and author of *Reformation of a Catholike Deformed by W. Perkins* (two parts, 1604–7), to say that he had 'not seene any book of like quality, published by a Protestant, to contain either more matter, or delivered in better method' (Merrill, xvii).

Perkins's *De praedestinationis modo et ordine* (1598), while positively received by most Calvinists, drew fire from Jacob Arminius, the controversial Dutch Reformed theologian and opponent of the Calvinist doctrine of predestination, who charged Perkins with returning protestant theology to scholasticism. Nor was Arminius satisfied with Perkins's treatise *God's Free Grace and Man's Freewill* (1602). His refutation of Perkins, completed in the year of the latter's death, takes issue not only with the Calvinist interpretation of predestination which Perkins taught, in which God by immutable decree before creation has arbitrarily elected some for salvation and condemned the rest, but also his doctrine of limited atonement which, following Beza and other Calvinist scholastics, taught that Jesus Christ did not die for all humanity, but for the elect alone. Such controversies did nothing to hinder the dissemination of Perkins's writings abroad. They were usually translated into Dutch, German (as much for circulation in Switzerland as in Germany itself), and Latin, sometimes into French and even Czech. This process continued into the last quarter of the seventeenth century, when a number of his works appeared in Welsh.

The list of students influenced by Perkins reads like a who's who of seventeenth-century Calvinism. William Ames, probably his most important pupil, embraced the more extreme elements of puritan thought and eventually left England for the Netherlands, where he took up the post of professor of theology at Franeker. As J. D. Eusden observes, while 'Amesian theology reworked much of the old and explored areas not entered by his respected teacher' (Ames, 4), Ames's theology none the less reflects both the practical aspects of Perkins's moral thought and the latter's doctrine on such issues as predestination. John Robinson, the founder of congregationalism in Leiden, extended Perkins's influence when he published his own catechism there. Other heirs of Perkins's thought included the elder Thomas Goodwin, Paul Baynes, Samuel Ward, later master of Sidney Sussex College, Cambridge, the poet Phineas Fletcher, Thomas Draxe, Thomas Taylor, James Ussher, the celebrated archbishop of Armagh, and his close friend Richard Montagu, master of Sidney Sussex and later bishop of Winchester. His practical and theological works (many of which were first published only after his death) remained popular in England throughout the seventeenth century. In the words of William Haller: 'No books, it is fair to say, were more often to be found upon the shelves of succeeding generations of preachers, and the name of no preacher recurs more often in later Puritan literature' (Haller, 65).

Perkins's writings are notoriously lacking in autobiographical statements, and it is difficult to glean from contemporary sources a reliable picture of the company he kept. He knew the Yorkshire puritans Sir Thomas and Lady Margaret Hoby, and the dedications of his books suggest that he was acquainted with Edward Russell, seventh earl of Bedford, Valentine Knightley, whose father, Sir Richard Knightley of Fawsley, was a leading figure among the Northamptonshire godly, Robert Beale, clerk of the council, Sir Edward Denny, who in 1626 became first earl of Norwich, Sir William Peryam, chief baron of the exchequer, and Margaret Clifford, countess of Cumberland. But there is nothing in them to explain Perkins's relationships with those to whom these dedications were given.

A portrait of Perkins hangs in the combination room of Christ's College; he looks heavy-faced, and his right hand is visibly maimed. It is known that he married Timothye Cradocke of Grantchester on 2 July 1595, and that together they had seven children, three of whom died in childhood. Immediately after his marriage Perkins resigned his fellowship, and largely for that reason almost nothing is recorded of the last seven years of his life, though his theological output continued unabated. He died in Cambridge on 22 October 1602, aged forty-four, after suffering intensely for several weeks from the stone. James Montagu preached at his funeral, which took place three days later, on Joshua 1: 2—'Moses my servant is dead'. Perkins was interred in St Andrew's Church at his college's expense. In his will he bequeathed 10s. apiece to his father, mother, and each of his siblings, and left his small property in Cambridge to his wife, who subsequently remarried. His library was purchased by William Bedell, a pupil of Perkins who in 1629 became bishop of Kilmore and Ardagh. MICHAEL JINKINS

Sources The works of William Perkins, ed. I. Breward (1970) · T. Fuller, The holy state and the profane state, ed. M. G. Walten (1642) · T. Fuller, 'Abel Redivivus, or, The dead yet speaking', Columbia University Studies in English and Comparative Literature, 2/136 (1938) · S. Clark, The marrow of ecclesiastical historie (1650) · S. Clarke, A generall martyrologie … whereunto are added, The lives of sundry modern divines (1651) · T. F. Merrill, ed., William Perkins, 1558–1602: English puritanist: his pioneer works on casuistry: 'A discourse of conscience' and 'The whole treatise of cases of conscience' (1966) · W. Haller, The rise of puritanism: … the New Jerusalem as set forth in pulpit and press from Thomas Cartwright to John Lilburne and John Milton, 1570–1643 (1938) · N. Pettit, The heart prepared: grace and conversion in puritan life (1966) · J. Arminius, Works: the London edition, trans. J. Nichols and W. Nichols, 3 vols. (1825–75) · P. Collinson, The Elizabethan puritan movement (1967) · P. Lake, Moderate puritans and the Elizabethan church (1982) · C. Durston and J. Eales, The culture of English puritanism, 1560–1700 (1996) · A. Delbanco, The puritan ordeal (1989) · M. Jinkins, 'Theodore Beza: continuity and regression in the reformed tradition', The Evangelical Quarterly: An International Review of Biblical Theology, 64 (April 1992), 144–54 · L. Wright, 'William Perkins: Elizabethan apostle for practical divinity', Huntington Library Quarterly, 3 (1939–40), 171–96, esp. 182 · P. Collinson, The religion of protestants (1982) · P. Lake, Anglicans and puritans? Presbyterianism and English conformist thought from Whitgift to Hooker (1988) · H. C. Porter, Reformation and reaction in Tudor Cambridge (1958) · J. Spurr, English puritanism, 1603–1689 (1998) · W. Ames, The marrow of theology, ed. J. D. Eusden (1968) · W. Bishop, Reformation of a Catholike deformed by W. Perkins, 2 vols. (1604–7)
Likenesses R. Elstrack, line engraving (after portrait), BM, NPG · oils, Christ's College, Cambridge · oils, DWL

Perks, Sir Robert William, first baronet (1849–1934),

industrialist and politician, was born at Old Brentford on 24 April 1849, the elder son of the Revd George Thomas Perks (1819–1877), president of the Wesleyan conference in 1873, and his wife, Mary (d. 1894), daughter of James Alexander Dodds, an Edinburgh architect of promise who died young.

Perks was educated at New Kingswood School, Bath (1858–65), which was then exclusively for Wesleyan ministers' sons, and at King's College, London (1867–71), where he gained honours in classics, English, and modern languages and won many open prizes. He competed for four years in succession for the Indian Civil Service, missing entrance each year by only a few places. This was a great disappointment at the time, but he lived to regard it as the most fortunate escape of his life. Turning to law he was

articled to the firm of Messrs De Jersey and Micklem in the City, and qualified as a solicitor in 1875. In the following year he became the partner in London of Henry Hartley Fowler (afterwards Viscount Wolverhampton), a fellow Wesleyan, with whom he remained for twenty-five years. The firm specialized in railway and parliamentary practice, and by sheer business acumen Perks made a reputation as a lawyer who could pilot company bills through parliament. He studied intensively all railway law, and had little difficulty in being appointed solicitor (1879–92) to the London Metropolitan District Railway Company; he was later (1901–5) chairman of the company during its transition from steam to electricity. He was associated with Messrs T. A. and C. Walker of Westminster, contractors, in various construction and engineering works, including Barry docks and railway, the Severn Tunnel, Manchester Ship Canal, Preston docks, the harbour works that created the port of Buenos Aires, the Rio de Janeiro harbour works, and a railway tunnel through the Andes. After leaving Messrs Walker in 1912 he joined Messrs Macarthur, Perks & Co., a firm of dock and railway contractors in Ottawa and New York.

His legal and business career established, Perks began his political life in 1886, serving as Liberal MP for the Louth division of Lincolnshire between July 1892 and January 1910, when he retired, somewhat disillusioned with the House of Commons (he subsequently said of his service there that 'there was no period of his life so fruitlessly spent, no time so absolutely wasted'). In this capacity he gained a reputation for his vigorous (not to say abrasive) advocacy of the interests of his rural electors and of nonconformist concerns, earning the sobriquet of Member for nonconformity. He was the moving spirit behind the nonconformist caucus in the house during these years, being co-founder (in 1898) and chairman (until 1908) of the Nonconformist Parliamentary Council (or Committee), which had 200 members in the 1906 parliament, although it was nowhere near as effective a pressure group as Perks liked to believe. He was closely identified with a number of legislative measures to redress nonconformist grievances, notably the Nonconformist Marriage Act of 1898 (which removed the need for the attendance of the civil registrar at weddings held in non-Anglican churches); he advocated passive resistance against the Education Act of 1902, supported disestablishment of the Church of England (which he regarded as the Anglo-Catholic church), and promoted the temperance cause. Of strongly imperialist views, which caused him to be known as 'Imperial Perks', he endorsed the Second South African War and was involved in the founding of both the Imperial Liberal Council in 1900 and the Liberal League in 1902, the latter under the presidency of Lord Rosebery, with Perks as treasurer and later vice-president.

Perks's business and political skills also found expression in his service of Methodism, both in the local church and at connexional level. Among the first lay members of the Wesleyan conference in 1878, he rose to become one of the denomination's most influential laymen, serving on many key committees, including the committee of privileges (to which he was lay secretary in 1882–92). An advocate of Methodist union from 1878, he worked tirelessly for its consummation, and, when the Wesleyan, Primitive, and United Methodists finally merged in 1932, Perks was elected unanimously as the first vice-president of the Methodist church. With similar success, he inaugurated the Wesleyan Twentieth Century Fund in 1898, which set out to raise 1 million guineas from one million Methodists, the intention being that nobody was to contribute more than 1 guinea in their own name. Through Perks's efforts as treasurer, and his personal contribution of over £10,000, when the fund closed in 1908 £1,074,000 had been raised. This was used for a variety of purposes, including the construction of the Westminster Central Hall (opened 1912) as Wesleyanism's connexional headquarters on the site of the Royal Aquarium, facing Westminster Abbey. Equally ambitious, but conspicuously less successful, was his Methodist Brotherhood, launched in 1907 as a sort of denominational welfare state, exploiting the worldwide Methodist family to provide facilities for emigration, employment, financial loans, and old-age support. Progressively watered down, the scheme was finally overtaken by the Liberal social reforms (which Perks regarded as socialism) and by the First World War.

Perks was created a baronet on 24 July 1908, but is believed to have declined a peerage as he disliked pomp and ceremony. He had married on 24 April 1878 Edith (*d.* 1943), youngest daughter of William Mewburn of Wykham Park, Banbury, and had one son and four daughters, of whom the eldest predeceased her father. Perks died at his home, 11 Kensington Palace Gardens, London, on 30 November 1934, and was succeeded as second baronet by his son, Robert Malcolm Mewburn (1892–1979).

O. A. RATTENBURY, *rev.* CLIVE D. FIELD

Sources R. W. Perks, *Sir Robert William Perks, baronet* (privately printed, London, 1936) · D. Crane, *The life-story of Sir Robert W. Perks* (1909) · *The Times* (1 Dec 1934) · *Methodist Recorder* (6 Dec 1934) · *Railway Gazette* (7 Dec 1934) · C. E. Lee, 'Perks, Sir Robert William', *DBB* · N. J. L. Lyons, 'Sir Robert Perks, liberal M.P. for Louth, 1892–1910', *Epworth Witness*, 2 (1971–6), 12–14, 27–30 · D. J. Jeremy, *Capitalists and Christians: business leaders and the churches in Britain, 1900–1960* (1990) · S. Koss, *Nonconformity in modern British politics* (1975) · D. W. Bebbington, *The nonconformist conscience: chapel and politics, 1870–1914* (1982) · R. Currie, *Methodism divided: a study in the sociology of ecumenicalism* (1968) · Burke, *Peerage* · H. C. G. Matthew, *The liberal imperialists: the ideas and politics of a post-Gladstonian élite* (1973)

Archives priv. coll. | Lincs. Arch., letters to R. W. Goulding · NL Scot., corresp. with Lord Rosebery · U. Newcastle, Robinson L., corresp. with Walter Runciman

Likenesses A. T. Nowell, portrait; formerly in possession of Sir Malcolm Perks · oils (after A. T. Nowell), Westminster Central Hall, London

Wealth at death £74,946 14s. 8d.: probate, 21 Feb 1935, *CGPLA Eng. & Wales*

Perley, Moses Henry (1804–1862), entrepreneur and naturalist in Canada, was born in Maugerville, Sunbury county, New Brunswick, on 31 December 1804, the son of Moses Perley and his cousin Mary, who were of an old Welsh family which had settled in Massachusetts in 1630. His father died before his birth. His mother took him to Saint John, New Brunswick, when he was very young and he went to school there, spending much of his free time with the local native people, in whose welfare he took a keen interest. On 6 September 1829 he married Jane, the daughter of Isaac Ketchum; they had eight children and took in two orphans. In 1828 he became an attorney and in 1830 was called to the bar, but soon entered business, particularly lumbering and coal mining, in which he was not conspicuously successful. Perley was critical of those who sought to restrict American investment in New Brunswick, and was accused in turn of being too pro-American.

Perley's knowledge of the area and interest in native people led to his being appointed honorary commissioner for Indian affairs at some point between 1839 and 1841, and in reports of 1842 and 1843 he protested against squatter encroachment on their lands, recommending that the crown hold these lands in trust and encourage them to settle in villages where education and health services could be provided. The native people of New Brunswick elected him 'chief over all' in 1842, and he frequently visited their settlements dressed in native clothes. Perley sharply criticized the 1844 New Brunswick Indian Act. The act enabled the government to sell wide tracts of native land, ostensibly for their benefit, but Perley, quite rightly, feared it would enable squatters to hold on to their land. Although he did his best to safeguard the interests of the native people after the passing of the act, he found that public opinion, squatter intransigence, and government indifference all conspired against them.

Perley continued to practise law and to cultivate his business interests, and by 1840 he was an authority on the province's natural resources. In 1843 and 1847 he was made New Brunswick emigrant agent for the provincial and British governments respectively, and as such supervised the arrival of and helped immigrants, many of whom arrived sick and destitute. His knowledge of the country prompted the government to turn to him for reports on timber resources (1847) and fisheries (1849) and to help negotiate the reciprocity treaty between the United States and the British North American colonies. In 1855 he was appointed fisheries commissioner to enforce the reciprocity treaty, and he also continued as emigration officer until 1858. In 1861 he bought a share in the *Colonial Empire* newspaper, which advocated intercolonial free trade and union. Perley became ill in the summer of 1862 on board the *Desperate* while inspecting the fisheries, died on board on 17 August, and was buried at Forteau, Labrador. As well as his many government reports, he left works on natural history and Indian legends, and, as founder of the Natural History Society of New Brunswick and an ichthyologist of note, laid the foundation of natural science in the province.

C. A. HARRIS, *rev.* ELIZABETH BAIGENT

Sources *DCB*, vol. 9 · private information (1895) · M. V. B. Perley, *History and genealogy of the Perley family* (1906) · P. Cox, 'Life of Moses

Henry Perley, writer and scientist', *Proceedings of the Miramichi Natural History Association*, 4 (1905), 33–40

Archives New Brunswick Natural History Society | Public Archives of New Brunswick

Perne, Andrew (1519?–1589), dean of Ely and college head, came from a family of minor Norfolk gentry with lands around Pudding Norton and was born in the village of East Bilney, the son of John Perne. He retained strong but troubled connections with what in Elizabethan times he was to call 'that great disordered diocese' of Norwich (Inner Temple Library, MS Petyt 538/47, fol. 494). He entered St John's College, Cambridge, and took his BA in 1539 and his MA in 1540, with the BTh following in 1547 and the DTh in 1552. In 1540 he was elected a fellow of St John's, but shortly afterwards migrated to Queens', where he served successively as bursar, dean, and vice-president, learning those managerial and political skills which he was to apply so effectively in a Cambridge career which included no fewer than five terms as vice-chancellor. He secured a number of parochial livings in Norfolk and Cambridgeshire, became a prebendary of Westminster in 1552, and dean of Ely in 1557. Perne was a fixture in Cambridge for more than fifty years, and seems to have regarded his deanery, which he may have visited only on the occasion of the annual audit and for somewhat meagre hospitality, as a sinecure (which technically it was). Unfortunately the good things which Perne did for his university have figured less prominently in his posthumous reputation than the ambidexterity with which he responded to the drastic religious changes and reversals of successive Tudor regimes and reformations.

As early as 1549, Perne had abandoned belief in transubstantiation. Evidently he was regarded by the protestant Edwardian ascendancy as one of themselves and was made one of six royal chaplains who were to divide their time between preaching at court and in the country. Although he began by opposing him, it seems likely that Perne, along with the future Archbishop Edmund Grindal, grew close to the famous Strasbourg reformer Martin Bucer who occupied the regius chair of divinity, and to whom he would, posthumously, play Judas. At the first convocation of Mary's reign, Perne again spoke against transubstantiation, earning a rebuke from the prolocutor to which the future Bishop John Aylmer responded with a defence of free speech. But Perne soon made his peace with the Marian regime, subscribing to articles which included a very explicit endorsement of the Catholic doctrine of the eucharist. He was the preferred candidate of Bishop Stephen Gardiner for the mastership of Peterhouse, to which he was elected in 1554. As vice-chancellor he served on a royal commission to inquire into heresy in Cambridge, but was not involved in any cases which led to burning at the stake, at least not the burning of any living persons. More notoriously, he was implicated as vice-chancellor in the macabre proceedings in which, in order to lift an interdict from the university church, the bones of Bucer and his colleague, the Hebraist Paul Fagius, were exhumed and burnt in Cambridge market, following an oration in which Perne had denounced the great reformer

Andrew Perne (1519?–1589), by unknown artist

and his doctrine, a speech which the martyrologist John Foxe described as 'a shameful railing' (Foxe, *Acts and Monuments*). According to Foxe, Perne in private deeply regretted his unconscientious conduct on this occasion. What is more certain is that Perne owned Foxe's *Acts and Monuments* in the 1576 edition, and that there is a hole burnt in the middle of the page which tells this story. In 1560, with Elizabeth on the throne, the university passed a grace restoring Bucer and Fagius to their degrees and other honours. The presiding vice-chancellor was again Perne.

In 1564 Elizabeth made a celebrated visit to Cambridge. Although Grindal, now bishop of London, was one of a small committee in charge of the arrangements, he was unable to prevent the choice of Perne to preach before the queen in King's College chapel. He told William Cecil that he hoped that Perne would not be well received, 'his apostacy being so notorious' (BL, Add. MS 35831, fol. 184). However, the sermon, on obedience to the higher powers, was a success. But later in the week Perne allowed himself, uncharacteristically, to be wrong-footed. In a theological disputation before the queen on the proposition that scripture carried more authority than tradition, Perne, who argued for tradition, was provoked by an outspoken attack on the Roman church as 'a shameless whore' by his opponent, Matthew Hutton, master of Pembroke College and regius professor, not only to assert the subordination of scripture to the church, but to insist that although it was not faultless, the Church of Rome was the most enduring of churches, from which the Church of England derived the essence of its doctrine and liturgy, not a meretricious whore but 'apostolica et matrix ecclesia' ('an apostolic church and our mother'; Collinson, McKitterick, and Leedham-Green, 9). Perne's library reveals the reading which informed these views: great folios of the fathers, extensively annotated, Thomas Aquinas and other scholastics perhaps not so closely read. Perne had to explain himself to Archbishop Matthew Parker, and not even the queen was best pleased. Perne was removed from the list of court preachers, and, apparently, from the number of those thought fit for a bishopric, which is no doubt why, although Archbishop John Whitgift recommended him for a mitre in 1584, he remained master of Peterhouse for the rest of his days.

In a constructive exchange of views with John Feckenham, formerly abbot of Westminster, Perne suggested that Feckenham could hardly find fault with the Book of Common Prayer without condemning his own mass book and other Catholic liturgies, since these were its sources. Was Perne a crypto-Catholic, a church papist? The Jesuit John Gerard alleged as much. Perne was rector of the Cambridgeshire parish of Balsham, where many of the leading men adhered to the mysterious and eclectic sect of the Family of Love. It appears that Perne knew all about their familism but did nothing, may even have felt at one with the familist strategy of keeping to themselves their true beliefs. In a letter to the lord chancellor, Sir Christopher Hatton, he advised a policy of pure equity, not respecting 'this or that profession, protestant, papist or puritan' (Westminster Abbey muniments, MS Book 15, fol. 86v).

Perne's ecumenical latitude kept the peace in Peterhouse, where it became a legend that in his time, Peterhouse men who became Catholic martyrs were hurried to the scaffold by Peterhouse judges after interrogation by Peterhouse inquisitors. The great 'parliament man' Thomas Norton, too much of a hot protestant to be religiously sympathetic, believed that there was 'not a better master for the helping of his house' than Perne (BL, Add. MS 48023, fol. 47). Not until the First World War would enrolments match the Perne years. The university was harder to manage, especially in the mid-1560s and early 1570s, when direct action by the younger dons against the supposedly 'popish' ceremonies retained in the Elizabethan church was followed by the presbyterian, anti-episcopal ideology advanced by Thomas Cartwright and his many supporters. Perne, together with his protégé Whitgift, initially a hot protestant whom he had protected in Mary's reign and whom he seems to have turned into a conformist, was the principal architect of new university statutes (they would remain in force until 1853) which restored discipline and replaced a kind of academic democracy with an oligarchy of the heads of houses resembling the constitution of Venice, a republic in which Perne himself regularly served as doge.

As such, Perne was a fierce and effective defender of the interests of the university against all comers, especially the town and the county. Perne's membership of the commission of the peace for Cambridgeshire proved to be a short-lived experiment. On one occasion he rather pointedly sent copies of the charter and statutes of the university to its chancellor, Lord Burghley, as a reminder of its privileges. But his relationship with Burghley was usually constructive, if formal, and twenty-four of the thirty letters from Perne which are known to survive were addressed to him. Perne was discretion itself, remembered even by his bitter enemy Gabriel Harvey for his 'grave and most eloquent silence' (*Works of Gabriel Harvey*, 2.302). When Perne read in his great folio edition of St Ambrose about uncharitable parsimony, he wrote in the margin 'R. Eliz.', but for his own eyes only. When Archbishop Parker on his deathbed proposed to write to the queen accusing Burghley and his brother-in-law Sir Nicholas Bacon of robbing the church, Perne advised against it. Among his other good deeds, it seems to have been Perne who devised the project which secured the solvency of Oxbridge colleges at a time of price inflation: an act of parliament requiring that in all leases of college property one third of the rent should be paid in kind, the so-called corn rent. Cambridge also had Perne to thank for the scheme later implemented as Hobson's Conduit, which brought water down from Trumpington to cleanse the fetid King's Ditch. He was dedicated to building up the university library, and was a predatory observer of the book market and a cultivator of potential donors. Perne was a reader, not a writer, and he published nothing. But he took care of Ecclesiastes and the Song of Songs for the version known as the Bishops' Bible.

In his last years, Perne was often at Lambeth as Whitgift's guest, and it was there that he died on 26 April 1589, suddenly, but not too soon to avoid the cruel fate of satirical vilification in the anti-episcopal Marprelate tracts, which not only dubbed him Old Andrew Turncoat but hinted at a homosexual relationship with the archbishop. This might not have happened if he had not, somewhat earlier, made enemies of Gabriel Harvey, who in 1593 would blacken his character as 'hypocrisy incarnate' in *Pierces Supererogation*, and of Harvey's friend Edmund Spenser who put him into the *Shepheardes Calender* as the worldly-wise Palinode. Thomas Nashe rallied to Perne's defence, no doubt on the grounds that my enemy's enemy is my friend.

Perne had died a wealthy bachelor, and in his will (in which he took his leave of 'this slippery earth'—Collinson, McKitterick, and Leedham-Green, 93) he generously remembered his brothers, brothers-in-law, nephews, and other more remote kin, as well as his college. He was buried in Lambeth parish church, where a monument was erected to his memory by his nephew, Richard Perne. But a more abiding monument is his library, much of it still preserved in Peterhouse. This was one of the largest private libraries of its day, the collection of a man of wide and diverse interests, who was perhaps more interested in medicine, cartography, and civil engineering than in theology, and of a connoisseur who valued the beauty of books and who set them off with a little museum of 'curiosities' to be shown to visiting VIPs. His panel portrait, also in Peterhouse, has been restored to reveal the inscription, in Greek, of what he called his 'posy', Ephesians 4: 15, 'Speaking the truth in love'.   PATRICK COLLINSON

Sources P. Collinson, D. McKitterick, and E. Leedham-Green, *Andrew Perne: quatercentenary studies*, Cambridge Bibliographical Society Monographs, 11 (1991) · T. A. Walker, *A biographical register of Peterhouse men*, 2 vols. (1927–30) · *The works of Gabriel Harvey*, ed. A. B. Grosart, 2 (1884) · Ely diocesan records, CUL, MS D/2/4 · *The acts and monuments of John Foxe*, ed. S. R. Cattley, 8 vols. (1837–41), vol. 8, pp. 258–86 · J. Nichols, *The progresses and public processions of Queen Elizabeth*, new edn, 3 vols. (1823) · Folger, MS V.a.176, fols. 69–77v · E. S. Leedham-Green, ed., *Books in Cambridge inventories: book-lists from the vice-chancellor's court probate inventories in the Tudor and Stuart periods*,

2 vols. (1986), vol. 1, pp. 419–79 • C. W. Marsh, 'Piety and persuasion in Elizabethan England: the Church of England meets the Family of Love', *England's long Reformation, 1500–1800*, ed. N. Tyacke (1998), 141–65 • G. E. Aylmer, 'The economics and finances of the collegiate university, c.1530–1640', *Hist. U. Oxf.* 3: *Colleg. univ.*, 535–43 • *The Marprelate tracts, 1588–1589*, ed. W. Pierce (1911) • R. J. Skaer, 'The panel portrait of Andrew Perne', *Peterhouse Annual Record, 1997–1998* (1999), 38, 41 • *DNB*

Archives Peterhouse, Cambridge
Likenesses oils, Peterhouse, Cambridge [*see illus.*]
Wealth at death estates with an annual rental value of approx. £150; library apparently valued at £300; goods about the same: will, Collinson, McKitterick, and Leedham-Green, *Andrew Perne*, 93–119

Perne, Andrew (c.1595–1654), Church of England clergyman, was the son of Thomas Perne. He was educated at Peterhouse, Cambridge, graduating BA in 1618 and proceeding MA in 1621, and was ordained a priest on 4 June 1622. From 1622 to 1627 he was fellow of St Catharine's College, where Richard Sibbes was the master; it was there he placed his conversion to the cause of true religion. In 1627 he was appointed to the rectory of Wilby in Northamptonshire by the patron, Thomas Pentlow. There is scant information concerning his family. With his wife, Mary, he had at least two daughters.

Perne became one of the leading clerical members of an influential puritan community centred on Northampton. As an evangelical Calvinist he made the main thrust of his ministry to awaken the elect saints to self-awareness by preaching the word:

> love to Christ, an earnest desire to encrease his Kingdom, pitty and compassion towards poor soules, a violent thirst after their salvation, and a burning zeale for the honour and glory of God were the motives that put him upon this worke. (Ainsworth, 39)

The opposite of this vision of true religion was popery, and in the decade before the civil war he was a prominent leader of Northamptonshire opposition to government policy, which he regarded as 'Popish' (PRO, SP 16/251/25). He was reported to have 'complained much of the overfloweings of Popery every where in this land, & wished or hoped, that God would raise up a standard to hinder it' (ibid.). His preference for preaching twice every Sunday led in 1633 to an interrogation by Bishop Augustine Lindsell of Peterborough—who denounced him as a 'hollow pillar of Puritanisme' (ibid.) for refusing to conduct a catechism class in the afternoon (as required by the *Instructions to Preachers* issued that year) at the expense of his second sermon. He was also accused of ceremonial nonconformity. About 1635 he was reported to the ecclesiastical courts for not publicly reading the Book of Sports, which puritans regarded as anti-sabbatarian, and in August 1640 for attending a meeting at The Swan inn in Kettering to co-ordinate opposition to the bishops' war and the revised *Book of Canons*.

Perne was chosen in 1643 one of the representatives from Northamptonshire to the Westminster assembly. He preached four sermons before the Long Parliament—including one on the occasion of a public fast, 31 May 1643, which was published as *Gospell Courage, or, Christian Resolution for God and his Truth*, and another on 23 April 1644 at

the 'thanksgiving' for Sir Thomas Fairfax's victory at Selby. In *Gospell Courage* Perne recognized that the civil war had both secular and religious causes but that the latter were more important. The Caroline regime had repressed the godly and true religion by discouraging preaching, stifling discussion of predestination, and permitting anti-sabbatarianism. The kingdom had degenerated into idolatry: 'the Popish language of Priests and Altars, and the superstitious bowing and gestures were brought in under a pretence of Authority' (Perne, 25). In these circumstances it was the duty of the people to be 'peremptory' (ibid., 15) in defence of their beliefs. When the sermon was delivered a vote of thanks was proposed by the puritan MP Sir Christopher Yelverton.

On 11 July 1643 Perne was admitted as vicar of St Dunstan-in-the-West, London, the previous incumbent James Marsh having been sequestered; six months later, on 14 January, Perne was readmitted on Marsh's death. In 1645 he was recommended by Robert Baillie as one of a number of eminent ministers who might give 'good satisfaction' as personal chaplains to Charles I (Paul, 120). Although Perne was officially established in 1646 as presbyterian minister at St Dunstan's, his relations with this most consistently radical of city parishes did not run smoothly, and in 1647 he resigned after controversy surrounding disputed churchwarden elections.

Perne died at Wilby on 13 December 1654 and was buried in the chancel of the church there. His funeral sermon, published in 1655, was delivered by his friend and former curate, Samuel Ainsworth, who claimed to have been converted by him. Perne was survived by his wife, Mary, who probably died in 1663.
J. FIELDING

Sources Venn, *Alum. Cant.* • correction book, Northants. RO, Peterborough diocesan records, A-63, fols. 177, 181, 202 • will, Northants. RO, Peterborough diocesan records, archdeaconry of Northampton wills, bk 10, 187 [Mary Perne] • PRO, SP16/251/25; 308/52, 461/86, 465/8, 12, 45 • R. Woodford, diary, 1637–41, New College, Oxford, MS 9502 • *DNB* • S. Ainsworth, *A sermon preached … at the funerall of Mr Andrew Pern* (1655) • A. Perne, *Gospell courage, or, Christian resolution for God and his truth* (1643), 9, 10, 15, 24, 25 • *Testimony of our reverend brethren ministers of the province of London to the truth of Jesus Christ and our solemn league and covenant etc. attested by other ministers of Christ in the county of Northampton* (1648), 4–6 • H. Isham-Longden, Peterborough institution book, 1542–1823, Northants. RO, HIL MS 2109.2 [esp. 1627] • A. J. Fielding, 'Conformists, puritans and the church courts: the diocese of Peterborough, 1603–1642', PhD diss., U. Birm., 1989, 186–8 • T. Webster, *Godly clergy in early Stuart England: the Caroline puritan movement, c.1620–1643* (1997), 229–31 • *Walker rev.*, 54 • R. S. Paul, *The assembly of the Lord: politics and religion in the Westminster assembly and the 'Grand debate'* (1985), 120 • Tai Liu, *Puritan London: a study of religion and society in the City parishes* (1986), 113–14 • K. Lindley, *Popular politics and religion in civil war London* (1997), 274

Pero [*known as* William Jones, Pero Jones] (1752/3–1798), slave and personal servant, was said to have been twelve years old when he was bought from Joanna Jones by John *Pinney on Nevis in the Leeward Islands, the West Indies, for £115 sterling on 4 July 1765, with his sisters Nancy (b. 1757?) and Sheba (b. 1759?), and an enslaved African woman, Harriott. Described as a Creole, he was born in the West Indies, probably on Nevis. Pero's father and another sister, Eve, were alive in 1798 but not on Pinney's plantation. Apart from this, nothing is known about Pero's parents or other siblings or whether he was married or had children.

Pero soon became Pinney's manservant at Mountravers plantation, chosen from about 150 slaves owned by Pinney at that time. Between August 1767 and July 1768 he was boarded out to Daniel Martin to learn the barber's trade, and in 1776 a man called Mial taught him to pull teeth. In 1772 Pero and his sister Nancy were taken as servants on Pinney's honeymoon to Philadelphia.

Pinney, who was less cruel to his slaves than some other Nevis planters, trusted Pero to deliver what, for slaves, would have been large amounts of cash to business partners, and to travel unaccompanied to neighbouring St Kitts where Pero's sister Nancy was trained as a seamstress. He showed an enterprising spirit from early on: in the 1770s he sold a sheep, a goat, and dungbaskets to Pinney, and he hired at his own expense an old enslaved woman, Soone, for a short period of time.

The Pinneys left Nevis for England in July 1783 with Pero and Mrs Pinney's mixed-race maidservant, Frances (Fanny) *Coker, a freed, or manumitted, slave. After a short stay in London and rural Dorset, in 1784 John Pinney moved his family to Bristol, first to a rented house at 5 Park Street and in 1791 to 7 Great George Street (now Bristol's Georgian House Museum). Here Pero would have met William and Dorothy Wordsworth, who stayed with the Pinneys in 1795; Horatio Nelson's wife, Fanny Nisbet; and, most likely, Robert Southey, Samuel Taylor Coleridge, and others in that circle.

Pero accompanied Pinney on two short visits to Nevis in 1790 and 1794. Pinney complained after the second Nevis visit that Pero's 'conduct has been very reprehensible—insomuch, that his mistress and every branch of my family have urged me to discharge him and send him back to Nevis with an annual allowance provided his behaviour there should have deserved it' (letter to Ann Weekes, letter-book 14). However, Pero remained in Bristol, probably increasingly unhappy with his situation. In May 1798 he was very ill and staying at Ashton, near Bristol, for a change of air. The Pinneys visited him three or four times a week but doubted he would recover.

Pero died between 23 May and 12 November 1798, probably at Ashton. Pinney wrote to his plantation manager that Pero's death

> was a great relief to himself and us: for he became so great a lover of liquor and connected with such abandoned characters, that we could not depend upon him a moment—his dissipation, at last, brought him to the Grave. (letter to James Williams, letter-book 14)

Mrs Pinney sent Pero's clothes to Nevis to be divided between his father and his nephew William Fisher (his sister Nancy's son), sold Pero's watch, and purchased each of his three sisters a pair of gold earrings. Also distributed to his family on Nevis were 10 guineas found on Pero when he died. It is known that he was literate because after his death it emerged that Pero had frequently lent money, at interest, but among his papers there was no record of his

debtors and the money was lost to his family. It appears that Pero was never manumitted.

Given Pero's alias of William Jones, used first in 1790, it is possible that he was buried at St Augustine-the-Less, Bristol, for the parish register notes the burial of a William Jones on 9 June 1798. As part of Bristol's growing awareness of its past links with slavery, and after a public campaign by the local minority ethnic community, in 1999 a new footbridge in Bristol's Harbourside was named after Pero to commemorate those enslaved by the city's merchant and planter community.

CHRISTINE EICKELMANN

Sources R. Pares, *A West India fortune* (1950) · D. Small and C. Eickelmann, *Pinney and Pero*, Bristol University Library, special collections, Pinney MSS, DM1867 · common records, 1764–9, Nevis court house, Charlestown, Nevis, fol. 255 · J. Pinney, letter-book 3, 5 Oct 1761–9 July 1775, University of Bristol Library, special collections, Pinney MSS · J. Pinney, letter-book 14, 28 Nov 1797–26 Feb 1799, University of Bristol Library, special collections, Pinney MSS · J. Pinney, account-book 17, 12 Nov 1762–5 July 1783, University of Bristol Library, special collections, Pinney MSS · J. Pinney, account-book 18, 31 July 1764–31 July 1779, University of Bristol Library, special collections, Pinney MSS · J. Pinney, account-book 21, 1 Jan 1768–31 Dec 1778, University of Bristol Library, special collections, Pinney MSS · J. Pinney, account-book 34, 15 Aug 1783–31 March 1802, University of Bristol Library, special collections, Pinney MSS · parish register, St Augustine-the-Less, 1798, Bristol RO, P/StAug/R/2(a) [burial] · M. Moorman, *William Wordsworth, a biography*, 1: *The early years, 1770–1803* (1957), 268–73 · B. Cottle, *Robert Southey and Bristol* (1980) · *Nelson's letters to his wife and other documents, 1785–1831*, ed. G. P. B. Naish, Navy RS, 100 (1958) · J. Pinney, letter-book 9, 1 Jan 1788–16 June 1792, University of Bristol Library, special collections, Pinney MSS · J. Pinney, account-book 15, 12 Nov 1760–14 May 1767, University of Bristol Library, special collections, Pinney MSS · J. Pinney, account-book 20, 1 March 1767–31 Dec 1777, University of Bristol Library, special collections, Pinney MSS · J. Pinney, account-book 26, 1 Jan 1777–26 Dec 1783, University of Bristol Library, special collections, Pinney MSS · J. Pinney, account-book 27, 5 April 1777–5 May 1785, University of Bristol Library, special collections, Pinney MSS

Archives Bristol University Library, Pinney MSS | FILM Bristol University Library, special collections, Pinney MSS, D. Small and C. Eickelmann, *Pinney and slavery*, DM 1867 [video] · Channel 4, *Untold: Britain's slave trade* (part 1)

Wealth at death a box of clothes, a watch, 10 guineas, and an unknown amount of money lent with interest: letter-book 14, 162–3, letter from John Pinney, Bristol, to James Williams, Nevis, 12 Nov 1798, Bristol University Library, special collections, Pinney MSS

Perowne, Edward Henry (1826–1906), college head, third son of the Revd John Perowne and his wife, Eliza Scott, and younger brother of John James Stewart *Perowne, was born at Burdwan, Bengal, where his parents were missionaries, on 8 January 1826. His family was of Huguenot descent. After private education, partly by his father, he was admitted pensioner of Corpus Christi College, Cambridge, in 1846 and scholar in 1847; he was Porson prizeman in 1848, members' prizeman in 1849 and 1852, and senior classic in 1850. He graduated BA in 1850, proceeding MA in 1853, BD in 1860, and DD in 1873. He was admitted *ad eundem* (MA) at Oxford in 1857. Ordained deacon in 1850 and priest in 1851, he was curate of Maddermarket, Norfolk (1850–51). He examined in the classical tripos several times between 1854 and 1863 and served as senior proctor in 1871–2. W. H. Thompson, master of Trinity, is alleged to have remarked, 'I presume God created Perowne in order to keep Senior Classics humble.' He was an unsuccessful candidate for the post of orator in 1857, when Joseph Romilly described him as 'a shy cold person'.

Perowne was elected fellow and tutor of Corpus in 1858 and became master in 1879. He was Whitehall preacher (1864–6); Hulsean lecturer in 1866; examining chaplain to the bishop of St Asaph (1874–88); prebendary of St Asaph (1877–90); vice-chancellor of Cambridge University (1879–81); honorary chaplain to Queen Victoria (1898–1900), and chaplain-in-ordinary (1900–01); examining chaplain to his brother the bishop of Worcester (1891–1901). Devoted to his college and university, a sound disciplinarian, a man of many friendships and wide interests, Perowne refused preferment to the deanery of Chester in 1886, despite a fondness for 'state and circumstance', and was long one of the most conspicuous figures in the academic and social life of Cambridge. He was a strong evangelical, and in politics a rigid Conservative. Under him the college became a nursery of bishops and missionaries; but its numbers diminished and it declined academically. Perowne resisted all change in the university, and as master and vice-chancellor vainly obstructed the royal commissioners in 1879–81. When they were done he wrote, 'My heart is very very sad, well-nigh broken. I could wish myself far away from Cambridge and its imminent evils' (Browne, 225).

Although, according to tradition, Perowne proposed more than once to Mrs Colvin Hutchinson, his successor's sister who became his residuary legatee, he died unmarried at Corpus Christi College, Cambridge, after a long illness, on 5 February 1906, and was buried at Grantchester on the 7th.

His principal works were: *The Christian's Daily Life, a Life of Faith* (1860); *Corporate Responsibility* (1862); *Counsel to Undergraduates on Entering the University* (1863); *The Godhead of Jesus* (1867); *Commentary on Galatians* in the Cambridge Bible for Schools series (1890); *Savonarola* (1900).

A. R. BUCKLAND, rev. JOHN D. PICKLES

Sources *The Times* (6 Feb 1906) · *The Guardian* (7 Feb 1906) · *The Record* (9 Feb 1906) · *Cambridge Review* (15 Feb 1906) · P. Bury, *The college of Corpus Christi and of the Blessed Virgin Mary: a history from 1822 to 1952* (1952) · *Cambridge Graphic* (3 Nov 1900) · J. P. C. Roach, 'Edward Henry Perowne', *Letter of the Corpus Association*, 59 (1980), 18–28 · G. F. Browne, *The recollections of a bishop* (1915) · *Romilly's Cambridge diary, 1848–1864*, ed. M. E. Bury and J. D. Pickles (2000) [5 Feb 1857] · *CGPLA Eng. & Wales* (1906) · Venn, *Alum. Cant.* · *Cambridge Chronicle* (9 Feb 1906)

Likenesses R. Lehmann, oils, 1885, CCC Cam. · photograph, repro. in Bury, *The college of Corpus Christi*, facing p. 84 · photograph, repro. in *Cambridge Graphic*, 11

Wealth at death £5772 17s. 11d.: resworn probate, 6 March 1906, *CGPLA Eng. & Wales*

Perowne, John James Stewart (1823–1904), bishop of Worcester, born at Durdawan, Bengal, on 13 March 1823, was the eldest of the three sons of the Revd John Perowne, a missionary of the Church Missionary Society, and his wife, Eliza, *née* Scott, of Heacham, Norfolk. His brothers were Edward Henry *Perowne, master of Corpus Christi College, Cambridge, and Thomas Thomason Perowne, archdeacon of Norwich from 1878 to 1910. The family was of Huguenot origin. Educated first by his father, and subsequently at Norwich grammar school, Perowne won a scholarship to Corpus Christi College, Cambridge. He was Bell university scholar in 1842; members' prizeman in 1844, 1846, and 1847; Crosse scholar in 1845; and Tyrwhitt scholar in 1848. He graduated BA in 1845, and proceeded MA in 1848, BD in 1856, and DD in 1873. In 1845 he became assistant master at Cheam School; he was ordained deacon in 1847 and priest in 1848; and he served the curacy of Tunstead, Norfolk, from 1847 to 1849. In 1849 he became a master at King Edward's School, Birmingham, and was elected to a fellowship at Corpus Christi College, Cambridge.

For a time Perowne served his college as assistant tutor, while also lecturing at King's College, London, acting as assistant preacher at Lincoln's Inn, and carrying out duties as examining chaplain to the bishop of Norwich. He examined for the classical tripos in 1851 and 1852, and was select preacher in 1853, an office he also filled in 1861, 1873, 1876, 1879, 1882, and 1897.

In 1862 following his marriage to Anna Maria Woolryche, daughter of Humphrey William Woolryche, Perowne moved to Wales. He was vice-principal of St David's College, Lampeter (1862–72); cursal prebendary of St David's (1867–72); canon of Llandaff (1869–78); and rector of Llandisilio, Montgomeryshire (1870–71). He became strongly influenced by the broad-churchman Connop Thirlwall, during his time at St David's, Lampeter.

Perowne's name as an Old Testament scholar was made by his two-volume commentary on, and translation of, the Psalms, published in 1864. In 1870 he was chosen one of the Old Testament Revision Company. In 1868 he had become Hulsean lecturer, and in 1872 he returned to Cambridge. From 1873 to 1875 he held a fellowship at Trinity College, Cambridge, and he was Lady Margaret preacher in 1874, and Whitehall preacher from 1874 to 1876. In 1875 he succeeded Joseph Barber Lightfoot as Hulsean professor, and he held office until 1878. For the same period (1875–8) he was one of the honorary chaplains to Queen Victoria, who was said to have commented that Bishop Perowne had the best legs of any prelate on the episcopal bench.

In 1878 Perowne was appointed dean of Peterborough. He developed the cathedral services, carried on the restoration of the fabric, and cultivated friendly relations with nonconformists. In 1881 he was appointed to the ecclesiastical courts commission, and he was one of seven commissioners who signed a protest against the exercise by the bishop of an absolute veto on proceedings. In 1889 he aided in founding a body known as Churchmen in Council, which aimed at uniting 'moderate' churchmen in a policy regarding ritual; he explained the aim of the society by issuing in the same year a proposal for authorizing both the maximum and the minimum interpretation of the 'ornaments rubric', which was widely discussed but led to no results.

Having turned down the bishopric of Bangor in 1889, Perowne accepted the see of Worcester and was consecrated bishop in Westminster Abbey on 2 February 1891. He obtained the appointment of a suffragan bishop, created a new archdeaconry, and summoned a diocesan conference. In 1892 and for several years following, he presided at some sessions of an informal conference on ecclesiastical reunion of nonconformists and Anglicans held at Grindelwald in Switzerland. Following a fire at the English church, Perowne celebrated communion in the Zwinglian chapel at Grindelwald and administered the sacrament to leading nonconformists at the conference. His action led to widespread censure by the high-church press. The church congress, hitherto excluded from the diocese, met at Birmingham in 1893, when the bishop announced his assent to the division of his diocese and his willingness to contribute £500 a year to the stipend of the new see from the income of Worcester. This was afterwards made contingent on his being allowed to give up Hartlebury Castle, to which the ecclesiastical commissioners refused consent. Attacked in the Birmingham press for his action in the matter in 1896, Perowne was presented with an address of approval by sixty beneficed clergy of three rural deaneries. He resigned the see in 1901, and retired to Southwick Park, near Tewkesbury in Gloucestershire, where he died on 6 November 1904. He was buried at Hartlebury churchyard. The Worcester diocese was divided under Perowne's successor and the see of Birmingham was founded in 1905. Perowne's wife, four sons, and one daughter all survived him.

Perowne's ecclesiastical position is not easily categorized. Although a lifelong evangelical, he took independent views of biblical criticism, home reunion, and proposals for meeting ritual difficulties. His theological writings, his dislike of sect and party within church matters, and the influence of the broad-churchman Connop Thirlwall suggest that he was closer to the broad-church position than the evangelical one. As a bishop he accepted a difficult see late in life, but showed himself an industrious, capable administrator willing to make courageous and unpopular decisions where necessary. A portrait of the bishop by the Hon. John Collier was given to Corpus Christi College, Cambridge, and another, by Henry Weigall, to Hartlebury Castle. Perowne's primary work remained his translation of and commentary on the Psalms, of which a sixth edition appeared in 1886. He produced several other articles and short books on the interpretation of the Old and New testaments, upholding the findings of biblical criticism. His 1868 Hulsean lectures on immortality were published in 1869.

As general editor of the Cambridge Bible for Schools (1877–) he was able to influence the degree to which the results of contemporary biblical scholarship were presented to Cambridge ordinands. He also edited Thomas Rogers in *Catholic Doctrine of the Church of England* (1854); *Remains of Connop Thirlwall, Bishop of St David's* (1877); *The Letters, Literary and Theological, of Connop Thirlwall* (1881); and *The Cambridge Greek Testament for Schools* (1881).

A. R. BUCKLAND, *rev.* STELLA WOOD

Sources LPL, Perowne MSS, 1961–5 · *The Times* (8 Nov 1904) · *Record* (11 Nov 1904) · S. M. Wood, 'Nonconformity, theology, and reunion', DPhil diss., U. Oxf., 1995 · *Worcester Times* (7 Nov 1904) · *CGPLA Eng. & Wales* (1905)
Archives CCC Cam., diary · LPL, corresp. and press cutting · Worcs. RO | CUL, letters to Sir George Stokes · LPL, corresp. with Archbishop Benson · LPL, corresp. with Archbishop Temple
Likenesses J. Collier, oils, 1892, CCC Cam. · H. Weigall, portrait, Hartlebury Castle, Worcestershire · print, NPG
Wealth at death £904 4s. 2d.: resworn probate, 7 Jan 1905, *CGPLA Eng. & Wales*

Perowne, Stewart Henry (1901–1989), diplomatist and author, was born on 17 June 1901 at the vicarage, North Hallow, Worcestershire, the third son of Arthur William Thomson Perowne (1867–1948), bishop of Worcester, and his wife, Helena Frances Oldnall-Russell. His grandfather John James Stewart *Perowne had also been bishop of Worcester, a circumstance in which he took much pride. He was educated at Haileybury College, where he was a champion sprinter, and Corpus Christi College, Cambridge, and then had a year at Harvard University. On going down he joined the education department of the government of Palestine, then a British mandate. Always ardent in his loyalty to the Church of England, he chose to teach at St George's School in Jerusalem, where he acquired the thorough knowledge of spoken and written Arabic which was to be so useful for his subsequent career. In 1930 he moved into the administrative branch of the government, working for a time as assistant district commissioner for Galilee.

In 1934 Perowne was for a time an assistant secretary in Malta, and in 1938 was briefly seconded to the BBC to help prepare talks and features in the overseas Arabic service which had been set up a couple of years previously. In the summer of 1939 he was appointed public information officer in Aden, which gave him an opportunity to pursue his abiding interest in archaeology, by inspecting and identifying two sites from the seventh century BC near the northern border of the protectorate. While in Yemen, Freya Madeline *Stark (1893?–1993), the traveller and writer, became his assistant. She described him at the time as 'long necked and bald-headed like a young vulture', but she added, 'Stewart likes bossing and organising and I find it rather pleasant to sit and watch him' (Izzard, 140). However, sitting and watching others was never to be one of Freya Stark's characteristic attitudes.

In the summer of 1941 Perowne was sent to Baghdad as public relations officer in the British embassy, moving in 1944 to become oriental counsellor in succession to the formidable scholar and sportsman Vyvyan Holt. These Baghdad years were perhaps Perowne's most satisfying: he was happy in the country and its people, in his work and his colleagues. His dedication to stage-management of the public appearances of the young king, it has been noted, was enhanced by the use of a secondhand landau from Buckingham Palace.

> This musical comedy effect, so different from traditional Arab procedure, elicited the designation 'Perownia' from a passing American journalist, while the flamboyance of his written reports, replete with every kind of historical reference analogy, were to amaze researchers and scholars

when the PRO archive was opened thirty-five years later. (Izzard, 209)

Perowne surprised his friends by proposing marriage to Freya Stark. She accepted, and the couple were married on 7 October 1947. Despite their having worked together and having many intellectual tastes in common, the chances of the marriage succeeding were not good. His career may have demanded a wife, but Stark's biographer has argued that she may not have realized that Perowne intended it to be a *mariage blanc*: 'In 1947 people's sexual proclivities were still part of their private lives and … no one among Freya's friends seemed able to warn her of the pitfalls of marriage to a homosexual' (Izzard, 210).

In 1947 Perowne was appointed colonial secretary to Barbados, a wholly new part of the world to him, which he did his best to get to know. However, in 1950 he was back again in more familiar surroundings as political adviser (interior) in Cyrenaica, newly freed from Italian rule and under the restored Senussis. However, Perowne's post was prematurely terminated in 1951, when Cyrenaica was merged with other adjacent territories to form what is now known as Libya.

No attractive colonial or Foreign Office posts presenting themselves, Perowne decided to take early retirement, although still aged only fifty. At the same time he and Freya Stark separated: they were divorced by mutual agreement in the spring of 1952. In that year Perowne returned to Palestine, joining the Anglican bishop in Jerusalem in working on model villages for the thousands of Arabs who had become refugees as a result of the 1948 war. He also embarked on what proved a most fruitful literary career. His first book, not surprisingly, was about Jerusalem, *The One Remains* (1954), a mixture of history and reminiscences. This was followed by *The Life and Times of Herod the Great* (1958), *The Later Herods* (1958), *Hadrian* (1960), *Caesars and Saints* (1962), *The End of the Roman World* (1966), and *The Death of the Roman Republic* (1969). Perowne was a man of wide erudition, fluent in many languages; he wrote with great clarity and was never dull. He challenged the Gibbonian thesis that the rise of Christianity was largely responsible for the collapse of the Roman empire.

Perowne was possessed of great wit and charm, a beguiling conversationalist and, as he was to prove on many a Mediterranean cruise, a most stimulating guide. He was equally at home in urban and country life, giving 'horses' as one of his recreations. Perowne was made OBE in 1944 and was a knight of St John. He died on 10 May 1989 in Charing Cross Hospital, Fulham, London. His was a generous spirit with, as was stated in his service of thanksgiving, 'an outstanding gift of Friendship' and the 'life-long practice of a quiet religious life'.   E. C. HODGKIN

Sources personal knowledge (2004) · M. Izzard, *Freya Stark: a biography* (1993) · b. cert. · m. cert. · d. cert. · *CGPLA Eng. & Wales* (1989) · *WWW* · *The Times* (15 May 1989) · private information (2004)
Archives St Ant. Oxf., Middle East centre, corresp. and papers | GL, corresp. with Hodder and Stoughton · Harvard University, near Florence, Center for Italian Renaissance Studies, letters to Bernard Berenson · Suffolk RO, Ipswich, letters to R. C. M. White
Wealth at death under £100,000: probate, 16 Aug 1989, *CGPLA Eng. & Wales*

Perreau, Daniel (*c*.1734–1776). *See under* Perreau, Robert (*c*.1734–1776).

Perreau, Louis de (1489?–1547×9), diplomat, was born probably in August 1489, the son of Jean Perreau, notary, secretary, and *clerc des comptes* of François I, and of Madeleine Laurens. Nothing is known of his life before February 1519, when he was appointed as a commissioner to receive the town of Tournai from the English. In March 1520 he was chosen to assist in arrangements for the Field of Cloth of Gold. His diplomatic activities then shifted to Italy. In September 1528 he was sent to Florence and in March 1529 to Venice. He conveyed sums of money to French commanders in Italy and treated of 'secret matters' with France's allies. He was back at the French court on 2 June. Meanwhile, he had become a gentleman of the French king's chamber, an office which he retained until at least the death of François I on 31 March 1547. In 1530 he entered the service of François's second queen, Eleanor, as a *valet de chambre*, an honorific title implying no domestic duties.

In 1533 Perreau succeeded Jean de Dinteville as resident ambassador in England. Although his credentials were issued on 10 September, he did not reach London until 6 November. François I was at this time trying to avert a final breach between Henry VIII and the Holy See. Perreau's first stay in London was apparently brief. A letter from him dated 6 March 1534 announced his impending return to France, yet he was still at his post ten days later. In 1536, after François had broken off relations with the emperor Charles V, Perreau was asked to escort the imperial ambassador out of France. On 6 May 1537 he was supplying fortresses in Picardy from Amiens. In June 1537 he was sent to England for the second time, again in succession to Dinteville. By then England's breach with Rome had taken place and the hope that it might be healed had faded, but François was keen to retain Henry's alliance. Perreau's embassy coincided with the death of Queen Jane Seymour, whose funeral he attended. Thereafter he worked hard to bring about an Anglo-French marriage, either between Henry's daughter Mary and a French prince or between Henry himself and a French princess. He gained the respect of Henry, who allowed him to use the house in Chelsea formerly owned by Sir Thomas More during a plague epidemic in London. Perreau was paid a daily wage of 20 livres during his embassy and also his expenses. His lively correspondence between December 1537 and August 1538 has been published: it sheds light on Henry VIII's fearful reaction to the rapprochement between François I and Charles V which was sealed by their meeting at Aigues-Mortes—'more ill pleased than I have found him for a long time', in Perreau's words (*LP Henry VIII*, 13/1, no. 1451).

Having failed in his efforts to bring about an Anglo-French entente, Perreau left London hurriedly without even waiting for his successor to arrive, thereby causing further anxiety at the English court. In 1541 he was in France, but still dealing with English affairs. It seems that Perreau, who was styled seigneur de Castillon et de

Villiers, was twice married; his first wife was Anne de Saint-Marsault, his second Jacqueline de Romersaville who outlived him. In June 1547 he became embroiled in a lawsuit with his stepson, Samson de Lespinay, which was referred to the *grand conseil*. Thereafter he disappears from view, but died before 8 October 1549, when his widow was mentioned in a lawsuit.   R. J. KNECHT

Sources J. Kaulek, ed., *Correspondance politique de MM. de Castillon et de Marillac, ambassadeurs de France en Angleterre (1537–1542)* (Paris, 1885) · *LP Henry VIII*, vols. 12/2–15 · *Catalogue des actes de François 1er*, 10 vols. (Paris, 1887–1908) · *Catalogue des actes de Henri II*, [6 vols.] (1979–), vols. 1, 3

Perreau, Robert (*c*.1734–1776), apothecary and forger, was born in St Kitts, West Indies. His father, Daniel, was born in Greenwich, the son of a Huguenot émigré from France who had been a large landowner and principal magistrate in La Rochelle before he left at the revocation of the edict of Nantes in 1685. Daniel, finding his prospects at home limited, eventually went to the West Indies to seek his fortune, becoming secretary to the governor of the Windward Islands. There he married a Miss Bretton, whose family had come from Northamptonshire, and whose father was attorney-general of the islands. They had fourteen children.

The focus of the family's hopes, Robert and **Daniel Perreau** (*c*.1734–1776), his twin and elder brother, were sent to England to be 'instructed in most branches of polite learning' (Theodosia, 7–28). Whatever the brothers might have hoped from this genteel upbringing, the early deaths of their parents made it necessary for them to find some sort of employment. In 1748 Robert was apprenticed to Mr Tribe, a London apothecary, for eight years, at a premium of £80, and soon became a favourite of his master. Daniel, on the other hand, had a less successful time: he engaged in various forms of trade, including acting as a merchant in Guadeloupe until his bankruptcy and return to England in 1769. By this time Robert, the epitome of the industrious apprentice, had taken over his master's business and established a growing reputation for skill in his trade. With his distinguished client list and a wide circle of acquaintances Robert had achieved a solid if unspectacular place in the life of late eighteenth-century London.

When Robert Perreau sought a spouse, he looked to his West Indian connections, and married, in 1757, Henrietta Thomas (*d*. 1798), whose father, originally from Wales, was now a rector of the parish of Basseterre, St Kitts, as well as a member of the privy council for the island. Robert and his wife lived in perfect harmony for eighteen years and had three children. While Robert may not have been at the very top of his profession, his assistant estimated that he earned at least £1000 and that 'the profits of so much business would have warranted a much greater expence than he appeared to allow himself in his way of living' (*The Trials of Robert and Daniel Perreau*, 32). He dressed well, had an elegant house and fine family, and owned a coach, the mark of social acceptance.

With Daniel Perreau's return from the West Indies the two brothers sought a speedier and more spectacular road to wealth than that which Robert had formerly trod.

Together they started 'playing the Alley', buying and selling stocks on the Exchange and speculating on windfall profits. It was at about the same time, in spring 1770, that Daniel first met Margaret Caroline *Rudd (*b*. *c*.1745, *d*. in or before 1798?) his common-law wife and the third party in the forgery ring. Daniel and Robert were then speculating on a coming war with Spain over the Falkland Islands. The losses they incurred from this mistaken gamble required them to find some major source of immediate revenue. Here they were caught in a classic double bind. If they sold their houses, carriages, and goods to raise the owed money, at the first sign of incipient financial difficulty their many creditors would descend and reclaim all their possessions to pay off outstanding debts. The only way to avoid this was to keep a steady and extravagant level of spending (to lull the creditors into false confidence) while searching for another expedient to pay off their losses. It is not known who first broached the possibility of forging bonds: both the brothers and Mrs Rudd blamed each other and swore they knew nothing of the larger scheme until its collapse. It is likely, however, that the three collaborated in such a pyramid forgery scheme for several years between 1771 and 1775, when their scheme came apart.

When Robert Perreau tried to use a bond, signed by the wealthy army agent William Adair at the bank of the Drummond brothers, as collateral for a loan the bankers refused to accept the note, claiming that it was forged. When Mrs Rudd admitted all the responsibility for this and argued that nothing had been lost, and that Robert knew nothing of the crime, the Drummonds decided not to prosecute. The three prepared to leave the country, knowing full well that now that their scheme had been found out their other dupes would be less generous. Robert, however, for reasons that do not appear entirely clear, felt that he could still clear his name, and that of his brother, by casting the forgeries (for several did in fact emerge over the next several weeks) as the sole work of Mrs Rudd. Appearing before the Bow Street magistrates he volunteered to tell of a nefarious plot in return for immunity from prosecution. The magistrates refused to comply, but instead compelled him to lay the story before them. Soon both Mrs Rudd and Robert were imprisoned, awaiting further examination by Sir John Fielding himself, the Blind Beak of Bow Street.

Not only was Robert Perreau's plan unfulfilled, but about three months later both he and Daniel stood on trial for their lives, for it was Mrs Rudd who had been given crown witness status and immunity. When both men were declared guilty, however, there was enough shock and horror at the possibility that Robert, at any rate—a hitherto highly respected and honest frequenter of the homes of London's fashionable families—would face the ultimate punishment, that their execution was delayed, and Mrs Rudd held over for trial.

In the next six months, while Mrs Rudd fought for her immunity from prosecution, Robert and Daniel awaited the decision in gaol. If Mrs Rudd were to be found guilty it was thought that the brothers would be pardoned, or at least have their sentences mitigated. Their supporters filled the daily newspapers with criticism of their imprisonment, though Mrs Rudd and her advocates were equally vocal and vociferous in her vindication. After several split decisions by the courts it was decided that she should go to trial. Unfortunately for Robert and Daniel she was found not guilty and released. Now only the possibility of royal pardon remained. Despite an extraordinary wave of campaigning to this end, a mustering of support for Robert, and to a lesser extent for Daniel, such pardon was rejected, and Robert and Daniel hanged, arm in arm, on 17 January 1776.

The scene of the execution was extraordinary. It was said there were 40,000 spectators and 300 constables employed to keep clear the space of the hangings (J. Villette, *A Genuine Account of the Behaviour and Dying Words of Daniel Perreau and Robert Perreau*, 1776, 12; *The Gazetteer*, 18 Jan 1776). At the end, in a familiar gesture Robert gave the hangman and his assistant some money. Then the two brothers kissed each other. 'At about five and thirty minutes after eleven the caps were drawn over their faces'. 'When the cart drew from under them they joined hands together, and in that manner launched into eternity'. 'When they had been turned off about two-thirds of a minute, their hands dropped from each other, and they died without the least apparent pain, amidst the prayers of an immense commiserating multitude'. 'Thus the two brothers', observed one paper, seeking to underline the melodramatic point, 'in the same moment quitted that world which they had entered together' (*Morning Chronicle*, 18 Jan 1776). They were buried at St Martin-in-the-Fields, London, on 20 January.

Robert Perreau's life and death seemed to many to be an almost too apt description of the dangers of overweening ambition and the lures of rampant speculation in an age of imperial expansion. To others he emerged from his death as victim of the arts of a depraved woman, another Circe or Eve. Dubbed by contemporaries 'the unfortunate Perreaus', Robert and Daniel presented the rare spectacle of men of fashion forced to pay for their crime with their lives. When later forgers, like William Dodd or Rylands, appealed for pardon, they too would have to live, and die, with the judgment passed on the Perreau brothers.

DONNA T. ANDREW

Sources Theodosia, *Genuine memoirs of the Mess. Perreau* (1775) · *An explicit account of the lives and trials of the twin brothers* (1775) · *The life, trials and dying words of the two unfortunate twin brothers* (1776) · *The diary of John Baker, barrister of the Middle Temple* (1931) · A. Knapp and W. Baldwin, *The Newgate calendar, comprising interesting memoirs of the most notorious characters*, 4 vols. (1824–8) · *The trials of Robert and Daniel Perreau* (1775) · *The Gazetteer* (18 Jan 1776) · *General Evening Post* · *Daily Advertiser* [London] · *Craftsman's Magazine* (20 Jan 1776) · *GM*, 1st ser., 79 (1809), 893

Likenesses portrait, NPG, Heinz Archive and Library

Perrers [*married name* Windsor], **Alice** (d. 1400/01), royal mistress, was probably the daughter of Sir Richard Perrers of Hertfordshire, who was imprisoned in 1350 and outlawed in 1359 following a land dispute with the abbey of St Albans—a fact which may explain the extreme hostility towards her of Thomas Walsingham, the St Albans chronicler, who claimed that she was the daughter of a thatcher,

and that she had no physical beauty, but gained her hold over the king through sorcery and the blandishments of her tongue. It has also been claimed that her father was a Devon weaver. Having served for some time as lady in waiting in the household of Queen Philippa (d. 1369), Alice seems to have become *Edward III's mistress around 1364: their son John was of age to be married in January 1377, and to accompany the earl of Cambridge on his Portuguese campaign of 1381–2. It was also in 1364 that the merchant and courtier Richard Lyons (d. 1381), later to become her friend, was ordered not to interfere with Alice's going where she wished on the king's business or her own.

It was not until after the queen's death, however, that her relationship with Edward III became public. During the last decade of the king's life Alice received numerous favours from the king in the form of wardships and marriages, grants of land, and jewels. In 1371 she was permitted to buy the royal manor of Wendover for £500, and in 1373 was given a selection of Queen Philippa's jewels. She also exploited her position to the full, accepting gifts from courtiers and others eager to curry favour with the king, and engaging in a series of enfeoffments-to-use and other land transactions with them, in the hope of protecting her acquisitions following Edward's death. Walsingham records that the abbot of St Albans, who was engaged in a property dispute with Alice, was advised in 1374 that she 'had such power and eminence in those days that no-one dared to prosecute a claim against her', and thus decided to abandon his suit until circumstances were more propitious (*Gesta abbatum*, 3.228).

In 1375 Edward held a tournament at Smithfield at which Alice was exhibited to the Londoners as the Lady of the Sun. Such disregard for conventional morality did not pass without criticism, however. Langland, in his *Piers Plowman*, is thought to have based his figure of Lady Meed—a personification of venality—on Alice, and in the Good Parliament of 1376 the speaker of the Commons, Sir Peter de la Mare, accused her of relieving the exchequer of £2000 or £3000 a year without profit to the realm. Walsingham added that the Dominican friar whom she employed to weave her spells over the king was apprehended at her manor of Pallenswick (Fulham) during this parliament, and brought before the king. The rolls of parliament merely record that an ordinance was passed forbidding women in general, and Alice in particular, to prosecute their quarrels in the royal courts 'by way of maintenance' (*RotP*, 2.329). As a result, she was told to absent herself from court and to desist from such practice in future, under pain of forfeiture and banishment from the realm.

During the Good Parliament it also emerged that Alice was not a single woman—as the king, when so informed, claimed to believe—but was married to Sir William *Windsor. Windsor, a Westmorland knight, had been appointed as royal lieutenant in Ireland in 1369, but was recalled in 1373 following complaints about the harshness of his rule there. He was reappointed in 1374, only to be recalled again in 1376, once more in the face of vociferous

Irish opposition. It was probably during his stay in England in 1373–4 that he and Alice were married—they certainly engaged in financial transactions together at this time—and it may be that she had a hand in his reappointment.

Alice's absence from court, if it was effective at all, was not prolonged. On 22 October 1376 she received a pardon from the king, and she remained with him until his death. In January 1377 her son by the king, John Southeray, was married to Mary, half-sister of Henry, Lord Percy, and on 17 June, four days before Edward's death, the king granted him a satin coat of arms. Walsingham claimed that she sat with the king until his voice began to fail, then seized the rings from his fingers and fled. Alice's moment of truth had now arrived. In November 1377 all those who wished to sue her for offences against the king and people were encouraged to bring their petitions to parliament. John of Gaunt, the king's son, presided at her trial, where she was accused on two counts: first, that in November 1376, after the council had ordered Sir Nicholas Dagworth to go to Ireland to investigate the charges against Windsor, she persuaded the king to countermand the order on the grounds that Dagworth was an enemy of Windsor; second, that she had persuaded the king, in May 1377, to grant a full pardon and a gift of 1000 marks to Richard Lyons, who like her had been attacked in the Good Parliament. Alice maintained her innocence on both counts, but was convicted and sentenced to banishment from the realm and forfeiture of all her goods and lands, including those with which she had enfeoffed others to her use, although this last clause, on account of its enormity (for such lands were normally regarded as exempt from confiscation), was not to be adopted as a precedent, but only 'for such an odious thing in this special case' (*RotP*, 3.12–14). On 3 December orders were issued to seize her lands. The resulting inquisitions reveal that she held properties in at least fifteen counties; it was also claimed later that following her conviction she had secretly passed jewels worth £20,000 to Windsor to prevent their being seized. This may be an exaggeration, but jewels worth over £3000 were certainly recovered from her after her arrest.

The remaining years of Alice's life were largely devoted to trying to recover as much as possible of what had been lost in 1377, a task in which she was initially aided by Windsor. He petitioned the parliament of October 1378 for a reversal of the judgment against her, and was given leave to pursue his suit. Apparently she had not left the realm, for when, following another petition from Windsor, her sentence of banishment was revoked on 14 December 1379, she was simultaneously pardoned for having remained in England, as was Windsor for having harboured her. On 15 March 1380, in return for a promise of military service to the crown, Windsor was granted some of the lands which Alice had forfeited in 1377, but the process of recovery was a slow one, and his death on 15 September 1384 brought new problems, for not only did he die in debt to the crown, but he had enfeoffed all his lands, including those which had once belonged to Alice, to a group of trustees, to be disposed of after his death

according to his last wishes. Alice claimed that he had intended her to have the lands, but the trustees asserted that he had nominated his nephew, John Windsor, as his beneficiary.

Her struggle with John Windsor dominated the rest of Alice's life. She submitted numerous petitions to parliament, and succeeded in 1393 in having Windsor committed briefly to Newgate gaol, but he was soon released. It was to little avail: she recovered only a few small properties, such as the manor of Gaines in Upminster (Middlesex), where she resided during her later years. Her will reveals her enduring bitterness: dated 15 August 1400, it bequeathed all the lands which John Windsor, or others with his consent, had 'usurped', to her daughters, Joan and Jane, 'for that I say, on pain of my soul, he hath no right to these, nor never had' (Nicolas, 153). She asked to be buried in Upminster church, Essex, leaving her manor of Gaines in Upminster to her younger daughter, Joan, and her remaining lands to be divided between Jane and Joan. What became of her son, John Southeray, is not clear. In 1380 he had been divorced by Mary Percy, who claimed never to have consented to their marriage, but after the Portuguese campaign of 1381–2 no more is heard of him; he probably died soon after. Since Alice's marriage to Windsor was certainly childless, the likelihood is that all three of her children were Edward III's, for there is no good evidence for the assertion that she had earlier been married to Sir Thomas Narford. Joan married Robert Skerne, a lawyer from Kingston (Surrey)—their memorial brasses may still be seen in All Saints' Church there—and Jane married Richard Northland. Alice died in the winter of 1400–01, her will being proved on 3 February 1401.

C. GIVEN-WILSON

Sources *Chancery records* · *Calendar of inquisitions miscellaneous* (*chancery*), 7 vols., PRO (1916–68) · *RotP*, vols. 2–3 · [T. Walsingham], *Chronicon Angliae, ab anno Domini 1328 usque ad annum 1388*, ed. E. M. Thompson, Rolls Series, 64 (1874) · V. H. Galbraith, ed., *The Anonimalle chronicle, 1333 to 1381* (1927) · *Gesta abbatum monasterii Sancti Albani, a Thoma Walsingham*, ed. H. T. Riley, 3 vols., pt 4 of *Chronica monasterii S. Albani*, Rolls Series, 28 (1867–9) · PRO · BL MSS, BL · *N&Q*, 7th ser., 7 (1889), 148, 215, 449–51 · *N&Q*, 7th ser., 8 (1889), 30, 97–8 · N. H. Nicolas, ed., *Testamenta vetusta: being illustrations from wills*, 2 vols. (1826) · G. Holmes, *The Good Parliament* (1975)

Perrin, Jean Baptiste (*fl.* 1767–1798), tutor and educational author, was born in France. He travelled to Dublin, where he settled and worked as a French teacher. He taught private pupils in their own homes and was often employed for several months at a time as a resident tutor in gentry families keen to master French. In the preface to *La bonne mère* (1786) he advertised his fees for teaching French as 2 guineas for eight lessons, plus 2 guineas for entrance or enrolment.

Perrin was a prolific author of educational books, particularly on the French language, nearly all of which were first published in London by the bookseller Bedwell Law. By 1770 he had five works to his name, each of which addressed different aspects of learning French, such as pronunciation, syntax, verbs, personal pronouns. His earliest work seems to have been *Essai sur l'origine et l'antiquité des langues*, which was published anonymously in 1767. As outlined in *The French student's vade-mecum* (1770), Perrin's method promised the student rapid results, and he unashamedly advised his readers how to cut corners and thereby avoid 'long and constant application to the rules of syntax and practice' (preface). He astutely compiled a volume of French conversations (with a parallel translation into English) on topics that would appeal to his teenage readers, such as trips to Vauxhall Gardens, buying a lottery ticket, going to hear a fashionable preacher, shopping in London's West End, and even playing a game of cricket. Like the majority of his works *The elements of French conversation, with new, familiar and easy dialogues, each preceded by a suitable vocabulary in French and English* (1774) proved popular, and reached its twenty-first edition in 1820. An Italian edition, in which the dialogues were also translated into Italian, was published in Naples in 1814, although without the dialogues on cricket. His other publications include a French grammar, which he dedicated to Lord Lyttelton, a new edition of Louis Chambaud's French–English dictionary, and a collection of moral dramas, *La bonne mère* (1786), which he dedicated to Queen Charlotte.

Perrin married an Irishwoman whose maiden name was Daly and they had at least one child, Louis *Perrin, a judge, who was born at Waterford in 1782. Perrin became involved in Irish patriot politics and on 26 April 1784 was elected an honorary member of the Sons of the Shamrock. He was a nationalist by the mid-1790s and apparently supported the plan to invite republican France to invade Ireland. In his later years he lived at Leinster Lodge, near Athy, co. Kildare, a house on the estate of the second duke of Leinster and formerly the home of Lord Edward Fitzgerald, who died in 1798; the house had been used for United Irish meetings leading up to the rising of 1798. It is not known when Perrin died; he was buried at the old church at Palmerstown.   S. J. SKEDD

Sources W. J. Fitzpatrick, *Secret service under Pitt* (1892), 199, 218, 245–6 · D. R. Plunket, *The life, letters and speeches of Lord Plunket*, 2 vols. (1867), 1.218 · J. B. Perrin, *La bonne mère* (1786), preface

Perrin, Louis (1782–1864), judge, was born at Waterford on 15 February 1782, the son of Jean Baptiste *Perrin (*fl.* 1767–1798), a teacher and author of school textbooks, and his Irish wife, whose maiden name was Daly. Perrin's father was born in France, but settled in Ireland, where he taught French to the Irish gentry. Perrin was educated at home and at the diocesan school at Armagh. On 7 November 1796 he entered Trinity College, Dublin, where he gained a scholarship in 1799 and graduated BA in 1801. During the court trial in which his fellow student and friend Robert Emmet was sentenced to death, he rushed forward to embrace the prisoner when the verdict was announced. Perrin studied mercantile law and was called to the Irish bar in Hilary term, 1806. In April 1815 he married Hester Connor Stewart; they had seven sons.

Perrin's father had been a supporter of nationalist ideals and Perrin soon distinguished himself as an uncompromising reformer, as well as an able barrister. When Watty Cox, the proprietor and publisher of *Cox's Magazine*, was prosecuted by the government for libel in 1811, three

defence lawyers—Daniel O'Connell, Isaac Burke Bethel, and Perrin—were hired, but the case was in effect conducted by Perrin who, though the most junior of the four, was clearly able. He was also junior counsel, in 1811, in the prosecution of Edward Sheridan, Thomas Kirwan, and the Catholic delegates, for violating the Convention Act. In 1832, he became a bencher of King's Inns, Dublin.

Perrin was a whig in politics, supported Catholic emancipation, and acquired the sobriquet of 'Honest Louis Perrin'. On 6 May 1831 he was elected MP for Dublin. He was unseated in August and returned for Monaghan on 24 December 1832, displacing Henry Robert Westenra, the previous tory member. At the next general election he was elected for the city of Cashel, on 14 January 1835, but he resigned in the following August in order to take his seat on the bench. At the bar Perrin was one of the recognized heads of the protestant liberal party, which advised and co-operated with Roman Catholics. While a third serjeant and MP Perrin wrote a report on the inquiry into municipal corporations, which was used as the foundation for the Irish Municipal Reform Act.

Perrin was made third serjeant on 7 February 1832. He later became first serjeant (from February to April 1835) and then attorney-general (29 April 1835). He was appointed a puisne justice of the king's bench, on 31 August 1835; and in the same year he became a privy councillor. He was remembered as an able and upright judge.

Perrin resigned on a pension in February 1860, and moved to Knockdromin, Lusk, near Rush, co. Dublin, where he frequently attended the petty sessions. He died at Knockdromin on 7 December 1864, and was buried at Rush on 10 December.

G. C. BOASE, *rev.* SINÉAD AGNEW

Sources F. E. Ball, *The judges in Ireland, 1221–1921*, 2 (1926), 275, 279–80, 292, 296, 325, 349 · Boase, *Mod. Eng. biog.* · J. S. Crone, *A concise dictionary of Irish biography*, rev. edn (1937), 205 · Burtchaell & Sadleir, *Alum. Dubl.* · *GM*, 3rd ser., 18 (1865), 123–4 · J. R. O'Flanagan, *The Irish bar*, 2nd edn (1879), 307–15 · W. J. Fitzpatrick, *Secret service under Pitt* (1892), 199, 218, 245, 246 · D. R. Plunket, *The life, letters, and speeches of Lord Plunket*, 1 (1867), 218 · *Freeman's Journal* [Dublin] (8 Dec 1864), 2 · *Freeman's Journal* [Dublin] (12 Dec 1864), 3
Likenesses C. Moore, marble bust, 1843, NG Ire.
Wealth at death under £40,000: probate, 7 Jan 1865, CGPLA Eng. & Wales

Perrin, Sir Michael Willcox (1905–1988), administrator and scientist, was born on 13 September 1905 in Victoria, British Columbia, the only son and elder child of William Willcox Perrin (1848–1934), Anglican bishop, and his wife, Isoline Harriet, daughter of James Bailey of Southampton. He moved to England in 1911 when his father exchanged the see of British Columbia for that of Willesden in London, and was educated at Winchester College and New College, Oxford, completing a degree in chemistry in 1928. Choosing a career in research, Perrin took a physics MA at Toronto University before joining Imperial Chemical Industries (ICI), which sent him to the Netherlands for four years to work under Professor Anton Michels.

ICI was eager to develop 'plastics' (the term was new) and Perrin was among those who saw promise in combining, or polymerizing, substances under high pressures. In

1932–3 at ICI laboratories in Winnington, Cheshire, Eric Fawcett and Reginald Gibson conducted experiments of this kind with ethylene and benzaldehyde, which yielded a waxy deposit. This was polythene, but the value of the discovery was not recognized and the pair were transferred to other work. Two years later Perrin, now working at Winnington, revived the project using more advanced apparatus and in December 1935 his team successfully produced a larger quantity of the new material, in powder form. On the patent application his was the first name of five (including those of Fawcett and Gibson) and a colleague later paid tribute to his dedication: 'He hung on like a bulldog, devoted his entire existence to the work for a year or two and talked about nothing else' (J. C. Swallow, quoted in 'Profile: Michael Perrin', 28). In the Second World War polythene found a military use, notably as an insulator for radar equipment; in time it became the world's most widely used plastic, most familiar as a packaging material.

By 1939 Perrin was assistant to ICI's research director, Wallace Akers, based in London, and in that capacity was among the first involved in secret British thinking on the atomic bomb. When in 1941 Akers became director of Tube Alloys, as the subsequent bomb project was codenamed, Perrin followed as his assistant and was made secretary to the main Tube Alloys committees. The following year Perrin visited the United States and witnessed the huge atomic effort undertaken there since Pearl Harbor (among other things he saw the world's first reactor under construction). His reports helped convince the London government of the urgency of merging Britain's efforts with the American programme; otherwise, he warned, Britain would be left behind.

In London Perrin took charge of efforts to establish the scale of the German atomic effort, working with the intelligence services. He it was who recommended the first raids intended to destroy the heavy water plant at Rjukan in Norway and he was involved in spiriting the physicist Niels Bohr to Britain after his escape from occupied Denmark—Bohr had been in contact with German physicists, notably Werner Heisenberg, and Perrin questioned him about this. The final phase of the European war found Perrin in British army uniform on the heels of advancing allied forces, confirming at first hand that the Germans had been behind the allies in atomic research. He then played a leading part in bringing Heisenberg and other German nuclear scientists to Britain, where they were sequestered for six months in a country house while their conversations were secretly recorded. Among Perrin's last war duties was to write, in a single twenty-four-hour session, the official statement issued in London after Hiroshima and Nagasaki. It told the story of Britain's role in making the bomb and proved a necessary complement to the similar American account which scarcely acknowledged British involvement.

With the peace, an atomic energy department was created inside the Ministry of Supply under the former chief of air staff, Lord Portal, who made Perrin his deputy controller (technical policy). The department had three branches, each run by a formidable personality equal in rank to Perrin: research under John Cockcroft; weapon development under William Penney; and reactor design and construction under Christopher Hinton. Since Portal wanted only a limited role, much of the co-ordination work fell to Perrin, and the task required all his skills. The most difficult moment came with the discovery in 1950 that Klaus Fuchs, a German-born physicist who had worked on the wartime bomb in Britain and the US before taking up a senior position under Cockcroft, was a Soviet spy. Perrin, with his intelligence connections, was deeply involved in handling this calamity and it was to him that Fuchs eventually spelt out the details of his espionage—an experience he said which left him feeling years older.

By 1951, with weapon development well advanced (the British bomb was successfully tested the following year), Portal and Perrin made the case for atomic energy to be taken out of ministry and civil-service structures. The idea was rejected and, with Portal retiring, Perrin chose that moment to leave too. Three years later the body they envisaged came into being as the Atomic Energy Authority but by then Perrin had moved into a different sphere. He first returned to ICI but in 1953 became chairman of Wellcome Foundation Ltd, the company which was the commercial, pharmaceutical side of Sir Henry Wellcome's legacy and was wholly owned by the charitable Wellcome Trust. In 1953 the foundation was emerging from a troubled period and, though Perrin did not seek an executive role, it fell to him to oversee reconstruction. For years the profits were ploughed back into the firm as new overseas markets were opened up, research was given more commercial focus, additional subsidiaries were acquired, and the company expanded into veterinary products. The turnaround was not quick but—especially after scientists at the American subsidiary discovered several important new drugs—it was dramatic. When Perrin retired in 1970 the company's sales were almost eight times their 1953 level and payments to the Wellcome Trust had risen in proportion. The trust went on to become one of the world's wealthiest charities and, while there is no doubt it owed that position primarily to Henry Wellcome, Perrin and his colleagues in the 1950s and 1960s deserved a share of the credit. On his departure the board paid warm tribute to his 'distinguished and statesmanlike contribution' to the group's prosperity (Wellcome Foundation Ltd, minute book no. 8, 20 Jan 1970).

Sir Michael Perrin (he was knighted in 1967) was a gifted administrator whose talents were ably deployed in three distinct worlds. A man of medium height and build, distinguished by heavy-framed glasses, he was at once businesslike and approachable. Blessed with the good chairman's knack of reconciling different views, he was also an effective operator in the corridors of power, at ease exploiting formal and informal connections alike. It was said of him that he loved power, not for its own sake but as a means of 'getting the right things done', and the senior positions he held are testimony to the trust he inspired ('Profile: Michael Perrin', 28). From 1960 onwards, besides his work at Wellcome he supported many bodies in the fields of science, education, and health. From 1960 to 1969 he was chairman of St Bartholomew's Hospital in London and president of its medical college. He was also chairman, board member or trustee of, among others, the Natural History Museum, the Royal London Veterinary College, Roedean School, and the Central Advisory Council for Science and Technology.

Perrin had married, on 12 April 1934, Nancy May Curzon (1910–1992), who was, like himself, the child of an Anglican bishop—Charles Edward Curzon, bishop of Stepney and later Exeter—and they had two children, Clare Ann, born in 1937, and Charles John, born in 1940. Since his arrival from Canada as a boy, Perrin's home for all but ten years had been in Hampstead, north London, and it was there, with his wife, that he lived out a quiet retirement. He died at 14 Christchurch Hill, Hampstead, London, on 18 August 1988.   BRIAN CATHCART

Sources M. Gowing, *Britain and atomic energy, 1939–45* (1964) · M. Gowing and L. Arnold, *Independence and deterrence: Britain and atomic energy, 1945–52* (1974) · W. J. Reader, *Imperial Chemical Industries: a history* (1970), vol. 1 · R. R. James, *Henry Wellcome* (1994) · B. Cathcart, *Test of greatness: Britain's struggle for the atom bomb* (1994) · 'Profile: Michael Perrin', *New Scientist* (24 Jan 1957) · *The Times* (22 Aug 1988), 12 · *The Independent* (22 Aug 1988) · WWW · *CGPLA Eng. & Wales* (1989) · m. cert. · d. cert.
Archives priv. coll., papers | CAC Cam., corresp. with James Chadwick · Glaxo Smith Kline, Greenford, Middlesex, archives of Wellcome Foundation · PRO, official atomic energy papers, AB1 to AB16: CAB
Likenesses R. L., line drawing, repro. in 'Profile', *New Scientist* · photograph, repro. in *The Times* · photograph, repro. in *The Independent* · photograph, repro. in *Foundation News* [pub. Wellcome Foundation] (1 Feb 1953)
Wealth at death under £70,000: probate, 1989, *CGPLA, Eng. & Wales* (1989)

Perrinchief, Richard (1620/21–1673), Church of England clergyman, was the son of Gabriel Perrinchief, a joiner of St Botolph, Aldersgate, London. He entered the school at Christ's Hospital, London, on 15 April 1625, aged four, and matriculated as a sizar at King's College, Cambridge, in the Lent term of 1638. He graduated BA from Magdalene College, Cambridge, early in 1642, proceeded MA in 1645, and was elected to a fellowship at Magdalene at some time thereafter. He was ordained deacon and priest at Lincoln on 3 July 1646 and ejected from his fellowship in 1650. In 1656 he was admitted by the triers to the rectory of Middleton in Hampshire. His first published work was *Nuntius a mortuis*, published in Paris in 1657 and in London two years later. Between the two editions he published in 1658 a version in English, *A Messenger from the Dead, or, Conference … between the Ghosts of Henry the 8. and Charls the First*. King Charles, 'the most moderate, and the most innocent' of Henry VIII's successors, was seen as the victim of the working out of divine providence punishing the sacrilege and tyranny of the Tudor sovereign to the third and fourth generations (p. 18); it concluded with Charles resolutely asserting his commitment to the Church of England.

Perrinchief dedicated *The Syracusan Tyrant … with some Reflexions on the Practices of our Modern Usurpers* (1661) to Thomas Wriothesley, earl of Southampton; this book was republished in 1676 as *The Sicilian Tyrant*. In both editions

an engraving showed 'Tyrannus', in the form of Oliver Cromwell dressed in dubious antique armour, being crowned with a laurel wreath by 'Perfidia' and 'Crudelitas'. Perrinchief was made rector of St Mildred Poultry, London, in 1661, to which the parish of St Mary Colechurch was annexed in February 1671. He was employed by the bookseller Richard Royston to finalize *Basilika: the Works of Charles I* (1662) after the original editor, William Fulham, died of smallpox. *Basilika* contained a biography of Charles I, which Perrinchief wrote with the aid of materials supplied by Silius Titus. This biography was republished as *The Royal Martyr* in 1676.

Perrinchief proceeded DD from Cambridge on 2 July 1663; his dissertations were published in *Potestas ecclesiae* (1663). In 1664 he published *Samaritanism*, an argument against 'Comprehending, Compounding, and Tolerating Several Religions in one Church'; a 'Revised' and 'Enlarged' edition of this title appeared in 1669. On 3 November 1664 he was made a prebendary of St Peter's, Westminster Abbey, and on 2 August 1667 he was installed as a prebendary of St Paul's Cathedral. He was also sub-almoner to Charles II. On 7 November 1666 he preached a sermon before the House of Commons which attacked those who denied that the plague was the result of divine punishment. In 1667 he published *A Discourse of Toleration* to refute the arguments of John Corbet's *A Discourse of the Religion of England*, and in the following year his *Indulgence Not Justified* was published. On 29 March 1670 he was collated to the archdeaconry of Huntingdon. In February 1672 John Evelyn heard him preach at Whitehall in the presence of the king on Acts 17: 31, and in September of the same year he heard him preach to the royal household in Whitehall on Ephesians 5: 2.

Perrinchief's will, dated 26 August 1673, five days before his death, expressed the desire to be buried as near as possible to his wife, who had been buried in Westminster Abbey two years earlier, on 15 June 1671. Under the terms of this will he bequeathed his divinity books to the library of Westminster Abbey, and gave £100 to Christ Church Hospital. He also made bequests to his 'worthy and good Friend' Dr John Dolben and to his 'very good friends' Dr William Clarke, dean of Winchester, and Mr Pocock, rector of Long Ditton in Surrey. He appointed Clarke and Pocock as executors of his estate and asked that they should use any money left after his debts had been settled to purchase 'some Impropriation or part of some Impropriation in some Great Markett Towne' in Huntingdonshire. If this did not happen within three years he nominated new executors who were to distribute the money to 'Prisoners for debt or others That by these Badd tymes have fallen to decay' (will, PRO, PROB 11/343, fol. 86r–v). He died at Westminster on 31 August 1673, and was buried two days later 'within the South monument door' (Chester, 181) of Westminster Abbey.   JASON McELLIGOTT

Sources *Walker rev.* · Venn, *Alum. Cant.*, 1/1–4 · Wood, *Ath. Oxon.*, new edn · *CSP dom.*, 1640–73 · Evelyn, *Diary* · will, PRO, PROB 11/343, fol. 86r–v · *Fifth report*, HMC, 4 (1876), 481 · R. Newcourt, *Repertorium ecclesiasticum parochiale Londinense*, 2 vols. (1708–10) · J. L.

Chester, ed., *The marriage, baptismal, and burial registers of the collegiate church or abbey of St Peter, Westminster*, Harleian Society, 10 (1876), 174, 181 · G. A. T. Allan, *Christ's Hospital exhibitioners to the universities of Oxford and Cambridge, 1566–1923* (1924)

Archives BL, Lansdowne MS 986, fol. 164 · BL, Lansdowne MS 988, fol. 258v

Wealth at death over £200: will, PRO, PROB 11/343, fol. 86r–v

Perring, John Shae (1813–1869), civil engineer and surveyor, was born at Boston, Lincolnshire, on 24 January 1813. He was educated at Donington grammar school, and then articled, on 28 March 1826, to Robert Reynolds, the surveyor of the port of Boston, under whom he was engaged in surveying, in the enclosure and drainage of the fens, in the improvements of Boston harbour and of Wainfleet haven, and the outfall of the East Fen, in the drainage of the Burgh and Croft marshes, and other works. In 1833 he moved to London, where he worked with various engineering establishments.

In March 1836 Perring went to Egypt, under contract with Galloway Brothers of London, as assistant engineer to Galloway Bey, then manager of public works for Mehmet Ali, viceroy of Egypt. One of the first undertakings on which Perring was engaged was the construction of a tramway from the quarries near El Mex to the sea. After the death of Galloway he became a member of the board of public works, was consulted on the Nile Embankment, advocated the establishment of stations in the desert between Cairo and Suez to facilitate overland transit, and was employed in constructing a road in order to carry out this scheme.

From January to August 1837 Perring was employed assisting Colonel R. W. H. Vyse and others in carrying out a survey of the pyramids at Giza, and in the production of plans, drawings, and maps of these monuments. He had already published, in 1835, a number of pamphlets, 'On the engineering of the ancient Egyptians'. During 1838 and 1839 he explored and surveyed the pyramids at Abu Roash, and those further south, including Fayyum. His contributions to the history of Egypt and the pyramids are described in a major work in three parts, *The Pyramids of Gizeh*, which was published in 1839. Perring's work is also referred to in a later publication by Colonel Vyse, *Operations Carried on at the Pyramids of Gizeh in 1837* (3 vols., 1840). Perring, before leaving Egypt, made a trigonometrical survey of 53 miles of country near the pyramids. The value of these researches, all made at Colonel Vyse's expense, are fully acknowledged in C. C. J. Bunsen's *Egypt's Place in Universal History* (5 vols., 1854) where it is stated that they supplied the names of six Egyptian kings until then unknown.

Perring returned to England in June 1840, and on 1 March 1841 entered upon the duties of engineering superintendent of the Llanelli railway docks and harbour. In April 1844 he was associated with the Manchester, Bury, and Rossendale Railway, which he helped to complete; after its amalgamation with other lines he was, from 1846 until 1859, resident engineer of the East Lancashire Railway. He was subsequently involved with the Railway,

Steel, and Plant Company, was engineer of the Ribblesdale Railway, and constructed the joint lines from Wigan to Blackburn. He was also engineer of the Oswaldtwistle and other waterworks. Finally, he was one of the engineers of the Manchester city railways. He was elected a member of the Institution of Civil Engineers on 6 December 1853, and in 1856 became a member of the Institution of Mechanical Engineers. He died of a stroke at his home, Broom Mount, Cheetham Hill, Manchester, on 26 January 1869. He was survived by his wife, Elizabeth Millard Perring.

G. C. BOASE, *rev.* R. C. COX

Sources *PICE*, 30 (1869–70), 455–6 · *Institution of Mechanical Engineers: Proceedings* (1870), 15–16 · d. cert. · CGPLA Eng. & Wales (1869)

Likenesses portrait, *c.*1840

Wealth at death under £8000: probate, 22 Feb 1869, CGPLA Eng. & Wales

Perring, William George Arthur (1898–1951), aerodynamicist and government scientist, was born on 16 December 1898 in Gillingham, Kent, the eldest son of John Richard Brooking Perring, a shipwright, and his wife, Alice Johns, both formerly of Devon. In 1913 he commenced a seven-year apprenticeship at the Royal Naval Dockyard, Chatham, after which he obtained a three-year scholarship from the Worshipful Company of Shipwrights to enter the Royal Naval College, Greenwich. In 1923 he gained a first-class professional certificate in naval architecture in his final examination, and was awarded an 1851 royal commission postgraduate scholarship for two years' research in the William Froude ship tank at the National Physical Laboratory (NPL), Teddington, where his research under G. S. Baker included the application of airscrew vortex theory to ships' propellers. During this time he became a member of the Institution of Naval Architects, who published his paper 'Form effect and form resistance', and also of the North-East Coast Institution of Engineers and Shipbuilders, who awarded him a £7 prize for his paper 'The influence of the type of engine on the running cost of ships', read to the institution in the 1923–4 session. After leaving the NPL he was briefly assistant to Sir George Hunter of Messrs Swan, Hunter, and Wigham Richardson in Newcastle upon Tyne, but with a depression in shipbuilding he turned to aviation and was appointed a junior scientific officer in the aerodynamics department at the Royal Aircraft Establishment (RAE), Farnborough, in December 1925.

In 1926 Perring married Joyce Carver, eldest daughter of John Carver (1852–1921), a seaman, and his wife, Alice Ann (1862–1947). Their three children were born at 52 Manor Road, Farnborough: Kenneth in 1927, Jean in 1929, and Wendy in 1930. However, family life was tragically interrupted in 1933 when Joyce Perring died during a serious operation, and again in 1939 when his son died from an infected minor injury. That year he moved to Samarkand, Ashley Road, Farnborough, and in 1942 he married May Elizabeth Willstrop (1901–1998), the widow of a former RAE metallurgist and friend, with one son, Roderick, later to become an astronomer at the Cambridge observatory. In 1949 they moved to Samarkand, Prior Road, Camberley.

William George Arthur Perring (1898–1951), by Bassano, 1946

From 1926 to 1930, under the leadership of G. P. Douglas, Perring carried out wind tunnel research at the RAE on numerous airfoil and prototype models, including research on multi-hinged flaps, induced drag from engine cooling systems, and high tip speed propellers, the latter particularly relevant to British Schneider Trophy seaplanes. In 1930 L. P. Coombes was transferred to Farnborough from the Marine Aircraft Experimental Establishment at Felixstowe to equip and run the new seaplane tank. Perring was appointed his assistant, but was first sent to Felixstowe for six months to gain practical water handling experience on flying boats. The new seaplane tank differed radically from ship tanks, which had been used previously. The speed, acceleration, and braking of the carriage, and the wing lift of the models required new methods of forced balance measurement and damping, and before model testing could begin on the hydrodynamic forces and stability of flying boat hulls, considerable test work was necessary to establish the wall, depth, and scale effect of the new tank. During these years, Perring published thirty Air Ministry reports and memoranda, and 'The Farnborough seaplane tank' in *Aircraft Engineering*, March 1934.

Perring returned to wind tunnel research in 1936, first on the 24 foot wind tunnel and later on the design and construction of the new high-speed tunnel, later renamed the 8 foot transonic tunnel. Many well-known scientists, including professors A. Thom, W. A. Mair, and A. R. Collar, and Sir Arnold Hall, later director of the RAE, were among the young scientists he recruited to the project. He was appointed superintendent of scientific research in 1940 and deputy director in 1941 following William Farren's appointment as director. In the wartime organization Farren initially looked after the electrical, armament, and instrument areas, leaving aerodynamics to Perring: work vital to improving the performance of allied aircraft and analysing the performance of enemy ones, including the reconstruction of a V 2 rocket from parts recovered when a prototype fell in Sweden. Some of this work was published in 'A critical review of German long-range rocket development' and, with Thom, 'The design and work of the Farnborough high speed tunnel' in the *Journal of the Royal Aeronautical Society*, 50 (1946) and 52 (1948) respectively. In 1946 Perring was appointed director of the RAE with John Serby as deputy director, to organize post-war research and development at Farnborough and to plan the new national aeronautical establishment at Bedford. From shipyard apprentice to director of a large government research establishment was a remarkable career achievement.

Slow of speech and slightly portly with ruddy complexion, Perring preferred to see specialist disciplines grouped together, with staff sharing experiences and able to move quickly from one problem to another, rather than placed in mixed discipline aircraft or missile departments. His prodigious workload and unfailing good humour were well known—reports stacked in his office, work carried home in a battered old suitcase, reading and commenting quickly on all RAE reports of consequence, and writing in the evening to leave the following day free for meetings. Nevertheless, there was always time to discuss and encourage the work of young scientists and engineers, and he was actively involved with education at Cranfield Aeronautical College and the RAE Technical College. He was a member of the Aeronautical Research Committee and of the Commonwealth Advisory Aeronautical Research Council, a member of council of the Royal Aeronautical Society, and was appointed CB in 1949.

This workload affected Perring's health and he died suddenly from a heart attack at his home in Camberley on 8 April 1951, aged fifty-two. He was buried in Ship Lane cemetery, Farnborough; a memorial service was held at Aldershot garrison church, at which addresses were given by Sir Archibald Rowlands and Sir Frederick Handley Page. The Royal Aeronautical Society posthumously awarded him their gold medal, but his early death denied him other civil honours he would undoubtedly have received. At the RAE a conference room was dedicated to his memory and the Perring memorial lecture was given in 1975 to mark the twenty-fifth anniversary of his death.

JOHN K. BRADLEY

Sources M. Morgan, 'Perring: the man', Royal Aeronautical Society, London · *The Times* (10 April 1951) · *The Times* (23 April 1951) · S. Jackson, 'Man with £20,000,000 air team', *Illustrated* (9 Nov 1946), 14–15 · W. G. A. Perring, 'High speed performance', *Aeronautical conference* [London 1947], ed. J. L. Pritchard and J. Bradbrooke (1948), 175–228 · 'The temple of the winds', *Flight* (21 April 1935) · W. G. A. Perring, 'Form effects and form resistance', *Transactions of the Institution of Naval Architects*, 67 (1925), 95–107 · R. Turnhill and H. Reed,

Farnborough: the story of the RAE (1980) · *DNB* · private information (2004) [family]
Likenesses Bassano, photograph, 1946 [*see illus.*] · J. Esten, photographs, repro. in Jackson, 'Man with £20,000,000 air team' · H. J. Proctor, oils (posthumous), Royal Aircraft Establishment, Farnborough, Hampshire
Wealth at death £5392 13s. 3d.: probate, 14 July 1951, *CGPLA Eng. & Wales*

Perrins, (Charles William) Dyson (1864–1958), book and porcelain collector and benefactor, was born in the parish of Claines, near Worcester, on 25 May 1864, the only son of James Dyson Perrins (1823–1887) and his wife and cousin, Frances Sarah (*d.* 1918), daughter of Charles Perrins. His father was one of the original partners in the firm of Lea and Perrins, makers of Worcestershire sauce, from which the family derived its wealth. Educated at Charterhouse School (1878–80) and the Queen's College, Oxford (where he matriculated in 1882), he served from 1888 in the 4th battalion of the Highland light infantry, but retired in 1892 with the rank of captain and began to devote himself to the family business and to public service.

On 16 October 1889 Perrins married Catherine Christina, daughter of Allan Gregory, corn merchant of Inverness. She died of a stroke in 1922 after suffering bad health for many years. They had two sons and two daughters. His second marriage, to Florence Winifred Midwood Milne, known as Frieda (*b. c.*1882), took place on 6 September 1923. They had no children.

Perrins served as mayor of Worcester in the jubilee year 1897, and high sheriff of Worcestershire two years later. His benefactions went hand in hand with his services to public life and to education; after twenty-six years as a member of the governing body of the Worcester Royal Grammar School, in 1916 he became its chairman, a post he held for the next thirty-four years, and built for the school the Perrins Hall, in memory of his father, who had been a governor before him, and a science laboratory. He maintained a continuing interest in education as a life governor of Birmingham University and a member of the council of Malvern College. To Malvern, where he lived, he presented Rose Bank house and gardens on his retirement in 1918 from the chairmanship of the urban district council, and also gave the town its hospital (himself providing the site, buildings, and equipment) and its public library, in conjunction with the Carnegie Trust. His own university received from him a large gift of money to foster the study of organic chemistry, and a further sum for the construction of the laboratory named in his honour, which was opened in 1916 and for which Oxford expressed its gratitude in 1919 by making him an honorary DCL.

Meanwhile Perrins's name had begun to become familiar in the world of the arts and of book collecting. His father had collected pictures—among them the great painting *Palestrina* from the middle period of J. M. W. Turner, which Dyson Perrins was to bequeath to the National Gallery—but his own tastes were as wide, as were his means to gratify them, while his choice was as sure as his generosity was public-spirited in buying treasures and presenting them to appropriate national institutions. Always a discriminating benefactor, he gave or

(**Charles William) Dyson Perrins** (1864–1958), by unknown photographer

bequeathed objects of the highest artistic value and historic interest to, for example, the Victoria and Albert Museum, the National Gallery, the Ashmolean Museum at Oxford, and the British Museum, which received by bequest two of his most splendid manuscripts, to which his heir allowed a further eight to be added by purchase at a specially reduced price. The main period of his book collecting lay in the two decades from 1900 to 1920, when he boldly took opportunities, the like of which will hardly recur, to acquire manuscripts and printed books of the finest quality from a series of great auction sales such as those of the libraries of Lord Amherst, Bishop Gott, and A. H. Huth. He was no less inspired in his purchases by private treaty: in 1906 he bought thirty-three manuscripts from Charles Fairfax Murray, and in the same year acquired en bloc, on the eve of its dispersal by public auction, the great collection of early woodcut books formed by Richard Fisher of Midhurst.

Perrins's prowess as a collector was recognized in 1908 by his election to the Roxburghe Club, and though he wrote nothing himself his patronage and his collections led to the publication of a notable series of volumes written by scholars who enjoyed his friendship. First among these was the monograph on the Gorleston psalter, published in 1907 by Sydney Cockerell, on whose advice Dyson Perrins had bought the manuscript in 1904, under the very nose of his friend and rival Henry Yates Thompson. His own presentation volume to the Roxburghe Club followed in 1910, the *Epistole et evangelii … in lingua toscana*, reproducing more than 500 Florentine woodcuts from an all but unique 1495 edition which he owned. This was edited by A. W. Pollard, who went on to publish in 1914 *Italian book-illustrations and early printing: a catalogue of early Italian books in the library of C. W. Dyson Perrins*, which has remained an important work of reference. In 1916 the Roxburghe Club members jointly issued *Topographical Study in Rome in 1581*, edited by Thomas Ashby from a manuscript in Dyson Perrins's library. Four years later came the sumptuous *Descriptive Catalogue* of his illuminated manuscripts, the work of Sir George Warner, in two volumes, describing in detail what has proved to be almost the last, and certainly one of the finest, gatherings of illuminated manuscripts formed by a single individual of the golden age of private collecting. The end of the series inspired by the Dyson Perrins collections came with a volume published in 1927 devoted to another single manuscript, the *Apocalypse in Latin*, described by M. R. James.

Only a few additions were made after the issue of the 1920 catalogue of Perrins's manuscripts, but one such purchase, made from a Yates Thompson sale, was the finest of the three surviving mid-twelfth-century bindings executed at Winchester; this he later presented, with characteristic generosity, to Winchester Cathedral Library. In 1946 Dyson Perrins decided to sell his printed books, in order to spend the proceeds on what had always been one of his special interests, the Royal Worcester porcelain factory. His own collection of Worcester china, probably the best in existence, and as strong in everyday pieces as in special ones, he eventually presented to the china works, which he had so long befriended and supported. After the First World War, when the factory was in economic difficulties and closure would have added to local unemployment as well as ending a historic enterprise, Dyson Perrins himself had for a time taken over the management and kept the china works in operation at his own expense. After the Second World War he determined to re-equip the factory to resume production up to the highest standard of the past, and the money raised by the auction of his printed books at four sales during 1946–7, which totalled £147,627, was earmarked for this purpose. After his death his illuminated manuscripts, with a few outstanding printed books, were dispersed in three auction sales during 1958–60, at which foreign national libraries competed with booksellers from all over the world to pay a record sum for only 154 lots. Including the earlier printed book sales and the British Museum's private purchases, the Dyson Perrins library brought nearly £1,100,000, the largest amount fetched to that time by a single individual's collection.

Despite the fame of his possessions and the publicity attendant on his numerous benefactions Dyson Perrins was personally extremely modest and deliberately shunned the limelight. Besides his various fields of collecting he enjoyed pursuits such as photography, and was a keen sportsman, for whom an estate in Ross-shire provided the stalking, fishing, and shooting in which he delighted. However, the estate was sold in 1937 when his other financial commitments meant he could no longer afford its upkeep. Perrins died at his home, Davenham, Malvern, on 29 January 1958. His second wife survived him.

DAVID ROGERS, *rev.*

Sources R. A. Pelik, *C. W. Dyson Perrins* (1983) · Burke, *Gen. GB* · Foster, *Alum. Oxon.* · *The Times* (30–31 Jan 1958) · F. K. W. Girdlestone, E. T. Hardman, and A. H. Tod, eds., *Charterhouse register, 1872–1900* (1904) · *Berrow's Worcester Journal* (31 Jan 1958)
Archives Dyson Perrins Museum, Davenham, Malvern, MSS
Likenesses A. Hacker, oils, *c.*1907, Worcester Royal Grammar School · photograph, 1951, repro. in Pelik, *C. W. Dyson Perrins*, 21 · photograph, NPG [*see illus.*]
Wealth at death £817,807 16s. 4d.: probate, 22 May 1958, *CGPLA Eng. & Wales*

Perrins, Isaac (1750×57–1801), pugilist and mechanical engineer, of whom few early details are known, appears, unusually for a member of the eighteenth-century boxing fraternity, to have been well educated and, as various extant letters in copperplate handwriting show, certainly extremely literate.

Perrins's enduring fame in the prize ring rests primarily on his memorable bout with the celebrated Tom Johnson. Before this he was credited with easily defeating every rival in the Birmingham area where he lived. Probably the most impressive of these provincial successes was at Coleshill against the locally renowned Jemmy Sargent (or Sargeant). The encounter, for 100 guineas, on 7 October 1782 was won by the underdog, Perrins, in about six minutes.

The Johnson battle, for 250 guineas a side, took place at Banbury on 22 October 1789. Such was the interest that there was almost unprecedented coverage of the build-up in the contemporary press. Perrins had overwhelming physical advantages but, owing to his naïvety, no clause was inserted in the articles of agreement to prevent 'shifting'. Johnson was therefore able to move around at will instead of standing his ground as was the customary practice. Moreover, Perrins was inexperienced in the subterfuges of the sport and found himself outwitted by his artful adversary. Eventually, having exhausted his strength pursuing Johnson around the stage, he became an easy victim of the smaller man's ferocious attacks. The contest lasted some seventy-five minutes during which sixty-two rounds were fought.

Perrins's last fistic engagement might have been an 85-minute victory over one Richards near Shrewsbury on 30 July 1790, which was widely reported in the London and provincial press but later refuted in some country newspapers. Thereafter, although the renowned Jewish pugilist Daniel Mendoza visited Birmingham in 1791 in an attempt to match Perrins with Johnson's recent conqueror, Ben Bryan (or Bryant, later erroneously recorded as Brain), this contest failed to materialize.

An upright handsome man, Perrins stood about 6 feet 2 inches tall and weighed between 17 and 18 stone. His strength was prodigious and his agility surprising. He was known to be able to carry over 800 pounds in weight and is said to have once leapt over a turnpike gate for a 10 guinea wager. As a fighter he lacked science but this was more

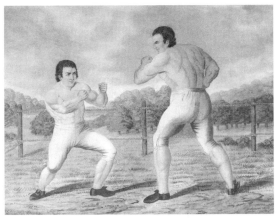

Isaac Perrins (1750x57–1801), by unknown artist [right, fighting Tom Johnson at Banbury on 22 November 1789]

than compensated for by his power and unquestionable courage. Despite his pugilistic background, Perrins was of a mild disposition. On one occasion, when challenged in a Manchester public house by George Frederick Cooke, he endured considerable provocation before calmly picking up the actor as though he were a child and gently depositing him outside.

Throughout his fistic career Perrins was employed at Soho near Birmingham by the engine manufactory of Boulton and Watt. Later he was sent to Manchester to construct their engines and subsequently took a public house, at 24 Leigh Street, while continuing his work on the company's behalf. Towards the end of 1794 he believed himself to be unfairly discharged from their service but thereafter appears still to have been called upon to work for them in the Manchester district.

On 27 December 1799 Perrins, now living in New Street, Hanover Street, was appointed inspector of engines and conductor of firemen by the police commissioners of Manchester. The position effectively put him in charge of the city's fire brigade. Late in the evening of 10 December 1800 a fire broke out in the centre of Manchester which raged until after daylight. As a result of his exertions that night Perrins became seriously ill, dying of a fever on 6 January 1801; different sources give his age at death as forty-four and fifty years old. He was buried the next day near the western door of St John's Church, Byrom Street, Manchester, in the same grave as his wife, Mary, who had died, aged forty, on 2 September of the previous year.

TONY GEE

Sources fight reports, etc., *St James's Chronicle, or, British Evening-Post*; *Diary, or, Woodfall's Register*; *Aris's Birmingham Gazette*; *The World*; *English Chronicle, or, Universal Evening Post*; *The Oracle: Bell's New World*; *Morning Post, and Daily Advertiser*; *Adams's Weekly Courant* [Chester]; *Derby Mercury* · I. Perrins, correspondence, Birm. CA, box 3/8/42, 4/13/22, 4/13/23, 4/13/24 · H. W. Dickinson and R. Jenkins, *James Watt and the steam engine* (1927), 282–3 · R. F. Bonner, *Manchester fire brigade* (1988), 10–12 · R. W. Procter, *Memorials of bygone Manchester* (1880), 273–4 · *Manchester Gazette, and Weekly Advertiser* (10 Jan 1801) · *Morning Chronicle* (13 Jan 1801) · *Courier and Evening Gazette* (13 Jan 1801) · S. W. Ryley, *The itinerant, or, Memoirs of an actor*, 2nd edn, 3 (1817), 66–71 · parish register (burial), St John's Church, Manchester, 1801, no. 16 · *Scholes's Manchester and Salford Directory* (1794) · *Scholes's Manchester and Salford Directory* (1797) · *Bancks's Manchester and Salford Directory* (1800)

Archives Birm. CA, Boulton and Watt collection, Boxes 3/8/42 and 4/13/22; 4/13/23; 4/13/24

Likenesses W. Allen, oils, 1789 (with Tom Johnson), Birmingham Museums and Art Gallery · J. Grozer, engraving, 1789 (with Tom Johnson; after C. M. Metz), BM · medal, 1789, Man. CL · drawing, priv. coll. [*see illus.*]

Perris, (George) Herbert (1866–1920), journalist and peace campaigner, was born on 29 January 1866 at 15 Tooke Street, Everton, Liverpool, the eldest of five children of the Revd Henry Woods Perris (1839–1926), a Unitarian minister, and his wife, Ellen Partington Perris (1839–1924), both of Liverpool. At sixteen, after elementary schooling at King Edward VI Commercial School in Norwich, Perris was apprenticed to a pharmaceutical chemist, but two years later joined the *Hull Express*, becoming its editor at nineteen. In 1888 he moved to London and was for ten years on *The Speaker*. On 24 July 1891 he married Mary Annie Robinson (1861–1929) of Hull; they had two daughters and a son, who was killed in the First World War.

A founding member of the Society of Friends of Russian Freedom (1890) and a regular contributor to its journal *Free Russia*, Perris visited Russia for the first time in 1896 and, increasingly interested in the ideas and beliefs of Tolstoy, wrote *Leo Tolstoy: the Grand Mujik* (1898), a study in personal evolution. However, after a visit to Tolstoy in 1904, he dissociated himself from the principle of absolute non-resistance. He became foreign editor of the Liberal newspaper *The Tribune* from its foundation in 1906, and provided space for repeated criticism of the tsar's regime, much to its annoyance. As joint secretary to the Memorial to the Duma Committee (1906), he visited St Petersburg to discuss the memorial and to help found the Anglo-Russian Friendship Society, and became caught up in events following the Duma's dissolution.

Perris is principally remembered for his contribution to the cause of international peace. However he was not a pacifist in the strict sense. As a strong internationalist the prevention of war was his highest political priority, but he did not exclude the use of force in the last resort. On the one hand he campaigned for the creation and strengthening of institutions to serve peace, such as arrangements for international arbitration and the spread of democratic government, and on the other against imperialism and the international arms trade. He summarized his views in *A Short History of War and Peace* (1911), and *The War Traders* (1914). In 1896 he formed the Increased Armaments Protest Committee; in 1898 he was chairman of the press committee of W. T. Stead's Peace Crusade; he attended the first Hague peace conference (1899) and published an account of it. Thereafter, he was a regular participant at national and international peace conferences. From 1906 Perris was a prominent critic of the Liberal government's foreign policy and rearmament plans; and in 1908 he left the party to join the Labour Party over the issue of the Anglo-Russian convention. He maintained regular contacts with peace leaders in Europe and the USA (where he went three times on speaking tours), and was active in promoting international understanding; for example, in 1905 he took a leading role in fostering friendship with Germany through the Anglo-German Friendship Society, of which he was joint secretary, at a time when relations between the two countries were strained. He was editor of *Concord*, journal of the International Arbitration and Peace Association, from 1898 to 1906 and briefly again in 1914; and a member of the executive committee of the National Peace Council from its establishment in 1904. He was also active in related fields, such as the Cobden Club (secretary, 1903–5), the Ethical Movement, and the Rainbow Circle.

After the collapse of *The Tribune* Perris became foreign editor of the *Daily News* (1908), and in 1910 assistant editor of the Home University Library, which he originated. This series provided specially commissioned, cheap, authoritative introductions to academic subjects for general readers, and in its first two and a half years sold over one million copies of eighty titles. In 1899 he had founded the Literary Agency of London, which was in existence until 1916; its clients included Edward Thomas, Stephen Crane, A. T. Mahon, Jean de Bloch, and Aylmer Maude.

On the outbreak of war in 1914 Perris joined the *Daily Chronicle* as its correspondent with the French armies. With some of his radical friends he became a reluctant supporter of a war he believed to have been caused by unprovoked and ferocious German aggression on Belgium and France. Accordingly, defeat of the Germans was a prerequisite to a new world order, and he particularly singled out the Kaiser and the Prussian governing class as having 'gone mad'.

Perris was appointed chevalier of the Légion d'honneur in 1918 and made a CBE in 1919. Worn out by years of overwork he died in London at 5 Ashburn Place, Kensington, on 23 December 1920, from influenza that turned to pneumonia, contracted while he was attending a conference of the League of Nations at Geneva, and was cremated at Golders Green crematorium six days later. He was a characteristic figure of his time, tireless in pursuit of what he thought right, writing, lecturing, and attending meetings, often after a day earning his living. He was a prolific writer: on his fortieth birthday he recorded having written at least 200,000 words each year since the age of twenty on matters of peace and war. His simple and clear prose style had a vigorous, memorable quality when he was moved to indignation. He loved poetry and had a gift for friendship. He was a slightly built figure, 5 feet 9 inches tall, with brown hair and hazel eyes. One of his brothers, Harry Shaw Perris (1870–1933), was also a campaigner for peace, making important contributions to pacifist and radical writings, and the first full-time secretary (1908) to the National Peace Council; another brother, Ernest Alfred Perris (1874–1961), was a journalist, chiefly remembered as the last editor (1918–1930) of the *Daily Chronicle*.

ROBERT GOMME

Sources R. A. Gomme, *George Herbert Perris, 1866–1920: the life and times of a radical* (2003) • *The Inquirer* (1 Jan 1921) • M. Ceadel, *Semi-detached idealists: the British peace movement and international relations, 1854–1945* (2000) • S. E. Cooper, *Patriotic pacifism* (1991) • *Concord* [International Arbitration and Peace Association] (1895–1917) • B. Hollingsworth, 'The Society of Friends of Russian Freedom: English liberals and Russian socialists, 1890–1917', *Oxford Slavonic Papers*, new ser., 3 (1970), 45–64 • *Free Russia* [Journal of the Society of Friends of Russian Freedom] (1890–1914) • B. Hollingsworth, 'British memorial to the Russian Duma, 1906', *Slavonic and East European Review*, 53 (1975), 539–57 • B. Hollingsworth, 'David Soskice in Russia, 1917', *European Studies Review*, 6/1 (1976), 73–9 • *Literary Year Book* (1899–1918) • M. Freeden, ed., *Minutes of the Rainbow Circle, 1894–1924*, CS, 4th ser., 38 (1989) • H. Josephson, ed., *Biographical dictionary of modern peace leaders* (1985) • B. Hollingsworth, 'Benckendorff's bête noire: The Tribune and Russian internal affairs, 1906–8', *Poetry, prose, and public opinion … essays presented in memory of Dr N. E. Andreyev*, ed. W. Harrison and A. Pyman (1984), 106–32 • A. J. A. Morris, *Radicalism against war, 1906–14* (1972) • P. Laity, *The British peace movement, 1870–1914* (2001) • private knowledge (2004) • b. cert. • d. cert.

Archives LUL, papers • NL Scot., corresp. incl. Sir Patrick Geddes | BLPES, National Peace Council MSS • Bodl. Oxf., letters to Gilbert Murray • Bodl. Oxf., corresp. with J. L. Myers • Bodl. Oxf., MSS Edward Thomas • HLRO, letters to David Soskice • U. Durham, Edward Thomas MSS

Likenesses photograph, repro. in *The diary of Olive Garnett*, ed. B. Johnson, 2 (1893–5) • photograph, repro. in *XVIIth Universal Peace Congress Record* (1908)

Wealth at death £1012 14s. 8d.: probate, 25 May 1921, *CGPLA Eng. & Wales*

Perronet, Edward (1721–1792). *See under* Perronet, Vincent (1693–1785).

Perronet, Vincent (1693–1785), Church of England clergyman, was born in the parish of St Giles-in-the-Fields, London, on 11 December 1693, the third and youngest son of David Perronet (1664–1717), a surgeon, and Philothea Arther, first cousin to the countess dowager of Dartmouth. Perronet was descended from a well-to-do Swiss family. His father had been born in Château d'Oex, then in the canton of Bern, and had come to England in 1680, being naturalized on 20 March 1708. A cousin, Jean Rodolphe Perronet (1708–1794), later achieved celebrity in France as the engineer of thirteen bridges, including the Pont de Neuilly and the Pont de la Concorde in Paris.

Vincent Perronet's mother had been brought up by Sir Philip Howard, uncle of the earl of Carlisle. Probably because of her connection with Lord Carlisle, Perronet was educated at St Bees School in Cumberland and the Queen's College, Oxford, from which he matriculated in December 1714 and graduated BA in 1718. On 4 December 1718 he married Charity (1688–1763), daughter of Thomas and Margaret Goodhew, at St Mary Magdalen, Old Fish Street, London. They had twelve children, the first of whom, Daniel, was baptized at St James's, Clerkenwell, on 2 October 1719. In the same year Perronet was ordained and began a nine-year curacy at Sundridge, in Kent. In 1724 he graduated MA from Corpus Christi College, Cambridge. Four years later he became the vicar of Shoreham, Kent, where he remained for the rest of his life.

From childhood onward Perronet experienced terrifying dreams, visions, mystical conflicts, and spiritual distress. He received some comfort from reading John Locke's *Essay Concerning Human Understanding*, which

Vincent Perronet (1693–1785), by unknown engraver

ensured that his religious outlook was never divorced from rational thought. He saw in Locke 'the most affectionate regard for truth, sound morality and divine revelation', and defended him first against the Anglican divine Joseph Butler in his *A Vindication of Mr Locke* (1736), and then in *A Second Vindication* (1738) against the dissenter Isaac Watts.

In 1744 Perronet was introduced to John Wesley by Henry Piers, a friend and fellow clergyman. Perronet, like other members of his family, had initially considered the Methodists a threat to the established church. Though increasingly attracted by Methodism, Perronet refused to embrace the movement before he had received a full statement about its origin and purpose. This Wesley famously set out in a letter of 1748, published as *A Plain Account of the People called Methodists* (1749), and thus began Perronet's lifelong friendship with the Wesleys and his support for Methodism through the pulpit and the press.

By the late 1740s the Wesley brothers had been excluded from preaching in many Anglican pulpits. Perronet's decision to allow them to preach in his church went against the wishes of his parishioners, and on the first occasion Charles Wesley spoke he was protected from missiles by Perronet's son Charles (1723–1776). Other members of the Perronet family also supported the Methodists. His eldest daughter, Damaris (d. 1782), became a Methodist class leader and a mainstay of the Shoreham Methodists. Another daughter, Elizabeth, married William Briggs, a class leader and John Wesley's book steward in 1749.

Perronet's connection with Methodism appears to have lessened his interest in philosophy, and his published works between 1745 and 1767 reflect a theology of grace and an advocacy of religious life as exemplified by Methodist teaching. From the beginning of their friendship the Wesleys looked to Perronet for guidance in personal as well as theological matters. He took part in the Methodist conference of 1747 which discussed the difficult subject of the doctrine of entire sanctification. In 1748 he encouraged Charles Wesley in his love for Sarah Gwynne and subsequently became a trustee of their marriage settlement. John Wesley, after his failed pursuit of Grace Murray, consulted him in 1751 about marriage and was advised to marry, though there is no indication that Wesley's disastrous union with Marie Vazeille can be blamed on Perronet.

In January 1770 Perronet was visited by Selina, countess of Huntingdon, who described him as 'a most heavenly man, with the most lively piety joined with the profoundest humility' (Seymour, 1.317). Later that year John Wesley outraged Huntingdon's followers by purging Methodist preaching of an association with Calvinism which, in Wesley's opinion, played down the necessity of holy living. Perronet, appalled as he was at the fury of the Calvinists' personal attacks, nevertheless tried to judge the matter on the truth it proposed, as he had done in his earlier defence of Locke. He distinguished the false belief (often laid at the Methodists' door) that a person could build up merit with God because of his good works from the scriptural command to do them simply as the inevitable concomitant of a Christian life.

> With regard to the merit of good works … I could not conceive how an unprofitable servant could merit anything from a holy God. But then … Christ came to purify unto himself a peculiar people, zealous of good works … though even our best works can have no merit in them. (*Arminian Magazine*, 253)

In later life rheumatism (possibly rheumatoid arthritis) left Perronet painfully disabled. From the end of 1778 he never left his home, though he continued to preach there every Sunday morning. With his wife and ten of his children now dead, Perronet was cared for by his granddaughter Elizabeth (Betsy) Briggs, daughter of Elizabeth. John Wesley continued to visit Perronet, whom in 1783 he found 'full of love'. In these years of confinement Perronet pursued his favourite subject, the application of scripture prophecies to the second coming of Christ and to the natural events in which he saw signs of the impending end of the world.

On 7 May 1785 Perronet became ecstatic in contemplation of the glorious happiness to come, and two days later died at the Shoreham vicarage in his sleep. He was buried at Shoreham on 14 May. Betsy, who later married Peard Dickinson, Perronet's curate, wrote a memoir of her grandfather which was published in the *Methodist Magazine* (1799), interspersed with her husband's reflections on Perronet's character. Dickinson spoke of Perronet's manly piety, Christian courtesy and hospitality, cheerful and sweet disposition, fervour of spirit, simplicity of manners, and frankness and generosity of temper. Those who knew him delighted in this happy, holy man whom Wesley called a 'saint'; an anonymous verse among the Perronet manuscripts ends 'Men loved in thee the image of their Lord'. Yet as his second son, Edward [see below], looked back over his father's life, he also saw an 'unwearied toil' with only 'minute gains' (Perronet, 198). Dickinson was similarly of the opinion that 'the success, which he ardently wished for, did not follow his labours' (Briggs and Dickinson, 161), at least in Shoreham. It was his decisive influence on the Wesleys, and therefore on Methodism, which gave Perronet's life historical importance. His reason, affection, and loyalty steered them through difficulties caused by their own characters and by religious opposition.

One of only two children to outlive their father, **Edward Perronet** (1721–1792), Independent minister and hymn writer, was born at Sundridge, Kent. He was educated at Sevenoaks School and entered St John's College, Cambridge, in 1741, though he did not graduate. Having joined Charles Wesley in 1746, he endured 'rough treatment' at Penkridge, Staffordshire, but continued with him on his tour of the north (1746–7). He married Duriah Clarke (d. 1792) at St Bartholomew-the-Great, London, on 10 September 1748; the couple had no children. Perronet preached with John Wesley in 1749, supported him in his misery after Grace Murray rejected him, and was attacked by critics of Methodists at Bolton. By 1750 difficulties caused by Perronet's independent-mindedness were becoming apparent. He and his brother Charles refused to preach where Wesley requested, although they remained committed to his message.

By then many Methodists who had been refused sacrament by clergy were asking to receive it from their own preachers. To accede implied a separation from the church which the Wesleys were determined to avoid. Nevertheless by 1755 Edward and his brother had administered the sacrament, believing that their calling gave them the right to do so, and that the Wesleys' opposition was a denial of their liberty to act according to their conscience. In 1756 Perronet published *The Mitre*, a ferocious attack in verse on the Church of England. The notes to the verse constitute a valuable theological commentary. Perronet claimed that the sacrament of the Lord's Supper was not a priestly rite, and that a handful of private individuals, or a single family, could celebrate it as had the early Christians.

The disagreement over *The Mitre* further worsened relations with the Wesleys. In November 1756 Charles Wesley wrote of Perronet:

> I love both him and Charles, and the whole family … but must we, therefore, suffer this madman to cast firebrands down and to tear our whole flock to pieces? … at Canterbury I saw our Sacrament Hymns, which Ted has scratched out and blotted, hardly leaving twenty entire lines … his own soul can never recover while he wanders from house to house in such a lounging way of life. Therefore let him go home to his wife, and do as much good and as little harm as he can at Canterbury. (C. Wesley to J. Wesley, 16 Nov 1756, Tyerman, *Life and Times*, 2.254)

Thus Perronet's connection with organized Methodism

came to an end. For a short time he preached in the Countess of Huntingdon's Connexion until his open aversion to the established church led to his becoming the minister of an Independent congregation.

Little is known of Perronet in later life, though he is said to have become the editor of a local newspaper in which he censured and ridiculed 'those whom he thought enthusiastic supporters of Church and State' (Smith, 1.209). He published, anonymously, collections of hymns and poems in 1756, 1782, and 1785, of which the last, *Occasional Verses*, was the most important. It contains his enduring memorial, the great hymn 'On the Resurrection' ('All hail the power of Jesu's name'), which has a place in most English-language hymnbooks; many other poems which reflect the Calvinist–Arminian quarrel also deserve recognition.

Edward Perronet probably separated from his family after the affair of *The Mitre*, and apart from £10 for 'mourning' for him and Duriah, he was excluded from Vincent Perronet's final will because he had inherited his sister Damaris's property at Wandsworth. The Wesleys continued to think affectionately of their former supporter. 'Where is your Uncle Ned?', Charles asked Betsy Briggs, 'I retain all my old love for him and trust he will be given at last to his blessed father's prayers' (*Journal of the Rev. Charles Wesley*, 2.284). Perronet died at Canterbury on 2 January 1792 and was buried six days later in the south cloister of Canterbury Cathedral.   MARGARET BATTY

Sources letters of Vincent Perronet and some of his children, JRL, Methodist Archives and Research Centre, photocopy no. SG 000 LL-0808 · [E. Briggs and P. Dickinson], 'Memoirs of the Rev. Vincent Perronet A.M.', *Methodist Magazine*, 22 (1799), 1–8, 53–8, 105–10, 157–62 · *The journal of the Rev. Charles Wesley*, ed. T. Jackson, 2 vols. [1849] · *The works of John Wesley*, [another edn], 21–3, ed. F. Baker and others (1992–5) · *The journal of the Rev. John Wesley*, ed. N. Curnock and others, 8 vols. (1909–16); repr. (1938) · *The letters of the Rev. John Wesley*, ed. J. Telford, 8 vols. (1931) · L. Tyerman, *The life and times of the Rev. John Wesley*, 4th edn, 3 vols. (1878) · J. Whitehead, *Life of Rev. John Wesley, and the life of Rev. Charles Wesley*, 2 vols. (1793) · L. Tyerman, *Wesley's designated successor: the life, letters, and literary labours of the Rev. John William Fletcher* (1882) · *GM*, 1st ser., 19 (1749) · *GM*, 1st ser,. 41 (1771) · Canterbury diocesan visitation, 1758, LPL · *Arminian Magazine*, 20 (1797), 253 · C. Atmore, *The Methodist memorial* (1801) · *The minutes of the annual conference of the Methodist church* (1812) · [A. C. H. Seymour], *The life and times of Selina, countess of Huntingdon*, 2 vols. (1840) · G. Smith, *History of Wesleyan Methodism*, 3 vols. (1863) · A. Stevens, *History of the life and times of John Wesley* (1864) · J. A. Vickers, *The story of Canterbury Methodism* (1961) · *The letters of John Pawson*, ed. J. C. Bowmer and J. A. Vickers, 3 vols. (1994–5) · 'La famille Perronet de Chateau-D'Oex', *Journal de Chateau D'Oex* (22 Dec 1950) · J. R. Gregory, 'The Perronets of Shoreham', *Wesleyan Methodist Magazine*, 125 (1902), 52–6, 215–20, 373–9, 603–8, 660–64 · A. W. Harrison, 'The Perronets of Shoreham', *Proceedings of the Wesley Historical Society*, 16 (1928), 41–7 · [E. Perronet], *Occasional verses, moral and sacred* (1785), 198 · IGI · Venn, *Alum. Cant.* · R. F. Scott, ed., *Admissions to the College of St John the Evangelist in the University of Cambridge*, 3: *July 1715 – November 1767* (1903) · A. R. B. Robinson, *The counting house: Thomas Thompson of Hull (1754–1828) and his family* (1992) · A. B. G. [A. B. Grossart], 'Perronet, Edward', *A dictionary of hymnology*, ed. J. Julian, rev. edn (1907); repr. (1908) · parish register, Château D'Oex, Switzerland, 29 Dec 1698
Archives Duke U., Perkins L., family letters and papers · JRL, Methodist Archive and Research Centre, letters, photocopy no. SG 000 LL-0808

Likenesses J. Spilsbury, mezzotint, 1787, BM, NPG · portrait, repro. in *Methodist Magazine* (Nov 1799) · stipple and line engraving, NPG [*see illus.*]

Wealth at death trust set up to administer moveable goods, securities, estates, premises, mainly at manor of Westgate, Canterbury: will, PRO, PROB 11/1139, fols. 86r–88v

Perrot, George (1710–1780), judge, was baptized on 24 June 1710 at Barwick in Elmet, in the West Riding of Yorkshire, the second son in the family of eleven children of the Revd Thomas Perrot—prebendary of Ripon and rector of Welbury in the North Riding of Yorkshire, and of St Martin-in-Micklegate, York—and his wife, Anastasia, daughter of the Revd George Plaxton, rector of Barwick in Elmet. He went to Westminster School in 1722, was admitted to the Inner Temple in November 1728, and was called to the bar in 1732. In 1742 he married Mary (c.1702–1784), daughter of William Bower of Bridlington, Yorkshire, and widow of Peter Whitton, lord mayor of York in 1728. They had no children.

In May 1757 he was elected a bencher of the Inner Temple, and in 1759 was made a king's counsel. On 16 April 1760 he opened the case against Laurence Shirley, fourth Earl Ferrers, on trial in the House of Lords for murder. On 24 January 1763 he was created a serjeant-at-law and appointed fourth baron of the exchequer. He was taken ill in Maidstone, Kent, during the Lent assizes in 1775, and retired from the bench on 15 May 1775 with a pension of £1200 a year.

Perrot moved to Pershore, Worcestershire, where he had extensive estates, including the River Avon from Tewkesbury to Evesham, and there he died on 28 January 1780. A monument was erected in his memory in the parish church at Laleham, Middlesex.

G. F. R. BARKER, *rev.* ANNE PIMLOTT BAKER

Sources Foss, *Judges*, vol. 8 · Baker, *Serjeants* · *Old Westminsters*, 2.735 · E. L. Barnwell, *Perrott notes, or, Some account of the various branches of the Perrot family* (1867) · *GM*, 1st ser., 50 (1780), 102 · [J. T. Fowler], ed., *Memorials of the church of SS Peter and Wilfrid, Ripon*, 2, SurtS, 78 (1886) · J. E. Martin, ed., *Masters of the bench of the Hon. Society of the Inner Temple, 1450–1883, and masters of the Temple, 1540–1883* (1883) · *IGI*

Perrot, Sir James (1571/2–1637), politician, was probably born in Munster, the third (but sole illegitimate) son of Sir John *Perrot (1528–1592), lord deputy of Ireland, and his mistress, Sybil Jones of Radnorshire. His father owned the Haroldston estate, near Haverfordwest in Pembrokeshire, but James may have spent his boyhood at Westmead in Carmarthenshire, one of Sir John's lesser Welsh properties. On 29 May 1584, shortly before Sir John's departure for Dublin to take up office as Ireland's lord deputy, Perrot was recognized by his father, who granted him full rights of inheritance. Six years later he confirmed these rights by a second conveyance after discovering that the first had been legally flawed.

Early years and inheritance Perrot matriculated at Jesus College, Oxford, aged fourteen on 8 July 1586 but did not graduate. He received a sound classical education, publishing in 1600 a short treatise on Greek philosophy, The

First Part of the Consideration of Humane Condition. After leaving university he is said by Anthony Wood to have travelled abroad for a few years. He entered the Middle Temple in January 1591. The following year witnessed the imprisonment, attainder, and death of his father. His family's fortunes were rescued by the queen's favourite, Robert Devereux, second earl of Essex, whose sister had married Perrot's sole surviving half-brother, Sir Thomas Perrot. The latter was restored by statute to his patrimony in March 1593, but died without male issue in February 1594, leaving James as heir to the Perrot estates. Despite the conveyances of 1584 and 1590, James's illegitimacy impeded his smooth succession. For the next fifteen years he was locked in a series of legal battles, first with Sir Thomas's widow, who was ultimately bought off with an annuity, and then with his erstwhile ally, Thomas Perrot of London, a descendant of a younger brother of Perrot's paternal grandfather. James ultimately triumphed, but the ordeal caused him to fall back on a deeply held religious faith; about this time he composed a series of prayers to help him through his 'adversities', which he later published (NL Wales, J. Perrot, *An Invitation unto Prayer*, 1624, preface).

In 1596 Perrot wrote a tract aimed at discouraging soldiers and scholars from settling abroad, where they might plot invasion. Entitled *Discovery of Discontented Minds*, it was dedicated to Essex, to whom Perrot continued to look for protection despite his dispute with the earl's sister. In the following year Perrot was returned to parliament for Haverfordwest, but played no recorded part in its activity. Appointed to the Pembrokeshire bench in November 1598, he successfully petitioned to become its chairman in 1601. In January 1599 he sought permission to accompany Essex to Ireland, but the earl evidently declined his offer of service, although he helped Perrot to several stewardships of crown lands in south Wales which had previously been held by Perrot's father. Perrot took no part in Essex's abortive rising, nor does he appear to have sought election to the 1601 parliament. An esquire of the body at the funeral of Queen Elizabeth in April 1603, he was knighted by James I a few months later. About this time he married Mary (d. 1639), daughter of Robert Ashfield of Chesham, in Buckinghamshire; they had two daughters, neither of whom reached adulthood. In March 1604 he was once more returned to parliament for Haverfordwest. On 5 May he made his first recorded speech in the house, 'a long and learned discourse touching matters of religion', which the underclerk described as 'very good' (*JHC, 1547–1628*, 1.199).

Early Jacobean parliaments—and Ireland In the summer of 1605, while parliament was in recess, Perrot renewed his offer of service in Ireland, where his brother-in-law Sir Arthur Chichester was the new lord deputy. However, he did not take ship, as he was elected mayor of Haverfordwest. During the second and third sessions of parliament Perrot earned a reputation at Westminster for godly protestant zeal; he took almost no recorded part in the union debates of 1607. Following the prorogation of July 1607, he at last travelled to Ireland from where, in June 1608, he conveyed to London Robert, fourth Lord Delvin, who was suspected of treason. On his return to Ireland he was given command of a company of foot; he was subsequently assigned to guard the border town of Newry, where he styled himself 'governor', apprehending and killing several rebels, for which he was commended to the English privy council. At the beginning of 1610 he offered to help plant escheated lands in Ulster with protestant settlers, but the reconvening of the English parliament caused him to sell his captaincy and return to Westminster, where he took little interest in the great contract but continued to seek reform of the church.

Following parliament's dissolution Perrot became deputy vice-admiral for Pembrokeshire under William Herbert, third earl of Pembroke, a major landowner in south Wales and leading privy councillor, who shared Perrot's firmly protestant outlook. Early in 1614 Pembroke helped persuade the king to summon a new parliament, arguing that a fresh assembly would remedy James's desperate financial condition if in return the king offered parliament various bills of grace, which had been laid before the Commons in 1610. Once at Westminster, sitting again for Haverfordwest, Perrot initially avoided the contentious issue of impositions, but instead spoke in favour of the grace bills, presumably at Pembroke's behest. However, on 3 June he reacted angrily to the king's threat to dissolve parliament unless the Commons debated supply rather than impositions. Declaring that the royal need for impositions stemmed from James's squandering of £70,000 each year on pensions to courtiers, he warned that if royal overspending was not curbed it would be pointless to vote subsidies. When parliament was dissolved four days later the council summoned him to explain this outburst. Possibly thanks to Pembroke's influence, Perrot was merely detained in London for a week, while several others who had delivered inflammatory speeches were committed to the Tower. Nevertheless, in August 1615 Perrot was struck off the Pembrokeshire bench.

Parliaments and anti-popery, 1621–1625 By 1619 Perrot was engaged in a project to continue the official history of Ireland from 1584, where it then ended, to 1608. He hoped to shed light on the nature of the Irish problem to enable English governments to avoid the pitfalls of their predecessors. Compiled from official records, Perrot's 'The chronicle of Ireland' was dedicated to Pembroke but, being never entirely completed, went unpublished in its author's lifetime. Re-elected for Haverfordwest in December 1620, Perrot displayed the virulent anti-popery which was his hallmark. He complained that the penal laws were being laxly implemented, and in February and March 1621 he spearheaded the attack on the exchequer official responsible for collecting recusancy fines, Sir Henry Spiller, for enriching himself at the king's expense. However, in seeking to gather incriminating evidence in the records of the exchequer Perrot neglected to obtain the signatures of his fellow committee members to his search warrants, thereby enabling Spiller to complain to the house. Subsequent attempts to have Spiller investigated

proved futile. Perrot's hostility to popery resurfaced on the final day of the parliamentary sitting (4 June), when he delivered an impassioned speech on the imperilled state of the Palatinate. He reminded his listeners that at the beginning of the parliament James had pledged to spend his own life and that of his son in the defence of the Palatinate. Now, when continental protestantism faced extinction, was it therefore not appropriate, he asked, that members of the Commons should follow James's lead by declaring that unless the elector had been restored to his possessions by the time parliament reconvened in November, they 'would be ready to adventure the lives and estates of all that belong unto us, or wherein we have interest, for the maintenance of the cause of God, and of his Majesty's royal issue' (Nicholas, 1.169)? The effect of this speech was electric. Members cheered and waved their hats, a gesture which, as Edward Nicholas recorded, 'had scarce ever been seen in parliament' (ibid.). After the din subsided the Commons drafted a declaration along the lines proposed by Perrot. This so pleased the king that he had the text translated and sent abroad.

Perrot was among the first to revisit the palatine question when parliament reassembled. On 26 November he argued that war against Spain was affordable despite a slump in the cloth trade, but he may have harmed his case by suggesting that subsidy-payers should not contribute less than they were rated. Two days later Perrot, whose fears for the fate of true religion abroad were exceeded only by his anxiety for the state of protestantism at home, regaled the Commons with lurid tales of the increasing boldness of England's Catholic community. In his eyes the growth in popery stemmed from a lax enforcement of the penal laws and a failure to prevent Catholics from sending their children abroad to be educated. Perrot clearly believed the new-found boldness of the papists to be closely connected to the negotiations for a Spanish bride for Prince Charles. On 3 December he proposed that the house should petition James to abandon the Spanish match, recalling the king's earlier pledge to match his son 'for the glory of God, his church and the realm' (Nicholas, 2.270), which would be broken if the prince married a Catholic. His views were widely shared in the Commons, which accordingly called upon the king to marry his son to a protestant. James was so incensed at this invasion of his prerogative that he reproached the house by letter, whereupon Perrot lamented that the king had been misinformed and that 'our religion is not so safe as we desire it to be'. Five days later the parliament was adjourned, never to reconvene.

Shortly after the parliament broke up Perrot was named to a commission to inquire into the ecclesiastical and temporal affairs of Ireland. Members of this commission may have received their places as punishment for their role in the final stages of the 1621 parliament, but Perrot undoubtedly welcomed the opportunity to help remould Irish institutions and may even have volunteered his services. He arrived in Dublin in April 1622, and in July he and Sir Francis Annesley were assigned counties Cavan and Fermanagh. His task completed, he returned to England at the beginning of 1623, when James rewarded him by restoring him to the Pembrokeshire bench. In 1623–4 he served a second term as mayor of Haverfordwest, ordering the bells rung in October 1623 to celebrate the safe return from Spain of Prince Charles. His mayoralty coincided with the summons of the last Jacobean parliament, and—since mayors could not return themselves—he was technically ineligible for election. However, he evaded parliamentary censure by getting himself elected for Pembrokeshire rather than Haverfordwest, in the process defeating John Wogan of Wiston, who had represented the shire in the previous two parliaments. On taking his seat Perrot reiterated his concern at the lax treatment of recusants and underlined his reputation for puritan fervour: notably he was one of just five members who, on 13 May, were required to alert Archbishop Abbot to the contents of Richard Mountague's recently published *A New Gagg for an Old Goose*, which highlighted the allegedly Catholic elements of Anglicanism. However, he probably astounded many of his colleagues on 27 April, when, during a debate on recusant officeholders, he admitted that his wife of more than twenty years was a papist. Perrot played no noticeable part in the impeachment of Lord Treasurer Middlesex, perhaps because one of his relatives was employed in the latter's service, but he did join the attack on Lord Keeper Williams, who had declared himself opposed to war with Spain.

The parliaments of Charles I Perrot's antagonism of John Wogan in 1624 returned to haunt him in 1625, for at the general election in that year Wogan, employing a variety of underhand practices, defeated him in a contest for the county seat. A despondent Perrot appealed to the Commons for redress. However, the matter remained unresolved at the August dissolution. When a new parliament was summoned in 1626 Perrot endeavoured to revive his earlier interest at Haverfordwest, but he discovered that the seat was no longer his for the taking. His long-standing local rival, the crypto-Catholic Sir Thomas Canon, who had filled the seat in 1625, was unwilling to make way for Perrot. In mid-January Perrot reported Canon to the government for electoral malpractice, and set out for London apparently confident of victory. However, when parliament assembled in February he was left once again without a seat. In despair Perrot considered a belated resumption of his military career in Ireland, but by mid-April he was once again in the Commons, almost certainly as member for Camelford, replacing the previously elected member who had been found to be incapable of sitting. Perrot undoubtedly owed his seat to Pembroke, who may have hoped that he would participate in the parliamentary assault on the royal favourite, the duke of Buckingham. Perrot, however, was more interested in defending true religion and in reiterating his concern at the writings of Richard Mountague, now a royal chaplain.

Some time in 1626 Perrot published an account of his father's rule in Ireland; he considered returning there but over the summer he was kept busy collecting the forced loan in Pembrokeshire. He returned to Westminster once again in 1628 as member for Haverfordwest. In the chamber he highlighted the threat of popery at home, drawing particular attention to the presence of Irish troops at strategic points along the south coast and of Catholic officers among the companies in Ireland. He played only a modest role in the debates which culminated in the formulation of the petition of right, but he supported the petition and hoped that the king would accord it the force of law. Unlike many in the house he professed not to desire Buckingham's ruin but merely a reduction in his power, an expression of relative moderation which reflected the rapprochement between the favourite and Pembroke which had existed since July 1626. During the 1629 session Perrot accused bishops Richard Mountague and William Laud of holding Arminian opinions, for by now he was convinced of the existence of a high-level conspiracy to subvert the fundamental doctrines of the Anglican church. In his final parliamentary speech (23 February) he warned his colleagues that 'the enemies of our religion are in agitation to break this Parliament' (Notestein and Relf, 236).

Following the dissolution Perrot became embroiled in a lengthy dispute over his vice-admiralty accounts with Sir Thomas Canon. In 1630 he published his *Meditation and Prayers on the Lords' Prayer and Ten Commandments*, which had been circulating in manuscript form for at least two years. He served as mayor of Haverfordwest for the last time in 1633–4, and died at Haroldston on 4 February 1637; he was buried in the chancel of St Mary's, Haverfordwest. In his will, dated 26 January 1637, he bequeathed the bulk of his property to Herbert Perrot of Moreton-on-Lugg in Herefordshire, with whose family he claimed kinship. Following the death of Perrot's widow on 9 May 1639 Herbert's claims were unsuccessfully disputed by Perrot's nephew, John Laugharne of St Bride's, in Pembrokeshire. Perrot's works also included 'A discourse of lawes', a 58-page unpublished treatise dedicated to Charles I, and a life of Sir Philip Sidney.　　　　ANDREW THRUSH

Sources HoP, *Commons, 1604–29* [draft] · HoP, *Commons, 1558–1603* · E. L. Barnwell, 'Notes on the Perrot family', *Archaeologia Cambrensis*, 3rd ser., 11 (1865), 1–32, 101–32, 228–60, 371–81 · E. L. Barnwell, 'Notes on the Perrot family', *Archaeologia Cambrensis*, 3rd ser., 12 (1866), 64–72, 167–82, 311–58, 478–515 · W. Notestein, F. H. Relf, and H. Simpson, eds., *Commons debates, 1621*, 7 vols. (1935) · [E. Nicholas], *Proceedings and debates of the House of Commons, in 1620 and 1621*, ed. [T. Tyrwhitt], 2 vols. (1766) · W. B. Bidwell and M. Jansson, eds., *Proceedings in parliament, 1626*, 4 vols. (1991–6) · R. C. Johnson and others, eds., *Proceedings in parliament, 1628*, 2–4 (1977–8) · W. Notestein and F. H. Relf, eds., *Commons debates for 1629* (1921) · Wood, *Ath. Oxon.*, new edn, 2.605–6 · Foster, *Alum. Oxon.* · H. A. C. Sturgess, ed., *Register of admissions to the Honourable Society of the Middle Temple, from the fifteenth century to the year 1944*, 3 vols. (1949) · W. A. Shaw, *The knights of England*, 2 (1906), 112 · B. G. Charles, ed., *Calendar of the records of the borough of Haverfordwest, 1539–1660*, University of Wales, Board of Celtic Studies, History and Law Series, 24 (1967) · *CSP dom., 1591–1637* · *CSP Ire., 1606–10; 1625–32* · *Calendar of the manuscripts of the most hon. the marquis of Salisbury*, 4, HMC, 9 (1892); 7 (1899); 9–11 (1902–6); 15–20 (1930–68) · *Third report*, HMC, 2 (1872), 205 · *APC, 1613–14, 1621–3, 1625–6* · V. Treadwell, *Buckingham and Ireland, 1616–28: a study in Anglo-Irish politics* (1998) · BL, Add. MS 10397 · PRO, E112/277/45; E133/10/1651; E133/8/1132 · F. J. Warren, *History and antiquities of S. Mary's, Haverfordwest* (1914), 41–2 · PRO,

E315/309, fols. 137, 145 · J. R. S. Phillips, ed., *The justices of the peace in Wales and Monmouthshire, 1541 to 1689* (1975) · R. K. Turvey, 'A note on the date of birth of Sir John Perrot', *National Library of Wales Journal*, 28 (1993–4), 233–8, esp. 235–7 · *Archaeologia Cambrensis*, 3rd ser., 9 (1863), 128

Archives BL, collections for chronicle of Ireland, Add MSS 4763, 4819 · Bodl. Oxf., MSS | CKS, letters to Lionel Cranfield relating to Irish affairs

Perrot, Sir John (1528–1592), lord deputy of Ireland, was born between 7 and 11 November 1528, probably at Haroldston in Pembrokeshire, the principal seat of the Perrot family since its acquisition in 1442. He was possibly the youngest of the three children of Thomas Perrot (1504/5–1531), landowner, and his wife, Mary (c.1511–c.1586), daughter of James Berkeley (d. c.1515) of Thornbury, Gloucestershire, and Hilton, Cambridgeshire, and his wife, Susan (d. c.1521), widow of William Vele. His sisters Jane and Elizabeth married, respectively, William Philipps of Picton and John Price of Gogerddan.

Early life Contrary to the popular and oft-quoted myth (the origin of which may be attributed to the work of Sir Robert Naunton), Perrot's mother was never a mistress of Henry VIII and he, consequently, was not the king's bastard son. His parents' marriage was arranged at great cost by Maurice, Lord Berkeley, who had purchased the wardship and marriage of both Mary, his niece, and Thomas Perrot two years after the death of Thomas's father, Sir Owen, in December 1521. Upon their marriage, some time after Thomas came of age in August 1526, and contingent on the will of Maurice, Lord Berkeley, the considerable sum of 500 marks was settled on the young couple. Like his father (Sir Owen died aged forty-one) and elder brother (Robert died aged eighteen in 1522), Thomas died tragically young, aged twenty-six years, on 19 September 1531.

Within a year of the death of his father, Perrot's mother had married Sir Thomas Jones (d. 1559) of Llanegwad and (from 1546) Abermarlais, Carmarthenshire, who then settled at Haroldston. The marriage (the second for both) produced five children, the eldest of whom, Sir Henry Jones (d. 1586), formed a particularly close relationship with his half-brother Perrot. Having acquired his stepson's wardship in February 1533, Jones set about the task of managing the Perrot estates and seeing to his ward's education and upbringing. We know little about Perrot's early life apart from the fact that he was brought up in a large household of ten children (his stepfather having two daughters from a previous marriage) and which seems to have been cosmopolitan in culture and religion and bilingual in speech. His Welsh-speaking stepfather patronized the bards, one of whom, Dafydd Fynglwyd, composed a poem (probably in the late 1530s or early 1540s) in praise of a clearly young Perrot, and, despite his own strong adherence to the Catholic faith, procured his stepson a place at the cathedral school at St David's, then in the care of the protestant bishop William Barlow. Here Perrot was introduced to what became a lifelong attachment to the protestant faith, and he also developed his flair for languages, becoming fluent, on his own admission and by the reports of contemporaries, in French, Spanish, Italian, and Latin.

London and the court Aged eighteen Perrot proceeded to London where his stepfather's connections at court (he was groom of the chamber in 1513 and gentleman usher in 1532) secured him a place in the house of William Paulet, Lord St John, later first marquess of Winchester and lord treasurer of England. Here, in the company of Henry Neville, sixth Lord Bergavenny, and John de Vere, sixteenth earl of Oxford, Perrot completed his formal education. However, he soon gained an unenviable reputation for violence which, added to his arbitrary disposition, ensured a turbulent apprenticeship. He twice fell out with Neville, with whom he brawled once so violently that they reportedly broke glasses 'about one another's ears' so that 'blood besprinkled … the chamber'. It was to a fracas, in which he was injured, with two yeomen of the guard when going 'into Southwarke (as it was supposed to a place of pleasure) taking but a page with him' (Perrot, *History*, 26) that Perrot owed his introduction to Henry VIII. Unfortunately, owing to the king's untimely death, a promise of preferment never materialized, though Perrot need not have worried, for his connections were such as almost to guarantee him a place at the court of Edward VI. Besides the influence of his stepfather and of his patron, Paulet, who as lord president of the council may have been instrumental in securing Perrot's election to parliament (for Carmarthenshire) on the death of Sir Richard Devereux in November 1547, his uncle Rhys or Rice Perrot (d. 1571) was reader in Greek to the young king. Knighted by King Edward within a week of attaining his majority on 17 November 1549, Perrot had evidently aligned himself with John Dudley, earl of Warwick—with whose eldest son, Ambrose, he established a lifelong friendship—in the *coup d'état* against Protector Somerset. In February 1550 Perrot's stepfather formally relinquished his interest in his stepson's estates though it was not until May that process had been completed. The attractions of the court and the distractions of London life conspired to delay Perrot's first step into local administration and it was not until September 1552 that he was pricked, succeeding his cousin John Perrot (d. 1569) of Scotsborough, near Tenby, as sheriff of Pembrokeshire.

Chivalry and debts As a result of his connections at court and his perceived skill in knightly exercises, in May 1551 Perrot accompanied the lord chamberlain, William Parr, marquess of Northampton, to France to negotiate a marriage between the teenage King Edward and the infant daughter of the French king, Princess Elizabeth. Perrot's reckless courage and passion for the hunt attracted the attention of a grateful king, Henri II, whom he saved from a life-threatening encounter with a wounded boar. Declining an invitation and generous pension to serve the French king, Perrot returned to England having enhanced his reputation for gallantry but denuded his purse of funds. At home his profligacy continued unabated and within a short time he found himself in considerable pecuniary difficulties. In a letter to a friend Perrot admitted to his reckless spending on 'the tilt and other toys I am ashamed to tell' (BL, Harley MS 5992, fol. 9). Forced to mortgage part of his Pembrokeshire estates to meet debts, reported by his biographer and son Sir James *Perrot (1571/2–1637) to have been between £7000 and £8000, Sir John is said also to have sought the aid of a sympathetic King Edward, who persuaded the council to grant him a minimum £100 per annum from concealed lands which he might discover. The king's generosity notwithstanding, salvation for Perrot came in the shape of his mother and stepfather who between them made over a number of properties in Pembrokeshire, some of which were held in dower.

Marriage, too, may have eased the burden of debt inasmuch as Perrot could expect his bride, Ann, to be well provided for, she being the daughter of Sir Thomas Cheyney of Shurland, Kent. Tragically, his wife died in September 1553 while giving birth to a son, Thomas (d. 1594), who survived briefly to succeed his father in 1592. Unusually for the time, Perrot remained unmarried for some ten years until in 1563 or 1564 he took as his second wife Jane (d. 1593), daughter of Hugh Prust of Thornery, Devon, and widow of Lewis Pollard (d. 1563) of Oakford, Devon. Together they had three children, a son, William (d. 1587), and daughters Lettice and Ann. An active libido ensured that further children were born to Perrot in less legitimate circumstances, of whom the following are known: Sir James, John (b. c.1565), Elizabeth, and an unnamed daughter.

Religion and military service Cheyney's influence served Perrot well, and it was his father-in-law who, as lord warden of the Cinque Ports, ensured his return as member for Sandwich, Kent, in the Marian parliaments of 1553 and 1555. Unsurprisingly, the Marian restoration was not to Perrot's liking. The fact of his being a protestant did not at first militate against him with Queen Mary, who:

> did favor hym very well, and would say that she did lyke exceedinge well of hym, and had a hope he would prove a worthy subject but that (as hir words were) he did smell of the smoake, meaninge thereby his religion. (Perrot, *History*, 36)

However, he soon fell foul of the new regime. In January 1554 he clashed with the servants of William Somerset, third earl of Worcester, for which he was briefly imprisoned in the Fleet. Soon after he refused a commission by William Herbert, earl of Pembroke, to hunt down his co-religionists in south-west Wales, preferring instead to risk the wrath of the government by sheltering heretics in his home at Haroldston. Among those who had cause to thank Perrot for his protection were his uncle Rhys, Laurence Nowell and possibly his brother Alexander Nowell, and an otherwise unknown Mr Banister. Sure enough Perrot was denounced by a neighbour, Thomas Catherne of Prendergast, and was again briefly imprisoned in the Fleet. Undeterred, he continued to live dangerously by aligning himself with the opposition in parliament, resulting in another violent quarrel with Pembroke when the latter objected to his support of Sir Anthony Kingston and Sir Edward Hastings, closely followed by his arrest in April 1556 on suspicion of complicity in the Dudley conspiracy.

Lack of evidence and court connections saved Perrot from a longer spell of imprisonment, or worse, in the Fleet, but even he came to realize that the government was fast running out of patience and he out of luck. He thought it best to remove himself from the kingdom and, having made up his quarrel with Pembroke, he set sail with the earl's forces for France. Pembroke's earlier magnanimous gesture in supporting Perrot's suit for the castle and lordship of Carew, which won the queen's approval, and the fact of his younger son Sir Edward Herbert's friendship with Perrot, did much to heal the rift between them, but it was to be their service together at the siege and capture of St Quentin in July to August 1557 which set the seal on their reconciliation. On his return from military service Perrot was plunged yet again into bitter dispute with Catherne whom he took, after breaking into his house, into custody at Carew Castle. Both were summoned to appear before the council in June 1558 where Perrot was found to be at fault having 'exceeded his commission and misused himself'. After a brief period in the Fleet, Perrot was released on condition he agreed to be bound over in a recognizance of £200 to keep the peace.

Rising fortunes Mary's death in November 1558 proved fortuitous for Perrot. A commission convened in September to investigate Catherne's accusations against him was allowed to lapse and on the accession of Elizabeth he was freed from yet another prison sentence, this time in the Marshalsea, to which he had been committed for non-appearance at court on an attachment for debt. Elizabeth favoured him, and as a mark of her trust he was appointed to be one of the four gentlemen chosen to carry the canopy of state at her coronation. In a remarkable series of appointments between 1559 and 1562—which included the stewardships of the manors of Carew, Coedra, and Narberth, the constableship of Narberth and Tenby castles, the gaolership of Haverfordwest prison (1559), election as mayor of Haverfordwest (1560), and by 1562 *custos rotulorum* of the county borough of Haverfordwest and vice-admiralship of the coast of south Wales—Perrot consolidated his hold on the government and administration of Pembrokeshire. In addition to investing Perrot with profitable crown offices, the regime also showered him with grants of land and advowsons in south-west Wales and elsewhere in England. His commissionership in 1561 of concealed lands (principally those formerly belonging to the priory of Haverfordwest) added considerably to his own landed wealth but inevitably brought him into conflict with his neighbours, whose titles were thus challenged, and among those pursued was his old adversary Catherne. Perrot's relentless pursuit of power in Pembrokeshire during the 1560s and 1570s made him very unpopular and gave rise to an anti-Perrot faction which attempted to block, and not without a little success, his progress. In 1572, while Perrot was away in Ireland, they wrested control of the town of Haverfordwest from him and succeeded in having their man, Catherne's son-in-law Alban Stepney, elected to serve the borough as its MP. However, in the face of Perrot's increasing wealth and influence (he counted Robert Dudley, earl of Leicester, Thomas Radcliffe, earl of Sussex, Sir Henry Sidney, and Sir

Francis Walsingham among his friends and patrons), it never amounted to more than a rearguard action. Never shy of resorting to law to browbeat his enemies into submission, Perrot is said by his contemporary the antiquarian squire of Henllys, George Owen, to have ruined a number of gentlemen in the process of prosecuting, and being prosecuted by, them.

Ireland, 1571–1573 Although not the regime's first choice for service in Ireland to head the newly created presidency of Munster, Perrot's growing political and administrative experience, added to his rugged individualism and uncompromising approach to resolving problems, was thought fit for the task of settling this disturbed region of the realm. Plagued by rebellion since 1569, led by James fitz Maurice Fitzgerald, the province had first to be pacified before its reformation and plantation could properly begin. Offered the post in December 1570, Perrot reluctantly accepted, and in February 1571, in the company of his friend Thomas Butler (Black Tom), tenth earl of Ormond and (since 1559) treasurer of Ireland, he set sail for Waterford. On taking the oath before Lord Deputy Sidney, who departed Dublin for home within weeks of Perrot's being sworn in, the president made haste for Cork. Perrot continued the reign of terror initiated in Munster by his predecessor Sir Humphrey Gilbert, and in the space of two years he dispatched to the gallows over 800 rebels. But fitz Maurice proved to be a resourceful opponent and, hampered by lack of resources and manpower, Perrot took fully two years to bring the rebel to heel. Constant campaigning took its toll on Perrot, who complained in a letter to Walsingham that for every white hair he had brought over with him he could now show sixty. Dissatisfied with the level of support given him by the privy council, and angered by accusations of dishonesty and malpractice in his seizure of a Portuguese merchantman, the *Peter and Paul*, laden with valuable spices (for which a Parisian grocer attempted to sue him in court), Perrot took his leave of Ireland in July 1573.

Wales, 1573–1579 Since he had left Ireland without permission, Perrot's enemies fully expected the queen to issue a severe and public reprimand, but none came. Pleading ill health as an excuse for not returning to Munster, though the queen wished him to do so, Perrot retired home to Carew. In a letter to the queen's chief secretary, William Cecil, Lord Burghley, Perrot declared that it was his intention 'to lead a countryman's life and to keep out of debt' (*CSP Ire.*, 1574–85, 62). His retirement from public office had lasted a little less than eighteen months when in September 1574 Perrot was appointed to the council in the marches of Wales. In Pembrokeshire too he was busy consolidating his power, being joined by his son and heir, Thomas, whom he invested with the house and manor of Haroldston not long after the latter attained his majority. Serving consecutive terms as mayor of Haverfordwest (1575–7) finally put paid to the anti-Perrot faction, the scale of whose defeat can best be appreciated by the fact that of the thirteen mayors elected in the fourteen years after Perrot's mayoralty (1577–91), all but three can be

closely connected either with him or with his son Thomas.

Perrot's years at home, during which time he attended court infrequently, were well spent inasmuch as he busied himself with enlarging and better managing his estates. However, not everyone appreciated his agricultural improvements, nor the means he employed to increase significantly his income from his estates. Accusations of rack-renting, encroachments, and enclosures were upheld by his biographer and son Sir James who, while admitting that his father 'was somewhat complained of in his life-time', said that he had nevertheless 'improved his lands to a high rate' and in mitigation stated that 'there are none of his tenants but would be glad to takes leases thereof now, and pay somewhat more for it' (Perrot, *History*, 22). That Perrot did maintain 'the part rather of a nobleman than of a knight … in retinue, in house-keeping and in all other respects' (ibid., 21) is made manifest by the fact that he was able to take thirty-four servants kitted out in his livery, sporting the family's distinctive crest (namely 'parrot with pear in claw'), to serve him in Ireland. Of greater and lasting significance in respect of Perrot's public demonstration of his wealth and power were his ambitious building projects which involved the conversion of the medieval castles of Laugharne (granted him by the queen in 1575) and Carew into mansions of some architectural pretension. That neither was fully completed by the time of his death owed more to his political difficulties after 1590 than to any loss of interest on his part. Nor had he overreached himself financially, a more prudent man than in his youth; in April 1590 he managed to raise £1500 from current rents alone. Not without good reason did contemporaries credit him with being wealthy, but they tended also to exaggerate his riches.

Piracy It was a restless Perrot—he had been badgering the privy council for some months with ideas on how Ireland might be better governed—that was called upon once again to serve the crown in a martial capacity, but this time at sea. In August 1579 he was given command of a squadron of ships and entrusted with the task of intercepting and destroying any Spanish or pirate vessel appearing off the southern coast of Ireland. Taking his son Thomas with him, Perrot cruised offshore for some weeks, occasionally putting into port and spending time ashore at Baltimore, Cork, and Waterford. At Waterford they met Perrot's successor as lord president of Munster, Sir William Drury, who shortly before his untimely death knighted his son, and Sir William George and Sir William Pelham.

Thinking that the danger of invasion had passed and with the closing of the season, in mid-October 1579 Perrot turned for home, but as he did so he came across a notorious pirate called Deryfold whom he determined to apprehend. Perrot gave chase and overtook his quarry near the Flemish coast, after which he made for the Thames. Unfortunately, his ship ran aground on the Kentish Knocks and as he and his companions struggled to cope with the storm that threatened to break up their vessel they prepared to die. As Perrot's:

> nearest followers and friends came to take their last farewell of him, amongst the rest his son Sir Thomas was one to whom he said 'Well Boy, God bless you and I give you my blessing. I wish to God that you were ashore and the Queen's ship safe then I should care the less about myself.' (Perrot, *History*, 114–15)

In fact Perrot, his son, and shipmates were spared when their ship, on the advice of Deryfold, righted itself and they sailed into the Thames and on to Greenwich Palace. Calls for his arrest on charges of misconduct and failure in his mission were ignored by the queen who reacted sympathetically to Perrot's request that Deryfold be pardoned for his exceptional and life-saving seamanship. However, such gallantry was viewed with suspicion by his enemies who had not long before accused him of trafficking with pirates in Welsh waters. Attempts by his successor as vice-admiral of south Wales, Sir William Morgan of Pen-coed, and his deputy, Richard Vaughan of Whitland, to have Perrot arrested and charged came to nothing. Although Perrot cannot be declared entirely innocent in respect of his dealings with pirates, the extent to which he has been credited with becoming involved with them has been exaggerated.

Ireland again, 1584–1588 In 1584 the call for Perrot's services once again echoed within the walls of the court. The queen, determined to deal effectively but cheaply with Ireland, was sufficiently impressed by Perrot's treatise of 1581 on the better government of the island to offer him the opportunity to put his ideas into practice. Service in Ireland, that graveyard of reputations of which the wise steered clear, called to the ambitious, and, through a combination of his own ego, the queen's flattery, and the prestige that came with the position and influence of the lord deputyship of Ireland (and despite the earnest advice of his stepbrother Sir Henry Jones not to go), Perrot was seduced into accepting the appointment on 17 January 1584. Five months later, on 21 June, he arrived in Dublin where he received the sword of state from the chancellor, Adam Loftus. Perrot began his work with energy and enthusiasm, setting off on a tour of the country within days of his arrival. His aim was to see and to be seen, to overawe both native and Old English with a public demonstration of royal power which he hoped might foster a healthier respect for English law. He established his provincial presidents in Connaught and in Munster, Sir Richard Bingham and Sir John Norris respectively, sought, and was offered in Connaught, the submission of native Irish leaders, and prepared for the subjugation and plantation of Ulster.

Perrot was less an administrator than a soldier, and when an opportunity arose to take to the field against an invasion of Scots, acting in concert with a dissident Irish leader, Sorley Boy Mac Donnell, he did not hesitate. Perrot, together with the earl of Ormond and Donough O'Brien, earl of Thomond, hastened to meet the incursion in Ulster only to be disappointed to find the Scots departed. Nevertheless, he determined on the pacification of the region and took the submission of Turlough Luineach O'Neill, together with his only son as hostage. But his chief purpose was in evicting the Mac Donnells from their territory along the Antrim coast. A three-day siege of Dunluce Castle in September 1584 resulted in its fall and the capture of much booty, particularly valuable pieces of which he presented to Walsingham, Lady Walsingham, and Lord Burghley. Frustrated at his failure either to apprehend or assassinate Sorley Boy Mac Donnell, Perrot questioned the commitment of those around him.

Perrot's ambitious projects for Ireland—reforming the revenue system, the plantation and shiring of Ulster, the enforcement, and in some areas introduction, of English law, and the foundation of a university in Dublin—largely failed. His failure to get Poynings' law suspended, and to heal the differences between the Gaelic Irish, the Old English, and the New English, meant that his parliament (1585–6) and most of its intended legislation had to be abandoned. On the other hand, his military campaigns proved rather more successful and though he was forced, on the outbreak of war with Spain, to reach an accommodation with Sorley Boy Mac Donnell, Perrot had largely pacified Ireland. His four years in Ireland proved to be a mixture of some achievements, bitter disappointments, increasing ill health (he was suffering kidney- and gall-stones), and a growing fear of dying in that 'slimy country'. It was a crestfallen Perrot who wrote to Walsingham informing him of the death of his second son, William, in July 1587 and asking to be relieved of his duties as lord deputy. In his final months in office Perrot was displaying signs of a more violent and tempestuous disposition, resulting in several brawls with his ministers and in utter frustration on Perrot's part, expressed in oaths. He had alienated former friends and supporters such as the earl of Ormond, who resorted to his usual practice of undermining the position of serving lord deputies at court, and Secretary Sir Geoffrey Fenton, who at first had found him 'affable and pleasing' but had since changed his opinion. Worse still, he had quarrelled with his provincial presidents, Bingham and Norris, and had made avowed enemies in Chancellor Loftus, Treasurer Sir Henry Wallop, and marshal Sir Nicholas Bagnal. Nevertheless, when he handed on the sword of state to his successor, Sir William Fitzwilliam, the latter was compelled to admit that he left the country in a state of peace.

Final years and downfall Perrot returned from Ireland in July 1588 with his reputation intact, quite a feat in the Elizabethan period, and within days had been appointed lieutenant-general of the three south-west shires of Wales under Henry Herbert, second earl of Pembroke, and entrusted with the task of organizing their defence in the face of a possible Spanish invasion. Before the end of the year Perrot had secured his election as member for Haverfordwest and as he prepared to attend the opening of parliament, on 4 February 1589, he was summoned by the queen, who confirmed his appointment to the privy council. This proved to be the high point of his career for, unbeknown to him, the foundations of his position and influence at court were soon to be undermined. As early as 25 March 1589 Thomas Widebank wrote to Walsingham that he had had his audience with the queen immediately after Sir John Perrot had left her: 'what had passed he knows not, but he found her out of tune' (*CSP dom.*, *1584–91*, 584). The agenda for their discussion concerned the queen's request for a bill against the embezzling of her armour and weapons which, for some unknown reason, had caused them to fall out.

Perrot's Irish service, and continuing influence in directing Irish affairs, as revealed by the council book entry 'Lord Buckhurst, Sir John Perrot, Mr. Fortescue did sit to hear Irish causes' (*APC*, 18.76), proved to be the catalyst for his enemies to bring him down. Perrot's successor as lord deputy, Sir William Fitzwilliam, came to resent his influence on Irish affairs within the privy council which he believed might end in his own disgrace. To exacerbate the situation an increasing number of Irish nobles, and even members of the Irish council, were either ignoring or bypassing Fitzwilliam and writing directly to Perrot. A disgruntled Fitzwilliam wrote to his patron Burghley, 'My credit and service is already in the balance and cannot stand long overthrown' (PRO, SP 63/147, no. 35).

Unsurprisingly, by October 1589 resentment had turned to open hostility as the two men traded insults, with Perrot alleging bribery and corruption on the part of Fitzwilliam. In February 1590 Fitzwilliam hit back hard when he accused Perrot of treason, in that he had consorted with known traitors, notably Brian O'Rourke and Sir William Stanley, and conspired with the king of Spain to remove the queen, for which he expected to be granted Wales! The queen ordered an investigation which made slow progress, mainly on account of the dubious quality of the evidence and the general unreliability of the chief witness for the prosecution, an Irish ex-priest called Denis O'Roughan. Nothing daunted, Perrot's accusers persisted and the case against him gathered momentum, particularly so after the death of his patron Sir Francis Walsingham in April 1590. By the end of the following month Perrot was placed under house arrest at Burghley's Strand residence while the charges were further investigated. A clearly distraught Perrot wrote to a friend, 'I do here … grow to utter contempt and no thing hath so much hurt me as wind whispered in corners' (Evans, 220–21). This whispering campaign soon turned into an avalanche of calls for his head. He was formally charged in December 1590 and in March 1591 he was removed to the Tower.

More than a year elapsed before Perrot's trial, and in a letter written in December 1591 he complained that his memory was becoming impaired through grief and close confinement. Eventually, on 27 April 1592, he was tried at Westminster on a charge of high treason before the court of queen's bench. According to the indictment he was charged with using contemptuous words about the queen, helping known traitors and Romish priests, encouraging the rebellion of O'Rourke, and lastly, writing

treasonable letters to Philip of Spain and the traitor Stanley. The prosecution concentrated upon the first charge, in which the evidence of Perrot's former secretary Philip Williams, who now served Fitzwilliam in the same capacity, proved decisive. The following remarks were attributed to the accused:

> Stick not so much upon Her Majesty's letter, she may command what she will, but we will do what we list
>
> Ah, silly woman, now she shall not curb me, she shall not rule me now
>
> God's wounds, this it is to serve a base bastard pissing kitchen woman, if I had served any prince in Christendom I have not been so dealt withal

(Bodl. Oxf., MS Willis 58, fols. 247–8, 263–305; Bodl. Oxf., MS Tanner 299, fol. 477)

Perrot, who was extremely agitated throughout his trial, did not deny that he might have spoken the words attributed to him but he resented the interpretation placed upon them. In spite of a spirited defence, and to his utter astonishment, Perrot was found guilty and condemned to death on 26 June 1592; thereafter he languished in the Tower awaiting his fate. Even towards the end Perrot never believed that he would be found guilty, much less executed. He took comfort from the fact that the queen had stayed judgement against him on six occasions. However, unbeknown to him the architect of his downfall was no less a man than Burghley who, before and throughout the trial, presented himself in public as a friend and ally but in secret wrought his destruction.

Death and reputation Perrot's last will and testament, dated 3 May 1592 (an earlier will made in August 1584 is still extant), is over three pages long and, in reality, is nothing more than a vindication of his conduct and an appeal for mercy; none came. Perrot died on 3 November 1592 and was buried on 10 November in the church of St Peter ad Vincula within the Tower. He died before sentence could be carried out or, as seems likely in view of the crown's favourable treatment of his family, before the queen could issue a pardon. Certainly, his widow was granted Carew for a term of years and his son Sir Thomas was, with the active support of his brother-in-law Robert Devereux, second earl of Essex, restored in blood to the family's estates in March 1593, less than four months after the death of his father. Despite the long accepted story of his natural death, there are grounds for believing that Perrot may in fact have been poisoned; this lends credence to the idea that his pardon was imminent since his enemies could ill afford to risk his wrath upon release.

Contemporaries were not slow to offer reasons why Sir John Perrot fell from grace and died in the ignominious way that he did. Naunton, who had married his granddaughter Penelope, suggested that it was in part due to the fact that he was 'a person that loved to stand too much alone, and on his own legs' (Naunton, 44). Perrot's son Sir James was more direct, stating that he was, 'more apt to give offence unto great ones than to creep or crouch unto them which in the end procured his ruin' (BL, Add. MS 4819, fol. 118b). It is generally agreed that Perrot's choleric nature and haughty pride, combined with the envy and competition of others, contributed to his downfall. He was too blunt and arrogant a man, 'as far from flattery as from fear' (ibid.), to fit easily into the polite ways and manners of the Elizabethan court. His scornful dismissal of Sir Christopher Hatton as someone who had made his way to the queen's favour 'by the galliard' reveals much about the attitude of the man. The words of one who knew him well, Sir Francis Walsingham, might perhaps serve as a fitting epitaph:

> It cannot be doubted that Sir John Perrot's intentions and purpose … were very honourable, but his course has not been agreeable to our humour. He might have lived in better season in the time of King Henry VIII, when princes were resolute to persist in honourable attempts, whereunto [Perrot] must be content to conform himself as other men do. (ibid.)

ROGER TURVEY

Sources P. C. C. Evans, 'Sir John Perrot', MA diss., U. Wales, Cardiff, 1940 · E. L. Barnwell, 'Notes on the Perrot family', *Archaeologia Cambrensis*, 3rd ser., 11 (1865), 1–32, 101–32, 228–60, 371–81 · E. L. Barnwell, 'Notes on the Perrot family', *Archaeologia Cambrensis*, 3rd ser., 12 (1866), 64–72, 167–82, 311–58, 478–515 · E. L. Barnwell, *Perrot notes* (1867) · J. Perrot, *The history of that most eminent statesman Sir John Perrott*, ed. [R. Rawlinson] (1728) · Bodl. Oxf., MS Perrot 1; MS Wood D. 33 · letters and papers, archive of the duke of Northumberland, Alnwick Castle, MS 476, vol. 6 · archive of the duke of Northumberland, Alnwick Castle, Perrot papers, Syon MS Y III 1 · BL, Add. MS 4819; Lansdowne MS 72 · R. K. Turvey, 'A note on the date of birth of Sir John Perrot', *National Library of Wales Journal*, 28 (1993–4), 233–8 · R. K. Turvey, 'Sir John Perrot, Henry VIII's bastard? The destruction of a myth', *Transactions of the Honourable Society of Cymmrodorion* (1992), 79–94 · R. K. Turvey, 'Sir John Perrot (1528–92): a fourth centenary retrospective', *Journal of the Pembrokeshire Historical Society*, 5 (1992–3), 15–30 · H. Morgan, 'The fall of Sir John Perrot', *The reign of Elizabeth: court and culture in the last decade*, ed. J. Guy (1995), 109–25 · HoP, *Commons, 1509–58* · HoP, *Commons, 1558–1603* · *DWB* · BL, Add. MS 32091 · Irish state papers, BL, Cottonian MS, Titus F v · BL, Harleian MSS 35, 3292 · BL, Lansdowne MSS 68, 111, 156 · state papers, Ireland, PRO, SP 63; SP 65 · *A descriptive catalogue of ancient deeds in the Public Record Office*, 6 vols. (1890–1915) · R. Naunton, *Fragmenta regalia, or, Observations on the late Queen Elizabeth, her times and favorits*, 3rd edn (1653); repr. (1895) · R. K. Turvey, 'The Perrot family and their circle in south-west Wales during the later middle ages', PhD diss., U. Wales, Swansea, 1988 · R. Bagwell, *Ireland under the Tudors*, 3 vols. (1885–90) · C. Brady, *The chief governors: the rise and fall of reform government in Tudor Ireland, 1536–1588* (1994) · H. Morgan, *Tyrone's rebellion: the outbreak of the Nine Years' War in Tudor Ireland*, Royal Historical Society Studies in History, 67 (1993) · C. McNeill, ed., 'The Perrot papers: the letter-book of Lord Deputy Sir John Perrot between 9 July 1584 and 26 May 1586', *Analecta Hibernica*, 12 (1943), 1–67 · V. Treadwell, 'Sir John Perrot and the Irish parliament of 1585–6', *Proceedings of the Royal Irish Academy*, 85C (1985), 259–308 · *Heraldic visitations of Wales and part of the marches … by Lewys Dwnn*, ed. S. R. Meyrick, 2 vols. (1846) · E. C. S., *The government of Ireland under the honest, just, and wise governor Sir John Perrot* (1626) · J. Perrot, *The chronicle of Ireland, 1584–1608*, ed. H. Wood, IMC (1933) · Carmarthenshire RO, Cawdor (Lort) MS 1/61 · W. A. Shaw, *The knights of England*, 2 (1906); repr. (1971), 64 · Tower chapel burial register · PRO, C 142/119/114; 121/102; wards, 51/150 · PRO, PROB 11/42B · PRO, C 142/235/91

Archives Alnwick Castle, Northumberland, papers · Alnwick Castle, Northumberland, archive of the duke of Northumberland, papers; letters and papers, vol. 6; MS 476; Syon MS Y III 1 | BL, Add. MS 4819 · Bodl. Oxf., MS Wood D. 33 · Bodl. Oxf., letters to the queen and her ministers relating to Ireland · PRO, Exchequer, ancient deeds, series D and DD · Worcs. RO, Pakington papers

Likenesses stone carved head, c.1575–1590, Carmarthen Museum, Old Bishop's Palace, Abergwili · V. Green, mezzotint, pubd 1776, BM, NPG · W. Tringham, line engraving, BM · mezzotint (after V. Green, 1776), NMG Wales · oils, priv. coll.

Wealth at death personal and household possessions valued at between £1000 and £2000; rental income from estate est. to be a little short of £2000 p.a.: Evans, 'Sir John Perrot', 301–56

Perrot, John (*d.* 1665), Quaker schismatic, was born in Ireland. The *Dictionary of National Biography* suggested that he may have been a descendant of one of the illegitimate sons of Sir John Perrot (1528–1592), lord deputy of Ireland; however, his name does not seem to appear in the nineteenth-century account of the family by Edward Barnwell. It was also claimed that he was a blacksmith from Sedbergh although this too has since been discounted.

Perrot was living 2 miles outside Waterford when, in 1655, he became a Quaker following a convincement by Edward Burrough; Perrot's wife and children were noted as still living there in 1659. Like many other early Quakers, Perrot had previously been a Baptist. In 1656 he was active as a Quaker missionary in Ireland, preaching in Limerick, where he was imprisoned twice in April, and in Kilkenny, where he was also incarcerated. He also suffered a spell in gaol in Dublin in May 1656, during which he wrote a work—never published—against the 'loathsome Abominacons' of lawyers (Carroll, 4). On his return to Kilkenny he intervened on behalf of a large group of imprisoned Irish Roman Catholics who were facing deportation, successfully gaining them their freedom. For his efforts in Ireland Perrot was described by Burrough—himself expelled from the country early in 1656—as 'Eminent in the nation' (Ingle, 198). Among the most prominent figures who knew Perrot at this time was the physician and friend of Samuel Hartlib, Benjamin Worsley, the surveyor-general of forfeited estates in Ireland; Perrot corresponded with Worsley and sought financial support for him for his later mission to the Mediterranean.

On 17 August 1656 Perrot experienced a vision at Cathrelagh:

> The word of the Lord came unto me … saying … behold I the Lord who have chosen thee from amongst men, doe Send thee into a farr country having given thee a sharpe Instrum[en]tt to thresh upon the Mountaines of Turkey. (Carroll, 9)

At some point after this he left for England where on 25 December he signed one of the many petitions seeking the mitigation of the sentence of James Nayler, the Quaker who had notoriously re-enacted Jesus's entry into Jerusalem at Bristol in October. It is not known whether Perrot ever met Nayler, but as a letter of Perrot's written in early 1657 describes Nayler's 'agents' as 'creeping upon their Bellyes' and Martha Simmonds as 'their Miserable Mother', it is clear that he was not sympathetic to Nayler's views (Carroll, 10). During his stay in England Perrot spent periods in London and the west country.

In May or June 1657, with the full support and financial backing of the Quaker movement, Perrot embarked on a mission, with five others, to the Ottoman empire to convert the sultan and to Rome to convert the pope. His companions were Beatrice Beckley, Mary Prince, Mary Fisher,

John Luffe, and John Buckley. They reached Leghorn (Livorno) via Lyons on 6 August 1657, and after holding services there for two weeks and meeting with the local Jewish community—using Latin as a common language—they were examined by the Inquisition. While in Leghorn, Perrot wrote *Immanuel, the Salvation of Israel*, which was published in London the following year. Following an interview with the local governor on 17 August, the group sailed for the island of Zante, just off the Turkish coast, on 20 August. Shortly after their arrival there on 6 September, the party divided. One group, including Fisher and Beckley, headed for Crete, while Perrot and Buckley travelled overland, via Corinth and Athens, to the island of Negroponte (Evvoia) and to Smyrna, where the group was to reunite. In Athens Perrot wrote *To All the Baptists*, later published in 1660. The two men also preached in the city on 27 September and debated with two Greek priests. They were held for a time at Negroponte where, during that same month, Perrot wrote *An Epistle to the Greeks*, later published in 1661. The two arrived in Smyrna (now Izmir) very late in 1657, the rest of their group having been there since 18 November. The English consul, learning of their plans to meet with the sultan, advised them to turn back; shortly afterwards all but Mary Prince left Smyrna for Venice, but weather forced them to return to Zante. Here the group again divided: Fisher and Beckley travelled on to Adrianople (where they would meet the sultan) via the Peloponnese; Buckley headed for Constantinople; and Perrot and Luffe sailed to Venice, intending to reach Jerusalem.

After enduring treacherous weather (two passengers were killed during an electric storm) and the hostility of both crew and other passengers, Perrot and Luffe arrived in the Gulf of Venice on 25 February 1658. Disembarking on 22 March, the two men were quarantined in the leper colony of Lazzaretto for forty days. In total the men spent only about six or seven weeks in Venice, during which time they met with members of the Jewish community; Perrot also either had a meeting with the doge or sent him a document of some sort, which formed the occasion for *To the Prince of Venice* (1661), which Perrot wrote at this time. On 7 May they left for Rome, arriving at the city on 6 June and taking up lodgings in the Piazza Farnese. Perrot intended to meet with the pope, and so approached Thomas Courtney, a Jesuit and the English confessor in St Peter's Basilica; Perrot was referred to the pope's chaplain, John Crey, a fellow Irishman to whom Perrot explained his purpose 'as an unfolded sheet upon a smooth floor' (Carroll, 24). Two days later Perrot was arrested at his lodgings and interrogated by the city governor, who promised him 'a sudden, fair and public Tryal' (Carroll, 25). Luffe too seems to have been imprisoned at this time. After a week Perrot and Luffe were transferred to the Inquisition prison, where they were held for a further eighteen weeks. Upon further interrogation, Perrot was deemed mad and was taken to the 'Pazzarella', or 'Prison of Madmen'; here both men were held in solitary confinement. By the end of 1658 Luffe was dead, officially

from starvation through fasting although other evidence suggested that he may have been hanged—by one account, upon the orders of the pope himself.

Perrot spent three years in the Pazzarella in squalid conditions. He was chained by the neck for the first few days, and then by the ankle for the next fourteen weeks. He reported being regularly tortured—including being beaten with a pizzle, presumably in the belief that the insane could be beaten into sense. Support and sympathy came from Quakers in England, some of whom travelled to Rome to intercede on Perrot's behalf; George Fox himself expressed approval of Perrot's work in 1658. Eventual release came in late May or early June 1661, following the intervention of two other Quakers, Jane Stokes and Charles Bayly. The ill-fated mission prompted two Catholic accounts in the later 1660s—one by the German Jesuit Theodore Rhay, the other by Cosimo de' Medici's secretary, Lorenzo Magalotti—both of which record the story of Perrot and his companions with extensive refutation of their theology.

Perrot wrote numerous letters and works during his imprisonment, many of which were published after his release in 1661. The most notable were *Battering Rams Against Rome* (1661), a detailed account of his sufferings at the hands of the Roman Catholic authorities, dedicated 'To the tender, moderate, Roman-Catholick reader' (sig. A2r), and *A Sea of the Seed's Sufferings, through which Runs a River of Rich Rejoycing* (1661), an extraordinary series of contemplations and songs in a variety of poetic forms, totalling some 1448 lines. The latter, a significant and unusual example of radical religious writing, indicated that Perrot was well read and familiar with poetic technique, and in its sublimation of his experiences of torture and abuse into a spiritual allegory built out of natural imagery (especially about the sea), the work bears some comparison with Milton's *Paradise Lost*. However, it was an unpublished letter sent from Rome that caused the most immediate sensation within the Quaker movement; in it Perrot argued that—contrary to Quaker practice—men should not remove their hats during prayer.

After a journey through Italy and France that saw Bayly imprisoned in Bourg-d'Ault for confronting some local priests, Perrot returned to England by late July and arrived in London in mid-August. Fox met with him at once in a series of meetings aimed at tempering Perrot's increasingly divergent Quaker views. Perrot was accused of financial extravagance during his mission in the Mediterranean, and his writings, especially his poetry, were regarded as an offence to the principle of plainness; moreover, Fox and other prominent Quakers saw Perrot's stance on hats as vain and lacking in humility, but, as St Paul had indicated that women should cover their head when praying, they found it difficult to oppose Perrot's argument without undermining the traditional Quaker hostility to social forms or appearing fundamentally inequitable. Undaunted, Perrot spent the next few months preaching in London, Canterbury (where he was imprisoned in September), and East Anglia; at some point before the following summer he also made a brief trip to Ireland. However, despite some support from Isaac Penington, Edward Burrough, and John Crook among others, leading Friends were unrelenting in their disapproval of Perrot: his enthusiastic preaching, his growing popularity particularly with women Friends, and even his Rabbinic-like beard reminded them uncomfortably of Nayler. It was averred that he had taken on his ministerial role too soon, a point underlined when Perrot began to hold his own meetings in London which only helped to enhance his reputation as a schismatic. It is also possible that Fox in particular feared Perrot's continuing influence over Quaker Mediterranean missions, for which Perrot continued to find funds for the support of Friends, especially if they had been imprisoned, and acted as mediator between Quakers and Italian Roman Catholics. A meeting between Perrot and senior Quaker figures in London on new year's eve 1661 prompted a final breach. By the time that Perrot was arrested and imprisoned in Newgate in June 1662 for attending a Quaker meeting at the Bull and Mouth in London, he had been roundly condemned by the Quaker leadership.

In return for his release, Perrot agreed to become a voluntary exile in Barbados. He left England with the strong disapproval of Fox, especially after his advocacy of unity among nonconformists—a view sustained by the clustering of several Perrot followers in Barbados. In the summer or autumn of 1663 Perrot visited Maryland and Virginia, where Quakers had been active since 1656, but was rejected by the Friends there who had possibly received warning letters from Fox. In Virginia Perrot advocated following no set or regular times for meetings but only as the spirit willed. In early 1664 he returned to Barbados and on 10 May the governor, Thomas Modyford, appointed him a captain. Thereafter, Perrot was famous for wearing a splendid satin coat and a sword though, more importantly, he received at the same time a 300 ton ship for transporting immigrants to Jamaica. In Barbados and Jamaica he then worked as a court clerk and, despite remaining a Friend, accepted payment for extracting the oaths that the Quakers refused to give. By this time Perrot had become firmly convinced of universalist principles (the belief that redemption is extended to all humankind), but the paper war with Fox continued unabated while others alleged that Perrot had renounced his faith for the sake of profit. Perrot continued to publish occasionally and became associated with Robert Rich, another Quaker separatist and sometime follower of Nayler who had emigrated to Barbados in the immediate aftermath of the Nayler affair. It may be that Perrot fell ill early in 1665 as he was certainly thinking of his death at that time; this finally occurred between 30 August, when he drew up his will, and 7 September 1665, when it was proved. In his will he mentioned a wife, Elizabeth, and two children. However, it was not until the following year, with the publication by eleven senior Quakers in May of the 'Testimony from the brethren', the recantation of several leading Perrot supporters at a London meeting hosted by Fox, and

the establishment of regular monthly and quarterly meetings across the Quaker movement as a whole, that the Perrotian controversy was effectively quelled.

After Perrot's death Rich collected Perrot's letters to Fox and others, and these were published just after Rich's death as *Hidden Things Brought to Light* (1680).

Nigel Smith

Sources DNB · H. J. Cadbury, 'John Perrot in Virginia', *Journal of the Friends' Historical Society*, 31 (1934), 36–7 · H. J. Cadbury, 'John Perrot in Rome: a Jesuit account', *Journal of the Friends' Historical Society*, 31 (1934), 37–8 · E. L. Barnwell, *Perrot notes, or, Some account of the various branches of the Perrot family* (1867) · K. L. Carroll, *John Perrot: early Quaker schismatic* (1971) · N. Smith, *Perfection proclaimed: language and literature in English radical religion, 1640–1660* (1989) · N. Smith, *Literature and revolution in England, 1640–1660* (1994) · H. L. Ingle, *First among Friends: George Fox and the creation of Quakerism* (1994) · N. Smith, 'Exporting enthusiasm: John Perrot and the Quaker epic', *Literature and the English civil war*, ed. T. Healey and J. Sawday (1990), 248–64 · R. Rich, ed., *Hidden things brought to light* (1680)
Archives RS Friends, Lond., letters and material

Perrot, Robert (*c*.1478–1550), church musician and land speculator, was the second son of George Perrot, gentleman, of Haroldston, near Haverfordwest, Pembrokeshire, and Isabel Langdale of Langdale, near Scarborough, Yorkshire. He was born at Hackness, immediately neighbouring Langdale. Of his education and musical training nothing is known, though an early connection with Oxford is rendered conceivable through the possibility that Robert Parret, organ player in 1474–5 of All Saints', Oxford, was of his family. For a suitably talented younger son of gentry stock a career in church music was perfectly honourable in pre-Reformation times, and between Michaelmas 1504 and Michaelmas 1506 Perrot was appointed a lay singing-man of the choir of King's College, Cambridge, and remained so until June 1509. At Michaelmas 1510 he was admitted master of the choristers of Magdalen College, Oxford, where his duties were to train the singing-boys and direct all performances of polyphonic music sung during the chapel services; he did not undertake the duties of organist, which were discharged by a separate individual. On 28 April 1512 he was appointed cantor and master of the lady chapel choir at Durham Cathedral, but chose not to accept; a certain streak of financial opportunism may be perceived in his exploiting this offer merely to negotiate better terms for his remaining at Magdalen.

As a musician Perrot enjoyed much distinction. During 1507–8 he obtained the Cambridge degree of bachelor of music (a non-residential degree generally conferred for expertise in composition), and in February 1516 he supplicated the University of Oxford for admission to the doctorate. This was granted, conditional upon his composing a mass and a companion piece of sacred music. There is no record of the degree having been conferred, and it is probable that Perrot did not proceed; never was he accorded the title 'Doctor' in the Magdalen archives. At Michaelmas 1529 he added to his duties those of chapel organ player. His career at Magdalen appears to have been entirely uneventful, his appearances in the surviving records being of only the most routine kind. No compositions have been preserved.

During 1531–2 Perrot undertook an extraordinary change of occupation. He surrendered his office of master of the choristers, retaining among his chapel duties only those of organist, which—evidently as merely a hobby occupying him for but a few hours per week—he retained for the rest of his life. He ventured upon a new career as a financial agent and speculator in landed property, especially properties formerly mendicant and monastic. Through this he achieved such prosperity that by 1543 he was among the wealthiest of Oxford's taxpayers, dwelling in a large house adjacent to Magdalen College known until the nineteenth century as Perrot's House. Of his first wife, Joan, nothing is known. By 1505 he had married his second wife, Alice Gardiner (c.1487–1557), the daughter of a minor family of Berkshire/Oxfordshire gentry; they had seven sons and six daughters. Having made his will on 18 April, he died aged seventy-two 'or thereabouts', at Oxford, probably at his home, on 20 April 1550. He was buried in the north aisle of the parish church of St Peter-in-the-East, Oxford, where once stood a memorial window depicting 'Robertus Porret, Bacalaureus Musices', kneeling at his devotions. He bequeathed numerous properties and leases, all located in Oxford and its immediate vicinity.

Perhaps through lack of sympathy with the Edwardian Reformation, Perrot made no bequest to Magdalen College. However, the restoration of Catholicism under Mary I gave his widow the opportunity in 1555 to found in his memory exhibitions for two poor scholars, and both an annual obit and twice-weekly intercessory prayers in the college chapel. In recognition of Robert's service as master of the choristers, special financial provision was made for the attendance of the boys and their master at his obit, and stringent penalties upon the college attended any failure to pay. In consequence of the abolition of the Latin service (1559), the terms of Alice Perrot's provisions had eventually to be reformulated. She had died on 1 May 1557, and it seems entirely likely that Magdalen College's annual 'May morning' observance by the choristers and their master on top of Magdalen tower, picturesque and now very celebrated, has its origin in a post-Reformation secularization of Alice Perrot's memorial benefaction for her husband. ROGER BOWERS

Sources Magd. Oxf. · King's Cam. · Emden, *Oxf.*, 4.442 · E. L. Barnwell, *Perrot notes, or, Some account of the various branches of the Perrot family* (1867), 4, 79–90, 194–5, 205–6 · T. Warton, *The life of Sir Thomas Pope, founder of Trinity College, Oxford*, 2nd edn (1780), 339–65 · J. R. Bloxam, *A register of the presidents, fellows … of Saint Mary Magdalen College*, 8 vols. (1853–85), vol. 2, pp. 182–7 · *VCH Oxfordshire*, 4.96–7, 106, 111, 269 · C. F. Abdy Williams, *A short historical account of the degrees in music at Oxford and Cambridge* [1893], 66, 121 · H. E. Salter, ed., *A cartulary of the Hospital of St John the Baptist*, 1, OHS, 69 (1914), 149 · *The life and times of Anthony Wood*, ed. A. Clark, 3, OHS, 26 (1894), 181–2, 254 · *The antient and present state of the city of Oxford* (1773), 46, 81 · H. E. Salter, ed., *Surveys and tokens*, OHS, 75 (1923), 142 · F. L. Harrison, 'Music at Oxford before 1500', *Hist. U. Oxf. 2: Late med. Oxf.*, 347–71

Archives Trinity College, Oxford, MS collection, 'The Perrot register'

Wealth at death considerable; bequeathed leases in Oxford and its vicinity, including Binsey, Horspath rectory, and North Stoke; property in Long Hanborough, Stonesfield, Woodstock (Oxfordshire), and Harwell (Berkshire): will, 1550, Bloxam, *Register*, 2.184–6

Perrott, Sir Richard, second baronet (1716–1796), army officer, was reportedly born in Shrewsbury, Shropshire, the eldest son of Richard Perrott of Broseley, Shropshire, and his wife, Rebecca, the daughter of J. Wyke of Wacton Court, Herefordshire, and was probably a descendant of the church musician and land speculator Robert Perrot (c.1478–1550). Reliable information on Richard Perrott is sparse: the few sources provide the following account. He succeeded his uncle Sir Robert Perrott, first baronet (created 1 July 1716), diplomatist, in 1759. He was present at the battle of Culloden (16 April 1746) in personal attendance on William Augustus, duke of Cumberland. Later he entered the service of Frederick II of Prussia, served in the Seven Years' War (1756–63), and was awarded the order of the Red Eagle. In October 1758 Frederick appointed Perrott lord high admiral with authority to establish a fleet, but the British government vetoed the appointment. Frederick used him in secret negotiations and awarded him the order of the Black Eagle, and Louis XIV created him a baron. In 1770, during the Wilkite disturbances, Perrott brought up the loyal Flint address and was thanked by the king. His support for the latter led to a mob demolishing his house at Gloucester View, Park Lane, London, and burning its costly contents in front of it. He was awarded a medal, a grant of the manor of Cheslemore, and other marks of royal approbation. On 3 March 1782 he married Margaret Jemima, the daughter of Captain William Fordyce, gentleman of the bedchamber to George III, and the great-grandniece of Archibald Campbell, first duke of Argyll. Their son Edward Bindloss Perrott succeeded as third baronet at Perrott's death in 1796. The baronetcy became extinct on the death of the sixth baronet, Sir Herbert Charles Perrott, on 15 February 1922.

In 1770 the scandalous and polemical *The Life, Adventures, and Amours of Sir R— P—* was published anonymously in London. It criticized the duke of Grafton for making 'such a wretch' as Perrott his 'newly created favourite' and alleged that Perrott was an adventurer of obscure origin, a thief, confidence trickster, and heartless reprobate, who was briefly in the slave trade. It also said that he befriended a rich widow, cheated her, and seduced and left pregnant both her and her daughter; the former went mad and the latter died in a workhouse. Attempting an elopement, he took 'some rather alarming liberties' with his victim, so she rejected him. Exploiting his baronetcy and Prussian knighthood to impress the gullible, after further cheating, attempts to marry heiresses, and 'breaches of honour and hospitality', he became Grafton's protégé through a mistress, a Sadler's Wells rope dancer. The biography of 1770 may have been 'an ebullition of private malice' (*DNB*). ROGER T. STEARN

Sources Burke, *Peerage* (1857); (1879); (1924) · *DNB* · Boase, *Mod. Eng. biog.* · *The life, adventures, and amours of Sir R— P—, who so recently had the honour to present the F— address at the English court* (1770) ·

G. Rudé, *Wilkes and liberty: a social study of 1763 to 1774* (1962) · P. D. G. Thomas, *John Wilkes: a friend to liberty* (1996)
Likenesses V. Green, mezzotint, pubd 1770, BM, NPG

Perry, Charles (1698/9–1730). *See under* Perry, Charles (d. 1780).

Perry, Charles (d. **1780**), traveller and medical writer, studied medicine at Leiden and graduated from Utrecht on 5 February 1723. Between 1739 and 1742 he travelled in France and Italy, and in the Middle East he visited Constantinople, Egypt, Palestine, and Greece. On his return he published a *View of the Levant, particularly of Constantinople, Syria, Egypt and Greece in which their antiquities, government, politics, maxims, manners and customs … are described* (1743). This was an important early work on Egypt; it contained much interesting information particularly on Upper Egypt, which until then was relatively little known. The handsome volume was illustrated with thirty-three fine plates engraved by George Bickham the younger, a noted contemporary engraver. In the preface Perry admitted to having bought some representations of the carvings, though he did verify their accuracy in person. The scale plans of various temples were, however, his own work. The work was dedicated to John Montagu, fourth earl of Sandwich, whom he had met in the Levant; he, like Perry, made something of a name for himself as a traveller and antiquary, bringing back new information from the region. Through Sandwich, who evidently continued to notice Perry after their return, Perry's volume attracted a large and distinguished list of subscribers. In it he described a mummy which was later acquired by Richard Cosway, and then by Thomas Joseph Pettigrew, who in turn described it in his *History of Egyptian Mummies* (1834). Perry's *View* was translated into German and reissued in English.

Perry practised as a physician in Norwich and perhaps Canterbury after his return to Britain in 1742, and both before and after his visit to the Middle East published extensively on medical subjects, particularly on spa waters. Perry died in 1780 and was buried at the east end of the nave of Norwich Cathedral. His elder brother was buried in 1795 near to him.

This Charles Perry has been often confused with a second **Charles Perry** (1698/9–1730), physician, who was born in Norwich and baptized there in the church of St Peter Mancroft on 23 October 1699 and was the younger son of John Perry, a Norwich attorney, and his wife, Francis. He spent four years at Mr Pate's school in Norwich and four years following at Mr Tuke's school at Bishop's Stortford, Hertfordshire. On 28 May 1717 he was admitted at Gonville and Caius College, Cambridge, as a pensioner, was a scholar in 1717–22, and graduated MB in 1722 and MD in 1727. He was a junior fellow of the college from Michaelmas 1723 to his death. He practised in Norwich and Cambridge. His will was dated 4 March 1730 and was proved at Norwich on 18 December 1730. In it he expressed his wish to be buried with his father in St Peter Mancroft, Norwich. ELIZABETH BAIGENT

Sources Venn, *Alum. Cant.* · J. Venn and others, eds., *Biographical history of Gonville and Caius College*, 8 vols. (1897–1998), vol. 1; vol. 2, p. 8 · W. R. Dawson and E. P. Uphill, *Who was who in Egyptology*, 3rd edn, rev. M. L. Bierbrier (1995) · P. J. Wallis and R. V. Wallis, *Eighteenth century medics*, 2nd edn (1988) · IGI

Perry, Charles (1807–1891), bishop of Melbourne, was born on 17 February 1807, the third son of John Perry of Harlow, sheriff of Essex and shipbuilder, and his second wife, Mary (*née* Green). After Harrow School (1819–23) Charles followed his brothers to Trinity College, Cambridge; he graduated BA (1828) with first-class honours as senior wrangler, seventh classic, and first Smith's prizeman. He began legal studies at the Inner Temple in London in 1828 but returned to Trinity after his health collapsed in 1831; he had already qualified for a Trinity fellowship in 1829 and he graduated MA in 1831, and was a tutor between 1832 and 1840.

Perry's assiduous attendance at Trinity College chapel reflected a strong maternal religious influence, and later his introduction to wider evangelical circles helped to clarify his religious uncertainties. Perry sought ordination and was made deacon by Bishop J. H. Monk of Gloucester on 16 June 1833; he was ordained priest on 26 November 1836 by Bishop J. Allen of Ely. To academic duties Perry added pastoral enterprise: he bought the advowson to St Andrew-the-Less, Cambridgeshire, and built two churches—Christchurch, Barnwell (1839), and St Paul's New Town (1842), of which he became the first vicar in 1845. In 1840 he resigned his Trinity fellowship to marry Frances (1815–1892), daughter of Samuel Cooper, a Hull merchant. They married on 14 October 1841; there were no children.

Perry advocated the Church Missionary Society (CMS) and better theological education within English universities; this attracted attention, and Lord Grey, then colonial secretary, followed the recommendation of the CMS secretary, Henry Venn, to nominate Perry to the new see of Melbourne. Archbishop Howley agreed, and Perry was consecrated in Westminster Abbey on 29 June 1847, along with William Tyrrell (Newcastle, New South Wales), Augustus Short (Adelaide), and Robert Gray (Cape Town). Perry was installed in St James's pro-cathedral on 28 January 1848, and his letters patent designated Melbourne a city and made his territorial jurisdiction coterminous with Victoria (which was given self-government in 1851). The population of his diocese was 43,000, and half was Anglican, served by three clergy. Perry's extensive use of lay readers attracted criticism but it helped to remedy severe shortages of clergy and funds.

Perry's legal training soon gauged the limits of applying the English established church's laws, which he had inherited along with the religious pluralism of the new British settlement. Exercising his potentially despotic powers as a colonial bishop rendered him vulnerable to criticism by ardent local democrats. In urging fellow bishops and home authorities to modify the church laws, he argued that the Anglican laity warranted a greater (if unaccustomed) share both in parochial appointments and

Charles Perry (1807–1891), by Samuel Alexander Walker, pubd 1890

in their denomination's wider government. Here he disagreed with his metropolitan, Bishop Broughton of Sydney, but found a strong ally in Bishop Selwyn of New Zealand. Six Australasian bishops met in Sydney in October 1850 to promote greater colonial church self-government, though they disagreed on how to achieve it. Accused of Erastianism, Perry recommended that colonial church constitutions be based on imperial or local legislation rather than on consensual compact alone. After the Commons rejected Archbishop Sumner's Church Regulation Bill (1853), Perry incorporated its provisions into a bill exclusively for the Church of England in Victoria. It passed Victoria's legislative council in November 1854, and Perry and his wife then brought it to England, where it received royal assent on 12 December 1855. The bill became a model, giving many Australian and Canadian dioceses a legislative autonomy that still kept them an integral part of the Church of England, fully sharing in its standards of faith, order, and discipline.

During Perry's episcopate, responsibility for education in Victoria shifted from church to state. Perry disliked the state system, which minimized religious education, yet he recognized how rival denominational schools misused scarce resources. Personally preferring a voluntary system for supporting both clergy and schools, he publicly conceded that the survival of Anglican parishes and schools depended on state aid. Victoria abolished state aid

between 1872 and 1875; many Anglican elementary day schools closed. Perry's own diocese, with its active synod, at first struggled for financial survival, but then grew solidly, and his greatest contribution to education in Victoria lay in establishing Melbourne grammar school (1849) and Geelong grammar school (1857) to train young male colonial leaders in sound liberal learning and the Christian faith. Perry also encouraged the foundation of Trinity College at Melbourne's university in 1860.

The discovery of gold in August 1851 transformed Victoria (its population increased tenfold between 1850 and 1860) and reinforced Perry's drive for church self-government to help the church to adapt. Acclimatization had limits, and Perry's churchmanship and sense of Anglican order frustrated his laity's wish to co-operate with the presbyterians in sustaining ministry in a vast rural hinterland. By 1869, however, the diocese warranted subdivision, its 113 clergy, 162 churches, and 75 parsonages reflecting wider support than state aid or Perry's pocket could ever have given. The bishopric of Ballarat goldfields became financially viable, and Perry and his wife left for England in 1874, ostensibly to help choose its new bishop. Samuel Thornton was appointed. In 1876 Perry resigned the Melbourne see, and helped to find his own successor, James Moorhouse, and to consecrate him on 22 October 1876.

In 1878 Perry became Bishop Selwyn's successor as prelate of the Order of St Michael and St George. He was also appointed a residential canon of Llandaff Cathedral and was an active CMS vice-president and a committee member of both the Society for the Propagation of the Gospel and the Society for the Promotion of Christian Knowledge; between 1874 and 1888 he regularly and earnestly advocated colonial and evangelical viewpoints at church congresses. His upbringing and later evangelical conviction made him abhor 'Romanism' and regard Anglo-Catholic ritualism as corrupting, opposed to the literal meaning of the articles and the prayer book, contrary to law, and subversive of church unity and growth. Concerned for the reformed Catholic, or protestant, character of his former diocese, his attempts to impose doctrinal tests on potential successors angered Archbishop Benson and other nominators in 1886. Never obscurantist, Perry's sermons openly discussed biblical criticism and scientific issues, and seeking an informed clergy he had helped to found Ridley Hall, Cambridge, in 1881, and chaired its council, submitting its new members to doctrinal tests.

Perry's church statesmanship regarded respect for court-interpreted church law as the necessary bond of Anglican unity and integrity. Accordingly he opposed Bishop Gray of Cape Town in 1869 in the latter's determination to flout privy council decisions by appointing a successor to Bishop Colenso in Natal. However, his adamant doctrinal and ecclesial convictions made Perry unpopular and isolated, and his strong intellect and opinions went unmatched by force of personality. His stern exterior nevertheless concealed affection and a willingness to sacrifice personal interests for higher goals. Scrupulously impartial, he rarely nursed bitterness, and his moral example remained unquestioned.

Perry died on 2 December 1891 at his home at 33 Avenue Road, Regent's Park, London, and was buried three days later at Harlow, Essex. His widow Frances died exactly twelve months afterwards.

ROBERT S. M. WITHYCOMBE

Sources A. Q. Robin, *Charles Perry, bishop of Melbourne: the challenges of a colonial episcopate, 1847–76* (1967) · A. Q. Robin, 'Perry, Charles', *AusDB*, vol. 5 · LPL, archbishops' MSS [especially Howley, Longley, Tait, Benson] · G. Goodman, *The church in Victoria* (1892) · G. R. Quaife, 'Money and men: aspects of the Anglican crisis in Victoria, 1850–65', *Journal of Religious History*, 5 (1968–9), 45–61 · F. Perry, *Australian sketches: the journals and letters of Frances Perry*, ed. A. de Q. Robin (1983) · *The Times* (6 Dec 1892)
Archives NRA, priv. coll. | CUL, letters to Sir George Stokes · LPL, corresp. with first earl of Selborne · LPL, Howley MSS · LPL, Longley MSS · LPL, corresp. with A. C. Tait · LPL, Benson MSS · Melbourne Diocesan Registry, bishop of Melbourne's MSS · NL Aus., Bishop Broughton's letters · Trinity Cam., corresp. with William Whewell · U. Durham, corresp. with third Earl Grey · United Society for the Propagation of the Gospel, London, bishop of Melbourne's letters
Likenesses print, 1851? (after wood-engraving by HE), NL Aus. · engraving, *c*.1855, repro. in Robin, *Charles Perry*, frontispiece · photograph, 1858, repro. in Robin, *Charles Perry*, 119 · medallions, *c*.1870 (with his wife Frances), Royal Women's Hospital, Melbourne; repro. in Robin, *Charles Perry*, 151 · photograph, 1872, State Library of Victoria, Melbourne; repro. in Robin, *Charles Perry*, 266 · print, 1874? (after wood-engraving by S. Calvert), NL Aus. · S. A. Walker, photograph, pubd 1890, NPG [*see illus.*] · H. Weigall, oils, State Library of Victoria, Melbourne, La Trobe picture collection
Wealth at death £46,627 10s. 4d.: resworn probate, 1892/3, *CGPLA Eng. & Wales*

Perry, Sir (Edwin) Cooper (1856–1938), physician and medical administrator, was born at Castle Bromwich, Warwickshire, on 10 September 1856, the only son of Edwin Cresswell Perry (1828–1899), who became vicar of Seighford, Staffordshire, in 1861, and his wife, Esther Cooper, daughter of Joseph Cockram, of Darlaston, Staffordshire. Perry's father, an all-round scholar and mathematician, was responsible for his entire education until he was thirteen. Then in 1870 Perry won a scholarship at Eton College, where he became head of school and was awarded the Newcastle scholarship in 1876. He left that year to become a scholar of King's College, Cambridge, where he gained the Bell university scholarship (1876), the Browne scholarship and medal (1878), and the Pitt scholarship (1879); he was senior classic in the tripos of 1880. While at Cambridge he was joint editor with A. H. Mann, the organist of King's, of the King's College anthem book, revised between 1879 and 1882.

In 1880, having been elected into a fellowship at his college, Perry set aside classics and the prospect of a career in the church to become a medical student. In 1883 he was appointed assistant lecturer in medical subjects at King's and assistant demonstrator of anatomy in the Cambridge medical school. In 1885 he entered the London Hospital; he qualified MRCS in October, and in 1886–7 held the posts of house surgeon to Frederick Treves and house physician to Stephen Mackenzie. In 1887 his fellowship ran out and Perry was appointed an assistant physician, demonstrator

of morbid anatomy, and physician to the dermatological department at Guy's Hospital, London. In the following year he became dean of the medical school. Now his formidable administrative energies came into play, and he reorganized the system of junior appointments and built a residential medical college for the students, of which he became the first warden. In conjunction with Frederick Newland-Pedley he was responsible for the establishment in 1889 of a dental school at Guy's. Even while primarily an administrator he retained his skill as a physician, and he acted as examiner on several subjects for the London, Cambridge, and the Conjoint boards.

Perry married in 1890 Caroline Matilda (*d*. 1935), second daughter of James MacManus, of Killeaden House, Kiltimagh, co. Mayo; they had one daughter. In 1892, on the death of John Charles Steele, he was appointed superintendent of Guy's Hospital, an office which he held until 1920; he was a governor of the hospital from 1920 to 1937. Perry went twice to Egypt, in 1897 and 1926, in order to assist in the reorganization of the teaching of medicine in the University of Cairo; on the second occasion he became director of the faculty of medicine, in his seventy-first year. Also in 1897 Perry was appointed one of the first visitors for the Prince of Wales's Hospital Fund (later King Edward's Hospital Fund); he served for many years as a member of its distribution committee and was its chairman from 1921 until his death. He was appointed GCVO in 1935 in recognition of his services to the fund.

Perry was elected in 1900 to the senate of the University of London as a representative of the faculty of medicine. He resigned in 1905 but was re-elected in 1915. From 1917 to 1919 he was vice-chancellor, and in 1920, on retiring from Guy's, he was appointed principal of the university; he held this post until 1926. In 1929 he became a member of the committee which redrafted the statutes of the university and he was a crown member of the court from 1930 until his death. In 1916 he was involved with the initiative that led to the formation of the College of Nursing. In accordance with the recommendations of the Athlone committee on postgraduate medical education in London, in 1921, he took a leading part in the foundation of the London School of Hygiene and Tropical Medicine, instituted by royal charter in 1924, and for many years he was the chairman of the council.

After the Second South African War, Perry served on a commission appointed to reorganize the Army Medical Service. For his assistance in helping to found the Royal Army Medical College at Millbank he was knighted, in 1903. He received the honorary degree of LLD from the University of London and that of MD from the University of Egypt.

At the end of 1938 Perry suffered a complete right-sided paralysis and he died at his home, Seighford, 25 Mill Road, West Worthing, twelve days later, on 17 December. His body was cremated and his ashes were interred in the church of his old home at Seighford, Staffordshire.

Perry's life was full and many-sided. A classical scholar, a musician, a sound physician and morbid anatomist, and an administrator of unusual quality, he would have made an ideal civil servant. Weighty, wise, deliberate in judgement, knowing just when to wait and watch and when to take decisive action, he could draft a document that could be subtle without deceit, and uncompromising yet courteous. He was a master of concise and lucid English prose. When in doubt as to the clarity of a sentence he had a habit of translating it into the more compact confines of Latin and then retranslating it.

Perry was little known to the public, for he was shy and had few social gifts. He cared little who received the credit for any task as long as it was done, usually by himself. He published practically nothing; his life's work is embodied in minutes, memoranda, and charters. Those who worked behind the scenes knew his value, his intellect, and his constructive capacity. 'Bulky, even ungainly, in figure, he was possessed of the most dextrous fingers. No one who ever saw him perform an autopsy could doubt it' (Cameron, 302).   H. L. Eason, *rev.* Patrick Wallis

Sources Munk, *Roll* · Venn, *Alum. Cant.* · H. C. Cameron, *Mr Guy's Hospital, 1726–1948* (1954) · H. A. Ripman, ed., *Guy's Hospital, 1725–1948* (1951) · *WWW, 1929–40* · *The Lancet* (24 Dec 1938) · *BMJ* (24 Dec 1938), 1339–40 · *The Times* (19 Dec 1938) · B. Abel-Smith, *A history of the nursing profession* (1960) · F. K. Prochaska, *Philanthropy and the hospitals of London: the King's Fund, 1897–1990* (1992) · private information (1949) · personal knowledge (1949) · *CGPLA Eng. & Wales* (1939)

Archives Bodl. Oxf., corresp. with Sir Henry Burdett

Wealth at death £30,806 1s. 9d.: probate, 23 Jan 1939, *CGPLA Eng. & Wales*

Perry [*née* Everett], **Frances Mary** (1907–1993), horticulturist, was born on 19 February 1907 at Bulls Cross, Enfield, Middlesex, the daughter of Richard Albert Everett, journeyman plumber, and his wife, Isabel Kate, *née* Hewitt. Enfield then was still a rural village and the family lived among fields and pastures where Frances grew up as a young countrywoman. Their next-door neighbour was the distinguished plantsman and vice-president of the Royal Horticultural Society (RHS), E. A. Bowles, and it was largely his influence that set Frances Everett on her life's work. When as a young girl she took him wild flowers for identification, Bowles encouraged her in horticulture, speaking of her as 'one of my boys' (*The Times*, 13 Oct 1993). Until very late in her life Enfield was the centre of Frances Perry's activities. She attended Enfield county school and then Swanley Horticultural College (an institution that was later to become famous as Wye College, part of the University of London, but in her day was for women only) where she received the diploma in horticulture.

Frances Everett's first paid employment was at the Hardy Plant Farm, owned by Amos Perry, and in 1930 she married his son, Gerald (d. 1964), also a horticulturist. They had two sons, one of whom died young in an accident. Within eight years of starting work with Perry, she published *Water Gardening*, the first of four books on the subject and one which is still read for its authority. In 1943 she was appointed horticultural organizer for agricultural and horticultural education for Middlesex county council, a position she occupied for ten years until 1953 when she was invited to apply for the post of principal of Norwood

Frances Mary Perry (1907–1993), by unknown photographer, 1966

Hall Institute and College of Horticulture, where she remained until her retirement fourteen years later.

Frances Perry began a long and intimate association with the RHS during her early days with the Perry nursery, and at a time when women were still relative strangers to the world of plant shows, at least as exhibitors. Women visitors dressed as if for Ascot and men wore grey morning suits. She became a regular and very familiar figure at RHS events, with her gently smiling but ever so slightly steely face and, as years passed, an unmistakable shock of white hair, the sight of which in a crowd always presaged the sound of the slightly rustic burr and the countrywoman's style of straight talking that never left her. She was appointed MBE for her services to horticulture in 1962, and this was followed by the RHS Veitch memorial medal in 1964; the crown, as so often, was ahead of the RHS with such recognition.

The Victoria medal of honour arrived in 1971, a justly deserved accolade but one that was undoubtedly facilitated by the events of 1968 when Frances Perry became the first woman ever to join the RHS council, a formidably male bastion for all of its previous 164 years. The events that preceded this election have become part of horticultural folklore. A vigorous correspondence and a leading article in *The Times* had fiercely debated the absence of women from the council. When Frances Perry was subsequently proposed for election to the council by Roy Hay, and then invited to join by the president, Lord Aberconway, she responded: 'If you want me because I am a woman, the answer is no, but if you want me because of anything I have done in horticulture, the answer is yes'

(*The Times*, 13 Oct 1993). Later she became a vice-president of the society, and her expertise was also recognized in the award of the Sara Francis Chapman medal of the Garden Club of America in 1971. She travelled widely to lecture and to study, and acquired a deep knowledge of tropical plants (she published her book *Flowers of the World* in 1972). In her travels she gained the admiration of gardeners internationally and also took great pride in her son Roger, a zoologist, becoming director of the Charles Darwin Research Centre in the Galápagos Islands.

In addition to her nineteen books (she was working on a twentieth at the time of her death), Frances Perry was an active journalist. She became the gardening correspondent of *The Observer* early in the 1970s and continued the column for about twenty years. Her articles were models of clarity and information, and displayed that rare quality of being of interest to experienced and inexperienced gardeners alike. She had an endearing turn of phrase: the day-lily, for example, she called one of 'the rentpayers of the garden' (Perry, 'Herbaceous plants'). The broadcasting media also recognized her abilities and she contributed regularly to both radio and television, most famously to the radio programme *Home Grown*, presented by Roy Hay and Fred Streeter and broadcast in the two o'clock slot on Sunday afternoon that was later to be occupied by *Gardeners' Question Time*.

Gerald Perry died in 1964 and thirteen years later, on 27 July 1977, much to the pleasure of their many horticultural friends, Frances Perry married her long-time colleague and champion, Robert Edwin (Roy) *Hay (1910–1989). They continued to live in Enfield, their own garden well stocked and a conservatory packed with the exotica that continued to fascinate them both. The garden was enlivened by their fondness for such gadgets as chain-driven devices to raise and lower hanging baskets. Roy Hay died in 1989, and only then and with failing health did Frances Perry leave her beloved Enfield to live with her son and his family in the exquisite Devon village of Lustleigh, where she continued to pursue her interests in photography and flower postage stamps. She still worked tirelessly to support the garden at Capel Manor Horticultural College, close by her old Enfield home, which she had championed against the intentions of Enfield council in the 1960s. She died in Lustleigh on 11 October 1993.

STEFAN BUCZACKI

Sources *The Times* (13 Oct 1993) · *The Independent* (15 Oct 1993) · personal knowledge (2004) · private information (2004) · b. cert. · *WWW*, 1996–2000 · F. Perry, 'Herbaceous plants in the modern garden', *Home grown*, ed. R. Hay (1956), 17–24
Archives SOUND BL NSA
Likenesses photograph, 1966, Royal Horticultural Society, Lindley Library [*see illus.*] · J. Wildgoose, photograph, repro. in *The Independent* · photograph, repro. in *The Times*
Wealth at death under £125,000: probate, 1993, *CGPLA Eng. & Wales*

Perry, Francis (*d.* 1765), engraver, was born at Abingdon, Berkshire, and apprenticed to a hosier, but, showing some aptitude for art, he was placed first with one of the Vanderbanks, and afterwards with Richardson, to study painting. Having made no progress in this he became clerk to a

commissary, whom he accompanied to Lichfield, and there made drawings of the cathedral, which he subsequently etched. Eventually he devoted himself to drawing and engraving topographical views and antiquities, working chiefly for magazines. He engraved two views of the cloisters of St Katharine by the Tower for Dr A. C. Ducarel's paper of 1790 on that church in Nichols's *Bibliotheca Topographica Britannica*, *A Collection of Eighteen Views of Antiquities in the County of Kent*, and portraits of Matthew Hutton, archbishop of York; of Dr Ducarel, after A. Soldi; and of Dr Thomas Hyde, after Cipriani.

Perry is best known, however, for his engravings of coins and medals, which he executed with great neatness and accuracy. The sixteen plates in Ducarel's *Anglo-Gallic Coins* (1757) are by Perry, and he also worked for the numismatist Thomas Snelling. In 1762 he began publication of a series of gold and silver British medals, of which three parts, containing ten plates, appeared before his death and a fourth posthumously. In 1764 he exhibited with the Free Society of Artists his print of Dr Hyde and a pen-and-ink view at Walworth. Perry had the use of only one eye and habitually etched on a white ground, which facilitated his working by candlelight. Though painstaking and industrious he could only earn a precarious living. At the time of his death, on 3 January 1765, he was unmarried and living in Carter Lane, south of St Paul's Cathedral. He was buried in Bunhill Fields on 7 January. His prints, coins, and medals, and some china were auctioned on 8 April, his estate being administered by a cousin.

F. M. O'DONOGHUE, *rev.* ANITA MCCONNELL

Sources Redgrave, *Artists* · J. Strutt, *A biographical dictionary, containing an historical account of all the engravers, from the earliest period of the art of engraving to the present time*, 2 vols. (1785–6) · H. Bromley, *A catalogue of engraved British portraits* (1793) · burials at Bunhill Fields, PRO, RG4/4654 · admon, PRO, PROB 6/141, fol. 309r
Wealth at death earned a precarious living; prints, coins, medals, and china auctioned after death

Perry, Frederick John [Fred] (1909–1995), lawn tennis player, was born on 18 May 1909 at 33 Carrington Road, Stockport, the son of Samuel Frederick Perry (1877–1954), a cotton spinner and lay preacher, and his first wife, Hannah Birch (*d.* 1930). His father became the first secretary of the Co-operative Party in 1918, and was Co-operative and Labour MP from 1920 to 1931. The family moved to London and lived in the Brentham Garden Suburb, near Ealing, and Fred Perry attended the Ealing county school. There he played the usual team games of cricket and football, but one of the crazes of the 1920s was the revival of table tennis, which Fred practised alone, having pushed the kitchen table up against a wall. He also joined the YMCA, where the game was popular, and soon became a seriously good player: with C. H. Bull he won the English open men's doubles title three years in succession between 1928 and 1930. The year 1929 was something of an *annus mirabilis* on the table for Perry: he also won the English open mixed doubles with Miss W. H. Land and the world championship in Budapest. But by then he was being distracted by his growing interest in lawn tennis.

On a family holiday in Eastbourne in 1924 Perry had

stumbled on the game in Devonshire Park. His father encouraged him by giving him an old racket and soon he was playing on the courts of the Brentham Institute and practising hard. One of the Brentham members was dressing-room supervisor at the Queen's Club and, seeing Perry's potential, helped him to join a better club, the Herga in Harrow. He quickly reached the final of the Middlesex junior championships and others began to take notice, among them A. R. Summers. He worked for the Slazenger sports goods company and not only arranged for Perry to benefit from their equipment but also became the young player's tennis adviser. Perry also joined the superior Chiswick Park club and was soon selected to play for Middlesex.

By this time Perry was working, first for the English and Scottish Joint Co-operative Wholesale Society in the tea department, and later for the sports goods manufacturers and retailers Spaldings. But it was tennis on which he was concentrating all his spare time and much of his energy. In 1929 he qualified for Wimbledon, where he lost to the former public schoolboy John Olliff. The year 1930 was a turning point. Spaldings refused him time off to play in the British hard court championships. His father agreed to support him for a year while he tried to reach the top in what was still an amateur sport. It involved paying out at least £10 a week for entrance fees, fares, and hotel expenses. Sam Perry had also promised his son £100 if he abstained from alcoholic drink before he was twenty-one. In May 1930 Perry collected the sum. Again he had to qualify for Wimbledon, where he knocked out the fourth seed, Umberto de Morpurgo, on the same day that the selection committee of the Lawn Tennis Association (LTA) was choosing a four-man British team to play in tournaments in North and South America. He took the last place. His next match was his first on the centre court but he lost in five sets to Colin Gregory.

The final recognition of Perry as one of the best players in British tennis came in 1931, when he was selected to play in the Davis cup. Moreover the Great Britain team reached the final against a French squad which was in the middle of a six-year winning streak. Though beaten by three matches to two, Perry played impressively. Nineteen thirty-one was the first of twenty Davis cup matches he played for the British team, winning 34 out of 38 singles and 11 out of 14 doubles. Two years later Great Britain defeated France in Paris in the final 3–2, with Perry winning the deciding rubber. It had become a tradition for large crowds to welcome home the FA cup winners, but an astonishing 10,000 turned up at Victoria Station to carry the tennis players on their shoulders in triumph. George V sent a message of congratulation. The team of Austin, Hughes, Lee, and Perry retained the Davis cup for the next three years. The British have never won it since.

Nineteen thirty-three was probably Fred Perry's greatest year in tennis, although 1934 ran it close. Not only was he a member of a winning Davis cup team, he also won the first of his three American championships by beating the Australian Jack Crawford in five sets. This was the first time for thirty years that the title had been won by a Briton. Moreover Crawford had already won the Australian, French, and Wimbledon championships and led Perry by two sets to one at Forest Hills. Perry won the last two sets for the loss of only one game. In 1934 Perry won Wimbledon for the first time, the US title again, and the Australian championship together with the men's doubles. He won the British hard court championship for the third year in succession. In 1935 he won the French title and Wimbledon again and in 1936 he completed a hat-trick of Wimbledon wins, won the American championship for a third time, and was the beaten finalist in Paris.

Frederick John Perry (1909–1995), by Edward G. Malindine, 1935 [playing against Godfried Von Cramm in the men's singles final at Wimbledon on 5 July 1935]

Remarkably, Perry seems to have transferred unchanged on to the courts the strokes he played on the table tennis table. The flicked forehand and the stabbed backhand became the running forehand and the sliced backhand down the line. Both were the result of hours of practice. His trademark running forehand was adapted from the game of the French wizard Henri Cochet and he spent months of practice, in 1929–30, at taking the ball early. He was also very fast about the court and very fit when it was not fashionable to be so in amateur sports, especially in Britain. These qualities enabled him to reach many drop shots and retrieve many lobs. But allied to speed, strength, stamina, and a good technique were those mental qualities which were coming to be recognized as essential in the make-up of any champion. He had a powerful will to win and was very confident, keen to exploit any psychological edge or weakness of an opponent. He was not a 'gentleman', and his lack of social polish when added to his obvious love of victory did not always go down well in the snobbery-flecked world of British tennis. He was fond of telling how after his first Wimbledon win, against Jack Crawford, he overheard while in the shower a Wimbledon committee member congratulate Crawford and then say 'the best man didn't win today'. The traditional club tie, normally presented to the winner, was left lying over the back of a chair for Perry to collect. Perry admitted later that he could be bloody-minded, but he was from the wrong side of the tracks in a sport which in Britain had already erected social barriers to entry. For a man born into the working class to win Wimbledon in 1934 was like a mongrel winning Crufts.

Perry turned professional in 1936. He needed the money, although it meant going to America where the only serious professional game existed. America also appeared to be more welcoming to talent whatever its origins and offered a lifestyle which he had sampled on his visits and came to enjoy, particularly in California and Florida. He played against a small group of challenging Americans: Bill Tilden, Ellsworth Vines, and Donald Budge. With Vines he bought in 1937 a major interest in the Beverly Hills tennis club, which mainly attracted a rich show business clientele. In the following year he took American citizenship. During the Second World War he served as a physical training and rehabilitation officer in the United States Air Force.

None of this helped to improve Perry's relationship with the British tennis establishment. He visited Britain to play in the professional championship sponsored by Slazenger, winning it for the third time in 1951, but it was played at Wembley rather than Wimbledon. In 1947, in an attempt to promote the recovery of British tennis after the war, the Slazenger company sponsored a visit to Britain during which Perry played exhibitions with Dan Maskell. The two toured the country with a tennis roadshow, trying to stimulate interest in the sport, especially among the children of the less well off, but entrenched attitudes in the clubs and associations made it a thankless task. He later worked with British Davis cup teams but his position as manager was ended after ten months in 1963 because

the only non-player to be allowed on the court during a match had to be an amateur. This was only five years before Wimbledon opened its courts to professionals.

If his career as a player was winding down after the war, Perry's role as businessman and commentator developed rapidly. In 1950 Perry met a Leicester businessman, Theodore Wegner. The eventual outcome was Fred Perry Sportswear, with what became the famous green laurel wreath emblem borrowed from the embroidered silk ribbon given to winners of the Wimbledon mixed doubles. Some of the earliest sweatbands were produced by the firm but it was the shirts which became a popular fashion item even attracting the 'mods' of the 1970s and 1980s. The business did so well that Perry and Wegner sold their interest in it to Charles McIntosh in 1961. It was later acquired by the Figgie Corporation of Cleveland, Ohio, with Perry continuing to play an important role in advertising and marketing. To later generations the Perry name was better known for the sportswear than the tennis.

On the other hand Perry's role as expert summarizer for BBC radio during the Wimbledon fortnight, the only time when the British really care about tennis, brought his informal and pungent verdicts to a wide audience. Delivered with an American accent but with English irony, his comments provoked up to sixty letters a day from listeners in the 1980s and 1990s. He could be severe about the modern game, and once pointed out that in spite of the improvements in fitness and technique, the time allowed between each point and for changing ends had become so extended that the famous Borg–McEnroe final of 1980, which took four and a half hours, would have lasted barely one and three-quarter hours in his day. But he recognized the virtues of the modern game and never complained that everything was better when he played. He also wrote on tennis for a number of newspapers, including the *Daily Telegraph*.

With social change and the passing of time, with the abolition of the old amateur–professional distinctions, the British tennis establishment began to look more fondly on their erstwhile rebel son. In 1984, fifty years after Perry's first Wimbledon victory, the All England club renamed the Somerset Road entrance to the courts the Fred Perry gates and then commissioned a statue by David Wynne which stands in a rose garden opposite the members' enclosure. In a typical Perry mixture of pride and wit he pointed out that whenever he turned up at Wimbledon without a pass, 'I just point to the statue and tell the gateman "That's me"' (*The Times*, 3 Feb 1995). He published his autobiography in 1984.

Fred Perry married four times. In 1935 he married the film actress Helen Vinson, *née* Rulfs (1907–1999), from whom he was divorced in 1938. He married the American fashion model Sandra Breaux in 1941 but later divorced her; he was married for the third time in 1945, to Lorraine Walsh, sister of the actor Walter Pidgeon. After this marriage also ended in divorce, in 1952 he married Barbara (Bobby) Friedman, *née* Riese, formerly the wife of Hollywood director Seymour Friedman, and sister of the British movie actress Patricia Roc. They had a daughter and Perry adopted her son.

Fred Perry was always fit. Apart from a broken rib, which probably stopped him winning the US title for the third year running in 1935, and a serious elbow injury in 1941, which restricted his subsequent professional career, he suffered no serious injuries nor illness. But in 1983 he suffered a major heart attack, which he survived only because he was in hospital for tests at the time. Heart surgery followed in 1992 but he was soon back travelling to the world's big tournaments and offering his forthright but often humorous opinions on the pampered élite of the modern game. He died in hospital in Melbourne, Australia, after falling and breaking his ribs in his hotel on 2 February 1995, having attended the Australian open championships. His fourth wife survived him.

TONY MASON

Sources F. Perry, *An autobiography* (1984) · *The Independent on Sunday* (8 July 2001) · *The Times* (3 Feb 1995) · *The Independent* (3 Feb 1995) · *Daily Telegraph* (3 Feb 1995) · WWBMP, vol. 3 · b. cert.
Likenesses photographs, 1931–78, Hult. Arch. · E. G. Malindine, photograph, 1935, NPG [*see illus.*] · D. Wynne, statue, 1984, All England lawn tennis and croquet club, Wimbledon · photograph, repro. in *The Times* · photograph, repro. in *The Independent* · photograph, repro. in *Daily Telegraph*

Perry, George Frederick (1793–1862), composer, born at Norwich, was the son of a turner, an amateur bass singer who took part in the annual performance of an oratorio at the cathedral under John Christmas Beckwith. Through Beckwith's instrumentality Perry became a chorister in the cathedral choir. His voice, if not refined, was powerful, and his musical talent very marked. After leaving the choir he learned the violin with Joseph Parnell, a lay clerk of the cathedral; piano with Parnell's son John; harmony, it is supposed, with Bond, a pupil of William Jackson, organist of Exeter Cathedral; and composition with a clever amateur, James Taylor. On 3 August 1817 his overture to *The Persian Hunters* was performed at the Lyceum Theatre, London.

About 1818 Perry succeeded Binfield as leader of the band at the Royal Theatre at Norwich, then an institution enjoying a considerable reputation. While still resident in his native town he wrote an oratorio, *The Death of Abel* (text by George Bennett of the Norwich Theatre), which was first performed at one of the Hall concerts in Norwich, and afterwards repeated in London by the Sacred Harmonic Society in 1841 and 1845. Shortly after his appointment to the theatre he wrote another oratorio, *Elijah and the Priests of Baal*, to a text by James Plumptre, which was first performed in Norwich on 12 March 1819. In 1822 Perry was appointed musical director of the Haymarket Theatre in London, where he wrote a number of operas. One of them, *Family Jars* (sometimes called *Family Quarrels*), a farce to a libretto by J. Lunn, was produced on 26 August 1822. Another, *Morning, Noon, and Night*, a comedy with a libretto by T. J. Dibdin, was first performed, with Madame Vestris in the cast, on 9 September 1822.

From opera, however, Perry soon turned again to oratorio, and on 30 February 1830, at the Hanover Square Rooms, he produced *The Fall of Jerusalem*, the text compiled by Edward Taylor (1784–1863) from Henry Hart Milman's poem. While still holding his appointment at the Haymarket, he became organist of the Quebec Chapel, a post he resigned in 1846 for that of Trinity Church, Gray's Inn Road.

When the Sacred Harmonic Society was founded in 1832, Perry was chosen leader of the band, and at their first concert, on 15 January 1833, the programme contained a selection from his oratorios *The Fall of Jerusalem* and *The Death of Abel*. Perry assiduously supported this society, and during his sixteen years' connection with it was never absent from a performance, and only once from a rehearsal. In 1848 Joseph Surman, the conductor, was removed from his post, and Perry performed the duties until the close of the season, when he severed his connection with the society on the election of Michael Costa to the conductorship.

In addition to the works already mentioned, Perry wrote an oratorio, *Hezekiah* (1847), a sacred cantata, *Belshazzar's Feast* (1836), and a festival anthem with orchestral accompaniment, 'Blessed be the Lord God of Israel', for the queen's accession (1838). His thanksgiving anthem for the birth of the princess royal ('The Queen Shall Rejoice', 1840) was performed with great success by the Sacred Harmonic Society, the orchestra and chorus numbering five hundred, Maria Caradori-Allan being the solo vocalist. He also wrote additional accompaniments to a number of Handel's works and made piano scores of several more. Some of his works were published in London. Perry died of bronchitis on 4 March 1862 at 4 Great Marylebone Street, London, and was buried at Kensal Green cemetery.

Perry's undoubted gifts enabled him to imitate rather than to create, and his musical style was based chiefly on that of Haydn as exemplified in *The Creation*, with other elements borrowed from Handel and Mozart. His fluency proved detrimental to the character of his work. It is said that he was in the habit of writing out the instrumental parts of his large compositions from memory before he had made a full orchestral score, and he frequently composed as many as four or five works simultaneously, writing a page of one while the ink of another was drying.

R. H. LEGGE, *rev.* ROSEMARY FIRMAN

Sources N. Temperley, 'Perry, George Frederick', *New Grove* · *Norfolk News* (19 April 1862) · Brown & Stratton, *Brit. mus.* · 'Mr Perry's new oratorio', *The Harmonicon*, 10 (1832), 57 · P. A. Scholes, *The mirror of music, 1844–1944: a century of musical life in Britain as reflected in the pages of the Musical Times*, 1 (1947), 66 · private information (1895) · d. cert.

Perry, George Gresley (1820–1897), ecclesiastical historian, born at Churchill in Somerset on 21 December 1820, was the twelfth and youngest child of William Perry, an intimate friend and neighbour of Hannah More. He was educated at Ilminster under the Revd John Allen, and in 1837 he won a scholarship on the Bath and Wells foundation at Corpus Christi College, Oxford. In 1840 he graduated BA with a second class in *literae humaniores*. His scholarship would have entitled him to a fellowship at Corpus in due course, but meanwhile a vacancy occurred in the Wells fellowship at Lincoln College, for which Perry was the successful competitor, Mark Pattison, who was then just beginning his intellectual reform of the college, strongly pressing his claims. He graduated MA in 1843, and was ordained by the bishop of Oxford: deacon in 1844 and priest in 1845. He held for a short time, first, the curacy of Wick on the coast of Somerset, and then that of Combe Florey, near Taunton; but in 1847 he returned to Oxford as college tutor at Lincoln, which office he held until 1852. During the last year of his fellowship occurred the memorable contest for the rectorship, described with such painful vividness in Pattison's *Memoirs*. In this contest Perry took a leading and characteristically straightforward part. It was he who first told Pattison that the junior fellows wished to have him for their head, and from first to last he supported Pattison heartily.

In 1852 Perry accepted the college living of Waddington, near Lincoln, and there he remained to the end of his days. He entered upon his duties on Low Sunday, 1852, and the next October married Eliza, sister of George Salmon, at one time provost of Trinity College, Dublin; it was a most happy union. They had three sons and four daughters, five of his children surviving him. His wife died in 1877.

The life of a country clergyman suited Perry. He was always fond of country pursuits, understood the minds of country people, and could profitably employ the leisure which such a life afforded. He attended well to his country parish, and also threw himself heartily into the work of the diocese, which showed, as far as it could, its appreciation of him. In 1861 Bishop Jackson made him a non-residentiary canon and rural dean of Longoboby; in 1867 his brother clergy elected him as their proctor in convocation; and they continued to re-elect him (more than once after a contest) until he voluntarily retired in 1893. In 1894 Bishop King appointed him to the archdeaconry of Stow, which he held until his death.

Perry's parochial and diocesan work still left him time for study, which he used for the benefit of the church. The earliest work which brought him into notice in the literary world was his *History of the Church of England* (3 vols., 1860–64). Its fairness and accuracy were at once recognized, and its value was increased by the fact that it was the first general history which included the then unfashionable period of the eighteenth century, previous historians, as a rule, having stopped short at the revolution of 1688. In the 1860s he published several minor works and in 1868 short lives of Henry Hammond and Robert Boyle. In 1872 came a book which greatly enhanced his reputation, the *Life of Bishop Grosseteste*. His intimate knowledge of the University of Oxford and also of the diocese of Lincoln, with both of which Grosseteste was so closely connected, made the task a labour of love to him, and enabled him to carry it out successfully. This was followed in 1879 by an equally good *Life of St Hugh of Avalon, Bishop of Lincoln*, though of course he had here to come into competition with the *Magna vita* (Rolls Series). His *History of the Reformation in England* (1886), written for the Epochs of Church History series edited by Mandell Creighton, gave scope for the

development of Perry's most characteristic merits—his power of condensation and of seizing the salient points of a subject, his fairness, and his accuracy. Moreover, although Perry was a competent all-round historian, the Reformation period was that with which he was most familiar. The volume ranks among the best of the series. The same merits are found in his larger publication, *The Student's English Church History* (3 vols., 1878–87). He also left two posthumous works. One was the *Diocesan History of Lincoln* for the series published by SPCK. This he took up after the death of Edmund Venables, and incorporated in it the work which Venables had done. It was not published until after his death, in 1897; but he lived just long enough to correct the final proofs. The other was the *Lives of the Bishops of Lincoln from Remigius to Wordsworth*, written in collaboration with J. H. Overton and finished by the latter for publication in 1900. Perry was also a contributor to periodical literature and to the *Dictionary of National Biography*. He died on 10 February 1897 in his rectory, and was buried in Waddington churchyard. A tablet to his memory in Waddington church and a window in the chapter house of Lincoln Cathedral were erected by public subscription.

J. H. OVERTON, *rev.* H. C. G. MATTHEW

Sources *The Times* (11 Feb 1897) · *The Athenaeum* (13 Feb 1897), 217 · M. Pattison, *Memoirs*, ed. Mrs Pattison (1885) · private information (1901) · *CGPLA Eng. & Wales* (1897)

Wealth at death £3952 15s. 3d.: resworn probate, Sept 1897, *CGPLA Eng. & Wales*

Perry [Parry], **Henry** (1560/61–1617), linguistic scholar, was born at Greenfield, Flintshire. Through his father, Harri Owen, he was descended from the Tudor family of Penmynydd, Anglesey, and could trace descent from Llewellyn ap Gruffudd, last native prince of Wales (d. 1282). His name is also given as Parry, and he was possibly the elder brother of Robert Parry, rector of Llanfair Pwllgwyngyll (1603). He matriculated at Balliol College, Oxford, on 20 March 1579, aged eighteen, graduated BA from Gloucester Hall on 14 January 1580, and proceeded MA on 23 March 1583 and BTh from Jesus College on 6 June 1597. He is recorded in Bishop Rowlands' register as holding the degree of DTh in 1601, but there is no corroboration of this. After leaving the university about 1583 he spent some years abroad and married for the first time, but little is known of him until he returned to north Wales as chaplain to Sir Richard Bulkeley of Baron Hill, near Beaumaris. After his first wife's death he married about 1600 Elizabeth, daughter of Robert Vaughan, gentleman, of Beaumaris. Through Bulkeley's influence he secured a succession of benefices in Anglesey—rector of Rhoscolyn (21 August 1601), of Trefdraeth (3 December 1606), and of Llanfachraeth (5 March 1614). On 6 February 1613 he was installed as a canon and prebendary of Bangor Cathedral.

The lexicographer John Davies describes Perry as a man very skilled in languages who worked towards the compiling of a Welsh dictionary, but his only published work was *Egluryn ffraethineb* ('The elucidator of eloquence'). Published in 1595, this was a pioneer work in Welsh on rhetoric which drew on earlier work by William Salesbury and treatises by English writers of the period. The thirteen poems which preface this edition, variously in Greek, Latin, English, and Welsh, show the esteem in which Perry was held by his contemporaries. A second edition, with omissions, was published in 1807 and reprinted in 1829. A reprint of the original was published in 1930; the introduction (in Welsh) by G. J. Williams contains a valuable assessment of Perry's work.

Perry had a daughter from either his first or his second marriage who married Thomas Maurice, curate of Llangristiolus, Anglesey, and they were the parents of Henry Maurice, Lady Margaret professor of divinity at Oxford. Perry died some time before 30 December 1617, when a successor was appointed to his prebend. His widow, Elizabeth, married William Owen, his successor as rector of Llanfachraeth. BARRIE WILLIAMS

Sources Wood, *Ath. Oxon.*, new edn · J. E. Griffith, *Pedigrees of Anglesey and Carnarvonshire families* (privately printed, Horncastle, 1914) · H. Perry, *Egluryn ffraethineb, sef, dosbarth ar retoreg*, ed. G. J. Williams (1930), introduction · Foster, *Alum. Oxon.* · *DWB* · A. I. Pryce, *The diocese of Bangor in the sixteenth century* (1923)

Perry [*formerly* Pirie], **James** (1756–1821), journalist, was born James Pirie at Aberdeen on 30 October 1756, son of a joiner and house builder. He was educated at Gairloch Chapel, at Aberdeen high school, and at Marischal College, Aberdeen, where he matriculated in 1771, but three years later his father's business failed and he had to leave without a degree to earn his living.

Early years Perry spent a year in the office of a local advocate, and may have worked as an assistant in a draper's shop in Aberdeen before attempting a career on the stage with a company led by Tate Wilkinson. There he met Thomas Holcroft, who later was a close friend. He gave up this venture, possibly as the result of an affair with an actress, but more probably because of his broad Scots accent which, he was warned, would not be understood south of the border. He nevertheless moved to Manchester, where he spent two years as a clerk in the office of a cotton manufacturer. During this time he read books to educate himself and spoke in debates at a local literary and philosophical society.

In 1777 at the age of twenty-one Perry moved to London to try to break into the literary world. According to Thomas Holcroft, he hoped to 'get a place in some counting house, or public office' (Holcroft, 1.211), but the friends to whom he bore letters of recommendation were slow in helping him. He passed the time in writing short essays and pieces of poetry which eventually attracted the notice of one of the proprietors of the *General Advertiser*, who offered Perry a post as writer and parliamentary reporter at a guinea a week, with an extra half-guinea for helping with the *London Evening-Post*. He devoted himself enthusiastically to his work and in 1778 he was sent to Portsmouth on a special assignment, to cover the proceedings at the court martial of Admiral Augustus Keppel over his conduct in the naval battle of Ushant. This was his opportunity and he took it eagerly. He sent in to London daily for six weeks reports which reputedly sometimes ran to a length of eight columns, and raised the circulation of the paper

James Perry (1756–1821), by John Jackson

to several thousands a day, making his reputation as a thorough reporter with a clear and lively style. He also published anonymously several political pamphlets and poems, and became a well-known speaker at several London debating societies. By his own later account, the younger Pitt and Lord Shelburne were so impressed that they offered to help to bring him into parliament, but Perry's political sympathies lay elsewhere. He had grown up in a period when, after the cases surrounding the activities of John Wilkes, the press was fighting fiercely for the freedom of reporting and comment against government attempts to restrict it, and he supported their campaigns. His attitude was confirmed by his growing admiration for Charles James Fox as the champion of popular liberties. Henceforward he never wavered in his allegiance.

Editorial apprenticeship Parry's first editorial venture was the conduct of the *European Magazine*, which was founded in January 1782 for a partnership of London booksellers. Twelve months later the same proprietors offered him the editorship of the *Gazetteer* on the death of its previous editor. He made his position clear at the outset, stipulating that he 'was to be left to the free exercise of his political opinions, which were those asserted by Mr Fox' (Christie, 338). The paper's readers were soon left in no doubt: in the autumn of 1783 he declared that it was to be 'the Paper of the People'—echoing Fox's title of 'the Man of the People'. Political news was prominent from the start. Perry employed two assistants to enable him to provide the fullest, earliest, and most accurate available reports of parliamentary debates, rivalling and soon surpassing the feats of William 'Memory' Woodfall of the *Morning Chronicle*, who was said to have produced his extensive reports alone and from memory, as note-taking by reporters in the gallery was forbidden by both houses. Perry was also one of the originators of the 'leading article' in which the editor commented at length, and in his case from the Foxite viewpoint, on the news of the day.

Perry did not stop at political news. He recognized that endless columns of parliamentary debates could deter the general reader who might not be committed to politics, and he determined to make the *Gazetteer* an all-round newspaper, catering for all tastes, literary and social as well as political. Consequently he reduced the amount of space devoted to advertisements, the lifeblood of most newspapers, and increased the proportion of news content. This policy, however, alarmed his proprietors, and it was probably due to disagreement over this, rather than the purchase of the paper by some tories, that Perry decided to leave in November 1790, although he was still negotiating for the purchase of a half-share of the paper and a partnership. His ambition was to own and control his own newspaper, and he saw his opportunity to purchase, in partnership with James Gray, another young Scot and parliamentary reporter, the once-dominant but now ailing *Morning Chronicle* which Perry's own superior parliamentary reports had forced into decline. Through the good offices of two booksellers who negotiated for them, Perry and Gray were able to buy the *Morning Chronicle* for a mere £210, and to raise a further £1000 for working capital, partly from Ransome's bank. They were provided with an office at 474 Strand, on the corner of Lancaster Court by St Martin-in-the-Fields, by the duke of Norfolk, one of Fox's friends. The paper was clearly intended to be the mouthpiece of the Foxite whigs, and in return for their substantial subsidy Perry was able to give a larger proportion of space to political news to serve the party's interest.

Political crusader The moment was propitious, for the outbreak of the revolution in France, which was thought by many Englishmen at the time to be in imitation of the English revolution of 1688, the anniversary of which they had been celebrating, had created a voracious appetite for news. In the summer of 1791 Perry himself went to Paris, accredited to several of the French leaders of the revolution as a 'deputy' from the English Revolution Society. He stayed for almost a year, providing the fullest reports of the proceedings of the constituent assembly and the events of the revolution. However, as matters became more extreme and the mob more violent, sympathy in England evaporated and the whigs themselves became divided. Perry followed Fox in maintaining sympathy for the revolution, but Burke rallied the right wing and centre of the party to the 'cause of order' and the reaction against radical ideas, fearing the spread of revolution to England. As Fox's rapport with the party leaders diminished, so they became less favourable towards the *Morning Chronicle*, and at the instance of Portland and Fitzwilliam, both influenced by Burke, the party's subsidy to the paper was withdrawn. The increasingly radical tone of Perry's articles convinced them that he and Gray were paid agents of the French national assembly, employed to introduce revolution on this side of the channel.

The government also became concerned at the tone of the *Morning Chronicle*'s reports from France, and in 1793 a prosecution was instituted by the attorney-general following the printing of an advertisement for a meeting of the Society for Constitutional Information in Derby in July 1792. After some delay owing to difficulties in empanelling a special jury, the case was finally heard by Lord Chief Justice Kenyon on 9 December 1793 and the defendants were charged with seditious libel. As with other notable 'state trials' of this period, they were represented by Thomas Erskine against the attorney-general, John Scott (later Lord Eldon), and were acquitted after lengthy deliberation by the jury.

The trial nevertheless marked a decline in the *Morning Chronicle*'s popularity. Interest in Perry's reports from Paris had helped by December 1793 to raise its circulation from barely enough to keep it afloat in 1790 to a position where, according to Joseph Farington, it had made a profit over the year of about £6000 (Farington, *Diary*, 1.115). Burke, who was campaigning against its influence, referred to its 'amazing' circulation (*The Correspondence of Edmund Burke*, ed. T. W. Copeland and others, 10 vols., 1958–78, 6.451). After the trial, and principally no doubt owing to the swing of opinion in England against the French Revolution and the outbreak of war with France in February 1793, the circulation declined. At the same time Gray's health gave way, and a rival journalist, Daniel Stuart, purchased the *Morning Post* and built it up as another leading opposition paper, with more moderate political views. A further blow fell in 1797 when the government, determined to hamper the expression of dissident views, and partly also to raise extra revenue, increased the newspaper stamp duty, which helped to restrict circulations. The average daily issue of the *Morning Chronicle* in March 1797 was little over 1000.

Prominence and prosperity However, the *Morning Chronicle* was too well established as a leading London daily newspaper to succumb entirely to these difficulties, and Perry survived. This was largely due to the paper's reputation for accurate and responsible reporting in general, and there was still a public for a paper whose views were critical of Pitt's regime. It was important that the paper was well written and that Perry had recruited a staff and contributors of high literary calibre. They included at various times Richard Porson, professor of Greek at Cambridge, the poet Thomas Campbell, Coleridge, Sheridan, Thomas Moore, Charles Lamb, and William Hazlitt, together with James Mackintosh, David Ricardo, J. R. McCulloch, and John Campbell, later lord chancellor of England: several of these were fellow Scots and personal friends. He was concerned for the moral reputation of the paper, and he avoided vulgarity and political abuse in an age when newspapers and newspapermen in general had a low reputation in these respects. According to one unnamed contemporary thirty years after his death, he was 'a thorough gentleman, who attracted every man to him with whom he was connected' (Hunt, 2.105–6).

The *Morning Chronicle*'s circulation recovered from the low point of 1797, which was the worst year of the war for the country in general, and during the next decade fluctuated between 3000 and 4000 copies (its readership in an age when people shared newspapers because of the high stamp duties would have been several times that number). The profits from advertisements were crucial to the paper's financial success. They rose from about £3000 in the first decade of the nineteenth century to £12,400 in 1819 and it has been calculated that out of an average profit of £200 per week in 1815, £150 represented a personal profit to Perry (Asquith, 'Advertising', 706–7).

In 1798 Perry had another brush with the law. He appeared before the House of Lords on 22 March for allegedly libelling the house, and despite pleading that he had not seen the offending article before publication he was sentenced to three months in Newgate. His incarceration was not onerous: he gave several parties to his friends in the prison and on his release he was presented with a silver-gilt vase at a party in the London tavern. On a third occasion in 1810 he was acquitted over a paragraph copied from Hunt's *Examiner* against the prince regent.

Perry's financial position was stable enough for him to contemplate matrimony, and on 23 August 1798 he married Anne Hull (1773–1815), 'a woman of pleasing manners and intelligent countenance' (Holcroft, 2.180); they had eight children, including Sir Thomas Erskine *Perry and Anne Horatia (d. 1855), who married the diplomatist John *Crawfurd (1783–1868). Anne Perry died in February 1815 after having resided for some time at Lisbon to recover from consumption, only to be carried off by pirates on her voyage back to England and kept prisoner in Africa for several weeks. She died at Bordeaux after her release and on her way home. Perry had saved her life on 26 December 1798 when her clothes caught fire; he put out the flames with his hands, burning them badly.

After Pitt's resignation in 1801 and the peace of Amiens in 1802, the Foxites recovered some of their reputation and popular support, which helped the *Morning Chronicle* to prosper. When they came briefly into office in 1806 Perry was given a place as a commissioner with a salary of £600, but their efforts to secure him a baronetcy were unsuccessful. He seems to have been relieved to give up the post when his friends lost power in 1807 and though he continued to support them, they began to lose faith in his efforts. Henry Brougham accused him of being too favourable towards the prince regent rather than following the party line of support for the cause of Princess Caroline, and of cutting down political news in their favour in order to preserve his advertising revenues. Perry was a newspaperman first and a politician second, and his energies were devoted to maintaining the paper's reputation and circulation by the quality of its reports rather than to scoring political points. During the Peninsular War he printed reports based on Wellington's dispatches before they even reached London by official channels, from a secret source at the duke's headquarters—probably Colonel Willoughby-Gordon, one of his staff. He was also alleged in 1818 to have been supplied with foreign intelligence by the duke of Kent on the continent.

Retirement and achievement In 1817 Perry's health forced him into semi-retirement and he gradually handed over the management of the paper to John Black, one of his assistants, who became editor after Perry's death. He underwent several painful operations and never fully recovered. He died on 5 December 1821 at his house at Brighton. His income at the end of his life was £12,000 a year and his paper's circulation was steady at 4000. When it was sold after his death it fetched £42,000. Perry also owned several properties in and around London which were valued at £130,000, a substantial fortune by contemporary standards. He was buried near one of them at Wimbledon church on 12 December, and the members of the Fox Club subscribed to a memorial to him in the church.

Perry was one of the most notable journalists of the age when the newspaper press was becoming established as a force in the country, and he did much to make it so. He was a lively companion, 'full of fire and energy' (Gordon, 241), honest and trustworthy, kindly and convivial. He lived a full social life, belonged to several clubs, and entertained at his house a wide circle of writers, artists, and politicians. Mary Russell Mitford remarked that he was 'a man so genial and so accomplished that even when Erskine, Romilly, Tierney and Moore were present, he was the most charming talker at his own table' (L'Estrange, 3.254). He has been described as 'the first journalist to gain general social acceptance among the upper classes' (Asquith, 'Advertising', 721) and he did much to establish journalism as a respectable profession. Brougham wrote in 1821 that 'he was very faithful, and far superior to the ordinary tribe of newspaper folks' (Aspinall, 304). In 1805 he wrote: 'I have never deviated from the principles of Whiggism and never outraged the decorums of private life.' It might be a fitting epitaph. E. A. SMITH

Sources I. R. Christie, 'James Perry of the *Morning Chronicle*, 1756–1821', *Myth and reality in late-eighteenth-century British politics, and other papers* (1970) · I. Asquith, 'James Perry and the *Morning Chronicle*, 1790–1821', PhD diss., U. Lond., 1973 · A. Aspinall, *Politics and the press, c.1780–1850* (1949) · I. Asquith, 'Advertising and the press in the late 18th and early 19th centuries: James Perry and the *Morning Chronicle*, 1790–1821', *HJ*, 18 (1975), 703–24 · J. Grant, *The newspaper press: its origin, progress, and present position*, 3 vols. (1871–2) · F. K. Hunt, *The fourth estate: contributions towards a history of newspapers, and of the liberty of the press*, 2 vols. (1850) · P. L. Gordon, *Personal memoirs, or, Reminiscences of men and manners at home and abroad*, 2 vols. (1830) · [T. Holcroft], *Life of Thomas Holcroft*, ed. E. Colby, 2 vols. (1925) · *The life of Mary Russell Mitford, related in a selection from her letters to her friends*, ed. A. G. K. L'Estrange, [2nd edn], 3 vols. (1870) · Farington, *Diary*, vol. 1 · *GM*, 1st ser., 68 (1798), 722 · *GM*, 1st ser., 91/2 (1821), 565–6

Archives Northants. RO, Fitzwilliam MSS · NRA, priv. coll., letters to William Adam · Sheffield Central Library, Fitzwilliam MSS · U. Durham, Grey MSS · UCL, Brougham MSS

Likenesses R. Dighton, etching, pubd 1824 (after his earlier work), NPG · R. Dighton, caricature, coloured etching, NPG · J. Jackson, pencil and watercolour drawing, BM [*see illus.*] · J. Lawrence, oils, repro. in *European Magazine* (1818) · J. Thompson, stipple (after A. Wivell), BM, NPG; repro. in *European Magazine* (1818)

Wealth at death £130,000–£190,000: *DNB*; Asquith, 'Advertising', 721n.

Perry, John (1669/70–1733), hydraulic engineer and writer, was born at Sinklow farmhouse in Rodborough, Gloucestershire, the second eldest son of Samuel Perry (1638?–*c*.1690) and his wife, Sarah, daughter of Sir Thomas Nott. He joined the Royal Navy in his teens and was commissioned lieutenant in April 1689. While serving with the *Montague* in January 1690 he lost his right arm after remaining at his post for over an hour with an undressed wound during combat with a French privateer off Ushant. Over the next two years Perry designed a dry dock for large ships at Portsmouth Dockyard, constructing a powerful engine to pump water from it, and made a technically proficient dam gate which was tested in August 1691. Although the results are not clear, his efforts secured him the captaincy in February 1692 of the *Owner's Love* fireship, whose activities he described in eleven letters to the Navy Board.

After sailing to the West Indies early in 1693 under Admiral Sir Francis Wheler, Perry transferred to the *Cygnet* fireship attached to the *Diamond*, a frigate commanded by Captain Wickham, his superior officer. Cruising near Cape Clear on 20 September 1693, the *Diamond* was attacked and captured by two French privateers and Perry surrendered the *Cygnet*. On 30 April 1694 both captains were sentenced by court martial to ten years' imprisonment and a £1000 fine for dereliction of duties. At the Marshalsea prison Perry wrote *A Regulation for Seamen* (1695), advocating the replacement of impressment by registering men as naval and merchant seamen for a maximum year's paid service followed by immunity from recall. In an appendix to this pamphlet, in his July 1694 petition to the Board of Admiralty, and in his court martial evidence (ADM 1/5254), he defended his actions on the *Cygnet*: Wickham's swift capitulation and failure to signal orders had left him with no alternative but to surrender. Pardoned and acquitted by the lords justices in June 1697, he immediately designed a dry dock for Flushing port. In April 1698 Lord Carmarthen and the navy's surveyor-general introduced him to the visiting tsar of Russia, who recruited him for hydraulic engineering projects. Perry made a verbal agreement with the Russian ambassador for an annual salary of £300, his expenses, and a bonus for each work completed. Arriving in Holland with the tsar on 26 April, he spent a week studying Dutch technology before travelling to Moscow.

Perry's first assignment, at Astrakhan, was to build a canal between the rivers Volga and Don to link the Caspian with the Black Sea. He surveyed a new cut through dry land, and work on the Volga–Don Canal continued for three years. Hampered by a shortage of materials and manpower, it was finally halted by war in 1701. Perry was recalled to Moscow and appointed comptroller of the Russian maritime works. His next two projects centred on Voronezh: first between 1702 and 1703 he built a dam across the Voronezh River, above its junction with the Don, with a lock and draw-doors to float warships onto the bank for reconditioning. Then, between 1704 and 1705, he constructed a large lock further upstream, rendering the river navigable for even larger ships into the Don. While laying the foundations for his locks and sluices, he made an improved version of his Portsmouth pump to overcome problems of spring flooding. Perry's proposal (BL, Add. MS 37359, fols. 132–5) for dry-docking and rot-proofing different classes of ships at Voronezh was initially approved and he carried out a survey in September 1706. In October that year Charles Whitworth, Britain's envoy to Russia, forwarded a similar scheme adapted by Perry for the British navy (BL, Add. MS 37359, fols. 136–7 and 37355, fol. 133) to the Admiralty in London, via the secretary of state (ADM 1/4091, fols. 89–95). During 1710 Perry prospected a canal to link the rivers Neva and Volga so that corn and timber could be shipped from Kazan to St Petersburg. His proposed route followed the great lakes and interconnecting riverways, with a 3 mile cut which he proposed for the river watershed between lakes Onega and Beloye, down to the River Sheksna flowing into the Volga at Rybinsk (BL, Add. MS 37359, fols. 248–52). The project faltered when Perry's petition for salary arrears was blocked by unreasonable conditions and dire threats, resulting in his departure from Russia at the end of June 1712 under the protection of Whitworth, then ambassador-extraordinary and -plenipotentiary, without 'Money, Pass or Discharge', as he explains in his book, *The State of Russia, under the Present Czar* (1716, 55). Widely read and translated into several European languages in numerous editions (1717–36 and 1871), this uniquely influential work is of great interest in reflecting the contemporary views of a foreigner directly engaged in Peter the Great's attempts to reform and Westernize Russia. Written originally in hopes of employment and redress for thirteen years' unpaid Russian service, which he describes in detail, Perry's wide-ranging account paints a vivid picture of Russian life, dynamically contrasting the tsar's progressive, expansionist aims with the reactionary opposition of bureaucratic officialdom, the Orthodox church, and a corrupt nobility.

In 1716 Perry secured a contract to stem the breach in the Thames Embankment at Dagenham with a scheme characterized by innovative use of dovetailed piles. Perry's book *An Account of the Stopping of Daggenham Breach* (1721), graphically describes his epic feat of engineering and his outstanding technical success in surmounting two breaches, caused by a storm and by a negligent watchman, between 1716 and 18 June 1719, when the tide was finally removed from the levels. The £15,000 granted him by parliament in 1721 for additional costs barely covered his expenses. In 1724 Perry moved from London to Rye, where he was appointed engineer to the planned new harbour works; his proposed works there were partly executed, but suspended for lack of funds. His more ambitious consulting and contracting engineering work for Dover harbour is evidenced by his 1718 survey, extensive correspondence (1722–4) with the duke of Dorset, lord warden of the Cinque Ports, and the Dover harbour commissioners, as well as by his detailed and costed reports, proposals, maps, and assignments (BL, Add. MS 42075, fols. 43–52).

Perry spent over eighteen months in Dublin between 1713 and 1726, planning to improve its harbour. Despite an offer to work for a foreign prince he renewed his proposals during 1721 on the recommendation of an Irish House of Commons' harbour committee, revisiting Dublin in 1725 at the earl of Carteret's invitation, when he carried out a further survey for the port's ballast office with Thomas Burgh, surveyor-general of the ordnance, costing the projected works at £13,001. He published an account in his Dagenham book, three pamphlets (1721 and 1725), and his map of Dublin Bay and harbour, reproduced in Gerry Daly's *Early Maps from the Dublin Port Board Collection* (Dublin port and docks board, pp. 5, 7–8). Nevertheless nothing tangible seems to have resulted from his endeavours, and Perry continued to be perilously short of money.

In 1727 Perry was paid for his recommendations to make the Yorkshire Ouse navigable as far as York. From 1724 until 1729 when he settled in Spalding, Lincolnshire, as engineer to the Adventurers of Deeping Fen, Perry issued reports and published proposals in 1725 and 1727 for draining the fens. On 16 April 1730, when nearly 6000 acres of fenland were conveyed to him for financing his enterprises, Perry was elected an honorary member of the Spalding Gentlemen's Society. 'Some account of the works done by Captain Perry' (1796), a substantial and fully indexed manuscript by its treasurer, Thomas Hawkes, documents more of Perry's activities during his last years. He died, unmarried, aged sixty-three, on 11 February 1733 and was buried two days later in Spalding's parish church where he was commemorated by a monumental inscription. An exceptionally able engineer, with views ahead of his times, Perry stands out for his indomitable spirit and resilience. JOHN H. APPLEBY

Sources S. B. Hamilton, 'Captain John Perry, 1670–1732', *Transactions* [Newcomen Society], 27 (1949–51), 241–53 · BL, Add. MSS 37355, fol. 133; 37358, fols. 282–3; 37359, fols. 132–5, 136–7, 249–52; 42075, fols. 36–52; Sloane MS 1731A, fol. 73; Stowe MS 164, fols. 22–32 · PRO, ADM 106/399, fols. 277–81, 106/409, 106/422; ADM 1/4091, fols. 80–95; ADM 1/5254; PC 1/4/9/1, 3, 5, 7; PROB 11/595, sig. 15 · Russian state naval archives, St Petersburg, Fond 233, op. 1, d. 45, fols. 419, 422, 423 · *JHC*, 18 (1714–18), 440–43 · *JHC*, 19 (1718–21), 554–5 · *JHC*, 20 (1722–7), 151, 269 · *JHC*, 22 (1732–7), 432 · *Sbornik imperatorskago Russkago Istoricheskago Obshchestva* [Compendium of the Imperial Russian Historical Society], 61 (1888), 224–6 · *J. Perry, appellant. W. Boswell, respondent. The appellant's case* (1725) · J. A. Collard, *A maritime history of Rye* (1978), 37–8 · H. A. Gilligan, *A history of the port of Dublin* (1988), 18–25 · B. F. Duckham, *The Yorkshire Ouse* (1967), 63 · C. Halliday, *The Scandinavian kingdom of Dublin* (1884), cvi–cvii, cxiii, 249 [Perry's map, 1728] · P. Putnam, *Seven Britons in imperial Russia, 1698–1812* (1952), 3–20 · S. Smiles, *Lives of the engineers*, 1 (1862); repr. with introduction by L. T. C. Rolt (1968), 69–82 · monument, Spalding church · *GM*, 1st ser., 3 (1733), 101

Archives BL, MSS, Add. MSS 37355, fol. 133; 37358, fols. 282–3; 37359, fols. 132–5, 136–7, 249–52 · PRO, ADM 106/399, fols. 277–81; 106/409; 106/422; 1/4091, fols. 80–95; 1/5254; PC 1/4/9/1, 3, 5, 7; PROB 11/595, sig. 15 · Russian state naval archives, St Petersburg, Fond 233, op. 1, d. 45, fols. 419, 422, 423

Perry, John (1850–1920), electrical engineer and university professor, was born on 14 February 1850 at Garvagh, co. Londonderry, the second son of Samuel Perry and his Scottish-born wife. His early education was inauspicious. At the model school in Belfast (1860–64) his persistent failure at first to do any homework led to his being 'more caned than praised' (*Engineering*, 110, 1920, 192), though he showed some precocity by gaining a silver medal for proficiency in science. He then spent four years as an apprentice in the drawing office and pattern shops of the Lagan foundry of Coates Ltd in Belfast, while attending evening classes and winning prizes from the Department of Science and Art. After surprising himself by securing a Whitworth exhibition in 1868 (and then again in 1869), he was able to return full-time to the world of learning. He enrolled to study engineering under Professor James Thomson at Queen's College, and graduated early as Bachelor of Engineering in 1870 with first-class honours, a gold medal, and the Peel prize, followed soon afterwards by a Whitworth scholarship.

Perry's first teaching post as physics and mathematics master at Clifton College, Bristol, commenced in January 1871. Here, in addition to composing his textbook *An Elementary Treatise on Steam*, he established the first physics laboratory and the second mechanics workshop in an English school. Although at the age of twenty-one he was a lively and inspirational teacher, he evidently had difficulties upholding discipline; once, overwhelmed by requests from his boys to leave the class, he snapped back, 'You may not. You should go out before you come in' (*Journal of the Institution of Electrical Engineers*, 58, 1920, 901–2). From 1874 he was elevated to be honorary assistant to Professor Sir William Thomson (Lord Kelvin), the brother of James Thomson, at the University of Glasgow. After working alongside him in the laboratory for just one year, Perry received Sir William's support in winning his next position—a professorship in civil engineering at the Imperial College in Tokyo.

This college was a core component of the Meiji administration's plans for a new industrial era in Japan. Both the college and the country's engineering concerns were ultimately to be managed exclusively by the Japanese themselves, with only initial assistance from foreign professors; hence, Perry was employed only for a fixed term, from 9 September 1875 to 8 September 1878. He lectured on steam power, mechanical structures, and hydrodynamics to Japanese student engineers, including those who would later act as his successors. When not teaching he undertook collaborative research with W. E. Ayrton, resulting in the communication of dozens of papers (chiefly on electrical subjects) to British scientific journals. So impressed was James Clerk-Maxwell by Ayrton and Perry's efforts—if not always by their results—that he declared their 'scientific energy' threatened 'to displace the centre of electrical development … quite out of Europe and America to a point much nearer to Japan' (*The Electrician*, 2, 1879, 271–2). Perry's brief but highly active period in Tokyo left him with an abiding interest in matters Japanese, particularly in the seismological study of the nation's endemic earthquakes.

On returning to London in 1879, Perry married Alice (*d.* 1904), the daughter of Thomas Jowitt of Sheffield. They had no children. Perry was employed to reorganize the machinery of Clark and Muirhead's telegraphic works, and also by the City and Guilds Institute in 1881 as its national examiner in mechanical engineering. In 1882 this institute appointed Perry to its chair of mechanical engineering at Finsbury Technical College, at which Ayrton had earlier been appointed to the chair of applied physics. Here the reunited pair translated their unique Japanese experience of laboratory-based technical education into a rather more frugal English form. In response to the fast-growing electrical light and power industry, Ayrton and Perry also collaborated, until about 1889, in a number of inventions, including the electric tricycle and rather speculative plans for 'seeing by electricity'. Among their myriad innovative measuring instruments, the ammeter and voltmeter were the most widely adopted, although by omitting to patent their clock-based domestic power-meter the partnership reputedly lost a substantial fortune. They did enjoy successful patents, however, relating to their magnifying springs for accurate proportional calibration of electrical measurement devices (1883) and their block system for the safe management of multi-vehicle electrical haulage and traction (1882). During this period the pair worked as consultants for the Faure [*sic*] Accumulator Company, arranged the lighting of the Grand Hotel at Charing Cross, and, with Fleeming Jenkin, co-founded the Telepherage Company. This last venture was established to exploit their collective patents in the 'telepherage' system for transporting goods by wires, which came to be widely adopted in the USA.

Although a busy textbook writer, and an avid reader of novels, Perry enjoyed a vigorous social life. The Perrys' London home was the regular meeting place for some of the most distinguished physicists of the day: Joseph Larmor, Oliver Lodge, and, especially, a fellow Irishman, George Fitzgerald. Perry was thus often at the centre of wide-ranging discussions, relishing the controversies—usually good-natured—into which he was often drawn by his characteristically unorthodox or outspoken views. Although protestant by upbringing, he rarely commented on religious matters, not even in the eirenic pamphlet *On the Age of the Earth* that he privately circulated in 1894 as his contribution to the theologically charged battle then raging between Kelvin and the Darwinists. More heartfelt was the complaint succinctly phrased in the title of his 1901 polemic *England's Neglect of Science*.

As professor of mathematics and mechanics from 1896 to 1913 at the Royal College of Science and School of Mines

in London (part of Imperial College from 1907), Perry pursued his most colourful campaign: the reform of mathematics teaching. At Finsbury he and Ayrton had developed the pragmatic use of squared paper and mechanical models to teach elementary calculus to engineering students who had little prior knowledge of geometry or algebra. Their successful experience of this approach was epitomized in Perry's series of widely read textbooks, especially *Calculus for Engineers* (1896), which went through several editions. Perry persistently fought the prevailing view that a thorough mastery of Euclid was essential for all students of mathematics, contending rather that, for non-specialists, the subject should be taught primarily with a view to its 'utility'. The short volume he edited for the British Association for the Advancement of Science in 1901, *Discussion on the Teaching of Mathematics*, reveals both the passion of Perry's convictions and the tenor of the opposition that these provoked. His reforming zeal undoubtedly had a major impact on the evolution of mathematical pedagogy in twentieth-century Britain.

As the culmination of his long-term involvement with the British Association for the Advancement of Science, Perry became its general treasurer in 1904, a year that also saw the death of his wife. On retiring nine years later from active teaching he became a leading member of the South African University Commission. He continued to pursue his interest in spinning tops, a subject on which he had lectured and published often since 1890, and which embodied his wide-ranging concerns from engineering to cosmology. Perry was a member of the Athenaeum and was elected to a fellowship of the Royal Society in 1885; he was also the recipient of many honorary degrees and awards. He died suddenly but peacefully at his London home, 25 Stanley Crescent, Bayswater, on 4 August 1920, and was buried on 8 August next to his wife at Wendover churchyard in Buckinghamshire. An affably disputatious man, Perry was remembered fondly by both allies and one-time opponents. His beaming, leonine, charismatic personality made its mark not only on thousands of engineering students, but also on the Institution of Electrical Engineers and on the Physical Society, of both of which he was an active member and also president (1900–01 and 1910–11 respectively). GRAEME J. N. GOODAY

Sources 'John Perry', *Cassier's Magazine*, 19 (1900), 158–60 • H. H. T. [H. H. Turner], *PRS*, 111A (1926), i–vii • H. H. Turner, 'Prof. John Perry', *Electrical Review*, 87 (1920), 211 • *The Electrician* (13 Aug 1920), 184–5 • *Journal of the Institution of Electrical Engineers*, 58 (1920), 901–2 • H. E. Armstrong, 'Prof. John Perry', *Nature*, 105 (1920), 751–2 • *Engineering* (6 Aug 1920), 192 • D. W. Jordan, 'The cry for useless knowledge: education for a new Victorian technology', *IEE Proceedings*, A132 (1985), 587–601 • S. Hong, 'Controversy over voltaic contact phenomena, 1862–1900', *Archive for History of Exact Sciences*, 47 (1994), 233–89 • W. H. Brock and M. H. Price, 'Squared paper in the nineteenth century', *Educational Studies in Mathematics*, 11 (1980), 365–81 • J. D. Burchfield, *Lord Kelvin and the age of the earth* (1975) • G. Gooday, 'The morals of energy metering', *The values of precision*, ed. M. N. Wise (1995), 239–82 • 'The mechanics laboratory of the Imperial College of Science and Technology', *Nature*, 78 (1908), 128–9

Archives ICL | CUL, Kelvin collection, Add. MS 7342

Likenesses photograph, *c.*1875, ICL, archives · Elliott & Fry, photograph, *c.*1900, repro. in 'John Perry', *Cassier's Magazine*, frontispiece of Dec issue · A. Tear, photograph, *c.*1910, ICL, archives, supplement to Old Students Association Magazine · photograph, *c.*1920, repro. in Turner, *PRS*, facing p. i · silver medal (Perry memorial medal), ICL, archives

Wealth at death £10,343 18s. 5d.: probate, 4 Oct 1920, *CGPLA Eng. & Wales*

Perry [*formerly* Pery], **Micaiah** (*bap.* 1641, *d.* 1721), merchant, was born in New Haven, in what was to become Connecticut, where he was baptized at the First Church on 31 October 1641. His grandfather Richard Pery (1580–1650), from a family of small merchants in Exeter, settled in 1615 in London, where he invested in the Virginia Company and, after its dissolution, traded privately to the colony. He participated in many ultra-puritan activities, culminating in his being named an 'assistant' (director) in the charter of the Massachusetts Bay Company. But, when the other officers emigrated with the charter to the planned colony, he remained in London, sending his eldest son, Richard, in his place. This Richard Pery settled provisionally at Charlestown, near Boston, but, dissatisfied, soon joined the group around John Davenport and Theophilus Eaton, which left in 1639 to found the colony of New Haven on Long Island Sound. About the time of the move, Richard Pery married Mary, daughter of Richard Malbon, a ship's captain and a kinsman of Eaton and original member of the Davenport–Eaton group. The register of the First Church in New Haven records the baptisms of five children of Richard and Mary Pery between 1640 and 1649.

The triumph of the parliamentary cause gave some of the New England settlers reason to reconsider their abandonment of England, and a considerable number of them returned, including Richard Malbon, about 1648 or 1649, and Richard Pery and family, about 1651 or 1652. Many of the returning New Englanders were rewarded by the Cromwellian regime, Richard Pery becoming collector of customs and excise in Glasgow and 'messenger itinerant for the country accompts' in Scotland. He lost these places about the time of Cromwell's death and withdrew to Ireland, where he became a merchant and cattle grazier near Clonmel in co. Tipperary. Before this last move, however, his eldest son, Micaiah, was apprenticed in 1656 in London to a merchant member of the Haberdashers' Company. Immediately following the end of his apprenticeship in 1663, Micaiah Perry (as he now spelt his name) married on 20 October Ann Owen (*d.* 1689), daughter of Dr Richard Owen, the recently restored rector of St Swithin, London, and prebendary of St Paul's Cathedral. This Anglican-royalist marriage suggests that Perry was consciously turning his back on a major part of his own family's deep puritan commitments.

Once out of his apprenticeship Perry began to trade on his own to Virginia, whither his grandfather Richard Pery had traded before 1640. By about 1670 he had formed a partnership in this trade with Thomas Lane, who was from a Northamptonshire minor gentry family. It is likely that in the early years of the firm both Perry and Lane would have visited Virginia. From twelfth in 1676 they were by 1686 to become the second largest London firm importing tobacco. Following the death in 1688 of their great rival John Jeffreys, they moved into first place, a rank which Perry retained, even after Lane's death in 1710, until his own demise in 1721. Given the importance of tobacco in British–American trade, his leadership in this trade made Perry the most important British merchant trading to North America in the period between 1689 and 1720.

The success of Perry and Lane owed much to its efficiency, dependability, and adaptability. In most areas of the Chesapeake, it began by trading directly with small and middling planters through factors acting for them on commission. As the number of indigenous merchants in the Chesapeake increased, many of the greatest preferred dealing with the Perry house. A class of larger planters also emerged towards the end of the seventeenth century who found it in their interest to deal directly with merchants in England. Many of this element preferred Perry and Lane, which then had a relatively good reputation for acting in its correspondents' interest in selling tobacco, buying return goods, and avoiding long delays in shipping. (In 1719 the firm imported tobacco in space chartered on fifty different vessels.) To support its Chesapeake business, the firm also had some Madeira, West Indies, and North Carolina trade and occasionally ventured on the servant and slave trades. In the 1680s Perry contracted with the Royal African Company for slave deliveries to Virginia and in 1707 he attempted one slaving voyage on his own.

Perry's success in attracting business from the largest planters made it inevitable that he would also be asked to perform political tasks, including solicitation for places in the gift of the crown and for desired legislation and orders. He acted as both political and financial agent for the colony of Virginia and sometimes represented Maryland as well. He and Robert Carter of Virginia managed the 'northern neck' of that colony for the proprietor, Lady Fairfax. He also handled the London business of Governor Francis Nicholson and of the College of William and Mary. His more charitable activities included raising funds for the college and for the refugees in the 1690s from the war-ravaged Palatinate; he was employed too by the archbishop of Canterbury to remit funds to America for the relief of Huguenot refugees there. He appears with striking frequency in the minutes of the Treasury and the Board of Trade. The board consulted him (more than fifty times between 1704 and 1713) about such matters as convoys and American conditions. In the City of London, however, he avoided all participation in municipal or guild affairs until 1708, when he was named to the lieutenancy (militia) commission.

Perry and his wife appear to have had two sons only. The younger, Micaiah, died in 1693 at the age of twenty-two. The elder, Richard, in 1694 married Sarah Richards, daughter and ultimate heir of the recently deceased merchant George Richards, a major competitor in the Chesapeake trade. By this marriage the Perrys in effect took over the Richards business. Perry was a commissioner for taking the £2 million subscription that led to the creation of the new East India Company, but did not himself invest in that venture. Richard Perry, his son and partner, who had acquired some wealth with his wife, bought shares in the Bank of England and became a director, in 1699–1701. But the family, like many others, came to prefer safer investments in real property, including the manor of Little Stanbridge in Essex. In London their realty holdings included large storage warehouses and two of the three quays along the Thames between the Tower of London and the Customs House. In Ireland Perry helped his brother John acquire a substantial estate near Clonmel during the forced sales of the 1690s. Perry's son Richard predeceased him in 1720 and he himself died at Leadenhall Street, London, on 1 October 1721. His business as the leading tobacco-importing firm in Britain passed to his grandsons, Richard's sons Micajah *Perry and Philip. They also inherited most of the family's other property though their mother and sisters were provided for. Perry was buried on 10 October 1721 at St Botolph without Bishopsgate.

Perry is a striking example of the fairly numerous cohort of merchants from nonconformist backgrounds who found it possible to reach a considerable level of commercial success after 1660—particularly in the American trades—without conspicuous political participation and concomitant government contracts.   JACOB M. PRICE

Sources J. M. Price, *Perry of London: a family and a firm on the seaborne frontier, 1615–1753* (1992) • J. L. Chester and J. Foster, eds., *London marriage licences, 1521–1869* (1887), 1046 • V. L. Oliver, *The history of the island of Antigua*, 3 vols. (1894–9), 24 • A. W. C. Hallen, ed., *The registers of St Botolph, Bishopsgate, London*, 2 (1889), 474 • will, PRO, PROB 11/581, sig. 185

Perry, Micajah (*bap.* **1694**, *d.* **1753**), merchant and politician, was baptized on 30 April 1694 at St Katharine Cree in London, the son of Richard Perry, merchant of London, and his wife, Sarah, daughter of George Richards, likewise a merchant. His grandfather, Micaiah *Perry, was one of the founders of the leading English firm in the tobacco-importing and North American trades between 1690 and 1720. His father, a partner in that concern, died in 1720, so that when Micaiah Perry died in 1721 this major house, with commitments all over the Atlantic trading world, passed into the hands of his two grandsons, Micajah, aged twenty-six, and his younger brother, Philip, aged eighteen. Having previously spent some time as a clerk in a Philadelphia merchant's counting-house, Micajah Perry was thus reasonably familiar with American business conditions and practices. On 19 September 1721 he married Elizabeth (*d.* 1738), daughter of Richard Cocke, a prosperous London linen draper. They lived in St Mary Axe in the City and at a villa at Epsom. They had no children.

In Micaiah Perry's day, Perry and Lane used all the principal trading modes known in the Chesapeake trade. As a commission house, it conducted business for both planters and merchants in the colonies, but also traded on its own through stores and factors there. It avoided unnecessary shipping risks and delays by chartering limited space on many vessels. After taking over the firm (now known as Perry & Co.), Micajah Perry simplified operations by eliminating stores and factors, by reducing correspondence with merchants, and by sending out a limited number of ships of his own rather than chartering partial freight on a larger number of vessels. Almost immediately his firm began to lose money on shipping, because, without the assistance of dependable agents in every river, his captains were detained for longer periods in the tobacco colonies looking for cargoes, and, even so, frequently returned without full freights. Moreover, the firm antagonized many of the larger planters on whom it was now particularly dependent by suing aggressively for sums owed with compound interest.

The time liberated by simplifying the operations of his firm came increasingly to be devoted by Perry to politics. This marked a sharp break with the practice of his father and grandfather who, though known whigs, had avoided any conspicuous involvement in national, municipal, or guild affairs—except for membership in the lieutenancy commission (in charge of the militia trained bands). In 1719, however, Perry's sister Sarah married William Heysham the younger, MP, a London West Indies merchant. The Heyshams were a politically active whig family, three of whose members had since 1698 been members of parliament for Lancaster or London. The death of his brother-in-law in 1727 very probably encouraged Perry to attempt to lead the surviving Heysham interest in the City. Merchants like the Heyshams and Perrys gave much business to London dealers in export goods as well as to the port's numerous ship carpenters, chandlers, sailmakers, ropeworks, and other maritime crafts and trades. The death of George I in June 1727 made it necessary to hold an election that year and the hitherto inactive Perry quickly became a liveryman and 'assistant' of the Haberdashers' Company and announced his candidacy for parliament. He was able to stand as part of a pro-ministerial grouping when the aged alderman Sir Gilbert Heathcote withdrew as a candidate for London. Perry came in third (out of the four elected) in the poll of November 1727. This was quickly followed by his selection as master of the Haberdashers' Company in December and as alderman for Aldgate ward in February 1728.

In parliament Perry appears to have devoted most of his efforts to commercial and colonial questions. (He was also agent for Pennsylvania in the 1720s.) On many of these issues he could co-operate with the ministry, most noticeably in obtaining the 1732 act facilitating the collection of debts in the colonies—a measure as strongly desired by merchants as loathed by colonists. On other issues he was impelled by feeling in the City to oppose the ministry, particularly on the question of Britain's reaction to the 'Spanish depredations' in the West Indies. His total break with the ministry came over Walpole's 1733 Tobacco Excise Bill, intended to curb fraud in collecting customs on tobacco, the opposition to which he led both in the City and in the house. As one of the very few tobacco merchants in the house, his leading role in the debates was both necessary and effective.

Perry's success in stopping the Excise Bill was a costly victory. In the City he was a hero, triumphantly returned to parliament in the general election of 1734 and elected sheriff for 1734–5 and lord mayor for 1738–9. But his private affairs suffered, for his Virginia correspondents were offended both by the passage of the Colonial Debts Act and by the failure of the Excise Bill. (Consigning planters had hoped that it would mean lower commissions on their sales accounts.) Many there felt, too, that his political involvements meant that he was devoting too little time to his business, from which his brother, Philip, withdrew in 1739. The Treasury also harassed him with an exchequer suit to recover customs duties repaid to him on tobacco not properly exported. Perry found it necessary to reach some sort of political understanding with the ministry in order to effect a 'composition' on the customs claim. This compromised him in the eyes of the ever more numerous ardently anti-Walpole City voters and helped secure his defeat in the parliamentary election of 1741. By that time both his business and his health were in ruins. Suffering from 'dropsy', he withdrew to Bath in 1743 and subsequently avoided bankruptcy only by turning over all his effects to his English creditors. He resigned his aldermanship on 25 November 1746 and received a pension of £200 per annum from the court of aldermen. In his last years he was so 'utterly incapable of Transacting any Business whatsoever' that the court of chancery had to appoint a guardian for him. He died intestate on 22 or 25 January 1753, either at East Greenwich in Kent, or at Epsom in Surrey. JACOB M. PRICE

Sources J. M. Price, *Perry of London: a family and a firm on the seaborne frontier, 1615–1753* (1992) · P. Langford, *The excise crisis: society and politics in the age of Walpole* (1975) · J. M. Price, 'The excise affair revisited', *England's rise to greatness, 1660–1763*, ed. S. B. Baxter (1983), 257–321 · V. L. Oliver, 'The aldermen of Aldgate', *N&Q*, 8th ser., 8 (1895), 17 · *GM*, 1st ser., 23 (1753), 53 · *London Magazine*, 22 (1753), 93 · *IGI* · administration, PRO, PROB 6/129, fols. 99r–101v

Perry, Percival Lee Dewhurst, Baron Perry (1878–1956),

motor vehicle manufacturer, was born on 18 March 1878, at Bristol, the third son of Alfred Thomas Perry, clerk, and his wife, Elizabeth, daughter of Revd Henry Wheeler. He won a scholarship to King Edward VI's Grammar School, Birmingham, which he attended from 1889 to 1894. His earliest jobs were in a bicycle shop and a solicitor's office, but his hope of studying law was frustrated by lack of funds. At the age of seventeen he sold his stamp collection to pay for a rail ticket to London, where he was employed by the motoring pioneer Harry Lawson. He married in 1902 Catherine, daughter of John Meals, postmaster, of Hull. They were childless.

In 1903 Perry was commissioned to write a technical report on the earliest Ford Model A cars imported to Britain. He was afterwards involved in an agency importing Ford cars, and during 1906 visited Detroit to meet Henry Ford. It was Perry who envisioned Ford's manufacturing motor vehicles outside the USA for sale across the British empire and Europe. He raced the company's cars, and in 1907, on the occasion of the motoring exhibition at Olympia, published *The O.K. Verses*, a pastiche on 'Umar Khayyam, giving a boisterous account of contemporary motoring and its cars, racing drivers, chauffeurs, makers, and touts. After being appointed in 1909 to run Ford's new showroom in London he organized a national network of exclusive dealers and superintended an assembly plant at Trafford Park which began production in 1911. The Ford Motor Company (England) Ltd was established in that year as a wholly owned subsidiary of the Detroit business, and proved indispensable after the imposition of McKenna import duties in 1915 enforced the need for the company to manufacture in Britain. Perry broke trade unionism at his factory and imposed job mobility, time wages, and direct managerial control over production, while paying his workers more than was usual in his sector. Ford's mechanized chassis assembly system, which was inaugurated in 1914, was the first in Britain.

Perry worked without remuneration as deputy controller of the food production department of the Board of Agriculture and Fisheries in 1916, and then as director of the agricultural machinery department of the Ministry of Munitions in 1917–18. He was deputy controller of the mechanical warfare department and director of traction at the same ministry in 1918–19. His wartime experiences gave him a rooted objection to state controls over manufacturing. He was appointed CBE in 1917 and knighted in 1918.

After the war Henry Ford wanted to run British operations from Detroit despite Perry's determination to direct all European business himself. Their differences could not be reconciled, and in May 1919 Perry resigned. He led a group which in April 1920 bought the Slough motor car repair depot (comprising 600 acres and 15,000 vehicles) from the Ministry of Munitions for £3.35 million. This property was converted into a model manufacturing estate based on Trafford Park. In 1922 Perry resigned as chairman and managing director of Slough Estates (although remaining on its board) having acquired the lease of the 300 acre Isle of Herm, in the Channel Islands, from the writer Compton Mackenzie. Perry lived for several years on Herm, where with his wife he wrote *The Island of Enchantment* (1926).

Ford's American managers having failed in Britain, he offered Perry the chairmanship of the newly formed Ford Motor Company Limited in 1928. Perry accepted, taking responsibility for Ford's new Dagenham factory, which was the largest automobile factory in the world outside the USA and by 1936 produced over 94,000 vehicles annually. The Dagenham plant in 1932 launched an 8 hp model costing £120 which was the first Ford car specifically made for European markets; it sustained the business through the depression. There was much less interference from Detroit under this new regime, and the policy of using British rather than American managers was soon vindicated. Perry in 1928 devised a new European strategy, which was, however, frustrated by deteriorating political and fiscal conditions. He superintended factories and assembly plants in Éire, Denmark, Spain, France, the

Netherlands, Belgium, and Germany, and maintained an English suzerainty over Ford's European operations.

Perry, who was interested in agriculture, instituted an experiment in co-operative farming, the Fordson farms, at Boreham in Essex during the 1930s. He was business adviser to the minister of food in 1939–40, and held outside directorships with the Firestone Tyre and Rubber Company and the National Provincial Bank. He enjoyed literary dabbling, and wrote *New Songs* (1925) and *The International Balance of Trade* (1932), as well as pamphlets advocating 'free enterprise' published by the Individualist Bookshop in the early 1940s. In 1943 he led the formation of the propagandist body Aims of Industry, of which he was first president.

Perry was stocky and genial-looking; heavy spectacles masked granite grey eyes of a rather designing hardness. He was keen, energetic, independent-minded, and personable, with an aptitude for selecting and motivating his staff. In the motor industry he was considered urbane and even intellectual; by contrast, the memoirs of his literary neighbour Sir Compton Mackenzie depict him as vulgar, pawky, penny-pinching, and complacent. He received an honorary LLD from Birmingham University in 1937 and was awarded several foreign decorations. He was raised to the peerage in 1938. Having retired from Ford in 1948, Perry died on 17 June 1956, at New Providence Island in the Bahamas, when his peerage became extinct. His wife died in the Bahamas in December 1956.

RICHARD DAVENPORT-HINES

Sources A. Nevins and F. E. Hill, *Ford*, 3 vols. (1954–62) · C. Mackenzie, *My life and times*, 10 vols. (1963–71), vol. 5 · M. Wilkins and F. E. Hill, *American business abroad: Ford on six continents* (1964) · *The Times* (19 June 1956) · *The Times* (21 June 1956) · *The Times* (22 June 1956) · *The Times* (8 May 1920) · A. C. Fox-Davies, ed., *Armorial families: a directory of gentlemen of coat-armour*, 7th edn, 2 vols. (1929) · GEC, *Peerage*
Archives Ford Archives, Dagenham, letters and unpublished memoir · Ford Archives, papers | PRO, Ministry of Munitions MSS
Likenesses W. Stoneman, photograph, 1921, NPG · photograph, 1930–39, repro. in Nevins and Hill, *Ford*, facing p. 141
Wealth at death £77,698 14*s*. 2*d*. in England: probate, 27 Aug 1956, *CGPLA Eng. & Wales*

Perry, Philip Mark (1720–1774), Roman Catholic priest and scholar, was born on 5 March 1720 at Bilston, Staffordshire, the son of Peter Perry and his wife, Joan Westwood. The family had resided in the area for many years and the name Perry occurs in the recusant lists of 1641 and 1705. In 1740 he went to the English College at Douai, where he completed the two-year philosophy course. In 1742 he was sent to St Gregory's English College, Paris, to join the select band of students who were following the demanding theological course at the Sorbonne. His studies were interrupted by ill health and he returned to England for two years. He resumed the course in 1746, obtained his MA in 1748, was ordained priest on 18 December 1751, proceeded to the licentiate, and finally gained his doctorate in theology on 22 May 1754.

On his return to England Perry took up residence as chaplain to Rowland Eyre at Hassop Hall, Bakewell, Derbyshire. After eight years he moved to Heythrop Park, Oxfordshire, to be chaplain to the earl of Shrewsbury. From 1765 he resided at Longbirch, Brewood, Staffordshire. On the expulsion of the Jesuits from Spain in 1767 Bishop Challoner appointed him rector of the English College of St Alban, Valladolid. Having arrived in Spain with no previous experience of the country or language, Perry succeeded in putting into effect the agreement that had been reached between Challoner and the Spanish court that the three English seminaries at Valladolid, Madrid, and Seville should be amalgamated into one establishment at Valladolid and administered by the English secular clergy. He negotiated the sale and transfer of college properties and established good relations with both the civil and ecclesiastical authorities.

Perry had hoped that his appointment to Spain might enable him to further his researches into the life of John Fisher and the divorce of Katherine of Aragon, and he obtained permission to visit Spanish libraries. However, his administrative duties curtailed these activities. He had a lifetime friendship with Alban Butler, the author of *Lives of the Saints*, with whom he corresponded and who expressed the wish that Perry would be his literary heir. The wide range of his interests is shown in his acquisitions for the college library at Valladolid and the numerous manuscripts on historical topics that are to be found among his papers. After his death John Geddes, whom he had assisted in the re-establishment of the Scots College in Spain, brought some of his works to Britain with a view to publication. They included lives of John Fisher and Robert Grosseteste and a continuation of Bede's *History*. Perry's activities on behalf of the college meant that he had to make prolonged visits to Madrid. In his absence he corresponded with his vice-rector in Valladolid, and these letters afford an insight into the domestic situation as well as his scholarly concern for precision and accuracy.

It was during a stay in Madrid in the very hot summer of 1774 that Perry caught a fever and died on 4 September, in the Hospice of San Andrès de la Nacion Flamenca. He was buried in its chapel the following day. In his will he left any goods and property in England to his surviving brother and two sisters in Staffordshire and his possessions in Spain to the college at Valladolid. During his lifetime his contemporaries remarked on his moroseness and rigidity; at his death they praised his learning, zeal, and prudence. We are told that he looked older than his fifty-four years and this is attributed to the time he had spent in study. John Kirk, in *Biographies of English Catholics* (1909), relates that Perry's nephew, the Revd John Perry, told him that after his death his uncle had appeared to him to prevent his taking evil ways.

MICHAEL E. WILLIAMS

Sources archives, St Alban's College, Valladolid, Spain, Perry MSS [including will] · E. Henson, ed., *The registers of the English College at Valladolid, 1589–1862*, Catholic RS, 30 (1930) · J. Kirk, *Biographies of English Catholics in the eighteenth century*, ed. J. H. Pollen and E. Burton (1909) · M. E. Williams, 'Philip Perry, rector of the English College, Valladolid', *Recusant History*, 17 (1984–5), 48–66 · M. E. Williams, 'English manuscripts in Scottish archives', *Innes Review*,

34 (1983), 93–6 · M. E. Williams, *St Alban's College, Valladolid: four centuries of English Catholic presence in Spain* (1986), 71–108 · G. Anstruther, *The seminary priests*, 4 (1977)
Archives Scottish Catholic Archives, Edinburgh · St Alban's College, Valladolid, Spain, archives

Perry, Sampson (1747–1823?), radical and newspaper proprietor, was born at Aston, near Birmingham; nothing is known of his parents. Perry trained as a physician and practised as a surgeon in Aldersgate Street, London, in the 1760s and early 1770s. He claimed to have invented a cure for kidney stones, which he marketed as Adams Solvent. Perry published *A Disquisition* on bladder and kidney diseases (eight editions, 1772–95), with *Observations* and *Further Observations* in 1789, and a dissertation on venereal diseases in 1786. He joined the East Middlesex militia in 1765, rising to lieutenant in 1777, surgeon in 1778, and captain in 1780. Though sympathetic to the American cause, on two occasions during the American War of Independence he raised volunteer companies to face the threat of invasion.

In early 1789 Perry and Jonathan King became the proprietors of *The Argus*, a new, moderate opposition newspaper. In 1792, as sole proprietor, Perry introduced a more radical stance, associating with the London Corresponding Society (LCS) and publishing contributions by Thomas Paine, John Horne Tooke, Maurice Margarot, and Jonathan King. Perry faced several prosecutions for libel on the government between June and September 1792, and was twice sentenced to a term of imprisonment. He continued to edit *The Argus* from prison, and his release was followed by further prosecutions for libel. An article, arguing that the House of Commons did not represent the people, led to a warrant's being issued for his arrest. Perry left for France in late September 1792, to avoid prosecution, was tried for libel in his absence, and found guilty in December. He was outlawed and his property seized in January 1793, and a £100 reward offered for his capture.

Perry considered emigrating to America but, through Paine, had many connections in Paris and soon became closely involved with émigré groups. He gave evidence at the trial of Jean-Paul Marat and was called to give evidence at the trial of the Dantonists on their connections with the English whigs, though the defence witnesses were not heard. With other enemy aliens Perry was arrested in August 1793 and gaoled for fourteen months. He believed he was lucky to have escaped execution and on his release in late 1794 he remained in Paris for a further five months. He returned clandestinely to Britain in early 1795 but was betrayed to the authorities and arrested on the charges of 1792. He was imprisoned in Newgate until the change of ministry in 1801. There he detailed his persecution by the government in the pamphlet *Oppression!!! The Appeal of Captain Perry … to the People of England*, published in 1795. That year he wrote his most substantial work, *An Historical Sketch of the French Revolution*, published in two volumes in 1796. Perry relaunched *The Argus* as a magazine in early 1796, and in the same year published *The Argus … a Political Miscellany*; the following year he published a pamphlet, *The Origin of Government, Compatible with, and Founded on the*

Rights of Man, in which he set out the objectives of the LCS. He had come close to death with gaol fever in 1796, and on his release in 1801 he wrote for a variety of radical periodicals. Around 1809 Perry became joint proprietor of *The Statesman*, an independent newspaper, which he made more radical. He was forced to sell his interest in the paper about 1812 because of the cost of cross-suits for libel, in 1811, with Lewis Goldsmith, editor of the *Anti-Gallican Monitor*.

Perry's first wife, details of whom are unknown, died in 1813 and later he married again. He continued to publish radical articles but was declared an insolvent debtor. He probably died in prison on 4 July 1823, of a ruptured artery, apparently just before he was to be released. His property was seized but his third wife, Barbara, and seven children were supported by a public subscription raised by a group of Perry's old radical friends. AUSTIN GEE

Sources I. D. McCalman, 'Sampson Perry', *British reform writers, 1789–1832*, ed. G. Kelly and E. Applegate, DLitB, 158 (1996), 275–8 · B. B. Schnorrenberg, 'Perry, Sampson', BDMBR, vol. 1 · DNB · S. Perry, *Oppression!!! The appeal of Captain Perry, (late editor of The Argus) to the people of England, containing a justification of his principles and conduct* (1795)
Likenesses Maddan, stipple (after R. Cosway), BM, NPG
Wealth at death died imprisoned for debt

Perry, Stephen Joseph (1833–1889), astronomer, was born on 26 August 1833 in London, the son of Stephen Perry, a steel pen-nib manufacturer of Red Lion Square, Holborn. As an infant he was seriously ill with inflammation of the brain, and his mother died when he was seven. He was educated by the Benedictines, first at Giffords Hall, Suffolk, then at St Edmund's College, Douai, in France. There he developed a vocation for the priesthood, and he went to the English College at Rome for his theological studies. His sister, who was in a convent, had lent him a life of St Ignatius to read, and this may have reinforced his decision to enter the Society of Jesus on 12 November 1853. In 1856 he went to Stonyhurst College for training in philosophy and physical science. His mathematical ability led to his being appointed assistant to Father Weld in the observatory; he matriculated in 1858 at the University of London, studied mathematics for a year under Augustus De Morgan, then went to Paris for training in higher mathematics and natural philosophy. On his return to Stonyhurst in 1860, he was appointed professor of mathematics and director of the observatory, but as he was obliged to spend the three years previous to his ordination, on 23 September 1866, at St Beuno's College, north Wales, followed by the Jesuits' customary two years' probation, he resumed his former duties only in 1868. He was a very able lecturer who usually illustrated his talks with lantern slides, and he was in constant demand to address not only learned societies, but artisans and working men in several towns and cities of northern England.

During the course of an exceptionally adventurous life, Perry 'undertook more astronomical expeditions than any man now living' (*The Observatory*, 13, 1890, 64). Terrestrial magnetism was another of his enduring interests,

Perry's most valuable work was undoubtedly in the field of solar physics. He was quick to make use of two new scientific techniques: photography and spectroscopy. In 1879, with John Couch Adams of Cambridge and Charles Pritchard of Oxford, he served on a physics committee set up to secure a complete daily record of the sun's disc by photography. From 1880 he made daily drawings of sunspots, and was able to confirm Schwabe's postulated eleven-year sunspot cycle, as well as the correlation of sunspot activity with solar prominences, magnetic storms, and aurorae. In the field of general astronomy he found time to study planetary and lunar occultations and comets; these activities were in addition to his obligations to attend to his religious offices and to his daytime teaching.

In 1866 the Board of Trade selected Stonyhurst as one of the seven principal meteorological stations in Britain. The observatory was provided with photographic self-recording instruments, and it contributed its results both nationally and to local newspapers. Perry was a member of the Meteorological Society and on its council. The parliamentary commission of 1883 investigating water supplies also drew on his rainfall records.

Perry's last expedition was to French Guiana, for the solar eclipse of 21 December 1889. A similar expedition was dispatched to Angola, the intention being to see if the shape of the solar corona changed during the two and a half hours between its sighting at the two stations. Unfortunately this question was unanswered, as the Angolan sky did not clear. Perry was camped on one of the Salut Islands, where dysentery was rife in the nearby convict settlement; he contracted the ailment, which soon developed into gangrene of the bowel. Despite his severe illness, he managed to command operations during the 120 seconds of totality, even taking a few photographs. Afterwards he collapsed, and his mind began to wander. His colleagues took him on board ship, and he died six days later, on 27 December 1889.

A. M. CLERKE, *rev.* ANITA McCONNELL

Sources G. Bishop, 'Stephen Perry, forgotten Jesuit', *Journal of the British Astronomical Association*, 89 (1978–9), 473–84 · E. B. K. [E. B. Knobel], *Monthly Notices of the Royal Astronomical Society*, 50 (1889–90), 168–75 · *PRS*, 48 (1890), xii–xv · *Nature*, 41 (1889–90), 279–80 · *The Observatory*, 13 (1890), 64, 81–86 · C. M. Charropin, *Sidereal Messenger*, 9 (1890), 197–200 · *Men of the time* (1887) · *The Times* (8 Jan 1890) · B. Vaughan, *The Tablet* (11 Jan 1890) · B. Vaughan, *The Tablet* (25 Jan 1890) · B. Vaughan, *The Tablet* (1 Feb 1890) · B. Vaughan, *The Tablet* (22 Feb 1890) · A. L. Cortie, 'Father Stephen Joseph Perry, SJ', *The Month* (1890), 305–23 · A. L. Cortie, 'The scientific work of Father Perry', *The Month* (1890), 474–88
Archives CUL, letters to Sir George Stokes · RAS, letters to Royal Astronomical Society
Likenesses Maull & Fox, photograph, RS [*see illus.*] · photograph, repro. in Bishop, 'Stephen Perry, forgotten Jesuit'

Stephen Joseph Perry (1833–1889), by Maull & Fox

starting with his first magnetic surveys in France in 1868 and 1869 and in Belgium in 1871. His results, with magnetic data from Stonyhurst, were presented to the Royal Society, which elected him a fellow on 4 June 1874—one of the few Catholic priests to be thus honoured; he later served on its council.

Perry was elected to the Royal Astronomical Society on 9 April 1869 and led its party sent to observe the solar eclipse of 22 December 1870 from San Antonio, near Cadiz, but cloud frustrated his intended work with the spectroscope. His next journey was to Kerguelen Island, in the Southern Ocean, to observe the transit of Venus across the sun's disc (8 December 1874). Again cloudy skies marred the value of both observations and photographs. The expedition remained a further five months in this desolate place in order to obtain its exact latitude, but on the way home Perry disembarked at Malta and was received by the pope at Rome. Despite being prone to seasickness, Perry led the party observing the second transit of Venus on 6 December 1882 from Madagascar, where they were favoured by good weather. Poor conditions again impeded his spectroscopic work during the solar eclipse of 19 August 1886, seen from the West Indies; the expedition to Pogost on the Volga, for the solar eclipse of 19 August 1887, was also fruitless, as dense cloud obscured the skies.

Perry, Sir Thomas Erskine (1806–1882), judge in India and politician, was born at Wandlebank House, Wimbledon, Surrey, on 20 July 1806, the second son of James *Perry (1756–1821), proprietor and editor of the *Morning Chronicle*, and his wife, Anne (1773–1815), daughter of John Hull of

Sir Thomas Erskine Perry (1806–1882), by John Linnell

Wilson Street, Finsbury Square, London. He was educated at Charterhouse and Trinity College, Cambridge, where he graduated BA in 1829. In 1827 he had been admitted to Lincoln's Inn, but after his graduation he went instead to Munich and attended the university there.

Upon returning to England in the early part of 1831 Perry joined the reform agitation. He became honorary secretary of the National Political Union of London and founded the Parliamentary Candidate Society, which aimed to promote reform by encouraging 'the return of fit and proper members of parliament'. He was an ardent supporter of the ballot, not because he put great store by popular opinion, but because he saw it as society's best means for avoiding political intimidation and coercion. At the general election of December 1832 Perry unsuccessfully contested the seat of Chatham.

In May 1832 Perry left Lincoln's Inn for the Inner Temple, whence he was called to the bar on 21 November 1834. Though he joined the home circuit, he appears to have devoted himself to law reporting. With Sandford Nevile he published *Reports of Cases Relating to the Office of Magistrates Determined in the Court of the King's Bench* (1837) and *Reports of Cases Argued and Determined in the Court of the King's Bench, and upon Writs of Error from that Court to the Exchequer*

Chamber (3 vols., 1837–9). He jointly wrote four more volumes of the latter work with Henry Davison in the years 1839 to 1842.

Having lost the greater part of his fortune by the failure of a bank in 1840, Perry turned to his friends in the government for assistance and was appointed a judge of the supreme court of Bombay and, on 11 February 1841, was knighted at Buckingham Palace. Two months later he was sworn into his judicial office at Bombay. His early months in India were marred by the death of his first wife, Louisa (1813–1841), only child of James M'Elkiney of Brighton and a niece of Madame Jérôme Bonaparte, whom he had married in 1834. Louisa died at Byculla on 12 October 1841 and was buried in St Thomas's Cathedral, Bombay.

In May 1847 Perry was appointed chief justice in the place of Sir David Pollock and continued to preside over the court until his retirement from the bench in the autumn of 1852. For the ten years prior to 1852 he also served as president of the Indian board of education. His liberalism and his enthusiastic advocacy of educational and employment opportunities for Indians made him popular with the small but articulate community of Western-educated Indians in Bombay, and upon his departure they contributed generously to the fund collected in his honour; the £5000 thus raised was, at his request, devoted to the establishment of a Perry professorship in law at Elphinstone College. His Indian experiences inspired several publications, including *Cases Illustrative of Oriental Life and the Application of English Law to India Decided in H.M. Supreme Court at Bombay* (1853) and *A Bird's-Eye View of India* (1855).

Upon his return to England Perry wrote several letters to *The Times* under the pseudonym Hadji advocating the abolition of the East India Company. In a by-election in June 1853 he unsuccessfully contested Liverpool, but in the following May was returned for the Liberals at Devonport, which borough he continued to represent until appointed to the Council of India in 1859. On 6 June 1855 Perry married Elizabeth Margaret, second daughter of Sir John Vanden Bempde-Johnstone, bt, and sister of Harcourt, first Lord Derwent.

As an MP Perry frequently addressed the house on the imperfections of the East India Company's government of India. He condemned the annexation of Oudh and, despairing at the repetition of history, argued that Lord Dalhousie, like Wellesley fifty years before him, had both exaggerated the misgovernment of the king of Oudh and ignored the extent to which his difficulties were attributable to conditions forced on him by the British. Perry accepted the essentially despotic nature of British rule in India, but hoped nevertheless for a display of benevolent liberalism from the British. He repeatedly called for the employment of Indians in the higher levels of the government service.

Perry also advocated improved property rights for married women, deprecating as unjust and injurious the rules of common law by which the personal property and earnings of a married woman accrued to her husband. On 14 May 1857, as chairman of the civil laws committee, he brought in a bill to amend the law of property as it affected married women; it was afforded a second reading, on 15 July, before being forced off the parliamentary timetable by the Divorce Bill.

On 8 August 1859 Perry was appointed a member of the Council of India, in which post he remained for over twenty years. His liberalism was undiminished, although he always tempered his enthusiasm for projects of public good with an eye to their cost. By the early 1880s he was instructing Lord Ripon, whom he greatly admired, that it was his duty as viceroy to prepare Indians for self-rule; it might, Perry conceded, seem a utopian project but it was undeniably a noble one.

In November 1881 Perry's health began to fail and he retired from the council early in the new year. A few months before his death the queen approved his admission to the privy council, but he was too ill to be sworn in. He died at his residence, 36 Eaton Place, London, on 22 April 1882, aged seventy-five. His second wife, Elizabeth, survived him for over thirty years; she died on 11 April 1913. G. F. R. BARKER, rev. KATHERINE PRIOR

Sources ILN (6 May 1882), 448 · WWBMP, vol. 1 · BL, Bright MSS · BL, Ripon MSS, 2nd ser. · W. W. Rouse Ball and J. A. Venn, eds., *Admissions to Trinity College, Cambridge*, 4 (1911) · W. A. Bartlett, *The history and antiquities of the parish of Wimbledon, Surrey* (1865); repr. (1971) · *Revised list of tombs and monuments of historical or archaeological interest in Bombay*, Government of Bombay [1912] · *CGPLA Eng. & Wales* (1883)
Archives BL OIOC, minutes, notes, and corresp., MS Eur. D 776 | BL, Bright MSS · BL, letters to Lord Ripon, Add. MS 43617 · BL, corresp. with Charles Wood, Add. MS 49552, *passim* · BL OIOC, corresp. with Sir G. R. Clerk, MS Eur. D 538 · Borth. Inst., corresp. with Lord Halifax · Som. ARS, letters from him and his wife to Lady Waldegrave · W. Yorks. AS, Leeds, letters to Lord Clamricarde
Likenesses J. Linnell, pencil and chalk drawing, NPG [*see illus.*]
Wealth at death £61,013 6s. 9d.: resworn probate, March 1883, *CGPLA Eng. & Wales* (1882)

Perry, Walter Copland (1814–1911), writer and collector of casts, born in Norwich on 24 July 1814, was the second son of Isaac Perry (1777–1837), a Congregational minister at Cherry Lane, Norwich (1802–14), who later became a Unitarian minister at Ipswich (1814–25) and at Edinburgh (1828–30), and then a schoolmaster at Liverpool. Walter's mother was Elizabeth, daughter of John Dawson Copland. He received his early education from his father, a fine scholar. In 1831 he was entered, as Walter Coupland Perry, at Manchester College, York, where he remained until 1836. He distinguished himself as a classical scholar, and on the advice of John Kenrick, tutor at Manchester College, who had studied at Göttingen, he went there in 1836; in August 1837 he gained a PhD with high honours for a thesis on Ephesus.

On returning to York, Perry replaced Kenrick as classical tutor in 1837–8, while the latter was ill. From 1838 to 1844 he was Unitarian minister at George's Meeting, Exeter, as colleague with Henry Acton. His pulpit services were more scholarly than popular. In 1844 he conformed to the Anglican church as a layman; his *Prayer Bell* (1843) suggests that his views were more evangelical than was common among Unitarians. He married on 23 June 1841 Hephzibah Elizabeth (d. 1880), second daughter of Samuel Shaen of

Crix Hall, Hatfield Peverel, Essex, with whom he had five sons, who all survived him, and one daughter (d. 1898).

On 12 January 1844 Perry entered as a student at the Middle Temple; he was called to the bar on 31 January 1851. After settling in Bonn at the end of 1844, he and his wife obtained great reputations as teachers and he came to act as the 'organ and representative of the English visitors at Bonn', as he expressed it. Among Perry's pupils were Edward Robert Bulwer, first earl of Lytton, Sir Francis Bertie, British ambassador in Paris, and Sir Eric Barrington.

On returning to Britain in 1875, Perry settled in London, where he was a member of the Athenaeum, and continued to write. He had already published on German universities (1845) and the Franks (1857) and now turned his hand to subjects as diverse as classical sculpture, Homer, Sicily, and the French Revolution, as well as fiction, of which he published some works anonymously and one pseudonymously as John Copland. In 1880 his first wife died and on 12 November 1889 he married Emma Evelyn, daughter of Robert Stopford. By his efforts, initiated at a meeting in Grosvenor House on 16 May 1877, followed by his paper 'On the formation of a gallery of casts from the antique in London' (1878), Perry gathered a large collection of casts, installed at first in a special gallery at the South Kensington Museum and after 1909 at the British Museum. He produced a catalogue of the collection in 1887. Such collections of casts had long been desired to enable students to trace the progress of classical sculpture, but Perry's creation was belated and short-lived. The British Museum, short of space for original sculptures, did not consider the cast gallery space well used and by 1939 the collection had been entirely dismantled and dispersed.

Perry, who had great personal charm, enjoyed blood sports and was a good amateur actor. He died at his residence, 25 Manchester Square, London, on 28 December 1911 and was buried in Hendon parish churchyard. He was survived by his wife.

ALEXANDER GORDON, rev. ELIZABETH BAIGENT

Sources *The Times* (1 Jan 1912) · *The Times* (3 Jan 1912) · private information (1912) · *Christian Life* (6 Jan 1912) · J. Browne, *A history of Congregationalism and memorials of the churches in Norfolk and Suffolk* (1877) · *Roll of students entered at the Manchester Academy* (1868) · J. Foster, *Men-at-the-bar: a biographical hand-list of the members of the various inns of court*, 2nd edn (1885) · *The trial of the English residents at Bonn* (1861) · I. Jenkins, *Archaeologists and aesthetes* (1992) · *CGPLA Eng. & Wales* (1912)
Wealth at death £2908 8s. 4d.: resworn probate, 20 May 1912, *CGPLA Eng. & Wales*

Perryn, Sir Richard (*bap.* 1723, *d.* 1803), judge, was baptized in the parish church of Flint on 16 August 1723, the son of Benjamin Perryn (d. 1761), merchant, and his wife, Jane (*bap.* 1701, *d.* 1781), eldest daughter of Richard Adams, town clerk of Chester. He was educated at Ruthin grammar school and matriculated from Queen's College, Oxford, on 13 March 1741, but did not take a degree. He had been admitted to Lincoln's Inn on 6 November 1740 and migrated on 27 April 1746 to the Inner Temple, where he was called to the bar on 3 July 1747. On 30 November

1752 he married Mary (1721/2–1795), daughter of Henry Browne of Skelbrooke, in the West Riding of Yorkshire; they had several children, including Richard, who became rector of Standish, Lincolnshire, and John and James, both of whom became army officers.

A character of Perryn published during his lifetime stated that 'it is well known that he was held *cheap* by the great Contemporaries with whom he practised' (Rede, 178), but in 1769 he was described by an attorney as 'one of the ablest Draftsmen attending the Chancery Barr' (Lemmings, 183n.) and in 1770 he was one of the busiest barristers in both the court of chancery and on the equity side of the exchequer. On 20 July 1770 he was appointed vice-chamberlain of Chester. He became a king's counsel on 28 January 1771, and also joined the bench of the Inner Temple in that year. He was made a baron of the exchequer in succession to Sir John Burland on 26 April 1776, and was knighted on the same day.

As a judge in criminal cases Perryn seems to have been inclined to ameliorate the law's harshness, although he could be severe when he felt normal process was evaded. When he was one of the judges at the trial of the hapless Dr William Dodd, for forgery, in February 1777 he complained of 'too great and an improper lenity to the prisoner at the bar in not putting him on the footing of other prisoners' by permitting him to avoid transferral to Newgate prison until the day before, contrary to the rules of sessions (*Old Bailey Proceedings*, 106). By July 1778 he was living in Twickenham, where Horace Walpole recorded that he was robbed at his own door; Walpole also said that one of Perryn's sons was imprisoned for debt in that month. In his charge to the grand jury of Sussex at the Lent assizes in 1785 he commented on Martin Madan's *Thoughts on Executive Justice with Respect to our Criminal Laws, Particularly on the Circuits* (1785), which had inveighed against the widespread practice of reprieving capital convicts from execution. Perryn was reported as saying that leaving them to hang 'would be making our laws like *Draco*, which, from their severity, were said to be written in blood' (Madan, 26), and made critical observations on the number of capital crimes in the statute book. He presided at the two trials of the Baptist preacher William Winterbotham for seditious words, held at Exeter in July 1793. The juries appear to have been strongly prejudiced against the defendant, and he was found guilty on both occasions, although at the second trial Perryn pointed out deficiencies in the evidence for the prosecution and stated that he was not convinced of Winterbotham's guilt. When the counsel for the defence argued in mitigation before the court of king's bench they reflected critically on Perryn's report of the trial for allegedly leaving out much of the evidence.

Perryn retired from the bench on 28 June 1799, and died at his home in Twickenham, Middlesex, on 2 January 1803. He was buried on 10 January in 'the new burial-ground' in Twickenham. In private life he was said to have been 'very much the Gentleman, and Man of Fashion; perfectly easy in his deportment, and amiable in his manners' (Rede, 179). DAVID LEMMINGS

Sources DNB · private information (2004) [Richard Morgan] · *State trials*, 22.905–6 · E. Foss, *Biographia juridica: a biographical dictionary of the judges of England … 1066–1870* (1870) · [M. Madan], *Thoughts on executive justice* (1785), appx · *Strictures on the lives and characters of the most eminent lawyers of the present day* (1790) · *Old Bailey proceedings* (1984), Feb 1777 [microfilm] · D. Lemmings, *Professors of the law* (2000) · G. Howson, *The Macaroni Parson* (1973) · Sainty, *Judges* · Sainty, *King's counsel* · Walpole, *Corr.*, 33.29–30 · Foster, *Alum. Oxon.* · GM, 1st ser., 65 (1795), 440; 73 (1803), 89
Likenesses G. Dupont, mezzotint, pubd 1779 (after Gainsborough), BM, NPG · print, Inner Temple, London

Persall [*alias* Harcourt], **John** (1633–1701), Jesuit, was born on 23 January 1633, a member of an old Catholic family and a native of Staffordshire. He studied humanities at the Jesuit college at St Omer (1648–53) and entered the Society of Jesus at Watten on 7 September 1653 under the name John Harcourt. After study at the Jesuit college at Liège and teaching at St Omer he was ordained about 1666. From about 1668 he taught philosophy at Liège, was professed of the four vows on 2 February 1671, and taught theology at Liège from 1672 to 1679. By 1683 he was a missioner in the Hampshire district of St Thomas. Two sermons of his, preached before James II and his queen in 1685–6, were subsequently published on royal authority, and reprinted in 1741. The first, preached in the chapel at St James's on 25 October 1685, used Christ's healing of the ruler's son (John 4) to address the sickness of the sinful soul and the means of cure. The second, preached at Windsor on Trinity Sunday, 30 May 1686, suggested in passing that heresies arose through failure to observe the principle 'That God can reveal more than we can understand' (*Catholick Sermons*, 2.266) and discussed the doctrine of the Trinity as an object of faith, love, and imitation. He was appointed one of the preachers in ordinary to James II and lived in the Jesuit college which opened in the Savoy, London, on 24 May 1687. Following the revolution of 1688 he escaped to the continent but appears to have been in Ireland during the time of James II's residence there. In 1694 he was declared rector of the Jesuit college of higher studies at Liège. He was appointed vice-provincial in England in 1696, and in that capacity attended the fourteenth annual congregation of the society held at Rome in the same year. He was again a missioner in the London district from 1699. The date of his death is usually given as 9 September 1701.

THOMPSON COOPER, *rev.* R. M. ARMSTRONG

Sources H. Foley, ed., *Records of the English province of the Society of Jesus*, 7 vols. in 8 (1875–83) · G. Holt, *The English Jesuits, 1650–1829: a biographical dictionary*, Catholic RS, 70 (1984) · Gillow, *Lit. biog. hist.* · *A select collection of Catholick sermons preach'd before … King James II*, 2 vols. (1741)

Perscrutator. *See* York, Robert (*fl.* 1313–1325).

Perse, Stephen (1547/8–1615), physician and benefactor, was born in either 1547 or 1548, the son of John Perse, landowner, of Great Massingham, Norfolk. He was educated at a school in Norwich before being admitted, aged seventeen, as a pensioner of Gonville and Caius College, Cambridge, on 29 October 1565. He graduated BA in 1569, and proceeded MA in 1572 and MD in 1581. Perse was elected to a fellowship of Caius in 1571 and, at university level, was elected to the *caput senatus* in 1589. He was ordained deacon and priest of Peterborough on 7 May 1573.

In 1582 Perse was implicated in a dispute between the master of Caius, Thomas Legge, and a majority of the fellows. Legge was accused of advancing Catholicism, maladministration, and acting without the consent of the fellows. Perse was held up as an example of the master's favouritism, having been allowed by Legge, without consultation, to change from a divinity to a medical fellowship and back again, and then to study medicine while holding a divinity fellowship. He was among those who supported Legge, and served alongside him and his successor as college bursar intermittently between 1586 and 1614. In 1603 he contributed to a collection of verses by members of the university celebrating James I's accession, *Threno-thriambeuticon*. He also composed the verse which was to be inscribed on his tomb.

Perse practised medicine in Cambridge, but it was as a result of investments in property and moneylending that he built up a personal fortune, which at the time of his death included £600 in property and leases, £10,000 in good debts, and over £3,000 in 'desperate debts' (CUL, university archives, records of the vice-chancellor's court, probate records, Perse's inventory, 1615). In his will he set out a scheme whereby small sums of money were to be lent out to local tradesmen, the interest so generated to be used in support of his charitable causes. The scheme fell through, but is illustrative of the connection Perse made between investment and charity. Two yeomen from Haddenham, Berkshire, who brought an unsuccessful petition against Perse for demanding excessive repayment between 1611 and 1613 in the court of chancery, seem to have viewed his efforts less favourably.

Perse died on 30 September 1615 and was buried in the college chapel. He and Legge were commemorated in effigy in near identical tombs. By a will dated 27 September, Perse divided his estate between charitable causes and his family. In one of the few clues as to his religion he named Valentine Carey, dean of St Paul's Cathedral and a noted supporter of the established church, as one of his executors. His will provided for the foundation of a free grammar school in Cambridge for local boys. It also established six fellowships and six scholarships at Caius, as well as the construction of a new building for the college, roads, and almshouses for local poor. Caius still celebrates Perse in an annual feast in his honour. Bequests to Mrs Ellvin, describing her as his 'mother-in-law', have given rise to the misapprehension that Perse was married. However, by the terms of his fellowship, he was required to remain celibate; and it is more likely that the expression was contemporary usage for stepmother.

Perse's will was precise, distributing a fixed income according to a rigid formula without regard for inflation. The master and fellows of Gonville and Caius, the administrators of the trust, became the sole beneficiaries of the increasing surplus which eventually developed, while the school itself was decaying by 1805. A chancery suit brought against the trustees in 1837 was heard by Henry Bickersteth, Baron Langdale, master of the rolls, who as a Perse fellow himself in 1830 drew attention to the iniquities of the scheme and paid back the excess he had received as a result. His judgment resulted in a new scheme for distribution of the trust's income, while further reform in 1873 resulted in the foundation of the Perse School for Girls in 1881. The school became a highly successful establishment as a result and moved to Hills Road in 1888.

ELLIE CLEWLOW

Sources C. N. L. Brooke, *A history of Gonville and Caius College* (1985) · S. J. D. Mitchell, *A history of the Perse School, 1615–1976* (1976) · J. Heywood and T. Wright, *Cambridge University transactions during the puritan controversies of the sixteenth and seventeenth centuries*, 2 vols. (1854) · BL, Lansdowne MS 33 · J. Venn, ed., *Biographical history of Gonville and Caius College*, 4 vols. (1897–1912), vols. 1, 3 · will, CUL, department of manuscripts and university archives, vice-chancellor's court will register III (1602–58), fols. 87v–94v · inventory, CUL, department of manuscripts and university archives, vice-chancellor's court, probate records · roll of Perse's debtors, Gon. & Caius Cam., LXIV, 4 · C. H. Cooper and J. W. Cooper, *Annals of Cambridge*, 5 vols. (1842–1908), vol. 3 · liber matriculationis, 1560–1678, Gon. & Caius Cam. · Venn, *Alum. Cant.* · J. M. Gray, *A history of the Perse School, Cambridge* (1921)

Archives Gon. & Caius Cam., papers and deeds relating to the administration of the Perse Trust

Likenesses attrib. M. Colte, tomb effigy, Gon. & Caius Cam.

Wealth at death approx. £11,000—£600 in leases and property; furniture and plate; £360 in cash; £10,000 in good debts; £3,300 in bad debts: inventory, 1615, and roll of debtors

Persons [Parsons], **Robert** (1546–1610), Jesuit, was born in Nether Stowey, Somerset, on 24 June 1546, the sixth of eleven children of Henry and Christina Persons. The religious affiliation of the family during his childhood is obscure. According to Anthony Wood, Henry Persons was converted to Roman Catholicism by the Jesuit Alexander Briant some time after 1579. Christina Persons later became part of the underground Catholic network. At least two brothers, George and Richard, became Catholics, while two others, John and Thomas, were protestant. John Persons became a clergyman of the Church of England and robustly defended his parents' reputation against the rumours of Robert Persons's illegitimacy that were spread by his detractors from 1598 onwards. Robert's niece Mary was one of the founding members of the English Benedictine abbey in Brussels.

Early career and vocation Persons won early distinction as a scholar and teacher. As a boy he attended the local grammar school at Stogursey and the free school at Taunton, where, after initial protests against ill treatment, he began to develop his lifelong habits of diligence and industry. After entering St Mary Hall, Oxford, in 1564, he migrated to Balliol College in 1566. He graduated BA on 31 May 1568, became a probationer fellow of Balliol, and in due course proceeded to the status of fellow (1569), lecturer in rhetoric (1571), bursar (1572), MA (3 December 1572), and dean (1573). On 13 February 1574 he resigned his fellowship under pressure from the master, Adam Squire, and another fellow, Christopher Bagshaw, who accused him of financial irregularity as bursar. Although he was given leave to stay until Easter, he was forced to retreat to London after attempting to enforce Lenten abstinence.

Robert Persons [Parsons] (1546–1610), by Johannes Valdor the elder

The reasons for this conflict at Balliol are still unclear. By all accounts Persons was an extremely popular and influential tutor. Bagshaw appears to have been motivated by personal rivalry and resentment; in the attempt to discredit Persons he suborned one of his pupils, James Hawley. He remained a bitter opponent of Persons throughout his career, even (and especially) after his own conversion to Catholicism. Persons may have provoked hostility by unwelcome signs of attachment to the Catholic faith during his Balliol career: although at first he showed an interest in studying Calvin, he was reluctant to subscribe to the oath of supremacy at his graduation, was impressed by the Catholic-leaning Edmund Campion, and distressed by the deprivation of his friend Richard Garnet, fellow of Balliol, for Catholicism in 1570.

Soon after his expulsion from Balliol, Persons decided to study medicine at Padua, possibly influenced by Lord Buckhurst, whose protection he enjoyed at this time. *En route* for Padua via Frankfurt he was delayed at Louvain in June 1574, where he performed the spiritual exercises of Ignatius of Loyola under the direction of the Jesuit William Good. His profound response to this experience was worked out over the next thirteen months: twice he visited Rome, the second time abandoning his studies at Padua and walking the road from Venice to Rome as an act of penance. He entered the Society of Jesus as a postulant on 4 July 1575. Making rapid progress in his studies at the Roman College, he was ordained priest in July 1578. Almost immediately he began an involvement with the conflicts within the English College, Rome, that was to last the rest of his life. The college, which had only recently developed from a hospice, was in turmoil over allegations of discrimination against English students by the Welsh rector, Maurice Clynnog. As a gifted scholar and teacher, already charged with the second year novices at the Roman College, Persons was approached for help by some of the students and tried to play a conciliatory role. The college was placed under Jesuit control in early 1579 with Alfonso Agazzari, a close associate of Persons, as rector.

The English mission Out of a correspondence over the controversy at the English College developed a highly influential lifelong collaboration between Persons and William Allen, founder of the seminary at Douai–Rheims and regarded as the leader of the English Catholics in exile. Allen came to Rome in October 1579 to consult with the Jesuit general, Everard Mercurian, about a possible Jesuit mission to England. Mercurian's initial reluctance was overcome largely by the enthusiasm of a friend of Persons, the Italian Jesuit Claudio Acquaviva. Persons was duly appointed superior of the mission, and Edmund Campion was summoned from Prague to Rome to join it. The group left for England on 18 April 1580, only nine days after Campion's arrival.

The aim of the mission was to strengthen the resolve of the Catholic faithful, forestall gradual absorption into the state church, and establish a network of support. Its political status was, however, ambivalent from the start. Pope Pius V's excommunication of Queen Elizabeth was still in force and, although Persons and Campion were strictly instructed not to involve themselves in political discussion and were empowered to release English Catholics from the duty of resisting Elizabeth's authority, the terms of the suspension of Elizabeth's deposition *rebus sic stantibus* ('so long as present conditions obtain') were open to sinister interpretation. It is probable that negotiations over the marriage of Queen Elizabeth to the French duke of Anjou also affected the timing and agenda of the mission. Moreover, the missionaries were compromised by a simultaneous Spanish military expedition to Ireland accompanied by Nicholas Sander, a prominent English Catholic apologist. Persons and Campion had to exercise extreme caution throughout their sojourn in England.

For safety's sake Campion and Persons entered England separately. Persons arrived in London on 17 June 1580, disguised as an army captain, and immediately made contact with the Catholic underground through Thomas Pounde, prisoner at the Marshalsea. His first act was to convene, in July, a synod of Catholic clergy at St Saviour, Southwark, at which the chief issue was recusancy. Persons firmly opposed church papism (occasional conformity by Catholics) at this synod and defended his position in his pamphlet *Reasons of Refusal*. Both Campion and Persons, anticipating arrest on charges of treason, now prepared declarations of intent; Campion's, which was prematurely released by Pounde as *Campion's Brag*, has become the more famous, especially in the light of his martyrdom, but Persons's *Confessio fidei* is of comparable interest.

Persons's activities on the mission in England included a missionary tour to the midlands and the west country, liaison with prominent Catholics in the London area, writing pamphlets, and setting up a secret printing press. This press, which was chiefly used for intervention in the controversy that blew up over *Campion's Brag*, was forced to change location at least twice. Eventually, in the spring of 1581, it was established at Stonor Park, near Henley, for the most daring propaganda initiative of the mission: the printing of Campion's apology for the Catholic faith, *Decem rationes*, to be distributed at St Mary's, the university church of Oxford, on 27 June, in time for the commencement exercises. Thereafter events turned against the Jesuits. Soon after parting from Persons, Campion, neglecting his superior's cautionary instructions, was captured at Lyford Grange (17 July), the press was seized, and Stephen Brinkley, the printer, arrested (4–13 August). Persons withdrew to Michaelgrove, Sussex, to review the situation and subsequently fled to France, taking refuge with the archdeacon Michael de Monsi (a connection of the Guise faction) in Rouen. Campion was executed for high treason on 1 December 1581, while Persons's place as superior was filled by Jasper Heywood, and later by William Weston (1584) and Henry Garnet (1588).

Persons's flight laid him open to accusations of cowardice; he remained in exile for the rest of his life, subject to the criticism of those who observed that Catholics in England had to pay the price of his uncompromising stance towards the Elizabethan government. Exile provided him with the freedom to exercise his apostolate of writing, while Campion's fate impelled him to work untiringly to build up the resources of the English mission and to secure, if possible, a political dispensation in England that would favour the growth of the Roman Catholic church. During his first months at Rouen he wrote his most influential work, *The First Booke of the Christian Exercise, Appertayning to Resolution* (Rouen, 1582; revised editions of 1585 and 1607 were known as *The Christian Directory*), urging his reader to 'resolve hym selfe to serve God in deed' (sig. A1v). This persuasive and forceful work guided the reader informally along a line of argument roughly equivalent to the initial stages of the Ignatian spiritual exercises. It was immediately recognized by protestants as a dangerously effective means of advancing the recusant cause, to the extent that a Calvinist divine, Edmund Bunny, felt it necessary to issue a heavily edited version, free of all specifically Roman Catholic doctrine and idiom. Bunny's version, *A Book of Christian Exercise, Appertaining to Resolution*, enjoyed phenomenal success as one of the most frequently reprinted of Elizabethan books, while the Catholic version, invariably called the *Resolution*, was a standard item in lists of Catholic books secretly distributed in England.

Invasion plans Opportunities for political intervention in support of a Catholic restoration soon presented themselves. Acquaviva, who succeeded Mercurian as general of the Jesuits, sent William Crichton to Scotland with a view to establishing a Scottish mission; his return to Paris in April 1582 issued in a plan devised by Henry, duke of Guise, Archbishop Beaton of Glasgow, and William Allen for a Spanish expedition to Scotland from Flanders. This would lead to an invasion of England in support of Mary Stuart or her son James VI. Persons was dispatched to Portugal to engage the interest of Philip II of Spain, who had recently secured the Portuguese succession. The invasion plan, which depended largely on the influence of the Catholic duke of Lennox on James, collapsed following the seizure of the king by protestants at the raid of Ruthven (23 August), but Persons remained in the Iberian peninsula until May 1583. For much of this time he was convalescing from a severe fever at Balbao and Ornate; nevertheless, he succeeded in striking up a fruitful relationship with Philip II, who promised financial aid to the seminary at Rheims.

On Persons's return to Paris, a second invasion plan was mooted; he now travelled to Rome to obtain papal briefs for the excommunication of Elizabeth and the appointment of Allen to a bishopric. This he achieved in August, but in the following months it became apparent that there would be little support from Spain. Persons turned his attention to the Spanish forces in Flanders under the command of Alessandro Farnese, prince of Parma; he spent time ministering to English Catholic soldiers in Parma's army and tried to promote interest in an invasion. Simultaneously he was active in organizing the communication lines for both the English and Scottish missions. When the immediate prospect of military intervention faded, he declared in October 1584 that he would devote his efforts, for the time being at least, to spiritual means alone. It appears that the new general, Acquaviva, urged him away from direct involvement in politics towards a more apostolic manner of proceeding.

Although Persons ultimately distanced himself from the Guise faction and the Catholic League, he made lifelong enemies among those Catholic exiles whose hopes were fixed on an alliance with the French monarchy. He was associated with (although he almost certainly did not write) the notorious pamphlet *The Copie of a Leter, Wryten by a Master of Arte of Cambridge Concerning the Erle of Leycester*, nicknamed *Parsons Greencoat* or *Leicester's Commonwealth* (1584), a scabrous attack on the earl of Leicester which the Guises used to embarrass Anglophiles at the French court. In response Charles Paget and Thomas Morgan used every opportunity to stir up hostility against Persons and discredit his activities. They found ready support in William Gifford, dean of Lille, and Oliver Mannaerts, the French provincial of the Jesuits.

In September 1585 Persons journeyed to Rome with William Allen. There he campaigned for Allen's elevation to cardinal, which was duly effected in August 1587. As plans for the Spanish Armada took shape Allen and Persons devised a strategy for Catholic restoration: they hushed up Philip II's claim to the English throne and composed a broadside for distribution by the invading forces, justifying the use of force against an illegitimate and heretical ruler. Persons was optimistic about the degree of support that Catholics in England would give to the invasion, with the result that his credit in Rome suffered after the failure of the Armada.

Late in 1588 Acquaviva sent Persons, together with Jose de Acosta, a Jesuit missionary to Peru and former provincial, to negotiate the Jesuit constitution in Spain. This followed a dispute between the Spanish Jesuits and the Inquisition over freedom of movement and the use of prohibited books. A creditable compromise was reached in March 1589. Persons's close association with Philip II led to a vigorous defence of the Spanish monarch's foreign policy in the work entitled *Elizabethae Angliae reginae in Catholicos edictum, cum responsione*, commonly known as the *Philopater* after the pseudonym Andreas Philopater. In it Persons responded satirically to the royal proclamation of October 1591 accusing Jesuits and seminarians of a treasonable alliance with Spain. It formed part of a propaganda campaign against Lord Burghley orchestrated by Persons and his agent in Antwerp, Richard Verstegan, who wrote two short English tracts in anticipation of Persons's Latin *Philopater*. Philip sponsored the publication of the *Philopater* in Antwerp, Lyons, Cologne, Naples, and Rome. Thomas Stapleton and Joseph Creswell also produced Latin treatises in defence of Philip's record, while the royal proclamation was supported by an unpublished work of Francis Bacon, *Certain Observations Made upon a Libel Published this Present Year, 1592*. Prospects of renewed Spanish invasion attempts in 1592 and 1596 temporarily raised Persons's hopes for an early end to persecution and protestant rule in England, but he was frequently frustrated by the priority given to Spanish domestic interests over the fate of the Roman church in England.

The seminaries During Persons's sojourn in Spain (1589–96) he negotiated for better treatment of English Catholic exiles in Spain and converted many English sailors held prisoner in Spanish ports. Most of his energy, however, was devoted to the establishment of seminaries, to prepare over a longer term for eventual restoration of the Roman church in England. On his arrival in Spain in early 1589 he appealed to Philip for funds for the overstretched college at Rheims. Later that year he founded a new seminary at Valladolid, followed by a hospice at Sanlúar (1591) and a seminary in Seville (1592); Philip honoured the English College at Valladolid with a royal visit in 1592. The colleges at Valladolid and Seville grew rapidly in the initial stages, but unrest grew when Persons himself had to leave their administration to others, such as the less tactful Joseph Creswell. The seminaries suffered from tensions with the Spanish Jesuits and were regarded as unwelcome competition for charity.

It was also through Persons's intervention, supported by Philip II, that a school for the sons of recusants was founded at St Omer in 1593. This was prompted by legislation planned for the parliament, due to open on 19 February, that would have placed severe restrictions on the children of recusant families. William Flack was sent from Valladolid to be the first headmaster. This school grew to over a hundred pupils by 1598, and gained an international reputation in the seventeenth century for its schoolboy drama. In the late eighteenth century, as a result of the expulsion of the Jesuits from France, it was transferred first to Liège and then to Stonyhurst, Lancashire.

All these foundations pursued a broad humanist curriculum rather than an agenda based on contemporary controversy: they reflected Persons's confidence that learning was firmly on the side of the Catholic faith. In the *Philopater*, and in the subsequent *Newes from Spayne and Holland* (1593, sometimes attributed to Henry Walpole), he defended the seminaries against charges of sedition, arguing that the students were being equipped to succour the Catholic community through depth of learning and readiness for self-sacrifice. He contrasted the supposed decline of Oxford and Cambridge with the vigour of all the Catholic English colleges abroad, including Rome and Douai–Rheims. In an account of the royal visit to Valladolid he praised the accomplishments of the students, especially in the ancient and modern languages. His educational philosophy thus coincided with Jesuit principles later codified in the *Ratio studiorum* of 1599.

The English succession Persons's hopes for a more favourable political dispensation now depended on the succession to the crown: James VI of Scotland might convert to the Catholic faith; the Spanish royal family had strong claims through the house of Lancaster; other contenders such as Ferdinand Stanley, Lord Strange, heir to the Derby title, had Catholic connections. Even if the successor were not Catholic, concessions might be won by offering Catholic support or by playing off the Cecil and Essex parties. Making use of genealogical researches by William Allen and Sir Francis Englefield, and taking advantage of a field left open by the official ban on public discussion of the issue, Persons produced, under the name of Doleman, the *Conference about the Next Succession to the Crowne* (Antwerp, 1595), mischievously dedicated to Essex. This work, which created a minor sensation in England, affected an entirely neutral and objective assessment of the rival claims, concluding that there was no clear favourite. It argued further, against the developing trend of absolutist political theory, that hereditary right had to be weighed against other considerations of beneficial rule, particularly the maintenance of religious orthodoxy. Despite Persons's vigorous denials, he was assumed to be covertly promoting the claim of Isabella, the infanta of Spain. Some doubt still remains over the authorship of the *Conference*, which was the subject of heated debate both in London and Rome.

In his writing Persons developed a clear policy for a Catholic restoration, determined to avoid the mistakes made during the reign of Mary Tudor; he elaborated the policy in some detail in a *Memorial for the Reformation of England*, composed in 1596 and circulated in manuscript, partly for the benefit of Isabella. His opponents saw in this a recipe for a clerical state dominated by the Jesuits, but its emphasis was on the reconstruction of all aspects of public life, especially education and justice. The work was first published by protestants in 1690 after the deposition of

James II as a warning against the return of a Catholic monarch.

Over the next few years Persons courted both the chief rivals to the throne: he exerted pressure on James VI to favour the Catholics, and he urged Philip II and, after his demise in 1598, Philip III, to support Isabella's claim publicly. Robert Cecil approached Persons indirectly about the succession from June to October 1600, but this was probably a manoeuvre to probe the intentions of Philip III rather than a genuine recognition of the English Catholics' role in the succession struggle. In the event, Persons's diplomacy foundered on the reluctance of Isabella to put herself forward as a serious candidate, the caution displayed by Philip III, and the superior strategy of Robert Cecil, who secured a Scottish succession with no obligations to the recusants.

Persons's intervention in the succession debate signalled an intensification of conflict within the English Catholic community. In 1594, even before the *Conference* was published, hostile rumours were spreading; the general, Acquaviva, at first expressed his alarm, especially in view of the recent resolution of the third general congregation of the Society of Jesus to ban all political involvement. Cardinal Allen died on 16 October 1594, further accelerating the fragmentation among the exiles. Persons's opponents almost immediately began to dissociate Allen from him, fearful that he would be next to be raised to the cardinalate. Matters came to a head in the unrest at the English College, Rome, as students supporting the anti-Jesuit party of Bishop Owen Lewis, another prime candidate to succeed Allen, rebelled against the Jesuit rector, Agazzari. Strong criticism of the *Conference* became commonplace at the college. Persons was eventually recalled from Spain in September 1596; by a combination of impassioned speeches and skilful private conferences he succeeded in pacifying the college during the course of the following year. He remained there as rector for the rest of his life.

The archpriest and 'watchword' controversies In Rome Persons wielded considerable influence through the patronage of the cardinal–nephew, Aldobrandino, and the friendship of Cardinal Camillo Borghese. When he was consulted about the most suitable hierarchy for the Catholic church in England for the time being, Persons ultimately approved the creation of an archpriest to assume authority over secular priests (that is priests who did not belong to a religious order) working in England. George Blackwell was accordingly appointed early in 1598. A group of secular priests, predominantly those connected with the 'Wisbech stirs', where imprisoned priests divided into pro- and anti-Jesuit factions, appealed to Pope Clement VIII against this arrangement on the grounds that it had been authorized only by the cardinal–protector of England, Cajetan. A bitter conflict ensued, lasting at least until 1602. In the course of several delegations to Rome the so-called appellants enlisted the diplomatic support of France and accused Persons of unfairly obstructing the appeal process. In fact Persons sometimes behaved in a conciliatory way, but Blackwell acted heavy-handedly,

accusing the appellant party of schism. The English government, through the bishop of London, Richard Bancroft, wooed the appellants with prospects of toleration and assisted in the printing of numerous pamphlets, many of which abused Persons in the most vituperative language. For his part Persons wrote two lofty denunciations, *A briefe apologie, or defence of the Catholike ecclesiastical hierarchie, and subordination in England* (Antwerp, 1601) and *A manifestation of the great folly and bad spirit of certayne in England calling themselves secular priestes* (Antwerp, 1602). Finally, in October 1602, Clement VIII upheld the archpriest's office but without severely censuring the appellants; Blackwell's personal authority was substantially weakened as a result.

Throughout the period of the archpriest controversy and for several years afterwards Persons was also engaged in a series of acrimonious controversies with protestant opponents over the question of the treasonableness of recusancy. Persecution of English Catholics had diminished during the period 1595–8 when England was informally allied with France in the latter's war with Spain. It was hoped that Henri IV might be able to negotiate a degree of toleration, but nothing came of the peace of Vervins (May 1598). Alarmist characterization of Catholics as seditious and unpatriotic was on the increase again after the republication in 1596 of Foxe's *Actes and Monuments*. Sir Francis Hastings excitedly warned against the Catholic threat in his *Watch-Word to All Religious, and True Hearted English-Men* (1598). For his part Persons planned a full-scale counter to Foxe by compiling an ecclesiastical history of England from the Catholic point of view. His interest in this subject was first shown when he worked on revising Nicholas Sander's incomplete *De schismate*, published in 1585; he drew up a scheme while in Valladolid in 1594, and now he collected material from various correspondents in England and Europe. The results were transcribed into the voluminous *Certamen ecclesiae Anglicanae*, which bears the date 24 June 1599 on the title-page of the first volume. In the same year he responded directly to Hastings with his *Temperate Ward-Word, to the Turbulent and Seditious Wach-Word*, drawing into the fray a rather more evenly matched opponent, Matthew Sutcliffe, dean of Exeter.

It was not until 1602 that Persons, distracted by appellant affairs, produced his next rejoinder, his extensive *Warn-Word to Sir Francis Hastinges*. This he designed as a compendium of all controversy over the character of the English church, to settle the issue in the minds of his readers. On the more specifically historical issue he appears to have abandoned the Latin *Certamen* at this stage in favour of a more polemical reply to Foxe, published in three volumes in 1603–4 as *A Treatise of Three Conversions of England from Paganisme to Christian Religion*. Here Persons attempted to demonstrate the English church's debt to Rome, and the compatibility of the doctrine and practice of the modern Roman church with that of the Christian religion in England from the earliest days. He dismissed the so-called calendar of Foxe's martyrs (a non-authorial embellishment of the *Actes and Monuments*) satirically month by month. Since so many of Foxe's narratives centred on commonsensical objections to the mass, *Three Conversions* concluded with a lucid exposition of Tridentine teaching on this subject.

Treason and toleration: the final years Following the accession of James I in June 1603 Persons gave up hope of a new Catholic order but wrote to the new king to put the case for toleration, based on what he took to be Elizabeth's sorry experience. He also warned him against an assassination plot by Rollino, to the amusement of the prescient Sir Robert Cecil. The possibility now arose of better collaboration with secular priests, whose more violent attacks on the Jesuits ceased with the execution for treason of two of Persons's chief calumniators, Watson and Clarke, on 9 December 1603. Despite a new royal proclamation against Jesuits, seminarians, and priests in February 1604, Persons continued to hope for a new climate of mitigation under James; the election of his friend Cardinal Borghese to the papacy in April 1605 also strengthened his position in Rome. In a memorandum written for Pope Paul V on how best to combat protestantism in the northern countries he was content to advocate the use of spiritual weapons only.

This moderately optimistic state of affairs was rudely interrupted by the Gunpowder Plot of Robert Catesby and his fellow conspirators. Persons had first to deal with the backlash against the Jesuits. For the information of General Acquaviva he translated the royal proclamation against John Gerard, Oswald Tesimond, and Henry Garnet, and after the execution of Garnet on 3 May 1606 he wrote to comfort his brethren in England. Conflict with the anti-Jesuit party among the Catholics continued as Persons saw to it that William Gifford, dean of Lille and his old enemy, was expelled from the Netherlands; he also approached the pope in an attempt to lift the prohibition on the archpriest's consulting with Jesuits, one of the concessions to the appellants. John Cecil and Anthony Champney, now the most prominent of the appellants, returned to Rome in mid-1606 for yet another appeal.

Persons now became deeply involved in the printed controversy over Catholic treason and the new oath of allegiance drawn up in consequence of the Catesby plot. In his *Answere to the Fifth Part of Reportes Lately Set Forth by Syr Edward Cooke* (St Omer, 1606) he denounced the tactics used against Garnet at his trial. The critique of these procedures was linked to a questioning of Coke's celebration of English freedom from canon law; in Persons's view, the state of English justice was in serious decline.

Persons's writings on the issues raised by the Gunpowder Plot were engaged in two interlocking controversies. Against what he regarded as seditious attacks on the recusants' loyalty by the king's chaplain, Thomas Morton, he wrote *A Treatise Tending to Mitigation Towardes Catholicke-Subjectes in England* (St Omer, 1608) and *A Quiet and Sober Reckoning with M. Thomas Morton* (St Omer, 1609), in which he argued that two religions could coexist peacefully in one country. This position reflected a pragmatic shift from his earlier political writings, which demanded uniformity in religion as the basis of the national welfare. The

vehemency and, as he saw it, the puerility of his opponent's writing allowed him to present himself as magisterial, a character which his reputation as a consummate polemicist now seemed to sustain. On the narrower question of the new oath of allegiance proposed in 1606, which represented the most determined effort yet to secure the political loyalty of English Catholics to the crown, Persons wrote a manuscript *Discourse Against Taking the Oath in England*. He also devised a memorial for Cardinal Robert Bellarmine, who was charged with giving the official Roman response. This drew him into an exchange with the king himself, whose anonymous *Triplici nodo, triplex cuneus* (1607) he countered with *The Judgment of a Catholicke English-Man* (St Omer, 1608). His chief argument was that recusants needed only the smallest concession from the government on the matter of the pope's authority to justify swearing their allegiance to the crown. The plotters, he claimed, had been exasperated by James's failure to make any of the concessions he had hinted at.

Both Jesuits and seculars were united against the oath of allegiance, but Persons's position was weakened by the decision of the archpriest, Blackwell, to take the oath on 7 July 1607. Although Blackwell was deposed by the pope the following February, his successor, George Birkhead, proved lukewarm to Persons, desiring to replace the Jesuit's close associate, Thomas Fitzherbert, as the archpriest's agent in Rome. Richard Smith, who was formally appointed to this office in March 1609, was overtly hostile to Persons. His determination to eclipse the Jesuit's influence in Rome dominated the final year of Persons's life, culminating in rival attempts to suppress each other's works by delating them to the curia. Persons was somewhat embittered by this continued conflict, which, despite a brief reconciliation, confirmed the archpriest Birkhead's attitude to Persons and so diminished Jesuit influence among the recusants. In early 1610 he also came under attack from the former seminarian William Alabaster, who accused him of complicity in the Gunpowder Plot. Persons was further frustrated by the appearance of William Barlow's *Answer to a Catholicke English-Man* (1608), which he felt obliged to savage in his *Discussion of the Answere of M. William Barlow*, completed after his death by Fitzherbert in 1612. He would much rather, he claimed, have spent the time on the long-postponed expansion of *The Christian Directory*.

From April 1608 Persons complained of almost continual indisposition, but despite his declining health he continued to provide leadership for the Catholic exiles. He dispatched John Blackfan to settle the troubles at Valladolid in November 1608, and advised on the administration of women's religious houses in Flanders, including the Benedictine convent in Brussels to which his niece Mary Persons belonged. Illness overtook him on 6 April 1610, Tuesday of holy week, and he died an exemplary death at the English College, Rome, the following Thursday, 15 April, after enduring several attacks which, according to contemporary reports, he bore with edifying fortitude and unabridged piety. Tributes were paid by Pope Paul V and Cardinal Bellarmine. He was buried next to

Cardinal Allen before the high altar of the chapel at the English College, Rome, where his epitaph inscription is still to be found.

Persons's achievements As a Jesuit leader and administrator Persons showed exceptional energy and organizational skill. On the English mission of 1580–81 he was more prudent than the older Campion, whose arrest followed his disregarding of Persons's instructions. He built up an efficient network of support for subsequent missionaries to England: approach routes, supplies of books and religious objects, lines of communication, and funds. He encouraged Weston and Garnet, his successors as superior in England, with frequent letters. From his vantage points on the continent, in Flanders, Spain, and Rome, he laid the foundation for the establishment of the English province of the Society of Jesus, whose first provincial, Henry More, wrote admiringly of him in his *History of the English Jesuits* (1660). The correspondence of contemporary Jesuits bears ample witness to his readiness to help wherever needed. He was, wrote his contemporary Pedro de Ribadeneira, 'the martyr not of a moment but of a lifetime' ('non semel tantum, sed per totam vitam quodammodo Martyr'; 725). His epitaph at the Venerable English College, Rome, includes the phrases: 'always ready, always steadfast, always plunging into the middle of the flame of the most dangerous conflict' ('semper paratus, semper erectus, semper in mediam flammam periculosissimae concertationis irrumpens'). His force of character, which impressed those he met, is recorded in this early description: 'Father *Parsons*, as to his person, was of middle size; his complexion rather swarthy; which, with his strong features, made his countenance somewhat forbidding. But his address, and the agreeableness of his conversation, quickly worked off the aversion' (Dodd, 2.404).

Strategically, Persons's interventions had mixed fortunes. His steadfast rejection of occasional conformity to the established religion may have ensured the survival of the English Catholic church as a distinct community, but also contributed to the increased harshness of recusancy laws. To find the funds and personnel for seminaries at Valladolid, Seville, and St Omer, as well as the hospice at Sanlúcar, was itself a considerable and lasting achievement, marked today by Stonyhurst College and St Alban's College, Valladolid. But too often the men to whom he entrusted the colleges lacked his authority and diplomatic skills, with the result that internal strife was endemic at Valladolid and Seville. At the English College, Rome, he played the part of peacemaker and then rector with aplomb, but even there divisions were never fully healed. The decision to support the appointment of an archpriest, and the subsequent conflict with the appellants, long drawn out, demonstrated both his strength and his weakness. He believed passionately in the necessity for unity among English Catholics and so, although he was prepared to act in a conciliatory and even at times generous manner towards the appellants, he was uncompromising in his opposition to dissent and used all his

power and influence, sometimes (it seems) unscrupulously, to block appeals to the papacy. Ultimately he was outmanoeuvred by the second archpriest, Birkhead.

Persons has conventionally been blamed for the pro-Spanish political alliances that proved disastrous for the recusants. Charges of treason and lack of patriotism are largely beside the point: he represented a persecuted minority that the English authorities were determined to neutralize by fair means or foul, and he believed that England's health as a nation depended on her reconversion to Rome. The strategic wisdom of his political activities, from the alliance with the duke of Guise (1582–4) to the close association with Philip of Spain (1588–96), is open to question. He alternated between optimism and pessimism and between military force and spiritual means. It should, however, be remembered that he had very patchy information on English domestic affairs, that he was in continual exile from 1581 to the end of his life, and that he never enjoyed the wholehearted support and confidence of Philip II. These factors placed him at a distinct disadvantage *vis-à-vis* his chief opponents, Lord Burghley and his son Robert Cecil.

Although Persons's fame—or notoriety—rests on his exploits as missionary and strategist of the Catholic reformation, his most enduring achievement, arguably, was literary. 'Persons the mission priest could easily be replaced by another, but the works of Persons the author could only be written by a few' (Meyer, 199). He was a prolific controversialist, feared by his opponents for his satirical wit and powers of logical demolition, and welcomed by his co-religionists for the confidence he imparted to the Catholic cause. The conviction of contemporary recusants and priests that doctrinal orthodoxy and moral probity were firmly on the side of Rome can in large measure be attributed to his reputation as a polemical writer. Although he was not a profound or original theologian, he had a gift for lucid expression and powerful exhortation; lacking the analytical erudition of the famous preachers of his day such as Donne and Andrewes, he nevertheless used scripture freely and persuasively. His spirituality was marked not so much by veneration for Roman tradition as a belief that Catholic doctrine, especially as defined by the Council of Trent, was eminently reasonable. His writings were for the most part occasional, responding to events such as the leaking of *Campion's Brag*, the post-Armada proclamations, and the framing of oaths of allegiance. Yet none is without some literary interest, because of Persons's skill at choosing techniques and genres to enhance his polemic: he used dialogue, satire, imaginative scenario, newsletter, epistle, and narrative to striking effect. His flexibility of tone also gives his prose a decidedly modern flavour. 'The writings of *Hooker*, who was a Country Clergyman, and of *Parsons* the Jesuit', wrote Jonathan Swift in *The Tatler*, 28 September 1710, 'are in a style that, with very few Allowances, would not offend any present Reader; much more clear and intelligible than … several others who wrote later' (*Prose Writings*, 2.177).

Several of Persons's works, such as *The Christian Directory*, *A Conference about the Next Succession*, and *A Treatise of*

Three Conversions, remained current for a century and more, probably because they represent, in a particularly readable form, the convictions of a brilliant and articulate English Roman Catholic coming to terms with religious pluralism. *The Christian Directory* was admired by Gabriel Harvey, Thomas Nashe, Sir John Harington, and Thomas Middleton, and was instrumental in the conversions of Robert Greene, Benet of Canfield, and Richard Baxter. Numerous young men in late Elizabethan England were impelled by its rhetoric to choose a Jesuit vocation. A foreign contemporary, Leon Coquaeus, claimed that his forcible arguments were as convincing as the resurrection of a dead man. In the early seventeenth century it was translated into German as *Guldenes Kleinod der Kinder Gottes* and often reprinted. *The Christian Directory* has thus been reckoned one of the most widely dispersed and influential English books of spirituality of the post-Reformation period.

The *Conference about the Next Succession* had a curious afterlife. During the revolutionary debates in the 1640s it was partially reprinted at least twice as anti-royalist propaganda, and, even more ironically, Algernon Sidney reprinted it in 1681 in his attempt to exclude the Catholic James, duke of York, from the succession. This version was known to Jonathan Swift, while Edward Gibbon possessed a copy of the *Treatise of Three Conversions* and imputed his youthful, temporary conversion to Catholicism to Persons's arguments.

Persons's reputation has suffered from what has come to be known as the 'black legend': a long English tradition of anti-Jesuit propaganda in which his figure was for many years the most prominent target. The appellants, encouraged by the authorities, systematically vilified him as a bastard, an ambitious 'Machiavel', and an 'Hispaniolated chameleon' consistent only in his promotion of the narrow interests of Spain and the Jesuits. Protestant propagandists, especially Matthew Sutcliffe, echoed these charges in an attempt to smear all Catholic recusants. 'Father Parsons the Jesuit' continued to feature at times of national outcry against popery, as in the late seventeenth century when Edward Gee published his *Memorial* as a warning against any future popish succession. Charles Kingsley, the nineteenth-century novelist who had a celebrated clash with Newman, offered an extremely unflattering portrait of Persons in *Westward Ho!* (1855). Late twentieth-century historiography has shown more sympathy with the complexities of his predicament as a leader in exile, and a higher estimation of his gifts as an organizer and polemicist. VICTOR HOULISTON

Sources F. Edwards, *Robert Persons: the biography of an Elizabethan Jesuit, 1546–1610* (1995) • L. Hicks, ed., *Letters and memorials of Father Robert Persons*, Catholic RS, 39 (1942) • 'The memoirs of Father Robert Persons', ed. J. H. Pollen, *Miscellanea, II*, Catholic RS, 2 (1906), 12–218 • 'The memoirs of Father Persons', ed. J. H. Pollen, *Miscellanea, IV*, Catholic RS, 4 (1907), 1–161 • A. Kenny, 'Reform and reaction in Elizabethan Balliol, 1559–1588', *Balliol studies*, ed. J. Prest (1982), 17–51 • T. M. McCoog, *The Society of Jesus in Ireland, Scotland, and England, 1541–1588* (1996) • A. F. Allison and D. M. Rogers, eds., *The contemporary printed literature of the English Counter-Reformation between 1558 and 1640*, 2 vols. (1989–94) • P. Milward, *Religious controversies of the*

Elizabethan age (1977) • P. Milward, *Religious controversies of the Jacobean age* (1978) • J. Bossy, 'The heart of Robert Persons', *The reckoned expense: Edmund Campion and the early English Jesuits*, ed. T. M. McCoog (1996), 141–58 • *The Elizabethan Jesuits: Historia missionis Anglicanae Societatis Jesu (1660) of Henry More*, ed. and trans. F. Edwards (1981) • C. Dodd [H. Tootell], *The church history of England, from the year 1500, to the year 1688*, 3 vols. (1737–42) • P. de Ribadeneira, *Bibliotheca scriptorum Societatis Jesu opus inchoatum* (Rome, 1676) • A. O. Meyer, *England and the Catholic church under Queen Elizabeth*, trans. J. R. McKee (1916); repr. with introduction by J. Bossy (1967) • T. M. McCoog, ed., 'Robert Parsons and Claudio Acquaviva: correspondence', *Archivum Historicum Societatis Jesu*, 68 (1999), 79–182 • *The prose writings of Jonathan Swift*, ed. H. Davis and others, 2 (1941), 177

Archives Archives of the British Province of the Society of Jesus, London, corresp. • Berks. RO, corresp. • Bodl. Oxf., corresp. • LUL, papers • NL Scot., 'A memoriall for the reformation of England' • Pembroke Cam., notes for succession | Archives of the British province of the Society of Jesus, London, Collectanea P • Archives of the English College, Valladolid, series II • Archivum Romanum Societatis Iesu, Rome, Epistolae selectae ex Anglia, Fondo Gesuitico MS 651

Likenesses H. Wierix, print, *c*.1619, Rome • J. Neeffs, line engraving, 1669, NPG; repro. in C. Hazart, *Kerklyche historie* (Antwerp, 1669) • line engraving, pubd 1794, BM, NPG • C. Gregori, line engraving, BM • J. Valdor the elder, line engraving, Stonyhurst College, Lancashire [*see illus.*]

Perth. For this title name *see* Drummond, James, fourth earl of Perth and Jacobite first duke of Perth (1648–1716); Drummond, James, styled fifth earl of Perth and Jacobite second duke of Perth (1674–1720); Drummond, James, styled sixth earl of Perth and Jacobite third duke of Perth (1713–1746); Drummond, John, styled seventh earl of Perth and Jacobite fourth duke of Perth (*c*.1714–1747); Drummond, (James) Eric, seventh earl of Perth (1876–1951).

Pertinax (126–193). *See under* Roman emperors (*act.* 55 BC–AD 410).

Pertwee, Jon Devon Roland (1919–1996), actor, was born on 7 July 1919 at 3 Sheffield Terrace, Kensington, London. He was the second son of the playwright, painter, and actor Roland Pertwee and his actress wife, Avice Scholtz. His parents separated when he was still an infant, and he and his brother Michael were brought up by their paternal grandmother.

He had a chequered school career, being expelled from his preparatory school and from Sherborne School before attending the progressive school Frensham Heights and finally the Royal Academy of Dramatic Art, where the principal considered him without talent. In 1936 Pertwee secured a place in the final tour of the Arts League of Service Travelling Theatre, directed by Donald Wolfit. In 1937 he joined J. Baxter-Somerville's Repertory Players at the Springfield Theatre in Jersey, and then toured with the Rex Lesley-Smith repertory company for a year before returning to London. During 1938 and 1939 Pertwee obtained several small parts in theatre before the actor John Salew gave him a break into commercial radio, where he stayed for the next two years. To supplement his income, he also worked as an extra at Denham film studios, appearing in productions including *Dinner at the Ritz*

Jon Devon Roland Pertwee (1919–1996), by unknown photographer, 1971 [as Dr Who, with Daleks]

(1936), *A Yank at Oxford* (1938), *Young Man's Fancy* (1939), and *The Four Just Men* (1939).

When the Second World War broke out Pertwee joined the navy as a wireless operator. On 29 November 1940 he was drafted on to *HMS Hood*, but he was transferred to the *Dunluce Castle* to train as an officer cadet just before *HMS Hood* had its fateful battle with the *Bismarck* on 24 May 1941. Following an incendiary bomb attack on Portsmouth barracks, he suffered a severe blow to the head and was dropped from the officer cadet course to be posted to the Isle of Man as a divisional officer. There he formed a small company of local amateurs and servicemen which became known as the Service Players. In 1946 Pertwee joined the cast of Eric Barker's forces radio show *Mediterranean Merry-Go-Round*, and in 1948 the fictional *HMS Waterlogged* became the subject of a spin-off show entitled *Waterlogged Spa*, for which Pertwee created a memorable radio character, the Postman, with the catch-phrase 'What does it matter what you do as long as you tear 'em up?'

Pertwee received star billing for a film for the first time in 1953, with George Cole in *Will any Gentleman …?*, filming which he met the actress Jean (Jeann Lindsey Torren) Marsh (*b.* 1934). They were married on 2 April 1955, but the marriage quickly broke down. It was on a skiing holiday in Kitzbühel in February 1958 that Pertwee met Ingeborg Renate Rhösa (*b.* 1934/5), a young German dress designer, and immediately fell in love. Pertwee was divorced from Marsh in 1960 and married Ingeborg on 13 August the

same year. They had two children, who both became actors. In 1958 Pertwee was asked by the BBC's head of light entertainment if he had any ideas for a new radio comedy series in which he might be interested in starring. Out of these discussions came *The Navy Lark*, a show which ran for eighteen years and 240 episodes, and took full advantage of Pertwee's range of funny voices.

During the sixties Pertwee continued working in film, including three of the popular *Carry on* films: *Carry on Cleo* (1964), *Carry on Cowboy* (1965), and *Carry on Screaming* (1966). He also enjoyed successful stage tours in *A Funny Thing Happened on the Way to the Forum* (1963–6) and *There's a Girl in my Soup* (1966–7).

In 1969 Pertwee succeeded Patrick Troughton as the star of the long-running BBC science fiction series *Dr Who*. Following William Hartnell's original creation of the Doctor as a crotchety old man and Troughton's humorous, somewhat fey interpretation, Pertwee played the Doctor rather more straight, as a flamboyant man of action complete with Edwardian roadster and clothes to match. This Doctor, earthbound by sentence of the Time Lords, confronted and defeated a weekly array of hostile aliens in the English countryside and metropolis, with the help of a team of United Nations soldiers and a girl assistant. The show frequently attracted audiences of over eight million viewers, and for a whole generation Pertwee was simply 'the Doctor'. He stayed with the show for five seasons, his character physically regenerating in 1974 into the irrepressible Tom Baker. After leaving *Dr Who*, Pertwee for five years hosted the successful quiz *Whodunnit?* for Thames Television and appeared in the film *One of our Dinosaurs is Missing* (1975). In 1976–7 he returned to the theatre in the musical *Irene*. In 1979 he was cast as the scarecrow Worzel Gummidge in Southern Television's series of that name, and he played the part with a fruity Devonian accent for four seasons. It won him another loyal audience of young children, both in Britain and abroad.

Pertwee continued to work on stage, appearing as Jacob Marley in *Scrooge—the Musical* in 1991–2. He returned to the role of the Doctor for several Dr Who stories and appeared in other television programmes including *Young Indiana Jones* (1994). He provided character voices for a computer game based on Terry Pratchett's *Discworld* in 1995.

Pertwee was in constant demand for appearances at science fiction conventions and in cabaret, for after-dinner speaking, and for guest appearances on television and radio and for charity: he was ever ready to don the costumes of the parts which had brought him celebrity, to please the fans and raise funds. In the early part of 1996 he was touring in two different productions, one an evening of music and comedy, the other his popular one-man show *Who is Jon Pertwee?* Throughout his career of more than five decades, Pertwee was a staunch supporter of and fund-raiser for the Grand Order of Water Rats, a charity caring for elderly and retired members of the acting profession.

Jon Pertwee died in his sleep on 20 May 1996 from a heart attack while on holiday in Connecticut, USA, weeks after completing work on his second volume of autobiography, *I am the Doctor* (1996). He was cremated at Putney Vale crematorium.   DAVID J. HOWE

Sources D. J. Howe, S. J. Walker, and M. Stammers, *Doctor Who: the seventies* (1994) · J. Pertwee, *Moon boots and dinner suits* (1984) · J. Pertwee and D. J. Howe, *I am the Doctor* (1996) · *The Times* (21 May 1996) · *The Independent* (21 May 1996) · *The Independent* (23 May 1996) · *Daily Telegraph* (21 May 1996) · b. cert. · m. certs. · personal knowledge (2004) · private information (2004) · *CGPLA Eng. & Wales* (1996)
Likenesses photographs, *c.*1950–1980, Hult. Arch. · photograph, 1971, Hult. Arch. [*see illus.*] · photograph, repro. in *The Times* · photograph, repro. in *The Independent* · photograph, repro. in *Daily Telegraph*
Wealth at death £420,149: probate, 1996, *CGPLA, Eng. & Wales* (1996)

Pertz, Dorothea Frances Matilda [Dora] (1859–1939), botanist, was born in London on 14 March 1859, the third and youngest daughter of Georg Heinrich Pertz (1795–1876), royal librarian in Berlin, and his second wife, Leonora Horner (*b.* 1818). There were three half-brothers, married with children, from her father's first marriage. Dora Pertz (as she was usually called) could claim scientifically distinguished antecedents in that her maternal grandfather was Leonard Horner, geologist, antiquary, and friend of Charles Darwin. Her aunts Mary, Katherine, and Frances Horner were married to Charles Lyell, Henry Lyell, and Charles James Fox Bunbury, respectively, and the two remaining aunts, Susan and Joanna Horner, wrote and travelled widely. All these Horner women, including her mother, had active intellectual lives, studying plants, shells and minerals, writing, translating, editing, and helping their menfolk with their researches. Her father was, moreover, a distinguished historian with a wide acquaintance among European literary scholars of the day, the author of *Monumenta Germanica* and editor of Leibniz's papers (1843–63). Dora Pertz remembered meeting these relations and other notable figures as a girl.

Dora Pertz's early life in Berlin was punctuated by annual visits to England. When her father died in 1876 she moved with her mother to Florence. In 1882 she entered Newnham College, Cambridge, where she sat Cambridge higher local examinations. The following year she interrupted her studies to spend time in Italy, returning to Cambridge late in 1884 for another year in which she took part one of the natural sciences tripos. When titular degrees for women were allowed she made up the required time with a final period of residence (1917–18), eventually graduating MA in 1932. At Newnham she showed great ability in botany and soon was introduced to Francis Darwin, a university reader in botany. The introduction was probably made through Ellen Wordsworth Crofts, lecturer at Newnham and Darwin's wife from 1883. Pertz subsequently settled in Cambridge and became one of a small group of women on the fringes of professional science in the early years of the twentieth century. She researched plant physiology under Francis Darwin and taught botany at Newnham, although never formally appointed either at the college or the university's botany school. Her researches mostly supplemented Francis Darwin's work on water movements in plants, and from 1892

to 1900 she published five papers jointly with him. The best known is on plant rhythms, delivered at the British Association in 1891 and published in *Annals of Botany*. She produced two short papers in her own right, including one on gravitational effects on plants. She also worked for William Bateson for a while from 1895, a connection again facilitated through the Newnham network, and in 1900 co-authored a paper with him on the inheritance of variations.

In 1905 Dora Pertz was elected fellow of the Linnean Society in the first group of women to be admitted, although the struggle for admittance was orchestrated by others. For this, and indeed for much of her career, she was indebted to Francis Darwin, who actively pushed for recognition of her merits. Like several of his scientific contemporaries, Darwin liked to gather intelligent female researchers around him. After Darwin's retirement, Dora Pertz continued to experiment on plants but eventually abandoned her researches. Her friend Edith Saunders said this was due to disappointing results with germinating seeds (*Proceedings of the Linnean Society*, 151, 1938–9, 246), although Agnes Arber claimed instead that botany was getting too mathematical for her (*Nature*, 143, 1939, 590). Either way, Frederick Blackman enlisted her services in cataloguing pamphlets held at the botany school, followed by indexing and abstracting papers from German journals. The magnitude of the task was very great and Saunders afterwards felt Pertz's achievement was insufficiently appreciated. At this time in her life Pertz also provided illustrations of floral anatomy for Saunders's important text on that topic.

During the First World War Dora Pertz trained as a masseuse in order to work at St Chad's Roman Catholic convalescent hospital in Cambridge, and her charitable work continued quietly afterwards. She was ill for several years before her death in Cambridge on 6 March 1939. She was cremated in Cambridge on 9 March and her ashes buried in Brookwood cemetery, Surrey.   JANET BROWNE

Sources A. B. White and others, eds., *Newnham College register, 1871–1971*, 2nd edn, 3 vols. (1979) · *Nature*, 143 (1939), 590–91 · E. R. Saunders, *Proceedings of the Linnean Society of London*, 151st session (1938–9), 245–6
Likenesses photograph, Newnham College, Cambridge
Wealth at death £18,816 19s. 8d.: probate, 1 June 1939, *CGPLA Eng. & Wales*

Pérussel, François (*fl.* 1534–1567), Reformed minister and theologian, was a native of Orléans but nothing is known about his parents or birth. About 1534 he entered the local Franciscan convent, and as a religious adopted the name Jean Perruceau. He moved to Paris, where by 1542 he was master of novices at the Franciscan house. At about this time he was converted to the Reformation. On 4 February 1545 the faculty of theology at the Sorbonne banned him from preaching because of his evangelical sympathies. Although proceedings were started against him, Pérussel left before the *parlement* of Paris delivered its judgment. He fled to Geneva but received a cool reception from Calvin; after two months he moved to Strasbourg. By December 1546 Pérussel had also married, his wife (whose name is unknown) originating from Picardy. In 1547 Pérussel arrived in Basel where Calvin recommended him to Jacques de Bourgogne, seigneur de Falais, as a tutor to his children and also as a preacher. It was in Basel that he met and became a friend of Sebastien Castellion. After a disagreement he left for Lausanne, and then with a recommendation from François Dryander returned to Strasbourg where he worked in the French church. In November 1548, following the interim of Augsburg, he fled to England.

Pérussel initially served the newly formed French congregation which was established in Canterbury with Jan Utenhove. On 24 July 1550 Edward VI granted a charter establishing the London exile churches under the superintendence of John à Lasco. The charter appointed Pérussel and Richard Vauville as the first ministers of the French congregation. Pérussel provided the congregation with an abridged account of Reformed teachings; on the eucharist this leaned more towards Zürich than Geneva, but it did recognize the importance of church discipline. A Latin translation, *Summa Christianae religionis*, was published in 1551. He also drew upon the liturgies of Strasbourg and Geneva for his *Forme des prières ecclesiastique* in 1552 and his *Doctrine de la pénitence publicque* was published in the same year. On the accession of Mary Tudor, the foreign congregations folded and went into exile. Pérussel initially remained to minister to the surviving French community, but in November 1553 he left for Antwerp.

In early 1554 Pérussel took up the ministry of the French congregation in Wesel, where he became embroiled in a dispute with Lutheran town authorities. The congregation were allowed to worship separately and in October 1555 were granted the use of the Heiliggeistkapelle, but they were repeatedly refused permission to hold their own communion service. The dispute led to an ultimatum that the congregation should conform to the confession of Augsburg, the authoritative summary of Lutheran doctrine, or leave. As a result the Wesel church was closed in the spring of 1557. Pérussel succeeded Valérand Poullain as minister of the French congregation in Frankfurt. However, here his ministry was marred by a quarrel with the minister Guillaume Houbraque.

In 1561 Pérussel went to Paris, where he joined Theodore Beza and other Reformed ministers at the colloquy of Poissy, where the issues separating Catholics and Huguenots were debated, and the subsequent discussions at St Germain. However, Beza viewed Pérussel with suspicion, even though he had subscribed to the French confession of faith and the *Discipline ecclesiastique* of 1559, because of his friendship with the tolerant humanist Castellion and his reputed opposition to the rigorous system of ecclesiastical discipline exercised in Geneva. This had been reflected in his dispute with Houbraque. However, the rift with Beza had been settled by February 1564 when the reformer defended Pérussel, commenting that since coming to France he had accepted the practices of Geneva. By October 1561 Pérussel had become chaplain to Louis de Bourbon, prince de Condé, and administered the Lord's supper to him on Easter Sunday 1562. During the first war of religion the prince was captured at the battle of Dreux on 19 December 1562. Although Pérussel initially escaped in the company of the English ambassador Nicholas Throckmorton, he was arrested at Nogent and imprisoned with Condé. He was presumably released with the prince when peace was established in March 1563. As a member of Condé's household and living in Picardy, Pérussel liaised between the Huguenots and their co-religionists in the Netherlands and preached there during 1563. He may have been the French preacher who was described as an 'homme de petite stature, petite barbe blonde, porte manteau noir, un petit bonnet de velour et une grand chappeau de feutre noir' ('a small man, a little fair beard, wearing a black coat, a small black velvet bonnet and a big black felt hat'; Moreau, 228). In October 1565 Condé accompanied Charles IX on that part of his extended royal progress which took him to Nantes, where Pérussel preached.

As Condé's chaplain, Pérussel had a significant role in the French Reformed churches. In April 1564 he attended the provincial synod of the Reformed churches of Brie, Champagne, Île-de-France, and Picardy at La Ferté-sous-Jouarre. Among routine business, the synod dealt with Jean Morély's plea to be reconciled with the Huguenot church. The following year Charles du Moulin's *Collatio et unio quatuor evangelistarum* was submitted to Pérussel and Jean de l'Espine for censure; the book was condemned by the national synod in December 1565. Pérussel's testimony against the claims made in *La défense du Ch. du Moulin contre les calomnies des Calvinistes et ministres de leur secte* was forwarded to Beza in January 1567. Pérussel probably died before 1572, when his daughter and her husband were killed during the St Bartholomew's day massacre.

ANDREW SPICER

Sources P. Denis, *Les églises d'étrangers en pays rhénans, 1538–1564* (Paris, 1984) · E. Haag and E. Haag, *La France protestante*, 10 vols. (Paris, 1846–59) · E. Haag and E. Haag, *La France protestante*, 2nd edn, 6 vols. (Paris, 1877–88) · A. Pettegree, 'The London exile community and the second sacramentarian controversy', in A. Pettegree, *Marian protestantism: six studies* (1996), 55–85 · A. Pettegree, *Foreign protestant communities in sixteenth-century London* (1986) · P. Denis, 'Les églises d'étrangers à Londres jusqu'à la mort de Calvin', Licence diss., University of Liège, 1973–4 · G. Baum and E. Cunitz, *Histoire ecclésiastique des églises reformées au royaume de France*, 3 vols. (1883–9) · G. Moreau, *Histoire du protestantisme à Tournai jusqu'à la veille de la révolution des Pays-Bas* (Paris, 1962) · F. W. Cross, *History of the Walloon and Huguenot church at Canterbury*, Huguenot Society of London, 15 (1898) · F. de Schickler, *Les églises du réfuge en Angleterre*, 3 vols. (Paris, 1892) · J. Pannier, 'La plus ancienne église des réfugiés en Angleterre: Canterbury, ses fondateurs Utenhove et Perrucel', *Bulletin Historique et Littéraire* [Société de l'Histoire du Protestantisme Français], 41 (1892), 513–18 · J. Crespin, *Histoire des martyrs*, ed. D. Benoit, 3 vols. (Toulouse, 1885–9) · N. Weiss, 'Le cordelier Jean Perrucel devant le Parlement de Paris', *Bulletin Historique et Littéraire* [Société de l'Histoire du Protestantisme Français], 41 (1892), 633–7

Pery [*née* Trotter], **Angela Olivia**, **countess of Limerick** (**1897–1981**), leader of the British and International Red Cross movements, was born in Folkestone on 27 August 1897, the younger daughter (there were no sons) of Lieutenant-Colonel Sir Henry Trotter KCMG, soldier, explorer, and diplomat, and his wife, Olivia Georgiana, daughter of Admiral Sir George Wellesley and a great-niece of the first duke of Wellington.

Angela was educated at North Foreland Lodge at Broadstairs, which she left in 1915 at the age of seventeen to train as a Red Cross voluntary aid detachment nurse. Being too young to serve overseas, she falsified her age to get to France, and there nursed the wounded in both French and British hospitals. After the war she took a diploma in social science and administration at the London School of Economics, and she travelled extensively in Europe, and also in areas of the Middle East where European women were almost unknown.

In 1926 Angela Trotter married Edmund Colquhoun (Mark) Pery (1888–1967), who succeeded his half-brother in 1929 as fifth earl of Limerick. They had two sons and a daughter. After her marriage Angela worked in the London branch of the British Red Cross Society (BRCS) and was also a poor-law guardian (1928–30). She served on the Kensington borough council (1929–35) and was chairman of both its maternity and child welfare and its public health committees, and she represented South Kensington on the London county council (1936–46). She was also a pioneer campaigner for family planning, to the extent of being pelted with stones at a meeting in Glasgow.

By 1939 Angela Limerick was president (having been director) of the London branch of the BRCS, and thus in charge of its services during the blitz. As a deputy chairman of the joint war organization of Red Cross and St John (1941–7) she visited fourteen countries, including several battle fronts. In addition she served on several government committees and was privy council representative on the General Nursing Council (1933–50). Immediately after the war she was closely involved with Red Cross rehabilitation work overseas.

In the years 1946 to 1963, as vice-chairman of the executive committee of the BRCS in charge of its international operations, Angela Limerick visited most of its branches in Africa, the Far East, and the Caribbean, encouraging the expansion of services and their preparation for transition into independent national societies. She also visited twenty-six other national Red Cross societies, including those in the USSR and China. She was a most active and articulate leader of the British delegation at all International Red Cross conferences and meetings: uncompromising in support of the fundamental principles and integrity of the movement, she was heard with ever-growing respect.

Lady Limerick's increasing contribution to the international work of the Red Cross was recognized by her election first as a vice-chairman of the League of Red Cross Societies (1957–73), and then in 1965 to the standing commission, the supreme co-ordinating committee of the International Red Cross, which promptly made her its chairman. Exceptionally, she was invited to preside at the quadrennial international conference in Istanbul in 1969, in which year she was re-elected chairman of the standing commission for a second four-year term, following joint persuasion from the Americans and Russians; in 1973, at the age of seventy-six, she refused further nomination.

Age notwithstanding, Lady Limerick was persuaded to succeed the duke of Edinburgh in 1974 as the first non-royal chairman of council of the BRCS (she was a vice-chairman from 1963) to preside over the transition to a more democratic constitution. When she retired in 1976 the queen approved her appointment as the first non-royal vice-president of the BRCS.

Angela Limerick was a much loved figure with great breadth of vision, humour, a remarkable memory and grasp of detail, and an endearing ability to establish close and lasting relationships after brief acquaintance; above all, she had the gift of bringing out the best in others by her encouragement and inspiration. Her role in the many organizations with which she was involved was invariably active. She was president or vice-president of the Multiple Sclerosis Society, St Giles's Hospital for Leprosy Patients, the International Social Service of Great Britain, the Family Planning Association, the Family Welfare Association, the Star and Garter Home, and Trinity Hospice. She was made honorary LLD by Manchester (1945) and Leeds (1951) universities, and in 1977 was appointed a deputy lieutenant for West Sussex.

Lady Limerick was appointed CBE in 1942, DBE in 1946, GBE in 1954, and CH in 1974. The last two awards gave her particular pleasure because, uniquely in each case, they matched awards to her husband, who died in 1967 after equally distinguished public service. Their harmonious partnership was exemplified in the beautiful garden they created at their Sussex home, which offered a happy haven for family and friends alike. Lady Limerick was fully active until a few days before her death at her home, Chiddinglye, West Hoathly, Sussex, on 25 April 1981.

A. M. BRYANS, rev.

Sources personal knowledge (1990) · *The Times* (27 April 1981) · *The Times* (2 June 1981), 14a · J. F. Hutchinson, *Champions of charity: war and the rise of the Red Cross* (1966) · CGPLA Eng. & Wales (1981)
Archives Bodl. Oxf., corresp. with Lord Woolton
Wealth at death £89,709: probate, 11 Aug 1981, CGPLA Eng. & Wales

Pery, Edmond Henry, first earl of Limerick (1758–1845), politician, was born on 8 January 1758 in Ireland, the only son of William Cecil Pery, first Baron Glentworth of Mallow (1721–1794), Church of Ireland bishop successively of Killaloe and Limerick, and his first wife, Jane Walcott. He was educated by a private tutor before entering Trinity College, Dublin, in 1773, but did not take a degree. He trained at Lincoln's Inn from December 1775. He travelled on the continent to France and Italy (1777–9) and on 29 January 1783 married Mary Alice Ormsby (1762/3–1850), only daughter and heir of Henry Ormsby and Mary Hartstonge.

In 1786 Pery entered the Irish House of Commons as member for the county of Limerick. He retained this seat until 4 July 1794, when he succeeded to the Irish peerage on the death of his father. Though of overbearing manners and small talent, he was a successful politician. His political importance and his success were largely due to his family connections and location. He was the heir not only of his father but also of his uncle, Edmond Sexton Pery, speaker of the Irish House of Commons, who was noted for his 'head well filled with Machiavellian brains' (Bodkin, 202). His second asset was the Pery family's interest in Limerick city and county. He closely attached himself to the protestant ascendancy party, which dominated the government after Lord Fitzwilliam's recall in 1794. For his services to the government he was made keeper of the signet in 1795, and in 1797 clerk of the crown and hanaper. On the outbreak of the rising of 1798 he raised a regiment of dragoons for service against the rebels at his own expense. He strongly supported the chancellor, Lord Clare, another co. Limerick magnate, in furthering the scheme for a union between England and Ireland. He spoke frequently on its behalf in the Irish House of Lords, and did much to obtain the support of the influential citizens of Limerick. In return for these services he was created Viscount Limerick in 1800, with the promise of an earldom, and was one of the twenty-eight temporal lords elected to represent the peerage of Ireland in the parliament of the United Kingdom after the legislative union had been carried out.

Limerick continued to exercise political influence after the union, for Limerick city, which had previously returned two MPs to the Irish parliament, now returned one to the imperial parliament. It a was county-borough constituency comprising both burgesses and freeholders, and the Perys controlled the freeholders. On 11 February 1803 he was raised to the dignity of earl of Limerick in the peerage of Ireland, and on 11 August 1815 he was made a United Kingdom peer, with the title Baron Foxford. Subsequently Limerick resided mainly in England. He took a prominent part in Irish debates in the House of Lords and steadily opposed any concession to the Irish Catholics. He died on 7 December 1845 at Southill Park, near Bracknell in Berkshire, and was buried on 23 December in Limerick Cathedral. Barrington described him as 'always crafty, sometimes imperious, and frequently efficient', and added, 'He had a sharp, quick, active intellect, and generally guessed right in his politics' (Barrington, 2.122). He was succeeded in his titles and property by his second grandson, William Henry Tennison Pery.

G. P. MORIARTY, rev. E. M. JOHNSTON-LIIK

Sources E. M. Johnston-Liik, *History of the Irish parliament, 1692–1800*, 6 vols. (2002) · M. MacDonagh, *The viceroy's post-bag* (1904), 50, 83–5, 195, 365 · M. Bodkin, ed., 'Notes on the Irish parliament in 1773', *Proceedings of the Royal Irish Academy*, 48C (1942–3), 145–232 · GEC, *Peerage* · A. J. Webb, *A compendium of Irish biography* (1878) · J. Barrington, *Historic memoirs of Ireland*, 2nd edn, 2 vols. (1833) · *Correspondence of Charles, first Marquis Cornwallis*, ed. C. Ross, 3 vols. (1859)

Archives NL Ire., corresp. and papers | BL, corresp. with Sir Robert Peel, Add. MSS 40230–40278

Likenesses T. A. Dean, stipple and line engraving, pubd after 1803, NG Ire. · T. A. Dean, stipple, pubd 1840 (after G. Dawe), BM, NPG · G. Hayter, group portrait, oils (*The trial of Queen Caroline, 1820*), NPG

Wealth at death £6000 p.a. excl. rents from Limerick city: E. Wakefield, *Account of Ireland: statistical and political* (1812)

Pery, Edmond Sexton, Viscount Pery (1719–1806), speaker of the Irish House of Commons, eldest son of Stackpole Pery (*c.*1688–1739), Church of Ireland clergyman, of Stackpole Court, co. Clare, and his wife, Jane Twigg, daughter of William Twigg, archdeacon of Limerick, was born in Limerick on 9 April 1719. The family originally came from Brittany and rose to prominence during the reign of Henry VIII. Edmond was educated at Trinity College, Dublin (1736–9), and was admitted as a student of the Middle Temple on 30 June 1739. He was called to the Irish bar in Hilary term 1745 and quickly achieved distinction within the profession. In 1751 he was elected MP for the borough of Wicklow. Initially he acted with the government, aligning himself with the administration of the duke of Dorset, and followed the party line by voting for the altered money bill on 17 December 1753.

The journals of the Irish House of Commons reveal Pery's activity in promoting the interests of Ireland, in particular the city of Dublin, of which he was a common councillor. On 7 January 1756 he presented heads of a bill for the encouragement of tillage; on 28 February heads of a bill for the improved supply of corn and flour to the city of Dublin; and on 2 March heads of a bill to prevent unlawful combination to raise the price of coals in the city of Dublin. Most of his measures gradually found their way into the statute book, but at the time he experienced considerable opposition from government, and at the close of the session of 1756 he thought himself justified in opposing the usual vote of thanks to the lord lieutenant, the duke of Devonshire. On 11 June 1756 Pery married Patty (*d.* 1757), youngest daughter of John Martin of Dublin. They had no children during their brief marriage.

In the 1756/7 parliamentary session Pery took part in the attack on the pension list, and, in order to secure proper parliamentary control of the revenue of the country, he supported a proposal to limit supply to one year, with the object of insuring the annual meeting of parliament. During the mid-1750s Pery virtually single-handedly agitated the issues that were to become central to patriot concerns during the late eighteenth century. As a result he was regarded in some quarters as the embodiment of the 'new' patriot opposition. The fact that he declined the prime serjeantcy, the third law office of the crown, enhanced his credibility and popularity. However, he declined it not because of patriotic interest but from an 'undeserved friendship' with the first earl of Belvedere, who was in a sulk with Dublin Castle (Emly (Pery) MS T/3087/16). In 1757 he published anonymously his *Letters from an Armenian in Ireland*, which contains some interesting and valuable reflections on the political situation.

Pery displayed great interest in the prosperity of his native city, and secured a grant of £27,000 from the government between 1755 and 1761 for construction in Limerick. In 1760, when Limerick was declared to be no longer a fortress, he was instrumental in causing the walls to be levelled, new roads to be made, and a new bridge and spacious quays to be built. At the general election of 1761 he was returned unopposed for the city of Limerick, which he continued to represent in successive parliaments until

Edmond Sexton Pery, Viscount Pery (1719–1806), by Gilbert Stuart, c.1788

his retirement in 1785. On 27 October 1762 he married his second wife, Elizabeth Handcock (1732/3–1821), widow of Robert Handcock of Waterstown, co. Westmeath, and eldest daughter of John Denny Vesey, first Baron Knapton, and Elizabeth Brownlow. They had two daughters: Diana Jane, who married Thomas Knox, and Frances, who married Nicholas Calvert of Hunsdon, Hertfordshire.

In 1761 Pery had had a serious illness, but on his return to parliament he resumed his place as the dominant opposition figure. He was the *de facto* leading spokesman of the 'flying squadron'—a group of patriot and independent-minded MPs who voted according to issues and were not averse to supporting measures sponsored by the administration if they perceived them to have some merit. During the parliamentary session Pery recommenced his onslaught on the pension list. An amendment to the address, moved by him at the opening of the session in October 1763, opposing the view that the 'ordinary establishment' included pensions, was adopted by the house, and was the means of wresting a promise from the government that no new pension should be granted on the civil list 'except upon very extraordinary occasions'. During November 1763 when debate commenced in the committee of supply Pery took the lead in challenging the administration's economic policies and sustained a critique of the national debt. He graphically highlighted the deterioration in the kingdom's finances by comparing the current national debt of £520,000 with the situation in the late 1740s, when the Treasury ran a surplus. But all the efforts to obtain an unqualified condemnation of the system ended in failure.

In the early winter of 1769 Pery was prominent in successfully opposing the main money bill on the grounds that it had originated not with the Irish House of Commons but with the British privy council. When the House of Commons adopted the usual face-saving formula of reintroducing the same money bill as a measure of its own, he proposed or was associated with successful amendments. In 1770 efforts were made by Pery and other patriots concerning the need to unite all the opponents of the administration to act as 'an Association'. However, these came to nothing. Then, when parliament reassembled after its long prorogation in February 1771, Pery carried an amendment to the address to the king which Lord Townshend described, in an official dispatch, as 'an artful justification of what the House voted last session, and a fresh, though indirect, assertion of their [sole] right to originate Money Bills' (R. A. Roberts, ed., *Calendar of Home Office Papers of the Reign of George III, 1770–72*, 216–22).

On the resignation of John Ponsonby, Pery was elected speaker of the Irish House of Commons on 7 March 1771. He had not been the choice of most patriots: Henry Flood and other independents lobbied on behalf of another candidate. However, it had been an avowed ambition of Pery since at least 1767. He did not, as was usual, affect to decline the honour conferred upon him, but on being presented for the approbation of the crown he admitted that it was the highest point of his ambition, and that he had not been more solicitous to obtain it than he would be to discharge the duties of the post. On 1 May he was sworn a member of the privy council.

It is unclear to what extent Pery's election as speaker changed his political course. From 1771 until his retirement from the house, he was speaker and as such had only limited opportunities for public pronouncements on political subjects. However, during the next session, on 19 February 1772, the house was equally divided on a motion censuring an increase in the number of commissioners of the revenue, a measure which was vital to Townshend's policy. Pery gave his casting vote in favour of the motion. 'This', said he:

> is a question which involves the privileges of the commons of Ireland. The noes have opposed the privilege: the noes have been wrong; let the privileges of the commons of Ireland stand unimpeached, therefore I say the ayes have it. (Grattan, 1.109)

Again, he was a source of great embarrassment to the succeeding administration, in the course of which he delivered in December 1773 his most outspoken presenting speech of all, in which he expressed the hope 'that the restrictions, which narrow and short-sighted policy of former times, equally injurious to Great Britain and to us, imposed upon the manufactures and commerce of this kingdom, will be remitted' (*Journals of the Irish House of Commons*, 9, 1773–8, 74). In March 1774 he made a further, unscheduled speech in the house that was designed to widen the definition of what was a money bill, and so extend the authority of the House of Commons at the expense, almost certainly, of the British privy council. The bill which he endeavoured to define as a money bill was a bill amending the Tontine Act passed earlier in the same session, the amendment being designed to make it easier for English capital to participate in the Irish tontine. It is clear that Pery warmly espoused the House of Commons view that the British privy council had no power to amend money bills, even when its amendments did not alter the level of tax.

After the general election of 1776 the administration exerted itself to get Pery re-elected speaker, holding a two-day session of parliament purely for that purpose and returning to it three people who sat for those two days only and were raised to the peerage as soon as their votes for Pery were cast. However, there is no suggestion that any pledge of good behaviour had been forthcoming from Pery. Indeed, his conduct as speaker of the 1776 parliament was very far from that of a ministerial hireling, particularly over free trade in 1779, and the constitution of 1782 which resulted in Ireland's legislative independence. In 1778 he travelled to England to press for concessions over free trade and had some success in clarifying the issue for doubting and suspicious ministers.

Pery was re-elected to the speakership in 1783 and played an active part in opposing Pitt's commercial propositions of 1785. These were an attempt to rationalize the laws governing trade between Great Britain and Ireland by reducing or eliminating tariffs. His original enthusiasm for the commercial arrangements waned visibly as it emerged that the resolutions were seen to threaten the legislative autonomy of the Irish parliament. Pitt's resolutions were simply unacceptable and opposition MPs began to bond together in what Thomas Orde (Irish chief secretary) termed 'murmurs and cabals' led by Pery, who 'with more warmth than usual declaimed against your propositions as unions to Ireland and intended to force this country into a rejection of them' (Kelly, *Prelude*, 145). Pery's discontent derived from his conviction that the changes Pitt had introduced represented 'a departure from the system of reciprocity which is the professed principle of the intended settlement' (NL Ire., Bolton MS 16351, fol. 23). The actions of Pery, who, Orde claimed, furnished Grattan 'privately with materials for discontent and remonstrance' and 'make[s] up perpetual doses of poison and puts some of it into almost every man's mess', combined with rumours of the unhappiness of other MPs with the terms of the arrangement, underlined the importance of the administration's search for concessions to appease the growing opposition (NL Ire., Bolton MS 16358, fols. 106–8, 223–8). Pitt worked on a compromise, and although Pery gave no firm indication that he supported the arrangement he did keep in close contact with the government and regularly suggested amendments. Pery's absence during the debate of the Commercial Bill in the Irish House of Commons during August 1785 has to be taken as an indication of his disapproval.

Pery's retirement followed closely on the abandonment of Pitt's commercial propositions after their near defeat in the Irish House of Commons. For some time prior to this, Pery, who was now sixty-six, had been negotiating with the government over the terms of his retirement

from the speakership. However, his decision to resign the chair on 4 September 1785 in the immediate aftermath of the rejection of the Commercial Bill shocked Dublin Castle. In recognition of his service he was granted a pension of £3000 p.a. and raised to the peerage by the title of Viscount Pery of Newtown-Pery in the county of Limerick.

Predictably, Pery was strongly opposed to the union. The impression that Pery's opposition was not uncompromising, as quoted in Lecky's *History of England* (8.295), was a probably somewhat optimistic interpretation of his sentiments by Dublin Castle. Before the start of the 1799 session of parliament, when the union was first introduced, it was at Pery's Dublin house that the anti-unionists met to discuss tactics. He ultimately voted against the act.

Pery died at his house in Park Street, London, on 24 February 1806 and was buried in the Calvert family vault at Furneaux Pelham, Hunsdon, Hertfordshire, on 4 March. He was survived by his widow, who died on 4 April 1821, and by his daughters, who inherited his personal property; the family estate, worth £8000 p.a., descended to his nephew, Edmond Henry Pery, earl of Limerick. His papers were later catalogued and published by the Historical Manuscripts Commission.

Pery's contemporaries' reactions concerning him ranged from veneration to contempt. In particular, his critics disputed his superiority over the attractions of patronage and power. However, his surviving correspondence establishes his reputation as a statesman and as a great Irishman. He was unquestionably one of the most influential members of parliament from 1751 to 1785. During the twenty years prior to his election to the speakership he had generally followed an individualistic course, judging questions on their merits and glorying in the fact that he was not a party man. He was of course looked to for leadership but this was largely a matter of spontaneous deference to his ability. He always worked to diminish what was bad in legislation and increase what was good. He was the only Irish politician of the second half of the eighteenth century who continued to strike a balance between government and opposition, and he was in effect a 'patriot' in power. Yet it must be recognized that Pery crucially entered the Irish House of Commons at just the right time. Nearly all the causes which he espoused—an Irish Habeas Corpus Act, a limitation in the duration of parliaments, annual parliamentary sessions, a change in the tenure of judges, the modification of Poynings' law—came to fruition during his time as an MP. Nevertheless, Pery was undoubtedly one of the leading political figures of eighteenth-century Ireland.   DAVID HUDDLESTON

Sources A. P. W. Malcolmson, 'Speaker Pery and the Pery papers', *North Munster Antiquarian Journal*, 16 (1973–4), 33–60 • PRO NIre., Emly (Pery) MSS • *Eighth report*, 3 vols. in 5, HMC, 7 (1881–1910) • *The manuscripts of the earl of Buckinghamshire, the earl of Lindsey ... and James Round*, HMC, 38 (1895) • J. Kelly, *Prelude to Union: Anglo-Irish politics in the 1780s* (1992) • J. Kelly, *Henry Flood: patriots and politics in eighteenth-century Ireland* (1998) • GEC, *Peerage* • H. Grattan, *Memoirs of the life and times of the Rt Hon. Henry Grattan*, 5 vols. (1839–46), vol. 1, pp. 104–12 • M. Lenihan, *Limerick: its history and antiquities*

(1866), 322 • J. Hill, *The building of Limerick* (1991) • *GM*, 1st ser., 76 (1806), 287–8 • *Annual Register* (1808), 517–18 • *Hibernian Magazine* (1777–8) • *Journals of the Irish House of Commons* (1749–85), vols.5–11, pt.2 • Burke, *Peerage* (1970), 2.1611 • D. Lammey, 'The free trade crisis', *Parliament, politics and people: essays in eighteenth century Irish history*, ed. G. O'Brien (1989), 69–92 • *The correspondence of the Right Hon. John Beresford, illustrative of the last thirty years of the Irish parliament*, ed. W. Beresford, 2 vols. (1854) • A. J. Webb, *A compendium of Irish biography* (1878) • *N&Q*, 3rd ser., 12 (1867), 295 • *DNB*

Archives Hunt. L., corresp. and papers • NRA, priv. coll., corresp. and papers [photocopies] • PRO NIre., MSS | BL, corresp. with first earl of Liverpool, Add. MSS 38213–38226, 38306–38310 • NL Ire., Limerick MSS • Sheff. Arch., corresp. with Edmund Burke

Likenesses line engraving, pubd 1777, NG Ire.; repro. in Walker, *Hibernian Magazine* (1777) • G. Stuart, oils, *c.*1788, NG Ire. [*see illus.*] • H. D. Hamilton, pastel drawing, 1790–99, repro. in Malcolmson, 'Speaker Pery' • J. C. F. Rossi, marble bust, 1807, TCD • W. Say, mezzotint, pubd 1809 (after G. C. Stuart), NG Ire. • W. Mossop, silver medal, National Museum of Ireland, Dublin • F. Wheatley, group portrait, oils (*The Irish House of Commons, 1780*), Leeds City Art Gallery • F. Wheatley, group portrait, watercolour (*Entry of the speaker into the Irish House of Commons, 1782*), NG Ire.

Wealth at death £8000 p.a.: *GM*, 287

Peryam, Sir William (1534–1604), judge, was the eldest son of John Peryam (*d.* 1572) and his wife, Elizabeth, a daughter of Robert Hone of Ottery St Mary, Devon. He was born at Exeter and was a cousin of Sir Thomas *Bodley. His father, a man of means, was twice mayor of Exeter, and his brother, Sir John, was also an alderman of that town and a benefactor of Exeter College, Oxford. William Peryam was educated at Exeter College, Oxford, and at Clifford's Inn. He was elected fellow of Exeter on 25 April 1551, but resigned on 7 October and sat for Plymouth in the parliament of 1563. In 1553 he joined the Middle Temple, where his arms are placed in the hall; he was called to the bar in 1565, became a serjeant-at-law in Michaelmas term 1580, and on 13 February 1581 was appointed a judge of the common pleas.

Peryam was thrice married: first, to Margery, daughter of John Holcot of Berkshire; second, in or before 1574, to Anne, daughter of John Parker of North Molton, Devon; third, in or after 1593, to Elizabeth Neville (1541–1621), a daughter of the lord keeper, Sir Nicholas *Bacon. He left four daughters, of whom the eldest, Mary, was married to Sir William *Pole (*d.* 1635) of Colcombe, Devon, on 20 July 1583, and Elizabeth to Sir Robert Basset of Heanton-Punchardon, Devon; Jane married Thomas Poyntz of Hertfordshire; and Anne, William Williams of Herringstone, Dorset.

Peryam was frequently in commissions for trials of political crimes, particularly those of Mary, queen of Scots, the earls of Arundel and Essex, and Sir John Perrot, and was a commissioner to hear causes in chancery. He was knighted in 1592. In January 1593 he was promoted to be chief baron of the exchequer, in which court he presided for nearly twelve years. On 9 October 1604 he died at his house at Little Fulford, near Crediton, Devon, and was buried at Holy Cross Church, where there is a tomb effigy; he had bought large estates in the neighbourhood. He had also built a 'fayre dwelling house' at Credy Peitevin or Wiger, which he left to his daughters, and they sold it to his brother John. A picture, supposed to be his portrait,

Sir William Peryam (1534–1604), by unknown artist, *c.*1600

and ascribed to Holbein, is in the National Portrait Gallery, London; another portrait, with a view of a country house, is at Exeter College, Oxford. Peryam's widow, in 1620, endowed a fellowship and two scholarships at Balliol College, Oxford, out of lands at Hambleden and Princes Risborough in Buckinghamshire.

J. A. HAMILTON, *rev.* DAVID IBBETSON

Sources J. Prince, *Danmonii orientales illustres, or, The worthies of Devon* (1701), 501 • HoP, *Commons, 1558–1603*, 2.53; 3.124, 209 • C. W. Boase, ed., *Registrum Collegii Exoniensis*, new edn, OHS, 27 (1894), 66 • J. L. Vivian, ed., *The visitations of the county of Devon, comprising the herald's visitations of 1531, 1564, and 1620* (privately printed, Exeter, [1895]), 603 • *State trials* • C. H. Hopwood, ed., *Middle Temple records*, 4 vols. (1904–5) • *CSP dom.* • Baker, *Serjeants*, 74 • Sainty, *Judges*, 74 • inquisition post mortem, PRO, WARDS 7/37/72; C142/289/63

Likenesses portrait, 1599, Exeter College, Oxford; version, Middle Temple • portrait, *c.*1600, priv. coll. [*see illus.*] • H. Holbein?, portrait, NPG • tomb effigy, Holy Cross Church, Crediton, Devon • watercolour drawing, NPG

Wealth at death over £130 p.a. in lands: PRO, C 142/289/63

Peryn, William (*d.* 1558), prior of St Bartholomew's, Smithfield, and theologian, was connected with the Perins of Brockton in Shropshire, a family which itself originated in Derbyshire. He became a Dominican early in life, and was educated at Blackfriars, in Oxford, where his presence was recorded in 1529, and again in 1531, the year in which he was ordained. He then went to London, where he was a vigorous preacher against heresy. He also served as chaplain to Sir John Port. Following the declaration of the royal supremacy in 1534 he went into exile, but returned in 1543, when he supplicated for the degree of BTh at Oxford. He also became a chantrist in St Paul's. Early in 1547 he preached in favour of images. Following the accession of Edward VI, however, he is said to have recanted on 19 June

1547 in the church of St Mary Undershaft, but soon went into exile once more. After several years in Louvain he returned to England in 1553, when he was made prior of the Dominican house of St Bartholomew in Smithfield, the first of the religious houses to be founded by Queen Mary. On 8 February 1556 he preached at Paul's Cross, while Sir Thomas Sampson, priest, did public penance in a sheet and bearing a taper, for having had two wives. Henry Machyn records this and other sermons that Peryn delivered in London.

Peryn published three books. During the latter part of Henry VIII's reign he published a work entitled *Thre Godly Sermons of the Sacrament of the Aulter* (1546), sermons that had originally been preached in the hospital of St Anthony in London. This work is dedicated to Edmund Bonner, bishop of London, and in a preface that conceals the extent to which his material was borrowed from John Fisher's *De veritate corporis et sanguinis Christi in eucharistia* the author explains that he has compiled the sermons:

> in homely and playne sentens, by cause that I have cheflye prepared them … for the unlearned. And the veryte (beyng delectable and bewtifull of herselfe) nedeth not, the gorgius ornamentes, of eloquens. Also the matters of our fayth, hath moche lesse nede of rethoricall perswacyons, havynge theyr grond, and fundacyon, upon the infallyble veritie, of goddes holy worde. (sig. *iiiv)

He also published *Spirituall exercyses and goostly meditacions, and a neare waye to come to perfection and lyfe contemplatyve* (1557), which was based on the *Exercitia theologiae mysticae* of Nicolaus van Ess, and dedicated to two English nuns in exile. A book close to the heart of the Catholic martyr Margaret Clitherow, it was reprinted at Caen in 1598. There is also record of a third work, *De frequenter celebranda missa*, of which no copy survives. Peryn died in 1558, and was buried in St Bartholomew's on 22 August, at the high altar.

L. E. C. WOODING

Sources *The diary of Henry Machyn, citizen and merchant-taylor of London, from AD 1550 to AD 1563*, ed. J. G. Nichols, CS, 42 (1848), 100, 119, 131, 171–2, 365n. · J. Strype, *Ecclesiastical memorials*, 3 vols. (1822), vol. 3, pt 1, pp. 471, 507; vol. 3, pt 2, pp. 2, 116 · A. B. Emden, *A survey of Dominicans in England* (1967), 422–3 · Emden, *Oxf.*, 4.444 · F. A. Gasquet and E. Bishop, *Edward VI and the Book of Common Prayer* (1890); rev. edn (1928), 25 · Foster, *Alum. Oxon.* · J. Pits, *Relationum historicarum de rebus Anglicis*, ed. [W. Bishop] (Paris, 1619), 751 · S. Brigden, *London and the Reformation* (1989) · C. Haigh, ed., *The English Reformation revised* (1987) · R. Rex, *The theology of John Fisher* (1991)

Peshall [*formerly* Pearsall], **John** [styled Sir John Peshall, sixth baronet] (**1718–1778**), antiquary, was born John Pearsall at Hawn, Shropshire, on 27 January 1718, the eldest son of Thomas Pearsall (1694–1759) of Eccleshall, Staffordshire, and his wife, Anne (d. 1770), daughter of Samuel Sanders of Ombersley, Worcestershire. He matriculated from Pembroke College, Oxford, on 15 April 1736 and graduated BA (1739) and MA (1745). He worked for a time as a schoolmaster in Highgate and was ordained. On 12 July 1753 he married Mary, daughter and coheir of James Allen, vicar of Thaxted, Essex, and Anne Peers. They had three sons and one daughter. Although he had been preferred to the living of Stoke Bliss in Herefordshire, he spent much

of his time in Oxford, where he was active as a county JP and in the philanthropic activities around the city. In or shortly before 1770 (probably after his mother's death on 6 July 1770), he assumed the baronetcy (created in 1611 but which had become extinct in 1712 on the death of the third baronet) and changed his name to Peshall, styling himself sixth baronet. In 1770 he was listed among the subscribers to the Radcliffe Infirmary and in 1772 he laid the foundation-stone for the new workhouse. He was among the most active of the paving commissioners from its inception in 1771 until 1775.

Peshall wrote *The History of the University of Oxford to the Death of William the Conqueror* (1772), a short pamphlet of thirty-two pages, which traced the foundation of Oxford from druidical times to the Norman conquest. He also edited Anthony Wood's *Antient and Present State of the City of Oxford* (1773) from the manuscript in the Bodleian Library, with additions of his own, and dedicated it to the mayor and aldermen. He preserved the structure of a topographical, parochial survey and the extensive lists of monumental inscriptions and material from parish registers, but his interest in the contemporary improvements initiated in recent years is also reflected in the effusive introductory description of the town and the inclusion of a history of the Holywell Music Room by William Hayes. Peshall died on 9 November 1778 at Halesowen, and was buried at Hawn. He was survived by his widow, whose will was proved in 1801. After his death Richard Gough wrote to John Price, Bodley's librarian, asking him to inquire after Peshall's collections towards the history of Oxford, but it is not known what their subsequent fate was; Gough did not, apparently, trace them.

R. H. SWEET

Sources DNB · *Jackson's Oxford Journal* (1778) · minutes of Oxford paving commissioners, 1771–7, Oxfordshire Archives, R/6/25 · GEC, *Baronetage* · Foster, *Alum. Oxon.* · C. R. J. Currie and C. P. Lewis, eds., *English county histories: a guide* (1994)

Pessagno, Sir Antonio (b. c.1280, d. in or after 1334), financier and administrator, was a native of Genoa, where he was born probably about 1280. His historical importance lies in his position as the chief financier of Edward II between 1312 and 1319. His massive loans and furnishing of commodities for the royal household and of supplies for the war against Scotland kept the king financially afloat during much of the period when the opposition of the lords ordainer severely limited his power. Between April 1312 and January 1319 royal indebtedness to Pessagno (exclusive of interest) amounted to at least £143,579. His annual average of advances amounted to approximately £20,500, which was higher than the annual average of any other royal banker between 1272 and 1337. Promises of 'gifts' to him (that is, interest) amounted to at least £6782.

Pessagno is known almost exclusively for his activities in England and France, though much of his large capital and financial credit presumably derived from the support of other Genoese merchants. His agents in England were other Genoese or Italians, but he was associated in transactions with some important Londoners. His family were long-established Genoese notables. His wife, Leona Fieschi, came from a Genoese family boasting two popes in the thirteenth century. His brother Manuel became in 1317 the hereditary admiral of Portugal.

Pessagno's high social rank and his naval activities made him eminently acceptable to the English royal court. He was responsible for arranging indentured contracts with commanders of castles on the Scottish border. On 17 November 1317 he was appointed seneschal of Gascony (that is, head of the administration of English Gascony) and held this office until November 1318.

Pessagno appears in records for the first time in 1306–7 as an exporter of English wool. By 1311 he was supplying spices to the royal household. An exchequer inquiry later in 1311 into foreign money owned by alien merchants in England revealed that Pessagno held 12,000 Florentine florins (£2000)—more than any other Italian firm.

The Frescobaldi of Florence, bankers to Edward II at the start of his reign, were ruined by the latter's opponents, the lords ordainer, in order to cripple Edward financially. They were bankrupt by the second half of 1311. Giovanni Frescobaldi later warned Italians: 'do not have any dealings with the men of the court' (Fryde and Fryde, 458). However, Pessagno was already in 1311 supplying the king's household with goods and loans on a modest scale. He was officially styled 'the king's merchant' on 5 April 1312 and by then the royal debt to him amounted to at least £2086. An agent of the Frescobaldi wrote in a letter of 16 February 1313 that Pessagno 'is now in such a condition that he fears nobody … and is so generous in the court … that everybody likes him' (Kaeuper, 82–3).

In 1313 Pessagno received on Edward II's behalf the large loan advanced by Philippe IV of France. In March 1314 he similarly received £25,000 advanced to Edward II by Pope Clement V. That money was destined to finance the invasion of Scotland in June 1314. Pessagno provided more than half the supplies needed for that army as well as much cash. He furnished at least £21,000 between March and June 1314. It was not through lack of resources that the English army was on 24 June disastrously defeated at Bannockburn.

In November 1314 Pessagno acknowledged that he had recovered from the king £104,900, while a balance of £6605 was still due to him. He was knighted by Edward II on 1 November 1315. During the terrible famine of 1315–17 he was importing corn from the Mediterranean, partly destined for the castles on the Scottish border. But, though popular at court, he was a heavy-handed administrator. His monopoly of the purchase of tin in Cornwall and Devon had to be cancelled in 1316 because of complaints against him. His year's tenure of the seneschalcy of Gascony was abruptly terminated in November 1318, partly because of his conflicts with Gascon notables. He appears to have left England after April 1320, possibly because of enmity towards the king's ruthless new favourites, the Despensers.

During the Anglo-French war of 1323–5 Pessagno was rumoured to be preparing a naval attack on England with Genoese and Portuguese galleys. But in the royal household list at Christmas 1330, the earliest after the overthrow of the government of Queen Isabella and Roger Mortimer masterminded by William Montagu (19 October 1330), Pessagno reappears as a banneret, the highest knightly dignity. Perhaps he had played some part in Montagu's conspiracy: it was through Montagu that Pessagno now secured his claim for the repayment of a balance of £8141 due to him. He is last heard of as an English envoy to the pope in 1334, and it is not known when he died.

E. B. Fryde

Sources E. B. Fryde, 'Italian merchants in medieval England, c.1270–1500', *Aspetti della vita economica medievale: atti del convegno di studi nel x anniversario della morte Federigo Melis* [Florence, Pisa, and Prato 1984] (Florence, 1985), 215–42 • N. Fryde, 'Antonio Pessagno of Genoa, king's merchant of Edward II', *Studi in memoria di Federigo Melis*, 2 ([Naples], 1978), 159–79 • P. Chaplais, ed., *The War of Saint-Sardos (1323–1325): Gascon correspondence and diplomatic documents*, CS, 3rd ser., 87 (1954) • Y. Renouard, *Études d'histoire médiévale*, 2 vols. (1968) • R. W. Kaeuper, 'The Frescobaldi of Florence and the English crown', *Studies in Medieval and Renaissance History*, 10 (1973), 41–95 • E. B. Fryde and M. M. Fryde, 'Public credit, with special reference to north-western Europe', *Economic organisation and politics in the middle ages*, ed. M. M. Postan, E. E. Rich, and E. Miller (1963), vol. 3 of *The Cambridge economic history of Europe*, ed. J. H. Clapham and others (1941–78), 430–553

Pestell, Thomas (*bap.* 1586, *d.* 1667), Church of England clergyman and poet, was baptized on 9 October 1586 at St Martin's, Leicester, the eldest of five children of Thomas Pestell, tailor, and Sarah Fawkoner (*d.* 1610), who had married the previous April. He matriculated from Queens' College, Cambridge, in 1602, graduated BA in 1606 and proceeded MA in 1609. Two years later he was presented by Sir Thomas Beaumont to the rectory of Coleorton, Leicestershire. Probably in 1612 he married Sarah Carr (*d.* in or after 1647), daughter of an Essex clergyman, thereby 'disappointing' a Mistress Stacy and initiating a lengthy feud with her family. The Pestells' eldest son, **Thomas Pestell** (1613–1690), was born at Coleorton on 1 May 1613; their other children included William (1615–1696), Margaret, Mary (*bap.* 1623), Lettice (*bap.* 1627), and Walter (*bap.* 1628).

Over the next decade Pestell published *The Good Conscience* (1615) and two assize sermons which castigated the love of money and the oppression of the poor, *Morbus epidemicus, or, The Churles Sicknesse* (1615), dedicated to Beaumont, and *The Poore Mans Appeale* (1620), dedicated to Sir Henry Hobart, chief justice of common pleas. In 1615 he became chaplain to Robert Devereux, third earl of Essex, and may have written the Spenserian 'Coleorton Masque' performed in 1618 to celebrate the wedding of Essex's sister. About this time he was mocked in a verse letter by Edward Catlin for the enthusiasm with which he sought the patronage of Elizabeth Hastings, countess of Huntingdon, through whose influence he also became vicar of Packington in 1622. Regarding himself as 'a poor retired Vicar in an obscure angle of the Countrey' he published nothing more until persuaded by Alderman James Ellis of Leicester to issue a sermon preached at an ordinary visitation of the town; *Gods Visitation* (1630) was dedicated to his friends the mayor, recorder, and corporation. In 1633 he produced two elegies for the countess of Huntingdon, and his work must have had a wider currency since in 1636 he acknowledged Queen Henrietta Maria's appreciation of his poetry.

Pestell was a controversial figure, capable of arrogance and even violence. By 1633 he had been accused of ecclesiastical irregularities before the court of high commission by Joseph Johnson and one of the Stacy family, but charges against him in the 1640s point to at least a degree of conformity in the previous decade, and Pestell was acquitted, although ordered to apologize to his patrons and pay damages to others. His credit was sufficient to gain him a royal chaplaincy: between 1641 and 1644 he appeared on the monthly rota for September.

Pestell's two older sons followed him into the ministry. Thomas the younger matriculated from Christ's College, Cambridge, on 29 August 1628, moved to Queens' College, graduated BA in 1633, and proceeded MA in 1636. He may have written the Latin play *Versipellis*, performed at Queens' in 1632, as well as other writings usually attributed to his father. William matriculated from Queens' in 1631, graduated BA in 1634, and proceeded MA in 1638. In or before 1644 Pestell resigned the Packington and Coleorton rectories to Thomas and William respectively, remaining as curate in the former parish.

The villages were at the heart of civil-war engagements in Leicestershire: Pestell's house was apparently looted eleven times. In April 1646 he and his elder son were charged before the parliamentary committee, on the accusation of Johnston and Stacy, among others, with a variety of offences including officiating according to the prayer book, employing scandalous curates, keeping hunting beagles which damaged neighbours' property, and living in the royalist garrison at Ashby-de-la-Zouch. Both denied many of the charges and the younger Thomas explained his presence at Ashby as necessitated by his being chaplain to the earl of Huntingdon. None the less, they were sequestered, and Thomas senior was ejected from Packington by soldiers; William suffered the same fate at Coleorton in 1652. Several times imprisoned, Pestell senior was dependent thereafter on charity, assuming the pointed pseudonym Perditus. Both he and Thomas the younger contributed to *Lachrymae musarum* (1649), in memory of Henry Hastings, Lord Hastings, and the father went on to write prefatory verse for Edward Benlowes's *Theophila, or, Loves Sacrifice* (1652). His *Sermons and Devotions Old and New* (1659), published 'as an oblation of gratitude to all such of the nobility, gentry and clergy as retain the noble conscience of having ministred to the weak condition of the author, now aged 73', also contained a discourse on duels. In 1658 he had acquired the patronage of Sir Justinian Isham, and the following year he became vicar of St Mary's, Leicester.

At the Restoration Pestell became rector of Lutterworth, Leicestershire, and confrator of Wigston's Hospital, Leicester. He died there about 30 June 1667 and was buried in the chapel there on 2 July. Thomas Pestell the younger was restored to Packington in 1662, became rector of

Markfield on 1 October 1677, and died in 1690. William was restored to Coleorton in 1660, published *A Congratulation to his Sacred Majesty* (1661), and became rector of Ravenstone, Leicestershire, in 1667. He died in 1696 and was buried at Coleorton on 31 January.   GORDON MCMULLAN

Sources *The poems of Thomas Pestell*, ed. H. Buchan (1940) · J. Nichols, *The history and antiquities of the county of Leicester*, 3 (1800–04) · A. Pritchard, 'Unpublished poems by Thomas Pestell', *English Literary Renaissance*, 10 (1980), 133–47 · IGI · Venn, *Alum. Cant.* · *Walker rev.*, 241–2 · N. W. S. Cranfield, 'Chaplains in ordinary at the early Stuart court: the purple road', *Patronage and recruitment in the Tudor and early Stuart church*, ed. C. Cross (1996), 120–47, esp. 145 · G. E. Bentley, *The Jacobean and Caroline stage*, 7 vols. (1941–68), vol. 4, pp. 952–5 · P. J. Finkelpearl, 'The authorship of the anonymous "Coleorton Masque"', *N&Q*, 238 (1993), 224–6

Archives Lincs. Arch., MS letters | Northants. RO, MSS Isham (Lamport), corresp.

Wealth at death see will, Buchan, ed., *Poems*

Pestell, Thomas (1613–1690). *See under* Pestell, Thomas (*bap.* 1586, *d.* 1667).

Petavel, Sir Joseph Ernest (1873–1936), engineer and physicist, was born in London on 14 August 1873, the younger son of Emmanuel Petavel DD and his wife, Susanna, daughter of William Olliff, of Great Missenden, Buckinghamshire. An eminent Hebrew scholar, Emmanuel Petavel moved to England from Neuchâtel in 1863 to become minister of the Swiss church in Endell Street, London. In 1876 the family left England for Geneva, later settling in Lausanne where Joseph attended school and read engineering at the university. In 1893 he returned to England to study science and engineering at University College, London.

In 1896 Petavel published his first paper, written in collaboration with John Ambrose Fleming, of University College, on the alternating current arc. With the award for three years of an 1851 Exhibition grant he was able to work in the laboratories of the Royal Institution, where he made, for Fleming and James Dewar, accurate measurements of the physical properties of materials at low temperatures. His skill in design and measurement was also evident in the work he carried out as John Harling research fellow at Manchester University in 1901–3, working in the new physics laboratory of Arthur Schuster. This work included the development of the 'Petavel gauge' for measuring the variation in pressure caused by the explosion of gases, and the construction of electrical furnaces and apparatus for studying chemical action at high pressures and temperatures.

In 1904 Petavel spent a year in charge of the British scientific contribution to the St Louis International Exhibition where he built and operated a reproduction of Dewar's plant at the Royal Institution for the liquefaction of gases. Petavel returned in 1905 to the University of Manchester as a lecturer in mechanics. Three years later he was appointed to the Beyer chair of engineering, held from 1868 to 1905 by Osborne Reynolds, which he combined with the post of director of the Whitworth and later the John Hopkinson Engineering Laboratories. His work at Manchester was chiefly concerned with standards of light, ventilation, structural stresses, the theory of gas engines, and aeronautics, and Petavel showed himself to be a capable and efficient administrator. During the First World War not only was his laboratory working at high pressure on the design of instruments and on testing of materials, but he also spent much of his time in London serving on committees for aeronautics, on which he became a recognized authority.

In 1919 Petavel was appointed director of the National Physical Laboratory as successor to Sir Richard Glazebrook and he remained in this post until his death. During his directorship the laboratory grew steadily as new buildings were constructed for the study of physics, high-tension electricity, acoustics, and aeronautics. Petavel greatly extended the national and international authority and influence of his institution and successfully managed the often difficult relationship with the Department of Scientific and Industrial Research which had assumed financial responsibility for the laboratory from the Royal Society at the end of the war. Those who worked with him at the laboratory recalled his hospitality, and his afternoon and moonlight parties were remembered fondly by his staff and friends. He will also be remembered for the beautifying of Bushy House and its grounds, for which he left the Royal Society a large sum.

Petavel, who had been elected FRS in 1907, was appointed KBE in 1920. He died, unmarried, at Bushy House, Teddington, on 31 March 1936 and was buried at Highgate cemetery.   R. ROBERTSON, *rev.* RUSSELL MOSELEY

Sources R. Robertson, *Obits. FRS*, 2 (1936–8), 183–203 • *The Times* (1 April 1936) • R. Moseley, 'Science, government and industrial research: the origins and development of the National Physical Laboratory', DPhil diss., U. Sussex, 1976 **Archives** Royal Institution of Great Britain, London, papers | California Institute of Technology Archives, Pasadena, corresp. with G. E. Hale **Likenesses** A. Hayward, oils, National Physical Laboratory, Teddington, Middlesex • photograph, RS; repro. in Robertson, *Obits. FRS*, 182 • photograph, RS • photograph, National Physical Laboratory, Teddington, Middlesex **Wealth at death** £61,161 12s. 4d.: probate, 27 May 1936, CGPLA Eng. & Wales

Peter (d. 1085), bishop of Lichfield, was a chaplain of William I, and custodian of the see of Lincoln in 1066. When Leofwine, the last Anglo-Saxon bishop of Lichfield, resigned in 1070, Lanfranc committed Lichfield to the care of Wulfstan, bishop of Worcester, for two years. Lanfranc finally consecrated Peter to the see in May 1072.

In 1075, at a synod held by Lanfranc in London, a decree was passed which allowed Peter to remove the see of Lichfield to Chester. There he made the church of St John's his cathedral church, instituting a dean and canons. The see was situated at Chester only until 1106 when Peter's successor, Robert de Limesey, returned it to Lichfield. However, some of the canonries inaugurated by Peter remained there until 1541, when the modern see of Chester was created. The Latin continuation of text A of the Anglo-Saxon Chronicle relates that, in 1076, Peter was sent by Lanfranc to assist the archbishop of York in certain consecrations. Peter died in 1085 and was buried at Chester, being the only bishop of the earlier foundation who

was interred there. A lead seal matrix bearing the legend 'SIGILLVM PETRI CESTRENSIS EPISCOPI' ('the seal of Peter, bishop of Chester'), which was found at Chester during excavations in 1967–9, may give a contemporary representation of Peter.

ALICE M. COOKE, *rev.* MARIOS COSTAMBEYS

Sources F. Barlow, *The English church, 1066–1154: a history of the Anglo-Norman church* (1979) • J. Cherry, 'The lead seal matrix of Peter, bishop of Chester', *Antiquaries Journal*, 65 (1985), 472–3 and pl. CVI b • *Ann. mon.*, vol. 1 • J. Stevenson, ed., *Chronicon monasterii de Abingdon*, 2 vols., Rolls Series, 2 (1858) • D. Wilkins, ed., *Concilia Magnae Britanniae et Hiberniae*, 1 (1737) • D. Dumville and S. Keynes, eds., *The Anglo-Saxon Chronicle: a collaborative edition*, 3, ed. J. M. Bately (1983) • E. B. Fryde and others, eds., *Handbook of British chronology*, 3rd edn, Royal Historical Society Guides and Handbooks, 2 (1986) • J. Le Neve, *Fasti ecclesiae anglicanae* (1716) **Likenesses** lead seal matrix, BM; repro. in Cherry, 'The lead seal matrix of Peter', pl. CVI a, CVI b

Peter de Montfort. *See* Montfort, Peter de (c.1205–1265).

Peter of Blois. *See* Blois, Peter of (1125x30–1212).

Peter of Cornwall. *See* Cornwall, Peter of (1139/40–1221).

Peter of Savoy. *See* Savoy, Peter of, count of Savoy and *de facto* earl of Richmond (1203?–1268).

Peter the Wild Boy (c.**1712–1785**), curiosity, was found in 1724 in the woods near Hamelin, about 25 miles from Hanover. In the words of contemporary pamphleteers, he was observed 'walking on his hands and feet, climbing trees like a squirrel, and feeding on grass and moss'. In November 1725 he was taken to the house of correction at Zell, and in the same month was presented to George I, who was visiting Hanover. Peter then escaped and took refuge in a tree, which had to be cut down before he was recaptured. In the spring of 1726, by the king's command, he was brought to England and, according to contemporary accounts, was exhibited to the nobility. The boy, who appeared to be about fourteen years old, was baptized and committed to the care of the physician and satirist John Arbuthnot. Attempts were made to teach Peter to speak, without success. The question of how Peter came to be in the woods was fiercely debated in chapbooks and pamphlets. There was also much speculation about what sort of creature had nurtured him; possible animals included a sow, wolf, and bear.

Jonathan Swift, who arrived in London at about the same time, wrote to Thomas Tickell that Peter 'hath been half our Talk this fortnight' (16 April 1726, *Correspondence*, 3.128). Swift also wrote a satirical pamphlet, *It Cannot Rain but it Pours*, which commented on London's fascination with the boy; Arbuthnot and Defoe provided similar investigations in their *The Most Wonderful Wonder* (1726) and *Mere Nature Delineated* (1726). Some of the more bizarre features of Swift's description, including Peter's neighing to express joy, were later applied by James Burnett, Lord Monboddo, for his theory of human development in *Of the Origin and Progress of Language* (1773–92). Monboddo compared the wild boy with an orang-utang—a species which he famously regarded as an uncivilized type of human being.

Peter the Wild Boy (*c*.1712–1785), by Valentine Green (after Pierre Étienne Falconet, exh. Society of Artists 1767)

Following the death of Queen Caroline, who had taken an interest in Peter's education, he was boarded with a farmer at the king's expense. He grew up strong and muscular and was able to do manual labour under careful supervision. Each spring he would wander away from the farm. In 1751 he walked as far as Norfolk, where he was apprehended as a vagrant and committed to the Norwich city bridewell. After his release he was given a brass collar which was inscribed 'Peter the Wild Boy, Broadway Farm, Berkhamsted'. He returned to the farm where he was visited by Monboddo in 1782, and where he died on 22 February 1785 (*GM*, 236). He was buried at Northchurch, Hertfordshire.

THOMAS SECCOMBE, *rev.* DAVID TURNER

Sources H. Wilson, *Wonderful characters*, 3 vols. (1821) · *N&Q*, 6th ser., 10 (1884), 248, 287–94 · *The correspondence of Jonathan Swift*, ed. H. Williams, 5 vols. (1963–5) · C. H. Timperley, *A dictionary of printers and printing* (1839) · *VCH Hertfordshire*, 2.246, 249 · M. Newton, 'Bodies without souls: the case of Peter the Wild Boy', *At the borders of the human*, ed. E. Fudge, R. Gilbert, and S. Wiseman (1999) · *GM*, 1st ser., 55 (1785), 236

Likenesses R. Cooper, engraving, repro. in Wilson, *Wonderful characters*, vol. 2 · V. Green, engraving (after P. É. Falconet, exh. Society of Artists 1767), NPG [*see illus.*] · engraving (after unknown portrait), repro. in J. Caulfield, *Portraits, memoirs and characters of remarkable persons*, 4 vols. (1819–20)

Peter, David (1765–1837), Independent minister and ecclesiastical historian, was born at Aberystwyth, Cardiganshire, on 5 August 1765, the son of David and Margaret Peter. When he was seven years old his father, who was a ship's carpenter, moved to New Quay, Cardiganshire. He

received his early education at the school of Evan Davies, Troed-y-rhiw, and later with the Revd David Davies of Castellhywel. His father, who was a churchman, wished him to become a clergyman. However, under the influence of the Revd Benjamin Evans of Tre-wen, Peter joined the Independents, and in March 1783 became a member of the church at Penrhiw-galed. In August 1783 he entered the Presbyterian Carmarthen Academy at Rhyd-y-groes and by the following year was keeping a school at St Ishmaels, Carmarthenshire. During this time he began to preach at Penrhiw-galed and in August 1786 he enrolled as a student at the Swansea Academy. In October 1789 he was appointed assistant tutor to the Revd William Howell at this institution, a position he resigned in 1792, in order to take the pastorate of Lammas Street Church, Carmarthen, where he was ordained on 8 June. The academy at Swansea was dissolved in 1794, but in the following year it was re-established at Carmarthen, and Peter was appointed president. He held this office, in conjunction with his pastorate, until his death. Peter married twice: his first wife was Sarah Lewis (*b.* 1755), *née* Llywelyn, a widow from Carmarthen, whom he married in October 1795; after her death in 1820 he married Charlotte Nott (*c*.1783–1834) on 18 July 1822.

Peter was highly regarded as an evangelical preacher who found great success in his ministry at Carmarthen. He was responsible for translating Samuel Palmer's *Protestant Dissenters' Catechism* (1803), but he is best known as the author of *Hanes crefydd yng Nghymru* (1816), an account of Welsh religion from the times of the druids to the beginning of the nineteenth century. The book, which shows fairly wide reading and is free from sectarian bias, remained for many years the main history of religion in Wales. Peter died on 4 May 1837 at Carmarthen and was buried at the Lammas Street Church.

MARI A. WILLIAMS

Sources W. H. Lewis, *Memoir of the life and labours of the Revd David Peter* (1846) · J. D. Owen, *Hanes eglwys Heol Awst, Caerfyrddin* (1926) · T. Rees and J. Thomas, *Hanes eglwysi annibynol Cymru*, 3 (1873) · *DWB*

Archives NL Wales

Likenesses stipple, *c*.1840, NL Wales · T. Blood, engraving, repro. in *Evangelical Magazine* (1812) · S. J. Lander, engraving, NL Wales · photograph, repro. in Owen, *Hanes eglwys Heol Awst*

Wealth at death under £1500: will, NL Wales, Aberystwyth, SD 1837/135

Peter [Peters], **Hugh** (*bap.* 1598, *d.* 1660), Independent minister, was born in Fowey, Cornwall, and baptized there on 11 June 1598, the third child and second son of Thomas Dickwoode or Peter (1571–1625), merchant, and his first wife, Martha Treffry (*bap.* 1572, *d.* 1598), daughter of John Treffry of Place and Emblem Tresithney; Thomas *Peter (1597–1654/5) was his brother. His father's family, probably originally named Dykeveldt, emigrated from Antwerp about 1543 and at the end of the sixteenth century adopted the name Peter, subsequently often rendered Peters. He matriculated sizar at Trinity College, Cambridge, in 1613, graduating BA early in 1618. Two years later he was in London, where he heard a sermon that initiated his conversion. Shortly thereafter he took a post

Veri Effigies HUGH PETERS Æt 57.

Printed by Peter Cole.

Hugh Peter (*bap.* 1598, *d.* 1660), by unknown engraver, *c.*1655

teaching school in Laindon, Essex. He was ordained deacon in London on 23 December 1621, but returned to Cambridge, where he proceeded MA in 1622. Ordained priest on 18 June 1623, he became curate at Rayleigh, Essex, through the patronage of the earl of Warwick; he remained at Rayleigh until 1626. About 1625 he married Elizabeth (*née* Cooke), widow of Edmund Reade of Wickford, Essex; she was a generation older than himself, with adult children.

London and the Netherlands In 1626 Peter returned to London, possibly to organize opposition to royal policies, particularly the forced loan, on behalf of Warwick. He was also active in the effort to buy up lay impropriations. He preached regularly at St Sepulchre, Holborn. In November, preaching at a private day in the neighbouring parish of Christ Church, he prayed for the queen to forsake her 'idolatry and superstition' (*CSP dom.*, *1625–49*, 175). He was imprisoned, but Warwick posted bail. In August 1627 Peter composed a statement to prove his orthodoxy for the bishop of London, but later that year his licence to preach was suspended. For the next year and a half he moved back and forth between the Low Countries and England. He served briefly as the minister at Amelant, an island off Friesland. He preached at Rayleigh, where the rector and wardens claimed to be ignorant of his suspension. When he prayed for the salvation of the queen at St Sepulchre his audacity landed him in prison for six months without bail. After his release he became proctor at Friesland University under its rector, William Ames. In

1628 Peter subscribed £50 to the precursor to the Massachusetts Bay Company; he attended company meetings as late as May 1629.

After that Peter stayed on the continent, taking a position as chaplain to one of the four English regiments in the army of Frederick Henry, stadholder of the United Provinces, possibly that of Sir Edward Harwood. He published an account of the army's successes, *Digitus Dei* [1631]. He eventually became pastor of the church at Rotterdam, and in 1633 set out to reform it along congregationalist lines. He introduced a church covenant and made subscription to it a condition of continued membership. The covenant unchurched a sizeable portion—one opponent alleged two-thirds—of the members. The congregation then proceeded to 'call' Peter as its minister, a ceremony that implied a renunciation of his Anglican ordination, a fact that was duly brought to the attention of the authorities in England. Later that year Ames joined Peter at Rotterdam but died soon after, in November 1633. Ames left his papers to Peter, who saw two works into print. In October 1633 Charles I put the English churches in Holland under the direct supervision of Archbishop William Laud. Henceforth, Peter found his activities increasingly scrutinized and many of his colleagues departing for New England. William Brereton visited Rotterdam in May 1634, describing Peter as 'a right zealous and worthy man'. He further opined that the church, 'formerly intended for a playhouse [was] now converted to a better use to a church' (*Travels in Holland*, 1844, 6). In 1635 the Merchant Adventurers relocated their court to Rotterdam and commandeered the English church. By agreement with local officials, who had heretofore supported Peter, the church was to conform to the Church of England discipline.

New England Peter and his wife returned to England in June 1635. The following month he sailed for New England, along with his stepdaughter Elizabeth, her new husband John Winthrop (1606–1676), and Sir Henry Vane. The three men were employed as agents by a group of investors interested in the Connecticut River valley, and for the first year of his sojourn in New England Peter worked on its behalf. He soon became involved in the affairs of the Bay Colony, helping to organize a January meeting to deal with differences between magistrates John Winthrop (1588–1649) and Thomas Dudley. He became a freeman in Massachusetts in March 1636. In July he travelled to Saybrook, on the Connecticut River, but that visit apparently ended his work for the patentees. Peter also worked to improve the region's economy, advocating the development of the fishery and shipbuilding, and persuaded a group to join with him in financing the construction of a ship. He suggested increased co-operation between congregations and a programme to readdress seasonal underemployment of women and children. He served on the colony's committee to develop a law code and as an overseer for Harvard College.

Peter became minister at Salem on 21 December 1636. The previous minister, Roger Williams, had been banished for his controversial views on separatism and other matters. Peter immediately wrote a new church covenant and, as in Rotterdam, required all church members to subscribe. During the same winter the so-called 'Antinomian controversy', centring on the religious teachings of Anne Hutchinson, generated considerable contention. At least from the moment he became Salem's minister, Peter took a leading role in the effort to root out the Hutchinsonians. He participated in clerical conferences, met with the general court, and attended both the civil and ecclesiastical trials of Hutchinson. He publicly confronted her and her supporters, including the young governor, Sir Henry Vane. At her church trial he lectured Hutchinson that she knew neither her catechism nor her place. His own congregation was divided at this time. A few of Williams's supporters remained in Salem, and they were joined by a number of Hutchinson's defenders. Peter laboured, in private conferences and eventually in a church trial, to eliminate opposition. His wife, who during his absence from Europe had returned to Rotterdam and been reportedly ill-treated by the church, had joined Peter in Salem in 1637. Williams's supporters questioned her admission to the church on the grounds that she lacked a proper dismissal from the Rotterdam church.

During his sojourn in New England Peter began to experience chronic health problems. His correspondence and that of others mention his debility, which occasionally became acute enough to affect his work. John Endecott, his friend at Salem, wrote that he 'hath bene very ill. But I hope the worst is past, though hee be as sick in his thoughts as ever' (*Winthrop Papers*, 4.30). Peter reported in September 1640 'that deep melancholy is getting fast upon mee agayne' (ibid., 4.285). Despite his infirmity, however, he was a popular minister, credited with bringing a measure of harmony to the town. On one occasion his romantic entanglements gave rise to controversy. His first wife having died within the previous two months, Peter was in April 1638 accused of misleading Ruth Ames, daughter of his former colleague, about his intentions. Her uncle John Phillips—minister at Dedham, Massachusetts—claimed that Peter had caused her to dismiss a marriage prospect in London. About the same time Peter was negotiating marriage with a widow, Deliverance Sheffield. Letters between Peter and various New England friends about these negotiations indicated that they were strained and that he felt himself committed to the marriage regardless of his own inclinations. How the Ames imbroglio was resolved is not known, but by mid-1639 Peter was married to Sheffield. She was dismissed from Boston and admitted to Salem church in January 1640. The couple's only child, a daughter, was born in October 1640.

Civil war England In 1641 Peter returned to England as one of three agents of the Massachusetts government. Their assignment was:

> to negotiate for us, as occasion should be offered, both in furthering the work of reformation of the churches there which was now like to be attempted, and to satisfy our countrymen of the true cause our engagements there have not been satisfied this year. (*Journal of John Winthrop*, 346)

Salem church was dismayed by the prospect of Peter's going, but relented under pressure from the general court. His wife and child remained behind in New England, where his absence was widely lamented.

Peter's work for the colony included raising £500, sent in 'Useful commodities for the country' (*Journal of John Winthrop*, 402). He also raised money to send poor children to New England. These funds became the subject of controversy, and it seems clear that some was misspent. Peter compiled and composed the introduction for a defence of the New England church way, *Church-Government and Church-Covenant Discussed* (1643), which appeared just as the Westminster assembly convened. Overlooking the Massachusetts agents, leaders in parliament wrote to New England to ask that John Cotton, Thomas Hooker, and John Davenport attend, but, partly on the advice of Peter, they declined. Peter was featured in a satirical pamphlet, purporting to be written by William Laud, in which the archbishop pleaded that he 'not be transported beyond the seas into New England with Master Peters' (*Copy of the Petition*, 1643). The satire appeared shortly after Laud heard apparently unfounded rumours of 'a plot laid by Peters, Wel[d], and others' that he be sent to New England (*The Works of … William Laud*, ed. J. Bliss and W. Scott, 7 vols., 1847–60, 3.251).

Resuming the role he had held in the United Provinces as chaplain, Peter served from May to September 1642 with the naval forces under Lord Forbes sent to reduce Ireland. He wrote an up-beat account of that unsuccessful campaign, *A True Relation of the Passages of God's Providence* (1642). In it he suggested that Ireland be reduced through the use of physical force as well as the civilizing force of a godly protestant ministry. Upon Peter's return to England, he took the lead in a petition against peace overtures and accommodation on religious issues. He emerged as an advocate of co-operation among the godly and embraced toleration in pursuit of shared goals. A zealous advocate of the Independent cause, he became a target of the more conservative presbyterians. He occasionally traded insults with them. He attended Laud's trial. Enraged over Laud's claim to have converted many, Peter accosted him, and Laud believed that only the intervention of the earl of Essex prevented Peter from laying hands on him. Later Peter preached against Laud at Lambeth, singling out his claim for ridicule. By this time his wife had joined him in England. She was suffering from some sort of mental problem, and her 'distraction' had led to her excommunication from the Salem church, which Peter judged to be uncharitable.

Peter emerged as a major promoter of parliament's cause, combining his inspiring preaching, his gift for practical organization, and his vision of a reformed England. Important parliamentarian military leaders—especially Sir Thomas Fairfax and Cromwell—relied upon him for counsel and to promote their activities. S. R. Gardiner wrote of him:

> It is easy to imagine how he could chat and jest with the soldiers, and yet could seize an opportunity to slip in a word on higher matters. His influence must have been such as

Cromwell loved—an influence which in every word and action made for concord. (Gardiner, *Great Civil War*, 2.326)

Considered a conciliator by his friends, he was also an accomplished polemicist who made many enemies among those he opposed. Peter was present at various military campaigns: the expedition to Lyme (May 1644), Bridgwater (July 1645), Bristol (August, although he left before the main attack), Winchester Castle (October), and Dartmouth (January 1646). He was at Fowey when the remnant of Essex's army under Major-General Philip Skippon surrendered in September 1644 and back in his native Cornwall in 1646 when parliament subdued it. He saw Oxford capitulate in June 1646 and Worcester in July. He repeatedly hurried to Westminster to deliver reports of the army's doings—often to announce victories and request more aid. Warwick sent him from Lyme in June 1644, and he conveyed money back to the army. When Bridgwater was taken and Prince Charles's papers captured, Peter carried the news. He brought word of the surrender of Winchester Castle on 7 October 1645. A week later he returned to report the storming of Basing House (where he reportedly tarried long enough to harangue the aged marquess of Winchester, whom he tried to argue out of his royalism). The following January he brought news of victory at Dartmouth, and in March he announced Sir Ralph Hopton's surrender in Cornwall. His reports were often published. At the close of the war, in *The Last Report of the English Wars* (1646), he warned: 'This is the misery of England whilst others are beaten into slavery, they are apt to be complemented into it' (p. 9).

Peter also rallied support through his preaching. Exhortations delivered in his capacity as a chaplain were described as extremely effective at pivotal moments. He was frequently dispatched to win support in crucial areas. In July 1643 he raised support for parliament in Kent and Sussex. Somerset clubmen heard him preach in August 1645, and Peter claimed to have won many recruits for Fairfax's forces at the siege of Bristol. He temporarily left the army to travel around the home counties to garner support for parliament's war effort later that month. In September his preaching in the market of Torrington reportedly 'convinced many of their Errors in adhering to the King's Party' (Whitelocke, 194). He preached of the royalist intention to invade Cornwall with Irish papists, thereby turning the people against the king. In addition to these recurrent efforts, Peter received special assignments. In September 1643 he went to the Netherlands to raise money for protestants in Ireland and for parliament. The efforts yielded £30,000. There he also collected information on royalists' efforts to organize support. He was appointed in March 1645 to seek out delinquents' estates. In 1646 Peter negotiated terms with leading royalists in his native Cornwall, dissuading them from coming into the war against parliament. That November he readied regiments to send to Ireland. He occasionally ministered to men condemned by the state. He acted as chaplain at the execution of Richard Challoner in July 1643 and through the condemned man's confession gathered evidence against his accomplices. In January 1644 Peter attended Sir John Hotham, receiving his thanks on the scaffold.

All of these efforts were rewarded. The house voted Peter an occasional monetary payment for his services. In March 1644, after he returned from the Netherlands, he received £100 and some of Laud's books. In 1646 £200 a year from the earl of Worcester's estate was settled on him. Other gifts were reported in the press, and Peter was derided for enriching himself through the suffering of others. He denied these charges in 1660, stating 'By the War, I never enriched my self, I have often offer'd my personal Estate for £200 and for Lands, I never had any but that part of a Noble mans, which I never laid up peny of' (*Case of Mr. Hugh Peters*, 5). Parliament also rewarded him with opportunities to preach before it. He delivered his best-known sermon, *God's Doings and Mans Duty* (1646), at a thanksgiving for the conquest of the west.

That autumn, the war over, Peter considered returning to New England—a move he often discussed. He sent his wife ahead in September but never followed her. He participated in the campaign against presbyterians in London, including drawing up a petition that received 20,000 signatures. Together with 'his London friends', he was frequently blamed for the radicalization of the army in this period (Gentles, 141). That winter Peter again experienced debilitating illness, but by late spring 1647 he was much improved. He then championed the Independents and the army, whereas earlier he had worked for co-operation among Charles's foes. John Lilburne characterized Peter as 'the grand Journey or Hackney-man of the Army' (*Clarke Papers*, 2.259). With Cromwell he fled London for the army in June 1647. Some accounts state that on that journey he worked on Cromwell to support the demand to bring the king to justice. When the king fell into the army's hands Peter had several conversations with him in Newmarket (June 1647), and Charles was reported to have said 'that he had often heard talk of him, but did not believe he had that solidity in him he found by his discourse' (*A Conference betwixt the Kings most Excellent Majesty, and Mr. Peters*, 1647). The king, however, declined to hear Peter preach. That October Peter defended the army's refusal to disband and put forward his own proposals for reform in *A Word for the Army and Two Words to the Kingdom* (1647). Later that month he attended the Putney debates, speaking only briefly.

In the short but sharp second war, Peter resumed his former duties. He was with Cromwell at the siege of Pembroke Castle. After the castle finally surrendered, Cromwell and Peter went to Preston. Subsequently Peter joined in the pursuit of the duke of Hamilton. His news report exaggerated his own role in the duke's surrender, and in New England the tale was further embellished so that it was rumoured that Peter alone had captured him.

Peter's role in the king's death Peter was extremely active in the months between the war's end and the king's execution. He preached to fortify the army before it marched on London for Pride's Purge. In the aftermath of the purge, Peter carried a list of the forty-one imprisoned members to Fairfax, then brought back word that two were to be freed. He gave one long speech at the Whitehall debates, in which he argued for involving the people in discussions of liberty of conscience and favourably cited the Dutch example of toleration. Ian Gentles describes Peter, in the weeks before the king's trial, dashing frenetically between various parties, working with Ireton and Cromwell to confound those opposed to regicide. He was one of only two ministers (John Goodwin being the other) publicly to support the army after its invasion of London. On the day before the execution he preached a 'grisly' sermon on Isaiah 14: 19–20 (Gentles, 309). As in other periods of intense activity, Peter fell ill. He missed the king's execution, sick in his lodgings. His absence led to rumours that he was the masked executioner. His prominent place in these events—both real and rumoured—contributed much to his fate at the Restoration. Lilburne accused him of recognizing no law but the sword, but Gardiner declared the charge clearly untrue (Gardiner, *Commonwealth and Protectorate*, 1.50). When, in the aftermath of the regicide, the duke of Hamilton was to be executed for his support of the king (March 1649), he publicly embraced Peter and bid him farewell.

Interregnum activities For some years after the regicide Peter remained active in public affairs. He advocated naval expansion before the new committee for the navy. He was temporarily given charge of the confiscated royal property at St James's Palace, a responsibility that led him to be blamed later for its dispersal. He quelled a mutiny in the navy at Sandwich in one powerful sermon, preached on 24 April 1649. A parody of the sermon was published as *A Most Pithy Exhortation Delivered in Eloquent Oration to the Watry Generation* (1649). The effort seems to have exhausted him once more, and he became ill. Upon his recovery he gained an interview with Lilburne, now in the Tower, accusing him of fomenting mutiny. Their conversation provided the basis for a number of Lilburne's pamphlets, attacking Peter and his circle. As those who had once supported parliament began fighting among themselves, Peter became an object of attack by his erstwhile allies. As with earlier royalist parody, much of these were sexual in nature. His wife having returned to England in ill health again that spring, the opposition press ridiculed her mental instability as well as his own.

Despite these attacks, Peter continued to receive major responsibilities. He managed the transport of a large contingent of men and troops intended to follow Cromwell's forces into Ireland. He again posted reports of the war. Cromwell commissioned him colonel, possibly to facilitate his provisioning efforts. Illness cut short his stint in Ireland, however, and he returned to Milford Haven, where parliament dispatched a physician to attend him. Dr William Yonge later testified against Peter and published an opprobrious biography, *England's Shame, or, The Unmasking of a Politick Atheist* (1663). Peter claimed that Yonge's animosity arose when he received no advancement through Peter's connections. After his recovery Peter became governor of Milford Haven, from whence he continued to supply the Irish expedition and worked to

persuade the Welsh to subscribe to the engagement. Having long thought the Welsh border counties ripe for the gospel, as is evident in *Mr. Peters Last Report* (1646), he worked closely with the commissioners for the propagation of the gospel in Wales.

Peter returned to London from Wales in September 1650, just after the battle of Dunbar. Before the end of the year he was appointed chaplain to the council of state, with lodgings in Whitehall and a salary of £200 a year. His wide-ranging plans for social reform received a hearing, as he was closest of the would-be reformers to the seat of power. He sat on Mathew Hale's legal reform committee in 1651. Bulstrode Whitelocke said of this effort that 'none was more forward or lyable to mistakes then Mr Hugh Peters' (*Diary*, 1990, 274). He continued to advance his reform agenda, as he had in the 1640s, by publishing pamphlets, including *Good Work for a Good Magistrate* (1651). He hurried up to Worcester after Cromwell's victory and preached to the soldiers. Colonist William Coddington visited Peter in 1651, and reported: 'I was mery with him and called him, the Arch BB: [Archbishop] of Canterberye, in regard of his adtendance by ministers and gentelmen and it passed very well' (*Winthrop Papers*, 6.173). Roger Williams noted that Peter had lodgings that had formerly belonged to Laud, along with his portion of Laud's books. Peter used his connections to find positions for his acquaintants, especially young New England men who came seeking their fortunes in the new republic. Although named an overseer of the Corporation for the Propagation of the Gospel in New England, he did not support efforts to convert Native Americans. Long an advocate of the Dutch model, which along with New England served as his major source of reform ideas, Peter abhorred the Anglo-Dutch War. When he tried to persuade Sir George Ayscue not to participate, Ayscue turned him in. Peter fell into disfavour briefly, although Cromwell intervened on his behalf.

Peter appears then to have sided with the army, which had become openly critical of the republican government. When the Barebone's Parliament convened Peter was restored to his former influence. He worked to bring the war to an end, intervening to smooth the peace negotiations. In the autumn of 1653 he was among those appointed to prepare Whitelocke's embassy to Sweden. He not only prayed over the departing retinue, but also sent along gifts of a cheese and an English mastiff to Queen Kristina. Whitelocke thought the gesture inappropriate but when the queen learned of it, she scolded Whitelocke for withholding her goods.

Although Peter had good relations with Cromwell personally, he apparently felt misgivings about the turn away from a republic to protectorate. Yet he served the protector faithfully, continuing as chaplain to the council of state. Under Cromwell, Peter served as one of thirty-eight 'triers' responsible to oversee the English ministry. Still, the later 1650s saw Peter less often in the centre of public affairs, perhaps owing to his ill health. He may have fallen again into disfavour. His correspondence with the Netherlands was suspected as the source of a leak of confidential information. Cromwell apparently reprimanded him for meddling in naval affairs in 1656, and his duties may have been limited to council chaplain after that. In 1658 he was called out of this semi-retirement to smooth over tensions between French and English forces at Dunkirk, which he performed with his previous energy and ability. Shortly thereafter, at Cromwell's funeral, Peter preached on the text Joshua 1: 2, 'Moses my servant is dead'. He served as a chaplain at army meetings plotting to bring down Richard Cromwell and reinstitute the republic, but later claimed not to have understood the intention. He published an open letter to the officers of the army, attempting to save the protectorate, but to no avail. Unsurprisingly, he was not active in public affairs after its fall. He was reviled in the press as an associate of Cromwell.

His death and the fate of his family When George Monck approached London, Peter went to join him. Although he preached before Monck, the general did nothing to promote or protect Peter, and he was turned out of his chambers at Whitehall. Then or shortly thereafter he retired to Southwark, where an obscure family sheltered him. Although technically not a regicide, Peter was exempt from royal pardon and was listed by parliament for revenge to be exacted for his prominent if largely unofficial role. His arrest was ordered on 7 June 1660, and he was caught on 31 August, reportedly betrayed by his servant. His daughter, by then aged twenty, visited him daily in prison. A committee also visited him to investigate what had become of the contents of St James's Palace. In a petition to the House of Lords Peter argued that due to the illness that kept him away from the execution he had had no hand in the king's death. While in prison, he wrote perhaps his best work, *A Dying Fathers Last Legacy to an Onely Child* (1660). It includes an autobiographical statement and denies the charge of sedition. 'Sedition is the heating of mans minds against the present Authority, in that I never was, yet sorry, Authority should have had any thoughts of me, or know so inconsiderable a creature as myself' (p. 111). At his trial on October 12 he responded angrily to Yonge's testimony. He averred that he had been guided by his concern for 'sound Religion ... Learning and Laws ... and that the poor might be cared for' (Stephen, 1.155). He was duly sentenced to a traitor's death. On 16 October he was made to watch the execution of his friend, John Cooke, before meeting his own death with dignity. His head was placed on London Bridge. The news weeklies averred 'there never was a person suffered death so unpitied and (which is more) whose Execution was the delight of the people' than he (Stearns, *The Strenuous Puritan*, 418). He was reviled in the press, and the tradition of depicting him as a buffoon was given a boost by the publication of *Tales and Jests of Hugh Peters* (1660).

Peter's wife, who lived apart from him in England for some years before his death, was in 1677 living on the charity of George Cokayne's Independent church in London. Their daughter remained in England and in 1665 married Robert Barker; eventually they lived in Deptford

and had eight children. Peter's estate in England was confiscated, but not that in New England. Later, the royal official Edmund Randolph, while damning the Massachusetts government for its association with Peter, tried to acquire Peter's estate, arguing that he had forfeited it by his treason. Elizabeth eventually won a suit for a Marblehead farm she claimed as the inheritance from her father.

Views of Hugh Peter Opinion about Hugh Peter was sharply divided from his own day at least through to the mid-nineteenth century. His contemporaries among royalists and religious conservatives roundly hated him. Thomas Edwards dubbed him 'Vicar Generall and Metropolitane of the Independents both in New and Old England' (*Second Part of Gangraena*, 1646, 61). His most recent modern biographer, Raymond Phineas Stearns, asserted that, except for C. H. Firth's *Dictionary of National Biography* entry on Peter, all accounts followed either the hagiographic tradition of Peter's own *A Dying Fathers Last Legacy* or the unfounded attacks of William Yonge's *Englands Shame* (1663). This overstates the case somewhat, although there has been a tendency to champion or revile Peter depending on one's political leanings. In nineteenth-century New England, defending Hugh Peter became a point of honour. The editor of the *New England Historical and Genealogical Register* fulminated:

> Mr. Peters perished by the hand of the mercenary murderer, but his memory should be safe in the hands of a faithful historian of New England ... The cause of Peters was the cause of New England and he perished for doing more than many others had courage to do. (8, 1854, 85–6)

Many modern scholars have attempted to come to terms with this charismatic, practical, and naïve man. To Gardiner he was the 'prince of army chaplains', almost capable of 'real, if somewhat incoherent, eloquence' and 'entirely without fear of giving offence to any of his hearers' (Gardiner, *Great Civil War*, 3.84). Bernard Bailyn characterized him as 'that ambitious, worldly cleric whose fascination with the things of Caesar was to cost him his head' (*New England Merchant*, 1955, 76), Austin Woolrych called him 'voluble and self-important' (*Commonwealth to Protectorate*, 1982, 119), and C. V. Wedgwood described him as an 'eloquent, resolute, bustling little man' (*King's War*, 1958, 111). Unlike many fellow ministers, Peter was no intellectual. He cared little for doctrine or theology. His tendency toward melancholy suits the stereotypical 'puritan' temperament, and his theology was no doubt central to his personal psychology. But in his public life religion seems to have mattered most as a guide to social and political action. He expected religious reformation to yield concrete results, and he supported causes from suppression of the Hutchinsonians to civil war and regicide because such position seemed conducive to the change he sought. He spoke especially to the common person, so that his preaching was highly effective in rallying soldiers or turning the mood of a crowd. This same common appeal no doubt earned his reputation for buffoonery. His flair for the dramatic and his willingness to take the lead at controversial moments thrust him into the centre of things in the 1640s. These tendencies, his mastery of the barbed insult slung at his foe, and his close association with the reviled Cromwell ensured his place on the scaffold in 1660.   CARLA GARDINA PESTANA

Sources R. P. Stearns, *The strenuous puritan: Hugh Peter, 1598–1660* (1954) · J. M. Patrick, 'Hugh Peters, a study in puritanism', *University of Buffalo Studies*, 17 (March 1946), 137–207 · *DNB* · I. Gentles, *The New Model Army in England, Ireland, and Scotland, 1645–1653* (1992) · *The Winthrop papers*, ed. W. C. Ford and others, 4–6 (1944–92) · R. P. Stearns, ed., 'Letters and documents by or relating to Hugh Peter', *Essex Institute Historical Collections*, 71 (1935), 303–18; 72 (1936), 43–72, 117–34, 208–32, 303–49; 73 (1937), 130–57 · R. Brenner, *Merchants and revolution: commercial change, political conflict, and London's overseas traders, 1550–1653* (1993) · *The journal of John Winthrop, 1630–1649*, ed. R. S. Dunn, J. Savage, and L. Yeandle (1996) · A. Laurence, *Parliamentary army chaplains, 1642–1651*, Royal Historical Society Studies in History, 59 (1990) · *Case of Mr. Hugh Peters* [1660] · S. R. Gardiner, *History of the great civil war, 1642–1649*, new edn, 4 vols. (1893) · S. R. Gardiner, *History of the Commonwealth and protectorate, 1649–1656*, 4 vols. (1894–1903) · B. Whitelocke, *Memorials of the English affairs*, new edn (1732) · H. L. Stephen, ed., *State trials: political and social*, 2 vols. (1899) · *The Clarke papers*, ed. C. H. Firth, [new edn], 2 vols. in 1 (1992) · P. M. Zall, ed., *'A nest of ninnies' and other English jestbooks of the seventeenth century* (1970), 187–8 · S. E. Morison, 'Sir Charles Firth and Master Hugh Peter: with a Hugh Peter bibliography', *Harvard Graduates' Magazine*, 39 (Dec 1930), 120–40 [partial bibliography] · Boase & Courtney, *Bibl. Corn.* · A. Rideout, *The Treffry family* (1984), 57–8 · Venn, *Alum. Cant.*

Archives BL, Sloane and Stowe MSS · Mass. Hist. Soc., Winthrop papers · Massachusetts Archives, Boston

Likenesses oils, *c.*1650, priv. coll. · line engraving, *c.*1655, NPG [*see illus.*] · print, *c.*1655, repro. in Gentles, *New model army* · oils, *c.*1658, Queens' College, Cambridge · etching, 1660, NPG · pen-and-ink drawing, 1660, NPG · attrib. P. Lely, oils, Courtauld Inst. · B. Moula, Indian ink drawing, Bodl. Oxf. · caricatures, repro. in Stearns, *Strenuous puritan* · engraving, BM · line engraving, BM, NPG; repro. in H. Peters, *Don Pedro de Quixot* (1660) · line engraving, NPG; repro. in H. Peters, *A dying fathers last legacy* (1660) · oils · print, facsimile, BM, NPG; repro. in W. Yonge, *Englands shame ... the life and death of ... Hugh Peters* (1663)

Wealth at death lost all as a result of traitor's death: Stearns, *Strenuous puritan*

Peter [Peters], **Thomas** (1597–1654/5), Church of England clergyman and colonist in America, was born at Fowey in Cornwall and baptized there in June 1597, the second child and elder son among the three children of Thomas Peter or Dickwoode (1571–1625), merchant, and his first wife, Martha (*bap.* 1572, *d.* 1598), daughter of John Treffry of Place and Emblem Tresithney; Hugh *Peter (*bap.* 1598, *d.* 1660) was his younger brother. Admitted to Brasenose College, Oxford, on 12 November 1610, Peter graduated BA on 30 June 1614 and proceeded MA on 6 April 1625. By 1628 he was serving as vicar of Mylor in Kerrier hundred, Cornwall. On 25 September 1632 he married Anne Rawe; they had a son, John, and four daughters, Mary, Sarah, Ann, and Elizabeth, living at the time he drew up his will in 1654.

At the time the Long Parliament was called, Peter was numbered among the few puritan ministers in Cornwall. The county became a royalist stronghold during the first civil war, and, probably in 1643, Peter was driven out by Sir Ralph Hopton. He arrived in New England in 1644, apparently without his wife and children, and by the next year was living at Saybrook Fort, possibly serving as chaplain to

George Fenwick there. Peter was related to the Winthrop clan (John Winthrop the younger having married his brother, Hugh's, stepdaughter Elizabeth Reade) and became involved with young Winthrop's plan to create an independent plantation at Pequot (later New London, Connecticut). When a church was gathered there in 1646, he was called as its first minister. During his time in New England he was involved with Native Americans in the Connecticut River region, especially the Pequot leader, Uncas. His earliest surviving letter relates a visit to Uncas in spring 1645; the following year he complained of Uncas for 'a plott etc & for some iniurious and hostil insolencies' and in 1647 he sparked a confrontation with Uncas over hunting rights and tributary Indians (N. B. Shurtleff, ed., *Records of the Colony of New Plymouth*, vol. 9, 1859, 71, 99–100). His household at Pequot included another stepdaughter of Hugh Peter (Margaret Lake) as well as her daughter. His correspondence reveals that he practised medicine, although he seems to have deferred to Winthrop on such matters.

Peter's decision to return to England appears to have been made suddenly in the autumn of 1646 and he travelled to Boston to await a ship. Initially he contracted to go home in the *Supply* but, after John Cotton preached a sermon predicting that the voyage would be troubled if a petition (known as the remonstrance) was taken to London aboard the vessel, he changed his plans and travelled on another ship by way of Spain. The voyages of the *Supply* and of his new ship were difficult, but both reached London safely. Upon his arrival Peter reported finding his brother Hugh 'sad afflicted' (*Winthrop Papers*, 150). Before leaving London to resume his duties in Cornwall he raised money for the school in Roxbury, Massachusetts.

Peter then returned to Mylor, serving as minister there until his death. During these years he engaged in a long drawn-out controversy with Samson Bond, rector of Mawgan in Meneague, Cornwall, whom he accused of plagiarizing sermons and of unsound doctrine. According to Peter's own account, published as an appendix to *A Remedie Against Ruine* (1652), a sermon preached at Launceston assizes, he got the better of this confrontation. At the end of his life he seems to have been discouraged about the effects of his preaching, describing his ministry at Cornwall as 'with little successe to soules' (PRO, PROB 11/243, fols. 238*v*–239*v*). He died at an unknown date between 26 October 1654, when, 'having some of deaths sentences upon my Body', he drew up his will, and 19 January 1655, when it was proved. He was buried in Mylor churchyard. Anne Peter survived her husband.

CARLA GARDINA PESTANA

Sources R. P. Stearns, *The strenuous puritan: Hugh Peter, 1598–1660* (1954) · E. B. Peters, 'Thomas Peter of Saybrook and Mylor', *New England Historical and Genealogical Register*, 54 (1900), 539–40 · *The Winthrop papers*, ed. W. C. Ford and others, 5 (1947) · E. Winslow, *New-Englands salamander* (1647) · *DNB* · [C. B. Heberden], ed., *Brasenose College register, 1509–1909*, 1, OHS, 55 (1909), 116 · F. L. Weis, *The colonial clergy and colonial churches of New England* (1936) · PRO, PROB 11/243, fols. 238*v*–239*v*

Archives Mass. Hist. Soc., Winthrop MSS, letters

Peter, William [*pseud.* Ralph Ferrars] (1788–1853), poet and writer, was born at Harlyn, St Merryn, Cornwall, on 22 March 1788, the eldest son of Henry Peter (*d.* 1821), an army officer, and his wife, Anna Maria, youngest daughter of Thomas Rous of Piercefield, Monmouthshire. He matriculated from Christ Church, Oxford, on 27 January 1803, and graduated BA on 19 March 1807 and MA on 7 December 1809. On 12 January 1811, he married Frances (*d.* 1836), only daughter and heir of John Thomas of Chiverton in Perranzabuloe, Cornwall; they had ten children.

After living for a few years in London, where he was called to the bar at Lincoln's Inn on 28 May 1813, Peter returned to his native county and settled on his property, which had been greatly increased by his marriage. He became a JP and deputy lieutenant for Cornwall, and was prominent among the country gentlemen who campaigned for electoral reform. When the close boroughs in Cornwall were abolished by the first Reform Act, he was invited to stand for the enlarged constituency of Bodmin, and was elected on 11 December 1832. He sat until the dissolution of parliament on 29 December 1834; but the enthusiasm for reform had then died away, and he did not stand again. His political interests are reflected in *Thoughts on the Present Crisis* (1815), a memoir of Sir Samuel Romilly in an edition of his speeches (1820), and *A Letter from an ex-M.P. to his Late Constituents* (1835).

Peter shortly retired to the continent to read, and to enjoy the company of, and to translate, German authors. His translations included Schiller's *William Tell* (1839), and *Mary Stuart* (1841). His own poetry includes *Sacred Songs*, paraphrases of selected psalms (1828), *Poems by Ralph Ferrars* (that is William Peter, new edn 1833), and some specimens in Griswold's *Poets and Poetry* (1875 edn, 240–43).

In 1840 Peter was appointed British consul in Pennsylvania and New Jersey. His first wife had died on 21 August 1836 and in 1844 in Philadelphia he married his second wife, Sarah King (1800–1877), daughter of Thomas Worthington of Ohio and widow of Edward King, son of Rufus King of New York. She was described as 'one of the most distinguished women in American society', the founder of a school of design for women at Philadelphia.

Peter's compilation *Specimens of the Poets and Poetry of Greece and Rome*, by various translators (1847), was well received. He died in Philadelphia on 6 February 1853 and was buried in the churchyard of St Peter there, where a monument to his memory was erected by a number of the leading citizens.

Peter's eldest son, John Thomas Henry Peter, fellow of Merton College, Oxford, died in July 1873. The third son, Robert Godolphin Peter, formerly fellow of Jesus College, Cambridge, became rector of Cavendish, Suffolk.

W. P. COURTNEY, rev. JOHN D. HAIGH

Sources *GM*, 2nd ser., 39 (1853), 441–2 · 'Peter, William', *DAB* · Allibone, *Dict.* · Foster, *Alum. Oxon.* · S. J. B. Hale, *Woman's record, or, Sketches of all distinguished women*, 2nd edn (1855), 870–71 · D. Giddy, *The parochial history of Cornwall*, 4 (1838), 54–9 · will, PRO, PROB 11/2176, sig. 557

Wealth at death second wife was wealthy; house was cultural showpiece: 'Peter, William', *DAB*: will, PRO, PROB 11/2176, sig. 557

Peterborough. For this title name *see* Mordaunt, John, first earl of Peterborough (*bap.* 1599, *d.* 1643) [*see under* Mordaunt, Henry, second earl of Peterborough (*bap.* 1623, *d.* 1697)]; Mordaunt, Henry, second earl of Peterborough (*bap.* 1623, *d.* 1697); Mordaunt, Charles, third earl of Peterborough and first earl of Monmouth (1658?–1735); Robinson, Anastasia, countess of Peterborough and Monmouth (*d.* 1755).

Peterborough, John of (*supp. fl.* 1369), supposed chronicler and Benedictine monk, is the name that has sometimes been given to the author of the so-called Peterborough chronicle contained in BL, Cotton MS Claudius A.v, fols. 2–45. The attribution, to John, abbot of Peterborough, is made at the beginning of the chronicle, but in a hand appreciably later than that of the greater part of the text, which starts with the foundation of Peterborough and concludes with the plague epidemic of 1369, and which is said only to have belonged to the abbey. In the past efforts have been made to identify this Abbot John with Abbot John de Caux (*d.* 1263), but the closing date rules out this identification, and since there was no other abbot of Peterborough called John until John Depyng, who succeeded about 1408, the attribution must be regarded as fanciful. In any case, it seems unlikely that the chronicle did originate at Peterborough, since it pays more attention to the affairs of the neighbouring Benedictine priory of Spalding in Lincolnshire, giving an account of its foundation, and providing obituaries of its thirteenth- and fourteenth-century priors listing their achievements. The chronicle has been published twice, by Joseph Sparke in his *Historiae Anglicanae scriptores varii* (1723), pages 1–114, and by J. A. Giles, who reissued Sparke's text as *Chronicon Angliae Petroburgense* (Caxton Society, 2, 1845). HENRY SUMMERSON

Sources BL, Cotton MS Claudius A.v, fols. 2–45 · J. Sparke, ed., *Historiae Anglicanae scriptores varii*, 2 (1723), 1–114 · J. A. Giles, ed., *Chronicon Angliae Petroburgense*, Caxton Society, 2 (1845) · *VCH Northamptonshire*, vol. 2

Archives BL, Cotton MS Claudius A.v, fols. 2–45

Peterborough, William of (*fl. c.*1190), Benedictine monk and theologian, was a native of Peterborough and a monk of Ramsey Abbey. He was a prolific author of works of popular theology, of which the following are known from the bibliographers Henry Kirkestede, John Leland, and John Bale: *Distinctiones theologiae*; *Sermones notabiles*, in two volumes; *Homeliae in cantica*; *Euphrastica*; *Opus partium*; and *Interpretaciones vocabulorum s. scripturae*. The title of the first of these works indicates a use of the scholastic method, and his own title *magister* confirms that he had studied in the schools. The only work that survives is *Euphrastica*, an explanation of difficult passages in the scriptures. 100 problems are taken, starting with the Old Testament and working through to the New Testament. They include: 'whether the impossible is possible to God, or not' (no. 31); 'how it was that one evangelist said "before the cock crows you will denounce me thrice", while another said "… twice"' (no. 60); and 'where Christ was in the forty days after his Passion' (no. 80). The work secures William's place among a group of monastic writers who 'wrote elaborate and lengthy commentaries on the Bible that contain little that is original' (Hunt, 27).   EDMUND KING

Sources Bale, *Index* · Tanner, *Bibl. Brit.-Hib.* · R. W. Hunt, 'English learning in the late twelfth century', *TRHS*, 4th ser., 19 (1936), 19–42, esp. 27 · F. Madan and H. H. E. Craster, *A summary catalogue of Western manuscripts in the Bodleian Library at Oxford*, 2/1 (1922) · R. Sharpe, *A handlist of the Latin writers of Great Britain and Ireland before 1540* (1997), no. 2145
Archives Bodl. Oxf., MS Bodley 833
Likenesses drawing, Bodl. Oxf., Bodley MS 833, fol. 123v

Peterkin, Alexander (1781–1846), writer, was born on 26 March 1781 at Macduff, Banffshire, the fifth of eight children of William Peterkin (d. 1792), minister of the chapel of ease there, and his wife, Isabel Irvine (d. 1810). After education at the parish school in Ecclesmachan, Linlithgowshire, to which his father was translated in 1787 after a brief ministry in Leadhills (1785–7), Alexander went on to attend classes at Edinburgh University, where he studied law. In 1803 he enrolled in the first regiment of Royal Edinburgh volunteers. Peterkin married, on 20 December 1807, Charlotte Giles, with whom he had two sons and five daughters. After training in the office of a writer to the signet, Peterkin qualified as a solicitor before the supreme courts and he began his professional career in Peterhead some time before 1811. In 1814 he was appointed sheriff-substitute of Orkney. Peterkin developed a great interest in the affairs of Orkney and his antiquarian researches resulted in the publication of *Rentals of the Ancient Earldom and Bishoprick of Orkney* (1820) and *Notes on Orkney and Zetland* (1822). However, it was not his views on Orkney's past, but his reflections on its present circumstances, that proved so offensive to many, and the latter work provoked an indignant response in the form of a *Vindication of Orkney* (1823). This railed against his depiction of landowners as tyrants and the system of agriculture as barbarous, concluding 'remove all its egotism and malevolence against Orkney, and you expunge all its contents' (Traill, 56). The reaction culminated in his dismissal as sheriff-substitute in 1823. Peterkin was not disposed to let the matter rest, and raised an action of damages against Samuel Laing of Papdale and James Baikie of Tankerness as the persons he held responsible for the libels which led to his dismissal. The action ground on inconclusively for years. From 1824 to 1826 Peterkin published the *Orkney and Zetland Chronicle* from Edinburgh, 'a very able but short-lived magazine, extending only to nineteen numbers' (Hossack, 109), with the aim of winning the parliamentary vote for Shetlanders.

Peterkin now combined journalism with legal work and was connected with newspapers in Belfast and Perth. From 1833 to 1835 he edited the *Kelso Chronicle*. He distinguished himself as the editor of *The Booke of the Universalle Kirk of Scotland* (1839) and with *The Records of the Church of Scotland* (1838) and *The Constitution of the Church of Scotland as Established at the Revolution, 1689–90* (1841). As a spirited controversialist, Peterkin advanced the views of a 'whig of 1688'. His special expertise in ecclesiastical history and law was naturally drawn upon during the years of conflict that preceded the Disruption in the Church of Scotland in 1843. He opposed the claims of the non-intrusion party throughout and acted as agent for the seven suspended ministers in the presbytery of Strathbogie.

Among Peterkin's earlier publications were an edition, with biographical sketch, of Robert Fergusson's *Works* (1807) and a reprint, with critical preface, of James Currie's *The Life and Works of Robert Burns* (1815), in which he took issue with Currie's view of Burns's supposed over-indulgence in alcohol. Peterkin died at his home, 27 Buccleuch Place, Edinburgh, on 9 November 1846. His elder son, **Alexander Peterkin** (1814–1889), was successively editor of the *Berwick Advertiser*, sub-editor of the *Edinburgh Advertiser*, and on the staff of *The Times*, from which he retired about 1853 on health grounds.

LIONEL ALEXANDER RITCHIE

Sources S. Maunder, *The biographical treasury* (1873), 792 · *Fasti Scot.*, 1.204 · *The Scotsman* (14 Nov 1846) · W. Traill, *Vindication of Orkney, in answer to 'Notes on Orkney' by Alex Peterkin* (1823) · W. P. L. Thomson, *History of Orkney* (1987), 237 · B. H. Hossack, *Kirkwall in the Orkneys* (1900) · Orkney Archives · private information (1895) · *DNB* · bap. reg. Scot. · m. reg. Scot.
Archives Orkney Archives, Kirkwall, notebooks and printed volumes relating to the history of Orkney | U. Edin., New Coll. L., Chalmers papers

Peterkin, Alexander (1814–1889). *See under* Peterkin, Alexander (1781–1846).

Petermann, August Heinrich (1822–1878), geographer and cartographer, was born in April 1822 (probably on the 1st) in Bleicherode am Eichsfelde, Prussia, the second of six children born to Katherine Henrietta and August Rudolf Petermann. He attended elementary school in Bleicherode and, from 1836 to 1839, the *Gymnasium* in Nordhausen. Maps drawn during his school days survive, and it was a map of South America that won him admittance to Heinrich Berghaus's Geographische Kunstschule in Potsdam in 1839, the year of its foundation, after plans that he should enter the church had been abandoned. Fees at the school were waived because of his parents' poverty. Clearly the most gifted student in the school, Petermann was employed on several important projects, notably Alexander von Humboldt's *Asie centrale* (1843), which contained the first map to be published as Petermann's independent work, and the *Physikalischer Atlas* (1838–48), the first thematic atlas of the world. The work met with acclaim and, when Alexander Keith Johnston was granted leave to produce an English version of it, Petermann moved to Johnston's cartographical institute in Edinburgh in 1845 to work on it and other atlases. In 1847 Petermann moved to London where, from his cartographic institute at 5 Carrington Street and later 9 Charing Cross, he produced maps for scholarly journals, newspapers, and other publications, sometimes in collaboration with Ernst Ravenstein and John Bartholomew, the younger. His

August Heinrich Petermann (1822–1878), by unknown photographer

In 1854 Petermann returned to Germany to Justus Pertes's publishing house in Gotha, which was being reshaped as a geographical institute under the influence of Wilhelm and Bernhardt Pertes; the status of professor was conferred on him by Ernst XI of Saxe-Gotha. From Gotha in 1855 he founded *Petermanns Geographische Mitteilungen*—an important journal still continuing in the late twentieth century—the contents of which reflected Petermann's cartographic skills, and his interest in both scientific geography and exploration. His work in encouraging exploration in Africa and the polar regions, cartographic innovations, and geographical education in universities and among the general public led in 1868 to his being awarded the founder's medal of the Royal Geographical Society, then the highest accolade for a geographer. His personal life was less happy than his professional. His first marriage in 1856 to Clara Mildred Leslie, with whom he had three children, was dissolved in 1877, and his second marriage, to Tony Pfister in 1878, lasted only four months before his death, by suicide, on 25 September 1878 in Gotha.

Petermann's maps were remarkable technically (for example, in their use of a modified lithography and of new projections), aesthetically (for example, in their use of colour), and intellectually (for example, in his development of thematic maps, which promoted understanding of phenomena by showing their distribution). His writings reflected the scientific nature of German geography and combined detailed observations and imaginative hypotheses. Through his pupils, who dominated the next generation of German cartographers, and his *Mitteilungen* he continued to influence geography, exploration, and cartography long after his death.

ELIZABETH BAIGENT

Sources M. Hoffmann, 'August Heinrich Petermann, 1822–1878', *Geographers: biobibliographical studies*, 12, ed. T. W. Freeman (1988), 133–8 · H. Wichmann, 'Petermann, August', *Allgemeine deutsche Biographie*, ed. R. von Liliencron and others, 26 (Leipzig, 1888), 795–805 · J. J. Kettler, 'August Petermann: eine biographische Skizze', *Aus allen Welt-theilen*, 10 (1879), 41–5, 110–14
Archives RGS, letters to Royal Geographical Society
Likenesses monument, Gotha, Germany · photograph, NPG [*see illus.*] · portrait, repro. in Kettler, 'August Petermann' · portrait, repro. in Hoffmann, 'August Heinrich Petermann' · portrait, RGS

map of 1852 showing the progress of the cholera epidemics of the 1830s is a remarkable early medical map with perceptive 'statistical notes'.

Petermann became interested in geographical discovery: in 1846 he was elected fellow of the Royal Geographical Society and in 1849 became a corresponding member of the Berlin Gesellschaft für Erdkunde with the support of Karl Ritter. As a result of his influence the German scientists Heinrich Barth and Adolf Overweg were invited to join James Richardson's expedition to central Africa in 1849, and Petermann published English and later German accounts of the expedition. He also made knowledgeable contributions (for example, on polar routes influenced by the Gulf Stream) to the debate about the fate of Sir John Franklin. Petermann was active as a lecturer on geographical topics to the Royal Geographical Society and the British Association. In 1852 he was granted the title 'physical geographer and engraver on stone in ordinary to the queen' and his maps were held in high regard in Britain. However, economic difficulties and personal differences with his English colleagues led him to renounce his intention of settling permanently in England.

Peters, Augustus Dudley [*formerly* August Detlef] (1892–1973), literary agent, was born in Schleswig-Holstein on 25 August 1892, the fourth of the seven children of Georg Peters, farmer and, later, civil servant. His father was born Danish, but by 1892 Prussia had annexed Schleswig-Holstein and Peters therefore was born Prussian. When he was three his father, then working as a farmer, went bankrupt and four aunts took charge of the young children until their father's fortunes improved. But Peters did not live with his father again. His aunt (Marie) Lisette de Wasgindt, his father's sister, adopted Peters. She ran a girls' school in Brighton, so he began life in England as the only boy in a girls' school. His name was probably Anglicized to Augustus Dudley Peters at about this time. About 1900 his aunt moved to a boarding-house in Hampstead, and in due course Peters went to the Haberdashers' Aske's School, Hampstead. In 1911 he went up to St John's College, Cambridge, where he obtained a second class in medieval and modern languages in 1913 and a third in part two of the economics tripos in 1914.

Peters was with the college cricket team on tour in Kent when war broke out. He left to join the Artists' Rifles but his German citizenship made him an enemy alien. He was handed over to the police but was told that he could do anything he liked except join the armed forces. He worked for a Manchester cotton merchant and a lead mine in north Wales until 1917, when the shortage of troops brought a change in the rules whereby aliens could join up. But he was only allowed into a labour battalion, and served in Belgium from 1917 until June 1919. On 2 March 1921 Peters married Helen Agatha MacGregor. They had a son, Richard (who was killed on active service in Burma in 1945), and a daughter, Catherine, who married the psychiatrist and writer Anthony Storr. After the war Peters became first assistant editor of *The World* and then editor of this and other magazines at Odhams Press until 1923. But he was already more interested in the theatre and in the early 1920s was a regular contributor to the drama page of the *Daily Telegraph*. In 1923 he was appointed the new drama critic for the *Daily Chronicle* but was bored by the job and disillusioned about the future. In May of the following year, partly as a result of pressure from writer friends who were unprotected against their publishers, he found his true vocation and started a literary agency. He realized, or perhaps imagined, that he did not have the makings of a first-class writer, and throughout his life maintained that in order to be a good agent you first had to be a writer *manqué*. The kind of insight which, in Arthur Koestler's words, 'turns many a bitter young man into a jaundiced literary critic, had the opposite effect on Peters. He gave up his job as a critic and became a catalyst'.

In 1924 there were few literary agencies, and even fewer with good reputations. Peters prospered in this role from the start. W. N. Roughead, a Scottish rugby international, joined the firm in 1927. In 1929 Peters bought the Andrew Dakers agency, and Dakers's secretary Margaret Stephens agreed to stay with him. She became his right hand and a pillar of the agency. Already his list of authors included J. C. Squire, Hilaire Belloc, Edmund Blunden, Alec Waugh, J. B. Priestley, Gerald Bullett, Martin Armstrong, Rebecca West, and Sheila Kaye-Smith. In the early 1930s these were joined by Terence Rattigan, James Agate, Eric Linklater, C. S. Forester, A. E. Coppard, Evelyn Waugh, C. Day Lewis, Margaret Irwin, John Moore, Frank O'Connor, Margery Sharp, J. L. Hodson, Norman Collins, and others who joined as clients and became friends.

Throughout his career Peters probably did more than anyone else to secure and defend the rights and standing of authors, having started as an agent at a time when publishers were notorious for the harshness of their contracts and the arrogance of their business dealings. In so doing, in the words of Arthur Koestler at his eightieth birthday

dinner, 'he conferred upon the profession of literary agent an aura of integrity, humanity and dignity which it had not possessed before.' Margaret Stephens commented that his 'work was his hobby and because his love of good writing, or the germ of good writing, never left him, his enjoyment in his work never diminished'. He was easy to like, yet difficult to know, and his reserve was legendary. The steady growth and success of the agency was of course based in the main on his talent for furthering and enhancing his authors' careers financially. He was never happier than when encouraging and guiding young authors, on whom he would lavish great pains, sometimes for little material return. He believed that an agent's loyalty was due first and last to his author, and as a result his professional relationships almost invariably became close personal ties. He was known almost universally as Peter or Pete. On 18 February 1933 he married Margaret Lucy Mayne; they had one daughter, Hilary.

At the same time Peters's work dovetailed with a wide variety of interests. Cricket was a great passion. Throughout the 1920s and 1930s he played with Alec Waugh, J. C. Squire, and Clifford Bax in a team known as the Invalids, and a fictional version of Peters may be found in Archibald Macdonell's *England, their England*. He retained a lifelong passion for the theatre, in and around which he worked effectively for a time. He launched Terence Rattigan after *French without Tears* had been repeatedly rejected and in the 1930s was responsible for the series of J. B. Priestley plays at the Duchess Theatre. He also produced a number of films, notably *An Inspector Calls* (1953). He was a great lover of the arts and a discerning collector of pictures, sculpture, and furniture. He was an undercover philanthropist, who gave time and money to various causes, such as the abolition of the death penalty, a fund-raising campaign for refugee writers, and towards the end of his life the Arthur Koestler award for prisoners, for which he was for seven years chairman of the board of trustees.

During the Second World War Peters worked in various capacities for the Ministry of Information, the Board of Trade, and the Ministry of Food, while at the same time keeping his business going. During the 1950s he was associated with Norman Collins and Lew Grade in forming the company which as Associated Television (ATV) was successful in the first round of bids for commercial television franchises.

Peters worked with undiminished enthusiasm until only six weeks before his death, having made over his by now very successful and profitable business to his junior partners without profit to himself. His mellow private life was reflected in a quite unusual style of enjoyment without ostentation, or, as Sir V. S. Pritchett put it, 'satisfaction without exhaustion'. He shared the last twenty-five years of his life with Margot Grahame (1911–1982), the actress and film star. He literary, she theatrical, they complemented each other well. He died a contented and much loved man, of pneumonia, at his London flat, 26 Barrie House, Lancaster Gate, on 3 February 1973. He was cremated.

CLARE L. TAYLOR

Sources *The Bookseller* (10 Feb 1973) · *The Times* (5 Feb 1973) · private information (2004) · m. certs. · d. cert.
Likenesses photograph, repro. in *The Bookseller*
Wealth at death £61,506: probate, 15 June 1973, *CGPLA Eng. & Wales*

Peters, Charles (1690–1774), Hebraist and Church of England clergyman, born at Tregony, Cornwall, on 1 December 1690, was the eldest child of Richard Peters. He was educated at Tregony School under a Mr Daddow, and matriculated from Exeter College, Oxford, on 3 April 1707; he graduated BA (27 October 1710), MA (5 June 1713), and was a batteler of his college from 8 April 1707 to 20 July 1713. Having been ordained into the Anglican church, he was curate of St Just in Roseland, Cornwall, from 1710 to 1715, when he was appointed by Elizabeth, Lady Mohun, to the rectory of Boconnoc in the same county. He remained there until 1723, and during his incumbency built the south front of the old parsonage-house. On 10 December 1723 Peters was instituted to the rectory of Bratton-Clovelly, Devon, and in November 1726 was appointed to the rectory of St Mabyn, Cornwall, holding both preferments until his death. To the poor of St Mabyn he was very charitable; and, being himself unmarried, he educated the two eldest sons, John and Jonathan, of his brother, John.

Peters knew Hebrew well (he was, according to the literary chronicler Richard Polwhele, 'the first Hebrew scholar in Europe'), and at St Mabyn he was able to pursue his studies without interruption. In 1751 he published *A Critical Dissertation on the Book of Job*, in which he criticized Bishop William Warburton's account, proved the book's antiquity, and demonstrated that a future state was the popular belief of the ancient Jews or Hebrews. A second edition, corrected and with a lengthy preface of ninety pages, appeared in 1757; the preface was also issued separately. Warburton, in the notes to his *Divine Legation of Moses*, always wrote contemptuously of Peters. The retort of Bishop Robert Lowth on the latter's behalf, in his printed letter to Warburton (1765), was that 'the very learned and ingenious person', Mr Peters, had given his antagonist 'a Cornish hug', from which he would be sore as long as he lived. Peters published in 1760 *An appendix to the critical dissertation on Job, giving a further account of the book of Ecclesiastes*, with a reply to some of Warburton's notes; and in 1765 he was engaged in finishing a more elaborate reply which was never published but descended to his nephew with his other manuscripts.

Peters died at St Mabyn on 11 February 1774 and was buried in the chancel of the parish church. In accordance with his desire—expressed two years previously—a volume of his sermons was printed in 1776 by his nephew Jonathan, vicar of St Clement, near Truro. Some extracts from Peters's private prayers, meditations, and letters are printed in Polwhele's *Biographical Sketches in Cornwall* (1831). W. P. COURTNEY, *rev.* PHILIP CARTER

Sources Nichols, *Illustrations*, 8.633 · *GM*, 1st ser., 65 (1795), 1085 · Boase & Courtney, *Bibl. Corn.*, 1.464–5, 474–5 · G. C. Boase, *Collectanea Cornubiensia: a collection of biographical and topographical notes relating to the county of Cornwall* (1890) · R. Lowth, *A letter to*

[*W. Warburton*] *the … author of the divine legation of Moses demonstrated* (1765) · PRO, PROB 11/996, fols. 132v–134v [will]
Likenesses oils; in possession of Arthur Cowper Ranyard, 1895

Peters, Charles (1695–1746?), physician, was the son of John Peters of London, where he was born. He matriculated at Christ Church, Oxford, on 31 March 1710, and graduated BA in 1713 and MA in 1724.

Richard Mead encouraged Peters to study medicine, and lent him a copy of the rare first edition, printed at Verona in 1530, of the Latin poem by Hieronymus Frascatorius entitled *Syphilis, sive, Morbus Gallicus*, which has provided a scientific name for a long series of pathological phenomena. Peters published an edition of *Syphilis* in 1720. It is a quarto finely printed by Jonah Bowyer at the Rose in St Paul's Churchyard, and has a portrait of Frascatorius engraved by Vertue for frontispiece. The contents of the dedication to Mead show that Peters was more occupied with literary than with scientific questions, for the only allusion he makes to the contents of the poem is to offer emendations of three lines. He is said to have graduated MD at Leiden in 1724, but his name does not appear in Innes-Smith.

Peters was elected a Radcliffe travelling fellow on 12 July 1725, and graduated BM and DM at Oxford on 8 November 1732. In 1733 he was appointed physician-extraordinary to the king, and was elected a fellow of the Royal College of Physicians of London on 16 April 1739, in which year he was also appointed physician-general to the army, an office he retained until his death. He was physician to St George's Hospital from April 1735 to February 1746, and was a censor in the College of Physicians in 1744, but illness prevented him from serving his full period. He published in the *Philosophical Transactions* in 1744–5 'The case of a person bit by a mad dog', a paper on hydrophobia, in which he suggests the use of warm baths in such a case. He probably died in 1746.

NORMAN MOORE, *rev.* PATRICK WALLIS

Sources Munk, *Roll* · Foster, *Alum. Oxon.* · *GM*, 1st ser., 16 (1746), 273 · *London Magazine*, 15 (1746), 209 · C. Peters, 'The case of a person bit by a mad dog', *PTRS*, 43 (1744–5), 257–62 · N. Cantlie, *A history of the army medical department*, 2 vols. (1974)
Archives BL, Sloane MSS 4054, fol. 187; 4060, fol. 101 · BL, Add. MS 4055, fol. 136–7

Peters, Ellis. *See* Pargeter, Edith Mary (1913–1995).

Peters, Hugh. *See* Peter, Hugh (*bap.* 1598, *d.* 1660).

Peters, James (1879–1954), rugby player, was born on 7 August 1879 at 32 Queen Street, Salford, the elder of two children of George Peters, a showman born in the West Indies, and his wife, Hannah, *née* Gough, of Shropshire. He is remembered by posterity as the first black player to be selected for England at rugby union, but his life was also a remarkable vignette of sport in the Edwardian era. As a young boy Peters worked in the circus as a bareback rider. However, a riding accident when he was aged eleven or twelve resulted in a broken arm. Being unable to support him, his parents sent him to stay in Dorset. From there he went to an orphanage in Greenwich, where he first began to demonstrate his outstanding sporting talent. By the age of fifteen he was captain of the orphanage's rugby and cricket teams, as well as being its champion for the 100 yards, the mile, the long jump, and the high jump. He began playing rugby for Bristol in the 1900–01 season and made thirty-five appearances for the club before moving to Plymouth, where he established a reputation as an outstanding stand-off half, who possessed elusive speed, sure handling skills, and exceptional kicking abilities. In 1903 he made the first of his twenty-one appearances for Devon, and he was instrumental in Devon's winning the 1906 and 1907 county championships. He eventually scored fourteen tries and twelve goals in his county career.

In March 1906 Peters was selected to play for England against Scotland at Inverleith, the first of his five appearances for the national side. His performance helped England to a 9–3 victory, but it was an open secret that not everyone in the sport approved of the selection of a black man to play for England. Indeed, rumours persisted that he would have been selected sooner had it not been for the colour of his skin. His colour again became an issue seven months later, when the touring South African side played Devon in Plymouth. On discovering that the Devon stand-off was black, the South Africans at first refused to play against him but eventually relented. He was not chosen to play for England against the Springboks later that season but did play against Ireland and Scotland. He played his last international against Wales in January 1908 at the Ashton Gate ground in Bristol.

In 1909 Peters suffered a serious hand injury at work and, assuming that this meant the end of his rugby career, he received a benefit from the Plymouth club. However, the injury was not as serious as first thought and he continued to play, although his status under Rugby Football Union regulations was unclear, as receiving a benefit was an expellable act of professionalism. Peters found himself thrust into prominence once again in 1912. Faced with the burgeoning popularity of soccer, a number of rugby clubs in Devon and the south-west sought to rekindle interest in rugby by joining the professional Northern Union, the precursor of the Rugby Football League. To counter the threat, on 30 November 1912 the rugby union authorities expelled or suspended twenty officials and players, including Peters, for acts of professionalism. On Christmas day 1912 he made his début for the newly formed Plymouth Northern Union side against Coventry. A western league of the Northern Union was formed by clubs in the region, but a combination of financial and travelling difficulties conspired to kill off the project in the summer of 1913. Along with a number of other players, Peters then moved north and signed to play for Barrow in the Northern Union. He made his début on 4 October 1913 against Swinton, but made only a handful of appearances for the club. In the summer of 1914 he transferred to St Helens, although he never appeared in a senior match for the club.

Following his retirement from St Helens, Peters moved back to Plymouth, where he continued in his trade as a builder's carpenter until his retirement. He died on 26 March 1954 in Plymouth City Hospital from heart failure brought on by bronchial pneumonia and was buried at Plymouth old cemetery on 31 March. TONY COLLINS

Sources A. Pallant, *A sporting century, 1863–1963* (1997) · F. A. Davey, *The story of the Devon Rugby Football Union* (1964) · *The Bristol F.C. jubilee book, 1888–1938* (1938) · G. Williams, 'How the west was (almost) won', *Open Rugby*, 52 (April 1983), 37–8 · *Football Herald* (13 Jan 1906) · *Football Herald* (28 April 1906) · *Western Morning Herald* (1 April 1954) · *Yorkshire Post* (17 March 1906) · *Yorkshire Post* (19 March 1906) · *North West Daily Mail* (6 Oct 1913) · *Barrow News* (29 Nov 1913) · Northern Rugby Football Union player registers, 1909–14, Rugby Football League, Red Hall Lane, Leeds · b. cert. · d. cert.

Peters, James Henry [Jim] (1918–1999), athlete, was born on 24 October 1918 at 81 Church Road, Homerton, London, the son of Percy Henry Peters, railway clerk, and his wife, Emma Harlow. Early in life Peters moved with his parents to Becontree in Essex. He soon found that he was good at cricket, football, and running, and became champion of Essex over one mile before 1939. Peters's athletics career was interrupted by the Second World War. He joined the Royal Army Medical Corps, where he trained as an optician, and it was this work which he would continue after demobilization. On 7 July 1940 he married Frieda Maud Howls (b. 1920/21), daughter of John James Howls, a fitter. They had a son and a daughter. After the war Peters returned to running, and won the Essex county cross-country title over 7 miles and the 3-mile championship on the track in 1946. He also surprised himself and the critics by winning the Amateur Athletics Association (AAA) 6-mile race at the White City by a wide margin. In the following year he won the 10-mile title. These performances got him selected for the Great Britain team for the Olympic games at London in 1948. But his experience of running at Wembley was very disappointing. Not only did he finish ninth in the 10,000 metres but he was lapped by the new phenomenon of distance running, Emil Zatopek. Peters was tempted to retire at the age of thirty but H. A. Johnston, his coach, convinced him that he could run in another Olympics if he transferred to the marathon.

Both Johnston and Peters believed that training of a greater quantity and quality could transform performance at the longer distances. At this time few long-distance runners trained every day. Nor were speed sessions common. Peters began to keep a record of both the number of his runs and the distance covered. In 1949–50 his 190 runs totalled 1400 miles; in 1950–51 his number of runs went up to 224 and the distance to 1737 miles; 1951–2 saw the runs increase to 410 and the mileage to 3287½; the next year his runs exceeded 500 and the total distance 4000 miles. Forty runs a month at over 300 miles brought criticism of over-training from athletic commentators such as Harold Abrahams. Certainly Peters's programme was not only pushing back the boundaries of athletic achievement: it was also exploring the limits of amateur sport as it had been traditionally defined.

Peters was a typical British amateur who fitted training, travel, and competition around his job and family life. He even raced in simple Dunlop gym shoes rather than the more sophisticated spikes. He trained fifty weeks a year, five or six times each week, together with a three-hour walk on Sunday pushing his son Robin in the pram. He spent eight hours a day working at his shop, eight hours sleeping, three and a half hours travelling from his home in Chadwell Heath to Mitcham and back, and one hour getting ready and eating each morning, which left three and a half hours for training. 'All social life is out and it's just plain work and slogging', he said. But he loved the sport and had no intention of giving it up while he could juggle all his responsibilities. And all this intense work did pay off eventually.

In 1951 Peters set a British best time in the Polytechnic marathon from Chiswick to Windsor. In 1952 he broke the British all-comers' record by five minutes. He also won the AAA's marathon four years in succession between 1951 and 1954. His best year was probably 1953, when he won four competitive marathons and only just failed to run 12 miles in one hour, a feat which only Viljo Heino and Emil Zatopek had achieved. Peters became the first man to run under 2 hours 20 minutes for the marathon. He broke the world record three times, lowering it from 2 hours 25 minutes 39 seconds to 2 hours 17 minutes 30.4 seconds, a degree of improvement not matched since. But he never won a major title.

At the Helsinki Olympics in 1952 Peters set a fast pace, but dropped out after about 19 miles with severe cramp. The race was won by Zatopek, in his first marathon. But it was the marathon at the Commonwealth games in Vancouver in 1954 which was to inscribe the name of Jim Peters on the British sports roll of heroic defeats. Peters was the English team captain and the favourite. The race began in the middle of a hot August day, with the temperature around 75 °F in the shade. Peters set his usual fast pace and was actually 3 miles ahead of what was left of the sixteen-strong field as he began the final two hills up to the stadium. They proved a struggle. By the time he reached the stadium he had become dangerously dehydrated. Peters did not normally take drinks during a marathon because he felt that slowing down would break his rhythm. Now he began swaying from side to side as he tried to cover the last 385 yards. He fell down at least six times. He said later that he tried to reach the shade of the stand roof and that he was determined to finish so as not to disgrace his wife and children. He took eleven minutes to cover 200 yards, almost as painful for those who watched as for himself. His struggle was captured for future generations by Movietone news. Peters failed to complete the last lap and was taken to hospital to spend the next seven hours in an oxygen tent being fed half a gallon of saline solution and dextrose intravenously. He never raced again. Peters harboured the suspicion that the course was too long. Before the race he, together with his team-mate Stan Cox, had travelled the course by car and found it to be not 26 miles 385 yards but 27 miles. At Christmas 1954 the duke of Edinburgh sent Peters a Commonwealth games gold medal 'as a token of admiration to a most gallant marathon runner'.

Peters remained in touch with his club, Essex Beagles, and continued work as an optician. He was later a Rotary

club member near his Thorpe Bay home. He was an old-style amateur who nevertheless recognized the same qualities that he had had in today's professional athletes: 'When the gun sounds you go out there to kill or be killed' (*The Times*, 13 Jan 1999). Peters suffered from cancer for six years before his death at 126 Chalkwell Avenue, Westcliff-on-Sea, Essex, on 9 January 1999. He was survived by his wife and children.   TONY MASON

Sources *World Sports* (April 1953) · *The Independent* (14 Jan 1999) · *The Scotsman* (14 Jan 1999) · *The Guardian* (18 Jan 1999) · *The Times* (13 Jan 1999) · b. cert. · m. cert. · d. cert.
Likenesses photograph, repro. in *The Guardian*

Peters [*née* Bowly], **Mary** (1813–1856), hymn writer, was born in Cirencester, Gloucestershire, on 17 April 1813, the daughter of Richard Bowly and his wife, Mary. According to the *Dictionary of National Biography* and John Julian's *Dictionary of Hymnology*, while very young she married John McWilliam Peters, rector of Quenington in Gloucestershire and later vicar of Langford in Oxfordshire, who left her a widow in 1834. If, as seems virtually certain, he was the John William Peters (*b.* 1791) mentioned in Venn's *Alumni Cantabrigienses*, who held the same cures, it appears likelier that he seceded from the Church of England in that year, as he did not die until 11 September 1861, when he was described as a fundholder.

Whatever the source of her troubles in 1834, Mary Peters reputedly found solace in literary pursuits, writing a seven-volume work entitled *The World's History from the Creation to the Accession of Queen Victoria* (n.d.). It is, however, as a hymn writer that she was best-known. She contributed hymns to the Plymouth Brethren's *Psalms, Hymns, and Spiritual Songs* (1842). Fifty-eight of her poems appeared in 1847 under the title *Hymns Intended to Help the Communion of Saints*. Selections from this volume were used in various hymnals, both of the established and nonconformist churches. E. F. Hatfield described her poetry as 'both pleasing and impressive': 'Around thy table, Holy Lord' and 'Through the love of God our Saviour' seem to have been the most popular of her hymns. Mary Peters died of pulmonary consumption at 7 The Mall, Clifton, Bristol, on 29 July 1856.

W. B. LOWTHER, *rev.* ROSEMARY MITCHELL

Sources J. Julian, ed., *A dictionary of hymnology*, rev. edn (1907), 891–2 · E. F. Hatfield, *The poets of the church: a series of biographical sketches of hymn writers* (1884) · Venn, *Alum. Cant.* · private information (1895) · d. cert. · d. cert. [J. W. Peters]

Peters, Sir Rudolph Albert (1889–1982), biochemist, was born on 13 April 1889 in Kensington, London, the only son and elder child of Albert Edward Duncan Ralph Peters (1863–1945), a general practitioner in Midhurst, Sussex, and his wife, Agnes Malvina Watts (1867–1950). Between the ages of nine and thirteen he attended Warden House preparatory school. He then moved to Wellington College, which he entered as a classical scholar, though intending to study medicine. His early interest in science was encouraged by private reading and by a mathematics master. From another master he received encouragement in music. He became a competent violinist and throughout his life enjoyed playing chamber music with friends.

In 1908 Peters entered Gonville and Caius College, Cambridge, where, under the influence of Joseph Barcroft, A. V. Hill, and others, he obtained first-class honours in part one of the natural sciences tripos (1910). He went on to spend two years on part two, in physiology including 'physiological chemistry' taught by F. Gowland Hopkins, but he was unable to take the examination because he had typhoid fever. Peters assisted Barcroft in research on haemoglobin, and in 1912 joined A. V. Hill in work on the chemistry of muscular contraction.

On the outbreak of the First World War in 1914 Peters, though awarded a fellowship at Caius, decided to complete his medical studies at St Bartholomew's Hospital, qualifying MB, BChir, in 1915. In November 1915 he joined the Royal Army Medical Corps and left for France to serve for six months with a field ambulance, then transferring to the 60th rifles as medical officer. He was awarded the MC and bar (1917) and was mentioned in dispatches. In 1917 Peters married Frances Williamina, daughter of Francis William Vérel, of Glasgow. They had two sons. Early in the same year he was recalled to the physiological laboratory at Porton, to carry out research under Barcroft on problems of chemical warfare; he remained there for the rest of the war. He gained his MD in 1919.

In 1918 Peters took up his fellowship at Caius, together with a lectureship in biochemistry. He maintained an interest in work begun at Porton but also started what was to become a major line of research, on the vitamin B complex. In 1923 Peters was appointed to the recently established Whitley chair of biochemistry in Oxford and occupied it until 1954. He was a fellow of Trinity College, Oxford, from 1925 to 1954. Then, immediately following his retirement, he accepted an appointment, under Ivan de Burgh Daly, to the Agricultural Research Council's Institute of Animal Physiology, where he built up a strong research group while continuing his own work. Following a second retirement in 1959, Peters settled in Cambridge where he was given facilities for laboratory work. He continued this until 1976, publishing his last paper in 1981.

Peters's researches fall into three periods. Throughout these he was interested in general and cellular metabolism. In the first, 1923–39, he began a search for the antineuritic component of vitamin B which led him to the first isolation of thiamine. He made important contributions to the understanding of its metabolic function as co-carboxylase. During the Second World War he directed his own and colleagues' attention to the biochemistry of chemical warfare agents. This led to the discovery (by L. A. Stocken and R. H. S. Thompson) of British anti-lewisite. Peters was also active in advising on research into human nutritional requirements. Finally, following 1945, he extended work begun during the war on the toxicity of fluoro compounds, showing how, by what he termed 'lethal synthesis', they become converted into metabolically inert analogues of normal metabolites.

Peters was a kind and friendly man, though capable of beneficial severity. His speech, apt to come in rapid bursts, expressed enthusiasm, alertness, and a sense of fun. Though his first love was biochemistry, Peters was more than merely an able biochemist. He was careful of the interests of all his associates, from first-year students to senior colleagues. Concerned as much with his department's teaching as with its research, he saw his subject in relationship with other sciences, physical, biological, and social, and its study as part of the whole matrix of academic fields of learning. His mind was quick, but tended to move elliptically in a way that could confuse. His style of writing was apt to be loose and sometimes unclear, but at the same time he was an artist in choosing the right word and striking phrase.

Peters was elected a fellow of the Royal Society in 1935, received its royal medal in 1949, and delivered its Croonian lecture in 1952. In that year he was knighted and became FRCP. He was elected honorary fellow of Gonville and Caius College, of Trinity College, Oxford, and of a number of professional organizations. Peters was awarded eight honorary degrees and gave many invited lectures. As well as his university duties in research, teaching, and administration, he was adviser to the Medical Research Council, the Ministry of Supply, and St Bartholomew's Hospital. From 1958 to 1961 he served as president of the International Council of Scientific Unions, travelling worldwide on its business. Peters died in Cambridge on 29 January 1982. He was survived by his wife and children.   ALEXANDER G. OGSTON, *rev.*

Sources R. H. S. Thompson and A. G. Ogston, *Memoirs FRS*, 29 (1983), 495–523 · personal knowledge (1990)
Archives Bodl. Oxf., corresp. and papers · Wellcome L., corresp. and papers relating to jaundice | CAC Cam., Hill MSS · CAC Cam., Mellanby MSS · CUL, corresp. with Joseph Needham · RS, corresp. with Sir Robert Robinson · Wellcome L., corresp. with Sir Ernst Chain · Wellcome L., letters to Sir Edward Mellanby
Likenesses Ramsey & Muspratt, photograph, 1935, repro. in Thompson and Ogston, *Memoirs FRS* · W. Stoneman, photograph, c.1950, RS
Wealth at death £184,428: probate, 25 March 1982, *CGPLA Eng. & Wales*

Peters, Thomas. See Peter, Thomas (1597–1654/5).

Peters, Thomas (1737/8?–1792), campaigner for black rights and slavery abolitionist, was, according to some sources, born in Africa, belonging to Egba royalty. He was kidnapped in the 1760s and enslaved in Louisiana. The earliest surviving documentation identifies him in 1776 as aged thirty-eight and a fugitive from his master, William Campbell of Wilmington, North Carolina. After the British offered sanctuary to any slave 'able and willing to bear arms' and owned by an American rebel, Peters fled to New York where he enlisted in the black pioneers on 14 November 1776 and soon became company sergeant. Black pioneers were told that after the 'rebellion' they would be given 'land and provisions the same as the Rest of the Disbanded Soldiers'. Britain's apparent intent to treat black loyalists equally was reinforced in 1779 by General Sir Henry Clinton, who promised freedom with no requirement of military service to any slave who deserted a rebel master. The belief spread among the slaves that a British victory would mean an end to slavery in America and equality for the former slaves. Thousands of

African Americans fled to the British as a result, including 26-year-old Sally (*b. c.*1757, *d.* in or after 1792) and her eight-year-old daughter, Clara. Sally joined the black pioneers, where she and Peters married about 1779. In 1782 their son, John, was 'born within the lines'.

After the war Peters, his wife, and children were among the 3000 black loyalists evacuated from New York to Nova Scotia, arriving at Annapolis Royal in May 1784. With Peters in charge, over two hundred former pioneers and their families established Brindley Town, near Digby, and in August they applied for the free land they had been promised. But farm lots were not granted to the black families, and to obtain provisions they were required to work on the county roads. They survived by cultivating their 1 acre town lots and hiring their labour to white employers. Frustrated at the betrayal of the wartime promises, Peters moved to New Brunswick in July 1785 and applied there for farms on behalf of his colleagues. Again he was unsuccessful and had to take paid labour. Like the other black loyalists in New Brunswick and Nova Scotia, Peters could not vote or serve on juries, and it was difficult to obtain justice through the courts, to collect unpaid wages, or even to seek protection against kidnappers. Peters witnessed several free black people returned to slavery, with compliance from the courts. Still confident that George III would uphold the promise of equality, Peters obtained power of attorney from several hundred black loyalists in order to present their grievances directly to authorities in London.

By 4 November 1790 Peters was in London, where he obtained references from his wartime commander and from General Clinton, endorsing his plea to the government. Perhaps through them Peters met Granville Sharp and other directors of the Sierra Leone Company, proprietors of a colony for liberated slaves in west Africa. In December Peters submitted two petitions to the British cabinet, both showing the unmistakable influence of his abolitionist sponsors. The first was a description of the black loyalists' failure to receive land, and stated that some of them would be willing to accept their promised grants in another part of the British empire. Though unmentioned, Sierra Leone was the obvious location. The second petition complained that the free black loyalists were denied legal equality and attributed this to the continued existence in Nova Scotia of slavery, whose cruelties the petition recounted. The government responded by instructing the governors of Nova Scotia and New Brunswick to inquire into Peters's complaint and to issue land grants if they had been withheld. Alternatively, black people would be offered passage to Sierra Leone at government expense. The second petition, imploring the abolition of slavery, was ignored.

Lieutenant John Clarkson was appointed to lead the Sierra Leone expedition, landing in Halifax in October 1791. He was preceded by Peters, who took responsibility for recruitment in the St John and Annapolis regions. Despite concerted interference and intimidation from white employers, the black response was overwhelming: 1196 declared for the Sierra Leone alternative, including almost 500 from Peters's area. The inquiry, meanwhile, confirmed the details in Peters's petition but blamed them on his 'hasty' departure for New Brunswick in 1785. No remedial action was deemed necessary.

When the black loyalists arrived in Sierra Leone in March 1792 they discovered that the company had instituted an all-white government, with Lieutenant Clarkson as superintendent. Bad weather, a fever epidemic, and incompetence delayed the distribution of land grants, generating discontent among the settlers. Although he had no official position, Peters articulated settler concerns and a public meeting delegated him to present their complaints to the superintendent. Clarkson feared an insurrection and threatened dire punishment, but Peters continued to agitate until he was convicted of unlawfully retrieving goods from a deceased settler. Clarkson reported that Peters's credibility was destroyed, though petitions bearing his mark continued to demand full rights for the black settlers right up until the night of 25 June 1792 when Peters too succumbed to the fever. Evidently he had not been entirely discredited, for the colony held a public funeral in his honour and his widow was granted a company pension. Peters was buried in Freetown on 27 June. He is remembered as a founding father of Sierra Leone and as an indefatigable fighter for recognition of former slaves as equal British subjects.

JAMES W. ST G. WALKER

Sources J. W. St G. Walker, *The black loyalists: the search for a promised land in Nova Scotia and Sierra Leone, 1783–1870* (1976); repr. (1992) · C. Fyfe, 'Thomas Peters: history and legend', *Sierra Leone Studies*, new ser., 1 (1953), 4–13 · C. B. Fergusson, ed., *Clarkson's mission to America, 1791–1792* (1971) · G. R. Hodges, ed., *The black loyalist directory* (1996) · E. G. Wilson, *John Clarkson and the African adventure* (1980) · BL, John Clarkson MSS vols. 1–4, Add. MSS 41262A–41264 · journal of James Strand, BL, Add. MSS 12131 · petitions of Thomas Peters, received 24 and 26 Dec 1790, PRO, FO 4/1 · 'Enquiry into the complaint of Thomas Peters, a black man', PRO, CO 217/63 · petitions of Thomas Peters, Public Archives of Nova Scotia · petitions of Thomas Peters, Public Archives of New Brunswick · Thomas Peters to Henry Dundas, received 6 July 1792, PRO, CO 267/9
Archives PRO · Public Archives of Nova Scotia, Halifax

Peters, (Matthew) William (1742–1814), portrait and genre painter and Church of England clergyman, was born at Freshwater, Isle of Wight. His father, Matthew Peters (*b.* 1711), was described on the 1778 engraving by Murphy after his son's portrait as 'Member of the Dublin Society and author of several treatises on tillage and agriculture'. His mother was the daughter of George Young of Dublin. Shortly after the birth of William (as he became known early in life, signing himself W. Peters) the family moved to Dublin, where Matthew Peters advised on the improvement of loughs and rivers for navigation.

William Peters was trained as an artist by Robert West in the first School of Design in Dublin; he received prizes in 1756 and 1758. The Dublin Society sent him to London where, when a pupil of Thomas Hudson in 1759, he won a premium from the Society of Arts. The Dublin Society paid for him to go to Italy (£30 per annum) and he arrived in Rome on 6 May 1762, having by his own account left Dublin for Cadiz in August 1761. He was delayed at sea 'beating about in the … equinoctial storms' (Ingamells, 763), and was then stranded for three months in Gibraltar. In Rome he studied life drawing at the Accademia del Nudo and at Pompeo Batoni's private academy. He was elected to the Accademia del Disegno in Florence on 23 September 1762.

Peters left Italy at the end of 1764, and was back in England in 1765. He exhibited at the Society of Artists from 1766 to 1769 from Tavistock Row (1766), Bond Street (1767), Suffolk Street (1768), and Welbeck Street (1769). On 27 February 1769 he became a freemason (Somerset House Lodge No. 2): he was made grand portrait painter of the Freemasons and first provincial grand master of Lincolnshire in 1792. The final works that Peters exhibited at the Royal Academy in 1785 were portraits of the duke of Manchester and Lord Petre as grand master.

Peters exhibited at the Royal Academy from 1769, and was elected associate in 1771 and academician in 1777. He was back in Florence by 5 November 1771 but by 1773 he was in Venice, from where he sent works to the Royal Academy exhibition that year and the next, and where he presumably painted *Edward Wortley Montagu in his Dress as an Arabian Prince* (NPG) in 1775. He exhibited in 1776 from Great Newport Street, Horace Walpole noting that he was 'just returned from Rome' (Ingamells). Peters also spent time in Paris, including (probably) 1783–4, where he was friendly with L.-P. Boilly and Antoine Vestier, and was influenced by Greuze.

However, no British contemporary had such an Italian manner of painting as Peters, reflecting the old masters he copied: for example Correggio's *Madonna of St Jerome* in Parma (parish church of Saffron Walden, Essex) and Barocci's *Madonna della scudella* in Perugia (1774), for which he was paid the substantial sum of 100 guineas by Robert, first Baron Clive. Peters's copy of Titian's *Venus of Urbino* is probably 'the Couchant Venus' attributed to Titian in the sale of the pictures of Richard, first Earl Grosvenor, following his death in 1802. The next lot in the same sale was Peters's most notorious composition, *Lydia* (exh. RA, 1777; Tate collection) showing a woman in bed, her prominent breasts and erect nipples frankly revealed. The *Morning Chronicle* (26 April 1777) commented in laboured *doubles entendres*:

> [the picture] makes every gentleman *stand* for some time … the inviting leer of the lady and her still more inviting bosom, ought to be consigned to the bed chamber of a *bagnio*, where each would doubtless *provoke* a proper effect.

It did Peters no harm: he was elected Royal Academician the same year. He made numerous compositions of a similar kind, all with the principal erotic charge of bare breasts, uncovered on one pretext or another, and all of these works were engraved and popular. Peters later regretted these *jeux d'esprit*: in 1781 he was ordained deacon and subsequently priest in 1782, having gone up to Exeter College, Oxford, in 1779 with this purpose. He was chaplain to the Royal Academy from 1784 to 1788 (when he resigned from the academy) and chaplain to the prince of Wales (he was also founding secretary of the Prince of Wales's Lodge, 1787).

Charles Manners, fourth duke of Rutland, presented Peters to the living of Scalford, Leicestershire, in 1784, and Peters became an enthusiastic but conscientious pluralist. In 1788 the dowager duchess (whom he had portrayed in 1783 as *An Angel Carrying the Spirit of a Child to Paradise*, priv. coll.) added the living of Knipton, when Peters also gained Woolsthorpe, both close to Belvoir Castle, where he became curator of pictures. He became prebendary of Lincoln Cathedral in 1795, at first with the stall of St Mary, Crackpool, quickly exchanged for the better living of Langford Ecclesia, Oxfordshire, to which he added Eaton (near Knipton) in the same year. He lived variously at Woolsthorpe, Knipton, and Langford, scrupulously maintaining the parish registers in Woolsthorpe and Knipton until 1806, and building a new church at Woolsthorpe in 1791 (replaced 1845). He painted numerous religious works, including a 10 by 5 feet *Annunciation* for Lincoln Cathedral (1799; subdeanery, Lincoln) and *The Resurrection of a Pious Family*, a picture won by the father of the future Cardinal Manning in a sovereign raffle and given to the church in Totteridge, Hertfordshire (sold in 1886). He painted five Shakespearian subjects for Boydell's Shakespeare Gallery from 1786, six for the Irish Shakespeare Gallery, and continued to paint portraits, charging 80 guineas for a full length in 1794. He married Margaret Susannah Knowsley, daughter and co-heir of the Revd John Fleming of Burton Fleming, Yorkshire, on 28 April 1790 at St James's, Piccadilly, London; there were five children.

Masonic quarrels persuaded Peters to live chiefly in Langford from about 1800. Other old habits perhaps died hard, for in 1810–11 he upset the locals with a 'certain sketch' (Hodgson and Eaton), and took refuge at Brasted Place, Kent, where he died, a rich man, on 20 March 1814.

ROBIN SIMON

Sources V. Manners, *Matthew William Peters* (1913) · J. Ingamells, ed., *A dictionary of British and Irish travellers in Italy, 1701–1800* (1997) · W. G. Strickland, *A dictionary of Irish artists*, 2 vols. (1913); facs. edn with introduction by T. J. Snoddy (1969) · Waterhouse, *18c painters* · *Illustrated catalogue of acquisitions, 1986–88*, Tate Gallery · J. E. Hodgson and F. A. Eaton, *The Royal Academy and its members, 1768–1830* (1905)
Likenesses W. Leney, engraving, 1795 (after self-portrait) · M. W. Peters, self-portrait

Petersdorff, Charles Erdman (1800–1886), legal writer, was born in London on 4 November 1800, the third son of Christian Frederick Petersdorff, furrier, who began trading in London in the 1790s and later lived at Ivy House, Tottenham. He became a student of the Inner Temple on 24 September 1818, and after practising as a special pleader and going on the home circuit, was called to the bar on 25 January 1833.

Petersdorff was for some time one of the counsel to the Admiralty, and by order of the lords of the Admiralty he compiled a complete collection of the statutes relating to the navy, to shipping, ports, and harbours. He had already, when only twenty, produced *A General Index to the Precedents in Civil and Criminal Proceedings from the Earliest Period*, followed in 1824 by *A Practical Treatise on the Law of Bail* and between 1825 and 1830 the fifteen volumes of *A practical and elementary abridgement of cases in the king's bench, common pleas, exchequer and at nisi prius from the Restoration*. Among his later writings, the most important was *A Practical and Elementary Abridgement of the Common Law* (five vols., 1841–4). In its synthesis of common law and statutory modifications, this work looked ahead to later legal encyclopaedias such as *Halsbury's Laws*.

On 15 November 1847 Petersdorff married Mary Anne, widow of James Mallock, a London solicitor. He was created a serjeant-at-law on 14 June 1858, and on 1 January 1863 nominated a judge of the county courts for north Devon and Somerset, an appointment which he resigned in December 1885 at the age of eighty-five. He died from a fall into the area of his house, 23 Harley Street, London, on 29 July 1886. G. C. BOASE, rev. PATRICK POLDEN

Sources *Law Journal* (7 Aug 1886), 467 · *Solicitors' Journal*, 30 (1885–6), 691 · Boase, *Mod. Eng. biog.* · Holdsworth, *Eng. law*, vols. 12, 13, 15 · A. W. B. Simpson, ed., *Biographical dictionary of the common law* (1984) · J. Whishaw, *Synopsis of the members of the English bar* (1835) · Baker, *Serjeants* · *Law Times* (5 June 1886), 103 · *Bibliography: a legal bibliography of the British commonwealth of nations*, 2 (1957) · *London Directory* [various dates]

Wealth at death £84 6s. 1d.: administration, 17 March 1887, CGPLA Eng. & Wales

Petersen, Jack. *See* Peterson, John Charles (1911–1990).

Peterson, Alexander Duncan Campbell (1908–1988), educational reformer, was born in Edinburgh on 13 September 1908, the third of five sons, but the second to survive childhood (there were no daughters), of John Carlos Kennedy Peterson (1876–1955), of the Indian Civil Service, under-secretary in the finance department, government of Bengal, and his wife, Flora Campbell (d. 1953). One of his brothers was Sir Arthur William *Peterson. He and his brothers were brought up largely by aunts and uncles. His parents had no home leave between 1915 and 1919, and when his mother eventually arrived at his preparatory school he failed to recognize her. He won scholarships to Radley College and to Balliol College, Oxford, liking the second as much as he had disliked the first. At Oxford he showed the breadth of interest and taste for experiment which marked him throughout life. His activities as an undergraduate were multifarious, and in 1930 he missed a first in *literae humaniores*, apparently by a very narrow margin. He had received a second class in classical honour moderations in 1928.

Peterson's flair for communication did not stay hidden for long. His ascent up the teacher's ladder (as assistant master, Shrewsbury School, 1932–40; and as headmaster of Adams' Grammar School, Newport, 1946–52, and of Dover College, 1954–7) was punctuated by two periods of psychological warfare in the Far East. The first (1943–5), under Lord Louis Mountbatten, earned him an OBE (1946); during the second (1952–4), under Sir Gerald Templer in Malaya, his formidable chief judged him 'absolutely first class'.

The directorship of Oxford University's department of education, which Peterson held from 1958 until his retirement in 1973, left him time for writing on educational

problems and for outside activities. As the chairman of the Farmington Trust's council from 1964 to 1971 he helped to found the *Journal of Moral Education*. He acted for a time as the Liberal Party's spokesman on education, and stood without any chance of success for Oxford in the 1966 election. He served from 1959 to 1966 as chairman of the Army Education Advisory Board. It was, however, as the advocate of broader sixth form studies that he became well known. He opened the campaign with a broadcast early in 1956 (*Listener*, 16 February), continued it in his Estlin Carpenter lectures at Oxford in 1957 (published as *Educating our Rulers*, 1957), and brought it to a remarkable climax with the Oxford department's report, 'Arts and science sides in the sixth form', in 1960. This established beyond reasonable doubt that the early specialization characterizing English secondary schools not merely precluded sixth form courses appropriate to a scientific age, but reduced the flow of science graduates. About 40 per cent of the English sixteen-year-olds questioned for the report would have liked to combine arts with mathematics or science: under 6 per cent were actually doing so. When more than 700 pupils in French *lycées* and German *Gymnasia* were asked what subjects they would have chosen for the *baccalauréat* or *Abitur* had there been no restrictions on choice, only five chose entirely from mathematics or science. Peterson had won the argument; but, like many others in the decades which followed, he found that this did not open the road to the needed reforms.

Frustrated in England, Peterson turned abroad. The international sixth form which he had started at Dover brought him into contact with Kurt Hahn, and in 1962, when Atlantic College was founded, he helped to plan its curriculum. No single syllabus could be made to conform to university entrance requirements, which varied from country to country; and in the same year plans for an international baccalaureate were being discussed in Geneva. The Oxford department, which was then embarking on an investigation for the Council of Europe, was soon involved in the planning for this; and Peterson was the director of the International Baccalaureate Office during the crucial phase of growth, from 1966 to 1977. In the year of his death an international baccalaureate, based on a balanced curriculum of six subjects, was in use in fifty-six countries and 2643 diplomas were awarded. Eleven years later this figure had grown to 13,089, and the system had been extended to include younger pupils, the total entry for the diplomas and certificates being 38,129. The United World Colleges, headed by Atlantic College, needed the international baccalaureate and nourished it. Peterson, who was chairman of the United World Colleges (1978–80), helped with both organizations until he died. In *Schools across Frontiers* (1987) he recorded the struggle to establish them. He was made an honorary doctor of the University of Trieste (1985).

Peterson was tall and good looking. In December 1939 he married Ruth Pauline, daughter of William Anderson Armstrong, solicitor. This marriage ended in divorce in 1946, and in the same year he married Corinna May, daughter of Sir Arthur William Steuart Cochrane, Clarenceux king of arms. There were two sons and a daughter of the second marriage. Peterson, who lived latterly at 107A Hamilton Terrace, London, died of a heart attack in St Mary's Hospital, Paddington, London, on 17 October 1988. He was survived by his wife. MICHAEL BROCK, rev.

Sources B. Sweet-Escott, *Baker Street irregular* (1965) · R. J. Leach, *International schools and their role in the field of international education* (1969) · T. J. Leasor, *Boarding party* (1978) · J. Cloake, *Templer, tiger of Malaya: the life of Field Marshal Sir Gerald Templer* (1985) · P. Ziegler, *Mountbatten: the official biography* (1985) · R. Blackburn, memorial tribute, 1988, Council of Foundation, Geneva, International Baccalaureate Office · *The Times* (19 Oct 1988) · *The Independent* (28 Nov 1988) · private information (1996) · personal knowledge (1996) · *CGPLA Eng. & Wales* (1990)

Likenesses H. Lamb, portrait, Dover College, Dover

Wealth at death £49,455: probate, 31 Jan 1990, *CGPLA Eng. & Wales*

Peterson, Sir Arthur William (1916–1986), public servant, was born in Calcutta on 22 May 1916, one of four surviving sons of John Carlos Kennedy Peterson CIE (1876–1955), of the Indian Civil Service (who was himself born in India), and his wife, Flora Campbell (*d*. 1953). Alexander *Peterson was his elder brother. He was sent from India to a preparatory school in England at the age of four, going on to Shrewsbury School, where he was head boy, and then to Merton College, Oxford. At Oxford he took a full part in literary and dramatic societies and was captain of the college boat club, and still took firsts in classical moderations (1936) and in Greats (1938), the latter with a special concentration on philosophy.

After passing the administrative class examination for the civil service Peterson joined the Home Office in 1938. He spent most of the Second World War in the Ministry of Home Security, his poor eyesight making him unfit for military service. On 19 September 1940 he married Mary Isabel Maples (*b*. 1919), daughter of Ernest Edgar Maples, doctor of medicine; they had a son and two daughters. After the war Peterson quickly reached the very centre of the Home Office, serving from 1946 to 1949 as principal private secretary to the home secretary, James Chuter Ede. From 1949 to 1951 he had another personal role as secretary of the royal commission on betting, lotteries and gaming.

In 1957 Peterson became special assistant to R. A. Butler, who was home secretary and lord privy seal. Butler's unusual position in the government, and his personal style, were well served by Peterson's genial efficiency and breadth of experience. Peterson was in turn stimulated by Butler's interest in penal reform and later in 1957 was appointed deputy chairman of the Prison Commission and in 1960 chairman. His fresh, businesslike approach gave new impetus to the caring, humane traditions of the prison service.

In 1964, with the arrival of Wilson's Labour government, Peterson's safe pair of hands were transferred to the often turbulent affairs of the new Department of Economic Affairs, under George Brown. As a deputy secretary in the department he supervised policies and institutions to correct uneven regional economic development. His next move would naturally have been to take charge of a government department, but the right vacancy was not obvious. It is a measure of his unstuffy adaptability that in 1968 he accepted an invitation to become director-general of the newly created Greater London council. Some civil servants were surprised that anyone could welcome a move from the top of the civil service into local government, but Peterson's talents and style were just as valuable at the Greater London council as in the Department of Economic Affairs, and his move was vindicated in 1972 when he became permanent secretary at the Home Office. This post brought together all the elements of his experience—dealing with ministers, a large staff, and a multitude of volatile topics of great political and social significance. He retired in 1977, staying on for a year after normal retirement age, and took charge of the committee of officials concerned with the celebration that year of the queen's silver jubilee (having been involved in 1953 with aspects of the coronation arrangements).

Peterson was a public servant of considerable distinction working mainly in the Home Office, and usually close to ministers. His intellectual ability, common sense, and a bluff personal presence gave him authority and influence. His contribution often lay in encouraging the ideas of others, and applying calm and reason to difficult situations. He did not seek personal credit, and it is difficult to point to particular policies or operations where he was a pioneer or indispensable. In keeping with his family background in the Indian Civil Service he was an administrator, and not a missionary.

Peterson's interventions in government business, deft, wise, and economical, could still be decisive. At the end of a long meeting with ministers about a proposed course of action, when others had offered a detailed analysis and a balanced recommendation, Peterson might stop puffing his pipe and simply say 'I wouldn't do it'; and that was then the decision. He brought out the best in his staff, showing them great consideration and trust. He commanded respect and affection on the wider stage, with politicians and at international gatherings on crime. In retirement, as well as being chairman of the Mersey Docks and Harbour Company (1977–80), he took on a number of public service posts. He was a wise and steadying member of the royal commission on criminal procedure (1978–80) and was chairman of the joint committee on refugees from Vietnam (1979–82). As chairman, from 1981, of the British Refugee Council he brought together the voluntary agencies working with the Vietnamese refugees.

Peterson was always cheerful and courteous; he enjoyed his family, and food and drink. He was sustained by his ready outlets away from London. Over many years he lived in a number of unusual houses in the country, including a pub and the gatehouse of a former house of correction, both in Lincolnshire. He was honoured with a MVO in 1953, a CB in 1963, and a KCB in 1973. He died on 8 May 1986, survived by his wife. BRIAN CUBBON

Sources *The Times* (13 May 1986) · Lord Allen of Abbeydale, address at memorial service, priv. coll. · Home Office departmental records · *WW* · *WWW*, 1951–60 · m. cert. · *CGPLA Eng. & Wales* (1986)
Wealth at death £75,479: probate, 5 Aug 1986, *CGPLA Eng. & Wales*

Peterson, John Charles [*known as* Jack Petersen] (1911–1990), boxer, was born in Cardiff on 2 September 1911, the only son (there was also a daughter) of John Thomas Peterson, massage specialist, and his wife, Melinda Laura Rossiter. The family's name was Peterson, but Jack was known professionally as Petersen. It was a sporting family—his father (whom the press called 'Pa') had trained south Wales boxers who were near-British champions. The younger Peterson was never a 'mountain' fighter (a bare-knuckle boxer who fought illegally). He did well at school and was an enthusiastic boy scout. Not surprisingly, he took up amateur boxing, and by the age of eighteen had reached the Welsh Amateur Boxing Association (ABA) finals at both middle and light heavyweight. In the following season he won Welsh titles at light heavy and heavyweight (1931), and the national ABA championships at the lighter weight.

Petersen immediately turned professional, managed by his father and backed by a syndicate of Welsh sportsmen. He won his first nine contests within the space of ten weeks at the stadium in Holborn, London. Cardiff was considered by professionals not to be a boxing city, though the Petersons lived in Whitchurch and Jack trained at St John Square, taking the train to go up for his Monday evening matches. Cardiff's Greyfriars Hall was soon used to display this stylish, hard punching boxing prospect to his home supporters, and they became vociferously excited when he rescued a contest by a knockout in the fifteenth round.

The British light heavyweight championship fell to Petersen at Holborn, and seven weeks later (July 1932), at Wimbledon stadium, he knocked out Reggie Meen, of Leicester, to become the British heavyweight champion, in his eighteenth professional contest, aged twenty. He was the first Welshman, and the youngest man, ever to win that title, and it was accomplished in ten months. The Cardiff press and the people of Wales glowed with pride. The light heavyweight division did not draw crowds to boxing matches, and though Petersen could still weigh 12 stones and 7 pounds he relinquished this title. As the champion at catchweights he became extraordinarily popular, partly because his opponents often outweighed him by 1 or 2 stones. He was an attacking boxer, a dark haired good-looking man, and the adjective 'gallant' appeared frequently in boxing reporters' commentary. On cinema newsreels his modesty and pride in his own locality registered with the general public. Petersen was the most popular British boxer since Bombardier Billy Wells.

In 1933 an even younger man emerged as a contender. Jack Doyle, from co. Cork via the Irish Guards, had won his ten fights by knockouts within two rounds, and he and Petersen were matched at the White City stadium in July.

The largest crowd at a boxing match in Britain at that time (some 30,000) assembled, only to watch Doyle repeatedly punch Petersen below the belt and be disqualified in the second round. Petersen ignored the fouls, did not go down, and honourably matched the bigger man blow for blow. In his next contest Petersen unexpectedly lost the British title to Len Harvey on points at the Royal Albert Hall (December 1933). It was his first defeat in twenty-five professional contests, and to a smaller, though exceptionally clever, man.

Six months later (June 1934) Petersen beat Harvey to regain this title and also win the heavyweight championship of the British empire, for which black men were allowed to box. One such contender, Larry Gains from Canada, was the next boxer that Petersen defeated. The man from Cardiff defended both championships successfully until August 1936, when he lost heavily to Ben Foord, a Leicester based white South African, who was qualified by residence for both titles. While champion for the second time, however, Petersen had suffered international reverses. In 1935 he boxed only twice, and was beaten both times by a strong, young, 14 stone heavyweight from Germany, Walter Neusel. Petersen retired from boxing in February 1937, at the early age of twenty-five, after losing bruisingly to Neusel for a third time.

During the Second World War Petersen was a physical training instructor in the Royal Air Force, and subsequently was heavily involved in Welsh affairs of the British Boxing Board of Control. In 1986 he became president of the board and was appointed OBE for his services to sport. He was also vice-chairman of the Sports Council for Wales. Petersen lifted the low prestige of British heavyweights in the inter-war years, and retired from boxing gracefully. In October 1935 he married Annie Elizabeth (Betty), daughter of Thomas Baker Williams, auctioneer, of Cardiff. His parents did not attend the long planned ceremony. 'Pa' had been in his son's corner throughout his career, but the boxer–manager relationship stopped after the second contest with Neusel, and Petersen managed himself for the last four matches of his six years' career. He died on 22 November 1990 at the Princess of Wales Hospital, Bridgend, of cancer of the lung.

STAN SHIPLEY, *rev.*

Sources *Western Mail* [Cardiff] (1930–39) · *South Wales Echo* (1930–39) · *Boxing* · *The Times* (23 Nov 1990) · *CGPLA Eng. & Wales* (1991)
Wealth at death £115,000: probate, 20 Feb 1991, *CGPLA Eng. & Wales*

Peterson, Sir Maurice Drummond (1889–1952), diplomatist, was born on 10 March 1889 in Dundee, the younger son of Sir William *Peterson (1856–1921), classical scholar and educationist, and his wife, Lisa Gibb, eldest daughter of William Ross, shipowner, of Glenearn, Perthshire. He was educated in Canada, after his father's appointment as principal of McGill University, and then at Rugby School and Magdalen College, Oxford, where he took a first in modern history in 1911. He entered the Foreign Office in December 1913, and between then and his retirement in June 1949 he had a varied career as a clerk and diplomatist,

Sir Maurice Drummond Peterson (1889–1952), by Walter Stoneman

and particularly made his mark in Egypt and the Soviet Union and in the Foreign Office in London during part of the Second World War.

The high point of Peterson's early career in the Foreign Office came in May 1917, when he was appointed a member of Arthur Balfour's mission to Washington. Three years later, in January 1920, he was transferred to Washington as second secretary. In February 1921 he was promoted first secretary, and between October 1921 and February 1922 he was attached to the British delegation to the Washington naval conference, as Balfour's private secretary. He returned to London in October 1922, but was transferred to Prague in June 1923. There he acted at various times as chargé d'affaires. In December 1924 he was transferred to Tokyo, where he made a serious study of the Japanese language, and concluded that the Japanese ruling élite was both jealous of and fundamentally hostile towards the British empire. On his return to England he married, on 27 April 1927, Eleanor Angel (b. 1903/4), the second daughter of the Revd Henry William Leycester O'Rorke, rector of Woodstock, Oxfordshire. They had three sons.

Shortly after his marriage, Peterson was transferred to Cairo, still as first secretary. After two years he was moved to Madrid, where he was promoted counsellor in November 1929 and remained until July 1931; he despised his ambassador, Sir George Grahame, admired Alfonso XIII,

and witnessed with sadness the passing of the Spanish monarchy, not to be restored during his lifetime. From July 1931 to October 1936 he was head of the Egyptian department in the Foreign Office and was sent out to Cairo for four months in 1934 as acting high commissioner. A mission to Rome in late 1933 to negotiate a border agreement between Libya and the Anglo-Egyptian Sudan, which failed in the face of excessive Italian demands, convinced him of Italian enmity to Britain. He was intimately involved in the negotiations surrounding the Abyssinian crisis in 1936, and although he was closely associated with what came to be known as the Hoare-Laval plan to stop the war in Abyssinia, he favoured a hard line against Mussolini during the later stages of the war, including barring the Suez Canal to Italian shipping.

Peterson's first headship of a mission was in Sofia from October 1936 to March 1938, as minister, to be followed by his first embassy, Baghdad, from March 1938 to March 1939. These years involved him in dealings with two royal autocrats: Boris III, for whom he had mixed feelings; and King Ghazi, who exasperated him and whose deposition by Britain he had come to regard as inevitable before Ghazi's death in a car accident accomplished the same purpose. Peterson was appointed KCMG in February 1938, having been made a CMG in January 1933. In February 1939 a meeting of senior officials decided that Peterson should become ambassador to Spain following the end of the civil war, as being 'our most energetic man: we hope to organise a regular drive—commercial missions, propaganda, etc—to get Franco over to our side or at least back to neutrality' (Harvey, 252). This was to lead to a humiliation that would blight the remainder of Peterson's life. His conviction that he was making a success of his mission was not shared by the Foreign Office, which decided in late April 1940 to replace him by Sir Samuel Hoare, bluntly informing Peterson that, in their estimation, he had failed. He spent most of the rest of the war in London, including six months during which the *Foreign Office List* described him as 'unemployed', before being placed in charge of the Egyptian, eastern and far eastern departments from January 1942 until September 1944. He worked hard to restore Anglo-American relations over the Middle East, but annoyed some by appearing too ready to endorse American views on the future of Palestine.

From September 1944 until May 1946 Peterson was ambassador to Turkey. In his memoirs, written when Turkey had become a cold war ally, he exaggerated his cordiality to the country. He went to Ankara feeling emotional contempt for Turkish neutrality in the war while understanding the intellectual case for it. In May 1946 Bevin offered him one of the most important embassies, Moscow, while informing him that for humane reasons he would only remain there for two years; it was a city where 'you can never have a night out' (*Diaries of Sir Robert Bruce Lockhart*, 532). In this case Peterson's memoirs provided a more reasonable guide to his stewardship. He was not convinced by the very pessimistic briefing about Soviet intentions provided by the Foreign Office before his departure;

indeed, he went to Russia full of goodwill and gratitude for its part in defeating Hitler. His spurning in 1948 of the offer of a visit to Stalingrad was, in his words, 'a measure of the distance I had traversed since May 1946' (Peterson, 275). He had become convinced that Russia was not part of European civilization, and that its foreign policy was motivated by militant ideological communism in combination with revived tsarist imperialism. His specific advice could be bad, including the claim in 1947 that Stalin was a 'failing force' within the Politburo, and the proposal that the west should launch 'political warfare against Communism' (PRO, FO 371) at the very time when western governments were trying to make it appear that Russia was sincerely being offered Marshall economic aid and was spurning the offer. Health troubles in the form of heart disease resulted in his retirement in June 1949. Afterwards he served on the board of the Midland Bank and wrote a volume of memoirs. He had been promoted GCMG in 1947.

Peterson's characteristics may be summarized under seven headings. The first was real eccentricity, exemplified by his use of dog biscuits for the cheese course when he was entertaining the foreign secretary in Moscow in 1947. The second was a high degree of touchiness and an inability to set aside a slight, especially if it emanated from the Foreign Office. This produced, third, a feeling of being in the Foreign Office but not of it. Fourth, he enjoyed exercising power and regretted that only once, in Egypt in 1934, was he able to bring about an important political change in the country to which he was accredited. Fifth, he was a passionate imperialist, a characteristic which, during the 1930s, caused him to regard Italy as a greater threat than Germany. Sixth, he could admire democracy abroad, as in Czechoslovakia in the 1920s, but saw no reason to object to autocracies 'so long as they did not become mere organisations for war' (Peterson, 42). Finally, he was a strong protestant and was convinced, *inter alia*, that intrigue by pro-Franco Anglo-Catholics had been an important factor in his recall from Madrid. He died at his home, Inglewood Lodge, Kintbury, Berkshire, on 15 March 1952.   VICTOR ROTHWELL

Sources The diaries of Sir Alexander Cadogan, ed. D. Dilks (1971) · The diplomatic diaries of Oliver Harvey, 1937–40, ed. J. Harvey (1970) · H. M. G. Jebb [Lord Gladwyn], The memoirs of Lord Gladwyn (1972) · W. R. Louis, Imperialism at bay, 1945–1951: the United States and the decolonization of the British empire (1977) · W. R. Louis, The British empire in the Middle East, 1945–1951 (1984) · M. Peterson, Both sides of the curtain: an autobiography (1950) · N. Rose, Vansittart: study of a diplomat (1978) · V. Rothwell, Britain and the cold war, 1941–1947 (1982) · The diaries of Sir Robert Bruce Lockhart, ed. K. Young, 2 (1980) · J. Zametica, ed., British officials and British foreign policy, 1945–50 (1990) · DNB · The Times (17 March 1952) · CGPLA Eng. & Wales (1952) · m. cert. · WW
Archives BL, corresp. with Lord Cecil, Add. MSS 51091 · Bodl. RH, corresp. with Lord Lugard · PRO, Foreign Office records, FO 371 | FILM BFI NFTVA, news footage | SOUND BL NSA, oral history interview
Likenesses W. Stoneman, photograph, NPG [see illus.] · photograph, repro. in Young, ed., Diaries of Sir Robert Bruce Lockhart, facing p. 81 · photographs, repro. in Peterson, Both sides of the curtain

Wealth at death £65,581 16s. 5d.: probate, 6 May 1952, CGPLA Eng. & Wales

Peterson, Peter (1847–1899), Sanskritist, was born in Edinburgh on 12 January 1847, the son of John Peterson, merchant of Leith, and Grace Montford Anderson. Sir William *Peterson, classical scholar and educationist, was his brother. His father and grandfather were natives of Shetland, and hence Peterson often described himself as a Shetlander. He was educated at Edinburgh high school and Edinburgh University, where he graduated MA with first-class honours in classics in 1867. It was there that he began to study Sanskrit, under the professor Simon Theodor Aufrecht. After a visit, partly for study, to Berlin, he proceeded in 1869 to Lincoln College, Oxford, to continue Sanskrit under Monier Williams and Friedrich Max Müller, gaining the Boden Sanskrit scholarship in 1870, and then moving to Balliol College, from which he graduated BA in 1872. Peterson married, on 29 October 1872, Agnes Christall (d. September 1900). Several children of the marriage survived him; a son entered the India civil service.

On 2 January 1873 Peterson joined the Indian educational service, and went to Bombay as professor of Sanskrit in Elphinstone College, where he remained until his death, except for the period from September 1874 to November 1876, in which he spent a year's sick leave in Europe and another year teaching at the Deccan College, Poona. During his first nine years in India Peterson did little research, thus contravening the terms of his post; accordingly in 1881 the government proposed to transfer him to a chair of English which did not require him to produce original work, and to give the Sanskrit chair to Professor Bhandarkar of Poona, who had been acting professor at Elphinstone from 1867 until Peterson's appointment. In 1882, however, it was agreed that the two would retain their posts and jointly lead the government-funded search for Sanskrit manuscripts in the Bombay 'circle' (western and central India). Many of Peterson's discoveries in the libraries of Gujarat, Rajputana, and elsewhere were of high literary value, and his six reports on the search (1883–99) were highly praised, as displaying his ability to identify what was most important out of a large mass of material; his exploration of Jain literature was especially appreciated. He edited several Sanskrit texts, mostly for the Bombay Sanskrit Series, of which he and Bhandarkar had joint charge. The most important were the romance *Kâdambarî* (1883) and the poetry anthology *The Subhâshitâvali of Vallabhadeva* (1886), the latter edited jointly with Pandit Durgaprasada; in these his main aim was to convey his appreciation of the literary qualities of the Sanskrit, and he frequently made comparisons with Western literature. Others included the *Hitopadeśa* (1887) and selections from the Ramayana (1883) and the Rigveda (4 vols., 1888–92). For the Bibliotheca Indica he edited (1889) *The Nyayabindutika of Dharmottaracharya*, a Buddhist text he had discovered himself. Much of Peterson's success was due to his tact and respect for Indians and their traditions. This is made clear in an obituary speech made by Bhandarkar, who remained not only a colleague but one of his closest friends (Bhandarkar, xlvi–l). To this also was due his success in unearthing the jealously concealed manuscripts of the Jains at Cambay and elsewhere.

Peterson also taught and examined English for Bombay University and produced editions of *The Merchant of Venice* and book 4 of Palgrave's *Golden Treasury* designed for Indian students. He was much admired for his mastery of different styles of English, displayed mainly in his frequent contributions to the Bombay dailies and the *Times of India*.

For some time Peterson was a popular member of the Bombay municipal corporation, and for a long time he was registrar of Bombay University. He often served as secretary of the Bombay branch of the Royal Asiatic Society, and he was its president from 1895 until his death. In 1883 he received a DSc in philology from Edinburgh University, and he was a candidate for the Boden chair of Sanskrit in Oxford at the time of his unexpected death from heart disease in Bombay on 28 August 1899.

CECIL BENDALL, rev. R. S. SIMPSON

Sources E. J. Rapson, *Journal of the Royal Asiatic Society of Great Britain and Ireland* (1899), 917–19 · R. G. Bhandarkar, *Journal of the Bombay Branch of the Royal Asiatic Society*, 20 (1898–1900), xlvi–lii · *The Times* (6 Sept 1899), 7f · *The Athenaeum* (9 Sept 1899), 356 · Foster, *Alum. Oxon.* · C. E. Buckland, *Dictionary of Indian biography* (1906) · personal knowledge (1901) · private information (1901)

Peterson, Robert (*fl.* 1562–1606), translator, was admitted to Lincoln's Inn on 14 April 1562. Nothing else is known of him.

Peterson's two translations demonstrate two different facets of Italian cultural influence, *Galateo* from the Italian of Giovanni della Casa, archbishop of Beneventa (1576) and *A Treatise Concerning the Causes of the Magnificence and Greatness of Cities* (1606) from Giovanni Botero's original. *Galateo* is a manual of polite conversation proper to court circles. Peterson sought to instruct the general public, and his version had a fair influence. Social graces were a preoccupation of the Renaissance, and the Italian codification of manners acted as a social bond right across Europe. Social conduct was governed by the desire to please, a skill best taught 'where the mind and the eye, precept and experience joined hands together', as Peterson writes in his dedication to Robert Dudley, earl of Leicester. This is clearly a selling-point: Dudley's reputation for elegance and *savoir-faire* made him an excellent example for Peterson's readers. The book is prefaced by laudatory verses by Francesco Pucci and Alessandro Citolini in Italian, and in English by Thomas Cradock, the Lady Margaret professor, and Thomas Drant, archdeacon of Lewes, and two unknowns, Thomas Browne of Lincoln's Inn, and I. Stoughton, 'a student'. Spingarn claims without good evidence that Peterson worked almost entirely from the French version of 1577 which had the Italian on facing pages.

Peterson's translation of Botero is a textbook in statecraft, discussing the political, social, and economic causes for the rise and fall of cities. His dedication of the translation to Sir Thomas Egerton, lord high chancellor of England, implies that this was translated from interest, and was not commissioned by the dedicatee. Both have been published in modern editions.

L. G. KELLY

Sources R. Peterson, *A Renaissance courtesy book*, ed. J. E. Spingarn (1914) · R. Peterson, *A treatise of the manners and behaviours it behoveth a man to use*, ed. H. Reid (1892) · W. P. Baildon, ed., *The records of the Honorable Society of Lincoln's Inn: admissions*, 1 (1896)

Peterson, Sir William (1856–1921), classical scholar and educationist, the fifth son of John Peterson, a merchant of Leith, and his wife, Grace Montford, *née* Anderson, was born in Edinburgh on 29 May 1856. He was educated at the high school there and the University of Edinburgh; graduating in 1875, he went with a travelling fellowship to Göttingen in Germany; in 1876 he entered Corpus Christi College, Oxford, as Ferguson scholar, graduating in 1879. From 1879 to 1882 he was assistant professor of the humanities at Edinburgh, and from 1882 to 1895 first principal of the newly founded University College, Dundee. Successful as an administrator, he secured excellent terms for his institution in the long negotiations leading to union with the University of St Andrews. He also continued his classical studies, editing book x of Quintilian's *Institutio oratoria* (1891), the *Dialogus de oratoribus* of Tacitus (1893), and Cicero's *Pro Cluentio* (1895). Peterson married in 1885 Lisa Gibb, eldest daughter of William Ross, shipowner, of Glenearn, Perthshire; they had two sons, the younger of whom was the diplomatist Sir Maurice Drummond *Peterson.

In May 1895 Peterson was appointed principal of McGill University, Montreal, Canada, in succession to Sir William Dawson. There his talent as administrator had ample scope. He found a group of largely autonomous schools and transformed it into a university. He won the confidence of the wealthy men of Montreal—especially Lord Strathcona and Sir William Macdonald (1831–1917), the head of the Canadian tobacco industry—and obtained from them buildings and endowments, especially for agriculture, applied science, and medicine. Faculties of law, medicine, commerce, education, and social service were added to the university; but Peterson's constant endeavours to strengthen the faculty of arts found less sympathy in a great commercial city.

As principal of McGill, Peterson continued his own classical studies and publications. In 1901 he discovered in the library of Holkham Hall a ninth-century manuscript (formerly belonging to Cluny) of Cicero's speeches; and in 1907 he produced an edition of the *Verrines*, based on this text. He also took an active part in educational work in Quebec, and throughout Canada and the United States, and was a very distinct personality among North American university presidents. He was for some years chairman of the protestant committee of the council of public instruction in Quebec, and a most influential trustee, and for a time chairman, of the Carnegie foundation for the advancement of teaching. He received many honorary degrees, and in 1915 was made KCMG. In politics he was an imperialist, and in his later years spoke and wrote much in favour of the continued and closer connection between Canada and Great Britain. Though devoted to McGill and to Canada, Peterson always remained half-Scot, half-cosmopolitan. He could show a salutary hauteur on occasion, and he did not suffer fools gladly, but he had also great personal charm and distinction.

During the First World War, Peterson spoke and worked unceasingly, and on 12 January 1919, while presiding at a meeting on behalf of the dependants of dead or disabled Scottish soldiers and sailors, he was stricken with paralysis. In May he resigned, and returned to England; he died in London at his home, Wildwood, North End, Hampstead, on 4 January 1921, his wife surviving him.

W. L. GRANT, rev. ROGER T. STEARN

Sources C. MacMillan, McGill and its story, 1821–1921 (1921) · personal knowledge (1927) · WWW, 1916–28 · CGPLA Eng. & Wales (1921)
Archives NL Scot., corresp. with Sir Patrick Geddes · University of Toronto, letters to James Mavor
Wealth at death £15,186 9s. 1d.: probate, 23 Feb 1921, CGPLA Eng. & Wales

Pether, Abraham (1756–1812), landscape painter, a cousin of William *Pether, was born at Chichester. As a child he showed a great talent for music, and at the age of nine played the organ in one of the Chichester churches. Adopting art as his profession, he became a talented pupil of George Smith (1713/14–1776). He painted river and mountain scenery, with classical buildings, in a style somewhat resembling that of Richard Wilson; but his reputation rests on moonlight subjects, which earned him the sobriquet of Moonlight Pether. He painted, with attention to harmony of colour, the combination of moonlight and firelight, as in Eruption of Vesuvius, Ship on Fire in a Gale at Night, and An Ironfoundry by Moonlight. Pether was a frequent exhibitor at both the free and the incorporated societies from 1773 to 1791, and at the Royal Academy from 1784 to 1811. His Harvest Moon, which was shown at the academy in 1795, was highly praised. He had an extensive knowledge of scientific subjects, and in his moonlight pictures the astronomical conditions are always correctly observed. He was also a skilled mechanic, constructing optical instruments for his own use, and lectured on electricity. Although his art was popular, Pether was never able to do more than supply the daily needs of his large family, and, incapacitated by a lingering disease which eventually caused his death, he was reduced to great poverty. He died at Southampton on 13 April 1812, leaving destitute a widow, Elizabeth (d. in or after 1812), and nine children; the fact that they were unable to obtain any assistance from the Artists' Benevolent Fund provoked a fierce attack upon the management of the society. Abraham Pether is sometimes known as Old Pether, to distinguish him from his son Sebastian *Pether.

Thomas Pether (fl. 1772–1781), who was probably a brother of Abraham—as, according to exhibition catalogues, they at one time lived together—was a wax modeller, and exhibited portraits in wax with the Free Society of Artists from 1772 to 1781. Nothing else is known of his life as work.

F. M. O'DONOGHUE, rev. J. DESMARAIS

Sources M. Pilkington, A general dictionary of painters: containing memoirs of the lives and works, ed. A. Cunningham and R. A. Davenport, new edn (1857) · Bryan, Painters (1886–9) · J. Pye, Patronage of British art: an historical sketch (1845) · The works of the late Edward Dayes, ed. E. W. Brayley (privately printed, London, 1805) · The exhibition of the Royal Academy (1773–1811) [exhibition catalogues] · exhibition catalogues (1773–1811) [Free Society of Artists] · exhibition catalogues (1773–1811) [Incorporated Society of Artists] · Waterhouse, 18c painters · C. Knight, ed., The English cyclopaedia: biography, 6 vols. (1856–8) [suppl. (1872)] · R. N. James, Painters and their works, 3 vols. (1896–7) · Graves, Artists, 1st edn · GM, 1st ser., 82/1 (1812), 491

Pether, Henry (fl. 1828–1865). See under Pether, Sebastian William Thomas (1790–1844).

Pether, Sebastian William Thomas (1790–1844), landscape painter, was baptized on 31 August 1794 at St Luke's, Chelsea, the eldest son of Abraham *Pether (1756–1812), landscape painter, and his wife, Elizabeth (d. in or after 1812). He was a pupil of his father and, like him, painted moonlight views and nocturnal conflagrations. The realism and preoccupation with colour harmonies in these works should have brought him success, but early in life the necessity of providing for a large family forced him into the hands of the dealers, who purchased his pictures for small sums for copying purposes, to which they readily lent themselves, and consequently they were rarely seen at exhibitions. In 1814 Pether sent to the Royal Academy View from Chelsea Bridge of the Destruction of Drury Lane Theatre, and in 1826 A Caravan Overtaken by a Whirlwind. The latter was a commission from Sir John Fleming Leicester, but as the subject was not suited to the painter's talent this solitary commission was of no real benefit to him. His life was one long struggle with adversity, which reached its climax when, in 1842, three pictures, which with the help of a frame-maker friend he had sent to the Royal Academy, were rejected.

Pether resembled his father in his taste for mechanical pursuits, and is said to have suggested the idea of the stomach-pump to a surgeon named Jukes. He died, of consumption, at Battersea on 14 March 1844, on which date a subscription was raised for his family.

Pictures attributed to Sebastian Pether frequently appear at sales but often they are copies of his work. **Henry Pether** (fl. 1828–1865), whose landscapes, including moonlight scenes along the Thames, are frequently confused with Pether's, was probably his son.

It is not always easy to see where Sebastian's pictures end and Henry's begin, unless they are signed. Henry more frequently used a signature, and his pictures, if less inventive in romantic imagery, are painted with more refinement, and show a sense of topography and local atmosphere. (Maas, 51)

F. M. O'DONOGHUE, rev. J. DESMARAIS

Sources Bryan, *Painters* (1886–9) · R. N. James, *Painters and their works*, 3 vols. (1896–7) · C. Knight, *Biography*, 7 vols. (1856) · Redgrave, *Artists*, 2nd edn · Thieme & Becker, *Allgemeines Lexikon* · *Art Union*, 6 (1844), 144–5 · F. P. Seguier, *A critical and commercial dictionary of the worth of painters* (1870) · Graves, *RA exhibitors* · Graves, *Brit. Inst.* · J. Johnson, ed., *Works exhibited at the Royal Society of British Artists, 1824–1893, and the New English Art Club, 1888–1917*, 2 vols. (1975) · *IGI* · J. Maas, *Victorian painters* (1969)

Pether, Thomas (*fl.* 1772–1781). *See under* Pether, Abraham (1756–1812).

Pether, William (*c.*1738–1821), mezzotint engraver and painter, one of the three sons and two daughters of William Pether (*d.* 1781), an organ and harpsichord builder, and his wife, Mary, was born at Carlisle. He became a pupil of the artist and porcelain manufacturer Thomas Frye of Stratford, Middlesex. Between 1756 and 1762 he won four prizes for drawing and two for mezzotints from the Society for the Encouragement of Arts, Manufactures, and Commerce. He became Frye's partner in 1761 and in the following year he engraved Frye's portrait of George III in three sizes. Pether regarded himself as a painter, and it was in that capacity that in 1765 he was elected a foundation fellow of the Incorporated Society of Artists; he served as a director in 1771–2 and 1773–4. Between 1761 and 1780 he exhibited crayon paintings of portraits and fancy heads, together with portrait miniatures and occasional mezzotints. He continued to exhibit portraits and other heads with the Royal Academy in 1781–3, 1789, and 1793–4. Although he presented himself as a candidate for election as ARA in 1781, he failed resoundingly, both then and again in 1783, to find support among the academicians.

Pether's mezzotints have survived better than his crayon paintings, and it is on mezzotint that his enduring reputation is based. In 1763 John Boydell published Pether's first print after Rembrandt, *Rembrandt's Wife in the Character of a Jew Bride*. This was the first of nine mezzotints of Rembrandt's paintings, executed for Boydell, or occasionally on his own account. The print called *A Jew Rabbi* (1764, now thought to represent Uzziah struck with leprosy), was well reviewed in the *Critical Review* and was selected by William Gilpin in *An Essay on Prints* (1768) to exemplify the excellence of contemporary mezzotint. The mastery of the distribution of light that made Pether such a fine interpreter of Rembrandt was perfectly suited to the work of Joseph Wright of Derby, and Pether scraped a series of fine mezzotints after Wright, with whom he seems also to have enjoyed a close friendship. *A Philosopher Giving a Lecture on the Orrery* (1768), *Three Persons Viewing the Gladiator by Candlelight* (1769), *A Farrier's Shop* (1771), *An Academy* (1772), and Pether's three other mezzotints after Wright are among the finest produced in Britain. Pether published the majority of his own plates, the remainder being issued by Boydell. Very few were portraits, but he interpreted a variety of subjects by English, Dutch, and Italian masters.

Pether's pupils included Robert Dunkarton, Edward Dayes, and Henry Edridge, and he employed the crippled dwarf John Jehner as an assistant. Edward Dayes found Pether 'a kind master, and polite gentleman', considering his rare oil portraits 'painted with a firm, broad pencil and great force of light and shade', his landscapes 'tolerable', and his miniatures 'clear, firm and spirited'. On the strength of his interpretations of Rembrandt and Wright, Dayes reckoned that in mezzotint he was 'unquestionably the first' (Dayes, 343–4). Miller considered Pether 'amiable, but an unsteady and unfortunate man ... he wanted *stability* in his pursuits; this defect in his nature rendered abortive the application of his excellent abilities' (Miller, 125).

Pether lived at various addresses in the Soho and Bloomsbury areas of London, and from the mid-1770s he also had a home in Church Row, Richmond. He was in Nottingham in 1780. His last plate published in London was dated 1793, and he exhibited at the Royal Academy for the last time in 1794. About ten years later he had settled at Bristol and was working as a drawing-master and cleaner of pictures; while there, he engraved the portraits of Samuel Seyer, the historian of Bristol (1816), and Edward Colston the philanthropist (1817), after Richardson. He died, aged eighty-two, in Montague Street, Bristol, on 19 July 1821, and was buried on 27 July in the churchyard at Horfield, where Seyer was rector. Elizabeth Pether, who was buried there on 25 June 1833 aged eighty-four, was possibly his widow.

TIMOTHY CLAYTON and ANITA MCCONNELL

Sources W. Miller, *Biographical sketches of British characters lately deceased* (1826), 125–6 · M. Huber and C. G. Martini, *Manuel des curieux et des amateurs de l'art*, 9 (Zürich, 1808), 220–4 · J. C. Smith, *British mezzotinto portraits*, 4 vols. in 5 (1878–84) · E. Dayes, *The works of the late Edward Dayes containing an excursion through the principal parts of Derbyshire and Yorkshire … and professional sketches of modern artists* (1805) · D. Rodgers, 'Pether, William', *The dictionary of art*, ed. J. Turner (1996) · J. Pye, *Patronage of British art: an historical sketch* (1845) · T. Clayton, 'The engraving and publication of prints of Joseph Wright's paintings'; T. Clayton, 'A catalogue of the engraved works of Joseph Wright of Derby', *Wright of Derby*, ed. J. Egerton (1990) [exhibition catalogue, Tate Gallery, London, 1990] · D. Alexander, 'Rembrandt and the reproductive print in eighteenth-century England', in C. White and others, *Rembrandt in eighteenth-century England* (New Haven, CT, 1983) [exhibition catalogue, Yale Center for British art, 1983] · W. Gilpin, *An essay on prints* (1768) · B. S. Long, *British miniaturists* (1929) · 'Engraving', *Critical Review*, 17 (1764), 298–9

Petheram, John (1807–1858), antiquary and publisher, was born at Oldmixon, near Weston-super-Mare, on 11 May 1807, the eldest in a family of four boys and three girls; his parents were Wesleyan Methodists. In 1830–31 he travelled to America with his family, who settled in New York state. From 1831 to 1834 he was a clerk with Brown, Roper & Co., Falcon Square, Aldersgate, London, in the wholesale drug trade. From July 1834 to autumn 1835 he spent some time in New York and travelling in the United States, supporting himself partly by trading in antiquarian books. An intermittent diary from his twenties shows him devoted to self-improvement and industrious reading at the London Institution (which he had joined in 1831), to collecting historical books for resale, and to preparing bibliographical compilations on English history.

Petheram returned to the druggists' warehouse in London but left it in 1839 to work for Edward Lumley of 56 Chancery Lane, remainder and second-hand bookseller, for whose catalogues he wrote discursive bibliographical articles. By the autumn of 1841 he had set up shop in his own premises at 71 Chancery Lane, and by 1848 had moved to 48 High Holborn. From these addresses he issued 207 catalogues and published several historical works. These included reprints (1843–7), with his own introductions and notes, of seven of the Elizabethan Marprelate tracts, intended as part of a longer series of 'puritan discipline tracts'. In 1853–4 he added five parts of a *Bibliographical Miscellany* to his catalogues, and he had earlier compiled a competent *Historical Sketch of the Progress and Present State of Anglo-Saxon Literature in England* (1840).

Petheram married Elizabeth Bickham, of Sherborne, Dorset, and they had six children, the eldest of whom was only fourteen when Petheram died on 18 December 1858 at 94 High Holborn, 'harassed in mind as well as body' (*The Bookseller*, 24 Feb 1859), suffering from typhus fever and pulmonary disease. Sales of his general books took place on 18 February 1859, and his extensive stock of old music books on 28 March, both dispersals handled by Southgate and Barrett. There seems to have been little left over to support his young family.

ALAN BELL and JOANNE POTIER

Sources diaries, 1831–2, and 1834–5, Bodl. Oxf., MSS Lyell · Bodl. Oxf., MSS Phillipps · T. A. Birrell, 'The making of a bookseller: the journals of John Petheram (1807–1858)', *Bodleian Library Record*, 15 (1996), 455–67 · K. Thomson, introduction, in J. Petheram, *An historical sketch of the progress and present state of Anglo-Saxon literature in England* (2000) · Boase, *Mod. Eng. biog.* · W. Maskell, *A history of the Martin Marprelate controversy* (1845) · *Publishers' Circular* (31 Dec 1858) · Allibone, *Dict.* · d. cert. · *The Bookseller* (24 Feb 1859)

Archives Bodl. Oxf., diaries

Wealth at death under £1500: administration, 15 Feb 1859, *CGPLA Eng. & Wales*

Pethick-Lawrence. For this title name *see* Lawrence, Emmeline Pethick-, Lady Pethick-Lawrence (1867–1954); Lawrence, Frederick William Pethick-, Baron Pethick-Lawrence (1871–1961).

Petillius Cerialis [Petillius Cerialis Caesius Rufus], **Quintus** (*fl. c.*AD 60–*c.*74), Roman governor of Britain, was related by marriage to the emperor Vespasian, almost certainly as the husband of Vespasian's only daughter, Flavia Domitilla. The consul of AD 83, Quintus Petillius Rufus, is generally considered to be his son from a previous marriage; another possible son is a senator called Petillius Firmus, who came from Arretium (Arezzo)—if the conjectured relationship is correct, this was Cerialis's home town. From the presumed marriage with Domitilla there was a daughter of the same names as her mother. Cerialis's presumed father, Petillius Rufus, was a senator in the reign of Tiberius, when 'he stooped to a shameful deed in the hope of becoming consul, but later met his just deserts' (Tacitus, *Annals*, iv.68 ff). This story in the *Annals*, combined with the tone of numerous references in the *Histories* and the account in *Annals* xiv. of Cerialis's conduct in AD 60, suggests that Tacitus heartily disliked

Cerialis, the former chief of his own father-in-law, Agricola. In the fashion of the time, Cerialis himself had two extra names, which indicate kinship with a family of Caesii. One of his predecessors as legate of the ninth legion, Caesius Nasica, might well have been a kinsman.

Cerialis's first known appointment was as legate of the ninth at the time of the great rebellion in AD 60 or 61. After the destruction of the Roman capital, Camulodunum (Colchester), by Queen Boudicca's forces, Cerialis, 'coming to help, was routed and his infantry was slaughtered; he himself with the cavalry escaped to his base [presumably Longthorpe near Peterborough], where he was protected by the fortifications', according to Tacitus, who further described his defeat as 'a disaster' (*clades*) (Tacitus, *Annals*, xiv.32). The ninth legion had to be brought up to strength after the revolt by the dispatch of two thousand men from the Rhine army. In spite of this débâcle, Cerialis had 'a not inglorious military reputation' (Tacitus, *Histories*, iii.59) nine years later (his activity in the intervening years is unknown), when he was chosen to command a special force of one thousand cavalry in the Flavian advance guard's assault on Rome in December of AD 69, the so-called 'year of the four emperors'. Further reasons for his selection, mentioned by Tacitus, were his kinship with Vespasian and his local knowledge, suggesting that he had property in Etruria or Umbria (which accords with the probable origin at Arretium). As it turned out, he bungled the task, being heavily defeated by the Vitellians in the outskirts of Rome and failing to prevent the burning of the Capitol, 'the most shameful deed in the history of Rome' (Tacitus, *Histories*, iii.72). Shortly afterwards, when a delegation from the senate arrived to negotiate, Cerialis was unable to prevent his men from mishandling the senators.

No doubt because of his kinship with Vespasian, Cerialis was none the less within a few weeks given an important new mission. He was made consul (presumably *in absentia*) or perhaps simply given the rank of ex-consul, the necessary qualification for appointment as governor and commander-in-chief of the Lower German army, with the task of suppressing the dangerous revolt of the Batavians and other German or north Gallic peoples. His operations in the Rhineland are described in detail by Tacitus in his *Histories*. A famous speech before an assembly of rebellious Gauls, put in the mouth of Cerialis, who begins with the immortal phrase 'neque ego umquam facundiam exercui' ('unaccustomed as I am to public speaking'; Tacitus, *Histories*, iv.73), has been called the finest justification of Roman imperialism ever written. There is of course no guarantee that it represents anything that Cerialis himself actually said. He is also given some credit for his tactful handling of the embarrassing attempt by Vespasian's younger son, Domitian, then only nineteen, to assume command of the campaign. But in general the impression conveyed is that Cerialis succeeded rather by good luck than by good generalship. On one occasion he narrowly escaped capture by the enemy, who seized the flagship of the Rhine flotilla during the night in the belief that the Roman commander was on board. However, Cerialis 'was sharing a bed on land with an Ubian woman, named Claudia Sacrata' (as Tacitus drily reports in *Histories*, v.22). The final outcome of the campaign is not recorded; the last surviving page of Tacitus's account has Cerialis negotiating on an island with the rebel leader Julius Civilis in the second half of AD 70. Cerialis's settlement evidently guaranteed the maintenance of certain privileges for the Batavians, whose fighting qualities continued to be highly prized by Rome, in return for them laying down their arms.

Cerialis proceeded straight from the northern Rhineland to take over the governorship of Britain from Marcus Vettius Bolanus, who had been struggling to keep the peace with a diminished garrison. Cerialis brought extra troops and at once began a forward policy, aimed at subduing the Brigantes of the Pennines, who had overthrown their pro-Roman ruler, Cartimandua (Bolanus had had to rescue the queen), and were now openly hostile under her ex-husband, Venutius. The archaeological record shows that Cerialis established bases at Eburacum (York) for his old legion, the ninth, and a forward post at Luguvalium (Carlisle); he probably penetrated into southern Scotland as well. The other legions were now based at Lindum (Lincoln), at Viroconium (Wroxter) or Deva (Chester), and at Isca (Caerleon). Cerialis's governorship of Britain is only briefly described by Tacitus, in the *Agricola*, the sole source. He is said to have overrun, if not to have completely conquered, the Brigantes; and Gnaeus Julius Agricola, serving under Cerialis as legate of the twentieth legion, had the opportunity for gaining distinction, even if 'the glory had to be reserved for his chief' (Tacitus, *Agricola*, 17). Cerialis had probably been replaced by the summer of AD 73; he was at any rate back at Rome by the spring of 74, when he held a second consulship (the record of which is the sole evidence for his full names). Nothing is heard of him thereafter. That the consul of AD 83, Quintus Petillius Rufus, Cerialis's presumed son, was one of the first consular colleagues of the new emperor Domitian (*r.* AD 81–96), suggests that the family enjoyed that ruler's favour, at least initially. But Cerialis's presumed daughter, Domitilla, a niece of Domitian, was married to the emperor's cousin Titus Flavius Clemens, who was executed in AD 95; and Cerialis and his family seem to have disappeared from the scene by the early second century, for the poet Martial refers to the 'Petillian mansion' (Martial, *Epigrams*, xii.57, 19) at Rome as the residence of another senator at this time.   A. R. BIRLEY

Sources C. Tacitus, *The histories [and] the annals*, ed. and trans. C. H. Moore and J. Jackson, 2 (1931) · C. Tacitus, *The histories [and] the annals*, ed. and trans. C. H. Moore and J. Jackson, 1 (1925) · Tacitus, *Agricola*, ed. and trans. M. Mutton (1914), 8, 17 · A. R. Birley, 'Petillius Cerialis and the conquest of Brigantia', *Britannia*, 4 (1973), 179–90 · A. R. Birley, *The fasti of Roman Britain* (1981)

Petit, Sir Dinshaw Manockjee, first baronet (1823–1901), cotton merchant and philanthropist in India, was born at Bombay on 30 June 1823, the elder of two sons of Manockjee Nasarwanji Petit (1803–1859), a Parsi merchant, and his wife, Bai Humabai (1809–1851), daughter of J. D. Mooghna. In 1805 his grandfather, Nasarwanji Cowasjee Bomanjee,

Sir Dinshaw Manockjee Petit, first baronet (1823–1901), by unknown photographer

migrated from Surat to Bombay, where he acted as agent to French vessels and those of the East India Company. On account of his small stature, his French clients gave him the cognomen of Petit, and, in accordance with Parsi custom, this, pronounced in the English manner, became the family surname. Dinshaw was educated in Bombay. He went, at the age of nine, to a school run by a pensioned sergeant named Sykes, and later to a more ambitious seminary kept by messrs Mainwaring and Corbet. At the age of seventeen he became a clerk on a monthly salary of 15 rupees (then the equivalent of £1 10s.) in the mercantile office of Dirom, Richmond & Co., of which his father was Indian manager. He married on 27 February 1837 Sakerbai (*d.* 1890), daughter of Framjee Bhikhajee Panday, of Bombay, and they had three sons and eight daughters. Subsequently his father built up a large broker's business, in which Dinshaw and his younger brother, Nasarwanjee, became partners in 1852, carrying it on after their father's death in May 1859 until 1864, when they divided a fortune of about Rs 2.5 million and separated by mutual consent.

Meanwhile Dinshaw inaugurated the cotton manufacturing industry which made Bombay the Manchester of India. A cotton mill was started for the first time in Bombay in 1854 by another Parsi, Cowasjee Nanabhai Davur, but it spun yarns only. In 1855 Dinshaw persuaded his father to erect a similar mill with additional machinery for weaving cloth. This mill commenced work as the Oriental Spinning and Weaving Mill in 1857. In 1860 he and his brother started the Manockjee Petit mill, which they converted into a joint-stock company.

The problems encountered by the Lancashire cotton industry during the cotton famine of 1861–5 encouraged wild speculation in Bombay, but Dinshaw Petit maintained his self-control and reaped colossal gains. Other mills were soon built by him, or came under his management, and he led the way in the manufacture of hosiery, damask, other fancy cloths, sewing thread, and also in machine dyeing on a large scale. Before his death he had the major shareholding in six joint-stock mills, aggregating nearly a quarter of a million spindles and 2340 looms, and employing 10,000 workers. He was thus mainly responsible for the conversion of the town and island of Bombay into a great industrial centre.

In addition to his entrepreneurial activities, Dinshaw Petit played a prominent role in early nationalist politics in Bombay. He was a founder member of the influential Bombay Presidency Association in 1869 and became its president in 1883. In 1888 the association split, with radicals supporting the newly formed Indian National Congress, and moderates, including Petit and most of the Parsi merchant community, maintaining a more pro-British stance.

Dinshaw Petit was also a co-founder of the powerful Bombay Mill-Owners' Association in 1874, of which he became chairman from 1878 until 1883. This body, composed, unusually, of both Indian and European businessmen, was formed to represent employers' views on industrial relations. Petit had conservative opinions on this subject and opposed the introduction of factory legislation to regulate the Bombay mill industry in 1875.

Dinshaw Petit served on the board of the Bank of Bombay; he was a justice of the peace for the city, and for a short time a member of the municipal corporation; he was sheriff of the city, 1886–7. He served on the legislative council of the governor-general, 1886–8, being the first Parsi to receive that honour. Knighted in February 1887, he was created a baronet of the United Kingdom on 1 September 1890, with special limitation to his second son. Petit was the second native Indian to receive this hereditary title, the first being Sir Jamsetjee Jeejeebhoy.

Throughout western India, Dinshaw Petit showed public spirit in the disposal of his great wealth. He arranged for the housing of the Bombay technical institute—a memorial of Queen Victoria's jubilee of 1887—in the manufacturing district of the city. He founded the Petit Hospital for Women and Children; gave 100,000 rupees (equivalent to nearly £7000) towards building a home for lepers; erected a hospital for animals as a memorial to his wife; and presented property both in Bombay and Poona for research laboratories. A devout Parsi, he was always attentive to the claims of his own community, and in various places where small colonies of them were to be found, he erected for their use fire temples and towers of silence (places for the disposal of the dead).

Petit died at his Bombay residence, Petit Hall, on 5 May 1901, and his remains were committed to the towers of silence, Hill, the same day. At the *oothumna*, or third day obsequies, charities were announced amounting to Rs 638,551. Petit's second son, Framjee Dinshaw, on whom the baronetcy had been entailed, predeceased his father on 8 August 1895, and his eldest son, Jeejeebhoy Framjee (*b.* 7 June 1873), became second baronet under the name of Sir Dinshaw Manockjee Petit.

F. H. Brown, rev. A.-M. Misra

Sources *Times of India* (6 May 1901) • C. E. Dobbin, *Urban leadership in western India: politics and communities in Bombay city, 1840–1885* (1972) • A. Seal, *The emergence of Indian nationalism: competition and collaboration in the later nineteenth century* (1968) • G. Johnson, *Provincial politics and Indian nationalism: Bombay and the Indian National Congress, 1880–1915* (1973) • S. D. Mehta, *The cotton mills of India, 1854–1954* (1954) • R. H. Jalbhoy, *The portrait gallery of western India*, 1st edn (1886)
Likenesses J. Linton, portrait, after 1901 (posthumous); last known at Petit Hall, Bombay, India, 1912 • T. Brock, marble statue, 1912, Bombay, India • photograph, NPG [*see illus.*]
Wealth at death charities at death totalled Rs638,551 (£42,270)

Petit, John Lewis (1736–1780). *See under* Petit, John Louis (1801–1868).

Petit, John Louis (1801–1868), architectural historian and watercolour painter, was born on 31 May 1801 in Ashton under Lyne, Lancashire, the only son of John Hayes Petit (1771–1822), a Church of England clergyman and JP, and his wife, Harriet Astley.

The family was descended from Lewis *Petit, also known as Lewis Petit des Etans (1665?–1720), a Huguenot refugee and military engineer. Petit's grandfather was **John Lewis Petit** (1736–1780), the son of John Petit of Little Aston Hall, Shenstone, Staffordshire. He graduated from Queens' College, Cambridge (BA 1756, MA 1759, and MD 1766), was elected fellow of the College of Physicians in 1767, was Gulstonian lecturer in 1768, and was censor in that year, 1774, and 1777. From 1770 to 1774 he was physician to St George's Hospital, then on the death of Dr Anthony Askew in 1774 he was elected physician to St Bartholomew's Hospital. In November 1769 he married Katherine Laetitia Serces, the daughter of one of the preachers of the French Chapel Royal in London. He died on 27 May 1780 and was buried at St Anne's, Soho.

John Louis Petit was educated at Eton College and contributed to *The Etonian*, then in its heyday. He was elected to a scholarship at Trinity College, Cambridge, in 1822, and graduated BA in 1823 and MA in 1826. On 17 June 1828 he married Louisa Elizabeth, the daughter of George Reid of Trelawny, Jamaica. He had been ordained deacon in 1824 and priest the year after, but it was not until 1840 that he took up his sole church appointment, as curate of Bradfield in Essex, which he held until 1848. By this time he had written and illustrated several works of architectural history, the main occupation of his career.

Petit had shown a taste for sketching in his early years and he made many hundreds of drawings in pencil and ink. These were often finished in watercolour, though in a limited palette. His favourite subject was old buildings, particularly churches, and he spent much time visiting and sketching them. His drawings were rapidly and adeptly executed on the spot, his style in the tradition of English topographical watercolour painters of the previous generation, such as Samuel Prout (1783–1852).

Although his works display an instinct for the picturesque setting and the telling viewpoint, his aim was less to produce finished paintings for their own sake than to record historic buildings and architectural details. Many were reproduced in his profusely illustrated books. He occasionally painted in oils. In almost all of these respects he resembles John Ruskin (1819–1900), whose concern for the conservation of old buildings was Petit's too.

In 1839 Petit made his first extensive tour on the continent, which informed his *Remarks on Church Architecture* (1841), part travelogue, part discursive survey of architectural styles since the Roman. Subsequent works provide more detailed analyses of individual buildings, including Tewkesbury Abbey, Sherborne Abbey, and Southwell Minster. Petit's credentials as an antiquary are reflected in his co-founding of the British Archaeological Institute in 1844 and his elections as fellow of the Society of Antiquaries and honorary member of the Institute of British Architects. He lectured to the Oxford society for promoting the study of Gothic architecture, a body which mirrored the Cambridge Camden Society and whose membership similarly took a deep interest in the way churches old and new should be laid out and used. This Oxford connection was fruitful academically for Petit, who was admitted to the university *ad eundem* in 1850, and personally too, as his sister, Maria, married a classics don, William *Jelf (1811–1875), in 1849. *Architectural Studies in France*, Petit's principal work, appeared in 1854 (new edition 1890). It is a detailed survey of French Gothic, profusely illustrated by Petit and by his companion on the research tour, Philip Delamotte (1820/21–1889), an artist, engraver, and early exponent of photography. Petit does not seem to have used photography for recording buildings; nevertheless, some of the illustrations were reproduced using a new technique, that of anastatic drawing.

Petit's books come from a rich period in England for research, publication, and debate on architectural history. His writing style was accessible and the illustrations attractive, but he lacked the intellectual rigour of others in the field, such as his Cambridge contemporaries William Whewell (1794–1866) and Robert Willis (1800–1875). His judgements could be shaky and, with his genteel admiration of almost anything old, he could elicit harsh reviews at a time when attitudes were hardening in favour of particular styles as models for revival. While he had a taste for the Romanesque, for example, just before it became fashionable as a style for new churches in the 1840s, he did not make himself its champion. He was not a polemicist like A. W. N. Pugin or George Gilbert Scott; besides, he had a distaste for debates that smacked of religious controversy. This was the tendency from the 1840s, particularly in the pages of *The Ecclesiologist*, the organ of the Cambridge Camden Society.

When Petit did turn his attention to contemporary architectural practice, he encountered spirited opposition. In 1841 Scott's designs for the remodelling of St Mary's, Stafford, were exhibited. This was a church close to Petit's heart (his brother-in-law was a benefactor) and

he objected in writing to the proposal for the thorough-going redesign of the south transept. He could accept Scott's interventions elsewhere in the building but not so the replacement of Gothic fabric, albeit sixteenth-century. Scott accepted the principle but argued that it could be ignored if the style was 'debased'. Their debate by correspondence was eventually put to a panel of experts from the Cambridge Camden Society and the Oxford society noted above. Scott won and Petit gamely published the papers.

As galling was the reception of Petit's only executed architectural design. His sister and brother-in-law moved to Cae'rdeon, near Barmouth, Merioneth, in 1854. Jelf took exception to the fact that most of the services in the Anglican parish church were said in Welsh, so in 1862 he asked his brother-in-law to design him a church, to be built at his own expense, where he could officiate in English. Petit designed him a rugged and muscular church for the mountainous setting. *The Ecclesiologist* lambasted it in a pithy review, attacking the design on practical grounds (roof pitches too shallow) and on theoretical grounds (pilasters for show, not structural necessity). The critic is clearly exasperated that Petit preferred picturesque effect to the application of formal principles: the alpine-style stone hut is simply not appropriate for an Anglican church on a turnpike road. There may also be a difference of churchmanship here. Petit and Jelf (for all his belligerence on the language issue) had avoided the febrile excesses of the Oxford Movement. Happily, St Philip Cae'rdeon still stands, somewhat altered but recently repaired.

During 1864–5 Petit travelled to Syria, Palestine, and Egypt. He continued to draw and paint avidly. He died in Lichfield on 1 December 1868 from a cold caught or aggravated while out sketching, and was buried in St Michael's churchyard. An exhibition of 339 of his sketches, including two views of the church at Cae'rdeon, was shown by the Architectural Exhibition Society in London during 1869. That year also saw the posthumous publication of a volume of his poetry.

Sir Nikolaus Pevsner gives a characteristically pungent account of Petit in his survey of nineteenth-century architectural writers. As an artist, his modest talent was given almost unlimited scope, producing a corpus of architectural impressions which is impressive, if slight as individual works of art. As a critic of contemporary practice, he is probably most significant as a spokesman for tolerance: he valued buildings and styles of many eras and favoured, if not consistently or dogmatically, repair over rebuilding.   GUY BRAITHWAITE

Sources Venn, *Alum. Cant.* · N. Pevsner, *Some architectural writers of the nineteenth century* (1972) · C. Miele, 'Re-presenting the Church Militant', *'A Church as it should be': the Cambridge Camden Society and its influence*, ed. C. Webster and J. Elliott (2000), esp. 274–6 · P. Howell, 'Church and chapel in Wales', *The Victorian church, architecture and society*, ed. C. Brooks and A. Saint (1995), 118–32, esp. 127 · *The Ecclesiologist*, new ser., 123 (Dec 1863), 374–5 · A. Hartshorne, *The Architect* (2 Jan 1869) · *Proceedings of the Society of Antiquaries of London*, 2nd ser., 4 (1867–70), 305 · *Architectural Exhibition Society catalogue of sketches* (1869) [V&A NAL catalogues collection, shelfmark

200.B.6] • R. L. Brown, 'Mr Jelf's proprietary chapel at a Welsh watering-place', *Journal of the Merioneth Historical and Records Society*, 12 (1994), 43–51
Archives RIBA BAL, lectures
Wealth at death under £25,000: resworn probate, Aug 1870, *CGPLA Eng. & Wales* (1869)

Petit, Lewis [Lewis Petit des Etans] (1665?–1720), military engineer and army officer, was (according to notes made by his descendant John Louis *Petit) a member of the family of Petit des Etans of Caen in Normandy, but rarely used the toponym. He arrived in England after the revocation of the edict of Nantes in 1685, and entered the service of the Board of Ordnance. He served with the ordnance train in Ireland from 19 June 1691 until the following May, when he was employed in the ordnance train with the Channel Fleet on the summer expeditions of 1692 and 1693. These attacks against the French coast produced little result, and in July 1693, having landed at Ostend, the train took part in the capture of Furnes, Dixmude, and Ghent. On 1 April 1697 Petit was appointed an engineer on the English establishment and may have been on half-pay until, in May 1700, he was warranted to fill a vacancy on the peace train, so called because the existence of a train of artillery in peacetime was a novelty. At about this time, perhaps in 1698, Petit married Marianne, daughter of John Meslin of Glatigny in Normandy.

Early campaigns in the War of the Spanish Succession In 1702 Petit served as engineer with the train that accompanied the expedition to Cadiz and subsequently to Vigo. He was among the engineers in the ordnance train created by royal warrant dated 24 July 1703 to proceed to Portugal in support of the pretensions of the archduke Charles of Austria to the Spanish throne, in opposition to the French-born Philip V, of the Bourbon dynasty. In 1704 he was present at Portalegre as engineer and was taken prisoner when James Fitzjames, duke of Berwick, commanding the Bourbon forces, laid siege and captured it. Henri Massue de Ruvigny, earl of Galway, complaining of the difficulty of finding good engineers, wrote on 30 November 1704 that Petit was very capable, and ought to be among the first to be exchanged and returned to Portugal. Petit was with the ordnance train arriving at Gibraltar in mid-February 1705.

The siege of Gibraltar was raised by the end of April and Petit was appointed chief engineer of the ordnance train accompanying the forces directed against Barcelona under Charles Mordaunt, third earl of Peterborough. The fleet arrived before Barcelona on 22 August. The outlying fort of Montjuic capitulated on 18 September. The attack on the town itself began with Petit erecting batteries on the side previously protected by the guns of Montjuic, ordnance from the fleet being hauled up from the beach by seamen. Eight guns and three mortars opened fire on 24 September, and four days later the whole complement of fifty-eight were in action. Petit was slightly wounded on 25 September but was out of action only briefly. His ceaseless energy was rewarded when on 3 October a breach was made and the following day negotiations for the capitulation began.

The loss of Barcelona was keenly felt in Versailles and Madrid, where preparations were made to mount a massive expeditionary force by land and sea to recover it. Peterborough had dispersed his forces across Catalunya leaving the fortress of Barcelona with a garrison of 1400 men and a small ordnance train under Petit, though the garrison was augmented at the last moment. In the first days of April 1706 the besiegers, amounting to 21,000 men, with King Philip and Marshal Tessé at their head, had surrounded the city. Petit had exerted himself in repairing and strengthening the defences, including Montjuic, where the Bourbon attack commenced on 4 April. After heavy fighting, on 25 April the garrison of Montjuic was forced to withdraw into Barcelona, leaving the fort to Tessé and his forces. Within a few days guns were playing on the walls of the town and breaches were soon made. Petit now constructed retrenchments to isolate the weak points. On 3 May the besiegers began mining operations which Petit met with countermines, blowing in the enemy's galleries and checking their advance. Nevertheless, matters were now desperate for the defenders and only the arrival on 8 May of the van of a relieving squadron from Lisbon caused the siege to be lifted.

The two sieges established Petit's reputation as a resourceful engineer and an officer of spirit. James Stanhope later referred to Petit's 'eminent services in both sieges of Barcelona the good success of which may chiefly be imparted to him' (Stanhope of Chevening MSS, U1590 O132/1, Centre for Kentish Studies, Maidstone, Kent). Archduke Charles, who had been present throughout the second siege, wrote to Queen Anne praising Petit's zeal and application, and appointed him his chief engineer. Petit was present at the disastrous allied defeat at Almanza on 25 April 1707 when the earl of Galway was overcome by a much superior force. Galway sent away the ordnance train ahead of his own retreat and it arrived safely at Valencia. Galway apparently conferred on Petit the rank of 'premier ingenieur en Espagne' with effect from 1 May 1707.

On 11 May the field train from Almanza arrived at Tortosa where Petit, now promoted colonel, was directed to put the works into condition to withstand a siege. Tortosa was attacked on 11 June 1708 when the duke of Orléans invested it with a force of 22,000 men. A spirited defence and heavy French casualties were insufficient to defer the inevitable surrender of the town on 10 July. Petit had been energetic in the defence and was conducted to Barcelona with the rest of the garrison under the terms of the capitulation. By the end of July he was at Tarragona.

Minorca At the end of August, Petit joined Stanhope, now in command in Spain, as chief engineer on the expedition to capture the island of Minorca. An allied force sailed from Barcelona on 3 September, met Admiral Sir John Leake off Minorca, and effected a landing. The unfortified town of Mahón submitted immediately, as did the remainder of the island. Resistance would come only from the fortress of St Philip's Castle, a substantial stronghold commanding the entrance to Port Mahón. The greatest problem for Petit was to transport the siege equipment from the landing place to the vicinity of St Philip's. By 23 September the guns had been brought up and emplacements were begun. On 28 September they began to fire and within five hours some of the defenders' guns were put out of action, at which Stanhope ordered a general advance. The besiegers gained a strong position near the fortress, and on the following day the French governor sent to ask for terms. On 30 September Stanhope, who could hardly have expected so easy a victory, marched into St Philip's.

Stanhope established Petit in command of the new possession, his eventual appointment by royal warrant being as 'lieutenant-governor of the town and garrison of Port Mahon … and of the castles, forts and all other military works and fortifications thereunto belonging' (PRO, SP 44/173, 74). Stanhope conferred the civil governorship of the island on a Spanish adherent of Archduke Charles to buttress the pretence that Minorca was held by the archduke as Carlos III of Spain, while Petit's warrant specifically commanded him to admit none but her majesty's own troops into the garrison and forts belonging to it. No doubt Petit's profession made him particularly suitable to command, for Stanhope had ambitious projects in mind for the fortification of Port Mahón.

Stanhope next gave Petit the rank of brigadier in the archduke's service. Petit was also made inspector-general of the fortifications, her majesty's chief engineer, paymaster of the works, commissary of the train, and furnisher of bread for the garrison, and in addition he was chief engineer for Archduke Charles. His emoluments amounted to £2 10s. a day.

Stanhope soon returned to Barcelona leaving Petit with the urgent task of measuring and costing the extensive projects for fortifications they had discussed. Work on the fortifications was funded by Stanhope from the extraordinaries of the war, and regular payments were sent to Petit throughout 1709. His first project was to build a 30-gun battery commanding the mouth of the harbour and linked to St Philip's. The estimates for enlarging St Philip's totalled about £100,000. Money ran out in the middle of 1710, when work slowed considerably.

Petit somehow found time to enter into commercial speculations on his own account. In partnership with two Spaniards and Stanhope's secretary Arent Furley, Petit purchased a French prize at Mahón for 7800 dollars with which to trade between Minorca, Majorca, Sardinia, and the Spanish and Barbary coasts. He advised Furley that he had found it necessary to use funds supplied for the fortifications to complete the purchase, and urgently requested capital from his partners to repay this misappropriation. Petit's participation was valuable to the enterprise owing to his ability to land cargoes at Mahón without paying duty, an activity much objected to by the local town government.

In May 1711 John Campbell, second duke of Argyll, arrived in Spain as commander-in-chief. It marked a sea change in Petit's fortunes. Argyll never acknowledged Petit's rank of brigadier, it being a foreign commission,

and in little more than a fortnight of his arrival at Barcelona and before having set foot in Minorca he wrote: 'I am more and more dissatisfied every day with Colonel Petit's behaviour at Port Mahon and am therefore resolved to put Colonel Farmer … in his place of Lieutenant Governour of Mahon' (Argyll to Earl Poulett, 17 June 1711, CUL, Add. MS 6570). Argyll objected that Petit had accepted a commission as lieutenant-governor from the king of Spain and made use of the Spanish colours, though such matters were approved by Stanhope. However, the replacement of Petit as lieutenant-governor was delayed until, as Argyll put it, 'our affairs are in less disorder'.

Petit was soon to find himself under the scrutiny of the inspectors sent from London to investigate irregularities in the expenditure of the army in Spain, as an attempt to disgrace the previous ministry. Stanhope was foremost in their sights, but Petit, having had at his discretion the disposal of such large sums, inevitably figured largely in the inquiry. The accusations against him concerned imperfections in his accounts, including allegations of missing vouchers, irregularities, and overcharging in the numbers of workmen and mules, and alleged differences between prices contracted and prices paid, among other charges. Petit was at the commissioners' disposal for these investigations from 26 January 1712, which he gives as the date of his supersession by Argyll, until 20 November following when he left for England. His accounts remained unresolved until July 1726, six years after his death. Adjustments in favour of the commissioners were small; few of the accusations against him stuck.

Later career and death Petit returned to England via France, landing in late November at Toulon, where he had a brother. His journey overland to Paris and the channel ports was tracked by the French authorities, who were aware of his identity. He next headed the list of engineers for home service dated 14 May 1714. In September he was sent to advise on the state of the works at Fort William and the other forts and castles in Scotland. Returning to London on 24 November, he laid his report before the board. In August 1715 he was ordered to Portsmouth to assist in putting it into a proper posture of defence. On 27 November a warrant was issued for the formation of an ordnance train for Scotland and Petit was appointed chief engineer, but the Jacobite rising was soon over and the train arrived too late for active service. After the rebellion Petit surveyed the head of Loch Ness for a fort, and he was in Scotland until the summer of 1716.

On 3 July 1716 a warrant was issued appointing Petit chief engineer at Minorca in the place of Brigadier Peter Durand, who had died there the previous December. Petit's Minorca accounts for 1708 to 1712, which had been investigated, remained outstanding in the hands of the Treasury: certain debts he had contracted in connection with the fortifications at Mahón had not been settled. Petit could not go to Minorca while these matters were pending. A royal warrant was issued on 5 September 1717 authorizing the auditor to make up and pass his accounts, but with no immediate result. On 22 April of that year Petit had become director of engineers at Minorca at 20s. a day. He eventually proceeded to the island in 1718, and work at St Philip's commenced by his authority on 21 June. On 18 November 1718 a royal warrant was issued appointing him lieutenant-governor of Fort St Philip. In the absence of the governor and lieutenant-governor of Minorca the command devolved on him, as occurred for a period in 1719.

Petit went to Naples in January 1720, but whether for his health or seeking materials for the works at Mahón is uncertain. He died in Naples on or after 24 May 1720 (the date of his will)—and probably before the end of May as he was not paid thereafter. He was buried in Naples, and survived by his wife. Petit also left two sons, John Peter (1699–1747) and Peter John (1700–1768), who were captains in regiments of foot and sub-engineers and who served at Minorca under their father from 1718 and for a period after his death; and four daughters, Henrietta, Judith, Susanna, and Clara. John Lewis Petit (1736–1780) and John Louis Petit (1801–1868) were descendants.

PAUL LATCHAM

Sources J. Armstrong, History of the island of Minorca (1752) · The answers of several persons concerned in the report of the commissioners sent into Spain (1714) · J. W. S. Conolly, 'Notitia historica of the corps of royal engineers, c.1860', MS, Royal Engineers Corps Library, Chatham, Kent · C. Dalton, George the First's army, 1714–1727, 2 vols. (1910–12) · F. Fornals, Castillo de San Felipe del Puerto de Mahón: siglos XVI–XVII–XVIII (Mahón, 1996) · A. D. Francis, The First Peninsular War, 1702–1713 (1975) · D. Gregory, Minorca, the illusory prize (1990) · J. J. Howard, ed., Miscellanea Genealogica et Heraldica, new ser., 4 (1884), 13–15 · B. Laurie, Life of Richard Kane (1994) · M. Mata, Menorca: Franceses, Ingleses, y la Guerra de Sucesión (Mahón, 1980) · M. Mata, Menorca Británica: pugna, pasividad y progreso (Mahón, 1994) · A. Parnell, The war of the succession in Spain during the reign of Queen Anne, 1702–1711 (1888); repr. (1905) · W. Porter, History of the corps of royal engineers, 2 vols. (1889) · J. Sloss, Richard Kane, governor of Minorca (1995) · P. H. Stanhope, History of the war of the succession in Spain (1836) · N. Taubman, Memoirs of the British fleets and squadrons in the Mediterranean, anno 1708 and 1709 (1710) · B. Williams, Stanhope: a study in eighteenth-century war and diplomacy (1932) · accounts, PRO, AO1/2521/620 [L. Petit] · correspondence relating to Minorca, PRO, CO 174/15 [L. Petit] · report on the petition of Raymondo Canter about payments due to him from Brigadier Petit, 1727, PRO, PC 1/4/60 · secretary of state entry books, military, 1706–1714, PRO, SP 44/173 · state papers foreign, Spain, 1712, PRO, SP 94/79 · secretary of state's letter book, 1721–1727, PRO, SP 104/132 · papers of the commissioners for inspecting the accounts of the allied army in Spain, Portugal, and Italy during the War of the Spanish Succession, 1708–1713, PRO, SP 109/1 · minutes of the board of ordnance, PRO, WO 47/27–33 · ordnance office entry books and papers, PRO, WO 55/133–43, 348 · Duke of Argyll, letter book, CUL, Add. MS 6570 · correspondence with J. Stanhope, CKS, Stanhope of Chevening papers, 01590, 0132, 0137, 1038, 1039, 0140, 0142

Archives CKS, corresp. with James Stanhope · CUL, duke of Argyll letter-book · NL Scot., surveys · PRO, accounts, AO 1/2521/620 · PRO, corresp. relating to Minorca, CO 174/1 · PRO, corresp., secretary of state entry books, military, SP 44/173 · PRO, corresp., state papers foreign, SP 94/79 · PRO, corresp., secretary of state's letter-book, SP104/132 · PRO, corresp., papers of commissioners for inspecting accounts of allied army in Spain, Portugal, and Italy during War of Spanish Succession, SP 109/1 · PRO, corresp., minutes of the board of ordnance, WO 47/27–33 · PRO, corresp., ordnance office entry books and papers, WO 55/133–43, 348

Wealth at death over £1300: will, PRO, PROB, 11/576, fols. 314r–314v

Petit, Thomas. See Petyt, Thomas (b. in or before 1494, d. 1565/6).

Petit, William (d. 1213), justiciar of Ireland, was a follower of Hugh de Lacy, first lord of Meath (d. 1186), and probably went over to Ireland with him in 1171. Between 1184 and 1186 Lacy granted him the barony of Magheradernon in Westmeath and Mullingar became the chief Petit manor. Lacy also granted him land in the barony of Shrule in Longford and Rathkenny and possibly Dunboyne in Meath. Petit's subsequent grants of land in Westmeath and Meath to the houses of St Mary, Dublin, and Llanthony in Gloucester were made for Lacy's soul. Between 1206 and 1210 Petit was also granted Dromin and part of Dromiskin in Louth by the archbishop of Armagh.

In 1185 Petit defeated an Irish force raiding Meath and killed its leader Máel Sechlainn Mac Lochlainn, king of Cenél nEógain. He served as justiciar of Ireland in the early 1190s. On 26 March 1204 he was appointed, with three others, to hear the complaint of Meiler fitz Henry, justiciar of Ireland, against William de Burgh. On 20 March 1208 he was sent by John with messages to the justiciar of Ireland. On 28 June 1210 Petit appeared at Dublin, with others, as a messenger from Walter de Lacy, second lord of Meath, praying the king to relax his ire and suffer Walter to approach his presence. This plea was unsuccessful and Meath was taken into the king's hands. Before 1210 Petit had served as constable of Meath for Lacy and subsequently served as steward of Meath on the king's behalf. In 1211 he was again justiciar and, along with Simon de Rochefort, bishop of Meath, Master Gerard de Cusack, and his own brother Ralph Petit, archdeacon of Meath and from 1227 to 1230 bishop of Meath, he served as an arbitrator in the matter of the division of their Irish lands between the two houses of Llanthony. In 1212 he and other Irish barons supported John against Innocent III.

Petit died in 1213. His son was taken by King John as a hostage for Richard de Faipo. His widow in February 1215 offered 100 marks for liberty to remarry as she pleased, and for the replacement of her son as hostage by Faipo's own son. Many members of his family came with Petit to Ireland, including his brothers Ralph and Nicholas and his nephew Henry.

W. E. RHODES, rev. B. SMITH

Sources CClR · CPR · H. S. Sweetman and G. F. Handcock, eds., Calendar of documents relating to Ireland, 5 vols., PRO (1875–86) · J. T. Gilbert, ed., Chartularies of St Mary's Abbey, Dublin: with the register of its house at Dunbrody and annals of Ireland, 2 vols., Rolls Series, 80 (1884) · E. St J. Brooks, ed., The Irish cartularies of Llanthony prima and secunda, IMC (1953) · G. H. Orpen, Ireland under the Normans, 4 vols. (1911–20), vol. 2 · D. A. Chart, ed., The register of John Swayne, archbishop of Armagh and primate of Ireland, 1418–1439 (1935) · Giraldus Cambrensis, Expugnatio Hibernica / The conquest of Ireland, ed. and trans. A. B. Scott and F. X. Martin (1978)

Petiver, James (c.1665–1718), botanist and entomologist, was one of at least three sons and a daughter of James Petiver, of Hillmorton, near Rugby, Warwickshire (where James was born), and Mary, daughter of Richard Elborow. His father, a freeman of the Haberdashers' Company in London, died during Petiver's childhood and he and his younger brothers were sent to the grammar school at

Rugby at the expense of their mother's wealthy father. Already on the threshold of adolescence, he had the benefit of just one year there before entering an eight-year apprenticeship in 1677 to a prominent London apothecary. This select training he no doubt owed again to his grandfather's benevolence, but he was later to express regret at not having been allowed any further 'academical learning'.

After completing his apprenticeship Petiver set up in practice on his own account at White Cross Street, Aldersgate, which was also to be his home for the rest of his life. By then he had already formed a small collection of London plants, doubtless the result of attending the 'herbarizings' traditionally laid on by the Society of Apothecaries for apprentices. This seems soon to have developed into a broader passion for natural history, in which entomology enduringly competed with botany as his dominant concern. By as early as 1690 Petiver's reputation was such that he was in frequent correspondence with the country's leading naturalists and a member of a circle of fellow enthusiasts who met informally in and around London. Sir Hans Sloane later drew on this group in his attempt to reinvigorate the Royal Society by recruiting active investigators who were not necessarily highly educated. Petiver and his friend Samuel Doody were invited to one of the society's meetings in June 1693 and allowed to take part in the discussions, an experiment sufficiently well received to gain them election as fellows some two years later. Petiver fully justified Sloane's belief in him by taking an active part in the society's affairs in subsequent years, presenting it with numerous specimens, reading before it several papers, and communicating many letters from his correspondents. Later he was also elected to its council several times.

It seems that this attainment of learned eminence brought occupational advancement in its train, for in 1700, significantly with Sloane again as one of his sponsors, Petiver secured the prestigious appointment of apothecary to the Charterhouse. His ordinary practice also flourished, his meticulously kept prescription books revealing numerous London merchants among his patients. By 1706 he was affluent enough to have lent nearly £800 to a friend. A lifelong bachelor, without a family to support, he also had the good fortune at that point to be left a large sum by a wealthy uncle. The legacy, however, was never paid and the friend, too, went bankrupt, but severe though those reverses were they did not curtail his spending on his collections.

By 1697 Petiver's herbarium alone amounted, on his own reckoning, to between 5000 and 6000 specimens, and he was ready to start reaping some scientific acclaim for the huge investment of time and effort by describing in print some of the contents of the by then famous Museum Petiverianum. The first and most notable of what was to prove a stream of publications to that end appeared in parts in 1695–1703, each part comprising plates and descriptions of either 100 or 200 different animals, plants, shells, or fossils, accompanied by copious notes on contributors of the specimens (as well as cutting remarks on his

rival, Leonard Plukenet). This was followed by his *Gazophylacium naturae et artis* (1702–9), again in several parts, illustrating with folio plates a further large number of natural history items, in no order and in many cases based on very imperfect material. There were many shorter lists, catalogues, and directions for collecting, all privately printed, most apparently in short runs and many undated, evidently rushed out by Petiver as a means of keeping his correspondents busy on his behalf and assured that what they sent him was duly studied and of value. In 1707 this extraordinary industry even led to the production of a periodical, the *Monthly Miscellany*, which survived for several years. Throughout, Petiver was also writing to a great assortment of people in many parts of the world, often at considerable length. The copies he kept of these, now among the Sloane MSS, fill nine volumes and together with his catalogues are a precious source of information on the provenance of specimens and the identity of collectors.

For Petiver, acquisition was virtually all: he had scant inclination to document or arrange his collections with the care that they deserved. A large proportion of his plant specimens have lost such labels as they may have possessed and the labels that survive are often illegible and vague about localities. Many of the specimens, too, are so fragmentary as to be indeterminable. As Sloane was to remark, despairingly, Petiver 'put them into heaps … where they were many of them injured by dust, insects, rain, etc' (Sloane, vol. 2, introduction). One visiting savant from Germany, Zacharias von Uffenbach, found everything 'in prodigious confusion in one wretched cabinet and in boxes', with no proper attempt at display. To make matters worse, Petiver offered samples of his collections to wealthy connoisseurs at exorbitant prices and advertised for sale sets of named specimens (the first person known to have followed this later widespread practice). Allegedly, too, he abused his appointment (by 1709) as demonstrator to the Society of Apothecaries by exploiting its Chelsea garden remorselessly to enrich his personal herbarium.

Though the first to record many English plants and author of a work, in 1713–15, which usefully remedied the lack of plates in Ray's great *Historia plantarum*, it was in English entomology that Petiver made his most significant contribution to learning, a greater one indeed than anyone before except for Ray. His manuscripts are a primary source for the methods of collecting insects at that period and also provide a datum-line for the distribution of many species. By the time he and Ray were in correspondence, to great mutual benefit, in the mid-1690s, he had reared a large number of Lepidoptera, and his *Papilionum Britanniae icones* (1717), the first publication devoted exclusively to English butterflies, was to feature more than eighty of these.

Petiver's own travels were not extensive. In England he seems to have ventured no further than the midlands (in 1692, to visit his married sister), Bristol (in 1712), and Cambridge (in 1715, with his kinsman James Sherard). A projected trip to France probably came to nothing, but in 1711 the auction of Paul Hermann's collections took him on Sloane's behalf to the Netherlands, where he met Boerhaave and many other leading Dutch naturalists and had the degree of doctor of medicine conferred on him by the University of Leiden. On 15 October 1716 the younger James Bobart wrote to congratulate Petiver on his marriage, but no supporting evidence has come to light and it is possible that Bobart was misinformed. Early in 1717 serious illness rendered him incapable of any exertion and that August he made his will, bequeathing most of his possessions to his sister. He died at his home in White Cross Street in April 1718 and was buried in St Botolph, Aldersgate, London, on 10 April. On his death Sloane, who had already offered a reputed £4000 for the collections and manuscripts (his books were but few, according to William Sherard), achieved their purchase; the plants alone, filling over 100 volumes, constituted far and away the single largest acquisition of that hardly less acquisitive man. Sloane was also one of six physicians who paid Petiver the final, signal honour of acting as pall-bearers at his funeral. Petiver is commemorated in a genus of plants named after him by Plumier.

D. E. ALLEN

Sources R. P. Stearns, 'James Petiver, promoter of natural science, c. 1663–1718', *Proc. Amer. Antiq. Soc.*, new ser., 62 (1953), 243–365 · W. W. Newbould, appendix, in H. Trimen and W. T. Thiselton Dyer, *Flora of Middlesex* (1869), 379–86 · J. Britten and J. E. Dandy, eds., *The Sloane herbarium* (1958), 175–82 · J. Petiver, autobiography, 1713, BL, Sloane MS 3339, fol. 10 · R. Pulteney, *Historical and biographical sketches of the progress of botany in England*, 2 (1790), 31–43 · S. [J. E. Smith], 'Petiver, James', in A. Rees and others, *The cyclopaedia, or, Universal dictionary of arts, sciences, and literature*, 45 vols. (1819–20) · G. F. Frick and others, 'Botanical explorations and discoveries in colonial Maryland, 1688 to 1753', *Huntia*, 7 (1987), 5–59 · C. R. Broome and others, 'A 1698 Maryland florula by the London apothecary James Petiver (ca. 1663–1718)', *Huntia*, 7 (1987), 61–90 · R. S. Wilkinson, 'Early English entomological methods in the seventeenth and eighteenth centuries: part 1, to 1720', *Entomologist's Record*, 78 (1966), 143–51 · *London in 1710: from the travels of Zacharias Conrad von Uffenbach*, ed. and trans. W. H. Quarrell and M. Mare (1934) · B. Henrey, *British botanical and horticultural literature before 1800*, 2 (1975), 77–88 · M. Hunter, *The Royal Society and its fellows, 1660–1700: the morphology of an early scientific institution* (1982), 77 · F. N. Egerton III, 'Richard Bradley's illicit excursion into medical practice in 1714', *Medical History*, 14 (1970), 53–62 · H. Sloane, *A voyage to the islands Madera, Barbados, Nieves, S. Christopher and Jamaica*, 2 (1725) · parish records, London, St Botolph, Aldersgate [burial]

Archives BL, corresp., journals, and papers, Add. MSS 433, 968–969, 5267, 5291 · NHM, drawings and papers · RS, papers | NHM, letters to Johann Jacob Scheuchzer [copies]

Peto, Henry (1774–1830), builder and contractor, was born on 4 May 1774, the fourth son in a family of nine children of James Peto and his wife, Mary, in the parish of Cobham in Kent. Documentary sources variously describe Henry as a carpenter, bricklayer, and builder, but nothing is known of his training or early working life as a builder until 1806 when he was thirty-two. Over the next two decades he emerged as one of a new breed of builder—the general contractor whose firm executed most branches of the work and contracted 'in gross'.

In 1806 Peto submitted drawings and a tender to the City corporation to build an extension to the sessions house in the Old Bailey, a late eighteenth-century court house designed by George Dance, the younger. Peto won the contract to build the two-storey addition within two years at a total cost of £5179. It was his first known commission. The building consisted of an open colonnaded area on the ground floor with 'Grecian Doric fluted columns of Portland stone' (CLRO, City Lands Contracts, 3), with rooms and offices above, a competent and scholarly classical design.

In 1809 Peto successfully tendered to build the naval hospital (St Nicholas's) at Yarmouth. The building was completed in 1811, again under a contract for the whole works. Peto's next undertaking, in partnership with John Miles and based at 31 Little Britain in the City of London, was the building of the foundations and carcass of a new London custom house in the City. The construction of the custom house was begun in 1813 to the designs of the city surveyor of the day, David Laing. Peto's partner died the following year. The project turned out to be a disaster from the moment it was finished in 1815, and became a professional scandal. When the Long Room in the central portion of the building collapsed in 1824 Sir Sidney Smirke was called in to investigate. He found a catalogue of building errors, the most serious of which was the failure by Peto to supply proper foundation piling in the crucial places. Peto was sued and found guilty of greed and cutting corners in a way 'inconsistent with the character of a fair and respectable tradesman' (PRO Works 12/100/2, fols. 69–71). Laing was blamed for not having supervised the work properly. Both would fight in and out of court for their fortunes and reputations for the rest of their lives.

Remarkably, notwithstanding these setbacks, Peto continued in business. Cash flow was undoubtedly a problem; money bequeathed to Peto in 1818 by Samuel Barber, a plumber and presumably a business associate, was offset by another building collapse. At this time Peto was involved in the building of Park Crescent, part of Nash's urban scheme for Regent's Park begun in 1816. Speculator Charles Mayor had begun to build six houses on the southeast quadrant of a proposed circus, and following Mayor's bankruptcy in 1817, Peto was brought in to complete them. One of the six had been damaged by fire and collapsed after Peto's rebuilding in March 1818. Investigations found more evidence of shoddy workmanship. Perhaps thanks to Nash's covering for him, Peto continued to work: at Bryanston Square on the Portman estate from 1821, and at Raymond's Buildings, a block of lawyers' chambers, from 1825 (the year in which he went into partnership with his nephew Thomas Grissell). He also designed Wood's Hotel, built on the site of Furnival's Inn; and from 1827 worked on another Nash scheme at Carlton Gardens.

For the latter part of his life, Peto lived in Highbury Terrace overlooking Highbury Fields. His builders' yards were extensive and based in Lambeth. Peto died on 15 September 1830 having recouped some of his fee for building the custom house (later rebuilt to Smirke's designs). Unmarried and without heirs, he left most of his estate, including his business, in equal parts, to his nephew and partner Thomas *Grissell (son of his sister Anne and Thomas De La Garde Grissell) and another nephew, Samuel Morton *Peto, both of whom had been apprenticed to him. Peto had taken a great interest in the education of (Samuel) Morton Peto and donated prize money to his school, but once responsible for Samuel's training, Peto was apparently very strict and did not allow his nephew many holidays. After Henry Peto's death the young men took over their uncle's works at York Road and Edward Street in Lambeth and formed a new company, Grissell and Peto, well known as builders of the houses of parliament and of railways later in the century.

SUSIE BARSON

Sources J. M. Crook and M. H. Port, 'The custom house, London', *The history of the king's works*, ed. H. M. Colvin, 6 (1973), 422–30 · H. B. Hodson, 'Holland, the architect', *The Builder*, 13 (1855) [letter] · PRO, crest 24/5 · PRO, Wrks, 12/100, fols. 69–71 · J. M. Crook, 'The custom house scandal', *Architectural History*, 6 (1963), 91–102 · will, LMA, BRA/747/77–84 [Samuel Barber] · H. Peto, *Sir Morton Peto: a memorial sketch* (1893) · City lands contracts, CLRO, vol. 3, fols. 10–13b · plans, CLRO, 76, fols. 1–7 · Henry Peto's will, PRO, PROB 11/1788, No. 51
Wealth at death see will, PRO, PROB 11/1788, No. 51

Peto, Sir (Samuel) Morton, first baronet (1809–1889), contractor for railways and public works, was born on 4 August 1809 at Whitmoor House, Woking, Surrey, the eldest son of William Peto (*d.* 1849) of Cookham, Berkshire, farmer, and his wife, Sophia, daughter of Ralph Alloway of Dorking. Educated first at a Cobham village school, he then spent two years at Jardine's boarding-school at Brixton Hill, Surrey.

Apprenticeship When he was fourteen he was apprenticed to his uncle, Henry *Peto, public works contractor, with whom he lived at 31 Little Britain, City of London. He also attended a technical school. His talent for drawing was developed by a draughtsman, George Maddox of Furnival's Inn, and an architect, either Charles or Samuel Beazley. Under his uncle, he learnt the practical side of building in the carpenter's shop and as a bricklayer and mason, before acting as a superintendent, work that gave him 'an insight into the mechanism of labour … [and] the idiosyncrasy of the English mechanic' (*Men of the time*).

On his uncle's death in 1830, Peto and his cousin Thomas *Grissell each inherited a half share in his business and heavily mortgaged estate. As partners they conducted one of the leading firms of public works contractors, in a period when competitive tendering for lump-sum contracts was becoming the norm for major building works. Their control of a wide range of building trades, even leasing their own stone quarries, enabled them to win contracts on terms that their close site controls made profitable to them. Their 1832 tender for Hungerford Market, London (designed by Charles Fowler) was, at £42,400, only £400 below their nearest competitor. It was the first in a notable series that included Charles Barry's Birmingham grammar school (1833), the Reform (also Barry, 1836), Conservative (1840), and Oxford and Cambridge (1836–8) clubs, Samuel Beazley's Lyceum (1831–4, in sixteen weeks) and St James's (1835, in thirteen weeks) theatres, and his Studley Castle, Warwickshire (1834), Bushall's Olympic

Sir (Samuel) Morton Peto, first baronet (1809–1889), by Camille Silvy, 1861

Theatre (1849), and Nelson's Column (1843). They also constructed Fowler's St John's Church, Hyde Park Crescent (1830–31).

Peto recalled that:

> our *ordinary* business coming regularly from the large breweries and fire offices, and the work of our own connection with the architects, netted on the average £11,000 or £12,000 a year, and with only £50,000 capital engaged in that department. (Peto, 13)

Well placed to benefit from new contracting opportunities, they engaged in railway construction, beginning with two stations in Birmingham, followed by the Hanwell to Langley section of the Great Western (1840)—where Peto successfully referred his disputed £162,000 account directly to the determination of Isambard Kingdom Brunel, the engineer—as well as the Woolwich graving dock. But their most celebrated work was the superstructure of Barry's houses of parliament, begun in 1840 on a lump-sum contract for the river front, and continued in a series of contracts based on their schedule of prices. Young men in their employ included George Gilbert Scott and the Lucas brothers, Charles Thomas and Thomas.

Railway building Peto was more enthusiastic than Grissell about developing the risky but profitable railway-building side of the business, which had the added advantage that he would then be able to stand for parliament, from which as a government contractor he was barred. He dissolved the partnership on 2 March 1846, taking over the railway works (including some in Norfolk), a substantial 'clear capital' and £25,000 worth of plant. He was returned as MP for Norwich in July 1847. Among his contracts were those for portions of the South Eastern Railway adjoining others being executed by Edward Ladd *Betts, who in 1843 had married Peto's sister. Having run into difficulties with the Saltwood Tunnel, where Betts had the contract for the permanent way, in 1846 they agreed to join forces, and subsequently formed a partnership that lasted until Betts's death in 1872. Peto worked on securing contracts, raising finance, and carrying out a modern company chairman's role, while Betts performed that of chief executive, actually conducting the works.

Peto and Betts's highly organized operations covered many parts of England, but especially the east, with contracts for the Great Northern loop line through Boston to Doncaster, the East Lincolnshire, and the Eastern Counties Railway for which alone their several contracts totalled over £1.12 million. Writing from Boston in 1847, Peto referred to the thirteen engines and 8000 men they had on the works. As a feeder for East Anglia, they developed the London, Tilbury, and Southend Railway (1854–6), which they also leased as operators, a costly speculation. They were also responsible for the London, Cambridge, and Ely line; the Oxford and Birmingham Railway (contracts including the Harbury cuttings, the largest in the country, requiring the removal of 1.5 million cu. yd of soil); and the Oxford, Worcester, and Wolverhampton. Other contracts included the Dorset sections of the London and South Western (at a cost of £420,000, partly paid in shares), and the Hereford, Ross and Gloucester, as well as for the Severn Valley and the Chester and Holyhead railway companies of which Peto was chairman. In the 1840s Peto had thirty-three railway contracts worth £20 million, the largest number held in the kingdom; according to Brunel he was the largest contractor in the world.

Beyond the scale of his operations, Peto's insistence on paying his men weekly in cash was unusual. He recommended this practice to the select committee on railway labourers in 1846, and it was endorsed in their report. In 1854 Peto, supporting an amendment of the Truck Act, claimed always to have paid in cash the wages of the 30,000 men his firm had employed throughout the world. Peto was also interested in the physical and moral well-being of his employees, building barrack huts for them where necessary, each under the charge of a married couple, and paying for chaplains, Bibles, and uplifting tracts. His system of management combined 'discipline, personal freedom, moral admonition reduced to practice, and a total avoidance of ostentatious pietism' (*Men of the time*).

Several of Peto's undertakings were 'contractors' lines', projected 'not because the district wanted a railway, but because the contractor wanted a job' (*The Times*, 25 April 1868, 9). Such companies paid their contractors by issuing them with stock at a discount, to sell at a profit when possible. Peto's name was a byword for this practice. In 1857,

after parliament sanctioned the London, Chatham, and Dover Railway, an author going under the pseudonym 'Tooth of the Dragon' published a pamphlet, *Petovia*, attacking 'Petoism': 'There was concoction of companies by contractors in order to make their own terms for construction of the works, or, bribery of directors in order to sacrifice the shareholders' (Popplewell, 9). As early as 1847, having been paid extensively in securities, Peto was experiencing serious cash flow difficulties, eventually resolved by the connection he developed with the Quaker Gurney banks in Norfolk and thence with the discounting house of Overend Gurney. In the late 1840s and early 1850s Peto's plans were largely focused on developing Lowestoft as a port for Norwich and its hinterland, and its establishment as a holiday resort.

When the major domestic routes had been completed, Peto and Betts looked abroad: in co-operation with Thomas Brassey, their only equal, they extended their operations into Norway (1851) and Denmark (in 1853, 1860, and 1863, totalling 350 miles). They even undertook projects in Canada from 1852, embarking on the Grand Trunk Railway (539 miles in length); this required the bridging of the St Lawrence River at Montreal, which proved so expensive that they had to be rescued by the Canadian government. Peto found one-third of the £270,000 capital for their Birkenhead Canada works to provide the metal parts and rolling stock needed. Other enterprises in which they joined Brassey included the Lyons and Avignon Railway (1852) and extensive lines in Australia (from 1859), and at home, the Victoria docks, London, in 1852 at a cost of £870,000. In the Crimean War, Peto offered to construct a railway at Balaklava at cost, but this necessitated his resignation of his parliamentary seat in December 1854; he was compensated with a baronetcy the following February. Peto and Betts were also responsible for the Algiers to Blidah line, the first railway in Algeria, and the Algiers quays; the Dünaberg and Vitebsk Railway in Russia (220 miles long); the Buenos Aires to Rosario; and a land drainage scheme in the Netherlands. At Sir John Rennie's suggestion, the firm made an agreement in 1857 for building the Coimbra to Oporto line, abandoned after disputes with the Portuguese government; Rennie thought that the real cause 'was that their resources were swallowed up by a great variety of speculations' (Rennie, 366).

Bankruptcy It was, however, essentially their involvement at home with the controversial and insecure London, Chatham, and Dover Railway (LCDR) that brought about their collapse. Peto and Betts, in partnership with the engineer T. R. Crampton from 1862, concluded a lump-sum contract at £5.979 million (including more than £1 million for land) for its metropolitan extension into Victoria Station. They were to be paid not in cash, but in shares and debentures of the heavily indebted company, to which in December 1863 Peto offered his services as financial adviser. He undertook to fund a floating debt of £1.25 million which enabled the company to issue more stock, taken by Peto at a heavy discount. By improperly certifying that the majority of this stock had been subscribed for, the company was then able to raise cash on debentures, a not unusual, but illegal, proceeding. It was exposed by Peto's borrowings, and on 11 May 1866 the partners went down, following their bankers, Overend, Gurney & Co., with liabilities estimated at £4 million. Though denouncing the essential unsoundness of 'contractors' lines', *The Times* lamented:

> It is not without a sense of national humiliation that we contemplate the failure of a house which is identified with some of the grandest mechanical achievements of the present century. Perhaps no one, save Mr Brassey, has filled so high a position among English contractors as Sir Morton Peto … a leading pioneer of the railway system, and a great master in the art of organizing labour. (26 July 1867, 9)

Gladstone and Disraeli alike paid him similar tributes in the Commons.

In the subsequent bankruptcy proceedings, the transactions between Peto and the LCDR were left undetermined: although the firm's books 'had been admirably kept' according to the LCDR's solicitor (*The Times*, 7 July 1868, 11), another viewpoint was that the accounts 'were both contradictory and most difficult to unravel' (Peto, 47). The firm claimed a balance due to them of £380,000, and the LCDR counter-claimed for £6,661,941. The affairs of the partners, too, were almost inextricable: £800,000 belonging to Peto, Betts, and Crampton had been applied to discharge Peto and Betts's liabilities, leaving a deficiency of over £1 million. The LCDR received a dividend of 1*s*. 10*d*. from the bankrupts' estate on their discharge. Peto had meanwhile resumed his parliamentary activities, being returned first for Finsbury in 1859 and then becoming member for Bristol in 1865, but as a bankrupt was once again obliged to step down, which he did in April 1868. Nevertheless he evidently had hopes of re-election, and his election committee in June 1868 rejected his offer to resign as a candidate; his subsequent 'involved and prolix exposition' to his former constituents of his affairs 'obscured rather than elucidated' in the view of *The Times* (7 July 1868), which thought that the ordinary reader would conclude that in Peto's opinion there were people involved who were more to blame than himself (a view shared by *The Builder*); but he could not 'be held as irresponsible as he claims' (*The Times*, 25 Oct 1868, 6). Peto did not, however, again contest Bristol.

Family life and religious activities On 18 May 1831 Peto married Thomas Grissell's oldest sister, Mary (*c*.1811–1842); the couple, who had two sons and three daughters, lived in Albany Terrace, York Road, Lambeth. After her death he married, on 12 July 1843, Sarah Ainsworth (*c*.1822–1892), eldest daughter of Henry Kelsall of Rochdale, a textile manufacturer and leading Baptist layman; they had another six sons, of whom Harold became a partner in the leading architectural practice of Sir Ernest George and Peto, and four daughters.

Peto, who had been brought up an evangelical Anglican, joined the Baptists about 1844, influenced by his second wife; from the mid-1840s until his bankruptcy he was the leading Baptist layman, serving in 1853–5 and again in 1863–7 as chairman of the dissenting deputies. He was treasurer of the Baptist Missionary Society from 1846 to 1867. Peto's omnibus, conveying family and servants (the sexes segregated) to worship in Bloomsbury, was a familiar Sunday sight between 1849 and 1873. He was in favour of complete religious freedom for every denomination, and this was one of the few topics on which he spoke in the Commons.

As an MP, Peto acted independently on the radical wing of the Liberal Party, expressing his confidence in the fourth earl of Aberdeen's coalition ministry in June 1854, during the Crimean War. Membership of the Commons for him offered a means of promoting his interests; he did not seek a career in politics. Peto was naturally active in discussion of religious questions: in 1850 he secured a non-contentious Trustee Act to safeguard nonconformist chapel trusts, but in 1861 his Burials Bill (to allow nonconformist services in parochial graveyards) was rejected. He encouraged a non-aggressive attitude towards the Church of England but attacked compulsory church rates, arguing that they were unnecessary. Apart from religious and public works topics, his speeches principally concerned the condition of the working classes, on which he regarded himself as peculiarly well informed: he 'believed he had been more extensively engaged with the industrious classes of this country than any Member' (*Hansard 3*, 121, 1862, 698). He was indeed seen as a philanthropic employer, endeavouring to make all in his employ 'feel that the interests of employer and employed are identical, … that the master cares for the comfort and welfare of his men, and is really … anxious that they should be helped in every way to rise in the world' (*Cassell's Illustrated Family Paper*, 39–40). Peto set out his political views in seconding the Address in the Commons on 4 February 1851, when he praised the reduction of import duties and the repeal of the Navigation Acts; pointed to the thriving state of stock farming as a result of the consequent improved working-class living standards; urged the building of more railways to benefit Ireland, and to open up India as a market for cotton manufactures; approved anti-papal legislation; and recommended the universal registration of property deeds. He served on a number of select committees (including that on masters and operatives, 1860) and official commissions, particularly the metropolitan commission of sewers (1849), of which he was deputy chairman in 1851–2, and the royal commission for the 1851 exhibition.

Peto published, in addition to religious tracts, *Observations on the Report of the Defence Commissioners, with an Analysis of the Evidence* (1862); *Taxation, its Levy and Expenditure, Past and Future* (1863)—a 400 page criticism of British financial policy; and *Resources and prospects of America ascertained during a visit to the States in the Autumn of 1865* (1866), a lengthy, generally admiring, analysis, but advocating the merits of free trade.

Although Peto spent liberally, his income was not as large as might be expected. In 1861 he said £10,000 was his best for seven years past, and in 1862 he realized assets in real estate worth several thousands annually. He was a generous benefactor to charity, funding the building of Bloomsbury Baptist Chapel (at a cost of £18,000) and, when repaid, buying the Regent's Park diorama for conversion to a chapel; he also restored the parish church on the estate he had bought at Somerleyton, Lowestoft, Suffolk, where he built a model village, with a school for the children of the men in his Lowestoft works. In 1850 he came forward as guarantor of the £50,000 required for the Great Exhibition of 1851.

In London, Peto and his family lived at 47 Russell Square, and then in 1853–63 in great style at 12 Kensington Palace Gardens (built by Thomas Grissell), supported by a governess, three male and twelve female indoor servants. In 1863–5, while he was temporarily living at 9 Great George Street, Lucas Brothers built him a new mansion on the adjoining garden plot, at a cost of nearly £50,000, complete with remarkable stables that accommodated nine coaches and twelve stalls. In consequence of Peto's bankruptcy, this house was bought by Thomas Lucas. At Lowestoft, Peto employed John Thomas to rebuild Somerleyton Hall for him (1844), described by Pevsner as 'more Jacobean than any original Jacobean house' (*Buildings of England, Suffolk*, 1961, 390). He became a JP and deputy lieutenant for Suffolk (and JP for Norfolk, and later Middlesex), but in 1862 moved to Chipstead, Sevenoaks, Kent. After his bankruptcy, Peto moved almost annually, until settling at Eastcote House, Pinner, Middlesex, in 1877. He moved for the last time in 1884, to Blackhurst, Tunbridge Wells, Kent.

After their discharge from bankruptcy in July 1868, the only contract undertaken by Peto and Betts was for minor works on the Metropolitan Railway. However, they had hopes of an abortive scheme for regulating the Danube at Budapest, where Peto spent much of 1868–9, moving on to Paris in hope of French contracts. After Betts's death he undertook construction of the Cornish mineral railways. His health deteriorated in the mid-1880s and he spent two winters at Cannes, but from November 1888 became increasingly ill. He died at Blackhurst on 13 November 1889, and was buried in Pembury churchyard, Kent. He was survived by his wife.   M. H. PORT

Sources H. Peto, *Sir Morton Peto: a memorial sketch* (1893) • J. L. Chown, *Sir Samuel Morton Peto: the man who built the houses of parliament* [1943] • *ILN* (8 Feb 1851), 106 • 'Select committee on railway labourers', *Parl. papers* (1846), 13.454ff., no. 530 • P. L. Cottrell, 'Railway finance and the crisis of 1866', *Journal of Transport History*, new ser., 3 (1975–6), 20–40 • L. Popplewell, *Contractors' lines* (1988) • *Hansard* 3 (1850–54); (1859–68) • *The Economist* (8 Sept–24 Nov 1866) • *The Economist* (19 Oct 1867) • *The Economist* (14 March 1868) • *The Economist* (25 April 1868) • *The Economist* (15–22 Aug 1868) • *The Times* (23 April 1868) • *The Times* (25 April 1868) • *The Times* (30 April 1868) • *The Times* (14 June 1868) • *The Times* (7 July 1868) • *The Times* (23 July 1868) • *The Times* (28 Aug 1868) • *The Times* (29 Aug 1868) • *The Times* (25 Oct 1868) • 'A sore in the body politic', *The Builder*, 25 (1867), 503–4 • 'Railway boards, contractors, and shareholders', *The Builder*, 26 (1868), 186–7 • *The Builder*, 26 (1868), 330–31 • census returns, 1841, 1861 • *PICE*, 99 (1889–90), 400–03 • *Men of the time* (1856) • J. Rennie, *Autobiography of Sir John Rennie, FRS* (1875) • *Cassell's Illustrated Family Paper* (1857)
Archives BL, letters
Likenesses W. H. Mote, stipple, pubd 1848 (after A. Wivell), NPG • C. Silvy, photograph, 1861, NPG [see illus.] • J. Beattie, carte-de-visite, NPG • G. R. Black, lithograph (after photograph by Mayall), NPG • H. Weigall, oils, Regent's Park College, Oxford • engraving, repro. in *ILN* (8 Feb 1851), 106 • photograph (in middle age), repro. in Peto, *Sir Morton Peto* • photograph (in middle age), repro. in Chown, *Sir Samuel Morton Peto* • prints, NPG • stipple, NPG

Peto [Peyto], **William** (*c*.1485–1558), cardinal, was a younger son of Edward Peyto of Chesterton, Warwickshire, and Godith Throckmorton (*d.* 1502), although it has been much more commonly said that 'the acts of his life were so obscure that in some respects Petow might be compared to Melchizedek, as no one knew who his parents were, nor where he was born' (*CSP Venice*, 1556–7, no. 937). One of four children, his brothers included John *Peyto [see under Peyto family]. After graduating BA at Oxford in 1502, Peto was incorporated in the following year at Cambridge, where he proceeded MA in 1505. In 1507/8 he was paid £4 to lecture on mathematics, and seems to have become briefly a fellow of Queens' College in 1511 (probably through John Fisher's patronage), immediately before his ordination to the priesthood on 15 March that year. He had been incorporated MA at Oxford on 16 June 1510 and held the office of university preacher at Cambridge in 1510–11. Peto was vice-warden of the Observant Franciscans at Richmond, Surrey, by December 1520, warden in 1522, and provincial minister of the Observants. In 1524 the Carthusians of Axholme presented him to the living of Sharnford, Leicestershire; he failed to keep the church in repair, which suggests that he did not reside.

Nothing further is known of Peto until the time of the divorce crisis, when he was again provincial and apparently also acting as confessor to Katherine of Aragon and her ladies, as well as to Princess Mary. He defended the queen, preaching a sermon before Henry at Easter 1532 in which he denounced those who repudiated their wives, threatened excommunication for the king since flatterers always ruined kingdoms, and observed that princes' affections obscured the truth. Nicholas Harpsfield later claimed that Peto had warned Henry that, like Ahab, dogs would lick his blood. An angry king summoned Peto before him, and Peto flatly told Henry that he would lose his kingdom because of his subjects' opposition. According to Sir George Throckmorton's confession of 1537, Peto offered Henry a detailed refutation of his case, arguing that he could have no other wife while Katherine lived unless he could prove that Prince Arthur had intercourse with her, something the king could not do, as the only evidence was Arthur's 'light word' about having been 'in the midst of Spain'. Peto also insisted that Henry could not marry Anne Boleyn, since he had 'meddled with the mother and the sister' (*LP Henry VIII*, 12/2, no. 952), probably the origin of Nicholas Sander's famous canard to the same effect. Peto helped to organize parliamentary opposition to the divorce, telling Throckmorton to stay the course for his soul's sake, and in convocation attacked Richard Curwen for having preached in the convent of Greenwich without the brothers' permission—Curwen had by royal order delivered a sermon confuting Peto.

The chronology of Peto's career becomes confusing

after 1532. According to one story, he had asked and received Henry's permission to retire to Toulouse, but the king had changed his mind and had him arrested. Nevertheless, Peto seems to have reached the continent before returning to England. It is certain that when he accused Curwen he was in the custody of Bishop Standish (where he remained at least into May 1532) and that he was in the Franciscan house at Pontoise in January 1533. Most sources agree that during this time he had a book published in Antwerp (suppositiously at Lüneburg) against the divorce, *Philalethae hyerborie … in Anticatoptrum suum … paresceve* ('Lover of truth from the north …') a reply to *A Glasse of the Truthe*. Although the book cannot have been his, both because of the pseudonym and also because its author refers to himself as having studied in Paris, Peto was frequently accused of having written it. There is a single copy in the Grenville collection in the British Library. Peto and his companion Friar Henry Elston may have brought the work back to England, or perhaps they merely forwarded it.

Once Peto had fled, various English agents, especially John Hutton, ambassador to the court of Mary of Hungary in the Low Countries, kept a close eye on him. In 1533 and 1534 he was in Antwerp in company with Elston, who was spreading the rumour that Spain was about to invade England. Stephen Vaughan, Thomas Cromwell's representative in the Low Countries, who once solemnly proclaimed that he would capture Peto, whom he called 'a hypocrite, a tiger clad in a sheepskin, a perilous knave' (*LP Henry VIII*, 6, no. 1324), wrote in March 1535 that Peto was at Bergen-op-Zoom (where he seems mainly to have stayed during the rest of his time in the Netherlands) and that Mary would have him arrested if Henry wrote to her personally. Peto was variously said to be supported by the Spanish or from England, and seems to have kept very close ties with home, notably with Sir Thomas More, who sent him several books including his own *Confutation of Tyndale's 'Answer'*.

Two years later, in 1537, Peto was involved in one of the more curious episodes in Reginald Pole's first legation against England. Hutton had recruited one William Vaughan, offering him a pardon in exchange for insinuating himself with Pole. Vaughan had a letter of introduction from Peto to his relative Michael Throckmorton. Pole greeted Vaughan cordially, according to Hutton, as a fellow exile and Welshman, gave him money and asked him to go to Antwerp to gather news. He left with a letter for Peto from Throckmorton. This may have been Peto's first contact with Pole, of whom he would later be described as one of the principal followers. He acted as go-between for Hutton with Throckmorton, Pole's representative, and often conferred with Hutton in person. Peto helped to cover Pole's escape from Flanders, possibly on the latter's instructions, recommending to Hutton that Nicholas Wilson be sent on the king's behalf to confer with Pole 'to stop such things as were likely to be put forth shortly' (PRO, SP 1/124, fol. 167r), probably a reference to the planned publication of Pole's *Pro ecclesiasticae unitatis defensione*, which borrowed Peto's argument that flattery

was at the root of Henry's actions. Peto probably had a copy, although Pole denied any knowledge of it. It apparently reached Hutton, who burnt it.

Peto still held out hope that the change in the pope's status in England was not permanent, and at least as late as December 1537, after Pole had returned to Rome, offered his allegiance to the king and his service to Cromwell, and said he would try to prevent the publication of a book against Henry, probably another reference to *Pro ecclesiasticae unitatis defensione*. About the same time, Peto told Hutton that if peace were concluded and a council called, he would go to Italy, but that he found many abuses among monks and nuns in England and thought the monasteries could be put to better uses. Thus except for the status of the pope, Peto wished he were in England. Shortly afterwards, however, Peto acted on his resolve to go to Italy, encountering Hutton's brother-in-law at Mainz as he made his way in secular attire to Rome. In August 1538 Peto was in the Observant convent at Venice, 'by Mr Pole's means' (*LP Henry VIII*, 13/1, no. 115), and he spent the winter there, Thomas Theobald describing him as 'somewhat babbling and very open' (Ellis, 2.128). He stayed against his wishes, since he had wanted to go to Rome, but had been prevented by the Franciscan general's orders. Pole wrote on Peto's behalf, asking the general to give Peto permission to join Pole whenever he chose.

This was now Peto's only good option, since he had been indicted for having traitorously gone to Rome, and then included in the massive bill of attainder against Pole and his allies of 19 May 1539. On 30 March 1543 Paul III nominated Peto as bishop of Salisbury with Marcello Cervini as referendary, after Pole had refused the see four years earlier. Henry did not recognize the election, and by the time Pole was in a position to implement it in 1555 Peto no longer wished to have the see and never took possession. He next became successively a chamberlain and warden of the English Hospice in Rome in 1544; he last appears as warden in November 1548. A gap of six years ensues until Peto appears in a Franciscan house in Mantua, according to the somewhat garbled testimony of the Mantuan envoy to the imperial court. It may have been thence that he wrote to Mary Tudor, probably in early 1554, advising her to remain single, supporting his argument with numerous quotations from the Bible, and warning her that she would be dominated by her husband and suffer dangerous pregnancies. Peto offered to come to England to tell the queen more.

On 4 January 1555 Peto's attainder was reversed, and by then he had probably returned home. Once there, he led the attempt to destroy Christ's Hospital, which had been founded on the site of the Greyfriars' convent in London, until persuaded to abandon his efforts by the intervention of the Spanish Friar John, probably Juan de Villagarcia. In November 1555 he was among twenty-five friars in the restored convent of Greenwich, and was possibly correctly identified as Mary's confessor and certainly incorrectly as a recent nominee for cardinal. That did not occur until 14 June 1557 when Paul IV, acting out of divine inspiration, or so he claimed, surprised the whole College of

Cardinals; the pope did not even give Peto a cardinal's title. More importantly, Paul did transfer to him Pole's legation to England. Sir Edward Carne, Mary's ambassador in Rome, rejected the nomination of a 'blockhead' and a dotard, and told the pope that he would have to report the news to the queen himself. Paul replied that Peto had been a great help to the congregation of the Inquisition (under unknown circumstances), and that he was certain Peto had been Mary's confessor despite Carne's attempt to prove he was not. Other observers put the nomination bluntly down to Paul's proceedings against Pole for heresy.

The pope's nomination, dated 20 June, went off to England on the 28th. Within a month Peto wrote back rejecting the appointment as legate, although Mary had refused to allow the courier to cross from Calais where he was put up at royal expense, and tried to keep the news from Pole. When the latter found out, he sought entry for the messenger. Carne secured a papal audience to present Peto's and the queen's letters, and Paul replied that the matter needed consultation with the cardinals. Peto's letter was read under the strictest secrecy in consistory on 12 August, but the absence of four leading imperialist cardinals gave the pope an excuse for further delay. In December Paul tried to summon Peto to Rome via Cardinal Carlo Carafa, probably to make it appear that the general summons of cardinals was not merely a cover to get Pole into the pope's hands. Peto may have formally resigned his bishopric in early 1558 and probably died late in the year. He was still alive and in England shortly before 17 November, when he attended the deathbed of Pole's brother Geoffrey.   T. F. MAYER

Sources Emden, *Oxf.*, 3.1474–5 · W. Dugdale, *The antiquities of Warwickshire illustrated* (1656); repr. (1765) · *LP Henry VIII*, 5, no. 989; 6, nos. 726, 836, 899–900, 917, 934, 1324, 1369; 7, no. 440; 9, no. 524; 12/2, nos. 209, 619, 952, 1172, 1303; 13/1, nos. 115, 827; 13/2, nos. 117, 813, 979(7), 1034; 14/1, nos. 190, 867(15); 18/1, no. 336 · *CSP Venice, 1527–33*, no. 760; *1556–7*, (no. 937), 54v (no. 938), 75v (no. 955), 79r–v (no. 959), 107r–v (no. 981), 113v (no. 983), 168r (no. 1024) · C. Eubel and others, eds., *Hierarchia Catholica medii et recentioris aevi*, 2nd edn, 3, ed. W. van Gulik, C. Eubel, and L. Schmitz-Kallenberg (Münster, 1923), 36, 292 · *CSP Spain, 1531–3*, 427; *1554–8*, 297–9, nos. 311, 315 · Bodl. Oxf., MS Ital. C. 25, fol. 303r · Archivio di Stato, Mantua, Archivio Gonzaga, b. 569 (Fiandra) [unfoliated], Guglielmo Cavagliate, duke of Mantua, Brussels, 12 Feb 1555 · Archivio di Stato, Mantua, Archivio Gonzaga, b. 578 (Inviati Inghilterra/Scozia), fols. 169–70 · Pole's register, LPL, fol. 49r · S. E. Lehmberg, *The Reformation Parliament, 1529–1536* (1970), 146n. · *John Howes' MS 1582*, ed. W. Lempriere (1904) · H. Ellis, ed., *Original letters illustrative of English history*, 3rd ser., 2 (1846), 128 · R. Rex, *The theology of John Fisher* (1991), 180 · A. Kenny, 'From hospice to college', *The Venerabile*, 21 (1962), 218–73, 269–70 [sexcentenary issue: *The English hospice in Rome*] · *CSP for.*, 1553–8, nos. 658, 693 · Biblioteca Apostolica Vaticana, Vatican City, MS Vat. lat. 5826, fols. 66r–69r [A. M. Querini, ed., *Epistolarum Reginaldi Poli … collectio*, 1744–57, 2, no. 80] · Biblioteca Apostolica Vaticana, Vatican City, Vat. lat. 5967, fols. 235r–v, 236r–v [A. M. Querini, ed., *Epistolarum Reginaldi Poli … collectio*, 1744–57, 3, no. 19; A. Torres, *As cartas latinas de Damiao de Góis*, 1982, no. 25; Querini, no. 20] · Biblioteca Apostolica Vaticana, Vatican City, Vat. lat. 6754, fol. 259v [*CSP Venetian*, 6/3, no. 1287] · Biblioteca Apostolica Vaticana, Vatican City, Barb. lat. 5115, fol. 145v · state papers, general series Henry VIII, PRO, SP 1/120, fols. 136r–137r [*LPH*, 12/2, no. 107]; 1/124, fol. 167r [*LPH*, 12/2, no. 635] · Archivio Segreto Vaticano, Vatican City, Arm. 42:9, fols. 269r–270r · N. Harpsfield, *A treatise on the pretended divorce between Henry VIII and Catharine of Aragon*, ed. N. Pocock, CS, new ser., 21 (1878), 202–3 · Worcs. RO, b. 716.093 BA 1648/8 (i), p. 307

Petowe, Henry (1575/6–1636?), poet, was made free of the Company of Clothworkers on 13 August 1600, so he would have passed a minimum age that was probably twenty-three. He did not inherit his freedom (despite the suggestion of Eccles, 105), for no earlier Petowe appears in the Clothworkers' freedoms' list, which begins in 1528. Neither was he elected to the livery of the Clothworkers' Company. Insights into the clothiers' trade in the 1603 pamphlet *Londoners, their Entertainment in the Countrie* indicate that the writer was once active in this trade.

A chancery record dated 1613 contains two autograph signatures of Henrie Petowe, identified as a scrivener thirty-seven years of age of the parish of St Michael, Wood Street (PRO, C24/81/74). These match exactly the 1613 signature of a Henrie Petowe identified as a 'Clothworker', who witnessed an obligation (Corporation of London RO, journal 29, fol. 65; Petowe is identified as clothworker also in the record of this obligation, Corporation of London RO, report 31, fol. 112v; Petowe's slightly different 1618 signature appears on a bond in PRO, REQ 2/243). Thus the poet, clothworker, and scrivener were one man. Petowe's name does not appear in surviving documents of the Scriveners' Company, but the company's records are not intact (Woudhuysen, 53–4; Guildhall Library, MS 5370).

As a clothworker Petowe was free of the City, and so eligible for the London volunteer infantry company known as the artillery garden. He was admitted to the artillery garden between 15 August and October 1611 and later became marshal (The vellum book). There is an unascribed note at the Honourable Artillery Company indicating that Petowe was 'Marshall T[rained] B[ands] 1622–26'. The writer's work after 1622 is often identified to be by Marshall Petowe.

The poet may have been same Henry Petowe who married Ann Burt on 16 April 1604 at St Bartholomew by the Exchange (Eccles, 105). But similar names are also found: a different Henrie Petto married Alse Harison on 14 January 1604 at St Bride's, Fleet Street, and a Humphrei Petto married on 12 March 1604, also at St Bride's, Fleet Street.

The parish records of St Michael, Wood Street, show that Henry Petowe, scrivener, with a wife identified from 1616 onwards as Anne, fathered twelve children between 1605 and 1622. At least seven of these died by 1625. Petowe's children were baptized and (where recorded) buried at St Michael's: Richard (bap. 1605, d. 1611); Thomas (bap. 1607); Henry (bap. 1609, d. 1610); Henrye (bap. 1610, d. 1613); Marie (bap. 1612, d. 1625); Anne (bap. 1613, d. in or before 1619?); Benjamin (bap. 1615); Catherine (bap. 1616, d. 1625); Thomas (bap. 1617); Anne (bap. 1619); and Francisse (bap. 1622, d. 1624). In addition, William, son of Henrie Petowe, scrivener, was buried on 4 February 1618. Two daughters and their mother died on 15, 25, and 29 August 1625, probably owing to an outbreak of plague.

Petowe's first publication, *The Second Part of Hero and Leander, Conteyning their Further Fortunes* (1598), continued

Marlowe's epyllion. An address 'To the quicke-sighted Reader' excuses this as 'the first fruits of an unripe wit, done at certaine vacant howers'. It begins with high praises of Marlowe, and then describes chivalric adventures leaving many corpses, but a happy ending for the hero and heroine. Leander is exiled on arbitrary charges of treason, a topic with a political edge. Hero's constancy withstands repeated assaults; one makes a villain 'hoarse', and he dies of heartbreak. Leander is not discredited when, in disguise, he tests Hero's chastity. A connection of the text with an image in *Hamlet* is proposed by B. L. Joseph. Taylor argues it takes its Ovidian allusions directly from Golding. The text is edited in N. Alexander, *Elizabethan Narrative Verse* (1967) and in Stephen Orgel's edition of Marlowe.

Petowe regrets his continuation of Marlowe in a not entirely conventional manner in the introductory matter to his next book, *Philochasander and Elanira* (1599). Introductory verses describe the earlier work using images of a 'snare', a 'gin', 'the pit', and 'The sinke of misconceite, and errors Cell'. Admitting the late 'head-long' fall of his 'wandering *Muse*', Petowe says his muse now 'hath prunde her wings', and hopes his new effort will 'live eternallie'. *Philochasander* is dismissed by most nineteenth- and twentieth-century critics (see, for example, Shapiro, 25–6; Zocca, 177, being a partial exception). Yet it is not 'prunde', but more daring. Following an introductory poem, it consists of forty poems of fifteen lines. Poem 2, 'From *Tuskane* came my ladies worthy race', deliberately echoes Surrey (as does most of poem 9), and poem 5 identifies the lady as '*White* by name'. The sequence becomes erotic from poem 8.

Petowe's next work, *Elizabetha quasi vivens: Eliza's Funerall* (1603), is composed of an 'Induction', then eight sonnets, six prose pages listing 'the order and formall proceeding at the Funerall', and a final verse. The fifth sonnet strikingly evokes massed black-clad mourners. The last sonnet names King James.

The queen is lamented also in Petowe's next book, of twenty-three sonnets, *Englands Caesar: his majesties most royall coronation … Eliza her coronation in heaven; and Londons sorrow for her visitation* (1603). The plague of 1603 is attributed to London's sins; the nineteenth sonnet rues James's by-passing of the expensive pageantry put on by the City to receive him, as the king had travelled by water purportedly to avoid infection.

Next appeared *Londoners, their Entertainment in the Countrie*, entered as by Henry Petoe on 26 December 1603 (Arber corrects 26 November). This argues that 'sin' caused the 1603 plague equally in London, the suburbs, and the countryside. It describes escaping Londoners' poor reception in the country, and paints a lively picture of country towns during the visitation (claiming that, unlike London, the country does not bury its dead). The last section of the book contains two pastoral poems allegorizing the London plague, 'An Aelegie' (sig. C3r–v) and 'The Aeglogue' (sig. C4r), then affectingly realistic reportage of the economic impact of London's disasters on the countryside (sig. C4r–D1r), and finally a summarizing

poem (sig. D2r–D4r), the sixth stanza of which contains further economic reflections.

The only later longer work of Petowe preserved also concerns a plague year: *The Countrie Ague, or, London her Welcome Home to her Retired Children* (1626). Most of the pamphlet is spoken in sorrow by London personified, who enjoins mercy and charity, and sharply condemns Londoners in authority who remained away from their posts when 'my Poore cryed out for reliefe'. A penultimate section, including an epitaph, describes the 'Funerall of Captaine Richard Robins' to prove the diminished artillery garden company and city authorities were still functioning. The pamphlet followed multiple deaths in Petowe's family (especially closely if the overprinting '1625' in the unique BL copy is accurate), which may account for its softened tone as compared with Petowe's book on the 1603 plague.

In the dedicatory epistle of *The Countrie Ague*, Petowe identifies a work, now lost, of 'some ten Weekes since' titled *London Sicke at Heart, or, A Caveat for Run-Awayes*. This would seem another plague pamphlet, yet Petowe writes that in comparison with it *The Countrie Ague* is 'in another kinde and Garbe of writing, yet to purpose and according as these dayes and times require … [for] I write no Fables, nor Imaginary Toyes, but lamentable Experience shall justifie my writ'. This differentiation implies that *London Sicke at Heart* was not a work of reportage.

Corser (9.147) claims a bookseller advertised a manuscript: 'A Description of the Countie of Surrey, containing a geographicall account of the said countrey or shyre, with other things thereunto apertaining. Collected and written by Henry Pattowe, 1611.' This is not likely to be by the London Henry Petowe; one or more contemporary Henry Petowes appear in the records of Farnham, Godalming, and Chiddingfold, Surrey.

'Marescallus Petowe' signed a poem in Anthony Munday's edition of Stowe, *The Survey of London* (1633, 754–5), 'The foundation of the armory of that remarkable nursery of military discipline, called the Artillery Garden London'. This commemorates improvements made between 1 May and 30 November 1622, and is not a separate broadside as sometimes thought. Petowe similarly signed a folio broadsheet preserved uniquely at the Society of Antiquaries entitled *An honourable president for great men by an elegiecall monument to the memory of that worthy gentleman Mr. John Bancks* (1630). Mr Banckes, a mercer, had given generously to the artillery garden. The Barber–Surgeons' Company thereafter gave 'to Marshall Petoe for his elegies on Mr Banckes his funerall' either 5s. or 10s. (Young, 211, 398). The following July Petowe was paid 20s. by the Goldsmiths' Company for an elegy on one Mr Crownshawe (now lost).

A broadside signed 'Henricus Petowe area militaris Londinensis marciscallus composuit' is headed *The Artillery Garden London, Magnificent and Tryumphant* (1635; Bodl. Oxf., Douce prints 6.12, fol. 83). It illustrates a coat of arms newly 'assigned to the Gentlemen of the same Societie'. There follow seventy-six couplets. These include recollections of English civil wars that may seem ominous in a poem dedicated to Charles I by a London citizen given to outbreaks of imagination.

Eccles suggests that Petowe later remarried and relocated. One Henry Petowe of the parish of All Hallows, London Wall, and his wife, Mary, baptized Sara on 19 October 1632 and Nycholas on 21 August 1634. In the plague year of 1635–6, first Mary, then Sara, and then Henry Petowe died, on 22 January, 27 September, and 10 October respectively. The administration of the estate of this Henry Petowe is noted in the act book of the archdeaconry court of London (London, Guildhall Library, MS 9050/7, fol. 10v).

B. J. SOKOL

Sources N. Alexander, *Elizabethan narrative verse* (1967) · Arber, *Regs. Stationers* · T. Corser, *Collectanea Anglo-poetica, or, A … catalogue of a … collection of early English poetry*, 9, ed. J. Crossley, Chetham Society, 106 (1879), 144–7 · A. T. Crathern, 'A romanticized version of Hero and Leander', *Modern Language Notes*, 46 (1931), 382–5 · M. Eccles, *Brief lives: Tudor and Stuart authors* (1982) · B. L. Joseph, *English*, 8 (1950), 47–8 · R. Lemon, ed., *Catalogue of a collection of broadsides in possession of the Society of Antiquaries of London* (1866) · C. Marlowe, *The complete poems and translations*, ed. S. Orgel (1979) · G. A. Raikes, *The history of the Honourable Artillery Company*, 2 vols. (1878) · G. A. Raikes, *The ancient vellum book of the Honourable Artillery Company … from 1611 to 1682* (1890) · J. Robertson and D. J. Gordon, eds., 'A calendar of dramatic records in the books of the livery companies of London, 1485–1640', *Malone Society Collections*, 3 (1954) · G. P. Shannon, 'Petowe's continuation of "Hero and Leander"', *Modern Language Notes*, 44 (1929), 383 · J. Shapiro, *Rival playwrights: Marlowe, Jonson, Shakespeare* (New York, 1991) · F. W. Steer, *Scrivener's Company common paper, 1357–1628* (1968) · J. Stow, *A survey of the cities of London and Westminster and the borough of Southwark*, ed. J. Strype, new edn, 2 vols. (1720) · A. B. Taylor, '"Shakespeare's Ovid": Golding's *Metamorphoses* and two minor Elizabethan writers', *N&Q*, 222 (1977), 133–4 · S. van den Berg, 'The passing of the Elizabethan court', *Ben Jonson Journal*, 1 (1994), 31–61 · H. R. Woudhuysen, *Sir Philip Sidney and the circulation of manuscripts, 1558–1640* (1996) · S. Young, *The annals of the Barber–Surgeons of London: compiled from their records and other sources* (1890) · L. R. Zocca, *Elizabethan narrative poetry* (1970) · parish register, London, St Michael, Wood Street [baptism; burial of children] · parish register, London, All Hallows, London Wall, 10 Oct 1636 [burial] · Scriveners' company records, GL, MS 5370 · The vellum book of the Honourable Artillery Company

Petre family (*per.* 1633–1801), Roman Catholic nobility, in the eighteenth century were owners of the most extensive estates in Essex and were among the leaders of English Roman Catholic society, intermarrying with most other similar families. A succession of minor heirs gave dowagers (usually occupying the family homes at Thorndon Hall, near Brentwood, and Ingatestone Hall) lengthy periods of authority. Two members of a junior branch of the family became vicars apostolic; the sixth baron ventured briefly and ineffectively into local politics; otherwise the family kept quiet and no doubt prayed for better times, their position in county society securing them against the strict application of the penal laws.

Thomas Petre, sixth Baron Petre (*bap.* 1633, *d.* 1707), was born at Ingatestone and baptized on 5 December 1633, the fourth of the five sons of Robert, third Baron Petre (1599–1638), and his wife, Mary Browne (*c.*1604–1685). He was a nephew of the translator William *Petre (1602–1678). Thomas's elder brothers William *Petre, fourth

Baron Petre (*d.* 1684), and John, fifth Baron Petre (*d.* 1685), having died without male heirs, he succeeded to the title in January 1685. In the following year he married the sixteen-year-old Mary (*d.* 1730), daughter of Sir Thomas Clifton, of Latham, Lancashire. In February 1688 James II appointed him lord lieutenant of Essex in place of Aubrey de Vere, twentieth earl of Oxford, following the latter's refusal to give unconditional support to the king. The warrant dispensed with the need for Petre to take the oaths of supremacy and allegiance, or to receive the Anglican sacrament. At about the same time nine other Essex Catholics were appointed justices of the peace: it appears that although none of those appointed was unworthy of the office, James could not have gone on to appoint more Catholics without lowering the social standing and influence of the Essex bench. Following publication of the declaration of indulgence in April, Lord Petre visited some fifty deputy lieutenants and justices to ask whether they would support abolition of the penal laws and the Test Act. The response was generally equivocal, only twelve of those questioned being prepared to comply with the king's wishes. Members of the gentry began refusing to accept militia commissions at his hands, and Lord Petre, finding his position untenable, relinquished office by October and retired from political life. He died on 5 January 1707, and was buried on 10 January at Ingatestone. His widow died at Ghent on 15 February 1730 and was buried in the chapel of the English Benedictine convent there.

Robert Petre, seventh Baron Petre (*bap.* 1690, *d.* 1713), was baptized at Ingatestone, Essex, on 17 March 1690, the eldest child of Thomas, sixth baron, and his wife, Mary. Reputedly one of the handsomest young noblemen in London, he defied current fashion by keeping his own long hair instead of wearing a wig. He was already celebrated as the original of the 'adventurous Baron' of Pope's *Rape of the Lock* when, on 1 March 1712, he married Catherine Walmesley [**Catherine Petre**, Lady Petre (1697–1785)]. Born on 4 January 1697, Catherine was the youngest of the four children of Bartholomew Walmesley (*d.* 1701), heir of the family estate created by the judge Sir Thomas Walmesley (1537–1612) at Dunkenhalgh, Lancashire, and enlarged by his descendants. Orphaned as a small child, her brother and sisters all predeceased her, leaving her (at fifteen) heiress to a fortune of £50,000 and an estate possibly worth £5000 a year. On one occasion the family account books record five suitors visiting her house simultaneously. She seems to have made her own choice of the seventh Baron Petre as a husband. Their marriage was brief: he died on 22 March 1713 in Arlington Street, London, of smallpox, and was buried on 30 March at Ingatestone. Ten weeks later the widowed Lady Petre gave birth to their son, Robert James *Petre, eighth Baron Petre (1713–1742). She devoted herself to his upbringing, and to a wide range of charitable activities. She made large donations to convents in Europe, not only in return for prayers on behalf of her late husband but also as dowries for young ladies entering them; she paid for boys' education or apprenticeships, and also (especially after the

1715 rising) sent money to prisoners. In 1717 she was proposed as a wife for James Francis Edward Stuart, the Pretender, but the plan was rejected despite her wealth. By 1720 she had founded schools for Catholic children at Ingatestone and nearby; Defoe commented that the family's 'constant series of beneficent actions to the poor and bounty upon all occasions, have gained an affectionate esteem throughout all that part of the country, such as no prejudice of religion could wear out' (Defoe, 141). Many years later, when her first and second husbands' heirs were again admitted to the House of Lords, they searched in vain for their ancestors' parliamentary robes: they had been cut up by Catherine 'to make petticoats for old women' (Petre).

Having resisted proposals of a second marriage until her son came of age, on 2 April 1733 Catherine married Charles Stourton, fifteenth Baron Stourton (1702–1753), one of her earlier suitors and a lawyer. They lived first at Dunkenhalgh and then in Cheam, Surrey, but he died childless in 1753 and Catherine embarked on another thirty-two years of widowhood. Her letters and accounts reveal a life that, while characterized by religious fervour (with daily mass and long evening prayers), was far from joyless. Cards, concerts, exchanging visits, and purchasing lottery tickets feature regularly; her admirer Ralph Standish wrote in 1727 'I never had so mutch innocent mirth and satisfaction as here [at Ingatestone], where they are not apt to take things amiss and never mean harme, always gay and merry without excess' (Foley, 'Catherine Walmesley', 18). She died at Ingatestone on 31 January 1785, and was buried there on 5 February.

Her son, the eighth baron, was more interested in plants than in his role as a leading Roman Catholic peer, but his marriage on 2 May 1732 to Lady Anna Radcliffe provided him with a wife more suited to that position. **Anna Maria Barbara Petre**, Lady Petre (1716–1760) was (after 1731) the only surviving child of James *Radcliffe, third earl of Derwentwater (1689–1716), who was executed for his part in the 1715 rising (and who had been another of Catherine's disappointed suitors in 1711–12). Her mother was Mary Tudor (d. 1723), daughter of Charles II. Anna was passionately devoted to her father's memory, and ordered her children to keep his apparel with respect and veneration in the mahogany chest she had had specially made. Derwentwater's body was eventually reburied at Thorndon Hall in October 1874. Her only son (following three daughters), Robert Edward *Petre, ninth Baron Petre (1742–1801), was about five months old when his father died, and she was his guardian until she too died, on 31 March 1760; she was buried on 4 April 1760 at Ingatestone. Her son became a leading figure in the campaign for Catholic emancipation.

Benjamin Petre [*alias* White] (1672–1758), vicar apostolic of the London district, was born on 10 August 1672, the sixth son of John Petre (1617–1690), of Writtle, Essex, and his second wife, Elizabeth Pincheon (d. 1678). He was a grandson of John, first Baron Petre, and a cousin of William Petre, the translator. He studied at the English College, Douai, and was ordained priest, probably in 1696.

After returning to England in 1697 he was chaplain to members of the Radcliffe family, notably James, third earl of Derwentwater. In 1721 Petre was nominated by Bishop Bonaventure Giffard, vicar apostolic of the London district, as his coadjutor and eventual successor. He protested that this nomination had been made without his knowledge, claiming that he had been chosen only because of his high birth and private wealth, and asserted that he had little theology and could hardly read Latin without a dictionary. Giffard however was insistent: he saw the appointment as a way of resisting Bishop John Talbot Stonor's attempts to secure another episcopal appointment for a member of the regular clergy, and Petre was consecrated bishop of Prusa on 11 November 1721. His reluctance was more than the conventional humility of a potential bishop, for he continued to protest and threaten resignation until 1730. Giffard continued to resist his arguments, despite complaining that Petre was more of a burden to him than the hoped-for 'comfort to me in my old age' (Anstruther, 3.166). When Giffard died in 1734 Petre succeeded him as vicar apostolic and hastened to secure the appointment of a coadjutor. The person chosen was Richard Challoner, who was appointed bishop of Debra in September 1739 and who was thenceforward largely responsible for episcopal duties in the district. He noted, for example, when visiting Bishop Benjamin's own congregation at Writtle in 1742 that fifteen of its forty members were awaiting confirmation. Petre appears to have spent much of his time on one or other of the Petre family estates in Essex. Among the family portraits at Ingatestone Hall is a painting of a large mongrel dog which 'saved Benjamin Bishop Petre's Life when he was attacked by Robbers whilst saying his Office in the Lime Walk at Ingatestone Hall' (Piper, 22), where he was living in 1733. In 1739 he consecrated the chapel at Thorndon Hall: the text of the service survives among the family papers, and is thought to be the earliest service of benediction used in England. The attached 'Rules for the keeping of the sacristy' give a vivid picture of religious observance in a devout eighteenth-century Roman Catholic household.

Although the London district covered the ten southeastern counties and the Channel Islands, Petre seems to have confined his activities to Essex and the capital, and it was at his London house in King Street, Golden Square, that he died on 22 December 1758. He was buried in St Pancras old churchyard on 27 December 1758; his remains were moved to St Edmund's, Ware, Hertfordshire, in 1908.

Francis Petre [*alias* Andrews] (1692–1775), vicar apostolic of the northern district, was born on 2 October 1692, at Fithlers, Writtle, Essex, the third son of Joseph Petre of Fithlers (1666–1722), and his wife, Catherine Andrews (d. 1700). He was grandson of Bishop Benjamin's father's eldest surviving son by his first marriage. He studied at the English College, Douai, and was ordained priest on 31 March 1720. He spent 1722 to 1726 partly in England and partly in Paris, sometimes as tutor to John Wolf. In 1750 he was made bishop of Armoria and coadjutor to Bishop

Edward Dicconson, whom he succeeded in 1752 as vicar apostolic of the northern district. As with his cousin Benjamin, his personal wealth did much to recommend him to his church, but unlike him he seems to have applied himself willingly to his episcopal duties. He died on 24 December 1775 at his principal residence, Showley Hall, Clayton-le-Dale, Blackburn, Lancashire, and was buried on 27 December 1775 at an 'ancient chapel' in Stydd Lodge, Dutton, Ribchester, Lancashire.   ROBERT G. E. WOOD

Sources GEC, *Peerage* · C. T. Kuypers, MS pedigree of the Petre family, 15th century to 1935, Essex RO, T/G 39/1 · [M. A. Petre], 'The pictures at Thorndon', Essex RO, MS D/DP/F232B · B. C. Foley, 'Catherine Walmesley (1698–1785) later Lady Petre and Lady Stourton', *Some other people of the penal times* (1992), 1–22, 188–9 · G. Anstruther, *The seminary priests*, 4 vols. (1969–77), vol. 3, pp. 165–7; vol. 4, 211–12 · R. B. Colvin, 'Thomas Petre, 6th Baron Petre: lord lieutenant & custos rotulorum, 1687–88', *The lieutenants and keepers of the rolls of the county of Essex* (1934), 109–14 · J. G. O'Leary, 'The declaration of indulgence in 1687/8 and the county of Essex', *Essex Recusant*, 3 (1961), 89–93 · N. C. Elliott, 'The Roman Catholic community in Essex, 1625–1701', *Essex Recusant*, 25/26 (1983–4), 1–70 · N. C. Elliott, 'The Roman Catholic community in Essex, 1625–1701', *Essex Recusant*, 27 (1985), 1–75 · P. Coverdale, 'Ralph Standish Howard's wooing of Lady Catherine Petre', *Essex Recusant*, 22 (1979), 60–78 · F. J. A. Skeet, *The life of the Right Honourable James Radcliffe, third earl of Derwentwater* (1929) · J. Stephan, 'Notes on household management in the 18th century: transcript of a MS notebook', *N&Q*, 203 (1958), 349–51; 204 (1959), 97–172 · D. Shanahan, 'Benjamin Petre, bishop of Prusa and vicar apostolic of the London district, 1672–1758', *Essex Recusant*, 17 (1975), 39–41 · W. V. Smith, 'Benjamin Petre and the earl of Derwentwater', *Essex Recusant*, 18 (1976), 106–7 · B. C. Foley, 'Bonaventure Giffard (1642–1734)', *Some people of the penal times* (1991), 67 · D. Piper, *Petre family portraits* (1956) · E. S. Worrall, 'Bishop Challoner's visitations in Essex', *Essex Recusant*, 24 (1982), 16 · S. Foster, 'The reluctant shepherd: the episcopal appointment of Bishop Benjamin Petre', *Opening the scrolls*, ed. D. A. Bellenger (1987), 115–34 · D. Defoe, *A tour through the eastern counties of England*, ed. R. A. N. Dixon (1984), 141 · P. Morant, *The history and antiquities of the county of Essex*, 2 (1768)

Archives Westm. DA, papers of Benjamin Petre

Likenesses J. Kerseboom (Thomas Petre), Ingatestone Hall, Essex · portrait (Catherine Petre), Ingatestone Hall, Essex · portrait (Anna Maria Barbara Petre), Ingatestone Hall, Essex · portraits (Robert Petre), Ingatestone Hall, Essex

Petre, Anna Maria Barbara, Lady Petre (1716–1760). *See under* Petre family (*per.* 1633–1801).

Petre, Benjamin (1672–1758). *See under* Petre family (*per.* 1633–1801).

Petre, Catherine, Lady Petre (1697–1785). *See under* Petre family (*per.* 1633–1801).

Petre, Sir Edward, **third baronet** (1630×33–1699), Jesuit and courtier, was born in London, possibly on 4 March 1633, the second son of Sir Francis Petre (*c.*1605–1658), first baronet, of Cranham Hall, Essex, and his wife, Elizabeth (*d.* in or before 1655), daughter of Sir John Gage, first baronet, of Firle Place, Sussex. However, his apparent age at death suggests that he may have been born in 1630/31. His great-grandfather was John, first Baron Petre. Petre was educated at the college at St Omer from about 1644 until 1652. He entered the Society of Jesus at Watten on 1 March 1653 under the name of Spencer. He then studied philosophy and theology at Liège, 1655–64, during which time

he was ordained a priest, on 22 October 1662. After spending some time in England he professed the four vows on 2 February 1671. He seems to have returned to England in 1672, and served as rector of the Hampshire district in 1678–9.

At this point Petre became embroiled in the Popish Plot. It was a letter from Petre which gave credence to the claim made by Titus Oates that a Jesuit consult had been held in London in April 1678. Petre was arrested, brought before the privy council, and committed to Newgate in September 1678. By January 1679 Petre had succeeded his elder brother, Francis, to the baronetcy. Petre was not tried with other alleged conspirators in June 1679, some people later claiming that he was under the protection of the duke of York, possibly for services rendered in the upbringing of York's illegitimate children, but it was probably because Petre was slated for trial with the Staffordshire plotters which had been delayed as there was only a single witness against Lord Aston. Petre was released on bail in June 1680. In August 1680 he became rector of the London district and vice-provincial of England until a new one could safely be appointed, but in October 1680 he again found himself in prison, being released on 6 February 1683.

The accession of James II in February 1685 transformed Petre's situation. He was called to court and appointed dean of the new Chapel Royal in St James's Palace. Petre possessed 'a fair smooth tongue, and a very affable way of flattery', both attributes useful at court (Marshall, 144). However, Petre had no experience of court politics and was 'to state affairs a perfect novice' (*Memoirs of … Ailesbury*, 1.128). This made him an easy target for the machinations of a shrewd political operator like Robert Spencer, second earl of Sunderland, who used Petre as an ally in his pursuit of power and more specifically the dismissal from office of his rivals the Hyde brothers. Further, Petre was 'puffed up with … vanity and ambition', which made him yearn for recognition within the church (Marshall, 144). Initially Petre wanted James II to procure him a bishopric but in November 1685 Pope Innocent XI refused the king's request, noting that Jesuits were not allowed to hold high office. Not that this rebuff deterred James as he continued to instruct his representative in Rome, Roger Palmer, first earl of Castlemaine, to press the pope in the matter. Eventually in June 1687 James accepted that a bishopric was out of the question and changed his request to ask for a cardinal's hat for Petre instead. Again he met without success.

Petre's perceived influence at court was evinced by the number of requests for patronage he received. One observer noted that Petre's 'antechambers were crowded with petitioners, for they found by experience if he undertook their business it seldom failed to prosper' (Marshall, 145). More formal recognition followed when on 5 November 1687 Petre was named to succeed Thomas Sprat as clerk of the closet. On 11 November he was sworn a member of the privy council. However, this merely regularized his position as an adviser and did not enhance his influence. Petre was also a member of the commission charged with regulating the corporations of the parliamentary boroughs in order to influence the composition of any new parliament. Gradually he moved beyond Sunderland's influence and supported the court faction grouped around the more extreme Catholics such as the earl of Melfort. Petre was a proponent of severe measures being taken against the fellows of Magdalen College, Oxford, in 1687–8.

The birth of the prince of Wales in June 1688 led to a host of scurrilous diatribes accusing Petre of involvement in a plot to switch babies in order to produce a male heir for the king. Petre advised a conciliatory approach to the petition of the seven bishops as he foresaw that punitive action would rebound against the government. With a Dutch invasion expected James refused to banish Petre from court, and as late as 22 October 1688 the king told the earls of Clarendon and Nottingham that should they return to the privy council he would ensure that Petre would not attend its meetings, but would not dismiss him. By the end of November 1688 Narcissus Luttrell reported that Petre had sent 'several great chests from Whitehall' ready for his departure (Luttrell, 1.480). He soon made his escape from London and fled to France. He never saw James II again.

Petre soon left France, for he was reported to be in Rome in December 1689, 'but is not much looked on there' (Luttrell, 1.616). In both 1691 and 1692 he was back in France, at Abbeville. In 1693 he was appointed rector at St Omer. In 1697 he retired to Watten, where he died on 15 May 1699, apparently aged sixty-eight. His sister, Mary Petre, took out administration of his will on 17 May 1699. As baronet Petre was succeeded in turn by his brothers Thomas and William; following the death of the latter in 1722 the baronetcy became extinct. His younger brother Charles (1644–1712) had most closely followed Petre's career, being educated at St Omer and serving the Jesuits in the English mission.

Petre's importance at the court of James II arose from his closeness to the king. The earl of Sunderland was able to utilize Petre's influence in order to manoeuvre the Anglican earl of Rochester from office. Gradually Petre moved free from Sunderland's influence, particularly as he felt that the earl was responsible for his failure to secure that which he coveted the most: preferment in the church. Indeed the earl of Ailesbury characterized him as 'a hot-headed ignorant churchman', who 'had nothing in view but a cardinal's hat' (Miller, *Popery*, 235–6). For the English he remained a 'bogey-man', commonly being burnt in effigy on 5 November each year. His papers were transferred from St Omer to Bruges but were lost in October 1773 when the Austrian government suppressed the Jesuits.   STUART HANDLEY

Sources GEC, *Peerage* • H. Foley, ed., *Records of the English province of the Society of Jesus*, 7 vols. in 8 (1875–83), vol. 5, pp. 34, 105, 148, 272–7; vol. 7, pp. 591–3 • J. J. Howard and H. F. Burke, eds., *Genealogical collections illustrating the history of Roman Catholic families of England* (1887), 38–9 • B. Basset, *The English Jesuits from Campion to Martindale* (1967) • J. C. Sainty and R. Bucholz, eds., *Officials of the royal household, 1660–1837*, 1: *Department of the lord chamberlain and associated offices* (1997), 153 • J. Miller, *James II: a study in kingship* (1989) • G. Holt, *The English Jesuits, 1650–1829: a biographical dictionary*, Catholic RS, 70 (1984), 191 • J. Kenyon, *The Popish Plot* (1972) • A. Marshall, *The age of faction: court politics, 1660–1702* (1999) • *Memoirs of Thomas, earl of Ailesbury*, ed. W. E. Buckley, 1, Roxburghe Club, 122 (1890), 121, 128 • J. Miller, *Popery and politics in England, 1660–1688* (1973) • N. Luttrell, *A brief historical relation of state affairs from September 1678 to April 1714*, 6 vols. (1857), vol. 1

Archives Essex RO, Chelmsford, papers

Likenesses line engraving (after caricature), BM, NPG; repro. in *La belle Constance dragonée arlequin déodat* • medals, BM

Petre, Francis (1692–1775). *See under* Petre family (*per.* 1633–1801).

Petre, (Edward Oswald) Gabriel Turville- (1908–1978), Icelandic scholar, was born on 25 March 1908 at Bosworth Hall, Husbands Bosworth, Leicestershire, younger son of Lieutenant-Colonel Oswald Henry Philip Turville-Petre (1862–1941), high sheriff of Leicestershire, and his wife, Margaret Lucy, *née* Cave (d. 1954). He was educated at Ampleforth College and in 1926 entered Christ Church, Oxford, where he read English, taking a third in 1930, before working for a research degree (BLitt, 1936). After some years spent teaching and studying in Iceland, Germany, and Scandinavia, he returned to Oxford as Vigfússon reader in ancient Icelandic literature and antiquities in 1941. He held this post, having been given the title of professor in 1953, and elected to a studentship of Christ Church in 1964, until his retirement in 1975. He also held honorary appointments at the universities of Leeds, London, and Melbourne. In 1943, he married Joan Elizabeth Blomfield (b. 1911), herself a distinguished scholar in the field of Old Norse–Icelandic studies, and they had three sons.

Gabriel Turville-Petre became interested in Iceland and its medieval literary culture when still a child, and his links with Iceland, both professional and personal, remained strong throughout his life. He formed close friendships with Icelandic scholars, among them Einar Ólafur Sveinsson, who wrote an affectionate memoir in the Festschrift for Turville-Petre's seventieth birthday, praising his command of modern Icelandic, his devotion to Icelandic culture, and the contribution he made to the growth of Icelandic studies in Britain. He was lektor in English in the University of Iceland, 1936–8, and served also as British pro-consul in Reykjavík during this time. In 1956 he was awarded the title of officer of the order of the Falcon, and commander in 1963, prestigious honours conferred by the president of Iceland, and received honorary degrees from the universities of Iceland (1961) and Uppsala (1977). He was elected FBA in 1973.

Turville-Petre's achievement and influence as a scholar of Old Norse–Icelandic studies can hardly be overestimated. One of the earliest of a large number of articles in scholarly journals, his 'Notes on the intellectual history of Icelanders' (*History*, 27, 1942) was a decisive intervention setting straight the vague misconceptions then current among English-speaking scholars about Icelandic literacy and scholarship after Iceland's conversion to Christianity in AD 1000. Turville-Petre definitively dispelled romantic assumptions about late Germanic pre-literacy in Iceland,

(Edward Oswald) **Gabriel Turville-Petre** (1908–1978), by Merlin Turville-Petre

and modern Icelandic, other Scandinavian languages, and German, enabled Turville-Petre to draw illuminating parallels between early Celtic verse, especially the poetry of the Irish *filid*, and Old Norse–Icelandic *dróttkvætt*, the intricate and cryptic court poetry which flourished in Iceland and Norway from about AD 800 to AD 1200. Articles published throughout his career, some bringing together these two difficult kinds of early poetry, and others formulating his conviction that the literary qualities of skaldic verse might have particular appeal for late twentieth-century readers, culminated in his anthology of skaldic verse, *Scaldic Poetry* (1976). This volume too is an impressive blend of his scholarly gifts—the careful editing of often corrupt strophes, with translations and explanatory notes—and, in his choice of poets and poems, his opinion-forming authority, born of a lifetime's study of and delight in this literature.

A selection of Turville-Petre's papers was published as *Nine Norse Studies* (1972) and presented to him by the Viking Society for Northern Research, of which he was an honorary life member, and whose scholarly journal, the *Saga Book*, he had jointly edited for many years. The papers in *Nine Norse Studies* give a good indication of the range and quality of his scholarship. Notable among them are pieces on the poetry of the Icelandic skald Gísli Súrsson, on the cult of Óðinn, and his still celebrated 'On the poetry of the scalds and of the filid', translated from an Icelandic version first published in 1954.

During his career at Oxford, Gabriel Turville-Petre was the influential teacher of many generations of Old Norse–Icelandic scholars. His command of the subject was such that his students only had to listen to learn, but although his authority was extraordinary, he was always courteous and kindly, and never derided the shortcomings of either his students or other scholars in the field. None the less, his standards were deeply rigorous and he expected from his students the absolute commitment to scholarship he had himself. He died on 17 February 1978, of cancer, at The Court, The Croft, Old Headington, Oxford, his home since 1948. At Oxford, an annual prize for distinguished work in Old Norse–Icelandic studies by a graduate or undergraduate is given in his name, and the room which houses the university's collection of books in the subject is named after him.   HEATHER O'DONOGHUE

Sources P. Foote, 'Gabriel Turville-Petre', *PBA*, 64 (1978), 467–81 • E. Ól. Sveinsson, 'Um Gabriel Turville-Petre', *Speculum Norroenum: Norse studies in memory of Gabriel Turville-Petre*, ed. U. Dronke and others (1981), 1–5 • 'A Gabriel Turville-Petre bibliography', ed. J. Turville-Petre, *Speculum Norroenum: Norse studies in memory of Gabriel Turville-Petre*, ed. U. Dronke and others (1981), 506–8 • Burke, *Gen. GB* (1937) • private information (2004) • personal knowledge (2004) • m. cert. • d. cert.

Archives U. Oxf., faculty of English language and literature, Icelandic collection

Likenesses M. Turville-Petre, photograph, British Academy [*see illus.*]

Wealth at death £117,566: probate, 31 May 1978, *CGPLA Eng. & Wales*

and his piece remains an authoritative summary of early Icelandic literary history. His edition of *Víga-Glúms saga* (1940), based on his BLitt thesis, drew on what was already a remarkable range of learning, especially with regard to textual criticism (demonstrating the complex literary prehistory of a saga which had been both shortened and lengthened before being written down in its extant form), pagan religion, and Icelandic topography, which he had explored first-hand during his many visits to Iceland.

Turville-Petre's later works reflect these strengths. His *Myth and Religion of the North* (1964) is the best account of Old Norse–Icelandic mythology in English, especially valuable because it presents a comprehensive survey of mythological references in Icelandic and related literatures without attempting to impose narrative pattern or religious cohesion on the material. *The Heroic Age of Scandinavia* (1951) is a similarly compendious and judicious account of a period whose sources mostly date from much later times, and derive from fictionalized texts. But his major contribution to Old Norse–Icelandic studies is his *Origins of Icelandic Literature* (1953; 2nd edn, 1967), in many ways an expansion of his 1942 article on Icelandic intellectual history, which seeks to show the roots of Icelandic saga writing—one of the most remarkable literary phenomena of the middle ages—in the earliest Christian literary productions of medieval Iceland. In its epilogue, his measured assessments of what constitutes excellence in the Icelandic canon have formed the taste of generations of later readers.

Knowledge of Irish and Welsh, in addition to medieval

Petre, Sir George Glynn (1822–1905), diplomatist, born on 4 September 1822 at Twickenham, was the great-grandson of Robert Edward Petre, ninth Baron Petre, and the second son of Henry William Petre of Dunkenhalgh, Clayton-le-Moors, and his first wife, Elizabeth Anne, daughter of Edmund John Glynn, of Glynn, Cornwall. Raised as a Roman Catholic, he was educated at Stonyhurst College and Prior Park College, near Bath.

Petre entered the diplomatic service in 1846 as attaché to the British legation at Frankfurt, then the seat of the diet of the German confederation; he was thus in Frankfurt during the revolutions of 1848. He was transferred to Hanover in 1852 and to Paris in 1853, and was appointed paid attaché at The Hague in 1855 and at Naples in March 1856. When the Neapolitan government ignored the Anglo-French remonstrance on its anti-libertarian behaviour, diplomatic relations were broken off in the summer. Ill health caused Sir William Temple, the British minister, to leave Naples in July, and Petre assumed charge of the legation until it was withdrawn at the end of October. Petre performed his duties with judgement and ability; his reports laid before parliament give an interesting narrative of the course of events. In 1857 he was temporarily attached to the embassy at Paris, and in June 1859 he accompanied Sir Henry Elliot on his special mission to Naples, diplomatic relations having been resumed on the accession of Francis II. He then went as secretary of legation to Hanover, and acted as chargé d'affaires there from December 1859 until February 1860. He was transferred in 1864 to Copenhagen (where, in the following year, he assisted at the investiture of Christian IX with the Order of the Garter), and in 1866 to Brussels, and was promoted to be secretary of embassy at Berlin in 1868. After four years of service at Berlin, covering the period of the Franco-Prussian War, he became chargé d'affaires at Stuttgart in 1872, and in April 1881 he was appointed British envoy at Buenos Aires. In 1882 he was also accredited to the republic of Paraguay as minister-plenipotentiary. In January 1884 he was appointed British envoy at Lisbon, where he remained until his retirement on a pension (1 January 1893).

During the latter years of his service in Portugal the obstacles offered by the Portuguese authorities to free communication with the British missions and settlements established on the Shire River and the shores of Lake Nyassa, and the seizure of British vessels while passing through Portuguese waters on their way to the lake, led to a state of acute tension between the two governments. A convention for the settlement of these and related questions was signed by Lord Salisbury and the Portuguese minister in London on 20 August 1890, but in consequence of popular and parliamentary opposition the Portuguese government resigned office without obtaining the authority of the Cortes to ratify it, and their successors found themselves equally unable to carry it through. The negotiations had therefore to be resumed *de novo*. A *modus vivendi* was agreed upon and signed by Lord Salisbury and the new Portuguese minister, Senhor Luiz de Soveral, on 14 November 1890, by which Portugal granted free transit over the waterways of the Zambezi, Shire, and Pungwe

rivers and a satisfactory settlement was finally placed on record in the convention signed by Petre and the Portuguese minister for foreign affairs on 11 June 1891. Petre's naturally calm and conciliatory disposition and the excellent personal relations which he succeeded in maintaining with the Portuguese ministers did much to keep the discussions on a friendly basis and to procure acceptance of the British demands. He was made CB in 1886 and KCMG in 1890.

Petre married on 10 April 1858 Emma Katharine Julia, fifth daughter of Major Ralph Henry Sneyd; they had six sons and a daughter. One son and the daughter predeceased him. He died at 6 Queen's Gardens, Hove, on 17 May 1905, and was buried at Odiham, Hampshire. His wife survived him. T. H. SANDERSON, rev. H. C. G. MATTHEW

Sources *The Times* (23 May 1905) • *FO List* (1906) • A. Loftus, *The diplomatic reminiscences of Lord Augustus Loftus, 1862–1879*, 2 vols. (1894), vol. 1, p. 374 • *CGPLA Eng. & Wales* (1905) • R. Robinson, J. Gallagher, and A. Denny, *Africa and the Victorians* (1961)
Likenesses oils, 1912; formerly at Dunkenhalgh, Clayton-le-Moors, Lancashire • portrait, 1912; formerly in priv. coll.
Wealth at death £29,244 16s. 4d.: probate, 10 Aug 1905, *CGPLA Eng. & Wales*

Petre, Maude Dominica (1863–1942), author and writer on religion, was born on 4 August 1863 at Coptfold Hall near the village of Margaretting in Essex, the seventh of eleven children of Arthur Petre (1828–1882), younger son of the thirteenth Lord Petre, and Lady Catherine Howard (1831–1882), fifth daughter of the earl of Wicklow. Her mother was a convert to Roman Catholicism and her father, a gentleman farmer and justice of the peace, belonged to one of the old Roman Catholic families. Her parents died within two months of each other when Maude was nineteen. She was educated at home. In her memoirs, *My Way of Faith* (1937), she described her Victorian Catholic childhood and adolescence and reflected on her spiritual journey. She saw herself as 'passionately religious' and 'innately sceptical' (Petre, 187). When she was twenty-two, at the suggestion of her confessor as a remedy for her religious doubts, she studied scholastic philosophy under private instruction in Latin from professors of the college of the *propaganda fide* in Rome. This unusual educational opportunity for a Roman Catholic woman at that time did not solve her religious doubts but it provided a philosophical foundation for her writing. Although she did not consider herself a scholar she read widely and was fluent in French, Italian, and Latin.

On 13 March 1890 Maude Petre entered the London noviciate of the Society of the Daughters of Mary, a religious congregation founded in France during the French Revolution. Unlike most women's religious congregations at the time which followed a monastic lifestyle, the Filles de Marie did not wear a religious habit, retained their own names, maintained their place in secular society, and had the option of remaining in their own homes rather than living in a community. In February 1896 Maude Petre professed vows for five years in the society and shortly after was selected as local superior in London (June 1896–1900).

She also served as provincial superior for the society in England and Ireland (1900–05) and as a provincial councillor (1905–8). In addition to duties within her religious congregation she continued to write on religious topics. Her first book, *Aethiopum servus: a Study in Christian Altruism* (1896), was an exploration of the difference between the philanthropist and the saint using the example of Peter Claver's ministry to African slaves. It was followed by *Devotional Essays* (1902), *The Temperament of Doubt* (1903), and *Where Saints have Trod: some Studies in Asceticism* (1903). These early works show Petre as critic and apologist.

In 1897 Maude Petre met George *Tyrrell (1861–1909), an English Jesuit priest and writer. Following a retreat preached by Tyrrell in 1900 a friendship developed which was the beginning of a long-term committed celibate relationship that had a profound effect on her life. Sharing his concerns about renewal within the Roman Catholic church and believing that he had a special calling within the church, she determined to help him in whatever ways she could. Petre, who already knew Friedrich von Hügel, joined him and Tyrrell in an informal network of persons in England, France, and Italy, who through their publications were working for change within the Roman Catholic church. When Tyrrell's writings were condemned and he was dismissed from the Society of Jesus in February 1906, Petre provided a home for him in Storrington, Sussex.

In September 1907 Pius X condemned modernism as 'the synthesis of errors' in the encyclical *Pascendi dominici gregis* (1907). Tyrrell responded with a critical letter in *The Times*, an action which brought upon him excommunication. Petre's book, *Catholicism and Independence: being Studies in Spiritual Liberty* (1907) was published just after the condemnation of modernism. Archbishop Bourne wanted it withdrawn but Petre was unwilling to do so. Her involvement in Roman Catholic modernism led to her departure from the Daughters of Mary on 2 February 1908.

Petre's home in Storrington became a gathering place for modernists, a matter of grave concern to the ecclesiastical authorities. There Tyrrell died of Bright's disease on 15 July 1909 at the age of forty-eight. Petre and von Hügel tried unsuccessfully to obtain a Roman Catholic funeral for their friend. He was buried in the parish churchyard in Storrington.

Petre was Tyrrell's literary executor. She prepared his last book, *Christianity at the Crossroads* (1909), for publication. In 1912 she published the *Autobiography and Life of George Tyrrell*, a two-volume work which was placed on the index of forbidden books. She was one of the first to write a history of modernism, *Modernism: its Failures and its Fruits* (1918). Her last book, *Alfred Loisy: his Religious Significance* (1944), published after her death, was about another modernist and friend. Petre continued to write and speak on modernism which she described in *My Way of Faith* as 'a movement of genuine Catholic believers … who held to their religious faith, and were endeavouring to answer their own difficulties as well as those of others' (Petre, 238). Peter Amigo, the Roman Catholic bishop of Southwark diocese, requested that Petre take the anti-

modernist oath. Petre refused, insisting that 'if one's life did not bear sufficient testimony to one's faith an oath would not do so' (ibid., 246). Her refusal to renounce modernism led to a partial excommunication which deprived her of the sacraments in her own diocese, a deprivation that caused her great suffering. She continued to believe in the modernist cause that the truths of religion and science could be reconciled and to hope that the Roman Catholic church would open itself to the modern world.

Petre was active in both the areas expected of women of her class and in a variety of progressive causes. During the First World War she nursed wounded soldiers in France and England. After the war she was involved in setting up a branch of the Labour Party in Storrington. She served as chair of the elected municipal council of Storrington for several years and as president of the Women's Institute pioneered a local housing scheme and founded a cottage hospital. For many years she participated in international summer gatherings of students and writers who met in Pontigny, France, to discuss political, religious, and social issues. Although she remained a committed Roman Catholic she was open to other churches and faiths. Toward the end of her life she was involved in the World Congress of Faith, delivering a paper in June 1941.

Despite her engagement in community activities Petre considered writing to be her real work. She published fourteen books and over ninety articles as well as edited essays and letters of Tyrrell. Her publications reflected a critical approach to authority, an insistence on spiritual independence, and a respect for pluralism. These characteristics were particularly evident in her study of her ancestor, *The Ninth Lord Petre: Pioneer of Roman Catholic Emancipation* (1928), whom she saw as 'a religious type which has almost disappeared—the old English Catholics, marked in religious and civil life by strength and determination' (p. xiii).

Petre herself exemplified these characteristics. Her aristocratic background and financial independence gave her certain privileges, including opportunities to travel. Besides frequent visits to friends in France and Italy, she visited her nephew in South Africa in 1926. The world was changing rapidly and Petre believed that new political and religious answers were needed. With courage she accepted change and developed her way of faith which respected authority while recognizing its limitations.

In 1939 Petre moved to London in the archdiocese of Westminster, where she was able to receive the sacraments. During the bombing of London she took her turn fire-watching. She died suddenly in her home at 15 Campden Grove, Kensington, on 16 December 1942. A requiem mass was celebrated at the Assumption Convent, Kensington Square, London. At her request she was buried in the parish churchyard of St Mary's Church, Storrington, in the same plot as her friend George Tyrrell.

ELLEN M. LEONARD

Sources M. Petre, *My way of faith* (1937) • E. M. Leonard, *Unresting transformation: the theology and spirituality of Maude Petre* (1991) • J. A. Walker, 'Maude Petre (1863–1942): a memorial tribute', *Hibbert*

Journal, 41 (April 1943), 340–46 · C. F. Crews, *English Catholic modernism: Maude Petre's Way of faith* (1984)
Archives BL, corresp. and papers, Add. MSS 44927–44931, 45361–45362, 45744–45745, 52367–52382 · CUL, collection of press cuttings · Emory University, Atlanta, Georgia, Pitts Theology Library, papers | Diocese of Southwark archive, London, Vigilance Committee file · U. St Andr. L., letters to Canon A. L. Lilley · U. St Andr. L., Wilfrid Ward family MSS, letters to Ward · Westm. DA, Bourne MSS, 1903–1935 · Westm. DA, Hinsley MSS, 1935–1943 · Westm. DA, Vaughan MSS, 1892–1903
Likenesses photograph, repro. in Crews, *English Catholic modernism* · photographs, repro. in Leonard, *Unresting transformation*; priv. coll.
Wealth at death £6634 19s. 6d.: resworn probate, 13 Feb 1943, CGPLA Eng. & Wales

Petre, Robert, seventh Baron Petre (*bap.* 1690, *d.* 1713). See under Petre family (*per.* 1633–1801).

Petre, Robert Edward, ninth Baron Petre (1742–1801), Roman Catholic leader, was born about February 1742 in London, the only son (he had three older sisters) of Robert James *Petre, eighth Baron Petre (1713–1742), of Ingatestone, Essex, a botanist and garden designer, and his wife, Anna Maria Barbara *Petre (1716–1760) [see under Petre family], daughter of James *Radcliffe, third earl of Derwentwater. He succeeded to his barony as a minor in July 1742 and may have been educated at the English Jesuit college at St Omer in France.

Petre was the principal representative of an enlightened, tolerant, rather tepid English Catholicism shared by the small but powerful grouping of 'old' Catholic families. His wealth made him one of the principal paymasters of the English Catholic community, and in political circles he was generally seen as the leader of Catholic opinion. He was one of the central figures in the Catholic Committee, a self-appointed body formed in 1778, predominately lay in character and noble in membership, which saw itself as speaking for 'informed' Catholic opinion (Petre always protected radicals among the clergy, such as Alexander Geddes), and which agitated for the freeing of the English Catholics from civil disabilities. It had considerable influence in negotiating the Catholic Relief Acts of 1778 and 1791 and in preparing a new oath of allegiance.

The visit of George III to Thorndon in October 1778 gave a royal seal of approval to Petre's efforts. Not all his co-religionists were so enthusiastic. Petre paid little attention either to the Irish dimension of Catholic relief or to the changing constituency of English Catholicism. The Cisalpine Club, formed in 1792 from the leading members of the Catholic Committee, looked very out of date by 1830 when its meetings finished. Ultramontanism was becoming more vigorous, and initiative among the English Catholics was moving away from the old Catholic families to the increasing Catholic population of towns. It was priests, not peers, who were now providing leadership in the church. Many of the disputes in which the English Catholics were involved during Petre's lifetime were about the place of lay power in an increasingly clericalized church or, as John Milner, bishop of Castabala, one of Petre's most bitter critics, put it, 'whether the

nomination of our Pastors shall be with *Lord Petre* or *the successors of St Peter*' (Duffy, 'Doctor Douglass', 249).

Petre married twice. In 1762 he married Anne (*d.* 1787), younger daughter and coheir of Philip Howard of Buckenham, Norfolk. They had four sons, two of whom died in infancy, and one daughter. In 1788 he married Juliana Barbara (*d.* 1833), sister of Bernard Edward Howard, later twelfth duke of Norfolk, and daughter of Henry Howard of Glossop, Derbyshire. They had one son and two daughters.

Elected FSA and FRS in 1780, Petre was also a leading freemason and grand master of the English freemasons in 1772–6 (the last Catholic to hold that office). James Paine designed his new residence at Thorndon Hall, Essex, and Lancelot (Capability) Brown laid out the grounds. Lord Petre died at his home in Park Lane, London, on 2 July 1801. He was succeeded in the barony by his eldest son, Robert Edward (*b.* 1763). DOMINIC AIDAN BELLENGER, *rev.*

Sources M. D. Petre, *The ninth Lord Petre, or, Pioneers of Roman Catholic emancipation* (1928) · B. Ward, *The dawn of the Catholic revival in England, 1781–1803*, 2 vols. (1909) · E. Duffy, 'Ecclesiastical democracy detected [pt 2]', *Recusant History*, 10 (1969–70), 309–31 · E. Duffy, 'Doctor Douglass and Mister Berington: an eighteenth-century retraction', *Downside Review*, 88 (1970), 246–69, esp. 249 · Burke, *Peerage*
Archives PRO, private papers, E 192/19–20

Petre, Robert James, eighth Baron Petre (1713–1742), patron of botany and garden designer, was born at Thorndon Hall, Ingatestone, Essex, on 3 June 1713. He was the posthumous son of Robert *Petre, seventh Baron Petre (*bap.* 1690, *d.* 1713) [see under Petre family], a man who was very much a part of the close-knit society of Roman Catholic families at the time, and famous as the original of the 'lock-raper' in Pope's poem. Petre's mother, Catherine Walmesley (1697–1785)—Catherine *Petre [see under Petre family]—was a wealthy Lancashire heiress. He was probably educated at home by Roman Catholic tutors. In 1732 he married Lady Anna Maria Barbara (Anne) Radcliffe (1716–1760)—Anna Maria Barbara *Petre [see under Petre family]—the wealthy heir of the estate of her father, the third earl of Derwentwater, who was beheaded for his part in the 1715 Jacobite rising. More important for Petre's subsequent botanical interests, his guardian was the father of Philip Southcote (*d.* 1758), the distinguished gardener and friend of Pope.

Petre's life was largely given over to nothing more eventful than the propagation of large numbers of exotic trees and shrubs. In this, however, he was famous in his time. Having become the chief supporter of a scheme by Peter Collinson (1694–1768) to support the botanizing of the pioneer American farmer John Bartram (1699–1777), Petre had by 1742 planted 40,000 American trees at Thorndon, his estate that he had redesigned with the assistance of the distinguished engraver, Hubert Gravelot (1699–1773). He was also a subscriber to Mark Catesby's *Natural History of Carolina* and a supporter of a fund for the improvement of botany in Georgia.

In the 1720s Petre met Philip Miller (1691–1771), keeper of the Chelsea Physic Garden, and John Martyn (1699–

1768), who was to be the first professor of botany at Cambridge. Martyn in 1731 sponsored Petre (then still a minor) as a fellow of the Royal Society, where he would have met Hans Sloane (1660–1753) whose work he had already read. Indeed, he had been planting and cultivating trees since boyhood, probably encouraged by his grandmother who was also a keen botanist. By the time of his return from a continental tour in 1730, he had amassed a considerable library of botanical and gardening books, now largely in the Sutro Library in San Francisco. Even before becoming the chief early supporter in the late 1730s of Collinson's scheme to import seeds and plants from America, Petre had subscribed to the botanizing of Mark Catesby (1683–1749) and William Houston (1695–1733) in the Carolinas and Georgia. He cultivated some of the novelties from both states at Thorndon, and by 1739 he was sending Sloane bananas from his 'stove' (greenhouse).

Famous by this time for his virtue and good nature, and as one of the most munificent botanists in England, Petre had already commissioned Miller in 1736 to make a catalogue of the plants at Thorndon. This catalogue, along with the extensive '*hortus siccus*' compiled chiefly from the American botanizing of Bartram and Houston, is still extant. The woods at Thorndon were themselves an anthology of the greatest collection of exotic trees ever naturalized.

Petre was part of a circle of planters that included the dukes of Richmond and Argyll, but he was no mere planter. Collinson described his plantings at Thorndon as 'painting with Living pencils' (Chambers, 107), and singled out Petre's 'skill in all the liberal arts, particularly architecture, statuary, planning and designing, planting and embellishing his large parks and gardens' (ibid., 118). Petre also worked on the estate of the eighth duke of Norfolk at Worksop, Nottinghamshire, and at Notley and Gisburn in Yorkshire. The still extant plans of Worksop show an extraordinary attention to detail in planting, both in the great forecourt of the house and in the 'clumps' designed for the landscape. In this, Petre was the first to put into practice the recommendations of Dezallier d'Argenville (1680–1765), Thomas Fairchild (1667?–1729), and Batty Langley (1696–1751). He also preceded Capability Brown in the moving of mature trees.

When Petre died suddenly at his seat in Essex of smallpox, on 2 July 1742, Collinson described his passing as 'the greatest loss to botany or gardening ever felt in this island' (*Selection of the Correspondence of Linnaeus*, 1.9). He was survived by his wife, three daughters, Catherine, Barbara, and Julia, and a son, Robert Edward *Petre, ninth Baron Petre (1742–1801), who went on to become a keen advocate of Catholic emancipation. But Petre's immortality must be with botany, where the camellia was his introduction, and one of about thirty species of American *Verbenaceae* was named *Petrea* after him by Linnaeus.

DOUGLAS D. C. CHAMBERS

Sources H. Grieve, 'A transatlantic gardening friendship, 1694–1777', *Historical Association, Essex Branch* (1981) · J. Britten, 'The eighth Lord Petre', *Dublin Review*, 155 (1914), 307–21 · *A selection of the correspondence of Linnaeus, and other naturalists, from the original manuscripts*, ed. J. E. Smith, 2 vols. (1821) · G. Clutton and C. Mackay, 'Old Thorndon Hall, Essex', *Garden History Society*, Occasional Paper 2 (1970), 27–37 · M. Binney, 'Worksop Manor, Nottinghamshire', *Country Life*, 153 (1973), 678–82 · E. P. McLean, 'An 18th century herbarium at the Sutro Library', *California State Library Foundation Bulletin*, 6 (1984) · D. C. Chambers, *The planters of the English landscape garden* (1993) · N. G. Brett-James, *The life of Peter Collinson* [1926] · M. Mack, *Alexander Pope: a life* (1985) · G. Jellicoe and S. Jellicoe, eds., *Oxford companion to gardens* (1986)

Archives BL, Add. MSS 15800, 14727 · Devon RO, family MSS · Essex RO · Glos. RO, estate MSS | Linn. Soc., Peter Collinson MSS · Passmore Edwards Museum, Stratford, P. Miller MS of Thorndon Plants · Sutro Library, San Francisco, California, Newham; Bartram/Petre MS

Petre, Thomas, sixth Baron Petre (*bap.* 1633, *d.* 1707). *See under* Petre family (*per.* 1633–1801).

Petre, Sir William (1505/6–1572), administrator, was the son of John Petre, a prosperous cattle farmer and tanner whose family had long been settled at Tor Newton in Torbryan, Devon. John had married Alice, daughter of John Colling of the neighbouring parish of Woodland. Both families occupied that intermediate station between yeomanry and gentility then known as that of franklin. William may have been the eldest son, though his brother John (*d.* 1568) inherited the main family property; another brother, also John, became customer of Dartmouth and Exeter, and sat for Dartmouth in the parliament of November 1554; the youngest brothers, Richard and Robert, became respectively archdeacon of Buckingham and an auditor of the exchequer.

Beginning a career Petre entered Oxford as a law student in 1519. He has been claimed for Exeter College, of which he was later a considerable benefactor, but there is no evidence of his undergraduate membership, which would have been irregular in a college restricted to arts students. He was admitted fellow of All Souls in 1523, retaining this place until 1535 and serving as law bursar in 1528/9. He graduated bachelor in both laws on 2 July 1526, and during 1527 and 1528 he practised in the Oxford chancellor's court. He is believed to have been made tutor to Sir Thomas Boleyn's son George (brother of Anne). Through this connection, supposedly, he came to Henry VIII's notice, and was one of the junior counsel representing the king in his matrimonial suit before the legatine court at Blackfriars (May–July 1529). Petre played no active part in these proceedings, and his presence is deduced only from the imprecise recollection of Cavendish in his life of Wolsey.

On 19 January 1530 Petre advanced his Oxford career by becoming principal of Peckwater Inn, a position he vacated by February 1534. On 17 February 1533 he incepted DCL. It is difficult to see how an alleged residence of several years abroad, chiefly in France, in the service of Boleyn father or son, can be accommodated in these years. Possibly Petre attended George Boleyn (now Viscount Rochford) on a mission to France between October 1529 and February 1530. If Petre spent further time overseas, he must have returned by the start of 1533; on 8 March he was admitted to Doctors' Commons, and in the course of the

Sir William Petre (1505/6–1572), by unknown artist, 1567

year began work as a chancery clerk. About this time he married Gertrude, daughter of John Tyrrell of Little Warley, Essex.

During the summer of 1535 Petre submitted proposals for the reorganization of ecclesiastical jurisdiction under the crown, and from October he presided over Cromwell's vice-gerential court. On 2 November Cranmer recommended him for the deanery of arches ('no man so meet'; *Miscellaneous Writings*, 315); this particular appointment eluded him, but on 13 January 1536 Cromwell made Petre his deputy in probate and other matters. In this capacity, though still a very junior official, he controversially presided at a session of convocation in June. Perhaps feeling that his status would be enhanced by an ecclesiastical dignity, Petre accepted a canonry of Lincoln Cathedral, with the prebend of Langford Ecclesia, to which he was installed by proxy on 11 December. The presentation was in the crown's gift by the attainder of the previous incumbent; Petre resigned by the following April. More importantly he had in 1536 been promoted to a mastership in chancery, and as such was on 25 November appointed to scrutinize papal bulls in the light of recent legislation. He may also have entered parliament this year as MP for Downton, Wiltshire, though the only evidence is an inconclusive scrap in Cromwell's hand.

Between 1535 and 1540 Petre was principally occupied with the visitation and dissolution of religious houses, tasks he performed with efficiency and fairness, avoiding the unsavoury reputation of his fellow commissioners. Nevertheless he used his position to amass a substantial landholding, mainly in his native Devon and in Essex. By

1540 he had a rent-roll in excess of £500. Like others he secured favourable leases from houses on the point of surrender, including (May 1538) that of the manor of Gyng Abbess, Essex, from Barking Abbey. On 15 December 1539, following the abbey's dissolution, he received a grant of the property from the crown. Here he built his seat, Ingatestone Hall, which his heirs still occupy.

Senior administrator During 1540 Petre first showed that adroitness in high politics which marked his career thereafter. He had been deputed to travel to Cleves to negotiate Henry VIII's marriage to the duke's daughter Anne, but he escaped this responsibility and so emerged from the resultant fiasco untainted by too close an association with Cromwell's failed scheme. On the minister's fall no new vicar-general was appointed, and Petre's deputyship necessarily lapsed. But on 5 October he was sworn of the king's council and appointed to preside over the conciliar court of White Hall.

Petre's wife died on 28 May 1541. By the following March he had married Anne, daughter of John Tyrrell of Heron (of another branch of the Essex gentry family from which Petre's first wife had come). She was the widow of William Browne of Flambard's Hall, and brought a healthy portion of £280 per annum.

During 1543–4 Petre deputized for Sir Ralph Sadler as keeper of the seal of the duchy of Lancaster. On 21 January 1544 he was appointed one of the principal secretaries (of state) in succession to Sir Thomas Wriothesley and as junior to Sir William Paget; at the same time he acquired a knighthood, membership of the privy council, and an *ex officio* seat in the House of Lords. By this year also he sat on the Essex bench; he would be appointed to numerous other local commissions. When in the summer of 1545 Henry VIII went to campaign in France, Petre was one of the queen regent's small advisory council, and (because the king took Paget with him) he was for the first time in charge of the national bureaucracy. From April to July 1545 he was one of five ambassadors sent to discuss commercial affairs at the imperial diet of Bourbourg. In September 1546 he paid a brief visit to France in an attempt to persuade the French to honour an ancient debt. He was unsuccessful, but this in itself cannot explain why Henry VIII excluded him from the regency council which he designed for his son's minority. Petre was appointed only to the outer group of assistant executors, and was the only one of the whole body of executors who did not receive a personal legacy from the king.

Royal secretary Notwithstanding this apparent disappointment, Petre and Paget were reappointed secretaries on 13 February 1547, Edward VI's coronation day, but for the moment Paget, as a privy councillor, was markedly the senior partner. Not until 18 March, when Somerset had expanded the privy council, did Petre regain a place there. However, on 29 June he was promoted to the comptrollership; he was then sole secretary until April 1548, and remained senior secretary until retirement in 1557. The secretaryship was his life's work; to it he brought a sharp mind and an easy command of paperwork; his handwriting, though not particularly neat, has a fluency which demonstrates the confidence with which he handled the multifarious duties of his office. Unsurprisingly he found little time for his position of *custos rotulorum* for Essex, also acquired in 1547, and he rarely sat as JP for the county. On 18 August 1547 he was made keeper of the *ad causas* seal which authenticated the crown's ecclesiastical jurisdiction. On 9 October he was awarded a £200 'bequest' from the late king (in reality compensation for the legacy he had been denied).

If Petre found Somerset's administration increasingly arbitrary he did not (as Paget did) make his feelings known. He developed a rapport with William Cecil, whose function as Somerset's secretary to some extent undercut the principal secretaries' work. Petre played a key part in the events leading to the end of the protectorate. He was with Somerset and the king at Hampton Court on 5 October 1549 when the protector, alarmed by the opposition of councillors left in London, appealed for military assistance. On the next day Petre was sent to London to parley with the councillors there. When he had not returned by nightfall, Somerset hustled the king away to Windsor. He supposed that Petre had been detained against his will; in fact he had been won over, and he drafted much of the correspondence which then flowed from opposition headquarters at Ely House, including the separate letters of 10 October to Somerset and to the latter's colleagues, the one conciliatory and the other disclosing the conspirators' true purpose. This manoeuvre succeeded in forcing Somerset's peaceful capitulation; when he was removed to the Tower, Petre composed the new government's official explanation. His role in the affair is not enlightened by any personal account, and he has been much criticized for it. Hayward, writing at the end of the century, said that 'under pretence of gravity [he] covered much untrustinesse of heart' (Hayward, 108). Subsequent better understanding of the ineptness of Somerset's regime makes it easier to condone Petre's defection.

In the succeeding administration Petre was (20 October 1549) given the further office of treasurer of first fruits and tenths, which he held until 25 January 1553. From January to May 1550 he was among the commissioners who negotiated the return of Boulogne to the French. During this mission Petre was said to have been described by Gaspard de Coligny as 'the man who said nothing' by whom the French were denied an additional 200,000 crowns in compensation (Emmison, *Tudor Secretary*, 88). The report is not contemporary, but it has fixed Petre with a reputation for shrewd silence, though it may be that his hesitancy in French contributed to this impression. In the remaining years of Edward VI's reign Petre served on taxation and chantry commissions for Essex, and in 1551 he was named a governor of Chelmsford grammar school. As the king was introduced into affairs of state, Petre assisted his political education; among Edward's surviving papers is a scheme in the king's hand for improving the privy council's routine, which was revised by Petre for submission to the council on 15 January 1553. The appointment of

Cheke as a third principal secretary on 2 June was thought to signal Petre's imminent removal. But, although he was later reported by Cecil to have had misgivings, he remained senior secretary and, though excluded from part of the deliberations, drafted some of the documents by which the succession was altered in favour of Lady Guildford Dudley. He was one of those who swore allegiance to her as Queen Jane on 9 July, three days after Edward's death. He and Cecil were sent to explain matters to the imperial ambassadors on the 10th. By 19 July the coup had collapsed, and Petre was among the councillors in London who changed sides and proclaimed Mary. On 30 July he was received by the queen at New Hall in Essex, and admitted to her council. The queen spent the night of 31 July at Ingatestone; there, if not before, Petre was reappointed secretary. Lady Petre's presence in the new queen's household may have assisted his re-engagement, but Mary was in no position to form a government from her own affinity, and Petre was among those of her brother's councillors she would have employed anyway.

Petre at once busied himself with the varied business the accession involved, and was soon rewarded with honours and service. With effect from 29 September he became chancellor of the Order of the Garter (though never a knight companion), charged with restoring religious elements in the statutes which Edward had personally expunged. On 1 January 1554 Petre was among the commissioners appointed to negotiate the queen's marriage to the prince of Spain. He was active in suppressing the disorders which the marriage provoked, and was among those who interrogated Princess Elizabeth over her alleged involvement in Wyatt's rising. When Philip arrived Petre was naturally in attendance, and received an annuity appropriate to his rank. After the king's departure in 1555, he became one of a group of 'select' councillors on whom Philip relied for information, and through whom he channelled his directives for his English realm. Petre drafted most of this body's reports, and so played a pivotal role in the Tudor–Habsburg monarchy. Meanwhile the English ambassador in France, Nicholas Wotton, frequently wrote dispatches to Petre alone, confident in his ability to digest news and present it to the government as a whole.

Parliamentary services Petre may have wanted to retire as early as September 1554, but in November that year Paget had told the emperor that he should not be allowed to do so because 'he had been there so long that he was as good as a council register' (*CSP Spain, 1554–8*, 89). No doubt this was meant as a compliment, though it could have seemed patronizing from one who had moved on from the secretaryship to higher office and a peerage. Petre was in fact by no means chained to his desk, but was also active in parliament. He sat as a member for Essex in every assembly from 1547 to 1563—which gave him a seat in the Commons as well as his *ex officio* place in the Lords. During Edward's reign he was employed on at least seven Commons' committees, and in the more frequent sessions of Mary's parliaments he came to be something like the modern leader of the house. Two months before the meeting of April 1554 he was among those deputed to plan the legislative programme and to appoint drafters of bills. In the first Marian parliament he had carried up two bills to the Lords, and in that of April 1554 he did so six times. In the crucial parliament of November 1554, when the reconciliation deal with Rome was hammered out, Petre was the chief mediator between legislature and legate; as Christmas approached he was almost daily on the river, plying the diplomatic shuttle between Westminster and Lambeth. He also had to introduce the new Treasons Bill in the Commons when the government's original proposals were thrown out by the Lords. In the 1555 parliament he was again busy on the floor of the house and in committee. In the final Marian parliament (1558) he was on the committee to examine the revived sanctuary claims of Westminster Abbey—an awkward by-product of the restoration of Catholicism.

Petre was probably sympathetic to the reunion with Rome; back in 1539 he had drafted the conservative Act of Six Articles, and now he was able to help implement Mary's comprehensive reaction. He was given to pious reflection, and in a letter to Cecil in 1551, discussing the many who were 'angling' for a particular church preferment, observed that:

> We which talk moch of Christ and his holy worde have I feare me used a moch contrary way, for we leave fysshing for men and fyssh agayn in the tempestuous seas of this world for gayne and wycked mammon.   (PRO, SP 10/13, no. 43)

Nevertheless, like all conservatives who had a share of appropriated church lands, he was not minded to part with his new acres to save his conscience. The deal made between Cardinal Pole and parliament in December 1554 had only been achieved because the current owners were left in possession. A bull issued by the new Pope Paul IV in July 1555 apparently rescinded that concession, to the consternation of Mary's council. Petre appears to have had secret knowledge of the issue, and expressed his anxieties to King Philip. He then secured for himself a personal papal bull confirming his property rights. By the time this was issued (28 November) a general confirmation of Pole's settlement had been received from Rome, but the incident is a notable indication of Petre's ability to make the papal bureaucracy work for his private purposes.

Retirement and death Dutiful son of the church he may now have become, but Petre probably thought the queen's firm policy against heretics was misguided, and this may help to explain his resignation. Another factor was Philip's return to England in March 1557, determined to bring the country into his war against France and the papacy. Unlike Paget, Petre had never been an ardent Habsburg imperialist, and he now voiced his opposition to English involvement in the continental war. For whatever reason, Petre vacated the secretaryship by the end of March. That he nevertheless continued to draft a good deal of the routine correspondence in the office shows that his retirement was unforced, and highlights the inexperience of those whom the queen had to employ in his place. Mary named Petre one of her executors but, by her successor's general order, he did not receive his designated legacy. Elizabeth retained him as a councillor, but he does not seem to have been a candidate for any office of state. He did, however, return to duty as acting secretary when Cecil was in Scotland in the summer of 1559.

In July 1561 Petre entertained the queen at Ingatestone for a few days, at a cost of £136. During 1564–6 he had another, though involuntary, royal guest, the queen's cousin Lady Catherine Grey, under house arrest because of her unauthorized marriage. Petre continued to attend council meetings until February 1567. He died at his house in Essex on 13 January 1572 and was buried on 1 February in the church at Ingatestone, where his memorial stands. He had already made substantial charitable bequests—a fellowship endowed at All Souls in 1557 and an almshouse founded at Ingatestone in the same year, and seven fellowships endowed at Exeter College in 1566, and another in 1568, these benefactions earning him recognition as the second founder of the college. By these and other gifts in his will he disposed of about £5000.

Petre's widow lived until 10 March 1582. The surviving children of his first marriage, Dorothy [see Wadham, Dorothy] and Elizabeth, had married Nicholas Wadham, founder of the eponymous Oxford college, and John Gostwick respectively; Catherine and Thomasine, daughters of Petre's second marriage, married respectively William Talbot and Ludovick, son of Sir Edward Greville. Petre's only surviving son, from his second marriage, inherited Ingatestone; he was knighted in 1576 and in 1603 was created Baron Petre of Writtle. He and his descendants made their chief residence at Thorndon Hall near Brentwood, as a result of which (and some conscious twentieth-century restoration) Ingatestone remains much as it was in Sir William's time. His life there is also richly documented by a substantial household archive, amply drawn on in F. G. Emmison's biography. Petre established a reputation for handsome hospitality, though perhaps of the contrived kind to which the *nouveaux* are reputedly inclined. As far as can be judged he lived within his means at the level appropriate to his station. Unlike his colleagues Cecil, Paget, and Russell he did not found a political dynasty. His family's firm adherence to the Catholic religion [see Petre family] largely impeded his heirs from following the path of royal and public service which he had himself so successfully negotiated.   C. S. KNIGHTON

Sources Emden, *Oxf.*, 4.445–6 • HoP, *Commons, 1509–58*, 3.92–6 • F. G. Emmison, *Tudor secretary: Sir William Petre at court and home* (1961) • F. G. Emmison, 'A plan of Edward VI and Secretary Petre for reorganizing the privy council's work, 1552–1553', *BIHR*, 31 (1958), 203–10 • F. G. Emmison, ed., *Elizabethan life: wills of Essex gentry and merchants* (1978), 28–36 [wills of Petre and his 2nd wife] • D. E. Hoak, *The king's council in the reign of Edward VI* (1976), esp. 163–4 • C. S. Knighton, 'The principal secretaries in the reign of Edward VI', in J. J. Scarisbrick, *Law and government under the Tudors: essays presented to Sir Geoffrey Elton*, ed. C. Cross and D. Loades (1988), 163–75 • G. A. Lemasters, 'The privy council in the reign of Queen Mary I', PhD diss., U. Cam., 1972 • *Fasti Angl., 1300–1541*, [Lincoln], 75 • *Miscellaneous writings and letters of Thomas Cranmer*, ed. J. E. Cox, Parker Society, [18] (1846), 315 • *The chronicle and political papers of King Edward VI*, ed. W. K. Jordan (1966) • J. Hayward, *The life and raigne of King Edward the sixth*, ed. B. L. Beer (1993), 108 • G. R. Elton, *Policy and* *police* (1972), 248 · G. R. Elton, *Reform and renewal* (1973), 134–4 · *LP Henry VIII*, 9, no. 1071; 10, nos. 40(ii), 88; 11, no. 1217(22); 14/1, no. 1193; 14/2, no. 780(26); 16, no. 124; 19/1, no. 1036 · *CPR*, 1549–51, 24; 1553–4, 160 · *CSP dom.*, 1547–53, 141–9, 288–9 · *CSP for.*, 1547–62 · *CSP Scot.*, 1547–63 · *CSP Spain*, 1553–8 · *APC*, 1547–50 · PRO, SP 10/13, no. 43

Archives Essex RO, Chelmsford, archives, legal and family papers, D/DP | PRO, SP (esp. 1, 10, 11)

Likenesses oils, *c.*1545, Ingatestone Hall, Essex; repro. in Emmison, *Tudor secretary*, p. 16 · formerly attrib. Holbein, oils, 1567, Ingatestone Hall, Essex; repro. in Emmison, *Tudor secretary*, frontispiece · attrib. S. van der Meulen, oils, 1567, Ingatestone Hall, Essex; version, NPG · attrib. S. van der Meulen, oils, 1567, Exeter College, Oxford · oils, 1567, NPG [*see illus.*] · C. Cure?, tomb effigy (with his wife), St Edmund and St Mary's Church, Ingatestone, Essex

Wealth at death £792 15s. 9¾d. p.a.: Emmison, *Tudor secretary*, 291

Petre, William (1602–1678), translator, was born on 28 July 1602 in his father's house at Ingatestone, Essex, the third son of William, second Lord Petre (1575–1637), and his wife, Catherine (d. 1624), second daughter of Edward Somerset, fourth earl of Worcester (*c.*1550–1628), and his wife, Elizabeth (*fl.* 1571–1621). He was the great-grandson of Sir William Petre (1505?–1572), secretary of state and benefactor of Exeter College, Oxford, where Petre matriculated as a gentleman commoner on 5 February 1613, at the early age of ten. The strength of the family's association with the college is marked by the fact that when Petre's eldest brother, John, died on 11 October 1613, the society of Exeter dedicated a threnody to the family. However, Petre's own connection with Exeter was short. When Wadham College was completed by his great-aunt, Dame Dorothy Wadham (1535–1618), later in 1613, both he and his elder brother, Robert, became members of that college; as Wood records, Petre was entered as 'the first gentleman commoner or nobleman thereof' (Wood, *Ath. Oxon.*, 3.1144–5). Both brothers left without taking a degree, but as fellow-commoners they presented the college with two silver tankards, which survived until 26 January 1643, when they were melted down at Charles I's mint in New Inn Hall Street.

After leaving Oxford, Petre joined the Inner Temple. He went on to travel in the south of Europe, and 'became a gentleman of many accomplishments' (Wood, *Ath. Oxon.*, 3.1145). He married Lucy (d. 1679), daughter of Sir Richard Fermor, of Somerton, Oxfordshire, with whom he had four sons and two daughters. Like the rest of his family, he remained a Roman Catholic, as is reflected in his translation work; later generations became leaders of English Roman Catholic society [*see* Petre family (*per.* 1633–1801)]. In 1669 he had published at St Omer a translation of the then popular *Flos sanctorum* of the Jesuit Pedro de Ribadeneira, originally published at Barcelona in 1643. His translation, *Lives of the Saints, with other Feasts of the Year According to the Roman Calendar*, extends the calendar as far as 1669. The first edition soon became scarce, and a second, corrected and amended, was published in London in 1730. This too appears to have been popular; Petre's translation was commended by Southey and by Isaac Disraeli in his

Curiosities of Literature. Petre died on 16 January 1678 at his house in Stanford Rivers in Essex, and was buried in the chancel of Stanford Rivers church.

THOMAS SECCOMBE, *rev.* JANE GRIFFITHS

Sources Wood, *Ath. Oxon.*, new edn · *Reg. Oxf.* · R. B. Gardiner, ed., *The registers of Wadham College, Oxford*, 1 (1889) · Wing, *STC* · T. H. Clancy, *English Catholic books, 1641–1700: a bibliography* [1974] · F. Blom and others, *English Catholic books, 1701–1800: a bibliography* (1996) · Burke, *Peerage* (1970) · GEC, *Peerage*, new edn, vol. 12/2 · F. Madan, *The early Oxford press: a bibliography of printing and publishing in Oxford, 1468–1640*, OHS, 29 (1895), vol. 1 of *Oxford books: a bibliography of printed works* (1895–1931) · *IGI*

Wealth at death bequeathed £110 in gold; 2 sums of 40s.; gold ring worth 40s.; disposes of estate of Stanford Rivers and two other 'manors' in Essex: will, PRO, PROB 11/357

Petre, William, fourth Baron Petre (1625/6–1684), nobleman and victim of the Popish Plot, was the eldest son of Robert Petre, third Baron Petre (1599–1638), and Mary (1603–1685), daughter of Anthony Browne, second Viscount Montagu. Although his twin brother, John, quickly sickened and died William appears to have been a fairly robust infant, upon whom the hopes of his house were settled. A full-length portrait of him, aged six, was commissioned from J. Parker in 1632, and shows him as an anxious, self-possessed child, who still had the need for a coral suckling stick or dummy. He came into his title and estates after the premature death of his father, in October 1638, and—at the outbreak of the civil war—was made a ward of the king. It is possible that he watched the battle of Edgehill, on 23 October 1642, from the comparative safety of the royalist baggage train, before returning to Charles I's wartime capital at Oxford. Upon his arrival he was placed under the care and supervision of the earl of Northampton, who chose to put him to his studies under the careful eye of a protestant tutor. Petre could not, however, be shaken from his attachment to the Roman Catholic faith in which he had been raised. Though he and his devoted servants continued to mask his beliefs—until the Restoration—in an attempt to prevent the total sequestration of his estates, there is every reason to believe that the heady atmosphere of ultra-royalism that he imbibed while at Oxford was of far more significance to his subsequent intellectual development than the admonitions of his rather ineffectual and pedestrian tutor.

In the summer of 1655 Petre was arrested at Westminster and imprisoned on suspicion that he was planning to take part in a projected royalist rebellion. Held until August he anxiously petitioned Secretary Thurloe for his release, declaring that it was impossible to find another man 'that hath lesse crime upon him' (Thurloe, *State papers*, 3.699). Despite his subsequent release Petre found that life under the republican government was becoming increasingly uncongenial. Consequently, he sought—and obtained—passes to go to France in March and November 1658, and 'beyond the seas' in June that year (*CSP dom.*, 1658–9, 583). However, it is not certain if he made use of them, for in the summer of 1659 he was arrested and taken into custody in Sussex in order to prevent his possible involvement in a fresh cycle of royalist insurrection. It was only after the collapse of Booth's rising that the council of state finally ordered his release, on 13 August 1659.

Denied a significant role at the heart of national government on account of his religion Petre seems, at the Restoration, to have been content to live in quiet seclusion, overseeing the administration of his large Essex estates from his seat at Ingatestone Hall. However, the state of his troubled marriage to Elizabeth (d. 1665), eldest daughter of John Savage, second Earl Rivers, whom he married in or before 1655, returned him to the public eye. Though handsome and high spirited in her youth Elizabeth's infidelities and heavy drinking had caused the couple to separate at some point before the spring of 1664. Faced by a warrant for her arrest for debt she claimed that she was exempt from the charges on account of her privilege as a peeress of the realm. William Joyce, the unfortunate chaloner who had attempted to recoup his losses through the prosecution, was subsequently reported by her to the House of Lords' committee of privileges, and was imprisoned for contempt in April 1664 in a remarkable reversal of fortune. Joyce was released upon bail and was compelled to apologize to both the house and to Lady Petre upon bended knee. This, however, did not satisfy Elizabeth, who declared 'that Revenge was sweeter to her than milk' and provoked a public row with her husband, who thought that the conduct of his estranged wife was bringing him nothing but disgrace (Pepys, 5.128). Despite her vow to continue pursuing Joyce 'if she lived [to] the age of Methusalem' Elizabeth died, still unsatisfied, on 19 July 1665, and was denied burial in the traditional Petre burial vault, her body being relegated to the New Chapel at Ingatestone (Pepys, 5.126).

Having married, by 15 April 1675, Bridget (1652/3–1695), daughter and coheir of his neighbours, John and Anne Pincheon of Writtle, Petre was unprepared for the storm that broke over him, in late 1678, as the result of Titus Oates's fevered allegations of a popish plot which aimed to overthrow the state and murder the king. Petre was named in Oates's initial deposition, sworn before Sir Edmund Berry Godfrey on 6 September 1678, and the justice's mysterious death, shortly afterwards, served to lend credence to the story, which might otherwise have been entirely lacking. Despite his having had no formal military training it was claimed that Petre was one of a number of leading Catholic magnates who aimed forcibly to reimpose their faith upon the peoples of the British Isles, and that he had received a commission as the lieutenant-general of an invading army, stamped and sealed by Johannes Paulus d'Olivia, the head of the Jesuit order. Further corroboration appeared to be provided by the testimony of Miles Prance, who swore that he had heard that Petre was intent upon levying war, that he had already appointed officers for the task, and that 'there would very shortly be Fifty thousand men in Arms' awaiting his command (A True Narrative and Discovery, 4–5). Following Oates's repetition of his allegations before the Commons in October, Petre was arrested along with four other Roman Catholic lords, Belasyse, Powis, Arundel, and Stafford, and charged with high treason. Committed to the Tower of London on 28 October, he was finally permitted to seek legal counsel in early December, and on 8 April 1679 he was summoned to appear before the bar of the Lords in order to hear the indictment read against him. However, despite the repeated pleas of his friends and the incessant clamouring of Oates and his following, further charges and a firm date for the trial were not forthcoming. Fortunately his plea of not guilty had been entered and accepted by the Lords as a legal answer to the charges brought, and he was allowed permission to visit his wife, who was still recovering after the difficult delivery of their only child, Mary (1679–1704), who had been born a month before.

In November 1679 royal assent was given to the bill stripping Petre of his membership of the Lords, while the hapless Viscount Stafford was found guilty and sent to the block in December 1680. However, the lack of a second prosecution witness, in addition to Prance, and the resurgence of the tories' political strength in 1681–2, increasingly rendered the chances of Petre's successful conviction an unlikely event. As the scaffolding erected in Westminster Hall to accommodate spectators for his projected trial began to decay, the threat under which Petre had laboured began to evaporate and his spirits began to rise. His confinement in the Tower had never been particularly harsh and, having taken lodgings in the home of one of the warders, he was often permitted to dine with noble visitors. On 19 August 1683 it was reported that during a game of 'nine pins in the bowling green' he had been 'very merry' and had declared that he expected to be 'cleared about next spring … by parliament' (CSP dom., 1683, 308). Sadly, at precisely the moment when deliverance appeared to be close at hand, his health finally broke down. He had suffered occasional bouts of illness throughout his imprisonment, but in October 1683 he suddenly sickened and was in 'danger of speedy death'. In December his wife desperately petitioned the king that he needed a 'change of air, which his physicians are ready to attest' and that he was prepared to offer a bond for his good conduct (CSP dom., 1683–4, 145). However, Charles II chose to ignore her pleas and Petre's condition continued to worsen. Knowing that his end was upon him Petre composed a final declaration in which he vigorously defended the Roman Catholic church from charges that it promoted regicide, and proclaimed his own continuing innocence as: 'a Dying but Dutiful Subject … [who had] lain so long under a false and injurious Calumny of a horrid Plot' (Declaration, 1). On 4 January 1684 the lord lieutenant of the Tower wrote that reports of the prisoner's death were still premature, 'though we expect it every hour' (CSP dom., 1683–4, 199). In the event, he had not long to wait, for Petre died in the Tower the very next day. Having been permitted to claim the body of her husband Lady Petre had his remains taken back to Essex and buried them in the family vault at Ingatestone church, on 10 January 1684. She died on 5 January 1695, aged forty-two, and was buried with him.

Yet even in death controversy continued to attach itself to Petre's name, and the publication of his *Declaration* sparked the exchange of rival, and bitterly polemical, pamphlets. While the anonymous author of *Observations on a Paper Intituled, 'The Declaration of the Lord Petre'* (1684) chose to cast doubt upon the authorship of his last statement, arguing that it smelt 'rank of a Popish Priests Contrivance' (p. 2), the writer of *A Pair of Spectacles for Mr. Observer* (1684) attested to its provenance and capably refuted the idea of a highly organized and covert Catholic plot, stating that 'his *Lordship* [had] to hundreds ... of very *Worthy Protestants* (who during his Confinement came often to him) *most solemnly declar'd his Innocence*' (p. 1). It is clear that Petre's sufferings aroused considerable public sympathy, and the duke of York was quick to take advantage of the sudden sea change, successfully pressing for the release of the surviving Catholic lords at the next session of the king's bench, on 18 February 1684. Petre was succeeded in his peerage by his brothers John (*bap.* 1629, *d.* 1685) and Thomas *Petre (*bap.* 1633, *d.* 1707) [*see under* Petre family].

JOHN CALLOW

Sources *The declaration of the Lord Petre upon his death touching the plot* (1684) · GEC, *Peerage* · J. J. Howard and H. F. Burke, eds., *Genealogical collection illustrating the history of Roman Catholic families of England*, pt 1 (1887) · *Fifth report*, HMC, 4 (1876) · *Observations on a paper intituled, 'The declaration of the Lord Petre'* (1684) · M. Prance, *A true narrative and discovery of several very remarkable passages relating to the horrid Popish Plot as they fell within the knowledge of Mr Miles Prance* (1679) · T. Oates, *A true narrative of the horrid plot and conspiracy of the popish party* (1679) · Thurloe, *State papers* · Pepys, *Diary* · Evelyn, *Diary* · *A pair of spectacles for Mr. Observer* (1684) · P. Morant, *The history and antiquities of the county of Essex*, 2 vols. (1768) · *The reasons and narrative of proceedings betwixt the two houses ... at the conference touching the tryal of the lords in the Tower* (1679) · N. Luttrell, *A brief historical relation of state affairs from September 1678 to April 1714*, 1 (1857) · S. A. H. Burne, *The trial of William Howard, viscount Stafford* (privately published, 1964) · D. Piper, *Petre family portraits on view to the public at Ingatestone Hall* (1956) · J. Lane [E. Dakers], *Titus Oates* (1949) · J. Kenyon, *The Popish Plot* (1972) · CSP dom., 1553–9; 1683–4 · PRO, PROB 11/375, fols. 51v–52r
Archives CUL, family estate accounts, Ee. III 27 · Devon RO, family estates at Axminster and Shute, deeds and manorial records, 517/M · Essex RO, Chelmsford, family estate deeds, D/DP · Essex RO, Chelmsford, Ingatestone Estate, deeds and papers, D/DZf
Likenesses attrib. J. Parker, oils, 1632, Ingatestone Hall, Essex · school of Van Dyck, oils, 1655? (of William Petre?), Ingatestone Hall, Essex · oils, c.1660–1670 (after P. Borsselaer), Ingatestone Hall, Essex · attrib. P. Borsselaer, oils, c.1663, Ingatestone Hall, Essex · W. Petre?, self-portrait, mezzotint, BM

Petrie, Alexander (*c.*1594–1662), Presbyterian minister in the Netherlands, was born in Montrose, the third son of Alexander Petrie, merchant burgess of that town. He graduated MA from St Andrews University in 1615 and from 1620 to 1630 was master of the grammar school of Montrose. He was presented to the parish of Rhynd, Perthshire, by Charles I and was ordained in July 1632. According to Robert Baillie, he wrote against corrupt episcopal practices and was appointed to a committee to consider such practices by the 1638 Glasgow general assembly.

In 1642 a Scottish church was founded in Rotterdam for the many expatriates who lived there, and Petrie was selected as the first minister by the presbytery of Edinburgh. He arrived in Rotterdam in July 1643 and was inducted by the local Dutch *classis* in the presence of William Spang, minister of Veere, on 30 August. The Dutch states and city authorities provided the salary and building (initially a former warehouse belonging to a wine merchant), and the church formed part of the Dutch Reformed church, though it was exempt from some aspects of normal Dutch practice.

Petrie's incumbency came during a period when the fledgeling kirk faced disruption from independency and millenarianism in the Netherlands. Soon after his arrival Petrie published *Chiliasto-mastix* (1644) to refute the millenarianism of Robert Maton's *Israel's Redemption* (1642); there were also heated disputes within the congregation on the exposition of scripture, which were only resolved when Petrie appealed directly to the Church of Scotland authorities. In April 1645 Robert Baillie and George Gillespie, who had been driven to the Dutch coast by a storm, advised Petrie on how to deal with Robert Nasmyth, a troublesome member of the church, and on the same visit they asked the Scots conservator to support the minister and elders in their efforts to maintain discipline. Nevertheless, as late as 1650 Petrie was appealing to the local Dutch church authorities for help in restoring peace to his disordered congregation. He was a strong disciplinarian, not known for his patience, and complained to the authorities of the work involved in caring for such a 'Rouwe Gemeente' ('raw congregation'); his portrait, still displayed in the Rotterdam kirk at the beginning of the twenty-first century, depicts a man of stern and determined temperament. Keen to have responsibility for the spiritual care of all Scots in Rotterdam, he sought to ensure that all Scottish marriages and baptisms took place in his kirk (between 1643 and 1660 there are records of 734 baptisms and more than 1100 new members) and a poor fund was established to assist the less fortunate. The ultimate success of the new kirk was largely his, and he gained respect from his congregation and from fellow theologians.

Petrie kept the church as close as possible to developments in Scotland: in January 1644 the solemn league and covenant was subscribed publicly in the church, and throughout the 1640s there were several fast days in support of the Scottish armies. Petrie was also in touch with developments taking place in the Westminster assembly and in 1649 was involved in negotiations with Charles II, who was then in exile in the United Provinces.

Petrie's *magnum opus* was *A compendious history of the Catholick church, from the year 600 untill the year 1600, showing her deformation and reformation*, published in 1662. It was a well-researched history of the Christian church, dedicated to the prince of Orange and containing extracts from the records of the early general assemblies of the Church of Scotland. Petrie did not long survive the publication: his meticulous reports in the church register had been deteriorating since 1654, and he died after a protracted illness on 6 September 1662. He was married (his wife's name is unknown) and was survived by two sons and three daughters, including Alexander (c.1622–1683), minister of the Scottish church at Delft from 1645 to 1668 and 1669 to 1683, and Christian, who married Andrew Snype, minister of the Scots church at Veere.

GINNY GARDNER

Sources Fasti Scot., new edn, 4.243, 7.543, 7.550 · W. Steven, The history of the Scottish church, Rotterdam (1832, 1833) · K. L. Sprunger, Dutch puritanism: a history of English and Scottish churches of the Netherlands in the sixteenth and seventeenth centuries (1982) · J. Morrison, Scots on the Dijk: the story of the Scots church, Rotterdam (1981) · DSCHT, 655 · The letters and journals of Robert Baillie, ed. D. Laing, 3 vols., Bannatyne Club, 73 (1841–2) · DNB
Archives Scots Church, Rotterdam, church records
Likenesses portrait (after engraving), Scots church, Rotterdam; repro. in Steven, The history of the Scottish church

Petrie, Alexander Gordon (1847/8–1909), rugby player, was born in Liverpool, the son of Alexander Petrie, a bleacher, and his wife, Betsy Gordon. His childhood was spent in Birkenhead and Chester before he moved to Edinburgh, where he enrolled for a special French class at the Royal High School, Edinburgh, in 1870. At 6 foot 3 inches tall and weighing some 13 stone, he was a giant of a man by nineteenth-century standards. He was quickly snapped up by Royal High School former pupils' club and within two seasons represented Scotland, gaining the first of his eleven caps in 1873. A man of exceptional strength, he excelled at other sports where his upper body strength gave him an advantage over his opponents, such as weightlifting, hammer throwing, rowing, and cricket (where his fast bowling caught the eye).

In total, Petrie won eleven caps for Scotland between 1873 and 1880 and this would have been undoubtedly more but for the rapid rise to Scotland's senior administrative position. It was customary at this time in Scotland for the senior cap (the person with the most representative appearances) to be chosen as captain. In 1881 Petrie, as the senior cap, was not selected as captain, and the position passed from R. W. Irvine to J. H. S. Graham, another member of the Edinburgh Academicals club. Petrie and other Edinburgh forwards withdrew from the Scottish team, which then lost to Ireland for the first time. At the next annual general meeting of the then Scottish Football Union (SFU), several changes were made in the composition of the SFU committee and Petrie was duly elected president for the 1881–2 season. The following year he took charge of the Scotland v. Ireland rugby union fixture in his only match as an international rugby referee.

Like many early Scottish rugby internationals, Petrie was a lawyer by profession and was a senior partner in the Edinburgh legal practice Gordon, Petrie, and Shand. He died from pneumonia at his home, 4 Dalrymple Crescent, Edinburgh, on 4 February 1909. He was survived by his widow, Annette (formerly Cooper). Petrie was one of Scotland's most prominent forwards, whose size and physical strength intimidated his opponents. However, he was very much the gentle giant, who viewed the game as one for gentlemen and for recreation. His elevation to the role of president of the SFU may have satisfied his friends and colleagues that justice had been done, but it deprived Scotland of their best forward for another two seasons.

WALTER ALLAN

Sources J. McI. Davidson, A compendium of Scotland's matches (1994) · A. M. C. Thorburn, The Scottish rugby union (1985) · d. cert.

Petrie, Sir David (1879–1961), police officer in India and head of the security service, was born on 9 September 1879 at Inveravon, Banffshire, the second surviving son of Thomas Petrie, master millwright, and his wife, Jane Allan. After taking an MA degree at Aberdeen University, Petrie entered the Indian police in December 1900. He served for three years in the Punjab and was then seconded (1904–8) to the north-west frontier as quartermaster and adjutant of the Samana Rifles (Kohat border military police). An essay by him on civil–military co-operation won a prize from the United Services Institution in India (1911). After acting as assistant to the deputy inspector-general of the Punjab criminal investigation department (1909–11), he was moved to the department of criminal intelligence (DCI), responsible to the home department of the government of India, and there became assistant to its assistant director.

Petrie faced a crucial test when chosen to investigate the bomb attack on the viceroy, Lord Hardinge, in Delhi in December 1912. The reputation of the DCI was at stake until he finally arrested the terrorists in February 1914; he received the king's police medal. The outbreak of the First World War emboldened militant Indian nationalists. In a gun battle with Sikh revolutionaries at Budge-Budge on 29 September 1914 Petrie was wounded, and a subsequent infection warranted convalescence in Britain.

When Petrie returned to India in summer 1915, the DCI was worried about contacts between Indian rebels and German agents in neutral Siam. He therefore spent six months as an intelligence officer at the British legation in Bangkok from August 1915, with results that convinced the government of India that it needed its own overseas intelligence network. Petrie recruited agents during a tour of Singapore, the Dutch East Indies, the Philippines, Hong Kong, China, and Japan, and directed their operations from August 1916 to November 1919, while ostensibly vice-consul in Shanghai. He was honoured with the CIE (1915), OBE (1918), and CBE (1919).

Petrie turned down the directorship of the DCI in 1919, pleading exhaustion. In the following year he married Edris Naida (d. 1945), daughter of W. Henry Elliston Warrall, a sea captain; there were no children. He escorted the duke of Connaught and the prince of Wales during their visits to India (1921–2) and worked again in the Punjab as senior superintendent of police in Lahore (1923). As a member of the royal commission on the public services in India (1923–4), he pondered the rate at which Indian personnel should be admitted to the higher echelons.

In 1924, when Cecil Kaye retired, Petrie this time consented to become director of the DCI, renamed the intelligence bureau of the home department of the government of India. It co-ordinated the efforts of provincial police forces to combat terrorism and communal violence and used informers to monitor the activity of the non-co-operation movement. Attempts by M. N. Roy to establish communist cells were comprehensively thwarted, for which Petrie received much credit. Knighted in June 1929, he left the intelligence bureau in 1931 to become first a member and then chairman (1932–6) of the Indian public services commission. He also chaired the Indian Red Cross Society.

On his retirement from Indian service in 1936 Petrie passed some time in east Africa and the Levant. He assisted his old friend and colleague Sir Charles Tegart in reporting on reorganization of the Palestine police (December 1937–January 1938) before settling in Britain. His career appeared to be at an end until the Second World War saw him commissioned into the intelligence corps and posted to Cairo in May 1940. Six months later he was recalled to London and asked to become director-general of the Security Service (still commonly known as MI5, its designation prior to 1931). Petrie hesitated to accept.

MI5, responsible for defence against espionage, subversion, and sabotage, was near collapse in 1940, riven by internal feuds and overwhelmed with reports of suspected 'fifth columnist' activity and demands for security 'vetting'. Churchill had dismissed its long-serving chief, Sir Vernon Kell, in June, but his temporary successor, A. W. A. (Jasper) Harker, had made little difference. It was Stewart Menzies, head of the Secret Intelligence Service (SIS or MI6), who now put forward Petrie, but Sir David refused to take charge without examining the situation for himself. His report, dated 13 February 1941, revealed that rapid expansion of MI5 (from thirty officers in 1938 to more than 200) had produced haphazard recruitment, inadequate supervision, confusion in the chain of command, and general demoralization. Having emphasized the seriousness of the problem, he agreed to tackle it—on the understanding that the director-general should be master in his own house. Petrie suspected that interference by Lord Swinton, chairman of the security executive, had exacerbated factional struggles. He formally took over on 24 April 1941.

The mere presence of Petrie appeared to improve the atmosphere inside MI5. A powerfully built man, with a steady gaze, square jaw, and military moustache, he was straightforward, firm, and decisive, combining a thorough grasp of practical intelligence work with the skills of an unspectacular but effective manager. His manner with subordinates was rather formal; he called even those closest to him by their surnames, and some sensed an air of Scottish puritanism about him. Very industrious, he briefed himself with great care for meetings, where he generally spoke little but to the point. His writing style could be long-winded and pompous, and he made scant effort to cultivate influential people, yet his reliability helped restore official confidence in his top-secret department.

Petrie ended wrangling within MI5 over the new Hollerith punch-card filing method by ruling in its favour, and reorganized the divisional structure of the service to allow its B division to concentrate on counter-espionage. Since autumn 1940 Guy Liddell had been successfully developing the 'double cross system', whereby captured German spies were used to feed false information to Berlin. There was much friction between MI5 and the SIS over access to decrypted signals intelligence from the Radio Security Service, and Petrie grew exasperated. The two secret services seemed competitive rather than complementary in some matters. MI5 did not operate more than 3 miles outside the British empire, while the SIS managed British intelligence and counter-intelligence in foreign countries. Petrie proposed in April 1942 that the SIS counter-intelligence section should be incorporated into B division of MI5, but prolonged negotiations came to nothing, despite his argument that the ideal demarcation between MI5 and the SIS was functional (defensive–offensive) rather than geographical.

In 1944, after the D-day landings surprised the Germans, Petrie claimed that MI5 had totally defeated enemy espionage in Britain. Post-war study of German archives confirmed this. In retrospect, however, this triumph had to be set alongside a serious failure: inadequate surveillance of Soviet spies. Petrie sensed that the Russian espionage which MI5 uncovered was the tip of an iceberg, but the Foreign Office urged restraint and MI5 had itself already been penetrated (by Anthony Blunt).

Petrie was awarded the KCMG in 1945, as well as American, Dutch, and Czechoslovak orders. Though the new Labour government viewed MI5 with some suspicion, he succeeded in resisting any reduction in its powers or remit. Attlee disregarded his recommendation of Liddell as a successor, however, and appointed Percy Sillitoe as director-general when Petrie retired in 1946. Shooting, fishing, and the countryside remained his pleasures. He died at Sidmouth, Devon, on 7 August 1961.

People routinely described Petrie as solid, sound, and trustworthy—with some clearly insinuating that he was neither intellectually brilliant nor inspiring. Historians of the secret services focused on more flamboyant characters, yet none denied that his plain merits had stabilized MI5 at a critical juncture.   JASON TOMES

Sources DNB · The Times (8 Aug 1961) · C. Andrew, introduction, in J. Curry, The security service, 1908–1945 (1999) · R. Popplewell, Intelligence and imperial defence: British intelligence and the defence of the Indian empire, 1904–1924 (1995) · F. H. Hinsley and C. A. G. Simkins, British intelligence in the Second World War, 4: Security and counter-intelligence (1990) · J. Masterman, On the chariot wheel (1975) · D. Petrie, Communism in India, 1924–27 (1972) · T. Bower, The perfect English spy: Sir Dick White and the secret war, 1935–90 (1995) · CGPLA Eng. & Wales (1961)

Archives BL OIOC, Indian police files · PRO, MI5 files

Likenesses photograph, repro. in P. Griffiths, To guard my people: the history of the Indian police (1971)

Wealth at death £25,034 18s. 11d.: probate, 10 Oct 1961, CGPLA Eng. & Wales

Petrie, Sir (William Matthew) Flinders (1853–1942), Egyptologist, was born at Ecclesbourne Cottage, Maryon Road, Charlton, near Greenwich, on 3 June 1853, the only child of William *Petrie (1821–1908) and his wife, Anne (1812–1892), the daughter of Captain Matthew *Flinders

Sir (William Matthew) Flinders Petrie (1853–1942), by Philip
A. de Laszlo

RN, the navigator and explorer of Australia. Too delicate
to be sent to school, he was educated at home by his
father, a skilled engineer and surveyor, and his mother
who taught him history, music, and French, and encouraged him to collect minerals and coins. His mother was
herself a scholar and published a work on the relationship
between mythology and scripture under the pseudonym
'Philomathes'. Petrie showed precocity in mathematics
and science, and by the time he was sixteen he was often
in the galleries of the British Museum, sometimes buying
for their coin department Greek and Roman coins picked
up in antique shops and country sales. His father taught
him surveying, and in his early twenties he would travel
about the south of England with measuring tape and theodolite, planning earthworks and ancient monuments;
with his father's help he measured Stonehenge, setting a
new standard of accuracy for that much surveyed
antiquity. The result of these expeditions was a portfolio
of plans which he deposited in the British Museum, and a
book, *Inductive Metrology* (1877), in which he sought to
determine the ancient linear standards of antiquity; the
experience gained by his surveys, and the natural accuracy of his eye, served him in good stead for the rest of his
life.

During the 1870s Petrie senior, a deeply religious man,
became interested in the theories of Piazzi Smyth concerning the supposed eschatological symbolism of the
Great Pyramid. Flinders himself was at first tempted to
believe, but felt that more accurate measurements were
needed. In 1880, after careful preparations, he set out for
Egypt; his father, who was to have accompanied him,

never plucked up courage to go. Flinders spent two winters of solitary, sometimes dangerous work in Giza, tri-
angulating the whole pyramid field and minutely investigating the outer structure and inner plan of the Great
Pyramid; his meticulously accurate measurements dis-
proved the existence of Smyth's 'pyramid inch' and
demolished his theories. He had now formed the resolution to spend the rest of his life, if that were possible, in
rescuing the antiquities which he saw everywhere in
Egypt pillaged by treasure-hunters and wrecked by
clumsy excavators who destroyed more evidence than
they obtained. 'Egypt was like a fire', he wrote later, 'so
rapid was the destruction going on. My duty was that of a
salvage man: to get all I could quickly gathered in' (Petrie,
Seventy Years in Archaeology, 19). His book *The Pyramids and
Temples of Gizeh*, published by the Royal Society in 1883,
brought him to the attention of Amelia Edwards, the novelist and traveller whose enthusiasm for Egypt's antiquities had led her, with the help of influential friends, to
found the Egypt Exploration Fund. With her encouragement and support Petrie was sent out by the fund in 1883
to excavate at Tanis, in the Nile delta. Single-handed in
command of a workforce of over 200, he uncovered huge
statuary but also insisted that small broken objects and
pottery, hitherto discarded by archaeologists as useless
for museum display, had their story to tell. Previously
excavators had employed labour gangs, driven by overseers and interested only in recovering monumental
remains and museum pieces; all else was discarded. Petrie
chose his own workmen, supervised them himself, and
rewarded them for their finds, which otherwise might
have gone to dealers, their context destroyed. In 1884 he
found the city of Naucratis; here and at Defennah, the
ancient Daphnae, he found quantities of Greek pottery,
confirming the identity of these places as Greek trading
colonies.

Petrie soon quarrelled with the Egypt Exploration Fund,
whose officials he found dilatory and extravagant, and for
the next few years he worked on his own. Two wealthy
businessmen, at Amelia Edwards's instigation, agreed to
finance his work: in 1887 they formed a syndicate, Petrie
to dig, and the three of them to share what finds he was
permitted to bring home. The next two years, of work in
the Faiyûm, were among the most rewarding, and certainly the most arduous, of his life: they brought the pene-
tration of the waterlogged pyramid chambers of the Middle Kingdom, the excavation of a whole Middle Kingdom
town, the discovery of the Labyrinth, and the unexpected
finding of a cemetery of Roman date in which, day after
day, more mummy portraits came to light. Those which
he was allowed to bring home to England caused a sensation when they were exhibited in London. Petrie also
imported twelve complete mummies and sixty-five skulls.
In the 1990s the British Museum commissioned the foren-
sic reconstruction of heads from two of the skulls; the
resulting casts in wax and bronze demonstrated the realism of the associated mummy portraits.

In the spring of 1890 Petrie was engaged by the Palestine
Exploration Fund to dig on its behalf; he chose Tell

al-Hesy, which he (wrongly) identified with ancient Lachish, and in only six weeks cut a vertical slice through the mound in steps, noting the level at which each type of pottery was found; to some wares he could give a date because he had found them in a dated context in Egypt. It was the first stratigraphic excavation in the Near East. Petrie had noted, and admired, the work of Pitt Rivers in England, and had read of the 'immense cutting' of Schliemann's work in Troy, but Schliemann himself had denied the possibility that pottery could be used as a guide to chronology. Petrie wrote:

> Once settle the pottery and the key is in our hands for all future explorations. A single glance at a mound of ruins … will show as much to anyone who knows the style of the pottery as weeks of work may reveal to a beginner.
> (*Palestine Exploration Fund Quarterly Statement*, 22, 1890, 329)

Although later work has revised some of his conclusions, Petrie is regarded as the founding father of Palestinian archaeology.

Amelia Edwards's death in 1892, while Petrie was excavating the site of the palace of Tell al-Amarna with its painted pavement, brought an alteration to his fortunes. In her will she left her library and her collection of Egyptian antiquities to University College, London, together with a capital sum enough to endow the first chair of Egyptology in England; she let it be known that she wished Petrie to be the first Edwards professor. His appointment in 1892 gave him the academic status he needed; out of his small stipend he paid an assistant to teach the language; by the terms of his appointment he himself was expected to dig every winter and train students to dig. With his first assistant, James Quibell, he found archaic statuary at Coptos and, in the following year, a large predynastic cemetery at Negada; later he devised a chronological sequence for the contents of the graves by a remarkable statistical method of his own devising, which he called sequence dating. On 29 November 1896 Petrie married Hilda Mary Isabel (1871–1957), daughter of Richard Denny Urlin, of Rustington Grange, Worthing, Sussex. They had a son and a daughter.

Petrie's greatest contribution to the study of Egypt's history was the revelation of its earliest phases. When he first began to dig, textbooks began with the pyramid builders: Manetho's early dynasties were regarded as semimythical. During three seasons (1899–1903), working again for the Egypt Exploration Fund, his careful excavation of a necropolis at Abydos, near Balliana, revealed the graves of kings of the first two dynasties. At Sinai in the winter of 1905 he found a Middle Kingdom temple with inscriptions in a hitherto unknown script, the earliest known alphabet. In the following year, leaving the fund again, he formed the British School of Archaeology in Egypt, a society whose members were to support his work financially for the rest of his life. His wife laboured as secretary to raise funds and recruit new subscribers. Except for a few years while their son and daughter were small, she accompanied her husband every year in the field; his autobiography is dedicated 'to my wife, on whose toil most of the work has depended'. Their archaeological

camps, run on a shoestring for students and helpers, became a byword for austerity.

In 1904 Petrie published a small but epoch-making book, *Methods and Aims in Archaeology*, in which he described his management of his workforce, his techniques of excavation, of recording, and of restoration, the packing and transport of antiquities, and the publication of results. Each spring, after his return from the field, he would hold an exhibition of his finds, which were then distributed, some to subscribing museums and some for his own collection. The latter was later purchased for University College by public subscription. Known as the Petrie Museum, it is the finest Egyptological teaching collection in Britain. Petrie founded the journal *Ancient Egypt* and edited it for twenty years. He published over a hundred books and articles; besides the annual excavation report which came out promptly every autumn, he issued catalogues of different types of objects and a number of more popular books for a wider audience. These and his lectures, delivered all over England, roused public interest for Egyptology and financial help for his work. During his absences abroad, students were taught the elements of Egyptology by Margaret Murray, one of his first students. After two years they would join the professor in the field; many of them became well-known archaeologists.

In 1926 Petrie decided to move his work to Palestine. He excavated three *tells*, Jemma, Far'a, and Ajjul, south of Gaza, but unfamiliarity with the stratigraphical advances made by excavators since his work at Tell al-Hesy detracted from the value of his findings; after the season of 1934 he was denied a permit to dig. In 1933 he had retired from the Edwards chair and made his home in Jerusalem. Unable to obtain a permit to dig in Syria, he worked for two seasons on a windswept site in Sinai; it was not until 1939 that he finally admitted that his digging days were over.

Those who dug with Petrie were agreed that he had an almost uncanny 'flair'. In the Faiyûm he found polychrome sherds which he guessed at once must be Aegean; Kamares ware of the Middle Minoan period had not yet been discovered but later, with the Mycenaean pottery he found at Tell al-Amarna, he, Arthur Evans, and Ernest Gardner were able to work out a chronology for Bronze Age Greece. The men from Quft whom he trained to be foremen passed on their skills to their descendants, who were still employed as professional diggers in Egypt at the end of the century. He has been accused of undue haste in publication; better that, he maintained, than to sit on one's material for years, hoping to elucidate every problem: the records were there for future archaeologists to consult. In all he wrote over a hundred books and some nine hundred reviews and articles; he dug over fifty sites and trained a generation of archaeologists. It has been said that he found Egyptology a treasure hunt, and left it a science. Essentially a fieldworker and not an armchair scholar, he was not a linguist, and his theories sometimes met with ridicule, in particular the impossibly long chronology of Egyptian civilization, to which he clung until the end of his life; but his mistakes were small compared with the services which he rendered to the still nascent science of archaeology.

Petrie was knighted in 1923, and was elected a fellow of the Royal Society in 1902 and a fellow of the British Academy in 1904. He received honorary degrees from the universities of Oxford (1892), Edinburgh (1896), Strasbourg (1897), and Cambridge (1900). He was a member of the Royal Irish Academy, of the American Philosophical Society, and of many other foreign learned societies. He died in the government hospital, Jerusalem, on 29 July 1942 and was buried the next day in the protestant cemetery on Mount Zion. His library was donated by his widow to the new department of antiquities in the Sudan.

MARGARET S. DROWER

Sources W. M. F. Petrie, *Seventy years in archaeology* (1931) · E. P. Uphill, 'A bibliography of Sir William Matthew Flinders Petrie (1853–1942)', *Journal of Near Eastern Studies*, 31 (1972), 356ff. · W. M. F. Petrie, journals, U. Oxf., Griffith Institute [reports from the field written by Petrie or his wife to friends and colleagues in England during each season's work] · corresp., priv. coll. · notebooks, pocket diaries, UCL, Petrie Museum of Egyptian Archaeology · M. S. Drower, *Flinders Petrie: a life in archaeology* (1985) · M. A. Murray, *The splendour that was Egypt* (1949) · S. Smith, 'Sir Flinders Petrie, 1853–1942', *PBA*, 28 (1942), 307–24 · O. Tufnell, *Palestine Exploration Quarterly* (1943), 5–8 · W. F. Allbright, *The archaeology of Palestine* (1949) · R. E. M. Wheeler, *Archaeology from the earth* (1954), esp. 29–30 · W. R. Dawson, *Journal of Egyptian Archaeology*, 29 (1943), 67–70 · *The Times* (26 June 1997) · personal knowledge (2004)

Archives Egypt Exploration Society, London, corresp. and papers relating to the Egypt Exploration Society · NMM, letters to his wife and papers · S. Antiquaries, Lond. · U. Oxf., Griffith Institute, journals (on loan), notebooks, photographs · U. Oxf., Sackler Library, notebooks · UCL, Institute of Archaeology, notebooks, journals, and papers · Wellcome L., lecture notes | BLPES, letters to C. G. Seligman relating to Sudan · Bodl. Oxf., corresp. with J. L. Myers · U. Oxf., Griffith Institute, letters to Aquila Dodgson · UCL, letters to Sir Francis Galton

Likenesses G. F. Watts, oils, 1900, NPG · W. Brunton, watercolour drawing, 1912, UCL · W. Stoneman, photographs, 1917, NPG · photograph, 1921, UCL · photograph, 1930 · P. A. de Laszlo, oils, 1934, NPG · P. A. de Laszlo, oils, UCL · P. A. de Laszlo, oils, unknown collection; copyprint, Courtauld Inst. [*see illus.*] · H. Wallis, watercolour drawing, UCL

Petrie, George (1790–1866), antiquary and painter, was born in Dublin on 1 January 1790, the only child of James Petrie, a portrait painter. His mother was a daughter of Sacheverel Simpson of Edinburgh. His paternal grandfather, also named James, had moved from Aberdeen to settle in Ireland. In 1799 Petrie was sent to Samuel Whyte's school in Dublin. From childhood he helped his father to paint miniatures, and he attended the art school of the Dublin Society. Before he was fourteen he was awarded the society's silver medal for drawing a group of figures. He early became interested in Irish antiquities, and in 1808 travelled round co. Wicklow, making notes of Irish music, ecclesiastical architecture, and ancient earthworks and pillar-stones. In 1810 he visited Wales, where he made landscape sketches, and in 1813 he visited London, where he was kindly treated by Benjamin West, to whom he had an introduction.

After his return to Ireland, Petrie painted landscapes, mainly in Dublin, co. Wicklow, co. Kildare, the King's county, and co. Kerry; in 1816 he exhibited at Somerset House pictures of Glendalough and Glenmalure, both in co. Wicklow. In 1820 he contributed illustrations to a number of guidebooks on Ireland. At the first exhibition of the Royal Hibernian Academy in 1826, Petrie exhibited a large picture of Ardfinane, a castle standing above a many-arched bridge on the north bank of the Suir. The next year he exhibited *The Round Tower of Kilbannon*, co. Galway, and *Dun Aengus*, a great cashel in Aranmor, co. Galway. He was elected an academician in 1828, and exhibited *The Twelve Pins in Connemara* and *The Last Round of the Pilgrims at Clonmacnoise*. In 1829 he painted *The Knight and the Lady* and *Culdean Abbey*. He was appointed librarian to the Hibernian Academy in 1830, and exhibited six pictures that year and nine in 1831. In the course of his studies for these works he made many tours throughout Ireland, travelled along the whole course of the Shannon, and explored Clonmacnoise, Cong, Kilfenora, the Aran Islands, and many other ecclesiastical ruins.

When Caesar Otway (1780–1842) began the *Dublin Penny Journal* in June 1832, Petrie joined him, and wrote many antiquarian articles in the fifty-six weekly numbers that appeared. He was also the sole editor of the *Irish Penny Journal*, which appeared for a year in 1842. Its aim was to describe to the Irish people the importance of their history and antiquities, their legends and traditions. John O'Donovan was a fellow contributor. Petrie joined the Royal Irish Academy in 1828, was elected onto its council in 1829, and worked hard to improve its museum and library. In 1831 he discovered and purchased the autograph copy of the second part of the 'Annals of the kingdom of Ireland', called by John Colgan the annals of the four masters. For the academy's museum he bought the cross of Cong, the Ardagh Chalice, and some torcs from Tara. Petrie's work on the collection made the museum a centre for the study of Ireland's past. The pieces he purchased now form the nucleus of the National Museum of Ireland.

From 1833 to 1846 Petrie worked for the Ordnance Survey of Ireland. Here his assistants were John O'Donovan and Eugene O'Curry. After O'Donovan, Petrie was the member of the staff who did most to preserve local history and historical topography through the publication of memoirs to accompany the maps. His work on Tara, written in 1837, was published by the Royal Irish Academy. The first memoir of the survey on Londonderry appeared in 1839. Here Petrie, who was a Catholic and a nationalist, charged the early Scottish settlers with fanaticism, and suggested that since the union the cultural life of the area had deteriorated. An anonymous letter to Dublin Castle accused him of prejudice and of wasting money by devoting too much time to investigating the ancestry of the peasantry.

The government soon after decided to stop the survey on the grounds of expense. A commission appointed in 1843 recommended its continuance, after examining Petrie and other witnesses, but it was never resumed. The Royal Irish Academy awarded Petrie a gold medal for his essay on Tara. Sir William Betham (1779–1853), the Ulster king of arms, whose theories on Irish antiquities had been demolished by Petrie, fiercely opposed the award and resigned his seat on the council. In 1833 Petrie was awarded a gold medal for an 'Essay on the origin and uses of the round towers of Ireland', which was later published as *The Ecclesiastical Architecture of Ireland* (1845). The round towers in Ireland—of which there are approximately 120—had been variously (and sometimes comically) identified by other scholars as Phoenician fire-temples, sorcerers' towers, astronomical observatories, centres for religious dances, temples of Vesta, minarets for proclaiming anniversaries, Danish watch-towers, tombs, gnomons, homes of Persian magi, and phallic emblems. Petrie put paid to all these theories, showing that the towers were Christian ecclesiastical buildings of varying dates. His evidence was abundant and well presented, and although modern research has refined his theory—suggesting that the towers date from the period of the viking raids and may have served a defensive purpose (although attached to ecclesiastical establishments)—the substance of his findings is established scholarly opinion.

Petrie also wrote numerous papers on Irish art, mainly careful descriptions of various antiquities. He also made a collection of Irish inscriptions, which was edited after his death, with additions, by Margaret Stokes, under the title of *Christian Inscriptions in the Irish Language*. In 1816 he wrote an 'Essay on music' in the *Dublin Examiner*: a devotee of Irish music, he collected airs wherever he travelled, and learned to play them on his violin. In 1855 he published *The Ancient Music of Ireland*, a collection of songs and airs made in all parts of Ireland. In the introduction he lamented the loss of a national memory of the past, the result of successive disasters, death, and emigration.

Petrie received the honorary degree of LLD from the University of Dublin in 1847, and in 1849 was given a civil-list pension. He continued to tour Ireland in his later years; in 1857 he again visited the Isles of Aran, and in the autumn of 1864 he made his last journey to the one region he had never seen, the Old Glen in the parish of Glencolumbkille in Donegal. Petrie, who was married to a Miss Mills, died at his house at 7 Charlemont Place, Dublin, on 17 January 1866, and was buried in Mount Jerome cemetery, Dublin. He was survived by at least one daughter. A disinterested student of medieval Irish architecture, decorative art, music, and topography all his life, he made permanent and important contributions in these fields, and, tangentially, in others. His work in tracing and illustrating Irish decorated churches from the seventh century was, for example, extremely influential on the designs of church architects in nineteenth-century Ireland. His sole object was the advancement of his research: he gave generous help to many other scholars, and attracted a large circle of friends. MARIE-LOUISE LEGG

Sources W. Stokes, *The life and labours in art and archaeology of George Petrie* (1868) · J. Sheehy, *The rediscovery of Ireland's past: the Celtic revival, 1830–1930* (1980) · C. Graves, 'Loss sustained by archaeological science in the death of George Petrie', *Proceedings of the Royal Irish Academy*, 9 (1864–6), 325–36 · J. H. Andrews, *A paper landscape: the ordnance survey in nineteenth-century Ireland* (1975) · T. Flanagan, 'Literature in English', *A new history of Ireland*, ed. T. W. Moody and others, 5: *Ireland under the Union, 1801–1870* (1989), 482–522, esp. 495–6
Archives PRO NIre. · Royal Irish Acad. · TCD, field notebooks of Irish ruins · TCD, musical collection · University of Limerick Library, corresp. | NL Ire., letters from John O'Donovan
Likenesses J. Kirkwood, etching, pubd 1839, NPG · J. Slattery, oils, 1857, Royal Irish Acad. · Irish school, charcoal and wash drawing, NG Ire. · Irish school, sculpture, NG Ire. · B. Mulrenin, oils, NG Ire. · J. Petrie, miniature, NG Ire. · J. Petrie, watercolour on ivory, NG Ire. · sculpture, NG Ire.
Wealth at death under £300: resworn administration, 14 April 1866, CGPLA Ire.

Petrie, (Frederick) Henry (*bap.* 1772, *d.* 1842), antiquary, was baptized on 28 April 1772 at St Mary's, Lambeth, the son of Henry Petrie, a schoolmaster in Stockwell, Surrey, and his wife, Elizabeth. He was intended to follow in his father's profession, but soon showed a marked preference for antiquarian research. He was a faithful topographical artist, and before 1810 carried out a large number of sketches of historic buildings in southern England and northern France. Between about 1800 and 1809 he also painted several hundred watercolours, mostly of churches and castles in Kent, Sussex, Surrey, and Bedfordshire. He had taught French and drawing to Thomas Dibdin, a pupil at his father's school, and the two remained close friends. Dibdin introduced Petrie to George John, second Earl Spencer, who warmly encouraged his researches. Petrie assisted Dibdin with his bibliographical works, leading his friend to claim that 'his knowledge of ancient manuscripts, places him second to none' (Dibdin, *Reminiscences*, 716). On the death of Samuel Lysons in 1819, Petrie was appointed keeper of the records in the Tower of London, and in 1830 his edition of the *Magni rotuli scaccarii Normanniae* was published. He was elected fellow of the Society of Antiquaries of London in 1820. After prolonged study of the materials for early English history, Petrie saw the need for the publication of a complete 'corpus historicum' for the period. A similar scheme had been suggested by the Scottish antiquary John Pinkerton, about 1790, and keenly advocated by Edward Gibbon, but after Gibbon's death it had lapsed. Petrie was the first to revive it. During 1818 and 1819 various meetings were held at Earl Spencer's house to further the scheme, at which it was agreed that a project of such national significance should be publicly funded. An appeal was made for government aid, and Petrie was chosen to draw up a plan. He aimed to make the body of materials to be published absolutely complete, and to include extracts from Greek and Roman authors containing references to early Britain, as well as copies of inscriptions on stone or marble, letters, charters, bulls, proceedings of councils and synods, laws, engravings of coins, medals, and seals, in addition to general histories, annals, and chronicles of England, and histories of particular monasteries.

The plan was presented to the record commission in 1821, and was sanctioned by the government and parliament. Work began in 1823, with Petrie as chief editor, assisted by his brother-in-law the Revd John Sharpe (1769–1859). The Welsh portion was entrusted to John Humffreys

Parry (1786–1825) and to Aneurin Owen, and was published in 1841. Petrie's section progressed steadily until 1832, when it was interrupted by his illness. But in 1834, when the whole text of the first volume had been completed, and a large collection of materials made for further volumes, the work was suspended by an order of the record commissioners. It had been criticized by Francis Palgrave as intrinsically defective, because the project was based on the methods of Dom Bouquet, the French historian, who advocated dispersing extracts in chronological order instead of printing entire texts.

Petrie was retired in 1840, and awarded compensation for loss of office. He died unmarried at his house at Stockwell Place, Stockwell Road, Stockwell, Surrey, on 17 March 1842, before the project was revived. His large collection of books was sold at auction by Evans over three days from 23 June 1842. One volume was finally completed and published in 1848 by Sir Thomas Duffus Hardy (who had been trained by Petrie), bearing the title *Monumenta historica Britannica, or, Materials for the history of Great Britain from the earliest period to the Norman conquest*. Hardy acknowledged valuable aid derived from Petrie's manuscripts in his *Descriptive Catalogue of Materials*, published in 1862.

A. F. POLLARD, rev. BERNARD NURSE

Sources GM, 2nd ser., 18 (1842), 661–2 · V. Smith, *Sussex churches: the Sharpe collection of watercolours and drawings, 1797–1809, mainly by Henry Petrie FSA* (1979) · T. F. Dibdin, *The bibliographical decameron*, 1 (1817) · T. F. Dibdin, *Reminiscences of a literary life*, 2 vols. (1836) · J. D. Cantwell, *The Public Record Office, 1838–1958* (1991) · T. D. Hardy, preface, in H. Petrie and J. Sharpe, *Monumenta historica Britannica* (1848) · T. D. Hardy, *Descriptive catalogue of materials relating to the history of Great Britain and Ireland*, 3 vols. in 4, Rolls Series, 26 (1862–71) · parish register (baptisms), St Mary's, Lambeth, 28 April 1772 **Archives** PRO, corresp., notes, and transcripts, PRO 30/17; PRO 31/5 | BL, letters to Philip Bliss, Add. MSS 34567–34568, 34570–34571, 34581, *passim* · BL, corresp. with Sir Frederic Madden, Egerton MSS 2837–2838, *passim* · BL, letters to second Earl Spencer · Bodl. Oxf., corresp. with Sir Thomas Phillipps · Hunt. L., letters to Charles O'Conor **Likenesses** S. P. Denning, portrait, 1835, BM, department of prints and drawings

Petrie, Irene Eleanora Verita (1864–1897), missionary, was born probably in October 1864 at Hanover Lodge, 14 Hanover Terrace, Kensington Park, London, the youngest of three daughters of Colonel Martin *Petrie (1823–1892) and his wife, Eleanora Grant Macdowall (d. 1886), youngest daughter of William Macdowall of Woolmet House, Midlothian. Both parents were of Scottish descent. Having been educated at home, unlike her sister, who had gone away to finishing school, from 1880 to 1882 she attended, at her own request, Notting Hill high school, Norland Square, London, one of the Girls' Public Day School Company schools. In 1884 she passed the Cambridge higher local examination, distinguishing herself especially in history. She painted, played the piano and guitar, and sang. Having been presented at court in March 1885, she enjoyed her coming out parties and balls. After her mother's death in January 1886 she occupied herself with philanthropic and religious work, including Sunday school teaching, through her parish, St Mary Abbots, Kensington, and in various charitable groups, locally and in the East End, including the National Health Society, the Prison Mission, the Scripture Union, and the Factory Helpers' Union. She had taken the pledge in July 1884 and was active in the Church of England Temperance Society and the Band of Hope. She also taught courses in scripture and hygiene in a correspondence school, the 'college by post', operated by her sister Mary (later Mrs Ashley Carus-Wilson).

A member of the St Mary Abbots Missionary Union from the age of fifteen, Irene Petrie became even more interested in foreign missions while pursuing her philanthropic work, lecturing, writing articles for the Ladies' Union of the Church Missionary Society (CMS), and singing in the CMS ladies' choir at Exeter Hall. After receiving a 'call' to be a missionary in 1891, she wrote to the CMS requesting appointment. Her father encouraged her choice of philanthropic and religious work over marriage but opposed her becoming a missionary, and she remained at home until after his death in November 1892. After a short period (9–23 October 1893) at the CMS training institute, The Willows (part of the Mildmay Institution), Stoke Newington, London, encouraged by her sister she sailed for India in October 1893.

Irene Petrie began her work in India as an unpaid volunteer at St Hilda's Diocesan Home in Lahore, which provided parochial care to poor European and Eurasian Christians employed by the railway and the post office. In April 1894 she was accepted by the Punjab and Sind corresponding committee of the CMS as an 'honorary missionary in local connexion', and joined the CMS's Kashmir mission in Srinagar for several months' intensive language study. In the severe winter of 1894–5 she lived in Srinagar with the head of the Kashmir women's mission, Miss Charlotte Hull, who remained a frequent companion in work and travel. Following language examinations in the spring of 1895 she returned to England for the summer to find 'friends for Kashmir' and to persuade the CMS to enrol her as a missionary in 'full connexion'. Having succeeded in these aims she returned to Srinagar in October 1895 to begin teaching Bible classes at the CMS schools and visiting women in their homes. Her career in Kashmir was cut short, however, during a holiday in Leh in the Ladakh region of the Himalayas, where she died of fever (probably typhoid) on 6 August 1897. She was buried in the Moravian cemetery at Leh. Memorial tablets were placed in St Mary Abbots Church, Kensington, and at St Luke's, Srinagar; the Irene Petrie Memorial Fund was established to support CMS work in Kashmir.

JEFFREY COX

Sources A. Carus-Wilson [M. L. G. Petrie], *Irene Petrie: missionary to Kashmir*, 2nd edn (1900) [pubd in the USA as *A woman's life for Kashmir: Irene Petrie, a biography* (1901)] · N. B. Harte and K. G. Ponting, *Cloth and clothing in medieval Europe: essays in memory of Professor E. M. Carus-Wilson* (1983), 1–3 · Church Missionary Society, *Register of missionaries (clerical, lay and female) and native clergy, from 1804 to 1904* (1905), 295 · *Church Missionary Intelligencer* (July 1892), 561–71 · DNB · Boase, *Mod. Eng. biog.* · J. Kamm, *Indicative past: a hundred years of the Girls' Public Day School Trust* (1971) · J. E. Sayers, *The fountain unsealed: a history of the Notting Hill and Ealing high school* (privately printed, Broadwater Press, 1973) · I. E. V. Petrie, 'Light bearers and light sharers', *Notting Hill High School Magazine* (June 1987), 22–5

Archives U. Birm. L., Church Missionary Society archives, records of the Punjab Mission
Likenesses portraits, repro. in Carus-Wilson, *Irene Petrie*, frontispiece, 18

Petrie, Martin (1823–1892), army officer, was born on 1 June 1823 at the Manor House, Kings Langley, Hertfordshire, the second son of Commissary-General William Petrie (1783/4–23 Dec 1842), who had seen active service in Egypt, Italy, and France. His mother, Margaret, was daughter and coheir of Henry Mitton of the Chase, Enfield. Colonel Petrie was sixth in descent from Alexander Petrie DD. His infancy was spent in Portugal and his childhood at the Cape of Good Hope, where his father held appointments. In youth he was chiefly in France, Italy, and Germany. On 14 April 1846 he entered the army as ensign in the Royal Newfoundland corps, and served for several years in North America, becoming lieutenant on 7 January 1848 and captain on 5 May 1854. On 26 January 1855 he was transferred to the 14th foot, and left Newfoundland on 20 March in the small steamer *Vesta*, which carried twenty-four passengers, seven of them, including Petrie, officers travelling to the Crimea. Some 300 miles off St John's the vessel, already damaged by ice floes, was caught in a terrific storm, and the engine-room was flooded. Petrie's mechanical skill and great courage enabled him to save the ship. He was called the 'hero of the *Vesta*', but his hands were so lacerated and frostbitten that he was invalided and could not go to the Crimea.

In May 1856 Petrie joined the Staff College at Camberley, and in December 1858 he passed the final examination, first on the list. He was attached to the topographical and statistical department (established 1855) of the War Office from 10 March 1859 to 30 June 1864, and in 1860 he brought out a standard work in three volumes, *The Strength, Composition, and Organisation of the Armies of Europe*, showing the annual revenue and military expenditure of each state, with its total forces in peace and war. In 1863 he published a volume of more detailed information on the British army, *The Organisation, Composition, and Strength of the Army of Great Britain* (5th edn, 1867). He also compiled two important volumes, *Equipment of Infantry* and *Hospital Equipment* (1865–6), part of a series on army equipment. For eighteen years (1864–82) he was examiner in military administration at the Staff College, and latterly also at the Royal Military College, Sandhurst. He became major on 13 July 1867 and exchanged to the 97th foot on 18th December; in July 1872 he retired on half pay, in 1876 became colonel, and in 1882 withdrew from the service. He presented papers at the Royal United Service Institution, of which he was a member; and as an enthusiastic freemason he was master of the St John's, Newfoundland, lodge, and a member of the Quatuor Coronati Lodge in London. He was active in philanthropic and religious work, and was a trustee of the Princess Mary Village Homes.

Petrie married Eleanora Grant (d. 31 Jan 1886), youngest daughter of William Macdowall of Woolmet House, Midlothian, and granddaughter of Sir William Dunbar of Durn, baronet, and they had three daughters. Petrie died on 19 November 1892 at his house, Hanover Lodge, Kensington Park, London, and was buried at Kensal Green cemetery, London. His elder daughter, Mary Louisa Georgina (d. 1935), author of *The Best Methods of Promoting Temperance among Educated Women* (1901) and of many religious books, married in 1893 Charles Ashley Carus-Wilson (1860–1942), an electrical engineer. The younger daughter, Irene Eleonora Verita *Petrie, joined the Church Missionary Society in Kashmir: after her death her sister published a memoir of her, *The Missions of the Church Missionary Society: the Kashmir Mission* (1901). G. A. AITKIN, rev. ROGER T. STEARN

Sources PRO, War Office MSS · private information (1895) · T. G. Fergusson, *British military intelligence, 1870–1914* (1984) · *WWW*, 1941–50 · Boase, *Mod. Eng. biog.* · *GM*, 2nd ser., 19 (1843) · *CGPLA Eng. & Wales* (1893)
Wealth at death £32 19s. 2d.: administration, 3 Jan 1893, *CGPLA Eng. & Wales*

Petrie, William (1821–1908), electrical engineer, was born on 21 January 1821 at Kings Langley, Hertfordshire, the eldest of four sons of William Petrie (b. 1784), a War Office official, and his wife, Margaret, daughter of Henry Mitton, banker, of The Chase, Enfield, Middlesex. From 1829 to 1837 the family lived at the Cape of Good Hope, where Petrie's father was deputy commissary-general. After an early education at home, Petrie and his brother Martin entered the South African College in Cape Town. He had early shown a liking for mechanics and chemistry, and his youthful studies were fostered by the friendly encouragement of their near neighbour, the astronomer Sir William Herschel.

In 1836 Petrie began studying for the medical profession at Cape Town Hospital, but abandoned that course when his family returned to London. He enrolled at King's College, London, taking chemistry under Professor Daniell, and also mathematics, and in 1840 went to study at Frankfurt am Main, devoting himself to magnetism and electricity. When he returned to England in 1841 he published 'Results of some experiments in electricity and magnetism' in the *Philosophical Magazine*, the first of many scientific papers, and took out a patent for a magneto-electric generator.

From 1846 to 1853 Petrie worked assiduously on electric lighting problems in collaboration with William Edwards Staite. In the course of this work he studied the magnetic properties of varieties of steel, presenting his results to the British Association. He also considered the principle of the arc lamp, where an electric spark or 'arc' is drawn between two pieces of carbon. The resulting heat produces light, but also burns up the carbon. A mechanism was needed to move the carbons together as they burnt, and Petrie was able to devise such a self-regulating arc lamp, supervising its manufacture at the works in Long Acre, in London, established by the mechanic Charles Holtzapffel. Under test, Petrie's lamp yielded a light of between 600 and 700 standard candle-power, with a consumption of one-third of a pound of zinc per 100 candle-power per hour. The lamp was displayed at the Hanover Square Rooms on 1 November 1848. Petrie gave a demonstration out of doors, on 28 November, with a lamp of 700 candle-power on the portico of the National Gallery, and on various nights in 1849 from the old Hungerford Bridge in London. These demonstrations were witnessed by Charles Wheatstone and other prominent scientists. On 6 February 1850 Petrie and Staite described their achievements to the Society of Arts. Unfortunately, however, their efforts to promote electric lighting brought financial disaster; indeed they could not have been successful until practical electrical generators became available in the 1870s.

Petrie married on 2 August 1851 Anne (1812–1892), only child of Matthew *Flinders, a naval hydrographer. She was a competent linguist and Egyptologist. Under the pseudonym 'Philomathes' she published a work on the relation between mythology and scripture, and as 'X.Q.' contributed essays to periodical literature. Their only child, (William Matthew) Flinders *Petrie (1853–1942), achieved fame as an archaeologist and professor of Egyptology at University College, London.

In later years Petrie turned his attention to electrochemistry, designing and equipping chemical works in France, Australia, and the United States. For many years he worked for Johnson, Matthey & Co., for whom he designed and patented a platinum-iridium boiler for concentrating sulphuric acid. He died at his home, 30 Crescent Road, Bromley, Kent, on 16 March 1908, survived by a second wife, Cecilia. He was buried at Bromley.

T. E. JAMES, rev. BRIAN BOWERS

Sources J. J. Fahie, 'Biographical sketch of Mr William Petrie', *Electrical Engineer* (29 Aug 1902) · J. J. Fahie, 'Biographical sketch of Mr William Petrie', *Electrical Engineer* (6 Feb 1903) · volume of press cuttings on electric lighting, Inst. EE, Staite collections · D. McDonald and L. B. Hunt, *A history of platinum and its allied metals* (1982), 301–4 · private information (1912) · *The Times* (2 Nov 1848), 3f · *CGPLA Eng. & Wales* (1908)
Archives Inst. EE, corresp. with John Joseph Fahie and notes
Likenesses photograph, repro. in McDonald and Hunt, *History of platinum*, 303 · portrait, repro. in Fahie, 'Biographical sketch of Mr William Petrie' (29 Aug 1902); (6 Feb 1903)
Wealth at death £4125 13s. 9d.: probate, 1 May 1908, *CGPLA Eng. & Wales*

Petroc [St Petroc, Pedrog] (*fl.* **6th cent.**), monk, was the founder of the church of Padstow and patron saint of Bodmin, Cornwall. His earliest life was probably written in Cornwall in the eleventh century; it survives in the Obituary of St Méen, Brittany (Paris, Bibliothèque Nationale, MS Lat. 9889). A number of texts concerning St Petroc, including a twelfth-century life partly derived from the St Méen life but containing much independent material, are preserved in the fourteenth-century Gotha manuscript compilation of British hagiographies, and an abridgement of the St Méen text was included by John Tynemouth in his fourteenth-century collection of lives of British saints (rearranged in *Nova legenda Anglie*). Petroc is also mentioned in several Welsh manuscripts of saints' lives and genealogies.

Unfortunately all these materials are legendary in character. They make Petroc a Welshman, son of King Glywys of Glamorgan (according to one genealogy, an uncle of St Cadog), or alternatively a son of a prince of Cornwall. The lives relate how he gave up his inheritance to become a monk, travelled to Ireland, Cornwall, Rome, the Holy Land, and India, and finally returned to Cornwall and led a life of ever-increasing solitude, abstinence, and miraculous power until his death at Treravel, near Padstow (commemorated on 4 June). An episode in which he visited a mysterious island in a glass boat recalls early Irish legend.

Historically, the most interesting details concern Petroc's relations with two other Cornish holy men, Wethenoc and Guron, who departed from their hermitages at Padstow and Bodmin to make way for him; this may reflect the takeover of independent monasteries by Petroc's expanding church after his death rather than events during his lifetime. The earliest centre of his cult, where he was buried, was Padstow, the site of his first landing in Cornwall. His relics had been transferred to Bodmin by the late eleventh century. In 1177, according to a vivid narrative in the Gotha manuscript, they were stolen by a Bodmin canon and taken to St Méen, Brittany, whence they were restored by the intervention of Henry II. They disappeared at the Reformation but the ivory casket in which they had been kept was rediscovered in the nineteenth century and is now in Bodmin church.

The wealth and importance of Bodmin church, and Petroc's status as co-patron of the diocese of Cornwall, caused his cult to spread more widely than those of most Cornish saints. He was the patron of many churches in south-west England, south Wales, and Brittany; already in the eleventh century his name was invoked in the litanies of Exeter and perhaps of Winchester and Salisbury, and in the middle ages his feast day was widely celebrated, eventually entering the Sarum calendar.

CAROLINE BRETT

Sources private information (2004) · P. Grosjean, ed., 'Vies et miracles de S. Petroc', *Analecta Bollandiana*, 74 (1956), 131–88, 470–96 · C. Horstman, ed., *Nova legenda Anglie, as collected by John of Tynemouth, J. Capgrave, and others*, 2 (1901), 317–20 · P. Grosjean, ed., 'De codice hagiographico Gothano', *Analecta Bollandiana*, 58 (1940), 90–103 · G. Doble, *St Petrock*, 3rd edn, Cornish Saints Series, 11 (1938) · G. Doble, 'The relics of St Petroc', *Antiquity*, 13 (1939), 403–15 · L. Olson, *Early monasteries in Cornwall* (1989), 66–78 · R. H. Pinder-Wilson and C. N. L. Brooke, 'The reliquary of St. Petroc and the ivories of Norman Sicily', *Archaeologia*, 104 (1973), 261–306 · M. Förster, 'Die Freilassungsurkunden des Bodmin-Evangeliars', *A grammatical miscellany offered to Otto Jespersen on his seventieth birthday*, ed. N. Bogholm, A. Brusendorff, and C. A. Bodelsen (1930), 77–99 · E. R. Henken, *Traditions of the Welsh saints* (1987), 199–205

Petronius (*d.* 654?), abbot of St Peter's and St Paul's, Canterbury, was probably born in or near Rome. All that is known about him comes from a late medieval Canterbury tradition recorded by William Thorne and Thomas Elmham. According to this, Archbishop Honorius consecrated him abbot of the monastery of St Peter and St Paul, Canterbury, in 640, two years after the death of his predecessor Gratiosus. Petronius probably died in 654. There was no record of his place of burial in the late fourteenth and early fifteenth centuries.

WILLIAM HUNT, rev. MARIOS COSTAMBEYS

Sources *William Thorne's chronicle of St Augustine's Abbey, Canterbury*, trans. A. H. Davis (1934) · Thomas of Elmham, *Historia monasterii S. Augustini Cantuariensis*, ed. C. Hardwick, Rolls Series, 8 (1858)

Petrucci, Ludovico (*b. c.*1575, *d.* in or after 1619), poet and soldier, was born at Pitigliano, near Siena, son of an Italian nobleman, Ariodante Petrucci. In 1597 he was arrested by the inquisition, accused of a number of crimes relating to necromancy, including possession of magic books and summoning of spirits. In particular, he had allegedly persuaded the son of a member of the Neapolitan aristocracy to sell his soul to the devil, and provided another Neapolitan nobleman with a familiar spirit to ensure success in love. It is unclear which members of the aristocracy of Naples were implicated in this matter, though Gabrieli (p. 300) suggests the duke of Amalfi as a plausible candidate.

Petrucci protested his innocence, claiming that he was being punished for offences committed by others. He remained incarcerated by the inquisition in Padua for four years, a horrifying experience later discussed in his published work. In 1601 he was released, and began a career as a soldier, serving first for the Venetians in Candia (Crete). Between 1603 and 1610 he worked as a soldier in the wars in Hungary, Austria, Moravia, and Germany: his employers during this period included the holy Roman emperor, the duke of Brandenburg, and the duke of Neuburg.

In April 1609, in Dusseldorf, the wandering soldier encountered two English merchants, Thomas Stone and James Higgins, and this may have persuaded him to try his luck in England. His arrival in London was noted in a report of 19 August 1610 from the Venetian ambassador, and he is next heard of in Oxford, where he was registered as a student of St Edmund Hall on 27 April 1611. He was later associated with Balliol College, New College, and perhaps others: it seems at least possible that he taught Italian in Oxford. Chronically short of money, Petrucci later wrote warmly of the hospitality provided by the university. In 1613 the university printer published Petrucci's *Raccolta d'alcune rime*, a collection of poems in Latin and Italian, containing numerous dedications to royalty and to British notables including Bacon and Archbishop Abbot. The collection is interspersed with letters and testimonials received by Petrucci from patrons across Europe.

Petrucci left Oxford about 1616. Anthony Wood's statement that anti-Catholic feeling forced his departure is perhaps corroborated by Petrucci's repeated attempts to prove by certificates his adherence to the Church of England. On 10 July 1619, incarcerated in the Fleet prison, he wrote the epistle to his second book, *Apologia equitis Ludovici Petrucci contra calumniatores suos*. The contents of this book include, once again, a dedication to King James, numerous Latin and Italian poems and prose addresses, and dedications to and testimonials from numerous British and European luminaries. The book also includes emblems, and an engraved portrait of Petrucci by Thomas Pothecary.

In a Latin epistle, Petrucci describes his current plight—which is, presumably, imprisonment for debt—as the culmination of a secret Catholic operation against him which has been active since his first encounter with the inquisition. Throughout his career, he writes, he has been beset by 'innumerable enemies of almost every nation and condition' employed by them, including 'certain booksellers' who seem to be responsible for his imprisonment (Gabrieli, 313), and he dwells at some length on this conspiracy.

Nothing is known of Petrucci's career after this. As Gabrieli notes, he may have died in the Fleet, but it is just possible that he escaped to further, unknown adventures across Europe. Petrucci's fame lived on in Oxford long enough for Wood to write a note on the unlucky knight, whom he considered 'phantasticall' and mentally unbalanced: in a broader sense his work is interesting as part of the story of the British reception of Italian culture.

MATTHEW STEGGLE

Sources V. Gabrieli, 'Ludovico Petrucci soldato e poeta', *English Miscellany*, 11 (1960), 287–315 · Wood, *Ath. Oxon.*, 1st edn, 1.387–8 · *DNB*
Archives BL, commonplace book, Lansdowne MS 704 | BL, Royal MS A14 A VII
Likenesses T. Pothecary, engraving, 1619, repro. in Gabrieli, 'Ludovico Petrucci'

Petrus [St Petrus] (*d.* 605×11), abbot of St Peter's and St Paul's, Canterbury (later St Augustine's), was both a monk and a priest, and was one of the companions of St Augustine on his mission to England in 596–7. Probably in late 600, Augustine sent him in company with Laurence, afterwards archbishop of Canterbury, to Pope Gregory to announce the success of the mission and to lay before him certain questions. He brought back the pope's replies in 601. Æthelberht, king of Kent, was building the monastery of St Peter and St Paul at the time of Augustine's death, and Petrus was appointed its first abbot. Bede is the principal witness for Petrus, probably deriving his information from Albinus, abbot of St Peter's and St Paul's, via the priest Nothelm. He recounts that Petrus was drowned in a creek of the sea at 'Amfleat' (Ambleteuse), a short distance north of Boulogne, while fulfilling a mission to Gaul on which he had been sent by Æthelberht. He was given an unworthy burial by the local inhabitants, but a heavenly light appeared above his grave every night, revealing to the people that it was a saint who was buried there. Having discovered his identity, they removed his body and buried it with due honour in a church in Boulogne.

According to the Benedictine martyrology, Petrus's death occurred on 30 December, though the English martyrology (reproduced by the Bollandists) places it on 6 January. William Stubbs suggested that this may have been the day of his translation. The year of his death probably depends on that assigned to Augustine, since Thomas Elmham, the early fifteenth-century chronicler of St Augustine's (as St Peter's and St Paul's became in 978), states that Petrus died one year, seven months, and three weeks after Augustine. Augustine's death occurred at some time between 604 and 609. Elmham gives an epitaph on Petrus.

There is an unprinted and unreliable life of Petrus, written in the twelfth century by Eadmer, in Cambridge, Corpus Christi College, MS 371, fol. 416.

WILLIAM HUNT, rev. MARIOS COSTAMBEYS

Sources Bede, *Hist. eccl.*, 1.27, 33 · T. Elmham, *Historia Monasteri Sancti Augustini Cantuariensis*, ed. C. Hardwick, Rolls Series, 8 (1858) · *Acta sanctorum: Januarius*, 1 (Antwerp, 1643), 334–5 · M. R. James, *A descriptive catalogue of the manuscripts in the library of Corpus Christi College, Cambridge*, 2 (1912), no. 371

Pett, (William) Norman (1891–1960), cartoonist, was born at 203 Windmill Lane, Smethwick, Staffordshire, on 12 April 1891, the son of John Ernest Pett, a journeyman jeweller, and his wife, Elizabeth, née Cooper. He studied at the Press Art School in Forest Hill, London, run from 1905 by Percy Venner Bradshaw. Pett then turned teacher, first at the Moseley Road Junior Art School in Birmingham, where one of his pupils was the cartoonist Peter Maddocks, and subsequently at the Birmingham Central School of Art. He contributed cartoons to *Punch* and *Passing Show* and drew strips for children's comics, *Comet*, *Knockout*, and *Girl*.

Pett's fame, however, rests on the creation of Jane. She made her first appearance, with her dog, in the *Daily Mirror* on 5 December 1932 in a single-panel weekly series, 'Jane's Journal—or the Diary of a Bright Young Thing'. Initially the series focused on fripperies and fashion, which made it popular with contemporary young women. Jane was modelled after Pett's first wife, Mary Wade, but love of golf decided her to plump for plus fours rather than posing. Don Freeman was engaged by the *Daily Mirror* as Pett's scenario writer in December 1938, and in 1940 a professional model, Christabel Jane Drury (d. 2000), whom Pett met posing in front of a class of students at his old art school, took over as Jane. A new, racier strip was born. Although a rather severe, schoolmasterish-looking man, not at all resembling the creator of naughty cartoons, Pett brought a new meaning to the term 'strip cartoon'. Living in a cottage in the Cotswolds, he took his work to London by train, travelling every few weeks to the newspaper office for a conference involving eighteen strips at a time, planned to concoct fascinating situations designed for a mass cult following.

Although she was curiously sexless, Jane's career spanned nearly three decades but she never aged a day. In retrospect Pett's heroine seems remarkably prim: just a pretty, decent English girl with a steady but rather wet boyfriend—whom she eventually married—who just happened to lose her clothes in the most unlikely circumstances. While she was engaged on a number of secret missions of national importance, any gust of wind, unexpected sharp object, foreign villain, or errant barrage balloon ropes promptly reduced her to camiknickers. Always accompanied by her faithful dachshund Fritz (named after one of the dachshunds bred by the artist), Jane was widely credited with helping the war effort: the more garments shed the greater the advances by HM forces. It was claimed that submarines were allocated advance supplies of the strip when they left port and that her picture adorned the first tank ashore on D-day; she appeared nude for the first time on the day after D-day in June 1944. There was shock, outrage even, but the armed forces loved her. She was adopted as the RAF's mascot and appeared emblazoned on aircraft, tanks, and submarines. Even in places where most people would not have been caught dead reading the *Mirror*, Jane was considered essential reading and her exploits were followed more closely than those of Rommel. Specially drawn whole-page Janes appeared as educational features in the combined operations magazine *Bulldozer* as well as appearances in *Union Jack* and *Stars and Stripes*. Her calendars were mass-produced between 1947 and 1949 along with booklets, commemorative belts, and ties. After the war it was suggested by Conservative loyalists that she attracted readers who moved from the cartoons to the pro-Labour *Mirror*'s news stories and helped to win the general election for Labour in 1945. On the other hand, the influential opinion canvassers, Mass-Observation, suggested that she was dismissed by most of those consulted as 'piffle', 'tripe', 'silly and stupid'.

Pett's assistant Michael Hubbard took over from 1 May 1948 and Pett turned to a new striptease character, Susie, whom he drew for the *Sunday Dispatch*. Although blessed with a pet poodle, the appeal of her tantalizing naughtiness vanished with the swinging sixties and she never really caught on. Christabel Leighton-Porter, as she was to become, toured the music halls in a revue called *Jane in the Mirror*, causing the lord chamberlain to voice concern about the amount of clothing removed. Christabel appeared also in a Keystone–New World film, *The Adventures of Jane* (1949), and a BBC South television documentary film, *Jane* (1989). Another film, *Jane and the Lost City* (1987), a 'tatty, low budget romp of no perceptible interest' involving a struggle in Africa with Nazis, left *Halliwell's Film and Video Guide 2000* unamused.

At least eight spin-off publications akin to *Pett's Annual* (1944) and *Jane at War* (1976) kept the duo in the public eye, but the strip itself was axed in October 1959, the last episodes written by Ian Berwick Gammidge, another joke and strip cartoonist. Jane was retired (age twenty-six), and the nation, along with other newspapers, mourned. Interest in Pett's inimitable creation, revived after the fortieth anniversary of the battle of Britain in the 1980s, led to a television series starring Glynis Barber. A member of the Bullfrogs Club, Pett married as his second wife a widow, Dora Mason, née Keay (d. 1991), and continued to draw for children's comics until his death at Oldland Cottage, Ockley Lane, Keymer, Sussex, on 16 February 1960.

GORDON PHILLIPS

Sources M. Bryant, *Dictionary of twentieth-century British cartoonists and caricaturists* (2000) · R. Allen and J. Frost, *Daily Mirror* (1981) · *Farewell to Jane*, Daily Mirror [1960] · L. Thomas, ed., *Jane* [n.d., c.1983], incl. introduction by L. Thomas · N. Pett and D. Freeman, *Jane at war* (1976) · *Pett's annual* (1944) · b. cert. · d. cert.
Likenesses watercolour, NAAFI Museum, Camberwell, London
Wealth at death £1535 7s.: probate, 22 March 1960, CGPLA Eng. & Wales

Pett, Peter (d. 1589), shipwright, was the son of Peter Pett of Harwich, Essex (d. c.1554) and Elizabeth Paynter. The details of his life until his appointment as a royal shipwright, from Michaelmas 1543, at a fee of 6*d*. per day for life 'in consideration of good and faithful service done and to be done' (*Autobiography of Phineas Pett*, xxi) are unknown. However, he may just have been the boy of the same name who was swept up in a press of East Anglian shipwrights in 1523 to work at Portsmouth. In April 1558 he was granted a patent advancing his fee to 1*s*. per day, which he surrendered in July 1582 for a new patent giving him the title of master shipwright for the first time.

Pett trained Richard Chapman, and probably also Matthew Baker, both of whom eventually joined him as the principal royal master shipwrights. Practically all the important shipbuilding of Elizabeth's reign was carried out by this triumvirate, and it is difficult to establish individual responsibility for the construction of particular vessels. William Borough, comptroller of the navy, held the opinion that, of the three, Baker built the better ships. In 1579 bargains were made between the queen and Sir John Hawkins, treasurer of the navy, and with Pett and Baker, for maintaining twenty-five named vessels in a seaworthy condition. Pett and Baker were to have £1000 a year between them, for which they were regularly to service ships' hulls, repair or replace defective upper spars and masts, provide all materials, and pay the workers. Perhaps in expectation of enhanced status from this arrangement, Pett obtained a grant of arms in 1583, but Hawkins's enforcement of the contract to his own advantage severely reduced the anticipated profit to Pett and Baker. In January 1588 they accused the treasurer of dishonesty. These charges seem not to have damaged Hawkins, nor indeed to have affected the positions of Pett or Baker, both of whom continued in their posts.

Faced with the Armada threat of 1588, the earl of Leicester called Pett to advise on the construction of a defensive barrier across the Thames between Tilbury and Gravesend to prevent Spanish ships reaching London. Pett inspected the site with Leicester on 23 July, and was not impressed by the proposed boom constructed from lighters chained together. He recommended that this should be strengthened with a number of ship's masts, which he would have sent down from Deptford. Leicester reported to Walsingham that the fort at Tilbury was lacking gun platforms, and that Pett had been sent 'for provision of such thinges as are most necessary for the platforms, as also touching the defence uppon this water'. That Pett discharged this mission is confirmed by a warrant dated 15 August 1588, ordering the payment of £150 to him, Matthew Baker, and Richard Chapman 'or any of them' towards charges incurred at Gravesend and Tilbury, pending detailed examination of their accounts (Cruden, 237, 247).

Peter Pett married twice. Nothing is known of his first wife, but they had at least five children, of whom William (*d*. 1587), Joseph (*d*. 1605), and Peter (*d*. c.1631) became master shipwrights with their own commercial yards. Joseph also succeeded to his father's post at Deptford. The date of Pett's second marriage, to Elizabeth Thornton (*d*. 1597), is unknown; there were at least eight children of this union,

of whom Phineas *Pett (1570–1647), yet another royal master shipwright, was the most notable. Through his offspring and their descendants Peter Pett founded a dynasty of shipwrights that dominated both royal and private Thames dockyards throughout most of the seventeenth century. Even eight generations after his death one descendant, Peter Rolt (1798–1882) was chairman of the Thames ironworks and Shipbuilding Company, which in 1912 was destined to launch the last new ship constructed on the Thames. Pett died, still working, at Deptford on or about 6 September 1589. STUART RANKIN

Sources *The autobiography of Phineas Pett*, ed. W. G. Perrin, Navy RS, 51 (1918) · M. Oppenheim, *A history of the administration of the Royal Navy* (1896) · N. Dews, 'Abstract of the pedigree of the family of Pett', *The history of Deptford*, 2nd edn (1884) · J. K. Laughton, ed., *State papers relating to the defeat of the Spanish Armada, anno 1588*, 2nd edn, 1, Navy RS, 1 (1895); facs. edn (1987) · R. P. Cruden, *The history of Gravesend in the county of Kent, and of the port of London* (1843) · P. Banbury, *Shipbuilders of the Thames and Medway* (1971)
Archives PRO, state papers, 'An opinion of Peter Pett and Mathew Baker the shipwright upon certain articles of Mr. J. Hawkyns', dom. Eliz., ccviii.18 · PRO, state papers, 'A survey of the navy', dom. Eliz. ccxvi.40

Pett, Peter (*b*. 1610, *d*. in or before 1672), naval administrator, was born at Woolwich on 6 August 1610, the fifth son of Phineas *Pett (1570–1647) and Anne Nicholls (*d*. 1627). He was brought up by his father as a shipwright, while still very young was his father's assistant at Deptford and Woolwich, and in 1635–7 built the *Sovereign of the Seas* under his father's supervision. On 8 September 1633 he married Katharine Cole of Woodbridge (*d*. 1651); they had seven sons and four daughters. In 1647 parliament ordered him a gratuity of £10 for building the *Phoenix* at Woolwich. He was then appointed master-shipwright at Chatham, and in 1648 he both warned parliament of the threat to the ships at Chatham from the royalist revolt in Kent, and subsequently repossessed the ships when the revolt began to collapse. In the same year he became the resident commissioner of the navy at Chatham. Pett excited a strong feeling of animosity by filling all the more important posts in the yard with his near relatives. As early as November 1651 complaints were laid by some of the subordinate officials, including the chaplain, William Adderley, that members of the family worked into each other's hands, that stores were wasted or misappropriated, that higher wages were charged than were paid, and that false musters were kept. A special inquiry was ordered in the following January, when Pett had little difficulty in proving that the charges were malicious; but it is clear that there were great opportunities for fraud and reasonable grounds for suspicion and Pett's running battle with Adderley continued intermittently throughout the 1650s. The commissioner's cousin, Joseph Pett, was master shipwright at Chatham; another cousin, Peter Pett, was master shipwright at Deptford; a younger brother, Christopher, assistant master shipwright at Woolwich; another brother, Phineas, clerk of the check at Chatham, and a cousin, Richard Holborne, master mastmaker. When, in the following summer, his cousin Peter at Deptford died, he was able to have his brother Christopher promoted to the vacancy, and Peter's son Phineas appointed assistant. Pett was also permitted to undertake private contracts for building ships of war.

Pett had, following his first wife's death in July 1651, married Mary Smith (d. c.1664) daughter of the serjeant-at-arms to Charles I. In 1665 he married his third wife, Elizabeth Hatton, née Pitt, widow of Sir Henry Hatton. Pett served as MP for Rochester in Richard Cromwell's parliament in 1659 and the convention in 1660. Due, in part, to the urging of his brother Phineas, he was won over to support the Restoration and retained his office as a result. He was elected a fellow of the Royal Society in 1662. He remained commissioner at Chatham until 29 September 1667, when he was charged with being the main cause of the disaster there in June, when the Dutch had attacked the English fleet, and was summarily superseded. He was accused, in detail, of having neglected or disobeyed orders from the duke of York, the duke of Albemarle, and the navy commissioners to moor the *Royal Charles* in a place of safety, to block the channel of the Medway by sinking a vessel inside the chain, to provide boats for the defence of the river, and to see that the officers and seamen were on board their ships. On 18 June he was sent a prisoner to the Tower, on the 19th was examined before the council, and on 22 October before the House of Commons. Impeachment proceedings began in November, but when parliament adjourned for two months the matter was dropped. The accusation was merely the outcome of a desire to make him answerable for the failings of those in high places, and Pett was also vulnerable because of his republican past and alleged links to nonconformity. The general feeling was clearly put by Marvell, in the lines:

> All our misfortunes upon Pett must fall
> His name alone seems fit to answer all.
> Pett, the sea-architect, in making ships
> Was the first cause of all these naval slips.
> (A. Marvell, *The Last Instructions to a Painter*; Lord, 1.131–2)

Pett's convenience as a scapegoat was enhanced by the realization that the commissioner's nepotism and corruption had seriously damaged the efficiency of Chatham yard: Pepys's papers of the 1660s are full of references to Pett's 'hypocrisy', 'false dealing' and 'villainy', and to his being 'as very a knave as lives upon earth … a false-hearted fellow' (*Samuel Pepys and the Second Dutch War*, 18, 19, 21, 383). Pett lived in obscure retirement after his dismissal until his death; his will was proved on 2 December 1672, at which time he was lord of two manors in Suffolk. None of Pett's sons pursued significant careers in the navy, despite the fact that the two eldest were bequeathed their father's ship models in his will. However, many other members of the extended Pett family did serve in the navy throughout the seventeenth and eighteenth centuries, leading to long-standing confusion between an abundance of naval Peter and Phineas Petts.

J. K. LAUGHTON, rev. J. D. DAVIES

Sources M. W. Helms and B. D. Henning, 'Pett, Peter', HoP, *Commons, 1660–90*, 3.229–30 • H. F. Burke and O. Baron, 'The builders of the navy: a genealogy of the family of Pett', *The Ancestor*, 10 (1904), 147–78 • *The autobiography of Phineas Pett*, ed. W. G. Perrin, Navy RS, 51 (1918) • *Samuel Pepys and the Second Dutch War: Pepys's navy white book and Brooke House papers*, ed. R. Latham, Navy RS, 133 (1995) [transcribed by W. Matthews and C. Knighton] • G. de F. Lord and others, eds., *Poems on affairs of state: Augustan satirical verse, 1660–1714*, 7 vols. (1963–75), vol. 1, pp. 131–2 • W. B. Cogar, 'The politics of naval administration, 1649–1660', DPhil diss., U. Oxf., 1983 • B. Capp, *Cromwell's navy: the fleet and the English revolution, 1648–1660* (1989) • J. D. Davies, *Gentlemen and tarpaulins: the officers and men of the Restoration navy* (1991)

Archives PRO, SP 46
Likenesses P. Lely, painting, c.1645, NMM; copy, NPG
Wealth at death two manors in Suffolk: will, Burke and Baron, 'Builders of the navy'

Pett, Sir Peter (*bap.* 1630, *d.* 1699), lawyer and author, was baptized on 31 October 1630 at St Nicholas's Church, Deptford Green, Kent, the son of Peter Pett (1592–1652), master shipwright at Deptford, and his wife, Elizabeth Johnson (*fl.* 1623–1652). He was the grandson of Peter Pett of Wapping, shipbuilder, and great-grandson of Peter Pett (*d.* 1589), the Elizabethan royal master shipwright. Having been educated at Greenwich School and St Paul's School, he was admitted as a pensioner to Sidney Sussex College, Cambridge, in 1645. After graduating BA in 1648 he migrated to Pembroke College, Oxford, and in 1649 was intruded into a fellowship at All Souls (from which he was ejected in 1660). He graduated BCL in 1650, was entered as a student at Gray's Inn, and settled there 'for good and all' about a year before the Restoration.

When the Royal Society was formed, in 1663, Pett was one of the original fellows, elected on 20 May, but was expelled on 18 November 1675 for 'not performing his obligation to the society'. He was probably absorbed in other interests. From 1661 to 1666 he sat in the Irish parliament as MP for Askeaton. He also participated profitably in the farm of Irish tax, and obtained Dutch property confiscated there. A protégé of Arthur Annesley, first earl of Anglesey, he was appointed advocate-general for Ireland, where he was knighted by the duke of Ormond in 1663.

Back in London in the 1670s, Pett acted as the earl of Anglesey's man of business, entering politics under the earl of Danby. He opposed exclusion and moved closer to the political centre with the accession of James II, but became 'badly tarred with the brush of popery' in the process (Goldie, 251).

The editor of the memoirs of the first earl of Anglesey and Thomas Barlow, bishop of Lincoln, Pett is best known as a polemicist. In a *Discourse Concerning Liberty of Conscience* (1661) he argued for the comprehension of protestant 'dissent' within an Anglican establishment broadened along the lines proposed by Archbishop James Ussher before the civil wars. Although intolerant of the kind of radical protestant ideology which had issued in regicide, he was prepared to accept peaceful unorthodoxy, and was generally latitudinarian in his belief in the passing of the age of religious controversy. He defended James II's declaration of indulgence in his *Obligation Resulting from the Oath of Supremacy* in 1687, albeit largely on pragmatic grounds. His most famous work is *The Happy Future State of England*, begun in 1681 and published in 1688, in which he followed the lead of Halifax and Anglesey in exploring the possibility of tory pragmatism. He was sceptical in his thinking, an Erastian ultimately indifferent to the theological differences between protestant and Catholic, believing first and foremost that the menace of popery must be eradicated from within both churches as a threat to the authority of the civil magistrate.

Pett died, unmarried, on 1 April 1699, and was buried on 19 April at St Martin-in-the-Fields, Westminster. In his will he bequeathed to his old school friend Samuel Pepys the ring given to Howard of Effingham by the admiral of the Spanish fleet in 1588. Pett has been often confused with his father's first cousin Peter *Pett, commissioner of the navy at Chatham, who is separately noticed.

J. K. LAUGHTON, *rev.* SEAN KELSEY

Sources H. F. Burke and O. Baron, 'The builders of the navy: a genealogy of the family of Pett', *The Ancestor*, 10 (1904), 147–78, esp. 164–5 · M. Goldie, 'Sir Peter Pett, sceptical toryism and the science of toleration in the 1680s', *Persecution and toleration*, ed. W. J. Sheils, SCH, 21 (1984), 247–74 · W. A. Shaw, *The knights of England*, 2 vols. (1906), 2 · M. McDonnell, ed., *The registers of St Paul's School, 1509–1748* (privately printed, London, 1977) · All Souls Oxf., archives · Foster, *Alum. Oxon.* · will, PRO, PROB 11/451, fols. 114–15 · PRO, PROB 11/453, fols. 311–12
Archives BL, Add. MSS · Bodl. Oxf., letters to A. Wood, Add. MS 25271, fols. 211 ff. · University College, Oxford, letters to Anthony Wood, ref. P2/C3
Wealth at death see will, PRO, PROB 11/451, fols. 114–15; PRO, PROB 11/453, fols. 311–12

Pett, Phineas (1570–1647), shipbuilder and naval administrator, was born at Deptford on 1 November 1570, the eldest son of Peter *Pett (*d.* 1589), master shipwright, of Deptford and his second wife, Elizabeth Thornton (*d.* 1597). He attended school at Rochester and Greenwich before entering Emmanuel College, Cambridge, in 1586. It would appear that he was intended for a career in the law or the church but his father's death and his mother's subsequent marriage to 'a most wicked husband' forestalled his future plans (*Autobiography*, 2). He was, however, awarded the degrees of BA in 1592 and MA in 1595.

Lack of prospects and funds obliged Pett, with his mother's encouragement, to become apprenticed to Richard Chapman, a master shipwright at Deptford, thereby following in an established family tradition. Once again Pett's plans were aborted with the death of Chapman after only three years of service, during which time he claimed to have learned little. Desperation obliged him to join the privateer *Gallion Constance* as a humble carpenter's mate, but its Mediterranean cruise proved unproductive and in 1594 Pett once again found himself facing destitution in London and dependent on his brothers Peter and Joseph.

The preparation of the *Defiance* and the *Triumph* for what was to be Drake's last voyage provided Pett with employment as a common workman. He also embarked on a deliberate campaign to advance his career by establishing contact 'with men of good rank far better than myself' (*Autobiography*, lv). This practice was to serve Pett admirably throughout his career. He was employed in the same humble capacity during the construction of the *Repulse* for

Phineas Pett (1570–1647), by unknown artist, *c.*1612

the earl of Essex's Cadiz expedition while at the same time studying mathematics and ship construction in the evenings under the tutelage of the master shipwright Matthew Baker. It was during this period that Pett came under the notice of the earl of Nottingham, the lord high admiral, who became his patron. From this point his star began to ascend, first as purveyor of timber in Norfolk and Suffolk in 1599–1600, and then as keeper of the stores at Chatham in June 1600. He used the role of purveyor to some financial gain and the navy treasurer, Sir Fulke Greville, questioned his accounts and withheld £20 from him. In March 1601 he became assistant to the master shipwright at Chatham. He quarrelled with and discarded Baker, having found more prestigious patrons. This breach reveals one of the less attractive sides of Pett who throughout his life believed that those who disagreed with him were conspiring maliciously against him.

In accordance with contemporary practice Pett was on the look-out for patrons and associated himself with Sir Robert Mansell, Greville's successor as navy treasurer, and Sir John Trevor, the navy surveyor. Unfortunately, in a period when naval administration was at its most corrupt, Mansell was arguably its most corrupt officer, with Trevor his willing accomplice. It was therefore highly likely that Pett would be drawn into dubious practices, as proved to be the case. As early as 1602 it was alleged (in an anonymous account preserved by Pepys) that Pett had sold the fore-topmast of the *Repulse*, for which offence Sir Henry Palmer sen., comptroller of the navy, struck him with a cudgel. Pepys also provides a list of items allegedly stolen by Pett, including timber sufficient to build a bridge and a sluice, and to run a small business selling posts (painted with naval paint) on which to hang clothes.

None the less Pett's position was secure and in 1604 he was ordered to build a miniature ship for Prince Henry, whose pleasure in it further assured Pett's future. In the following year he was granted the reversion of the positions held by Baker and his brother Joseph, and the latter's death in the same year allowed Pett's succession to the post of master shipwright at Deptford. In 1604 he had embarked on a shady construction project, in partnership with Mansell and Trevor. This was the construction of the *Resistance*, a small vessel of about 160 tons laid down in a private yard at Gillingham belonging to David Duck, a fellow shipwright at Chatham. The vessel was built entirely from timber, rigging, and sails which had been 'borrowed', or purchased at discounted rates, from the dockyard at Chatham on warrants from the principal officers, two of whom were Mansell and Trevor. She was then hired to the state as a transport for Nottingham's embassy of 1605 to Spain and rated as 300 tons (almost double her actual size). Not content with the excessive freight payment the owners also loaded a cargo for trade in Spain and Pett, in command, also sold a demi-culverin plus shot to the Spanish for £300, together with some of the ship's victuals (also 'borrowed' from Chatham). Pett's brother even managed to sell some of the vessel's sails during the voyage.

The extent of corruption in naval affairs finally forced James I to act and in 1608 a commission of inquiry was established under Nottingham and Henry Howard, earl of Northampton, to investigate the matter. It quickly emerged that Pett was one of the main offenders, his name appearing a number of times, notably in the *Resistance* affair. Other offences in which he was implicated were the acceptance of poor timber and the continuous repair for personal gain of vessels that were no longer serviceable. An example of this was the *Anne Royal* the estimate for which was £3576 but which in fact under Pett's supervision cost £7600. He also allegedly received bribes for the delivery of short loads of stores and used naval timber to build an extension to his house. Pett's response to these accusations was less than convincing but equally he seems to have been taking an undue proportion of the blame, much of which should have fallen on his superiors, Mansell and Trevor. Fortunately for Pett the king decided in 1609 to judge the matter personally. A condemnation of Pett would have damned the principal officers and even Nottingham, so ignoring the evidence James let all parties off with only a lecture. As a result the navy was condemned to an indefinite future of malpractice.

In 1607 Pett built a scale model of a substantial ship which so impressed the lord admiral that he in turn presented it to the king. James agreed to the construction of a ship based on the lines of the model. This is perhaps the first instance of a scale model being presented for approval before construction began, the vessel being the *Prince Royal*. The laying of the keel in October 1608 coincided with the commission of inquiry and thereby raised doubts as to the suitability of Pett as a builder, both morally and professionally. Baker stated 'that he never saw

any work of his doing whereby he should so think him sufficient for that work, but rather thinketh the contrary' (*Autobiography*, lxviii). Baker also estimated the cost of constructing such a large ship (1187 tons old measurement) at £7000. The actual cost came to almost £20,000.

The *Prince Royal* was in fact only the third vessel fully built by Pett (he had rebuilt three and contributed to others) and undoubtedly there was a considerable amount of envy in the opposition of his fellow shipwrights, accentuated by Pett's rapid rise. An investigation of her construction, instigated by Northampton but under the direction of Nottingham, together with the earls of Worcester and Suffolk (both of whom were ignorant of ship design), decided in Pett's favour, as did the king. By contrast a survey by six shipwrights together with Captain George Waymouth provided a detailed list of her defects. It is important to note that many of the misdemeanours of which Pett was accused were common practice among his colleagues and his patrons ensured that he survived the commission of inquiry and the launch of the *Prince Royal*. One charge, of having used insufficient and unsuitable timber, does appear to have had substance for by December 1621 the navy commissioners were complaining that the vessel was unfit for service having been built of decayed or green timber. Almost £1000 was spent in repairs although they felt more was required (£6000). In 1641 the ship was completely rebuilt by Peter Pett at a total cost of over £18,000.

A further commission of inquiry was instituted in 1618 and yielded much the same results as that of 1608–9, although this time Pett did not emerge as the chief villain. One outcome of the inquiry was the recommendation to concentrate shipbuilding at Deptford, whereas Pett was employed at Chatham. William Burrell, the East India Company's chief shipwright, was contracted to build two ships a year for five years at Deptford, much to Pett's anger. He maintained a characteristic enmity towards Burrell despite the fact that Burrell had supported him in the *Prince Royal* affair.

Pett's career continued to prosper despite the damage to his reputation. In 1612 he was appointed first master of the Shipwrights' Company and in the following year was present when the elector palatine was escorted to Flanders. He was present on the 1620–21 expedition against the Algiers pirates and in 1623 sailed to Santander to collect the infanta. Marks of royal favour continued when Charles I succeeded to the throne, the new king awarding him a gold chain and allowing him to be present when Henrietta Maria embarked at Boulogne in June 1625. In February 1630 he became an assistant to the principal officers and in late December that same year a full principal officer.

In 1620 Pett built two vessels for a consortium of London merchants but, as was common practice, he exceeded his instructions by more than doubling their dimensions in order to increase profits. The merchants refused to pay the extra costs, which consequently had to be borne by Pett (a total of £900). To meet his debts (he was arrested briefly in 1628) he borrowed £325 from his brother Peter, who died about 1631. After his death Peter's widow relentlessly pursued the debt until eventually Pett was arrested in December 1634 despite going into hiding. He appears eventually to have cleared the debt. A similar instance of exceeding instructions may have occurred when Pett built the *Destiny*, on which he lost £700, for Sir Walter Ralegh in 1617. In 1633 Pett was again accused of graft, along with Sir Henry Palmer jun., over the sale of old cordage ('brown paper stuff'). In February 1634 he and a number of others were suspended from office only for Pett to receive a personal pardon from Charles. Throughout his career he relied on patronage from the highest levels at times of crisis.

In 1634 Pett prepared a model for what was to be the largest ship in the navy, the *Sovereign of the Seas* (1522 tons). Despite opposition from the masters of Trinity House, much of it transparently wrong, the keel was laid in December 1635 and the ship launched in October 1637, six months late. Once again the budget proved inadequate. Despite Pett's original estimate of £13,860, and assurance to complete her for £16,000, the final cost was a staggering £40,833. Pett continued to work at Chatham, where, following the defection of the fleet to the earl of Warwick in July 1642, he handed the dockyard over to parliament's control. For this he was rewarded with appointment as a navy commissioner on the same allowances as he already held, higher than the £100 allowed the other commissioners. He was not an active commissioner, perhaps owing to his age, and lived out his remaining years quietly at Chatham.

Pett was married three times: on 15 May 1598 to Anne (*d.* 1627), daughter of Richard Nicholls of Highwood Hill, Middlesex; in July 1627 to Susan, *née* Eaglefield (*d.* 1636), widow of Robert Yardley; and in 1638 to Mildred Byland, *née* Etherington (*d.* 1638). He had three daughters and eight sons with his first wife. His eldest son, John (who married Katharine Yardley, daughter of Robert Yardley, in 1625), was lost in his ship the *Sixth Whelp* when returning from the Rochelle expedition in 1628; Peter *Pett (*b.* 1610, *d.* in or before 1672) was a shipwright and navy commissioner; Phineas (1619–1666) was killed in the *Tiger*; and Christopher (1620–1668) was a master shipwright at Woolwich and Deptford. Their father died at Chatham, where he was buried on 21 August 1647.   ROY MCCAUGHEY

Sources *The autobiography of Phineas Pett*, ed. W. G. Perrin, Navy RS, 51 (1918) • *The naval tracts of Sir William Monson*, ed. M. Oppenheim, 5 vols., Navy RS, 22–3, 43, 45, 47 (1902–14) • *CSP dom.* • A. P. McGowan, 'The Royal Navy under the first duke of Buckingham', PhD diss., U. Lond., 1971 • A. P. McGowan, ed., *The Jacobean commissions of enquiry, 1608 and 1618*, Navy RS, 116 (1971) • M. Oppenheim, *A history of the administration of the Royal Navy* (1896) • declared accounts, PRO, audit office • declared accounts, PRO, pipe office • admiralty bill books, PRO • *DNB* • R. McCaughey, 'The English navy, politics and administration c.1640–1649', PhD diss., University of Ulster, 1983 • Pepys, *Diary*
Archives BL, Add. MS 9298
Likenesses oils, c.1612, NPG [*see illus.*]

Petter, (William) Edward Willoughby (1908–1968), aircraft designer, was born on 8 August 1908 at Highgate, Middlesex, the oldest in the family of three sons and one daughter of Ernest Willoughby *Petter (1873–1954),

(William) Edward Willoughby Petter (1908–1968), by Elliott & Fry, 1951

co-founder and chairman of Petters Ltd, oil engine and aircraft manufacturers of Yeovil, Somerset, and his wife, Angela Emma (*d.* 1934), daughter of Henry Petter of Calcutta. He was educated at Marlborough College and Gonville and Caius College, Cambridge, where he was awarded a first class in the mechanical sciences tripos in 1929 and shared the John Bernard Seely prize in aeronautics after concentrating on aerodynamics and aircraft engineering in his third year. Cambridge University had established a chair in aeronautical engineering in 1919, and most of the leading British aeronautical engineers were Cambridge graduates.

After leaving Cambridge, Teddy Petter, as he was commonly known, joined Westland Aircraft Works, the subsidiary of Petters Ltd, and after two and a half years as a graduate apprentice working in the machine and assembly shops and in the design office he became personal assistant to the managing director, Robert Bruce, in 1932. Also in 1932 he married Claude Marguerite Juliette (*d.* 1975), daughter of Louis Munier of Geneva, a Swiss League of Nations official; they had three daughters. When Sir Ernest Petter decided that his son should be co-opted onto the board of directors of Westland Aircraft Works as technical director in 1934, Bruce and several other older members of the firm resigned. In 1935 Westland Aircraft Works was detached from its parent company, becoming Westland Aircraft Ltd.

At first the Air Ministry lacked confidence in Petter's designs because of his youth and inexperience, and he had no success in tendering for Air Ministry specifications. However, he had powerful friends, including Roy Fedden at Bristol, who convinced the ministry of Petter's technical brilliance, and Westland was invited to tender for specification A.39/34 for an army co-operation aircraft. This led to a contract for two prototypes, designed by Arthur Davenport, the chief engineer, under Petter's technical direction, followed by an order for 169 aircraft in 1936. This plane was later named the Lysander, and between 1935 and 1942 more than 1400 were built at Yeovil. To cope with the production of the Lysanders Petter successfully challenged his father's proposal that the firm should merge with British Marine Aircraft Ltd, and instead persuaded it to build a large new assembly shop in Yeovil. When John Brown Ltd, the Clydeside shipbuilding firm, took over Westland in 1938, Teddy Petter remained as technical director.

Petter's other most successful designs were the Whirlwind, a four-cannon fighter, which won a contract for 175 planes in 1937 with the first planes delivered to the RAF in 1940, and the Welkin, a high altitude fighter, accepted in 1941. Although more than a hundred of these were built, there was little call for them as there turned out to be very few attacks at high altitude. Most of the Westland production during the Second World War consisted of subcontracted Spitfire and Seafire aircraft. At the peak of its production Westland was building twenty Spitfires a week. Meanwhile Petter was working on the early stages of an Admiralty specification for a strike fighter to be launched from an aircraft-carrier.

In December 1944 Petter resigned from Westland Aircraft Ltd after failing to obtain the board's agreement to his taking over responsibility for production as well as design. He had begun work on a government specification for a twin-engined jet fighter bomber to replace the Mosquito, and was allowed by the managing director, Eric Mensforth, to take the designs with him, to the English Electric Company in Preston, Lancashire, where he was appointed chief engineer of the aircraft division. English Electric had re-entered the aircraft manufacturing business in 1938, subcontracting the mass production of airframes, and had been making Halifax bombers. The company had been without a design office since 1923, but in 1944 the decision was taken to continue to build aircraft after the end of the war, and as there would be little subcontract work, a design team and development centre were needed. In 1944 English Electric was one of the companies invited by the government to develop a jet bomber, and the managing director, George Nelson (later first Baron Nelson of Stafford), approached Petter, asking him to form and head a design team. The government specification had changed, as the Air Ministry decided it wanted a high altitude jet bomber, and Petter's design won a Ministry of Supply contract for four prototypes in 1946. Later named the Canberra, this made its first flight in 1949, and its first public display at that year's Farnborough Air Show generated great excitement, as it flew at double the speed of previous bombers. This was the first British jet bomber, and its success moved English Electric to the forefront of British aviation. The Canberra was chosen by the United States Air Force: known as the B 57, it was the first British military aircraft to be built in the United States for over forty years. More than 1300 Canberras were built in Britain, the United States, and Australia, and it was still being used by the RAF in the 1980s and served in the Falklands War. Petter's other important design for English Electric was a supersonic fighter, with swept back wings, which developed into the Lightning.

In 1950 Petter resigned from English Electric, just as suddenly as he had previously resigned from Westland, and for the same reason, that he found it difficult to work with colleagues in other departments and wanted to be in charge of production as well as design, and to have his own experimental shop. When this was refused, he joined Folland Aircraft Ltd, a small subcontractor company in Hamble, Hampshire, as chief engineer, taking several members of his English Electric design team with him. After the death of Henry Folland in 1954 Petter became managing director. At Folland he designed a small jet fighter, the Gnat. More than three hundred were sold to the Ministry of Aviation, as well as sales to India, Finland, and Yugoslavia, and a later version, the Gnat trainer, became standard equipment in the RAF Flying Training Command. In 1962 Folland Aircraft Ltd was taken over by the Hawker Siddeley Group; Petter resigned as he did not want to work in a large organization again, and he left the aircraft industry altogether.

Petter was a brilliant designer, one of the leading aeronautical engineers of his time, but his eccentricity and authoritarian approach alienated his colleagues. He was conceited and had a reputation for rejecting any idea that he had not originated. Harald Penrose, chief test pilot at Westland, described him as 'poetical looking', and he had intellectual interests, particularly in philosophy. He never learned to fly.

Petter was elected a fellow of the Royal Aeronautical Society in 1944 and was awarded its silver medal in 1950. In 1951 he was made a CBE. When he left Folland he decided to devote the rest of his life to prayer and meditation, and moved with his family to Switzerland. In an attempt to cure his wife of Parkinson's disease, Petter, his wife, and youngest daughter joined a small religious community which practised faith healing, and, dressed in a monk's habit, he continually prayed for her recovery. They later moved to the same order in France. Petter died in Beruges, France, on 1 May 1968.

ANNE PIMLOTT BAKER

Sources H. Penrose, *Adventure with fate* (1984) · S. Ransom and R. Fairclough, *English Electric aircraft and their predecessors* (1987) · D. N. James, *Westland Aircraft since 1915* (1991) · D. Mondey, *Westland* (1982) · R. Beamont and A. Reed, *English Electric Canberra* (1984) · A. H. Lukins, *The book of Westland Aircraft* (1944) · P. King, *Knights of the air: the life and times of the extraordinary pioneers who first built British aeroplanes* (1989) · *The Times* (27 May 1968) · T. J. N. Hilken, *Engineering at Cambridge University, 1783–1965* (1967) · *DNB*

Likenesses group portrait, photograph, 1940–49, repro. in Ranson and Fairclough, *English Electric aircraft*, 50 · Elliott & Fry, photograph, 1951, NPG [*see illus.*] • photograph, repro. in Beamont and Reed, *English Electric Canberra*, 12

Petter, Sir Ernest Willoughby (1873–1954), engine and aircraft manufacturer, and his business partner, **Percival Waddams Petter** (1873–1955), were identical twins born on 26 May 1873 in High Street, Yeovil, Somerset, the third and fourth of the fifteen children of James Bazeley Petter, ironmonger, of Yeovil, and his wife, Charlotte Waddams, *née* Branscombe, of Bristol, the daughter of a rubber merchant. They were educated at Yeovil grammar school, and after two years at Mount Radford School, Exeter, they left school in 1890 at the age of sixteen to start apprenticeships in their father's business.

The ironmongery firm of Harman and Gillett in Yeovil had been given to James Petter by his father as a wedding present. He later acquired the Yeovil Foundry and Engineering Works, making agricultural machinery, and also started the Nautilus Stove Company, making grates and kitchen ranges, much in demand after Queen Victoria had installed Nautilus fire grates at Balmoral Castle and Osborne House. Percival, Percy as he was generally known, became manager of the foundry in 1895, and he, in particular, became interested in the new horseless carriages being designed on the continent. With the help of the foreman he designed and built a single-cylinder 1 hp oil engine and installed it in a chassis built by the local carriage builders, Hill and Boll. Demonstrated in 1895, this was one of the first vehicles propelled by internal combustion to be produced in Great Britain. The Yeovil Motor Car and Cycle Company Ltd was established and twelve motor cars were built following the appearance of a technical description of the Petter horseless carriage in *The Engineer* in 1896. But the company did not prosper, and the Petters decided to concentrate on small oil engines for agricultural use. The Petter Patent Oil Engine (1.25 hp) was exhibited at the Royal Show in 1899, and in 1901 the brothers bought the business from their father, and it was reorganized as James B. Petter & Sons Ltd, with Ernest and Percy Petter as joint managing directors. The range of oil engines was expanded, with power outputs from 1.25 to 22 hp, and in 1902 they produced an agricultural tractor powered by a 30 hp oil engine.

After its registration as a public company in 1910 Petters Ltd continued to expand and by 1912 had over 500 employees and was producing 1500 engines a year. The existing foundry could not cope with this level of production, and in 1913 a site was found at West Hendford, west of Yeovil, for a new foundry and a garden village for the employees, which became known as Westland.

With the outbreak of the First World War the demand for engines increased but in 1915 Ernest Petter, the new chairman of Petters Ltd, persuaded the board to put its manufacturing resources at the disposal of the government. As a result, Petters was asked to build aeroplanes, beginning with an order for twelve Short seaplanes. Westland Aircraft Works was founded as a subsidiary of Petters with R. A. Bruce, former managing director of the British and Colonial Aeroplane Company in Bristol, as managing director. The seaplanes were followed by Sopwith fighters and Airco De Havilland bombers, and nearly a thousand planes were built by the end of the war. By then Westland Aircraft Works had built up a design office and converted neighbouring farmland into an airfield in order to be able to test planes, and when the DH 9 bomber was found to have shortcomings in its design, Westland's drawing office was asked to redesign it to enable it to take the American Liberty engine. The success of the DH 9A bomber brought Westland recognition.

Meanwhile Petters, with Percy Petter as managing director, continued to make engines together with shell cases and gun carriage equipment. After the war, it concentrated on the production of diesel and petrol engines, which were used throughout the world as agricultural engines, electricity generators, and marine engines. A venture in association with Vickers, Vickers Petters Ltd, in Ipswich, formed to produce large diesel engines and managed by Ernest Petter, was less successful.

The Petters continued to regard the aircraft works very much as a sideline to the oil engine business. Westland Aircraft Works, like other aircraft manufacturers, suffered after the war from the cancellation of military contracts. The design office produced seventeen new designs but none was accepted until 1927, when the works won the government contract for the Wapiti, a replacement for the DH 9A. More than a thousand Wapitis had been sold all over the world by the early 1930s, including more than five hundred to the RAF, and they accounted for most of the Westland production between 1927 and 1934. In the early 1930s exports of Petter oil engines fell, and it was the aircraft works which kept the firm going.

In 1935 the Petters decided to separate the engine and aircraft businesses completely, and Westland Aircraft Ltd was registered as a public company, with Petters Ltd retaining half the shares. In 1938, John Brown Ltd, the Clydeside shipbuilding firm, bought a controlling interest in Westland. Ernest Petter, who had been knighted in 1925, resigned as chairman of Petters Ltd and Westland Aircraft Ltd, sold his aircraft shares to Associated Electrical Industries Ltd, and emigrated to Victoria, British Columbia; Percy Petter resigned as vice-chairman. The Petters Ltd engine business was sold to Brush Electrical Engineering Ltd, and moved to Loughborough.

Ernest Petter stood unsuccessfully for parliament three times, twice contesting Bristol North as a Conservative, in 1918 and 1923, and St George's, Westminster, in a 1931 by-election. He published a number of pamphlets on industrial economics, including *The Disease of Unemployment and the Cure* (1925). He was president of the British Engineers' Association from 1923 to 1925, and was knighted after organizing the engineering section of the British Empire Exhibition at Wembley in 1925. In 1907 he married Angela Emma (d. 1934), daughter of Henry Petter of Calcutta; they had three sons, the eldest of whom, (William) Edward Willoughby *Petter, became an aircraft designer, and one daughter. After her death he married, in 1935, Lucy Ellen, daughter of Charles Hopkins of Portsmouth. Petter returned to England from Canada in 1953, and died at his home, Bywell, Spencer Road, New Milton, Hampshire, on 18 July 1954, survived by his wife.

Percy Petter, in contrast to his extrovert brother, was shy and withdrawn, and a teetotaller. A devout Anglican and a member of the Christian Brethren, in 1919 he was one of the 'Pilgrim preachers' who preached on a journey between Bath and London. He retained his interest in invention, and as late as 1932 designed a desk calculating machine, the Petometer, which sold in small numbers. Percy Petter was active in local politics, and was mayor of Yeovil 1925–7. He married in 1904 Emily Kennan of Dublin, daughter of one of the selling agents for Petter engines in Ireland. They had two sons and four daughters. After her death he married Ruth Penson-Harris. Percy Petter died at his home, Heather Lawn, Seaway Avenue, Christchurch, Hampshire, on 15 September 1955, and was buried at Yeovil cemetery on 19 September. His wife survived him.   ANNE PIMLOTT BAKER

Sources D. Mondey, *Westland* (1982) · D. N. James, *Westland Aircraft since 1915* (1991) · A. H. Lukins, *The book of Westland Aircraft* (1944) · D. J. Jeremy and F. Goodall, 'Petter, Sir Ernest Willoughby, and Petter, Percival Waddams', *DBB* · H. Penrose, *Adventure with fate* (1984) · P. King, *Knights of the air: the life and times of the extraordinary pioneers who first built British aeroplanes* (1989) · *The Times* (19 July 1954) · *The Engineer* (23 July 1954) · *Engineering* (23 July 1954) · *The Times* (16 Sept 1955) [Percival Waddams Petter] · *Engineering* (23 Sept 1955) [Percival Waddams Petter] · d. cert. · d. cert. [Percival Waddams Petter] · b. cert. · b. cert. [Percival Waddams Petter]
Likenesses double portrait, photograph (of the twins), repro. in James, *Westland Aircraft since 1915*, 5 · double portrait, photograph (of the twins), repro. in Jeremy and Goodall, 'Petter'
Wealth at death £859 1s. 6d.: probate, 1955, *CGPLA Eng. & Wales* · £23,502 8s. 1d.—Percival Waddams Petter: probate, 1956, *CGPLA Eng. & Wales*

Petter, Percival Waddams (1873–1955). *See under* Petter, Sir Ernest Willoughby (1873–1954).

Pettie, George (c.1548–1589), writer of romances, was the fourth son of John Pettie (or Le Petite or Petty) of Tetsworth and Stoke Talmage, Oxfordshire, and Mary, daughter of William Charnell of Snareston, Leicestershire. He became a scholar of Christ Church, Oxford, in 1564 and graduated BA on 29 March 1569. He was uncle of Mary Pettie, the mother of Anthony Wood, and it is Wood who records that during his time at Oxford Pettie formed a literary friendship with the Latin dramatist William Gager, also of Christ Church. Upon leaving Oxford, Pettie travelled in continental Europe and saw military service abroad.

Pettie's best-known work is a story collection entitled *A Petite Pallace of Pettie his Pleasure: contaynyng many pretie hystories by him set foorth in comely colours, and most delightfully discoursed*, which acknowledges the book's debt to *The Palace of Pleasure* (1566 and 1567) of William Painter. The *Petite Pallace* was licensed to Richard Watkins on 6 August 1576 but was published undated. Its dedication, 'To the gentle Gentlewomen Readers', is signed 'R. B.' Hazlitt, in his edition of Thomas Warton's *History of English Poetry* (1871, 4.336), proposes that these are the reversed initials of Barnaby Riche but Hartman favours the unknown 'R. B.' who wrote *A New Tragicall Comedie of Apius and Virginia* (1575).

The possibility remains that 'R. B.' is an authorial alias used by Pettie; the prefatory matter to George Gascoigne's *Adventures of Master F. J.* (1573) employs a similar strategy, if such this is. 'R. B.' confesses to supplying the stories without the author's permission, a scenario supported by the letter of the printer to the reader. The preliminary matter also includes 'The letter of G[eorge] P[ettie] to R. B. concerning this woorke', dated from Holborn, 12 July, which urges R. B. to keep the stories 'to your owne private pleasure' because they 'touch neerely divers of my nere friendes'.

Subsequent editions were published c.1578 and c.1585, the latter omitting the prefatory material, as does the edition of c.1590. Editions by George Eld appeared in 1608 and 1613. Modern editions have been undertaken by Israel Gollancz (1908) and Herbert Hartman (1938). The significance of the *Petite Pallace* lies in its prioritizing of a female readership, and its role in the development of the literary style called euphuism: it influenced the early euphuistic romances of Robert Greene and acted as a storehouse of proverbs for John Lyly in the writing of his romance *Euphues*. Pettie himself was not averse to literary borrowing: the influence of George Gascoigne and George Turberville can be detected in his work. The overwhelmingly Ovidian and euphuistic character of the collection is remarked in *Le prince d'amour* (1660), in which one of the offences against the prince is described as being to 'deprave the books of *Ovid de Arte amandi*, *Euphues* and his *England*, *Petite Pallace*, or other laudable discourses of love' (*Le Prince*, 57).

Pettie also translated the first three books of Guazzo's *Civile Conversation*, using the French of George Chappuys. The translation was licensed to Richard Watkins on 11 November 1579, with another mention in the Stationers' register on 27 February 1581. It was published later that year with a dedication addressed from Pettie's lodging near St Paul's, London, to Marjorie, wife of Henry Norris, Baron Norris of Rycote. In his preface to the *Civile Conversation* Pettie explains that he intends this translation to counterbalance the frivolity of the *Petite Pallace*: he hopes 'to purchase to my selfe some better fame by some better woorke, and to countervayle my former Vanitie, with some formal gravitie' (*Civile Conversation*, 1.7). A second issue, by Thomas East, was dated 1586, and included Guazzo's fourth book, translated from the Italian by Bartholomew Young.

According to Wood, Pettie died in July 1589 at Plymouth, 'being then a captain and a man of note', and was buried in the 'great church' (Wood, *Ath. Oxon.*, 1.555) there. He left to his brother Christopher the lands at Aston-Rowant, Kingston, and Tetsworth, Oxfordshire, which he had himself received from his father. Wood is in two minds about the literary merits of Pettie's *Petite Pallace*: his relative's 'passionate penning of amorous stories' made him 'as much commended for his neat stile as any of his time', but in Wood's own time the *Petite Pallace* seemed 'more fit to be read by a schoolboy, or rustical amoratto, than by a gent. of mode or language' (ibid., 1.553).   HELEN MOORE

Sources The life and times of Anthony Wood, ed. A. Clark, 1, OHS, 19 (1891), 32–7 · Wood, Ath. Oxon., new edn, 1.552–5 · Foster, Alum. Oxon., 1500–1714, 3.1153 · Arber, Regs. Stationers, 2.301, 361, 389 · G. Pettie, A petite pallace of Pettie his pleasure, ed. H. Hartman (1938) · STC, 1475–1640 · C. J. Vincent, 'Pettie and Greene', Modern Language Notes, 54 (1939), 105–11 · M. P. Tilley, Elizabethan proverb lore in Lyly's 'Euphues' and in Pettie's 'Petite pallace', with parallels from Shakespeare (New York, 1926) · D. J. N. Bush, 'Pettie's petty pilfering from poets', Philological Quarterly, 5 (1926), 325–9 · J. L. Lievsay, Stefano Guazzo and the English Renaissance, 1575–1675 (Chapel Hill, 1961) · G. Pettie, A petite pallace of Pettie his pleasure containing many pretie histories by him set forth in comely colours and most delightfully discovered, ed. I. Gollancz, 2 vols. (1908) · E. Sullivan, Introduction, in The 'Civile conversation' of M. Steeven Guazzo, ed. C. Whibley, 2 vols. (1925)

Pettie, John (1839–1893), painter, was born in Edinburgh on 17 March 1839, the eldest of the three sons and two daughters of Alexander Pettie, a prosperous shopkeeper, and his wife, Alison Frier. At the age of thirteen he moved with his family to East Linton, East Lothian, and it was here that he began to show artistic promise by making copies of reproductions of paintings with household paints from his father's shop. On 16 October 1855 he enrolled at the Trustees' Academy, Edinburgh, where he studied for five years under Robert Scott Lauder. Among his contemporaries were William Quiller Orchardson, William MacTaggart, and George Paul Chalmers, all of whom later became distinguished painters.

An ambitious and conscientious student, Pettie began exhibiting at the Royal Scottish Academy, Edinburgh, in 1858, and two years later had his first picture accepted by the Royal Academy in London. Among his early successes were numerous interpretations of incidents from the novels of Sir Walter Scott, including Scene from 'The Monastery' (1859), as well as historical subjects, such as The Prison Pet (1859; priv. coll.). His gift for visual narrative was recognized by the publishers Blackie & Son, who commissioned him to produce illustrations for their devotional part-work Family Worship (1862–3). Commercial assignments of this kind were to provide a lucrative source of income in the early stage of Pettie's career, and throughout the 1860s he regularly contributed illustrations to several other popular periodicals, among them Good Words and the Sunday Magazine.

The financial security provided by his work as an illustrator enabled Pettie to move to London in 1862. Here he shared lodgings at 62 Stanley Street, Pimlico, with his former student colleague Orchardson, with whom he moved in 1863 to 37 Fitzroy Square (a house later occupied by Ford Madox Brown). On 24 August 1865 he married Elizabeth Ann Bossom, the sister-in-law of the Scottish painter C. E. Johnson, and lived with her in Regent's Park before moving to St John's Wood Road in 1869. They had three sons, Graham, Ralph, and Norman, and a daughter, Alison, who later married the Scottish composer Hamish *MacCunn. In 1882 the family finally settled in The Lothians, a house in Fitzjohn's Avenue designed for Pettie by his friend the architect William Wallace.

On his arrival in London, Pettie quickly established himself as the leader of a group of expatriate Scottish painters, whose work was distinguished by the vividness of its narrative content and the brilliance of its visual style. Pettie himself was strongly influenced by the earlier work of Sir David Wilkie, from whom he developed an interest in physical gesture and facial expression. Much of his subject matter was historical, with the turbulent events of the English civil war and the Jacobite rising providing his principal source material. His approach to the representation of history was not, however, a rigorously academic one, and in most cases the scenes he depicted were intended merely to embody the 'spirit and romance of history' (Hardie, 1908, 76) rather than illustrate documented historical occurrences. Typical examples of such historical fictions are The Drumhead Court-Martial (1862; Sheffield Galleries and Museums Trust), Treason (1867; Sheffield Galleries and Museums Trust), and The Vigil (1884; Tate collection). In many cases the narrative is focused on a single dramatic moment, as in The Disgrace of Cardinal Wolsey (1869; Sheffield Galleries and Museums Trust), a psychologically charged study of political humiliation, or The Sally (1870; Sheffield Galleries and Museums Trust), in which suspense is created by the skilful massing of a group of soldiers huddled behind a castle door. Apart from the clarity and force of his narrative technique, Pettie's great strength as a painter lay in his ability to evoke the atmosphere of a historical period through the effective use of costume and background accessories. He was also a fine colourist, and in many of his mature paintings the composition is organized around a dominant figure, or group of figures, dressed in brilliantly coloured costumes. Examples of this tendency are Ho! Ho! Old Noll (1874; Glasgow Art Gallery and Museum) and The Chieftain's Candlesticks (1886; Forbes Magazine Collection, New York).

Towards the end of his career Pettie began to concentrate on studies of social manners, with works such as Two Strings to her Bow (1887; Glasgow Art Gallery and Museum) and The World Went Very Well Then (1890; Dundee City Art Gallery) typifying his fondness for idealizing the day-to-day life of rural communities. It is significant, however, that these are almost invariably set in the Regency period, rather than Pettie's own day, despite his frequent use of friends and relatives as models. His reluctance to engage with contemporary history extended to his portraits, many of which present the sitter in period costume or in the manner of earlier artists such as Rembrandt. In his portrait of the novelist William Black, for example, the subject is depicted as A Knight of the Seventeenth Century (1877; Glasgow Art Gallery and Museum).

One of the most critically and commercially successful artists of his day, Pettie became an associate of the Royal Academy in 1866 and a Royal Academician eight years later. He himself attributed his success to an almost superhuman capacity for hard work, and there is little doubt that his lifelong dedication to painting left little time for other pursuits. As a student his principal leisure activity was participating in the meetings of an informal sketching club, a practice which he continued after his arrival in London. Similarly, his involvement with the National Volunteer Association in Edinburgh in 1859, and his consequent role in the establishment of the Artists' company of the City artillery volunteers, may be seen as an extension of the passion for military matters which inspired much of his creative output. Towards the end of 1892 he began to suffer from an abscess of the ear, and on 10 January 1893 he was found unconscious on his studio floor. The abscess was later removed, but he failed to recover and died at 47 Eversfield Place, Hastings, on 21 February. He was buried in Paddington cemetery six days later.

RAY McKENZIE

Sources M. Hardie, *John Pettie, R.A., H.R.S.A.* (1908) · L. Errington, *Master class: Robert Scott Lauder and his pupils* (1983), 39–44, 68ff. [exhibition catalogue, NG Scot., 15 July – 2 Oct 1983, and Aberdeen Art Gallery, 15 Oct – 12 Nov 1983] · D. Macmillan, *Scottish art, 1460–1990* (1990), 233–5 · W. M. Gilbert, *Art Journal*, new ser., 13 (1893), 206–10 · E. Pinnington, *George Paul Chalmers RSA and the art of his time, 1833–1878* (1896) · J. L. Caw, *Scottish painting past and present, 1620–1908* (1908), 240–43 · D. Irwin and F. Irwin, *Scottish painters at home and abroad, 1700–1900* (1975), 342–4 · W. Armstrong, *Scottish painters* (1888), 84–5 · M. Hardie, *John Pettie, R.A., H.R.S.A.: sixteen examples in colour of the artist's work* (1910) · W. Hardie, *Scottish painting, 1837–1939* (1976), 47–51 · b. cert. · m. cert. · d. cert. · *CGPLA Eng. & Wales* (1893) · will, Probate Department of the Principal Registry of the Family Division, London

Archives NL Scot., corresp. | NL Scot., letters to William McTaggart

Likenesses J. Pettie, self-portrait, oils, 1881, Aberdeen Art Gallery · Lock & Whitfield, woodburytype photograph, 1882, NPG · J. Pettie, self-portrait, oils, 1882, Tate collection · R. W. Robinson, photograph, 1891, NPG · J. Archer, oils, Scot. NPG · G. P. Chalmers, oils, Scot. NPG · R. Cleaver, group portrait, pen-and-ink drawing (*Hanging committee, Royal Academy, 1892*), NPG · Elliott & Fry, carte-de-visite, NPG · G. A. Lawson, bronze bust, Scot. NPG · G. A. Lawson, bronze bust, Glasgow Art Gallery · G. G. Manton, group portrait, watercolour drawing (*Conversazione at the Royal Academy, 1891*), NPG · woodcuts (after photographs), BM, NPG

Wealth at death £11,688 0s. 8d.: probate, 17 March 1893, *CGPLA Eng. & Wales*

Pettigrew, James Bell (1834–1908), comparative anatomist, born on 26 May 1834 at Roxhill, Lanarkshire, was the son of Robert Pettigrew and Mary Bell. He was related on his father's side to Thomas Joseph *Pettigrew, surgeon, and on his mother's side to Henry *Bell, the builder of the *Comet* steamship. Educated at the Free West Academy of Airdrie, he studied arts at the University of Glasgow from 1850 to 1855. He then migrated to Edinburgh, where he pursued medical studies. In 1858–9 he was awarded Professor John Goodsir's senior anatomy gold medal for the best treatise 'On the arrangement of the muscular fibres in the ventricles of the vertebrate heart' (*Philosophical Transactions*, 1864). This treatise gained him the appointment of Croonian lecturer at the Royal Society of London in 1860. He received at Edinburgh in 1860 the annual gold medal in the class of medical jurisprudence with an essay 'On the presumption of survivorship' (*British and Foreign Medico-Chirurgical Review*, January 1865). He graduated MD at Edinburgh in 1861, obtaining the gold medal for his inaugural dissertation on 'the ganglia and nerves of the heart and their connection with the cerebrospinal and sympathetic systems in mammalia' (*Proceedings of the Royal Society of Edinburgh*, 1865).

In 1861 Pettigrew acted as house surgeon to Professor James Syme at the Royal Infirmary, Edinburgh, and in

James Bell Pettigrew (1834–1908), by Walter William Ouless, 1902

1862 he was appointed assistant in the Hunterian Museum at the Royal College of Surgeons of England. Here he remained until 1867, adding dissections to the collection and writing papers on various anatomical subjects. In 1867 he contributed a paper to the *Transactions of the Linnean Society* entitled 'On the mechanical appliances by which flight is maintained in the animal kingdom', and in the same year he left the Hunterian Museum in order to spend two years in the south of Ireland so as to extend his knowledge of the flight of insects, birds, and bats. He also experimented largely on the subject of artificial flight. His *Animal Locomotion, or, Walking, Swimming, and Flying, with a Dissertation on aëronautics* appeared in 1873 and was translated into French (1874) and German (1879).

Elected FRS in 1869, in the autumn of that year Pettigrew became curator of the museum of the Royal College of Surgeons of Edinburgh and pathologist at the Royal Infirmary. He continued his anatomical, physical, and physiological researches, especially those on flight, and in 1870 he published a memoir 'On the physiology of wings, being an analysis of the movements by which flight is produced in the insect, bird and bat' (*Transactions of the Royal Society of Edinburgh*, 26).

At Edinburgh Pettigrew was elected FRSE and FRCP (Edin.) in 1873. He was appointed in the same year lecturer on physiology at the College of Surgeons of Edinburgh. In 1874 he was awarded the Godard prize of the French Académie des Sciences for his anatomico-physiological researches and was made a laureate of the Institut de France. In 1875 he was appointed Chandos professor of medicine and anatomy and dean of the medical faculty in the University of St Andrews. In 1875–7 he delivered special courses of lectures on physiology in Dundee, and University College, Dundee, owes its origin largely to his efforts. In 1877 he was elected by the universities of Glasgow and St Andrews to represent them on the General Medical Council. After 1886, when a new medical act enabled each of the Scottish universities to return its own member, Pettigrew represented St Andrews alone on the council. In 1883 he received the honorary degree of LLD at Glasgow. He married, in 1890, Elsie, second daughter of Sir William *Gray, of Greatham, co. Durham, but left no family.

Pettigrew died at his home, the Swallowgate, St Andrews, on 30 January 1908. A museum for the botanic gardens was erected in his memory by his widow as an adjunct to the Bute medical buildings of St Andrews University. Pettigrew's *Design in Nature*, the work which occupied the last ten years of his life, was published posthumously in three volumes in 1908.

D'A. POWER, rev. MICHAEL BEVAN

Sources *Men and women of the time* (1899) · *The Lancet* (8 Feb 1908), 471 · *BMJ* (8 Feb 1908), 357 · private information (1912) · F. Bennet and M. Melrose, *Index of fellows of the Royal Society of Edinburgh: elected November 1783 – July 1883*, ed. H. Frew, rev. edn (1984) · WWW
Likenesses W. W. Ouless, oils, 1902, U. Edin. [*see illus.*]

Pettigrew, Thomas Joseph (1791–1865), surgeon and antiquary, was born on 28 October 1791 at 128 Fleet Street, London, son of William Pettigrew (1739–1825), surgeon-apothecary, a Scot and former naval surgeon, and his second wife, Elizabeth (*née* Cranford). Thomas showed an interest in anatomy from the age of twelve. He attended a local school until the age of fourteen, assisted his father for two years in his duties as surgeon to St Bride's parish, and was then apprenticed to the surgeon John Taunton. He attended the United Borough Hospitals' medical schools and assisted Taunton as demonstrator in his anatomy school. In 1808 he was one of the founders of the City Philosophical Society, later the Philosophical Society of London. Also in 1808 he was elected a fellow of the Medical Society of London and in 1809 he published his first book, *Views of the Basis of the Brain and Cranium*, a precocious work which attracted suspicions of plagiarism—the first of many controversies. In 1811 he married Elizabeth Reed (1786–1854). They had twelve children, of whom five sons and three daughters reached adult life. Two of the sons followed their father into the medical profession.

In 1812, at Taunton's instigation, Pettigrew was elected secretary of the Medical Society of London, defeating the eminent physician George Birkbeck, a contest which led to some subsequent ill feeling. He also took on the post of registrar with residential accommodation at the society's house in Bolt Court, Fleet Street, but forgoing the salary. He qualified as MRCS in 1812. In 1813, through the influence of the Medical Society's founder, John Coakley Lettsom, Pettigrew became secretary to the Royal Humane Society, holding the post until 1820 and in 1818 receiving the society's medal for life-saving. On Lettsom's death in 1815 Pettigrew delivered a eulogy before the Philosophical

Society of London, printed in 1816, and in 1817 produced *Memoirs of the Life and Writings of the Late John Coakley Lettsom*, in three volumes. From 1816 to 1819 he was surgeon to the Dispensary for the Treatment of Diseases of Children, St Andrew's Hill, Doctors' Commons, later the Royal Universal Dispensary for Children. In 1818 he left the Medical Society and moved to 22 Spring Gardens.

Through his connection with the Royal Humane Society, Pettigrew was appointed surgeon to the duke of Kent and vaccinated his daughter Princess Victoria. He also became surgeon to the duke of Sussex and, in 1819, his librarian. Under the duke's influence he was initiated as a freemason. The first volume of an ambitious catalogue of the duke's library, *Bibliotheca Sussexiana*, was published in two parts in 1827, containing the religious manuscripts and printed editions of the Bible. Pettigrew's reward was a doctorate in philosophy from the University of Göttingen, conferred on 7 November 1826. Meanwhile his professional career continued: in 1819 he became surgeon to the Asylum for Female Orphans, a post which he retained until 1848, and in 1822 surgeon to the Royal West London Infirmary and Dispensary which in 1827 became the Charing Cross Hospital. He published regularly in the medical journals and in 1819 delivered the annual oration of the Medical Society of London, on medical jurisprudence (MS in Wellcome Library). In 1824 he moved to 8 Savile Row, where he later held popular soirées. His connection with the duke of Sussex came to an untimely end. Pettigrew, who had been elected a fellow of the Royal Society in 1827, was involved in the negotiations leading to the controversial election of the duke as president on the resignation of Davies Gilbert in 1830. The duke found the unexpected contest embarrassing and soon afterwards severed relations with Pettigrew, following his repetition of the duke's private comments about an unsuccessful fellowship candidate. Pettigrew was never restored as librarian but a partial reconciliation made possible publication of volume 2 of the *Bibliotheca Sussexiana* in 1839. In 1835 Pettigrew also lost his position at Charing Cross Hospital on a charge of receiving £500 from John Howship for securing him the post of assistant surgeon, though Pettigrew in his *Address to the Governors and Subscribers of the Charing Cross Hospital* (1836) maintained that the payment was part of an agreement for the sharing of anticipated fees. Thereafter he devoted himself to private practice and, increasingly, to his antiquarian interests.

Pettigrew had been interested in Egyptology since the 1820s; he published in 1834 *A History of Egyptian Mummies* (having himself unrolled numerous specimens) and in 1842 the first part only of *Encyclopaedia Aegyptiana*. In 1836 he published *The pauper farming system: a letter … on the condition of the pauper children of St James Westminster*. As a diversion after the death of his eldest son, Thomas Lettsom, an officer in the Madras army, in 1837 he compiled *The Medical Portrait Gallery* (4 vols., 1838–40), including his own autobiography. He also contributed 540 biographies to H. J. Rose's *A New General Biographical Dictionary* (12 vols., 1840–57), and in 1849 published *The Life of Vice-Admiral Lord Nelson*, in two volumes. He was appointed to the council of the Historical Society of Science in 1840 and to the council of the Percy Society in 1841. In 1843 he was elected one of the first fellows of the Royal College of Surgeons and over the years was elected to various foreign medical and antiquarian societies. His publications in medical history include *On Superstitions Connected with … Medicine and Surgery* (1844) and an edition for the Percy Society of John Halle's *An Historiall Expostulation Against the Beastlye Abusers both of Chyrurgerie and Physyke* (1844). He had been an active fellow of the Society of Antiquaries since 1824 and was one of the founders of the British Archaeological Association in 1843, serving as treasurer until his death and allowing meetings to be held at his house. He declined an offer of the presidency in 1854.

Pettigrew continued to court controversy: in 1852 his *Letter to the Lord Viscount Mahon* criticized the management of the Society of Antiquaries, and in 1854 he successfully defended his conduct at the British Archaeological Association against an attack by Thomas Hugo. His antiquarian writings appeared mainly in periodicals. A revised edition of Richard Gough's *Sepulchral Monuments* was projected in 1852 but abandoned on grounds of cost. His last book was *Chronicles of the Tombs* (1857). On the death of his wife in 1854 he retired from practice and moved to 16 Onslow Crescent, Brompton, London. He continued to attend the British Archaeological Association's annual conferences, in spite of failing health, but made only a token appearance at Durham in 1865. Pettigrew died at his home on 23 November 1865 and was buried on 30 November at Brompton cemetery. His library was sold at Sothebys on 10 May 1866. There had been an earlier sale on 13 February 1856, and a final sale at Knight, Frank, and Rutley on 23 August 1905 included his collections of paintings, engravings, Egyptian antiquities, shells, and minerals, as well as books and manuscripts.   JOHN SYMONS

Sources W. R. Dawson, 'Memoir of Thomas Joseph Pettigrew', *Medical Life*, 38 (1931), 1–136 · A. Lister, 'The duke of Sussex and T. J. Pettigrew's *Bibliotheca Sussexiana*', *Antiquarian Book Monthly Review*, 14 (1987), 58–65 · T. J. Pettigrew, 'Autobiographical sketch', *Medical portrait gallery: biographical memoirs of the most celebrated physicians, surgeons … who have contributed to the advancement of medical science*, 4 (1840) · M. B. Hall, *All scientists now: the Royal Society in the nineteenth century* (1984) · J. Evans, *A history of the Society of Antiquaries* (1956) · M. Gillen, *Royal duke, Augustus Frederick duke of Sussex* (1976) · R. J. Minney, *The two pillars of Charing Cross* (1967) · F. Hart, *The roots of service: history of Charing Cross Hospital* (1985) · T. Hunt, ed., *The Medical Society of London, 1773–1973* (1972) · J. J. Abraham, *Lettsom, his life, times, friends and descendants* (1933) · W. R. Dawson and E. P. Uphill, *Who was who in Egyptology*, 2nd edn (1972) · *DNB* · *CGPLA Eng. & Wales* (1866)
Archives BL, corresp., Add. MSS 56229–56230 · Exeter Cathedral, dean and chapter library, corresp. · Wellcome L., commonplace books, corresp., and papers · Yale U., Beinecke L., corresp. and papers | Bodl. Oxf., letters to Sir Thomas Phillipps · Royal Arch., Duke of Sussex MSS · U. Edin. L., corresp. with James Halliwell-Phillipps
Likenesses G. G. Adams, marble medallion, c.1850 · C. Baugniet, lithograph, 1856 (after his drawing), repro. in Dawson, 'Memoir', 2 · photograph, 1863, repro. in Dawson, 'Memoir', 125 · W. Holl and F. Holl, stipple (after oil painting by H. Room, 1838), Wellcome L.; repro. in Pettigrew, 'Autobiographical sketch' · A. W. Skelton, watercolour drawing (after H. Room), Scot. NPG · H. S. Turner,

lithograph (aged 40; after sketch by E. U. Eddis, 1831), repro. in Dawson, 'Memoir', 78
Wealth at death under £3000: probate, 22 Feb 1866, *CGPLA Eng. & Wales*

Pettingall, John (1707/8–1781), Church of England clergyman and antiquary, was born in Newport, Monmouthshire, the son of the Revd Francis Pettingall. He attended the grammar school in Newport before matriculating from Jesus College, Oxford, on 15 March 1725, aged seventeen. He graduated BA in 1728 and was later incorporated at Corpus Christi College, Cambridge, where he received the degree of MA (1740); he later proceeded DD from Lambeth. He was ordained priest at Llandaff on 5 March 1732 and for a while served as chaplain to the bishop of Llandaff, Richard Watson. He was rector of Whitsun, and vicar of Christchurch, both in Monmouthshire, until 1756. On 3 June 1757 he was appointed a prebendary of St Paul's Cathedral and on 28 July 1758 was installed prebendary of Lincoln. He appears to have been the incumbent preacher at Duke Street Chapel in Westminster until his preferment to the rectory of Stoke Hammond, Buckinghamshire, which he held until his death.

Pettingall was a keen antiquarian and in 1752 he was elected a fellow of the Society of Antiquaries. He wrote several works on Roman artefacts and early British coins, and published a study of the use of the jury system in Greek and Roman society. He read three papers before the Society of Antiquaries which were later published in *Archaeologia*, together with another paper on a deed issued by Bishop Odo of Bayeux. He also translated A. C. F. Houtteville's *Discours historique et critique sur la méthode des principaux auteurs qui ont écrit pour ou contre le Christianisme*, which he published in 1739 with an appendix entitled 'A dissertation on the life of Apollonius Tyaneus, with some observations on the Platonists of the later school'. Pettingall, who was married to Susanna Long of the parish of St Margaret's, Westminster, died at Stoke Hammond on 30 June 1781 and was buried in the churchyard there on 2 July. His son **Thomas Pettingall** (1744/5–1826), a Church of England clergyman and tutor, was educated at Westminster School from about 1756, where he became a king's scholar in 1758, and at Christ Church, Oxford, whence he matriculated on 9 June 1762, aged seventeen. He graduated BA (1766) and proceeded MA (1769) and BD (1778). He was briefly an usher at his old school (1770–73) but returned to his college to take up a post as tutor and censor from 1774 to 1779. He was appointed rector of East Hampstead, Berkshire, in 1782 and died at Bagshot, Surrey, on 8 April 1826.

G. LE G. NORGATE, *rev.* M. J. MERCER

Sources Venn, *Alum. Cant.*, 1/3.352 · Foster, *Alum. Oxon.*, 1715–1886, 3.1103 · *Old Westminsters*, 2.737 · *GM*, 1st ser., 51 (1781), 442 · *GM*, 1st ser., 91/1 (1821), 379 · Watt, *Bibl. Brit.* · M. E. C. Walcott, *The memorials of Westminster*, new edn (1851), 72
Archives BL, corresp. with W. Cole, Add. MSS 5834, 5886, 5993, 6401

Pettingall, Thomas (1744/5–1826). *See under* Pettingall, John (1707/8–1781).

Pettitt, Henry Alfred (1848–1893), playwright, was born on 7 April 1848 at Cape Hill, Smethwick, near Birmingham, the son of Edwin Pettitt, a civil engineer, and his wife, Lucy, *née* Hart. Pettitt was educated at a school kept by the Revd William Smerdon, but was thrown on his own resources at the age of thirteen, as a result of the failure of his father's investment in cotton patent machinery, which forced him to leave England and live abroad. Henry Pettitt tried various professions, including an attempt on the stage at Sadler's Wells, and he was for two years clerk in the head offices in London of Messrs Pickford & Co., the carriers. He wrote without remuneration for various periodicals, and tried his hand at writing novels, producing *The Cotton Lord* (1862) and *Uncle Crotty's Relations* (1864) under the pseudonym Herbert Glyn. About 1869 he obtained a post as junior English master in the North London Collegiate School, High Street, Camden Town.

Still writing for periodicals and for the stage, Pettitt reached a turning point when he was paid £5 for *Golden Fruit*, a drama produced at the East London Theatre (14 July 1873). Before this time he had written, in collaboration with Paul Merritt, *British Born*, in a prologue and three acts, produced on 17 October 1872 at the Grecian Theatre, of which Merritt had been a principal support. Between 1875 and 1893 Pettitt went on to produce (singly and with collaborators) an extraordinary number of plays for the London stage and touring companies. At one time, twenty-two companies were on tour in England and six in America, performing his pieces. According to one authority, 'Six dramas in which he had collaborated were on in London the same evening', although no specifics are given as to the date involved (Boase, *Mod. Eng. biog.*, 2.1486).

Pettit was to collaborate with writers such as Merritt, George Conquest, Augustus Harris, Charles Reade, George R. Sims, and Sydney Grundy. His partnership with Conquest was the most productive in the early stages of his career: in 1875, for instance, they worked together on *Dead to the World* and *Sentenced to Death* at the Grecian Theatre, and they continued their partnership in the following year with *Snatched from the Grave* and *The Sole Survivor*. They continued to produce plays together until 1879. As the titles indicate, Pettitt favoured melodrama, and his work in the genre was inventive. He also wrote comedies, however, and in 1880 he supplied the Grecian with a pantomime, *Harlequin King Frolic*, which was said to have had the longest run of any pantomime of the nineteenth century.

Pettit's star was rising. On 31 July 1880 *The World*, by Paul Merritt, Henry Pettitt, and Augustus Harris, was staged at Drury Lane, and marked the beginning of a very prosperous era both for Pettitt and the playhouse. In 1880 and 1881 Pettitt visited the United States to look after his royalties, and to superintend the production of a version of *Le voyage en Suisse*, which he wrote for the Hanlon-Lee troupe. While in America, he became involved in a legal case in Boston concerning the copyright of his play *The World*. Pettitt's return to England was followed by increased writing activity, which continued until his death. He began to collaborate to a greater extent with Harris, producing plays such as *A Run of Luck* (Drury Lane, 28 August 1886), which was

aptly named, as it brought in £25,000 in only twelve weeks. He also worked more extensively with Reade, Sims, and Grundy in this later part of his career. His penultimate play, *A Woman's Revenge*, was described by William Archer as a 'beautifully symmetrical fable' marred by a 'ridiculously wound up' ending (Archer, 188). *The Life of Pleasure*, a drama written with Harris, was his last work and was performed on 21 September 1893.

Pettit's many plays were thought by his contemporaries to show considerable knowledge of dramatic effect, a sense of situation, and general deftness of execution, although the critics also found his characters to be conventional, and largely forgettable. He enjoyed great popular success, however, and managed to accumulate considerable wealth in a few years, while remaining a generous and open-handed man. He died of typhoid fever at Chestnuts, 352 Goldhawk Road, London, on 24 December 1893 and was buried in Brompton cemetery on 29 December.

JOSEPH KNIGHT, rev. MEGAN A. STEPHAN

Sources *Daily Telegraph* (25 Dec 1893), 6 · Boase, *Mod. Eng. biog.*, 2.1485–6 · W. Archer, *The theatrical 'World' for 1893* (1894), 187–8 · b. cert. · d. cert. · personal knowledge (1895)
Archives JRL, corresp., papers, and play scripts
Wealth at death £44,935 1s. 5d.: resworn probate, April 1894, CGPLA Eng. & Wales

Pettiward, Roger Gamelyn [*pseud.* Paul Crum] (1906–1942), artist, was born at Onehouse Lodge, Onehouse, near Stowmarket, Suffolk, on 25 November 1906 into a well-to-do landowning family. Roger Pettiward was the eldest son in the family of two sons and two daughters of Charles Terry (1855–1933) and his wife, Eliza Mary Gamlen (1880–1952). Charles Terry took the surname Pettiward by royal licence in 1908 in order to inherit the estate of his cousin, Robert John Pettiward of Finborough Hall, Suffolk. Roger Pettiward was educated at Wixenford School (1915–19), Eton College (1919–25), and Christ Church, Oxford (1925–8), and was athletic (good at rowing and boxing in particular). He took a degree in agriculture and later a course in farm management, aiming to take over his father's estate at Finborough, but he finally decided on art. He studied art at Vienna (1928–9), Munich (1929–30), the Slade School of Fine Art, London (1930–32), and in Paris. At intervals he wandered off, walking and touring in Czechoslovakia, Italy, Spain, Hungary, and Romania; he also sailed, became an expert skier, and learned to fly. He was 6 feet 5 inches tall and red-haired.

In his short life Pettiward had two claims to fame: he played an important part in the expedition to find the lost explorer Colonel Fawcett in the Matto Grosso, described in Peter Fleming's best-seller *Brazilian Adventure* (1932); and for about four years, between 1935 and the beginning of the war in 1939, he contributed humorous drawings regularly to *Punch*, *Night and Day*, and *London Week*. These drawings showed to the discerning that here was a major artist. When he began publishing humorous drawings, he signed them with a whorl, because he wanted his name to be associated only with fine art. But the editor of *Punch* advised him to sign his work with a name; he chose Paul

Crum, but many of his drawings continued to be signed with the whorl or not at all.

Pettiward continued all the time to paint, from models and from nature, exhibiting principally at the Leicester Galleries in London. His drawings seem to have been a sideline, but one which gave him a small income. It can be noted that the captions to his drawings were always very important: without them, many of the drawings seem to have no particular point. The captions are often odd, very English, and original.

The British humorous artist with whom Pettiward can perhaps be most easily compared is Nicolas Bentley, born one year after Pettiward. They were both drawing for *Punch* and other papers at the same time, and often their jokes were nearly identical. Their draughtsmanship was however very different: Bentley's was tight, Pettiward's often wildly free and flowing. He was brilliant at portraying the essential character and likeness of the people he was drawing: he was particularly successful at delineating the often subtle facial expressions which illustrate his captions. The only collection of Pettiward's drawings so far published is *The Last Cream Bun* (the title taken from one of the captions), published by Chatto and Windus in 1984. It contains over 100 drawings in black and white, some never published before, and eight in colour.

A comment by Osbert Lancaster in the introduction to the catalogue for the posthumous exhibition of Pettiward's drawings and paintings at the Leicester Galleries (1943) is apt:

> The element of freshness in the artist's work, quickened and fortified by a keen observation, is a direct reflection of his personality, for Roger Pettiward was never one for the ivory studio. His art only absorbed a portion of his energies; like Goya, who dashed from his easel to appear in the bull-ring, he never hesitated, whether as a rowing man at Oxford, a student at the Slade, or an explorer on the Amazon, to accept any demands that life might make. For his friends his charm lay in the ironic, deprecatory attitude he maintained about all his activities; an attitude that gives to his art itself its peculiar distinction.

Pettiward was married on 1 July 1935 in St Bartholomew's Church, Smithfield, to Diana Berners-Wilson (1910–2000), whom he had met at the Slade; she was the daughter of Frederick Berners-Wilson, of The Hardwick, Abergavenny, Monmouthshire. Their honeymoon was spent in the wilds of Labrador. They had one son and two daughters.

Roger Pettiward was killed in the Dieppe raid on 19 August 1942 leading a troop of no. 4 commando attacking the German heavy gun battery at Varengeville to the west of Dieppe. (Leadership of his unit in the successful assault was taken over by Captain Pat Porteous, a liaison officer between the two commando detachments, who was wounded and later awarded the VC.) Pettiward has no known grave but was commemorated, together with fifteen other commando dead, on a plaque in the village square of Ste Marguerite, near Varengeville. His early death was as grievous a loss to British art as the deaths in war of Eric Ravilious and Rex Whistler, and of 'Pont' (Gravin Graham Laidler), whose name was linked with

Pettiward by Kenneth Bird ('Fougasse', the art editor and later editor of *Punch*). Bird wrote:

> these two, Pont and Pettiward, probably did more during this period to carry the development of modern pictorial humour a whole stage further than two, ten or twenty others put together and it is sad that neither of them survived to see how post-war pictorial humour developed.   (Fougasse, *The Good-Tempered Pencil*, 1976)

RUARI McLEAN

Sources private information (2004) · Burke, *Gen. GB* (1937) [Pettiward, formerly of Finborough Hall] · m. cert.
Wealth at death £15,018 12s. 10d.—save and except settled land: probate, 22 April 1943, *CGPLA Eng. & Wales* · £137,894—limited to settled land: probate, 27 Aug 1943, *CGPLA Eng. & Wales*

Pettman, Charles (1851–1935), Methodist minister and lexicographer, was born on 14 August 1851 at Seasalter, Whitstable, Kent, the eldest son of Richard Pettman, baker, and his wife, Mary Wells. Having been brought up as a Baptist, Pettman was attracted to Methodism as a young man. After becoming a local preacher while in business in Folkestone, he was accepted as a candidate for the ministry in 1873. He attended Richmond College in Surrey until 1876, when he left on the *Windsor Castle* for missionary work in South Africa. His arrival was dramatic: the ship struck a reef 2 miles west of Dassen Island in the early hours of 19 October 1876, in clear, calm weather, the passengers finally arriving by coaster in Cape Town in 'forlorn condition' (*Methodist Churchman*, 15 April 1935, 2).

Pettman was one of the first English ministers appointed to the East London circuit, on the south-eastern Cape coast. He established the Methodist presence there during the first year (1877) of the Ngqika–Gcaleka frontier war. He then moved to Port Elizabeth (1878–80), where in 1880 he married Annie Alicia Glanville (1852–1926), daughter of Thomas B. Glanville (1822–1878), Methodist missionary, editor, member of the Cape parliament, and Cape emigration commissioner. Charles and Annie Pettman had six children that reached adulthood—four sons and two daughters. At least three children died in infancy, one after falling into a fire. Pettman's third son died in 1918 while serving in France; his eldest son predeceased him.

Pettman's ministry was spent predominantly in the Eastern Cape circuits of the Methodist church, where in the early years he visited his parishioners on horseback and travelled between circuits by ox-wagon and Cape cart. His third posting was to Grahamstown (1881–2), where he was ordained to 'full work' in the Commemoration Methodist church on 19 January 1881. He subsequently served congregations in the Uitenhage, Durban, and Cape Town circuits (1883–95). The family spent 1896 in England, and returned to work in the eastern Cape—in Graaff-Reinet (1897–1901), Pettman serving as chaplain to General French's imperial troops during the Second South African War; King William's Town (1902–6); and Queenstown (1907–12). Pettman served as chairman of the Queenstown Methodist district in 1908, 1910, and 1912, and was secretary of conference from 1905 to 1909 and president in

1910. After five years in the diamond-mining city of Kimberley (1913–17), he returned to Port Elizabeth for his final posting (1918–19).

Described as a natural leader, and an excellent conversationalist, speaker, and debater, 'a man of striking appearance and commanding personality', Pettman was 'beloved of his brethren', possessing 'a strong humorous vein' and 'a merry twinkle in his eye' (*Methodist Churchman*, 15 April 1935, 2). His interests and accomplishments were many, including botany and horticulture, astronomy, and onomastics. He was a German and Xhosa scholar, a philatelist, and a collector of Africana books—he left his considerable collection to the Queenstown Public Library, of which he was chairman. He also served as town councillor for Queenstown. However, he is remembered for his documentation of the South African English vocabulary, and for his researches into local place names.

Pettman compiled the earliest dictionary of South African English—the 579-page *Africanderisms, a glossary of South African colloquial words and phrases and of place and other names* (1913). Lexicography, he wrote, was an interest

which could … only be indulged in as a relaxation from duties that always had the first claim. The Glossary was begun on the day of the author's landing in Cape Town in October 1876, when he jotted down in his notebook a few of the strange words that then fell upon his ear.   (Pettman, v)

Recognizing the need for supplementing the documentation of local English in the *Oxford English Dictionary*, Pettman gained assistance from people such as Rudolf Marloth and E. E. Galpin (eminent botanists), Sir William Bisset Berry (physician and MP), and Thomas Muir (Cape superintendent-general of education).

Sometimes eccentric and idiosyncratic, 'half a glossary and half an encyclopaedia' (*TLS*), and including some fanciful etymologies, *Africanderisms* is nevertheless a pioneering work, offering insights into even subtle local linguistic peculiarities. A rich mine of raw material, the *Glossary* proved an invaluable resource for *A Dictionary of South African English on Historical Principles* (1996), supplying rare early examples of colloquial language, and definitions of many vanished words and expressions.

Pettman's researches into local place names resulted in lectures to the South African Association for the Advancement of Science (1916 and 1920). He published several books and monographs, including *Notes on South African Place Names* (1914), *Hottentot Place Names* (*c*.1920), *Place Names in the Orange Free State* (1922), *South African Methodist Place Names* (1923), and his main onomastic work, *South African Place Names, Past and Present* (1931). He also contributed regularly to newspapers such as *The Friend* (Bloemfontein), the *Queenstown Daily Representative*, and the *East London Dispatch* (authoring 'Nature notes' as Umfuni, 1902–12).

The Pettmans retired to Queenstown in 1920, where they lived until their deaths. Annie died on 18 October 1926, aged seventy-four, and Charles thereafter lived 'a very quiet and somewhat lonely life' (*Methodist Churchman*, 22 April 1935, 2). He died of pleurisy at his home, 45 Prince Alfred Street, on 4 April 1935, in his eighty-fourth year,

and was buried in Queenstown the following day. His publications clearly supplemented his clerical income, for he left an estate of £3178 3*s*. 2*d*. to his four surviving children.   PENNY SILVA

Sources *DSAB*, 1.611–12 · burial register, Rhodes University, Grahamstown, South Africa, Cory Library, Methodist Archives, PR 3832, Pie/M 3660/18 · South African Methodist conference minutes, 1883–1935, Rhodes University, Grahamstown, Methodist Church of South Africa Archives, esp. 1935, pp. 7–8 · *Report of the Wesleyan Methodist Missionary Society* (1877–82) · *Methodist Churchman* (22 April 1935), 2 · *Methodist Churchman* (15 April 1935), 2 · *Methodist Churchman* (25 Oct 1926), 4–5 · death notice, Rhodes University, Grahamstown, South Africa, Cory Library · will, Master's Office, Cape Town, no. 45837 · b. cert. · *Graham's Town Journal* (21 Jan 1881) · *TLS* (24 July 1913), 309 · M. Murray, *Ships and South Africa* (1933), 333 · C. Pettman, preface, *Africanderisms* (1913)
Archives Queenstown Public Library, Eastern Cape, South Africa, collection of Africana books · Rhodes University, Grahamstown, South Africa, MSS
Likenesses photograph, *c*.1890, Rhodes University, Grahamstown, South Africa, Cory Library · photograph, *c*.1910, repro. in *South African who's who*, 368 · photograph, *c*.1930, repro. in *Methodist Churchman* (15 April 1935), 2 · group portraits, photographs, Rhodes University, Grahamstown, South Africa, Cory Library
Wealth at death £3178 3*s*. 2*d*.—divided equally between his four surviving children (two male, two female): estate papers, 1935, Cape Archives, Cape Town, MOOC vol. 6/9/4587, ref. 45331, part 1

Petto, Samuel (*c*.1624–1711), clergyman and ejected minister, may possibly have been connected with the Peyto family of Chesterton, near Leamington, Warwickshire. He was admitted as a sizar at St Catharine's College, Cambridge, on 15 June 1644, matriculated on 19 March 1645, and graduated MA. In 1648 he was admitted as rector of Sandcroft, in the deanery of South Elmham, Suffolk. Perhaps a little later he married; his wife's name was Mary, and they baptized a son, Samuel, at South Elmham St Cross on 27 April 1654, but Mary died the next year. In the summer of 1654 Petto was reported to be paid £36 a year for his services at Sandcroft, and to give a sermon every second Sunday at nearby Homersfield. He was at Sandcroft when on 4 May 1658 the council of state recommended that he be granted an augmentation of £50 per annum. In a letter of 17 August 1658 to Samuel Slater, of the Independent church at St Katharine by the Tower, Petto reported that while many Suffolk Independents opposed or doubted infant baptism, none had themselves been rebaptized and all were happily in communion with the majority who differed in the matter. His own congregational views embraced the practice of lay preaching, and on this subject he engaged in 1658–9 with Frederick Woodall of Woodbridge, Suffolk, and John Martin of Edgfield, Nottinghamshire, against Matthew Pool's *Quo warranto*, a work commissioned by the London Provincial Assembly, and *Vindiciae ministerii evangelici revindicate* (1658) by John Collinges, who conceded in his foreword that their efforts were the work of 'grave and sober persons, with a good show of argument'. After ejection from Sandcroft in 1660 Petto moved to nearby Wortwell-cum-Alburgh, Norfolk, and continued his ministry in the area. In 1669 he was preaching in Norfolk at Yarmouth, at Denton, and to an auditory of over 300 at Gillingham. On 8 May 1672 he was licensed as a congregational teacher at his own house at Wortwell, and at the house of John Wesgate at Redenhall. About two years later Petto began his long association with the town of Sudbury, Suffolk.

A Sudbury corporation document of 5 October 1669 reported that 'there is no settled minister' in the town and that services depended 'upon the goodwill and benevolence of the people' of whom the greater part 'meet in conventicles and absent themselves' (*Short History*, 152–3); it was resolved to seek an act of parliament to provide proper maintenance. This evidently this did not materialize for in 1684 local tories alleged that the former mayor John Catesby had so favoured dissenters, that 'Mr Petto the Nonconformist preacher in the barn' had been unmolested there for ten years, only once having been brought before the quarter sessions, and then not punished. Petto had, moreover, with his wife and family 'constantly lived within the said Corporation for ten years last past, in no more private place than in the Vicarage House belonging to All Saints Church' (Hodson, *Independents*, 53–4). Petto had other problems at Sudbury. On 31 August 1677 he wrote to Increase Mather that:

> lately one of my daughters is become a prodigal, & about 10 dayes ago resolved to go beyond sea, hath obscured herself in order to that end, so as I have been searching for her all this week in London & cannot find her; she was a sempster in the city and might have lived well, but on a suddain is bent to ramble and hath sinned greatly against the Lord by falsehoods. ('Letters of Samuel Petto', 341)

Before the following 14 May the prodigal had returned. In 1690 Petto was reported still to be a preacher at Sudbury, with his second wife, Martha, and twelve children to support and in receipt of £45 per annum.

Petto was a firm believer in the power of witchcraft and in 1693 published *A faithful narrative of the wonderful and extraordinary fits, which Mr Thomas Spatchett, minister of Dunwich and Cockley, was under by witchcraft*, in which he claimed that despite hearing her confession in 1665 the justices refused to punish the alleged culprit because she bewitched only Spatchett and another local puritan, one Manning. Petto did not see his belief in occult powers as incompatible with his interest in science. He wrote in *Philosophical Transactions* of the appearance in the sky over Sudbury on 28 December 1698 of three 'suns', and was aware that these were 'really one true sun; the reflections of its beams cause such images' (*PTRS*, 21, 1699, 107). Petto was greatly respected by dissenters in the district. He died in Sudbury in 1711 and was buried in the churchyard of All Saints, Sudbury, on 21 September. His son-in-law, the Revd Josias Maultby, had been appointed as his copastor in 1707; after Petto's death he continued as pastor until emigrating to Rotterdam in 1719.   STEPHEN WRIGHT

Sources *Calamy rev.* · 'Letters of Samuel Petto', *Collections of the Massachusetts Historical Society*, 4th ser., 8 (1868), 341–50 · F. Peck, ed., *Desiderata curiosa*, new edn, 2 vols. in 1 (1779) · *A short history of the borough of Sudbury ... compiled from materials collected by W. W. Hodson*, ed. C. Sperling (1896) · W. Hodson, *The Independents of Sudbury* (1893) · Venn, *Alum. Cant.*

Pettus, Sir John (*c*.1613–1685), natural philosopher and politician, was the second son of Sir Augustine Pettus (d. 1613) of Rackheath, Norfolk, and his second wife, Abigail (1592–1673), third daughter of Sir Arthur *Heveningham of Ketteringham in the same county. In 1632 he matriculated as a fellow-commoner at Pembroke College, Cambridge, where his tutor was Thomas Boswell. He probably attended the college from about 1627 and may have graduated BA in 1631. When he was seventeen Pettus undertook the first of three summer tours around England in the company of Sir Thomas Bendish. Each tour lasted two months and they continued until he left Cambridge. They were designed to give Pettus a wide knowledge of England before he travelled on the continent, and the first included a visit to a lead mine in Derbyshire. Pettus was admitted to Lincoln's Inn on 13 May 1635. In 1637 he married Elizabeth, daughter of Sir Richard *Gurney of Cheapside, London, who became lord mayor in 1641–2, and his wife, Ebigail, daughter of Henry Sandford of Birchington, Kent. John's and Elizabeth's only son, Richard, died in 1662. Their daughter, Elizabeth, married Samuel Sandys, son of Samuel Sandys of Ombersley, Worcestershire, and his wife, Mary, *née* Barker, in 1657. Elizabeth Sandys died on 25 May 1714 aged seventy-four.

Pettus entered the service of Charles I in 1639, and was knighted on 25 November 1641 as a mark of the king's favour to Gurney. In March 1643 he was among those captured by Oliver Cromwell's forces at Lowestoft, suspected of trying to fortify the town for the king. Pettus reportedly told Cromwell of his intention of joining the royalists. He was first imprisoned at Cambridge before being transferred to unpleasantly overcrowded quarters in Windsor Castle. He was released on an exchange early in 1644 and then served in Oxford, Bath, and Bristol. He and his wife were in Bristol at the surrender of the city to the New Model Army in September 1645, when they were helped by Charles Fleetwood, who was related to Pettus by marriage. The fine for Pettus's delinquency was first set at £1300, but was later reduced to £866 13s. 4d., one-tenth the value of his estate. He was also involved in settling the estate of Sir Richard Gurney, who died in October 1647, in conjunction with Thomas Richardson, later Baron of Cramond, who had married Gurney's other daughter, Anne.

Pettus was imprisoned in 1650 on suspicion of corresponding with Charles II, being questioned by the council of state over a period of three weeks before being released on bail of £4000. Presumably this was when he felt that his life had been in danger and he had again been indebted to Fleetwood for intervening on his behalf. He also acknowledged Fleetwood's help with preserving his estates and in protecting him from being required to take oaths and renunciations. In 1656 he protested to the lord protector of his loyalty to the regime, but after the fall of the protectorate he was approached in 1659 by Francis Finch, an ironmonger, to act as an intermediary between the royalists and Fleetwood.

Pettus's wife left him in 1657, taking some of his possessions, including jewels which he valued at £900. He attributed her action to her conversion to Roman Catholicism. A reconciliation in 1662, when she restored his jewels and he paid her debts, which totalled more than £800, did not long outlast the death of their son in that year. She left

Pettus once more in 1662, again taking possessions with her, including pictures, books, and 'rarities', and entered a nunnery abroad. Although she returned to England after five years they were not reconciled, and disputes over her alimony led to his excommunication and an appearance before the privy council in 1672, when the king personally ordered him to pay £2 per week. The case was brought before the privy council again in 1673 and 1674. In 1674 Pettus published a justification, *A Narrative of the Excommunication of Sir John Pettus*.

Pettus's interest in metallurgy and mining led to him becoming a member of the Society of Mines Royal and Battery Works in 1651 and he acted as deputy governor of the royal mines from then until his death, apart from one brief interval. He was elected a fellow of the Royal Society in 1663. He published, in 1670, *Fodinae regales, or, The history, laws and places of the chief mines and mineral works in England, Wales and the English pale in Ireland* and, in 1683, *Fleta minor: the laws of art and nature, in knowing, judging, assaying, fining, refining and inlarging the bodies of confin'd metals*. The latter consists of a translation of a sixteenth-century work in German by Lazarus Erckern, with a dictionary of metallurgical terms by Pettus.

Pettus was chosen as MP for Dunwich at a by-election in March 1670. He was named to 109 committees of the Cavalier Parliament and was listed as a member of the court party. He made four attempts to obtain a bill regulating charitable stock in the parish of Kelsale, Suffolk, and also presented a bill for settling the estate of Henry Smith, for whom Sir Richard Gurney had acted as executor. *The Case and Justification of Sr J. Pettus* (1678) was his defence against claims that he was introducing needless bills and disturbing charities which were functioning satisfactorily. He was blacklisted in the 'unanimous club' of court supporters and did not seek re-election after the dissolution of the Cavalier Parliament.

Pettus was involved in affairs in East Anglia, visiting Norwich after the explosion of the magazine there in 1648 and providing for the prisoners taken during the Third Anglo-Dutch War in 1672, in his capacity as deputy to the vice-admiral, as well as mediating between the military and the inhabitants. He was a JP for Suffolk from July 1660 until his death, and deputy lieutenant from 1671. He held the rank of captain of the foot in the militia by 1665 and was a colonel from 1671. Pettus was made a freeman of Dunwich in 1670 and served as bailiff in 1671–2 and 1675–6, and as coroner in 1677–8. He was made a gentleman of the privy chamber in 1670 and retained the position until his death.

Pettus succeeded his grandfather as tenant of land in South Walsham, Norfolk, and before his marriage he bought the manor of Chediston, Suffolk. He used his wife's jointure to acquire the manor of Winbaston and a nearby farm, also in Suffolk, but sold them in the late 1640s to pay his composition fine and debts incurred during the civil war. At the Restoration he claimed that he had lost £25,000 in the royal service and in 1674 that he had not been paid by Charles I or Charles II. His debts were reported at £5960 in 1651 and in 1674 he wrote that he had

discharged debts of £28,000 since about 1664. His circumstances were exacerbated by the dispute with his wife and his finances continued to deteriorate. In 1679 he was in a debtors' prison and appealed to William Sancroft, archbishop of Canterbury, for a loan of £20 to release him. He was in the Fleet prison for debt in 1683, hence the punning title of *Fleta minor*.

Pettus's other publications were *Volatiles from the History of Adam and Eve* (1674) and *The Constitution of Parliaments in England* (1680), and he contributed a preface to *England's Independency upon the Papal Power* by Sir John Davis and Sir Edward Coke (1674). The attribution to Pettus of *St Foine Improved* (1674) is doubtful. He died in 1685 and was buried in the Temple Church in London on 12 July. A portrait of him, aged fifty-seven, engraved by W. Sherwin, is the frontispiece of *Fodinae regales* and another of him, aged seventy, engraved by R. White, is the frontispiece to *Fleta minor*.   STEPHEN PORTER

Sources HoP, *Commons, 1660–90*, 3.230–32 · *DNB* · privy council registers, PRO, PC2/63, pp. 301, 316, 342, 345; PC2/64, pp. 16, 75, 204 · B. Schofield, ed., *The Knyvett letters, 1620–1644*, Norfolk RS, 20 (1949), 33–4, 47, 115 · M. A. E. Green, ed., *Calendar of the proceedings of the committee for compounding … 1643–1660*, 1, PRO (1889), 1291 · M. A. E. Green, ed., *Calendar of the proceedings of the committee for advance of money, 1642–1656*, 2, PRO (1888), 1378 · A. W. Hughes Clarke and A. Campling, eds., *The visitation of Norfolk … 1664, made by Sir Edward Bysshe*, 2, Harleian Society, 86 (1934), 164–5 · D. Underdown, *Royalist conspiracy in England, 1649–1660* (1960), 310, 318 · R. W. Ketton-Cremer, *Norfolk in the civil war: a portrait of a society in conflict* (1969), 181, 186

Likenesses R. White, line engraving, 1683, NPG · W. Sherwin, line engraving (aged fifty-seven), BM, NPG; repro. in J. Pettus, *Fodinae regales* (1670)

Petty [Pettus], **Maximilian** (*bap.* 1617, *d.* in or after 1661?), Leveller, was probably the child of an Oxfordshire gentry family who was baptized on 3 June 1617 at Tetsworth. If so he was the second surviving son of John Petty (*d.* 1619×22) of Stoke Talmage, near Tetsworth, and his second wife, Anne (*d.* 1622), widow of Thomas Webley, clothier, of Witney in Oxfordshire, and daughter of one Johnson of Witney. He was apprenticed to London Grocers' Company in 1634 and gained his freedom in 1642. At an unknown date he married Mary, daughter of his uncle Leonard Petty; the couple had a single child, Mary, who married one Blackwell. The Pettys were connected by marriage to the Hampdens and the Ingoldsbys; one of Maximilian's uncles, another Maximilian, was MP for Westbury, Wiltshire, in 1628–9. The MP Maximilian was probably acquainted with the puritan martyr Alexander Leighton, and his son, Edmund, sat for parliament in 1660.

Petty is renowned for his contribution to the Putney debates, the discussions of the New Model Army and civilians in autumn 1647 concerning the settlement of the nation. That summer he attended talks over the army's terms for settlement, *The Heads of the Proposals*. Soon afterwards, as he described at Putney, it 'pleased God to raise a company of men that do stand up for the power of the House of Commons' (Woodhouse, 89). Petty became acquainted with these men and a cipher key suggests his involvement over the summer in their attempts to forge links with and influence the New Model's agitator organization. By autumn this civilian effort to secure a platform within the army reached its zenith when Petty and John Wildman brought a counter-proposal for settlement, the *Agreement of the People*, to the army general council on 28 October. Possibly the work of Wildman on behalf of his and Petty's associates in London the *Agreement* was a written constitution calling for a new social compact between the people and their rulers, far more radical terms for settlement than those of the army. None the less the paper split the general council and became the focus of fierce debate, during which Petty (or Pettus as the clerks recorded his name) expressed hostility to the negative voice of king and lords. However, his comments on the franchise, which dominated debate on 29 October, have attracted most attention. The *Agreement*, with its demand for a more equal redistribution of the electorate 'according to the number of the inhabitants' and Petty's remark that 'We judge that all inhabitants that have not lost their birthright should have an equal voice in elections' were interpreted (perhaps correctly) by the generals and their supporters as a call for manhood suffrage (ibid., 444, 53). Yet towards the end of the debate and in an attempt to reach a compromise position on the franchise Petty referred to his willingness to 'exclude apprentices, or servants, or those that take alms' (ibid., 83). The *Agreement* would never be realized without the support of the New Model, and compromise on the franchise, probably not the most important proposal, was an attempt to secure it. The tactic failed when in committee the army addressed the majority of concerns voiced by soldiers who supported the *Agreement*. The outcome in November was an army *Remonstrance*, based on the New Model's terms for settlement, which excluded the civilian proposals. The generals subsequently turned on Petty and his disruptive associates, identifying as Levellers those who sought to 'take away all kind of distinction of [king or lords] from other men' (ibid., 123).

By contriving a second civil war in 1648 Charles I turned the New Model's generals against him. Although parliament resumed negotiations with the defeated king the army vehemently opposed the discussions and courted support from well-affected Londoners. In November, meetings between Levellers and City Independents saw their proposals for settlement sent to army headquarters. Later that month Petty, Wildman, John Lilburne, and William Wetton journeyed to Windsor to express the Levellers' remaining concerns to the commissary-general, Henry Ireton. As a result it was agreed that a committee of sixteen, consisting of four MPs, army officers, City Independents, and Levellers, would draw up a second *Agreement of the People* as the basis for a settlement. Petty was chosen as a Leveller representative and attended the committee's meetings at Windsor and at Whitehall, which produced a draft document. When in December the draft was submitted for debate by the council of officers it is unclear whether he sided with those Levellers who protested at the conduct of the talks. He is not listed among the large Leveller delegation that presented Sir Thomas Fairfax with a petition critical of proceedings, yet neither was he among the Levellers who attended the council's debates after the precipitate withdrawal of the Leveller leader Lilburne. When in March 1649 Leveller criticism of the new military regime prompted the arrest of their leading figures Petty was not among them. Nevertheless Thomas Scott, the Commonwealth's intelligencer, considered him one of the principal Levellers who remained at liberty and questioned him regarding their activities.

The Levellers' demise during 1649 brought a temporary halt to Petty's political pursuits. By April 1650 he, Wildman, and Wetton were employed in administering the estates of the republican MP Henry Marten. Marten was a member of the 1648 committee of sixteen and his close ties with the Levellers during the late 1640s suggest that he may have known all three men earlier. Alongside Wetton, Petty was a co-administrator of Marten's Derbyshire estates and also assisted in administering the MP's Berkshire lands. By autumn 1659 his political activities resumed in London where both he and Wildman attended James Harrington's republican club, the Rota. This select debating society of metropolitan intellectuals discussed and voted on issues of popular government. John Aubrey described Petty as 'a very able man in these matters, and who had more then once turn'd the councill-board of Oliver Cromwell' (*Brief Lives*, 1.290). Although the Rota was short-lived Petty's republican ties may have been of longer duration. In 1661 a Mr Pretty reportedly met in London with a small group of republicans, including Wildman. Under questioning that November Wildman denied knowing a Mr Pretty but offered that he knew a Mr Petty, an associate of the duke of Buckingham. Buckingham was involved in intrigue with Wildman and Lilburne in the 1650s and could conceivably have known Petty through them. If Wildman was referring to Maximilian Petty it is the last surviving record of him, his place and date of death being unknown.

BETH R. HOWARD and P. R. S. BAKER

Sources *DNB* · A. S. P. Woodhouse, ed., *Puritanism and liberty: being the army debates (1647–49) from the Clarke manuscripts*, 3rd edn (1986), 22–3, 48, 53, 61–2, 78–9, 83, 89, 344–9 · C. Thompson, 'Maximilian Petty and the Putney debate on the franchise', *Past and Present*, 88 (1980), 63–9 · J. Morrill and P. Baker, 'The case of the armie truly re-stated', *The Putney debates of 1647: the army, the Levellers, and the English state*, ed. M. Mendle (2001), 103–24 · *The life and times of Anthony Wood*, ed. A. Clark, 1, OHS, 19 (1891), 32–5 · S. Barber, *A revolutionary rogue: Henry Marten and the English republic* (2000), 14, 30, 98, 113 · G. Aylmer, 'Gentleman levellers?', *Past and Present*, 49 (1970), 120–25 · F. G. Lee, *The history, description and antiquities of the prebendal church of the Blessed Virgin Mary of Thame* (1883), 85, 206, 215–18 · Grocers' Company admissions, etc., 1345–c.1670, alphabet book (photostat), GL, MS 11592A, unfol. entry for 1642 · C. H. Firth, 'Thomas Scot's account of his actions as intelligencer during the Commonwealth', *EngHR*, 12 (1897), 116–26, esp. 118 · *Brief lives, chiefly of contemporaries, set down by John Aubrey, between the years 1669 and 1696*, ed. A. Clark, 1 (1898), 289–90 · BL, Egerton MS 2543, fols. 65r–66r · *The manuscripts of Rye and Hereford corporations*, HMC, 31 (1892), 401–2 · M. Gimelfarb-Brack, 'Petty, Maximilian', Greaves & Zaller, *BDBR*, 3.34 · B. Taft, 'The council of officers', *Agreement of the people, 1648/9', HJ*, 28 (1985), 169–85, esp. 171–4 · S. Foster, *Notes from the Caroline underground: Alexander Leighton, the puritan triumvirate, and the Laudian reaction to nonconformity* (1978), 35 and n. 24 · M. W.

Helms, L. Naylor, and G. Jaggar, 'Petty, Edmund', HoP, *Commons, 1660–90*, 3.232

Petty, Sir William (1623–1687), natural philosopher and administrator in Ireland, was born at Romsey, Hampshire, on 26 May 1623, the third child of Anthony Petty (1587–1654), clothier, and his wife, Francesca (d. 1663). In later life Petty was keen to stress the obscurity of his origins in order to exaggerate his spectacular success.

Education and early career After a conventional education in Romsey, Petty did not follow his father's calling in the textile trade, but instead went to sea as a mariner. An accident on board ship led to his being abandoned in Normandy in 1637. This mishap was apparently put to good use when he enrolled in a Jesuit college at Caen. There he refined his mathematical proficiency and developed a voracious appetite for learning. On returning to London he continued his studies. However, once the civil war broke out he returned to the continent. His intention was to acquire medical qualifications. To this end he went to Amsterdam, Leiden, Utrecht, and Paris. In Paris he met and quizzed Thomas Hobbes, Gassendi, and Mersenne, and was put in touch with prime exponents of experimental science. He was back in England by 1646 and continued his education at Oxford. The victory of parliament and consequent purge of royalists and episcopalians from the university speeded Petty's advance. Happy enough to comply with the political and ecclesiastical principles of the new order he accepted a fellowship of Brasenose College, probably in 1648, and was created DM on 7 March 1650. In 1651 he served as vice-principal of the college, and was elected to the professorship of anatomy. He attended assiduously to the duties of the post. Some of his lecture notes—in Latin—have survived and reveal the methodical manner in which he approached his responsibilities.

As well as lecturing Petty conducted chemical experiments and built up a private medical practice. It was as a doctor that he first achieved wider fame. He resuscitated the corpse of Anne Greene, which had been cut down from the gallows and was intended for dissection. This wonder was soon publicized in pamphlets, and brought Petty's name before a larger public. He was admitted to a fellowship of the College of Physicians, and elected as one of the readers at Gresham's College in London.

Surveyor in Ireland, 1650s Petty's medical skills secured his next appointment, in September 1652, as physician to the army in Ireland. Contacts in Oxford, as well as the recent publicity over Anne Greene, probably secured the post. Paid £1 daily it was financially attractive. It also brought additional fees through attending officers of the English army and administration. Petty's talents, which he never hid, were soon in demand in other spheres. In particular the complex task of surveying the lands forfeited by the defeated Irish insurgents and of allotting them to their new owners among the English soldiery and investors overstretched the resources of the administration. Petty derided the scheme of the surveyor-general, Worsley, and sketched a better of his own. In December 1654, a grateful government accepted his proposal for the 'down survey',

Sir William Petty (1623–1687), by Isaac Fuller, c.1649–50

as it became known. Its chief attraction was its lower cost. The circumstances in which Petty had ousted Worsley rankled. Not only had he impugned Worsley's technical abilities, but he differed from his competitor in religion and politics. Worsley had identified with the republicans and sectaries who thrived under the lax regime of Lord Deputy Charles Fleetwood. This group felt beleaguered when in the summer of 1655 Fleetwood was effectively superseded by his brother-in-law, Henry Cromwell. Petty, for his part, gravitated towards Henry Cromwell, becoming one of his secretaries and a confidant. As a result, he was regarded as a prime target by the aggrieved republicans and officers. These alignments help to explain why Petty's survey was fiercely criticized. Inevitable mistakes, especially when he had to rely on soldiers for much of the detailed surveying, led to the available lands being underestimated by 10 per cent. This deficiency embarrassed a government which intended that the confiscations surveyed by Petty should reward thousands of creditors. The latter, civilians in England and soldiers in Ireland, had expected more and better than they were now allocated. However, the undoubted shortcomings in the down survey pale beside its achievement. The mapping was based on the administrative unit of the barony, and combined other man-made features with the staples of the physical terrain. On the basis of Petty's work 8,400,000 acres were redistributed to new (and usually protestant) owners.

Any final distribution of the lands took time. The impatient and disappointed blamed Petty. Moreover their often meagre returns were contrasted with the evident plenty which Petty himself had secured. He conceded that he had made at least £9000 from the undertaking. Soon allegations of chicanery as well as incompetence were voiced. In the parliament of 1659 a direct attack was launched when Sir Jerome Sankey, an MP from Ireland and sectarian supporter of Fleetwood, sought to have Petty impeached. More than the detail of the down survey was at stake. Strenuous efforts had been made to have Petty elected to this parliament, with the result that he was returned for both the Cornish constituency of West Looe and an Irish one. He chose to sit for the first. Petty had been selected for attack not just because he was the architect of the land settlement and could be blamed for its inadequacies. He personified the more conservative tenor of Henry Cromwell's government, and as such antagonized the supporters of 'the good old cause': in the Irish context, the regime of Fleetwood. The parliament was dissolved before Petty suffered any serious retribution. Belatedly, in 1660, he published his own riposte to Sankey.

The protracted dispute with Worsley was the more embarrassing because both he and Petty belonged to the circle of Samuel Hartlib, the refugee from Bohemia anxious to advance learning and protestantism. Petty embraced the empirical and utilitarian philosophy of the group, having been introduced to many of its principles while he was on the continent during the 1640s. He first showed his commitment publicly in 1648 when he addressed a printed manifesto on the advancement of learning to Hartlib. The same principles underpinned the down survey, and assorted practical and utopian schemes which Petty (and others) promoted in Cromwellian Ireland. His many talents, including a taste for controversy, endeared him to Henry Cromwell. The clerkship to the council, to which the latter had promoted him, added £400 to Petty's annual income.

Politics, public office, and Ireland, 1660–1685 The collapse of the protectorate at first presented the agnostic Petty with opportunities. He was in England during 1659, and frequented the Rota Club, a group of republican idealists. What soon followed, the restoration of Charles II, offered both challenges and chances. Petty, supple and opportunistic, seized the chances and met the challenges. He had not been concerned in the representative body, the general convention, which assembled in Dublin briefly in the spring of 1660. But he was returned to the Irish parliament of 1661 for the Wexford borough of Enniscorthy and the Kilkenny town of Inistioge. He opted for the second.

Petty's experience and his considerable stake in Ireland—more than 18,000 acres in five counties—gave him a continuing role there. His usefulness explained his being chosen as an MP. At the same time, closely involved in the Cromwellian regime, he was naturally suspected. Persistent doubts about his reliability meant that he was never again entrusted with the same responsibilities as in the 1650s. Relegated to the Irish council of trade Petty was unwearyingly inventive in the suggestions with which he bombarded the government in Dublin. But few of his schemes were adopted. Also, he felt victimized when his large holdings of Irish lands were subjected to heavy taxes. This was an issue with which Petty became

obsessed. The estates were to serve as a showcase for his rational methods. By increasing their yield and value he would show others how best to proceed. Much of what he hoped to do still derived from the philosophy and designs of his and Hartlib's friends. The informal discussions and plans of the 1650s were systematized, notably in the Royal Society. Not only had Petty joined the groups of the 1650s, but was a founding member of the Royal Society when it was established in 1662. Because he divided his time between Ireland and England, participation in the London society was erratic until the early 1670s, when he became (temporarily) a stalwart.

Petty exemplified the continuities between the earlier devotees of the Baconian method, the utilitarianism of Hartlib's followers, and the wider constituency of the fashionable and altruistic to which the infant Royal Society appealed. Reading, interpreting, and communicating 'the book of nature' preoccupied him. His wit and asperity entertained the king. Petty was unabashed in seeking a profitable outlet for his manifold talents. He impressed and amused the important, including the king, by his verbal and intellectual dexterity. Unfortunately, he also irritated and bored them. Although knighted in 1661 he felt undervalued and underemployed. A peerage proffered in acknowledgement of his wealth—estimated at more than £6000 p.a., principally from Irish lands—was spurned. Rationally enough he objected to the extra expenditure that such a rank would involve. He sought in vain a seat in the privy council.

Petty's claims to fresh public employment were seconded with a series of disquisitions. These built on his work in the 1650s. Maps which had first been drawn to assist the down survey were corrected and reworked until they could be issued in 1685 as the first atlas of Irish counties, *Hiberniae delineatio*. Before that Petty regarded the originals of the maps as his own property and charged those who wished to consult them. At the same time he composed apparently authoritative surveys of the topography, demography, and potential of Ireland. In these writings he returned many times to the obvious gap between the ideal and the real Ireland. If some of these tracts had arisen from his official role in the council of trade, others, such as *A Treatise of Taxes and Contributions* (1662) backed his unsuccessful bid to farm the Irish customs revenues. The majority remained in manuscript but circulated freely among those who governed Ireland and England. In addition to serving personal and topical purposes Petty was developing a mathematical approach to the problems confronting government. With access to official data about mortality, housing, imports, and exports, he collected and then analysed much. In particular, interest in matters relating to production and employment led him to elaborate a theory of economic surplus, through which human beings would be freed from the drudgery of constant labour. He was also consciously promoting the discipline of 'political arithmetic', entailing a more rigorously statistical approach to running the state.

Petty's interest in the problems and opportunities specific to Ireland was encouraged anew by his appointment in 1676 as judge and registrar of the admiralty court in Dublin. His authority derived from James, duke of York, who, although obliged by the Test Act of 1673 to relinquish the post of lord high admiral in England, evidently retained an Admiralty jurisdiction over Ireland. Petty went to work enthusiastically. He hoped through his court to assist poor mariners against arbitrary masters. However, he was obstructed both by common lawyers and landowners resentful of the Admiralty. Petty planned to rout these adversaries by investigating the origins and extent of the court's powers. This ambition, along with his aim that the Admiralty advance commerce and shipping, was not realized.

Political arithmetic and commercial schemes The accession of James II, his erstwhile patron, revived Petty's hopes. After 1685 he deluged the new monarch with proposals. What Petty wrote, about both Ireland and England, blended exact statistical information with fanciful projections. True to his belief in the empirical method, learned on the continent early in the 1640s, he aimed to end idle speculation by expressing all in 'number, weight and measure'. This statistical precision certainly added to the novelty and authority of *The Political Arithmetic* and *Anatomy of Ireland*. The precision owed much to his access to the cadastral data which had been collected under his own auspices during the down survey, and later when poll and hearth taxes were levied in Ireland and as bills of mortality enumerated and classified the dead both in London and Dublin. In addition he gathered information from his own estates, particularly those in co. Kerry, from which he then constructed his larger theories. These offered estimates of the proportions and absolute totals of those involved in different occupations and living in houses of different sizes. He also speculated about the mean sizes of households in Ireland, again distinguishing between the various social orders.

Petty did not confine his advice and reflections to Ireland. In England, he concerned himself with agriculture, industry, technology, population, architecture, and medicine. He also interested himself in the demography of London, now more clearly revealed in the weekly bills of mortality. In association with John Graunt he analysed this material and used it to predict future trends. During the 1680s these analytical techniques were applied to Dublin. Petty examined the wealth, potential and actual, of England. He saw labour as the key to increased national prosperity. Like other commentators he sought lessons from the evident successes of the United Provinces and France under Colbert. The novelty in Petty's approach was to quantify. Yet sometimes his willingness to give numbers invested his calculations with a spurious authority. Just as the down survey was found wanting as to its accuracy, so in his later endeavours too often he seemed to pluck numbers from the air, usually when solid figures were lacking. Nevertheless, by abstracting numbers and using these as the basis of calculation, whether of profit and loss in his own Irish ironworks or English trades and industries, he constructed the method known as political

arithmetic which was widely copied in the later seventeenth century (and beyond). In addition, by isolating such issues as the velocity of circulation, the difference between the natural and market price of a commodity, and the theory of economic surplus, he established important themes and methods for classical economists.

Intimates venerated Petty. Sceptical and droll, when relaxed he delighted and charmed. On occasion he composed scabrous and indecent verses. Others merely encountered a combative and abrasive character. Detractors revelled in his discomfiture when certain of his highly advertised ventures foundered. Notable among these was the double-hulled ship—a novel catamaran—which turned turtle and sank in Dublin Bay. The wearisome struggle to overcome the impersonal and human obstacles to immediate improvement of his Irish estates disillusioned him and cautioned his contemporaries. Yet something of the respect in which he was held was shown in 1684 when he was chosen as first president of the Dublin Philosophical Society. This was appropriate as the institution sought to realize the objectives which Petty and his associates had espoused since the 1650s. Its rules insisted on a preference for experiment and observation rather than for tradition, the free communication of discoveries, and more intensive researches into the physical resources of Ireland.

Family life and last years After 1660 the bulk of Petty's income came from Ireland. He hoped to use it to finance an English career. To this end he investigated the purchase of an English country estate. In the event, he remained in London, where he owned a house and dabbled in the redevelopment after the fire of 1666. On Trinity Sunday 1667 he married Elizabeth (*c*.1636–1708/10), daughter of Sir Hardress *Waller (*c*.1604–1666), the regicide, a prominent landowner in co. Limerick. She was the widow of another prosperous settler in Munster, Sir Maurice Fenton (*d.* 1664). Care of a young son gave her interests which were multiplied after her marriage to Petty. Her new husband deputed oversight and management of his scattered Irish concerns to her, especially during his absences in London. Together they attended to the upbringing of three children, John (*bap.* 1669, *d.* 1670), Charles (*c*.1653–1696), and Henry (1675–1751). The needs of his family and household prompted Petty to reflect more generally on education. True to his questioning approach he rejected as useless some parts of the traditional scholastic curriculum, and instead urged more practical and vocational studies, akin to those which he had had. At the same time he was sensitive to the compromises and conventions necessary to succeed in public life. His own failures cautioned him against too cavalier a dismissal of these requirements.

James II failed to adopt Petty's programme. It included constitutional union of England with Ireland and the enforced transfer of peoples from one island to the other. These proposals, redolent of what had been attempted in the interregnum, belonged to a tradition in which Ireland was treated simply as a colony akin to North America. On other occasions he accepted as axiomatic that Ireland was a kingdom with its own sophisticated institutions, albeit one which had been conquered and subordinated to England. Petty's stated indifference to questions of religious confession ought to have endeared him to the Catholic monarch eager to help his co-religionists. However, Petty's willingness to contemplate greater generosity to Catholics combined with a fierce and occasionally irreverent anti-clericalism. Clerical power, especially as exercised by the papacy and Catholic priesthood, conflicted with Petty's idea of a well-governed state in which the church was firmly subordinated to the secular authorities. Nor could Petty escape from the logic of a situation in which he, in common with other recent gainers of Irish lands, benefited directly from the expropriation of the Irish Catholics. He never proposed a wholesale reversal of the land transfers which his own work had facilitated and from which he had profited so handsomely. In addition, although many of his schemes rested on a belief that the indigenous Irish could be trained for a variety of crafts and tasks, he did not altogether shed the English sense of cultural superiority.

From 1685 Petty lived continuously in London. Easier access to the king and court did not in the end bring any greater influence over policies. His health deteriorated sharply, and on 16 December 1687 he died at his London residence in Piccadilly. He was buried at St James's, Piccadilly, on 31 December. His ample fortune, suspected by contemporaries, was fully disclosed in his will. It was further recognized when, in 1688, his widow was ennobled as Baroness Shelburne, and the barony of the same name conferred on his eldest surviving son, Charles. The scope of Petty's interests and scale of his achievements were enlarged after his death: first, with the publication of his *Political Arithmetic* in 1690 and *Political Anatomy* in 1691, and then of other papers. This process has still to be completed. The writings, if sometimes repetitive and frequently utopian, provide abundant detail of the physical and human geography of seventeenth-century Ireland and England. They also show Petty's formidable intellectual prowess, especially as the originator of statistical analysis under the name of political arithmetic.

TOBY BARNARD

Sources BL, Add. MSS 72850–72908 · McGill University Library, Osler MS 7608 · *A brief of proceedings between Sir Hierome Sankey and Dr. William Petty* (1659) · W. Petty, notebook, TCD, MS 2947 · W. Petty, *Reflections upon some persons and things in Ireland* (1660) · *The advice of W. P[etty] to Mr. Samuel Hartlib: for the advancement of some particular parts of learning* (1648) · W. Petty, *The history of the survey of Ireland: commonly called the down survey, AD 1655-6*, ed. T. A. Larcom (1851) · *The Petty papers: some unpublished writings of Sir William Petty*, ed. marquis of Lansdowne [H. W. E. Petty-Fitzmaurice], 2 vols. (1927) · *The Petty–Southwell correspondence, 1676-1687*, ed. marquis of Lansdowne [H. E. W. Petty-Fitzmaurice] (1928) · C. H. Hull, ed., *The economic writings of Sir William Petty*, 2 vols. (1899) · E. Fitzmaurice, *The life of Sir William Petty, 1623-1687* (1895) · C. Webster, *The great instauration: science, medicine and reform, 1626-1660* (1975) · K. T. Hoppen, *The common scientist in the seventeenth century* (1970) · L. G. Sharp, 'Sir William Petty and some aspects of seventeenth-century natural philosophy', DPhil diss., U. Oxf., 1977 · T. C. Barnard, *Cromwellian Ireland* (1975) · T. C. Barnard, 'Sir William Petty, Irish landowner', *History and imagination: essays in honour of H. R. Trevor-Roper*, ed. H. Lloyd-Jones, V. Pearl, and B. Worden (1981) · T. C.

Barnard, 'Sir William Petty as Kerry ironmaster', *Proceedings of the Royal Irish Academy*, 82 sect. C (1982) · M. D. Slatter, *Calendar of the literary and personal papers of Sir William Petty (1623-1687) at Bowood House* (1980) · J. H. Andrews, *Shapes of Ireland: maps and their makers, 1564-1839* (Dublin, 1998), chap. 5 · F. Harris, 'Ireland as a laboratory: the archive of Sir William Petty', *Archives of the scientific revolution*, ed. M. C. W. Hunter (1998) · T. Aspromourgos, *On the origins of classical economics* (1996) · T. Aspromourgos, 'Political economy, political arithmetic and political medicine in the thought of William Petty', *Physicians and political economy*, ed. P. D. Groenewegen (2001) · T. Aspromourgos, 'The mind of the oeconomist: an overview of the "Petty Papers" archive', *History of Economic Ideas*, 9 (2001), 39–101 · GEC, *Peerage*

Archives BL, corresp. and papers, incl. Down Survey of Ireland, Add. MSS 72850–72908 · BL, letters and papers relating to double-hulled ships, Lyell MS emft 32 · BL, political tracts on Ireland, Add. MSS 21127–21128 · McGill University, Montreal, Osler Library of the History of Medicine, account and letter-books · McGill University, Montreal, Osler Library of the History of Medicine, Osler MS 7608 · NMM, papers relating to double-hulled ships · RS, papers | Nuffield Oxf., Hartlib papers · TCD, MS 2947

Likenesses I. Fuller, oils, *c*.1649–1650, NPG [*see illus.*] · E. Sandys, line engraving, 1683, BM, NPG · E. Sandys, line engraving, 1685 (after lost drawing by D. Luggan, 1680), NG Ire. · J. Smith, mezzotint, 1696 (after J. Closterman), NG Ire. · photogravure, pubd 1895 (after I. Fuller), NPG · J. Closterman, oils, Bowood, Wiltshire

Wealth at death £6700 p.a.; £46,412 personal estate: will, 2 May 1685, repr. in Fitzmaurice, *The life*, 318–24

Petty [*formerly* Fitzmaurice], **William, second earl of Shelburne and first marquess of Lansdowne** (1737–1805), prime minister, was born on 2 May 1737 in Dublin, the elder son of John Fitzmaurice (later Petty; 1706–1761), a landowner, and his wife, Mary Fitzmaurice (*d.* 1780), who was a cousin. His father's family had dominated co. Kerry for generations; his paternal grandmother was the daughter of Sir William Petty, whose estates at High Wycombe, carrying with them electoral influence over one seat, were inherited in 1751 by his father, who thereupon changed his name to Petty. His father was created earl of Shelburne in 1753 and in 1760 was raised to the British peerage, an honour which the duke of Newcastle believed was obtained only by his wealth and Henry Fox's patronage.

William, who was styled Viscount Fitzmaurice from 1753, believed his childhood had been peculiarly wretched and talked of it with horror, according to his friend Jeremy Bentham. Brought up in co. Kerry by his grandfather, the first earl of Kerry, whom he thought a tyrant by nature, he described his experience of childhood as 'domestic brutality and ill-usage', since his father had 'no notion of governing his children except by fear' (Fitzmaurice, 1.9, 12). He was educated at Dr Ford's school in Dublin and was instructed by a private tutor before going to Christ Church, Oxford, whence he matriculated on 11 March 1755. He summarized his position on leaving Christ Church: 'it became necessary for me to take some resolution for myself; home detestable, no prospect of a decent allowance to go abroad, neither happiness nor quiet' (ibid., 1.92). Having joined the army, he served in the 20th regiment and was present at the attack upon Rochefort in 1757. He was then appointed to Lord Granby's staff in Germany and distinguished himself at Minden (1759) and Kloster Kampen (1760). His reward was immediate. By

William Petty, second earl of Shelburne and first marquess of Lansdowne (1737–1805), by Sir Joshua Reynolds, 1767?

the end of 1760 he had been promoted colonel and appointed aide-de-camp to the new king, George III. His prospects were transformed. In June 1760, after his father had been given a British barony, Fitzmaurice succeeded to the parliamentary seat at Wycombe, and at the general election of 1761 he was returned to the Westminster parliament for Wycombe and to the Dublin parliament for County Kerry.

This spectacular progress aroused envy. The duke of Richmond resigned his place in the royal bedchamber in protest at the slight which Fitzmaurice's army promotions implied for his brother, Lord George Lennox. Before Fitzmaurice could take his seat in either House of Commons, his father's death in May 1761 transported him to the House of Lords at Westminster as Baron Wycombe and at Dublin as second earl of Shelburne. His initial political contacts were with Henry Fox, a distant relative and his father's patron, and with Fox's new ally Lord Bute. Despite his promising military début, Shelburne now resolved on a political career, though he continued to hold army rank. As early as March 1761 he had applied to the king for the comptrollership of the household, in what must have been a maladroit letter: the king, disliking the suggestion that his aide-de-camp sought 'real business', took offence, leaving Shelburne to make awkward apologies through Bute. Next he acted as broker in the complex negotiations by which Bute obtained Fox's support. His credit with the king was further damaged by an injudicious speech and protest on 5 February 1762, when he joined the duke of Bedford in deploring any continuation of the war in Germany (a move against Newcastle) and voted against the

previous motion which Bute himself had moved. Bute was irritated, and the king pointedly ignored Shelburne at the next levée. By June 1762 George III was describing Shelburne as a man who 'once dissatisfied will go any lengths' (*Letters ... to Lord Bute*, no. 163).

Shelburne declined to take part in Bute's ministry, despite Fox's urgent entreaty to 'get your harness on immediately' (Fitzmaurice, 1.143). He remained on good terms with Bute and Fox, and in December 1762 moved the acceptance of the peace preliminaries in the Lords. But when in the reshuffle in the spring of 1763, following Bute's decision to retire, Fox proposed Shelburne as one of the two secretaries of state, the king objected strongly. George Grenville, who finished up in the reshuffle as prime minister, warned Bute that Shelburne's promotion would disgust many people: 'from Lord Shelburne's youth, his inexperience in business, by having never held any civil office whatever, and from his situation and family, so lately raised to the peerage' (*Grenville Papers*, 2.35). The problem was compounded by an acrimonious quarrel with his patron Fox, who accused him, without any authority from Fox himself, of spreading the impression that Fox wished to retire from the paymastership. The mutual recriminations in which the affair ended deprived Fox of two of his closest supporters, John Calcraft and Richard Rigby, who sided with Shelburne. It is not easy to see what Shelburne stood to gain by misrepresenting Fox's views, but the episode lost nothing in the retelling, and enhanced Shelburne's growing reputation as a slippery fellow.

Cabinet office Shelburne was also extremely ambitious. Before he had held any political office, and while negotiations were still continuing, his friends spoke of his prospects in lofty terms. On 15 March 1763 Calcraft wrote assuming that Shelburne would be made secretary and dismissing the question of prime minister somewhat airily: 'with our hold on Lord Northumberland, is it possible to think of placing him as a great lord ... at the head of the Treasury, either for some short time, or till you could take it?' (Fitzmaurice, 1.195–6). In the end, Shelburne had to be content to be first lord at the Board of Trade, with a seat in the cabinet, and proved at once a difficult colleague. A demarcation dispute over American policy arose immediately with Lord Egremont, secretary of state for the south, and Shelburne demanded equal access to the king; American issues, brought to the forefront of politics by the Seven Years' War, dominated Shelburne's public life for the next twenty years. For good measure, he was also at odds with the other secretary, Lord Halifax, doubting both the wisdom and the legality of prosecuting Wilkes for no. 45 of the *North Briton* under a general warrant. Within two months of taking office Shelburne was threatening resignation. But Bute dissuaded him, pointing out that, at his age, the office which he held was one with which 'ambition ought to be satisfied' (Fitzmaurice, 1.276).

By the summer of 1763 the king was finding Grenville intolerable, and Shelburne was employed to negotiate with Pitt and Bedford. His admiration for Pitt dates from this period. When the negotiations broke down Shelburne tendered his resignation from the Board of Trade, though assuring the king of his continued support. George III regarded it as desertion in the midst of battle: he reported to Grenville, not one of Shelburne's admirers, that 'he finds the business of the board disagreeable to him … and subjecting him to too close an attendance' (*Grenville Papers*, 2.203). This may have been unfair to Shelburne, but he had held office for only four months: great noblemen with large incomes and estates to supervise often found the routine of administration tedious, and Shelburne had already declared that 'emolument' was no consideration with him (Fitzmaurice, 1.142). On 29 November 1763, in a debate on the expulsion of Wilkes, he spoke strongly against the government line that privilege of parliament did not extend to seditious libel. Grenville, temporarily reconciled with George III, reminded him that Shelburne was still an aide-de-camp and should be disciplined. 'A worthless man' was the king's terse reply, and Shelburne was dismissed, together with his parliamentary lieutenants Isaac Barré and Calcraft (*Grenville Papers*, 2.230, 236). Horace Walpole presumed that Shelburne was making up to Pitt as the man of the future. It was not, however, at all obvious in 1763 that Pitt had much political future, unless a new war should break out, which might sweep him to power by popular demand. Shelburne prided himself on his independence from party connection and his devotion to the monarch (which does not seem to have been reciprocated). He was now able to devote himself to that rural retirement he had previously commended: he employed Capability Brown to construct the lake at Bowood and Robert Adam to enlarge the house, and he turned his attention to the neglected Wycombe estates. In April 1764 he visited Ireland and took his seat in the Dublin House of Lords. On 2 or 3 February 1765 his marriage to Sophia Carteret (1745–1771), the daughter of John *Carteret, Earl Granville (1690–1763), and his second wife, Lady Sophia Fermor, brought him large estates near Bath, including much of Lansdowne Hill. They had two sons, John Henry, who succeeded as second marquess of Lansdowne, and William Granville, who died on 28 January 1778.

Pitt's disciple For a time it looked as though Shelburne's rapprochement with Pitt had been unwise. When the king's patience with Grenville finally ran out in the summer of 1765 it was the marquess of Rockingham who formed a ministry. Shelburne was offered his former post at the Board of Trade, but declined, pleading to Rockingham 'a real consciousness of my own inability in so active an office, to which the domestic habits I have lately fallen into add not a little' (Fitzmaurice, 1.334). His reliance was now totally upon Pitt: ''tis you, Sir, alone, in everybody's opinion', he wrote to the great man in December 1765, 'can put an end to this anarchy' (*Correspondence of William Pitt*, 2.357).

Shelburne followed Pitt's line on America: he spoke and voted on 3 February 1766 for the repeal of the Stamp Act but, disapproving strongly of the Declaratory Act which accompanied it, he warned the Lords that it was unwise to raise abstract constitutional questions, and voted in a minority of 5 to 125 against it. When Pitt, by then elevated to the Lords as earl of Chatham, formed his second ministry in July 1766 in succession to Rockingham, Shelburne was appointed secretary of state for the south. His responsibilities included India, Ireland, and America, as well as diplomatic relations with France, Spain, and the south of Europe. Three factors enhanced his standing still more. His colleague in the northern department was Henry Seymour Conway, one of the more conciliatory politicians of the day; Grafton, officially first lord of the Treasury, was young, inexperienced, and in thrall to Pitt: moreover, Pitt himself succumbed to a mysterious breakdown, which rendered him incapable of business or even human contact, and left Shelburne as his main representative in the deserted cabinet.

The absence of its real head made for an acrimonious and inept administration. Shelburne was soon at odds with a number of his colleagues. His sharpest differences were with Charles Townshend, chancellor of the exchequer, who made all the running in Chatham's absence. Shelburne's attitude towards the American colonies was circumspect, and he hoped that the issue of taxation could be avoided by reducing expenditure and by exploiting the quit-rents on virgin land. Townshend, who was not fond of the Americans, approved of the Stamp Act, and in January 1767 he pledged himself to raise an adequate revenue from the colonies. Shelburne appealed by letter to Chatham, recuperating at Bath, but his reply was painfully inexplicit. Townshend's position was strengthened by Lord North's refusal to replace him, and he carried the day; the Townshend duties were introduced in June. Shelburne's ineffective retort was to stop attending cabinet meetings.

The post-war financial difficulties would also be helped if a revenue could be raised from India. The role of the East India Company moved to the forefront and, again, Shelburne and Townshend clashed. Shelburne was deeply interested in the matter, publicly and privately, since he had invested heavily in company stock, which fluctuated according to government intentions, and was supporting Laurence Sulivan in the company against Lord Clive. Chatham and Shelburne denied the right of the company to a territorial revenue and favoured instead a searching review which would lead to a measure of government control and a substantial subsidy to the exchequer: Townshend hoped to achieve a similar end through negotiation with the directors. While matters drifted, Townshend's proposals went through.

Though Shelburne's rivalry with Charles Townshend was ended by the latter's sudden death in September 1767, it continued with his elder brother, Lord Townshend, appointed lord lieutenant of Ireland in August 1767. Within weeks of his arrival in Dublin he was complaining of a 'very severe letter' from Shelburne, and later of 'the propensity Lord Shelburne always expresses to condemn my conduct' (*Rutland MSS*, 2.293, 298). With the duke of Grafton, Shelburne was on better terms, since both admired Chatham; however, neither had a high opinion of the other, and there were sharp clashes over patronage.

Nor were Shelburne's relations with the king himself much warmer than they had been during his first spell in office. Before the ministry had been in power a year, George III was writing to Chatham that he and Grafton regarded Shelburne as 'a secret enemy' and suggesting his removal (*Correspondence*, ed. Fortescue, 1.480, no. 521). Shelburne survived, but suffered a significant setback when the supervision of the American colonies was removed from his department and given to a newly created American secretary, Lord Hillsborough. The king clearly hoped that Shelburne would resign in dudgeon, but he held on, waiting for Chatham's return. The junction with the Bedford group was yet another misfortune for him, since their views rarely coincided with his.

To these differences was added a major one in April 1768, when it became necessary for the ministry to decide its attitude towards Wilkes's election for Middlesex. At first Grafton and the cabinet inclined to a gentle approach to avoid giving Wilkes the crown of martyrdom, but in the course of time opinion hardened. Camden and Shelburne continued to urge caution, but the Bedfords were for strong measures, and the king wrote in April that 'the expulsion of Mr. Wilkes appears to be very essential and must be effected' (*Correspondence*, ed. Fortescue, 2.21, no. 613). But before the issue came to parliament Shelburne's fate had been sealed. Whateley reported to Grenville in May that Shelburne's dismissal was 'expected every day' (*Grenville Papers*, 4.296). In September the king warned Grafton that 'Lord Shelburne manifestly still attempted to thwart every measure that originated from you, and seemed resolved to propose none himself' (*Correspondence*, ed. Fortescue, 2.43, no. 651). But Camden, to whom this was confided, reminded the king that Shelburne was still under Chatham's protection, even if he had lost the good opinion 'of every one of the other active members of the cabinet' (ibid.). The following month the king again urged Grafton to sound out Chatham, believing that he would acquiesce in Shelburne's dismissal. He did not, but tendered his own resignation. Shelburne's resignation followed a week later.

Opposition During 1769, Grafton's administration, assaulted by Junius, fell to pieces, while Shelburne joined Rockingham and Grenville in opposition. The Wilkes issue rumbled on, with the momentous decision to seat the government candidate, Colonel Henry Luttrell, for Middlesex. Shelburne was a valuable recruit to opposition in the Lords, particularly since Rockingham was a notoriously poor and reluctant speaker. In his speech of 15 December 1768 Shelburne sniped at his former colleagues, for he was still waiting to see whether Chatham would return and what his line would be. In January 1770 Chatham, amazingly restored, appeared once more in the Lords, denounced the ministers for their policies on both America and Wilkes, declared that the liberty of the subject was in danger at home and abroad, and hinted darkly at a secret influence, 'a mysterious power', that lurked behind the scenes. This salvo carried away Camden, who resigned the chancellorship, and it appeared that the government was doomed: 'the seals would go a begging', said Shelburne, but he 'hoped there would not be found in the kingdom a wretch so base and mean-spirited as to accept of them' (Cobbett, *Parl. hist.*, 16, 1765–71, 665). By the end of the month Grafton, too, had resigned. But the advantage did not fall to Chatham and Shelburne. Lord North took over as prime minister, and, while he was at first regarded as a mere stopgap, he established an administration which condemned Chatham to opposition for the rest of his life and Shelburne for the next twelve years.

Shelburne's private life was also difficult. He invested heavily in East India Company stock through his undersecretary Lauchlin Macleane and admitted losing £40,000 in the 1769 crash, in which Macleane was completely ruined: though Shelburne gave up interfering in company matters, the suspicion of insider dealing did little for his reputation. His building programme at Bowood, at Wycombe Abbey, and at the large house in Berkeley Square, which he had purchased half-finished from Bute, made severe demands upon even his ample fortune. His way of life was lavish, with great hospitality extended to the remarkable coterie of friends and advisers whom he gathered round him. In addition, on 5 January 1771 his wife died in childbirth at the age of twenty-five. Shelburne left in May for a continental tour with Barré to assuage his grief, during which he made the acquaintance of a large number of *philosophes*, including Beccaria, Turgot, Malesherbes, and Morellet, and became a convert to the new free-trade doctrine.

The hopes of opposition for a speedy return to power depended upon war with Spain over the Falkland Islands, which, they believed, must lead to Chatham's recall. While the issue was still in doubt, Shelburne declared that 'whether we commence a war with Spain or tamely crouch under the insults of that haughty kingdom', power could not remain 'in such feeble, in such incompetent hands' (Cobbett, *Parl. hist.*, 16, 1765–71, 1113–14). North negotiated a peaceful settlement of the dispute in January 1771, which the opposition naturally denounced as craven and cowardly. On 14 February 1771, in an attack upon the settlement, Shelburne spoke, according to Horace Walpole, 'better than he had ever done' (Walpole, *Memoirs of … George III*, 4.275). On his return from the continental tour he took up the proposal of Dr Richard Price, one of his closest followers, that dissenting clergy should be released from the obligation to subscribe to the Thirty-Nine Articles. The ministers decided to let the measure through the Commons but kill it in the Lords, where it was rejected by 102 votes to 29. The East India Company, despite the settlement of 1767, got into further difficulty, and in 1772 was obliged to approach the government for a substantial loan. North agreed to rescue it, but subject to the appointment of a governor-general and a considerable degree of governmental control. Though the Rockinghams condemned the bill as a gross violation of charters, Shelburne gave it general support. William Lyttelton reported that Shelburne had 'never spoken better in his life', though his enemies hinted that he was angling for a return to office (*Correspondence of William Pitt*, 4.284).

Shelburne was by now a leading member of the opposition and more than a mere mouthpiece for the ageing Chatham. He had a considerable following in the City of London, where he worked closely with James Townsend and the more moderate radicals. His electoral interest was useful. After spending £100,000 on property in the neighbourhood, he controlled two seats at Calne and one at Wycombe and had influence in Wiltshire and Buckinghamshire. His parliamentary following, though small, was able, with John Dunning a rising lawyer and Barré a formidable debater. His own parliamentary speeches were frequently informed and impressive, though he was sometimes tempted into lurid and melodramatic language, and he had a penchant for threatening severe punishment. Not only did this lay him open to easy retorts from the more adroit lords, it built up a residue of dislike which, in the end, proved costly.

Increasingly in the 1770s the political scene was dominated by the American troubles. Shelburne was perhaps handicapped by his strict adherence to Chatham's line, which, from 1773 onwards, looked unrealistic and sentimental. In January 1775 he supported Chatham's motion to withdraw British troops from Boston, condemning 'the madness, injustice and infatuation of coercing the Americans into a blind and servile submission': it was defeated by sixty-eight votes to eighteen (Cobbett, *Parl. hist.*, 18, 1774–6, 163). In a debate in February on an address urging the king to enforce obedience on the colonists, Shelburne clashed violently with Lord Mansfield, whom he accused of being the secret influence behind the American policy. In return he was attacked for 'uttering the most gross falsehoods' (ibid., 18.282). Once shots had been exchanged at Lexington, events developed their own momentum, and it was hard for the opposition not to appear factious and disloyal: 'the popular tide', Shelburne admitted, 'was against him' (ibid., 18.449). In November 1775 he paid handsome tribute to Chatham as 'the most efficient servant of the crown, and while he had life in him, the nerve of Great Britain' (ibid., 18.923–4). It was not clear, however, how much life Chatham did have left in him, and his argument that the colonists were not really seeking independence looked more and more implausible. On 5 March 1776 Shelburne was said by Walpole to have made 'a great figure in the debate' on Richmond's motion against the employment of German mercenaries in America (*Last Journals of Horace Walpole*). On 14 March he made a major effort in support of Grafton's motion for some gesture of goodwill towards the colonists, pleading that a middle path was the only hope of avoiding disaster. It was defeated by ninety-one votes to twenty-eight. There was little chance that Shelburne and the opposition could change the direction of policy, but the possibility remained that Chatham might be invited to join the government, bringing Shelburne with him, especially after the news of Burgoyne's surrender at Saratoga had been received in December 1777, carrying with it the probability that France and Spain would intervene. An important

speech of 5 March 1778 on the American conciliation bills suggested a change of emphasis, if not of policy, on Shelburne's part. He told the Lords that he would:

> never consent that America should be independent ... Great Britain should superintend the interests of the whole ... as soon as that event should take place, the sun of Great Britain is set, and we shall no longer be a powerful or respectable people. (Cobbett, *Parl. hist.*, 19, 1777–8, 850)

A week later North obtained the king's grudging permission to sound out Chatham through Shelburne: 'I do not expect Lord Chatham and his crew will come to your assistance', George warned North (*Correspondence*, ed. Fortescue, 4.58, no. 2221). The proposal, put forward by William Eden, was for Chatham to receive the Garter and join the cabinet, while Shelburne took his old post as secretary of state. Shelburne replied that Chatham 'must be dictator' and would bring in the Rockinghams. The king's relief at the failure of the negotiations with Chatham, 'that perfidious man', was total (ibid., 4.59, no. 2224). Three weeks later Chatham suffered his dramatic collapse in the House of Lords, and by May he was dead. Shelburne's motion that the House of Lords as an order should attend the funeral in Westminster Abbey was lost by one vote. But his final verdict on his former idol, recorded many years later, was much cooler:

> he was always acting, always made up, and never natural, incapable of friendship, and constantly upon the watch and never unbent ... I was in the most intimate political habits with him for ten years ... without drinking a glass of water in his house or company, or five minutes conversation out of the way of business. (Fitzmaurice, 1.72–9)

Chatham's death, though depriving Shelburne of a diminishing asset, liberated him from the need to consult and report. But his political behaviour became somewhat erratic. In a rambling speech of 26 November 1778, which contained veiled threats against the king, Shelburne called for a union of all parties to bring 'condign punishment' on wicked and evil ministers; he would 'cheerfully cooperate with any set of men to drag them from their present situations', and bring them to justice (Cobbett, *Parl. hist.*, 19, 1777–8, 1318–19). The following month he repeated his view that, without America, Britain would be but a petty state: 'he would never serve with any man who would consent to acknowledge the independence of America' (ibid., 20, 1779–80, 40). This drove a wedge between him and his Rockingham allies and suggested that he was a man the court might approach. With North still anxious to lay down the burden of office, fresh negotiations took place. In February 1779 Grafton was entrusted with discussions for a general coalition, which got nowhere, though he recorded that Shelburne had promised not to contest the premiership with Rockingham. There were further discussions in November 1779 when Gower and Weymouth left the ministry. Shelburne attempted to inject some vigour into the proceedings by moving on 1 December a motion on the state of Ireland, which North feared would be the prelude to his own impeachment. Shelburne obliged with a strong personal attack, insisting that North's conduct was 'highly criminal' (ibid., 20.1169). North had suggested to the king that

Shelburne could be 'easily induced' (*Correspondence*, ed. Fortescue, 4.501, no. 2855) to make up an administration with Gower and Thurlow. But Thurlow's conversation with Shelburne found him more inexplicit than ever: 'the more connection that could be preserved with America the better; but he did not say what the nature of that connection should be' (ibid., 4.521, no. 2882). Nor could he say whether the opposition would take part in a coalition. The king found this reply 'cold and distant' (ibid.), the negotiations came to nothing, and North was persuaded to soldier on.

Several episodes at this time throw light upon Shelburne's character and reputation. In 1777 an Irish adventurer, David Brown Dignam, accused him and other lords of a bizarre conspiracy to assassinate the king. Though Dignam was soon unmasked and sent to the hulks, he would not have picked on Shelburne had not the latter's French connections and his correspondence with Franklin and other Americans rendered him suspect. In 1778 Shelburne's engagement was announced to Frances Molesworth, a young, attractive, and wealthy heiress. But Eleanor Elliot wrote to her brother Hugh: 'she dined at his house and sat at the head of the table and was seen to cry all dinner-time … she sent Lady Lucan a letter and begged she would break off the detested match' (Minto, 147). Horace Walpole, no friend to Shelburne, conceded that he had been an 'admirable husband' to his first wife, but there were reports that Miss Molesworth complained that Shelburne did nothing but talk politics to her (Walpole, *Corr.*, 33.115). Shelburne's disappointment soon passed, and the following year he married Louisa Fitzpatrick (1755–1789), the daughter of John Fitzpatrick, first earl of Upper Ossory, and his wife, Evelyn Leveson-Gower. They had two children, Henry Petty-*Fitzmaurice, third marquess, and a daughter who died in infancy. On 22 March 1780, as a consequence of some characteristically sharp remarks in debate, Shelburne fought a duel with the Scottish MP William Fullarton. Shelburne behaved with military courage, was slightly wounded in the groin, and achieved fleeting popularity, since the Scots were even more disliked than he was. In 1778 he became acquainted with the young Jeremy Bentham, whose reminiscences of the Bowood circle are of value, but who repaid considerable hospitality and kindness from Shelburne with a verdict far from flattering.

The weight of wartime taxation and the development of the Yorkshire Association's campaign for economical reform put wind into the sails of the opposition during the winter of 1779–80. Shelburne responded by moving on 8 February 1780 for a committee to examine the public accounts with a view to economy and a reduction in the influence of the crown. After a long debate the motion was rejected, though Shelburne was supported by fifty of the peers attending, eighty-one being against. But a further difference with Lord Rockingham arose when the economical reformers moved on to embrace parliamentary reform. Rockingham was mistrustful, but Shelburne, following the line chalked out by Chatham in the 1770s, favoured an increase in the number of county seats and

shorter parliaments. The gap between the two groups widened dramatically with the Gordon riots in June 1780: the Rockinghams were strong supporters of law and order, while Shelburne's sympathy for the rioters was so great that he was accused of encouraging them. He was also, like Charles James Fox and many others, impatient at Rockingham's sluggish leadership. On 3 June 1780 he declared that, though he would not pledge himself, he would attend the House of Lords no more until there was 'a greater likelihood of speaking to some purpose' (Christie, 112–13). The well-publicized split in the ranks of the opposition and the swing to the political right caused by the riots prompted a fresh negotiation for a government of national unity, but in the discussions held with Rockingham in July 1780 Shelburne was neither consulted nor mentioned. Shelburne was understandably nettled: 'I owe nothing to them', he wrote of the Rockinghams, 'and much to others … The conduct of others during the summer will abundantly justify silence and inaction' (Fitzmaurice, 3.105–6). Of Rockingham himself, he wrote: 'there he stands obstinately stopping the free course of popular spirit which alone can ever oppose the court' (ibid., 3.107). When he spoke in January 1781 on the breach with Holland, he began by telling the house that 'he had long determined to absent himself from his attendance there' (Cobbett, *Parl. hist.*, 21, 1780–81, 1023). From this dangerous split the opposition was rescued by the news of Cornwallis's surrender at Yorktown in October 1781.

Shelburne attended the opening of parliament on 27 November 1781 and moved an amendment to the address, arguing that financial debility and shortage of recruits made any further prosecution of the war in America impossible. In a debate of 7 February 1782 on the surrender of Yorktown, he took the opportunity to repeat that 'he would never consent, under any possible given circumstances, to acknowledge the independency of America' (ibid., 22, 1781–2, 987). To the king this represented a signal that Shelburne was the least implacable of his opponents. Consequently, when Lord North insisted on resigning on 20 March, the king sent for Shelburne and expressed 'his preference of me compared to the rest of the opposition' (Fitzmaurice, 3.131). This was not saying much, but the king was in a very difficult position and contemplating abdication. Shelburne declined to try to form an administration, telling Rockingham, 'you can stand without me, but I could not without you' (ibid., 3.131). The king refused categorically to deal directly with Rockingham but agreed to negotiate through Shelburne: in that decision were many of the seeds of the subsequent resentments. Buttressed by Dunning, to be brought into the cabinet as Lord Ashburton, and supported by Thurlow, to be retained as lord chancellor at the king's insistence, Shelburne would be in a powerful position. On 26 March George III wrote to him:

> Lord Shelburne's note I look upon as an instance of *personal* attention, and feel it as such: I trust from it, he has stood firm, and will have remembered that the powers intrusted to him in the ministerial line … gives him strength with more

vigour to resist all others. (*Correspondence*, ed. Fortescue, 5.412–13, no. 3582)

Rockingham accordingly took the Treasury, with Fox and Shelburne as the two secretaries of state. On 19 April Shelburne was given the Garter.

First minister The second Rockingham ministry was brief and unpleasant. The rifts in it were apparent before it took office—indeed, they were built into it. Within a week of kissing hands, Shelburne and Rockingham were at odds about patronage: George III told Thurlow that 'Lord Shelburne expressed an uneasiness lest I should yield to the importunities of Lord Rockingham, which would reduce him to a Secretary of State, acting under the former, instead of a colleague' (*Correspondence*, ed. Fortescue, 5.443, no. 3632). The king composed a bland formula, suggesting joint recommendations. Fox and Shelburne disputed in whose department negotiations with the Americans lay and finished up with rival plenipotentiaries in Paris. The implementation of economic reform also caused trouble. Of the debate in the Lords on 15 April, Shelburne reported to the king that 'I insisted that the proposed reduction of ministerial influence must make the struggle within and without doors who should contribute most to Your Majesty's dignity, comfort and splendour' (ibid., 5.463, no. 3665). This interpretation had occurred to no one before, but George III, not surprisingly, replied that 'nothing could be more proper than Lord Shelburne's language' (ibid., 5.464, no. 3666). Shelburne was already building up support, sending Thurlow to sound out Henry Dundas as early as April in case 'a breach of administration should ever happen as to leave him in possession of government'. At a later meeting Dundas, a blunt Scot, found Shelburne's 'civility and courtship a little overdone upon so slight an acquaintance' (Cannon, *Fox–North Coalition*, 12–13).

One of Shelburne's main responsibilities was for Ireland, where the armed volunteers were demanding the immediate acknowledgement of legislative independence. In public, Shelburne declared handsomely that 'the voice of a people … ought to be attended to': in letters to his brother-in-law Richard Fitzpatrick, now chief secretary, he urged firmness and delay. To the king he confessed that, while it was 'a subject through which I do not see some sort of way', it was 'never off my mind'. On American independence he was equally delphic. In cabinet and to the commanders in the field he accepted that independence was not a condition of peace, but a categorical offer: to the king he reported to the contrary—that peace would be 'the price of independence' (Cannon, *Fox–North Coalition*, 12–13, 17–18). Fox was considering resigning on the issue when rumours spread that Rockingham was gravely ill. Shelburne at once began making plans, discussing with the king what role, if any, Fox should play in the new government: 'it may not be necessary to remove him at once' (*Correspondence*, ed. Fortescue, 6.70, no. 3825). As soon as Rockingham's death was known, the king offered Shelburne the Treasury.

Shelburne's ministry, the peak of his career, lasted eight months, for five of which parliament was in recess. His strongest card was his new chancellor of the exchequer, young William Pitt. But Pitt, who had already raised eyebrows with his declaration that he would never accept a junior post, was also a potential rival—an obvious successor to an unpopular first minister. Lord Grantham became foreign secretary, Lord Temple went to Dublin as viceroy, and Thomas Townshend took the Home Office: the new recruits, thought Thurlow, who remained as lord chancellor, were 'not all of the most promising sort' (*Fifth Report*, HMC, 211). Dundas was brought in to augment the Commons team, John Robinson was recruited to give electoral advice, and in August the king wrote personally to beg North to use his influence on behalf of the ministry. Challenged by Fox to deny that his resignation was not pique but policy, Shelburne produced one of his classic responses: 'he made no such assertion; but he had certainly said, that "in his opinion", that was the cause, and the exclusive cause, but he had not asserted it as a fact' (Cobbett, *Parl. hist.*, 23, 1782–3, 200–01).

Most of Shelburne's time in the summer was devoted to the peace negotiations, over which he exercised very close supervision. Until a late stage he entertained hopes of some form of federal union. The first setback was the American declaration that, if independence was not unconditionally acknowledged, negotiations were at an end: though the king grumbled that he did not see 'how the present ministry can consent to it', Shelburne gave way. A second problem was the American refusal to compensate the loyalists, insisting that this was a matter for the individual colonies—a palpable evasion, which was bound to go down badly with the British public. At the same time Shelburne continued the complex process of economical reform, and though he wriggled out of any commitment to parliamentary reform, it meant that he was seriously overloaded. He had neither the time, nor probably the inclination, to consult widely or to carry his colleagues with him. Grafton, Camden, Richmond, Keppel, and Conway rebelled on a proposal to cede Gibraltar, and it had to be abandoned. Temple, in Dublin, was outraged that Shelburne could not find time to talk to his younger brother William Grenville, the chief secretary, about Irish problems. On 27 November 1782 Shelburne fell back on one of his stock phrases: 'the subject was never off his mind … and a great deal of such verbiage' (*Memoirs of the Court*, 1.67). On 7 December Grenville was mortified when Shelburne walked out while he was talking, and concluded that 'Lord Shelburne's evident intention is to make cyphers of his colleagues' (ibid., 1.84). A week later Shelburne produced another classic: 'he was *inclined to think*', Grenville reported to Temple, 'not that he *thought*, your government would go on there more easily than you expected' (ibid., 1.87). With that serene assurance, Temple had to be satisfied, and began to contemplate resignation.

Peace preliminaries with America were signed on 30 November, and Shelburne approached the meeting of parliament in a mood of unintelligible confidence. He had always shared Chatham's conviction that the support of the king was everything, but he possessed neither Chatham's oratory to fall back on nor his experience of the Commons. On 13 November he assured Lord Carmarthen that his opponents in the Lower House would not exceed sixty—'which he had reason to be assured of, tho' it appeared scarce credible' (*Political Memoranda*, 76). Next he told Fitzpatrick that he understood nothing of the Commons, 'but that they show him *a very good list*' (*Memorials and Correspondence*, 2.10). This was Robinson's estimate of probable voting, itself based upon the assumption that the king would bring North and his troops to the support of the ministry. On 18 December 1782 Grenville reported another meeting with Shelburne:

> I never heard any man, in the whole course of my life, affirm any one thing more distinctly, positively and unequivocally, than he did, when he told me that Government were on a sure foundation here—there was a moral certainty … Either Lord Shelburne is … the most abandoned and direct liar upon the face of the earth, or he is deceived himself, too grossly to be imagined. (*Memoirs of the Court*, 1.89)

Nor had the opening day in parliament gone well. The issue of recognition of American independence returned to haunt him. In the Commons, Pitt declared that it was unconditional: in the Lords, Shelburne declared the opposite. Fox and his friends made the most of their advantage, and though the king suggested that Pitt must have got it wrong and could correct himself, Pitt did not take kindly to the idea. It was, Shelburne admitted, 'awkward', and in the Lords he was forced to take refuge in refusing to answer questions on the subject (*Correspondence*, ed. Fortescue, 6.175, no. 4014). Worst of all were signs that the king was beginning to harbour doubts about his new first minister. Deploring the administration's poor showing in the Lords on 5 December, he remarked that these mishaps would not occur 'if there was any energy or discipline in government' (ibid., 6.173, no. 4012). On the 8th he declared that 'it is highly material that Lord Shelburne should not by any language in the House of Lords appear to change his conduct, let the blame fall where it may. I do not wish that he should appear but in a dignified light' (ibid., 6.175–6, no. 4015).

With Fox and Shelburne quite irreconcilable, the fate of the ministry turned on North and his friends. But North was by no means a free agent, and it is doubtful whether he could have carried most of his followers in support of the peace. Setting aside personalities, the failure to secure compensation for the loyalists was bound to be a sticking point for men who had, for seven years, supported the American war. Preoccupied with the peace negotiations, Shelburne left his approach to North far too late, partly because Pitt remained opposed to any such move. In the meantime Shelburne scarcely seemed to notice that his government was disintegrating. Keppel resigned from the Admiralty on 23 January 1783, Carlisle gave up the lord high stewardship, Richmond left the cabinet, and Grafton, always unsteady, resigned on the day of the debate on the peace. North's understanding with Fox was agreed on 14 February and announced in parliament on the 18th. In

the Lords, Shelburne offered a rather rambling and theatrical defence but carried the day, in a very full house, by seventy-two votes to fifty-nine. In the Commons, despite surprise at the new coalition, Fox and North held most of their supporters and defeated the ministry by 224 to 208. At this point Shelburne's unpopularity came into play. A rearguard action was not out of the question, but hardly any of his colleagues wished Shelburne to continue, and he seems himself to have been exhausted, bewildered, and demoralized. Carmarthen, who dined with him on the 20th, found him 'totally devoid of spirit' (*Political Memoranda*, 82). He had been so convinced that the king's support would be decisive that he had no contingency plans and could scarcely comprehend what had happened. His friends hinted at treachery at court. Orde reported the opinion of John Hatsell, clerk to the Commons, that 'the stability or downfall to your administration depends solely (as Your Lordship has always said) upon the *Highest* … It is his will' (Fitzmaurice, 3.361). This was arrant nonsense. Nor is it clear why the opinion of a Commons clerk on such a matter should carry much weight, but it was perhaps easier for Shelburne to believe that he had been betrayed than to admit that he had totally misjudged the situation. In a second debate on 21 February, Pitt acquitted himself magnificently. However, that was of little comfort for Shelburne since it established Pitt firmly as the heir apparent, and much of his speech sounded like a political obituary for Shelburne, abandoned to the admiration of posterity: 'when stripped of his power and emoluments, he once more descends to private life … men will see him through a different medium' (Cobbett, *Parl. hist.*, 23, 1782–3, 551). The opposition won again by 207 to 190, and the following day Shelburne was told that he must resign.

Shelburne stayed in office until 26 March to enable a new administration to be formed. Though he remained active in the Lords for more than twenty years, his political career was over. He spoke bitterly afterwards of the king as a man who 'obtained your confidence, procured from you your opinion of different public characters, and then availed himself of this knowledge to sow dissension' (Fitzmaurice, 3.363). Hardly any of his associates mourned his departure. Horace Walpole's vituperation may be ascribed to Shelburne's threat to his sinecures: 'he was so well known that he could only deceive by speaking truth … He was so fond of insincerity as if he had been the inventor' (*Last Journals of Horace Walpole*, 2.465). But few found him pleasant to work with. George Rose declared he would never be in the same room with him again: 'the alternate violence and flattery of Lord Shelburne … made my situation so thoroughly unpleasant to me that I felt the certain removal from office as a relief' (*Diaries and Correspondence*, 1.25–8). William Knox wrote that 'those who served with him in office abhorred him as a principal', and Sir Stanier Porten claimed to have told him 'God be thanked I am not going to be under you again' (*Various Collections*, 6.283). He might perhaps have found a niche as a reforming minister under some enlightened despot, but, in a parliamentary system which called for some capacity to work with other people, his basic insecurity meant that he found it almost impossible to establish tolerable relations.

Aftermath Since at the time of his resignation Shelburne was only forty-five, a return to power was not impossible. A strange speech in May 1783 did little to restore his reputation. He denied that the House of Commons had the sole right to consider money bills, and added: 'with regard to the argument that he had lost the confidence of the House of Commons, he did not believe he had lost it, but let the House of Commons beware or they would lose my confidence'. The House of Commons bore this threat with equanimity, the House of Lords declined to pick a quarrel on money bills, and Shelburne's comeback finished with an acrimonious exchange with his former colleague Keppel (Cobbett, *Parl. hist.*, 23, 1782–3, 824). The coalition ministry which followed lasted only until December 1783 and was succeeded by Pitt's. But Pitt, according to George Rose, was 'as little disposed to further connexion with Lord Shelburne as myself' (*Diaries and Correspondence*, 1.32), and Townshend (now Lord Sydney) confided to Orde that to bring back Shelburne would be as alarming as bringing back Lord Bute. At a later date Bentham reported a conversation with Shelburne who 'complained repeatedly of Pitt and Thurlow for breach of faith … it seemed to sit very heavy on him' (Bentham, 10.214). Nursing his resentments, he did not attend to vote against Fox's India Bill. In August 1784 Daniel Pulteney wrote that the only thing that could endanger Pitt's government would be to give a place to Shelburne 'where he can be credited to be prime minister' (*Rutland MSS*, 3.132). Pitt's solution was to obtain for Shelburne promotion to a marquessate in November 1784. This did not mollify him for long. In October 1785 Orde found him at Bowood 'not in the most satisfactory temper with the ministers', and in March 1786 Shelburne—now Lord Lansdowne—admitted that he found the ministry's attitude towards him 'unaccountable' (ibid., 250, 287). Meanwhile the coalition wits pilloried him in *The Rolliad* as 'the sylvan sage, whom Bowood guards to rule a purer age', and made fun of his contorted language. His small following collapsed. Dunning died in August 1783, Townsend followed in July 1787, and Barré went blind. The duke of Rutland, lord lieutenant of Ireland, who had lobbied Pitt on Lansdowne's behalf, died in October 1787 at the age of thirty-three. Of his newer associates, Bentham was unfitted for parliamentary life and Samuel Romilly did not enter parliament until after Lansdowne's death.

Lansdowne continued to speak in the Lords, but as a commentator, or even a lecturer, rather than a leading politician. In June 1785 he took the opportunity of Pitt's Irish commercial propositions to reiterate his belief in free trade, and he repeated the argument when he gave strong support to the commercial treaty with France in March 1787, denying that France was a natural enemy of Britain. Even then he became involved in another angry exchange with a former colleague, Richmond, which smouldered on for several days. In 1788 he spoke and voted on the government side over the proposed regency.

It is possible that the death of his second wife on 7 August 1789 would have pushed Lansdowne back into politics in any case, but the advent of the French Revolution was certain to call him into action. His close contacts with French writers and statesmen, among them Mirabeau and Talleyrand, made him sympathetic, and he was convinced that the French sought only a liberal constitution. His judgement was not noticeably better than that of his colleagues. He greatly approved of the French nobility abandoning their separate order and joining the Third Estate, which, he insisted, would give them vast influence. He believed that the revolution would grow less violent and that the continental powers would not intervene. Most obvious was his growing antipathy towards Pitt, with whom he had already had differences over Indian affairs and the impeachment of Hastings. The first public evidence of the breach came in his speech of 13 December 1790 on the settlement with Spain at the end of the Nootka Sound crisis. In a long survey of the foreign policy of Pitt's government he claimed that, as soon as Frederick the Great had died in 1786, ministers had abandoned their pacific stance and sought to terrify and intimidate every court in Europe. By 1791 he was in persistent opposition, joining the strong censure of Pitt's handling of the Ochakov crisis with Russia, which forced the minister into a humiliating withdrawal. Lansdowne, reported Sydney in June 1791, was 'in a state of great and extraordinary political violence' (*Correspondence of … Cornwallis*, 2.142). The diplomatic rebuff forced the resignation of the foreign secretary and shook Pitt's position, and in the spring of 1792 there were negotiations for a coalition, in which Lansdowne played some part. Gillray produced a caricature, entitled *Malagrida's Driving Post*, which showed him entering St James's Palace while Fox and Sheridan begged a lift, and the Bowood archives include a rather strange memo by Lansdowne, more of a disquisition than a working paper, on the possibilities of a change of ministry. The negotiations failed, but in the summer Thurlow was dismissed and Loughborough took his place as lord chancellor.

Under these circumstances, Fox and Lansdowne edged closer. Their rapprochement was assisted by Fox's friendly treatment in the House of Commons of Lansdowne's son Lord Wycombe, which contrasted with Pitt's scorn. Some more formal understanding was needed in 1793 after the outbreak of war hardened the divisions in parliament. To Fox's initiative, Lansdowne responded by asking whether a mere reconciliation or an avowed junction was intended. Lord Spencer wrote in February 1794 that 'Lord Lansdowne stands as clearly at the head of the opposition in one house as Mr Fox does at the head of that in the House of Commons' (Mitchell, 232), but wondered whether a formal coalition would do much to improve Fox's popularity. The following year Fox admitted that 'I never can have a good opinion of him, and still less a great one. However, we are upon terms of the greatest civility' (*Memorials and Correspondence*, 3.112–13). They agreed to consult in the unlikely event of an approach from the court. In the meantime Lansdowne's opposition to the war led to a fresh campaign of vilification in the newspapers as a friend of the Jacobins. Caricaturists had a field day, portraying him as a French agent or a sans-culotte, shouting 'Ça ira!', wearing the cap of liberty, and working the guillotine, usually with a bland smile. His parliamentary activity increased considerably. He insisted that any attempt to invade France would be doomed to failure, warned of the danger of turning France into 'a military republic … impossible to extinguish', and predicted that France might produce a military genius—'great moments have always produced great men' (Cobbett, *Parl. hist.*, 30, 1792–4, 1395). His motion was rejected by 103 votes to thirteen. In May 1794 he protested strongly against the suspension of habeas corpus, complaining that the committee of secrecy was made up of alarmists, and in January 1795 he supported the duke of Bedford's motion for peace with France. But his renewed activity made it less rather than more likely that he would be recalled to active service, and he admitted ruefully that 'the tide of popularity was against him' (ibid., 31, 1794–5, 973). In a debate on the Seditious Meetings Bill in December 1795 he agreed that precautions against subversion were needed—'an admission which, he trusted, would at least be sufficient to exempt him from the charge of Jacobinism' (ibid., 32, 1795–7, 534). But he was trapped in the same position as in the 1770s when he had opposed the American war, and he conceded that he attended reluctantly, when all he could do was to issue warnings of dire disaster. 'Not one session had passed since 1793', he declared in 1797 in a rare moment of wry humour, 'in which he had not bored their lordships with his prophetic admonitions' (ibid., 32, 1795–7, 1564). The isolation of the leaders of the opposition forced them closer. In February 1796 Fox wrote that

the circumstances of the times will of themselves bring me and Lansdowne together … we are indeed now upon a very good footing and quite sufficiently so to enable us to act cordially together, if any occasion offers to doing so usefully. (*Memorials and Correspondence*, 3.129)

There was a flurry of excitement in February 1801 when a recurrence of the king's illness made possible a regency for the prince of Wales, an ardent admirer of Fox. Lansdowne and Fox agreed to serve as secretaries of state under Lord Moira, which would have reconstituted the unhappy partnership of the spring of 1782, and Lord Wycombe was pencilled in for the Admiralty. But the king recovered within four weeks, and Lansdowne's last moment had passed. He lived to see his younger son, Lord Henry Petty, lay the foundations of a distinguished parliamentary career, and he made his last speech on 23 May 1803, arguing that none of Napoleon's provocations justified a resumption of the war. The motion was lost by 142 votes to ten. He died at his house in Berkeley Square on 7 May 1805 and was buried at High Wycombe.

A good and ready speaker, a formidable debater, more persistent and better informed than almost all his contemporaries, particularly among the peerage, Lansdowne was in the centre of politics for forty years, held high office on four occasions, was awarded the Garter (1782) and was raised in the peerage (1784). Nevertheless, his career was a failure and he felt it dearly: 'his mind is soured', wrote Thomas Orde in 1786 (*Rutland MSS*, 3.324). At the end of his life, in a fragment of autobiography, he reflected on the causes of his lack of success. He deplored his education; complained that as a child only one aunt, Lady Arabella Denny, had shown him any real affection; and lamented that 'it has been my fate through life to fall in with clever but unpopular connections' (Fitzmaurice, 1.17). In all of this there was a certain amount of self-deception. He was certainly not worse educated than most of his aristocratic contemporaries, and his later circle at Bowood included such distinguished men as Dunning, Price, Priestley, and Bentham. Early in his political career he was associated with Bute and Henry Fox, who were certainly disliked. But men can choose their associates. His patrons were out of active politics by 1766, and soon Shelburne himself was the unpopular connection other people shunned, collecting more than his share of political abuse as 'Malagrida' (arch-dissembler) or 'the Jesuit of Berkeley Square'. There are other and more plausible explanations of the mistrust he aroused and the disappointment he suffered. His uneasiness prompted him to alternate flattery and hectoring, which most of his colleagues found unpleasant, and to suspiciousness, of which his son complained forcefully while abroad in 1785. In debate he was frequently vituperative and sarcastic—Daniel Pulteney referred in 1787 to his 'sneering manner' (*Rutland MSS*, 3.376)—and Lord Holland, in a very fair assessment, wrote that his speeches 'were not only animated and entertaining, but embittered the contest' (Holland, 1.42). His early success was resented by his fellow peers, who regarded him as a pushy Irish upstart, and his very brief membership of the Commons (he never took his seat) left him seriously underestimating the importance of that house. His advocacy of popular and reformist policies—free trade, religious toleration, economical reform, and parliamentary reform—while commending him to some later historians, won little praise from the governing élite of Hanoverian Britain. Bentham thought that Lansdowne was muddle-headed, with a tendency to embrace grand schemes without fully understanding them, and though it would be difficult for anyone to attain Bentham's standards of rigour and logic, Lansdowne could become confused. His reluctance to delegate meant that he was often overworked: 'of all ministers', wrote one subordinate, 'he was the most difficult to please, never satisfied with what anyone did, or even what he did himself' (*Various Collections*, 6.283).　　JOHN CANNON

Sources *Life of William, earl of Shelburne … with extracts from his papers and correspondence*, ed. E. G. P. Fitzmaurice, 3 vols. (1875–6) • *The correspondence of King George the Third from 1760 to December 1783*, ed. J. Fortescue, 6 vols. (1927–8) • *The later correspondence of George III*, ed. A. Aspinall, 5 vols. (1962–70) • *The Grenville papers: being the correspondence of Richard Grenville … and … George Grenville*, ed. W. J. Smith, 4 vols. (1852–3) • Cobbett, *Parl. hist.*, 15.1251; 16.165–6, 181, 350, 477, 665, 1113–14; 17.905–17; 18.163, 282, 449, 923–4, 1220–21, 1270–72; 19.850, 1306–19; 20.40, 1156–69; 21.293–5, 319–27, 677, 682, 1023; 22.987, 1273–5; 23.200–01, 305–11, 551, 824; 25.855–64; 26.554–66, 573–84, 587–95; 28.939–48; 29.46–52, 441–8; 30.10–12, 1395;

31.598–602, 1269–74, 973; 32.534–9, 1564; 36.1505–7 · *Letters from George III to Lord Bute, 1756–1766*, ed. R. Sedgwick (1939) · J. Norris, *Shelburne and reform* (1963) · *Additional Grenville papers, 1763–1765*, ed. J. R. G. Tomlinson (1962) · Walpole, *Corr.* · J. Brooke, 'Calne', HoP, *Commons, 1754–90*, 1.408 · L. B. Namier, 'Petty, William, Viscount Fitzmaurice', HoP, *Commons, 1754–90* · J. Brooke, 'Petty, John Henry, Earl Wycombe', HoP, *Commons, 1754–90* · H. Van Thal, ed., *The prime ministers*, 2 vols. (1974) · J. Brooke, *King George the Third* (1972) · *The last journals of Horace Walpole*, ed. Dr Doran, rev. A. F. Steuart, 2 vols. (1910) · *The journal and correspondence of William, Lord Auckland*, ed. [G. Hogge], 4 vols. (1861–2) · *Diaries and correspondence of James Harris, first earl of Malmesbury*, ed. third earl of Malmesbury [J. H. Harris], 4 vols. (1844) · J. A. Cannon, *The Fox–North coalition* (1969) · J. A. Cannon, *Parliamentary reform* (1973) · *The Jenkinson papers, 1760–66*, ed. N. Jucker (1949) · *Autobiography and political correspondence of Augustus Henry, third duke of Grafton*, ed. W. R. Anson (1898) · Duke of Buckingham and Chandos [R. Grenville], *Memoirs of the court and cabinets of George the Third*, 4 vols. (1853–5) · *The political memoranda of Francis, fifth duke of Leeds*, ed. O. Browning, CS, new ser., 35 (1884) · *The diaries and correspondence of the Right Hon. George Rose*, ed. L. V. V. Harcourt, 2 vols. (1860) · H. Walpole, *Memoirs of the reign of King George the Third*, ed. D. Le Marchant, 4 vols. (1845) · *Correspondence of William Pitt, earl of Chatham*, ed. W. S. Taylor and J. H. Pringle, 4 vols. (1838–40) · G. Thomas, earl of Albemarle [G. T. Keppel], *Memoirs of the marquis of Rockingham and his contemporaries*, 2 vols. (1852) · Earl of Ilchester [G. S. Holland Fox-Strangways], *Henry Fox, first Lord Holland, his family and relations*, 2 vols. (1920) · H. R. Vassall, Lord Holland, *Memoirs of the whig party during my time*, ed. H. E. Vassall, Lord Holland, 2 vols. (1852–4) · J. Bentham, *Works*, ed. J. Bowring, new edn, 11 vols. (1962) · J. H. Jesse, *Memoirs of the life and reign of George III*, 3 vols. (1867) · G. B. Dodington, *Diary*, ed. H. P. Wyndham, 4th edn (1809) · I. R. Christie, *Myth and reality in late-eighteenth-century British politics, and other papers* (1970) · *The manuscripts of his grace the duke of Rutland*, 4 vols., HMC, 24 (1888–1905) · *The manuscripts of J. B. Fortescue*, 10 vols., HMC, 30 (1892–1927) · *Report on manuscripts in various collections*, 8 vols., HMC, 55 (1901–14), vol. 6 · *Third report*, HMC, 2 (1872) · *Fifth report*, HMC, 4 (1876) · *Sixth report*, HMC, 5 (1877–8) · L. S. Sutherland, 'Lord Shelburne and East India Company politics, 1766–9', *EngHR*, 49 (1934), 523–35 · *Correspondence of Charles, first Marquis Cornwallis*, ed. C. Ross, 3 vols. (1859) · A. Mitchell, *The whigs in opposition, 1815–1830* (1967) · F. G. Stephens and M. D. George, eds., *Catalogue of prints and drawings in the British Museum, division 1: political and personal satires*, 11 vols. in 12 (1870–1954), vol. 7, nos. 8440, 8624, 8648, 8681, 8826 · *Correspondence of John, fourth duke of Bedford*, ed. J. Russell, 3 vols. (1842–6) · Lord Kerry, 'King's Bowood Park', *Wiltshire Archaeological and Natural History Society Magazine*, 41–2 (1920) · *Memorials and correspondence of Charles James Fox*, ed. J. Russell, 4 vols. (1853–7) · *Passages from the diaries of Mrs Philip Lybbe Powys*, ed. C. Powys (1899) · countess of Minto [E. E. E. E. Murray Kynynmound], *A memoir of Rt Hon. Hugh Elliot* (1868)

Archives BL, corresp., Add. MS 9242 · BL, corresp. and papers · Bowood House, Wiltshire, Bowood MSS · priv. coll., political, personal, financial, and estate corresp., and papers [microfilm copy, Bodl. Oxf. MS films 1988–2032] · U. Mich., Clements L., corresp. and papers | Beds. & Luton ARS, corresp. with Lord Grantham · Beds. & Luton ARS, letters to Thomas Robinson · Birm. CA, letters to Matthew Boulton · BL, letters to Lord Auckland, Add. MSS 34418, 34461 · BL, corresp. with Jeremy Bentham, Add. MSS 33539–33542 · BL, letters to Lord Hardwicke and Sir R. M. Keith, Add. MSS 35526–35661, *passim* · BL, letters to Warren Hastings, Add. MSS 29134–29193, *passim* · BL, corresp. with Lord Holland, Add. MS 51682 · BL, corresp. with earl of Liverpool, Add. MSS 38192, 38309 · Bodl. Oxf., letters to Richard Price · CKS, corresp. with Lord Stanhope · College of William and Mary, Williamsburg, Virginia, letters to earl of Dunmore · Glos. RO, corresp. with Granville Sharp · Hunt. L., letters to Elizabeth Montagu · ING Barings, London, corresp. with Sir Francis Baring [copies] · Mount Stuart Trust, Isle of Bute, corresp. with Lord Bute · N. Yorks. CRO, corresp. with Christopher Wyvill · NL Ire., corresp. with Lord Bolton · NL Ire.,

letters to Lord Upper Ossory · NMM, corresp. with Sir Charles Middleton · NMM, corresp. with Earl St Vincent · priv. coll., corresp. with Lord Burke · PRO, corresp. with Sir Guy Carleton, PRO 30/55 · PRO, letters to earl of Chatham, PRO 30/8 · Sheff. Arch., corresp. with Lord Rockingham · Suffolk RO, Bury St Edmunds, corresp. with duke of Grafton

Likenesses J. Reynolds, oils, 1767?, Bowood House, Wiltshire [*see illus.*] · J. S. Copley, group portrait, oils, 1779–80 (*The collapse of the earl of Chatham in the House of Lords, 7 July 1778*), Tate collection; on loan to NPG · J. Sayers, caricatures, etchings, 1780–1800, NPG · F. Bartolozzi, stipple, pubd 1787 (after T. Gainsborough), BM, NPG · J. Reynolds, group portrait, oils, 1787–8 (with John Dunning and Colonel Barré), priv. coll. · etching, pubd 1794, NPG · S. W. Reynolds, mezzotint, pubd 1824 (after J. Reynolds, 1764), BM, NPG · G. F. Storm, group portrait, mezzotint, 1848 (after J. Reynolds), BM, NPG · J. Gillray, caricatures, etchings, NPG · J. Reynolds, oils (reduced copy of portrait, 1767?), NPG · Riley, stipple, NPG

Wealth at death income of approx. £50,000 p.a.: Fitzmaurice, *Life*

Pettyt, Thomas (*d.* 1556), surveyor and military engineer, is of unknown origins; all that is known of his family is that an Edmund Pettyt who was at Calais while Thomas was surveyor there may well have been related. Thomas appears first in 1542 'riding to Barwike about the King's affairs' (*LP Henry VIII*, 17, no. 482), and the next year was sent north again to inspect the conditions of Wark Castle at a time when Anglo-Scottish conflict threatened: probably he also resumed work on the defences of Berwick. He then appears to have accompanied the English army in its drive north in 1544 and 1545, when he was required to report on the potential of Ross Castle on the Isle of Bute to control Scotland's western approaches. In autumn 1545, however, he was in Calais, drawing up a map of the English holdings around the city, completed and signed in October. Early the next year he was appointed surveyor of Calais, a post he held until his death.

Towards the end of 1547 Pettyt was dispatched north again to survey and examine various fortified or fortifiable sites in the west marches of Scotland, and subsequently to advise on the further improvement of the defences of Berwick. It seems that he was not the official architect or consultant but rather the on-site manager; in this role he ensured that instructions from the principal engineers were carried out despite the shortage of money and manpower and the difficulty of the ground, all of which figure in his reports. In this capacity and as surveyor he was to remain in the borders or in Scotland during the English invasions.

When required to advise on a suitable site for an inland fort to protect English lines of communication, Pettyt proposed Lauder, and spent some months there in 1548. Although he did not stay long enough to complete the work, it was at least in an advanced state at his departure in June. This seems to be the only case where he supplied the design as well as organizing building operations, although it is possible that he was involved in fortifying Eyemouth. His structure at Lauder is now largely buried under later buildings, but a plan drawn up shortly after he left suggests that he had absorbed well the ideas of Italian engineers and the leading English engineers who were adopting their principles, notably in the modern form of the bastions. Merriman comments that the design shows 'sophistication and eccentricity' (Merriman and Summerson, 4.715). Lord Grey, the English commander, claimed that the whole Scottish army would not be able to capture such a strong fortress, whatever foreign aid they might have. His report was apparently accompanied by Pettyt's own plan, which has not survived.

In July Pettyt accompanied an English force that set out to reinforce Haddington, then besieged by the joint Franco-Scottish army. Finding the allied forces had given up the siege for the time being, and were retreating, the English sought to harass them; the allies then turned on them, pursuing them for several miles. Pettyt was among those captured, and wrote from prison in Edinburgh, to ask for an exchange. After his release he remained on the borders until almost the end of 1549. A substantial bonus was awarded him for his services over the two years. Once the English army had evacuated Haddington late in that year, Lauder was an obvious target. The allies were preparing to besiege it when, by the terms of peace signed at Boulogne in 1550, the whole area had to be returned to Scottish control; the fortress was abandoned and apparently dismantled.

Meanwhile Pettyt had returned to Calais, where he remained for the rest of his life apart from official visits to London. He was given instructions for improving the defences of Calais and outlying strongholds, including the replacement of a rounded bastion by one apparently more Italianate. These instructions were sufficiently important for Pettyt to have to report directly to Somerset, the lord protector, and even to be recorded in some detail in Edward VI's own chronicle for 1550. In such cases it is never clear how far these instructions may not have been his own recommendations, which he laid before the council, who then ordered him to carry them out; and how far he simply had to report on the state of particular structures, and then act on plans laid down by his superiors. Another map of Calais and the surroundings dating from this time is probably also by him. A few later references in 1552–3 mention his work as surveyor, carrying out various improvements to the fortifications, notably at the outlying stronghold of Guînes, but he died before December 1556, when John Rogers was appointed in his place. As Rogers was to be paid 'from the tyme of Petyte's death' (CPR, 1555–7, 527), and to have the same house for his residence, Pettyt's death must have been quite recent.

Pettyt's role as surveyor evidently included inspection and overseeing construction and repair of fortifications. Except at Lauder, however, he was a manager and supervisor rather than original designer. His two maps of the Calais territory of 1545 and c.1550 are in the British Library (Cotton MS Augustus I.ii.57B and Cotton MS Augustus I.ii.71 respectively). Plans and maps he made in Scotland are lost, although a plan of Lauder is now at Belvoir Castle.   A. G. KELLER

Sources H. M. Colvin, 'The king's works in France', *The history of the king's works*, ed. H. M. Colvin, D. R. Ransome, and J. Summerson, 3 (1975), 337–93 · M. Merriman and J. Summerson, 'The Scottish border', *The history of the king's works*, ed. H. M. Colvin and others, 4 (1982), 607–728 · *LP Henry VIII*, vols. 17–21 · *CSP Scot. ser., 1509–89* · *CSP dom., addenda, 1547–65* · *CPR, 1555–7* · *APC, 1547–52* · I. McIvor, 'Artillery and major places of strength in the Lothians', *Scottish weapons and fortifications*, ed. D. Caldwell (1981), 94–154
Archives BL, maps, Cotton MS

Petyt [Petit], **Thomas** (*b.* in or before **1494**, *d.* **1565/6**), printer and bookseller, was born in England but may have been related to the Parisian printer John Petit, who is said to have had printed books 'in thaundes of Thomas Petytt' in exchequer receipts (Duff, *Century*, 120). Nothing further is known of Petyt's origins, although he had property in Greenstead and Stanford Rivers, Essex, and a kinswoman named Agnes Vincent, in Sheppey, Kent. In his will he also describes himself as kinsman to Anthony Kitson, a former apprentice and a fellow bookseller in London. Petyt was freed as a member of the Drapers' Company by John Hutton in 1519, and was the first member of that company to become a printer. His shop was at St Paul's Churchyard at the sign of the Maiden's Head, from which he issued books from 1536 until at least 1561. He may have leased the property as early as 1523, when he was assessed for £10 in a lay subsidy as a resident of St Faith's parish. In 1547 he also freed the draper Thomas Raynald, who took over operation of his press while Petyt continued to publish and sell books from Maiden's Head. By 1548, some of his printing material had passed to William Hill.

Copies of fifty-nine editions printed by or for Petyt are extant. His name first appears in a 1536 edition of *The Rutter of the Sea*. His output was varied: he printed law books, including George Ferrers's translation of Magna Carta and royal proclamations; devotional material in Latin and English; and popular, vernacular works, including jest books, short chronicles, and herbals. He took a share in an edition of Chaucer's *Works* (1550?) with William Bonham, Richard Kele, and Robert Toy, and an edition of *Four Sons of Aymon* with Toy and John Walley (1554). These editions give some indication of his dealings with his close neighbours in Paul's Cross. His shop was next to that of Toy, who bequeathed property at the sign of the Bell 'adioinynge to Master Petitts house' to his widow in 1556 (Plomer, 12). Petyt was among those present in 1526 when the bishop of London issued his second set of injunctions to the booksellers (Reed, 173–5). Petyt is named, along with Bonham, John Reynes, Thomas Dockwray, Henry Tab, and Henry Pepwell, as one of the booksellers in arrears for his Paul's Cross property in September 1539, and with Toy again in the 1543–4 lay subsidy roll. More intriguing is a record of a case that came before the lord mayor in 1546, in which Petyt's servant Elizabeth Harwood confessed to attempting to murder her master and mistress by putting 'Ratsbane in her master's potte' (CLRO, Rep. 11, fol. 282v).

Petyt's career as a book producer began at the time of the Reformation, and his own religious affiliations apparently shifted with official policy. He printed Tyndale bibles for the king's printer, Thomas Berthelet, in 1539, and further editions under Edward IV, but issued works on behalf of the Catholic cause under Mary, including an edition of Richard Smith's *Brief Treatyse Settynge Forth Diuers Truthes*.

In 1543 the privy council imprisoned a bookseller by the name of Petye with Edward Whitchurch, Richard Grafton, John Byddell, William Middleton, John Mayler, Richard Lant, and Kele in Poultry Compter for producing and distributing unlawful books. If this was Petyt there is no way of determining the specific nature of his transgression, as the lists of 'Englisshe bokes off ill matter' each man was to produce have not survived (*APC*, 1542–7, 117).

By the time of his death Petyt was a powerful member of the Drapers' Company. Among his apprentices was Christopher Munday, father of the writer Anthony Munday. He was admitted to its livery in 1535 and was warden of the company for 1545–6, 1551–2, 1554–5, and 1561–2. Between 1545 and 1561 his name frequently appears in the company's records of assessments for gifts, loans, and subsidies, usually as one of the wealthiest men assessed.

Petyt died at some point between 18 May 1565 when he drew up his will and 13 February 1566 when it was proved by his wife and sole executor, Joanne (whose previous married name was Wood). Gefferey Finche of Greenstead is named supervisor. Petyt makes bequests to his wife's children by a former marriage: Marie, Margaret, Dennys, Elizabeth, William, and John Wood. He also makes bequests to a number of London stationers in addition to Kitson: William Riddell's widow, Abraham Veale, John Wight (whom Petyt freed in 1540), Thomas Wight (John's son and Petyt's godson), and the queen's printer, John Cawood. Notable among his other legatees is Steven Tenaunte, the lord treasurer's chaplain.

ALEXANDRA GILLESPIE

Sources STC, 1475–1640 · LP Henry VIII, 14/2.241 · APC, 1542–47, 107, 117, 125 · DNB · E. G. Duff, *A century of the English book trade* (1905) · will, PRO, PROB 11/48, sig. 4 · P. Blayney, *The Stationers' Company before the charter, 1403–1557* (2003) · P. W. M. Blayney, *The bookshops in Paul's Cross churchyard* (1990) · W. H. Phelps, 'Some sixteenth-century stationers' wills', *Studies in Bibliography*, 32 (1989), 48–59 · P. W. M. Blayney, *The bookshops in Paul's Cross churchyard* (1990) · E. G. Duff, 'Notes on stationers from the lay subsidy rolls of 1523–4', *The Library*, new ser., 9 (1908), 257–66 · H. S. Bennett, *English books and readers, 1475–1557* (1969), 195 · Arber, *Regs. Stationers*, 1.394 · M. Eccles, 'Anthony Munday', *Studies in the English Renaissance drama: in memory of Karl Julius Holzknecht*, ed. J. W. Bennett, O. Cargill, and V. Hall jr (1959), 97 · P. Boyd, *Rolls of the Drapers' Company of London* (1934), 144 · A. H. Johnson, *The history of the Worshipful Company of the Drapers of London* (1914–22), vol. 2, appxs 6, 10–14, 27, 31 · H. Plomer, *Abstracts from the wills of English printers and stationers from 1492 to 1630* (1903) · A. W. Reed, *Early Tudor drama* (1926)

Petyt [Petit], **William** (1641?–1707), lawyer and political propagandist, was born at Storiths, near Bolton Abbey, Skipton in Craven, Yorkshire, the son of William Petyt, a landowner and lawyer of Bolton Abbey and Barnard's Inn. He was educated at Skipton School and matriculated from Christ's College, Cambridge, in April 1660. He was admitted to the Middle Temple in 1664, called to the bar in February 1670, and appointed autumn reader in 1694. In 1701 he became treasurer of the Middle Temple. His brother Silvester (d. 1719) also enjoyed a career in law, serving as principal of Barnard's Inn (1715).

Known throughout his adult life as an assiduous student of English historical records, Petyt learned at the feet of the high tory archivist and lawyer Fabian Philipps. But his own political inclinations ran in a different direction. By the late 1670s he had become an active proponent of excluding Charles II's brother, the Catholic James, duke of York, from the throne, and he counted among his close associates some of the most radical whigs of the period. Thus he was the friend, protégé, and legal adviser of Arthur Capel, earl of Essex, who committed suicide while imprisoned for alleged complicity in the Rye House Plot. This relationship gave him access to the group of people around Essex's friend the earl of Shaftesbury, including James Tyrrell and perhaps John Locke. Petyt's circle also included such like-minded whig lawyers as William Atwood, whom he tutored in the ways of the historical archives, and Sir George Treby and Sir Francis Pollexfen, whom he supplied with legal precedents in Charles II's *quo warranto* proceedings against the City of London. In addition, Petyt was in touch with Gilbert Burnet, bishop of Salisbury, Henry Neville, William Post-Script Hunt, and Samuel Johnson—all associated with spirited and sometimes violent opposition to the late Stuart kingship.

Petyt's reputation rested upon his polemical contributions to this opposition, and, in particular, his service to the radical ancient constitutionalist cause during the exclusion crisis and at the revolution of 1688. Indeed, his powerful briefs on its behalf made him one of the most highly valued—and feared—of whig writers. This particular ideology, which was based upon medieval chronicles and manufactured texts such as the so-called laws of St Edward the Confessor, the *Modus tenendi parliamentum*, and the *Mirror of Justices*, had grown out of the civil wars of the 1640s, where it served, along with theories of natural law, to justify rebellion, regicide, and the establishment of a republic. Ancient constitutionalist theorizing, to which Petyt fully subscribed, began with the assumption that the governmental arrangements of pre-Norman England were the same as those that existed in Stuart England.

Although modern scholarship has shown that this whiggish version of the past, based as it was on spurious texts such as St Edward's laws, the *Modus*, and the *Mirror*, was wrong, most sixteenth- and seventeenth-century writers found both its sources and its stories of institutional continuity credible. In the late 1670s and early 1680s, however, the ancient constitutionalist construction fell under serious attack, as tories scrambled to repair the damage it did to the principle of indefeasible hereditary succession. First came the publication of Sir Robert Filmer's *Patriarcha* (1679), which was soon followed by the republication of his *Freeholder's Grand Inquest* (1680). The *Freeholder's* proved particularly dangerous to the ancient constitutionalist cause because it presented a wide range of arguments against the antiquity of the House of Commons, including evidence that the earliest extant writ to the house dated from 1265. If this line of reasoning, which would soon be reinforced by the powerful polemics of the high-tory historian Dr Robert Brady, went unrefuted, the ancient constitution would lose its claim to antiquity and the Commons would forfeit its right to participate as an equal with the king and the House of Lords. Put differently, this particular tory version of English history seriously undermined the whig argument for excluding the future James II from the throne.

It was in this charged and risky ideological atmosphere that Petyt wrote his immensely influential *The Antient Right of the Commons of England Asserted* (1680). One of the most effective and powerful of the radical ancient constitutionalist tracts published in the late seventeenth century, the work was deemed sufficiently weighty to warrant extended response from Brady, and it was cited approvingly by whigs such as Atwood and Tyrrell throughout the rest of the Stuart period. In his tract Petyt turned to medieval chroniclers such as Matthew Paris, Roger Hoveden, and Henry Huntingdon, and, above all, to St Edward's laws, the *Modus*, and the *Mirror*, to make his case for a legally sovereign parliament that now possessed the power to alter the succession because it had anciently done so. Although there was nothing new in the story Petyt told, he presented his arguments for the ancient constitution in a particularly powerful and compelling manner. To the tory denial of the Commons' antiquity, Petyt responded that St Edward's laws told how St Edward collected and reformed 'the ancient Saxon laws and added new ones *a Rege, Baronibus, & Populo*, that is, by king, barons, and people'. Thus, concluded Petyt:

> it is apparent and past all contradiction that the Commons in those days were an essential part of the legislative power, in making and ordaining laws, by which themselves and their posterity were to be governed, and that the law was then the golden metwand and rule which measured out and allowed the prerogative of the prince and the liberty of the subject.
> (W. Petyt, *The Antient Right*, 1680, 11–12)

Nor was this arrangement changed in 1066 or its aftermath, for William I and his successors kept St Edward's laws alive through a series of confirmations made in the coronation oath and in Magna Carta. This historical evidence gave the lie to tory claims that a Norman conquest had obliterated Saxon laws and institutions. Indeed, what else could the repeated confirmations of Saxon laws mean other than:

> that in the British, Saxon, and Norman governments, the commons (as we now phrase them) had votes, and a share in the making and enacting of laws for the government of the kingdom, and that they were an essential part of the *Commune Concilium Regni*, WittenaGemot, or parliament, before and after the supposed conquest of William the First.
> (W. Petyt, *The Antient Right*, 1680, 73)

Petyt also turned to the *Modus* and the *Mirror* to prove the high power of parliament and the king's subservience to the law made there. The *Mirror*'s message was particularly appropriate to his discussion of parliament's right to exclude the duke of York from the throne, for it told how 'parliaments were instituted *pur oyer & terminer les plaintes de tort de la Roy, de la Roigne & de lour Infans* … against whom the subject otherwise could not have common justice' (W. Petyt, *The Antient Right*, 1680, 40–41). Since the reign of a Catholic king would surely wrong the people of England, parliament necessarily possessed the power to alter

the succession. Moreover, this right was not merely theoretical. Indeed, Petyt wrote, it had been previously exercised on many occasions, as in, for example, the cases of William II, Henry I, and King John, who 'were elected kings of England having no hereditary right' (ibid., 46–7).

Although Petyt wrote several other political tracts in which he argued the ancient constitutionalist position (*Miscellanea parliamentaria*, 1680; *The Pillars of Parliament Struck at by the Hands of a Cambridge Doctor*, 1681; *Jus parliamentum*, 1739), none came close to attaining the status of *The Antient Right*. Its persuasive power gave Petyt a presence at the revolution of 1688. He was called, along with the leading common lawyers and judges of the day, to give counsel about what had happened in 1688 and 1689. When queried by the Lords about the Commons' resolution concerning the original contract, most members of the long robe admitted that English law had little to say. Petyt was less reticent. Turning to the radical ancient constitutionalist version of history, he told the Lords that in Germanic and Saxon times kings, who were elected by people and parliament, swore an oath at their coronation to uphold the law. This practice continued after the Norman invasion and characterized their present governmental arrangements. Here in the oath, Petyt strongly implied, could be found the contract that bound kings to the law, a contract which James II had presumably broken.

Although the Convention Parliament eventually reached a compromise in which the Bill of Rights contained no mention of contract, the radical ancient constitutionalism that Petyt had so well articulated constituted a primary, though by no means the only, justification for the revolution settlement.

Petyt was duly rewarded for his service to the cause. On 25 July 1689 William III appointed him keeper of the Tower records, in which position he replaced Brady, the favourite historian of late Stuart kings. There Petyt 'reigned … as a respectable scholar until the end of his days' (Pocock, 229).

Petyt died, unmarried, on 3 October 1707 at Chelsea and was buried in the west part of the Temple Church. In his will he provided for the building of a library in the Inner Temple to house his enormous collection of manuscripts and tracts, but his brother Silvester removed about 2000 pieces to his Yorkshire home (*A Catalogue of the Petyt Library at Skipton*, 1964). A monument to his memory and a portrait were placed in the Inner Temple.

JANELLE GREENBERG

Sources J. G. A. Pocock, *The ancient constitution and the feudal law*, 2nd edn (1987) · C. Weston and J. Greenberg, *Subjects and sovereigns: the grand controversy over legal sovereignty in Stuart England* (1981) · M. S. Zook, *Radical whigs and conspiratorial politics in late Stuart England* (1999) · J. Greenberg, *The radical face of the ancient constitution: St Edward's laws in early modern political thought* (2001) · H. Nenner, *By colour of law: legal culture and constitutional politics in England, 1660–1689* (1977) · H. Nenner, *The right to be king: the succession to the crown of England, 1603–1714* (1995) · *DNB* · Inner Temple Library, London, Petyt MS 512, vols. L, M, N, T · Inner Temple Library, London, Petyt MS 533, vol. 15 · Inner Temple Library, London, Petyt MS 535, vols. 1–3 · Inner Temple Library, London, Petyt MS 538, vol. 17 · Inner

Temple Library, London, Petyt miscellaneous MSS 61, 152 · L. G. Schwoerer, *The declaration of rights, 1689* (1981) · will, PRO, PROB 11/497, sig. 235 · Venn, *Alum. Cant.*
Archives BL, parliamentary collections, notes and papers, Lansdowne MSS 510–521 · BL, treatise on Saxon parliaments in reply to Robert Brady, Add. MSS 28600–28601 · Inner Temple, London, MS collection · NRA, priv. coll., cash book | PRO, catalogues of state papers, SP 46/165–167
Likenesses R. van Bleeck, oils, PRO, Gov. Art Coll. · R. van Bleeck, oils, Inner Temple, London · R. White, line engraving, BM, NPG
Wealth at death see will, PRO, PROB 11/497, sig. 235

Petzold, Gertrude von (1876–1952), Unitarian minister and public lecturer, was born in Thorn, East Prussia, of aristocratic ancestry. Her father was an officer in the Prussian army, while her mother instructed her thoroughly in the Lutheran catechism. After teacher training at a seminary, she soon became impatient of the limited opportunities afforded to women in Germany, and at the same time grew increasingly critical of the literal interpretation of Lutheran dogma. Not yet twenty, she made her way first to St Andrews University in Scotland (1895–7), then to Edinburgh University, where she spent four years, and thence in 1901 to Manchester College, Oxford, where she became the first woman to train for the ministry in England, and so qualified in 1904.

In order to pursue her vocation, von Petzold needed a church both sufficiently liberal in its theological stance and willing to accept a woman as its minister. The Free Christian (Unitarian) church in Leicester was to fulfil this role when—in competition with seven male candidates—the church's 150 members, determined to rise above convention, invited her unanimously to their pulpit. R. A. Armstrong wrote in *The Inquirer* (10 September 1904): 'We recognize the courage of her who tonight breaks a perverse and mischievous tradition'; while Joseph Wood at her induction as the first woman minister in England wondered if women might not have special qualities for ministry, 'considering that there were some 100,000 sermons delivered every Sunday by men' (*The Inquirer*, 8 Oct 1904).

Eloquent in the pulpit and on many a suffragist platform, von Petzold became a *cause célèbre* and her photo was sold on the streets of Leicester. She visited Berlin in 1906, lecturing on liberal Christianity, and conducted a German service in the American church there, the first woman ever to do so in Berlin. In 1907 she was the only European woman delegate to attend the Fourth International Congress of Religious Liberals in Boston, and in a lecture which outlined the role of women in the early Christian church she argued powerfully that in the twentieth century women's right to prophesy and minister should be restored.

In 1908 Gertrude von Petzold left Leicester for the United States and allied herself to a group of radical Unitarian women ministers working in Iowa and Illinois; she deputized for the Revd Mary Safford as chaplain in the state legislature in Des Moines. On returning to England in 1910, she became minister at Small Heath in Birmingham, where she declared her conviction 'There is no work in the world, except perhaps the slaughtering of other

Gertrude von Petzold (1876–1952), by Burton & Sons, 1904

people, that a woman cannot do as efficiently as a man if she is given the same training and opportunity' (*Christian Life*, 7 Jan 1911). She attracted large congregations and was much in demand as a speaker: notably at King's Weigh House Church in London, where she lectured on Luther, Calvin, and Wycliffe; and in 1911, on another visit to Germany, when she preached at the Lutheran church in Bremen and at the Swiss Reformed churches in Zürich and Basel, speaking generally on the ministry of women. In England R. J. Campbell, proponent of the New Theology, thought her 'one of the most brilliant women speakers of the day, a scholar of repute' (newsletter of Macclesfield Congregational Church, 1911). She freely associated with religious liberals of all denominations and stated that she was keen to unite 'Trinitarians, Unitarians, Baptists, Methodists, Swedenborgians, Churchmen, Agnostics and avowed Atheists'. Unitarians, she thought, were sometimes too conservative!

By now the First World War was in progress and von Petzold's application for naturalization had lapsed because of her time in America. Despite the support of civic leaders in Leicester and Birmingham both for her and 'her friend and helper' Rosa Widmann, her application and Rosa's were turned down and they had to return to Germany. Here, at length (1917), she became pastor of the Free Evangelical congregations in Königsberg and

Tilsit—the only free churches in East Prussia—before taking a PhD and becoming a lecturer in English at Frankfurt University.

As a committed internationalist von Petzold promoted Anglo-German relations whenever possible, even in the first year of the First World War before she was deported, and anti-German feeling resulted in arson at the Small Heath church. Between the wars she made several trips to England motivated by the desire for reconciliation. And soon after the Second World War she wrote an article for *The Inquirer* (9 August 1947) entitled 'English refugees in Germany', having observed among the bombed ruins of Frankfurt the shell of the Weissfrauenkirche, which in the sixteenth century had sheltered a congregation of English refugees of the reformed faith who had fled persecution in the reign of Mary Tudor and had found there 'a large-minded benevolence and understanding which would never be wiped out of the hearts of the English people' (*Christian Register*, Sept 1952)—a silver goblet presented by the English community in 1558 still testifies to the fact. Gertude von Petzold saw it as a significant reminder of the deep-rooted associations between England and Germany. Her large sympathies remained clear at the time of her death in 1952, when she was devoting her energies to the cause of refugees then flocking into West Germany from eastern Europe. She died at Bad Homberg, near Frankfurt, West Germany, on 14 March 1952.

Gertude von Petzold's involvement as a woman in liberal religious developments in Britain, Germany, and America in the first half of the twentieth century, and in the women's movement, especially with regard to suffrage, earns her a niche of no little significance and interest.   KEITH GILLEY

Sources K. Gilley, 'Gertrude von Petzold', *Transactions of the Unitarian Historical Society*, 21/3 (1995–8), 157–72 · *The Inquirer* (1904–15) · *Christian Life* (1904–15) · C. Wendte, ed., *Freedom and fellowship in religion* (1907) · A. Clarke, *The first woman minister* (c.1940) · C. Lyttle, *Freedom moves west* (1952) · *Forty portraits and biographical sketches for the 4th International Congress of Religious Liberals* (1907) · *Christian Register* (24 Sept 1908) · *Christian Register* (Sept 1952) · R. V. Holt, *The Unitarian contribution to social progress in England* (1938) · A. Ruston, *The Hibbert Trust: a history* (1984) · *Growing together: feminist theology* (1983) [Unitarian report] · I. ap Nicholas, *Heretics at large* (1977)
Likenesses Burton & Sons, photograph, 1904, priv. coll. [*see illus.*]

Peulan [St Peulan, Paulinus] (*fl.* **6th cent.**), holy man, was known in the middle ages as a famous teacher, but remains largely a shadowy figure of probable Carmarthenshire origins. His feast day is celebrated on 22 November. No explicit account of his life and deeds survives, although he is noticed occasionally in the twelfth-century lives of other Welsh saints. However, it has been argued that the first book of the *Vita sancti Pauli Aureliani*, composed by the Breton monk Wrmonoc in 884, which describes the supposed Welsh origins of St *Paul of St Pol-de-Léon (sometimes called Paulus Aurelianus or Paulinus), is based in part on traditions about the Carmarthenshire Peulan whom the author sought to identify with his subject—whether correctly or incorrectly is not certain.

Although the *Vita* begins by attempting to identify its subject with yet another Welsh saint, Paul of Penychen in Glamorgan, it immediately shifts to locate Paul's origins in Llandingad, near Llandovery, in Carmarthenshire. Following a period of study under St Illtud at Llantwit Major, he is said to have become a hermit at Llanddeusant (also in Carmarthenshire), before moving to Cornwall and eventually migrating to Brittany with his twelve disciples. The second book of the *Vita* describes Paul's arrival on the island of Ushant off the coast of Finistère and his subsequent move inland to found the monastery at St Pol-de-Léon, of which he was ordained bishop. This apparently confuses the seventh-century Frankish saint Philibert, who might ordain, with the Merovingian king Childebert I (*r.* 511–58), who could not.

How much of Wrmonoc's narrative, especially the exclusively Breton material, can be associated with the Carmarthenshire Peulan is difficult to determine. Some later Welsh saints' lives also preserve traditions relating to Peulan, often contradicting those given by Wrmonoc. For example, Rhigyfarch's *Vita sancti Davidis* (*Rhigyfarch's Life*, chap. 10) claims that St David spent a number of years studying under Paulinus 'the scribe' or 'teacher' on an unidentified island called 'Wincdi-lantquendi'; and it is claimed (ibid., chap. 49) that it was he who would later urge the other bishops to invite David to attend the Synod of Llanddewibrefi. This Paulinus is said to have previously been a disciple of 'Germanus the bishop', that is Germanus of Auxerre, who visited Britain in 429 and c.445. This connection with St Germanus is incredible chronologically, given the approximate dates of St David's life. On the other hand, the *Vita sancti Kebii* refers to a Peulan as a disciple of St Cybi, whom some have therefore identified with the Carmarthenshire Peulan, though this appears to be a different saint of alleged Manx origins and patron of Llanbeulan on Anglesey. Furthermore, the *Vita sancti Teliaui* in the Book of Llandaff names St Teilo among the disciples of the 'wise man' Poulinus. Whether Peulan was a disciple of Illtud, Germanus, or even Cybi, or of none of them, is impossible to determine with any certainty; and similarly, the traditions that saints David and Teilo were among his own disciples may reveal more about his later reputation as a teacher than historical fact.

Nevertheless, that there had been a St Peulan underlying these various later notices seems probable, given the existence of a handful of dedications to a saint of that name in Carmarthenshire, including the churches of Capel Peulin and Nant-bai and a holy well known as Ffynnon Beulin all in the parish of Llandingad; and in addition, at Llan-gors in neighbouring Brecknockshire lie the churches of Llanbeulan and of Llan y Deuddeg Sant ('Church of the Twelve Saints', perhaps echoing the twelve disciples of Paul Aurelian). In Brittany, there are various dedications to Paul Aurelian, mostly but not wholly in Finistère, an area which also contains a concentration of dedications to the Brecknockshire saints of the family of Brychan. Finally, it has been argued that the Carmarthenshire St Peulan may be identifiable with the Pavlinvs, 'Preserver of the Faith, constant lover of his country, ... the devoted champion of righteousness', whose grave is marked by one of the early Christian memorial stones found at Maes Llanwrthwl in Cynwyl Gaeo, near Llandovery. The location of the inscription would certainly support the identification, though if correct, it would undermine an identification with Paul Aurelian as described in the second book of Wrmonoc's *Vita*, since he is said there to have died and been buried in Brittany.   DAVID E. THORNTON

Sources A. W. Wade-Evans, ed. and trans., *Vitae sanctorum Britanniae et genealogiae* (1944) · C. Cuissard, ed., 'Vie de S. Paul de Léon en Bretagne d'après un manuscrit de Fleury-sur-Loire', *Revue Celtique*, 5 (1881–3), 413–60 · *Rhigyfarch's Life of St David*, ed. J. W. James (1967) · J. G. Evans and J. Rhys, eds., *The text of the Book of Llan Dâv reproduced from the Gwysaney manuscript* (1893) · V. E. Nash-Williams, *The early Christian monuments of Wales* (1950) · G. H. Doble, *Lives of the Welsh saints*, ed. D. S. Evans (1971) · G. H. Doble, *The saints of Cornwall*, pt 1 (1960) · E. G. Bowen, *Saints, seaways, and settlements in the Celtic lands* (1969) · inscription on memorial stone, Maes Llanwrthwl, Cynwyl Gaeo, Dyfed, Wales

Peulevé, Henri Leonard Thomas [Harry] (1916–1963), secret operations officer, the only son of Leonard Otho Peulevé and his wife, Eva Juliet Dallison, both of British nationality, was born on 29 January 1916 at Worthing, where his mother and sister were temporarily in refuge from the German invasion of France. The family home was in Paris where Leonard Peulevé represented a firm of British seedsmen until the outbreak of war in 1914 when he joined the British army. At the time of his son's birth he was a staff sergeant-major in the Army Service Corps. When the fighting in France became stabilized as trench warfare, his wife returned with the two children, moving from one place to another as her husband's unit was posted from this sector to that.

The Peulevé agency in France was not revived after the war and the family's wanderings continued while Peulevé sought to make a living, shuttling back and forth between France and England, with a period in Algiers where for a time he was British vice-consul. Thus Harry Peulevé's upbringing was as unsettled as his education was varied. His many schools included a nuns' kindergarten in Algiers, the Shakespeare School at Stratford upon Avon, Rye grammar school, private schools and tutors in England and France, and finally a technical college in London where he took courses in telegraphy and wireless which led him to his first job, as technical assistant in the Baird Television Company. From this he went on to the British Broadcasting Corporation in the early days of television, became a cameraman, and was so employed at the outbreak of war in 1939 when he joined the army.

Peulevé was commissioned in the Royal Army Ordnance Corps, worked on the first radar equipment, and later transferred with the rank of captain to the Royal Electrical and Mechanical Engineers (REME), whence in 1942, as one of the earliest volunteers, he was seconded to Special Operations Executive (SOE), the paramilitary body created by the British joint chiefs of staff to organize and conduct clandestine warfare in enemy-occupied territories. Peulevé could not have been better fitted for such a task: he was bilingual and could pass as a Frenchman in France; his loyalties to that country and to Britain were equal, indivisible, and dedicated; he had an ingrained ability to make the best, even to take advantage, of the unpredictable; and he was already a specialist in wireless communication as both technician and operator. As though these qualifications were insufficient, nature had provided him with a well built body, broad-shouldered and suggestive of considerable physical strength. Large grey-green eyes which could on occasion compel without frightening were allied with a persuasiveness remarkable in that it was always muted and made acceptable by his charm of personality. These attributes came together in developing his powers of leadership in circumstances where difference and independence in the men he commanded in the field were uncontained by the disciplines of military training. A final gift stood him in great stead in outwitting and escaping his enemies: he was able to withdraw mentally, to make his mind still in the presence of those he did not want to notice him—a surer disguise than any false beard or dark glasses.

After training in a secret agent's special skills by SOE, Peulevé parachuted into the Pyrenees area on the night of 30 July 1942, but, by the pilot's error, he was too low for safe landing and broke a leg. He escaped across the mountains on crutches into Spain where he was imprisoned; he got away and reached England in very poor physical condition. After recuperating he volunteered to try again. In September 1943 he was landed safely by light aircraft and established himself in the Corrèze area and extended his influence to the northern Dordogne. He trained and armed a large group of resistance fighters which in the course of the following months reached some 3000 men whom he led in extensive sabotage operations, on occasions joining battle in running fights with German occupation troops and inflicting considerable casualties. He acted throughout as his own radio operator in maintaining contact with SOE in London, organizing regular airdrops of supplies of arms and equipment for his increasing forces, as well as agents to assist him.

Despite the Gestapo's determined efforts to find and capture him, Peulevé evaded them until by a stroke of bad luck he was erroneously denounced as a black marketeer and arrested while operating his radio set, on 21 March 1944. Interrogated under torture he refused to talk, and the enemy never discovered who he was and the important part he had played in the clandestine war. Imprisoned in solitary confinement at Fresnes for almost a year, he attempted escape, was shot and wounded in the thigh, and, since he was refused medical treatment, himself removed the bullet with the aid of a spoon. Eventually he was taken to Buchenwald where, on the eve of his execution, he was chosen by F. F. E. Yeo-Thomas as one of the two agents who with himself changed identities with Frenchmen dying of typhus. As one of the prison's forced labour group Peulevé was more easily able to escape (11 April 1945); but he was recaptured almost within sight of an advancing American unit by two Belgian SS. He persuaded the two men of the danger of being captured in uniform, suggested they undress, and while they were doing so seized one of their pistols and made them his prisoners, then delivered them to the Americans. He was appointed to the DSO, made a chevalier of the Légion d'honneur, and received the MC and Croix de Guerre.

After the war Peulevé worked for the Shell Oil Company in several European countries, Egypt, and Tunis. In 1952 he married Marie-Louise Tetens John, a Danish woman; they had a son and a daughter. Peulevé died at the Hotel Alfonso XIII in Seville, of a heart attack on 18 March 1963.

SELWYN JEPSON, rev.

Sources *The Times* (25 March 1963) · M. R. D. Foot, *SOE in France: an account of the work of the British Special Operations Executive in France, 1940–1944*, 2nd edn (1968) · M. R. D. Foot, *Six faces of courage* (1978) · private information (1981) · personal knowledge (1981) · CGPLA Eng. & Wales (1963)
Wealth at death £3116 13s. 0d.: administration, 9 Sept 1963, CGPLA Eng. & Wales

Peverel [Peverell], **Thomas** (d. 1419), bishop of Worcester, was said by John Bale in the sixteenth century to have been of good birth, but no connection has been established with any of the several notable families with his surname. He was a member of the Carmelite friary at Bishop's Lynn, Norfolk, by 1377, and became BTh of Oxford University. On 31 July 1387 he was summoned before the lord mayor and aldermen of London, for reasons unknown. On 17 June 1392 he attended the trial of the heretic Henry Crump at Stamford, and in the following year was appointed second *socius* to the prior-general of his order. On 25 October or 3 November 1395 he was papally provided to the see of Ossory in Ireland, with restitution of temporalities on 4 February following. This was a see under English control, but Peverel secured licence to live in England on 19 May 1396, and nominated attorneys in Ireland on 30 July. His translation on 12 July 1398 to Llandaff was said by the pope to be from Leighlin, another see in the English pale, but this seems a simple error. The temporalities were restored on 16 November.

Although there is no explicit evidence, it seems very probable that he was among the handful of monks and friars whom Richard II kept around his court in his last years, to considerable criticism. Indeed, on 17 March 1399 he was appointed chancellor to the child Queen Isabella. The fall of the king ended any such role at court, but Peverel was never implicated in any die-hard Ricardian plotting. Probably, he devoted himself quietly to his little Welsh diocese, whence in the summer of 1402 he was forced to flee by Owain Glyn Dŵr's rebels. This at least would have ensured any necessary reconciliation with the Lancastrian crown, and on 12 May 1405 he received letters of protection to go with Henry IV on a projected expedition into Wales. However, his diocese remained too dangerous to occupy, especially as Glyn Dŵr had now developed firm plans for an all-Welsh episcopate under the Clementist obedience. Peverel was obliged to mark time as a suffragan for Bishop Henry Beaufort, performing ordinations at Winchester on 6 March 1406, and on 12 March and 5 May 1407.

On 4 July 1407 Peverel was translated to Worcester, receiving his temporalities on 20 November. This was quite notable preferment for a man of his background, especially from a dynasty that had usurped his original patron. Presumably the crown wished to make plain its firm support for anyone who had fallen foul of rebellion against itself. The promotion did not mean that Peverel now had any active public role under the dynasty, although he attended parliaments regularly. He settled down to run his diocese. Archbishop Thomas Arundel once had occasion to remind him formally to observe the constitutions of the province, but his register suggests that he was a conventionally conscientious diocesan, willing and able to move around between his residences. His register ends in 1417—both the general *acta* (April) and his record of ordinations (August)—but this seems more likely to be a misfortune of survival than sure evidence of suddenly failing powers. He died intestate (as his order required) on 1 March 1419 and was buried in the Carmelite house in Oxford. He seems to have had an equivocal reputation. While John Bale described him 150 years later as a scholar of long standing and an admired preacher, an opponent in the papal curia in 1407 said he was 'of evil life and bad character … a simple-minded man, ignorant of law and insufficient in learning' (Bodl. Oxf., Arch. Selden B.23, fols. 113v–114). With Peverel, it was very much a matter of the light in which he was viewed.

R. G. DAVIES

Sources R. G. Davies, 'The episcopate in England and Wales, 1375–1443', PhD diss., University of Manchester, 1974, 3, ccxviii–ccxix · Emden, *Oxf.* · episcopal register, Herefs. RO, b.716.093 – BA.2648/5(ii) · BL, Harley MS 3838 fol. 91r–v [John Bale] · William Swan's letter-book, Bodl. Oxf., MS Arch. Selden B.23
Archives Worcs. RO, register

Peverel, William (b. c.1090, d. after 1155), baron, was the son of a father of the same name, an important Domesday tenant-in-chief in the north midlands, and Adeline. His father, who had custody of Nottingham Castle from 1068, and of the Castle of the Peak in Derbyshire (later named Peveril Castle), died on 28 January 1114; his mother was still alive in 1130. Their children were William, Adelise (b. c.1080), who married Richard de Revières, and Matilda. Peverel witnessed c.1109 his father's foundation charter for the Cluniac priory at Lenton, near Nottingham, and some royal charters in the 1120s. He was twice married, first, c.1115, to Oddona, and second, c.1145, to Avice, daughter of William of Lancaster. William of Lancaster was one of the honorial barons of the honour of Lancaster, then controlled by Ranulf (II) of Chester. With Oddona, Peverel had a son William (described as his heir in a charter for Garendon Abbey), who predeceased him, a son Henry, who may also have predeceased him, and a daughter, Margaret, who married Robert de Ferrers, earl of Derby.

Peverel, like his father, served as a royal agent under Henry I, particularly in forest matters, though he was less frequently at court. At Northampton in September 1131, if not earlier, he would have sworn to accept the succession of the empress; but he attached himself to Stephen on his accession, and witnessed his charter of liberties of April 1136. He took a prominent part in the civil war of Stephen's reign, and ultimately suffered forfeiture for backing the wrong side. He fought for Stephen at the battle of the Standard in August 1138 and at the battle of Lincoln in

February 1141, when he was captured. He thereby lost control of Nottingham Castle, which was given to Ralph Paynel, who had instigated an attack on it by Robert of Gloucester in the previous year. About this time Robert de Ferrers took the title of earl of Nottingham. In 1142 Peverel's knights recaptured the castle and town of Nottingham, and expelled from it 'all who were in favour of the empress' (Symeon of Durham, 2.312). These events were not forgotten when the civil war drew to its close. When Duke Henry landed in England in 1153 he granted Ranulf (II), earl of Chester, the lands of William Peverel, 'unless in my court he is able to clear himself of charges of wickedness and treason' (*Reg. RAN*, 3, no. 180). The reference is to the charge that Peverel had earlier attempted to poison Ranulf of Chester while a guest in his house. When Ranulf did die later in the year, the story was not forgotten.

Nottingham Castle had been burnt in the summer of 1153, and it may be presumed that William Peverel lost control at that time, for no security in respect of it was asked for in the peace settlement later in the year. Peverel's lands were forfeit in February 1155 when Henry, by now king, marched against him. Peverel, who had earlier taken the cowl in one of his religious houses, probably Lenton Priory, fled the area, and was not heard of again. 'The lands of William Peverel' were accounted for separately in the pipe rolls throughout Henry II's reign.

EDMUND KING

Sources GEC, *Peerage* · W. Farrer, *Honors and knights' fees … from the eleventh to the fourteenth century*, 1 (1923) · *Reg. RAN* · K. R. Potter and R. H. C. Davis, eds., *Gesta Stephani*, OMT (1976) · John of Hexham, 'Historia regum continuata', Symeon of Durham, *Opera*, vol. 2 · *The historical works of Gervase of Canterbury*, ed. W. Stubbs, 2 vols., Rolls Series, 73 (1879–80) · John of Worcester, *Chron.* · *Pipe rolls* · J. A. Green, 'Earl Ranulf II and Lancashire', *Journal of the Chester Archaeological Society*, 71 (1991), 97–108 [G. Barraclough issue, *The earldom of Chester and its charters*, ed. A. T. Thacker] · M. Jones, 'The charters of Robert II de Ferrers, earl of Nottingham, Derby and Ferrers', *Nottingham Medieval Studies*, 24 (1980), 7–26 · D. Williams, 'The Peverils and the Essebies, 1066–1166', *England in the twelfth century* [Harlaxton 1988], ed. D. Williams (1990), 241–59

Wealth at death £315—value at which 'the lands of William Peverel' were farmed in the approximate year of his death

Peverell, Thomas. *See* Peverel, Thomas (*d.* 1419).

Peverell, William, of Nottingham. *See* Peverel, William (*b. c.*1090, *d.* after 1155).

Pevsner, Sir Nikolaus Bernhard Leon (1902–1983), architectural historian, was born in Leipzig on 30 January 1902 into a Russian-Jewish family, the younger son (there were no daughters) of Hugo Pewsner, later Pevsner (1869–1940), a successful fur trader, and his wife, Annie Perlmann (*d.* 1942). Pevsner's parents had migrated to Leipzig some time before 1900, and took German citizenship in 1914 (when they also changed the spelling of their surname from Pewsner to Pevsner). Nikolaus's elder brother died in 1919, his father in 1940; his mother committed suicide two years later to avoid internment in a concentration camp.

Sir Nikolaus Bernhard Leon Pevsner (1902–1983), by Paul Joyce, 1975

Early years: 1902–1933 Pevsner was educated at St Thomas's School, Leipzig, became a Lutheran convert in 1921, and attended the universities of Leipzig, Munich, Berlin, and Frankfurt. In 1923 he married Karola (Lola) Kurlbaum, also a Lutheran, and 'the most important influence on his life' (Murray, 501); her mother was of Jewish descent, but not her father, the distinguished appeal lawyer Alfred Adolf Kurlbaum. The Pevsners had two sons and a daughter, all of whom survived him, but Lola died of an embolism on the lung in 1963.

With his doctoral thesis on the baroque merchant houses of Leipzig completed in 1924, Pevsner was subsidized by his father and father-in-law and so could combine regular reviewing with holding an unpaid post from 1924 to 1928 as assistant keeper at the Dresden Gallery. Pevsner's *Leipziger Barock* (1928) grew out of his thesis, and in the same year he contributed on mannerist and baroque Italian painting to the *Handbuch der Kunstwissenschaft*; this series was a precedent for the multi-volumed Pelican History of Art, which he edited from 1953. It was in the 1920s that Pevsner acquired the approach to art history from which he never publicly retreated. It owed much to the influence of Wilhelm Pinder, whose Hegelian determinist perspective emphasized the impact on art and architecture of both national character and the 'spirit of the age'.

Pevsner often later described himself as a 'general practitioner' among art historians, as distinct from the more specialist 'consultants', but it was indeed an achievement to unite the study of art, architecture, and design; to relate all three to social context; and to cover so long a time-span. His range soon broadened still further, both intellectually and geographically, for in 1925 he had been deeply impressed by the modern style in visits to Gropius's Bauhaus in Dessau and to Le Corbusier's Pavillon de l'Esprit Nouveau at the Paris Exhibition. Discussing William Morris, Gropius in the late 1920s told Pevsner 'I owe him so very much'—a remark which enhanced Pevsner's interest in English architecture. Already fluent in Italian, he now set about mastering English language and culture, and made a research trip to Britain in 1930. Attached to the University of Göttingen as a self-funded lecturer from 1928, he lectured on English architecture in the art history department and occasionally in the philosophy faculty.

An English refuge: 1933–1942 Events in Germany in 1933 unexpectedly lent a new priority to Pevsner's English research, for in that year the Nazi race laws forced him out of his lectureship. In later years he did not publicly discuss what view he had then taken of Nazism. Suffice it to say that later in the year he left Germany for Britain, but not until 1935 did he bring his wife and three children from Göttingen to England. Given that his father's fur-trading business had suffered in the recession after 1931, Pevsner was now in several respects on his own. But at crucial stages in his career his eye for opportunity was alert, and he made the most of the two-year fellowship (1934–5), funded by the Academic Assistance Council and by supporters at Birmingham University, which he held under Philip Sargant Florence in the university's department of commerce. Francesca Wilson, Pevsner's landlady in Edgbaston, gave him crucially important moral support at this time, and eventually became a friend. It was Florence who suggested that Pevsner investigate English industrial design. From this came Pevsner's *An Enquiry into Industrial Art in England* (1937), dedicated to Lola and with a quotation from William Morris as epigraph: 'what business have we with art at all, unless all can share it?' The question of design, Pevsner insisted, 'is a social question', and the elimination of shoddy goods 'becomes a moral duty' (N. B. L. Pevsner, *An Enquiry into Industrial Art in England*, 1937, 11). 'Appalling', 'shocking', 'depressing', and 'meretricious' are words which recur in the book.

Pevsner believed that in the relatively egalitarian context of the machine age, art must reflect the needs of the mass consumer, not the tastes of the rich patron. In catering for the consumer, the role of the state would be central: state planning, town planning, and social engineering would now come into their own. With standardized products and buildings commissioned by anonymous patrons marshalled in committees, architects and designers would become servants of the public, driving out the sham materials and technique of traditionalist ornamentation. And if, as Pevsner believed, the consumer as well as the manufacturer and the retailer needed a voice in design, a further role for the state opened up, for both artist and consumer needed educating—with help from art schools slanted more firmly towards the practical and the vocational. Pevsner viewed Herbert Read's *Art in Industry* (1934), linking good design to the pursuit of economic justice, as 'the most outstanding book on the subject … his approach is arresting, his outlook European' (N. B. L. Pevsner, *An Enquiry into Industrial Art in England*, 1937, 173). Pevsner saw a role, too, for the employer with a sense of social responsibility, and in 1935 met the distinguished furniture maker Gordon Russell, in whose Wigmore Street showroom he became a buyer, thereby obtaining his only secure income for several years. Cambridge University Press wanted a second edition of the *Enquiry* in 1948; Pevsner thought that by then the book needed rewriting, so made his inter-war notes and much guidance available to Michael Farr for his *Design in British Industry: a Mid-Century Survey* (1955).

At this remarkably creative period in his career, Pevsner was in a position to draw together his diverse interests into the broad-ranging and moralistic analysis of modern architectural history which in two influential books laid the foundation for his career in England as an architectural historian. The first was his amply illustrated and much translated *Pioneers of the Modern Movement from William Morris to Walter Gropius* (1936), which carried forward the research he had begun in the early 1930s on English architecture; it went through several editions and revisions. His analysis was not original; as so often during his career, Pevsner was exploiting the refugee's prize asset: alertness to cultural contrast. He was familiarizing Britain with art-historical ideas already widely accepted in Germany.

The modern style seemed, for Pevsner in 1936, as he later recalled, 'the coming of the Millennium' (3 Dec 1966; Games, 295). He believed that industrial society required entirely new types of building, new approaches to the architect's profession, and new patterns of patronage; funding by committee, inevitable in the mass society, entailed new materials and a modern utilitarian and impersonal style. The English contribution to the modern style had been crucial, he thought, for the architectural tradition that ran from Pugin to Ruskin to Morris to Voysey, and Lethaby had at last cultivated a social conscience among designers and architects, encouraging pride in workmanship and preoccupation with everyday needs. Furthermore, English engineers—most notably in the Crystal Palace (1851)—had demonstrated what new materials could achieve.

Yet architecturally, about 1900, said Pevsner, England 'gave up' (25 July 1951; Games, 125). It was not, he thought, sufficient merely to repudiate the machine: new techniques, materials, and styles must be embraced, not shunned, otherwise mass demand could never be satisfied. Art nouveau transferred to the continent Morris's concern with craftsmanship while at the same time freeing the architect from period styles, and also occasionally drawing architect and engineer together in the use of new materials. England's timid neo-classical alternative, dominant between 1900 and 1940, Pevsner dismissed as sometimes pleasant, sometimes pretentious, but as leading nowhere. Yet even art nouveau focused unduly on surface decoration, and before the modern style could prevail, the heroic effort of 'my giants' (11 Feb 1961; Games, 272) was required—Behrens, Gropius, and others from Europe, but also Frank Lloyd Wright. By 1914 these courageous and imaginative pioneers had fused the English arts and crafts tradition with machine production to launch the modern style: rational, economical, orderly, healthy, moral, international, inevitable. In this new style for a new age, form must reflect function, and in Frank Pick, proponent of modern design on London's underground in the 1930s, Pevsner saw the English Morris tradition revived through effective teaching by example: some might see Pick, 'the ideal patron of our age' (1942; N. B. L. Pevsner, *Studies in Art, Architecture and Design II*, 1968, 209), as authoritarian, but Pevsner felt there was a place for humane dictatorship, and if the passenger did not see the good in Pick's improvements, 'he must be made to see it, gently but firmly' (ibid., 208).

War lent Pevsner the label 'enemy alien', and in 1940 he was interned in Huyton under wartime regulation 18B. This was ironic, given his inclusion in that anti-Nazi pantheon the 'Black Book', for there the chief of the German counter-espionage bureaucracy listed those designated for 'protective custody' after a successful German invasion. Pevsner's friends, including Pick, quickly secured his release and he was among the first commissioned to write for the Ministry of Information's *Die Zeitung*, an anti-Nazi organ for Germans in England. Also in 1940 Pevsner published his *Academies of Art, Past and Present*. It was dedicated to Pinder, a Nazi sympathizer who had remained in Nazi Germany. This dedication can be variously interpreted—as Pevsner's politically naïve expression of deeply felt personal obligation to his mentor, or as a regrettable compromise with a detestable regime.

Popular educator: 1942–1955 After briefly working as a labourer clearing rubble from bombed London streets, Pevsner consolidated his position. He contributed regularly to the pace-setting *Architectural Review*, and consolidated a link with Penguin Books by editing, from 1941 (following the death in an air raid of Elisabeth Senior, the founding editor), the series of King Penguins. These miniature picture books had short texts by distinguished scholars, and included his own *The Leaves of Southwell* (1945), on the carved foliage in the chapter house. In 1942 he was appointed part-time lecturer at Birkbeck College, University of London; he accepted the offer of work from the Architectural Press, so that from 1942 to 1945 the editorship of the *Architectural Review* was largely in his hands; and he tightened his Penguin link by publishing his Pelican paperback, *An Outline of European Architecture*. Even more influential than *Pioneers*, it pushed back to the sixth century AD the argument he had set out in 1936, while retaining all the cultural breadth of the earlier book; only 160 pages long and modestly priced, it went into seven editions and was translated into sixteen languages. Modernist architects had shed the nineteenth-century role of designing façades in outdated historical styles for uncultivated patrons, he said, and the 'new kind of beauty and order' that industrialization had made possible was now

within their grasp (N. B. L. Pevsner, *An Outline of European Architecture*, 1942, 138).

Pevsner lectured at Birkbeck until he retired in 1969, and from 1959 was professor of the history of art. He was naturalized in 1946, and became a star in the galaxy of German scholarly talent that took refuge in the United Kingdom. The imprints Phaidon and Thames and Hudson constitute a reminder that Jewish refugees were revolutionizing art publishing in Britain during Pevsner's prime. But whereas for some German refugee art historians the Warburg Institute became a haven from British life, Pevsner was remarkable for the completeness of his assimilation. He grew to love the variety of the English scene, and in a feat of cultural adaptation he became thoroughly fluent as an English stylist. Although his accent never lost its foreign tinge, this if anything enhanced his appeal, and he became a familiar, attractive, and respected radio personality around whom affectionate anecdotes clustered. This was a time when the Reithian improving ideal of BBC radio had yet to be abandoned, when the Third Programme was an important scholarly medium, when there were high hopes of adult education in Britain, and when Penguin paperbacks eagerly catered for them. Pevsner was in tune with all these trends.

Following the success of his *Outline*, the publisher Sir Allen Lane asked Pevsner what he would like to tackle next. This evoked two suggestions, both immediately accepted. One was for an ambitious historical series on art and architecture, which he would edit; the Pelican History of Art, launched in 1953, covered a huge span. But it is Pevsner's other suggestion, for a series of county-by-county guides to British architecture, that made him a household name. The *Buildings of England* series was inspired by the *Handbuch der deutschen Kunstdenkmaler* founded by Georg Dehio in 1900, and Pevsner agreed to produce two volumes a year, a target usually achieved, though not always with ease. Work began in 1945, and the series was launched with its first three volumes in 1951. It was completed in forty-six volumes, latterly with help from collaborators, in 1974; others later extended it to Scotland, Wales, and Northern Ireland. Following popular usage, the name Pevsner Architectural Guides was adopted for the series in 1998.

By the late 1950s a regular pattern of publication, one or two volumes in the series per year, had been established. Much help came from Pevsner's wife, who established the annual Pevsner working cycle. Two refugee German ladies, succeeded by graduate assistants, gathered published material on a county's buildings, then Lola drove Pevsner all over the country to view them. If anything, her death increased his determination, and graduate students took over the driving. The working day began early and ended late, meals were snatched, accommodation was modest, organization was tight. 'He worked as if quietly but very surely possessed', Michael Taylor recalled. 'Our record was nineteen parishes in a day, that is nineteen churches, say some forty other buildings and an assortment of other features of interest.' In the evening, while his assistant prepared for the next day's visits, 'the Professor went to his room and wrote up everything he had seen that day … so when we got back to London the book was finished and needed only the introduction' (Bradley and Cherry, 13–14). Pevsner thought it essential to write up on the day, 'with iron determination; otherwise all would go dim and dead. No lunch or dinner invitations are accepted' (Pevsner, 240). Sheer lack of time may be one reason why, as some later complained, he neglected social contact with the owners of country houses who might have helped his studies.

Convenient, informative, incisive, sometimes amusing, and even quirky in their vocabulary, these volumes were a revelation even to those who knew and loved English towns and villages. The pre-war Little Guides series published by Methuen, insular and antiquarian, was immediately supplanted by Pevsner's comprehensive coverage: buildings of every type featured from all periods, and were seen in European perspective. By the 1970s his guides had become a national institution—'mentioned in Pevsner' being a weapon deployed in planning enquiries and official reports. Error was inevitable in volumes so speedily produced, and some important buildings were omitted, but here as elsewhere Pevsner's scholarship was unusual in reconciling itself to temporary imperfection. It was important to get the volumes out: revised and ampler editions could later polish them up, for Pevsner readily learned from his critics and made adjustments. 'Don't be deceived, gentle reader', he wrote on completing the *Buildings* series, 'the first editions are only *ballons d'essai*; it is the second editions which count' (Murray, 508). Furthermore, selections from *The Buildings of England* could be published later, as *The Cathedrals of England* (ed. Priscilla Metcalf, 1988) demonstrated—bringing together as it did his lucid and authoritative accounts of their development and place in European architecture. Yet *The Buildings of England* never paid: Allen Lane once introduced Pevsner at a prize-giving dinner as his best-losing author, and from 1955 subsidies proved necessary from the Leverhulme Trust and other funding bodies.

John Betjeman was among the critics of the series, grumbling privately to James Lees-Milne in 1952 about 'that dull pedant from Prussia' (Betjeman, *Letters*, 23), publicly complaining in the same year that 'the Herr-Professor-Doktors are writing everything down for us, sometimes throwing in a little hurried pontificating too' (Betjeman, *First and Last Loves*, 15), and anonymously and damagingly reviewing Pevsner's volume on Durham in the *Times Literary Supplement* for 3 July 1953. Pevsner did indeed match some aspects of the Germanic professorial stereotype: spectacled, bright-eyed, and with a puckish smile, he lived simply, worked incessantly, and was wholly dedicated to scholarship and the arts—walking and swimming constituting his only recreations. Yet he belied the stereotype with his self-deprecating sense of humour, his lively and responsive conversation, his concise and often witty letters, and his capacity for relating to the young. He was no dryasdust chronicler and categorizer: his writings breathe enthusiasm for art and architecture, and words and phrases such as 'delicious', 'delightful', 'impeccably satisfactory' abound. Furthermore it was to Pevsner among others that Betjeman turned for help when defending Victorian buildings against demolition in the 1960s. The preservationist Victorian Society, of which Pevsner was a founder member and chairman from 1963 to 1976 and life president thereafter, could weld into a powerful combination both Betjeman's romantic nostalgia and Pevsner's vision of the Victorians as modernist pioneers.

Pevsner in 1946 had referred to the Victorians' 'complete ethical blackout … in matters of aesthetics' (N. B. L. Pevsner, *Visual Pleasures from Everyday Things*, 1946, 10). His view mellowed, but he retained his concern of the late 1920s at the artist's precarious situation in modern society. Through studying the social history of art he hoped to find a way out, and Birkbeck College constituted for him a congenially earnest environment. His was a sustained attempt to overcome the suspicion of art, widespread in mid-twentieth-century England, by alerting ordinary people through his lectures and writings to the role of art and architecture in their everyday life. Between 1945 and 1977 he gave seventy-eight talks to the BBC's domestic audience and another fifteen in its German-language service. He was Slade professor of fine art at Cambridge in 1949–55 and at Oxford in 1968–9, but the high point in his broadcasting career was 1955, when he delivered the BBC's annual Reith lectures on 'The Englishness of English art', revised for publication in 1956.

Pevsner was a skilful broadcaster, well able to generate in the listener a sense of shared discovery, and cultivating the slightly colloquial intimacy appropriate to a one-to-one conversation. His subject-matter, 'national character as it is expressed in terms of art' (16 Oct 1955; Games, 175), involved complementing his historical approach to art and architecture with a geographical slant. Echoing the somewhat complacent English national self-image prevalent at the time, he tried to link distinctive traits in English art and architecture not only to environmental factors such as the English climate, but to such alleged English social-psychological characteristics as reasonableness, compromise, detachment, empiricism, understatement, and belief in continuity. The argument was complex and at times confusing, and many of the alleged linkages were questionable; there were too many internal contradictions and admitted exceptions to generalization for any clear interpretation to stand out or carry conviction. But the lectures made a considerable impact at the time, securing Pevsner's objective of encouraging deeper thought about art, as well as about the importance of the English contribution to it.

Achievements and challenge: 1955–1983 Pevsner's flow of books, talks, and articles was unceasing, and though he was selective in his social engagements he was active and effective on numerous time-consuming public committees. He accumulated several honorary degrees at home and abroad, was appointed CBE in 1953, elected FBA in 1965, and knighted 'for services to art and architecture' in 1969. His career coincided with the remarkable boom in the serious study of art and architecture in Britain after 1945. Several of its leading practitioners contributed to *Concerning Architecture*, a book of essays edited by Sir John Summerson and presented to Pevsner on his birthday in 1968. Its affectionate introductory note likens the book to a family album whose members 'honour you for what you have achieved among us and in the world at large'.

Pevsner also seemed to be riding on the crest of a modernist wave. 'I was an ardent modern in the 1930s', he declared in 1961, 'and I still am' (11 Feb 1961; Games, 274). From the start *The Buildings of England* had innovated by including modern-style buildings among its illustrations. 'Today only the weaker hearts are attracted to the past', he wrote in 1954, referring to fashions in contemporary architecture, whereas 'the exploring and the consistent' had for twenty years been gathering under the modernist banner (N. B. L. Pevsner, 'Originality', *Architectural Review*, June 1954, 369). In successfully backing Holford's relatively informal plan for rebuilding the area round St Paul's Cathedral in London, Pevsner helped his adopted country to resume its one-time central role in advancing the modern style, and by the late 1950s in the City of London he was championing the excitements of the Barbican against neo-Georgian timidities. The Coldstream reports were guiding British art schools towards the vocationalism and the accommodation between art and industry that Pevsner had recommended late in the 1930s, and new buildings 'designed by Georgian-Palladian diehards' could, he said, 'be left to die of old age' (N. B. L. Pevsner, 'Modern architecture and the historian, or, The return of historicism', *Journal of the Royal Institute of British Architects*, April 1961, 230). As a member of the Historic Buildings Council's listing committee in 1967–8, he took care to ensure that the most vulnerable among significant modern-style buildings were on the list, subsequently endorsed, which he had himself originated. In the discussion following his lecture in April 1961 on 'Modern architecture and the historian' at the Royal Institute of British Architects, nobody questioned his assumption that the modern style was in some sense 'rational', and in the preface to the third (Pelican, 1960) edition of his *Pioneers of the Modern Movement* he could claim that 'the main theses of, and the principal accents in, this book did not call for recantation or revision, which is a happy thought for an author looking back over twenty-five years' (N. B. L. Pevsner, *Pioneers of the Modern Movement*, 3rd edn, 1960, 18).

He had thought it necessary, however, while retaining the sub-title 'From William Morris to Walter Gropius', to modify the book's title. Its second edition (1949) had become *Pioneers of Modern Design*, for 'historical fairness … made it imperative to show up the line which runs from Gaudi and the Art Nouveau to the present Neo-Art-Nouveau—by way of the Expressionism of the years immediately after the First World War'; indeed, he went on, 'now we are surrounded once again by fantasts and freaks' (N. B. L. Pevsner, *Pioneers of the Modern Movement*, 3rd edn, 1960, 17). His lecture of 1961 was prompted by a schism within the modernist camp. The fact that some modernists were diluting the pure functionalist gospel

was for him 'an alarming recent phenomenon' (N. B. L. Pevsner, 'Modern architecture and the historian, or, The return of historicism', *Journal of the Royal Institute of British Architects*, April 1961, 230); some were even displaying 'undisciplined individualism' and doing 'funny turns', seeking to be 'original at all costs' (11 Feb 1961; Games, 276–7). The bold collaboration between James Stirling and James Gowan in their influential engineering building at Leicester University was among the modernist ventures which worried him, and by 1966 he feared that architects' personality cults were, as in the case of the 'expressionists'—art nouveau's architects and the expressionist architects of 1917–27—obscuring the functionalism which was at the heart of modernism.

By the 1970s, modernist buildings which Pevsner had praised for their honesty, utility, and rationality were, at least in the British context, proving less practical than had been expected, and, according to Reyner Banham, 'Pevsner-bashing' had become 'an accepted academic field-sport', especially among his pupils (Banham). David Watkin, a young fellow of Peterhouse, Cambridge, included Pevsner among the influential moralizing high priests of secularism who were less tolerant and benign than they appeared. Watkin's influential *Morality and Architecture* (1977) detected in the early Pevsner an 'essentially determinist approach to art and architecture' (Watkin, *Morality and Architecture Revisited*, 86), whereby the architect becomes the mere instrument of the prevailing socialistic intellectual and social climate, his repertoire constricted, his creativity devalued, his autonomy cramped. In a letter to Watkin, Sir John Summerson praised Watkin's book, though this perception did not influence Summerson's article on Pevsner for the *Dictionary of National Biography*. Pevsner, who suffered a minor heart attack in August 1977, did not reply to Watkin. In his last published work—his amply illustrated *A History of Building Types* (1976)—Pevsner had pursued somewhat mechanistically what had long been an important modernist concern, consistent also among his own interests since the 1920s, when few had shared it: that is, a preoccupation with how social change prompts architects and others to cater for new functions with new designs.

Pevsner's last years, marred by Parkinson's disease, were spent at 2 Wildwood Terrace, Hampstead, which had long been his home. He died there on 18 August 1983, and was buried in the churchyard of Clyffe Pypard, the village near the Pevsners' family cottage. His tombstone, shared with his wife, characteristically wastes no words: 'Lola Pevsner born Kurlbaum 1902–1963 and Nikolaus her husband 1902–1983'.

Concluding assessment Pevsner's energies carried him through decades as a productive scholar and skilful educator into a world that the young admirer of Gropius in 1925 had not envisaged. Late twentieth-century architectural historians became less concerned to explain (with Pevsner) why the modern style had failed to arrive earlier—more preoccupied with understanding how that style could ever have been embraced with such fervour, and how it could ever have been seen as architecture's final destination and culmination. The English pedigree which Pevsner lent to the modern style can as readily be seen to anticipate the 'period' twenty-first-century starter-home as any modernist structure of the 1960s. In later life he came to see virtues in some of the significant British architects whom with his modernist perspective he had earlier dismissed; as early as April 1951, for example, he reached a more nuanced view of Lutyens in the *Architectural Review*, and in 1976 he was ready to assign listed status to twentieth-century buildings not in modern mainstream—they were, after all, he said, 'also part of history' (Cherry, 'The "Pevsner 50"', 106).

The modern style's history and evolution were inevitably central in any synoptic interpretation of recent architectural history, and the publishing history of his books shows in itself how effectively Pevsner's analysis stimulated a generation thirsting for guidance in this area. Yet he was never an original theorist, and for all his enthusiasm for 'reason' in style and design, his strength lay elsewhere: in patiently accumulating and classifying information over an impressive span in time and space. In decades of substantial books, broadcasts, and articles for the *Architectural Review*, Pevsner accumulated an unrivalled grasp of European art and architecture, and generously encouraged others to do the same. The edifice was crowned by his formidable *Buildings of England*, a work which Watkin himself pronounced 'almost incredible', for which 'our debt of gratitude can never be adequately expressed' (prefatory note of 1975; Watkin, *Morality and Architecture Revisited*, 4). Others might be visually more discerning, more assiduous in pursuing archival sources, more alert to the interaction between great houses and their contents, but none was as encyclopaedic, energetic, and evangelical in promoting architectural and aesthetic appreciation in the country of his adoption.

Nor should Pevsner's achievements of character and personality be neglected: not just his industry, but also his capacity for uniting an exhaustive preoccupation with detail to the broadest and most fearless generalization, his skill at moving easily between the library and the public forum, his willingness to complement private study with carrying out public responsibilities, his concern to make his scholarship readily accessible, and his courage in drawing the utmost cultural benefit from his enforced move in his thirties from Germany to England. Whatever debt he owed to his island refuge was more than amply repaid.   BRIAN HARRISON

Sources DNB · *The Times* (19 Aug 1983) · N. Pevsner, 'Pevsner in the car pocket', *The Bookseller* (28 Jan 1967), 240–42 · J. Summerson, ed., *Concerning architecture: essays on architectural writers and writing presented to Nikolaus Pevsner* (1968) · R. Banham, 'Pevsner's progress', *TLS* (17 Feb 1978), 191–2 · P. Murray, *PBA*, 70 (1984), 501–14 · D. Watkin, 'Sir Nikolaus Pevsner: a study in "historicism"', *Apollo*, 136 (1992), 169–72 · G. Stamp, 'Pevsner e l'Inghilterra', *Nikolaus Pevsner: la trama della storia*, ed. F. Irace (Milan, 1992) · B. Cherry, *The buildings of England, Ireland, Scotland and Wales: a short history and bibliography*, 2nd edn (1998) · T. Mowl, *Stylistic cold wars: Betjeman versus Pevsner* (2000) · S. Bradley and B. Cherry, *The buildings of England: a celebration compiled to mark fifty years of the Pevsner architectural guides* (2001) · D. Watkin, *Morality and architecture revisited* (2001) [rev. edn of *Morality and architecture* (1977) with new preface, prologue, and epilogue] · M. Rosso, *La storia utile: patrimonio e modernità nel lavoro di John Summerson e Nikolaus Pevsner: Londra 1928–1955* (Turin, 2001) · S. Games, ed., *Pevsner on art and architecture: the radio talks* (2002) · B. Cherry, 'The "Pevsner 50": Nikolaus Pevsner and the listing of modern buildings', *Transactions of the Ancient Monuments Society*, new ser., 46 (2002) · J. Betjeman, 'Love is dead', *First and last loves* (1952); pbk edn (1960) · *John Betjeman: letters*, 2: *1951 to 1984*, ed. C. Lycett Green (1995) · d. cert. · private information (2004)
Archives Tate collection, corresp. with Lord Clark
Likenesses photograph, 1954, Hulton Getty · P. Joyce, photograph, 1975, NPG [*see illus.*]
Wealth at death £292,968: probate, 10 Nov 1983, *CGPLA Eng. & Wales*

Pevzner, Neyemiya Borisovich. *See* Gabo, Sir Naum (1890?–1977).

Peyronnet, Frances de [*née* Frances Whitfield], **Viscountess de Peyronnet in the French nobility** (1815–1895), journalist, was born on 15 April 1815 in the West Indies, the daughter of George Whitfield, a lawyer and West Indian sugar plantation proprietor, and his wife, Georgina Pauline, *née* Ross (b. 1791). The family were originally from Scotland. Not long after her birth Frances was taken to England by her mother, along with her sister and brother, to live in Feltham, Middlesex. Her father remained in the British West Indies, where he died at St Vincent in 1819. He had been a classical scholar and a lover of literature; an early sign that Frances shared similar propensities came on her fifth birthday, when her mother presented her with a prayer book and was surprised to find her able to read it immediately.

In 1822 or 1823 the family left England, perhaps for reasons of economy, to live in Boulogne, where Frances attended a school run by a Miss Cruikshanks. She already knew some French, having been taught by a refugee curé from the terror. About three years later the Whitfields moved to Paris, and Frances's mother married the Vicomte Monod de Béranger. Frances herself soon married into the French aristocracy; her wedding to the Vicomte Jules de Peyronnet (1804–1872) took place in the first half of the 1830s, and they had a son, who died young, and three daughters. Her father-in-law was Comte Pierre-Denis de Peyronnet, an author and a minister of the lately deposed Charles X. He disapproved of his son's marriage to an English protestant, and stopped his allowance; thanks to the income from the Whitfield sugar plantations, however, they were able to tour Europe in style. Later, with the gradual abolition of slavery in the English West Indies, this source of revenue began to dry up, and they (and her mother) moved to St Vincent in 1840. Alarmed that their two elder daughters were starting to speak Creole, they returned to France about 1844.

After the revolutions of 1848 the de Peyronnets started to suffer real financial hardship, and it must have been necessity that drove Frances to journalism. She wrote—chiefly reviews of French books—for *The Athenaeum* (c.1851–2), and for the *Edinburgh Review* (1852–69); a review of Victor Hugo's *Les misérables* was among her contributions. Henry Reeve, the latter journal's editor, became a friend, and once lent her his London home for a visit. From 1863 she also wrote for the *Pall Mall Gazette* and the

Journal de Débats. She probably did much of the translation work for her husband's French edition of Macaulay's *History of England* (1861).

Frances de Peyronnet is now best known for her work as a correspondent of *The Times* during the Franco-Prussian War (1870–71). Her identity was kept secret at the time, and there was much speculation as to who the author was. As the articles were strongly critical of the French government and people, she feared for her safety if her authorship were revealed. A second reason for the concealment was that one of her daughters, Laura, had married Arthur Russell, MP for Tavistock, and brother of Odo Russell, a British diplomat attached to Bismarck's headquarters at Versailles. The first of her columns, signed 'A French Correspondent', appeared on 11 July 1870. She dealt mainly with social life in Paris during the conflict and siege, but was not shy of expressing her hostility to the French government of Napoleon III (her husband's sympathies, certainly, had been with the second republic) and her admiration for Bismarck, whom she compared to Richelieu and Pitt. She recognized the difficulties of achieving due impartiality: 'I catch myself involuntarily grasping my pen like a sword, with which it would be sweet to smite and utterly destroy all those who, by pandering to popular passions and popular ignorance, have brought us to our present pass' (Pitman). She earned £5 per column, paid into Arthur Russell's bank account. At times during the siege the de Peyronnets subsisted on boiled rice and red wine, which she used to make sauces; to file her copy, she resorted to balloon post, to carrier pigeons, and once to training a servant to pass as English so that he might get through the lines. Her last column, a retrospective, was published on 7 February 1871, three weeks before the Prussians entered Paris.

In the late 1880s Frances de Peyronnet and her unmarried daughter Madeleine took a house in Brighton. She died in London on 8 July 1895.   MARTIN RUSSELL

Sources press cuttings of articles by Frances de Peyronnet, corresp., MSS, priv. coll. • papers of Lady Mary Isobel Browne, priv. coll. • correspondence of Frances de Peyronnet, News Int. RO, *The Times* archive • J. Pitman, 'Secret despatches from Paris by balloon', *The Times* (22 Dec 1994) • [S. Morison and others], *The history of The Times*, 2 (1939), 415, 422 • *Wellesley index* • 'The Athenaeum index of reviews and reviewers, 1830–1870', www.soi.city.ac.uk/~asp/v2/home.html, Sept 2002 • *CGPLA Eng. & Wales* (1895)

Archives priv. coll., press cuttings of articles, corresp., MSS | News Int. RO, *The Times* archive • priv. coll., papers of Lady Mary Isobel Browne

Wealth at death £5892 15s. 3d.: probate, 29 July 1895, *CGPLA Eng. & Wales*

Peyto family (*per.* 1487–1658), gentry, held land in Warwickshire from the reign of Edward I and acquired the manor of Chesterton by marriage in the fourteenth century. They established their seat there, rebuilding the manor house with a fine collection of armorial glass (later recorded by William Dugdale) in order to emphasize the position of the family among the county élite. They also held land in the vicinity of Sowe, near Coventry. The misfortunes of Sir William Peyto (*d.* 1464) in the 1440s, when he was captured and ransomed in France and returned to

England heavily in debt, led to the mortgaging of his family's three manors in Warwickshire, and their fortunes had not fully recovered when his son and grandson died within a month of each other in 1487, leaving a nine-year-old heir **John Peyto** (1477/8–1542). John's mother, Godith, was the daughter of Sir Thomas Throgmorton of Fladbury, Worcestershire, a marriage with a local gentry family which indicates the lowering of the Peytos' horizons [*see* Throgmorton family]. It was at Fladbury that his father, Edward, died, apparently while living with his brother-in-law Robert Throgmorton—he had not entered, indeed had refused to enter, on his father's estate. John's wardship was acquired by his uncle. He had three brothers, including Cardinal William *Peto, and one sister. The manor of Barton on the Heath had apparently passed out of the family's hands in the 1470s, but Godith (who lived until 1502) continued to claim the advowson as dower. She also claimed forty-two virgates of the manor of Chesterton, worth 20 marks, and a third of the manor of Wolfhamcote. John retained five messuages and six virgates of Chesterton, also worth 20 marks.

John Peyto married Anna, daughter of Richard Cooke of Coventry, mercer, with whom he had two sons, John and William. The family kept extensive flocks of sheep and these, combined with a marriage to mercantile wealth, helped to restore their fortunes. After the death of his first wife John married Margaret, daughter of Sir John Baynham, with whom he had several more children. The manor of Wolfhamcote was divided between the sons of his second marriage for their lives, and by John's will the lease of the tithes of Harbury parsonage was left to their mother for her life, granting her the power to bequeath them to any of their children. Apart from bequests to servants and the poor the remainder of his goods were left to his wife. As overseer of his will he appointed William Whorwood, the solicitor-general. Despite being the brother of a cardinal the wording of his will suggests that he was an enthusiastic protestant. His widow lived until 1554 and was survived by two sons and five daughters. Apart from small bequests to her two stepsons she left the goods from the clearly well-furnished house at Chesterton, her money, and her sheep to her own children and other relatives.

John died in 1542 and was succeeded by his eldest son, **John Peyto** (*d.* 1558). About 1541 he married Anne, daughter of Sir John Ferrers of Tamworth, Staffordshire, with whom he had a son. The misfortune of his father's succeeding as a minor was compounded by the younger John's being declared mad in 1553, five years before his death on 11 September 1558. Consequently the manor of Chesterton was settled on the latter's son **Humphrey Peyto** (*c.*1542–1585) on his marriage to Anne, daughter of Basil Fielding of Newnham, in 1553. It appears that Anne already had a son, John, at the time of her marriage; he is referred to in Humphrey's will as 'my Sonne and Freinde John Fildinge alias Peyto' (PRO, PROB 11/68, fol. 175r). Humphrey Peyto died in March 1585. The funeral monument erected at Chesterton according to the instructions in his will shows that Humphrey and Anne had six sons, of whom one died in childhood, and four daughters. In the will itself Humphrey refers to three sons, including John, and three daughters, of whom Godith was married to John Wyrley of Hampsted, Staffordshire, and the other two were left marriage portions of 1000 marks. Anne lived until 1604. Humphrey had clearly inherited his grandfather's staunch protestantism, expressed in the preamble of this will and reflected in his concern for the sermons to be preached at his funeral and at a memorial service a year later by a 'learned preacher'.

Humphrey was succeeded by his son **William Peyto** (b. before 1564, d. 1619), who married Elianor, the daughter of Sir Walter Aston of Tixall, Staffordshire, about 1582. She was the aunt of Sir Walter Aston (1584–1639), James I's ambassador to Spain in 1620, and it may have been this connection that led to their elder son, Edward, receiving part of his education abroad. A younger son, William, entered the Middle Temple and became a barrister, while their daughter Anne married Edward Ferrers of Baddesley Clinton, Warwickshire. Despite their staunch protestantism the Peytos seem to have been influenced more by considerations of property and kinship than by religion in their choice of marriage partners. The Astons, Ferrers, and Wyrleys were all families with Catholic connections. The family occupied a position just below the élite of Warwickshire society, but there were indications that their fortunes were improving. William served as sheriff in 1603–4 and his son **Sir Edward Peyto** (c.1591–1643) was knighted on 4 February 1611. The manor of Wolfhamcote was sold to its tenant in 1613, the year in which Sir Edward obtained permission to travel abroad for three years to learn languages. The latter succeeded his father on his death in 1619. Once more the wealth of the family was affected by the survival of a widow, as Elianor lived until 1636.

Although Sir Edward's wealth and status would have been sufficient to have secured him appointment as a JP had his estate been in the north of the county, the concentration of gentry in southern Warwickshire and his frequent absences from the county ensured that he was never selected. His yearly income was at least £500, and he was an energetic landowner who undertook various schemes of improvement such as brick making and woad growing. He was also a man of wide intellectual interests, reflected in a library of more than 600 books. Among these was a notable collection of architectural works, indicating an interest manifested in his construction of a classical watermill and circular windmill at Chesterton in 1632. He also commissioned Nicholas Stone to design his father's tomb in 1639 and repaired an ancestral monument in the collegiate church at Warwick. His marriage to Elizabeth (d. after 1658), daughter of Sir Adam *Newton of Charlton, Kent, and niece of Sir Thomas Puckering of Warwick, drew him into the most significant kinship network within the Warwickshire gentry in this period. There were two sons of the marriage. He was staunchly protestant and following the outbreak of the civil war he acted as an inspiring second in command to Lord Brooke. He commanded the garrison of Warwick Castle, which refused to yield when the town fell in 1642. When summoned, a red flag of defiance was hung out, to which Sir Edward added a bible and a winding sheet to symbolize his willingness to die in defence of holy scripture. His role as lieutenant-general of the artillery in Essex's army until his death on 21 September 1643 suggests that he had some military experience, possibly gained during his education abroad.

Unlike his father, **Edward Peyto** (1625–1658) was educated at Oxford, where he graduated BA in 1641. He subsequently entered the Middle Temple (in 1646). In the civil war he held a short-lived command as a colonel in Denbigh's army. He was a JP from July 1646 until his death and served as sheriff in 1654–5. When the Warwickshire militia was reformed in 1650 he was one of the four colonels appointed. However, he was comparatively uninvolved in local politics and was inactive as a justice after serving as sheriff, although he did sit as a county MP in 1656. The evidence suggests that during the interregnum he became suspicious of the government and increasingly unsympathetic to the regime. Following his death in 1658 the aggressively anti-Calvinist Thomas Pierie, who preached at his funeral, described as the only blemish on Edward's otherwise exemplary life his having been persuaded by his father to become an active parliamentarian, to his later regret. He had married Elizabeth (b. 1622), daughter of Greville Verney of Compton Verney, Warwickshire, in 1647 and they had three sons and three daughters. The house at Chesterton had been damaged during the civil war and had 'mushrumps growing in the top of the chambers for want of tiling' (Shakespeare Birthplace Trust, DR 37/88/65). Inheriting his father's architectural interests, Edward initiated its rebuilding in a classical style by John Stone, in the process of which the armorial glass recorded by Dugdale was destroyed. He died shortly afterwards, directing in his will that this work should be completed.

The fortunes of the Peyto family were yet again adversely affected by the comparatively early death of its head, which left an underage heir, younger children, a mother and a widow to be supported. This lack of an adult male representative prevented the Peytos from fully establishing their position within the Warwickshire gentry at the time of the Restoration. Chesterton does not appear in the hearth tax returns, presumably because the rebuilding was then unfinished; its cost, amounting to more than £2000, represented a further significant drain on the family's resources. Nevertheless the family once again gradually recovered their fortunes. Edward's heir, also Edward, died young and was succeeded by his brother William (d. 1699), who served as sheriff in 1695. His son William (d. 1734) lived in some state at Chesterton, sat in parliament for Warwickshire from 1715, and kept a pack of foxhounds. He never married, whether from lack of inclination or because his estate was insufficient to support both a taste for good living and a wife and children is unclear. He died intestate, apparently strangled by his own neckcloth after over-indulging at a dinner at Warwick Castle. As his brother Edward had also died without an heir they were succeeded in the estate by their aunt

Margaret, the last of the direct Peyto line, from whom it passed to her Verney relations at her death in 1746. The legacy was sufficient to induce John Verney, Lord Willoughby de Broke, to alter his family's name to Peyto-Verney as had been stipulated by his cousin.

JAN BROADWAY

Sources A. Hughes, *Politics, society and civil war in Warwickshire, 1620–1660* (1987) · C. Carpenter, *Locality and polity* (1992) · *VCH Warwickshire*, vol. 5 · 'Chesterton, Warwickshire', *ArchR*, 118 (1955), 115–18 · W. Dugdale, *The antiquities of Warwickshire illustrated* (1656) · G. Tyack, *The making of the Warwickshire country house, 1500–1650*, Warwickshire Local History Society, occasional paper, 4 (1982) · G. Tyack, *Warwickshire country houses in the age of classicism, 1650–1800*, Warwickshire Local History Society, occasional paper, 3 (1980) · wills, PRO, PROB 11/29, fol. 167r [John Peyto]; PROB 11/37, fols. 43v–44r [Margaret Peyto]; PROB 11/68, fols. 174r–177r [Humphrey Peyto]; PROB 11/298, fol. 88r–88v [Edward Peyto] · Shakespeare Birthplace Trust RO, Stratford upon Avon, DR 37/88/65, 473/293
Archives Shakespeare Birthplace Trust, Willoughby de Broke collection
Wealth at death manor of Chesterton valued at 40 marks late fifteenth century; income approx. £500 p.a. mid-seventeenth century: *VCH Warwickshire*; Hughes, *Politics* · wills, PRO, PROB 11/29, fol. 167r [John Peyto]; PROB 11/37, fols. 43v–44r [Margaret Peyto]; PROB 11/68, fols. 174r–177r [Humphrey Peyto]; PROB 11/298, fol. 88r–88v [Edward Peyto]

Peyto, Sir Edward (c.1591–1643). *See under* Peyto family (*per.* 1487–1658).

Peyto, Edward (1625–1658). *See under* Peyto family (*per.* 1487–1658).

Peyto, Humphrey (c.1542–1585). *See under* Peyto family (*per.* 1487–1658).

Peyto, John (1477/8–1542). *See under* Peyto family (*per.* 1487–1658).

Peyto, John (d. 1558). *See under* Peyto family (*per.* 1487–1658).

Peyto, William (b. before 1564, d. 1619). *See under* Peyto family (*per.* 1487–1658).

Peyton, Sir Edward, second baronet (1587/8–1657), parliamentarian political writer, was the eldest of the five sons (there were also six daughters) of Sir John Peyton (d. 1616) of Isleham, Cambridgeshire, and his wife, Alice (1563–1626), daughter of Sir Edward Osborne, lord mayor of London in 1565. A nephew of Robert, Lord Rich, the future second earl of Warwick, Sir John held various political offices in Cambridgeshire, was knighted in 1596, and created a baronet on 22 May 1611. Edward studied at the grammar school in Bury St Edmunds and then, according to Anthony Wood, at Cambridge. He also pursued legal studies at Gray's Inn, where he was admitted on 16 August 1611. Although he had no bachelor's degree, he was allowed to proceed MA at Cambridge in 1618.

At Streatham, Surrey, on 24 April 1604 Peyton married Martha (d. 1613), daughter of Robert Livesay of Tooting, Surrey, on which occasion Peyton's father gave him the manor of Great Bradley, Suffolk. Peyton and his first wife had five children, John (1607–1693), Edward, Robert (b. 1611), Thomas (bur. 1 Jan 1614), and Amy (b. 1605). James I knighted Peyton at Whitehall on 18 March 1611, and he succeeded to the baronetcy and the family estate at Isleham when his father died in December 1616. Following his wife's death in October 1613, Peyton married on 6 June 1614 Jane, daughter of Sir James Calthorpe of Crockthorpe, Norfolk, and widow of Sir Edmond Thimelthorpe (or Sir Henry Thomelthorpe); they had three children, James (d. November 1620), Thomas (1617–1683), and Jane (d. February 1633).

In 1621 Peyton represented Cambridgeshire in parliament, reporting to the house for the recess subcommittee on petitions, including those dealing with patents. In later speeches he argued that bishops should not try capital cases in the Lords, and he opposed a bill for enclosing more commons, which he did not think 'fitt now when Christendom is a garboile' (Notestein, Relf, and Simpson, 3.186). Peyton served as sheriff of Cambridgeshire and Huntingdonshire in 1622–3. In January 1624 he defeated Sir John Cuts, a client of the duke of Buckingham, in a hotly contested election to represent Cambridgeshire in parliament. Responding to a petition from Cuts and Toby Palavicini, who had been defeated by Peyton's electoral partner, Sir Simeon Steward, the House of Commons invalidated the election, but Peyton prevailed in a second election on 18 March.

As MP for Cambridgeshire in Charles I's first parliament Peyton served on various committees, including those that dealt with privileges, fraudulently held estates, inebriety, and petty larceny. Sitting again for Cambridgeshire in the parliament of 1626, he was appointed to numerous committees, including those for religion, recusancy, and purveyance, and those that considered Lords' bills regarding adultery and fornication, the export of ordnance, and outlaws. In the Commons he spoke against the bill to drain 360,000 acres of fens, a third of which would have gone to the crown, and he presented a petition against William Gyles, vicar of Elm, Cambridgeshire, for drunkenness, recourse to prostitutes, and slandering Martin Luther, Theodore Beza, and William Perkins. About 1627 Buckingham dismissed Peyton as *custos rotulorum* for Cambridgeshire, replacing him with Cuts. For instigating a fight with neighbours Peyton was summoned before Star Chamber on 10 October 1632. Despite these difficulties he was not yet a staunch critic of the royal court, for his unpublished manuscript, 'A discourse of court and courtiers' (1633), acknowledges that favourites have served the crown by commanding military forces, undertaking embassies, and raising revenue, and are thus entitled to advance their families and augment their estates. However, Peyton was again in trouble in 1638, when Archbishop William Laud and the high commission ordered him to appear before them, presumably for his puritan views. By this time Peyton's second wife had died, and in December 1638 he married the spinster Dorothy Minshawe (c.1617–1681) at St James's, Clerkenwell, Middlesex (according to Burke, his new wife was Dorothy, daughter of Edward Ball of Stockwell).

Although Peyton did not serve in the Short or Long parliaments, his sympathies were clearly with the country, as reflected in his book, *The King's Violation of the Rights of Parliament* (1641), criticizing Charles I's attempt to arrest the five MPs. Yet Peyton also insisted that the people had no right to destroy the monarchy. The following year he published *A discourse concerning the fitnesse of the posture necessary to be used in taking the bread and wine at the sacrament*, in which he defended his right to partake standing or sitting. To buttress his argument he cited Augustine, Tertullian, Calvin, Bullinger, Beza, Perkins, and others. Roger Cocks responded in *An Answer to a Book Set Forth by Sir Edward Peyton* (1642). Peyton would subsequently write prefatory verse for Humphrey Mill's *The Second Part of the Nights Search*.

During the first civil war Peyton fought with the parliamentary forces at Edgehill, serving as a captain in the earl of Peterborough's regiment of foot. Captured, he was incarcerated in Banbury Castle. He claimed to have fought against the royalists at Newbury and Naseby, but Joshua Sprigge does not include his name in the list of officers who served under Sir Thomas Fairfax. Beginning in 1644 Peyton's second son, Edward, served under the earl of Denbigh as a lieutenant-colonel of horse in the parliamentary army. Sir Edward offered suggestions to resolve the disputes between Charles, parliament, and the army in *The High-Way to Peace* (1647). Peyton's family had suffered financially during the war. Royalist troops had seized household goods worth £400 from Peyton at Broad Chalk, Wiltshire, where his brother Robert was vicar, and because Peyton's son Thomas had fought for the royalists in Wales, he was fined £338 in December 1646. Convinced Sir Edward had conveyed his estates to Thomas during the war, the committee for compounding sequestered them, an action that prompted Sir Edward to protest that his son only had a reversionary interest in the property. The committee reduced Thomas's fine to £169 in February 1649, but the fine to reclaim Rougham Manor, Norfolk, which his wife had inherited from her father, Sir William Yelverton, was set at £1500 in November 1650, though reduced by a third in June 1651. Thomas paid the fine two months later, having raised the money by selling Greenhall Manor, Norfolk.

The bitterness Peyton now felt toward the Stuarts is evident in *The Divine Catastrophe of the Kingly Family of the House of Stuarts*, issued by the radical printer Giles Calvert in 1652. In it Peyton defended the regicide and the abolition of monarchy as actions that conformed to the divine will. Underlying this work are Peyton's millenarian convictions and belief in the role of divine providence in ordering human affairs. Peyton even thought God might destroy all the monarchs in Christendom. As a prisoner in the Tower of London in 1655 Peyton received a furlough in August to take the waters at Tunbridge Wells. The pass was provided by Henry Lawrence, lord president of the council of state, who had married Peyton's elder daughter, Amy, on 21 October 1628.

Peyton died intestate at Wicken, Cambridgeshire, in April 1657 and was buried at St Clement Danes, London.

On 1 July 1657 his widow, Dorothy, was empowered to settle his estate. His eldest son, John, succeeded him as baronet. Dorothy subsequently married Edward Lowe, vicar of Brighton; she was buried at Brighton on 10 April 1681.

RICHARD L. GREAVES

Sources R. E. C. Waters, *Genealogical memoirs of the extinct family of Chester of Chicheley*, 2 vols. (1878) · J. Burke and J. B. Burke, *A genealogical and heraldic history of the extinct and dormant baronetcies of England, Ireland, and Scotland* (1838) · Venn, *Alum. Cant.*, 1/3.353–4 · HoP, *Commons, 1558–1603* · *CSP dom.*, 1619–23; 1631–3; 1638–9; 1644; addenda, 1625–49 · R. E. Ruigh, *The parliament of 1624: politics and foreign policy* (1971) · W. B. Bidwell and M. Jansson, eds., *Proceedings in parliament, 1626*, 4 vols. (1991–6) · Wood, *Ath. Oxon.*, new edn, 3.321 · W. Notestein, F. H. Relf, and H. Simpson, eds., *Commons debates, 1621*, 7 vols. (1935) · J. L. Chester and G. J. Armytage, eds., *Allegations for marriage licences issued by the bishop of London*, 2, Harleian Society, 26 (1887), 239 · M. A. E. Green, ed., *Calendar of the proceedings of the committee for compounding … 1643–1660*, 2, PRO (1890), 1491–2 · PRO, PROB 6/33, fol. 156r · *The list of the army raised under the command of his excellency, Robert Earle of Essex and Ewe* (1642), sig. B1r
Archives PRO, state papers, domestic
Wealth at death see administration, PRO, PROB 6/33, fol. 156r

Peyton, Edward (d. 1749), naval officer, details of whose parents and upbringing are unknown, entered the navy in 1707 as a volunteer per order on the *Scarborough*. Afterwards he served as a volunteer in the *Kingston* for over four years, during which he participated in the abortive expedition to the St Lawrence in 1711. Peyton went on to serve as midshipman in the *Aldborough* and the *Elizabeth*. He passed his lieutenant's examination on 4 August 1715, but seems not to have gained a commission. On 6 February 1716 he married Ester Higgins at the church of St Mary, Lewisham, Kent. What he did during the next eleven years is unclear, but he was given a commission as fourth lieutenant in the *Royal Oak* on 30 April 1727 by Sir Charles Wager, whose squadron was cruising off the Spanish coast. The commission was confirmed on 6 February 1728 and he was promoted third lieutenant on 22 May. On 26 July he became lieutenant on the *Gibraltar* and seems to have joined the ship with her new captain, John Stanley, at Lisbon. Peyton left the ship when she refitted at Deptford and was not recommissioned when the *Gibraltar* left for America under Captain Henry Medley. However, Peyton rejoined the *Gibraltar* on 23 November 1733 and went with Medley to the Mediterranean. Peyton was commissioned lieutenant in the *Dursley Galley* on 18 June 1734, and stayed with this ship on cruising and convoy duties in the Mediterranean until 20 January 1738, when the muster book notes that he 'quitted' the ship. He seems to have made his way back to England and on 24 April 1738 he was commissioned lieutenant of the *Chatham*, which was fitting out for Newfoundland under Captain Vanburgh. The *Chatham* spent the summer at Newfoundland and in October escorted the fisheries trade to the markets of Lisbon and Leghorn. At Leghorn, on 24 February 1739, Vanburgh left the ship and Peyton was commissioned first lieutenant of the *Somerset*, flagship of the commander of the Mediterranean squadron, Rear-Admiral Nicholas Haddock.

Peyton's first command, from 27 June 1739, was as master and commander of the sloop *Grampus* in which he resumed the familiar convoy and cruising work between

Port Mahon and Gibraltar. On 17 January 1740 he was put in command of the bomb-vessel *Salamander*. On 20 January Captain Ambrose of the *Greyhound* was suspended after complaints by the Lisbon merchants and on 4 April Haddock gave Peyton a commission as captain of the *Greyhound*—he had thus at last achieved post rank. On 16 July Peyton took command of the *Kennington*. Operations in the *Kennington* took Peyton to the West Indies, where he saw the remnants of the expeditionary force return from the failure to take Cartagena de las Indias. After returning to Portsmouth for a refit he convoyed trade to Ireland and on to Gibraltar. The new commander in the Mediterranean, Vice-Admiral Thomas Mathews, promoted Peyton to the *Rochester* on 10 June 1743. He stayed in the *Rochester* only until 3 August, when Mathews chose him to take dispatches to the king in Hanover and then on to the ministry and Admiralty in London.

Peyton had gained considerable experience at sea and evidence of high regard from his commanders when he arrived in London. However, he heard that Captain Ambrose had been acquitted at a court martial and was to be paid as captain of the *Greyhound* during his suspension. This called into question both Peyton's pay and seniority. Peyton wrote to the Admiralty: 'I believe there is no precedent of any Gentleman having served without a commission from any admiral on board his majesty's ships (especially in time of war) without being confirmed from it. I therefore hope their Lordships will not make me a precedent' (Peyton to the secretary of the Admiralty board, 7 Oct 1743, PRO, ADM 1/2285). He heard nothing and wrote again requesting the confirmation of his commission. He feared 'being commanded by so many gentlemen that I must always look on as juniors to me. I must also beg their Lordships to consider my service on board the *Greyhound* was in time of war on a station where I might have lost my life and limbs and surely I deserv'd something for my service'. He offered to give up the pay if only they would confirm his rank (ibid., 21 Jan 1744). Although he received no reply from the Admiralty it appears that this compromise was accepted and his post rank was dated from 4 April 1740 (PRO, ADM 6/424).

On 19 March 1744 Peyton was given command of the *Medway* (60 guns); she was under two years old, but already plagued with a serious leak that could not be located. He sailed as part of Commodore Curtis Barnett's small squadron for the East Indies in May 1744. After leaving Madagascar the *Medway* and the frigate *Diamond* were sent to cruise the straits of Malacca, where Peyton captured a large French merchant ship, which was added to the squadron as the *Medway Prize* (40 guns). Peyton later joined Barnett at Batavia, where the *Medway* was cleaned and the problem of the ship's leak became more pronounced. The force later sailed for the Bay of Bengal. Throughout the following months rumours of a French squadron reaching this coast forced Barnett to keep his force together despite diminishing stores, fouled bottoms, and the serious leak in the *Medway*.

On 29 April 1746 Barnett died at Fort St David, Cuddalore, and Peyton, as senior captain, assumed command of the force. By June the *Medway* was taking in so much water that he decided to take the whole force to Trincomalee to repair her. On 25 June he fell in with the long-expected French squadron off Negapatam. The force that La Bourdonnais, the governor of Mauritius, had managed to assemble consisted of nine large ships. Peyton drew up his vessels into line of battle and by late afternoon there was a general cannonading along the line. The following day, calms and light winds precluded renewing the action. Three British ships had severely damaged masts and a council of war decided it was best to seek repairs at Trincomalee, so the British force bore away. On 27 July Peyton's squadron was at sea again in search of the French. On 7 August he sighted them in Negapatam Road and bore down. The following day, as the two squadrons closed, Peyton believed that the French were now considerably reinforced and decided not to pursue the action. Instead he stood off to remain in a position to protect a convoy expected from England. With the French close to Madras, provisions short, and the *Medway's* leak causing great concern he sailed to re-provision in the Hooghly River, south of Calcutta. La Bourdonnais unexpectedly captured Madras on 10 September while Peyton's squadron was careening and victualling. Peyton was still effecting these repairs when Commodore Thomas Griffin arrived with reinforcements in December 1746.

Although there were no immediate repercussions news of the loss of Madras reached England by the end of 1747. The secret committee of the East India Company, the principal executive body of the company, complained to the Admiralty about Peyton on 8 December that year and the board reacted by ordering Griffin to arrest Peyton. Peyton had been ill since the end of 1747; his health suffered further when he was confined aboard the *Pearl*, which, with Peyton and his witnesses, returned with Griffin to England and arrived at Spithead on 6 July 1749. Peyton remained confined aboard the *Winchester* until the end of the month and was eventually allowed to return to London to await events. Although too ill to travel, Peyton considered himself a prisoner and pleaded for his case to be brought to trial. However, by then the East India Company had made it clear to the Admiralty that it would not proceed as the principal complainant against Peyton. On 16 September 1749 Peyton informed the Admiralty that his condition had become so bad that he hoped

> their Lordships will excuse me that I have at last put myself into his hands [his surgeon, Mr Sharp] and shall tomorrow undergo an operation for the stone. If I survive it as soon as I am able to go out I will acquaint their Lordships and be ready to attend their commands. (Peyton to the secretary of the Admiralty board, PRO, ADM 1/2289)

He survived the operation, but died on 26 October of 'a mortification in his foot' (PRO, ADM 6/424). He was buried at St Alfege, Greenwich, on 31 October 1749.

Peyton was an officer with great experience in keeping ships at sea for long periods in difficult circumstances. The need to keep his squadron seaworthy and a threat to the French until reinforcements arrived led to decisions that ended with the loss of Madras. Although never formally condemned for this, he was never able to justify his behaviour and the result was to end his career and probably to shorten his life.   RICHARD HARDING

Sources captains' letters, P, 1739–50, PRO, ADM 1/2284–2289 · commander-in-chief correspondence, East Indies, 1744–53, PRO, ADM 1/160 · seniority list, PRO, ADM 6/424 · correspondence, Admiral Nicholas Haddock, PRO, SP 42/86 · lieutenants' passing certificates, PRO, ADM 107/3, p. 26 · commission and warrant registers, PRO, ADM 6/9, fol. 52; ADM 6/13, fol. 205v; ADM 6/13, fols. 210v, 211v; ADM 6/14, fol. 191; ADM 6/15, fol. 109 · will, PRO, PROB 11/774, sig. 351 · PRO, ADM 51 613 (*Medway*); 781 (*Rochester*); 509 (*Kennington*); 838 (*Salamander*); 820 (*Ruby*); 410 (*Grampus*); 289 (*Dursley Galley*); 390 (*Gibraltar*); 190 (*Chatham*) [captain's logs] · ships' disposition lists, 1726–40, PRO, ADM 8/18–21 · muster book of the *Dursley Galley*, 1734–7, PRO, ADM 36/960
Archives PRO, ADM MSS
Wealth at death £17,200—and residence and other chattels: will, PRO, PROB 11/774, sig. 351

Peyton, Sir Henry (*d.* 1623), army officer, was the son of Thomas Peyton of Bury St Edmunds, customer of Plymouth, and his wife, Cecilia, daughter of John Bourchier, second earl of Bath. He attended Emmanuel College, Cambridge, where he matriculated in 1594. He probably went straight from there to serve in the army of the Dutch republic, though the date and circumstances of his first service in the Netherlands is uncertain. He was given command of a company of foot in 1605, an office which he kept until at least 1614.

Peyton was knighted by James I in 1606 and joined the household of his namesake, Henry, prince of Wales, the same year. Peyton married Mary (*d.* 1619/20), the daughter of Edward *Seymour, duke of Somerset, and widow of Andrew Rogers of Bryanstone, Dorset, at Long Ditton, Surrey, on 22 September 1607. She must have been more than twenty years older than her new husband. Peyton wrote in his will (which he made in April 1618) of the 'singular love which I beare unto … my wife' (PRO, PROB 11/143, fol. 142).

In 1610 Peyton was given charge of a 'kind lettre' from Prince Henry's secretary to Sir Horace Vere, the preeminent English commander in Dutch service (Trim, 347); this marked the beginning of an attempt by the prince to establish a circle of military men. In 1613 Peyton and another English soldier, Sir William Constable, were rivals for a subordinate office in the 'cautionary town' of Brill: such posts were prized because they were a foothold in the English establishment, though it did not necessitate surrendering existing commissions in the Dutch army. The following year Peyton served as a captain in Vere's regiment in the Cleves–Jülich campaign.

Early in 1618 Peyton expanded his horizon when he went to the Adriatic in command of a force of 500 infantry hired by the Venetian republic as part of an Anglo-Dutch force raised to counter the threat posed by the aggression of the Spanish viceroy of Naples. Peyton was, the Venetian ambassador-extraordinary assured his masters, 'an English gentleman, one of the good soldiers of Flanders, where he yet has a company in the service of the States' (*CSP Venice, 1617–19*, 123). Conceding that Peyton had no

experience of naval affairs, the ambassador was convinced that his courage on land would make him worthy of the republic's favour. Peyton was made a colonel to give him the same rank as the senior Dutch officer. Having reached the Adriatic in July 1618 after a hard voyage, Peyton was unable to prevent his troops mutinying over pay. Any breach caused by the ruthless action of the Venetian admiral in hanging the ringleaders was later papered over by the Venetian authorities paying Peyton the money due to him and giving him a gold chain in token of their respect. Peyton's force formed only a small part of the foreign troops aboard the Venetian fleet—a mere 350 men by the summer of 1619 after the depletions of long months at sea, compared with over 3000 Dutchmen—but his three companies were praised by the new captain-general at sea as brave troops under a brave and prudent leader. Peyton had command of his own ship.

In December 1619 Peyton's force went into winter quarters at Zara in Dalmatia; from the following summer they were stationed partly in Venice's mainland territories, partly at sea. Peyton himself seems never to have returned to England, despite his or the English ambassador's suggesting on three occasions—in August 1620, February 1621, and January 1622—that he go back to recruit more men. In March 1621 the Venetian ambassador to England reported to the doge and senate stories that returning officers and soldiers were complaining of the ill treatment that they had received at Peyton's hands. By early 1622 Peyton, when he was stationed at Brescia, was reported as heavily in debt. In July of that year Peyton offered to serve with Venice's allies, the Grisons—the protestant 'grey leagues' whose lands which controlled the alpine passes into Italy had recently been partly occupied by Habsburg forces—either openly as an officer of the republic or covertly in a deniable role. The suggestion was turned down.

Peyton's wife, Mary, died in his absence and was buried in Westminster Abbey on 18 January 1620. Later, in Venice, Peyton married a daughter of Vicenzo Gritti, who survived him. He died of a fever on 13 October 1623.

D. J. B. TRIM

Sources D. J. B. Trim, 'Sir Horace Vere in Holland and the Rhineland, 1610–1612', *Historical Research*, 72 (1999), 334–51 · *CSP dom.*, 1611–18 · will, PRO, PROB 11/143, fol. 142 · *DNB* · F. T. Colby, ed., *The visitation of the county of Devon in the year 1620*, Harleian Society, 6 (1872) · Nationaal Archief, The Hague, Archief van de Staten-Generaal, 8043–8045 · Nationaal Archief, The Hague, Archief van de Raad van State, 1235–1238 · Nationaal Archief, The Hague, Collectie Goldberg, 51, 295–6 · Nationaal Archief, The Hague, Generaliteits Rekenkamer, 1232 · Venn, *Alum. Cant.* · J. P. Rylands, ed., *The visitation of the county of Dorset, taken in the year 1623*, Harleian Society, 20 (1885) · *CSP Venice, 1617–25* · J. L. Chester, ed., *The marriage, baptismal, and burial registers of the collegiate church or abbey of St Peter, Westminster*, Harleian Society, 10 (1876) · H. Peacham, *A most true relation of the affaires of Cleve and Gulick* (1615) · W. A. Shaw, *The knights of England*, 2 vols. (1906) · M. Mallet and J. R. Hale, *The military organisation of a renaissance state: Venice, c.1400 to 1617* (1984) · G. Parker, *Europe in crisis, 1598–1648*, rev. edn (1984)
Likenesses D. Mytens, oils, 1621, Courteenhall, Northamptonshire
Wealth at death expected the sale of his goods would only meet his debts: will, PRO, PROB 11/143, fol. 142

Peyton, Sir John (1544–1630), soldier and administrator, born between February and December 1544, was the second son of John Peyton of Knowlton, Kent (*d.* 1558), and his wife, Dorothy, daughter of Sir John Tyndale. Before 1564 Peyton served in Ireland under his father's friend and neighbour Sir Henry Sidney of Penshurst, and in 1568 he was again in Ireland with Sidney, then lord deputy. He became a member of Sidney's household and sometimes bore dispatches to England for him. On 8 June 1578 he married Dorothy, the only child of Edward Beaupré of Beaupré Hall, Outwell, Norfolk, and his second wife, Catherine Beddingfield, and the widow of Sir Robert Bell (*d.* 1577). From his wife's large property, Peyton gained a position in the county of Norfolk. She died in February 1603.

In 1586 Peyton served under the earl of Leicester with the expedition to the Netherlands. In 1586–7 he was lieutenant-governor of Bergen op Zoom, and was often effectively in command there in Willoughby's absence. He was knighted in 1586, and in 1588 was appointed colonel in the forces for the defence of the queen's person against the threatened attack of the Spanish Armada. He was granted the receivership of the counties of Norfolk and Huntingdon and of the city of Norwich in 1593. In 1596 he was appointed one of three deputy lieutenants of Cambridgeshire under Roger, Lord North, treasurer of the household, and in 1602 he was appointed deputy lieutenant of the same county under Thomas, Lord Howard de Walden.

Peyton was appointed lieutenant of the Tower of London in June 1597, and it was in that capacity that he examined several witnesses in the trial of Essex and was present at Essex's execution. On 10 December 1600 he was appointed to the commission to investigate controversies and abuses in the ordnance office. A report was written detailing the abuses and proposing wide-ranging reforms. Peyton was discharged from the lieutenancy of the Tower on 30 July 1603 and appointed, apparently in accordance with his own wishes, governor of Jersey, a post forfeited by attainder of its previous holder, Sir Walter Ralegh. Ralegh had been under Peyton's care as a prisoner in the Tower, and his 'strange and dejected mind' had caused concern to Peyton, for whom he would send several times a day in his passions of grief (BL, Add. MS 6177, fols. 127–8). Later, in January 1604, Peyton was, according to a letter from Dudley Carleton to John Chamberlain, disgraced for entertaining intelligence between Cobham and Ralegh.

Peyton took the usual form of oath as governor before the royal court of Jersey on 10 September 1603. Peter Heylyn states that Peyton tried to do away with the Calvinist form of church government then current in Jersey and to introduce the established church there, but that does not seem to have been his intention immediately upon his appointment. In fact, James I, believing it to have been sanctioned by Elizabeth, expressly permitted the continuation of the French Calvinist form of church government in Jersey and Guernsey. There was a dispute between Peyton and the Jersey colloquy in 1604 over the manner of the appointment of a minister to a benefice, but generally Peyton seems to have been on good terms with the ministers during his early years in office, and sometimes attended and participated in the colloquy meetings. His relationship with the colloquy deteriorated when they took issue with his appointment of a chaplain in 1609. Following a dispute in 1613 over the refusal of Peyton's episcopally ordained candidate for a vacant benefice in Jersey to submit to the laying on of hands of the ministers, delegations were summoned to England in 1614, one favouring the continuation of the *status quo* and another supporting the introduction of the usages of the Church of England to Jersey. The final outcome was the appointment of David Bandinel as dean in 1620 and the promulgation of the ecclesiastical canons for Jersey in 1623: these together represented the end of the Calvinist form of church government in the island and its bringing into the reformed Church of England.

The period of Peyton's governorship saw much strife in Jersey over civil matters, and Peyton was involved in constant disputes with Sir Philippe de Carteret, with Philippe Maret, and, most of all, with the bailiff Jean *Herault. The dispute between Peyton and Herault over the relationship of the bailiff and governor led to a suit resulting in the judgment of 1617 declaring that the charge of the military forces rested only in the governor: this judgment has ever since been regarded as a principle fundamental to the government of the island. During the time of his residence in Jersey, Peyton seems to have conscientiously supervised the defence and fortifications of the island, and many of his records relating to the military care of the island survive in the state papers.

Peyton's friends included Sir Philip Sidney, Peregrine Bertie, Lord Willoughby de Eresby, and Henry Cuffe, Essex's secretary. He died on 4 November 1630 and was buried on 15 December at Doddington in the Isle of Ely, where he had had his private residence since his wife's death. Though it was stated by John Lewis Peyton that he was ninety-nine at the time of his death, and the monument of his great-granddaughter Mrs Alice Lowe, in Christ Church, Oxford, gives his age at death as 105, from his own statements of his age as seventy-nine in February 1624 and eighty in December 1624 it appears that Peyton was in fact eighty-six.

Peyton's only son, **Sir John Peyton** (1579–1635), matriculated as a fellow-commoner of Queens' College, Cambridge, in 1594. From 1598 to 1600 he travelled extensively in Germany, Bohemia, Poland, Switzerland, and Italy: the detailed account of these travels which he addressed to his father survives in manuscript in Cambridge University Library. He married, on 25 November 1602, a relative, Alice, the second daughter of Sir John Peyton of Isleham in Cambridgeshire. They had at least three sons, Robert (*b.* 1626), Algernon (*b.* 1632), and Henry, and at least two daughters, Anne and Alice (*b.* 1635/6), who married, in 1659 or 1660, Edward Lowe, a gentleman of Salisbury and master of the choristers and organist of Christ Church, Oxford. Peyton served as lieutenant to his father as governor of Jersey in 1607 and intermittently from 1618 until his father's death. He was knighted on 28 March 1603. He died early in 1635; his wife was the sole executor of his will, dated 24 February 1635. She was buried at Doddington on 28 March 1637. HELEN M. E. EVANS

Sources DNB · J. L. Peyton, Memoir of William Madison Peyton (1873) · M. Syvret and J. Stevens, Balleine's history of Jersey (1981) · CSP dom., 1558–1625; addenda, 1547–1625 · CSP for., 1557–95 · APC, 1558 · 'The first part of the observations of Sir John Peyton the younger, knt., lieutenant-governor of Jersey, during his travailes', CUL, MS Kk.5,2 · Venn, Alum. Cant. · R. W. Stewart, The English ordnance office (1996) · J. A. Messervy, 'Liste des gouverneurs, lieut.-gouverneurs et députés gouverneurs de l'Île de Jersey', Annual Bulletin [Société Jersiaise], 4 (1897–1901), 373–94 · minutes of the Jersey Calvinist colloquy, 1577–1614, CUL, MS Dd.11.43 · BL, Add. MS 6177 · P. Heylyn, Aerius redivivus (1670), 396

Archives Bodl. Oxf., declaration on the state of the Tower of London

Peyton, Sir John (1579–1635). *See under* Peyton, Sir John (1544–1630).

Peyton, Sir John Strutt (1786–1838), naval officer, born in London on 14 January 1786, was the third son of William Peyton, chief clerk of the Navy Office, grandson of Admiral Joseph Peyton (d. 1804), and great-grandson of Commodore Edward Peyton. His father's three brothers were also all in the navy; one of them, John, who died a rear-admiral in 1809, was captain of the *Defence* in the battle of the Nile. His grandmother was a daughter of Commander John Strutt; his mother was the daughter of Commander Jacob Lobb, who died in command of the sloop *Kingfisher* in 1773, and was sister of Captain William Granville Lobb, afterwards a commissioner of the navy.

Peyton first went to sea in October 1797, on the *Hector*, off Cadiz; he was then for three years in the *Emerald* in the Mediterranean, and in January 1801 was appointed to the *San Josef*, Nelson's flagship in the channel. With Nelson, his patron, he was moved to the *St George*, in which he was in the Baltic and afterwards off Cadiz and in the West Indies, for part of the time under his uncle, Captain Lobb. During 1802–3 he served, in quick succession, in several frigates in the channel or in the North Sea, and in August 1803 was sent out to the *Victory*, Nelson's flagship off Toulon. In March 1805 he was appointed acting lieutenant of the *Canopus*, from which he was moved in May to the frigate *Ambuscade*, with Captain William Durban, employed during the next two years in the Adriatic. Peyton's commission as lieutenant was dated 7 October 1805. In July 1807, having been sent to destroy a vessel which ran herself ashore near Ortona, he was wounded in the right elbow by a musket bullet; the arm had to be amputated, and he was invalided.

On 1 December 1807 Peyton was promoted commander, and from June 1809 to February 1811 he commanded the brig *Ephira* in the North Sea, in the Walcheren expedition, and afterwards off Cadiz. He was then appointed to the *Weazle* (18 guns), in the Aegean archipelago; and on 26 September 1811 was posted to the *Minstrel* (20 guns), in which, and afterwards in the *Thames*, he was employed on the coast of Valencia and Catalonia until near the end of the war. During this time he repeatedly fought coastal batteries and privateers, and received the thanks of Sir Edward Pellew, the commander-in-chief. In September 1813 the *Thames* returned to England and was paid off. In October 1814 Peyton married a daughter of Lieutenant Woodyear RN, of St Kitts, and they had three daughters and two sons.

On 25 January 1836 Peyton was made a KCH, and in June 1836 was appointed to the *Madagascar* (46 guns), in which he went out to the West Indies. In the spring of 1838 he had to be invalided, returned in extreme ill health, and died at his lodgings in Somerset Street, Portman Square, London, on 20 May.

J. K. LAUGHTON, *rev.* ANDREW LAMBERT

Sources D. Syrett and R. L. DiNardo, The commissioned sea officers of the Royal Navy, 1660–1815, rev. edn, Occasional Publications of the Navy RS, 1 (1994) · J. M. Collinge, Navy Board officials, 1660–1832 (1978) · GM, 2nd ser., 10 (1838)

Peyton, Sir Robert (c.1633–1689), politician and conspirator, was the fourth son of Henry Peyton (d. 1656), examiner in chancery (1632–54), of Chancery Lane, London, where his son was born. Peyton was admitted to Lincoln's Inn in 1655, having also succeeded his father as an examiner in chancery in 1654. He married Jane Robinson (d. 1684), daughter of Lionel Robinson of Cowton Grange, Yorkshire. They had at least one son and one daughter. He was knighted in 1670, served as deputy lieutenant for Middlesex from 1670 to 1676 and again in 1689, as JP from 1672 to 1676, and as MP for Middlesex in the parliaments of spring 1679 and autumn 1680.

Despite holding these positions of responsibility in the 1670s, Peyton was a leading member of the opposition to Charles II. He was a political associate of both the main opposition leaders, George Villiers, second duke of Buckingham, and Anthony Ashley Cooper, first earl of Shaftesbury. By the mid-1670s Peyton had become the leader of a republican group, 'Peyton's gang', and it has been argued that this group had a hand in the murder of the JP Sir Edmund Berry Godfrey in 1678, which provoked widespread belief in the bogus Popish Plot. Godfrey was a member of Peyton's gang, but after receiving, in his capacity as a JP, the Popish Plot depositions of the false informer Titus Oates, Godfrey promptly warned one of the accused Catholics and the court itself. Peyton may have decided to have Godfrey killed both because of his 'betrayal' and to stir up hatred against the Catholics, on whom suspicion would inevitably fall.

Peyton's heavy involvement in opposition plotting had already been noted by the government. In 1676 Peyton and a number of his fellow JPs for Middlesex were removed abruptly from the bench. This was an unusual step, because Charles II—at least prior to 1681—was notoriously tolerant towards his political opponents (much to the chagrin of his supporters). Although most of those removed were members of Peyton's gang, there is also some evidence to suggest that Peyton and his friends were removed for being involved in the distribution of seditious literature.

Peyton was one of the most active members in the turbulent parliament of spring 1679. In the same year he became the chairman of the radical Green Ribbon Club, having been a founder member of the club some six years earlier. However, by the end of 1679 Peyton had briefly and secretly come over to the court interest. This remains rather a shadowy affair. Peyton appears to have been won over by the renowned Catholic midwife Elizabeth Cellier. Peyton later claimed that his motives were sexual, and certainly both of them, Peyton in particular, had a reputation for sexual licentiousness. There is also, however, some evidence to suggest that Peyton was partly motivated by fear. When Charles II had fallen seriously ill at the end of summer 1679, Peyton and some of his opposition colleagues, including fellow London radicals such as Sir Thomas Player and Francis Jenks, had apparently discussed rising in revolt against James, duke of York, should he become king. However, Charles had recovered, James was experiencing a temporary resurgence of his fortunes, and Peyton appears to have been afraid of the repercussions. Whatever Peyton's reasons for his temporary defection, he was discovered and bitterly attacked by his former friends in the next parliamentary session.

Peyton did move back into some degree of opposition (now called whig) contact, and he was involved on the peripheries of the 1682–3 Rye House plot. In 1685 he planned to raise London for James Scott, duke of Monmouth, during the Monmouth rebellion. Peyton, however, vacillated, being unsure of support, and Monmouth was defeated in the west while Peyton was still holding meetings. Peyton's plotting was discovered, and, charged with high treason, he fled abroad to the Netherlands.

In 1686 the English envoy to the states general, Bevil Skelton, and some of James II's army officers attempted to kidnap Peyton and bring him back to England, but failed, and the affair caused a diplomatic incident. Two years later, Peyton commanded a regiment in William of Orange's invasion force against James II. However, Peyton died in London less than a year later, on 3 May 1689, reportedly of a fever two days after drinking bad claret. He was buried in London on 8 May.

Peyton had a violent character, behaving viciously in the frequent private quarrels in which he became embroiled. He may well, though, have had a magnetic side to his personality, to be able to rise to such a high position in opposition circles.   ALAN HOBSON

Sources PRO, State Papers, SP 29, Charles II · *CSP dom.*, 1665–78 · HoP, *Commons, 1660–90* · S. Knight, *The killing of Justice Godfrey* (1984) · J. Miller, 'Extravagant counsel', *TLS* (18 Jan 1985) [review] · *The life and times of Anthony Wood*, ed. A. Clark, 3, OHS, 26 (1894) · *The manuscripts of the House of Lords*, 4 vols., HMC, 17 (1887–94), vol. 2 · MSS concerning deputy lieutenants for Middlesex, LMA, MS Acc 351/631 · 'A letter from Amsterdam 30 Aug [16]72 [*sic*, actually late 1672 or early 1673] to Sir R[obert] P[eyton] at the Green Ribbon Club', Bodl. Oxf., MS Rawl. letters 73 · A. Marshall, *Intelligence and espionage in the reign of Charles II, 1660–1685* (1994) · *Report on the manuscripts of Allan George Finch*, 5 vols., HMC, 71 (1913–2003) · will, PRO, PROB 11/395, sig. 69
Wealth at death over £4000: will, 1689, PRO, PROB 11/395, sig. 69

Peyton, Thomas (1595–1626), poet, was born at Royston, Hertfordshire, the son and heir of Thomas Peyton. On 26 November 1613 he was admitted a student of Lincoln's Inn. He was a studious and devout young man who published the first part of a poem entitled *The Glasse of Time in the First Age, Divinely Handled by Thomas Peyton of Lincolnes Inne, Gent* (1620), with every intention of a continuation. The volume opens with addresses in verse to King James, Prince Charles, Lord Chancellor Bacon, and the reader. The poem consists of 168 stanzas, of varying lengths, in heroic verse and relates the story of the Fall, as told in the Bible. There are many classical allusions and digressions into contemporary religious topics. Peyton writes as a champion of the established church and a warm opponent of the puritans.

In 1623 Peyton continued the work in a second volume, entitled *The Glasse of Time in the Second Age*, and brought the scriptural narrative up to Noah's entrance into the ark. A further continuation was promised but never written. The two parts together are titled *The Glasse of Time in the Two First Ages* and consist of 164 pages, interspersed with woodcuts. Some of the episodes in Peyton's poem—notably his descriptions of paradise and of Lucifer—very faintly suggest some masterly passages on the same subject in Milton's *Paradise Lost* but the resemblances are not close enough to render it probable that Milton was acquainted with his predecessor's efforts (see *North American Review*, October 1860). Peyton died in 1626.

[ANON.], *rev.* JOANNA MOODY

Sources BL cat. · Watt, *Bibl. Brit.*, 2.752 · W. T. Lowndes, *The bibliographer's manual of English literature*, ed. H. G. Bohn, [new edn], 3 (1864), 1847 · STC, *1475–1640*, no. 19824 · F. W. Bateson, *The Cambridge bibliography of English literature*, 1 (1940), 479 · W. P. Baildon, ed., *The records of the Honorable Society of Lincoln's Inn: admissions*, 1 (1896)

Pfander, Karl Gottlieb (1803–1865), missionary, was born on 3 November 1803 in Waiblingen, Württemberg, the son of Johann Friedrich Pfander, a master baker, and Elisabeth Margaretha Bürcklin. The family's strong Lutheran pietist connections ensured a sound education, first in a local Latin school, then at a Moravian boarding-school in Stuttgart. Pfander's studies from 1821 to 1825 at the Missionsinstitut in Basel (the recently established evangelical mission seminary) confirmed his strong missionary vocation, rooted in a conservative understanding of biblical revelation, and also prepared him, particularly through the study of Arabic and the Koran, for his subsequent evangelistic activities among Muslims in the Middle East and India.

Pfander's first missionary posting, in 1825, was to Shusha in the Russian Caucasus, recently annexed from Persia. For twelve years he preached to Muslims as well as to Armenian Christians, and he also travelled to Baghdad and throughout Persia. In an effort to overcome the apathy, sometimes hostility, of his audiences, he drafted in German an evangelical explanation of Christianity and refutation of Islam, entitled 'Waage der Wahrheit', which was translated into Persian as the *Mizan ul-haqq* or 'Balance of truth' (Shusha, 1835), and subsequently into Urdu, Arabic, Turkish, and other languages used by Muslims. He also prepared several other books on specific aspects of

Christianity and Islam. The diaries of his travels, published in German evangelical journals in the 1820s and 1830s, provide an important source for European perceptions of Muslim, particularly Shi'i, society. On 11 July 1834 he married Sophie Reuss; she died in Shusha in 1835, within a year of their marriage.

In 1837 the tsar's closure of the Shusha mission caused Pfander to be transferred to the north India mission of the Anglican Church Missionary Society (CMS). On 19 January 1841 he married for a second time, taking Emily Emma Swinburne, of Richmond, as his wife. In the same year he was posted to Agra, a former capital of the Muslim Mughal empire but by then a British provincial capital. Optimistic that this colonial context offered new opportunities for evangelism, Pfander prepared vernacular editions of his various books, and sent invitations to the 'ulama' class of Muslim religious leaders to engage in religious discussion. At first ignored, Pfander's outspoken criticism of the prophet Muhammad eventually caused an 'ulama'-led reaction against him, based on rationalist objections to Christian doctrines. This came to a head in 1854 at a public debate in Agra where, witnessed by a large audience, the Muslims used arguments from recent biblical criticism rather than rational arguments to counter Pfander's defence of key Christian doctrines—notably concerning the divinity of Christ and the Trinity. Local Muslim leaders used the occasion to publicize the perceived missionary threat to their religion and culture. Some commentators have linked Pfander's name and activities to the escalation of civil rebellion which centred on this region of India in 1857–8 (the Indian mutiny), but the question of missionary provocation is complex, and there is no consensus. The CMS had by then transferred Pfander: first, in 1855, to the north-west frontier town of Peshawar; then, in 1858, to Turkey, where the resumption of his provocative methods of evangelism was proscribed by the Ottoman authorities, this time with British diplomatic support. Pfander had succeeded, however, in arousing a hostile reaction among Muslim religious leaders in the heartlands of Islam, particularly in Mecca and Constantinople.

Pfander died on 1 December 1865 during a visit to Richmond, Surrey, the home of his second wife. She and his six children remained in Britain, first at Great Coggeshall, Essex, and then at Richmond. Although Pfander had intended to return to Turkey, missionary opinion was by then divided on the efficacy of his methods, and the subsequent reception of mild biblical criticism undermined some of his claims about the biblical text. Yet Pfander's publications, seemingly superseded, have attracted intermittent attention, particularly since the 1970s when, in the context of Islamic revival movements in the Middle East, the writings of his Indian 'ulama' opponents have been reprinted in Arabic, Urdu, and English. A conservative evangelical group in Württemberg also began to redistribute in the 1980s Pfander's major work on Islam, the *Mizan ul-haqq*, thereby confirming his place among the most influential of the nineteenth century's Christian missionaries to the Muslim world.   AVRIL A. POWELL

Sources C. F. Eppler, *D. Karl Gottlieb Pfander, ein Zeuge der Wahrheit unter den Bekennern des Islam* (Basel, 1888) • A. A. Powell, *Muslims and missionaries in pre-mutiny India* (1993) • S. M. Zwemer, 'Karl Gottlieb Pfander', *Moslem World*, 31 (1941), 217–26 • Ledderhose, 'Pfander, Karl Gottlieb', *Allgemeine deutsche Biographie*, ed. R. von Liliencron and others, 25 (Leipzig, 1887), 597–600 • *Magazin für die neueste Geschichte der evangelischen Missions und Bibel-Gesellschaften* (1820x29–1830x39) • *CGPLA Eng. & Wales* (1866)
Archives Basel Mission archive, Basel, Switzerland • U. Birm. L., Church Missionary Society archive, North India and Mediterranean Mission archives
Likenesses portrait, repro. in C. F. Eppler, *D. Karl Gottlieb Pfander, ein Zeuge der Wahrheit unter den Bekennern des Islam* (Basel, 1888), frontispiece
Wealth at death under £7000: probate, 12 March 1866, *CGPLA Eng. & Wales*

Pfeiffer [*née* Davis], **Emily Jane** (1827–1890), poet, was born on 26 November 1827 in Montgomeryshire, Wales, eldest of the three daughters of (Thomas) Richard Davis, who was in his early years an army officer, and his wife, Emily, the youngest daughter of the Tilsley family of Milford Hall, Montgomeryshire. Davis once owned considerable property in Oxfordshire but lost his fortune when his father-in-law's bank, the chief banking institution in Montgomeryshire, failed in 1831. The family's straitened circumstances prevented Emily from receiving any regular education, but her father encouraged her to study and practise painting and poetry. Flower painting and embroidery were lifelong pastimes, and her first book, *The Holly Branch, an Album for 1843*, was published as early as 1842. A friend took her on tour to the Rhineland, and she spent a season in London before marrying Jurgen Edward Pfeiffer (d. 1889) on 26 January 1850. He was a German tea merchant resident in London, and the marriage, though childless, was a happy one. In 1858 they bought 2 acres on West Hill, just south of Richmond Road in Putney, London, and they built a house on it called Mayfield where they lived for the rest of their lives.

Throughout her life Pfeiffer suffered from bouts of ill health and insomnia, but she remained a prolific writer. Her first mature work, *Valisneria* (1857), prompted comparisons with Sara Coleridge. Conscious of the imperfection of her education, she worked hard at improving herself, and she did not publish again until 1873, when *Gerard's Monument* appeared. Thereafter she published a full-length work every two or three years throughout her life. Her writings varied widely in form and style, from collections of miscellaneous poems to the complex narrative structure of *The Rhyme of the Lady of the Rock, and how it Grew* (1884) and the full-length blank verse drama *The Wynnes of Wynhavod* (1881). The long prose work *Flying Leaves from East and West* (1885) is a narrative of her travels in 1884 in eastern Europe, Asia, and the United States and has been described as 'a collection of political and artistic commentaries in travelogue form' (Todd, 536). However, her sonnets were generally regarded as her best work and were praised by contemporary critics for their delicacy. Later, feminist critics highlighted the theme of female disempowerment which runs throughout her œuvre. Her contributions to the *Cornhill Magazine* and the *Contemporary Review* demonstrate her interest in the position of women in society. The essays collected in *Women and Work* (1887) assessed and attacked theories concerning women's inherent weakness: ironically, *The Spectator* commented of her case that 'few men could have stated it more ably' (p. 112).

Pfeiffer's husband died in January 1889 and she never recovered from the blow. She wrote and published *Flowers of the Night* later that year, but she survived him by only just over a year, dying of pneumonia at their home in Putney on 23 January 1890. She asked that her property be disposed of according to the wishes of her husband, as expressed in a letter of 1884 composed before a journey to the United States. Thus, although she left some money to her two sisters, most of her wealth went towards charity and education. Funds were provided to endow a school of dramatic art for women and to establish an orphanage. The remainder was left to trustees to further women's higher education: £2000 of this was used to build Aberdare Hall, the first dormitory for women at the University College of South Wales, Cardiff, which was opened in 1895.   JESSICA HININGS

Sources J. Todd, ed., *Dictionary of British women writers* (1989) · Blain, Clements & Grundy, *Feminist comp.* · A. H. Japp, 'Emily Pfeiffer, 1841–1890', *The poets and poetry of the century*, ed. A. H. Miles, 7 (1892), 555–6; *The poets and poetry of the nineteenth century*, 9 (1907), 161–4 · *The Athenaeum* (1 Feb 1890), 80–81 · *The Times* (18 June 1831) · *The Times* (21 March 1890) · *Western Mail* [Cardiff] (8 Oct 1895) · E. C. Stedman, *Victorian poets*, 13th edn (1887) · *The Spectator*, xii/x, 112 · private information (1895) · B. Herbertson, *The Pfeiffer bequest and the education of women: a centenary review* (privately printed, Cambridge, 1993) · m. cert. · d. cert.

Archives NL Scot., letters and poems to J. S. Blackie

Wealth at death £63,611 10s. 8d.: probate, 11 March 1890, *CGPLA Eng. & Wales*

Pfeiffer, Rudolf Carl Franz Otto (1889–1979), classical scholar, was born in the house in Augsburg, Germany, which had belonged in the sixteenth century to the humanist Conrad Peutinger, on 28 September 1889, the son of Carl Philip Jacob Pfeiffer, a printing office proprietor, and his wife, Elizabeth Naegele. He was educated at the Benedictine abbey of St Stephan, remaining a devout Roman Catholic throughout his life, and then at the University of Munich. While there he married, in 1913, Lili (d. 1969), daughter of Sigmund Beer. His doctoral dissertation of 1914 on Johannes Spreng, the Augsburg Meistersinger and translator of Homer, combined the history of Augsburg with the study of Greek poetry and the history of classical scholarship, the two themes that informed the whole of his work.

After military service in the First World War, in which Pfeiffer was severely wounded, he returned to the University of Munich as librarian. In 1920 he was given leave to study for a year in Berlin, editing in 1921 the newly discovered fragments of the Hellenistic poet Callimachus and earning his *Habilitation*. He returned to Munich as a *Privat-Dozent*, but in 1923 accepted a call as professor, to Berlin, and then in the same year to Hamburg; the appointment evoked the surprise of the Latinist Eduard Norden, who described Pfeiffer in a letter to Fritz Saxl, of

Rudolf Carl Franz Otto Pfeiffer (1889–1979), by Gabriele, Gräfin von Arnim

the Warburg Institute, as still no more than promising ('nur eine Hoffnung'; 18 July 1923, Saxl MSS).

Pfeiffer was not at home in the north, and through illness missed lectures at the Warburg Institute. The desire of the institute, whose library Pfeiffer evidently used, that he should lecture on Erasmus took fifteen months to come to fruition: 'Humanitas Erasmiana' was delivered on 27 November 1926, and published in 1931 without significant change, despite Saxl's optimistic suggestion that Pfeiffer might add material about Erasmus and England (*Humanitas Erasmiana*, Studien der Bibliothek Warburg, 22, 1931). It was presumably because Pfeiffer was known to be thinking of a new edition of the *Antibarbari* that Saxl had thought of the subject for the lecture; in the event, Pfeiffer was informed by P. S. Allen that a new manuscript of an early version existed, and abandoned his plans. His work concentrated on Hellenistic poetry in general and on Callimachus in particular; he accepted a call in 1927 to Freiburg im Breisgau and in 1929 to Munich. He remained in touch with the Warburg Institute, accepting in 1931 an invitation to be responsible for the bibliography on the legacy of the survival and transmission of classical scholarship ('Nachleben der Antike in der klassischen Gelehrsamkeit').

Both Pfeiffer's beliefs and the Jewish origin of his wife made it in due course impossible for him to remain in Germany, and he resigned his chair in 1937. He arrived in Oxford in the following year. The Warburg Institute had arrived in London in 1933, and the classical scholar Eduard

Fraenkel in Oxford in 1935, and Pfeiffer was at once in contact with both: Saxl was soon once more trying to persuade Pfeiffer to lecture. Pfeiffer lived, like most refugees of the period, from a variety of sources, until in 1946 he was offered a post by Oxford as university lecturer in the history of classical scholarship. He became reader in Greek literature in 1950. During his time in Oxford he was a member of the senior common room of Corpus Christi College, of which he was elected an honorary fellow in 1959.

The most important consequence of Pfeiffer's exile was access to unpublished papyri of Callimachus and the agreement of Oxford University Press to publish his *Callimachus* (1949, 1953); his obituarist for the British Academy, Hugh Lloyd-Jones, said of the first volume that it was 'hard to think of a critical edition of an ancient text that comes nearer to perfection' (Lloyd-Jones, 776). Pfeiffer was elected a fellow of the British Academy in 1949.

Pfeiffer returned to his chair in Munich in 1951 and retired in 1957; in retirement he concentrated on the history of classical scholarship, his first volume appearing in 1968 and covering the beginning down to the end of the Hellenistic period, the second in 1976, beginning with the Italian Renaissance. The core ideas had already been laid out in an article of 1938 and in a lecture to the Bayerische Akademie der Wissenschaften in 1960, 'Philologia perennis'. Both volumes appeared in English. The second volume should be regarded as unfinished, and reads like a series of sketches. Pfeiffer died in Munich on 6 May 1979.

For Pfeiffer, 'philology in the proper sense begins with scholar poets, who are impelled by their love of poetry to preserve the poetry of the past' (Lloyd-Jones, 777), beginning in the Hellenistic period. He regarded the study of the ancient world as having moral value and as essentially the study of great literature, in particular poetry, Greek poetry, and Homer. Like Erasmus, on whom he expressed his views in a paper of 1955, he too believed that the scriptures were a proper study for philology. Pfeiffer saw the two volumes on the history of classical scholarship as an essentially historical exercise, concerned with the continuity of knowledge and with truth that once established lasts forever, like the truth of Christianity. But the truth in which he was interested was internal to the activity of scholarship, an interest that led him to take a favourable view of the 'Augustan peace'; and a phrase used in agreeing to lecture at the Warburg Institute in 1950, but in refusing to do so in a series devoted to religious festivals, is revealing: 'I am, unfortunately, no historian of religion, but only a simple classical scholar, and I would not feel entitled to deal with a festival as such' (14 May 1949, Saxl MSS).

MICHAEL H. CRAWFORD

Sources *Rudolf Pfeiffer: ausgewählte Schriften*, ed. W. Bühler (1960) • A. Fingerle, ed., *Zum 80. Geburtstage von Rudolf Pfeiffer: Rudolf Pfeiffer, von der Liebe zur Antike. Auswahl und Einleitung von Anton Fingerle* (1969) • H. Lloyd-Jones, *PBA*, 65 (1979), 771–81 • *Biographisches Handbuch der deutsch-sprachigen Emigration* • *Deutsche biographische Enzyklopädie* • Saxl MSS, U. Lond., Warburg Institute • *WWW* • K. J. Dover, *Pelican Record* [Corpus Christi College, Oxford] (1978–9), 47– 8 • P. A. Hunt, *Corpus Christi College biographical register*, ed. N. A. Flanagan (1988)
Likenesses G. von Arnim, photograph, British Academy, London [see illus.]

Phaer [Phayer], **Thomas** (1510?–1560), translator and physician, was the son of Thomas Phaer of Norwich and his wife, Clara, daughter of either Sir Richard or Sir William Godier. He was educated at Oxford University and Lincoln's Inn. Early in his career he became attached to the household of William Paulet, first marquess of Winchester, whom he described as 'my first brynger up and patrone' (Phaer, sig. A2r). With his patron's backing, Phaer was appointed solicitor to the council in the marches of Wales in or about 1547. Winchester was also apparently instrumental in arranging Phaer's marriage to Anne Revel, the prosperous widow of a Pembrokeshire merchant, Thomas Revel. The marriage took place between 18 June 1548, when Agnes was granted the wardship of her late husband's heir, and 21 December 1551, when Richard, Lord Rich, ceased to be lord chancellor. In 1549 he was granted a lease in the Forest of Cilgerran in Pembrokeshire, and lived there for the remainder of his life. Thomas and Anne had two daughters, whom they named Mary and Elizabeth, after the two daughters of Henry VIII. Thomas Phaer had another daughter, Eleanor, who was married by 1560, and may have been the product of a previous marriage.

Phaer's first professional activities were in the field of law, and he published two legal handbooks in the English language, *Natura brevium* (1530?) and *A Newe Book of Presidentes* (1543). The latter proved enduringly popular, with twenty-seven editions up to 1656. From about 1540 Phaer embarked on a second career as a doctor and writer on medical matters. In 1544 he published in one volume *The Regiment of Lyfe*, a translation of the work by Jehan Goeurot, together with three medical works of his own, *A Goodly Bryefe Treatise of the Pestylence*, *A Declaration of the Veynes*, and *The Boke of Chyldren*. An enlarged edition appeared in 1553, and the volume would prove one of the most widely read and frequently reprinted medical texts of the Tudor era. While early readers may have been primarily interested in Goeurot, Phaer's own importance as a paediatrician is now widely recognized. He has been called the 'Father of English Pediatrics' (Ruhräh, 147). There is reason to suppose that he was responsible for the introduction of a bill 'for the nursing of Children in Wales' in the 1547 parliament. Although he published no further medical works, Phaer continued to practise medicine. On 6 February 1559 he graduated MB from Oxford, with leave to practise, proceeding MD on 21 March of the same year. In his supplication for the first degree he stated that he had practised medicine for twenty years, and had conducted experiments involving poisons and antidotes.

Alongside his professional activities Phaer was an author and translator of verse. He contributed commendatory verses to Peter Betham's *Preceptes of Warre* (1544), and a lament in the person of Owen Glendour (Owain

Glyn Dŵr) to *The Mirror for Magistrates*. (Phaer's poem is found on the only surviving page of the suppressed first edition of the *Mirror*, printed in the reign of Mary.) In addition Warton attributed to Phaer a ballad he had seen on the famous Gad's Hill robbery; if the poem was indeed Phaer's, it may also have been intended for inclusion in the *Mirror*, as the incident belongs to the same era as the Glyn Dŵr rising. Another lost work, 'Certen Verses of Cupydo, by M. Fayre', received licence for publication by Thomas Purfoot in 1566, after Phaer's death.

Phaer is remembered above all as the first Englishman to attempt a full translation of Virgil's *Aeneid*. He began the work on 9 May 1555 and made it, as he explained in his dedication to Queen Mary, 'my pastyme in all my vacations' (Phaer, sig. A2r). *The Seven First Bookes of the Eneidos of Virgill* was published in 1558, with a note at the end of each book of the number of days (averaging around twenty) spent in translating it. Phaer went on to translate the eighth and ninth books, and to begin work on the tenth, before receiving an injury to his right hand in 1560 that stopped his work and led to his death. In 1562 Phaer's friend and literary executor William Wightman, 'receptour of Wales', arranged the publication of *The nyne fyrst bookes of the Eneidos of Virgil converted into Englishe vearse by Thomas Phaer doctour of phisike, with so muche of the tenthe booke, as since his death coulde be founde in unperfit papers at his house in Kilgarran forest in Penbroke shyre*. The volume was dedicated, as Phaer had apparently requested, to Sir Nicholas Bacon, lord keeper of the great seal. Phaer's translation was finally completed by his friend Thomas Twyne in 1573. In 1584 the work was reissued, with the addition of Twyne's translation of the 'thirteenth book' added to Virgil's twelve by Maffeo Veggio.

Phaer's translation, in rhyming lines of fourteen syllables, is fairly readable and generally faithful to the original. The work was held in high esteem by the Elizabethans. George Puttenham, in numbering the best English poets, declared that 'In Queenes Maries time florished above any other Doctour Phaer' (Puttenham, *Arte of English Poesie*, ed. E. Arber, 1906, 75). Thomas Nashe too praised Phaer's 'heavenly verse' while complaining that it was 'blemished by his hautie thoghts' (*The Works of Thomas Nashe*, ed. R. B. McKerrow, rev. F. P. Wilson, 1958, 3.319). The precise nature of the charge is unclear, but Nashe may have been referring to Phaer's ambitiousness as a would-be Renaissance polymath, devoting himself simultaneously to law, medicine, and poetry. The same point was later made by Wood, rather more gently, when he noted that Phaer was remembered as 'a person of mutable mind' (Wood, *Ath. Oxon.*, 315).

However disparate their subject matter, all of Phaer's published works are united by use of the English language, and the author's often aggressive pride in that tongue. In his legal and medical works Phaer associated the use of the vernacular with social reform and the popularization of vital knowledge. Describing medical lore as a treasure, he announced his intention 'to declare that to the use of many, which ought not to be secrete for lucre of

a fewe' (Phaer, *The Regiment of Lyfe*, 1546, sig. Aiiv). At the same time, in keeping with the mood of post-Reformation England, Phaer was concerned to uphold the worthiness of English on patriotic grounds. He claimed to have undertaken his translation of the *Aeneid* in part 'for defence of my countrey language (which I have heard discommended of many, and estemyd of some to be more than barbarous)' (Phaer, sig. X2r).

It is a paradox of Phaer's career that he devoted himself to the defence of the English language on populist and patriotic grounds while living in a region of west Wales where English was not widely spoken. Whether or not he ever learned Welsh, Phaer was clearly committed both politically and poetically to his adopted country. Significantly, he chose a Welsh subject for his one avowed contribution to *The Mirror for Magistrates*, and his collaborators found it noteworthy 'that a Saxon would speake so mutch for a Brytton' (Campbell, 131). Given that the Welsh in this era claimed descent from Aeneas and the Trojans, Phaer's decision to translate Virgil's epic may also have owed something to his local situation.

In addition to serving as solicitor to the council in the marches, Phaer represented Welsh constituencies in four parliaments under three monarchs, being returned first for Carmarthen Boroughs (1547) and subsequently for Cardigan Boroughs (1555, 1558, 1559). He also held a variety of local offices, serving as steward of Cilgerran and constable of Cilgerran Castle from 1548 until his death, as justice of the peace in Cardiganshire, and as customs officer in Milford Haven and other ports. His 'Report on his perambulation around the coast of Wales', prepared in the reign of Edward VI, remains a valuable source of information about Welsh ports and customs administration in the mid-sixteenth century. Phaer's career as a public servant was not marked by controversy, though there is an intriguing reference at the end of the fifth book of *Eneidos*, completed on 4 May 1557, to his having escaped some kind of personal danger in Carmarthen.

In 1560 Phaer suffered the injury, possibly involving a fall from a horse, which deprived him of the use of his right hand and led to his death. His will is dated 12 August 1560, and his death, at his home in the Forest of Cilgerran, followed within a few weeks; on 26 September 1560 John Vaughan succeeded him as steward of Cilgerran. He left his Cilgerran estate, which had been regranted to him in 1558 for a term of forty years, to his wife. He also instructed her to bestow the sum of £5 'where she doth knowe, by an appointemente betwene her and me' (Cunningham, 4). This bequest has been taken as indication that Phaer remained privately faithful to the Catholic church. The inference is supported by his dedication of the *Eneidos* to Queen Mary, and by an approving reference in the preface to Rome's abiding spiritual authority.

On the day before he died, according to William Wightman, Phaer translated and sent to Wightman two lines from the tenth book of the *Aeneid*:

> Ech mans day stands prefixt, time short & swift with cureles bretche

Is lotted al mankind, but by their deedes their fame to
     stretche
That privilege vertue gives.
(*Nyne First Bookes*, sig. Gg3r)

Phaer's death was mourned in verse by Thomas Chaloner
and Barnabe Googe. George Ferrers selected the scriptural
verses for Phaer's memorial in Cilgerran church, where
he was buried. The memorial has long since disappeared,
but a new commemorative tablet was erected at Cilgerran
in 1986, following an appeal in the *British Medical Journal*.

PHILIP SCHWYZER

Sources R. Bowers, *Thomas Phaer and 'The boke of chyldren'* (1544)
(1999) · W. R. B. Robinson, 'Dr Thomas Phaer's report on the har-
bours and customs administration of Wales under Edward VI',
BBCS, 24 (1970–72), 485–90 · J. Ruhräh, *Pediatrics of the past* (1925) ·
DNB · L. B. Campbell, ed., *The mirror for magistrates* (1938) · T. Phaer,
The seven first bookes of the Eneidos of Virgill (1558) · P. Cunningham,
'The will of Thomas Phaer', *Shakespeare Society Papers*, 4 (1849), 1–5 ·
Wood, *Ath. Oxon.*, new edn, vol. 1 · J. R. Phillips, *The history of Cilger-
ran* (1867), 98–102 · R. Fenton, *A historical tour through Pembrokeshire*
(1811)
Archives PRO, exchequer king's remembrancer in memoranda
rolls, 4 Elizabeth 1, E 160
Wealth at death lease on lands in forest of Cilgerran left to wife
(lease had been renewed for forty years' term in 1558): will, 12 Aug
1560, PRO, PROB 11/44/23; Robinson, 'Dr Thomas Phaer's report'

Phayre, Sir Arthur Purves (1812–1885), administrator in
Burma, born at Shrewsbury on 7 May 1812, was the second
son of Richard Phayre, of Claremont, Shrewsbury, and his
wife, Maria, daughter of James Leech Ridgeway, publisher, of 169 Piccadilly, London. Sir Robert *Phayre was
his brother. Educated at Shrewsbury School, he entered
the Indian army and was gazetted ensign in the 7th Bengal
native infantry in August 1828, serving in Gorakhpur and
Azamgarh. His first connection with Burma, the country
with which his life was mainly associated, came in 1834,
when he was sent to Moulmein to raise a Mon corps of
military police for service in Tenasserim which, together
with the province of Arakan, had been ceded to the British
in 1826 at the close of the First Anglo-Burmese War. Promoted lieutenant in 1835, Phayre was appointed senior
assistant to the commissioner of Arakan in 1837, and
served as a district officer at Akyab, Kyaukpyu, and Sando-
way. In 1846 he became principal assistant to the commissioner of Tenasserim, and after volunteering to serve with
his regiment in the Punjab campaign of 1848, returned to
Burma in April 1849 as captain and commissioner of Arakan, in succession to his former chief, Captain Archibald
Bogle. The foundations of Phayre's administrative abilities and of his intimate knowledge of Burmese language
and history were laid during these early years in Burma.
His talents caught the attention of Lord Dalhousie,
governor-general of India, who selected him in December
1852 to become commissioner of the Lower Burma province of Pegu, annexed at the close of the Second Anglo-
Burmese War. Phayre was promoted major in 1855 and
lieutenant-colonel in 1859. He was responsible for planning the early development and lay-out of Rangoon as the
capital of the new province of Pegu, which flourished
under his administration. In late 1854 he accompanied a
Burmese mission to Calcutta and the following year, as

envoy of the governor-general, led a return mission to the
court of King Mindon for the purpose of establishing
treaty relations. He was accompanied on the 1855 mission
to Amarapura by, among others, Thomas Oldham, superintendent of the geological survey of India, the photographer Captain Linnaeus Tripe, Colesworthy Grant as official artist, and Captain Henry Yule as secretary. Phayre's
mission, although it did not succeed in obtaining a treaty,
collected much valuable information about Burma, its
people, and its government, and achieved fame through
Yule's report, published in 1858 as *A Narrative of the Mission
Sent by the Governor-General of India to the Court of Ava in 1855*.
In 1862 the three provinces of Tenasserim, Arakan, and
Pegu were formed into a united administration and
Phayre was appointed first chief commissioner of British
Burma. Phayre led a second mission to the Burmese court
at Mandalay in 1862, when a commercial treaty was nego-
tiated, and a third mission in 1866 when he was promoted
colonel. Owing to ill health, he retired as chief commis-
sioner in February 1867 and the following month left
Burma, never to return.

Phayre, having declined Sir Stafford Northcote's offer of
the prestigious post of resident at Hyderabad, travelled
extensively in India, the Far East, and America. After
returning to Britain in 1870, he settled at Bray, near Dublin, for four years. In November 1874 he was appointed by
Lord Carnarvon to the governorship of Mauritius. His
administration was both successful and popular, and he
held office until the end of 1878, when he in effect retired
from the Indian army, though remaining on the supernumerary list of the Bengal staff corps. In recognition of
his distinguished services he was made a CB in 1863, KCSI
in 1867, and GCMG in 1877, and he received military promotion to major-general in 1870 and to lieutenant-general
in 1877. On his return from Mauritius he settled again at
Bray, and occupied himself in compiling his *History of
Burma, including Burma proper, Pegu, Taungnu, Tenasserim and
Arakan, from the earliest time to the end of the first war with
British India* (1883; repr. 1969). This pioneering work was
based substantially on the *Mahayazawin* or 'royal chronicles' and other Burmese sources. One of his last public
acts was to write a letter to *The Times* (13 October 1885)
expressing his approval of military intervention in and
annexation of independent Upper Burma. He died,
unmarried, at 12 Goldsmith Terrace, Queensborough
Road, Bray on the night of 14–15 December 1885, and was
buried at Enniskerry.

As a soldier–administrator, Phayre had a deep devotion
to duty and was a zealous official correspondent, while his
understanding of Burmese matters was exceptional. His
firm and just administration laid the foundations of the
prosperity of the lower Burma provinces under British
rule, and his scholarly knowledge of Burmese language,
literature, and history made an important contribution to
Anglo-Burmese relations and to the historiography of
Burma.

Phayre's publications, besides *The History of Burma*, were
Coins of Arakan, of Pegu and of Burma (part of the International Numismata Orientalia, 1882), and many articles

in the *Journal of the Asiatic Society of Bengal* as detailed in the *Proceedings of the Royal Geographical Society* (8, 1886, 111) and the *British Library Journal* (1975, 69).

PATRICIA M. HERBERT

Sources H. Yule, *Proceedings* [Royal Geographical Society], new ser., 8 (1886), 103–12 · H. Yule, *A narrative of the mission sent by the governor-general of India to the court of Ava in 1855* (1968) [repr. of 1858 orig.] · D. G. E. Hall, ed., *The Dalhousie–Phayre correspondence, 1852–1856* (1932) · P. M. Herbert, 'The Sir Arthur Phayre collection of Burmese manuscripts', *British Library Journal*, 1 (1975), 62–70 · *East-India Register and Directory* (1830), 52 · *India List, Civil and Military* (March 1877), 291
Archives BL OIOC | BL OIOC, letters to Sir E. B. Sladen, MS Eur. E 290 · NA Scot., letters to Lord Dalhousie · W. Yorks. AS, Leeds, letters, when commissioner of Pegu, to Lord Canning
Likenesses C. Grant, portrait, 1855, BL OIOC · photograph, c.1862, BL OIOC, Bowring collection · T. N. Maclean, bronze statue, exh. RA 1889, Gov. Art Coll. · T. Jones, portrait, East India Club, London · woodcut, NPG
Wealth at death £16,566 15s. 8d.: administration, 13 May 1886, CGPLA Eng. & Wales

Phayre [Phaire], **Robert** (1618/19–1682), parliamentarian army officer, was almost certainly the son of the Revd Emmanuel Phayre. The father had migrated, probably from Devon, to Ireland, where he held ecclesiastical livings in co. Cork. Both father and son sustained losses during the uprising of 1641, when they were living near Duhallow in the north of the county. Robert Phayre was then farming in a modest way. In 1642 he asserted that he had endured losses totalling £51 10s. Like neighbours among the protestant settlers he enlisted in the force commanded by Inchiquin in an effort to contain the Irish Catholic insurgents and recover possessions. By September 1646 he had risen to the rank of lieutenant-colonel in the regiment of Richard Townshend. Phayre did not follow his general, the earl of Inchiquin, in defecting to the king, and was arrested by Inchiquin in the spring of 1648.

Freed after an exchange of prisoners, Phayre next made his way to England where he appeared as a volunteer in Thomas Fairfax's parliamentarian force. Shortly afterwards, in January 1649, he was one of the officers in London to whom the warrant for Charles I's execution was directed. He was among the halberdiers who guarded Whitehall while the sentence was carried out. In the autumn of 1649 he returned to Ireland to assist in the reconquest. Serving under Roger Boyle, Lord Broghill, he fought chiefly in his own province of Munster, taking part in the victory in Macroom on 10 April 1650. His enthusiasm for and prominence in the cause of the English Commonwealth led to his appointment in 1651 as governor of co. Cork. As well as overseeing numerous administrative tasks in the aftermath of warfare, he supported religious and political radicals. This offended the more orthodox within the local protestant community. At the same time he treated some defeated Catholics, notably Lord and Lady Muskerry, compassionately. Phayre's loyalties lay with the Commonwealth: reservations about the 'Instrument of government' and Cromwell's advance to the position of protector may explain his retirement from the governorship of Cork in 1654. In the same year, however, at the age of thirty-five, he was appointed to the commission of the

peace in that county. The authorities were perturbed when he protected Quakers, whom he credited with doing more to advance godliness than any other group during the past century.

Phayre's army service was rewarded with the grant of lands confiscated from the defeated Irish Catholics. To these he added through private transactions. In particular he became involved in the exploitation of the dense woodlands and iron ore deposits around Enniscorthy, co. Wexford, where he and other soldiers from his regiment had been allocated lands. Earlier, in 1654, he had been charged by the state with preserving the depleted woods in co. Cork and settled at Rostellan, where he was still living in 1664. These private and profitable projects occupied him during the time of Henry Cromwell's government in Ireland, the conservative tenor of which did not please Phayre. Between 1657 and 1658 he was in London to negotiate a partnership to exploit the Enniscorthy property. Phayre had married, probably a woman named Houghton, by 10 March 1653, when a letter to him referred to his 'wife and little babes'; they are known to have had two sons (both of whom predeceased Phayre) and two daughters (Welply, 30.22). Following his first wife's death Phayre married on 16 August 1658 at St Werburgh's, Dublin, Elizabeth (d. 1698?), daughter of Thomas *Herbert, attendant to Charles I in 1647–9. Together they had three sons and three daughters.

The fall of the protectorate and the advent of a more radical regime both in Ireland and England led to his receiving a new commission, on 8 July 1659, as a colonel of foot under Edmund Ludlow. Phayre had been on hand in London on 27 June 1659 to present a petition from republican officers in Ireland to parliament. In Ireland, he again acted as governor of Cork. But once the restoration of Charles II became inevitable, he was vulnerable on account alike of his opinions and record. He had been seized during the coup engineered by more conservative officers in December 1659. He was arrested again at Cork on 18 May 1660, and then transported to England. Although imprisoned in the Tower of London, he escaped trial thanks to the intercession of royalists whom he had befriended during the interregnum and of his father-in-law, Herbert. However, he was not released until 1662, when he was permitted to return to Ireland. There he soon came under fresh suspicion of complicity in a plot to surprise Dublin Castle in 1663. He had not severed his links with republican comrades of the 1650s. Indeed John Lisle was assassinated while visiting Edmund Ludlow in his Swiss exile in 1664 when allegedly he was mistaken for Phayre.

In Ireland, though he was watched closely, Phayre was not ostracized. He continued to develop iron-works in co. Wexford and his own estate at Grange, near Ovens in co. Cork, where he settled in his later years. He was also still involved in the timber trade. Nor had he forsaken his search for spiritual satisfaction. He patronized the co. Waterford healer Valentine Greatorex (who had earlier served in Phayre's own regiment), and still kept the company of the Quakers. He entertained William Penn, the son of another settler in co. Cork, when the Quaker visited Ireland in 1669–70. But it was as a disciple of Lodowick Muggleton, encountered in London in 1662 while under restraint, that Phayre ended his idiosyncratic quest for religious truth. In worldly terms, to judge from his will, he had prospered. He died at Grange between his making it, on 13 September 1682, and its proof on 13 November 1682, and was probably buried in the family plot belonging to his son-in-law, the Cork merchant, Quaker, and former Muggletonian George Gamble, in the parish of St John of Jerusalem in the south liberties of Cork.

TOBY BARNARD

Sources depositions of E. and R. Phayre, 23 May 1642, TCD, MS 825, fols. 60, 275 · R. T. Dunlop, *Ireland under the Commonwealth*, 2 vols. (1913) · *The memoirs of Edmund Ludlow*, ed. C. H. Firth, 2 vols. (1894) · T. C. Barnard, *Cromwellian Ireland* (1975) · BL, Lansdowne MS 821 · J. C., 'Robert Phaire, regicide', *Journal of the Cork Historical and Archaeological Society*, 2nd ser., 20 (1914), 146–50, 199–203 · W. H. Welply, 'Colonel Robert Phaire, "regicide"', *Journal of the Cork Historical and Archaeological Society*, 2nd ser., 30 (1925), 20–26; 31 (1926), 31–6, 78–86; 32 (1927), 24–33 · Bodl. Oxf., MS Carte 32, fol. 653; 66, fol. 215 · diary of the second earl of Cork, Chatsworth House, Derbyshire, Lismore MSS · St J. Brodrick to Lady Orrery, 12 Oct 1668, W. Sussex RO, Orrery MSS, general series, 28 · J. Reeve and L. Muggleton, *A volume of spiritual epistles* (1755), 91, 104 · C. H. Firth and G. Davies, *The regimental history of Cromwell's army*, 2 (1940), 654–6 · R. Caulfield, ed., *The council book of the corporation of the city of Cork* (1876), 1164–5 · *Report on the manuscripts of the earl of Egmont*, 2 vols. in 3, HMC, 63 (1905–9), vol. 1, p. 523 · W. Penn, *My Irish journal, 1669–70*, ed. I. Grubb (1952) · T. C. Barnard, 'An Anglo-Irish industrial venture: iron-making at Enniscorthy, 1657–92', *Proceedings of the Royal Irish Academy*, 85C (1985), 101–44

Wealth at death over £9000: will, Welply, 'Colonel Robert Phaire' (1926), 35

Phayre, Sir Robert (1820–1897), army officer, born at Shrewsbury on 22 January 1820, was the third son of Richard Phayre of Claremont Buildings, Shrewsbury, and brother of General Sir Arthur Purves *Phayre. He was educated at Shrewsbury School, and commissioned ensign in the East India Company service on 26 January 1839, being posted to the 25th Bombay native infantry, and became lieutenant on 1 December 1840. He served with his regiment in the First Anglo-Afghan War, was engaged with the Baluchis under Nasir Khan at Kotra and Gandava in December 1840, and was mentioned in dispatches. He took part in the 1843 Sind War, was severely wounded at Miani, and was again mentioned in dispatches for bravery. In 1844 he was appointed assistant quartermaster-general in Sind. In 1846 he married Diana Bunbury (d. 1904), daughter of Captain Arnold Thompson, formerly paymaster of the 81st regiment.

From 1851 to 1856 Phayre was specially employed in clearing mountain roads in the southern Maratha country. In 1856–7 he was involved in the organization of the expeditionary force to Persia. From March 1857 and throughout the Indian mutiny he was quartermaster-general to the Bombay army, his services being highly commended by Sir Hugh Rose (later Lord Strathnairn) on 15 May 1860. He held this appointment until 1868. He had become captain in his regiment on 28 December 1848, and

was made brevet major on 16 June 1857, and major in the Bombay staff corps on 18 February 1861.

Phayre became brevet lieutenant-colonel on 6 January 1863, and colonel five years later. He took part in the Abyssinian expedition as quartermaster-general, was mentioned in dispatches, and was made CB and aide-de-camp to the queen. From 1868 to 1872 he was political superintendent of the Sind frontier, and commandant of the frontier force. In March 1873 he was appointed resident at Baroda. He made strong representations of the misgovernment of the Maharaja Gaikwar, Malhar Rao, and a commission which investigated his charges found that they were substantially proved. The Gaikwar was warned and advised to change his minister, but matters did not improve. The friction between Phayre and the Gaikwar increased, and at the instigation of the latter an attempt was made on 9 November 1874 to poison Phayre, by putting arsenic and diamond dust in his sherbet. The Baroda trial followed, and led to the deposition of the Gaikwar on 23 April 1875. But the Indian government had previously decided to change the resident at Baroda, and Phayre, declining to resign, was superseded by Sir Lewis Pelly on 25 November 1874.

Reverting to military employment, Phayre commanded a brigade, first in Bombay and afterwards in Rajputana, from 10 May 1875 to 4 May 1880. Having been promoted major-general on 1 January 1880, he was then appointed to command the reserve division of the army engaged in the second campaign of the Second Anglo-Afghan War, and had charge of the line of communication by Quetta to Kandahar. After the disaster of Maiwand (27 July 1880), Phayre was directed to push forward to Kandahar, which was being besieged by Ayub Khan, but was delayed by a lack of troops and transport, as well as by tribal uprising as a result of Maiwand, and Kandahar was relieved by Roberts before his arrival. Phayre was mentioned in dispatches, and made KCB on 22 February 1881. He commanded with distinction a division of the Bombay army from 1 March 1881 to 2 March 1886, and for some months acted as commander-in-chief at Bombay. On 22 January 1887 he was placed on the unemployed supernumerary list. He had become lieutenant-general on 1 November 1881, and became general on 22 January 1889. He received the GCB on 26 May 1894.

Phayre was active in religious and philanthropic movements, and published pamphlets including *The Bible versus Corrupt Christianity* (1890) and *Monasticism Unveiled* (1890). He died at his home, 64 St George's Square, Pimlico, London, on 28 January 1897.

E. M. LLOYD, rev. JAMES LUNT

Sources *The Times* (29 Jan 1897) · Lord Roberts [F. S. Roberts], *Forty-one years in India*, 2 vols. (1897) · T. H. Thornton, *General Sir Richard Meade and the feudatory states of central and southern India* (1898) · official record of the expedition to Abyssinia · B. Robson, *The road to Kabul: the Second Afghan War, 1878–1881* (1986) · V. C. P. Hodson, *List of officers of the Bengal army, 1758–1834*, 4 vols. (1927–47) · J. W. Kaye, *History of the war in Afghanistan*, 3rd edn, 3 vols. (1874) · J. A. Norris, *The First Afghan War, 1838–1842* (1967) · CGPLA Eng. & Wales (1897)

Likenesses engraving, repro. in *The Graphic* (1875) · engraving, repro. in *ILN* (6 Feb 1897) · woodcuts, NPG

Wealth at death £905 2s. 11d.: resworn probate, March 1898, *CGPLA Eng. & Wales* (1897)

Phear, Sir John Budd (1825–1905), judge in India and author, was born at Earl Stonham, Suffolk, on 9 February 1825, the eldest son of John Phear (1794–1869), fellow of Pembroke College, Cambridge, and rector of Earl Stonham from 1823 to 1869, and his wife, Catherine Wreford, only daughter of Samuel Budd, doctor, of North Tawton, Devon. Of his two brothers, Henry Carylon Phear (1826–1880) was a fellow of Gonville and Caius College, Cambridge, and a chancery barrister, and the Revd Samuel George Phear (1829–1918) was master of Emmanuel College, Cambridge, from 1871 to 1895.

Educated privately by his father, John entered Pembroke College, Cambridge, in March 1843 and graduated BA as sixth wrangler in 1847. In April 1847 he was elected a fellow of Clare College and shortly thereafter mathematical lecturer. While at Cambridge he published two textbooks, *Elementary Mechanics* (1850) and *Elementary Hydrostatics with Numerous Examples* (1852), and in 1856 was moderator of the mathematical tripos. He left Cambridge in 1854, but retained his fellowship until his marriage in 1865. In 1854 Phear was called to the bar by the Inner Temple and joined the western circuit, subsequently transferring himself to the Norfolk circuit. In 1859 he published *A Treatise on Rights of Water*, which remained the standard legal text on the topic for many years.

In 1864 Phear was appointed a judge of the high court of Bengal, and on 16 October 1865, at Madras, married the widowed Emily Tabart (d. 1897), daughter of John Bolton of Burnley House, Stockwell, with whom he had two daughters.

As a judge Phear prided himself on his freedom from racial prejudice and was particularly noted for his refusal to trivialize cases of assault brought by Indians against Europeans. In Calcutta's insular Anglo-Indian community such behaviour was soon translated into the perceived sin of 'a partiality for the natives'—a view heightened in 1867, when Phear and his wife gave an Indian name to their first-born daughter, Ethel Kamini.

In addition to his judicial duties, Phear was variously president of the Asiatic Society of Bengal, the Bengal Social Science Association, and the Bengal Photographic Society. In particular, as long-term president of the Bethune Society, dedicated to the education of Bengalis, he established himself as a prominent commentator on Indian domestic life. He was respected by many Westernized Bengalis but his belief that India's social and political advancement hinged on the processes of Anglicization and female emancipation alienated the more radical members of Bengal's intelligentsia. Phear only moved comfortably among those Bengalis who acknowledged the superiority of Western achievements; it was beyond doubt to him that Bengal's indigenous culture, which he described in *The Aryan Village in India and Ceylon* (1880), represented a lesser, primitive stage of civilization.

Phear left Calcutta in August 1876 and in the following year was knighted and appointed chief justice of Ceylon, in which post he revised the civil and criminal code for the colony. He returned to England in 1879 and settled at Marpool Hall, Exmouth, Devon, and, as in Bengal, threw himself into local public life. He chaired the quarter sessions for fourteen years from October 1881 and served as an alderman of Devon county council from 1889 until his death. An ardent Liberal, he thrice contested unsuccessfully Devon county divisions in the Liberal interest: Honiton in 1885, Tavistock in 1886, and Tiverton in 1892. In 1886 he was president of the Devonshire Association for the Advancement of Science, Literature, and Art. He was a good cricketer and a life member of the London Skating Club, and, from 1852, a fellow of the Geological Society.

Phear died at Marpool Hall, Exmouth, on 7 April 1905 and was buried at Littleham. His wife, Emily, a member of the Exmouth school board, had died in 1897.

T. C. HUGHES, rev. KATHERINE PRIOR

Sources *The Times* (8 April 1905), 6 · *Charivari's album* (1875) · *Friend of India* (5 Aug 1876) · *Friend of India* (12 Aug 1876) · *The Englishman* (3 Aug 1876) · *The Englishman* (4 Aug 1876) · *The Englishman* (9 Aug 1876) · ecclesiastical records, BL OIOC · Venn, *Alum. Cant.*, 2/5
Likenesses Isca, lithograph, c.1875, repro. in *Charivari's album*
Wealth at death £67,800 9s. 10d.: probate, 22 May 1905, *CGPLA Eng. & Wales*

Phelip, William, Baron Bardolf (1383/4–1441), nobleman and soldier, was the son and heir of Sir William Phelip of Dennington, Suffolk (d. 1407) and his wife, Juliana, daughter of Sir Robert Erpingham of Erpingham, Norfolk. His early political career was shaped by his close association with his maternal uncle, Sir Thomas Erpingham, a leading figure at court and in East Anglia after 1399. Phelip entered the service of Thomas Beaufort, duke of Exeter, with whom Erpingham was closely connected, and who was the leading magnate in East Anglia from 1405 when he was granted the Norfolk estates forfeited by Thomas, Lord Bardolf, because of his involvement in the Scrope rebellion. It was presumably through Beaufort's influence that Phelip married Joan (1390–1447), younger daughter and coheir of Lord Bardolf, by June 1408.

Their connections with Erpingham and Beaufort led Phelip and his younger brother John into royal service under Henry IV, and both rose to greater prominence under Henry V. Both fought in the French campaign of 1415; John Phelip died at Harfleur, but William went on to serve at Agincourt. He spent the years from 1417 to 1422 mostly in France, and served as captain of Harfleur from July 1421 to November 1422. He had been knighted in 1413, and became a knight of the Garter in 1418. From October 1421 until November 1422 he also held office as treasurer of Henry V's household. This eminence in central government continued under Henry VI; Phelip was appointed to the royal council in May 1432, and became chamberlain of the king's household in November of that year, appointments that he held until his death.

Phelip's influence in East Anglia was also increasing. He was MP for Suffolk in both parliaments of 1414; he became a regular member of the peace commission in Suffolk from 1423, and in Norfolk from 1429, and served on a wide variety of other local commissions. The childless deaths of Beaufort in 1426 and Erpingham in 1428 offered Phelip the opportunity, as Erpingham's heir and Beaufort's chief executor, to take their place at the head of the broad political connection that had developed under their leadership in East Anglia since 1399. However, the farm of the Bardolf estates which Beaufort had held was secured in 1431 not by Phelip but by William de la Pole, earl of Suffolk (1396–1450), who was seeking to establish his own regional lordship after his return from France in 1430.

Phelip had, with Erpingham, held the custody of Suffolk's lands during his minority from 1415 to 1418, but there is little evidence of further association between Phelip and Suffolk in a local context in the years immediately after the earl's return to England. Their respective authorities seem to have developed in parallel until 1437, when a series of manoeuvres resulted in an accommodation which allowed their regional interests to be assimilated into a single political connection. In November 1437 Suffolk surrendered his farm of the Bardolf lands in Norfolk so that a hereditary grant could finally be made to Phelip; two days later Phelip surrendered the lordship of Swaffham in Norfolk, the farm of which he had recently acquired, so that it could be granted to Suffolk. Phelip had therefore succeeded in recovering his wife's inheritance, in recognition of which he was thereafter styled Baron Bardolf, while Suffolk's regional authority had been safeguarded. Accommodation was again reached between Suffolk and Phelip in the reorganization of the duchy of Lancaster administration in the same year; the earl became chief steward of the north parts of the duchy, and Phelip was granted the equivalent office in the south.

Phelip died on 6 June 1441, and was buried at Dennington, as was his wife, who died six years later. Their only child, Elizabeth, wife of John Beaumont, Viscount Beaumont, died shortly after her father (certainly by October 1441). Her heir was her son William, during whose minority Beaumont had custody of the estates.

HELEN CASTOR

Sources Chancery records · HoP, Commons, 1386–1421 · CIPM, vols. 19–20 · PRO · E. F. Jacob, ed., The register of Henry Chichele, archbishop of Canterbury, 1414–1443, 2, CYS, 42 (1937), 598–605 · CPR, 1405–8, 448 · PRO, Inquisitions Post Mortem, C139/30
Wealth at death will, Jacob, ed., Register of Henry Chichele · £400 p.a., 'conservative valuation': HoP, Commons, 1386–1421, 4.71–4

Phelippes, Thomas (c.1556–1625×7), cryptographer and intelligence gatherer, was the first son of William Philipps (d. 1590), a cloth merchant and customs officer for wool in the port of London, and his wife, Joan (d. 1613), daughter of Thomas Houghton. Little is known of Phelippes's early life, though he may have been the matriculant who entered Trinity College, Cambridge, in 1569 and graduated BA in 1574, proceeding MA in 1577. Certainly he was schooled in languages, Latin and Italian in particular but also French, Spanish, and German. He was described by his father as 'being of a stayd and secrett nature' (PRO, SP 12/194/21), and by 1578 he was known to Thomas Wilson, the principal secretary, as skilled in deciphering codes. Already employed by Sir Francis Walsingham—probably as an intelligence agent—Phelippes was a frequent visitor during 1578–83 to the English embassy in Paris and visited

Bruges in August 1582. At home in London he was by now, like his father, 'of the custom house' (Diaries of John Dee, 46) and in 1580 had to defend himself from the first of many subsequent allegations that he diverted crown revenues to his own use. From this period also can be dated Phelippes's reputation as an accomplished mimic, as well as his association with Francis Bacon, who during 1584–6 'brought upp' one of his younger brothers (Hammer, 154).

During the mid-1580s Phelippes became central to Walsingham's intelligence system. His expertise was varied—as cryptographer, forger, and gatherer of secret correspondence. His extensive correspondence with overseas agents is recorded from January 1584 and during the winter of 1584–5 he was said by another of Walsingham's servants, Thomas Harrison, to have 'wrought' the evidence upon which the queen's would-be assassin William Parry was condemned and executed (Hicks, 69). He may have been MP for Hastings in 1584 and 1586.

More certain is Phelippes's role in the downfall of Mary, queen of Scots. In December 1585 he visited her at Chartley, Staffordshire, where she had been placed under the supervision of Sir Amias Paulet, one of his former employers in Paris. Mary recorded her impression of Phelippes: 'of low stature, slender every way, dark yellow haired on the head, and clear yellow bearded, eaten in the face with smallpox [and] of short sight' (Pickering, 3.219). Mary was distrustful. 'Although he has promised to do me service', she reported, 'I know that he is playing a double game' (Hicks, 245). Phelippes now changed tack and set about establishing how her confidential correspondence might be intercepted secretly. Between May and July 1586 Mary incriminated herself through coded letters intercepted and deciphered by Phelippes—first in London, then at Chartley itself—in which she supported invasion plans and Anthony Babington's assassination plot against Elizabeth. For his efforts Phelippes received a pension of 100 marks from Elizabeth for the remainder of her reign, Walsingham assuring him that he would 'not believe in how good part she accepteth of your service' (Smith, 127).

By 1586 Phelippes had married his wife, Mary. It seems there were no children, and throughout their married life Mary supported and assisted her husband in his work. For the next four years he was the linchpin in Walsingham's extensive intelligence service: paying agents; drafting copious memoranda and dispatches; collecting examples of codes and alphabets; maintaining an extensive correspondence with agents in Scotland, France, and the Netherlands; deciphering and encrypting secret correspondence; and handling letters intercepted by the government. The sum of £2000 was allocated for the secretarial costs of this aspect of government business in 1588 alone. In much of the sensitive correspondence that Phelippes decoded numbers or symbols were used to disguise proper names. Informed readers could readily guess such meanings. However, in the ciphers used by Mary and her correspondents the letters of each word were encrypted using a system of substitutes or symbols which required for their decoding the construction of a parallel alphabet of letters. To establish such cipher keys Phelippes employed frequency analysis in which individual letters were identified in the order of those most commonly used in English and the less frequent substitutes deduced in the manner of a modern crossword puzzle.

When Walsingham died in April 1590 Phelippes's work came to an abrupt halt as William Cecil, Lord Burghley, reined in government costs. To maintain a personal network of overseas spies and correspondents Phelippes had to draw on fresh resources: the income from the London property he now inherited from his father but also substantial appropriation of the crown revenues he handled as a customs official. This was risky, for under Robert Cecil and Robert Devereux, second earl of Essex, during 1592–5 his employment in intelligence was sporadic. Furthermore, a blunder by one of his agents in September 1593 saw the queen impute 'weakness of judgement' to him (*Salisbury MSS*, 6.511) and once his services in uncovering the alleged plot against Elizabeth led by Rodrigo Lopez were concluded, Burghley intervened again. With Phelippes's debts to the crown estimated at £10,000, his income from the customs was suspended in December 1594 and he was ordered to make monthly repayments. Unable to do so, he lost his job at the customs and was imprisoned in the Marshalsea and then in the Fleet as a debtor from the end of 1595 to mid-1597.

Yet such was the value placed on Phelippes's expertise that Essex sent him papers to decipher in his prison cell. So too did Cecil, and when he and the queen complained that Phelippes's work was slow, he reminded them of the technical obstacles, pointing out that the Spanish continually deployed new codes in 'such kind as will ask time to tread it out', while imprisonment had damaged him 'in body and mind' and denied him access to his records (*Salisbury MSS*, 7.96–7). Phelippes was at liberty by June 1597 through the intervention of Anthony Bacon, who offered to discharge his debts, now officially calculated at £11,683. He was in prison again in the summer of 1598, however, no doubt at Burghley's behest; his renewed release in August 'for better finding means of paying his debt' (*CSP dom.*, 1598–1601, 104) came within a week of the lord treasurer's death. Cecil, now principal secretary, was more accommodating. From mid-1597, with Essex overseas, he had changed tack by expanding the intelligence budget, and he retained Phelippes as his personal intelligencer for the rest of the reign.

The accession of James I proved an irreversible set-back for Phelippes. Stripped of his pension as part-repayment of his debt to the crown, he was imprisoned in the Gatehouse in January 1605 at the instigation of Henry Howard, earl of Northampton. Trunks were removed from his house 'and all his papers seased' (*Letters of John Chamberlain*, 1.202) to allow investigation of his contacts with the fugitive Catholic Hugh Owen in Brussels, a correspondence that went back to at least 1593. Released after ten weeks, Phelippes resumed intelligence duties and was involved in apprehending the conspirators in the Gunpowder Plot. However, when in January 1606 Guy Fawkes

admitted Owen's involvement, and when Phelippes continued to correspond with Owen, Cecil had Phelippes reimprisoned in the Gatehouse, considering that his integrity was now decisively brought 'into question' (*Salisbury MSS*, 18.51). Phelippes was subsequently moved to the Tower and remained in prison for at least four and half years. Mary took on her husband's correspondence. This included her attempts to secure from old contacts in Brussels the formula 'for converting iron into steel … as a mean to relieve our decayed estate' (ibid., 19.393) and in 1609 she appealed to Cecil successfully for the moiety of two of her husband's suspended crown annuities. Thereafter Phelippes's fortunes deteriorated further. From 1610 until 1620 he was involved in litigation over the revenues from his principal provincial estate, at Kirkby Misperton in Yorkshire. Even more protracted was his feud with Sir Anthony Ashley, conducted over at least fifteen years from 1596. Phelippes was at liberty by 1612 but in May 1622 was once more in the Marshalsea 'upon an old quarrel between me and one Tyttyn' (*Letter-Books*, 375).

Despite his fractious temperament, Phelippes had established himself in the 1580s and 1590s as the master of his art in England. In his own assessment the work presented four technical challenges: cipher writers were often semi-literate, making the codes used inconsistent; very often encrypted correspondence was fraudulent in content, provenance, authorship, and recipient; sustained mental stamina was required—a single Armada paper had, he declared, 'held me twenty days in work'; and each time the Spanish realized he had broken a code, a new cipher was devised and this made essential the keeping of precise records of known codes and alphabets (*Salisbury MSS*, 7.96–7). Multiple aliases were also essential and he was known to correspondents at various times as Peter Halins, John Morice, Henry Willsdon, and John Wystand. In 1622 Phelippes was described by the Venetian ambassador in London as being still 'unequalled in deciphering' (*CSP Venice*, 1621–3, 289); however, failing eyesight and his disuse of Italian meant that when the Venetians used Phelippes that year to test the security of diplomatic correspondence their ciphers defeated him. In 1624 more work for the Venetians arose and Phelippes, now almost blind, imparted the key of a cipher to a friend. This so concerned the incoming ambassador, Zuane Pesaro, that in January 1625 George Villiers, first duke of Buckingham, agreed to Phelippes's being placed in solitary confinement in king's bench even though, in Pesaro's view, Phelippes 'dealt sincerely' and should be paid by the Venetian state 'as he has certainly rendered services' (ibid., 1623–5, 601). In April Sir Edward Conway told the ambassador that 'the laws did not allow of his close confinement any longer' (ibid., 1625–6, 6) but Phelippes was still in prison in December. Whether he was ever released is unknown: his wife was a widow by March 1627.

WILLIAM RICHARDSON

Sources *CSP dom.*, 1582–1627 · *Calendar of the manuscripts of the most hon. the marquis of Salisbury*, 24 vols., HMC, 9 (1883–1976), vols. 5–7, 10, 12–15, 17–19, 21, 24 · *CSP for.*, 1577–89 · *CSP Venice*, 1621–6 · M. R. Pickering, 'Phillips, Thomas', HoP, *Commons*, 1558–1603, 3.219–20 ·

P. E. J. Hammer, *The polarisation of Elizabethan politics: the political career of Robert Devereux, 2nd earl of Essex, 1585–1597* (1999) · A. G. Smith, *The Babington plot* (1936) · R. B. Wernham, *The return of the armadas: the last years of the Elizabethan war against Spain, 1595–1603* (1994) · *The letter-books of Sir Amias Poulet*, ed. J. Morris (1874) · *The diaries of John Dee*, ed. E. Fenton (1998) · *The letters of John Chamberlain*, ed. N. E. McClure, 1 (1939) · F. Collins, ed., *Feet of fines of the Tudor period*, 4: *1594–1603*, Yorkshire Archaeological and Topographical Association, 8 (1890) · L. Hicks, *An Elizabethan problem: some aspects of the careers of two exile adventurers* (1964) · P. M. Handover, *The second Cecil* (1959) · S. Singh, *The code book: the secret history of codes and code breakers* (1999) · J. H. Pollen and W. MacMahon, eds., *The Ven. Philip Howard, earl of Arundel, 1557–1595: English martyrs*, Catholic RS, 21 (1919) · State papers domestic, Elizabeth I, PRO, SP 12/194/21
Archives BL, Bagot MSS · BL, Cotton MS Julius C.iii · BL, Lansdowne MSS 31, 82, 83, 84 · Hatfield House, Hertfordshire, marquess of Salisbury MSS · PRO, State papers, foreign · PRO, SP 46/19, fol. 38 · PRO, SP 46/20, fols. 229–30 · PRO, SP 46/38, fols. 16 and 141 · PRO, SP 46/40, fol. 127

Phelips, Sir Edward (*c.*1555–1614), speaker of the House of Commons, was the fourth and youngest son of Thomas Phelips (*c.*1500–1590) of Montacute, Somerset, and Corfe Mullen, Dorset, and his wife, Elizabeth Smyth (*d.* 1598), daughter of Matthew *Smyth [see under Smyth family (*per. c.*1500–1680)], a merchant, of Bristol. His father, former servant to Thomas Cromwell and Protector Somerset, was a successful grazier in Somerset and Dorset, whose own parliamentary service provided the political base for three of his sons. Phelips's education at New Inn and Middle Temple was sponsored by his cousin, the treasurer, Matthew Smyth. Called to the bar in 1579, he established a lucrative career in chancery and in the court of Star Chamber, where his political connections proved crucial. He was appointed autumn reader in the Middle Temple in 1596.

Phelips's legal career was synonymous with his political life. His first seat, Bere Alston, in the 1584 parliament, was under the patronage of his legal client the marchioness of Winchester. His 1586 seat for Weymouth had been previously held by his father, grandfather, and a cousin. He sat for Penryn in 1593, and Robert, second earl of Essex, married to a Somerset connection, was his likely patron for the 1597 seat for Andover. In 1601 he was selected junior knight of the shire for Somerset, just as his impressive mansion at Montacute was being completed alongside the public highway which connected the county seat at Ilchester and the muster grounds on Ham Hill. The intersection of his legal and political careers was evident in his selection as queen's serjeant-at-law in February 1603. When the group of fourteen serjeants were invested in May 1603, Phelips was chosen as James I's serjeant-meane, with 'precedence before all others'. His patrons were Thomas Sackville, earl of Dorset, and Thomas Egerton, then lord chancellor, both supporters of the accession of James I; he was knighted in July that year. In February 1604 he was returned again for Somerset and he was elected speaker on 19 March. Both honours recognized his service to the new sovereign and his chief ministers.

Phelips's political and legal career was devoted to the preservation of governmental order: as justice of common pleas in the county palatine of Lancaster from 1604, he was noted for his prosecution of recusancy; as king's serjeant he opened the indictment against the gunpowder plotters in 1606; as speaker he effectively represented the crown interests. He was rewarded with the reversion of the mastership of the rolls in 1608, succeeding in January 1611, the chancellorship of Prince Henry's re-established duchy of Cornwall in 1610, and the rangership of all royal forests, parks, and chases in 1613. He was also a minor literary patron. He sponsored his father's godson, Thomas Coryate, in Prince Henry's household, and paid Thomas Chapman and Inigo Jones for their Middle Temple masque written for the marriage of Princess Elizabeth. However, the cost of such a public career was high. His expenses, such as the lavish house at Montacute and the entertainment of James I at his leased house at Wanstead, required more funds than the rewards from his political career. The untimely death of Prince Henry in 1612 may have deprived him of future grants.

By the time of his sudden death at Rolls House in London on 11 September 1614, Phelips was £12,000 in debt. His political credit had been eroded, with James I due to his objections to the *post nati* issue and among his peers in Somerset over the contested election in March 1614 when his son, Sir Robert *Phelips, failed to secure a seat. With his first wife, Margaret Newdigate (*d.* 1590), daughter of Robert Newdigate of Hawnes, Bedfordshire, he had two sons, Sir Robert and Francis. By his second marriage, to Elizabeth Pigott (*d.* 1638), daughter of Thomas Pigott of Dodershall, Buckinghamshire, he had one son, Edward. He was buried at St Catherine's Church, Montacute, on 25 September 1614. The family held the mansion at Montacute until 1931, when it was donated to the National Trust.

REBECCA S. MORE

Sources DNB · P. W. Hasler, 'Phelips, Edward', HoP, *Commons, 1558–1603*, 3.216–17 · S. D'Ewes, ed., *The journals of all the parliaments during the reign of Queen Elizabeth, both of the House of Lords and House of Commons* (1682) · *Les reportes del cases in camera stellata, 1593 to 1609, from the original ms. of John Hawarde*, ed. W. P. Baildon (privately printed, London, 1894) · *The letters of John Chamberlain*, ed. N. E. McClure, 2 vols. (1939) · *Calendar of the manuscripts of the most hon. the marquis of Salisbury*, 24 vols., HMC, 9 (1883–1976) · N. Briggs, 'The foundation of Wadham College, Oxford', *Oxoniensia*, 21 (1956), 61–81 · J. H. Bettey, *The rise of a gentry family, the Smyths of Ashton Court, c. 1500–1642* (1978) · R. S. More, 'The rewards of virtue: gentility in early modern England', PhD diss., Brown University, 1998 · VCH *Somerset*, vol. 3 · Baker, *Serjeants* · J. S. Cockburn, 'The spoils of the law: the trial of Sir John Hele, 1604', *Tudor rule and revolution*, ed. D. Guth and J. W. McKenna (1982) · M. A. Kishlansky, *Parliamentary selection: social and political choice in early modern England* (1986) · M. Rogers, *Montacute House* (1991) · G. Haslam, 'Jacobean phoenix: the duchy of Cornwall in the principates of Henry Frederick and Charles', *The estates of the English crown, 1558–1640*, ed. R. W. Hoyle (1992) · E. Skelton, 'The court of star chamber in the reign of Queen Elizabeth', MA diss., U. Lond., 1931 · W. Notestein, *The House of Commons, 1604–1610* (1971) · T. L. Moir, *The Addled Parliament of 1614* (1958) · C. H. Hopwood, ed., *Middle Temple records*, 4 vols. (1904–5) · PRO, C/142/366/190 · Som. ARS, DD/PH5b; DD/PH 221/6 · parish registers, Montacute, St Catherine, Som. ARS, D/P/Mont. 2/1/1
Archives Som. ARS, personal and family papers, incl. Gunpowder Plot legal papers | BL, Hargrave MSS · BL, Lansdowne MSS · Bristol RO, Smyth MSS · Duchy of Cornwall Archive, London, Rolls Series MSS · Essex RO, Chelmsford, Petre MSS · Hunt. L., Ellesmere

MSS · PRO, Chancery Patent Rolls, C66 · PRO, Court of Star Chamber MSS

Likenesses oils, c.1611, Palace of Westminster, London · oils, c.1786, Montacute House, Somerset

Wealth at death £94 6s. 28d. p.a.: PRO, C/142/366/190; Som. ARS, DD/PH 221/6; · £1363 p.a.; debts of approx. £12,000: Chamberlain, *Letters*, ed. McClure, vol. 1, p. 555

Phelips, Sir Robert (1586?–1638), politician and landowner, was the elder son of Sir Edward *Phelips (c.1555–1614) and his first wife, Margaret (d. 1590), daughter of Robert Newdigate of Newdigate, Surrey. There is no record of his early education. He entered the Middle Temple in 1606 as son and heir apparent of Sir Edward, serjeant-at-law, but was never called to the bar. He had already been knighted (with his father) at James I's coronation in 1603. From 1604 to 1611 he sat for East Looe, Cornwall, in James's first parliament, of which his father was speaker. By 1613 he married Bridget, daughter of Sir Thomas Gorges of Longford Castle, Wiltshire. In the parliament of 1614, he failed to win a county seat for Somerset thanks to the organizational skill of another Somerset squire, John Poulett, who became his inveterate enemy. Phelips scrambled to be returned for the Cornish seat of Saltash. He was one of the more eloquent and aggressive MPs, attacking undertakers, demanding satisfaction of grievances before supply, and hotly pursuing Bishop Richard Neile of Lincoln for his speech in the Lords which demeaned the Commons. He moved into the first rank of the growing parliamentary opposition, and suffered for his prominence: by James's command he was sacked as a JP and as *custos rotulorum* for Somerset (in which office he had succeeded his father two years before). Though restored to the commission in 1616, he was never again *custos*.

While his father had secured for him the reversion of one of the three clerkships of the petty bag in chancery in 1613, and he later pursued (unsuccessfully) a mastership of requests, Phelips does not appear to have held any central office. His ambition lay elsewhere. The experience of the grand tour in 1613 promoted his inclusion in Sir John Digby's 1615 embassy to Spain for negotiation of the Spanish match. His journal and papers in his near-illegible hand (Somerset Archive and Record Service, DD/PH, family letters) indicate his early distaste for the alliance. He carried that distaste to parliament in 1621, when he sat for Bath, Somerset, and emerged as one of the half-dozen leaders of the new and strident opposition. But only in the second session, after mistakenly perceiving the marquess of Buckingham's opposition to the alliance, did he attack it in the house and subsequently in a paper entitled 'A Discourse … betweene a counsellor of state and a country gentleman' (Somerset Archive and Record Service, DD/PH 227/16). Attacking Spain as the paymaster of the Catholic powers against the elector palatine and as the destroyer of English trade, he proposed withholding supply until there was a thorough preparation for war in defence of the elector. In 1621 every targeted grievance of the Commons saw Phelips in hot pursuit, leading the chase against monopolists, particularly Sir Giles Mompesson, and against

Lord Chancellor Francis Bacon. He went after smaller game, notably the hapless recusant lawyer, Edward Floyd (Flud)—giving point to S. R. Gardiner's disdainful 'Gifted with an elegant tongue, and with every virtue except discretion' (Gardiner, *History*, 4.248). With parliament's dissolution Phelips was arrested on 1 January 1622; he remained in the Tower until 10 August.

In the 1621 parliament Phelips had led in restoring the franchise of a number of ancient boroughs, including Ilchester, Somerset, of which he was steward and in which he had considerable, though not ineluctable, influence; he meant to avoid another Saltash. In 1624 he carried one of the Somerset seats and had enough sway to put his friend and fellow radical John Symes in the other. While the king wished to exclude Phelips, influence stopped any attempt to bar him. The initial common cause joining Buckingham and the opposition in carrying out war against Spain, the 'blessed revolution' (Cogswell, 139–65), deteriorated by the end of the parliament, and Phelips's mounting bellicosity, given edge by the favourite's passing him over for ambassador to The Hague, cost him Buckingham's indulgence. With the first parliament of Charles's reign in 1625, Phelips again won a county seat, though the other knight for Somerset was Sir John Stawell, protégé of John Poulett. Stawell, no less inimical towards Phelips, was very young and impetuous and cut no figure in the Commons. At Westminster and on adjournment at Oxford, Phelips was pre-eminently the leader of the opposition, in full cry against Buckingham, insisting on withholding supply until grievances were addressed, attacking impositions, and railing against court toleration of Catholics. Gardiner concluded that 'the history of the Parliament of 1625 is summed up in the name of Phelips', that at Oxford he 'virtually assumed that unacknowledged leadership which was all that the traditions of Parliament at that time permitted. It was Phelips who placed the true issue of want of confidence before the House' (Gardiner, *History*, 4.432).

Like Sir Edward Coke and Sir Thomas Wentworth, Phelips was made sheriff (in his case of Somerset) in November 1625 to disable him from sitting in the next parliament. He lost his deputy lieutenancy and his militia colonelcy in 1625 for his opposition to the privy-seal loans. He was put out of the Somerset commission of the peace in 1626 for his vehement opposition to the free gift. The loss of these offices—on the delation of John Poulett, according to Phelips—put him at considerable political disadvantage in the county in his rivalry with Poulett, whose star rose to the heights of a peerage (as Baron Poulett) as Phelips's descended at court. In the two years of his eclipse before the next parliament, Phelips responded to Poulett's challenge by reining in any tendency to court popularity, such as might be considered dangerous by fellow members of the élite, or to trade on the fact he was one of those to be 'thought their countries only freindes' (BL, Royal MS 17 A.xxxvii, fols. 17–33) as the undertakers for draining King's Sedgmoor put it. In fact, while he might have been expected to lead the opposition to that ambitious scheme, he was silent. Phelips managed an advantageous exchange of his Neroche Forest property with the commissioners for its disafforestation and had the satisfaction of seeing the forest's keeper, Poulett, lose his hunting there. During the forced loan of 1626–7 Phelips was much in London and raised no voice against the loan in the county. He could not resist troubling the reform of militia mustering, both in revenge for being excluded from militia matters and as a means to annoy Poulett and his adherents. But his sallies were sufficiently oblique that they could be dissembled by protestations of being wronged by his adversaries and merely defending the just interests of his countrymen threatened by the deputy lieutenants' undue proceedings. In the process he maintained his constituency against the next county election.

Phelips's last election to parliament for Somerset, in February 1628, was at the cost of Sir John Stawell and came upon another victory. Stawell had accused the sheriff of partiality at the 1625 elections, had pressed one of his bailiffs as a soldier, and had slandered Phelips and other JPs at quarter sessions. Phelips had prosecuted him in Star Chamber, and the dismissal with heavy costs of Stawell's countersuit a couple of months before the new election gave Phelips added satisfaction. Though somewhat overshadowed by both Wentworth's purposeful management of the debate on the petition of right and Sir John Eliot's soaring rhetoric if not always clear policy direction in leadership of the opposition, Phelips yet played a crucial role in the debates over lieutenancy and billeting in April 1628, not only casting the question higher than it had been before but bringing to the issues a convincing, principled, albeit pragmatic, realism.

The 1629 session proved difficult for Phelips. John Pym's single-minded and unprecedentedly vehement pursuit of Arminianism devalued the grand issues—foreign affairs, privileges, prerogative, taxation, the liberties of the subject—which were always central in Phelips's politics. He now followed rather than led. Though he was 'as intense' in his 'religious alarm' as Pym, he was 'less settled in it' (Russell, 407). Having distanced himself from the hysteria with which the session ended, he was not arrested with Eliot and eight other MPs the day after parliament adjourned.

With the advent of Charles I's personal rule Phelips's political ambit—but not his political ambition—was limited to Somerset. He was certain there would be another parliament, and he sought supremacy in the county in order to assure the political base for his election. It has been suggested that 'Phelips in the 1630s perhaps served his county's interests more effectively for the fact that he was able to use discretion about when it was expedient to do so' (Russell, 425). Expediency dictated Phelips's assiduous execution of various enclosure and disafforestation schemes and of the Somerset commission for distraint of knighthood, his vigorous implementation of the Book of Orders, and his strident support for the Book of Sports (where he scored against both Poulett and the hapless chief justice Sir Thomas Richardson). Expediency was

overborne in 1636 in the matter of the militia, when Phelips adroitly manoeuvred Poulett into an abuse of his authority as chief deputy lieutenant, resulting in Poulett's severe reprimand by the lord lieutenant and other privy councillors. And with the 1634 writ of ship money, Phelips raised the first opposition to the tax in what would be a sustained campaign to cripple it by disputing the rates for its collection. Where Phelips led other county magnates followed, and by 1638 ship money was virtually uncollectable in Somerset. Phelips's victory was complete, for he had become truly his 'countries only freinde', had defeated Poulett and Stawell at every juncture, and could reasonably claim that those principles for which he had stood so prominently in the parliaments of the 1620s he had advanced in county governance in the 1630s.

Phelips's victory was short-lived. He died in 1638 and was buried on 13 April in the parish church at Montacute, leaving his widow, Bridget, his sons Edward (1612/13–1680) and Robert (1619–1707), and three daughters. He had been a poor manager of his estates and had not advanced his fortune. He cleared his debts and settled Edward's inheritance by a marriage alliance between Edward and Sir Walter Pye's daughter, Anne, that compromised Bridget's dower and deprived their three daughters of their portions. Sir Robert had not lived long enough to see another parliament—or, for that matter, a revolution. Edward did, being elected to both the Short and the Long parliaments for his father's pocket borough, Ilchester. Disabled in 1644, Edward was a royalist colonel and governor of Bristol after it fell to the king. There is little reason to suppose that had he lived Sir Robert's pilgrimage would have been any different.

THOMAS G. BARNES

Sources Som. ARS, Phelips MSS, DD/PH · Som. ARS, Sandford MSS, DD/SF · quarter sessions order books, Som. ARS, DD/SF · sessions rolls, Som. ARS, DD/SF · inquisition post mortem, PRO, C 142/571/157 and 366/190 · PRO, PC2; SP14 and SP16 · S. R. Gardiner, ed., *Parliamentary debates in 1610*, CS, 81 (1862) · E. R. Foster, ed., *Proceedings in parliament, 1610*, 2 vols. (1966) · M. Jansson, ed., *Proceedings in parliament, 1614 (House of Commons)* (1988), 172 · W. Notestein, F. H. Relf, and H. Simpson, eds., *Commons debates, 1621*, 7 vols. (1935) · M. Jansson and W. B. Bidwell, eds., *Proceedings in parliament, 1625* (1987) · R. C. Johnson and others, eds., *Commons debates, 1628*, 6 vols. (1977–83) · W. Notestein and F. H. Relf, eds., *Commons debates for 1629* (1921) · T. G. Barnes, *Somerset, 1625–1640: a county's government during the personal rule* (1961) · C. Russell, *Parliaments and English politics, 1621–1629* (1979) · R. E. Ruigh, *The parliament of 1624: politics and foreign policy* (1971) · R. Zaller, *The parliament of 1621: a study in constitutional conflict* (1971) · S. R. Gardiner, *History of England from the accession of James I to the outbreak of the civil war, 1603–1642*, 10 vols. (1883–4) · E. de Villiers, 'Parliamentary boroughs restored by the House of Commons, 1621–1641', *EngHR*, 67 (1952), 175–202 · J. P. Ferris, 'Phelips, Edward', HoP, *Commons, 1660–90* · T. Cogswell, *The blessed revolution: English politics and the coming of war, 1621–1624* (1989) · S. W. Bates-Harbin, *Members of parliament for the county of Somerset* (1939), 135, 140

Archives Som. ARS, corresp. and papers

Likenesses attrib. H. G. Pot, oils, 1632, Montacute House, Somerset; on loan from NPG

Wealth at death modest estate: IPM, PRO, C 142/571/157, 22 Aug 1638, in Taunton

PICTURE CREDITS

Pater, Walter Horatio (1839–1894)—© National Portrait Gallery, London

Paterson, Andrew Barton (1864–1941)—by permission of the National Library of Australia

Paterson, John (1632–1708)—Christie's Images Ltd. (2004)

Paterson, (James) Ralston Kennedy (1897–1981)—by courtesy of Dr Elspeth Russell

Paterson, William (1658–1719)—© National Portrait Gallery, London

Patmore, Coventry Kersey Deighton (1823–1896)—© National Portrait Gallery, London

Paton, Alexander Allan (1874–1934)—© National Portrait Gallery, London

Paton, George (1721–1807)—National Museums of Scotland

Paton, John Brown (1830–1911)—Phillips Picture Library

Paton, John Gibson (1824–1907)—© National Portrait Gallery, London

Paton, Sir William Drummond MacDonald (1917–1993)—Godfrey Argent Studios / Royal Society

Patrick, Robert William Cochran- (1842–1897)—Scottish National Portrait Gallery

Patrick, Simon (1626–1707)—© National Portrait Gallery, London

Patteson, John Coleridge (1827–1871)—© National Portrait Gallery, London

Patti, Adelina (1843–1919)—© National Portrait Gallery, London

Patti, Carlotta (1835–1889)—© National Portrait Gallery, London

Pattison, Dorothy Wyndlow [Sister Dora] (1832–1878)—© National Portrait Gallery, London

Pattison, Mark (1813–1884)—© National Portrait Gallery, London

Pattle, Marmaduke Thomas St John (1914–1941)—The Imperial War Museum, London

Pattrick, George (1746–1800)—© National Portrait Gallery, London

Paul, Sir George Onesiphorus, second baronet (1746–1820)—The Conway Library, Courtauld Institute of Art, London

Paul, Herbert Woodfield (1853–1935)—© National Portrait Gallery, London

Paul, (Charles) Kegan (1828–1902)—© National Portrait Gallery, London

Paul, William Francis (1850–1928)—courtesy of BOCM Pauls; photograph © Eric Palmer

Paulet, John, fifth marquess of Winchester (1598?–1675)—© National Portrait Gallery, London

Paulet, William, first marquess of Winchester (1474/5?–1572)—© National Portrait Gallery, London

Pauncefote, Julian, Baron Pauncefote (1828–1902)—© National Portrait Gallery, London

Pavlova, Anna Pavlovna (1881–1931)—by courtesy of Felix Rosenstiel's Widow & Son Ltd., London, on behalf of the Estate of Sir John Lavery; © Tate, London, 2004

Paxton, Sir Joseph (1803–1865)—by permission of the Linnean Society of London

Paye, Richard Morton (bap. 1750, d. 1821)—National Trust Photographic Library

Payne, Ernest Alexander (1902–1980)—© National Portrait Gallery, London

Payne, Joseph (1808–1876)—© National Portrait Gallery, London

Payne, Thomas (1716x18–1799)—© Collection of The New-York Historical Society. Negative no. 6647

Peabody, George (1795–1869)—© National Portrait Gallery, London

Peacock, Sir Edward Robert (1871–1962)—Estate of the Artist; ING Bank, NV, London Branch

Peacock, George (1791–1858)—Christie's Images Ltd. (2004)

Peacock, Thomas Love (1785–1866)—© National Portrait Gallery, London

Peake, Frederick Gerard (1886–1970)—© National Portrait Gallery, London

Peake, Mervyn Laurence (1911–1968)—© Estate of Mervyn Peake; photograph National Portrait Gallery, London

Pearce, Stephen (1819–1904)—© National Portrait Gallery, London

Pearce, Zachary (1690–1774)—© National Portrait Gallery, London

Pears, Sir Peter Neville Luard (1910–1986)—Reg Wilson / Rex Features

Pearsall, William Harold (1891–1964)—© National Portrait Gallery, London

Pearse, Patrick Henry (1879–1916)—Getty Images – Hulton Archive

Pearson, Charles Henry (1830–1894)—© National Portrait Gallery, London

Pearson, John (1613–1686)—© National Portrait Gallery, London

Pearson, John Loughborough (1817–1897)—© National Portrait Gallery, London

Pearson, Karl (1857–1936)—© National Portrait Gallery, London

Pearson, Lester Bowles (1897–1972)—Karsh / Camera Press

Pease, Edward (1767–1858)—© National Portrait Gallery, London

Pease, Joseph Albert, first Baron Gainford (1860–1943)—© National Portrait Gallery, London

Peat, Stanley (1902–1969)—Godfrey Argent Studios / Royal Society

Peate, Iorwerth Cyfeiliog (1901–1982)—by courtesy of the National Library of Wales

Peel, Arthur Wellesley, first Viscount Peel (1829–1912)—© National Portrait Gallery, London

Peel, John (1776–1854)—© National Portrait Gallery, London

Peel, Jonathan (1799–1879)—by permission of Huntingdon Town Council

Peel, Sir Robert, first baronet (1750–1830)—private collection; © reserved in the photograph

Peel, Sir Robert, second baronet (1788–1850)—private collection;

photograph National Portrait Gallery, London

Peel, Sir Robert, third baronet (1822–1895)—Howarth-Loomes Collection; photograph National Portrait Gallery, London

Peers, Sir Charles Reed (1868–1952)—© National Portrait Gallery, London

Pegge, Samuel (1704–1796)—© National Portrait Gallery, London

Peierls, Sir Rudolf Ernst (1907–1995)—© National Portrait Gallery, London

Pelham, Henry (1694–1754)—© National Portrait Gallery, London

Pelham, Henry Francis (1846–1907)—Trinity College, Oxford; photograph © National Portrait Gallery, London

Pellegrini, Carlo [Ape] (1839–1889)—National Gallery of Ireland

Pellett, Thomas (c.1671–1744)—by permission of the Royal College of Physicians, London

Pellew, Edward, first Viscount Exmouth (1757–1833)—© National Portrait Gallery, London

Pembridge, Sir Richard (c.1320–1375)—by permission of the Dean and Chapter of Hereford Cathedral

Pengelly, Sir Thomas (1675–1730)—© National Portrait Gallery, London

Penn, Sir William (bap. 1621, d. 1670)—© National Maritime Museum, London, Greenwich Hospital Collection

Penn, William (1644–1718)—courtesy of the Historical Society of Pennsylvania Collection, Atwater Kent Museum of Philadelphia

Pennant, Thomas (1726–1798)—© National Portrait Gallery, London

Pennefather, William (1816–1873)—© National Portrait Gallery, London

Pennell, Joseph (1857–1926)—© Copyright The British Museum

Penney, William George, Baron Penney (1909–1991)—Getty Images – Hulton Archive; photograph National Portrait Gallery, London

Penny, Thomas (c.1530–1589)—© National Portrait Gallery, London

Penrose, Dame Emily (1858–1942)—© National Portrait Gallery, London

Penrose, Francis Cranmer (1817–1903)—RIBA Library Photographs Collection

Penrose, (Elizabeth) Lee [Lee Miller], Lady Penrose (1907–1977)—© Estate of Lee Miller; collection National Portrait Gallery, London

Pentland, Joseph Barclay (1797–1873)—© National Portrait Gallery, London

Pentreath, Dorothy (bap. 1692, d. 1777)—© National Portrait Gallery, London

Pepler, Sir George Lionel (1882–1959)—© National Portrait Gallery, London

Pepler, Harry Douglas Clarke [Hilary] (1878–1951)—private collection

Peploe, Hanmer William Webb- (1837–1923)—© National Portrait Gallery, London

Peploe, Samuel (bap. 1667, d. 1752)—Ashmolean Museum, Oxford

Pepperrell, Sir William, first baronet (1696–1759)—photography courtesy Peabody Essex Museum

Pepusch, John Christopher (1666/7–1752)—© National Portrait Gallery, London

Pepys, Charles Christopher, first earl of Cottenham (1781–1851)—© National Portrait Gallery, London

Pepys, Samuel (1633–1703)—© National Portrait Gallery, London

Perceval, John, first earl of Egmont (1683–1748)—© National Portrait Gallery, London

Perceval, John, second earl of Egmont (1711–1770)—© National Portrait Gallery, London

Perceval, Spencer (1762–1812)—© National Portrait Gallery, London

Percy, Algernon, tenth earl of Northumberland (1602–1668)—Collection of the Duke of Northumberland. Photograph: Photographic Survey, Courtauld Institute of Art, London

Percy, Elizabeth, duchess of Northumberland and suo jure Baroness Percy (1716–1776)—Collection of the Duke of Northumberland. Photograph: Photographic Survey, Courtauld Institute of Art, London

Percy, Henry, first earl of Northumberland (1341–1408)—The British Library

Percy, Henry, ninth earl of Northumberland (1564–1632)—© Rijksmuseum, Amsterdam

Percy, Henry, Baron Percy of Alnwick (c.1604–1659)—National Trust Photographic Library / Derrick E. Witty

Percy, Hugh, first duke of Northumberland (bap. 1712, d. 1786)—Collection of the Duke of Northumberland. Photograph: Photographic Survey, Courtauld Institute of Art, London

Percy, Hugh, second duke of Northumberland (1742–1817)—Collection of the Duke of Northumberland. Photograph: Photographic Survey, Courtauld Institute of Art, London

Percy, Hugh, third duke of Northumberland (1785–1847)—© National Portrait Gallery, London

Percy, John (1817–1889)—Heritage Images Partnership

Percy, Sidney Richard (1821–1886)—© Jan Reynolds; photograph © National Portrait Gallery, London

Percy, Thomas, seventh earl of Northumberland (1528–1572)—National Trust Photographic Library

Percy, Thomas (1560–1605)—© National Portrait Gallery, London

Percy, Thomas (1729–1811)—© National Portrait Gallery, London

Pereira, Jonathan (1804–1853)—© National Portrait Gallery, London

Oxford dictionary of
national biography